W9-BUO-779

Official 1997
National Football League

Record
& Fact Book

A National Football League Book.
Workman Publishing Co., New York.

NATIONAL FOOTBALL LEAGUE
280 Park Avenue, New York, N.Y. 10017 (212) 450-2000. NFL Internet Address: http://nfl.com

Copyright © 1997 by the National Football League. All rights reserved. The information in this publication has been compiled for use by the news media to aid in reporting of the games and teams of the National Football League. No part of this book may be reproduced or transmitted in any form or by any means, electronic or mechanical, including photocopying, recording, or by any information storage and retrieval system, without permission in writing from the National Football League.

Printed in the United States of America.

A National Football League Book.

Compiled by the NFL Communications Department and Seymour Siwoff, Elias Sports Bureau.

Edited by Chris McCloskey, NFL Communications Department and Matt Marini, NFLP Publishing Group. Assisted by William Tham and Lee Balint. Cover designed by Helen Choy Whang.
Statistics by Elias Sports Bureau.
Produced by NFL Properties, Inc., Publishing Group, Los Angeles.

Cover Photograph by Glen James.

Workman Publishing Co.
708 Broadway, New York, N.Y. 10003
Manufactured in the United States of America.
First printing, July 1997.
10 9 8 7 6 5 4 3 2 1

(All times local except American Bowl games, which are EDT.)
Nationally televised games in parentheses.

PRESEASON/FIRST WEEK

Saturday, July 26   Pro Football Hall of Fame Game at Canton, Ohio

     Minnesota _____ vs. Seattle _____   (ABC) 2:30

     Buffalo _____ at Denver _____   7:00

     Miami_____ at Green Bay _____   5:30

Sunday, July 27   American Bowl at Dublin, Ireland

     Chicago _____ vs. Pittsburgh _____   (FOX) 1:00*

Thursday, July 31   New England _____ at Green Bay _____   (ESPN) 7:00

Friday, August 1   Atlanta _____ at Detroit _____   7:30

     Cincinnati _____ at Indianapolis _____   6:30

Saturday, August 2   Arizona _____ at Seattle _____   7:00

     Chicago _____ at Buffalo _____   7:00

     New York Giants _____ at Baltimore _____   8:00

     Philadelphia _____ at New York Jets _____   8:00

     Pittsburgh _____ at Kansas City _____   7:00

     St. Louis _____ at Minnesota _____   7:00

     San Francisco _____ at San Diego _____   7:00

     Tennessee _____ vs. New Orleans _____ at Memphis, Tenn.   7:00

     Washington _____ at Tampa Bay _____   7:30

Sunday, August 3   Carolina _____ at Jacksonville _____   (NBC) 3:00

     Oakland _____ at Dallas _____   (TNT) 7:00

Monday, August 4   American Bowl at Mexico City, Mexico

     Denver _____ vs. Miami _____   (ABC) 8:00

     *Dublin game actual kickoff 6:00 P.M.

PRESEASON/SECOND WEEK

Friday, August 8   Arizona _____ at St. Louis _____   7:00

     Baltimore _____ at New York Jets _____   8:00

     Cincinnati _____ at Detroit _____   7:30

     Dallas _____ at New England _____   8:00

     Green Bay _____ at Oakland _____   7:00

     Minnesota _____ at Buffalo _____   7:30

Saturday, August 9   Denver _____ at Carolina _____   8:00

     Indianapolis _____ at San Diego _____   7:00

     Jacksonville _____ at New York Giants _____   8:00

     Kansas City _____ at New Orleans _____   7:00

     Seattle _____ at San Francisco _____   6:00

     Tampa Bay _____ at Atlanta _____   7:30

     Tennessee _____ vs. Washington _____ at Nashville, Tenn.   7:00

Sunday, August 10   Chicago _____ at Miami _____   (TNT) 8:00

Monday, August 11   Philadelphia _____ at Pittsburgh _____   (ABC) 8:00

PRESEASON/THIRD WEEK

Thursday, August 14   Carolina _____ at Kansas City _____   (ESPN) 7:00

Friday, August 15   St. Louis _____ at Dallas _____   (FOX) 7:00

Saturday, August 16   American Bowl at Toronto, Canada

     Buffalo _____ vs. Green Bay _____   (NBC) 4:00

     Arizona _____ at Chicago _____   7:00

     Baltimore _____ at Philadelphia _____   8:00

     Indianapolis _____ at Seattle _____   7:00

     Miami _____ at Tampa Bay _____   7:30

     Minnesota _____ at Cincinnati _____   7:30

     New Orleans _____ at Oakland _____   1:00

     New York Jets _____ at New York Giants _____   8:00

     Tennessee _____ vs. San Diego _____ at Nashville, Tenn.   7:00

     Washington _____ at Atlanta _____   7:30

Sunday, August 17   Denver _____ at New England _____   (NBC) 1:00

     Detroit _____ at Pittsburgh _____   (TNT) 8:00

Monday, August 18   Jacksonville _____ at San Francisco _____   (ABC) 5:00

PRESEASON/FOURTH WEEK

Thursday, August 21
Detroit _____ at Indianapolis _____		7:30
New England _____ at Philadelphia _____		8:00
Washington _____ at Miami _____	(ESPN)	8:00

Friday, August 22
Atlanta _____ at Jacksonville _____		7:30
Buffalo _____ at Baltimore _____		7:30
Kansas City _____ at St. Louis _____		7:00
New Orleans _____ at Chicago _____		7:30
New York Giants _____ vs. Green Bay _____ at Madison, Wis.		7:00
New York Jets _____ vs. Tampa Bay _____ at Orlando, Fla.		7:30
Oakland _____ at Arizona _____		7:00
Pittsburgh _____ at Carolina _____		8:00
San Diego _____ at Minnesota _____		7:00
Seattle _____ at Cincinnati _____		7:30
Tennessee _____ at Dallas _____		7:00

Saturday, August 23
San Francisco _____ at Denver _____	(FOX)	6:00

KICKOFF WEEKEND

Sunday, August 31
(NBC-TV National Weekend)
Arizona _____ at Cincinnati _____		1:00
Atlanta _____ at Detroit _____		1:00
Dallas _____ at Pittsburgh _____		1:00
Indianapolis _____ at Miami _____		1:00
Jacksonville _____ at Baltimore _____		4:00
Kansas City _____ at Denver _____		2:00
Minnesota _____ at Buffalo _____		1:00
New Orleans _____ at St. Louis _____		12:00
New York Jets _____ at Seattle _____		1:00
Oakland _____ at Tennessee _____		12:00
Philadelphia _____ at New York Giants _____		1:00
San Diego _____ at New England _____		1:00
San Francisco _____ at Tampa Bay _____		4:00

Sunday Night
Washington _____ at Carolina _____	(TNT)	8:00

Monday, September 1
Chicago _____ at Green Bay _____	(ABC)	8:00

SECOND WEEK

Sunday, September 7
(FOX-TV National Weekend)
Buffalo _____ at New York Jets _____		1:00
Carolina _____ at Atlanta _____		1:00
Cincinnati _____ at Baltimore _____		1:00
Denver _____ at Seattle _____		1:00
Green Bay _____ at Philadelphia _____		4:00
Minnesota _____ at Chicago _____		12:00
New England _____ at Indianapolis _____		12:00
New York Giants _____ at Jacksonville _____		4:00
San Diego _____ at New Orleans _____		12:00
San Francisco _____ at St. Louis _____		12:00
Tampa Bay _____ at Detroit _____		1:00
Tennesee _____ at Miami _____		1:00
Washington _____ at Pittsburgh _____		1:00

Sunday Night
Dallas _____ at Arizona _____	(TNT)	5:00

Monday, September 8
Kansas City _____ at Oakland _____	(ABC)	6:00

THIRD WEEK
Open Dates:
Cincinnati, Jacksonville,
Pittsburgh, Tennessee

Sunday, September 14
(FOX-TV National Weekend)
Arizona _____ at Washington _____		1:00
Baltimore _____ at New York Giants _____		1:00
Buffalo _____ at Kansas City _____		12:00
Carolina _____ at San Diego _____		1:00
Detroit _____ at Chicago _____		12:00
Miami _____ at Green Bay _____		12:00
New Orleans _____ at San Francisco _____		1:00
Oakland _____ at Atlanta _____		1:00
St. Louis _____ at Denver _____		2:00
Seattle _____ at Indianapolis _____		3:00
Tampa Bay _____ at Minnesota _____		12:00

Sunday Night
New York Jets _____ at New England _____	(TNT)	8:00

Monday, September 15
Philadelphia _____ at Dallas _____	(ABC)	8:00

FOURTH WEEK Open Dates: Arizona, Dallas, Philadelphia, Washington	**Sunday, September 21** **(NBC-TV National Weekend)**	Atlanta _____ at San Francisco _____ Baltimore _____ at Tennessee _____ Chicago _____ at New England _____ Cincinnati _____ at Denver _____ Detroit _____ at New Orleans _____ Indianapolis _____ at Buffalo _____ Kansas City _____ at Carolina _____ Minnesota _____ at Green Bay _____ New York Giants _____ at St. Louis _____ Oakland _____ at New York Jets _____ San Diego _____ at Seattle _____	1:00 12:00 1:00 2:00 12:00 4:00 1:00 12:00 3:00 1:00 1:00
	Sunday Night **Monday, September 22**	Miami _____ at Tampa Bay _____ Pittsburgh _____ at Jacksonville _____	(TNT) 8:00 (ABC) 9:00
FIFTH WEEK Open Dates: Buffalo, Indianapolis, Miami, New England	**Sunday, September 28** **(FOX-TV National Weekend)**	Arizona _____ at Tampa Bay _____ Baltimore _____ at San Diego _____ Chicago _____ at Dallas _____ Denver _____ at Atlanta _____ Green Bay _____ at Detroit _____ Jacksonville _____ at Washington _____ New Orleans _____ at New York Giants _____ New York Jets _____ at Cincinnati _____ St. Louis _____ at Oakland _____ Seattle _____ at Kansas City _____ Tennessee _____ at Pittsburgh _____	1:00 1:00 3:00 1:00 1:00 1:00 1:00 4:00 1:00 3:00 1:00
	Sunday Night **Monday, September 29**	Philadelphia _____ at Minnesota _____ San Francisco _____ at Carolina _____	(TNT) 7:00 (ABC) 9:00
SIXTH WEEK Open Dates: Atlanta, Carolina, St. Louis, San Francisco	**Sunday, October 5** **(NBC-TV National Weekend)**	Cincinnati _____ at Jacksonville _____ Dallas _____ at New York Giants _____ Detroit _____ at Buffalo _____ Kansas City _____ at Miami _____ Minnesota _____ at Arizona _____ New York Jets _____ at Indianapolis _____ Pittsburgh _____ at Baltimore _____ San Diego _____ at Oakland _____ Tampa Bay _____ at Green Bay _____ Tennessee _____ at Seattle _____ Washington _____ at Philadelphia _____	1:00 1:00 1:00 1:00 1:00 3:00 1:00 1:00 12:00 1:00 1:00
	Sunday Night **Monday, October 6**	New Orleans _____ at Chicago _____ New England _____ at Denver _____	(TNT) 7:00 (ABC) 7:00
SEVENTH WEEK Open Dates: Baltimore, Denver, Kansas City, Oakland, San Diego, Seattle	**Sunday, October 12** **(FOX-TV National Weekend)**	Atlanta _____ at New Orleans _____ Buffalo _____ at New England _____ Carolina _____ at Minnesota _____ Cincinnati _____ at Tennessee _____ Detroit _____ at Tampa Bay _____ Green Bay _____ at Chicago _____ Miami _____ at New York Jets _____ New York Giants _____ at Arizona _____ Philadelphia _____ at Jacksonville _____ St. Louis _____ at San Francisco _____	12:00 1:00 3:00 12:00 1:00 12:00 1:00 1:00 1:00 1:00
	Sunday Night **Monday, October 13**	Indianapolis _____ at Pittsburgh _____ Dallas _____ at Washington _____	(TNT) 8:00 (ABC) 9:00

EIGHTH WEEK
Open Dates:
Chicago, Green Bay,
Minnesota, Tampa Bay

Thursday, October 16
San Diego _____ at Kansas City _____ (TNT) 7:00

Sunday, October 19
(NBC-TV National Weekend)
Arizona _____ at Philadelphia _____ 1:00
Carolina _____ at New Orleans _____ 12:00
Denver _____ at Oakland _____ 1:00
Jacksonville _____ at Dallas _____ 12:00
Miami _____ at Baltimore _____ 4:00
New England _____ at New York Jets _____ 1:00
New York Giants _____ at Detroit _____ 4:00
Pittsburgh _____ at Cincinnati _____ 4:00
San Francisco _____ at Atlanta _____ 1:00
Seattle _____ at St. Louis _____ 12:00
Washington _____ at Tennessee _____ 12:00

Monday, October 20
Buffalo _____ at Indianapolis _____ (ABC) 8:00

NINTH WEEK
Open Dates:
Detroit,
New York Jets

Sunday, October 26
(NBC-TV National Weekend)
Baltimore _____ at Washington _____ 1:00
Chicago _____ at Miami _____ 4:00
Cincinnati _____ at New York Giants _____ 1:00
Dallas _____ at Philadelphia _____ 1:00
Denver _____ at Buffalo _____ 1:00
Indianapolis _____ at San Diego _____ 1:00
Jacksonville _____ at Pittsburgh _____ 4:00
Kansas City _____ at St. Louis _____ 12:00
Minnesota _____ at Tampa Bay _____ 1:00
Oakland _____ at Seattle _____ 1:00
San Francisco _____ at New Orleans _____ 12:00
Tennessee _____ at Arizona _____ 2:00

Sunday Night
Atlanta _____ at Carolina _____ (TNT) 8:00

Monday, October 27
Green Bay _____ at New England _____ (ABC) 9:00

TENTH WEEK
Open Dates:
New Orleans,
New York Giants

Sunday, November 2
(FOX-TV National Weekend)
Baltimore _____ at New York Jets _____ 1:00
Dallas _____ at San Francisco _____ 1:00
Jacksonville _____ at Tennessee _____ 3:00
Miami _____ at Buffalo _____ 1:00
New England _____ at Minnesota _____ 12:00
Oakland _____ at Carolina _____ 1:00
Philadelphia _____ at Arizona _____ 2:00
St. Louis _____ at Atlanta _____ 1:00
San Diego _____ at Cincinnati _____ 1:00
Seattle _____ at Denver _____ 2:00
Tampa Bay _____ at Indianapolis _____ 1:00
Washington _____ at Chicago _____ 12:00

Sunday Night
Detroit _____ at Green Bay _____ (ESPN) 7:00

Monday, November 3
Pittsburgh _____ at Kansas City _____ (ABC) 8:00

ELEVENTH WEEK

Sunday, November 9
(NBC-TV National Weekend)
Arizona _____ at Dallas _____ 12:00
Carolina _____ at Denver _____ 2:00
Chicago _____ at Minnesota _____ 12:00
Cincinnati _____ at Indianapolis _____ 1:00
Detroit _____ at Washington _____ 1:00
Kansas City _____ at Jacksonville _____ 1:00
New England _____ at Buffalo _____ 4:00
New Orleans _____ at Oakland _____ 1:00
New York Giants _____ at Tennessee _____ 3:00
New York Jets _____ at Miami _____ 1:00
St. Louis _____ at Green Bay _____ 12:00
Seattle _____ at San Diego _____ 1:00
Tampa Bay _____ at Atlanta _____ 1:00

Sunday Night
Baltimore _____ at Pittsburgh _____ (ESPN) 8:00

Monday, November 10
San Francisco _____ at Philadelphia _____ (ABC) 9:00

TWELFTH WEEK

Sunday, November 16
(FOX-TV National Weekend)

Arizona _____ at New York Giants _____		1:00
Atlanta _____ at St. Louis _____		12:00
Carolina _____ at San Francisco _____		1:00
Cincinnati _____ at Pittsburgh _____		1:00
Denver _____ at Kansas City _____		12:00
Green Bay _____ at Indianapolis _____		1:00
Minnesota _____ at Detroit _____		1:00
New England _____ at Tampa Bay _____		1:00
New York Jets _____ at Chicago _____		3:00
Philadelphia _____ at Baltimore _____		1:00
Seattle _____ at New Orleans _____		12:00
Tennessee _____ at Jacksonville _____		1:00
Washington _____ at Dallas _____		12:00

Sunday Night Oakland _____ at San Diego _____ (ESPN) 5:00
Monday, November 17 Buffalo _____ at Miami _____ (ABC) 9:00

THIRTEENTH WEEK

Sunday, November 23
(NBC-TV National Weekend)

Arizona _____ at Baltimore _____		1:00
Buffalo _____ at Tennessee _____		12:00
Carolina _____ at St. Louis _____		3:00
Dallas _____ at Green Bay _____		12:00
Indianapolis _____ at Detroit _____		1:00
Jacksonville _____ at Cincinnati _____		4:00
Kansas City _____ at Seattle _____		1:00
Miami _____ at New England _____		1:00
Minnesota _____ at New York Jets _____		1:00
New Orleans _____ at Atlanta _____		1:00
Pittsburgh _____ at Philadelphia _____		1:00
San Diego _____ at San Francisco _____		1:00
Tampa Bay _____ at Chicago _____		12:00

Sunday Night New York Giants _____ at Washington _____ (ESPN) 8:00
Monday, November 24 Oakland _____ at Denver _____ (ABC) 7:00

FOURTEENTH WEEK

Thursday, November 27

Chicago _____ at Detroit _____		(FOX) 12:30
Tennessee _____ at Dallas _____		(NBC) 3:00

Sunday, November 30
(NBC-TV National Weekend)

Atlanta _____ at Seattle _____		1:00
Baltimore _____ at Jacksonville _____		1:00
Cincinnati _____ at Philadelphia _____		1:00
Indianapolis _____ at New England _____		1:00
Miami _____ at Oakland _____		1:00
New Orleans _____ at Carolina _____		1:00
New York Jets _____ at Buffalo _____		1:00
Pittsburgh _____ at Arizona _____		2:00
St. Louis _____ at Washington _____		1:00
San Francisco _____ at Kansas City _____		12:00
Tampa Bay _____ at New York Giants _____		4:00

Sunday Night Denver _____ at San Diego _____ (ESPN) 5:00
Monday, December 1 Green Bay _____ at Minnesota _____ (ABC) 8:00

FIFTEENTH WEEK

Thursday, December 4 Tennessee _____ at Cincinnati _____ (ESPN) 8:00

Sunday, December 7
(FOX-TV National Weekend)

Atlanta _____ at San Diego _____		1:00
Buffalo _____ at Chicago _____		12:00
Denver _____ at Pittsburgh _____		1:00
Green Bay _____ at Tampa Bay _____		1:00
Indianapolis _____ at New York Jets _____		4:00
Minnesota _____ at San Francisco _____		1:00
New England _____ at Jacksonville _____		1:00
New York Giants _____ at Philadelphia _____		1:00
Oakland _____ at Kansas City _____		12:00
St. Louis _____ at New Orleans _____		12:00
Seattle _____ at Baltimore _____		1:00
Washington _____ at Arizona _____		2:00

Sunday Night Detroit _____ at Miami _____ (ESPN) 8:00
Monday, December 8 Carolina _____ at Dallas _____ (ABC) 8:00

SIXTEENTH WEEK

Saturday, December 13

Pittsburgh ____ at New England ____	(NBC)	4:00
Washington ____ at New York Giants ____	(FOX)	12:30

Sunday, December 14
(FOX-TV National Weekend)

Arizona ____ at New Orleans ____	3:00
Dallas ____ at Cincinnati ____	1:00
Detroit ____ at Minnesota ____	12:00
Green Bay ____ at Carolina ____	4:00
Jacksonville ____ at Buffalo ____	1:00
Kansas City ____ at San Diego ____	1:00
Miami ____ at Indianapolis ____	1:00
Philadelphia ____ at Atlanta ____	1:00
Seattle ____ at Oakland ____	1:00
Tampa Bay ____ at New York Jets ____	1:00
Tennessee ____ at Baltimore ____	1:00

Sunday Night

Chicago ____ at St. Louis ____	(ESPN)	7:00

Monday, December 15

Denver ____ at San Francisco ____	(ABC)	6:00

SEVENTEENTH WEEK

Saturday, December 20

Buffalo ____ at Green Bay ____	(NBC)	11:30A.M.
St. Louis ____ at Carolina ____	(FOX)	4:00

Sunday, December 21
(NBC-TV National Weekend)

Atlanta ____ at Arizona ____	2:00
Baltimore ____ at Cincinnati ____	1:00
Chicago ____ at Tampa Bay ____	1:00
Indianapolis ____ at Minnesota ____	12:00
Jacksonville ____ at Oakland ____	1:00
New Orleans ____ at Kansas City ____	12:00
New York Giants ____ at Dallas ____	12:00
New York Jets ____ at Detroit ____	4:00
Philadelphia ____ at Washington ____	1:00
Pittsburgh ____ at Tennessee ____	12:00
San Diego ____ at Denver ____	2:00

Sunday Night

San Francisco ____ at Seattle ____	(ESPN)	5:00

Monday, December 22

New England ____ at Miami ____	(ABC)	9:00

Wild Card Playoff Games
Site Priorities

Three Wild Card teams (division non-champions with best three records) from each conference and the division champion with the third-best record in each conference will enter the first round of the playoffs. The division champion with the third-best record will play host to the Wild Card team with the third-best record. The Wild Card team with the best record will play host to the Wild Card team with the second-best record. There are no restrictions on intra-division games.

Saturday, December 27, 1997 American Football Conference

_____ at _____ (ABC)

National Football Conference

_____ at _____ (ABC)

Sunday, December 28, 1997 American Football Conference

_____ at _____ (NBC)

National Football Conference

_____ at _____ (FOX)

Divisional Playoff Games
Site Priorities

In each conference, the two division champions with the highest won-lost-tied percentage during the regular season will play host to the Wild Card winners. The division champion with the best record in each conference is assured of playing the lowest seeded Wild Card survivor. There are no restrictions on intra-division games.

Saturday, January 3, 1998 American Football Conference

_____ at _____ (NBC)

National Football Conference

_____ at _____ (FOX)

Sunday, January 4, 1998 American Football Conference

_____ at _____ (NBC)

National Football Conference

_____ at _____ (FOX)

Championship Games
Site Priorities
for Championship Games
The home teams will be the surviving playoff winners with the best won-lost-tied percentage during the regular season. A Wild Card team cannot play host unless two Wild Card teams are in the game, in which case the Wild Card team that was seeded highest in the first round of the playoffs will be the home team.

Sunday, January 11, 1998   American Football Conference

_____ at _____ (NBC)

National Football Conference

_____ at _____ (FOX)

Super Bowl XXXII

Sunday, January 25, 1998   Super Bowl XXXII at Qualcomm Stadium, Jack Murphy Field, San Diego, California

_____ vs. _____ (NBC)

AFC-NFC Pro Bowl

Sunday, February 1, 1998   AFC-NFC Pro Bowl at Honolulu, Hawaii

AFC _____ vs. NFC _____ (ABC)

POSTSEASON GAMES

Saturday, December 27	AFC and NFC Wild Card Playoffs (ABC)
Sunday, December 28	AFC and NFC Wild Card Playoffs (NBC and FOX)
Saturday, January 3	AFC and NFC Divisional Playoffs (NBC and FOX)
Sunday, January 4	AFC and NFC Divisional Playoffs (NBC and FOX)
Sunday, January 11	AFC and NFC Championship Games (NBC and FOX)
Sunday, January 25	Super Bowl XXXII at Qualcomm Stadium, Jack Murphy Field, San Diego (NBC)
Sunday, February 1	AFC-NFC Pro Bowl at Honolulu, Hawaii (ABC)

1997 NATIONALLY TELEVISED GAMES

Regular Season

Sunday, August 31	Kansas City at Denver (day, NBC)
	Washington at Carolina (night, TNT)
Monday, September 1	Chicago at Green Bay (night, ABC)
Sunday, September 7	Green Bay at Philadelphia (day, FOX)
	Dallas at Arizona (night, TNT)
Monday, September 8	Kansas City at Oakland (night, ABC)
Sunday, September 14	St. Louis at Denver (day, FOX)
	New York Jets at New England (night, TNT)
Monday, September 15	Philadelphia at Dallas (night, ABC)
Sunday, September 21	Cincinnati at Denver (day, NBC)
	Miami at Tampa Bay (night, TNT)
Monday, September 22	Pittsburgh at Jacksonville (night, ABC)
Sunday, September 28	Chicago at Dallas (day, FOX)
	Philadelphia at Minnesota (night, TNT)
Monday, September 29	San Francisco at Carolina (night, ABC)
Sunday, October 5	San Diego at Oakland (day, NBC)
	New Orleans at Chicago (night, TNT)
Monday, October 6	New England at Denver (night, ABC)
Sunday, October 12	Carolina at Minnesota (day, FOX)
	Indianapolis at Pittsburgh (night, TNT)
Monday, October 13	Dallas at Washington (night, ABC)
Thursday, October 16	San Diego at Kansas City (night, TNT)
Sunday, October 19	Denver at Oakland (day, NBC)
Monday, October 20	Buffalo at Indianapolis (night, ABC)
Sunday, October 26	Oakland at Seattle (day, NBC)
	Atlanta at Carolina (night, TNT)
Monday, October 27	Green Bay at New England (night, ABC)
Sunday, November 2	Dallas at San Francisco (day, FOX)
	Detroit at Green Bay (night, ESPN)
Monday, November 3	Pittsburgh at Kansas City (night, ABC)
Sunday, November 9	New England at Buffalo (day, NBC)
	Baltimore at Pittsburgh (night, ESPN)
Monday, November 10	San Francisco at Philadelphia (night, ABC)
Sunday, November 16	Carolina at San Francisco (day, FOX)
	Oakland at San Diego (night, ESPN)
Monday, November 17	Buffalo at Miami (night, ABC)
Sunday, November 23	San Diego at San Francisco (day, NBC)
	New York Giants at Washington (night, ESPN)
Monday, November 24	Oakland at Denver (night, ABC)
Thursday, November 27	Chicago at Detroit (day, FOX)
	Tennessee at Dallas (day, NBC)
Sunday, November 30	Miami at Oakland (day, NBC)
	Denver at San Diego (night, ESPN)
Monday, December 1	Green Bay at Minnesota (night, ABC)
Thursday, December 4	Tennessee at Cincinnati (night, ESPN)
Sunday, December 7	Minnesota at San Francisco (day, FOX)
	Detroit at Miami (night, ESPN)
Monday, December 8	Carolina at Dallas (night, ABC)

Saturday, December 13	Washington at New York Giants (day, FOX)
	Pittsburgh at New England (day, NBC)
Sunday, December 14	Green Bay at Carolina (day, FOX)
	Chicago at St. Louis (night, ESPN)
Monday, December 15	Denver at San Francisco (night, ABC)
Saturday, December 20	Buffalo at Green Bay (day, NBC)
	St. Louis at Carolina (day, FOX)
Sunday, December 21	San Diego at Denver (day, NBC)
	San Francisco at Seattle (night, ESPN)
Monday, December 22	New England at Miami (night, ABC)

NATIONAL PRIMETIME TELEVISION GAMES AT A GLANCE

(All times local; Sunday and Thursday on TNT and ESPN, Monday on ABC; all on CBS radio)

Sunday, August 31	Washington at Carolina (TNT)	8:00
Monday, September 1	Chicago at Green Bay (ABC)	8:00
Sunday, September 7	Dallas at Arizona (TNT)	5:00
Monday, September 8	Kansas City at Oakland (ABC)	6:00
Sunday, September 14	New York Jets at New England (TNT)	8:00
Monday, September 15	Philadelphia at Dallas (ABC)	8:00
Sunday, September 21	Miami at Tampa Bay (TNT)	8:00
Monday, September 22	Pittsburgh at Jacksonville (ABC)	9:00
Sunday, September 28	Philadelphia at Minnesota (TNT)	7:00
Monday, September 29	San Francisco at Carolina (ABC)	9:00
Sunday, October 5	New Orleans at Chicago (TNT)	7:00
Monday, October 6	New England at Denver (ABC)	7:00
Sunday, October 12	Indianapolis at Pittsburgh (TNT)	8:00
Monday, October 13	Dallas at Washington (ABC)	9:00
Thursday, October 16	San Diego at Kansas City (TNT)	7:00
Monday, October 20	Buffalo at Indianapolis (ABC)	8:00
Sunday, October 26	Atlanta at Carolina (TNT)	8:00
Monday, October 27	Green Bay at New England (ABC)	9:00
Sunday, November 2	Detroit at Green Bay (ESPN)	7:00
Monday, November 3	Pittsburgh at Kansas City (ABC)	8:00
Sunday, November 9	Baltimore at Pittsburgh (ESPN)	8:00
Monday, November 10	San Francisco at Philadelphia (ABC)	9:00
Sunday, November 16	Oakland at San Diego (ESPN)	5:00
Monday, November 17	Buffalo at Miami (ABC)	9:00
Sunday, November 23	New York Giants at Washington (ESPN)	8:00
Monday, November 24	Oakland at Denver (ABC)	7:00
Sunday, November 30	Denver at San Diego (ESPN)	5:00
Monday, December 1	Green Bay at Minnesota (ABC)	8:00
Thursday, December 4	Tennessee at Cincinnati (ESPN)	8:00
Sunday, December 7	Detroit at Miami (ESPN)	8:00
Monday, December 8	Carolina at Dallas (ABC)	8:00
Sunday, December 14	Chicago at St. Louis (ESPN)	7:00
Monday, December 15	Denver at San Francisco (ABC)	6:00
Sunday, December 21	San Francisco at Seattle (ESPN)	5:00
Monday, December 22	New England at Miami (ABC)	9:00

1997

July 7 — Claiming period of 24 hours begins in waiver system. All waiver requests for the rest of the year are no-recall and no-withdrawal.

Mid-July — Training camps open. Veteran players cannot be required to report earlier than 15 days prior to club's first preseason game or July 15, whichever is later.

July 15 — Signing period ends at 4 P.M., Eastern Time, for Unrestricted Free Agents to whom June 1 tender was made by Old Club, and for Transition Players and Franchise Players who are subject to the rules for Transition Players. After this date and through 4 P.M., Eastern Time, on November 4, Old Club has exclusive negotiating rights with its unsigned Unrestricted Free Agents.

July 26 — Hall of Fame Game, Canton, Ohio: Minnesota vs. Seattle.

July 27 — American Bowl, Dublin, Ireland: Chicago vs. Pittsburgh

August 1 — If a drafted rookie has not signed with his club by this date, he may not be traded to any other club in 1997.

August 1 — Deadline for players under contract to report in order to earn a season of free agency credit.

August 4 — American Bowl, Mexico City, Mexico: Denver vs. Miami.

August 16 — American Bowl, Toronto, Canada: Buffalo vs. Green Bay.

August 19 — Roster cutdown to maximum of 60 players on Active List by 4 P.M., Eastern Time.

August 24 — Roster cutdown to maximum of 53 players on Active/Inactive List by 4 P.M., Eastern Time. Clubs may dress minimum of 42 and maximum of 45 players and third quarterback for each regular-season and postseason game.

August 25 — After 4 P.M., Eastern Time, clubs may establish a Practice Squad of five players by signing free agents who do not have an accrued season of free-agency credit, unless that season was achieved by spending an entire regular season on Reserve/Injured or Reserve/Physically Unable to Perform.

August 29 — All clubs are required to identify their 49-player Active List by 7:00 P.M., Eastern Time, on this Friday and thereafter on each Friday before a regular-season Sunday game. No later than one hour and 30 minutes prior to kickoff, clubs must identify their 45-player Active List and third quarterback, if any.

August 31-September 1 — Regular season opens.

September 16 — Priority on multiple waiver claims is now based on the current season's standing.

October 7 — All trading ends at 4 P.M., Eastern Time.

October 8 — Players with at least four previous pension-credited seasons are subject to the waiver system for the remainder of the regular season and postseason.

October 14-15 — NFL Fall Meeting, Washington, D.C.

November 4 — Deadline for clubs to sign by 4 P.M., Eastern Time, their Franchise and Transition players. If still unsigned after this date, such players are prohibited from playing in NFL in 1997.

November 4 — Deadline for clubs to sign by 4 P.M., Eastern Time, their Unrestricted and Restricted Free Agents to whom June 1 tender was made. If still unsigned after this date, such players are prohibited from playing in NFL in 1997.

November 4 — Deadline for clubs to sign drafted players by 4 P.M., Eastern Time. If such players remain unsigned, they are prohibited from playing in NFL in 1997.

November 22 — Deadline for reinstatement of players in Reserve List categories of Retired and Did Not Report.

December 19 — Deadline for waiver requests in 1997, except for "special waiver requests" which have a 10-day claiming period, with termination or assignment delayed until after the Super Bowl.

December 23 — Clubs may begin signing free-agent players for the 1998 season.

December 27-28 — Wild-Card Playoff Games.

1998

January 3-4 — Divisional Playoff Games.

January 11 — AFC and NFC Championship Games.

January 25 — Super Bowl XXXII, Qualcomm Stadium, Jack Murphy Field, San Diego, California.

February 1 — AFC-NFC Pro Bowl, Honolulu, Hawaii.

February 2 — Waiver system begins for 1998. Players with at least four previous pension-credited seasons that a club desires to terminate are not subject to the waiver system until after the trading deadline.

February 5-9 — Combine Timing and Testing, RCA Dome, Indianapolis, Indiana.

February 12 — Deadline for clubs to designate Franchise and Transition Players.

February 12 — Expiration date of all player contracts due to expire in 1998.

February 13 — Free Agency period begins.

February 13 — Trading period begins for 1998 after expiration of all 1997 contracts.

March 22-27 — NFL Annual Meeting, Orlando, Florida.

*April 13 — Deadline for signing of Offer Sheets by Restricted Free Agents.

*April 18-19 — Annual player selection meeting, New York, New York.

May 18-21 — NFL Spring Meeting, St. Louis, Missouri.

June 1 — Deadline for Old Club to send tender to its unsigned Restricted Free Agents or to extend Qualifying Offer, whichever is greater, in order to retain rights.

June 1 — Deadline for Old Club to send tender to its unsigned Unrestricted Free Agents to retain rights if player is not signed by another club by July 15.

*August 2 — Hall of Fame Game, Canton, Ohio.

*September 6-7 — Regular season opens.

1999

*January 2-3 — Wild-Card Playoff Games.

*January 9-10 — Divisional Playoff Games.

*January 17 — AFC and NFC Championship Games.

*January 31 — Super Bowl XXXIII, Pro Player Stadium, Miami, Florida.

2000

*January 30 — Super Bowl XXXIV, Georgia Dome, Atlanta, Georgia.

2001

*January 28 — Super Bowl XXXV, Tampa, Florida.

*Tentatively scheduled.

The NFL is online to provide fans and media quick and easy access to all the latest professional football information.

NFL.COM—(http://nfl.com)

NFL.COM is the league's year-round home page on the Internet, providing information on the NFL during the regular season, post-season and offseason. The site is easily navigable for the following information:

NEWS: Includes up-to-the-minute news from around the league, plus game previews, injury reports, statistics, game photos, and breaking developments.

STATS: Statistics organized by players, teams, and rankings.

FANS: Features information and activities for fans off the field including an online merchandise catalog, upcoming television specials, youth programs, events, and chat sessions.

TEAM AREAS: Customized areas for all 31 clubs featuring updated rosters, depth charts, and all the latest news from the teams.

GAMEDAY: Real-time game coverage with live play-by-play, scores, and statistics from stadiums around the league.

CYBERSPACE SHOWDOWNS: Chat sessions presented by the Quarterback Club featuring top NFL stars.

PLAY FOOTBALL: An area dedicated to the younger football fan including interactive games, contests, and information on how kids can get involved in events such as Punt, Pass & Kick.

TEAM NFL on America Online-Keyword: NFL

The NFL's area on America Online features daily news updates, scores and statistics, team and player information, game previews and recaps, and weekly chat sessions with NFL players. Fans can vote to send their favorite players to the Pro Bowl through exclusive online balloting on AOL.

SUPERBOWL.COM—(http://superbowl.com)

Look for superbowl.com in late December for complete coverage of the playoffs and Super Bowl XXXII. The multimedia site follows all postseason action and features audio and video clips of past Super Bowls.

During the week leading up to Super Bowl XXXII, the site will go 'live' from San Diego, providing coverage of events, press conferences, and chats with Super Bowl players.

On Super Bowl Sunday, superbowl.com will showcase a live Internet cybercast, complete with online commentators calling the action. The site also features digital photos from the game, live public address audio and press-box announcements, and live audio from foreign broadcasts.

WORLDLEAGUE.COM—(http://worldleague.com)

The official Internet site of the World League provides game previews and recaps, player profiles, statistics, and individual team information. In addition, the site will feature live video from FX's broadcast coverage of one game each week during the 10-week regular season as well as live audio play-by-play from all 30 regular-season games.

NFL PLAYER SITES

Following are addresses for some current and former NFL players who have their own Web sites:

Darren Bennett, Chargers (www.nflaussie.com)
Doug Brien, Saints (www.kicking.com)
Toi Cook, Panthers (www.bltpro.com/cookbook/)
Jim Flanigan, Bears (www.jimflanigan.com)
Jim Kelly, Bills (www.jimkelly.com)
Jerry Rice, 49ers (www.sportsline.com/u/jrice/)
Reggie Rivers, Broncos (http://www.reggierivers.com)
Junior Seau, Chargers (www.juniorseau.org/)
Fran Tarkenton, Vikings-Giants (www.tarkenton.com)
Mike Utley, Lions (www.imageone.com/mikeutley/)

OFFICIAL NFL TEAM SITES

In addition to a dedicated area on NFL.COM, several teams have created their own Web sites, which have separate URLs, and are hot linked from NFL.COM.

Atlanta Falcons (www.atlantafalcons.com)
Buffalo Bills (www.buffalobills.com)
Cleveland Browns (www.clevelandbrowns.com)
Dallas Cowboys (www.dallascowboys.com)
Denver Broncos (www.denverbroncos.com)
Detroit Lions (www.detroitlions.com)
Jacksonville Jaguars (www.jaguarsnfl.com)
Kansas City Chiefs (www.kcchiefs.com)
Miami Dolphins (www.pwr.com/dolphins)
New England Patriots (www.patriots.com)
Oakland Raiders (www.raiders.com)
Philadelphia Eagles (www.eaglesnet.com)
St. Louis Rams (www.stlouisrams.com)
San Francisco 49ers (www.sf49ers.com)

At the conclusion of the 1997 NFL regular season, it will be possible to determine the 1998 opponents of the 30 teams.

Each 1997 team schedule is based on a "common-opponent" formula initiated for the 1978 season and most recently modified in 1995. Under the common-opponent format, all teams in a division play at least 11 of their 16 games the following season against common opponents. It is not a position scheduling format in which the strong play the strong and the weak play the weak.

In creating a schedule, the NFL seeks an easily understood and balanced formula that provides both competitive equality and a variety of opponents. Under the rotation scheduling system in effect from 1970-77, non-division opponents were determined by a pre-set formula. This often resulted in competitive imbalances.

With common opponents as the basis for scheduling, a more competitive and equitable method of determining division champions and postseason playoff representatives has developed. Teams battling for a division title are playing more than two-thirds of their games against common opponents.

In 1987, NFL owners passed a bylaw proposal designed to modify the common-opponent scheduling format and create greater equity. And in 1995, with the addition of two expansion teams, the 1987 changes were modified to include fifth-place teams in the common-opponent scheduling format for each division. The following chart shows a history of the pairings in non-division games within the conference since the change to a common-opponent format in 1978:

Prior Year's Finish in Division	Current Pairings in Non-Division Games Within Conference	Previous Pairings 1987-94	Previous Pairings 1978-86
1	1-1-2-3	1-1-2-3	1-1-4-4
2	1-2-2-4	1-2-2-4	2-2-3-3
3	1-3-3-5	1-3-3-4	2-2-3-3
4	2-4-4-5	2-3-4-4	1-1-4-4
5	3-4-5-5		

Under the common-opponent format, schedules of all NFL teams are figured according to the following formula. (The reference point for the figuring is the team's final division standing. Ties in divisions are broken according to the tie-breaking procedures outlined on page 16.)

1. Home-and-away round-robin **within the division** (8 games).
2. In the **interconference games,** each team plays four teams in a division of the other conference (4 games). In 1998, the AFC East will play the NFC West, the AFC Central will play the NFC Central, and the AFC West will play the NFC East (see chart on following page).

   Individual interconference matchups for the 1998 season are listed since they reflect a rotation of interconference games put in place prior to the 1995 seaon. This rotation will result in each team playing all teams in the opposing conference four times over 15 seasons (twice at home and twice away), barring future expansion.
3. **Within the conference,** the first-place team plays the first-place teams in the other divisions plus a second- and third-place team in the conference. The second-place team plays the second-place teams in the other divisions plus a first- and fourth-place team in the conference. The third-place team plays the third-place teams in the other divisions plus a first- and fifth-place team in the conference. The fourth-place team plays the fourth-place teams in the other divisions plus a second- and fifth-place team in the conference. The fifth-place team plays the fifth-place teams in the other divisions plus a third- and fourth-place team in the conference (4 games, see chart).

This completes the 16-game schedule.

The 1998 Opponent Breakdown chart on the following page does not include the round-robin games within the division. Those are automatically scheduled on a home-and-away basis.

NOTES

1997 NFL Standings

AFC	NFC
EAST AE	**EAST NE**
1	1
2	2
3	3
4	4
5	5
CENTRAL AC	**CENTRAL NC**
1	1
2	2
3	3
4	4
5	5
WEST AW	**WEST NW**
1	1
2	2
3	3
4	4
5	5

A Team's 1998 Schedule

Team Name _____

OPPONENTS

1 _____
2 _____
3 _____
4 _____
5 _____
6 _____
7 _____
8 _____
9 _____
10 _____
11 _____
12 _____
13 _____
14 _____
15 _____
16 _____

1998 Non-Divisional Opponent Breakdown
INTRACONFERENCE GAMES

American Football Conference

AFC East Home	Away	AFC Central Home	Away	AFC West Home	Away
AE1 AW1	AC1	**AC1** AE1	AW1	**AW1** AC1	AE1
AC3	AW2	AW3	AE2	AE3	AC2
AE2 AW2	AC2	**AC2** AE2	AW2	**AW2** AC2	AE2
AC1	AW4	AW1	AE4	AE1	AC4
AE3 AW3	AC3	**AC3** AE3	AW3	**AW3** AC3	AE3
AC5	AW1	AW5	AE1	AE5	AC1
AE4 AW4	AC4	**AC4** AE4	AW4	**AW4** AC4	AE4
AC2	AW5	AW2	AE5	AE2	AC5
AE5 AW5	AC5	**AC5** AE5	AW5	**AW5** AC5	AE5
AC4	AW3	AW4	AE3	AE4	AC3

National Football Conference

NFC East Home	Away	NFC Central Home	Away	NFC West Home	Away
NE1 NC1	NW1	**NC1** NW1	NE1	**NW1** NE1	NC1
NW3	NC2	NE3	NW2	NC3	NE2
NE2 NC2	NW2	**NC2** NW2	NE2	**NW2** NE2	NC2
NW1	NC4	NE1	NW4	NC1	NE4
NE3 NC3	NW3	**NC3** NW3	NE3	**NW3** NE3	NC3
NW5	NC1	NE5	NW1	NC5	NE1
NE4 NC4	NW4	**NC4** NW4	NE4	**NW4** NE4	NC4
NW2	NC5	NE2	NW5	NC2	NE5
NE5 NC5	NW5	**NC5** NW5	NE5	**NW5** NE5	NC5
NW4	NC3	NE4	NW3	NC4	NE3

INTRACONFERENCE GAMES

Team	Home	Away	Team	Home	Away	Team	Home	Away	Team	Home	Away	Team	Home	Away	Team	Home	Away
BUF	STL	CAR	**BAL**	DET	CHI	**DEN**	DAL	NYG	**ARZ**	OAK	KC	**CHI**	BAL	HOU	**ATL**	IND	NE
	SF	NO		MIN	GB		PHI	WAS		SD	SEA		JAX	PIT		MIA	NYJ
IND	CAR	ATL	**CIN**	GB	DET	**KC**	ARZ	NYG	**DAL**	OAK	DEN	**DET**	CIN	BAL	**CAR**	BUF	IND
	NO	SF		TB	MIN		DAL	PHI		SEA	KC		PIT	JAX		MIA	NYJ
MIA	NO	ATL	**HOU**	CHI	GB	**OAK**	NYG	ARZ	**NYG**	DEN	OAK	**GB**	BAL	CIN	**NO**	BUF	IND
	STL	CAR		MIN	TB		WAS	DAL		KC	SD		HOU	PIT		NE	MIA
NE	ATL	NO	**JAX**	DET	CHI	**SD**	NYG	ARZ	**PHI**	KC	DEN	**MIN**	CIN	BAL	**STL**	NE	BUF
	SF	STL		TB	MIN		PHI	WAS		SEA	SD		JAX	HOU		NYJ	MIA
NYJ	ATL	STL	**PIT**	CHI	DET	**SEA**	ARZ	DAL	**WAS**	DEN	OAK	**TB**	HOU	CIN	**SF**	IND	BUF
	CAR	SF		GB	TB		WAS	PHI		SD	SEA		PIT	JAX		NYJ	NE

The following procedures will be used to break standings ties for postseason playoffs and to determine regular-season schedules. NOTE: Tie games count as one-half win and one-half loss for both clubs.

TO BREAK A TIE WITHIN A DIVISION

If, at the end of the regular season, two or more clubs in the same division finish with identical won-lost-tied percentages, the following steps will be taken until a champion is determined.

TWO CLUBS

1. Head-to-head (best won-lost-tied percentage in games between the clubs).
2. Best won-lost-tied percentage in games played within the division.
3. Best won-lost-tied percentage in games played within the conference.
4. Best won-lost-tied percentage in common games, if applicable.
5. Best net points in division games.
6. Best net points in all games.
7. Strength of schedule.
8. Best net touchdowns in all games.
9. Coin toss.

THREE OR MORE CLUBS

(Note: If two clubs remain tied after third or other clubs are eliminated during any step, tie breaker reverts to step 1 of the two-club format).

1. Head-to-head (best won-lost-tied percentage in games among the clubs).
2. Best won-lost-tied percentage in games played within the division.
3. Best won-lost-tied percentage in games played within the conference.
4. Best won-lost-tied percentage in common games.
5. Best net points in division games.
6. Best net points in all games.
7. Strength of schedule.
8. Best net touchdowns in all games.
9. Coin toss.

TO BREAK A TIE FOR THE WILD-CARD TEAM

If it is necessary to break ties to determine the three Wild-Card clubs from each conference, the following steps will be taken.

1. If the tied clubs are from the same division, apply division tie breaker.
2. If the tied clubs are from different divisions, apply the following steps.

TWO CLUBS

1. Head-to-head, if applicable.
2. Best won-lost-tied percentage in games played within the conference.
3. Best won-lost-tied percentage in common games, minimum of four.
4. Best net points in conference games.
5. Best net points in all games.
6. Strength of schedule.
7. Best net touchdowns in all games.
8. Coin toss.

THREE OR MORE CLUBS

(Note: If two clubs remain tied after third or other clubs are eliminated, tie breaker reverts to step 1 of applicable two-club format.)

1. Apply division tie breaker to eliminate all but the highest ranked club in each division prior to proceeding to step 2. The original seeding within a division upon application of the division tie breaker remains the same for all subsequent applications of the procedure that are necessary to identify the three Wild-Card participants.

2. Head-to-head sweep. (Applicable only if one club has defeated each of the others or if one club has lost to each of the others).
3. Best won-lost-tied percentage in games played within the conference.
4. Best won-lost-tied percentage in common games, minimum of four.
5. Best net points in conference games.
6. Best net points in all games.
7. Strength of schedule.
8. Best net touchdowns in all games.
9. Coin toss.

When the first Wild-Card team has been identified, the procedure is repeated to name the second Wild-Card, i.e., eliminate all but the highest-ranked club in each division prior to proceeding to step 2, and repeated a third time, if necessary, to identify the third Wild Card. In situations where three or more teams from the same division are involved in the procedure, the original seeding of the teams remains the same for subsequent applications of the tie breaker if the top-ranked team in that division qualifies for a Wild-Card berth.

OTHER TIE-BREAKING PROCEDURES

1. Only one club advances to the playoffs in any tie-breaking step. Remaining tied clubs revert to the first step of the applicable division or Wild-Card tie breakers. As an example, if two clubs remain tied in any tie-breaker step after all other clubs have been eliminated, the procedure reverts to step one of the two-club format to determine the winner. When one club wins the tie breaker, all other clubs revert to step 1 of the applicable two-club or three-club format.
2. In comparing division and conference records or records against common opponents among tied teams, the best won-lost-tied percentage is the deciding factor since teams may have played an unequal number of games.
3. To determine home-field priority among division titlists, apply Wild-Card tie breakers.
4. To determine home-field priority for Wild-Card qualifiers, apply division tie breakers (if teams are from the same division) or Wild-Card tie breakers (if teams are from different divisions).

TIE-BREAKING PROCEDURE FOR SELECTION MEETING

If two or more clubs are tied in the selection order, the strength-of-schedule tie breaker is applied, subject to the following exceptions for playoff clubs:

1. The Super Bowl winner is last and the Super Bowl loser next-to-last.
2. Any non-Super Bowl playoff club involved in a tie shall be assigned priority within its segment below that of non-playoff clubs and in the order that the playoff clubs exited from the playoffs. Thus, within a tied segment a playoff club that loses in the Wild-Card game will have priority over a playoff club that loses in the Divisional playoff game, which in turn will have priority over a club that loses in the Conference Championship game. If two tied clubs exited the playoffs in the same round, the tie is broken by strength of schedule.

If any ties cannot be broken by strength of schedule, the divisional or conference tie breakers, whichever are applicable, are applied. Any ties that still exist are broken by a coin flip.

The NFL rates its passers for statistical purposes against a fixed performance standard based on statistical achievements of all qualified pro passers since 1960. The current system replaced one that rated passers in relation to their position in a total group based on various criteria. The current system, which was adopted in 1973, removes inequities that existed in the former method and, at the same time, provides a means of comparing passing performances from one season to the next.

It is important to remember that the system is used to rate **passers,** not **quarterbacks.** Statistics do not reflect leadership, play-calling, and other intangible factors that go into making a successful professional quarterback. Four categories are used as a basis for compiling a rating:

—Percentage of completions per attempt
—Average yards gained per attempt
—Percentage of touchdown passes per attempt
—Percentage of interceptions per attempt

The **average** standard, is 1.000. The bottom is .000. To earn a 2.000 rating, a passer must perform at exceptional levels, i.e., 70 percent in completions, 10 percent in touchdowns, 1.5 percent in interceptions, and 11 yards average gain per pass attempt. The **maximum** a passer can receive in any category is 2.375.

For example, to gain a 2.375 in completion percentage, a passer would have to complete 77.5 percent of his passes. The NFL record is 70.55 by Ken Anderson (Cincinnati, 1982). To earn a 2.375 in percentage of touchdowns, a passer would have to achieve a percentage of 11.9. The record is 13.9 by Sid Luckman (Chicago, 1943). To gain 2.375 in percentage of interceptions, a passer would have to go the entire season without an interception. The 2.375 figure in average yards is 12.50, compared with the NFL record of 11.17 by Tommy O'Connell (Cleveland, 1957).

In order to make the rating more understandable, the point rating is then converted into a scale of 100. In rare cases, where statistical performance has been superior, it is possible for a passer to surpass a 100 rating. For example, take Steve Young's record-setting season in 1994 when he completed 324 of 461 passes for 3,969 yards, 35 touchdowns, and 10 interceptions. The four calculations would be:

—**Percentage of Completions**—324 of 461 is 70.28 percent. Subtract 30 from the completion percentage (40.28) and multiply the result by 0.05. The result is a point rating of **2.014**.
Note: If the result is less than zero (Comp. Pct. less than 30.0), award zero points. If the results are greater than 2.375 (Comp. Pct. greater than 77.5), award 2.375.

—**Average Yards Gained Per Attempt**—3,969 yards divided by 461 attempts is 8.61. Subtract three yards from yards-per-attempt (5.61) and multiply the result by 0.25. The result is **1.403**.
Note: If the result is less than zero (yards per attempt less than 3.0), award zero points. If the result is greater than 2.375 (yards per attempt greater than 12.5), award 2.375 points.

—**Percentage of Touchdown Passes**—35 touchdowns in 461 attempts is 7.59 percent. Multiply the touchdown percentage by 0.2. The result is **1.518**.
Note: If the result is greater than 2.375 (touchdown percentage greater than 11.875), award 2.375.

—**Percentage of Interceptions**—10 interceptions in 461 attempts is 2.17 percent. Multiply the interception percentage by 0.25 (0.542) and subtract the number from 2.375. The result is **1.833**.
Note: If the result is less than zero (interception percentage greater than 9.5), award zero points.

The sum of the four steps is (2.014 + 1.403 + 1.518 + 1.833) **6.768**. The sum is then divided by six (1.128) and multiplied by 100. In this case, the result is **112.8**. This same formula can be used to determine a passer rating for any player who attempts at least one pass.

The following is a list of qualifying passers who had a single-season passer rating of 100 or higher:

Player, Team	Season	Rating	Att.	Comp.	Pct.	Yds.	Avg.	TD	TD Pct.	Int.	Int. Pct.
Steve Young, San Francisco	1994	112.8	461	324	70.2	3,969	8.61	35	7.6	10	2.2
Joe Montana, San Francisco	1989	112.4	386	271	70.2	3,521	9.12	26	6.7	8	2.1
Milt Plum, Cleveland	1960	110.4	250	151	60.4	2,297	9.19	21	8.4	5	2.0
Sammy Baugh, Washington	1945	109.9	182	128	70.3	1,669	9.17	11	6.0	4	2.2
Dan Marino, Miami	1984	108.9	564	362	64.2	5,084	9.01	48	8.5	17	3.0
Sid Luckman, Chicago Bears	1943	107.5	202	110	54.5	2,194	10.86	28	13.9	12	5.9
Steve Young, San Francisco	1992	107.0	402	268	66.7	3,465	8.62	25	6.2	7	1.7
Bart Starr, Green Bay	1966	105.0	251	156	62.2	2,257	8.99	14	5.6	3	1.2
Roger Staubach, Dallas	1971	104.8	211	126	59.7	1,882	8.92	15	7.1	4	1.9
Y.A. Tittle, N.Y. Giants	1963	104.8	367	221	60.2	3,145	8.57	36	9.8	14	3.8
Bart Starr, Green Bay	1968	104.3	171	109	63.7	1,617	9.46	15	8.8	8	4.7
Ken Stabler, Oakland	1976	103.4	291	194	66.7	2,737	9.41	27	9.3	17	5.8
Joe Montana, San Francisco	1984	102.9	432	279	64.6	3,630	8.40	28	6.5	10	2.3
Charlie Conerly, N.Y. Giants	1959	102.7	194	113	58.2	1,706	8.79	14	7.2	4	2.1
Bert Jones, Baltimore	1976	102.5	343	207	60.3	3,104	9.05	24	7.0	9	2.6
Joe Montana, San Francisco	1987	102.1	398	266	66.8	3,054	7.67	31	7.8	13	3.3
Steve Young, San Francisco	1991	101.8	279	180	64.5	2,517	9.02	17	6.1	8	2.9
Len Dawson, Kansas City	1966	101.7	284	159	56.0	2,527	8.90	26	9.2	10	3.5
Steve Young, San Francisco	1993	101.5	462	314	68.0	4,023	8.71	29	6.3	16	3.5
Jim Kelly, Buffalo	1990	101.2	346	219	63.3	2,829	8.18	24	6.9	9	2.6
Jim Harbaugh, Indianapolis	1995	100.7	314	200	63.7	2,575	8.20	17	5.4	5	1.6

TOP ACTIVE PASSERS

1,000 or more attempts

	Yrs.	Att.	Comp.	Pct. Comp.	Yards	Avg. Gain	TD	Pct. TD	Had Int.	Pct. Int.	Rating Pts.
1.Steve Young, S.F.	12	3192	2059	64.5	25,479	7.98	174	5.5	85	2.7	96.2
2.Brett Favre, G.B.	6	2693	1667	61.9	18,724	6.95	147	5.5	79	2.9	88.6
3.Dan Marino, Mia.	14	6904	4134	59.9	51,636	7.48	369	5.3	209	3.0	88.3
4.Troy Aikman, Dall.	8	3178	2000	62.9	22,733	7.15	110	3.5	98	3.1	83.0
5.Jeff Hostetler, Oak.	13	2194	1278	58.2	15,531	7.08	89	4.1	61	2.8	82.1
6.Dave Krieg, Tenn.	17	5288	3092	58.5	37,946	7.18	261	4.9	199	3.8	81.5
7.Warren Moon, Sea.	13	6000	3514	58.6	43,787	7.30	254	4.2	208	3.5	81.0
8.Neil O'Donnell, NYJ	7	2059	1179	57.3	14,014	6.81	72	3.5	46	2.2	80.5
9.Scott Mitchell, Det.	7	1507	853	56.6	10,516	6.98	71	4.7	49	3.3	80.5
10.Boomer Esiason, Cin.	13	5019	2851	56.8	36,442	7.26	234	4.7	182	3.6	80.1
11.Jeff Blake, Cin.	5	1431	794	55.5	9,640	6.74	66	4.6	41	2.9	79.8
12.Mark Rypien, St.L.	9	2565	1442	56.2	18,146	7.07	115	4.5	86	3.4	79.4
13.Erik Kramer, Chi.	8	1431	813	56.8	9,715	6.79	67	4.7	48	3.4	79.3
14.Jim Everett, S.D.	11	4848	2805	57.9	34,380	7.09	202	4.2	171	3.5	79.0
15.Randall Cunningham, Minn.	11	3362	1874	55.7	22,877	6.80	150	4.5	105	3.1	78.7
16.John Elway, Den.	14	6392	3633	56.8	45,034	7.05	251	3.9	205	3.2	78.5
17.Jim Harbaugh, Ind.	10	2680	1580	59.0	18,212	6.80	89	3.3	78	2.9	78.5
18.Bobby Hebert, *	11	3121	1839	58.9	21,683	6.95	135	4.3	124	4.0	78.0
19.Jeff George, Oak.	7	2712	1588	58.6	18,126	6.68	91	3.4	78	2.9	77.9
20.Stan Humphries, S.D.	7	2291	1310	57.2	15,703	6.85	84	3.7	78	3.4	76.3
21.Steve Bono, K.C.	11	1554	860	55.3	9,603	6.18	57	3.7	38	2.4	76.0
22.Wade Wilson, Dall.	16	2319	1327	57.2	16,600	7.16	92	4.0	98	4.2	75.2
23.Chris Chandler, Atl.	9	1918	1102	57.5	12,680	6.61	74	3.9	71	3.7	74.9
24.Craig Erickson, Mia.	5	1064	578	54.3	7,460	7.01	41	3.9	37	3.5	74.9
25.Steve Beuerlein, Car.	8	1548	821	53.0	10,921	7.05	61	3.9	54	3.5	74.3
26.John Friesz, Sea.	6	1258	690	54.8	8,086	6.43	43	3.4	36	2.9	74.0
27.Rich Gannon, K.C.	8	1229	696	56.6	7,709	6.27	49	4.0	44	3.6	73.8
28.Don Majkowski, *	10	1905	1056	55.4	12,700	6.67	66	3.5	67	3.5	72.9
29.Rodney Peete, Phil.	8	1690	969	57.3	11,952	7.07	53	3.1	69	4.1	72.8
30.Vinny Testaverde, Balt.	10	3707	2029	54.7	26,252	7.08	157	4.2	168	4.5	72.4

TOP ACTIVE SCORERS

	Yrs.	TD	FG	PAT	TP
1.Nick Lowery, *	18	0	383	562	1711
2.Gary Anderson, *	15	0	356	488	1556
3.Morten Andersen, Atl.	15	0	355	472	1537
4.Norm Johnson, Pitt.	15	0	300	552	1452
5.Kevin Butler, Ariz.	12	0	257	404	1175
6.Al Del Greco, Tenn.	13	0	236	403	1111
7.Jerry Rice, S.F.	12	165	0	4	994
8.Chip Lohmiller, *	9	0	204	301	913
9.Pete Stoyanovich, K.C.	8	0	193	280	859
10.Jeff Jaeger, Chi.	9	0	185	267	822
11.Chris Jacke, *	8	0	173	301	820
12.Marcus Allen, K.C.	15	134	0	2	806
13.Greg Davis, Minn.	10	0	181	228	771
14.John Carney, S.D.	9	0	181	226	769
15.Steve Christie, Buff.	7	0	164	232	724
16.Emmit Smith, Dall.	7	115	0	0	690
17.John Kasay, Car.	6	0	145	156	591
18.Matt Stover, Balt.	6	0	127	190	571
19.Barry Sanders, Det.	8	91	0	0	546
20.Jason Hanson, Det.	5	0	113	181	520
21.Thurman Thomas, Buff.	9	82	0	0	492
Herschel Walker, Dall.	11	82	0	0	492
23.Jason Elam, Den.	4	0	108	155	479
24.Cris Carter, Minn.	10	77	0	4	466
25.Andre Reed, Buff.	12	76	0	0	456
26.Irving Fryar, Phil.	13	73	0	4	442
27.Earnest Byner, Balt.	13	72	0	0	432
28.Doug Pelfrey, Cin.	4	0	104	112	424
29.Andre Rison, *	8	66	0	2	398
30.Henry Ellard, Wash.	14	65	0	0	390

TOP ACTIVE INTERCEPTORS

	Yrs.	No.	Yards	TD
1.Eugene Robinson, G.B.	12	48	693	0
2.Darrell Green, Wash.	14	43	434	5
3.Albert Lewis, Oak.	14	40	329	0
4.Rod Woodson, *	10	38	779	5
5.Kevin Ross, K.C.	13	38	654	2
6.Eric Allen, N.O.	9	37	543	5
7.Eugene Daniel, *	13	35	423	3
8.Lionel Washington, *	14	35	374	3
9.Deion Sanders, Dall.	8	34	860	6
10.Terry McDaniel, Oak.	9	33	607	5
11.Aeneas Williams, Ariz.	6	32	436	4
12.Tim McKyer, *	11	32	235	2
13.Donnell Woolford, Pitt.	8	32	212	1
14.Tim McDonald, S.F.	10	31	566	4
15.Tyrone Braxton, Den.	10	31	432	3
16.Cris Dishman, Wash.	9	31	348	1
17.Mike Prior, G.B.	11	30	368	1
18.Louis Oliver, *	8	27	605	2
19.Brian Washington, K.C.	8	27	449	4
20.James Hasty, K.C.	9	27	340	2
21.LeRoy Butler, G.B.	7	26	501	1
22.Darren Perry, Pitt.	5	26	428	1
23.Mark Collins, *	11	26	343	2
24.Nate Odomes, *	8	26	224	1
25.Gene Atkins, *	10	25	348	0
26.Don Griffin, *	11	25	51	0
27.Seth Joyner, *	11	24	307	2
28.Greg Jackson, *	8	24	242	1
29.Ricky Reynolds, *	10	23	198	2
30.Darren Carrington, *	8	22	377	1
31.Brett Maxie, *	12	22	300	3
32.Eric Turner, Oak.	6	22	273	2

TOP ACTIVE RUSHERS

	Yrs.	Att.	Yards	TD
1. Marcus Allen, K.C.	15	2898	11738	112
2. Barry Sanders, Det.	8	2384	11725	84
3. Thurman Thomas, Det.	9	2566	10762	62
4. Emmitt Smith, Dall.	7	2334	10160	108
5. Herschel Walker, Dall.	11	1948	8205	61
6. Earnest Byner, Balt.	13	2011	7948	56
7. Rodney Hampton, NYG	7	1801	6816	48
8. Chris Warren, Sea.	7	1359	5859	44
9. Ricky Watters, Phil.	5	1343	5524	49
10. Terry Allen, Wash.	5	1326	5457	54
11. Jerome Bettis, Pitt.	4	1116	4522	24
12. Randall Cunningham, Minn.	11	677	4482	32
13. Harold Green, *	7	1095	4250	12
14. Craig Heyward, St.L.	9	991	4202	29
15. Leonard Russell, *	6	1164	3973	29
16. Reggie Cobb, *	7	1065	3743	25
17. Steve Young, S.F.	12	591	3529	34
18. Harvey Williams, Oak.	6	875	3386	15
19. Edgar Bennett, G.B.	5	936	3353	19
20. Erric Pegram, Pitt.	6	827	3303	11
21. Natrone Means, Jax.	4	841	3232	27
22. John Elway, Den.	14	687	3095	31
23. Keith Byars, N.E.	11	850	3051	23
24. Derrick Fenner, *	8	797	2972	32
25. Marshall Faulk, Ind.	3	801	2947	29
26. Errict Rhett, T.B.	3	792	2757	21
27. Ronnie Harmon, Tenn.	11	605	2738	10
28. Leroy Hoard, Minn.	7	675	2695	13
29. Terrell Davis, Den.	2	582	2655	20
30. Curtis Martin, N.E.	2	684	2639	28

TOP ACTIVE PASS RECEIVERS

	Yrs.	No.	Yards	TD
1.Jerry Rice, S.F.	12	1050	16377	154
2.Henry Ellard, Wash.	14	775	13177	61
3.Andre Reed, Buff.	12	766	10884	75
4.Cris Carter, Minn.	10	667	8367	76
5.Irving Fryar, Phil.	13	650	10111	69
6.Michael Irvin, Dall.	9	591	9500	52
7.Bill Brooks, *	11	583	8001	46
8.Marcus Allen, K.C.	15	576	5325	21
9.Andre Rison, *	8	569	7747	66
10.Ronnie Harmon, Tenn.	11	564	5879	24
11.Keith Byars, N.E.	11	564	5214	25
12.Webster Slaughter, NYJ	11	555	8018	44
13.Anthony Miller, Dall.	9	549	8503	59
14.Brian Blades, Sea.	9	536	7117	32
15.Haywood Jeffires, N.O.	10	535	6334	50
16.Mark Carrier, *	10	517	8026	44
17.Brett Perriman, *	9	500	6197	29
18.Herschel Walker, Dall.	11	498	4710	19
19.Tim Brown, Oak.	9	495	7180	55
20.Earnest Byner, Balt.	13	491	4477	15
21.Eric Metcalf, S.D.	8	455	4520	29
22.Rob Moore, Ariz.	7	427	6181	31
23.Herman Moore, Det	6	424	6191	44
24.Jay Novacek, Dall.	11	422	4630	30
25.Michael Haynes, *	9	416	6434	46
26.Larry Centers, Ariz.	7	412	3571	16
27.Thurman Thomas, Buff.	9	397	3876	20
28.Shannon Sharpe, Den.	7	393	4884	31
29.Brent Jones, S.F.	10	388	4812	31
30.Quinn Early, Buff.	9	375	5295	34

TOP ACTIVE PUNT RETURNERS
50 or more punt returns

	Yrs.	No.	Yards	Avg.	TD
1. Darrien Gordon, Den.	3	103	1407	13.7	3
2. Desmond Howard, Oak.	5	92	1230	13.4	4
3. Winslow Oliver, Car.	1	52	598	11.5	1
4. Henry Ellard, Wash.	14	135	1527	11.3	4
5. Darrell Green, Wash.	14	51	576	11.3	0
6. Brian Mitchell, Wash.	7	195	2196	11.3	6
7. Mel Gray, Tenn.	11	233	2592	11.1	3
8. Jeff Burris, Buff.	3	79	847	10.7	0
9. David Meggett, N.E.	8	299	3201	10.7	7
10. Eric Metcalf, S.D.	8	193	2020	10.5	6
11. Tim Brown, Oak.	9	301	3083	10.2	2
12. Joey Galloway, Sea.	2	51	518	10.2	2
13. Arthur Marshall, *	5	59	590	10.0	0
14. Irving Fryar, Phil.	13	206	2055	10.0	3
15. Glyn Milburn, Det.	4	146	1442	9.9	0
16. Dexter Carter, *	7	138	1358	9.8	2
17. Kelvin Martin, *	10	261	2567	9.8	3
18. Tamarick Vanover, K.C.	2	68	656	9.6	1
19. Corey Sawyer, Cin.	3	50	482	9.6	1
20. David Palmer, Minn.	3	78	751	9.6	2
21. Kevin Williams, Dall.	4	95	913	9.6	3
22. Todd Kinchen, Atl.	5	106	1009	9.5	2
23. Dale Carter, K.C.	5	83	787	9.5	2
24. Anthony Parker, St.L.	7	46	431	9.4	0
25. Ronnie Harris, Sea.	4	48	444	9.3	0
26. Rod Woodson, *	10	257	2362	9.2	2
27. Tyrone Hughes, Chi.	4	116	1060	9.1	2
28. Don Griffin, Phil.	11	74	667	9.0	1
29. Deion Sanders, Dall.	8	95	847	8.9	2
30. Robert Brooks, G.B.	5	67	589	8.8	1

TOP ACTIVE KICKOFF RETURNERS
50 or more kickoff returns

	Yrs.	No.	Yards	Avg.	TD
1. Tamarick Vanover, K.C.	2	76	1949	25.6	3
2. Tim Brown, Oak.	9	48	1228	25.6	1
3. Anthony Miller, Den.	9	50	1269	25.4	2
4. Tyrone Hughes, Chi.	4	229	5717	25.0	3
5. Mel Gray, Tenn.	11	412	10057	24.4	6
6. Derrick Witherspoon, Phil.	2	71	1730	24.4	3
7. Robert Brooks, G.B.	5	51	1237	24.3	2
8. Glyn Milburn, Det.	4	160	3877	24.2	0
9. Aaron Bailey, Ind.	3	64	1536	24.0	2
10. Napoleon Kaufman, Oak.	2	47	1120	23.8	1
11. Tony Smith, *	3	61	1453	23.8	1
12. Herschel Walker, Dall.	11	165	3917	23.7	2
13. Kevin Williams, Dall.	4	144	3416	23.7	1
14. Andre Coleman, S.D.	3	166	3914	23.6	4
15. Michael Bates, Car.	4	98	2285	23.3	1
16. Eric Moulds, Buff.	1	52	1205	23.2	1
17. Ernie Mills, Car.	6	76	1753	23.1	0
18. Brian Mitchell, Wash.	7	272	6262	23.0	0
19. Deion Sanders, Dall.	8	148	3403	23.0	3
20. Irving Spikes, Mia.	3	65	1493	23.0	0
21. Steve Broussard, Sea.	7	96	2203	22.9	0
22. O.J. McDuffie, Mia.	4	91	2086	22.9	0
23. Vaughn Hebron, Den.	3	69	1577	22.9	0
24. Corey Harris, Sea.	5	104	2354	22.6	0
25. J.T. Thomas, St.L.	2	62	1395	22.5	0
26. Randy Baldwin, *	6	117	2607	22.3	1
27. Qadry Ismail, G.B.	4	147	3273	22.3	0
28. Rod Woodson, *	10	220	4894	22.2	2
29. David Dunn, Cin.	2	85	1874	22.0	1
30. Ryan Terry, *	2	41	892	21.8	0

TOP ACTIVE QUARTERBACK SACKERS (since 1982)

	Yrs.	No.
1. Reggie White, G.B.	12	165.0
2. Bruce Smith, Buff.	12	140.0
3. Richard Dent, *	14	133.0
4. Kevin Greene, Car.	12	122.5
5. Chris Doleman, S.F.	12	115.5
6. Leslie O'Neal, St.L.	10	112.5
7. Pat Swilling, Oak.	11	105.5
8. Jim Jeffcoat, Buff.	14	102.0
9. Clyde Simmons, Jax.	11	100.5
10. Derrick Thomas, K.C.	8	98.0
11. Charles Haley, Dall.	11	97.5
12. William Fuller, S.D.	11	94.5
13. Neil Smith, Den.	9	85.5
14. Ken Harvey, Wash.	9	77.5
15. Henry Thomas, Det.	10	72.5
16. John Randle, Minn.	7	70.0
17. Freddie Joe Nunn, *	12	67.5
18. Wayne Martin, N.O.	8	64.5
19. Jumpy Geathers, Den.	13	62.0
20. Tony Bennett, Ind.	7	61.5
21. Michael Dean Perry, Den.	9	61.0
22. Jeff Cross, *	8	59.5
23. Trace Armstrong, Mia.	8	58.5
24. Bryce Paup, Buff.	7	56.0
25. Cornelius Bennett, Atl.	10	55.5
26. Tony Tolbert, Dall.	8	54.0
27. Duane Bickett, *	12	53.0
28. Anthony Smith, Oak.	6	51.0
29. Danny Stubbs, Mia.	8	50.5
30. Greg Lloyd, Pitt.	9	50.0

TOP ACTIVE PUNTERS
50 or more punts

	Yrs.	No.	Avg.	LG
1. Darren Bennett, S.D.	2	159	45.2	66
2. Matt Turk, Wash.	2	149	43.8	63
3. Greg Montgomery, Balt.	8	441	43.7	77
4. Sean Landeta, St.L.	12	807	43.7	71
5. Reggie Roby, Tenn.	14	859	43.5	77
6. Rick Tuten, Sea.	8	566	43.5	73
7. Rohn Stark, Car.	15	1121	43.4	72
8. Tom Rouen, Den.	4	260	43.0	62
9. Tom Hutton, Phil.	2	158	43.0	63
10. Rich Camarillo, Oak.	16	1027	42.7	76
11. Tommy Barnhardt, T.B.	10	619	42.7	65
12. Tommy Thompson, S.F.	2	130	42.5	65
13. Lee Johnson, Cin.	12	834	42.4	70
14. Tom Tupa, N.E.	8	214	42.3	65
15. Brian Hansen, NYJ	12	946	42.3	73
16. Mike Horan, NYG	12	860	42.2	75
17. Bryan Barker, Jax.	7	489	42.1	67
18. Craig Hentrich, G.B.	3	214	41.9	70
19. Todd Sauerbrun, Chi.	2	133	41.9	72
20. John Jett, Det.	4	253	41.9	60
21. Mark Royals, N.O.	8	552	41.5	69
22. John Kidd, Mia	13	864	41.4	67
23. Chris Gardocki, Ind.	6	366	41.3	69
24. Jeff Gossett, *	15	982	41.3	65
25. Louie Aguiar, K.C.	5	474	41.3	71
26. Jeff Feagles, Ariz.	9	724	41.2	77
27. Josh Miller, Pitt.	1	55	41.0	61
28. Chris Mohr, Buff.	7	526	40.7	80
29. Klaus Wilmsmeyer, *	5	305	40.6	63
30. Mitch Berger, Minn.	2	113	40.4	63

Free agent; subject to developments.

COACHES RECORDS

ACTIVE COACHES' CAREER RECORDS (Order Based on Career Victories)

Start of 1997 Season

Coach	Team(s)	Yrs.	Regular Season Won	Lost	Tied	Pct.	Postseason Won	Lost	Tied	Pct.	Career Won	Lost	Tied	Pct.
Dan Reeves	Denver Broncos, New York Giants, Atlanta Falcons	16	141	106	1	.571	8	7	0	.533	149	113	1	.568
Marv Levy	Kansas City Chiefs, Buffalo Bills	16	137	102	0	.573	11	8	0	.579	148	110	0	.574
Marty Schottenheimer	Cleveland Browns, Kansas City Chiefs	13	125	73	1	.631	5	10	0	.333	130	83	1	.610
Bill Parcells	New York Giants, New England Patriots, New York Jets	12	109	81	1	.573	10	5	0	.667	119	86	1	.580
Mike Ditka	Chicago Bears, New Orleans Saints	11	106	62	0	.631	6	6	0	.500	112	68	0	.622
Ted Marchibroda	Baltimore-Indianapolis Colts, Baltimore Ravens	10	75	79	0	.487	2	4	0	.333	77	83	0	.481
Jimmy Johnson	Dallas Cowboys, Miami Dolphins	6	52	44	0	.542	7	1	0	.875	59	45	0	.567
Mike Holmgren	Green Bay Packers	5	51	29	0	.638	7	3	0	.700	58	32	0	.644
Bill Cowher	Pittsburgh Steelers	5	53	27	0	.663	4	5	0	.444	57	32	0	.640
Dick Vermeil	Philadelphia Eagles, St. Louis Rams	7	54	47	0	.535	3	4	0	.429	57	51	0	.528
Bobby Ross	San Diego Chargers, Detroit Lions	5	47	33	0	.588	3	3	0	.500	50	36	0	.581
Dennis Green	Minnesota Vikings	5	47	33	0	.588	0	4	0	.000	47	37	0	.560
Barry Switzer	Dallas Cowboys	3	34	14	0	.708	5	2	0	.714	39	16	0	.709
Bruce Coslet	New York Jets, Cincinnati Bengals	5	33	40	0	.452	0	1	0	.000	33	41	0	.446
Lindy Infante	Green Bay Packers, Indianapolis Colts	5	33	47	0	.413	0	1	0	.000	33	48	0	.407
Dave Wannstedt	Chicago Bears	4	32	32	0	.500	1	1	0	.500	33	33	0	.500
Mike Shanahan	Los Angeles Raiders, Denver Broncos	4	29	23	0	.558	0	1	0	.000	29	24	0	.547
Ray Rhodes	Philadelphia Eagles	2	20	12	0	.625	1	2	0	.333	21	14	0	.600
Joe Bugel	Arizona Cardinals, Oakland Raiders	4	20	44	0	.313	0	0	0	.000	20	44	0	.313
Dom Capers	Carolina Panthers	2	19	13	0	.594	1	1	0	.500	20	14	0	.588
Norv Turner	Washington Redskins	3	18	30	0	.375	0	0	0	.000	18	30	0	.375
Jeff Fisher	Tennessee Oilers	3	16	22	0	.421	0	0	0	.000	16	22	0	.421
Tom Coughlin	Jacksonville Jaguars	2	13	19	0	.406	2	1	0	.667	15	20	0	.429
Dennis Erickson	Seattle Seahawks	2	15	17	0	.469	0	0	0	.000	15	17	0	.469
Vince Tobin	Arizona Cardinals	1	7	9	0	.438	0	0	0	.000	7	9	0	.438
Pete Carroll	New York Jets, New England Patriots	1	6	10	0	.375	0	0	0	.000	6	10	0	.375
Tony Dungy	Tampa Bay Buccaneers	1	6	10	0	.375	0	0	0	.000	6	10	0	.375
Jim Fassel	New York Giants	0	0	0	0	.000	0	0	0	.000	0	0	0	.000
Kevin Gilbride	San Diego Chargers	0	0	0	0	.000	0	0	0	.000	0	0	0	.000
Steve Mariucci	San Francisco 49ers	0	0	0	0	.000	0	0	0	.000	0	0	0	.000

COACHES WITH 100 CAREER VICTORIES (Order Based on Career Victories)

Start of 1997 Season

Coach	Team(s)	Yrs.	Regular Season Won	Lost	Tied	Pct.	Postseason Won	Lost	Tied	Pct.	Career Won	Lost	Tied	Pct.
Don Shula	Baltimore Colts, Miami Dolphins	33	328	156	6	.676	19	17	0	.528	347	173	6	.665
George Halas	Chicago Bears	40	318	148	31	.671	6	3	0	.667	324	151	31	.671
Tom Landry	Dallas Cowboys	29	250	162	6	.605	20	16	0	.556	270	178	6	.601
Earl (Curly) Lambeau	Green Bay Packers, Chicago Cardinals, Washington Redskins	33	226	132	22	.624	3	2	0	.600	229	134	22	.623
Chuck Noll	Pittsburgh Steelers	23	193	148	1	.566	16	8	0	.667	209	156	1	.572
Chuck Knox	Los Angeles Rams, Buffalo Bills, Seattle Seahawks	22	186	147	1	.558	7	11	0	.389	193	158	1	.550
Paul Brown	Cleveland Browns, Cincinnati Bengals	21	166	100	6	.621	4	8	0	.333	170	108	6	.609
Bud Grant	Minnesota Vikings	18	158	96	5	.620	10	12	0	.455	168	108	5	.607
Steve Owen	New York Giants	23	151	100	17	.595	2	8	0	.200	153	108	17	.581
Dan Reeves	Denver Broncos, New York Giants, Atlanta Falcons	16	141	106	1	.571	8	7	0	.533	149	113	1	.568
Marv Levy	Kansas City Chiefs, Buffalo Bills	16	137	102	0	.573	11	8	0	.579	148	110	0	.574
Joe Gibbs	Washington Redskins	12	124	60	0	.674	16	5	0	.762	140	65	0	.683
Hank Stram	Kansas City Chiefs, New Orleans Saints	17	131	97	10	.571	5	3	0	.625	136	100	10	.573
Weeb Ewbank	Baltimore Colts, New York Jets	20	130	129	7	.502	4	1	0	.800	134	130	7	.507
Marty Schottenheimer	Cleveland Browns, Kansas City Chiefs	13	125	73	1	.631	5	10	0	.333	130	83	1	.610
Sid Gillman	Los Angeles Rams, Los Angeles-San Diego Chargers, Houston Oilers	18	122	99	7	.550	1	5	0	.167	123	104	7	.541
Bill Parcells	New York Giants, New England Patriots, New York Jets	12	109	81	1	.573	10	5	0	.667	119	86	1	.580
George Allen	Los Angeles Rams, Washington Redskins	12	116	47	5	.705	2	7	0	.222	118	54	5	.681
Don Coryell	St. Louis Cardinals, San Diego Chargers	14	111	83	1	.572	3	6	0	.333	114	89	1	.561
Mike Ditka	Chicago Bears, New Orleans Saints	11	106	62	0	.631	6	6	0	.500	112	68	0	.622
John Madden	Oakland Raiders	10	103	32	7	.750	9	7	0	.563	112	39	7	.731
George Seifert	San Francisco 49ers	8	98	30	0	.766	10	5	0	.667	108	35	0	.755
Ray (Buddy) Parker	Chicago Cardinals, Detroit Lions, Pittsburgh Steelers	15	104	75	9	.577	3	1	0	.750	107	76	9	.581
Tom Flores	Oakland-Los Angeles Raiders, Seattle Seahawks	12	97	87	0	.527	8	3	0	.727	105	90	0	.538
Vince Lombardi	Green Bay Packers, Washington Redskins	10	96	34	6	.728	9	1	0	.900	105	35	6	.740
Bill Walsh	San Francisco 49ers	10	92	59	1	.609	10	4	0	.714	102	63	1	.617

Active coaches in bold.

The **Chicago Bears** need two victories to become the first franchise in NFL history to record 600 regular-season victories.

The **Miami Dolphins** need three victories and the **Kansas City Chiefs** need six victories to become the second and third teams from the AFL to record 300 total victories.

Dan Reeves, Atlanta, and **Marv Levy**, Buffalo, can become the 10th and 11th head coaches to record 150 career victories. In 16 seasons each, Reeves has 149 wins, while Levy has 148.

Dan Marino, Miami, needs 31 touchdown passes to become the first player in NFL history to record 400. Marino has recorded 369 TD passes in 14 seasons.

John Elway, Denver, needs 54 completions, 76 attempts, and 1,970 yards passing to move into second place on the all-time list, surpassing Fran Tarkenton in all three categories.

Elway can become the third player (Dan Marino and Fran Tarkenton) in NFL history to reach 50,000 yards of total offense. Elway has recorded 48,176 yards of total offense in 14 seasons.

Elway needs 23 touchdown passes to move into fourth place on the all-time list, surpassing Warren Moon, Dan Fouts, Sonny Jurgensen, Dave Krieg, and Joe Montana. Elway has thrown 251 TD passes. (See Moon and Krieg note.)

Dave Krieg, Tennessee, needs 13 touchdown passes to move into fourth place on the all-time list, surpassing Joe Montana. Krieg has thrown 261 TD passes in 17 seasons. (See Elway and Moon note.)

Warren Moon, Seattle, needs 20 touchdown passes to move into fourth place on the all-time list, surpassing Dan Fouts, Sonny Jurgensen, Dave Krieg, and Joe Montana. Moon has thrown 254 TD passes in 13 seasons. (See Elway and Krieg note.)

Jim Everett, San Diego, needs 620 yards passing to become the 11th player in NFL history to reach 35,000 yards. Everett has recorded 34,380 yards passing in 11 seasons.

Brett Favre, Green Bay, needs six touchdown passes to become the Packers' all-time leader, surpassing Bart Starr (152). Favre has thrown 147 touchdown passes in five seasons with the Packers.

Jerry Rice, San Francisco, needs a reception in each of his first nine games to become the NFL's all-time leader in consecutive games with a reception, surpassing Art Monk (183). Rice has recorded a reception in 175 consecutive games.

Rice needs six points to become the first non-kicker in NFL history to record 1,000. He has recorded 994 points in 12 seasons.

Rice and quarterback **Steve Young** need to connect for six touchdown passes to become the all-time leading QB-receiver duo, surpassing Dan Marino and Mark Clayton (79). Rice and Young have connected for 74 touchdowns.

Henry Ellard, Washington, needs 828 receiving yards to move into second place on the all-time list, surpassing James Lofton (14,004). Ellard has recorded 13,177 receiving yards in 14 seasons.

Ellard can also become the fourth player in NFL history to record 800 receptions. He has 775 receptions. (See Reed note.)

Andre Reed, Buffalo, can become the fourth player in NFL history to record 800 receptions. Reed has recorded 766 receptions in 12 seasons. (See Ellard note.)

Reed can also become the eighth player in league history to record 11,000 career receiving yards. He has 10,884 yards.

Isaac Bruce, St. Louis, needs 85 receptions to become the NFL's all-time reception leader after the first four seasons of a career, surpassing Andre Rison (308). Bruce has recorded 224 receptions in three seasons.

Michael Irvin, Dallas, needs 500 receiving yards to become the 14th player in NFL history to record 10,000 yards. Irvin has 9,500 receiving yards in nine seasons.

Anthony Miller, Dallas, can become the 16th player in NFL history to record 600 career receptions. Miller has recorded 549 receptions in nine NFL seasons.

Cris Carter, Minnesota, needs 720 receiving yards to become the Vikings' all-time leader, surpassing Anthony Carter (7,636). Cris Carter has 6,917 receiving yards in seven seasons with the Vikings.

Marcus Allen, Kansas City, needs 1,002 rushing yards to move into third place all-time, surpassing Franco Harris (12,120), Jim Brown (12,312), and Tony Dorsett (12,739). Allen has recorded 11,738 yards in 15 NFL seasons. (See Sanders note.)

Allen needs 262 rushing yards to become the sixth player in league history to record 12,000 career rushing yards. (See Sanders note.)

Barry Sanders, Detroit, needs 1,015 rushing yards to move into third place all-time, surpassing Marcus Allen (11,738), Franco Harris (12,120), Jim Brown (12,312) and Tony Dorsett (12,739). Sanders has recorded 11,725 yards in eight NFL seasons. (See Allen note.)

Sanders needs 275 rushing yards to become the sixth player in league history to record 12,000 career rushing yards. (See Allen note.)

Sanders also can become the first player in NFL history to record nine-straight 1,000-yard rushing seasons. (See Thomas note.)

Thurman Thomas, Buffalo, can become the first player in NFL history to record nine-straight 1,000-yard rushing seasons. (See Sanders note.)

Thomas can become the first player to record 65 rushing touchdowns and 25 receiving touchdowns with an additional three rushing TDs and five receiving TDs.

Thomas needs 238 rushing yards to become the 10th player in league history to record 11,000 career rushing yards. (See E. Smith note.)

Emmitt Smith, Dallas, needs five rushing touchdowns to become the NFL's all-time leader, surpassing Marcus Allen (112). Smith has recorded 108 rushing touchdowns in seven seasons.

Smith needs 840 rushing yards to become the 10th player in NFL history to record 11,000 career rushing yards. (See Thomas note.)

Smith can also become the fourth player in NFL history to rush for seven-straight 1,000-yard seasons.

Chris Warren, Seattle, needs 847 rushing yards to become the Seahawks' all-time leader, surpassing Curt Warner (6,705). Warren has rushed for 5,859 yards in seven seasons with the Seahawks.

Bruce Smith, Buffalo, needs 10 sacks to become the first player in NFL history to record at least 10 sacks in each of 11 seasons. (See White note.)

Reggie White, Green Bay, can become the first player in NFL history to record 11 10-sack seasons. (See B. Smith note.)

Kevin Greene, Carolina, needs 10.5 sacks to become the league's all-time linebacker sack leader, surpassing Rickey Jackson (128.0) and Lawrence Taylor (132.5). Greene has recorded 122.5 sacks in 12 seasons.

Darrell Green, Washington, needs to play in 15 games to become the Redskins' all-time leader, surpassing Monte Coleman (216). He has played in 202 games in 14 seasons with the Redskins.

Eugene Daniel, Indianapolis, needs to play in 16 games to become the Colts' all-time leader, surpassing Johnny Unitas (213). He has played in 198 games in 13 seasons with the Colts.

Richmond Webb, Miami, needs to start 16 consecutive games to become the Dolphins' all-time leader, surpassing Jim Langer (109). Webb has started 94 consecutive games for Miami.

David Meggett, New England, needs 117 punt return yards to become the NFL's all-time leader, surpassing Billy (White Shoes) Johnson (3,317). Meggett has recorded 3,201 punt return yards in eight NFL seasons.

Morten Andersen, Atlanta, needs 29 field goals to move into first place on the all-time list, surpassing Gary Anderson (356), Jan Stenerud (373), and Nick Lowery (383). Andersen has recorded 355 field goals in 15 NFL seasons.

Andersen also needs 100 points to tie Nick Lowery for the most 100-point seasons with 11.

Chris Boniol, Philadelphia, needs five consecutive field goals to break Fuad Reveiz's NFL record of 31.

61st Annual NFL Draft, April 19-20, 1997
*Denotes Compensatory Selection

ARIZONA CARDINALS
1. Tom Knight—9, DB, Iowa
2. Jake Plummer—42, QB, Arizona State
3. Choice to Philadelphia
   Ty Howard—84, DB, Ohio State, from Philadelphia
4. Chris Dishman—106, G, Nebraska
5. Chad Carpenter—139, WR, Washington State
6. Rod Brown—175, RB, North Carolina State
   Tony McCombs—188, LB, Eastern Kentucky, from Philadelphia
7. Mark Smith—212, DE, Auburn

ATLANTA FALCONS
1. Choice to Seattle
   Michael Booker—11, DB, Nebraska, from Chicago through Seattle
2. Nathan Davis—32, DE, Indiana
   Byron Hanspard—41, RB, Texas Tech, from Seattle
3. Choice to Tampa Bay through Seattle
   O.J. Santiago—70, TE, Kent State, from Seattle
4. Choice to Tennessee
   Henri Crockett—100, LB, Florida State, from Baltimore through Seattle
5. Marcus Wimberly—133, DB, Miami
6. Choice to New Orleans through Tennessee
   Calvin Collins—180, C, Texas A&M, from Washington
7. Tony Graziani—204, QB, Oregon
   Chris Bayne—222, DB, Fresno State, from Washington

BALTIMORE RAVENS
1. Peter Boulware—4, DE, Florida State
2. Jamie Sharper—34, LB, Virginia
   Kim Herring—58, DB, Penn State, from Denver
3. Jay Graham—64, RB, Tennessee
4. Choice to Atlanta through Seattle
   Tyrus McCloud—118, LB, Louisville, from Dallas
5. Jeff Mitchell—134, C, Florida
6. Steve Lee—167, RB, Indiana
   *Cornell Brown—194, LB, Virginia Tech
7. Chris Ward—205, DE, Kentucky
   *Wally Richardson—234, QB, Penn State
   *Ralph Staten—236, DB, Alabama
   *Leland Taylor—238, DT, Louisville

BUFFALO BILLS
1. Antowain Smith—23, RB, Houston
2. Marcellus Wiley—52, DE, Columbia
3. Choice to Oakland
4. Jamie Nails—120, T, Florida A&M
5. Sean Woodson—153, DB, Jackson State
6. Marcus Spriggs—185, T, Houston
7. Pat Fitzgerald—226, TE, Texas

CAROLINA PANTHERS
1. Rae Carruth—27, WR, Colorado
2. Mike Minter—56, DB, Nebraska
3. Kinnon Tatum—87, LB, Notre Dame
4. Tarek Saleh—122, LB, Wisconsin
5. Choice to Miami through Oakland
6. Matt Finkes—189, LB, Ohio State
7. Kris Mangum—228, TE, Mississippi

CHICAGO BEARS
1. Choice to Atlanta through Seattle
2. John Allred—38, TE, Southern California, from St. Louis
   Choice to St. Louis
3. Bob Sapp—69, G, Washington
4. Darnell Autry—105, RB, Northwestern, from Seattle
   Marcus Robinson—108, WR, South Carolina
5. Van Hiles—141, DB, Kentucky
6. Choice to Miami through St. Louis
   *Shawn Swayda—196, DE, Arizona State
   *Richard Hogans—200, LB, Memphis
   *Ricky Parker—201, DB, San Diego State
7. Mike Miano—210, DT, Southwest Missouri State
   *Marvin Thomas—233, DE, Memphis

CINCINNATI BENGALS
1. Reinard Wilson—14, LB, Florida State
2. Corey Dillon—43, RB, Washington
3. Rod Payne—76, C, Michigan
4. Tremain Mack—111, DB, Miami
5. Andre Purvis—144, DT, North Carolina
6. Canute Curtis—176, LB, West Virginia
7. William Carr—217, DT, Michigan

DALLAS COWBOYS
1. David LaFleur—22, TE, Louisiana State, from Philadelphia
   Choice to Philadelphia
2. Choice to Detroit
3. Dexter Coakley—65, LB, Appalachian State, from Detroit
   Steve Scifres—83, T, Wyoming
   *Kenny Wheaton—94, DB, Oregon
4. Antonio Anderson—101, DT, Syracuse, from Detroit
   Choice to Baltimore
   *Macey Brooks—127, WR, James Madison
   *Nicky Sualua—129, RB, Ohio State
5. Choice to Philadelphia
6. Lee Vaughn—187, DB, Wyoming
7. Omar Stoutmire—224, DB, Fresno State

DENVER BRONCOS
1. Trevor Pryce—28, DT, Clemson
2. Choice to Baltimore
3. Dan Neil—67, G, Texas, from St. Louis through New York Jets
   Choice to New York Jets
4. Cory Gilliard—124, DB, Ball State
5. Choice to St. Louis
6. Choice to New York Jets
7. Choice to New York Jets

DETROIT LIONS
1. Bryant Westbrook—5, DB, Texas
2. Juan Roque—35, G, Arizona State
   Kevin Abrams—54, DB, Syracuse, from Dallas
3. Choice to Dallas
4. Choice to Dallas
   *Matt Russell—130, LB, Colorado
5. Pete Chryplewicz—135, TE, Notre Dame
   *Duane Ashman—161, DE, Virginia
6. Tony Ramirez—168, T, Northern Colorado
7. Terry Battle—206, RB, Arizona State
   *Marcus Harris—232, WR, Wyoming
   *Richard Jordan—239, LB, Missouri Southern

GREEN BAY PACKERS
1. Ross Verba—30, T, Iowa
2. Darren Sharper—60, DB, William & Mary
3. Brett Conway—90, K, Penn State
4. Jermaine Smith—126, DT, Georgia
5. Anthony Hicks—160, LB, Arkansas
6. Choice to Oakland
7. Chris Miller—213, WR, Southern California, from Oakland
   Jerald Sowell—231, RB, Tulane
   *Ronnie McAda—240, QB, Army

INDIANAPOLIS COLTS
1. Tarik Glenn—19, T, California
2. Adam Meadows—48, T, Georgia
3. Choice to San Francisco
   Bert Barry—86, LB, Notre Dame, from San Francisco
4. Delmonico Montgomery—117, DB, Houston
5. Nate Jacquet—150, WR, San Diego State
   Carl Powell—156, DE, Louisville, from San Francisco
6. Scott Von Der Ahe—182, LB, Arizona State
7. Clarence Thompson—219, DB, Knoxville

JACKSONVILLE JAGUARS
1. Renaldo Wynn—21, DT, Notre Dame
2. Mike Logan—50, DB, West Virginia
3. James Hamilton—79, LB, North Carolina
4. Seth Payne—114, DT, Cornell
5. Damon Jones—147, TE, Southern Illinois
6. Daimon Shelton—184, RB, Cal State-Sacramento
7. Jon Hesse—221, LB, Nebraska

KANSAS CITY CHIEFS
1. Tony Gonzalez—13, TE, California, from Tennessee
   Choice to Tennessee
2. Kevin Lockett—47, WR, Kansas State
3. Choice to Tennessee
4. Pat Barnes—110, QB, California, from Tennessee
   Choice to New Orleans through Tennessee
5. Choice to Miami
   *June Henley—163, RB, Kansas
6. Choice to Tennessee
   *Isaac Byrd—195, WR, Kansas
7. Nathan Park—214, T, Stanford, from Miami
   Choice to San Diego through Pittsburgh

MIAMI DOLPHINS
1. Yatil Green—15, WR, Miami
2. Sam Madison—44, DB, Louisville
3. Jason Taylor—73, DE, Akron
   *Derrick Rodgers—92, LB, Arizona
   *Ronnie Ward—93, LB, Kansas
   *Brent Smith—96, T, Mississippi State
4. Choice to St. Louis
   Jerome Daniels—121, T, Northeastern, from Pittsburgh through St. Louis
5. Choice to New York Jets
   Barron Tanner—149, DT, Oklahoma, from Kansas City
   Nicholas Lopez—157, DE, Texas Southern, from Carolina through Oakland
6. John Fiala—166, LB, Washington, from New Orleans through Oakland
   Brian Manning—170, WR, Stanford, from St. Louis
   Mike Crawford—173, LB, Nevada, from Chicago through St. Louis
   Ed Perry—177, TE, James Madison
7. Hudhaifa Ismaeli—203, DB, Northwestern, from New Orleans through Oakland
   Choice to Kansas City

MINNESOTA VIKINGS
1. Dwayne Rudd—20, LB, Alabama
2. Torrian Gray—49, DB, Virginia Tech
3. Stalin Colinet—78, DE, Boston College
4. Antonio Banks—113, DB, Virginia Tech
5. Tony Williams—151, DT, Memphis
6. Robert Tate—183, WR, Cincinnati
7. Artie Ulmer—220, LB, Valdosta State
   *Matthew Hatchette—235, WR, Langston

NEW ENGLAND PATRIOTS
1. Chris Canty—29, DB, Kansas State
2. Brandon Mitchell—59, DT, Texas A&M
3. Sedrick Shaw—61, RB, Iowa, from New York Jets
   Chris Carter—89, DB, Texas
4. Damon Denson—97, G, Michigan, from New York Jets
   Ed Ellis—125, T, Buffalo
5. Vernon Crawford—159, LB, Florida State
6. Tony Gaiter—192, WR, Miami
7. Scott Rehberg—230, T, Central Michigan

NEW ORLEANS SAINTS
1. Choice to Oakland
   Chris Naeole—10, G, Colorado, from Oakland
2. Rob Kelly—33, DB, Ohio State
   Jared Tomich—39, DE, Nebraska, from Oakland
3. Troy Davis—62, RB, Iowa State
4. Danny Wuerffel—99, QB, Florida
   Keith Poole—116, WR, Arizona State, from Kansas City through Tennessee
5. Choice to Washington
6. Nicky Savoie—165, TE, Louisiana State, from Atlanta through Tennessee
   Choice to Miami through Oakland
7. Choice to Miami through Oakland

NEW YORK GIANTS
1. Ike Hilliard—7, WR, Florida
2. Tiki Barber—36, RB, Virginia
3. Ryan Phillips—68, LB, Idaho
   *Brad Maynard—95, P, Ball State
4. Pete Monty—103, LB, Wisconsin
5. Sam Garnes—136, DB, Cincinnati
6. Mike Cherry—171, QB, Murray State
7. Matt Keneley—208, DT, Southern California

NEW YORK JETS
1. Choice to St. Louis
   James Farrior—8, LB, Virginia, from Tampa Bay
2. Rick Terry—31, DT, North Carolina
3. Choice to New England
   Dedric Ward—88, WR, Northern Iowa, from Denver
4. Choice to New England
   Terry Day—102, DE, Mississippi State, from St. Louis
   Leon Johnson—104, RB, North Carolina, from Tampa Bay
5. Lamont Burns—131, G, East Carolina
   Raymond Austin—145, DB, Tennessee, from Miami
6. Tim Scharf—164, LB, Northwestern
   Chuck Clements—191, QB, Houston, from Denver
7. Steve Rosga—202, DB, Colorado
   Jason Ferguson—229, DT, Georgia, from Denver

OAKLAND RAIDERS
1. Darrell Russell—2, DT, Southern California, from New Orleans
   Choice to New Orleans
2. Choice to New Orleans
3. Adam Treu—72, G, Nebraska
   Tim Kohn—85, G, Iowa State, from Buffalo
4. Choice to Tennessee through New Orleans
   Chad Levitt—123, RB, Cornell, from San Francisco through Miami
5. Choice to Washington through Atlanta
6. Calvin Branch—172, RB, Colorado State
   Grady Jackson—193, DE, Knoxville, from Green Bay
7. Choice to Green Bay

PHILADELPHIA EAGLES
1. Choice to Dallas
   Jon Harris—25, DE, Virginia, from Dallas
2. Choice to San Francisco
   James Darling—57, LB, Washington State, from San Francisco
3. Duce Staley—71, RB, South Carolina, from Arizona
   Choice to Arizona
4. Damien Robinson—119, DB, Iowa
5. Ndukwe Kalu—152, DE, Rice
   Luther Broughton—155, TE, Furman, from Dallas
6. Choice to Arizona
   Antwuan Wyatt—190, WR, Bethune-Cookman, from San Francisco
   *Edward Jasper—198, DT, Texas A&M
7. Koy Detmer—207, QB, Colorado, from St Louis through New York Jets
   Byron Capers—225, DB, Florida State
   Deauntae Brown—227, DB, Central State, Ohio, from San Francisco

PITTSBURGH STEELERS
1. Chad Scott—24, DB, Maryland
2. Will Blackwell—53, WR, San Diego State
3. Paul Wiggins—82, T, Oregon
   *Mike Vrabel—91, DE, Ohio State
4. Choice to Miami through St. Louis
5. George Jones—154, RB, San Diego State
6. Daryl Porter—186, DB, Boston College
   *Rod Manuel—199, DE, Oklahoma
7. Michael Adams—223, WR, Texas

ST. LOUIS RAMS
1. Orlando Pace—1, T, Ohio State, from New York Jets
   Choice to Seattle through New York Jets and Tampa Bay
2. Choice to Chicago
   Dexter McCleon—40, DB, Clemson, from Chicago
3. Choice to Denver through New York Jets
4. Choice to New York Jets
   Ryan Tucker—112, C, Texas Christian, from Miami
5. Choice to San Diego
   Taje Allen—158, DB, Texas, from Denver
6. Choice to Miami
   Muadianvita Kazadi—179, LB, Tulsa, from Tennessee
7. Choice to Philadelphia through New York Jets
   Cedric White—215, DE, North Carolina A&T, from San Diego

SAN DIEGO CHARGERS
1. Choice to Tampa Bay
2. Freddie Jones—45, TE, North Carolina
3. Michael Hamilton—74, LB, North Carolina A&T
4. Raleigh Roundtree—109, T, South Carolina State
5. Kenny Bynum—138, RB, South Carolina State, from St. Louis
   Paul Bradford—146, DB, Portland State
6. Daniel Palmer—178, C, Air Force
7. Choice to St. Louis
   Toran James—218, LB, North Carolina A&T, from Kansas City through Pittsburgh
   *Tony Corbin—237, QB, Cal State-Sacramento

SAN FRANCISCO 49ERS
1. Jim Druckenmiller—26, QB, Virginia Tech
2. Marc Edwards—55, RB, Notre Dame, from Philadelphia
   Choice to Philadelphia
3. Greg Clark—77, TE, Stanford, from Indianapolis
   Choice to Indianapolis
4. Choice to Oakland through Miami
5. Choice to Indianapolis
6. Choice to Philadelphia
7. Choice to Philadelphia

SEATTLE SEAHAWKS
1. Shawn Springs—3, DB, Ohio State, from Atlanta
   Walter Jones—6, T, Florida State, from St. Louis through New York Jets and Tampa Bay
   Choice to Tampa Bay
2. Choice to Atlanta
3. Choice to Atlanta
4. Choice to Chicago
5. Eric Stokes—142, DB, Nebraska
6. Itula Mili—174, TE, Brigham Young
7. Carlos Jones—211, DB, Miami

TAMPA BAY BUCCANEERS
1. Choice to New York Jets
   Warrick Dunn—12, RB, Florida State, from Seattle
   Reidel Anthony—16, WR, Florida, from San Diego
2. Jerry Wunsch—37, T, Wisconsin
3. Frank Middleton—63, G, Arizona, from Atlanta through Seattle
   Ronde Barber—66, DB, Virginia
4. Choice to New York Jets
   *Alshermond Singleton—128, LB, Temple
5. Patrick Hape—137, TE, Alabama
6. Al Harris—169, DB, Texas A&M-Kingsville
   *Nigea Carter—197, WR, Michigan State
7. Anthony DeGrate—209, DT, Stephen F. Austin

TENNESSEE OILERS
1. Choice to Kansas City
   Kenny Holmes—18, DE, Miami, from Kansas City
2. Joey Kent—46, WR, Tennessee
3. Denard Walker—75, DB, Louisiana State
   Scott Sanderson—81, T, Washington State, from Kansas City
4. Derrick Mason—98, WR, Michigan State, from Atlanta
   Pratt Lyons—107, DE, Troy State, from Oakland through New Orleans
   Choice to Kansas City
5. George McCullough—143, DB, Baylor
6. Choice to St. Louis
   Dennis Stallings—181, LB, Illinois, from Kansas City
7. Armon Williams—216, DB, Arizona

WASHINGTON REDSKINS
1. Kenard Lang—17, DE, Miami
2. Greg Jones—51, LB, Colorado
3. Derek Smith—80, LB, Arizona State
4. Albert Connell—115, WR, Texas A&M
5. Jamel Williams—132, DB, Nebraska, from New Orleans
   Keith Thibodeaux—140, DB, Northwestern St., La., from Oakland through Atlanta
   Twan Russell—148, LB, Miami
   *Brad Badger—162, G, Stanford
6. Choice to Atlanta
7. Choice to Atlanta

NUMBER OF PLAYERS DRAFTED—1997

BY POSITION:

Defensive Backs 50
Linebackers 39
Wide Receivers 25
Defensive Ends 23
Running Backs 23
Defensive Tackles .18
Tackles 18
Tight Ends 15
Guards 11
Quarterbacks 11
Centers 5
Kickers 1
Punters 1

BY COLLEGE:

Arizona State 8
Miami 8
Nebraska 8
Florida State 7
Ohio State 7
Colorado 6
Texas 6
Virginia 6
North Carolina 5
Notre Dame 5
Florida 4
Houston 4
Iowa 4
Louisville 4
San Diego State 4
Southern California .4
Stanford 4
Texas A&M 4
Virginia Tech 4
Alabama 3
California 3
Georgia 3
Kansas 3
Louisiana State 3
Memphis 3
Michigan 3
North Carolina A&T .3
Northwestern 3
Oregon 3
Penn State 3
Tennessee 3
Washington 3
Washington State 3
Wisconsin 3
Wyoming 3
Arizona 2
Ball State 2
Boston College 2
Cal State-Sacramento 2
Cincinnati 2
Clemson 2
Cornell 2
Fresno State 2
Indiana 2
Iowa State 2
James Madison 2
Kansas State 2
Kentucky 2
Knoxville 2
Michigan State 2
Mississippi State 2
Oklahoma 2
South Carolina 2

South Carolina State .2
Syracuse 2
West Virginia 2
Air Force 1
Akron 1
Appalachian State 1
Arkansas 1
Army 1
Auburn 1
Baylor 1
Bethune-Cookman 1
Brigham Young 1
Buffalo 1
Central Michigan 1
Central State, Ohio .1
Colorado State 1
Columbia 1
East Carolina 1
Eastern Kentucky 1
Florida A&M 1
Furman 1
Idaho 1
Illinois 1
Jackson State 1
Kent State 1
Langston 1
Maryland 1
Mississippi 1
Missouri Southern 1
Murray State 1
Nevada 1
North Carolina State .1
Northeastern 1
Northern Colorado 1
Northern Iowa 1
Northwestern State, La. 1
Portland State 1
Rice 1
Southern Illinois 1
Southwest Missouri State 1
Stephen F. Austin 1
Temple 1
Texas A&M-Kingsville 1
Texas Christian 1
Texas Southern 1
Texas Tech 1
Troy State 1
Tulane 1
Tulsa 1
Valdosta State 1
William & Mary 1

BY CONFERENCE:

Big 12 35
Pac 10 30
Big 10 28
SEC 25
ACC 22
Big East 19
WAC 15
Conference USA 14
Independent 11
MEAC 7
MAC 5
Yankee 4
Big Sky 3
Gateway 3
Ivy 3
Southland 3
Big West 2
Ohio Valley 2
Southern 2
SWAC 2
Gulf South 1
Lone Star 1
Mid-America Intercollegiate 1
North Central Intercollegiate 1
Oklahoma Intercollegiate 1

UNDERCLASSMEN AND THE DRAFT

Year	Entered	Drafted	In Top 10
1989	25	12	3
1990	38	18	5
1991	29	22	2
1992	34	25	5
1993	37	24	5
1994	29	26	6
1995	33	22	2
1996	46	21	4
1997	44	27	7

WAIVERS

The waiver system is a procedure by which player contracts or NFL rights to players are made available by a club to other clubs in the League. During the procedure, the 29 other clubs either file claims to obtain the players or waive the opportunity to do so—thus the term "waiver." Claiming clubs are assigned players on a priority based on the inverse of won-and-lost standing. The claiming period normally is 10 days during the offseason and 24 hours from early July through December. In some circumstances, another 24 hours is added on to allow the original club to rescind its action (known as a recall of a waiver request) and/or the claiming club to do the same (known as withdrawal of a claim). If a player passes through waivers unclaimed and is not recalled by the original club, he becomes a free agent. All waivers from July through December are no recall and no withdrawal. Under the Collective Bargaining Agreement, from the beginning of the waiver system each year through the trading deadline (October 7, 1997), any veteran who has acquired four years of pension credit is not subject to the waiver system if the club desires to release him. After the trading deadline, such players are subject to the waiver system.

ACTIVE/INACTIVE LIST

The Active/Inactive List is the principal status for players participating for a club. It consists of all players under contract who are eligible for preseason, regular-season, and postseason games. Teams are permitted to open training camp with no more than 80 players under contract and thereafter must meet two mandatory roster reductions prior to the season opener. Teams will be permitted an Active List of 45 players and an Inactive List of eight players for each regular-season and postseason game during the season. Provided that a club has two quarterbacks on its 45-player Active List, a third quarterback from its Inactive List is permitted to dress for the game, but if he enters the game during the first three quarters, the other two quarterbacks are thereafter prohibited from playing. Teams also are permitted to establish Practice Squads of up to five players who are eligible to participate in practice, but these players remain free agents and are eligible to sign with any other team in the league.

August 20 ....Roster reduction to 60 players
August 25 ....Roster reduction to 53 players
August 26 ....Teams establish a Practice Squad of up to five players

In addition to the squad limits described above, the overall roster limit of 80 players remains in effect throughout the regular season and postseason. The overall limit is applicable to players on a team's Active, Inactive, and Exempt Lists, players on the Practice Squad, and players on the Reserve List as Injured, Physically Unable to Perform, Non-Football Illness/Injury, and Suspended by Club.

RESERVE LIST

The Reserve List is a status for players who, for reasons of injury, retirement, military service, or other circumstances, are not immediately available for participation with a club. Players on Reserve/Injured are not eligible to practice or return to the Active/Inactive List in the same season that they are placed on Reserve. Players in the category of Reserve/Retired or Reserve/Did Not Report may not be reinstated during the period from 30 days before the end of the regular season through the postseason.

TRADES

Unrestricted trading between the AFC and NFC is allowed in 1997 through October 7, after which trading will end until 1998.

ANNUAL ACTIVE PLAYER LIMITS

NFL

Year(s)	Limit
1991-97	45**
1985-90	45
1983-84	49
1982	45†-49
1978-81	45
1975-77	43
1974	47
1964-73	40
1963	37
1961-62	36
1960	38
1959	36
1957-58	35
1951-56	33
1949-50	32
1948	35
1947	35*-34
1945-46	33
1943-44	28
1940-42	33
1938-39	30
1936-37	25
1935	24
1930-34	20
1926-29	18
1925	16

**45 plus a third quarterback
† 45 for first two games
* 35 for first three games

AFL

Year(s)	Limit
1966-69	40
1965	38
1964	34
1962-63	33
1960-61	35

NFL FREE AGENCY MOVEMENT

The following chart details veteran free agents who signed with new teams:

	1993	1994	1995	1996
Unrestricted	108	121	171	99
Restricted	8	7	6	4
Transition	4	4	2	2
Franchise	1	0	0	0
TOTALS	121	132	179	105

The AFC

BALTIMORE RAVENS

American Football Conference
Central Division
Team Colors: Black, Purple, and Metallic Gold
11001 Owings Mills Boulevard
Owings Mills, Maryland 21117
Telephone: (410) 654-6200

CLUB OFFICIALS

President and Owner: Arthur B. Modell
Executive Vice President/Legal and
    Administration: Jim Bailey
Executive Vice President/Assistant to the President:
    David Modell
Vice President/Public Relations: Kevin Byrne
Vice President/Sales and Marketing: David Cope
Vice President/Player Personnel: Ozzie Newsome
Chief Financial Officer: Pat Moriarty
Treasurer: Steven F. Costa
Director of Ticket Operations: Roy Sommerhof
Director of Operations/Information: Bob Eller
Director of Publications/Assistant Director of
    Public Relations: Francine Lubera
Director of Broadcasting: Lisa Bercu
Director of Pro Personnel: James Harris
Director of College Scouting: Phil Savage
Scouts: George Kokinis, Ron Marciniak,
    Terry McDonough, Vince Newsome, Ernie Plank,
    Ellis Rainsberger
Head Trainer: Bill Tessendorf
Facilities Manager: Chuck Cusick
Equipment Manager: Ed Carroll
Video Director: Jon Dube
Stadium: Memorial Stadium • **Capacity:** 64,522
    1000 East 33rd Street
    Baltimore, Maryland 21218
Playing Surface: SportGrass
Training Camp: Western Maryland College
    2 College Hill
    Westminster, Maryland 21157

RECORD HOLDERS
INDIVIDUAL RECORDS—CAREER

Category	Name	Performance
Rushing (Yds.)	Byron (Bam) Morris, 1996	737
Passing (Yds.)	Vinny Testaverde, 1996	4,177
Passing (TDs)	Vinny Testaverde, 1996	33
Receiving (No.)	Michael Jackson, 1996	76
Receiving (Yds.)	Michael Jackson, 1996	1,201
Interceptions	Antonio Langham, 1996	5
	Eric Turner, 1996	5
Punting (Avg.)	Greg Montgomery, 1996	43.8
Punt Return (Avg.)	Jermaine Lewis, 1996	9.4
Kickoff Return (Avg.)	Jermaine Lewis, 1996	21.5
Field Goals	Matt Stover, 1996	19
Touchdowns (Tot.)	Michael Jackson, 1996	14
Points	Matt Stover, 1996	91

INDIVIDUAL RECORDS—SINGLE SEASON

Category	Name	Performance
Rushing (Yds.)	Byron (Bam) Morris, 1996	737
Passing (Yds.)	Vinny Testaverde, 1996	4,177
Passing (TDs)	Vinny Testaverde, 1996	33
Receiving (No.)	Michael Jackson, 1996	76
Receiving (Yds.)	Michael Jackson, 1996	1,201
Interceptions	Antonio Langham, 1996	5
	Eric Turner, 1996	5
Punting (Avg.)	Greg Montgomery, 1996	43.8
Punt Return (Avg.)	Jermaine Lewis, 1996	9.4
Kickoff Return (Avg.)	Jermaine Lewis, 1996	21.5
Field Goals	Matt Stover, 1996	19
Touchdowns (Tot.)	Michael Jackson, 1996	14
Points	Matt Stover, 1996	91

INDIVIDUAL RECORDS—SINGLE GAME

Category	Name	Performance
Rushing (Yds.)	Earnest Byner, 9-29-96	149
Passing (Yds.)	Vinny Testaverde, 10-27-96	429
Passing (TDs)	Vinny Testaverde, 10-20-96	4
Receiving (No.)	Michael Jackson, 11-24-96	9
	Brian Kinchen, 11-24-96	9
Receiving (Yds.)	Derrick Alexander, 12-1-96	198
Interceptions	Antonio Langham, 12-15-96	2
Field Goals	Matt Stover, 11-24-96	4
Touchdowns (Tot.)	Michael Jackson, 12-22-96	3
Points	Michael Jackson, 12-22-96	18

1997 SCHEDULE
PRESEASON

Aug. 2	**N.Y. Giants**	8:00
Aug. 8	at N.Y. Jets	8:00
Aug. 16	at Philadelphia	8:00
Aug. 22	**Buffalo**	7:30

REGULAR SEASON

Aug. 31	**Jacksonville**	4:00
Sept. 7	**Cincinnati**	1:00
Sept. 14	at New York Giants	1:00
Sept. 21	at Tennessee	12:00
Sept. 28	at San Diego	1:00
Oct. 5	**Pittsburgh**	1:00
Oct. 12	Open Date	
Oct. 19	**Miami**	4:00
Oct. 26	at Washington	1:00
Nov. 2	at New York Jets	1:00
Nov. 9	at Pittsburgh	8:00
Nov. 16	**Philadelphia**	1:00
Nov. 23	**Arizona**	1:00
Nov. 30	at Jacksonville	1:00
Dec. 7	**Seattle**	1:00
Dec. 14	**Tennessee**	1:00
Dec. 21	at Cincinnati	1:00

COACHING HISTORY
(4-12-0)

1996	Ted Marchibroda	4-12-0

MEMORIAL STADIUM

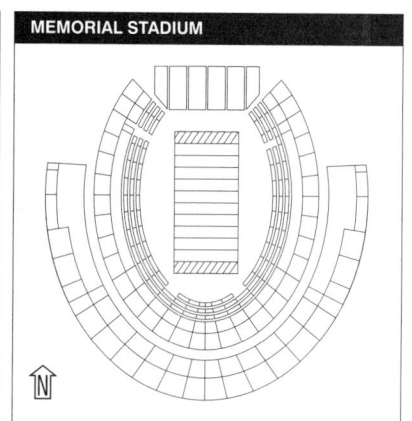

1996 TEAM RECORD

PRESEASON (3-1)

Date	Result		Opponents
8/3	W	17-9	Philadelphia
8/10	W	37-27	at N.Y. Giants
8/17	L	15-17	Green Bay
8/23	W	37-14	at Buffalo

REGULAR SEASON (4-12)

Date	Result		Opponents	Att.
9/1	W	19-14	Oakland	64,124
9/8	L	17-31	at Pittsburgh	57,241
9/15	L	13-29	at Houston	20,082
9/29	W	17-10	New Orleans	61,063
10/6	L	38-46	New England	63,569
10/13	L	21-26	at Indianapolis	56,978
10/20	L	34-45	at Denver	70,453
10/27	W	37-31	St. Louis (OT)	60,256
11/3	L	21-24	Cincinnati	60,743
11/10	L	27-30	at Jacksonville	64,628
11/17	L	20-38	at San Francisco	51,596
11/24	L	25-28	Jacksonville (OT)	57,384
12/1	W	31-17	Pittsburgh	51,822
12/8	L	14-21	at Cincinnati	43,022
12/15	L	16-27	at Carolina	70,075
12/22	L	21-24	Houston	52,704

(OT) Overtime

SCORE BY PERIODS

Ravens	70	129	64	102	6	—	371
Opponents	88	128	92	130	3	—	441

ATTENDANCE

Home 471,665   Away 434,075   Total 905,740
Single-game home record, 64,124 (9/1/96)
Single-season home record, 471,665 (1996)

1996 TEAM STATISTICS

	Ravens	Opp.
Total First Downs	338	351
Rushing	108	115
Passing	208	213
Penalty	22	23
Third Down: Made/Att	88/201	108/224
Third Down Pct.	43.8	48.2
Fourth Down: Made/Att	4/10	7/13
Fourth Down Pct.	40.0	53.8
Total Net Yards	5723	5889
Avg. Per Game	357.7	368.1
Total Plays	1024	1075
Avg. Per Play	5.6	5.5
Net Yards Rushing	1745	1920
Avg. Per Game	109.1	120.0
Total Rushes	416	508
Net Yards Passing	3978	3969
Avg. Per Game	248.6	248.1
Sacked/Yards Lost	38/296	30/146
Gross Yards	4274	4115
Att./Completions	570/335	537/350
Completion Pct.	58.8	65.2
Had Intercepted	20	15
Punts/Avg.	69/43.2	68/42.4
Net Punting Avg.	69/37.8	68/35.6
Penalties/Yards Lost	94/818	104/744
Fumbles/Ball Lost	23/13	23/7
Touchdowns	45	50
Rushing	10	18
Passing	34	27
Returns	1	5
Avg. Time of Possession	27:05	32:55

1996 INDIVIDUAL STATISTICS

PASSING	Att.	Comp.	Yds.	Pct.	TD	Int.	Tkld.	Rate
Testaverde	549	325	4177	59.2	33	19	34/270	88.7
Zeier	21	10	97	47.6	1	1	4/26	57.0
Ravens	570	335	4274	58.8	34	20	38/296	87.6
Opponents	537	350	4115	65.2	27	15	30/146	93.4

SCORING	TD R	TD P	TD Rt	PAT	FG	Saf	PTS
Stover	0	0	0	34/35	19/25	0	91
Jackson	0	14	0	0/0	0/0	0	88
Alexander	0	9	0	0/0	0/0	0	56
Byner	4	1	0	0/0	0/0	0	30
Morris	4	1	0	0/0	0/0	0	30
Testaverde	2	0	0	0/0	0/0	0	14
F. Turner	0	2	0	0/0	0/0	0	12
Arvie	0	1	0	0/0	0/0	0	6
Caldwell	0	0	1	0/0	0/0	0	6
Green	0	1	0	0/0	0/0	0	6
J. Jones	0	1	0	0/0	0/0	0	6
Kinchen	0	1	0	0/0	0/0	0	6
J. Lewis	0	1	0	0/0	0/0	0	6
Ogden	0	1	0	0/0	0/0	0	6
C. Williams	0	1	0	0/0	0/0	0	6
Gardner	0	0	0	0/0	0/0	0	2
Ravens	10	34	1	34/35	19/25	0	371
Opponents	18	27	5	41/41	28/31	1	441

2-Point conversions: Jackson 2, Alexander, Gardner, Testaverde. Team: 5-9, Opponents: 7-9.

RUSHING	Att.	Yds.	Avg.	LG	TD
Morris	172	737	4.3	19	4
Byner	159	634	4.0	42	4
Testaverde	34	188	5.5	22	2
Gardner	26	108	4.2	19	0
Hoard	15	61	4.1	10	0
F. Turner	2	12	6.0	6	0
Zeier	2	8	4.0	5	0
Alexander	3	0	0.0	12	0
E. Hunter	1	0	0.0	0	0
Montgomery	1	0	0.0	0	0
J. Lewis	1	-3	-3.0	-3	0
Ravens	416	1745	4.2	42	10
Opponents	508	1920	3.8	71t	18

RECEIVING	No.	Yds.	Avg.	LG	TD
Jackson	76	1201	15.8	86t	14
Alexander	62	1099	17.7	64t	9
Kinchen	55	581	10.6	29	1
F. Turner	38	461	12.1	27t	2
Byner	30	270	9.0	40	1
Morris	25	242	9.7	52t	1
Green	15	150	10.0	23	1
C. Williams	13	85	6.5	19	1
Gardner	7	28	4.0	7	0
J. Lewis	5	78	15.6	24	1
Ethridge	2	24	12.0	15	0
Bishop	2	22	11.0	13	0
E. Hunter	1	25	25.0	25	0
Hoard	1	4	4.0	4	0
J. Jones	1	2	2.0	2t	1
Arvie	1	1	1.0	1t	1
Ogden	1	1	1.0	1t	1
Ravens	335	4274	12.8	86t	34
Opponents	350	4115	11.8	55	27

INTERCEPTIONS	No.	Yds.	Avg.	LG	TD
Langham	5	59	11.8	28	0
E. Turner	5	1	0.2	1	0
Caldwell	1	45	45.0	45t	1
Adams	1	16	16.0	16	0
Croel	1	16	16.0	16	0
Moore	1	10	10.0	10	0
R. Lewis	1	0	0.0	0	0
Ravens	15	147	9.8	45t	1
Opponents	20	349	17.5	68t	3

PUNTING	No.	Yds.	Avg.	In 20	LG
Montgomery	68	2980	43.8	23	67
Ravens	69	2980	43.2	23	67
Opponents	68	2881	42.4	27	64

PUNT RETURNS	No.	FC	Yds.	Avg.	LG	TD
J. Lewis	36	13	339	9.4	46	0
Alexander	1	0	15	15.0	15	0
Ethridge	1	0	3	3.0	3	0
E. Hunter	0	1	0	—	—	0
Ravens	38	14	357	9.4	46	0
Opponents	27	14	273	10.1	47	0

KICKOFF RETURNS	No.	Yds.	Avg.	LG	TD
J. Lewis	41	883	21.5	44	0
Baldwin	20	405	20.3	34	0
E. Hunter	9	178	19.8	29	0
Ethridge	8	171	21.4	29	0
Byner	4	61	15.3	19	0
Alexander	1	13	13.0	13	0
Isaia	1	2	2.0	2	0
Kinchen	1	19	19.0	19	0
Morris	1	3	3.0	3	0
Frederick	0	-1	—	-1	0
Ravens	86	1734	20.2	44	0
Opponents	70	1402	20.0	51	0

SACKS	No.
Caldwell	4.5
Pleasant	4.0
Burnett	3.0
Croel	3.0
Goad	3.0
Thompson	3.0
J. Williams	3.0
R. Lewis	2.5
Fortune	1.0
J. Jones	1.0
Lyle	1.0
Brady	0.5
Footman	0.5
Ravens	30.0
Opponents	38.0

1997 DRAFT CHOICES

Round	Name	Pos.	College
1	Peter Boulware	DE	Florida State
2	Jamie Sharper	LB	Virginia
	Kim Herring	DB	Penn State
3	Jay Graham	RB	Tennessee
4	Tyrus McCloud	LB	Louisville
5	Jeff Mitchell	C	Florida
6	Steve Lee	RB	Indiana
	Cornell Brown	LB	Virginia Tech
7	Chris Ward	DE	Kentucky
	Wally Richardson	QB	Penn State
	Ralph Staten	DB	Alabama
	Leland Taylor	DT	Louisville

BALTIMORE RAVENS

1997 VETERAN ROSTER

No.		Name	Pos.	Ht.	Wt.	Birthdate	NFL Exp.	College	Hometown	How Acq.	'96 Games/ Starts
82		Alexander, Derrick	WR	6-2	195	11/6/71	4	Michigan	Detroit, Mich.	D1b-'94	15/14
23		Baldwin, Randy	RB	5-10	216	8/19/67	7	Mississippi	Griffin, Ga.	FA-'96	9/0
69		Blackshear, Jeff	G	6-6	323	3/29/69	5	Northeast Louisiana	Fort Pierce, Fla.	T(Sea)-'96	16/12
24		Brady, Donny	CB-S	6-2	195	11/24/73	2	Wisconsin	North Bellmore, N.Y.	FA-'95	16/13
22		Brew, Dorian	CB	5-10	182	7/19/74	2	Kansas	Florissant, Mo.	FA-'96	7/0
77		Brown, Orlando	G-T	6-7	340	11/12/70	5	South Carolina State	Washington, D.C.	FA-'93	16/16
90		Burnett, Rob	DE	6-4	280	8/27/67	8	Syracuse	Coram, N.Y.	D5-'90	6/6
21		Byner, Earnest	RB	5-10	215	9/15/62	14	East Carolina	Milledgeville, Ga.	UFA(Wash)-'94	16/8
56	#	Caldwell, Mike	LB	6-2	235	8/31/71	5	Middle Tennessee State	Oak Ridge, Tenn.	D3-'93	9/9
85		Ethridge, Ray	WR	5-10	180	12/12/68	2	Pasadena City	San Diego, Calif.	FA-'95	14/1
78		Footman, Dan	DE	6-5	290	1/13/69	5	Florida State	Tampa, Fla.	D2-'93	10/8
94		Frederick, Mike	DE	6-5	280	8/6/72	3	Virginia	Neshaminy, Pa.	D3b-'95	16/11
72		Goad, Tim	DT	6-3	280	2/28/66	10	North Carolina	Stuart, Va.	UFA(NE)-'95	16/5
62		Goeas, Leo	G	6-4	300	8/15/66	8	Hawaii	Honolulu, Hawaii	UFA(StL)-'97	16/13*
50	#	Goganious, Keith	LB	6-3	245	12/7/68	6	Penn State	Virginia Beach, Va.	FA-'96	13/8
86	#	Green, Eric	TE	6-5	285	6/22/67	8	Liberty	Savannah, Ga.	FA-'96	6/3
64		Isaia, Sale	G-T	6-5	315	6/13/72	3	UCLA	Oceanside, Calif.	FA-'95	9/0
81		Jackson, Michael	WR	6-4	195	4/12/69	7	Southern Mississippi	Kentwood, La.	D6-91	16/16
25		Jenkins, Deron	CB	5-11	190	11/14/73	2	Tennessee	St. Louis, Mo.	D2-'96	15/2
97		Jones, James	DT	6-2	290	2/6/69	7	Northern Iowa	Davenport, Iowa	FA-'96	16/11
31		Jones, Rondell	S	6-2	210	5/7/71	5	North Carolina	Sunderland, Md.	UFA(Sea)-'97	16/0*
88		Kinchen, Brian	TE	6-2	240	8/6/65	10	Louisiana State	Baton Rouge, La.	FA-'91	16/16
38		Langham, Antonio	CB	6-0	180	7/31/72	4	Alabama	Town Creek, Ala.	D1a-'94	15/14
84		Lewis, Jermaine	WR-KR	5-7	172	10/16/74	2	Maryland	Lanham, Md.	D5-'96	16/1
52		Lewis, Ray	LB	6-1	235	5/15/75	2	Miami	Lakeland, Fla.	D1b-'96	14/13
99		McCrary, Michael	DE	6-4	270	7/7/70	5	Wake Forest	Vienna, Va.	UFA(Sea)-'97	16/13*
9		Montgomery, Greg	P	6-4	215	10/29/64	9	Michigan State	Little Silver, N.J.	FA-'96	16/0
27		Moore, Stevon	S	5-11	210	2/9/67	9	Mississippi	Wiggins, Miss.	PB(Mia)-'92	16/16
33		Morris, Byron (Bam)	RB	6-0	245	1/13/72	4	Texas Tech	Cooper, Tex.	FA-'96	11/7
67		Neujahr, Quentin	G-T	6-4	285	1/30/71	3	Kansas State	Seward, Neb.	FA-'94	5/0
75		Ogden, Jonathan	G-T	6-8	318	7/31/74	2	UCLA	Washington, D.C.	D1a-'96	16/16
6		Otis, Scott	QB	6-5	230	9/28/72	2	Glenville State	Southington, Conn.	FA-'96	0*
98	#	Pleasant, Anthony	DE	6-5	280	1/27/68	8	Tennessee State	Century, Fla.	D3-'90	12/12
59		Powell, Craig	LB	6-4	235	11/13/71	3	Ohio State	Youngstown, Ohio	D1-'95	9/0
83		Roe, James	WR	6-1	187	8/23/73	2	Norfolk State	Richmond, Va.	D6b-'96	1/0
96		Siragusa, Tony	DT	6-3	320	5/14/67	8	Pittsburgh	Kenilworth, N.J.	UFA(Ind)-'97	10/10*
3		Stover, Matt	K	5-11	178	1/27/68	8	Louisiana Tech	Dallas, Tex.	PB(NYG)-'91	16/0
12		Testaverde, Vinny	QB	6-5	227	11/13/63	11	Miami	Floral Park, N.Y.	UFA(TB)-'93	16/16
37		Thompson, Bennie	S	6-0	214	2/10/63	8	Grambling State	New Orleans, La.	UFA(NO)-'94	16/0
87	#	Turner, Floyd	WR	5-11	199	5/29/66	9	Northwestern State, La.	Shreveport, La.	UFA-'96	11/6
57	#	Williams, Jerrol	LB	6-4	245	7/5/67	8	Purdue	Las Vegas, Nev.	FA-'96	9/6
63		Williams, Wally	G-C	6-2	305	2/19/71	5	Florida A&M	Tallahassee, Fla.	FA-'93	15/13
10		Zeier, Eric	QB	6-0	205	9/6/72	3	Georgia	Marietta, Ga.	D3a-95	1/0

* Goeas played 16 games with St. Louis in '96; R. Jones played 16 games with Seattle; McCrary played 16 games with Seattle; Otis was inactive for 14 games; Siragusa played 10 games with Indianapolis.

\# Unrestricted free agent; subject to developments.

Traded—T Tony Jones (15 games in '96) to Denver.

Players lost through free agency (4): LB Mike Croel (Atl; 16 games in '96), C Steve Everitt (Phil; 8), RB Carwell Gardner (SD; 13), LB Eddie Sutter (Cin; 16).

Also played with Ravens in '96—S Vashone Adams (16 games), T Herman Arvie (14), TE Harold Bishop (8), CB Isaac Booth (11), LB Sedric Clark (6), LB Dexter Daniels (4), DB Corey Dowden (3), DE-DT Elliott Fortune (14), TE Frank Hartley (8), RB Leroy Hoard (2), RB Earnest Hunter (5), DE-DT Rick Lyle (11), S Eric Turner (14), WR Calvin Williams (7).

COACHING STAFF

Head Coach,
Ted Marchibroda

Pro Career: Marchibroda enters his second year after being named the first-ever head coach of the Baltimore Ravens in 1996. The Ravens held a second-half lead in 10 of their final 11 games, winning only two. Four division losses (Cincinnati and Jacksonville, twice each) were decided in the final minute of play or overtime. Even with a 4-12 record, Baltimore finished third in the league in total offense, second in passing. QB Vinny Testaverde completed his best season with a trip to the Pro Bowl after throwing for 4,177 yards and 33 touchdowns. Prior to his return to Baltimore, Marchibroda originally coached the Baltimore Colts from 1975-79 (41-36) and the Indianapolis Colts from 1992-94 (32-35), and owns a 77-83 overall record. His 1995 Colts came within one "Hail Mary" pass of going to Super Bowl XXX in the thrilling 20-16 loss to the Pittsburgh Steelers at Three Rivers Stadium. Twice in his career he has improved his team by a margin of eight victories. Inheriting a 2-12 Colts team when he was named head coach in 1975, he led Baltimore to a 10-4 record and the AFC East title and was named NFL Coach of the Year. The Colts followed with two more division titles, earning 11-3 and 10-4 records in 1976 and 1977. Those are the most titles won by any coach in Colts' history. From October 26, 1975, through November 20, 1977, Marchibroda's Colts won 29 of 33 regular-season games. Marchibroda left the Colts following the 1979 season and was rehired as the team boss on January 28, 1992. Marchibroda achieved the eight-game swing the second time in 1992, taking Indianapolis to a 9-7 mark after the team finished 1-15 in 1991. Prior to returning to the Colts, Marchibroda served five years as an assistant with the Buffalo Bills (1987-1991), the last three as offensive coordinator. He began his career as backfield coach with the Washington Redskins in 1961. Marchibroda joined George Allen's staff with the Los Angeles Rams in 1966 and moved with Allen to the Redskins in 1971, where he served as offensive coordinator through the 1974 season. After his stint with the Colts, Marchibroda served as quarterback coach with the Chicago Bears in 1981, then moved on to Detroit as offensive coordinator with the Lions from 1982-83. He served in that same role with the Philadelphia Eagles from 1984-85 before joining Buffalo in 1987. Marchibroda was the first draft pick of the Pittsburgh Steelers in 1953 and played one year before serving in the Army. He returned to Pittsburgh for the 1955-56 seasons. His top season was 1956, when he completed 124 of 275 passes for 1,585 yards and 12 touchdowns. His playing career ended with the Chicago Cardinals in 1957. Career record: 77-83.

Background: Quarterback at St. Bonaventure 1950-51 and University of Detroit 1952. Led nation in total offense at Detroit. He was a football, basketball (all-state selection), and baseball player at Franklin (Pa.) High School.

Personal: Born March 15, 1931, Franklin, Pa. Ted and his wife Ann reside in Timonium, Md. They have two daughters, Jodi and Lonni and two sons, Ted Jr. and Robert.

ASSISTANT COACHES

Maxie Baughan, linebackers; born August 3, 1938, Forkland, Ala., lives in Reisterstown, Md. Center-linebacker Georgia Tech 1957-60. Pro linebacker Philadelphia Eagles 1960-65, Los Angeles Rams 1966-70, Washington Redskins 1971, 1974. College coach: Georgia Tech 1972-73, Cornell 1983-88 (head coach). Pro coach: Baltimore Colts 1975-79, Detroit Lions 1980-82, Minnesota Vikings 1990-91, Tampa Bay Buccaneers, 1992-95, joined Ravens in 1996.

Jacob Burney, defensive line; born January 24, 1959, Chattanooga, Tenn., lives in Reisterstown, Md. Defensive tackle Tennessee-Chattanooga 1977-80. No pro playing experience. College coach: New Mexico 1983-86, Tulsa 1987, Mississippi State 1988, Wisconsin 1989, UCLA 1990-92, Tennessee 1993.

1997 FIRST-YEAR ROSTER

Name	Pos.	Ht.	Wt.	Birthdate	College	Hometown	How Acq.
Alvarado, Richard	LB	6-2	240	5/10/74	Jackson State	Boligee, Ala.	FA
Arrington, Rusty	LB	6-1	235	7/4/74	Indian Univ., Pa.	Penn Hills, Pa.	FA
Bernstein, Alex	DL	6-3	325	8/11/75	Amherst	Aspen Co.	FA
Boulware, Peter	DE-LB	6-4	255	12/18/74	Florida State	Columbia, S.C.	D1
Brown, Bryon	DB	5-9	180	11/19/74	Texas A&I	Corpus Christi Tex.	FA
Brown, Cornell	LB	6-0	240	3/15/75	Virginia Tech	Lynchburg, Va.	D6b
Bruce, Clint	LB	6-0	240	1/16/74	Navy	Garland, Tex.	FA
Cotton, Kenyon	RB	6-0	255	2/23/74	Southwestern Louisiana	Minden, La.	FA
Epps, James	WR	6-0	185	9/5/73	East Texas State	Atlanta, Tex.	FA
Flynn, Mike	G-T	6-3	295	6/15/74	Maine	Agawam, Ma.	FA
Folau, Spencer (1)	T	6-5	300	4/5/73	Idaho	Sequoia, Calif.	FA
Graham, Jay	RB	5-11	220	7/14/75	Tennessee	Concord, N. C.	D3
Guidry, Paul	CB-S	5-9	175	8/20/74	UCLA	Cerritos, Calif.	FA
Herring, Kim	S	5-11	210	9/10/75	Penn State	Solon, Ohio	D2b
Holmes, Priest	RB	5-9	205	10/7/73	Texas	San Antonio, Tex.	FA
Howard, Richard	G-T	6-6	340	10/4/73	Carson-Newman	Oak Ridge, Tenn.	FA
Ivey, Mike	DE-DT	6-5	275	1/3/75	Wisconsin-LaCrosse	Eagle, Wisc.	FA
Khayat, Bill (1)	TE	6-4	225	3/26/73	Duke	York, Pa.	FA
King, Charles	DE-DT	6-0	275	2/2/71	Memphis State	Okeechobee, Fla.	FA
Lee, Steve	RB	6-0	265	4/16/74	Indiana	Indianapolis, Ind.	D6a
McCloud, Tyrus	LB	6-1	250	11/23/74	Louisville	Pompano Beach, Fla.	D4
Mitchell, Jeff	C	6-4	300	1/29/74	Florida	Clearwater, Fla.	D5
Moore, Kelvin	DE	6-3	270	2/20/74	Alabama	Daphne, Ala.	FA
Ofodile, A J (1)	TE	6-4	260	10/10/73	Missouri	Detroit, Mich.	FA
Olsommer, Keith	TE	6-3	245	11/7/73	Penn State	Moscow, Pa.	FA
Richard, Donald	WR	6-0	180	11/18/72	Southwestern Louisiana	Kaplan, La.	FA
Richardson, Wally	QB	6-4	225	2/11/74	Penn State	Sumter, S.C.	D7b
Russ, Bernard	LB	6-0	225	11/4/73	West Virginia	Utica, N.Y.	FA
Sharper, Jamie	LB	6-3	240	11/23/74	Virginia	Glen Allen, Va.	D2a
Staten, Ralph	S	6-3	205	12/3/74	Alabama	Montgomery, Al.	D7c
Taylor, Leland	DT	6-3	305	10/25/72	Louisville	Louisville, Ky.	D7d
Trent, Jermaine	CB-S	6-0	200	6/14/74	Cincinnati	Bartlesville, Okla.	FA
Walker, Robert	DT	6-1	330	5/13/75	Southern	Baton Rouge, La.	FA
Ward, Chris	DE	6-3	275	2/4/74	Kentucky	Decatur, Ga.	FA
Ward, Shawn	WR	5-8	175	8/6/73	Towson State	Somers Point, N.J.	D7a
Williams, John	CB-S	5-7	180	7/26/74	Southern	Hammond, La.	FA

The term <u>NFL Rookie</u> is defined as a player who is in his first season of professional football and has not been on the roster of another professional football team for any regular-season or postseason games. A <u>Rookie</u> is designated by an "R" on NFL rosters. Players who have been active in another professional football league or players who have NFL experience, including either preseason training camp or being on an Active List or Inactive List, or on Reserve/Injured or Reserve/Physically Unable to Perform for fewer than six regular-season games, are termed <u>NFL First-Year Players</u>. An <u>NFL First-Year Player</u> is designated by a "1" on NFL rosters. Thereafter, a player is credited with an additional year of experience for each season in which he accumulates six games on the Active List or Inactive List, or on Reserve/Injured or Reserve/Physically Unable to Perform.

NOTES

Pro coach: Joined Ravens/Browns in 1994.

Kirk Ferentz, assistant head coach-offense; born August 1, 1955, Royal Oak, Mich., lives in Baldwin, Md. Linebacker Connecticut 1973-76. No pro playing experience. College coach: Connecticut 1977, Pittsburgh 1980, Iowa 1981-89, Maine 1990-92 (head coach). Pro coach: Joined Ravens/Browns in 1993.

Al Lavan, running backs; born September 13, 1946, Pierce, Fla., lives in Reisterstown, Md. Defensive back Colorado State 1965-67. Pro defensive back Philadelphia Eagles 1968, Atlanta Falcons 1969-70. College coach: Colorado State 1972, Louisville 1973, Iowa State 1974, Georgia Tech 1977-78, Stanford 1979, Washington 1992-95. Pro coach: Atlanta Falcons 1975-76, Dallas Cowboys 1980-88, San Francisco 49ers 1989-90, joined Ravens in 1996.

Marvin Lewis, defensive coordinator; born September 23, 1958, McDonald, Pa., lives in Finksburg, Md. Linebacker Idaho State 1977-80. No pro playing experience. College coach: Idaho State 1981-84, Long Beach State 1985-86, New Mexico, 1987-89, Pittsburgh 1990-91. Pro coach: Pittsburgh Steelers, 1992-95, joined Ravens in 1996.

Richard Mann, receivers; born April 20, 1947, Aliquippa, Pa., lives in Owings Mills, Md. Wide receiver Arizona State 1966-68. No pro playing experience. College coach: Arizona State 1974-79, Louisville 1980-81. Pro coach: Baltimore/Indianapolis Colts 1982-84, Cleveland Browns 1985-93, New York Jets 1994-96, joined Ravens in 1997.

Scott O'Brien, special teams; born June 25, 1957,

Superior, Wis., lives in Reisterstown, Md. Defensive end Wisconsin-Superior 1975-78. Pro defensive end Green Bay Packers 1979, Toronto Argonauts (CFL) 1979. College coach: Wisconsin-Superior 1980-82, Nevada-Las Vegas 1983-85, Rice 1986, Pittsburgh 1987-90. Pro coach: Joined Ravens/Browns in 1991.

Alvin Reynolds, secondary; born June 24, 1959, Pineville, La., lives in Owings Mills, Md. Safety Indiana State 1978-81. No pro playing experience. College coach: Indiana State 1982-92. Pro coach: Denver Broncos 1993-95, joined Ravens in 1996.

Jerry Simmons, strength and conditioning; born June 15, 1954, Elkhart, Kan., lives in Reisterstown, Md. Linebacker Fort Hays State 1976-77. No pro playing experience. College coach: Fort Hays State 1978, Clemson 1980, Rice 1981-82, Southern California 1983-87. Pro coach: New England Patriots 1988-90, joined Ravens/Browns in 1991.

Don Strock, quarterbacks; born November 27, 1950, Pottstown, Pa., lives in Pikesville, Md. Quarterback Virginia Tech 1970-72. Pro quarterback Miami 1973-87, Cleveland 1988, Indianapolis 1988. Pro coach: Miami (Arena Football League) 1993 (head coach), Mass Marauders (Arena Football League) 1994 (head coach), Rhein Fire (World League) 1995, joined Ravens in 1996.

Ken Whisenhunt, tight ends; born February 28, 1962, Atlanta, Ga., lives in Reisterstown, Md. End Georgia Tech 1980-1984. Pro tight end Atlanta Falcons 1985-1988, Washington Redskins 1989-1990, New York Jets 1991-1993. College coach: Vanderbilt 1995-1996. Pro coach: Joined Ravens in 1997.

American Football Conference
Eastern Division
Team Colors: Royal Blue, Scarlet Red, and White
One Bills Drive
Orchard Park, New York 14127-2296
Telephone: (716) 648-1800

CLUB OFFICIALS

President: Ralph C. Wilson, Jr.
Exec. V.P./General Manager: John Butler
Corporate V.P.: Linda Bogdan
V.P./Head Coach: Marv Levy
Treasurer: Jeffrey C. Littmann
Vice President/Administration: Jim Miller
Director of Ticket Sales: Jerry Foran
Asst. G.M./Business Operations: Bill Munson
Director of Business Operations: Jim Overdorf
Director of Marketing and Sales: John Livsey
Asst. Director of Marketing and Sales: Jeff Hall
Director of Merchandising: Christy Wilson Hofmann
Director of Player Personnel: Dwight Adams
Director of Pro Personnel: A.J. Smith
Director of Player/Alumni Relations: Jerry Butler
Director of Public/Community Relations: Denny Lynch
Director of Media Relations: Scott Berchtold
Asst. Director of Media Relations: Joseph Assad
Director of Stadium Operations: George Koch
Engineering and Operations Manager:
   Joseph Frandina
Director of Security: Bill Bambach
Ticket Director: June Foran
Equipment Manager: Dave Hojnowski
Asst. Equipment Manager: Randy Ribbeck
Strength/Conditioning Coordinator: Rusty Jones
Conditioning Assistant: Joe Torine
Trainers: Ed Abramoski, Bud Carpenter,
   Melvin Lewis, Greg McMillen
Video Director: Henry Kunttu
Video Assistant: Chris Prevet
Scouts: Brad Forsyth, Tom Gibbons, Doug Majeski,
   Buddy Nix, Bob Ryan, George (Chink) Sengel,
   Jim Shofner, David G. Smith, David W. Smith
Stadium: Rich Stadium •**Capacity:** 80,024
   One Bills Drive
   Orchard Park, New York 14127-2296
Playing Surface: AstroTurf
Training Camp: Fredonia State University
   Fredonia, New York 14063

1997 SCHEDULE

PRESEASON

July 26	at Denver	7:00
Aug. 2	**Chicago**	7:00
Aug. 8	**Minnesota**	9:30
Aug. 16	vs. Green Bay at Toronto	4:00
Aug. 22	at Baltimore	7:30

REGULAR SEASON

Aug. 31	**Minnesota**	1:00
Sept. 7	at New York Jets	1:00
Sept. 14	at Kansas City	12:00
Sept. 21	**Indianapolis**	4:00
Sept. 28	Open Date	

RECORD HOLDERS

INDIVIDUAL RECORDS—CAREER

Category	Name	Performance
Rushing (Yds.)	Thurman Thomas, 1988-1996	10,762
Passing (Yds.)	Jim Kelly, 1986-1996	35,467
Passing (TDs)	Jim Kelly, 1986-1996	237
Receiving (No.)	Andre Reed, 1985-1996	766
Receiving (Yds.)	Andre Reed, 1985-1996	10,884
Interceptions	George (Butch) Byrd, 1964-1970	40
Punting (Avg.)	Paul Maguire, 1964-1970	42.1
Punt Return (Avg.)	Jeff Burris, 1994-96	10.7
Kickoff Return (Avg.)	Wallace Francis, 1973-74	27.2
Field Goals	Scott Norwood, 1985-1991	133
Touchdowns (Tot.)	Thurman Thomas, 1988-1996	82
Points	Scott Norwood, 1985-1991	670

INDIVIDUAL RECORDS—SINGLE SEASON

Category	Name	Performance
Rushing (Yds.)	O.J. Simpson, 1973	2,003
Passing (Yds.)	Jim Kelly, 1991	3,844
Passing (TDs)	Jim Kelly, 1991	33
Receiving (No.)	Andre Reed, 1994	90
Receiving (Yds.)	Andre Reed, 1989	1,312
Interceptions	Billy Atkins, 1961	10
	Tom Janik, 1967	10
Punting (Avg.)	Billy Atkins, 1961	44.5
Punt Return (Avg.)	Keith Moody, 1977	13.1
Kickoff Return (Avg.)	Ed Rutkowski, 1963	30.2
Field Goals	Scott Norwood, 1988	32
Touchdowns (Tot.)	O.J. Simpson, 1975	23
Points	O.J. Simpson, 1975	138

INDIVIDUAL RECORDS—SINGLE GAME

Category	Name	Performance
Rushing (Yds.)	O.J. Simpson, 11-25-76	273
Passing (Yds.)	Joe Ferguson, 10-9-83	419
Passing (TDs)	Jim Kelly, 9-8-91	6
Receiving (No.)	Andre Reed, 11-20-94	15
Receiving (Yds.)	Jerry Butler, 9-23-79	255
Interceptions	Many Times	3
	Last time by Jeff Nixon, 9-7-80	
Field Goals	Steve Christie, 10-20-96	6
Touchdowns (Tot.)	Cookie Gilchrist, 12-8-63	5
Points	Cookie Gilchrist, 12-8-63	30

Oct. 5	**Detroit**	1:00
Oct. 12	at New England	1:00
Oct. 20	at Indianapolis (Mon.)	8:00
Oct. 26	**Denver**	1:00
Nov. 2	**Miami**	1:00
Nov. 9	**New England**	4:00
Nov. 17	at Miami (Mon.)	9:00
Nov. 23	at Tennessee	12:00
Nov. 30	**New York Jets**	1:00
Dec. 7	at Chicago	12:00
Dec. 14	**Jacksonville**	1:00
Dec. 20	at Green Bay (Sat.)	12:30

COACHING HISTORY

(275-292-8)

1960-61	Buster Ramsey	11-16-1
1962-65	Lou Saban	38-18-3
1966-68	Joe Collier*	13-17-1
1968	Harvey Johnson	1-10-1
1969-70	John Rauch	7-20-1
1971	Harvey Johnson	1-13-0
1972-76	Lou Saban**	32-29-1
1976-77	Jim Ringo	3-20-0
1978-82	Chuck Knox	38-38-0
1983-85	Kay Stephenson***	10-26-0
1985-86	Hank Bullough****	4-17-0
1986-96	Marv Levy	117-68-0

*Released after two games in 1968
**Resigned after five games in 1976
***Released after four games in 1985
****Released after nine games in 1986

RICH STADIUM

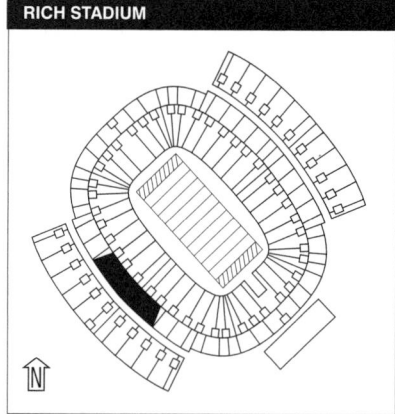

1996 TEAM RECORD

PRESEASON (2-2)

Date	Result		Opponents
8/2	L	7-17	Washington
8/8	W	35-12	at Minnesota
8/17	W	24-0	at Carolina
8/23	L	14-37	Baltimore

REGULAR SEASON (10-6)

Date	Result		Opponents	Att.
9/1	W	23-20	at N.Y. Giants (OT)	74,218
9/8	W	17-10	New England	78,104
9/16	L	6-24	at Pittsburgh	59,002
9/22	W	10-7	Dallas	78,098
10/6	W	16-13	Indianapolis (OT)	79,401
10/13	L	7-21	Miami	79,642
10/20	W	25-22	at N.Y. Jets	49,775
10/27	L	25-28	at New England	58,858
11/3	W	38-13	Washington	78,002
11/10	W	24-17	at Philadelphia	66,613
11/17	W	31-17	Cincinnati	75,549
11/24	W	35-10	N.Y. Jets	60,854
12/1	L	10-13	at Indianapolis (OT)	53,804
12/8	L	18-26	at Seattle	41,373
12/16	L	14-16	at Miami	67,016
12/22	W	20-9	Kansas City	68,671

POSTSEASON (0-1)

12/28	L	27-30	Jacksonville	70,213

(OT) Overtime

SCORE BY PERIODS

Bills	37	110	77	89	6	—	319
Opponents	70	63	39	91	3	—	266

ATTENDANCE

Home 598,321   Away 470,659   Total 1,068,980
Single-game home record, 80,368 (10/4/92)
Single-season home record, 635,899 (1991)

1996 TEAM STATISTICS

	Bills	Opp.
Total First Downs	294	283
Rushing	128	94
Passing	149	168
Penalty	17	21
Third Down: Made/Att	83/238	92/259
Third Down Pct.	34.9	35.5
Fourth Down: Made/Att	9/14	5/17
Fourth Down Pct.	64.3	29.4
Total Net Yards	5119	4737
Avg. Per Game	319.9	296.1
Total Plays	1094	1105
Avg. Per Play	4.7	4.3
Net Yards Rushing	1901	1669
Avg. Per Game	118.8	104.3
Total Rushes	563	495
Net Yards Passing	3218	3068
Avg. Per Game	201.1	191.8
Sacked/Yards Lost	48/340	48/341
Gross Yards	3558	3409
Att./Completions	483/279	562/292
Completion Pct.	57.8	52.0
Had Intercepted	24	14
Punts/Avg.	101/41.5	102/43.2
Net Punting Avg.	101/36.5	102/36.7
Penalties/Yards Lost	106/831	86/607
Fumbles/Ball Lost	25/13	23/14
Touchdowns	35	28
Rushing	14	12
Passing	18	11
Returns	3	5
Avg. Time of Possession	28:40	31:20

1996 INDIVIDUAL STATISTICS

PASSING	Att.	Comp.	Yds.	Pct.	TD	Int.	Tkld.	Rate
Kelly	379	222	2810	58.6	14	19	37/287	73.2
Collins	99	55	739	55.6	4	5	11/53	71.9
Van Pelt	5	2	9	40.0	0	0	0/0	47.9
Bills	483	279	3558	57.8	18	24	48/340	72.6
Opponents	562	292	3409	52.0	11	14	48/341	66.8

SCORING	TD R	TD P	TD Rt	PAT	FG	Saf	PTS
Christie	0	0	0	33/33	24/29	0	105
Thomas	8	0	0	0/0	0/0	0	48
Reed	0	6	0	0/0	0/0	0	36
Holmes	4	1	0	0/0	0/0	0	32
Early	0	4	0	0/0	0/0	0	26
Moulds	0	2	1	0/0	0/0	0	18
Tasker	0	3	0	0/0	0/0	0	18
Kelly	2	0	0	0/0	0/0	0	12
Brantley	0	1	0	0/0	0/0	0	6
Cline	0	1	0	0/0	0/0	0	6
Northern	0	0	1	0/0	0/0	0	6
White	0	0	1	0/0	0/0	0	6
Bills	14	18	3	33/33	24/29	0	319
Opponents	12	11	5	25/26	23/36	1	266

2-Point conversions: Early, Holmes. Team: 2-2,
Opponents: 1-2.

RUSHING	Att.	Yds.	Avg.	LG	TD
Thomas	281	1033	3.7	36	8
Holmes	189	571	3.0	37	4
Kelly	19	66	3.5	22	2
Tindale	14	49	3.5	15	0
Moulds	12	44	3.7	11	0
Collins	21	43	2.0	10	0
Early	3	39	13.0	29	0
Tasker	9	31	3.4	11	0
Reed	8	22	2.8	13	0
Bratton	4	8	2.0	5	0
Van Pelt	3	-5	-1.7	-1	0
Bills	563	1901	3.4	37	14
Opponents	495	1669	3.4	51	12

RECEIVING	No.	Yds.	Avg.	LG	TD
Reed	66	1036	15.7	67t	6
Early	50	798	16.0	95t	4
Johnson	46	457	9.9	33	0
Thomas	26	254	9.8	69	0
Tasker	21	372	17.7	62	3
Moulds	20	279	14.0	47	2
Cline	19	117	6.2	15	1
Holmes	16	102	6.4	20	1
Copeland	7	85	12.1	31	0
Brantley	5	47	9.4	22t	1
Coons	1	12	12.0	12	0
Louchiey	1	0	0.0	0	0
Tindale	1	-1	-1.0	-1	0
Bills	279	3558	12.8	95t	18
Opponents	292	3409	11.7	61	11

INTERCEPTIONS	No.	Yds.	Avg.	LG	TD
Schulz	4	24	6.0	19	0
Martin	2	35	17.5	31	0
Stevens	2	0	0.0	0	0
Burris	1	28	28.0	28	0
Spielman	1	14	14.0	14	0
Kerner	1	6	6.0	6	0
Perry	1	6	6.0	6	0
Jackson	1	0	0.0	0	0
T. Smith	1	0	0.0	0	0
Bills	14	113	8.1	31	0
Opponents	24	498	20.8	91t	4

PUNTING	No.	Yds.	Avg.	In 20	LG
Mohr	101	4194	41.5	27	80
Bills	101	4194	41.5	27	80
Opponents	102	4406	43.2	27	66

PUNT RETURNS	No.	FC	Yds.	Avg.	LG	TD
Burris	27	7	286	10.6	45	0
Copeland	14	7	119	8.5	19	0
Tasker	2	1	18	9.0	12	0
Bills	43	15	423	9.8	45	0
Opponents	40	25	246	6.2	87t	1

KICKOFF RETURNS	No.	Yds.	Avg.	LG	TD
Moulds	52	1205	23.2	97t	1
Copeland	6	136	22.7	47	0
Bills	58	1341	23.1	97t	1
Opponents	65	1255	19.3	32	0

SACKS	No.
B. Smith	13.5
Hansen	8.0
Paup	6.0
Jeffcoat	5.0
Northern	5.0
Rogers	3.5
Washington	3.5
Irvin	2.0
Kerner	1.0
White	0.5
Bills	48.0
Opponents	48.0

1997 DRAFT CHOICES

Round	Name	Pos.	College
1	Antowain Smith	RB	Houston
2	Marcellus Wiley	DE	Columbia
4	Jamie Nails	T	Florida A&M
5	Sean Woodson	DB	Jackson State
6	Marcus Spriggs	T	Houston
7	Pat Fitzgerald	TE	Texas

BUFFALO BILLS

1997 VETERAN ROSTER

No.	Name	Pos.	Ht.	Wt.	Birthdate	NFL Exp.	College	Hometown	How Acq.	'96 Games/ Starts
76	Albright, Ethan	G-T	6-5	283	5/1/71	3	North Carolina	Greensboro, N.C.	FA-'96	16/0
81	Armour, Justin	WR	6-4	209	1/1/73	3	Stanford	Colorado Springs, Colo.	D4b-'95	0*
82	Brantley, Chris	WR	5-10	180	12/12/70	3	Rutgers	Teaneck, N.J.	FA-'96	10/0
79	Brown, Ruben	G	6-3	304	2/13/72	3	Pittsburgh	Lynchburg, Va.	D1-'95	14/14
22	Burris, Jeff	CB	6-0	204	6/7/72	4	Notre Dame	Rock Hill, S.C.	D1-'94	15/15
2	Christie, Steve	K	6-0	185	11/13/67	8	William & Mary	Oakville, Ontario	PB(TB)-'92	16/0
86	Cline, Tony	TE	6-4	247	11/24/71	3	Stanford	Davis, Calif.	D4c-'95	16/7
15	Collins, Todd	QB	6-4	224	11/5/71	3	Michigan	Walpole, Mass.	D2-'95	7/3
87	Coons, Robert	TE	6-5	249	9/18/69	4	Pittsburgh	Anaheim, Calif.	FA-'95	16/0
85	# Copeland, Russell	WR	6-0	200	11/4/71	5	Memphis State	Tupelo, Miss.	D4-'93	11/0
57	Covington, Damien	LB	5-11	236	12/4/72	3	North Carolina State	Berlin, N.J.	D3b-'95	9/2
88	Early, Quinn	WR	6-0	190	4/13/65	10	Iowa	West Hempstead, N.Y.	FA(NO)-'96	16/13
70	Fina, John	T	6-4	285	3/11/69	6	Arizona	Tucson, Ariz.	D1-'92	15/15
90	Hansen, Phil	DE	6-5	278	5/20/68	7	North Dakota State	Ellendale, N.D.	D2-'91	16/16
8	t- Hobert, Billy Joe	QB	6-3	230	1/8/71	5	Washington	Puyallup, Wash.	T(Oak)-'97	8/3*
44	Holmes, Darick	RB	6-0	226	7/1/71	3	Portland State	Pasadena, Calif.	D7b-'95	16/1
27	Irvin, Ken	CB	5-10	182	7/11/72	3	Memphis	Rome, Ga.	D4a-'95	16/16
31	Jackson, Raymond	CB-S	5-10	189	2/17/73	2	Colorado State	Denver, Colo.	D5-'96	16/1
77	Jeffcoat, Jim	DE	6-5	280	4/1/61	15	Arizona State	Cliffwood, N.J.	FA(Dall)-'95	12/0
84	Johnson, Lonnie	TE	6-3	240	2/14/71	4	Florida State	Miami, Fla.	D2b-'94	16/15
20	Jones, Henry	S	5-11	197	12/29/67	7	Illinois	St. Louis, Mo.	D1-'91	5/5
46	Kerner, Marlon	CB	5-10	187	3/18/73	3	Ohio State	Columbus, Ohio	D3a-'95	15/0
68	Lacina, Corbin	G	6-4	297	11/2/70	4	Augustana	Woodbury, Minn.	D6-'93	12/2
72	Louchiey, Corey	T	6-8	305	10/10/71	4	South Carolina	Greenville, S.C.	D3b-'94	16/4
55	Maddox, Mark	LB	6-1	233	3/23/68	7	Northern Michigan	Milwaukee, Wis.	D9-'91	14/14
21	Martin, Manny	CB	5-11	184	7/31/69	2	Alabama State	Miami, Fla.	FA-'96	16/1
9	Mohr, Chris	P	6-5	215	5/11/66	8	Alabama	Thompson, Ga.	FA-'91	16/0
98	Moran, Sean	DE	6-3	255	6/5/73	2	Colorado State	Aurora, Colo.	D4-'96	16/0
80	Moulds, Eric	WR	6-0	204	7/17/73	2	Mississippi State	Lucedale, Miss.	D1-'96	16/5
99	Northern, Gabe	DE	6-2	240	6/8/74	2	Louisiana State	Baton Rouge, La.	D2-'96	16/2
60	Ostroski, Jerry	G	6-4	310	7/12/70	3	Tulsa	Collegeville, Pa.	FA-'93	16/16
74	Parker, Glenn	T	6-5	305	4/22/66	8	Arizona	Huntington Beach, Calif.	D3-'90	14/13
95	Paup, Bryce	LB	6-5	247	2/29/68	8	Northern Iowa	Jefferson, Ia.	FA(GB)-'95	12/11
58	Perry, Marlo	LB	6-4	250	8/25/72	4	Jackson State	Forest, Miss.	D3a-'94	13/0
94	Pike, Mark	DE	6-4	272	12/27/63	12	Georgia Tech	Villa Hills, Ky.	D7b-'86	16/0
91	Price, Shawn	DE	6-5	260	3/28/70	5	Pacific	Woodland Hills, Calif.	FA-'96	15/0
83	Reed, Andre	WR	6-2	190	1/29/64	13	Kutztown	Allentown, Pa.	D4a-'85	16/16
59	Rogers, Sam	LB	6-3	245	5/30/70	4	Colorado	Pontiac, Mich.	D2c-'94	14/14
24	Schulz, Kurt	S	6-1	208	12/12/68	6	Eastern Washington	Yakima, Wash.	D7-'92	15/15
40	Smedley, Eric	CB-S	5-11	199	7/23/73	2	Indiana	Charleston, W. Va.	D7c-'96	6/0
78	Smith, Bruce	DE	6-4	273	6/18/63	13	Virginia Tech	Norfolk, Va.	D1a-'85	16/16
28	Smith, Thomas	CB	5-11	188	12/5/70	5	North Carolina	Gates, N.C.	D1-'93	16/16
54	Spielman, Chris	LB	6-0	247	10/11/65	10	Ohio State	Massillon, Ohio	FA(Det)-'96	16/16
23	Stevens, Matt	CB	6-0	206	6/15/73	2	Appalachian State	Chapel Hill, N.C.	D3-'96	13/11
89	Tasker, Steve	WR	5-9	183	4/10/62	13	Northwestern	Leoti, Kan.	W(Hou)-'86	8/5
34	Thomas, Thurman	RB	5-10	198	5/16/66	10	Oklahoma State	Missouri City, Tex.	D2-'88	15/15
33	Tindale, Tim	RB	5-10	220	4/15/71	3	Western Ontario	London, Ontario	FA-'94	14/3
10	Van Pelt, Alex	QB	6-0	220	5/1/70	3	Pittsburgh	Pittsburgh, Pa.	FA-'94	1/0
92	Washington, Ted	NT	6-4	325	4/13/68	7	Louisville	Tampa, Fla.	UFA(Den)-'95	16/16
51	† White, David	LB	6-2	235	2/27/70	4	Nebraska	New Orleans, La.	FA-'95	16/5

* Armour was inactive for 11 games in '96; Hobert played 8 games with Oakland in '96.

\# Unrestricted free agent; subject to developments.

† Restricted free agent; subject to developments.

t- Bills traded for Hobert (Oakland).

Retired—Jim Kelly, 11-year quarterback, 13 games in '96.

Also played with Bills in '96—RB Jason Bratton (2 games), C-G Dusty Zeigler (2).

COACHING STAFF

Head Coach,
Marv Levy

Pro Career: Begins his twelfth season as Bills head coach. Guided Buffalo to its eighth postseason appearance in its past nine seasons. Led Bills to four consecutive AFC Championships in 1990-93. Under Levy, the Bills recorded 13-3 records in 1990 and 1991, the best regular-season marks in club history. He guided the Bills to their second consecutive AFC East title with a 9-7 record in 1989. Finished 1988 season with a 12-4 record and a berth in the AFC Championship Game. In his first full year with Bills in 1987, he led team to a 7-8 record. Replaced Hank Bullough on November 3, 1986, and compiled a 2-5 record over the final seven weeks of the season. Previously served as head coach of the Kansas City Chiefs from 1978-1982 and produced a 31-42 mark. Levy began his pro coaching career in 1969 as an assistant with the Philadelphia Eagles. He joined George Allen and the Los Angeles Rams as an assistant one-year later and followed Allen to Washington, where he remained with the Redskins through the 1972 season when Washington played in Super Bowl VII. He was named head coach of the Montreal Alouettes (CFL) in 1973 and posted a 50-34-4 record and two Grey Cup victories (1974, 1977) in five seasons in Canada. After two seasons away from football, he became head coach of the Chicago Blitz of the USFL in 1984. No pro playing experience. Career record: 148-110.

Background: Running back at Coe College 1948-50. Coached at high school level for two years before returning to alma mater from 1953-55. Joined New Mexico staff in 1956 and served as head coach there in 1958-59. Head coach of California from 1960-63 before becoming head coach at William & Mary from 1964-68.

Personal: Born August 3, 1925, Chicago, Ill. Levy was Phi Beta Kappa at Coe College and earned master's degree in English history from Harvard. He lives with his wife Mary Frances in Hamburg, N.Y.

ASSISTANT COACHES

Tom Bresnahan, offensive line; born January 21, 1935, Springfield, Mass., lives in Orchard Park, N.Y. Tackle Holy Cross 1953-55. No pro playing experience. College coach: Williams 1963-67, Columbia 1968-72, Navy 1973-80. Pro coach: Kansas City Chiefs 1981-82, New York Giants 1983-84, St. Louis/Phoenix Cardinals 1986-88, joined Bills in 1989.

Ted Cottrell, linebackers; born June 13, 1947, Chester, Pa., lives in Orchard Park, N.Y. Linebacker Delaware Valley College 1966-68. Pro linebacker Atlanta Falcons 1969-70, Winnepeg Blue Bombers (CFL) 1971. College coach: Rutgers 1973-80, 1983. Pro coach: Kansas City Chiefs 1981-82, New Jersey Generals (USFL) 1983-84, Buffalo Bills 1986-89, Arizona Cardinals 1990-94, rejoined Bills in 1995.

Bruce DeHaven, special teams; born September 6, 1952, Trousdale, Kan., lives in East Aurora, N.Y. No college or pro playing experience. College coach: Kansas 1979-81, New Mexico State 1982. Pro coach: New Jersey Generals (USFL) 1983, Pittsburgh Maulers (USFL) 1984, Orlando Renegades (USFL) 1985, joined Bills in 1987.

Dan Henning, offensive coordinator-quarterbacks; born June 21, 1942, Bronx, N.Y., lives in Orchard Park, N.Y. Quarterback William & Mary 1962-64. Pro quarterback San Diego Chargers 1964, 1966-67. College coach: Florida State 1968-70, 1974, Virginia Tech 1971, 1973, Boston College 1994-96 (head coach). Pro coach: Houston Oilers 1972, New York Jets 1976-78, Miami Dolphins 1979-80, Washington Redskins 1981-82, 1987-88, Atlanta Falcons 1983-86 (head coach), San Diego Chargers 1989-91 (head coach), Detroit Lions 1992-93, joined Bills in 1997.

Charlie Joiner, receivers; born October 14, 1947, Many, La., lives in Orchard Park, N.Y. Wide receiver Grambling 1965-68. Defensive back-wide receiver Houston Oilers 1969-72, Cincinnati Bengals 1972-75, San Diego Chargers 1976-86. Inducted

into Pro Football Hall of Fame in 1996. Pro coach: San Diego Chargers 1987-91, joined Bills in 1992.

Rusty Jones, strength and conditioning; born August 14, 1953, Berwick, Maine, lives in Hamburg, N.Y. No college or pro playing experience. College coach: Springfield 1978-79. Pro coach: Pittsburgh Maulers (USFL) 1983-84, joined Bills in 1985.

Don Lawrence, offensive quality control-tight ends; born June 4, 1937, Cleveland, Ohio, lives in Orchard Park, N.Y. Offensive-defensive lineman Notre Dame 1957-58. Pro offensive-defensive lineman Washington Redskins 1959-61. College coach: Notre Dame 1961-63, Kansas State 1964-65, Cincinnati 1966, Virginia 1970-73 (head coach 1971-73), Texas Christian 1974-75, Missouri 1976-77. Pro coach: British Columbia Lions (CFL) 1978-79, Kansas City Chiefs 1980-82, 1987-88, Buffalo Bills 1983-84, Tampa Bay Buccaneers 1985-86, Winnipeg Blue Bombers (CFL) 1989, rejoined Bills in 1990.

Chuck Lester, administrative assistant to head coach, assistant linebackers coach; born May 18, 1955, Chicago, Ill., lives in Orchard Park, N.Y. Linebacker Oklahoma 1974. No pro playing experience. College coach: Iowa State 1980-81, Oklahoma 1982-84. Pro coach: Kansas City Chiefs 1984-86 (scout), joined Bills in 1987.

Wade Phillips, defensive coordinator; born June 21, 1947, Orange, Tex., lives in Orchard Park, N.Y. Linebacker Houston 1966-68. No pro playing experience. College coach: Houston, 1969, Oklahoma State 1973-74, Kansas 1975. Pro coach: Houston Oilers 1976-80, New Orleans Saints 1981-85 (head coach last four games of 1985), Philadelphia Eagles 1986-88, Denver Broncos 1989-94 (head coach 1993-94), joined Bills in 1995.

Elijah Pitts, assistant head coach-running backs; born February 3, 1938, Mayflower, Ark., lives in Orchard Park, N.Y. Running back Philander Smith 1957-60. Pro running back Green Bay Packers 1961-69, 1971, Los Angeles Rams 1970, Chicago Bears 1970, New Orleans Saints 1970. Pro coach: Los Angeles Rams 1974-77, Buffalo Bills 1978-80, Houston Oilers 1981-83, Hamilton Tiger-Cats (CFL) 1984, rejoined Bills in 1985.

Dick Roach, defensive backs; born August 23, 1937, Rapid City, S.D., lives in Orchard Park, N.Y. Defensive back Black Hills State 1952-55. No pro playing experience. College coach: Montana State 1966-69, Oregon State 1970, Wyoming 1971-72, Fresno State 1973, Washington State 1974-75. Pro coach: Montreal Alouettes (CFL) 1976-77, Kansas City Chiefs 1978-80, New England Patriots 1981, Michigan Panthers (USFL) 1983-84, Tampa Bay Buccaneers 1985-86, joined Bills in 1987.

Dan Sekanovich, defensive line; born July 27, 1933, West Hazelton, Pa., lives in Depew, N.Y. End Tennessee 1951-53. Pro defensive end Montreal Alouettes (CFL) 1954. College coach: Susquehanna 1961-63, Connecticut 1964-67, Pittsburgh 1968, Navy 1969-70, Kentucky 1971-72. Pro coach: Montreal Alouettes (CFL) 1973-76, New York Jets 1977-82, Atlanta Falcons 1983-85, Miami Dolphins 1986-91, joined Bills in 1992.

1997 FIRST-YEAR ROSTER

Name	Pos.	Ht.	Wt.	Birthdate	College	Hometown	How Acq.
Ballard, Jim (1)	QB	6-3	223	4/16/72	Mount Union	Cuyahoga, Ohio	FA
Bender, Carey (1)	RB	5-8	185	1/28/72	Coe College	Marion, Iowa	FA-'95
Brandenburg, Dan (1)	LB	6-2	255	2/2/73	Indiana State	Rensselaor, Ind.	D7a-'96
Bratton, Jason (1)	RB	6-1	252	10/19/72	Grambling State	Longview, Tex.	FA-'96
Brown, Doug	DT	6-7	280	9/29/74	Simon Fraser	Coquitlam, Canada	FA
Buckner, Tyrell	LB	6-0	250	6/5/75	Alabama	Denison, Tex.	FA
Collins, Marc (1)	P	6-4	209	4/24/74	Eastern Kentucky	Covington, Ky.	FA
Conaty, Bill	G-T	6-2	306	3/8/73	Virginia Tech	Pennsuken, N.J.	FA
Cunningham, Jimmy (1)	WR-KR	5-7	170	1/1/73	Howard	Houston, Tex.	FA-'96
Fitzgerald, Pat	TE	6-2	228	12/4/74	Texas	Van Nuys, Calif.	D7
Galloway, Mitchell	WR	5-8	178	10/8/74	East Carolina	Bennettsville, S.C.	FA
Green, Clifford	CB	5-8	185	4/14/75	Tennessee State	Decatur, Ga.	FA
Hack, Dave (1)	G-T	6-6	277	4/22/72	Maryland	Holland, N.Y.	FA
Hammonds, Juan (1)	DE	6-3	260	3/5/72	Michigan State	Louisville, Ky.	FA
Holecek, John (1)	LB	6-2	238	5/7/72	Illinois	Steger, Ill.	D5-'95
Huerta, Carlos (1)	K	5-7	185	6/29/69	Miami	Coral Gables, Fla.	FA
Ingoglia, Rene	RB	5-10	202	5/23/72	Massachusetts	Rochester, N.Y.	FA
James, Kendall	WR	6-0	195	1/4/73	Carson Newman	Miami, Fla.	FA
Jeffcoat, Jerold (1)	DT	6-2	315	8/30/69	Temple	Cliffwood, N.J.	FA-'96
Lacoste, Paul	LB	6-1	225	9/3/74	Mississippi State	Jackson, Miss.	FA
Nails, Jamie	T	6-6	354	6/3/75	Florida A&M	Baxley, Ga.	D4
Provo, Dwayne (1)	CB	5-9	180	10/7/70	St. Marys	North Preston, Canada	FA
Reese, Jerry (1)	WR-KR	5-11	190	3/1/73	San Jose State	Pittsburg, Calif.	FA
Riemersma, Jay (1)	TE	6-5	254	5/17/73	Michigan	Leeland, Mich.	D7b-'96
Rockwood, Mike (1)	G-T	6-10	345	6/5/73	Nevada-Reno	Mira Loma, Calif.	FA
Smith, Antowain	RB	6-2	224	3/14/72	Houston	Montgomery, Ala.	D1
Spriggs, Marcus	T	6-3	295	5/17/74	Houston	Hattiesburg, Miss.	D6
Wiley, Marcellus	DE	6-5	271	11/30/74	Columbia	Los Angeles, Calif.	D2
Williams, Pat	DT	6-3	270	10/24/72	Texas A&M	Monroe, La.	FA
Woodson, Sean	S	6-0	214	8/27/74	Jackson State	Jackson, Miss.	D5
Zeigler, Dusty (1)	C-G	6-5	298	9/27/73	Notre Dame	Rincon, Ga.	D6b-'96

The term NFL Rookie is defined as a player who is in his first season of professional football and has not been on the roster of another professional football team for any regular-season or postseason games. A Rookie is designated by an "R" on NFL rosters. Players who have been active in another professional football league or players who have NFL experience, including either preseason training camp or being on an Active List or Inactive List, or on Reserve/Injured or Reserve/Physically Unable to Perform for fewer than six regular-season games, are termed NFL First-Year Players. An NFL First-Year Player is designated by a "1" on NFL rosters. Thereafter, a player is credited with an additional year of experience for each season in which he accumulates six games on the Active List or Inactive List, or on Reserve/Injured or Reserve/Physically Unable to Perform.

NOTES

CINCINNATI BENGALS

American Football Conference
Central Division
Team Colors: Black, Orange, and White
One Bengals Drive
Cincinnati, Ohio 45204
Telephone: (513) 621-3550

CLUB OFFICIALS

President/General Manager: Michael Brown
Chairman of the Board: Austin E. Knowlton
Vice President: John Sawyer
Assistant General Manager/Director of
  Player Personnel: Pete Brown
General Counsel/Corporate Secretary:
  Katherine Blackburn
Director of Stadium Development: Troy Blackburn
Assistant Secretary/Treasurer;
  Scouting/Player Personnel: Paul H. Brown
Business Manager: Bill Connelly
Director of Community Affairs: Jeff Berding
Stadium Sales/Marketing: Jennifer L. McNally
Director of Pro Personnel/Scouting: Jim Lippincott
Comptroller: Jay Reis
Director of Finance: Bill Scanlon
Public Relations Director: Jack Brennan
Assistant Public Relations Director:
  Patrick J. Combs
Director of Marketing: Mike Hoffbauer
Entertainment Director/Assistant Director
  of Marketing: Dave Slyby
Ticket Manager: Paul Kelly
Trainer: Paul Sparling
Assistant Trainers: Billy Brooks, Rob Recker
Equipment Manager: Tom Gray
Video Director: Al Davis
Assistant Video Director: Travis Brammer
Stadium: Cinergy Field • **Capacity:** 60,389
  200 Cinergy Field
  Cincinnati, Ohio 45202
Playing Surface: AstroTurf-8
Training Camp: Georgetown College
  Georgetown, Kentucky 40324

1997 SCHEDULE
PRESEASON
Aug. 1	at Indianapolis	6:30
Aug. 8	at Detroit	7:30
Aug. 16	**Minnesota**	7:30
Aug. 22	**Seattle**	7:30

REGULAR SEASON
Aug. 31	**Arizona**	1:00
Sept. 7	at Baltimore	1:00
Sept. 14	Open Date	
Sept. 21	at Denver	2:00
Sept. 28	**New York Jets**	4:00
Oct. 5	at Jacksonville	1:00
Oct. 12	at Tennessee	12:00
Oct. 19	**Pittsburgh**	4:00
Oct. 26	at New York Giants	1:00
Nov. 2	**San Diego**	1:00
Nov. 9	at Indianapolis	1:00
Nov. 16	at Pittsburgh	1:00
Nov. 23	**Jacksonville**	4:00
Nov. 30	at Philadelphia	1:00
Dec. 4	**Tennessee** (Thurs.)	8:00
Dec. 14	**Dallas**	1:00
Dec. 21	**Baltimore**	1:00

COACHING HISTORY
(205-242-1)
1968-75	Paul Brown	55-59-1
1976-78	Bill Johnson*	18-15-0
1978-79	Homer Rice	8-19-0
1980-83	Forrest Gregg	34-27-0
1984-91	Sam Wyche	64-68-0
1992-96	Dave Shula**	19-52-0
1996	Bruce Coslet	7-2-0

* Resigned after five games in 1978
** Released after seven games in 1996

RECORD HOLDERS
INDIVIDUAL RECORDS—CAREER
Category	Name	Performance
Rushing (Yds.)	James Brooks, 1984-1991	6,447
Passing (Yds.)	Ken Anderson, 1971-1986	32,838
Passing (TDs)	Ken Anderson, 1971-1986	197
Receiving (No.)	Cris Collinsworth, 1981-88	417
Receiving (Yds.)	Isaac Curtis, 1973-1984	7,101
Interceptions	Ken Riley, 1969-1983	65
Punting (Avg.)	Dave Lewis, 1970-73	43.9
Punt Return (Avg.)	Mitchell Price, 1990-92	10.4
Kickoff Return (Avg.)	Lemar Parrish, 1970-77	24.7
Field Goals	Jim Breech, 1980-1992	225
Touchdowns (Tot.)	Pete Johnson, 1977-1983	70
Points	Jim Breech, 1980-1992	1,151

INDIVIDUAL RECORDS—SINGLE SEASON
Category	Name	Performance
Rushing (Yds.)	James Brooks, 1989	1,239
Passing (Yds.)	Boomer Esiason, 1986	3,959
Passing (TDs)	Ken Anderson, 1981	29
Receiving (No.)	Carl Pickens, 1996	100
Receiving (Yds.)	Eddie Brown, 1988	1,273
Interceptions	Ken Riley, 1976	9
Punting (Avg.)	Dave Lewis, 1970	46.2
Punt Return (Avg.)	Mike Martin, 1984	15.7
Kickoff Return (Avg.)	Lemar Parrish, 1970	30.2
Field Goals	Doug Pelfrey, 1995	29
Touchdowns (Tot.)	Carl Pickens, 1995	17
Points	Doug Pelfrey, 1995	121

INDIVIDUAL RECORDS—SINGLE GAME
Category	Name	Performance
Rushing (Yds.)	James Brooks, 12-23-90	201
Passing (Yds.)	Boomer Esiason, 10-7-90	490
Passing (TDs)	Boomer Esiason, 12-21-86	5
	Boomer Esiason, 10-29-89	5
Receiving (No.)	James Brooks, 12-25-89	12
	Carl Pickens, 11-10-96	12
Receiving (Yds.)	Eddie Brown, 11-6-88	216
Interceptions	Many times	3
	Last time by David Fulcher, 12-17-89	
Field Goals	Doug Pelfrey, 11-6-94	6
Touchdowns (Tot.)	Larry Kinnebrew, 10-28-84	4
Points	Larry Kinnebrew, 10-28-84	24

CINERGY FIELD

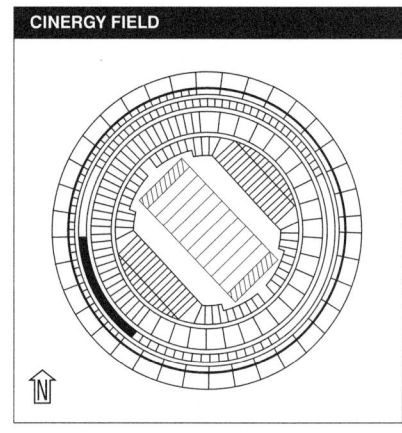

1996 TEAM RECORD

PRESEASON (2-2)

Date	Result		Opponents
8/3	W	28-25	Indianapolis
8/10	L	10-13	at Arizona
8/16	W	28-7	at Washington
8/23	L	17-24	Detroit

REGULAR SEASON (8-8)

Date	Result		Opponents	Att.
9/1	L	16-26	at St. Louis	62,659
9/8	L	14-27	at San Diego	55,880
9/15	W	30-15	New Orleans	45,412
9/29	L	10-14	Denver	51,798
10/6	L	27-30	Houston (OT)	44,680
10/13	L	10-20	at Pittsburgh	58,875
10/20	L	21-28	at San Francisco	63,218
10/27	W	28-21	Jacksonville	45,890
11/3	W	24-21	at Baltimore	60,743
11/10	W	34-24	Pittsburgh	57,265
11/17	L	17-31	at Buffalo	75,549
11/24	W	41-31	Atlanta	44,868
12/1	L	27-30	at Jacksonville	57,408
12/8	W	21-14	Baltimore	43,022
12/15	W	21-13	at Houston	15,131
12/22	W	31-24	Indianapolis	49,389

(OT) Overtime

SCORE BY PERIODS

Bengals	57	111	65	139	0	—	372
Opponents	67	105	86	108	3	—	369

ATTENDANCE

Home 382,324   Away 449,463   Total 831,787
Single-game home record, 60,284 (10/17/71)
Single-season home record, 473,288 (1990)

1996 TEAM STATISTICS

	Bengals	Opp.
Total First Downs	332	317
Rushing	114	109
Passing	190	196
Penalty	28	12
Third Down: Made/Att	102/236	94/214
Third Down Pct.	43.2	43.9
Fourth Down: Made/Att	5/12	8/13
Fourth Down Pct.	41.7	61.5
Total Net Yards	5225	5469
Avg. Per Game	326.6	341.8
Total Plays	1088	1047
Avg. Per Play	4.8	5.2
Net Yards Rushing	1793	1643
Avg. Per Game	112.1	102.7
Total Rushes	478	444
Net Yards Passing	3432	3826
Avg. Per Game	214.5	239.1
Sacked/Yards Lost	47/294	32/202
Gross Yards	3726	4028
Att./Completions	563/316	571/319
Completion Pct.	56.1	55.9
Had Intercepted	16	34
Punts/Avg.	82/44.3	61/44.4
Net Punting Avg.	82/34.0	61/38.5
Penalties/Yards Lost	90/678	102/768
Fumbles/Ball Lost	19/9	16/10
Touchdowns	43	42
Rushing	14	15
Passing	25	22
Returns	4	5
Avg. Time of Possession	31:33	28:27

1996 INDIVIDUAL STATISTICS

PASSING	Att.	Comp.	Yds.	Pct.	TD	Int.	Tkld.	Rate
Blake	549	308	3624	56.1	24	14	44/278	80.3
Wilhelm	13	7	90	53.8	1	2	3/16	61.9
Pickens	1	1	12	100.0	0	0	0/0	116.7
Bengals	563	316	3726	56.1	25	16	47/294	79.4
Opponents	571	319	4028	55.9	22	34	32/202	66.1

SCORING	TD R	TD P	TD Rt	PAT	FG	Saf	PTS
Pelfrey	0	0	0	41/41	23/28	0	110
Pickens	0	12	0	0/0	0/0	0	74
Carter	8	1	0	0/0	0/0	0	54
Scott	0	5	0	0/0	0/0	0	30
McGee	0	4	0	0/0	0/0	0	24
Bieniemy	2	0	0	0/0	0/0	0	12
Blake	2	0	0	0/0	0/0	0	12
Dunn	0	1	1	0/0	0/0	0	12
Hearst	0	1	0	0/0	0/0	0	8
Ambrose	0	0	1	0/0	0/0	0	6
Cothran	1	0	0	0/0	0/0	0	6
Francis	0	0	1	0/0	0/0	0	6
Hundon	0	1	0	0/0	0/0	0	6
Milne	1	0	0	0/0	0/0	0	6
Spencer	0	0	1	0/0	0/0	0	6
Bengals	14	25	4	41/41	23/28	0	372
Opponents	15	22	5	40/40	25/30	0	369

2-Point conversions: Hearst, Pickens. Team: 2-2,
Opponents: 1-2.

RUSHING	Att.	Yds.	Avg.	LG	TD
Hearst	225	847	3.8	24	0
Blake	72	317	4.4	18	2
Bieniemy	56	269	4.8	33t	2
Carter	91	264	2.9	31t	8
Cothran	15	44	2.9	9	1
Wilhelm	6	24	4.0	18	0
Milne	8	22	2.8	5	1
Scott	3	4	1.3	8	0
Pickens	2	2	1.0	2	0
Bengals	478	1793	3.8	33t	14
Opponents	444	1643	3.7	45t	15

RECEIVING	No.	Yds.	Avg.	LG	TD
Pickens	100	1180	11.8	61t	12
Scott	58	833	14.4	50t	5
McGee	38	446	11.7	22	4
Dunn	32	509	15.9	40	1
Bieniemy	32	272	8.5	42	0
Carter	22	169	7.7	20	1
Hearst	12	131	10.9	40	1
Battaglia	8	79	9.9	17	0
Cothran	7	49	7.0	14	0
Milne	3	29	9.7	15	0
Sadowski	3	15	5.0	8	0
Hundon	1	14	14.0	14t	1
Bengals	316	3726	11.8	61t	25
Opponents	319	4028	12.6	57	22

INTERCEPTIONS	No.	Yds.	Avg.	LG	TD
Ambrose	8	63	7.9	31t	1
Spencer	5	48	9.6	34	0
Tovar	4	42	10.5	24	0
Francis	3	61	20.3	42t	1
Walker	2	35	17.5	35	0
Myers	2	10	5.0	10	0
Rod W. Jones	2	2	1.0	2	0
Orlando	2	0	0.0	0	0
Sawyer	2	0	0.0	0	0
Rog. Jones	1	30	30.0	30	0
Dixon	1	10	10.0	10	0
Wilkinson	1	7	7.0	7	0
Langford	1	0	0.0	0	0
Bengals	34	308	9.1	42t	2
Opponents	16	172	10.8	61	1

PUNTING	No.	Yds.	Avg.	In 20	LG
L. Johnson	80	3630	45.4	16	67
Pelfrey	1	4	4.0	0	4
Bengals	82	3634	44.3	16	67
Opponents	61	2706	44.4	20	65

PUNT RETURNS	No.	FC	Yds.	Avg.	LG	TD
Sawyer	15	5	117	7.8	62	0
Myers	9	2	51	5.7	12	0
Dunn	7	1	54	7.7	20	0
Hundon	1	0	-7	-7.0	-7	0
Pickens	1	0	2	2.0	2	0
Bengals	33	8	217	6.6	62	0
Opponents	38	6	502	13.2	64	0

KICKOFF RETURNS	No.	Yds.	Avg.	LG	TD
Dunn	35	782	22.3	90t	1
Sawyer	12	241	20.1	33	0
Hundon	10	237	23.7	31	0
Hill	9	173	19.2	29	0
Sadowski	2	7	3.5	7	0
Battaglia	1	8	8.0	8	0
Cothran	1	11	11.0	11	0
Bengals	70	1459	20.8	90t	1
Opponents	69	1642	23.8	95t	1

SACKS	No.
Wilkinson	6.5
McDonald	5.0
Copeland	3.0
Francis	3.0
Tovar	3.0
T. Johnson	2.5
Langford	2.0
Stallings	2.0
Sawyer	1.5
Orlando	1.0
Smith	1.0
Von Oelhoffen	1.0
Morabito	0.5
Bengals	32.0
Opponents	47.0

1997 DRAFT CHOICES

Round	Name	Pos.	College
1	Reinard Wilson	LB	Florida State
2	Corey Dillon	RB	Washington
3	Rod Payne	C	Michigan
4	Tremain Mack	DB	Miami
5	Andre Purvis	DT	North Carolina
6	Canute Curtis	LB	West Virginia
7	William Carr	DT	Michigan

CINCINNATI BENGALS

1997 VETERAN ROSTER

No.		Name	Pos.	Ht.	Wt.	Birthdate	NFL Exp.	College	Hometown	How Acq.	'96 Games/ Starts
33		Ambrose, Ashley	CB	5-10	192	9/17/70	6	Mississippi Valley State	New Orleans, La.	UFA(Ind)-'96	16/16
71		Anderson, Willie	T	6-5	325	7/11/75	2	Auburn	Mobile, Ala.	D1-'96	16/10
89		Battaglia, Marco	TE	6-3	250	1/25/73	2	Rutgers	Howard Beach, N.Y.	D2-'96	16/0
21		Bieniemy, Eric	RB	5-7	198	8/15/69	7	Colorado	New Orleans, La.	UFA(SD)-'95	16/0
66		Blackman, Ken	G	6-6	315	11/8/72	2	Illinois	Abilene, Tex.	D3-'96	14/10
8		Blake, Jeff	QB	6-0	202	12/4/70	6	East Carolina	Sanford, Fla.	W(NYJ)-'94	16/16
38		Borgella, Jocelyn	CB	5-10	180	8/26/71	4	Cincinnati	Miami, Fla.	FA-'97	11/0*
74		Braham, Rich	C-G	6-4	290	11/6/70	4	West Virginia	Morgantown, W. Va.	W(Ariz)-'94	16/16
65		Brilz, Darrick	C	6-3	295	2/14/64	11	Oregon State	Pinole Valley, Calif.	UFA(Sea)-'94	13/13
75		Brown, Anthony	T-G	6-5	310	11/6/72	3	Utah	Salt Lake City, Utah	FA-'95	7/0
72		Brumfield, Scott	G	6-8	320	8/19/70	5	Brigham Young	Spanish Fork, Utah	FA-'94	9/8
32		Carter, Ki-Jana	RB	5-10	227	9/12/73	3	Penn State	Westerville, Ohio	D1-'95	16/4
55	#	Collins, Andre	LB	6-1	231	5/4/68	8	Penn State	Cinaminson, N.J.	FA-'95	14/0
92		Copeland, John	DE	6-3	286	9/20/70	5	Alabama	Lanett, Ala.	D1-'93	13/13
29		Cothran, Jeff	RB	6-1	249	6/28/71	4	Ohio State	Middletown, Ohio	D3-'94	11/11
51		Dixon, Gerald	LB	6-3	250	6/20/69	6	South Carolina	Rock Hill, S.C.	UFA(Balt)-'96	16/1
80		Dunn, David	WR	6-3	210	6/10/72	3	Fresno State	San Diego, Calif.	D5-'95	16/0
7		Esiason, Boomer	QB	6-5	224	4/17/61	14	Maryland	Islip, N.Y.	UFA(Ariz)-'97	10/8*
50		Francis, James	LB	6-5	252	8/4/68	8	Baylor	Houston, Tex.	D1-'90	16/15
41		Graham, Scottie	RB	5-9	222	3/28/69	5	Ohio State	Long Island, N.Y.	UFA(Minn)-'97	11/0*
62		Gutierrez, Brock	C	6-3	300	9/25/73	2	Central Michigan	Charlotte, Mich.	FA-'96	0*
84		Hill, Jeff	WR	5-11	178	9/24/72	3	Purdue	Cincinnati, Ohio	FA-'94	10/0
11		Johnson, Lee	P-K	6-2	200	11/27/61	13	Brigham Young	Conroe, Tex.	W(Clev)-'88	16/0
90		Johnson, Tim	DT	6-3	286	1/29/65	11	Penn State	Sarasota, Fla.	UFA(Wash)-'96	14/13
25	#	Jones, Rod	CB	6-0	185	3/31/64	12	Southern Methodist	Dallas, Tex.	FA-'96	6/1
60		Jones, Rod	G	6-4	315	1/11/74	2	Kansas	Detroit, Mich.	D7-'96	5/1
24		Jones, Roger	CB	5-9	175	4/22/69	7	Tennessee State	Nashville, Tenn.	W(TB)-'94	14/1
83		Jordan, Kevin	WR	6-1	188	12/14/72	2	UCLA	Washington, D.C.	W(Ariz)-'96	0*
94		Langford, Jevon	DE	6-3	275	2/16/74	2	Oklahoma State	Washington, D.C.	D4-'96	12/3
40		McCullough, Deland	RB	5-11	195	12/1/72	2	Miami, Ohio	Youngstown, Ohio	FA-'96	0*
56		McDonald, Ricardo	LB	6-2	235	11/8/69	6	Pittsburgh	Kingston, Jamaica	D4-'92	16/15
82		McGee, Tony	TE	6-3	246	4/21/71	5	Michigan	Terre Haute, Ind.	D2-'93	16/16
44		Milne, Brian	RB	6-3	254	1/7/73	2	Penn State	Waterford, Pa.	W(Ind)-'96	6/5
93		Morabito, Tim	DT	6-3	288	10/12/73	2	Boston College	Garnerville, N.Y.	FA-'96	7/1
31		Myers, Greg	S	6-1	197	9/30/72	2	Colorado State	Tampa, Fla.	D5-'96	14/0
26		Orlando, Bo	S	5-10	180	4/3/66	8	West Virginia	Berwick, Pa.	UFA(SD)-'96	16/16
9		Pelfrey, Doug	K	5-11	185	9/25/70	5	Kentucky	Ft. Thomas, Ky.	D8-'93	16/0
81		Pickens, Carl	WR	6-2	206	3/23/70	6	Tennessee	Murphy, N.C.	D2-'92	16/16
87		Sadowski, Troy	TE	6-5	250	12/8/65	8	Georgia	Atlanta, Ga.	UFA(NYJ)-'94	16/0
77		Sargent, Kevin	T	6-6	284	3/31/69	6	Eastern Washington	Bremerton, Wash.	FA-'92	0*
23		Sawyer, Corey	CB	5-11	171	10/4/71	4	Florida State	Key West, Fla.	D4-'94	15/2
86	†	Scott, Darnay	WR	6-1	180	7/7/72	4	San Diego State	St. Louis, Mo.	D2-'94	16/16
35		Shade, Sam	S	6-1	191	6/14/73	3	Alabama	Birmingham, Ala.	D4-'95	12/0
70		Smith, Artie	DE	6-4	285	5/15/70	5	Louisiana Tech	Stillwater, Okla.	W(SF)-'94	16/12
22		Spencer, Jimmy	CB	5-9	180	3/29/69	6	Florida	South Bay, Fla.	UFA(NO)-'96	15/14
79		Stallings, Ramondo	DE	6-7	285	11/21/71	4	San Diego State	Winston-Salem, N.C.	D7-'94	13/3
57		Sutter, Eddie	LB	6-3	235	10/3/69	5	Northwestern	Peoria, Ill.	UFA(Balt)-'97	16/4*
58		Tovar, Steve	LB	6-3	244	4/25/70	5	Ohio State	Elyria, Ohio	D3-'93	13/13
59		Truitt, Greg	LS	6-0	235	12/8/65	4	Penn State	Sarasota, Fla.	FA-'94	16/0
53		Tumulty, Tom	LB	6-2	242	2/11/73	2	Pittsburgh	Penn Hills, Pa.	D6-'96	16/3
61		Tuten, Melvin	T	6-6	305	11/11/71	3	Syracuse	Washington, D.C.	D3-'95	16/7
67		Von Oelhoffen, Kimo	DT	6-4	300	1/30/71	4	Boise State	Molokai, Hawaii	D6-'94	11/1
27		Walker, Bracey	S	6-0	200	10/28/70	4	North Carolina	Pine Forest, N.C.	W(KC)-'94	16/16
91	#	Wallerstedt, Brett	LB	6-1	240	11/24/70	4	Arizona State	Manhattan, Kan.	W(Den)-'94	0*
63		Walter, Joe	T	6-7	292	6/18/63	13	Texas Tech	Dallas, Tex.	D7a-'85	15/15
37	#	Wheeler, Leonard	CB-S	6-0	198	1/15/69	6	Troy State	Taccoa, Ga.	D3-'92	13/0
4		Wilhelm, Erik	QB	6-3	217	11/9/65	8	Oregon State	Lake Oswego, Ore.	UFA-'96	3/0
99		Wilkinson, Dan	DT	6-5	313	3/13/73	4	Ohio State	Dayton, Ohio	D1-'94	16/16

* Borgella played 11 games with Detroit in '96; Esiason played 10 games with Arizona; Graham played 11 games with Minnesota; Gutierrez was inactive for 14 games; Jordan was inactive for 5 games; McCullough, Sargent, and Wallerstedt missed '96 season because of injury; Sutter played 16 games with Baltimore.

\# Unrestricted free agent; subject to developments.

† Restricted free agent, subject to developments.

Players lost through free agency (1): RB Garrison Hearst (SF; 16 games in '96).

Also played with Bengals in '96—DE Kenny Davidson (3 games), DE Todd Kelly (2), S Chris Shelling (1), WR Tydus Winans (2).

COACHING STAFF

Head Coach,
Bruce Coslet

Pro Career: Coslet is entering his first full season as head coach of the Cincinnati Bengals after spending the previous two and a half seasons as the team's offensive coordinator. He was named the team's seventh head coach seven games into the 1996 season, leading the team to an impressive 7-2 record over the final nine games after its 1-6 start. This is the second head coaching position held by Coslet, who was head coach of the New York Jets for four seasons from 1990-93. Coslet began his coaching career as an assistant coach with the San Francisco 49ers in 1980. He joined the Bengals as an assistant coach in 1981. Coslet coached with Cincinnati for nine seasons from 1981-89, including four as offensive coordinator from 1986-89, before becoming head coach of the Jets. After four seasons with the Jets, he again returned to Cincinnati as offensive coordinator in 1994. Coslet played tight end for the Bengals for eight seasons from 1969-76. Career record: 33-41.

Background: Coslet is a native of Oakdale, Calif., and played football for Joint H.S. He was a tight end for the University of the Pacific from 1965-67.

Personal: Born August 5, 1946, Coslet and his wife, Kathy, live in Cincinnati and have two children, son J.J., and daughter Amy.

ASSISTANT COACHES

Paul Alexander, offensive line; born February 12, 1960, Rochester, N.Y., lives in Cincinnati. Tackle Cortland State 1979-81. No pro playing experience. College coach: Penn State 1982-84, Michigan 1985-86, Central Michigan 1987-91. Pro coach: New York Jets 1992-93, joined Bengals in 1994.

Jim Anderson, running backs; born March 27, 1948, Harrisburg, Pa., lives in Cincinnati. Linebacker-defensive end Cal Western 1967-70. No pro playing experience. College coach: Cal Western 1970-71, Scottsdale (Ariz.) Community College 1973, Nevada-Las Vegas 1974-75, Southern Methodist 1976-80, Stanford 1981-83. Pro coach: Joined Bengals in 1984.

Ken Anderson, offensive coordinator; born February 15, 1949, Batavia, Ill., lives in Highland Heights, Ky. Quarterback Augustana (Ill.) 1967-70. Pro quarterback Cincinnati Bengals 1971-86. Pro coach: Joined Bengals in 1992.

Louie Cioffi, defensive staff asst.; born September 21, 1973, Greenlawn, N.Y., lives in Cincinnati. No pro playing experience. College coach: C.W. Post 1995-96. Pro coach: New York Jets 1993-94, joined Bengals in 1997.

Mark Duffner, linebackers; born July 19, 1953, Annandale, Va., lives in Cincinnati. Defensive lineman William & Mary 1973-74. No pro playing experience. College coach: Ohio State 1975-76, Cincinnati 1977-80, Holy Cross 1981-91 (head coach 1986-91), Maryland 1992-96 (head coach). Pro coach: Joined Bengals in 1997.

John Garrett, offensive staff asst.; born March 2, 1965, Danville, Pa., lives in Cincinnati. Wide receiver Columbia 1983-84, Princeton 1987. Pro wide receiver Cincinnati Bengals 1989, San Antonio Riders (World League) 1991. Pro coach: Joined Bengals in 1995.

Ray Horton, defensive backs; born April 12, 1960, Tacoma, Wash., lives in Cincinnati. Defensive back Washington 1979-82. Pro defensive back Cincinnati Bengals 1983-88, Dallas Cowboys 1989-92. Pro coach: Washington Redskins 1994-96, joined Bengals in 1997.

Tim Krumrie, defensive line; born May 20, 1960, Menomonie, Wis., lives in Cincinnati. Defensive tackle Wisconsin 1979-82. Pro defensive tackle Cincinnati Bengals 1983-94. Pro coach: Joined Bengals in 1995.

Dick LeBeau, assistant head coach-defensive coordinator; born September 9, 1937, London, Ohio, lives in Cincinnati. Offensive-defensive back Ohio State 1954-57. Pro cornerback Detroit Lions 1959-72. Pro coach: Philadelphia Eagles 1973-75, Green Bay Packers 1976-79, Cincinnati Bengals 1980-91,

Pittsburgh Steelers 1992-96, rejoined Bengals in 1997.

Al Roberts, special teams; born January 6, 1944, Fresno, Calif., lives in Cincinnati. Running back Washington 1964-65, Puget Sound 1967-68. No pro playing experience. College coach: Washington 1977-82, 1996, Purdue 1986-87. Pro coach: Los Angeles Express (USFL) 1983-84, Houston Oilers 1984-85, Philadelphia Eagles 1988-90, New York Jets 1991-93, Arizona Cardinals 1994-95, joined Bengals in 1997.

Kim Wood, strength; born July 12, 1945, Barrington, Ill., lives in Cincinnati. Running back Wisconsin 1965-68. No pro playing experience. Pro coach: Joined Bengals in 1975.

Bob Wylie, tight ends; born February 16, 1951, West Warwick, R.I., lives in Cincinnati. Linebacker Colorado 1969-71. No pro playing experience. College coach: Brown 1980-82, Holy Cross 1983-84, Ohio University 1985-87, Colorado State 1988-89, Cincinnati 1996. Pro coach: New York Jets 1990-91, Tampa Bay Buccaneers 1992-95, joined Bengals in 1997.

1997 FIRST-YEAR ROSTER

Name	Pos.	Ht.	Wt.	Birthdate	College	Hometown	How Acq.
Bush, Steve	TE	6-3	258	7/4/74	Arizona State	Phoenix, Ariz.	FA
Carr, William	NT	6-0	269	1/13/75	Michigan	Dallas, Tex.	D7
Cottrell, Dana	LB	6-3	238	1/11/74	Syracuse	Billerica, Mass.	FA
Curtis, Canute	LB	6-2	250	8/4/74	West Virginia	Amityville, N.Y.	D6
Daniels, Damon	WR	5-10	175	12/13/74	Delaware State	Wilmington, Del.	FA
Dillon, Corey	RB	6-2	220	10/24/75	Washington	Seattle, Wash.	D2
Douthard, Ty	RB	6-1	215	5/27/73	Illinois	Cincinnati, Ohio	FA
Granville, Billy	LB	6-3	245	3/11/74	Duke	Lawrenceville, N.J.	FA
Groover, Chad	T	6-6	298	5/23/74	Appalachian State	Winston-Salem, N.C.	FA
Hundon, James (1)	WR	6-1	195	4/9/71	Portland State	Daly City, Calif.	FA-'96
Jenkins, Mike	WR	6-4	200	8/25/74	Hampton	Portsmouth, Va.	FA
Kresser, Eric	QB	6-2	209	2/6/73	Marshall	Palm Beach Gardens, Fla.	FA
Lott, Anthone	CB	5-9	192	7/22/74	Florida	Gainesville, Fla.	FA
Mack, Tremain	S	6-0	195	11/21/74	Miami	Tyler, Tex.	D4
Medley, Darrell	RB	6-2	235	1/3/74	Virginia	South Boston, Va.	FA
Messam, Wayne	WR	6-4	208	6/7/74	Florida State	South Bay, Fla.	FA
Neal, Randy (1)	LB	6-3	236	12/29/72	Virginia	Hackensack, N.J.	FA-'96
Payne, Rod	C	6-4	305	6/14/74	Michigan	Miami, Fla.	D3
Purvis, Andre	NT	6-5	290	7/14/73	North Carolina	Jacksonville, N.C.	D5
Simon, Geroy	WR	6-0	183	9/11/75	Maryland	Johnstown, Pa.	FA
Terry, Tim	LB	6-3	235	7/26/74	Temple	Hempstead, N.Y.	FA
Twyner, Gunnard (1)	WR	5-10	167	7/14/73	Western Illinois	Bettendorf, Ill.	FA-'96
Wilkins, Kenny	S	6-3	215	4/11/73	Colorado	Mesa, Ariz.	FA
Wilson, Reinard	LB	6-2	259	12/12/73	Florida State	Lake City, Fla.	D1
Wright, Lawrence	S	6-0	209	9/6/73	Florida	Miami, Fla.	FA

The term NFL Rookie is defined as a player who is in his first season of professional football and has not been on the roster of another professional football team for any regular-season or postseason games. A Rookie is designated by an "R" on NFL rosters. Players who have been active in another professional football league or players who have NFL experience, including either preseason training camp or being on an Active List or Inactive List, or on Reserve/Injured or Reserve/Physically Unable to Perform for fewer than six regular-season games, are termed NFL First-Year Players. An NFL First-Year Player is designated by a "1" on NFL rosters. Thereafter, a player is credited with an additional year of experience for each season in which he accumulates six games on the Active List or Inactive List, or on Reserve/Injured or Reserve/Physically Unable to Perform.

NOTES

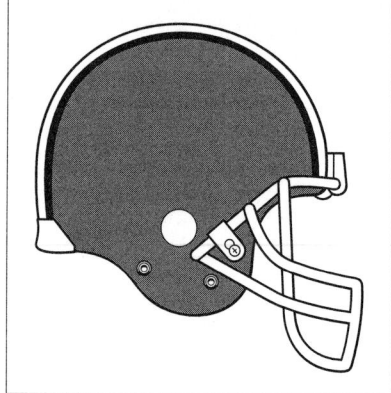

Team Colors: Brown, Orange, and White
80 First Avenue
Berea, Ohio 44017
Telephone: (216) 891-5000

TRUST OFFICIALS

President: William F. Futterer, III
Communications Manager: Laura Paquelet
Communications Assistant: Jason Ferrante
Customer Relations Manager: Marylin McGrath
Customer Relations Coordinators:
  Monica Donahue, Jamie Koechley, Kerry Sayers
Facilities Manager: Dean Phillips
Sales Associates: Eddie Johnson, Dino Lucarelli,
  Gerald McNeil, Maria Shaheen
Special Events Manager: Ella Fong
Special Events Coordinator: Vicki Dansby
Permanent Seat License Consultant:
  Muhleman Marketing
Stadium Consultant: Clark Sports
Marketing Consultant: I.M.S. Properties, Inc.
Advertising Consultant: Marcus Advertising
Stadium: 1999 New Cleveland Stadium
  •**Capacity:** 70,300
  West 3rd Street
  Cleveland, Ohio 44114
Playing Surface: Grass
Headquarters/Training Camp: 80 First Avenue
  Berea, Ohio 44017

HALL OF FAMERS

Jim Brown	RB	Inducted 1971
Paul Brown	Coach	Inducted 1967
Len Ford	DE	Inducted 1976
Frank Gatski	C	Inducted 1985
Otto Graham	QB	Inducted 1965
Lou Groza	T-K	Inducted 1974
Leroy Kelly	RB	Inducted 1994
Dante Lavelli	E	Inducted 1975
Mike McCormack	T	Inducted 1984
Bobby Mitchell	RB	Inducted 1983
Marion Motley	RB	Inducted 1968
Paul Warfield	WR	Inducted 1983
Bill Willis	G	Inducted 1977

RECORD HOLDERS
INDIVIDUAL RECORDS—CAREER

Category	Name	Performance
Rushing (Yds.)	Jim Brown, 1957-1965	12,312
Passing (Yds.)	Brian Sipe, 1974-1983	23,713
Passing (TDs)	Brian Sipe, 1974-1983	154
Receiving (No.)	Ozzie Newsome, 1978-1990	662
Receiving (Yds.)	Ozzie Newsome, 1978-1990	7,980
Interceptions	Thom Darden, 1972-74, 1976-1981	45
Punting (Avg.)	Horace Gillom, 1950-56	43.8
Punt Return (Avg.)	Greg Pruitt, 1973-1981	11.8
Kickoff Return (Avg.)	Greg Pruitt, 1973-1981	26.3
Field Goals	Lou Groza, 1950-59, 1961-67	234
Touchdowns (Tot.)	Jim Brown, 1957-1965	126
Points	Lou Groza, 1950-59, 1961-67	1,349

INDIVIDUAL RECORDS—SINGLE SEASON

Category	Name	Performance
Rushing (Yds.)	Jim Brown, 1963	1,863
Passing (Yds.)	Brian Sipe, 1980	4,132
Passing (TDs)	Brian Sipe, 1980	30
Receiving (No.)	Ozzie Newsome, 1983	89
	Ozzie Newsome, 1984	89
Receiving (Yds.)	Webster Slaughter, 1989	1,236
Interceptions	Thom Darden, 1978	10
Punting (Avg.)	Gary Collins, 1965	46.7
Punt Return (Avg.)	Leroy Kelly, 1965	15.6
Kickoff Return (Avg.)	Billy Reynolds, 1954	29.5
Field Goals	Matt Stover, 1995	29
Touchdowns (Tot.)	Jim Brown, 1965	21
Points	Jim Brown, 1965	126

INDIVIDUAL RECORDS—SINGLE GAME

Category	Name	Performance
Rushing (Yds.)	Jim Brown, 11-24-57	237
	Jim Brown, 11-19-61	237
Passing (Yds.)	Bernie Kosar, 1-3-87	489
Passing (TDs)	Frank Ryan, 12-12-64	5
	Bill Nelsen, 11-2-69	5
	Brian Sipe, 10-7-79	5
Receiving (No.)	Ozzie Newsome, 10-14-84	14
Receiving (Yds.)	Ozzie Newsome, 10-14-84	191
Interceptions	Many times	3
	Last time by Frank Minnifield, 11-22-87	
Field Goals	Don Cockroft, 10-19-75	5
Touchdowns (Tot.)	Dub Jones, 11-25-51	*6
Points	Dub Jones, 11-25-51	36

*NFL Record

COACHING HISTORY
(385-285-10)

1950-62	Paul Brown	115-49-5
1963-70	Blanton Collier	79-38-2
1971-74	Nick Skorich	30-26-2
1975-77	Forrest Gregg*	18-23-0
1977	Dick Modzelewski	0-1-0
1978-84	Sam Rutigliano**	47-52-0
1984-88	Marty Schottenheimer	46-31-0
1989-90	Bud Carson***	12-14-1
1990	Jim Shofner	1-6-0
1991-95	Bill Belichick	37-45-0

  *Resigned after 13 games in 1977
  **Released after eight games in 1984
  ***Released after nine games in 1990

CLEVELAND STADIUM

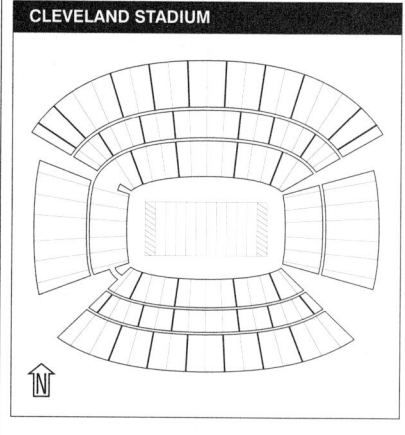

AGREEMENT BETWEEN THE NFL AND THE CITY OF CLEVELAND

On June 12, 1996, the city of Cleveland and the NFL announced the terms of an historic public-private partnership that continues the Browns franchise in Cleveland and guarantees a new state-of-the-art stadium in Cleveland by 1999.

On July 1, 1996 the Cleveland Browns Trust began operating in Cleveland to oversee the return of the Browns.

The Cleveland Browns operate as a franchise front office that actively participates in special events, charitable work, alumni and fan relations, and facilities management.

The first Browns game in the new stadium is currently scheduled for August 21, 1999.

The agreement includes the following key points:

•Cleveland Browns Franchise: The Browns franchise will remain in Cleveland and is scheduled to resume play in 1999. This team will be either an expansion franchise or a relocated club from another city.

•Cleveland Browns' Logo, Colors, and Heritage: The heritage and records, including the Browns' name, logo, colors, history, playing records, trophies, and memorabilia, will remain in Cleveland as property of the Cleveland Browns franchise.

•New Cleveland Stadium: The new stadium will be owned by the city of Cleveland and will have a 30-year lease with the NFL franchise.

On January 21, 1997, the city of Cleveland announced it had met and exceeded the premium seating sales goal required by the agreement between the city of Cleveland and the National Football League. This announcement secured the league's contribution on behalf of the Browns' future ownership for construction of the new Cleveland stadium.

The official ground-breaking for the new Cleveland Stadium was May 15, 1997. The new open-air, natural grass stadium was designed by HOK Architects.

ALL-TIME LEADERS

PASSER RATING (minimum 1000 attempts)	Att.	Comp.	Yds.	TD	Int.	Rate
Plum, Milt	1,083	627	8,914	66	39	89.9
Kosar, Bernie	3,150	1,853	21,904	116	81	81.6
Ryan, Frank	1,755	907	13,361	134	88	81.4
Graham, Otto	1,565	872	13,499	88	94	78.2
Sipe, Brian	3,439	1,944	23,713	154	149	74.8
Nelsen, Bill	1,314	689	9,725	71	71	72.1
Phipps, Mike	1,317	633	7,700	40	81	51.0

SCORING	PTS
Groza, Lou	1,349
Cockroft, Don	1,080
Brown, Jim	756
Bahr, Matt	677
Kelly, Leroy	540
Stover, Matt	480
Collins, Gary	420
Renfro, Ray	330
Mack, Kevin	324
Warfield, Paul	318

RUSHING	Att.	Yds.	TD
Brown, Jim	2,359	12,312	106
Kelly, Leroy	1,727	7,274	74
Pruitt, Mike	1,593	6,540	47
Pruitt, Greg	1,158	5,496	25
Mack, Kevin	1,291	5,123	46
Byner, Earnest	862	3,364	27
Green, Ernie	668	3,204	15
Mitchell, Bobby	423	2,297	16
Miller, Cleo	546	2,286	16
Metcalf, Eric	592	2,229	11

RECEIVING	No.	Yds.	TD
Newsome, Ozzie	662	7,980	47
Collins, Gary	331	5,299	70
Pruitt, Greg	323	3,022	17
Brennan, Brian	315	4,148	19
Rucker, Reggie	310	4,953	32
Slaughter, Webster	305	4,834	27
Metcalf, Eric	297	2,732	15
Renfro, Ray	281	5,508	50
Byner, Earnest	276	2,630	10
Morin, Milt	271	4,208	16
Warfield, Paul	271	5,210	52

RECEIVING YARDAGE	Yds.	No.	TD
Newsome, Ozzie	7,980	662	47
Renfro, Ray	5,508	281	50
Collins, Gary	5,299	331	70
Warfield, Paul	5,210	271	52
Rucker, Reggie	4,953	310	32
Slaughter, Webster	4,834	305	27
Logan, Dave	4,247	262	24
Morin, Milt	4,208	271	16
Brennan, Brian	4,148	315	19
Lavelli, Dante	3,908	244	33

INTERCEPTIONS	No.	Yds.	TD
Darden, Thom	45	820	2
Lahr, Warren	40	530	5
Scott, Clarence	39	407	2
Konz, Ken	30	392	4
Parrish, Bernie	29	557	3
Fichtner, Ross	27	581	3
Howell, Mike	27	252	0
Dixon, Hanford	26	225	0
James, Tommy	26	208	0
Wright, Felix	26	469	2

PUNT RETURNS (minimum 50 returns)	No.	Yds.	Avg.	TD
Pruitt, Greg	56	659	11.8	0
Mitchell, Bobby	54	607	11.2	3
Metcalf, Eric	127	1,341	10.6	5
Kelly, Leroy	94	990	10.5	3
McNeil, Gerald	161	1,545	9.6	1
Konz, Ken	68	556	8.2	1
Hall, Dino	111	901	8.1	0
Brennan, Brian	55	435	7.9	1
Wright, Keith	78	467	6.0	0
Reynolds, Billy	67	363	5.4	0

KICKOFF RETURNS (minimum 50 returns)	No.	Yds.	Avg.	TD
Pruitt, Greg	58	1,523	26.3	1
Roberts, Walt	62	1,608	25.9	0
Wright, Keith	70	1,767	25.2	0
Mitchell, Bobby	62	1,550	25.0	3
Lefear, Billy	60	1,461	24.4	0
Young, Glen	87	2,079	23.9	0
Kelly, Leroy	76	1,784	23.5	0
Baldwin, Randy	82	1,872	22.8	1
Hall, Dino	151	3,185	21.1	0
McNeil, Gerald	64	1,301	20.3	1

DENVER BRONCOS

American Football Conference
Western Division
Team Colors: Orange, Broncos Navy Blue, and
White
13655 Broncos Parkway
Englewood, Colorado 80112
Telephone: (303) 649-9000

CLUB OFFICIALS

President-Chief Executive Officer: Pat Bowlen
General Manager: John Beake
Vice President of Business Operations: David Wass
Director of Player Personnel: Neal Dahlen
Chief Financial Officer: Allen Fears
Director of Ticket Operations/Business
    Development: Rick Nichols
Executive Assistant to the President: Yolanda Saltus
Director of Media Relations: Jim Saccomano
Director of Stadium Operations: Gail Stuckey
Director of Operations: Bill Harpole
Director of Marketing: Sara Gilbertson
Assistant to the General Manager/Community
    Relations: Fred Fleming
Director of Player Relations: Bill Thompson
Community Relations Coordinator: Steve Sewell
Trainer: Steve Antonopulos
Equipment Manager: Doug West
Video Director: Kent Erickson
Stadium: Denver Mile High Stadium
    •**Capacity:** 76,082
    1900 West Eliot
    Denver, Colorado 80204
Playing Surface: Grass (PAT)
Training Camp: University of Northern Colorado
    Greeley, Colorado 80639

1997 SCHEDULE

PRESEASON

July 26	**Buffalo**	7:00
Aug. 4	vs. Miami at Mexico City, Mexico	6:00
Aug. 9	at Carolina	8:00
Aug. 17	at New England	1:00
Aug. 23	**San Francisco**	6:00

REGULAR SEASON

Aug. 31	**Kansas City**	2:00
Sept. 7	at Seattle	1:00
Sept. 14	**St. Louis**	2:00
Sept. 21	**Cincinnati**	2:00
Sept. 28	at Atlanta	1:00
Oct. 6	**New England** (Mon.)	7:00
Oct. 12	Open Date	
Oct. 19	at Oakland	1:00
Oct. 26	at Buffalo	1:00
Nov. 2	**Seattle**	2:00
Nov. 9	**Carolina**	2:00
Nov. 16	at Kansas City	12:00
Nov. 24	**Oakland** (Mon.)	7:00
Nov. 30	at San Diego	5:00
Dec. 7	at Pittsburgh	1:00
Dec. 14	at San Francisco (Mon.)	6:00
Dec. 21	**San Diego**	2:00

RECORD HOLDERS

INDIVIDUAL RECORDS—CAREER

Category	Name	Performance
Rushing (Yds.)	Floyd Little, 1967-1975	6,323
Passing (Yds.)	John Elway, 1983-1996	45,034
Passing (TDs)	John Elway, 1983-1996	251
Receiving (No.)	Lionel Taylor, 1960-66	543
Receiving (Yds.)	Lionel Taylor, 1960-66	6,872
Interceptions	Steve Foley, 1976-1986	44
Punting (Avg.)	Jim Fraser, 1962-64	45.2
Punt Return (Avg.)	Rick Upchurch, 1975-1983	12.1
Kickoff Return (Avg.)	Abner Haynes, 1965-66	26.3
Field Goals	Jim Turner, 1971-79	151
Touchdowns (Tot.)	Floyd Little, 1967-1975	54
Points	Jim Turner, 1971-79	742

INDIVIDUAL RECORDS—SINGLE SEASON

Category	Name	Performance
Rushing (Yds.)	Terrell Davis, 1996	1,538
Passing (Yds.)	John Elway, 1993	4,030
Passing (TDs)	John Elway, 1995, 1996	26
Receiving (No.)	Lionel Taylor, 1961	100
Receiving (Yds.)	Steve Watson, 1981	1,244
Interceptions	Goose Gonsoulin, 1960	11
Punting (Avg.)	Jim Fraser, 1963	46.1
Punt Return (Avg.)	Floyd Little, 1967	16.9
Kickoff Return (Avg.)	Bill Thompson, 1969	28.5
Field Goals	Jason Elam, 1995	31
Touchdowns (Tot.)	Terrell Davis, 1996	15
Points	Gene Mingo, 1962	137

INDIVIDUAL RECORDS—SINGLE GAME

Category	Name	Performance
Rushing (Yds.)	Terrell Davis, 10-20-96	194
Passing (Yds.)	Frank Tripucka, 9-15-62	447
Passing (TDs)	Frank Tripucka, 10-28-62	5
	John Elway, 11-18-84	5
Receiving (No.)	Lionel Taylor, 11-29-64	13
	Bobby Anderson, 9-30-73	13
Receiving (Yds.)	Lionel Taylor, 11-27-60	199
Interceptions	Goose Gonsoulin, 9-18-60	*4
	Willie Brown, 11-15-64	*4
Field Goals	Gene Mingo, 10-6-63	5
	Rich Karlis, 11-20-83	5
	Jason Elam, 9-3-95	5
Touchdowns (Tot.)	Many times	3
	Last time by Terrell Davis, 11-17-96	
Points	Gene Mingo, 12-10-60	21

*NFL Record

COACHING HISTORY

(278-280-10)

1960-61	Frank Filchock	7-20-1
1962-64	Jack Faulkner*	9-22-1
1964-66	Mac Speedie**	6-19-1
1966	Ray Malavasi	4-8-0
1967-71	Lou Saban***	20-42-3
1971	Jerry Smith	2-3-0
1972-76	John Ralston	34-33-3
1977-80	Robert (Red) Miller	42-25-0
1981-92	Dan Reeves	117-79-1
1993-94	Wade Phillips	16-17-0
1995-96	Mike Shanahan	21-12-0

*Released after four games in 1964
**Resigned after two games in 1966
***Resigned after nine games in 1971

DENVER MILE HIGH STADIUM

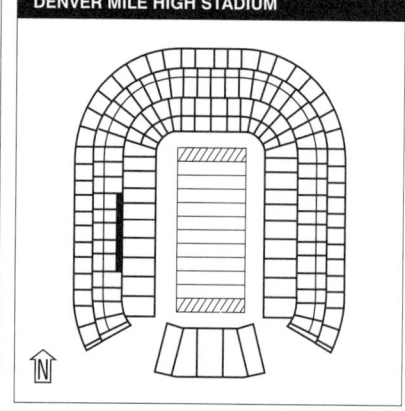

1996 TEAM RECORD

PRESEASON (3-1)

Date	Result		Opponents
8/3	W	20-17	at San Francisco
8/10	W	40-28	Carolina
8/17	W	20-3	at Dallas
8/23	L	24-31	Jacksonville

REGULAR SEASON (13-3)

Date	Result		Opponents	Att.
9/1	W	31-6	N.Y. Jets	70,595
9/8	W	30-20	at Seattle	43,671
9/15	W	27-23	Tampa Bay	71,535
9/22	L	14-17	at Kansas City	79,439
9/29	W	14-10	at Cincinnati	51,798
10/6	W	28-17	San Diego	75,058
10/20	W	45-34	Baltimore	70,453
10/27	W	34-7	Kansas City	75,652
11/4	W	22-21	at Oakland	61,179
11/10	W	17-12	Chicago	75,555
11/17	W	34-8	at New England	59,452
11/24	W	21-17	at Minnesota	59,142
12/1	W	34-7	Seattle	74,982
12/8	L	6-41	at Green Bay	60,712
12/15	W	24-19	Oakland	75,466
12/22	L	10-16	at San Diego	46,801

POSTSEASON (0-1)

1/4	L	27-30	Jacksonville	75,678

SCORE BY PERIODS

Broncos	131	132	65	63	—	391
Opponents	52	77	78	68	—	275

ATTENDANCE

Home 589,296   Away 462,194   Total 1,051,490
Single-game home record, 76,089 (10/26/86)
Single-season home record, 598,224 (1981)

1996 TEAM STATISTICS

	Broncos	Opp.
Total First Downs	336	261
Rushing	134	67
Passing	180	165
Penalty	22	29
Third Down: Made/Att	112/229	78/217
Third Down Pct.	48.9	35.9
Fourth Down: Made/Att	6/11	7/16
Fourth Down Pct.	54.5	43.8
Total Net Yards	5791	4470
Avg. Per Game	361.9	279.4
Total Plays	1092	951
Avg. Per Play	5.3	4.7
Net Yards Rushing	2362	1331
Avg. Per Game	147.6	83.2
Total Rushes	525	345
Net Yards Passing	3429	3139
Avg. Per Game	214.3	196.2
Sacked/Yards Lost	31/233	40/274
Gross Yards	3662	3413
Att./Completions	536/327	566/302
Completion Pct.	61.0	53.4
Had Intercepted	17	23
Punts/Avg.	65/41.8	83/46.1
Net Punting Avg.	65/36.2	83/37.4
Penalties/Yards Lost	109/949	119/834
Fumbles/Ball Lost	27/15	26/9
Touchdowns	47	31
Rushing	20	5
Passing	26	22
Returns	1	4
Avg. Time of Possession	33:17	26:43

1996 INDIVIDUAL STATISTICS

PASSING	Att.	Comp.	Yds.	Pct.	TD	Int.	Tkld.	Rate
Elway	466	287	3328	61.6	26	14	26/194	89.2
Musgrave	52	31	276	59.6	0	2	4/32	57.9
Lewis	17	9	58	52.9	0	1	1/7	35.9
Craver	1	0	0	0.0	0	0	0/0	39.6
Broncos	536	327	3662	61.0	26	17	31/233	84.3
Opponents	566	302	3413	53.4	22	23	40/274	67.7

SCORING	TD R	TD P	TD Rt	PAT	FG	Saf	PTS
Elam	0	0	0	46/46	21/28	0	109
Davis	13	2	0	0/0	0/0	0	90
Sharpe	0	10	0	0/0	0/0	0	60
McCaffrey	0	7	0	0/0	0/0	0	42
Elway	4	0	0	0/0	0/0	0	24
Miller	1	3	0	0/0	0/0	0	24
Craver	2	1	0	0/0	0/0	0	18
R. Smith	0	2	0	0/0	0/0	0	12
Braxton	0	0	1	0/0	0/0	0	6
Sherrard	0	1	0	0/0	0/0	0	6
Broncos	20	26	1	46/46	21/28	0	391
Opponents	5	22	4	25/25	20/23	0	275

2-Point conversions: 0. Team: 0-1, Opponents: 2-6.

RUSHING	Att.	Yds.	Avg.	LG	TD
Davis	345	1538	4.5	71t	13
Hebron	49	262	5.3	47	0
Elway	50	249	5.0	22	4
Craver	59	232	3.9	28	2
Lewis	4	39	9.8	18	0
Miller	3	39	13.0	26t	1
Rivers	2	6	3.0	3	0
R. Smith	1	1	1.0	1	0
Musgrave	12	-4	-.3	6	0
Broncos	525	2362	4.5	71t	20
Opponents	345	1331	3.9	56	5

RECEIVING	No.	Yds.	Avg.	LG	TD
Sharpe	80	1062	13.3	51	10
Miller	56	735	13.1	46	3
McCaffrey	48	553	11.5	39t	7
Craver	39	297	7.6	39t	1
Davis	36	310	8.6	23	2
R. Smith	16	237	14.8	49t	2
Sherrard	16	185	11.6	25t	1
Carswell	15	85	5.7	11	0
Chamberlain	12	129	10.8	17	0
Hebron	7	43	6.1	11	0
Kinchen	1	27	27.0	27	0
Rivers	1	-1	-1.0	-1	0
Broncos	327	3662	11.2	51	26
Opponents	302	3413	11.3	51t	22

INTERCEPTIONS	No.	Yds.	Avg.	LG	TD
Braxton	9	128	14.2	69t	1
Atwater	3	11	3.7	11	0
Romanowski	3	1	0.3	1	0
Crockett	2	34	17.0	34	0
Washington	2	17	8.5	23	0
James	2	15	7.5	15	0
Hilliard	1	27	27.0	27	0
Mobley	1	8	8.0	8	0
Broncos	23	241	10.5	69t	1
Opponents	17	171	10.1	34	0

PUNTING	No.	Yds.	Avg.	In 20	LG
Rouen	65	2714	41.8	16	57
Broncos	65	2714	41.8	16	57
Opponents	83	3825	46.1	18	67

PUNT RETURNS	No.	FC	Yds.	Avg.	LG	TD
Kinchen	26	4	300	11.5	40	0
R. Smith	23	15	283	12.3	36	0
Broncos	49	19	583	11.9	40	0
Opponents	23	22	261	11.3	88t	1

KICKOFF RETURNS	No.	Yds.	Avg.	LG	TD
Hebron	45	1099	24.4	59	0
Chamberlain	3	49	16.3	21	0
Jeffers	1	18	18.0	18	0
R. Smith	1	29	29.0	29	0
Broncos	50	1195	23.9	59	0
Opponents	76	1602	21.1	97t	1

SACKS	No.
A. Williams	13.0
Geathers	5.0
Tanuvasa	5.0
Crockett	4.0
Perry	3.5
Romanowski	3.0
Hasselbach	2.0
Lodish	1.5
Mobley	1.5
D. Williams	1.0
Robinson	0.5
Broncos	40.0
Opponents	31.0

1997 DRAFT CHOICES

Round	Name	Pos.	College
1	Trevor Pryce	DT	Clemson
3	Dan Neil	G	Texas
4	Cory Gilliard	DB	Ball State

DENVER BRONCOS

1997 VETERAN ROSTER

No.	Name	Pos.	Ht.	Wt.	Birthdate	NFL Exp.	College	Hometown	How Acq.	'96 Games/ Starts
73	Adams, Scott	G-T	6-6	315	9/28/66	6	Georgia	Lake City, Fla.	FA-'97	7/2*
57	Aldridge, Allen	LB	6-1	245	5/30/72	4	Houston	Houston, Tex.	D2-'94	16/16
54	Ale, Arnold	LB	6-2	245	6/17/70	3	UCLA	Carson, Calif.	FA-'97	8/0*
76	Alex, Keith	OL	6-4	307	6/9/69	3	Texas M&M	Hardin County, Tex.	FA-'97	0*
27	Atwater, Steve	S	6-3	217	10/28/66	9	Arkansas	Chicago, Ill.	D1-'89	16/16
92	Barber, Kurt	DE	6-4	260	1/5/69	5	Southern California	Paducah, Ky.	FA-'97	0*
34	Braxton, Tyrone	S	5-11	185	12/17/64	11	North Dakota State	Madison, Wis.	FA-'95	16/16
6	Brister, Bubby	QB	6-3	207	8/15/62	11	Northeast Louisiana	Monroe, La.	FA-'97	0*
70	Brown, Jamie	T	6-8	320	4/24/72	3	Florida A&M	Miami, Fla.	D4a-'95	12/2
55	Brown, Ken	LB	6-1	235	5/5/71	2	Virginia Tech	Richmond, Va.	D4b-'95	0*
56	† Burns, Keith	LB	6-2	245	5/16/72	4	Oklahoma State	Greeleyville, S.C.	D7a-'94	16/0
59	Cadrez, Glenn	LB	6-3	245	1/2/70	6	Houston	El Centro, Calif.	FA-'95	16/0
67	Campbell, Mark	DT	6-1	290	9/12/72	2	Florida	Miami, Fla.	D3b-'96	0*
89	Carswell, Dwayne	TE	6-3	261	1/18/72	3	Liberty	Jacksonville, Fla.	FA-'94	16/2
50	Carter, Bernard	LB	6-3	238	8/22/71	2	East Carolina	Miami, Fla.	FA-'97	0*
86	Chamberlain, Byron	TE	6-1	240	10/17/71	2	Wayne State	Fort Worth, Tex.	D7b-'95	11/0
39	Crockett, Ray	CB	5-10	185	1/5/67	9	Baylor	Dallas, Tex.	UFA(Det)-'94	15/15
30	Davis, Terrell	RB	5-11	200	10/28/72	3	Georgia	San Diego, Calif.	D6b-'95	16/16
63	Diaz-Infante, David	G	6-3	292	3/31/64	2	San Jose State	San Jose, Calif.	FA-'95	9/2
33	Dodge, Dedrick	S	6-2	184	6/14/67	6	Florida State	Neptune, N.J.	FA-'97	16/3*
1	Elam, Jason	K	5-11	192	3/8/70	5	Hawaii	Ft. Walton Beach, Fla.	D3b-'93	16/0
7	Elway, John	QB	6-3	215	6/28/60	15	Stanford	Port Angeles, Wash.	T(Balt)-'83	15/15
79	Geathers, Jumpy	DT	6-7	300	6/26/60	14	Wichita State	Georgetown, S.C.	FA-'96	16/0
23	Gordon, Darrien	CB	5-11	182	11/14/70	5	Stanford	Shawnee, Okla.	UFA(SD)-'97	16/6*
86	Green, Willie	WR	6-4	188	4/2/66	8	Mississippi	Athens, Ga.	UFA(Car)-'97	15/11*
29	Griffith, Howard	RB	6-0	240	11/17/67	5	Illinois	Chicago, Ill.	UFA(SF)-'97	16/14*
75	Habib, Brian	G	6-7	299	12/2/64	10	Washington	Ellensburg, Wash.	UFA(Minn)-'93	16/16
96	Hasselbach, Harald	DE	6-6	280	9/22/67	4	Washington	Amsterdam, Holland	FA-'94	16/1
37	# Hauck, Tim	S	5-10	185	12/20/66	9	Montana	Big Timber, Mont.	UFA(GB)-'95	16/0
22	Hebron, Vaughn	RB	5-8	195	10/7/70	5	Virginia Tech	Baltimore, Md.	FA-'96	16/0
21	Hilliard, Randy	CB	5-11	165	2/6/67	8	Northwestern State, La.	Metairie, La.	FA-'94	13/3
20	James, Tory	CB	6-1	188	5/18/73	2	Louisiana State	New Orleans, La.	D2-'96	16/2
81	Jeffers, Patrick	WR	6-3	217	2/2/72	2	Virginia	Fort Campbell, Ky.	D5-'96	4/0
25	Johnson, Darrius	CB	5-9	175	9/17/72	2	Oklahoma	Terrell, Tex.	D4b-'96	13/0
72	Jones, Ernest	DE	6-2	255	4/1/71	3	Oregon	Utica, N.Y.	FA-'96	6/0
77	t- Jones, Tony	T	6-5	295	5/24/66	10	Western Carolina	Royston, Ga.	T(Balt)-'97	15/15*
43	Joseph, Vance	CB	6-0	202	9/20/72	2	Colorado	Marrero, La.	FA-'97	0*
8	Lewis, Jeff	QB	6-2	217	4/17/73	2	Northern Arizona	Columbus, Ohio	D4a-'96	2/0
97	# Lodish, Mike	DT	6-3	280	8/11/67	8	UCLA	Birmingham, Mich.	UFA(Buff)-'95	16/16
45	Loville, Derek	RB	5-10	205	7/4/68	7	Oregon	San Francisco, Calif.	UFA(SF)-'97	12/6*
37	Lynn, Anthony	RB	6-3	230	12/21/68	4	Texas Tech	McKinney, Tex.	UFA(SF)-'97	16/1*
87	McCaffrey, Ed	WR	6-5	215	8/17/68	7	Stanford	Allentown, Pa.	UFA(SF)-'95	15/15
68	# McElroy, Reggie	T	6-6	290	3/4/60	14	West Texas State	Beaumont, Tex.	FA-'95	7/0
51	Mobley, John	LB	6-1	230	10/10/73	2	Kutztown	Chester, Pa.	D1-'96	16/16
14	# Musgrave, Bill	QB	6-3	215	11/11/67	7	Oregon	Grand Junction, Colo.	UFA(SF)-'95	6/1
52	Myles, Godfrey	LB	6-1	240	9/22/68	7	Florida	Miami, Fla.	FA-'97	16/0*
66	Nalen, Tom	C	6-2	280	5/13/71	4	Boston College	Foxboro, Mass.	D7c-'94	16/16
61	Nutten, Tom	G-T	6-4	276	6/8/71	2	Western Michigan	Kalamazoo, Mich.	FA-'97	0*
95	Perry, Michael Dean	DT	6-1	285	8/27/65	10	Clemson	Aiken, S.C.	FA-'95	15/15
38	# Rivers, Reggie	RB	6-1	215	2/22/68	7	Southwest Texas State	Dayton, Ohio	FA-'91	16/0
53	Romanowski, Bill	LB	6-4	241	4/2/66	10	Boston College	Vernon, Conn.	UFA(Phil)-'96	16/16
16	Rouen, Tom	P	6-3	215	6/9/68	5	Colorado	Hinsdale, Ill.	FA-'93	16/0
11	# Rubley, T.J.	QB	6-3	212	11/29/68	6	Tulsa	Davenport, Iowa	FA-'96	0*
69	Schlereth, Mark	G	6-3	278	1/25/66	9	Idaho	Anchorage, Alaska	UFA(Wash)-'95	14/14
84	Sharpe, Shannon	TE	6-2	230	6/26/68	8	Savannah State	Glennville, Ga.	D7-'90	15/15
42	Smith, Detron	RB	5-9	231	2/25/74	2	Texas A&M	Dallas, Tex.	D3a-'96	13/0
99	Smith, Neil	DE	6-4	273	4/10/66	10	Nebraska	New Orleans, La.	UFA(KC)-'97	16/16*
80	Smith, Rod	WR	6-0	190	5/15/70	3	Missouri Southern	Texarkana, Ark.	FA-'95	10/1
74	Swayne, Harry	T	6-5	295	2/2/65	10	Rutgers	Philadelphia, Pa.	UFA(SD)-'97	16/3*
64	# Tamm, Ralph	G	6-4	280	3/11/66	10	West Chester	Bensalem, Pa.	FA-'95	9/0
98	Tanuvasa, Maa	DT	6-2	277	11/6/70	4	Hawaii	Mililani, Hawaii	FA-'95	16/1
94	Traylor, Keith	DT	6-2	315	9/3/69	6	Central State, Okla.	Little Rock, Ark.	UFA(KC)-'97	15/1*
91	Williams, Alfred	DE	6-6	265	11/6/68	7	Colorado	Houston, Tex.	UFA(SF)-'96	16/16
90	Williams, Dan	DE	6-4	290	12/15/69	5	Toledo	Ypsilanti, Mich.	D1-'93	15/15
24	Willis, Jamal	RB	6-2	218	12/12/73	2	Brigham Young	Las Vegas, Nev.	FA-'97	0*
65	# Zimmerman, Gary	T	6-6	294	12/13/61	12	Oregon	Walnut, Calif.	T(Minn)-'94	14/14

* Adams played 7 games with Tampa Bay in '96; Ale played 8 games with San Diego; Alex last active with Minnesota in '95; Barber, Brister, and Joseph last active with N.Y. Jets in '95; K. Brown last active with Denver in '95; Campbell inactive for 16 games; Carter last active with Jacksonville in '95; Dodge and Lynn played 16 games with San Francisco; Gordon and Swayne played 16 games with San Diego; Green played 15 games with Carolina; Griffith played 16 games with Carolina; T. Jones played 15 games with Baltimore; Loville played 12 games with San Francisco; Myles played 16 games with Dallas; Nutten last active with Buffalo in '95; Rubley last active with Green Bay in '95; N. Smith played 16 games with Kansas City; Traylor played 15 games with Kansas City; Willis last active with San Francisco in '95.

\# Unrestricted free agent; subject to developments.

† Restricted free agent; subject to developments.

t- Broncos traded for T. Jones (Baltimore).

Players lost to free agency (3): RB Aaron Craver (SD; 15 games in '96), S Rondell Jones (Balt; 16), DE Jeff Robinson (StL; 16).

Also played with Broncos in '96—LB Britt Hager (2 games), WR Anthony Miller (16), WR Mike Sherrard (15), T Broderick Thompson (16), CB Lionel Washington (14).

COACHING STAFF

Head Coach,
Mike Shanahan

Pro Career: Became the eleventh head coach in Broncos history on January 31, 1995, coming to Denver from the 1994 world champion San Francisco 49ers, where he served as offensive coordinator from 1992-94. In 1996 Shanahan led the Broncos to a 13-3 record and the AFC Western Division title, tying the club record for wins in a season and leading the NFL in total offense, that after having rewritten the Denver record books in Shanahan's first year. In 1995 he improved the Broncos to an 8-8 mark while stamping the Denver offense with his signature as the most productive unit in the AFC, finishing third in the NFL. The two seasons under Shanahan have produced the most prolific two-year total offense statistics in Broncos history. San Francisco's three-year average under Shanahan's direction was the most-productive offense in the history of pro football. San Francisco's quarterback Steve Young rewrote many NFL passing records and was named the NFL most valuable player twice in his three years under Shanahan's guidance. During his NFL career, Shanahan has been a part of teams that have played in seven AFC or NFC Championship Games, in addition to his four Super Bowl appearances, three with Denver and Super Bowl XXIX with San Francisco. In his 22 seasons coaching in the NFL and at the college level, Shanahan's teams have participated in postseason playoffs or bowl games 16 times. A driving force behind the Broncos' offense for all three of the team's most recent Super Bowl appearances (following the 1986, 1987, and 1989 seasons), he first came to Denver in 1984 as wide receivers coach. Shanahan was Broncos' offensive coordinator from 1985-87, and then returned to Denver as quarterbacks coach on October 16, 1989, after serving as head coach of the Los Angeles Raiders in 1988 and through the first four games of the 1989 campaign. His record with the Raiders was 8-12. Career record: 29-24.

Background: Shanahan began his coaching career at Oklahoma in 1975-76, also coaching at Northern Arizona (1977), Eastern Illinois (1978), and Minnesota (1979), before moving on to Florida (1980-83), where he led the Gators to an NCAA-record 4,540 yards as assistant head coach in 1983. During his tenure on the college level, Shanahan's teams had a combined record of 77-29-3 (.720), including national championship seasons at Oklahoma in 1975 and at Eastern Illinois in 1978.

Personal: Shanahan was born in Oak Park, Illinois, on August 24, 1952. He attended East Leyden High School in Franklin Park and was a wishbone quarterback/defensive back at Eastern Illinois, graduating in 1974 with a degree in physical education. He earned a master's degree there in 1975. Mike and his wife, Peggy, have two children, son Kyle and daughter Krystal.

ASSISTANT COACHES

Frank Bush, linebackers; born January 10, 1963, Athens, Ga., lives in Englewood, Colo. Linebacker North Carolina State 1981-84. Pro linebacker Houston Oilers 1985-86. Pro coach: Houston Oilers 1992-94, joined Broncos in 1995.

Barney Chavous, assistant offensive line-assistant strength and conditioning; born March 22, 1951, Aiken, S.C., lives in Englewood, Colo. Defensive end South Carolina State 1969-72. Pro defensive end Denver Broncos 1973-85. Pro coach: Joined Broncos in 1989.

Rick Dennison, special teams; born June 22, 1958, in Kalispel, Mont., lives in Englewood, Colo. Tight end Colorado State 1976-79. Pro linebacker Denver Broncos 1982-90. Pro coach: Joined Broncos in 1995.

Ed Donatell, special teams; born February 4, 1957, Akron, Ohio, lives in Littleton, Colo. Safety Glenville State 1975-78. No pro playing experience. College coach: Kent State 1979-80, Washington 1981-82, Pacific 1983-85, Idaho 1986-88, Cal State-Fullerton

1997 FIRST-YEAR ROSTER

Name	Pos.	Ht.	Wt.	Birthdate	College	Hometown	How Acq.
Abdullah, Joe (1)	RB	5-11	212	2/21/73	Pacific	Stockton, Calif.	FA
Banks, Chris	G	6-1	286	4/4/73	Kansas	Lexington, Mo.	FA
Beck, Tom	QB	6-1	188	5/5/74	Northern Colorado	Castro Valley, Calif.	FA
Branch, Darrick (1)	WR	6-0	196	2/10/70	Hawaii	Dallas, Tex.	FA
Burkett, Jeremy (1)	RB	6-1	215	4/15/73	Colorado State	Denver, Colo.	FA
Ellis, Jamal (1)	CB	5-11	190	6/21/72	Duke	Dallas, Tex.	FA
Gamble, David (1)	WR	6-1	190	6/14/71	New Hampshire	Albany, N.Y.	FA
Gilliard, Cory	S	6-0	210	10/10/74	Ball State	Bronx, N.Y.	D4
Jones, John (1)	G	6-1	309	12/8/72	Kansas	Los Angeles, Calif.	FA
Jones, K.C.	C	6-1	260	3/28/74	Miami	Midland, Tex.	FA
Lepsis, Matt	TE	6-4	265	1/13/74	Colorado	Conroe, Tex.	FA
Mackey, Chad	WR	6-0	204	3/21/74	Louisiana Tech	Longview, Tex.	FA
Morreale, Nathan	P	5-11	190	5/6/74	Utah State	Irvine, Calif.	FA
Morris, Luther (1)	TE	6-3	235	1/30/73	Northwestern	Chicago, Ill.	FA
Neil, Dan	G-C	6-2	291	10/21/73	Texas	Cypress Creek, Tex.	D3
Pryce, Trevor	DT	6-5	285	8/3/75	Clemson	Winter Park, Fla.	D1
Richie, David	DT	6-2	270	9/26/73	Washington	Orange, Calif.	FA
Russ, Steve (1)	LB	6-4	237	9/16/72	Air Force	Stetsonville, Wis.	D7a-'95
Simmons, Dalton	CB	6-0	180	9/14/73	Colorado	New Orleans, La.	FA
Talanoa, Ken (1)	DE-DT	6-4	267	12/14/72	Arizona State	Inglewood, Calif.	FA
Turner, Robert (1)	CB	6-2	206	9/5/70	Washington State	Oakland, Calif.	FA
Veland, Tony (1)	S	6-0	205	3/11/73	Nebraska	Omaha, Neb.	D6-'96
Wallace, Larry (1)	WR	6-1	185	9/9/70	Southern California	Stockton, Calif.	FA

The term NFL Rookie is defined as a player who is in his first season of professional football and has not been on the roster of another professional football team for any regular-season or postseason games. A Rookie is designated by an "R" on NFL rosters. Players who have been active in another professional football league or players who have NFL experience, including either preseason training camp or being on an Active List or Inactive List, or on Reserve/Injured or Reserve/Physically Unable to Perform for fewer than six regular-season games, are termed NFL First-Year Players. An NFL First-Year Player is designated by a "1" on NFL rosters. Thereafter, a player is credited with an additional year of experience for each season in which he accumulates six games on the Active List or Inactive List, or on Reserve/Injured or Reserve/Physically Unable to Perform.

NOTES

1989. Pro coach: New York Jets 1990-94, joined Broncos in 1995.

George Dyer, defensive line; born May 4, 1940, Alhambra, Calif., lives in Aurora, Colo. Center-linebacker U.C. Santa Barbara 1961-63. No pro playing experience. College coach: Humboldt State 1964-66, Coalinga (Calif.) J.C. 1967 (head coach), Portland State 1968-71, Idaho 1972, San Jose State 1973, Michigan State 1977-79, Arizona State 1980-81. Pro coach: Winnipeg Blue Bombers (CFL) 1974-76, Buffalo Bills 1982, Seattle Seahawks 1983-91, Los Angeles Rams 1992-94, joined Broncos in 1995.

Alex Gibbs, assistant head coach-offensive line; born February 11, 1941, Morganton, N.C., lives in Greenwood Village, Colo. Running back-defensive back Davidson College 1959-63. No pro playing experience. College coach: Duke 1969-70, Kentucky 1971-72, West Virginia 1973-74, Ohio State 1975-78, Auburn 1979-81, Georgia 1982-83. Pro coach: Denver Broncos 1984-87, Los Angeles Raiders 1988-89, San Diego Chargers 1990-91, Indianapolis Colts 1992, Kansas City Chiefs 1993-94, rejoined Broncos in 1995.

Mike Heimerdinger, wide receivers; born October 13, 1952, DeKalb, Ill., lives in Englewood, Colo. Wide receiver Eastern Illinois 1970-74. No pro playing experience. College coach: Florida 1980, Air Force 1981, North Texas State 1982, Florida 1983-87, Cal State-Fullerton 1988, Rice 1989-93, Duke 1994. Pro coach: Joined Broncos in 1995.

Gary Kubiak, offensive coordinator-quarterbacks; born August 15, 1961, Houston, Tex., lives in Englewood, Colo. Quarterback Texas A&M 1979-82. Pro quarterback Denver Broncos 1983-91. College coach: Texas A&M 1992-93. Pro coach: San Francisco 49ers 1994, joined Broncos in 1995.

Brian Pariani, tight ends; born July 2, 1965, San Francisco, Calif., lives in Castle Pines, Colo. No college or pro playing experience. College coach: UCLA 1989. Pro coach: San Francisco 49ers 1991-94, joined Broncos in 1995.

Ricky Porter, offensive assistant; born January 14, 1960, Sylacaga, Ala., lives in Englewood, Colo. Running back Slippery Rock 1978-81. Pro running back Detroit Lions 1982, Baltimore Colts 1983, Memphis

Showboats (USFL) 1985, Montreal Alouettes (CFL) 1986-87, Buffalo Bills 1987. College coach: Slippery Rock 1990-91, Kent 1992-93. Pro coach: Tampa Bay Buccaneers 1996, joined Broncos in 1997.

Greg Robinson, defensive coordinator; born October 9, 1951, Los Angeles, Calif., lives in Aurora, Colo. Linebacker-tight end Pacific 1972-74. No pro playing experience. College coach: Pacific 1975-76, Cal State-Fullerton 1977-79, North Carolina State 1980-81, UCLA 1982-89. Pro coach: New York Jets 1990-94, joined Broncos in 1995.

Greg Saporta, assistant strength and conditioning; born February 2, 1957, New York, N.Y., lives in Englewood, Colo. Wide receiver Buffalo State 1977-79. No pro playing experience. College coach: Florida 1981-88, 1993-94, North Carolina 1989-92. Pro coach: Joined Broncos in 1995.

Rick Smith, defensive assistant; born September 3, 1969, Petersburg, Va., lives in Aurora, Colo. Safety Purdue 1987-91. No pro playing experience. College coach: Purdue 1992-95. Pro coach: Joined Broncos in 1996.

John Teerlinck, pass rush specialist; born April 9, 1951, Rochester, N.Y., lives in Englewood, Colo. Defensive lineman Western Illinois 1970-73. Pro defensive tackle San Diego Chargers 1974-76. College coach: Iowa Lakes J.C. 1977, Eastern Illinois 1978-79, Illinois 1980-82. Pro coach: Chicago Blitz (USFL) 1983, Arizona Wranglers/Outlaws (USFL) 1984-85, Cleveland Browns 1989-90, Los Angeles Rams 1991, Minnesota Vikings 1992-94, Detroit Lions 1995-96, joined Broncos in 1997.

Bobby Turner, running backs; born May 6, 1949, East Chicago, Ind., lives in Englewood, Colo. Defensive back Indiana State 1968-71. No pro playing experience. College coach: Indiana State 1975-82, Fresno State 1983-88, Ohio State 1989-90, Purdue 1991-94. Pro coach: Joined Broncos in 1995.

Rich Tuten, strength and conditioning; born December 30, 1953, Columbia, S.C., lives in Englewood, Colo. Nose guard Clemson 1976-78. No pro playing experience. College coach: Florida 1979-88, 1993-94, North Carolina 1989-92. Pro coach: Joined Broncos in 1995.

American Football Conference
Eastern Division
Team Colors: Royal Blue and White
P.O. Box 535000
Indianapolis, Indiana 46253
Telephone: (317) 297-2658

CLUB OFFICIALS

Owner and CEO: James Irsay
Executive Vice President and Chief Financial
   Officer: Michael G. Chernoff
Vice President-Director of Football Operations:
   Bill Tobin
Vice President: Bob Terpening
Director of Pro Player Personnel: Clyde Powers
Director of College Player Personnel:
   George Boone
Controller: Kurt Humphrey
Executive Director of Operations: Pete Ward
Director of Public Relations: Craig Kelley
Director of Ticket Operations and Sales: Larry Hall
Director of Corporate Sales: Rene Longoria
Director of Marketing: Patrick Coyle
Asst. Director of Public Relations: Todd Stewart
Purchasing Administrator: David Filar
Community Relations Manager: Nicole Kucharski
Assistant Director of Ticket Operations:
   Kristi Dorman
Equipment Manager: Jon Scott
Assistant Equipment Manager: Mike Mays
Video Director: Marty Heckscher
Assistant Video Director: John Starliper
Head Trainer: Hunter Smith
Assistant Trainer: Dave Hammer
Team Physician and Orthopedic Surgeon:
   K. Donald Shelbourne
Orthopedic Surgeon: Arthur C. Rettig
Physician: Douglas Robertson
Stadium: RCA Dome •**Capacity:** 60,599
      100 South Capitol Avenue
      Indianapolis, Indiana 46225
Playing Surface: AstroTurf
Training Camp: Anderson University
         Anderson, Indiana 46011

1997 SCHEDULE

PRESEASON

Aug. 1	**Cincinnati**	6:30
Aug. 9	at San Diego	7:00
Aug. 16	at Seattle	7:00
Aug. 21	**Detroit**	7:30

REGULAR SEASON

Aug. 31	at Miami	1:00
Sept. 7	**New England**	12:00
Sept. 14	**Seattle**	3:00
Sept. 21	at Buffalo	4:00
Sept. 28	Open Date	
Oct. 5	**New York Jets**	3:00
Oct. 12	at Pittsburgh	8:00
Oct. 20	**Buffalo** (Mon.)	8:00
Oct. 26	at San Diego	1:00
Nov. 2	**Tampa Bay**	1:00

RECORD HOLDERS

INDIVIDUAL RECORDS—CAREER

Category	Name	Performance
Rushing (Yds.)	Lydell Mitchell, 1972-77	5,487
Passing (Yds.)	Johnny Unitas, 1956-1972	39,768
Passing (TDs)	Johnny Unitas, 1956-1972	287
Receiving (No.)	Raymond Berry, 1955-1967	631
Receiving (Yds.)	Raymond Berry, 1955-1967	9,275
Interceptions	Bob Boyd, 1960-68	57
Punting (Avg.)	Rohn Stark, 1982-1994	43.8
Punt Return (Avg.)	Wendell Harris, 1964	12.6
Kickoff Return (Avg.)	Jim Duncan, 1969-1971	32.5
Field Goals	Dean Biasucci 1984, 1986-1994	176
Touchdowns (Tot.)	Lenny Moore, 1956-1967	113
Points	Dean Biasucci, 1984, 1986-1994	783

INDIVIDUAL RECORDS—SINGLE SEASON

Category	Name	Performance
Rushing (Yds.)	Eric Dickerson, 1988	1,659
Passing (Yds.)	Johnny Unitas, 1963	3,481
Passing (TDs)	Johnny Unitas, 1959	32
Receiving (No.)	Reggie Langhorne, 1993	85
Receiving (Yds.)	Raymond Berry, 1960	1,298
Interceptions	Tom Keane, 1953	11
Punting (Avg.)	Rohn Stark, 1985	45.9
Punt Return (Avg.)	Clarence Verdin, 1989	12.9
Kickoff Return (Avg.)	Jim Duncan, 1970	35.4
Field Goals	Cary Blanchard, 1996	36
Touchdowns (Tot.)	Lenny Moore, 1964	20
Points	Cary Blanchard, 1996	135

INDIVIDUAL RECORDS—SINGLE GAME

Category	Name	Performance
Rushing (Yds.)	Norm Bulaich, 9-19-71	198
Passing (Yds.)	Johnny Unitas, 9-17-67	401
Passing (TDs)	Gary Cuozzo, 11-14-65	5
	Gary Hogeboom, 10-4-87	5
Receiving (No.)	Lydell Mitchell, 12-15-74	13
	Joe Washington, 9-2-79	13
Receiving (Yds.)	Raymond Berry, 11-10-57	224
Interceptions	Many times	3
	Last time by Mike Prior, 12-20-92	
Field Goals	Many times	5
	Last time by Dean Biasucci, 9-25-88	
Touchdowns (Tot.)	Many times	4
	Last time by Eric Dickerson, 10-31-88	
Points	Many times	24
	Last time by Eric Dickerson, 10-31-88	

Nov. 9	**Cincinnati**	1:00
Nov. 16	**Green Bay**	1:00
Nov. 23	at Detroit	1:00
Nov. 30	at New England	1:00
Dec. 7	at New York Jets	4:00
Dec. 14	**Miami**	1:00
Dec. 21	at Minnesota	12:00

COACHING HISTORY

BALTIMORE 1953-1983
(317-325-7)

1953	Keith Molesworth	3-9-0
1954-62	Weeb Ewbank	61-52-1
1963-69	Don Shula	73-26-4
1970-72	Don McCafferty*	26-11-1
1972	John Sandusky	4-5-0
1973-74	Howard Schnellenberger**	4-13-0
1974	Joe Thomas	2-9-0
1975-79	Ted Marchibroda	41-36-0
1980-81	Mike McCormack	9-23-0
1982-84	Frank Kush***	11-28-1
1984	Hal Hunter	0-1-0
1985-86	Rod Dowhower****	5-24-0
1986-91	Ron Meyer#	36-36-0
1991	Rick Venturi	1-10-0
1992-95	Ted Marchibroda	32-35-0
1996	Lindy Infante	9-7-0

  *Released after five games in 1972
  **Released after three games in 1974
  ***Resigned after 15 games in 1984
  ****Released after 13 games in 1986
    #Released after five games in 1991

RCA DOME

1996 TEAM RECORD

PRESEASON (3-2)

Date	Result		Opponents
7/27	W	10-3	vs. New Orleans at Canton, Ohio
8/3	L	25-28	at Cincinnati
8/10	L	12-16	at Houston
8/17	W	15-13	Seattle
8/24	W	30-6	Green Bay

REGULAR SEASON (9-7)

Date	Result		Opponents	Att.
9/1	W	20-13	Arizona	48,133
9/8	W	21-7	at N.Y. Jets	63,534
9/15	W	25-24	at Dallas	63,021
9/23	W	10-6	Miami	60,891
10/6	L	13-16	at Buffalo (OT)	79,401
10/13	W	26-21	Baltimore	56,978
10/20	L	9-27	New England	58,725
10/27	L	16-31	at Washington	54,254
11/3	L	19-26	San Diego	58,484
11/10	L	13-37	at Miami	66,623
11/17	W	34-29	N.Y. Jets	48,322
11/24	L	13-27	at New England	58,226
12/1	W	13-10	Buffalo (OT)	53,804
12/5	W	37-10	Philadelphia	52,689
12/15	W	24-19	at Kansas City	71,136
12/22	L	24-31	at Cincinnati	49,389

POSTSEASON (0-1)

12/29	L	14-42	at Pittsburgh	58,078

(OT) Overtime

SCORE BY PERIODS

Colts	57	94	65	98	3	—	317
Opponents	60	123	66	82	3	—	334

ATTENDANCE

Home 438,026   Away 505,584   Total 943,610
Single-game home record, 60,891 (9/23/96)
Single-season home record, 481,305 (1984)

1996 TEAM STATISTICS

	Colts	Opp.
Total First Downs	288	305
Rushing	89	108
Passing	172	189
Penalty	27	8
Third Down: Made/Att	81/215	88/221
Third Down Pct.	37.7	39.8
Fourth Down: Made/Att	5/12	11/15
Fourth Down Pct.	41.7	73.3
Total Net Yards	4744	5403
Avg. Per Game	296.5	337.7
Total Plays	1000	1022
Avg. Per Play	4.7	5.3
Net Yards Rushing	1448	1760
Avg. Per Game	90.5	110.0
Total Rushes	420	459
Net Yards Passing	3296	3643
Avg. Per Game	206.0	227.7
Sacked/Yards Lost	43/248	29/182
Gross Yards	3544	3825
Att./Completions	537/311	534/318
Completion Pct.	57.9	59.6
Had Intercepted	11	13
Punts/Avg.	68/45.7	81/43.5
Net Punting Avg.	68/39.0	81/36.3
Penalties/Yards Lost	76/615	121/970
Fumbles/Ball Lost	24/13	20/10
Touchdowns	30	38
Rushing	9	12
Passing	16	25
Returns	5	1
Avg. Time of Possession	30:44	29:16

1996 INDIVIDUAL STATISTICS

PASSING	Att.	Comp.	Yds.	Pct.	TD	Int.	Tkld.	Rate
Harbaugh	405	232	2630	57.3	13	11	36/190	76.3
Justin	127	74	839	58.3	2	0	7/58	83.4
Bell	5	5	75	100.0	1	0	0/0	158.3
Colts	537	311	3544	57.9	16	11	43/248	79.2
Opponents	534	318	3825	59.6	25	13	29/182	87.0

SCORING	TD R	TD P	TD Rt	PAT	FG	Saf	PTS
Blanchard	0	0	0	27/27	36/40	0	135
Harrison	0	8	0	0/0	0/0	0	48
Faulk	7	0	0	0/0	0/0	0	42
Dilger	0	4	0	0/0	0/0	0	24
Belser	0	0	2	0/0	0/0	0	12
Bailey	0	0	1	0/0	0/0	0	6
Crockett	0	1	0	0/0	0/0	0	6
Daniel	0	0	1	0/0	0/0	0	6
Dawkins	0	1	0	0/0	0/0	0	6
Harbaugh	1	0	0	0/0	0/0	0	6
Herrod	0	0	1	0/0	0/0	0	6
Pollard	0	1	0	0/0	0/0	0	6
Stablein	0	1	0	0/0	0/0	0	6
Warren	1	0	0	0/0	0/0	0	6
Dent	0	0	0	0/0	0/0	1	2
Colts	9	16	5	27/27	36/40	1	317
Opponents	12	25	1	33/34	23/28	1	334

2-Point conversions: 0. Team: 0-3, Opponents: 1-4.

RUSHING	Att.	Yds.	Avg.	LG	TD
Faulk	198	587	3.0	43	7
Warren	67	230	3.4	53	1
Harbaugh	48	192	4.0	21	1
Groce	46	184	4.0	24	0
Crockett	31	164	5.3	25	0
Workman	24	70	2.9	11	0
Harrison	3	15	5.0	15	0
Justin	2	7	3.5	6	0
Bell	1	-1	-1.0	-1	0
Colts	420	1448	3.4	53	9
Opponents	459	1760	3.8	32t	12

RECEIVING	No.	Yds.	Avg.	LG	TD
Harrison	64	836	13.1	41	8
Faulk	56	428	7.6	30	0
Dawkins	54	751	13.9	42	1
Dilger	42	503	12.0	51	4
Warren	22	174	7.9	17	0
Bailey	18	302	16.8	40	0
Stablein	18	192	10.7	30t	1
Groce	13	106	8.2	24	0
Crockett	11	96	8.7	32	1
Pollard	6	86	14.3	48t	1
Workman	4	36	9.0	18	0
Stock	2	24	12.0	13	0
Doering	1	10	10.0	10	0
Colts	311	3544	11.4	51	16
Opponents	318	3825	12.0	95t	25

INTERCEPTIONS	No.	Yds.	Avg.	LG	TD
Belser	4	81	20.3	44t	2
Daniel	3	35	11.7	35t	1
Buchanan	2	32	16.0	32	0
Herrod	1	68	68.0	68t	1
Watts	1	21	21.0	21	0
Morrison	1	20	20.0	20	0
Alberts	1	19	19.0	19	0
Colts	13	276	21.2	68t	4
Opponents	11	133	12.1	36	0

PUNTING	No.	Yds.	Avg.	In 20	LG
Gardocki	68	3105	45.7	23	61
Colts	68	3105	45.7	23	61
Opponents	81	3525	43.5	22	65

PUNT RETURNS	No.	FC	Yds.	Avg.	LG	TD
Harrison	18	9	177	9.8	31	0
Buchanan	12	3	201	16.8	82	0
Stablein	6	2	56	9.3	30	0
Stock	5	1	13	2.6	9	0
Colts	41	15	447	10.9	82	0
Opponents	38	15	413	10.9	71	0

KICKOFF RETURNS	No.	Yds.	Avg.	LG	TD
Bailey	43	1041	24.2	95t	1
Stock	12	254	21.2	28	0
Warren	3	54	18.0	18	0
Buchanan	1	20	20.0	20	0
Groce	1	18	18.0	18	0
Hetherington	1	16	16.0	16	0
Stablein	0	0	—	—	0
Colts	61	1403	23.0	95t	1
Opponents	67	1666	24.9	70	0

SACKS	No.
Dent	6.5
Bennett	6.0
McCoy	5.0
Whittington	3.0
Siragusa	2.0
Alexander	1.0
Belser	1.0
Grant	1.0
Martin	1.0
Tate	1.0
Buchanan	0.5
Colts	29.0
Opponents	43.0

1997 DRAFT CHOICES

Round	Name	Pos.	College
1	Tarik Glenn	T	California
2	Adam Meadows	T	Georgia
3	Bert Berry	LB	Notre Dame
4	D. Montgomery	DB	Houston
5	Nate Jacquet	WR	San Diego State
	Carl Powell	DE	Louisville
6	Scott Von Der Ahe	LB	Arizona State
7	Clarence Thompson	DB	Knoxville

INDIANAPOLIS COLTS

1997 VETERAN ROSTER

No.	Name	Pos.	Ht.	Wt.	Birthdate	NFL Exp.	College	Hometown	How Acq.	'96 Games/ Starts
51	Alberts, Trev	LB	6-4	245	8/8/70	4	Nebraska	Cedar Falls, Iowa	D1b-'94	9/4
50	Alexander, Elijah	LB	6-2	233	8/2/70	6	Kansas State	Fort Worth, Tex.	FA-'96	14/3
75	Auzenne, Troy	T	6-7	300	6/26/69	6	California	El Monte, Calif.	UFA(Chi)-'96	12/5
80	† Bailey, Aaron	WR	5-10	183	10/24/71	4	Louisville	Ann Arbor, Mich.	FA-'94	14/2
83	Banta, Bradford	TE	6-6	260	12/14/70	4	Southern California	Baton Rouge, La.	D4-'94	13/0
12	Bell, Kerwin	QB	6-3	210	6/15/65	3	Florida	Mayo, Fla.	FA-'96	1/0
29	Belser, Jason	DB	5-9	188	5/28/70	6	Oklahoma	Kansas City, Mo.	D8a-'92	16/16
56	Bennett, Tony	LB	6-2	250	7/1/67	8	Mississippi	Clarksdale, Miss.	FA-'94	14/13
14	Blanchard, Cary	K	6-1	227	11/5/68	5	Oklahoma State	Hurst, Tex.	FA-'95	16/0
53	Burroughs, Sammie	LB	6-0	215	6/21/73	2	Portland State	Pomona, Calif.	FA-'96	16/1
55	Coryatt, Quentin	LB	6-3	250	8/1/70	6	Texas A&M	St. Croix, Virgin Islands	D1b-'92	8/7
32	Crockett, Zack	RB	6-2	246	12/2/72	3	Florida State	Pompano Beach, Fla.	D3-'95	5/5
38	# Daniel, Eugene	CB-S	5-11	178	5/4/61	14	Louisiana State	Baton Rouge, La.	D8-'84	16/9
87	Dawkins, Sean	WR	6-4	211	2/3/71	5	California	Red Bank, N.J.	D1-'93	15/14
96	# Dent, Richard	DE	6-5	265	12/13/60	13	Tennessee State	Atlanta, Ga.	FA-'96	16/1
85	Dilger, Ken	TE	6-5	259	2/2/71	3	Illinois	Mariah Hill, Ind.	D2-'95	16/16
28	Faulk, Marshall	RB	5-10	211	2/26/73	4	San Diego State	New Orleans, La.	D1-'94	13/13
99	Fontenot, Albert	DE	6-4	275	9/17/70	5	Baylor	Houston, Tex.	UFA(Chi)-'97	16/16*
17	Gardocki, Chris	P	6-1	200	2/7/70	7	Clemson	Stone Mountain, Ga.	UFA(Chi)-'95	16/0
59	Grant, Stephen	LB	6-0	240	12/23/69	6	West Virginia	Miami, Fla.	D10-'92	11/11
23	Gray, Carlton	CB	6-0	200	6/26/71	5	UCLA	Cincinnati, Ohio	UFA(Sea)-'97	16/16*
30	Gray, Derwin	CB-S	5-11	210	4/9/71	5	Brigham Young	San Antonio, Tex.	D4a-'93	10/1
33	Groce, Clif	RB	5-11	245	7/30/72	2	Texas A&M	College Station, Tex.	FA-'95	15/8
4	Harbaugh, Jim	QB	6-3	215	12/23/63	11	Michigan	Ann Arbor, Mich.	FA-'94	14/14
88	Harrison, Marvin	WR	6-0	181	8/25/72	2	Syracuse	Philadelphia, Pa.	D1-'96	16/15
54	Herrod, Jeff	LB	6-0	249	7/29/66	10	Mississippi	Birmingham, Ala.	D9-'88	14/14
44	Hetherington, Chris	RB	6-3	233	11/27/72	2	Yale	North Branford, Conn.	FA-'96	6/0
62	Johnson, Ellis	DE-DT	6-2	292	10/30/73	3	Florida	Wildwood, Fla.	D1-'95	12/6
11	Justin, Paul	QB	6-4	211	5/19/68	3	Arizona State	Schaumburg, Ill.	FA-'95	8/2
58	Leeuwenburg, Jay	C-G	6-3	297	6/18/69	6	Colorado	St. Louis, Mo.	UFA(Chi)-'96	15/7
63	# Lowdermilk, Kirk	C	6-4	284	4/10/63	13	Ohio State	Canton, Ohio	UFA(Minn)-'93	16/16
65	Mahlum, Eric	G	6-4	289	12/6/70	4	California	San Diego, Calif.	D2-'94	13/9
79	Mandarich, Tony	T	6-5	317	9/23/66	6	Michigan State	Ontario, Canada	FA-'96	15/6
90	Martin, Steve	DT	6-4	292	5/31/74	2	Missouri	Jefferson City, Mo.	D5-'96	14/5
67	Mathews, Jason	T	6-5	290	2/9/71	4	Texas A&M	Orange, Tex.	D3-'94	16/15
26	Mathis, Dedric	CB-S	5-10	196	9/26/73	2	Houston	Cuero, Tex.	D2-'96	16/6
61	McCoy, Tony	DT	6-0	282	6/10/69	6	Florida	Orlando, Fla.	D4b-'92	15/15
40	McElroy, Ray	S	5-11	207	7/31/72	3	Eastern Illinois	Bellwood, Ill.	D4-'95	16/5
52	Morrison, Steve	LB	6-3	243	12/28/71	3	Michigan	Birmingham, Mich.	FA-'95	16/8
81	Pollard, Marcus	TE	6-4	257	2/8/72	3	Bradley	Valley, Ala.	FA-'95	16/4
42	Potts, Roosevelt	RB	6-0	250	1/8/71	4	Northeast Louisiana	Rayville, La.	D2-'93	0*
97	Shello, Kendel	DE-DT	6-3	301	11/24/73	2	Southern	New Iberia, La.	FA-'96	1/0
84	Slutzker, Scott	TE	6-4	254	12/20/72	2	Iowa	Hasbrouck Heights, N.J.	D3-'96	15/0
86	† Stablein, Brian	WR	6-1	193	4/14/70	4	Ohio State	Erie, Pa.	FA-'94	16/0
10	Stock, Mark	WR	5-11	173	4/27/66	6	Virginia Military Institute	Canton, Ohio	FA-'96	14/0
49	Tate, David	CB-S	6-1	209	11/22/64	10	Colorado	Buffalo Grove, Ill.	FA-'94	10/10
71	Vickers, Kipp	T-G	6-2	297	8/27/69	3	Miami	Holiday, Fla.	FA-'94	10/6
21	Warren, Lamont	RB	5-11	211	1/4/73	4	Colorado	Indianapolis, Ind.	D6-'94	13/3
36	† Watts, Damon	CB-S	5-10	175	4/8/72	4	Indiana	Indianapolis, Ind.	FA-'94	10/0
72	West, Derek	T	6-8	312	3/28/72	3	Colorado	Indianapolis, Ind.	D5-'95	1/0
95	† Whittington, Bernard	DE	6-6	283	8/20/71	4	Indiana	St. Louis, Mo.	FA-'94	16/14
64	Widell, Doug	G	6-4	291	9/23/66	9	Boston College	Hartford, Conn.	UFA(Det)-'96	16/16
46	# Workman, Vince	RB	5-10	215	5/9/68	9	Ohio State	Buffalo, N.Y.	FA-'95	9/0

* Fontenot played 16 games with Chicago in '96; C. Gray played 16 games with Seattle; Potts last active with Indianapolis in '95.

\# Unrestricted free agent; subject to developments.

† Restricted free agent; subject to developments.

Players lost through free agency (2): CB-S Ray Buchanan (Atl; 13 games in '96), DT Tony Siragusa (Balt; 10).

Also played with Colts in '96—CB-S Derrick Frazier (6 games), G-T Steve Hardin (1), CB-S Vance Joseph (4), RB Arnold Mickens (3), DE Freddie Joe Nunn (5), WR Bobby Olive (1), LB Phil Yeboah-Kodie (2).

COACHING STAFF

Head Coach,
Lindy Infante

Pro Career: Infante is in his second season as the Colts' head coach and his third with the team. The Colts' 4-0 start in 1996 made Infante the only head coach in club history to win his first four games. He became the sixth head coach to lead the Colts to the playoffs and joined Don McCafferty (1970) and Ted Marchibroda (1975) as the only Colts' coaches to reach the postseason in their inaugural campaign. The Colts reached the 1996 postseason despite having 19 starters miss a total of 78 starts due to injury, the highest total in the league. Infante previously served as the Colts offensive coordinator in 1995. Under Infante's tutelage, three offensive players (Marshall Faulk, Jim Harbaugh, Will Wolford) earned Pro Bowl spots, and Harbaugh led the NFL in passing rating (100.7) and became the first Colts quarterback named to the Pro Bowl since 1976 (Bert Jones). Harbaugh's rating was the second-highest in club history (Jones, 102.5, 1976) and matched Johnny Unitas (1958, 1965) as the only Colts quarterbacks to top the NFL in passing rating. Infante previously served as head coach of the Green Bay Packers from 1988-1991. He was named NFL Coach of the Year in 1989 by the *Associated Press* and *The Sporting News* and NFC Coach of the Year by *United Press International,* the Pro Football Writers Association of America, *Football News,* and *College and Pro Football Newsweekly* after guiding Green Bay to a 10-6 record. He entered the coaching ranks as an assistant on the staff of Miami Senior High School in 1965. He served as freshman coach at Florida from 1966-68 and coached the Gators' defensive backs from 1969-71. Infante served as offensive coordinator and assistant head coach at Memphis State from 1972-74 before joining the staff of the Charlotte Hornets of the World Football League in 1975. He was offensive coordinator at Tulane in 1976 and 1979, a tenure sandwiched around a two-year stint as receivers coach with the New York Giants (1977-78). Infante left Tulane for the Cincinnati Bengals (1980-82). He served as quarterbacks/receivers coach in 1980-81 and was named the team's first-ever offensive coordinator prior to the 1982 season. Infante served as head coach of the Jacksonville Bulls of the United States Football League in 1984-85. He served as offensive coordinator/quarterbacks coach with the Cleveland Browns in 1986-87. Career record: 33-48.

Background: Was three-year letterman (1960-62) as running back at Florida. In 1963, he was a twelfth-round selection of the Cleveland Browns and an eleventh-round choice of the Buffalo Bills of the American Football League. He signed with Buffalo, was released before the season began, and then played briefly with the Hamilton Tiger Cats of the Canadian Football League.

Personal: Born May 27, 1940, Miami, Fla. Lindy and his wife, Stephanie, live in Indianapolis, and have two sons, Brett and Brad.

ASSISTANT COACHES

Tom Batta, tight ends-quality control; born October 6, 1942, Youngstown, Ohio, lives in Indianapolis. Offensive-defensive line Kent State 1961-63. No pro playing experience. College coach: Akron 1973, Colorado 1974-78, Kansas 1979-82, North Carolina State 1983. Pro coach: Minnesota Vikings 1984-93, joined Colts in 1994.

Greg Blache, defensive line; born March 9, 1949, New Orleans, La., lives in Indianapolis. No college or pro playing experience. College coach: Notre Dame 1973-75, 1981-83, Tulane 1976-80, Southern University 1986, Kansas 1987. Pro coach: Jacksonville Bulls (USFL) 1984-85, Green Bay Packers 1988-93, joined Colts in 1994.

Ron Blackledge, offensive line; born April 15, 1938, Canton, Ohio, lives in Indianapolis. Tight end-defensive end Bowling Green 1957-59. No pro playing experience. College coach: Ashland 1968-69, Cincinnati 1970-72, Kentucky 1973-75, Princeton 1976, Kent State 1977-81 (head coach 1979-81). Pro coach: Pittsburgh Steelers 1982-91, joined Colts in 1992.

Chuck Bresnahan, linebackers; born September 8, 1960, Springfield, Mass., lives in Indianapolis. Linebacker Navy 1979-83. No pro playing experience. College coach: Navy 1983-84, 1986-87, Georgia Tech 1987-91, Maine 1992-93. Pro coach: Cleveland Browns 1994-95, joined Colts in 1996.

Charlie Davis, asst. offensive line; born August 7, 1944, San Diego, Calif., lives in Indianapolis. Linebacker UCLA 1962-64. No pro playing experience. College coach: UCLA 1966, San Francisco State 1967-68, San Diego City College 1969-70, Xavier 1971-73, Ball State 1974-75, Tulane 1976-80. Pro coach: Jacksonville Bulls (USFL) 1984-85, Cleveland Browns 1986-87, Green Bay Packers 1988-91, joined Colts in 1996.

Wayne (Buddy) Geis, offensive assistant-asst. quarterbacks; born September 18, 1946, Altoona, Pa., lives in Indianapolis. Wide receiver Northern Arizona 1965. No pro playing experience. College coach: Arizona 1974-76, Tulane 1977-82, Memphis State 1986-87, Duke 1993, Tulane 1994. Pro coach: Jacksonville Bulls (USFL) 1984-85, Green Bay Packers 1988-91, Memphis Mad Dogs (CFL) 1995, joined Colts in 1996.

Gene Huey, running backs; born July 20, 1947, Uniontown, Pa., lives in Indianapolis. Defensive back-wide receiver Wyoming 1966-69. No pro playing experience. College coach: Wyoming 1970-74, New Mexico 1975-77, Nebraska 1978-87, Ohio State 1988-91. Pro coach: Joined Colts in 1992.

Jim Johnson, defensive coordinator; born May 26, 1941, Maywood, Ill., lives in Indianapolis. Quarterback Missouri 1959-62. Pro tight end Buffalo Bills 1963-64. College coach: Missouri Southern 1967-68 (head coach), Drake 1969-72, Indiana 1973-76,

Notre Dame 1977-80. Pro coach: Oklahoma Outlaws (USFL) 1984, Jacksonville Bulls (USFL) 1985, Phoenix Cardinals 1986-93, joined Colts in 1994.

Hank Kuhlmann, special teams; born October 6, 1937, Webster Groves, Mo., lives in Indianapolis. Running back Missouri 1956-59. No pro playing experience. College coach: Missouri 1962-71, Notre Dame 1975-77. Pro coach: Green Bay Packers 1972-74, Chicago Bears 1978-82, Birmingham Stallions (USFL) 1983-85, St. Louis/Phoenix Cardinals 1986-1989, Tampa Bay Buccaneers 1991, joined Colts in 1994.

Jay Robertson, defensive assistant; born February 20, 1940, Chicago, Ill., lives in Indianapolis. Center Northwestern 1959-62. No pro playing experience. College coach: Northwestern 1967-75, Northern Illinois 1976-79, Wisconsin 1980-81, Notre Dame 1982-83, Army 1984-91. Pro coach: Indianapolis Colts 1992-93, rejoined Colts in 1997.

Jimmy Robinson, wide receivers; born January 3, 1953, Atlanta, Ga., lives in Indianapolis. Wide receiver Georgia Tech 1972-74. Pro wide receiver Atlanta Falcons 1975, New York Giants 1976-79, San Francisco 49ers 1980, Denver Broncos 1981. College coach: Georgia Tech 1982-83. Pro coach: Memphis Showboats (USFL) 1984-85, Atlanta Falcons 1990-93, joined Colts in 1994.

Pat Thomas, secondary; born September 1, 1954, Plano, Tex., lives in Indianapolis. Cornerback Texas A&M 1972-75. Pro cornerback Los Angeles Rams 1976-82. College coach: Houston 1987-89. Pro coach: Houston Gamblers (USFL) 1984-85, Houston Oilers 1990-92, joined Colts in 1994.

Tom Zupancic, strength and conditioning; born September 14, 1955, Indianapolis, lives in Indianapolis. Defensive tackle-offensive tackle Indiana Central 1975-78. No pro playing experience. Pro coach: Joined Colts in 1984.

1997 FIRST-YEAR ROSTER

Name	Pos.	Ht.	Wt.	Birthdate	College	Hometown	How Acq.
Allen, Eric	CB-S	6-0	205	12/4/74	Indiana	Indianapolis, Ind.	FA
Berry, Bert	LB	6-2	243	8/15/75	Notre Dame	Houston, Tex.	D3
Cravens, Matt	C	6-3	280	1/8/74	Miami, Ohio	Spring Valley, Ohio	FA
Daniels, Juan	WR	6-1	210	12/10/73	Georgia	Norcross, Ga.	FA
Drexler, Darren	TE	6-5	257	11/26/73	Northwestern	Kirkwood, Mo.	FA
Gagliano, Mark	K	6-2	195	5/8/74	Southern Illinois	Collierville, Tenn.	FA
Glenn, Tarik	T	6-5	335	5/25/76	California	Cleveland, Ohio	D1
Haynes, Gary	DT	6-0	298	4/23/74	Houston	Palacios, Tex.	FA
Jacquet, Nate	WR	6-0	173	9/2/75	San Diego State	Duarte, Calif.	D5a
Johnson, Jason	C	6-3	288	2/6/74	Kansas State	Gladstone, Mo.	FA
Kidd, Brannon	G	6-3	294	8/19/73	Southern Methodist	Dallas, Tex.	FA
Lanier, Tony	WR	5-11	172	12/10/71	Virginia State	Danville, Va.	FA
Lusk, Harold	CB-S	5-11	197	12/29/73	Utah	Seaside, Calif.	FA
McTyer, Tim	CB-S	5-11	181	12/14/75	Brigham Young	Los Angeles, Calf.	FA
Meadows, Adam	T	6-5	297	1/25/74	Georgia	Powder Springs, Ga.	D2
Montgomery, Delmonico	CB-S	5-11	193	12/8/73	Houston	Dallas, Tex.	D4
Neil, Owen	T	6-3	275	4/6/74	Florida A&M	Louisville, Kan.	FA
Osborne, Dedric	LB	6-1	225	9/24/75	Miami, Ohio	Olympia Fields, Ill.	FA
Pickett, Booker	DE	6-1	242	8/7/74	Miami	Zephyrhills, Fla.	FA
Powell, Carl	DE	6-3	257	1/4/74	Louisville	Detroit, Mich.	D5b
Smith, Alex	RB	5-11	208	11/12/74	Indiana	Brookville, Ind.	FA
Thomas, Malcom	RB	5-7	199	5/15/74	Syracuse	Jacksonville, Fla.	FA
Thompson, Clarence	CB-S	6-1	198	1/5/75	Knoxville College	Detroit, Mich.	D7
Von Der Ahe, Scott	LB	5-11	251	10/12/75	Arizona State	Lancaster, Calif.	D6
West, Lorenzo	DE	6-3	257	5/5/73	East Carolina	Atlanta, Ga.	FA
Wilson, Abu	RB	6-0	214	1/2/73	Utah State	San Francisco, Calif.	FA

The term NFL Rookie is defined as a player who is in his first season of professional football and has not been on the roster of another professional football team for any regular-season or postseason games. A Rookie is designated by an "R" on NFL rosters. Players who have been active in another professional football league or players who have NFL experience, including either preseason training camp or being on an Active List or Inactive List, or on Reserve/Injured or Reserve/Physically Unable to Perform for fewer than six regular-season games, are termed NFL First-Year Players. An NFL First-Year Player is designated by a "1" on NFL rosters. Thereafter, a player is credited with an additional year of experience for each season in which he accumulates six games on the Active List or Inactive List, or on Reserve/Injured or Reserve/Physically Unable to Perform.

NOTES

_____

_____

_____

_____

JACKSONVILLE JAGUARS

American Football Conference
Central Division
Team Colors: Teal, Black, and Gold
ALLTEL Stadium
One ALLTEL Stadium Place
Jacksonville, Florida 32202
Telephone: (904) 633-6000

CLUB OFFICIALS

Chairman, President and Chief Executive Officer:
  Wayne Weaver
Senior Vice President/Football Operations:
  Michael Huyghue
Senior Vice President/Marketing: Dan Connell
Chief Financial Officer/Vice President: Bill Prescott
General Counsel/Vice President, Administration:
  Paul Vance
Vice President/Ticket Operations: Judy Seldin
Executive Director of Communications:
  Dan Edwards
Director of Pro Personnel: Ron Hill
Director of College Scouting: Rick Reiprish
Director of Finance: Kim Dodson
Director of Facilities: Jeff Cannon
Director of Computer Services: Bruce Swindell
Director of Security: Skip Richardson
Director of Team Operations: Daren Anderson
Director of Broadcasting: Jennifer Kumik
Head Athletic Trainer: Michael Ryan
Video Director: Mike Perkins
Equipment Manager: Bob Monica
Corporate Sponsorship Manager: Macky Weaver
Special Events Manager: Roddy White

Chair & Chief Executive Officer, Jaguars Foundation:
  Delores Barr Weaver
President, Jaguars Foundation: Dr. Gregory Gross
Stadium: ALLTEL Stadium
  •**Capacity:** 73,000
  One ALLTEL Stadium Place
  Jacksonville, Florida 32202
Playing Surface: Grass
Training Camp: ALLTEL Stadium
  One ALLTEL Stadium Place
  Jacksonville, Florida 32202

RECORD HOLDERS

INDIVIDUAL RECORDS—CAREER

Category	Name	Performance
Rushing (Yds.)	James Stewart, 1995-96	1,248
Passing (Yds.)	Mark Brunell, 1995-96	6,535
Passing (TDs)	Mark Brunell, 1995-96	34
Receiving (No.)	Jimmy Smith, 1995-96	105
Receiving (Yds.)	Jimmy Smith, 1995-96	1,532
Interceptions	Harry Colon, 1995	3
Punting (Avg.)	Bryan Barker, 1995-96	43.8
Punt Return (Avg.)	Chris Hudson, 1996	10.9
Kickoff Return (Avg.)	Jimmy Smith, 1995-96	22.7
Field Goals	Mike Hollis, 1995-96	50
Touchdowns (Tot.)	James Stewart, 1995-96	13
Points	Mike Hollis, 1995-96	204

INDIVIDUAL RECORDS—SINGLE SEASON

Category	Name	Performance
Rushing (Yds.)	James Stewart, 1996	723
Passing (Yds.)	Mark Brunell, 1996	4,367
Passing (TDs)	Mark Brunell, 1996	19
Receiving (No.)	Keenan McCardell, 1996	85
Receiving (Yds.)	Jimmy Smith, 1996	1,244
Interceptions	Harry Colon, 1995	3
Punting (Avg.)	Bryan Barker, 1995	43.8
Punt Return (Avg.)	Chris Hudson, 1996	10.9
Kickoff Return (Avg.)	Bucky Brooks, 1996	24.2
Field Goals	Mike Hollis, 1996	30
Touchdowns (Tot.)	James Stewart, 1996	10
Points	Mike Hollis, 1996	117

INDIVIDUAL RECORDS—SINGLE GAME

Category	Name	Performance
Rushing (Yds.)	James Stewart, 10-20-96	112
Passing (Yds.)	Mark Brunell, 9-22-96	432
Passing (TDs)	Mark Brunell, 10-15-95, 12-10-95, 9-22-96	3
Receiving (No.)	Keenan McCardell, 10-20-96	16
Receiving (Yds.)	Keenan McCardell, 10-20-96	232
Interceptions	Many times	1
	Last time by Tony Brackens, 12-15-96	
Field Goals	Mike Hollis, 12-1-96	5
Touchdowns (Tot.)	Jimmy Smith, 12-3-95	3
Points	Jimmy Smith, 12-3-95	18

1997 SCHEDULE

PRESEASON

Aug. 3	**Carolina**	3:00
Aug. 9	at N.Y. Giants	8:00
Aug. 18	at San Francisco	5:00
Aug. 22	**Atlanta**	7:30

REGULAR SEASON

Aug. 31	at Baltimore	4:00
Sept. 7	**New York Giants**	4:00
Sept. 14	Open Date	
Sept. 22	**Pittsburgh** (Mon.)	9:00
Sept. 28	at Washington	1:00
Oct. 5	**Cincinnati**	1:00
Oct. 12	**Philadelphia**	1:00
Oct. 19	at Dallas	12:00
Oct. 26	at Pittsburgh	4:00
Nov. 2	at Tennessee	3:00
Nov. 9	**Kansas City**	1:00
Nov. 16	**Tennessee**	1:00
Nov. 23	at Cincinnati	4:00
Nov. 30	**Baltimore**	1:00
Dec. 7	**New England**	1:00
Dec. 14	at Buffalo	1:00
Dec. 21	at Oakland	1:00

COACHING HISTORY

(15-20-0)

1995-96	Tom Coughlin	15-20-0

ALLTEL STADIUM

1996 TEAM RECORD

PRESEASON (2-2)

Date	Result		Opponents
8/2	L	17-24	N.Y. Giants
8/9	L	10-17	at St. Louis
8/18	W	38-10	San Francisco
8/23	W	31-24	at Denver

REGULAR SEASON (9-7)

Date	Result		Opponents	Att.
9/1	W	24-9	Pittsburgh	70,210
9/8	L	27-34	Houston	66,468
9/15	L	3-17	at Oakland	46,291
9/22	L	25-28	at New England (OT)	59,446
9/29	W	24-14	Carolina	71,537
10/6	L	13-17	at New Orleans	34,231
10/13	W	21-17	N.Y. Jets	65,699
10/20	L	14-17	at St. Louis	60,066
10/27	L	21-28	at Cincinnati	45,890
11/10	W	30-27	Baltimore	64,628
11/17	L	3-28	at Pittsburgh	58,879
11/24	W	28-25	at Baltimore (OT)	57,384
12/1	W	30-27	Cincinnati	57,408
12/8	W	23-17	at Houston	20,196
12/15	W	20-13	Seattle	66,134
12/22	W	19-17	Atlanta	71,449

POSTSEASON (2-1)

12/28	W	30-27	at Buffalo	70,213
1/4	W	30-27	at Denver	75,678
1/12	L	6-20	at New England	60,190

(OT) Overtime

SCORE BY PERIODS

Jaguars	68	80	80	94	3	—	325
Opponents	70	117	65	80	3	—	335

ATTENDANCE

Home 533,533   Away 382,383   Total 915,916
Single-game home record, 72,363 (9/3/95)
Single-season home record, 554,814 (1995)

1996 TEAM STATISTICS

	Jaguars	Opp.
Total First Downs	325	315
Rushing	90	110
Passing	208	180
Penalty	27	25
Third Down: Made/Att	87/208	93/211
Third Down Pct.	41.8	44.1
Fourth Down: Made/Att	5/8	3/8
Fourth Down Pct.	62.5	37.5
Total Net Yards	5760	5085
Avg. Per Game	360.0	317.8
Total Plays	1038	992
Avg. Per Play	5.5	5.1
Net Yards Rushing	1650	1781
Avg. Per Game	103.1	111.3
Total Rushes	431	447
Net Yards Passing	4110	3304
Avg. Per Game	256.9	206.5
Sacked/Yards Lost	50/257	37/237
Gross Yards	4367	3541
Att./Completions	557/353	508/290
Completion Pct.	63.4	57.1
Had Intercepted	20	13
Punts/Avg.	69/43.7	71/42.0
Net Punting Avg.	69/35.6	71/34.5
Penalties/Yards Lost	127/1006	97/800
Fumbles/Ball Lost	29/10	26/14
Touchdowns	33	37
Rushing	13	9
Passing	19	24
Returns	1	4
Avg. Time of Possession	31:18	28:42

1996 INDIVIDUAL STATISTICS

PASSING	Att.	Comp.	Yds.	Pct.	TD	Int.	Tkld.	Rate
Brunell	557	353	4367	63.4	19	20	50/257	84.0
Jaguars	557	353	4367	63.4	19	20	50/257	84.0
Opponents	508	290	3541	57.1	24	13	37/237	83.8

SCORING	TD R	TD P	TD Rt	PAT	FG	Saf	PTS
Hollis	0	0	0	27/27	30/36	0	117
Stewart	8	2	0	0/0	0/0	0	60
Smith	0	7	0	0/0	0/0	0	42
Brunell	3	0	0	0/0	0/0	0	22
McCardell	0	3	0	0/0	0/0	0	22
Jackson	0	3	0	0/0	0/0	0	20
Means	2	1	0	0/0	0/0	0	18
Rison	0	2	0	0/0	0/0	0	12
Mitchell	0	1	0	0/0	0/0	0	6
Washington	0	0	1	0/0	0/0	0	6
Jaguars	13	19	1	27/27	30/36	0	325
Opponents	9	24	4	33/35	26/34	0	335

2-Point conversions: Brunell 2, McCardell 2, Jackson. Team: 5-6, Opponents: 1-2.

RUSHING	Att.	Yds.	Avg.	LG	TD
Stewart	190	723	3.8	34	8
Means	152	507	3.3	35	2
Brunell	80	396	5.0	33	3
Maston	8	22	2.8	7	0
Jackson	1	2	2.0	2	0
Jaguars	431	1650	3.8	35	13
Opponents	447	1781	4.0	76	9

RECEIVING	No.	Yds.	Avg.	LG	TD
McCardell	85	1129	13.3	52	3
Smith	83	1244	15.0	62	7
Mitchell	52	575	11.1	30	1
Rison	34	458	13.5	61t	2
Jackson	33	486	14.7	58	3
Stewart	30	177	5.9	21t	2
Brown	17	141	8.3	16	0
Means	7	45	6.4	11t	1
Maston	6	54	9.0	17	0
Griffith	5	53	10.6	18	0
Hallock	1	5	5.0	5	0
Jaguars	353	4367	12.4	62	19
Opponents	290	3541	12.2	63t	24

INTERCEPTIONS	No.	Yds.	Avg.	LG	TD
Hudson	2	25	12.5	21	0
Hardy	2	19	9.5	13	0
Thomas	2	7	3.5	8	0
T. Davis	2	0	0.0	0	0
Brackens	1	27	27.0	27	0
Hall	1	20	20.0	20	0
V. Clark	1	15	15.0	15	0
Washington	1	1	1.0	1	0
Beasley	1	0	0.0	0	0
Jaguars	13	114	8.8	27	0
Opponents	20	370	18.5	92t	3

PUNTING	No.	Yds.	Avg.	In 20	LG
Barker	69	3016	43.7	16	62
Jaguars	69	3016	43.7	16	62
Opponents	71	2979	42.0	19	70

PUNT RETURNS	No.	FC	Yds.	Avg.	LG	TD
Hudson	32	12	348	10.9	60	0
McCardell	1	1	2	2.0	2	0
Thomas	1	0	1	1.0	1	0
Jaguars	34	13	351	10.3	60	0
Opponents	44	7	400	9.1	40	0

KICKOFF RETURNS	No.	Yds.	Avg.	LG	TD
Jordan	26	553	21.3	73	0
Brooks	17	412	24.2	36	0
Bullard	7	157	22.4	36	0
Jackson	7	149	21.3	27	0
Bell	6	119	19.8	28	0
Griffith	2	24	12.0	16	0
Smith	2	49	24.5	29	0
Jaguars	67	1463	21.8	73	0
Opponents	71	1674	23.6	62	0

SACKS	No.
Simmons	7.5
Brackens	7.0
Hardy	5.5
Smeenge	5.0
Lageman	4.5
Pritchett	2.0
Beasley	1.0
Jurkovic	1.0
Robinson	1.0
Davey	0.5
T. Davis	0.5
Hudson	0.5
Jaguars	*37.0
Opponents	50.0

Jaguars were credited with 1 team sack.

1997 DRAFT CHOICES

Round	Name	Pos.	College
1	Renaldo Wynn	DT	Notre Dame
2	Mike Logan	DB	West Virginia
3	James Hamilton	LB	North Carolina
4	Seth Payne	DT	Cornell
5	Damon Jones	TE	Southern Illinois
6	Daimon Shelton	RB	Cal State-Sacramento
7	Jon Hesse	LB	Nebraska

JACKSONVILLE JAGUARS

1997 VETERAN ROSTER

No.	Name	Pos.	Ht.	Wt.	Birthdate	NFL Exp.	College	Hometown	How Acq.	'96 Games/ Starts
4	Barker, Bryan	P	6-2	191	6/28/64	8	Santa Clara	Orinda, Calif.	UFA(Phil)-'95	16/0
84	Barlow, Reggie	WR	5-11	186	1/22/73	2	Alabama State	Montgomery, Ala.	D4-'96	7/0
21	Beasley, Aaron	CB	5-11	206	7/7/73	2	West Virginia	Pottstown, Pa.	D3-'96	9/7
42	Bell, Ricky	CB	5-10	186	10/2/74	2	North Carolina State	Columbia, S.C.	W(Pitt)-'96	12/0
71	Boselli, Tony	T	6-7	322	4/17/72	3	Southern California	Boulder, Colo.	D1a-'95	16/16
52	Boyer, Brant	LB	6-1	231	6/27/71	3	Arizona	Hooper, Utah	FA-'96	12/0
90	Brackens, Tony	DE	6-4	266	12/26/74	2	Texas	Fairfield, Tex.	D2a-'96	16/1
22	Brooks, Bucky	CB	6-0	195	1/22/71	3	North Carolina	Raleigh, N.C.	W(GB)-'96	6/1
86	Brown, Derek	TE	6-6	267	3/31/70	6	Notre Dame	Fairfax, Va.	ED24(NYG)-'95	16/14
8	Brunell, Mark	QB	6-1	216	9/17/70	5	Washington	Santa Maria, Calif.	T(GB)-'95	16/16
88	Bullard, Kendricke	WR	6-2	190	4/30/72	2	Arkansas State	Pine Bluff, Ark.	FA-'96	12/0
63	Cheever, Michael	C	6-3	298	6/24/73	2	Georgia Tech	Newnan, Ga.	D2b-'96	11/2
62	Coleman, Ben	G-T	6-6	325	5/18/71	5	Wake Forest	South Hill, Va.	W(Ariz)-'95	16/16
92	Davey, Don	DT	6-4	270	4/8/68	7	Wisconsin	Manitowoc, Wis.	UFA(GB)-'95	16/12
77	Davis, Andre	DT	6-3	330	10/7/75	2	Southern	Baton Rouge, La.	FA-'96	2/0
45	Davis, Travis	S	6-0	203	1/10/73	3	Notre Dame	Wilmington, Calif.	FA-'95	16/7
73	DeMarco, Brian	G	6-7	325	4/9/72	3	Michigan State	Lorain, Ohio	D2a-'95	10/9
27	Figures, Deon	CB	6-0	192	1/20/70	5	Colorado	Bellflower, Calif.	UFA(Pitt)-'97	14/0*
24	Fisher, John	S	5-10	204	7/28/73	2	Missouri Western	Oakland, Calif.	D6a-'96	0*
91	Frase, Paul	DE	6-5	271	5/5/65	9	Syracuse	Barrington, N.H.	ED9(NYJ)-'95	14/0
85	Griffith, Rich	TE	6-5	256	7/31/69	4	Arizona	Tucson, Ariz.	FA-'95	16/2
28	Hall, Dana	S	6-2	209	7/8/69	6	Washington	Bellflower, Calif.	FA-'96	16/10
49	† Hallock, Ty	LB	6-3	256	4/30/71	4	Michigan State	Greenville, Mich.	T(Det)-'95	7/0
51	Hardy, Kevin	LB	6-4	246	7/24/73	2	Illinois	Evansville, Ind.	D1-'96	16/15
74	Herndon, Jimmy	T	6-8	316	8/30/73	2	Houston	Baytown, Tex.	D5-'96	0*
1	Hollis, Mike	K	5-7	178	5/5/72	3	Idaho	Spokane, Wash.	FA-'95	16/0
37	Hudson, Chris	S	5-10	200	10/6/71	3	Colorado	Houston, Tex.	D3-'95	16/16
66	Huntington, Greg	C-G	6-4	302	9/22/70	4	Penn State	Mountain Brook, Ala.	FA-'96	2/0
80	Jackson, Willie	WR	6-1	208	8/16/71	4	Florida	Gainesville, Fla.	ED11(Dall)-'95	16/2
11	Johnson, Rob	QB	6-3	212	3/18/73	3	Southern California	El Toro, Calif.	D4a-'95	2/0
23	Jordan, Randy	RB	5-10	213	6/6/70	4	North Carolina	Manson, N.C.	FA-'94	15/0
64	Jurkovic, John	DT	6-2	295	8/18/67	6	Eastern Illinois	Calumet City, Ill.	UFA(GB)-'96	16/14
57	Kopp, Jeff	LB	6-3	243	7/8/71	3	Southern California	Danville, Calif.	FA-'96	12/0
56	Lageman, Jeff	DE	6-6	267	7/18/67	9	Virginia	Sterling, Va.	UFA(NYJ)-'95	12/9
89	Marsh, Curtis	WR	6-2	201	11/24/70	3	Utah	Simi Valley, Calif.	D7-'95	1/0
40	Massey, Robert	CB	5-11	200	2/27/67	9	North Carolina Central	Charlotte, N.C.	FA-'96	16/0
35	Maston, Le'Shai	RB	6-0	237	10/7/70	5	Baylor	Dallas, Tex.	ED18(Hou)-'95	15/7
87	McCardell, Keenan	WR	6-1	186	1/6/70	6	Nevada-Las Vegas	Houston, Tex.	UFA(Balt)-'96	16/15
55	McManus, Tom	LB	6-2	247	7/30/70	3	Boston College	Edgewater, Fla.	FA-'95	16/11
20	Means, Natrone	RB	5-10	240	4/26/72	5	North Carolina	Harrisburg, N.C.	W(SD)-'96	14/4
83	Mitchell, Pete	TE	6-2	238	10/9/71	3	Boston College	Birmingham, Mich.	T(Mia)-'95	16/7
3	Moore, Will	WR	6-2	180	2/21/70	2	Texas Southern	Dallas, Tex.	FA-'97	2/1*
67	Novak, Jeff	G-T	6-5	298	7/27/67	4	Southwest Texas State	Arlington Heights, Ill.	ED3(Mia)-'95	5/0
7	O'Neill, Pat	P	6-1	200	2/9/71	3	Syracuse	Harrisburg, Pa.	FA-'97	0*
5	Philcox, Todd	QB	6-4	218	9/25/66	7	Syracuse	Norwalk, Conn.	UFA(TB)-'96	0*
94	Pritchett, Kelvin	DT	6-3	296	10/24/69	7	Mississippi	Atlanta, Ga.	UFA(Det)-'96	13/4
50	Robinson, Eddie	LB	6-1	238	4/13/70	6	Alabama State	New Orleans, La.	UFA(Hou)-'96	16/15
58	Schwartz, Bryan	LB	6-4	253	12/5/71	3	Augustana	St. Lawrence, S.D.	D2b-'95	4/3
72	Searcy, Leon	T	6-3	315	12/21/69	6	Miami	Washington, D.C.	UFA(Pitt)-'96	16/16
96	Simmons, Clyde	DE	6-6	281	8/4/64	12	Western Carolina	Lanes, S.C.	FA-'96	16/14
99	Smeenge, Joel	LB	6-6	270	4/1/68	8	Western Michigan	Grand Rapids, Mich.	UFA(NO)-'95	10/10
82	Smith, Jimmy	WR	6-1	204	2/9/69	5	Jackson State	Jackson, Miss.	FA-'95	16/9
33	Stewart, James	RB	6-1	224	12/27/71	3	Tennessee	Morristown, Tenn.	D1b-'95	13/11
30	Studstill, Darren	S	6-1	190	8/9/70	3	West Virginia	Palm Beach Gardens, Fla.	FA-'95	7/0
41	Thomas, Dave	CB	6-3	215	8/25/68	5	Tennessee	Miami, Fla.	ED16(Dall)-'95	9/5
76	Tylski, Rich	G	6-4	304	2/27/71	2	Utah State	San Diego, Calif.	W(NE)-'95	16/7
79	Widell, Dave	C	6-7	312	5/14/65	10	Boston College	Hartford, Conn.	UFA(Den)-'95	15/14

* Figures played 14 games with Pittsburgh in '96; Fisher missed '96 season because of injury; Herndon inactive for 8 games; Moore played 2 games with New England; O'Neill last active with Chicago and New England in '95; Philcox inactive for 16 games.

† Restricted free agent; subject to developments.

Players lost through free agency (1): DE Ernie Logan (NYJ; 4 games in '96).

Also played with Jaguars in '96—RB Ryan Christopherson (2 games), LB Reggie Clark (5), CB Vinnie Clark (4), LB Nate Dingle (2), CB Rashid Gayle (2), RB Roger Graham (1), WR Andre Rison (10), CB Mickey Washington (16).

COACHING STAFF

Head Coach,
Tom Coughlin

Pro Career: In just two seasons, Coughlin directed the young Jaguars to the AFC Championship Game in only the thirty-fifth game of the franchise's history. With a five-game winning streak at the end of the 1996 season, the Jaguars became the first team in NFL history to play in—and win—2 playoff games in only its second season. En route to the 1996 AFC Championship Game, the Jaguars became the first visiting team to win a playoff game at Buffalo's Rich Stadium, and only the second to win a playoff game at Denver's Mile High Stadium. Coughlin became the first head coach of the NFL's newest franchise on February 21, 1994, following a successful three seasons as head coach at Boston College. A veteran of 27 years in coaching, including 17 at the collegiate level and seven as an NFL assistant, Coughlin previously coached wide receivers for the Philadelphia Eagles (1984-85), Green Bay Packers (1986-87), and New York Giants (1988-1990). He was a member of the Giants' Super Bowl XXV champion coaching staff prior to being named head coach at Boston College in 1991. In three seasons at Boston College, he turned a struggling program into a top-20 team, posting a 21-13-1 record. His final season at Boston College was highlighted by eight consecutive wins, including a 41-39 victory over top-ranked Notre Dame, and a 9-3 finish. Despite an 0-2 start to the season, Boston College ranked thirteenth in the *Associated Press* poll and twelfth in the *USA Today/CNN* coaches poll at the end of the 1993 season. Coughlin's previous 14 seasons as a college coach were at Rochester Institute of Technology 1970-73 (head coach), Syracuse 1974-80, and Boston College 1981-83. No pro playing experience. Career record: 15-20.

Background: Played wingback for Syracuse from 1965-67 under legendary coach Ben Schwartzwalder, along with teammates Larry Csonka and Floyd Little. Received Syracuse 1967 Orange Key Award as outstanding scholar athlete, and graduated in 1968 with bachelor's degree in education. Received master's degree in education from Syracuse in 1969.

Personal: Born August 31, 1947, Waterloo, N.Y. Was standout scholastic star for Waterloo Central High School. Tom and his wife, Judy, reside in Jacksonville. They have two daughters, Keli and Katie, and two sons, Tim and Brian.

ASSISTANT COACHES

Joe Baker, assistant special teams; born June 29, 1969, Glen Ridge, N.J., lives in Jacksonville. Wide receiver Princeton 1987-90. No pro playing experience. College coach: Samford 1993. Pro coach: Joined Jaguars in 1995.

Pete Carmichael, wide receivers; born March 4, 1941, North Plainfield, N.J., lives in Jacksonville. Quarterback Dayton 1961, Montclair State College 1962-63. No pro playing experience. College coach: Virginia Military 1965-66, New Hampshire 1967, Boston College 1968-72, 1981-93, Trenton State College 1973 (head coach), Columbia 1974-77, Merchant Marine Academy 1977-80 (head coach). Pro coach: Joined Jaguars in 1995.

Randy Edsall, secondary; born August 27, 1958, Glen Rock, Pa., lives in Jacksonville. Quarterback Syracuse 1976-79. No pro playing experience. College coach: Syracuse 1983-90, Boston College 1991-93. Pro coach: Joined Jaguars in 1995.

Fred Hoaglin, tight ends; born January 28, 1944, Alliance, Ohio, lives in Jacksonville. Center Pittsburgh 1962-65. Pro center Cleveland Browns 1966-72, Baltimore Colts 1973, Houston Oilers 1974-75, Seattle Seahawks 1976. Pro coach: Detroit Lions 1978-84, New York Giants 1985-92, New England Patriots 1993-96, joined Jaguars in 1997.

Jerald Ingram, running backs; born December 24, 1960, Beaver, Pa., lives in Jacksonville. Fullback Michigan 1979-84. No pro playing experience. College coach: Ball State 1985-90, Boston College 1991-93. Pro coach: Joined Jaguars in 1995.

Dick Jauron, defensive coordinator; born October 7, 1950, Peoria, Ill., lives in Jacksonville. Defensive back Yale 1970-72. Pro defensive back Detroit Lions 1973-77, Cincinnati Bengals 1978-80. Pro coach: Buffalo Bills 1985, Green Bay Packers 1986-94, joined Jaguars in 1995.

Mike Maser, offensive line; born March 2, 1947, Clayton, N.Y., lives in Jacksonville. Guard Buffalo 1967-70. No pro playing experience. College coach: Marshall 1973, Bluefield State College 1974-78, Maine 1979-80, Boston College 1981-93. Pro coach: Joined Jaguars in 1995.

Chris Palmer, offensive coordinator; born September 23, 1949, Mt. Kisco, N.Y., lives in Jacksonville. Quarterback Southern Connecticut State 1968-71. No pro playing experience. College coach: Connecticut 1972-74, Lehigh 1975, Colgate 1976-82, New Haven 1986-87 (head coach), Boston University 1988-89 (head coach). Pro coach: Montreal Concordes (CFL) 1983, New Jersey Generals (USFL) 1984-85, Houston Oilers 1990-92, New England Patriots 1993-96, joined Jaguars in 1997.

Jerry Palmieri, strength and conditioning; born October 30, 1958, Englewood, N.J., lives in Jacksonville. No college or pro playing experience. College coach: Oklahoma State 1984-87, Kansas State 1988-92, Boston College 1993-94. Pro coach: Joined Jaguars in 1995.

Larry Pasquale, special teams coordinator; born April 21, 1941, Brooklyn, N.Y., lives in Jacksonville. Quarterback Bridgeport 1961-63. No pro playing experience. College coach: Slippery Rock State 1967, Boston University 1968, Navy 1969-70, Massachusetts 1971-75, Idaho State 1976. Pro coach: Montreal Alouettes (CFL) 1977-78, Detroit Lions 1979, New York Jets 1980-89, San Diego Chargers 1990-91, Philadelphia Eagles 1992-94, joined Jaguars in 1995.

John Pease, defensive line; born October 14, 1943, Pittsburgh, Pa., lives in Jacksonville. Wingback Utah 1963-64. No pro playing experience. College coach: Fullerton, Calif., J.C. 1970-73, Long Beach State 1974-76, Utah 1977, Washington 1978-83. Pro coach: Philadelphia/Baltimore Stars (USFL) 1983-85, New Orleans Saints 1986-94, joined Jaguars in 1995.

Lucious Selmon, outside linebackers; born March 15, 1951, Muskogee, Okla., lives in Jacksonville. Defensive tackle Oklahoma 1970-73. Pro defensive tackle Memphis Southmen (WFL) 1974-75. College coach: Oklahoma 1976-94. Pro Coach: Joined Jaguars in 1995.

Steve Szabo, inside linebackers; born September 11, 1943, Chicago, Ill., lives in Jacksonville. Halfback/defensive back Navy 1961-64. No pro playing experience. College coach: Johns Hopkins 1969, Toledo 1970, Iowa 1971-72, Syracuse 1974-76, Iowa State 1977-78, Ohio State 1979-81, Western Michigan 1982-84, Edinboro 1985-87 (head coach), Northern Iowa 1988, Colorado State 1989-90, Boston College 1991-93. Pro coach: Joined Jaguars in 1995.

1997 FIRST-YEAR ROSTER

Name	Pos.	Ht.	Wt.	Birthdate	College	Hometown	How Acq.
Anderson, Curtis	CB	6-0	193	9/29/73	Pittsburgh	Lynchburg, Va.	FA
Askew, Chad (1)	WR	6-4	200		Pittsburgh	Aliquippa, Pa.	FA
Baisley, Jamie	LB	6-2	242	3/1/74	Indiana	Glencoe, Ill.	FA
Church, Johnie (1)	LB	6-3	259	1/1/74	Florida	Fort Myers, Fla.	FA
Curtis, Isaac	TE	6-3	251	1/30/74	Kentucky	Cincinnati, Ohio	FA
Devine, Kenny	CB	5-0	184	12/11/74	California	West Covina, Calif.	FA
Fordham, Todd	T	6-5	302	10/9/73	Florida State	Tifton, Ga.	FA
Funderburk, Lance	QB	6-4	227	8/18/74	Valdosta State	Blackshear, Ga.	FA
Hamilton, James	LB	6-4	237	4/17/74	North Carolina	Hamlet, N.C.	D3
Hesse, Jon	LB	6-4	250	6/6/73	Nebraska	Lincoln, Neb.	D7
Jones, Damon	TE	6-5	282	9/18/74	Southern Illinois	Evanston, Ill.	D5
Kidd, James	WR	5-8	160	3/4/74	Colorado	Elk Grove, Calif.	FA
Logan, Mike	CB-S	6-0	203	9/15/74	West Virginia	McKeesport, Pa.	D2
Oltmanns, Chris (1)	T	6-5	315	11/21/72	Kansas State	Delmar, Iowa	FA
Parker, Chris (1)	RB	5-10	201	12/31/72	Marshall	Lynchburg, Va.	FA
Payne, Seth	DT	6-4	306	2/12/75	Cornell	Victor, N.Y.	D4
Price, Marcus (1)	T	6-6	318	3/3/72	Louisiana State	Port Arthur, Tex.	FA
Shelton, Daimon	RB	6-0	250	9/15/72	Cal. St.-Sacramento	Fresno, Calif.	D6
Thompson, David	RB	5-8	196	1/13/75	Oklahoma State	Okmulgee, Ga.	FA
Wallace, Al	DE	6-5	243	3/25/74	Maryland	Del Ray Beach, Fla.	FA
Warren, Graig	T	6-5	337	7/26/74	Stephen F. Austin	Plano, Tex.	FA
West, Marcell	WR	5-10	180	5/24/73	Alabama	Niceville, Fla.	FA
White, Jose (1)	DE	6-3	274	3/2/73	Howard	Washington, D.C.	FA
Wynn, Renaldo	DT	6-2	296	9/3/74	Notre Dame	Chicago, Ill.	D1

The term NFL Rookie is defined as a player who is in his first season of professional football and has not been on the roster of another professional football team for any regular-season or postseason games. A Rookie is designated by an "R" on NFL rosters. Players who have been active in another professional football league or players who have NFL experience, including either preseason training camp or being on an Active List or Inactive List, or on Reserve/Injured or Reserve/Physically Unable to Perform for fewer than six regular-season games, are termed NFL First-Year Players. An NFL First-Year Player is designated by a "1" on NFL rosters. Thereafter, a player is credited with an additional year of experience for each season in which he accumulates six games on the Active List or Inactive List, or on Reserve/Injured or Reserve/Physically Unable to Perform.

NOTES

_____

_____

_____

_____

_____

_____

_____

_____

KANSAS CITY CHIEFS

American Football Conference
Western Division
Team Colors: Red, Gold, and White
One Arrowhead Drive
Kansas City, Missouri 64129
Telephone: (816) 924-9300

CLUB OFFICIALS

Founder: Lamar Hunt
Chairman of the Board: Jack Steadman
President/General Manager and Chief Executive
    Officer: Carl Peterson
Executive Vice President, Assistant General
    Manager: Dennis Thum
Vice President of Administration: Dennis Watley
Secretary: Jim Seigfreid
Director of Finance/Treasurer: Dale Young
Director of Public Relations: Bob Moore
Director of Sales and Marketing: Wallace Bennett
Director of Player Personnel: Terry Bradway
Director of College Scouting: Chuck Cook
Director of Operations: Steve Schneider
Director of Development: Ken Blume
Assistant Director of Public Relations: Jim Carr
Director of Corporate Sponsorships: Anita McDonald
Community Relations Manager: Brenda Sniezek
Director of Ticket Operations: Doug Hopkins
Equipment Manager: Mike Davidson
Asst. Equipment Managers: Allen Wright, Darin Kerns
Trainer: Dave Kendall
Assistant Trainer: Bud Epps
Director of Video Operations: John Wuehrmann
Assistant Video Directors: Mike Kirk, Mike Portz
Stadium: Arrowhead Stadium •**Capacity:** 79,409
        One Arrowhead Drive
        Kansas City, Missouri 64129
Playing Surface: Grass
Training Camp: University of
        Wisconsin-River Falls
        River Falls, Wisconsin 54022

1997 SCHEDULE
PRESEASON

Aug. 2	**Pittsburgh**	7:00
Aug. 9	at New Orleans	7:00
Aug. 14	**Carolina**	7:00
Aug. 22	at St. Louis	7:00

REGULAR SEASON

Aug. 31	at Denver	2:00
Sept. 8	at Oakland (Mon.)	6:00
Sept. 14	**Buffalo**	12:00
Sept. 21	at Carolina	1:00
Sept. 28	**Seattle**	3:00
Oct. 5	at Miami	1:00
Oct. 12	Open Date	
Oct. 16	**San Diego** (Thurs.)	7:00
Oct. 26	at St. Louis	12:00
Nov. 3	**Pittsburgh** (Mon.)	8:00
Nov. 9	at Jacksonville	1:00
Nov. 16	**Denver**	12:00
Nov. 23	at Seattle	1:00
Nov. 30	**San Francisco**	12:00

RECORD HOLDERS
INDIVIDUAL RECORDS—CAREER

Category	Name	Performance
Rushing (Yds.)	Christian Okoye, 1987-1992	4,897
Passing (Yds.)	Len Dawson, 1962-1975	28,507
Passing (TDs)	Len Dawson, 1962-1975	237
Receiving (No.)	Henry Marshall, 1976-1987	416
Receiving (Yds.)	Otis Taylor, 1965-1975	7,306
Interceptions	Emmitt Thomas, 1966-1978	58
Punting (Avg.)	Jerrel Wilson, 1963-1977	43.5
Punt Return (Avg.)	J.T. Smith, 1979-1984	10.6
Kickoff Return (Avg.)	Noland Smith, 1967-69	26.8
Field Goals	Nick Lowery, 1980-1993	329
Touchdowns (Tot.)	Otis Taylor, 1965-1975	60
Points	Nick Lowery, 1980-1993	1,466

INDIVIDUAL RECORDS—SINGLE SEASON

Category	Name	Performance
Rushing (Yds.)	Christian Okoye, 1989	1,480
Passing (Yds.)	Bill Kenney, 1983	4,348
Passing (TDs)	Len Dawson, 1964	30
Receiving (No.)	Carlos Carson, 1983	80
Receiving (Yds.)	Carlos Carson, 1983	1,351
Interceptions	Emmitt Thomas, 1974	12
Punting (Avg.)	Jerrel Wilson, 1965	46.0
Punt Return (Avg.)	Abner Haynes, 1960	15.4
Kickoff Return (Avg.)	Dave Grayson, 1962	29.7
Field Goals	Nick Lowery, 1990	34
Touchdowns (Tot.)	Abner Haynes, 1962	19
Points	Nick Lowery, 1990	139

INDIVIDUAL RECORDS—SINGLE GAME

Category	Name	Performance
Rushing (Yds.)	Barry Word, 10-14-90	200
Passing (Yds.)	Len Dawson, 11-1-64	435
Passing (TDs)	Len Dawson, 11-1-64	6
Receiving (No.)	Ed Podolak, 10-7-73	12
Receiving (Yds.)	Stephone Paige, 12-22-85	309
Interceptions	Bobby Ply, 12-16-62	*4
	Bobby Hunt, 12-4-64	*4
	Deron Cherry, 9-29-85	*4
Field Goals	Many times	5
	Last time by Nick Lowery, 9-20-93	
Touchdowns (Tot.)	Abner Haynes, 11-26-61	5
Points	Abner Haynes, 11-26-61	30

*NFL Record

Dec. 7	**Oakland**	12:00
Dec. 14	at San Diego	1:00
Dec. 21	**New Orleans**	12:00

COACHING HISTORY
DALLAS TEXANS 1960-62
(294-260-12)

1960-74	Hank Stram	129-79-10
1975-77	Paul Wiggin*	11-24-0
1977	Tom Bettis	1-6-0
1978-82	Marv Levy	31-42-0
1983-86	John Mackovic	30-35-0
1987-88	Frank Gansz	8-22-1
1989-96	Marty Schottenheimer	84-52-1

*Released after seven games in 1977

ARROWHEAD STADIUM

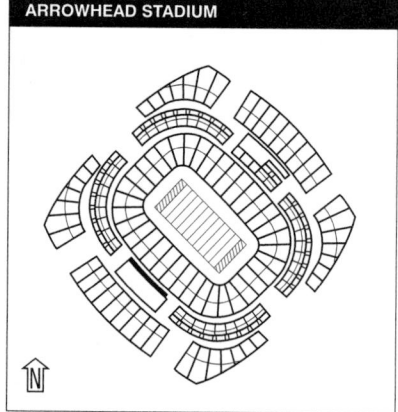

1996 TEAM RECORD

PRESEASON (3-1)

Date	Result		Opponents
8/5	W	32-6	vs. Dallas at Monterrey, Mexico
8/10	W	42-6	New Orleans
8/17	L	30-34	St. Louis
8/22	W	14-10	at Chicago

REGULAR SEASON (9-7)

Date	Result		Opponents	Att.
9/1	W	20-19	at Houston	27,725
9/8	W	19-3	Oakland	79,281
9/15	W	35-17	at Seattle	39,790
9/22	W	17-14	Denver	79,439
9/29	L	19-22	at San Diego	59,384
10/7	L	7-17	Pittsburgh	79,189
10/17	W	34-16	Seattle	76,057
10/27	L	7-34	at Denver	75,652
11/3	W	21-6	at Minnesota	59,552
11/10	W	27-20	Green Bay	79,281
11/17	W	14-10	Chicago	76,762
11/24	L	14-28	San Diego	69,472
11/28	W	28-24	at Detroit	75,079
12/9	L	7-26	at Oakland	57,082
12/15	L	19-24	Indianapolis	71,136
12/22	L	9-20	at Buffalo	68,671

SCORE BY PERIODS

Chiefs	61	108	38	90	—	297
Opponents	81	76	72	71	—	300

ATTENDANCE

Home 610,617   Away 462,935   Total 1,073,552
Single-game home record, 82,094 (11/5/72)
Single-season home record, 620,180 (1995)

1996 TEAM STATISTICS

	Chiefs	Opp.
Total First Downs	312	296
Rushing	111	84
Passing	168	184
Penalty	33	28
Third Down: Made/Att	77/221	92/218
Third Down Pct.	34.8	42.2
Fourth Down: Made/Att	8/17	3/10
Fourth Down Pct.	47.1	30.0
Total Net Yards	4899	5204
Avg. Per Game	306.2	325.3
Total Plays	1045	1008
Avg. Per Play	4.7	5.2
Net Yards Rushing	2009	1666
Avg. Per Game	125.6	104.1
Total Rushes	488	441
Net Yards Passing	2890	3538
Avg. Per Game	180.6	221.1
Sacked/Yards Lost	27/203	31/193
Gross Yards	3093	3731
Att./Completions	530/290	536/289
Completion Pct.	54.7	53.9
Had Intercepted	14	17
Punts/Avg.	88/41.7	71/41.8
Net Punting Avg.	88/33.8	71/36.2
Penalties/Yards Lost	122/901	103/876
Fumbles/Ball Lost	17/10	23/10
Touchdowns	35	32
Rushing	15	11
Passing	18	19
Returns	2	2
Avg. Time of Possession	30:39	29:21

1996 INDIVIDUAL STATISTICS

PASSING	Att.	Comp.	Yds.	Pct.	TD	Int.	Tkld.	Rate
Bono	438	235	2572	53.7	12	13	22/161	68.0
Gannon	90	54	491	60.0	6	1	5/42	92.4
Allen	1	0	0	0.0	0	0	0/0	39.6
Hughes	1	1	30	100.0	0	0	0/0	118.8
Chiefs	530	290	3093	54.7	18	14	27/203	72.3
Opponents	536	289	3731	53.9	19	17	31/193	74.6

SCORING	TD R	TD P	TD Rt	PAT	FG	Saf	PTS
Stoyanovich	0	0	0	34/34	17/24	0	85
Allen	9	0	0	0/0	0/0	0	54
Hill	4	1	0	0/0	0/0	0	30
Penn	0	5	0	0/0	0/0	0	30
Anders	2	2	0	0/0	0/0	0	24
LaChapelle	0	2	0	0/0	0/0	0	12
Vanover	0	1	1	0/0	0/0	0	12
Carter	0	1	0	0/0	0/0	0	6
Dawson	0	1	0	0/0	0/0	0	6
Hasty	0	0	1	0/0	0/0	0	6
Hughes	0	1	0	0/0	0/0	0	6
R. Johnson	0	1	0	0/0	0/0	0	6
McNair	0	1	0	0/0	0/0	0	6
Richardson	0	1	0	0/0	0/0	0	6
Walker	0	1	0	0/0	0/0	0	6
Saleaumua	0	0	0	0/0	0/0	1	2
Chiefs	15	18	2	34/34	17/24	1	297
Opponents	11	19	2	29/29	25/36	1	300

2-Point conversions: 0. Team: 0-1, Opponents: 1-3.

RUSHING	Att.	Yds.	Avg.	LG	TD
Allen	206	830	4.0	35	9
Hill	135	645	4.8	28	4
Anders	54	201	3.7	15t	2
Bennett	36	166	4.6	34	0
Gannon	12	81	6.8	19	0
McNair	9	32	3.6	9	0
Bono	26	27	1.0	17	0
Richardson	4	10	2.5	4	0
Horn	1	8	8.0	8	0
Vanover	4	6	1.5	6	0
Carter	1	3	3.0	3	0
Chiefs	488	2009	4.1	35	15
Opponents	441	1666	3.8	65t	11

RECEIVING	No.	Yds.	Avg.	LG	TD
Anders	60	529	8.8	45	2
Penn	49	628	12.8	22	5
LaChapelle	27	422	15.6	69	2
Allen	27	270	10.0	59	0
Vanover	21	241	11.5	24	1
McNair	21	181	8.6	29	1
R. Johnson	18	189	10.5	26	1
Hughes	17	167	9.8	26	1
Cash	14	80	5.7	20	0
Walker	9	73	8.1	24	1
Bennett	8	21	2.6	10	0
Carter	6	89	14.8	46t	1
Dawson	5	83	16.6	25	1
Hill	3	60	20.0	34t	1
Horn	2	30	15.0	21	0
Richardson	2	18	9.0	17	1
Bailey	1	12	12.0	12	0
Chiefs	290	3093	10.7	69	18
Opponents	289	3731	12.9	55	19

INTERCEPTIONS	No.	Yds.	Avg.	LG	TD
Collins	6	45	7.5	23	0
Washington	3	39	13.0	34	0
Carter	3	17	5.7	17	0
A. Davis	2	37	18.5	30	0
Edwards	1	22	22.0	22	0
Stargell	1	9	9.0	9	0
Simien	1	2	2.0	2	0
Chiefs	17	171	10.1	34	0
Opponents	14	68	4.9	21	0

PUNTING	No.	Yds.	Avg.	In 20	LG
Aguiar	88	3667	41.7	25	68
Chiefs	88	3667	41.7	25	68
Opponents	71	2969	41.8	21	60

PUNT RETURNS	No.	FC	Yds.	Avg.	LG	TD
Vanover	17	12	116	6.8	24	0
Penn	14	4	148	10.6	20	0
Carter	2	0	18	9.0	15	0
Chiefs	33	16	282	8.5	24	0
Opponents	42	23	492	11.7	81t	1

KICKOFF RETURNS	No.	Yds.	Avg.	LG	TD
Vanover	33	854	25.9	97t	1
Woods	25	581	23.2	66	0
Anders	2	37	18.5	20	0
Hughes	2	42	21.0	22	0
Manusky	2	32	16.0	17	0
McNair	2	21	10.5	16	0
Chiefs	66	1567	23.7	97t	1
Opponents	64	1300	20.3	86	0

SACKS	No.
Thomas	13.0
N. Smith	6.0
A. Davis	2.5
Browning	2.0
Phillips	2.0
Bayless	1.0
Booker	1.0
Collins	1.0
Hasty	1.0
Traylor	1.0
Washington	0.5
Chiefs	31.0
Opponents	27.0

1997 DRAFT CHOICES

Round	Name	Pos.	College
1	Tony Gonzalez	TE	California
2	Kevin Lockett	WR	Kansas State
4	Pat Barnes	QB	California
5	June Henley	RB	Kansas
6	Isaac Byrd	WR	Kansas
7	Nathan Parks	T	Stanford

KANSAS CITY CHIEFS

1997 VETERAN ROSTER

No.	Name	Pos.	Ht.	Wt.	Birthdate	NFL Exp.	College	Hometown	How Acq.	'96 Games/ Starts
5	Aguiar, Louie	P	6-2	218	6/30/66	7	Utah State	Livermore, Calif.	FA-'94	16/0
32	Allen, Marcus	RB	6-2	210	3/26/60	16	Southern California	San Diego, Calif.	UFA(Raid)-'93	16/15
76	Alt, John	T	6-8	307	5/30/62	14	Iowa	Columbia Hts., Minn.	D1b-'84	12/11
38	Anders, Kimble	RB	5-11	230	9/10/66	7	Houston	Galveston, Tex.	FA-'91	16/15
44	Anderson, Darren	CB	5-10	189	1/11/69	5	Toledo	Cincinnati, Ohio	T(TB)-'94	11/3
71	Barndt, Tom	G	6-3	295	3/14/72	2	Pittsburgh	Mentor, Ohio	D6b-'95	13/0
30	Bennett, Donnell	RB	6-0	240	9/14/72	4	Miami	Ft. Lauderdale, Fla.	D2-'94	16/0
99	Booker, Vaughn	DE	6-5	295	2/24/68	4	Cincinnati	Cincinnati, Ohio	FA-'94	14/12
93	Browning, John	DE	6-4	272	9/30/73	2	West Virginia	Miami, Fla.	D3-'96	13/2
96	t- Buckner, Brentson	DE-DT	6-2	305	9/30/71	4	Clemson	Columbus, Ga.	T(Pitt)-'97	15/14*
26	Cade, Eddie	S	6-1	210	8/4/73	2	Arizona State	Eloy, Ariz.	FA-'97	0*
34	Carter, Dale	CB	6-1	188	11/28/69	6	Tennessee	Covington, Ga.	D1-'92	14/14
69	Criswell, Jeff	T	6-7	294	3/7/64	10	Graceland	Searsboro, Iowa	UFA(NYJ)-'95	15/5
50	Davis, Anthony	LB	6-0	235	3/7/69	4	Utah	Pasco, Wash.	FA-'94	16/15
80	† Dawson, Lake	WR	6-1	207	1/2/72	4	Notre Dame	Federal Way, Wash.	D3a-'94	4/0
55	Dumas, Troy	LB	6-3	242	9/30/72	3	Nebraska	Cheyenne, Wyo.	D3b-'95	6/0
59	Edwards, Donnie	LB	6-2	236	4/6/73	2	UCLA	Chula Vista, Calif.	D4-'96	15/1
64	Gaines, Wendall	G	6-4	293	1/17/72	3	Oklahoma State	Frederick, Okla.	FA-'97	0*
12	Gannon, Rich	QB	6-3	210	1/20/65	10	Delaware	Philadelphia, Pa.	FA-'95	4/3
11	Grbac, Elvis	QB	6-5	232	8/13/70	4	Michigan	Cleveland, Ohio	UFA(SF)-'97	15/4*
61	Grunhard, Tim	C	6-2	307	5/17/68	8	Notre Dame	Chicago, Ill.	D2-'90	16/16
40	Hasty, James	CB	6-0	208	5/23/65	10	Washington State	Seattle, Wash.	UFA(NYJ)-'95	15/14
27	Hill, Greg	RB	5-11	207	2/23/72	4	Texas A&M	Dallas, Tex.	D1-'94	15/1
84	Horn, Joe	WR	6-1	195	1/16/72	2	Itawamba J.C.	Fayetteville, N.C.	D5-'96	9/0
83	Hughes, Danan	WR	6-2	211	12/11/70	5	Iowa	Bayonne, N.J.	D7-'93	15/2
74	Jenkins, Trezelle	T	6-7	317	3/13/73	3	Michigan	Chicago, Ill.	D1-'95	6/0
9	Jones, Reggie	WR	6-0	175	5/5/71	2	Louisiana State	Kansas City, Mo.	FA-'97	0*
18	LaChapelle, Sean	WR	6-3	217	7/29/70	3	UCLA	Sacramento, Calif.	FA-'96	12/8
51	Manusky, Greg	LB	6-1	234	8/12/66	10	Colgate	Dallas, Pa.	FA-'94	16/1
15	Matthews, Steve	QB	6-3	220	10/13/70	2	Memphis State	Tullahoma, Tenn.	D7a-'94	0*
98	Maumalanga, Chris	DT	6-2	292	12/15/71	3	Kansas	Hawthorne, Calif.	FA-'97	1/0*
91	McBride, Oscar	TE	6-5	266	7/23/72	2	Notre Dame	Chiefland, Fla.	FA-'97	0*
77	McDaniels, Pellom	DE	6-3	285	2/21/68	5	Oregon State	San Jose, Calif.	FA-'93	9/1
81	† Penn, Chris	WR	6-0	200	4/20/71	4	Tulsa	Lenapah, Okla.	D3b-'94	16/16
75	Phillips, Joe	DT	6-5	310	7/15/63	11	Southern Methodist	Vancouver, Wash.	FA-'92	16/16
49	Richardson, Tony	RB	6-1	232	12/17/71	3	Auburn	Daleville, Ala.	FA-'95	13/0
95	Roberts, Tim	DE	6-6	318	4/14/69	5	Southern Mississippi	Atlanta, Ga.	FA-'97	0*
97	Saleaumua, Dan	DT	6-0	309	11/25/64	11	Arizona State	San Diego, Calif.	PB(Det)-'89	15/14
68	Shields, Will	G	6-3	305	9/15/71	5	Nebraska	Lawton, Okla.	D3-'93	16/16
66	# Siglar, Ricky	T	6-7	308	6/14/66	6	San Jose State	Albuquerque, N.M.	FA-'93	16/16
54	Simien, Tracy	LB	6-1	255	5/21/67	7	Texas Christian	Sweeney, Tex.	FA-'91	16/13
65	Smith, Jeff	C	6-3	322	5/25/73	2	Tennessee	Decatur, Tenn.	D7b-'96	0*
22	Smith, J.J.	RB	6-0	203	10/14/72	3	Kansas State	Kansas City, Mo.	FA-'95	0*
45	Stargell, Tony	CB	5-11	186	8/7/66	8	Tennessee State	LaGrange, Ga.	FA-'96	8/4
10	Stoyanovich, Pete	K	5-11	195	4/28/67	9	Indiana	Dearborn Heights, Mich.	T(Mia)-'96	16/0
79	Szott, Dave	G	6-4	293	12/12/67	8	Penn State	Clifton, N.J.	D7-'90	16/16
58	Thomas, Derrick	LB	6-3	247	1/1/67	9	Alabama	Miami, Fla.	D1-'89	16/13
41	Tongue, Reggie	S	6-0	201	4/11/73	2	Oregon State	Fairbanks, Alaska	D2-'96	16/0
87	Vanover, Tamarick	WR	5-11	218	2/25/74	3	Florida State	Tallahassee, Fla.	D3a-'95	13/6
82	Walker, Derrick	TE	6-0	250	6/23/67	8	Michigan	Chicago Heights, Ill.	FA-'94	11/9
29	Washington, Brian	S	6-1	210	9/10/65	9	Nebraska	Richmond, Va.	FA-'95	16/16
6	Winans, Tydus	WR	5-11	180	7/26/72	4	Fresno State	Los Angeles, Calif.	FA-'97	0*
90	Wooden, Terry	LB	6-3	239	1/14/67	8	Syracuse	Farmington, Conn.	UFA(Sea)-'97	9/9*
31	Woods, Jerome	S	6-2	200	3/17/73	2	Memphis	Memphis, Tenn.	D1-'96	16/0

* Buckner played 15 games with Pittsburgh in '96; Cade last active with Miami in '95; Gaines and McBride last active with Arizona in '95; Grbac played 15 games with San Francisco; Jones last active with Carolina in '95; Matthews inactive for 16 games; Maumalanga played 1 game with Arizona; Roberts last active with New England in '95; Jeff Smith inactive for 15 games; J.J. Smith missed '96 season because of injury; Winans last active with Redskins in '95; Wooden played 9 games with Seattle.

\# Unrestricted free agent; subject to developments.

† Restricted free agent; subject to developments.

t- Chiefs traded for Buckner (Pittsburgh).

Players lost through free agency (3): DE Neil Smith (Den; 16 games), DT Keith Traylor (Den; 15), S William White (Atl; 12).

Also played with Chiefs in '96—WR Victor Bailey (2 games), S Martin Bayless (16), TE Keith Cash (9), LB George Jamison (5), TE Reggie Johnson (11), RB Todd McNair (16), LB Tracy Rogers (3), G Danny Villa (16).

COACHING STAFF

Head Coach,
Marty Schottenheimer

Pro Career: In eight seasons as head coach of the Kansas City Chiefs, Schottenheimer has established the highest regular-season winning percentage in franchise history (.633). In directing the Chiefs to eight of their ten winning seasons since 1974, Schottenheimer led the club to six consecutive postseason berths and his teams have been in the playoffs 10 of his 12 full seasons as an NFL head coach. He is also the only NFL coach who has taken his club to the playoffs 10 times since 1985, accumulating more regular season victories (125) than any other NFL coach during that span. In 1995, he became just the eighth coach in NFL history to direct his club into the playoffs six straight seasons. Schottenheimer's career winning percentage (.631) is highest among active NFL coaches with at least six full seasons of experience. As head coach of the Cleveland Browns from midseason in 1984 through 1988, he led the club to four playoff berths, three AFC Central Division titles, two AFC Championship Game appearances, and captured AFC coach of the year honors (1986). He first joined the Browns in 1980 as defensive coordinator after serving as linebackers coach of the Detroit Lions in 1978-79. His first coaching job came with the New York Giants, where he was linebackers coach and later defensive coordinator from 1975-77. He also served as an assistant coach with the Portland Storm (WFL) in 1974. A seventh-round draft choice of the Buffalo Bills in 1965, he played linebacker with the Bills until 1968 and finished his pro playing career with the Boston Patriots in 1969-70. Career record: 130-83-1.

Background: Schottenheimer was an All-America linebacker at the University of Pittsburgh from 1962-64. Following his retirement from pro football, he worked as a real estate developer in both Miami and Denver from 1971-74.

Personal: Born September 23, 1943, Canonsburg, Pa. Marty and his wife, Patricia, live in Overland Park, Kan., and have one daughter, Kristen, and one son, Brian.

ASSISTANT COACHES

Russ Ball, administrative assistant to the head coach; born August 28, 1959, Moberly, Mo., lives in Kansas City. Center Central Missouri State 1977-80. No pro playing experience. College coach: Missouri 1981-88. Pro coach: Joined Chiefs in 1989.

Gunther Cunningham, defensive coordinator-linebackers; born December 6, 1944, Munich, Germany, lives in Leawood, Kan. Linebacker-placekicker Oregon 1966-68. No pro playing experience. College coach: Oregon 1969-71, Arkansas 1972, Stanford 1973-76, California 1977-80. Pro coach: Hamilton Tiger-Cats (CFL) 1981, Baltimore-Indianapolis Colts 1982-84, San Diego Chargers 1985-90, Los Angeles Raiders 1991-94, joined Chiefs in 1995.

Jim Erkenbeck, tight ends-offensive assistant; born September 10, 1933, Los Angeles, Calif., lives in Kansas City. Linebacker-end San Diego State 1949-51. No pro playing experience. College coach: San Diego State 1961-63, Grossmont (Calif.) J.C. 1964-67 (head coach), Utah State 1968, Washington State 1969-71, California 1972-76. Pro coach: Winnepeg Blue Bombers (CFL) 1977, Montreal Alouettes (CFL) 1978-81, Calgary Stampeders (CFL) 1982, Philadelphia/Baltimore Stars (USFL) 1983-85, New Orleans Saints 1986, Dallas Cowboys 1987-88, Kansas City Chiefs 1989-91, Los Angeles Rams 1992-94, rejoined Chiefs in 1995.

Paul Hackett, offensive coordinator; born July 5, 1947, Burlington, Vt., lives in Overland Park, Kan. Quarterback Cal-Davis 1965-68. No pro playing experience. College coach: Cal-Davis 1970-71, California 1972-75, Southern California 1976-80, Pittsburgh 1989-92 (head coach 1990-92). Pro coach: Cleveland Browns 1981-82, San Francisco 49ers 1983-85, Dallas Cowboys 1986-88, joined Chiefs in 1993.

Bob Karmelowicz, defensive line; born July 22,

1949, New Britain, Conn., lives in Kansas City, Mo. Nose tackle Bridgeport 1972. No pro playing experience. College coach: Arizona State 1974-79, Massachusetts 1979-80, Texas-El Paso 1980-81, Illinois 1982-86, Washington State 1987-88, Miami 1989-91. Pro coach: Cincinnati Bengals 1992-93, Washington Redskins 1994-96, joined Chiefs in 1997.

Woodrow Lowe, assistant linebackers; born June 9, 1954, Columbus, Ga., lives in Lenexa, Kan. Linebacker Alabama 1973-75. Pro linebacker San Diego Chargers 1976-86. Pro coach: Joined Chiefs in 1995.

Mike McCarthy, quarterbacks; born November 10, 1963, Pittsburgh, Pa., lives in Lenexa, Kan. Tight end Baker University 1985-86. No pro playing experience. College coach: Fort Hays State 1987-88, Pittsburgh 1989-92. Pro coach: Joined Chiefs in 1993.

Jimmy Raye, running backs; born March 26, 1946, Fayetteville, N.C., lives in Kansas City. Quarterback Michigan State 1965-67. Pro defensive back Philadelphia Eagles 1969. College coach: Michigan State 1971-75, Wyoming 1976. Pro coach: San Francisco 49ers 1977, Detroit Lions 1978-79, Atlanta Falcons 1980-82, 1987-89, Los Angeles Rams 1983-84, 1991, Tampa Bay Buccaneers 1985-86, New England Patriots 1990, joined Chiefs in 1992.

Dave Redding, strength and conditioning; born June 14, 1952, North Platte, Neb., lives in Lee's Summit, Mo. Defensive end Nebraska 1972-75. No pro playing experience. College coach: Nebraska 1976, Washington State 1977, Missouri 1978-81. Pro coach: Cleveland Browns 1982-88, joined Chiefs in 1989.

Al Saunders, assistant head coach-receivers; born February 1, 1947, London, England, lives in Overland Park, Kan. Defensive back San Jose State 1966-68. No pro playing experience. College coach:

Southern California 1970-71, Missouri 1972, Utah State 1973-75, California 1976-81, Tennessee 1982. Pro coach: San Diego Chargers 1983-88 (head coach 1986-88), joined Chiefs in 1989.

Kurt Schottenheimer, defensive backs; born October 1, 1949, McDonald, Pa., lives in Leawood, Kan. Defensive back Miami 1969-70. No pro playing experience. College coach: William Patterson 1974, Michigan State 1978-82, Tulane 1983, Louisiana State 1984-85, Notre Dame 1986. Pro coach: Cleveland Browns 1987-88, joined Chiefs in 1989.

Mike Solari, offensive line; born January 16, 1955, Daly City, Calif., lives in Kansas City, Mo. Offensive lineman San Diego State 1975-76. No pro playing experience. College coach: Mira Vista (Calif.) J.C. 1977-78, U.S. International 1979, Boise State 1980, Cincinnati 1990-91. Pro coach: Dallas Cowboys 1987-88, Phoenix Cardinals 1989, San Francisco 49ers 1992-96, joined Chiefs in 1997.

Mike Stock, special teams; born September 29, 1939, Barberton, Ohio, lives in Overland Park, Kan. Fullback Northwestern 1957-60. Pro running back Saskatchewan Roughriders (CFL) 1961. College coach: Northwestern 1961, Buffalo 1966-67, Navy 1968, Notre Dame 1969-74, Wisconsin 1975-78, Eastern Michigan 1979-83 (head coach), Notre Dame 1984-86, Ohio State 1992-94. Pro coach: Cincinnati Bengals 1987-91, joined Chiefs in 1995.

Darvin Wallis, special assistant-quality control; born February 14, 1949, Ft. Branch, Ind., lives in Overland Park, Kan. Defensive end Arizona 1970-71. No pro playing experience. College coach: Adams State 1976-77, Tulane 1978-79, Mississippi 1980-81. Pro coach: Cleveland Browns 1982-88, joined Chiefs in 1989.

1997 FIRST-YEAR ROSTER

Name	Pos.	Ht.	Wt.	Birthdate	College	Hometown	How Acq.
Baker, Clayton	CB	5-9	178	11/4/74	Missouri	Denison, Tex.	FA
Barnard, David (1)	DT	6-2	310	11/26/74	Florida	Miami, Fla.	FA
Barnes, Pat	QB	6-3	215	2/23/75	California	Trabuco Hills, Calif.	D4
Blair, Michael	RB	6-1	240	11/26/74	Ball State	Dolton, Ill.	FA
Burgess, James	LB	5-11	230	3/31/74	Miami	Homestead, Fla.	FA
Byrd, Isaac	WR	6-1	173	11/11/74	Kansas	St. Louis, Mo.	D6
Davis, Terence (1)	WR	5-10	195	2/27/73	McNeese State	Jasper, Tex.	FA
DeGraffenreid, Byran	DE	6-6	275	6/3/74	Vanderbilt	Dunwoody, Ga.	FA
Dorsey, Tommy	LB	6-2	241	3/3/73	North Carolina Central	Fayetteville, N.C.	FA
Dritlein, Michael (1)	WR	6-1	185	1/14/74	Washburn	Olathe, Kan.	FA
Florine, Ron (1)	T	6-6	305	9/27/71	Central Missouri State	Marceline, Mo.	FA
Gallery, Nick	P	6-4	239	2/15/75	Iowa	Masonville, Iowa	FA
Gonzalez, Tony	TE	6-4	244	2/27/76	California	Huntington Beach, Calif.	D1
Haynes, Jesse	RB	5-9	210	8/8/72	Northwest Missouri	Fort Worth, Tex.	FA
Henley, June	RB	5-10	226	9/4/75	Kansas	Columbus, Ohio	D5
Hernandez, Jesus	G	6-2	300	10/16/71	Florida State	Miami, Fla.	FA
Hicks, Kerry (1)	DE-DT	6-6	283	12/29/72	Colorado	Salt Lake City, Utah	FA-'96
Johnson, Clyde	CB	5-10	191	5/22/70	Kansas State	Austin, Tex.	FA
Lockett, Kevin	WR	6-1	177	9/8/74	Kansas State	Tulsa, Okla.	D2
Lyon, Billy	DE	6-5	292	12/10/73	Marshall	Erlanger, Ky.	FA
Parks, Nathan	T	6-5	303	10/24/74	Stanford	Durham, Calif.	D7
Ratliffe, Leslie (1)	T	6-7	296	5/22/73	Tennessee	Newport, Ark.	FA
Richards, Scott	TE	6-4	244	1/7/74	East Carolina	North Augusta, S.C.	FA
Senters, Michael (1)	CB	5-11	186	12/14/71	Northwestern	Dallas, Tex.	FA
Smith, Eric (1)	WR	5-11	183	1/5/71	Louisiana State	Vero Beach, Fla.	FA
Smith, Mark	LB	6-3	242	1/27/74	Arkansas	Webb City, Mo.	FA
Swanson, Pete	T	6-5	307	3/26/74	Stanford	Hollister, Calif.	FA
Walker, Larry	LB	6-1	239	12/3/74	Texas A&M	Rusk, Tex.	FA
Walters, Shawn	RB	5-11	244	10/25/73	Southern California	Arlington, Tex.	FA
Washington, Vann	S	6-1	212	5/18/74	West Virginia	Monticello, Fla.	FA

The term NFL Rookie is defined as a player who is in his first season of professional football and has not been on the roster of another professional football team for any regular-season or postseason games. A Rookie is designated by an "R" on NFL rosters. Players who have been active in another professional football league or players who have NFL experience, including either preseason training camp or being on an Active List or Inactive List, or on Reserve/Injured or Reserve/Physically Unable to Perform for fewer than six regular-season games, are termed NFL First-Year Players. An NFL First-Year Player is designated by a "1" on NFL rosters. Thereafter, a player is credited with an additional year of experience for each season in which he accumulates six games on the Active List or Inactive List, or on Reserve/Injured or Reserve/Physically Unable to Perform.

NOTES

MIAMI DOLPHINS

American Football Conference
Eastern Division
Team Colors: Aqua, Coral, Blue, and White
7500 S.W. 30th Street
Davie, Florida 33314
Telephone: (954) 452-7000

CLUB OFFICIALS

Owner/Chairman of the Board: H. Wayne Huizenga
President/Chief Operating Officer: Eddie J. Jones
General Manager/Head Coach: Jimmy Johnson
Vice President-Administration: Bryan Wiedmeier
Vice President-Finance: Jill R. Strafaci
Director of Football Operations: Bob Ackles
Director of Pro Personnel: Tom Heckert
Director of College Scouting: Tom Braatz
Senior Director-Media Relations: Harvey Greene
Media Relations Coordinator: Neal Gulkis
Director of Publications: Scott Stone
Senior Director-Marketing: David Evans
Senior Director-Information Systems: Burt Gilner
Community Relations Director: Fudge Browne
Ticket Director: Bill Galante
Head Athletic Trainer: Kevin O'Neill
Equipment Manager: Tony Egues
Stadium: Pro Player Stadium • **Capacity:** 75,192
2269 N.W. 199th Street
Miami, Florida 33056
Playing Surface: Grass (PAT)
Training Camp: Nova University
7500 S.W. 30th Street
Davie, Florida 33314

1997 SCHEDULE

PRESEASON

Jul. 26	at Green Bay	5:30
Aug. 4	vs. Denver at Mexico City, Mexico	8:00
Aug. 10	**Chicago**	8:00
Aug. 16	at Tampa Bay	7:30
Aug. 21	**Washington**	8:00

REGULAR SEASON

Aug. 31	**Indianapolis**	1:00
Sept. 7	**Tennessee**	1:00
Sept. 14	at Green Bay	12:00
Sept. 21	at Tampa Bay	8:00
Sept. 28	Open Date	
Oct. 5	**Kansas City**	1:00
Oct. 12	at New York Jets	1:00
Oct. 19	at Baltimore	4:00
Oct. 26	**Chicago**	4:00
Nov. 2	at Buffalo	1:00
Nov. 9	**New York Jets**	1:00
Nov. 17	**Buffalo** (Mon.)	9:00
Nov. 23	at New England	1:00
Nov. 30	at Oakland	1:00
Dec. 7	**Detroit**	8:00
Dec. 14	at Indianapolis	1:00
Dec. 22	**New England** (Mon.)	9:00

RECORD HOLDERS

INDIVIDUAL RECORDS—CAREER

Category	Name	Performance
Rushing (Yds.)	Larry Csonka, 1968-1974, 1979	6,737
Passing (Yds.)	Dan Marino, 1983-1995	*51,636
Passing (TDs)	Dan Marino, 1983-1995	*369
Receiving (No.)	Mark Clayton, 1983-1992	550
Receiving (Yds.)	Mark Duper, 1982-1992	8,869
Interceptions	Jake Scott, 1970-75	35
Punting (Avg.)	John Kidd, 1994-96	44.6
Punt Return (Avg.)	Freddie Solomon, 1975-77	11.4
Kickoff Return (Avg.)	Mercury Morris, 1969-1975	26.5
Field Goals	Pete Stoyanovich, 1989-1995	176
Touchdowns (Tot.)	Mark Clayton, 1983-1992	82
Points	Garo Yepremian, 1970-78	830

INDIVIDUAL RECORDS—SINGLE SEASON

Category	Name	Performance
Rushing (Yds.)	Delvin Williams, 1978	1,258
Passing (Yds.)	Dan Marino, 1984	*5,084
Passing (TDs)	Dan Marino, 1984	*48
Receiving (No.)	Mark Clayton, 1988	86
Receiving (Yds.)	Mark Clayton, 1984	1,389
Interceptions	Dick Westmoreland, 1967	10
Punting (Avg.)	John Kidd, 1996	46.3
Punt Return (Avg.)	Freddie Solomon, 1975	12.3
Kickoff Return (Avg.)	Duriel Harris, 1976	32.9
Field Goals	Pete Stoyanovich, 1991	31
Touchdowns (Tot.)	Mark Clayton, 1984	18
Points	Pete Stoyanovich, 1992	124

INDIVIDUAL RECORDS—SINGLE GAME

Category	Name	Performance
Rushing (Yds.)	Mercury Morris, 9-30-73	197
Passing (Yds.)	Dan Marino, 10-23-88	521
Passing (TDs)	Bob Griese, 11-24-77	6
	Dan Marino, 9-21-86	6
Receiving (No.)	Jim Jensen, 11-6-88	12
Receiving (Yds.)	Mark Duper, 11-10-85	217
Interceptions	Dick Anderson, 12-3-73	*4
Field Goals	Garo Yepremian, 9-26-71	5
Touchdowns (Tot.)	Paul Warfield, 12-15-73	4
	Mark Ingram, 11-27-94	4
Points	Paul Warfield, 12-15-73	24
	Mark Ingram, 11-27-94	24

*NFL Record

COACHING HISTORY

(297-194-4)

1966-69	George Wilson	15-39-2
1970-95	Don Shula	274-147-2
1996	Jimmy Johnson	8-8-0

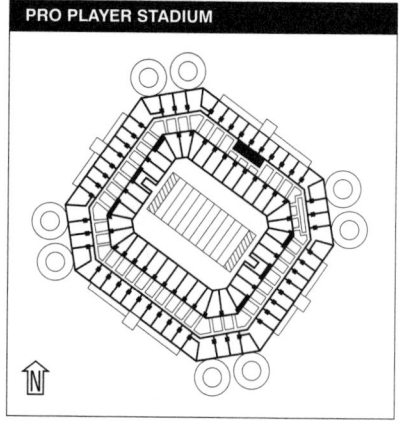

1996 TEAM RECORD

PRESEASON (3-1)

Date	Result		Opponents
8/3	W	13-10	Tampa Bay
8/11	L	21-24	at Chicago
8/19	W	24-17	Minnesota
8/23	W	19-7	at Tampa Bay

REGULAR SEASON (8-8)

Date	Result		Opponents	Att.
9/1	W	24-10	New England	71,542
9/8	W	38-10	at Arizona	55,444
9/15	W	36-27	N.Y. Jets	68,137
9/23	L	6-10	at Indianapolis	60,891
10/6	L	15-22	Seattle	59,539
10/13	W	21-7	at Buffalo	79,642
10/20	L	28-35	at Philadelphia	66,240
10/27	L	10-29	Dallas	75,283
11/3	L	23-42	at New England	58,942
11/10	W	37-13	Indianapolis	66,623
11/17	W	23-20	at Houston	47,358
11/25	L	17-24	Pittsburgh	73,489
12/1	L	7-17	at Oakland	60,591
12/8	L	7-17	N.Y. Giants	63,889
12/16	W	16-14	Buffalo	67,016
12/22	W	31-28	at N.Y. Jets	47,271

SCORE BY PERIODS

Dolphins	57	102	84	78	0	—	339
Opponents	72	89	71	93	0	—	325

ATTENDANCE

Home 545,518   Away 476,379   Total 1,021,897
Single-game home record, 75,283 (10/27/96)
Single-season home record, 560,917 (1995)

1996 TEAM STATISTICS

	Dolphins	Opp.
Total First Downs	294	306
Rushing	92	91
Passing	173	191
Penalty	29	24
Third Down: Made/Att	89/221	65/193
Third Down Pct.	40.3	33.7
Fourth Down: Made/Att	8/19	11/24
Fourth Down Pct.	42.1	45.8
Total Net Yards	5165	5191
Avg. Per Game	322.8	324.4
Total Plays	1000	987
Avg. Per Play	5.2	5.3
Net Yards Rushing	1622	1536
Avg. Per Game	101.4	96.0
Total Rushes	460	411
Net Yards Passing	3543	3655
Avg. Per Game	221.4	228.4
Sacked/Yards Lost	36/240	37/233
Gross Yards	3783	3888
Att./Completions	504/300	539/337
Completion Pct.	59.5	62.5
Had Intercepted	11	20
Punts/Avg.	78/46.3	75/43.8
Net Punting Avg.	78/38.8	75/38.3
Penalties/Yards Lost	111/852	98/786
Fumbles/Ball Lost	31/13	29/16
Touchdowns	41	41
Rushing	14	10
Passing	22	29
Returns	5	2
Avg. Time of Possession	31:08	28:52

1996 INDIVIDUAL STATISTICS

PASSING	Att.	Comp.	Yds.	Pct.	TD	Int.	Tkld.	Rate
Marino	373	221	2795	59.2	17	9	18/131	87.8
Erickson	99	55	780	55.6	4	2	11/72	86.3
Kosar	32	24	208	75.0	1	0	6/34	102.1
Abdul-Jabbar	0	0	0	—	0	0	1/3	—
Dolphins	504	300	3783	59.5	22	11	36/240	88.4
Opponents	539	337	3888	62.5	29	20	37/233	86.7

SCORING	TD R	TD P	TD Rt	PAT	FG	Saf	PTS
Nedney	0	0	0	35/36	18/29	0	89
Abdul-Jabbar	11	0	0	0/0	0/0	0	66
McDuffie	0	8	0	0/0	0/0	0	48
R. Hill	0	4	0	0/0	0/0	0	24
Spikes	3	1	0	0/0	0/0	0	24
Barnett	0	3	0	0/0	0/0	0	18
Pritchett	0	2	0	0/0	0/0	0	12
Buckley	0	0	1	0/0	0/0	0	6
Carolan	0	1	0	0/0	0/0	0	6
S. Hill	0	0	1	0/0	0/0	0	6
Jackson	0	0	1	0/0	0/0	0	6
Miller	0	0	1	0/0	0/0	0	6
L. Thomas	0	1	0	0/0	0/0	0	6
Z. Thomas	0	0	1	0/0	0/0	0	6
Wainright	0	1	0	0/0	0/0	0	6
R. Wilson	0	1	0	0/0	0/0	0	6
Drayton	0	0	0	0/0	0/0	0	2
Dolphins	14	22	5	35/36	18/29	*1	339
Opponents	10	29	2	38/39	13/17	0	325

2-Point conversions: Drayton. Team: 1-5,
Opponents: 1-2.
*Dolphins were credited with 1 team safety.

RUSHING	Att.	Yds.	Avg.	LG	TD
Abdul-Jabbar	307	1116	3.6	29	11
Spikes	87	316	3.6	49	3
Parmalee	25	80	3.2	17	0
McPhail	6	28	4.7	10	0
Pritchett	7	27	3.9	16	0
Izzo	1	26	26.0	26	0
Erickson	11	16	1.5	12	0
McDuffie	2	7	3.5	7	0
Kosar	1	6	6.0	6	0
Kidd	1	3	3.0	3	0
R. Wilson	1	0	0.0	0	0
Marino	11	-3	-0.3	7	0
Dolphins	460	1622	3.5	49	14
Opponents	411	1536	3.7	49t	10

RECEIVING	No.	Yds.	Avg.	LG	TD
McDuffie	74	918	12.4	36	8
Barnett	36	562	15.6	66	3
Pritchett	33	354	10.7	74t	2
Drayton	26	320	12.3	51	0
Abdul-Jabbar	23	139	6.0	23	0
R. Hill	21	409	19.5	61	4
Parmalee	21	189	9.0	17	0
McPhail	20	282	14.1	52	0
L. Thomas	10	166	16.6	34	1
Miller	9	116	12.9	22	0
Spikes	8	81	10.1	19	1
Jordan	7	152	21.7	43	0
Byars	5	40	8.0	16	0
Carolan	4	48	12.0	21	1
R. Wilson	2	5	2.5	3t	1
Wainright	1	2	2.0	2t	1
Dolphins	300	3783	12.6	74t	22
Opponents	337	3888	11.5	84t	29

INTERCEPTIONS	No.	Yds.	Avg.	LG	TD
Buckley	6	164	27.3	91t	1
Oliver	3	110	36.7	60	0
Jackson	3	82	27.3	61t	1
Z. Thomas	3	64	21.3	27	1
Wooden	2	15	7.5	15	0
J. Brown	1	29	29.0	29	0
Hollier	1	11	11.0	11	0
S. Hill	1	0	0.0	0	0
Dolphins	20	475	23.8	91t	3
Opponents	11	256	23.3	100t	1

PUNTING	No.	Yds.	Avg.	In 20	LG
Kidd	78	3611	46.3	26	63
Dolphins	78	3611	46.3	26	63
Opponents	75	3283	43.8	13	80

PUNT RETURNS	No.	FC	Yds.	Avg.	LG	TD
McDuffie	22	24	212	9.6	19	0
Buckley	3	1	24	8.0	13	0
Miller	1	0	15	15.0	15	0
Dolphins	26	25	251	9.7	19	0
Opponents	48	7	368	7.7	26	0

KICKOFF RETURNS	No.	Yds.	Avg.	LG	TD
Spikes	28	681	24.3	59	0
McPhail	15	335	22.3	40	0
Dar Dar	7	132	18.9	25	0
Jordan	4	81	20.3	22	0
R. Hill	2	4	2.0	4	0
Buckley	1	48	48.0	48	0
Z. Thomas	1	17	17.0	17	0
Wainright	1	10	10.0	10	0
R. Wilson	1	12	12.0	12	0
Dolphins	60	1320	22.0	59	0
Opponents	48	1058	22.0	54	0

SACKS	No.
Armstrong	12.0
Stubbs	9.0
Bowens	3.0
Burton	3.0
Emtman	2.0
Z. Thomas	2.0
Jackson	1.5
Bailey	1.0
Gardener	1.0
S. Hill	1.0
Hollier	1.0
Hand	0.5
Dolphins	37.0
Opponents	36.0

1997 DRAFT CHOICES

Round	Name	Pos.	College
1	Yatil Green	WR	Miami
2	Sam Madison	DB	Louisville
3	Jason Taylor	DE	Akron
	Derrick Rodgers	LB	Arizona State
	Ronnie Ward	LB	Kansas
	Brent Smith	T	Mississippi State
4	Jerome Daniels	T	Northeastern
5	Barron Tanner	DT	Oklahoma
	Nicholas Lopez	DE	Texas Southern
6	John Fiala	LB	Washington
	Brian Manning	WR	Stanford
	Mike Crawford	LB	Nevada
	Ed Perry	TE	James Madison
7	Hudhaifa Ismaeli	DB	Northwestern

MIAMI DOLPHINS

1997 VETERAN ROSTER

No.	Name	Pos.	Ht.	Wt.	Birthdate	NFL Exp.	College	Hometown	How Acq.	'96 Games/ Starts
33	Abdul-Jabbar, Karim	RB	5-10	194	6/28/74	2	UCLA	Los Angeles, Calif.	D3b-'96	16/14
93	Armstrong, Trace	DE	6-4	266	10/5/65	9	Florida	Birmingham, Ala.	T(Chi)-'95	16/9
80	Barnett, Fred	WR	5-11	210	6/17/66	8	Rosedale, Miss.	Arkansas State	UFA(Phil)-'96	9/7
60	Bock, John	G	6-3	295	2/11/71	3	Indiana State	Crystal Lake, Ill.	FA-'96	2/0
95	Bowens, Tim	DT	6-4	310	2/7/73	4	Mississippi	Okolona, Miss.	D1-'94	16/16
57	Brigance, O.J.	LB	6-0	223	9/29/69	2	Rice	Sugarland, Tex.	FA-'96	12/0
76	Brown, James	T	6-6	329	11/30/70	5	Virginia State	Philadelphia, Pa.	T(NYJ)-'96	16/16
77	Buckey, Jeff	T	6-5	300	8/7/74	2	Stanford	Bakersfield, Cailf.	D7a-'96	15/1
27	Buckley, Terrell	CB	5-9	176	6/7/71	6	Florida State	Pascagoula, Miss.	T(GB)-'95	16/16
75	Burton, Shane	DT	6-6	300	1/18/74	2	Tennessee	Catawba, N.C.	D5b-'96	16/8
89	Dar Dar, Kirby	WR	5-9	183	3/27/72	2	Syracuse	Tampa, Fla.	FA-'95	11/0
26	Davis, Cedric	CB	5-9	172	9/7/72	2	Tennessee State	Brandon, Fla.	FA-'97	0*
86	Dawsey, Lawrence	WR	6-0	192	11/16/67	7	Florida State	Dothan, Ala.	UFA(NYG)-'97	16/4*
63	Dixon, Cal	C	6-4	302	10/11/69	6	Florida	Merrit Island, Fla.	FA-'96	11/0
84	Drayton, Troy	TE	6-3	255	6/29/70	5	Penn State	Steelton, Pa.	T(StL)-'96	13/13*
7	Erickson, Craig	QB	6-2	209	5/17/69	6	Miami	West Palm Beach, Fla.	FA-'96	7/3
92	Gardener, Daryl	DT	6-6	320	2/25/73	2	Baylor	Lawton, Okla.	D1-'96	16/12
62	Gray, Chris	G	6-4	296	6/19/70	5	Auburn	Birmingham, Ala.	D5-'93	11/11
98	Hand, Norman	DT	6-3	329	9/4/72	3	Mississippi	Waterboro, S.C.	D5-'95	9/0
51	Harris, Anthony	LB	6-1	224	1/25/73	2	Auburn	Fort Pierce, Fla.	FA-'96	7/3
40	Harris, Corey	S	5-11	199	10/25/69	6	Vanderbilt	Indianapolis, Ind.	UFA(Sea)-'97	16/16*
31	Hill, Sean	S	5-10	179	8/14/71	4	Montana State	Colorado Springs, Colo.	D7-'94	12/5
50	Hollier, Dwight	LB	6-2	250	4/21/69	6	North Carolina	Hampton, Va.	D4-'92	16/15
47	Holmes, Clayton	CB	5-10	181	8/23/69	5	Carson-Newman	Florence, S.C.	FA-'97	0*
53	Izzo, Larry	LB	5-10	220	9/26/74	2	Rice	Houston, Tex.	FA-'96	16/0
38	Jackson, Calvin	CB	5-9	185	10/28/72	3	Auburn	Ft. Lauderdale, Fla.	FA-'95	16/15
34	Jacobs, Tim	CB	5-10	185	4/5/70	4	Delaware	Greenbelt, Md.	FA-'96	12/0
88	Jordan, Charles	WR	5-11	183	10/9/69	5	Long Beach City College	Inglewood, Calif.	RFA(GB)-'96	6/0
17	Kidd, John	P	6-3	214	8/22/61	14	Northwestern	Findlay, Calif.	FA-'94	16/0
13	Marino, Dan	QB	6-4	224	9/15/61	15	Pittsburgh	Pittsburgh, Pa.	D1-83	13/13
81	McDuffie, O.J.	WR	5-10	188	12/2/69	5	Penn State	Gate Mills, Ohio	D1-'93	16/16
66	McIver, Everett	G	6-6	315	8/5/70	4	Elizabeth City State	Fayetteville, N.C.	FA-'96	7/5
32	McPhail, Jerris	RB	5-11	201	6/26/72	2	East Carolina	Clinton, N.C.	D5a-'96	9/1
6	Nedney, Joe	K	6-4	205	3/22/73	2	San Jose State	San Jose, Calif.	FA-'96	16/0
30	Parmalee, Bernie	RB	5-11	196	9/16/67	6	Ball State	Jersey City, N.J.	FA-'92	16/0
36	Pritchett, Stanley	RB	6-1	232	12/12/73	2	South Carolina	College Park, Ga.	D4b-'96	16/16
83	Reeves, Walter	TE	6-4	270	12/16/65	9	Auburn	Eufaula, Ala.	UFA(SD)-'97	9/2*
61	Ruddy, Tim	C	6-3	290	4/27/72	4	Notre Dame	Dunmore, Pa.	D2b-'94	16/16
69	Sims, Keith	G	6-3	309	6/17/67	8	Iowa State	Watchung, N.J.	D2-'90	15/15
35	Spikes, Irving	RB	5-8	206	12/21/70	4	Northeast Louisiana	Ocean Springs, Miss.	FA-'94	15/1
96	Stubbs, Daniel	DE	6-4	272	1/3/65	9	Miami	Red Bank, N.J.	UFA(Dall)-'97	16/15
97	Sturgis, Oscar	DE	6-5	278	1/12/71	2	North Carolina	Richmond City, N.C.	FA-'96	0*
23	Teague, George	S	6-1	196	2/18/71	5	Alabama	Montgomery, Ala.	UFA(Dall)-'97	16/8*
85	Thomas, Lamar	WR	6-2	173	2/12/70	5	Miami	Gainsville, Fla.	FA-'96	9/3
54	Thomas, Zach	LB	5-11	231	9/1/73	2	Texas Tech	Pampa, Tex.	D5c-'96	16/16
82	Wainright, Frank	TE	6-3	245	10/10/67	7	Northern Colorado	Arvada, Colo.	FA-'95	16/0
78	Webb, Richmond	T	6-6	303	1/11/67	8	Texas A&M	Dallas, Tex.	D1-'90	16/16
24	Wilson, Jerry	CB	5-10	184	7/17/73	3	Southern	Lake Charles, La.	FA-'96	2/0
20	Wilson, Robert	RB	6-0	255	1/13/69	5	Texas A&M	Houston, Tex.	FA-'94	15/0
22	Wooden, Shawn	S	5-11	186	10/23/73	2	Notre Dame	Abington, Pa.	D6-'96	16/11

* Davis last active with Arizona in '95; Dawsey played 16 games with the Giants in '96; Drayton played 3 games with St. Louis; Harris played 16 games with Seattle; Holmes last active with Miami in '95; Reeves played 9 games with San Diego; Sturgis inactive for 1 game; Teague played 16 games with Dallas.

Retired—Bernie Kosar, 12-year quarterback, 3 games in '96.

Players lost through free agency (1): WR Randal Hill (NO; 14 games in '96).

Also played with Dolphins in '96—S Gene Atkins (5 games), CB Robert Bailey (14), CB J.B. Brown (14), RB Keith Byars (4), TE Brett Carolan (6), DT Steve Emtman (13), DE Aaron Jones (8), WR Scott Miller (12), T Billy Milner (4), S Louis Oliver (16), LB Chris Singleton (14), S Michael Stewart (9).

COACHING STAFF

Head Coach,
Jimmy Johnson

Pro Career: Begins his seventh season as an NFL head coach and his second with the Miami Dolphins after going 8-8 in his first year with the club. Named general manager/head coach of the Dolphins on January 11, 1996, becoming the third head coach in club history. Became the first, and one of only two head coaches ever in football history, to win both a Super Bowl title (Dallas Cowboys - 1992 and 1993) and a national collegiate championship (University of Miami - 1987). Served as head coach of the Cowboys from 1989 through 1993. Became only the third man in NFL history to coach consecutive Super Bowl winners, winning Super Bowl XXVII in 1992 and following that with a victory in Super Bowl XXVIII in 1993. In his five years in Dallas, Johnson led the Cowboys to two NFL championships, with their first title in 1992 coming just three years after the franchise produced a 1-15 mark in 1989. In addition, Johnson's postseason winning percentage of .875 (7-1 record) is the second best in NFL history, behind only Vince Lombardi's mark of .900 (9-1). Career record: 59-45.

Background: At the University of Miami (1984-88), Johnson led the Hurricanes to a 52-9 (.853) record, including a 44-4 mark over the final four seasons. His Hurricane teams also captured two Orange Bowl titles, a national championship in 1987, and two number two finishes (1986, 1988). In his first head coaching job, Johnson took over a losing program at Oklahoma State in 1979 and brought it to national prominence, compiling a 29-25 record in five seasons, including two bowl appearances. Johnson was named Big Eight Coach of the Year following his first season. Served as assistant head coach/defensive coordinator at Pittsburgh (1977-78), defensive coordinator at Arkansas (1973-76), defensive line coach at Oklahoma (1970-72), defensive coordinator at Iowa State (1968-69), assistant coach at Wichita State (1967), and defensive line coach at Louisiana Tech (1965). Before beginning his coaching career, Johnson was an All-Southwest Conference defensive lineman at Arkansas and helped lead the Razorbacks to the 1964 national championship. A three-year letterman, Johnson was named to Arkansas' All-Decade Team of the 1960s.

Personal: Born July 16, 1943, in Port Arthur, Texas. Lives in Miami. He has two sons, Brent and Chad.

ASSISTANT COACHES

Larry Beightol, assistant head coach-offensive line; born November 21, 1942, Morrisville, Pa., lives in Plantation, Fla. Guard-linebacker Catawba College 1961-63. No pro playing experience. College coach: William & Mary 1968-71, North Carolina State 1972-75, Auburn 1976, Arkansas 1977-78, 1980-82, Louisiana Tech 1979 (head coach), Missouri 1983-84. Pro coach: Atlanta Falcons 1985-86, Tampa Bay Buccaneers 1987-88, San Diego Chargers 1989, New York Jets 1990-94, Houston Oilers 1995, joined Dolphins in 1996.

Kippy Brown, running backs; born March 6, 1955, Sweetwater, Tenn., lives in Plantation, Fla. Quarterback Memphis State 1974-77. No pro playing experience. College coach: Memphis State 1978-80, Louisville 1982, Tennessee 1983-89, 1993-94. Pro coach: New York Jets 1990-92, Tampa Bay Buccaneers 1995, joined Dolphins in 1996.

Joel Collier, defensive staff assistant; born December 25, 1963, Buffalo, N.Y., lives in Plantation, Fla. Linebacker Northern Colorado 1984-87. No pro playing experience. College coach: Syracuse 1988-89. Pro coach: Tampa Bay Buccaneers 1990, New England Patriots 1991-93, joined Dolphins in 1994.

John Gamble, strength and conditioning; born June 26, 1957, Richmond, Va., lives in Weston, Fla. Linebacker Hampton Institute 1975-78. No pro playing experience. College coach: Virginia 1982-93. Pro coach: Joined Dolphins in 1994.

Cary Godette, defensive line; born March 20, 1954, New Bern, N.C., lives in Plantation, Fla. Defensive end East Carolina 1973-76. No pro playing experience. College coach: East Carolina 1977-79, 1990-91, Wyoming 1980-82, Cincinnati 1983-88, Georgia Tech 1992-93, North Carolina State 1994. Pro coach: Carolina Panthers 1995, joined Dolphins in 1996.

George Hill, defensive coordinator-linebackers; born April 28, 1933, Bay Village, Ohio, lives in Plantation, Fla. Tackle-fullback Denison 1954-57. No pro playing experience. College coach: Findlay 1959, Denison 1960-64, Cornell 1965, Duke 1966-70, Ohio State 1971-78. Pro coach: Philadelphia Eagles 1979-84, Indianapolis Colts 1985-88, joined Dolphins in 1989.

Pat Jones, tight ends; born November 4, 1947, Memphis, Tenn., lives in Ft. Lauderdale, Fla. Nose guard Arkansas Tech 1965, linebacker-nose guard Arkansas 1966-67. No pro playing experience. College coach: Arkansas 1974-75, Southern Methodist 1976-77, Pittsburgh 1978, Oklahoma State 1979-94 (1984-94 head coach). Pro coach: Joined Dolphins in 1996.

Les Koenning, offensive staff assistant; born February 10, 1959, San Antonio, Tex., lives in Ft. Lauderdale, Fla. Wide receiver Texas 1978-90. No pro playing experience. College coach: Texas 1981-83, Alabama 1984, Southwestern Louisiana 1985, Mississippi State 1986-89, Rice 1990-93, Texas A&M 1994-96. Pro coach: Joined Dolphins in 1997.

Bill Lewis, defensive nickel package; born August 5, 1941, Bristol, Pa., lives in Ft. Lauderdale, Fla. Quarterback East Stroudsburg State 1959-62. No pro playing experience. College coach: East Stroudsburg State 1963-65, Pittsburgh 1966-68, Wake Forest 1969-70, Georgia Tech 1971-72, 1992-94 (head coach), Arkansas 1973-76, Wyoming 1977-79, Georgia 1980-88, East Carolina 1989-91 (head coach). Pro coach: Joined Dolphins in 1996.

Rich McGeorge, assistant offensive line; born September 14, 1948, Roanoke, Va., lives in Plantation, Fla. Tight end Elon College 1966-69. Pro tight end Green Bay Packers 1970-78. College coach: Duke 1992-93, North Carolina State 1994. Pro coach: Carolina Panthers 1995, joined Dolphins in 1996.

1981-82, 1987-89, Florida 1990-92. Pro coach: Birmingham Stallions (USFL) 1983-84, Tampa Bay Bandits (USFL) 1985, joined Dolphins in 1993.

Mel Phillips, secondary; born January 6, 1942, Shelby, N.C., lives in Miami Lakes, Fla. Defensive back-running back North Carolina A&T 1964-65. Pro defensive back San Francisco 49ers 1966-77. Pro coach: Detroit Lions 1980-84, joined Dolphins in 1985.

Brad Roll, assistant strength and conditioning; born July 4, 1958, Houston, Tex., lives in Ft. Lauderdale, Fla. Center Blinn (Tex.) J.C. 1976-77, Stephen F. Austin 1978-79. No pro playing experience. College coach: Stephen F. Austin 1980, Southwestern Louisiana 1981-86, Kansas 1987-88, Miami 1989-92. Pro coach: Tampa Bay Buccaneers 1993-95, joined Dolphins in 1996.

Larry Seiple, wide receivers; born February 14, 1945, Allentown, Pa., lives in Pembroke Pines, Fla. Running back-receiver-punter Kentucky 1964-66. Pro punter-tight end-receiver-running back Miami Dolphins 1966-77. College coach: Miami 1978-79. Pro coach: Detroit Lions 1980-84, Tampa Bay Buccaneers 1985-86, joined Dolphins in 1988.

Gary Stevens, offensive coordinator; born March 19, 1943, Cleveland, Ohio, lives in Ft. Lauderdale, Fla. Running back John Carroll 1963-65. No pro playing experience. College coach: Louisville 1971-74, Kent State 1975, West Virginia 1976-79, Miami 1980-88. Pro coach: Joined Dolphins in 1989.

Mike Westhoff, special teams; born January 10, 1948, Pittsburgh, Pa., lives in Plantation, Fla. Center-linebacker Wichita State 1967-69. No pro playing experience. College coach: Indiana 1974-75, Dayton 1976, Indiana State 1977, Northwestern 1978-80, Texas Christian 1981. Pro coach: Baltimore/Indianapolis Colts 1982-84, Arizona Outlaws (USFL) 1985, joined Dolphins in 1986.

1997 FIRST-YEAR ROSTER

Name	Pos.	Ht.	Wt.	Birthdate	College	Hometown	How Acq.
Bennett, Brandon (1)	RB	5-11	210	2/3/73	South Carolina	Taylors, S.C.	FA-'96
Bruno, Vince	LB	6-2	231	6/4/74	Western Illinois	Westlake Village, Calif.	FA
Crawford, Mike	LB	6-1	230	10/29/74	Nevada	Zephyr Cover, Nev.	D6c
Cunningham, Melvin	CB	5-10	177	12/16/76	Marshall	Red Jacket, W. Va.	D6a
Daniels, Jerome	G	6-5	355	9/13/74	Northeastern	Bloomfield, Conn.	D4
Deignan, Rob	P	6-4	225	1/8/74	Purdue	Ft. Lauderdale, Fla.	FA
Dye, James	WR	5-9	160	12/9/73	Brigham Young	Los Angeles, Calif.	FA
Elmore, John (1)	G	6-3	320	3/23/73	Texas	Sherman, Tex.	FA
Fiala, John	LB	6-1	230	11/25/73	Washington	Bellevue, Wash.	D6a
Fischer, Spence (1)	QB	6-4	220	11/30/72	Duke	Atlanta, Ga.	FA
Frazier, Daryl (1)	WR	6-1	181	1/23/71	Florida	Winter Haven, Fla.	FA
Green, Yatil	WR	6-2	205	11/25/73	Miami	Lake City, Fla.	D1
Huard, Damon (1)	QB	6-3	220	7/9/73	Washington	Puyallup, Wash.	FA
Ismaeli, Hudhaifa	CB	5-11	197	7/30/75	Northwestern	Pittsburgh, Pa.	D7
Jackson, Larry (1)	DE	6-3	262	10/7/71	Texas A&M	Rockdale, Tex.	FA
Lillibridge, Marc (1)	LB	6-1	240	2/19/72	Iowa State	Marion, Iowa	FA-'96
Little, Earl	S	6-0	183	3/10/73	Miami	Miami, Fla.	FA
Lopez, Nicholas	DE	6-4	250	7/17/72	Texas Southern	Houston, Tex.	D5b
Madison, Sam	CB	5-11	180	4/23/74	Louisville	Monticello, Fla.	D2
Manning, Brian	WR	5-11	180	4/22/75	Stanford	Kansas City, Mo.	D6b
Mare, Olindo (1)	K	5-10	178	6/6/73	Syracuse	Cooper City, Fla.	FA
McClinton, Lee (1)	RB	5-11	252	8/2/72	New Hampshire	Highland, N.Y.	FA
Mohring, Mike	DT	6-5	275	3/22/74	Pittsburgh	West Chester, Pa.	FA
Nealy, Ray	RB	5-11	220	4/30/75	Arkansas-Pine Bluff	Little Rock, Ark.	FA
Perry, Ed	TE	6-4	245	9/1/74	James Madison	Richmond, Va.	D6d
Rodgers, Derrick	LB	6-1	223	10/14/71	Arizona State	New Orleans, La.	D3b
Sheldon, Mike (1)	G	6-4	295	6/8/73	Grand Valley State	Villa Park, Ill.	FA
Smith, Brent	T	6-5	300	11/21/73	Mississippi State	Pontotoc, Miss.	D3d
Stanley, Dimitrious	WR	5-10	184	9/19/74	Ohio State	Worthington, Ohio	FA
Tanner, Barron	DT	6-3	318	9/14/73	Oklahoma	Athens, Tex.	D5a
Taylor, Jason	DE	6-6	243	9/1/74	Akron	Woodland Hills, Pa.	D3a
Ward, Ronnie	LB	6-0	225	2/11/74	Kansas	St. Louis, Mo.	D3c
Wheeler, Randy	G	6-2	320	5/4/75	South Carolina	Hartsville, S.C.	FA
Workman, Latori	DE	6-3	280	9/14/72	Winston-Salem	Winston-Salem, N.C.	FA
Young, Donnie	G	6-4	315	11/17/73	Florida	Venice, Fla.	FA

The term NFL Rookie is defined as a player who is in his first season of professional football and has not been on the roster of another professional football team for any regular-season or postseason games. A Rookie is designated by an "R" on NFL rosters. Players who have been active in another professional football league or players who have NFL experience, including either preseason training camp or being on an Active List or Inactive List, or on Reserve/Injured or Reserve/Physically Unable to Perform for fewer than six regular-season games, are termed NFL First-Year Players. An NFL First-Year Player is designated by a "1" on NFL rosters. Thereafter, a player is credited with an additional year of experience for each season in which he accumulates six games on the Active List or Inactive List, or on Reserve/Injured or Reserve/Physically Unable to Perform.

1992-93, North Carolina State 1994. Pro coach: Carolina Panthers 1995, joined Dolphins in 1996.

NEW ENGLAND PATRIOTS

American Football Conference
Eastern Division
Team Colors: Blue, Red, Silver, and White
Foxboro Stadium
60 Washington Street
Foxboro, Massachusetts 02035
Telephone: (508) 543-8200

CLUB OFFICIALS

Owner/Chief Executive Officer: Robert K. Kraft
Vice President-Owner's Representative:
　Jonathan A. Kraft
Vice President-Business Operations:
　Andrew Wasynczuk
Vice President of Player Personnel: Bobby Grier
Vice President of Marketing and Broadcast Sales:
　Daniel A. Kraft
Vice President-Finance: James Hausmann
Vice President of Public and Community Relations:
　Donald Lowery
Director of Media Relations: Stacey James
Director of Football Operations: Ken Deininger
Director of Player Resources: Andre Tippett
Controller: Jim Nolan
Director of College Scouting: Charles Armey
Director of Ticketing: Mike Nichols
Director of Stadium Operations: Dan Murphy
Building Services Manager: Bernie Reinhart
Head Trainer: Ron O'Neil
Equipment Manager: Don Brocher
Video Director: Jimmy Dee
Stadium: Foxboro Stadium •**Capacity:** 60,292
　　　　　60 Washington Street
　　　　　Foxboro, Massachusetts 02035
Playing Surface: Grass
Training Camp: Bryant College
　　　　　Route 7
　　　　　Smithfield, Rhode Island 02917

1997 SCHEDULE
PRESEASON

July 31	at Green Bay	7:00
Aug. 8	**Dallas**	8:00
Aug. 17	**Denver**	1:00
Aug. 21	at Philadelphia	8:00

REGULAR SEASON

Aug. 31	**San Diego**	1:00
Sept. 7	at Indianapolis	12:00
Sept. 14	**New York Jets**	8:00
Sept. 21	**Chicago**	1:00
Sept. 28	Open Date	
Oct. 6	at Denver (Mon.)	7:00
Oct. 12	**Buffalo**	1:00
Oct. 19	at New York Jets	1:00
Oct. 27	**Green Bay** (Mon.)	9:00
Nov. 2	at Minnesota	12:00
Nov. 9	at Buffalo	4:00
Nov. 16	at Tampa Bay	1:00
Nov. 23	**Miami**	1:00
Nov. 30	**Indianapolis**	1:00
Dec. 7	at Jacksonville	1:00
Dec. 13	**Pittsburgh** (Sat.)	4:00
Dec. 22	at Miami (Mon.)	9:00

RECORD HOLDERS
INDIVIDUAL RECORDS—CAREER

Category	Name	Performance
Rushing (Yds.)	Sam Cunningham, 1973-79, 1981-82	5,453
Passing (Yds.)	Steve Grogan, 1975-1990	26,886
Passing (TDs)	Steve Grogan, 1975-1990	182
Receiving (No.)	Stanley Morgan, 1977-1989	534
Receiving (Yds.)	Stanley Morgan, 1977-1989	10,352
Interceptions	Raymond Clayborn, 1977-1989	36
Punting (Avg.)	Rich Camarillo, 1981-87	42.6
Punt Return (Avg.)	Mack Herron, 1973-75	12.0
Kickoff Return (Avg.)	Allen Carter, 1975-76	27.2
Field Goals	Gino Cappelletti, 1960-1970	176
Touchdowns (Tot.)	Stanley Morgan, 1977-1989	68
Points	Gino Cappelletti, 1960-1970	1,130

INDIVIDUAL RECORDS—SINGLE SEASON

Category	Name	Performance
Rushing (Yds.)	Curtis Martin, 1995	1,487
Passing (Yds.)	Drew Bledsoe, 1994	4,555
Passing (TDs)	Vito (Babe) Parilli, 1964	31
Receiving (No.)	Ben Coates, 1994	96
Receiving (Yds.)	Stanley Morgan, 1986	1,491
Interceptions	Ron Hall, 1964	11
Punting (Avg.)	Rich Camarillo, 1983	44.6
Punt Return (Avg.)	Mack Herron, 1974	14.8
Kickoff Return (Avg.)	Raymond Clayborn, 1977	31.0
Field Goals	Tony Franklin, 1986	32
Touchdowns (Tot.)	Curtis Martin, 1996	17
Points	Gino Cappelletti, 1964	155

INDIVIDUAL RECORDS—SINGLE GAME

Category	Name	Performance
Rushing (Yds.)	Tony Collins, 9-18-83	212
Passing (Yds.)	Drew Bledsoe, 11-13-94	426
Passing (TDs)	Vito (Babe) Parilli, 11-15-64	5
	Vito (Babe) Parilli, 10-15-67	5
	Steve Grogan, 9-9-79	5
Receiving (No.)	Ben Coates, 11-27-94	12
Receiving (Yds.)	Stanley Morgan, 11-8-81	182
Interceptions	Many times	3
	Last time by Roland James, 10-23-83	
Field Goals	Gino Cappelletti, 10-4-64	6
Touchdowns (Tot.)	Many times	3
	Last time by Curtis Martin, 11-3-96	
Points	Gino Cappelletti, 12-18-65	28

COACHING HISTORY
BOSTON 1960-1970
(254-299-9)

1960-61	Lou Saban*	7-12-0
1961-68	Mike Holovak	53-47-9
1969-70	Clive Rush**	5-16-0
1970-72	John Mazur***	9-21-0
1972	Phil Bengtson	1-4-0
1973-78	Chuck Fairbanks****	46-41-0
1978	Hank Bullough-Ron Erhardt#	0-1-0
1979-81	Ron Erhardt	21-27-0
1982-84	Ron Meyer##	18-16-0
1984-89	Raymond Berry	51-41-0
1990	Rod Rust	1-15-0
1991-92	Dick MacPherson	8-24-0
1993-96	Bill Parcells	34-34-0

*Released after five games in 1961
**Released after seven games in 1970
***Resigned after nine games in 1972
****Suspended for final regular-season game in 1978
#Co-coaches
##Released after eight games in 1984

FOXBORO STADIUM

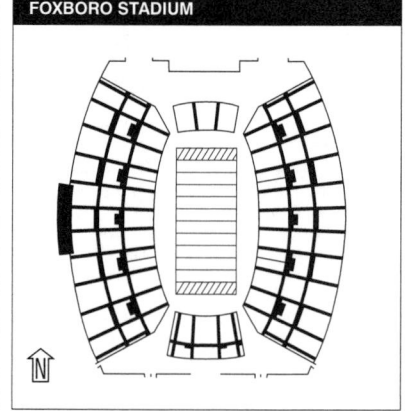

1996 TEAM RECORD

PRESEASON (3-1)

Date	Result		Opponents
8/2	L	7-24	at Green Bay
8/12	W	31-7	at Dalles
8/18	W	37-10	Philadelphia
8/23	W	27-19	Washington

REGULAR SEASON (11-5)

Date	Result		Opponents	Att.
9/1	L	10-24	at Miami	71,542
9/8	L	10-17	at Buffalo	78,104
9/15	W	31-0	Arizona	59,118
9/22	W	28-25	Jacksonville (OT)	59,446
10/6	W	46-38	at Baltimore	63,569
10/13	L	22-27	Washington	59,638
10/20	W	27-9	at Indianapolis	58,725
10/27	W	28-25	Buffalo	58,858
11/3	W	42-23	Miami	58,942
11/10	W	31-27	at N.Y. Jets	61,715
11/17	L	8-34	Denver	59,452
11/24	W	27-13	Indianapolis	58,226
12/1	W	45-7	at San Diego	59,209
12/8	W	34-10	N.Y. Jets	54,621
12/15	L	6-12	at Dallas	64,578
12/21	W	23-22	at N.Y. Giants	65,387

POSTSEASON (2-1)

Date	Result		Opponents	Att.
1/5	W	28-3	Pittsburgh	60,188
1/12	W	20-6	Jacksonville	60,190
1/26	L	21-35	vs. Green Bay	72,301
(OT) Overtime				

SCORE BY PERIODS

Patriots	79	123	108	105	3	—	418
Opponents	59	105	75	74	0	—	313

ATTENDANCE

Home 468,301   Away 522,829   Total 991,130
Single-game home record, 61,457 (12/5/71)
Single-season home record, 482,572 (1986)

1996 TEAM STATISTICS

	Patriots	Opp.
Total First Downs	339	305
Rushing	103	102
Passing	206	178
Penalty	30	25
Third Down: Made/Att	84/228	82/228
Third Down Pct.	36.8	36.0
Fourth Down: Made/Att	19/34	12/22
Fourth Down Pct.	55.9	54.5
Total Net Yards	5369	5305
Avg. Per Game	335.6	331.6
Total Plays	1085	1063
Avg. Per Play	4.9	5.0
Net Yards Rushing	1468	1502
Avg. Per Game	91.8	93.9
Total Rushes	427	434
Net Yards Passing	3901	3803
Avg. Per Game	243.8	237.7
Sacked/Yards Lost	30/190	33/252
Gross Yards	4091	4055
Att./Completions	628/374	596/322
Completion Pct.	59.6	54.0
Had Intercepted	15	23
Punts/Avg.	64/43.2	82/42.5
Net Punting Avg.	64/35.8	82/33.6
Penalties/Yards Lost	97/716	139/1189
Fumbles/Ball Lost	25/12	23/11
Touchdowns	48	34
Rushing	15	14
Passing	27	17
Returns	6	3
Avg. Time of Possession.	30:11	29:49

1996 INDIVIDUAL STATISTICS

PASSING	Att.	Comp.	Yds.	Pct.	TD	Int.	Tkld.	Rate
Bledsoe	623	373	4086	59.9	27	15	30/190	83.7
Tupa	2	0	0	0.0	0	0	0/0	39.6
Grier	1	0	0	0.0	0	0	0/0	39.6
Meggett	1	0	0	0.0	0	0	0/0	39.6
Zolak	1	1	5	100.0	0	0	0/0	87.5
Patriots	628	374	4091	59.6	27	15	30/190	83.2
Opponents	596	322	4055	54.0	17	23	33/252	68.9

SCORING	TD R	TD P	TD Rt	PAT	FG	Saf	PTS
Vinatieri	0	0	0	39/42	27/35	0	120
Martin	14	3	0	0/0	0/0	0	104
Coates	0	9	0	0/0	0/0	0	56
Glenn	0	6	0	0/0	0/0	0	36
Jefferson	0	4	0	0/0	0/0	0	24
Byars	0	2	0	0/0	0/0	0	14
Gash	0	2	0	0/0	0/0	0	14
McGinest	0	0	2	0/0	0/0	0	12
Bartrum	0	1	0	0/0	0/0	0	6
C. Brown	0	0	1	0/0	0/0	0	6
Bruschi	0	0	1	0/0	0/0	0	6
Grier	1	0	0	0/0	0/0	0	6
Law	0	0	1	0/0	0/0	0	6
Meggett	0	0	1	0/0	0/0	0	6
Patriots	15	27	6	39/42	27/35	1	418
Opponents	14	17	3	28/28	23/29	1	313

2-Point conversions: Byars, Coates, Gash, Martin.
Team: 4-6, Opponents: 5-6.
*Patriots were credited with 1 team safety.

RUSHING	Att.	Yds.	Avg.	LG	TD
Martin	316	1152	3.6	57	14
Meggett	40	122	3.1	12	0
Grier	27	105	3.9	26	1
Glenn	5	42	8.4	26	0
Bledsoe	24	27	1.1	8	0
Gash	8	15	1.9	3	0
Jefferson	1	6	6.0	6	0
Byars	2	2	1.0	3	0
Zolak	4	-3	-0.7	0	0
Patriots	427	1468	3.4	57	15
Opponents	434	1502	3.5	36	14

RECEIVING	No.	Yds.	Avg.	LG	TD
Glenn	90	1132	12.6	37t	6
Coates	62	682	11.0	84t	9
Jefferson	50	771	15.4	42	4
Martin	46	333	7.2	41	3
Meggett	33	292	8.8	26	0
Gash	33	276	8.4	28	2
Byars	27	249	9.2	27	2
T. Brown	21	222	10.6	38	0
Graham	5	64	12.8	23	0
W. Moore	3	37	12.3	16	0
Burke	1	19	19.0	19	0
Grier	1	8	8.0	8	0
Jells	1	5	5.0	5	0
Bartrum	1	1	1.0	1t	1
Patriots	374	4091	12.6	84t	27
Opponents	322	4055	12.6	63t	17

INTERCEPTIONS	No.	Yds.	Avg.	LG	TD
Clay	4	50	12.5	35	0
Law	3	45	15.0	38t	1
Smith	2	20	10.0	11	0
Hitchcock	2	14	7.0	14	0
Milloy	2	14	7.0	14	0
Henderson	2	7	3.5	7	0
Reynolds	2	7	3.5	7	0
McGinest	1	46	46.0	46t	1
Ray	1	43	43.0	43	0
Collins	1	7	7.0	7	0
Slade	1	2	2.0	2	0
Johnson	1	0	0.0	0	0
Sabb	1	0	0.0	0	0
Patriots	23	255	11.1	46t	2
Opponents	15	191	12.7	60	1

PUNTING	No.	Yds.	Avg.	In 20	LG
Tupa	63	2739	43.5	14	62
Vinatieri	1	27	27.0	1	27
Patriots	64	2766	43.2	15	62
Opponents	82	3483	42.5	18	58

PUNT RETURNS	No.	FC	Yds.	Avg.	LG	TD
Meggett	52	9	588	11.3	60t	1
Patriots	52	9	588	11.3	60t	1
Opponents	34	8	334	9.8	36	0

KICKOFF RETURNS	No.	Yds.	Avg.	LG	TD
Meggett	34	781	23.0	54	0
T. Brown	29	634	21.9	51	0
Gisler	1	9	9.0	9	0
Patriots	64	1424	22.3	54	0
Opponents	81	1683	20.8	70	0

SACKS	No.
McGinest	9.5
Slade	7.0
Bruschi	4.0
Sagapolutele	3.0
Jones	2.0
Eaton	1.0
Milloy	1.0
Ray	1.0
Smith	1.0
Wheeler	1.0
Wyman	1.0
Collons	0.5
McGruder	0.5
Sabb	0.5
Patriots	33.0
Opponents	30.0

1997 DRAFT CHOICES

Round	Name	Pos.	College
1	Chris Canty	DB	Kansas State
2	Brandon Mitchell	DT	Texas A&M
3	Sedrick Shaw	RB	Iowa
	Chris Carter	DB	Texas
4	Damon Denson	G	Michigan
	Ed Ellis	T	Buffalo
5	Vernon Crawford	LB	Florida State
6	Tony Gaiter	WR	Miami
7	Scott Rehberg	T	Central Michigan

1997 VETERAN ROSTER

No.	Name	Pos.	Ht.	Wt.	Birthdate	NFL Exp.	College	Hometown	How Acq.	'96 Games/ Starts
78	Armstrong, Bruce	T	6-4	295	9/7/65	11	Louisville	Miami, Fla.	D1-'87	16/16
46	Barber, Kantroy	RB	6-1	243	10/4/73	2	West Virginia	Miami, Fla.	D4c-'96	0*
86	Bartrum, Mike	TE	6-5	245	6/23/70	4	Marshall	Pomeroy, Ohio	T(GB)-'96	16/0
11	Bledsoe, Drew	QB	6-5	233	2/14/72	5	Washington State	Walla Walla, Wash.	D1-'93	16/16
82	Brisby, Vincent	WR	6-2	188	1/25/71	5	Northeast Louisiana	Lake Charles, La.	D2c-'93	3/0
30	Brown, Corwin	S	6-1	200	4/25/70	5	Michigan	Chicago, Ill.	D4b-'93	14/0
93	Brown, Monty	LB	6-1	240	4/13/70	5	Ferris State	Bridgeport, Mich.	RFA(Buff)-'96	11/7
80	Brown, Troy	WR	5-9	190	7/2/71	5	Marshall	Blackville, S.C.	FA-'94	16/0
54	Bruschi, Tedy	LB	6-1	245	6/9/73	2	Arizona	Roseville, Calif.	D3-'96	16/0
85	† Burke, John	TE	6-3	248	9/7/71	4	Virginia Tech	Holmdel, N.J.	D4-'94	11/2
41	Byars, Keith	RB	6-1	255	10/14/63	12	Ohio State	Dayton, Ohio	FA-'96	10/6
32	Clay, Willie	S	5-10	198	9/5/70	6	Georgia Tech	Pittsburgh, Pa.	UFA-'96	16/16
87	Coates, Ben	TE	6-5	245	8/16/69	7	Livingstone College	Greenwood, S.C.	D5b-'91	16/15
59	Collins, Todd	LB	6-2	242	5/27/70	5	Carson-Newman	New Market, Tenn.	D3a-'92	16/9
92	Collons, Ferric	DE	6-6	285	12/4/69	4	California	Sacramento, Calif.	T(GB)-'95	15/5
33	Gash, Sam	RB	6-1	235	3/7/69	6	Penn State	Hendersonville, N.C.	D8-'92	14/9
67	Gisler, Mike	C	6-4	300	8/26/69	5	Houston	Range, Tex.	FA-'93	14/0
88	Glenn, Terry	WR	5-10	184	7/23/74	2	Ohio State	Columbus, Ohio	D1-'96	15/15
81	Graham, Hason	WR	5-10	176	3/21/71	3	Georgia	Decatur, Ga.	FA-'95	9/0
34	Grant, Rupert	RB	6-1	233	11/5/73	3	Howard	Washington, D.C.	FA-'95	0*
35	Grier, Marrio	RB	5-10	225	12/5/71	2	Tennessee-Chattanooga	Charlotte, N.C.	D6b-'96	16/0
31	Hitchcock, Jimmy	CB	5-10	188	11/9/71	3	North Carolina	Concord, N.C.	D3b-'95	13/5
63	Irwin, Heath	G	6-4	300	6/27/73	2	Colorado	Boulder, Colo.	D4a-'96	0*
37	Israel, Steve	CB	5-11	186	3/16/69	6	Pittsburgh	Haddon Heights, N.J.	UFA(SF)-'97	14/2*
84	Jefferson, Shawn	WR	5-11	180	2/22/69	7	Central Florida	Jacksonville, Fla.	UFA-'96	15/15
83	Jells, Dietrich	WR	5-10	186	4/11/72	2	Pittsburgh	Erie, Pa.	W(KC)-'96	7/1
52	Johnson, Ted	LB	6-3	240	12/4/72	3	Colorado	Carlsbad, Calif.	D2-'95	16/16
96	Jones, Mike	DE	6-4	295	8/25/69	7	North Carolina State	Columbus, S.C.	FA-'94	16/12
68	† Lane, Max	T	6-6	305	2/22/71	4	Navy	Norborne, Mo.	D6b-'94	16/16
24	Law, Ty	CB	5-11	196	2/10/74	3	Michigan	Aliquippa, Pa.	D1-'95	13/12
43	# Lewis, Vernon	CB	5-10	192	10/27/70	5	Pittsburgh	Houston, Tex.	FA-'93	7/0
15	Lucas, Ray	WR	6-2	201	8/6/72	2	Rutgers	Harrison, N.J.	FA-'96	2/0
28	Martin, Curtis	RB	5-11	203	5/1/73	3	Pittsburgh	Pittsburgh, Pa.	D3a-'95	16/15
55	McGinest, Willie	DE	6-5	255	12/11/71	4	Southern California	Long Beach, Calif.	D1-'94	16/16
27	McGruder, Scooter	CB	5-11	184	5/6/64	8	Kent State	Cleveland Heights, Ohio	UFA(TB)-'96	14/0
22	Meggett, David	RB	5-7	195	4/30/66	9	Towson State	Charleston, S.C.	UFA(NYG)-'95	16/1
36	Milloy, Lawyer	S	6-1	208	11/14/73	2	Washington	Tacoma, Wash.	D2-'96	16/10
58	† Moore, Marty	LB	6-1	244	3/19/71	4	Kentucky	Fort Thomas, Ky.	D7b-'94	16/0
77	Moss, Zefross	T	6-6	324	8/17/66	9	Alabama State	Holt, Ala.	UFA(Det)-'97	15/15*
48	Purnell, Lovett	TE	6-2	250	4/7/72	2	West Virginia	Seaford, Del.	D7a-'96	2/0
23	# Ray, Terry	S	6-1	200	10/12/69	6	Oklahoma	Killeen, Tex.	W(Atl)-'93	16/7
21	# Reynolds, Ricky	CB	5-11	190	1/19/65	11	Washington State	Sacramento, Calif.	UFA(TB)-'94	11/9
62	# Richards, Dave	T	6-5	315	4/11/66	10	UCLA	Dallas, Tex.	W(Atl)-'96	5/0
76	# Roberts, William	G	6-5	298	8/5/62	14	Ohio State	Miami, Fla.	FA-'95	16/16
71	Rucci, Todd	G	6-5	291	7/4/70	5	Penn State	Upper Darby, Pa.	D2b-'93	16/12
18	Ryans, Larry	WR	5-11	182	7/28/71	2	Clemson	Greenwood, S.C.	FA-'97	3/0*
95	# Sabb, Dwayne	LB	6-4	248	10/9/69	6	New Hampshire	Union, N.J.	D5-'92	16/7
75	Sagapolutele, Pio	DT	6-6	297	11/28/69	7	San Diego State	American Samoa	UFA(Balt)-'96	15/10
53	Slade, Chris	LB	6-5	245	1/30/71	5	Virginia	Newport News, Va.	D2a-'93	16/9
74	Sullivan, Chris	DE	6-4	279	3/14/73	2	Boston College	North Attleboro, Mass.	D4b-'96	16/0
19	Tupa, Tom	P-QB	6-4	220	2/6/66	9	Ohio State	Cleveland, Ohio	UFA(Balt)-'96	16/0
4	Vinatieri, Adam	K	6-1	200	12/28/72	2	South Dakota State	Rapid City, S.D.	FA-'96	16/0
97	Wheeler, Mark	DT	6-3	285	4/1/70	6	Texas A&M	San Marcos, Tex.	UFA(TB)-'96	16/15
25	Whigham, Larry	S	6-2	205	6/23/72	4	Northeast Louisiana	Hattiesburg, Miss.	FA-'94	16/1
50	Williams, James	LB	6-1	240	10/10/68	7	Mississippi State	Natchez, Miss.	FA-'97	0*
64	Wohlabaugh, Dave	C	6-3	292	4/13/72	3	Syracuse	Hamburg, N.Y.	D4-'95	16/16
72	Wyman, Devin	DT	6-7	307	8/29/73	2	Kentucky State	East Palo Alto, Calif.	D6c-'96	9/4
16	Zolak, Scott	QB	6-5	235	12/13/67	7	Maryland	Monongahela, Pa.	D4-'91	2/0

* Barber inactive for 6 games in '96; Grant last active with New England in '95; Irwin inactive for 16 games; Israel played 14 games with San Francisco in '96; Moss played 15 games with Detroit; Ryans played 3 games with Tampa Bay; Williams last active for Jacksonville in '94.

\# Unrestricted free agent; subject to developments.

† Restricted free agent; subject to developments.

Players lost through free agency (1): CB Otis Smith (NYJ; 11 games in '96).

Also played with Patriots in '96—DT Troy Barnett (1 game), C Jeff Dellenbach (2), CB-S Jerome Henderson (7), WR Will Moore (2), DE Walter Scott (1).

COACHING STAFF

Head Coach,
Pete Carroll

Pro Career: Pete Carroll was named head coach of the New England Patriots on February 3, 1997, to become just the thirteenth head coach in franchise history. He joins the Patriots after serving two seasons as the defensive coordinator for the San Francisco 49ers, where he instructed one of the premier defensive units in the league. While in San Francisco, the 49ers' defense allowed just 283.1 yards per game. Only Pittsburgh boasted a lower net average (278.8 yards per game) during that two-year span. Under Carroll's guidance, the 1995 49ers defense was one of the best in the history of the franchise. The unit finished the season ranked first in the league in total defense, rushing defense and scoring defense. They grabbed a league-leading 26 interceptions. Carroll joined the 49ers after five seasons with the New York Jets. His tenure in New York began in 1990 when he was named defensive coordinator. During the next four years, Carroll established a reputation for being one of the game's most innovative defensive minds. His attacking style of defense annually placed the Jets defense among the league leaders in forced turnovers and total defense. In 1994, the Jets named Carroll as their ninth head coach in franchise history. That year, the Jets were in contention for the AFC East title through the first 11 games of the season (6-5 record), but lost their final five games of the season. Despite the early success the Jets enjoyed that year, Carroll was relieved of his duties after just one rebuilding season. He began his NFL coaching career in 1984 with the Buffalo Bills. The following year he joined Bud Grant's staff in Minnesota and spent the next five seasons (1985-89) as the defensive back coach for the Vikings. During that time, the Vikings totaled 126 interceptions and scored 10 touchdowns on their returns. Career record: 6-10.

Background: Carroll began his coaching career at Pacific in 1974 at the age of 22. He coached three seasons at Pacific before moving on, gaining coaching experience at Arkansas (1977), Iowa State (1978) and Ohio State (1979) before settling in at North Carolina State in 1980. For the next three seasons (1980-82) Carroll directed the Wolfpack's defense before returning to his alma mater for one year as the assistant head coach in 1983.

Personal: Carroll was born September 15, 1951, in San Francisco, Calif. He was a football standout at Redwood High School prior to a stellar collegiate career at the University of the Pacific, where he twice earned All-Pacific Coast Conference honors as a defensive back. He had a tryout with the Hawaiians of the World Football League before pursuing a coaching career. He and his wife, Glena live in Medfield, Mass., and have two sons, Brennan and Nathan and a daughter, Jaime.

ASSISTANT COACHES

Paul Boudreau, offensive line; born December 30, 1949, Arlington, Mass., lives in Wrentham, Mass. Guard Boston College 1971-73. No pro playing experience. College coach: Boston College 1975-76, Maine 1977-79, Dartmouth 1980-82, Navy 1983. Pro coach: Edmonton Eskimos (CFL) 1983-86, New Orleans Saints 1987-93, Detroit Lions 1984-86, joined Patriots in 1997.

Jeff Davidson, tight ends; born October 3, 1967, Akron, Ohio, lives in Franklin, Mass. Offensive lineman Ohio State 1986-89. Pro offensive lineman Denver Broncos 1990-92, New Orleans Saints 1994. Pro coach: New Orleans Saints 1995-96, joined Patriots in 1997.

Ray Hamilton, defensive line; born January 20, 1951, Omaha, Neb., lives in Sharon, Mass. Nose tackle Oklahoma 1969-72. Pro nose tackle-defensive end New England Patriots 1973-81. College coach: Tennessee 1992. Pro coach: New England Patriots 1985-89, Tampa Bay Buccaneers 1991, Los Angeles Raiders 1993-94, New York Jets 1995-96, rejoined Patriots in 1997.

Larry Kennan, offensive coordinator; born June 13,

1997 FIRST-YEAR ROSTER

Name	Pos.	Ht.	Wt.	Birthdate	College	Hometown	How Acq.
Bivins, Marquin (1)	G	6-2	317	7/24/72	Alcorn State	Laurel, Miss.	FA
Bresnahan, Chris	QB	6-5	230	9/30/74	New Hampshire	Syracuse, N.Y.	FA
Canty, Chris	CB	5-9	194	3/30/76	Kansas State	Voorhees, N.J.	D1
Carter, Chris	S	6-1	201	9/27/74	Texas	Tyler, Tex.	D3b
Claro, Tom (1)	G	6-5	300	12/14/74	Holy Cross	Floral Park, N.Y.	FA
Conrad, J.R. (1)	T	6-3	300	2/2/74	Oklahoma	Fairland, Okla.	FA
Crawford, Vernon	LB	6-3	250	6/25/74	Florida State	Texas City, Tex.	D5
Cullors, Derrick (1)	RB	5-11	181	12/26/72	Murray State	Dallas, Tex.	FA
Denson, Damon	G	6-3	304	2/8/75	Michigan	Pittsburgh, Pa.	D4a
Ellis, Edward	T	6-7	340	10/13/75	Buffalo	Hamden, Conn.	D4b
Gaiter, Tony	WR	5-8	169	7/15/74	Miami	Miami, Fla.	D6
Jones, Curtis	CB	6-0	180	6/22/74	Howard	Sussex, Va.	FA
Miles, Jermaine	DE	6-5	265	8/16/74	Gergoia Tech	Brooklyn, N.Y.	FA
Mitchell, Brandon	DT	6-3	289	6/19/75	Texas A&M	Abbeville, La.	D2
Parker, Jason	S	5-11	192	8/6/74	Tennessee	Garland, Tex.	FA
Porter, Juan	C	6-3	294	11/26/73	Ohio State	Cleveland, Ohio	FA
Reeves, Chad (1)	LB	6-2	250	4/29/73	McNeese State	Lake Charles, La.	FA
Rehberg, Scott	T	6-8	336	11/17/73	Central Michigan	Kalamazoo, Mich.	D7
Shaw, Sedrick	RB	6-0	214	11/16/73	Iowa	Austin, Tex.	D3a
Tate, Mark	CB	5-11	185	3/20/74	Penn State	Erie, Pa.	FA
Taves, Josh (1)	DE	6-7	285	5/3/72	Northeastern	Yarmouth, Mass.	FA
Turner, Shawn	WR	6-1	200	5/18/73	Utah State	Nampa, Idaho	FA
Warren, Michael (1)	TE	6-3	270	11/11/72	McNeese State	Sour Lake, Tex.	FA
Wing, Chris	LB	6-2	235	5/28/71	Boise State	Redmond, Wash.	FA

The term NFL Rookie is defined as a player who is in his first season of professional football and has not been on the roster of another professional football team for any regular-season or postseason games. A Rookie is designated by an "R" on NFL rosters. Players who have been active in another professional football league or players who have NFL experience, including either preseason training camp or being on an Active List or Inactive List, or on Reserve/Injured or Reserve/Physically Unable to Perform for fewer than six regular-season games, are termed NFL First-Year Players. An NFL First-Year Player is designated by a "1" on NFL rosters. Thereafter, a player is credited with an additional year of experience for each season in which he accumulates six games on the Active List or Inactive List, or on Reserve/Injured or Reserve/Physically Unable to Perform.

NOTES

1944, Pomona, Calif., lives in Norfolk, Mass. Quarterback LaVerne College 1962-65. No pro playing experience. College coach: Colorado 1969-71, Nevada-Las Vegas 1973-75, Southern Methodist 1976-77, Lamar 1978-81 (head coach). Pro coach: Los Angeles-Oakland Raiders 1982-87,1996, Denver Broncos 1988, Indianapolis Colts 1989-90, London Monarchs (World League) 1991, Seattle Seahawks 1992-94, New Orleans Saints 1995, joined Patriots in 1997.

Ron Lynn, defensive backs; born December 6, 1944, Youngstown, Ohio, lives in Dover, Mass. Quarterback-defensive back Mt. Union (Ohio) 1963-65. No pro playing experience. College coach: Toledo 1966, Mt. Union (Ohio) 1967-73, Kent State 1974-76, San Jose State 1977-78, Pacific 1979, California 1980-82. Pro coach: Oakland Invaders (USFL) 1983-85, San Diego Chargers 1986-91, Cincinnati Bengals 1992-93, Washington Redskins 1994-96, joined Patriots in 1997.

Johnny Parker, strength and conditioning; born February 1, 1947, Greenville, S.C., lives in Foxboro, Mass. Attended Mississippi. No college or pro playing experience. College coach: South Carolina 1974-76, Indiana 1977-79, Louisiana State 1980, Mississippi 1981-83. Pro coach: New York Giants 1984-92, joined Patriots in 1993.

Andre Patterson, defensive assistant; born June 12, 1960, lives in Attleboro, Mass. Offensive lineman Contra Costa J.C. 1978-80, offensive lineman Montana 1981. No pro playing experience. College coach: Montana 1982, Weber State 1988-89, Western Washington 1989-90, Cornell 1990-91, Washington State 1992-93, California Polytechnical State 1993-96. Pro coach: Joined Patriots in 1997.

Bo Pelini, linebackers; born December 13, 1967, Youngstown, Ohio, lives in Attleboro, Mass. Defensive back Ohio State 1986-90. No pro playing experience. College coach: Iowa 1991-92. Pro coach: San Francisco 49ers 1994-96, joined Patriots in 1997.

Dante Scarnecchia, special teams; born February 15, 1948, Los Angeles, Calif., lives in Wrentham,

Mass. Center-guard California Western 1968-70. No pro playing experience. College coach: California Western (now U.S. International) 1970-72, Iowa State 1973, Southern Methodist 1975-76, 1980-81, Pacific 1977-78, Northern Arizona 1979. Pro coach: New England Patriots 1982-89, Indianapolis Colts 1990, rejoined Patriots in 1991.

Steve Sidwell, defensive coordinator; born August 30, 1944, Winfield, Kansas, lives in Wrentham, Mass. Linebacker Colorado 1962-65. No pro playing experience. College coach: Colorado 1966-73, Nevada-Las Vegas 1974-75, Southern Methodist 1976-81. Pro coach: New England Patriots 1982-84, Indianapolis Colts 1985, New Orleans Saints 1986-94, Houston Oilers 1995-96, joined Patriots in 1997.

Carl Smith, assistant head coach-quarterbacks; born April 26, 1948, Wasco, Calif., lives in Franklin, Mass. Defensive back Cal Poly-SLO 1968-70. No pro playing experience. College coach: Cal Poly SLO 1971, Colorado 1972-73, Southwestern Louisiana 1974-78, Lamar 1979-81, North Carolina State 1982. Pro coach: Philadelphia/Baltimore Stars (USFL) 1983-85, New Orleans Saints 1986-96, joined Patriots in 1997.

Steve Walters, wide receivers; born June 16, 1948, Jonesboro, Arkansas. Quarterback-defensive back Arkansas 1967-70. No pro playing experience. College coach: Tampa 1973, Northeast Louisiana 1974-75, Morehead State 1976, Tulsa 1977-78, Memphis State 1979, Southern Methodist 1980-81, Alabama 1985. Pro coach: New England Patriots 1982-84, New Orleans Saints 1986-96, rejoined Patriots in 1997.

Kirby Wilson, running backs; born August 24, 1961, Los Angeles, Calif., lives in Norwood, Mass. Running back-wide receiver Pasadena C.C. 1979-80, wide receiver-kick returner Illinois 1981-82. Pro defensive back-kick returner Winnipeg (CFL) 1983, Toronto (CFL) 1984. College coach: Pasadena C.C. 1985, L.A. Southwest C.C. 1989-90, Southern Illinois 1991-92, Wyoming 1993-94, Iowa State 1995-96. Pro coach: Joined Patriots in 1997.

American Football Conference
Eastern Division
Team Colors: Kelly Green and White
1000 Fulton Avenue
Hempstead, New York 11550
Telephone: (516) 560-8100

CLUB OFFICIALS

Chairman of the Board: Leon Hess
President: Steve Gutman
Head Coach and Chief Football Operations Officer:
  Bill Parcells
Director of Player Personnel: Dick Haley
Director of Pro Personnel: Scott Pioli
Director of Player Contract Negotiations:
  Mike Tannenbaum
Director of Player Development: Carl Banks
Director of Player Administration: Pat Kirwan
Director of Public Relations: Frank Ramos
Treasurer & C.F.O.: Mike Gerstle
Director of Operations: Mike Kensil
Executive Director of Business Operations:
  Bob Parente
Talent Scouts: Joey Clinkscales, Sid Hall,
  Jesse Kaye, Bob Schmitz, Marv Sunderland,
  Lionel Vital
Travel Coordinator: Kevin Coyle
College Scouting Coordinator: John Griffin
Asst. Director of Public Relations: Doug Miller
Public Relations Assistants: Sharon Czark,
  Berj Najarian
Coordinator of Special Projects: Ken Ilchuk
Controller: Mike Minarczyk
Senior Marketing Manager: Mark Riccio
Marketing Manager: Beth Conroy
Director of Ticket Operations: John Buschhorn
Computer Ticket Operations Manager: Carol Anne
  Coppola
Director of Computer Technology: Hal Masure
Video Director: Jim Pons
Assistant Video Director: John Seiter
Head Trainer: David Price
Assistant Head Coach: John Mellody
Equipment Manager: Bill Hampton
Equipment Director: Clay Hampton
Stadium: Giants Stadium •**Capacity:** 77,803
        East Rutherford, New Jersey 07073
Playing Surface: AstroTurf
Training Center: 1000 Fulton Avenue
        Hempstead, New York 11550

1997 SCHEDULE
PRESEASON

Aug. 2	**Philadelphia**	8:00
Aug. 8	**Baltimore**	8:00
Aug. 16	at New York Giants	8:00
Aug. 22	vs. Tampa Bay at Orlando	7:30

REGULAR SEASON

Aug. 31	at Seattle	1:00
Sept. 7	**Buffalo**	1:00
Sept. 14	at New England	8:00
Sept. 21	**Oakland**	1:00
Sept. 28	at Cincinnati	4:00
Oct. 5	at Indianapolis	3:00
Oct. 12	**Miami**	1:00
Oct. 19	**New England**	1:00
Oct. 26	Open Date	
Nov. 2	**Baltimore**	1:00
Nov. 9	at Miami	1:00
Nov. 16	at Chicago	3:00
Nov. 23	**Minnesota**	1:00
Nov. 30	at Buffalo	1:00
Dec. 7	**Indianapolis**	4:00
Dec. 14	**Tampa Bay**	1:00
Dec. 21	at Detroit	4:00

RECORD HOLDERS
INDIVIDUAL RECORDS—CAREER

Category	Name	Performance
Rushing (Yds.)	Freeman McNeil, 1981-1992	8,074
Passing (Yds.)	Joe Namath, 1965-1976	27,057
Passing (TDs)	Joe Namath, 1965-1976	170
Receiving (No.)	Don Maynard, 1960-1972	627
Receiving (Yds.)	Don Maynard, 1960-1972	11,732
Interceptions	Bill Baird, 1963-69	34
Punting (Avg.)	Curley Johnson, 1961-68	42.8
Punt Return (Avg.)	Dick Christy, 1961-63	16.2
Kickoff Return (Avg.)	Bobby Humphery, 1984-89	22.8
Field Goals	Pat Leahy, 1974-1991	304
Touchdowns (Tot.)	Don Maynard, 1960-1972	88
Points	Pat Leahy, 1974-1991	1,470

INDIVIDUAL RECORDS—SINGLE SEASON

Category	Name	Performance
Rushing (Yds.)	Freeman McNeil, 1985	1,331
Passing (Yds.)	Joe Namath, 1967	4,007
Passing (TDs)	Al Dorow, 1960	26
	Joe Namath, 1967	26
Receiving (No.)	Al Toon, 1988	93
Receiving (Yds.)	Don Maynard, 1967	1,434
Interceptions	Dainard Paulson, 1964	12
Punting (Avg.)	Curley Johnson, 1965	45.3
Punt Return (Avg.)	Dick Christy, 1961	21.3
Kickoff Return (Avg.)	Bobby Humphery, 1984	30.7
Field Goals	Jim Turner, 1968	34
Touchdowns (Tot.)	Art Powell, 1960	14
	Don Maynard, 1965	14
	Emerson Boozer, 1972	14
Points	Jim Turner, 1968	145

INDIVIDUAL RECORDS—SINGLE GAME

Category	Name	Performance
Rushing (Yds.)	Freeman McNeil, 9-15-85	192
Passing (Yds.)	Joe Namath, 9-24-72	496
Passing (TDs)	Joe Namath, 9-24-72	6
Receiving (No.)	Clark Gaines, 9-21-80	17
Receiving (Yds.)	Don Maynard, 11-17-68	228
Interceptions	Many times	3
	Last time by Marcus Turner, 11-20-94	
Field Goals	Jim Turner, 11-3-68	6
	Bobby Howfield, 12-3-72	6
Touchdowns (Tot.)	Wesley Walker, 9-21-86	4
Points	Wesley Walker, 9-21-86	24

COACHING HISTORY
New York Titans 1960-62
(236-315-8)

1960-61	Sammy Baugh	14-14-0
1962	Clyde (Bulldog) Turner	5-9-0
1963-73	Weeb Ewbank	73-78-6
1974-75	Charley Winner*	9-14-0
1975	Ken Shipp	1-4-0
1976	Lou Holtz**	3-10-0
1976	Mike Holovak	0-1-0
1977-82	Walt Michaels	41-49-1
1983-89	Joe Walton	54-59-1
1990-93	Bruce Coslet	26-39-0
1994	Pete Carroll	6-10-0
1995-96	Rich Kotite	4-28-0

*Released after nine games in 1975
**Resigned after 13 games in 1976

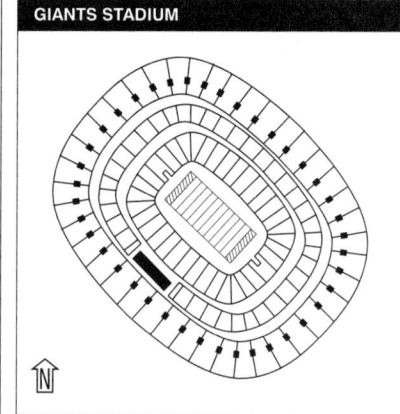

1996 TEAM RECORD

PRESEASON (1-3)

Date	Result		Opponents
8/3	L	13-31	vs. Houston
			at Jackson, Miss.
8/9	L	16-30	at Philadelphia
8/17	W	13-6	N.Y. Giants
8/23	L	27-44	at Oakland

REGULAR SEASON (1-15)

Date	Result		Opponents	Att.
9/1	L	6-31	at Denver	70,595
9/8	L	7-21	Indianapolis	63,534
9/15	L	27-36	at Miami	68,137
9/22	L	6-13	N.Y. Giants	58,339
9/29	L	16-31	at Washington	52,068
10/6	L	13-34	Oakland	63,611
10/13	L	17-21	at Jacksonville	65,699
10/20	L	22-25	Buffalo	49,775
10/27	W	31-21	at Arizona	28,088
11/10	L	27-31	New England	61,715
11/17	L	29-34	at Indianapolis	48,322
11/24	L	10-35	at Buffalo	60,854
12/1	L	10-35	Houston	21,731
12/8	L	10-34	at New England	54,621
12/14	L	20-21	Philadelphia	29,178
12/22	L	28-31	Miami	47,271

SCORE BY PERIODS

Jets	54	100	50	75	—	279
Opponents	51	144	107	152	—	454

ATTENDANCE

Home 395,154   Away 448,384   Total 843,538
Single-game home record, 75,606 (11/27/94)
Single-season home record, 541,832 (1985)

1996 TEAM STATISTICS

	Jets	Opp.
Total First Downs	319	304
Rushing	94	119
Passing	191	157
Penalty	34	28
Third Down: Made/Att	95/232	86/215
Third Down Pct.	40.9	40.0
Fourth Down: Made/Att	9/22	7/12
Fourth Down Pct.	40.9	58.3
Total Net Yards	5208	5564
Avg. Per Game	325.5	347.8
Total Plays	1077	1023
Avg. Per Play	4.8	5.4
Net Yards Rushing	1583	2200
Avg. Per Game	98.9	137.5
Total Rushes	407	539
Net Yards Passing	3625	3364
Avg. Per Game	226.6	210.3
Sacked/Yards Lost	41/286	28/178
Gross Yards	3911	3542
Att./Completions	629/339	456/257
Completion Pct.	53.9	56.4
Had Intercepted	30	11
Punts/Avg.	74/44.5	75/42.1
Net Punting Avg.	74/36.5	75/38.4
Penalties/Yards Lost	110/819	107/902
Fumbles/Ball Lost	25/16	26/15
Touchdowns	33	55
Rushing	8	19
Passing	22	33
Returns	3	3
Avg. Time of Possession	29:26	30:34

1996 INDIVIDUAL STATISTICS

PASSING	Att.	Comp.	Yds.	Pct.	TD	Int.	Tkld.	Rate
Reich	331	175	2205	52.9	15	16	14/94	68.9
O'Donnell	188	110	1147	58.5	4	7	18/127	67.8
Foley	110	54	559	49.1	3	7	9/65	46.7
Jets	629	339	3911	53.9	22	30	41/286	64.7
Opponents	456	257	3542	56.4	33	11	28/178	95.5

SCORING	TD R	TD P	TD Rt	PAT	FG	Saf	PTS
Lowery	0	0	0	26/27	17/24	0	77
Johnson	0	8	0	0/0	0/0	0	50
Murrell	6	1	0	0/0	0/0	0	42
Graham	0	6	0	0/0	0/0	0	36
Chrebet	0	3	0	0/0	0/0	0	18
Glenn	0	0	2	0/0	0/0	0	12
Slaughter	0	2	0	0/0	0/0	0	12
Brady	0	1	0	0/0	0/0	0	8
Anderson	1	0	0	0/0	0/0	0	6
Cobb	1	0	0	0/0	0/0	0	6
Douglas	0	0	1	0/0	0/0	0	6
Van Dyke	0	1	0	0/0	0/0	0	6
Jets	8	22	3	26/27	17/24	0	279
Opponents	19	33	3	51/52	23/28	1	454

2-Point conversions: Brady, Johnson. Team: 2-6, Opponents: 1-3.

RUSHING	Att.	Yds.	Avg.	LG	TD
Murrell	301	1249	4.1	78	6
Anderson	47	150	3.2	11	1
Cobb	25	85	3.4	9	1
Foley	7	40	5.7	12	0
Reich	18	31	1.7	10	0
O'Donnell	6	30	5.0	17	0
Hansen	1	1	1.0	1	0
Moore	1	1	1.0	1	0
Bailey	1	-4	-4.0	-4	0
Jets	407	1583	3.9	78	8
Opponents	539	2200	4.1	53	19

RECEIVING	No.	Yds.	Avg.	LG	TD
Chrebet	84	909	10.8	44	3
Johnson	63	844	13.4	50	8
Graham	50	788	15.8	78t	6
Anderson	44	385	8.8	48	0
Slaughter	32	434	13.6	53	2
Van Dyke	17	118	6.9	12	1
Murrell	17	81	4.8	30	1
Brady	15	144	9.6	25	1
Baxter	7	114	16.3	23	0
Bailey	5	65	13.0	28	0
Cobb	4	23	5.8	12	0
Davis	1	6	6.0	6	0
Jets	339	3911	11.5	78t	22
Opponents	257	3542	13.8	83t	33

INTERCEPTIONS	No.	Yds.	Avg.	LG	TD
Glenn	4	113	28.3	100t	2
Green	2	27	13.5	18	0
Houston	2	3	1.5	3	0
Coleman	1	23	23.0	23	0
Young	1	0	0.0	0	0
Spindler	1	-1	-1.0	-1	0
Jets	11	165	15.0	100t	2
Opponents	30	384	12.8	45	2

PUNTING	No.	Yds.	Avg.	In 20	LG
Hansen	74	3293	44.5	13	69
Jets	74	3293	44.5	13	69
Opponents	75	3158	42.1	27	61

PUNT RETURNS	No.	FC	Yds.	Avg.	LG	TD
Chrebet	28	16	139	5.0	15	0
Jets	28	16	139	5.0	15	0
Opponents	40	14	429	10.7	31	0

KICKOFF RETURNS	No.	Yds.	Avg.	LG	TD
Bailey	24	470	19.6	34	0
Cobb	23	488	21.2	34	0
Van Dyke	15	289	19.3	37	0
Moore	8	118	14.8	28	0
Carpenter	6	107	17.8	21	0
Brady	2	26	13.0	16	0
Glenn	1	6	6.0	6	0
Murrell	0	0	—	—	0
Jets	79	1504	19.0	37	0
Opponents	58	1485	25.6	97t	1

SACKS	No.
Douglas	8.0
B. Hamilton	4.5
Cascadden	3.0
Washington	2.5
Brock	2.0
Green	2.0
Gunn	2.0
R. Hamilton	1.5
M. Jones	1.0
Chalenski	0.5
Lewis	0.5
Spindler	0.5
Jets	28.0
Opponents	41.0

1997 DRAFT CHOICES

Round	Name	Pos.	College
1	James Farrior	LB	Virginia
2	Rick Terry	DT	North Carolina
3	Dedric Ward	WR	Northern Iowa
4	Terry Day	DE	Mississippi State
	Leon Johnson	RB	North Carolina
5	Lamont Burns	G	East Carolina
	Raymond Austin	DB	Tennessee
6	Tim Scharf	LB	Northwestern
	Chuck Clements	QB	Houston
7	Steve Rosga	DB	Colorado
	Jason Ferguson	DT	Georgia

NEW YORK JETS

1997 VETERAN ROSTER

No.	Name	Pos.	Ht.	Wt.	Birthdate	NFL Exp.	College	Hometown	How Acq.	'96 Games/ Starts
20	Anderson, Richie	RB	6-2	225	9/13/71	5	Penn State	Sandy Spring, Md.	D6-'93	16/13
84	Baxter, Fred	TE	6-3	260	6/14/71	5	Auburn	Brundidge, Ala.	D5a-'93	16/4
88	Brady, Kyle	TE	6-6	260	1/14/72	3	Penn State	New Cumberland, Pa.	D1a-'95	16/16
23	Brown, Lance	CB	6-0	200	2/2/72	3	Indiana	Jacksonville, Fla.	FA-'96	0*
53	Cascadden, Chad	LB	6-1	235	5/14/72	3	Wisconsin	Chippewa Fallas, Wis.	FA-'95	16/8
80	Chrebet, Wayne	WR	5-10	185	8/14/73	3	Hofstra	Garfield, N.J.	FA-'95	16/9
28	Cobb, Reggie	RB	6-1	212	7/7/68	7	Tennessee	Knoxville, Tenn.	FA-'96	15/0
42	Coleman, Marcus	S-CB	6-2	205	5/24/74	2	Texas Tech	Dallas, Tex.	D5-'96	13/4
27	D'Agostino, Lou	RB	6-0	235	12/12/73	2	Rhode Island	Atlantic Beach, N.Y.	FA-'96	9/0
83	Davis, Tyrone	TE	6-4	255	6/30/72	2	Virginia	Halifax, Va.	D4b-'95	2/0
98	t- Dixon, Ronnie	DT	6-3	310	5/10/71	4	Cincinnati	Clinton, N.C.	T(Phil)-'97	16/4*
99	Douglas, Hugh	DE	6-2	270	8/23/71	3	Central State	Mansfield, Ohio	D1b-'95	10/10
56	DuBose, Demetrius	LB	6-1	235	3/23/71	5	Notre Dame	Seattle, Wash.	UFA(TB)-'97	14/0*
62	Duffy, Roger	C-G	6-3	305	7/16/67	8	Penn State	Canton, Ohio	D8-'90	16/16
76	Elliott, John	T	6-7	308	4/1/65	10	Michigan	Lake Ronkonkoma, N.Y.	UFA(NYG)-'96	14/14
68	Fiore, Dave	G-C-T	6-4	275	8/10/74	2	Hofstra	Waldwick, N.J.	W(SF)-'96	0*
4	Foley, Glenn	QB	6-2	210	10/10/70	4	Boston College	Cherry Hill, N.J.	D7-'94	5/3
64	Galbreath, Harry	G	6-1	295	1/1/65	10	Tennessee	Nashville, Tenn.	FA-'96	15/8
31	Glenn, Aaron	CB	5-9	185	7/16/72	4	Texas A&M	Aldine, Tex.	D1-'94	16/16
81	Graham, Jeff	WR	6-2	200	2/14/69	7	Ohio State	Kettering, Ohio	UFA(Chi)-'96	11/9
21	Green, Victor	S	5-11	205	12/8/69	5	Akron	Americus, Ga.	FA-'93	16/16
34	Greewood, Carl	CB	5-11	186	3/11/72	3	UCLA	Corpus Christi, Tex.	D5-'95	14/2
92	Hamilton, Bobby	DE	6-5	280	1/7/71	3	Southern Mississippi	Columbia, Miss.	FA-'96	15/11
11	Hansen, Brian	P	6-4	215	10/26/60	13	Sioux Falls	Hawarden, Iowa	UFA(Cle)-'94	16/0
26	Henderson, Jerome	CB	5-10	188	8/8/69	7	Clemson	Statesville, N.C.	UFA(NE)-'97	7/0*
55	Houston, Bobby	LB	6-2	245	10/26/67	7	North Carolina State	Hyattsville, Md.	PB(Atl)-'91	15/15
65	Hudson, John	C-G	6-2	276	1/29/68	8	Auburn	Paris, Tenn.	UFA(Phil)-'96	16/0
19	Johnson, Keyshawn	WR	6-3	215	7/22/72	2	Southern California	Los Angeles, Calif.	D1-'96	14/11
52	Johnson, Pepper	LB	6-3	248	7/29/64	12	Ohio State	Detroit, Mich.	UFA(Det)-'97	15/11*
54	Jones, Marvin	LB	6-2	250	6/28/72	5	Florida State	Miami, Fla.	D1-'93	12/12
57	Lewis, Mo	LB	6-3	255	10/21/69	7	Georgia	Peachtree, Ga.	D3-'91	9/9
93	Logan, Ernie	DE	6-3	290	5/18/68	6	East Carolina	Fayetteville, N.C.	UFA(Jax)-'97	4/0*
95	Lyle, Rick	DT-DE	6-5	280	2/26/71	4	Missouri	Hickman Hills, Mo.	UFA(Balt)-'97	13/3*
75	Malamala, Siupeli	G-T	6-5	305	1/15/69	6	Washington	Kalaheo, Hawaii	D3-'92	4/1
24	Mickens, Ray	CB	5-8	180	1/4/73	2	Texas A&M	El Paso, Tex.	D3-'96	15/10
29	Murrell, Adrian	RB	5-11	214	10/16/70	5	West Virginia	Wahiawa, Hawaii	D5b-'93	16/16
22	Neal, Lorenzo	RB	5-11	240	12/27/70	5	Fresno State	Hanford, Calif.	UFA(NO)-'97	16/11*
14	O'Donnell, Neil	QB	6-3	228	7/3/66	8	Maryland	Madison, N.J.	UFA(Pitt)-'96	6/6
70	O'Dwyer, Matt	G	6-5	294	9/1/72	3	Northwestern	Lincolnshire, Ill.	D2-'95	16/16
10	Paci, John	QB	6-3	218	7/19/72	2	Indiana	Huntington, N.Y.	FA-'96	0*
66	Palelei, Lonnie	G	6-3	315	10/15/70	4	Nevada-Las Vegas	Blue Springs, Mo.	FA-'97	0*
5	Silvestri, Don	K	6-4	220	12/25/68	3	Pittsburgh	Perkasie, Pa.	FA-'95	12/0
45	Smith, Otis	CB	5-11	190	10/22/65	8	Missouri	New Orleans, La.	UFA(NE)-'97	13/6*
86	Van Dyke, Alex	WR	6-0	200	7/24/74	2	Nevada	Sacramento, Calif.	D2-'96	15/1
97	Washington, Marvin	DE-DT	6-6	280	10/22/65	9	Idaho	Dallas, Tex.	D6a-'89	14/14
96	White, Reggie	DT	6-5	310	3/22/70	5	North Carolina A&T	Balitmore, Md.	FA-'97	0*
60	Wiegmann, Casey	C	6-3	290	7/20/73	2	Iowa	Parkersburg, Iowa	W(Ind)-'96	0*
73	Williams, David	T	6-5	300	6/21/66	9	Florida	Lakeland, Fla.	FA-'96	14/14

* Brown inactive for 5 games in '96; Dixon played 16 games with Philadelphia; DuBose played 14 games with Tampa Bay; Fiore inactive for 9 games; Henderson played 7 games with New England; P. Johnson played 15 games with Detroit; Logan played 4 games with Jacksonville; Lyle played 13 games with Baltimore; Neal played 16 games with New Orleans; Paci inactive for 9 games; Palelei and White missed '96 season because of injury; Smith played 13 games with New England; Wiegmann inactive for 5 games.

t- Jets traded for Dixon (Philadelphia).

Players lost through free agency (2): T Harry Boatswain (Phil; 16 games in '96); RB Ron Moore (StL; 16).

Also played with Jets in '96—C Dave Alexander (7 games), WR Henry Bailey (8), LB Aubrey Beavers (7), T Harry Boatswain (16), DT Matt Brock (16), S Ron Carpenter (2), DE-DT Mike Chalenski (15), LB Kyle Clifton (16), CB Kwame Ellis (8), DT Jeff Faulkner (4), DE-DT Mark Gunn (9), LB Rick Hamilton (15), T Melvin Hayes (1), DE-DT Erik Howard (1),S Gary Jones (15), DT Brad Keeney (1), K Nick Lowery (16), RB Sherridan May (8), T James Parrish (1), QB Frank Reich (10), WR Phillip Riley (1), WR Webster Slaughter (10), CB Otis Smith (2), DT Mark Spindler (15), DE Brent Williams (5), S Lonnie Young (15), S Eric Zomalt (10).

COACHING STAFF

Head Coach,
Bill Parcells

Pro Career: On February 11, 1997, Parcells was named the Jets' eleventh full-time head coach. Parcells comes to the Jets after having led the New England Patriots to the 1996 AFC Championship and an appearance in Super Bowl XXXI versus the Green Bay Packers. In New England, Parcells inherited a team that went 2-14 in 1992 and began the rebuilding process with a 6-10 campaign in 1993. In just his second year at the helm, Parcells steered the Patriots into the playoffs on the heels of a franchise record seven consecutive victories and a wild-card matchup versus the Cleveland Browns. Over the course of his four year Patriots career, Parcells had a 34-34 record, including 2-2 in the postseason. Parcells made his NFL coaching debut with the Patriots as linebackers coach on Ron Erhardt's staff in 1980. He accepted the same position on the New York Giants staff in 1981 and was named the Giants head coach in 1983. In eight seasons at the helm of the Giants, Parcells led his teams to two Super Bowl championships. His first title came in 1986, with a 39-20 win over the Denver Broncos. Four years later, the Giants claimed another victory over the Buffalo Bills. On May 15, 1991 Parcells resigned from the Giants due to health reasons. During his two years away from coaching, Parcells served as a studio analyst in 1991 and as a color commentator in 1992 for NBC Sports. Career record: 119-86-1.

Background: Linebacker at Wichita State 1961-63. College assistant Hastings (Neb.) 1964, Wichita State 1965, Army 1966-69, Florida State 1970-72, Vanderbilt 1973-74, Texas Tech 1975-77, Air Force 1978 (head coach).

Personal: Born August 22, 1941, Englewood, N.J. Bill and his wife, Judy, live in Sea Girt, N.J., and have three daughters—Suzy, Jill, and Dallas.

ASSISTANT COACHES

Bill Belichick, assistant head coach-defensive backs; born April 16, 1952, Nashville, Tenn., lives on Long Island, N.Y. Center/tight end Wesleyan 1971-74. No pro playing experience. Pro coach: Baltimore Colts 1975, Detroit Lions 1976-77, Denver Broncos 1978, New York Giants 1979-90, Cleveland Browns 1991-95 (head coach), New England Patriots 1996, joined Jets in 1997.

Maurice Carthon, running backs; born April 24, 1961, Chicago, Ill., lives on Long Island, N.Y. Running back Arkansas State 1979-82. Pro running back New York Generals (USFL) 1983-85, New York Giants 1985-91, Indianapolis Colts 1992. Pro coach: New England Patriots 1994-96, joined Jets in 1997.

Romeo Crennel, defensive line; born June 18, 1947, Lynchburgh, Va., lives on Long Island, N.Y. Defensive-offensive tackle, linebacker Western Kentucky 1966-69. No pro playing experience. College coach: Western Kentucky 1970-74, Texas Tech 1975-77, Mississippi 1978-79, Georgia Tech 1980. Pro coach: New York Giants 1981-92, New England Patriots 1993-96, joined Jets in 1997.

Ron Erhardt, quarterbacks-special assistant coach; born February 27, 1931, Mandan, N.D., lives on Long Island, N.Y. Quarterback Jamestown (N.D.) College 1951-54. No pro playing experience. College coach: North Dakota State 1963-72 (head coach 1966-72). Pro coach: New England Patriots 1973-81 (head coach 1979-81), New York Giants 1982-91, Pittsburgh Steelers 1992-95, joined Jets in 1996.

Al Groh, linebackers; born July 13, 1944, New York, N.Y. Defensive end Virginia 1964-67. No pro playing experience. College coach: Army 1968-69, Virginia 1970-72, North Carolina 1973-77, Air Force 1978-79, Texas Tech 1980, Wake Forest 1981-86 (head coach), South Carolina 1988. Pro coach: Atlanta Falcons 1987, New York Giants 1989-91, Cleveland Browns 1992, New England Patriots 1993-96, joined Jets in 1997.

Todd Haley, offensive assistant-quality control; born February 28, 1967, Atlanta, Ga., lives on Long Island, N.Y. No college or pro playing experience. Pro coach: Joined Jets in 1997.

Pat Hodgson, tight ends; born January 30, 1944, Columbus, Ga., lives on Long Island, N.Y. Tight end Georgia 1963-65. Pro tight end Washington Redskins 1966, Minnesota Vikings 1967. College coach: Georgia 1968-70, 1972-77, Florida State 1971, Texas Tech 1978. Pro coach: San Diego Chargers 1978, New York Giants 1979-87, Pittsburgh Steelers 1992-95, joined Jets in 1996.

John Lott, strength and conditioning; born May 9, 1964 in Denton, Tex., lives on Long Island, N.Y. Offensive lineman North Texas State 1983-86. Offensive lineman Pittsburgh Steelers 1987. College coach: North Texas State 1989, Houston 1990-96. Pro coach: Joined Jets in 1997.

Eric Mangini, defensive assistant-quality control; born January 19, 1971, Hartford, Conn., lives on Long Island, N.Y. Defensive tackle Wesleyan 1990-93. No pro playing experience. No college coaching experience. Pro coach: Baltimore Ravens 1996, joined Jets in 1997.

Bill Muir, offensive line; born October 26, 1942, Pittsburgh, Pa., lives on Long Island, N.Y. Tackle Susquehanna 1962-64. No pro playing experience. College coach: Susquehanna 1965, Delaware Valley 1966-67, Rhode Island 1970-71, Idaho State 1972-73, Southern Methodist 1976-77. Pro coach: Orlando (Continental Football League) 1968-69, Houston-Shreveport Steamer (WFL) 1975, New England Patriots 1982-88, Indianapolis Colts 1989-91, Philadelphia Eagles 1992-94, joined Jets in 1995.

Charlie Weis, wide receivers; born March 30, 1956, Trenton, N.J., lives on Long Island, N.Y. No college or pro playing experience. College coach: South Carolina 1985-88. Pro coach: New York Giants 1990-92, New England Patriots 1993-96, joined Jets in 1997.

1997 FIRST-YEAR ROSTER

Name	Pos.	Ht.	Wt.	Birthdate	College	Hometown	How Acq.
Augafa, Patrick	C	6-2	326	11/12/73	Iowa State	American Samoa	FA
Austin, Raymond	CB-S	5-11	190	12/21/74	Tennessee	Lawton, Okla.	D5b
Bolach, Mark	TE	6-6	279	10/7/74	Michigan	Muskegon, Mich.	FA
Burns, Lamont	G	6-4	300	3/16/74	East Carolina	Greensboro, N.C.	D5a
Butler, Duane	S	6-1	203	11/29/73	Illinois State	Trotwood, Ohio	FA
Clements, Chuck	QB	6-3	214	9/29/73	Houston	Huntsville, Tex.	D6b
Cummins, Jeff (1)	DE	6-6	270	6/25/69	Oregon	Torrance, Calif.	FA
Day, Terry	DE	6-4	280	9/18/74	Mississippi State	Pickens, Miss.	D4a
Douglass, Joe	WR	5-11	187	1/21/74	Montana	Salem, Ore.	FA
Doxzon, Todd	WR	6-0	186	3/28/75	Iowa State	Omaha, Neb.	FA
Farmer, Robert	RB	5-11	209	3/4/74	Notre Dame	Bolingbrook, Ill.	FA
Farrior, James	LB	6-2	240	1/6/75	Virginia	Ettrick, Va.	D1
Ferguson, Jason	DT	6-3	305	11/28/74	Georgia	Nettleton, Miss.	D7b
Fogle, Anthony	CB	6-0	191	2/23/75	Oklahoma	Houston, Tex.	FA
Gaine, Brian (1)	TE	6-5	260	4/20/73	Maine	Pearl River, N.Y.	FA
Grooms, Terry	DE	6-4	272	9/18/74	Cincinnati	Rochester, N.Y.	FA
Guest, Craig	LB	6-1	232	12/10/75	Buffalo	North Haven, Conn.	FA
Hagood, Jay	T	6-4	306	8/9/73	Virginia Tech	Easley, S.C.	FA
Hall, John	K	6-3	223	3/17/74	Wisconsin	Port Charlotte, Fla.	FA
Hines, Tyrone	LB	6-1	233	3/14/73	Tennessee	Brownsville, Tenn.	FA
Johnson, Alonzo	WR	5-11	186	4/18/73	Central State, Ohio	Tuscaloosa, Ala.	FA
Johnson, Eric	LB	6-1	238	2/4/74	Illinois State	Pittsburgh, Pa.	FA
Johnson, Ezra	RB	6-0	240	12/19/72	Rutgers	Orange, N.J.	FA
Johnson, Leon	RB	6-0	209	7/13/74	North Carolina	Morganton, N.C.	D4b
Jones, Casey	G	6-4	295	8/22/73	Texas Tech	Shepherd, Tex.	FA
Jones, Jay	WR	6-1	188	2/25/74	James Madison	Richmond, Va.	FA
Kinszer, Zatish (1)	S	6-2	212	8/16/71	Cincinnati	Montclair, NJ	FA
MacInnis, Chris (1)	P	5-11	190	12/19/71	Air Force	North Agusta, S.C.	FA
Rosga, Steve	S	6-1	215	7/10/74	Colorado	Roseville, Minn.	D7a
Scharf, Tim	LB	6-1	244	3/20/75	Northwestern	Rockford, Ill.	D6a
Stark, Troy (1)	T	6-6	305	1/2/73	Georgia	Canandaigua, N.Y.	FA
Terry, Rick	DT	6-4	309	4/5/74	North Carolina	Lexington, N.C.	D2
Walker, Anthony	CB-S	6-0	200	12/6/73	Syracuse	Linthicum, Md.	FA
Ward, Dedric	WR	5-9	180	9/29/74	Northern Iowa	Cedar Rapids, Iowa	D3

The term NFL Rookie is defined as a player who is in his first season of professional football and has not been on the roster of another professional football team for any regular-season or postseason games. A Rookie is designated by an "R" on NFL rosters. Players who have been active in another professional football league or players who have NFL experience, including either preseason training camp or being on an Active List or Inactive List, or on Reserve/Injured or Reserve/Physically Unable to Perform for fewer than six regular-season games, are termed NFL First-Year Players. An NFL First-Year Player is designated by a "1" on NFL rosters. Thereafter, a player is credited with an additional year of experience for each season in which he accumulates six games on the Active List or Inactive List, or on Reserve/Injured or Reserve/Physically Unable to Perform.

NOTES

_____
_____
_____
_____
_____
_____
_____
_____
_____
_____

OAKLAND RAIDERS

**American Football Conference
Western Division
Team Colors:** Silver and Black
**1220 Harbor Bay Parkway
Alameda, California 94502
Telephone:** (510) 864-5000

CLUB OFFICIALS

President of the General Partner: Al Davis
Executive Assistant: Al LoCasale
Senior Assistant: Bruce Allen
Pro Football Scout: George Karras
Personnel Executive: Ken Herock
Legal Affairs: Jeff Birren, Amy Trask,
 Roxanne Critchlow
Finance: Mark Fletcher, Tom Blanda, Marc Badain
Senior Administrator: Morris Bradshaw
Senior Executive: John Herrera
Public Relations: Mike Taylor
Public Relations Assistants: Mario Perez,
 Marc McKinney
Special Projects: Jim Otto
Ticket Operations: Peter Eiges
Trainers: H. Rod Martin, Jonathan Jones,
 Scott Touchet
Equipment Manager: Bob Romanski
Video Director: Dave Nash
Stadium: Oakland-Alameda County Coliseum
 •**Capacity:** 63,026
Playing Surface: Grass
Training Camp: Napa Valley Marriott
 Napa, California 94558

1997 SCHEDULE

PRESEASON

Aug. 3	at Dallas	7:00
Aug. 8	**Green Bay**	7:00
Aug. 16	**New Orleans**	1:00
Aug. 22	at Arizona	7:00

REGULAR SEASON

Aug. 31	at Tennessee	12:00
Sep. 8	**Kansas City** (Mon.)	6:00
Sep. 14	at Atlanta	1:00
Sep. 21	at New York Jets	1:00
Sep. 28	**St. Louis**	1:00
Oct. 5	**San Diego**	1:00
Oct. 12	Open Date	
Oct. 19	**Denver**	1:00
Oct. 26	at Seattle	1:00
Nov. 2	at Carolina	1:00
Nov. 9	**New Orleans**	1:00
Nov. 16	at San Diego	5:00
Nov. 24	at Denver (Mon.)	7:00
Nov. 30	**Miami**	1:00
Dec. 7	at Kansas City	12:00
Dec. 14	**Seattle**	1:00
Dec. 21	**Jacksonville**	1:00

RECORD HOLDERS

INDIVIDUAL RECORDS—CAREER

Category	Name	Performance
Rushing (Yds.)	Marcus Allen, 1982-1992	8,545
Passing (Yds.)	Ken Stabler, 1970-79	19,078
Passing (TDs)	Ken Stabler, 1970-79	150
Receiving (No.)	Fred Biletnikoff, 1965-1978	589
Receiving (Yds.)	Fred Biletnikoff, 1965-1978	8,974
Interceptions	Willie Brown, 1967-1978	39
	Lester Hayes, 1977-1986	39
Punting (Avg.)	Ray Guy, 1973-1986	42.5
Punt Return (Avg.)	Claude Gibson, 1963-65	12.6
Kickoff Return (Avg.)	Jack Larscheid, 1960-61	28.4
Field Goals	Chris Bahr, 1980-88	162
Touchdowns (Tot.)	Marcus Allen, 1982-1992	98
Points	George Blanda, 1967-1975	863

INDIVIDUAL RECORDS—SINGLE SEASON

Category	Name	Performance
Rushing (Yds.)	Marcus Allen, 1985	1,759
Passing (Yds.)	Ken Stabler, 1979	3,615
Passing (TDs)	Daryle Lamonica, 1969	34
Receiving (No.)	Todd Christensen, 1986	95
Receiving (Yds.)	Art Powell, 1964	1,361
Interceptions	Lester Hayes, 1980	13
Punting (Avg.)	Ray Guy, 1973	45.3
Punt Return (Avg.)	Claude Gibson, 1964	14.4
Kickoff Return (Avg.)	Harold Hart, 1975	30.5
Field Goals	Jeff Jaeger, 1993	35
Touchdowns (Tot.)	Marcus Allen, 1984	18
Points	Jeff Jaeger, 1993	132

INDIVIDUAL RECORDS—SINGLE GAME

Category	Name	Performance
Rushing (Yds.)	Bo Jackson, 11-30-87	221
Passing (Yds.)	Jeff Hostetler, 10-31-93	424
Passing (TDs)	Tom Flores, 12-22-63	6
	Daryle Lamonica, 10-19-69	6
Receiving (No.)	Dave Casper, 10-3-76	12
	Tim Brown, 12-19-95	12
Receiving (Yds.)	Art Powell, 12-22-63	247
Interceptions	Many times	3
	Last time by Terry McDaniel, 10-9-94	
Field Goals	Jeff Jaeger, 12-11-94	5
Touchdowns (Tot.)	Art Powell, 12-22-63	4
	Marcus Allen, 9-24-84	4
Points	Art Powell, 12-22-63	24
	Marcus Allen, 9-24-84	24

COACHING HISTORY

**OAKLAND 1960-1981
LOS ANGELES 1982-1994
(349-224-11)**

1960-61	Eddie Erdelatz*	6-10-0
1961-62	Marty Feldman**	2-15-0
1962	Red Conkright	1-8-0
1963-65	Al Davis	23-16-3
1966-68	John Rauch	35-10-1
1969-78	John Madden	112-39-7
1979-87	Tom Flores	91-56-0
1988-89	Mike Shanahan***	8-12-0
1989-94	Art Shell	56-41-0
1995-96	Mike White	15-17-0

 *Released after two games in 1961
**Released after five games in 1962
***Released after four games in 1989

OAKLAND-ALAMEDA COUNTY COLISEUM

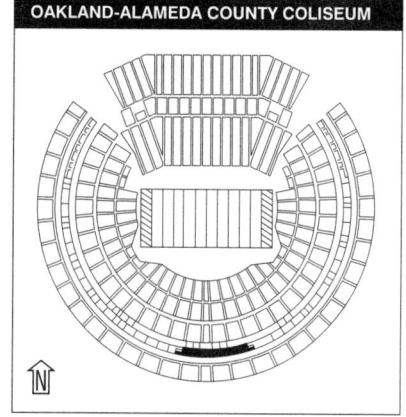

1996 TEAM RECORD

PRESEASON (2-3)

Date	Result		Opponents
7/27	L	34-35	at Dallas
8/2	W	26-3	at Arizona
8/8	L	19-24	Seattle
8/15	L	6-27	at Atlanta
8/23	W	44-27	N.Y. Jets

REGULAR SEASON (7-9)

Date	Result		Opponents	Att.
9/1	L	14-19	at Baltimore	64,124
9/8	L	3-19	at Kansas City	79,281
9/15	W	17-3	Jacksonville	46,291
9/22	L	34-40	San Diego	49,097
9/29	L	17-19	at Chicago	57,062
10/6	W	34-13	at N.Y. Jets	63,611
10/13	W	37-21	Detroit	50,037
10/21	W	23-14	at San Diego	62,350
11/4	L	21-22	Denver	61,179
11/10	L	17-20	at Tampa Bay (OT)	45,392
11/17	L	13-16	Minnesota (OT)	41,183
11/24	W	27-21	at Seattle	47,506
12/1	W	17-7	Miami	60,591
12/9	W	26-7	Kansas City	57,082
12/15	L	19-24	at Denver	75,466
12/22	L	21-28	Seattle	33,455

(OT) Overtime

SCORE BY PERIODS

Raiders	42	128	83	87	0	— 340
Opponents	69	65	65	88	6	— 293

ATTENDANCE

Home 398,915   Away 494,792   Total 893,707
Single-game home record, 61,179 (11/4/96)
Single-season home record, 398,915 (1996)

1996 TEAM STATISTICS

	Raiders	Opp.
Total First Downs	306	292
Rushing	98	97
Passing	172	162
Penalty	36	33
Third Down: Made/Att	91/224	74/217
Third Down Pct.	40.6	34.1
Fourth Down: Made/Att	9/14	7/14
Fourth Down Pct.	64.3	50.0
Total Net Yards	5252	4697
Avg. Per Game	328.3	293.6
Total Plays	1034	1010
Avg. Per Play	5.1	4.7
Net Yards Rushing	2174	1676
Avg. Per Game	135.9	104.8
Total Rushes	456	463
Net Yards Passing	3078	3021
Avg. Per Game	192.4	188.8
Sacked/Yards Lost	45/249	34/252
Gross Yards	3327	3273
Att./Completions	533/311	513/284
Completion Pct.	58.3	55.4
Had Intercepted	19	17
Punts/Avg.	79/40.1	85/41.9
Net Punting Avg.	79/34.6	85/35.3
Penalties/Yards Lost	156/1266	113/965
Fumbles/Ball Lost	30/12	18/9
Touchdowns	38	31
Rushing	7	7
Passing	28	22
Returns	3	2
Avg. Time of Possession	30:39	29:21

1996 INDIVIDUAL STATISTICS

PASSING

	Att.	Comp.	Yds.	Pct.	TD	Int.	Tkld.	Rate
Hostetler	402	242	2548	60.2	23	14	32/181	83.2
Hobert	104	57	667	54.8	4	5	9/52	67.3
Klingler	24	10	87	41.7	0	0	4/16	51.9
Williams	2	1	18	50.0	1	0	0/0	120.8
Hobbs	1	1	7	100.0	0	0	0/0	95.8
Raiders	533	311	3327	58.3	28	19	45/249	79.4
Opponents	513	284	3273	55.4	22	17	34/252	75.3

SCORING

	TD R	TD P	TD Rt	PAT	FG	Saf	PTS
Ford	0	0	0	36/36	24/31	0	108
T. Brown	0	9	0	0/0	0/0	0	54
Fenner	4	4	0	0/0	0/0	0	48
Dudley	0	4	0	0/0	0/0	0	24
Jett	0	4	0	0/0	0/0	0	24
Hobbs	0	3	0	0/0	0/0	0	18
Kaufman	1	1	0	0/0	0/0	0	12
Shedd	0	1	0	0/0	0/0	1	8
Aska	1	0	0	0/0	0/0	0	6
Ball	0	0	1	0/0	0/0	0	6
Cunningham	0	1	0	0/0	0/0	0	6
A. Glover	0	1	0	0/0	0/0	0	6
Hostetler	1	0	0	0/0	0/0	0	6
Johnstone	0	0	1	0/0	0/0	0	6
McDaniel	0	0	1	0/0	0/0	0	6
Raiders	7	28	3	36/36	24/31	*2	340
Opponents	7	22	2	26/26	25/34	1	293

2-Point conversions: 0. Team: 0-2, Opponents: 2-5.
* Raiders were credited with 1 team safety.

RUSHING

	Att.	Yds.	Avg.	LG	TD
Kaufman	150	874	5.8	77	0
Williams	121	431	3.6	44	0
Aska	62	326	5.3	38	1
Fenner	67	245	3.7	17	4
Hostetler	37	179	4.8	17	1
Klingler	4	36	9.0	14	0
T. Brown	6	35	5.8	15	0
Gossett	3	28	9.3	18	0
Hobert	2	13	6.5	14	0
Hall	3	7	2.3	4	0
Araguz	1	0	0.0	0	0
Raiders	456	2174	4.8	77	7
Opponents	463	1676	3.6	42	7

RECEIVING

	No.	Yds.	Avg.	LG	TD
T. Brown	90	1104	12.3	42t	9
Hobbs	44	423	9.6	29	3
Jett	43	601	14.0	58t	4
Dudley	34	386	11.4	62t	4
Fenner	31	252	8.1	23t	4
Kaufman	22	143	6.5	19	1
Williams	22	143	6.5	20	0
A. Glover	9	101	11.2	25	1
Aska	8	63	7.9	22	0
Davison	4	21	5.3	8	0
Shedd	3	87	29.0	51	1
Cunningham	1	3	3.0	3t	1
Raiders	311	3327	10.7	62t	28
Opponents	284	3273	11.5	82t	22

INTERCEPTIONS

	No.	Yds.	Avg.	LG	TD
McDaniel	5	150	30.0	56t	1
Lynch	3	75	25.0	35	0
Morton	2	13	6.5	13	0
Lewis	2	0	0.0	0	0
Ball	1	66	66.0	66t	1
Trapp	1	23	23.0	23	0
Carrington	1	21	21.0	21	0
L. Brown	1	4	4.0	4	0
Kidd	1	1	1.0	1	0
Biekert	0	0	—	0	0
Raiders	17	353	20.8	66t	2
Opponents	19	257	13.5	83t	1

PUNTING

	No.	Yds.	Avg.	In 20	LG
Gossett	57	2264	39.7	19	64
Araguz	13	534	41.1	4	52
Hobert	9	371	41.2	1	53
Raiders	79	3169	40.1	24	64
Opponents	85	3562	41.9	23	68

PUNT RETURNS

	No.	FC	Yds.	Avg.	LG	TD
T. Brown	32	21	272	8.5	36	0
Hobbs	10	3	84	8.4	35	0
Kidd	0	0	47	—	47	0
Raiders	42	24	403	9.6	50	0
Opponents	38	21	272	7.2	35	0

KICKOFF RETURNS

	No.	Yds.	Avg.	LG	TD
Kidd	29	622	21.4	48	0
Kaufman	25	548	21.9	39	0
Shedd	3	51	17.0	19	0
Aska	1	17	17.0	17	0
T. Brown	1	24	24.0	24	0
Gossett	1	0	0.0	0	0
Hobbs	1	14	14.0	14	0
Raiders	61	1276	20.9	48	0
Opponents	55	1129	20.5	55	0

SACKS

	No.
McGlockton	8.0
Swilling	6.0
Bruce	4.0
Ball	3.0
Lewis	3.0
Harrison	2.0
Maryland	2.0
Smith	2.0
Holmberg	1.0
Johnstone	1.0
M. Jones	1.0
Morton	1.0
Raiders	34.0
Opponents	45.0

1997 DRAFT CHOICES

Round	Name	Pos.	College
1	Darrell Russell	DT	Southern California
3	Adam Treu	G	Nebraska
	Tim Kohn	G	Iowa State
4	Chad Levitt	RB	Cornell
6	Calvin Branch	DB	Colorado State
	Grady Jackson	DT	Knoxville

OAKLAND RAIDERS

1997 VETERAN ROSTER

No.	Name	Pos.	Ht.	Wt.	Birthdate	NFL Exp.	College	Hometown	How Acq.	'96 Games/ Starts
33	Anderson, Eddie	S	6-1	210	7/22/63	12	Fort Valley State	Warner Robbins, Ga.	FA-'87	7/5
35	Aska, Joe	RB	5-11	240	7/14/72	3	Central Oklahoma	Putnam City, Okla.	D3-'95	15/2
54	Biekert, Greg	LB	6-2	240	3/14/69	5	Colorado	Longmont, Colo.	D7-93	16/15
24	Brown, Larry	CB	5-11	185	11/30/69	7	Texas Christian	Los Angeles, Calif.	UFA(Dall)-'96	8/1
81	Brown, Tim	WR	6-0	195	7/22/66	10	Notre Dame	Dallas, Tex.	D1-'88	16/16
99	Bruce, Aundray	DE	6-5	265	4/30/66	10	Auburn	Montgomery, Ala.	PB(Atl)-'92	16/0
59	# Butcher, Paul	LB	6-0	225	11/8/63	11	Wayne State	Dearborn, Mich.	FA-'96	16/0
21	# Carrington, Darren	S	6-2	200	10/10/66	9	Northern Arizona	Bronx, N.Y.	UFA(Jax)-'96	14/9
20	Carter, Perry	CB	6-0	190	8/5/71	3	Southern Mississippi	Magnolia, Miss.	FA-'96	4/0
68	Cunningham, Rick	G	6-7	315	1/4/69	7	Texas A&M	Beverly Hills, Calif.	FA-'96	13/0
83	Dudley, Rickey	TE	6-6	245	7/15/72	2	Ohio State	Hendersonville, Tex.	D1-'96	13/0
95	Faumui, Taase	DT	6-3	290	3/19/71	3	Hawaii	Honolulu, Hawaii	FA-'97	0*
55	Folston, James	LB	6-3	235	8/14/71	4	Northeast Louisiana	Cocoa, Fla.	D2-'94	12/0
5	Ford, Cole	K	6-2	210	12/31/72	3	Southern California	Tucson, Ariz.	FA-'95	16/0
53	Fredrickson, Rob	LB	6-4	240	5/13/71	4	Michigan State	St. Joseph, Mich.	D1-'94	10/10
3	George, Jeff	QB	6-4	215	12/8/67	7	Illinois	Indianapolis, Ind.	FA-'97	3/3*
87	# Glover, Andrew	TE	6-6	250	8/12/67	7	Grambling State	Geismar, La.	D10-'91	14/4
75	Harlow, Pat	T	6-6	295	3/16/69	7	Southern California	Norco, Ill.	T(NE)-'96	10/9
12	Hollas, Don	QB	6-3	215	11/22/67	5	Rice	Rosenberg, Tex.	FA-'97	0*
57	Holmberg, Rob	LB	6-3	230	5/6/71	4	Penn State	Mt. Pleasant, Pa.	D7-'94	13/1
71	Holmes, Lester	G	6-4	315	9/27/69	5	Jackson State	Tylertown, Miss.	UFA(Phil)-'97	16/14*
15	Hostetler, Jeff	QB	6-3	220	4/22/61	14	West Virginia	Davidsville, Pa.	UFA(NYG)-'93	13/13
21	Howard, Desmond	KR	5-10	180	5/15/70	6	Michigan	Cleveland, Ohio	UFA(GB)-'97	16/0*
64	Jenkins, Robert	T	6-5	295	12/30/63	11	UCLA	Dublin, Calif.	FA-'94	10/6
82	Jett, James	WR	5-10	165	12/28/70	5	West Virginia	Kearneysville, W. Va.	FA-'93	16/16
98	Johnson, Kevin	DT	6-1	305	10/30/70	3	Texas Southern	Los Angeles, Calif.	FA-'97	12/5*
51	Johnstone, Lance	DE	6-4	245	6/11/73	2	Temple	Philadelphia, Pa.	D2-'96	16/10
26	Kaufman, Napoleon	RB	5-9	185	6/7/73	3	Washington	Lompoc, Calif.	D1-'95	16/9
72	Kennedy, Lincoln	T	6-6	335	2/12/71	5	Washington	San Diego, Calif.	T(Atl)-'96	16/16
46	Kidd, Carl	CB	6-1	200	6/14/73	3	Arkansas	Pine Bluff, Ark.	FA-'95	16/0
7	Klingler, David	QB	6-3	210	2/17/69	6	Houston	Stratford, Tex.	UFA(Cin)-'96	1/0
79	Kysar, Jeff	T	6-7	335	6/14/72	3	Arizona State	San Diego, Calif.	D5-'95	0*
25	Land, Dan	S	6-0	195	7/3/65	9	Albany State	Donalsonville, Ga.	FA-'89	16/2
29	Lewis, Albert	CB	6-2	205	10/6/60	15	Grambling State	Mansfield, La.	UFA(KC)-'94	16/13
43	Lynch, Lorenzo	S	5-11	200	4/6/63	11	Cal State-Sacramento	Oakland, Calif.	FA-'96	16/16
44	Lyons, Lamar	S	6-3	210	3/25/63	2	Washington	Santa Monica, Calif.	FA-'96	6/0
97	Maryland, Russell	DT	6-1	290	3/22/69	7	Miami	Chicago, Ill.	UFA(Dall)-'96	16/16
36	McDaniel, Terry	CB	5-10	180	2/8/65	10	Tennessee	Saginaw, Mich.	D1-'88	16/15
91	McGlockton, Chester	DT	6-4	320	9/16/69	6	Clemson	Whiteville, N.C.	D1-'92	16/16
50	Morton, Mike	LB	6-4	235	3/28/72	3	North Carolina	Kannapolis, N.C.	D4-'95	16/16
63	Robbins, Barret	C	6-3	305	8/26/73	3	Texas Christian	Houston, Tex.	D2-'95	14/14
84	Shedd, Kenny	WR	5-10	170	2/14/71	3	Northern Iowa	Davenport, Iowa	FA-'96	16/1
94	Smith, Anthony	DE	6-3	270	6/28/67	8	Arizona	Elizabeth City, N.C.	D1-'90	6/4
80	Smith, Kevin	TE	6-4	265	7/25/69	3	UCLA	Oakland, Calif.	FA-'97	0*
77	# Stephens, Rich	G	6-7	315	1/1/65	4	Tulsa	House Springs, Mo.	FA-'92	0*
56	Swilling, Pat	DE	6-3	250	10/25/64	12	Georgia Tech	Toccoa, Ga.	UFA(Det)-'95	16/16
37	Trapp, James	S	6-0	190	12/28/69	5	Clemson	Lawton, Okla.	D3-'93	12/4
88	Truitt, Olanda	WR	6-0	195	1/4/71	5	Mississippi State	Birmingham, Ala.	FA-'06	10/0
67	# Turk, Dan	C	6-4	295	8/25/62	13	Wisconsin	Milwaukee, Wis.	FA-'89	16/2
42	Turner, Eric	S	6-1	205	9/20/68	7	UCLA	Ventura, Calif.	FA-'97	14/14*
73	Villa, Danny	C	6-5	310	9/21/64	11	Arizona State	Nogales, Ariz.	FA-'97	16/0*
22	Williams, Harvey	RB	6-2	215	4/22/67	7	Louisiana State	Hempstead, Tex.	UFA(KC)-'94	13/5
76	Wisniewski, Steve	G	6-2	290	4/7/67	9	Penn State	Houston, Tex.	D2-'89	16/16

* Faumui last active with Pittsburgh in '95; George played 3 games with Atlanta in '96; Hollas last active with Cincinnati in '94; Holmes played 16 games with Philadelphia; Howard played 16 games with Green Bay; Johnson played 12 games with Philadelphia; Kysar missed '96 season because of injury; K. Smith last active with Oakland in '94; Stephens last active with Oakland in '95; Turner played 14 games with Baltimore; Villa played 16 games with Kansas City.

\# Unrestricted free agent; subject to developments.

Traded—WR Daryl Hobbs (16 games in '96) to New Orleans; QB Billy Joe Hobert (8) to Buffalo.

Retired—Charles McRae, 6-year tackle, 13 games in '96.

Players lost through free agency (2): Kevin Gogan (SF; 16 games in '96), LB Mike Jones (StL; 15).

Also played with Raiders in '96—DT Jerry Ball (16 games), P Rich Camarillo (1), RB Jerone Davison (2), RB Derrick Fenner (16), DT La Roi Glover (2), P Jeff Gossett (12), RB Tim Hall (2), DT Nolan Harrison (15), TE Marcus Hinton (2), TE Trey Junkin (6).

COACHING STAFF

Head Coach,
Joe Bugel

Pro Career: Became the eleventh head coach in Raider history on January 30, 1997, after two years as assistant head coach/offense for the organization. First joined Raiders in that capacity in 1995, also directing the offensive line. First came into pro coaching as an assistant with Detroit Lions in 1975-76. From 1977-80 was offensive line coach with Houston Oilers. From 1981-89 was assistant head coach for Washington Redskins on Joe Gibbs' staff, with three Super Bowl appearances, including World Championships in 1982 and 1987. In 17 seasons as NFL assistant coach his teams were 159-99 for a .616 winning percentage. Head coach Phoenix Cardinals, 1990-93, with 20-44 record, including 7-9 in his final season. Career record: 20-44.

Background: Offensive guard and linebacker at Western Kentucky 1960-63 while earning degree in physical education. Received a master's degree in counseling from Western Kentucky in 1964. Began his 32-year coaching career at Western Kentucky in 1964, remaining there through 1968. In 1969 began four-year stint as an assistant at United States Naval Academy before moving to Iowa State in 1973. His final year as a college assistant coach was at Ohio State under legendary head coach Woody Hayes in 1974.

Personal: Born March 10, 1940, Pittsburgh, Pa. Joe and wife, Brenda, live in Alameda, Calif. Their family includes daughters Holly, Jennifer, and Angela.

ASSISTANT COACHES

Dave Adolph, linebackers; born June 6, 1937, Akron, Ohio, lives in Alameda, Calif. Guard-linebacker Akron 1955-58. No pro playing experience. College coach: Akron 1963-64, Connecticut 1965-68, Kentucky 1969-72, Illinois 1973-76, Ohio State 1977-78. Pro coach: Cleveland Browns 1979-84, 1986-88, San Diego Chargers 1985, 1995-96, Los Angeles Raiders 1989-91, Kansas City Chiefs 1992-94, rejoined Raiders in 1997.

Fred Biletnikoff, wide receivers; born February 23, 1943, Erie, Pa., lives in Danville, Calif. Wide receiver Florida State 1962-64. Pro wide receiver Oakland Raiders 1965-78, Montreal Alouettes (CFL) 1980. College coach: Palomar, (Calif.), J.C. 1983, Diablo Valley, (Calif.), J.C. 1984, 1986. Pro coach: Oakland Invaders (USFL) 1985, Calgary Stampeders (CFL) 1987-88, joined Raiders in 1989.

Willie Brown, cornerbacks and squad development; born December 2, 1940, Yazoo City, Miss., lives in San Ramon, Calif. Defensive back Grambling 1959-62. Pro defensive back Denver Broncos 1963-66, Oakland Raiders 1967-78. College coach: Long Beach State 1990-91 (head coach 1991). Pro coach: Oakland/Los Angeles Raiders 1979-88, re-joined Raiders in 1995.

Garrett Giemont, strength and conditioning; born August 31, 1957, Fullerton, Calif., lives in Alameda, Calif. No college or pro playing experience. Pro coach: Los Angeles Rams 1990-91, joined Raiders in 1995.

John Guy, defensive line; born May 26, 1951, Greensboro, N.C., lives in Alameda, Calif. Defensive back-kicker North Carolina A&T 1969-72. No pro playing experience. College coach: North Carolina 1973-77, Virginia Tech 1978, Duke 1978-80, Georgia Tech 1981-86, Alabama 1987-89, Kentucky 1990-91. Pro coach: Pittsburgh Steelers 1992-93, joined Raiders in 1995.

Bishop Harris, running backs; born November 23, 1941, Phenix City, Ala., lives in Alameda, Calif. Running back and defensive back North Carolina College 1960-63. No pro playing experience. College coach: Duke 1972-75, North Carolina State 1977-79, Louisiana State 1980-83, Notre Dame 1984-85, Minnesota 1986-90, North Carolina Central 1991-92 (head coach). Pro coach: Denver Broncos 1993-94, joined Raiders in 1995.

Bill Meyers, tight ends; born October 8, 1946, Chippewa Falls, Wis., lives in Alameda, Calif. Tackle Stanford 1970-71. No pro playing experience. College coach: California 1972-73, 1977-78, Santa Clara 1974-76, Notre Dame 1979-81, Missouri 1985-86, Pittsburgh 1987-92. Pro coach: Green Bay Packers 1982-83, Pittsburgh Steelers 1984, joined Raiders in 1993.

Ray Perkins, offensive coordinator; born November 6, 1941, Mount Olive, Miss., lives in Alameda, Calif. Wide receiver Alabama 1964-66. Pro wide receiver Baltimore Colts 1967-71. College coach: Mississippi State 1973, Alabama 1983-86 (head coach), Arkansas State 1992 (head coach). Pro coach: New England Patriots 1974-77, 1993-96, San Diego Chargers 1978, New York Giants 1979-82 (head coach), Tampa Bay Buccaneers 1987-90 (head coach), joined Raiders in 1997.

Keith Rowen, assistant head coach-offense/offensive line; born September 2, 1952, New York, N.Y., lives in San Ramon, Calif. Offensive tackle Stanford 1972-74. No pro playing experience. College coach: Stanford 1975-76, Long Beach State 1977-78, Arizona 1979-82. Pro coach: Boston/New Orleans Breakers (USFL) 1983-84, Cleveland Browns 1984, Indianapolis Colts 1985-88, New England Patriots 1989, Atlanta Falcons 1990-93, Minnesota Vikings 1994-96, joined Raiders in 1997.

Steve Shafer, safeties; born December 8, 1940, Glendale, Calif., lives in Alameda, Calif. Quarterback-defensive back Utah State 1961-62. Pro defensive back British Columbia Lions (CFL) 1963-67. College coach: San Mateo (Calif.) J.C. 1968-74 (head coach 1973-74), San Diego State 1975-82, 1994. Pro coach: Los Angeles Rams 1983-90, Tampa Bay Buccaneers 1991-93, joined Raiders in 1995.

Kevin Spencer, quality control-defense; born November 2, 1953, Queens, N.Y., lives in Danville, Calif. No college or pro playing experience. College coach: State University of New York 1975-76, Cornell 1979-80, Ithaca 1981-86, Wesleyan 1987-91 (head coach). Pro coach: Cleveland Browns 1991-94, joined Raiders in 1995.

Rusty Tillman, special teams; born February 27, 1946, Beloit, Wis., lives in Alameda, Calif. Linebacker Arizona 1966-67, Northern Arizona 1968-69. Pro linebacker Washington Redskins 1970-77. Pro coach: Seattle Seahawks 1979-94, Tampa Bay Buccaneers 1995, joined Raiders in 1996.

Bill Urbanik, defensive line; born December 27, 1946, Donora, Pa., lives in Castro Valley, Calif. Lineman Ohio State 1965-68. No pro playing experience. College coach: Marshall 1971-73, 1975, Northern Illinois 1976-78, Wake Forest 1979-83. Pro coach: Cincinnati Bengals 1984-88, Los Angeles Raiders 1989-90, Sacramento Goldminers (CFL) 1993-94, rejoined Raiders in 1997.

Fred Whittingham, defensive coordinator; born February 4, 1939, Boston, Mass., lives in Alameda, Calif. Tight end-linebacker Brigham Young 1957-58, Cal Poly-SLO 1961-62. Pro linebacker Los Angeles Rams 1963-64, Philadelphia Eagles 1965-66, 1971, New Orleans Saints 1967-70. College coach: Brigham Young 1973-81, Utah 1992-94. Pro coach: Los Angeles Rams 1982-91, joined Raiders in 1995.

1997 FIRST-YEAR ROSTER

Name	Pos.	Ht.	Wt.	Birthdate	College	Hometown	How Acq.
Araguz, Leo (1)	P	5-11	185	1/18/70	Stephen F. Austin	Harlington, Tex.	FA-'96
Branch, Calvin	CB	5-11	200	5/8/74	Colorado State	Spring, Tex.	D6
Branscomb, Kenyon (1)	WR	6-2	200	6/13/70	Oregon State	Beaverton, Ore.	FA
Cooper, Obadiah	WR	5-8	160	3/8/70	Eastern Illinois	San Bernardino, Calif.	FA
Davis, Jason	QB	6-4	220	1/11/73	Western State	Springerville, Ariz.	FA
Davison, Jerone (1)	RB	6-1	235	9/16/70	Arizona State	Picayune, Miss.	FA
Glover, La'Roi (1)	DT	6-1	285	7/4/74	San Diego State	San Diego, Calif.	D5-'96
Grace, Kenny (1)	WR	5-10	165	12/29/72	Southern California	El Sobrante, Calif.	FA
Hall, Tim (1)	RB	5-11	220	2/15/74	Robert Morris	Kansas City, Mo.	D6-'96
Hervey, Ed (1)	WR	6-2	190	5/4/73	Southern California	Compton, Calif.	FA
Hinton, Marcus (1)	TE	6-4	260	12/27/71	Alcorn State	Wiggins, Miss.	FA-'95
Ioja, Adrian	LB	6-2	245	10/17/74	San Diego State	Garden Grove, Calif.	FA
Jackson, Grady	DT	6-2	320	1/21/73	Knoxville	Greensboro, Ala.	D6
Kirkman, Darron	RB	5-11	235	4/4/73	Oregon State	Chicago, Ill.	FA
Kohn, Tim	G	6-5	315	12/6/73	Iowa State	Wadsworth, Ill.	D3
Levitt, Chad	RB	6-1	230	11/21/75	Cornell	Melrose Park, Pa.	D4
Montez, Alfred (1)	QB	6-2	235	10/18/72	Western New Mexico	Grenada, Colo.	FA-'96
Muirbrook, Shay	LB	6-0	230	11/15/73	Brigham Young	Norco, Calif.	FA
Rosenstiel, Robert	TE	6-3	240	2/7/74	Eastern Illinois	Junction City, Ore.	FA
Russell, Darrell	DT	6-5	320	5/27/76	Southern California	San Diego, Calif.	D1
Sargeant, Shatony	DE	6-5	285	9/27/75	Fresno City	Long Beach, Calif.	FA
Thompson, Chris (1)	DE	6-4	260	6/17/70	Bowie State	Clinton, Md.	FA
Treu, Adam	G	6-5	300	6/24/74	Nebraska	Lincoln, Neb.	D3
Whittaker, Scott	T	6-7	305	5/7/74	Kansas	Alta Loma, Calif.	FA
Wylie, Joey (1)	C	6-3	305	4/25/74	Stephen F. Austin	Santa Fe, Tex.	D7-'96

The term NFL Rookie is defined as a player who is in his first season of professional football and has not been on the roster of another professional football team for any regular-season or postseason games. A Rookie is designated by an "R" on NFL rosters. Players who have been active in another professional football league or players who have NFL experience, including either preseason training camp or being on an Active List or Inactive List, or on Reserve/Injured or Reserve/Physically Unable to Perform for fewer than six regular-season games, are termed NFL First-Year Players. An NFL First-Year Player is designated by a "1" on NFL rosters. Thereafter, a player is credited with an additional year of experience for each season in which he accumulates six games on the Active List or Inactive List, or on Reserve/Injured or Reserve/Physically Unable to Perform.

NOTES

PITTSBURGH STEELERS

American Football Conference
Central Division
Team Colors: Black and Gold
Three Rivers Stadium
300 Stadium Circle
Pittsburgh, Pennsylvania 15212
Telephone: (412) 323-0300

CLUB OFFICIALS
President: Daniel M. Rooney
Vice President: John R. McGinley
Vice President: Arthur J. Rooney, Jr.
Vice President/General Counsel: Arthur J. Rooney II
Administration Advisor: Charles H. Noll
Director of Marketing: Mark Fuhrman
Public Relations Coordinator: Rob Boulware
Director of Business: Mark Hart
Business Controller: Dan Ferens
Accounts Controller: Jim Ellenberger
Director of Football Operations: Tom Donahoe
College Personnel Director: Tom Modrak
Pro Personnel Coordinator: Charles Bailey
College Scouts: Mark Gorscak, Phil Kreidler,
   Bob Lane, Max McCartney
Office/Ticket Manager: Geraldine R. Glenn
Player Development Coordinator: Anthony Griggs
Trainers: John Norwig, Rick Burkholder
Equipment Manager: Rodgers Freyvogel
Stadium: Three Rivers Stadium
   •**Capacity:** 59,600
   300 Stadium Circle
   Pittsburgh, Pennsylvania 15212
Playing Surface: AstroTurf
Training Camp: St. Vincent College
   Latrobe, Pennsylvania 15650

1997 SCHEDULE
PRESEASON
July 27	vs. Chicago at Dublin, Ireland	1:00
Aug. 2	at Kansas City	7:00
Aug. 11	**Philadelphia**	8:00
Aug. 17	**Detroit**	8:00
Aug. 22	at Carolina	8:00

REGULAR SEASON
Aug. 31	**Dallas**	1:00
Sept. 7	**Washington**	1:00
Sept. 14	Open Date	
Sept. 22	at Jacksonville (Mon.)	9:00
Sept. 28	**Tennessee**	1:00
Oct. 5	at Baltimore	1:00
Oct. 12	**Indianapolis**	8:00
Oct. 19	at Cincinnati	4:00
Oct. 26	**Jacksonville**	4:00
Nov. 3	at Kansas City (Mon.)	8:00
Nov. 9	**Baltimore**	8:00
Nov. 16	**Cincinnati**	1:00
Nov. 23	at Philadelphia	1:00
Nov. 30	at Arizona	2:00
Dec. 7	**Denver**	1:00
Dec. 13	at New England (Sat.)	4:00
Dec. 21	at Tennessee	12:00

RECORD HOLDERS
INDIVIDUAL RECORDS—CAREER
Category	Name	Performance
Rushing (Yds.)	Franco Harris, 1972-1983	11,950
Passing (Yds.)	Terry Bradshaw, 1970-1983	27,989
Passing (TDs)	Terry Bradshaw, 1970-1983	212
Receiving (No.)	John Stallworth, 1974-1987	537
Receiving (Yds.)	John Stallworth, 1974-1987	8,723
Interceptions	Mel Blount, 1970-1983	57
Punting (Avg.)	Bobby Joe Green, 1960-61	45.7
Punt Return (Avg.)	Bobby Gage, 1949-1950	14.9
Kickoff Return (Avg.)	Lynn Chandnois, 1950-56	29.6
Field Goals	Gary Anderson, 1982-1994	309
Touchdowns (Tot.)	Franco Harris, 1972-1983	100
Points	Gary Anderson, 1982-1994	1,343

INDIVIDUAL RECORDS—SINGLE SEASON
Category	Name	Performance
Rushing (Yds.)	Barry Foster, 1992	1,690
Passing (Yds.)	Terry Bradshaw, 1979	3,724
Passing (TDs)	Terry Bradshaw, 1978	28
Receiving (No.)	Yancey Thigpen, 1995	85
Receiving (Yds.)	John Stallworth, 1984	1,395
Interceptions	Mel Blount, 1975	11
Punting (Avg.)	Bobby Joe Green, 1961	47.0
Punt Return (Avg.)	Bobby Gage, 1949	16.0
Kickoff Return (Avg.)	Lynn Chandnois, 1952	35.2
Field Goals	Norm Johnson, 1995	34
Touchdowns (Tot.)	Louis Lipps, 1985	15
Points	Norm Johnson, 1995	141

INDIVIDUAL RECORDS—SINGLE GAME
Category	Name	Performance
Rushing (Yds.)	John Fuqua, 12-20-70	218
Passing (Yds.)	Bobby Layne, 12-3-58	409
Passing (TDs)	Terry Bradshaw, 11-15-81	5
	Mark Malone, 9-8-85	5
Receiving (No.)	J.R. Wilburn, 10-22-67	12
Receiving (Yds.)	Buddy Dial, 10-22-61	235
Interceptions	Jack Butler, 12-13-53	*4
Field Goals	Gary Anderson, 10-23-88	6
Touchdowns (Tot.)	Ray Mathews, 10-17-54	4
	Roy Jefferson, 11-3-68	4
Points	Ray Mathews, 10-17-54	24
	Roy Jefferson, 11-3-68	24

*NFL Record

COACHING HISTORY
Pittsburgh Pirates 1933-1940
(427-444-20)
1933	Forrest (Jap) Douds	3-6-2
1934	Luby DiMelio	2-10-0
1935-36	Joe Bach	10-14-0
1937-39	Johnny (Blood) McNally*	6-19-0
1939-40	Walt Kiesling	3-13-3
1941	Bert Bell**	0-2-0
	Aldo (Buff) Donelli***	0-5-0
1941-44	Walt Kiesling****	13-20-2
1945	Jim Leonard	2-8-0
1946-47	Jock Sutherland	13-10-1
1948-51	Johnny Michelosen	20-26-2
1952-53	Joe Bach	11-13-0
1954-56	Walt Kiesling	14-22-0
1957-64	Raymond (Buddy) Parker	51-48-6
1965	Mike Nixon	2-12-0
1966-68	Bill Austin	11-28-3
1969-91	Chuck Noll	209-156-1
1992-96	Bill Cowher	57-32-0

*Released after three games in 1939
**Resigned after two games in 1941
***Released after five games in 1941
****Co-coach with Earle (Greasy) Neale in Philadelphia-
   Pittsburgh merger in 1943 and with Phil Handler in
   Chicago Cardinals-Pittsburgh merger in 1944

THREE RIVERS STADIUM

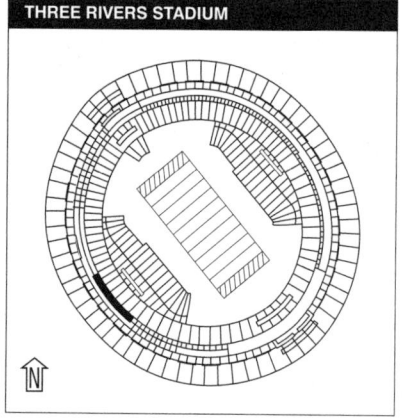

1996 TEAM RECORD

PRESEASON (2-3)

Date	Result		Opponents
7/27	L	10-20	vs. San Diego at Tokyo, Japan
8/3	W	16-10	St. Louis
8/11	L	17-24	at Green Bay
8/17	W	13-3	Tampa Bay
8/23	L	19-20	at Philadelphia

REGULAR SEASON (10-6)

Date	Result		Opponents	Att.
9/1	L	9-24	at Jacksonville	70,210
9/8	W	31-17	Baltimore	57,241
9/16	W	24-6	Buffalo	59,002
9/29	W	30-16	Houston	58,608
10/7	W	17-7	at Kansas City	79,189
10/13	W	20-10	Cincinnati	58,875
10/20	L	13-23	at Houston	50,337
10/27	W	20-17	at Atlanta	58,760
11/3	W	42-6	St. Louis	58,148
11/10	L	24-34	at Cincinnati	57,265
11/17	W	28-3	Jacksonville	58,879
11/25	W	24-17	at Miami	73,489
12/1	L	17-31	at Baltimore	51,822
12/8	W	16-3	San Diego	56,368
12/15	L	15-25	San Francisco	59,823
12/22	L	14-18	at Carolina	72,217

POSTSEASON (1-1)

Date	Result		Opponents	Att.
12/29	W	42-14	Indianapolis	58,078
1/5	L	3-28	at New England	60,188

SCORE BY PERIODS

Steelers	84	115	92	53	—	344
Opponents	67	85	42	63	—	257

ATTENDANCE

Home 466,944   Away 513,289   Total 980,233
Single-game home record, 60,608 (12/18/94)
Single-season home record, 466,944 (1996)

1996 TEAM STATISTICS

	Steelers	Opp.
Total First Downs	296	286
Rushing	138	80
Passing	146	174
Penalty	12	32
Third Down: Made/Att	84/208	77/213
Third Down Pct.	40.4	36.2
Fourth Down: Made/Att	4/10	4/11
Fourth Down Pct.	40.0	36.4
Total Net Yards	5140	4362
Avg. Per Game	321.3	272.6
Total Plays	1002	1009
Avg. Per Play	5.1	4.3
Net Yards Rushing	2299	1415
Avg. Per Game	143.7	88.4
Total Rushes	525	411
Net Yards Passing	2841	2947
Avg. Per Game	177.6	184.2
Sacked/Yards Lost	21/149	51/369
Gross Yards	2990	3316
Att./Completions	456/246	547/322
Completion Pct.	53.9	58.9
Had Intercepted	19	23
Punts/Avg.	72/40.7	86/43.8
Net Punting Avg.	72/33.7	86/38.1
Penalties/Yards Lost	83/665	97/746
Fumbles/Ball Lost	27/14	28/17
Touchdowns	39	27
Rushing	18	7
Passing	15	17
Returns	6	3
Avg. Time of Possession	30:08	29:52

1996 INDIVIDUAL STATISTICS

PASSING	Att.	Comp.	Yds.	Pct.	TD	Int.	Tkld.	Rate
Tomczak	401	222	2767	55.4	15	17	16/105	71.8
Stewart	30	11	100	36.7	0	2	3/37	18.8
Ji. Miller	25	13	123	52.0	0	0	2/7	65.9
Steelers	456	246	2990	53.9	15	19	21/149	68.0
Opponents	547	322	3316	58.9	17	23	51/369	69.2

SCORING	TD R	TD P	TD Rt	PAT	FG	Saf	PTS
N. Johnson	0	0	0	37/37	23/30	0	106
Bettis	11	0	0	0/0	0/0	0	66
Stewart	5	3	0	0/0	0/0	0	48
Hastings	0	6	0	0/0	0/0	0	36
C. Johnson	0	3	0	0/0	0/0	0	20
Lake	0	0	2	0/0	0/0	0	12
Pegram	1	0	1	0/0	0/0	0	12
Thigpen	0	2	0	0/0	0/0	0	12
Woodson	0	0	2	0/0	0/0	0	12
Lester	1	0	0	0/0	0/0	0	6
Mills	0	1	0	0/0	0/0	0	6
Perry	0	0	1	0/0	0/0	0	6
Bruener	0	0	0	0/0	0/0	0	2
Steelers	18	15	6	37/37	23/30	0	344
Opponents	7	17	3	26/26	21/26	3	257

2-Point conversions: Bruener, C. Johnson.
Team: 2-2, Opponents: 0-1.

RUSHING	Att.	Yds.	Avg.	LG	TD
Bettis	320	1431	4.5	50t	11
Pegram	97	509	5.2	27	1
Stewart	39	171	4.4	80t	5
Hastings	4	71	17.8	37	0
Witman	17	69	4.1	15	0
Mills	2	24	12.0	15	0
Lester	8	20	2.5	5t	1
McAfee	7	17	2.4	5	0
Richardson	5	17	3.4	8	0
Arnold	1	-3	-3.0	-3	0
Ji. Miller	2	-4	-2.0	0	0
Tomczak	22	-7	-0.3	6	0
Edge	1	-16	-16.0	-16	0
Steelers	525	2299	4.4	80t	18
Opponents	411	1415	3.4	33t	7

RECEIVING	No.	Yds.	Avg.	LG	TD
Hastings	72	739	10.3	38	6
C. Johnson	60	1008	16.8	70t	3
Bettis	22	122	5.5	16	0
Stewart	17	293	17.2	48	3
Pegram	17	112	6.6	14	0
Thigpen	12	244	20.3	39	2
Bruener	12	141	11.8	36	0
Mills	7	92	13.1	22	1
Lester	7	70	10.0	19	0
Arnold	6	76	12.7	26	0
McAfee	5	21	4.2	9	0
Botkin	4	36	9.0	17	0
Witman	2	15	7.5	11	0
Hayes	2	14	7.0	7	0
Holliday	1	7	7.0	7	0
Steelers	246	2990	12.2	70t	15
Opponents	322	3316	10.3	53	17

INTERCEPTIONS	No.	Yds.	Avg.	LG	TD
Woodson	6	121	20.2	43t	1
Perry	5	115	23.0	28	1
Kirkland	4	12	3.0	6	0
Brown	2	20	10.0	16	0
Figures	2	13	6.5	13	0
Lake	1	47	47.0	47t	1
Olsavsky	1	5	5.0	5	0
Williams	1	1	1.0	1	0
Fuller	1	0	0.0	0	0
Steelers	23	334	14.5	47t	3
Opponents	19	234	12.3	61t	2

PUNTING	No.	Yds.	Avg.	In 20	LG
Jo. Miller	55	2256	41.0	18	61
Edge	17	675	39.7	7	48
Steelers	72	2931	40.7	25	61
Opponents	86	3771	43.8	25	64

PUNT RETURNS	No.	FC	Yds.	Avg.	LG	TD
Hastings	37	12	242	6.5	33	0
Arnold	2	0	6	3.0	6	0
Jones	1	0	3	3.0	3	0
Steelers	40	12	251	6.3	33	0
Opponents	32	15	284	8.9	46	0

KICKOFF RETURNS	No.	Yds.	Avg.	LG	TD
Arnold	19	425	22.4	30	0
Pegram	17	419	24.6	91t	1
Mills	8	146	18.3	27	0
C. Johnson	6	111	18.5	31	0
Hastings	1	42	42.0	42	0
Perry	1	8	8.0	8	0
Witman	1	20	20.0	20	0
Steelers	53	1171	22.1	91t	1
Opponents	69	1509	21.9	90t	1

SACKS	No.
Brown	13.0
Gildon	7.0
Kirkland	4.0
Buckner	3.0
Emmons	2.5
Gibson	2.5
M. Bell	2.0
Lake	2.0
Oldham	2.0
Ravotti	2.0
Henry	1.5
Holmes	1.0
B. Johnson	1.0
Jones	1.0
Lloyd	1.0
Perry	1.0
Raybon	1.0
Williams	1.0
Woodson	1.0
Olsavsky	0.5
Steelers	51.0
Opponents	21.0

1997 DRAFT CHOICES

Round	Name	Pos.	College
1	Chad Scott	DB	Maryland
2	Will Blackwell	WR	San Diego State
3	Paul Wiggins	T	Oregon
	Mike Vrabel	DE	Ohio State
5	George Jones	RB	San Diego State
6	Daryl Porter	DB	Boston College
	Rod Manuel	DE	Oklahoma
7	Michael Adams	WR	Texas

1997 VETERAN ROSTER

No.	Name	Pos.	Ht.	Wt.	Birthdate	NFL Exp.	College	Hometown	How Acq.	'96 Games/ Starts
80	Arnold, Jahine	WR	6-0	187	6/19/73	2	Fresno State	Cupertino, Calif.	D4b-'96	9/0
14	Bailey, Henry	WR	5-8	176	2/28/73	2	Nevada-Las Vegas	Chicago, Ill.	FA-'97	8/0*
40	Bell, Myron	S	5-11	203	9/15/71	4	Michigan State	Toledo, Ohio	D5a-'94	16/4
36	Bettis, Jerome	RB	5-11	243	2/16/72	5	Notre Dame	Detroit, Mich.	T(StL)-'96	16/12
84	Botkin, Kirk	TE	6-3	245	3/19/71	3	Arkansas	Baytown, Tex.	FA-'96	16/0
21	Brown, J.B.	CB	6-0	191	1/5/67	9	Maryland	Washington, D.C.	FA-'97	14/1*
87	Bruener, Mark	TE	6-4	258	9/16/72	3	Washington	Aberdeen, Wash.	D1-'95	12/12
53	Conley, Steven	LB	6-5	235	1/18/72	2	Arkansas	Chicago, Ill.	D3a-'96	2/0
72	Dafney, Bernard	T-G	6-5	335	11/1/68	6	Tennessee	Los Angeles, Calif.	FA-'96	14/1
63	Dawson, Dermontti	C	6-2	288	6/17/65	10	Kentucky	Lexington, Ky.	D2-'88	16/16
51	Emmons, Carlos	LB	6-5	246	9/3/73	2	Arkansas State	Greenwood, Miss.	D7-'96	15/0
86	Farquhar, John	TE	6-6	278	3/22/72	2	Duke	Stanford, Calif.	FA-'96	4/0
41	Flowers, Lethon	CB-S	6-0	213	1/14/73	3	Georgia Tech	Spring Valley. N.C.	D5a-'95	16/0
29	† Fuller, Randy	CB-S	5-10	185	6/2/70	4	Tennessee State	Columbus, Ga.	FA-'95	14/1
98	Gibson, Oliver	DE-DT	6-3	298	3/15/72	3	Notre Dame	Romeoville, Ill.	D4a-'95	16/0
92	† Gildon, Jason	LB	6-3	245	7/31/72	4	Oklahoma State	Altus, Okla.	D3a-'94	14/13
74	Harrison, Nolan	DE	6-5	280	1/25/69	7	Indiana	Chicago, Ill.	UFA(Oak)-'97	15/2*
87	Hawkins, Courney	WR	5-9	183	12/12/69	6	Michigan State	Flint, Mich.	UFA(TB)-'97	16/16*
85	# Hayes, Jonathan	TE	6-5	248	8/11/62	13	Iowa	Oxford, Ohio	FA-'94	16/6
76	Henry, Kevin	DE	6-4	282	10/23/68	5	Mississippi State	Mound Bayou, Miss.	D4-'93	12/10
83	Holliday, Corey	WR	6-2	208	1/31/71	2	North Carolina	Richmond, Va.	FA-'95	11/0
50	Holmes, Earl	LB	6-2	246	4/28/73	2	Florida A&M	Tallahassee, Fla.	D4a-'96	3/1
65	Jackson, John	T	6-6	297	1/4/65	10	Eastern Kentucky	Cincinnati , Ohio	D10-'88	16/16
90	# Johnson, Bill	DL	6-4	311	12/9/68	6	Michigan State	Chicago, Ill.	FA-'95	15/8
81	Johnson, Charles	WR	6-0	193	1/3/72	4	Colorado	San Bernardino, Calif.	D1-'94	16/12
9	Johnson, Norm	K	6-2	202	5/31/60	16	UCLA	Garden Grove, Calif.	UFA(Atl)-'95	16/0
54	Jones, Donta	LB	6-2	226	8/27/72	3	Nebraska	Pomfret, Md.	D4b-'95	15/2
99	Kirkland, Levon	LB	6-1	264	2/17/69	6	Clemson	Lamar, S.C.	D2-'92	16/16
37	Lake, Carnell	S	6-1	210	7/15/67	9	UCLA	Inglewood, Calif.	D2-'89	13/13
34	Lester, Tim	RB	5-10	233	6/15/68	6	Eastern Kentucky	Miami, Fla.	FA-'95	16/13
95	Lloyd, Greg	LB	6-2	228	5/26/65	11	Fort Valley State	Fort Valley, Ga.	D6b-'87	1/1
85	Lyons, Mitch	TE	6-5	265	5/13/70	5	Michigan State	Grand Rapids, Mich.	UFA(Atl)-'97	145/8*
94	Mayfield, Corey	NT	6-3	302	2/25/70	3	Oklahoma	Tyler, Tex.	FA-'97	0*
25	McAfee, Fred	RB	5-10	193	6/20/68	7	Mississippi College	Philadelphia, Miss.	FA-'94	14/0
16	Miller, Jim	QB	6-2	216	2/9/71	4	Michigan State	Waterford, Mich.	D6a-'94	2/1
4	Miller, Josh	P	6-3	215	7/14/70	2	Arizona	East Brunswick, N.J.	FA-'96	12/0
62	Myslinski, Tom	T-G	6-3	287	12/7/68	5	Tennessee	Rome, N.Y.	FA-'96	8/6
24	Oldham, Chris	CB	5-9	193	10/26/68	7	Oregon	Sacramento, Calif.	UFA(Ariz)-'95	16/0
55	Olsavsky, Jerry	LB	6-1	224	3/29/67	9	Pittsburgh	Youngstown, Ohio	FA-'94	15/13
20	Pegram, Erric	RB	5-10	195	1/7/69	7	North Texas State	Dallas, Tex.	UFA(Atl)-'95	12/4
39	Perry, Darren	S	5-11	196	12/29/68	6	Penn State	Deep Creek, Va.	D8a-'92	16/16
33	Phillips, Bobby	RB	5-9	187	12/8/69	2	Virginia Union	Richmond, Va.	FA-'97	0*
91	Raybon, Israel	DE	6-6	293	2/5/73	2	North Alabama	Lee, Ala.	D5-'96	3/0
57	Ravotti, Eric	LB	6-2	250	3/16/71	4	Penn State	Freeport, Pa.	D6b-'94	16/2
44	Richardson, Terry	RB	6-0	204	10/8/71	1	Syracuse	Ft. Lauderdale, Fla.	D6a-'96	1/0
71	Roye, Orpheus	DE	6-4	290	1/21/74	2	Florida State	Miami Springs, Fla.	D6a-'96	13/1
56	Scott, Patrick	LB	6-4	229	6/4/71	2	South Carolina State	Durham, N.C.	FA-'96	0*
68	Stai, Brenden	G	6-4	305	3/30/72	3	Nebraska	Anaheim, Calif.	D3-'95	9/9
93	Steed, Joel	NT	6-2	300	2/17/69	6	Colorado	Denver, Colo.	D3-'92	16/14
67	Stephens, Jamain	T	6-6	330	1/9/74	2	North Carolina A&T	Lumberton, N.C.	D1-'96	0*
10	Stewart, Kordell	QB	6-1	212	10/16/72	3	Colorado	Marrero, La.	D2-'95	16/2
73	Strzelczyk, Justin	T-G	6-6	302	8/18/68	8	Maine	Seneca, N.Y.	D11-'90	16-16
66	Sweeney, Jim	C-G	6-4	295	8/8/62	14	Pittsburgh	Pittsburgh, Pa.	FA-'96	16/0
82	Thigpen, Yancey	WR	6-1	202	8/15/69	6	Winston-Salem State	Tarboro, N.C.	FA-'92	6/2
18	Tomczak, Mike	QB	6-1	201	10/23/62	13	Ohio State	Calumet City, Ill.	UFA(Clev)-'93	16/15
38	Witman, Jon	RB	6-1	240	6/1/72	2	Penn State	Wrightsville, Pa.	D3b-'96	16/4
77	Wolford, Will	G-T	6-5	300	5/18/64	12	Vanderbilt	Louisville, Ky.	UFA(Ind)-'96	16/16
26	# Woodson, Rod	CB	6-0	200	3/10/65	11	Purdue	Fort Wayne, Ind.	D1-'87	16/16

* Bailey played 8 games with N.Y. Jets in '96; Brown played 14 games with Miami; Harrison played 15 games with Oakland; Hawkins played 16 games with Tampa Bay; Lyons played 14 games with Atlanta; Mayfield last active with Jacksonville in '95; Phillips last active with Minnesota in '95; Scott missed '96 season because of injury; Stephens inactive for 16 games.

\# Unrestricted free agent; subject to developments.

† Restricted free agent; subject to developments.

Traded—DT Brentson Buckner (15 games in '96) to Kansas City.

Players lost through free agency (6): LB Chad Brown (Sea; 14 games in '96), CB Deon Figures (Jax; 16), WR Andre Hastings (NO; 16), WR Ernie Mills (Car; 9), DE Ray Seals (Car; 0), CB Willie Williams (Sea; 15).

Also played with Steelers in '96—P Shayne Edge (4 games).

COACHING STAFF

Head Coach,
Bill Cowher

Pro Career: Begins his sixth season as the fifteenth head coach in Steelers' history, replacing Chuck Noll on January 21, 1992. Cowher led the Steelers, to an 11-5 regular-season record in 1995 and, at age 38, became the youngest coach to lead his team to a Super Bowl. Cowher is only the third coach in NFL history to lead his team to the playoffs during his first five seasons as head coach. During Cowher's 12-year coaching career, teams he has been associated with have made the postseason 11 times. Began his NFL career as a free-agent linebacker with the Philadelphia Eagles in 1979, and then signed with the Cleveland Browns the following year. Cowher played three seasons (1980-82) in Cleveland before being traded back to the Eagles, where he played two more years (1983-84). Cowher began his coaching career in 1985 at age 28 under Marty Schottenheimer with the Cleveland Browns. He was the Browns' special teams coach in 1985-86 and secondary coach in 1987-88 before following Schottenheimer to the Kansas City Chiefs in 1989 as defensive coordinator. Career record: 57-32.

Background: Excelled in football, basketball, and track for Carlynton High in Crafton, Pa. Was a three-year starter at linebacker for North Carolina State, serving as captain and earning team MVP honors as senior. Graduated in 1979 with education degree.

Personal: Born in Pittsburgh, Pa., on May 8, 1957. His wife Kaye, also a North Carolina State graduate, played professional basketball for the New York Stars of the Women's Professional Basketball League with twin sister Faye. Bill and Kaye live in Pittsburgh and have three daughters—Meagan Lyn, Lauren Marie, and Lindsay Morgan.

ASSISTANT COACHES

Mike Archer, linebackers; born July 26, 1953, State College, Pa., lives in Pittsburgh. Safety/punter Miami 1972-75. No pro playing experience. College coach: Miami 1978-83, Louisiana State 1984-90, Virginia 1991-92, Kentucky 1993-95. Pro coach: Joined the Steelers in 1996.

Dave Culley, receivers; born September 17, 1955, Sparta, Tenn., lives in Pittsburgh. Quarterback Vanderbilt 1973-77. No pro playing experience. College coach: Austin Peay 1978, Vanderbilt 1979-81, Middle Tennessee State 1982, Tennessee-Chattanooga 1983, Western Kentucky 1984, Southwestern Louisiana 1985-88, Texas-El Paso 1989-90, Texas A&M 1991-93. Pro coach: Tampa Bay Buccaneers 1994-95, joined Steelers in 1996.

Chan Gailey, offensive coordinator; born January 5, 1952, Gainesville, Ga., lives in Pittsburgh. Quarterback Florida 1970-73. No pro playing experience. College coach: Troy State 1976-78, 1983-84, Air Force 1979-82, Samford (head coach) 1992. Pro coach: Denver Broncos 1985-90, Birmingham Fire (World League) 1991-92, joined Steelers in 1994.

Jim Haslett, defensive coordinator; born December 9, 1955, Pittsburgh, Pa., lives in Pittsburgh. Defensive end Indiana University (Pa.) 1975-78. Linebacker Buffalo Bills 1979-86, New York Jets 1987. College coach: Buffalo 1988-90. Pro coach: Sacramento Surge (World League) 1991-92, Los Angeles Raiders 1993-94, New Orleans Saints 1995-96, joined Steelers in 1997.

Dick Hoak, running backs; born December 8, 1939, Jeannette, Pa., lives in Greensburg, Pa. Halfback-quarterback Penn State 1958-60. Pro running back Pittsburgh Steelers 1961-70. Pro coach: Joined Steelers in 1972.

Tim Lewis, defensive backs; born December 18, 1961, Quakertown, Pa., lives in Pittsburgh. Defensive back Pittsburgh 1979-82. Pro cornerback Green Bay Packers 1983-86. College coach: Texas A&M 1987-88, Southern Methodist 1989-92, Pittsburgh 1993-94. Pro coach: Joined Steelers in 1995.

Mike Mularkey, tight ends; born November 19, 1961, Ft. Lauderdale, Fla., lives in Pittsburgh. Tight end Florida 1979-82. Pro tight end Minnesota Vikings 1983-88, Pittsburgh Steelers 1989-91. College coach: Concordia 1993. Pro coach: Tampa Bay Buccaneers 1994-95, joined Steelers in 1996.

John Mitchell, defensive line; born October 14, 1951, Mobile, Ala., lives in Pittsburgh. Defensive end Eastern Arizona J.C. 1969-70, Alabama 1971-72. No pro playing experience. College coach: Alabama 1973-76, Arkansas 1977-82, Temple 1986, Louisiana State 1987-90. Pro coach: Birmingham Stallions (USFL) 1983-85, Cleveland Browns 1991-93, joined Steelers in 1994.

Kent Stephenson, offensive line; born February 4, 1942, Anita, Iowa, lives in Pittsburgh. Guard-nose tackle Northern Iowa 1962-64. No pro playing experience. College coach: Wayne State 1965-68, North Dakota 1969-71, Southern Methodist 1972-73, Iowa 1974-76, Oklahoma State 1977-78, Kansas 1979-82. Pro coach: Michigan Panthers (USFL) 1983-84, Seattle Seahawks 1985-91, joined Steelers in 1992.

Ron Zook, special teams; born April 28, 1954, Ashland, Ohio, lives in Pittsburgh. Defensive back Miami (Ohio) 1972-75. No pro playing experience. College coach: Murray State 1978-80, Cincinnati 1981-82, Kansas 1983, Tennessee 1984-86, Virginia Tech 1987, Ohio State 1988-90, Florida 1991-95. Pro coach: Joined the Steelers in 1996.

1997 FIRST-YEAR ROSTER

Name	Pos.	Ht.	Wt.	Birthdate	College	Hometown	How Acq.
Adams, Mike	WR	5-11	184	3/25/74	Texas	Arlington, Tex.	D7
Blackwell, Will	WR	6-0	184	7/6/75	San Diego State	Capitol Heights, Md.	D2
Chabot, Justin	G-T	6-5	295	11/14/74	Northwestern	Oxford, Ohio	FA
Evers, Marcus	DE-DT	6-2	298	8/10/72	Clark College	Memphis, Tenn.	FA
Filardi, Gerald	LB	6-0	241	12/30/74	Penn State	Huntington, N.Y.	FA
Gadsden, Oronde (1)	WR	6-3	218	8/20/71	Winston-Salem	Charleston, S.C.	FA
Jacobs, Andy	LB	6-3	249	7/22/74	California	Benicia, Calif.	FA
Jones, D.J.	TE	6-3	253	8/15/74	Ohio State	Lebanon, Ohio	FA
Jones, George	RB	5-9	204	12/31/73	San Diego State	Greenville, S.C.	D5
Kearney, Jay (1)	WR	6-1	195	9/29/71	West Virginia	Piscataway, N.J.	FA
Manuel, Rod	DE	6-5	281	10/8/74	Oklahoma	Fort Worth, Tex.	D6b
Martin, Emerson (1)	G-T	6-3	316	5/6/70	Hampton	Elizabeth, N.C.	FA
McCann, David	RB	5-11	210	7/27/75	Murray State	Elizabethtown, Ky.	FA
Miles, Baron (1)	CB	5-8	165	1/1/72	Nebraska	Roselle, N.J.	FA
Nori, Mark	G-T	6-3	307	1/1/74	Boston College	Philadelphia, Pa.	FA
Pointer, Kirk (1)	CB	5-11	178	2/13/74	Austin Peay	Memphis, Tenn.	FA-'96
Porter, Daryl	CB-S	5-9	188	1/16/74	Boston College	Ft. Lauderdale, Fla.	D6a
Quinn, Mike	QB	6-3	226	4/15/74	Stephen F. Austin	Houston, Tex.	FA
Reali, Sean	K-P	5-11	202	1/20/74	Syracuse	Bay Village, Ohio	FA
Richardson, Terry (1)	RB	6-0	204	10/8/71	Syracuse	Ft. Lauderdale, Fla.	FA-'96
Samuel, Cedric	CB-S	5-9	183	9/26/74	Alabama	Demopolis, Ala.	FA
Scott, Chad	CB-S	6-1	203	9/6/74	Maryland	Capitol Heights, Md.	D1
Storm, Matt (1)	G-T	6-3	297	9/23/72	Georgia	Edmonds, Wash.	FA-'96
Vrabel, Mike	DE	6-4	270	8/14/75	Ohio State	Stow, Ohio	D3b
Wiggins, Paul	G-T	6-3	303	8/17/73	Oregon	Portland, Ore.	D3a

The term NFL Rookie is defined as a player who is in his first season of professional football and has not been on the roster of another professional football team for any regular-season or postseason games. A Rookie is designated by an "R" on NFL rosters. Players who have been active in another professional football league or players who have NFL experience, including either preseason training camp or being on an Active List or Inactive List, or on Reserve/Injured or Reserve/Physically Unable to Perform for fewer than six regular-season games, are termed NFL First-Year Players. An NFL First-Year Player is designated by a "1" on NFL rosters. Thereafter, a player is credited with an additional year of experience for each season in which he accumulates six games on the Active List or Inactive List, or on Reserve/Injured or Reserve/Physically Unable to Perform.

NOTES

_____
_____
_____
_____
_____
_____
_____
_____
_____
_____
_____
_____
_____
_____
_____
_____

American Football Conference
Western Division
Team Colors: Navy Blue, White, and Gold
Qualcomm Stadium, Jack Murphy Field
P.O. Box 609609
San Diego, California 92160-9609
Telephone: (619) 874-4500

CLUB OFFICIALS

Chairman of the Board: Alex G. Spanos
President-Vice Chairman: Dean A. Spanos
Executive Vice President: Michael A. Spanos
General Manager: Bobby Beathard
Vice President-Finance: Jeremiah T. Murphy
Chief Financial and Administrative Officer:
  Jeanne Bonk
Director of Player Personnel: Billy Devaney
Director of Pro Personnel: Rudy Feldman
Coordinator of Football Operations: Marty Hurney
Director of Executive Sales: Lynn Abramson
Business Manager: John Hinek
Director of Marketing: Rich Israel
Director of Public Relations: Bill Johnston
Director of Ticket Operations: Ron Tuck
Director of Video Operations: Dusty Alves
Head Trainer: Keoki Kamau
Equipment Manager: Sid Brooks
Stadium: Qualcomm Stadium, Jack Murphy Field
  •**Capacity:** 71,000
  9449 Friars Road
  San Diego, California 92108
Playing Surface: Grass
Training Camp: University of California-San Diego
  Third College
  La Jolla, California 92037

1997 SCHEDULE
PRESEASON

Aug. 2	**San Francisco**	7:00
Aug. 9	**Indianapolis**	7:00
Aug. 16	vs. Tennessee at Nashville	7:00
Aug. 22	at Minnesota	7:00

REGULAR SEASON

Aug. 31	at New England	1:00
Sept. 7	at New Orleans	12:00
Sept. 14	**Carolina**	1:00
Sept. 21	at Seattle	1:00
Sept. 28	**Baltimore**	1:00
Oct. 5	at Oakland	1:00
Oct. 12	Open Date	
Oct. 16	at Kansas City (Thurs.)	7:00
Oct. 26	**Indianapolis**	1:00
Nov. 2	at Cincinnati	1:00
Nov. 9	**Seattle**	1:00
Nov. 16	**Oakland**	5:00
Nov. 23	at San Francisco	1:00
Nov. 30	**Denver**	5:00
Dec. 7	**Atlanta**	1:00
Dec. 14	**Kansas City**	1:00
Dec. 21	at Denver	2:00

RECORD HOLDERS
INDIVIDUAL RECORDS—CAREER

Category	Name	Performance
Rushing (Yds.)	Paul Lowe, 1960-67	4,963
Passing (Yds.)	Dan Fouts, 1973-1987	43,040
Passing (TDs)	Dan Fouts, 1973-1987	254
Receiving (No.)	Charlie Joiner, 1976-1986	586
Receiving (Yds.)	Lance Alworth, 1962-1970	9,585
Interceptions	Gill Byrd, 1983-1992	42
Punting (Avg.)	Ralf Mojsiejenko, 1985-88	42.9
Punt Return (Avg.)	Leslie (Speedy) Duncan, 1964-1970	12.3
Kickoff Return (Avg.)	Leslie (Speedy) Duncan, 1964-1970	25.2
Field Goals	John Carney, 1990-96	179
Touchdowns (Tot.)	Lance Alworth, 1962-1970	83
Points	Rolf Benirschke, 1977-1986	766

INDIVIDUAL RECORDS—SINGLE SEASON

Category	Name	Performance
Rushing (Yds.)	Natrone Means, 1994	1,350
Passing (Yds.)	Dan Fouts, 1981	4,802
Passing (TDs)	Dan Fouts, 1981	33
Receiving (No.)	Tony Martin, 1995	90
Receiving (Yds.)	Lance Alworth, 1965	1,602
Interceptions	Charlie McNeil, 1961	9
Punting (Avg.)	Darren Bennett, 1996	45.6
Punt Return (Avg.)	Leslie (Speedy) Duncan, 1965	15.5
Kickoff Return (Avg.)	Keith Lincoln, 1962	28.4
Field Goals	John Carney, 1994	34
Touchdowns (Tot.)	Chuck Muncie, 1981	19
Points	John Carney, 1994	135

INDIVIDUAL RECORDS—SINGLE GAME

Category	Name	Performance
Rushing (Yds.)	Gary Anderson, 12-18-88	217
Passing (Yds.)	Dan Fouts, 10-19-80, 12-11-82	444
Passing (TDs)	Dan Fouts, 11-22-81	6
Receiving (No.)	Kellen Winslow, 10-7-84	15
Receiving (Yds.)	Wes Chandler, 12-20-82	260
Interceptions	Many times	3
	Last time by Dwayne Harper, 11-27-95	
Field Goals	John Carney, 9-5-93, 9-18-93	6
Touchdowns (Tot.)	Kellen Winslow, 11-22-81	5
Points	Kellen Winslow, 11-22-81	30

COACHING HISTORY
Los Angeles 1960
(280-275-11)

1960-69	Sid Gillman*	83-51-6
1969-70	Charlie Waller	9-7-3
1971	Sid Gillman**	4-6-0
1971-73	Harland Svare***	7-17-2
1973	Ron Waller	1-5-0
1974-78	Tommy Prothro****	21-39-0
1978-86	Don Coryell#	72-60-0
1986-88	Al Saunders	17-22-0
1989-91	Dan Henning	16-32-0
1992-96	Bobby Ross	50-36-0

  *Retired after nine games in 1969
  **Resigned after 10 games in 1971
  ***Resigned after eight games in 1973
  ****Resigned after four games in 1978
  #Resigned after eight games in 1986

QUALCOMM STADIUM, JACK MURPHY FIELD

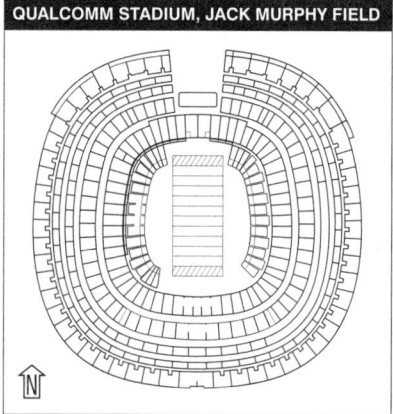

1996 TEAM RECORD

PRESEASON (2-3)

Date	Result		Opponents
7/27	W	20-10	vs. Pittsburgh at Tokyo, Japan
8/3	L	20-23	at Minnesota (OT)
8/10	L	12-16	at San Francisco (OT)
8/17	W	32-10	Arizona
8/23	L	34-37	at St. Louis

REGULAR SEASON (8-8)

Date	Result		Opponents	Att.
9/1	W	29-7	Seattle	58,780
9/8	W	27-14	Cincinnati	55,880
9/15	L	10-42	at Green Bay	60,584
9/22	W	40-34	at Oakland	49,097
9/29	W	22-19	Kansas City	59,384
10/6	L	17-28	at Denver	75,058
10/21	L	14-23	Oakland	62,350
10/27	L	13-32	at Seattle	38,143
11/3	W	26-19	at Indianapolis	58,484
11/11	W	27-21	Detroit	60,425
11/17	L	17-25	Tampa Bay	57,526
11/24	L	28-14	at Kansas City	69,472
12/1	L	7-45	New England	59,209
12/8	L	3-16	at Pittsburgh	56,368
12/14	L	14-27	at Chicago	49,763
12/22	W	16-10	Denver	46,801

(OT) Overtime

SCORE BY PERIODS

Chargers	113	79	45	73	—	310
Opponents	71	125	71	109	—	376

ATTENDANCE
Home 460,355   Away 456,969   Total 917,324
Single-game home record, 63,381 (1/8/95)
Single-season home record, 479,842 (1994)

1996 TEAM STATISTICS

	Chargers	Opp.
Total First Downs	272	321
Rushing	80	92
Passing	168	199
Penalty	24	30
Third Down: Made/Att	78/230	102/243
Third Down Pct.	33.9	42.0
Fourth Down: Made/Att	9/16	9/19
Fourth Down Pct.	56.3	47.4
Total Net Yards	4670	5421
Avg. Per Game	291.9	338.8
Total Plays	1022	1100
Avg. Per Play	4.6	4.9
Net Yards Rushing	1312	1755
Avg. Per Game	82.0	109.7
Total Rushes	412	431
Net Yards Passing	3358	3666
Avg. Per Game	209.9	229.1
Sacked/Yards Lost	33/296	33/201
Gross Yards	3654	3867
Att./Completions	577/314	636/369
Completion Pct.	54.4	58.0
Had Intercepted	21	22
Punts/Avg.	87/45.6	71/44.3
Net Punting Avg.	87/37.2	71/34.2
Penalties/Yards Lost	110/969	115/991
Fumbles/Ball Lost	30/11	29/14
Touchdowns	32	43
Rushing	7	10
Passing	23	28
Returns	2	5
Avg. Time of Possession	27:35	32:25

1996 INDIVIDUAL STATISTICS

PASSING	Att.	Comp.	Yds.	Pct.	TD	Int.	Tkld.	Rate
Humphries	416	232	2670	55.8	18	13	63t	76.7
Salisbury	161	82	984	50.9	5	8	56	59.6
Team	577	314	3654	54.4	23	21	63t	71.9
Opponents	636	369	3867	58	28	22	60	76.0

	TD	TD	TD					
SCORING	R	P	Rt	PAT		FG	Saf	PTS
Carney	0	0	0	31/31		29/36	0	118
Martin	0	14	0	0/0		0/0	0	84
Russell	7	0	0	0/0		0/0	0	42
Jones	0	4	0	0/0		0/0	0	24
A. Coleman	0	2	0	0/0		0/0	0	12
Fletcher	0	2	0	0/0		0/0	0	12
Clark	0	0	1	0/0		0/0	0	6
Da. Gordon	0	0	1	0/0		0/0	0	6
Pupunu	0	1	0	0/0		0/0	0	6
Chargers	7	23	2	31/31		29/36	0	310
Opponents	10	28	5	40/40		26/33	0	376

2-Point conversions: 0. Team: 0-1, Opponents 0-3.

RUSHING	Att.	Yds.	Avg.	LG	TD
Russell	219	713	3.3	21	7
Fletcher	77	282	3.7	19	0
Hayden	55	166	3.0	13	0
Bradley	32	109	3.4	17	0
Humphries	21	28	1.3	7	0
Salisbury	6	14	2.3	11	0
A. Coleman	2	0	0.0	7	0
Chargers	412	1312	3.2	21	7
Opponents	431	1755	4.1	77	10

RECEIVING	No.	Yds.	Avg.	LG	TD
Martin	85	1171	13.8	55	14
Fletcher	61	476	7.8	41	2
Jones	41	524	12.8	63t	4
A. Coleman	36	486	13.5	50	2
Pupunu	24	271	11.3	41	1
May	19	188	9.9	39	0
Russell	13	180	13.8	35	0
Roche	13	111	8.5	19	0
Mitchell	10	57	5.7	25	0
Still	6	142	23.7	56	0
Ellison	3	15	5.0	6	0
Bradley	1	20	20.0	20	0
Hayden	1	10	10.0	10	0
Reeves	1	3	3.0	3	0
Chargers	314	3654	11.6	63t	23
Opponents	369	3867	10.5	60	28

INTERCEPTIONS	No.	Yds.	Avg.	LG	TD
Harrison	5	56	11.2	29	0
Shaw	3	78	26.0	36	0
Gouveia	3	41	13.7	21	0
Clark	2	83	41.5	83t	1
Da. Gordon	2	55	27.5	55	0
Seau	2	18	9.0	10	0
Ross	2	7	3.5	7	0
Harper	1	0	0.0	0	0
Lee	1	-1	-1.0	-1	0
Young	1	-1	-1.0	-1	0
Chargers	22	336	15.3	83t	1
Opponents	21	320	15.2	90t	2

PUNTING	No.	Yds.	Avg.	In 20	LG
Bennett	87	3967	45.6	23	66
Chargers	87	3967	45.6	23	66
Opponents	71	3145	44.3	23	63

PUNT RETURNS	No.	FC	Yds.	Avg.	LG	TD
Da. Gordon	36	13	537	14.9	81t	1
Jones	1	1	21	21.0	21	0
Still	1	0	1	1.0	1	0
Chargers	38	14	559	14.7	81t	1
Opponents	51	15	612	12.0	82	1

KICKOFF RETURNS	No.	Yds.	Avg.	LG	TD
A. Coleman	55	1210	22.0	57	0
Still	4	113	28.3	37	0
Edwards	1	0	0.0	0	0
Harrison	1	10	10.0	10	0
Pupunu	1	15	15.0	15	0
Russell	1	10	10.0	10	0
Chargers	63	1358	21.6	57	0
Opponents	59	1497	25.4	66	0

SACKS	No.
Seau	7.0
Mims	6.0
M. Coleman	4.0
R. Davis	3.0
Johnson	3.0
Da. Gordon	2.0
Parrella	2.0
Bush	1.0
Edwards	1.0
Gouveia	1.0
Harrison	1.0
Lee	1.0
Chargers	*33.0
Opponents	33.0

*Chargers were credited with 1 team sack.

1997 DRAFT CHOICES

Round	Name	Pos.	College
2	Freddie Jones	TE	North Carolina
3	Michael Hamilton	LB	North Carolina A&T
4	Raleigh Roundtree	T	South Carolina State
5	Kenny Bynum	RB	South Carolina State
	Paul Bradford	DB	Portland State
6	Daniel Palmer	C	Air Force
7	Toran James	LB	North Carolina A&T
	Tony Corbin	QB	Cal State-Sacramento

SAN DIEGO CHARGERS

1997 VETERAN ROSTER

No.	Name	Pos.	Ht.	Wt.	Birthdate	NFL Exp.	College	Hometown	How Acq.	'96 Games/ Starts
2	Bennett, Darren	P	6-5	235	1/9/65	3	No College	Western, Australia	FA-'95	16/0
75	Berti, Tony	G-T	6-6	300	6/21/72	3	Colorado	Thornton, Colo.	D6d-'95	16/14
50	Binn, David	LS	6-3	240	2/6/72	4	California	San Mateo, Calif.	FA-'94	16/0
33	Bouie, Kevin	RB	6-1	230	8/18/71	3	Mississippi	Pohokee, Fla.	FA-'96	1/0
35	Bradley, Freddie	RB	5-10	208	6/12/70	2	Sonoma State	Oxnard, Calif.	D7-'96	10/1
32	Brown, Gary	RB	5-11	233	7/1/69	6	Penn State	Williamsport, Pa.	FA-'97	0*
58	Bush, Lewis	LB	6-2	245	12/2/69	5	Washington State	Tacoma, Wash.	D4b-'93	16/16
3	Carney, John	K	5-11	170	4/20/64	8	Notre Dame	West Palm Beach, Fla.	FA-'90	16/0
44	Castle, Eric	S	6-3	212	3/15/70	5	Oregon	Lebanon, Ore.	D6-'93	16/0
31	Clark, Willie	CB	5-10	186	1/6/72	4	Notre Dame	Wheatland, Calif.	D3b-'94	16/4
68	Cocozzo, Joe	G	6-4	300	8/7/70	5	Michigan	Mechanicville, N.Y.	D3-'93	16/11
83	† Coleman, Andre	WR-KR	5-9	165	9/19/72	4	Kansas State	Hermitage, Pa.	D3a-'94	16/10
90	Coleman, Marco	DE	6-3	267	12/18/69	6	Georgia Tech	Dayton, Ohio	UFA(Mia)-'96	16/15
39	Craver, Aaron	RB	6-0	220	12/18/68	7	Fresno State	Compton, Calif.	UFA(Den)-'97	15/15*
51	Cummings, Joe	LB	6-3	240	6/8/74	2	Wyoming	Stevensville, Mont.	FA-'96	3/0
73	Davis, Isaac	G	6-3	320	4/8/72	4	Arkansas	Malvern, Ark.	D2a-'94	14/5
93	Davis, Reuben	DT	6-5	320	5/7/65	10	North Carolina	Greensboro, N.C.	UFA(Ariz)-'94	15/15
20	Dumas, Mike	S	6-0	195	3/18/69	6	Indiana	Lowell, Mich.	FA-'97	0*
95	Edwards, Vernon	DE	6-4	255	6/23/72	2	Southern Methodist	Houston, Tex.	FA-'96	5/1
84	Ellison, 'OMar	WR	6-1	200	10/8/71	3	Florida State	Griffin, Ga.	D5-'95	10/1
60	Engel, Greg	C	6-3	285	1/18/71	4	Illinois	Bloomington, Ill.	FA-'94	12/9
41	Fletcher, Terrell	RB	5-8	196	9/14/73	3	Wisconsin	St. Louis, Mo.	D2b-'95	16/0
95	Fuller, William	DE	6-3	280	3/8/62	12	North Carolina	Chesapeake, Va.	UFA(Phil)-'97	16/16*
35	Gardner, Carwell	RB	6-2	240	11/27/66	9	Louisville	Louisville, Ky.	UFA(Balt)-'97	13/3*
54	Gouveia, Kurt	LB	6-1	240	9/14/64	12	Brigham Young	Honolulu, Hawaii	UFA(Phil)-'96	16/16
28	Harper, Dwayne	CB	5-11	175	3/29/66	10	South Carolina State	Orangeburg, S.C.	UFA(Sea)-'94	6/6
37	Harrison, Rodney	S	6-0	201	12/15/72	4	Western Illinois	Marion, Ill.	D5b-'94	16/16
24	Hayden, Aaron	RB	5-11	218	4/13/73	3	Tennessee	Detroit, Mich.	D4b-'95	11/0
38	Hendrix, David	S	6-1	213	5/29/72	3	Georgia Tech	Norcross, Ga.	FA-'95	14/0
12	Humphries, Stan	QB	6-2	223	4/14/65	9	Northeast Louisiana	Shreveport, La.	T(Wash)-'92	13/13
99	Johnson, Raylee	DE	6-3	265	6/1/70	5	Arkansas	Fordyce, Ark.	D4a-'93	16/1
82	Jones, Charlie	WR	5-8	175	12/1/72	2	Fresno State	Hanford, Calif.	D4-'96	14/4
98	Lee, Shawn	DT	6-2	300	10/24/66	10	North Alabama	Brooklyn, N.Y.	FA-'92	15/7
81	Martin, Tony	WR	6-0	181	9/5/65	8	Mesa, Colorado	Miami, Fla.	T(Mia)-'94	16/16
63	McKenzie, Raleigh	C-G	6-2	283	2/8/63	13	Tennessee	Knoxville, Tenn.	UFA(Phil)-'97	16/16*
21	Metcalf, Eric	WR	5-10	188	1/23/68	9	Texas	Seattle, Wash.	UFA(Atl)-'97	16/11*
66	Mills, Jim	G-T	6-4	290	3/30/73	2	Idaho	Marysville, Wash.	D6a-'96	1/0
89	† Mitchell, Shannon	TE	6-2	245	3/28/72	4	Georgia	Alcoa, Tenn.	FA-'94	16/11
40	Montreuil, Mark	CB	6-1	200	12/29/71	3	Concordia, Canada	Montreal, Canada	D7-'95	13/0
85	Oliver, Jimmy	WR	5-10	173	1/30/73	3	Texas Christian	Dallas, Tex.	D2c-'95	0*
70	† Parker, Vaughn	T	6-3	296	6/5/71	4	UCLA	Buffalo, N.Y.	D2b-'94	16/16
97	Parrella, John	DT	6-3	290	11/22/69	5	Nebraska	Topeka, Kan.	FA-'94	16/9
86	Pupunu, Alfred	TE	6-2	265	10/17/69	6	Weber State	Salt Lake City, Utah	W(KC)-'92	9/8
87	Roche, Brian	TE	6-4	255	5/5/73	2	San Jose State	LaVerne, Calif.	D3-'96	13/0
8	Salisbury, Sean	QB	6-5	225	3/9/63	9	Southern California	Escondido, Calif.	FA-'96	16/3
56	Sapp, Patrick	LB	6-4	258	5/11/73	2	Clemson	Jacksonville, Fla.	D2b-'96	16/0
96	Sasa, Don	DT	6-2	286	9/16/72	3	Washington State	Long Beach, Calif.	D3a-'95	4/1
55	Seau, Junior	LB	6-3	250	1/19/69	8	Southern California	Oceanside, Calif.	D1-'90	15/15
29	Shaw, Terrance	CB	5-11	190	11/11/73	3	Stephen F. Austin	Marshall, Tex.	D2a-'95	16/16
65	Sienkiewicz, Troy	G-T	6-5	310	5/27/72	3	New Mexico State	Alamogordo, N.M.	D6a-'96	7/0
80	Still, Bryan	WR	5-11	174	6/3/74	2	Virginia Tech	Richmond, Va.	D2a-'96	16/0
64	Stoltenberg, Bryan	C	6-1	293	8/25/72	2	Colorado	Sugarland, Tex.	D6b-'96	9/0
26	Thomas, Johnny	CB	5-9	191	8/3/64	10	Baylor	Houston, Tex.	UFA(Phil)-'97	9/0*
5	Whelihan, Craig	QB	6-5	204	4/15/71	3	Pacific	San Jose, Calif.	D6c-'95	0*

* Brown last active with Houston in '95; Craver played 15 games with Denver in '96; Dumas last active with Jacksonville in '95; Fuller and McKenzie played 16 games with Philadelphia; Gardner played 13 games with Baltimore; Metcalf played 16 games with Atlanta; Oliver inactive for 6 games; Thomas played 9 games with Philadelphia; Whelihan inactive for 13 games.

† Restricted free agent; subject to developments.

Players lost through free agency (4): CB Darrien Gordon (Den, 16 games in '96); TE Deems May (Sea); TE Walter Reeves (Mia; 9); T Harry Swayne (Den, 16).

Also played with Chargers in '96—LB Arnold Ale (7 games), LB Dwayne Gordon (13), C Courtney Hall (7), DE Chris Mims (15), G Eric Moten (15), S Kevin Ross (16), RB Leonard Russell (15), LB Glen Young (6).

COACHING STAFF

Head Coach,
Kevin Gilbride

Pro Career: Begins first season as San Diego's head coach after spending past two seasons (1995-96) as offensive coordinator of Jacksonville Jaguars. In 1996, Gilbride led Jacksonville to top ranking in NFL by averaging 256.9 yards passing per game. Jacksonville also ranked second overall in NFL total offense in 1996. Named tenth head coach in Chargers' history on January 19, 1997. First professional coaching job was for Ottawa Rough Riders of Canadian Football League where he was quarterbacks/receivers coach in 1985 and offensive coordinator in 1986. Gilbride began his NFL coaching career in Houston in 1989 as quarterbacks coach before being named the Oilers' offensive coordinator in 1990. Remained Oilers' offensive coordinator through 1993 before spending the 1994 season as the team's assistant head coach/offense. Under Gilbride's direction, the Oilers' offense ranked first in the NFL in passing yards from 1990 through 1992 and was third in 1993. For four consecutive seasons (1990-93), the Oilers ranked among the NFL's top three teams in total offense (including No. 1 in 1990). No pro playing experience.

Background: Played quarterback and tight end for Southern Connecticut State. Began coaching career at Idaho State in 1974. After two seasons at Idaho State, Gilbride was the linebackers coach for two seasons at Tufts University (1976-77) and the defensive coordinator for two years (1978-79) at American International. Spent five seasons (1980-84) as head coach at Southern Connecticut State, compiling career collegiate head coaching record of 35-14-2. During his tenure as Southern Connecticut State's head coach, Gilbride was named New England Coach of the Year and the NCAA Division II Coach of the Year by various groups, including the ECAC Officials, the Walter Camp Foundation and the New Haven Gridiron Club. After two years in the Canadian Football League, Gilbride coached for two years (1987-88) at East Carolina, the first season as passing game coordinator and second as offensive coordinator.

Personal: Born August 27, 1951, in New Haven, Conn. Kevin and his wife, Deborah, have three children—Kelly, Kristen, and Kevin.

ASSISTANT COACHES

George DeLeone, offensive line; born May 9, 1948, in New Haven, Conn., lives in San Diego. Guard-linebacker Connecticut 1966-68. No pro playing experience. College coach: Southern Connecticut State 1970-79 (head coach 1976-79), Rutgers 1980-83, Holy Cross 1984, Syracuse 1985-96. Pro coach: Joined Chargers in 1997.

Tyrone Dixon, wide receivers; born October 22, 1964, Aliquippa, Pa., lives in San Diego. Safety Indiana University (Pa.) 1982-85. No pro playing experience. College coach: Indiana (Pa.) 1986-89, Akron 1990-91, Temple 1992, James Madison 1993, Houston 1994-96. Pro coach: Joined Chargers in 1997.

Bill Macdermott, tight ends; born May 14, 1936, Providence, R.I., lives in San Diego. Guard-tackle Trinity College (Hartford, Conn.) 1955, 1957-59. No pro playing experience. College coach: Wesleyan University 1966-86 (head coach 1981-86), Cal Poly-San Luis Obispo 1987-89. Pro coach: Montreal Alouettes (CFL) 1987, Toronto Argonauts (CFL) 1990, Orlando Thunder (World League) 1991-92, Edmonton Eskimos (CFL) 1992-96, Winnipeg Blue Bombers (CFL) 1997, joined Chargers in 1997.

Nick Nicolau, assistant head coach; born May 5, 1933, New York, N.Y., lives in San Diego. Running back Southern Connecticut State 1957-59. No pro playing experience. College coach: Southern Connecticut State 1960, Springfield 1961, Bridgeport 1962-69 (head coach 1965-69), Massachusetts 1970, Connecticut 1971-72, Kent State 1973. Pro coach: Hamilton Tiger-Cats (CFL) 1977, Montreal Alouettes (CFL) 1978-79, New Orleans Saints 1980, Denver Broncos 1981-87, Los An-

geles Raiders 1988, Buffalo Bills 1989-91, Indianapolis Colts 1992-94, Jacksonville Jaguars 1995-96, joined Chargers in 1997.

Frank Novak, special teams; born May 18, 1938, Leominster, Mass., lives in San Diego. Quarterback Northern Michigan 1959-61. No pro playing experience. College coach: Northern Michigan 1966-72, East Carolina 1973, Virginia 1974-75, Western Illinois 1976-77, Holy Cross 1978-83, Massachusetts 1986, Missouri 1988. Pro coach: Oklahoma Outlaws (USFL) 1984, Birmingham Stallions (USFL) 1985, Houston Oilers 1989-94, Detroit Lions 1995-96, joined Chargers in 1997.

Wayne Nunnely, defensive line; born March 29, 1952, Los Angeles, Calif., lives in San Diego. Fullback Nevada-Las Vegas 1972-75. No pro playing experience. College coach: Nevada-Las Vegas 1976, 1982-89 (head coach 1986-89), Cal Poly-Pomona 1977-78, Cal State-Fullerton 1979, Pacific 1980-81, Southern California 1991-92, UCLA 1993-94. Pro coach: New Orleans Saints 1995-96, joined Chargers in 1997.

Joe Pascale, defensive coordinator; born April 4, 1946, New York, N.Y., lives in San Diego. Linebacker Connecticut 1963-66. No pro playing experience. College coach: Connecticut 1967-68, Rhode Island 1969-73, Idaho State 1974-76 (head coach 1976), Princeton 1977-79. Pro coach: Montreal Alouettes (CFL) 1980-81, Ottawa Rough Riders (CFL) 1982-83, New Jersey Generals (USFL) 1984-85, St. Louis/Phoenix Cardinals 1986-93, Cincinnati Bengals 1994-96, joined Chargers in 1997.

Rod Perry, defensive backs; born September 11,

1953, Fresno, Calif., lives in San Diego. Defensive back Colorado 1972-74. Pro cornerback Los Angeles Rams 1975-82, Cleveland Browns 1983-84. College coach: Columbia 1985, Fresno City College 1986, Fresno State 1987-88. Pro coach: Seattle Seahawks 1989-91, Los Angeles Rams 1992-94, Houston Oilers 1995-96, joined Chargers in 1997.

Mike Sheppard, offensive coordinator; born October 29, 1951, Tulsa, Okla., lives in San Diego. Wide receiver Cal Lutheran 1969-72. No pro playing experience. College coach: Cal Lutheran 1974-76, Brigham Young 1977-78, U.S. International 1979, Idaho State 1980-81, Long Beach State 1982, 1984-86 (head coach), Kansas 1983, New Mexico 1987-91, California 1992. Pro coach: Cleveland Browns 1993-95/Baltimore Ravens 1996, joined Chargers in 1997.

Jim Vechiarella, linebackers; born February 20, 1937, Youngstown, Ohio, lives in San Diego. Linebacker Youngstown State 1955-57. No pro playing experience. College coach: Youngstown State 1964-74, Southern Illinois 1976-77, Tulane 1978-80. Pro coach: Charlotte (WFL) 1975, Los Angeles Rams 1981-82, Kansas City Chiefs 1983-85, New York Jets 1986-89, Cleveland Browns 1990, Philadelphia Eagles 1991-94, joined Chargers in 1997.

Ollie Wilson, running backs; born March 3, 1951, Worcester, Mass., lives in San Diego. Wide receiver Springfield 1971-73. No pro playing experience. College coach: Springfield 1975, Northeastern 1976-82, California 1983-90. Pro coach: Atlanta Falcons 1991-96, joined Chargers in 1997.

1997 FIRST-YEAR ROSTER

Name	Pos.	Ht.	Wt.	Birthdate	College	Hometown	How Acq.
Bell, Robert	T	6-5	317	1/25/75	Howard	Philadelphia, Pa.	FA
Bordelon, Ben	T	6-4	291	4/9/74	Louisiana State	Mathews, La.	FA
Boyd, Sterling	RB	5-11	200	6/1/74	Texas Christian	Sherman, Tex.	FA
Boyer, Wayne	K-P	5-10	170	6/15/74	Southwest Missouri	St. Louis, Mo.	FA
Bradford, Paul	CB	5-8	185	4/20/74	Portland State	Palo Alto, Calif.	D5b
Brown, Matt (1)	G	6-2	309	10/27/71	Rutgers	Trenton, N.J.	FA
Bynum, Kenny	RB	5-11	191	5/29/74	South Carolina State	Gainesville, Fla.	D5a
Carter, Grant (1)	LB	6-3	250	12/30/70	Pacific	Lake Oswego, Ore.	FA
Chancey, Robert	RB	6-0	258	9/7/72	No College	Millbrook, Ala.	FA
Corbin, Tony	QB	6-2	215	3/21/74	Sacramento State	Turlock, Calif.	D7b
Daniels, Steve	WR	5-11	185	12/2/70	Arkansas Tech	Tulsa, Okla.	FA
DiBernado, Joe	LB	6-0	230	2/6/74	Appalachian State	Miami, Fla.	FA
Filer, Rodney	RB	6-1	220	6/14/74	Iowa	Houston, Tex.	FA
Gibson, Nate	C	6-4	305	10/15/75	Mansfield	Philadelphia, Pa.	FA
Green, Ryan	TE	6-2	246	10/30/74	Hawaii	Turlock, Calif.	FA
Hamilton, Michael	LB	6-1	244	12/3/73	North Carolina A&T	Greenville, S.C.	D3
Hamlet, Sean	S	5-11	211	3/24/74	Florida State	Hampton, Va.	FA
Hicks, Anthony	LB	6-1	246	7/30/74	Middle Tenn. State	Mufressboro, Tenn.	FA
Hinchen, Shad	CB-PR	5-9	177	11/10/75	Washington State	Indio, Calif.	FA
Hippler, Werner (1)	TE	6-5	262	7/30/70	Sacramento State	Cologne, Germany	FA
Ivey, Pat (1)	DE	6-4	255	12/27/72	Missouri	Detroit, Mich.	FA
James, Toran	LB	6-3	247	3/8/74	North Carolina A&T	Ahoskie, N.C.	D7a
Johnson, Damion	WR	6-1	190	10/18/74	Houston	Temple, Tex.	FA
Jones, Freddie	TE	6-4	260	9/16/74	North Carolina	Landover, Md.	D2
Maslowski, Mike	LB	6-1	246	7/11/74	Wisconsin-LaCrosse	Stanley, Wis.	FA
Palmer, Daniel	T	6-4	290	8/24/73	Air Force Academy	Anderson, S.C.	D6
Poumele, Pulu (1)	G	6-4	300	1/31/72	Arizona	Oceanside, Calif.	FA
Rachal, Latario	WR	5-11	183	1/31/73	Fresno State	Los Angeles, Calif.	FA
Rodgers, Anthony	WR	6-3	190	12/11/73	Cal State-Northridge	Los Angeles, Calif.	FA
Roundtree, Raleigh	T	6-4	295	8/31/75	South Carolina State	Augusta, Ga.	D4
Soli, Junior (1)	DT	6-2	290	11/15/74	Arkansas	Ft. Benning, Ga.	D5
Spain, Connel	DT	6-2	285	6/9/74	Florida State	Melbourne, Fla.	FA
Stallworth, Larry (1)	WR	5-10	187	8/9/73	Sacramento C.C.	Sacramento, Calif.	FA
Swift, Michael (1)	CB	5-10	165	2/28/74	Austin Peay	Tiptonville, Tenn.	FA
Swinger, Rashod	DT	6-2	286	11/27/74	Rutgers	Patterson, N.J.	FA
Tuinei, Van	DE	6-3	266	2/16/71	Arizona	Westminster, Calif.	FA
Williams, Gerome	S	6-2	210	7/9/73	Houston	Houston, Tex.	FA

The term NFL Rookie is defined as a player who is in his first season of professional football and has not been on the roster of another professional football team for any regular-season or postseason games. A Rookie is designated by an "R" on NFL rosters. Players who have been active in another professional football league or players who have NFL experience, including either preseason training camp or being on an Active List or Inactive List, or on Reserve/Injured or Reserve/Physically Unable to Perform for fewer than six regular-season games, are termed NFL First-Year Players. An NFL First-Year Player is designated by a "1" on NFL rosters. Thereafter, a player is credited with an additional year of experience for each season in which he accumulates six games on the Active List or Inactive List, or on Reserve/Injured or Reserve/Physically Unable to Perform.

NOTES

American Football Conference
Western Division
Team Colors: Blue, Green, and Silver
11220 N.E. 53rd Street
Kirkland, Washington 98033
Telephone: (425) 827-9777

CLUB OFFICIALS

Administration
Executive Vice President: Mickey Loomis
Vice President/Football Operations: Randy Mueller
Vice President/Administration and Communications:
    Gary Wright
Player Personnel Director: Mike Allman
Public Relations Director: Dave Neubert
Community Relations Director: Sandy Gregory
Player Programs Director: Reggie McKenzie
Assistant Public Relations Director: Steve Wright
Information Systems Director: Sterling Monroe
Ticket Manager: James Nagaoka
Trainer: Jim Whitesel
Equipment Manager: Terry Sinclair
Team Physicians: Dr. Kevin Auld, Dr. Stan Herring,
    Dr. Ed Khalfayan, Dr. Brad Shoup
Stadium: Kingdome • **Capacity:** 66,400
        201 South King Street
        Seattle, Washington 98104
Playing Surface: AstroTurf
Training Camp: Eastern Washington University
        Cheney, Washington 99004

1997 SCHEDULE

PRESEASON

July 26	vs. Minnesota at Canton, Ohio	2:30
Aug. 2	**Arizona**	7:00
Aug. 9	at San Francisco	6:00
Aug. 16	**Indianapolis**	7:00
Aug. 22	at Cincinnati	7:30

REGULAR SEASON

Aug. 31	**New York Jets**	1:00
Sept. 7	**Denver**	1:00
Sept. 14	at Indianapolis	3:00
Sept. 21	**San Diego**	1:00
Sept. 28	at Kansas City	3:00
Oct. 5	**Tennessee**	1:00
Oct. 12	Open Date	
Oct. 19	at St. Louis	12:00
Oct. 26	**Oakland**	1:00
Nov. 2	at Denver	2:00
Nov. 9	at San Diego	1:00
Nov. 16	at New Orleans	12:00
Nov. 23	**Kansas City**	1:00
Nov. 30	**Atlanta**	1:00
Dec. 7	at Baltimore	1:00
Dec. 14	at Oakland	1:00
Dec. 21	**San Francisco**	5:00

RECORD HOLDERS

INDIVIDUAL RECORDS—CAREER

Category	Name	Performance
Rushing (Yds.)	Curt Warner, 1983-89	6,705
Passing (Yds.)	Dave Krieg, 1980-1991	26,132
Passing (TDs)	Dave Krieg, 1980-1991	195
Receiving (No.)	Steve Largent, 1976-1989	819
Receiving (Yds.)	Steve Largent, 1976-1989	13,089
Interceptions	Dave Brown, 1976-1986	50
Punting (Avg.)	Rick Tuten, 1991-96	44.0
Punt Return (Avg.)	Paul Johns, 1981-84	11.4
Kickoff Return (Avg.)	Steve Broussard, 1995-96	23.8
Field Goals	Norm Johnson, 1982-1990	159
Touchdowns (Tot.)	Steve Largent, 1976-1989	101
Points	Norm Johnson, 1982-1990	810

INDIVIDUAL RECORDS—SINGLE SEASON

Category	Name	Performance
Rushing (Yds.)	Chris Warren, 1994	1,545
Passing (Yds.)	Dave Krieg, 1984	3,671
Passing (TDs)	Dave Krieg, 1984	32
Receiving (No.)	Brian Blades, 1994	81
Receiving (Yds.)	Steve Largent, 1985	1,287
Interceptions	John Harris, 1981	10
	Kenny Easley, 1984	10
Punting (Avg.)	Rick Tuten, 1995	45.0
Punt Return (Avg.)	Bobby Joe Edmonds, 1987	12.6
Kickoff Return (Avg.)	Steve Broussard, 1995	24.7
Field Goals	Todd Peterson, 1996	28
Touchdowns (Tot.)	Chris Warren, 1995	16
Points	Todd Peterson, 1996	111

INDIVIDUAL RECORDS—SINGLE GAME

Category	Name	Performance
Rushing (Yds.)	Curt Warner, 11-27-83	207
Passing (Yds.)	Dave Krieg, 11-20-83	418
Passing (TDs)	Dave Krieg, 12-2-84, 9-15-85, 11-28-88	5
Receiving (No.)	Steve Largent, 10-18-87	15
Receiving (Yds.)	Steve Largent, 10-18-87	261
Interceptions	Kenny Easley, 9-3-84	3
	Eugene Robinson, 12-6-92	3
Field Goals	Norm Johnson, 9-20-87, 12-18-88	5
Touchdowns (Tot.)	Daryl Turner, 9-15-85	4
	Curt Warner, 12-11-88	4
Points	Daryl Turner, 9-15-85	24
	Curt Warner, 12-11-88	24

COACHING HISTORY

(151-180-0)

1976-82	Jack Patera*	35-59-0
1982	Mike McCormack	4-3-0
1983-91	Chuck Knox	83-67-0
1992-94	Tom Flores	14-34-0
1995-96	Dennis Erickson	15-17-0

*Released after two games in 1982

KINGDOME

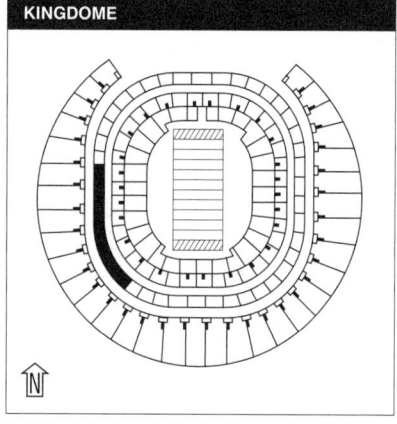

1996 TEAM RECORD

PRESEASON (3-1)

Date	Result		Opponents
8/3	W	19-17	Atlanta
8/8	W	24-19	at Oakland
8/17	L	13-15	at Indianapolis
8/23	W	20-3	San Francisco

REGULAR SEASON (7-9)

Date	Result		Opponents	Att.
9/1	L	7-29	at San Diego	58,780
9/8	L	20-30	Denver	43,671
9/15	L	17-35	Kansas City	39,790
9/22	W	17-13	at Tampa Bay	30,212
9/29	L	10-31	Green Bay	59,973
10/6	W	22-15	at Miami	59,539
10/17	L	16-34	at Kansas City	76,057
10/27	W	32-13	San Diego	38,143
11/3	W	23-16	Houston	36,320
11/10	W	42-23	Minnesota	50,794
11/17	L	16-17	at Detroit	51,194
11/24	L	21-27	Oakland	47,506
12/1	L	7-34	at Denver	74,982
12/8	W	26-18	Buffalo	41,373
12/15	L	13-20	at Jacksonville	66,134
12/22	W	28-21	at Oakland	33,455

SCORE BY PERIODS

Seahawks	53	117	57	90	—	317
Opponents	85	111	64	116	—	376

ATTENDANCE

Home 357,570   Away 450,353   Total 807,923
Single-game home record, 64,411 (12/4/84)
Single-season home record, 514,984 (1992)

1996 TEAM STATISTICS

	Seahawks	Opp.
Total First Downs	268	325
Rushing	94	114
Passing	147	181
Penalty	27	30
Third Down: Made/Att	64/212	80/211
Third Down Pct.	30.2	37.9
Fourth Down: Made/Att	7/17	7/15
Fourth Down Pct.	41.2	46.7
Total Net Yards	5024	5437
Avg. Per Game	314.0	339.8
Total Plays	974	1066
Avg. Per Play	5.2	5.1
Net Yards Rushing	1997	2098
Avg. Per Game	124.8	131.1
Total Rushes	442	506
Net Yards Passing	3027	3339
Avg. Per Game	189.2	208.7
Sacked/Yards Lost	38/189	48/285
Gross Yards	3216	3624
Att./Completions	494/261	512/303
Completion Pct.	52.8	59.2
Had Intercepted	17	14
Punts/Avg.	86/43.6	76/42.3
Net Punting Avg.	86/34.5	76/34.0
Penalties/Yards Lost	112/879	98/804
Fumbles/Ball Lost	24/12	37/18
Touchdowns	33	40
Rushing	16	15
Passing	14	25
Returns	3	0
Avg. Time of Possession	28:01	31:59

1996 INDIVIDUAL STATISTICS

PASSING	Att.	Comp.	Yds.	Pct.	TD	Int.	Tkld.	Rate
Mirer	265	136	1546	51.3	5	12	22/84	56.6
Friesz	211	120	1629	56.9	8	4	12/77	86.4
Torretta	16	5	41	31.3	1	1	3/17	35.4
Gelbaugh	2	0	0	0.0	0	0	1/11	39.6
Seahawks	494	261	3216	52.8	14	17	38/189	68.3
Opponents	512	303	3624	59.2	25	14	48/285	85.8

SCORING	TD R	TD P	TD Rt	PAT	FG	Saf	PTS
Peterson	0	0	0	27/27	28/34	0	111
Smith	8	0	0	0/0	0/0	0	54
Galloway	0	7	1	0/0	0/0	0	48
Warren	5	0	0	0/0	0/0	0	32
Blades	0	2	0	0/0	0/0	0	12
Mirer	2	0	0	0/0	0/0	0	12
Proehl	0	2	0	0/0	0/0	0	12
Blackmon	0	0	1	0/0	0/0	0	6
Broussard	1	0	0	0/0	0/0	0	6
Fauria	0	1	0	0/0	0/0	0	6
Pritchard	0	1	0	0/0	0/0	0	6
D. Williams	0	0	1	0/0	0/0	0	6
R. Williams	0	1	0	0/0	0/0	0	6
Seahawks	16	14	3	27/27	28/34	0	317
Opponents	15	25	0	35/35	31/34	1	376

2-Point conversions: Smith 3, Warren. Team: 4-5, Opponents: 3-5.

RUSHING	Att.	Yds.	Avg.	LG	TD
Warren	203	855	4.2	51	5
Smith	153	680	4.4	29	8
Mirer	33	191	5.8	33	2
Galloway	15	127	8.5	51	0
Broussard	15	106	7.1	26t	1
Pritchard	2	13	6.5	7	0
Torretta	2	12	6.0	13	0
Strong	5	8	1.6	4	0
O. Gray	2	4	2.0	2	0
Friesz	12	1	0.1	3	0
Seahawks	442	1997	4.5	51	16
Opponents	506	2098	4.1	40	15

RECEIVING	No.	Yds.	Avg.	LG	TD
Galloway	57	987	17.3	65t	7
Blades	43	556	12.9	80t	4
Warren	40	273	6.8	33	0
Crumpler	26	258	9.9	26	0
Proehl	23	309	13.4	56	2
Pritchard	21	328	15.6	44	1
Fauria	18	214	11.9	23t	1
Strong	9	78	8.7	20	0
Smith	9	58	6.4	22	0
Broussard	6	26	4.3	9	0
R. Williams	5	25	5.0	11	1
R. Harris	2	26	13.0	21	0
McKnight	1	73	73.0	73	0
O. Gray	1	5	5.0	5	0
Seahawks	261	3216	12.3	80t	14
Opponents	303	3624	12.0	65t	25

INTERCEPTIONS	No.	Yds.	Avg.	LG	TD
D. Williams	5	148	29.6	79t	1
Blackmon	3	48	16.0	38	0
Bellamy	3	18	6.0	16	0
C. Harris	1	25	25.0	25	0
Wooden	1	13	13.0	13	0
Moss	1	1	1.0	1	0
C. Gray	0	3	—	3	0
Seahawks	14	256	18.3	79t	1
Opponents	17	305	17.9	63	0

PUNTING	No.	Yds.	Avg.	In 20	LG
Tuten	85	3746	44.1	20	66
Seahawks	86	3746	43.6	20	66
Opponents	76	3214	42.3	23	57

PUNT RETURNS	No.	FC	Yds.	Avg.	LG	TD
R. Harris	19	10	194	10.2	35	0
Galloway	15	5	158	10.5	88t	1
Seahawks	34	15	352	10.4	88t	1
Opponents	52	17	640	12.3	50	0

KICKOFF RETURNS	No.	Yds.	Avg.	LG	TD
Broussard	43	979	22.8	86	0
R. Harris	12	240	20.0	29	0
C. Harris	7	166	23.7	41	0
Brown	4	51	12.8	24	0
McKnight	3	86	28.7	55	0
Barber	1	12	12.0	12	0
Fauria	1	8	8.0	8	0
Crumpler	0	0	—	—	0
Seahawks	71	1542	21.7	86	0
Opponents	72	1642	22.8	60	0

SACKS	No.
McCrary	13.5
Sinclair	13.0
Kennedy	8.0
Adams	5.5
Daniels	2.0
Edwards	2.0
Blackmon	1.0
C. Harris	1.0
Moss	1.0
Wells	1.0
Seahawks	48.0
Opponents	38.0

1997 DRAFT CHOICES

Round	Name	Pos.	College
1	Shawn Springs	DB	Ohio State
	Walter Jones	T	Florida State
5	Eric Stokes	DB	Nebraska
6	Itula Mili	TE	Brigham Young
7	Carlos Jones	DB	Miami

SEATTLE SEAHAWKS

1997 VETERAN ROSTER

No.	Name	Pos.	Ht.	Wt.	Birthdate	NFL Exp.	College	Hometown	How Acq.	'96 Games/ Starts
98	Adams, Sam	DT	6-3	297	6/13/73	4	Texas A&M	Houston, Tex.	D1-'94	16/15
74	Atkins, James	T	6-6	306	1/28/70	4	Southwestern Louisiana	Amite, La.	FA-'93	16/16
75	Ballard, Howard	T	6-6	325	11/3/63	10	Alabama A&M	Ashland, Ala.	UFA(Buff)-'94	16/16
54	Barber, Michael	LB	6-1	246	11/9/71	3	Clemson	Edgemore, S.C.	FA-'95	13/7
64	Barr, Robert	T	6-4	316	6/7/73	2	Rutgers	Hanover, Penn.	D3a-'96	0*
63	Beede, Frank	C	6-4	296	5/1/73	2	Panhandle State	Antioch, Calif.	FA-'96	14/2
20	Bellamy, Jay	S	5-11	199	7/8/72	4	Rutgers	Aberdeen, N.J.	FA-'94	16/0
48	Benford, Clarence	TE	6-3	249	8/18/73	2	Albany State	Windsor Forrest, Ga.	FA-'96	0*
36	Blades, Bennie	S	6-1	221	9/3/66	10	Miami	Ft. Lauderdale, Fla.	UFA(Det)-'97	15/15*
89	Blades, Brian	WR	5-11	190	7/24/65	10	Miami	Ft. Lauderdale, Fla.	D2-'88	11/9
31	Broussard, Steve	RB	5-7	201	2/22/67	8	Washington State	Los Angeles, Calif.	FA-'95	12/0
99	Brown, Chad	LB	6-2	240	7/12/70	4	Colorado	Altadena, Calif.	UFA(Pitt)-'97	14/14*
34	Brown, Reggie	RB	6-0	244	6/26/73	2	Fresno State	Detroit, Mich.	D3b-'96	7/0
91	Bryant, Keif	DT	6-4	287	3/12/73	2	Rutgers	Largo, Fla.	D7-'95	0*
59	Cain, Joe	LB	6-1	242	6/11/65	9	Oregon Tech	Compton, Calif.	UFA(Chi)-'97	16/15*
87	Crumpler, Carlester	TE	6-6	260	9/5/71	4	East Carolina	Greenville, N.C.	D7-'94	16/7
21	Cunningham, T.J.	S	6-0	197	10/24/72	2	Colorado	Aurora, Colo.	D6b-'96	9/0
93	Daniels, Phillip	DE	6-5	263	3/4/73	2	Georgia	Donalsonville, Ga.	D4a-'96	15/0
94	Edwards, Antonio	DE	6-3	271	3/10/70	5	Valdosta State	Moultrie, Ga.	D8b-'93	13/3
86	Fauria, Christian	TE	6-4	245	9/22/71	3	Colorado	Encino, Calif.	D2-'95	10/9
17	Friesz, John	QB	6-4	219	5/19/67	8	Idaho	Coeur d'Alene, Idaho	UFA(Wash)-'95	8/6
84	Galloway, Joey	WR	5-11	188	11/20/71	3	Ohio State	Bellaire, Ohio	D1-'95	16/16
19	Goines, Eddie	WR	6-0	186	8/16/72	3	North Carolina State	Lakeland, Fla.	D6b-'95	0*
77	Graham, Derrick	G	6-4	315	3/18/67	8	Appalachian State	Groveland, Fla.	FA-'96	16/16
32	Gray, Oscar	RB	6-1	255	8/7/72	2	Arkansas	Houston, Tex.	FA-'96	9/0
68	Greene, Andrew	G	6-3	304	9/24/69	2	Indiana	Ontario, Canada	FA-'97	0*
81	Harris, Ronnie	WR	5-11	179	6/4/70	4	Oregon	San Jose, Calif.	FA-'94	16/0
67	Harrison, Martin	DE	6-5	257	9/20/67	7	Washington	Bellevue, Wash.	UFA(Minn)-'97	16/8*
28	Innocent, Dou	RB	5-11	212	7/9/72	2	Mississippi	Pompano Beach, Fla.	FA-'96	4/0
66	Kendall, Pete	G	6-5	292	7/9/73	2	Boston College	Weymouth, Mass.	D1-'96	12/11
96	Kennedy, Cortez	DT	6-3	306	8/23/68	8	Miami	Wilson, Ark.	D1-'90	16/16
57	Kyle, Jason	LB	6-3	242	5/12/72	3	Arizona State	Tempe, Ariz.	D4b-'95	16/0
97	LaBounty, Matt	DE	6-4	275	1/3/69	5	Oregon	Novato, Calif.	T(GB)-'96	3/0
56	Logan, James	LB	6-2	225	12/6/72	3	Memphis	Opp, Ala.	W(Cin)-'95	6/0
52	Mawae, Kevin	C	6-4	296	1/23/71	4	Louisiana State	Leesville, La.	D2-'94	16/16
46	May, Deems	TE	6-4	263	3/6/69	6	North Carolina	Lexington, N.C.	UFA(SD)-'97	16/12*
82	McKnight, James	WR	6-0	194	6/17/72	3	Liberty	Apopka, Fla.	FA-'94	16/0
92	McMillian, Henry	DT	6-3	290	10/17/71	3	Florida	Folkston, Ga.	D6a-'95	3/0
1	Moon, Warren	QB	6-3	213	11/18/56	14	Washington	Los Angeles, Calif.	FA-'97	8/8*
55	Moss, Winston	LB	6-3	245	12/24/65	11	Miami	Miami, Fla.	UFA(Oak)-'95	16/16
2	Peterson, Todd	K	5-10	171	2/4/70	3	Georgia	Valdosta, Ga.	FA-'95	16/0
85	Pritchard, Mike	WR	5-10	193	10/26/69	6	Colorado	Las Vegas, Nev.	FA-'96	16/5
29	Richardson, C.J.	S	5-10	209	6/10/72	2	Miami	Dallas, Tex.	FA-'97	0*
78	Riley, Pat	DT	6-5	290	3/8/72	2	Miami	Marrero, La.	FA-'96	0*
23	Seigler, Dexter	CB	5-9	178	1/11/72	2	Miami	Miami, Fla.	FA-'95	12/0
70	Sinclair, Michael	DE	6-4	267	1/31/68	7	Eastern New Mexico	Beaumont, Tex.	D6-'91	16/16
25	† Smith, Lamar	RB	5-11	218	11/29/70	4	Houston	Fort Wayne, Ind.	D3-'94	16/2
38	Strong, Mack	RB	6-0	235	9/11/71	4	Georgia	Columbus, Ga.	FA-'93	14/8
22	Thomas, Fred	CB	5-9	172	9/11/73	2	Tennessee-Martin	Bruce, Miss.	D2-'96	15/0
13	Torretta, Gino	QB	6-3	215	8/10/70	4	Miami	Pinole, Calif.	W(SF)-'96	1/0
14	Tuten, Rick	P	6-2	221	1/5/65	9	Florida State	Ocala, Fla.	FA-'91	16/0
53	Unverzagt, Eric	LB	6-1	241	12/18/72	2	Wisconsin	Central Islip, N.Y.	D4c-'96	8/0
42	Warren, Chris	RB	6-2	228	1/24/68	8	Ferrum	Burke, Va.	D4-'90	14/14
95	Wells, Dean	LB	6-3	248	7/20/70	5	Kentucky	Louisville, Kent.	D4-'93	16/15
33	Williams, Darryl	S	6-0	202	1/7/70	6	Miami	Hialeah, Fla.	UFA(Cin)-'96	16/16
79	Williams, Grant	T	6-7	323	5/10/74	2	Louisiana Tech	Clinton, Miss.	FA-'96	8/0
83	Williams, Ronnie	TE	6-3	258	1/19/66	6	Oklahoma State	Wichita Falls, Tex.	FA-'96	13/3
27	Williams, Willie	CB	5-9	180	12/26/70	5	Western Carolina	Columbia, S.C.	UFA(Pitt)-'97	15/14*

* Barr inactive for 16 games; Benford, Bryant, Goines, and Stowe missed '96 season because of injury; Blades played 15 games with Detroit; Brown played 14 games with Pittsburgh; Cain played 16 games with Chicago; Greene last active with Miami in '95; Harrison played 16 games with Minnesota; May played 16 games with San Diego; Moon played 8 games with Minnesota; Richardson last active with Arizona in '95; Riley active for 2 games with Seattle; W. Williams played 15 games with Pittsburgh.

† Restricted free agent; subject to developments.

Traded—QB Rick Mirer (11 games in '96) to Chicago.

Players lost through free agency (4): CB Carlton Gray (Ind; 16 games in '96); CB Corey Harris (Mia; 16); DE Michael McCrary (Balt; 16); LB Terry Wooden (KC; 9).

Also played for Seahawks in '96—S Robert Blackmon (16 games), C Ed Cunningtham (11), QB Stan Gelbaugh (1), CB Selwyn Jones (16), DT Glenn Montgomery (7), DT Joe Nash (8), WR Ricky Proehl (16).

COACHING STAFF

Head Coach,
Dennis Erickson

Pro Career: Named the fifth head coach in franchise history on January 12, 1995. Career record: 15-17-0.
Background: Started his coaching career at Montana State as a graduate assistant in 1969. Also served as a graduate assistant at Washington State in 1970. Was an assistant at Montana State, Idaho, and Fresno State before becoming the head coach at Idaho in 1982. Twice advanced to NCAA I-AA playoffs and was a two-time All-Big Sky Conference coach of the year. Head coach one season (1986) at Wyoming before moving to Washington State in 1987. Took Cougars to their first bowl game since 1981 and posted their first bowl game win in 72 years in 1988. Finished the season with a national ranking of sixteenth, the school's best ever. Spent the last six seasons at the University of Miami, where he won national championships in 1989 (his first season) and in 1991, compiling an undefeated (12-0) record. Played in six New Year's Day bowl games, including five with national championship implications. Twice finished third in the country and once sixth in addition to the two national titles. Posted an NCAA-best 63-9 record during tenure at Miami and reached 100 career wins in just 137 games, the fourth fastest among Division I coaches active in 1994. Was 35-2 at the Orange Bowl, including being part of an NCAA-record 58-game winning streak. Played quarterback collegiately at Montana State from 1966-68. Career record: 137-40-1.
Personal: Born March 24, 1947, in Everett, Washington. Graduated from Montana State with a bachelor of arts degree in Physical Education. Dennis and his wife, Marilyn, have two sons, Bryce and Ryan, and live in Redmond, Washington.

ASSISTANT COACHES

Dave Arnold, special teams; born September 18, 1944, Jackson, Mich., lives in Bellevue, Wash. Tight end Drake 1963-66. No pro playing experience. College coach: Michigan State 1980-81, Montana State 1982-86 (head coach 1983-86), Washington State 1987-88, Miami 1989-94. Pro coach: Joined Seahawks in 1995.
Tommy Brasher, defensive line; born December 30, 1940, El Dorado, Ark., lives in Redmond, Wash. Linebacker Arkansas 1962-63. No pro playing experience. College coach: Arkansas 1970, Virginia Tech 1971, Northeast Louisiana 1974, 1976, Southern Methodist 1977-81. Pro coach: Shreveport Steamer (WFL) 1975, New England Patriots 1982-84, Philadelphia Eagles 1985, Atlanta Falcons 1986-89, Tampa Bay Buccaneers 1990, joined Seahawks in 1992.
Bob Bratkowski, offensive coordinator-wide receivers; born December 2, 1955, San Angelo, Tex., lives in Redmond, Wash. Wide receiver Washington State 1974, 1976-77. No pro playing experience. College coach: Missouri 1978-80, Weber State 1981-85, Wyoming 1986, Washington State 1987-88, Miami 1989-91. Pro coach: Joined Seahawks in 1992.
Dave Brown, defensive assistant; born January 16, 1953, Akron, Ohio, lives in Woodinville, Wash. Defensive back Michigan 1972-74. Pro defensive back Pittsburgh Steelers 1975, Seattle Seahawks 1976-86, Green Bay Packers 1987-90. Pro coach: Joined Seahawks in 1992.
Keith Gilbertson, tight ends; born May 15, 1948, Snohomish, Wash., lives in Kirkland, Wash. Lineman Hawaii 1969-70. No pro playing experience. College coach: Idaho State 1971-73, Western Washington 1974, Washington 1976, 1989-91, Utah State 1977-81, Idaho 1982, 1985-88 (head coach 1986-88), California 1992-95 (head coach). Pro coach: Joined Seahawks in 1996.
Ned James, defensive assistant; born January 18, 1964, Syracuse, N.Y., lives in Kirkland, Wash. Quarterback New Mexico 1965-66. Pro quarterback Montreal Alouettes (CFL) 1987, Dallas Texans (Arena Football) 1990. College coach: Arizona State 1987-88, Long Beach State 1988-89, Texas Christian 1989-90, Winona State 1992-94. Pro coach: London

Monarchs (World League) 1991-92, joined Seahawks in 1995.
Darren Krein, assistant strength and conditioning; born July 7, 1971, Aurora, Colo., lives in Kirkland, Wash. Linebacker/defensive end Miami 1989-93. Pro defensive end San Diego Chargers 1994, Barcelona Dragons (World League) 1996. Pro coach: Joined Seahawks in 1997.
Dana LeDuc, strength and conditioning; born March 22, 1953, Tacoma, Wash., lives in Bellevue, Wash. No college or pro playing experience. College coach: Texas 1977-92, Miami 1993-94. Pro coach: Joined Seahawks in 1995.
Greg McMakin, defensive coordinator; born April 24, 1947, Springfield, Ore., lives in Redmond, Wash. Defensive back Southern Oregon 1964-68. No pro playing experience. College coach: Arizona 1968-69, Southern Oregon State 1973-76, Idaho 1976-78, San Jose State 1978-83, Stanford 1984-85, Oregon Tech 1986-90, Utah 1990-92, Miami 1993-94. Pro coach: Denver Gold (USFL) 1985-86, joined Seahawks in 1995.
Howard Mudd, offensive line; born February 10, 1942, Midland, Mich., lives in Kirkland, Wash. Guard Hillsdale College 1961-63. Pro guard San Francisco 49ers 1964-69, Chicago Bears 1969-71. College coach: California 1972-73. Pro coach: San Diego Chargers 1974-76, San Francisco 49ers 1977, Seattle Seahawks 1978-82, Cleveland Browns 1983-88, Kansas City Chiefs 1989-92, rejoined Seahawks in 1993.
Mike Murphy, linebackers; born September 25, 1944, New York City, N.Y., lives in Bellevue, Wash. Guard-linebacker Huron College 1963-1965. No pro

playing experience. College coach: Vermont 1970-73, Idaho State 1974-76, Western Illinois 1977-78. Pro coach: Saskatchewan Roughriders (CFL) 1979, Chicago Blitz (USFL) 1984, Detroit Lions 1985-89, Arizona Cardinals 1990-93, joined Seahawks in 1995.
Rich Olson, quarterbacks; born July 7, 1948, Wilmington, Calif., lives in Bellevue, Wash. Quarterback/free safety Washington State 1968-69. No pro playing experience. College coach: Washington State 1970, Fresno State 1976, Southern California 1977, Southern Methodist 1978-80, Arkansas 1981-83, Fresno State 1984-91, Miami 1992-94. Pro coach: Joined Seahawks in 1995.
Willy Robinson, defensive backs; born February 10, 1956, Fort Carson, Colo., lives in Bellevue, Wash. No college or pro playing experience. College coach: Fresno State 1978, 1980-93, San Jose State 1979, Miami 1994. Pro coach: Joined Seahawks in 1995.
Clarence Shelmon, running backs; born September 17, 1952, Bossier City, La., lives in Kirkland, Wash. Running back Houston 1971-75. No pro playing experience. College coach: Army 1978-80, Indiana 1981-83, Arizona 1984-86, Southern California 1987-90. Pro coach: Los Angeles Rams 1991, joined Seahawks in 1992.
Gregg Smith, assistant head coach-offensive line; born October 28, 1946, Oklahoma City, Okla., lives in Bellevue, Wash. Tight end Idaho 1965-66. No pro playing experience. College coach: Idaho 1967-68, 1982-85, Wyoming 1986, Washington State 1987-88, Miami 1989-94. Pro coach: Joined Seahawks in 1995.

1997 FIRST-YEAR ROSTER

Name	Pos.	Ht.	Wt.	Birthdate	College	Hometown	How Acq.
Arellanes, Jim	QB	6-3	217	1/30/74	Fresno State	Pico River, Calif.	FA
Bloedorn, Greg (1)	G	6-6	278	11/15/72	Cornell	Glen Ellyn, Ill.	FA-'96
Burton, Paul	P	5-11	191	7/8/73	Northwestern	Framingham, Mass.	FA
Clark, Jamal	TE	6-5	250	8/20/74	UCLA	Davis, Calif.	FA
Cooper, Andre	WR	6-2	190	6/21/75	Florida State	Jacksonville, Fla.	FA
DiMario, Pete	T	6-4	285	8/3/72	Alabama	Tuscaloosa, Ala.	FA
Elzy, Myron	DT	6-3	308	3/8/72	Central State, Ohio	Warren, Ohio	FA
Gianacakos, Nick	DE	6-4	262	9/9/74	Boston College	Lyons, Ill.	FA
Hampton, Alonzo	CB	5-11	170	10/9/73	Northeast Louisiana	Warren, Ark.	FA
Ina, J.	G	6-3	290	7/7/74	Miami	Franklin, La.	FA
Jones, Carlos	CB	5-10	180	8/31/73	Miami	Marrero, La.	D7
Jones, Walter	T	6-5	300	1/19/74	Florida State	Aliceville, Ala.	D1b
Kempfert, David	C	6-4	288	5/11/74	Montana	Missoula, Mont.	FA
Kitna, Jon (1)	QB	6-2	217	9/21/72	Central Washington	Tacoma, Wash.	FA-'96
McQueen, Le Vance	LB	6-0	242	10/3/76	Duke	Dunn, N.C.	FA
Mili, Itula	TE	6-4	265	4/20/73	Brigham Young	Laie, Hawaii	D6
Moore, Larry	G	6-3	291	6/1/75	Brigham Young	Spring Valley, Calif.	FA
Parker, Riddick (1)	DT	6-3	274	11/20/72	North Carolina	Southampton, Va.	FA-'96
Peters, Tyrell	LB	6-0	230	8/4/74	Oklahoma	Norman, Okla.	FA
Shillingford, Grayson (1)	WR	6-0	192	12/25/74	British Columbia	Toronto, Ontario	FA-'96
Springs, Shawn	CB	6-0	195	3/11/75	Ohio State	Silver Springs, Md.	D1a
Stokes, Eric	S	5-11	200	12/18/73	Nebraska	Lincoln, Neb.	D5
Wilson, Robert	WR	5-11	176	6/23/74	Florida A&M	Monticello, Fla.	FA

The term NFL Rookie is defined as a player who is in his first season of professional football and has not been on the roster of another professional football team for any regular-season or postseason games. A Rookie is designated by an "R" on NFL rosters. Players who have been active in another professional football league or players who have NFL experience, including either preseason training camp or being on an Active List or Inactive List, or on Reserve/Injured or Reserve/Physically Unable to Perform for fewer than six regular-season games, are termed NFL First-Year Players. An NFL First-Year Player is designated by a "1" on NFL rosters. Thereafter, a player is credited with an additional year of experience for each season in which he accumulates six games on the Active List or Inactive List, or on Reserve/Injured or Reserve/Physically Unable to Perform.

NOTES

TENNESSEE OILERS

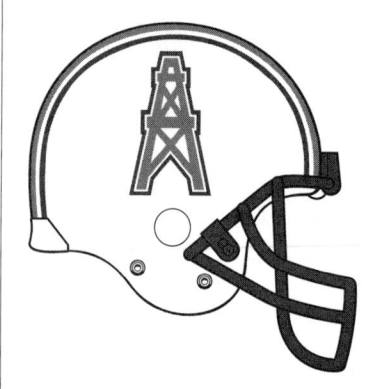

American Football Conference
Central Division
Team Colors: Columbia Blue, Scarlet, and White
Baptist Sports Park
7640 Hwy 70 South
Nashville, Tennessee 37221
Telephone: (615) 673-1500

CLUB OFFICIALS

President: K.S. (Bud) Adams, Jr.
Exec. Assistant to President: Thomas S. Smith
Exec. V.P./General Manager: Floyd Reese
Exec. V.P./Administration: Mike McClure
Vice President/General Counsel: Steve Underwood
Vice President/Player Personnel and Scouting:
  Mike Holovak
Senior Vice President/Marketing and Broadcasting:
  Don MacLachlan
Director of Player Personnel: Rich Snead
Director of Business Operations: Lewis Mangum
Director of Media Services: Dave Pearson
Director of Public and Community Relations:
  Rod St. Clair
Assistant Ticket Manager: Ralph Stolarski
Director of Security: Grady Sessums
Director of Player Relations: Willie Alexander
Head Trainer: Brad Brown
Assistant Trainers: Don Moseley, Geoff Kaplan
Equipment Manager: Paul Noska
Video Coordinator: Ken Sparacino
Stadium: Liberty Bowl Memorial Stadium
  •**Capacity:** 62,380
  335 South Hollywood
  Memphis , Tennessee 38104
Playing Surface: Grass
Training Camp: Hale Hall
  Tennessee State University
  Nashville, Tennessee 37209-1561

1997 SCHEDULE
PRESEASON

Aug. 2	vs. New Orleans at Memphis	7:00
Aug. 9	vs. Washington at Nashville	7:00
Aug. 16	vs. San Diego at Nashville	7:00
Aug. 22	at Dallas	7:00

REGULAR SEASON

Aug. 31	**Oakland**	12:00
Sept. 7	at Miami	1:00
Sept. 14	Open Date	
Sept. 21	**Baltimore**	12:00
Sept. 28	at Pittsburgh	1:00
Oct. 5	at Seattle	1:00
Oct. 12	**Cincinnati**	12:00
Oct. 19	**Washington**	12:00
Oct. 26	at Arizona	2:00
Nov. 2	**Jacksonville**	3:00
Nov. 9	**New York Giants**	3:00
Nov. 16	at Jacksonville	1:00
Nov. 23	**Buffalo**	12:00
Nov. 27	at Dallas (Thurs.)	3:00
Dec. 4	at Cincinnati (Thurs.)	8:00
Dec. 14	at Baltimore	1:00

RECORD HOLDERS
INDIVIDUAL RECORDS—CAREER

Category	Name	Performance
Rushing (Yds.)	Earl Campbell, 1978-1984	8,574
Passing (Yds.)	Warren Moon, 1984-1993	33,685
Passing (TDs)	Warren Moon, 1984-1993	196
Receiving (No.)	Ernest Givins, 1986-1994	542
Receiving (Yds.)	Ernest Givins, 1986-1994	7,935
Interceptions	Jim Norton, 1960-68	45
Punting (Avg.)	Greg Montgomery, 1988-1993	43.6
Punt Return (Avg.)	Billy Johnson, 1974-1980	13.2
Kickoff Return (Avg.)	Bobby Jancik, 1962-67	26.5
Field Goals	Al Del Greco, 1991-96	135
Touchdowns (Tot.)	Earl Campbell, 1978-1984	73
Points	George Blanda, 1960-66	596

INDIVIDUAL RECORDS—SINGLE SEASON

Category	Name	Performance
Rushing (Yds.)	Earl Campbell, 1980	1,934
Passing (Yds.)	Warren Moon, 1991	4,690
Passing (TDs)	George Blanda, 1961	36
Receiving (No.)	Charlie Hennigan, 1964	101
Receiving (Yds.)	Charlie Hennigan, 1961	1,746
Interceptions	Fred Glick, 1963	12
	Mike Reinfeldt, 1979	12
Punting (Avg.)	Greg Montgomery, 1992	46.9
Punt Return (Avg.)	Billy Johnson, 1977	15.4
Kickoff Return (Avg.)	Ken Hall, 1960	31.3
Field Goals	Al Del Greco, 1996	32
Touchdowns (Tot.)	Earl Campbell, 1979	19
Points	Al Del Greco, 1996	131

INDIVIDUAL RECORDS—SINGLE GAME

Category	Name	Performance
Rushing (Yds.)	Billy Cannon, 12-10-61	216
Passing (Yds.)	Warren Moon, 12-16-90	527
Passing (TDs)	George Blanda, 11-19-61	*7
Receiving (No.)	Charlie Hennigan, 10-13-61	13
	Haywood Jeffires, 10-13-91	13
Receiving (Yds.)	Charlie Hennigan, 10-13-61	272
Interceptions	Many times	3
	Last time by Marcus Robertson, 11-21-93	
Field Goals	Roy Gerela, 9-28-69	5
Touchdowns (Tot.)	Billy Cannon, 12-10-61	5
Points	Billy Cannon, 12-10-61	30

*NFL Record

Dec. 21	**Pittsburgh**	12:00

COACHING HISTORY
HOUSTON 1960-1996
(260-304-6)

1960-61	Lou Rymkus*	12-7-1
1961	Wally Lemm	10-0-0
1962-63	Frank (Pop) Ivy	17-12-0
1964	Sammy Baugh	4-10-0
1965	Hugh Taylor	4-10-0
1966-70	Wally Lemm	28-40-4
1971	Ed Hughes	4-9-1
1972-73	Bill Peterson**	1-18-0
1973-74	Sid Gillman	8-15-0
1975-80	O.A. (Bum) Phillips	59-38-0
1981-83	Ed Biles***	8-23-0
1983	Chuck Studley	2-8-0
1984-85	Hugh Campbell****	8-22-0
1985-89	Jerry Glanville	35-35-0
1990-94	Jack Pardee#	44-35-0
1994-96	Jeff Fisher	16-22-0

  * Released after five games in 1961
 ** Released after five games in 1973
*** Resigned after six games in 1983
**** Released after 14 games in 1985
 # Released after 10 games in 1994

LIBERTY BOWL MEMORIAL STADIUM

N

1996 TEAM RECORD
PRESEASON (2-2)

Date	Result		Opponents
8/3	W	31-13	vs. N.Y. Jets at Jackson, Miss.
8/10	W	16-12	Indianapolis
8/16	L	23-34	Detroit
8/24	L	19-24	vs. Dallas at Orlando, Fla.

REGULAR SEASON (8-8)

Date	Result		Opponents	Att.
9/1	L	19-20	Kansas City	27,725
9/8	W	34-27	at Jacksonville	66,468
9/15	W	29-13	Baltimore	20,082
9/29	L	16-30	at Pittsburgh	58,608
10/6	W	30-27	at Cincinnati (OT)	44,680
10/13	W	23-13	at Atlanta	35,401
10/20	W	23-13	Pittsburgh	50,337
10/27	L	9-10	San Francisco	53,664
11/3	L	16-23	at Seattle	36,320
11/10	W	31-14	at New Orleans	34,121
11/17	L	20-23	Miami	47,358
11/24	L	6-31	Carolina	20,107
12/1	W	35-10	at N.Y. Jets	21,731
12/8	L	17-23	Jacksonville	20,196
12/15	L	13-21	Cincinnati	15,131
12/22	W	24-21	at Baltimore	52,704

(OT) Overtime

SCORE BY PERIODS

Oilers	105	79	67	91	3	—	345
Opponents	64	78	48	129	0	—	319

ATTENDANCE
Home 254,600   Away 350,033   Total 604,633
Single-game home record, 63,713 (9/6/92)
Single-season home record, 482,726 (1991)

1996 TEAM STATISTICS

	Oilers	Opp.
Total First Downs	287	271
Rushing	110	78
Passing	157	169
Penalty	20	24
Third Down: Made/Att	79/206	70/199
Third Down Pct.	38.3	35.2
Fourth Down: Made/Att	7/11	4/12
Fourth Down Pct.	63.6	33.3
Total Net Yards	5048	4610
Avg. Per Game	315.5	288.1
Total Plays	972	956
Avg. Per Play	5.2	4.8
Net Yards Rushing	1950	1385
Avg. Per Game	121.9	86.6
Total Rushes	475	397
Net Yards Passing	3098	3225
Avg. Per Game	193.6	201.6
Sacked/Yards Lost	34/198	35/242
Gross Yards	3296	3467
Att./Completions	463/272	524/312
Completion Pct.	58.7	59.5
Had Intercepted	15	12
Punts/Avg.	68/43.7	75/41.0
Net Punting Avg.	68/38.0	75/35.1
Penalties/Yards Lost	91/812	88/672
Fumbles/Ball Lost	26/15	29/14
Touchdowns	35	35
Rushing	12	5
Passing	22	24
Returns	1	6
Avg. Time of Possession	33:02	27:58

1996 INDIVIDUAL STATISTICS

PASSING	Att.	Comp.	Yds.	Pct.	TD	Int.	Tkld.	Rate
Chandler	320	184	2099	57.5	16	11	25/153	79.7
McNair	143	88	1197	61.5	6	4	9/45	90.6
Oilers	463	272	3296	58.7	22	15	34/198	83.0
Opponents	524	312	3467	59.5	24	12	35/242	85.0

SCORING	TD R	TD P	TD Rt	PAT	FG	Saf	PTS
Del Greco	0	0	0	35/35	32/38	0	131
George	8	0	0	0/0	0/0	0	48
Davis	0	6	0	0/0	0/0	0	36
Wycheck	0	6	0	0/0	0/0	0	36
Sanders	0	4	0	0/0	0/0	0	24
Harmon	1	2	0	0/0	0/0	0	18
McNair	2	0	0	0/0	0/0	0	12
Russell	0	2	0	0/0	0/0	0	12
Floyd	0	1	0	0/0	0/0	0	6
D. Lewis	0	0	1	0/0	0/0	0	6
Norgard	0	1	0	0/0	0/0	0	6
Thomas	1	0	0	0/0	0/0	0	6
Jackson	0	0	0	0/0	0/0	1	2
Oilers	12	22	1	35/35	32/38	*2	345
Opponents	5	24	6	32/32	25/33	0	319

2-Point conversions: 0. Team: 0-0, Opponents: 1-3.
*Oilers were credited with 1 team safety.

RUSHING	Att.	Yds.	Avg.	LG	TD
George	335	1368	4.1	76	8
McNair	31	169	5.5	24t	2
Thomas	49	151	3.1	24t	1
Harmon	29	131	4.5	25	1
Chandler	28	113	4.0	16	0
Davis	1	15	15.0	15	0
Wycheck	2	3	1.5	3	0
Oilers	475	1950	4.1	76	12
Opponents	397	1385	3.5	26	5

RECEIVING	No.	Yds.	Avg.	LG	TD
Wycheck	53	511	9.6	29	6
Sanders	48	882	18.4	83t	4
Harmon	42	488	11.6	43	2
Davis	39	464	11.9	49	6
Russell	34	421	12.4	29	2
George	23	182	7.9	17	0
Thomas	13	128	9.8	33	0
Floyd	10	145	14.5	63t	1
R. Lewis	7	50	7.1	18	0
Wilson	2	24	12.0	14	0
Norgard	1	1	1.0	1t	1
Oilers	272	3296	12.1	83t	22
Opponents	312	3467	11.1	86t	24

INTERCEPTIONS	No.	Yds.	Avg.	LG	TD
D. Lewis	5	103	20.6	53	1
Robertson	4	44	11.0	27	0
Dishman	1	7	7.0	7	0
Bishop	1	6	6.0	6	0
Robinson	1	2	2.0	2	0
Oilers	12	162	13.5	53	1
Opponents	15	222	14.8	42t	3

PUNTING	No.	Yds.	Avg.	In 20	LG
Roby	67	2973	44.4	25	68
Oilers	68	2973	43.7	25	68
Opponents	75	3073	41.0	16	62

PUNT RETURNS	No.	FC	Yds.	Avg.	LG	TD
Gray	22	15	205	9.3	40	0
Floyd	7	3	74	10.6	32	0
Oilers	29	18	279	9.6	40	0
Opponents	31	14	251	8.1	46	0

KICKOFF RETURNS	No.	Yds.	Avg.	LG	TD
Gray	50	1224	24.5	88	0
Thomas	5	80	16.0	35	0
Harmon	4	69	17.3	20	0
Archie	2	24	12.0	13	0
McKeehan	2	6	3.0	6	0
Wycheck	2	5	2.5	5	0
Roan	1	13	13.0	13	0
Oilers	66	1421	21.5	88	0
Opponents	78	1675	21.5	47	0

SACKS	No.
Cook	7.5
Barrow	6.0
Walker	5.5
Young	4.0
Bowden	3.0
Roberson	3.0
Jackson	2.0
Wortham	2.0
Ford	1.0
Mix	1.0
Oilers	35.0
Opponents	34.0

1997 DRAFT CHOICES

Round	Name	Pos.	College
1	Kenny Holmes	DE	Miami
2	Joey Kent	WR	Tennessee
3	Denard Walker	DB	Louisiana State
	Scott Sanderson	T	Washington State
4	Derrick Mason	WR	Michigan State
	Pratt Lyons	DE	Troy State
5	George McCullough	DB	Baylor
6	Dennis Stallings	LB	Illinois
7	Armon Williams	DB	Arizona

TENNESSEE OILERS

1997 VETERAN ROSTER

No.	Name	Pos.	Ht.	Wt.	Birthdate	NFL Exp.	College	Hometown	How Acq.	'96 Games/ Starts
22	Archie, Mike	RB	5-8	205	10/14/72	2	Penn State	Sharon, Pa.	D7-'96	2/0
23	Bishop, Blaine	S	5-9	197	7/24/70	5	Ball State	Indianapolis, Ind.	D8-'93	15/15
58	Bowden, Joe	LB	5-11	230	2/25/70	6	Oklahoma	Mesquite, Tex.	D5a-'92	16/16
94	Burton, Kendrick	DE	6-5	288	9/7/73	2	Alabama	Hartselle, Ala.	D4a-'96	4/2
78	Cook, Anthony	DE-DT	6-3	293	5/30/72	3	South Carolina State	Bennettsville, S.C.	D2-'95	12/11
84	Davis, Willie	WR	6-0	181	10/10/67	6	Central Arkansas	Little Rock, Ark.	UFA(KC)-'96	16/14
3	Del Greco, Al	K	5-10	200	3/2/62	14	Auburn	Coral Gables, Fla.	FA-'91	16/0
77	Donnalley, Kevin	G-T	6-5	305	6/10/68	7	North Carolina	Raleigh, N.C.	D3b-'91	16/16
30	Dorsett, Anthony	CB	5-11	203	9/14/73	2	Pittsburgh	Dallas, Tex.	D6-'96	8/0
75	Eatman, Irv	T	6-7	305	1/1/61	12	UCLA	Dayton, Ohio	UFA(Atl)-'95	16/16
60	El-Mashtoub, Hicham	C	6-2	288	5/11/72	3	Arizona	Laval, Canada	D6-'95	1/0
91	Evans, Josh	DE-DT	6-0	280	9/6/72	3	Alabama-Birmingham	West Shawmut, Ala.	FA-'95	8/0
83	† Floyd, Malcolm	WR	6-0	194	12/29/72	4	Fresno State	Sacramento, Calif.	D3-'94	16/0
92	Ford, Henry	DE-DT	6-3	284	10/30/71	4	Arkansas	Ft. Worth, Tex.	D1-'94	15/14
27	George, Eddie	RB	6-3	232	9/24/73	2	Ohio State	Philadelphia, Pa.	D1-'96	16/16
21	Gray, Mel	KR-RB	5-9	171	3/16/61	12	Purdue	Williamsburg, Va.	UFA(Det)-'95	14/0
93	Halapin, Mike	DT	6-4	294	7/1/73	2	Pittsburgh	Apollo, Pa.	FA-'96	9/0
51	Hall, Lemanski	LB	6-0	229	11/24/70	3	Alabama	Valley, Ala.	D7-'94	3/0
33	Harmon, Ronnie	RB	5-11	200	5/7/64	12	Iowa	Queens, N.Y.	UFA(SD)-'96	16/6
71	Hayes, Melvin	T	6-6	325	4/28/73	3	Mississippi State	New Orleans, La.	FA-'96	1/0*
72	Hopkins, Brad	T	6-3	306	9/5/70	5	Illinois	Moline, Ill.	D1-'93	16/16
24	Jackson, Steve	CB	5-8	182	4/8/69	7	Purdue	Houston, Tex.	D3a-'91	16/1
57	Jones, Lenoy	LB	6-1	232	9/25/74	2	Texas Christian	Groesbeck, Tex.	FA-'96	11/0
50	Killens, Terry	LB	6-1	232	3/24/74	2	Penn State	Cincinnati, Ohio	D3-'96	14/0
17	Krieg, Dave	QB	6-1	202	10/20/58	18	Milton College	Schofield, Wis.	UFA(Chi)-'97	13/12*
66	Layman, Jason	T-G	6-5	306	7/29/73	2	Tennessee	Sevierville, Tenn.	D2b-'96	16/0
29	Lewis, Darryll	CB	5-9	183	12/16/68	7	Arizona	La Puente, Calif.	D2b-'91	16/16
88	† Lewis, Roderick	TE	6-5	254	6/9/71	4	Arizona	Dallas, Tex.	D5a-'94	16/7
56	Marts, Lonnie	LB	6-2	240	11/10/68	8	Tulane	New Orleans, La.	UFA(TB)-'97	16/13*
74	Matthews, Bruce	G-C	6-5	298	8/8/61	15	Southern California	Arcadia, Calif.	D1-'83	16/16
87	McKeehan, James	TE	6-3	251	8/9/73	2	Texas A&M	Willis, Tex.	FA-'95	14/0
9	McNair, Steve	QB	6-2	224	2/14/73	3	Alcorn State	Mt. Olive, Miss.	D1-'95	9/4
55	# Mills, John Henry	LB	6-0	222	10/31/69	5	Wake Forest	Tallahassee, Fla.	D5-'93	16/0
97	Mix, Bryant	DE-DT	6-3	301	7/28/72	2	Alcorn State	Water Valley, Miss.	D2a-'96	6/2
64	Norgard, Erik	G-C	6-1	282	11/4/65	8	Colorado	Arlington, Wash.	FA-'90	13/0
16	Ritchey, James	QB	6-2	218	7/10/73	2	Stephen F. Austin	Copperas Cove, Tex.	FA-'96	1/0
80	Roan, Michael	TE	6-3	251	8/29/72	3	Wisconsin	Iowa City, Iowa	D4-'95	15/1
90	Roberson, James	DE	6-3	275	5/3/71	2	Florida State	Lake Wales, Fla.	FA-'96	15/5
31	Robertson, Marcus	S	5-11	197	10/2/69	7	Iowa State	Pasadena, Calif.	D4b-'91	16/16
37	Robinson, Rafael	S	5-11	200	6/19/69	6	Wisconsin	Jefferson, Tex.	UFA(Sea)-'96	16/2
7	Roby, Reggie	P	6-3	258	7/30/61	15	Iowa	East Waterloo, Iowa	UFA(TB)-'96	16/0
69	Runyan, Jon	T	6-7	308	11/27/73	2	Michigan	Flint, Mich.	D4b-'96	10/0
85	Russell, Derek	WR	6-0	195	7/22/69	7	Arkansas	Little Rock, Ark.	UFA(Den)-'95	16/5
81	Sanders, Chris	WR	6-1	184	5/8/72	3	Ohio State	Denver, Colo.	D3a-'95	16/15
54	Smith, Al	LB	6-1	244	11/26/64	11	Utah State	Los Angeles, Calif.	D6a-'87	1/1
53	Stepnoski, Mark	C	6-2	269	1/20/67	9	Pittsburgh	Erie, Pa.	UFA(Dall)-'95	16/16
26	Stewart, Rayna	CB-S	5-10	192	6/18/73	2	Northern Arizona	Chatsworth, Calif.	D5-'96	15/0
20	Thomas, Rodney	RB	5-10	213	3/30/73	3	Texas A&M	Groveton, Tex.	D3b-'95	16/0
96	Walker, Gary	DE-DT	6-2	285	2/28/73	3	Auburn	Lavonia, Ga.	D5-'95	16/16
82	Wilson, Sheddrick	WR	6-2	210	11/23/73	2	Louisiana State	Thomasville, Ga.	FA-'96	11/0
52	† Wortham, Barron	LB	5-11	244	11/1/69	4	Texas-El Paso	Everman, Tex.	D6b-'94	15/14
89	Wycheck, Frank	TE	6-3	247	10/14/71	5	Maryland	Philadelphia, Pa.	W(Wash)-'95	16/16

* Hayes played 1 game with N.Y. Jets in '96; Krieg played 13 games with Chicago; Marts played 16 games with Tampa Bay.

Unrestricted free agent; subject to developments.

† Restricted free agent; subject to developments.

Traded—QB Chris Chandler (12 games in '96) to Atlanta.

Players lost through free agency (2): LB Micheal Barrow (Car; 16 games in '96), CB Cris Dishman (Wash; 16).

Also played with Oilers in '96—CB Tomur Barnes (5 games), DE Robert Young (15).

COACHING STAFF

Head Coach,
Jeff Fisher

Pro Career: Officially named as Oilers' fifteenth head coach on January 5, 1995. Holds record of 15-17 in first two full seasons as head coach, missing the playoffs by just one game in 1996. Was elevated to head coach-defensive coordinator on November 14, 1994, after head coach Jack Pardee and assistant head coach-offense Kevin Gilbride were relieved of their duties. Took over a 1-9 team and guided them through the final six games of the season, picking up his first victory against the New York Jets in the season finale. Originally joined the Oilers on February 9, 1994, as defensive coordinator after spending two seasons as defensive backs coach for the San Francisco 49ers (1992-93). Prior to stint with the 49ers, worked as defensive coordinator for the Los Angeles Rams (1991). From 1986-1990, was an assistant for Buddy Ryan's Philadelphia Eagles, serving as defensive backs coach from 1986-88 before becoming the NFL's youngest defensive coordinator in 1989. Drafted by Chicago in seventh round in 1981, spent five seasons as a cornerback and kick returner for the Bears (1981-85). Did not play in Bears' 1985 Super Bowl championship season after being placed on injured reserve with an ankle injury. That season he assisted defensive coordinator Buddy Ryan. Career record: 16-22.

Background: Played at Southern California (1977-1980) for John Robinson in a star-studded defensive backfield that included Ronnie Lott, Dennis Smith, and Joey Browner. Member of the USC team that won the national championship in 1978. Also served as the Trojans' backup placekicker and was a Pac-10 All-Academic selection in 1980.

Personal: Born February 25, 1958, in Culver City, Calif. Jeff and his wife, Juli, have three children, sons Brandon and Trenton, and daughter Tara. The family resides in Sugar Land, Tex.

ASSISTANT COACHES

Bart Andrus, offensive assistant-quality control; born March 30, 1958, Logan, Utah, lives in Houston, Tex. Quarterback Montana 1978-81. No pro playing experience. College coach: Humboldt State 1986-89, Montana State 1990-91, Southern Utah 1993-95, Rocky Mountain College 1996 (head coach). Pro coach: Joined Oilers in 1997.

Greg Brown, defensive backs; born October 10, 1957, Denver, Colo., lives in Houston, Tex. Defensive back Texas-El Paso 1978-79. No pro playing experience. College coach: Wyoming 1987-88, Purdue 1989-90, Colorado 1991-93. Pro coach: Denver Gold (USFL) 1983-84, Tampa Bay Buccaneers 1984-86, Atlanta Falcons 1994, San Diego Chargers 1995-96, joined Oilers in 1997.

O'Neill Gilbert, linebackers; born March 29, 1965, Monroe, La., lives in Houston, Tex. Linebacker Texas A&M 1985-88. Pro linebacker San Francisco 49ers 1990, Montreal Machine (WFL) 1991. College coach: Navarro (Tex.) J.C. 1991, Nevada-Las Vegas 1992-94, Illinois 1995-96. Pro coach: Joined Oilers in 1997.

Jerry Gray, defensive assistant-quality control; born December 16, 1962, Lubbock, Tex., lives in Houston, Tex. Defensive back Texas 1981-84. Pro safety-cornerback Los Angeles Rams 1985-91, Houston Oilers 1992, Tampa Bay Buccaneers 1993. College coach: Southern Methodist 1995-96. Pro coach: Joined Oilers in 1997.

George Henshaw, offensive line-tight ends; born January 22, 1948, Richmond, Va., lives in Houston, Tex. Defensive tackle West Virginia 1967-69. No pro playing experience. College coach: West Virginia 1970-75, Florida State 1976-82, Alabama 1983-86, Tulsa 1987 (head coach). Pro coach: Denver Broncos 1988-92, New York Giants 1993-96, joined Oilers in 1997.

Alan Lowry, wide receivers; born November 21, 1950, Miami, Okla., lives in Houston, Tex. Defensive back-quarterback Texas 1970-72. No pro playing experience. College coach: Virginia Tech 1974, Wyoming 1975, Texas 1977-81. Pro coach: Dallas Cowboys 1982-90, Tampa Bay Buccaneers 1991, San Francisco 49ers 1992-95, joined Oilers in 1996.

Mike Munchak, offensive line; born March 5, 1960, Scranton, Pa., lives in Sugar Land, Tex. Guard-tackle Penn State 1979-81. Pro guard Houston Oilers 1982-93. Pro coach: Joined Oilers in 1994.

Rex Norris, defensive line; born December 10, 1939, Tipton, Ind., lives in Sugar Land, Tex. Linebacker San Angelo (Tex.) J.C. 1959-60, East Texas State 1961-62. No pro playing experience. College coach: Navarro (Tex.) J.C. 1970-71, Texas A&M 1972, Oklahoma 1973-83, Arizona State 1984, Florida 1988-89, Tennessee 1990-91, Texas 1992-93. Pro coach: Detroit Lions 1985-87, Denver Broncos 1994, joined Oilers in 1995.

Russ Purnell, special teams; born June 12, 1948, Chicago, Ill., lives in Sugar Land, Tex. Center Orange Coast (Calif.) J.C. 1966-67, Whittier College 1968-69. No pro playing experience. College coach: Whittier College 1970-71, Southern California 1982-84. Pro coach: Seattle Seahawks 1986-94, joined Oilers in 1995.

Sherman Smith, running backs; born November 1, 1954, Youngstown, Ohio, lives in Missouri City, Tex. Quarterback Miami (Ohio) 1972-75. Pro running back Seattle Seahawks 1976-82, San Diego Chargers 1983-84. College coach: Miami (Ohio) 1990-91, Illinois 1992-94. Pro coach: Joined Oilers in 1995.

Les Steckel, offensive coordinator-quarterbacks; born July 1, 1946, North Hampton, Pa., lives in Sugar Land, Tex. Running back Kansas 1964-68. No pro playing experience. College coach: Colorado 1972-76, 1991-92, Navy 1977, Brown 1989. Pro coach: San Francisco 49ers 1978, Minnesota Vikings 1979-84 (head coach 1984), New England Patriots 1985-88, Denver Broncos 1993-94, joined Oilers in 1995.

Steve Watterson, strength and rehabilitation; born November 27, 1956, Newport, R.I., lives in Sugar Land, Tex. Attended Rhode Island. No college or pro playing experience. Pro coach: Philadelphia Eagles 1984-85, joined Oilers in 1986.

Gregg Williams, defensive coordinator; born July 15, 1958 in Excelsior Springs, Mo., lives in Katy, Tex. Quarterback Northeast Missouri State 1976-79. No pro playing experience. College coach: Houston 1988-89. Pro coach: Joined Oilers in 1990.

1997 FIRST-YEAR ROSTER

Name	Pos.	Ht.	Wt.	Birthdate	College	Hometown	How Acq.
Adams, Louis	LB	6-1	231	7/8/74	Oklahoma State	Pontiac, Mich.	FA
Alderson, Winston	T	6-4	344	12/27/73	Arkansas	El Dorado, Ark.	FA
Allen, James	RB	5-10	212	3/28/75	Oklahoma	Wynnewood, Okla.	FA
Atteberry, Ty	P-K	6-0	199	8/11/73	Baylor	Kingwood, Tex.	FA
Barnes, Derrick	LB	6-1	261	9/11/74	Oregon	San Jose, Calif.	FA
Burnstein, Brent	DE	6-7	268	11/21/73	Arizona State	Glendale, Ariz.	FA
Byrd, Rodney	RB	6-2	240	4/28/74	Illinois	O'Fallon, Ill.	FA
Cole, Lee	CB	5-11	188	6/25/74	Arizona State	Riverside, Calif.	FA-'96
Dulick, Jason	WR	6-4	200	5/26/74	Illinois	St. Louis, Mo.	FA
Emery, John	DE	6-2	255	8/28/73	Nicholls State	Norco, La.	FA
George, Spencer	RB	5-9	202	10/28/73	Rice	Beaumont, Tex.	FA
Gilbert, Aaron	QB	6-4	220	3/30/73	Northern Illinois	Rochelle, Ill.	FA
Hemsley, Nate	LB	6-0	219	5/15/74	Syracuse	Delran, N.J.	D1
Holmes, Kenny	DE	6-4	270	10/24/73	Miami	Vero Beach, Fla.	D1
Jackson, Chris (1)	S	6-0	202	9/21/73	Iowa	Missouri City, Tex.	FA
Jennings, Bryan	TE	6-3	257	1/22/75	Virginia Tech	Forest, Va.	FA
Kent, Joey	WR	6-1	186	4/23/74	Tennessee	Huntsville, Ala.	D2
Lyons, Pratt	DE-DT	6-5	278	9/17/74	Troy State	Ft. Worth, Tex.	D4b
Mason, Derrick	WR	5-10	193	1/17/74	Michigan State	Detroit, Mich.	D4a
McCullough, George	CB	5-10	187	2/18/75	Baylor	Galveston, Tex.	D5
McElmurry, Blaine	S	6-0	188	10/23/73	Montana	Troy, Mont.	FA
Moore, Jim	TE	6-3	262	4/29/73	Kansas	Garden City, Kan.	FA
Mustafa, Isaiah	WR	6-2	204	2/11/74	Arizona State	Oxnard, Calif.	FA
Sanderson, Scott	T	6-6	290	7/25/74	Washington State	Concord, Calif.	D3b
Smith, Kyle	G	6-5	297	8/11/73	Colorado	Torrington, Wyo.	FA
Stallings, Dennis	LB	6-0	234	5/25/74	Illinois	East St. Louis, Ill.	D6
Walker, Denard	CB	6-1	186	8/9/73	Louisiana State	Garland, Tex.	D3a
Wells, Sean	G-T	6-4	288	11/22/73	Louisiana State	Jenks, Okla.	FA
Williams, Armon	S-LB	6-0	223	8/13/73	Arizona	Tempe, Ariz.	D7
Williams, Devron	DE-DT	6-3	280	7/26/74	West Texas A&M	Houston, Tex.	FA

The term NFL Rookie is defined as a player who is in his first season of professional football and has not been on the roster of another professional football team for any regular-season or postseason games. A Rookie is designated by an "R" on NFL rosters. Players who have been active in another professional football league or players who have NFL experience, including either preseason training camp or being on an Active List or Inactive List, or on Reserve/Injured or Reserve/Physically Unable to Perform for fewer than six regular-season games, are termed NFL First-Year Players. An NFL First-Year Player is designated by a "1" on NFL rosters. Thereafter, a player is credited with an additional year of experience for each season in which he accumulates six games on the Active List or Inactive List, or on Reserve/Injured or Reserve/Physically Unable to Perform.

NOTES

The NFC

National Football Conference
Eastern Division
Team Colors: Cardinal Red, Black, and White
P.O. Box 888
Phoenix, Arizona 85001-0888
Telephone: (602) 379-0101

CLUB OFFICIALS

President: William V. Bidwill
Vice President: Larry Wilson
Vice President of Sales and Marketing: John Shean
Secretary and General Counsel:
  Thomas J. Guilfoil
Treasurer and Chief Financial Officer:
  Charley Schlegel
Vice President/General Counsel: Michael Bidwill
Vice President-Player Personnel: Bob Ferguson
Assistant to the General Manager: Joe Woolley
Assistant to the President: Rod Graves
Public Relations Director: Paul Jensen
Media Coordinator: Greg Gladysiewski
Director of NFL Programs and Community
  Outreach: Earl Edwards
Director of Community Relations: Adele Harris
Director of Marketing: Joe Castor
Business Manager: Steve Walsh
Ticket Manager: Steve Bomar
Trainer: John Omohundro
Assistant Trainers: Jim Shearer, Jeff Herndon
Equipment Manager: Mark Ahlemeier
Assistant Equipment Manager: Steve Christensen
Stadium: Sun Devil Stadium • **Capacity:** 73,273
  Fifth Street
  Tempe, Arizona 85287
Playing Surface: Grass
Training Camp: Northern Arizona University
  Flagstaff, Arizona 86011

1997 SCHEDULE

PRESEASON

Aug. 2	at Seattle	7:00
Aug. 8	at St. Louis	7:00
Aug. 16	at Chicago	7:00
Aug. 22	**Oakland**	7:00

REGULAR SEASON

Aug. 31	at Cincinnati	1:00
Sept. 7	**Dallas**	5:00
Sept. 14	at Washington	1:00
Sept. 21	Open Date	
Sept. 28	at Tampa Bay	1:00
Oct. 5	**Minnesota**	1:00
Oct. 12	**New York Giants**	1:00
Oct. 19	at Philadelphia	1:00
Oct. 26	**Tennessee**	2:00
Nov. 2	**Philadelphia**	2:00
Nov. 9	at Dallas	12:00
Nov. 16	at New York Giants	1:00
Nov. 23	at Baltimore	1:00
Nov. 30	**Pittsburgh**	2:00
Dec. 7	**Washington**	2:00
Dec. 14	at New Orleans	3:00
Dec. 21	**Atlanta**	2:00

RECORD HOLDERS

INDIVIDUAL RECORDS—CAREER

Category	Name	Performance
Rushing (Yds.)	Ottis Anderson, 1979-1986	7,999
Passing (Yds.)	Jim Hart, 1966-1983	34,639
Passing (TDs)	Jim Hart, 1966-1983	209
Receiving (No.)	Roy Green, 1979-1990	522
Receiving (Yds.)	Roy Green, 1979-1990	8,497
Interceptions	Larry Wilson, 1960-1972	52
Punting (Avg.)	Jerry Norton, 1959-1961	44.9
Punt Return (Avg.)	Charley Trippi, 1947-1955	13.7
Kickoff Return (Avg.)	Ollie Matson, 1952, 1954-58	28.5
Field Goals	Jim Bakken, 1962-1978	282
Touchdowns (Tot.)	Roy Green, 1979-1990	70
Points	Jim Bakken, 1962-1978	1,380

INDIVIDUAL RECORDS—SINGLE SEASON

Category	Name	Performance
Rushing (Yds.)	Ottis Anderson, 1979	1,605
Passing (Yds.)	Neil Lomax, 1984	4,614
Passing (TDs)	Charley Johnson, 1963	28
	Neil Lomax, 1984	28
Receiving (No.)	Larry Centers, 1995	101
Receiving (Yds.)	Roy Green, 1984	1,555
Interceptions	Bob Nussbaumer, 1949	12
Punting (Avg.)	Jerry Norton, 1960	45.6
Punt Return (Avg.)	John (Red) Cochran, 1949	20.9
Kickoff Return (Avg.)	Ollie Matson, 1958	35.5
Field Goals	Greg Davis, 1995	30
Touchdowns (Tot.)	John David Crow, 1962	17
Points	Jim Bakken, 1967	117
	Neil O'Donoghue, 1984	117

INDIVIDUAL RECORDS—SINGLE GAME

Category	Name	Performance
Rushing (Yds.)	LeShon Johnson, 9-22-96	214
Passing (Yds.)	Boomer Esiason, 11-10-96 (OT)	522
Passing (TDs)	Jim Hardy, 10-2-50	6
	Charley Johnson, 9-26-65, 11-2-69	6
Receiving (No.)	Sonny Randle, 11-4-62	16
Receiving (Yds.)	Sonny Randle, 11-4-62	256
Interceptions	Bob Nussbaumer, 11-13-49	*4
	Jerry Norton, 11-20-60	*4
Field Goals	Jim Bakken, 9-24-67	*7
Touchdowns (Tot.)	Ernie Nevers, 11-28-29	*6
Points	Ernie Nevers, 11-28-29	*40

*NFL Record

COACHING HISTORY

Chicago 1920-1959, St. Louis 1960-1987
(405-555-39)

1920-22	John (Paddy) Driscoll	17-8-4
1923-24	Arnold Horween	13-8-1
1925-26	Norman Barry	16-8-2
1927	Guy Chamberlin	3-7-1
1928	Fred Gillies	1-5-0
1929	Dewey Scanlon	6-6-1
1930	Ernie Nevers	5-6-2
1931	LeRoy Andrews*	0-1-0
1931	Ernie Nevers	5-3-0
1932	Jack Chevigny	2-6-2
1933-34	Paul Schissler	6-15-1
1935-38	Milan Creighton	16-26-4
1939	Ernie Nevers	1-10-0
1940-42	Jimmy Conzelman	8-22-3
1943-45	Phil Handler**	1-29-0
1946-48	Jimmy Conzelman	27-10-0
1949	Phil Handler-Buddy Parker***	2-4-0
1949	Raymond (Buddy) Parker	4-1-1
1950-51	Earl (Curly) Lambeau****	7-15-0
1951	Phil Handler-Cecil Isbell#	1-1-0
1952	Joe Kuharich	4-8-0
1953-54	Joe Stydahar	3-20-1
1955-57	Ray Richards	14-21-1
1958-61	Frank (Pop) Ivy##	17-29-2
1961	Chuck Drulis-Ray Prochaska-Ray Willsey###	2-0-0
1962-65	Wally Lemm	27-26-3
1966-70	Charley Winner	35-30-5
1971-72	Bob Hollway	8-18-2
1973-77	Don Coryell	42-29-1
1978-79	Bud Wilkinson####	9-20-0
1979	Larry Wilson	2-1-0
1980-85	Jim Hanifan	39-50-1

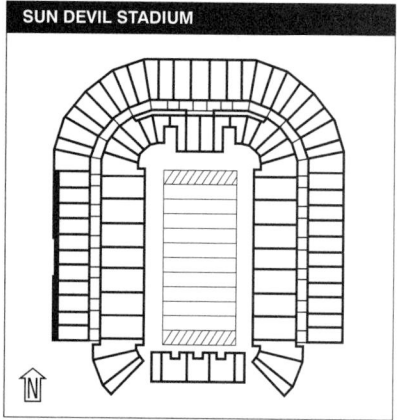

1986-89	Gene Stallings@	23-34-1
1989	Hank Kuhlmann	0-5-0
1990-93	Joe Bugel	20-44-0
1994-95	Buddy Ryan	12-20-0
1996	Vince Tobin	7-9-0

  * Resigned after one game in 1931
 ** Co-coach with Walt Kiesling in Chicago Cardinals-
      Pittsburgh merger in 1944
*** Co-coaches for first six games in 1949
**** Resigned after 10 games in 1951
    # Co-coaches
   ## Resigned after 12 games in 1961
  ### Co-coaches
 #### Released after 13 games in 1979
    @ Released after 11 games in 1989

1996 TEAM RECORD

PRESEASON (1-3)

Date	Result		Opponents
8/2	L	3-26	Oakland
8/10	W	13-10	Cincinnati
8/17	L	10-32	at San Diego
8/23	L	30-31	at Atlanta

REGULAR SEASON (7-9)

Date	Result		Opponents	Att.
9/1	L	13-20	at Indianapolis	48,133
9/8	L	10-38	Miami	55,444
9/15	L	0-31	at New England	59,118
9/22	W	28-14	at New Orleans	34,316
9/29	W	31-28	St. Louis (OT)	33,116
10/13	L	3-17	at Dallas	64,096
10/20	W	13-9	Tampa Bay	27,738
10/27	L	21-31	N.Y. Jets	28,088
11/3	L	8-16	at N.Y. Giants	68,262
11/10	W	37-34	at Washington (OT)	51,929
11/17	W	31-23	N.Y. Giants	34,924
11/24	W	36-30	Philadelphia	36,175
12/1	L	17-41	at Minnesota	45,767
12/8	L	6-10	Dallas	70,763
12/15	W	27-26	Washington	34,260
12/22	L	19-29	at Philadelphia	63,658

(OT) Overtime

SCORE BY PERIODS

Cardinals	39	70	51	134	6	—	300
Opponents	56	130	90	121	0	—	397

ATTENDANCE

Home 320,508   Away 435,279   Total 755,787
Single-game home record, 73,025 (9/19/93)
Single-season home record, 497,330 (1994)

1996 TEAM STATISTICS

	Cardinals	Opp.
Total First Downs	308	337
Rushing	70	120
Passing	214	192
Penalty	24	25
Third Down: Made/Att	95/228	90/218
Third Down Pct.	41.7	41.3
Fourth Down: Made/Att	11/17	5/10
Fourth Down Pct.	64.7	50.0
Total Net Yards	5190	5361
Avg. Per Game	324.4	335.1
Total Plays	1050	1062
Avg. Per Play	4.9	5.0
Net Yards Rushing	1502	1862
Avg. Per Game	93.9	116.4
Total Rushes	401	514
Net Yards Passing	3688	3499
Avg. Per Game	230.5	218.7
Sacked/Yards Lost	36/229	28/185
Gross Yards	3917	3684
Att./Completions	613/336	520/311
Completion Pct.	54.8	59.8
Had Intercepted	21	11
Punts/Avg.	77/43.2	69/43.8
Net Punting Avg.	77/36.4	69/36.2
Penalties/Yards Lost	106/873	104/841
Fumbles/Ball Lost	29/14	24/14
Touchdowns	33	44
Rushing	8	18
Passing	23	21
Returns	2	5
Avg. Time of Possession	28:45	31:15

1996 INDIVIDUAL STATISTICS

PASSING	Att.	Comp.	Yds.	Pct.	TD	Int.	Tkld.	Rate
Esiason	339	190	2293	56.0	11	14	17/109	70.6
K. Graham	274	146	1624	53.3	12	7	19/120	75.1
Cardinals	613	336	3917	54.8	23	21	36/229	72.6
Opponents	520	311	3684	59.8	21	11	28/185	86.1

SCORING	TD R	TD P	TD Rt	PAT	FG	Saf	PTS
Butler	0	0	0	17/19	14/17	0	59
Centers	2	7	0	0/0	0/0	0	54
Davis	0	0	0	12/12	9/14	0	39
R. Moore	0	4	0	0/0	0/0	0	26
L. Johnson	3	1	0	0/0	0/0	0	24
Sanders	0	4	0	0/0	0/0	0	24
Dowdell	0	2	0	0/0	0/0	0	12
McElroy	1	1	0	0/0	0/0	0	12
C. Smith	1	1	0	0/0	0/0	0	12
Esiason	1	0	0	0/0	0/0	0	8
Carter	0	1	0	0/0	0/0	0	6
Edwards	0	1	0	0/0	0/0	0	6
McWilliams	0	1	0	0/0	0/0	0	6
Miller	0	0	1	0/0	0/0	0	6
Williams	0	0	1	0/0	0/0	0	6
Cardinals	8	23	2	29/31	23/31	0	300
Opponents	18	21	5	41/43	30/37	0	397

2-Point conversions: Esiason, R. Moore. Team: 2-2,
Opponents: 1-1.

RUSHING	Att.	Yds.	Avg.	LG	TD
L. Johnson	141	634	4.5	70t	3
Centers	116	425	3.7	24	2
McElroy	89	305	3.4	32	1
K. Graham	21	87	4.1	19	0
Esiason	15	52	3.5	13	1
C. Smith	14	15	1.1	3	1
Feagles	1	0	0.0	0	0
McKinnon	1	-4	-4.0	-4	0
Sanders	2	-4	-2.0	1	0
Edwards	1	-8	-8.0	-8	0
Cardinals	401	1502	3.7	70t	8
Opponents	514	1862	3.6	78	18

RECEIVING	No.	Yds.	Avg.	LG	TD
Centers	99	766	7.7	39	7
Sanders	69	813	11.8	34	4
R. Moore	58	1016	17.5	69	4
Edwards	29	311	10.7	31	1
Carter	26	329	12.7	36	1
Dowdell	20	318	15.9	64t	2
L. Johnson	15	176	11.7	35	1
McWilliams	7	80	11.4	21	1
McElroy	5	41	8.2	22t	1
Anderson	4	64	16.0	19	0
C. Smith	3	3	1.0	2	1
Terry	1	0	0.0	0	0
Williams	0	0	—	—	0
Cardinals	336	3917	11.7	69	23
Opponents	311	3684	11.8	55	21

INTERCEPTIONS	No.	Yds.	Avg.	LG	TD
Williams	6	89	14.8	65t	1
Alexander	2	3	1.5	3	0
Lassiter	1	20	20.0	20	0
Joyner	1	10	10.0	10	0
Bradford	1	0	0.0	0	0
Cardinals	11	122	11.1	65t	1
Opponents	21	186	8.9	33	0

PUNTING	No.	Yds.	Avg.	In 20	LG
Feagles	76	3328	43.8	23	68
Cardinals	77	3328	43.2	23	68
Opponents	69	3022	43.8	26	63

PUNT RETURNS	No.	FC	Yds.	Avg.	LG	TD
Dowdell	34	8	297	8.7	35	0
Edwards	5	1	46	9.2	20	0
Cardinals	39	9	343	8.8	35	0
Opponents	37	19	403	10.9	66t	1

KICKOFF RETURNS	No.	Yds.	Avg.	LG	TD
McElroy	54	1148	21.3	92	0
L. Johnson	10	198	19.8	27	0
Dowdell	5	122	24.4	31	0
Terry	4	84	21.0	30	0
McCleskey	1	18	18.0	18	0
McDonald	1	16	16.0	16	0
C. Smith	1	14	14.0	14	0
Cardinals	75	1582	21.1	92	0
Opponents	61	1290	21.1	95t	1

SACKS	No.
Rice	12.5
Joyner	5.0
Swann	5.0
Miller	1.0
Ottis	1.0
B. Smith	1.0
Williams	1.0
Wilson	1.0
Bankston	0.5
Cardinals	28.0
Opponents	36.0

1997 DRAFT CHOICES

Round	Name	Pos.	College
1	Tom Knight	DB	Iowa
2	Jake Plummer	QB	Arizona State
3	Ty Howard	DB	Ohio State
4	Chris Dishman	G	Nebraska
5	Chad Carpenter	WR	Washington State
6	Rod Brown	RB	North Carolina State
	Tony McCombs	LB	Eastern Kentucky
7	Mark Smith	DE	Auburn

ARIZONA CARDINALS

1997 VETERAN ROSTER

No.	Name	Pos.	Ht.	Wt.	Birthdate	NFL Exp.	College	Hometown	How Acq.	'96 Games/ Starts
46	Alexander, Brent	DB	5-10	184	7/10/71	4	Tennessee State	Gallatin, Tex.	FA-'95	16/15
82	Anderson, Stevie	WR	6-5	215	5/12/70	4	Grambling State	Monroe, La.	W(NYJ)-'95	8/0
63	Bankston, Michael	DE-DT	6-3	280	3/12/70	6	Sam Houston State	East Bernard, Tex.	D4b-'92	16/16
28	Bennett, Tommy	S	6-1	204	2/19/73	2	UCLA	San Diego, Calif.	FA-'96	16/1
3	Brown, Lomas	T	6-4	275	3/30/63	13	Florida	Miami, Fla.	UFA(Det)-'96	16/16
75	Butler, Kevin	K	6-1	200	7/24/62	13	Georgia	Stone Mountain, Ga.	FA-'96	7/0
80	# Carter, Pat	TE	6-4	258	8/1/66	10	Florida State	Sarasota, Fla.	UFA(StL)-'96	16/16
15	Case, Stoney	QB	6-2	206	7/7/72	3	New Mexico	Odessa, Tex.	D3-'95	0*
37	Centers, Larry	RB	5-11	215	6/1/68	8	Stephen F. Austin	Tatum, Tex.	D5-'90	16/14
36	Christopherson, Ryan	RB	5-11	246	7/26/72	2	Wyoming	Sioux Falls, S.D.	FA-'96	6/0
43	# Darby, Matt	S	6-1	200	11/19/68	6	UCLA	Virginia Beach, Va.	UFA(Buff)-'96	15/15
62	Devlin, Mike	C	6-2	300	11/16/69	5	Iowa	Marlton, N.J.	UFA(Buff)-'96	11/11
64	Dexter, James	G-T	6-5	300	3/3/73	2	South Carolina	Springfield, Va.	D5-'96	6/1
76	Drake, Jerry	DT	6-4	292	7/9/69	2	Hastings College	Kingston, N.Y.	FA-'95	11/0
65	# Dye, Ernest	G	6-6	325	7/15/71	4	South Carolina	Greenwood, S.C.	D1b-'93	8/0
83	# Edwards, Anthony	WR	5-10	190	5/26/66	8	New Mexico Highlands	Casa Grande, Ariz.	FA-'91	16/1
92	England, Eric	DE	6-2	283	3/25/71	4	Texas A&M	Sugarland, Tex.	D3b-'94	11/1
10	Feagles, Jeff	P	6-1	205	3/7/66	10	Miami	Scottsdale, Ariz.	UFA-'94	16/0
89	Gedney, Chris	TE	6-5	265	8/9/70	5	Syracuse	Liverpool, N.Y.	UFA-'97	0*
54	Graham, Aaron	C	6-1	295	5/22/73	2	Nebraska	Denton, Tex.	D4-'96	16/7
11	Graham, Kent	QB	6-5	242	11/1/68	6	Ohio State	Wheaton, Ill.	UFA(Det)-'96	10/8
49	Hayes, Jarius	TE	6-3	255	3/23/73	2	North Alabama	Muscle Shoals, Ala.	D7-'96	4/0
58	Hill, Eric	LB	6-2	255	11/14/66	9	Louisiana State	Galveston, Tex.	D1-'89	16/16
56	Irving, Terry	LB	6-0	224	7/3/71	4	McNeese State	Galveston, Tex.	D4c-'94	16/0
32	† Johnson, LeShon	RB	5-11	195	1/15/71	4	Northern Illinois	Haskell, Okla.	W(GB)-'95	15/8
66	Jonassen, Eric	G-T	6-5	310	8/16/68	4	Bloomsburg	Glen Burnie, Md.	FA-'96	0*
73	Joyce, Matt	G	6-7	316	3/30/72	2	Richmond	St. Petersburg, Fla.	FA-'96	2/0
59	Joyner, Seth	LB	6-2	235	11/18/64	12	Texas-El Paso	Spring Valley, N.Y.	UFA(Phil)-'94	16/16
86	Junkin, Trey	LS-TE	6-2	240	1/23/61	15	Louisiana Tech	North Little Rock, Ark.	W(Oak)-'96	10/0
42	Lassiter, Kwamie	CB-S	5-11	180	12/3/69	3	Kansas	Newport News, Va.	FA-'95	14/0
52	Leasy, Wesley	LB	6-2	234	9/7/71	3	Mississippi State	Greenville, Miss.	D7b-'95	16/0
5	May, Chad	QB	6-1	220	9/28/71	3	Kansas State	West Covina, Calif.	FA-'96	0*
47	† McCleskey, J.J.	CB	5-7	177	4/10/70	4	Tennessee	Knoxville, Tenn.	W(NO)-'96	5/0
55	# McDonald, Devon	LB	6-4	240	11/8/69	5	Notre Dame	Kingston, Jamaica	FA-'96	16/0
30	McElroy, Leeland	RB	5-9	198	6/25/74	2	Texas A&M	Beaumont, Tex.	D2-'96	16/6
57	McKinnon, Ronald	LB	5-11	230	9/20/73	2	North Alabama	Elba, Ala.	FA-'96	16/0
89	McWilliams, Johnny	TE	6-4	261	12/14/72	2	Southern California	Ontario, Calif.	D3-'96	12/0
95	Miller, Jamir	LB	6-4	242	11/19/73	4	UCLA	Oakland, Calif.	D1-'94	16/16
40	Moore, Derrick	RB	6-1	227	10/13/67	6	Northeastern Oklahoma St.	Albany, Ga.	FA-'96	0*
85	Moore, Rob	WR	6-3	205	9/27/68	8	Syracuse	Hempstead, N.Y.	T(NYJ)-'95	16/16
96	† Ottis, Brad	DT	6-4	280	3/2/72	4	Wayne State	Fremont, Neb.	FA-'96	11/1
27	Paul, Tito	CB-S	6-0	195	5/24/72	3	Ohio State	Kissimmee, Fla.	D5c-'95	16/3
60	† Redmon, Anthony	G	6-4	308	4/6/71	4	Auburn	Brewton, Ala.	D5b-'94	16/16
79	Rice, Simeon	DE	6-5	265	2/24/74	2	Illinois	Chicago, Ill.	D1-'96	16/15
81	Sanders, Frank	WR	6-1	202	2/17/73	3	Auburn	Fort Lauderdale, Fla.	D2-'95	16/16
70	Scott, Lance	G-T	6-3	285	2/15/72	3	Utah	Salt Lake City, Utah	D5b-'95	0*
74	# Selby, Rob	G	6-3	286	10/11/67	7	Auburn	Birmingham, Ala.	FA-'95	13/4
45	Smith, Cedric	RB	5-10	222	5/27/68	6	Florida	Enterprise, Fla.	FA-'96	15/2
98	Swann, Eric	DT	6-5	295	8/16/70	7	No College	Swann Station, N.C.	D1-'91	16/15
35	Williams, Aeneas	CB	5-10	190	1/29/69	7	Southern	New Orleans, La.	D3-'91	16/16
94	Wilson, Bernard	DT	6-2	295	8/17/70	5	Tennessee State	Nashville, Tenn.	W(TB)-'94	16/16
68	# Wolf, Joe	G-T	6-6	296	12/28/66	9	Boston College	Allentown, Pa.	D1b-'89	16/16

* Case inactive for 13 games in '96; Gedney missed '96 season because of injury with Chicago; Jonassen inactive for 2 games; May inactive for 7 games; D. Moore inactive for 14 games; Scott inactive for 6 games.

Unrestricted free agent; subject to developments.

† Restricted free agent; subject to developments.

Player lost through free agency (1): CB Ronnie Bradford (Atl; 15 games in '96).

Also played with Cardinals in '96—CB-S Lance Brown (1 game), K Greg Davis (9), WR Marcus Dowdell (15), QB Boomer Esiason (10), S Terry Hoage (5), CB D.J. Johnson (7), WR Kevin Jordan (1), G Duval Love (9), DT Chris Maumalanga (1), TE Oscar McBride (2), G Joe Staysniak (9), RB Ryan Terry (5).

COACHING STAFF

Head Coach,
Vince Tobin

Pro Career: Named Cardinals' head coach on February 7, 1996. Became thirty-third coach in the history of the franchise dating back to 1920. In his first season, Arizona rebounded from an 0-3 start to claim a 7-4 record in final 11 games and remain in playoff contention until the final week of the season. Arizona improved from twenty-fourth (1995) to twelfth in offense, from twenty-sixth (1995) to twenty-first in defense, and forged the club's first winning November (3-1) since 1987. As a defensive coordinator of the Indianapolis Colts from 1994-95, oversaw a defense that was a principal reason Indianapolis finished 9-7 during the 1995 regular season before defeating San Diego (35-10) and Kansas City (10-7) in the first two rounds of postseason play. Tobin earned credit for rebuilding a Colts defense he inherited that ranked last in overall defense in 1993. Tobin's first unit improved to twentieth in 1994 and tied for seventh with Carolina in 1995 at 314.2 yards per game. In four seasons prior to Tobin's arrival, the Colts' defense finished twenty-fourth or lower against the run. In 1994, Tobin's first Indianapolis defense ranked twelfth against the rush, then improved to sixth in 1995 at 91.1 yards per game, the second lowest figure in team history. It also was just the third time in Colts history the opposition averaged less than 100 yards per game on the ground. Over the past two seasons, Tobin's defensive unit did not allow an individual to rush for 100 yards in 24 consecutive games (final 13 games in 1994, first 11 games in 1995). His 1994 Colts' defense also boasted the lowest red-zone touchdown percentage (40) in the NFL and did not allow a touchdown at home in the final 12 quarters of the season. Tobin previously served as defensive coordinator of the Chicago Bears (1986-1992), tutoring a Bears' defense that set an NFL record for fewest points allowed in a 16-game season (187 in 1986). His 1986 Chicago unit topped the league by allowing just 258 yards per contest. The 1987 Bears surrendered the league's fewest points (215) and sported the best rushing defense (82.9). Tobin also earned victories over Tampa Bay and Washington as Chicago's interim head coach for Mike Ditka. Tobin's other coaching stops have been with the USFL Philadelphia/Baltimore Stars (1983-85), the CFL British Columbia Lions (1977-1982), and his alma mater, the University of Missouri (1967-1976). Tobin's defensive units in the CFL ranked second overall during his six seasons, while his defensive schemes in the USFL helped the Stars rank first defensively in 1983 and 1984 and second in 1985 while allowing the fewest points all three seasons. The Stars reached the league championship game each season, winning the final two times. Career record: 7-9.

Background: Tobin played defensive back at Missouri from 1961-64. He joined the Missouri coaching staff as a defensive assistant from 1967-1976, serving the final six years as defensive coordinator. Tobin owns a bachelor's degree in education and a master's degree in guidance and counseling.

Personal: Born September 29, 1943, in Burlington Junction, Missouri. He and his wife, Kathy, have two children—son Ryan and daughter Shannon.

ASSISTANT COACHES

George (Geep) Chryst, tight ends-quality control; born June 25, 1962, Madison, Wis., lives in Phoenix. Linebacker Princeton 1981-84. Pro linebacker Orlando Thunder (World League) 1991. College coach: Wisconsin-Platteville 1987, Wisconsin 1988-90. Pro coach: Orlando Thunder (World League) 1991, Chicago Bears 1991-95, joined Cardinals in 1996.

Alan Everest, special teams; born August 22, 1950, Santa Barbara, Calif., lives in Phoenix. Safety Southern Methodist 1970-71. No pro playing experience. College coach: Southern Methodist 1972, North Texas State 1973-74, Cameron (Okla.) 1974-75, U.S. International 1981-87. Pro coach: Arkansas Miners (PSFL) 1991-92, Birmingham Barracudas (CFL)

1997 FIRST-YEAR ROSTER

Name	Pos.	Ht.	Wt.	Birthdate	College	Hometown	How Acq.
Bentley, Scott	K	5-11	205	4/10/74	Florida State	Aurora, Co.	FA
Berger, Blaine (1)	DT	6-5	292	12/28/70	Utah	Idaho Falls, Idaho	FA-'96
Brock, Fred (1)	WR	5-10	175	11/15/74	Southern Mississippi	Montgomery, Ala.	FA-'96
Brown, Rod	RB	5-11	245	2/28/74	North Carolina State	Lithonia, Ga.	D6a
Carpenter, Chad	WR	5-11	197	7/17/73	Washington State	Weiser, Idaho	D5
Cobbins, Lyron	LB	5-11	240	9/17/74	Notre Dame	Kansas City, Kan.	FA
Cobbs, Anthony	CB	6-0	182	1/9/74	UCLA	Long Beach, Calif.	FA
Comer, Micheal	LB	5-9	250	10/25/74	Texas-El Paso	Odessa, Tex.	FA
DeGraffenreid, Allen	G	6-4	300	6/3/74	Vanderbilt	Dunwoody, Ga.	FA
Dishman, Chris	G	6-3	322	2/27/74	Nebraska	Cozad, Neb.	D4
Felder, Darrius	DE	6-4	282	10/10/73	Cincinnati	Akron, Ohio	FA
Fisher, Ta'boris	WR	5-8	175	1/1/75	Mississippi	Jackson, Miss.	FA
Guynes, Thomas	T	6-4	302	9/9/74	Michigan	Kankakee, Ill.	FA
Harris, Kenny	S	6-1	198	4/27/75	North Carolina State	Durham, N.C.	FA
Howard, Ty	CB	5-9	177	11/30/73	Ohio State	Columbus, Ohio	D3
Ihegborow, Best	DE	6-2	260	12/29/74	Texas-El Paso	Houston, Tex.	FA
Irons, Jarrett	LB	6-0	235	12/14/73	Michigan	The Woodlands, Tex.	FA
Jackson, Kevin	S	6-0	200	10/27/73	Alabama	Dothan, Ala.	FA
Kaufman, Ben	G	6-4	288	10/25/74	Texas Tech	Edinburg, Tex.	FA
Kealaluhi, K.O.	WR	6-1	200	12/22/72	Brigham Young	Makawao, Hawaii	FA
Knight, Tom	CB	5-11	195	12/29/74	Iowa	Marlton, N.J.	D1
Larsen, Atle (1)	K	5-11	201	3/24/73	Virginia Tech	Sola, Norway	FA-'96
Leahy, Ryan (1)	G-T	6-3	290	8/30/72	Notre Dame	Yakima, Wash.	FA-'96
McCombs, Tony	LB	6-2	240	8/24/74	Eastern Kentucky	Hopkinsville, Ken.	D6b
McGee, Dell (1)	CB	5-8	180	9/7/73	Auburn	Columbus, Ga.	D5c-'96
Mostella, Marcellus	LB	6-3	234	2/13/75	Auburn	Gadsden, Ala.	FA
Perryman, Nathan	CB	5-9	191	8/30/75	Georgia Tech	Columbia, S.C.	FA
Peyton, Matt	P	6-1	184	3/20/74	Arizona	Tucson, Ariz.	FA
Plummer, Jake	QB	6-2	195	12/19/74	Arizona State	Boise, Idaho	D2
Price, J.C. (1)	G	6-4	291	1/13/72	Virginia Tech	Dunkirk, N.C.	FA-'96
Rice, Matt	DT	6-2	287	11/7/74	Northwestern	Middleton, Wis.	FA
Smith, Mark	DE	6-4	273	8/28/74	Auburn	Vicksburg, Miss.	D7
Thomas, Erik	RB	6-0	180	10/16/74	Marshall	Washington, D.C.	FA
Watkins, Michael (1)	WR	5-10	176	12/28/71	Northeast Louisiana	Hickory, N.C.	FA-'96
Wilfork, Rory	LB	6-1	240	8/17/75	Columbia	Miami, Fla.	FA
Williams, C.J.	RB	6-0	240	8/29/75	Georgia Tech	West Point, Ga.	FA

The term NFL Rookie is defined as a player who is in his first season of professional football and has not been on the roster of another professional football team for any regular-season or postseason games. A Rookie is designated by an "R" on NFL rosters. Players who have been active in another professional football league or players who have NFL experience, including either preseason training camp or being on an Active List or Inactive List, or on Reserve/Injured or Reserve/Physically Unable to Perform for fewer than six regular-season games, are termed NFL First-Year Players. An NFL First-Year Player is designated by a "1" on NFL rosters. Thereafter, a player is credited with an additional year of experience for each season in which he accumulates six games on the Active List or Inactive List, or on Reserve/Injured or Reserve/Physically Unable to Perform.

NOTES

1995, joined Cardinals in 1996.

Joe Greene, defensive line; born September 24, 1946, Temple, Tex., lives in Phoenix. Defensive tackle North Texas State 1966-68. Pro defensive tackle Pittsburgh Steelers 1969-81. Inducted into Pro Football Hall of Fame in 1987. Pro coach: Pittsburgh Steelers 1987-91, Miami Dolphins 1992-95, joined Cardinals in 1996.

Dick Jamieson, offensive coordinator; born November 13, 1937, Peoria, Ill., lives in Phoenix. Quarterback Bradley 1955-58. Pro quarterback Baltimore Colts 1959, New York Titans (AFL) 1960. College coach: Bradley 1962-64, Missouri 1972-1977, Indiana State 1978-79, Northwestern 1990-91, Rutgers 1992-94. Pro coach: St. Louis Cardinals 1980-85, Houston Oilers 1986-87, Philadelphia Eagles 1995-96, rejoined Cardinals in 1997.

Larry Marmie, defensive backs; born October 17, 1942, Barnesville, Ohio, lives in Phoenix. Quarterback Eastern Kentucky 1962-65. No pro playing experience. College coach: Eastern Kentucky 1967-68, 1972-76, Morehead State 1968-71, Tulsa 1977-78, North Carolina 1979-82, Tennessee 1983-84, 1992-94, Arizona State 1988-91 (head coach), UCLA 1995. Pro coach: Joined Cardinals in 1996.

Carl Mauck, offensive line; born July 7, 1947, McLeansboro, Ill., lives in Phoenix. Linebacker-center Southern Illinois 1966-68. Pro center Baltimore Colts 1969, Miami Dolphins 1970, San Diego Chargers 1971-74, Houston Oilers 1975-81. Pro coach: New Orleans Saints 1982-85, Kansas City Chiefs 1986-88, Tampa Bay Buccaneers 1991, San Diego Chargers 1992-95, joined Cardinals in 1996.

Dave McGinnis, defensive coordinator; born August

7, 1951, Independence, Kan., lives in Phoenix. Defensive back Texas Christian 1970-72. No pro playing experience. College coach: Texas Christian 1973-74, 1982, Missouri 1975-77, Indiana State 1978-81, Kansas State 1983-85. Pro coach: Chicago Bears 1986-95, joined Cardinals in 1996.

Glenn Pires, linebackers; born September 13, 1958, New Bedford, Mass., lives in Phoenix. Linebacker Springfield College 1978-80. No pro playing experience. College coach: Syracuse 1983-84, Dartmouth 1985-88, Michigan State 1989-95. Pro coach: Joined Cardinals in 1996.

Vic Rapp, wide receivers; born December 23, 1935, Marionville, Mo., lives in Phoenix. Running back Southwest Missouri State 1954-57. No pro playing experience. Pro coach: Edmonton Eskimos (CFL) 1972-76, British Columbia Lions (CFL) 1977-82 (head coach), Houston Oilers 1983, Los Angeles Rams 1984, Tampa Bay Buccaneers 1985-86, Detroit Lions 1987, Chicago Bears 1989-92, joined Cardinals in 1996.

Bob Rogucki, strength and conditioning; born September 27, 1953, Clarksburg, W.Va., lives in Phoenix. No college or pro playing experience. College coach: Penn State 1981, Weber State 1982, Army 1983-89. Pro coach: Joined Cardinals in 1990.

Johnny Roland, running back; born May 21, 1943, Corpus Christi, Tex., lives in Phoenix. Running back Missouri 1961-65. Pro running back St. Louis Cardinals 1966-72, New York Giants 1973. College coach: Notre Dame 1975. Pro coach: Green Bay Packers 1974, Philadelphia Eagles 1976-78, Chicago Bears 1983-92, New York Jets 1993-94, St. Louis Rams 1995-96, joined Cardinals in 1997.

National Football Conference
Western Division
Team Colors: Black, Red, Silver, and White
One Falcon Place
Suwanee, Georgia 30174
Telephone: (770) 945-1111

CLUB OFFICIALS

Chairman of the Board: Rankin M. Smith, Sr.
President: Taylor Smith
Executive Vice President/Football Operations &
   Head Coach: Dan Reeves
Vice President & Chief Financial Officer: Jim Hay
Vice President of Administration: Rob Jackson
Director of Public Relations: Charlie Taylor
Asst. Director of Public Relations: Frank Kleha
Public Relations Assistant: Gary Glenn
Sales & Marketing: Todd Marble, Chris Demos,
   Trisha Williamson, Spencer Treadwell
Director of Community Relations: Carol Breeding
Director of Player Programs: Billy Johnson
Director of Ticket Operations: Jack Ragsdale
Asst. Director of Ticket Operations: Mike Jennings
Administrative Assts./Finance: Kevin Anthony,
   John Knox
Administrative Asst./Player Personnel: Danny Mock
Scouts: Bill Baker, Ken Blair, Dick Corrick,
   Elbert Dubenion, Bill Groman, Bob Harrison
Director of Player Personnel/College:
   Reed Johnson
Director of Player Personnel/Pro: Chuck Connor
Director of Player Development: Tommy Nobis
Controller: Wallace Norman
Director of Information Systems: Randy Kopp
Trainer: Ron Medlin
Assistant Trainers: Arnold Gamber, Matt Smith
Equipment Manager: Brian Boigner
Senior Equipment Manager: Horace Daniel
Video Director: Tom Atcheson
Assistant Video Director: Lou Crocker
Stadium: Georgia Dome • **Capacity:** 71,228
   One Georgia Dome Drive
   Atlanta, Georgia 30313
Playing Surface: Artificial turf
Training Camp: One Falcon Place
           Suwanee, Georgia 30174

1997 SCHEDULE
PRESEASON

Aug. 1	at Detroit	7:30
Aug. 9	**Tampa Bay**	7:30
Aug. 16	**Washington**	7:30
Aug. 22	at Jacksonville	7:30

REGULAR SEASON

Aug. 31	at Detroit	1:00
Sept. 7	**Carolina**	1:00
Sept. 14	**Oakland**	1:00
Sept. 21	at San Francisco	1:00
Sept. 28	**Denver**	1:00
Oct. 5	Open Date	
Oct. 12	at New Orleans	12:00
Oct. 19	**San Francisco**	1:00
Oct. 26	at Carolina	8:00
Nov. 2	**St. Louis**	1:00
Nov. 9	**Tampa Bay**	1:00
Nov. 16	at St. Louis	12:00
Nov. 23	**New Orleans**	1:00
Nov. 30	at Seattle	1:00
Dec. 7	at San Diego	1:00
Dec. 14	**Philadelphia**	1:00
Dec. 21	at Arizona	2:00

COACHING HISTORY
(177-289-5)

1966-68	Norb Hecker*	4-26-1
1968-74	Norm Van Brocklin**	37-49-3
1974-76	Marion Campbell***	6-19-0
1976	Pat Peppler	3-6-0
1977-82	Leeman Bennett	47-44-0
1983-86	Dan Henning	22-41-1
1987-89	Marion Campbell****	11-32-0
1989	Jim Hanifan	0-4-0
1990-93	Jerry Glanville	28-38-0
1994-96	June Jones	19-30

  *Released after three games in 1968
  **Released after eight games in 1974
 ***Released after five games in 1976
****Retired after 12 games in 1989

RECORD HOLDERS
INDIVIDUAL RECORDS—CAREER

Category	Name	Performance
Rushing (Yds.)	Gerald Riggs, 1982-88	6,631
Passing (Yds.)	Steve Bartkowski, 1975-1985	23,468
Passing (TDs)	Steve Bartkowski, 1975-1985	154
Receiving (No.)	Andre Rison, 1990-94	423
Receiving (Yds.)	Andre Rison, 1990-94	5,635
Interceptions	Rolland Lawrence, 1973-1980	39
Punting (Avg.)	Rick Donnelly, 1985-89	42.6
Punt Return (Avg.)	Al Dodd, 1973-74	11.8
Kickoff Return (Avg.)	Tony Smith, 1992-94	24.9
Field Goals	Mick Luckhurst, 1981-87	115
Touchdowns (Tot.)	Andre Rison, 1990-94	56
Points	Mick Luckhurst, 1981-87	558

INDIVIDUAL RECORDS—SINGLE SEASON

Category	Name	Performance
Rushing (Yds.)	Gerald Riggs, 1985	1,719
Passing (Yds.)	Jeff George, 1995	4,143
Passing (TDs)	Steve Bartkowski, 1980	31
Receiving (No.)	Terance Mathis, 1994	111
Receiving (Yds.)	Alfred Jenkins, 1981	1,358
Interceptions	Scott Case, 1988	10
Punting (Avg.)	Billy Lothridge, 1968	44.3
Punt Return (Avg.)	Gerald Tinker, 1974	13.9
Kickoff Return (Avg.)	Sylvester Stamps, 1987	27.5
Field Goals	Morten Andersen, 1995	31
Touchdowns (Tot.)	Andre Rison, 1993	15
Points	Morten Andersen, 1995	122

INDIVIDUAL RECORDS—SINGLE GAME

Category	Name	Performance
Rushing (Yds.)	Gerald Riggs, 9-2-84	202
Passing (Yds.)	Steve Bartkowski, 11-15-81	416
Passing (TDs)	Wade Wilson, 12-13-92	5
Receiving (No.)	William Andrews, 11-15-81	15
Receiving (Yds.)	Alfred Jackson, 12-2-84	193
	Andre Rison, 9-4-94	193
Interceptions	Many times	2
	Last time by Vinnie Clark, 10-9-94	
Field Goals	Norm Johnson, 11-13-94	6
Touchdowns (Tot.)	Many times	3
	Last time by Terance Mathis, 11-19-95	
Points	Norm Johnson, 11-13-94	20

GEORGIA DOME

1996 TEAM RECORD

PRESEASON (2-2)

Date	Result		Opponents
8/3	L	17-19	at Seattle
8/10	L	0-16	at Tampa Bay
8/15	W	27-6	Oakland
8/23	W	31-30	San Diego

REGULAR SEASON (3-13)

Date	Result		Opponents	Att.
9/1	L	6-29	at Carolina	69,522
9/8	L	17-23	Minnesota	42,688
9/22	L	18-33	Philadelphia	40,107
9/29	L	17-39	at San Francisco	62,995
10/6	L	24-28	at Detroit	58,666
10/13	L	13-23	Houston	35,401
10/20	L	28-32	at Dallas	64,091
10/27	L	17-20	Pittsburgh	58,760
11/3	W	20-17	Carolina	42,726
11/10	L	16-59	at St. Louis	58,776
11/17	W	17-15	New Orleans	43,119
11/24	L	31-41	at Cincinnati	44,868
12/2	L	10-34	San Francisco	46,318
12/8	W	31-15	at New Orleans	32,923
12/15	L	27-34	St. Louis	26,519
12/22	L	17-19	at Jacksonville	71,449

SCORE BY PERIODS

Falcons	52	82	82	93	—	309
Opponents	100	157	87	117	—	461

ATTENDANCE

Home 335,638   Away 463,290   Total 798,928
Single-game home record, 70,089 (10/29/95)
Single-season home record, 553,979 (1992)

1996 TEAM STATISTICS

	Falcons	Opp.
Total First Downs	292	309
Rushing	67	102
Passing	202	182
Penalty	23	25
Third Down: Made/Att	79/200	87/206
Third Down Pct.	39.5	42.2
Fourth Down: Made/Att	4/10	2/6
Fourth Down Pct.	40.0	33.3
Total Net Yards	5116	5786
Avg. Per Game	319.8	361.6
Total Plays	971	994
Avg. Per Play	5.3	5.8
Net Yards Rushing	1461	2041
Avg. Per Game	91.3	127.6
Total Rushes	329	473
Net Yards Passing	3655	3745
Avg. Per Game	228.4	234.1
Sacked/Yards Lost	42/254	36/208
Gross Yards	3909	3953
Att./Completions	600/356	485/302
Completion Pct.	59.3	62.3
Had Intercepted	30	6
Punts/Avg.	75/42.0	64/42.1
Net Punting Avg.	75/35.5	64/35.3
Penalties/Yards Lost	111/961	106/816
Fumbles/Ball Lost	23/11	27/17
Touchdowns	35	48
Rushing	9	18
Passing	26	26
Returns	0	4
Avg. Time of Possession	29:52	30:08

1996 INDIVIDUAL STATISTICS

Passing	Att.	Comp.	Yds.	Pct.	TD	Int.	Tkld.	Rate
Hebert	488	294	3152	60.2	22	25	27/150	72.9
J. George	99	56	698	56.6	3	3	11/84	76.1
Nagle	13	6	59	46.2	1	2	4/20	45.5
Falcons	600	356	3909	59.3	26	30	42/254	72.3
Opponents	485	302	3953	62.3	26	6	36/208	100.6

SCORING	TD R	TD P	TD Rt	PAT	FG	Saf	PTS
Andersen	0	0	0	31/31	22/29	0	97
Mathis	0	7	0	0/0	0/0	0	44
Anderson	5	1	0	0/0	0/0	0	36
Emanuel	0	6	0	0/0	0/0	0	36
Metcalf	0	6	0	0/0	0/0	0	36
Heyward	3	0	0	0/0	0/0	0	18
Birden	0	2	0	0/0	0/0	0	12
T. Brown	0	1	0	0/0	0/0	0	6
Hebert	1	0	0	0/0	0/0	0	6
Lyons	0	1	0	0/0	0/0	0	6
Preston	0	1	0	0/0	0/0	0	6
Tobeck	0	1	0	0/0	0/0	0	6
Falcons	9	26	0	31/31	22/29	0	309
Opponents	18	26	4	43/43	42/44	1	461

2-Point conversions: Mathis. Team: 1-4, Opponents: 1-5.

RUSHING	Att.	Yds.	Avg.	LG	TD
Anderson	232	1055	4.5	32t	5
Heyward	72	321	4.5	34	3
Hebert	15	59	3.9	25	1
J. George	5	10	2.0	5	0
Huntley	2	8	4.0	5	0
Metcalf	3	8	2.7	4	0
Falcons	329	1461	4.4	34	9
Opponents	473	2041	4.3	67	18

RECEIVING	No.	Yds.	Avg.	LG	TD
Emanuel	75	921	12.3	53	6
Mathis	69	771	11.2	55	7
Metcalf	54	599	11.1	67	6
Anderson	49	473	9.7	34	1
Birden	30	319	10.6	57	2
T. Brown	28	325	11.6	38	1
Preston	21	208	9.9	17t	1
Heyward	16	168	10.5	25	0
Scott	7	80	11.4	27	0
Lyons	4	16	4.0	5	1
Tobeck	2	15	7.5	14	1
Huntley	1	14	14.0	14	0
Falcons	356	3909	11.0	67	26
Opponents	302	3953	13.1	77t	26

INTERCEPTIONS	No.	Yds.	Avg.	LG	TD
Edwards	2	15	7.5	15	0
Smith	1	21	21.0	21	0
Bennett	1	3	3.0	3	0
Bush	1	2	2.0	2	0
Walker	1	0	0.0	0	0
Falcons	6	41	6.8	21	0
Opponents	30	324	10.8	55t	2

PUNTING	No.	Yds.	Avg.	In 20	LG
Stryzinski	75	3152	42.0	22	58
Falcons	75	3152	42.0	22	58
Opponents	64	2697	42.1	19	68

PUNT RETURNS	No.	FC	Yds.	Avg.	LG	TD
Metcalf	27	9	296	11.0	39	0
Mathis	3	1	19	6.3	10	0
Heyward	1	0	0	0.0	0	0
Falcons	31	10	315	10.2	39	0
Opponents	32	25	413	12.9	78t	1

KICKOFF RETURNS	No.	Yds.	Avg.	LG	TD
Metcalf	49	1034	21.1	55	0
Preston	32	681	21.3	50	0
Anderson	4	80	20.0	27	0
Heyward	1	18	18.0	18	0
Styles	1	12	12.0	12	0
Falcons	87	1825	21.0	55	0
Opponents	53	1314	24.8	97t	1

SACKS	No.
Matthews	6.5
Hall	6.0
Smith	6.0
Owens	5.5
Bennett	3.0
Archambeau	2.0
R. George	2.0
Brandon	1.0
McKyer	1.0
Riddick	1.0
Tuggle	1.0
Zgonina	1.0
Falcons	36.0
Opponents	42.0

1997 DRAFT CHOICES

Round	Name	Pos.	College
1	Michael Booker	DB	Nebraska
2	Nathan Davis	DE	Indiana
	Byron Hanspard	RB	Texas Tech
3	O.J. Santiago	TE	Kent State
4	Henri Crockett	LB	Florida State
5	Marcus Wimberly	DB	Miami
6	Calvin Collins	C	Texas A&M
7	Tony Graziani	QB	Oregon
	Chris Bayne	DB	Fresno State

ATLANTA FALCONS

1997 VETERAN ROSTER

No.		Name	Pos.	Ht.	Wt.	Birthdate	NFL Exp.	College	Hometown	How Acq.	'96 Games/ Starts
5		Andersen, Morten	K	6-2	225	8/19/60	16	Michigan State	Struer, Denmark	UFA(NO)-'95	16/0
32		Anderson, Jamal	RB	5-11	234	9/30/72	4	Utah	El Camino, Calif.	D7-'94	16/12
92		Archambeau, Lester	DE	6-5	275	6/27/67	8	Stanford	Montville, N.J.	T(GB)-'93	15/15
97		Bennett, Cornelius	LB	6-2	238	8/25/65	11	Alabama	Birmingham, Ala.	UFA(Buff)-'96	13/13
43		Bolden, Juran	CB	6-2	201	6/27/74	2	Mississippi Delta	Tampa, Fla.	D4-'96	9/0
23		Bradford, Ronnie	CB	5-10	188	10/1/70	5	Colorado	Minot, N.D.	UFA(Ariz)-'97	15/11*
51		Brandon, David	LB	6-4	234	2/9/65	11	Memphis State	Memphis, Tenn.	UFA(SD)-'96	16/2
80		Brown, Tyrone	WR	5-11	168	1/3/73	3	Toledo	Cincinnati, Ohio	FA-'95	9/4
34		Buchanan, Ray	CB	5-9	195	9/29/71	5	Louisville	Chicago, Ill.	UFA(Ind)-'97	13/13*
91		Burrough, John	DT	6-5	275	5/17/72	3	Wyoming	Pinedale, Wyo.	D7-'95	16/1
25		Bush, Devin	S	5-11	210	7/3/73	3	Florida State	Miami, Fla.	D1-'95	16/15
12	t-	Chandler, Chris	QB	6-4	225	10/12/65	10	Washington	Everett, Wash.	T(Hou)-'97	12/12*
44		Christian, Bob	RB	5-11	230	11/14/68	5	Northwestern	Florissant, Mo.	UFA(Car)-'96	0*
56		Croel, Mike	LB	6-3	235	6/6/69	7	Nebraska	Detroit, Mich.	UFA(Balt)-'97	16/16*
76		Davis, Antone	T	6-4	330	2/28/67	7	Tennessee	Fort Valley, Ga.	UFA(Phil)-'96	16/10
95		Davis, Paschall	LS	6-2	225	7/5/69	2	Texas A&M-Kingsville	Bryan, Tex.	FA-'97	10/0*
45		Downs, Gary	RB	6-1	212	6/6/72	4	North Carolina State	Columbus, Ga.	FA-'97	6/1*
87	†	Emanuel, Bert	WR	5-10	180	10/26/70	4	Rice	Houston, Tex.	D2-'94	14/13
65		Fortin, Roman	C	6-5	297	2/26/67	8	San Diego State	Ventura, Calif.	PB(Det)-'92	16/16
53		Fountaine, Jamal	LB	6-2	236	1/29/71	3	Washington	Wilmington, N.C.	FA-'97	0*
98		Hall, Travis	DE	6-5	287	8/3/72	3	Brigham Young	Kenai, Alaska	D6-'95	14/13
33		Huntley, Richard	RB	5-11	224	9/18/72	2	Winston-Salem State	Monroe, N.C.	D4-'96	1/0
96		Kelly, Todd	DE	6-2	259	11/27/70	5	Tennessee	Hampton, Va.	FA-'96	2/0
89		Kinchen, Todd	WR	5-11	187	1/7/69	6	Louisiana State	Baton Rouge, La.	UFA(Den)-'97	7/0*
49		Kozlowski, Brian	TE	6-3	255	10/4/70	4	Connecticut	Rochester, N.Y.	FA-'97	5/0*
68		Loneker, Keith	G	6-3	325	6/21/71	4	Kansas	Roselle Park, N.J.	FA-'96	0*
8		Maddox, Tommy	QB	6-4	218	9/2/71	5	UCLA	Hurst, Tex.	UFA(NYG)-'97	0*
81		Mathis, Terance	WR	5-10	180	6/7/67	8	New Mexico	Stone Mountain, Ga.	UFA(NYJ)-'94	16/16
28		McGill, Lenny	CB	6-1	198	5/31/71	4	Arizona State	Escondido, Calif.	T(GB)-'96	16/8
93		Owens, Dan	DT	6-3	280	3/16/67	8	Southern California	Whittier, Calif.	UFA(Det)-'96	16/9
64		Pahukoa, Jeff	G-T	6-2	298	2/9/69	6	Washington	Vancouver, Wash.	FA-'95	14/3
26		Phillips, Anthony	CB	6-2	209	10/5/70	4	Texas A&M-Kingsville	Galveston, Tex.	D3-'94	7/5
85		Preston, Roell	WR	5-10	185	6/23/72	3	Mississippi	Miami, Fla.	D5-'95	15/2
52		Sauer, Craig	LB	6-1	232	12/13/72	2	Minnesota	Sartell, Minn.	D6-'96	16/1
84		Scott, Freddie	WR	5-10	189	8/26/74	2	Penn State	Southfield, Mich.	FA-'96	10/0
37	#	Shelley, Elbert	S	5-11	190	12/24/64	11	Arkansas State	Tyronza, Ark.	D11-'87	12/0
90		Smith, Chuck	DE	6-2	262	12/21/69	6	Tennessee	Athens, Ga.	D2-'92	15/15
4		Stryzinski, Dan	P	6-2	200	5/15/65	8	Indiana	Vincennes, Ind.	UFA(TB)-'95	16/0
59		Styles, Lorenzo	LB	6-1	245	1/31/74	3	Ohio State	Columbus, Ohio	D3-'95	16/0
61		Tobeck, Robbie	G-C	6-4	295	3/6/70	4	Washington State	Tarpon Springs, Fla.	FA-'93	16/16
11		Tolliver, Billy Joe	QB	6-1	217	2/7/66	8	Texas Tech	Boyd, Tex.	FA-'96	0*
58		Tuggle, Jessie	LB	5-11	230	4/4/65	11	Valdosta State	Spalding, Ga.	FA-'87	16/16
83		West, Ed	TE	6-1	250	8/2/61	14	Auburn	Leighton, Ala.	UFA(Phil)-'97	16/4*
35		White, William	S	5-10	205	2/19/66	10	Ohio State	Lima, Ohio	FA-'97	12/2*
70		Whitfield, Bob	T	6-5	310	10/18/71	6	Stanford	Carson, Calif.	D1a-'92	16/16
69		Williams, Gene	G-T	6-2	306	10/14/68	7	Iowa State	Omaha, Neb.	T(Clev)-'95	10/0
77		Willig, Matt	G-T	6-8	317	1/21/69	5	Southern California	La Mirada, Calif.	T(NYJ)-'96	12/0

* Bradford played 15 games with Arizona in '96; Buchanan played 13 games with Indianapolis; Chandler played 12 games with Houston; Christian and Fountaine last active with Carolina in '95; Croel played 16 games with Baltimore; P. Davis played 10 games with St. Louis; Downs played 6 games with N.Y. Giants; Kinchen played 7 games with Denver; Kozlowski played 5 games with N.Y. Giants; Loneker inactive for 2 games; Maddox last active with N.Y. Giants in '95; Tolliver inactive for 9 games; West played 16 games with Philadelphia; White played 12 games with Kansas City.

Unrestricted free agent; subject to developments.

† Restricted free agent; subject to developments.

t- Falcons traded for Chandler (Houston).

Retired—Clay Mathews, 19-year linebacker, 15 games in '96.

Players lost to free agency (7): S Brad Edwards (GB; 16 games in '96), TE Harper Le Bel (GB; 16), TE Mitch Lyons (Pitt; 14), WR Eric Metcalf (SD; 16), CB Darnell Walker (SF; 15), G Mike Zandofsky (Phil; 14), DT Jeff Zgonina (StL; 8).

Also played with Falcons in '96—WR J.J. Birden (12 games), T Ethan Brooks (2), DE Shane Dronett (5), LB Scott Fields (6), DT Moe Gardner (10), QB Jeff George (3), LB Ron George (16), QB Bobby Hebert (14), RB Craig Heyward (15), CB D.J. Johnson (2), CB Tim McKyer (8), QB Browning Nagle (5), CB Nate Odomes (7), T Dave Richards (6), S Louis Riddick (16).

COACHING STAFF

Head Coach,
Dan Reeves

Pro Career: Named the eighth coach in Falcons history on January 20, 1997. Reeves enters the 1997 season as the NFL's winningest active coach with a career record of 149-113-1 in 16 years, ranking tenth on the league's all-time list. Reeves had been the head coach of the New York Giants from 1993-96. Prior to that, he compiled a 117-79-1 record as head coach of the Denver Broncos from 1981-92, earning NFL Coach of the Year honors in 1982, 1988, and 1991. He led the Broncos to three Super Bowl berths, four AFC Championship games, five AFC West Division titles, and eight winning seasons. In his first year in New York, he earned NFL Coach of the Year honors for a fourth time, taking the Giants from 6-10 to an 11-5 mark, including a wild-card playoff victory. Overall, Reeves has accumulated ten winning seasons as head coach, participated in 45 playoff games and eight Super Bowls as an NFL player, assistant coach, and head coach. He was the only NFL coach in the 1980's to take his team to back-to-back Super Bowls. Reeves, whose teams have won at least 10 games eight different times, was very successful at Mile High Stadium, where he compiled a 72-21 (.774) record. His Broncos teams finished in first place five times and in second place three times in the AFC West. In 1984, Denver set a team record with 10 straight wins en route to a franchise-best 13-win season. The following season (1985), the Broncos set a team record for total offense and points scored. In 1986, they started out 6-0 and established thirty-five team and individual club marks. Career record: 149-113-1.

Background: Prior to obtaining his first NFL head coaching job in 1981, Reeves had been a member of the Dallas Cowboys coaching staff since 1970, spending a total of 16 years under Tom Landry as a player and coach. In 1977 he was named offensive coordinator of Landry's staff. Reeves began his pro career as a free agent running back for Dallas in 1965. Prior to that he was a quarterback at South Carolina from 1962-64, passing for 2,561 yards and 16 TD's. He totaled 3,376 yards during his career with the Gamecocks, leading to his induction into the school's hall of fame in 1978. Reeves later was inducted into the state of Georgia Sports Hall of Fame.

Personal: Born January 19, 1944, Americus, Ga. Dan and his wife, Pam, live in Atlanta, and have three children — Dana, Laura, and Lee.

ASSISTANT COACHES

Don Blackmon, linebackers; born March 14, 1958, Pompano Beach, Fla., lives in Atlanta. Linebacker Tulsa 1977-80. Pro linebacker New England Patriots 1981-87. Pro coach: New England Patriots 1988-90, Cleveland Browns 1991-92, New York Giants 1993-96, joined Falcons in 1997.

Rich Brooks, assistant head coach-defensive coordinator; born August 10, 1941, Forest, Calif., lives in Atlanta. Tailback, defensive back, and quarterback Oregon State 1959-62. No pro playing experience. College coach: Oregon State 1965-69, 1973, UCLA 1970, 1976, Oregon 1977-94 (head coach). Pro coach: Los Angeles Rams 1971-72, San Francisco 49ers 1974-75, St. Louis Rams 1995-96 (head coach), joined Falcons in 1997.

Jack Burns, quarterbacks, born January 3, 1949, Tampa, Fla., lives in Atlanta. Safety Florida, 1967-70. No pro playing experience. College coach: Florida 1971-73, 1975, Louisville 1974, 1985-88, Texas 1976, Vanderbilt 1977-78, Auburn 1979-80. Pro coach: Tampa Bay Bandits (USFL) 1983, Washington Redskins 1989-91, Minnesota Vikings 1992-93, joined Falcons in 1997.

James Daniel, tight ends; born January 17, 1953, Wetumpka, Ala., lives in Atlanta. Offensive guard Alabama State 1970-73. No pro playing experience. College coach: Auburn 1981-92. Pro coach: New York Giants 1993-96, joined Falcons in 1997.

Joe DeCamillis, special teams; born June 29, 1965, Arvada, Colo., lives in Alpharetta, Ga. No college or pro playing experience. College coach: Wyoming

1997 FIRST-YEAR ROSTER

Name	Pos.	Ht.	Wt.	Birthdate	College	Hometown	How Acq.
Akers, Jeremy	T	6-5	304	1/9/74	Notre Dame	Washington, D.C.	FA
Allen, Demetrius (1)	WR	5-10	160	7/8/74	Virginia	Norfolk, Va.	FA
Baldwin, Robert (1)	RB	5-11	230	9/1/72	Duke	Deland, Fla.	FA
Bayne, Chris	S	6-1	205	3/22/75	Fresno State	Riverside, Calif.	D7b
Booker, Michael	CB	6-2	203	12/19/72	Nebraska	Oceanside, Calif.	D1
Boyd, Sean (1)	S	6-2	206	12/19/72	North Carolina	Gastonia, N.C.	FA
Brown, Shannon (1)	DT	6-5	290	5/23/72	Alabama	Milbrook, Ala.	D3-'96
Collins, Calvin	C-G	6-2	307	1/5/74	Texas A&M	Beaumont, Tex.	D6
Crockett, Henri	LB	6-2	249	10/28/74	Florida State	Whittier, Calif.	D4
Davis, Nathan	DT	6-5	312	2/6/74	Indiana	Richmond, Ind.	D2a
Denton, Tim (1)	CB	5-11	180	2/2/73	Sam Houston State	Galveston, Tex.	FA
Embra, Donnie	DT	6-3	288	8/26/74	Baylor	Houston, Tex.	FA
Goltra, Bob	T	6-7	315	9/30/73	Pittsburg State	Ft. Scott, Kan.	FA
Graziani, Tony	QB	6-2	195	12/23/73	Oregon	Modesto, Calif.	D7a
Grenier, Geoff (1)	RB	6-2	240	1/25/73	Oklahoma State	Fullerton, Calif.	FA
Grier, Derek	CB	6-3	183	3/4/70	Marshall	Altanta, Ga.	FA
Hanspard, Bryon	RB	5-10	198	1/23/76	Texas Tech	DeSoto, Tex.	D2b
Keeney, Brad (1)	RB	6-3	295	11/20/73	The Citadel	Oakland, Calif.	FA
Kushner, Bill (1)	P	6-0	203	1/13/70	Boston College	San Diego, Calif.	FA
Ladd, Anthony	WR	6-1	193	12/23/73	Cincinnati	Homestead, Fla.	FA
Lauder, David	K	6-2	226	2/18/69	Bringham Young	Centerville, Utah	FA
Lester, Fred (1)	RB	6-1	244	8/1/71	Alabama A&M	Miami, Fla.	FA
Miller, Nate (1)	T	6-3	310	10/8/71	Louisiana State	Tuscaloosa, Ala.	FA
Mitchell, Barry	DE	6-3	268	3/18/74	Idaho	Aurora, Colo.	FA
Pegross, Pearce	WR	5-7	171	8/12/73	Baylor	Port Arthur, Tex.	FA
Perkins, Barry	G	6-3	293	7/10/73	Texas A&M-Kingsville	Mt. Pleasant, Tex.	FA
Santiago, O.J.	TE	6-7	267	4/4/74	Kent State	Whitby, Canada	D3
Smith, Darius (1)	C	6-2	275	10/9/72	Sam Houston State	Dallas, Tex.	FA
Smith, Ed (1)	TE	6-4	253	6/5/69	No College	Trenton, N.J.	FA
Thornal, Kevin	WR	6-2	186	11/28/73	Southern Methodist	DeSoto, Tex.	FA
Vavao, Mathias	DT	6-4	295	11/14/74	Murray State	Laie, Hawaii	FA
Wimberly, Marcus	S	5-11	192	7/8/74	Miami	Memphis, Tenn.	D5

The term NFL Rookie is defined as a player who is in his first season of professional football and has not been on the roster of another professional football team for any regular-season or postseason games. A Rookie is designated by an "R" on NFL rosters. Players who have been active in another professional football league or players who have NFL experience, including other preseason training camp or being on an Active List or Inactive List, or on Reserve/Injured or Reserve/Physically Unable to Perform for fewer than six regular-season games, are termed NFL First-Year Players. An NFL First-Year Player is designated by a "1" on NFL rosters. Thereafter, a player is credited with an additional year of experience for each season in which he accumulates six games on the Active List or Inactive List, or on Reserve/Injured or Reserve/Physically Unable to Perform.

NOTES

1988. Pro coach: Denver Broncos 1989, Miami Dolphins 1990, New York Giants 1993-96, joined Falcons in 1997.

Tim Jorgensen, assistant strength and conditioning; born April 21, 1955, St. Louis, Mo., lives in Snellville, Ga. Guard Southwest Missouri State 1974-76. No pro playing experience. College coach: Southwest Missouri State 1977-78, Alabama 1979, Louisiana State 1980-83. Pro coach: Philadelphia Eagles 1984-86, joined Falcons in 1987.

Bill Kollar, defensive line; born November 27, 1952, Warren, Ohio, lives in Duluth, Ga. Defensive end Montana State 1971-74. Pro defensive end Cincinnati Bengals 1974-76, Tampa Bay Buccaneers 1977-81. College coach: Illinois 1985-87, Purdue 1988-89. Pro coach: Tampa Bay Buccaneers 1984, joined Falcons in 1990.

Ron Meeks, secondary; born August 27, 1954, Jacksonville, Fla., lives in Atlanta. Defensive back Arkansas State 1975-76. Pro defensive back Hamilton Tiger-Cats (CFL) 1977-79, Ottawa Rough Riders (CFL) 1979, Toronto Argonauts (CFL) 1980-81. College coach: Arkansas State 1984-85, Miami 1986-87, New Mexico State 1988, Fresno State 1989-90. Pro coach: Dallas Cowboys 1991, Cincinnati Bengals 1992-96, joined Falcons in 1997.

Al Miller, strength and conditioning; born August 29, 1947, El Dorado, Ark., lives in Atlanta. Wide receiver Northeast Louisiana 1965-69. No pro playing experience. College coach: Northwestern State (La.) 1974-78, Mississippi State 1980, Northeast Louisiana 1981, Alabama 1982-84. Pro coach: Denver Broncos 1987-92, New York Giants 1993-96, joined Falcons in 1997.

Harold Richardson, assistant head coach-football operations; born September 27, 1944, Houston,

Texas, lives in Atlanta. Tight end Southern Methodist 1964-67. No pro playing experience. College coach: Southern Methodist 1971-72, Oklahoma State 1973-76, Texas Christian 1977-78, North Texas State 1979-80, Colorado State 1986-88. Pro coach: New Orleans Saints 1981-85, Denver Broncos 1989-92, joined Falcons in 1997.

George Sefcik, offensive coordinator-running backs; born December 27, 1939, Cleveland, Ohio, lives in Atlanta. Halfback Notre Dame 1959-61. No pro playing experience. College coach: Notre Dame 1963-68, Kentucky 1969-72. Pro coach: Baltimore Colts 1973-74, Cleveland Browns 1975-77, 1989-90, Cincinnati Bengals 1978-83, Green Bay Packers 1984-87, Kansas City Chiefs 1988, New York Giants 1991-96, joined Falcons in 1997.

Art Shell, offensive line; born November 26, 1946, Charleston, S.C., lives in Atlanta. Offensive-defensive tackle Maryland State 1965-67. Pro offensive tackle Oakland/Los Angeles Raiders 1968-82. Inducted into Pro Football Hall of Fame 1989. Pro coach: Los Angeles Raiders 1983-94 (head coach 1989-94), Kansas City Chiefs 1995-96, joined Falcons in 1997.

Warren "Rennie" Simmons, wide receivers; born February 25, 1942, Poughkeepsie, N.Y., lives in Atlanta. Center San Diego State 1961-65. No pro playing experience. College coach: Cal State-Fullerton 1974-78, Cerritos (Calif.) J.C. 1978-80, Vanderbilt 1995. Pro coach: Washington Redskins 1981-93, Los Angeles Rams 1994, Houston Oilers 1996, joined Falcons in 1997.

Brian Xanders, defensive quality control; born April 10, 1971, East Stroudsburg, Pa., lives in Atlanta. Linebacker Florida State 1989-92. No pro playing experience. Pro coach: Joined Falcons in 1997.

CAROLINA PANTHERS

National Football Conference
Western Division
Team Colors: Black, Panther Blue, and Silver
800 South Mint Street
Charlotte, North Carolina 28202-1502
Telephone: (704) 358-7000

CLUB OFFICIALS

Founder/Owner: Jerry Richardson
President: Mark Richardson
President Carolina Stadium Corps.: Jon Richardson
General Manager: Bill Polian
Assistant Director of Business Operations:
  Charles Waddell
Counsel: Richard Thigpen, Jr.
Chief Financial Officer: Dave Olsen
Controller: Lisa Garber
Director Player Personnel: Dom Anile
Pro Personnel Cordinator: Chris Polian
Pro Scouts: Hal Hunter
Regional Scouts: Jack Bushofsky, Ralph Hawkins
Area Scouts: Hal Athon, Joe Bushofsky,
  Bob Guarini, Tony Softli, Todd Vasvari
Scouting Assistant: Tom Telesco
Director of Communications: Charlie Dayton
Media Relations Assistant: Lex Sant
Communications and Marketing Assistant:
  Bruce Speight
Director of Ticket Sales: Phil Youtsey
Assistant Ticket Manager: Kati Hynes
Director of Player Relations: Donnie Shell
Director of Community Relations/Family Programs:
  B.J. Harrison Waymer
Director of Special Events: Leslie Matz
Director of Information Systems: Roger Goss
Football Systems: Rob Rogers
Programmer: Troy Bigelow
Video Director: Dave Sutherby
Assistant Video Director: Mark Hobbs
Head Trainer: John Kasik
Assistant Trainers: Al Shuford, Dan Ruiz
Head Equipment Manager: Jackie Miles
Assistant Equipment Manager: Don Toner
Equipment Assistant: Matt Grupp
Director of Football Security: Ed Stillwell
Manager of Football Administration: Mark Koncz
Director of Facilities: Tom Fellows
Director of Stadium Security: Gene Brown
Stadium Operations Coordinator: Mitch Silverman
Office Manager: Jackie Jeffries
Stadium: Ericsson Stadium •**Capacity:** 75,248
        Charlotte, North Carolina 28202-1502
Playing Surface: Grass
Training Camp: Wofford College
        Spartanburg, South Carolina
        29303

RECORD HOLDERS
INDIVIDUAL RECORDS—CAREER

Category	Name	Performance
Rushing (Yds.)	Anthony Johnson, 1995-96	1,230
Passing (Yds.)	Kerry Collins, 1995-96	5,171
Passing (TDs)	Kerry Collins, 1995-96	28
Receiving (No.)	Mark Carrier, 1995-96	124
Receiving (Yds.)	Mark Carrier, 1995-96	1,810
Interceptions	Brett Maxie, 1995-96	7
Punting (Avg.)	Tommy Barnhardt, 1995	41.1
Punt Return (Avg.)	Winslow Oliver, 1996	11.5
Kickoff Return (Avg.)	Michael Bates, 1996	30.2
Field Goals	John Kasay, 1995-96	63
Touchdowns (Tot.)	Wesley Walls, 1996	10
Points	John Kasay, 1995-96	250

INDIVIDUAL RECORDS—SINGLE SEASON

Category	Name	Performance
Rushing (Yds.)	Anthony Johnson, 1996	1,120
Passing (Yds.)	Kerry Collins, 1995	2,717
Passing (TDs)	Kerry Collins 1995, 1996	14
Receiving (No.)	Mark Carrier, 1995	66
Receiving (Yds.)	Mark Carrier, 1995	1,002
Interceptions	Brett Maxie, 1995	6
Punting (Avg.)	Tommy Barnhardt, 1995	41.1
Punt Return (Avg.)	Winslow Oliver, 1996	11.5
Kickoff Return (Avg.)	Michael Bates, 1996	30.2
Field Goals	John Kasay, 1996	37
Touchdowns (Tot.)	Wesley Walls, 1996	10
Points	John Kasay, 1996	145

INDIVIDUAL RECORDS—SINGLE GAME

Category	Name	Performance
Rushing (Yds.)	Anthony Johnson, 10-13-96	126
Passing (Yds.)	Kerry Collins, 11-26-95	335
Passing (TDs)	Kerry Collins, 11-26-95, 10-13-96, 12-8-96	3
	Steve Beverlein, 11-24-96	3
Receiving (No.)	Willie Green, 11-3-96	9
Receiving (Yds.)	Willie Green, 11-12-95, 12-8-96	157
Interceptions	Brett Maxie, 10-22-95	2
	Pat Terrell, 11-10-96	2
Field Goals	John Kasay, 9-1-96, 9-8-96	5
Touchdowns (Tot.)	Howard Griffith, 10-22-95	2
	Mark Carrier, 11-26-95, 9-29-96	2
	Wesley Walls, 9-22-96, 10-13-96, 12-8-96	2
Points	John Kasay, 9-1-96	17

1997 SCHEDULE
PRESEASON

Aug. 3	at Jacksonville	3:00
Aug. 9	**Denver**	8:00
Aug. 14	at Kansas City	7:00
Aug. 22	**Pittsburgh**	8:00

REGULAR SEASON

Aug. 31	**Washington**	8:00
Sept. 7	at Atlanta	1:00
Sept. 14	at San Diego	1:00
Sept. 21	**Kansas City**	1:00
Sept. 29	**San Francisco** (Mon.)	9:00
Oct. 5	Open Date	
Oct. 12	at Minnesota	3:00
Oct. 19	at New Orleans	12:00
Oct. 26	**Atlanta**	8:00
Nov. 2	**Oakland**	1:00
Nov. 9	at Denver	2:00
Nov. 16	at San Francisco	1:00
Nov. 23	at St. Louis	3:00
Nov. 30	**New Orleans**	1:00
Dec. 8	at Dallas (Mon.)	8:00
Dec. 14	**Green Bay**	4:00
Dec. 20	**St. Louis** (Sat.)	4:00

ERICSSON STADIUM

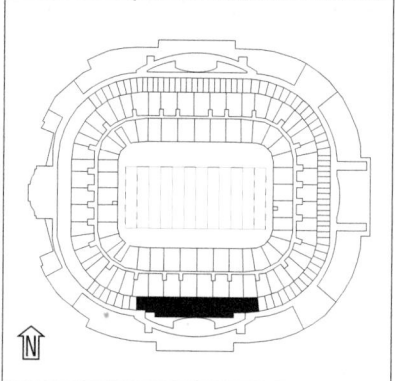

COACHING HISTORY
(20-14-0)

1995-96	Dom Capers	20-14-0

1996 TEAM RECORD

PRESEASON (2-2)

Date	Result		Opponents
8/3	W	30-12	Chicago
8/10	L	28-40	at Denver
8/17	L	0-24	Buffalo
8/23	W	34-7	at N.Y. Giants

REGULAR SEASON (12-4)

Date	Result		Opponents	Att.
9/1	W	29-6	Atlanta	69,522
9/8	W	22-20	at New Orleans	43,288
9/22	W	23-7	San Francisco	72,224
9/29	L	14-24	at Jacksonville	71,537
10/6	L	12-14	at Minnesota	60,894
10/13	W	45-13	St. Louis	70,535
10/20	W	19-7	New Orleans	70,888
10/27	L	9-20	at Philadelphia	65,982
11/3	L	17-20	at Atlanta	42,726
11/10	W	27-17	N.Y. Giants	70,298
11/17	W	20-10	at St. Louis	60,652
11/24	W	31-6	at Houston	20,107
12/1	W	24-0	Tampa Bay	57,623
12/8	W	30-24	at San Francisco	66,291
12/15	W	27-16	Baltimore	70,075
12/22	W	18-14	Pittsburgh	72,217

POSTSEASON (1-1)

Date	Result		Opponents	Att.
1/5	W	26-17	Dallas	72,808
1/12	L	13-30	at Green Bay	60,215

SCORE BY PERIODS

Panthers	74	102	107	84	—	367
Opponents	62	100	23	33	—	218

ATTENDANCE

Home 553,382   Away 431,477   Total 984,859
Single-game home record, 72,224 (9/22/96)
Single-season home record, 553,382 (1996)

1996 TEAM STATISTICS

	Panthers	Opp.
Total First Downs	292	251
Rushing	93	69
Passing	160	167
Penalty	39	15
Third Down: Made/Att	84/226	71/219
Third Down Pct.	37.2	32.4
Fourth Down: Made/Att	6/13	7/22
Fourth Down Pct.	46.2	31.8
Total Net Yards	4812	4776
Avg. Per Game	300.8	298.5
Total Plays	1025	990
Avg. Per Play	4.7	4.8
Net Yards Rushing	1729	1562
Avg. Per Game	108.1	97.6
Total Rushes	502	374
Net Yards Passing	3083	3214
Avg. Per Game	192.7	200.9
Sacked/Yards Lost	36/250	60/371
Gross Yards	3333	3585
Att./Completions	487/273	556/307
Completion Pct.	56.1	55.2
Had Intercepted	11	22
Punts/Avg.	78/40.5	95/43.8
Net Punting Avg.	78/35.7	95/35.3
Penalties/Yards Lost	94/638	133/1155
Fumbles/Ball Lost	25/14	25/16
Touchdowns	36	24
Rushing	9	6
Passing	22	17
Returns	5	1
Avg. Time of Possession	30:48	29:12

1996 INDIVIDUAL STATISTICS

PASSING

	Att.	Comp.	Yds.	Pct.	TD	Int.	Tkld.	Rate
Collins	364	204	2454	56.0	14	9	18/114	79.4
Beuerlein	123	69	879	56.1	8	2	18/136	93.5
Panthers	487	273	3333	56.1	22	11	36/250	83.0
Opponents	556	307	3585	55.2	17	22	60/371	68.7

SCORING

	TD R	TD P	TD Rt	PAT	FG	Saf	PTS
Kasay	0	0	0	34/35	37/45	0	145
Walls	0	10	0	0/0	0/0	0	60
Carrier	0	6	0	0/0	0/0	0	36
Johnson	6	0	0	0/0	0/0	0	36
Green	0	3	0	0/0	0/0	0	18
Griffith	1	1	0	0/0	0/0	0	12
Bates	0	0	1	0/0	0/0	0	6
K. Greene	0	0	1	0/0	0/0	0	6
S. Greene	0	1	0	0/0	0/0	0	6
Ismail	1	0	0	0/0	0/0	0	6
King	0	0	1	0/0	0/0	0	6
Mills	0	0	1	0/0	0/0	0	6
Muhammad	0	1	0	0/0	0/0	0	6
Oliver	0	0	1	0/0	0/0	0	6
Philyaw	1	0	0	0/0	0/0	0	6
Collins	0	0	0	0/0	0/0	0	2
Panthers	9	22	5	34/35	37/45	*2	367
Opponents	6	17	1	23/24	17/20	0	218

2-Point conversions: Collins. Team: 1-1, Opponents: 0-0.
*Panthers were credited with 2 team safeties.

RUSHING

	Att.	Yds.	Avg.	LG	TD
Johnson	300	1120	3.7	29	6
Biakabutuka	71	229	3.2	17	0
Oliver	47	183	3.9	16	0
Ismail	8	80	10.0	35t	0
Collins	32	38	1.2	14	0
Philyaw	12	38	3.2	8	1
Beuerlein	12	17	1.4	13	0
Hoard	5	11	2.2	5	0
Griffith	12	7	0.6	3	1
Stone	1	6	6.0	6	0
Green	1	1	1.0	1	0
Muhammad	1	-1	-1.0	-1	0
Panthers	502	1729	3.4	35t	9
Opponents	374	1562	4.2	80t	6

RECEIVING

	No.	Yds.	Avg.	LG	TD
Walls	61	713	11.7	40t	10
Carrier	58	808	13.9	39	6
Green	46	614	13.3	50	3
Griffith	27	223	8.3	21	1
Johnson	26	192	7.4	55	0
Muhammad	25	407	16.3	54t	1
Oliver	15	144	9.6	29	0
Ismail	12	214	17.8	51	0
S. Greene	2	7	3.5	6	1
Stone	1	11	11.0	11	0
Panthers	273	3333	12.2	55	22
Opponents	307	3585	11.7	55	17

INTERCEPTIONS

	No.	Yds.	Avg.	LG	TD
Cota	5	63	12.6	35	0
Davis	5	57	11.4	36	0
Cook	3	28	9.3	22	0
Terrell	3	6	2.0	6	0
Lofton	1	42	42.0	42	0
Maxie	1	35	35.0	35	0
Poole	1	35	35.0	35	0
Mills	1	10	10.0	10	0
King	1	1	1.0	1	0
Pieri	1	0	0.0	0	0
Panthers	22	277	12.6	42	0
Opponents	11	41	3.7	22t	1

PUNTING

	No.	Yds.	Avg.	In 20	LG
Stark	77	3128	40.6	21	60
Kasay	1	30	30.0	0	30
Panthers	78	3158	40.5	21	60
Opponents	95	4159	43.8	18	68

PUNT RETURNS

	No.	FC	Yds.	Avg.	LG	TD
Oliver	52	17	598	11.5	84t	1
Poole	3	0	26	8.7	12	0
Panthers	55	17	624	11.3	84t	1
Opponents	32	25	173	5.4	25	0

KICKOFF RETURNS

	No.	Yds.	Avg.	LG	TD
Bates	33	998	30.2	93t	1
Oliver	7	160	22.9	33	0
Ismail	5	100	20.0	30	0
S. Greene	2	10	5.0	6	0
Baker	1	11	11.0	11	0
Bickett	1	12	12.0	12	0
Hoard	1	19	19.0	19	0
Panthers	50	1310	26.2	93t	1
Opponents	71	1429	20.1	33	0

SACKS

	No.
K. Greene	14.5
Lathon	13.5
Mills	5.5
Cook	4.0
Thomas	4.0
King	3.0
Kragen	3.0
Miller	3.0
Bailey	2.5
Bickett	2.0
Fox	2.0
Cota	1.0
R. Smith	1.0
Williams	1.0
Panthers	60.0
Opponents	36.0

1997 DRAFT CHOICES

Round	Name	Pos.	College
1	Rae Carruth	WR	Colorado
2	Mike Minter	DB	Nebraska
3	Kinnon Tatum	LB	Notre Dame
4	Tarek Saleh	LB	Wisconsin
6	Matt Finkes	LB	Ohio State
7	Kris Mangum	TE	Mississippi

CAROLINA PANTHERS

1997 VETERAN ROSTER

No.	Name	Pos.	Ht.	Wt.	Birthdate	NFL Exp.	College	Hometown	How Acq.	'96 Games/ Starts
24	Abraham, Clifton	CB	5-9	185	12/9/71	3	Florida State	Dallas, Tex.	W(Chi)-'97	2/0*
54	# Bailey, Carlton	LB	6-3	242	12/15/64	10	North Carolina	Baltimore, Md.	FA-'95	16/14
66	# Baker, Myron	LB	6-1	234	1/6/71	5	Louisiana Tech	Haughton, La.	W(Chi)-'96	16/0
11	Barker, Jay	QB	6-3	220	4/20/72	3	Alabama	Birmingham, Ala.	W(NE)-'96	0*
56	Barrow, Micheal	LB	6-2	236	4/19/70	5	Miami	Homestead, Fla.	UFA(Hou)-'97	16/16*
82	Bates, Michael	WR	5-10	189	12/19/69	5	Arizona	Tucson, Ariz.	FA-'96	14/0
7	Beuerlein, Steve	QB	6-3	220	3/7/65	11	Notre Dame	Anaheim, Calif.	UFA(Jax)-'96	8/4
21	Biakabutuka, Tshimanga	RB	6-0	210	1/24/74	2	Michigan	Lonqueuil, Canada	D1-'96	4/4
50	# Bickett, Duane	LB	6-5	251	12/1/62	13	Southern California	Glendale, Calif.	UFA(Sea)-'96	16/0
68	Brockermeyer, Blake	T	6-4	300	4/11/73	3	Texas	Fort Worth, Tex.	D1c-'95	12/12
66	Campbell, Mathew	T	6-4	270	7/14/72	3	South Carolina	North Augusta, S.C.	FA-'95	9/8
83	# Carrier, Mark	WR	6-0	186	10/28/65	11	Nicholls State	Church Point, La.	ED16(Clev)-'95	16/15
12	Collins, Kerry	QB	6-5	240	12/30/72	3	Penn State	Lebanon, Pa.	D1a-'95	13/12
41	# Cook, Toi	CB	5-11	188	12/3/64	11	Stanford	Van Nuys, Calif.	FA-'96	15/1
37	Cota, Chad	S	6-1	195	8/13/71	3	Oregon	Ashland, Ore.	D7a-'95	16/2
76	Davidds-Garrido, Norberto	T	6-6	313	10/4/72	2	Southern California	La Puente, Calif.	D4a-'96	12/8
25	Davis, Eric	CB	5-11	185	1/26/68	8	Jacksonville State	Anniston, Ala.	UFA(SF)-'96	16/16
52	Elliott, Matt	G	6-3	295	10/1/68	5	Michigan	Carmel, Ind.	FA-'95	16/12
93	Fox, Mike	DE	6-8	295	8/5/67	8	West Virginia	Akron, Ohio	UFA(NYG)-'95	11/11
65	Garcia, Frank	G	6-1	295	1/28/72	3	Washington	Phoenix, Ariz.	D4-'95	14/8
60	Greeley, Bucky	C-G	6-2	270	7/30/72	2	Penn State	Wilkes-Barre, Pa.	FA-'96	0*
91	Greene, Kevin	LB	6-3	247	7/31/62	13	Auburn	Granite City, Ill.	UFA(Pitt)-'96	16/16
43	Greene, Scott	RB	5-11	225	6/1/72	2	Michigan State	Canandaigua, N.Y.	FA-'96	8/0
67	Hayes, Brandon	G	6-4	305	3/11/73	3	Central State	Muncie, Ind.	FA-'95	7/0
81	Ismail, Raghib	WR	5-11	175	11/18/69	5	Notre Dame	Wilkes-Barre, Pa.	TR(Oak)-'96	13/5
23	Johnson, Anthony	RB	6-0	225	10/15/67	8	Notre Dame	South Bend, Ind.	W(Chi)-'95	16/11
4	Kasay, John	K	5-10	198	10/27/69	7	Georgia	Athens, Ga.	UFA(Sea)-'95	16/0
96	King, Shawn	DE	6-3	278	6/24/72	3	Northeast Louisiana	Monroe, La.	D2-'95	16/0
71	Kragen, Greg	NT	6-3	267	3/4/62	13	Utah State	Pleasanton, Calif.	ED9(KC)-'95	16/16
57	Lathon, Lamar	LB	6-3	260	12/23/67	8	Houston	Wharton, Tex.	UFA(Hou)-'95	16/16
27	# Lofton, Steve	CB	5-9	177	11/26/68	6	Texas A&M	Alto, Tex.	FA-'95	11/3
26	McDaniel, Emmanuel	CB	5-9	178	7/27/72	2	East Carolina	Jonesboro, Ga.	D4b-'96	2/0
89	Mills, Ernie	WR	5-11	192	10/28/68	7	Florida	Dunnellon, Fla.	UFA(Pitt)-'97	2/0*
51	Mills, Sam	LB	5-9	232	6/3/59	12	Montclair State	Long Branch, N.J.	UFA(NO)-'95	16/16
87	Muhammad, Muhsin	WR	6-2	217	5/5/73	2	Michigan State	Lansing, Mich.	D2-'96	9/5
20	Oliver, Winslow	RB	5-7	180	3/3/73	2	New Mexico	Houston, Tex.	D3a-'96	16/0
90	† Philion, Ed	NT	6-2	277	3/27/70	4	Ferris State	Essex, Canada	W(Buff)-'96	0*
27	Pieri, Damon	S	6-0	186	9/25/70	3	San Diego State	Phoenix, Ariz.	FA-'95	16/1
38	Poole, Tyrone	CB	5-8	188	2/3/72	3	Fort Valley State	La Grange, Ga.	D1b-'95	15/15
88	† Rasby, Walter	TE	6-3	247	9/7/72	4	Wake Forest	Washington, N.C.	FA-'95	16/1
45	Reed, Michael	CB	5-9	182	8/16/72	2	Boston College	Wilmington, Del.	FA-'97	2/0
63	Rodenhauser, Mark	C	6-5	280	6/1/61	10	Illinois State	Addison, Ill.	ED17(Det)-'95	16/0
58	Royal, Andre	LB	6-2	288	12/1/72	3	Alabama	Tuscaloosa, Ala.	FA-'95	16/0
99	Seals, Ray	DE	6-3	306	6/17/65	10	No College	Syracuse, N.Y.	UFA(Pitt)-'97	0*
75	Skrepenak, Greg	G	6-7	325	1/31/70	6	Michigan	Wilkes-Barre, Pa.	UFA(Oak)-'96	16/16
22	Smith, Marquette	RB	5-7	190	7/14/72	2	Central Florida	Lake Howell, Fla.	D5-'96	0*
31	Smith, Rod	CB	5-11	194	3/12/70	6	Notre Dame	St. Paul, Minn.	FA-'96	8/1
3	# Stark, Rohn	P	6-3	203	5/4/59	16	Florida State	Pine River, Minn.	FA-'96	16/0
80	# Stone, Dwight	WR	6-0	195	1/28/64	11	Middle Tennessee State	Florala, Ala.	UFA(Pitt)-'95	16/0
40	Terrell, Pat	S	6-2	210	3/18/68	8	Notre Dame	St. Petersburg, Fla.	FA-'95	16/16
89	Tucker, Syii	TE	6-4	236	7/31/73	2	Miami	Oklahoma City, Okla.	FA-'96	0*
85	Walls, Wesley	TE	6-5	250	2/26/66	9	Mississippi	Pontotoc, Miss.	UFA(NO)-'96	16/15
53	Whitley, Curtis	C	6-1	295	5/10/69	6	Clemson	Smithfield, N.C.	ED7(SD)-'95	11/8
98	Williams, Gerald	DE	6-3	290	9/8/63	12	Auburn	Valley, Ala.	UFA(Pitt)-'95	16/14

* Abraham played 2 games with Chicago in '96; Barker inactive for 16 games; Barrow played 16 games with Houston; Greeley inactive for 6 games; E. Mills played 2 games with Pittsburgh; Philion inactive for 10 games; Seals and Smith missed '96 season because of injury; Tucker inactive for 16 games.

\# Unrestricted free agent; subject to developments.

† Restricted free agent; subject to developments.

Players lost through free agency (4): RB Bob Christian (Atl; 0 games in '96); WR Willie Green (Den; 16); RB Howard Griffith (Den; 16); DE Mark Thomas (Chi; 12).

Also played with Panthers in '96—NT Tim Colston (2 games), T Mark Dennis (16), RB Leroy Hoard (3), DT Tommy Jeter (1), RB Dino Philyaw (9).

COACHING STAFF

Head Coach,
Dom Capers

Pro Career: Enters his third season as head coach of the Carolina Panthers after receiving NFL Coach of the Year honors from AP, UPI, PFWA, The Sporting News, Pro Football Weekly, USA Today and Sports Illustrated among others for directing the Panthers to 12-4 regular season record, NFC Western Divison championship, and a berth in the NFC Championship Game in only the franchise's second season. Led team that had seven players selected to the Pro Bowl and defense that set an NFL record, allowing only 56 second-half points. Team established another NFL record by posting fewer penalty yards than its opponents in 20 consecutive games. Guided team from an 0-5 start to a 7-9 finish in 1995, the best expansion record in NFL history. Capers also directed the Panthers to other expansion records including the first to win four consecutive games; the first to defeat the reigning world champions; the first to win four games in a row at home; the first to win two straight on the road; and the first team to post a winning record at home (5-3). Also, the Panthers were just the third team in NFL history to begin the season 0-5 and win the next four games. He was named first head coach in Carolina Panthers history on January 23, 1995 after spending three seasons as defensive coordinator for the Pittsburgh Steelers where he oversaw a unit that allowed the fewest points in the league from 1992-94. Capers entered the professional coaching ranks as an assistant with the USFL Baltimore/Philadelphia Stars (1984-85). He then coached the New Orleans Saints secondary from 1986-1991. Career record: 20-14.

Background: Capers played defensive back for Mount Union College. He was a graduate assistant at Kent State (1972-74) and served full-time coaching stints at Hawaii (1975-76), San Jose State (1977), California (1978-79), Tennessee (1980-81), and Ohio State (1982-83).

Personal: Born August 5, 1950, in Cambridge, Ohio. Capers and his wife, Karen, were married in June, 1994. They live in Davidson, N.C.

ASSISTANT COACHES

Don Breaux, tight ends; born August 3, 1940, Jennings, La., lives in Charlotte, N.C. Quarterback McNeese State 1959-61. Pro quarterback Denver Broncos 1963, San Diego Chargers 1964-65. College coach: Florida State 1966-67, Arkansas 1968-71, 1977-80, Florida 1973-74, Texas 1975-76. Pro coach: Houston Oilers 1972, Washington Redskins 1981-1993, New York Jets 1994, joined Panthers in 1995.

Blair Bush, assistant offensive line; born November 25, 1956, Palos Verdes, Calif., lives in Charlotte, N.C. Center University of Washington 1977-79. Pro center Cincinnati Bengals 1979-82, Seattle Seahawks 1983-88, Green Bay Packers 1989-91, Los Angeles Rams 1992-94. No college coaching experience. Pro coach: Joined Panthers in 1995.

George Catavolos, defensive backs; born May 8, 1945, Chicago, Ill., lives in Charlotte, N.C. Defensive back Purdue 1963-67. No pro playing experience. College coach: Purdue 1967-68, 1971-76, Middle Tennessee State 1969, Louisville 1970, Kentucky 1977-81, Tennessee 1982-83. Pro coach: Indianapolis Colts 1984-93, joined Panthers in 1995.

Billy Davis, outside linebackers; born November 5, 1965, Youngstown, Ohio, lives in Charlotte, N.C. Quarterback Cincinnati 1984-88. No pro playing experience. College coach: Michigan State 1990-91. Pro coach: Pittsburgh Steelers 1992-94, joined Panthers in 1995.

Vic Fangio, defensive coordinator; born August 22, 1958, Dunmore, Pa., lives in Charlotte, N.C. Defensive back East Stroudsburg State 1976-78. No pro playing experience. College coach: North Carolina 1983. Pro coach: Philadelphia/Baltimore Stars (USFL) 1984-85, New Orleans Saints 1986-94, joined Panthers in 1995.

Ted Gill, defensive line; born October 3, 1948, Washington, D.C., lives in Charlotte, N.C. Defensive tackle

1997 FIRST-YEAR ROSTER

Name	Pos.	Ht.	Wt.	Birthdate	College	Hometown	How Acq.
Akers, David	K	5-10	174	12/9/74	Louisville	Lexington, Ky.	FA
Benning, Damon	RB	5-10	211	3/2/74	Nebraska	Omaha, Neb.	FA
Carruth, Rae	WR	5-11	194	1/20/74	Colorado	Sacramento, Calif.	D1
Colston, Tim (1)	NT	6-0	275	12/18/73	Kansas State	Tampa, Fla.	FA
Denton, Robert (1)	G	6-3	315	6/3/73	Michigan State	Martinsville, Ind.	FA
Estes, Brian	T	6-4	265	6/20/74	Presbyterian	Fairburn, Ga.	FA
Evjen, Jon	LB	6-4	234	10/14/73	Hofstra	Mountville, Conn.	FA
Finkes, Matt	LB	6-3	272	2/12/75	Ohio State	Piqua, Ohio	D6
Gragert, Brian (1)	P	6-1	228	8/14/72	Wyoming	Elkhorn, Neb.	FA
Herrin, Errik (1)	LB	6-2	235	4/3/69	Southern California	Akron, Ohio	FA
Hunter, Todd	T	6-6	315	9/15/74	Tulane	Kingwood, Tex.	FA
Jackson, Waverly	DE-DT	6-2	299	12/19/72	Virginia Tech	South Hill, Va.	FA
Johnson, Chad	QB	6-3	210	3/19/74	West Virginia	Peterson, W. Va.	FA
Jurewicz, Bryan	DE	6-5	278	2/23/74	Wisconsin	Deerfield, Ill.	FA
Kubiak, Jim (1)	QB	6-2	211	5/12/72	Navy	Buffalo, N.Y.	FA
Lane, Fred	RB	5-10	205	9/6/75	Lane College	Franklin, Tenn.	FA
Mangum, Kris	TE	6-4	249	8/15/73	Mississippi	Magee, Miss.	D7
Minter, Mike	S	5-10	188	1/15/74	Nebraska	Lawton, Okla.	D2
Newsome, Myron	LB	5-9	218	5/13/74	Virginia Tech	Hampton, Va.	FA
Ogard, Jeff	DE	6-6	310	9/1/73	Nebraska	St. Paul, Neb.	FA
Palmer, Mitchell	LB	6-4	245	9/2/73	Colorado State	San Diego, Calif.	FA
Reddick, Nakia	S	6-1	215	9/29/74	Central Florida	Miami, Fla.	FA
Running, Mitch (1)	WR	5-11	184	9/7/72	Kansas State	Decorah, Iowa	FA
Saleh, Tarek	LB	6-1	240	11/7/74	Wisconsin	Woodbridge, Conn.	D4
Schuster, Brian	RB	5-11	225	9/19/73	Nebraska	Fullerton, Neb.	FA
Sensley, Tim (1)	CB	5-9	165	1/15/73	Southwestern La.	Ethel, La.	FA
Staley, Maurice	WR	6-1	195	6/15/76	Tennessee	Charlotte, N.C.	FA
Tatum, Kinnon	LB	6-0	222	7/19/75	Notre Dame	Fayetteville, N.C.	D3
Thomas, Ratcliff	LB	6-1	238	1/2/74	Maryland	Alexandria, Va.	FA
Vance, Eric	S	6-2	215	7/14/75	Vanderbilt	Hurst, Tex.	FA
Walter, Ken	P	6-1	195	8/15/72	Kent State	Euclid, Ohio	FA
Wiggins, Brian (1)	WR	5-11	187	6/14/68	Texas Southern	San Antonio, Tex.	FA
Wilson, Jamie	T	6-7	283	6/6/73	Marshall	Gloucester, Va.	FA
Zachery, Cedric (1)	WR	6-0	178	11/10/72	Georgia Tech	Decatur, Ga.	FA

The term NFL Rookie is defined as a player who is in his first season of professional football and has not been on the roster of another professional football team for any regular-season or postseason games. A Rookie is designated by an "R" on NFL rosters. Players who have been active in another professional football league or players who have NFL experience, including either preseason training camp or being on an Active List or Inactive List, or on Reserve/Injured or Reserve/Physically Unable to Perform for fewer than six regular-season games, are termed NFL First-Year Players. An NFL First-Year Player is designated by a "1" on NFL rosters. Thereafter, a player is credited with an additional year of experience for each season in which he accumulates six games on the Active List or Inactive List, or on Reserve/Injured or Reserve/Physically Unable to Perform.

NOTES

Idaho State. No pro playing experience. College coach: Utah 1974-76, New Mexico State 1977, Ball State 1978-81, Cornell 1982, Army 1983, North Carolina 1984-87, Rice 1988-89, Iowa 1990-94, Oklahoma State 1995. Pro coach: Joined Panthers in 1996.

Chick Harris, running backs; born September 21, 1945, Durham, N.C., lives in Charlotte, N.C. Running back Northern Arizona 1966-69. No pro playing experience. College coach: Colorado State 1970-72, Long Beach State 1973-74, Washington 1975-80. Pro coach: Buffalo Bills 1981-82, Seattle Seahawks 1983-91, Los Angeles Rams 1992-94, joined Panthers in 1995.

Jim McNally, offensive line; born December 13, 1943, Buffalo, N.Y., lives in Charlotte, N.C. Guard Buffalo 1961-65. No pro playing experience. College coach: Buffalo 1966-69, Marshall 1973-75, Boston College 1976-78, Wake Forest 1979. Pro coach: Cincinnati Bengals 1980-94, joined Panthers in 1995.

Chip Morton, strength and conditioning; born November 27, 1962, Hamden, Conn., lives in Charlotte, N.C. No college or pro playing experience. College coach: Ohio State 1985-86, Penn State 1987-91. Pro coach: San Diego Chargers 1992-94, joined Panthers in 1995.

Joe Pendry, offensive coordinator; born August 5, 1947, Matheny, W. Va., lives in Charlotte, N.C. Tight end West Virginia 1966-67. No pro playing experience. College coach: West Virginia 1967-74, 1976-77, Kansas State 1975, Pittsburgh 1978-79, Michigan State 1980-81. Pro coach: Philadelphia Stars (USFL) 1983, Pittsburgh Maulers (USFL) 1984 (head coach), Cleveland Browns 1985-88, Kansas City Chiefs 1989-92, Chicago Bears 1993-94, joined Panthers in 1995.

Greg Roman, asst. strength and conditioning; born August 19, 1972, Atlantic City, N.J. Defensive lineman-linebacker John Carroll. No pro playing experience. No college coaching experience. Pro coach: Joined Panthers in 1995.

Brad Seely, special teams; born September 6, 1956, Vinton, Iowa, lives in Charlotte, N.C. Tackle-guard South Dakota State 1974-77. No pro playing experience. College coach: Colorado State 1980, Southern Methodist 1981, North Carolina State 1982, Pacific 1983, Oklahoma State 1984-88. Pro coach: Indianapolis Colts 1989-93, New York Jets 1994, joined Panthers in 1995.

John Shoop, quarterbacks; born August 1, 1969, Pittsburgh, Pa., lives in Charlotte, N.C. Quarterback University of the South 1987-91. No pro playing experience. College coach: Dartmouth 1991, Vanderbilt 1992-94. Pro coach: Joined Panthers in 1995.

Kevin Steele, linebackers; born March 17, 1958, La Jolla, Calif., lives in Matthews, N.C. Linebacker Tennessee 1976-79. No pro playing experience. College coach: Tennessee 1981-82, 1987-88, New Mexico State 1983, Oklahoma State 1984-86, Nebraska 1989-94. Pro coach: Joined Panthers in 1995.

Richard Williamson, wide receivers; born April 13, 1941, Ft. Deposit, Ala., lives in Charlotte, N.C. Receiver Alabama 1961-62. No pro playing experience. College coach: Alabama 1963-67, 1970-71, Arkansas 1968-69, 1972-74, Memphis State 1975-80 (head coach). Pro coach: Kansas City Chiefs 1983-86, Tampa Bay Buccaneers 1987-91 (interim head coach final three games of 1990 season, head coach 1991), Cincinnati Bengals 1992-94, joined Panthers in 1995.

CHICAGO BEARS

National Football Conference
Central Division
Team Colors: Navy Blue, Orange, and White
Halas Hall at Conway Park
1000 Football Drive
Lake Forest, Illinois 60045
Telephone: (847) 295-6600

CLUB OFFICIALS

Chairman of the Board: Edward W. McCaskey
President and CEO: Michael B. McCaskey
Secretary: Virginia H. McCaskey
Vice President: Tim McCaskey
Vice President of Operations: Ted Phillips
Vice President of Player Personnel: Mark Hatley
Director of Administration: Tim LeFevour
Ticket Manager: George McCaskey
Director of Community Relations: Pat McCaskey
Player Liaison: Brian McCaskey
Director of Marketing/Communications:
 Ken Valdiserri
Manager of Promotions: John Bostrom
Manager of Sales: Jack Trompeter
Director of Public Relations: Bryan Harlan
Asst. Directors of Public Relations: Phil Handler,
 Scott Hagel
Computer Systems: Greg Gershuny
Controller: Scott Worthem
Video Director: Dean Pope
Head Athletic Trainer: Tim Bream
Assistant Trainers: Jeff Hay, Eric Sugarman
Physical Development Coordinator: Russ Riederer
Assistant Physical Development Coordinator:
 Steve Little
Head Equipment Manager: Tony Medlin
Quality Control: Eric Studesville
Assistant Equipment Managers: Randy Knowles,
 Carl Piekarski
Scouts: Gary Smith, Jeff Shiver, Bobby Riggle,
 Mike McCartney, Charles Garcia
Stadium: Soldier Field •**Capacity:** 66,944
 425 McFetridge Place
 Chicago, Illinois 60605
Playing Surface: Grass
Training Camp: University of Wisconsin-Platteville
 Platteville, Wisconsin 53818

1997 SCHEDULE
PRESEASON

July 27	vs. Pittsburgh at Dublin, Ireland	1:00
Aug. 2	at Buffalo	7:00
Aug. 10	at Miami	8:00
Aug. 16	**Arizona**	7:00
Aug. 22	**New Orleans**	7:30

REGULAR SEASON

Sept. 1	at Green Bay (Mon.)	8:00
Sept. 7	**Minnesota**	12:00
Sept. 14	**Detroit**	12:00
Sept. 21	at New England	1:00
Sept. 28	at Dallas	3:00
Oct. 5	**New Orleans**	7:00
Oct. 12	**Green Bay**	12:00

RECORD HOLDERS
INDIVIDUAL RECORDS—CAREER

Category	Name	Performance
Rushing (Yds.)	Walter Payton, 1975-1987	*16,726
Passing (Yds.)	Sid Luckman, 1939-1950	14,686
Passing (TDs)	Sid Luckman, 1939-1950	137
Receiving (No.)	Walter Payton, 1975-1987	492
Receiving (Yds.)	Johnny Morris, 1958-1967	5,059
Interceptions	Gary Fencik, 1976-1987	38
Punting (Avg.)	George Gulyanics, 1947-1952	44.5
Punt Return (Avg.)	Ray (Scooter) McLean, 1940-47	14.8
Kickoff Return (Avg.)	Gale Sayers, 1965-1971	30.6
Field Goals	Kevin Butler, 1985-1995	243
Touchdowns (Tot.)	Walter Payton, 1975-1987	125
Points	Kevin Butler, 1985-1995	1,116

INDIVIDUAL RECORDS—SINGLE SEASON

Category	Name	Performance
Rushing (Yds.)	Walter Payton, 1977	1,852
Passing (Yds.)	Erik Kramer, 1995	3,838
Passing (TDs)	Erik Kramer, 1995	29
Receiving (No.)	Johnny Morris, 1964	93
Receiving (Yds.)	Jeff Graham, 1995	1,301
Interceptions	Mark Carrier, 1990	10
Punting (Avg.)	Bobby Joe Green, 1963	46.5
Punt Return (Avg.)	Harry Clark, 1943	15.8
Kickoff Return (Avg.)	Gale Sayers, 1967	37.7
Field Goals	Kevin Butler, 1985	31
Touchdowns (Tot.)	Gale Sayers, 1965	22
Points	Kevin Butler, 1985	144

INDIVIDUAL RECORDS—SINGLE GAME

Category	Name	Performance
Rushing (Yds.)	Walter Payton, 11-20-77	*275
Passing (Yds.)	Johnny Lujack, 12-11-49	468
Passing (TDs)	Sid Luckman, 11-14-43	*7
Receiving (No.)	Jim Keane, 10-23-49	14
Receiving (Yds.)	Harlon Hill, 10-31-54	214
Interceptions	Many times	3
	Last time by Mark Carrier, 12-9-90	
Field Goals	Roger LeClerc, 12-3-61	5
	Mac Percival, 10-20-68	5
Touchdowns (Tot.)	Gale Sayers, 12-12-65	*6
Points	Gale Sayers, 12-12-65	36

*NFL Record

Oct. 19	Open Date	
Oct. 26	at Miami	4:00
Nov. 2	**Washington**	12:00
Nov. 9	at Minnesota	12:00
Nov. 16	**New York Jets**	3:00
Nov. 23	**Tampa Bay**	12:00
Nov. 27	at Detroit (Thurs.)	12:30
Dec. 7	**Buffalo**	12:00
Dec. 14	at St. Louis	7:00
Dec. 21	at Tampa Bay	1:00

COACHING HISTORY
Decatur Staleys 1920,
Chicago Staleys 1921
(612-408-42)

1920-29	George Halas	84-31-19
1930-32	Ralph Jones	24-10-7
1933-42	George Halas*	88-24-4
1942-45	Hunk Anderson- Luke Johnsos**	24-12-2
1946-55	George Halas	76-43-2
1956-57	John (Paddy) Driscoll	14-10-1
1958-67	George Halas	76-53-6
1968-71	Jim Dooley	20-36-0
1972-74	Abe Gibron	11-30-1
1975-77	Jack Pardee	20-23-0
1978-81	Neill Armstrong	30-35-0
1982-92	Mike Ditka	112-68-0
1993-96	Dave Wannstedt	33-33-0

 *Retired after five games to enter U.S. Navy
**Co-coaches

SOLDIER FIELD

1996 TEAM RECORD
PRESEASON (1-3)

Date	Result		Opponents
8/3	L	12-30	at Carolina
8/11	W	24-21	Miami
8/17	L	21-31	at New Orleans
8/22	L	10-14	Kansas City

REGULAR SEASON (7-9)

Date	Result		Opponents	Att.
9/2	W	22-6	Dallas	63,076
9/8	L	3-10	at Washington	52,711
9/15	L	14-20	Minnesota	61,301
9/22	L	16-35	at Detroit	70,022
9/29	L	19-17	Oakland	57,062
10/6	L	6-37	Green Bay	65,480
10/13	L	24-27	at New Orleans	43,512
10/28	W	15-13	at Minnesota	60,774
11/3	W	13-10	Tampa Bay	58,727
11/10	L	12-17	at Denver	75,555
11/17	L	10-14	at Kansas City	76,762
11/24	W	31-14	Detroit	55,864
12/1	L	17-28	at Green Bay	59,682
12/8	W	35-9	St. Louis	66,944
12/14	W	27-14	San Diego	49,763
12/22	L	19-34	at Tampa Bay	51,572

SCORE BY PERIODS

Bears	70	89	57	67	—	283
Opponents	48	140	62	55	—	305

ATTENDANCE
Home 456,348   Away 490,590   Total 946,938
Single-game home record, 66,900 (9/5/93)
Single-season home record, 495,484 (1986)

1996 TEAM STATISTICS

	Bears	Opp.
Total First Downs	300	295
Rushing	104	87
Passing	176	183
Penalty	20	25
Third Down: Made/Att	78/231	79/206
Third Down Pct.	33.8	38.3
Fourth Down: Made/Att	20/28	8/14
Fourth Down Pct.	71.4	57.1
Total Net Yards	4905	4884
Avg. Per Game	306.6	305.3
Total Plays	1046	981
Avg. Per Play	4.7	5.0
Net Yards Rushing	1720	1617
Avg. Per Game	107.5	101.1
Total Rushes	472	427
Net Yards Passing	3185	3267
Avg. Per Game	199.1	204.2
Sacked/Yards Lost	23/165	30/209
Gross Yards	3350	3476
Att./Completions	551/318	524/314
Completion Pct.	57.7	59.9
Had Intercepted	18	17
Punts/Avg.	78/44.8	76/40.1
Net Punting Avg.	78/34.9	76/34.0
Penalties/Yards Lost	103/808	113/849
Fumbles/Ball Lost	25/9	29/11
Touchdowns	31	37
Rushing	9	13
Passing	19	21
Returns	3	3
Avg. Time of Possession	30:51	29:09

1996 INDIVIDUAL STATISTICS

PASSING	Att.	Comp.	Yds.	Pct.	TD	Int.	Tkld.	Rate
Krieg	377	226	2278	59.9	14	12	14/104	76.3
Kramer	150	73	781	48.7	3	6	7/53	54.3
Matthews	17	13	158	76.5	1	0	1/3	124.1
Stenstrom	4	3	37	75.0	0	0	1/5	103.1
Sauerbrun	2	2	63	100.0	0	0	0/0	118.8
Conway	1	1	33	100.0	1	0	0/0	158.3
Bears	551	318	3350	57.7	19	18	23/165	73.4
Opponents	524	314	3476	59.9	21	17	30/209	79.5

SCORING	TD R	TD P	TD Rt	PAT	FG	Saf	PTS
Jaeger	0	0	0	23/23	19/23	0	80
Conway	0	7	0	0/0	0/0	0	42
Engram	0	6	0	0/0	0/0	0	36
R. Harris	4	1	0	0/0	0/0	0	30
Salaam	3	1	0	0/0	0/0	0	24
Huerta	0	0	0	3/3	4/7	0	15
Cox	0	0	1	0/0	0/0	0	6
Faulkerson	0	1	0	0/0	0/0	0	6
Flanigan	0	1	0	0/0	0/0	0	6
Krieg	1	0	0	0/0	0/0	0	6
Lowery	0	0	1	0/0	0/0	0	6
Matthews	1	0	0	0/0	0/0	0	6
Spears	0	1	0	0/0	0/0	0	6
Wetnight	0	1	0	0/0	0/0	0	6
Woolford	0	0	1	0/0	0/0	0	6
Bears	9	19	3	26/26	23/30	*1	283
Opponents	13	21	3	35/36	16/23	0	305

2-Point conversions: 0. Team: 0-5, Opponents: 0-1.
*Bears were credited with 1 team safety.

RUSHING	Att.	Yds.	Avg.	LG	TD
R. Harris	194	748	3.9	23	4
Salaam	143	496	3.5	32	3
Green	60	249	4.2	19	0
Hicks	27	92	3.4	23	0
Conway	8	50	6.3	19	0
T. Carter	11	43	3.9	23	0
Timpson	3	21	7.0	13	0
Krieg	16	12	0.8	2	1
Kramer	8	4	0.5	3	0
Sauerbrun	1	3	3.0	3	0
Matthews	1	2	2.0	2t	0
Bears	472	1720	3.6	32	9
Opponents	427	1617	3.8	63	13

RECEIVING	No.	Yds.	Avg.	LG	TD
Conway	81	1049	13.0	58t	7
Timpson	62	802	12.9	49	0
T. Carter	41	233	5.7	29	0
Engram	33	389	11.8	24	6
R. Harris	32	296	9.3	47	1
Wetnight	21	223	10.6	38	1
Green	13	78	6.0	18	0
Neely	9	92	10.2	21	0
Salaam	7	44	6.3	11t	1
Jennings	6	56	9.3	20	0
Cash	4	42	10.5	14	0
Ja. Jackson	4	39	9.8	14	0
Krieg	1	5	5.0	5	0
Faulkerson	1	1	1.0	1t	1
Flanigan	1	1	1.0	1t	1
Spears	1	1	1.0	1t	1
Hicks	1	-1	-1.0	-1	0
Bears	318	3350	10.5	58t	19
Opponents	314	3476	11.1	62t	21

INTERCEPTIONS	No.	Yds.	Avg.	Long	TD
Woolford	6	37	6.2	28t	1
M. Carter	3	34	11.3	29	0
Marshall	2	20	10.0	20	0
Carrier	2	0	0.0	0	0
W. Harris	2	0	0.0	0	0
Burton	1	11	11.0	11	0
Minter	1	5	5.0	5	0
Bears	17	107	6.3	29	1
Opponents	18	94	5.2	27	0

PUNTING	No.	Yds.	Avg.	In 20	LG
Sauerbrun	78	3491	44.8	15	72
Bears	78	3491	44.8	15	72
Opponents	76	3047	40.1	25	60

PUNT RETURNS	No.	FC	Yds.	Avg.	LG	TD
Engram	31	19	282	9.1	34	0
Bears	31	19	282	9.1	34	0
Opponents	42	12	527	12.5	88t	2

KICKOFF RETURNS	No.	Yds.	Avg.	LG	TD
Ja. Jackson	27	619	22.9	60	0
Engram	25	580	23.2	45	0
Faulkerson	4	63	15.8	20	0
Marshall	0	75	—	75	0
Bears	56	1337	23.9	88	0
Opponents	52	1115	21.4	90t	1

SACKS	No.
Spellman	8.0
Flanigan	5.0
A. Fontenot	4.5
Cox	3.0
Thierry	2.0
Miniefield	1.5
Minter	1.5
Simpson	1.5
Cain	1.0
Mangum	1.0
Smith	1.0
Bears	30.0
Opponents	23.0

1997 DRAFT CHOICES

Round	Name	Pos.	College
2	John Allred	TE	Southern California
3	Bob Sapp	G	Washington
4	Darnell Autry	RB	Northwestern
	Marcus Robinson	WR	South Carolina
5	Van Hiles	DB	Kentucky
6	Shawn Swayda	DE	Arizona State
	Richard Hogans	LB	Memphis
	Ricky Parker	DB	San Diego State
7	Mike Miano	DT	Southwest Missouri State
	Marvin Thomas	DE	Memphis

1997 VETERAN ROSTER

No.	Name	Pos.	Ht.	Wt.	Birthdate	NFL Exp.	College	Hometown	How Acq.	'96 Games/ Starts
63	Burger, Todd	G	6-3	303	3/20/70	4	Penn State	Clark, N.J.	FA-'93	11/8
35	Burton, James	CB	5-9	184	4/27/71	4	Fresno State	Long Beach, Calif.	W(KC)-'94	16/3
10	† Butterfield, Mark	QB	6-4	215	7/14/73	2	Stanford	Antioch, Calif.	FA(Ariz)-'96	0*
20	Carrier, Mark	S	6-1	192	4/28/68	8	Southern California	Long Beach, Calif.	D1-'90	13/13
23	Carter, Marty	S	6-1	212	12/17/69	7	Middle Tennessee St.	La Grange, Ga.	UFA(TB)-'95	16/16
25	Carter, Tom	CB	6-1	187	9/5/72	5	Notre Dame	St. Petersburgh, Fla.	RFA(Wash)-'97	16/16*
30	† Carter, Tony	RB	5-11	236	8/23/72	4	Minnesota	Columbus, Ohio	FA-'94	16/11
72	Clark, Jon	T	6-6	345	4/11/73	2	Temple	Philadelphia, Pa.	D6a-'96	1/0
80	Conway, Curtis	WR	6-1	194	3/13/71	5	Southern California	Hawthorne, Calif.	D1-'93	16/16
52	Cox, Bryan	LB	6-4	250	2/17/68	7	Western Illinois	East St. Louis, Ill.	UFA(Mia)-'96	9/9
60	† Davis, Rob	DT-LS	6-3	271	12/10/68	2	Shippensburg	District Heights, Md.	FA(KC)-'96	16/0
38	Dulaney, Mike	RB	6-1	245	9/9/70	2	North Carolina	Kingsport, Tenn.	FA(Cin)-'95	16/0
81	Engram, Bobby	WR	5-10	192	1/7/73	2	Penn State	Camden, S.C.	D2-'96	16/2
99	Flanigan, Jim	DT	6-2	286	8/27/71	4	Notre Dame	Green Bay, Wis.	D3-'94	14/14
46	Forbes, Marlon	S	6-1	205	12/25/71	2	Penn State	Long Island, N.Y.	FA-'95	15/0
93	Grasmanis, Paul	DT	6-2	298	8/2/74	2	Notre Dame	Jenison, Mich.	D4-'96	14/3
29	† Harris, Raymont	RB	6-1	225	12/23/70	4	Ohio State	Lorain, Ohio	D4-'94	12/10
57	Harris, Sean	LB	6-3	245	2/25/72	3	Arizona	Magnet, Ariz.	D3a-'95	15/0
27	Harris, Walt	CB	5-11	194	8/10/74	2	Mississippi State	La Grange, Ga.	D1-'96	15/13
64	Heck, Andy	T	6-6	298	1/1/67	9	Notre Dame	Fairfax, Va.	RFA(Sea)-'94	16/16
95	Howard, Dana	LB	6-1	244	2/25/72	3	Illinois	East St. Louis, Ill.	FA(StL)-'96	3/0
33	Hughes, Tyrone	KR	5-9	175	1/14/70	5	Nebraska	New Orleans, La.	FA(NO)-'97	16/1*
88	Jackson, Jack	WR	5-8	174	11/11/72	3	Florida	Moss Point, Miss.	D4-'95	12/0
1	Jaeger, Jeff	K	5-11	190	11/26/64	11	Washington	Kent, Wash.	FA(Oak)-'96	13/0
85	Jennings, Keith	TE	6-4	275	5/19/66	8	Clemson	Summerville, S.C.	FA-'94	6/5
32	† Joseph, Dwayne	CB	5-9	186	6/2/72	3	Syracuse	Carol City, Fla.	FA-'94	0*
73	Keyes, Marcus	DT	6-3	303	10/20/73	2	North Alabama	Taylorville, Miss.	D7a-'96	2/0
12	Kramer, Erik	QB	6-1	200	11/6/64	8	North Carolina State	Burbank, Calif.	UFA(Det)-'94	4/4
53	Lowery, Michael	LB	6-1	224	2/14/74	2	Mississippi	McComb, Miss.	FA-'96	16/0
26	Mangum, John	S	5-10	190	3/16/67	8	Alabama	Magee, Miss.	D7-'90	16/2
36	† Marshall, Anthony	S	6-1	212	9/16/70	3	Louisiana State	Mobile, Ala.	FA-'94	13/3
24	Miniefield, Kevin	CB	5-9	182	3/2/70	5	Arizona State	Phoenix, Ariz.	FA(Det)-'93	13/3
92	Minter, Barry	LB	6-2	242	1/28/70	5	Tulsa	Mt. Pleasant, Tex.	T(Dall)-'93	16/7
13	t- Mirer, Rick	QB	6-2	214	3/19/70	5	Notre Dame	Goshen, Ind.	T(Sea)-'96	11/9*
87	† Neely, Bobby	TE	6-3	255	3/22/74	2	Virginia	Atlanta, Ga.	FA-'96	11/5
79	Parrish, James	T	6-5	292	5/19/68	5	Temple	Dundalk, Md.	FA(Pitt)-'96	0*
75	Perry, Todd	G	6-5	312	11/28/70	5	Kentucky	Elizabethtown, Ky.	D4a-'93	16/16
54	Peterson, Anthony	LB	6-1	223	1/23/72	4	Notre Dame	Monogahela, Pa.	UFA(SF)-'96	16/0*
65	Pilgrim, Evan	G	6-4	304	8/14/72	3	Brigham Young	Antioch, Calif.	D3b-'95	6/0
69	Polk, Octus	G	6-3	345	9/17/71	2	Stephen F. Austin	Sulphur Springs, Tex.	FA-'95	0*
83	Proehl, Ricky	WR	6-1	190	3/7/68	8	Wake Forest	Hillsborough, N.J.	FA(Sea)-'97	16/7*
68	Reeves, Carl	DE	6-4	265	12/17/71	3	North Carolina State	Northern Durham, N.C.	D6b-'95	5/0
31	Salaam, Rashaan	RB	6-1	224	10/8/74	3	Colorado	La Jolla, Calif.	D1-'95	12/6
16	Sauerbrun, Todd	P	5-10	209	1/4/73	3	West Virginia	Setauket, N.Y.	D2b-'95	16/0
98	Simpson, Carl	DT	6-2	292	4/18/70	5	Florida State	Appling County, Ga.	D2-'93	16/16
55	# Smith, Vinson	LB	6-2	248	7/3/65	10	East Carolina	Statesville, N.C.	T(Dall)-'93	15/12
90	Spellman, Alonzo	DE	6-4	292	9/27/71	6	Ohio State	Rancocas, N.J.	D1-'92	16/15
18	Stenstrom, Steve	QB	6-1	202	12/23/71	3	Stanford	El Toro, Calif.	W(KC)-'95	1/0
91	Thierry, John	DE	6-4	265	9/4/71	4	Alcorn State	Opelousas, La.	D1-'94	16/2
74	Thomas, Mark	DE	6-5	275	5/6/69	6	North Carolina State	Lilburn, Ga.	UFA(Car)-'97	12/0*
58	Villarrial, Chris	C-G	6-4	305	6/9/73	2	Indiana, Pa.	Hershey, Pa.	D5-'96	14/8
89	Wetnight, Ryan	TE	6-2	235	11/5/70	5	Stanford	Fresno, Calif.	FA-'93	11/5
71	Williams, James	T	6-7	340	3/29/68	7	Cheyney State	Allerdice, Pa.	FA-'91	16/16
97	Zorich, Chris	DT	6-1	282	3/13/69	7	Notre Dame	Chicago, Ill.	D2-'91	0*

* Butterfield inactive for 11 games in '96; Tom Carter started 16 games for Washington; Hughes played 16 games for New Orleans; Joseph and Zorich missed '96 season because of injury; Mirer played 11 games with Seattle; Parrish inactive for 3 games in '96; Peterson played 16 games for San Francisco; Polk inactive for 11 games; Proehl played 16 games for Seattle; Thomas played 12 games with Carolina.

\# Unrestricted free agent; subject to developments.

† Restricted free agent; subject to developments.

t- Bears traded for Mirer (Seattle).

Players lost through free agency (5): LB Joe Cain (Sea; 16 games in '96), DE Al Fontenot (Ind; 16), C Jerry Fontenot (NO; 16), TE Chris Gedney (Ariz; 0), QB Dave Krieg (Tenn; 13).

Also played with Bears in '96—CB Clifton Abraham (2 games), LB Greg Briggs (14), TE Kerry Cash (4), RB Mike Faulkerson (16), RB Robert Green (10), K Carlos Huerta (3), WR John Jackson (5), CB Chris Martin (1), QB Shane Matthews (2), T Marcus Spears (9), WR Michael Timpson (15), CB Donnell Woolford (15).

COACHING STAFF

Head Coach,
Dave Wannstedt

Pro Career: Has guided Bears to a 32-32 regular season record, 1-1 in the playoffs, since being named Chicago's head coach on January 19, 1993. He was an integral part of one of the most successful turnarounds in NFL history, helping to turn the 1989 Dallas Cowboys, which finished the season 1-15, into Super Bowl champions four years later. In January, 1992, he was named Dallas's assistant head coach and defensive coordinator. He was the defensive coordinator for the Cowboys in 1989. Selected by the Green Bay Packers in the fifteenth round of the 1974 draft, but spent the entire season on injured reserve. Career record: 33-33.

Background: Played offensive tackle at the University of Pittsburgh from 1970-73. Began coaching career at Pittsburgh in 1975 and was part of the staff that led the Panthers to a 12-0 record and the NCAA championship in 1976. In 1979, he took a job with Jimmy Johnson at Oklahoma State as defensive line coach. After two seasons, he was promoted to defensive coordinator. In 1983, Wannstedt was the defensive line coach for Southern California before rejoining Johnson at the University of Miami as the Hurricanes' defensive coordinator. In his first year (1986), Miami went 11-0 before losing to Penn State in the Fiesta Bowl. The following season Miami was crowned NCAA champion with a perfect 12-0 record.

Personal: Born May 21, 1952, Pittsburgh, Pa. Dave and his wife, Jan, live in Lake Forest, Ill. and have two children—Keri and Jami.

ASSISTANT COACHES

Keith Armstrong, special teams; born December 15, 1963, Trenton, N.J., lives in Lake Forest, Ill. Running back-defensive back Temple 1983-86. No pro playing experience. College coach: Temple 1986, Miami 1987-88, Akron 1989, Oklahoma State 1990-92, Notre Dame 1993. Pro coach: Atlanta Falcons 1994-96, joined Bears in 1997.

Clarence Brooks, defensive line; born May 20, 1951, New York, N.Y., lives in Lake Forest, Ill. Guard Massachusetts 1970-73. No pro playing experience. College coach: Massachusetts 1976-80, Syracuse 1981-89, Arizona 1990-92. Pro coach: Joined Bears in 1993.

Matt Cavanaugh, offensive coordinator-quarterbacks; born October 27, 1956, Youngstown, Ohio, lives in Riverwoods, Ill. Quarterback Pittsburgh 1974-77. Pro quarterback New England Patriots 1978-82, San Francisco 49ers 1983-85, Philadelphia Eagles 1986-89, New York Giants 1990-91. College coach: Pittsburgh 1993. Pro coach: Arizona Cardinals 1994-95, San Francisco 49ers 1996, joined Bears in 1997.

Ivan Fears, wide receivers; born November 15, 1954, Portsmouth, Va., lives in Lake Forest, Ill. Running back William and Mary 1973-75. No pro playing experience. College coach: William and Mary 1977-80, Syracuse 1981-90. Pro coach: New England Patriots 1991-92, joined Bears in 1993.

Carlos Mainord, defensive backs; born August 26, 1944, Greenville, Tex., lives in Lake Forest, Ill. Linebacker Navarro (Tex.) Junior College 1962-63, McMurry College 1964-65. No pro playing experience. College coach: McMurry College 1966-68, Texas Tech 1969, 1983-85, 1987-92, Ranger (Tex.) Junior College 1970-71, 1972-77 (head coach), Rice 1978-82, Miami 1986. Pro coach: Joined Bears in 1993.

Willie Peete, running backs; born July 14, 1937, Mesa, Ariz., lives in Chicago. Fullback Arizona 1956-59. No pro playing experience. College coach: Arizona 1960-62, 1971-82. Pro coach: Kansas City Chiefs 1983-86, Green Bay Packers 1987-91, Tampa Bay Buccaneers 1992-94, joined Bears in 1995.

Ted Plumb, receivers-tight ends; born August 20, 1939, Reno, Nev., lives in Lake Forest, Ill. Wide receiver Baylor 1960-61. Pro wide receiver Buffalo Bills 1962. College coach: Cerritos, Calif., J.C. 1966-67, Texas Christian 1968-70, Tulsa 1971, Kansas 1972-73. Pro coach: New York Giants 1974-76, Atlanta Falcons 1977-79, Chicago Bears 1980-85, Philadelphia

1997 FIRST-YEAR ROSTER

Name	Pos.	Ht.	Wt.	Birthdate	College	Hometown	How Acq.
Allen, Tremayne	TE	6-2	234	8/9/74	Florida	Nashville, Tenn.	FA
Allred, John	TE	6-4	246	9/9/74	Southern California	Del Mar, Calif.	D2
Augustino, Jason (1)	T	6-6	290	3/31/73	Virginia	Wexford, Pa.	FA
Autry, Darnell	RB	5-10	210	6/19/76	Northwestern	Tempe, Ariz.	D4a
Bownes, Fabien (1)	WR	5-11	186	2/29/72	Western Illinois	Aurora, Ill.	FA
Carter, Daryl	LB	6-2	222	2/24/75	Wisconsin	Milwaukee, Wis.	FA
Clements, Jimmy	LB	6-3	228	12/28/73	Georgia Tech	Marietta, Ga.	FA
Coleman, Mill (1)	WR	5-9	178	6/19/72	Michigan State	Farmington, Mich.	FA
Cousin, Terry	CB	5-9	176	4/11/75	South Carolina	Miami Beach, Fla.	FA
Ferguson, Danyell	RB	5-10	205	7/7/74	Miami	Miami, Fla.	FA
Hicks, Michael (1)	RB	6-0	194	2/1/73	South Carolina State	Barnsville, Ga.	FA
Hiles, Van	S	6-0	195	11/1/75	Kentucky	Baton Rouge, La.	D5
Hogans, Richard	LB	6-2	249	7/8/75	Memphis	Columbus, Ga.	D6b
Holloway, Bobby	DT	6-3	280	7/17/73	Ohio	Decatur, Tex.	FA
Jefferson, Tafa	T	6-5	295	10/16/74	Pacific	Garden Grove, Calif.	FA
Jenkins, Kerry	T	6-6	320	9/6/73	Troy State	Tuscaloosa, Ala.	FA
Martin, Chris (1)	CB	5-9	181	9/1/74	Northwestern	Tampa, Fla.	FA
Miano, Mike	DT	6-3	303	12/17/73	Southwest Missouri State	St. Louis, Mo.	D7a
Parker, Ricky	S	6-1	205	12/4/74	San Diego State	Sacramento, Calif.	D6c
Randolph, Charles (1)	TE	6-1	287	7/29/72	Northeast Louisiana	New Orleans, La.	FA
Riley, Phillip (1)	WR	5-11	189	9/24/72	Florida State	Orlando, Fla.	FA
Robinson, Marcus	WR	6-3	213	2/27/75	South Carolina	Ft. Valley, Ga.	D4b
Sapp, Bob	G	6-4	303	9/22/73	Washington	Colorado Springs, Colo.	D3
Soward, Marcus	CB	5-11	175	5/29/74	Arizona State	Rialto, Calif.	FA
Swayda, Shawn	DT	6-5	279	9/4/74	Arizona State	Phoenix, Ariz.	D6a
Swayne, Kevin	WR	6-2	175	1/17/75	Wayne State	Riverside, Calif.	FA
Thomas, Marvin	DE	6-5	264	10/19/73	Memphis	Bay Minette, Ala.	D7b
Washington, Shawn	RB	6-1	230	1/8/74	Baylor	Waco, Tex.	FA
Zitelli, Emmett	C	6-3	295	3/13/74	Purdue	McKees Rocks, Pa.	FA

The term NFL Rookie is defined as a player who is in his first season of professional football and has not been on the roster of another professional football team for any regular-season or postseason games. A Rookie is designated by an "R" on NFL rosters. Players who have been active in another professional football league or players who have NFL experience, including either preseason training camp or being on an Active List or Inactive List, or on Reserve/Injured or Reserve/Physically Unable to Perform for fewer than six regular-season games, are termed NFL First-Year Players. An NFL First-Year Player is designated by a "1" on NFL rosters. Thereafter, a player is credited with an additional year of experience for each season in which he accumulates six games on the Active List or Inactive List, or on Reserve/Injured or Reserve/Physically Unable to Perform.

NOTES

Eagles 1986-89, Arizona Cardinals 1990-95, rejoined Bears in 1996.

Greg Schiano, defensive assistant; born June 1, 1966, Paterson, N.J., lives in Lake Forest, Ill. Linebacker Bucknell 1984-88. No pro playing experience. College coach: Rutgers 1989, Penn State 1990-95. Pro coach: Joined Bears in 1996.

Bob Slowik, defensive coordinator-linebackers; born May 16, 1954, Pittsburgh, Pa., lives in Lake Forest, Ill. Cornerback Delaware 1973-76. No pro playing experience. College coach: Delaware 1977, Florida 1978-81, Drake 1982, Rutgers 1983, East

Carolina 1984-91. Pro coach: Dallas Cowboys 1992, joined Bears in 1993.

Tony Wise, assistant head coach-offensive line; born December 28, 1951, Albany, N.Y., lives in Lake Forest, Ill. Offensive lineman Ithaca College 1971-72. No pro playing experience. College coach: Albany State 1973, Bridgeport 1974, Central Connecticut State 1975, Washington State 1976, Pittsburgh 1977-78, Oklahoma State 1979-83, Syracuse 1984, Miami 1985-88. Pro coach: Dallas Cowboys 1989-92, joined Bears in 1993.

National Football Conference
Eastern Division
Team Colors: Royal Blue, Metallic Silver
Blue, and White
Cowboys Center
One Cowboys Parkway
Irving, Texas 75063
Telephone: (972) 556-9900

CLUB OFFICIALS

Owner/President/General Manager:
Jerry Jones
Executive Vice President-Player Personnel:
Stephen Jones
Vice President/Marketing: George Hays
Vice President/Director of Marketing and Special
Events: Charlotte Anderson
Vice President/Legal Operations: Jerry Jones, Jr.
Public Relations Director: Rich Dalrymple
Assistant Director of Public Relations:
Brett Daniels
Director of College and Pro Scouting:
Larry Lacewell
Director of Operations: Bruce Mays
Director of Human Resources: Debbie Ross
Treasurer: Robert Nunez
Ticket Manager: Carol Padgett
Trainer: Jim Maurer
Equipment Manager: Mike McCord
Video Director: Robert Blackwell
Cheerleader Director: Kelli Finglass
Stadium: Texas Stadium •**Capacity:** 65,675
Irving, Texas 75062
Playing Surface: Sportfield Turf
Training Camp: St. Edward's University
Austin, Texas 78704

1997 SCHEDULE

PRESEASON
Aug. 3	**Oakland**	7:00
Aug. 8	at New England	8:00
Aug. 15	**St. Louis**	7:00
Aug. 22	**Tennessee**	7:00

REGULAR SEASON
Aug. 31	at Pittsburgh	1:00
Sept. 7	at Arizona	5:00
Sept. 15	**Philadelphia** (Mon.)	8:00
Sept. 21	Open Date	
Sept. 28	**Chicago**	3:00
Oct. 5	at New York Giants	1:00
Oct. 13	at Washington (Mon.)	9:00
Oct. 19	**Jacksonville**	12:00
Oct. 26	at Philadelphia	1:00
Nov. 2	at San Francisco	1:00
Nov. 9	**Arizona**	12:00
Nov. 16	**Washington**	12:00
Nov. 23	at Green Bay	12:00
Nov. 27	**Tennessee** (Thurs.)	3:00
Dec. 8	**Carolina** (Mon.)	8:00
Dec. 14	at Cincinnati	1:00
Dec. 21	**New York Giants**	12:00

RECORD HOLDERS

INDIVIDUAL RECORDS—CAREER
Category	Name	Performance
Rushing (Yds.)	Tony Dorsett, 1977-1987	12,036
Passing (Yds.)	Troy Aikman, 1989-1996	22,733
Passing (TDs)	Danny White, 1976-1988	155
Receiving (No.)	Michael Irvin, 1988-1996	591
Receiving (Yds.)	Michael Irvin, 1988-1996	9,500
Interceptions	Mel Renfro, 1964-1977	52
Punting (Avg.)	Mike Saxon, 1985-1992	41.5
Punt Return (Avg.)	Bob Hayes, 1965-1974	11.1
Kickoff Return (Avg.)	Mel Renfro, 1964-1977	26.4
Field Goals	Rafael Septien, 1978-1986	162
Touchdowns (Tot.)	Emmitt Smith, 1990-96	115
Points	Rafael Septien, 1978-1986	874

INDIVIDUAL RECORDS—SINGLE SEASON
Category	Name	Performance
Rushing (Yds.)	Emmitt Smith, 1995	1,773
Passing (Yds.)	Danny White, 1983	3,980
Passing (TDs)	Danny White, 1983	29
Receiving (No.)	Michael Irvin, 1995	111
Receiving (Yds.)	Michael Irvin, 1995	1,603
Interceptions	Everson Walls, 1981	11
Punting (Avg.)	Sam Baker, 1962	45.4
Punt Return (Avg.)	Bob Hayes, 1968	20.8
Kickoff Return (Avg.)	Mel Renfro, 1965	30.0
Field Goals	Chris Boniol, 1996	32
Touchdowns (Tot.)	Emmitt Smith, 1995	*25
Points	Emmitt Smith, 1995	150

INDIVIDUAL RECORDS—SINGLE GAME
Category	Name	Performance
Rushing (Yds.)	Emmitt Smith, 10-31-93	237
Passing (Yds.)	Don Meredith, 11-10-63	460
Passing (TDs)	Many times	5
	Last time by Danny White, 10-30-83	
Receiving (No.)	Lance Rentzel, 11-19-67	13
Receiving (Yds.)	Bob Hayes, 11-13-66	246
Interceptions	Herb Adderley, 9-26-71	3
	Lee Roy Jordan, 11-4-73	3
	Dennis Thurman, 12-13-81	3
Field Goals	Chris Boniol, 11-18-96	*7
Touchdowns (Tot.)	Many times	4
	Last time by Emmitt Smith, 9-4-95	
Points	Many times	24
	Last time by Emmitt Smith, 9-4-95	

*NFL Record

COACHING HISTORY

(360-231-6)
1960-88	Tom Landry	270-178-6
1989-93	Jimmy Johnson	51-37-0
1994-96	Barry Switzer	39-16-0

TEXAS STADIUM

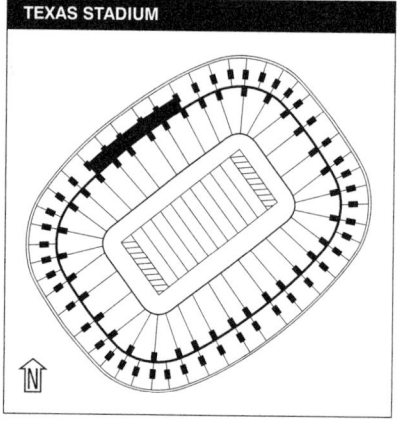

1996 TEAM RECORD

PRESEASON (2-3)

Date	Result		Opponents
7/27	W	35-34	Oakland
8/5	L	6-32	vs. Kansas City
			at Monterrey, Mexico
8/12	L	7-31	New England
8/17	L	3-20	Denver
8/24	W	24-19	vs. Houston at Orlando, Fla.

REGULAR SEASON (10-6)

Date	Result		Opponents	Att.
9/2	L	6-22	at Chicago	63,076
9/8	W	27-0	N.Y. Giants	63,069
9/15	L	24-25	Indianapolis	63,021
9/22	L	7-10	at Buffalo	78,098
9/30	W	23-19	at Philadelphia	67,201
10/13	W	17-3	Arizona	64,096
10/20	W	32-28	Atlanta	64,091
10/27	W	29-10	at Miami	75,283
11/3	L	21-31	Philadelphia	64,952
11/10	W	20-17	at San Francisco (OT)	68,919
11/18	W	21-6	Green Bay	65,032
11/24	L	6-20	at N.Y. Giants	77,081
11/28	W	21-10	Washington	64,955
12/8	W	10-6	at Arizona	70,763
12/15	W	12-6	New England	64,578
12/22	L	10-37	at Washington	56,454

POSTSEASON (1-1)

Date	Result		Opponents	Att.
12/28	W	40-15	Minnesota	64,682
1/5	L	17-26	at Carolina	72,808

(OT) Overtime

SCORE BY PERIODS

Cowboys	60	85	57	81	3	—	286
Opponents	52	80	51	67	0	—	250

ATTENDANCE

Home 513,794   Away 556,875   Total 1,070,669
Single-game home record, 65,180 (11/12/95)
Single-season home record, 518,167 (1995)

1996 TEAM STATISTICS

	Cowboys	Opp.
Total First Downs	286	260
Rushing	105	89
Passing	163	144
Penalty	18	27
Third Down: Made/Att	89/213	73/212
Third Down Pct.	41.8	34.4
Fourth Down: Made/Att	4/8	12/20
Fourth Down Pct.	50.0	60.0
Total Net Yards	4763	4382
Avg. Per Game	297.7	273.9
Total Plays	981	958
Avg. Per Play	4.9	4.6
Net Yards Rushing	1641	1576
Avg. Per Game	102.6	98.5
Total Rushes	475	437
Net Yards Passing	3122	2806
Avg. Per Game	195.1	175.4
Sacked/Yards Lost	19/127	37/219
Gross Yards	3249	3025
Att./Completions	487/307	484/271
Completion Pct.	63.0	56.0
Had Intercepted	14	19
Punts/Avg.	74/42.6	75/46.1
Net Punting Avg.	74/36.8	75/39.5
Penalties/Yards Lost	103/832	94/717
Fumbles/Ball Lost	24/15	26/14
Touchdowns	27	24
Rushing	14	10
Passing	12	10
Returns	1	4
Avg. Time of Possession	30:53	29:07

1996 INDIVIDUAL STATISTICS

PASSING	Att.	Comp.	Yds.	Pct.	TD	Int.	Tkld.	Rate
Aikman	465	296	3126	63.7	12	13	18/120	80.1
Wilson	18	8	79	44.4	0	1	1/7	34.3
Garrett	3	3	44	100.0	0	0	0/0	118.8
Sh. Williams	1	0	0	0.0	0	0	0/0	39.6
Cowboys	487	307	3249	63.0	12	14	19/127	78.6
Opponents	484	271	3025	56.0	10	19	37/219	65.3

SCORING	TD R	TD P	TD Rt	PAT	FG	Saf	PTS
Boniol	0	0	0	24/25	32/36	0	120
E. Smith	12	3	0	0/0	0/0	0	90
Bjornson	0	3	0	0/0	0/0	0	20
Irvin	0	2	0	0/0	0/0	0	14
Sanders	0	1	1	0/0	0/0	0	12
Aikman	1	0	0	0/0	0/0	0	6
Johnston	0	1	0	0/0	0/0	0	6
Martin	0	1	0	0/0	0/0	0	6
Walker	1	0	0	0/0	0/0	0	6
K. Williams	0	1	0	0/0	0/0	0	6
Cowboys	14	12	1	24/25	32/36	0	286
Opponents	10	10	4	20/20	28/32	1	250

2-Point conversions: Bjornson, Irvin. Team: 2-2, Opponents 0-4.

RUSHING	Att.	Yds.	Avg.	LG	TD
E. Smith	327	1204	3.7	42	12
Sh. Williams	69	269	3.9	27	0
Walker	10	83	8.3	39t	1
Johnston	22	48	2.2	7	0
Aikman	35	42	1.2	10	1
K. Williams	4	11	2.8	9	0
Wilson	4	5	1.3	8	0
Sanders	3	2	0.7	3	0
Jett	1	-23	-23.0	-23	0
Cowboys	475	1641	3.5	42	14
Opponents	437	1576	3.6	37	10

RECEIVING	No.	Yds.	Avg.	LG	TD
Irvin	64	962	15.0	61	2
Bjornson	48	388	8.1	25	3
E. Smith	47	249	5.3	21	3
Johnston	43	278	6.5	23	1
Sanders	36	475	13.2	41	1
K. Williams	27	323	12.0	31	1
Martin	25	380	15.2	60t	1
Walker	7	89	12.7	24	0
Sh. Williams	5	41	8.2	13	0
Armstrong	2	10	5.0	6	0
St. Williams	1	32	32.0	32	0
Mitchell	1	17	17.0	17	0
Ware	1	5	5.0	5	0
Cowboys	307	3249	10.6	61	12
Opponents	271	3025	11.2	52	10

INTERCEPTIONS	No.	Yds.	Avg.	LG	TD
K. Smith	5	45	9.0	24	0
Woodson	5	43	8.6	21	0
Teague	4	47	11.8	22	0
Harper	2	30	15.0	15	0
Sanders	2	3	1.5	2	0
Strickland	1	0	0.0	0	0
W. Davis	0	0	—	0	0
Cowboys	19	168	8.8	24	0
Opponents	14	250	17.9	104t	1

PUNTING	No.	Yds.	Avg.	In 20	LG
Jett	74	3150	42.6	22	60
Cowboys	74	3150	42.6	22	60
Opponents	75	3459	46.1	22	67

PUNT RETURNS	No.	FC	Yds.	Avg.	LG	TD
Martin	41	10	373	9.1	22	0
K. Williams	2	0	17	8.5	9	0
Sanders	1	1	4	4.0	4	0
Cowboys	44	11	394	9.0	22	0
Opponents	32	23	249	7.8	52	0

KICKOFF RETURNS	No.	Yds.	Avg.	LG	TD
Walker	27	779	28.9	89	0
K. Williams	21	471	22.4	39	0
Marion	3	68	22.7	37	0
C. Williams	2	21	10.5	21	0
Cowboys	53	1339	25.3	89	0
Opponents	70	1431	20.4	50	0

SACKS	No.
Tolbert	12.0
Hennings	4.5
Thomas	4.5
Lett	3.5
Carver	3.0
Woodson	3.0
McCormack	2.5
Childress	1.0
Haley	1.0
D. Smith	1.0
Strickland	1.0
Cowboys	37.0
Opponents	19.0

1997 DRAFT CHOICES

Round	Name	Pos.	College
1	David LaFleur	TE	Louisiana State
3	Dexter Coakley	LB	Appalachian State
	Steve Scifres	T	Wyoming
	Kenny Wheaton	DB	Oregon
4	Antonio Anderson	DT	Syracuse
	Macey Brooks	WR	James Madison
	Nicky Sualua	RB	Ohio State
6	Lee Vaughn	DB	Wyoming
7	Omar Stoutmire	DB	Fresno State

DALLAS COWBOYS

1997 VETERAN ROSTER

No.	Name	Pos.	Ht.	Wt.	Birthdate	NFL Exp.	College	Hometown	How Acq.	'96 Games/ Starts
8	Aikman, Troy	QB	6-4	219	11/21/66	9	UCLA	Henryetta, Okla.	D1-'89	15/15
73	Allen, Larry	G	6-3	326	11/27/71	4	Sonoma State	Napa, Calif.	D2-'94	16/16
40	Bates, Bill	S	6-1	213	6/6/61	15	Tennessee	Knoxville, Tenn.	FA-'83	14/0
91	Benson, Darren	DT	6-7	308	8/25/74	3	Trinity Valley	Memphis, Tenn.	SD3-'95	0*
86	Bjornson, Eric	TE	6-4	236	12/15/71	3	Washington	Oakland, Calif.	D4a-'95	14/10
29	Brice, Alundis	CB	5-10	178	5/1/70	3	Mississippi	Brookhaven, Miss.	D4b-'95	14/1
59	Campos, Alan	LB	6-3	236	3/3/73	2	Louisville	Miami, Fla.	D5b-'96	15/0
98	Carver, Shante	DE	6-5	253	2/12/71	4	Arizona State	Stockton, Calif.	D1-'94	10/7
75	Casillas, Tony	DT	6-3	278	10/26/63	12	Oklahoma	Tulsa, Okla.	FA-'96	16/3
87	Davis, Billy	WR	6-1	205	7/6/72	3	Pittsburgh	El Paso, Tex.	FA-'95	13/0
35	Davis, Wendell	CB	5-10	183	6/27/73	2	Oklahoma	Wichita, Kan.	D6-'96	13/0
63	Flannery, John	C-G	6-3	304	1/13/69	6	Syracuse	Pottsville, Pa.	FA-'96	1/0
17	Garrett, Jason	QB	6-2	195	3/28/66	5	Princeton	Chagrin, Ohio	FA-'93	1/0
56	Godfrey, Randall	LB	6-2	237	4/6/73	2	Georgia	Valdosta, Ga.	D2b-'96	16/6
94	Haley, Charles	DE	6-5	260	1/6/64	12	James Madison	Campbell County, Va.	T(SF)-'92	5/5
64	Hannah, Shane	G	6-5	360	10/21/71	2	Michigan State	Germantown, Ohio	D2c-'95	0*
24	Harper, Roger	S	6-2	223	10/26/70	5	Ohio State	Columbus, Ohio	T(Atl)-'96	14/0
69	Hegamin, George	T	6-7	331	2/14/73	4	North Carolina State	Camden, N.J.	D3-'94	16/1
70	Hellestrae, Dale	C-G	6-5	291	7/11/62	13	Southern Methodist	Scottsdale, Ariz.	T(Raid)-'90	16/0
95	Hennings, Chad	DT	6-6	291	10/20/65	6	Air Force	Elberon, Iowa	D11-'88	15/15
88	Irvin, Michael	WR	6-2	207	3/5/66	10	Miami	Ft. Lauderdale, Fla.	D1-'88	11/11
48	Johnston, Daryl	RB	6-2	242	2/10/66	9	Syracuse	Youngstown, N.Y.	D2-'89	16/15
78	Lett, Leon	DT	6-6	295	10/12/68	7	Emporia State	Fair Hope, Ala.	D7-'91	13/13
31	Marion, Brock	S	5-11	197	6/11/70	5	Nevada-Reno	Bakersfield, Calif.	D7-'93	10/10
83	# Martin, Kelvin	WR	5-9	162	5/14/65	11	Boston College	Jacksonville, Fla.	FA-'96	16/1
99	McCormack, Hurvin	DE-DT	6-5	284	4/6/72	4	Indiana	Brooklyn, N.Y.	FA-'94	16/4
83	Miller, Anthony	WR	5-11	190	4/15/65	10	Tennessee	Pasadena, Calif.	FA-'97	16/16*
61	Newton, Nate	G	6-3	320	12/20/61	12	Florida A&M	Orlando, Fla.	FA-'86	16/16
84	Novacek, Jay	TE	6-4	234	10/24/62	13	Wyoming	Gothenburg, Neb.	PB(Phx)-'90	0*
97	Pittman, Kavika	DE	6-6	267	10/9/74	2	McNeese State	Leesville, La.	D2a-'97	15/0
62	Renfro, Leonard	DT	6-3	308	6/29/70	3	Colorado	Orchard Lake, Mich.	FA-'97	0*
21	Sanders, Deion	CB-WR	6-1	195	8/9/67	9	Florida State	Ft. Myers, Fla.	UFA(SF)-'95	16/15
50	Shiver, Clay	C	6-2	294	12/7/72	2	Florida State	Tifton, Ga.	D3a-'96	14/0
22	Smith, Emmitt	RB	5-9	209	5/15/69	8	Florida	Escambia, Fla.	D1-'90	15/15
26	Smith, Kevin	CB	5-11	190	4/7/70	6	Texas A&M	Orange, Tex.	D1a-'92	16/16
55	Strickland, Fred	LB	6-2	251	8/15/66	10	Purdue	Wanaque, N.J.	UFA(GB)-'96	16/16
51	Thomas, Broderick	DE	6-4	254	2/20/67	9	Nebraska	Houston, Tex.	FA-'96	16/9
92	Tolbert, Tony	DE	6-6	263	12/29/67	9	Texas-El Paso	Englewood, N.J.	D4-'89	16/16
71	Tuinei, Mark	T	6-5	314	3/31/60	15	Hawaii	Honolulu, Hawaii	FA-'83	15/15
93	Ulufale, Mike	DT	6-4	284	2/1/72	2	Brigham Young	Honolulu, Hawaii	D3c-'96	3/0
34	Walker, Herschel	RB	6-1	225	3/3/62	12	Georgia	Wrightsville, Ga.	FA-'96	16/1
82	Watkins, Kendell	TE	6-1	282	3/8/73	3	Mississippi State	Jackson, Miss.	D2b-'95	0*
42	Williams, Charlie	S	6-1	189	2/2/72	3	Bowling Green	Detroit, Mich.	D3-'95	7/0
79	Williams, Erik	T	6-6	328	9/7/68	7	Central State, Ohio	Philadelphia, Pa.	D3c-'91	16/16
85	# Williams, Kevin	WR	5-9	194	1/25/71	5	Miami	Dallas, Tex.	D2a-'93	10/9
20	Williams, Sherman	RB	5-8	202	8/13/73	3	Alabama	Mobile, Ala.	D2a-'95	16/1
80	Williams, Stepfret	WR	6-0	170	6/14/73	2	Northeast Louisiana	Minden, La.	D3b-'96	5/1
18	Wilson, Wade	QB	6-3	208	2/1/59	17	East Texas State	Commerce, Tex.	FA-'95	3/1
28	Woodson, Darren	S	6-1	219	4/25/69	6	Arizona State	Phoenix, Ariz.	D2b-'92	16/16

*   Benson, Novacek, and Watkins missed '96 season because of injury; Hannah last active with Dallas in '95; Miller played 16 games with Denver; Renfro last active with Philadelphia in '94.

\# Unrestricted free agent; subject to developments.

Players lost through free agency (6): K Chris Boniol (Phil; 16 games in '96), P John Jett (Det; 16), LB Godfrey Myles (Den; 16), LB Jim Schwartz (SF; 16), LB Darrin Smith (Phil; 16), S George Teague (Mia; 16).

Also played with Cowboys in '96—TE Tyji Armstrong (16 games), DT Ray Childress (3), C Ray Donaldson (16), C-G Derek Kennard (1), TE Johnny Mitchell (4), RB Dominique Ross (2), TE Derek Ware (5).

COACHING STAFF

Head Coach,
Barry Switzer

Pro Career: Led Cowboys to Super Bowl XXX victory over the Pittsburgh Steelers in January, 1996. In three seasons with Dallas, Switzer has claimed three NFC East titles, reached two NFC title games, and captured a Super Bowl win. Named the third head coach in Cowboys history on March 30, 1994. No pro playing experience. Career record: 39-16.

Background: Played at Arkansas from 1955-59 before beginning his assistant coaching career at his alma mater in 1962. Moved on to Oklahoma in 1966, and was named the Sooners' offensive coordinator in 1967. As head coach at Oklahoma from 1973-88, Switzer registered a career record of 157-29-4. His .837 winning percentage at Oklahoma is the fourth highest mark in college history, behind only Notre Dame's Knute Rockne (.881) and Frank Leahy (.864) and Carlisle's George Woodruff (.846). He guided the Sooners to 28 consecutive wins from 1973-75 and went 37 straight games without a defeat. Switzer's Oklahoma teams won three national championships (1974, 1975, and 1985) and 12 Big Eight Conference championships.

Personal: Born October 5, 1937, Crossett, Arkansas. Switzer lives in Coppell, Texas. He has two sons—Greg and Doug and one daughter Kathy.

ASSISTANT COACHES

Hubbard Alexander, wide receivers; born February 14, 1939, Winston-Salem, N.C., lives in Coppell, Tex. Center Tennessee State 1958-61. No pro playing experience. College coach: Tennessee State 1962-63, Vanderbilt 1974-78, Miami 1979-88. Pro coach: Joined Cowboys in 1989.

Joe Avezzano, special teams; born November 17, 1943, Yonkers, N.Y., lives in Coppell, Tex. Guard Florida State 1961-65. Pro center Boston Patriots 1966. College coach: Florida State 1968, Iowa State 1969-72, Pittsburgh 1973-76, Tennessee 1977-79, Oregon State 1980-84 (head coach), Texas 1985-88. Pro coach: Joined Cowboys in 1990.

Jim Bates, linebackers; born May 31, 1946, Pontiac, Mich., lives in Irving, Tex. Linebacker Tennessee 1964-67. No pro playing experience. College coach: Tennessee 1968, Southern Mississippi 1972, Villanova 1973-74, Kansas State 1975-76, West Virginia 1977, Texas Tech 1978-83, Tennessee 1989, Florida 1990. Pro coach: San Antonio Gunslingers (USFL) 1984-85 (head coach 1985), Arizona Outlaws (USFL) 1986, Detroit Drive (AFL) 1988, Cleveland Browns 1991-93, 1995, Atlanta Falcons 1994, joined Cowboys in 1996.

Craig Boller, defensive tackles; born January 29, 1948, Belmond, Iowa, lives in Irving, Tex. Defensive tackle Iowa State 1966-70. No pro playing experience. College coach: William Penn College 1974-76 (head coach 1976), Tennessee 1977, Memphis State 1978-79, Oregon State 1980-86, Iowa State 1987-94. Pro coach: Joined Cowboys in 1995.

Joe Brodsky, running backs; born June 9, 1934, Miami, Fla., lives in Coppell, Tex. Fullback-linebacker Florida 1953-56. No pro playing experience. College coach: Miami 1978-88. Pro coach: Joined Cowboys in 1989.

Dave Campo, defensive coordinator; born July 18, 1947, New London, Conn., lives in Coppell, Tex. Defensive back Central Connecticut State 1967-70. No pro playing experience. College coach: Central Connecticut State 1971-72, Albany State 1973, Bridgeport 1974, Pittsburgh 1975, Washington State 1976, Boise State 1977-79, Oregon State 1980, Weber State 1981-82, Iowa State 1983, Syracuse 1984-86, Miami 1987-88. Pro coach: Joined Cowboys in 1989.

Robert Ford, tight ends; born June 21, 1951, Belton, Tex., lives in Coppell, Tex. Wide receiver Houston 1970-72. No pro playing experience. College coach: Western Illinois 1974-76, New Mexico 1977-79, Oregon State 1980-81, Mississippi State 1982-83, Kansas 1986, Texas Tech 1987-88, Texas A&M 1989-90. Pro coach: Houston Gamblers (USFL) 1985, joined Cowboys in 1991.

Tommy Hart, defensive ends; born November 11, 1944, Macon, Ga., lives in Irving, Tex. Offensive guard/defensive end Morris Brown 1964-67. Pro defensive end San Francisco 49ers 1968-77, Chicago Bears 1978-79, New Orleans Saints 1980. Pro coach: San Francisco 49ers 1983-91, joined Cowboys in 1996.

Steve Hoffman, kickers-research and development; born September 8, 1958, Camden, N.J., lives in Coppell, Tex. Quarterback-running back-wide receiver Dickinson College 1979-82. Pro punter Washington Federals (USFL) 1983. College coach: Miami 1985-87. Pro coach: Joined Cowboys in 1989.

Hudson Houck, assistant head coach/offensive line; born January 7, 1943, Los Angeles, Calif., lives in Irving, Tex. Center Southern California 1962-64. No pro playing experience. College coach: Southern California 1970-72, 1976-82, Stanford 1973-75. Pro coach: Los Angeles Rams 1983-91, Seattle Seahawks 1992, joined Cowboys in 1993.

Joe Juraszek, strength and conditioning; born June 8, 1958, Chicago, Ill., lives in Coppell, Tex. Linebacker-defensive end New Mexico 1976-80. No pro playing experience. College coach: Oklahoma 1981-86, 1993-96, Texas Tech 1987-92. Pro coach: Joined Cowboys in 1997.

Clancy Pendergast, defensive assistant; born November 29, 1967, Phoenix, Ariz., lives in Irving, Tex. No college or pro playing experience. College coach: Mississippi State 1991, Southern California 1992, Oklahoma 1993-94. Pro coach: Houston Oilers 1995, joined Cowboys in 1996.

Jack Reilly, quarterbacks; born May 22, 1945, Boston, Mass., lives in Irving, Tex. Quarterback Washington State 1963, Santa Monica (Calif.) J.C. 1964, Long Beach State 1965-66. No pro playing experience. College coach: El Camino (Calif.) J.C. 1980-84 (head coach 1981-84), Utah 1985-89. Pro coach: San Diego Chargers 1990-93, Los Angeles Raiders 1994, St. Louis Rams 1995-96, joined Cowboys in 1997.

Ernie Zampese, offensive coordinator; born March 12, 1936, Santa Barbara, Calif., lives in Coppell, Tex. Halfback Southern California 1956-58. No pro playing experience. College coach: Hancock, Calif., J.C. 1962-65, Cal Poly-SLO 1966, San Diego State 1967-75. Pro coach: San Diego Chargers 1976, 1979-86, Los Angeles Rams 1987-93, joined Cowboys in 1994.

Mike Zimmer, defensive backs; born June 5, 1956, Peoria, Ill., lives in Grapevine, Tex. Quarterback-linebacker Illinois State 1974-76. No pro playing experience. College coach: Missouri 1979-80, Weber State 1981-88, Washington State 1989-93. Pro coach: Joined Cowboys in 1994.

1997 FIRST-YEAR ROSTER

Name	Pos.	Ht.	Wt.	Birthdate	College	Hometown	How Acq.
Anderson, Antonio	DT	6-6	318	6/4/73	Syracuse	Milford, Conn.	D4a
Bates, James	LB	6-1	236	8/3/73	Florida	Sevierville, Tenn.	FA
Brooks, Macey	WR	6-5	220	2/2/75	James Madison	Hampton, Va.	D4b
Calicchio, Lonny (1)	P	6-3	249	10/24/72	Mississippi	Plantation, Fla.	FA
Coakley, Dexter	LB	5-10	215	10/20/72	Appalachian State	Mt. Pleasant, S.C.	D3a
Culberson, Quincy	WR	6-1	184	10/1/73	Jackson State	Springfield Gardens, N.Y.	FA
Cunningham, Richie (1)	K	5-10	167	8/18/70	Southwestern Louisiana	Houma, La.	FA
Fitzgerald, Pat	LB	6-2	237	12/2/74	Northwestern	Orland Park, Ill.	FA
Gowin, Toby	P	5-10	167	3/30/75	North Texas	Jacksonville, Tex.	FA
Henry, Rocky	WR	6-0	187	4/25/75	Utah	Columbia, Mo.	FA
Hutson, Tony (1)	G	6-3	313	3/13/74	Northeast Oklahoma State	Houston, Tex.	FA
Jackson, Keith	WR	6-1	185	2/24/72	Wisconsin	Sicklerville, N.J.	FA
Kesi, Pat	G	6-3	319	9/10/73	Washington	Honolulu, Hawaii	FA
Kight, Danny (1)	K	6-1	200	8/18/71	Augusta State	Atlanta, Ga.	FA
Knake, Max	QB	6-1	205	4/11/73	Texas Christian	McKinney, Tex.	FA
LaFleur, David	TE	6-7	280	1/29/74	Louisiana State	Westlake, La.	D1
Mathis, Kevin	CB	5-9	172	4/9/74	East Texas State	Kansas City, Mo.	FA
Mobley, Singor	S	5-11	195	10/12/72	Washington State	Tacoma, Wash.	FA
Mock, Kerry (1)	LB	6-1	232	8/17/73	North Carolina	Thomasville, N.C.	FA
Morgan, Beau	RB	5-10	192	8/4/75	Air Force	Carrollton, Tex.	FA
Odumuyiwa, Mike	DE	6-6	260	1/9/74	Eastern Illinois	Aurora, Ill.	FA
Parks, Odell (1)	LB	6-2	250	9/5/72	Navarro J.C.	Corsicana, Tex.	FA
Perry, Jarvis (1)	RB	6-0	205	2/3/69	Rowan	Camden, N.J.	FA
Scifres, Steve	G-T	6-4	300	1/22/72	Wyoming	Colorado Springs, Colo.	D3b
Simms, Sean	TE	6-2	245	7/5/74	Nevada	Santa Barbara, Calif.	FA
Stoutmire, Omar	S	5-11	198	7/9/74	Fresno State	Long Beach, Calif.	D7
Sualua, Nicky	RB	5-11	257	4/16/75	Ohio State	Santa Ana, Calif.	D4c
Talley, Charles	RB	5-11	228	2/12/74	Northern Illinois	Pontiac, Mich.	FA
Vaughn, Lee	CB	5-11	184	11/27/74	Wyoming	Cheyenne, Wyo.	D6
Washington, T.J.	T	6-4	335	7/1/74	Virginia Tech	Melfa, Va.	FA
Wheaton, Kenny	CB	5-10	190	3/8/75	Oregon	Phoenix, Ariz.	D3c
Williams, Brett	DE	6-4	263	10/15/73	Clemson	Albany, Ga.	FA
Williams, Montrell	CB-S	6-0	193	4/2/74	Idaho	Amarillo, Tex	FA
Young, Marshall	K	5-10	195	3/13/74	Texas-El Paso	The Woodlands, Tex.	FA

The term NFL Rookie is defined as a player who is in his first season of professional football and has not been on the roster of another professional football team for any regular-season or postseason games. A Rookie is designated by an "R" on NFL rosters. Players who have been active in another professional football league or players who have NFL experience, including either preseason training camp or being on an Active List or Inactive List, or on Reserve/Injured or Reserve/Physically Unable to Perform for fewer than six regular-season games, are termed NFL First-Year Players. An NFL First-Year Player is designated by a "1" on NFL rosters. Thereafter, a player is credited with an additional year of experience for each season in which he accumulates six games on the Active List or Inactive List, or on Reserve/Injured or Reserve/Physically Unable to Perform.

NOTES

_____

_____

_____

_____

_____

DETROIT LIONS

National Football Conference
Central Division
Team Colors: Honolulu Blue and Silver
Pontiac Silverdome
1200 Featherstone Road
Pontiac, Michigan 48342
Telephone: (248) 335-4131

CLUB OFFICIALS

Chairman and President: William Clay Ford
Vice Chairman: William Clay Ford, Jr.
Executive Vice President and Chief Operating
    Officer: Chuck Schmidt
Vice President of Player Personnel: Ron Hughes
Vice President of Communications, Sales and
    Marketing: Bill Keenist
Vice President of Football Administration: Larry Lee
Vice President of Finance and Chief Financial
    Officer: Tom Lesnau
Vice President-General Counsel: David Potts
Secretary: David Hempstead
Director of Salary Cap and Stadium Development:
    Tom Lewand
Director of Pro Personnel: Kevin Colbert
Scouts: Russ Bolinger, Dirk Dierking, Thomas
    Dimitroff, Allen Hughes, Scott McEwen, Jim
    Owens, Rick Spielman
Executive Director of Marketing: Steve Harms
Director of Media Relations: Mike Murray
Media Services Coordinator: James Petrylka
Executive Director of Ticket Sales and Customer
    Service: Duane McLean
Box Office Manager: Mark Graham
Director of Community Relations and Detroit Lions
    Charities: Tim Pendell
Head Athletic Trainer: Kent Falb
Equipment Manager: Dan Jaroshewich
Video Director: Steve Hermans
Stadium: Pontiac Silverdome •**Capacity:** 80,368
    1200 Featherstone Road
    Pontiac, Michigan 48342
Playing Surface: AstroTurf
Training Camp: Pontiac Silverdome
    1200 Featherstone Road
    Pontiac, Michigan 48342

1997 SCHEDULE
PRESEASON

Aug. 1	**Atlanta**	7:30
Aug. 8	**Cincinnati**	7:30
Aug. 17	at Pittsburgh	8:00
Aug. 21	at Indianapolis	7:30

REGULAR SEASON

Aug. 31	**Atlanta**	1:00
Sept. 7	**Tampa Bay**	1:00
Sept. 14	at Chicago	12:00
Sept. 21	at New Orleans	12:00
Sept. 28	**Green Bay**	1:00
Oct. 5	at Buffalo	1:00
Oct. 12	at Tampa Bay	1:00
Oct. 19	**New York Giants**	4:00
Oct. 26	Open Date	

Nov. 2	at Green Bay	7:00
Nov. 9	at Washington	1:00
Nov. 16	**Minnesota**	1:00
Nov. 23	**Indianapolis**	1:00
Nov. 27	**Chicago** (Thurs.)	12:30
Dec. 7	at Miami	8:00
Dec. 14	at Minnesota	12:00
Dec. 21	**New York Jets**	4:00

COACHING HISTORY
Portsmouth Spartans 1930-33
(433-447-32)

1930	Hal (Tubby) Griffen	5-6-3
1931-36	George (Potsy) Clark	49-20-6
1937-38	Earl (Dutch) Clark	14-8-0
1939	Elmer (Gus) Henderson	6-5-0
1940	George (Potsy) Clark	5-5-1
1941-42	Bill Edwards*	4-9-1
1942	John Karcis	0-8-0
1943-47	Charles (Gus) Dorais	20-31-2
1948-50	Alvin (Bo) McMillin	12-24-0
1951-56	Raymond (Buddy) Parker	50-24-2
1957-64	George Wilson	55-45-6
1965-66	Harry Gilmer	10-16-2
1967-72	Joe Schmidt	43-35-7
1973	Don McCafferty	6-7-1
1974-76	Rick Forzano**	15-17-0
1976-77	Tommy Hudspeth	11-13-0
1978-84	Monte Clark	43-63-1

RECORD HOLDERS
INDIVIDUAL RECORDS—CAREER

Category	Name	Performance
Rushing (Yds.)	Barry Sanders, 1989-1996	11,725
Passing (Yds.)	Bobby Layne, 1950-58	15,710
Passing (TDs)	Bobby Layne, 1950-58	118
Receiving (No.)	Brett Perriman, 1991-96	428
Receiving (Yds.)	Herman Moore, 1991-96	6,191
Interceptions	Dick LeBeau, 1959-1972	62
Punting (Avg.)	Yale Lary, 1952-53, 1956-1964	44.3
Punt Return (Avg.)	Jack Christiansen, 1951-58	12.8
Kickoff Return (Avg.)	Pat Studstill, 1961-67	25.7
Field Goals	Eddie Murray, 1980-1991	243
Touchdowns (Tot.)	Barry Sanders, 1989-1996	91
Points	Eddie Murray, 1980-1991	1,113

INDIVIDUAL RECORDS—SINGLE SEASON

Category	Name	Performance
Rushing (Yds.)	Barry Sanders, 1994	1,883
Passing (Yds.)	Scott Mitchell, 1995	4,338
Passing (TDs)	Scott Mitchell, 1995	32
Receiving (No.)	Herman Moore, 1995	*123
Receiving (Yds.)	Herman Moore, 1995	1,686
Interceptions	Don Doll, 1950	12
	Jack Christiansen, 1953	12
Punting (Avg.)	Yale Lary, 1963	48.9
Punt Return (Avg.)	Jack Christiansen, 1952	21.5
Kickoff Return (Avg.)	Tom Watkins, 1965	34.4
Field Goals	Jason Hanson, 1993	34
Touchdowns (Tot.)	Barry Sanders, 1991	17
Points	Jason Hanson, 1995	132

INDIVIDUAL RECORDS—SINGLE GAME

Category	Name	Performance
Rushing (Yds.)	Barry Sanders, 11-13-94	237
Passing (Yds.)	Scott Mitchell, 11-23-95	410
Passing (TDs)	Gary Danielson, 12-9-78	5
Receiving (No.)	Herman Moore, 12-4-95	14
Receiving (Yds.)	Cloyce Box, 12-3-50	302
Interceptions	Don Doll, 10-23-49	*4
Field Goals	Garo Yepremian, 11-13-66	6
Touchdowns (Tot.)	Dutch Clark, 10-22-34	4
	Cloyce Box, 12-3-50	4
	Barry Sanders, 11-24-91	4
Points	Dutch Clark, 10-22-34	24
	Cloyce Box, 12-3-50	24
	Barry Sanders, 11-24-91	24

*NFL Record

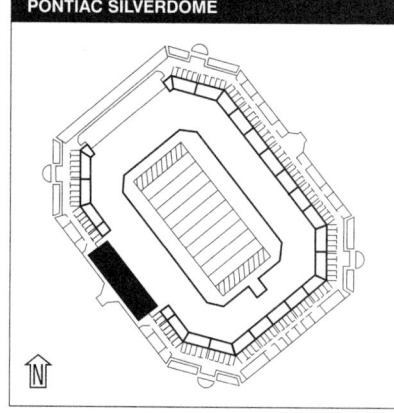

PONTIAC SILVERDOME

1985-88	Darryl Rogers***	18-40-0
1988-96	Wayne Fontes	67-71-0

* Released after three games in 1942
** Resigned after four games in 1976
*** Released after 11 games in 1988

1996 TEAM RECORD

PRESEASON (3-1)

Date	Result		Opponents
8/2	L	22-23	New Orleans
8/9	W	34-25	Washington
8/16	W	34-23	at Houston
8/23	W	24-17	at Cincinnati

REGULAR SEASON (5-11)

Date	Result		Opponents	Att.
9/1	L	13-17	at Minnesota	52,972
9/8	W	21-6	Tampa Bay	54,229
9/15	L	17-24	at Philadelphia	66,007
9/22	W	35-16	Chicago	70,022
9/29	W	27-0	at Tampa Bay	34,961
10/6	W	28-24	Atlanta	58,666
10/13	L	21-37	at Oakland	50,037
10/27	L	7-35	New York Giants	63,501
11/3	L	18-28	at Green Bay	60,695
11/11	L	21-27	at San Diego	60,425
11/17	W	17-16	Seattle	51,194
11/24	L	14-31	at Chicago	55,864
11/28	L	24-28	Kansas City	75,079
12/8	L	22-24	Minnesota	46,043
12/15	L	3-31	Green Bay	73,214
12/23	L	14-24	at San Francisco	61,921

SCORE BY PERIODS

Lions	52	124	69	57	—	302
Opponents	81	130	79	78	—	368

ATTENDANCE

Home 491,948   Away 442,882   Total 934,830
Single-game home record, 80,444 (12/20/81)
Single-season home record, 622,593 (1980)

1996 TEAM STATISTICS

	Lions	Opp.
Total First Downs	317	324
Rushing	105	126
Passing	180	172
Penalty	32	26
Third Down: Made/Att	73/190	95/220
Third Down Pct.	38.4	43.2
Fourth Down: Made/Att	9/20	8/15
Fourth Down Pct.	45.0	53.3
Total Net Yards	5013	5351
Avg. Per Game	313.3	334.4
Total Plays	976	1044
Avg. Per Play	5.1	5.1
Net Yards Rushing	1810	2007
Avg. Per Game	113.1	125.4
Total Rushes	389	510
Net Yards Passing	3203	3344
Avg. Per Game	200.2	209.0
Sacked/Yards Lost	46/260	32/233
Gross Yards	3463	3577
Att./Completions	541/309	502/311
Completion Pct.	57.1	62.0
Had Intercepted	21	11
Punts/Avg.	71/42.9	71/41/2
Net Punting Avg.	71/33.3	71/35.3
Penalties/Yards Lost	108/863	114/938
Fumbles/Ball Lost	21/5	26/8
Touchdowns	38	44
Rushing	15	12
Passing	20	28
Returns	3	4
Avg. Time of Possession	27:06	32:54

1996 INDIVIDUAL STATISTICS

PASSING	Att.	Comp.	Yds.	Pct.	TD	Int.	Tkld.	Rate
Mitchell	437	253	2917	57.9	17	17	36/199	74.9
Majkowski	102	55	554	53.9	3	3	10/61	67.2
Royals	1	1	-8	100.0	0	0	0/0	79.2
Sanders	1	0	0	0.0	0	1	0/0	0.0
Lions	541	309	3463	57.1	20	21	46/260	72.5
Opponents	502	311	3577	62.0	28	11	32/233	92.9

SCORING	TD R	TD P	TD Rt	PAT	FG	Saf	PTS
Hanson	0	0	0	36/36	12/17	0	72
Sanders	11	0	0	0/0	0/0	0	66
Moore	0	9	0	0/0	0/0	0	56
Morton	0	6	0	0/0	0/0	0	36
Perriman	0	5	0	0/0	0/0	0	30
Mitchell	4	0	0	0/0	0/0	0	24
Blades	0	0	1	0/0	0/0	0	6
Raymond	0	0	1	0/0	0/0	0	6
Wells	0	0	1	0/0	0/0	0	6
Lions	15	20	3	36/36	12/17	0	302
Opponents	12	28	4	40/41	20/25	1	368

2-Point conversions: Moore. Team: 1-2, Opponents: 1-3.

RUSHING	Att.	Yds.	Avg.	LG	TD
Sanders	307	1553	5.1	54t	11
Rivers	19	86	4.5	26	0
Mitchell	37	83	2.2	9	4
Majkowski	14	38	2.7	12	0
Morton	9	35	3.9	18	0
Perriman	1	13	13.0	13	0
Lynch	2	2	1.0	2	0
Lions	389	1810	4.7	54t	15
Opponents	510	2007	3.9	52	12

RECEIVING	No.	Yds.	Avg.	LG	TD
Moore	106	1296	12.2	50t	9
Perriman	94	1021	10.9	44	5
Morton	55	714	13.0	62t	6
Sanders	24	147	6.1	28	0
Metzelaars	17	146	8.6	20	0
Sloan	7	51	7.3	18	0
Matthews	3	41	13.7	21	0
Rivers	2	28	14.0	19	0
Price	1	14	14.0	14	0
Roberts	0	5	—	5	0
Lions	309	3463	11.2	62t	20
Opponents	311	3577	11.5	73	28

INTERCEPTIONS	No.	Yds.	Avg.	LG	TD
McNeil	5	14	2.8	15	0
Blades	2	112	56.0	98t	1
Raymond	1	24	24.0	24t	1
Stewart	1	14	14.0	14	0
Malone	1	5	5.0	5	0
Jeffries	1	0	0.0	0	0
Lions	11	169	15.4	98t	2
Opponents	21	313	14.9	37	3

PUNTING	No.	Yds.	Avg.	In 20	LG
Royals	69	3020	43.8	11	60
Hanson	1	24	24.0	1	24
Lions	71	3044	42.9	12	60
Opponents	71	2927	41.2	23	62

PUNT RETURNS	No.	FC	Yds.	Avg.	LG	TD
Milburn	34	19	284	8.4	33	0
Lions	34	19	284	8.4	33	0
Opponents	42	12	519	12.4	92t	1

KICKOFF RETURNS	No.	Yds.	Avg.	LG	TD
Milburn	64	1627	25.4	65	0
Lynch	1	15	15.0	15	0
Matthews	1	10	10.0	10	0
Metzelaars	1	1	1.0	1	0
Rivers	1	8	8.0	8	0
Washington	1	14	14.0	14	0
Lions	69	1675	24.3	65	0
Opponents	52	1298	25.0	88	0

SACKS	No.
Porcher	10.0
Elliss	6.5
Thomas	6.0
London	3.0
Waldroup	2.5
Bonham	2.0
Scroggins	2.0
Lions	32.0
Opponents	46.0

1997 DRAFT CHOICES

Round	Name	Pos.	College
1	Bryant Westbrook	DB	Texas
2	Juan Roque	G	Arizona State
	Kevin Abrams	DB	Syracuse
4	Matt Russell	LB	Colorado
5	Pete Chryplewicz	TE	Notre Dame
	Duane Ashman	DE	Virginia
6	Tony Ramirez	T	Northern Colorado
7	Terry Battle	RB	Arizona State
	Marcus Harris	WR	Wyoming
	Richard Jordan	LB	Missouri Southern

DETROIT LIONS

1997 VETERAN ROSTER

No.	Name	Pos.	Ht.	Wt.	Birthdate	NFL Exp.	College	Hometown	How Acq.	'96 Games/ Starts
42	Baxter, Brad	RB	6-1	235	5/5/67	7	Alabama State	Slocomb, Ala.	FA-'97	0*
51	Beer, Tom	LB	6-1	237	3/27/69	4	Wayne State	Bay Port, Mich.	D7-'94	16/1
12	Blundin, Matt	QB	6-8	233	3/7/69	5	Virginia	Folsom, Pa.	FA-'97	0*
96	Bonham, Shane	DE-DT	6-4	260	10/18/70	4	Tennessee	Fairbanks, Alaska	D3-'94	15/2
57	Boyd, Stephen	LB	6-0	247	8/22/72	3	Boston College	Valley Stream, N.Y.	D5a-'95	8/5
59	Brown, Reggie	LB	6-2	241	9/28/74	2	Texas A&M	Austin, Tex.	D1a-'96	10/10
29	Colon, Harry	S	6-0	203	2/14/69	6	Missouri	Kansas City, Kan.	FA-'97	0*
77	Compton, Mike	C-G	6-6	297	9/18/70	5	West Virginia	Richland, Va.	D3b-'93	15/15
76	Conover, Scott	T	6-4	285	9/27/68	7	Purdue	Freehold, N.J.	D5-'91	10/7
92	Dronett, Shane	DT	6-6	288	1/12/71	6	Texas	Orange, Tex.	FA-'96	7/0
94	Ellis, Luther	DT	6-5	291	3/22/73	3	Utah	Mancos, Colo.	D1-'95	14/14
44	Ford, Brad	CB	5-10	170	1/11/74	2	Alabama	Alexander City, Ala.	D4-'96	14/0
53	Glover, Kevin	C	6-2	282	6/17/63	13	Maryland	Upper Marlboro, Md.	D2-'85	16/16
50	Hamilton, Rick	LB	6-1	241	4/19/70	3	Central Florida	Inverness, Fla.	FA-'97	15/4*
4	Hanson, Jason	K	5-11	183	6/17/70	6	Washington State	Spokane, Wash.	D2b-'92	16/0
64	Hartings, Jeff	G	6-3	283	9/7/72	2	Penn State	St. Henry, Ohio	D1b-'96	11/10
74	Harrison, Chris	G	6-3	290	2/25/72	2	Virginia	Washington, D.C.	FA-'96	2/0
68	Hempstead, Hessley	C-G	6-1	295	1/29/72	3	Kansas	Upland, Calif.	D7-'95	13/0
81	Hickman, Kevin	TE	6-4	258	8/20/71	3	Navy	Delran, N.J.	D6a-'95	0*
58	Jamison, George	LB	6-1	235	9/30/62	12	Cincinnati	Bridgeton, N.J.	FA-'97	1/0*
25	Jeffries, Greg	CB	5-9	184	10/16/71	5	Virginia	High Point, N.C.	D6-'93	16/4
18	Jett, John	P	6-0	199	11/11/68	5	East Carolina	Reedville, Va.	UFA-'97	16/0*
13	Johnson, Johnny	QB	6-1	202	1/21/73	2	Illinois	North Chicago, Ill.	FA-'96	0*
70	Jones, Jeff	T	6-6	310	5/30/72	3	Texas A&M	Killeen, Tex.	FA-'95	7/0
52	Kowalkowski, Scott	LB	6-2	228	8/23/68	7	Notre Dame	Orchard Lake, Mich.	FA-'94	16/1
55	London, Antonio	LB	6-2	234	4/14/71	5	Alabama	Tullahoma, Tenn.	D3a-'93	14/12
26	Lynch, Eric	RB	5-10	224	5/16/70	4	Grand Valley State	Woodhaven, Mich.	FA-'92	16/0
17	Macik, Miles	WR	6-4	210	9/15/73	2	Pennsylvania	Mayfield Heights, Ohio	FA-'96	0*
39	† Malone, Van	S	5-11	186	7/1/70	4	Texas	Houston, Tex.	D2-'94	15/15
10	McCorvey, Kez	WR	6-0	180	1/23/72	3	Florida State	Pascagoula, Miss.	D5b-'95	1/0
89	Metzelaars, Pete	TE	6-7	254	5/24/60	16	Wabash	Portage, Mich.	UFA(Car)-'96	15/11
33	Milburn, Glyn	RB-KR	5-8	177	1/2/68	5	Stanford	Santa Monica, Calif.	T(Den)-'96	16/0
19	Mitchell, Scott	QB	6-6	230	1/2/68	8	Utah	Springville, Utah	UFA(Mia)-'94	14/14
84	Moore, Herman	WR	6-3	210	10/20/69	7	Virginia	Danville, Va.	D1-'91	16/16
87	Morton, Johnnie	WR	6-0	190	10/7/71	4	Southern California	Torrance, Calif.	D1-'94	16/15
91	Porcher, Robert	DE	6-3	283	7/30/69	6	South Carolina State	Wando, S.C.	D1-'92	16/16
82	Price, Derek	TE	6-3	240	8/12/72	2	Iowa	Tempe, Ariz.	FA-'96	13/1
31	Raymond, Corey	CB	5-11	185	7/28/69	6	Louisiana State	New Iberia, La.	T(NYG)-'95	13/13
14	Reich, Frank	QB	6-4	210	12/4/61	13	Maryland	Lebanon, Pa.	FA-'97	10/7*
28	Rice, Ron	S	6-1	206	11/9/72	3	Eastern Michigan	Detroit, Mich.	FA-'95	13/2
34	Rivers, Ron	RB	5-8	205	11/13/71	3	Fresno State	Highland, Calif.	FA-'94	15/0
72	Roberts, Ray	T	6-6	308	6/3/69	6	Virginia	Asheville, N.C.	UFA(Sea)-'96	16/16
20	Sanders, Barry	RB	5-8	203	7/16/68	9	Oklahoma State	Wichita, Kan.	D1-'89	16/16
30	Schlesinger, Cory	RB	6-0	230	6/23/72	3	Nebraska	Duncan, Neb.	D6b-'95	16/1
97	Scroggins, Tracy	LB	6-2	255	9/11/69	6	Tulsa	Checotah, Okla.	D2a-'92	6/6
62	† Semple, Tony	G	6-4	286	12/20/70	4	Memphis State	Lincoln, Ill.	D5-'94	15/1
86	Sloan, David	TE	6-6	254	6/8/72	3	New Mexico	Tollhouse, Calif.	D3-'95	4/4
69	Solomon, Ariel	T	6-5	290	7/16/68	7	Colorado	Boulder, Colo.	UFA(Minn)-'97	16/0*
38	Stewart, Ryan	S	6-1	207	9/30/73	2	Georgia Tech	Moncks Corner, S.C.	D3-'96	14/2
49	Stocz, Eric	TE	6-4	278	5/25/74	2	Westminster	Trumbull, Ohio	FA-'96	1/0
79	Tharpe, Larry	T	6-4	300	11/19/70	6	Tennessee State	Macon, Ga.	FA-'97	0*
44	Vardell, Tommy	RB	6-2	230	2/20/69	6	Stanford	El Cajon, Ca.	UFA(SF)-'97	11/7*
93	Waldroup, Kerwin	DE-DT	6-3	260	8/1/74	2	Central State, Ohio	Country Club Hills, Ill.	D5-'96	16/10
90	Washington, Keith	DE	6-4	268	12/18/72	3	Nevada-Las Vegas	Dallas, Tex.	FA-'96	12/0
95	Wells, Mike	DE	6-3	287	1/6/71	4	Iowa	Arnold, Mo.	FA-'94	16/1

* Baxter last active with N.Y. Jets in '95; Blundin last active with Kansas City in '95; Colon last active with Jacksonville in '95; Hamilton played 15 games with N.Y. Jets; Hickman missed '96 season because of injury; Jamison played 1 game with Kansas City; Jett played 16 games with Dallas; J. Johnson inactive for 15 games; Macik inactive for 7 games; Reich played 10 games with N.Y. Jets; Solomon played 16 games with Minnesota; Tharpe inactive for 6 games; Vardell played 11 games with San Francisco.

† Restricted free agent; subject to developments.

Players lost to free agency (4): S Bennie Blades (Sea; 15 games in '96), LB Pepper Johnson (NYJ; 15), T Zefross Moss (NE; 15), P Mark Royals (NO; 16).

Also played with Lions in '96—CB Jocelyn Borgella (11 games), LB Michael Brooks (4), TE Steve Brooks (1), G Chris Harrington (2), QB Don Majkowski (5), WR Aubrey Matthews (16), CB Ryan McNeil (16), WR Brett Perriman (16), CB Richard Woodley (1).

COACHING STAFF

Head Coach,
Bobby Ross

Pro Career: Named the Lions' head coach January 13, 1997. Joined the Lions following five seasons as the head coach of the San Diego Chargers. Led the Chargers to three playoff appearances in five years, including two AFC Western Division titles and the club's first-ever AFC Championship and an appearance in Super Bowl XXIX. Hired as the ninth coach of the Chargers January 2, 1992. He began his pro coaching career as an assistant with the Kansas City Chiefs in 1978. He coached the Chiefs special teams and defense in 1978-79 and offensive backs in 1980-81. No pro playing experience. Career record: 50-36.

Background: Played quarterback and defensive back for Virginia Military Institute. Began coaching career at VMI in 1965. Moved on as an assistant at William & Mary 1967-70, Rice 1971, and Maryland 1972. Head coach at The Citadel 1973-77. Compiled 39-19-1 record at Maryland (1982-86) as he led the Terrapins to three Atlantic Coast Conference titles and made four bowl game appearances in five seasons. Guided Georgia Tech (1987-91) to first ACC title in school history. Under Ross, the Yellow Jackets won first national championship as country's only undefeated team (11-0-1) in 1990. Named consensus national coach of the year in 1990. Career collegiate record: 94-76-2.

Personal: Born December 23, 1935, Richmond, Va. Bobby and wife, Alice, live in West Bloomfield, Mich. and have five children—Chris, Kevin, Robbie, Mary, and Teresa.

ASSISTANT COACHES

Brian Baker, defensive line; born June 20, 1962, Baltimore, Md., lives in Rochester, Mich. Linebacker Maryland 1980-83. No pro playing experience. College coach: Maryland 1984-85, Army 1986, Georgia Tech 1987-95. Pro coach: San Diego Chargers 1996, joined Lions in 1997.

Don Clemons, defensive asst. & asst. strength coach; born February 15, 1954, Newark, N.J., lives in Rochester, Mich. Defensive end Muhlenberg College 1973-76. No pro playing experience. College coach: Kutztown State 1977-78, New Mexico 1979, Arizona State 1980-84. Pro coach: Joined Lions in 1985.

Sylvester Croom, offensive coordinator; born September 25, 1954, Tuscaloosa, Ala., lives in Rochester, Mich. Center Alabama 1971-74. Pro center New Orleans Saints 1975. College coach: Alabama 1976-86. Pro coach: Tampa Bay Buccaneers 1987-90, Indianapolis Colts 1991, San Diego Chargers 1992-96, joined Lions in 1997.

Frank Falks, running backs; born March 9, 1943, Tampa, Fla., lives in Rochester Hills, Mich. Linebacker Joplin (Mo.) J.C. 1963-64, Parsons College 1965-66. No pro playing experience. College coach: Parsons College 1967-69, Kansas State 1970-72, Arkansas 1973-77, Wyoming 1978-79, San Diego State 1980, Oklahoma State 1981-82, Southern California 1983-86, Arizona State 1987-91, Ohio State 1992-93. Pro coach: San Diego Chargers 1994-96, joined Lions in 1997.

Jack Henry, offensive line; born March 14, 1946, Wilmington, Pa., lives in Rochester Hills, Mich. Linebacker Penn State 1964-65, guard Indiana (Pa.) University 1967-68. No pro playing experience. College coach: West Virginia 1970, 1978-79, Edinboro 1973, Louisville 1974, Millersville 1975-76, Southern Illinois 1977, Appalachian State 1980, Wake Forest 1981-85, Indiana (Pa.) University 1986-89, Pittsburgh 1993-95. Pro coach: Pittsburgh Steelers 1990-91, San Diego Chargers 1996, joined Lions in 1997.

Bert Hill, strength and conditioning; born January 25, 1958, Montgomery, Ala., lives in Rochester Hills, Mich. Linebacker Marion (Ala.) Military Institute 1976-77, Wichita State 1978. No pro playing experience. College coach: Nicholls State 1981-82, Auburn 1983, Texas A&M 1984-88, Ohio State 1989. Pro coach: Joined Lions in 1990.

Stan Kwan, offense and special teams asst.; born November 2, 1967, Phoenix, Ariz., lives in Rochester Hills, Mich. No college or pro playing experience. Pro coach: San Diego Chargers 1991-96, joined Lions in 1997.

John Misciagna, quality control-offense & administrative asst.; born December 11, 1954, Brooklyn, N.Y., lives in Auburn Hills, Mich. Guard Dickinson College 1973-76. No pro playing experience. College coach: Indiana (Pa.) University 1977, Columbia 1978-79, Maryland 1980-88, Georgia Tech 1989-91. Pro coach: San Diego Chargers 1992-96, joined Lions in 1997.

Gary Moeller, linebackers; born January 26, 1941, Lima, Ohio, lives in Ann Arbor, Mich. Center-linebacker Ohio State 1960-62. No pro playing experience. College coach: Miami (Ohio) 1967-68, Michigan 1969-76, 1980-94 (head coach 1990-94), Illinois 1977-79 (head coach). Pro coach: Cincinnati Bengals 1995-96, joined Lions in 1997.

Dennis Murphy, quality control-defense; born October 22, 1940, Endicott, N.Y., lives in Rochester, Mich. Tight end-defensive lineman Notre Dame 1959-61. No pro playing experience. College coach: Notre Dame 1968-74, Colgate 1975, Holy Cross 1976-77, Eastern Michigan 1978-81, Maryland 1982-91, Navy 1992-93. Pro coach: San Diego Chargers 1994-96, joined Lions in 1997.

Bob Palcic, tight ends; born July 2, 1948, Gowanda, N.Y., lives in Rochester, Mich. Linebacker Dayton 1968-70. No pro playing experience. College coach: Dayton 1974-75, Ball State 1976-77, Wisconsin 1978-81, Arizona 1984-85, Ohio State 1986-91, Southern California 1992, UCLA 1993. Pro coach: Atlanta Falcons 1994-96, joined Lions in 1997.

Larry Peccatiello, defensive coordinator; born December 21, 1937, Newark, N.J., lives in Rochester, Mich. Receiver William & Mary 1955-58. No pro playing experience. College coach: William & Mary 1961-68, Navy 1969-70, Rice 1971. Pro coach: Houston Oilers 1972-75, Seattle Seahawks 1976-80, Washington Redskins 1981-93, Cincinnati Bengals 1994-96, joined Lions in 1997.

Chuck Priefer, special teams; born July 26, 1944, Cleveland, Ohio, lives in Rochester Hills, Mich. No college or pro playing experience. College coach: Miami (Ohio) 1977, North Carolina 1978-83, Kent State 1986, Georgia Tech 1987-91. Pro coach: Green Bay Packers 1984-85, San Diego Chargers 1992-96, joined Lions in 1997.

Richard Selcer, defensive backs; born August 22, 1937, Cincinnati, Ohio, lives in Rochester, Mich. Running back Notre Dame 1955-58. No pro playing experience. College coach: Xavier 1962-64, 1970-71 (head coach), Cincinnati 1965-66, Brown 1967-69, Wisconsin 1972-74, Kansas State 1975-77, Southwestern Louisiana 1978-80. Pro coach: Houston Oilers 1981-83, Cincinnati Bengals 1984-91, Los Angeles-St. Louis Rams 1992-96, joined Lions in 1997.

Jerry Sullivan, wide receivers; born July 13, 1944, Miami, Fla., lives in Rochester Hills, Mich. Quarterback Florida State 1963-64. No pro playing experience. College coach: Kansas State 1971-72, Texas Tech 1973-75, South Carolina 1976-82, Indiana 1983, Louisiana State 1984-90, Ohio State 1991. Pro coach: San Diego Chargers 1992-96, joined Lions in 1997.

Marc Trestman, quarterbacks; born January 15, 1956, Minneapolis, Minn., lives in Rochester, Mich. Quarterback Minnesota 1975-77, Moorhead (Minn.) 1978. Pro quarterback Minnesota Vikings 1979. College coach: Miami (Fla.) 1981-84. Pro coach: Minnesota Vikings 1985-86, 1990-91, Tampa Bay Buccaneers 1987, Cleveland Browns 1988-89, San Francisco 49ers 1995-96, joined Lions in 1997.

1997 FIRST-YEAR ROSTER

Name	Pos.	Ht.	Wt.	Birthdate	College	Hometown	How Acq.
Abrams, Kevin	CB	5-8	175	2/28/74	Syracuse	Tampa, Fla.	Db2
Ashman, Duane	DE	6-4	274	12/29/73	Virginia	Silver Springs, Md.	D5b
Ball, Raphael	CB	5-10	179	12/9/74	Ball State	Cincinnati, Ohio	FA
Battle, Terry	RB	5-11	197	2/7/76	Arizona State	San Diego, Calif.	D7a
Beverly, Eric	T	6-3	279	3/28/74	Miami, Ohio	Bedford Heights, Ohio	FA
Boyd, Tommie	WR	6-0	195	12/21/71	Toledo	Lansing, Mich.	FA
Caflisch, Andy	P	6-3	200	7/19/68	Wisconsin-Stout	River Falls, Wis.	FA
Chryplewicz, Pete	TE	6-5	253	4/27/74	Notre Dame	Sterling Heights, Mich.	D5a
Davis, Chuck	WR	6-0	189	5/17/75	Saginaw Valley State	Genessee, Mich.	FA
Davis, Jerome	DE	6-4	275	3/4/74	Minnesota	Detroit, Mich.	FA
Harris, Marcus	WR	6-2	213	10/11/74	Wyoming	Minneapolis, Minn.	D7b
Jordan, Richard	LB	6-1	265	12/1/74	Missouri Southern	Vlan, Okla.	D7c
Kirschke, Travis	DT	6-3	286	9/8/74	UCLA	Yorba Linda, Calif.	FA
Martin, Tim	WR	5-9	180	2/12/74	Marshall	Soddy-Daisy, Tenn.	FA
Milton, Eldren	WR	6-0	191	9/14/72	Arkansas-Monticello	Pontiac, Mich.	FA
Pulsipher, Dan	K	6-0	175	4/17/78	Utah	Carlsbad, Calif.	FA
Ramirez, Tony	T	6-6	296	1/26/73	Northern Colorado	Lincoln, Neb.	D6
Roque, Juan	T	6-8	333	1/8/74	Arizona State	Ontario, Calif.	D2a
Russell, Matt	LB	6-2	245	7/5/73	Colorado	Belleville, Ill.	D4
Sheahan, Kevin	DT	6-1	286	6/19/75	Carroll College	Reno, Nev.	FA
Thomas, Tre	S	6-1	211	9/12/75	Texas	Houston, Tex.	FA
Vandervelt, Jamie	G	6-4	305	4/23/74	Wisconsin	Waukesha, Wis.	FA
Weems, Cyril	CB	6-2	207	8/1/74	Wisconsin	Detroit, Mich.	FA
Westbrook, Bryant	CB	6-0	199	12/19/74	Texas	Oceanside, Calif.	D1
Williams, Allen	RB	5-10	205	9/17/72	Maryland	Thomasville, Ga.	FA

The term NFL Rookie is defined as a player who is in his first season of professional football and has not been on the roster of another professional football team for any regular-season or postseason games. A Rookie is designated by an "R" on NFL rosters. Players who have been active in another professional football league or players who have NFL experience, including either preseason training camp or being on an Active List or Inactive List, or on Reserve/Injured or Reserve/Physically Unable to Perform for fewer than six regular-season games, are termed NFL First-Year Players. An NFL First-Year Player is designated by a "1" on NFL rosters. Thereafter, a player is credited with an additional year of experience for each season in which he accumulates six games on the Active List or Inactive List, or on Reserve/Injured or Reserve/Physically Unable to Perform.

NOTES

National Football Conference
Central Division
Team Colors: Dark Green, Gold, and White
1265 Lombardi Avenue
Green Bay, Wisconsin 54304
Telephone: (920) 496-5700

CLUB OFFICIALS

President, CEO: Bob Harlan
Vice President: John Fabry
Secretary: Peter Platten
Treasurer: John Underwood
Vice President-Administration/
  Chief Financial Officer: Mike Reinfeldt
Exec. V.P. and General Manager: Ron Wolf
Exec. Assistant to the President: Phil Pionek
General Counsel: Lance Lopes
Exec. Director of Public Relations: Lee Remmel
Director of Marketing: Jeff Cieply
Assistant Director of Public Relations: Jeff Blumb
Assistant Director of Public Relations/Travel
  Coordinator: Mark Schiefelbein
Director of Family Programs/Player Speakers
  Bureau: Sherry Schuldes
Director of Player Personnel: Ted Thompson
Director of College Scouting: John Dorsey
Director of Pro Personnel: Reggie McKenzie
Personnel Assistant: Matt Boockmeier
College Scouts: Shaun Herock, Will Lewis,
  Johnny Meads, Scot McCloughan, Sam Seale,
  Red Cochran
Scouting Administrator: Bryan Broaddus
Administrative Assistant-Football: Gary Reynolds
Ticket Director: Mark Wagner
Accountants: Duke Copp, Vicki Vannieuwenhoven
Director of Computer Services: Wayne Wichlacz
Video Director: Al Treml
Trainer: Pepper Burruss
Equipment Manager: Gordon Batty
Corporate Security Officer: Jerry Parins
Stadium Supervisor: Ted Eisenreich
Stadium: Lambeau Field •**Capacity:** 60,790
  1265 Lombardi Avenue
  Green Bay, Wisconsin 54304
Playing Surface: Grass
Training Camp: St. Norbert College
  De Pere, Wisconsin 54115

1997 SCHEDULE

PRESEASON

July 26	**Miami**	5:30
July 31	**New England**	7:00
Aug. 8	at Oakland	7:00
Aug. 16	vs. Buffalo at Toronto	4:00
Aug. 22	vs. New York Giants at Madison, Wis.	7:00

REGULAR SEASON

Sept. 1	**Chicago** (Mon.)	8:00
Sept. 7	at Philadelphia	4:00
Sept. 14	**Miami**	12:00
Sept. 21	**Minnesota**	12:00
Sept. 28	at Detroit	1:00
Oct. 5	**Tampa Bay**	12:00
Oct. 12	at Chicago	12:00
Oct. 19	Open Date	
Oct. 27	at New England (Mon.)	9:00
Nov. 2	**Detroit**	7:00
Nov. 9	**St. Louis**	12:00
Nov. 16	at Indianapolis	1:00
Nov. 23	**Dallas**	12:00
Dec. 1	at Minnesota (Mon.)	8:00
Dec. 7	at Tampa Bay	1:00
Dec. 14	at Carolina	4:00
Dec. 20	**Buffalo** (Sat.)	11:30 A.M.

RECORD HOLDERS

INDIVIDUAL RECORDS—CAREER

Category	Name	Performance
Rushing (Yds.)	Jim Taylor, 1958-1966	8,207
Passing (Yds.)	Bart Starr, 1956-1971	24,718
Passing (TDs)	Bart Starr, 1956-1971	152
Receiving (No.)	Sterling Sharpe, 1988-1994	595
Receiving (Yds.)	James Lofton, 1978-1986	9,656
Interceptions	Bobby Dillon, 1952-59	52
Punting (Avg.)	Dick Deschaine, 1955-57	42.6
Punt Return (Avg.)	Desmond Howard 1996	15.1
Kickoff Return (Avg.)	Travis Williams, 1967-1970	26.7
Field Goals	Chris Jacke, 1989-1996	173
Touchdowns (Tot.)	Don Hutson, 1935-1945	105
Points	Don Hutson, 1935-1945	823

INDIVIDUAL RECORDS—SINGLE SEASON

Category	Name	Performance
Rushing (Yds.)	Jim Taylor, 1962	1,474
Passing (Yds.)	Lynn Dickey, 1983	4,458
Passing (TDs)	Brett Favre, 1996	39
Receiving (No.)	Sterling Sharpe, 1993	112
Receiving (Yds.)	Robert Brooks, 1995	1,497
Interceptions	Irv Comp, 1943	10
Punting (Avg.)	Jerry Norton, 1963	44.7
Punt Return (Avg.)	Billy Grimes, 1950	19.1
Kickoff Return (Avg.)	Travis Williams, 1967	*41.1
Field Goals	Chester Marcol, 1972	33
Touchdowns (Tot.)	Jim Taylor, 1962	19
Points	Paul Hornung, 1960	*176

INDIVIDUAL RECORDS—SINGLE GAME

Category	Name	Performance
Rushing (Yds.)	Jim Taylor, 12-3-61	186
Passing (Yds.)	Lynn Dickey, 10-12-80	418
Passing (TDs)	Many times.	5
	Last time by Brett Favre, 11-12-95	
Receiving (No.)	Don Hutson, 11-22-42	14
Receiving (Yds.)	Bill Howton, 10-21-56	257
Interceptions	Bobby Dillon, 11-26-53	*4
	Willie Buchanon, 9-24-78	*4
Field Goals	Chris Jacke, 11-11-90, 10-14-96	5
Touchdowns (Tot.)	Paul Hornung, 12-12-65	5
Points	Paul Hornung, 10-8-61	33

*NFL Record

COACHING HISTORY

(547-445-36)

1921-49	Earl (Curly) Lambeau	212-106-21
1950-53	Gene Ronzani*	14-31-1
1953	Hugh Devore-	
	Ray (Scooter) McLean**	0-2-0
1954-57	Lisle Blackbourn	17-31-0
1958	Ray (Scooter) McLean	1-10-1
1959-67	Vince Lombardi	98-30-4
1968-70	Phil Bengtson	20-21-1
1971-74	Dan Devine	25-28-4
1975-83	Bart Starr	53-77-3
1984-87	Forrest Gregg	25-37-1
1988-91	Lindy Infante	24-40-0
1992-96	Mike Holmgren	58-32-0

*Resigned after 10 games in 1953
**Co-coaches

LAMBEAU FIELD

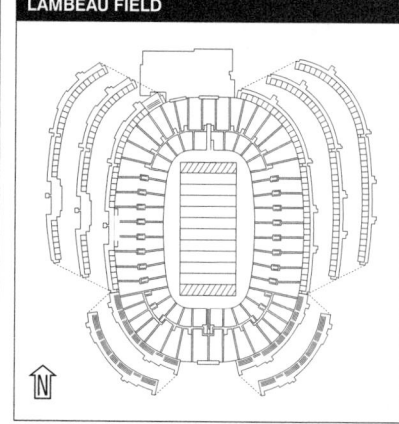

1996 TEAM RECORD

PRESEASON (3-1)

Date	Result		Opponents
8/2	W	24-7	New England
8/11	W	24-17	Pittsburgh
8/17	W	17-15	at Baltimore
8/24	L	6-30	at Indianapolis

REGULAR SEASON (13-3)

Date	Result		Opponents	Att.
9/1	W	34-3	at Tampa Bay	54,102
9/9	W	39-13	Philadelphia	60,666
9/15	W	42-10	San Diego	60,584
9/22	L	21-30	at Minnesota	64,168
9/29	W	31-10	at Seattle	59,973
10/6	W	37-6	at Chicago	65,480
10/14	W	23-20	San Francisco (OT)	60,716
10/27	W	13-7	Tampa Bay	60,627
11/3	W	28-18	Detroit	60,695
11/10	L	20-27	at Kansas City	79,281
11/18	L	6-21	at Dallas	65,032
11/24	W	24-9	at St. Louis	61,499
12/1	W	28-17	Chicago	59,682
12/8	W	41-6	Denver	60,712
12/15	W	31-3	at Detroit	73,214
12/22	W	38-10	Minnesota	59,306

POSTSEASON (3-0)

Date	Result		Opponents	Att.
1/4	W	35-14	San Francisco	60,787
1/12	W	30-13	Carolina	60,215
1/26	W	35-21	vs. New England	72,301

(OT) Overtime

SCORE BY PERIODS

Packers	76	125	136	116	3	—	456
Opponents	32	96	25	57	0	—	210

ATTENDANCE

Home 482,988   Away 522,749   Total 1,005,737
Single-game home record, 60,716 (10/14/96)
Single-season home record, 482,988 (1996)

1996 TEAM STATISTICS

	Packers	Opp.
Total First Downs	338	248
Rushing	118	74
Passing	197	151
Penalty	23	23
Third Down: Made/Att	97/219	74/226
Third Down Pct.	44.3	32.7
Fourth Down: Made/Att	5/11	14/22
Fourth Down Pct.	45.5	63.6
Total Net Yards	5535	4156
Avg. Per Game	345.9	259.8
Total Plays	1053	981
Avg. Per Play	5.3	4.2
Net Yards Rushing	1838	1416
Avg. Per Game	114.9	88.5
Total Rushes	465	400
Net Yards Passing	3697	2740
Avg. Per Game	231.1	171.3
Sacked/Yards Lost	40/241	37/202
Gross Yards	3938	2942
Att./Completions	548/328	544/283
Completion Pct.	59.9	52.0
Had Intercepted	13	26
Punts/Avg.	68/42.4	90/43.1
Net Punting Avg.	68/36.3	90/32.5
Penalties/Yards Lost	92/714	107/797
Fumbles/Ball Lost	33/11	25/13
Touchdowns	56	19
Rushing	9	7
Passing	39	12
Returns	8	0
Avg. Time of Possession	31:44	28:16

1996 INDIVIDUAL STATISTICS

PASSING	Att.	Comp.	Yds.	Pct.	TD	Int.	Tkld.	Rate
Favre	543	325	3899	59.9	39	13	40/241	95.8
McMahon	4	3	39	75.0	0	0	0/0	105.2
Hentrich	1	0	0	0.0	0	0	0/0	39.6
Packers	548	328	3938	59.9	39	13	40/241	95.7
Opponents	544	283	2942	52.0	12	26	37/202	55.4

SCORING	TD R	TD P	TD Rt	PAT	FG	Saf	PTS
Jacke	0	0	0	51/53	21/27	0	114
Jackson	0	10	0	0/0	0/0	0	60
Levens	5	5	0	0/0	0/0	0	60
Freeman	0	9	0	0/0	0/0	0	54
Beebe	0	4	2	0/0	0/0	0	36
R. Brooks	0	4	0	0/0	0/0	0	24
Bennett	2	1	0	0/0	0/0	0	22
Howard	0	0	3	0/0	0/0	0	18
Favre	2	0	0	0/0	0/0	0	12
Mayes	0	2	0	0/0	0/0	0	12
Mickens	0	2	0	0/0	0/0	0	12
Butler	0	0	1	0/0	0/0	0	6
Evans	0	0	1	0/0	0/0	0	6
Henderson	0	1	0	0/0	0/0	0	6
Koonce	0	0	1	0/0	0/0	0	6
Rison	0	1	0	0/0	0/0	0	6
Packers	9	39	8	51/53	21/27	*1	456
Opponents	7	12	0	17/17	25/27	1	210

*2-Point conversion: Bennett 2. Team: 2-3,
Opponents: 1-2.*
*Packers were credited with 1 team safety.

RUSHING	Att.	Yds.	Avg.	LG	TD
Bennett	222	899	4.0	23	2
Levens	121	566	4.7	24	5
Favre	49	136	2.8	23	2
Henderson	39	130	3.3	14	0
Jervey	26	106	4.1	12	0
R. Brooks	4	2	0.5	6	0
McMahon	4	-1	-.2	2	0
Packers	465	1838	4.0	24	9
Opponents	400	1416	3.5	37t	7

RECEIVING	No.	Yds.	Avg.	LG	TD
Freeman	56	933	16.7	51t	9
Jackson	40	505	12.6	51t	10
Beebe	39	699	17.9	80t	4
Levens	31	226	7.3	49	5
Bennett	31	176	5.7	25t	1
Chmura	28	370	13.2	29	0
Henderson	27	203	7.5	27	1
R. Brooks	23	344	15.0	38	4
Mickens	18	161	8.9	19	2
Rison	13	135	10.4	22t	1
Howard	13	95	7.3	12	0
Mayes	6	46	7.7	12	2
Thomason	3	45	15.0	24	0
Packers	328	3938	12.0	80t	39
Opponents	283	2942	10.4	69	12

INTERCEPTIONS	No.	Yds.	Avg.	LG	TD
E. Robinson	6	107	17.8	39	0
Butler	5	149	29.8	90t	1
Evans	5	102	20.4	63	1
Koonce	3	84	28.0	75t	1
Newsome	2	22	11.0	20	0
White	1	46	46.0	46	0
Prior	1	7	7.0	7	0
Dowden	1	5	5.0	5	0
Hollinquest	1	2	2.0	2	0
Simmons	1	0	0.0	0	0
Packers	26	524	20.2	90t	3
Opponents	13	98	7.5	41	0

PUNTING	No.	Yds.	Avg.	In 20	LG
Hentrich	68	2886	42.4	28	65
Packers	68	2886	42.4	28	65
Opponents	90	3876	43.1	15	63

PUNT RETURNS	No.	FC	Yds.	Avg.	LG	TD
Howard	58	16	875	15.1	92t	3
Prior	0	1	0	—	—	0
Packers	58	17	875	15.1	92t	3
Opponents	29	15	237	8.2	26	0

KICKOFF RETURNS	No.	Yds.	Avg.	LG	TD
Howard	22	460	20.9	40	0
Beebe	15	403	26.9	90t	1
Levens	5	84	16.8	29	0
Henderson	2	38	19.0	23	0
Freeman	1	16	16.0	16	0
Jervey	1	17	17.0	17	0
Thomason	1	20	20.0	20	0
Packers	47	1038	22.1	90t	1
Opponents	76	1649	21.7	45	0

SACKS	No.
White	8.5
Butler	6.5
Dotson	5.5
S. Jones	5.0
Evans	3.0
Wilkins	3.0
Simmons	2.5
Gi. Brown	1.0
McKenzie	1.0
Clavelle	0.5
B. Williams	0.5
Packers	37.0
Opponents	40.0

1997 DRAFT CHOICES

Round	Name	Pos.	College
1	Ross Verba	T	Iowa
2	Darren Sharper	DB	William & Mary
3	Brett Conway	K	Penn State
4	Jermaine Smith	DT	Georgia
5	Anthony Hicks	LB	Arkansas
7	Chris Miller	WR	Southern California
	Jerald Sowell	RB	Tulane
	Ronnie McAda	QB	Army

GREEN BAY PACKERS

1997 VETERAN ROSTER

No.	Name	Pos.	Ht.	Wt.	Birthdate	NFL Exp.	College	Hometown	How Acq.	'96 Games/ Starts
82	Beebe, Don	WR	5-11	183	12/18/64	9	Chadron State	Maple Park, Ill.	UFA(Car)-'96	16/6
34	Bennett, Edgar	RB	6-0	217	2/15/69	6	Florida State	Jacksonville, Fla.	D4-'92	16/15
13	Bono, Steve	QB	6-4	215	5/11/62	13	UCLA	Norristown, Pa.	FA-'97	14/13*
43	Bostic, James	RB	5-11	225	3/13/72	3	Auburn	Ft. Lauderdale, Fla.	FA-'96	0*
87	Brooks, Robert	WR	6-0	180	6/23/70	6	South Carolina	Greenwood, S.C.	D3-'92	7/7
68	Brown, Gary	T-G	6-4	315	6/25/71	4	Georgia Tech	Brentwood, N.Y.	W(Pitt)-'94	8/5
93	Brown, Gilbert	DT	6-2	325	2/22/71	5	Kansas	Detroit, Mich.	W(Minn)-'93	16/16
36	Butler, LeRoy	S	6-0	200	7/19/68	8	Florida State	Jacksonville, Fla.	D2-'90	16/16
89	Chmura, Mark	TE	6-5	250	2/22/69	6	Boston College	South Deerfield, Mass.	D6-'92	13/13
69	Chung, Eugene	G	6-5	295	6/14/69	5	Virginia Tech	Vienna, Va.	FA-'97	0*
48	Clark, Reggie	LB	6-2	240	10/17/67	3	North Carolina	Charlotte, N.C.	FA-'97	0*
91	Clavelle, Shannon	DE	6-2	287	10/12/72	3	Colorado	New Orleans, La.	FA-'95	8/0
61	Cummings, Joe	LB	6-2	242	6/8/72	2	Wyoming	Stevensville, Mont.	FA-'97	3/0*
44	Darkins, Chris	RB	6-0	215	4/30/74	2	Minnesota	Houston, Tex.	D4-'96	0*
67	# Dellenbach, Jeff	C	6-6	300	2/14/63	12	Wisconsin	Wausau, Wis.	FA-'96	3/0
23	Dorsett, Matthew	CB	5-11	190	8/23/73	3	Southern	New Orleans, La.	FA-'95	0*
72	Dotson, Earl	T	6-4	315	12/17/70	5	Texas A&I	Beaumont, Tex.	D3-'93	15/15
71	Dotson, Santana	DT	6-5	285	12/19/69	6	Baylor	Houston, Tex.	UFA(TB)-'96	16/15
45	Edwards, Brad	S	6-2	208	2/22/66	9	South Carolina	Fayetteville, N.C.	UFA(Atl)-'97	16/7*
33	Evans, Doug	CB	6-1	190	5/13/70	5	Louisiana Tech	Haynesville, La.	D6a-'93	16/16
4	Favre, Brett	QB	6-2	225	10/10/69	7	Southern Mississippi	Kiln, Mass.	T(Atl)-'92	16/16
58	Flanagan, Mike	C	6-5	290	11/10/73	2	UCLA	Sacramento, Calif.	D3a-'96	0*
86	Freeman, Antonio	WR	6-1	190	5/27/72	3	Virginia Tech	Baltimore, Md.	D3d-'95	12/12
55	Harris, Bernardo	LB	6-2	243	10/15/71	3	North Carolina	Chapel Hill, N.C.	FA-'95	16/0
30	Henderson, William	RB	6-1	248	2/19/71	3	North Carolina	Chester, Va.	D3b-'95	16/11
17	Hentrich, Craig	P	6-3	200	5/18/71	4	Notre Dame	Alton, Ill.	FA-'93	16/0
90	Holland, Darius	DT	6-5	310	11/10/73	3	Colorado	Las Cruces, N.M.	D3a-'95	16/0
56	† Hollinquest, Lamont	LB	6-3	243	10/24/70	4	Southern California	Downey, Calif.	FA-'96	16/0
81	Ismail, Qadry	WR	6-0	196	11/8/70	5	Syracuse	Wilkes-Barre, Pa.	FA-'97	16/2*
57	Jefferson, Kevin	LB	6-2	240	1/14/74	3	Lehigh	Greensburg, Pa.	FA-'97	0*
32	Jervey, Travis	RB	6-0	225	5/5/72	3	The Citadel	Mt. Pleasant, S.C.	D5b-'95	16/0
65	Knapp, Lindsay	G	6-6	300	2/25/70	5	Notre Dame	Deerfield, Ill.	T(KC)-'95	9/0
53	Koonce, George	LB	6-1	243	10/15/68	6	East Carolina	Vanceboro, N.C.	FA-'92	16/16
94	Kuberski, Bob	DT	6-4	295	4/5/71	3	Navy	Folsom, Pa.	D7-'93	1/0
54	Le Bel, Harper	LS	6-4	250	7/14/63	9	Colorado State	Sherman Oaks, Calif.	UFA(Atl)-'97	16/0*
25	† Levens, Dorsey	RB	6-1	235	5/21/70	4	Georgia Tech	Syracuse, N.Y.	D5b-'94	16/1
80	Mayes, Derrick	WR	6-0	200	1/28/74	2	Notre Dame	Indianapolis, Ind.	D2-'96	7/0
95	McKenzie, Keith	LB-DE	6-3	242	10/17/73	2	Ball State	Highland Park, Mich.	D7b-'96	10/0
77	Michels, John	T	6-7	290	3/19/73	2	Southern California	La Jolla, Calif.	D1-'96	15/9
85	† Mickens, Terry	WR	6-0	198	2/21/71	4	Florida A&M	Tallahassee, Fla.	D5a-'94	8/5
28	Mullen, Roderick	CB-S	6-1	204	12/5/72	3	Grambling State	St. Francisville, La.	FA-'95	14/0
21	Newsome, Craig	CB	6-0	190	8/10/71	3	Arizona State	Rialto, Calif.	D1-'95	16/16
18	Pederson, Doug	QB	6-3	215	1/31/68	5	Northeast Louisiana	Ferndale, Wash.	FA-'95	1/0
60	Peterson, Andrew	T	6-5	300	6/11/72	2	Washington	Port Orchard, Wash.	FA-'97	0*
46	Pinkney, Lovell	TE	6-5	255	8/18/72	2	Texas	Washington, D.C.	FA-'97	0*
39	Prior, Mike	S	6-0	208	11/14/63	12	Illinois State	Chicago Heights, Ill.	UFA(Ind)-'93	16/0
62	Rivera, Marco	G	6-4	295	4/26/72	2	Penn State	Elmont, N.Y.	D6-'96	0*
41	Robinson, Eugene	S	6-0	195	5/28/63	13	Colgate	Hartford, Conn.	T(Sea)-'96	16/16
19	Schroeder, Bill	WR	6-2	198	1/9/71	2	Wisconsin-LaCrosse	Sheboygan, Wis.	FA-'97	0*
74	Scott, Walter	DE	6-3	285	5/18/73	2	East Carolina	Johnston, S.C.	FA-'97	1/0*
59	Simmons, Wayne	LB	6-2	248	12/15/69	5	Clemson	Hilton Head, S.C.	D1a-'93	16/16
76	Spears, Marcus	T	6-4	302	9/28/71	4	Northwestern State, La.	Scotlandville, La.	FA-'97	9/0*
73	Taylor, Aaron	G	6-4	305	11/14/72	4	Notre Dame	Concord, Calif.	D1-'94	16/16
83	Thomason, Jeff	TE	6-5	250	12/30/69	5	Oregon	Newport Beach, Calif.	FA-'95	16/1
97	Thompson, Mike	DT	6-4	290	12/22/71	2	Wisconsin	Portage, Wis.	FA-'97	0*
63	Timmerman, Adam	G	6-4	295	8/14/71	3	South Dakota State	Cherokee, Iowa	D7-'95	16/16
92	White, Reggie	DE	6-5	300	12/19/61	13	Tennessee	Chattanooga, Tenn.	UFA(Phil)-'93	16/16
64	Wilkerson, Bruce	T	6-5	305	7/28/64	11	Tennessee	Loudon, Tenn.	FA-'96	14/2
98	Wilkins, Gabe	DE	6-5	305	9/1/71	4	Gardner-Webb	Spartanburg, S.C.	D4-'94	16/1
51	Williams, Brian	LB	6-1	235	12/17/72	3	Southern California	Dallas, Tex.	D3c-'95	16/16
37	Williams, Tyrone	CB	5-11	195	5/31/73	2	Nebraska	Brandenton, Fla.	D3b-'95	16/0
52	Winters, Frank	C	6-3	295	1/23/64	11	Western Illinois	Union City, N.J.	PB(KC)-'92	16/16
20	Yarborough, Ryan	WR	6-2	195	4/26/71	3	Wyoming	Park Forest, Ill.	T(NYJ)-'96	0*

* Bono played 14 games for Kansas City; Bostic, Darkins, Dorsett, and Flanagan missed '96 season because of injury; Chung and Thompson last active with Jacksonville in '95; Clark and Peterson last active with Carolina in '95; Cummings played 3 games for San Diego; Edwards and Le Bel played 16 games for Atlanta; Ismail played 16 games for Minnesota; Jefferson last active with Cincinnati in '94; Pinkney last active with St. Louis in '95; Rivera was inactive for 16 games; Schroeder last active with Green Bay in '94; Scott played 1 game with New England; Spears played 9 games with Chicago; Yarborough last active with N.Y. Jets in '95.

\# Unrestricted free agent; subject to developments.

† Restricted free agent; subject to developments.

Retired—Keith Jackson, 9-year tight end, 16 games in '96; Jim McMahon, 15-year quarterback, 5 games; Sean Jones, 13-year defensive end, 15 games.

Players lost through free agency (1): WR Desmond Howard (Oak; 16 games in '96).

Also played with Packers in '96—C Mike Arthur (5 games), CB Bucky Brooks (2), LB Ron Cox (16), CB Corey Dowden (9), K Chris Jacke (16), Calvin Jones (1), C Gene McGuire (8), WR Anthony Morgan (3), WR Andre Rison (7), CB Michael Robinson (6), T Ken Ruettgers (4), RB Brian Satterfield (1), RB Kevin Smith (1).

COACHING STAFF

Head Coach,
Mike Holmgren

Pro Career: Became Packers' eleventh head coach on January 11, 1992. Since that time, he has directed Green Bay to its first NFL championship in 29 years, five consecutive winning seasons, four straight playoff berths for the first time in club history, two NFC Central titles (the first since 1972), and two appearances in the NFC Championship Game. In 1996, he brought the Packers their league-high twelfth NFL championship with a 35-21 victory over the New England Patriots in Super Bowl XXXI. En route, Green Bay won more games (16) than any other team in the organization's 78-year history and captured a second consecutive division crown with a 13-3 regular-season record, including a perfect 8-0 mark at home (10-0 counting playoffs). His previous Packer teams went 9-7, 9-7, and 9-7 from 1992-94 and 11-5 in 1995. Holmgren was offensive coordinator for the San Francisco 49ers under George Seifert (1989-91) after spending three previous seasons (1986-88) as quarterbacks coach under Bill Walsh. During his six-year tenure with San Francisco, the 49ers won five consecutive NFC Western Division championships (1986-1990) and back-to-back Super Bowls (XXIII and XXIV). The 49ers never ranked lower than third overall in his three years as offensive coordinator. Career record: 58-32.

Background: Quarterback at Southern California (1966-69) and was drafted by the St. Louis Cardinals in the eighth round of the 1970 NFL draft. He served as an assistant coach at San Francisco State (1981) and Brigham Young (1982-85) before his tenure with the 49ers. Earned his bachelor of science degree in business finance at Southern California (1970).

Personal: Born June 15, 1948, in San Francisco. He and his wife, Kathy, live in Green Bay and have four daughters—Calla, Jenny, Emily, and Gretchen.

ASSISTANT COACHES

Larry Brooks, defensive line; born June 10, 1950, Prince George, Va., lives in De Pere, Wis. Defensive lineman Virginia State 1968-71. Pro defensive tackle Los Angeles Rams 1972-82. College coach: Virginia State 1992-93. Pro coach: Los Angeles Rams 1983-90, joined Packers in 1994.

Nolan Cromwell, special teams; born January 30, 1955, Smith Center, Kan., lives in Green Bay. Quarterback-safety Kansas 1973-76. Pro defensive back Los Angeles Rams 1977-87. Pro coach: Los Angeles Rams 1991, joined Packers in 1992.

Gil Haskell, wide receivers; born September 24, 1943, San Francisco, Calif., lives in Green Bay. Defensive back San Francisco State 1961, 1963-65. No pro playing experience. College coach: Southern California 1978-82. Pro coach: Los Angeles Rams 1983-91, joined Packers in 1992.

Johnny Holland, defensive assistant-quality control; born March 11, 1965, Hempstead, Tex., lives in Green Bay. Linebacker Texas A&M 1983-86. Pro linebacker Green Bay Packers 1987-1993. Pro coach: Joined Packers in 1995.

Kent Johnston, strength and conditioning; born February 21, 1956, Mexia, Tex., lives in Green Bay. Defensive back Stephen F. Austin 1974-77. No pro playing experience. College coach: Northwestern State (Louisiana) 1979, Northeast Louisiana 1980-81, Alabama 1983-86. Pro coach: Tampa Bay Buccaneers 1987-91, joined Packers in 1992.

Sherman Lewis, offensive coordinator; born June 29, 1942, Louisville, Ky., lives in Green Bay. Running back Michigan State 1961-63. Pro running back Toronto Argonauts (CFL) 1964-65, New York Jets 1966. College coach: Michigan State 1969-82. Pro coach: San Francisco 49ers 1983-91, joined Packers in 1992.

Jim Lind, linebackers; born November 11, 1947, Isle, Minn., lives in Green Bay. Linebacker Bethel College 1965-66; defensive back Bemidji State 1971-72. No pro playing experience. College coach: St. Cloud State 1977-78, St. John's (Minn.) 1979-80, Brigham Young 1981-82, Minnesota-Morris 1983-86 (head coach), Wisconsin-Eau Claire 1987-91 (head coach). Pro coach: Joined Packers in 1992.

Tom Lovat, offensive line; born December 28, 1938, Bingham, Utah, lives in Green Bay. Guard-linebacker Utah 1958-60. No pro playing experience. College coach: Utah 1967, 1972-76 (head coach 1974-76), Idaho State 1968-70, Stanford 1977-79, Wyoming 1989. Pro coach: Saskatchewan Roughriders (CFL) 1971, Green Bay Packers 1980, St. Louis-Phoenix Cardinals 1981-84, 1990-91, Indianapolis Colts 1985-88, rejoined Packers in 1992.

Andy Reid, quarterbacks; born March 19, 1958, Los Angeles, Calif., lives in Green Bay. Offensive tackle-guard Brigham Young 1978-80. No pro playing experience. College coach: Brigham Young 1982, San Francisco State 1983-85, Northern Arizona 1986, Texas-El Paso 1987, Missouri 1988-91. Pro coach: Joined Packers in 1992.

Mike Sherman, tight ends-assistant offensive line; born December 19, 1954, Norwood, Mass., lives in Green Bay. Linebacker-offensive guard-tackle Central Connecticut State 1974, 1976-77. No pro playing experience. College coach: Pittsburgh 1981-82, Tulane 1983-84, Holy Cross 1985-88, Texas A&M 1989-93, 1995-96, UCLA 1994. Pro coach: Joined Packers in 1997.

Fritz Shurmur, defensive coordinator; born July 15, 1932, Riverview, Mich., lives in Suamico, Wis. No pro playing experience. College coach: Albion 1956-61, Wyoming 1962-74 (head coach 1971-74). Pro coach: Detroit Lions 1975-77, New England Patriots 1978-81, Los Angeles Rams 1982-90, Phoenix Cardinals 1991-93, joined Packers in 1994.

Harry Sydney, running backs; born June 26, 1959, Petersburg, Va., lives in Green Bay. Quarterback/running back Kansas 1978-81. Pro running back Denver Gold (USFL) 1983-84, Memphis Showboats (USFL) 1985, Montreal Alouettes (CFL) 1986, San Francisco 49ers 1987-91, Green Bay Packers 1992. Pro coach: Joined Packers in 1994.

Bob Valesente, defensive backs; born July 19, 1940, Seneca Falls, N.Y., lives in Green Bay. Halfback Ithaca College 1958-61. No pro playing experience. College coach: Cornell 1964-74, Cincinnati 1975-76, Arizona 1977-79, Mississippi State 1980-81, Kansas 1984-87 (head coach 1986-87), Maryland 1988, Pittsburgh 1989. Pro coach: Baltimore Colts 1982-83, Pittsburgh Steelers 1990-91, joined Packers in 1992.

1997 FIRST-YEAR ROSTER

Name	Pos.	Ht.	Wt.	Birthdate	College	Hometown	How Acq.
Anderson, Ronnie	WR	6-1	190	2/27/75	Allegheny College	Cleveland, Ohio	FA
Andruzzi, Joe	G	6-3	313	8/23/75	Southern Connecticut State	Staten Island, N.Y.	FA
Conway, Brett	K	6-2	191	3/8/75	Penn State	Lilburn, Ga.	D3
Hayes, Chris (1)	S	6-0	200	5/7/72	Washington State	San Bernardino, Calif.	FA-'96
Hicks, Anthony	LB	6-1	242	3/31/74	Arkansas	Arkadelphia, Ark.	D5
Johnson, Eric (1)	DE	6-5	260	3/31/73	Texas Southern	Decatur, Ga.	FA
Kinder, Randy	RB	6-1	213	4/4/75	Notre Dame	East Lansing, Mich.	FA
Krueger, John	P	6-5	226	9/10/75	Duke	Hackensack, N.J.	FA
Matthews, Eric (1)	WR	5-11	170	3/22/72	Indiana	Lantana, Fla.	FA
McAda, Ronnie	QB	6-3	205	12/6/73	Army	Mesquite, Tex.	D7c
Miller, Chris	WR	5-10	192	7/10/73	Southern California	Los Angeles, Calif.	D7a
Pettigrew, Jay	TE	6-3	240	6/30/75	DePauw	Indianapolis, Ind.	FA
Richter, Jim	K	6-5	209	6/1/74	Furman	Columbia, S.C.	FA
Salina, Adam	RB	6-3	257	2/7/75	Stanford	Berlin, Conn.	FA
Sharper, Darren	CB-S	6-2	206	11/3/75	William & Mary	Glen Allen, Va.	D2
Smith, Emory	RB	6-0	246	5/21/74	Clemson	Pensacola, Fla.	FA
Smith, Jermaine	DT	6-3	289	2/3/72	Georgia	Augusta, Ga.	D4
Sowell, Jerald	RB	6-0	248	1/21/74	Tulane	Baker, La.	D7b
Verba, Ross	T	6-4	299	10/31/73	Iowa	West Des Moines, Iowa	D1
Wachholtz, Kyle (1)	TE	6-4	235	5/17/72	Southern California	Norco, Calif.	D7a-'96

The term NFL Rookie is defined as a player who is in his first season of professional football and has not been on the roster of another professional football team for any regular-season or postseason games. A Rookie is designated by an "R" on NFL rosters. Players who have been active in another professional football league or players who have NFL experience, including either preseason training camp or being on an Active List or Inactive List, or on Reserve/Injured or Reserve/Physically Unable to Perform for fewer than six regular-season games, are termed NFL First-Year Players. An NFL First-Year Player is designated by a "1" on NFL rosters. Thereafter, a player is credited with an additional year of experience for each season in which he accumulates six games on the Active List or Inactive List, or on Reserve/Injured or Reserve/Physically Unable to Perform.

NOTES

_____

_____

_____

_____

_____

_____

_____

_____

_____

_____

_____

_____

National Football Conference
Central Division
Team Colors: Purple, Gold, and White
9520 Viking Drive
Eden Prairie, Minnesota 55344
Telephone: (612) 828-6500

CLUB OFFICERS

Chairman of the Board: John C. Skoglund
Vice Chairmen: Jaye F. Dyer, Philip S. Maas
Directors: James Binger, N. Bud Grossman,
    Roger L. Headrick, James R. Jundt, Elizabeth
    MacMillan, Carol S. Sperry, Wheelock Whitney

CLUB OFFICIALS

President/CEO: Roger L. Headrick
Vice President Administration/Team Operations:
    Jeff Diamond
Vice President Player Personnel: Frank Gilliam
Vice President of Marketing and Business
    Development: Stew Widdess
Assistant General Manager/National Scouting:
    Jerry Reichow
Assistant General Manager/Pro Personnel:
    Paul Wiggin
Director of Finance: Nick Valentine
Director of Research and Development: Mike Eayrs
Director of Sales: Kernal Buhler
Director of Public Relations: David Pelletier
Director of Team Operations: Breck Spinner
Ticket Manager: Gina Dillon
Director of Security: Steve Rollins
Player Personnel Coordinator: Scott Studwell
Equipment Manager: Dennis Ryan
Trainer: Fred Zamberletti
Video Director: Larry Kohout
Stadium: Hubert H. Humphrey Metrodome
    •**Capacity:** 64,182
    500 11th Avenue South
    Minneapolis, Minnesota 55415
Playing Surface: AstroTurf
Training Camp: Mankato State University
    Mankato, Minnesota 56001

1997 SCHEDULE

PRESEASON

July 26	vs. Seattle at Canton, Ohio	2:30
Aug. 2	**St. Louis**	7:00
Aug. 8	at Buffalo	7:30
Aug. 16	at Cincinnati	7:30
Aug. 22	**San Diego**	7:00

REGULAR SEASON

Aug. 31	at Buffalo	1:00
Sept. 7	at Chicago	12:00
Sept. 14	**Tampa Bay**	12:00
Sept. 21	at Green Bay	12:00
Sept. 28	**Philadelphia**	7:00
Oct. 5	at Arizona	1:00
Oct. 12	**Carolina**	3:00
Oct. 19	Open Date	
Oct. 26	at Tampa Bay	1:00
Nov. 2	**New England**	12:00
Nov. 9	**Chicago**	12:00
Nov. 16	at Detroit	1:00
Nov. 23	at New York Jets	1:00
Dec. 1	**Green Bay** (Mon.)	8:00
Dec. 7	at San Francisco	1:00
Dec. 14	**Detroit**	12:00
Dec. 21	**Indianapolis**	12:00

RECORD HOLDERS

INDIVIDUAL RECORDS—CAREER

Category	Name	Performance
Rushing (Yds.)	Chuck Foreman, 1973-79	5,879
Passing (Yds.)	Fran Tarkenton, 1961-66, 1972-78	33,098
Passing (TDs)	Fran Tarkenton, 1961-66, 1972-78	239
Receiving (No.)	Cris Carter, 1990-96	578
Receiving (Yds.)	Anthony Carter, 1985-1993	7,636
Interceptions	Paul Krause, 1968-1979	53
Punting (Avg.)	Harry Newsome, 1990-93	43.8
Punt Return (Avg.)	David Palmer, 1994-96	9.6
Kickoff Return (Avg.)	Charlie West, 1968-1973	25.5
Field Goals	Fred Cox, 1963-1977	282
Touchdowns (Tot.)	Bill Brown, 1962-1974	76
Points	Fred Cox, 1963-1977	1,365

INDIVIDUAL RECORDS—SINGLE SEASON

Category	Name	Performance
Rushing (Yds.)	Terry Allen, 1992	1,201
Passing (Yds.)	Warren Moon, 1994	4,264
Passing (TDs)	Warren Moon, 1995	33
Receiving (No.)	Cris Carter, 1994, 1995	122
Receiving (Yds.)	Cris Carter, 1995	1,371
Interceptions	Paul Krause, 1975	10
Punting (Avg.)	Bobby Walden, 1964	46.4
Punt Return (Avg.)	David Palmer, 1995	13.2
Kickoff Return (Avg.)	John Gilliam, 1972	26.3
Field Goals	Fuad Reveiz, 1994	34
Touchdowns (Tot.)	Chuck Foreman, 1975	22
Points	Chuck Foreman, 1975	132
	Fuad Reveiz, 1994	132

INDIVIDUAL RECORDS—SINGLE GAME

Category	Name	Performance
Rushing (Yds.)	Chuck Foreman, 10-24-76	200
Passing (Yds.)	Tommy Kramer, 11-2-86	490
Passing (TDs)	Joe Kapp, 9-28-69	*7
Receiving (No.)	Rickey Young, 12-16-79	15
Receiving (Yds.)	Sammy White, 11-7-76	210
Interceptions	Many times	3
	Last time by Jack Del Rio, 12-5-93	
Field Goals	Rich Karlis, 11-5-89	*7
Touchdowns (Tot.)	Chuck Foreman, 12-20-75	4
	Ahmad Rashad, 9-2-79	4
Points	Chuck Foreman, 12-20-75	24
	Ahmad Rashad, 9-2-79	24

*NFL Record

VIKINGS COACHING HISTORY

(302-255-9)

1961-66	Norm Van Brocklin	29-51-4
1967-83	Bud Grant	161-99-5
1984	Les Steckel	3-13-0
1985	Bud Grant	7-9-0
1986-91	Jerry Burns	55-46-0
1992-96	Dennis Green	47-37-0

METRODOME

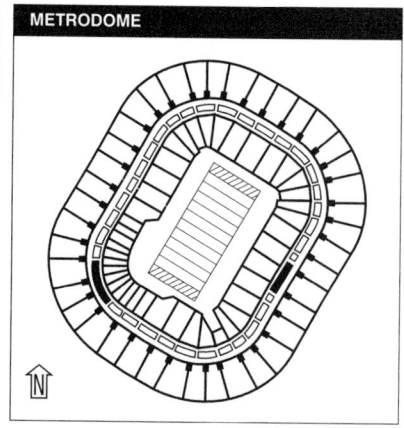

1996 TEAM RECORD

PRESEASON (1-3)

Date	Result		Opponents
8/3	W	23-20	San Diego (OT)
8/8	L	12-35	Buffalo
8/19	L	17-24	at Miami
8/23	L	13-16	at New Orleans

REGULAR SEASON (9-7)

Date	Result		Opponents	Att.
9/1	W	17-13	Detroit	52,972
9/8	W	23-17	at Atlanta	42,688
9/15	W	20-14	at Chicago	61,301
9/22	W	30-21	Green Bay	64,168
9/29	L	10-15	at N.Y. Giants	70,970
10/6	W	14-12	Carolina	60,894
10/13	L	13-24	at Tampa Bay	32,175
10/28	L	13-15	Chicago	60,774
11/3	L	6-21	Kansas City	59,552
11/10	L	23-42	at Seattle	50,794
11/17	W	16-13	at Oakland (OT)	41,183
11/24	L	17-21	Denver	59,142
12/1	W	41-17	Arizona	45,767
12/8	W	24-22	at Detroit	46,043
12/15	W	21-10	Tampa Bay	49,302
12/22	L	10-38	at Green Bay	59,306

POSTSEASON (0-1)

12/28	L	15-40	at Dallas	64,682

(OT) Overtime

SCORE BY PERIODS

Vikings	50	93	51	101	3	—	298
Opponents	53	88	80	94	0	—	315

ATTENDANCE

Home 452,571   Away 407,327   Total 859,898
Single-game home record, 64,168 (9/22/96)
Single-season home record, 474,244 (1994)

1996 TEAM STATISTICS

	Vikings	Opp.
Total First Downs	284	309
Rushing	75	117
Passing	186	169
Penalty	23	23
Third Down: Made/Att	101/240	70/211
Third Down Pct.	42.1	33.2
Fourth Down: Made/Att	3/5	10/17
Fourth Down Pct.	60.0	58.8
Total Net Yards	5204	5087
Avg. Per Game	325.3	317.9
Total Plays	1030	1025
Avg. Per Play	5.1	5.0
Net Yards Rushing	1546	1966
Avg. Per Game	96.6	122.9
Total Rushes	435	445
Net Yards Passing	3658	3121
Avg. Per Game	228.6	195.1
Sacked/Yards Lost	34/241	43/263
Gross Yards	3899	3384
Att./Completions	561/331	537/314
Completion Pct.	59.0	58.5
Had Intercepted	19	22
Punts/Avg.	90/40.2	84/42.8
Net Punting Avg.	90/32.4	84/37.6
Penalties/Yards Lost	106/835	105/840
Fumbles/Ball Lost	26/13	27/13
Touchdowns	33	36
Rushing	7	15
Passing	24	18
Returns	2	3
Avg. Time of Possession	30:14	29:46

1996 INDIVIDUAL STATISTICS

PASSING	Att.	Comp.	Yds.	Pct.	TD	Int.	Tkld.	Rate
B. Johnson	311	195	2258	62.7	17	10	15/119	89.4
Moon	247	134	1610	54.3	7	9	19/122	68.7
Walker	2	2	31	100.0	0	0	0/0	118.8
Walsh	1	0	0	0.0	0	0	0/0	39.6
Vikings	561	331	3899	59.0	24	19	34/241	80.4
Opponents	537	314	3384	58.5	18	22	43/263	71.2

SCORING	TD R	TD P	TD Rt	PAT	FG	Saf	PTS
Sisson	0	0	0	30/30	22/29	0	96
Carter	0	10	0	0/0	0/0	0	60
Reed	0	7	0	0/0	0/0	0	42
Hoard	3	0	0	0/0	0/0	0	18
Ismail	0	3	0	0/0	0/0	0	18
Rob. Smith	3	0	0	0/0	0/0	0	18
Lee	0	2	0	0/0	0/0	0	12
Walsh	0	1	0	0/0	0/0	0	8
Frisch	0	1	0	0/0	0/0	0	6
B. Johnson	1	0	0	0/0	0/0	0	6
Palmer	0	0	1	0/0	0/0	0	6
Washington	0	0	1	0/0	0/0	0	6
Jordan	0	0	0	0/0	0/0	0	2
Vikings	7	24	2	30/30	22/29	0	298
Opponents	15	18	3	33/33	20/30	2	315

2-Point conversions: Jordan, Walsh. Team: 2-3,
Opponents: 1-3.

RUSHING	Att.	Yds.	Avg.	LG	TD
Rob. Smith	162	692	4.3	57	3
Hoard	105	420	4.0	25	3
Lee	51	161	3.2	12	0
Graham	57	138	2.4	12	0
B. Johnson	34	90	2.6	13	1
Evans	13	29	2.2	9	0
Palmer	2	9	4.5	8	0
Moon	9	6	0.7	5	0
R. McDaniel	2	1	0.5	1	0
Vikings	435	1546	3.6	57	7
Opponents	445	1966	4.4	39	15

RECEIVING	No.	Yds.	Avg.	LG	TD
Carter	96	1163	12.1	43t	10
Reed	72	1320	18.3	82t	7
Lee	54	422	7.8	21	2
Ismail	22	351	16.0	54t	3
Evans	22	135	6.1	16	0
Jordan	19	128	6.7	15	0
Hoard	10	129	12.9	37	0
DeLong	8	34	4.3	9	0
Graham	7	48	6.9	18	0
Rob. Smith	7	39	5.6	16	0
Palmer	6	40	6.7	20	0
Walsh	4	39	9.8	17	1
Frisch	3	27	9.0	21	1
Goodwin	1	24	24.0	24	0
Vikings	331	3899	11.8	82t	24
Opponents	314	3384	10.8	80t	18

INTERCEPTIONS	No.	Yds.	Avg.	LG	TD
Thomas	5	57	11.4	34	0
Griffith	4	67	16.8	41	0
Brady	3	20	6.7	8	0
Fuller	3	3	1.0	2	0
Washington	2	27	13.5	27t	1
Jackson	2	4	2.0	4	0
Edwards	1	18	18.0	18	0
Talley	1	10	10.0	10	0
Fisk	1	0	0.0	0	0
Vikings	22	206	9.4	41	1
Opponents	19	339	17.8	75t	3

PUNTING	No.	Yds.	Avg.	In 20	LG
Berger	88	3616	41.1	26	63
Vikings	90	3616	40.2	26	63
Opponents	84	3596	42.8	37	68

PUNT RETURNS	No.	FC	Yds.	Avg.	LG	TD
Palmer	22	20	216	9.8	69t	1
Lee	10	11	84	8.4	18	0
Vikings	32	31	300	9.4	69t	1
Opponents	37	28	577	15.6	72	0

KICKOFF RETURNS	No.	Yds.	Avg.	LG	TD
Ismail	28	527	18.8	32	0
Palmer	13	292	22.5	60	0
Morrow	6	117	19.5	26	0
Lee	5	85	17.0	18	0
Brown	3	35	11.7	12	0
Carter	1	3	3.0	3	0
DeLong	1	3	3.0	3	0
Gerak	1	13	13.0	13	0
Vikings	58	1075	18.5	60	0
Opponents	53	1314	24.8	47	0

SACKS	No.
Randle	11.5
F. Smith	9.5
Harrison	7.0
Alexander	3.5
Edwards	3.5
Tuaolo	2.5
Griffith	2.0
Brady	1.5
Barnett	1.0
Fisk	1.0
Vikings	43.0
Opponents	34.0

1997 DRAFT CHOICES

Round	Name	Pos.	College
1	Dwayne Rudd	LB	Alabama
2	Torrian Gray	DB	Virginia Tech
3	Stalin Colinet	DE	Boston College
4	Antonio Banks	DB	Virginia Tech
5	Tony Williams	DT	Memphis
6	Robert Tate	WR	Cincinnati
7	Artie Ulmer	LB	Valdosta State
	Matthew Hatchette	WR	Langston

1997 VETERAN ROSTER

No.	Name	Pos.	Ht.	Wt.	Birthdate	NFL Exp.	College	Hometown	How Acq.	'96 Games/ Starts
90	Alexander, Derrick	DE	6-4	271	11/3/73	3	Florida State	Jacksonville, Fla.	D1a-'95	12/9
56	Bercich, Pete	LB	6-1	238	12/23/71	3	Notre Dame	Joliet, Ill.	D7-'94	15/1
17	Berger, Mitch	P	6-2	220	6/24/72	2	Colorado	Vancouver, Canada	FA-'96	16/0
50	Brady, Jeff	LB	6-1	243	11/9/68	7	Kentucky	Melbourne, Ky.	UFA(TB)-'95	16/16
54	Briggs, Greg	LB	6-3	212	10/1/68	4	Texas Southern	Meadville, Miss.	FA-'97	14/0*
80	Carter, Cris	WR	6-3	208	11/25/65	11	Ohio State	Middletown, Ohio	W(Phil)-'90	16/16
62	Christy, Jeff	C	6-3	282	2/3/69	5	Pittsburgh	Freeport, Pa.	FA-'93	16/16
92	Clemons, Duane	DE	6-5	285	5/23/74	2	California	Riverside, Calif.	D1-'96	13/0
7	Cunningham, Randall	QB	6-4	205	3/27/63	12	Nevada-Las Vegas	Santa Barbara, Calif.	FA-'97	0*
5	Davis, Greg	K	6-0	205	10/29/65	11	The Citadel	Atlanta, Ga.	FA-'97	9/0*
85	DeLong, Greg	TE	6-4	251	4/3/73	3	North Carolina	Orefield, Pa.	FA-'95	16/8
76	Dill, Scott	T	6-5	294	4/5/66	10	Memphis	Birmingham, Ala.	FA-'96	9/1
71	Dixon, David	G	6-5	348	1/5/69	4	Arizona State	Auckland, New Zealand	FA-'94	13/6
59	Edwards, Dixon	LB	6-1	228	3/25/68	7	Michigan State	Cincinnati, Ohio	UFA(Dall)-'96	14/13
38	Ellis, Kwame	CB	5-10	188	2/27/74	2	Stanford	Oakland, Calif.	FA-'96	8/0*
29	Evans, Charles	RB	6-1	244	4/16/67	5	Clark	Augusta, Ga.	D11-'92	16/6
72	Fisk, Jason	DT	6-3	291	9/4/72	3	Stanford	Davis, Calif.	D7b-'95	16/6
83	Frisch, David	TE	6-7	260	6/22/70	5	Colorado State	House Springs, Mo.	FA-'96	10/1
27	Fuller, Corey	CB	5-10	205	5/11/71	3	Florida State	Rickards, Fla.	D2b-'95	16/14
87	Goodwin, Hunter	TE	6-5	274	10/10/72	2	Texas A&M	Bellville, Tex	D4-'96	9/6
24	Griffith, Robert	S	5-11	189	11/30/70	4	San Diego State	San Diego, Calif.	FA-'94	14/14
51	Hanks, Ben	LB	6-2	222	7/31/72	2	Florida	Miami, Fla.	FA-'96	12/0
44	Hoard, Leroy	RB	5-11	225	5/15/68	8	Michigan	New Orleans, La.	FA-'96	6/6
14	Johnson, Brad	QB	6-5	219	9/13/68	6	Florida State	Black Mountain, N.C.	D9a-'92	12/8
35	Johnson, Chris	S	6-0	199	8/7/71	2	San Diego State	San Diego, Calif.	FA-'96	5/0
89	Jordan, Andrew	TE	6-4	254	6/21/72	4	Western Carolina	Charlotte, N.C.	D6-'94	13/9
61	Lindsay, Everett	G-C	6-4	290	9/18/70	4	Mississippi	Raleigh, N.C.	D5'-93	0*
48	Maddox, Markco	CB	6-2	214	9/2/71	2	Albany State	Albany, Ga.	FA-'96	0*
75	Manley, James	DT	6-2	305	7/11/74	2	Vanderbilt	Birmingham, Ala.	D2-'96	0*
58	McDaniel, Ed	LB	5-11	230	2/23/69	6	Clemson	Battesburgh, S.C.	D5-'92	0*
64	McDaniel, Randall	G	6-3	278	12/19/64	10	Arizona State	Avondale, Ariz.	D1-'88	16/16
97	McIntosh, Toddrick	DL	6-3	270	1/22/72	3	Florida State	Richardson, Tex.	FA-'97	0*
68	Morris, Mike	C	6-5	276	2/22/61	11	Northeast Missouri State	Centerville, Iowa	FA-'91	16/0
33	Morrow, Harold	RB	5-11	210	2/24/73	2	Auburn	Maplesville, Ala.	W(Dall)-'96	8/0
22	Palmer, David	WR	5-8	169	11/19/72	4	Alabama	Birmingham, Ala.	D2a-'94	11/1
40	Prior, Anthony	CB	5-11	185	3/27/70	4	Washington State	Riverside, Calif.	FA-'97	3/0
93	Randle, John	DT	6-1	282	12/12/67	8	Texas A&I	Hearne, Tex.	FA-'90	16/16
86	Reed, Jake	WR	6-3	216	9/28/67	7	Grambling State	Covington, Ga.	D3b-'91	16/15
9	Sisson, Scott	K	6-0	196	7/21/71	3	Georgia Tech	Marietta, Ga.	FA-'96	16/0
95	Smith, Fernando	DE	6-6	277	8/2/71	4	Jackson State	Flint, Mich.	D2b-'94	16/16
26	Smith, Robert	RB	6-2	212	3/4/72	5	Ohio State	Euclid, Ohio	D1-'93	8/7
73	Steussie, Todd	T	6-6	309	12/1/70	4	California	Canoga Park, Calif.	D1b-'94	16/16
28	Stewart, James	RB	6-2	246	12/8/71	3	Miami	Vero Beach, Fla.	D5-'95	0*
77	Stringer, Korey	T	6-4	353	5/8/74	3	Ohio State	Warren, Ohio	D1b-'95	16/15
43	Thomas, Orlando	S	6-1	211	10/21/72	3	Southwestern Louisiana	Crowley, La.	D2a-'95	16/16
6	Walker, Jay	QB	6-3	229	1/24/72	3	Howard	Los Angeles, Calif.	FA-'96	1/0
81	Walsh, Chris	WR	6-1	198	12/12/68	5	Stanford	Concord, Calif.	FA-'94	15/0
20	Washington, Dewayne	CB	5-11	186	12/27/72	4	North Carolina State	Durham, N.C.	D1a-'94	16/16
21	Williams, Moe	RB	6-1	196	7/26/74	2	Kentucky	Columbus, Ga.	D3-'96	9/0

* Briggs played in 14 games with Chicago in '96; Cunningham last active with Philadelphia in '95; Davis played 9 games with Arizona; Ellis played 8 games with N.Y. Jets; Lindsay, Maddox, E. McDaniel and Stewart missed '96 season because of injury; Manley was inactive for 2 game; McIntosh last active with Tampa Bay in '95.

Players lost through free agency (4): G John Gerak (StL; 14 games in '96), RB Scottie Graham (Cin; 11), DE Martin Harrison (Sea; 16), T Ariel Solomon (Det; 16).

Also played with Vikings in '96—CB Tomur Barnes (2 games), S Harlon Barnett (16), LB Richard Brown (14), LB Dave Garnett (12), DL Robert Goff (5), DB Steve Hall (1), WR Qadry Ismail (16), CB Alfred Jackson (14), RB Amp Lee (16), QB Warren Moon (8), LB Darryl Talley (12), NT Esera Tuaolo (14), CB Sean Vanhorse (9).

COACHING STAFF

Head Coach
Dennis Green

Pro Career: Named the fifth head coach in Vikings history on January 10, 1992, Green is one of only seven people in the history of the league to lead his team to the playoffs in each of his first three seasons as an NFL head coach. He also won two NFC Central titles in his first three seasons in Minnesota. In 1994, NFL Commissioner Paul Tagliabue appointed Green to the league's Competition Committee. His best coaching job may have come in 1996, when he made key lineup changes with six games remaining that propelled Minnesota to win four of five games and earn a wild-card playoff berth. In '92, Green led the Vikings to their best record (11-5) and first division title under a first-year head coach. He earned NFL coach of the year honors from the Washington Touchdown Club and NFC coach of the year honors from *United Press International* and *College & Pro Football Newsweekly*. As receivers coach at San Francisco from 1986-88, Green developed Pro Bowl players Jerry Rice and John Taylor. Green's first pro coaching opportunity came as special teams coach for the 49ers in 1979. Green briefly played defensive back with British Columbia (CFL) in 1971. Career record: 47-37.

Background: A running back at Iowa from 1968-70, Green began his coaching career as a graduate assistant for Iowa in 1972. He coached running backs and receivers at Dayton in 1973 then running backs and receivers at Iowa from 1974-76. Green worked with running backs at Stanford in 1977-78. He returned to Stanford as offensive coordinator in 1980 then was head coach at Northwestern from 1981-85. Green was named Big Ten coach of the year in 1982. As head coach at Stanford from 1989-91, he led the school to the 1991 Aloha Bowl, its first bowl game since 1986.

Personal: Born February 17, 1949 in Harrisburg, Pa., Green earned his degree in recreation from Iowa. He and his wife, Marie, live in Minnetonka, Minn. with their daughter Vanessa. Green also has a daughter Patti and a son Jeremy.

ASSISTANT COACHES

Dave Atkins, tight ends; born May 18, 1949, Victoria, Tex., lives in Eden Prairie, Minn. Running back Texas-El Paso 1970-72. Pro running back San Francisco 49ers 1973, Honolulu Hawaiians (WFL) 1974, San Diego Chargers 1975. College coach: Texas-El Paso 1979-80, San Diego State 1981-85. Pro coach: Philadelphia Eagles 1986-92, New England Patriots 1993, Arizona Cardinals 1994-95, New Orleans Saints 1996, joined Vikings in 1997.

Brian Billick, offensive coordinator; born February 28, 1954, Redlands, Calif., lives in Eden Prairie, Minn. Tight end Brigham Young 1974-76. Pro tight end Dallas Cowboys 1977. College coach: Brigham Young 1977, Redlands 1979, San Diego State 1981-85, Utah State 1986-88, Stanford 1989-91. Pro coach: Joined Vikings in 1992.

Foge Fazio, defensive coordinator; born February 28, 1939, Dawmont, W.Va., lives in Eden Prairie, Minn. Linebacker-center Pittsburgh 1957-60. No pro playing experience. College coach: Boston University 1967, Harvard 1968, Pittsburgh 1969-72, 1977-81, 1982-85 (head coach), Cincinnati 1973-76, Notre Dame 1986-87. Pro coach: Atlanta Falcons 1988-89, New York Jets 1990-94, joined Vikings in 1995.

Jeff Friday, assistant strength and conditioning; born October 11, 1966, Milwaukee, Wis., lives in Eden Prairie, Minn. No college or pro playing experience. College coach: Illinois State 1991-92, Northwestern 1992-95. Pro coach: Joined Vikings in 1996.

Carl Hargrave, running backs; born November 8, 1954, Frankfurt, Germany, lives in Eden Prairie, Minn. Defensive back Upper Iowa 1972-75. No pro playing experience. College coach: Upper Iowa 1977-80, Northwestern 1981-85, Pittsburgh 1986, Houston 1987-91, Iowa 1992-93. Pro coach: Joined Vikings in 1994.

Wade Harman, coaching asst.; born October 1, 1963, Corydon, Ia., lives in Eden Prairie, Minn. Linebacker Drake 1985, Utah State 1986. College coach: Utah State 1987-91, Pacific 1992-95, Morningside 1996. Pro coach: Joined Vikings in 1997.

John Levra, defensive line; born October 2, 1937, Arma, Kan., lives in Eden Prairie, Minn. Guard-linebacker Pittsburg (Kan.) State 1963-65. No pro playing experience. College coach: New Mexico Highlands 1966-70, Stephen F. Austin 1971-74, Kansas 1975-78, North Texas State 1979. Pro coach: British Columbia Lions (CFL) 1980, New Orleans Saints 1981-85, Chicago Bears 1986-92, Denver Broncos 1993-94, joined Vikings in 1995.

Chip Myers, wide receivers; born July 9, 1945, Panama City, Fla., lives in Eden Prairie, Minn. Receiver Northwestern Oklahoma 1964-66. Pro receiver San Francisco 49ers 1967, Cincinnati Bengals 1969-76. College coach: Illinois 1980-82. Pro coach: Tampa Bay Buccaneers 1983-84, Indianapolis Colts 1985-88, New York Jets 1990-93, New Orleans Saints 1994, joined Vikings in 1995.

Tom Olivadotti, inside linebackers; born September 22, 1945, Long Branch, N.J., lives in Eden Prairie, Minn. Defensive back-wide receiver Upsala 1963-66. No pro playing experience. College coach: Princeton 1975-77, Boston College 1978-79, Miami 1980-83. Pro coach: Cleveland Browns 1985-86, Miami Dolphins 1987-95, joined Vikings in 1996.

Ray Sherman, quarterbacks; born November 27, 1951, Berkeley, Calif., lives in Eden Prairie, Minn. Wide receiver Laney (Calif.) J.C. 1969-70, Fresno State 1971-72. Pro defensive back Green Bay Packers 1973. College coach: San Jose State 1974, California 1975, 1981, Michigan State 1976-77, Wake Forest 1978-80, Purdue 1982-85, Georgia 1986-87. Pro coach: Houston Oilers 1988-89, San Francisco 49ers 1991-93, New York Jets 1994, joined Vikings in 1995.

Richard Solomon, defensive backs; born December 8, 1949, New Orleans, La., lives in Eden Prairie, Minn. Running back-defensive back Iowa 1970-73. No pro playing experience. College coach: Dubuque 1973-75, Southern Illinois 1976, Iowa 1977-78, Syracuse 1979, Illinois 1980-86. Pro coach: New York Giants 1987-91 (scout), joined Vikings in 1992.

Mike Tice, offensive line; born February 2, 1959, Bayshore, N.Y., lives in Eden Prairie, Minn. Quarterback Maryland 1977-80. Pro tight end Seattle Seahawks 1981-88, 1990-91, Washington Redskins 1989, Minnesota Vikings 1992-93, 1995. Pro coach: Joined Vikings in 1996.

Trent Walters, outside linebackers; born November 20, 1943, Knoxville, Tenn., lives in Eden Prairie, Minn. Defensive back Indiana 1963-65. Pro defensive back Edmonton Eskimos (CFL) 1966-67. College coach: Indiana 1968-71, Louisville 1972, Indiana 1973-80, Washington 1981-83, Pittsburgh 1985, Louisville 1986-90, Texas A&M 1991-93. Pro coach: Cincinnati Bengals 1984, joined Vikings in 1994.

Steve Wetzel, strength and conditioning; born May 11, 1963, Washington D.C., lives in Eden Prairie, Minn. No college or pro playing experience. College coach: Maryland 1985-89, George Mason 1990. Pro coach: Washington Redskins 1990-91, joined Vikings in 1996.

Gary Zauner, special teams; born November 2, 1950, Milwaukee, Wis., lives in Eden Prairie, Minn. Kicker Wisconsin-LaCrosse 1968-72. No pro playing experience. College coach: Brigham Young 1979-80, San Diego State 1981-86, New Mexico 1987-88, Long Beach State 1990-91. Pro coach: Joined Vikings in 1994.

1997 FIRST-YEAR ROSTER

Name	Pos.	Ht.	Wt.	Birthdate	College	Hometown	How Acq.
Alexander, Rod (1)	WR	6-0	195	10/30/71	Northern Arizona	San Diego, Calif.	FA
Ayanbadejo, Obafemi	RB	6-2	230	3/5/75	San Diego State	Santa Cruz, Calif.	FA
Banks, Antonio	CB	5-10	195	3/12/73	Virginia Tech	Newport News, Va.	D4
Bland, Tony (1)	WR	6-3	213	12/12/72	Florida A&M	St. Petersburg, Fla.	FA-'96
Bobo, Orlando (1)	G	6-3	304	2/9/74	Northeast Louisiana	West Point, Miss.	FA-'96
Bouman, Todd	QB	6-2	195	8/1/72	St. Cloud State	Ruthton, Minn.	FA
Bussey, Kendall (1)	RB	6-1	230	2/14/73	Northeast Louisiana	Marrero, La.	FA
Colinet, Stalin	DE	6-6	288	7/19/74	Boston College	New York, N.Y.	D3
Daniels, LeShun	G	6-1	304	5/30/74	Ohio State	Warren, Ohio	FA
Davis, Robert (1)	CB	5-9	188	8/6/72	Vanderbilt	Nashville, Tenn.	FA
Emanuel, Charles	S	6-0	196	6/3/73	West Virginia	Indiantown, Fla.	FA
Gray, Torrian	S	6-0	200	3/18/74	Virginia Tech	Lakeland, Fla.	D2
Hatchette, Matthew	WR	6-2	195	5/1/74	Langston	Cleveland, Ohio	D7b
Jones, Clarence (1)	WR	6-0	184	3/12/73	Tennessee State	Vero Beach, Fla.	FA
Kurz, Todd	P	6-3	218	4/20/74	Illinois State	Bloomington, Ill.	FA
Lynch, Ben (1)	C	6-3	291	11/18/71	California	Sebastapol, Calif.	FA
McDaniel, Kenneth (1)	G-T	6-3	322	12/20/73	Norfolk State	Mechanicsville, Va.	FA-'96
McKinney, Anthony	TE	6-2	240	12/8/74	Connecticut	Fairfield, Conn.	FA
Ned, Kevin	G	6-3	338	7/19/74	New Mexico	Houston, Tex.	FA
Rudd, Dwayne	LB	6-2	241	2/3/76	Alabama	South Panola, Miss.	D1
Stansberry, Allen	LB	6-0	225	9/10/74	Louisiana State	Baton Rouge, La.	FA
Tate, Robert	WR	5-10	185	10/19/73	Cincinnati	Harrisburg, Pa.	D6
Ulmer, Artie	LB	6-2	239	7/20/73	Valdosta State	Rincon, Ga.	D7a
Wilcox, Josh	TE	6-2	253	6/5/74	Oregon	Junction City, Ore.	FA
Williams, Tony	DT	6-5	292	7/9/75	Memphis	Germantown, Tenn.	D5

The term NFL Rookie is defined as a player who is in his first season of professional football and has not been on the roster of another professional football team for any regular-season or postseason games. A Rookie is designated by an "R" on NFL rosters. Players who have been active in another professional football league or players who have NFL experience, including either preseason training camp or being on an Active List or Inactive List, or on Reserve/Injured or Reserve/Physically Unable to Perform for fewer than six regular-season games, are termed NFL First-Year Players. An NFL First-Year Player is designated by a "1" on NFL rosters. Thereafter, a player is credited with an additional year of experience for each season in which he accumulates six games on the Active List or Inactive List, or on Reserve/Injured or Reserve/Physically Unable to Perform.

NOTES

_____

_____

_____

_____

_____

_____

National Football Conference
Western Division
Team Colors: Old Gold, Black, and White
5800 Airline Highway
Metairie, Louisiana 70003
Telephone: (504) 733-0255

CLUB OFFICIALS

Owner: Tom Benson
President, General Manager,
  & Chief Operating Officer: Bill Kuharich
Senior Vice President of Marketing &
  Administration: Greg Suit
Vice President & Director of Football Operations:
  Chet Franklin
Director of College Scouting: Bruce Lemmerman
Treasurer: Bruce Broussard
Administrative Coordinator/Director of Player
  Programs: Austin Dejan
Comptroller: Charleen Sharpe
Director of Corporate Sales: Bill Ferrante
Director of Media and Public Relations:
  Greg Bensel
Assistant Director of Media and Public Relations:
  Robert Gunn
Data Processing Manager: Jay Romig
Director of Travel/Entertainment/Special Projects:
  Barra Birrcher
Player Personnel Scouts: Marty Barrett,
  Hamp Cook, Hokie Gajan, Tom Marino
Director of Ticket Sales: Greg Seeling
Trainer: Dean Kleinschmidt
Equipment Manager: Dan Simmons
Video Director: Joe Malota
Stadium: Louisiana Superdome
  •Capacity: 69,420
  1500 Poydras Street
  New Orleans, Louisiana 70112
Playing Surface: AstroTurf
Training Camp: University of Wisconsin-La Crosse
  La Crosse, Wisconsin 54601

1997 SCHEDULE
PRESEASON

Aug. 2	vs. Tennessee at Memphis, Tenn.	7:00
Aug. 9	**Kansas City**	7:00
Aug. 16	at Oakland	1:00
Aug. 22	at Chicago	7:30

REGULAR SEASON

Aug. 31	at St. Louis	12:00
Sept. 7	**San Diego**	12:00
Sept. 14	at San Francisco	1:00
Sept. 21	**Detroit**	12:00
Sept. 28	at New York Giants	1:00
Oct. 5	at Chicago	7:00
Oct. 12	**Atlanta**	12:00
Oct. 19	**Carolina**	12:00
Oct. 26	**San Francisco**	12:00
Nov. 2	Open Date	
Nov. 9	at Oakland	1:00
Nov. 16	**Seattle**	12:00
Nov. 23	at Atlanta	1:00
Nov. 30	at Carolina	1:00
Dec. 7	**St. Louis**	12:00
Dec. 14	**Arizona**	3:00
Dec. 21	at Kansas City	12:00

RECORD HOLDERS
INDIVIDUAL RECORDS—CAREER

Category	Name	Performance
Rushing (Yds.)	George Rogers, 1981-84	4,267
Passing (Yds.)	Archie Manning, 1971-1982	21,734
Passing (TDs)	Archie Manning, 1971-1982	115
Receiving (No.)	Eric Martin, 1985-1993	532
Receiving (Yds.)	Eric Martin, 1985-1993	7,854
Interceptions	Dave Waymer, 1980-89	37
Punting (Avg.)	Tommy Barnhardt, 1987, 1989-1994	43.0
Punt Return (Avg.)	Mel Gray, 1986-88	13.4
Kickoff Return (Avg.)	Walter Roberts, 1967	26.3
Field Goals	Morten Andersen, 1982-1994	302
Touchdowns (Tot.)	Dalton Hilliard, 1986-1993	53
Points	Morten Andersen, 1982-1994	1,318

INDIVIDUAL RECORDS—SINGLE SEASON

Category	Name	Performance
Rushing (Yds.)	George Rogers, 1981	1,674
Passing (Yds.)	Jim Everett, 1995	3,970
Passing (TDs)	Jim Everett, 1995	26
Receiving (No.)	Eric Martin, 1988	85
Receiving (Yds.)	Eric Martin, 1989	1,090
Interceptions	Dave Whitsell, 1967	10
Punting (Avg.)	Tommy Barnhardt, 1992	44.0
Punt Return (Avg.)	Mel Gray, 1987	14.7
Kickoff Return (Avg.)	Don Shy, 1969	27.9
	Mel Gray, 1986	27.9
Field Goals	Morten Andersen, 1985	31
Touchdowns (Tot.)	Dalton Hilliard, 1989	18
Points	Morten Andersen, 1987	121

INDIVIDUAL RECORDS—SINGLE GAME

Category	Name	Performance
Rushing (Yds.)	George Rogers, 9-4-83	206
Passing (Yds.)	Archie Manning, 12-7-80	377
Passing (TDs)	Billy Kilmer, 11-2-69	6
Receiving (No.)	Tony Galbreath, 9-10-78	14
Receiving (Yds.)	Wes Chandler, 9-2-79	205
Interceptions	Tommy Myers, 9-3-78	3
	Dave Waymer, 10-6-85	3
	Reggie Sutton, 10-18-87	3
	Gene Atkins, 12-22-91	3
Field Goals	Many times	5
	Last time by Morten Andersen, 12-11-94	
Touchdowns (Tot.)	Many times	3
	Last time by Mario Bates, 12-4-94	
Points	Many times	18
	Last time by Mario Bates, 12-4-94	

COACHING HISTORY
(177-272-5)

1967-70	Tom Fears*	13-34-2
1970-72	J.D. Roberts	7-25-3
1973-75	John North**	11-23-0
1975	Ernie Hefferle	1-7-0
1976-77	Hank Stram	7-21-0
1978-80	Dick Nolan***	15-29-0
1980	Dick Stanfel	1-3-0
1981-85	O.A. (Bum) Phillips****	27-42-0
1985	Wade Phillips	1-3-0
1986-96	Jim Mora#	93-78-0
1996	Rick Venturi	1-7-0

  *Released after seven games in 1970
 **Released after six games in 1975
***Released after 12 games in 1980
****Resigned after 12 games in 1985
  #Resigned after 8 games in 1996

LOUISIANA SUPERDOME

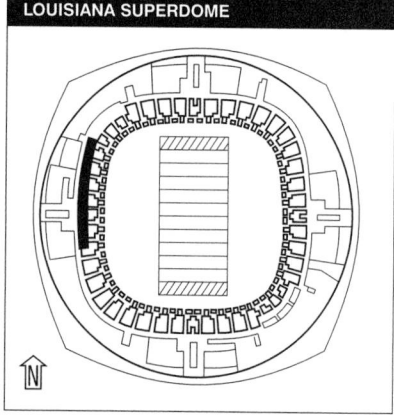

1996 TEAM RECORD

PRESEASON (3-2)

Date	Result		Opponents
7/27	L	3-10	vs. Indianapolis at Canton, Ohio
8/2	W	23-22	at Detroit
8/10	L	6-42	at Kansas City
8/17	W	31-21	Chicago
8/23	W	16-13	Minnesota

REGULAR SEASON (3-13)

Date	Result		Opponents	Att.
9/1	L	11-27	at San Francisco	63,970
9/8	L	20-22	Carolina	43,288
9/15	L	15-30	at Cincinnati	45,412
9/22	L	14-28	Arizona	34,316
9/29	L	10-17	at Baltimore	61,063
10/6	W	17-13	Jacksonville	34,231
10/13	W	27-24	Chicago	43,512
10/20	L	7-19	at Carolina	70,888
11/3	L	17-24	San Francisco	53,297
11/10	L	14-31	Houston	34,121
11/17	L	15-17	at Atlanta	43,119
11/24	L	7-13	at Tampa Bay	40,203
12/1	L	10-26	St. Louis	26,310
12/8	L	15-31	Atlanta	32,923
12/15	W	17-3	at N.Y. Giants	52,530
12/21	L	13-14	at St. Louis	57,681

SCORE BY PERIODS

Saints	42	58	38	91	—	229
Opponents	80	105	78	76	—	339

ATTENDANCE

Home 301,998   Away 434,866   Total 736,864
Single-game home record, 70,940 (9/2/79)
Single-season home record, 548,728 (1992)

1996 TEAM STATISTICS

	Saints	Opp.
Total First Downs	232	287
Rushing	77	104
Passing	135	152
Penalty	20	31
Third Down: Made/Att	65/207	85/232
Third Down Pct.	31.4	36.6
Fourth Down: Made/Att	6/19	9/16
Fourth Down Pct.	31.6	56.3
Total Net Yards	4206	4910
Avg. Per Game	262.9	306.9
Total Plays	923	1027
Avg. Per Play	4.6	4.8
Net Yards Rushing	1308	2076
Avg. Per Game	81.8	129.8
Total Rushes	386	521
Net Yards Passing	2898	2834
Avg. Per Game	181.7	177.1
Sacked/Yards Lost	22/171	41/283
Gross Yards	3069	3117
Att./Completions	515/295	465/267
Completion Pct.	57.3	57.4
Had Intercepted	17	12
Punts/Avg.	87/40.8	74/43.0
Net Punting Avg.	87/32.5	74/40.1
Penalties/Yards Lost	114/853	102/823
Fumbles/Ball Lost	30/20	25/10
Touchdowns	24	34
Rushing	10	11
Passing	13	22
Returns	1	1
Avg. Time of Possession	27:33	32:27

1996 INDIVIDUAL STATISTICS

PASSING

	Att.	Comp.	Yds.	Pct.	TD	Int.	Tkld.	Rate
Everett	464	267	2797	57.5	12	16	19/154	69.4
Nussmeier	50	28	272	56.0	1	1	3/17	69.8
Ea. Hunter	1	0	0	0.0	0	0	0	39.6
Saints	515	295	3069	57.3	13	17	22/171	69.3
Opponents	465	267	3117	57.4	22	12	41/283	82.9

SCORING

	TD R	TD P	TD Rt	PAT	FG	Saf	PTS
Brien	0	0	0	18/18	21/25	0	81
Haynes	0	4	0	0/0	0/0	0	26
Bates	4	0	0	0/0	0/0	0	24
Zellars	4	0	0	0/0	0/0	0	24
Jeffries	0	3	0	0/0	0/0	0	18
Small	1	2	0	0/0	0/0	0	18
Neal	1	1	0	0/0	0/0	0	12
DeRamus	0	1	0	0/0	0/0	0	6
Guess	0	1	0	0/0	0/0	0	6
T. Johnson	0	1	0	0/0	0/0	0	6
B. Jones	0	0	1	0/0	0/0	0	6
Wilmsmeyer	0	0	0	0/0	0/0	0	2
Saints	10	13	1	18/18	21/25	0	229
Opponents	11	22	1	32/32	33/42	0	339

2-Point conversions: Haynes, Wilmsmeyer. Team: 2-6, Opponents: 2-2.

RUSHING

	Att.	Yds.	Avg.	LG	TD
Bates	164	584	3.6	33	4
Zellars	120	475	4.0	63	4
Neal	21	58	2.8	11	1
Whittle	20	52	2.6	15	0
Small	4	51	12.8	22	1
Ea. Hunter	14	44	3.1	9	0
Brown	13	30	2.3	12	0
Hayes	2	7	3.5	5	0
Nussmeier	3	6	2.0	6	0
Everett	22	3	0.1	3	0
DeRamus	1	2	2.0	2	0
Guess	2	-4	-2.0	-1	0
Saints	386	1308	3.4	63	10
Opponents	521	2076	4.0	70t	11

RECEIVING

	No.	Yds.	Avg.	LG	TD
Small	50	558	11.2	41	2
Haynes	44	786	17.9	51	4
Neal	31	194	6.3	23	1
Lusk	27	210	7.8	24	0
Whittle	26	162	6.2	28	0
Jeffries	20	215	10.8	27t	3
Ea. Hunter	17	138	8.1	22	0
DeRamus	15	182	12.1	28t	1
I. Smith	15	144	9.6	37	0
Bates	13	44	3.4	15	0
Zellars	9	45	5.0	12	0
Brown	8	54	6.8	18	0
Green	7	91	13.0	23	0
T. Johnson	7	76	10.9	17	1
Hayes	4	101	25.3	50	0
Guess	2	69	34.5	57t	1
Saints	295	3069	10.4	57t	13
Opponents	267	3117	11.7	70	22

INTERCEPTIONS

	No.	Yds.	Avg.	LG	TD
Newman	3	40	13.3	21	0
Jackson	3	24	8.0	10	0
McMillian	2	4	2.0	4	0
Molden	2	2	1.0	2	0
Allen	1	33	33.0	33	0
Tubbs	1	11	11.0	11	0
Saints	12	114	9.5	33	0
Opponents	17	93	5.5	35	0

PUNTING

	No.	Yds.	Avg.	In 20	LG
Wilmsmeyer	87	3551	40.8	16	63
Saints	87	3551	40.8	16	63
Opponents	74	3184	43.0	25	67

PUNT RETURNS

	No.	FC	Yds.	Avg.	LG	TD
Hughes	30	20	152	5.1	16	0
Guess	1	0	7	7.0	7	0
Saints	31	20	159	5.1	16	0
Opponents	43	21	546	12.7	84t	1

KICKOFF RETURNS

	No.	Yds.	Avg.	LG	TD
Hughes	70	1791	25.6	58	0
Hayes	2	30	15.0	17	0
B. Smith	2	14	7.0	8	0
Brown	1	10	10.0	10	0
Ea. Hunter	1	20	20.0	20	0
Lusk	1	16	16.0	16	0
McCleskey	1	18	18.0	18	0
Saints	78	1899	24.3	58	0
Opponents	52	1155	22.2	71	0

SACKS

	No.
Martin	11.0
J. Johnson	7.5
Turnbull	6.5
Mickell	3.0
Broughton	2.0
Fields	2.0
Harvey	2.0
Molden	2.0
B. Smith	2.0
Robbins	1.0
Stokes	1.0
Tubbs	1.0
Saints	41.0
Opponents	22.0

1997 DRAFT CHOICES

Round	Name	Pos.	College
1	Chris Naeole	G	Colorado
2	Rob Kelly	DB	Ohio State
	Jared Tomich	DE	Nebraska
3	Troy Davis	RB	Iowa State
4	Danny Wuerffel	QB	Florida
	Keith Poole	WR	Arizona State
6	Nicky Savoie	TE	Louisiana State

1997 VETERAN ROSTER

No.	Name	Pos.	Ht.	Wt.	Birthdate	NFL Exp.	College	Hometown	How Acq.	'96 Games/ Starts
69	Ackerman, Tom	C-G	6-3	290	9/6/72	2	Eastern Washington	Nooksack, Wash.	D5b-'96	2/0
27	Adams, Vashone	CB-S	5-10	196	9/12/73	2	Eastern Michigan	Aurora, Colo.	FA-'97	15/2*
21	Allen, Eric	CB	5-10	180	11/22/65	10	Arizona State	San Diego, Calif.	UFA(Phil)-'95	16/16
24	† Bates, Mario	RB	6-1	217	1/16/73	4	Arizona State	Tucson, Ariz.	D2-'94	14/10
75	Belin, Chuck	G	6-2	305	10/27/70	5	Wisconsin	Milwaukee, Wis.	FA-'97	1/0*
40	Bender, Wes	RB	5-10	230	8/2/70	2	Southern California	Burbank, Calif.	FA-'97	0*
10	† Brien, Doug	K	6-0	180	11/24/70	4	California	Concord, Calif.	FA-'95	16/0
99	Broughton, Willie	DT	6-5	285	9/9/64	11	Miami	Ft. Pierce, Fla.	T(Oak)-'95	14/5
22	Brown, Derek	RB	5-9	205	4/15/71	5	Nebraska	Anaheim, Calif.	D4b-'93	11/0
37	Cherry, Je'Rod	S	6-0	196	5/30/73	2	California	Berkely, Calif.	D2-'96	13/0
53	Davis, Don	LB	6-1	240	12/17/72	2	Kansas	Olathe, Kan.	FA-'96	11/0
87	DeRamus, Lee	WR	6-0	205	8/24/72	3	Wisconsin	Atco, N.J.	D6-'95	15/4
55	Fields, Mark	LB	6-2	244	11/9/72	3	Washington State	Cerritos, Calif.	D1-'95	16/15
60	Fontenot, Jerry	C	6-3	290	11/21/66	8	Texas A&M	Lafayette, La.	UFA(Chi)-'97	16/16*
62	Gammon, Kendall	C	6-4	288	10/23/68	6	Pittsburg State	Rose Hill, Kan.	FA-'96	16/0
85	Green, Paul	TE	6-3	253	10/8/66	5	Southern California	Clovis, Calif.	FA-'96	14/5
18	Guess, Terry	WR	6-0	200	9/22/74	2	Gardner-Webb	Orangeburg, S.C.	D5c-'96	3/2
84	Guliford, Eric	WR	5-8	165	10/25/69	4	Arizona State	Peoria, Ariz.	FA-'97	0*
52	Harvey, Richard	LB	6-1	242	9/11/66	8	Tulane	Pascagoula, Miss.	UFA(Den)-'95	14/7
88	Hastings, Andre	WR	6-1	190	11/7/70	4	Georgia	Morrow, Ga.	UFA(Pitt)-'97	16/10*
89	Hayes, Mercury	WR	5-11	195	1/1/73	2	Michigan	Houston, Tex.	D5a-'96	7/0
81	Hill, Randal	WR	5-11	180	9/21/69	6	Miami	Miami, Fla.	UFA(Mia)-'97	14/5*
76	Hills, Keno	T	6-6	305	6/13/72	2	Southwestern Lousiana	Tampa, Fla.	D6a-'96	1/0
80	t- Hobbs, Daryl	WR	6-2	175	5/23/68	5	Pacific	Los Angeles, Calif.	T(Oak)-'97	16/1*
32	Hunter, Earnest	RB	5-8	201	12/21/70	3	Southeast Oklahoma	Longview, Tex.	FA-'96	6/0
94	Johnson, Joe	DT	6-4	270	7/11/72	4	Louisville	St. Louis, Mo.	D1-'94	13/13
86	Johnson, Tony	TE	6-5	255	2/5/72	2	Alabama	Como, Miss.	FA-'96	9/7
58	Jones, Brian	LB	6-1	250	1/22/68	4	Texas	Lubbock, Tex.	FA-'95	16/1
74	Jones, Clarence	T	6-6	280	5/6/68	7	Maryland	Central Islip, N.Y.	UFA(StL)-'96	16/16
61	King, Ed	G	6-4	300	12/3/69	6	Auburn	Phoenix City, Ala.	FA-'95	16/16
93	Martin, Wayne	DT	6-5	275	10/26/65	9	Arkansas	Cherry Valley, Ark.	D1-'89	16/16
67	McCollum, Andy	C-G	6-4	295	6/2/70	4	Toledo	Akron, Ohio	FA-'94	16/16
44	McCrary, Fred	RB	6-0	219	9/19/72	2	Mississippi State	Naples, Fla.	FA-'97	0*
92	Mickell, Darren	DE	6-4	291	8/3/70	6	Florida	Miami, Fla.	UFA(KC)-'96	12/12
30	Newman, Anthony	S	6-0	200	11/21/65	10	Oregon	Beaverton, Ore.	FA-'95	16/16
13	† Nussmeier, Doug	QB	6-3	211	12/11/70	4	Idaho	Lake Oswego, Ore.	D4-'94	2/1
77	Roaf, William	T	6-5	300	4/18/70	5	Lousiana Tech	Pine Bluff, Ark.	D1a-'93	13/13
95	† Robbins, Austin	DT	6-6	290	3/1/71	4	North Carolina	Washington, D.C.	T(Oak)-'96	15/7
3	Royals, Mark	P	6-5	215	6/22/64	8	Appalachian State	Mathews, Va.	FA-'97	16/0*
5	t- Shuler, Heath	QB	6-2	221	12/31/71	4	Tennessee	Bryson City, N.C.	T(Wash)-'97	1/0*
51	Sims, William	LB	6-4	271	12/30/70	2	Southwestern Louisiana	Quitman, Ga.	FA-'97	0*
91	Smith, Brady	DE	6-5	260	6/5/73	2	Colorado State	Barrington, Ill.	D3-'96	16/4
82	Smith, Irv	TE	6-3	246	10/13/71	5	Notre Dame	Pemberton, N.J.	D1b-'93	7/7
41	# Strong, William	CB	5-10	191	11/3/71	2	North Carolina State	Lewisville, S.C.	D5-'95	9/0
54	† Tubbs, Winfred	LB	6-4	250	9/24/70	4	Texas	Fairfield, Tex.	D3-'94	16/13
97	Turnbull, Renaldo	DE	6-4	250	1/5/66	8	West Virginia	St. Thomas, Virgin Islands	D1-'90	12/7
66	Verstegen, Mike	G-T	6-6	311	10/24/71	3	Wisconsin	Kimberly, Wis.	D3-'95	8/4
26	Washington, Mickey	CB	5-10	191	7/8/68	7	Texas A&M	Beaumont, Tex.	UFA(Jax)-'97	16/16*
23	Whittle, Ricky	RB	5-9	200	12/21/71	2	Oregon	Fresno, Calif.	D4-'96	10/0
63	Willis, Donald	C-G	6-3	330	7/15/73	3	North Carolina A&T	Lompoc, Calif.	FA-'96	4/0
34	Zellars, Ray	RB	5-11	233	3/25/73	3	Notre Dame	Pittsburgh, Pa.	D2-'95	9/6

* Adams played 15 games with Baltimore in '96; Belin played 1 game with St. Louis; Bender last active with Oakland in '95; Fontenot played 16 games with Chicago; Guliford last active with Carolina in '95; Hastings played 16 games with Pittsburgh; Hill played 14 games with Miami; Hobbs played 16 games with Oakland; McCrary last active with Philadelphia in '95; Royals played 16 games with Detroit; Shuler played 1 game with Washington; Sims last active with Minnesota in '95; Washington played 16 games with Jacksonville.

\# Unrestricted free agent; subject to developments.

† Restricted free agent; subject to developments.

t- Saints traded for Hobbs (Oakland) and Shuler (Washington).

Players lost through free agency (2): CB Tyrone Hughes (Chi; 16 games in '96), RB Lorenzo Neal (NYJ; 16).

Also played with Saints in '96—LB Ernest Dixon (16), G Jim Dombrowski (10), QB Jim Everett (15), WR Michael Haynes (16), S Derrick Hoskins (1), S Greg Jackson (16), WR Haywood Jeffires (9), S Sean Lumpkin (7), TE Hendrick Lusk (16), S J.J. McCleskey (5), CB Mark McMillan (16), G Craig Novitsky (16), DT Emile Palmer (1), LB Rufus Porter (13), WR Torrance Small (16), DE Fred Stokes (9), P Klaus Wilmsmeyer (16).

COACHING STAFF

Head Coach,
Mike Ditka

Pro Career: Named the twelfth head coach in Saints history in January. Ditka's 112 career victories are the fifth-most among active head coaches entering the 1997 season. He is one of just two people (Tom Flores) to have won a Super Bowl ring as a head coach, assistant coach, and player. All three of Ditka's Super Bowl triumphs have taken place in New Orleans. Came to New Orleans after a four-year stint as a broadcaster with NBC. Was head coach of the Chicago Bears for eleven seasons (1982-92). The Bears won the NFC Central Division five consecutive seasons (1984-88) and reached the playoffs seven times during his tenure. The 1985 Bears finished with a 15-1 record and won Super Bowl XX at the Superdome when they defeated the New England Patriots 46-10. Ditka began his pro coaching career as an assistant with the Dallas Cowboys (1973-81). The Cowboys won Super Bowl XII, at the Superdome, when they defeated the Denver Broncos 27-10. As a NFL player, Ditka was chosen in the first round with the fifth overall pick of the 1961 draft by the Chicago Bears. The tight end earned rookie of the year honors by hauling in 56 receptions. Was traded to Philadelphia and played for two seasons (1967-68). From 1969-72 Ditka played for the Cowboys. Dallas defeated Miami 24-3 to capture Super Bowl VI at Tulane Stadium in New Orleans. In that game, Ditka caught a 7-yard touchdown pass from Roger Staubach. Career record: 112-68.

Background: Played tight end at Pittsburgh (1958-60), where he earned all-America honors his senior season. Also played defensive end, linebacker, and ranked among the nation's top punters. Attended Aliquippa High School, where he lettered in football, baseball, and basketball.

Personal: Born October 18, 1939, in Carneige, Pa. Mike and his wife, Diana, live in Metairie, La., and have four children—sons Mike, Mark, and Matthew, and daughter Megan.

ASSISTANT COACHES

Danny Abramowicz, offensive coordinator; born July 13, 1945, Steubenville, Ohio, lives in New Orleans, La. Wide receiver Xavier 1964-66. Wide receiver New Orleans 1967-72, San Francisco 49ers 1973-74. No college coaching experience. Pro coach: Chicago Bears 1992-96, joined Saints in 1997.

Bobby April, special teams; born April 15, 1953, New Orleans, lives in Mandeville, La. Linebacker-defensive end Nicholls State 1972-75. College coach: Southern Mississippi 1978, Tulane 1979, Arizona 1980-86, Southern California 1987-90. Pro coach: Atlanta Falcons 1991-93, Pittsburgh Steelers 1994-95, joined Saints in 1996.

Tom Clements, quarterbacks; born June 18, 1953, McKees Rocks, Pa., lives in Harahan, La. Quarterback Notre Dame 1972-74. Pro quarterback Ottawa Rough Riders (CFL) 1975-78, Saskatchewan Roughriders (CFL) 1979, Hamilton Tiger-Cats (CFL) 1979, 1981-83, Kansas City Chiefs 1980, Winnipeg Blue Bombers (CFL) 1983-87. College coach: Notre Dame 1992-95. Pro coach: Joined Saints in 1996.

Walt Corey, defensive line; born May 9, 1938, Latrobe, Pa., lives in River Ridge, La. Defensive end Miami 1956-59. Pro linebacker Dallas Texans/Kansas City Chiefs 1960-66. College coach: Utah State 1967-69, Miami 1970, Coast Guard Academy 1995. Pro coach: Kansas City Chiefs 1971-74, 1978-86, Cleveland Browns 1975-77, Buffalo Bills 1987-94, joined Saints in 1997.

Jack Del Rio, asst. strength and conditioning; born April 4, 1963, Castro Valley, Calif., lives in New Orleans, La. Linebacker Southern California 1981-84. Pro linebacker New Orleans Saints 1985-86, Kansas City Chiefs 1987-88, Dallas Cowboys 1989-91, Minnesota Vikings 1992-95. No college coaching experience. Pro coach: Joined Saints in 1997.

Judd Garrett, offensive assistant; born June 25, 1967, Abington, Pa., lives in La Place, La. Running back Princeton 1987-89. Pro running back London

Monarchs (WLAF) 1991-92, Dallas Cowboys 1993, Las Vegas Posse (CFL) 1994, San Antonio Texans (CFL) 1995. College coach: Princeton 1990. Pro coach: Joined Saints in 1997.

Harold Jackson, wide receivers; born January 6, 1946, Hattiesburg, Miss., lives in River Ridge, La. Wide receiver Jackson State 1964-67. Pro wide receiver Los Angeles Rams 1968, 1973-77, Philadelphia Eagles 1969-72, New England Patriots 1978-81, Seattle Seahawks 1983. College coach: North Carolina Central 1990, Virginia Union 1994 (head coach), Benedict College 1995-96 (head coach). Pro coach: New England Patriots 1985-89, New Orleans Night (Arena League) 1991, Tampa Bay Buccaneers 1992-93, joined Saints in 1997.

Tom Moore, running backs; born November 7, 1938, Owatanna, Minn., lives in River Ridge, La. Quarterback Iowa 1957-60. No pro playing experience. College coach: Iowa 1961-62, Dayton 1965-68, Wake Forest 1969, Georgia Tech 1970-71, Minnesota 1972-73, 1975-76. Pro coach: New York Stars (WFL) 1974, Pittsburgh Steelers 1977-89, Minnesota Vikings 1990-93, Detroit Lions 1994-96, joined Saints in 1997.

Dan Neal, tight ends; born August 30, 1949, Corbin, Ky., lives in Harahan, La. Center Kentucky 1969-72. Pro center Baltimore Colts 1973-74, Chicago Bears 1975-83. College coach: Western Illinois 1996. Pro coach: Philadelphia Eagles 1986-91, Arizona Cardinals 1994-95, joined Saints in 1997.

John Pagano, defensive assistant; born March 30, 1967, Boulder, Colo., lives in Harahan, La. Linebacker Mesa College 1985-88. No pro playing experience. College coach: Mesa College 1989, Nevada-Las Vegas 1990-91, Louisiana Tech 1994, Mississippi 1995. Pro coach: Bergamo Lions (Italian League) 1992, joined Saints in 1996.

Willie Shaw, defensive backs; born January 11, 1944, Glenmora, La., lives in Kenner, La. Cornerback

New Mexico 1966-68. College coach: San Diego C.C. 1970-73, Stanford 1974-76, 1989-91, Long Beach State 1977-78, Oregon 1979, Arizona State 1980-84. Pro coach: Detroit Lions 1985-88, Minnesota Vikings 1992-93, San Diego Chargers 1994, St. Louis Rams 1995-96, joined Saints in 1997.

Dick Stanfel, offensive guard; born July 20, 1927, San Francisco, Calif., lives in River Ridge, La. Guard San Francisco 1948-50. Pro guard Detroit Lions 1951-55, Washington Redskins 1956-58. College coach: Notre Dame 1959-62, California 1963. Pro coach: Philadelphia Eagles 1964-70, San Francisco 49ers 1971-75, New Orleans Saints 1976-80 (interim head coach for four games, 1980), Chicago Bears 1981-92, rejoined Saints in 1997.

Rick Venturi, asst. head coach-linebackers; born February 23, 1946, Taylorville, Ill., lives in Destrehan, La. Quarterback-defensive back Northwestern 1965-67. No pro playing experience. College coach: Northwestern 1968-72, 1978-80 (head coach), Purdue 1973-76, Illinois 1977. Pro coach: Hamilton Tiger-Cats (CFL) 1981, Indianapolis Colts 1982-93 (interim head coach for final 11 games of 1991), Cleveland Browns 1994-95, joined Saints in 1996 (interim head coach for final eight games, 1996).

Mike Woicik, strength and conditioning; born September 26, 1956, Baltimore, Md., lives in Kenner, La. Attended Boston College. No college or pro playing experience. College coach: Springfield College 1978-79, Syracuse 1980-89. Pro coach: Dallas Cowboys 1990-96, joined Saints in 1997.

Zaven Yaralian, defensive coordinator; born February 5, 1952, Syria, lives in Metairie, La. Cornerback Nebraska 1972-73. Pro cornerback Green Bay Packers 1974, Philadelphia Bell (WFL) 1975. College coach: Nebraska 1975, Washington State 1976-77, Missouri 1978-82, Florida 1983-87, Colorado 1988-89. Pro coach: Chicago Bears 1990-92, New York Giants 1993-96, joined Saints in 1997.

1997 FIRST-YEAR ROSTER

Name	Pos.	Ht.	Wt.	Birthdate	College	Hometown	How Acq.
Aleaga, Ink	LB	6-1	225	4/4/73	Washington	Honolulu, Hawaii	FA
Bagley, Marvin	WR	6-5	220	9/26/74	North Carolina A&T	Winston-Salem, N.C.	FA
Bech, Brett (1)	WR	6-1	184	8/20/71	Louisiana State	Slidell, La.	FA-'96
Becksvoort, John (1)	K	6-1	177	2/26/73	Tennessee	Chattanooga, Tenn.	FA
Bowman, Brian	CB	5-9	190	12/25/72	Penn State	Donora, Penn.	FA
Carter, Eric (1)	CB	6-0	195	1/23/69	Knoxville College	Wayne, Ga.	FA-'96
Davis, Troy	RB	5-7	191	9/14/75	Iowa State	Miami, Fla.	D3
Edge, Shayne (1)	P	5-11	174	8/21/71	Florida	Lake City, Fla.	FA
Europe, Tom	S	6-0	200	7/27/70	Bishops University	Toronto, Ontario	FA
Fickell, Luke	DT	6-4	284	8/18/73	Ohio State	Columbus, Ohio	FA
Greer, Donovan	CB	5-9	178	9/11/74	Texas A&M	Alief, Tex.	FA
Harvey, Lee	S	5-11	210	6/2/70	Texas Southern	Houston, Tex.	FA
Hewitt, Chris	S	6-0	210	7/22/74	Cincinnati	Englewood, N.J.	FA
Jerich, Mike (1)	G	6-5	300	7/10/72	Stanford	LaGrange, Ill.	FA
Kelly, Rob	S	6-0	199	6/21/74	Ohio State	Newark, Ohio	D2a
Knight, Sammy	S	6-0	205	9/10/75	Southern California	Riverside, Calif.	FA
Lattimore, Michael	DE	6-3	265	2/10/74	North Carolina Central	Shelby, N.C.	FA
Leshinski, Ron	RB	6-2	248	3/6/74	Army	Vermillion, Ohio	FA
Mitchell, Keith	LB	6-2	240	7/24/74	Texas A&M	Garland, Tex.	FA
Naeole, Chris	G	6-3	313	12/25/74	Colorado	Kaaava, Hawaii	D1
O'Brien, Joe (1)	LS-DT	6-2	275	11/16/72	Boise State	Pittsburg, Calif.	FA
Palmer, Emile (1)	DT	6-3	320	4/5/73	Syracuse	Cheverly, Md.	FA-'96
Poole, Keith	WR	6-0	188	6/18/74	Arizona State	Clovis, Calif.	D4b
Ray, Leonard (1)	T	6-3	300	8/23/71	Louisville	Port St. Joe, Fla.	FA
Savoie, Nicky	TE	6-5	253	9/21/73	Louisiana State	Cut Off, La.	D6
Tomich, Jared	DE	6-2	258	4/24/74	Nebraska	St. John, Ind.	D2b
Williams, Tashe	T	6-4	300	9/23/72	Northern Colorado	Colorado Springs, Colo.	FA
Wuerffel, Danny	QB	6-1	212	5/27/74	Florida	Fort Walton, Fla.	D4a

The term NFL Rookie is defined as a player who is in his first season of professional football and has not been on the roster of another professional football team for any regular-season or postseason games. A Rookie is designated by an "R" on NFL rosters. Players who have been active in another professional football league or players who have NFL experience, including either preseason training camp or being on an Active List or Inactive List, or on Reserve/Injured or Reserve/Physically Unable to Perform for fewer than six regular-season games, are termed NFL First-Year Players. An NFL First-Year Player is designated by a "1" on NFL rosters. Thereafter, a player is credited with an additional year of experience for each season in which he accumulates six games on the Active List or Inactive List, or on Reserve/Injured or Reserve/Physically Unable to Perform.

NOTES

NEW YORK GIANTS

National Football Conference
Eastern Division
Team Colors: Blue, Red, and White
Giants Stadium
East Rutherford, New Jersey 07073
Telephone: (201) 935-8111

CLUB OFFICIALS

President/Co-CEO: Wellington T. Mara
Chairman/Co-CEO: Preston Robert Tisch
Executive Vice President/General Counsel:
  John K. Mara, Esq.
Treasurer: Jonathan Tisch
Senior Vice President-General Manager:
  George Young
Vice President-Chief Financial Officer:
  John Pasquali
Vice President-Marketing: Rusty Hawley
Vice President-Public Relations: Pat Hanlon
Assistant General Manager: Ernie Accorsi
Special Assistant to the General Manager:
  Harry Hulmes
Director of Player Personnel: Tom Boisture
Director of Pro Personnel: Tim Rooney
Assistant Director of Player Personnel:
  Rick Donohue
Director of Administration: Tom Power
Director of Promotion: Frank Mara
Ticket Manager: John Gorman
Controller: Christine Procops
Assistant Director of Public Relations: Aaron Salkin
Assistant Director of Marketing: Bill Smith
Manager of Creative Services: Doug Murphy
Community Relations Coordinator:
  Allison Stangeby
Head Trainer: Ronnie Barnes
Assistant Trainers: John Johnson, Michael Colello,
  Steve Kennelly
Equipment Manager: Ed Wagner, Jr.
Stadium: Giants Stadium •**Capacity:** 78,148
  East Rutherford, New Jersey 07073
Playing Surface: AstroTurf
Training Camp: University at Albany
        1400 Washington Avenue
        Albany, N.Y. 12222

1997 SCHEDULE
PRESEASON
Aug. 2	at Baltimore	8:00
Aug. 9	**Jacksonville**	8:00
Aug. 16	**New York Jets**	8:00
Aug. 22	vs. Green Bay at Madison, Wis.	7:00

REGULAR SEASON
Aug. 31	**Philadelphia**	1:00
Sept. 7	at Jacksonville	4:00
Sept. 14	**Baltimore**	1:00
Sept. 21	at St. Louis	3:00
Sept. 28	**New Orleans**	1:00
Oct. 5	**Dallas**	1:00
Oct. 12	at Arizona	1:00
Oct. 19	at Detroit	4:00
Oct. 26	**Cincinnati**	1:00
Nov. 2	Open Date	
Nov. 9	at Tennessee	3:00
Nov. 16	**Arizona**	1:00
Nov. 23	at Washington	8:00
Nov. 30	**Tampa Bay**	4:00
Dec. 7	at Philadelphia	1:00
Dec. 13	**Washington** (Sat.)	12:30
Dec. 21	at Dallas	12:00

RECORD HOLDERS
INDIVIDUAL RECORDS—CAREER
Category	Name	Performance
Rushing (Yds.)	Rodney Hampton, 1990-96	6,816
Passing (Yds.)	Phil Simms, 1979-1993	33,462
Passing (TDs)	Phil Simms, 1979-1993	199
Receiving (No.)	Joe Morrison, 1959-1972	395
Receiving (Yds.)	Frank Gifford, 1952-1960, 1962-64	5,434
Interceptions	Emlen Tunnell, 1948-1958	74
Punting (Avg.)	Don Chandler, 1956-1964	43.8
Punt Return (Avg.)	David Meggett, 1989-1994	11.0
Kickoff Return (Avg.)	Rocky Thompson, 1971-72	27.2
Field Goals	Pete Gogolak, 1966-1974	126
Touchdowns (Tot.)	Frank Gifford, 1952-1960, 1962-64	78
Points	Pete Gogolak, 1966-1974	646

INDIVIDUAL RECORDS—SINGLE SEASON
Category	Name	Performance
Rushing (Yds.)	Joe Morris, 1986	1,516
Passing (Yds.)	Phil Simms, 1984	4,044
Passing (TDs)	Y.A. Tittle, 1963	36
Receiving (No.)	Earnest Gray, 1983	78
Receiving (Yds.)	Homer Jones, 1967	1,209
Interceptions	Otto Schnellbacher, 1951	11
	Jim Patton, 1958	11
Punting (Avg.)	Don Chandler, 1959	46.6
Punt Return (Avg.)	Merle Hapes, 1942	15.5
Kickoff Return (Avg.)	John Salscheider, 1949	31.6
Field Goals	Ali Haji-Sheikh, 1983	35
Touchdowns (Tot.)	Joe Morris, 1985	21
Points	Ali Haji-Sheikh, 1983	127

INDIVIDUAL RECORDS—SINGLE GAME
Category	Name	Performance
Rushing (Yds.)	Gene Roberts, 11-12-50	218
Passing (Yds.)	Phil Simms, 10-13-85	513
Passing (TDs)	Y.A. Tittle, 10-28-62	*7
Receiving (No.)	Mark Bavaro, 10-13-85	12
Receiving (Yds.)	Del Shofner, 10-28-62	269
Interceptions	Many times	3
	Last time by Terry Kinard, 9-27-87	
Field Goals	Joe Danelo, 10-18-81	6
Touchdowns (Tot.)	Ron Johnson, 10-2-72	4
	Earnest Gray, 9-7-80	4
	Rodney Hampton, 9-24-95	4
Points	Ron Johnson, 10-2-72	24
	Earnest Gray, 9-7-80	24
	Rodney Hampton, 9-24-95	24

*NFL Record

COACHING HISTORY
(527-442-32)
1925	Bob Folwell	8-4-0
1926	Joe Alexander	8-4-1
1927-28	Earl Potteiger	15-8-3
1929-30	LeRoy Andrews*	24-5-1
1930	Benny Friedman	2-0-0
1930-53	Steve Owen	155-108-17
1954-60	Jim Lee Howell	55-29-4
1961-68	Allie Sherman	57-54-4
1969-73	Alex Webster	29-40-1
1974-76	Bill Arnsparger**	7-28-0
1976-78	John McVay	14-23-0
1979-82	Ray Perkins	24-35-0
1983-90	Bill Parcells	85-52-1
1991-92	Ray Handley	14-18-0
1993-96	Dan Reeves	32-34-0

*Released after 15 games in 1930
**Released after seven games in 1976

GIANTS STADIUM

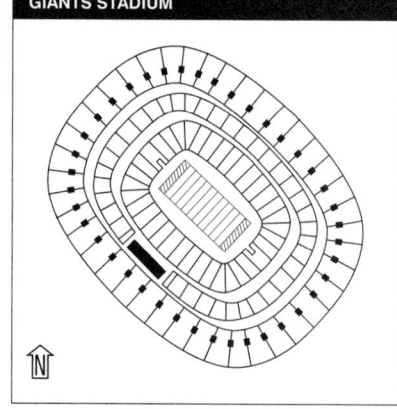

1996 TEAM RECORD

PRESEASON (1-3)

Date	Result		Opponents
8/2	W	24-17	at Jacksonville
8/10	L	27-37	Baltimore
8/17	L	6-13	at N.Y. Jets
8/23	L	7-34	Carolina

REGULAR SEASON (6-10)

Date	Result		Opponents	Att.
9/1	L	20-23	Buffalo (OT)	74,218
9/8	L	0-27	at Dallas	63,069
9/15	L	10-31	Washington	71,693
9/22	W	13-6	at N.Y. Jets	58,339
9/29	W	15-10	Minnesota	70,970
10/13	L	10-19	Philadelphia	72,729
10/20	L	21-31	at Washington	52,684
10/27	W	35-7	at Detroit	63,501
11/3	W	16-8	Arizona	68,262
11/10	L	17-27	at Carolina	70,298
11/17	L	23-31	at Arizona	34,924
11/24	W	20-6	Dallas	77,081
12/1	L	0-24	at Philadelphia	51,468
12/8	W	17-7	at Miami	63,889
12/15	L	3-17	New Orleans	52,530
12/21	L	22-23	New England	65,387

(OT) Overtime

SCORE BY PERIODS

Giants	37	107	45	53	0	—	242
Opponents	75	90	39	90	3	—	297

ATTENDANCE

Home 552,870   Away 458,172   Total 1,011,042
Single-game home record, 77,454 (9/4/95)
Single-season home record, 599,570 (1990)

1996 TEAM STATISTICS

	Giants	Opp.
Total First Downs	248	285
Rushing	82	98
Passing	145	174
Penalty	21	13
Third Down: Made/Att	61/220	76/222
Third Down Pct.	27.7	34.2
Fourth Down: Made/Att	9/20	7/18
Fourth Down Pct.	45.0	38.9
Total Net Yards	3942	5047
Avg. Per Game	246.4	315.4
Total Plays	1000	1050
Avg. Per Play	3.9	4.8
Net Yards Rushing	1603	1748
Avg. Per Game	100.2	109.3
Total Rushes	485	487
Net Yards Passing	2339	3299
Avg. Per Game	146.2	206.2
Sacked/Yards Lost	56/324	30/178
Gross Yards	2663	3477
Att./Completions	459/238	533/317
Completion Pct.	51.9	59.5
Had Intercepted	21	22
Punts/Avg.	102/42.0	92/41.3
Net Punting Avg.	102/35.9	92/33.7
Penalties/Yards Lost	85/666	100/781
Fumbles/Ball Lost	27/13	27/13
Touchdowns	24	33
Rushing	4	14
Passing	14	15
Returns	6	4
Avg. Time of Possession	29:48	30:12

1996 INDIVIDUAL STATISTICS

PASSING

	Att.	Comp.	Yds.	Pct.	TD	Int.	Tkld.	Rate
Brown	398	214	2412	53.8	12	20	49/276	61.3
Kanell	60	23	227	38.3	1	1	7/48	48.4
Wheatley	1	1	24	100.0	1	0	0/0	158.3
Giants	459	238	2663	51.9	14	21	56/324	60.6
Opponents	533	317	3477	59.5	15	22	30/178	71.0

SCORING

	TD R	TD P	TD Rt	PAT	FG	Saf	PTS
Daluiso	0	0	0	22/22	24/27	0	94
Calloway	0	4	0	0/0	0/0	0	24
Lewis	0	4	0	0/0	0/0	0	24
Wheatley	1	2	0	0/0	0/0	0	18
Pierce	1	1	0	0/0	0/0	0	12
Toomer	0	0	2	0/0	0/0	0	12
Way	1	1	0	0/0	0/0	0	12
Wooten	0	0	1	0/0	0/0	1	8
Agnew	0	0	1	0/0	0/0	0	6
Cross	0	1	0	0/0	0/0	0	6
Douglass	0	0	1	0/0	0/0	0	6
Hampton	1	0	0	0/0	0/0	0	6
Kozlowski	0	1	0	0/0	0/0	0	6
Sehorn	0	0	1	0/0	0/0	0	6
Giants	4	14	6	22/22	24/27	*2	242
Opponents	14	15	4	31/31	22/26	0	297

2-Point conversions: 0 Team: 0-2, Opponents: 1-2
*Giants were credited with 1 team safety.

RUSHING

	Att.	Yds.	Avg.	LG	TD
Hampton	254	827	3.3	25	1
Wheatley	112	400	3.6	37	1
Brown	50	170	3.4	18	0
Downs	29	94	3.2	27	0
Way	22	79	3.6	18	1
Elias	9	24	2.7	8	0
Kanell	7	6	0.9	13	0
Calloway	1	2	2.0	2	0
Pierce	1	1	1.0	1t	1
Giants	485	1603	3.3	37	4
Opponents	487	1748	3.6	39t	14

RECEIVING

	No.	Yds.	Avg.	LG	TD
Calloway	53	739	13.9	36	4
Lewis	53	694	13.1	34	4
Way	32	328	10.3	37t	1
Cross	22	178	8.1	19	1
Dawsey	18	233	12.9	28	0
Hampton	15	82	5.5	16	0
Wheatley	12	51	4.3	13	2
Pierce	11	144	13.1	30	1
Elias	8	51	6.4	11	0
Alexander	4	88	22.0	35	0
Saxton	4	31	7.8	14	0
Downs	3	20	6.7	13	0
Toomer	1	12	12.0	12	0
Douglas	1	8	8.0	8	0
Kozlowski	1	4	4.0	4t	1
Giants	238	2663	11.2	37t	14
Opponents	317	3477	11.0	66	15

INTERCEPTIONS

	No.	Yds.	Avg.	LG	TD
Sehorn	5	61	12.2	24	1
Ellsworth	3	62	20.7	33	0
Sparks	3	23	7.7	19	0
Armstead	2	23	11.5	23	0
Campbell	2	14	7.0	14	0
Widmer	2	8	4.0	4	0
Wooten	1	35	35.0	35	0
Agnew	1	34	34.0	34t	1
Douglass	1	32	32.0	32t	1
C. Hamilton	1	29	29.0	29	0
Beamon	1	20	20.0	20	0
Giants	22	341	15.5	35	3
Opponents	21	225	10.7	68t	1

PUNTING

	No.	Yds.	Avg.	In 20	LG
Horan	102	4289	42.0	32	63
Giants	102	4289	42.0	32	63
Opponents	92	3801	41.3	22	69

PUNT RETURNS

	No.	FC	Yds.	Avg.	LG	TD
Toomer	18	10	298	16.6	87t	2
Marshall	13	9	144	11.1	36	0
Lewis	10	4	36	3.6	8	0
Sehorn	1	0	0	0.0	0	0
Giants	42	23	478	11.4	87t	2
Opponents	45	22	432	9.6	69t	2

KICKOFF RETURNS

	No.	Yds.	Avg.	LG	TD
Wheatley	23	503	21.9	43	0
C. Hamilton	19	382	20.1	29	0
Toomer	11	191	17.4	25	0
Lewis	4	107	26.8	47	0
Saxton	3	31	10.3	12	0
Alexander	2	27	13.5	14	0
Way	2	19	9.5	10	0
Douglas	1	11	11.0	11	0
Kozlowski	1	16	16.0	16	0
Giants	66	1287	19.5	47	0
Opponents	42	948	22.6	65	0

SACKS

	No.
Bratzke	5.0
Strahan	5.0
Harris	4.5
Armstead	3.0
K. Hamilton	3.0
Sehorn	3.0
Miller	2.0
Widmer	2.0
Rudolph	1.0
Agnew	0.5
Giants	*30.0
Opponents	56.0

*Giants were credited with 1 team sack.

1997 DRAFT CHOICES

Round	Name	Pos.	College
1	Ike Hilliard	WR	Florida
2	Tiki Barber	RB	Virginia
3	Ryan Phillips	LB	Idaho
	Brad Maynard	P	Ball State
4	Pete Monty	LB	Wisconsin
5	Sam Garnes	DB	Cincinnati
6	Mike Cherry	QB	Murray State
7	Matt Keneley	DT	Southern California

NEW YORK GIANTS

1997 VETERAN ROSTER

No.		Name	Pos.	Ht.	Wt.	Birthdate	NFL Exp.	College	Hometown	How Acq.	'96 Games/ Starts
93		Agnew, Ray	DT	6-3	285	12/9/67	8	North Carolina State	Winston-Salem, N.C.	FA-'95	13/2
86		Alexander, Kevin	WR	5-9	184	1/23/75	2	Utah State	Phoenix, Ariz.	FA-'96	4/0
98		Armstead, Jessie	LB	6-1	232	10/26/70	5	Miami	Dallas, Tex.	D8-'93	16/16
78		Bishop, Greg	T	6-5	300	5/2/71	5	Pacific	Lodi, Calif.	D4-'93	16/16
77		Bratzke, Chad	DE	6-4	273	9/15/71	4	Eastern Kentucky	Brandon, Fla.	D5-'94	16/16
17		Brown, Dave	QB	6-5	223	2/25/70	6	Duke	Westfield, N.J.	SD1-'92	16/16
55		Buckley, Marcus	LB	6-3	240	2/3/71	5	Texas A&M	Fort Worth, Tex.	D3-'93	15/2
80		Calloway, Chris	WR	5-10	191	3/29/68	8	Michigan	Chicago, Ill.	FA-'92	16/15
58		Colman, Doug	LB	6-2	252	6/4/73	2	Nebraska	Somers Point, N.J.	D6-'96	13/0
87		Cross, Howard	TE	6-5	265	8/8/67	9	Alabama	Huntsville, Ala.	D6-'89	16/16
3		Daluiso, Brad	K	6-2	210	12/31/67	7	UCLA	San Diego, Calif.	FA-'93	16/0
62	#	Davis, Scott	G	6-3	292	1/29/70	5	Iowa	Glenwood, Iowa	D6-'93	0*
82		Douglas, Omar	WR	5-10	182	6/3/72	4	Minnesota	New Orleans, La.	FA-'94	4/0
24	#	Douglass, Maurice	S	5-11	210	2/12/64	12	Kentucky	Dayton, Ohio	UFA(Chi)-'95	15/0
96		Duff, Jamal	DE	6-7	271	3/11/72	3	San Diego State	Tustin, Calif.	D6a-95	0*
43		Ellsworth, Percy	S	6-2	199	10/19/74	2	Virginia	Drewryville, Va.	FA-'96	14/4
52		Galyon, Scott	LB	6-2	237	3/23/74	2	Tennessee	Seymour, Tenn.	D6-'96	16/0
74		Gragg, Scott	T	6-8	325	2/28/72	3	Montana	Silverton, Ore.	D2-'95	16/16
41		Hamilton, Conrad	CB	5-10	184	11/5/74	2	Eastern New Mexico	Alamogordo, N.M.	D7-'96	15/1
75		Hamilton, Keith	DE	6-6	285	5/25/71	6	Pittsburgh	Lynchburg, Va.	D4-'92	14/14
27		Hampton, Rodney	RB	5-11	230	4/3/69	8	Georgia	Houston, Tex.	D1-'90	15/15
97		Harris, Robert	DE	6-4	295	6/13/69	6	Southern	Riviera Beach, Fla.	RFA(Minn)-'95	16/16
79		Holsey, Bernard	DT	6-2	284	12/10/73	2	Duke	Cave Spring, Ga.	FA-'96	16/0
94		Jones, Cedric	DE	6-4	275	4/30/74	2	Oklahoma	Houston, Tex.	D1-'96	16/0
13		Kanell, Danny	QB	6-3	222	11/21/73	2	Florida State	Ft. Lauderdale, Fla.	D4-'96	4/0
68		Kline, Alan	T	6-5	290	5/25/71	2	Ohio State	Tiffin, Ohio	FA-'97	0*
81		Lewis, Thomas	WR	6-1	195	1/10/72	4	Indiana	Akron, Ohio	D1-'94	13/11
57		Miller, Corey	LB	6-2	245	10/25/68	7	South Carolina	Pageland, S.C.	D6-'91	14/13
72		Oben, Roman	T	6-4	297	10/9/72	2	Louisville	Washington, D.C.	D3-'96	2/0
70		Okoli, Ramon	DE-DT	6-5	300	3/15/73	2	Murray State	Little Rock, Ark.	FA-'96	0*
84		Pierce, Aaron	TE	6-5	250	9/6/69	6	Washington	Seattle, Wash.	D3-'92	10/3
23		Randolph, Thomas	CB	5-9	178	10/5/70	4	Kansas State	Norfork, Va.	D2a-'94	16/2
66	†	Reynolds, Jerry	G-T	6-6	315	4/2/70	4	Nevada-Las Vegas	Ft. Thomas, Ky.	FA-'95	8/0
83		Saxton, Brian	TE	6-6	256	3/13/72	2	Boston College	Whippany, N.J.	FA-'96	16/2
67	#	Schreiber, Adam	C	6-4	298	2/20/62	14	Texas	Galveston, Tex.	FA-'94	15/2
31		Sehorn, Jason	S	6-2	210	4/15/71	4	Southern California	Mt. Shasta, Calif.	D2b-'94	16/15
61	#	Smith, Lance	G	6-3	282	1/1/63	13	Louisiana State	Kannapolis, N.C.	UFA(Ariz)-'94	16/10
22		Sparks, Phillippi	CB	5-11	190	4/15/69	6	Arizona State	Glendale, Calif.	D2-'92	14/14
65		Stone, Ron	G	6-5	325	7/20/71	5	Boston College	Roxbury, Mass.	RFA(Dall)-'96	16/16
92		Strahan, Michael	DE	6-4	268	11/21/71	5	Texas Southern	Westbury, Tex.	D2-'93	16/16
54		Talley, Ben	LB	6-3	245	7/14/72	3	Tennessee	Griffin, Fla.	D4b-'95	0*
89		Toomer, Amani	WR	6-3	202	9/8/74	2	Michigan	Berkeley, Calif.	D2-'96	7/1
30		Way, Charles	RB	6-0	245	12/27/72	3	Virginia	Philadelphia, Pa.	D6b-'95	16/12
28		Wheatley, Tyrone	RB	6-0	228	1/19/72	3	Michigan	Inkster, Mich.	D1-'95	14/0
8		White, Stan	QB	6-2	218	8/14/71	4	Auburn	Birmingham, Ala.	FA-'94	0*
90		Widmer, Corey	LB	6-3	250	12/25/68	6	Montana State	Bozeman, Mont.	D7-'92	16/16
59		Williams, Brian	C	6-5	300	6/8/66	9	Minnesota	Mt. Lebanon, Pa.	D1-'89	14/14
29	†	Wooten, Tito	S	6-0	195	12/12/71	4	Northeast Louisiana	Goldsboro, N.C.	SD4-'94	13/12
47		Young, Rodney	S	6-1	212	1/25/73	3	Louisiana State	Grambling, La.	D3-'95	12/0
73		Zatechka, Rob	G	6-4	315	12/1/71	3	Nebraska	Lincoln, Neb.	D4a-'95	15/6

* Davis was inactive for 14 games in '96; Duff, Okoli, and Talley missed '96 season because of injury; Kline last active with New Orleans in '95; White was inactive for 10 games.

\# Unrestricted free agent; subject to developments.

† Restricted free agent; subject to developments.

Players lost to free agency (1): WR Lawrence Dawsey (Mia; 1 game).

Also played with Giants in '96—CB Willie Beamon (5 games), S Jesse Campbell (16), RB Gary Downs (6), RB Keith Elias (9), TE Brian Kozlowski (5), WR Arthur Marshall (5), LB Moses Regular (3), LB Coleman Rudolph (16), RB Robert Walker (1).

COACHING STAFF

Head Coach,
Jim Fassel

Pro Career: Jim Fassel was introduced by general manager George Young on January 15, 1997 as the fifteenth head coach in Giants' history. Fassel spent two seasons as an assistant coach with the Giants, first as quarterbacks coach in 1991, then as offensive coordinator in 1992. Following his service with the Giants, Fassel spent two campaigns as assistant head coach/offensive coordinator for the Denver Broncos in 1993 and 1994. He spent the 1995 season as quarterbacks coach for the Oakland Raiders and was the offensive coordinator and the quarterbacks coach for the Arizona Cardinals last season. Fassel, who brings 24 years of coaching experience to the Giants, has been credited with an ability to develop quarterbacks. Under Fassel's guidance, Broncos quarterback John Elway enjoyed his finest season as a pro in 1993, earning honors that included the American Football Conference player-of-the-year and most valuable player. Elway was the starting quarterback in the Pro Bowl and led the AFC in all six major passing categories. Last season with the Cardinals, Fassel helped tutor former Giants quarterback Kent Graham into a solid player and helped rejuvenate veteran Boomer Esiason. The Cardinals finished sixth in passing offense in 1996.

Background: A former collegiate quarterback, Fassel began coaching in 1973 at his alma mater, Fullerton Community College, then was a player-coach for the Hawaii Hawaiians of the World Football League in 1974. He coached quarterbacks and receivers at Utah in 1976, then served seven seasons as offensive coordinator at both Weber State (1977-78) and Stanford (1979-83). At Stanford, Fassel was credited with recruiting and coaching Elway, who finished second in the balloting for the Heisman Trophy as a senior in 1982. Fassel entered the pro arena in 1984 as offensive coordinator for the New Orleans Breakers of the USFL, then returned to Utah as the school's head coach from 1985-89 where he recruited and coached current Detroit Lions quarterback Scott Mitchell. En route to the NFL under Fassel's tutelage, Mitchell set 10 NCAA and five additional Western Athletic Conference records along with virtually every school passing record.

Personal: A native of Anaheim, California, Fassel was a standout quarterback at Anaheim High School before leading Fullerton Community College to a 25-1 record over two seasons and winning the junior college national championship in 1967. He also played collegiately at Southern California, with Green Bay Packers head coach Mike Holmgren, and at Long Beach State. He was drafted by Chicago in the seventh round of the 1972 NFL Draft. Born August 31, 1949 in Anaheim, Fassel and his wife, Kitty, have four children, John, Brian, Jana, and Mike. John is a junior quarterback at Weber State.

ASSISTANT COACHES

Dave Brazil, defensive quality control; born March 25, 1936, Detroit, Mich., lives in East Rutherford, N.J. No college or pro playing experience. College coach: Holy Cross 1968, Tulsa 1969-70, Eastern Michigan 1971-73, Boston College 1980, Kent State 1981-82. Pro coach: Detroit Wheels (WFL) 1974, Chicago Wind (WFL) 1975, Kansas City Chiefs 1984-88, Pittsburgh Steelers 1989-91, joined Giants in 1992.

Rod Dowhower, quarterbacks; born April 15, 1943, Ord, Neb. Quarterback San Diego State 1963-65. No pro playing experience. College coach: San Diego State 1966-72, UCLA 1974-75, Boise State 1976, Stanford 1977-79 (head coach 1979), Vanderbilt 1995-96 (head coach). Pro coach: St. Louis Cardinals 1973, 1982-84, Denver Broncos 1980-1981, Indianapolis Colts 1985-86 (head coach), Atlanta Falcons 1987-89, Washington Redskins 1990-93, joined Giants in 1997.

John Dunn, strength and conditioning; born July 22, 1956, Hillsdale, N.Y. Guard Penn State 1974-77. No pro playing experience. College coach: Penn State 1978. Pro coach: Washington Redskins 1984-86, Los Angeles Raiders 1987-89, San Diego Chargers

1990-96, joined Giants in 1997.

John Fox, defensive coordinator; born February 8, 1955, Virginia Beach, Va. Defensive back San Diego State 1975-77. No pro playing experience. College coach: U.S. International 1979, Boise State 1980, Long Beach State 1981, Utah 1982, Kansas 1983, 1985, Iowa State 1984, Pittsburgh 1986-88. Pro coach: Los Angeles Express (USFL) 1985, Pittsburgh Steelers 1989-1991, San Diego Chargers 1992-93, Los Angeles/Oakland Raiders 1994-95, St. Louis Rams 1996, joined Giants in 1997.

Mike Gillhamer, offensive quality control; born February 20, 1954. Defensive back Humbolt State. No pro playing experience. College coach: College of the Sequoias 1979-83, Weber State 1984, Utah 1985-89, San Jose State 1990-93, Nevada 1994-95, Rutgers 1996. Pro coach: Joined Giants in 1997.

Mike Haluchak, linebackers; born November 28, 1949, Concord, Calif. Linebacker Southern California 1967-70. No pro playing experience. College coach: Southern California 1976-77, Cal State-Fullerton 1978, Pacific 1979-80, California 1981, North Carolina State 1982. Pro coach: Oakland Invaders (USFL) 1983-85, San Diego Chargers 1986-91, Cincinnati Bengals 1992-93, Washington Redskins 1994-96, joined Giants in 1997.

Milt Jackson, wide receivers; born October 16, 1943, Groesbeck, Tex. Defensive back Tulsa 1965-66. Pro defensive back San Francisco 49ers 1967. College coach: Oregon State 1973, Rice 1974, California 1975-76, Oregon 1977-78, UCLA 1979. Pro coach: San Francisco 49ers 1980-82, Buffalo Bills 1983-84, Philadelphia Eagles 1985, Houston Oilers 1986-88, Indianapolis Colts 1989-91, Los Angeles Rams 1992-93, Atlanta Falcons 1994-96, joined Giants in 1997.

Johnnie Lynn, defensive backs; born December 19, 1956, Los Angeles, Calif. Defensive back UCLA 1975-78. Pro defensive back New York Jets 1979-86. College coach: Arizona 1988-93. Pro coach: Tampa Bay Buccaneers 1994-95, San Francisco 49ers 1996,

joined Giants in 1997.

Larry MacDuff, special teams; born June 22, 1948, Clinton, Iowa. Defensive end Fullerton Community College 1966-67, Oklahoma 1968-69. No pro playing experience. College coach: Fullerton Community College 1970, 1974-79, Stanford 1980-83, Hawaii 1984-86, Arizona 1987-96. Pro coach: Joined Giants in 1997.

Denny Marcin, defensive line; born April 24, 1942, Cleveland, Ohio. Defensive and offensive line Miami (Ohio) 1961-64. No pro playing experience. College coach: Miami (Ohio) 1974-77, North Carolina 1978-87, Illinois 1988-96. Pro coach: Joined Giants in 1997.

John Matsko, offensive line; born February 2, 1951, Cleveland, Ohio. Fullback Kent State 1970-73. No pro playing experience. College coach: Kent State 1973, Miami (Ohio) 1974-75, 1977, North Carolina 1978-84, Navy 1985, Arizona 1986, Southern California 1987-91. Pro coach: Phoenix Cardinals 1992-93, New Orleans Saints 1994-96, joined Giants in 1997.

Dick Rehbein, tight ends; born November 22, 1955, Green Bay, Wis., lives in Wayne, N.J. Center Ripon 1973-77. No pro playing experience. Pro coach: Green Bay Packers 1979-83, Los Angeles Express (USFL) 1984, Minnesota Vikings 1984-91, joined Giants in 1992.

Jim Skipper, offensive coordinator-running backs; born January 23, 1949, Breaux Bridge, La. Defensive back Whittier College 1971-72. No pro playing experience. College coach: Cal Poly-Pomona 1974-76, San Jose State 1977-78, Pacific 1979, Oregon 1980-82. Pro coach: Philadelphia/Baltimore Stars (USFL) 1983-85, New Orleans Saints 1986-95, Arizona Cardinals 1996, joined Giants in 1997.

Craig Stoddard, assistant strength and conditioning; born February 8, 1972, North Terrytown, N.Y. Linebacker Springfield College 1990-93. No pro playing experience. College coach: Penn State 1995-96. Pro coach: San Diego Chargers 1994, joined Giants in 1997.

1997 FIRST-YEAR ROSTER

Name	Pos.	Ht.	Wt.	Birthdate	College	Hometown	How Acq.
Barber, Tiki	RB	5-10	200	4/7/75	Virginia	Montgomer County, Va.	D2
Blackwell, Kory	CB	5-11	185	8/3/72	Massachusetts	Queens, N.Y.	FA
Calhoun, Matt	RB	6-0	250	12/31/73	Ohio State	Heath, Ohio	FA
Castro, Cayetano	G	6-6	305	11/27/74	Wisconsin	Bronx, N.Y.	FA
Cherry, Mike	QB	6-3	222	12/15/73	Murray State	Texarkana, Ark.	D6
Engler, Derek	C	6-5	301	7/11/74	Wisconsin	St. Paul, Minn.	FA
Estes, Charles	DE	6-3	257	9/30/75	Army	Georgetown, Ky.	FA
Garnes, Sam	S	6-3	225	7/12/74	Cincinnati	Bronx, N.Y.	D5
Gilliard, Darnell (1)	DT	6-5	304	3/24/73	Troy State	Anderson, S.C.	FA
Gragg, Harold	DE	6-4	273	5/17/74	Wake Forest	Black Mountain, N.C.	FA
Hilliard, Ike	WR	5-11	189	4/5/76	Florida	Patterson, La.	D1
Hurley, Brion	K	6-4	215	3/13/74	Iowa	Iowa City, Iowa	FA
Jessie, Brandon	TE	6-6	255	5/20/74	Utah	Huntington Beach, Calif.	FA
Johnson, James	S	6-0	180	10/23/72	Nevada	Las Vegas, Nev.	FA
Keneley, Matt	DT	6-4	286	12/1/73	Southern California	Laguna Hills, Calif.	D7
Lane, Eric	RB	6-2	217	3/17/74	Tennessee	East Orange, N.J.	FA
Maynard, Brad	P	6-1	185	2/9/74	Ball State	Atlanta, Ind.	D3b
McMullen, Typail	S	6-2	197	9/3/73	Middle Tennessee St.	Lubbock, Tex.	FA
Monty, Pete	LB	6-2	253	7/13/74	Wisconsin	Ft. Collins, Colo.	D4
Nelson, Picasso (1)	S	6-0	208	5/1/73	Jackson State	Hattiesburg, Miss.	FA
Patten, David (1)	WR	5-9	182	8/19/74	Western Carolina	Hopkins, S.C.	FA
Peter, Christian	DT	6-3	304	10/5/72	Nebraska	Locust, N. J.	FA
Phillips, Ryan	LB	6-4	250	2/7/74	Idaho	Auburn, Wash.	D3a
Player, Scott (1)	P	6-0	220	12/17/69	Florida State	St. Augustine, Fla.	FA
Rilatt, Dave	T	6-6	315	10/16/73	Maine	West Chester, Pa.	FA
Roberson, Brian	WR	5-10	170	1/8/74	Fresno State	Sylmar, Calif.	FA
Sanders, Brandon (1)	S	5-9	185	6/10/73	Arizona	San Diego, Calif.	FA
Sumner, Jamie	G	6-4	320	11/14/73	Ohio State	Wichita, Kan.	FA
Thorp, Deron (1)	T	6-8	330	8/31/73	Nevada	Santa Clara, Calif.	FA
Walker, Robert (1)	RB	5-10	197	6/26/72	West Virginia	Huntington, W. Va.	FA
Washington, John	WR	5-9	160	7/8/74	Texas Christian	Longview, Tex.	FA
William, Marc	CB-S	5-9	173	11/4/74	Oregon State	Dallas, Tex.	FA

The term NFL Rookie is defined as a player who is in his first season of professional football and has not been on the roster of another professional football team for any regular-season or postseason games. A Rookie is designated by an "R" on NFL rosters. Players who have been active in another professional football league or players who have NFL experience, including either preseason training camp or being on an Active List or Inactive List, or on Reserve/Injured or Reserve/Physically Unable to Perform for fewer than six regular-season games, are termed NFL First-Year Players. An NFL First-Year Player is designated by a "1" on NFL rosters. Thereafter, a player is credited with an additional year of experience for each season in which he accumulates six games on the Active List or Inactive List, or on Reserve/Injured or Reserve/Physically Unable to Perform.

National Football Conference
Eastern Division
Team Colors: Midnight Green, Silver, Black, and
White
Veterans Stadium
3501 South Broad Street
Philadelphia, Pennsylvania 19148
Telephone: (215) 463-2500

CLUB OFFICIALS

Owner/Chief Executice Officer: Jeffrey Lurie
Senior Vice President: Joe Banner
Senior Vice President-Chief Financial Officer:
  Mimi Box
Vice President-Sales and Marketing: Len Komoroski
Vice President of Sales: Vic Gregovits
Director of Football Operations: Dick Daniels
Executive Direcotor of Eagles Youth Partnership:
  Sarah Helfman
Director of College Scouting: John Wooten
Director of Administration: Vicki Chatley
Director of Corporate Sales: Dave Rowan
Director of Public Relations: Ron Howard
Assistant Director of Public Relations: Derek Boyko
Ticket Manager: Leo Carlin
Director of Business Development: David Perry
Director of Merchandising: Steve Strawbridge
Director of Advertising and Promotions: Kim Babiak
Office Manager/Travel Coordinator: Tracey Bucher
Head of Security: Anthony Buchanico
Director of Penthouse Operations: Christiana Noyalas
Trainer: James Collins
Assistant Trainers: Scottie Patton, Scott Trulock
Peak Performance Specialist: Baron Baptiste
Video Director: Mike Dougherty
Equipment Manager: Rusty Sweeney
Stadium: Veterans Stadium •**Capacity:** 65,352
  3501 South Broad Street
  Philadelphia, Pennsylvania 19148
Playing Surface: AstroTurf-8
Training Camp: Lehigh University
  Bethlehem, Pennsylvania 18015

1997 SCHEDULE
PRESEASON

Aug. 2	at New York Jets	8:00
Aug. 11	at Pittsburgh	8:00
Aug. 16	**Baltimore**	8:00
Aug. 22	**New England**	8:00

REGULAR SEASON

Aug. 31	at New York Giants	1:00
Sept. 7	**Green Bay**	4:00
Sept. 15	at Dallas (Mon.)	9:00
Sept. 21	Open Date	
Sept. 28	at Minnesota	8:00
Oct. 5	**Washington**	1:00
Oct. 12	at Jacksonville	1:00
Oct. 19	**Arizona**	1:00
Oct. 26	**Dallas**	1:00
Nov. 2	at Arizona	4:00
Nov. 10	**San Francisco** (Mon.)	9:00
Nov. 16	at Baltimore	1:00
Nov. 23	**Pittsburgh**	1:00
Nov. 30	**Cincinnati**	1:00
Dec. 7	**New York Giants**	1:00
Dec. 14	at Atlanta	1:00
Dec. 21	at Washington	1:00

RECORD HOLDERS
INDIVIDUAL RECORDS—CAREER

Category	Name	Performance
Rushing (Yds.)	Wilbert Montgomery, 1977-1984	6,538
Passing (Yds.)	Ron Jaworski, 1977-1986	26,963
Passing (TDs)	Ron Jaworski, 1977-1986	175
Receiving (No.)	Harold Carmichael, 1971-1983	589
Receiving (Yds.)	Harold Carmichael, 1971-1983	8,978
Interceptions	Bill Bradley, 1969-1976	34
Punting (Avg.)	Tom Hutton, 1995-96	43.0
Punt Return (Avg.)	Steve Van Buren, 1944-1951	13.9
Kickoff Return (Avg.)	Steve Van Buren, 1944-1951	26.7
Field Goals	Paul McFadden, 1984-87	91
Touchdowns (Tot.)	Harold Carmichael, 1971-1983	79
Points	Bobby Walston, 1951-1962	881

INDIVIDUAL RECORDS—SINGLE SEASON

Category	Name	Performance
Rushing (Yds.)	Wilbert Montgomery, 1979	1,512
Passing (Yds.)	Randall Cunningham, 1988	3,808
Passing (TDs)	Sonny Jurgensen, 1961	32
Receiving (No.)	Irving Fryar, 1996	88
Receiving (Yds.)	Mike Quick, 1983	1,409
Interceptions	Bill Bradley, 1971	11
Punting (Avg.)	Joe Muha, 1948	47.2
Punt Return (Avg.)	Steve Van Buren, 1944	15.3
Kickoff Return (Avg.)	Al Nelson, 1972	29.1
Field Goals	Paul McFadden, 1984	30
Touchdowns (Tot.)	Steve Van Buren, 1945	18
Points	Paul McFadden, 1984	116

INDIVIDUAL RECORDS—SINGLE GAME

Category	Name	Performance
Rushing (Yds.)	Steve Van Buren, 11-27-49	205
Passing (Yds.)	Randall Cunningham, 9-17-89	447
Passing (TDs)	Adrian Burk, 10-17-54	*7
Receiving (No.)	Don Looney, 12-1-40	14
Receiving (Yds.)	Tommy McDonald, 12-10-60	237
Interceptions	Russ Craft, 9-24-50	*4
Field Goals	Tom Dempsey, 11-12-72	6
Touchdowns (Tot.)	Many times	4
	Last time by Irving Fryar, 10-20-96	
Points	Bobby Walston, 10-17-54	25

*NFL Record

COACHING HISTORY
(391-457-24)

1933-35	Lud Wray	9-21-1
1936-40	Bert Bell	10-44-2
1941-50	Earle (Greasy) Neale*	66-44-5
1951	Alvin (Bo) McMillin**	2-0-0
1951	Wayne Millner	2-8-0
1952-55	Jim Trimble	25-20-3
1956-57	Hugh Devore	7-16-1
1958-60	Lawrence (Buck) Shaw	20-16-1
1961-63	Nick Skorich	15-24-3
1964-68	Joe Kuharich	28-41-1
1969-71	Jerry Williams***	7-22-2
1971-72	Ed Khayat	8-15-2
1973-75	Mike McCormack	16-25-1
1976-82	Dick Vermeil	57-51-0
1983-85	Marion Campbell****	17-29-1
1985	Fred Bruney	1-0-0
1986-90	Buddy Ryan	43-38-1
1991-94	Rich Kotite	37-29-0
1995-96	Ray Rhodes	21-14-0

  *Co-coach with Walt Kiesling in Philadelphia-Pittsburgh
    merger in 1943
  **Retired after two games in 1951
  ***Released after three games in 1971
****Released after 15 games in 1985

VETERANS STADIUM

1996 TEAM RECORD

PRESEASON (2-2)

Date	Result		Opponents
8/3	L	9-17	at Baltimore
8/8	W	30-16	N.Y. Jets
8/18	L	10-37	at New England
8/23	W	20-19	Pittsburgh

REGULAR SEASON (10-6)

Date	Result		Opponents	Att.
9/1	W	17-14	at Washington	53,415
9/9	L	13-39	at Green Bay	60,666
9/15	W	24-17	Detroit	66,007
9/22	W	33-18	at Atlanta	40,107
9/30	L	19-23	Dallas	67,201
10/13	W	19-10	at N.Y. Giants	72,729
10/20	W	35-28	Miami	66,240
10/27	W	20-9	Carolina	65,982
11/3	W	31-21	at Dallas	64,952
11/10	L	17-24	Buffalo	66,613
11/17	L	21-26	Washington	66,834
11/24	L	30-36	at Arizona	36,175
12/1	W	24-0	N.Y. Giants	51,468
12/5	L	10-37	at Indianapolis	52,689
12/14	W	21-20	at N.Y. Jets	29,178
12/22	W	29-19	Arizona	63,658

POSTSEASON (0-1)

Date	Result		Opponents	Att.
12/29	L	0-14	at San Francisco	56,460

SCORE BY PERIODS

Eagles	98	88	64	113	—	363
Opponents	64	119	73	85	—	341

ATTENDANCE

Home 514,003   Away 409,911   Total 923,914
Single-game home record, 72,111 (11/1/81)
Single-season home record, 557,325 (1980)

1996 TEAM STATISTICS

	Eagles	Opp.
Total First Downs	319	264
Rushing	107	87
Passing	196	150
Penalty	16	27
Third Down: Made/Att	83/219	84/215
Third Down Pct.	37.9	39.1
Fourth Down: Made/Att	6/15	5/14
Fourth Down Pct.	40.0	35.7
Total Net Yards	5627	4562
Avg. Per Game	351.7	285.1
Total Plays	1076	961
Avg. Per Play	5.2	4.7
Net Yards Rushing	1882	1583
Avg. Per Game	117.6	98.9
Total Rushes	489	421
Net Yards Passing	3745	2979
Avg. Per Game	234.1	186.2
Sacked/Yards Lost	39/234	40/264
Gross Yards	3979	3243
Att./Completions	548/328	500/271
Completion Pct.	59.9	54.2
Had Intercepted	18	19
Punts/Avg.	74/42.0	74/44.4
Net Punting Avg.	74/35.1	74/37.5
Penalties/Yards Lost	117/963	99/710
Fumbles/Ball Lost	24/14	26/12
Touchdowns	41	35
Rushing	16	12
Passing	19	18
Returns	6	5
Avg. Time of Possession	32:12	27:48

1996 INDIVIDUAL STATISTICS

PASSING	Att.	Comp.	Yds.	Pct.	TD	Int.	Tkld.	Rate
Detmer	401	238	2911	59.4	15	13	27/171	80.8
Peete	134	80	992	59.7	3	5	11/53	74.6
Rypien	13	10	76	76.9	1	0	0/0	116.2
Hoying	0	0	0	—	0	0	1/10	—
Eagles	548	328	3979	59.9	19	18	39/234	80.1
Opponents	500	271	3243	54.2	18	19	40/264	70.4

SCORING	TD R	TD P	TD Rt	PAT	FG	Saf	PTS
Anderson	0	0	0	40/40	25/29	0	115
Watters	13	0	0	0/0	0/0	0	78
Fryar	0	11	0	0/0	0/0	0	66
Jones	0	5	0	0/0	0/0	0	30
Dunn	0	2	0	0/0	0/0	0	12
Witherspoon	0	0	2	0/0	0/0	0	12
Detmer	1	0	0	0/0	0/0	0	6
Garner	1	0	0	0/0	0/0	0	6
Hall	0	0	1	0/0	0/0	0	6
Mamula	0	0	1	0/0	0/0	0	6
Peete	1	0	0	0/0	0/0	0	6
W. Thomas	0	0	1	0/0	0/0	0	6
Turner	0	1	0	0/0	0/0	0	6
Vincent	0	0	1	0/0	0/0	0	6
Eagles	16	19	6	40/40	25/29	*1	363
Opponents	12	18	5	30/32	31/36	1	341

2-Point conversions: 0. Team: 0-1, Opponents: 3-3.
*Eagles were credited with 1 team safety.

RUSHING	Att.	Yds.	Avg.	LG	TD
Watters	353	1411	4.0	56t	13
Garner	66	346	5.2	46	1
Detmer	31	59	1.9	9	1
Turner	18	39	2.2	7	0
Peete	20	31	1.6	11	1
Fryar	1	-4	-4.0	-4	0
Eagles	489	1882	3.8	56t	16
Opponents	421	1583	3.8	49t	12

RECEIVING	No.	Yds.	Avg.	LG	TD
Fryar	88	1195	13.6	42	11
Jones	70	859	12.3	38	5
Watters	51	444	8.7	36	0
Turner	43	409	9.5	41	1
Seay	19	260	13.7	35	0
Dunn	15	332	22.1	58	2
Williams	2	8	4.0	4	0
Garner	14	92	6.6	13	0
Solomon	8	125	15.6	23	0
West	8	91	11.4	29	0
J. Johnson	7	127	18.1	31	0
Ingram	2	33	16.5	20	0
McIntyre	1	4	4.0	4	0
Eagles	328	3979	12.0	62	19
Opponents	271	3243	12.0	67	18

INTERCEPTIONS	No.	Yds.	Avg.	LG	TD
Zordich	4	54	13.5	28	0
Vincent	3	144	48.0	90t	1
W. Thomas	3	47	15.7	37	0
Dawkins	3	41	13.7	30	0
Taylor	3	-1	-.3	0	0
Willis	1	14	14.0	14	0
J. Fuller	1	4	4.0	4	0
Farmer	1	0	0.0	0	0
Hall	0	0	—	—	0
Eagles	19	303	15.9	104t	1
Opponents	18	265	14.7	65t	3

PUNTING	No.	Yds.	Avg.	In 20	LG
Hutton	73	3107	42.6	17	60
Eagles	74	3107	42.0	17	60
Opponents	74	3287	44.4	16	61

PUNT RETURNS	No.	FC	Yds.	Avg.	LG	TD
Seay	35	14	305	8.7	56	0
Solomon	5	3	27	5.4	9	0
Vincent	0	0	-2	—	-2	0
Eagles	40	17	330	8.3	56	0
Opponents	36	12	330	9.2	65t	1

KICKOFF RETURNS	No.	Yds.	Avg.	LG	TD
Witherspoon	53	1271	24.0	97t	2
Garner	6	117	19.5	28	0
Seay	4	51	12.8	22	0
Brooks	1	0	0.0	0	0
Eagles	64	1439	22.5	97t	2
Opponents	73	1715	23.5	86	0

SACKS	No.
W. Fuller	13.0
Mamula	8.0
W. Thomas	5.5
Hall	4.5
Jefferson	2.5
Dawkins	1.0
Farmer	1.0
Harmon	1.0
K. Johnson	1.0
Taylor	1.0
H. Thomas	1.0
Griffin	0.5
Eagles	40.0
Opponents	39.0

1997 DRAFT CHOICES

Round	Name	Pos.	College
1	Jon Harris	DE	Virginia
2	James Darling	LB	Washington State
3	Duce Staley	RB	South Carolina
4	Damien Robinson	DB	Iowa
5	Ndukwe Kalu	DE	Rice
	Luther Broughton	TE	Furman
6	Antwuan Wyatt	WR	Bethune-Cookman
	Edward Jasper	DT	Texas A&M
7	Koy Detmer	QB	Colorado
	Byron Capers	DB	Florida State
	Deauntae Brown	DB	Central State, Ohio

PHILADELPHIA EAGLES

1997 VETERAN ROSTER

No.	Name	Pos.	Ht.	Wt.	Birthdate	NFL Exp.	College	Hometown	How Acq.	'96 Games/ Starts
62	Beckles, Ian	G	6-1	304	7/20/67	7	Indiana	Montreal, Canada	UFA(TB)-'97	13/13
69	Boatswain, Harry	T-G	6-4	310	6/26/69	7	New Haven	Brooklyn, N.Y.	UFA(NYJ)-'97	16/4*
18	Boniol, Chris	K	5-11	167	12/9/71	4	Louisiana Tech	Alexandria, La.	RFA(Dall)-'97	16/0*
25	Boykin, Deral	S	5-11	198	9/2/70	5	Louisville	Kent, Ohio	FA-'96	10/0
76	Brooks, Barrett	T	6-4	309	5/5/72	3	Kansas State	Florissant, Mo.	D2b-'95	16/5
19	Caldwell, Mike	WR	6-2	200	3/28/71	2	California	Danville, Calif.	FA-'97	1/0*
93	# Conner, Darion	DE-LB	6-2	250	9/28/67	8	Jackson State	Prairie Point, Miss.	FA-'96	7/0
77	Cooper, Richard	T	6-5	290	11/1/64	8	Tennessee	Memphis, Tenn.	UFA(NO)-'96	16/16
85	Copeland, Russell	WR	6-0	200	11/4/71	5	Memphis State	Tupelo, Miss.	UFA(Buff)-'97	11/0*
29	Croom, Corey	RB	5-11	208	5/22/71	4	Ball State	Sandusky, Ohio	FA-'97	0*
20	Dawkins, Brian	S	5-11	190	10/13/73	2	Clemson	Jacksonville, Fla.	D2b-'96	14/13
14	Detmer, Ty	QB	6-0	194	10/30/67	6	Brigham Young	San Antonio, Tex.	UFA(GB)-'96	13/11
74	DeVries, Jed	T	6-6	300	1/6/71	2	Utah State	Ogden, Utah	FA-'97	0*
96	Dillard, Stacey	DT	6-5	290	9/17/68	5	Oklahoma	Clarksville, Tex.	FA-'97	0*
75	Drake, Troy	T	6-6	305	5/15/72	3	Indiana	Byron, Ill.	FA-'95	11/0
94	Duff, John	DE	6-8	282	7/31/67	3	New Mexico	Tustin, Calif.	FA-'97	0*
87	Dunn, Jason	TE	6-4	257	11/15/73	2	Eastern Kentucky	Harrodsburg, Ky.	D2a-'96	16/12
61	Everitt, Steve	C	6-5	290	8/21/70	5	Michigan	Miami, Fla.	UFA(Balt)-'97	8/7*
55	Farmer, Ray	LB	6-3	225	7/1/72	2	Duke	Kernersville, N.C.	D4-'96	16/11
80	Fryar, Irving	WR	6-0	200	9/28/62	14	Nebraska	Mount Holly, N.J.	UFA(Mia)-'96	16/16
22	Fuller, James	S	5-11	208	8/5/69	4	Portland State	Tacoma, Wash.	FA-'96	13/2
30	† Garner, Charlie	RB	5-9	187	2/13/72	4	Tennessee	Falls Church, Va.	D2b-'94	15/1
97	Hall, Rhett	DT	6-2	276	12/5/68	7	California	Morgan Hill, Calif.	UFA(SF)-'95	16/16
91	Harmon, Andy	DT	6-4	278	4/6/69	7	Kent State	Centerville, Ohio	D6-'91	2/2
42	Harris, Rudy	RB	6-2	257	9/18/70	3	Clemson	Brockton, Mass.	FA-'97	0*
7	Hoying, Bobby	QB	6-3	221	9/20/72	2	Ohio State	St. Henry, Ohio	D3-'96	1/0
4	Hutton, Tom	P-K	6-1	193	7/8/72	3	Tennessee	Memphis, Tenn.	FA-'95	16/0
79	Jefferson, Greg	DE	6-3	257	8/31/71	3	Central Florida	Bartow, Fla.	D3a-'95	11/0
88	Johnson, Jimmie	TE	6-2	257	10/6/66	9	Howard	Augusta, Ga.	FA-'95	16/3
82	Jones, Chris T.	WR	6-3	209	8/7/71	3	Miami	West Palm Beach, Fla.	D3b-'95	16/16
37	Jones, Larry	RB	6-0	232	2/16/71	2	Miami	Gainesville, Fla.	FA-'97	0*
26	Jourdain, Yonel	RB	5-11	204	4/20/71	3	Southern Illinois	Evanston, Ill.	FA-'97	0*
59	Mamula, Mike	LB-DE	6-4	252	8/14/73	3	Boston College	Lackawana, N.Y.	D1-'95	16/16
71	Mayberry, Jermane	G-T	6-4	325	8/29/73	2	Texas A&M-Kingsville	Floresville, Tex.	D1-'96	3/1
65	Miller, Bubba	C	6-1	300	1/24/73	2	Tennessee	Franklin, Tenn.	FA-'96	0*
72	† Panos, Joe	G-C	6-2	293	1/24/71	4	Wisconsin	Brookfield, Wis.	D3a-'94	16/16
9	Peete, Rodney	QB	6-0	225	3/16/66	9	Southern California	Tucson, Ariz.	UFA(Dall)-'95	5/5
48	President, Andre	TE	6-3	255	6/16/71	2	Angelo State	Fort Worth, Tex.	FA-'97	0*
16	Rhem, Steve	WR	6-2	212	11/9/71	4	Minnesota	Ocala, Fla.	FA-'97	0*
98	Samson, Michael	DT	6-3	294	2/17/73	2	Grambling State	Heidelberg, Miss.	FA-'96	2/0
81	# Seay, Mark	WR	6-0	175	4/1/71	6	Long Beach State	San Bernardino, Calif.	FA-'96	16/0
89	Singleton, Nate	WR	5-11	190	7/5/68	5	Grambling State	Morrero, La.	UFA(SF)-'97	2/0*
56	Smith, Darrin	LB	6-1	230	4/15/70	5	Miami	Miami, Fla.	UFA(Dall)-'97	16/16*
84	Solomon, Freddie	WR	5-10	180	8/15/72	2	South Carolina State	Alachua, Fla.	FA-'95	12/0
21	Taylor, Bobby	CB	6-3	216	12/28/73	3	Notre Dame	Longview, Tex.	D2a-'95	16/16
78	Thomas, Hollis	DT	6-0	306	1/10/74	2	Northern Illinois	St. Louis, Mo.	FA-'96	16/5
51	Thomas, William	LB	6-2	223	8/13/68	7	Texas A&M	Amarillo, Tex.	D4-'91	16/16
83	Timpson, Michael	WR	5-10	180	6/6/67	9	Penn State	Maimi Lakes, Fla.	FA-'97	15/15
34	Turner, Kevin	RB	6-1	231	6/12/69	6	Alabama	Prattville, Ala.	RFA(NE)-'95	16/12
68	Unutoa, Morris	C	6-1	284	3/10/71	2	Brigham Young	Carson, Calif.	FA-'96	16/0
23	Vincent, Troy	CB	6-0	194	6/8/70	6	Wisconsin	Trenton, N.J.	RFA(Mia)-'96	16/16
33	Watson, Tim	S	6-2	221	8/13/70	4	Howard	Fort Valley, Ga.	FA-'97	0*
32	Watters, Ricky	RB	6-1	217	4/7/69	7	Notre Dame	Harrisburg, Pa.	RFA(SF)-'95	16/16
50	Willis, James	LB	6-2	237	9/2/72	5	Auburn	Huntsville, Ala.	FA-'95	16/13
31	Witherspoon, Derrick	RB	5-10	196	2/14/71	3	Clemson	Sumter, S.C.	FA-'95	16/0
52	Wright, Sylvester	DE-LB	6-2	258	12/30/71	3	Kansas	Detroit, Mich.	FA-'95	16/0
66	Zandofsky, Mike	G	6-2	308	11/30/65	9	Washington	Corvallis, Ore.	UFA(Atl)-'97	14/14*
36	Zordich, Michael	S	6-1	212	10/12/63	11	Penn State	Youngstown, Ohio	FA-'94	16/16

* Beckles played 13 games with Tampa Bay in '96; Boatswain played 16 games with N.Y. Jets; Boniol and Smith played 16 games with Dallas; Caldwell played 1 game with San Francisco; Copeland played 11 games with Buffalo; Croom last active with New England in '95; DeVries last active with Cleveland in '95; Dillard and Watson last active with N.Y. Giants in '95; Duff last active with LA Raiders in '94; Everitt played 8 games with Baltimore; Harris last active with Tampa Bay in '94; L. Jones last active with Washington in '95; Jourdain last active with Buffalo in '95; Miller inactive for 16 games; President last active with Chicago in '95; Rhem spent '96 season on New Orleans' injured reserve list; Singleton played 2 games with San Francisco; Timpson played 15 games with Chicago; Zandofsky played 14 games with Atlanta.

\# Unrestricted free agent; subject to developments.

† Restricted free agent; subject to developments.

Traded—DT Ronnie Dixon (16 games in '96) to N.Y. Jets.

Players lost through free agency (6): DE William Fuller (SD; 16 games in '96), T Lester Holmes (Oak; 16), C Raleigh McKenzie (SD; 16), QB Mark Rypien (StL; 1), CB Johnny Thomas (SD; 9), TE Ed West (Atl; 16).

Also played with Eagles in '96—K Gary Anderson (16 games), DE Mark Gunn (3), WR Mark Ingram (5), DT Kevin Johnson (12), LB Joe Kelly (16), G Guy McIntyre (15), RB Adam Walker (13), CB Barry Wilburn (7), WR Calvin Williams (1), LB Marc Woodard (16), S Eric Zomalt (3).

COACHING STAFF

Head Coach,
Ray Rhodes

Pro Career: Named the nineteenth head coach in Eagles history on February 2, 1995, after serving as the defensive coordinator for the San Francisco 49ers. After being named the 1995 NFL coach of the year in his inaugural season at the Eagles' helm, Rhodes led the Eagles to another 10-6 season and a wild card playoff berth in 1996. As such, Rhodes became the first coach in team history to lead his team to the playoffs in each of his first two seasons. In 1995, Rhodes battled through major roster turnover, a slew of injuries to key personnel, an early season quarterback change, and a sluggish 1-3 start to post a 10-6 record, the top wild card berth in the NFC, and a record-setting 58-37 postseason defeat of the Detroit Lions. In 1996, Rhodes' troops again finished second in the NFC East behind the Dallas Cowboys. Philadelphia then closed the '96 season as the fifth of six seeds in the NFC playoffs and fell to the host 49ers in a wild card game. Rhodes came to Philadelphia after assisting George Seifert and the 49ers to that franchise's unprecedented fifth Super Bowl championship. In fact, Rhodes was an assistant on each of the 49ers' championship teams, making him one of only four men in NFL history to have served on the staffs of five Super Bowl winners. Before his most recent stint with San Francisco, Rhodes served two seasons in Green Bay as defensive coordinator under ex-49ers assistant Mike Holmgren, where he elevated the Packers' defense to the second-ranked unit overall in just two seasons. Rhodes ended his seven-year NFL playing career with San Francisco in 1980 and then joined Bill Walsh's coaching staff as an assistant defensive backs coach the following season. In 1982, he was promoted to defensive backs coach and held that position through 1991. Over that period, he developed four Pro Bowl defenders, cornerbacks Ronnie Lott and Eric Wright, and safeties Dwight Hicks and Carlton Williamson. Career record: 21-14.

Background: After spending two years at Texas Christian University, Rhodes finished his collegiate career at the University of Tulsa and was selected by the New York Giants in the tenth round of the 1974 NFL draft. He played wide receiver for his first three seasons with the Giants but was switched to defensive back in 1977. In 1979, he was traded to San Francisco in a deal that also saw 49ers defensive back Tony Dungy, presently the head coach of the Tampa Bay Buccaneers, sent to the Giants.

Personal: Born October 20, 1950, in Mexia, Tex. Rhodes and his wife, Carmen, have four daughters: Detra, Candra, Tynesha, and Raven, and reside in Marlton, New Jersey.

Assistant Coaches

Bill Callahan, offensive line; born July 31, 1956, Chicago, Ill., lives in Mt. Laurel, N.J. Quarterback Illinois Benedictine 1975-77. No pro playing experience. College coach: Illinois 1980-87, Northern Arizona 1987-88, Southern Illinois 1989, Wisconsin 1990-94. Pro coach: Joined Eagles in 1995.

Gerald Carr, wide receivers; born June 28, 1959, Davidson, N.C., lives in Siclerville, N.J. Quarterback Southern Illinois 1977-80. No pro playing experience. College coach: Southern Illinois 1982, Davidson 1983-85, Akron 1986-88, Washington State 1989-90, Arizona 1991, North Carolina 1992-94. Pro coach: Joined Eagles in 1995.

Juan Castillo, tight ends; born October 8, 1959, Port Isabel, Tex., lives in Moorestown, N.J. Linebacker Texas A&M-Kingsville (formerly Texas A&I) 1978-80. Pro linebacker San Antonio Gunslingers (USFL) 1984-85. College coach: Texas A&M-Kingsville 1982-85, 1990-94. Pro coach: Joined Eagles in 1995.

Jon Gruden, offensive coordinator; born August 17, 1963, Sandusky, Ohio, lives in Mt. Laurel, N.J. Quarterback Dayton 1983-85. No pro playing experience. College coach: Tennessee 1986-87, Southeast Missouri 1988, Pacific 1989, Pittsburgh 1991. Pro coach:

1997 FIRST-YEAR ROSTER

Name	Pos.	Ht.	Wt.	Birthdate	College	Hometown	How Acq.
Broughton, Luther	TE	6-2	248	11/30/74	Furman	Huger, S.C.	D5b
Brown, Deauntae	CB	5-10	195	4/28/74	Central State, Ohio	Detroit, Mich.	D7c
Burks, Dialleo (1)	WR	6-2	181	7/7/74	Eastern Kentucky	LaGrange, Ga.	FA
Capers, Byron	CB	6-1	194	3/21/74	Florida State	Marietta, Ga.	D7b
Cavil, Ben (1)	G	6-2	310	1/31/72	Oklahoma	Lamarque, Tex.	W(SD)
Cooper, Damion	DE	6-3	260	7/14/71	Central State, Ohio	Denver, Colo.	FA
Crespina, Keita (1)	CB	5-8	184	2/25/71	Temple	Philadelphia, Pa.	FA
Darling, James	LB	6-0	250	12/28/74	Washington State	Kettle Falls, Wash.	D2
Detmer, Koy	QB	6-0	180	7/5/73	Colorado	San Antonio, Tex.	D7a
Fogle, DeShawn	LB	6-1	220	4/1/75	Kansas State	Manhattan, Kan.	FA
Ford, Fredric (1)	CB	6-3	196	1/2/73	Mississippi Valley State	Greenwood, Miss.	FA
Harris, Jon	DE	6-7	280	6/9/74	Virginia	Inwood, N.Y.	D1
Heyward, Anthony	G	6-3	291	9/20/74	Howard	Largo, Md.	FA
Hoover, Dan	C	6-5	278	1/8/74	Mississippi State	Fairhope, Ala.	FA
Jasper, Edward	DT	6-2	295	1/18/73	Texas A&M	Troop, Tex.	D6b
Kalu, Ndukwe	DE	6-3	248	8/3/75	Rice	San Antonio, Tex.	D5a
Knox, Kevin (1)	WR	6-2	199	1/30/71	Florida State	Niceville, Fla.	FA
Lewis, Chad	TE	6-6	252	10/5/71	Brigham Young	Orem, Utah	FA
McGaughey, Thomas (1)	S	6-0	207	5/8/73	Houston	Houston, Tex.	FA
McGregor, Maurice	LB	6-1	243	5/31/74	North Carolina	Marietta, Ga.	FA
Rice, Anthony	CB-S	5-9	185	11/29/73	Laverne	Pomona, Calif.	FA
Robinson, Damien	S	6-2	210	12/22/73	Iowa	Dallas, Tex.	D4
Staley, Duce	RB	5-11	220	2/27/75	South Carolina	Columbia, S.C.	D3
Swinton, Kireem	G	6-2	305	11/7/75	Howard	Forestville, Md.	FA
Thrash, James	WR	6-0	197	4/28/75	Missouri Southern	Wewoka, Okla.	FA
Walker, Corey	RB	5-10	188	6/4/73	Arkansas State	Memphis, Tenn.	FA
Wyatt, Antwuan	WR	5-10	199	7/18/75	Bethune-Cookman	Daytona Beach, Fla.	D6a

The term NFL Rookie is defined as a player who is in his first season of professional football and has not been on the roster of another professional football team for any regular-season or postseason games. A Rookie is designated by an "R" on NFL rosters. Players who have been active in another professional football league or players who have NFL experience, including either preseason training camp or being on an Active List or Inactive List, or on Reserve/Injured or Reserve/Physically Unable to Perform for fewer than six regular-season games, are termed NFL First-Year Players. An NFL First-Year Player is designated by a "1" on NFL rosters. Thereafter, a player is credited with an additional year of experience for each season in which he accumulates six games on the Active List or Inactive List, or on Reserve/Injured or Reserve/Physically Unable to Perform.

NOTES

_____

_____

_____

_____

_____

_____

San Francisco 49ers 1990, Green Bay Packers 1992-94, joined Eagles in 1995.

Chuck Knox, Jr., defensive assistant; born June 19, 1965, Englewood, N.J., lives in Mt. Laurel, N.J. Running back Arizona 1984-85. No pro playing experience. Pro coach: Los Angeles Rams 1993-94, joined Eagles in 1995.

Sean Payton, quarterbacks; born December 29, 1963, San Mateo, Calif., lives in Marlton, N.J. Quarterback Eastern Illinois 1982-86. Pro quarterback Chicago Bears 1987. College coach: San Diego State 1988-89, 1992-93, Indiana State 1990-91, Miami (Ohio) 1994-95, Illinois 1996. Pro coach: Joined Eagles in 1997.

David Shaw, offensive assistant; born July 31, 1972, San Diego Calif., lives in Philadelphia, Pa. Wide receiver Stanford 1990-94. No pro playing experience. College coach: Western Washington 1995-96. Pro coach: Joined Eagles in 1997.

Danny Smith, defensive backs; born November 7, 1953, Pittsburgh, Pa., lives in Mt. Laurel, N.J. Defensive back Edinboro State 1972-75. No pro playing experience. College coach: Edinboro State 1976, Clemson 1979, William & Mary 1980-83, Citadel 1984-86, Georgia Tech 1987-94. Pro coach: Joined Eagles in 1995.

Emmitt Thomas, defensive coordinator; born June 3, 1943, Angleton, Tex., lives in Voorhees, N.J. Quarterback-wide receiver Bishop (Tex.) College 1963-65. Pro defensive back Kansas City Chiefs 1966-78. College coach: Central Missouri State 1979-80. Pro coach: St. Louis Cardinals 1981-85, Washington

Redskins 1986-94, joined Eagles in 1995.

Mike Trgovac, defensive line; born February 27, 1959, Youngstown, Ohio, lives in Marlton, N.J. Defensive lineman Michigan 1977-80. No pro playing experience. College coach: Michigan 1984-85, Ball State 1986-88, Navy 1989, Colorado State 1990-91, Notre Dame 1992-94. Pro coach: Joined Eagles in 1995.

Joe Vitt, linebackers; born August 23, 1954, Camden, N.J., lives in Mt. Laurel, N.J. Linebacker Towson State 1973-75. No pro playing experience. Pro coach: Baltimore Colts 1979-81, Seattle Seahawks 1982-91, Los Angeles Rams 1992-94, joined Eagles in 1995.

Joe Wessel, special teams; born January 5, 1962, Miami, Fla., lives in Philadelphia, Pa. Quarterback-safety Florida State 1981-84. No pro playing experience. College coach: Louisiana State 1985-90, Notre Dame 1991-93. Pro coach: Cincinnati Bengals 1994-96, joined Eagles in 1997.

Ted Williams, running backs; born November 17, 1943, Lyons, Tex., lives in Siclerville, N.J. No college or pro playing experience. College coach: UCLA 1980-89, Washington State 1991-93, Arizona 1994. Pro coach: Joined Eagles in 1995.

Mike Wolf, strength and conditioning; born May 15, 1965, Allentown, Pa., lives in Marlton, N.J. Center Penn State 1983-87. No pro playing experience. College coach: Vanderbilt 1988-89, Lehigh 1990, Penn State 1991. Pro coach: Minnesota Vikings 1992-94, joined Eagles in 1995.

National Football Conference
Western Division
Team Colors: Royal Blue, Gold, and White
One Rams Way
St. Louis County, Missouri 63045
Telephone: (314) 982-7267

CLUB OFFICIALS

Owner/Chairman: Georgia Frontiere
Owner/Vice Chairman: Stan Kroenke
President: John Shaw
President-Football Operations and Head Coach:
  Dick Vermeil
Executive Vice President: Jay Zygmunt
Senior Vice President-Administration and
  General Counsel: Bob Wallace
Treasurer: Jeff Brewer
Vice President-Finance: Adrian Barr
Vice President-Player Personnel: John Becker
Vice President-Media and Community Relations:
  Marshall Klein
Vice President-Football Operations: Lynn Stiles
Vice President-Marketing: Phil Thomas
Vice President-Sales: Brian Ulione
Director of Pro Personnel: Charlie Armey
Director of Player Development: Les Miller
Vice President/Player Development: Jackie Slater
Director of Operations: John Oswald
Director of Public Relations: Rick Smith
Assistant Director of Public Relations: Tony Wyllie
Head Trainer: Jim Anderson
Assistant Trainers: Dake Walden, Ron DuBuque
Equipment Manager: Todd Hewitt
Scouts: Billy Campfield, Greg Gaines,
  Kevin McCabe, Lawrence McCutcheon,
  David Razzano, Paul Russell, Harley Sewell
Stadium: Trans World Dome at America's Center
  •**Capacity:** 66,000
  701 Convention Plaza
  St. Louis County, Missouri 63101
Playing Surface: AstroTurf
Training Camp: Western Illinois University
  Thompson Hall
  Macomb, Illinois 61455

1997 SCHEDULE
PRESEASON
Aug. 2	at Minnesota	7:00
Aug. 8	**Arizona**	7:00
Aug. 15	at Dallas	7:00
Aug. 22	**Kansas City**	7:00

REGULAR SEASON
Aug. 31	**New Orleans**	12:00
Sept. 7	**San Francisco**	12:00
Sept. 14	at Denver	2:00
Sept. 21	**New York Giants**	3:00
Sept. 28	at Oakland	1:00
Oct. 5	Open Date	
Oct. 12	at San Francisco	1:00
Oct. 19	**Seattle**	12:00
Oct. 26	**Kansas City**	12:00
Nov. 2	at Atlanta	1:00
Nov. 9	at Green Bay	12:00
Nov. 16	**Atlanta**	12:00
Nov. 23	**Carolina**	3:00
Nov. 30	at Washington	1:00
Dec. 7	at New Orleans	12:00
Dec. 14	**Chicago**	7:00
Dec. 20	at Carolina (Sat.)	4:00

RECORD HOLDERS
INDIVIDUAL RECORDS—CAREER
Category	Name	Performance
Rushing (Yds.)	Eric Dickerson, 1983-87	7,245
Passing (Yds.)	Jim Everett, 1986-1993	23,758
Passing (TDs)	Roman Gabriel, 1962-1972	154
Receiving (No.)	Henry Ellard, 1983-1993	593
Receiving (Yds.)	Henry Ellard, 1983-1993	9,761
Interceptions	Ed Meador, 1959-1970	46
Punting (Avg.)	Danny Villanueva, 1960-64	44.2
Punt Return (Avg.)	Henry Ellard, 1983-1992	11.3
Kickoff Return (Avg.)	Tom Wilson, 1956-1961	27.1
Field Goals	Mike Lansford, 1982-1990	158
Touchdowns (Tot.)	Eric Dickerson, 1983-87	58
Points	Mike Lansford, 1982-1990	789

INDIVIDUAL RECORDS—SINGLE SEASON
Category	Name	Performance
Rushing (Yds.)	Eric Dickerson, 1984	*2,105
Passing (Yds.)	Jim Everett, 1989	4,310
Passing (TDs)	Jim Everett, 1988	31
Receiving (No.)	Isaac Bruce, 1995	119
Receiving (Yds.)	Isaac Bruce, 1995	1,781
Interceptions	Dick (Night Train) Lane, 1952	*14
Punting (Avg.)	Danny Villanueva, 1962	45.5
Punt Return (Avg.)	Woodley Lewis, 1952	18.5
Kickoff Return (Avg.)	Verda (Vitamin T) Smith, 1950	33.7
Field Goals	David Ray, 1973	30
Touchdowns (Tot.)	Eric Dickerson, 1983	20
Points	David Ray, 1973	130

INDIVIDUAL RECORDS—SINGLE GAME
Category	Name	Performance
Rushing (Yds.)	Eric Dickerson, 1-4-86	248
Passing (Yds.)	Norm Van Brocklin, 9-28-51	*554
Passing (TDs)	Many times.	5
	Last time by Jim Everett, 9-25-88	
Receiving (No.)	Tom Fears, 12-3-50	*18
Receiving (Yds.)	Willie Anderson, 11-26-89	*336
Interceptions	Many times.	3
	Last time by Keith Lyle, 12-15-96	
Field Goals	Bob Waterfield, 12-9-51	5
Touchdowns (Tot.)	Bob Shaw, 12-11-49	4
	Elroy (Crazylegs) Hirsch, 9-28-51	4
	Harold Jackson, 10-14-73	4
Points	Bob Shaw, 12-11-49	24
	Elroy (Crazylegs) Hirsch, 9-28-51	24
	Harold Jackson, 10-14-73	24

*NFL Record

COACHING HISTORY
Cleveland 1937-1945, Los Angeles 1946-1994
(424-388-20)
1937-38	Hugo Bezdek*	1-13-0
1938	Art Lewis	4-4-0
1939-42	Earl (Dutch) Clark	16-26-2
1944	Aldo (Buff) Donelli	4-6-0
1945-46	Adam Walsh	16-5-1
1947	Bob Snyder	6-6-0
1948-49	Clark Shaughnessy	14-8-3
1950-52	Joe Stydahar**	19-9-0
1952-54	Hamp Pool	23-11-2
1955-59	Sid Gillman	28-32-1
1960-62	Bob Waterfield***	9-24-1
1962-65	Harland Svare	14-31-3
1966-70	George Allen	49-19-4
1971-72	Tommy Prothro	14-12-2
1973-77	Chuck Knox	57-20-1
1978-82	Ray Malavasi	43-36-0
1983-91	John Robinson	79-74-0
1992-94	Chuck Knox	15-33-0
1995-96	Rich Brooks	13-19-0

*Released after three games in 1938
**Resigned after one game in 1952
***Resigned after eight games in 1962

TRANS WORLD DOME

1996 TEAM RECORD

PRESEASON (3-1)

Date	Result		Opponents
8/3	L	10-16	at Pittsburgh
8/9	W	17-10	Jacksonville
8/17	W	34-30	at Kansas City
8/23	W	37-34	San Diego

REGULAR SEASON (6-10)

Date	Result		Opponents	Att.
9/1	W	26-16	Cincinnati	62,659
9/8	L	0-34	at San Francisco	63,624
9/22	L	10-17	Washington	62,303
9/29	L	28-31	at Arizona (OT)	33,116
10/6	L	11-28	San Francisco	61,260
10/13	L	13-45	at Carolina	70,535
10/20	W	17-14	Jacksonville	60,066
10/27	L	31-37	at Baltimore (OT)	60,256
11/3	L	6-42	at Pittsburgh	58,148
11/10	W	59-16	Atlanta	58,776
11/17	L	10-20	Carolina	60,652
11/24	L	9-24	Green Bay	61,499
12/1	W	26-10	at New Orleans	26,310
12/8	L	9-35	at Chicago	45,075
12/15	W	34-27	at Atlanta	26,519
12/21	W	14-13	New Orleans	57,681

(OT) Overtime

SCORE BY PERIODS

Rams	55	102	60	86	0	—	303
Opponents	68	112	120	100	9	—	409

ATTENDANCE

Home 484,896   Away 405,452   Total 890,348
Single-game home record, 65,598 (11/12/95)
Single-season home record, 496,486 (1995)

1996 TEAM STATISTICS

	Rams	Opp.
Total First Downs	255	329
Rushing	93	114
Passing	141	191
Penalty	21	24
Third Down: Made/Att	84/224	95/226
Third Down Pct.	37.5	42.0
Fourth Down: Made/Att	9/19	13/21
Fourth Down Pct.	47.4	61.9
Total Net Yards	4372	5529
Avg. Per Game	273.3	345.6
Total Plays	986	1068
Avg. Per Play	4.4	5.2
Net Yards Rushing	1607	1854
Avg. Per Game	100.4	115.9
Total Rushes	448	478
Net Yards Passing	2765	3675
Avg. Per Game	172.8	229.7
Sacked/Yards Lost	57/379	32/181
Gross Yards	3144	3856
Att./Completions	481/249	558/341
Completion Pct.	51.8	61.1
Had Intercepted	23	26
Punts/Avg.	78/44.8	69/40.6
Net Punting Avg.	78/36.1	69/32.5
Penalties/Yards Lost	133/1015	111/832
Fumbles/Ball Lost	42/21	26/13
Touchdowns	34	50
Rushing	10	22
Passing	18	23
Returns	6	5
Avg. Time of Possession	27:58	32:02

1996 INDIVIDUAL STATISTICS

PASSING	Att.	Comp.	Yds.	Pct.	TD	Int.	Tkld.	Rate
Banks	368	192	2544	52.2	15	15	48/306	71.0
Walsh	77	33	344	42.9	0	5	4/27	29.4
Martin	34	23	241	67.6	3	2	4/34	92.9
Bruce	2	1	15	50.0	0	1	0/0	35.4
Phillips	0	0	0	—	0	0	1/12	—
Rams	481	249	3144	51.8	18	23	57/379	65.0
Opponents	558	341	3856	61.1	23	26	32/181	76.1

	TD	TD	TD				
SCORING	R	P	Rt	PAT	FG	Saf	PTS
Lohmiller	0	0	0	28/29	21/25	0	91
Kennison	0	9	2	0/0	0/0	0	66
Bruce	0	7	0	0/0	0/0	0	42
Green	4	1	0	0/0	0/0	0	32
Phillips	4	1	0	0/0	0/0	0	30
Parker	0	0	2	0/0	0/0	0	12
Lyght	0	0	1	0/0	0/0	0	6
Robinson	1	0	0	0/0	0/0	0	6
Ross	1	0	0	0/0	0/0	0	6
T. Wright	0	0	1	0/0	0/0	0	6
Banks	0	0	0	0/0	0/0	0	2
Huerta	0	0	0	2/2	0/0	0	2
Lyle	0	0	0	0/0	0/0	0	0
Rams	10	18	6	30/31	21/25	*1	303
Opponents	22	23	5	46/47	19/27	2	409

2-Point conversions: Banks, Green. Team: 2-3,
Opponents: 1-2.
*Rams were credited with 1 team safety.

RUSHING	Att.	Yds.	Avg.	LG	TD
Phillips	193	632	3.3	38	4
Green	127	523	4.1	35t	4
Banks	61	212	3.5	22	0
Robinson	32	134	4.2	24	1
Lyle	3	39	13.0	20	0
Moore	11	32	2.9	14	0
Martin	7	14	2.0	11	0
Walsh	6	10	1.7	13	0
D. Harris	3	5	1.7	3	0
Bruce	1	4	4.0	4	0
Ross	1	3	3.0	3t	1
Landeta	2	0	0.0	0	0
Thomas	1	-1	-1.0	-1	0
Rams	448	1607	3.6	38	10
Opponents	478	1854	3.9	66	22

RECEIVING	No.	Yds.	Avg.	LG	TD
Bruce	84	1338	15.9	70	7
Kennison	54	924	17.1	77t	9
Green	37	246	6.6	19	1
Conwell	15	164	10.9	26	0
Ross	15	160	10.7	28	0
Laing	13	116	8.9	22	0
Phillips	8	28	3.5	11t	1
Thomas	7	46	6.6	11	0
Clay	4	51	12.8	34	0
D. Harris	4	17	4.3	8	0
Moore	3	14	4.3	7	0
A. Wright	2	24	12.0	13	0
Drayton	2	11	5.5	6	0
Robinson	1	6	6.0	6	0
Rams	249	3144	12.6	77t	18
Opponents	341	3856	11.3	54t	23

INTERCEPTIONS	No.	Yds.	Avg.	LG	TD
Lyle	9	152	16.9	68	0
Lyght	5	43	8.6	25t	1
Parker	4	128	32.0	92t	2
Dorn	1	40	40.0	40	0
T. Wright	1	19	19.0	19t	1
Farr	1	5	5.0	5	0
Lincoln	1	3	3.0	3	0
McBurrows	1	3	3.0	3	0
R. Jones	1	0	0.0	0	0
Walker	1	0	0.0	0	0
Jenkins	1	-3	-3.0	-3	0
Rams	26	390	15.0	92t	4
Opponents	23	252	11.0	42	1

PUNTING	No.	Yds.	Avg.	In 20	LG
Landeta	78	3491	44.8	23	70
Rams	78	3491	44.8	23	70
Opponents	69	2801	40.6	20	61

PUNT RETURNS	No.	FC	Yds.	Avg.	LG	TD
Kennison	29	16	423	14.6	78t	2
O'Berry	5	0	16	3.2	8	0
Figaro	1	0	0	0.0	0	0
P. Davis	0	0	0	—	—	0
Rams	35	16	439	12.5	78t	2
Opponents	41	13	495	12.1	62	0

KICKOFF RETURNS	No.	Yds.	Avg.	LG	TD
Thomas	30	643	21.4	43	0
Kennison	23	454	19.7	44	0
Crawford	4	47	11.8	19	0
Phillips	4	74	18.5	35	0
Laing	1	15	15.0	15	0
Rams	62	1233	19.9	44	0
Opponents	58	1290	22.2	93t	2

SACKS	No.
Carter	9.5
O'Neal	7.0
J. Jones	5.5
Farr	4.5
J. Harris	2.0
Phifer	1.5
Goss	1.0
Osborne	1.0
Rams	32.0
Opponents	57.0

1997 DRAFT CHOICES

Round	Name	Pos.	College
1	Orlando Pace	T	Ohio State
2	Dexter McCleon	DB	Clemson
4	Ryan Tucker	C	Texas Christian
5	Taje Allen	DB	Texas
6	Muadianvita Kazadi	LB	Tulsa
7	Cedric White	DE	North Carolina A&T

1997 VETERAN ROSTER

No.	Name	Pos.	Ht.	Wt.	Birthdate	NFL Exp.	College	Hometown	How Acq.	'96 Games/ Starts
12	Banks, Tony	QB	6-4	225	4/5/73	2	Michigan State	San Diego, Calif.	D2a-'96	14/13
61	Brostek, Bern	C	6-3	300	9/11/66	8	Washington	Honolulu, Hawaii	D1-'90	16/16
80	Bruce, Isaac	WR	6-0	186	11/10/72	4	Memphis State	Ft. Lauderdale, Fla.	D2a-'94	16/16
93	Carter, Kevin	DE	6-5	280	9/21/73	3	Florida	Tallahassee, Fla.	D1-'95	16/16
89	Clay, Hayward	TE	6-3	260	7/25/73	2	Texas A&M	Snyder, Tex.	D6b-'96	11/4
84	Conwell, Ernie	TE	6-1	255	8/17/72	2	Washington	Kent, Wash.	D2b-'97	10/8
20	Crawford, Keith	WR	6-2	185	11/21/70	4	Howard Payne	Palestine, Tex.	W(GB)-'96	16/0
69	Dye, Ernest	T	6-6	325	7/15/71	5	South Carolina	Greenwood, S.C.	UFA(Ariz)-'97	8/0*
75	Farr, D'Marco	DT	6-1	280	6/9/71	4	Washington	Richmond, Calif.	FA-'94	16/16
9	Furrer, Will	QB	6-3	215	2/5/68	5	Virginia Tech	Pullman, Wash.	FA-'97	0*
70	Gandy, Wayne	T	6-4	300	2/10/71	4	Auburn	Haines City, Fla.	D1-'94	16/16
54	Gaskins, Percell	LB	6-0	226	4/25/72	2	Kansas State	Daytona Beach, Fla.	D4-'96	15/1
66	Gerak, John	G	6-3	269	1/6/70	5	Penn State	Struthers, Ohio	UFA(Minn)-'97	14/10*
60	Gruttadauria, Mike	C	6-3	295	12/26/72	2	Central Florida	Tarpon Springs, Fla.	FA-'96	9/4
51	Hager, Britt	LB	6-1	225	2/20/66	9	Texas	Odessa, Tex.	UFA(Den)-'97	2/0*
33	Harris, Derrick	RB	6-0	250	8/18/72	2	Miami	Houston, Tex.	D6a-'96	11/6
99	Harris, James	DE	6-6	285	5/13/68	5	Temple	East St. Louis, Ill.	FA-'96	16/0
34	Heyward, Craig	RB	5-11	250	9/26/66	10	Pittsburgh	Passaic, N.J.	UFA(Atl)-'97	15/5*
57	Homco, Thomas	LB	6-1	242	1/8/70	5	Northwestern	Highland, Ind.	FA-'92	1/0
68	James, Jesse	C	6-4	311	9/16/71	3	Mississippi State	Mobile, Ala.	D2b-'95	1/0
52	Jones, Mike	LB	6-1	230	4/15/69	7	Missouri	Kansas City, Mo.	UFA(Oak)-'97	13/9*
55	Jones, Robert	LB	6-3	242	9/27/69	6	East Carolina	Reedville, Va.	UFA(Dall)-'96	16/13
88	Kennison, Eddie	WR	6-0	195	1/20/73	2	Louisiana State	Lake Charles, La.	D1b-'97	15/14
65	Kirksey, Jon	DT	6-4	345	2/21/71	2	Sacramento State	Greenville, S.C.	FA-'95	10/1
86	Laing, Aaron	TE	6-3	255	7/19/71	3	New Mexico State	Houston, Tex.	FA-'96	12/8
17	Lee, Kevin	WR	6-1	190	1/1/71	3	Alabama	Mobile, Ala.	FA-'97	2/0*
41	Lyght, Todd	CB	6-0	189	2/9/69	7	Notre Dame	Flint, Mich.	D1-'91	16/16
35	Lyle, Keith	S	6-2	204	4/17/72	3	Virginia	Vienna, Va.	D3a-'94	16/16
94	Mack, Rico	LB	6-2	250	2/22/71	4	Appalachian State	Stratham, Ga.	FA-'96	0*
10	Martin, Jamie	QB	6-2	210	2/8/70	4	Weber State	Arroyo Grande, Calif.	FA-'94	6/0
23	McBurrows, Gerald	S	5-11	206	10/7/73	3	Kansas	Detroit, Mich.	D7a-'95	16/7
73	Miller, Fred	T	6-7	306	2/6/73	2	Baylor	Houston, Tex.	D7a-'96	14/0
79	Milner, Billy	T	6-4	304	6/21/72	3	Houston	Atlanta, Ga.	T(Mia)-'96	10/0
44	Moore, Jerald	RB	5-9	229	11/20/74	2	Oklahoma	Houston, Tex.	D3-'96	11/4
29	Moore, Ron	RB	5-10	225	1/26/70	5	Pittsburg State	Spencer, Okla.	UFA(NYJ)-'97	15/0*
91	O'Neal, Leslie	DE	6-4	270	5/7/64	12	Oklahoma State	Little Rock, Ark.	UFA(SD)-'96	16/16
97	Osborne, Chuck	DT	6-2	295	11/2/73	2	Arizona	Canyon Country, Calif.	D7-'96	15/1
27	Parker, Anthony	CB	5-10	185	2/1/66	7	Arizona State	Tempe, Ariz.	UFA(Minn)-'95	14/14
58	Phifer, Roman	LB	6-2	239	3/5/68	7	UCLA	Pineville, N.C.	D2-'91	15/15
21	Phillips, Lawrence	RB	6-0	212	5/12/75	2	Nebraska	West Covina, Calif.	D1a-'96	15/11
28	Philyaw, Dino	RB	5-10	203	10/6/70	3	Oregon	Dudley, N.C.	FA-'97	10/0*
77	Robinson, Jeff	DE	6-4	265	2/20/70	5	Idaho	Spokane, Wash.	UFA(Den)-'97	16/0*
82	† Ross, Jermaine	WR	6-0	196	4/27/71	3	Purdue	Jeffersonville, Ind.	FA-'94	15/0
11	Rypien, Mark	QB	6-4	231	10/2/62	12	Washington State	Spokane, Wash.	UFA(Phil)-'97	1/0*
22	Scurlock, Mike	S	5-10	199	2/26/72	3	Arizona	Tucson, Ariz.	D5-'95	16/0
87	Thomas, J.T.	WR	5-10	182	7/11/71	3	Arizona State	San Bernardino, Calif.	D7d-'95	16/1
38	Walker, Marquis	CB	5-10	173	7/6/72	2	Southeast Missouri	St. Louis, Mo.	FA-'96	8/4
67	White, Dwayne	G	6-2	315	2/10/67	8	Alcorn State	Philadelphia, Pa.	UFA(NYJ)-'95	16/16
72	Wiegert, Zach	T	6-4	315	8/16/72	3	Nebraska	Fremont, Neb.	D2a-'95	16/16
14	Wilkins, Jeff	K	6-2	192	4/9/72	4	Youngstown State	Austintown, Ohio	FA(SF)-'97	16/0*
19	Williams, Billy	WR	5-11	185	6/7/71	2	Tennessee	Alcoa, Tenn.	FA-'96	1/0
96	Williams, Jay	DT	6-3	280	10/13/71	2	Wake Forest	Washington, D.C.	FA-'94	2/0
92	Wilson, Troy	DE-DT	6-2	263	11/22/70	3	Pittsburg State	Tecumseh, Kan.	FA-'97	0*
32	Wright, Toby	S	5-11	215	11/19/70	4	Nebraska	Phoenix, Ariz.	D2b-'94	12/12
90	Zgonina, Jeff	DT	6-2	285	5/24/70	5	Purdue	Mundolein, Ill.	UFA(Atl)-'97	8/0*

* Dye played 8 games with Arizona in '96; Furrer last active with Houston in '95; Gerak played 14 games with Minnesota; Hager played 2 games with Denver; Heyward played 15 games with Atlanta; M. Jones played 13 games with Oakland; Lee played 2 games with San Francisco; Mack missed '96 season because of injury; R. Moore played 15 games with N.Y. Jets; Philyaw played 10 games with Carolina; Robinson played 16 games with Denver; Rypien played 1 game with Philadelphia; Wilkins played 16 games with San Francisco; Wilson last active with San Francisco in '95; Zgonina played 8 games with Atlanta.

† Restricted free agent; subject to developments.

Retired—Alexander Wright, 7-year wide receiver, 3 games in '96.

Players lost through free agency (3): G Chuck Belin (NO; 1 game in '96), T Leo Goeas (Balt; 16), QB Steve Walsh (TB; 3).

Also played with Rams in '96—T Darryl Ashmore (6 games), LB Paschall Davis (10), CB Torin Dorn (9), TE Troy Drayton (3), LB Cedric Figaro (15), LB Antonio Goss (8), RB Harold Green (16), RB Marcus Holiday (1), K Carlos Huerta (1), LB Carlos Jenkins (13), DT Jimmie Jones (14), P Sean Landeta (16), CB Jeremy Lincoln (13), K Chip Lohmiller (15), CB Herman O'Berry (9), RB Greg Robinson (11), G Joe Valerio (1), DE Alberto White (3), LB Mark Williams (2).

COACHING STAFF

Head Coach,
Dick Vermeil

Pro Career: Named twentieth head coach of the Rams on January 22, 1997. Was designated the first special teams coach in NFL history in 1969 for the Los Angeles Rams. After one year of coaching in college, he returned to the Rams as the quarterbacks coach from 1971-73. In 1976, he was named head coach of the Philadelphia Eagles. In 1978, he led the Eagles to their first playoff appearance in eighteen seasons. In 1980, he led the Eagles to Super Bowl XV before losing to the Oakland Raiders. He concluded his stint in Philadelphia in 1982 after piloting the Eagles to four playoff appearances in seven seasons. Career record: 57-51.

Background: Played quarterback at San Jose State from 1956-57 after transferrng from Napa Junior College. Began his head coaching career in 1960 at Hillsdale High School in San Mateo, California, then moved on to San Mateo College in 1963. The following year he became head coach at Napa College. In 1965, joined John Ralston's staff at Stanford where he was an assistant for four years. Returned to college coaching in 1970 when he became the offensive coordinator at UCLA. Vermeil was named head coach at UCLA in 1974 where he earned national recognition during his two seasons. In 1975, the Bruins capped off an improbable season by upsetting No. 1 Ohio State in the Rose Bowl. Has been named Coach of the Year on four levels: high school, junior college, Division I, and NFL. Is the only coach who has guided his team to a Super Bowl and a Rose Bowl.

Personal: Born October 30, 1936, in Calistoga, Calif. Graduated from San Jose State in 1958 with a bachelor of science degree in physical education and in 1959 with a master's degree in physical education. Vermeil and his wife, Carol, reside in Chesterfield, Mo., and have three children and ten grandchildren.

Assistant Coaches

Nick Aliotti, defensive asst.; born May 29, 1954, Pittsburg, Calif., lives in St. Louis. Running back U.C.-Davis 1972-75. No pro playing experience. College coach: U.C.-Davis 1976-77, Oregon 1978-79, 1988-94, Oregon State 1980-83, Chico State 1984-87. Pro coach: Joined Rams in 1995.

Steve Brown, defensive asst.; born March 20, 1960, Sacramento, Calif., lives in St. Louis. Defensive back Oregon 1978-82. Pro cornerback Houston Oilers 1983-90. Pro coach: Joined Rams in 1995.

John Bunting, linebackers; born July 15, 1950, Portland, Maine, lives in St. Louis. Linebacker North Carolina 1968-71. Pro linebacker Philadelphia Eagles 1972-82, Philadelphia Stars (USFL) 1983-84. College coach: Brown 1986, Rowan College 1987-92. Pro coach: Baltimore Stars (USFL) 1985, Kansas City Chiefs 1993-96, joined Rams in 1997.

Bud Carson, defensive coordinator; born April 28, 1931, Freeport, Pa., lives in St. Louis. Running back-safety North Carolina 1948-51. No pro playing experience. College coach: North Carolina 1957-64, South Carolina 1965, Georgia Tech 1966-71. Pro coach: Pittsburgh Steelers 1972-77, Los Angeles Rams 1978-81, Baltimore Colts 1982, Kansas City Chiefs 1983, New York Jets 1985-88, Cleveland Browns 1989-90 (head coach), Philadelphia Eagles 1991-94, re-joined Rams in 1997.

Chris Clausen, strength and conditioning coordinator; born February 21, 1958, Evergreen Park, Ill., lives in St. Louis. Cornerback Indiana 1976-79. No pro playing experience. College coach: San Diego State 1987-88. Pro coach: San Diego Chargers 1989-91, joined Rams in 1992.

Dick Coury, wide receivers; born September 29, 1929, Athens, Ohio, lives in St. Louis. No college or pro playing experience. College coach: Southern California 1967-69, Cal State-Fullerton 1970-71. Pro coach: Denver Broncos 1972-73, Portland Storm (WFL) 1974 (head coach), San Diego Chargers 1975, Philadelphia Eagles 1976-81, Boston/New Orleans/Portland Breakers (USFL) 1983-85 (head

1997 FIRST-YEAR ROSTER

Name	Pos.	Ht.	Wt.	Birthdate	College	Hometown	How Acq.
Allen, Taje	CB	5-10	180	11/6/73	Texas	Lubbock, Tex.	D5
Baker, Donnell (1)	WR	6-0	180	12/21/73	Southern	Baton Rouge, La.	FA
Baynham, Grant	TE	6-5	250	10/11/73	Georgia Tech	North Augusta, S.C.	FA
Brice, Will	P	6-4	225	10/24/74	Virginia	Lancaster, S.C.	FA
Cochran, Nate	P	6-5	215	2/26/75	Pittsburgh	Greenville, S.C.	FA
Clemons, Charlie (1)	LB	6-2	250	7/4/72	Georgia	Griffin, Ga.	FA
Ford, Peter	CB-S	5-11	178	2/3/75	Clemson	Sumter, S.C.	FA
Gordon, Joe	CB	5-8	180	11/27/73	Kansas State	Arlington, Tex.	FA
Henne, Aaron	G	6-5	299	7/16/75	Maryland	Allison Park, Pa.	FA
Hitson, Don	RB	6-1	200	12/8/73	Murray State	Valdosta, Ga.	FA
Ivy, Greg (1)	P	6-0	210	9/28/72	Oklahoma State	Atlanta, Tex.	FA
Jacoby, Mitch	TE	6-4	252	12/8/73	Northern Illinois	Frenonia, Wis.	FA
Kazadi, Muadianvita	LB	6-2	236	12/20/73	Tulsa	Newton, Kan.	D6
Knuckles, Brian	RB	5-10	206	11/12/72	Western Illinois	Charlotte, N.C.	FA
Locker, Joel	LB	6-2	240	1/5/74	Tulane	Slidell, La.	FA
McCleon, Dexter	CB	5-10	198	10/9/73	Clemson	Meridian, Miss.	D2
McEntyre, Kenny (1)	CB	5-11	185	12/2/70	Kansas City	Plano, Tex.	FA
Pace, Orlando	T	6-7	334	11/4/75	Ohio State	Sandusky, Ohio	D1
Regular, Moses	TE	6-2	265	10/31/71	Missouri Valley	Osceola, Fla.	FA
Robinson, Bryan	DE-DT	6-4	283	6/22/74	Fresno State	Fresno, Calif.	FA
Rowe, Joe	CB-S	6-0	195	12/8/73	Virginia	Emporia, Va.	FA
Sellers, Donald	WR	6-0	185	12/30/74	New Mexico	Birmingham, Ala.	FA
Swann, Charles (1)	CB	6-1	188	10/29/70	Indiana	South Bend, Ind.	FA
Tillman, Buster	WR	6-0	190	9/16/74	Ohio State	Steubenville, Ohio	FA
Tellison, A.C. (1)	WR	6-2	208	9/5/71	Miami	Bay City, Tex.	FA
Tucker, Ryan	C	6-5	285	6/12/75	Texas Christian	Lubbock, Tex.	D4
Wood, Joe	K	6-2	210	12/3/68	Air Force	Mission Viejo, Calif.	FA
White, Cedric	DT	6-2	298	10/22/74	North Carolina A&T	Los Angeles, Calif.	D7
Williams, Tyrone (1)	DE	6-4	282	10/22/72	Wyoming	Papillion, Neb.	FA

The term NFL Rookie is defined as a player who is in his first season of professional football and has not been on the roster of another professional football team for any regular-season or postseason games. A Rookie is designated by an "R" on NFL rosters. Players who have been active in another professional football league or players who have NFL experience, including either preseason training camp or being on an Active List or Inactive List, or on Reserve/Injured or Reserve/Physically Unable to Perform for fewer than six regular-season games, are termed NFL First-Year Players. An NFL First-Year Player is designated by a "1" on NFL rosters. Thereafter, a player is credited with an additional year of experience for each season in which he accumulates six games on the Active List or Inactive List, or on Reserve/Injured or Reserve/Physically Unable to Perform.

NOTES

coach), Los Angeles Rams 1986-90, New England Patriots 1991-92, Minnesota Vikings 1993, Houston Oilers 1994-96, re-joined Rams in 1997.

Frank Gansz, special teams-offensive asst.; born November 22, 1938, Altoona, Pa., lives in St. Louis. Guard-linebacker Navy 1957-59. No pro playing experience. College coach: Air Force 1964-66, Colgate 1968, Navy 1969-72, Oklahoma State 1973, 1975, Army 1974, UCLA 1976-77. Pro coach: San Francisco 49ers 1978, Cincinnati Bengals 1979-80, Kansas City Chiefs 1981-82, 1986-88 (head coach 1987-88), Philadelphia Eagles 1983-85, Detroit Lions 1989-93, Atlanta Falcons 1994-96, joined Rams in 1997.

Peter Giunta, defensive backs; born August 11, 1956, Salem, Mass., lives in Chesterfield, Mo. Running back-defensive back Northeastern 1974-77. No pro playing experience. College coach: Penn State 1981-83, Brown 1984-87, Lehigh 1988-90. Pro coach: Philadelphia Eagles 1991-94, New York Jets 1995-96, joined Rams in 1997.

Kerry Goode, strength and conditioning coordinator; born July 28, 1965; lives in St. Louis. Tailback Alabama 1983-1987. Pro running back Tampa Bay Buccaneers 1988, Denver Broncos 1989, Miami Dolphins 1990. No college coaching experience. Pro coach: New York Giants 1993-1996, joined Rams in 1997.

Jim Hanifan, offensive line; born September 21, 1933, Compton, Calif., lives in St. Louis. Wide receiver California 1952-54. Pro wide receiver Toronto Argonauts (USFL) 1955. College Coach: Yuba City J.C. (Calif.) 1959-61, Glendale J.C. (Calif.) 1964-65, Utah 1966-69, California 1970-71, San Diego State 1972. Pro coach: St. Louis Cardinals 1973-78, 1980-85 (head coach), San Diego Chargers 1979, Atlanta Falcons 1987-89, Washington Redskins 1990-96, joined Rams in 1997.

Carl Hairston, defensive line; born December 15, 1952, Martinsville, Va., lives in St. Louis. Defensive end Maryland-Eastern Shore 1972-75. Pro defensive end Philadelphia Eagles 1976-83, Cleveland Browns

1984-89, Phoenix Cardinals 1990. Pro coach: Kansas City Chiefs 1995-96, joined Rams in 1997.

Wilbert Montgomery, running backs; born September 16, 1954, Greenville, Miss., lives in Chesterfield, Mo. Running back Abilene Christian 1973-76. Pro running back Philadelphia Eagles 1977-84. Pro coach: joined Rams in 1997.

John Ramsdell, tight ends; born August 16, 1954, Lafayette, Ind., lives in St. Louis. Running back Springfield (Mass.) College 1972-75. No pro playing experience. College coach: San Francisco State 1976-77, Long Beach State 1978, Pacific 1979-82, Oregon 1983-94. Pro coach: Joined Rams in 1995.

Jerry Rhome, offensive coordinator-quarterbacks; born March 6, 1942, in Dallas, Tex., lives in St. Louis. Quarterback Southern Methodist 1960-61, Tulsa 1963-64. Pro quarterback Dallas Cowboys 1965-68, Cleveland Browns 1969, Houston Oilers 1970, Los Angeles Rams 1971-72. College coach: Tulsa 1973-74. Pro coach: Seattle Seahawks 1976-82, Washington Redskins 1983-87, San Diego Chargers 1988, Dallas Cowboys 1989, Arizona Cardinals 1990-93, Minnesota Vikings 1994, Houston Oilers 1995-96, re-joined Rams in 1997.

George Warhop, offensive line; born September 19, 1961, Riverside, Calif., lives in St. Louis. Guard Mt. San Jacinto (Calif.) J.C. 1979-80. Pro center Cincinnati 1981-82. No pro playing experience. College coach: Cincinnati 1983, Kansas 1984-86, Vanderbilt 1987-89, New Mexico 1990, Southern Methodist 1993, Boston College 1994-95. Pro coach: London Monarchs (World League) 1991-92, joined Rams in 1996.

Mike White, assistant head coach-tight ends; born January 4, 1936, Berkeley, Calif., lives in St. Louis. Wide receiver California 1955-57. No pro playing experience. College coach: California 1958-63, 1972-1977 (head coach), Stanford 1964-71, Illinois 1980-87 (head coach). Pro coach: San Francisco 49ers 1978-79, Los Angeles-Oakland Raiders 1990-96 (head coach) 1995-96, joined Rams in 1997.

National Football Conference
Western Division
Team Colors: Forty Niners Gold and Cardinal
4949 Centennial Boulevard
Santa Clara, California 95054
Telephone: (408) 562-4949

CLUB OFFICIALS

Owner: Edward J. DeBartolo, Jr.
President: Carmen Policy
Vice President /Director of Football Operations:
   Dwight Clark
Vice President/Business Operations & C.F.O.:
   Bill Duffy
Director of Player Personnel: Vinny Cerrato
Pro Personnel/NFC: Joe Collins
Pro Personnel/AFC: George Streeter
Director of Public/Community Relations:
   Rodney Knox
Ticket Manager: Lynn Carrozzi
Director of Stadium Operations:
   Murlan (Mo) Fowell
Video Director: Robert Yanagi
Trainer: Lindsy McLean
Equipment Manager: Bronco Hinek
Stadium: 3Com Park •**Capacity:** 70,140
           San Francisco, California 94124
Playing Surface: Grass
Training Camp: Sierra Community College
           Rocklin, California 95677

1997 SCHEDULE

PRESEASON

Aug. 2	at San Diego	7:00
Aug. 9	**Seattle**	6:00
Aug. 18	**Jacksonville**	5:00
Aug. 23	at Denver	6:00

REGULAR SEASON

Aug. 31	at Tampa Bay	4:00
Sept. 7	at St. Louis	12:00
Sept. 14	**New Orleans**	1:00
Sept. 21	**Atlanta**	1:00
Sept. 29	at Carolina (Mon.)	9:00
Oct. 5	Open Date	
Oct. 12	**St. Louis**	1:00
Oct. 19	at Atlanta	1:00
Oct. 26	at New Orleans	12:00
Nov. 2	**Dallas**	1:00
Nov. 10	at Philadelphia (Mon.)	9:00
Nov. 16	**Carolina**	1:00
Nov. 23	**San Diego**	1:00
Nov. 30	at Kansas City	12:00
Dec. 7	**Minnesota**	1:00
Dec. 15	**Denver** (Mon.)	6:00
Dec. 21	at Seattle	5:00

RECORD HOLDERS

INDIVIDUAL RECORDS—CAREER

Category	Name	Performance
Rushing (Yds.)	Joe Perry, 1950-1960, 1963	7,344
Passing (Yds.)	Joe Montana, 1979-1992	35,124
Passing (TDs)	Joe Montana, 1979-1992	244
Receiving (No.)	Jerry Rice, 1985-1996	*1,050
Receiving (Yds.)	Jerry Rice, 1985-1996	*16,377
Interceptions	Ronnie Lott, 1981-1990	51
Punting (Avg.)	Tommy Davis, 1959-1969	44.7
Punt Return (Avg.)	Dana McLemore, 1982-87	10.8
Kickoff Return (Avg.)	Abe Woodson, 1958-1964	29.4
Field Goals	Ray Wersching, 1977-1987	190
Touchdowns (Tot.)	Jerry Rice, 1985-1996	*165
Points	Jerry Rice, 1985-1996	994

INDIVIDUAL RECORDS—SINGLE SEASON

Category	Name	Performance
Rushing (Yds.)	Roger Craig, 1988	1,502
Passing (Yds.)	Steve Young, 1993	4,023
Passing (TDs)	Steve Young, 1994	35
Receiving (No.)	Jerry Rice, 1995	122
Receiving (Yds.)	Jerry Rice, 1995	*1,848
Interceptions	Dave Baker, 1960	10
	Ronnie Lott, 1986	10
Punting (Avg.)	Tommy Davis, 1965	45.8
Punt Return (Avg.)	Dana McLemore, 1982	22.3
Kickoff Return (Avg.)	Joe Arenas, 1953	34.4
Field Goals	Jeff Wilkins, 1996	30
Touchdowns (Tot.)	Jerry Rice, 1987	23
Points	Jerry Rice, 1987	138

INDIVIDUAL RECORDS—SINGLE GAME

Category	Name	Performance
Rushing (Yds.)	Delvin Williams, 10-31-76	194
Passing (Yds.)	Joe Montana, 10-14-90	476
Passing (TDs)	Joe Montana, 10-14-90	6
Receiving (No.)	Jerry Rice, 11-20-94	16
Receiving (Yds.)	Jerry Rice, 12-18-95	289
Interceptions	Dave Baker, 12-4-60	*4
Field Goals	Ray Wersching, 10-16-83	6
	Jeff Wilkins, 9-29-96	6
Touchdowns (Tot.)	Jerry Rice, 10-14-90	5
Points	Jerry Rice, 10-14-90	30

*NFL Record

COACHING HISTORY

(390-298-13)

1950-54	Lawrence (Buck) Shaw	33-25-2
1955	Norman (Red) Strader	4-8-0
1956-58	Frankie Albert	19-17-1
1959-63	Howard (Red) Hickey*	27-27-1
1963-67	Jack Christiansen	26-38-3
1968-75	Dick Nolan	56-56-5
1976	Monte Clark	8-6-0
1977	Ken Meyer	5-9-0
1978	Pete McCulley**	1-8-0
1978	Fred O'Connor	1-6-0
1979-88	Bill Walsh	102-63-1
1989-96	George Seifert	108-35-0

*Resigned after three games in 1963
**Released after nine games in 1978

3COM PARK

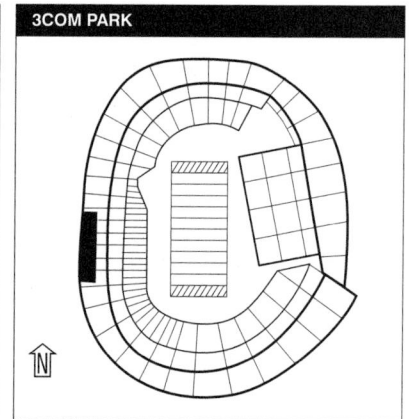

1996 TEAM RECORD

PRESEASON (1-3)

Date	Result		Opponents
8/3	L	17-20	Denver
8/10	W	16-13	San Diego (OT)
8/18	L	10-38	at Jacksonville
8/23	L	3-20	at Seattle

REGULAR SEASON (12-4)

Date	Result		Opponents	Att.
9/1	W	27-11	New Orleans	63,970
9/8	W	34-0	St. Louis	63,624
9/22	L	7-23	at Carolina	72,224
9/29	W	39-17	Atlanta	62,995
10/6	W	28-11	at St. Louis	61,260
10/14	L	20-23	at Green Bay (OT)	60,716
10/20	W	28-21	Cincinnati	63,218
10/27	W	10-9	at Houston	53,664
11/3	W	24-17	at New Orleans	53,297
11/10	L	17-20	Dallas (OT)	68,919
11/17	W	38-20	Baltimore	51,596
11/24	W	19-16	at Washington (OT)	54,235
12/2	W	34-10	at Atlanta	46,318
12/8	L	24-30	Carolina	66,291
12/15	W	25-15	at Pittsburgh	59,823
12/23	W	24-14	Detroit	61,921

POSTSEASON (1-1)

Date	Result		Opponents	Att.
12/29	W	14-0	Philadelphia	56,460
1/4	L	14-35	at Green Bay	60,787

(OT) Overtime

SCORE BY PERIODS

49ers	85	153	50	107	3	—	398
Opponents	60	63	55	73	6	—	257

ATTENDANCE

Home 502,534   Away 461,537   Total 964,071
Single-game home record, 69,014 (11/13/94)
Single-season home record, 518,928 (1995)

1996 TEAM STATISTICS

	49ers	Opp.
Total First Downs	315	269
Rushing	108	76
Passing	188	164
Penalty	19	29
Third Down: Made/Att	76/216	78/232
Third Down Pct.	35.2	33.6
Fourth Down: Made/Att	12/19	9/20
Fourth Down Pct.	63.2	45.0
Total Net Yards	5506	4661
Avg. Per Game	344.1	291.3
Total Plays	1046	1021
Avg. Per Play	5.3	4.6
Net Yards Rushing	1847	1497
Avg. Per Game	115.4	93.6
Total Rushes	454	418
Net Yards Passing	3659	3164
Avg. Per Game	228.7	197.8
Sacked/Yards Lost	42/200	45/297
Gross Yards	3859	3461
Att./Completions	550/358	558/287
Completion Pct.	65.1	51.4
Had Intercepted	16	20
Punts/Avg.	75/42.9	88/42.0
Net Punting Avg.	75/38.2	88/35.5
Penalties/Yards Lost	119/925	97/819
Fumbles/Ball Lost	16/8	29/14
Touchdowns	43	25
Rushing	17	4
Passing	24	21
Returns	2	0
Avg. Time of Possession	31:28	28:32

1996 INDIVIDUAL STATISTICS

PASSING	Att.	Comp.	Yds.	Pct.	TD	Int.	Tkld.	Rate
S. Young	316	214	2410	67.7	14	6	34/160	97.2
Grbac	197	122	1236	61.9	8	10	6/30	72.2
Brohm	34	21	189	61.8	1	0	2/10	86.5
Kirby	2	1	24	50.0	1	0	0/0	133.3
Rice	1	0	0	0.0	0	0	0/0	39.6
49ers	550	358	3859	65.1	24	16	42/200	88.0
Opponents	558	287	3461	51.4	21	20	45/297	68.4

SCORING	TD R	TD P	TD Rt	PAT	FG	Saf	PTS
Wilkins	0	0	0	40/40	30/34	0	130
Rice	1	8	0	0/0	0/0	0	54
Popson	0	6	0	0/0	0/0	0	36
S. Young	4	0	0	0/0	0/0	0	26
Kirby	3	1	0	0/0	0/0	0	24
Loville	2	2	0	0/0	0/0	0	24
Owens	0	4	0	0/0	0/0	0	24
Floyd	2	1	0	0/0	0/0	0	18
Grbac	2	0	0	0/0	0/0	0	12
Vardell	2	0	0	0/0	0/0	0	12
Carter	1	0	0	0/0	0/0	0	6
Doleman	0	0	1	0/0	0/0	0	6
Jones	0	1	0	0/0	0/0	0	6
Pope	0	0	1	0/0	0/0	0	6
Uwaezuoke	0	1	0	0/0	0/0	0	6
B. Young	0	0	0	0/0	0/0	2	4
49ers	17	24	2	40/40	30/34	*4	398
Opponents	4	21	0	21/21	26/29	0	257

2-Point conversions: S. Young. Team: 1-3, Opponents: 4-4.
*49ers were credited with 2 team safeties.

RUSHING	Att.	Yds.	Avg.	LG	TD
Kirby	134	559	4.2	31	3
S. Young	52	310	6.0	33	4
Loville	70	229	3.3	16	2
Vardell	58	192	3.3	17	2
Floyd	47	186	4.0	12	2
Lynn	24	164	6.8	67	0
Rice	11	77	7.0	38	1
Carter	19	66	3.5	18	1
Brohm	16	43	2.7	22	0
Grbac	23	21	0.9	12	2
49ers	454	1847	4.1	67	17
Opponents	418	1497	3.6	54t	4

RECEIVING	No.	Yds.	Avg.	LG	TD
Rice	108	1254	11.6	39	8
Kirby	52	439	8.4	52	1
Owens	35	520	14.9	46t	4
Jones	33	428	13.0	39	1
Vardell	28	179	6.4	22	0
Popson	26	301	11.6	39t	6
Floyd	26	197	7.6	24	1
Stokes	18	249	13.8	40	0
Loville	16	138	8.6	44t	2
Uwaezuoke	7	91	13.0	29t	1
Manuel	3	18	6.0	7	0
Lynn	2	14	7.0	8	0
Caldwell	2	9	4.5	8	0
Cooper	1	11	11.0	11	0
Singleton	1	11	11.0	11	0
49ers	358	3859	10.8	52	24
Opponents	287	3461	12.1	65t	21

INTERCEPTIONS	No.	Yds.	Avg.	LG	TD
Pope	6	98	16.3	55t	1
Hanks	4	7	1.8	8	0
Dodge	3	27	9.0	26	0
McDonald	2	14	7.0	14	0
Doleman	2	1	0.5	1	0
Stubblefield	1	15	15.0	15	0
Drakeford	1	11	11.0	11	0
Israel	1	3	3.0	3	0
49ers	20	176	8.8	55t	1
Opponents	16	107	6.7	35	0

PUNTING	No.	Yds.	Avg.	In 20	LG
Thompson	73	3217	44.1	20	65
49ers	75	3217	42.9	20	65
Opponents	88	3695	42.0	23	62

PUNT RETURNS	No.	FC	Yds.	Avg.	LG	TD
Carter	36	17	317	8.8	52	0
Singleton	2	0	32	16.0	21	0
Kirby	1	4	3	3.0	3	0
49ers	39	21	352	9.0	52	0
Opponents	36	11	235	6.5	22	0

KICKOFF RETURNS	No.	Yds.	Avg.	LG	TD
Carter	41	909	22.2	71	0
Loville	10	229	22.9	35	0
Owens	3	47	15.7	18	0
Deese	2	20	10.0	12	0
Kirby	1	22	22.0	22	0
Singleton	1	10	10.0	10	0
Uwaezuoke	1	21	21.0	21	0
49ers	59	1258	21.3	71	0
Opponents	77	1414	18.4	58	0

SACKS	No.
Barker	12.5
B. Young	11.5
Doleman	11.0
Woodall	2.5
D. Brown	2.0
Drakeford	2.0
McDonald	1.0
Mitchell	1.0
Stubblefield	1.0
J. Bryant	0.5
49ers	45.0
Opponents	42.0

1997 DRAFT CHOICES

Round	Name	Pos.	College
1	Jim Druckenmiller	QB	Virginia Tech
2	Marc Edwards	RB	Notre Dame
3	Greg Clark	TE	Stanford

SAN FRANCISCO 49ERS

1997 VETERAN ROSTER

No.	Name	Pos.	Ht.	Wt.	Birthdate	NFL Exp.	College	Hometown	How Acq.	'96 Games/ Starts
47	Avery, Steve	RB	6-2	229	8/18/66	3	Northern Michigan	Milwaukee, Wis.	FA-'97	0*
92	Barker, Roy	DE	6-5	290	2/14/69	6	North Carolina	New York, N.Y.	UFA(Minn)-'96	15/15
17	Barr, Dave	QB	6-4	205	5/9/72	2	California	Concord, Calif.	FA-'97	0*
79	Barton, Harris	T	6-4	286	4/19/64	11	North Carolina	Atlanta, Ga.	D1a-'87	13/13
78	Brandon, Michael	DE	6-4	290	7/30/68	4	Florida	Perry, Fla.	FA-'95	4/0
11	Brohm, Jeff	QB	6-1	205	4/24/71	3	Louisville	Louisville, Ky.	FA-'95	3/0
65	Brown, Ray	G	6-5	315	12/12/62	12	Arkansas State	Marion, Ark.	UFA(Wash)-'96	16/16
90	Bryant, Junior	DE	6-4	275	1/16/71	3	Notre Dame	Omaha, Neb.	FA-'95	16/1
28	Buckley, Curtis	S	5-10	190	9/25/70	5	East Texas State	Silsbee, Tex.	RFA(TB)-'96	15/0
67	Dalman, Chris	C-G	6-3	285	3/15/70	5	Stanford	Salinas, Calif.	D6-'93	16/16
63	Deese, Derrick	G	6-3	275	5/17/70	6	Southern California	Culver City, Calif.	FA-'92	16/0
56	Doleman, Chris	DE	6-5	275	10/16/61	13	Pittsburgh	York, Pa.	UFA(Atl)-'96	16/16
25	Dowden, Corey	CB-S	5-11	190	10/18/68	2	Tulane	New Orleans, La.	FA-'97	9/0*
22	Drakeford, Tyronne	CB	5-9	185	6/21/71	4	Virginia Tech	Camden, S.C.	D2b-'94	16/16
43	Fann, Chad	RB	6-3	250	6/7/70	4	Florida A&M	Jacksonville, Fla.	FA-'97	0*
40	Floyd, William	RB	6-1	242	2/17/72	4	Florida State	St. Petersburg, Fla.	D1b-'94	9/6
66	Gogan, Kevin	G	6-7	325	11/2/64	11	Washington	San Francisco, Calif.	UFA(Oak)-'97	16/16*
36	Hanks, Merton	S	6-2	185	3/12/68	7	Iowa	Dallas, Tex.	D5a-'91	16/16
77	Hanshaw, Tim	G	6-5	300	4/27/70	3	Brigham Young	Spokane, Wash.	D4-'95	1/0
20	Hearst, Garrison	RB	5-11	215	1/4/71	5	Georgia	Lincolnton, Ga.	UFA(Cin)-'97	16/12*
64	Ifeanyi, Israel	DE	6-3	246	11/21/70	2	Southern California	Lagos, Nigeria	D2-'96	3/0
84	Jones, Brent	TE	6-4	230	2/12/63	11	Santa Clara	San Jose, Calif.	FA-'87	11/10
62	Keim, Mike	T	6-8	302	11/12/65	3	Brigham Young	Anaheim, Calif.	FA-'97	0*
41	Kirby, Terry	RB	6-1	223	1/20/70	5	Virginia	Tabb, Va.	T(Mia)-'96	14/10
57	Kirk, Randy	LB	6-2	235	12/27/64	10	San Diego State	San Diego, Calif.	UFA(Ariz)-'96	16/0
32	Levy, Chuck	RB	6-0	197	1/7/72	2	Arizona	Los Angeles, Calif.	FA-'96	0*
82	Manuel, Sean	TE	6-2	245	12/1/73	2	New Mexico State	Los Gatos, Calif.	D7a-'96	11/0
46	McDonald, Tim	S	6-2	215	1/6/65	11	Southern California	Fresno, Calif.	FA-'93	16/16
69	Milstead, Rod	G	6-2	290	11/10/69	6	Delawre State	Indian Head, Md.	FA-'94	11/0
55	Mitchell, Kevin	LB	6-1	260	1/1/71	4	Syracuse	Harrisburg, Pa.	D2a-'94	12/3
51	Norton, Ken Jr.	LB	6-2	241	9/29/66	10	UCLA	Los Angeles, Calif.	UFA(Dall)-'94	16/16
81	Owens, Terrell	WR	6-2	213	12/7/73	2	Tennessee-Chatanooga	Alexander City, Ala.	D3-'96	16/10
50	Plummer, Gary	LB	6-2	247	1/26/60	12	California	Fremont, Calif.	UFA(SD)-'94	13/11
75	Pollack, Frank	T	6-5	285	11/5/67	7	Northern Arizona	Phoenix, Ariz.	FA-'94	16/2
23	Pope, Marquez	CB	5-11	193	10/29/70	6	Fresno State	Long Beach, Calif.	RFA(Oak)-'95	16/16
91	Price, Daryl	DE	6-3	274	10/23/72	2	Colorado	Beaumont, Tex.	D4-'96	14/0
80	Rice, Jerry	WR	6-2	200	10/13/62	13	Mississippi Valley State	Crawford, Miss.	D1-'85	16/16
60	Rudolph, Joe	G	6-2	290	7/21/72	2	Wisconsin	Belle Vernon, Pa.	FA-'97	0*
30	Salmon, Mike	S	6-1	208	12/27/70	2	Southern California	Phoenix, Ariz.	FA-'96	0*
76	Scrafford, Kirk	T	6-6	275	3/15/67	8	Montana	Billings, Mont.	UFA(Den)-'95	7/1
52	Schwantz, Jim	LB	6-2	240	1/23/70	4	Purdue	Palatine, Ill.	RFA(Dall)-'97	16/0*
24	Smith, Frankie	CB	5-9	182	10/8/68	5	Baylor	Osceola, Ark.	FA-'96	14/0
83	Stokes, J.J.	WR	6-4	217	10/6/72	3	UCLA	San Diego, Calif.	D1-'95	6/6
94	Stubblefield, Dana	DT	6-2	290	11/14/70	5	Kansas	Cleves, Ohio	D1a-'93	15/15
3	Thompson, Tommy	P	5-10	192	4/27/72	3	Oregon	Lompoc, Calif.	FA-'95	16/0
89	Uwaezuoke, Iheanyi	WR	6-2	195	7/24/73	2	California	Inglewood, Calif.	D5-'96	14/0
38	Walker, Darnell	CB	5-8	168	1/17/70	5	Arizona State	St. Louis, Mo.	UFA(Atl)-'97	15/9*
54	Woodall, Lee	LB	6-0	220	10/31/69	4	West Chester	Carlisle, Pa.	D6-'94	16/13
97	Young, Bryant	DT	6-2	276	1/27/72	4	Notre Dame	Chicago Heights, Ill.	D1a-'94	16/16
8	Young, Steve	QB	6-2	205	10/11/61	13	Brigham Young	Greenwich, Conn.	T(TB)-'87	12/12

* Avery last active with Pittsburgh in '95; Barr last active with St. Louis in '95; Dowden played 9 with Green Bay; Fann last active with Arizona in '95; Gogan played 16 games with Oakland; Hearst played 16 games with Cincinnati; Keim last active with Seattle in '95; Levy last active with Arizona in '94; Rudolph last active with Philadelphia in '95; Salmon inactive for 2 games; Schwantz played 16 games with Dallas; Walker played 15 games with Atlanta.

Players lost through free agency (3): QB Elvis Grbac (KC; 15 games in '96), CB Steve Israel (NE; 14), WR Nate Singleton (Phil; 2).

Also played with the 49ers in '96—LB Daved Benefield (15 games), DE Dennis Brown (15), WR Mike Caldwell (1), RB Dexter Carter (16), CB-S Dedrick Dodge (16), WR Mark Harris (1), WR Kevin Lee (2), RB Derek Loville (12), RB Anthony Lynn (16), G Rod Milstead (11), LB Tony Peterson (13), TE Ted Popson (15), RB Tommy Vardell (11), T Steve Wallace (16), K Jeff Wilkins (16), CB James Williams (1).

COACHING STAFF

Head Coach,
Steve Mariucci

Pro Career: Considered one of the top young talents in the game today, Steve Mariucci was named as the head coach of the San Francisco 49ers January 16, 1997. He is the thirteenth head coach in 49ers' history. Mariucci replaces George Seifert (1989-96) after spending one season as head coach at the University of California. He served as the quarterbacks coach of the Green Bay Packers from 1992-95, tutoring the likes of two-time MVP Brett Favre, Mark Brunell, and Ty Detmer. His first pro position was in 1985 when he coached the receivers for the USFL's Orlando Renegades. Later that fall, he had a brief stint with the Los Angeles Rams as quality control coach. No pro playing experience.

Background: Three-time All-America quarterback at Northern Michigan University. Began his coaching career at his alma mater (1978-79), serving as the quarterbacks and running backs coach, then moved to Cal State-Fullerton as the quarterbacks and special teams coordinator (1980-82). In 1983 and 1984, Mariucci was the assistant head coach and offensive coordinator at Louisville. Joined the Southern California staff in 1986, then moved to the University of California as receivers and special teams coach in 1987. In 1990-91, he served as the Bears' offensive coordinator, helping California post a 10-2 record and a number seven national ranking in his final season at Berkeley. Became the head coach at California in 1996 and guided the squad to a 5-0 start and finally a berth in the Aloha Bowl. His offense averaged over 457 yards per game, including a school record 321.5 yards through the air.

Personal: Born November 4, 1955. He and his wife, Gayle, have four children—Tyler, Adam, Stephen, and Brielle—and live in Saratoga, Calif.

ASSISTANT COACHES

Jerry Attaway, physical development; born January 3, 1946, Susanville, Calif., lives in San Jose, Calif. Defensive back Yuba, Calif. J.C. 1964-65, Cal-Davis 1967. No pro playing experience. College coach: Cal-Davis 1970-71, Idaho 1972-74, Utah State 1975-77, Southern California 1978-82. Pro coach: Joined 49ers in 1983.

Mike Barnes, strength development; born March 13, 1966, Rochester, N.Y., lives in Dublin, Calif. No college or pro playing experience. College coach: Texas A&M 1990, California 1991-93. Pro coach: Joined 49ers in 1994.

Dwaine Board, defensive line; born November 29, 1956, Rocky Mount, Va., lives in Redwood City, Calif. Defensive lineman North Carolina A&T 1974-77. Pro defensive lineman San Francisco 49ers 1979-87, New Orleans Saints 1988. Pro coach: Joined 49ers in 1991.

Jaime Hill, defensive assistant; born July 6, 1963, Bakersfield, Calif., lives in Fremont, Calif. Wide receiver San Francisco State 1982-85. No pro playing experience. College coach: San Francisco State 1987, UTEP 1988, Northern Arizona 1989, Sonoma State 1990-91, Portland State 1992-96. Pro coach: Joined 49ers in 1997.

Larry Kirksey, wide receivers; born January 6, 1951, Harlan, Ky., lives in Pleasanton, Calif. Wide receiver Eastern Kentucky 1970-72. No pro playing experience. College coach: Miami (Ohio) 1974-76, Kentucky 1977-81, Kansas 1982, Kentucky State 1983 (head coach), Florida 1984-88, Pittsburgh 1989, Alabama 1990-93. Pro coach: Joined 49ers in 1994.

Greg Knapp, offensive assistant; born March 5, 1963, Long Beach, Calif., lives in Santa Clara, Calif. Quarterback Cal State-Sacramento 1982-85. No pro playing experience. College coach: Cal State-Sacramento 1986-94. Pro coach: Joined 49ers in 1995.

John Marshall, defensive coordinator; born October 2, 1945, Arroyo Grande, Calif., lives in Pleasanton, Calif. Linebacker Washington State 1964. No pro playing experience. College coach: Oregon 1970-76, Southern California 1977-79. Pro coach: Green Bay Packers 1980-82, Atlanta Falcons 1983-

85, Indianapolis Colts 1986-88, joined 49ers in 1989.

Bobb McKittrick, offensive line; born December 29, 1935, Baker, Ore., lives in San Mateo, Calif. Guard Oregon State 1955-57. No pro playing experience. College coach: Oregon State 1961-64, UCLA 1965-70. Pro coach: Los Angeles Rams 1971-72, San Diego Chargers 1974-78, joined 49ers in 1979.

Bill McPherson, defensive asst.; born October 24, 1931, Santa Clara, Calif., lives in San Jose, Calif. Tackle Santa Clara 1950-52. No pro playing experience. College coach: Santa Clara 1963-74, UCLA 1975-77. Pro coach: Philadelphia Eagles 1978, joined 49ers in 1979.

Jim Mora, defensive backs; born November 19, 1961, Los Angeles, Calif., lives in Sunnyvale, Calif. Defensive back Washington 1980-83. No pro playing experience. College coach: Washington 1984. Pro coach: San Diego Chargers 1985-91, New Orleans Saints 1992-96, joined 49ers in 1997.

Marty Mornhinweg, offensive coordinator; born March 29, 1962, Edmond, Okla., lives in Pleasanton, Calif. Quarterback Montana 1980-84. No pro playing experience. College coach: Montana 1985, UTEP 1986-87, Northern Arizona 1988, 1994, Southeast Missouri State 1989-90, Missouri 1991-93. Pro coach: Green Bay Packers 1995-96, joined 49ers in 1997.

Pat Morris, tight ends; born April 7, 1954, Cleveland,

Ohio, lives in Mountain View, Calif. Offensive lineman Southern California 1972-75. No pro playing experience. College coach: Southern California 1976-77, 1983-86, Northern Arizona 1978, Minnesota 1979-82, Michigan State 1987-94, Stanford 1995-96. Pro coach: Joined 49ers in 1997.

Tom Rathman, running backs; born October 7, 1962, Grand Island, Neb., lives in Redwood City, Calif. Running back Nebraska 1983-85. Pro running back San Francisco 49ers 1986-93, Los Angeles Raiders 1994. College coach: Menlo College 1996. Pro coach: Joined 49ers in 1997.

Richard Smith, linebackers; born October 17, 1955, Los Angeles, Calif., lives in Santa Clara, Calif. Offensive lineman Rio Hondo J.C. 1975-76, Fresno State 1977-78. No pro playing experience. College coach: Rio Hondo J.C. 1979-80, Cal State-Fullerton 1981-83, California 1984-86, Arizona 1987. Pro coach: Houston Oilers 1988-92, Denver Broncos 1993-96, joined 49ers in 1997.

George Stewart, special teams; born December 29, 1958, Little Rock, Ark., lives in Santa Clara, Calif. Guard Arkansas 1977-80. No pro playing experience. College coach: Minnesota 1984-85, Notre Dame 1986-88. Pro coach: Pittsburgh Steelers 1989-91, Tampa Bay Buccaneers 1992-95, joined 49ers in 1996.

1997 FIRST-YEAR ROSTER

Name	Pos.	Ht.	Wt.	Birthdate	College	Hometown	How Acq.
Baker, Jon (1)	K	6-1	170	8/13/72	Arizona	Bakersfield, Calif.	FA
Cavallo, Tom	LB	6-2	245	4/21/71	Louisville	St. Charles, Ill.	FA
Clark, Greg	TE	6-4	262	4/7/72	Stanford	Centerville, Utah	D3
Coleman, Herb (1)	DE	6-4	285	9/4/72	Trinity International	Country Club Hills, Ill.	D7-'95
Covington, John (1)	DB	6-0	206	8/1/70	Notre Dame	Winter Haven, Fla.	FA
Druckenmiller, Jim	QB	6-4	234	9/19/72	Virginia Tech	Allentown, Pa.	D1
Edwards, Marc	RB	6-0	236	11/17/74	Notre Dame	Norwood, Ohio	D2
Gordon Steve	C	6-4	290	4/15/69	California	Nevada City, Calif.	FA
Harris, Mark (1)	WR	6-4	197	4/28/70	Stanford	Brigham, Utah	FA
Longwell, Ryan	K	6-0	180	8/16/74	California	Bend, Ore.	FA
Makovicka, Jeff (1)	RB	5-11	245	9/24/72	Nebraska	Brainard, Neb.	FA
Manuel, Sam (1)	LB	6-2	235	12/1/73	New Mexico State	Los Gatos, Calif.	D7b-'96
McDaniel, Michael	WR	6-1	218	5/1/74	Oklahoma	Oklahoma City, Okla.	FA
Mitchell, Shon	RB	5-10	195	10/8/73	Texas	Austin, Tex.	FA
Moore, Andrew (1)	T	6-5	290	12/22/72	Sonoma State	San Diego, Calif.	FA
Phillips, Tucker	P	6-2	210	2/4/74	Rice	Houston Tex.	FA
Reese, Albert (1)	DT	6-6	275	4/29/72	Grambling State	Mobile, Ala.	FA
Shearer, Curtis (1)	WR	5-10	170	6/8/71	San Diego State	San Jose, Calif.	FA
Smith, Tyrone (1)	CB	5-11	184	9/29/72	Baylor	Missouri City, Tex.	FA
Swinson, Corey (1)	DT	6-5	355	12/15/69	Hampton	Bayshore, N.Y.	FA
Thorton, Carlos	DE	6-4	240	9/19/74	Alcorn State	Greenville, Miss.	FA
Young, Alan (1)	DE	6-3	252	1/20/71	Vanderbilt	Woodstock, N.Y.	FA
Gordon Steve	C	6-4	290	4/15/69	California	Nevada City, Calif.	FA

The term NFL Rookie is defined as a player who is in his first season of professional football and has not been on the roster of another professional football team for any regular-season or postseason games. A Rookie is designated by an "R" on NFL rosters. Players who have been active in another professional football league or players who have NFL experience, including either preseason training camp or being on an Active List or Inactive List, or on Reserve/Injured or Reserve/Physically Unable to Perform for fewer than six regular-season games, are termed NFL First-Year Players. An NFL First-Year Player is designated by a "1" on NFL rosters. Thereafter, a player is credited with an additional year of experience for each season in which he accumulates six games on the Active List or Inactive List, or on Reserve/Injured or Reserve/Physically Unable to Perform.

NOTES

TAMPA BAY BUCCANEERS

National Football Conference
Central Division
Team Colors: Buccaneer Red, Pewter, Black,
  and Orange
One Buccaneer Place
Tampa, Florida 33607
Telephone: (813) 870-2700

CLUB OFFICIALS

Owner/President: Malcolm Glazer
Executive Vice President: Bryan Glazer
Executive Vice President: Joel Glazer
General Manager: Rich McKay
Director of Player Personnel: Jerry Angelo
Director of College Scouting: Tim Ruskell
Director of Football Administration: John Idzik
Vice President of Marketing and Communications:
  Rick McNerney
Vice President of Sales Administration:
  Veronica (Roni) Costello
Director of Communications: Reggie Roberts
Director of Client Relations: Jim Overton
Director of Marketing: George Woods
Director of Special Events: Meredith Chimerine
Director of Ticket Operations: Kevin Brooks
Controller: Patrick Smith
Luxury Suite Managers: Cheryll Pritcher,
  Hillary Weber
Group Sales: Bill Butler
College Scouts: Mike Ackerley, Dave Boller,
  Ruston Webster, Mike Yowarsky
Pro Personnel Assistants: Mark Dominik,
  Dennis Hickey
Asst. Director/Ticket Operations: Dave Redus
Communications Managers: Scott Smith,
  Nelson Luis
Community Relations Managers: Stephanie Waller,
  Andre Thornton
Trainer: Todd Toriscelli
Assistant Trainer: Mark Shermansky
Equipment Manager: Darin Kerns
Video Director: Dave Levy
Assistant Video Director: Pat Brazil
Stadium: Houlihan's Stadium •**Capacity:** 74,301
  Tampa, Florida 33607
Playing Surface: Grass
Training Camp: University of Tampa
  Tampa, Florida 33606

1997 SCHEDULE
PRESEASON

Aug. 2	**Washington**	7:30
Aug. 9	at Atlanta	7:30
Aug. 16	**Miami**	7:30
Aug. 22	vs. N.Y. Jets at Orlando, Fla.	7:30

REGULAR SEASON

Aug. 31	**San Francisco**	4:00
Sept. 7	at Detroit	1:00
Sept. 14	at Minnesota	12:00
Sept. 21	**Miami**	8:00
Sept. 28	**Arizona**	1:00
Oct. 5	at Green Bay	12:00
Oct. 12	**Detroit**	1:00
Oct. 19	Open Date	
Oct. 26	**Minnesota**	1:00
Nov. 2	at Indianapolis	1:00
Nov. 9	at Atlanta	1:00
Nov. 16	**New England**	1:00
Nov. 23	at Chicago	12:00
Nov. 30	at New York Giants	4:00
Dec. 7	**Green Bay**	1:00
Dec. 14	at New York Jets	1:00
Dec. 21	**Chicago**	1:00

RECORD HOLDERS
INDIVIDUAL RECORDS—CAREER

Category	Name	Performance
Rushing (Yds.)	James Wilder, 1981-89	5,957
Passing (Yds.)	Vinny Testaverde, 1987-1992	14,820
Passing (TDs)	Vinny Testaverde, 1987-1992	77
Receiving (No.)	James Wilder, 1981-89	430
Receiving (Yds.)	Mark Carrier, 1987-1992	5,018
Interceptions	Cedric Brown, 1977-1984	29
Punting (Avg.)	Frank Garcia, 1983-87	41.1
Punt Return (Avg.)	Willie Drewrey, 1989-1992	9.4
Kickoff Return (Avg.)	Isaac Hagins, 1976-1980	21.9
Field Goals	Donald Igwebuike, 1985-89	94
Touchdowns (Tot.)	James Wilder, 1981-89	46
Points	Donald Igwebuike, 1985-89	416

INDIVIDUAL RECORDS—SINGLE SEASON

Category	Name	Performance
Rushing (Yds.)	James Wilder, 1984	1,544
Passing (Yds.)	Doug Williams, 1981	3,563
Passing (TDs)	Doug Williams, 1980	20
	Vinny Testaverde, 1989	20
Receiving (No.)	Mark Carrier, 1989	86
Receiving (Yds.)	Mark Carrier, 1989	1,422
Interceptions	Cedric Brown, 1981	9
Punting (Avg.)	Tommy Barnhardt, 1996	43.1
Punt Return (Avg.)	Karl Williams, 1996	21.1
Kickoff Return (Avg.)	Karl Williams, 1996	27.4
Field Goals	Michael Husted, 1994, 1996	25
Touchdowns (Tot.)	James Wilder, 1984	13
Points	Donald Igwebuike, 1989	99

INDIVIDUAL RECORDS—SINGLE GAME

Category	Name	Performance
Rushing (Yds.)	James Wilder, 11-6-83	219
Passing (Yds.)	Doug Williams, 11-16-80	486
Passing (TDs)	Steve DeBerg, 9-13-87	5
Receiving (No.)	James Wilder, 9-15-85	13
Receiving (Yds.)	Mark Carrier, 12-6-87	212
Interceptions	Many times	2
	Last time by Martin Mayhew, 12-3-95	
Field Goals	Many times	4
	Last time by Michael Husted, 11-17-96	
Touchdowns (Tot.)	Jimmie Giles, 10-20-85	4
Points	Jimmie Giles, 10-20-85	24

COACHING HISTORY
(101-226-1)

1976-84	John McKay	45-91-1
1985-86	Leeman Bennett	4-28-0
1987-90	Ray Perkins*	19-41-0
1990-91	Richard Williamson	4-15-0
1992-95	Sam Wyche	23-41-0
1996	Tony Dungy	6-10-0

*Released after 13 games in 1990

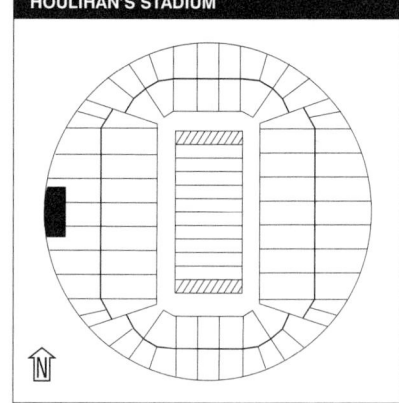

HOULIHAN'S STADIUM

1996 TEAM RECORD

PRESEASON (1-3)

Date	Result		Opponents
8/3	L	10-13	at Miami
8/10	W	16-0	Atlanta
8/17	L	3-13	at Pittsburgh
8/23	L	7-19	Miami

REGULAR SEASON (6-10)

Date	Result		Opponents	Att.
9/1	L	3-34	Green Bay	54,102
9/8	L	6-21	at Detroit	54,229
9/15	L	23-27	at Denver	71,535
9/22	L	13-17	Seattle	30,212
9/29	L	0-27	Detroit	34,961
10/13	W	24-13	Minnesota	32,175
10/20	L	9-13	at Arizona	27,738
10/27	L	7-13	at Green Bay	60,627
11/3	L	10-13	at Chicago	58,727
11/10	W	20-17	Oakland (OT)	45,392
11/17	W	25-17	at San Diego	57,526
11/24	W	13-7	New Orleans	40,203
12/1	L	0-24	at Carolina	57,623
12/8	W	24-10	Washington	44,733
12/15	L	10-21	at Minnesota	49,302
12/22	W	34-19	Chicago	51,572

(OT) Overtime

SCORE BY PERIODS

Buccaneers	46	76	38	58	3	—	221
Opponents	64	91	71	67	0	—	293

ATTENDANCE

Home 333,350   Away 437,307   Total 770,657
Single-game home record, 72,077 (10/8/89)
Single-season home record, 545,980 (1979)

1996 TEAM STATISTICS

	Buccaneers	Opp.
Total First Downs	260	296
Rushing	90	114
Passing	152	156
Penalty	18	26
Third Down: Made/Att	89/225	87/214
Third Down Pct.	39.6	40.7
Fourth Down: Made/Att	9/24	10/13
Fourth Down Pct.	37.5	76.9
Total Net Yards	4316	4814
Avg. Per Game	269.8	300.9
Total Plays	996	976
Avg. Per Play	4.3	4.9
Net Yards Rushing	1589	1889
Avg. Per Game	99.3	118.1
Total Rushes	472	438
Net Yards Passing	2727	2925
Avg. Per Game	170.4	182.8
Sacked/Yards Lost	30/217	35/207
Gross Yards	2944	3132
Att./Completions	494/274	503/311
Completion Pct.	55.5	61.8
Had Intercepted	20	17
Punts/Avg.	71/42.5	74/43.4
Net Punting Avg.	71/37.8	74/33.1
Penalties/Yards Lost	95/787	101/810
Fumbles/Ball Lost	28/14	31/12
Touchdowns	21	34
Rushing	8	13
Passing	12	17
Returns	1	4
Avg. Time of Possession	30:58	29:02

1996 INDIVIDUAL STATISTICS

PASSING

	Att.	Comp.	Yds.	Pct.	TD	Int.	Tkld.	Rate
Dilfer	482	267	2859	55.4	12	19	28/207	64.8
Weldon	9	5	76	55.6	0	1	2/10	44.0
Milanovich	3	2	9	66.7	0	0	0/0	70.1
Buccaneers	494	274	2944	55.5	12	20	30/217	64.4
Opponents	503	311	3132	61.8	17	17	35/207	76.7

SCORING

	TD R	TD P	TD Rt	PAT	FG	Saf	PTS
Husted	0	0	0	18/19	25/32	0	93
Alstott	3	3	0	0/0	0/0	0	36
Rhett	3	1	0	0/0	0/0	0	24
Moore	0	3	0	0/0	0/0	0	18
R. Brooks	2	0	0	0/0	0/0	0	12
Thomas	0	2	0	0/0	0/0	0	12
Harris	0	1	0	0/0	0/0	0	8
Harper	0	1	0	0/0	0/0	0	6
Hawkins	0	1	0	0/0	0/0	0	6
K. Williams	0	0	1	0/0	0/0	0	6
Buccaneers	8	12	1	18/19	25/32	0	221
Opponents	13	17	4	32/32	19/27	0	293

2-Point conversions: Harris. Team: 1-2, Opponents: 0-2.

RUSHING

	Att.	Yds.	Avg.	LG	TD
Rhett	176	539	3.1	35	3
Alstott	96	377	3.9	39	3
R. Brooks	112	368	3.3	56	2
Dilfer	32	124	3.9	19	0
Ellison	35	106	3.0	13	0
Lynch	1	40	40.0	40	0
Barnhardt	2	27	13.5	25	0
Thompson	14	25	1.8	10	0
Weldon	2	-1	-0.5	0	0
K. Williams	1	-3	-3.0	-3	0
Hawkins	1	-13	-13.0	-13	0
Buccaneers	472	1589	3.4	56	8
Opponents	438	1889	4.3	57	13

RECEIVING

	No.	Yds.	Avg.	LG	TD
Alstott	65	557	8.6	29	3
Hawkins	46	544	11.8	45	1
Thomas	33	427	12.9	31t	2
Harris	30	349	11.6	36	1
Moore	27	237	8.8	23	3
K. Williams	22	246	11.2	25	0
Harper	19	289	15.2	40t	1
Ellison	18	208	11.6	42	0
Thompson	5	36	7.2	12	0
Rhett	4	11	2.8	5t	1
R. Brooks	3	13	4.3	9	0
Marshall	2	27	13.5	20	0
Buccaneers	274	2944	10.7	45	12
Opponents	311	3132	10.1	63t	17

INTERCEPTIONS

	No.	Yds.	Avg.	LG	TD
Abraham	5	27	5.4	21	0
Lynch	3	26	8.7	25	0
M. Johnson	2	24	12.0	24	0
Nickerson	2	24	12.0	17	0
Dimry	2	1	0.5	1	0
Mincy	1	26	26.0	26	0
D. Brooks	1	6	6.0	6	0
Mayhew	1	5	5.0	5	0
Buccaneers	17	139	8.2	26	0
Opponents	20	326	16.3	98t	3

PUNTING

	No.	Yds.	Avg.	In 20	LG
Barnhardt	70	3015	43.1	24	62
Buccaneers	71	3015	42.5	24	62
Opponents	74	3210	43.4	14	63

PUNT RETURNS

	No.	FC	Yds.	Avg.	LG	TD
Silvan	14	5	113	8.1	17	0
Marshall	13	1	95	7.3	29	0
K. Williams	13	2	274	21.1	88t	1
Hawkins	1	1	-1	-1.0	-1	0
Buccaneers	41	9	481	11.7	88t	1
Opponents	38	22	248	6.5	22	0

KICKOFF RETURNS

	No.	Yds.	Avg.	LG	TD
Silvan	28	626	22.4	54	0
K. Williams	14	383	27.4	63	0
Marshall	12	264	22.0	37	0
Alstott	1	14	14.0	14	0
Ellison	0	0	—	0	0
Buccaneers	55	1287	23.4	63	0
Opponents	51	972	19.1	35	0

SACKS

	No.
Sapp	9.0
Marts	7.0
Ahanotu	5.5
Upshaw	4.0
Nickerson	3.0
Curry	2.0
Culpepper	1.5
M. Jones	1.0
Lynch	1.0
Mayhew	1.0
Buccaneers	35.0
Opponents	30.0

1997 DRAFT CHOICES

Round	Name	Pos.	College
1	Warrick Dunn	RB	Florida State
	Reidel Anthony	WR	Florida
2	Jerry Wunsch	T	Wisconsin
3	Frank Middleton	G	Arizona
	Ronde Barber	DB	Virginia
4	Alshermond Singleton	LB	Temple
5	Patrick Hape	TE	Alabama
6	Al Harris	DB	Texas A&M-Kingsville
	Nigea Carter	WR	Michigan State
7	Anthony DeGrate	DT	Stephen F. Austin

TAMPA BAY BUCCANEERS

1997 VETERAN ROSTER

No.	Name	Pos.	Ht.	Wt.	Birthdate	NFL Exp.	College	Hometown	How Acq.	'96 Games/ Starts
21	Abraham, Donnie	CB	5-10	181	10/8/73	2	East Tennessee State	Orangeburg, S.C.	D3-'96	16/12
72	Ahanotu, Chidi	DE	6-2	283	10/11/70	5	California	Berkeley, Calif.	D6-'93	13/13
40	Alstott, Mike	RB	6-1	244	12/21/73	2	Purdue	Joliet, Ill.	D2-'96	16/16
27	Austin, Eric	S	5-11	217	6/9/73	2	Jackson State	Moss Point, Miss.	D4b-'96	2/0
6	Barnhardt, Tommy	P	6-2	207	6/11/63	11	North Carolina	China Grove, N.C.	FA-'96	16/0
23	Bouie, Tony	S	5-10	193	8/7/72	3	Arizona	New Orleans, La.	FA-'95	16/0
55	Brooks, Derrick	LB	6-0	231	4/18/73	3	Florida State	Pensacola, Fla.	D1b-'95	16/16
41	Brooks, Reggie	RB	5-8	211	1/19/71	5	Notre Dame	Tulsa, Okla.	W(Wash)-'96	11/4
88	Copeland, Horace	WR	6-3	202	1/2/71	5	Miami	Orlando, Fla.	D4b-'93	0*
77	Culpepper, Brad	DT	6-1	275	5/8/69	6	Florida	Tallahassee, Fla.	W(Minn)-'94	13/13
75	Curry, Eric	DE	6-5	270	2/3/70	5	Alabama	Thomasville, Ga.	D1-'93	12/3
48	Davis, John	TE	6-4	257	5/14/73	2	Emporia State	Jasper, Tex.	FA-'97	0*
64	Diaz, Jorge	G	6-4	295	11/15/73	2	Texas A&M-Kingsville	Katy, Tex.	FA-'96	11/6
12	Dilfer, Trent	QB	6-4	235	3/13/72	4	Fresno State	Aptos, Calif.	D1-'94	16/16
39	Dimry, Charles	CB	6-0	176	1/31/66	10	Nevada-Las Vegas	Oceanside, Calif.	UFA(Den)-'94	16/7
37	Ellison, Jerry	RB	5-10	204	12/20/71	3	Tennessee-Chattanooga	Augusta, Ga.	FA-'94	16/2
29	Gant, Kenneth	S	5-11	203	4/18/67	8	Albany State	Lakeland, Fla.	UFA(Dall)-'95	16/0
50	Gooch, Jeff	LB	5-11	218	10/31/74	2	Austin Peay	Nashville, Tenn.	FA-'96	15/0
43	Greene, Tracy	TE	6-5	270	11/5/72	3	Grambling State	Grambling, La.	FA-'97	0*
74	Gruber, Paul	T	6-5	296	2/24/65	10	Wisconsin	Prairie du Sac, Wis.	D1-'88	13/13
81	Harris, Jackie	TE	6-4	246	1/4/68	8	Northeast Louisiana	Pine Bluff, Ark.	RFA(GB)-'94	13/12
5	Husted, Michael	K	6-0	195	6/16/70	5	Virginia	Hampton, Va.	FA-'93	16/0
67	Ingram, Stephen	T-G	6-4	320	5/8/71	3	Maryland	Seat Pleasant, Md.	D7a-'95	0*
97	Jackson, Tyoka	DE-DT	6-2	266	11/22/71	3	Penn State	Washington, D.C.	FA-'96	13/2
25	Johnson, Melvin	S	6-0	198	4/15/72	3	Kentucky	Cincinnati, Ohio	D2-'95	16/16
57	Jones, LaCurtis	LB	6-0	200	6/23/72	2	Baylor	Waco, Tex.	FA-'96	10/0
78	Jones, Marcus	DT	6-6	282	8/15/73	2	North Carolina	Jacksonville, N.C.	D1b-'96	16/3
45	Legette, Tyrone	CB	5-9	177	2/15/70	6	Nebraska	Columbia, S.C.	UFA(NO)-'96	15/0
66	Love, Sean	G	6-3	304	9/6/68	4	Penn State	Tamaqua, Pa.	FA-'97	0*
47	Lynch, John	S	6-2	210	9/25/71	5	Stanford	Solana Beach, Calif.	D3-'93	16/14
90	Maniecki, Jason	DT	6-4	295	8/15/72	2	Wisconsin	Wisconsin Dells, Wis.	D5-'96	5/0
89	Marshall, Marvin	WR-KR	5-10	162	6/21/72	2	South Carolina State	Augusta, Ga.	FA-'95	5/0
54	Mason, Eddie	LB	6-0	245	1/9/72	3	North Carolina	Silver City, N.C.	FA-'97	0*
61	Mayberry, Tony	C	6-4	292	12/8/67	8	Wake Forest	Springfield, Va.	D4b-'90	16/16
35 #	Mayhew, Martin	CB	5-8	178	10/8/65	10	Florida State	Tallahassee, Fla.	UFA(Wash)-'93	16/16
91	McKenzie, Rich	DE	6-2	265	4/15/71	2	Penn State	Fort Lauderdale, Fla.	FA-'97	0*
13	Milanovich, Scott	QB-P	6-3	212	1/29/73	2	Maryland	Butler, Pa.	FA-'96	1/0
79	Miller, Jeff	T	6-4	305	11/23/72	3	Mississippi	Vero Beach, Fla.	FA-'97	0*
22	Mincy, Charles	S	5-11	198	12/16/69	7	Washington	Los Angeles, Calif.	FA-'96	2/0
83	Moore, Dave	TE	6-2	248	11/11/69	5	Pittsburgh	Succasunna, N.J.	FA-'92	16/8
56	Nickerson, Hardy	LB	6-2	233	9/1/65	11	California	Compton, Calif.	UFA(Pitt)-'93	16/16
9	Nittmo, Bjorn	K	5-11	179	7/26/66	2	Appalachian State	Enterprise, Ala.	FA-'97	0*
70	Odom, Jason	T	6-5	296	3/31/74	2	Florida	Bartow, Fla.	D4a-'96	12/7
69	Pierson, Pete	T	6-5	295	2/4/71	3	Washington	Portland, Ore.	D5-'94	11/2
59	Porter, Rufus	LB	6-1	230	5/18/65	10	Southern	Baton Rouge, La.	FA-'97	13/9*
60	Pyne, Jim	G	6-2	290	11/23/71	4	Virginia Tech	Milford, Mass.	D7-'94	12/11
32	Rhett, Errict	RB	5-11	211	12/11/70	4	Florida	Pembroke Pines, Fla.	D2-'94	9/7
52	Rouse, Wardell	LB	6-2	235	6/9/72	3	Clemson	Clewiston, Fla.	D6-'95	0*
99	Sapp, Warren	DT	6-2	288	12/19/72	3	Miami	Apopka, Fla.	D1a-'95	15/14
38	Scott, Todd	S	5-11	205	1/23/68	7	Southwestern Louisiana	Galveston, Tex.	W(NYJ)-'95	2/2
87	Silvan, Nilo	WR-KR	5-9	184	10/2/73	2	Tennessee	Covington, La.	D6-'96	7/0
33	Staten, Robert	RB	5-11	240	11/23/69	2	Jackson State	Shubuta, Miss.	FA-'96	6/0
82	Tate, Willy	TE	6-3	243	9/7/72	2	Oregon	Elk Grove, Calif.	FA-'96	13/0
84	Thomas, Robb	WR	5-11	175	3/29/66	9	Oregon State	Corvallis, Ore.	FA-'96	12/8
73	Upshaw, Regan	DE	6-4	264	8/12/75	2	California	Pittsburg, Calif.	D1a-'96	16/16
4	Walsh, Steve	QB	6-3	200	12/1/66	9	Miami	St. Paul, Minn.	UFA(StL)-'97	3/3*
94	White, Steve	DE	6-2	246	10/25/73	2	Tennessee	Memphis, Tenn.	FA-'96	4/0
86	Williams, Karl	WR	5-10	163	4/10/71	2	Texas A&M-Kingsville	Rowlett, Tex.	FA-'96	16/0
58	Williams, Mark	LB	6-4	240	5/17/71	3	Ohio State	Forrestville, Md.	FA-'96	2/0*

* Copeland, Davis, Mason, Miller and Rouse missed '96 season because of injury; Greene last active with Pittsburgh in '95; Ingram inactive for 6 games; Love last active with Carolina in '95; McKenzie last active with Cleveland in '95; Nittmo last active with N.Y. Giants in '89; Porter played 13 games with New Orleans; Walsh played 3 games with St. Louis; M. Williams played 2 games with St. Louis.

\# Unrestricted free agent; subject to developments.

† Restricted free agent; subject to developments.

Players lost through free agency (4): G Ian Beckles (Phil; 13 games in '96); LB Demetrius DuBose (NYJ; 14); WR Courtney Hawkins (Pitt; 16); LB Lonnie Marts (Tenn; 16).

Also played with the Buccaneers in '96—G Scott Adams (7 games), C-G Joel Crisman (9), LB Kevin Dogins (1), TE John Farquhar (1), WR Alvin Harper (12), RB Tracy Johnson (10), T Doug Riesenberg (10), CB Reggie Rusk (1), WR Larry Ryans (3), DE Herman Smith (5), LB Darnell Stephens (1), RB LeRoy Thompson (5), QB Casey Weldon (3).

COACHING STAFF

Head Coach,
Tony Dungy

Pro Career: After 15 years as an NFL assistant coach, was named as the Buccaneers' sixth head coach on January 22, 1996, when he signed a six-year contract. Joined Tampa Bay after serving as Minnesota Vikings' defensive coordinator from 1992-95. Helped Vikings' defense lead NFL with 95 interceptions during his four years in Minnesota. Prior to going to Vikings, spent 1989-1991 as defensive backs coach for Kansas City Chiefs. Also worked eight years as an assistant coach for the Pittsburgh Steelers under Chuck Noll as a defensive assistant (1981), defensive backs coach (1982-83), and as defensive coordinator (1984-88). At 25, was NFL's youngest assistant coach when hired by Steelers in 1981, then became league's youngest coordinator at age of 28. Began coaching career coaching defensive backs at University of Minnesota in 1980. As an NFL player, signed with Pittsburgh as a free agent in 1977 and played safety for Steelers for two seasons (1977-78). Had nine interceptions (second in AFC with 6 in 1978) in 30 games for Pittsburgh and played in Super Bowl XIII victory over Dallas Cowboys. Had unusual distinction of making and throwing an interception in same 1977 game versus Houston Oilers. Traded to San Francisco 49ers during 1979 training camp and played 15 games for 49ers. Was traded again prior to 1980 season to New York Giants in multi-player deal that sent current Philadelphia Eagle head coach Ray Rhodes to 49ers. Career record: 6-10.

Background: Starred as quarterback at University of Minnesota from 1973-76. Finished career as school's all-time leader in attempts, completions, passing yards, and touchdown passes. Left Minnesota in fourth place in Big Ten history in total offense. Two-time team most valuable player, played in Hula Bowl, East-West Shrine Game, and Japan Bowl. Attended Parkside High School in Jackson, Michigan.

Personal: Born October 6, 1955, in Jackson, Michigan. Tony and his wife, Lauren, have three children including daughter Tiara (12), and sons James (10) and Eric (5). The family resides in Tampa.

ASSISTANT COACHES

Mark Asanovich, strength and conditioning; born May 20, 1959, Duluth, Minn., lives in Clearwater, Fla. No college or pro playing experience. College coach: Ohio State 1985, Citadel 1986. Pro coach: Minnesota Vikings 1995, joined Buccaneers in 1996.

Clyde Christensen, tight ends; born January 28, 1958, Corvine, Calif., lives in Tampa. Quarterback Fresno (Calif.) J.C. 1975, North Carolina 1976-78. No pro playing experience. College coach: East Tennessee State 1980-82, Temple 1983-85, East Carolina 1986-88, Holy Cross 1989-90, South Carolina 1991, Maryland 1992-93, Clemson 1994-95. Pro coach: Joined Buccaneers in 1996.

Herman Edwards, assistant head coach/defensive backs; born April 27, 1954, Monmouth, N.J., lives in Tampa. Defensive back California 1972, 1974, Monterey Peninsula (Calif.) J.C. 1973, San Diego State 1975-76. Pro defensive back Philadelphia Eagles 1977-85, Los Angeles Rams 1986, Atlanta Falcons 1986. College coach: San Jose State 1987-89. Pro coach: Kansas City Chiefs 1992-94 (scout 1990-91, 1995), joined Buccaneers in 1996.

Chris Foerster, offensive line; born October 12, 1961, Milwaukee, Wis., lives in Tampa. Center Colorado State 1979-82. No pro playing experience. College coach: Colorado State 1983-87, Stanford 1988-91, Minnesota 1992. Pro coach: Minnesota Vikings 1993-95, joined Buccaneers in 1996.

Monte Kiffin, defensive coordinator; born February 29, 1940, Lexington, Neb., lives in Tampa. Offensive/defensive tackle Nebraska 1959-63. Pro defensive end Winnipeg Blue Bombers (CFL) 1965. College coach: Nebraska 1966-76, Arkansas 1977-79, North Carolina State 1980-82 (head coach). Pro coach: Green Bay Packers 1983, Buffalo Bills 1984-

85, Minnesota Vikings 1986-89, 1991-94, New York Jets 1990, New Orleans Saints 1995, joined Buccaneers in 1996.

Joe Marciano, special teams; born February 10, 1954, Scranton, Pa., lives in Tampa. Quarterback Temple 1972-75. No pro playing experience. College coach: East Stroudsburg 1977, Rhode Island 1978-79, Villanova 1980, Penn State 1981, Temple 1982. Pro coach: Philadelphia/Baltimore Stars (USFL) 1983-85, New Orleans Saints 1986-95, joined Buccaneers in 1996.

Rod Marinelli, defensive line; born July 13, 1949, Rosemead, Calif., lives in Tampa. Offensive/defensive tackle California Lutheran 1970-72 (military service 1969-70). No pro playing experience. College coach: Utah State 1976-82, California 1983-91, Arizona State 1992-94, Southern California 1995. Pro coach: Joined Buccaneers in 1996.

Tony Nathan, running backs; born December 14, 1956, Birmingham, Ala., lives in Tampa. Running back Alabama 1975-78. Pro running back Miami Dolphins 1979-87. Pro coach: Miami Dolphins 1988-95, joined Buccaneers in 1996.

Kevin O'Dea, defensive assistant; born June 9, 1960, Williamsport, Va., lives in Tampa. Defensive back/wide receiver Lock Haven 1982-85. No pro playing experience. College coach: Lock Haven 1986, Cornell 1987, Virginia 1988-90, Penn State

1991-93. Pro coach: San Diego Chargers 1994-95, joined Buccaneers in 1996.

Mike Shula, offensive coordinator; born June 3, 1965, Baltimore, Md., lives in Tampa. Quarterback Alabama 1983-86. Pro quarterback Tampa Bay Buccaneers 1987. Pro coach: Tampa Bay Buccaneers 1988-90, Miami Dolphins 1991-92, Chicago Bears 1993-95, rejoined Buccaneers in 1996.

Lovie Smith, linebackers; born May 8, 1958, Gladewater, Tex., lives in Tampa. Linebacker Tulsa 1976-79. No pro playing experience. College coach: Tulsa 1983-86, Wisconsin 1987, Arizona State 1988-91, Kentucky 1992, Tennessee 1993-94, Ohio State 1995. Pro coach: Joined Buccaneers in 1996.

Ricky Thomas, offensive assistant; born March 29, 1965, London, England, lives in Tampa. Safety Alabama 1983-86. Pro safety Seattle Seahawks 1987. College coach: Kentucky 1996, Gardner-Webb 1996. Pro coach: Joined Buccaneers in 1997.

Charlie Williams, wide receivers; born January 31, 1958, Long Beach, Calif., lives in Tampa. Defensive back Long Beach City College 1977-78, Colorado State 1979-80. No pro playing experience. College coach: Colorado State 1981, Long Beach City College 1984-85, New Mexico State 1986-87, Texas Christian 1988-91, Minnesota 1992, Miami 1993-95. Pro coach: Joined Buccaneers in 1996.

1997 FIRST-YEAR ROSTER

Name	Pos.	Ht.	Wt.	Birthdate	College	Hometown	How Acq.
Anthony, Reidel	WR	5-11	183	10/20/76	Florida	Glades Central, Fla.	D1b
Barber, Ronde	CB	5-10	185	4/7/75	Virginia	Roanoke, Va.	D3b
Bellisari, Greg	LB	6-0	232	6/21/75	Ohio State	Boca Raton, Fla.	FA
Campbell, Chris	WR	6-0	199	5/12/74	Penn State	Akron, Ohio	FA
Carter, Nigea	WR	6-1	176	9/1/74	Michigan State	Coconut Creek, Fla.	D6b
Coleman, Shaston	WR	5-11	212	1/18/72	Mississippi State	Ackerman, Miss.	FA
DeGrate, Anthony	DT	6-1	333	11/15/73	Stephen F. Austin	Waco, Tex.	D7
Dittman, Seth (1)	T	6-7	295	7/23/72	Stanford	Tigard, Ore.	FA
Dogins, Kevin (1)	C	6-1	290	12/7/72	Texas A&M-Kingsville	Eagle Lake, Tex.	FA-'96
Dunn, Warrick	RB	5-8	176	1/5/75	Florida State	Baton Rouge, La.	D1a
Ekiyor, Emil (1)	DE	6-2	253	12/25/73	Central Florida	Port Orange, Fla.	FA-'96
Garth, Patrick	DE	6-4	282	12/25/74	South Carolina	Aberdeen, Miss.	FA
Gayle, Rashid (1)	CB	5-9	185	4/16/74	Boise State	Boise, Idaho	FA-'96
Hape, Patrick	TE	6-4	253	6/6/74	Alabama	Killen, Ala.	D5
Harris, Al	CB	6-0	178	12/7/74	Texas A&M-Kingsville	Coconut Creek, Fla.	D6a
Hunter, Brice (1)	WR	6-0	211	4/21/74	Georgia	Valdosta, Ga.	FA-'96
Martin, Jason	QB	6-2	234	12/12/74	Louisiana Tech	Oak Grove, La.	FA
Middleton, Frank	G	6-3	324	10/25/74	Arizona	Beaumont, Tex.	D3a
Newman, Brian	G	6-3	291	2/11/74	Tulsa	Stroud, Okla.	FA
Quarles, Shelton (1)	LB	6-1	236	9/11/71	Vanderbilt	Whites Creek, Tenn.	FA
Ross, Dominique (1)	RB	6-0	203	1/12/72	Valdosta State	Jacksonville, Fla.	FA
Rusk, Reggie (1)	CB	5-10	182	10/19/72	Kentucky	Texas City, Tex.	D7-'96
Shamburger, Cliff	CB	5-11	190	7/22/74	Troy State	Jasper, Ala.	FA
Singleton, Alshermond	LB	6-2	224	8/7/75	Temple	Irvington, N.J.	D4
Spann, Gregory (1)	WR	6-0	215	4/16/73	Jackson State	Macon, Miss.	FA
White, Cornelius	WR	6-0	193	6/28/73	Virginia Tech	Penndel, Pa	FA
Williams, Jermane	RB	6-0	228	8/14/73	Houston	Greenville, N.C.	FA
Wunsch, Jerry	T	6-6	327	1/21/74	Wisconsin	Wausau, Wis.	D2
Young, Floyd	LB	6-0	170	11/23/75	Texas A&M-Kingsville	New Orleans, La.	FA

The term NFL Rookie is defined as a player who is in his first season of professional football and has not been on the roster of another professional football team for any regular-season or postseason games. A Rookie is designated by an "R" on NFL rosters. Players who have been active in another professional football league or players who have NFL experience, including either preseason training camp or being on an Active List or Inactive List, or on Reserve/Injured or Reserve/Physically Unable to Perform for fewer than six regular-season games, are termed NFL First-Year Players. An NFL First-Year Player is designated by a "1" on NFL rosters. Thereafter, a player is credited with an additional year of experience for each season in which he accumulates six games on the Active List or Inactive List, or on Reserve/Injured or Reserve/Physically Unable to Perform.

NOTES

_____
_____
_____
_____
_____
_____
_____
_____
_____

National Football Conference
Eastern Division
Team Colors: Burgundy and Gold
Redskin Park
P.O. Box 17247
Washington, D.C. 20041
Telephone: (703) 478-8900

CLUB OFFICIALS

President: John Kent Cooke
House Counsel: Stuart Haney
Controller: Mark Francis
General Manager: Charley Casserly
Assistant General Manager: Bobby Mitchell
Director of Player Development: Joe Mendes
Director of College Scouting: George Saimes
Scouts: Gene Bates, Larry Bryan, Scott Cohen,
    Mike Hagen, Mike Maccagnan, Miller McCalmon
    Joel Patten
Coordinator of Scouting: Chuck Banker
Scouting Administrator: Dave Scars
Director of Public Relations: Mike McCall
Director of Media Relations: Chris Helein
Public Relations Assistants: Reggie Saunders,
    Scott McKeen
Community Relations Coordinator: Wendy Brinker
Director of Administration: Barry Asimos
VP Marketing: John Kent Cooke, Jr.
Asst. Marketing Director: John Wagner
Video Director: Donnie Schoenmann
Asst. Video Director: Hugh McPhillips
Video Analyst: Mike Bean
Ticket Manager: Jeff Ritter
Director of Stadium Operations: Jeff Klein
Head Trainer: Bubba Tyer
Assistant Trainers: Al Bellamy, Kevin Bastin
Equipment Manager: Jay Brunetti
Asst. Equipment Manager: Jeff Parsons
Stadium: Jack Kent Cooke Stadium
    •**Capacity:** 78,600
    Raljon, Maryland 20785-4236
Playing Surface: Grass
Training Camp: Frostburg State University
    Frostburg, Maryland 21532-1099

1997 SCHEDULE

PRESEASON

Aug. 2	at Tampa Bay	7:30
Aug. 9	vs. Tennessee at Nashville	7:00
Aug. 16	at Atlanta	7:30
Aug. 21	at Miami	8:00

REGULAR SEASON

Aug. 31	at Carolina	8:00
Sept. 7	at Pittsburgh	1:00
Sept. 14	**Arizona**	1:00
Sept. 21	Open Date	
Sept. 28	**Jacksonville**	1:00
Oct. 5	at Philadelphia	1:00
Oct. 13	**Dallas** (Mon.)	9:00
Oct. 19	at Tennessee	12:00
Oct. 26	**Baltimore**	1:00
Nov. 2	at Chicago	12:00
Nov.9	**Detroit**	1:00
Nov. 16	at Dallas	12:00
Nov. 23	**New York Giants**	8:00
Nov. 30	**St. Louis**	1:00
Dec. 7	at Arizona	2:00
Dec. 13	at New York Giants (Sat.)	12:30
Dec. 21	**Philadelphia**	1:00

RECORD HOLDERS

INDIVIDUAL RECORDS—CAREER

Category	Name	Performance
Rushing (Yds.)	John Riggins, 1976-79, 1981-85	7,472
Passing (Yds.)	Joe Theismann, 1974-1985	25,206
Passing (TDs)	Sammy Baugh, 1937-1952	187
Receiving (No.)	Art Monk, 1980-1993	888
Receiving (Yds.)	Art Monk, 1980-1993	12,028
Interceptions	Darrell Green, 1983-1995	40
Punting (Avg.)	Sammy Baugh, 1937-1952	*45.1
Punt Return (Avg.)	Johnny Williams, 1952-53	12.8
Kickoff Return (Avg.)	Bobby Mitchell, 1962-68	28.5
Field Goals	Mark Moseley, 1974-1986	263
Touchdowns (Tot.)	Charley Taylor, 1964-1977	90
Points	Mark Moseley, 1974-1986	1,206

INDIVIDUAL RECORDS—SINGLE SEASON

Category	Name	Performance
Rushing (Yds.)	Terry Allen, 1996	1,353
Passing (Yds.)	Jay Schroeder, 1986	4,109
Passing (TDs)	Sonny Jurgensen, 1967	31
Receiving (No.)	Art Monk, 1984	106
Receiving (Yds.)	Bobby Mitchell, 1963	1,436
Interceptions	Dan Sandifer, 1948	13
Punting (Avg.)	Sammy Baugh, 1940	*51.4
Punt Return (Avg.)	Johnny Williams, 1952	15.3
Kickoff Return (Avg.)	Mike Nelms, 1981	29.7
Field Goals	Mark Moseley, 1983	33
Touchdowns (Tot.)	John Riggins, 1983	24
Points	Mark Moseley, 1983	161

INDIVIDUAL RECORDS—SINGLE GAME

Category	Name	Performance
Rushing (Yds.)	Gerald Riggs, 9-17-89	221
Passing (Yds.)	Sammy Baugh, 10-31-43	446
Passing (TDs)	Sammy Baugh, 10-31-43, 11-23-47	6
	Mark Rypien, 11-10-91	6
Receiving (No.)	Art Monk, 12-15-85	13
	Kelvin Bryant, 12-7-86	13
	Art Monk, 11-4-90	13
Receiving (Yds.)	Anthony Allen, 10-4-87	255
Interceptions	Sammy Baugh, 11-14-43	*4
	Dan Sandifer, 10-31-48	*4
Field Goals	Many times	5
	Last time by Chip Lohmiller, 10-25-92	
Touchdowns (Tot.)	Dick James, 12-17-61	4
	Larry Brown, 12-4-73	4
Points	Dick James, 12-17-61	24
	Larry Brown, 12-4-73	24

*NFL Record

COACHING HISTORY

Boston 1932-36
(468-407-26)

1932	Lud Wray	4-4-2
1933-34	William (Lone Star) Dietz	11-11-2
1935	Eddie Casey	2-8-1
1936-42	Ray Flaherty	56-23-3
1943	Arthur (Dutch) Bergman	7-4-1
1944-45	Dudley DeGroot	14-6-1
1946-48	Glen (Turk) Edwards	16-18-1
1949	John Whelchel*	3-3-1
1949-51	Herman Ball**	4-16-0
1951	Dick Todd	5-4-0
1952-53	Earl (Curly) Lambeau	10-13-1
1954-58	Joe Kuharich	26-32-2
1959-60	Mike Nixon	4-18-2
1961-65	Bill McPeak	21-46-3
1966-68	Otto Graham	17-22-3
1969	Vince Lombardi	7-5-2
1970	Bill Austin	6-8-0
1971-77	George Allen	69-35-1
1978-80	Jack Pardee	24-24-0
1981-92	Joe Gibbs	140-65-0
1993	Richie Petitbon	4-12-0
1994-96	Norv Turner	18-30-0

*Released after seven games in 1949
**Released after three games in 1951

JACK KENT COOKE STADIUM

1996 TEAM RECORD

PRESEASON (1-3)

Date	Result		Opponents
8/2	W	17-7	at Buffalo
8/9	L	25-34	at Detroit
8/16	L	7-28	Cincinnati
8/23	L	19-27	at New England

REGULAR SEASON (9-7)

Date	Result		Opponents	Att.
9/1	L	14-17	Philadelphia	53,415
9/8	W	10-3	Chicago	52,711
9/15	W	31-10	at N.Y. Giants	71,693
9/22	W	17-10	at St. Louis	62,303
9/29	W	31-16	N.Y. Jets	52,068
10/13	W	27-22	at New England	59,638
10/20	W	31-21	N.Y. Giants	52,684
10/27	W	31-16	Indianapolis	54,254
11/3	L	13-38	at Buffalo	78,002
11/10	L	34-37	Arizona (OT)	51,929
11/17	W	26-21	at Philadelphia	66,834
11/24	L	16-19	San Francisco (OT)	54,235
11/28	L	10-21	at Dallas	64,955
12/8	L	10-24	at Tampa Bay	44,733
12/15	L	26-27	at Arizona	34,260
12/22	W	37-10	Dallas	56,454

(OT) Overtime

SCORE BY PERIODS

Redskins	56	123	97	88	0	—	364
Opponents	39	110	68	89	6	—	312

ATTENDANCE

Home 427,750   Away 482,418   Total 910,168
Single-game home record, 56,454 (12/22/96)
Single-season home record, 443,678 (1992)

1996 TEAM STATISTICS

	Redskins	Opp.
Total First Downs	307	358
Rushing	106	146
Passing	174	191
Penalty	27	21
Third Down: Made/Att	77/203	100/228
Third Down Pct.	37.9	43.9
Fourth Down: Made/Att	7/9	10/15
Fourth Down Pct.	77.8	66.7
Total Net Yards	5229	5723
Avg. Per Game	326.8	357.7
Total Plays	960	1114
Avg. Per Play	5.4	5.1
Net Yards Rushing	1910	2275
Avg. Per Game	119.4	142.2
Total Rushes	467	520
Net Yards Passing	3319	3448
Avg. Per Game	207.4	215.5
Sacked/Yards Lost	22/134	34/207
Gross Yards	3453	3655
Att./Completions	471/270	560/325
Completion Pct.	57.3	58.0
Had Intercepted	11	21
Punts/Avg.	77/45.1	68/44.0
Net Punting Avg.	77/38.9	68/36.4
Penalties/Yards Lost	95/740	102/867
Fumbles/Ball Lost	21/7	27/9
Touchdowns	41	33
Rushing	27	20
Passing	12	12
Returns	2	1
Avg. Time of Possession	27:29	32:31

1996 INDIVIDUAL STATISTICS

PASSING

	Att.	Comp.	Yds.	Pct.	TD	Int.	Tkld.	Rate
Frerotte	470	270	3453	57.4	12	11	22/134	79.3
Mitchell	1	0	0	0.0	0	0	0/0	39.6
Redskins	471	270	3453	57.3	12	11	22/134	79.2
Opponents	560	325	3655	58.0	12	21	34/207	69.2

SCORING

	TD R	TD P	TD Rt	PAT	FG	Saf	PTS
Allen	21	0	0	0/0	0/0	0	126
Blanton	0	0	0	40/40	26/32	0	118
Shepherd	2	3	0	0/0	0/0	0	30
Asher	0	4	0	0/0	0/0	0	24
Davis	2	0	0	0/0	0/0	0	12
Ellard	0	2	0	0/0	0/0	0	12
Galbraith	0	2	0	0/0	0/0	0	12
Logan	2	0	0	0/0	0/0	0	12
D. Green	0	0	1	0/0	0/0	0	6
Turner	0	0	1	0/0	0/0	0	6
Westbrook	0	1	0	0/0	0/0	0	6
Redskins	27	12	2	40/40	26/32	0	364
Opponents	20	12	1	31/31	27/38	0	312

2-Point conversions: 0. Team: 0-1, Opponents: 1-2.

RUSHING

	Att.	Yds.	Avg.	LG	TD
Allen	347	1353	3.9	49t	21
Mitchell	39	193	4.9	32	0
Davis	23	139	6.0	39t	2
Logan	20	111	5.6	36t	2
Shepherd	6	96	16.0	32t	2
Frerotte	28	16	0.6	17	0
Westbrook	2	2	1.0	2	0
Shuler	1	0	0.0	0	0
Turk	1	0	0.0	0	0
Redskins	467	1910	4.1	49t	27
Opponents	520	2275	4.4	57	20

RECEIVING

	No.	Yds.	Avg.	LG	TD
Ellard	52	1014	19.5	51	2
Asher	42	481	11.5	34	4
Westbrook	34	505	14.9	45	1
Mitchell	32	286	8.9	20	0
Allen	32	194	6.1	28	0
Shepherd	23	344	15.0	52t	3
Logan	23	269	11.7	26	0
Brooks	17	224	13.2	31	0
Galbraith	8	89	11.1	30t	2
Bell	3	23	7.7	12	0
Bowie	3	17	5.7	8	0
Jenkins	1	7	7.0	7	0
Redskins	270	3453	12.8	52t	12
Opponents	325	3655	11.2	64t	12

INTERCEPTIONS

	No.	Yds.	Avg.	LG	TD
Carter	5	24	4.8	24	0
D. Green	3	84	28.0	68t	1
Richard	3	47	15.7	42	0
M. Patton	2	26	13.0	23	0
Turner	2	16	8.0	12	0
Pounds	2	11	5.5	11	0
Morrison	1	4	4.0	4	0
Harvey	1	2	2.0	2	0
Boutte	1	0	0.0	0	0
Stephens	1	0	0.0	0	0
Redskins	21	214	10.2	68t	1
Opponents	11	154	14.0	40	0

PUNTING

	No.	Yds.	Avg.	In 20	LG
Turk	75	3386	45.1	24	63
Blanton	2	84	42.0	0	45
Redskins	77	3470	45.1	24	63
Opponents	68	2990	44.0	15	72

PUNT RETURNS

	No.	FC	Yds.	Avg.	LG	TD
Mitchell	23	16	258	11.2	71	0
Redskins	23	16	258	11.2	71	0
Opponents	35	5	235	6.7	28	0

KICKOFF RETURNS

	No.	Yds.	Avg.	LG	TD
Mitchell	56	1258	22.5	50	0
Bell	8	130	16.3	27	0
Asher	1	13	13.0	13	0
Redskins	65	1401	21.6	50	0
Opponents	76	1610	21.2	63	0

SACKS

	No.
Owens	11.0
Harvey	9.0
Nottage	5.0
Gilbert	3.0
M. Patton	2.0
Palmer	1.0
Stephens	1.0
B. Walker	1.0
Woods	1.0
Redskins	34.0
Opponents	22.0

1997 DRAFT CHOICES

Round	Name	Pos.	College
1	Kenard Lang	DE	Miami
2	Greg Jones	LB	Colorado
3	Derek Smith	LB	Arizona State
4	Albert Connell	WR	Texas A&M
5	Jamel Williams	DB	Nebraska
	Keith Thibodeaux	DB	Northwestern St., La.
	Twan Russell	LB	Miami
	Brad Badger	G	Stanford

WASHINGTON REDSKINS

1997 VETERAN ROSTER

No.	Name	Pos.	Ht.	Wt.	Birthdate	NFL Exp.	College	Hometown	How Acq.	'96 Games/ Starts
58	Alexander, Patrise	LB	6-1	247	10/23/72	2	Southwestern Louisiana	Galveston, Tex.	FA-'96	16/1
21	Allen, Terry	RB	5-10	208	2/21/68	8	Clemson	Commerce, Ga.	FA-'95	16/16
84	Asher, Jamie	TE	6-3	241	10/31/72	3	Louisville	Galveston, Tex.	D5a-'95	16/12
73	Ashmore, Darryl	T	6-7	310	11/1/69	6	Northwestern	Peoria, Ill.	FA-'96	5/0
72	Bandison, Romeo	DT	6-5	295	2/12/71	4	Oregon	Mill Valley, Calif.	FA-'95	10/0
23	Barnes, Tomur	CB	5-10	188	9/8/70	3	North Texas	McNair, Tex.	FA-'96	3/0
61	Batiste, Michael	G-T	6-3	325	12/24/70	2	Tulane	Beaumont, Tex.	FA-'97	0*
36	Bell, William	FB	5-11	214	7/22/71	4	Georgia Tech	Miami, Fla.	FA-'94	16/0
16	Blanton, Scott	K	6-2	221	7/1/73	3	Oklahoma	Norman, Okla.	FA-'95	16/0
93	Boutte, Marc	DT	6-4	301	7/26/69	6	Louisiana State	Lake Charles, La.	FA-'94	10/10
47	Bowie, Larry	RB	6-0	242	3/21/73	2	Georgia	Anniston, Ala.	FA-'96	3/0
37	Campbell, Jesse	S	6-1	211	4/11/69	7	North Carolina State	Vanceboro, N.C.	UFA(NYG)-'97	16/16*
75	Dahl, Bob	G	6-5	329	1/15/68	6	Notre Dame	Chagrin Falls, Ohio	UFA(Balt)-'96	15/15
48	Davis, Stephen	RB	6-0	230	3/1/74	2	Auburn	Spartanburg, S.C.	D4-'96	12/0
26	Dishman, Cris	CB	6-0	188	8/13/65	10	Purdue	Louisville, Ky.	UFA(Hous)-'97	16/16*
85	Ellard, Henry	WR	5-11	185	7/21/61	15	Fresno State	Fresno, Calif.	UFA(Rams)-'94	16/16
23	Evans, Gregory	CB-S	6-1	208	6/28/71	2	Texas Christian	Pittsburg, Tex.	FA-'97	0*
35	Evans, Leomont	S	6-1	200	7/12/74	2	Clemson	Abbeville, S.C.	D5-'96	12/0
12	† Frerotte, Gus	QB	6-2	228	7/3/71	4	Tulsa	Ford Cliff, Pa.	D7-'94	16/16
95	Gaines, William	DT	6-5	305	6/20/71	4	Florida	Jackson, Miss.	FA-'95	16/6
89	Galbraith, Scott	TE	6-2	254	1/7/67	8	Southern California	Sacramento, Calif.	UFA(Dall)-'95	16/6
94	Gilbert, Sean	DT	6-5	303	4/10/70	6	Pittsburgh	Aliquippa, Pa.	T(StL)-'96	16/16
28	Green, Darrell	CB	5-8	184	2/15/60	15	Texas A&I	Houston, Tex.	D1-'83	16/16
10	† Green, Trent	QB	6-3	213	7/9/70	4	Indiana	St. Louis, Mo.	FA-'95	0*
57	Harvey, Ken	LB	6-2	236	5/6/65	10	California	Austin, Tex.	UFA(Ariz)-'94	16/16
88	# Jenkins, James	TE	6-2	249	8/17/67	7	Rutgers	Staten Island, N.Y.	FA-'91	16/5
69	Johnson, Andre	T	6-5	311	8/25/73	2	Penn State	Long Island, N.Y.	D1-'96	0*
77	Johnson, Tré	G	6-2	337	8/30/71	4	Temple	Peekskill, N.Y.	D2-'94	15/15
70	Kinney, Kelvin	DE	6-6	252	12/31/72	2	Virginia State	Montgomery, W. Va.	D6-'96	0*
20	Logan, Marc	RB	6-0	220	5/9/65	10	Kentucky	Lexington, Ky.	UFA(SF)-'95	14/9
64	# Matich, Trevor	C	6-4	287	10/9/61	13	Brigham Young	Sacramento, Calif.	UFA(Ind)-'94	16/0
92	Mays, Damon	WR	5-9	170	5/20/68	4	Missouri	Phoenix, Ariz.	FA-'97	0*
30	Mitchell, Brian	RB	5-10	220	8/18/68	8	Southwestern Louisiana	Plaquemine, La.	D5-'90	16/2
92	Nottage, Dexter	DE	6-4	287	11/14/70	4	Florida A&M	Miami, Fla.	D6-'94	16/4
91	Olive, Bobby	WR	6-1	175	4/2/70	2	Ohio State	Paris, Tenn.	FA-'97	1/0*
96	Owens, Rich	DE	6-6	279	5/22/72	3	Lehigh	Philadelphia, Pa.	D5b-'95	16/16
97	Palmer, Sterling	DE	6-5	287	2/4/71	5	Florida State	Ft. Lauderdale, Fla.	D4-'93	6/5
68	† Patton, Joe	G	6-5	309	1/5/72	4	Alabama A&M	Birmingham, Ala.	D3b-'94	16/15
53	Patton, Marvcus	LB	6-2	241	5/1/67	8	UCLA	Lawndale, Calif.	UFA(Buff)-'95	16/16
31	Pounds, Darryl	CB-S	5-10	181	7/21/72	3	Nicholls State	Ft. Worth, Tex.	D3-'95	12/1
67	Pourdanesh, Shar	T	6-6	318	7/19/70	2	Nevada-Reno	Teheran, Iran	FA-'96	16/8
52	Raymer, Cory	C	6-2	292	3/3/73	3	Wisconsin	Fond du Lac, Wis.	D2-'95	6/5
71	Reem, Matt	T	6-6	270	12/23/72	2	Minnesota	Roseville, Minn.	FA-'96	0*
24	Richard, Stanley	S	6-2	197	10/21/67	7	Texas	Miniola, Tex.	FA-'95	16/15
99	Rucker, Keith	DT	6-3	331	11/20/68	5	Ohio Wesleyan	University Park, Ill.	FA-'97	0*
59	Sedoris, Chris	C	6-3	286	4/25/73	2	Purdue	Columbus, Ind.	FA-'96	9/0
86	Shepherd, Leslie	WR	5-11	180	11/3/69	4	Temple	Forestville, Md.	FA-'94	12/6
76	Simmons, Ed	T	6-5	333	12/31/63	11	Eastern Washington	Seattle, Wash.	D6-'87	11/11
6	Thomas, Chris	WR	6-2	190	7/16/71	2	Cal Poly-San Luis Obispo	Ventura, Calif.	FA-'97	0*
1	Turk, Matt	P	6-5	234	6/16/68	3	Wisconsin-Whitewater	Greenfield, Wis.	FA-'95	16/0
29	Turner, Scott	CB	5-10	180	2/26/72	3	Illinois	Richardson, Tex.	D7-'95	16/0
55	Uhlenhake, Jeff	C	6-3	284	1/28/66	9	Ohio State	Newark, Ohio	FA-'96	12/11
45	Walker, Brian	S	6-2	191	5/31/72	2	Washington State	Colorado Springs, Colo.	FA-'96	16/4
82	Westbrook, Michael	WR	6-3	220	7/7/72	3	Colorado	Detroit, Mich.	D1-'95	11/6

* Batiste last active with Dallas in '95; Campbell played 16 games with New York Giants; Dishman played 16 games with Houston; G. Evans last active with Buffalo in '95; T. Green inactive for 16 games; A. Johnson inactive for 16 games; Kinney missed '96 season due to injury; Mays inactive for 2 games; Olive played 1 game with Indianapolis; Reem inactive for 6 games; Rucker last active with Cincinnati in '95; Thomas last active with San Francisco in '95.

\# Unrestricted free agent; subject to developments.

† Restricted free agent; subject to developments.

Traded—QB Heath Shuler (1 game in '96) to New Orleans.

Players lost through free agency (1): CB Tom Carter (Chi;16 games in '96).

Also played with Redskins in '96—WR Flipper Anderson (2 games in '96), DT Troy Barnett (3), WR Bill Brooks (16), LB Darrick Brownlow (16), LB Al Catanho (15), S Darryl Morrison (12), LB Rod Stephens (16), CB Eric Sutton (4), S Keith Taylor (3), LB Matt Vanderbeek((1), CB Marquis Walker (1), DE Tony Woods (13).

COACHING STAFF

Head Coach,
Norv Turner

Pro Career: Enters his fourth season as head coach of the Washington Redskins after serving three years as the Dallas Cowboys' offensive coordinator. Turner guided the Cowboys' prolific offense during back-to-back Super Bowl championship seasons. He inherited a Cowboys offense that finished twenty-eighth in total offense in 1990, and a year later improved to ninth. The Cowboys finished fourth in the league offensively in 1992-93. In three seasons under Turner, quarterback Troy Aikman compiled a 91.7 rating, and running back Emmitt Smith won three consecutive NFL rushing titles. Prior to joining the Cowboys, Turner coached six seasons (1985-1990) with the Los Angeles Rams where he oversaw the passing game. Quarterback Jim Everett enjoyed his best seasons under Turner, while Willie Anderson led the NFL in yards per catch in 1989 and 1990, and Henry Ellard was the league's leading receiver in 1988. Career record: 18-30.

Background: Turner played quarterback for three seasons at the University of Oregon (1972-74). He began his coaching career as a graduate assistant at Oregon in 1975. A year later, he moved to the University of Southern California, where he coached from 1976-1984.

Personal: Born May 17, 1952, in LeJeune, N.C. Turner and his wife, Nancy, live in Oakton, Va., and have three children—Scott, Stephanie, and Drew.

ASSISTANT COACHES

Jason Arapoff, assistant conditioning; born July 8, 1965, Weymouth, Mass., lives in Centreville, Va. Defensive back Springfield College 1985-88. No pro playing experience. Pro coach: Joined Redskins in 1992.

Russ Grimm, offensive line; born May 2, 1959, Scottdale, Pa., lives in Fairfax, Va. Guard-center Pittsburgh 1977-80. Pro guard Washington Redskins 1981-91. Pro coach: Joined Redskins in 1992.

Tom Hayes, defensive backs; born March 26, 1949, Keokuk, Iowa, lives in Ashburn, Va. Defensive back Iowa 1968-71. No pro playing experience. College coach: Coe College 1973, Iowa 1977-78, Cal State-Fullerton 1979, UCLA 1980-88, Texas A&M 1989, Oklahoma 1990-94. Pro coach: Joined Redskins in 1995.

Bobby Jackson, running backs; born February 16, 1940, Forsyth, Ga., lives in Sterling, Va. Linebacker-running back Samford 1959-62. No pro playing experience. College coach: Florida State 1965-69, Kansas State 1970-74, Louisville 1975-76, Tennessee 1977-82. Pro coach: Atlanta Falcons 1983-86, San Diego Chargers 1987-91, Phoenix Cardinals 1992-93, joined Redskins in 1994.

Earl Leggett, defensive line; born March 5, 1935, Jacksonville, Fla., lives in Leesburg, Va. Defensive tackle Louisiana State. Pro defensive tackle Chicago Bears 1957-65, Los Angeles Rams 1966, New Orleans Saints 1967-68. Pro coach: Seattle Seahawks 1976-77, San Francisco 49ers 1978, Oakland/Los Angeles Raiders 1980-84, 1991-92, Denver Broncos 1989-90, New York Giants 1993-96, joined Redskins in 1997.

Dale Lindsey, linebackers; born January 18, 1943, Bedford, Ind., lives in Ashburn, Va. Pro linebacker Western Kentucky 1961-64. Pro linebacker Cleveland Browns 1965-73. College coach: Southern Methodist 1988-89. Pro coach: Green Bay Packers 1986-87, New England Patriots 1990, Tampa Bay Buccaneers 1991, San Diego Chargers 1994-96, joined Redskins in 1997.

Mike Martz, quarterbacks; born May 13, 1951, Sioux Falls, S.D., lives in Leesburg, Va. No college or pro playing experience. Pro coach: San Diego Mesa 1974, 1976-77, San Jose State 1975, Santa Ana College 1978, Fresno State 1979, Pacific 1980-81, Arizona State 1983-91. Pro coach: Los Angeles/St. Louis Rams 1992-96, joined Redskins in 1997.

LeCharls McDaniel, secondary assistant; born October 15, 1958, Fort Bragg, N.C., lives in Ashburn,

Va. Cornerback Cal Poly-San Luis Obispo 1976-80. Pro defensive back Washington Redskins 1981-82, New York Giants 1983-84. College coach: Hartnell College (Calif.) 1984-89, Cal Poly-San Luis Obispo 1992, San Diego State 1994-95. Pro coach: San Diego Chargers 1989-91, Phoenix Cardinals 1993, joined Redskins in 1997.

Michael Nolan, defensive coordinator; born March 7, 1959, Baltimore, Md., lives in Oakton, Va. Free safety Oregon 1977-80. No pro playing experience. College coach: Oregon 1981, Stanford 1982-83, Rice 1984-85, Louisiana State 1986. Pro coach: Denver Broncos 1987-92, New York Giants 1993-96, joined Redskins in 1997.

Michael Pope, tight ends; born March 15, 1942, Monroe, N.C., lives in Ashburn, Va. Quarterback Lenoir Rhyne 1962-64. No pro playing experience. College coach: Florida State 1970-74, Texas Tech 1975-77, Mississippi 1978-82. Pro coach: New York Giants 1983-91, Cincinnati Bengals 1992-93, New England Patriots 1994-96, joined Redskins in 1997.

Dan Riley, conditioning; born October 19, 1949,

Syracuse, N.Y., lives in Ashburn, Va. No college or pro playing experience. College coach: Army 1973-76, Penn State 1977-81. Pro coach: Joined Redskins in 1982.

Terry Robiskie, receivers; born November 12, 1954, New Orleans, La., lives in Clifton, Va. Running back Louisiana State 1973-76. Pro running back Oakland Raiders 1977-79, Miami Dolphins 1980-81. Pro coach: Los Angeles Raiders 1982-93, joined Redskins in 1994.

Pete Rodriguez, special teams; born July 25, 1940, Chicago, Ill., lives in Sterling, Va. Guard-linebacker Denver University 1959-60, Western State (Colo.) 1961-63. No pro playing experience. College coach: Western State (Colo.) 1964, Arizona 1968-69, Western Illinois 1970-73, 1979-82 (head coach), Florida State 1974-75, Iowa State 1976-78, Northern Iowa 1986. Pro coach: Michigan Panthers (USFL) 1983-84, Denver Gold (USFL) 1985, Jacksonville Bulls (USFL) 1986, Ottawa Rough Riders (CFL) 1987, Los Angeles Raiders 1988-89, Phoenix Cardinals 1990-93, joined Redskins in 1994.

1997 FIRST-YEAR ROSTER

Name	Pos.	Ht.	Wt.	Birthdate	College	Hometown	How Acq.
Anderson, Lance	P	6-1	212	3/7/74	Arizona State	Apple Valley, Calif.	FA
Asher, Jeremy	LB	6-0	234	10/5/72	Oregon	Medford, Ore.	D7a-'96
Badger, Brad	G	6-4	296	1/11/75	Stanford	Corvallis, Ore.	D5d
Bennett, Kerry	RB	5-11	214	10/31/73	Stephen F. Austin	Orange, Tex.	FA
Brooks, Steven	TE-LS	6-5	256	6/2/71	California-Santa Barbara	Burbank, Calif.	FA-'96
Connell, Albert	WR	6-0	184	5/13/71	Texas A&M	Ft. Lauderdale, Fla.	D4
Crawford, Melvin	S	6-0	193	2/18/73	Hampton	Rockville, Md.	FA
Echols, Larry	LB	6-1	227	1/25/74	Stephen F. Austin	Ennis, Tex.	FA
Foley, Mike	DT	6-3	290	11/12/71	New Hampshire	Worcester, Mass	FA
Hankton, Karl	WR	6-3	200	7/24/70	Louisiana State	New Orleans, La.	FA
Hartsell, Mark	QB	6-4	224	12/7/73	Boston College	Brockton, Mass	FA
Jones, Greg	LB	6-4	241	5/22/74	Colorado	Denver, Colo.	D2
Kennedy, Brannon	WR	6-2	192	2/23/73	Hawaii	North Augusta, S.C.	FA
Kitts, Jim	RB	6-2	243	12/28/72	Ferrum	Chesapeake, Va.	FA
Lang, Kenard	DE	6-4	277	1/31/75	Miami	Orlando, Fla.	D1
Lee, Mark	DE	6-4	260	6/4/72	Western Colorado State	Colorado Springs, Colo.	FA-'96
Maritz, Matt	T	6-6	315	11/25/72	Slippery Rock	Pittsburgh, Pa.	FA
Maxwell, Deandre	WR	6-1	213	4/6/73	San Diego State	Fresno, Calif.	FA-'96
Maxwell, Jonathan	CB	6-1	195	3/17/74	Louisiana Tech	Little Rock, Ark.	FA
Otton, Brad	QB	6-6	235	12/5/72	Southern California	Tunwater, Wash.	FA
Powell, Ozell	T	6-5	295	11/17/73	Alabama	Greenville, Ala.	FA
Robinson, Dwaine	DT	6-4	275	8/26/75	Virginia Union	Newton, Va.	FA
Russell, Twan	LB	6-1	230	4/25/74	Miami	Ft. Lauderdale, Fla.	D5c
Sanders, Christopher	TE	6-3	243	4/22/73	Texas A&M	Austin, Tex.	FA
Seagraves, Del	TE	6-3	245	2/12/72	Pittsburgh	Greensboro, N.C.	FA
Smith, Derek	LB	6-2	235	1/18/75	Arizona State	American Fork, Utah	D3
Thibodeaux, Keith	CB	5-11	185	5/16/74	Northwestern State, La.	Opelousas, La.	D5b
Truluck, R-Kal	LB	6-4	243	9/30/74	SUNY-Cortland	Brooklyn, N.Y.	FA
Westbrook, John	WR	5-9	176	9/1/71	Arkansas Tech	Parktin, Ark.	FA
Williams, Jamel	S	5-11	205	12/22/73	Nebraska	Merrillville, Ind.	D5a

The term NFL Rookie is defined as a player who is in his first season of professional football and has not been on the roster of another professional football team for any regular-season or postseason games. A Rookie is designated by an "R" on NFL rosters. Players who have been active in another professional football league or players who have NFL experience, including either preseason training camp or being on an Active List or Inactive List, or on Reserve/Injured or Reserve/Physically Unable to Perform for fewer than six regular-season games, are termed NFL First-Year Players. An NFL First-Year Player is designated by a "1" on NFL rosters. Thereafter, a player is credited with an additional year of experience for each season in which he accumulates six games on the Active List or Inactive List, or on Reserve/Injured or Reserve/Physically Unable to Perform.

NOTES

1996 Season in Review

1996 INTERCONFERENCE TRADES

Defensive end **Matt LaBounty** from Green Bay to Seattle for defensive back **Eugene Robinson**. (6/27)

Defensive end **Robert Young** from St. Louis to Houston for the Oilers' sixth-round selection in 1997. (7/17)

Wide receiver **Ryan Yarborough** from the N.Y. Jets to Green Bay for the Packers' seventh-round selection in 1997. (7/26)

Defensive back **Carlos Yancy** from New England to Green Bay for past considerations. (8/7)

Running back **Terry Kirby** from Miami to San Francisco for the 49ers' fourth-round selection in 1997. (8/19)

Tight end **Mike Bartrum** and defensive end **Walter Scott** from Green Bay to New England for past considerations. (8/25)

Defensive tackle **Austin Robbins** from Oakland to New Orleans for the Saints' seventh-round selection in 1997. (8/25)

Wide receiver **Raghib Ismail** from Oakland to Carolina for the Panthers' fifth-round selection in 1997. (8/25)

Wide receiver **Todd Kinchen** from St. Louis to Denver for the Broncos' fifth-round selection in 1997. (8/26)

Tight end **Troy Drayton** from St. Louis to Miami for tackle **Billy Milner**. (10/1)

1997 INTERCONFERENCE TRADES

Quarterback **Rick Mirer** and the Seahawks' fourth-round selection from Seattle to Chicago for the Bears' first-round selection. (2/19)

Quarterback **Chris Chandler** from Houston to Atlanta for the Falcons' fourth-round selection. (2/24)

Atlanta's first- and third-round selections in 1997 to Seattle for the Seahawks' first-, second-, third-, and fourth-round selections in 1997. (3/28)

Oakland's first-, second-, and fourth-round selections in 1997 to New Orleans for the Saints' first- and sixth-round selections in 1997. (4/1)

Wide receiver **Daryl Hobbs** from Oakland to New Orleans for past considerations. (4/1)

New York Jets' first-round selection in 1997 to St. Louis for the Rams' first-, third-, fourth-, and seventh-round selections in 1997. (4/17)

Defensive tackle **Ronnie Dixon** from Philadelphia to New York Jets for the Jets' seventh-round selection in 1997. (4/18)

New York Jets' first-round selection in 1997 to Tampa Bay for the Buccaneers' first- and fourth-round selections in 1997. Tampa Bay traded the first-round selection acquired from the Jets to Seattle. The Jets selected linebacker **James Farrior** (Virginia) and running back **Leon Johnson** (North Carolina). (4/19)

Tampa Bay's first-round selection in 1997 to Seattle for the Seahawks' first- and third-round selections in 1997. Seattle selected tackle **Walter Jones** (Florida State). Tampa Bay selected running back **Warrick Dunn** (Florida State) and guard **Frank Middleton** (Arizona). (4/19)

Indianapolis' third-round selection in 1997 to San Francisco for the 49ers' third- and fifth-round selections in 1997. San Francisco selected tight end **Greg Clark** (Stanford). Indianapolis selected linebacker **Bert Berry** (Notre Dame) and defensive end **Carl Powell** (Louisville). (4/19)

New Orleans' fourth-round selection in 1997 to Houston for the Oilers' fourth- and sixth-round selctions in 1997. Houston selected defensive end **Pratt Lyons** (Troy State). New Orleans selected wide receiver **Keith Poole** (Arizona State) and tight end **Nicky Savoie** (Louisiana State). (4/20)

Miami's fourth-round selection in 1997 to St. Louis for the Rams' fourth- and two sixth-round selections in 1997. St. Louis selected center **Ryan Tucker** (Texas Christian). Miami selected tackle **Jerome Daniels** (Northeastern), wide receiver **Brian Manning** (Stanford), and linebacker **Mike Crawford** (Nevada-Reno). (4/20)

St. Louis' fifth-round selection in 1997 to San Diego for the Chargers' seventh-round selection in 1997 and fourth-round selection in 1998. San Diego selected running back **Kenny Bynum** (South Carolina State). St. Louis selected defensive end **Cedric White** (North Carolina A&T). (4/20)

Green Bay's sixth-round selection in 1997 to Oakland for the Raiders' seventh-round selection in 1997. Oakland selected defensive end **Grady Jackson** (Knoxville). Green Bay selected wide receiver **Chris Miller** (Southern California). (4/20)

1996 AFC TRADES

Kicker **Pete Stoyanovich** from Miami to Kansas City for the Chiefs' fifth-round selection in 1997. (8/21)

1997 AFC TRADES

Tackle **Tony Jones** from Baltimore to Denver for the Broncos' second-round selection. (2/14)

Quarterback **Billy Joe Hobert** from Oakland to Buffalo for the Bills' third-round selection. (2/18)

Defensive end **Brentson Buckner** from Pittsburgh to Kansas City for the Chiefs' seventh-round selection in 1997. (4/4)

Houston's first- and fourth-round selections in 1997 to Kansas City for the Chiefs' first-, third-, fourth-, and sixth-round selections in 1997. The Chiefs selected tight end **Tony Gonzalez** (California) and quarterback **Pat Barnes** (California). Houston selected defensive end **Kenny Holmes** (Miami), tackle **Scott Sanderson** (Washington State), traded the fourth-round selection acquired from Kansas City to New Orleans, and linebacker **Dennis Stallings** (Illinois). (4/19)

New York Jets' third-round selection in 1997 to Denver for the Broncos' third-, sixth-, and seventh-round selections in 1997 and sixth-round selection in 1998. Denver selected guard **Dan Neil** (Texas). New York Jets selected wide receiver **Dedric Ward** (Northern Iowa), quarterback **Chuck Clements** (Houston) and defensive tackle **Jason Ferguson** (Georgia). (4/19)

Miami's fourth-round selection in 1997 to Oakland for the Raiders' fifth-, sixth-, and seventh-round selections in 1997. Oakland selected running back **Chad Levitt** (Cornell). Miami selected defensive end **Nicholas Lopez** (Texas Southern), linebacker **John Fiala** (Washington) and defensive back **Hudhaifa Ismaeli** (Northwestern). (4/20)

Pittsburgh's fifth- and seventh-round selections in 1997 to San Diego for the Chargers' third-round selection in 1998. San Diego selected defensive back **Paul Bradford** (Portland State) and linebacker **James Toran** (North Carolina A&T). (4/20)

1996 NFC TRADES

Running back **Robert Baldwin** from Atlanta to Green Bay for defensive back **Lenny McGill**. (6/6)

Defensive back **George Teague** from Green Bay to Atlanta for the Falcons' seventh-round selection in 1997. (7/17)

Defensive end **Wendall Gaines** from Green Bay to St. Louis for the Rams' seventh-round selection in 1997. (8/6)

Defensive tackle **Pat Riley** from Chicago to Atlanta for the Falcons' seventh-round selection in 1997. (8/20)

1997 NFC TRADES

Quarterback **Heath Shuler** from Washington to New Orleans for the Saints' third-round selection in 1997 and third-round selection in 1998. (4/18)

Dallas' first- and fifth-round selections in 1997 and third-round selection in 1998 to Philadelphia for the Eagles' first-round selection in 1997. Philadelphia selected defensive end **Jon Harris** (Virginia) and tight end **Luther Broughton** (Furman). Dallas selected tight end **David LaFleur** (Louisiana State). (4/19)

St. Louis' second-round selection in 1997 to Chicago for the Bears' second- and sixth-round selections in 1997. Chicago selected tight end **John Allred** (Southern California). St. Louis selected defensive back **Dexter McCleon** (Clemson) and traded the sixth-round selection acquired from Chicago to Miami. (4/19)

Dallas' second-round selection in 1997 to Detroit for the Lions' third- and fourth-round selections in 1997. Detroit selected cornerback **Kevin Abrams** (Syracuse). Dallas selected linebacker **Dexter Coakley** (Appalachian State) and defensive tackle **Antonio Anderson** (Syracuse). (4/19)

Philadelphia's second-round selection in 1997 to San Francisco for the 49ers' second-, sixth-, and seventh-round selections in 1997. San Francisco selected running back **Marc Edwards** (Notre Dame). Philadelphia selected linebacker **James Darling** (Washington State), wide receiver **Antwuan Wyatt** (Bethune-Cookman) and defensive back **Deauntae Brown** (Central State, Ohio). (4/19)

Philadelphia's third- and sixth-round selections in 1997 to Arizona for the Cardinals' third-round selection in 1997. Arizona selected defensive back **Ty Howard** (Ohio State) and linebacker **Tony McCombs** (Eastern Kentucky). Philadelphia selected running back **Duce Staley** (South Carolina). (4/19)

Atlanta's fifth-round selection in 1997 to Washington for the Redskins' sixth- and seventh-round selections in 1997. Washington selected defensive back **Keith Thibodeaux** (Northwestern State, La.). Atlanta selected center **Calvin Collins** (Texas A&M) and defensive back **Chris Bayne** (Fresno State). (4/20)

FINAL STANDINGS

AMERICAN FOOTBALL CONFERENCE
Eastern Division

	W	L	T	Pct.	Pts.	OP
Miami	3	1	0	.750	77	58
New England	3	1	0	.750	102	60
Indianapolis	3	2	0	.600	92	66
Buffalo	2	2	0	.500	80	66
N.Y. Jets	1	3	0	.250	69	111

Central Division

	W	L	T	Pct.	Pts.	OP
Baltimore	3	1	0	.750	106	67
Cincinnati	2	2	0	.500	83	69
Houston	2	2	0	.500	89	83
Jacksonville	2	2	0	.500	96	75
Pittsburgh	2	3	0	.400	75	77

Western Division

	W	L	T	Pct.	Pts.	OP
Denver	3	1	0	.750	104	79
Kansas City	3	1	0	.750	118	56
Seattle	3	1	0	.750	76	54
Oakland	2	3	0	.400	129	116
San Diego	2	3	0	.400	119	96

NATIONAL FOOTBALL CONFERENCE
Eastern Division

	W	L	T	Pct.	Pts.	OP
Philadelphia	2	2	0	.500	69	89
Dallas	2	3	0	.400	75	136
Arizona	1	3	0	.250	56	99
N.Y. Giants	1	3	0	.250	64	101
Washington	1	3	0	.250	68	96

Central Division

	W	L	T	Pct.	Pts.	OP
Detroit	3	1	0	.750	114	88
Green Bay	3	1	0	.750	71	69
Chicago	1	3	0	.250	67	96
Minnesota	1	3	0	.250	65	95
Tampa Bay	1	3	0	.250	36	45

Western Division

	W	L	T	Pct.	Pts.	OP
St. Louis	3	1	0	.750	98	90
New Orleans	3	2	0	.600	79	108
Atlanta	2	2	0	.500	75	71
Carolina	2	2	0	.500	92	83
San Francisco	1	3	0	.250	46	91

AFC PRESEASON RECORDS—TEAM BY TEAM

Eastern Division

BUFFALO (2-2)

7	WASHINGTON	17
35	at Minnesota	12
24	at Carolina	0
14	BALTIMORE	37
80		66

INDIANAPOLIS (3-2)

10	vs. New Orleans*	3
25	at Cincinnati	28
12	at Houston	16
13	SEATTLE	13
30	GREEN BAY	6
92		66

MIAMI (3-1)

13	TAMPA BAY	10
21	at Chicago	24
24	MINNESOTA	17
19	at Tampa Bay	7
77		58

NEW ENGLAND (3-1)

7	at Green Bay	24
31	at Dallas	7
37	PHILADELPHIA	10
27	WASHINGTON	19
102		60

N.Y. JETS (1-3)

13	vs. Houston (JAC)	31
16	at Philadelphia	30
13	N.Y. GIANTS	6
27	at Oakland	44
69		111

Central Division

BALTIMORE (3-1)

17	PHILADELPHIA	9
37	at N.Y. Giants	27
15	GREEN BAY	17
37	at Buffalo	14
106		67

CINCINNATI (2-2)

28	INDIANAPOLIS	25
10	at Arizona	13
28	at Washington	7
17	DETROIT	24
83		69

HOUSTON (2-2)

31	vs. N.Y. Jets (JAC)	13
16	INDIANAPOLIS	12
23	DETROIT	34
19	vs. Dallas (ORL)	24
89		83

JACKSONVILLE (2-2)

17	N.Y. GIANTS	24
10	at St. Louis	17
38	SAN FRANCISCO	10
31	at Denver	24
96		75

PITTSBURGH (2-3)

10	vs. San Diego**	20
16	ST. LOUIS	10
17	at Green Bay	24
13	TAMPA BAY	3
19	at Philadelphia	20
75		77

Western Division

DENVER (3-1)

20	at San Francisco	17
40	CAROLINA	28
20	at Dallas	3
24	JACKSONVILLE	31
104		79

KANSAS CITY (3-1)

32	vs. Dallas†	6
42	NEW ORLEANS	6
30	ST. LOUIS	34
14	at Chicago	10
118		56

OAKLAND (2-3)

34	at Dallas	35
26	at Arizona	3
19	SEATTLE	24
6	at Atlanta	27
44	N.Y. JETS	27
129		116

SAN DIEGO (2-3)

20	vs. Pittsburgh**	10
20	at Minnesota(OT)	23
13	at San Francisco(OT)	16
32	ARIZONA	10
34	at St. Louis	37
119		96

SEATTLE (3-1)

19	ATLANTA	17
24	at Oakland	19
13	at Indianapolis	15
20	SAN FRANCISCO	3
76		54

NFC PRESEASON RECORDS—TEAM BY TEAM

Eastern Division

ARIZONA (1-3)

3	OAKLAND	26
13	CINCINNATI	10
10	at San Diego	32
30	at Atlanta	31
56		99

DALLAS (2-3)

35	OAKLAND	34
6	vs. Kansas City†	32
7	NEW ENGLAND	31
3	DENVER	20
24	vs. Houston (ORL)	19
75		136

N.Y. GIANTS (1-3)

24	at Jacksonville	17
27	BALTIMORE	37
6	at N.Y. Jets	13
7	CAROLINA	34
64		101

PHILADELPHIA (2-2)

9	at Baltimore	17
30	N.Y. JETS	16
10	at New England	37
20	PITTSBURGH	19
69		89

WASHINGTON (1-3)

17	at Buffalo	7
25	at Detroit	34
7	CINCINNATI	28
19	at New England	27
68		96

Central Division

CHICAGO (1-3)

12	at Carolina	30
24	MIAMI	21
21	at New Orleans	31
10	KANSAS CITY	14
67		96

DETROIT (3-1)

22	NEW ORLEANS	23
34	WASHINGTON	25
34	at Houston	23
24	at Cincinnati	17
114		88

GREEN BAY (3-1)

24	NEW ENGLAND	7
24	PITTSBURGH	17
17	at Baltimore	15
6	at Indianapolis	30
71		69

MINNESOTA (1-3)

23	SAN DIEGO(OT)	20
12	BUFFALO	35
17	at Miami	24
13	at New Orleans	16
65		95

TAMPA BAY (1-3)

10	at Miami	13
16	ATLANTA	0
3	at Pittsburgh	13
7	MIAMI	19
36		45

Western Division

ATLANTA (2-2)

17	at Seattle	19
0	at Tampa Bay	16
27	OAKLAND	6
31	ARIZONA	30
75		71

CAROLINA (2-2)

30	CHICAGO	12
28	at Denver	40
0	BUFFALO	24
34	at N.Y. Giants	7
92		83

NEW ORLEANS (3-2)

3	vs. Indianapolis*	10
23	at Detroit	22
6	at Kansas City	42
31	CHICAGO	21
16	MINNESOTA	13
79		108

ST. LOUIS (3-1)

10	at Pittsburgh	16
17	JACKSONVILLE	10
34	at Kansas City	30
37	SAN DIEGO	34
98		90

SAN FRANCISCO (1-3)

17	DENVER	20
16	SAN DIEGO(OT)	13
10	at Jacksonville	38
3	at Seattle	20
46		91

(OT) denotes overtime game
* denotes Pro Football Hall of Fame game in Canton, Ohio
** denotes American Bowl in Tokyo, Japan
† denotes American Bowl in Monterrey, Mexico
(JAC) denotes game in Jackson, Miss.
(ORL) denotes game in Orlando, Fla.

FINAL STANDINGS

AMERICAN FOOTBALL CONFERENCE

Eastern Division

	W	L	T	Pct.	Pts.	OP
* New England	11	5	0	.688	418	313
# Buffalo	10	6	0	.625	319	266
# Indianapolis	9	7	0	.563	317	334
Miami	8	8	0	.500	339	325
N.Y. Jets	1	15	0	.063	279	454

Central Division

	W	L	T	Pct.	Pts.	OP
* Pittsburgh	10	6	0	.625	344	257
# Jacksonville	9	7	0	.563	325	335
Cincinnati	8	8	0	.500	372	369
Houston	8	8	0	.500	345	319
Baltimore	4	12	0	.250	371	441

Western Division

	W	L	T	Pct.	Pts.	OP
* Denver	13	3	0	.813	391	275
Kansas City	9	7	0	.563	297	300
San Diego	8	8	0	.500	310	376
Oakland	7	9	0	.438	340	293
Seattle	7	9	0	.438	317	376

NATIONAL FOOTBALL CONFERENCE

Eastern Division

	W	L	T	Pct.	Pts.	OP
* Dallas	10	6	0	.625	286	250
# Philadelphia	10	6	0	.625	363	341
Washington	9	7	0	.563	364	312
Arizona	7	9	0	.438	300	397
N.Y. Giants	6	10	0	.375	242	297

Central Division

	W	L	T	Pct.	Pts.	OP
* Green Bay	13	3	0	.813	456	210
# Minnesota	9	7	0	.563	298	315
Chicago	7	9	0	.438	283	305
Tampa Bay	6	10	0	.375	221	293
Detroit	5	11	0	.313	302	368

Western Division

	W	L	T	Pct.	Pts.	OP
* Carolina	12	4	0	.750	367	218
# San Francisco	12	4	0	.750	398	257
St. Louis	6	10	0	.375	303	409
Atlanta	3	13	0	.188	309	461
New Orleans	3	13	0	.188	229	339

*Division Champion; #Wild Card Team

Jacksonville finished ahead of Indianapolis and Kansas City based on better conference record (7-5 to Colts' 6-6 and Chiefs' 5-7). Indianapolis was third Wild Card based on head-to-head victory over Kansas City (1-0). Cincinnati finished ahead of Houston based on better net division points (19 to Oilers' 11). Oakland finished ahead of Seattle based on better division record (3-5 to Seahawks' 2-6). Dallas finished ahead of Philadelphia based on better record against common opponents (8-5 to Eagles' 7-6). Minnesota was third Wild Card based on better conference record than Washington (8-4 to Redskins' 6-6). Carolina finished ahead of San Francisco based on head-to-head sweep (2-0). Atlanta finished ahead of New Orleans based on head-to-head sweep (2-0).

WILD CARD PLAYOFFS
AFC
Jacksonville 30, BUFFALO 27; PITTSBURGH 42, Indianapolis 14
NFC
DALLAS 40, Minnesota 15; SAN FRANCISCO 14; Philadelphia 0

DIVISIONAL PLAYOFFS
AFC
Jacksonville 30, DENVER 27; NEW ENGLAND 28, Pittsburgh 3
NFC
GREEN BAY 35, San Francisco 14; CAROLINA 26, Dallas 17

CHAMPIONSHIP GAMES
AFC
NEW ENGLAND 20, Jacksonville 6
NFC
GREEN BAY 30, Carolina 13

SUPER BOWL XXXI
Green Bay (NFC) 35, New England (AFC) 21, at Louisiana Superdome, New Orleans, Louisiana

AFC-NFC PRO BOWL
AFC 26, NFC 23 (OT), at Aloha Stadium, Honolulu, Hawaii

Home teams in playoff games are indicated by capital letters

AFC SEASON RECORDS—TEAM BY TEAM

BALTIMORE (4-12)
19	OAKLAND	14
17	at Pittsburgh	31
13	at Houston	29
	OPEN DATE	
17	NEW ORLEANS	10
38	NEW ENGLAND	46
21	at Indianapolis	26
34	at Denver	45
37	ST. LOUIS (OT)	31
21	CINCINNATI	24
27	at Jacksonville	30
20	at San Francisco	38
25	JACKSONVILLE (OT)	28
31	PITTSBURGH	17
14	at Cincinnati	21
16	at Carolina	27
21	HOUSTON	24
371		**441**

BUFFALO (10-6)
23	at N.Y. Giants (OT)	20
17	NEW ENGLAND	10
6	at Pittsburgh	24
10	DALLAS	7
	OPEN DATE	
16	INDIANAPOLIS (OT)	13
7	MIAMI	21
25	at N.Y. Jets	22
25	at New England	28
38	WASHINGTON	13
31	CINCINNATI	17
35	N.Y. JETS	10
10	at Indianapolis (OT)	13
18	at Seattle	26
14	at Miami	16
20	KANSAS CITY	9
319		**266**

CINCINNATI (8-8)
16	at St. Louis	26
14	at San Diego	27
30	NEW ORLEANS	15
	OPEN DATE	
10	DENVER	14
27	HOUSTON (OT)	30
10	at Pittsburgh	20
21	at San Francisco	28
28	JACKSONVILLE	21
24	at Baltimore	21
34	PITTSBURGH	24
17	at Buffalo	31
41	ATLANTA	31
27	at Jacksonville	30
21	BALTIMORE	14
21	at Houston	31
31	INDIANAPOLIS	24
372		**369**

DENVER (13-3)
31	N.Y. JETS	6
30	at Seattle	20
27	TAMPA BAY	23
14	at Kansas City	17
14	at Cincinnati	10
28	SAN DIEGO	17
	OPEN DATE	
45	BALTIMORE	34
34	KANSAS CITY	7
22	at Oakland	21
17	CHICAGO	12
34	at New England	8
21	at Minnesota	17
34	SEATTLE	7
6	at Green Bay	41
24	OAKLAND	19
10	at San Diego	16
391		**275**

HOUSTON (8-8)
19	KANSAS CITY	20
34	at Jacksonville	27
29	BALTIMORE	13
	OPEN DATE	
16	at Pittsburgh	30
30	at Cincinnati (OT)	27
23	at Atlanta	13
23	PITTSBURGH	13
9	SAN FRANCISCO	10
16	at Seattle	23
31	at New Orleans	13
20	MIAMI	23
6	CAROLINA	31
35	at N.Y. Jets	10
17	JACKSONVILLE	23
13	CINCINNATI	21
24	at Baltimore	21
345		**319**

INDIANAPOLIS (9-7)
20	ARIZONA	13
21	at N.Y. Jets	7
25	at Dallas	24
10	MIAMI	6
	OPEN DATE	
13	at Buffalo (OT)	16
26	BALTIMORE	21
19	NEW ENGLAND	27
16	at Washington	31
19	SAN DIEGO	26
13	at Miami	37
34	N.Y. JETS	29
13	at New England	27
13	BUFFALO (OT)	10
37	PHILADELPHIA	10
24	at Kansas City	19
24	at Cincinnati	31
317		**334**

JACKSONVILLE (9-7)
24	PITTSBURGH	9
27	HOUSTON	34
3	at Oakland	17
25	at New England (OT)	28
10	CAROLINA	14
13	at New Orleans	14
21	N.Y. JETS	17
14	at St. Louis	17
21	at Cincinnati	28
	OPEN DATE	
30	BALTIMORE	27
3	at Pittsburgh	28
28	at Baltimore (OT)	25
30	CINCINNATI	27
23	at Houston	17
20	SEATTLE	13
19	ATLANTA	17
325		**335**

KANSAS CITY (9-7)
20	at Houston	19
19	OAKLAND	3
35	at Seattle	17
17	DENVER	14
19	at San Diego	22
7	PITTSBURGH	17
	OPEN DATE	
34	SEATTLE	16
7	at Denver	34
21	at Minnesota	6
27	GREEN BAY	20
14	CHICAGO	10
14	SAN DIEGO	28
28	at Detroit	24
7	at Oakland	26
19	INDIANAPOLIS	24
9	at Buffalo	20
297		**300**

MIAMI (8-8)
24	NEW ENGLAND	10
38	at Arizona	10
36	N.Y. JETS	27
6	at Indianapolis	10
	OPEN DATE	
15	SEATTLE	22
21	at Buffalo	7
28	at Philadelphia	35
10	DALLAS	29
23	at New England	42
37	INDIANAPOLIS	13
23	at Houston	20
17	PITTSBURGH	24
7	at Oakland	17
7	N.Y. GIANTS	17
16	BUFFALO	14
31	at N.Y. Jets	28
339		**325**

NEW ENGLAND (11-5)
10	at Miami	24
10	at Buffalo	17
31	ARIZONA	0
28	JACKSONVILLE (OT)	25
	OPEN DATE	
46	at Baltimore	38
22	WASHINGTON	27
27	at Indianapolis	9
28	BUFFALO	25
42	MIAMI	23
31	at N.Y. Jets	27
27	INDIANAPOLIS	13
45	at San Diego	7
34	N.Y. JETS	10
6	at Dallas	12
23	at N.Y. Giants	22
418		**313**

N.Y. JETS (1-15)
6	at Denver	31
7	INDIANAPOLIS	21
27	at Miami	36
6	N.Y. GIANTS	13
16	at Washington	31
22	BUFFALO	25
31	at Arizona	21
	OPEN DATE	
27	NEW ENGLAND	31
29	at Indianapolis	34
10	at Buffalo	35
10	HOUSTON	35
10	at New England	34
20	PHILADELPHIA	21
28	MIAMI	31
279		**454**

OAKLAND (7-9)
14	at Baltimore	19
3	at Kansas City	19
17	JACKSONVILLE	3
34	SAN DIEGO	40
17	at Chicago	19
34	at N.Y. Jets	13
37	DETROIT	21
23	at San Diego	14
	OPEN DATE	
21	DENVER	22
17	at Tampa Bay (OT)	20
13	MINNESOTA (OT)	16
27	at Seattle	21
17	MIAMI	7
26	KANSAS CITY	7
19	at Denver	24
21	SEATTLE	28
340		**293**

PITTSBURGH (10-6)
9	at Jacksonville	24
31	BALTIMORE	17
24	BUFFALO	6
	OPEN DATE	
30	HOUSTON	16
17	at Kansas City	7
20	CINCINNATI	10
13	at Houston	23
20	at Atlanta	17
42	ST. LOUIS	6
24	at Cincinnati	34
28	JACKSONVILLE	3
24	at Miami	17
17	at Baltimore	31
16	SAN DIEGO	3
15	SAN FRANCISCO	25
14	at Carolina	18
344		**257**

SAN DIEGO (8-8)
29	SEATTLE	7
27	CINCINNATI	14
10	at Green Bay	42
40	at Oakland	34
22	KANSAS CITY	19
17	at Denver	28
	OPEN DATE	
14	OAKLAND	23
13	at Seattle	32
26	at Indianapolis	19
27	DETROIT	21
7	TAMPA BAY	25
28	at Kansas City	14
7	NEW ENGLAND	45
3	at Pittsburgh	16
14	at Chicago	27
16	DENVER	10
310		**376**

SEATTLE (7-9)
7	at San Diego	29
20	DENVER	30
17	KANSAS CITY	35
17	at Tampa Bay	13
10	GREEN BAY	31
22	at Miami	15
	OPEN DATE	
16	at Kansas City	34
32	SAN DIEGO	13
23	HOUSTON	16
42	MINNESOTA	23
16	at Detroit	17
21	OAKLAND	27
7	at Denver	34
26	BUFFALO	18
13	at Jacksonville	20
28	at Oakland	21
317		**376**

(OT) denotes overtime

NFC SEASON RECORDS—TEAM BY TEAM

ARIZONA (7-9)
13	at Indianapolis	20
10	MIAMI	38
0	at New England	31
28	at New Orleans	14
31	ST. LOUIS (OT)	28
	OPEN DATE	
3	at Dallas	17
13	TAMPA BAY	9
21	N.Y. JETS	31
8	at N.Y. Giants	16
37	at Washington (OT)	34
31	N.Y. GIANTS	23
36	PHILADELPHIA	30
17	at Minnesota	41
6	DALLAS	10
27	WASHINGTON	26
19	at Philadelphia	29
300		**397**

ATLANTA (3-13)
6	at Carolina	29
17	MINNESOTA	23
	OPEN DATE	
18	PHILADELPHIA	33
17	at San Francisco	39
24	at Detroit	28
13	HOUSTON	23
28	at Dallas	32
17	PITTSBURGH	20
20	CAROLINA	17
16	at St. Louis	59
17	NEW ORLEANS	15
31	at Cincinnati	41
10	SAN FRANCISCO	34
31	at New Orleans	15
27	ST. LOUIS	34
17	at Jacksonville	19
309		**461**

CAROLINA (12-4)
29	ATLANTA	6
22	at New Orleans	20
	OPEN DATE	
23	SAN FRANCISCO	7
14	at Jacksonville	24
12	at Minnesota	14
45	ST. LOUIS	13
19	NEW ORLEANS	7
9	at Philadelphia	20
17	at Atlanta	31
27	N.Y. GIANTS	17
20	at St. Louis	10
31	at Houston	6
24	TAMPA BAY	0
30	at San Francisco	24
27	BALTIMORE	16
18	PITTSBURGH	14
367		**218**

CHICAGO (7-9)
22	DALLAS	6
3	at Washington	10
14	MINNESOTA	20
16	at Detroit	35
19	OAKLAND	17
6	GREEN BAY	37
24	at New Orleans	27
	OPEN DATE	
15	at Minnesota	13
13	TAMPA BAY	10
12	at Denver	17
10	at Kansas City	14
31	DETROIT	14
17	at Green Bay	28
35	ST. LOUIS	9
27	SAN DIEGO	14
19	at Tampa Bay	34
283		**305**

DALLAS (10-6)
6	at Chicago	22
27	N.Y. GIANTS	0
24	INDIANAPOLIS	25
7	at Buffalo	10
23	at Philadelphia	19
	OPEN DATE	
17	ARIZONA	3
32	ATLANTA	28
29	at Miami	10
21	PHILADELPHIA	31
20	at San Francisco (OT)	17
21	GREEN BAY	6
6	at N.Y. Giants	20
21	WASHINGTON	10
12	NEW ENGLAND	6
10	at Washington	37
286		**250**

DETROIT (5-11)
13	at Minnesota	17
21	TAMPA BAY	6
17	at Philadelphia	24
35	CHICAGO	16
27	at Tampa Bay	0
28	ATLANTA	24
21	at Oakland	37
	OPEN DATE	
7	N.Y. GIANTS	35
18	at Green Bay	28
21	at San Diego	27
17	SEATTLE	16
14	at Chicago	31
24	KANSAS CITY	28
22	MINNESOTA	24
3	GREEN BAY	31
14	at San Francisco	24
302		**368**

GREEN BAY (13-3)
34	at Tampa Bay	3
39	PHILADELPHIA	13
42	SAN DIEGO	10
21	at Minnesota	30
31	at Seattle	10
37	at Chicago	6
23	SAN FRANCISCO (OT)	20
	OPEN DATE	
13	TAMPA BAY	7
28	DETROIT	18
20	at Kansas City	27
6	at Dallas	21
24	at St. Louis	9
28	CHICAGO	17
41	DENVER	6
31	at Detroit	3
38	MINNESOTA	10
456		**210**

MINNESOTA (9-7)
17	DETROIT	13
23	at Atlanta	17
20	at Chicago	14
30	GREEN BAY	21
10	at N.Y. Giants	15
14	CAROLINA	12
13	at Tampa Bay	24
	OPEN DATE	
13	CHICAGO	15
6	KANSAS CITY	21
23	at Seattle	42
16	at Oakland (OT)	13
17	DENVER	21
41	ARIZONA	17
24	at Detroit	22
21	TAMPA BAY	10
10	at Green Bay	38
298		**315**

NEW ORLEANS (3-13)
11	San Francisco	27
20	CAROLINA	22
15	at Cincinnati	30
14	ARIZONA	28
10	at Baltimore	17
17	JACKSONVILLE	13
27	CHICAGO	24
7	at Carolina	19
	OPEN DATE	
17	SAN FRANCISCO	24
14	HOUSTON	31
15	at Atlanta	17
7	at Tampa Bay	13
10	ST. LOUIS	26
15	ATLANTA	31
17	at N.Y. Giants	3
13	at St. Louis	14
229		**339**

N.Y. GIANTS (6-10)
20	BUFFALO (OT)	23
0	at Dallas	27
10	WASHINGTON	31
13	at N.Y. Jets	6
15	MINNESOTA	10
	OPEN DATE	
10	PHILADELPHIA	19
21	at Washington	31
35	at Detroit	7
16	ARIZONA	8
17	at Carolina	27
23	at Arizona	31
20	DALLAS	6
0	at Philadelphia	24
17	at Miami	7
3	NEW ORLEANS	17
22	NEW ENGLAND	23
242		**297**

PHILADELPHIA (10-6)
17	at Washington	14
13	at Green Bay	39
24	DETROIT	17
33	at Atlanta	18
19	DALLAS	23
	OPEN DATE	
19	at N.Y. Giants	10
35	MIAMI	28
20	CAROLINA	9
31	at Dallas	21
17	BUFFALO	24
21	WASHINGTON	26
30	at Arizona	36
24	N.Y. GIANTS	0
10	at Indianapolis	37
21	at N.Y. Jets	20
29	ARIZONA	19
363		**341**

ST. LOUIS (6-10)
26	CINCINNATI	16
0	at San Francisco	34
	OPEN DATE	
10	WASHINGTON	17
28	at Arizona (OT)	31
11	SAN FRANCISCO	28
13	at Carolina	45
17	JACKSONVILLE	14
31	at Baltimore (OT)	37
6	at Pittsburgh	42
59	ATLANTA	16
10	CAROLINA	20
9	GREEN BAY	24
26	at New Orleans	10
9	at Chicago	35
34	at Atlanta	27
14	NEW ORLEANS	13
303		**409**

SAN FRANCISCO (12-4)
27	NEW ORLEANS	11
34	ST. LOUIS	0
	OPEN DATE	
7	at Carolina	23
39	ATLANTA	17
28	at St. Louis	11
20	at Green Bay (OT)	23
28	CINCINNATI	21
10	at Houston	9
24	at New Orleans	17
17	DALLAS (OT)	20
38	BALTIMORE	20
19	at Washington (OT)	16
34	at Atlanta	10
24	CAROLINA	30
25	at Pittsburgh	15
24	DETROIT	14
398		**257**

TAMPA BAY (6-10)
3	GREEN BAY	34
6	at Detroit	21
23	at Denver	27
13	SEATTLE	17
0	DETROIT	27
	OPEN DATE	
24	MINNESOTA	13
9	at Arizona	13
7	at Green Bay	13
10	at Chicago	13
20	OAKLAND (OT)	17
25	at San Diego	17
13	NEW ORLEANS	7
0	at Carolina	24
24	WASHINGTON	10
10	at Minnesota	21
34	CHICAGO	19
221		**293**

WASHINGTON (9-7)
14	PHILADELPHIA	17
10	CHICAGO	3
31	at N.Y. Giants	10
17	at St. Louis	10
31	N.Y. JETS	16
	OPEN DATE	
27	at New England	22
31	N.Y. GIANTS	21
31	INDIANAPOLIS	16
13	at Buffalo	38
34	ARIZONA (OT)	37
26	at Philadelphia	21
16	SAN FRANCISCO (OT)	19
10	at Dallas	21
10	at Tampa Bay	24
26	at Arizona	27
37	DALLAS	10
364		**312**

(OT) denotes overtime

Attendance figures as they appear in the following, and in the club-by-club sections starting on page 28, are turnstile counts and not paid attendance. Paid attendance totals are on page 235.

FIRST WEEK SUMMARIES

AMERICAN FOOTBALL CONFERENCE

Eastern Division	W	L	T	Pct.	Pts.	OP
Buffalo	1	0	0	1.000	23	20
Indianapolis	1	0	0	1.000	20	13
Miami	1	0	0	1.000	24	10
New England	0	1	0	.000	10	24
N.Y. Jets	0	1	0	.000	6	31
Central Division						
Baltimore	1	0	0	1.000	19	14
Jacksonville	1	0	0	1.000	24	9
Cincinnati	0	1	0	.000	16	26
Houston	0	1	0	.000	19	20
Pittsburgh	0	1	0	.000	9	24
Western Division						
Denver	1	0	0	1.000	31	6
Kansas City	1	0	0	1.000	20	19
San Diego	1	0	0	1.000	29	7
Oakland	0	1	0	.000	14	19
Seattle	0	1	0	.000	7	29

NATIONAL FOOTBALL CONFERENCE

Eastern Division	W	L	T	Pct.	Pts.	OP
Philadelphia	1	0	0	1.000	17	14
Arizona	0	1	0	.000	13	20
Dallas	0	1	0	.000	6	22
N.Y. Giants	0	1	0	.000	20	23
Washington	0	1	0	.000	14	17
Central Division						
Chicago	1	0	0	1.000	22	6
Green Bay	1	0	0	1.000	34	3
Minnesota	1	0	0	1.000	17	13
Detroit	0	1	0	.000	13	17
Tampa Bay	0	1	0	.000	3	34
Western Division						
Carolina	1	0	0	1.000	29	6
St. Louis	1	0	0	1.000	26	16
San Francisco	1	0	0	1.000	27	11
Atlanta	0	1	0	.000	6	29
New Orleans	0	1	0	.000	11	27

SUNDAY, SEPTEMBER 1

INDIANAPOLIS 20, ARIZONA 13—at RCA Dome, attendance 48,133. Jim Harbaugh threw 2 touchdown passes and the Colts held off the Cardinals' late charge. Arizona led 6-0 until Harbaugh tossed a 2-yard touchdown pass to fullback Zack Crockett to put Indianapolis ahead for good 7:36 before halftime. Harbaugh's second touchdown pass was a 35-yard strike to rookie Marvin Harrison to give the Colts a 20-6 advantage with just 1:54 left in the game. Arizona drove 81 yards in only 4 plays and pulled within seven points on quarterback Boomer Esiason's 2-yard run with 1:01 left. The Cardinals recovered the ensuing onside kick and eventually reached the Colts' 22, but Indianapolis cornerback Eugene Daniel broke up a pair of passes in the end zone in the final seconds. Esiason completed 25 of 38 passes for 237 yards in his first game with Arizona. Cardinals running back Larry Centers caught 11 passes for 108 yards. Harbaugh was 16 of 25 for 196 yards for the Colts. Indianapolis's victory was the first for new coach Lindy Infante, but spoiled the debut of new Cardinals head coach Vince Tobin, formerly the defensive coordinator for the Colts.

Arizona	3	3	0	7	—	13
Indianapolis	0	10	0	10	—	20

Ariz — FG G. Davis 24
Ariz — FG G. Davis 29
Ind — Crockett 2 pass from Harbaugh (Blanchard kick)
Ind — FG Blanchard 23
Ind — FG Blanchard 40
Ind — Harrison 35 pass from Harbaugh (Blanchard kick)
Ariz — Esiason 2 run (G. Davis kick)

CAROLINA 29, ATLANTA 6—at Ericsson Stadium, attendance 69,522. Kerry Collins threw 2 touchdown passes, John Kasay kicked 5 field goals, and the Panthers opened their new stadium by routing the Falcons, a playoff team in 1995. Carolina took the game's opening kickoff, marched 64 yards in nine plays to Collins's 12-yard touchdown pass to Mark Carrier, and never trailed. Kasay's field goals, including one from 53 yards in the third quarter, kept the game out of Atlanta's reach. The Falcons could muster little offense, managing only 12 first downs and 281 total yards. Jeff George completed only 16 of 35 passes for 215 yards and was under pressure most of the afternoon from the Panthers' pass rush. George was sacked 7 times, including 3 times by linebacker Lamar Lathon and twice by free-agent linebacker Kevin Greene.

Atlanta	3	3	0	0	—	6
Carolina	7	13	3	6	—	29

Car — Carrier 12 pass from Collins (Kasay kick)
Atl — FG Andersen 46
Car — FG Kasay 32
Atl — FG Andersen 33
Car — FG Kasay 36
Car — Walls 1 pass from Collins (Kasay kick)
Car — FG Kasay 53
Car — FG Kasay 38
Car — FG Kasay 42

ST. LOUIS 26, CINCINNATI 16—at Trans World Dome, attendance 62,659. The Rams won a mistake-filled game by scoring 16 points in the fourth quarter. Rookie Lawrence Phillips rushed for 2 touchdowns in his first NFL game and Chip Lohmiller kicked 4 field goals. Doug Pelfrey had 3 field goals and Jeff Blake tossed a 6-yard touchdown pass to Darnay Scott as the Bengals built a 16-10 advantage through three quarters. But Lohmiller kicked field goals of 20, 29, and 20 yards, and Phillips ran 1 yard for a touchdown to overcome the deficit. All 16 points were scored in a span of 9:28 as the Rams took advantage of 2 fumble recoveries, an interception, and a blocked punt. Cincinnati committed 5 turnovers and was penalized 16 times for 101 yards. St. Louis had 3 turnovers, 11 penalties, and only 209 total yards. Rams quarterback Steve Walsh completed just 13 of 35 passes for 154 yards and was intercepted once. Blake was 23 of 40 for 226 yards and was intercepted twice. He also was hampered by a running game that produced only 37 yards on 22 carries. Ki-Jana Carter, the top pick in the 1995 draft who missed all of his rookie season with a knee injury, rushed 14 times for 14 yards in his first NFL game.

Cincinnati	3	6	7	0	—	16
St. Louis	7	0	3	16	—	26

Cin — FG Pelfrey 27
StL — Phillips 1 run (Lohmiller kick)
Cin — FG Pelfrey 35
Cin — FG Pelfrey 47
Cin — Scott 6 pass from Blake (Pelfrey kick)
StL — FG Lohmiller 42
StL — FG Lohmiller 20
StL — FG Lohmiller 29
StL — Phillips 1 run (Lohmiller kick)
StL — FG Lohmiller 20

MINNESOTA 17, DETROIT 13—at Hubert H. Humphrey Metrodome, attendance 52,972. Brad Johnson's 31-yard touchdown pass to Cris Carter with 1:06 remaining gave the Vikings a dramatic victory. Johnson, Minnesota's backup quarterback who entered the game late in the first half after Warren Moon suffered an ankle injury, completed 16 of 23 passes for 157 yards. Jason Hanson's 39-yard field goal gave the Lions a 13-10 lead with 2:19 left in the fourth quarter. Qadry Ismail's kickoff return, and a subsequent 15-yard penalty added to the end of the play, gave Minnesota excellent field position. Johnson then drove his team 55 yards in only five plays, and threw the first touchdown pass of his five-year NFL career. Detroit's last chance ended when linebacker Jeff Brady intercepted Scott Mitchell's pass at Minnesota's 11-yard line with 20 seconds left. That was one of 4 interceptions for the Vikings, who forced 5 turnovers in all while committing none. The Lions finished with advantages in first downs (27-16) and total yards (435-311) but were undone by the interceptions and a fumble lost at Minnesota's 2-yard line. Barry Sanders rushed for 163 yards on 24 carries for Detroit. Robert Smith had 113 yards on 22 carries for the Vikings.

Detroit	0	10	0	3	—	13
Minnesota	7	0	0	10	—	17

Minn — Washington 27 lateral from Brady (Sisson kick)
Det — Moore 17 pass from Mitchell (Hanson kick)
Det — FG Hanson 24
Minn — FG Sisson 25
Det — FG Hanson 39
Minn — C. Carter 31 pass from B. Johnson (Sisson kick)

GREEN BAY 34, TAMPA BAY 3—at Houlihan's Stadium, attendance 54,102. Brett Favre threw 4 touchdown passes as the Packers ruined the head-coaching debut of the Buccaneers' Tony Dungy. Favre completed 20 of 27 passes for 247 yards. He tossed 3 touchdown passes to tight end Keith Jackson as Green Bay built a 24-3 lead by intermission, then closed the scoring with a 1-yard touchdown pass to running back Dorsey Levens in the third quarter. Tampa Bay quarterback Trent Dilfer, struggled throughout the day, completing only 13 of 30 passes for 123 yards. He was intercepted four times, twice by safety LeRoy Butler. The Packers piled up 406 total yards while limiting the Buccaneers to only 176.

Green Bay	10	14	10	0	—	34
Tampa Bay	0	3	0	0	—	3

GB — FG Jacke 23
GB — K. Jackson 1 pass from Favre (Jacke kick)
TB — FG Husted 48
GB — K. Jackson 4 pass from Favre (Jacke kick)
GB — K. Jackson 51 pass from Favre (Jacke kick)
GB — FG Jacke 40
GB — Levens 1 pass from Favre (Jacke kick)

KANSAS CITY 20, HOUSTON 19—at Astrodome, attendance 27,725. Steve Bono's 2 first-half touchdown passes erased an early 10-point deficit and helped lift the Chiefs to victory. Al Del Greco's 34-yard field goal and Chris Chandler's 34-yard touchdown pass to Willie Davis gave the Oilers a 10-0 advantage 8:58 into the game. But Kansas City took only three plays to counter, with the help of a 52-yard pass interference penalty on Darryll Lewis and a 10-yard unsportsmanlike conduct infraction added, with Bono's 11-yard touchdown pass to Tamarick Vanover to trim its deficit to 10-7. Then, late in the first half, Bono directed a seven-play, 68-yard drive in only 56 seconds, capping the march with a 23-yard touchdown pass to Lake Dawson to give the Chiefs their first lead at 17-16 just 26 seconds before halftime. It was 20-16 in the fourth quarter when Del Greco's fourth field goal of the game, from 22 yards, pulled Houston within a point again with 3:37 left in the game. The Oilers then forced a punt that was blocked by Ronnie Harmon, giving Houston possession on Kansas City's 34-yard line. But 2 incompletions and a penalty pushed the ball back to the 38, and Del Greco's 55-yard field-goal try fell short. Dale Carter's interception with 1:26 remaining ended the Oilers' last chance.

Kansas City	7	10	0	3	—	20
Houston	10	6	0	3	—	19

Hou — FG Del Greco 34
Hou — W. Davis 34 pass from Chandler (Del Greco kick)
KC — Vanover 11 pass from Bono (Stoyanovich kick)
KC — FG Stoyanovich 35
Hou — FG Del Greco 44
Hou — FG Del Greco 33
KC — Dawson 23 pass from Bono (Stoyanovich kick)
KC — FG Stoyanovich 43
Hou — FG Del Greco 22

MIAMI 24, NEW ENGLAND 10—at Pro Player Park, attendance 71,542. Jimmy Johnson debuted as the Dolphins' head coach with an easy victory over the Patriots. Miami took control of the game early when safety Sean Hill picked up teammate Louis Oliver's fumble and raced 10 yards for a touchdown only 3:54 into the game. Oliver had intercepted Drew Bledsoe's pass and returned it 60 yards before fumbling. The Dolphins led 17-3 at halftime, then put the game away by driving 96 yards for a touchdown to start the second half. Miami quarterback Dan Marino got his team out of a hole at its own 4-yard line with a 52-yard completion to rookie fullback Stanley Pritchett, and later connected with Pritchett on a 15-yard gain to the goal line. Pritchett fumbled when hit, but the ball was recovered by wide receiver Scott Miller in the end zone for a touchdown and a 24-3 advantage. Marino threw only 22 passes, completing 16 for 176 yards, as the Dolphins relied primarily

on their rushing game to win. Rookie Karim Abdul-Jabbar ran for 115 yards and a touchdown on 26 carries. New England managed only 29 yards on the ground. Bledsoe finished with 19 completions in 38 attempts for 222 yards and a touchdown, but also was intercepted twice.

New England	0	3	7	0	—	10
Miami	10	7	7	0	—	24

Mia — S. Hill 10 fumble return (Nedney kick)
Mia — FG Nedney 34
NE — FG Vinatieri 25
Mia — Abdul-Jabbar 3 run (Nedney kick)
Mia — Miller fumble recovery in end zone (Nedney kick)
NE — Coates 29 pass from Bledsoe (Vinatieri kick)

SAN FRANCISCO 27, NEW ORLEANS 11—at 3Com Park, attendance 63,970. Fullback Tommy Vardell, wide receiver Jerry Rice, and running back Derek Loville rushed for touchdowns in the first half as the 49ers built a 24-0 lead and cruised to victory over the Saints. San Francisco finished twenty-third in the NFL in rushing in 1995, but ran for 157 yards against the Saints. Loville gained 61 yards on 16 carries, while quarterback Steve Young added 52 yards on 6 rushes. Vardell ran 1 yard for a touchdown 6:41 into the game on his first carry as a 49er, and Rice capped a 69-yard drive with his touchdown run six minutes later. Rice, who caught 5 passes for 88 yards, had a 38-yard reception earlier on the march, which also was highlighted by Young's 21-yard run. Young completed 18 of 29 passes for 199 yards and was not intercepted. New Orleans managed only 231 total yards, much of it on a 75-yard drive to their lone touchdown, a 3-yard pass from Jim Everett to Haywood Jeffires with 8:39 left in the game.

New Orleans	0	0	3	8	—	11
San Francisco	14	10	0	3	—	27

SF — Vardell 1 run (Wilkins kick)
SF — Rice 2 run (Wilkins kick)
SF — FG Wilkins 29
SF — Loville 4 run (Wilkins kick)
NO — FG Brien 35
SF — FG Wilkins 29
NO — Jeffires 3 pass from Everett (Wilmsmeyer run)

DENVER 31, N.Y. JETS 6—at Mile High Stadium, attendance 70,595. John Elway threw 2 touchdown passes and the Broncos buried the Jets with a 24-point second quarter. Elway teamed with tight end Shannon Sharpe (13 yards) and wide receiver Ed McCaffrey (39 yards) on touchdown passes to give Denver a 14-0 lead one minute into the second quarter. The Broncos then took advantage of three Jets' turnovers to open a 31-0 bulge by halftime: cornerback Lionel Washington's interception set up a 1-yard run by Terrell Davis; defensive tackle Michael Dean Perry's fumble recovery was followed by Anthony Miller's 26-yard touchdown run on the next play; and defensive tackle Maa Tanuvasa's fumble recovery led to Jason Elam's 28-yard field goal. New York quarterback Neil O'Donnell was the victim of each of the turnovers. The free-agent signee completed only 7 of 13 passes for 50 yards in three quarters of play and suffered 8 sacks. Denver had 9 sacks in all, including 2 by Perry. The Jets, who were outgained 244 yards to 33 in the first half (the final tally was 367-188), averted a shutout when Frank Reich threw a 13-yard touchdown pass to Webster Slaughter with 2:07 left in the game.

N.Y. Jets	0	0	0	6	—	6
Denver	7	24	0	0	—	31

Den — Sharpe 13 pass from Elway (Elam kick)
Den — McCaffrey 39 pass from Elway (Elam kick)
Den — Davis 1 run (Elam kick)
Den — Miller 26 run (Elam kick)
Den — FG Elam 28
NYJ — Slaughter 13 pass from Reich (pass failed)

BALTIMORE 19, OAKLAND 14—at Memorial Stadium, attendance 64,124. Earnest Byner's 1-yard touchdown run capped a second-half rally that lifted the Ravens to victory in the first NFL game in Baltimore in 13 years. Billy Joe Hobert's 2 touchdown passes to Tim Brown in the first half staked the Raiders to a 14-7 lead. But the Ravens turned to a No-Huddle offense in the second half, and pulled within 14-13 on a pair of Matt Stover field goals in the third

quarter. In the fourth quarter, quarterback Vinny Testaverde keyed an 83-yard drive with a 25-yard completion to running back Earnest Hunter and a 12-yard scramble to set up Byner's winning touchdown. Testaverde finished with 19 completions in 33 attempts for 254 yards. He also scrambled for 42 yards. Hobert, starting in place of injured Jeff Hostetler, completed 17 of 26 passes for 192 yards. But the Ravens shut down Oakland's rushing attack, limiting the Raiders to only 60 yards on 21 attempts.

Oakland	0	14	0	0	—	14
Baltimore	7	0	6	6	—	19

Balt — Testaverde 9 run (Stover kick)
Oak — Brown 7 pass from Hobert (Ford kick)
Oak — Brown 10 pass from Hobert (Ford kick)
Balt — FG Stover 25
Balt — FG Stover 37
Balt — Byner 1 run (pass failed)

PHILADELPHIA 17, WASHINGTON 14—at RFK Stadium, attendance 53,415. Rodney Peete passed for 257 yards and 2 touchdowns in the first half as the Eagles built a 17-7 advantage before turning things over to their defense in the second half. Peete, who finished the game with 20 completions in 34 attempts for 269 yards, teamed with Irving Fryar on an 18-yard touchdown pass in the first quarter and with Chris T. Jones on a 9-yard pass in the second period. The Redskins' Terry Allen, who ran 2 yards for a touchdown in the first quarter, burst 49 yards for another touchdown on the second play of the third quarter to pull his team within three points. But Philadelphia thwarted each of Washington's efforts after that. The Eagles pass rush sacked Redskins quarterback Gus Frerotte 3 times and harassed him into only 12 completions in 25 attempts for 119 yards. Allen provided more than half of Washington's 220 total yards by rushing for 111 yards on 20 carries.

Philadelphia	7	10	0	0	—	17
Washington	7	0	7	0	—	14

Phil — Fryar 18 pass from Peete (Anderson kick)
Wash — Allen 2 run (Blanton kick)
Phil — C. Jones 9 pass from Peete (Anderson kick)
Phil — FG Anderson 26
Wash — Allen 49 run (Blanton kick)

JACKSONVILLE 24, PITTSBURGH 9—at Jacksonville Municipal Stadium, attendance 70,210. Mark Brunell's 2 touchdown passes helped the Jaguars stun the defending AFC champions. Jacksonville marched 80 yards in eight plays the first time it had the ball, taking a lead it would not relinquish on Brunell's 38-yard touchdown pass to Willie Jackson 6:34 into the game. The Jaguars' quarterback also teamed with Keenan McCardell on a 15-yard touchdown pass 16 seconds before halftime. Running back James Stewart delivered the decisive blow with a 1-yard touchdown run with 4:49 left in the game. Brunell completed 20 of 31 passes for 212 yards and Stewart rushed for 77 yards as Jacksonville, which ranked twenty-eighth in the league in total offense in 1995, amassed 313 total yards. The Steelers managed just 187 total yards on offense, and lost linebacker Greg Lloyd for the season with a torn tendon in his knee. Quarterback Jim Miller completed only 9 of 17 passes for 83 yards in his first NFL start.

Pittsburgh	3	3	3	0	—	9
Jacksonville	7	7	0	10	—	24

Jax — Jackson 38 pass from Brunell (Hollis kick)
Pitt — FG Johnson 48
Pitt — FG Johnson 23
Jax — McCardell 15 pass from Brunell (Hollis kick)
Pitt — FG Johnson 23
Jax — FG Hollis 52
Jax — J. Stewart 1 run (Hollis kick)

SAN DIEGO 29, SEATTLE 7—at San Diego Jack Murphy Stadium, attendance 58,780. John Carney kicked 5 field goals and the Chargers pounded the Seahawks for 185 yards on the ground. Carney's field goals included one of 53 yards on the last play of the first half and another of 50 yards to give San Diego a 19-7 lead early in the fourth quarter. The Chargers then put the game away by recovering a fumble on the ensuing kickoff and driving 16 yards for Leonard Russell's 6-yard touchdown run with 11:39 left in the game. San Diego scored 13 points in the fourth

quarter, all within a span of 3:06, and all following Seattle turnovers. Aaron Hayden rushed for 59 yards, Terrell Fletcher had 49, and Russell added 46 for the Chargers, who had 27 first downs and maintained possession for 34:30 of the game's 60 minutes. San Diego quarterback Stan Humphries completed 21 of 38 passes for 195 yards, including a 2-yard touchdown to Tony Martin to open the first-quarter scoring. Rick Mirer was 24 of 41 for 251 yards for the Seahawks, but also suffered a pair of interceptions.

Seattle	0	7	0	0	—	7
San Diego	7	6	3	13	—	29

SD — Martin 2 pass from Humphries (Carney kick)
Sea — Mirer 6 run (Peterson kick)
SD — FG Carney 35
SD — FG Carney 53
SD — FG Carney 22
SD — FG Carney 50
SD — Russell 6 run (Carney kick)
SD — FG Carney 31

SUNDAY NIGHT, SEPTEMBER 1

BUFFALO 23, N.Y. GIANTS 20 (OT)—at Giants Stadium, attendance 74,218. Steve Christie's 34-yard field goal 10:08 into overtime capped a 16-point rally by the Bills. Rookie Amani Toomer's 87-yard punt return helped the Giants build a 17-0 advantage midway through the second quarter. New York still led 20-7 in the third period before Christie kicked a 28-yard field goal at the 6:30 mark, and when Jim Kelly and Andre Reed teamed on a 60-yard touchdown pass just 1:45 later, Buffalo had narrowed the gap to three points. Christie's 39-yard field goal with 7:14 remaining in regulation sent the game into overtime. In the extra session, defensive end Bruce Smith sacked Giants quarterback Dave Brown, forcing a fumble that linebacker Chris Spielman recovered at New York's 33. Seven plays later, Christie's third field goal of the game won it. Kelly completed 24 of 41 passes for 313 yards for the Bills, who outgained the Giants 410-231. Thurman Thomas ran for 97 yards on 32 carries. Reed caught 5 passes for 138 yards.

Buffalo	0	7	10	3	3	—	23
N.Y. Giants	3	14	3	0	0	—	20

NYG — FG Daluiso 22
NYG — Toomer 87 punt return (Daluiso kick)
NYG — Way 37 pass from Brown (Daluiso kick)
Buff — Thomas 1 run (Christie kick)
NYG — FG Daluiso 34
Buff — FG Christie 28
Buff — Reed 60 pass from Kelly (Christie kick)
Buff — FG Christie 39
Buff — FG Christie 34

MONDAY, SEPTEMBER 2

CHICAGO 22, DALLAS 6—at Soldier Field, attendance 66,944. The Bears combined trick plays with a stingy defense to upset the defending Super Bowl-champion Cowboys. Dallas led 3-0 in the second quarter when Chicago wide receiver Curtis Conway took a handoff from quarterback Erik Kramer and tossed a 33-yard touchdown pass to running back Raymont Harris 3:31 before halftime. The next time the Bears had the ball, they apparently were forced to punt. But Todd Sauerbaun completed a 47-yard pass to Harris out of punt formation, and moments later Carlos Huerta kicked a 31-yard field goal to give Chicago a 10-6 advantage at the intermission. Two more field goals by Huerta and linebacker Bryan Cox's fumble recovery in the end zone kept the Cowboys from making a charge. Dallas, which failed to score a touchdown in three of its preseason games, did not reach the end zone in a regular-season game for the first time since 1991. The Cowboys converted only 4 of 13 third-down opportunities and managed only 256 total yards. They also got a scare when running back Emmitt Smith was carted off the field on a stretcher after injuring his shoulder and neck late in the game. Dallas's Deion Sanders extensively played wide receiver on offense and cornerback on defense. He led the Cowboys with 9 catches for 87 yards. Harris had 3 receptions for 103 yards for the Bears.

Dallas	3	0	0	3	—	6
Chicago	0	10	0	12	—	22

Dall — FG Boniol 28
Chi — Harris 33 pass from Conway (Huerta kick)
Chi — FG Huerta 31
Chi — FG Huerta 42

Chi — FG Huerta 34
Chi — Cox recovered fumble in end zone (pass failed)
Dall — FG Boniol 28

SECOND WEEK SUMMARIES
AMERICAN FOOTBALL CONFERENCE

Eastern Division	W	L	T	Pct.	Pts.	OP
Buffalo	2	0	0	1.000	40	30
Indianapolis	2	0	0	1.000	41	20
Miami	2	0	0	1.000	62	20
New England	0	2	0	.000	20	41
N.Y. Jets	0	2	0	.000	13	52
Central Division						
Baltimore	1	1	0	.500	36	45
Houston	1	1	0	.500	53	47
Jacksonville	1	1	0	.500	51	43
Pittsburgh	1	1	0	.500	40	41
Cincinnati	0	2	0	.000	30	53
Western Division						
Denver	2	0	0	1.000	61	26
Kansas City	2	0	0	1.000	39	22
San Diego	2	0	0	1.000	56	21
Oakland	0	2	0	.000	17	38
Seattle	0	2	0	.000	27	59

NATIONAL FOOTBALL CONFERENCE

Eastern Division	W	L	T	Pct.	Pts.	OP
Dallas	1	1	0	.500	33	22
Philadelphia	1	1	0	.500	30	53
Washington	1	1	0	.500	24	20
Arizona	0	2	0	.000	23	58
N.Y. Giants	0	2	0	.000	20	50
Central Division						
Green Bay	2	0	0	1.000	73	16
Minnesota	2	0	0	1.000	40	30
Chicago	1	1	0	.500	25	16
Detroit	1	1	0	.500	34	23
Tampa Bay	0	2	0	.000	9	55
Western Division						
Carolina	2	0	0	1.000	51	26
San Francisco	2	0	0	1.000	61	11
St. Louis	1	1	0	.500	26	50
Atlanta	0	2	0	.000	23	52
New Orleans	0	2	0	.000	31	49

SUNDAY, SEPTEMBER 8

PITTSBURGH 31, BALTIMORE 17—at Three Rivers Stadium, attendance 57,241. The Steelers forced 2 turnovers, which led to 14 points, and received a solid offensive performance to win their home opener. Rod Woodson, coming off last season's major reconstructive knee surgery, intercepted Vinny Testaverde's pass on the game's second play from scrimmage and raced 43 yards for a touchdown. With the Steelers leading 21-14, Woodson recovered Testaverde's fumble, forced by Carlos Emmons, which led to Andre Hastings's 20-yard touchdown reception and a commanding 28-14 lead. The Steelers' offense produced touchdown drives of 70, 83, and 40 yards in its first three possessions. Jerome Bettis rushed for 116 yards on 21 carries, while Mike Tomczak completed 18 of 25 pass attempts, including 14 consecutive, as Pittsburgh controlled the ball for more than 35 minutes.

Baltimore	7	10	0	0	—	17
Pittsburgh	14	14	3	0	—	31

Pitt — Woodson 43 interception return (N. Johnson kick)
Balt — Testaverde 6 run (Stover kick)
Pitt — Bettis 1 run (N. Johnson kick)
Balt — Alexander 17 pass from Testaverde (Stover kick)
Pitt — C. Johnson 5 pass from Tomczak (N. Johnson kick)
Pitt — Hastings 20 pass from Tomczak (N. Johnson kick)
Balt — FG Stover 29
Pitt — FG N. Johnson 35

CAROLINA 22, NEW ORLEANS 20—at Louisiana Superdome, attendance 43,288. John Kasay kicked 5 field goals for the second consecutive week, leading the Panthers to victory. The Saints' defense stifled the Panthers, permitting them just 83 rushing yards on 34 attempts. Carolina's only touchdown came on rookie Winslow Oliver's 84-yard punt return. New Orleans's offense scored touchdowns on two of its first three possessions, but kicked 2 field goals for its only points in the game's final 43 minutes. Trailing 20-19,

Carolina got the ball on its 33-yard line with 7:40 remaining. Kerry Collins guided the Panthers downfield with 3 passes that set up first downs. However, Collins sprained his knee and Steve Beuerlein took over the reins. Tshimanga Biakabutuka ran four times to set up Kasay's winning kick with 2:09 to play. Rookie Muhsin Muhammad had 4 key receptions in the second half, 2 on each of the drives that concluded with Kasay's final 2 field goals. The lead changed hands five times.

Carolina	7	6	3	6	—	22
New Orleans	7	7	3	3	—	20

NO — Small 9 pass from Everett (Brien kick)
Car — Oliver 84 punt return (Kasay kick)
NO — Jeffires 27 pass from Everett (Brien kick)
Car — FG Kasay 51
Car — FG Kasay 22
Car — FG Kasay 29
NO — FG Brien 48
Car — FG Kasay 51
NO — FG Brien 43
Car — FG Kasay 27

WASHINGTON 10, CHICAGO 3—at RFK Stadium, attendance 52,711. Terry Allen scampered 28 yards for a touchdown and the Redskins' defense held an opponent without a touchdown for the first time since 1993 in Washington's second victory. With the score 3-3, the Bears were driving in the third quarter. Michael Timpson made a third-down catch good enough for a first down, but Stanley Richard forced Timpson to fumble at the 25-yard line. Darrell Green returned the fumble 14 yards. The Redskins wasted no time, as Gus Frerotte hit Henry Ellard with 17- and 16-yard receptions on the next two plays. Allen scored one play later. Robert Green rushed for 107 yards for Chicago. The two teams combined to convert just 8 of 29 third-down situations.

Chicago	3	0	0	0	—	3
Washington	0	3	7	0	—	10

Chi — FG Huerta 37
Wash — FG Blanton 50
Wash — Allen 28 run (Blanton kick)

SAN DIEGO 27, CINCINNATI 14—at San Diego Jack Murphy Stadium, attendance 55,880. Leonard Russell scored 2 touchdowns to lead the Chargers to a home victory. The Chargers used two drives of more than 5:00 to score their first 2 touchdowns. After John Carney's second field goal early in the fourth quarter, Kurt Gouveia's 22-yard interception return to the 3-yard line set up Russell's second touchdown. San Diego dominated the game, outgaining the Bengals (383-249) and getting nearly twice as many first downs (25-14). The Chargers' defense held running backs Ki-Jana Carter and Garrison Hearst to a combined 29 yards on 14 carries. Jeff Blake completed just 14 of 33 passes, including 4 of his first 20 attempts. Stan Humphries completed 27 of 41 passes for 275 yards. Tony Martin had 9 receptions for 96 yards and a touchdown.

Cincinnati	0	7	0	7	—	14
San Diego	7	0	3	10	—	27

SD — Russell 1 run (Carney kick)
SD — Martin 21 pass from Humphries (Carney kick)
Cin — Pickens 27 pass from Blake (Pelfrey kick)
SD — FG Carney 47
SD — FG Carney 23
SD — Russell 1 run (Carney kick)
Cin — McGee 12 pass from Wilhelm (Pelfrey kick)

DENVER 30, SEATTLE 20—at Kingdome, attendance 43,671. John Elway, playing in his club-record 192nd game, threw 2 touchdown passes and ran for another to lead the Broncos. Bill Romanowski had 3 takeaways for the Broncos, including a fumble recovery that led to Jason Elam's third field goal and a 23-13 lead with 10:32 remaining. Seattle scored its first offensive touchdown when John Friesz, who replaced Rick Mirer at halftime after an ineffective first half, threw a 23-yard touchdown pass to Christian Fauria with 4:14 left. Elway and the Broncos responded with a 52-yard drive, set up by Vaughn Hebron's 40-yard kickoff return, that ended with Elway's 1-yard quarterback sneak with 2:00 to play. Denver led in first downs (22-10), total yards (374-211), and time of possession (36:44-23:16).

Denver	3	10	7	10	—	30
Seattle	3	3	7	7	—	20

Den — FG Elam 18
Sea — FG Peterson 27
Sea — FG Peterson 40
Den — Craver 39 pass from Elway (Elam kick)
Den — FG Elam 28
Sea — Galloway 88 punt return (Peterson kick)
Den — Miller 7 pass from Elway (Elam kick)
Den — FG Elam 33
Sea — Fauria 23 pass from Friesz (Peterson kick)
Den — Elway 1 run (Elam kick)

HOUSTON 34, JACKSONVILLE 27—at Jacksonville Municipal Stadium, attendance 66,468. Chris Chandler threw 3 touchdown passes, and Eddie George ran for 143 yards as the Oilers held off Jacksonville. Houston led 24-13 when Mike Hollis missed a 31-yard field goal for the Jaguars. After a penalty, the Oilers faced first-and-20 from their 11-yard line and called a running play. George avoided tacklers in the backfield and raced 76 yards down the right sideline before being dragged down at the 13-yard line. Chandler then found Willie Davis for an 11-yard touchdown to give Houston a 31-13 lead midway through the third quarter. Jacksonville did not give up, as Mark Brunell threw 2 touchdowns, the first set up by Chris Hudson's 46-yard punt return and the second a 3-yard pass to Keenan McCardell with 2:33 to play, to cut the deficit to 34-27. The Jaguars' Dave Thomas recovered the onside kick, and Jacksonville drove deep into Oilers' territory. However, Brunell's pass to Pete Mitchell on the first play after the two-minute warning bounced high off his hands and was intercepted by Marcus Robertson at the 10-yard line to preserve the victory. Brunell completed 27 of 38 passes for 302 yards, and McCardell had 8 receptions for 100 yards. Chandler attempted just 22 passes, but completed 14 of them for 226 yards, 3 touchdowns, and no interceptions.

Houston	10	14	7	3	—	34
Jacksonville	10	3	7	7	—	27

Jax — FG Hollis 38
Hou — FG Del Greco 32
Jax — Stewart 5 run (Hollis kick)
Hou — George 1 run (Del Greco kick)
Hou — Floyd 63 pass from Chandler (Del Greco kick)
Jax — FG Hollis 37
Hou — Wycheck 7 pass from Chandler (Del Greco kick)
Hou — W. Davis 11 pass from Chandler (Del Greco kick)
Jax — Smith 5 pass from Brunell (Hollis kick)
Hou — FG Del Greco 29
Jax — McCardell 3 pass from Brunell (Hollis kick)

INDIANAPOLIS 21, N.Y. JETS 7—at Giants Stadium, attendance 63,534. Ken Dilger had 7 receptions for 156 yards to lead the Colts to victory in a game that featured a 32-minute weather delay. With the Colts leading 21-7 with 11:10 remaining, referee Bob McElwee cleared the field due to the severe lightning and pelting rain that surrounded East Rutherford. The Jets flirted with the end zone following the delay, but Kyle Brady's fumble at the 2-yard line dashed the Jets' hopes. Marvin Harrison's 29-yard punt return set up Marshall Faulk's 1-yard touchdown run and gave the Colts a 7-0 lead. An unnecessary roughness penalty and a 51-yard pass to Dilger was followed by Dilger's 22-yard touchdown catch from Jim Harbaugh that put the Colts ahead 14-0. Keyshawn Johnson, the first pick of the 1996 draft, caught his first NFL touchdown 31 seconds before halftime to cut the deficit to 14-7. However, in the fourth quarter Harbaugh found Dilger again, this time for 28 yards, and Harbaugh's 12-yard run moments later ended the scoring. Neil O'Donnell completed 26 of 46 passes for 319 yards.

Indianapolis	7	7	0	7	—	21
N.Y. Jets	0	7	0	0	—	7

Ind — Faulk 1 run (Blanchard kick)
Ind — Dilger 22 pass from Harbaugh (Blanchard kick)
Jets — K. Johnson 11 pass from O'Donnell (Lowery kick)
Ind — Harbaugh 12 run (Blanchard kick)

MINNESOTA 23, ATLANTA 17—at Georgia Dome, attendance 42,688. Brad Johnson, making the first start of his five-year NFL career, completed 15 of 26 passes for 275 yards and 2 touchdowns to lead the Vikings to a come-from-behind victory. Johnson, who started due to ankle and foot injuries Warren Moon suffered the previous week, found Cris Carter with a 7-yard touchdown pass in the second quarter to give the Vikings a 10-3 lead. Atlanta's Terance Mathis caught just 2 passes in the game, but both were third-quarter touchdown receptions to give the Falcons a 17-10 advantage. Johnson hit Jake Reed with a 71-yard pass to set up a Scott Sisson field goal to cut the deficit to 17-13. Moments later, Harlon Barnett recovered Jamal Anderson's fumble at the Falcons' 34-yard line, setting up four-year tight end David Frisch's first NFL touchdown to give Minnesota a 20-17 lead with 10:27 left. Sisson tacked on a field goal just 17 seconds left to seal the victory. Reed totalled 148 yards on 4 catches. Jeff George completed 24 of 41 pass attempts for 266 yards. Bert Emanuel caught 9 passes for 116 yards.

Minnesota	3	7	13	—	23
Atlanta	3	0	14	0	—	17

Minn — FG Sisson 26
Atl — FG Andersen 20
Minn — Carter 7 pass from Johnson (Sisson kick)
Atl — Mathis 3 pass from George (Andersen kick)
Atl — Mathis 10 pass from George (Andersen kick)
Minn — FG Sisson 30
Minn — Frisch 3 pass from Johnson (Sisson kick)
Minn — FG Sisson 21

BUFFALO 17, NEW ENGLAND 10—at Rich Stadium, attendance 78,104. Quinn Early caught a 63-yard touchdown pass from Jim Kelly with 5:21 to play, and Phil Hansen stopped David Meggett inside the 5-yard line as time ran out to give the Bills a hard-earned victory. The Bills faced third-and-23 from their own 37-yard line and had gained just 160 total offensive yards in the game when Kelly found Early on a quick slant pass. Early outraced the coverage to the end zone to propel the Bills into the lead. The Patriots drove to the 16-yard line and Drew Bledsoe faked as if he was going to spike the ball to stop the clock. Instead, Bledsoe threw towards the end zone and drew a pass interference penalty on Marlon Kerner that put the ball at the 2-yard line. However, Hansen stuffed Meggett's rushing attempt behind the line of scrimmage to end the game. New England had plenty of opportunities in the first half as well. The Patriots had the ball inside the Bills' 11-yard line three times, but got just one Adam Vinatieri field goal to show for their work. The Patriots failed to convert a fake field-goal attempt and Vinatieri missed from 25 yards on another attempt. Vinatieri also missed from 45 and 47 yards. The defenses held each of their counterparts to under 300 yards. The Bills won despite committing 10 penalties and Kelly's 3 interceptions.

New England	3	0	7	0	—	10
Buffalo	3	7	0	7	—	17

NE — FG Vinatieri 42
Buff — FG Christie 33
Buff — Thomas 4 run (Christie kick)
NE — Glenn 37 pass from Bledsoe (Vinatieri kick)
Buff — Early 63 pass from Kelly (Christie kick)

DALLAS 27, N.Y. GIANTS 0—at Texas Stadium, attendance 63,069. Troy Aikman threw 3 touchdown passes, and the defense held the Giants to just 93 total yards, as the defending Super Bowl champions won their first game. Deion Sanders and Kevin Williams each caught first-quarter touchdown passes to put the Cowboys ahead 14-0. Later, the Cowboys started from their 29-yard line with 1:54 remaining in the half. Aikman found Kelvin Martin on a 39-yard pass to get into Giants' territory. Emmitt Smith, who ran for 94 yards on 25 carries despite a sore neck, caught Aikman's 5-yard touchdown with just 2 seconds left in the half to give Dallas a commanding 21-0 lead. The Cowboys defense was stifling, and didn't allow the Giants to cross midfield until the fourth quarter. Dallas outgained the Giants (368-93) and tripled their first-down total (21-7).

N.Y. Giants	0	0	0	0	—	0
Dallas	14	7	3	3	—	27

Dall — Sanders 8 pass from Aikman (Boniol kick)
Dall — K. Williams 19 pass from Aikman (Boniol kick)
Dall — E. Smith 5 pass from Aikman (Boniol kick)
Dall — FG Boniol 23
Dall — FG Boniol 29

KANSAS CITY 19, OAKLAND 3—at Arrowhead Stadium, attendance 79,281. Derrick Thomas forced 2 quarterback fumbles that led directly to 9 points and a victory. The win gave Kansas City 13 victories in its last 14 games against the Raiders. The Chiefs led 7-0 midway through the third quarter, but the Raiders had the ball at the Chiefs' 5-yard line on second and goal. Thomas hit quarterback Billy Joe Hobert from behind, knocking the ball loose. James Hasty scooped up the ball and raced 80 yards for a touchdown and 14-0 lead. The Raiders got the ball back trailing 17-3 with four minutes left when Thomas once again forced a Hobert fumble. Center Barret Robbins beat Dan Saleaumua to the ball in the end zone, but the Chiefs still recorded a safety for the game's final points. The Raiders had trouble on special teams as well, having one field-goal attempt thwarted by holder Jeff Gossett's inability to hold on to the snap, and another attempt blocked by the Chiefs' Keith Traylor.

Oakland	0	0	0	3	—	3
Kansas City	0	7	7	5	—	19

KC — T. Richardson 1 pass from Bono (Stoyanovich kick)
KC — Hasty 80 fumble return (Stoyanovich kick)
KC — FG Stoyanovich 23
Oak — FG Ford 38
KC — Safety, Saleaumua tackled Robbins in end zone

SAN FRANCISCO 34, ST. LOUIS 0—at 3Com Park, attendance 63,624. The 49ers' defense held the Rams to 6 first downs, 105 total yards, and forced 4 turnovers en route to a shutout. The 49ers scored 14 points in the second quarter on 2 safeties, a field goal, and a touchdown. Rams rookie quarterback Tony Banks made his NFL debut in the second quarter, with the Rams taking over possession on their 1-yard line. Bryant Young sacked Banks in the end zone for a safety on his second NFL play. San Francisco took the ensuing free kick and scored on Derek Loville's short run. After Jeff Wilkins' field goal, the 49ers' defense held the Rams once again. When St. Louis had to punt deep in its territory, Joe Valerio's snap sailed over Sean Landeta's head for the 49ers' second safety of the quarter. The Rams' defense held the 49ers to just 3.1 yards per carry, but they tired at the game's end (San Francisco had a 38:37-21:23 time of possession advantage) and gave up 2 touchdowns in the final seven minutes. The victory marked the 49ers' twelfth consecutive victory against the Rams.

St. Louis	0	0	0	0	—	0
San Francisco	0	14	3	17	—	34

SF — Safety, Banks tackled by B. Young in end zone
SF — Loville 2 run (Wilkins kick)
SF — FG Wilkins 38
SF — Safety, Landeta kicked ball out of end zone
SF — FG Wilkins 22
SF — FG Wilkins 21
SF — Vardell 1 run (Wilkins kick)
SF — Carter 1 run (Wilkins kick)

DETROIT 21, TAMPA BAY 6—at Pontiac Silverdome, attendance 54,229. The Lions used the legs of Barry Sanders and a couple of interceptions to defeat the Buccaneers. With Detroit trailing 6-0 in the second quarter, Sanders helped jump start the offense. Three of his carries, and a 16-yard pass from Scott Mitchell to David Sloan, put the ball at the Lions' 46-yard line. Sanders then raced 54 yards for a touchdown, and the Lions never gave back the lead. The Lions' defense intercepted Trent Dilfer twice. Corey Raymond's 24-yard interception return just 70 seconds after Sanders' touchdown run put the Lions ahead 14-6. Greg Jefferies' interception resulted in Herman Moore's 23-yard touchdown catch midway through the third quarter to end the scoring. Sanders finished with 125 yards. The Buccaneers were kept out of the end zone for the second consecutive game. Courtney Hawkins had 111 yards on 8 catches for Tampa Bay.

Tampa Bay	3	3	0	0	—	6
Detroit	0	14	7	0	—	21

TB — FG Husted 30
TB — FG Husted 41
Det — Sanders 54 run (Hanson kick)
Det — Raymond 24 interception return (Hanson kick)
Det — Moore 23 pass from Mitchell (Hanson kick)

SUNDAY NIGHT, SEPTEMBER 8

MIAMI 38, ARIZONA 10—at Sun Devil Stadium, attendance 55,444. Karim Abdul-Jabbar ran for 2 touchdowns and Dan Marino threw 2 touchdown passes to catapult the Dolphins to victory. With the game-time temperature reaching 101 degrees, it was the Cardinals who struggled early. Arizona allowed 8 first downs, including 3 third-down conversions, had a punt blocked, fumbled twice, and committed 4 penalties in the first quarter. Joe Nedney's 36-yard field goal five seconds before halftime staked the Dolphins to a 24-0 advantage. Kent Graham started the second half at quarterback for Arizona, having replaced Boomer Esiason, and the Cardinals quickly put 10 points on the scoreboard to cut the deficit to 24-10. However, Irving Spikes helped the Dolphins regain momentum with a 34-yard run and 10-yard reception that led to his 1-yard touchdown run. Zach Thomas's fumble recovery moments later led to Marino's second touchdown pass. Miami outgained the Cardinals (331-203) and had nearly twice as many first downs (25-13) while forcing 4 turnovers.

Miami	7	17	7	7	—	38
Arizona	0	0	10	0	—	10

Mia — Abdul-Jabbar 3 run (Nedney kick)
Mia — Abdul-Jabbar 3 run (Nedney kick)
Mia — Thomas 20 pass from Marino (Nedney kick)
Mia — FG Nedney 36
Ariz — C. Smith 1 pass from Graham (Davis kick)
Ariz — FG Davis 26
Mia — Spikes 1 run (Nedney kick)
Mia — McDuffie 5 pass from Marino (Nedney kick)

MONDAY, SEPTEMBER 9

GREEN BAY 39, PHILADELPHIA 13—at Lambeau Field, attendance 60,666. Brett Favre threw 3 touchdown passes, including 2 to Robert Brooks, in Green Bay's victory. The Packers scored 20 points in an 11:22 stretch of the first half to take a 23-0 lead. The Eagles' Ricky Watters's ran 1-yard run to cut the deficit to 23-7 with 1:56 left in the half. But Favre and the Packers countered with a drive that concluded with Brooks's second touchdown of the half just 26 seconds before halftime. Favre completed 17 of 31 attempts for 261 yards. Rodney Peete connected on just 10 of 25 passes for 142 yards for the Eagles. He was intercepted 3 times and sacked for a safety in the fourth quarter. Brooks finished with 130 yards on 5 receptions.

Philadelphia	0	7	0	6	—	13
Green Bay	10	20	7	2	—	39

GB — FG Jacke 29
GB — Brooks 25 pass from Favre (Jacke kick)
GB — FG Jacke 44
GB — Levens 1 run (Jacke kick)
GB — FG Jacke 38
Phil — Watters 1 run (Anderson kick)
GB — Brooks 20 pass from Favre (Jacke kick)
GB — Bennett 25 pass from Favre (Jacke kick)
GB — Safety, White and Dotson tackled Peete in end zone
Phil — Garner 1 run (pass failed)

THIRD WEEK SUMMARIES
AMERICAN FOOTBALL CONFERENCE

Eastern Division	W	L	T	Pct.	Pts.	OP
Indianapolis	3	0	0	1.000	66	44
Miami	3	0	0	1.000	98	47
Buffalo	2	1	0	.667	46	54
New England	1	2	0	.333	51	41
N.Y. Jets	0	3	0	.000	40	88

Central Division	W	L	T	Pct.	Pts.	OP
Houston	2	1	0	.667	82	60
Pittsburgh	2	1	0	.667	64	47
Baltimore	1	2	0	.333	49	74
Cincinnati	1	2	0	.333	60	68

	W	L	T	Pct.	Pts.	OP
Jacksonville	1	2	0	.333	54	60
Western Division						
Denver	3	0	0	1.000	88	49
Kansas City	3	0	0	1.000	74	39
San Diego	2	1	0	.667	66	63
Oakland	1	2	0	.333	34	41
Seattle	0	3	0	.000	44	94

NATIONAL FOOTBALL CONFERENCE

Eastern Division	W	L	T	Pct.	Pts.	OP
Philadelphia	2	1	0	.667	54	70
Washington	2	1	0	.667	55	30
Dallas	1	2	0	.333	57	47
Arizona	0	3	0	.000	23	89
N.Y. Giants	0	3	0	.000	30	81
Central Division						
Green Bay	3	0	0	1.000	115	26
Minnesota	3	0	0	1.000	60	44
Chicago	1	2	0	.333	39	36
Detroit	1	2	0	.333	51	47
Tampa Bay	0	3	0	.000	32	82
Western Division						
Carolina	2	0	0	1.000	51	26
San Francisco	2	0	0	1.000	61	11
St. Louis	1	1	0	.500	26	50
Atlanta	0	2	0	.000	23	52
New Orleans	0	3	0	.000	46	79

SUNDAY, SEPTEMBER 15

NEW ENGLAND 31, ARIZONA 0—at Foxboro Stadium, attendance 59,118. Curtis Martin scored 3 touchdowns to lead the Patriots to their first victory of the season. Drew Bledsoe threw 3 touchdown passes while completing 21 of 35 passes for 221 yards for New England. Bledsoe found Coates with a 2-yard touchdown pass 20 seconds before halftime to stake the Patriots to a 20-0 halftime lead. By halftime, New England had more first downs (18) than Arizona had plays (15). The Patriots permitted just 9 first downs and 170 total yards while forcing 4 turnovers.

Arizona	0	0	0	0	—	0
New England	7	13	8	3	—	31

NE — Martin 13 pass from Bledsoe (Vinatieri kick)
NE — Martin 1 run (Vinatieri kick)
NE — Coates 2 pass from Bledsoe (kick failed)
NE — Martin 7 pass from Bledsoe (Martin pass from Bledsoe)
NE — FG Vinatieri 31

HOUSTON 29, BALTIMORE 13—at Astrodome, attendance 20,082. Houston's defense intercepted 3 passes and Chris Chandler threw 2 touchdown passes to lead the Oilers. Darryll Lewis's interception on the Ravens' first possession led to Chandler's 3-yard touchdown pass to tight end Frank Wycheck. Marcus Robertson's 27-yard interception return later in the first quarter set up Chandler's 18-yard touchdown pass to Willie Davis. Testaverde completed 25 of 40 passes for 217 yards and 2 touchdowns, but could not overcome the 3 interceptions. Wycheck had 6 receptions for 64 yards.

Baltimore	0	7	0	6	—	13
Houston	14	3	9	3	—	29

Hou — Wycheck 3 pass from Chandler (Del Greco kick)
Hou — Davis 18 pass from Chandler (Del Greco kick)
Balt — Jackson 7 pass from Testaverde (Stover kick)
Hou — FG Del Greco 41
Hou — Safety, Montgomery stepped out of end zone
Hou — Harmon 2 run (Del Greco kick)
Hou — FG Del Greco 44
Balt — Arvie 1 pass from Testaverde (pass failed)

PHILADELPHIA 24, DETROIT 17—at Veterans Stadium, attendance 66,007. Ricky Watters ran for 153 yards and a touchdown as the Eagles defeated the Lions. Watters started the day with a 53-yard run on the first play from scrimmage. He ended the drive with an 11-yard touchdown run 4:41 into the game. Detroit drove downfield, but Bobby Taylor intercepted Scott Mitchell's pass at the goal line to stop the drive. Chris T. Jones, who led all receivers with 9 catches and 121 receiving yards, caught a 17-yard touchdown pass in the third quarter to increase the Eagles lead

to 17-3. Barry Sanders, despite gaining just 49 yards on 16 carries, scored 2 second-half touchdowns. The second one, set up by Glyn Milburn's 49-yard kickoff return, came just 1:42 after Rodney Peete's quarterback sneak put Philadelphia ahead 24-10. Peete completed 25 of 30 passes for 284 yards. The Eagles dominated the time of possession category (39:22-20:38).

Detroit	0	3	7	7	—	17
Philadelphia	7	3	7	7	—	24

Phil — Watters 11 run (Anderson kick)
Det — FG Hanson 50
Phil — FG Anderson 39
Phil — C. Jones 17 pass from Peete (Anderson kick)
Det — Sanders 8 run (Hanson kick)
Phil — Peete 1 run (Anderson kick)
Det — Sanders 1 run (Hanson kick)

INDIANAPOLIS 25, DALLAS 24—at Texas Stadium, attendance 63,021. Cary Blanchard's fourth field goal, from 43 yards with 51 seconds remaining, gave the Colts a come-from-behind victory on the road against the defending Super Bowl champions. The Cowboys had an opportunity to win on the game's final play, but Chris Boniol's 57-yard field goal attempt bounced off the crossbar. Trailing 3-0, the Cowboys ran off 21 consecutive points en route to a 21-9 halftime advantage: Daryl Johnston caught a 5-yard touchdown pass from Troy Aikman for the first score; Deion Sanders's 22-yard return of fumble, forced by Tony Tolbert, put Dallas ahead 14-3; and Emmitt Smith ran 2 yards for a touchdown. Jim Harbaugh threw 2 third-quarter touchdown passes for the Colts, to Marcus Pollard and Ken Dilger, to give Indianapolis the lead. Boniol's 52-yard field goal with 13:26 left put Dallas ahead 24-22. However, Boniol missed a 40-yard attempt with 2:48 left. Harbaugh found Dilger for 28 yards and running back Zack Crockett for 18 to set up Blanchard's heroics. Harbaugh was 19 of 28 for 244 yards despite being sacked 5 times.

Indianapolis	3	6	13	3	—	25
Dallas	3	14	0	3	—	24

Ind — FG Blanchard 23
Dall — Johnston 5 pass from Aikman (Boniol kick)
Dall — Sanders 22 fumble return (Boniol kick)
Dall — E. Smith 2 run (Boniol kick)
Ind — FG Blanchard 25
Ind — FG Blanchard 52
Ind — Pollard 48 pass from Harbaugh (Blanchard kick)
Ind — Dilger 8 pass from Harbaugh (pass failed)
Dall — FG Boniol 52
Ind — FG Blanchard 43

OAKLAND 17, JACKSONVILLE 3—at Oakland Coliseum, attendance 46,291. Jerry Ball's 66-yard fumble return for a touchdown with 2:15 left secured the victory for Oakland, which broke an eight-game losing streak dating back to last season. Rob Fredrickson forced Mark Brunell to fumble. Ball, with a convoy of teammates, lumbered into the end zone. Oakland had taken a 10-0 lead behind Jeff Hostetler's 19-yard touchdown pass to Tim Brown and a Cole Ford field goal 58 seconds before halftime. Mike Hollis's third-quarter field goal cut the deficit to 10-3 and the Jaguars drove down to the 26-yard line with just over 2:00 left when Fredrickson made his big play. The two teams combined for 18 penalties and 5 turnovers.

Jacksonville	0	0	3	0	—	3
Oakland	0	10	0	7	—	17

Oak — Brown 19 pass from Hostetler (Ford kick)
Oak — FG Ford 32
Jax — FG Hollis 33
Oak — Ball 66 interception return (Ford kick)

KANSAS CITY 35, SEATTLE 17—at Kingdome, attendance 39,790. Marcus Allen ran for 2 touchdowns and became just the eighth player in NFL history to surpass 11,000 rushing yards as the Chiefs won their eleventh consecutive AFC West game. Steve Bono threw 3 touchdown passes for the Chiefs, one of which went to cornerback Dale Carter. Carter, due to injuries to teammates, played wide receiver and caught the first 3 passes of his NFL career. Chris Penn caught 2 touchdown passes for the first multi-touchdown game of his career. The Chiefs led 28-17 in the fourth quarter, but the Seahawks drove deep into

Kansas City territory before Mark Collins's interception at the 7-yard line with 6:33 left kept the Seahawks from scoring. A 34-yard run by Donnell Bennett and 12-yard run by Greg Hill led to Allen's second touchdown with 3:19 left. Bono completed 18 of 27 passes for 185 yards. The Chiefs' defense sacked Rick Mirer 7 times and held Chris Warren to just 6 yards on 14 carries.

Kansas City	14	7	7	7	—	35
Seattle	0	10	0	7	—	17

KC — Penn 9 pass from Bono (Stoyanovich kick)
KC — D. Carter 46 pass from Bono (Stoyanovich kick)
Sea — FG Peterson 47
Sea — Smith 4 run (Peterson kick)
KC — Penn 1 pass from Bono (Stoyanovich kick)
KC — Allen 2 run (Stoyanovich kick)
Sea — Mirer 1 run (Peterson kick)
KC — Allen 1 run (Stoyanovich kick)

MINNESOTA 20, CHICAGO 14—at Soldier Field, attendance 61,301. Warren Moon returned to the Vikings' line-up and passed for 239 yards and a touchdown to give the Vikings their first 3-0 start since 1975. Moon, who had missed the previous 1½ games due to an ankle injury, completed 22 of 44 passes. Donnell Woolford's 28-yard interception return gave the Bears a 14-7 second-quarter lead. However Erik Kramer, who played with ace bandages wrapped around his back and left leg, threw interceptions on the Bears' next two possessions. The second interception, by Corey Fuller, led to Moon's 29-yard touchdown pass to Jake Reed that tied the game 14-14 at halftime. With the scored still tied in the fourth quarter, Chicago's Carlos Huerta missed a 44-yard field goal. The Vikings responded with a 51-yard drive to set up the first of 2 fourth-quarter Scott Sisson field goals. Robert Smith had 81 rushing yards and a touchdown for the Vikings.

Minnesota	0	14	0	6	—	20
Chicago	7	7	0	0	—	14

Chi — Engram 5 pass from Kramer (Huerta kick)
Minn — Rob.Smith 14 run (Sisson kick)
Chi — Woolford 28 interception return (Huerta kick)
Minn — Reed 29 pass from Moon (Sisson kick)
Minn — FG Sisson 33
Minn — FG Sisson 34

CINCINNATI 30, NEW ORLEANS 15—at Cinergy Field, attendance 45,412. Ki-Jana Carter scored his first NFL touchdown to lead the Bengals to their first victory. Carter's 31-yard run, the longest by a Cincinnati player in two years, gave the Bengals a 17-6 lead going into halftime. The Saints cut the deficit to 17-12 on Ray Zellars's 3-yard run 1:33 into the second half. However, New Orleans self-destructed: Jim Everett threw 3 interceptions; the Saints committed a roughing the punter penalty on a drive that led to the second of Doug Pelfrey's 3 field goals; and defensive penalties allowed the Bengals to score their final touchdown with 4:00 remaining. Cincinnati had more first downs (24-15) and a large edge in time of possession (36:32-23:28). Jeff Blake completed 22 of 39 passes for 225 yards. Jim Everett passed for 296 yards, but the Bengals held the Saints to just 27 rushing yards on 15 carries.

New Orleans	3	3	6	3	—	15
Cincinnati	3	14	3	10	—	30

Cin — FG Pelfrey 33
NO — FG Brien 51
Cin — Scott 24 pass from Blake (Pelfrey kick)
NO — FG Brien 37
Cin — Carter 31 run (Pelfrey kick)
NO — Zellars 3 run (pass failed)
Cin — FG Pelfrey 21
Cin — FG Pelfrey 35
NO — FG Brien 25
Cin — Bieniemy 5 run (Pelfrey kick)

MIAMI 36, N.Y. JETS 27—at Pro Player Stadium, attendance 68,137. Dan Marino celebrated his thirty-fifth birthday by throwing 3 touchdown passes, and the Dolphins scored a touchdown on four consecutive possessions to beat the Jets. Aaron Glenn's club-record 100-yard interception return threatened to blow out the candles on Marino's cake. Neil O'Donnell, who also threw 3 touchdown passes, found Webster Slaughter for a 30-yard touchdown

pass and a 14-0 lead with 6:52 left in the half. Undaunted, Marino threw a 74-yard touchdown pass to rookie running back Stanley Pritchett, the longest reception by a running back in club history, on the next play from scrimmage to begin a 33-point barrage. A pass interference penalty on the Dolphins' next possession led to Karim Abdul-Jabbar's game-tying 5-yard run. Marino included some not-so-familiar faces in the third quarter. He threw a 2-yard touchdown pass to Frank Wainright, his first reception since 1992, and a 12-yard touchdown pass to Brett Carolan, who made just his fifth reception in three NFL seasons. It was the first NFL touchdown for both players. O'Donnell threw 2 fourth-quarter touchdown passes just 2:55 apart to cut the deficit to 33-27. However, the Dolphins marched 63 yards, all on the ground, to set up Joe Nedney's 28-yard field goal with 1:45 left to end the scoring. Abdul-Jabbar ran for 124 yards as the Dolphins outgained the Jets on the ground 195-72.

N.Y. Jets	0	14	0	13	—	27
Miami	0	14	12	10	—	36

Jets — Glenn 100 interception return (Lowery kick)
Jets — Slaughter 30 pass from O'Donnell (Lowery kick)
Mia — Pritchett 74 pass from Marino (Nedney kick)
Mia — Abdul-Jabbar 4 run (Nedney kick)
Mia — Wainright 2 pass from Marino (kick failed)
Mia — Carolan 12 pass from Marino (pass failed)
Mia — Abdul-Jabbar 7 run (Nedney kick)
Jets — Graham 78 pass from O'Donnell (run failed)
Jets — K. Johnson 29 pass from O'Donnell (Lowery kick)
Mia — FG Nedney 29

GREEN BAY 42, SAN DIEGO 10—at Lambeau Field, attendance 60,584. Brett Favre threw 3 touchdown passes and the Packers tallied their highest point total in Mike Holmgren's five-year coaching tenure. Leading 14-3 in the second quarter, the Packers controlled the ball for 9:24 on a 17-play, 88-yard drive that concluded with William Henderson's 8-yard touchdown reception 1:13 before halftime. Favre's third touchdown pass, to Keith Jackson late in the third quarter, gave the Packers a 28-3 lead. San Diego cut the deficit to 28-10 on Tony Martin's 9-yard touchdown catch with 8:16 left. The Chargers threatened again less than two minutes later, but LeRoy Butler intercepted Stan Humphries's pass and raced 90 yards for the clinching touchdown. Desmond Howard ended the scoring with a 55-yard punt return moments later. The Packers outgained the Chargers 349-141 and held the ball for nearly two-thirds of the game (38:38-21:22). Favre completed 22 of 34 passes for 231 yards. Green Bay sacked Stan Humphries 4 times.

San Diego	3	0	0	7	—	10
Green Bay	7	14	7	14	—	42

GB — Bennett 10 run (Jacke kick)
SD — FG Carney 43
GB — Freeman 19 pass from Favre (Jacke kick)
GB — Henderson 8 pass from Favre (Jacke kick)
GB — Jackson 7 pass from Favre (Jacke kick)
SD — Martin 9 pass from Humphries (Carney kick)
GB — Butler 90 interception return (Jacke kick)
GB — Howard 65 punt return (Jacke kick)

WASHINGTON 31, N.Y. GIANTS 10—at Giants Stadium, attendance 71,693. Terry Allen rushed for 146 yards and a touchdown as the Redskins snapped a six-game losing streak against the Giants. The Redskins led 10-0 when they lined up for a potential 47-yard field goal. However the Redskins faked the field goal and holder Gus Frerotte threw a 30-yard touchdown pass to Scott Galbraith. The Giants cut the lead to 17-10 before Allen scored from 7 yards on the first play of the fourth quarter. Tom Carter intercepted Dave Brown twice in the final quarter and Stephen Davis raced 39 yards for a touchdown in the closing minutes to secure the victory. Frerotte completed 15 of 23 passes for 197 yards. Brown finished 17 of 31 for 201 yards, but threw 4 interceptions.

Washington	3	14	0	14	—	31
N.Y. Giants	0	7	3	0	—	10

Wash — FG Blanton 36
Wash — Logan 3 run (Blanton kick)
Wash — Galbraith 30 pass from Frerotte (Blanton kick)
Giants— Pierce 7 pass from Brown (Daluiso kick)
Giants— FG Daluiso 19
Wash — Allen 7 run (Blanton kick)
Wash — Davis 39 run (Blanton kick)

SUNDAY NIGHT, SEPTEMBER 15

DENVER 27, TAMPA BAY 23—at Mile High Stadium, attendance 71,535. Terrell Davis rushed for 137 yards and scored the winning touchdown with 3:32 left to give the Broncos a come-from-behind victory. After trailing 13-10 at halftime, the Broncos scored on their first 2 possessions of the second half with John Elway's 17-yard touchdown pass to Anthony Miller putting Denver ahead 20-13. The Buccaneers responded with a 40-yard touchdown pass from Trent Dilfer to Alvin Harper on a third-and-23 play to tie the game. Derrick Brooks's interception set up Michael Husted's 28-yard field goal that gave Tampa Bay a 23-20 lead with 11:43 left. However, the Broncos controlled the ball for more than eight minutes as they went 14 plays (12 rushing) and 80 yards to the winning score. Elway completed 25 of 34 passes for 180 yards. Dilfer was 12 of 30 for 200 yards. Reggie Brooks ran for 114 yards for Tampa Bay.

Tampa Bay	3	10	7	3	—	23
Denver	7	3	10	7	—	27

Den — Braxton 69 interception return (Elam kick)
TB — FG Husted 24
Den — FG Elam 45
TB — R. Brooks 8 run (Husted kick)
TB — FG Husted 35
Den — FG Elam 20
Den — Miller 17 pass from Elway (Elam kick)
TB — Harper 40 pass from Dilfer (Husted kick)
TB — FG Husted 28
Den — Davis 3 run (Elam kick)

MONDAY, SEPTEMBER 16

PITTSBURGH 24, BUFFALO 6—at Three Rivers Stadium, attendance 59,002. Jerome Bettis rushed for 133 yards and 2 touchdowns as Pittsburgh continued its recent Monday-night dominance. The Steelers improved their Monday-night record under coach Bill Cowher to 8-1, including 6-0 at home. Bettis compiled his second consecutive 100-yard rushing game to help the Steelers dominate possession of the clock (38:58-21:02). Kordell Stewart's 48-yard catch and run of a screen pass set up Bettis's first touchdown and put the Steelers ahead 7-3. In the closing seconds of the first half, Jim Kelly threw an out-pattern pass that Carnell Lake intercepted and returned 47 yards for a touchdown to give Pittsburgh a 24-3 halftime lead. The Steelers held the Bills to just 185 total yards. Kelly completed 15 of 31 passes for 116 yards and 4 interceptions.

Buffalo	3	0	3	0	—	6
Pittsburgh	7	17	0	0	—	24

Buff — FG Christie 31
Pitt — Bettis 1 run (N. Johnson kick)
Pitt — FG N. Johnson 30
Pitt — Bettis 43 run (N. Johnson kick)
Pitt — Lake 47 interception return (N. Johnson kick)
Buff — FG Christie 45

FOURTH WEEK SUMMARIES
AMERICAN FOOTBALL CONFERENCE

Eastern Division	W	L	T	Pct.	Pts.	OP
Indianapolis	4	0	0	1.000	76	50
Buffalo	3	1	0	.750	56	61
Miami	3	1	0	.750	104	57
New England	2	2	0	.500	79	66
N.Y. Jets	0	4	0	.000	46	101
Central Division						
Houston	2	1	0	.667	82	60
Pittsburgh	2	1	0	.667	64	47
Baltimore	1	2	0	.333	49	74
Cincinnati	1	2	0	.333	60	68
Jacksonville	1	3	0	.250	79	88
Western Division						
Kansas City	4	0	0	1.000	91	53
Denver	3	1	0	.750	102	66
San Diego	3	1	0	.750	106	97
Oakland	1	3	0	.250	68	81
Seattle	1	3	0	.250	61	107

NATIONAL FOOTBALL CONFERENCE

Eastern Division	W	L	T	Pct.	Pts.	OP
Philadelphia	3	1	0	.750	87	88
Washington	3	1	0	.750	72	40
Arizona	1	3	0	.250	51	103
Dallas	1	3	0	.250	64	57
N.Y. Giants	1	3	0	.250	43	87
Central Division						
Minnesota	4	0	0	1.000	90	65
Green Bay	3	1	0	.750	136	56
Detroit	2	2	0	.500	86	63
Chicago	1	3	0	.250	55	71
Tampa Bay	0	4	0	.000	45	99
Western Division						
Carolina	3	0	0	1.000	74	33
San Francisco	2	1	0	.667	68	34
St. Louis	1	2	0	.333	36	67
Atlanta	0	3	0	.000	41	85
New Orleans	0	4	0	.000	60	107

SUNDAY, SEPTEMBER 22

ARIZONA 28, NEW ORLEANS 14—at Louisiana Superdome, attendance 34,316. LeShon Johnson ran for 214 yards and 2 touchdowns to lead the Cardinals to their first victory. The third-year running back had just 101 career yards in 20 games entering the contest. The Saints led 7-6 at halftime on Ernest Dixon's blocked punt that was returned for a touchdown by Brian Jones. Arizona, who had scored only 23 points in three previous games, then got rolling. Kent Graham made his first start of the season and gave the Cardinals the lead with a 20-yard touchdown pass, and subsequent 2-point conversion to Rob Moore. Johnson then broke free for a 56-yard touchdown run 14 seconds into the fourth quarter. Less than two minutes later, Johnson ran 70 yards for a touchdown.

Arizona	3	3	8	14	—	28
New Orleans	0	7	0	7	—	14

Ariz — FG Davis 25
Ariz — FG Davis 25
NO — B. Jones 11 blocked punt return (Brien kick)
Ariz — Moore 20 pass from Graham (Moore pass from Graham)
Ariz — Johnson 56 run (Davis kick)
Ariz — Johnson 70 run (Davis kick)
NO — Jeffires 23 pass from Everett (Brien kick)

DETROIT 35, CHICAGO 16—at Pontiac Silverdome, attendance 70,022. Scott Mitchell threw 4 touchdown passes and ran for another as Detroit continued its home-field dominance. The win marked the Lions' ninth consecutive home victory. Mitchell completed 24 of 34 passes for 336 yards, with 20 of those completions finding the hands of his three wide receivers. Johnnie Morton caught 7 passes for a career-high 174 yards and 2 touchdowns. Brett Perriman also caught 2 touchdowns among his 6 catches, and Herman Moore contributed 7 receptions. Barry Sanders helped break open a tight game with a 30-yard run in the third quarter to set up Mitchell's 1-yard sneak that extended the Lions lead to 28-16. Curtis Conway had 8 catches for 126 yards for the Bears.

Chicago	0	16	0	0	—	16
Detroit	0	21	7	7	—	35

Det — Morton 15 pass from Mitchell (Hanson kick)
Det — Perriman 2 pass from Mitchell (Hanson kick)
Chi — FG Jaeger 46
Chi — Conway 58 pass from Kramer (Jaeger kick)
Det — Morton 62 pass from Mitchell (Hanson kick)
Chi — Flanigan 1 pass from Kramer (pass failed)
Det — Mitchell 1 run (Hanson kick)
Det — Perriman 24 pass from Mitchell (Hanson kick)

BUFFALO 10, DALLAS 7—at Rich Stadium, attendance 78,098. The Bills' defense limited the Cowboys to 192 total yards and forced 4 turnovers to defeat the defending Super Bowl champions. The Cowboys' 1-3 record equalled their worst start since 1990. Buffalo played without starting

quarterback Jim Kelly, who was out with a hamstring injury. Todd Collins, in just his second career start, completed 10 of 17 passes for 88 yards before leaving the game late in third quarter with a sprained ankle. Alex Van Pelt played the remainder of the game. The Bills scored on their first possession, with Thurman Thomas's 2-yard touchdown run completing a 17-play, 78-yard drive that took 10:40 off the clock. Emanuel Martin's third-quarter interception, the first of his 2 on the day, and subsequent 31-yard return led to Steve Christie's 32-yard field goal. Dallas did not score until Herschel Walker's 24-yard reception to the 1-yard line set up Emmitt Smith's touchdown with 5:53 remaining. The Cowboys' Troy Aikman completed 18 of 33 passes for 164 yards with 3 interceptions. The Bills limited the Cowboys to a 3 conversions in 12 third-down situations, and dominated time of possession (37:28-22:32).

Dallas	0	0	0	7	—	7
Buffalo	7	0	3	0	—	10

Buff — Thomas 2 run (Christie kick)
Buff — FG Christie 32
Dall — E. Smith 2 run (Boniol kick)

KANSAS CITY 17, DENVER 14—at Arrowhead Stadium, attendance 79,439. Marcus Allen's 2-yard touchdown run with 4:09 left gave the Chiefs their first 4-0 start in club history. The second of Terrell Davis's 2 first-half touchdown runs staked the Broncos to 14-10 lead 6:34 before halftime. The score remained the same until Steve Bono led the Chiefs on a 67-yard drive. Bono completed passes of 16 and 18 yards to Chris Penn and 16 yards to Danan Hughes before Allen tied Jim Brown's NFL record with his 106th career rushing touchdown. John Elway, who had beaten the Chiefs in the fourth quarter six times during his career, had a long pass intercepted by Dale Carter at the 4-yard line with three minutes to play. Deep in his own territory, Bono completed 2 third-down passes, one to Penn and another to Todd McNair, in the closing minutes to run out the clock. Bono was 20 of 35 for 242 yards. Shannon Sharpe had 9 receptions for 131 of Elway's 156 passing yards.

Denver	7	7	0	0	—	14
Kansas City	3	7	0	7	—	17

Den — Davis 6 run (Elam kick)
KC — FG Stoyanovich 37
KC — Hughes 8 pass from Bono (Stoyanovich kick)
Den — Davis 65 run (Elam kick)
KC — Allen 2 run (Stoyanovich kick)

MINNESOTA 30, GREEN BAY 21—at Metrodome, attendance 64,168. Robert Smith scored the go-ahead touchdown on a 37-yard run with 4:13 remaining, and the Vikings recorded 7 sacks to remain undefeated. The Vikings led 14-7 at halftime on 2 Warren Moon touchdown passes. Scott Sisson's third-quarter field goal increased the advantage to 17-7, but the Packers responded. Don Beebe raced 80 yards for a touchdown on the Packers' next play from scrimmage to cut the lead to 17-14. George Koonce returned an interception 75 yards for a touchdown to give Green Bay a 21-17 lead. Smith's touchdown run capped an 80-yard drive. Derrick Alexander then recovered a fumble, leading to a 44-yard field goal by Sisson and a 27-21 lead with 3:31 left. After the Vikings' defense stopped the Packers on downs, Sisson booted his third field goal with 31 seconds left to seal the victory. Minnesota outscored the Packers 13-0 in the fourth quarter, and had outscored their opponents 42-3 in the final quarter for the season. The Vikings' defense held the Packers to just 8 first downs and 217 total yards. The Packers lost their first game after having not even trailed in any of their first three games. The Vikings defeated the Packers at home for the fifth consecutive season.

Green Bay	7	0	14	0	—	21
Minnesota	7	7	3	13	—	30

GB — R. Brooks 13 pass from Favre (Jacke kick)
Minn — Reed 26 pass from Moon (Sisson kick)
Minn — Ismail 20 pass from Moon (Sisson kick)
Minn — FG Sisson 35
GB — Beebe 80 pass from Favre (Jacke kick)
GB — Koonce 75 interception return (Jacke kick)
Minn — Smith 37 run (Sisson kick)
Minn — FG Sisson 44
Minn — FG Sisson 33

NEW ENGLAND 28, JACKSONVILLE 25 (OT)—at Foxboro Stadium, attendance 59,446. Adam Vinatieri's 40-yard field goal in overtime gave the Patriots the victory. The Patriots dominated the first half and held a 22-0 lead before Mark Brunell's Hail Mary pass on the last play of the first half fell into Jimmy Smith's hands for a touchdown. The Jaguars received the second half's opening kickoff and drove 75 yards, the last 41 coming on Brunell's touchdown bomb to Andre Rison, to cut the deficit to 22-14. After Vinatieri's fourth field goal, Rison caught a 61-yard bomb from Brunell. Brunell ran in the 2-point conversion to cut the lead to three points. Mike Hollis erased the deficit with a 27-yard field goal midway through the fourth quarter. The Jaguars attempted another Hail Mary pass on the last play of regulation. Willie Jackson caught the pass for a 53-yard reception, but he was stopped inches short of the end zone. The Patriots won the coin toss going into overtime and never relinquished possession of the ball. Brunell completed 23 of 39 passes for 432 yards for Jacksonville. Drew Bledsoe completed 27 of 44 passes for 255 yards for New England. Rison caught 4 for 115 yards and Jackson had 4 catches for 101 yards. Jacksonville commmited a team-record 17 penalties for 148 yards, and was dominated in the time of possession category (37:38-24:58) and first downs (26-12).

Jacksonville	0	7	15	3	0	—	25
New England	9	13	3	0	3	—	28

NE — Coates 5 pass from Bledsoe (kick blocked)
NE — FG Vinatieri 23
NE — FG Vinatieri 30
NE — Martin 4 run (Vinatieri kick)
NE — FG Vinatieri 29
Jax — Smith 51 pass from Brunell (Hollis kick)
Jax — Rison 41 pass from Brunell (Hollis kick)
NE — FG Vinatieri 41
Jax — Rison 61 pass from Brunell (Brunell run)
Jax — FG Hollis 27
NE — FG Vinatieri 40

N.Y. GIANTS 13, N.Y. JETS 6—at Giants Stadium, attendance 58,339. Chris Calloway caught a 17-yard touchdown pass, and two fourth-quarter field goals by Brad Daluiso provided some breathing room as the visiting Giants won the battle of New York teams. Dave Brown completed all 4 of his passes on the touchdown-scoring drive. Two Nick Lowery field goals cut the deficit to 7-6. The Jets' defense stopped Rodney Hampton from the 1-yard line three consecutive plays, forcing the Giants to settle for Daluiso's first field goal less than two minutes into the fourth quarter. A couple of late-hit personal foul penalties and a 22-yard pass from Brown to Lawrence Dawsey led to Daluiso's second field goal with 4:35 left. The game was played in rain showers, including a torrential downpour in the final minutes. Both defenses excelled, as the Giants had 201 total yards and were 2 of 11 in third-down conversions, while the Jets had 208 yards and were forced to punt 7 times.

N.Y. Giants	0	7	0	6	—	13
N.Y. Jets	3	0	3	0	—	6

NYJ — FG Lowery 46
NYG — Calloway 17 pass from Brown (Daluiso kick)
NYJ — FG Lowery 39
NYG — FG Daluiso 20
NYG — FG Daluiso 20

SAN DIEGO 40, OAKLAND 34—at Oakland Coliseum, attendance 49,097. Stan Humphries threw 3 touchdown passes in a 3:05 span late in the first quarter to lead the Chargers to victory. Darrien Gordon's 35-yard punt return set up Humphries's first touchdown pass, a 6-yard toss to Terrell Fletcher with 4:03 left in the first quarter. Kurt Gouveia's interception led to Tony Martin's touchdown catch 58 seconds after Fletcher's scoring reception. Rodney Harrison recovered a fumble at the Raiders' 41-yard line, and the Chargers went deep on the first play as Humphries hit Martin to give San Diego a 21-0 lead. Jeff Hostetler threw 3 touchdown passes to pull the Raiders within 27-21 with 5:41 left in the third quarter, but Martin's third touchdown catch and Willie Clark's 83-yard interception return gave San Diego a 40-21 advantage with 3:40 left. Reserve Billy Joe Hobert threw 2 touchdown passes in the final 90 seconds, with Kenny Shedd's 28-yard touchdown catch with 12 seconds remaining cutting the deficit to 40-34. The Chargers, unable to recover an onside kick just over a minute earlier, recovered another kick with 10 seconds left to seal the win. Martin had 10 catches for 138 yards to go along with his 3 touchdowns. The Raiders gained 553 total yards, with their two quarterbacks combining to complete 34 of 56 passes for 400 yards. Tim Brown had 11 receptions for 120 yards and 2 touchdowns.

San Diego	21	6	0	13	—	40
Oakland	0	14	7	13	—	34

SD — Fletcher 6 pass from Humphries (Carney kick)
SD — Martin 7 pass from Humphries (Carney kick)
SD — Martin 41 pass from Humphries (Carney kick)
Oak — Fenner 4 pass from Hostetler (Ford kick)
SD — FG Carney 28
Oak — Dudley 6 pass from Hostetler (Ford kick)
SD — FG Carney 39
Oak — Brown 6 pass from Hostetler (Ford kick)
SD — Martin 19 pass from Humphries (run failed)
SD — Clark 83 interception return (Carney kick)
Oak — Brown 11 pass from Hobert (pass failed)
Oak — Shedd 28 pass from Hobert (Ford kick)

CAROLINA 23, SAN FRANCISCO 7—at Ericsson Stadium, attendance 72,224. Steve Beuerlein threw 2 touchdown passes to Wesley Walls, and the Panthers had 4 quarterback sacks to defeat the 49ers for the second time in the series' three-game history. Beuerlein, who started in place of injured Kerry Collins, completed 22 of 31 passes for 290 yards. The Panthers scored on their first three possesions: they drove 80 yards and scored on Walls's 19-yard touchdown reception; Beuerlein's 38-yard pass to Willie Green set up John Kasay's field goal; and Beuerlein completed 5 of 5 passes for 60 yards on an 81-yard drive that led to Walls's second touchdown catch and a 17-0 lead. Steve Young found a wide-open Derek Loville for a 44-yard touchdown pass midway through the third quarter for San Francisco's lone score. After another Kasay field goal increased the Panthers lead to 20-7, the 49ers' Tim McDonald intercepted a pass and returned it for an apparent touchdown that would have cut the lead to 20-13. However, the play was nullified due to a penalty. Kasay added a third field goal in the final minute to close out the scoring. The Panthers held the 49ers to just 2 of 11 third-down conversions. Jerry Rice had 10 receptions for 127 yards. The victory gave the Panthers lone possession of first place in the NFC West just 19 games into their existence.

San Francisco	0	0	7	0	—	7
Carolina	10	7	3	3	—	23

Car — Walls 19 pass from Beuerlein (Kasay kick)
Car — FG Kasay 28
Car — Walls 7 pass from Beuerlein (Kasay kick)
SF — Loville 44 pass from Young (Wilkins kick)
Car — FG Kasay 35
Car — FG Kasay 19

SEATTLE 17, TAMPA BAY 13—at Houlihan's Stadium, attendance 30,212. Rick Mirer guided the Seahawks to 2 touchdowns in the final three minutes for a comeback victory. Michael Husted's second field goal gave the Buccaneers a 13-3 lead with 9:20 left in the game. Seattle responded with an 83-yard drive capped by Mirer's 5-yard touchdown pass to Brian Blades. Mirer completed 8 of 9 passes on the drive. The Seahawks' defense then stopped the Buccaneers, forcing them to punt. Seattle started at its 39-yard line with 2:22 left and converted 3 third-down plays to set up Lamar Smith's 14-yard touchdown run. Tampa Bay's lone touchdown was set up by John Lynch's 40-yard run on a fake punt in the second quarter. Blades had 9 receptions for 92 yards.

Seattle	0	3	0	14	—	17
Tampa Bay	3	7	0	3	—	13

TB — FG Husted 33
Sea — FG Peterson 33
TB — R. Brooks 2 run (Husted kick)
TB — FG Husted 28
Sea — Blades 5 pass from Mirer

(Peterson kick)

Sea — L. Smith 14 run (Peterson kick)

WASHINGTON 17, ST. LOUIS 10—at Trans World Dome, attendance 62,303. Terry Allen rushed for 78 yards and a touchdown, and the Redskins intercepted 3 passes as they won their third consecutive game for the first time since 1992. The Redskins compiled only 257 total yards, but did not have to drive further than 51 yards on either of their touchdown drives. The Rams broke a seven-quarter streak without a touchdown when Jermaine Ross ran 3 yards for a score with 7:17 left. The Rams had a chance to tie the game in the closing minutes, but Tom Carter's interception at the 13-yard line with 2:40 left sealed the victory. Isaac Bruce had 11 receptions for 136 yards for St. Louis.

| Washington | 7 | 3 | 7 | 0 | — | 17 |
| St. Louis | 0 | 0 | 3 | 7 | — | 10 |

Wash — Galbraith 2 pass from Frerotte (Blanton kick)

Wash — FG Blanton 38

StL — FG Lohmiller 19

Wash — Allen 9 run (Blanton kick)

StL — Ross 3 run (Lohmiller kick)

SUNDAY NIGHT, SEPTEMBER 22

PHILADELPHIA 33, ATLANTA 18—at Georgia Dome, attendance 40,107. Ricky Watters ran for 121 yards and 2 touchdowns, and Gary Anderson booted 4 field goals to lead the Eagles to victory. Philadelphia took a 13-0 lead with 4:14 left in the first half before the Falcons responded. Jeff George found Eric Metcalf for 67 yards and Terance Mathis for a 12-yard scoring strike. Morten Andersen's 43-yard field goal with four seconds left cut the deficit to 13-10. The Eagles then scored 13 consecutive points to take a 26-10 lead. Bobby Hebert guided the Falcons to the end zone, finding Mathis from 12 yards for a touchdown and a 2-point conversion with 4:11 remaining to pull Atlanta within 26-18. However, Derrick Witherspoon dashed the Falcons' comeback hopes by returning the ensuing kickoff 97 yards for a touchdown. The Eagles allowed 391 total yards, but forced 6 turnovers, including 5 interceptions.

| Philadelphia | 3 | 10 | 10 | 10 | — | 33 |
| Atlanta | 0 | 10 | 0 | 8 | — | 18 |

Phil — FG Anderson 28

Phil — Watters 2 run (Anderson kick)

Phil — FG Anderson 33

Atl — Emanuel 23 pass from George (Andersen kick)

Atl — FG Andersen 43

Phil — Watters 56 run (Anderson kick)

Phil — FG Anderson 39

Phil — FG Anderson 25

Atl — Mathis 12 pass from Hebert (Mathis pass from Hebert)

Phil — Witherspoon 97 kickoff return

MONDAY, SEPTEMBER 23

INDIANAPOLIS 10, MIAMI 6—at RCA Dome, attendance 60,891. Jim Harbaugh threw a touchdown pass and had a key fourth-quarter fumble recovery as the Colts improved their record to 4-0. Miami took a 3-0 lead in the first quarter, but Dan Marino injured his ankle on the scoring drive and missed the remainder of the game. Backup Bernie Kosar completed 15 of 22 passes for 122 yards, but constantly was harrassed by a swarming Colts defense that recorded 5 sacks. Harbaugh threw a 1-yard touchdown pass to Ken Dilger midway through the second quarter to give Indianapolis the lead. Miami's best opportunity came with 9:00 left in the game trailing 10-6, when the Colts fumbled on their own 39-yard line. Harbaugh emerged from the scramble with the ball, and the Colts secured the victory. Zack Crockett had 81 yards on 9 carries and Harbaugh completed 19 of 25 passes. The Colts' defense, which was without five starters due to injury, allowed just 190 total yards and 12 first downs.

| Miami | 3 | 3 | 0 | 0 | — | 6 |
| Indianapolis | 0 | 7 | 0 | 3 | — | 10 |

Mia — FG Nedney 24

Ind — Dilger 1 pass from Harbaugh (Blanchard kick)

Mia — FG Nedney 39

Ind — FG Blanchard 18

FIFTH WEEK SUMMARIES

AMERICAN FOOTBALL CONFERENCE

Eastern Division	W	L	T	Pct.	Pts.	OP
Indianapolis	4	0	0	1.000	76	50
Buffalo	3	1	0	.750	56	61
Miami	3	1	0	.750	104	57
New England	2	2	0	.500	79	66
N.Y. Jets	0	5	0	.000	62	132
Central Division						
Pittsburgh	3	1	0	.750	94	63
Houston	2	2	0	.500	98	90
Baltimore	2	2	0	.500	66	84
Jacksonville	2	3	0	.400	103	102
Cincinnati	1	3	0	.250	70	82
Western Division						
Denver	4	1	0	.800	116	76
Kansas City	4	1	0	.800	110	75
San Diego	4	1	0	.800	128	116
Oakland	1	4	0	.200	85	100
Seattle	1	4	0	.200	71	138

NATIONAL FOOTBALL CONFERENCE

Eastern Division	W	L	T	Pct.	Pts.	OP
Washington	4	1	0	.800	103	56
Philadelphia	3	2	0	.600	106	111
Arizona	2	3	0	.400	82	131
Dallas	2	3	0	.400	87	76
N.Y. Giants	2	3	0	.400	58	97
Central Division						
Green Bay	4	1	0	.800	167	66
Minnesota	4	1	0	.800	100	80
Detroit	3	2	0	.600	113	63
Chicago	2	3	0	.400	74	88
Tampa Bay	0	5	0	.000	45	126
Western Division						
Carolina	3	1	0	.750	88	57
San Francisco	3	1	0	.750	107	51
St. Louis	1	3	0	.250	64	98
Atlanta	0	4	0	.000	58	124
New Orleans	0	5	0	.000	70	124

SUNDAY, SEPTEMBER 29

SAN FRANCISCO 39, ATLANTA 17—at 3Com Park, attendance 62,995. Jeff Wilkins kicked a club-record 6 field goals and the 49ers rattled off 33 consecutive points to defeat the Falcons. Atlanta controlled the ball for the first seven minutes of the game, with Morten Andersen's field goal capping the drive. But Wilkins kicked 2 field goals, Marquez Pope returned an interception 55 yards for a touchdown, running back Terry Kirby threw a touchdown pass to Jerry Rice, and reserve Elvis Grbac found backup tight end Ted Popson for a touchdown to give the 49ers a 27-3 halftime lead. Grbac, who was playing in place of injured Steve Young, completed 22 of 36 passes for 222 yards while improving his record to 4-2 as a starter. Popson was replacing injured starter Brent Jones in the lineup. Bobby Hebert made his first start of the year and completed 17 of 32 passes for 206 yards and 2 touchdowns, with 3 interceptions.

| Atlanta | 3 | 0 | 7 | 7 | — | 17 |
| San Francisco | 6 | 21 | 9 | 3 | — | 39 |

Atl — FG Andersen 20

SF — FG Wilkins 21

SF — FG Wilkins 43

SF — Pope 55 interception return (Wilkins kick)

SF — Rice 24 pass from Kirby (Wilkins kick)

SF — Popson 16 pass from Grbac (Wilkins kick)

SF — FG Wilkins 46

SF — FG Wilkins 29

Atl — T. Brown 22 pass from Hebert (Andersen kick)

SF — FG Wilkins 38

Atl — Preston 17 pass from Hebert (Andersen kick)

JACKSONVILLE 24, CAROLINA 14—at Jacksonville Municipal Stadium, attendance 71,537. The Jaguars jumped out to a 17-0 lead and their defense recorded 5 sacks while beating the previously undefeated Panthers. This was the first regular-season game between the 1995 expansion teams. The Jaguars scored on the game's first possession, with James Stewart, who ran for 96 yards on the day, rushing 1 yard for a touchdown. Jimmy Smith's 8-yard touchdown catch capped a 68-yard drive late in the first quarter. Mark Brunell, who completed 15 of 27 passes for 214 yards, scrambled for 20 yards just before halftime to set up

Mike Hollis's 53-yard field goal on the last play of the half. Carolina's Mark Carrier, who had 124 yards on 8 receptions, caught the first of his 2 touchdown receptions early in the third quarter. But the Jaguars had a 17-play, 80-yard drive that was capped by Stewart's second touchdown early in the fourth quarter. On offense, the Jaguars established the running game, averaging 4.7 yards per carry while permitting just 2.7. Defensively, Jacksonville harassed Panthers quarterback Steve Beuerlein, who played for the Jaguars last year and was starting due to a knee injury to Kerry Collins. Beuerlein was forced to leave the game in the fourth quarter with an injury. Collins replaced him and threw a late touchdown pass to Carrier.

| Carolina | 0 | 0 | 6 | 8 | — | 14 |
| Jacksonville | 14 | 3 | 0 | 7 | — | 24 |

Jax — Stewart 1 run (Hollis kick)

Jax — Smith 8 pass from Brunell (Hollis kick)

Jax — FG Hollis 53

Car — Carrier 24 pass from Beuerlein (kick failed)

Jax — Stewart 4 run (Hollis kick)

Car — Carrier 3 pass from Collins (Collins run)

DENVER 14, CINCINNATI 10—at Cinergy Field, attendance 51,798. John Elway passed for a season-high 335 yards and 2 touchdowns to lead the Broncos over the Bengals. Cincinnati led 10-7 at halftime on Jeff Blake's 2-yard touchdown run. Denver responded with an 80-yard drive late in the third quarter, with Elway finding Anthony Miller on a 23-yard touchdown pass. The combination of Elway (23 of 37 passing) and Terrell Davis (a franchise record-tying fourth consecutive 100-yard game) allowed the Broncos to convert 10 of 16 third-down opportunites. Both defenses made big plays, with Tyrone Braxton and Bracey Walker each intercepting a pass in the end zone. The Bengals could not drive further than their 37-yard line in the final minutes. Denver's defense permitted Blake just 5 completions out of 14 attempts in the second half.

| Denver | 7 | 0 | 7 | 0 | — | 14 |
| Cincinnati | 3 | 7 | 0 | 0 | — | 10 |

Cin — FG Pelfrey 44

Den — Sharpe 11 pass from Elway (Elam kick)

Cin — Blake 2 run (Pelfrey kick)

Den — Miller 23 pass from Elway (Elam kick)

DETROIT 27, TAMPA BAY 0—at Houlihan's Stadium, attendance 34,961. Scott Mitchell passed for 230 yards and 2 touchdowns to lead the Lions to a divisional victory. Tampa Bay trailed 17-0 at halftime despite outgaining the Lions and controlling the ball for more than 21 minutes. Bennie Blades returned an interception a career-long 98 yards for a touchdown late in the first quarter to begin the scoring. Johnnie Morton and Herman Moore each caught touchdown passes from Mitchell. Moore finished with 9 receptions for 104 yards. Detroit's defense dominated the second half, allowing just 74 yards after halftime and permitting the Lions to run 20 minutes off the clock.

| Detroit | 7 | 10 | 0 | 10 | — | 27 |
| Tampa Bay | 0 | 0 | 0 | 0 | — | 0 |

Det — Blades 98 interception return (Hanson kick)

Det — FG Hanson 20

Det — Morton 31 pass from Mitchell (Hanson kick)

Det — FG Hanson 29

Det — Moore 3 pass from Mitchell (Hanson kick)

GREEN BAY 31, SEATTLE 10—at Kingdome, attendance 59,973. Brett Favre threw 4 touchdown passes and the Packers' defense forced 5 turnovers that led to 24 points en route to a road victory. Antonio Freeman caught 2 of Favre's touchdown passes and finished with 7 receptions for 108 yards. Former Seahawk Eugene Robinson's 39-yard interception return set up Green Bay's first touchdown. Reggie White's 46-yard return of an interception led to Chris Jacke's field goal. Santana Dotson set up Dorsey Levens's touchdown run with a fumble recovery at the Seahawks' 28-yard line. With Green Bay leading 24-10 in the fourth quarter, Doug Evans intercepted a pass at the 9-yard line and returned it 63 yards. Favre threw his second touchdown pass of the game to Freeman five plays later to close out the scoring. The Packers' defense allowed Rick Mirer to complete just 10 of 30 passes. Chris Warren ran for 103 yards and scored the Seahawks' lone touchdown.

Green Bay	10	7	7	7	—	31
Seattle	0	7	3	0	—	10

GB — Freeman 13 pass from Favre (Jacke kick)
GB — FG Jacke 36
GB — Levens 4 pass from Favre (Jacke kick)
Sea — Warren 37 run (Peterson kick)
GB — Jackson 10 pass from Favre (Jacke kick)
Sea — FG Peterson 44
GB — Freeman 4 pass from Favre (Jacke kick)

PITTSBURGH 30, HOUSTON 16—at Three Rivers Stadium, attendance 58,608. Jerome Bettis recorded his third consecutive 100-yard rushing game, Mike Tomczak threw 2 touchdown passes, and the Steelers' defense forced 5 turnovers to take sole possession of first place in the AFC Central. After a fumble at the Oilers' 16-yard line, Kordell Stewart made a one-handed touchdown catch to give the Steelers a 7-0 lead. Then, Jason Gildon forced a fumble, and Jerry Olsavsky's recovery led to the first of 3 Norm Johnson field goals. Moments later, after a punt, Tomczak threw a 62-yard touchdown pass to Charles Johnson to give Pittsburgh a 17-0 lead just 7:36 into the game. Houston scored 2 touchdowns just 2:21 apart in the third quarter, with Darryll Lewis's 36-yard interception return cutting the deficit to 20-14. However, Darren Perry's 13-yard interception return for a touchdown with 5:17 to play clinched the victory. Tomczak completed 15 of 28 passes for 202 yards. Chris Chandler was 24 of 42 for 207 yards, with 2 interceptions.

Houston	0	0	14	2	—	16
Pittsburgh	17	3	0	10	—	30

Pitt — Stewart 16 pass from Tomczak (N. Johnson kick)
Pitt — FG N. Johnson 33
Pitt — C. Johnson 62 pass from Tomczak (N. Johnson kick)
Pitt — FG N. Johnson 36
Hou — Davis 4 pass from Chandler (Del Greco kick)
Hou — Lewis 36 interception return (Del Greco kick)
Pitt — FG N. Johnson 36
Pitt — Perry 13 interception return (N. Johnson kick)
Hou — Safety, Edge ran out of end zone

SAN DIEGO 22, KANSAS CITY 19—at San Diego Jack Murphy Stadium, attendance 59,384. Junior Seau intercepted 2 passes and Chris Mims blocked a last-minute field-goal attempt to give the Chargers a tough AFC West victory. Midway through the third quarter the score stood at 9-9. Then the Chiefs attempted a fake punt, with Louie Aguiar tucking the ball in and running 18 yards for a first down. A penalty was called, however, and the Chiefs had to punt. Darrien Gordon received the punt and returned it 81 yards for a touchdown. Kansas City responded immediately. Marcus Allen caught a short pass from Steve Bono on the next play from scrimmage and ran 59 yards down to the 3-yard line. Bono threw a touchdown pass to Reggie Johnson on the next play to tie the game. After an exchange of field goals, Seau grabbed his second interception, returning it 8 yards to the Chiefs' 20-yard line. Carney made his fifth field goal with 3:17 to play. The Chiefs drove to the Chargers' 30, but Mims got a hand on Pete Stoyanovich's fifth field-goal attempt of the day with 28 seconds to play. Stan Humphries was 19 of 41 for 238 yards. Bono completed 25 of 54 passes for 280 yards, with 2 interceptions.

Kansas City	0	9	7	3	—	19
San Diego	6	0	10	6	—	22

SD — FG Carney 33
SD — FG Carney 38
KC — FG Stoyanovich 44
KC — FG Stoyanovich 26
KC — FG Stoyanovich 26
SD — FG Carney 44
SD — Gordon 81 punt return (Carney kick)
KC — R. Johnson 3 pass from Bono (Stoyanovich kick)
SD — FG Carney 39
KC — FG Stoyanovich 32
SD — FG Carney 33

N.Y. GIANTS 15, MINNESOTA 10—at Giants Stadium, attendance 70,970. Brad Daluiso kicked 3 field goals and Phillippi Sparks intercepted a pass in the closing minutes to help the Giants beat the previously undefeated Vikings. Minnesota had won each of its first four games with fourth-quarter comebacks, and they were in position once again to rally. Trailing 15-10 with five minutes left, the Vikings took possession at their 45 after a short punt. A 28-yard run by Robert Smith got the Vikings deep into Giants' territory, but then Sparks intercepted Warren Moon's pass at the 4-yard line. The Giants controlled the ball for more than 37 minutes and ran 74 plays compared to 47 by the Vikings.

Minnesota	0	7	0	3	—	10
N.Y. Giants	3	3	6	3	—	15

NYG — FG Daluiso 25
Minn — Palmer 69 punt return (Sisson kick)
NYG — FG Daluiso 27
NYG — Pierce 1 run (pass failed)
Minn — FG Sisson 28
NYG — FG Daluiso 18

BALTIMORE 17, NEW ORLEANS 10—at Memorial Stadium, attendance 61,063. Earnest Byner had 149 yards rushing and Vinny Testaverde threw 2 touchdown passes to propel the Ravens to victory. Byner had his best rushing day since 1990, and his 42-yard run, which set up Matt Stover's second-quarter field goal, was his longest since his rookie season in 1984. The Ravens took a 10-7 lead into the fourth quarter when Jim Everett fired a 31-yard touchdown pass to Michael Haynes to complete a 12-play drive and tie the score. Baltimore responded on the next possesssion with a 75-yard drive, keyed by Testaverde's 26-yard pass to Michael Jackson and 29-yard pass to Brian Kinchen, that ended with Testaverde's 6-yard touchdown pass to Jackson with 10:23 left. The Ravens stopped Everett on a quarterback sneak attempt on fourth-and-1 at the Ravens' 30-yard line in the closing minutes. Everett completed 23 of 30 passes for 207 yards.

New Orleans	3	0	0	7	—	10
Baltimore	7	3	0	7	—	17

Balt — Alexander 64 pass from Testaverde (Stover kick)
NO — FG Brien 23
Balt — FG Stover 38
NO — Haynes 31 pass from Everett (Brien kick)
Balt — Jackson 6 pass from Testaverde (Stover kick)

CHICAGO 19, OAKLAND 17—at Soldier Field, attendance 57,062. Jeff Jaeger kicked 4 field goals, including the game-winner with 11 seconds left, to cap a 16-0 run by the Bears. Jaeger, who had been the Raiders' kicker the previous seven seasons before being cut in training camp and was playing just his second game with the Bears, connected on 3 fourth-quarter field goals. Oakland took a 17-3 lead on Jeff Hostetler's 5-yard touchdown pass to Tim Brown with 8:39 left in the third quarter. The Bears scored on their next possession, with Rashaan Salaam catching Dave Krieg's 11-yard touchdown pass. James Burton's interception led to Jaeger's second field goal, cutting the deficit to 17-13 less than a minute into the fourth quarter. Barry Minter then grabbed an interception to set up Jaeger's 41-yard kick. Chicago took possession on its own 21 with 5:44 left and took 13 plays, with Krieg finding Curtis Conway for 17- and 10-yard pass receptions, to lead to the winning kick. Hostetler was 19 of 35 for 172 yards and 4 interceptions.

Oakland	0	10	7	0	—	17
Chicago	0	3	7	9	—	19

Chi — FG Jaeger 44
Oak — Fenner 1 run (Ford kick)
Oak — FG Ford 28
Oak — Brown 5 pass from Hostetler (Ford kick)
Chi — Salaam 11 pass from Krieg (Jaeger kick)
Chi — FG Jaeger 24
Chi — FG Jaeger 41
Chi — FG Jaeger 30

ARIZONA 31, ST. LOUIS 28 (OT)—at Sun Devil Stadium, attendance 33,116. Kent Graham threw 4 touchdown passes and Greg Davis kicked the game-winning field goal as the Cardinals erased a 14-point fourth-quarter deficit to defeat the Rams. St. Louis, behind 3 long touchdown passes by Tony Banks and a 66-yard punt return for a touchdown by Eddie Kennison, took a 28-14 lead into the fourth quarter. The Cardinals battled back, with Graham throwing a short touchdown pass to Larry Centers with 6:19 left. After a Rams' punt, Graham completed 7 of 8 passes on a 62-yard drive, including a key fourth-and-9 completion to Frank Sanders to set up Sanders's game-tying touchdown grab with just 11 seconds remaining. After the Cardinals won the overtime coin toss, LeShon Johnson, who had been held to 31 yards during regulation, raced 66 yards down to the 8-yard line to set up Davis's winning kick. Graham completed 37 of 58 passes for 366 yards. Arizona dominated the game statistically, accumulating more first downs (27-10), yards (498-226), and time of possession (41:48-20:06). The Rams, who stayed in the game with big plays, were led by Isaac Bruce's 4 receptions for 117 yards and 2 touchdowns. Banks completed 10 of 18 pass attempts for 186 yards.

St. Louis	7	14	7	0	—	28
Arizona	0	14	0	14	3	—	31

StL — Kennison 66 punt return (Lohmiller kick)
StL — Bruce 46 pass from Banks (Lohmiller kick)
Ariz — R. Moore 24 pass from Graham (Davis kick)
StL — Kennison 34 pass from Banks (Lohmiller kick)
Ariz — Johnson 2 pass from Graham (Davis kick)
StL — Bruce 49 pass from Banks (Lohmiller kick)
Ariz — Centers 5 pass from Graham (Davis kick)
Ariz — Sanders 5 pass from Graham (Davis kick)
Ariz — FG Davis 24

SUNDAY NIGHT, SEPTEMBER 29

WASHINGTON 31, N.Y. JETS 16—at RFK Stadium, attendance 52,068. Leslie Shepherd ran for a touchdown and caught a touchdown pass off a flea-flicker to help the Redskins to a 4-0 start. Terry Allen gained 101 yards and ran for 2 touchdowns. Washington led 17-16 entering the fourth quarter when Shepherd caught a 52-yard touchdown pass from Gus Frerotte to extend the lead. The Jets, who had scored on four consecutive possessions, with the last 3 ending on field goals by Nick Lowery, drove deep into Redskins' territory. The Redskins' defense rose to the occasion when Tom Carter wrestled the ball away from Keyshawn Johnson in the end zone for an interception and the game's only turnover. With just under two minutes remaining, Allen raced 28 yards for his second touchdown to end the scoring. Adrian Murrell had 118 rushing yards and Neil O'Donnell completed 27 of 40 passes for 292 yards for the Jets.

N.Y. Jets	0	13	3	0	—	16
Washington	0	10	7	14	—	31

Wash — FG Blanton 28
NYJ — Murrell 9 run (Lowery kick)
NYJ — FG Lowery 26
Wash — Shepherd 12 run (Blanton kick)
NYJ — FG Lowery 35
Wash — Allen 8 run (Blanton kick)
NYJ — FG Lowery 33
Wash — Shepherd 52 pass from Frerotte (Blanton kick)
Wash — Allen 28 run (Blanton kick)

MONDAY, SEPTEMBER 30

DALLAS 23, PHILADELPHIA 19—at Veterans Stadium, attendance 67,201. Herschel Walker had a big kickoff return and the Cowboys' defense forced 5 turnovers to defeat their division rival. Ricky Watters's touchdown run gave the Eagles a 10-0 lead in the opening quarter. But Walker returned the ensuing kickoff 49 yards, sparking the Cowboys. Troy Aikman threw a 5-yard touchdown pass to Eric Bjornson to start a 20-0 Dallas run. Rhett Hall's 32-yard interception return cut the deficit to 20-17, but Chris Boniol's third field goal put Dallas back up by six points. The Eagles received 2 points with eight seconds left when punter John Jett ran out of the end zone for a safety. The Eagles not only lost the game, but starting quarterback Rodney Peete suffered a season-ending knee injury while dropping back to pass in the second quarter. Ty Detmer replaced Peete and completed 7 of 14 passes for 118 yards.

Dallas	7	13	3	0	—	23
Philadelphia	10	0	7	2	—	19

Phil — FG Anderson 46
Phil — Watters 2 run (Anderson kick)
Dall — Bjornson 5 pass from Aikman

(Boniol kick)
Dall — E. Smith 5 run (Boniol kick)
Dall — FG Boniol 46
Dall — FG Boniol 30
Phil — Hall 32 interception return (Anderson kick)
Dall — FG Boniol 21
Phil — Safety, Jett ran out of end zone

SIXTH WEEK SUMMARIES

AMERICAN FOOTBALL CONFERENCE

Eastern Division	W	L	T	Pct.	Pts.	OP
Buffalo	4	1	0	.800	72	74
Indianapolis	4	1	0	.800	89	66
Miami	3	2	0	.600	119	79
New England	3	2	0	.600	125	104
N.Y. Jets	0	6	0	.000	75	166
Central Division						
Pittsburgh	4	1	0	.800	111	70
Houston	3	2	0	.600	128	117
Baltimore	2	3	0	.400	104	130
Jacksonville	2	4	0	.333	116	119
Cincinnati	1	4	0	.200	97	112
Western Division						
Denver	5	1	0	.833	144	93
Kansas City	4	2	0	.667	117	92
San Diego	4	2	0	.667	145	144
Oakland	2	4	0	.333	119	113
Seattle	2	4	0	.333	93	153

NATIONAL FOOTBALL CONFERENCE

Eastern Division	W	L	T	Pct.	Pts.	OP
Washington	4	1	0	.800	103	56
Philadelphia	3	2	0	.600	106	111
Arizona	2	3	0	.400	82	131
Dallas	2	3	0	.400	87	76
N.Y. Giants	2	3	0	.400	58	97
Central Division						
Green Bay	5	1	0	.833	204	72
Minnesota	5	1	0	.833	114	92
Detroit	4	2	0	.667	141	87
Chicago	2	4	0	.333	80	125
Tampa Bay	0	5	0	.000	45	126
Western Division						
San Francisco	4	1	0	.800	135	62
Carolina	3	2	0	.600	100	71
St. Louis	1	4	0	.200	75	126
New Orleans	1	5	0	.167	87	137
Atlanta	0	5	0	.000	82	152

SUNDAY, OCTOBER 6

DETROIT 28, ATLANTA 24—at Pontiac Silverdome, attendance 58,666. Scott Mitchell threw 3 touchdown passes and the Lions held off a furious rally by the Falcons to remain a game out of first place in the NFC Central. The victory marked the Lions' tenth consecutive home win and 15 out of 16 at the Pontiac Silverdome. Detroit jumped out to a 28-0 lead in the first half. Little did anyone realize that Mitchell's third touchdown pass, a 50-yard connection with Herman Moore with 1:57 left in the half, would be the Lions' last points of the day. Atlanta swiftly drove downfield, and Jamal Anderson scored the first of his 3 touchdowns, from 9 yards with seven seconds left in the half. Anderson's second touchdown came 5:11 left in the third quarter, and his third on the last play of the third quarter to cut the deficit to 28-21. Ryan McNeil intercepted a Bobby Hebert pass in the end zone with 10:44 to play to halt a Falcons drive. Atlanta responded with a 20-yard punt return by Eric Metcalf to set up Morten Andersen's 47-yard field goal with 5:57 remaining. The Lions were able to maintain possession the remainder of the game, driving to the 1-yard line before letting the clock expire. Mitchell completed 20 of 37 passes for 276 yards. Anderson had 103 rushing yards for Atlanta.

Atlanta	0	7	14	3	—	24
Detroit	7	21	0	0	—	28

Det — Mitchell 2 run (Hanson kick)
Det — Perriman 9 pass from Mitchell (Hanson kick)
Det — Moore 25 pass from Mitchell (Hanson kick)
Det — Moore 50 pass from Mitchell (Hanson kick)
Atl — Anderson 9 run (Andersen kick)
Atl — Anderson 5 run (Andersen kick)
Atl — Anderson 14 run (Andersen kick)
Atl — FG Andersen 47

MINNESOTA 14, CAROLINA 12—at Metrodome, attendance 60,894. Cris Carter had 2 touchdown catches and the Vikings' defense forced 6 turnovers to give Minnesota a 5-1 record for the first time since 1992. Warren Moon found Carter twice in the end zone, the second of which came with 9:45 left in the third quarter to give the Vikins a 14-0 lead. Anthony Johnson had a 4-yard touchdown run with 2:12 left in the third quarter, and Michael Bates blocked a punt out of the end zone for a safety 1:09 later to cut the lead to five points. Carolina reached the Vikings 5-yard line midway through the fourth quarter, but had to settle for John Kasay's 22-yard field goal. Dewayne Washington's second interception of the game, with 3:08 remaining, ended the Panthers' comeback hopes. Both defenses played well, not allowing either team to exceed 300 yards. Robert Smith had 102 yards for the Vikings. Johnson set career-highs with 23 carries for 102 rushing yards.

Carolina	0	0	9	3	—	12
Minnesota	0	7	7	0	—	14

Minn — Carter 6 pass from Moon (Sisson kick)
Minn — Carter 3 pass from Moon (Sisson kick)
Car — Johnson 4 run (Kasay kick)
Car — Safety, Bates blocked punt out of end zone
Car — FG Kasay 22

GREEN BAY 37, CHICAGO 6—at Soldier Field, attendance 65,480. Brett Favre threw 4 touchdown passes and the Packers scored 2 touchdowns in the final 35 seconds of the first half to defeat the Bears. Following Jeff Jaeger's field goal with 2:12 left in the half, Favre threw a 2-yard touchdown pass to Keith Jackson with 35 seconds left to give the Packers a 14-3 advantage. Doug Evans's interception at midfield with 20 seconds left gave the Packers an opportunity for more. After two incompletions, Favre threw a 50-yard Hail Mary that Antonio Freeman caught in the end zone as the half expired. Jaeger kicked his second field goal on the Bears' first possession of the third quarter, but Don Beebe returned the ensuing kickoff 90 yards for a touchdown. Favre was 18 of 27 for 246 yards. Freeman caught 7 passes for 146 yards and 2 touchdowns. Dave Krieg completed 15 of 27 passes for 142 yards, but threw 3 interceptions.

Green Bay	0	20	14	3	—	37
Chicago	0	3	3	0	—	6

GB — Brooks 18 pass from Favre (Jacke kick)
Chi — FG Jaeger 40
GB — Jackson 2 pass from Favre (Jacke kick)
GB — Freeman 50 pass from Favre (kick failed)
Chi — FG Jaeger 41
GB — Beebe 90 kickoff return (Jacke kick)
GB — Freeman 35 pass from Favre (Jacke kick)
GB — FG Jacke 32

BUFFALO 16, INDIANAPOLIS 13 (OT)—at Rich Stadium, attendance 79,401. Doug Christie kicked a 39-yard field goal in overtime to defeat the Colts. Todd Collins, in just his third career start, completed 23 of 44 passes for 309 yards and a touchdown. Buffalo took a 10-0 lead five minutes into the third quarter. Cary Blanchard's field goal cut the deficit to 10-3, and the Colts drove 81 yards, with Jim Harbaugh connecting on 3 long passes to different receivers, before Marshall Faulk tied the game from a yard out on the opening play of the fourth quarter. Brian Stablein's punt return set up Blanchard's second field goal and gave the Colts the lead with 8:25 left. Buffalo got the ball on their own 22-yard line with 1:51 left. Collins led the Bills on a 58-yard drive, with a 21-yard pass to Quinn Early and 24-yard completion to Eric Moulds leading to Christie's tying field goal with 15 seconds left in regulation. Thurman Thomas gained 69 yards, and became just the eleventh player in NFL history to surpass 10,000 rushing yards in a career.

Indianapolis	0	0	3	10	0	—	13
Buffalo	0	7	3	3	3	—	16

Buff — Reed 30 pass from Collins (Christie kick)
Buff — FG Christie 42
Ind — FG Blanchard 44
Ind — Faulk 1 run (Blanchard kick)
Ind — FG Blanchard 41
Buff — FG Christie 37
Buff — FG Christie 39

NEW ORLEANS 17, JACKSONVILLE 13—at Louisiana Superdome, attendance 34,231. Jim Everett threw a 6-yard touchdown pass to Torrance Small with 1:45 remaining to give the Saints their first victory. The Saints jumped out to a 10-0 lead, but the Jaguars came back. With the scored tied 10-10, the Jaguars drove 64 yards down to the 2-yard line before having to settle for Mike Hollis's second field goal to take the lead with 5:15 left. Everett guided the Saints on the winning drive, with the big play being a 23-yard completion to Small on third-and-4 from their own 46-yard line. Mark Brunell completed 28 of 35 passes for 250 yards for Jacksonville. Each team committed 10 penalties.

Jacksonville	0	7	3	3	—	13
New Orleans	10	0	0	7	—	17

NO — Bates 1 run (Brien kick)
NO — FG Brien 27
Jack — Stewart 21 pass from Brunell (Hollis kick)
Jack — FG Hollis 36
Jack — FG Hollis 19
NO — Small 6 pass from Everett (Brien kick)

NEW ENGLAND 46, BALTIMORE 38—at Memorial Stadium, attendance 63,569. Drew Bledsoe threw for 4 touchdown passes to give the Patriots their first road victory.The game also marked the first-ever home defeat for the Ravens. The Ravens led 14-10 before the Patriots scored 24 points in a span of 9:24. After Bledsoe's touchdown pass to Ben Coates, Adam Vinatieri kicked a field goal as the first half expired to put the Patriots ahead 20-14. New England received the second half's opening kickoff and Bledsoe threw a touchdown pass to Mike Bartrum. The reception was the first of Bartrum's career. Bledsoe threw a 35-yard touchdown pass to Shawn Jefferson two plays after a Ravens punt to take a 35-14 lead. Bledsoe completed 7 of 7 passes for 104 yards on those first two drives of the second half. The Ravens scored 2 touchdowns in the final four minutes but were unable to recover an onside kick attempt for a chance to tie the game. Baltimore set an NFL record by recording 3 two-point conversions in the game. Bledsoe was 25 of 39 for 310 yards. Vinny Testaverde completed 29 of 45 passes for 353 yards. Michael Jackson had 8 receptions for 128 yards. The teams combined for 54 first downs and 827 total yards.

New England	3	17	15	11	—	46
Baltimore	0	14	0	24	—	38

NE — FG Vinatieri 22
Balt — Byner 4 run (Stover kick)
NE — Jefferson 7 pass from Bledsoe (Vinatieri kick)
Balt — Jackson 5 pass from Testaverde (Stover kick)
NE — Coates 1 pass from Bledsoe (Vinatieri kick)
NE — FG Vinatieri 35
NE — Bartrum 1 pass from Bledsoe (Gash pass from Bledsoe)
NE — Jefferson 35 pass from Bledsoe (Vinatieri kick)
NE — FG Vinatieri 50
Balt — Alexander 16 pass from Testaverde (Jackson pass from Testaverde)
NE — Bruschi 4 blocked punt return (Coates pass from Bledsoe)
Balt — Byner 5 run (Jackson pass from Testaverde)
Balt — Jackson 27 pass from Testaverde (Gardner run)

OAKLAND 34, N.Y. JETS 13—at Giants Stadium, attendance 63,611. Jeff Hostetler threw 3 touchdown passes and Joe Aska ran for a career-high 136 yards to propel the Raiders to victory. The Raiders compiled 222 rushing yards, and allowed just exactly half of that amount to the Jets. Derrick Fenner's 3-yard run to the 10-yard line on fourth-and-1 early in the fourth quarter set up Hostetler's 3-yard touchdown pass to Daryl Hobbs to give Oakland a 20-6 lead. Rickey Dudley caught his second touchdown pass of the day midway through the final quarter to give the Raiders a 27-6 advantage. Oakland's running game allowed it to control the ball (35:26-24:34), and their defense permitted just 5 first downs in 14 third-down attempts. Hostetler completed 17 of 28 for 188 yards. Neil O'Donnell separated his shoulder in the second quarter. His replacement, Frank Reich, was 15 of 31 for 177 yards and 2 interceptions. Adrian Murrell had 102 rushing yards for the Jets.

Nick Lowery kicked 2 field goals for the Jets, giving him 373 career field goals to tie him for first all-time with Pro Football Hall of Fame kicker Jan Steneurd.

Oakland	0	13	0	21	—	34
N.Y. Jets	0	3	3	7	—	13

Oak — FG Ford 26
Jets — FG Lowery 43
Oak — Dudley 23 pass from Hostetler (Ford kick)
Oak — FG Ford 35
Jets — FG Lowery 24
Oak — Hobbs 3 pass from Hostetler (Ford kick)
Oak — Dudley 2 pass from Hostetler (Ford kick)
Jets — Van Dyke 3 pass from Reich (Lowery kick)
Oak — Aska 30 run (Ford kick)

DENVER 28, SAN DIEGO 17—at Denver Mile High Stadium, attendance 75,058. John Elway threw 4 touchdown passes, 3 to Shannon Sharpe, to help the Broncos comeback from a 17-0 deficit to defeat the Chargers. Stan Humphries threw 2 touchdown passes just over four minutes apart in the second quarter as the Chargers bolted out to a 17-0 lead. Elway responded with 5-play, 80-yard drive in 1:32, capped by a 20-yard touchdown pass to Sharpe, to cut the deficit to 17-7 at halftime. After a second touchdown pass to Sharpe, Todd Kinchen's 26-yard punt return led to Elway's third touchdown pass to Sharpe and gave Denver its first lead of the game with 3:03 to play in the third quarter. Elway threw his fourth touchdown, a 9-yard pass to Ed McCaffrey, with 8:22 left to finish the scoring. Denver registered 23 first downs and 406 total yards. Elway completed 32 of 41 passes for 323 yards. Sharpe caught a career-high 13 passes for 153 yards. Humphries was 23 of 35 for 237 yards, with Terrell Fletcher hauling in 10 receptions.

San Diego	3	14	0	0	—	17
Denver	0	7	14	7	—	28

SD — FG Carney 27
SD — Fletcher 5 pass from Humphries (Carney kick)
SD — Martin 6 pass from Humphries (Carney kick)
Den — Sharpe 20 pass from Elway (Elam kick)
Den — Sharpe 20 pass from Elway (Elam kick)
Den — Sharpe 3 pass from Elway (Elam kick)
Den — McCaffrey 9 pass from Elway (Elam kick)

SAN FRANCISCO 28, ST. LOUIS 11—at Trans World Dome, attendance 61,260. Elvis Grbac threw 3 touchdown passes and the defense forced 2 turnovers that led to scores to put the 49ers back into first place. Grbac, who was playing for Steve Young could rest a nagging groin injury, completed 20 of 32 passes for 222 yards. Two of his touchdown passes went to Ted Popson. Leading 7-0 in the second quarter, Merton Hanks intercepted a pass near midfield. Grbac threw a 30-yard pass to Terry Kirby down to the 4-yard line before Kirby ran in from 1-yard out to put the 49ers ahead 14-0. Popson scored his second touchdown 1:06 later after Ken Norton, Jr. returned a fumble down to the 9-yard line. The 49ers outgained the Rams 389-202 and forced 4 turnovers. Jerry Rice had 7 receptions for 108 yards and a fourth-quarter touchdown catch.

San Francisco	7	14	0	7	—	28
St. Louis	0	0	3	8	—	11

SF — Popson 1 pass from Grbac (Wilkins kick)
SF — Kirby 1 run (Wilkins kick)
SF — Popson 9 pass from Grbac (Wilkins kick)
StL — FG Lohmiller 28
SF — Rice 31 pass from Grbac (Wilkins kick)
StL — Green 3 pass from Banks (Banks run)

SEATTLE 22, MIAMI 15—at Pro Player Stadium, attendance 59,539. In his first start of the season John Friesz threw 3 long touchdown passes, including an 80-yard connection with Brian Blades with 2:03 left, to win the game in the rain of southern Florida. Friesz beat the blitz on his first touchdown pass, throwing to Joey Galloway, who was facing one-on-one coverage and outjumped Calvin Jackson for the ball. Galloway came down with the ball and finished the 65-yard touchdown on the final play of the first quarter. Less than three minutes later the same combination hit again, as Galloway ran a crossing route and scored on a 51-yard play. Randal Hill caught a touchdown pass from Craig Erickson in the second quarter, and Irving Spikes's 2-yard touchdown run in the third quarter gave the Dolphins the lead. Facing third-and-10 with just over two minutes remaining in the game, Friesz found Blades on a crossing pattern for the winning points. Friesz was 18 of 32 passes for 301 yards. Galloway had 5 receptions for 139 yards. The game was played in rain, and contributed to four fumbles by Craig Erickson, who was making his first start of the season. Erickson completed 16 of 28 passes for 243 yards. Neither team averaged 3 yards per carry.

Seattle	7	7	0	8	—	22
Miami	3	6	6	0	—	15

Mia — FG Nedney 20
Sea — Galloway 65 pass from Friesz (Peterson kick)
Sea — Galloway 51 pass from Friesz (Peterson kick)
Mia — Hill 33 pass from Erickson (run failed)
Mia — Spikes 2 run (run failed)
Sea — Blades 80 pass from Friesz (L. Smith run)

SUNDAY NIGHT, OCTOBER 6

HOUSTON 30, CINCINNATI 27 (OT)—at Cinergy Field, attendance 44,680. Al Del Greco made a 49-yard field goal in overtime to propel the Oilers into second place in the AFC Central. Jimmy Spencer had a fumble return for a touchdown and an interception that led to Doug Pelfrey's second field goal and a 13-10 halftime lead for Cincinnati. Jeff Cothran's 2-yard touchdown run gave the Bengals a 20-10 lead with 9:49 left in the third quarter. The Oilers responded with the help of rookie running back Eddie George. The Heisman Trophy winner, who played his college ball at Ohio State, relished the return home by racing 45 yards for a touchdown. George finished with 152 yards. Mel Gray's punt return set up Del Greco's tying field goal early in the fourth quarter. Cincinnati responded with an 11-play, 66-yard drive that consumed more than six minutes and was capped by Jeff Blake's 1-yard touchdown pass to Darnay Scott. Mel Gray returned the ensuing kickoff 88 yards to set up Chris Chandler's 7-yard touchdown pass to Derek Russell to tie the game with 5:15 left. The Bengals had an opportunity to win in regulation, but Pelfrey's 41-yard field goal attempt sailed wide right. The Oilers held the Bengals to three plays and a punt at the start of overtime, and then put together a 51-yard drive, keyed by Chandler's 37-yard pass to Willie Davis, to allow Del Greco's winning kick. Chandler was 18 of 32 for 193 yards.

Houston	3	7	7	10	3	—	30
Cincinnati	0	13	7	7	0	—	27

Hou — FG Del Greco 40
Cin — FG Pelfrey 41
Hou — Wycheck 9 pass from Chandler (Del Greco kick)
Cin — Spencer 59 fumble return (Pelfrey kick)
Cin — FG Pelfrey 31
Cin — Cothran 2 run (Pelfrey kick)
Hou — George 45 run (Del Greco kick)
Hou — FG Del Greco 32
Cin — Scott 1 pass from Blake (Pelfrey kick)
Hou — Russell 7 pass from Chandler (Del Greco kick)
Hou — FG Del Greco 49

MONDAY, OCTOBER 7

PITTSBURGH 17, KANSAS CITY 7—at Arrowhead Stadium, attendance 79,189. Jerome Bettis ran for 103 yards and a touchdown to give the Steelers their fourth consecutive victory. Marcus Allen's 107th career touchdown, three shy of Walter Payton's record, gave the Chiefs a 7-0 lead. Pittsburgh drove to the 4-yard line twice in the final five minutes of the half before settling for 2 Norm Johnson field goals. The Steelers reached as far as the 2-yard line in the third quarter before being stopped. Johnson attempted another field goal, only to have it blocked by Derrick Thomas. The Steelers finally reached the end zone on Bettis's run and the combination of Mike Tomczak and Mark Bruener added the 2-point conversion. Tomczak completed 20 of 32 passes for 338 yards. Charles Johnson had 6 receptions for 125 yards. Johnson and Bettis's 100-yard performances were the first by a Steelers pair since 1992 (Barry Foster and Jeff Graham). The combination of the dual 100-yard efforts and Tomczak's 300-yard passing display marked the first time the Chiefs had allowed that trifecta since the Chargers did it in 1965. The defeat broke an NFL-best 11-game home-winning streak for the Chiefs.

Pittsburgh	0	6	8	3	—	17
Kansas City	0	7	0	0	—	7

KC — Allen 6 run (Stoyanovich kick)
Pitt — FG N. Johnson 21
Pitt — FG N. Johnson 32
Pitt — Bettis 5 run (Bruener pass from Tomczak)
Pitt — FG N.Johnson 43

SEVENTH WEEK SUMMARIES
AMERICAN FOOTBALL CONFERENCE

Eastern Division	W	L	T	Pct.	Pts.	OP
Indianapolis	5	1	0	.833	115	87
Buffalo	4	2	0	.667	79	95
Miami	4	2	0	.667	140	86
New England	3	3	0	.500	147	131
N.Y. Jets	0	7	0	.000	92	187

Central Division						
Pittsburgh	5	1	0	.833	131	80
Houston	4	2	0	.667	151	130
Jacksonville	3	4	0	.429	137	136
Baltimore	2	4	0	.333	125	156
Cincinnati	1	5	0	.167	107	132

Western Division						
Denver	5	1	0	.833	144	93
Kansas City	4	2	0	.667	117	92
San Diego	4	2	0	.667	145	144
Oakland	3	4	0	.429	156	134
Seattle	2	4	0	.333	93	153

NATIONAL FOOTBALL CONFERENCE

Eastern Division	W	L	T	Pct.	Pts.	OP
Washington	5	1	0	.833	130	78
Philadelphia	4	2	0	.667	125	121
Dallas	3	3	0	.500	104	79
Arizona	2	4	0	.333	85	148
N.Y. Giants	2	4	0	.333	68	116

Central Division						
Green Bay	6	1	0	.857	227	92
Minnesota	5	2	0	.714	127	116
Detroit	4	3	0	.571	162	124
Chicago	2	5	0	.286	104	152
Tampa Bay	1	5	0	.167	69	139

Western Division						
Carolina	4	2	0	.667	145	84
San Francisco	4	2	0	.667	155	85
New Orleans	2	5	0	.286	114	161
St. Louis	1	5	0	.167	88	171
Atlanta	0	6	0	.000	95	175

SUNDAY, OCTOBER 13

DALLAS 17, ARIZONA 3—at Texas Stadium, attendance 64,096. Dallas used a great defensive effort and Emmitt Smith's 100th and 101st career rushing touchdowns to defeat the Cardinals. The game also marked the return of Michael Irvin, who had finished serving a five-game suspension. Irvin caught 5 passes, 2 of which set up Chris Boniol's 23-yard field goal five seconds before intermission for the only scoring of the first half. Smith's 1-yard touchdown run late in third quarter capped a 7-minute, 25-second drive. His final touchdown, a 13-yard blast up the middle, clinched the Cowboys' victory with 2:03 remaining. The Cowboys' defense dominated, allowing the Cardinals just 178 total yards. Arizona was forced to punt its first seven possessions. A pass interference penalty on fourth down kept the Cardinals' eighth drive alive, with Greg Davis's 49-yard field goal putting Arizona on the board with 5:49 remaining. The game featured just 2 turnovers and 5 penalties, and was played in two hours and 35 minutes.

Arizona	0	0	0	3	—	3
Dallas	0	3	7	7	—	17

Dall — FG Boniol 23
Dall — E. Smith 3 run (Boniol kick)
Ariz — FG Davis 49
Dall — E. Smith 13 run (Boniol kick)

NEW ORLEANS 27, CHICAGO 24—at Louisiana Superdome, attendance 43,512. Doug Brien's career-long 54-yard field goal with 1:44 remaining gave the Saints their second consecutive victory. The winning drive began from the Saints' own 33 following a disputed missed field goal by Jeff Jaeger with 3:52 left. Ray Zellars, whose 3-yard run tied the game 24-24 with 10:12 remaining, had 4 carries for 39 yards to help the Saints get in Brien's range for the winning kick. Zellars ran for a career-high 174 yards on 20 carries. He had gained only 242 yards in his previous seven-

teen NFL games. New Orleans, which ranked last in the NFL in rushing, compiled 205 yards on the ground. Both quarterbacks were efficient: Chicago's Dave Krieg completed 19 of 28 pass attempts for 247 yards and 3 touchdowns; Jim Everett was 22 of 31 for 223 yards, 2 touchdowns, and 1 interception. Curtis Conway had 7 receptions for 111 yards and 2 touchdowns for Chicago. The Bears, who blew two 10-point leads during the game, lost despite forcing 4 turnovers while giving the ball up just once.

Chicago	3	14	7	0	—	24
New Orleans	0	7	10	10	—	27

Chi — FG Jaeger 28
Chi — Conway 18 pass from Krieg (Jaeger kick)
NO — DeRamus 28 pass from Everett (Brien kick)
Chi — Spears 1 pass from Krieg (Jaeger kick)
NO — FG Brien 34
NO — Haynes 5 pass from Everett (Brien kick)
Chi — Conway 53 pass from Krieg (Jaeger kick)
NO — Zellars 3 run (Brien kick)
NO — FG Brien 54

PITTSBURGH 20, CINCINNATI 10—at Three Rivers Stadium, attendance 58,875. The Steelers defense recorded 10 sacks and scored a game-clinching fourth quarter touchdown to give Pittsburgh its fifth consecutive victory. Leading 13-3 with 3:29 remaining, the Steelers' Levon Kirkland blitzed Jeff Blake on a fourth-and-1 play from midfield. Blake fumbled, and Rod Woodson picked up the ball and ran 42 yards to put Pittsburgh ahead 20-3. Blake, who connected on 23 of 30 pass attempts while facing an intense pass rush, threw a 3-yard touchdown pass to Carl Pickens with 1:20 remaining. Pittsburgh recovered the ensuing onside kick and ran out the clock. Trailing 3-0, the Bengals had a chance to take the lead, but tight end Tony McGee was stopped at the 2-yard line on a third-and-goal situation in the third quarter, thus settling for Doug Pelfrey's field goal. The Steelers answered with a two-minute, four-play drive, capped by Kordell Stewart's 32-yard touchdown on a screen pass to take the lead for good. Chad Brown had 4½ sacks, the most by any player since Derrick Thomas recorded an NFL-record 7 in 1991. Jerome Bettis gained 109 yards, eclipsing the 100-yard barrier for the fifth consecutive game.

Cincinnati	0	0	3	7	—	10
Pittsburgh	3	0	7	10	—	20

Pitt — FG Johnson 33
Cin — FG Pelfrey 19
Pitt — Stewart 32 pass from Tomczak (Johnson kick)
Pitt — FG Johnson 22
Pitt — Woodson 42 fumble return (Johnson kick)
Cin — Pickens 3 pass from Blake (Pelfrey kick)

OAKLAND 37, DETROIT 21—at Oakland-Alameda County Coliseum, attendance 50,037. Jeff Hostetler threw 4 touchdown passes, 2 to James Jett, as the Raiders held off the Lions. Staked to a 20-0 halftime lead, the Raiders took just six plays to score 2 touchdowns on bombs to Jett (58 yards) and Rickey Dudley (62 yards). Trailing 34-0, the Lions woke up. Scott Mitchell threw 3 touchdown passes in the final 7:51 of the third quarter to cut the deficit to 34-21. Detroit got the ball back twice, but was stopped on downs with 8:38 left. Larry Brown's interception with 3:45 remaining set up Cole Ford's third field goal to seal the victory. Hostetler completed 27 of 38 passes for 295 yards and 4 touchdowns. Mitchell had a great third quarter (14 of 18, 177 yards, and 3 touchdowns), but struggled the other quarters (17 for 32 for 176 yards, and 2 interceptions). Jett tallied 112 receiving yards on 7 receptions, while Herman Moore and Johnnie Morton each had 109 receiving yards for Detroit. Oakland's mistake-free offense controlled the ball for 36 minutes 15 seconds.

Detroit	0	0	21	0	—	21
Oakland	7	13	14	3	—	37

Oak — Jett 4 pass from Hostetler (Ford kick)
Oak — FG Ford 29
Oak — FG Ford 23
Oak — Kaufman 10 pass from Hostetler (Ford kick)
Oak — Jett 58 pass from Hostetler (Ford kick)
Oak — Dudley 62 pass from Hostetler (Ford kick)
Det — Moore 11 pass from Mitchell (Hanson kick)
Det — Moore 6 pass from Mitchell (Hanson kick)
Det — Morton 19 pass from Mitchell (Hanson kick)
Oak — FG Ford 33

HOUSTON 23, ATLANTA 13—at Georgia Dome, attendance 35,401. Rookie running back Eddie George ran for 109 yards, topping the 100-yard plateau for the third time, as the Houston Oilers defeated the winless Falcons. A 62-yard touchdown pass from Chris Chandler to Chris Sanders on a third-and-1 late in the first quarter staked the Oilers to a 7-0 lead. Chandler, however, had to leave the game before halftime with a strained groin. The Oilers' 1995 first-round draft pick, Steve McNair, did a solid job replacing Chandler. McNair's 10-yard run capped a 9-play, 63-yard drive in the third quarter to put Houston ahead 17-0. Al Del Greco aided the Oilers cause by booting 3 field goals. The first two followed Oilers interceptions, and the final kick was set up by 37- and 15-yard runs by George. Bobby Hebert, starting his third consecutive game, completed 31 of 46 passes for 279 yards. He threw 2 touchdown passes, both to Terance Mathis. Mathis' 3-yard reception with 10:27 remaining concluded a 24-yard drive after the Falcons recovered a fumbled punt return to cut the lead to 20-7. The second touchdown, with 1:56 remaining, gave the Falcons a chance to pull within a score of tying Houston, but Hebert's two-point conversion pass fell incomplete. The Oilers recovered the ensuing onside kick to run out the clock. The Falcons threw twice as many passes (46-23), but Houston outgained the Falcons 121-55 on the ground.

Houston	7	3	7	6	—	23
Atlanta	0	0	0	13	—	13

Hou — Sanders 62 pass from Chandler (Del Greco kick)
Hou — FG Del Greco 27
Hou — McNair 10 run (Del Greco kick)
Hou — FG Del Greco 35
Atl — Mathis 3 pass from Hebert (Andersen kick)
Hou — FG Del Greco 33
Atl — Mathis 1 pass from Hebert (pass failed)

MIAMI 21, BUFFALO 7—at Rich Stadium, attendance 79,642. Dolphins cornerback Terrell Buckley's 91-yard interception return with 47 seconds remaining gave Miami a big divisional road victory. Trailing 14-7, Andre Reed hauled in a Jim Kelly pass at the Dolphins' 30 and raced down the sideline before being dragged down by Buckley at the 2-yard line with 1:55 remaining. On first down, Kelly threw the ball out of the end zone, and was penalized for intentional grounding. From the 12-yard line, Kelly threw an incompletion, and Thurman Thomas ran 2 yards to set up fourth-and-goal. Kelly's pass was intended for Reed, but Buckley stepped in front of it at the goal line, bobbled the ball before grasping it at the nine, and raced down the left sideline with the game-clinching touchdown. The victory pulled the Dolphins into second place in the AFC East. It also broke the team's eight-game winless streak when playing without Dan Marino, who was still recovering from a broken ankle. In his place, Craig Erickson completed 14 of 29 passes for 192 yards for 0 touchdowns and, more importantly, 0 interceptions. His 61-yard pass to Randal Hill set up Irving Spikes's 1-yard run that put Miami ahead 14-0. Buffalo's defense held the Dolphins to just 239 total yards, including only 37 yards on 25 carries by rookie Karim Abdul-Jabbar. The Dolphins defense, despite starting four rookies, had a big game. They tallied 7 sacks, a game-high 2½ by Trace Armstrong, and forced 4 turnovers. Buffalo quarterback Jim Kelly, in his first game since returning from a right hamstring injury, completed 21 of 32 passes for 247 yards, but threw 3 interceptions. Reed caught 10 passes for 134 yards.

Miami	0	7	7	7	—	21
Buffalo	0	0	7	0	—	7

Mia — Abdul-Jabbar 3 run (Nedney kick)
Mia — Spikes 1 run (Nedney kick)
Buff — Thomas 19 run (Christie kick)
Mia — Buckley 91 interception return (Nedney kick)

TAMPA BAY 24, MINNESOTA 13—at Houlihan's Stadium, attendance 32,175. Trent Dilfer threw 3 touchdown passes to help put the Buccaneers in the win column. The victory served as coach Tony Dungy's first as a head coach. It came at the expense of his old team, the Vikings, where he had served as the defensive coordinator the previous four seasons. Dilfer, who was the second-lowest rated passer in the NFL going into the game, completed 22 of 35 pass attempts for 218 yards and 0 interceptions. It was the first time in eleven games he did not throw an interception, and only the second multi-touchdown passing game of the third-year quarterback's career. Two of Dilfer's scoring tosses went to Robb Thomas, the second of which gave the Bucs a 21-10 lead with 9:19 remaining. That touchdown was set up due to Dewayne Washington's 37-yard pass interference penalty on third-and-14 two plays earlier. The Vikings got the ball back on their own 30 with 2:12 left, trailing 21-13. But Warren Sapp sacked Warren Moon on the first play, forcing a fumble that Chidi Ahanotu recovered. Michael Husted's ensuing field goal with 43 seconds left iced the game and knocked the Vikings out of first place. Robert Smith gained a career-high 133 yards on 18 carries in defeat.

Minnesota	7	0	3	3	—	13
Tampa Bay	0	0	7	17	—	24

Minn — Smith 26 run (Sisson kick)
TB — R. Thomas 31 pass from Dilfer (Husted kick)
Minn — FG Sisson 33
TB — Alstott 12 pass from Dilfer (Husted kick)
TB — R. Thomas 11 pass from Dilfer (Husted kick)
Minn — FG Sisson 32
TB — FG Husted 35

JACKSONVILLE 21, N.Y. JETS 17—at Jacksonville Municipal Stadium, attendance 65,699. Mark Brunell threw 2 touchdown passes to lead the Jaguars to victory. The winless Jets took a 14-3 lead on Frank Reich's 2 touchdown passes. Reich started in place of the injured Neil O'Donnell. Rookie Kevin Hardy intercepted a pass to set up Mike Hollis's second field goal, cutting the deficit to 14-6. Jacksonville then took just six plays to go 93 yards, keyed by Jimmy Smith's 62-yard reception and ending with his 15-yard touchdown catch, to pull the Jaguars within two. Going for the two-point conversion with 1:51 still left in the first half, Brunell hit Willie Jackson with the tying points. On third-and-2 from the Jets' 41-yard line in the third quarter, Jackson took a short pass and raced down the left sideline for the go-ahead score. The Jets got close with 10:59 remaining when Nick Lowery booted his NFL-record 374th field goal, breaking the mark of Pro Football Hall of Fame kicker Jan Stenerud. Wayne Chrebet's career-high 12th reception got the Jets down to the Jaguars' 31-yard line with 1:17 left. However, four consecutive incompletions ended the Jets' chances. The Jets outgained Jacksonville, 367-289, and had more first downs, 24-10, in the losing cause. Brunell, the NFL passing yardage leader, threw for 248 yards on 14 of 23 attempts. Smith had 135 yards on 5 receptions. Chrebet totaled 162 receiving yards for the Jets. The win gave Jacksonville a 3-1 home record.

N.Y. Jets	7	7	0	3	—	17
Jacksonville	3	11	7	0	—	21

Jax — FG Hollis 35
NYJ — Murrell 14 pass from Reich (Lowery kick)
NYJ — Chrebet 12 pass from Reich (Lowery kick)
Jax — FG Hollis 40
Jax — Smith 15 pass from Brunell (Jackson pass from Brunell)
Jax — Jackson 41 pass from Brunell (Hollis kick)
NYJ — FG Lowery 20

PHILADELPHIA 19, N.Y. GIANTS 10—at Giants Stadium, attendance 72,729. William Thomas's 23-yard fumble return and 4 Gary Anderson field goals gave the Eagles a come-from-behind victory. Anderson booted 2 field goals in a 4:26 span that pulled the Eagles to within 10-9 of the Giants with 14:01 remaining in the game. The Eagles defense continued to stymie the Giants attack, forcing Mike Horan's ninth punt with 8:05 remaining. The Eagles went on a 14-play, 68-yard drive, featuring 8 carries by Ricky Watters for 40 of his game-high 110 yards, to set up Anderson's go-ahead 29-yard field goal with 2:12 left. On the

next play from scrimmage Dave Brown fumbled while attempting to throw the ball away. Thomas picked up the ball and ran into the end zone for the game-clinching score. The Giants mustered just 150 yards, 9 first downs, and did not run a play inside the Eagles' 20-yard line. The Giants put up a great defensive effort in which they did not allow an offensive touchdown for the third consecutive game. Ty Detmer, in his first NFL start, completed 18 of 33 passes for 170 yards. Brown, who was sacked 8 times, threw for just 105 yards on 11 of 25 passing. Rookie Amani Toomer's second punt return-touchdown of the season marked the only time the Giants reached the end zone.

| Philadelphia | 0 | 3 | 3 | 13 | — | 19 |
| N.Y. Giants | 3 | 7 | 0 | 0 | — | 10 |

NYG — FG Daluiso 39
Phil — FG Anderson 39
NYG — Toomer 65 punt return (Daluiso kick)
Phil — FG Anderson 46
Phil — FG Anderson 45
Phil — FG Anderson 29
Phil — W. Thomas 23 fumble return (Anderson kick)

CAROLINA 45, ST. LOUIS 13—at Ericsson Stadium, attendance 70,535. The Carolina Panthers scored a team-record 45 points as they handed the visiting St. Louis Rams their fifth consecutive loss. Following the San Francisco 49ers' loss on Monday, the Panthers vaulted into first place in the NFC West. Kerry Collins fired 3 touchdown passes, 2 to tight end Wesley Walls. Late in the first quarter, Rams rookie quarterback Tony Banks fumbled while scrambling out of the pocket. Kevin Greene scooped up the ball and lumbered 66 yards for his first touchdown since 1987, and just the second of his career. Collins then hit Muhsin Muhammad, a rookie wide receiver making his first career start, with a 54-yard touchdown pass to put the Panthers in front, 21-0. Rams cornerback Anthony Parker scored his fifth defensive touchdown in 2½ seasons to cut the Panthers' lead to 21-7. Michael Bates ran the ensuing kickoff back 15 yards, but the Rams were called for offside. St. Louis kicked off again, and Bates went 93 yards for a touchdown. The Panthers' defense, which allowed the Rams only 219 total yards, and compiled 5 sacks, held them scoreless in the second half to handily win the game. The Panthers averaged 8.9 yards per pass and permitted the Rams just 3.4 yards per attempt. Anthony Johnson, starting in place of running back Tim Biakabutuka (out for the season), ran for a club-record 126 yards. The win gave the Panthers a perfect 3-0 record at their new home, Ericsson Stadium. Combined with their performance at Clemson Stadium in 1995, the Panthers won eight of their last nine home games, allowing the oppositon to score just 12.1 points per game. Rams rookie Eddie Kennison had 8 receptions for 93 yards and 1 touchdown.

| St. Louis | 0 | 13 | 0 | 0 | — | 13 |
| Carolina | 14 | 14 | 10 | 7 | — | 45 |

Car — Walls 9 pass from Collins (Kasay kick)
Car — Greene 66 fumble return (Kasay kick)
Car — Muhammad 54 pass from Collins (Kasay kick)
StL — Parker 22 interception return (Lohmiller kick)
Car — Bates 93 kickoff return (Kasay kick)
StL — Kennison 12 pass from Banks (kick failed)
Car — FG Kasay 22
Car — Walls 19 pass from Collins (Kasay kick)
Car — Philyaw 2 run (Kasay kick)

WASHINGTON 27, NEW ENGLAND 22—at Foxboro Stadium, attendance 59,638. Henry Ellard caught 8 passes for 152 yards and 1 touchdown as the Redskins stayed in first place in the NFC East. Ellard's touchdown catch, from 13 yards, was the second of 2 Redskins touchdowns in the third quarter, increasing their lead to 24-16. Curtis Martin's second touchdown, from 2 yards with 5:33 remaining, cut the lead to 24-22. The Patriots stopped for the 2-point conversion, but the Redskins stopped Martin on a sweep play to the right. Ellard then kept the ensuing drive going with 2 third-down receptions. Scott Blanton's second field goal, from 24 yards with 56 seconds left, clinched the victory. Drew Bledsoe threw 4 consecutive incompletions from the Patriots' 33 to end New England's hopes. Gus Frerotte threw for 280 yards and 2 touchdowns. Terry Allen, who gained 71 yards, saw his streak of 10 consecutive games scoring a touchdown end. Martin ran for 164

yards on 17 carries, while Bledsoe completed just 23 of 48 pass attempts in a losing cause.

| Washington | 3 | 7 | 14 | 3 | — | 27 |
| New England | 6 | 10 | 0 | 6 | — | 22 |

NE — FG Vinatieri 24
Wash — FG Blanton 21
NE — FG Vinatieri 35
Wash — Shepherd 32 run (Blanton kick)
NE — Martin 3 run (Vinatieri kick)
NE — FG Vinatieri 29
Wash — Asher 13 pass from Frerotte (Blanton kick)
Wash — Ellard 14 pass from Frerotte (Blanton kick)
NE — Martin 2 run (run failed)
Wash — FG Blanton 24

SUNDAY NIGHT, OCTOBER 13

INDIANAPOLIS 26, BALTIMORE 21—at RCA Dome, attendance 56,978. Jeff Herrod's 68-yard interception return was the deciding factor as the Colts defeated the Ravens in the first game that featured the two teams with links to Baltimore. The Ravens, having moved from Cleveland during the offseason, took a 14-13 lead early in the third quarter on Derrick Alexander's second touchdown catch of the game. However the Colts, who moved from Baltimore to Indianapolis in 1984, responded with a 1-yard run by Marshall Faulk to retake the lead. On the next possession, Herrod intercepted Vinny Testaverde's pass, his first interception since 1993, and returned it into the end zone to put the Colts ahead 26-14. Testaverde's third touchdown pass, to Calvin Williams from 3 yards out with 4:09 left, cut the deficit to five. The Ravens got the ball back, but Alexander dropped a 40-yard pass that would have put the Ravens inside the Colts' 20 with 1:39 remaining. The Colts executed 38 rushing plays, passing just 19 times while controlling the ball for more than 34 minutes. It was a costly loss to the Ravens, who saw defensive linemen Dan Footman and Rob Burnett suffer season-ending injuries.

| Baltimore | 0 | 7 | 7 | 7 | — | 21 |
| Indianapolis | 3 | 10 | 7 | 6 | — | 26 |

Ind — FG Blanchard 27
Ind — Stablein 30 pass from Harbaugh (Blanchard kick)
Balt — Alexander 23 pass from Testaverde (Stover kick)
Ind — FG Blanchard 30
Balt — Alexander 5 pass from Testaverde (Stover kick)
Ind — Faulk 1 run (Blanchard kick)
Ind — Herrod 68 interception return (pass failed)
Balt — Williams 3 pass from Testaverde (Stover kick)

MONDAY, OCTOBER 14

GREEN BAY 23, SAN FRANCISCO 20 (OT)—at Lambeau Field, attendance 60,716. Chris Jacke's 53-yard field goal, the longest in overtime history, gave the Packers the best record in the NFL. Jacke's fifth field goal capped a wild game that saw the Packers outgain the 49ers 446-253 yards and gain an important edge for home-field advantage in the postseason. Brett Favre completed 28 of a career-high 61 pass attempts, for 395 yards, 1 touchdown, and 2 interceptions. Favre's touchdown pass was a 59-yard play to Don Beebe, who made a diving catch at the 30-yard line. After the catch, Beebe got up and ran into the end zone. The 49ers scored their only two touchdowns during a 1 minute, 57 seconds span late in the second quarter. Jerry Rice caught both touchdown passes, the latter one 23 seconds before halftime, was set up by Dana Stubblefield's second career interception. With the score tied 17-17, Marquez Pope intercepted a Favre pass, returning it to the Packers 13 with 2:07 remaining. The 49ers did not attempt a pass, and settled for Jeff Wikins' 28-yard field goal with 1:50 left. The Packers were then helped on a holding and subsequent unsportsmanlike conduct penalty on Steve Israel. The 20 yards of penalties, and 2 passes to Antonio Freeman, set up Jacke's tying boot with eight seconds left in regulation. After forcing the 49ers to punt to begin overtime, Favre hit Beebe with a 13-yard pass to get to the San Francisco 40. Jacke then converted the game-winning kick. Beebe, who caught 11 passes for 220 yards, was pressed into service after the Packers leading receiver, Robert Brooks, injured his knee on Green Bay's first play from scrimmage, knocking him out for the season.

| San Francisco | 0 | 17 | 0 | 3 | 0 | — | 20 |
| Green Bay | 6 | 0 | 8 | 6 | 3 | — | 23 |

GB — FG Jacke 30
GB — FG Jacke 25
SF — FG Wilkins 48
SF — Rice 7 pass from Grbac (Wilkins kick)
SF — Rice 13 pass from Grbac (Wilkins kick)
GB — Beebe 59 pass from Favre (Bennett pass from Favre)
GB — FG Jacke 35
SF — FG Wilkins 28
GB — FG Jacke 31
GB — FG Jacke 53

EIGHTH WEEK SUMMARIES

AMERICAN FOOTBALL CONFERENCE

Eastern Division	W	L	T	Pct.	Pts.	OP
Buffalo	5	2	0	.714	104	117
Indianapolis	5	2	0	.714	124	114
Miami	4	3	0	.571	168	121
New England	4	3	0	.571	174	140
N.Y. Jets	0	8	0	.000	114	212
Central Division						
Houston	5	2	0	.714	174	143
Pittsburgh	5	2	0	.714	144	103
Jacksonville	3	5	0	.375	151	153
Baltimore	2	5	0	.286	159	201
Cincinnati	1	6	0	.143	128	160
Western Division						
Denver	6	1	0	.857	189	127
Kansas City	5	2	0	.714	151	108
San Diego	4	3	0	.571	159	167
Oakland	4	4	0	.500	179	148
Seattle	2	5	0	.286	109	187

NATIONAL FOOTBALL CONFERENCE

Eastern Division	W	L	T	Pct.	Pts.	OP
Washington	6	1	0	.857	161	99
Philadelphia	5	2	0	.714	160	149
Dallas	4	3	0	.571	136	107
Arizona	3	4	0	.429	98	157
N.Y. Giants	2	5	0	.286	89	147
Central Division						
Green Bay	6	1	0	.857	227	92
Minnesota	5	2	0	.714	127	116
Detroit	4	3	0	.571	162	124
Chicago	2	5	0	.286	104	152
Tampa Bay	1	6	0	.143	78	152
Western Division						
Carolina	5	2	0	.714	164	91
San Francisco	5	2	0	.714	183	106
St. Louis	2	5	0	.286	105	185
New Orleans	2	6	0	.250	121	180
Atlanta	0	7	0	.000	123	207

THURSDAY, OCTOBER 17

KANSAS CITY 34, SEATTLE 16—at Arrowhead Stadium, attendance 76,057. Marcus Allen's 108th and 109th career rushing touchdowns helped lead the Kansas City Chiefs to a 34-16 victory over the Seattle Seahawks. Allen is just 1 touchdown shy of Walter Payton's record for rushing touchdowns. Steve Bono, over the course of the game's first two drives, completed 7 of his first 9 pass attempts as the Chiefs took a 10-0 lead. A 13-play, 81-yard drive, which featured 3 offside penalties on the Seahawks, ended with Allen's 1-yard touchdown run to put Kansas City ahead 17-0. Todd Peterson's 24-yard field goal 26 seconds before halftime pulled the Seahawks within 14 points. However, 2 pass completions and 2 more offside penalties put the Chiefs in field goal range, with Pete Stoyanovich's 43-yard kick ending the half. Chris Warren's 50-yard gallop after a Greg Hill fumble pulled Seattle within ten points, but the Chiefs added 2 touchdowns to pull away. Bono completed 17 of 26 passes for 194 yards, 1 touchdown, and his cadence helped baited during two scoring drives. John Friesz threw for 238 yards in defeat.

| Seattle | 0 | 3 | 7 | 6 | — | 16 |
| Kansas City | 10 | 10 | 7 | 7 | — | 34 |

KC — FG Stoyanovich 45
KC — Anders 15 run (Stoyanovich kick)
KC — Allen 1 run (Stoyanovich kick)
Sea — FG Peterson 24
KC — FG Stoyanovich 43
Sea — Warren 50 run (Peterson kick)
KC — Allen 1 run (Stoyanovich kick)
KC — Lachapelle 4 pass from Bono (Stoyanovich kick)

Sea — Galloway 16 pass from Friesz
(run failed)

SUNDAY, OCTOBER 20

DALLAS 32, ATLANTA 28—at Texas Stadium, attendance 64,091. Kelvin Martin's 60-yard touchdown reception with 1:42 remaining gave Dallas a come-from-behind victory. The play, in which Martin caught a slant pass over the middle and went untouched into the end zone, thwarted the winless Falcons upset bid of the Super Bowl champions. Atlanta had taken a 28-25 lead on Morten Andersen's fifth field goal, a 37-yard kick, with 7:09 remaining. Dallas started the winning drive at the 7-yard line after forcing a Falcons punt with 2:46 left. Troy Aikman completed 3 passes, including a 24-yard connection to Martin just prior to the touchdown. The Falcons reached their own 41 as time was running out. Browning Nagle, who has a stronger arm than starter Bobby Hebert, ran onto the field to take the final snap but Broderick Thomas sacked Nagle to end the game. Two long kickoff returns by Herschel Walker, an 89-yard return to start the game and a 43-yard effort after the Cowboys fell behind 25-17, led to two Dallas touchdowns. The Falcons scored 12 points in a 2 minute, 53 second span late in the first half, due to two Cowboys fumbles deep in their own territory, to take an 18-17 halftime lead. Hebert completed 25 of 40 passes for 272 yards, 101 of those yards going to Terance Mathis. Michael Irvin, in his second game since being suspended, caught 7 passes for 119 yards. Aikman threw just 24 passes, but had 17 completions for 265 yards. Atlanta lost despite controlling the ball for 41 minutes, 22 seconds.

Atlanta	3	15	7	3	—	28
Dallas	7	10	8	7	—	32

Dall — E. Smith 9 pass from Aikman
(Boniol kick)
Atl — FG Andersen 23
Dall — E. Smith 1 run (Boniol kick)
Atl — FG Andersen 54
Dall — FG Boniol 49
Atl — Hebert 1 run (run failed)
Atl — FG Andersen 32
Atl — FG Andersen 28
Atl — Emanuel 4 pass from Hebert
(Andersen kick)
Dall — E. Smith 3 run (Irvin pass from Aikman)
Atl — FG Andersen 37
Dall — Martin 60 pass from Aikman
(Boniol kick)

DENVER 45, BALTIMORE 34—at Mile High Stadium, attendance 70,453. John Elway threw 3 touchdown passes and ran in from the 9-yard line with 1:16 remaining as Denver rallied to remain in first place. Trailing 34-31 early in the fourth quarter, Elway threw his third touchdown pass to Ed McCaffrey to regain the lead. After forcing a punt, the Broncos drove to the Ravens' 1-yard line, but Terrell Davis was stopped on fourth-and-goal with 1:57 left. With the weather having changed from sunshine to sleet, Vinny Testaverde threw his only interception of the game, with Tyrone Braxton returning it to the Ravens' 15. On third-and-4, Elway bootlegged and ran untouched into the end zone to seal the Broncos' victory. Denver scored on each of its first 3 possessions to take a 21-3 advantage. After the Ravens cut the lead to 21-13, Elway drove the Broncos 75 yards on eight plays in 1:37, with McCaffrey's second touchdown catch 14 seconds before halftime giving Denver a 28-13 lead. The Ravens ran the no-huddle offense to perfection in the third quarter, scoring on all 3 of their drives to take a 34-31 lead. Both quarterbacks had big games: Elway completed 25 of 39 passes for 326 yards and 3 touchdowns; Testaverde was 27 of 45 for 338 yards and 4 touchdowns. Davis ran for a career-high 194 yards, and Shannon Sharpe caught 9 passes for 161 yards. The teams combined for 49 first downs and 940 total yards.

Baltimore	0	13	21	0	—	34
Denver	14	14	3	14	—	45

Den — McCaffrey 4 pass from Elway (Elam kick)
Den — Davis 71 run (Elam kick)
Balt — FG Stover 45
Den — Davis 4 run (Elam kick)
Balt — Byner 4 pass from Testaverde (Stover kick)
Balt — FG Stover 33
Den — McCaffrey 8 pass from Elway (Elam kick)

Balt — Turner 11 pass from Testaverde (Stover kick)
Balt — Jackson 25 pass from Testaverde (pass failed)
Den — FG Elam 34
Balt — Jackson 9 pass from Testaverde (Testaverde run)
Den — McCaffrey 6 pass from Elway (Elam kick)
Den — Elway 9 run (Elam kick)

BUFFALO 25, N.Y. JETS 22—at Giants Stadium, attendance 49,775. Steve Christie's club-record sixth field goal, from 47 yards with 10 seconds remaining, gave the Bills a hard-fought victory against the winless Jets. Christie's heroics capped a 9-play, 51-yard drive. Wayne Chrebet's diving touchdown catch with 1:43 remaining tied the game at 22-22. Buffalo had capitalized on 2 Jets turnovers: Jeff Burris' fumble recovery on the Jets' 5-yard line set up Darick Holmes 1-yard run; and Burris' interception led to Christie's fifth field goal and a 22-15 Bills lead. The Jets took a 15-9 lead on the strength of 2 touchdown catches by rookie Keyshawn Johnson, who was in his first game since returning from minor knee surgery. Johnson finished the day with 8 catches for 94 yards. Reich, who played his first 10 NFL seasons with the Bills, completed 21 of 36 passes for 253 yards, 3 touchdowns, and 2 interceptions. The Bills held onto the ball for 36 minutes, 24 seconds.

Buffalo	3	3	3	16	—	25
N.Y. Jets	7	0	8	7	—	22

NYJ — K. Johnson 16 pass from Reich (Lowery kick)
Buff — FG Christie 48
Buff — FG Christie 32
Buff — FG Christie 47
NYJ — K. Johnson 9 pass from Reich (Brady pass from Reich)
Buff — FG Christie 23
Buff — Holmes 1 run (Christie kick)
Buff — FG Christie 33
NYJ — Chrebet 20 pass from Reich (Lowery kick)
Buff — FG Christie 47

SAN FRANCISCO 28, CINCINNATI 21—at 3Com Park, attendance 63,218. Steve Young hobbled 15 yards into the end zone with 68 seconds left to give the 49ers a come-from-behind victory. The Bengals, who led 21-0, fired coach Dave Shula the next day. Young, suffering from a strained groin, scored the winning touchdown after Dedrick Dodge's interception at the Bengals' 32 with 1:40 remaining. The 49ers tied the score 21-21 with 2:08 left on a 45-yard post-pattern to Terrell Owens. Young started the game but was taken out after re-injuring his groin in the second quarter. Elvis Grbac came in and threw a touchdown pass to Ted Popson before injuring his left shoulder late in the first half. Young returned and led the second half comeback. Cincinnati jumped out to a 14-0 lead less than 10 minutes into the game. Jeff Blake threw 2 touchdown passes, the first set up by Ashley Ambrose's interception and the second by James Francis's fumble recovery. Blake's bomb to Darnay Scott put Cincinnati ahead 21-0, but the 49ers answered on the next drive with Popson's first touchdown. Popson finished with career-highs in receptions (8) and receiving yards (116). Young was 19 of 30 for 274 yards. Blake, who completed 11 of 21 first half-passes, connected on just 3 of 13 second half-attempts.

Cincinnati	14	7	0	0	—	21
San Francisco	0	7	7	14	—	28

Cin — McGee 5 pass from Blake (Pelfrey kick)
Cin — Hearst 15 pass from Blake (Pelfrey kick)
Cin — Scott 50 pass from Blake (Pelfrey kick)
SF — Popson 17 pass from Grbac (Wilkins kick)
SF — Popson 39 pass from Young (Wilkins kick)
SF — Owens 45 pass from Young (Wilkins kick)
SF — Young 15 run (Wilkins kick)

ST. LOUIS 17, JACKSONVILLE 14—at Trans World Dome, attendance 60,066. The St. Louis Rams intercepted 5 passes, and stopped Jacksonville at the 5-yard line as time expired, to defeat the Jaguars. Jacksonville dominated the game, outgaining the Rams 538-204 yards, and had more first downs (36-8), plays (87-39), and time of possession (41:34-18:26). Mark Brunell completed 37 of 52 attempts

for 421 yards, but all 5 interceptions he threw were in Rams territory. Two of the interceptions came in the fourth quarter, and three occurred inside the Rams' 20-yard line. Starting from their own 6 with 2:38 remaining and trailing 17-14, the Jaguars marched downfield. On third-and-5 from the Rams' 39 with 22 seconds left, Willie Jackson caught a short pass, spun out of a few tackles, and ran to the 5-yard line. With the clock running, Brunell attempted to spike the ball but the officials ruled there was no time left on the clock. Keenan McCardell caught 16 passes, equaling the third-highest total in NFL history, for 232 yards. James Stewart gained 112 yards and scored twice. Anthony Parker, who had 2 interceptions along with Keith Lyle, scored a defensive touchdown for the second consecutive week to give the Rams a 7-0 lead. Jacksonville fumbled the ensuing kickoff, which led to a Rams field goal and a 10-0 advantage. After falling behind 14-10 in the third quarter, the Rams responded with their only long drive of the game, with the rookie combination of Tony Banks and Eddie Kennison connecting for the winning touchdown.

Jacksonville	0	7	7	0	—	14
St. Louis	10	0	7	0	—	17

StL — Parker 92 interception return (Lohmiller kick)
StL — FG Lohmiller 25
Jax — Stewart 1 run (Hollis kick)
Jax — Stewart 8 run (Hollis kick)
StL — Kennison 29 pass from Banks (Lohmiller kick)

PHILADELPHIA 35, MIAMI 28—at Veterans Stadium, attendance 66,240. Irving Fryar caught a career-high 4 touchdowns from Ty Detmer, and Ricky Watters 49-yard touchdown run in the closing minutes led the Eagles to victory. Fryar, who played with Miami from 1993-95, also set an NFL record by catching a touchdown pass from his 14th different quarterback. His first touchdown was on a bomb, to put the Eagles ahead 7-0 just 1:41 into the game. Craig Erickson connected with Randal Hill on a touchdown pass and Troy Drayton on a 2-point conversion to cut the Eagles lead to 14-11 with 1:55 left in the first half. The Eagles quickly responded, as Fryar caught his third touchdown just 5 seconds before halftime to give Philadelphia a 21-11 lead. Joe Nedney's second field goal, from 39 yards with 6:56 left in the game, cut the lead to 28-21. With 2:38 remaining the Eagles got the ball on Miami's 49 after forcing a punt and Watters raced 49 yards on the Eagles first play. Bernie Kosar threw a touchdown pass to O.J. McDuffie with 1:04 left, but Mark Seay recovered the onside kick to seal the victory. Watters scoring run capped his 173-yard day. Detmer completed 18 of 24 passes for 226 yards and 4 touchdowns in his second career start. Fryar had 8 receptions for 116 yards. McDuffie had 7 catches for 121 yards and 2 touchdowns.

Miami	3	8	0	17	—	28
Philadelphia	14	7	7	7	—	35

Phil — Fryar 38 pass from Detmer (Anderson kick)
Phil — Fryar 2 pass from Detmer (Anderson kick)
Mia — FG Nedney 37
Mia — Hill 6 pass from Erickson (Drayton pass from Erickson)
Phil — Fryar 12 pass from Detmer (Anderson kick)
Phil — Fryar 36 pass from Detmer (Anderson kick)
Mia — McDuffie 24 pass from Erickson (Nedney kick)
Mia — FG Nedney 39
Phil — Watters 49 run (Anderson kick)
Mia — McDuffie 17 pass from Kosar (Nedney kick)

NEW ENGLAND 27, INDIANAPOLIS 9—at RCA Dome, attendance 58,725. The Patriots, aided by 2 Colts turnovers, scored 17 points in a 5-minute, 27-second span to hand the division-leading Colts their first home defeat of the season. After Indianapolis took a 6-0 lead, Clif Groce fumbled with 2:15 left in the first half. Willie Clay returned the fumble 16 yards to the Colts' 8-yard line, where Drew Bledsoe threw a touchdown pass to Terry Glenn on the next play to give the Patriots the lead for good. After New England's defense forced a punt, Adam Vinatieri's 44-yard field goal gave the Patriots a 10-6 halftime lead. The Colts defense stopped New England on its first drive of the second

half, but Marvin Harrison fumbled the punt return. The first of Curtis Martin's 2 third quarter touchdown runs capped the 17-yard drive. The Colts, who played without Marshall Faulk and lost Jim Harbaugh early in the fourth quarter to a broken nose, outgained the Patriots 368-222 total yards but lost 4 fumbles in defeat.

New England	0	10	14	3	—	27
Indianapolis	3	3	0	3	—	9

Ind — FG Blanchard 21
Ind — FG Blanchard 35
NE — Glenn 8 pass from Bledsoe (Vinatieri kick)
NE — FG Vinatieri 44
NE — Martin 1 run (Vinatieri kick)
NE — Martin 6 run (Vinatieri kick)
Ind — FG Blanchard 38
NE — FG Vinatieri 36

CAROLINA 19, NEW ORLEANS 7—at Ericsson Stadium, attendance 70,888. John Kasay's 4 field goals and Anthony Johnson's third consecutive 100-yard game sparked the Panthers to a home divisional victory. The win gave the Panthers a 4-0 record at Ericsson Stadium and signaled a home sweep of the NFC West for the second-year club. Kasay, who helped the Panthers defeat the Saints in week 2 with five field goals, had his first field goal set up by Tyrone Hughes's fumbled punt. The Saints responded midway through the second quarter with a 1-yard blast by Ray Zellars to take a 7-3 lead. Three third-down conversions kept alive a drive that ended with Kasay's 40-yard field goal just 50 seconds before halftime. The Panthers drove 72 yards in 13 plays, keyed by two Saints penalties that gave Carolina two automatic first downs, to take the lead 9-7 on Kasay's third field goal. On their next possession, a 31-yard screen pass to Johnson set up Kerry Collins's 13-yard touchdown pass to Mark Carrier to give the Panthers an insurmountable 16-7 advantage. Carolina's defense allowed just 10 first downs and 103 passing yards. The offense converted 8 of 18 third-down conversions and controlled the ball for 38 minutes, 22 seconds. Saints head coach Jim Mora resigned the following day, ending his 11-year tenure.

New Orleans	0	7	0	0	—	7
Carolina	3	3	10	3	—	19

Car — FG Kasay 23
NO — Zellars 1 run (Brien kick)
Car — FG Kasay 40
Car — FG Kasay 26
Car — Carrier 13 pass from Collins (Kasay kick)
Car — FG Kasay 39

WASHINGTON 31, N.Y. GIANTS 21—at RFK Stadium, attendance 52,684. The Redskins held off a furious second half-rally by the Giants to sweep their division rival for the first time since 1991. Terry Allen had 3 short touchdown runs to give him an NFL-high 10 touchdowns for the season. All three runs came following a big gain: Leslie Shepherd's 31-yard reverse; Brian Mitchell's 13-yard screen pass on third-and-10; and Henry Ellard's 48-yard reception. Darrell Green then intercepted a pass that bounced out of Thomas Lewis's hands and returned it 68 yards to give the Redskins a commanding 28-0 halftime lead. The Giants responded with touchdowns in their first two second half possessions to cut the lead in half. Tyrone Wheatley's 1-yard blast with 6:35 left cut the deficit to 28-21. The Redskins, which had gained just 34 yards in the second half, marched downfield, with Scott Blanton's 45-yard field goal with 2:33 left being the game's final points. Kicker Brad Daluiso missed from 41 yards with 1:39 left to end any Giants hopes of a comeback. Allen ran for 89 yards and Ellard had 119 receiving yards. The Redskins totaled 252 first half yards, but allowed 292 in the second half. Dave Brown threw for 298 yards on 26 of 43 passes. Lewis had 9 receptions for 125 yards.

N.Y. Giants	0	0	14	7	—	21
Washington	7	21	0	3	—	31

Wash — Allen 2 run (Blanton kick)
Wash — Allen 1 run (Blanton kick)
Wash — Allen 2 run (Blanton kick)
Wash — Green 68 interception return (Blanton kick)
NYG — Lewis 31 pass from Brown (Daluiso kick)
NYG — Calloway 13 pass from Brown (Daluiso kick)
NYG — Wheatley 1 run (Daluiso kick)
Wash — FG Blanton 45

HOUSTON 23, PITTSBURGH 13—at Astrodome, attendance 50,337. Willie Davis and Eddie George scored touchdowns less than 2 minutes apart to vault the Oilers into first place. Trailing 13-9, Davis beat Rod Woodson on a hitch-and-go pattern to put Houston ahead 16-13 with 5:01 left. On the next play from scrimmage, Mike Tomczak was sacked by Gary Walker, forcing a fumble. Barron Wortham recovered at the Steelers' 5. George scored from 2 yards out with 3:05 remaining to seal the victory. Al Del Greco booted 3 field goals, including a 48-yarder at the halftime gun that was set up by a 16-yard scramble by Chris Chandler. Charles Johnson played a big role in all of the Steelers' points. He caught a pass on a 20-yard crossing pattern one-handed, and ran into the end zone for a 70-yard touchdown. Johnson then was the intended receiver when Marcus Robertson was flagged for a 38-yard pass interference penalty. That set up the first of 2 Norm Johnson field goals, with the second one coming early in the fourth quarter after Johnson's 63-yard reception. Houston controlled the ball for 34 minutes, 17 seconds and tallied 23 first downs compared to the Steelers' 12.

Pittsburgh	7	3	0	3	—	13
Houston	3	6	0	14	—	23

Hou — FG Del Greco 22
Pitt — C. Johnson 70 pass from Tomczak (N. Johnson kick)
Pitt — FG N. Johnson 26
Hou — FG Del Greco 32
Hou — FG Del Greco 48
Pitt — FG N. Johnson 29
Hou — W. Davis 34 pass from Chandler (Del Greco kick)
Hou — George 2 run (Del Greco kick)

ARIZONA 13, TAMPA BAY 9—at Sun Devil Stadium, attendance 27,738. The Cardinals used 3 long scoring drives to record their third victory in their last four games. Greg Davis kicked his first of 2 field goals to conclude an 8:40 game-opening drive to put the Cardinals ahead 3-0. After forcing a punt, Arizona had another 16-play drive, this one lasting 8:11, with Larry Centers' 5-yard touchdown catch giving the Cardinals a 10-0 lead. The first half ended with Michael Husted, who had missed from 49 yards earlier, missing a 52-yard attempt. The Buccaneers took the second half kickoff and ran 6:32 off the clock before Husted connected from 41 yards to cut the deficit to 10-3. Arizona responded with a 14-play, 75-yard drive that lasted 6:21, ending with Davis's second field goal. Tampa Bay then drove 70 yards in 15 plays, with Mike Alstott's 1-yard dive ending the 9:33 drive. However, Matt Darby blocked Husted's extra point attempt. Tampa Bay got the ball back twice in the final 3:18, but never crossed midfield. The Buccaneers, who committed 14 penalties compared to just 2 by the Cardinals, had just 7 possessions. The game featured 0 turnovers and just 3 punts.

Tampa Bay	0	0	3	6	—	9
Arizona	3	7	3	0	—	13

Ariz — FG Davis 22
Ariz — Centers 5 pass from Graham (Davis kick)
TB — FG Husted 41
Ariz — FG Davis 37
TB — Alstott 1 run (kick blocked)

MONDAY, OCTOBER 21

OAKLAND 23, SAN DIEGO 14—at San Diego Jack Murphy Stadium, attendance 62,350. Jeff Hostetler completed 20 of 33 passes for 191 yards and 1 touchdown, and Cole Ford booted 3 field goals, to lead the Raiders. Oakland's victory gives them an NFL-best 32-13-1 (.711) record on Mondays. The Raiders took a 17-7 lead when Derrick Fenner caught a touchdown pass from Hostetler on a drive that began following a John Carney missed 44-yard field goal. The Chargers then drove to the Raiders' 24-yard line. On the next play, Chester McGlockton stripped Sean Salisbury. Pat Swilling scooped up the ball and ran 49 yards, setting up Ford's second field goal. Tony Martin caught his second touchdown pass of the game, and NFL-leading ninth of the season, to cut the lead to 20-14 with 13:05 remaining. With six minutes left Darrien Gordon was called for a 16-yard pass interference on a third-and-10 play, and had an unsportsmanlike conduct penalty tacked on, allowing the Raiders to run a few extra minutes off the clock. The Chargers stopped the Raiders, but Gordon dropped the punt and the Raiders recovered the ball at the 19 with 3:53 left. Ford's third field goal sailed through the uprights with 2:11 remaining to ice the game. Salisbury, who was 22 of 35 for 252 yards and 2 touchdowns, came into the game after a McGlockton first quarter hit separated the left shoulder of Stan Humphires.

Oakland	7	3	10	3	—	23
San Diego	7	0	0	7	—	14

Oak — Kaufman 12 run (Ford kick)
SD — Martin 11 pass from Salisbury (Carney kick)
Oak — FG Ford 36
Oak — Fenner 17 pass from Hostetler (Ford kick)
Oak — FG Ford 32
SD — Martin 12 pass from Salisbury (Carney kick)
Oak — FG Ford 34

NINTH WEEK SUMMARIES

AMERICAN FOOTBALL CONFERENCE

Eastern Division	W	L	T	Pct.	Pts.	OP
Buffalo	5	3	0	.625	129	145
Indianapolis	5	3	0	.625	140	145
New England	5	3	0	.625	202	165
Miami	4	4	0	.500	178	150
N.Y. Jets	1	8	0	.111	145	233
Central Division						
Pittsburgh	6	2	0	.750	164	120
Houston	5	3	0	.625	183	153
Baltimore	3	5	0	.375	196	232
Jacksonville	3	6	0	.333	172	181
Cincinnati	2	6	0	.250	156	181
Western Division						
Denver	7	1	0	.875	223	134
Kansas City	5	3	0	.625	158	142
Oakland	4	4	0	.500	179	148
San Diego	4	4	0	.500	172	199
Seattle	3	5	0	.375	141	200

NATIONAL FOOTBALL CONFERENCE

Eastern Division	W	L	T	Pct.	Pts.	OP
Washington	7	1	0	.875	192	115
Philadelphia	6	2	0	.750	180	158
Dallas	5	3	0	.625	165	117
Arizona	3	5	0	.375	119	188
N.Y. Giants	3	5	0	.375	124	154
Central Division						
Green Bay	7	1	0	.875	240	99
Minnesota	5	3	0	.625	140	131
Detroit	4	4	0	.500	169	159
Chicago	3	5	0	.375	119	165
Tampa Bay	1	7	0	.125	85	165
Western Division						
San Francisco	6	2	0	.750	193	115
Carolina	5	3	0	.625	173	111
New Orleans	2	6	0	.250	121	180
St. Louis	2	6	0	.250	136	222
Atlanta	0	8	0	.000	140	227

SUNDAY, OCTOBER 27

PHILADELPHIA 20, CAROLINA 9—at Veterans Stadium, attendance 65,982. Ty Detmer threw for a career-high 342 yards to spark the Eagles. In just his third start, Detmer completed 23 of 38 passes, 1 touchdown, and 1 interception. The touchdown pass, to rookie Jason Dunn for his first NFL score, capped a 5-play, 81-yard drive that consumed exactly 1 minute and gave the Eagles a 14-0 lead with 1:02 remaining before halftime. John Kasay kicked a field goal as the half expired, and 2 more field goals by Kasay cut the Eagles lead to 17-9. Early in the fourth quarter, Mike Mamula's near block of a Rohn Stark punt gave the Eagles excellent field position, setting up Anderson's second field goal with 9:29 left. The Panthers answered quickly, as a long pass to Muhsin Muhammad and a 25-yard pass interference penalty got the Panthers to the Eagles' 8. However, Troy Vincent forced Kerry Collins to fumble two plays later, and the Eagles recovered the ball with 7:54 left. Irving Fryar, who caught 4 touchdown passes the week before, caught 7 passes for 143 yards. Carolina was a combined 2 of 17 on third- or fourth-down conversions.

Carolina	0	3	6	0	—	9
Philadelphia	7	7	3	3	—	20

Phil — Watters 3 run (Anderson kick)
Phil — Dunn 9 pass from Detmer (Anderson kick)
Car — FG Kasay 47
Phil — FG Anderson 46
Car — FG Kasay 39

Car — FG Kasay 29
Phil — FG Anderson 21

DALLAS 29, MIAMI 10—at Pro Player Stadium, attendance 75,283. Troy Aikman threw for 363 yards and 3 second-half touchdown passes to spark the Cowboys against their former coach, Jimmy Johnson. Trailing 10-9 at halftime, the Cowboys marched 60 yards in 12 plays, culminating with Eric Bjornson's 4-yard touchdown reception to give the Cowboys a 16-10 lead. Later in the quarter, Aikman hit Michael Irvin with a 61-yard reception, setting up Irvin's 2-yard touchdown catch. Kevin Smith's interception at the Miami 31 put the Cowboys in position to go ahead 29-10 on Emmitt Smith's 10-yard touchdown catch with 12:49 remaining. Miami scored its only touchdown on a 7-play, 72-yard drive following Chris Boniol's second field goal. Dan Marino returned from a broken ankle to complete just 12 of 27 passes for 173 yards. Aikman's 33 of 41 effort included 12 catches and 186 receiving yards for Irvin. Dallas dominated, with more first downs (27-10), yards (482-221), and total plays (78-40).

Dallas	3	6	13	7	—	29
Miami	0	10	0	0	—	10

Dall — FG Boniol 33
Dall — FG Boniol 29
Mia — Pritchett 16 pass from Marino (Nedney kick)
Mia — FG Nedney 26
Dall — FG Boniol 24
Dall — Bjornson 4 pass from Aikman (Boniol kick)
Dall — Irvin 2 pass from Aikman (kick failed)
Dall — E. Smith 10 pass from Aikman (Boniol kick)

WASHINGTON 31, INDIANAPOLIS 16—at RFK Stadium, attendance 54,254. Terry Allen scored 3 touchdowns for the second consecutive week to keep the Redskins in first place. His 13 touchdowns lead the NFL. After falling behind, the Colts scored 10 points in the final 1:57 of the first half to cut the deficit to 17-13. Brian Mitchell returned a punt 71 yards to the 1-yard line to set up Allen's second touchdown. After Cary Blanchard's third field goal cut the Redskins lead to 24-16, Allen ran 32 yards for a touchdown with 10:23 left for the game's final points. The Redskins had 25 first downs and 215 rushing yards, including 124 yards by Allen, against an injured Colts defense.

Indianapolis	0	13	3	0	—	16
Washington	10	7	7	7	—	31

Wash — FG Blanton 20
Wash — Allen 4 run (Blanton kick)
Ind — FG Blanchard 21
Wash — Shepherd 7 pass from Frerotte (Blanton kick)
Ind — Faulk 1 run (Blanchard kick)
Ind — FG Blanchard 49
Wash — Allen 1 run (Blanton kick)
Ind — FG Blanchard 51
Wash — Allen 32 run (Blanton kick)

CINCINNATI 28, JACKSONVILLE 21—at Cinergy Field, attendance 45,890. Two touchdown runs by Ki-Jana Carter spearheaded a 21-point fourth quarter to lead the Bengals to victory. The Jaguars took a 14-7 third quarter-lead on Natrone Means's 8-yard reception. The Bengals responded with a quick drive, capped by Carl Pickens's second touchdown of the day on the first play of the fourth quarter to tie the score. Carter finished a 5:31 drive with his first touchdown with 6:10 remaining. Bo Orlando intercepted Mark Brunell's tipped pass, and Carter scored again to end the 22-yard drive with 3:32 left. Jimmy Smith caught an 11-yard strike from Brunell with 1:35 remaining to cut the lead to 28-21. The Bengals recovered the ensuing onside kick to clinch the victory for coach Bruce Coslet in his first game.

Jacksonville	0	7	7	7	—	21
Cincinnati	0	7	0	21	—	28

Jax — Brunell 14 run (Hollis kick)
Cin — Pickens 11 pass from Blake (Pelfrey kick)
Jax — Means 8 pass from Brunell (Hollis kick)
Cin — Pickens 10 pass from Blake (Pelfrey kick)
Cin — Carter 1 run (Pelfrey kick)
Cin — Carter 4 run (Pelfrey kick)
Jax — J. Smith 11 pass from Brunell (Hollis kick)

DENVER 34, KANSAS CITY 7—at Mile High Stadium, attendance 75,652. Three first-half touchdown passes by John Elway led Denver to its largest margin of victory in the 73-game series history between the teams. Rod Smith had punt returns of 20 and 36 yards to set up the Broncos first 2 scores. Trailing 10-0, Tamarick Vanover returned the ensuing kickoff for the Chiefs' lone score. The Broncos responded with Shannon Sharpe's second touchdown to give Denver a 17-7 lead. Mike Sherrard's 25-yard catch 46 seconds before halftime put the game out of reach. Denver led in first downs (26-10), yards (499-232), and time of possession (34:01-25:59). Elway threw for 286 yards, with Sharpe totaling 99 receiving yards and Anthony Miller 88. Steve Bono struggled, completing just 21 of 49 passes for 213 yards, and 2 interceptions.

Kansas City	7	0	0	0	—	7
Denver	17	7	7	3	—	34

Den — Sharpe 46 pass from Elway (Elam kick)
Den — FG Elam 40
KC — Vanover 97 kickoff return (Stoyanovich kick)
Den — Sharpe 10 pass from Elway (Elam kick)
Den — Sherrard 25 pass from Elway (Elam kick)
Den — Craver 1 run (Elam kick)
Den — FG Elam 29

N.Y. GIANTS 35, DETROIT 7—at Pontiac Silverdome, attendance 63,501. The Giants scored 23 points in a 4:54 span of the second quarter to defeat the Lions. Trailing 7-2, running back Tyrone Wheatley threw a 24-yard touchdown to Chris Calloway on his first NFL pass attempt. Corey Widmer intercepted Scott Mitchell on the Lions' third play, and Brad Daluiso's field goal gave the Giants an 11-7 lead with 7:59 left in the half. Three plays later, 11-year veteran Maurice Douglass intercepted Mitchell and ran 32 yards for his first NFL touchdown. On Detroit's next possession—again on the third play of the drive—Tito Wooten intercepted Mitchell and returned the ball 43 yards. Dave Brown threw a 23-yard touchdown pass to Thomas Lewis on the next play to give the Giants a 25-7 lead with 5:23 left in the half. Mitchell was then replaced by Don Majkowski, who threw 2 interceptions himself. In all, the Giants forced 6 turnovers and maintained possession for 35 minutes, and 39 seconds. The loss broke a 10-game home-winning streak for the Lions.

N.Y. Giants	2	23	0	10	—	35
Detroit	7	0	0	0	—	7

Det — Mitchell 1 run (Hanson kick)
NYG — Safety, Wooten blocked punt out of end zone
NYG — Calloway 24 pass from Wheatley (run failed)
NYG — FG Daluiso 38
NYG — Douglass 32 interception return (Daluiso kick)
NYG — Lewis 23 pass from Brown (Daluiso kick)
NYG — FG Daluiso 32
NYG — Agnew 34 interception return (Daluiso kick)

N.Y. JETS 31, ARIZONA 21—at Sun Devil Stadium, attendance 28,088. Adrian Murrell rushed for 199 yards and 1 touchdown to lead the Jets to their first victory of the season. Richie Anderson's 1-yard run with 16 seconds left in the first half gave the Jets a 17-0 halftime lead. Larry Centers caught 2 short touchdown passes 1 minute, 48 seconds apart in the third quarter to cut the deficit to 17-14. The Jets responded with a 13-play, 90-yard drive, capped by Murrell's 1-yard run. The key play was an 18-yard pass to Wayne Chrebet on third down to get to the Arizona 6. Leeland McElroy returned the ensuing kickoff 92 yards, and Kent Graham hit Rob Moore from 6 yards to pull the Cardinals within three points. However, Murrell had a 78-yard run, and Reggie Cobb scored from the 2-yard line with 4:55 left to end the scoring. The Jets had 27 first downs, and converted 10 of 14 third-down opportunities. Frank Reich completed 22 of 31 passes for 254 yards. Moore had 7 catches for 143 yards against his old team.

N.Y. Jets	3	14	0	14	—	31
Arizona	0	0	14	7	—	21

NYJ — FG Lowery 37
NYJ — Johnson 34 pass from Reich (Lowery kick)
NYJ — Anderson 1 run (Lowery kick)
Ariz — Centers 1 pass from Graham (Davis kick)
Ariz — Centers 2 pass from Graham (Davis kick)
NYJ — Murrell 1 run (Lowery kick)
Ariz — Moore 6 pass from Graham (Davis kick)
NYJ — Cobb 2 run (Lowery kick)

PITTSBURGH 20, ATLANTA 17—at Georgia Dome, attendance 58,760. Norm Johnson kicked a 20-yard field goal as time expired to give Pittsburgh the victory. Atlanta tied the score 17-17 with 5:55 left on Bert Emanuel's 4-yard touchdown reception. However, the Steelers did not allow the Falcons to get back the ball. The 13-play, 66-yard drive was keyed by Andre Hastings's 14-yard reception that put the Steelers at Atlanta's 21-yard line. A few carries by Jerome Bettis, who had 126 yards on the day, put Johnson in position for the winning kick. Atlanta took a 10-3 halftime lead on the strength of tackle-eligible Robbie Tobeck's first career touchdown. The Steelers scored on consecutive third quarter-drives to take a 17-10 lead. Charles Johnson caught 8 passes for 110 yards. Mike Tomczak completed 22 of 27 passes for 214 yards. Bobby Hebert countered with a 24 of 36 effort, for 234 yards.

Pittsburgh	3	0	14	3	—	20
Atlanta	7	3	0	7	—	17

Pitt — FG N. Johnson 27
Atl — Tobeck 1 run from Hebert (Andersen kick)
Atl — FG Andersen 41
Pitt — Hastings 12 pass from Tomczak (N. Johnson kick)
Pitt — Bettis 1 run (N. Johnson kick)
Atl — Emanuel 4 pass from Hebert (Andersen kick)
Pitt — FG N. Johnson 20

BALTIMORE 37, ST. LOUIS 31 (OT)—at Memorial Stadium, attendance 60,256. Michael Jackson caught a 22-yard touchdown pass from Vinny Testaverde with 10 seconds left in overtime to give the Ravens a dramatic victory. The 4-play, 55-second drive began when Tony Banks threw a fourth down incompletion from the Ravens' 40. The Rams had a chance to win with 5:49 left in overtime with a 33-yard field goal, but holder Jamie Martin mishandled the snap and Sale Isaia recovered the ball. The Ravens trailed until Derrick Alexander's 13-yard touchdown catch gave them a 24-23 lead with 13:17 remaining in regulation. Byron (Bam) Morris scored from 10 yards with 6:36 left to increase the Ravens lead to 31-23. The Rams answered with a 10-play, 87-yard drive, culminating with Harold Green's 1-yard run with 3:37 left and subsequent 2-point conversion. Matt Stover had a chance to win the game, but he hooked a 32-yard field-goal attempt, his second miss of the game, as time ran out in regulation. Testaverde completed 31 of 51 attempts for 429 yards, 3 touchdowns, and 2 interceptions. Jackson had 7 receptions for 113 yards, and Floyd Turner had 6 catches for 108 yards. Tony Banks was 26 of 40 for 353 yards, 1 touchdown, and 2 interceptions. Isaac Bruce caught 11 passes for 229 yards.

St. Louis	7	6	7	11	0	—	31
Baltimore	0	6	11	14	6	—	37

StL — Bruce 8 pass from Banks (Lohmiller kick)
StL — FG Lohmiller 50
StL — FG Lohmiller 38
Balt — Turner 27 pass from Testaverde (kick failed)
StL — Lyght 25 interception return (Lohmiller kick)
Balt — FG Stover 50
Balt — Morris 3 run (Alexander pass from Testaverde)
StL — FG Lohmiller 36
Balt — Alexander 13 pass from Testaverde (Stover kick)
Balt — Morris 10 run (Stover kick)
StL — Green 1 run (Green run)
Balt — Jackson 22 pass from Testaverde

SEATTLE 32, SAN DIEGO 13—at Kingdome, attendance 38,143. Seattle forced 5 turnovers, and Todd Peterson kicked 4 field goals, to lead the Seahawks. Chris Warren's 50-yard run set up Lamar Smith's 10-yard touchdown jaunt and gave Seattle a 13-6 lead with 6:42 remaining in the first half. Darryl Williams intercepted a Sean Salisbury pass and streaked 79 yards for the touchdown to give Seattle a 20-6 halftime lead. Peterson's fourth field goal, set up by Carlton

Gray's 62-yard fumble return, put Seattle ahead 26-6. Chris Warren's 37-yard touchdown with 4:48 left ended the scoring. Salisbury completed 21 of 43 passes for 291 yards, but threw 4 interceptions, 2 to Williams. Warren rushed for 146 yards.

San Diego	3	3	0	7	—	13
Seattle	3	17	3	9	—	32

Sea — FG Peterson 33
SD — FG Carney 41
SD — FG Carney 43
Sea — FG Peterson 44
Sea — L. Smith 10 run (Peterson kick)
Sea — D. Williams 79 interception return (Peterson kick)
Sea — FG Peterson 47
Sea — FG Peterson 27
SD — C. Jones 27 pass from Salisbury (Carney kick)
Sea — Warren 37 run (run failed)

SAN FRANCISCO 10, HOUSTON 9—at Astrodome, attendance 53,664. Terrell Owens's touchdown with 4:27 remaining gave the 49ers a hard-fought road victory. Trailing 9-3, Terry Kirby caught a screen pass and ran 49 yards to the Houston 33. Facing third-and-7, Jeff Brohm threw a 10-yard sideline pass to Owens, who spun away from Darryl Lewis and scored the game's only touchdown. Houston got the ball two more times, but Steve McNair threw an incompletion on fourth down with 2:18 left, and then, after a 49ers punt, Junior Bryant tipped a McNair pass that Chris Doleman intercepted to seal the victory. McNair entered the game in the third quarter after Chris Chandler reaggravated his injured groin. Brohm came in after Steve Young received a concussion on the third play of the game. The irony in Young's injury was that time out had been called just prior to the play, but no one heard the whistle. Each offense could only muster 12 first downs, and the Oilers converted only 1 of 13 third downs.

San Francisco	3	0	0	7	—	10
Houston	0	6	3	0	—	9

SF — FG Wilkins 27
Hou — FG Del Greco 38
Hou — FG Del Greco 56
Hou — FG Del Greco 39
SF — Owens 20 pass from Brohm (Wilkins kick)

GREEN BAY 13, TAMPA BAY 7—at Lambeau Field, attendance 60,627. Chris Jacke kicked 2 field goals to boost the Packers to a home victory. Jacke's first field goal was set up by Reggie White's blocked punt. Dorsey Levens's 1-yard plunge put Green Bay ahead 10-0 early in the second quarter. Michael Husted then missed a 27-yard field goal, and Green Bay responded with a long drive. However, the Buccaneers forced the Packers to punt from Tampa Bay's 35. However, the Buccaneers had 12 men on the field, and, taking advantage of the 5-yard penalty, Jacke trotted onto the field and made his second field goal 59 seconds before halftime. Dave Moore's fourth quarter touchdown cut the deficit to six points with 5:28 remaining. Tampa Bay stopped the Packers on fourth-and-2 from the Bucs' 31 with 1:55 left, but Trent Dilfer got sacked on fourth down from their own 35-yard line to end Tampa Bay's chances. It was a costly victory for Green Bay, as Antonio Freeman had to leave the game after suffering a broken arm in the first quarter. With a depleted receiving corps, Edgar Bennett gained 93 yards on 20 carries. The 13 points marked a season-low total for the NFL's highest-scoring team.

Tampa Bay	0	0	0	7	—	7
Green Bay	3	10	0	0	—	13

GB — FG Jacke 40
GB — Levens 1 run (Jacke kick)
GB — FG Jacke 48
TB — Moore 11 pass from Dilfer (Husted kick)

SUNDAY NIGHT, OCTOBER 27

NEW ENGLAND 28, BUFFALO 25—at Foxboro Stadium, attendance 58,858. The Patriots scored 2 touchdowns 44 seconds apart in the closing minutes to defeat their AFC East rival. Trailing 18-15, the Patriots got the ball on their own 16-yard line with 2:57 remaining. Drew Bledsoe orchestrated an 8-play, 84-yard drive, keyed by big catches by David Meggett and Troy Brown, that finished with Curtis Martin's second touchdown with 1:25 left. Adam Vinatieri missed the extra point, thus making the score

21-18. Buffalo attempted to drive into field-goal range, but Willie McGinest intercepted Jim Kelly's swing pass and raced 46 yards for a touchdown and a 28-18 advantage with 41 seconds left. Buffalo was not done, as Andre Reed caught Jim Kelly's tipped Hail-Mary pass on the next play from scrimmage to cut the deficit to 28-25 with 24 seconds remaining. The Patriots recovered the onside kick to seal the game. Bledsoe completed 32 of 45 passes for 373 yards. Thurman Thomas gained 119 yards on the ground and scored a touchdown in the losing effort.

Buffalo	0	0	10	15	—	25
New England	7	6	2	13	—	28

NE — Martin 4 pass from Bledsoe (Vinatieri kick)
NE — FG Vinatieri 40
NE — FG Vinatieri 32
Buff — FG Christie 33
Buff — Holmes 6 pass from Kelly (Christie kick)
NE — Safety, Kelly called for intentional grounding in end zone
Buff — Thomas 1 run (Holmes run)
NE — Martin 10 run (kick failed)
NE — McGinest 46 interception return (Vinatieri kick)
Buff — Reed 48 pass from Kelly (Christie kick)

MONDAY, OCTOBER 28

CHICAGO 15, MINNESOTA 13—at Metrodome, attendance 58,143. Bryan Cox's fumble recovery and the Bears excellent special-teams play helped them stave off the Vikings. Leading 5-3, Rashaan Salaam blasted in from the 1-yard line with 38 seconds left in the half. Mark Carrier then intercepted a Warren Moon pass at the Bears' 43-yard line with 23 seconds left, setting up Jeff Jaeger's second field goal just before halftime. With Chicago clinging to a 15-13 lead and 3:47 remaining in the game, Sean Harris blocked Scott Sisson's 48-yard field-goal attempt. It was the Bears second blocked kick of the game, with Kevin Miniefield having done the trick earlier. After a Jason Fisk interception gave the Vikings the ball back, Cox stripped Brad Johnson of the ball and recovered the fumble at the Bears' 35 to seal the victory. Johnson was playing because of a third quarter injury to Moon. Robert Smith suffered a season-ending knee injury in the first quarter. Jake Reed caught 11 passes for 153 yards. The Vikings hurt themselves, committing 12 penalties in addition to the 2 blocked kicks and 2 costly turnovers.

Chicago	2	13	0	0	—	15
Minnesota	3	0	10	0	—	13

Minn — FG Sisson 41
Chi — Safety, Miniefield blocked punt out of end zone
Chi — FG Jaeger 41
Chi — Salaam 1 run (Jaeger kick)
Chi — FG Jaeger 44
Minn — Ismail 54 pass from Moon (Sisson kick)
Minn — FG Sisson 43

TENTH WEEK SUMMARIES
AMERICAN FOOTBALL CONFERENCE

Eastern Division	W	L	T	Pct.	Pts.	OP
Buffalo	6	3	0	.667	167	158
New England	6	3	0	.667	244	188
Indianapolis	5	4	0	.556	159	171
Miami	4	5	0	.444	201	192
N.Y. Jets	1	8	0	.111	145	233
Central Division						
Pittsburgh	7	2	0	.778	206	126
Houston	5	4	0	.556	199	176
Baltimore	3	6	0	.333	217	256
Cincinnati	3	6	0	.333	180	202
Jacksonville	3	6	0	.333	172	181
Western Division						
Denver	8	1	0	.889	245	155
Kansas City	6	3	0	.667	179	148
San Diego	5	4	0	.556	198	218
Oakland	4	5	0	.444	200	170
Seattle	4	5	0	.444	164	216

NATIONAL FOOTBALL CONFERENCE

Eastern Division	W	L	T	Pct.	Pts.	OP
Philadelphia	7	2	0	.778	171	179
Washington	7	2	0	.778	205	153
Dallas	5	4	0	.556	186	148
N.Y. Giants	4	5	0	.444	140	162
Arizona	3	6	0	.333	127	204
Central Division						
Green Bay	8	1	0	.889	268	117
Minnesota	5	4	0	.556	146	152
Chicago	4	5	0	.444	132	175
Detroit	4	5	0	.444	187	187
Tampa Bay	1	8	0	.111	95	178
Western Division						
San Francisco	7	2	0	.778	217	132
Carolina	5	4	0	.556	190	131
New Orleans	2	7	0	.222	138	204
St. Louis	2	7	0	.222	142	264
Atlanta	1	8	0	.111	160	244

SUNDAY, NOVEMBER 3

N.Y. GIANTS 16, ARIZONA 8—at Giants Stadium, attendance 68,262. Brad Daluiso kicked 3 field goals, and rookie Danny Kanell played flawless in relief of Dave Brown, as the Giants defeated the Cardinals for the twelfth time in the last 13 games at Giants Stadium. Kanell entered the game in the first quarter after Brown injured his back on Simeon Rice's sack. Kanell completed 14 of 27 passes for 128 yards, with no interceptions, and threw a 24-yard touchdown pass to Thomas Lewis. That pass gave the Giants a 13-0 lead with 8:34 remaining. Jesse Campbell's second interception of the game put Daluiso in position for his third field goal with 5:30 to play. The Giants were 40 seconds away from their first shutout in 100 games, but Boomer Esiason threw a touchdown pass to Frank Sanders on fourth-and-goal. Omar Douglas recovered the onside kick to preserve the victory. Esiason came in after Kent Graham left in the first quarter with a knee injury. The Cardinals netted just 29 rushing yards and were only 2 for 14 on third-down conversions.

Arizona	0	0	0	8	—	8
N.Y. Giants	3	0	3	10	—	16

NYG — FG Daluiso 31
NYG — FG Daluiso 32
NYG — Lewis 24 pass from Kanell (Daluiso kick)
NYG — FG Daluiso 45
Ariz — Sanders 7 pass from Esiason (Esiason run)

ATLANTA 20, CAROLINA 17—at Georgia Dome, attendance 42,726. Jamal Anderson rushed for 109 yards to lead the Falcons to their first victory of the season. Anderson, who inked a new three-year contract extension earlier in the week, scored from 32 yards one play after Lenny McGill's fumble recovery of a kickoff return. The 2 scores, 23 seconds apart, gave the Falcons a 10-0 lead. After the Panthers tied the game, Morten Andersen booted a 45-yard field goal as time expired in the first half. Bobby Hebert, who completed 19 of 32 passes, fired a 15-yard touchdown pass to J.J. Birden with 13:41 remaining. Carolina cut the lead to three points on Mark Carrier's 12-yard touchdown pass from Steve Beuerlein with 2:22 left. The Falcons recovered the ensuing onside kick, but were forced to punt. The oldest player in the NFL, 40-year old Clay Matthews, recorded his third sack of the game as time ran out. Beuerlein replaced Kerry Collins, who suffered a knee injury in the third quarter.

Carolina	3	7	0	7	—	17
Atlanta	10	3	0	7	—	20

Atl — FG Andersen 25
Atl — J. Anderson 32 run (Andersen kick)
Car — FG Kasay 40
Car — A. Johnson 6 run (Kasay kick)
Atl — FG Andersen 45
Atl — Birden 15 pass from Hebert (Andersen kick)
Car — Carrier 12 pass from Beuerlein (Kasay kick)

CINCINNATI 24, BALTIMORE 21—at Memorial Stadium, attendance 60,743. Doug Pelfrey kicked 2 field goals in the final 1:49, including a game winner from 34 yards with no time left, to give interim head coach Bruce Coslet a 2-0 record. Moments earlier, Pelfrey kicked a 49-yard field goal to cap a 15-play, 45-yard drive that lasted 8 minutes and 45 seconds to tie the game 21-21. The Bengals got the ball back after 3 incompletions. Starting from their own 28, the Bengals gained yards on five consecutive plays, the longest a 17-yard pass to Darnay Scott, to set up Pelfrey's heroics. Michael Jackson's 26-yard touchdown catch 33 seconds before halftime gave the Ravens a 21-3 lead going into the locker room. Two consecutive scoring drives, capped by Jeff Blake's 4-yard run, cut the lead to 21-18

with 14:17 remaining. Ray Lewis kept the second drive alive with a defensive pass interference penalty in the end zone on fourth-and-2. Cincinnati tackle Scott Brumfield suffered a spinal cord injury in the third quarter when he collided with tight end Tony McGee on a running play. The Bengals scored the last four times they had the ball and totaled 33 first downs in the game. Floyd Turner caught 6 passes for 104 yards in the losing cause.

Cincinnati	0	3	7	14	—	24
Baltimore	7	14	0	0	—	21

Balt — Alexander 17 pass from Testaverde (Stover kick)
Cin — FG Pelfrey 41
Balt — Morris 1 run (Stover kick)
Balt — Jackson 20 pass from Testaverde (Stover kick)
Cin — Carter 1 run (Pelfrey kick)
Cin — Blake 4 run (Pickens pass from Blake)
Cin — FG Pelfrey 49
Cin — FG Pelfrey 34

GREEN BAY 28, DETROIT 18—at Lambeau Field, attendance 60,695. It was another ho-hum day at Lambeau Field, as Brett Favre threw 4 touchdown passes and the Packers won their twelfth consecutive home game. Terry Mickens, who entered the game without a catch in 1996 and was playing because of injuries to Robert Brooks and Antonio Freeman, caught 2 short touchdown passes to give the Packers a 21-10 lead. After being on the receiving end of two horrific hits earlier in the game, Don Beebe beat Ryan McNeil on a 65-yard bomb late in the third quarter to give the Packers an 18-point advantage. Former Packers quarterback Don Majkowski, playing in place of the injured Scott Mitchell, connected on an 8-yard touchdown pass to Brett Perriman and a 2-point conversion to Herman Moore to cut the deficit to 28-18 with 4:27 left. The Lions recovered the ensuing onside kick, but, on fourth-and-17 from the Packers' 48, Moore's reception could only garner 16 yards. Favre completed 24 of 35 attempts for 281 yards, and 1 interception. Mickens caught 7 passes, and Beebe had 4 receptions for 106 yards. Barry Sanders, whose 152 yards included a darting 18-yard touchdown run, broke the 100-yard barrier for the first time in seven games.

Detroit	3	7	0	8	—	18
Green Bay	7	7	14	0	—	28

Det — FG Hanson 48
GB — Levens 1 pass from Favre (Jacke kick)
Det — Sanders 18 run (Hanson kick)
GB — Mickens 1 pass from Favre (Jacke kick)
GB — Mickens 6 pass from Favre (Jacke kick)
GB — Beebe 65 pass from Favre (Jacke kick)
Det — Perriman 8 pass from Majkowski (Moore pass from Majkowski)

SEATTLE 23, HOUSTON 16—at Kingdome, attendance 36,320. Michael McCrary blocked Al Del Greco's field goal attempt and lateraled the ball to Robert Blackmon, who raced 61 yards with 4 seconds left for the game-winning touchdown. After Joey Galloway caught a 14-yard touchdown pass from John Friesz to tie the game 16-16 with 3:30 left, Houston took eight plays to drive 60 yards down to the Seahawks' 20. With Houston lined up for the game-winning field goal with 16 seconds remaining, McCrary barrelled through the middle of the line, blocking the ball with his chest. He scooped up the ball on one bounce and ran 7 yards before lateraling to Blackmon, who took the ball the rest of the way. With the game tied 9-9 early in the fourth quarter, Chris Sanders took a short pass from Steve McNair, made a few moves, and raced down the sideline for a 65-yard touchdown to take a 16-9 lead with 8:12 left. The Seahawks answered with a 56-yard drive, capped by Galloway's touchdown. Del Greco had not had a kick blocked since 1986. Rookie Eddie George ran for 91 yards, and McNair, playing for injured starter Chris Chandler, completed 12 of 18 passes for 225 yards. Friesz completed 24 of 38 passes for 323 yards. The attendance was the smallest non-strike crowd in Seahawks' history.

Houston	3	0	3	10	—	16
Seattle	3	3	3	14	—	23

Hou — FG Del Greco 35
Sea — FG Peterson 25
Sea — FG Peterson 35
Hou — FG Del Greco 36
Sea — FG Peterson 44
Hou — FG Del Greco 45
Hou — Sanders 65 pass from McNair (Del Greco kick)
Sea — Galloway 14 pass from Friesz (Peterson kick)
Sea — Blackmon 61 lateral from McCrary (Peterson kick)

KANSAS CITY 21, MINNESOTA 6—at Metrodome, attendance 59,552. Greg Hill scored 2 touchdowns 25 seconds apart late in the fourth quarter to help the Chiefs hand the Vikings their third consecutive defeat. Hill raced 17 yards for his first touchdown with 3:32 remaining. Brad Johnson, who started in place of an injured Warren Moon, threw an interception to Brian Washington on the Vikings' next play from scrimmage. Washington ran the ball back to the 10-yard line, where Hill banged it into the end zone on the following play. Cris Carter's short touchdown catch with 1:28 left helped the Vikings avoid their first shutout at home since 1962. The Chiefs scored the only points of the first three quarters by converting 3 third-down attempts to key an 83-yard drive that finished with Marcus Allen scoring from 1-yard out for his 110th rushing touchdown—tying him with Walter Payton for the all-time rushing touchdown record. Hill gained exactly 100 yards, while the Chiefs outgained the Vikings 202-48, controlling the ball for 36:33. The Vikings scored 14 points or fewer for the fifth consecutive game.

Kansas City	0	7	0	14	—	21
Minnesota	0	0	0	6	—	6

KC — Allen 1 run (Stoyanovich kick)
KC — Hill 17 run (Stoyanovich kick)
KC — Hill 10 run (Stoyanovich kick)
Minn — Carter 1 pass from Johnson (pass failed)

NEW ENGLAND 42, MIAMI 23—at Foxboro Stadium, attendance 58,942. Curtis Martin had 3 rushing touchdowns, and Drew Bledsoe threw for 419 yards and 3 touchdowns to lead the Patriots to victory. The game's turning point was in the third quarter. Leading 17-14, Shawn Wooden intercepted a Bledsoe pass. On the next play, Karim Abdul-Jabbar was tackled after an 8-yard run and fumbled. Ben Coates caught a 23-yard touchdown pass four plays later to complete a 78-yard drive. It still was a four-point game with 7:30 left when Coates took a short pass and rumbled 84 yards for a touchdown. Sam Gash caught a 5-yard touchdown pass less than 2 minutes later, after a Dan Marino fumble, and Martin scored his third touchdown with 2:36 remaining after the Patriots' defense stopped the Dolphins on downs. Rookie Terry Glenn set career-highs with 10 receptions for 112 yards. Coates added 135 receiving yards on just 5 catches. Bledsoe, 30 of 41 for 419 yards, 3 touchdowns, and 2 interceptions, outdueled Marino, 17 of 34 for 225 yards, no touchdowns, and 1 interception. Abdul-Jabbar gained 104 yards and recorded his third multi-touchdown game of the season.

Miami	7	7	3	6	—	23
New England	7	7	7	21	—	42

NE — Martin 1 run (Vinatieri kick)
Mia — Abdul-Jabbar 3 run (Nedney kick)
Mia — Abdul-Jabbar 3 run (Nedney kick)
NE — Martin 1 run (Vinatieri kick)
Mia — FG Nedney 39
NE — Coates 23 pass from Bledsoe (Vinatieri kick)
NE — Coates 84 pass from Bledsoe (Vinatieri kick)
NE — Gash 5 pass from Bledsoe (Vinatieri kick)
NE — Martin 2 run (Vinatieri kick)
Mia — McDuffie 29 pass from Erickson (pass failed)

PHILADELPHIA 31, DALLAS 21—at Texas Stadium, attendance 64,952. James Willis intercepted a Troy Aikman pass in the end zone, and lateralled to Troy Vincent who went 90 yards for a touchdown to seal the Eagles' upset victory. Michael Irvin's 19-yard reception on a third-and-2 play put the Cowboys on the Eagles' 3-yard line with 1:16 left. Vincent tackled Emmitt Smith on first down, and Sylvester Wright stuffed Smith on second down. On third-and-goal from the 3, Aikman forced a pass to Tyji Armstrong. Willis picked it off and ran 14 yards before flipping it to Vincent, who cut across the field and raced 90 yards to clinch the victory. Gary Anderson kicked a 30-yard field goal with 3:19 to play to give the Eagles the lead. His kick was set up when Aikman rolled right and threw back across the middle only to have James Fuller intercept his pass at the Cowboys' 41. The Cowboys had tied the game at 21-21 on Smith's 7-yard touchdown run and Eric Bjornson's 2-point conversion catch with 10:14 remaining. Ricky Watters compiled 116 rushing yards, and Irving Fryar caught 9 passes for 120 yards. Ty Detmer completed 19 of 33 for 217 yards, 1 touchdown, and no interceptions. Aikman connected on 21 of 33 attempts for 179 yards, but threw no touchdowns, and 2 interceptions. Smith rushed for 113 yards.

Philadelphia	7	7	7	10	—	31
Dallas	7	3	3	8	—	21

Dall — E. Smith 1 run (Boniol kick)
Phil — Watters 5 run (Anderson kick)
Dall — FG Boniol 19
Phil — Detmer 6 run (Anderson kick)
Dall — FG Boniol 37
Phil — Fryar 14 pass from Detmer (Anderson kick)
Dall — E. Smith 7 run (Bjornson pass from Aikman)
Phil — FG Anderson 30
Phil — Vincent 90 lateral from Willis (Anderson kick)

PITTSBURGH 42, ST. LOUIS 6—at Three Rivers Stadium, attendance 58,148. Two first-quarter touchdown runs by former Rams running back Jerome Bettis paved the Steelers' path to victory. Bettis's first touchdown, from 3 yards, capped a game-opening 11-play, 69-yard drive. St. Louis then went for a first down on fourth-and-6 from Pittsburgh's 37, but Tony Banks was sacked by Myron Bell for a 12-yard loss. Bettis chugged 50 yards into the end zone on the next play, giving the Steelers a 14-0 lead with 3:51 left in the first quarter. Chip Lohmiller's second field goal came after the Rams blew a first-and-goal at the 2-yard line. Erric Pegram took the following kickoff and went 91 yards to put Pittsburgh ahead 28-6. Eddie Kennison fumbled the ensuing kickoff, leading to Kordell Stewart's second touchdown of the day. The Rams only totaled 201 yards, as Banks completed 16 of 35 attempts for 184 yards, 2 interceptions, and was sacked 6 times. Isaac Bruce caught 7 passes for 108 yards. Bettis, who was traded to the Steelers on draft day, gained 129 yards, his seventh 100-yard game of the season. The Steelers outgained the Rams by 184 rushing yards (248-64).

St. Louis	0	3	3	0	—	6
Pittsburgh	14	7	14	7	—	42

Pitt — Bettis 3 run (N. Johnson kick)
Pitt — Bettis 50 run (N. Johnson kick)
StL — FG Lohmiller 25
Pitt — Stewart 7 run (N. Johnson kick)
StL — FG Lohmiller 27
Pitt — Pegram 91 kickoff return (N. Johnson kick)
Pitt — Stewart 2 run (N. Johnson kick)
Pitt — Pegram 17 run (N. Johnson kick)

SAN DIEGO 26, INDIANAPOLIS 19—at RCA Dome, attendance 58,484. The Chargers turned 5 Colts turnovers into 20 points to win an interconference road game against the team that knocked them out of the playoffs the previous year. Jim Harbaugh, who had thrown just 2 interceptions all season, threw 4 picks in the first half. Kurt Gouveia's interception led to Charlie Jones's 41-yard touchdown reception and gave the Chargers a 7-0 lead less than five minutes into the game. After a second interception did not tally any points, Terrance Shaw's 36-yard interception return set up the first of 4 John Carney field goals. Carney booted a second field goal with 10:43 to play in the second quarter after nine-year veteran Shawn Lee's second career interception. Cary Blanchard booted 4 field goals, the last of which was set up by Ray Buchanan's 82-yard punt return to the 9-yard line, to cut the lead to 19-12. Chris Mims recovered a Harbaugh fumble, and Tony Martin caught his NFL-leading tenth touchdown pass of the season to give the Chargers a 26-12 lead. Marvin Harrison caught a 9-yard touchdown pass from Harbaugh with 3:20 left, but the Chargers were able to nearly run out the clock to preserve the victory. Sean Salisbury, playing in place of injured starter Stan Humphries, completed 19 of 31 attempts for 237 yards, 2 touchdowns, and no interceptions. Martin caught 6 of those passes for 128 yards. Harbaugh finished the day 18 of 44 for 203 yards, 1 touchdown, and 4 interceptions.

San Diego	7	9	3	7	—	26
Indianapolis	0	6	6	7	—	19

SD — Jones 41 pass from Salisbury (Carney kick)
SD — FG Carney 28
SD — FG Carney 30
Ind — FG Blanchard 47
Ind — FG Blanchard 39
SD — FG Carney 47
SD — FG Carney 22
Ind — FG Blanchard 33
Ind — FG Blanchard 20
SD — Martin 22 pass from Salisbury (Carney kick)
Ind — Harrison 9 pass from Harbaugh (Blanchard kick)

CHICAGO 13, TAMPA BAY 10—at Soldier Field, attendance 58,727. Vinson Smith's fumble recovery set up Raymont Harris's 1-yard plunge to give Chicago its second consecutive victory. Smith recovered an Errict Rhett fumble and rumbled 35 yards to the Bucs 19-yard line. Most of the players thought the play had ended, but Smith picked up the ball before being tackled by Trent Dilfer. Harris barreled in from the 1-yard line three plays later to score the deciding points. The Buccaneers scored their only touchdown one play after Clifton Abraham's interception. Dave Moore's 17-yard touchdown reception gave Tampa Bay a 7-3 second quarter-lead. Dilfer's fourth-and-15 pass from his own 49-yard line fell incomplete with 1:52 remaining effectively ending the Bucs' comeback hopes. Harris ran for 118 yards to spark the Bears' offense.

Tampa Bay	0	10	0	0	—	10
Chicago	3	3	7	0	—	13

Chi — FG Jaeger 27
TB — Moore 17 pass from Dilfer (Husted kick)
Chi — FG Jaeger 23
TB — FG Husted 45
Chi — Harris 1 run (Jaeger kick)

BUFFALO 38, WASHINGTON 13—at Rich Stadium, attendance 78,002. Darick Holmes ran for 122 yards and 3 touchdowns, and Thurman Thomas added 107 yards and a score, to lead the Bills. Thomas scored Buffalo's first touchdown to tie the game 7-7. Mark Maddox's fumble recovery set up Steve Christie's 33-yard field goal to give Buffalo a 17-10 advantage with 7:31 left in the half, a lead they would not relinquish. Jim Kelly hit Eric Moulds with a 15-yard pass on third-and-10 to set up Darick Holmes's 3-yard touchdown and a 17-7 halftime lead. The Redskins got the ball to begin the second half, but Bryce Paup forced Gus Frerotte to fumble. Sam Rogers recovered the ball, and Holmes scored his second touchdown to give Buffalo a 24-7 lead. The Bills then drove 97 yards on their next possession, with Kelly ending the 13-play, 4-minute and 33-second drive with a 4-yard run with 1:08 left in the third quarter. Terry Allen had two short touchdown runs for the Redskins. Buffalo outgained the Redskins (476-234), had more first downs (31-16), and piled up 266 rushing yards. Kelly completed 19 of 23 passes for 206 yards. The loss ended a seven-game winning streak for the Redskins.

Washington	7	0	0	6	—	13
Buffalo	0	17	14	7	—	38

Wash — Allen 1 run (Blanton kick)
Buff — Thomas 10 run (Christie kick)
Buff — FG Christie 33
Buff — Holmes 3 run (Christie kick)
Buff — Holmes 5 run (Christie kick)
Buff — Kelly 4 run (Christie kick)
Wash — Allen 1 run (pass failed)
Buff — Holmes 13 run (Christie kick)

SUNDAY NIGHT, NOVEMBER 3

SAN FRANCISCO 24, NEW ORLEANS 17—at Superdome, attendance 53,297. Steve Young ran and threw for a touchdown to lead the 49ers to victory and ruin the debut of interim coach Rick Venturi. Jerry Rice set up Young's fourth-quarter touchdown run with a 9-yard reception to the 2-yard line. The catch was Rice's NFL-record 1,000th career reception. Young hit Jerry Rice with a 36-yard touchdown pass with 6:46 to go before halftime to give the 49ers a 14-7 advantage. Dedrick Dodge's interception set up Jeff Wilkins's third field goal to give the 49ers a 17-7 third-quarter lead. The Saints responded with a 6-play, 77-yard drive that just took 2 minutes, and 23 seconds, ending with Michael Haynes's circus catch of Jim Everett's pass for a

50-yard touchdown. Dexter Carter returned the ensuing kickoff 71 yards to set up Young's 2-yard run. Doug Brien's 37-yard field goal cut the deficit to 24-17 with 2:16 remaining. Rice recovered the Saints' onside kick attempt, but the 49ers could not pick up a first down and had to punt. However, Everett was sacked and fumbled the football away in Saints territory with five seconds left. Young was 12 of 23 for 149 yards, 1 touchdown, no interceptions, but was sacked 6 times. Everett was 20 of 40 for 260 yards, 1 touchdown, but threw 2 interceptions. Haynes had 121 receiving yards on 5 receptions.

San Francisco	3	11	3	7	—	24
New Orleans	0	7	0	10	—	17

SF — FG Wilkins 34
SF — FG Wilkins 35
NO — Zellars 1 run (Brien kick)
SF — Rice 36 pass from Young (Young run)
SF — FG Wilkins 27
NO — Haynes 50 pass from Everett (Brien kick)
SF — Young 2 run (Wilkins kick)
NO — FG Brien 37

MONDAY, NOVEMBER 4

DENVER 22, OAKLAND 21—at Oakland-Alameda County Coliseum, attendance 61,179. John Elway threw a 49-yard touchdown pass to Rod Smith with 4:14 remaining to give the Broncos a victory over AFC West-rival Oakland. The winning drive, which consisted of 6 plays and covered 73 yards in just 47 seconds, followed 2 fourth quarter-touchdowns by the Raiders. Jason Elam's third field goal staked the Broncos to a 16-7 lead with 10:08 remaining. The Raiders went to a no-huddle offense and drove 57 yards in just over 2½ minutes, with Derrick Fenner's 15-yard touchdown reception cutting the deficit to 16-14. After the Raiders forced a punt, Jeff Hostetler hit a wide-open Tim Brown from 42 yards to give the Raiders a 21-16 lead with 5:01 left. But on third-and-10, Elway pump-faked and then fired a 49-yard touchdown pass to Smith. The Raiders punted from their own 47 with 3:07 left, Denver ran out the clock. The victory marks the thirty-fifth time that Elway led the Broncos to a fourth-quarter victory drive. An illegal motion penalty nullified Cole Ford's 25-yard second-quarter field goal. After the penalty, he missed a 30-yard field-goal attempt. The Raiders committed 11 penalties and lost for the first time in franchise history in Oakland on Monday night.

Denver	7	6	0	9	—	22
Oakland	7	0	0	14	—	21

Oak — Hostetler 5 run (Ford kick)
Den — Sharpe 10 pass from Elway (Elam kick)
Den — FG Elam 36
Den — FG Elam 43
Den — FG Elam 28
Oak — Fenner 15 pass from Hostetler (Ford kick)
Oak — T. Brown 42 pass from Hostetler (Ford kick)
Den — R. Smith 49 pass from Elway (pass failed)

ELEVENTH WEEK SUMMARIES

AMERICAN FOOTBALL CONFERENCE

Eastern Division	W	L	T	Pct.	Pts.	OP
Buffalo	7	3	0	.700	191	175
New England	7	3	0	.700	275	215
Indianapolis	5	5	0	.500	172	208
Miami	5	5	0	.500	238	205
N.Y. Jets	1	9	0	.100	172	264
Central Division						
Pittsburgh	7	3	0	.700	230	160
Houston	6	4	0	.600	230	190
Cincinnati	4	6	0	.400	214	226
Jacksonville	4	6	0	.400	202	208
Baltimore	3	7	0	.300	244	286
Western Division						
Denver	9	1	0	.900	262	167
Kansas City	7	3	0	.700	206	168
San Diego	6	4	0	.600	225	239
Seattle	5	5	0	.500	206	239
Oakland	4	6	0	.400	217	190

NATIONAL FOOTBALL CONFERENCE

Eastern Division	W	L	T	Pct.	Pts.	OP
Philadelphia	7	3	0	.700	228	203
Washington	7	3	0	.700	239	190
Dallas	6	4	0	.600	206	165
Arizona	4	6	0	.400	164	238
N.Y. Giants	4	6	0	.400	157	189
Central Division						
Green Bay	8	2	0	.800	288	144
Minnesota	5	5	0	.500	169	194
Chicago	4	6	0	.400	144	192
Detroit	4	6	0	.400	208	214
Tampa Bay	2	8	0	.200	115	195
Western Division						
San Francisco	7	3	0	.700	234	152
Carolina	6	4	0	.600	217	148
St. Louis	3	7	0	.300	201	280
New Orleans	2	8	0	.200	152	235
Atlanta	1	9	0	.100	176	303

SUNDAY, NOVEMBER 10

ARIZONA 37, WASHINGTON 34 (OT)—at RFK Stadium, attendance 51,929. Boomer Esiason threw for the third-most yards in NFL history, and newly signed Kevin Butler got a second chance and kicked a 32-yard game-winning field goal in overtime to give the Cardinals an upset victory. Butler missed a 37-yard game-winning field goal, but Darryl Morrison was whistled for being offsides, allowing Butler to win the game with just 33 seconds left in overtime. Four minutes earlier, Washington's Scott Blanton made an apparent game-winning 38-yard field goal. However, Scott Galbraith was called for holding, and Blanton missed the ensuing 48-yard attempt. After Blanton's miss, Esiason hit Marcus Dowdell with a 13-yard pass on third-and-10 to get to the Redskins' 24. Butler, in his first game with Arizona, missed a 32-yard field goal earlier in overtime. The Redskins took a 34-20 lead with 10:37 remaining on Terry Allen's 1-yard run. The Cardinals drove 80 yards in exactly three minutes, with Johnny McWilliams's 14-yard touchdown reception cutting the lead to seven. Darryl Pounds intercepted an Esiason pass at the 6-yard line with 1:52 remaining. The Redskins had to punt, however, after Gus Frerotte's third-and-5 pass to Michael Westbrook fell incomplete with 1:39 left. Esiason drove the Cardinals 66 yards in 64 seconds, with Anthony Edwards's 12-yard reception tying the game. Esiason was 35 of 59 for 522 yards, 4 interceptions, and 3 touchdowns. The Cardinals outgained Washington (615-416), and converted 11 of 20 third-down conversions, compared to 4 of 14 for the Redskins. Terry Allen rushed for 124 yards and 2 touchdowns.

Arizona	3	10	0	21	3	—	37
Washington	3	10	14	7	0	—	34

Ariz — FG Butler 26
Wash — FG Blanton 53
Wash — Logan 36 run (Blanton kick)
Ariz — FG Butler 39
Ariz — Dowdell 64 pass from Esiason (Butler kick)
Wash — FG Blanton 24
Wash — Westbrook 17 pass from Frerotte (Blanton kick)
Wash — Allen 1 run (Blanton kick)
Ariz — Centers 1 run (Butler kick)
Wash — Allen 1 run (Blanton kick)
Ariz — McWilliams 13 pass from Esiason (Butler kick)
Ariz — Edwards 12 pass from Esiason (Butler kick)
Ariz — FG Butler 32

ST. LOUIS 59, ATLANTA 16—at Trans World Dome, attendance 58,776. Eddie Kennison's 78-yard punt return sparked the Rams to score the most points by a team in the 1990s. Kennison's return, less than three minutes into the game, began the onslaught. Lawrence Phillips's 1-yard run gave St. Louis a 21-0 lead 11:42 before halftime. Eighteen seconds later, Toby Wright scored on a 19-yard interception return. The Falcons pulled to 31-13 when Jamal Anderson caught a 2-yard pass from Bobby Hebert to cap the opening drive of the second half. Tony Banks drove the Rams downfield and threw a 1-yard touchdown pass to Kennison to give the Rams a 38-13 lead. After a Falcons field goal, Harold Green scored from 1 yard out to make it 45-16 with 10:50 remaining. Phillips and Green each rushed for 106 yards. The point total was the most scored by the Rams since they defeated the Falcons 59-0 in 1976. St. Louis, which entered the game ranked thirtieth in the NFL in offense and defense, outgained Atlanta (464-292) and had more first downs (29-15). The Rams averaged 7.3 yards per carry, gaining 279 rushing yards. Banks was 15 of 24 for 188 yards. Atlanta had just 2 rushing yards in the first half.

Atlanta	0	7	9	0	—	16
St. Louis	14	17	7	21	—	59

StL — Kennison 78 punt return (Lohmiller kick)
StL — Bruce 22 pass from Banks (Lohmiller kick)
StL — Phillips 1 run (Lohmiller kick)
StL — Wright 19 interception return (Lohmiller kick)
Atl — Birden 18 pass from Hebert (Andersen kick)
StL — FG Lohmiller 42
Atl — Anderson 2 pass from Hebert (kick failed)
StL — Kennison 1 run from Banks (Lohmiller kick)
Atl — FG Andersen 47
StL — Green 1 run (Lohmiller kick)
StL — Green 35 run (Lohmiller kick)
StL — Robinson 13 run (Lohmiller kick)

JACKSONVILLE 30, BALTIMORE 27—at Jacksonville Municipal Stadium, attendance 64,628. Mark Brunell's 1-yard bootleg with 41 seconds remaining catapulted the Jaguars to a comeback victory. The Ravens took a 27-16 lead with 6:23 left on Derrick Alexander's 21-yard catch. Jacksonville went 90 yards in just two minutes, 33 seconds to pull within five with 3:50 left, but Brunell was unable to complete the 2-point conversion attempt. The Ravens were forced to punt after three plays, and the Jaguars drove 60 yards in one minute, 50 seconds, capped by Brunell's run. He then successfully converted the 2-point play with a pass to Keenan McCardell giving them a 3-point lead. Baltimore reached its own 43-yard line, but Clyde Simmons sacked Vinny Testaverde, forced him to fumble, and recovered the loose ball to clinch the victory. Brunell completed 24 of 37 attempts for 354 yards. Testaverde was 17 of 27 for 253 yards and 3 touchdowns. Byron (Bam) Morris rushed for 109 yards on 26 carries.

Baltimore	7	10	3	7	—	27
Jacksonville	0	3	10	17	—	30

Balt — M. Jackson 5 pass from Testaverde (Stover kick)
Jax — FG Hollis 23
Balt — Morris 52 pass from Testaverde (Stover kick)
Balt — FG Stover 21
Jax — Stewart 10 run (Hollis kick)
Balt — FG Stover 21
Jax — FG Hollis 33
Jax — FG Hollis 24
Balt — Alexander 21 pass from Testaverde (Stover kick)
Jax — Stewart 8 pass from Brunell (pass failed)
Jax — Brunell 1 run (McCardell pass from Brunell)

BUFFALO 24, PHILADELPHIA 17—at Veterans Stadium, attendance 66,613. Buffalo scored 10 points in the final 2½ minutes of the first half and held off the Eagles in the final minute. Philadelphia scored on its first possession when Kevin Turner caught a 23-yard touchdown pass from Ty Detmer. Rookie defensive lineman Gabe Northern blocked Tommy Hutton's punt and returned it 18 yards to tie the game. Trailing 10-7, Thurman Thomas's 5-yard run completed a 16-play, 64-yard drive. Buffalo had another long drive, with Quinn Early's 5-yard touchdown catch capping a 15-play, 74-yard drive in the third quarter. Detmer hit his favorite target, Irving Fryar, from 10 yards to pull the Eagles within seven points with 10:27 remaining. The Eagles' defense forced Buffalo to punt after three plays. Philadelphia drove from its own 25 to the Bills 3, but on fourth-and-goal with 32 seconds left, Bruce Smith sacked Detmer to quell the threat. Detmer was 26 of 44 for 315 yards. The Bills held the NFC's leading rusher, Ricky Watters, to just 51 yards on 19 carries. The Eagles outgained Buffalo (385-252) and controlled the clock (36:14-23:46), but allowed the Bills to convert 9 of 13 third-down conversions.

Buffalo	7	10	7	0	—	24
Philadelphia	10	0	0	7	—	17

Phil — Turner 23 pass from Detmer (Anderson kick)
Buff — Northern 18 blocked punt return (Christie kick)
Phil — FG Anderson 23
Buff — Thomas 5 run (Christie kick)
Buff — FG Christie 38
Buff — Early 5 pass from Kelly (Christie kick)
Phil — Fryar 10 pass from Detmer (Anderson kick)

DENVER 17, CHICAGO 12—at Mile High Stadium, attendance 75,555. Denver's defense stopped the Bears on four plays inside the 5-yard line to end the game. Trailing 17-12, a pass interference penalty in the end zone on Randy Hilliard with 40 seconds left gave the Bears the ball on the 1-yard line. Raymont Harris lost 1 yard on first down and 2 yards on a second-down sweep. Defensive tackle Jim Flanigan, who lines up as a fullback in short-yardage situations, dropped a pass at the goal line on third down and Tyrone Braxton knocked down a pass intended for Curtis Conway on fourth down as time expired. The Bears consumed nearly the first nine minutes of the second half, with Harris carrying the ball 10 times, concluding with Conway's 11-yard touchdown catch. However, the 2-point conversion attempt fell incomplete and left the score 14-9. The teams traded field goals, with Jeff Jaeger cutting the deficit to 17-12 with 9:33 left. Chicago outgained Denver (346-284) but committed 3 turnovers while forcing none. John Elway, hobbled by a sore hamstring, was 19 of 32 for 198 yards. Harris gained 112 yards.

Chicago	3	0	6	3	—	12
Denver	7	7	0	3	—	17

Chi — FG Jaeger 35
Den — Sharpe 15 pass from Elway (Elam kick)
Den — Davis 1 run (Elam kick)
Chi — Conway 11 pass from Krieg (pass failed)
Den — FG Elam 24
Chi — FG Jaeger 48

DALLAS 20, SAN FRANCISCO 17 (OT)—at 3Com Park, attendance 68,919. Chris Boniol's 29-yard field goal in overtime broke Dallas's three-game losing streak to San Francisco. The 49ers took an early 10-0 lead, but Steve Young suffered his second concussion in three weeks when he was hit by Jim Schwantz in the second quarter. Boniol tied the game 10-10 three seconds into the fourth quarter, but the 49ers retook the lead on Terry Kirby's 27-yard run with 11:38 left. Driving for the tying touchdown, Troy Aikman threw an interception to Marquez Pope on the 6-yard line with 6:37 left. However, Elvis Grbac, who replaced Young, threw an interception to Fred Strickland on the next play. Eric Bjornson caught a 6-yard touchdown pass from Aikman with 2:45 left to tie the game. The Cowboys won the overtime coin toss and drove 66 yards in 12 plays, setting up Boniol's heroics. Aikman completed 24 of 39 passes for 230 yards, 1 interception, and 1 touchdown. Grbac was 10 of 17 for 88 yards and 2 interceptions.

Dallas	0	7	0	10	3	—	20
San Francisco	10	0	0	7	0	—	17

SF — FG Wilkins 28
SF — Uwaezuoke 29 pass from Young (Wilkins kick)
Dall — Aikman 3 run (Boniol kick)
Dall — FG Boniol 26
SF — Kirby 27 run (Wilkins kick)
Dall — Bjornson 6 pass from Aikman (Boniol kick)
Dall — FG Boniol 29

KANSAS CITY 27, GREEN BAY 20—at Arrowhead Stadium, attendance 79,281. Greg Hill scored 3 touchdowns, and the Chiefs held off a late Green Bay rally to defeat the Packers. Hill scored on an 8-yard run with 10:18 left in the first half to give Kansas City a 13-3 lead. Hill caught a 34-yard pass from Steve Bono less than three minutes later to give the Chiefs a 20-3 lead. Chris Jacke's second field goal, from 49 yards at the halftime gun, cut the deficit to 20-6. However, Neil Smith forced Brett Favre to fumble on the first play from scrimmage in the second half. Hill ran in from 24 yards out on the next play to give the Chiefs a commanding 27-6 lead 22 seconds into the third quarter. Favre's second touchdown pass, to Derrick Mayes with 1:02 left, cut the lead to seven. Kimble Anders recovered the onside kick, and the Chiefs ran out the clock. Kansas City ran for 182 yards against the league's number-one ranked defense. Favre was 27 of 49 for 310 yards.

Green Bay	3	3	7	7	—	20
Kansas City	3	17	7	0	—	27

KC — FG Stoyanovich 26
GB — FG Jacke 24
KC — FG Stoyanovich 22
KC — Hill 8 run (Stoyanovich kick)
KC — Hill 34 pass from Bono (Stoyanovich kick)
GB — FG Jacke 49
KC — Hill 24 run (Stoyanovich kick)
GB — Beebe 25 pass from Favre (Jacke kick)
GB — Mayes 6 pass from Favre (Jacke kick)

HOUSTON 31, NEW ORLEANS 14—at Louisiana Superdome, attendance 34,121. Chris Chandler threw 3 touchdown passes to help the Oilers end their two-game losing skid. Houston scored on its first two possessions, with Chandler hitting Chris Sanders on a slant pattern for 42 yards and running back Ronnie Harmon for 11 yards, to take a 14-0 lead 6:43 into the game. Chandler's final touchdown pass went to tackle-eligible Erik Norgard, who caught a 1-yard touchdown pass for his first reception in 88 career games, 1:11 before halftime. Jim Everett threw his 200th career touchdown pass, making him only the twentieth quarterback to reach that milestone, when he fired a 34-yard strike to Michael Haynes in the fourth quarter. Everett finished 16 of 33 for 169 yards. The Oilers held the ball for 35 minutes, 25 seconds and held the Saints to 227 total yards and just a 1 for 11 third-down conversion rate. Of Chandler's 13 completions for 173 yards, Harmon caught 7 for 108 yards.

Houston	14	7	7	3	—	31
New Orleans	3	3	0	8	—	14

Hou — Sanders 42 pass from Chandler (Del Greco kick)
Hou — Harmon 11 pass from Chandler (Del Greco kick)
NO — FG Brien 29
Hou — Norgard 1 pass from Chandler (Del Greco kick)
NO — FG Brien 49
Hou — George 1 run (Del Greco kick)
NO — Haynes 34 pass from Everett (Brien kick)
Hou — FG Del Greco 25

MIAMI 37, INDIANAPOLIS 13—at Pro Player Stadium, attendance 66,623. Fred Barnett and Karim Abdul-Jabbar each scored 2 touchdowns to lead Miami to a rout of the Colts. Dan Marino threw 3 touchdown passes and also reached a personal milestone when he became the first player to surpass 50,000 passing yards in an NFL career. After the Dolphins took a 7-3 lead, Larry Izzo's blocked punt gave the Dolphins good field position. Abdul-Jabbar scored from 1 yard out to give Miami a 14-3 lead with 8:06 left in the second quarter. On the next drive, in which Marino hit McDuffie with a 36-yard pass to reach 50,000 yards, Barnett caught his first touchdown pass to put Miami ahead 21-3. Danny Stubbs forced Jim Harbaugh into an intentional grounding penalty in the end zone just 1:38 into the second half. Barnett scored again after the ensuing free kick to give Miami a 30-6 lead with 8:16 left in the third quarter. J.B. Brown intercepted Harbaugh on the next possession, and Abdul-Jabbar scored his second touchdown. Harbaugh, who threw 2 interceptions, was replaced by Paul Justin in the fourth quarter. Marino finished his day 17 of 24 for 204 yards and 3 touchdowns. Barnett had 106 receiving yards on 6 catches.

Indianapolis	3	3	0	7	—	13
Miami	7	14	16	0	—	37

Ind — FG Blanchard 48
Mia — McDuffie 12 pass from Marino (Nedney kick)
Mia — Abdul-Jabbar 1 run (Nedney kick)
Mia — Barnett 15 pass from Marino (Nedney kick)
Ind — FG Blanchard 22
Mia — Safety, Harbaugh intentional grounding in the end zone
Mia — Barnett 12 pass from Marino (Nedney kick)
Mia — Abdul-Jabbar 3 run (Nedney kick)
Ind — Dawkins 16 pass from Justin (Blanchard kick)

SEATTLE 42, MINNESOTA 23—at Kingdome, attendance 50,794. Seattle scored 2 touchdowns in the final 55 seconds of the first half to rout the Vikings. Trailing 13-7, the Vikings attempted to drive downfield just before halftime. Jay Bellamy intercepted Warren Moon with 1:16 left in the half, setting up Joey Galloway's 7-yard touchdown reception with 55 seconds left to give Seattle a 21-7 lead. Win-

ston Moss intercepted Moon 31 seconds later, and Steve Broussard ran 26 yards for a touchdown with 11 seconds remaining in the half. Chris Warren's touchdown run on the Seahawks' first third-quarter possession gave them a commanding 35-7 lead. Seattle converted 4 turnovers into 29 points. John Friesz was 22 of 33 for 263 yards and 2 touchdowns. Cris Carter had 142 receiving yards for the Vikings, who scored 2 touchdowns in the final 2:40 after Brad Johnson came in at quarterback. Moon was 14 of 30 for 187 yards and 2 interceptions.

Minnesota	0	7	0	16	—	23
Seattle	10	18	7	7	—	42

Sea — FG Peterson 54
Sea — L. Smith 1 run (Peterson kick)
Sea — FG Peterson 38
Minn — Reed 38 pass from Moon (Sisson kick)
Sea — Galloway 7 pass from Friesz (L. Smith run)
Sea — Broussard 26 run (Peterson kick)
Sea — Warren 1 run (Peterson kick)
Sea — Proehl 22 pass from Friesz (Peterson kick)
Minn — Johnson 1 run (Jordan pass from Johnson)
Minn — Reed 14 pass from Johnson (Walsh pass from Johnson)

NEW ENGLAND 31, NEW YORK JETS 27—at Giants Stadium, attendance 61,843. Drew Bledsoe fired 3 touchdown passes to lead the Patriots to a come-from-behind victory. Trailing 21-0, Terry Glenn scored in the final two minutes of the first half, and Curtis Martin finished the opening drive of the second half with a touchdown to cut the deficit to 21-14. After an exchange of field goals, Bledsoe completed 6 of 7 passes on a 9-play, 72-yard drive capped by Ben Coates's 17-yard touchdown to tie the game 24-24 with 11:25 remaining. On the next drive Frank Reich hit Richie Anderson with a 48-yard pass to set up Lowery's second field goal. The Patriots responded with David Meggett's 32-yard kickoff return to put the ball at their own 41-yard line. On fourth-and-two, Bledsoe hit Coates with a pass to keep the drive alive. Keith Byars scored his first touchdown as a Patriot to give New England its first lead, 31-27, with 4:03 left. The Jets reached the Patriots' 11 in the final minute, but Reich threw 4 incompletions. The Jets lost despite outgaining the Patriots (422-343 total yards), and controlling the clock (35:45-24:15). Adrian Murrell rushed for 128 yards and 2 touchdowns. Reich was 22 of 44 passes for 281 yards, 1 touchdown, and 1 interception. Bledsoe completed 24 of 34 passes for 297 yards, 3 touchdowns, and 2 interceptions.

New England	0	7	10	14	—	31
N.Y. Jets	7	14	3	3	—	27

NYJ — Graham 26 from Reich (Lowery kick)
NYJ — Murrell 1 run (Lowery kick)
NYJ — Murrell 1 run (Lowery kick)
NE — Glenn 26 pass from Bledsoe (Vinatieri kick)
NE — Martin 1 run (Vinatieri kick)
NE — FG Vinatieri 30
NYJ — FG Lowery 26
NE — Coates 17 pass from Bledsoe (Vinatieri kick)
NYJ — FG Lowery 32
NE — Byars 2 pass from Bledsoe (Vinatieri kick)

TAMPA BAY 20, OAKLAND 17 (OT)—at Houlihan's Stadium, attendance 45,392. Michael Husted's 23-yard field goal with 3:04 left in overtime gave Tampa Bay the victory. The Buccaneers were fortunate overtime occurred. Cole Ford missed a 23-yard field goal at the end of regulation to allow the game to remain tied at 17-17. The Raiders had driven 62 yards down to the Bucs' 6, and then kneeled down three times, before Ford hooked his attempt. Husted's overtime field goal was set up by a 20-yard pass to Mike Alstott to the Raiders' 15, and a 10-yard run to the 5-yard line. Tampa Bay drove nine minutes, 32 seconds to open the game, with Errict Rhett's 5-yard touchdown catch capping the 13-play, 78-yard drive. Anthony Smith's recovery of Trent Dilfer's fumble led to Harvey Williams's 18-yard halfback-option touchdown pass to James Jett. Each team kicked field goals in the final minute of the first half to send the clubs into the locker room tied 10-10. After Darryl Hobbs's touchdown catch gave the Raiders their only lead, the Buccaneers responded with a 14-play, 73-yard drive that lasted seven minutes, 59 seconds, ending with Alstott's 2-yard touchdown catch. The drive was kept alive by an unnecessary roughness penalty on third-and-9. The Raiders committed 12 penalties and converted just 2 of 8 third-down situations, whereas Tampa Bay was 10 of 16 on third-down conversions. Tampa Bay controlled the ball twice as long as Oakland (48:09-23:47).

Oakland	0	10	7	0	0	—	17
Tampa Bay	7	3	0	7	3	—	20

TB — Rhett 5 pass from Dilfer (Husted kick)
Oak — Jett 18 pass from H. Williams (Ford kick)
TB — FG Husted 44
Oak — FG Ford 45
Oak — Hobbs 8 pass from Hostetler (Ford kick)
TB — Alstott 2 pass from Dilfer (Husted kick)
TB — FG Husted 23

CINCINNATI 34, PITTSBURGH 24—at Cinergy Field, attendance 57,265. The Bengals scored the game's final 17 points to upset the Steelers and give coach Bruce Coslet a 3-0 record. Pittsburgh led 10-3 before Ki-Jana Carter tied the game with 1:15 left in the first half. A 39-yard pass to Yancey Thigpen set up Kordell Stewart's 1-yard sneak to put the Steelers ahead 17-10 with five seconds left. However, David Dunn returned the kickoff 90 yards for a touchdown on the last play of the half to tie the game 17-17. After Jerome Bettis's second touchdown, Eric Bieniemy countered with a 33-yard run down the left side to tie the game 24-24. Carter caught a 12-yard pass to give the Bengals a 31-24 lead with 6:39 left. That drive was kept alive when Jason Gildon speared Jeff Blake after he was sacked on a third-and-9 play in Bengals territory. Jimmy Spencer intercepted Mike Tomczak at the Bengals' 30 with 5:48 left, and Doug Pelfrey's 34-yard field goal with 2:27 left iced the game. The Bengals recorded 34 first downs and had the ball for 35 minutes, 49 seconds of the game's 60 minutes. Under Coslet, the Bengals have outscored their opponents 59-21 in the second half.

Pittsburgh	0	17	7	0	—	24
Cincinnati	3	14	7	10	—	34

Cin — FG Pelfrey 32
Pitt — FG N. Johnson 46
Pitt — Bettis 6 run (N. Johnson kick)
Cin — Carter 1 run (Pelfrey kick)
Pitt — Stewart 1 run (N. Johnson kick)
Cin — Dunn 90 kickoff return (Pelfrey kick)
Pitt — Bettis 1 run (N. Johnson kick)
Cin — Bieniemy 33 run (Pelfrey kick)
Cin — Carter 12 pass from Blake (Pelfrey kick)
Cin — FG Pelfrey 34

SUNDAY NIGHT, NOVEMBER 10

CAROLINA 27, NEW YORK GIANTS 17—at Ericsson Stadium, attendance 70,298. A stifling second-half defense vaulted the Carolina Panthers to a comeback victory. The Giants, who scored on their first two drives, took a 17-10 lead on Brad Daluiso's field goal with 9:57 left in the third quarter. Pat Terrell intercepted Dave Brown, leading to Anthony Johnson's game-tying 1-yard run. Greg Kragen then forced and recovered Rodney Hampton's fumble. John Kasay's field goal gave Carolina a 20-17 lead. After forcing a punt, the Panthers drove and Kerry Collins found Howard Griffith for a 17-yard touchdown pass with 11:36 left to conclude the scoring. Following their field goal to begin the second half, the Giants gained just 40 yards on 19 plays in their last 7 possessions. Three possessions ended in punts, with the others ending with a fumble and 3 interceptions. The Panthers improved to 5-0 at home, with their defense having allowed just 10 second-half points in those games.

N.Y. Giants	14	0	3	0	—	17
Carolina	7	3	10	7	—	27

Car — Ismail 35 run (Kasay kick)
NYG — Calloway 13 pass from Brown (Daluiso kick)
NYG — Lewis 23 pass from Brown (Daluiso kick)
Car — FG Kasay 42
NYG — FG Daluiso 22
Car — A. Johnson 1 run (Kasay kick)
Car — FG Kasay 28
Car — Griffith 17 pass from Collins (Kasay kick)

MONDAY, NOVEMBER 11

SAN DIEGO 27, DETROIT 21—at San Diego Jack Murphy Stadium, attendance 60,425. Andre Coleman caught a 46-yard Hail Mary pass on the final play of the first half to help propel the Chargers. Trailing 14-10 two seconds before halftime, Stan Humphries heaved an extremely high pass into the end zone. Coleman managed to get behind the defense and caught his first NFL touchdown pass. The Chargers, who controlled the ball for 40 minutes, 39 seconds, had Alfred Pupunu's 9-yard touchdown catch cap a four and one-half-minute drive and John Carney's 20-yard field goal ended an eight minute, eight second drive to put the Chargers ahead 27-14 with 12:24 remaining. Don Majkowski, who replaced an injured Scott Mitchell in the third quarter, drove the Lions downfield late in the game, with Brett Perriman catching a 1-yard pass with 1:52 left. However, Junior Seau recovered the onside kick. The Lions got the ball back for one last play deep in their own territory, and Majkowski was sacked to end the game. Barry Sanders scored twice for the Lions, with each touchdown set up by two San Diego penalties. Humphries, who had missed the previous two weeks with a dislocated shoulder, was 24 of 32 for 311 yards and 3 touchdowns. The Lions lost for the fourth consecutive time. The victory was costly for the Chargers as both center Courtney Hall and Pupunu suffered season-ending injuries.

Detroit	7	7	0	7	—	21
San Diego	7	10	7	3	—	27

SD — Martin 32 pass from Humphries (Carney kick)
Det — Sanders 2 run (Hanson kick)
Det — Sanders 11 run (Hanson kick)
SD — FG Carney 29
SD — A. Coleman 46 pass from Humphries (Carney kick)
SD — Pupunu 9 pass from Humphries (Carney kick)
SD — FG Carney 20
Det — Perriman 1 pass from Majkowski (Hanson kick)

TWELFTH WEEK SUMMARIES

AMERICAN FOOTBALL CONFERENCE

Eastern Division	W	L	T	Pct.	Pts.	OP
Buffalo	8	3	0	.727	222	192
New England	7	4	0	.636	283	249
Indianapolis	6	5	0	.545	206	237
Miami	6	5	0	.545	261	225
N.Y. Jets	1	10	0	.091	201	298
Central Division						
Pittsburgh	8	3	0	.727	258	163
Houston	6	5	0	.545	250	213
Cincinnati	4	7	0	.364	231	257
Jacksonville	4	7	0	.364	205	236
Baltimore	3	8	0	.273	264	324
Western Division						
Denver	10	1	0	.909	296	175
Kansas City	8	3	0	.727	220	178
San Diego	6	5	0	.545	242	264
Seattle	5	6	0	.455	222	256
Oakland	4	7	0	.364	230	206

NATIONAL FOOTBALL CONFERENCE

Eastern Division	W	L	T	Pct.	Pts.	OP
Washington	8	3	0	.727	265	211
Dallas	7	4	0	.636	227	171
Philadelphia	7	4	0	.636	249	229
Arizona	5	6	0	.455	195	261
N.Y. Giants	4	7	0	.364	180	220
Central Division						
Green Bay	8	3	0	.727	294	165
Minnesota	6	5	0	.545	185	207
Detroit	5	6	0	.455	225	230
Chicago	4	7	0	.364	154	206
Tampa Bay	3	8	0	.273	140	212
Western Division						
San Francisco	8	3	0	.727	272	172
Carolina	7	4	0	.636	237	158
St. Louis	3	8	0	.273	211	300
Atlanta	2	9	0	.182	193	318
New Orleans	2	9	0	.182	167	252

SUNDAY, NOVEMBER 17

SAN FRANCISCO 38, BALTIMORE 20—at 3Com Park, attendance 51,596. Elvis Grbac ran for a touchdown and completed 26 of 31 passes for 268 yards and a touchdown to lead the 49ers to a come-from-behind victory. The Ravens took a 20-17 third-quarter lead when Eric Zeier, who replaced injured Vinny Testaverde, threw a 2-yard touchdown pass to defensive lineman James Jones, who was lined up as a fullback. Faced with fourth-and-5 from the Ravens 30, Grbac completed a pass to Jerry Rice for a first down. William Floyd finished the drive with a 1-yard

touchdown run with 4:21 left in the third quarter to give the 49ers the lead for good. Chris Doleman sacked Zeier, forced him to fumble and recovered the ball in the end zone to give the 49ers a 31-20 lead with 12:08 to play. Grbac added a late touchdown to finish the scoring.

Baltimore	7	6	7	0	—	20
San Francisco	10	7	7	14	—	38

Balt — Jackson 65 pass from Testaverde (Stover kick)
SF — Kirby 8 run (Wilkins kick)
SF — FG Wilkins 27
SF — Rice 34 pass from Grbac (Wilkins kick)
Balt — FG Stover 43
Balt — FG Stover 25
Balt — J. Jones 2 pass from Zeier (Stover kick)
SF — Floyd 1 run (Wilkins kick)
SF — Doleman fumble recovery in end zone (Wilkins kick)
SF — Grbac 1 run (Wilkins kick)

CAROLINA 20, ST. LOUIS 10—at Trans World Dome, attendance 60,652. Anthony Johnson had a 7-yard touchdown run and recorded his fourth 100-yard rushing game to give the Panthers a 6-1 record against their divisional opponents. After an exchange of field goals, the Rams took a 10-3 lead 1:53 before halftime on Tony Banks's 11-yard touchdown pass to Lawrence Phillips. Carolina scored on its first two possessions of the second half to take a 17-10 lead. The Rams were unable to drive inside the Panthers' 40-yard line in the final quarter, and John Kasay's second field goal, 2:43 to play, ended the scoring. An NFL record was set during the game, as Rohn Stark's 39-yard punt with 13:25 remaining in the game allowed him to surpass Dave Jennings's punting yardage record. The 15-year veteran finished the game with 47,575 yards compared to Jennings's 47,567. Johnson finished with 123 yards. In a defensive struggle, the two teams combined for fewer than 500 total yards, while the Panthers recorded 6 sacks.

Carolina	0	3	14	3	—	20
St. Louis	0	10	0	0	—	10

StL — FG Lohmiller 41
Car — FG Kasay 38
StL — Phillips 11 pass from Banks (Lohmiller kick)
Car — Walls 9 pass from Beuerlein (Kasay kick)
Car — A. Johnson 7 run (Kasay kick)
Car — FG Kasay 34

KANSAS CITY 14, CHICAGO 10—at Arrowhead Stadium, attendance 76,752. Mark Collins made 2 key defensive plays in the second half to give the Chiefs their third consecutive victory. Each team scored on its first possession. Dave Krieg's 31-yard pass to Curtis Conway set up Raymont Harris's 14-yard touchdown run. Steve Bono threw a 24-yard pass to Derrick Walker before finding Chris Penn for a 20-yard touchdown reception to tie the game 7-7. The Chiefs converted 2 third-down situations on their second-quarter scoring drive that was capped by Kimble Anders's 10-yard run. Jeff Jaeger kicked a 49-yard field goal 15 seconds before halftime to cut the deficit to 14-10. However, the second half was a scoreless battle. Collins forced a fumble and recovered the ball at the Chiefs' 32-yard line late in the third quarter, and his interception in the end zone with just under four minutes remaining thwarted the Bears' final scoring opportunity.

Chicago	7	3	0	0	—	10
Kansas City	7	7	0	0	—	14

Chi — R. Harris 14 run (Jaeger kick)
KC — Penn 20 pass from Bono (Stoyanovich kick)
KC — Anders 10 run (Stoyanovich kick)
Chi — FG Jaeger 49

BUFFALO 31, CINCINNATI 17—at Rich Stadium, attendance 75,549. Jim Kelly threw a touchdown pass and ran for one as well and the defense forced 4 turnovers and recorded 7 sacks in the Bills' victory. The loss marked the Bengals' first defeat in four games under interim head coach Bruce Coslet. Jeff Burris's 32-yard punt return set up Buffalo's first touchdown. Thurman Thomas had 2 big third-down runs, and Jim Kelly's 1-yard sneak capped a 19-play, 92-yard drive that took nearly eight minutes off the clock and gave the Bills a 14-0 lead. Ashley Ambrose scored his first career touchdown with a 31-yard intercep-

tion return to cut the lead to 14-7. After forcing a punt, the Bengals got the ball back but Chris Spielman forced Ki-Jana Carter to fumble a lateral, and David White picked up the ball and went 12 yards for his first NFL touchdown. Kelly threw a 22-yard touchdown pass to Steve Tasker on the opening drive of the second half to give the Bills a commanding 31-7 lead. The Bills throttled Jeff Blake, allowing him to complete just 8 of 22 passes for 95 yards before being replaced by Erik Wilhelm. Andre Reed had 105 receiving yards on 6 catches for the Bills.

Cincinnati	0	7	0	10	—	17
Buffalo	7	17	7	0	—	31

Buff — Thomas 1 run (Christie kick)
Buff — Kelly 1 run (Christie kick)
Cin — Ambrose 31 interception return (Pelfrey kick)
Buff — White 12 fumble return (Christie kick)
Buff — FG Christie 22
Buff — Tasker 22 from Kelly (Christie kick)
Cin — Carter 1 run (Pelfrey kick)
Cin — FG Pelfrey 30

DENVER 34, NEW ENGLAND 8—at Foxboro Stadium, attendance 59,457. Terrell Davis had 3 first-half touchdowns and compiled his sixth 100-yard rushing game of the season to propel the Broncos to their seventh consecutive victory. New England attempted a fake punt on fourth down of its opening possession, but Tedy Bruschi dropped a pass that would have given the Patriots a first down. Denver started at the Patriots' 32-yard line and John Elway threw a 15-yard touchdown pass to Davis less than five minutes into the game. Steve Atwater's interception led to a 42-yard touchdown drive, capped by Davis's 10-yard scoring run. Davis scored his third touchdown of the half on a 2-yard run in which he fumbled the ball before crossing the goal line, only to have it bounce right back into his hands. Denver dominated the game with more first downs (26-11), total yards (422-218), and time of possession (39:00-21:00). Davis had 32 carries for 154 yards. Elway was 14 of 23 for 175 yards. Drew Bledsoe completed 22 of 41 passes for 212 yards. Curtis Martin scored a touchdown in his club-record sixth consecutive game.

Denver	14	10	7	3	—	34
New England	0	0	8	0	—	8

Den — Davis 15 pass from Elway (Elam kick)
Den — Davis 10 run (Elam kick)
Den — Davis 2 run (Elam kick)
Den — FG Elam 28
NE — Martin 7 run (Byars pass from Bledsoe)
Den — Elway 1 run (Elam kick)
Den — FG Elam 47

PITTSBURGH 28, JACKSONVILLE 3—at Three Rivers Stadium, attendance 57,879. Yancey Thigpen caught his first 2 touchdown passes of the season and Carnell Lake scored a game-turning touchdown for the Steelers. Thigpen opened the scoring with a 12-yard touchdown grab of Mike Tomczak's pass early in the second quarter. Jason Gildon sacked Mark Brunell and forced a fumble on the next play from scrimmage. Joel Steed recovered the fumble, and Jerome Bettis scored on the following play to quickly give the Steelers a 14-0 lead. The Jaguars, trailing 14-3, drove nearly the length of the field early in the third quarter. However, Lake blitzed and sacked Brunell, forcing a fumble. Lake scooped up the ball and raced 85 yards to put the Steelers ahead 21-3. Chad Brown had 3 sacks and Gildon recorded 2 of the Steelers' 6 sacks. Pittsburgh also forced 4 turnovers, and permitted the Jaguars just 3 first downs in 13 third-down opportunites. The Jaguars fell to 0-6 on the road.

Jacksonville	0	3	0	0	—	3
Pittsburgh	0	14	14	0	—	28

Pitt — Thigpen 12 pass from Tomczak (N. Johnson kick)
Pitt — Bettis 3 run (N. Johnson kick)
Jax — FG Hollis 40
Pitt — Lake 85 fumble return (N. Johnson kick)
Pitt — Thigpen 28 pass from Tomczak (N. Johnson kick)

MIAMI 23, HOUSTON 20—at Astrodome, attendance 47,358. Joe Nedney kicked 3 field goals, including the game winner as time expired, to give the Dolphins a come-from-behind victory. The Oilers sprinted to a 14-0 lead less than 11 minutes into the game. Chris Chandler completed a combined 8 of 9 passes on the two drives and threw 2

touchdown passes. The Dolphins trailed 17-13 in the fourth quarter, when Larry Izzo went 26 yards with a fake punt to keep the Dolphins drive alive. However, Cris Dishman recovered Karim Abdul-Jabbar's fumble in the end zone for a touchback. On the next play, Zach Thomas intercepted Chandler's pass and went 26 yards for a touchdown and gave Miami a 20-17 lead with 10:42 left. O.J. McDuffie's fumble and the subsequent recovery by Steve Jackson led to Al Del Greco's tying field goal with 3:20 remaining. Marino completed a short pass to Troy Drayton, who went 51 yards down the left sideline to the 5-yard line. Miami ran the clock down and Nedney booted the game-winning 29-yard field goal as time ran out. Marino was 21 of 28 for 237 yards. Chandler finished 15 of 27 for 167 yards.

Miami	0	10	3	10	—	23
Houston	14	0	3	3	—	20

Hou — Russell 18 pass from Chandler (Del Greco kick)
Hou — Wycheck 15 pass from Chandler (Del Greco kick)
Mia — Spikes 10 pass from Marino (Nedney kick)
Mia — FG Nedney 34
Mia — FG Nedney 44
Hou — FG Del Greco 30
Mia — Z. Thomas 26 interception return (Nedney kick)
Hou — FG Del Greco 33
Mia — FG Nedney 29

ATLANTA 17, NEW ORLEANS 15—at Georgia Dome, attendance 43,119. Bobby Hebert threw 2 touchdown passes against his former team to lead the Falcons to their second victory of the season. Linebacker Ron George's fumble recovery set up the Falcons' first score, an 8-yard touchdown pass from Hebert to Eric Metcalf. Brad Edwards's interception on the Saints' next possession led to Morten Andersen's 38-yard field goal. After Doug Brien's field goal, the Falcons responded with a 78-yard drive, capped by Hebert's touchdown pass to Terance Mathis with 16 seconds left before halftime. Brien's second field goal and Jim Everett's 19-yard touchdown pass to Lorenzo Neal cut the deficit to 17-12, but the Saints could not convert the two-point conversion. Faced with a 4th-and-5 situation at the Falcons' 12-yard line with 2:38 to play and trailing 17-12, interim coach Rick Venturi chose to have Brien kick his third field goal. New Orleans got the ball back on its own 41 with 18 seconds left, but Everett threw an incompletion before throwing a 20-yard pass to Michael Haynes. However, Haynes was tackled as time expired. Hebert was 26 of 39 for 229 yards. Everett completed 23 of 33 passes for 244 yards and 2 interceptions. The win was Atlanta's sixth consecutive home victory against divisional opponents.

New Orleans	0	3	3	9	—	15
Atlanta	10	7	0	0	—	17

Atl — Metcalf 8 pass from Hebert (Andersen kick)
Atl — FG Andersen 38
NO — FG Brien 42
Atl — Mathis 5 pass from Hebert (Andersen kick)
NO — FG Brien 37
NO — FG Neal 19 pass from Everett (pass failed)
NO — FG Brien 30

ARIZONA 31, N.Y. GIANTS 23—at Sun Devil Stadium, attendance 34,924. Boomer Esiason threw 2 first-half touchdown passes and the Cardinals held on for a NFC Eastern Division victory. The Cardinals recorded consecutive games with 30 or more points for the first time since 1988. Arizona vaulted out to a 21-3 lead when Esiason threw a 2-yard touchdown pass to Frank Sanders with 10:36 left in the second quarter. A 16-play, 88-yard drive which consumed 8:40 off the clock resulted in Brad Daluiso's field goal and cut the deficit to 21-6 at halftime. Charles Way's fumble recovery of Marcus Dowdell's punt led to the Giants first touchdown, but the Cardinals responded with a touchdown of their own on their next possession. Percy Ellsworth's fourth quarter fumble recovery gave the Giants possession at the Cardinals' 42-yard line. A 33-yard pass play from Dave Brown to Kevin Alexander set up Tyrone Wheatley's second touchdown at cut the score to 28-20 with 9:56 left. The Cardinals were forced to punt on their next possession, but Jason Sehorn could not handle the

punt. Anthony Edwards recovered the ball and Kevin Butler kicked an 18-yard field goal with 4:26 to play. The Giants took 16 plays to drive 59 yards, but had to settle for Daluiso's third field goal with 1:25 remaining. Seth Joyner recovered the ensuing onside kick to preserve the victory for Arizona. Esiason completed 18 of 26 for 260 yards. Brown was 22 of 41 for 262 yards.

N.Y. Giants	0	6	7	10	—	23
Arizona	14	7	7	3	—	31

Ariz — Moore 18 pass from Esiason (Butler kick)
Ariz — C. Smith 1 run (Butler kick)
NYG — FG Daluiso 25
Ariz — Sanders 2 pass from Esiason (Butler kick)
NYG — FG Daluiso 22
NYG — Wheatley 4 pass from Brown (Daluiso kick)
Ariz — L. Johnson 1 run (Butler kick)
NYG — Wheatley 9 pass from Brown (Daluiso kick)
Ariz — FG Butler 18
NYG — FG Daluiso 27

INDIANAPOLIS 34, N.Y. JETS 29—at RCA Dome, attendance 48,322. Cary Blanchard booted 4 field goals and the Colts took advantage of 3 third-quarter Jets turnovers to win. The Colts trailed 15-10 entering the third quarter, but Quentin Coryatt began the comeback with a fumble recovery leading to Jim Harbaugh's 4-yard touchdown pass to Marvin Harrison. Eugene Daniel returned an interception 35 yards for a touchdown just over a minute later and the Colts had a 23-15 lead less than five minutes into the third quarter. After Murrell's touchdown run, Ray Buchanan's interception put Blanchard in position for his second field goal. Jeff Graham's third touchdown catch, from 32 yards less than a minute into the fourth quarter, and the subsequent 2-point conversion connection from Frank Reich to Keyshawn Johnson allowed the Jets to retake the lead. The Colts rallied as Richard Dent sacked Reich for a safety, and Blanchard added 2 field goals, the second coming with 1:24 left, to take a 34-29 lead. Faced with a fourth-and-16 situation from their own 37 and no time outs, Reich completed an 18-yard pass to Johnson. After an incompletion, Reich threw a Hail Mary pass on the game's final play. Johnson nearly caught the pass in the end zone, but Buchanan knocked the ball away to preserve the victory. Reich completed 20 of 42 passes for a career-high 352 yards, with 3 touchdowns and 4 interceptions. Graham had 9 receptions for a career-high 189 yards and 3 touchdowns.

N.Y. Jets	3	12	6	8	—	29
Indianapolis	3	7	16	8	—	34

NYJ — FG Lowery 23
Ind — FG Blanchard 25
Ind — Warren 1 run (Blanchard kick)
NYJ — Graham 52 pass from Reich (kick blocked)
NYJ — Graham 17 pass from Reich (pass failed)
Ind — Harrison 4 pass from Harbaugh (pass failed)
Ind — Daniel 35 interception return (Blanchard kick)
NYJ — Murrell 1 run (pass failed)
Ind — FG Blanchard 49
NYJ — Graham 32 pass from Reich (Johnson pass from Reich)
Ind — safety, Dent sacked Reich in end zone
Ind — FG Blanchard 37
Ind — FG Blanchard 50

DETROIT 17, SEATTLE 16—at Silverdome, attendance 51,194. Jason Hanson's 43-yard field goal with 4:32 remaining gave the Lions the victory and snapped Seattle's three-game winning streak. Seattle had an opportunity to win the game, but Todd Peterson missed a 42-yard field goal as time expired. Seattle had to settle for 3 short field goal's by Peterson to take a 16-14 lead with 9:05 to play. Detroit responded with a 51-yard drive to set up Hanson's winning kick. The Seahawks faced 4th-and-10 at the Lions' 49 when Rick Mirer threw a 17-yard pass to Carlester Crumpler. A short pass and a running play gave Seattle first down at its own 20, but Lamar Smith was tackled for a 5-yard loss, forcing Peterson to attempt a longer field goal. Don Majkowski, starting in place of injured Scott Mitchell,

completed 18 of 23 for 157 yards. Barry Sanders rushed for 134 yards and a touchdown on 16 carries. Smith had 148 yards on 33 carries, both career high's.

Seattle	7	3	3	3	—	16
Detroit	0	7	7	3	—	17

Sea — L. Smith 1 run (Peterson kick)
Sea — FG Peterson 24
Det — Sanders 11 run (Hanson kick)
Sea — FG Peterson 25
Det — Moore 6 pass from Majkowski (Hanson kick)
Sea — FG Peterson 21
Det — FG Hanson 43

TAMPA BAY 25, SAN DIEGO 17—at San Diego Jack Murphy Stadium, attendance 57,526. Trent Dilfer passed for a career-high 327 yards and Michael Husted kicked 4 field goals as the Buccaneers erased a 14-0 deficit and defeated the Chargers. The game marked only the Buccaneers' second victory on the west coast in their 21-year history. Trailing 17-13, Husted kicked his third field goal to cut the deficit to 17-16 with 8:32 to play. John Lynch's interception set up Errict Rhett's 1-yard touchdown and gave Tampa Bay its first lead with 6:02 remaining. After the Buccaneers' defense forced a punt, Marvin Marshall's 29-yard punt return allowed Husted to boot his fourth field goal of the day to give the Chargers an eight-point lead with 1:11 left. The Chargers reached Tampa Bay's 35 in the final seconds, but 2 pass attempts fell incomplete in the end zone as time expired. Dilfer was 30 of 40 for 327 yards. Humphries completed 15 of 33 passes for 203 yards and 3 interceptions. Tampa Bay won back-to-back games under first-year head coach Tony Dungy for the first time. The Buccaneers' defense permitted just 11 first downs and held the opponent to 17 points or fewer for the sixth consecutive game.

Tampa Bay	3	10	0	12	—	25
San Diego	14	0	3	0	—	17

SD — Jones 63 pass from Humphries (Carney kick)
SD — Russell 14 run (Carney kick)
TB — FG Husted 33
TB — Alstott 4 run (Husted kick)
TB — FG Husted 29
SD — FG Carney 42
TB — FG Husted 27
TB — Rhett 1 run (pass failed)
TB — FG Husted 19

WASHINGTON 26, PHILADELPHIA 21—at Veterans Stadium, attendance 66,834. Gus Frerotte and Jamie Asher connected for 2 touchdowns and Scott Blanton kicked 4 field goals to propel the Redskins back into first place in the NFC Eastern Division. Asher's second touchdown catch capped a 61-yard second-half opening drive to give the Redskins a 20-7 advantage. The Eagles answered with a 78-yard drive of their own, capped by Ty Detmer's 13-yard touchdown pass to Chris T. Jones. Blanton's third field goal put the Redskins ahead 23-14, but Philadelphia battled back to within two points when Jason Dunn's 21-yard reception down to the 1-yard line set up Ricky Watters's touchdown run with 7:45 left. Brian Mitchell's 23-yard punt return led to Blanton's 33-yard kick with 1:20 remaining. The Eagles drove to the Redskins' 21-yard line before Detmer threw 4 incompletions to give the ball back with five seconds left. Frerotte completed 18 of 33 passes for 212 yards. Detmer was 21 of 33 for 251 yards. Jones had 7 receptions and 103 receiving yards.

Washington	3	10	10	3	—	26
Philadelphia	0	7	7	7	—	21

Wash — FG Blanton 37
Wash — Asher 12 pass from Frerotte (Blanton kick)
Phil — Watters 1 run (Anderson kick)
Wash — FG Blanton 22
Wash — Asher 7 pass from Frerotte (Blanton kick)
Phil — Jones 13 pass from Detmer (Anderson kick)
Wash — FG Blanton 30
Phil — Watters 1 run (Anderson kick)
Wash — FG Blanton 33

SUNDAY NIGHT, NOVEMBER 17

MINNESOTA 16, OAKLAND 13 (OT)—at Oakland-Alameda County Coliseum, attendance 41,183. Scott Sisson

kicked a 31-yard field goal with 3:07 remaining in overtime to defeat the Raiders. Minnesota took a 10-0 lead, capped by Brad Johnson's 82-yard touchdown pass to Jake Reed. Terry McDaniel's 52-yard interception return cut the deficit to three points. Jeff Hostetler's 25-yard pass to Rickey Dudley on third down set up Cole Ford's game-tying field goal late in the third quarter. Both teams exchanged fourth-quarter field goals before Sisson missed a 38-yard attempt with 3:20 to play in regulation. After Oakland was forced to punt on the first possession of overtime, the Vikings drove 16 plays to set up Sisson's winning kick. The Vikings recorded 445 total yards, while permitting just 237 yards. Leroy Hoard recorded his third career 100-yard game with 108 yards. Johnson was 20 of 33 for 275 yards. Reed had 4 receptions for 134 yards.

Minnesota	10	0	0	3	3	—	16
Oakland	0	7	3	3	0	—	13

Minn — FG Sisson 22
Minn — Reed 82 pass from B. Johnson (Sisson kick)
Oak — McDaniel 52 interception return (Ford kick)
Oak — FG Ford 26
Minn — FG Sisson 24
Oak — FG Ford 41
Minn — FG Sisson 31

MONDAY, NOVEMBER 18

DALLAS 21, GREEN BAY 6—at Texas Stadium, attendance 65,032. Chris Boniol equalled an NFL record by kicking 7 field goals as Dallas defeated Green Bay for the fifth consecutive time in regular season action, and eighth consecutive time overall. Dallas lead 18-0 before Green Bay scored with 1:53 remaining on Brett Favre's 3-yard touchdown pass to Derrick Mayes. Dallas recovered the onside kick, and Boniol added the record-tying field goal as time expired. Troy Aikman completed 24 of 35 passes 206 yards. Favre completed 21 of 37 passes for 194 yards and was sacked 4 times. Dallas held an opponent to 10 points or fewer for the fifth time in eleven games.

Green Bay	0	0	0	6	—	6
Dallas	6	9	0	6	—	21

Dall — FG Boniol 45
Dall — FG Boniol 37
Dall — FG Boniol 42
Dall — FG Boniol 45
Dall — FG Boniol 35
Dall — FG Boniol 39
GB — Mayes 3 pass from Favre (pass failed)
Dall — FG Boniol 28

THIRTEENTH WEEK SUMMARIES

AMERICAN FOOTBALL CONFERENCE

Eastern Division	W	L	T	Pct.	Pts.	OP
Buffalo	9	3	0	.750	257	202
New England	8	4	0	.667	310	262
Indianapolis	6	6	0	.500	219	264
Miami	6	6	0	.500	278	249
N.Y. Jets	1	11	0	.083	211	333
Central Division						
Pittsburgh	9	3	0	.750	282	180
Houston	6	6	0	.500	256	244
Cincinnati	5	7	0	.412	272	288
Jacksonville	5	7	0	.412	233	261
Baltimore	3	9	0	.250	289	352
Western Division						
Denver	11	1	0	.917	317	192
Kansas City	8	4	0	.667	234	206
San Diego	7	5	0	.583	270	278
Oakland	5	7	0	.412	257	227
Seattle	5	7	0	.412	243	283

NATIONAL FOOTBALL CONFERENCE

Eastern Division	W	L	T	Pct.	Pts.	OP
Washington	8	4	0	.667	281	230
Dallas	7	5	0	.583	233	191
Philadelphia	7	5	0	.583	279	265
Arizona	6	6	0	.500	231	291
N.Y. Giants	5	7	0	.412	200	226
Central Division						
Green Bay	9	3	0	.750	318	174
Minnesota	6	6	0	.500	202	228
Chicago	5	7	0	.412	185	220
Detroit	5	7	0	.412	239	261
Tampa Bay	4	8	0	.333	153	219
Western Division						
San Francisco	9	3	0	.750	291	188

Carolina	8	4	0	.667	268	164
St. Louis	3	9	0	.250	220	324
Atlanta	2	10	0	.167	224	359
New Orleans	2	10	0	.167	174	265

SUNDAY, NOVEMBER 24

CINCINNATI 41, ATLANTA 31—at Cinergy Field, attendance 44,868. Jeff Blake threw 4 touchdown passes, including 3 to Carl Pickens, as Cincinnati improved to 4-1 under coach Bruce Coslet. Leading 3-0, Darnay Scott finished an 89-yard drive with a 20-yard touchdown catch. Less than two minutes later, Pickens hauled in a 61-yard bomb to give the Bengals a 17-0 lead. Pickens' touchdown came three plays after rookie Jevon Langford's first career interception. Atlanta twice cut the Cincinnati lead to three points, at 20-17 and 27-24. However, Brian Milne scored his first NFL touchdown with 11:00 remaining, and, after Steve Tovar's interception, Pickens caught his third touchdown of the game with 9:33 left. Blake was 21 of 36 for 349 yards, with 4 touchdowns and no interceptions. Pickens had 11 receptions for 176 yards. Bobby Hebert, who played with a stomach virus, completed 23 of 40 passes for 304 yards and 3 touchdowns, but threw 2 interceptions. Eric Metcalf caught 9 passes for 122 yards and 2 touchdowns. The loss was the tenth consecutive road defeat for Atlanta.

Atlanta	0	10	7	14	—	31
Cincinnati	17	3	7	14	—	41

Cin — FG Pelfrey 37
Cin — D. Scott 20 pass from Blake (Pelfrey kick)
Cin — Pickens 61 pass from Blake (Pelfrey kick)
Atl — FG Andersen 33
Atl — Emanuel 16 pass from Hebert (Andersen kick)
Cin — FG Pelfrey 20
Atl — J. Anderson 4 run (Andersen kick)
Cin — Pickens 7 pass from Blake (Pelfrey kick)
Atl — Metcalf 26 pass from Hebert (Andersen kick)
Cin — Milne 1 run (Pelfrey kick)
Cin — Pickens 14 pass from Blake (Pelfreykick)
Atl — Metcalf 27 pass from Hebert (Andersen kick)

CAROLINA 31, HOUSTON 6—at Astrodome, attendance 20,107. Steve Beuerlein threw 3 touchdown passes, and the Panthers scored their last 21 points off Oilers turnovers to lead Carolina to victory. Leading 10-7 in the third quarter, Eric Davis's 11-yard interception return to the Oilers' 25 set up Willie Green's second touchdown catch with 5:46 left in the third quarter. Al Del Greco's second field goal cut the deficit to 17-6, but Sam Mills picked up a bobbled snap by reserve quarterback Steve McNair and lumbered 41 yards to give the Panthers a commanding 24-6 lead with 7:18 remaining. Willie Davis's fumble on the next possession was followed by a 40-yard touchdown pass from Beuerlein to Wesley Walls. Beuerlein, who was a last minute starter for the still-injured Kerry Collins, completed 11 of 18 for 165 yards and 3 touchdowns. Mark Carrier, who had 3 catches, became the fiftieth player in NFL history with 500 receptions. McNair entered the game late in the third quarter after Chris Chandler severely sprained his ankle. Carolina won despite getting just 12 first downs.

Carolina	0	10	7	14	—	31
Houston	0	3	0	3	—	6

Car — Green 30 pass from Beuerlein (Kasay kick)
Hou — FG Del Greco 24
Car — FG Kasay 49
Car — Green 12 pass from Beuerlein (Kasay kick)
Hou — FG Del Greco 45
Car — Mills 41 fumble return (Kasay kick)
Car — Walls 40 pass from Beuerlein (Kasay kick)

N.Y. GIANTS 20, DALLAS 6—at Giants Stadium, attendance 77,081. The Giants' defense forced 5 turnovers to stun the defending Super Bowl champions. Dallas failed to score a touchdown for the second consecutive week, marking the first time they had done that since 1990. The Cowboys first turnover, an interception by Jason Sehorn, led to Brad Daluiso's first field goal. Leading 6-3, Corey Widmer stripped Michael Irvin of the ball. Tito Wooten picked it up and ran 54 yards for a touchdown and a 13-3 Giants lead with 1:53 left in the half. Deion Sanders caught a 41-yard pass from Troy Aikman in the third quarter, but Phillippi Sparks stripped him of the ball inside the 10-yard line. Chris Boniol's second field goal cut the deficit to 13-6 with 11:43 left. However, the Giants responded with a 10-play, nearly six-minute drive, capped by Brian Kozlowski's first NFL touchdown. Daryl Johnston fumbled, and Aikman threw another interception in the final minutes to secure the Giants' victory. Aikman completed 28 of 39 for 280 yards, but threw 2 interceptions and saw his receivers fumble away 3 of those completions.

Dallas	3	0	0	3	—	6
N.Y. Giants	0	13	0	7	—	20

Dall — FG Boniol 31
NYG — FG Daluiso 45
NYG — FG Daluiso 46
NYG — Wooten 54 fumble return (Daluiso kick)
Dall — FG Boniol 37
NYG — Kozlowski 4 pass from Brown (Daluiso kick)

DENVER 21, MINNESOTA 17—at Hubert H. Humphrey Metrodome, attendance 59,142. Ed McCaffrey caught a 5-yard touchdown, on a pass that was deflected twice, with 19 seconds left to give John Elway his thirty-fourth comeback victory. Faced with a third-and-2 situation from the 5-yard line, Elway forced a pass over the middle to Shannon Sharpe. Harlon Barnett deflected the pass at the goal line, but in attempting to intercept the pass he collided with teammate Orlando Thomas, knocking the ball into the air again. McCaffrey caught the ball on the 2-yard line and dove into the end zone for the winning score. The lead changed hands three times before McCaffrey's final catch. The Vikings took their last lead when Cris Carter caught a 10-yard touchdown pass from Brad Johnson with 23 seconds left in the third quarter. Jason Elam missed a gametying 42-yard field goal with 7:51 left. However, the Broncos forced the Vikings to punt after three plays. Denver drove 84 yards in 11 plays for the winning score, with Aaron Craver's short reception on fourth-and-1 to the Vikings' 13 allowing McCaffrey's heroics. Elway was 27 of 36 for 334 yards, 2 touchdowns, and 1 interception. Johnson, who started for an injured Warren Moon, was 24 of 35 for 266 yards, 2 touchdowns, and 2 interceptions.

Denver	7	7	0	7	—	21
Minnesota	0	10	7	0	—	17

Den — T. Davis 1 run (Elam kick)
Minn — FG Sisson 27
Minn — Walsh 7 pass from Johnson (Sisson kick)
Den — T. Davis 1 pass from Elway (Elam kick)
Minn — Carter 11 pass from Johnson (Sisson kick)
Den — McCaffrey 5 pass from Elway (Elam kick)

CHICAGO 31, DETROIT 14—at Soldier Field, attendance 55,864. Dave Krieg threw 3 touchdown passes to lead the Bears. Curtis Conway's 19-yard touchdown catch just 1:40 into the game began the scoring. After Scott Mitchell's 1-yard run, Anthony Marshall took a lateral from Bobby Engram on the ensuing kickoff and went 75 yards to the 10-yard line. Mike Faulkerson's first career touchdown gave the Bears a 14-7 lead. Barry Sanders scored from 22 yards out with 46 seconds left to complete a wild first quarter. Both Detroit touchdowns were set up by 22-yard pass interference penalties. Krieg's third touchdown pass, 5 yards to Engram, ended a 7-minute, two-second drive. Jeff Jaeger added a field goal 31 seconds before halftime, and Raymont Harris scored on the Bears' first possession of the second half to finish the scoring. The second half was played in sleet, contributing to the lack of offensive production. Harris gained 122 rushing yards. Krieg threw for 219 yards, 3 touchdowns, and no interceptions, while Scott Mitchell threw for 230 yards, but 0 touchdowns and 3 interceptions. Sanders rushed for 107 yards and became the first player in NFL history to gain at least 1,000 yards in each of his first eight seasons.

Detroit	14	0	0	0	—	14
Chicago	14	10	7	0	—	31

Chi — Conway 19 pass from Krieg (Jaeger kick)
Det — Mitchell 1 run (Hanson kick)
Chi — Faulkerson 1 pass from Krieg (Jaeger kick)
Det — Sanders 22 run (Hanson kick)
Chi — Engram 5 pass from Krieg (Hanson kick)
Chi — FG Jaeger 42
Chi — Harris 3 run (Jaeger kick)

NEW ENGLAND 27, INDIANAPOLIS 13—at Foxboro Stadium, attendance 58,226. Curtis Martin racked up 141 rushing yards and scored a touchdown to give the Patriots a season-sweep of the Colts. New England began the game with two scoring drives of more than six minutes. Shawn Jefferson's 13-yard touchdown reception gave the Patriots a 10-0 lead with 50 seconds left in the first quarter. Drew Bledsoe's second touchdown pass, to Terry Glenn, staked New England to a 17-0 lead with 4:37 remaining in the first half. Two Cary Blanchard field goals pulled the Colts within 11 points, but Jim Harbaugh injured his knee on Willie Clay's blitz, thus severely damaging the Colts' offense. Martin's 12-yard jaunt, which was his club-record sixteenth touchdown of the season, put the Patriots ahead 27-6 with 11:42 left and all but iced the game. New England dominated the game statistically, with more first downs (25-15), total yards (429-291), and time of possession (38:07-21:53). Bledsoe was 21 of 30 for 242 yards and 2 touchdowns.

Indianapolis	0	3	3	7	—	13
New England	10	7	3	7	—	27

NE — FG Vinatieri 26
NE — Jefferson 13 pass from Bledsoe (Vinatieri kick)
NE — Glenn 5 pass from Bledsoe (Vinatieri kick)
Ind — FG Blanchard 42
Ind — FG Blanchard 50
NE — FG Vinatieri 22
NE — Martin 12 run (Vinatieri kick)
Ind — Harrison 5 pass from Justin (Blanchard kick)

JACKSONVILLE 28, BALTIMORE 25 (OT)—at Memorial Stadium, attendance 57,384. Mark Brunell threw 4 fourth-quarter touchdown passes and ran in a 2-point conversion, and Mike Hollis kicked a 34-yard overtime field goal to give the Jaguars a come-from-behind victory. Trailing 25-10, Brunell threw an 11-yard touchdown pass to Pete Mitchell with 12:04 left. The 74-yard drive was kept alive by 3 third-down completions by Brunell. Baltimore stopped the Jaguars on downs at the Ravens' 30 with 2:49 left. However, a bad exchange between center Wally Williams and Vinny Testaverde on the next play from scrimmage allowed Eddie Robinson to recover the ball at the 19-yard line. Brunell gunned a 7-yard touchdown pass to Willie Jackson to cut the lead to 25-23 with 1:24 left. Going for two points, Brunell rolled left and then lunged into the end zone with the tying conversion. The Ravens drove downfield, but Matt Stover, who had made 4 field goals earlier, missed a 49-yard attempt with two seconds left. In overtime, Earnest Byner fumbled and Kelvin Pritchett recovered at the Jaguars' 37, allowing Hollis to kick the game-winning field goal. The loss marked the fifth time this season that Baltimore blew a fourth-quarter lead. Brunell was 28 of 46 for 306 yards, 2 touchdowns, and 2 interceptions. Testaverde completed 31 of 50 passes for 366 yards. Keenan McCardell (9 catches, 107 yards) and Jimmy Smith (8 catches, 131 yards) had big days for the Jaguars, while Michael Jackson had 9 receptions for 150 yards for Baltimore. The offenses dominated the game, with the Jaguars converting on 9 of 16 third-down conversions, and the Ravens 8 of 15.

Jacksonville	0	10	0	15	3	—	28
Baltimore	7	9	9	0	0	—	25

Balt — Caldwell 45 interception return (Stover kick)
Balt — FG Stover 21
Jax — Stewart 1 run (Hollis kick)
Balt — FG Stover 29
Jax — FG Hollis 29
Balt — FG Stover 41
Balt — Morris 1 run (run failed)
Balt — FG Stover 33
Jax — Mitchell 11 pass from Brunell (Hollis kick)
Jax — W. Jackson 7 pass from Brunell (Brunell run)
Jax — FG Hollis 34

TAMPA BAY 13, NEW ORLEANS 7—at Houlihan's Stadium, attendance 40,203. Tampa Bay forced 4 turnovers and held its seventh consecutive opponent to 17 or fewer points to win its third straight game. A 13-yard pass to Jackie Harris on fourth-and-1 set up Michael Husted's 43-yard field goal midway through the first quarter. Husted connected again with 2:31 left, giving Tampa Bay a 6-0 halftime lead. Tampa Bay took a 13-0 lead when it drove 80 yards to begin the second half, capped by Mike Alstott's 17-yard touchdown reception off a screen pass. The Saints responded when Jim Everett's 1-yard touchdown pass to Tony Johnson finishing a 13-play, 7-minute, 46-second drive. New Orleans could get no closer than the Buccaneers' 39 the remainder of the game. John Lynch's interception with 4:45 left ended the Saints' chances. Tampa Bay's defense held the Saints to just 3 of 11 third-down conversions. Trent Dilfer was 20 of 34 for 253 yards and 1 touchdown. Everett completed 20 of 31 passes for 196 yards, but threw 3 interceptions.

New Orleans	0	0	7	0	—	7
Tampa Bay	3	3	7	0	—	13

TB — FG Husted 43
TB — FG Husted 38
TB — Alstott 17 pass from Dilfer (Husted kick)
NO — T. Johnson 1 pass from Everett (Brien kick)

BUFFALO 35, N.Y. JETS 10—at Rich Stadium, attendance 60,854. A quick-striking Buffalo offense produced 4 touchdown passes, 3 by Jim Kelly, to lead the Bills to victory. Trailing 3-0, Steve Tasker raced 62 yards with a reception to set up Andre Reed's 3-yard touchdown to complete a 7-play, 75-yard drive. Early in the second quarter, Kurt Schulz intercepted Frank Reich, and Reed caught his second touchdown one minute, one second later. The Bills perfected the two-minute drill at the end of the first half, driving 69 yards in 6 plays, in one minute, 21 seconds, ending with Tasker's 19-yard touchdown. Kelly hurt his hamstring the play prior to the touchdown and left the game. In the third quarter Todd Collins directed a 5-play, 46-yard drive, which lasted one minute, 57 seconds, capped by Tasker's second touchdown. After Jeff Graham cut the deficit to eighteen points, rookie Eric Moulds returned the kickoff 97 yards. Tasker caught 6 passes for 160 yards. Former Bills quarterback Reich was 25 of 51 for 267 yards, 1 touchdown, but threw 3 interceptions. Adrian Murrell gained 103 rushing yards, while Graham caught 7 passes for 124 yards, and Wayne Chrebet hauled in 10 receptions.

N.Y. Jets	3	0	0	7	—	10
Buffalo	7	14	7	7	—	35

NYJ — FG Lowery 25
Buff — Reed 3 pass from Kelly (Christie kick)
Buff — Reed 22 pass from Kelly (Christie kick)
Buff — Tasker 19 pass from Kelly (Christie kick)
Buff — Tasker 18 pass from Collins (Christie kick)
NYJ — Graham 8 pass from Reich (Lowery kick)
Buff — Moulds 97 kickoff return (Christie kick)

OAKLAND 27, SEATTLE 21—at Kingdome, attendance 47,506. Jeff Hostetler threw 2 touchdown passes to lead the Raiders past Seattle and help end their 3-game skid. Oakland held a 14-10 halftime lead before each team scored on its first two second-half possessions. The final score of the frenzy, Chris Warren's 2-yard run and successful 2-point conversion, cut the Raiders lead to 24-21 with 11:10 remaining. After forcing the Raiders to punt, Seattle reached the Raiders' 42. But the drive stalled as Lamar Smith was stopped for no gain on third-and-1 and Rick Mirer was stuffed on a quarterback sneak attempt on fourth down with 6:36 left. The Raiders ran the next four minutes, 40 seconds, off the clock, with Cole Ford's field goal giving them a 6-point cushion with 1:56 left. Seattle reached the Raiders' 47 with 51 seconds remaining, but Mirer's fourth down pass to Joey Galloway fell incomplete. Seattle's touchdowns were set up on 40- and 42-yard passes to Galloway to the 2-yard line. Napoleon Kaufman rushed for 104 yards on just 15 carries.

Oakland	0	14	3	10	—	27
Seattle	3	7	3	8	—	21

Sea — FG Peterson 21
Oak — Jett 17 pass from Hostetler (Ford kick)
Sea — R. Williams 2 pass from Mirer (Peterson kick)
Oak — Cunningham 3 pass from Hostetler (Ford kick)
Oak — FG Ford 47
Sea — FG Peterson 32
Oak — Fenner 1 run (Ford kick)
Sea — Warren 2 run (Warren run)
Oak — FG Ford 26

ARIZONA 36, PHILADELPHIA 30—at Sun Devil Stadium, attendance 36,175. Boomer Esiason's 24-yard touchdown pass to Marcus Dowdell with 14 seconds remaining capped a wild fourth quarter, in which 24 points were scored in the final 2:45, to give Arizona a hard-earned victory. The Cardinals took a 24-13 lead with 10:58 remaining on Pat Carter's 6-yard touchdown catch. The Eagles responded with a 68-yard drive that ended with Ricky Watters's 4-yard jaunt. Arizona took the next five minutes, 38 seconds off the clock and scored when Larry Centers caught an Esiason swing pass from 2 yards with 2:45 left. Derrick Witherspoon returned the ensuing squib kick 95 yards down the left sideline to cut the deficit to 29-27. Johnny Thomas recovered the onside kick, and the Eagles got down to the Cardinals' 20 with 1:18 left, but Watters was only able to get 6 yards on three carries and, with Arizona using all three of its timeouts, Gary Anderson kicked a 32-yard field goal with 52 seconds left to put the Eagles ahead 30-29. Leeland McElroy returned the kickoff to the 35-yard line, and Esiason hit Dowdell with a 17-yard out pattern. On the Eagles' 48, with 29 seconds left, Esiason threw consecutive 12-yard out patterns to Rob Moore and Frank Sanders to get the Cardinals within field-goal range. Disdaining the kick however, Esiason found Dowdell on an out-and-up pattern to win the game. Esiason was 24 of 43 for 367 yards and 3 touchdowns. Ty Detmer completed 21 of 38 passes for 322 yards and an interception.

Philadelphia	7	3	3	17	—	30
Arizona	3	10	3	20	—	36

Phil — Watters 1 run (Anderson kick)
Ariz — FG Butler 21
Phil — FG Anderson 44
Ariz — McElroy 4 run (Butler kick)
Ariz — FG Butler 36
Phil — FG Anderson 25
Ariz — FG Butler 27
Ariz — P. Carter 6 pass from Esiason (pass failed)
Phil — Watters 4 run (Anderson kick)
Ariz — Centers 2 pass from Esiason (Butler kick)
Phil — Witherspoon 95 kickoff return (Anderson kick)
Phil — FG Anderson 32
Ariz — Dowdell 24 pass from Esiason (Butler kick)

SAN DIEGO 28, KANSAS CITY 14—at Arrowhead Stadium, attendance 69,472. Tony Martin caught 2 touchdown passes from Stan Humphries, and Leonard Russell scored twice as San Diego swept Kansas City. With the wind-chill measuring minus-5 degrees, Martin caught 2 first-half touchdown receptions, giving him an NFL-leading 13 touchdown receptions, and Russell scored from 4 yards to give the Chargers a 21-0 halftime lead. Russell plunged from the 1-yard line midway through the third quarter to give San Diego a 28-0 advantage. Rich Gannon replaced an ineffective Steve Bono late in the third quarter and drove the Chiefs to 2 fourth-quarter touchdowns. San Diego moved the ball on the Chiefs' defense, as the Chargers last three scoring drives went 97, 79, and 74 yards. Martin had 5 receptions for 148 yards.

San Diego	7	14	7	0	—	28
Kansas City	0	0	0	14	—	14

SD — Martin 20 pass from Humphries (Carney kick)
SD — Russell 4 run (Carney kick)
SD — Martin 10 pass from Humphries (Carney kick)
SD — Russell 1 run (Carney kick)
KC — Penn 17 pass from Gannon (Stoyanovich kick)
KC — McNair 10 pass from Gannon (Stoyanovich kick)

SAN FRANCISCO 19, WASHINGTON 16 (OT)—at RFK Stadium, attendance 54,235. Jeff Wilkins booted 4 field goals, including the game-winner in overtime, to lift the 49ers to a come-from-behind road victory. The teams traded field goals the first 3½ quarters before Jamie Asher broke over the plane with a 20-yard touchdown pass from Gus Frerotte with 7:28 remaining. On the ensuing kickoff, kick returner Dexter Carter was tackled by Darrick Brownlow and fumbled. Junior Bryant miraculously managed to dig the ball out of the pile, which allowed the 49ers to drive 73 yards and tie the game on William Floyd's 1-yard run with 1:57 left. The 49ers won the toss in overtime and, with the assistance of a 25-yard run by Terry Kirby, got in position for Wilkins's heroics. Kirby had 11 catches and 143 total yards. Steve Young, playing his first full game in four weeks, completed 20 consecutive passes and was 33 of 41 for 295 yards. Frerotte was 18 of 26 for 294 yards. Michael Westbrook caught 7 passes for 126 yards.

San Francisco	3	3	0	10	3	—	19
Washington	0	6	3	7	0	—	16

SF — FG Wilkins 19
Wash — FG Blanton 19
Wash — FG Blanton 22
SF — FG Wilkins 48
Wash — FG Blanton 31
SF — FG Wilkins 44
Wash — Asher 20 pass from Frerotte (Blanton kick)
SF — Floyd 1 run (Wilkins kick)
SF — FG Wilkins 38

SUNDAY NIGHT, NOVEMBER 24

GREEN BAY 24, ST. LOUIS 9—at Trans World Dome, attendance 61,499. The Packers used big defensive and special-teams plays to overcome a 9-0 deficit and defeat the Rams. Brett Favre was flagged for intentional grounding in the end zone, giving the Rams a 9-0 lead with 2:08 left in the half. The Rams failed to fall on the ensuing free kick, as Mike Prior recovered it to set up Chris Jacke's 37-yard field goal to end the first half. Doug Evans intercepted Tony Banks's pass and raced 32 yards for a touchdown to give the Packers a 10-9 lead 52 seconds into the second half. Later in the quarter, Brian Williams recovered Tony Banks's fumble, leading to Favre's 6-yard scoring toss to Keith Jackson. Desmond Howard had a 29-yard punt return to start a 38-yard Packers' drive, with Favre finding Dorsey Levens from 6 yards for the game's final points. Favre became only the second quarterback to have three seasons with at least 30 touchdown passes. Dan Marino has turned the trick four times. The teams combined for just 473 yards and 5 turnovers.

Green Bay	0	3	14	7	—	24
St. Louis	0	9	0	0	—	9

StL — Bruce 6 pass from Banks (Lohmiller kick)
StL — Safety, Favre called for intentional-grounding in end zone
GB — FG Jacke 37
GB — Evans 32 interception return (Jacke kick)
GB — K. Jackson 6 pass from Favre (Jacke kick)
GB — Levens 5 pass from Favre (Jacke kick)

MONDAY, NOVEMBER 25

PITTSBURGH 24, MIAMI 17—at Pro Player Stadium, attendance 73,489. Ernie Mills caught a 20-yard touchdown pass with 2:10 remaining to give the Steelers a hard-earned victory. The winning drive began when the Steelers' defense forced the Dolphins to punt, giving the offense the ball at the Dolphins' 45 with 6:06 remaining. Seven consecutive running plays, six by Jerome Bettis, gave Pittsburgh third-and-8 from the Dolphins' 20. Mike Tomczak then executed a play-action pass to a wide open Mills. Miami drove downfield, but Deon Figures's tackle on Bernie Parmalee forced the Dolphins into a fourth-and-1 situation from the Steelers' 7. Dan Marino threw an incomplete pass to Scott Miller in the end zone to end the Dolphins' chances. Miami drove nine minutes, 45 seconds, to start the game, ending with O.J. McDuffie's 2-yard reception, for its only offensive touchdown of the game. Calvin Jackson's 61-yard interception return gave Miami a 14-3 lead. However, the Steelers responded with an 80-yard touchdown drive, capped by Tim Lester's 5-yard run, and then drove the first seven minutes of the second half, with Kordell Stewart scoring from 1 yard out, to take a 17-14 lead. The victory gave coach Bill Cowher a career 11-1 record on Monday nights, the best record among coaches with at least 10 games. Bettis (119 yards) had his ninth 100-yard

rushing game of the season.

Pittsburgh	3	7	7	7	—	24
Miami	7	7	3	0	—	17

Mia — McDuffie 2 pass from Marino (Nedney kick)
Pitt — FG N. Johnson 47
Mia — Jackson 61 interception return (Nedney kick)
Pitt — Lester 5 run (N. Johnson kick)
Pitt — Stewart 1 run (N. Johnson kick)
Mia — FG Nedney 41
Pitt — Mills 20 pass from Tomczak (N. Johnson kick)

FOURTEENTH WEEK SUMMARIES

AMERICAN FOOTBALL CONFERENCE

Eastern Division	W	L	T	Pct.	Pts.	OP
New England	9	4	0	.692	355	269
Buffalo	9	4	0	.692	267	215
Indianapolis	7	6	0	.538	232	274
Miami	6	7	0	.462	285	266
N.Y. Jets	1	12	0	.077	221	368

Central Division	W	L	T	Pct.	Pts.	OP
Pittsburgh	9	4	0	.692	299	211
Houston	7	6	0	.538	291	254
Jacksonville	6	7	0	.462	263	288
Cincinnati	5	8	0	.385	299	318
Baltimore	4	9	0	.308	320	369

Western Division	W	L	T	Pct.	Pts.	OP
Denver	12	1	0	.923	351	199
Kansas City	9	4	0	.692	262	230
San Diego	7	6	0	.538	277	323
Oakland	6	7	0	.462	274	234
Seattle	5	8	0	.385	250	317

NATIONAL FOOTBALL CONFERENCE

Eastern Division	W	L	T	Pct.	Pts.	OP
Dallas	8	5	0	.615	254	201
Philadelphia	8	5	0	.615	303	265
Washington	8	5	0	.615	291	251
Arizona	6	7	0	.462	248	332
N.Y. Giants	5	8	0	.385	200	250

Central Division	W	L	T	Pct.	Pts.	OP
Green Bay	10	3	0	.769	346	191
Minnesota	7	6	0	.538	243	245
Chicago	5	8	0	.385	202	248
Detroit	5	8	0	.385	263	289
Tampa Bay	4	9	0	.308	153	243

Western Division	W	L	T	Pct.	Pts.	OP
San Francisco	10	3	0	.769	325	198
Carolina	9	4	0	.692	292	164
St. Louis	4	9	0	.308	246	334
Atlanta	2	11	0	.154	234	393
New Orleans	2	11	0	.154	184	291

THURSDAY, NOVEMBER 28

KANSAS CITY 28, DETROIT 24—at Pontiac Silverdome, attendance 75,079. Marcus Allen scored 2 touchdowns, including the game winner with 46 seconds remaining, to defeat the Lions on Thanksgiving Day. Allen's first touchdown run, which came with 3:49 left in the first quarter, allowed him to break Walter Payton's record of 110 career rushing touchdowns. Scott Mitchell's 16-yard touchdown pass to Johnnie Morton on the first play of the second quarter tied the game. Then, Robert Porcher stripped the ball from Rich Gannon to force a fumble. Mike Wells fell on the ball in the end zone to give Detroit its first lead. Donnie Edwards's interception set up Gannon's touchdown pass to Chris Penn to tie the score. The Chiefs reached the Lions 21 as time was running out in the first half, but were unable to stop the clock and the half ended 14-14. Barry Sanders capped a 14-play, 7:06 drive with a 13-yard touchdown run in the third quarter, but the Chiefs responded as Gannon threw a 9-yard touchdown pass to Derrick Walker. Glyn Miburn's 48-yard kickoff return and Mitchell's 44-yard pass to Brett Perriman set up Jason Hanson's go-ahead field goal with 8:41 left. However, the Chiefs mounted a 15-play, 76-yard drive that consumed 7:55 and was keyed by 37 yards from Greg Hill, to score the winning points. Gannon made his first start since 1993 and completed 15 of 18 passes for 120 yards. The Chiefs outgained the Lions 243-81 on the ground. Hill finished with 103 rushing yards. Mitchell completed 18 of 29 passes for 247 yards, with 2 interceptions. Perriman had 8 receptions for 131 yards.

Kansas City	7	7	0	14	—	28
Detroit	0	14	7	3	—	24

KC — Allen 1 run (Stoyanovich kick)
Det — Morton 16 pass from Mitchell (Hanson kick)
Det — Wells recovered fumble in end zone (Hanson kick)
KC — Penn 17 pass from Gannon (Stoyanovich kick)
Det — Sanders 13 run (Hanson kick)
KC — Walker 9 pass from Gannon (Stoyanovich kick)
Det — FG Hanson 21
KC — Allen 1 run (Stoyanovich kick)

DALLAS 21, WASHINGTON 10—at Texas Stadium, attendance 64,955. Emmitt Smith rushed for 155 yards and 3 touchdowns to propel the Cowboys into a tie for first place in the NFC East with the Redskins. Smith surpassed the 1,000-yard rushing mark for the sixth consecutive season. The Cowboys won for the seventh time in nine games, while the Redskins lost their fourth out of their last five. Fred Strickland recovered a fumbled snap at the Redskins' 33 that led to Smith's first touchdown, a 4-yard run 2:03 before halftime. Scott Blanton kicked a 21-yard field goal 23 seconds before halftime to cut the lead to 7-3. Washington scored on its first possession of the second half, as Frerotte completed 4 of 6 passes on a 54-yard drive that concluded with his 26-yard touchdown pass to Leslie Shepherd. The Cowboys responded on their next possession, helped by a 42-yard run by Smith, and scored on Smith's 4-yard run with 6:02 left in the third quarter to take the lead for good. Smith added a 3-yard run to cap a 14-play, 7:58 drive midway through the fourth quarter. Troy Aikman completed 9 of 19 passes for 63 yards. He did not have to pass often as Dallas had more rushing yards (201-46) and greater time of possession (36:35-23:25). Frerotte completed 17 of 33 passes for 175 yards and 2 interceptions.

Washington	0	3	7	0	—	10
Dallas	0	7	7	7	—	21

Dall — E. Smith 4 run (Boniol kick)
Wash — FG Blanton 21
Wash — Shepherd 26 pass from Frerotte (Blanton kick)
Dall — E. Smith 4 run (Boniol kick)
Dall — E. Smith 3 run (Boniol kick)

SUNDAY, DECEMBER 1

MINNESOTA 41, ARIZONA 17—at Metrodome, attendance 45,767. Brad Johnson threw touchdown passes to 4 different receivers as the Vikings maintained second place in the NFC Central. Johnson, making his third consecutive start for injured Warren Moon, completed 19 of 26 passes for 238 yards. The Vikings took advantage of turnovers in the first half as Corey Fuller's interception led to Scott Sisson's first field goal and Robert Griffith's interception set up Johnson's 19-yard touchdown pass to Amp Lee. Johnson threw a 40-yard touchdown pass to Jake Reed to finish a 96-yard drive midway through the third quarter. The Vikings increased their lead to 27-3 on Johnson's 13-yard touchdown pass to Qadry Ismail. Fernando Smith's fumble recovery set up Johnson's 4-yard touchdown pass to Cris Carter on the first play of the fourth quarter. The Vikings had more first downs (29-18) and controlled the clock (37:46-22:14). Boomer Esiason was 26 of 40 for 270 yards and 1 touchdown, with 2 interceptions for the Cardinals.

Arizona	0	3	0	14	—	17
Minnesota	3	10	14	14	—	41

Minn — FG Sisson 38
Minn — FG Sisson 26
Minn — Lee 19 pass from B. Johnson (Sisson kick)
Ariz — FG Butler 38
Minn — Reed 40 pass from B. Johnson (Sisson kick)
Minn — Ismail 13 pass from B. Johnson (Sisson kick)
Minn — Carter 4 pass from B. Johnson (Sisson kick)
Ariz — Centers 9 pass from Esiason (Butler kick)
Minn — Hoard 1 run (Sisson kick)
Ariz — Centers 1 run (Butler kick)

INDIANAPOLIS 13, BUFFALO 10 (OT)—at RCA Dome, attendance 53,804. Cary Blanchard kicked a 49-yard field goal with 4:14 left in overtime to defeat the Bills. Both teams were ravaged by injuries, as the Colts were without quarterback Jim Harbaugh, among others, and Buffalo was playing without quarterback Jim Kelly, running back Thurman Thomas, and linebacker Bryce Paup. With his team trailing 7-0, Buffalo's Todd Collins threw a club-record 95-yard touchdown pass to Quinn Early with 8:04 left in the second quarter to tie the score. Collins's 47-yard pass to Eric Moulds set up Steve Christie's field goal to give the Bills a 10-7 halftime lead. Blanchard booted a game-tying 25-yard field goal six seconds into the fourth quarter. Paul Justin's 28-yard pass to Aaron Bailey helped set up Blanchard's winning kick in overtime. Blanchard missed 33- and 41-yard field-goal attempts earlier in the game before making the winning kick. Buffalo was forced to punt after all seven of its possessions after halftime. Justin was 22 of 40 for 228 yards. Collins completed 9 of 17 passes for 204 yards, with 2 interceptions. Early had 3 receptions for 113 yards.

Buffalo	0	10	0	0	0	—	10
Indianapolis	7	0	0	3	3	—	13

Ind — Faulk 1 run (Blanchard kick)
Buff — Early 95 pass from Collins (Christie kick)
Buff — FG Christie 24
Ind — FG Blanchard 25
Ind — FG Blanchard 49

GREEN BAY 28, CHICAGO 17—at Lambeau Field, attendance 59,682. Desmond Howard had a 75-yard punt return for a touchdown and Antonio Freeman had a career-high 10 receptions for 156 yards as the Packers won their thirteenth consecutive home game. The game was scoreless until Chicago's Dave Krieg threw a 15-yard touchdown pass to Bobby Engram with 1:30 left in the first half. The Packers answered with a 4-play, 64-yard drive capped by Brett Favre's 19-yard touchdown pass to Keith Jackson to tie the score 7-7 at halftime. Howard's 75-yard punt return for a touchdown with 5:30 left in the third quarter gave the Packers their first lead. After Jeff Jaeger's field goal put Chicago ahead, Dorsey Levens's 10-yard touchdown run capped an 80-yard drive. Eugene Robinson's interception allowed the Packers to drive 47 yards and consume more than six minutes before Favre's 1-yard quarterback sneak gave Green Bay a commanding 28-10 lead with 5:39 left. Favre completed 19 of 27 passes for 231 yards. Krieg was 29 of 45 for 218 yards.

Chicago	0	7	3	7	—	17
Green Bay	0	7	7	14	—	28

Chi — Engram 15 pass from Krieg (Jaeger kick)
GB — K. Jackson 19 pass from Favre (Jacke kick)
GB — Howard 75 punt return (Jacke kick)
Chi — FG Jaeger 34
GB — Levens 10 run (Jacke kick)
GB — Favre 1 run (Jacke kick)
Chi — Engram 6 pass from Krieg (Jaeger kick)

JACKSONVILLE 30, CINCINNATI 27—at Jacksonville Municipal Stadium, attendance 57,408. Mike Hollis broke his own club record with 5 field goals as the Jaguars held off the Bengals. Jacksonville improved its home record to 5-1. Jeff Blake threw 2 touchdown passes to Carl Pickens to give the Bengals a 17-16 halftime lead. The scoring began in the first quarter when Jacksonville's Mickey Washington recovered Clyde Simmons's blocked field goal and returned it 64 yards for a touchdown. The two clubs exchanged field goals in the third quarter before Mark Brunell threw a 48-yard touchdown pass to Keenan McCardell, and the subsequent 2-point conversion to Willie Jackson, to give the Jaguars a 27-20 lead. Hollis's 20-yard field goal with 2:07 left gave the Jaguars a 30-20 lead. The Bengals went 83 yards in 1:41, with Blake and Pickens connecting for their third touchdown of the game with 15 seconds left. But the onside kick hopped out of bounds and the Jaguars ran out the clock. Brunell completed 21 of 34 passes for 356 yards, his sixth 300-yard passing game of the season. Jimmy Smith had 162 receiving yards to go along with his 7 receptions. Blake completed 23 of 39 passes for 313 yards, with 2 interceptions. Pickens had 7 receptions for 109 yards.

Cincinnati	7	10	3	7	—	27
Jacksonville	13	3	11	3	—	30

Jax — Washington 64 return of blocked field goal (Hollis kick)
Jax — FG Hollis 25

Cin — Pickens 23 pass from Blake (Pelfrey kick)
Jax — FG Hollis 46
Cin — FG Pelfrey 22
Cin — Pickens 8 pass from Blake (Pelfrey kick)
Jax — FG Hollis 40
Jax — FG Hollis 39
Cin — FG Pelfrey 34
Jax — McCardell 48 pass from Brunell (W. Jackson pass from Brunell)
Jax — FG Hollis 20
Cin — Pickens 25 pass from Blake (Pelfrey kick)

HOUSTON 35, N.Y. JETS 10—at Giants Stadium, attendance 21,731. Eddie George ran for 141 yards and 2 touchdowns and Steve McNair threw 2 first-quarter touchdown passes to lead the Oilers to victory. McNair, who started in place of injured Chris Chandler, threw a 23-yard touchdown pass to Frank Wycheck with 4:13 left in the first quarter. After forcing a punt, McNair threw an 83-yard touchdown pass to Frank Sanders. A couple of scrambles by McNair kept alive a drive that ended with George racing 35 yards for a touchdown to give Houston a 21-3 lead with 3:48 left in the half. Frank Reich threw an 18-yard touchdown pass to Keyshawn Johnson with 1:10 left before halftime to cut the score to 21-10, but the Jets could get no closer. Keeping the ball on the ground, the Oilers scored 2 fourth-quarter touchdowns, capped by Rodney Thomas's 24-yard run with 4:01 remaining. McNair completed 6 of 17 passes for 142 yards. Sanders had 102 yards on 3 receptions. Reich completed 13 of 27 passes for 154 yards.

Houston	14	7	0	14	— 35
N.Y. Jets	0	10	0	0	— 10

Hou — Wycheck 23 pass from McNair (Del Greco kick)
Hou — Sanders 83 pass from McNair (Del Greco kick)
NYJ — FG Lowery 30
Hou — George 35 run (Del Greco kick)
NYJ — K. Johnson 18 pass from Reich (Lowery kick)
Hou — George 1 run (Del Greco kick)
Hou — Thomas 24 run (Del Greco kick)

OAKLAND 17, MIAMI 7—at Oakland-Alameda County Coliseum, attendance 60,591. Jeff Hostetler completed 20 of 28 passes for 165 yards and a touchdown to give the Raiders a 9-0 home record against the Dolphins. Oakland's Tim Brown set an NFL record with 293 career punt returns, surpassing Vai Sikahema's mark. Derrick Fenner's 6-yard touchdown run midway through the second quarter opened the scoring. Terry McDaniel's interception at the Raiders' 24-yard line and subsequent 18-yard return set up Jeff Hostetler's 22-yard touchdown pass to Brown 42 seconds before halftime. Cole Ford added a field goal with 4:50 left to give the Raiders a 17-0 lead. Dan Marino threw a 4-yard touchdown pass to Randal Hill with 2:34 remaining for the Dolphins' lone points. The Raiders' defense recorded 4 sacks, forced 4 turnovers, and permitted just 34 yards rushing on 20 carries. Marino completed 22 of 39 passes for 290 yards, with 3 interceptions.

Miami	0	0	0	7	— 7
Oakland	0	14	0	3	— 17

Oak — Fenner 6 run (Ford kick)
Oak — T. Brown 22 pass from Hostetler (Ford kick)
Oak — FG Ford 38
Mia — R. Hill 4 pass from Marino (Nedney kick)

PHILADELPHIA 24, N.Y. GIANTS 0—at Veterans Stadium, attendance 51,468. Ty Detmer threw 3 first-half touchdown passes as the Eagles vaulted into a three-way tie for first place in the NFC East. The Eagles' defense permitted 9 first downs, forced 4 turnovers, recorded 5 sacks, and allowed just 131 total yards. Ray Farmer's interception set up Gary Anderson's 44-yard field goal. The Eagles scored on their next two possessions, the second one set up by Mike Mamula's fumble recovery at the Giants' 14-yard line. Detmer ended the scoring with a 2-yard touchdown pass to Chris T. Jones 28 seconds before halftime. Detmer completed 25 of 33 passes for 284 yards. Ricky Watters had 104 yards rushing and caught 6 passes for 77 yards. Giants quarterbacks Dave Brown and Danny Kanell were a combined 7 of 24 for 78 yards. It was the Eagles' first shutout since 1992.

N.Y. Giants	0	0	0	0	— 0
Philadelphia	10	14	0	0	— 24

Phil — FG Anderson 44
Phil — Dunn 14 pass from Detmer (Anderson kick)
Phil — Fryar 19 pass from Detmer (Anderson kick)
Phil — Jones 2 pass from Detmer (Anderson kick)

BALTIMORE 31, PITTSBURGH 17—at Memorial Stadium, attendance 51,822. Vinny Testaverde threw 3 touchdown passes and Baltimore scored 17 points in the final 3:25 of the first half to defeat the Steelers and snap a four-game losing streak. In a game played in a steady rain, Jermaine Lewis's 46-yard punt return led to Testaverde's 1-yard touchdown pass to tackle-eligible Jonathan Ogden. The Steelers took a 10-7 lead, but Testaverde completed a third-and-10 pass to Floyd Turner for a first down to set up his 24-yard touchdown pass to Derrick Alexander to give the Ravens a 14-10 lead. After Baltimore forced a punt, Testaverde threw a 44-yard pass to Alexander to set up Earnest Byner's 7-yard touchdown run with 1:24 left in the half. Mike Croel's interception led to Matt Stover's 40-yard field goal to give the Ravens a 24-10 lead as the half expired. Mike Tomczak and Andre Hastings connected for their second touchdown of the day, but Testaverde threw a 4-yard touchdown pass to Eric Green early in the fourth quarter to finish the scoring. Testaverde completed 17 of 24 passes for 259 yards. Alexander finished with 198 yards on 7 receptions. The Ravens' Byron (Bam) Morris played his first game against his former team and finished with 28 carries for 100 yards. Pittsburgh's Jerome Bettis had 105 rushing yards to surpass 100 yards for the tenth time this season.

Pittsburgh	7	3	7	0	— 17
Baltimore	7	17	0	7	— 31

Balt — Ogden 1 pass from Testaverde (Stover kick)
Pitt — Hastings 30 pass from Tomczak (N. Johnson kick)
Pitt — FG N. Johnson 22
Balt — Alexander 24 pass from Testaverde (Stover kick)
Balt — Byner 7 run (Stover kick)
Balt — FG Stover 40
Pitt — Hastings 5 pass from Tomczak (N. Johnson kick)
Balt — Green 3 pass from Testaverde (Stover kick)

ST. LOUIS 26, NEW ORLEANS 10—at Superdome, attendance 26,310. Tony Banks threw for 231 yards and a touchdown and Chip Lohmiller added 4 field goals as the Rams snapped a five-game road losing streak. Torrance Small gave the Saints a 10-6 lead in the second quarter with a 17-yard touchdown run on a reverse. However, Banks threw a 10-yard touchdown pass to Isaac Bruce to give the Rams a 13-10 halftime lead. After Lohmiller's third field goal, the Rams took advantage of Jimmie Jones's fumble recovery as Harold Green's 1-yard touchdown run put the Rams ahead 23-10. Lohmiller's final field goal with 4:07 to play ended the scoring. Bruce finished with 112 yards on 4 receptions to record his fifth 100-yard receiving game of the season. The Rams' defense allowed the Saints to convert just 4 of 13 third-down situations.

St. Louis	3	10	10	3	— 26
New Orleans	3	7	0	0	— 10

StL — FG Lohmiller 35
NO — FG Brien 30
StL — FG Lohmiller 32
NO — Small 17 run (Brien kick)
StL — Bruce 10 pass from Banks (Lohmiller kick)
StL — FG Lohmiller 49
StL — Green 1 run (Lohmiller kick)
StL — FG Lohmiller 27

DENVER 34, SEATTLE 7—at Mile High Stadium, attendance 74,982. John Elway threw 2 touchdown passes and ran for another as the Broncos became the first team to clinch a postseason berth and also earned home-field advantage throughout the playoffs. Elway's 2-yard touchdown run broke a 7-7 tie late in the first quarter. After 2 field goals by Jason Elam, Tory James's fumble recovery and subsequent 15-yard return set up Elway's 4-yard touchdown pass to Ed McCaffrey 30 seconds before halftime for a commanding 27-7 lead. Elway, who nursed a sore hamstring, completed 17 of 27 passes for 189 yards. Terrell Davis ran for 106 yards and scored the game's final points on a 5-yard touchdown run midway through the third quarter. Rick Mirer completed 13 of 28 passes for 177 yards, with 2 interceptions, for Seattle. Joey Galloway had 108 yards on 5 receptions. Denver had more first downs (31-13), total yards (441-277), and time of possession (41:24-18:36).

Seattle	7	0	0	0	— 7
Denver	14	13	7	0	— 34

Den — Sharpe 1 pass from Elway (Elam kick)
Sea — Pritchard 8 pass from Mirer (Peterson kick)
Den — Elway 2 run (Elam kick)
Den — FG Elam 44
Den — FG Elam 18
Den — McCaffrey 4 pass from Elway (Elam kick)
Den — Davis 5 run (Elam kick)

CAROLINA 24, TAMPA BAY 0—at Ericsson Stadium, attendance 57,623. Shawn King had a fumble return for a touchdown and an interception as the Panthers' defense forced 4 turnovers and was responsible for 21 points in recording the franchise's first shutout. Carolina won its fourth consecutive game and broke the Buccaneers' three-game winning streak. The Panthers had a 16-play, 78-yard drive that consumed 9:14 and culminated in John Kasay's 23-yard field goal for a 3-0 lead. On the first play of the second quarter, Toi Cook stripped Trent Dilfer of the ball and King scooped it up and went 12 yards for his first NFL touchdown. Eric Davis's 39-yard interception return set up Howard Griffith's 1-yard touchdown run, and King's interception at midfield led to Anthony Johnson's 25-yard touchdown run with 3:10 left. Tampa Bay drove to the Panthers' 1-yard line in the closing seconds, but the shutout was saved when Dilfer's fourth-down pass fell incomplete. Kerry Collins completed 14 of 24 passes for 83 yards. Johnson ran for 111 yards. Dilfer was 23 of 41 for 236 yards, but threw 2 interceptions and was sacked 4 times.

Tampa Bay	0	0	0	0	— 0
Carolina	3	7	7	7	— 24

Car — FG Kasay 23
Car — King 12 fumble return (Kasay kick)
Car — Griffith 1 run (Kasay kick)
Car — Johnson 25 run (Kasay kick)

SUNDAY NIGHT, DECEMBER 1

NEW ENGLAND 45, SAN DIEGO 7—at San Diego Jack Murphy Stadium, attendance 62,541. Drew Bledsoe threw 4 touchdown passes and the Patriots' defense forced 6 turnovers, which led to 31 points, and recorded 6 sacks to defeat the Chargers. Bledsoe threw touchdown passes to Terry Glenn and Keith Byars in the opening 9:32 of the game. Stan Humphries threw a 46-yard touchdown pass to cut the deficit to 14-7. Ted Johnson's interception and return to the Chargers' 7 set up Bledsoe's touchdown pass to Sam Gash with 13:20 left in the second quarter. Willie McGinest's fumble recovery with 2:32 left in the half increased the Patriots' lead to 28-7, and Lawyer Milloy's interception set up Adam Vinatieri's field goal in the half's final minute. Otis Smith's interception in the opening minute of the third quarter set up Bledsoe's fourth touchdown pass, and Corwin Brown's 42-yard fumble return ended the scoring. Bledsoe completed 19 of 29 passes for 232 yards. Humphries was 16 of 35 for 204 yards with 3 interceptions.

New England	14	17	14	0	— 45
San Diego	7	0	0	0	— 7

NE — Glenn 8 pass from Bledsoe (Vinatieri kick)
NE — Byars 19 pass from Bledsoe (Vinatieri kick)
SD — Martin 46 pass from Humphries (Carney kick)
NE — Gash 7 pass from Bledsoe (Vinatieri kick)
NE — McGinest recovered fumble in end zone (Vinatieri kick)
NE — FG Vinatieri 47
NE — Jefferson 11 pass from Bledsoe (Vinatieri kick)
NE — C. Brown 42 fumble return (Vinatieri kick)

MONDAY, DECEMBER 2

SAN FRANCISCO 34, ATLANTA 10—at Georgia Dome, attendance 46,318. Steve Young ran for 2 touchdowns and threw for another to guide the 49ers to victory. Along with the 2 touchdown runs, Young completed 23 of 30 passes for 255 yards. Terry Kirby gained 105 yards rushing and became the first 49ers player to surpass 100 rushing yards since Ricky Watters in 1994. The 49ers held a 6-3 lead when Marquez Pope's interception set up Young's 26-yard scramble for a touchdown to take a 13-3 lead. After another field goal, the 49ers drove 87 yards, with Young's 5-yard touchdown run giving them a 22-3 lead with 41 seconds left in the half. Dedrick Dodge's interception set up Jeff Wilkins's fourth field goal of the half and gave the 49ers a 25-3 halftime lead. Reserve Browning Nagle threw a 7-yard touchdown pass to Terance Mathis with 2:23 remaining for the Falcons' only touchdown. The 49ers had more first downs (25-9), outgained the Falcons (464-178), and consumed 40:19 off the clock. The 49ers' defense forced 4 turnovers and allowed Atlanta to convert just 1 of 11 third-down situations.

San Francisco	6	19	7	2	—	34
Atlanta	3	0	0	7	—	10

SF — FG Wilkins 39
Atl — FG Andersen 32
SF — FG Wilkins 26
SF — Young 26 run (Wilkins kick)
SF — FG Wilkins 43
SF — Young 5 run (pass failed)
SF — FG Wilkins 23
SF — Kirby 10 pass from Young (Wilkins kick)
SF — Safety, Nagle sacked by B. Young in end zone
Atl — Mathis 7 pass from Nagle (Andersen kick)

FIFTEENTH WEEK SUMMARIES

AMERICAN FOOTBALL CONFERENCE

Eastern Division	W	L	T	Pct.	Pts.	OP
New England	10	4	0	.714	389	279
Buffalo	9	5	0	.643	285	241
Indianapolis	8	6	0	.571	269	284
Miami	6	8	0	.429	292	283
N.Y. Jets	1	13	0	.071	231	402
Central Division						
Pittsburgh	10	4	0	.714	315	214
Jacksonville	7	7	0	.500	286	305
Houston	7	7	0	.500	308	277
Cincinnati	6	8	0	.429	320	332
Baltimore	4	10	0	.286	334	390
Western Division						
Denver	12	2	0	.857	357	240
Kansas City	9	5	0	.643	269	256
San Diego	7	7	0	.500	280	339
Oakland	7	7	0	.500	300	241
Seattle	6	8	0	.429	276	335

NATIONAL FOOTBALL CONFERENCE

Eastern Division	W	L	T	Pct.	Pts.	OP
Dallas	9	5	0	.643	264	207
Philadelphia	8	6	0	.571	313	302
Washington	8	6	0	.571	301	275
Arizona	6	8	0	.429	254	342
N.Y. Giants	6	8	0	.429	217	257
Central Division						
Green Bay	11	3	0	.786	387	197
Minnesota	8	6	0	.571	267	267
Chicago	6	8	0	.429	237	257
Detroit	5	9	0	.357	272	324
Tampa Bay	5	9	0	.357	177	253
Western Division						
Carolina	10	4	0	.714	322	188
San Francisco	10	4	0	.714	349	218
St. Louis	4	10	0	.286	255	369
Atlanta	3	11	0	.214	265	408
New Orleans	2	12	0	.143	199	322

THURSDAY, DECEMBER 5

INDIANAPOLIS 37, PHILADELPHIA 10—at RCA Dome, attendance 52,689. Marshall Faulk rushed for 101 yards and 2 touchdowns and the Colts' defense grabbed 3 interceptions as the Colts remained alive in the playoff chase. The Colts, who played without Jim Harbaugh and three defensive starters, took advantage of a 39-yard pass interference penalty to lead to Faulk's first touchdown. Jason Belser's 44-yard interception return for a touchdown gave the Colts a 17-3 lead with 6:48 left in the half. Trev Alberts's 19-yard interception return set up the first of 2 Cary Blanchard field goal's in the final two minutes of the half to take a commandeing 23-3 lead. Philadelphia scored its lone touchdown with five seconds remaining. Paul Justin completed 14 of 23 passes for 144 yards, and Kerwin Bell was 5 of 5 for 75 yards. Ty Detmer completed 17 of 34 passes for 182 yards, with 3 interceptions.

Philadelphia	3	0	0	7	—	10
Indianapolis	7	16	7	7	—	37

Ind — Faulk 13 run (Blanchard kick)
Phil — FG Anderson 31
Ind — FG Blanchard 30
Ind — Belser 44 interception return (Blanchard kick)
Ind — FG Blanchard 42
Ind — FG Blanchard 51
Ind — Harrison 20 pass from Bell (Blanchard kick)
Ind — Faulk 7 run (Blanchard kick)
Phil — Fryar 8 pass from Rypien (Anderson kick)

SUNDAY, DECEMBER 8

ATLANTA 31, NEW ORLEANS 15—at Louisiana Superdome, attendance 32,923. Bobby Hebert passed for 198 yards and 3 touchdowns to lead the Falcons to their second victory over the Saints in four weeks. The Saints lost their seventh consecutive game and fell to 0-6 under interim head coach Rick Venturi. Hebert threw a 10-yard touchdown pass to Eric Metcalf 29 seconds before halftime to take a 14-7 lead. Chuck Smith's fumble recovery led to Craig Heyward's 1-yard touchdown run just over three minutes into the second half to take a 21-7 lead. Heyward's 34-yard run led to Hebert's third touchdown pass with 10:07 left to pad the lead. Doug Nussmeier made his NFL debut, replacing injured Jim Everett, and completed 18 of 33 passes for 166 yards for the Saints.

Atlanta	7	7	7	10	—	31
New Orleans	3	0	6	6	—	15

NO — FG Brien 34
Atl — Lyons 3 pass from Hebert (Andersen kick)
Atl — Metcalf 4 pass from Hebert (Andersen kick)
Atl — Heyward 1 run (Andersen kick)
NO — Guess 57 pass from Nussmeier (pass failed)
Atl — Emanuel 3 pass from Hebert (Andersen kick)
Atl — FG Andersen 33
NO — Bates 4 run (pass failed)

CINCINNATI 21, BALTIMORE 14—at Cinergy Field, attendance 43,022. Jeff Blake threw 2 touchdown passes, including the game winner to Tony McGee with 3:09 left, and Sam Shade made a touchdown-saving tackle at the 1-yard line in the final minute to give the Bengals a season-series sweep of the Ravens. The victory gave the Bengals a 5-2 record under interim head coach Bruce Coslet. Doug Pelfrey's 2 field goals gave the Bengals a 13-7 lead with 13:03 to play. Baltimore scored on its next possession as Vinny Testaverde threw his second touchdown pass of the day, this one to Jermaine Lewis from 6 yards, to take a 14-13 lead. Cincinnati responded with an 11-play drive, capped by McGee's touchdown catch. Garrison Hearst ran in the 2-point conversion to give the Bengals a seven-point cushion. The Ravens reached the 5-yard line when Testaverde threw a 29-yard pass to Michael Jackson. Byron (Bam) Morris ran to the 1-yard line on first down, but was stopped the next to plays for no gain. On fourth down, Testaverde threw a swing pass to Carwell Gardner, who was immediately stopped by Shade. Blake completed 26 of 42 passes for 272 yards and 2 touchdowns. Testaverde was 21 of 39 for 205 yards. Morris rushed for 117 yards on 21 carries.

Baltimore	0	7	0	7	—	14
Cincinnati	0	10	0	11	—	21

Balt — Kinchen 23 pass from Testaverde (Stover kick)
Cin — Pickens 14 pass from Blake (Pelfrey kick)
Cin — FG Pelfrey 23
Cin — FG Pelfrey 26
Balt — Lewis 6 pass from Testaverde (Stover kick)
Cin — McGee 1 pass from Blake (Hearst run)

SEATTLE 26, BUFFALO 18—at Rich Stadium, attendance 41,373. Darryl Williams grabbed 2 interceptions and recovered a fumble to lead to 13 points and propel the Seahawks to victory. The loss prevented the Bills from clinching a postseason bid. Williams recovered a Thurman Thomas fumble in the opening minutes, and the Seahawks capitalized on Rick Mirer's 27-yard touchdown pass to Joey Galloway. Williams then had 39- and 34-yard interception returns to lead to 2 of Todd Peterson's 3 first-half field goals to give Seattle a 16-0 lead. Trailing 19-11 with 9:38 to play, Buffalo committed its fourth turnover as Sam Adams recovered Jim Kelly's fumble, and Lamar Smith's 12-yard touchdown run two plays later iced the game. The Bills outgained the Seahawks (382-302) and had more first downs (21-11), but committed 5 turnovers while forcing none. Mirer was 9 of 23 for 147 yards. Chris Warren ran for 116 yards. Kelly completed 24 of 41 passes for 324 yards, with 2 interceptions.

Buffalo	0	8	0	10	—	18
Seattle	10	6	3	7	—	26

Sea — Galloway 27 pass from Mirer (Peterson kick)
Sea — FG Peterson 41
Sea — FG Peterson 38
Sea — FG Peterson 22
Buff — Moulds 37 pass from Kelly (Early pass from Kelly)
Sea — FG Peterson 30
Buff — FG Christie 22
Sea — L. Smith 12 run (Peterson kick)
Buff — Brantley 22 pass from Collins (Christie kick)

CAROLINA 30, SAN FRANCISCO 24—at 3Com Park, attendance 66,291. Kerry Collins threw 3 touchdown passes as the Panthers became the first NFL franchise to clinch a postseason berth in just their second season. The Panthers' victory gave both clubs identical 10-4 records, but Carolina was in first place by virtue of its season-series sweep of the 49ers. Carolina scored on the game's opening possession, as Collins threw a 39-yard pass to Mark Carrier to set up Wesley Walls's touchdown grab. The two teams combined for 34 second-quarter points. Carolina scored its 2 second-quarter touchdowns due to a 58-yard kickoff return by Bates, a 50-yard pass from Collins to Willie Green, and set up John Kasay's field goal with Collins's 32-yard pass to Raghib Ismail. Steve Young's 52-yard pass to Terry Kirby set up Rick Wilkins's 31-yard field goal as the half expired. The defense's established order in the second half. Eric Davis's interception of a pass off Terrell Owens's hands at the Panthers' 21-yard line with 4:30 remaining clinched the victory. The Panthers recorded 5 sacks and forced 4 turnovers, while committing none. Collins was 22 of 37 for 327 yards. Green had 157 yards on 7 receptions. Young completed 27 of 41 passes for 393 yards, with 2 interceptions. Jerry Rice had 10 receptions for 129 yards, and Owens had 110 yards on 5 catches.

Carolina	10	17	3	0	—	30
San Francisco	0	17	0	7	—	24

Car — Walls 5 pass from Collins (Kasay kick)
Car — FG Kasay 18
SF — B. Jones 1 pass from Young (Wilkins kick)
Car — Walls 5 pass from Collins (Kasay kick)
SF — Owens 46 pass from Young (Wilkins kick)
Car — Green 20 pass from Collins (Kasay kick)
Car — FG Kasay 26
SF — FG Wilkins 31
Car — FG Kasay 33
SF — Rice 5 pass from Young (Wilkins kick)

DALLAS 10, ARIZONA 6—at Sun Devil Stadium, attendance 70,763. Michael Irvin caught 8 passes for 198 yards, including a 50-yard touchdown reception, and the Cowboys converted 2 turnovers into all 10 of their points to take over first place in the NFC Eastern Division. The victory marks the Cowboys' thirteenth consecutive victory over the Cardinals. Arizona put together 63- and 77-yard drives in the first half, but had to settle for Kevin Butler field goal's both times. Deion Sanders recovered a fumble at the Cowboys' 32 to set up Troy Aikman's touchdown pass to Irvin with 5:07 left in the third quarter. Darren Woodson's interception and 7-yard return to the Cardinals' 23 led to Chris Boniol's field goal with 8:41 remaining. Dallas got the ball back with 5:01 left and made a couple of big third-down

conversions to run out the clock. Aikman was 15 of 24 for 255 yards. Boomer Esiason completed 18 of 36 for 224 yards, with 2 interceptions.

Dallas	0	0	7	3	— 10
Arizona	3	3	0	0	— 6

Ariz — FG Butler 33
Ariz — FG Butler 28
Dall — Irvin 50 pass from Aikman (Boniol kick)
Dall — FG Boniol 31

GREEN BAY 41, DENVER 6—at Lambeau Field, attendance 60,712. Brett Favre threw 4 touchdown passes and Antonio Freeman had 3 touchdowns and a career-high 175 receiving yards as the Packers claimed the NFC Central Division title for the second consecutive season. The victory also snapped the Broncos' nine-game winning streak. The score was tied 3-3 when Chris Jacke kicked a 22-yard field goal 1:54 before halftime. Green Bay got the ball back and drove 73 yards in 34 seconds, with Favre throwing a 14-yard touchdown pass to Freeman 17 seconds before halftime. Favre threw 3 second-half touchdown passes to culminate drives of 88, 50, and 35 yards to take a 34-6 lead. Green Bay more than doubled the Broncos in first downs (22-9) and total yards (379-176). Favre was 20 of 38 for 280 yards. Denver, who had clinched a postseason berth the previous week, played without injured quarterback John Elway. Bill Musgrave completed 12 of 21 passes for 101 yards. The Packers' defense held the NFL's leading rusher, Terrell Davis, to 54 yards on 14 carries.

Denver	3	0	3	0	— 6
Green Bay	3	10	7	21	— 41

GB — FG Jacke 33
Den — FG Elam 40
GB — FG Jacke 22
GB — Freeman 14 pass from Favre (Jacke kick)
Den — FG Elam 39
GB — Freeman 51 pass from Favre (Jacke kick)
GB — Jackson 1 pass from Favre (Jacke kick)
GB — Freeman 25 pass from Favre (Jacke kick)
GB — Beebe fumble recovery in end zone (Jacke kick)

JACKSONVILLE 23, HOUSTON 17—at Astrodome, attendance 20,196. Natrone Means rushed for 2 touchdowns as the Jaguars remained in playoff contention with their third consecutive victory. Houston fell to 7-7 and lost for the fifth time in seven games. The game was tied 7-7 in the first half when John Jurkovic recovered Steve McNair's fumble to set up Mike Hollis's 34-yard field goal 1:49 before halftime. Chris Hudson's 21-yard interception return led to Means's 5-yard touchdown run. The Jaguars were clinging to a 20-14 lead with 3:21 remaining when Tony Brackens forced McNair to fumble. Don Davey recovered the ball, and Hollis's field goal gave the Jaguars a nine-point lead. Al Del Greco kicked a field goal with 11 seconds left, but the Jaguars recovered the ensuing onside kick. Brunell was 15 of 25 for 172 yards, ending his streak of consecutive games with at least 200 passing yards at 15, one shy of Dan Marino's NFL record. Keenan McCardell had 68 receiving yards and Jimmy Smith had 61 as the pair of Jaguars receivers each surpassed the 1,000-yard receiving barrier in a season for the first time. McNair completed 24 of 37 passes for 308 yards, with 1 interceptions and 2 fumbles. Chris Sanders had 7 receptions for 127 yards for the Oilers.

Jacksonville	7	3	7	6	— 23
Houston	0	7	0	10	— 17

Jax — Means 1 run (Hollis kick)
Hou — Harmon 23 pass from McNair (Del Greco kick)
Jax — FG Hollis 34
Jax — Means 5 run (Hollis kick)
Hou — George 6 run (Del Greco kick)
Jax — FG Hollis 38
Jax — FG Hollis 31
Hou — FG Del Greco 27

N.Y. GIANTS 17, MIAMI 7—at Pro Player Stadium, attendance 63,889. Dave Brown completed 21 of 28 passes for 169 yards and 1 touchdown to give the Giants a road victory. The Dolphins lost their third consecutive game. Rodney Hampton's 1-yard touchdown run capped the game's opening drive and tied Joe Morris's club-record with 48 ca-

reer rushing touchdowns. Dan Marino's 66-yard pass to Fred Barnett set up his 3-yard touchdown pass to Robert Wilson to tie the score. Brown directed a 16-play, 78-yard drive to take the lead on Howard Cross's touchdown catch 1:15 before halftime. The Giants' defense not only kept the Dolphins off the scoreboard the remainder of the game but set up the offense's final points when Conrad Hamilton intercepted a pass and returned it 29 yards to lead to Brad Daluiso's field goal. Marino was 16 of 30 for 209, with 2 interceptions. Barnett finished with 4 receptions for 139 yards.

N.Y. Giants	7	3	7	0	— 17
Miami	7	0	0	0	— 7

NYG — Hampton 4 run (Daluiso kick)
Mia — Wilson 3 pass from Marino (Nedney kick)
NYG — Cross 1 pass from Brown (Daluiso kick)
NYG — FG Daluiso 37

NEW ENGLAND 34, N.Y. JETS 10—at Giants Stadium, attendance 54,621. Curtis Martin ran for a touchdown and Ty Law returned an interception 38 yards for a score as the Patriots vaulted into first place in the AFC Eastern Division and earned a playoff berth. New England won for the seventh time in its last eight games. New England led 10-3 when Martin scored a 19-yard touchdown with 3:04 left in the half, and Adam Vinatieri kicked a field goal with two seconds left take a 20-3 halftime lead. Glenn Foley threw a 4-yard touchdown pass to Keyshawn Johnson, and the Jets began driving for more points on their next possession only to watch Law's interception return. Bledsoe was 24 of 42 for 251 yards, and, at age 24, became the youngest quarterback in NFL in history to have passed for 14,000 yards. Foley made his first career start and completed 22 of 45 passes for 227 yards, with 2 interceptions.

N.Y. Jets	0	3	7	0	— 10
New England	7	13	7	7	— 34

NE — Coates 2 pass from Bledsoe (Vinatieri kick)
NE — FG Vinatieri 19
NYJ — FG Lowery 27
NE — Martin 19 run (Vinatieri kick)
NE — FG Vinatieri 41
NYJ — K. Johnson 4 pass from Foley (Lowery kick)
NE — Law 38 interception return (Vinatieri kick)
NE — Grier 1 run (Vinatieri kick)

CHICAGO 35, ST. LOUIS 9—at Soldier Field, attendance 45,075. Rashaan Salaam rushed for 115 yards and 2 touchdowns to lead the Bears to victory. Chicago led 7-3 at halftime before Salaam broke off a 32-yard run to key an 81-yard drive, capped off by his 3-yard touchdown run. Dave Krieg's quarterback sneak on the Bears' next possession gave them a 21-3 lead. Michael Lowery's fumble recovery of Eddie Kennison's muffed punt early in the fourth quarter secured the victory. Jamie Martin replaced Tony Banks, who was ejected in the fourth quarter, and led the Rams to their lone touchdown. Krieg was 17 of 25 for 226 yards. Michael Timpson had 6 receptions for 111 yards. Banks completed 20 of 38 passes for 194 yards. Kennison had 102 receiving yards on 8 receptions.

St. Louis	0	3	0	6	— 9
Chicago	7	0	14	14	— 35

Chi — Conway 27 pass from Krieg (Jaeger kick)
StL — FG Lohmiller 25
Chi — Salaam 3 run (Jaeger kick)
Chi — Krieg 1 run (Jaeger kick)
Chi — Lowry recovers fumbled in end zone (Jaeger kick)
Chi — Salaam 4 run (Jaeger kick)
StL — Kennison 19 pass from Martin (pass failed)

PITTSBURGH 16, SAN DIEGO 3—at Three Rivers Stadium, attendance 56,368. Norm Johnson kicked 3 field goals and the Steelers' defense recorded 5 sacks, and permitted just 8 first downs and 148 total yards to defeat the Chargers. Mike Tomczak completed a 46-yard pass to Charles Johnson to set up Norm Johnson's first field goal less than five minutes into the game. Darrien Gordon intercepted a pass deep in Chargers territory to thwart a Steelers drive, but then fumbled the ball on the return. Ernie Mills recovered and Johnson kicked his second field goal moments

later. Pittsburgh drove 88 yards for their first touchdown, a 11-yard pass play from Tomczak to Andre Hastings. The Chargers scored their only points when Terrell Fletcher recovered a fumble at the Steelers' 27, but had to settle for John Carney's field goal. Kevin Henry's fumble recovery led to Johnson's final field goal. Tomczak was 15 of 31 for 153 yards, with 3 interceptions. Sean Salisbury, starting in place of injured Stan Humphries, was 10 of 29 for 125 yards.

San Diego	0	0	3	0	— 3
Pittsburgh	6	7	0	3	— 16

Pitt — FG N. Johnson 49
Pitt — FG N. Johnson 39
Pitt — Hastings 11 pass from Tomczak (N. Johnson kick)
SD — FG Carney 25
Pitt — FG N. Johnson 21

TAMPA BAY 24, WASHINGTON 10—at Houlihan's Stadium, attendance 44,733. Trent Dilfer threw a touchdown pass and Mike Alstott scored a touchdown to lead the Buccaneers to their fourth consecutive home victory. Tampa Bay allowed fewer than 18 points for the eighth time in their last nine games, and handed the Redskins their fifth loss in six games. Tampa Bay took advantage of the game's only 2 turnovers: Martin Mayhew's interception set up Dilfer's 22-yard touchdown pass to Jackie Harris; and Regan Upshaw's fumble recovery led to Michael Husted's field goal. Trailing 10-0, the Redskins quickly responded with Scott Blanton's field goal, but Husted added 2 more field goals and Alstott's 13-yard run put the game away. The Buccaneers did not allow a touchdown until there were less than three minutes left. Dilfer completed 8 of 15 passes for 112 yards. Gus Frerotte completed 20 of 39 passes for 219 yards.

Washington	0	3	0	7	— 10
Tampa Bay	10	3	11	0	— 24

TB — Harris 22 pass from Dilfer (Husted kick)
TB — FG Husted 42
Wash — FG Blanton 29
TB — FG Husted 35
TB — FG Husted 19
TB — Alstott 13 run (Harris pass from Dilfer)
Wash — Ellard 3 pass from Frerotte (Blanton kick)

SUNDAY NIGHT, DECEMBER 8

MINNESOTA 24, DETROIT 22—at Pontiac Silverdome, attendance 46,043. Brad Johnson threw 3 touchdown passes and Robert Griffith broke up a game-tying 2-point conversion attempt with 2:34 left to keep the Vikings' playoff hopes alive. Minnesota led the entire game, but the Lions cut the score to 17-16 on Jason Hanson's third field goal of the game with 8:31 left. The Lions had allowed Minnesota just 1 second-half first down until Johnson led a 7-play, 66-yard drive, culminating in his 30-yard touchdown pass to Cris Carter with 4:56 to play. Barry Sanders scored to cut the lead to 24-22, but Griffith batted down the 2-point conversion attempt pass at the goal line. Carter recovered the onside kick, and Vikings ran out the clock. Johnson was 19 of 29 for 195 yards. Scott Mitchell completed 21 of 31 passes for 250 yards. Herman Moore had 9 receptions for 126 yards. Sanders had 134 rushing yards and passed John Riggins to move into seventh place on the NFL's all-time rushing list.

Minnesota	3	14	0	7	— 24
Detroit	0	10	3	9	— 22

Minn — FG Sisson 31
Minn — Lee 3 pass from B. Johnson (Sisson kick)
Det — Morton 15 pass from Mitchell (Hanson kick)
Minn — J. Reed 13 pass from B. Johnson (Sisson kick)
Det — FG Hanson 30
Det — FG Hanson 48
Det — FG Hanson 31
Minn — Carter 30 pass from B. Johnson (Sisson kick)
Det — Sanders 2 run (pass failed)

MONDAY, DECEMBER 9

OAKLAND 26, KANSAS CITY 7—at Oakland-Alameda County Coliseum, attendance 57,082. Jeff Hostetler threw 3 touchdown passes and the Raiders allowed just 169 total yards to keep their playoff hopes alive. Napoleon Kaufman had 109 rushing yards on 8 carries for the Raiders, in-

cluding a 45-yard run to the 1-yard line to set up Oakland's first touchdown. The Raiders led 10-0 going into the third quarter when the defense forced Rich Gannon to intentionally ground the ball while in the end zone, resulting in a safety. Hostetler threw 2 touchdown passes within four minutes of each other late in the third quarter to take a commanding 26-0 lead. Hostetler completed 13 of 27 passes for 150 yards. Gannon completed 12 of 33 passes for 88 yards.

| Kansas City | 0 | 0 | 0 | 7 | — | 7 |
| Oakland | 10 | 0 | 16 | 0 | — | 26 |

Oak — Glover 1 pass from Hostetler (Ford kick)
Oak — FG Ford 43
Oak — Safety, Gannon called for intentional grounding in the end zone
Oak — Fenner 23 pass from Hostetler (Ford kick)
Oak — T.Brown 34 pass from Hostetler (Ford kick)
KC — Lachapelle 12 pass from Gannon (Stoyanovich kick)

SIXTEENTH WEEK SUMMARIES

AMERICAN FOOTBALL CONFERENCE

Eastern Division	W	L	T	Pct.	Pts.	OP
New England	10	5	0	.667	395	291
Indianapolis	9	6	0	.600	293	303
Buffalo	9	6	0	.600	299	257
Miami	7	8	0	.467	308	297
N.Y. Jets	1	14	0	.067	251	423
Central Division						
Pittsburgh	10	5	0	.667	330	239
Jacksonville	8	7	0	.533	306	318
Cincinnati	7	8	0	.467	341	345
Houston	7	8	0	.467	321	298
Baltimore	4	11	0	.267	350	417
Western Division						
Denver	13	2	0	.867	381	259
Kansas City	9	6	0	.600	288	280
San Diego	7	8	0	.467	294	366
Oakland	7	8	0	.467	319	265
Seattle	6	9	0	.400	289	355

NATIONAL FOOTBALL CONFERENCE

Eastern Division	W	L	T	Pct.	Pts.	OP
Dallas	10	5	0	.667	276	213
Philadelphia	9	6	0	.600	334	322
Washington	8	7	0	.533	327	302
Arizona	7	8	0	.467	281	368
N.Y. Giants	6	9	0	.400	220	274
Central Division						
Green Bay	12	3	0	.800	418	200
Minnesota	9	6	0	.600	288	277
Chicago	7	8	0	.467	264	271
Detroit	5	10	0	.333	288	3445
Tampa Bay	5	10	0	.333	187	274
Western Division						
Carolina	11	4	0	.733	349	204
San Francisco	11	4	0	.733	374	243
St. Louis	5	10	0	.333	289	396
Atlanta	3	12	0	.200	292	442
New Orleans	3	12	0	.200	216	325

SATURDAY, DECEMBER 14

PHILADELPHIA 21, N.Y. JETS 20—at Giants Stadium, attendance 29,176. Ty Detmer threw 3 second-half touchdown passes to give the Eagles a comeback victory. The Eagles earned a wild-card berth the following day when Washington lost at Arizona. The Jets led 10-7 late in the third quarter when Aaron Glenn returned an interception 13 yards for a touchdown. Hugh Douglas recovered a fumble moments later, and Nick Lowery's field goal gave the Jets a 20-7 lead. Detmer threw a 2-yard touchdown pass to Chris T. Jones with 7:04 left. Michael Zordich's interception less than a minute later put Detmer in position to throw his third touchdown pass. William Thomas's interception in Eagles' territory with less than four minutes left ended the Jets' comeback hopes. Detmer was 17 of 34 for 198 yards, with 2 interceptions. Foley completed 16 of 26 for 186 yards, with 4 interceptions.

| Philadelphia | 0 | 0 | 7 | 14 | — | 21 |
| N.Y. Giants | 7 | 3 | 10 | 0 | — | 20 |

NYJ — K. Johnson 46 pass from Foley (Lowery kick)
NYJ — FG Lowery 27
Phil — Fryar 40 pass from Detmer (Anderson kick)
NYJ — Glenn 13 interception return (Lowery kick)
NYJ — FG Lowery 29
Phil — Jones 2 pass from Detmer (Anderson kick)
Phil — Fryar 14 pass from Detmer (Anderson kick)

CHICAGO 27, SAN DIEGO 14—at Soldier Field, attendance 49,763. Dave Krieg threw 3 touchdown passes to all but knock the Chargers out of the playoff race. Indianapolis's victory over Kansas City the next day officially ended San Diego's postseason aspirations. Jeff Jaeger's 45-yard field goal midway through the third quarter broke a 14-14 tie. Krieg's third touchdown pass, to Ryan Wetnight on the first play of the fourth quarter, came on third-and-goal and capped a 51-yard drive. Krieg completed 24 of 38 passes for 217 yards. Stan Humphries was 23 of 38 for 217 yards for the Chargers.

| San Diego | 7 | 7 | 0 | 0 | — | 14 |
| Chicago | 14 | 0 | 3 | 10 | — | 27 |

SD — A. Coleman 20 pass from Humphries (Carney kick)
Chi — Engram 7 pass from Krieg (Jaeger kick)
Chi — Conway 7 pass from Krieg (Jaeger kick)
SD — Russell 1 run (Carney kick)
Chi — FG Jaeger 45
Chi — Wetnight 8 pass from Krieg (Jaeger kick)
Chi — FG Jaeger 40

SUNDAY, DECEMBER 15

CAROLINA 27, BALTIMORE 16—at Ericsson Stadium, attendance 70,075. Kerry Collins threw 2 touchdown passes as the Panthers won their sixth consecutive game. Carolina improved its home record to 7-0. The Panthers fell to 0-7 on the road. The Panthers trailed 13-10 when Collins threw a 6-yard touchdown pass to Mark Carrier midway through the third quarter to culminate a drive in which he completed all 5 of his pass attempts and also gained 2 yards on a fourth-and-1 quarterback sneak. Collins's second touchdown, to Scott Greene, came with 3:38 remaining and iced the game. Collins completed 26 of 39 passes for 268 yards. Antohny Johnson gained 81 yards and became the first player in Panthers history to surpass 1,000 rushing yards. Vinny Testaverde completed 20 of 37 passes for 240 yards for the Ravens.

| Baltimore | 7 | 6 | 0 | 3 | — | 16 |
| Carolina | 3 | 7 | 10 | 7 | — | 27 |

Car — FG Kasay 29
Balt — Jackson 23 pass from Testaverde (Stover kick)
Car — Johnson 2 run (Kasay kick)
Balt — FG Stover 37
Balt — FG Stover 46
Car — Carrier 6 pass from Collins (Kasay kick)
Car — FG Kasay 44
Balt — FG Stover 25
Car — S. Greene 1 pass from Collins (Kasay kick)

CINCINNATI 21, HOUSTON 13—at Astrodome, attendance 15,131. James Francis's 2 interceptions helped give the Bengals the victory. James Hundon's first career touchdown catch, from 14 yards in the third quarter, completed a 12-play, 79-yard drive and gave Cincinnati a 7-6 lead. Francis's interception return for a touchdown moments later gave Cincinnati a 14-6 lead with 2:07 left in the third quarter. His second interception led to Ki-Jana Carter's 9-yard touchdown run with 3:47 left in the game. Steve McNair entered the game and guided the Oilers to an 89-yard drive, capped by his touchdown pass to Frank Wycheck with 37 seconds left. Cincinnati recovered the onside kick to seal the victory. Jeff Blake completed 13 of 23 passes for 158 yards. Chris Chandler was 16 of 29 for 178 yards, with 3 interceptions, for the Oilers.

| Cincinnati | 0 | 0 | 14 | 7 | — | 21 |
| Houston | 3 | 3 | 0 | 7 | — | 13 |

Hou — FG Del Greco 46
Hou — FG Del Greco 42
Cin — Hundon 14 pass from Blake (Pelfrey kick)
Cin — Francis 42 interception return (Pelfrey kick)
Cin — Carter 9 run (Pelfrey kick)
Hou — Wycheck 16 pass from McNair (Del Greco kick)

GREEN BAY 31, DETROIT 3—at Pontiac Silverdome, attendance 73,214. Brett Favre threw a touchdown pass and ran for another, and Desmond Howard returned a punt 92 yards for a score to give Green Bay a first-round playoff bye. Howard set up the Packers' first-half scoring, as his 23-yard punt return set up Chris Jacke's field goal, and his touchdown return gave the Packers a 10-0 lead at the half. Favre's quarterback sneak culminated the opening drive of the second half, and Dorsey Levens's touchdown run came on the drive immediately following Jason Hanson's field goal. Favre completed 16 of 25 passes for 240 yards. Scott Mitchell was 23 of 40 for 207 yards for the Lions.

| Green Bay | 3 | 7 | 6 | 15 | — | 31 |
| Detroit | 0 | 0 | 3 | 0 | — | 3 |

GB — FG Jacke 20
GB — Howard 92 punt return (Jacke kick)
GB — Favre 1 run (kick failed)
Det — FG Hanson 39
GB — Levens 1 run (Bennett pass from Favre)
GB — Freeman 27 pass from Favre (Jacke kick)

INDIANAPOLIS 24, KANSAS CITY 19—at Arrowhead Stadium, attendance 71,136. Marvin Harrison caught 3 touchdown passes from Jim Harbaugh as the Colts remained in playoff contention with a road victory over the Chiefs. Harrison's third touchdown catch came with 3:48 to play and gave the Colts a 24-13 lead. Steve Bono, who had replaced injured Rich Gannon for the Chiefs, threw a touchdown pass to Kimble Anders with 1:17 left. Kansas City's Anthony Davis recovered the ensuing onside kick, and the Chiefs reached the 11-yard line before Bono threw 4 consecutive incompletions. Harbaugh, after missing the previous two games with a knee injury, completed 16 of 28 passes for 227 yards. Harrison finished with 6 receptions for 103 yards. Bono was 18 of 33 for 194 yards.

| Indianapolis | 14 | 0 | 0 | 10 | — | 24 |
| Kansas City | 0 | 10 | 0 | 9 | — | 19 |

Ind — Harrison 3 pass from Harbaugh (Blanchard kick)
Ind — Harrison 37 pass from Harbaugh (Blanchard kick)
KC — Anders 18 pass from Gannon (Stoyanovich kick)
Ind — FG Blanchard 22
KC — FG Stoyanovich 30
Ind — FG Blanchard 30
Ind — Harrison 5 pass from Harbaugh (Blanchard kick)
KC — Anders 5 pass from Bono (run failed)

DALLAS 12, NEW ENGLAND 6—at Texas Stadium, attendance 64,578. Chris Boniol kicked 4 field goals as Dallas captured its fifth consecutive NFC Eastern Division title. The Cowboys won for the fifth time in six games, while the Patriots lost for just the second time in their last nine games. The Patriots claimed the AFC Eastern Division title when Buffalo lost to Miami on Saturday night. New England entered the game as the NFL's top-scoring team, but was held to just 2 first-quarter field goals. After Boniol's third field goal, Darren Woodson's interception set up his fourth scoring kick. Ty Law's interception in the end zone early in the fourth quarter allowed the Patriots to stay within six points. But Drew Bledsoe threw an incompletion on fourth-and-2 from the Cowboys' 23 with six minutes left, and Woodson's second interception, at the Patriots' 35 with 2:22 left, iced the game. Aikman completed 16 of 28 passes for 169 yards, with 2 interceptions. Bledsoe was 20 of 40 for 178 yards, with 3 interceptions.

| New England | 6 | 0 | 0 | 0 | — | 6 |
| Dallas | 3 | 3 | 6 | 0 | — | 12 |

NE — FG Vinatieri 21
NE — FG Vinatieri 30
Dall — FG Boniol 23
Dall — FG Boniol 36
Dall — FG Boniol 35
Dall — FG Boniol 29

NEW ORLEANS 17, N.Y. GIANTS 3—at Giants Stadium, attendance 52,530. Mario Bates rushed for 129 yards and a touchdown and the Saints' defense forced 4 turnovers and allowed just 138 total yards in recording their first victory under interim head coach Rick Venturi. New Orleans had lost seven in a row, including their first six games with Venturi at the helm. The Giants scored their lone points after Chad Bratzke recovered a Saints' fumble at the

9-yard line, but had to settle for Brad Daluiso's field goal to trim the lead to 7-3. The Giants, trailing 10-3 midway through the fourth quarter, were driving when Je'Rod Cherry recovered a fumble at the Saints' 37-yard line. Bates capitalized on the turnover with a 22-yard touchdown run with 3:47 to play. Jim Everett completed 12 of 22 passes for 106 yards for New Orleans. Dave Brown, who left with a sprained shoulder, and Danny Kanell combined to complete 13 of 38 passes for 94 yards, with 3 interceptions, for the Giants.

New Orleans	0	7	0	10	—	17
N.Y. Giants	0	0	3	0	—	3

NO — Neal 1 run (Brien kick)
NYG — FG Daluiso 30
NO — FG Brien 51
NO — Bates 22 run (Brien kick)

DENVER 24, OAKLAND 19—at Mile High Stadium, attendance 75,466. John Elway threw for 206 yards and a touchdown and the Broncos' defense set up 2 touchdowns with interceptions as Denver vaulted to a 24-3 lead en route to defeating the Raiders. Tyrone Braxton's interception set up Terrell Davis's touchdown run, and Elway threw a 20-yard touchdown pass to Rod Smith after Steve Atwater's interception. Oakland took advantage of the Broncos' second-half turnovers, as Dan Land's fumble recovery set up Cole Ford's second field goal and Lance Johnstone scored on a fumble return. Jeff Hostetler's 7-yard touchdown pass to Daryl Hobbs with 3:38 left cut the lead to five points. Hostetler was injured on the play, and, after the Raiders regained possession in the final minute, Ray Crockett intercepted Billy Joe Hobert's pass to ice the victory. Elway completed 19 of 31 passes, while Hostetler was 18 of 36 for 146 yards, with 2 interceptions. The Raiders committed 4 turnovers and their 20 penalties were the most by a team in a game since 1976.

Oakland	3	0	9	7	—	19
Denver	7	17	0	0	—	24

Den — T. Davis 3 run (Elam kick)
Oak — FG Ford 38
Den — Craver 1 run (Elam kick)
Den — R. Smith 20 pass from Elway (Elam kick)
Den — FG Elam 28
Oak — FG Ford 35
Oak — Johnstone 1 fumble return (run failed)
Oak — Hobbs 7 pass from Hostetler (Ford kick)

ST. LOUIS 34, ATLANTA 27—at Georgia Dome, attendance 26,519. Tony Banks threw 3 long touchdown passes to Eddie Kennison and the Rams' defense forced 7 turnovers to give the Rams their first season-series sweep of the Falcons since 1989. Keith Lyle had 3 of the Rams' 6 interceptions, including one in the end zone on the final play of the game. In the second quarter, Todd Lyght's interception in the end zone allowed the Rams to maintain a 7-3 lead. Banks threw a 77-yard bomb to Kennison three plays later to give St. Louis a 14-3 advantage, which they increased to 24-3. However, Ron George's fumble recovery in the opening seconds of the second half led to Craig Heyward's 1-yard touchdown run and the Rams led just 24-17. Banks and Kennison hooked up for the third time midway through the fourth quarter, but Bobby Hebert threw a 2-yard touchdown pass to Eric Metcalf with 3:16 remaining to pull Atlanta within seven points again. The Falcons regained possession on their 41 with 56 seconds left, only to be thwarted by Lyle's third interception as time expired. Banks completed 11 of 16 passes for 304 yards. Kennison had 5 receptions for 226 yards. Lawrence Phillips recorded his second career 100-yard game, finishing with 112 yards and a touchdown on 22 carries. Hebert completed 28 of 49 passes for 363 yards and 2 touchdowns, with 6 interceptions. Bert Emanuel had 9 catches for 173 yards.

St. Louis	7	17	3	7	—	34
Atlanta	3	7	10	7	—	27

Atl — FG Andersen 34
StL — Kennison 72 pass from Banks (Lohmiller kick)
StL — Kennison 77 pass from Banks (Lohmiller kick)
StL — FG Lohmiller 25
StL — Phillips 6 run (Lohmiller kick)
Atl — Emanuel 5 pass from Hebert (Andersen kick)
Atl — Heyward 1 run (Andersen kick)

StL — FG Lohmiller 25
Atl — FG Andersen 31
StL — Kennison 41 pass from Banks (Lohmiller kick)
Atl — Metcalf 2 pass from Hebert (Andersen kick)

SAN FRANCISCO 25, PITTSBURGH 15—at Three Rivers Stadium, attendance 59,823. Steve Young threw 3 first-half touchdown passes as the 49ers bolted to a 22-0 halftime lead en route to defeating the Steelers. The victory snapped Pittsburgh's 13-game home winning streak. Daryl Price's fumble recovery at the 16-yard line in the opening moments set up Young's touchdown pass to Jerry Rice. After Bryant Young sacked Mike Tomczak for a safety, the 49ers quickly drove downfield, and Young threw a 4-yard touchdown pass to William Floyd to take a 16-0 lead less than six minutes into the game. Young completed 24 of 36 passes for 253 yards. Tomczak was 23 of 43 for 253 yards, with 2 interceptions. Erric Pegram rushed for 103 yards for the Steelers.

San Francisco	16	6	0	3	—	25
Pittsburgh	0	0	8	7	—	15

SF — Rice 4 pass from S. Young (Wilkins kick)
SF — Safety, B. Young sacked Tomczak in end zone
SF — Floyd 4 pass from S. Young (Wilkins kick)
SF — Owens 20 pass from S. Young (Wilkins kick)
Pitt — Bettis 1 run (C. Johnson pass from Tomczak)
SF — FG Wilkins 22
Pitt — Stewart 42 pass from Tomczak (N. Johnson kick)

MINNESOTA 21, TAMPA BAY 10—at Metrodome, attendance 49,202. Leroy Hoard rushed for 101 yards and 2 touchdowns and the Vikings' defense permitted just 8 first downs to win their third consecutive game. Minnesota claimed a wild-card playoff berth later in the afternoon by virtue of Washington's loss to Arizona. The game was tied 7-7 at halftime despite the fact that the Vikings outgained Tampa Bay 185-26 and had more first downs (12-1). Hoard's 22-yard scoring run late in the third quarter gave the Vikings the lead for good. Brad Johnson made his fourth consecutive start for injured Warren Moon and completed 25 of 35 passes for 221 yards, including a 36-yard touchdown pass to Cris Carter with 1:54 remaining to ice the game. Trent Dilfer completed 13 of 32 passes for 104 yards, with 2 interceptions for Tampa Bay.

Tampa Bay	7	0	3	0	—	10
Minnesota	0	7	7	7	—	21

TB — Rhett 5 run (Husted kick)
Minn — Hoard 5 run (Sisson kick)
TB — FG Husted 36
Minn — Hoard 22 run (Sisson kick)
Minn — Carter 36 pass from B. Johnson (Sisson kick)

ARIZONA 27, WASHINGTON 26—at RFK Stadium, attendance 34,260. Kevin Butler's 28-yard field goal as time expired gave the Cardinals a season-series sweep of the Redskins. The loss knocked the Redskins out of the playoffs and was their sixth loss in seven games. Washington led 16-14 at halftime and increased its lead to nine points on Terry Allen's touchdown run midway through the third quarter. However, Butler's field goal and Kent Graham's touchdown pass to Frank Sanders gave Arizona the lead with 12:38 to play. Tom Carter's interception return set up Scott Blanton's go-ahead field goal with 7:14 remaining. The Cardinals ran out the clock with a 15-play, 69-yard drive to set up Butler's heroics. Graham completed 20 of 46 passes for 232 yards. Gus Frerotte was 22 of 40 for 258 yards for Washington.

Washington	3	13	7	3	—	26
Arizona	7	7	3	10	—	27

Ariz — Centers 6 pass from Graham (Butler kick)
Wash — FG Blanton 20
Ariz — Miller 26 lateral from Swann (Butler kick)
Wash — Turner fumble recovery in end zone (Blanton kick)
Wash — FG Blanton 22

Wash — FG Blanton 23
Wash — Allen 14 run (Blanton kick)
Ariz — FG Butler 22
Ariz — Sanders 21 pass from Graham (Butler kick)
Wash — FG Blanton 35
Ariz — FG Butler 28

SUNDAY NIGHT, DECEMBER 15

JACKSONVILLE 20, SEATTLE 13—at Jacksonville Municipal Stadium, attendance 66,134. Mark Brunell threw 2 touchdown passes and Mike Hollis added 2 field goals as the Jaguars stayed alive for a playoff berth with a come-from-behind victory. After Todd Peterson's second field goal gave the Seahawks a 13-7 lead late in the third quarter, the Jaguars responded with Brunell's 39-yard touchdown pass to Jimmy Smith early in the fourth quarter. Tony Brackens's interception led to Hollis's first field goal, with the second successful boot with 2:48 left capping a 10-play drive. The Jaguars did not allow Seattle to cross midfield on its next possession and stopped them on downs. Mark Brunell completed 19 of 26 passes for 231 yards for the Jaguars. Brunell became the nineteenth player in NFL history to surpass 4,000 passing yards in a season, as he finished the night with 4,145 passing yards. Smith had 8 receptions for 124 yards. Rick Mirer was 16 of 31 for 156 yards for Seattle.

Seattle	0	10	3	0	—	13
Jacksonville	7	0	0	13	—	20

Jack — J. Smith 12 pass from Brunell (Hollis kick)
Sea — FG Peterson 27
Sea — Proehl 10 pass from Mirer (Peterson kick)
Sea — FG Peterson 24
Jack — J. Smith 39 pass from Brunell (Hollis kick)
Jack — FG Hollis 19
Jack — FG Hollis 39

MONDAY, DECEMBER 16

MIAMI 16, BUFFALO 14—at Pro Player Stadium, attendance 67,016. Joe Nedney kicked 3 field goals and Dan Marino threw a touchdown pass to give the Dolphins their first season-series sweep of the Bills since 1986. The New England Patriots clinched the AFC Eastern Division title by virtue of the Bills' defeat. Buffalo took a 7-6 lead on Jim Kelly's 67-yard touchdown pass to Andre Reed one play after Nedney's second field goal. After Nedney's third field goal, Buffalo had an opportunity to reclaim the lead, but a high snap forced Steve Christie to miss a 20-yard field goal late in the third quarter. The Bills, trailing 16-14, got the ball back on their 29 with 26 seconds remaining, but Kelly was sacked by Norman Hand and Daniel Stubbs on consecutive plays to end the game. Miami ran more plays (79-49) and dominated time of possession (41:55-18:05). Marino completed 26 of 37 passes for 263 yards. Kelly was 17 of 29 for 240 yards. Reed finished with 6 receptions for 127 yards.

Buffalo	0	7	0	7	—	14
Miami	3	3	3	7	—	16

Mia — FG Nedney 28
Mia — FG Nedney 41
Buff — Reed 67 pass from Kelly (Christie kick)
Mia — FG Nedney 18
Mia — McDuffie 5 pass from Marino (Nedney kick)
Buff — Moulds 16 pass from Kelly (Christie kick)

SEVENTEENTH WEEK SUMMARIES
AMERICAN FOOTBALL CONFERENCE

Eastern Division	W	L	T	Pct.	Pts.	OP
New England	11	5	0	.688	418	313
Buffalo	10	6	0	.625	319	266
Indianapolis	9	7	0	.563	317	334
Miami	8	8	0	.500	339	325
N.Y. Jets	1	15	0	.063	279	454
Central Division						
Pittsburgh	10	6	0	.625	344	257
Jacksonville	9	7	0	.563	325	335
Cincinnati	8	8	0	.500	372	369
Houston	8	8	0	.500	345	319
Baltimore	4	12	0	.250	371	441
Western Division						
Denver	13	3	0	.813	391	275

	W	L	T	Pct.	Pts.	OP
Kansas City	9	7	0	.563	297	300
San Diego	8	8	0	.500	310	376
Oakland	7	9	0	.438	340	293
Seattle	7	9	0	.438	317	376

NATIONAL FOOTBALL CONFERENCE

Eastern Division	W	L	T	Pct.	Pts.	OP
Dallas	10	6	0	.625	286	250
Philadelphia	10	6	0	.625	363	341
Washington	9	7	0	.563	364	312
Arizona	7	9	0	.438	300	397
N.Y. Giants	6	10	0	.375	242	297
Central Division						
Green Bay	13	3	0	.813	456	210
Minnesota	9	7	0	.563	298	315
Chicago	7	9	0	.438	283	305
Tampa Bay	6	10	0	.375	221	293
Detroit	5	11	0	.313	302	368
Western Division						
Carolina	12	4	0	.750	367	218
San Francisco	12	4	0	.750	398	257
St. Louis	6	10	0	.375	303	409
Atlanta	3	13	0	.188	309	461
New Orleans	3	13	0	.188	229	339

SATURDAY, DECEMBER 21

NEW ENGLAND 23, N.Y. GIANTS 22—at Giants Stadium, attendance 65,387. Drew Bledsoe's 13-yard touchdown pass to Ben Coates with 1:23 remaining capped a 22-point comeback and defeated the Giants. The Giants used an efficient offense, and nine points from the defense, to take a 22-0 halftime lead. However, the Patriots held the Giants to just 4 second-half first downs. Terry Glenn's 26-yard touchdown reception cut the deficit to 22-10 with 12:20 left. Just 71 seconds later, David Meggett returned a punt 60 yards for a touchdown to pull the Patriots within five points. The game-winning drive consisted of 13 plays for 75 yards and took 5:45 off the clock. Bledsoe completed 2 third-down passes to keep the drive alive, and then found Coates on fourth-and-7 for the go-ahead score. Needing just a field goal to win, the Giants got into New England territory, but Thomas Lewis dropped a Dave Brown pass near the 25-yard line, ending the Giants hopes. Bledsoe completed 31 of 47 passes for 301 yards. Glenn finished his rookie season with 8 catches for 124 yards. His 91 receptions for the year set a rookie record. With the loss, the Giants suffered back-to-back losing seasons for the first time since 1979-1980.

New England	0	0	3	20	—	23
N.Y. Giants	2	20	0	0	—	22

NYG — Safety, Bledsoe intentional grounding in end zone
NYG — Way 1 run (Daluiso kick)
NYG — FG Daluiso 30
NYG — FG Daluiso 27
NYG — Sehorn 23 interception return (Daluiso kick)
NE — FG Vinatieri 40
NE — Glenn 26 pass from Bledsoe (Vinatieri kick)
NE — Meggett 60 punt return (Vinatieri kick)
NE — Coates 13 pass from Bledsoe (pass failed)

ST. LOUIS 14, NEW ORLEANS 13—at Trans World Dome, attendance 57,681. Reserve quarterback Jamie Martin threw 2 touchdowns to give the Rams a come-from-behind victory. Martin, who had thrown just 15 passes the entire season, replaced injured starter Tony Banks in the second quarter. Isaac Bruce and Eddie Kennison each caught scoring tosses from Martin, who finished 12 of 19 for 132 yards. Kennison's game-winning 15-yard catch came with 5:30 remaining and concluded a 33-yard drive that included a key third-down reception by Harold Green. The two teams combined for just 428 total yards and 26 first downs. The game also served as the final one for head coaches Rick Venturi and Rich Brooks.

New Orleans	10	0	0	3	—	13
St. Louis	0	0	7	7	—	14

NO — Bates 1 run (Brien kick)
NO — FG Brien 43
StL — Bruce 22 pass from Martin (Huerta kick)
NO — FG Brien 35
StL — Kennison 15 pass from Martin (Huerta kick)

SUNDAY, DECEMBER 22

PHILADELPHIA 29, ARIZONA 19—at Veterans Stadium, attendance 63,658. Mike Mamula's fumble return for a touchdown 41 seconds into the game propelled the Eagles to victory. Mamula sacked Kent Graham, forcing the quarterback to fumble, and picked up the ball and ran 4 yards for his first NFL touchdown. Gary Anderson booted 3 of his 5 field goals and Ricky Watters scored on a 1-yard plunge 48 seconds before halftime to give the Eagles a commanding 23-3 halftime lead. Boomer Esiason replaced Graham and led the Cardinals to their lone offensive touchdown. The Eagles controlled the ball for 38 minutes, 40 seconds. Watters gained 99 rushing yards and Ty Detmer completed 20 of 32 pass attempts.

Arizona	0	3	3	13	—	19
Philadelphia	13	10	3	3	—	29

Phil — Mamula 4 fumble return (Anderson kick)
Phil — FG Anderson 23
Phil — FG Anderson 22
Phil — FG Anderson 43
Ariz — FG Butler 41
Phil — Watters 1 run (Anderson kick)
Ariz — FG Butler 41
Phil — FG Anderson 26
Phil — FG Anderson 39
Ariz — McElroy 22 pass from Esiason (kick failed)
Ariz — A. Williams 65 interception return (Butler kick)

JACKSONVILLE 19, ATLANTA 17—at Jacksonville Municipal Stadium, attendance 71,449. Jacksonville earned its first-ever playoff berth when Atlanta kicker Morten Andersen missed a 30-yard field-goal attempt with just four seconds remaining. The Jaguars led the entire game, on the strength of 4 Mike Hollis' field goals, before Craig Heyward cut the deficit to 2 points with his 2-yard run with 5:39 left. After forcing the Jaguars to punt after three plays, the Falcons drove, using a 23-yard pass to Tyrone Brown, deep in Jacksonville territory. With eight seconds left Andersen, who had a 92 percent success rate inside the 40-yard line for his career, lined up to kick the game winner and knock the Jaguars out of the playoffs. However, Andersen's plant foot slipped out from under him and the ball sailed left of the uprights, setting off a delirious celebration. Natrone Means gained 110 yards for the Jaguars, who finished the season with a five game-winning streak. Atlanta did not rehire head coach June Jones for the following season.

Atlanta	0	3	7	7	—	17
Jacksonville	7	6	3	3	—	19

Jax — Brunell 2 run (Hollis kick)
Atl — FG Anderson 46
Jax — FG Hollis 23
Jax — FG Hollis 26
Jax — FG Hollis 22
Atl — Metcalf 4 pass from Hebert (Andersen kick)
Jax — FG Hollis 42
Atl — Heyward 2 run (Andersen kick)

TAMPA BAY 34, CHICAGO 19—at Houlihan's Stadium, attendance 51,572. Tampa Bay established team records by scoring 24 points in the second quarter and 31 in the first half en route to a 34-19 victory over Chicago. Raymont Harris scored from 1-yard out to give the Bears a 7-0 lead, but Tampa Bay responded by scoring the next 31 points. With the score tied 7-7, Hardy Nickerson sacked Dave Krieg, forced him to fumble, and recovered the ball at the 4-yard line. Errict Rhett scored from the 3 to put the Buccaneers in front. Karl Williams' 88-yard punt return, the longest in Tampa Bay history, put the Bucs ahead 21-7. Dilfer's second touchdown pass, and Michael Husted's 50-yard field goal 22 seconds before halftime ended the scoring spree. Shane Matthews replaced Krieg and led the Bears to 2 late touchdowns. Tampa Bay had just 181 total yards, but won for the fifth time in its last seven games. Chicago's Curtis Conway had 9 catches for 120 yards.

Chicago	7	0	12	0	—	19
Tampa Bay	7	24	0	3	—	34

Chi — Harris 1 run (Jaeger kick)
TB — D. Moore 3 pass from Dilfer (Husted kick)
TB — Rhett 3 run (Husted kick)
TB — K. Williams 88 punt return (Husted kick)
TB — Hawkins 15 pass from Dilfer (Husted kick)
TB — FG Husted 50
TB — FG Husted 22
Chi — Engram 6 pass from Matthews (pass failed)
Chi — Matthews 2 run (pass failed)

WASHINGTON 37, DALLAS 10—at RFK Stadium, attendance 56,454. Terry Allen scored 3 touchdowns and Gus Frerotte threw for a career-high 346 yards to give the Redskins a victory in the last game played at RFK Stadium. The Redskins more than doubled the Cowboys in total yardage output (483-235) and first downs (32-14). Dallas played the game without Troy Aikman and Emmitt Smith, with both players being rested for the playoffs the following week. Besides Frerotte's performance, Allen gained 87 yards and Henry Ellard had 7 receptions for 155 yards. Wade Wilson, in his first start since 1993, completed just 8 of 18 passes for 79 yards.

Dallas	0	3	0	7	—	10
Washington	3	13	7	14	—	37

Wash — FG Blanton 45
Wash — FG Blanton 29
Dall — FG Boniol 34
Wash — Allen 1 run (Blanton kick)
Wash — FG Blanton 18
Wash — Allen 2 run (Blanton kick)
Wash — Allen 6 run (Blanton kick)
Wash — S. Davis 4 run (Blanton kick)
Dall — Walker 39 run (Boniol kick)

HOUSTON 24, BALTIMORE 21—at Memorial Stadium, attendance 52,704. Steve McNair threw a touchdown pass and ran 24 yards for a score to lead the Oilers to victory. He completed 19 of 24 passes for 238 yards. McNair's touchdown run late in the third quarter staked the Oilers to a 24-7 lead. Vinny Testaverde, who threw for 307 yards on 23 of 32 passing attempts, found Michael Jackson for 3 touchdowns. The final one, from 4 yards with 13 seconds left, cut the deficit to 24-21. However James McKeehan recovered the ensuing onside kick, ending the Ravens' threat. Houston's Eddie George ran for a touchdown and gained 85 rushing yards. Houston was outgained by 26 yards, and had 2 fewer first downs, but controlled the ball more than 13 minutes longer than the Ravens.

Houston	10	7	7	0	—	24
Baltimore	7	0	0	14	—	21

Hou — George 1 run (Del Greco kick)
Balt — M. Jackson 86 pass from Testaverde (Stover kick)
Hou — FG Del Greco 37
Hou — Davis 19 pass from McNair (Del Greco kick)
Hou — McNair 24 run (Del Greco kick)
Balt — M. Jackson 8 pass from Testaverde (Stover kick)
Balt — M. Jackson 4 pass from Testaverde (Stover kick)

CINCINNATI 31, INDIANAPOLIS 24—at Cinergy Field, attendance 49,389. Jeff Blake threw 3 touchdown passes, including the game winner to Tony McGee with 5:27 left, to defeat Indianapolis. Despite the loss, the Colts were given a playoff berth by virtue of Kansas City losing to Buffalo. Indianapolis tied the Bengals at 3-3, 10-10, 17-17, and 24-24, but were unable to score again following McGee's touchdown catch, which capped a 10-play, 73-yard drive following Aaron Bailey's 95-yard kickoff return that tied the game 24-24. The Bengals dominated the game offensively, outgaining the Colts 441-266 and amassing 10 more first downs (26-16). However, Jason Belser's 21-yard interception return for a touchdown in the first quarter, and Bailey's kickoff return, kept the Colts close. Following Blake's third touchdown pass, Indianapolis was forced to punt. But James Hundon fumbled and Belser recovered at the Bengals' 25-yard line. However, on fourth down Ashley Ambrose tackled Marvin Harrison two yards shy of a first down. The Colts got the ball with 16 seconds left, but Jim Harbaugh's Hail Mary pass was intercepted by Gerald Dixon at the 10-yard line on the game's final play. Cincinnati finished with its first non-losing season since 1990, and Bruce Coslet had a 7-2 record as the Bengals head coach.

Indianapolis	3	7	7	7	—	24
Cincinnati	7	3	7	14	—	31

Cin — Dunn 10 pass from Blake (Pelfrey kick)
Ind — Belser 21 interception return (Blanchard kick)

Cin — FG Pelfrey 25
Ind — FG Blanchard 32
Cin — Carter 1 run (Pelfrey kick)
Ind — Dilger 1 pass from Harbaugh (Blanchard kick)
Cin — Pickens 2 pass from Blake (Pelfrey kick)
Ind — Bailey 95 kickoff return (Blanchard kick)
Cin — McGee 9 pass from Blake (Pelfrey kick)

BUFFALO 20, KANSAS CITY 9—at Rich Stadium, attendance 68,671. Two fourth-quarter 4-yard scoring passes by Jim Kelly gave Buffalo a victory and knocked Kansas City out of the playoffs for the first time in the 1990s. The Chiefs got inside the Bills' 10-yard line three times, twice after Buffalo turnovers, but came away with just three field goals. Trailing 9-3 in the third quarter, Bruce Smith forced Steve Bono to fumble near midfield. Phil Hansen recovered the ball, and Steve Christie's field goal moments later cut the deficit to 9-6. After forcing a punt on the next possession, the Bills drove 72 yards in six plays. Kelly completed 3 consecutive passes of more than 20 yards, to Thurman Thomas, Andre Reed, and Lonnie Johnson, to set up Tony Cline's 4-yard scoring reception. Chris Spielman then intercepted Bono, beginning a 41-yard drive that concluded with Quinn Early's touchdown catch. Bono, who started for an injured Rich Gannon and finished 14 of 28 for 138 yards and 2 interceptions, completed just 1 pass in the first half on 7 attempts. Kelly completed 20 of 29 passes for 279 yards and 2 touchdowns.

Kansas City	3	3	3	0	—	9
Buffalo	0	3	3	14	—	20

KC — FG Stoyanovich 19
KC — FG Stoyanovich 24
Buff — FG Christie 41
KC — FG Stoyanovich 26
Buff — FG Christie 42
Buff — Cline 4 pass from Kelly (Christie kick)
Buff — Early 4 pass from Kelly (Christie kick)

MIAMI 31, N.Y. JETS 28—at Giants Stadium, attendance 49,933. Dan Marino fired 3 touchdown passes and Karim Abdul-Jabbar ran for 152 yards to lead the Dolphins. The loss gave the Jets the distinction of being the fifth team in NFL history to finish 1-15. The Jets took a 14-0 lead on Hugh Douglas' 62-yard fumble return and with Adrian Murrell capping an impressive 84-yard drive with a 1-yard run. The Jets stopped Miami three different times on a drive late in the first half, but hurt themselves with penalties. Miami finally scored on O.J. McDuffie's 1-yard catch with six seconds left in the half. Miami scored immediately in the third quarter, on Fred Barnett's 33-yard catch, to tie the game. The Jets responded with a scoring drive of their own, with Kyle Brady the scoring recepient of Glenn Foley's pass. The Dolphins answered on the next drive with an unnecessary roughness penalty and a fourth-down run by Irving Spikes setting up Abdul-Jabbar's tying tally. After a Miami field goal, the Dolphins scored again when they capitalized on the Jets' defensive holding call on third-and-8. Randal Hill caught a 50-yard touchdown pass to put Miami ahead 31-21 with 11:17 left. Wayne Chrebet caught a 9-yard pass from Frank Reich, who replaced Foley, with 4:45 left to cut the deficit to 3 points. The Jets forced Miami to punt, but Chrebet fumbled inside Dolphins' territory, and Miami ran out the clock.

Miami	0	7	17	7	—	31
N.Y. Jets	14	0	7	7	—	28

NYJ — Douglas 62 fumble return (Lowery kick)
NYJ — Murrell 1 run (Lowery kick)
Mia — McDuffie 1 pass from Marino (Nedney kick)
Mia — Barnett 33 pass from Marino (Nedney kick)
NYJ — Brady 11 pass from Foley (Lowery kick)
Mia — Abdul-Jabbar 17 run (Nedney kick)
Mia — FG Nedney 38
Mia — Hill 50 pass from Marino (Nedney kick)
NYJ — Chrebet 9 pass from Reich (Lowery kick)

GREEN BAY 38, MINNESOTA 10—at Lambeau Field, attendance 59,306. Brett Favre threw 3 touchdown passes, and Dorsey Levens scored twice, as the Packers earned home-field advantage throughout the NFC playoffs. Scott Sisson's 34-yard field goal as the half expired tied the game 10-10. Desmond Howard returned the opening kickoff of the second half 40 yards, leading to Levens' 13-yard touchdown reception three minutes into the second half. Howard had a 24-yard punt return, which led to Andre Rison's first touchdown as a Packers player. Favre threw his third touchdown pass, and team-record thirty-ninth of the season, to Keith Jackson five seconds into the fourth quarter. Howard's 47-yard punt return led to Levens' second touchdown to finish the scoring. Green Bay outgained the Vikings (440-252), had more first downs (29-12), and dominated time of possession (37:10-22:50). The Packers had 233 rushing yards, with 109 belonging to Edgar Bennett, and won their fifteenth consecutive home game.

Minnesota	7	3	0	0	—	10
Green Bay	7	3	14	14	—	38

GB — Bennett 5 run (Jacke kick)
Minn — Carter 43 pass from B. Johnson (Sisson kick)
GB — FG Jacke 35
Minn — FG Sisson 34
GB — Levens 13 pass from Favre (Jacke kick)
GB — Rison 22 pass from Favre (Jacke kick)
GB — Jackson 23 pass from Favre (Jacke kick)
GB — Levens 11 run (Jacke kick)

CAROLINA 18, PITTSBURGH 14—at Ericsson Stadium, attendance 72,217. Chad Cota's interception in the end zone with 29 seconds left clinched the NFC West title for Carolina. The Steelers had reached the Panthers' 1-yard line on a defensive holding penalty. However, the Steelers were penalized five yards for a false start, and Stewart threw an incompletion and was sacked for a 2-yard loss. On third-and-goal from the 8-yard line, Cota stepped in front of the pass intended for Ernie Mills, clinching the victory. Pittsburgh had an opportunity to take the lead with 3:54 to play, but Mills dropped Stewart's pass in the end zone on fourth-and-goal. Carolina grabbed an early 9-0 lead, but the Steelers answered with Andre Hastings' 6-yard scoring catch. Then Kordell Stewart, scrambling, raced 80 yards for a touchdown. It was the longest run by a quarterback in NFL history. John Kasay booted 3 field goals to put Carolina in front. The Panthers finished the season 8-0 at Ericsson Stadium.

Pittsburgh	0	14	0	0	—	14
Carolina	7	2	6	3	—	18

Car — Walls 9 pass from Collins (Kasay kick)
Car — Safety, Tomczak intentional grounding in end zone
Pitt — Hastings 6 pass from Tomczak (N. Johnson kick)
Pitt — Stewart 80 run (N. Johnson kick)
Car — FG Kasay 35
Car — FG Kasay 30
Car — FG Kasay 29

SEATTLE 28, OAKLAND 21—at Oakland-Alameda County Coliseum, attendance 33,456. Seattle benefited from 6 Raiders fumbles to defeat Oakland. Seattle won despite gaining just 129 total yards, including just 13 passing yards, and 8 first downs. Oakland accumulated 356 total yards, had the ball for 36:11 of the game's 60 minutes, and had 21 first downs. However they committed 7 turnovers while only causing 2 Seahawks miscues. The Raiders led 11-0 when Cortez Kennedy recovered Harvey Williams's fumble at the 22-yard line. After losing five yards, Todd Peterson booted a 45-yard field goal. Special teams trickery, a 52-yard punt return off a lateral from Tim Brown to Carl Kidd, set up Ford's fourth field goal with 1:12 left in the first half. However, Dennis McKnight's 54-yard kickoff return set up Lamar Smith's 27-yard touchdown run with 55 seconds left. Robert Blackmon intercepted Billy Joe Hobert, allowing Peterson to kick a 52-yard field goal as the half expired, cutting the Raiders lead to 14-13. At the beginning of the third quarter, Sam Adams sacked Hobert, forcing a fumble recovered by Michael McCrary. The play knocked Hobert out of the game and set up Gino Torretta's 32-yard touchdown toss to Joey Galloway. Later in the quarter, Corey Harris recovered Napoleon Kaufman's fumble and returned it 17 yards to the 7-yard line, setting up Smith's second touchdown run. The Raiders best opportunity of their four fourth-quarter possessions ended on a Kaufman fumble at the 20-yard line after Derrick Fenner cut the Seattle lead to 28-21.

Seattle	0	13	15	0	—	28
Oakland	8	6	7	0	—	21

Oak — FG Ford 47
Oak — Safety, blocked punt through end zone
Oak — FG Ford 23
Oak — FG Ford 28
Sea — FG Peterson 45
Oak — FG Ford 24
Sea — Smith 27 run (Peterson kick)
Sea — FG Peterson 52
Sea — Galloway 32 pass from Torretta (Smith run)
Sea — Smith 3 run (Peterson kick)
Oak — Fenner 2 run (Ford kick)

SUNDAY NIGHT, DECEMBER 22

SAN DIEGO 16, DENVER 10—at San Diego Jack Murphy Stadium, attendance 46,801. San Diego ended a three-game losing streak by scoring the game's final 16 points. The Broncos, who had already clinched home-field advantage throughout the AFC playoffs, only played John Elway in the first quarter, when they scored all 10 of their points. Bill Musgrave played the second and third quarters, with rookie Jeff Lewis guiding Denver in the fourth. San Diego used 57-yard and 78-yard drives to set up Carney's third-quarter field goals. The Broncos' best chance to win was thwarted when Rodney Harrison intercepted a Lewis pass, intended for Dwayne Carswell, in the end zone with 6:12 remaining in the game.

Denver	10	0	0	0	—	10
San Diego	7	3	6	0	—	16

Den — FG Elam 51
Den — Davis 1 run (Elam kick)
SD — Jones 9 pass from Humphries (Carney kick)
SD — FG Carney 50
SD — FG Carney 21
SD — FG Carney 22

MONDAY, DECEMBER 23

SAN FRANCISCO 24, DETROIT 14—at 3Com Park, attendance 61,921. The 49ers defeated Detroit, handing the Lions their fifth consecutive defeat and ninth in their last 10 games. Steve Young, who played the first half and clinched his fifth passing title in the last six seasons, threw 2 touchdown passes. Jerry Rice had 5 catches and ended the season with an NFL-best 108 receptions. Barry Sanders, who ran for 175 yards, including a 54-yard touchdown run, surpassed the 1,500-yard mark for an NFL-record third consecutive season and won the league's rushing title. The 49ers' and Lions' statistics were nearly identical, with both teams having 18 first downs and zero turnovers, and the 49ers gaining 4 more total yards and garnering possession for just eight more seconds than the Lions. The Lions converted just 4 of 14 third-down situations. This was the last regular-season game for both head coaches, Wayne Fontes and George Seifert.

Detroit	7	0	7	0	—	14
San Francisco	7	7	7	3	—	24

SF — Popson 1 pass from Young (Wilkins kick)
Det — Sanders 54 run (Hanson kick)
SF — Loville 1 pass from Young (Wilkins kick)
SF — Grbac 6 run (Wilkins kick)
Det — Moore 5 pass from Mitchell (Hanson kick)
SF — FG Wilkins 49

EIGHTEENTH WEEK SUMMARIES
SATURDAY, DECEMBER 28
AFC WILD CARD PLAYOFF GAME

JACKSONVILLE 30, BUFFALO 27—at Rich Stadium, attendance 70,213. Mike Hollis's third field goal, a 45-yard boot that caromed off the right upright before going through, with 3:07 remaining gave Jacksonville a playoff victory in its first-ever postseason game. The second-year franchise also pinned the Bills with their first-ever postseason home loss, after having won their first nine playoff games at Rich Stadium. Thurman Thomas scored two first-half touchdowns, but Jacksonville got a defensive touchdown from Clyde Simmons and a 30-yard run by Natrone Means. The teams entered the fourth-quarter tied 20-20 when Buffalo's Jeff Burris intercepted Mark Brunell's tipped pass and raced 38 yards to give the Bills a 27-20 advantage 43 seconds into the final quarter. The Jaguars put a 10-play, 65-yard drive together, keyed by 2 receptions by Keenan McCardell and a fourth-and-1 conversion by Means, to tie the game on Jimmy Smith's 2-yard pass with 8:40 remaining. On the ensuing possession, Chris Hudson sacked a scrambling Jim Kelly, forcing him to fumble and

injuring him on the play. Aaron Beasley recovered the ball at the Jaguars' 41 with 7:13 left. Facing third-and-7 from the Bills' 41, Brunell hit McCardell with an 11-yard passing play to set up Hollis's winning kick. Todd Collins replaced the injured Kelly on Buffalo's final two possessions, but the Bills could not move the ball. Means carried 31 times for 175 yards, with 21 carries coming in the second half as the Jaguars won the time of possession battle (33:06-26:54) and total yards (409-308).

Jacksonville	10	7	3	10	—	30
Buffalo	14	3	3	7	—	27

Buff — Thomas 7 pass from Kelly (Christie kick)
Jax — Simmons 20 interception return (Hollis kick)
Buff — Thomas 2 run (Christie kick)
Jax — FG Hollis 27
Jax — Means 30 run (Hollis kick)
Buff — FG Christie 33
Buff — FG Christie 47
Jax — FG Hollis 24
Buff — Burris 38 interception return (Christie kick)
Jax — Smith 2 pass from Brunell (Hollis kick)
Jax — FG Hollis 45

NFC WILD CARD PLAYOFF GAME

DALLAS 40, MINNESOTA 15—at Texas Stadium, attendance 64,682. Three big plays by George Teague catapulted Dallas to a 30-0 halftime lead en route to routing the Vikings. With the Cowboys leading 7-0, the Vikings Amp Lee caught a pass over the middle on this way to the end zone. However, Teague lunged at Lee from behind, slapping the ball through the end zone to give Dallas possession at their 20-yard line. Chris Boniol capped the 12-play drive with a 28-yard field goal to put Dallas ahead 10-0. On the next play from scrimmage, Teague forced Leroy Hoard to fumble the ball away. On the next play Emmitt Smith streaked 37 yards for a touchdown. Exactly one minute later, Teague intercepted Brad Johnson's pass and returned it 29 yards for a touchdown, giving the Cowboys 17 points in a one-minute, 32-second span and a 24-0 lead. It was the Vikings seventh consecutive playoff loss, and the fourth under coach Dennis Green. Dallas completely dominated the game statistically, compiling more first downs (27-12), total yards (438-268), time of possession (42:03-17:57), and committing fewer turnovers (5-2).

Minnesota	0	0	7	8	—	15
Dallas	7	23	7	3	—	40

Dall — Aikman 2 run (Boniol kick)
Dall — FG Boniol 28
Dall — E. Smith 37 run (Boniol kick)
Dall — Teague 29 interception return (Boniol kick)
Dall — FG Boniol 31
Dall — FG Boniol 22
Minn — Carter 30 pass from B. Johnson (Sisson kick)
Dall — E. Smith 1 run (Boniol kick)
Dall — FG Boniol 25
Minn — B. Johnson 5 run (Carter pass from B. Johnson)

SUNDAY, DECEMBER 29

AFC WILD CARD PLAYOFF GAME

PITTSBURGH 42, INDIANAPOLIS 14—at Three Rivers Stadium, attendance 58,078. Jerome Bettis scored 2 touchdowns, and the Steelers' defense permitted just 8 first downs, 146 yards, and compiled 4 sacks as they advanced to play the New England Patriots. The Colts led 14-13 at halftime on the strength of Eugene Daniel's 59-yard interception return and a 48-yard pass play from Jim Harbaugh to Marvin Harrison. The Steelers opened the second half with a 9:30 drive, with Bettis's first touchdown capping the 16-play march. Late in the third quarter, Carnell Lake forced Marshall Faulk to fumble and recovered the ball at the Colts' 18-yard line. Bettis scored his second touchdown moments later, and the rout was on. Pittsburgh scored a postseason-team record 42 points while totalling 407 yards and controlling the ball for 37:36. Bettis, who eleven times during the season broke the 100-yard barrier, had 25 carries for 102 yards.

Indianapolis	0	14	0	0	—	14
Pittsburgh	10	3	8	21	—	42

Pitt — FG N. Johnson 29
Pitt — Stewart 1 run (N. Johnson kick)
Pitt — FG N. Johnson 50
Ind — Daniel 59 interception return (Blanchard kick)
Ind — Bailey 9 pass from Harbaugh (Blanchard kick)
Pitt — Bettis 1 run (Farquhar pass from Stewart)
Pitt — Bettis 1 run (N. Johnson kick)
Pitt — Witman 31 run (N. Johnson kick)
Pitt — Stewart 3 run (N. Johnson kick)

NFC WILD CARD PLAYOFF GAME

SAN FRANCISCO 14, PHILADELPHIA 0—at 3Com Park, attendance 56,460. Steve Young ran for a touchdown and threw for one as the 49ers defeated the Eagles in the mud of 3Com Park. The Eagles blew three scoring chances in the first half. Gary Anderson missed a 40-yard field goal on the Eagles first possession. Trailing 7-0 after a scrambling touchdown run by Young in which he bruised his ribs, the Eagles drove deep into 49ers territory. On third-and-1 from the 8-yard line, Detmer attempted to throw the ball away on a pass attempt. However Marquez Pope grabbed the errant toss for the interception. After a punt, Philadelphia drove to the 49ers' 5-yard line, but Roy Barker intercepted Detmer's third-and-4 pass. Philadelphia got into 49ers territory only once the remainder of the game. Young, who left the game in the second quarter with a rib injury, threw a 36-yard pass to Jerry Rice, who made a spectacular one-handed catch, to set up the duo's third-quarter touchdown. San Francisco garnered its first postseason shutout since the 1984 NFC Championship Game.

Philadelphia	0	0	0	0	—	0
San Francisco	0	7	7	0	—	14

SF — S. Young 9 run (Wilkins kick)
SF — Rice 3 pass from S. Young (Wilkins kick)

NINETEENTH WEEK SUMMARIES

SATURDAY, JANUARY 4

AFC DIVISIONAL PLAYOFF GAME

JACKSONVILLE 30, DENVER 27—at Mile High Stadium, attendance 75,678. Mark Brunell passed for 245 yards and 2 touchdowns to lead the Jaguars to their second consecutive postseason victory. The Broncos, who finished the season 8-0 at home and had home-field advantage throughout the playoffs, blew a 12-0 lead. After Vaughn Hebron's short run began the scoring, Clyde Simmons blocked the extra point attempt. The Broncos failed to convert the 2-point conversion following Shannon Sharpe's touchdown catch late in the first quarter. The Jaguars responded by scoring on their next six possessions. Natrone Means, who carried the ball 21 times for 140 yards, pulled the Jaguars within two points before Mike Hollis's 42-yard field goal with 10 seconds left in the half put Jacksonville ahead 13-12. Brunell, rolling to his left, lofted a pefectly placed 31-yard touchdown pass to Keenan McCardell in the left corner of the end zone to put the Jaguars ahead 20-12. Jacksonville took 8 minutes, 32 seconds off the clock with its next possession, ending with Hollis's third field goal. The 17-play drive was kept alive when Michael Dean Perry failed to hustle off the field when the Jaguars were punting in a fourth-and-5 situation. Denver got the ball back with less than 11 minutes remaining, and Terrell Davis scored and tallied a 2-point conversion, to cut the deficit to 23-20. Jacksonville calmly marched down field, and Jimmy Smith caught a 16-yard touchdown pass on third-and-5 to put Jacksonville ahead by 10 points with 3:39 remaining. John Elway quickly led the Broncos to another touchdown, with Ed McCaffrey doing the honors with 1:50 left. However Le'Shai Maston recovered the onside kick and the Jaguars ended the Broncos postseason home-winning streak at 6 games. Neither team committed a turnover.

Jacksonville	0	13	7	10	—	30
Denver	12	0	0	15	—	27

Den — Hebron 1 run (kick blocked)
Den — Sharpe 18 pass from Elway (pass failed)
Jax — FG Hollis 46
Jax — Means 8 run (Hollis kick)
Jax — FG Hollis 42
Jax — McCardell 31 pass from Brunell (Hollis kick)
Jax — FG Hollis 22
Den — Davis 2 run (Davis run)
Jax — Smith 16 pass from Brunell (Hollis kick)
Den — McCaffrey 15 pass from Elway (Elam kick)

NFC DIVISIONAL PLAYOFF GAME

GREEN BAY 35, SAN FRANCISCO 14—at Lambeau Field, attendance 60,787. Desmond Howard had two big punt returns, one for a touchdown and one to set up another, and Edgar Bennett scored twice to lead the Packers to victory at muddy Lambeau Field. Howard's 71-yard punt return for a touchdown 2:15 into the game to gave the Packers an early lead. A 46-yard punt return by Howard set up Andre Rison's touchdown catch, Bennett completed a short 15-yard drive, set up by Craig Newsome's interception, with a touchdown to give Green Bay a commanding 21-0 advantage. Two careless turnovers brought the 49ers back into the game. Chris Hayes had a 49ers punt bounce off his foot. Curtis Buckley recovered the ball and Terry Kirby scored 24 seconds before halftime. As Green Bay prepared to receive the opening kickoff to the second half, Howard still was in the locker room changing his pants. Andre Rison ran onto the field as the ball was kicked. Steve Israel beat Rison to the ball, giving the 49ers possession at the 4-yard line. Elvis Grbac's 2-yard run cut the deficit to 21-14. The Packers responded with a long drive, but chaos ensued as they were about to score. Bennett, in his effort to break the end zone plane with the ball, fumbled at the goal line, causing a pileup in the end zone. After sifting through bodies, the referees ruled Antonio Freeman had recovered the ball for a touchdown. Bennett scored the game's final points after Kirby fumbled a punt return at his own 32-yard line. Brett Favre, tempered by the poor weather conditions, attempted just 15 passes, completing 11 for 79 yards. Grbac, who came in during the first quarter after Steve Young's bruised ribs inhibited his performance, completed 19 of 36 passes for 125 yards, 1 touchdown, and 3 interceptions. The teams combined for just 404 total yards and 6 turnovers.

San Francisco	0	7	7	0	—	14
Green Bay	14	7	7	7	—	35

GB — Howard 71 punt return (Jacke kick)
GB — Rison 4 pass from Favre (Jacke kick)
GB — Bennett 2 run (Jacke kick)
SF — Kirby 8 pass from Grbac (Wilkins kick)
SF — Grbac 2 run (Wilkins kick)
GB — Freeman recovered fumble in end zone (Jacke kick)
GB — Bennett 11 run (Jacke kick)

SUNDAY, JANUARY 5

AFC DIVISIONAL PLAYOFF GAME

NEW ENGLAND 28, PITTSBURGH 3—at Foxboro Stadium, attendance 60,188. Curtis Martin scored three touchdowns and New England's defense stifled Pittsburgh as the Patriots routed the Steelers in the fog in Foxboro. The Patriots broke Pittsburgh's back on their first play from scrimmage as Terry Glenn beat Rod Woodson and, despite heavy fog, caught a 53-yard bomb from Drew Bledsoe. Martin scored on the next play to start the rout. The Patriots next drive lasted 1:59, finishing with Keith Byars's 34-yard touchdown off a screen pass. Martin then raced 78 yards up the right sideline to stake New England to a 21-0 second-quarter lead. The Steelers were forced to punt after each of their first seven possessions. Chad Brown's interception in Patriots' territory set up Norm Johnson's field goal. Martin capped his 166-yard rushing day by scoring on a 23-yard jaunt. Pittsburgh shuffled quarterbacks throughout the game, with Mike Tomczak completing 16 of 29 pass attempts for 110 yards and 2 interceptions, while Kordell Stewart finished a dreadful 0 for 10. Jerome Bettis, hampered by a groin injury, gained just 43 yards. Pittsburgh converted just 3 of 18 third-down opportunities.

Pittsburgh	0	0	3	0	—	3
New England	14	7	0	7	—	28

NE — Martin 2 run (Vinatieri kick)
NE — Byars 34 pass from Bledsoe (Vinatieri kick)
NE — Martin 78 run (Vinatieri kick)
Pitt — FG N. Johnson 29
NE — Martin 23 run (Vinatieri kick)

NFC DIVISIONAL PLAYOFF GAME

CAROLINA 26, DALLAS 17—at Ericsson Stadium, attendance 72,808. The Panthers defense intercepted 3 passes, and John Kasay booted 4 field goals, as Carolina won its first playoff game in franchise history. Dallas, which had won the Super Bowl three of the previous four years, scored on its first possession and went ahead 3-0 on Chris Boniol's field goal. However, the scoring drive was costly because Michael Irvin separated his shoulder making a 23-

yard catch and missed the remainder of the game. Carolina responded with a 68-yard scoring drive, keyed by two Cowboys' penalties, and took the lead on Wesley Walls's touchdown catch. After forcing a punt, Collins threw his second touchdown pass, this one to Willie Green, to put the Panthers ahead 14-3. Dallas put its best drive of the game together, with Daryl Johnston's touchdown catch ending the 15-play, eight-minute, 21 second drive. A bad snap over Rohn Stark's head and through the end zone on the following possession pulled Dallas within three points and gave them momentum. However, Chad Cota's interception and 49-yard return set up Kasay's 24-yard field goal three seconds before halftime giving the Panthers a 17-11 lead. Four second-half field goals, 2 by each team, gave the Panthers a 23-17 lead. Dallas got the ball back on a Carolina punt, but with poor field position after Dwight Stone downed it at the 2-yard line. Just as the Cowboys were mounting a possible game-winning drive, Pat Terrell intercepted Aikman and returned the ball 49 yards to set up Kasay's final field goal. Sam Mills's interception in the final minute iced the game. Johnson totaled 104 yards, the first 100-yard rushing game by a Cowboys playoff opponent since Eric Dickerson in 1985.

Dallas	3	8	3	3 —	17
Carolina	7	10	3	6 —	26

Dall — FG Boniol 22
Car — Walls 1 pass from Collins (Kasay kick)
Car — W. Green 10 pass from Collins (Kasay kick)
Dall — Johnston 2 pass from Aikman (pass failed)
Dall — Safety, Carolina bad snap on punt went out of end zone
Car — FG Kasay 24
Dall — FG Boniol 21
Car — FG Kasay 40
Car — FG Kasay 23
Dall — FG Boniol 21
Car — FG Kasay 32

TWENTIETH WEEK SUMMARIES
SUNDAY, JANUARY 12
AFC CHAMPIONSHIP GAME

NEW ENGLAND 20, JACKSONVILLE 6—at Foxboro Stadium, attendance 60,190. Otis Smith's 47-yard fumble return with 2:24 remaining gave the Patriots their second Super Bowl berth in franchise history. The Patriots received a couple big plays from their special teams. Jacksonville punted after its opening possession, but the snap was high. Larry Whigham tackled the scrambling Bryan Barker at the 4-yard line, setting up Curtis Martin's 1-yard touchdown. After a Jacksonville field goal, Ray Lucas stripped punt returner Chris Hudson of the ball. Mike Bartrum recovered it at the 20-yard line, and Adam Vinatieri kicked a 29-yard field goal to put New England ahead 10-3. Shawn Jefferson hauled in a 38-yard pass to the Jaguars' 2-yard line with eight seconds left before halftime after Ben Coates's 5-yard reception on fourth-and-2 kept a Patriots drive alive. Vinatiei's field goal gave the Patriots a 10-point cushion. Eddie Robinson's fumble recovery led to Mike Hollis's 28-yard field goal to pull the Jaguars within 7 points. In the fourth quarter the Jaguars drove to the Patriots' 5-yard line, but Willie Clay intercepted Mark Brunell's pass in the end zone with 3:43 left to preserve the 13-6 lead. The Jaguars forced New England to punt, and Jacksonville got the ball on their own 42-yard line with 2:36 to play. However, Chris Slade stripped James Stewart of the ball, knocking it into Smith's hands. Smith streaked down the right sideline for the score. Tedy Bruschi intercepted Brunell near midfield to quell the pesky Jaguars' third consecutive upset bid.

Jacksonville	0	3	3	0 —	6
New England	7	6	0	7 —	20

NE — Martin 1 run (Vinatieri kick)
Jax — FG Hollis 32
NE — FG Vinatieri 29
NE — FG Vinatieri 20
Jax — FG Hollis 28
NE — Smith 47 fumble return (Vinatieri kick)

NFC CHAMPIONSHIP GAME

GREEN BAY 30, CAROLINA 13—at Lambeau Field, attendance 60,216. Dorsey Levens combined for 205 total yards of offense, and Brett Favre threw 2 touchdown passes, as the Packers earned their first Super Bowl berth in twenty-nine years. With the wind chill fluctuating between 17- and 25-degrees below zero, the Panthers scored first. Sam Mills intercepted Favre and returned the ball to the 2-yard line, setting up Howard Griffith's touchdown catch. Levens broke off a 35-yard run on third-and-1 late in the first quarter, and then made a spectacular diving catch in the end zone to open the second quarter and tie the game. Lamar Lathon recovered a Favre fumble, setting up John Kasay's go-ahead field goal. Green Bay then scored twice in the final 48 seconds of the first half to turn the game's momentum. Antonio Freeman caught a 6-yard touchdown pass on third-and-3 after Andre Rison's 22-yard catch put the Packers in position. Tyrone Williams then made a diving interception on the Packers' 38-yard line with 35 seconds left in the half. Favre fired a 23-yard pass to Rison and 25-yard bullet to Freeman to set up Chris Jacke's field goal and give Green Bay a 17-10 halftime lead. After an exchange of field goals, Levens turned a screen pass into a 66-yard play, setting up Edgar Bennett's touchdown run. LeRoy Butler recovered Anthony Johnson's fumble on Carolina's next possession, and set up Jacke's last field goal. Green Bay had 201 rushing yards, outgained Carolina 479-251 in total yards, and dominated time of possession (38:03-21:57). The victory gave Green Bay a 9-0 postseason record at Lambeau Field.

Carolina	7	3	3	0 —	13
Green Bay	0	17	10	3 —	30

Car — Griffith 3 pass from Collins (Kasay kick)
GB — Levens 29 pass from Favre (Jacke kick)
Car — FG Kasay 22
GB — Freeman 6 pass from Favre (Jacke kick)
GB — FG Jacke 31
GB — FG Jacke 32
Car — FG Kasay 23
GB — Bennett 4 run (Jacke kick)
GB — FG Jacke 28

TWENTY-FIRST WEEK SUMMARY
SUNDAY, JANUARY 26
SUPER BOWL XXXI
NEW ORLEANS, LOUISIANA

GREEN BAY 35, NEW ENGLAND 21—at Louisiana Superdome, attendance 72,301. Desmond Howard returned a kickoff 99 yards for a touchdown and Brett Favre threw 2 touchdown passes and ran for a score as the Packers won their first Super Bowl in twenty-nine years. Howard, en route to garnering the MVP trophy, established a Super Bowl record with 244 total return yards. It was Favre's arm that struck first, as he hit Andre Rison for a 54-yard touchdown on the Packers' second play from scrimmage to take a 7-0 lead. Two plays later Doug Evans made a diving interception of Drew Bledsoe's pass at the 28-yard line, setting up Chris Jacke's field goal and giving the Packers a 10-0 lead just 6:18 into the Super Bowl. The Patriots answered with touchdowns on their next two possessions with Craig Newsome's pass interference penalty setting up the first touchdown and a 44-yard completion from Bledsoe to Terry Glenn preceeding Ben Coates's touchdown gave New England its first and only lead. The 24 combined first quarter points were the most in Super Bowl history. Green Bay struck again 56 seconds into the second quarter as Favre hit Antonio Freeman with a Super Bowl-record 81-yard touchdown bomb. Jacke booted his second field goal on Green Bay's next possession. After a Mike Prior interception, Favre orchestrated a 74-yard, nearly 6-minute drive which concluded with a diving Favre stretching to touch the ball against the pylon to give Green Bay a 27-14 halftime lead. Curtis Martin brought the Patriots to within a score by running in from 18 yards out with 3:27 left in the third quarter. But Howard broke the Patriots' spirit by returning the ensuing kickoff a Super Bowl-record 99 yards. Favre found Mark Chmura for the 2-point conversion to finish the scoring. Bledsoe was intercepted twice in the fourth quarter as the Patriots never crossed midfield in 4 fourth-quarter possessions. Favre completed 14 of 27 passes for 246 yards, 2 touchdowns, 0 interceptions, and 1 rushing TD. Bledsoe completed 11 more passes than Favre, but for just 7 more yards and 4 interceptions.

New England	14	0	7	0 —	21
Green Bay	10	17	8	0 —	35

GB — Rison 54 pass from Favre (Jacke kick)
GB — FG Jacke 37
NE — Byars 1 pass from Bledsoe (Vinatieri kick)
NE — Coates 4 pass from Bledsoe (Vinatieri kick)

GB — Freeman 81 pass from Favre (Jacke kick)
GB — FG Jacke 31
GB — Favre 2 run (Jacke kick)
NE — Martin 18 run (Vinatieri kick)
GB — Howard 99 kickoff return (Chmura pass from Favre)

TWENTY-SECOND WEEK SUMMARY
SUNDAY, FEBRUARY 2
AFC-NFC PRO BOWL
HONOLULU, HAWAII

AFC 26, NFC 23 (OT)—at Aloha Stadium, attendance 50,031. Cary Blanchard's 37-yard field goal 8:16 into overtime gave the AFC a 26-23 victory. The field goal was an ironic ending to a game that saw Blanchard and NFC kicker John Kasay, who each broke the previous single-season record of 35 field goals, combine to miss 5 of 8 field-goal attempts. The NFC scored on its first two possessions, with Vikings guard Randall McDaniel, who lined up as a fullback, scoring his first professional touchdown to give the NFC a 9-3 lead. However, the follies of the kicking unit began as holder Matt Turk muffed the snap on the extra point attempt. Blanchard booted a 28-yard field goal with 27 seconds left in the half to cut the NFC's lead to 9-3. Barry Sanders scored from 6 yards out, but Kerry Collins was sacked on the 2-point attempt. A 41-yard pass from Drew Bledsoe to Tony Martin led to Curtis Martin's 3-yard run, and after Ashley Ambrose ran an interception back 54 yards for a touchdown 11 seconds into the fourth quarter, the AFC found itself with a 16-15 lead. The NFC drove for more than six minutes, only to have Kasay miss a 40-yard field goal attempt. After an AFC punt, Cris Carter caught a 47-yard touchdown bomb from Gus Frerotte to put the NFC ahead 23-16. After each team punted, the AFC got the ball on its own 20-yard line with 55 seconds left. Mark Brunell hit Tim Brown with an 80-yard bomb down the right sideline to tie the game with 44 seconds left. Wesley Walls caught a 33-yard pass to give the NFC a chance to win in regulation, but Kasay missed a 39-yard attempt and the game went to overtime. The AFC won the overtime toss, but Blanchard missed a 41-yard field goal attempt. The NFC had to punt after three plays, and Brunell hit Ben Coates with a 43-yard pass on the AFC's first play. After three running plays failed to gain a first down, Blanchard trotted onto the field and made the game-winning kick. The teams combined for 962 total yards. Brunell, who completed 12 of 22 pass attempts for 236 yards, was selected as the player of the game.

AFC	0	3	7	13	3 —	26
NFC	9	0	6	8	0 —	23

NFC — FG Kasay 20
NFC — McDaniel 5 pass from Favre (muffed snap)
AFC — FG Blanchard 28
NFC — B. Sanders 6 run (pass failed)
AFC — Martin 3 run (Blanchard kick)
AFC — Ambrose 54 interception return (pass failed)
NFC — C. Carter 53 pass from Frerotte (Walls pass from Frerotte)
AFC — T. Brown 80 pass from Brunell (Blanchard kick)
AFC — FG Blanchard 37

	NFL	AFC	NFC
PRO FOOTBALL WRITERS OF AMERICA			
Most Valuable Player	Brett Favre		
Rookie of the Year	Eddie George		
Coach of the Year	Dom Capers		
ASSOCIATED PRESS			
Most Valuable Player	Brett Favre		
Offensive Player of the Year	Terrell Davis		
Defensive Player of the Year	Bruce Smith		
Offensive Rookie of the Year	Eddie George		
Defensive Rookie of the Year	Simeon Rice		
Coach of the Year	Dom Capers		
UNITED PRESS INTERNATIONAL			
Offensive Player of the Year		Terrell Davis	Brett Favre
Defensive Player of the Year		Bruce Smith	Kevin Greene
Rookie of the Year		Terry Glenn	Simeon Rice
Coach of the Year		Tom Coughlin	Dom Capers
THE SPORTING NEWS			
Player of the Year	Brett Favre		
Rookie of the Year	Eddie George		
Coach of the Year	Dom Capers		
FOOTBALL NEWS			
Player of the Year		John Elway	Brett Favre
Coach of the Year	Dom Capers		
PRO FOOTBALL WEEKLY			
Most Valuable Player	Brett Favre		
Defensive Player of the Year	Bruce Smith		
Offensive Rookie of the Year	Eddie George		
Defensive Rookie of the Year	Simeon Rice		
Coach of the Year	Dom Capers		
Assistant Coach of the Year	Dave Campo		
Kicker of the Year	Cary Blanchard		
Comeback Player of the Year	Jerome Bettis		
Executive of the Year	Bill Polian		
FOOTBALL DIGEST			
Player of the Year	Brett Favre		
Defensive Player of the Year	Bruce Smith		
Offensive Rookie of the Year	Eddie George		
Defensive Rookie of the Year	Zach Thomas		
SPORTS ILLUSTRATED			
Most Valuable Player	Terrell Davis		
Coach of the Year	Dom Capers		
Rookie of the Year	Eddie George		
USA TODAY			
Coach of the Year	Dom Capers		
COLLEGE AND PRO FOOTBALL NEWSWEEKLY			
Offensive Player of the Year	Brett Favre		
Defensive Player of the Year	Bruce Smith		
Offensive Rookie of the Year	Eddie George		
Defensive Rookie of the Year	Simeon Rice		
Coach of the Year	Dom Capers		
Rookie Coach of the Year	Tony Dungy		
NEWSPAPER ENTERPRISE ASSOCIATION			
Tom Landry Award (Offensive Player of the Year)	Brett Favre		
George Halas Award (Defensive Player of the Year)	Kevin Greene		
Bert Bell Trophy (Rookie of the Year)	Eddie George		
MAXWELL CLUB PLAYER OF THE YEAR			
(Bert Bell Trophy)	Brett Favre		
MAXWELL CLUB COACH OF THE YEAR			
(Earle "Greasy" Neale Trophy)	Dom Capers		
MILLER LITE PLAYER OF THE YEAR	Brett Favre		
TRUE VALUE NFL MAN OF THE YEAR	Darrell Green		
SUPER BOWL MOST VALUABLE PLAYER			
(Pete Rozelle Trophy)	Desmond Howard		
AFC-NFC PRO BOWL PLAYER OF THE GAME			
(Dan McGuire Award)	Mark Brunell		
VISA/NFL COACH OF THE YEAR	Mike Holmgren		
FOOTACTION NFL QUARTERBACK OF THE YEAR	Brett Favre		

1996 PLAYERS OF THE WEEK/MONTH

1996 AFC PLAYERS OF THE WEEK

		Offense		Defense		Special Teams
Week	1	RB Karim Abdul-Jabbar, Miami	LB Ray Lewis, Baltimore	K John Carney, San Diego
Week	2	RB Eddie George, Houston	LB Derrick Thomas, Kansas City	PR Marvin Harrison, Indianapolis
Week	3	RB Marcus Allen, Kansas City	DE Alfred Williams, Denver	K Cary Blanchard, Indianapolis
Week	4	QB Stan Humphries, San Diego	S Manny Martin, Buffalo	K Adam Vinatieri, New England
Week	5	RB Earnest Byner, Baltimore	LB Junior Seau, San Diego	K John Carney, San Diego
Week	6	QB Drew Bledsoe, New England	DT Cortez Kennedy, Seattle	PR-KR Mel Gray, Houston
Week	7	QB Jeff Hostetler, Oakland	LB Chad Brown, Pittsburgh	K Nick Lowery, New York Jets
Week	8	RB Terrell Davis, Denver	DE Willie McGinest, New England	K Steve Christie, Buffalo
Week	9	QB Vinny Testaverde, Baltimore	S Darryl Williams, Seattle	P Tom Tupa, New England
Week	10	RB Darick Holmes, Buffalo	LB Junior Seau, San Diego	DE Michael McCrary, Seattle
Week	11	QB Mark Brunell, Jacksonville	DE Bruce Smith, Buffalo	KR David Dunn, Cincinnati
Week	12	RB Terrell Davis, Denver	S Mark Collins, Kansas City	K Cary Blanchard, Indianapolis
Week	13	WR Carl Pickens Cincinnati	S Kurt Schulz, Buffalo	P Bryan Barker, Jacksonville
Week	14	WR Derrick Alexander, Baltimore	DE Willie McGinest, New England	K Mike Hollis, Jacksonville
Week	15	QB Jeff Blake, Cincinnati	S Jason Belser, Indianapolis	P Rick Tuten, Seattle
Week	16	WR Marvin Harrison, Indianapolis	LB James Francis, Cincinnati	K Joe Nedney, Miami
Week	17	QB Jim Kelly, Buffalo	DE Michael McCrary, Seattle	PR David Meggett, New England

1996 AFC PLAYERS OF THE MONTH

	Offense	Defense	Special Teams
September	RB Terrell Davis, Denver	DE Bruce Smith, Buffalo	K John Carney, San Diego
October	QB John Elway, Denver	DE Willie McGinest, New England	K Al Del Greco, Houston
November	RB Jerome Bettis, Pittsburgh	DE Bruce Smith, Buffalo	K Cary Blanchard, Indianapolis
December	QB Mark Brunell, Jacksonville	DE Michael McCrary, Seattle	KR-PR David Meggett, New England

1996 NFC PLAYERS OF THE WEEK

		Offense	Defense	Special Teams
Week	1	QB Brett Favre, Green Bay	LB Jeff Brady, Minnesota	K John Kasay, Carolina
Week	2	QB Brad Johnson, Minnesota	DT Sean Gilbert, Washington	K John Kasay, Carolina
Week	3	RB Ricky Watters, Philadelphia	S LeRoy Butler, Green Bay	PR Desmond Howard, Green Bay
Week	4	RB LeShon Johnson, Arizona	DT John Randle, Minnesota	KR Derrick Witherspoon, Philadelphia
Week	5	QB Kent Graham, Arizona	DT Leon Lett, Dallas	K Jeff Jaeger, Chicago
Week	6	QB Scott Mitchell, Detroit	DT Bryant Young, San Francisco	KR Don Beebe, Green Bay
Week	7	WR Don Beebe, Green Bay	LB William Thomas, Philadelphia	K Chris Jacke, Green Bay
Week	8	WR Irving Fryar, Philadelphia	CB Anthony Parker, St. Louis	KR Herschel Walker, Dallas
Week	9	QB Troy Aikman, Dallas	DE Chris Doleman, San Francisco	KR Brian Mitchell, Washington
Week	10	RB Jamal Anderson, Atlanta	DE Roy Barker, San Francisco	K Brad Daluiso, New York Giants
Week	11	QB Boomer Esiason, Arizona	S Pat Terrell, Carolina	PR Eddie Kennison, St. Louis
Week	12	RB Anthony Johnson, Carolina	DE Chris Doleman, San Francisco	K Chris Boniol, Dallas
Week	13	QB Boomer Esiason, Arizona	S John Lynch, Tampa Bay	K Jeff Wilkins, San Francisco
Week	14	QB Brad Johnson, Minnesota	LB Ray Farmer, Philadelphia	PR Desmond Howard, Green Bay
Week	15	QB Kerry Collins, Carolina	DE Fernando Smith, Minnesota	K Brad Daluiso, New York Giants
Week	16	WR Eddie Kennison, St. Louis	DT Wayne Martin, New Orleans	PR Desmond Howard, Green Bay
Week	17	QB Brett Favre, Green Bay	DE William Fuller, Philadelphia	PR Karl Williams, Tampa Bay

1996 NFC PLAYERS OF THE MONTH

	Offense	Defense	Special Teams
September	QB Brett Favre, Green Bay	DT John Randle, Minnesota	K John Kasay, Carolina
October	RB Terry Allen, Washington	S Keith Lyle, St. Louis	K Chris Jacke, Green Bay
November	QB Boomer Esiason, Arizona	LB Sam Mills, Carolina	K Chris Boniol, Dallas
December	WR Antonio Freeman, Green Bay	DE William Fuller, Philadelphia	KR-PR Karl Williams, Tampa Bay

1996 PLAYOFF PLAYERS OF THE WEEK

	Offense	Defense	Special Teams
Wild Card	RB Natrone Means, Jacksonville	S George Teague, Dallas	K Chris Boniol, Dallas
Divisional	QB Mark Brunell, Jacksonville	LB Sam Mills, Carolina	KR Desmond Howard, Green Bay
Championship	RB Dorsey Levens, Green Bay	CB Otis Smith, New England	S Larry Whigham, New England

1996 ROOKIES OF THE MONTH

	Offense	Defense
September	RB Eddie George, Houston (Ohio State)	LB Simeon Rice, Arizona (Illinois)
October	WR Eddie Kennison, St. Louis (Louisiana State)	LB Zach Thomas, Miami (Texas Tech)
November	RB Mike Alstott, Tampa Bay (Purdue)	LB Gabe Northern, Buffalo (Louisiana State)
December	KR-PR Karl Williams, Tampa Bay (Texas A&M-Kingsville)	DE Tony Brackens, Jacksonville (Texas)

1996 PFW/PFWA ALL-PRO TEAM

Selected by Pro Football Weekly *and the* Professional Football Writers of America

Offense

Jerry Rice, San Francisco	Wide Receiver
Carl Pickens, Cincinnati	Wide Receiver
Shannon Sharpe, Denver	Tight End
William Roaf, New Orleans	Tackle
Gary Zimmerman, Denver	Tackle
Randall McDaniel, Minnesota	Guard
Larry Allen, Dallas	Guard
Dermontti Dawson, Pittsburgh	Center
Brett Favre, Green Bay	Quarterback
Barry Sanders, Detroit	Running Back
Terrell Davis, Denver	Running Back

Defense

Bruce Smith, Buffalo	End
Alfred Williams, Denver	End
John Randle, Minnesota	Tackle
Bryant Young, San Francisco	Tackle
Chad Brown, Pittsburgh	Linebacker
Kevin Greene, Carolina	Linebacker
Sam Mills, Carolina	Linebacker
Deion Sanders, Dallas	Cornerback
Aeneas Williams, Arizona	Cornerback
Darren Woodson, Dallas	Safety
LeRoy Butler, Green Bay	Safety

Specialists

Cary Blanchard, Indianapolis	Kicker
Chris Gardocki, Indianapolis	Punter
Michael Bates, Carolina	Kick Returner
Desmond Howard, Green Bay	Punt Returner
Jim Schwantz, Dallas	Special Teams Player

1996 ASSOCIATED PRESS ALL-PRO TEAM

Selected by the Associated Press

Offense

Jerry Rice, San Francisco	Wide Receiver
Herman Moore, Detroit	Wide Receiver
Shannon Sharpe, Denver	Tight End
Gary Zimmerman, Denver	Tackle
Erik Williams, Dallas	Tackle
Larry Allen, Dallas	Guard
Randall McDaniel, Minnesota	Guard
Dermontti Dawson, Pittsburgh	Center
Brett Favre, Green Bay	Quarterback
Terrell Davis, Denver	Running Back
Jerome Bettis, Pittsburgh	Running Back
Larry Centers, Arizona	Fullback

Defense

Bruce Smith, Buffalo	End
Alfred Williams, Denver	End
Bryant Young, San Francisco	Tackle
John Randle, Minnesota	Tackle
Kevin Greene, Carolina	Linebacker
Chad Brown, Pittsburgh	Linebacker
Sam Mills, Carolina	Linebacker
Junior Seau, San Diego	Linebacker
Deion Sanders, Dallas	Cornerback
Ashley Ambrose, Cincinnati	Cornerback
LeRoy Butler, Green Bay	Safety
Darren Woodson, Dallas	Safety

Specialists

Cary Blanchard, Indianapolis	Kicker
Chris Gardocki, Indianapolis/Matt Turk, Washington	Punter
Michael Bates, Carolina	Kick Returner

1996 ALL-NFL TEAM

Selected by the Associated Press, Pro Football Weekly, *and the* Professional Football Writers of America

Offense

Jerry Rice, San Francisco (AP, PFW/PFWA)	Wide Receiver
Herman Moore, Detroit (AP)	Wide Receiver
Carl Pickens, Cincinnati (PFW/PFWA)	Wide Receiver
Shannon Sharpe, Denver (AP, PFW/PFWA)	Tight End
Gary Zimmerman, Denver (AP, PFW/PFWA)	Tackle
Erik Williams, Dallas (AP)	Tackle
William Roaf, New Orleans (PFW/PFWA)	Tackle
Larry Allen, Dallas (AP, PFW/PFWA)	Guard
Randall McDaniel, Minnesota (AP, PFW/PFWA)	Guard
Dermontti Dawson, Pittsburgh (AP, PFW/PFWA)	Center
Brett Favre, Green Bay (AP, PFW/PFWA)	Quarterback
Terrell Davis, Denver (AP, PFW/PFWA)	Running Back
Jerome Bettis, Pittsburgh (AP)	Running Back
Barry Sanders, Detroit (PFW/PFWA)	Running Back
Larry Centers, Arizona (AP)	Fullback

Defense

Bruce Smith, Buffalo (AP, PFW/PFWA)	End
Alfred Williams, Denver (AP, PFW/PFWA)	End
John Randle, Minnesota (AP, PFW/PFWA)	Tackle
Bryant Young, San Francisco (AP, PFW/PFWA)	Tackle
Chad Brown, Pittsburgh (AP, PFW/PFWA)	Linebacker
Kevin Greene, Carolina (AP, PFW/PFWA)	Linebacker
Sam Mills, Carolina (AP, PFW/PFWA)	Linebacker
Junior Seau, San Diego (AP)	Linebacker
Deion Sanders, Dallas (AP, PFW/PFWA)	Cornerback
Ashley Ambrose, Cincinnati (AP)	Cornerback
Aeneas Williams, Arizona (PFW/PFWA)	Cornerback
LeRoy Butler, Green Bay (AP, PFW/PFWA)	Safety
Darren Woodson, Dallas (AP, PFW/PFWA)	Safety

Specialists

Cary Blanchard, Indianapolis (AP, PFW/PFWA)	Kicker
Chris Gardocki, Indianapolis (AP, PFW/PFWA)	Punter
Matt Turk, Washington (AP)	Punter
Michael Bates, Carolina (AP, PFW/PFWA)	Kick Returner
Desmond Howard, Green Bay (PFW/PFWA)	Punt Returner
Jim Schwantz, Dallas (PFW/PFWA)	Special Teams Player

1996 UPI ALL-AFC TEAM

Selected by United Press International

Offense

Carl Pickens, Cincinnati	Wide Receiver
Terry Glenn, New England	Wide Receiver
Shannon Sharpe, Denver	Tight End
Gary Zimmerman, Denver	Tackle
Bruce Armstrong, New England	Tackle
Steve Wisniewski, Oakland	Guard
Bruce Matthews, Houston	Guard
Dermontti Dawson, Pittsburgh	Center
John Elway, Denver	Quarterback
Terrell Davis, Denver	Running Back
Jerome Bettis, Pittsburgh	Running Back

Defense

Bruce Smith, Buffalo	End
Alfred Williams, Denver	End
Chester McGlockton, Oakland	Tackle
Cortez Kennedy, Seattle	Tackle
Chad Brown, Pittsburgh	Linebacker
Derrick Thomas, Kansas City	Linebacker
Junior Seau, San Diego	Linebacker
Dale Carter, Kansas City	Cornerback
Ashley Ambrose, Cincinnati	Cornerback
Steve Atwater, Denver	Safety
Carnell Lake, Pittsburgh	Safety

Specialists

Cary Blanchard, Indianapolis	Kicker
Chris Gardocki, Indianapolis	Punter
David Meggett, New England	Return Specialist

1996 UPI ALL-NFC TEAM

Selected by United Press International

Offense

Jerry Rice, San Francisco	Wide Receiver
Herman Moore, Detroit	Wide Receiver
Wesley Walls, Carolina	Tight End
William Roaf, New Orleans	Tackle
Lomas Brown, Detroit	Tackle
Larry Allen, Dallas	Guard
Randall McDaniel, Minnesota	Guard
Kevin Glover, Detroit	Center
Brett Favre, Green Bay	Quarterback
Barry Sanders, Detroit	Running Back
Terry Allen, Washington	Running Back

Defense

Tony Tolbert, Dallas	End
Reggie White, Green Bay	End
Bryant Young, San Francisco	Tackle
John Randle, Minnesota	Tackle
Kevin Greene, Carolina	Linebacker
Lamar Lathon, Carolina	Linebacker
Sam Mills, Carolina	Linebacker
Deion Sanders, Dallas	Cornerback
Aeneas Williams, Arizona	Cornerback
Darren Woodson, Dallas	Safety
LeRoy Butler, Green Bay	Safety

Specialists

John Kasay, Carolina	Kicker
Matt Turk, Washington	Punter
Desmond Howard, Green Bay	Return Specialist

1996 PFW/PFWA ALL-ROOKIE TEAM

Selected by Pro Football Weekly *and the Professional Football Writers of America*

Offense

Terry Glenn, New England	Wide Receiver
Eddie Kennison, St. Louis	Wide Receiver
Jason Dunn, Philadelphia	Tight End
Jonathan Ogden, Baltimore	Tackle
Jeff Hartings, Detroit	Tackle
Willie Anderson, Cincinnati	Guard
John Michels, Green Bay	Guard
Aaron Graham, Arizona	Center
Tony Banks, St. Louis	Quarterback
Eddie George, Houston	Running Back
Karim Abdul-Jabbar, Miami	Running Back

Defense

Simeon Rice, Arizona	End
Tony Brackens, Jacksonville	End
Daryl Gardener, Miami	Tackle
Devin Wyman, New England	Tackle
Kevin Hardy, Jacksonville	Linebacker
John Mobley, Denver	Linebacker
Zach Thomas, Miami	Linebacker
Walt Harris, Chicago	Cornerback
Donnie Abraham, Tampa Bay	Cornerback
Brian Dawkins, Philadelphia	Safety
Lawyer Milloy, New England	Safety

Specialists

Adam Vinatieri, New England	Kicker
Eric Moulds, Buffalo	Kick Returner
Eddie Kennison, St. Louis	Punt Returner
Larry Izzo, Miami	Special Teams Player

TEN BEST RUSHING PERFORMANCES, 1996

	Att.	Yards	TD
1. LeShon Johnson Arizona vs. New Orleans, Sept. 22	21	214	2
2. Adrian Murrell N.Y. Jets vs. Arizona, Oct. 27	31	199	1
3. Terrell Davis Denver vs. Baltimore, Oct. 20	28	194	2
4. Barry Sanders Detroit vs. San Francisco, Dec. 23	28	175	1
5. Ray Zellars New Orleans vs. Chicago, Oct. 13	20	174	1
6. Ricky Watters Philadelphia vs. Miami, Oct. 20	25	173	1
7. Curtis Martin New England vs. Washington, Oct. 13	17	164	2
8. Barry Sanders Detroit vs. Minnesota, Sept. 1	24	163	0
9. Emmitt Smith Dallas vs. Washington, Nov. 28	29	155	3
10. Terrell Davis Denver vs. New England, Nov. 17	32	154	2

100-YARD RUSHING PERFORMANCES, 1996

First Week
Barry Sanders, Detroit — 163 yards vs. Minnesota
Karim Abdul-Jabbar, Miami — 115 yards vs. New England
Robert Smith, Minnesota — 113 yards vs. Detroit
Terry Allen, Washington — 111 yards vs. Philadelphia
Jamal Anderson, Atlanta — 108 yards vs. Carolina

Second Week
Eddie George, Houston — 143 yards vs. Jacksonville
Barry Sanders, Detroit — 125 yards vs. Tampa Bay
Jerome Bettis, Pittsburgh — 116 yards vs. Baltimore
Terrell Davis, Denver — 111 yards vs. Seattle
Robert Green, Chicago — 106 yards vs. Washington

Third Week
Ricky Watters, Philadelphia — 153 yards vs. Detroit
Terry Allen, Washington — 146 yards vs. N.Y. Giants
Terrell Davis, Denver — 137 yards vs. Tampa Bay
Jerome Bettis, Pittsburgh — 133 yards vs. Buffalo
Karim Abdul-Jabbar, Miami — 124 yards vs. N.Y. Jets
Reggie Brooks, Tampa Bay — 114 yards vs. Denver
Emmitt Smith, Dallas — 101 yards vs. Indianapolis

Fourth Week
LeShon Johnson, Arizona — 214 yards vs. New Orleans
Terrell Davis, Denver — 141 yards vs. Kansas City
Ricky Watters, Philadelphia — 121 yards vs. Atlanta
Napoleon Kaufman, Oakland — 116 yards vs. San Diego

Fifth Week
Earnest Byner, Baltimore — 149 yards vs. New Orleans
Adrian Murrell, N.Y. Jets — 118 yards vs. Washington
Jerome Bettis, Pittsburgh — 115 yards vs. Houston
Terrell Davis, Denver — 112 yards vs. Cincinnati
Chris Warren, Seattle — 103 yards vs. Green Bay
Terry Allen, Washington — 101 yards vs. N.Y. Jets

Sixth Week
Eddie George, Houston — 152 yards vs. Cincinnati
Joe Aska, Oakland — 136 yards vs. N.Y. Jets
Jamal Anderson, Atlanta — 103 yards vs. Detroit
Jerome Bettis, Pittsburgh — 103 yards vs. Kansas City
Anthony Johnson, Carolina — 102 yards vs. Minnesota
Adrian Murrell, N.Y. Jets — 102 yards vs. Oakland
Robert Smith, Minnesota — 102 yards vs. Carolina

Seventh Week
Ray Zellars, New Orleans — 174 yards vs. Chicago
Curtis Martin, New England — 164 yards vs. Washington
Robert Smith, Minnesota — 133 yards vs. Tampa Bay
Anthony Johnson, Carolina — 126 yards vs. St. Louis
Emmitt Smith, Dallas — 112 yards vs. Arizona
Ricky Watters, Philadelphia — 110 yards vs. N.Y. Giants
Jerome Bettis, Pittsburgh — 109 yards vs. Cincinnati
Eddie George, Houston — 109 yards vs. Atlanta

Eighth Week
Terrell Davis, Denver — 194 yards vs. Baltimore
Ricky Watters, Philadelphia — 173 yards vs. Miami
Anthony Johnson, Carolina — 123 yards vs. New Orleans
James Stewart, Jacksonville — 112 yards vs. St. Louis

Ninth Week
Adrian Murrell, N.Y. Jets — 199 yards vs. Arizona
Chris Warren, Seattle — 146 yards vs. San Diego
Jerome Bettis, Pittsburgh — 126 yards vs. Atlanta
Terry Allen, Washington — 124 yards vs. Indianapolis
Thurman Thomas, Buffalo — 119 yards vs. New England

Tenth Week
Barry Sanders, Detroit — 152 yards vs. Green Bay
Jerome Bettis, Pittsburgh — 129 yards vs. St. Louis
Darrick Holmes, Buffalo — 122 yards vs. Washington
Raymont Harris, Chicago — 118 yards vs. Tampa Bay
Ricky Watters, Philadelphia — 116 yards vs. Dallas
Emmitt Smith, Dallas — 113 yards vs. Philadelphia
Jamal Anderson, Atlanta — 109 yards vs. Carolina
Thurman Thomas, Buffalo — 107 yards vs. Washington
Karim Abdul-Jabbar, Miami — 104 yards vs. New England
Greg Hill, Kansas City — 100 yards vs. Minnesota

Eleventh Week
Adrian Murrell, N.Y. Jets — 128 yards vs. New England
Terry Allen, Washington — 124 yards vs. Arizona
Raymont Harris, Chicago — 112 yards vs. Denver
Jerome Bettis, Pittsburgh — 111 yards vs. Cincinnati
Byron (Bam) Morris, Baltimore — 109 yards vs. Jacksonville
Harold Green, St. Louis — 106 yards vs. Atlanta
Lawrence Phillips, St. Louis — 106 yards vs. Atlanta

Twelfth Week
Terrell Davis, Denver — 154 yards vs. New England
Lamar Smith, Seattle — 148 yards vs. Detroit
Barry Sanders, Detroit — 134 yards vs. Seattle
Anthony Johnson, Carolina — 123 yards vs. St. Louis
Leroy Hoard, Minnesota — 108 yards vs. Oakland

Thirteenth Week
Curtis Martin, New England — 141 yards vs. Indianapolis
Raymont Harris, Chicago — 122 yards vs. Detroit
Jerome Bettis, Pittsburgh — 119 yards vs. Miami
Barry Sanders, Detroit — 107 yards vs. Chicago
Napoleon Kaufman, Oakland — 104 yards vs. Seattle
Adrian Murrell, N.Y. Jets — 103 yards vs. Buffalo

Fourteenth Week
Emmitt Smith, Dallas — 155 yards vs. Washington
Greg Hill, Kansas City — 103 yards vs. Detroit
Eddie George, Houston — 141 yards vs. N.Y. Jets
Anthony Johnson, Carolina — 111 yards vs. Tampa Bay
Terrell Davis, Denver — 106 yards vs. Seattle
Jerome Bettis, Pittsburgh — 105 yards vs. Baltimore
Terry Kirby, San Francisco — 105 yards vs. Atlanta
Ricky Watters, Philadelphia — 104 yards vs. N.Y. Giants
Byron (Bam) Morris, Baltimore — 100 yards vs. Pittsburgh

Fifteenth Week
Barry Sanders, Detroit — 134 yards vs. Minnesota
Byron (Bam) Morris, Baltimore — 117 yards vs. Cincinnati
Chris Warren, Seattle — 116 yards vs. Buffalo
Rashaan Salaam, Chicago — 115 yards vs. St. Louis
Napoleon Kaufman, Oakland — 109 yards vs. Kansas City
Marshall Faulk, Indianapolis — 101 yards vs. Philadelphia

Sixteenth Week

Mario Bates, New Orleans	129 yards vs. N.Y. Giants
Lawrence Phillips, St. Louis	112 yards vs. Atlanta
Erric Pegram, Pittsburgh	103 yards vs. San Francisco
Leroy Hoard, Minnesota	101 yards vs. Tampa Bay

Seventeenth Week

Barry Sanders, Detroit	175 yards vs. San Francisco
Karim Abdul-Jabbar, Miami	152 yards vs. N.Y. Jets
Natrone Means, Jacksonville	110 yards vs. Atlanta
Edgar Bennett, Green Bay	109 yards vs. Minnesota
Kordell Stewart, Pittsburgh	102 yards vs. Carolina

Times 100 or More (103)

Bettis, 10; Davis, Sanders, 7; Watters, 6; Allen, Johnson, Murrell, 5; Abdul-Jabbar, George, E. Smith, 4; Anderson, R. Harris, Kaufman, Morris, R. Smith, Warren, 3; Hill, Hoard, Martin, Phillips, Thomas, 2.

TEN BEST PASSING PERFORMANCES, 1996

		Att.	Comp.	Yards	TD
1.	Boomer Esiason Arizona vs. Washington, Nov. 10	59	35	522	3
2.	Mark Brunell Jacksonville vs. N.E., Sept. 22	39	23	432	3
3.	Vinny Testaverde Baltimore vs. St. Louis, Oct. 27	51	31	429	3
4.	Mark Brunell Jacksonville vs. St. Louis, Oct. 20	52	37	421	0
5.	Drew Bledsoe N.E. vs. Miami, Nov. 3	41	30	419	3
6.	Brett Favre Green Bay vs. S.F., Oct. 14	61	28	395	1
7.	Steve Young S.F. vs. Carolina, Dec. 8	41	27	393	3
8.	Drew Bledsoe N.E. vs. Buffalo, Oct. 27	45	32	373	1
9.	Boomer Esiason Arizona vs. Philadelphia, Nov. 24	43	24	367	3
10.	Vinny Testaverde Baltimore vs. Jacksonville, Nov. 24	50	31	366	0

300-YARD PASSING PERFORMANCES, 1996

First Week

Jim Kelly, Buffalo	313 yards vs. N.Y. Giants

Second Week

Neil O'Donnell, N.Y. Jets	319 yards vs. Indianapolis
Mark Brunell, Jacksonville	302 yards vs. Houston

Third Week

Neil O'Donnell, N.Y. Jets	325 yards vs. Miami

Fourth Week

Mark Brunell, Jacksonville	432 yards vs. New England
Scott Mitchell, Detroit	336 yards vs. Chicago

Fifth Week

Kent Graham, Arizona	366 yards vs. St. Louis
John Elway, Denver	335 yards vs. Cincinnati

Sixth Week

Vinny Testaverde, Baltimore	353 yards vs. New England
Mike Tomczak, Pittsburgh	338 yards vs. Kansas City
John Elway, Denver	323 yards vs. San Diego
Drew Bledsoe, New England	310 yards vs. Baltimore
Todd Collins, Buffalo	309 yards vs. Indianapolis

Seventh Week

Brett Favre, Green Bay	395 yards vs. San Francisco
Scott Mitchell, Detroit	343 yards vs. Oakland

Eighth Week

Mark Brunell, Jacksonville	421 yards vs. St. Louis
Vinny Testaverde, Baltimore	338 yards vs. Denver
John Elway, Denver	326 yards vs. Baltimore

Ninth Week

Vinny Testaverde, Baltimore	429 yards vs. St. Louis
Drew Bledsoe, New England	373 yards vs. Buffalo
Troy Aikman, Dallas	363 yards vs. Miami
Tony Banks, St. Louis	353 yards vs. Baltimore
Ty Detmer, Philadelphia	342 yards vs. Carolina

Tenth Week

Drew Bledsoe, New England	419 yards vs. Miami
John Friesz, Seattle	323 yards vs. Houston

Eleventh Week

Boomer Esiason, Arizona	522 yards vs. Washington
Mark Brunell, Jacksonville	354 yards vs. Baltimore
Ty Detmer, Philadelphia	315 yards vs. Buffalo
Stan Humphries, San Diego	311 yards vs. Detroit
Brett Favre, Green Bay	310 yards vs. Kansas City

Twelfth Week

Frank Reich, N.Y. Jets	352 yards vs. Indianapolis
Trent Dilfer, Tampa Bay	327 yards vs. San Diego

Thirteenth Week

Boomer Esiason, Arizona	367 yards vs. Philadelphia
Vinny Testaverde, Baltimore	366 yards vs. Jacksonville
Jeff Blake, Cincinnati	349 yards vs. Atlanta
John Elway, Denver	334 yards vs. Minnesota
Ty Detmer, Philadelphia	322 yards vs. Arizona
Mark Brunell, Jacksonville	306 yards vs. Baltimore
Bobby Hebert, Atlanta	304 yards vs. Cincinnati

Fourteenth Week

Mark Brunell, Jacksonville	356 yards vs. Cincinnati
Jeff Blake, Cincinnati	313 yards vs. Jacksonville

Fifteenth Week

Steve Young, San Francisco	393 yards vs. Carolina
Kerry Collins, Carolina	327 yards vs. San Francisco
Jim Kelly, Buffalo	324 yards vs. Seattle
Steve McNair, Houston	308 yards vs. Jacksonville

Sixteenth Week

Bobby Hebert, Atlanta	363 yards vs. St. Louis
Tony Banks, St. Louis	304 yards vs. Atlanta

Seventeenth Week

Gus Frerotte, Washington	346 yards vs. Dallas
Vinny Testaverde, Baltimore	307 yards vs. Houston
Drew Bledsoe, New England	301 yards vs. N.Y. Giants

Times 300 or More (50)
Brunell, 6; Testaverde, 5; Bledsoe, Elway, 4; Detmer, 3; Banks, Blake, Esiason, Favre, Hebert, Kelly, Mitchell, O'Donnell, 2.

TEN BEST RECEIVING PERFORMANCES, 1996

		No.	Yards	TD
1.	Keenan McCardell Jacksonville vs. St. Louis, Oct. 20	16	232	0
2.	Isaac Bruce St. Louis vs. Baltimore, Oct. 27	11	229	1
3.	Eddie Kennison St. Louis vs. Atlanta, Dec. 15	5	226	3
4.	Don Beebe Green Bay vs. San Francisco, Oct. 14	11	220	1
5.	Derrick Alexander Baltimore vs. Pittsburgh, Dec. 1	7	198	1
	Michael Irvin Dallas vs. Arizona, Dec. 8	8	198	1
7.	Jeff Graham N.Y. Jets vs. Indianapolis, Nov. 17	9	189	3
8.	Michael Irvin Dallas vs. Miami, Oct. 27	12	186	1
9.	Carl Pickens Cincinnati vs. Atlanta, Nov. 24	11	176	3
10.	Antonio Freeman Green Bay vs. Denver, Dec. 8	9	175	3

100-YARD RECEIVING PERFORMANCES, 1996

First Week

Herman Moore, Detroit	157 yards vs. Minnesota
Andre Reed, Buffalo	138 yards vs. N.Y. Giants
Terance Mathis, Atlanta	123 yards vs. Carolina
Larry Centers, Arizona	108 yards vs. Indianapolis
Raymont Harris, Chicago	103 yards vs. Dallas

Second Week

Ken Dilger, Indianapolis	156 yards vs. N.Y. Jets
Jake Reed, Minnesota	148 yards vs. Atlanta
Robert Brooks, Green Bay	130 yards vs. Philadelphia
Quinn Early, Buffalo	119 yards vs. New England
Bert Emanuel, Atlanta	116 yards vs. Minnesota
Courtney Hawkins, Tampa Bay	111 yards vs. Detroit
Keenan McCardell, Jacksonville	100 yards vs. Houston

Third Week

Michael Haynes, New Orleans	156 yards vs. Cincinnati
Jeff Graham, N.Y. Jets	136 yards vs. Miami
Chris T. Jones, Philadelphia	121 yards vs. Detroit
Robert Brooks, Green Bay	108 yards vs. San Diego

Fourth Week

Johnnie Morton, Detroit	174 yards vs. Chicago
Tony Martin, San Diego	138 yards vs. Oakland
Isaac Bruce, St. Louis	136 yards vs. Washington
Shannon Sharpe, Denver	131 yards vs. Kansas City
Jake Reed, Minnesota	129 yards vs. Green Bay
Jerry Rice, San Francisco	127 yards vs. Carolina
Curtis Conway, Chicago	126 yards vs. Detroit
Tim Brown, Oakland	120 yards vs. San Diego
Andre Rison, Jacksonville	115 yards vs. New England
Willie Jackson, Jacksonville	101 yards vs. New England

Fifth Week

Rob Moore, Arizona	143 yards vs. St. Louis
Anthony Miller, Denver	131 yards vs. Cincinnati
Mark Carrier, Carolina	124 yards vs. Jacksonville
Isaac Bruce, St. Louis	117 yards vs. Arizona
Antonio Freeman, Green Bay	108 yards vs. Seattle
Herman Moore, Detroit	104 yards vs. Tampa Bay

Sixth Week

Shannon Sharpe, Denver	153 yards vs. San Diego
Antonio Freeman, Green Bay	146 yards vs. Chicago
Joey Galloway, Seattle	137 yards vs. Miami
Michael Jackson, Baltimore	128 yards vs. New England
Charles Johnson, Pittsburgh	125 yards vs. Kansas City

Derrick Alexander, Baltimore	123 yards vs. New England
Thurman Thomas, Buffalo	111 yards vs. Indianapolis
Jerry Rice, San Francisco	108 yards vs. St. Louis
Herman Moore, Detroit	107 yards vs. Atlanta
Curtis Conway, Chicago	101 yards vs. Green Bay

Seventh Week

Don Beebe, Green Bay	220 yards vs. San Francisco
Wayne Chrebet, N.Y. Jets	162 yards vs. Jacksonville
Henry Ellard, Washington	152 yards vs. New England
Jimmy Smith, Jacksonville	135 yards vs. N.Y. Jets
Andre Reed, Buffalo	134 yards vs. Miami
James Jett, Oakland	112 yards vs. Detroit
Curtis Conway, Chicago	111 yards vs. New Orleans
Herman Moore, Detroit	109 yards vs. Oakland
Johnnie Morton, Detroit	109 yards vs. Oakland
Chris Sanders, Houston	100 yards vs. Atlanta

Eighth Week

Keenan McCardell, Jacksonville	232 yards vs. St. Louis
Shannon Sharpe, Denver	161 yards vs. Baltimore
Charles Johnson, Pittsburgh	155 yards vs. Houston
Derrick Alexander, Baltimore	126 yards vs. Denver
Thomas Lewis, N.Y. Giants	125 yards vs. Washington
O.J. McDuffie, Miami	121 yards vs. Philadelphia
Michael Irvin, Dallas	119 yards vs. Atlanta
Henry Ellard, Washington	119 yards vs. N.Y. Giants
Ted Popson, San Francisco	116 yards vs. Cincinnati
Irving Fryar, Philadelphia	116 yards vs. Miami
Chris Calloway, N.Y. Giants	108 yards vs. Washington
Terance Mathis, Atlanta	101 yards vs. Dallas

Ninth Week

Isaac Bruce, St. Louis	229 yards vs. Baltimore
Michael Irvin, Dallas	186 yards vs. Miami
Jake Reed, Minnesota	153 yards vs. Chicago
Rob Moore, Arizona	143 yards vs. N.Y. Jets
Irving Fryar, Philadelphia	143 yards vs. Carolina
Andre Reed, Buffalo	121 yards vs. New England
Michael Jackson, Baltimore	113 yards vs. St. Louis
Charles Johnson, Pittsburgh	110 yards vs. Atlanta
Floyd Turner, Baltimore	108 yards vs. St. Louis

Tenth Week

Ben Coates, New England	135 yards vs. Miami
Tony Martin, San Diego	128 yards vs. Indianapolis
Tim Brown, Oakland	126 yards vs. Denver
Michael Haynes, New Orleans	121 yards vs. San Francisco
Irving Fryar, Philadelphia	120 yards vs. Dallas
Terry Glenn, New England	112 yards vs. Miami
Qadry Ismail, Carolina	108 yards vs. Atlanta
Isaac Bruce, St. Louis	108 yards vs. Pittsburgh
Don Beebe, Green Bay	106 yards vs. Detroit
Floyd Turner, Baltimore	104 yards vs. Cincinnati

Eleventh Week

Cris Carter, Minnesota	142 yards vs. Seattle
Tony Martin, San Diego	113 yards vs. Detroit
Bert Emanuel, Atlanta	109 yards vs. St. Louis
Ronnie Harmon, Houston	108 yards vs. New Orleans
O.J. McDuffie, Miami	106 yards vs. Indianapolis
Carl Pickens, Cincinnati	103 yards vs. Pittsburgh

Twelfth Week

Jeff Graham, N.Y. Jets	189 yards vs. Indianapolis
Jake Reed, Minnesota	134 yards vs. Oakland
Andre Reed, Buffalo	105 yards vs. Cincinnati
Chris T. Jones, Philadelphia	103 yards vs. Washington

Thirteenth Week

Carl Pickens, Cincinnati	176 yards vs. Atlanta
Steve Tasker, Buffalo	160 yards vs. N.Y. Jets
Rob Moore, Arizona	156 yards vs. Philadelphia
Michael Jackson, Baltimore	150 yards vs. Jacksonville

Tony Martin, San Diego	148 yards vs. Kansas City
Jimmy Smith, Jacksonville	131 yards vs. Baltimore
Irving Fryar, Philadelphia	131 yards vs. Arizona
Michael Westbrook, Washington	126 yards vs. San Francisco
Jeff Graham, N.Y. Jets	124 yards vs. Buffalo
Eric Metcalf, Atlanta	122 yards vs. Cincinnati
Keenan McCardell, Jacksonville	107 yards vs. Baltimore

Fourteenth Week

Derrick Alexander, Baltimore	198 yards vs. Pittsburgh
Jimmy Smith, Jacksonville	162 yards vs. Cincinnati
Antonio Freeman, Green Bay	156 yards vs. Chicago
Brett Perriman, Detroit	131 yards vs. Kansas City
Charles Johnson, Pittsburgh	117 yards vs. Baltimore
Quinn Early, Buffalo	113 yards vs. Indianapolis
Isaac Bruce, St. Louis	112 yards vs. New Orleans
Carl Pickens, Cincinnati	109 yards vs. Jacksonville
Joey Galloway, Seattle	108 yards vs. Denver
Chris Sanders, Houston	102 yards vs. N.Y. Jets

Fifteenth Week

Michael Irvin, Dallas	198 yards vs. Arizona
Antonio Freeman, Green Bay	175 yards vs. Denver
Willie Green, Carolina	157 yards vs. San Francisco
Fred Barnett, Miami	139 yards vs. N.Y. Giants
Jerry Rice, San Francisco	129 yards vs. Carolina
Chris Sanders, Houston	127 yards vs. Jacksonville
Herman Moore, Detroit	126 yards vs. Minnesota
Michael Timpson, Chicago	111 yards vs. St. Louis
Terrell Owens, San Francisco	110 yards vs. Carolina
Marvin Harrison, Indianapolis	106 yards vs. Philadelphia
Darnay Scott, Cincinnati	103 yards vs. Baltimore
Eddie Kennison, St. Louis	102 yards vs. Chicago

Sixteenth Week

Eddie Kennison, St. Louis	226 yards vs. Atlanta
Bert Emanuel, Atlanta	173 yards vs. St. Louis
Andre Reed, Buffalo	127 yards vs. Miami
Jimmy Smith, Jacksonville	124 yards vs. Seattle
Marvin Harrison, Indianapolis	103 yards vs. Kansas City

Seventeenth Week

Henry Ellard, Washington	155 yards vs. Dallas
Terry Glenn, New England	124 yards vs. N.Y. Giants
Curtis Conway, Chicago	120 yards vs. Tampa Bay
Michael Jackson, Baltimore	117 yards vs. Houston

Times 100 or More (135)

Bruce, H. Moore, A. Reed, 5; Conway, Freeman, Fryar, M. Jackson, C. Johnson, Martin, J. Reed, J. Smith, 4; Alexander, Ellard, Emanuel, Graham, Irvin, McCardell, McDuffie, R. Moore, Pickens, Rice, Sanders, Sharpe, 3; Beebe, Brooks, T. Brown, Early, Galloway, Glenn, Harrison, Haynes, Jones, Kennison, Mathis, Morton, F. Turner, 2.

TOP QUARTERBACK SACK PERFORMANCES, 1996
(2.5 or More Sacks Per Game Needed to Qualify)

First Week
Lamar Lathon, Carolina — 3.0 vs. Atlanta

Second Week
Michael Sinclair, Seattle — 4.0 vs. Denver
Bruce Smith, Buffalo — 3.0 vs. New England

Third Week
Michael Sinclair, Seattle — 3.0 vs. Kansas City
Tony Tolbert, Dallas — 3.0 vs. Indianapolis

Fourth Week
John Randle, Minnesota — 3.5 vs. Green Bay

Fifth Week
None

Sixth Week
Bryant Young, San Francisco — 3.0 vs. St. Louis

Seventh Week
Chad Brown, Pittsburgh — 4.5 vs. Cincinnati
Trace Armstrong, Miami — 2.5 vs. Buffalo
Mike Mamula, Philadelphia — 2.5 vs. N.Y. Giants

Eighth Week
None

Ninth Week
Clyde Simmons, Jacksonville — 2.5 vs. Cincinnati

Tenth Week
Clay Matthews, Atlanta — 3.0 vs. Carolina
Roy Barker, San Francisco — 2.5 vs. New Orleans

Eleventh Week
Bennie Thompson, Baltimore — 3.0 vs. Jacksonville

Twelfth Week
Chad Brown, Pittsburgh — 3.0 vs. Jacksonville
Chris Doleman, San Francisco — 3.0 vs. Baltimore
Kevin Greene, Carolina — 2.5 vs. St. Louis

Thirteenth Week
None

Fourteenth Week
None

Fifteenth Week
Michael Sinclair, Seattle — 3.0 vs. Buffalo
Trace Armstrong, Miami — 2.5 vs. N.Y. Giants

Sixteenth Week
Hugh Douglas, N.Y. Jets — 3.0 vs. Philadelphia
Michael McCrary, Seattle — 3.0 vs. Jacksonville
Anthony Cook, Houston — 2.5 vs. Cincinnati
Joe Johnson, New Orleans — 2.5 vs. N.Y. Giants

Seventeenth Week
Michael McCrary, Seattle — 4.0 vs. Oakland
William Fuller, Philadelphia — 3.0 vs. Arizona

AMERICAN FOOTBALL CONFERENCE OFFENSE

	Balt	Buff	Cin	Den	Hou	Ind	Jax	KC	Mia	NE	NYJ	Oak	Pitt	SD	Sea
First Downs	338	294	332	336	287	288	325	312	294	339	319	306	296	272	268
Rushing	108	128	114	134	110	89	90	111	92	103	94	98	138	80	94
Passing	208	149	190	180	157	172	208	168	173	206	191	172	146	168	147
Penalty	22	17	28	22	20	27	27	33	29	30	34	36	12	24	27
Rushes	416	563	478	525	475	420	431	488	460	427	407	456	525	412	442
Net Yds. Gained	1745	1901	1793	2362	1950	1448	1650	2009	1622	1468	1583	2174	2299	1312	1997
Avg. Gain	4.2	3.4	3.8	4.5	4.1	3.4	3.8	4.1	3.5	3.4	3.9	4.8	4.4	3.2	4.5
Avg. Yds. per Game	109.1	118.8	112.1	147.6	121.9	90.5	103.1	125.6	101.4	91.8	98.9	135.9	143.7	82.0	124.8
Passes Attempted	570	483	563	536	463	537	557	530	504	628	629	533	456	577	494
Completed	335	279	316	327	272	311	353	290	300	374	339	311	246	314	261
% Completed	58.8	57.8	56.1	61.0	58.7	57.9	63.4	54.7	59.5	59.6	53.9	58.3	53.9	54.4	52.8
Total Yds. Gained	4274	3558	3726	3662	3296	3544	4367	3093	3783	4091	3911	3327	2990	3654	3216
Times Sacked	38	48	47	31	34	43	50	27	36	30	41	45	21	33	38
Yds. Lost	296	340	294	233	198	248	257	203	240	190	286	249	149	296	189
Net Yds. Gained	3978	3218	3432	3429	3098	3296	4110	2890	3543	3901	3625	3078	2841	3358	3027
Avg. Yds. per Game	248.6	201.1	214.5	214.3	193.6	206.0	256.9	180.6	221.4	243.8	226.6	192.4	177.6	209.9	189.2
Net Yds. per Pass Play	6.54	6.06	5.63	6.05	6.23	5.68	6.77	5.19	6.56	5.93	5.41	5.33	5.96	5.50	5.69
Yds. Gained per Comp.	12.76	12.75	11.79	11.20	12.12	11.40	12.37	10.67	12.61	10.94	11.54	10.70	12.15	11.64	12.32
Combined Net Yds. Gained	5723	5119	5225	5791	5048	4744	5760	4899	5165	5369	5208	5252	5140	4670	5024
% Total Yds. Rushing	30.5	37.1	34.3	40.8	38.6	30.5	28.6	41.0	31.4	27.3	30.4	41.4	44.7	28.1	39.7
% Total Yds. Passing	69.5	62.9	65.7	59.2	61.4	69.5	71.4	59.0	68.6	72.7	69.6	58.6	55.3	71.9	60.3
Avg. Yds. per Game	357.7	319.9	326.6	361.9	315.5	296.5	360.0	306.2	322.8	335.6	325.5	328.3	321.3	291.9	314.0
Ball Control Plays	1024	1094	1088	1092	972	1000	1038	1045	1000	1085	1077	1034	1002	1022	974
Avg. Yds. per Play	5.6	4.7	4.8	5.3	5.2	4.7	5.5	4.7	5.2	4.9	4.8	5.1	5.1	4.6	5.2
Avg. Time of Poss.	27:05	28:40	31:33	33:17	32:02	30:44	31:18	30:39	31:08	30:11	29:26	30:39	30:08	27:35	28:01
Third Down Efficiency	43.8	34.9	43.2	48.9	38.3	37.7	41.8	34.8	40.3	36.8	40.9	40.6	40.4	33.9	30.2
Had Intercepted	20	24	16	17	15	11	20	14	11	15	30	19	19	21	17
Yds. Opp Returned	349	498	172	171	222	133	370	68	256	191	384	257	234	320	305
Ret. by Opp. for TD	3	4	1	0	3	0	3	0	1	1	2	1	2	2	0
Punts	69	101	82	65	68	68	69	88	78	64	74	79	72	87	86
Yds. Punted	2980	4194	3634	2714	2973	3105	3016	3667	3611	2766	3293	3169	2931	3967	3746
Avg. Yds. per Punt	43.2	41.5	44.3	41.8	43.7	45.7	43.7	41.7	46.3	43.2	44.5	40.1	40.7	45.6	43.6
Punt Returns	38	43	33	49	29	41	34	33	26	52	28	42	40	38	34
Yds. Returned	357	423	217	583	279	447	351	282	251	588	139	403	251	559	352
Avg. Yds. per Return	9.4	9.8	6.6	11.9	9.6	10.9	10.3	8.5	9.7	11.3	5.0	9.6	6.3	14.7	10.4
Returned for TD	0	0	0	0	0	0	0	0	0	1	0	0	0	1	1
Kickoff Returns	86	58	70	50	66	61	67	66	60	64	79	61	53	63	71
Yds. Returned	1734	1341	1459	1195	1421	1403	1463	1567	1320	1424	1504	1276	1171	1358	1542
Avg. Yds. per Return	20.2	23.1	20.8	23.9	21.5	23.0	21.8	23.7	22.0	22.3	19.0	20.9	22.1	21.6	21.7
Returned for TD	0	1	1	0	0	1	0	1	0	0	0	0	1	0	0
Fumbles	23	25	19	27	26	24	29	17	31	25	25	30	27	30	24
Lost	13	13	9	15	15	13	10	10	13	12	16	12	14	11	12
Out of Bounds	2	2	3	2	1	0	2	1	3	2	2	2	1	4	2
Own Rec. for TD	0	0	0	0	0	0	0	0	2	0	0	0	0	0	0
Opp. Rec. by	7	14	10	9	14	10	14	10	16	11	15	9	17	14	18
Opp. Rec. for TD	0	1	1	0	0	0	0	1	0	2	1	1	2	0	0
Penalties	94	106	90	109	91	76	127	122	111	97	110	156	83	110	112
Yds. Penalized	818	831	678	949	812	615	1006	901	852	716	819	1266	665	969	879
Total Points Scored	371	319	372	391	345	317	325	297	339	418	279	340	344	310	317
Total TDs	45	35	43	47	35	30	33	35	41	48	33	38	39	32	33
TDs Rushing	10	14	14	20	12	9	13	15	14	15	8	7	18	7	16
TDs Passing	34	18	25	26	22	16	19	18	22	27	22	28	15	23	14
TDs on Ret. and Rec.	1	3	4	1	1	5	1	2	5	6	3	3	6	2	3
Extra Point Kicks	34	33	41	46	35	27	27	34	35	39	26	36	37	31	27
Extra Point Kicks Att.	35	33	41	46	35	27	27	34	36	42	27	36	37	31	27
2Pt Conversions	5	2	2	0	0	0	5	0	1	4	2	0	2	0	4
2Pt Conversions Att.	9	2	2	1	0	3	6	1	5	6	6	2	2	1	6
Safeties	0	0	0	0	2	1	0	1	1	1	0	2	0	0	0
Field Goals Made	19	24	23	21	32	36	30	17	18	27	17	24	23	29	28
Field Goals Attempted	25	29	28	28	38	40	36	24	29	35	24	31	30	36	34
% Successful	76.0	82.8	82.1	75.0	84.2	90.0	83.3	70.8	62.1	77.1	70.8	77.4	76.7	80.6	82.4

AMERICAN FOOTBALL CONFERENCE DEFENSE

	Balt	Buff	Cin	Den	Hou	Ind	Jax	KC	Mia	NE	NYJ	Oak	Pitt	SD	Sea
First Downs	351	283	317	261	271	305	315	296	306	305	304	292	286	321	325
Rushing	115	94	109	67	78	108	110	84	91	102	119	97	80	92	114
Passing	213	168	196	165	169	189	180	184	191	178	157	162	174	199	181
Penalty	23	21	12	29	24	8	25	28	24	25	28	33	32	30	30
Rushes	508	495	444	345	397	459	447	441	411	434	539	463	411	431	506
Net Yds. Gained	1920	1669	1643	1331	1385	1760	1781	1666	1536	1502	2200	1676	1415	1755	2098
Avg. Gain	3.8	3.4	3.7	3.9	3.5	3.8	4.0	3.8	3.7	3.5	4.1	3.6	3.4	4.1	4.1
Avg. Yds. per Game	120.0	104.3	102.7	83.2	86.6	110.0	111.3	104.1	96.0	93.9	137.5	104.8	88.4	109.7	131.1
Passes Attempted	537	562	571	566	524	534	508	536	539	596	456	513	547	636	512
Completed	350	292	319	302	312	318	290	289	337	322	257	284	322	369	303
% Completed	65.2	52.0	55.9	53.4	59.5	59.6	57.1	53.9	62.5	54.0	56.4	55.4	58.9	58.0	59.2
Total Yds. Gained	4115	3409	4028	3413	3467	3825	3541	3731	3888	4055	3542	3273	3316	3867	3624
Times Sacked	30	48	32	40	35	29	37	31	37	33	28	34	51	33	48
Yds. Lost	146	341	202	274	242	182	237	193	233	252	178	252	369	201	285
Net Yds. Gained	3969	3068	3826	3139	3225	3643	3304	3538	3655	3803	3364	3021	2947	3666	3339
Avg. Yds. per Game	248.1	191.8	239.1	196.2	201.6	227.7	206.5	221.1	228.4	237.7	210.3	188.8	184.2	229.1	208.7
Net Yds. per Pass Play	7.00	5.03	6.34	5.18	5.77	6.47	6.06	6.24	6.35	6.05	6.95	5.52	4.93	5.48	5.96
Yds. Gained per Comp.	11.76	11.67	12.63	11.30	11.11	12.03	12.21	12.91	11.54	12.59	13.78	11.52	10.30	10.48	11.96
Combined Net Yds. Gained	5889	4737	5469	4470	4610	5403	5085	5204	5191	5305	5564	4697	4362	5421	5437
% Total Yds. Rushing	32.6	35.2	30.0	29.8	30.0	32.6	35.0	32.0	29.6	28.3	39.5	35.7	32.4	32.4	38.6
% Total Yds. Passing	67.4	64.8	70.0	70.2	70.0	67.4	65.0	68.0	70.4	71.7	60.5	64.3	67.6	67.6	61.4
Avg. Yds. per Game	368.1	296.1	341.8	279.4	288.1	337.7	317.8	325.3	324.4	331.6	347.8	293.6	272.6	338.8	339.8
Ball Control Plays	1075	1105	1047	951	956	1022	992	1008	987	1063	1023	1010	1009	1100	1066
Avg. Yds. per Play	5.5	4.3	5.2	4.7	4.8	5.3	5.1	5.2	5.3	5.0	5.4	4.7	4.3	4.9	5.1
Avg. Time of Poss.	32:55	31:20	28:27	26:43	27:58	29:16	28:42	29:21	28:52	29:49	30:34	29:21	29:52	32:25	31:59
Third Down Efficiency	48.2	35.5	43.9	35.9	35.2	39.8	44.1	42.2	33.7	36.0	40.0	34.1	36.2	42.0	37.9
Intercepted By	15	14	34	23	12	13	13	17	20	23	11	17	23	22	14
Yds. Returned By	147	113	308	241	162	276	114	171	475	255	165	353	334	336	256
Returned for TD	1	0	2	1	1	4	0	0	3	2	2	2	3	1	1
Punts	68	102	61	83	75	81	71	71	75	82	75	85	86	71	76
Yds. Punted	2881	4406	2706	3825	3073	3525	2979	2969	3283	3483	3158	3562	3771	3145	3214
Avg. Yds. per Punt	42.4	43.2	44.4	46.1	41.0	43.5	42.0	41.8	43.8	42.5	42.1	41.9	43.8	44.3	42.3
Punt Returns	27	40	38	23	31	38	44	42	48	34	40	38	32	51	52
Yds. Returned	273	246	502	261	251	413	400	492	368	334	429	272	284	612	640
Avg. Yds. per Return	10.1	6.2	13.2	11.3	8.1	10.9	9.1	11.7	7.7	9.8	10.7	7.2	8.9	12.0	12.3
Returned for TD	0	1	0	1	0	0	0	1	0	0	0	0	0	1	0
Kickoff Returns	70	65	69	76	78	67	71	64	48	81	58	55	69	59	72
Yds. Returned	1402	1255	1642	1602	1675	1666	1674	1300	1058	1683	1485	1129	1509	1497	1642
Avg. Yds. per Return	20.0	19.3	23.8	21.1	21.5	24.9	23.6	20.3	22.0	20.8	25.6	20.5	21.9	25.4	22.8
Returned for TD	0	0	1	1	0	0	0	0	0	0	1	0	1	0	0
Fumbles	23	23	16	26	29	20	26	23	29	23	26	18	28	29	37
Lost	7	14	10	9	14	10	14	10	16	11	15	9	17	14	18
Out of Bounds	3	3	0	6	1	2	1	0	2	1	1	1	4	0	5
Own Rec. for TD	0	0	0	1	0	0	0	0	0	2	0	0	0	0	0
Opp. Rec. by	13	12	9	15	15	13	10	10	13	12	16	12	14	11	12
Opp. Rec. for TD	1	0	2	1	2	1	1	1	1	0	0	1	0	2	0
Penalties	104	86	102	119	88	121	97	103	98	139	107	113	97	115	98
Yds. Penalized	744	607	768	834	672	970	800	876	786	1189	902	965	746	991	804
Total Points Scored	441	266	369	275	319	334	335	300	325	313	454	293	257	376	376
Total TDs	50	28	42	31	35	38	37	32	41	34	55	31	27	43	40
TDs Rushing	18	12	15	5	5	12	9	11	10	14	19	7	7	10	15
TDs Passing	27	11	22	22	24	25	24	19	29	17	33	22	17	28	25
TDs on Ret. and Rec.	5	5	5	4	6	1	4	2	2	3	3	2	3	5	0
Extra Point Kicks	41	25	40	25	32	33	33	29	38	28	51	26	26	40	35
Extra Point Kicks Att.	41	26	40	25	32	34	35	29	39	28	52	26	26	40	35
2Pt Conversions	7	1	1	2	1	1	1	1	1	5	1	2	0	0	3
2Pt Conversions Att.	9	2	2	6	3	4	2	3	2	6	3	5	3	0	5
Safeties	1	1	0	0	0	1	0	1	0	1	1	1	3	0	1
Field Goals Made	28	23	25	20	25	23	26	25	13	23	23	25	21	26	31
Field Goals Attempted	31	36	30	23	33	28	34	36	17	29	28	34	26	33	34
% Successful	90.3	63.9	83.3	87.0	75.8	82.1	76.5	69.4	76.5	79.3	82.1	73.5	80.8	78.8	91.2

NATIONAL FOOTBALL CONFERENCE OFFENSE

	Ariz	Atl	Car	Chi	Dall	Det	GB	Minn	NO	NYG	Phi	StL	SF	TB	Wash
First Downs	308	292	292	300	286	317	338	284	232	248	319	255	315	260	307
Rushing	70	67	93	104	105	105	118	75	77	82	107	93	108	90	106
Passing	214	202	160	176	163	180	197	186	135	145	196	141	188	152	174
Penalty	24	23	39	20	18	32	23	23	20	21	16	21	19	18	27
Rushes	401	329	502	472	475	389	465	435	386	485	489	448	454	472	467
Net Yds. Gained	1502	1461	1729	1720	1641	1810	1838	1546	1308	1603	1882	1607	1847	1589	1910
Avg. Gain	3.7	4.4	3.4	3.6	3.5	4.7	4.0	3.6	3.4	3.3	3.8	3.6	4.1	3.4	4.1
Avg. Yds. per Game	93.9	91.3	108.1	107.5	102.6	113.1	114.9	96.6	81.8	100.2	117.6	100.4	115.4	99.3	119.4
Passes Attempted	613	600	487	551	487	541	548	561	515	459	548	481	550	494	471
Completed	336	356	273	318	307	309	328	331	295	238	328	249	358	274	270
% Completed	54.8	59.3	56.1	57.7	63.0	57.1	59.9	59.0	57.3	51.9	59.9	51.8	65.1	55.5	57.3
Total Yds. Gained	3917	3909	3333	3350	3249	3463	3938	3899	3069	2663	3979	3144	3859	2944	3453
Times Sacked	36	42	36	23	19	46	40	34	22	56	39	57	42	30	22
Yds. Lost	229	254	250	165	127	260	241	241	171	324	234	379	200	217	134
Net Yds. Gained	3688	3655	3083	3185	3122	3203	3697	3658	2898	2339	3745	2765	3659	2727	3319
Avg. Yds. per Game	230.5	228.4	192.7	199.1	195.1	200.2	231.1	228.6	181.1	146.2	234.1	172.8	228.7	170.4	207.4
Net Yds. per Pass Play	5.68	5.69	5.89	5.55	6.17	5.46	6.29	6.15	5.40	4.54	6.38	5.14	6.18	5.20	6.73
Yds. Gained per Comp.	11.66	10.98	12.21	10.53	10.58	11.21	12.01	11.78	10.40	11.19	12.13	12.63	10.78	10.74	12.79
Combined Net Yds. Gained	5190	5116	4812	4905	4763	5013	5535	5204	4206	3942	5627	4372	5506	4316	5229
% Total Yds. Rushing	28.9	28.6	35.9	35.1	34.5	36.1	33.2	29.7	31.1	40.7	33.4	36.8	33.5	36.8	36.5
% Total Yds. Passing	71.1	71.4	64.1	64.9	65.5	63.9	66.8	70.3	68.9	59.3	66.6	63.2	66.5	63.2	63.5
Avg. Yds. per Game	324.4	319.8	300.8	306.6	297.7	313.3	345.9	325.3	262.9	246.4	351.7	273.3	344.1	269.8	326.8
Ball Control Plays	1050	971	1025	1046	981	976	1053	1030	923	1000	1076	986	1046	996	960
Avg. Yds. per Play	4.9	5.3	4.7	4.7	4.9	5.1	5.3	5.1	4.6	3.9	5.2	4.4	5.3	4.3	5.4
Avg. Time of Poss.	28:45	29:52	30:48	30:51	30:53	27:06	31:44	30:14	27:33	29:48	32:12	27:58	31:28	30:58	27:29
Third Down Efficiency	41.7	39.5	37.2	33.8	41.8	38.4	44.3	42.1	31.4	27.7	37.9	37.5	35.2	39.6	37.9
Had Intercepted	21	30	11	18	14	21	13	19	17	21	18	23	16	20	11
Yds. Opp Returned	186	324	41	94	250	313	98	339	93	225	265	252	107	326	154
Ret. by Opp. for TD	0	2	1	0	1	3	0	3	0	1	3	1	0	3	0
Punts	77	75	78	78	74	71	68	90	87	102	74	78	75	71	77
Yds. Punted	3328	3152	3158	3491	3150	3044	2886	3616	3551	4289	3107	3491	3217	3015	3470
Avg. Yds. per Punt	43.2	42.0	40.5	44.8	42.6	42.9	42.4	40.2	40.8	42.0	42.0	44.8	42.9	42.5	45.1
Punt Returns	39	31	55	31	44	34	58	32	31	42	40	35	39	41	23
Yds. Returned	343	315	624	282	394	284	875	300	159	478	330	439	352	481	258
Avg. Yds. per Return	8.8	10.2	11.3	9.1	9.0	8.4	15.1	9.4	5.1	11.4	8.3	12.5	9.0	11.7	11.2
Returned for TD	0	0	1	0	0	0	3	1	0	2	0	2	0	1	0
Kickoff Returns	75	87	50	56	53	69	47	58	78	66	64	62	59	55	65
Yds. Returned	1582	1825	1310	1337	1339	1675	1038	1075	1899	1287	1439	1233	1258	1287	1401
Avg. Yds. per Return	21.1	21.0	26.2	23.9	25.3	24.3	22.1	18.5	24.3	19.5	22.5	19.9	21.3	23.4	21.6
Returned for TD	0	0	1	0	0	0	1	0	0	0	2	0	0	0	0
Fumbles	29	23	25	25	24	21	33	26	30	27	24	42	16	28	21
Lost	14	11	14	9	15	5	11	13	20	13	14	21	8	14	7
Out of Bounds	4	1	1	1	3	1	3	2	2	2	2	2	2	3	1
Own Rec. for TD	0	0	0	0	0	0	1	0	0	0	0	0	0	0	0
Opp. Rec. by	14	17	16	11	13	8	12	13	10	13	12	13	14	12	9
Opp. Rec. for TD	1	0	3	2	1	1	0	0	1	1	3	0	1	0	1
Penalties	106	111	94	103	103	108	92	106	114	85	117	133	119	95	95
Yds. Penalized	873	961	638	808	832	863	714	835	853	666	963	1015	925	787	740
Total Points Scored	300	309	367	283	286	302	456	298	229	242	363	303	398	221	364
Total TDs	33	35	36	31	27	38	56	33	24	24	41	34	43	21	41
TDs Rushing	8	9	9	9	14	15	9	7	10	4	16	10	17	8	27
TDs Passing	23	26	22	19	12	20	39	24	13	14	19	18	24	12	12
TDs on Ret. and Rec.	2	0	5	3	1	3	8	2	1	6	6	6	2	1	2
Extra Point Kicks	29	31	34	26	24	36	51	30	18	22	40	30	40	18	40
Extra Point Kicks Att.	31	31	35	26	25	36	53	30	18	22	40	31	40	19	40
2Pt Conversions	2	1	1	0	2	1	2	2	2	0	0	2	1	1	0
2Pt Conversions Att.	2	4	1	5	2	2	3	3	6	2	1	3	3	2	1
Safeties	0	0	2	1	0	0	1	0	0	2	1	1	4	0	0
Field Goals Made	23	22	37	23	32	12	21	22	21	24	25	21	30	25	26
Field Goals Attempted	31	29	45	30	36	17	27	29	25	27	29	25	34	32	32
% Successful	74.2	75.9	82.2	76.7	88.9	70.6	77.8	75.9	84.0	88.9	86.2	84.0	88.2	78.1	81.3

NATIONAL FOOTBALL CONFERENCE DEFENSE

	Ariz	Atl	Car	Chi	Dall	Det	GB	Minn	NO	NYG	Phil	StL	SF	TB	Wash
First Downs	337	309	251	295	260	324	248	309	287	285	264	329	269	296	358
Rushing	120	102	69	87	89	126	74	117	104	98	87	114	76	114	146
Passing	192	182	167	183	144	172	151	169	152	174	150	191	164	156	191
Penalty	25	25	15	25	27	26	23	23	31	13	27	24	29	26	21
Rushes	514	473	374	427	437	510	400	445	521	487	421	478	418	438	520
Net Yds. Gained	1862	2041	1562	1617	1576	2007	1416	1966	2076	1748	1583	1854	1497	1889	2275
Avg. Gain	3.6	4.3	4.2	3.8	3.6	3.9	3.5	4.4	4.0	3.6	3.8	3.9	3.6	4.3	4.4
Avg. Yds. per Game	116.4	127.6	97.6	101.1	98.5	125.4	88.5	122.9	129.8	109.3	98.9	115.9	93.6	118.1	142.2
Passes Attempted	520	485	556	524	484	502	544	537	465	533	500	558	558	503	560
Completed	311	302	307	314	271	311	283	314	267	317	271	341	287	311	325
% Completed	59.8	62.3	55.2	59.9	56.0	62.0	52.0	58.5	57.4	59.5	54.2	61.1	51.4	61.8	58.0
Total Yds. Gained	3684	3953	3585	3476	3025	3577	2942	3384	3117	3477	3243	3856	3461	3132	3655
Times Sacked	28	36	60	30	37	32	37	43	41	30	40	32	45	35	34
Yds. Lost	185	208	371	209	219	233	202	263	283	178	264	181	297	207	207
Net Yds. Gained	3499	3745	3214	3267	2806	3344	2740	3121	2834	3299	2979	3675	3164	2925	3448
Avg. Yds. per Game	218.7	234.1	200.9	204.2	175.4	209.0	171.3	195.1	177.1	206.2	186.2	229.7	197.8	182.8	215.5
Net Yds. per Pass Play	6.39	7.19	5.22	5.90	5.39	6.26	4.72	5.38	5.60	5.86	5.52	6.23	5.25	5.44	5.80
Yds. Gained per Comp.	11.85	13.09	11.68	11.07	11.16	11.50	10.40	10.78	11.67	10.97	11.97	11.31	12.06	10.07	11.25
Combined Net Yds. Gained	5361	5786	4776	4884	4382	5351	4156	5087	4910	5047	4562	5529	4661	4814	5723
% Total Yds. Rushing	34.7	35.3	32.7	33.1	36.0	37.5	34.1	38.6	42.3	34.6	34.7	33.5	32.1	39.2	39.8
% Total Yds. Passing	65.3	64.7	67.3	66.9	64.0	62.5	65.9	61.4	57.7	65.4	65.3	66.5	67.9	60.8	60.2
Avg. Yds. per Game	335.1	361.6	298.5	305.3	273.9	334.4	259.8	317.9	306.9	315.4	285.1	345.6	291.3	300.9	357.7
Ball Control Plays	1062	994	990	981	958	1044	981	1025	1027	1050	961	1068	1021	976	1114
Avg. Yds. per Play	5.0	5.8	4.8	5.0	4.6	5.1	4.2	5.0	4.8	4.8	4.7	5.2	4.6	4.9	5.1
Avg. Time of Poss.	31:15	30:08	29:12	29:09	29:07	32:54	28:16	29:46	32:27	30:12	27:48	32:02	28:32	29:02	32:31
Third Down Efficiency	41.3	42.2	32.4	38.3	34.4	43.2	32.7	33.2	36.6	34.2	39.1	42.0	33.6	40.7	43.9
Intercepted By	11	6	22	17	19	11	26	22	12	22	19	26	20	17	21
Yds. Returned By	122	41	277	107	168	169	524	206	114	341	303	390	176	139	214
Returned for TD	1	0	0	1	0	2	3	1	0	3	1	4	1	0	1
Punts	69	64	95	76	75	71	90	84	74	92	74	69	88	74	68
Yds. Punted	3022	2697	4159	3047	3459	2927	3876	3596	3184	3801	3287	2801	3695	3210	2990
Avg. Yds. per Punt	43.8	42.1	43.8	40.1	46.1	41.2	43.1	42.8	43.0	41.3	44.4	40.6	42.0	43.4	44.0
Punt Returns	37	32	32	42	32	42	29	37	43	45	36	41	36	38	35
Yds. Returned	403	413	173	527	249	519	237	577	546	432	330	495	235	248	235
Avg. Yds. per Return	10.9	12.9	5.4	12.5	7.8	12.4	8.2	15.6	12.7	9.6	9.2	12.1	6.5	6.5	6.7
Returned for TD	1	1	0	2	0	1	0	0	1	2	1	0	0	0	0
Kickoff Returns	61	53	71	52	70	52	76	53	52	42	73	58	77	51	76
Yds. Returned	1290	1314	1429	1115	1431	1298	1649	1314	1155	948	1715	1290	1414	972	1610
Avg. Yds. per Return	21.1	24.8	20.1	21.4	20.4	25.0	21.7	24.8	22.2	22.6	23.5	22.2	18.4	19.1	21.2
Returned for TD	1	1	0	1	0	0	0	0	0	0	0	2	0	0	0
Fumbles	24	27	25	29	26	26	25	27	25	27	26	26	29	31	27
Lost	14	17	16	11	14	8	13	13	10	13	12	13	14	12	9
Out of Bounds	2	0	3	3	1	1	1	1	0	6	4	0	4	1	2
Own Rec. for TD	0	0	0	0	0	0	0	0	0	0	0	0	0	0	0
Opp. Rec. by	14	11	14	9	15	5	11	12	20	13	13	14	21	8	14	7
Opp. Rec. for TD	3	0	0	0	3	0	0	0	0	1	0	2	0	1	1
Penalties	104	106	133	113	94	114	107	105	102	100	99	111	97	101	102
Yds. Penalized	841	816	1155	849	717	938	797	840	823	781	710	832	819	810	867
Total Points Scored	397	461	218	305	250	368	210	315	339	297	341	409	257	293	312
Total TDs	44	48	24	37	24	44	19	36	34	33	35	50	25	34	33
TDs Rushing	18	18	6	13	10	12	7	15	11	14	12	22	4	13	20
TDs Passing	21	26	17	21	10	28	12	18	22	15	18	23	21	17	12
TDs on Ret. and Rec.	5	4	1	3	4	4	0	3	1	4	5	5	0	4	1
Extra Point Kicks	41	43	23	35	20	40	17	33	32	31	30	46	21	32	31
Extra Point Kicks Att.	43	43	24	36	20	41	17	33	32	31	32	47	21	32	31
2Pt Conversions	1	1	0	0	0	1	1	1	2	1	3	1	4	0	1
2Pt Conversions Att.	1	5	0	1	4	3	2	3	2	2	3	2	4	2	2
Safeties	0	1	0	0	1	1	1	2	0	0	1	2	0	0	0
Field Goals Made	30	42	17	16	28	20	25	20	33	22	31	19	26	19	27
Field Goals Attempted	37	44	20	23	32	25	27	30	42	26	36	27	29	27	38
% Successful	81.1	95.5	85.0	69.6	87.5	80.0	92.6	66.7	78.6	84.6	86.1	70.4	89.7	70.4	71.1

AFC, NFC, AND NFL SUMMARY

	AFC Offense Total	AFC Offense Average	AFC Defense Total	AFC Defense Average	NFC Offense Total	NFC Offense Average	NFC Defense Total	NFC Defense Average	NFL Total	NFL Average
First Downs	4606	307.1	4538	302.5	4353	290.2	4421	294.7	8959	298.6
Rushing	1583	105.5	1460	97.3	1400	93.3	1523	101.5	2983	99.4
Passing	2635	175.7	2706	180.4	2609	173.9	2538	169.2	5244	174.8
Penalty	388	25.9	372	24.8	344	22.9	360	24.0	732	24.4
Rushes	6925	461.7	6731	448.7	6669	444.6	6863	457.5	13594	453.1
Net Yds. Gained	27313	1820.9	25337	1689.1	24993	1666.2	26969	1797.9	52306	1743.5
Avg. Gain	—	3.9	—	3.8	—	3.7	—	3.9	—	3.8
Avg. Yds. per Game	—	113.8	—	105.6	—	104.1	—	112.4	—	109.0
Passes Attempted	8060	537.3	8137	542.5	7906	527.1	7829	521.9	15966	532.2
Completed	4628	308.5	4666	311.1	4570	304.7	4532	302.1	9198	306.6
% Completed	—	57.4	—	57.3	—	57.8	—	57.9	—	57.6
Total Yds. Gained	54492	3632.8	55094	3672.9	52169	3477.9	51567	3437.8	106661	3555.4
Times Sacked	562	37.5	546	36.4	544	36.3	560	37.3	1106	36.9
Yds. Lost	3668	244.5	3587	239.1	3426	228.4	3507	233.8	7094	236.5
Net Yds. Gained	50824	3388.3	51507	3433.8	48743	3249.5	48060	3204.0	99567	3318.9
Avg. Yds. per Game	—	211.8	—	214.6	—	203.1	—	200.3	—	207.4
Net Yds. per Pass Play	—	5.89	—	5.93	—	5.77	—	5.73	—	5.83
Yds. Gained per Comp.	—	11.77	—	11.81	—	11.42	—	11.38	—	11.60
Combined Net Yds. Gained	78137	5209.1	76844	5122.9	73736	4915.7	75029	5001.9	151873	5062.4
% Total Yds. Rushing	—	35.0	—	33.0	—	33.9	—	35.9	—	34.4
% Total Yds. Passing	—	65.0	—	67.0	—	66.1	—	64.1	—	65.6
Avg. Yds. per Game	—	325.6	—	320.2	—	307.2	—	312.6	—	316.4
Ball Control Plays	15547	1036.5	15414	1027.6	15119	1007.9	15252	1016.8	30666	1022.2
Avg. Yds. per Play	—	5.0	—	5.0	—	4.9	—	4.9	—	5.0
Third Down Efficiency	—	39.1	—	39.0	—	37.7	—	37.8	—	38.4
Interceptions	269	17.9	271	18.1	273	18.2	271	18.1	542	18.1
Yds. Returned	3930	262.0	3706	247.1	3067	204.5	3291	219.4	6997	233.2
Returned for TD	23	1.5	23	1.5	18	1.2	18	1.2	41	1.4
Punts	1150	76.7	1162	77.5	1175	78.3	1163	77.5	2325	77.5
Yds. Punted	49766	3317.7	49980	3332.0	49965	3331.0	49751	3316.7	99731	3324.4
Avg. Yds. per Punt	—	43.3	—	43.0	—	42.5	—	42.8	—	42.9
Punt Returns	560	37.3	578	38.5	575	38.3	557	37.1	1135	37.8
Yds. Returned	5482	365.5	5777	385.1	5914	394.3	5619	374.6	11396	379.9
Avg. Yds. per Return	—	9.8	—	10.0	—	10.3	—	10.1	—	10.0
Returned for TD	3	0.2	4	0.3	10	0.7	9	0.6	13	0.4
Kickoff Returns	975	65.0	1002	66.8	944	62.9	917	61.1	1919	64.0
Yds. Returned	21178	1411.9	22219	1481.3	20985	1399.0	19944	1329.6	42163	1405.4
Avg. Yds. per Return	—	21.7	—	22.2	—	22.2	—	21.7	—	22.0
Returned for TD	5	0.3	4	0.3	4	0.3	5	0.3	9	0.3
Fumbles	382	25.5	376	25.1	394	26.3	400	26.7	776	25.9
Lost	188	12.5	188	12.5	189	12.6	189	12.6	377	12.6
Out of Bounds	29	1.9	30	2.0	30	2.0	29	1.9	59	2.0
Own Rec. for TD	2	0.1	3	0.2	1	0.1	0	0.0	3	0.1
Opp. Rec.	188	12.5	187	12.5	187	12.5	188	12.5	375	12.5
Opp. Rec. for TD	9	0.6	13	0.9	15	1.0	11	0.7	24	0.8
Penalties	1594	106.3	1587	105.8	1581	105.4	1588	105.9	3175	105.8
Yds. Penalized	12776	851.7	12654	843.6	12473	831.5	12595	839.7	25249	841.6
Total Points Scored	5084	338.9	5033	335.5	4721	314.7	4772	318.1	9805	326.8
Total TDs	567	37.8	564	37.6	517	34.5	520	34.7	1084	36.1
TDs Rushing	192	12.8	169	11.3	172	11.5	195	13.0	364	12.1
TDs Passing	329	21.9	345	23.0	297	19.8	281	18.7	626	20.9
TDs on Ret. and Rec.	46	3.1	50	3.3	48	3.2	44	2.9	94	3.1
Extra Point Kicks	508	33.9	502	33.5	469	31.3	475	31.7	977	32.6
Extra Point Kicks Att.	514	34.3	508	33.9	477	31.8	483	32.2	991	33.0
2Pt Conversions	27	1.8	27	1.8	17	1.1	17	1.1	44	1.5
2Pt Conversions Att.	52	3.5	56	3.7	40	2.7	36	2.4	92	3.1
Safeties	8	0.5	11	0.7	12	0.8	9	0.6	20	0.7
Field Goals Made	368	24.5	357	23.8	364	24.3	375	25.0	732	24.4
Field Goals Attempted	467	31.1	452	30.1	448	29.9	463	30.9	915	30.5
% Successful	—	78.8	—	79.0	—	81.3	—	81.0	—	80.0

CLUB LEADERS

	Offense	Defense
First Downs	NE 339	GB 248
Rushing	Pitt 138	Den 67
Passing	Ariz 214	Dall 144
Penalty	Car 39	Ind 8
Rushes	Buff 563	Den 345
Net Yds. Gained	Den 2362	Den 1331
Avg. Gain	Oak 4.8	Buff 3.4
Passes Attempted	NYJ 629	NYJ 456
Completed	NE 374	NYJ 257
% Completed	SF 65.1	SF 51.4
Total Yds. Gained	Jax 4367	GB 2942
Times Sacked	Dall 19	Car 60
Yds. Lost	Dall 127	Car 371
Net Yds. Gained	Jax 4110	GB 2740
Net Yds. per Pass Play	Jax 6.77	GB 4.72
Yds. Gained per Comp.	Wash 12.79	TB 10.07
Combined Net Yds. Gained	Den 5791	GB 4156
% Total Yds. Rushing	Pitt 44.7	NE 28.3
% Total Yds. Passing	NE 72.7	NO 57.7
Ball Control Plays	Buff 1094	Den 951
Avg. Yds. per Play	Balt 5.6	GB 4.2
Avg. Time of Poss.	Den 33:17	—
Third Down Efficiency	Den 48.9	Car 32.4
Interceptions	—	Cin 34
Yds. Returned	—	GB 524
Returned for TD	—	Ind & StL 4
Punts	NYG. 102	—
Yds. Punted	NYG 4289	—
Avg. Yds. per Punt	Mia 46.3	—
Punt Returns	GB 58	Den 23
Yds. Returned	GB 875	Car 173
Avg. Yds. per Return	GB 15.1	Car 5.4
Returned for TD	GB 3	—
Kickoff Returns	Atl 87	NYG 42
Yds. Returned	NO 1899	NYG 948
Avg. Yds. per Return	Car 26.2	SF 18.4
Returned for TD	Phi 2	—
Total Points Scored	GB 456	GB 210
Total TDs	GB 56	GB 19
TDs Rushing	Wash 27	SF 4
TDs Passing	GB 39	Dall 10
TDs on Ret. and Rec.	GB 8	Three tied 0
Extra Points	GB 51	GB 17
2-Point Conversions	Balt & Jax 5	—
Safeties	SF 4	—
Field Goals Made	Car 37	Mia 13
Field Goals Attempted	Car 45	Mia 17
% Successful	Ind 90.0	Buff 63.9

NFL CLUB RANKINGS BY YARDS

	Offense			Defense		
	Total	Rush	Pass	Total	Rush	Pass
Arizona	13	25	6	21	21	21
Atlanta	17	27	9	29	26	27
Baltimore	3	14	2	30	23	30
Buffalo	16	8	17	9	14	8
Carolina	23	15	22	10	8	12
Chicago	21	16	19	12	11	14
Cincinnati	10	13	12	25	12	29
Dallas	24	18	20	3	9	2
Denver	*1	*1	13	4	*1	10
Detroit	20	12	18	20	25	18
Green Bay	5	11	5	*1	4	*1
Houston	18	6	21	6	2	13
Indianapolis	25	28	16	22	18	23
Jacksonville	2	17	*1	15	19	16
Kansas City	22	4	26	18	13	22
Miami	14	19	11	17	7	24
Minnesota	12	24	8	16	24	9
New England	7	26	3	19	6	28
New Orleans	29	30	25	13	27	3
N.Y. Giants	30	21	30	14	16	15
N.Y. Jets	11	23	10	27	29	19
Oakland	8	3	23	8	15	7
Philadelphia	4	9	4	5	10	6
Pittsburgh	15	2	27	2	3	5
St. Louis	27	20	28	26	20	26
San Diego	26	29	14	23	17	25
San Francisco	6	10	7	7	5	11
Seattle	19	5	24	24	28	17
Tampa Bay	28	22	29	11	22	4
Washington	9	7	15	28	30	20

= League Leader

AFC TAKEAWAYS/GIVEAWAYS

	Takeaways			Giveaways			Net
	Int	Fum	Total	Int	Fum	Total	Diff.
Cincinnati	34	10	44	16	9	25	+19
Miami	20	16	36	11	13	24	+12
New England	23	11	34	15	12	27	+7
Pittsburgh	23	17	40	19	14	33	+7
San Diego	22	14	36	21	11	32	+4
Kansas City	17	10	27	14	10	24	+3
Seattle	14	18	32	17	12	29	+3
Denver	23	9	32	17	15	32	0
Indianapolis	13	10	23	11	13	24	-1
Jacksonville	13	14	27	20	10	30	-3
Houston	12	14	26	15	15	30	-4
Oakland	17	9	26	19	12	31	-5
Buffalo	14	14	28	24	13	37	-9
Baltimore	15	7	22	20	13	33	-11
N.Y. Jets	11	15	26	30	16	46	-20

NFC TAKEAWAYS/GIVEAWAYS

	Takeaways			Giveaways			Net
	Int	Fum	Total	Int	Fum	Total	Diff.
Green Bay	26	13	39	13	11	24	+15
Carolina	22	16	38	11	14	25	+13
Washington	21	9	30	11	7	18	+12
San Francisco	20	14	34	16	8	24	+10
Dallas	19	14	33	14	15	29	+4
Minnesota	22	13	35	19	13	32	+3
Chicago	17	11	28	18	9	27	+1
N.Y. Giants	22	13	35	21	13	34	+1
Philadelphia	19	12	31	18	14	32	-1
St. Louis	26	13	39	23	21	44	-5
Tampa Bay	17	12	29	20	14	34	-5
Detroit	11	8	19	21	5	26	-7
Arizona	11	14	25	21	14	35	-10
New Orleans	12	10	22	17	20	37	-15
Atlanta	6	17	23	30	11	41	-18

SCORING

Points
- NFC: 145—John Kasay, Carolina
- AFC: 135—Cary Blanchard, Indianapolis

Touchdowns
- NFC: 21—Terry Allen, Washington
- AFC: 17—Curtis Martin, New England

Extra Points
- NFC: 51—Chris Jacke, Green Bay
- AFC: 46—Jason Elam, Denver

Field Goals
- AFC: 37—John Kasay, Carolina
- NFC: 36—Cary Blanchard, Indianapolis

Field Goal Attempts
- AFC: 45—John Kasay, Carolina
- NFC: 40—Cary Blanchard, Indianapolis

Longest Field Goal
- NFC: 54—Doug Brien, New Orleans vs. Chicago, October 13
- 54—Morten Andersen, Atlanta at Dallas, October 20
- AFC: 56—Al Del Greco, Houston vs. San Francisco, October 27

Most Points, Game
- NFC: 24—Irving Fryar, Philadelphi vs. Miami, October 20 (4 TD)
- AFC: 20—Curtis Martin, New England vs. Arizona, September 15 (3 TD, 1 X2G)

Team Leaders, Points
- AFC: BALTIMORE: 91, Matt Stover; BUFFALO: 105, Steve Christie; CINCINNATI: 110, Doug Pelfrey; DENVER: 109, Jason Elam; HOUSTON: 131, Al Del Greco; INDIANAPOLIS: 135, Cary Blanchard; JACKSONVILLE: 117, Mike Hollis; KANSAS CITY: 85, Pete Stoyanovich; MIAMI: 89, Joe Nedney; NEW ENGLAND: 120, Adam Vinatieri; N.Y. JETS: 77, Nick Lowery; OAKLAND: 108, Cole Ford; PITTSBURGH: 106, Norm Johnson; SAN DIEGO: 118, John Carney; SEATTLE: 111, Todd Peterson
- NFC: ARIZONA: 59, Kevin Butler; ATLANTA: 97, Morten Andersen; CAROLINA: 145, John Kasay; CHICAGO: 80, Jeff Jaeger; DALLAS: 120, Chris Boniol; DETROIT: 72, Jason Hanson; GREEN BAY: 114, Chris Jacke; MINNESOTA: 96, Scott Sisson; NEW ORLEANS: 81, Doug Brien; N.Y. GIANTS: 94, Brad Daluiso; PHILADELPHIA: 115, Gary Anderson; ST. LOUIS: 91, Chris Lohmiller; SAN FRANCISCO: 130, Jeff Wilkins; TAMPA BAY: 93, Michael Husted; WASHINGTON: 126, Terry Allen

Team Champion
- NFC: 456—Green Bay
- AFC: 418—New England

AFC SCORING—TEAM

	TD	TDR	TDP	TDM	EXTRA PT. KICKS MADE	EXTRA PT. KICKS ATT.	2-POINT TRIES MADE	2-POINT TRIES ATT.	FG	FGA	SAF	PTS
New England	48	15	27	6	39	42	4	6	27	35	1	418
Denver	47	20	26	1	46	46	0	1	21	28	0	391
Cincinnati	43	14	25	4	41	41	2	2	23	28	0	372
Baltimore	45	10	34	1	34	35	5	9	19	25	0	371
Houston	35	12	22	1	35	35	0	0	32	38	2	345
Pittsburgh	39	18	15	6	37	37	2	2	23	30	0	344
Oakland	38	7	28	3	36	36	0	2	24	31	2	340
Miami	41	14	22	5	35	36	1	5	18	29	1	339
Jacksonville	33	13	19	1	27	27	5	6	30	36	0	325
Buffalo	35	14	18	3	33	33	2	2	24	29	0	319
Indianapolis	30	9	16	5	27	27	0	3	36	40	1	317
Seattle	33	16	14	3	27	27	4	6	28	34	0	317
San Diego	32	7	23	2	31	31	0	1	29	36	0	310
Kansas City	35	15	18	2	34	34	0	1	17	24	1	297
N.Y. Jets	33	8	22	3	26	27	2	6	17	24	0	279
AFC Total	567	192	329	46	508	514	27	52	368	467	8	5084
AFC Average	37.8	12.8	21.9	3.1	33.9	34.3	1.8	3.5	24.5	31.1	0.5	338.9

NFC SCORING—TEAM

	TD	TDR	TDP	TDM	EXTRA PT. KICKS MADE	EXTRA PT. KICKS ATT.	2-POINT TRIES MADE	2-POINT TRIES ATT.	FG	FGA	SAF	PTS
Green Bay	56	9	39	8	51	53	2	3	21	27	1	456
San Francisco	43	17	24	2	40	40	1	3	30	34	4	398
Carolina	36	9	22	5	34	35	1	1	37	45	2	367
Washington	41	27	12	2	40	40	0	1	26	32	0	364
Philadelphia	41	16	19	6	40	40	0	1	25	29	1	363
Atlanta	35	9	26	0	31	31	1	4	22	29	0	309
St. Louis	34	10	18	6	30	31	2	3	21	25	1	303
Detroit	38	15	20	3	36	36	1	2	12	17	0	302
Arizona	33	8	23	2	29	31	2	2	23	31	0	300
Minnesota	33	7	24	2	30	30	2	3	22	29	0	298
Dallas	27	14	12	1	24	25	2	2	32	36	0	286
Chicago	31	9	19	3	26	26	0	5	23	30	1	283
N.Y. Giants	24	4	14	6	22	22	0	2	24	27	2	242
New Orleans	24	10	13	1	18	18	2	6	21	25	0	229
Tampa Bay	21	8	12	1	18	19	1	2	25	32	0	221
NFC Total	517	172	297	48	469	477	17	40	364	448	12	4721
NFC Average	34.5	11.5	19.8	3.2	31.3	31.8	1.1	2.7	24.3	29.9	0.8	314.7
NFL Total	1084	364	626	94	977	991	44	92	732	915	20	9805
NFL Average	36.1	12.1	20.9	3.1	32.6	33.0	1.5	3.1	24.4	30.5	0.7	326.8

NFL TOP TEN SCORERS—NONKICKERS

	TD	TDR	TDP	TDM	2-PT	PTS
Allen, Terry, Was.	21	21	0	0	0	126
Martin, Curtis, N.E.	17	14	3	0	1	104
Davis, Terrell, Den.	15	13	2	0	0	90
Smith, Emmitt, Dal.	15	12	3	0	0	90
Jackson, Michael, Bal.	14	0	14	0	2	88
Martin, Tony, S.D.	14	0	14	0	0	84
Watters, Ricky, Phi.	13	13	0	0	0	78
Pickens, Carl, Cin.	12	0	12	0	1	74
Abdul-Jabbar, Karim, Mia.	11	11	0	0	0	66
Bettis, Jerome, Pit.	11	11	0	0	0	66
Fryar, Irving, Phi.	11	0	11	0	0	66
Kennison, Eddie, St.L	11	0	9	2	0	66
Sanders, Barry, Det.	11	11	0	0	0	66

NFL TOP TEN SCORERS—KICKERS

	XP	XPA	FG	FGA	PTS
Kasay, John, Car.	34	35	37	45	145
Blanchard, Cary, Ind.	27	27	36	40	135
Del Greco, Al, Hou.	35	35	32	38	131
Wilkins, Jeff, S.F.	40	40	30	34	130
Boniol, Chris, Dal.	24	25	32	36	120
Vinatieri, Adam, N.E.	39	42	27	35	120
Blanton, Scott, Was.	40	40	26	32	118
Carney, John, S.D.	31	31	29	36	118
Hollis, Mike, Jac.	27	27	30	36	117
Anderson, Gary, Phi.	40	40	25	29	115

AFC SCORERS—INDIVIDUAL

Kickers

	XP	XPA	FG	FGA	PTS
Blanchard, Cary, Ind.	27	27	36	40	135
Del Greco, Al, Hou.	35	35	32	38	131
Vinatieri, Adam, N.E.	39	42	27	35	120
Carney, John, S.D.	31	31	29	36	118
Hollis, Mike, Jac.	27	27	30	36	117
Peterson, Todd, Sea.	27	27	28	34	111
Pelfrey, Doug, Cin.	41	41	23	28	110
Elam, Jason, Den.	46	46	21	28	109
Ford, Cole, Oak.	36	36	24	31	108
Johnson, Norm, Pit.	37	37	23	30	106
Christie, Steve, Buf.	33	33	24	29	105
Stover, Matt, Bal.	34	35	19	25	91
Nedney, Joe, Mia.	35	36	18	29	89
Stoyanovich, Pete, K.C.	34	34	17	24	85
Lowery, Nick, NY-J	26	27	17	24	77

Nonkickers

	TD	TDR	TDP	TDM	2-PT	PTS
Martin, Curtis, N.E.	17	14	3	0	1	104
Davis, Terrell, Den.	15	13	2	0	0	90
Jackson, Michael, Bal.	14	0	14	0	2	88
Martin, Tony, S.D.	14	0	14	0	0	84
Pickens, Carl, Cin.	12	0	12	0	1	74
Abdul-Jabbar, Karim, Mia.	11	11	0	0	0	66
Bettis, Jerome, Pit.	11	11	0	0	0	66
Sharpe, Shannon, Den.	10	0	10	0	0	60
Stewart, James, Jac.	10	8	2	0	0	60
Alexander, Derrick, Bal.	9	0	9	0	1	56
Coates, Ben, N.E.	9	0	9	0	1	56
Allen, Marcus, K.C.	9	9	0	0	0	54
Brown, Tim, Oak.	9	0	9	0	0	54
Carter, Ki-Jana, Cin.	9	8	1	0	0	54
Smith, Lamar, Sea.	8	8	0	0	3	54
Johnson, Keyshawn, NY-J	8	0	8	0	1	50
Fenner, Derrick, Oak.	8	4	4	0	0	48
Galloway, Joey, Sea.	8	0	7	1	0	48
George, Eddie, Hou.	8	8	0	0	0	48
Harrison, Marvin, Ind.	8	0	8	0	0	48
McDuffie, O. J., Mia.	8	0	8	0	0	48
Stewart, Kordell, Pit.	8	5	3	0	0	48
Thomas, Thurman, Buf.	8	8	0	0	0	48
Faulk, Marshall, Ind.	7	7	0	0	0	42
McCaffrey, Ed, Den.	7	0	7	0	0	42
Murrell, Adrian, NY-J	7	6	1	0	0	42
Russell, Leonard, S.D.	7	7	0	0	0	42
Smith, Jimmy, Jac.	7	0	7	0	0	42
Davis, Willie, Hou.	6	0	6	0	0	36
Glenn, Terry, N.E.	6	0	6	0	0	36
Graham, Jeff, NY-J	6	0	6	0	0	36
Hastings, Andre, Pit.	6	0	6	0	0	36

	TD	TDR	TDP	TDM	2-PT	PTS
Reed, Andre, Buf.	6	0	6	0	0	36
Wycheck, Frank, Hou.	6	0	6	0	0	36
Holmes, Darick, Buf.	5	4	1	0	1	32
Warren, Chris, Sea.	5	5	0	0	1	32
Byner, Earnest, Bal.	5	4	1	0	0	30
Hill, Greg, K.C.	5	4	1	0	0	30
Morris, Bam, Bal.	5	4	1	0	0	30
Penn, Chris, K.C.	5	0	5	0	0	30
Scott, Darnay, Cin.	5	0	5	0	0	30
Early, Quinn, Buf.	4	0	4	0	1	26
Anders, Kimble, K.C.	4	2	2	0	0	24
Dilger, Ken, Ind.	4	0	4	0	0	24
Dudley, Rickey, Oak.	4	0	4	0	0	24
Elway, John, Den.	4	4	0	0	0	24
Hill, Randal, Mia.	4	0	4	0	0	24
Jefferson, Shawn, N.E.	4	0	4	0	0	24
Jett, James, Oak.	4	0	4	0	0	24
Jones, Charlie, S.D.	4	0	4	0	0	24
McGee, Tony, Cin.	4	0	4	0	0	24
Miller, Anthony, Den.	4	1	3	0	0	24
Sanders, Chris, Hou.	4	0	4	0	0	24
Spikes, Irving, Mia.	4	3	1	0	0	24
Brunell, Mark, Jac.	3	3	0	0	2	22
McCardell, Keenan, Jac.	3	0	3	0	2	22
Jackson, Willie, Jac.	3	0	3	0	1	20
Johnson, Charles, Pit.	3	0	3	0	1	20
Barnett, Fred, Mia.	3	0	3	0	0	18
Chrebet, Wayne, NY-J	3	0	3	0	0	18
Craver, Aaron, Den.	3	2	1	0	0	18
Harmon, Ronnie, Hou.	3	1	2	0	0	18
Hobbs, Daryl, Oak.	3	0	3	0	0	18
Means, Natrone, Jac.	3	2	1	0	0	18
Moulds, Eric, Buf.	3	0	2	1	0	18
Tasker, Steve, Buf.	3	0	3	0	0	18
Byars, Keith, N.E.	2	0	2	0	1	14
Gash, Sam, N.E.	2	0	2	0	1	14
Testaverde, Vinny, Bal.	2	2	0	0	1	14
Belser, Jason, Ind.	2	0	0	2	0	12
Bieniemy, Eric, Cin.	2	2	0	0	0	12
Blades, Brian, Sea.	2	0	2	0	0	12
Blake, Jeff, Cin.	2	2	0	0	0	12
Coleman, Andre, S.D.	2	0	2	0	0	12
Dunn, David, Cin.	2	0	1	1	0	12
Fletcher, Terrell, S.D.	2	0	2	0	0	12
Glenn, Aaron, NY-J	2	0	0	2	0	12
Kaufman, Napoleon, Oak.	2	1	1	0	0	12
Kelly, Jim, Buf.	2	2	0	0	0	12
LaChapelle, Sean, K.C.	2	0	2	0	0	12
Lake, Carnell, Pit.	2	0	0	2	0	12
McGinest, Willie, N.E.	2	0	0	2	0	12
McNair, Steve, Hou.	2	2	0	0	0	12
Mirer, Rick, Sea.	2	2	0	0	0	12
Pegram, Erric, Pit.	2	1	0	1	0	12
Pritchett, Stanley, Mia.	2	0	2	0	0	12
Proehl, Ricky, Sea.	2	0	2	0	0	12
Rison, Andre, Cin.	2	0	2	0	0	12
Russell, Derek, Hou.	2	0	2	0	0	12
Slaughter, Webster, NY-J	2	0	2	0	0	12
Smith, Rod, Den.	2	0	2	0	0	12
Thigpen, Yancey, Pit.	2	0	2	0	0	12
Turner, Floyd, Bal.	2	0	2	0	0	12
Vanover, Tamarick, K.C.	2	0	1	1	0	12
Woodson, Rod, Pit.	2	0	0	2	0	12
Brady, Kyle, NY-J	1	0	1	0	1	8
Hearst, Garrison, Cin.	1	0	1	0	1	8
Shedd, Kenny, Oak.	1	0	1	0	0	*8
Ambrose, Ashley, Cin.	1	0	0	1	0	6
Anderson, Richie, NY-J	1	1	0	0	0	6
Arvie, Herman, Bal.	1	0	1	0	0	6
Aska, Joe, Oak.	1	1	0	0	0	6
Bailey, Aaron, Ind.	1	0	0	1	0	6
Ball, Jerry, Oak.	1	0	0	1	0	6
Bartrum, Mike, N.E.	1	0	1	0	0	6
Blackmon, Robert, Sea.	1	0	0	1	0	6
Brantley, Chris, Buf.	1	0	1	0	0	6
Braxton, Tyrone, Den.	1	0	0	1	0	6
Broussard, Steve, Sea.	1	1	0	0	0	6
Brown, Corwin, N.E.	1	0	0	1	0	6
Bruschi, Tedy, N.E.	1	0	0	1	0	6
Buckley, Terrell, Mia.	1	0	0	1	0	6
Caldwell, Mike, Bal.	1	0	0	1	0	6
Carolan, Brett, Mia.	1	0	1	0	0	6

	TD	TDR	TDP	TDM	2-PT	PTS
Carter, Dale, K.C.	1	0	1	0	0	6
Clark, Willie, S.D.	1	0	0	1	0	6
Cline, Tony, Buf.	1	0	1	0	0	6
Cobb, Reggie, NY-J	1	1	0	0	0	6
Cothran, Jeff, Cin.	1	1	0	0	0	6
Crockett, Zack, Ind.	1	0	1	0	0	6
Cunningham, Rick, Oak.	1	0	1	0	0	6
Daniel, Eugene, Ind.	1	0	0	1	0	6
Dawkins, Sean, Ind.	1	0	1	0	0	6
Dawson, Lake, K.C.	1	0	1	0	0	6
Douglas, Hugh, NY-J	1	0	0	1	0	6
Fauria, Christian, Sea.	1	0	1	0	0	6
Floyd, Malcolm, Hou.	1	0	1	0	0	6
Francis, James, Cin.	1	0	0	1	0	6
Glover, Andrew, Oak.	1	0	1	0	0	6
Gordon, Darrien, S.D.	1	0	0	1	0	6
Green, Eric, Bal.	1	0	1	0	0	6
Grier, Marrio, N.E.	1	1	0	0	0	6
Harbaugh, Jim, Ind.	1	1	0	0	0	6
Hasty, James, K.C.	1	0	0	1	0	6
Herrod, Jeff, Ind.	1	0	0	1	0	6
Hill, Sean, Mia.	1	0	0	1	0	6
Hostetler, Jeff, Oak.	1	1	0	0	0	6
Hughes, Danan, K.C.	1	0	1	0	0	6
Hundon, James, Cin.	1	0	1	0	0	6
Jackson, Calvin, Mia.	1	0	0	1	0	6
Johnson, Reginald, K.C.	1	0	1	0	0	6
Johnstone, Lance, Oak.	1	0	0	1	0	6
Jones, James, Bal.	1	0	1	0	0	6
Kinchen, Brian, Bal.	1	0	1	0	0	6
Law, Ty, N.E.	1	0	0	1	0	6
Lester, Tim, Pit.	1	1	0	0	0	6
Lewis, Darryll, Hou.	1	0	0	1	0	6
Lewis, Jermaine, Bal.	1	0	1	0	0	6
McDaniel, Terry, Oak.	1	0	0	1	0	6
McNair, Todd, K.C.	1	0	1	0	0	6
Meggett, David, N.E.	1	0	0	1	0	6
Miller, Scott, Mia.	1	0	0	1	0	6
Mills, Ernie, Pit.	1	0	1	0	0	6
Milne, Brian, Cin.	1	1	0	0	0	6
Mitchell, Pete, Jac.	1	0	1	0	0	6
Norgard, Erik, Hou.	1	0	1	0	0	6
Northern, Gabe, Buf.	1	0	0	1	0	6
Ogden, Jonathan, Bal.	1	0	1	0	0	6
Perry, Darren, Pit.	1	0	0	1	0	6
Pollard, Marcus, Ind.	1	0	1	0	0	6
Pritchard, Mike, Sea.	1	0	1	0	0	6
Pupunu, Alfred, S.D.	1	0	1	0	0	6
Richardson, Tony, K.C.	1	0	1	0	0	6
Sherrard, Mike, Den.	1	0	1	0	0	6
Spencer, Jimmy, Cin.	1	0	0	1	0	6
Stablein, Brian, Ind.	1	0	1	0	0	6
Thomas, Lamar, Mia.	1	0	1	0	0	6
Thomas, Rodney, Hou.	1	1	0	0	0	6
Thomas, Zach, Mia.	1	0	0	1	0	6
Van Dyke, Alex, NY-J	1	0	1	0	0	6
Wainright, Frank, Mia.	1	0	1	0	0	6
Walker, Derrick, K.C.	1	0	1	0	0	6
Warren, Lamont, Ind.	1	1	0	0	0	6
Washington, Mickey, Jac.	1	0	0	1	0	6
White, David, Buf.	1	0	0	1	0	6
Williams, Calvin, Bal.	1	0	1	0	0	6
Williams, Darryl, Sea.	1	0	0	1	0	6
Williams, Ronnie, Sea.	1	0	1	0	0	6
Wilson, Robert, Mia.	1	0	1	0	0	6
Bruener, Mark, Pit.	0	0	0	0	1	2
Dent, Richard, Ind.	0	0	0	0	0	*2
Drayton, Troy, Mia.	0	0	0	0	1	2
Gardner, Carwell, Bal.	0	0	0	0	1	2
Jackson, Steve, Hou.	0	0	0	0	0	*2
Saleaumua, Dan, K.C.	0	0	0	0	0	*2

* Safety
Team safety credited to Houston, Oakland, Miami, and New England

NFC SCORERS—INDIVIDUAL
Kickers

	XP	XPA	FG	FGA	PTS
Kasay, John, Car.	34	35	37	45	145
Wilkins, Jeff, S.F.	40	40	30	34	130
Boniol, Chris, Dal.	24	25	32	36	120
Blanton, Scott, Was.	40	40	26	32	118
Anderson, Gary, Phi.	40	40	25	29	115
Jacke, Chris, G.B.	51	53	21	27	114
Andersen, Morten, Atl.	31	31	22	29	97
Sisson, Scott, Min.	30	30	22	29	96
Daluiso, Brad, NY-G	22	22	24	27	94
Husted, Michael, T.B.	18	19	25	32	93
Lohmiller, Chip, St.L	28	29	21	25	91
Brien, Doug, N.O.	18	18	21	25	81
Jaeger, Jeff, Chi.	23	23	19	23	80
Hanson, Jason, Det.	36	36	12	17	72
Butler, Kevin, Ariz	17	19	14	17	59
Davis, Greg, Ariz	12	12	9	14	39
Huerta, Carlos, Chi.-St.L	5	5	4	7	17

Nonkickers

	TD	TDR	TDP	TDM	2-PT	PTS
Allen, Terry, Was.	21	21	0	0	0	126
Smith, Emmitt, Dal.	15	12	3	0	0	90
Watters, Ricky, Phi.	13	13	0	0	0	78
Fryar, Irving, Phi.	11	0	11	0	0	66
Kennison, Eddie, St.L	11	0	9	2	0	66
Sanders, Barry, Det.	11	11	0	0	0	66
Carter, Cris, Min.	10	0	10	0	0	60
Jackson, Keith, G.B.	10	0	10	0	0	60
Levens, Dorsey, G.B.	10	5	5	0	0	60
Walls, Wesley, Car.	10	0	10	0	0	60
Moore, Herman, Det.	9	0	9	0	1	56
Centers, Larry, Ariz	9	2	7	0	0	54
Freeman, Antonio, G.B.	9	0	9	0	0	54
Rice, Jerry, S.F.	9	1	8	0	0	54
Mathis, Terance, Atl.	7	0	7	0	1	44
Bruce, Isaac, St.L	7	0	7	0	0	42
Conway, Curtis, Chi.	7	0	7	0	0	42
Reed, Jake, Min.	7	0	7	0	0	42
Alstott, Mike, T.B.	6	3	3	0	0	36
Anderson, Jamal, Atl.	6	5	1	0	0	36
Beebe, Don, G.B.	6	0	4	2	0	36
Carrier, Mark, Car.	6	0	6	0	0	36
Emanuel, Bert, Atl.	6	0	6	0	0	36
Engram, Bobby, Chi.	6	0	6	0	0	36
Johnson, Anthony, Car.	6	6	0	0	0	36
Metcalf, Eric, Atl.	6	0	6	0	0	36
Morton, Johnnie, Det.	6	0	6	0	0	36
Popson, Ted, S.F.	6	0	6	0	0	36
Green, Harold, St.L	5	4	1	0	1	32
Harris, Raymont, Chi.	5	4	1	0	0	30
Jones, Chris T., Phi.	5	0	5	0	0	30
Perriman, Brett, Det.	5	0	5	0	0	30
Phillips, Lawrence, St.L	5	4	1	0	0	30
Shepherd, Leslie, Was.	5	2	3	0	0	30
Haynes, Michael, N.O.	4	0	4	0	1	26
Moore, Rob, Ariz	4	0	4	0	1	26
Young, Steve, S.F.	4	4	0	0	1	26
Asher, Jamie, Was.	4	0	4	0	0	24
Bates, Mario, N.O.	4	4	0	0	0	24
Brooks, Robert, G.B.	4	0	4	0	0	24
Calloway, Chris, NY-G	4	0	4	0	0	24
Johnson, LeShon, Ariz	4	3	1	0	0	24
Kirby, Terry, S.F.	4	3	1	0	0	24
Lewis, Thomas, NY-G	4	0	4	0	0	24
Loville, Derek, S.F.	4	2	2	0	0	24
Mitchell, Scott, Det.	4	4	0	0	0	24
Owens, Terrell, S.F.	4	0	4	0	0	24
Rhett, Errict, T.B.	4	3	1	0	0	24
Salaam, Rashaan, Chi.	4	3	1	0	0	24
Sanders, Frank, Ariz	4	0	4	0	0	24
Zellars, Ray, N.O.	4	4	0	0	0	24
Bennett, Edgar, G.B.	3	2	1	0	2	22
Bjornson, Eric, Dal.	3	0	3	0	1	20
Floyd, William, S.F.	3	2	1	0	0	18
Green, Willie, Car.	3	0	3	0	0	18
Heyward, Craig, Atl.	3	3	0	0	0	18
Hoard, Leroy, Min.	3	3	0	0	0	18
Howard, Desmond, G.B.	3	0	0	3	0	18
Ismail, Qadry, Min.	3	0	3	0	0	18
Jeffires, Haywood, N.O.	3	0	3	0	0	18

	TD	TDR	TDP	TDM	2-PT	PTS
Moore, Dave, T.B.	3	0	3	0	0	18
Small, Torrance, N.O.	3	1	2	0	0	18
Smith, Robert, Min.	3	3	0	0	0	18
Wheatley, Tyrone, NY-G	3	1	2	0	0	18
Irvin, Michael, Dal.	2	0	2	0	1	14
Birden, J. J., Atl.	2	0	2	0	0	12
Brooks, Reggie, T.B.	2	2	0	0	0	12
Davis, Stephen, Was.	2	2	0	0	0	12
Dowdell, Marcus, Ariz	2	0	2	0	0	12
Dunn, Jason, Phi.	2	0	2	0	0	12
Ellard, Henry, Was.	2	0	2	0	0	12
Favre, Brett, G.B.	2	2	0	0	0	12
Galbraith, Scott, Was.	2	0	2	0	0	12
Grbac, Elvis, S.F.	2	2	0	0	0	12
Griffith, Howard, Car.	2	1	1	0	0	12
Lee, Amp, Min.	2	0	2	0	0	12
Logan, Marc, Was.	2	2	0	0	0	12
Mayes, Derrick, G.B.	2	0	2	0	0	12
McElroy, Leeland, Ariz	2	1	1	0	0	12
Mickens, Terry, G.B.	2	0	2	0	0	12
Neal, Lorenzo, N.O.	2	1	1	0	0	12
Parker, Anthony, St.L	2	0	0	2	0	12
Pierce, Aaron, NY-G	2	1	1	0	0	12
Sanders, Deion, Dal.	2	0	1	1	0	12
Smith, Cedric, Ariz	2	1	1	0	0	12
Thomas, Robb, T.B.	2	0	2	0	0	12
Toomer, Amani, NY-G	2	0	0	2	0	12
Vardell, Tommy, S.F.	2	2	0	0	0	12
Way, Charles, NY-G	2	1	1	0	0	12
Witherspoon, Derrick, Phi.	2	0	0	2	0	12
Esiason, Boomer, Ariz	1	1	0	0	1	8
Harris, Jackie, T.B.	1	0	1	0	1	8
Walsh, Chris, Min.	1	0	1	0	1	8
Wooten, Tito, NY-G	1	0	0	1	0	*8
Agnew, Ray, NY-G	1	0	0	1	0	6
Aikman, Troy, Dal.	1	1	0	0	0	6
Bates, Michael, Car.	1	0	0	1	0	6
Blades, Bennie, Det.	1	0	0	1	0	6
Brown, Tyrone, Atl.	1	0	1	0	0	6
Butler, LeRoy, G.B.	1	0	0	1	0	6
Carter, Dexter, S.F.	1	1	0	0	0	6
Carter, Pat, Ariz	1	0	1	0	0	6
Cox, Bryan, Chi.	1	0	0	1	0	6
Cross, Howard, NY-G	1	0	1	0	0	6
DeRamus, Lee, N.O.	1	0	1	0	0	6
Detmer, Ty, Phi.	1	1	0	0	0	6
Doleman, Chris, S.F.	1	0	0	1	0	6
Douglass, Maurice, NY-G	1	0	0	1	0	6
Edwards, Anthony, Ariz	1	0	1	0	0	6
Evans, Doug, G.B.	1	0	0	1	0	6
Faulkerson, Mike, Chi.	1	0	1	0	0	6
Flanigan, Jim, Chi.	1	0	1	0	0	6
Frisch, David, Min.	1	0	1	0	0	6
Garner, Charlie, Phi.	1	1	0	0	0	6
Green, Darrell, Was.	1	0	0	1	0	6
Greene, Kevin, Car.	1	0	0	1	0	6
Greene, Scott, Car.	1	0	1	0	0	6
Guess, Terry, N.O.	1	0	1	0	0	6
Hall, Rhett, Phi.	1	0	0	1	0	6
Hampton, Rodney, NY-G	1	1	0	0	0	6
Harper, Alvin, T.B.	1	0	1	0	0	6
Hawkins, Courtney, T.B.	1	0	1	0	0	6
Hebert, Bobby, Atl.	1	1	0	0	0	6
Henderson, William, G.B.	1	0	1	0	0	6
Ismail, Raghib, Car.	1	1	0	0	0	6
Johnson, Brad, Min.	1	1	0	0	0	6
Johnson, Tony, N.O.	1	0	1	0	0	6
Johnston, Daryl, Dal.	1	0	1	0	0	6
Jones, Brent, S.F.	1	0	1	0	0	6
Jones, Brian, N.O.	1	0	0	1	0	6
King, Shawn, Car.	1	0	0	1	0	6
Koonce, George, G.B.	1	0	0	1	0	6
Kozlowski, Brian, NY-G	1	0	1	0	0	6
Krieg, Dave, Chi.	1	1	0	0	0	6
Lowery, Michael, Chi.	1	0	0	1	0	6
Lyght, Todd, St.L	1	0	0	1	0	6
Lyons, Mitch, Atl.	1	0	1	0	0	6
Mamula, Mike, Phi.	1	0	0	1	0	6
Martin, Kelvin, Dal.	1	0	1	0	0	6
Matthews, Shane, Chi.	1	1	0	0	0	6
McWilliams, Johnny, Ariz	1	0	1	0	0	6
Miller, Jamir, Ariz	1	0	0	1	0	6

	TD	TDR	TDP	TDM	2-PT	PTS
Mills, Sam, Car.	1	0	0	1	0	6
Muhammad, Muhsin, Car.	1	0	1	0	0	6
Oliver, Winslow, Car.	1	0	0	1	0	6
Palmer, David, Min.	1	0	0	1	0	6
Peete, Rodney, Phi.	1	1	0	0	0	6
Philyaw, Dino, Car.	1	1	0	0	0	6
Pope, Marquez, S.F.	1	0	0	1	0	6
Preston, Roell, Atl.	1	0	1	0	0	6
Raymond, Corey, Det.	1	0	0	1	0	6
Rison, Andre, G.B.	1	0	1	0	0	6
Robinson, Greg, St.L	1	1	0	0	0	6
Ross, Jermaine, St.L	1	1	0	0	0	6
Sehorn, Jason, NY-G	1	0	0	1	0	6
Spears, Marcus, Chi.	1	0	1	0	0	6
Thomas, William, Phi.	1	0	0	1	0	6
Tobeck, Robbie, Atl.	1	0	1	0	0	6
Turner, Kevin, Phi.	1	0	1	0	0	6
Turner, Scott, Was.	1	0	0	1	0	6
Uwaezuoke, Iheanyi, S.F.	1	0	1	0	0	6
Vincent, Troy, Phi.	1	0	0	1	0	6
Walker, Herschel, Dal.	1	1	0	0	0	6
Washington, Dewayne, Min.	1	0	0	1	0	6
Wells, Mike, Det.	1	0	0	1	0	6
Westbrook, Michael, Was.	1	0	1	0	0	6
Wetnight, Ryan, Chi.	1	0	1	0	0	6
Williams, Aeneas, Ariz	1	0	0	1	0	6
Williams, Karl, T.B.	1	0	0	1	0	6
Williams, Kevin, Dal.	1	0	1	0	0	6
Woolford, Donnell, Chi.	1	0	0	1	0	6
Wright, Toby, St.L	1	0	0	1	0	6
Young, Bryant, S.F.	0	0	0	0	0	*4
Banks, Tony, St.L	0	0	0	0	1	2
Collins, Kerry, Car.	0	0	0	0	1	2
Jordan, Andrew, Min.	0	0	0	0	1	2
Wilmsmeyer, Klaus, N.O.	0	0	0	0	1	2

Safety

Team safety credited to Carolina (2), Chicago, Green Bay, N.Y. Giants, Philadelphia, St. Louis, and San Francisco (2).

FIELD GOALS

Field Goal Percentage

AFC:	.900—Cary Blanchard, Indianapolis	
NFC:	.889—Chris Boniol, Dallas	
	Brad Daluiso, N.Y. Giants	

Field Goals

NFC:	37—John Kasay, Carolina
AFC:	36—Caray Blanchard, Indianapolis

Field Goal Attempts

NFC:	45—John Kasay, Carolina
AFC:	40—Cary Blanchard, Indianapolis

Longest Field Goal

AFC:	56—Al Del Greco, Houston vs. San Francisco, October 27
NFC:	54—Doug Brien, New Orleans vs. Chicago, October 13
	Morten Andersen, Atlanta at Dallas, October 20

Average Yards Made

NFC:	37.9—Jeff Jaeger, Chicago
AFC:	36.1—Al Del Greco, Houston

AFC FIELD GOALS—TEAM

	FG	FGA	Pct.	Long
Indianapolis	36	40	.900	52
Houston	32	38	.842	56
Jacksonville	30	36	.833	53
Buffalo	24	29	.828	48
Seattle	28	34	.824	54
Cincinnati	23	28	.821	49
San Diego.	29	36	.806	53
Oakland	24	31	.774	47
New England	27	35	.771	50
Pittsburgh	23	30	.767	49
Baltimore.	19	25	.760	50
Denver.	21	28	.750	51
Kansas City	17	24	.708	45
N.Y. Jets.	17	24	.708	46
Miami	18	29	.621	44
AFC Total	368	467	—	56
AFC Average	24.5	31.1	.788	—

NFC FIELD GOALS—TEAM

	FG	FGA	Pct.	Long
Dallas.	32	36	.889	52
N.Y. Giants	24	27	.889	46
San Francisco	30	34	.882	49
Philadelphia	25	29	.862	46
New Orleans	21	25	.840	54
St. Louis.	21	25	.840	50
Carolina	37	45	.822	53
Washington	26	32	.813	53
Tampa Bay.	25	32	.781	50
Green Bay.	21	27	.778	53
Chicago	23	30	.767	49
Atlanta	22	29	.759	54
Minnesota.	22	29	.759	44
Arizona	23	31	.742	49
Detroit	12	17	.706	51
NFC Total	364	448	—	54
NFC Average	24.3	29.9	.813	—
League Total	732	915	—	56
League Average	24.4	30.5	.800	—

AFC FIELD GOALS—INDIVIDUAL

	1-19 Yards	20-29 Yards	30-39 Yards	40-49 Yards	50 or Longer	Totals	Avg. Yds. Att.	Avg. Yds. Made	Avg. Yds. Miss	Long
Blanchard, Cary, Ind.	1-1 1.000	11-11 1.000	8-9 .889	11-14 .786	5-5 1.000	36-40 .900	36.4	35.9	40.5	52
Del Greco, Al, Hou.	0-0 —	7-7 1.000	14-16 .875	10-12 .833	1-3 .333	32-38 .842	37.4	36.1	44.7	56
Hollis, Mike, Jac.	2-2 1.000	9-9 1.000	12-14 .857	5-8 .625	2-3 .667	30-36 .833	34.6	33.2	41.5	53
Christie, Steve, Buf.	0-0 —	5-6 .833	12-14 .857	7-8 .875	0-1 .000	24-29 .828	35.7	35.2	38.2	48
Peterson, Todd, Sea.	0-0 —	11-13 .846	7-7 1.000	8-11 .727	2-3 .667	28-34 .824	35.1	34.4	38.2	54
Pelfrey, Doug, Cin.	1-1 1.000	7-7 1.000	10-11 .909	5-9 .556	0-0 —	23-28 .821	34.1	32.2	43.0	49
Carney, John, S.D.	0-0 —	11-13 .846	8-8 1.000	7-12 .583	3-3 1.000	29-36 .806	35.9	34.7	41.1	53
Ford, Cole, Oak.	0-0 —	9-11 .818	10-11 .909	5-8 .625	0-1 .000	24-31 .774	34.9	33.6	39.4	47
Vinatieri, Adam, N.E.	1-1 1.000	9-10 .900	8-8 1.000	8-14 .571	1-2 .500	27-35 .771	35.1	32.7	43.1	50
Johnson, Norm, Pit.	0-0 —	10-12 .833	8-10 .800	5-7 .714	0-1 .000	23-30 .767	33.8	32.5	38.1	49
Stover, Matt, Bal.	0-0 —	8-8 1.000	5-6 .833	5-10 .500	1-1 1.000	19-25 .760	36.2	33.6	44.3	50
Elam, Jason, Den.	2-2 1.000	8-8 1.000	4-5 .800	6-10 .600	1-3 .333	21-28 .750	36.2	33.4	44.6	51
Lowery, Nick, NY-J	0-0 —	9-9 1.000	6-7 .857	2-8 .250	0-0 —	17-24 .708	35.0	30.7	45.4	46
Stoyanovich, Pete, K.C.	1-1 1.000	7-8 .875	5-7 .714	4-7 .571	0-1 .000	17-24 .708	33.8	31.2	40.1	45
Nedney, Joe, Mia.	1-1 1.000	7-7 1.000	7-11 .636	3-8 .375	0-2 .000	18-29 .621	36.3	32.6	42.5	44
AFC Totals	9-9 1.000	128-139 .921	124-144 .861	91-146 .623	16-29 .552	368-467 .788	35.4	33.7	41.8	56
League Totals	20-20 1.000	266-281 .947	244-288 .847	172-268 .642	30-58 .517	732-915 .800	35.2	33.5	42.2	56

Leader based on percentage, minimum 16 field goal attempts

NFC FIELD GOALS—INDIVIDUAL

	1-19 Yards	20-29 Yards	30-39 Yards	40-49 Yards	50 or Longer	Totals	Avg. Yds. Att.	Avg. Yds. Made	Avg. Yds. Miss	Long
Boniol, Chris, Dal.	1-1	13-13	12-13	5-7	1-2	32-36	34.1	32.9	44.0	52
	1.000	1.000	.923	.714	.500	.889				
Daluiso, Brad, NY-G	2-2	10-10	9-9	3-6	0-0	24-27	31.1	29.7	42.3	46
	1.000	1.000	1.000	.500	—	.889				
Wilkins, Jeff, S.F.	0-0	16-16	7-8	7-10	0-0	30-34	34.1	32.7	44.0	49
	—	1.000	.875	.700	—	.882				
Anderson, Gary, Phi.	0-0	10-11	8-9	7-9	0-0	25-29	34.6	33.8	39.8	46
	—	.909	.889	.778	—	.862				
Brien, Doug, N.O.	0-0	4-4	9-10	5-7	3-4	21-25	39.0	37.8	45.0	54
	—	1.000	.900	.714	.750	.840				
Lohmiller, Chip, St.L	1-1	11-11	4-5	4-7	1-1	21-25	33.3	31.4	43.0	50
	1.000	1.000	.800	.571	1.000	.840				
Jaeger, Jeff, Chi.	0-0	4-4	3-4	12-15	0-0	19-23	38.7	37.9	42.3	49
	—	1.000	.750	.800	—	.826				
Butler, Kevin, Ariz	1-1	6-6	5-8	2-2	0-0	14-17	31.2	30.7	33.7	41
	1.000	1.000	.625	1.000	—	.824				
Kasay, John, Car.	2-2	14-14	11-12	7-10	3-7	37-45	36.0	33.6	46.8	53
	1.000	1.000	.917	.700	.429	.822				
Blanton, Scott, Was.	2-2	13-13	7-7	2-7	2-3	26-32	32.9	29.8	46.3	53
	1.000	1.000	1.000	.286	.667	.813				
Husted, Michael, T.B.	2-2	7-8	8-11	7-8	1-3	25-32	35.3	33.9	40.0	50
	1.000	.875	.727	.875	.333	.781				
Jacke, Chris, G.B.	0-0	6-6	9-11	5-9	1-1	21-27	36.3	34.5	42.7	53
	—	1.000	.818	.556	1.000	.778				
Andersen, Morten, Atl.	0-0	5-5	9-11	7-8	1-5	22-29	38.2	35.8	45.9	54
	—	1.000	.818	.875	.200	.759				
Sisson, Scott, Min.	0-0	8-8	11-14	3-7	0-0	22-29	33.7	31.4	40.7	44
	—	1.000	.786	.429	—	.759				
Hanson, Jason, Det.	0-0	4-4	4-5	3-5	1-3	12-17	38.6	35.3	46.8	51
	—	1.000	.800	.600	.333	.706				
Nonqualifiers										
Davis, Greg, Ariz	0-0	7-9	1-2	1-3	0-0	9-14	31.9	29.2	36.6	49
	—	.778	.500	.333	—	.643				
Huerta, Carlos, Chi	0-0	0-0	3-5	1-2	0-0	4-7	37.4	36.0	39.3	42
	—	—	.600	.500	—	.571				
NFC Totals	11-11	138-142	120-144	81-122	14-29	364-448	35.0	33.2	42.7	54
	1.000	.972	.833	.664	.483	.813				
League Totals	20-20	266-281	244-288	172-268	30-58	732-915	35.2	33.5	42.2	56
	1.000	.947	.847	.642	.517	.800				

Leader based on percentage, minimum 16 field goal attempts

RUSHING

Yards
NFC: 1553—Barry Sanders, Detroit
AFC: 1538—Terrell Davis, Denver

Yards, Game
NFC: 214—LeShon Johnson, Arizona at New Orleans, September 22, (21 attempts, 2 TD)
AFC: 199—Adrian Murrell, N.Y. Jets at Arizona, October 27, (31 attempts, 1 TD)

Longest
AFC: 80—Kordell Stewart, Pittsburgh at Carolina, December 22 - TD
NFC: 70—LeShon Johnson, Arizona at New Orleans, September 22 - TD

Attempts
NFC: 353—Ricky Watters, Philadelphia
AFC: 345—Terrell Davis, Denver

Attempts, Game
AFC: 35—Curtis Martin, New England vs. Indianapolis, November 24 (141 yards - TD)
NFC: 33—Eric Rhett, Tampa Bay vs. Oakland, November 10 (95 yards)

Yards Per Attempt
NFC: 5.8—Napoleon Kaufman, Oakland
AFC: 5.1—Barry Sanders, Detroit

Touchdowns
NFC: 21—Terry Allen, Washington
AFC: 14—Curtis Martin, New England

Team Leaders, Yards
AFC: BALTIMORE: 737, Bam Morris; ARIZONA: 634, LeShon Johnson; BUFFALO: 1033, Thurman Thomas; ATLANTA: 1055, Jamal Anderson; CINCINNATI: 847, Garrison Hearst; CAROLINA: 1120, Anthony Johnson; DENVER: 1538, Terrell Davis; CHICAGO: 748, Raymont Harris; HOUSTON: 1368, Eddie George; DALLAS: 1204, Emmitt Smith; INDIANAPOLIS: 587, Marshall Faulk; DETROIT: 1553, Barry Sanders; JACKSONVILLE: 723, James Stewart; GREEN BAY: 899, Edgar Bennett; KANSAS CITY: 830, Marcus Allen; MINNESOTA: 692, Robert Smith; MIAMI: 1116, Karim Abdul-Jabbar; NEW ORLEANS: 584, Mario Bates; NEW ENGLAND: 1152, Curtis Martin; N.Y. GIANTS: 827, Rodney Hampton; N.Y. JETS: 1249, Adrian Murrell; PHILADELPHIA: 1411, Ricky Watters; OAKLAND: 874, Napoleon Kaufman; ST. LOUIS: 632, Lawrence Phillips; PITTSBURGH: 1431, Jerome Bettis; SAN FRANCISCO: 559, Terry Kirby; SAN DIEGO: 713, Leonard Russell; TAMPA BAY: 539, Errict Rhett; SEATTLE: 855, Chris Warren; WASHINGTON: 1353, Terry Allen

Team Champion
AFC: 2362—Denver
NFC: 1910—Washington

AFC RUSHING—TEAM

	Att.	Yards	Avg.	Long	TD
Denver	525	2362	4.5	71t	20
Pittsburgh	525	2299	4.4	80t	18
Oakland	456	2174	4.8	77	7
Kansas City	488	2009	4.1	35	15
Seattle	442	1997	4.5	51	16
Houston	475	1950	4.1	76	12
Buffalo	563	1901	3.4	37	14
Cincinnati	478	1793	3.8	33t	14
Baltimore	416	1745	4.2	42	10
Jacksonville	431	1650	3.8	35	13
Miami	460	1622	3.5	49	14
N.Y. Jets	407	1583	3.9	78	8
New England	427	1468	3.4	57	15
Indianapolis	420	1448	3.4	53	9
San Diego	412	1312	3.2	21	7
AFC Total	6925	27313	3.9	80t	192
AFC Average	461.7	1820.9	3.9	—	12.8

NFC RUSHING—TEAM

	Att.	Yards	Avg.	Long	TD
Washington	467	1910	4.1	49t	27
Philadelphia	489	1882	3.8	56t	16
San Francisco	454	1847	4.1	67	17
Green Bay	465	1838	4.0	24	9
Detroit	389	1810	4.7	54t	15
Carolina	502	1729	3.4	35t	9
Chicago	472	1720	3.6	32	9
Dallas	475	1641	3.5	42	14
St. Louis	448	1607	3.6	38	10
N.Y. Giants	485	1603	3.3	37	4
Tampa Bay	472	1589	3.4	56	8
Minnesota	435	1546	3.6	57	7
Arizona	401	1502	3.7	70t	8
Atlanta	329	1461	4.4	34	9
New Orleans	386	1308	3.4	63	10
NFC Total	6669	24993	3.7	70t	172
NFC Average	444.6	1666.2	3.7	—	11.5
League Total	13594	52306	—	80t	364
League Average	453.1	1743.5	3.8	—	12.1

NFL TOP TEN RUSHERS

	Att.	Yards	Avg.	Long	TD
Sanders, Barry, Det.	307	1553	5.1	54t	11
Davis, Terrell, Den.	345	1538	4.5	71t	13
Bettis, Jerome, Pit.	320	1431	4.5	50t	11
Watters, Ricky, Phi.	353	1411	4.0	56t	13
George, Eddie, Hou.	335	1368	4.1	76	8
Allen, Terry, Was.	347	1353	3.9	49t	21
Murrell, Adrian, NY-J	301	1249	4.1	78	6
Smith, Emmitt, Dal.	327	1204	3.7	42	12
Martin, Curtis, N.E.	316	1152	3.6	57	14
Johnson, Anthony, Car.	300	1120	3.7	29	6

AFC RUSHERS—INDIVIDUAL

	Att.	Yards	Avg.	Long	TD
Davis, Terrell, Den.	345	1538	4.5	71t	13
Bettis, Jerome, Pit.	320	1431	4.5	50t	11
George, Eddie, Hou.	335	1368	4.1	76	8
Murrell, Adrian, NY-J	301	1249	4.1	78	6
Martin, Curtis, N.E.	316	1152	3.6	57	14
Abdul-Jabbar, Karim, Mia.	307	1116	3.6	29	11
Thomas, Thurman, Buf.	281	1033	3.7	36	8
Kaufman, Napoleon, Oak.	150	874	5.8	77	1
Warren, Chris, Sea.	203	855	4.2	51	5
Hearst, Garrison, Cin.	225	847	3.8	24	0
Allen, Marcus, K.C.	206	830	4.0	35	9
Morris, Bam, Bal.	172	737	4.3	19	4
Stewart, James, Jac.	190	723	3.8	34	8
Russell, Leonard, S.D.	219	713	3.3	21	7
Smith, Lamar, Sea.	153	680	4.4	29	8
Hill, Greg, K.C.	135	645	4.8	28	4
Byner, Earnest, Bal.	159	634	4.0	42	4
Faulk, Marshall, Ind.	198	587	3.0	43	7
Holmes, Darick, Buf.	189	571	3.0	37	4
Pegram, Erric, Pit.	97	509	5.2	27	1

	Att.	Yards	Avg.	Long	TD
Means, Natrone, Jac.	152	507	3.3	35	2
Williams, Harvey, Oak.	121	431	3.6	44	0
Brunell, Mark, Jac.	80	396	5.0	33	3
Aska, Joe, Oak.	62	326	5.3	38	1
Blake, Jeff, Cin.	72	317	4.4	18	2
Spikes, Irving, Mia.	87	316	3.6	49	3
Fletcher, Terrell, S.D.	77	282	3.7	19	0
Bieniemy, Eric, Cin.	56	269	4.8	33t	2
Carter, Ki-Jana, Cin.	91	264	2.9	31t	8
Hebron, Vaughn, Den.	49	262	5.3	47	0
Elway, John, Den.	50	249	5.0	22	4
Fenner, Derrick, Oak.	67	245	3.7	17	4
Craver, Aaron, Den.	59	232	3.9	28	2
Warren, Lamont, Ind.	67	230	3.4	53	1
Anders, Kimble, K.C.	54	201	3.7	15t	2
Harbaugh, Jim, Ind.	48	192	4.0	21	1
Mirer, Rick, Sea.	33	191	5.8	33	2
Testaverde, Vinny, Bal.	34	188	5.5	22	2
Groce, Clif, Ind.	46	184	4.0	24	0
Hostetler, Jeff, Oak.	37	179	4.8	17	1
Stewart, Kordell, Pit.	39	171	4.4	80t	5
McNair, Steve, Hou.	31	169	5.5	24t	2
Bennett, Donnell, K.C.	36	166	4.6	34	0
Hayden, Aaron, S.D.	55	166	3.0	13	0
Crockett, Zack, Ind.	31	164	5.3	25	0
Thomas, Rodney, Hou.	49	151	3.1	24t	1
Anderson, Richie, NY-J	47	150	3.2	11	1
Harmon, Ronnie, Hou.	29	131	4.5	25	1
Galloway, Joey, Sea.	15	127	8.5	51	0
Meggett, Dave, N.E.	40	122	3.1	12	0
Chandler, Chris, Hou.	28	113	4.0	16	0
Bradley, Freddie, S.D.	32	109	3.4	17	0
Gardner, Carwell, Bal.	26	108	4.2	19	0
Broussard, Steve, Sea.	15	106	7.1	26t	1
Grier, Marrio, N.E.	27	105	3.9	26	1
Cobb, Reggie, NY-J	25	85	3.4	9	1
Gannon, Rich, K.C.	12	81	6.8	19	0
Parmalee, Bernie, Mia.	25	80	3.2	17	0
Hastings, Andre, Pit.	4	71	17.8	37	0
Workman, Vince, Ind.	24	70	2.9	11	0
Witman, Jon, Pit.	17	69	4.1	15	0
Kelly, Jim, Buf.	19	66	3.5	22	2
Tindale, Tim, Buf.	14	49	3.5	15	0
Cothran, Jeff, Cin.	15	44	2.9	9	1
Moulds, Eric, Buf.	12	44	3.7	11	0
Collins, Todd, Buf.	21	43	2.0	10	0
Glenn, Terry, N.E.	5	42	8.4	26	0
Foley, Glenn, NY-J	7	40	5.7	12	0
Early, Quinn, Buf.	3	39	13.0	29	0
Lewis, Jeff, Den.	4	39	9.8	18	0
Miller, Anthony, Den.	3	39	13.0	26t	1
Klingler, David, Oak.	4	36	9.0	14	0
Brown, Tim, Oak.	6	35	5.8	15	0
McNair, Todd, K.C.	9	32	3.6	9	0
Reich, Frank, NY-J	18	31	1.7	10	0
Tasker, Steve, Buf.	9	31	3.4	11	0
O'Donnell, Neil, NY-J	6	30	5.0	17	0
Gossett, Jeff, Oak.	3	28	9.3	18	0
Humphries, Stan, S.D.	21	28	1.3	7	0
McPhail, Jerris, Mia.	6	28	4.7	10	0
Bledsoe, Drew, N.E.	24	27	1.1	8	0
Bono, Steve, K.C.	26	27	1.0	17	0
Pritchett, Stanley, Mia.	7	27	3.9	16	0
Izzo, Larry, Mia.	1	26	26.0	26	0
Mills, Ernie, Pit.	2	24	12.0	15	0
Wilhelm, Erik, Cin.	6	24	4.0	18	0
Maston, Le'Shai, Jac.	8	22	2.8	7	0
Milne, Brian, Cin.	8	22	2.8	5	1
Reed, Andre, Buf.	8	22	2.8	13	0
Lester, Tim, Pit.	8	20	2.5	5t	1
McAfee, Fred, Pit.	7	17	2.4	5	0
Richardson, Terry, Pit.	5	17	3.4	8	0
Erickson, Craig, Mia.	11	16	1.5	12	0
Davis, Willie, Hou.	1	15	15.0	15	0
Gash, Sam, N.E.	8	15	1.9	3	0
Harrison, Marvin, Ind.	3	15	5.0	15	0
Salisbury, Sean, S.D.	6	14	2.3	11	0
Hobert, Billy Joe, Oak.	2	13	6.5	14	0
Pritchard, Mike, Sea.	2	13	6.5	7	0
Torretta, Gino, Sea.	2	12	6.0	13	0
Turner, Floyd, Bal.	2	12	6.0	6	0
Richardson, Tony, K.C.	4	10	2.5	4	0

	Att.	Yards	Avg.	Long	TD
Bratton, Jason, Buf.	4	8	2.0	5	0
Horn, Joe, K.C.	1	8	8.0	8	0
Strong, Mack, Sea.	5	8	1.6	4	0
Zeier, Eric, Bal.	2	8	4.0	5	0
Hall, Tim, Oak.	3	7	2.3	4	0
Justin, Paul, Ind.	2	7	3.5	6	0
McDuffie, O. J., Mia.	2	7	3.5	7	0
Jefferson, Shawn, N.E.	1	6	6.0	6	0
Kosar, Bernie, Mia.	1	6	6.0	6	0
Rivers, Reggie, Den.	2	6	3.0	3	0
Vanover, Tamarick, K.C.	4	6	1.5	6	0
Gray, Oscar, Sea.	2	4	2.0	2	0
Scott, Darnay, Cin.	3	4	1.3	8	0
Carter, Dale, K.C.	1	3	3.0	3	0
Kidd, John, Mia.	1	3	3.0	3	0
Wycheck, Frank, Hou.	2	3	1.5	3	0
Byars, Keith, N.E.	2	2	1.0	3	0
Jackson, Willie, Jac.	1	2	2.0	2	0
Pickens, Carl, Cin.	2	2	1.0	2	0
Friesz, John, Sea.	12	1	0.1	3	0
Hansen, Brian, NY-J	1	1	1.0	1	0
Moore, Ronald, NY-J	1	1	1.0	1	0
Smith, Rod, Den.	1	1	1.0	1	0
Alexander, Derrick, Bal.	3	0	0.0	12	0
Araguz, Leo, Oak.	1	0	0.0	0	0
Coleman, Andre, S.D.	2	0	0.0	7	0
Montgomery, Greg, Bal.	1	0	0.0	0	0
Wilson, Robert, Mia.	1	0	0.0	0	0
Bell, Kerwin, Ind.	1	-1	-1.0	-1	0
Arnold, Jahine, Pit.	1	-3	-3.0	-3	0
Lewis, Jermaine, Bal.	1	-3	-3.0	-3	0
Marino, Dan, Mia.	11	-3	-.3	7	0
Zolak, Scott, N.E.	4	-3	-.7	0	0
Bailey, Henry, NY-J	1	-4	-4.0	-4	0
Miller, Jim, Pit.	2	-4	-2.0	0	0
Musgrave, Bill, Den.	12	-4	-.3	6	0
Van Pelt, Alex, Buf.	3	-5	-1.7	-1	0
Tomczak, Mike, Pit.	22	-7	-.3	6	0
Edge, Shayne, Pit.	1	-16	-16.0	-16	0

t = Touchdown
Leader based on most yards gained

NFC RUSHERS—INDIVIDUAL

	Att.	Yards	Avg.	Long	TD
Sanders, Barry, Det.	307	1553	5.1	54t	11
Watters, Ricky, Phi.	353	1411	4.0	56t	13
Allen, Terry, Was.	347	1353	3.9	49t	21
Smith, Emmitt, Dal.	327	1204	3.7	42	12
Johnson, Anthony, Car.	300	1120	3.7	29	6
Anderson, Jamal, Atl.	232	1055	4.5	32t	5
Bennett, Edgar, G.B.	222	899	4.0	23	2
Hampton, Rodney, NY-G	254	827	3.3	25	1
Harris, Raymont, Chi.	194	748	3.9	23	4
Smith, Robert, Min.	162	692	4.3	57	3
Johnson, LeShon, Ariz	141	634	4.5	70t	3
Phillips, Lawrence, St.L	193	632	3.3	38	4
Bates, Mario, N.O.	164	584	3.6	33	4
Levens, Dorsey, G.B.	121	566	4.7	24	5
Kirby, Terry, S.F.	134	559	4.2	31	3
Rhett, Errict, T.B.	176	539	3.1	35	3
Green, Harold, St.L	127	523	4.1	35t	4
Salaam, Rashaan, Chi.	143	496	3.5	32	3
Hoard, Leroy, Bal.-Car.-Min.	125	492	3.9	25	3
Zellars, Ray, N.O.	120	475	4.0	63	4
Centers, Larry, Ariz	116	425	3.7	24	2
Wheatley, Tyrone, NY-G	112	400	3.6	37	1
Alstott, Mike, T.B.	96	377	3.9	39	3
Brooks, Reggie, T.B.	112	368	3.3	56	2
Garner, Charlie, Phi.	66	346	5.2	46	1
Heyward, Craig, Atl.	72	321	4.5	34	3
Young, Steve, S.F.	52	310	6.0	33	4
McElroy, Leeland, Ariz	89	305	3.4	32	1
Williams, Sherman, Dal.	69	269	3.9	27	0
Green, Robert, Chi.	60	249	4.2	19	0
Biakabutuka, Tim, Car.	71	229	3.2	17	0
Loville, Derek, S.F.	70	229	3.3	16	2
Banks, Tony, St.L	61	212	3.5	22	0
Mitchell, Brian, Was.	39	193	4.9	32	0
Vardell, Tommy, S.F.	58	192	3.3	17	2
Floyd, William, S.F.	47	186	4.0	12	2
Oliver, Winslow, Car.	47	183	3.9	16	0

	Att.	Yards	Avg.	Long	TD
Brown, Dave, NY-G	50	170	3.4	18	0
Lynn, Anthony, S.F.	24	164	6.8	67	0
Lee, Amp, Min.	51	161	3.2	12	0
Davis, Stephen, Was.	23	139	6.0	39t	2
Graham, Scottie, Min.	57	138	2.4	12	0
Favre, Brett, G.B.	49	136	2.8	23	2
Robinson, Greg, St.L	32	134	4.2	24	1
Henderson, William, G.B.	39	130	3.3	14	0
Dilfer, Trent, T.B.	32	124	3.9	19	0
Logan, Marc, Was.	20	111	5.6	36t	2
Ellison, Jerry, T.B.	35	106	3.0	13	0
Jervey, Travis, G.B.	26	106	4.1	12	0
Shepherd, Leslie, Was.	6	96	16.0	32t	2
Downs, Gary, NY-G	29	94	3.2	27	0
Hicks, Michael, Chi.	27	92	3.4	23	0
Johnson, Brad, Min.	34	90	2.6	13	1
Graham, Kent, Ariz	21	87	4.1	19	0
Rivers, Ron, Det.	19	86	4.5	26	0
Mitchell, Scott, Det.	37	83	2.2	9	4
Walker, Herschel, Dal.	10	83	8.3	39t	1
Ismail, Raghib, Car.	8	80	10.0	35t	1
Way, Charles, NY-G	22	79	3.6	18	1
Rice, Jerry, S.F.	11	77	7.0	38	1
Carter, Dexter, S.F.	19	66	3.5	18	1
Detmer, Ty, Phi.	31	59	1.9	9	1
Hebert, Bobby, Atl.	15	59	3.9	25	1
Neal, Lorenzo, N.O.	21	58	2.8	11	1
Esiason, Boomer, Ariz	15	52	3.5	13	1
Whittle, Ricky, N.O.	20	52	2.6	15	0
Small, Torrance, N.O.	4	51	12.8	22	1
Conway, Curtis, Chi.	8	50	6.3	19	0
Johnston, Daryl, Dal.	22	48	2.2	7	0
Hunter, Ernest, Bal.-N.O.	15	44	2.9	9	0
Brohm, Jeff, S.F.	16	43	2.7	22	0
Carter, Tony, Chi.	11	43	3.9	23	0
Aikman, Troy, Dal.	35	42	1.2	10	1
Lynch, John, T.B.	1	40	40.0	40	0
Lyle, Keith, St.L	3	39	13.0	20	0
Turner, Kevin, Phi.	18	39	2.2	7	0
Collins, Kerry, Car.	32	38	1.2	14	0
Majkowski, Don, Det.	14	38	2.7	12	0
Philyaw, Dino, Car.	12	38	3.2	8	1
Morton, Johnnie, Det.	9	35	3.9	18	0
Moore, Jerald, St.L	11	32	2.9	14	0
Peete, Rodney, Phi.	20	31	1.6	11	1
Brown, Derek, N.O.	13	30	2.3	12	0
Evans, Chuck, Min.	13	29	2.2	9	0
Barnhardt, Tommy, T.B.	2	27	13.5	25	0
Thompson, Leroy, T.B.	14	25	1.8	10	0
Elias, Keith, NY-G	9	24	2.7	8	0
Grbac, Elvis, S.F.	23	21	0.9	12	2
Timpson, Michael, Chi.	3	21	7.0	13	0
Beuerlein, Steve, Car.	12	17	1.4	13	0
Frerotte, Gus, Was.	28	16	0.6	17	0
Smith, Cedric, Ariz	14	15	1.1	3	1
Martin, Jamie, St.L	7	14	2.0	11	0
Perriman, Brett, Det.	1	13	13.0	13	0
Krieg, Dave, Chi.	16	12	0.8	2	1
Williams, Kevin, Dal.	4	11	2.8	9	0
George, Jeff, Atl.	5	10	2.0	5	0
Walsh, Steve, St.L	6	10	1.7	13	0
Palmer, David, Min.	2	9	4.5	8	0
Huntley, Richard, Atl.	2	8	4.0	5	0
Metcalf, Eric, Atl.	3	8	2.7	4	0
Griffith, Howard, Car.	12	7	0.6	3	1
Hayes, Mercury, N.O.	2	7	3.5	5	0
Kanell, Danny, NY-G	7	6	0.9	13	0
Moon, Warren, Min.	9	6	0.7	5	0
Nussmeier, Doug, N.O.	3	6	2.0	6	0
Stone, Dwight, Car.	1	6	6.0	6	0
Harris, Derrick, St.L	3	5	1.7	3	0
Wilson, Wade, Dal.	4	5	1.3	8	0
Bruce, Isaac, St.L	1	4	4.0	4	0
Kramer, Erik, Chi.	8	4	0.5	3	0
Everett, Jim, N.O.	22	3	0.1	3	0
Ross, Jermaine, St.L	1	3	3.0	3t	1
Sauerbrun, Todd, Chi.	1	3	3.0	3	0
Brooks, Robert, G.B.	4	2	0.5	6	0
Calloway, Chris, NY-G	1	2	2.0	2	0
DeRamus, Lee, N.O.	1	2	2.0	2	0
Lynch, Eric, Det.	2	2	1.0	2	0
Matthews, Shane, Chi.	1	2	2.0	2t	1

	Att.	Yards	Avg.	Long	TD
Sanders, Deion, Dal.	3	2	0.7	3	0
Westbrook, Michael, Was.	2	2	1.0	2	0
Green, Willie, Car.	1	1	1.0	1	0
McDaniel, Randall, Min.	2	1	0.5	1	0
Pierce, Aaron, NY-G	1	1	1.0	1t	1
Feagles, Jeff, Ariz	1	0	0.0	0	0
Landeta, Sean, St.L	2	0	0.0	0	0
Shuler, Heath, Was.	1	0	0.0	0	0
Turk, Matt, Was.	1	0	0.0	0	0
McMahon, Jim, G.B.	4	-1	-.2	2	0
Muhammad, Muhsin, Car.	1	-1	-1.0	-1	0
Thomas, J.T., St.L	1	-1	-1.0	-1	0
Weldon, Casey, T.B.	2	-1	-.5	0	0
Williams, Karl, T.B.	1	-3	-3.0	-3	0
Fryar, Irving, Phi.	1	-4	-4.0	-4	0
Guess, Terry, N.O.	2	-4	-2.0	-1	0
McKinnon, Ronald, Ariz	1	-4	-4.0	-4	0
Sanders, Frank, Ariz	2	-4	-2.0	1	0
Edwards, Anthony, Ariz	1	-8	-8.0	-8	0
Hawkins, Courtney, T.B.	1	-13	-13.0	-13	0
Jett, John, Dal.	1	-23	-23.0	-23	0

t = Touchdown
Leader based on most yards gained

PASSING

Highest Rating
NFC: 97.2—Steve Young, San Francisco
AFC: 89.2—John Elway, Denver

Completion Percentage
NFC: 67.7—Steve Young, San Francisco
AFC: 63.4—Mark Brunell, Jacksonville

Attempts
AFC: 623—Drew Bledsoe, New England
NFC: 543—Brett Favre, Green Bay

Completions
AFC: 373—Drew Bledsoe, New England
NFC: 325—Brett Favre, Green Bay

Yards
AFC: 4367—Mark Brunell, Jacksonville
NFC: 3899—Brett Favre, Green Bay

Yards, Game
NFC: 522—Boomer Eseason, Arizona at Washington, November 10 (35-59, 3 TD)
AFC: 432—Mark Brunell, Jacksonville at New England, September 22 (23-29, 3 TD)

Longest
AFC: 95—Todd Collins (to Quinn Early), Buffalo at Indianapolis, December 1 - TD
NFC: 82—Brad Johnson (to Jake Reed), Minnesota at Oakland, November 17 - TD

Yards Per Attempt
AFC: 7.84—Mark Brunell, Jacksonville
NFC: 7.63—Steve Young, San Francisco

Touchdown Passes
NFC: 39—Brett Favre, Green Bay
AFC: 33—Vinny Testaverde, Baltimore

Touchdown Passes, Game
NFC: 4—Stan Humphries, San Diego at Oakland, September 22 (18-25, 226 yards)
John Elway, Denver vs. San Diego, October 6, (32-41, 323 yards)
Drew Bledsoe, New England at Baltimore, October 6 (25-39, 310 yards)
Jeff Hostetler, Oakland vs. Detroit, October 13 (27-38, 295 yards)
Vinny Testaverde, Baltimore at Denver, October 20 (27-45, 338 yards)
Jeff Blake, Cincinnati vs. Atlanta, November 24 (21-36, 349 yards)
Drew Bledsoe, New England at San Diego, December 1 (19-29, 232 yards)
AFC: 4—Brett Favre, Green Bay at Tampa Bay, September 1 20-27, 247 yards)
Scott Mitchell, Detroit vs. Chicago, September 22 24-34, 336 yards)
Kent Graham, Arizona vs. St. Louis, September 29 37-58, 366 yards)
Brett Favre, Green Bay at Seattle, September 29 20-34, 209 yards)
Brett Favre, Green Bay at Chicago, October 6 18-27, 246 yards)
Ty Detmer, Philadelphia vs. Miami, October 20 18-24, 226 yards)
Brett Favre, Green Bay vs. Detroit, November 3 24-35, 281 yards)
Brad Johnson, Minnesota vs. Arizona, December 1 19-26, 238 yards)
Brett Favre, Green Bay vs. Denver, December 8 20-38, 280 yards)

Lowest Interception Percentage
NFC: 1.9—Steve Young, San Francisco
AFC: 2.4—Drew Bledsoe, New England

Team Champion (Most Net Yards)
AFC: 4110—Jacksonville
NFC: 3745—Philadelphia

AFC PASSING—TEAM

	Att.	Comp.	Pct. Comp.	Gross Yards	Sacked	Yds. Lost	Net Yards	Yds./ Att.	Yds./ Comp.	TD	Pct. TD	Long	Int.	Pct. Int.
Jacksonville	557	353	63.4	4367	50	257	4110	7.84	12.37	19	3.41	62	20	3.6
Baltimore	570	335	58.8	4274	38	296	3978	7.50	12.76	34	5.96	86t	20	3.5
New England	628	374	59.6	4091	30	190	3901	6.51	10.94	27	4.30	84t	15	2.4
N.Y. Jets	629	339	53.9	3911	41	286	3625	6.22	11.54	22	3.50	78t	30	4.8
Miami	504	300	59.5	3783	36	240	3543	7.51	12.61	22	4.37	74t	11	2.2
Cincinnati	563	316	56.1	3726	47	294	3432	6.62	11.79	25	4.44	61t	16	2.8
Denver	536	327	61.0	3662	31	233	3429	6.83	11.20	26	4.85	51	17	3.2
San Diego	577	314	54.4	3654	33	296	3358	6.33	11.64	23	3.99	63t	21	3.6
Buffalo	483	279	57.8	3558	48	340	3218	7.37	12.75	18	3.73	95t	24	5.0
Indianapolis	537	311	57.9	3544	43	248	3296	6.60	11.40	16	2.98	51	11	2.0
Oakland	533	311	58.3	3327	45	249	3078	6.24	10.70	28	5.25	62t	19	3.6
Houston	463	272	58.7	3296	34	198	3098	7.12	12.12	22	4.75	83t	15	3.2
Seattle	494	261	52.8	3216	38	189	3027	6.51	12.32	14	2.83	80t	17	3.4
Kansas City	530	290	54.7	3093	27	203	2890	5.84	10.67	18	3.40	69	14	2.6
Pittsburgh	456	246	53.9	2990	21	149	2841	6.56	12.15	15	3.29	70t	19	4.2
AFC Total	8060	4628	—	54492	562	3668	50824	—	—	329	—	95t	269	—
AFC Average	537.3	308.5	57.4	3632.8	37.5	244.5	3388.3	6.76	11.77	21.9	4.1	—	17.9	3.3

NFC PASSING—TEAM

	Att.	Comp.	Pct. Comp.	Gross Yards	Sacked	Yds. Lost	Net Yards	Yds./ Att.	Yds./ Comp.	TD	Pct. TD	Long	Int.	Pct. Int.
Philadelphia	548	328	59.9	3979	39	234	3745	7.26	12.13	19	3.47	62	18	3.3
Green Bay	548	328	59.9	3938	40	241	3697	7.19	12.01	39	7.12	80t	13	2.4
Arizona	613	336	54.8	3917	36	229	3688	6.39	11.66	23	3.75	69	21	3.4
Atlanta	600	356	59.3	3909	42	254	3655	6.52	10.98	26	4.33	67	30	5.0
Minnesota	561	331	59.0	3899	34	241	3658	6.95	11.78	24	4.28	82t	19	3.4
San Francisco	550	358	65.1	3859	42	200	3659	7.02	10.78	24	4.36	52	16	2.9
Detroit	541	309	57.1	3463	46	260	3203	6.40	11.21	20	3.70	62t	21	3.9
Washington	471	270	57.3	3453	22	134	3319	7.33	12.79	12	2.55	52t	11	2.3
Chicago	551	318	57.7	3350	23	165	3185	6.08	10.53	19	3.45	58t	18	3.3
Carolina	487	273	56.1	3333	36	250	3083	6.84	12.21	22	4.52	55	11	2.3
Dallas	487	307	63.0	3249	19	127	3122	6.67	10.58	12	2.46	61	14	2.9
St. Louis	481	249	51.8	3144	57	379	2765	6.54	12.63	18	3.74	77t	23	4.8
New Orleans	515	295	57.3	3069	22	171	2898	5.96	10.40	13	2.52	57t	17	3.3
Tampa Bay	494	274	55.5	2944	30	217	2727	5.96	10.74	12	2.43	45	20	4.0
N.Y. Giants	459	238	51.9	2663	56	324	2339	5.80	11.19	14	3.05	37t	21	4.6
NFC Total	7906	4570	—	52169	544	3426	48743	—	—	297	—	82t	273	—
NFC Average	527.1	304.7	57.8	3477.9	36.3	228.4	3249.5	6.60	11.42	19.8	3.8	—	18.2	3.5
League Total	15966	9198	—	106661	1106	7094	99567	—	—	626	—	95t	542	—
League Average	532.2	306.6	57.6	3555.4	36.9	236.5	3318.9	6.68	11.60	20.9	3.9	—	18.1	3.4

Leader based on net yards

NFL TOP TEN PASSERS

	Att.	Comp.	Pct. Comp.	Yds.	Avg. Gain	TD	Pct. TD	Long	Int.	Pct. Int.	Sack	Yds. Lost	Rating Points
Young, Steve, S.F.	316	214	67.7	2410	7.63	14	4.4	52	6	1.9	34	160	97.2
Favre, Brett, G.B.	543	325	59.9	3899	7.18	39	7.2	80t	13	2.4	40	241	95.8
Johnson, Brad, Min.	311	195	62.7	2258	7.26	17	5.5	82t	10	3.2	15	119	89.4
Elway, John, Den.	466	287	61.6	3328	7.14	26	5.6	51	14	3.0	26	194	89.2
Testaverde, Vinny, Bal.	549	325	59.2	4177	7.61	33	6.0	86t	19	3.5	34	270	88.7
Marino, Dan, Mia.	373	221	59.2	2795	7.49	17	4.6	74t	9	2.4	18	131	87.8
Brunell, Mark, Jac.	557	353	63.4	4367	7.84	19	3.4	62	20	3.6	50	257	84.0
Bledsoe, Drew, N.E.	623	373	59.9	4086	6.56	27	4.3	84t	15	2.4	30	190	83.7
Hostetler, Jeff, Oak.	402	242	60.2	2548	6.34	23	5.7	62t	14	3.5	32	181	83.2
Detmer, Ty, Phi.	401	238	59.4	2911	7.26	15	3.7	42	13	3.2	27	171	80.8

AFC PASSING—INDIVIDUAL

	Att.	Comp.	Pct. Comp.	Yds.	Avg. Gain	TD	Pct. TD	Long	Int.	Pct. Int.	Sack	Yds. Lost	Rating Points
Elway, John, Den.	466	287	61.6	3328	7.14	26	5.6	51	14	3.0	26	194	89.2
Testaverde, Vinny, Bal.	549	325	59.2	4177	7.61	33	6.0	86t	19	3.5	34	270	88.7
Marino, Dan, Mia.	373	221	59.2	2795	7.49	17	4.6	74t	9	2.4	18	131	87.8
Brunell, Mark, Jac.	557	353	63.4	4367	7.84	19	3.4	62	20	3.6	50	257	84.0
Bledsoe, Drew, N.E.	623	373	59.9	4086	6.56	27	4.3	84t	15	2.4	30	190	83.7
Hostetler, Jeff, Oak.	402	242	60.2	2548	6.34	23	5.7	62t	14	3.5	32	181	83.2
Blake, Jeff, Cin.	549	308	56.1	3624	6.60	24	4.4	61t	11	3.4	25	153	79.7
Chandler, Chris, Hou.	320	184	57.5	2099	6.56	16	5.0	63t	13	3.1	20	187	76.7
Humphries, Stan, S.D.	416	232	55.8	2670	6.42	18	4.3	63t	13	3.1	20	187	76.7
Harbaugh, Jim, Ind.	405	232	57.3	2630	6.49	13	3.2	51	11	2.7	36	190	76.3
Kelly, Jim, Buf.	379	222	58.6	2810	7.41	14	3.7	67t	19	5.0	37	287	73.2
Tomczak, Mike, Pit.	401	222	55.4	2767	6.90	15	3.7	70t	17	4.2	16	105	71.8
Reich, Frank, NY-J	331	175	52.9	2205	6.66	15	4.5	52t	16	4.8	14	94	68.9
Bono, Steve, K.C.	438	235	53.7	2572	5.87	12	2.7	69	13	3.0	22	161	68.0
Mirer, Rick, Sea.	265	136	51.3	1546	5.83	5	1.9	60	12	4.5	22	84	56.6
Nonqualifiers													
Kosar, Bernie, Mia.	32	24	75.0	208	6.50	1	3.1	20	0	0.0	6	34	102.1
Gannon, Rich, K.C.	90	54	60.0	491	5.46	6	6.7	25	1	1.1	5	42	92.4
McNair, Steve, Hou.	143	88	61.5	1197	8.37	6	4.2	83t	4	2.8	9	45	90.6
Friesz, John, Sea.	211	120	56.9	1629	7.72	8	3.8	80t	4	1.9	12	77	86.4
Erickson, Craig, Mia.	99	55	55.6	780	7.88	4	4.0	61	2	2.0	11	72	86.3
Justin, Paul, Ind.	127	74	58.3	839	6.61	2	1.6	38	0	0.0	7	58	83.4
Collins, Todd, Buf.	99	55	55.6	739	7.46	4	4.0	95t	5	5.1	11	53	71.9
O'Donnell, Neil, NY-J	188	110	58.5	1147	6.10	4	2.1	78t	7	3.7	18	127	67.8
Hobert, Billy Joe, Oak.	104	57	54.8	667	6.41	4	3.8	51	5	4.8	9	52	67.3
Miller, Jim, Pit.	25	13	52.0	123	4.92	0	0.0	17	0	0.0	2	7	65.9
Wilhelm, Erik, Cin.	13	7	53.8	90	6.92	1	7.7	38	2	15.4	3	16	61.9
Salisbury, Sean, S.D.	161	82	50.9	984	6.11	5	3.1	56	8	5.0	13	109	59.6
Musgrave, Bill, Den.	52	31	59.6	276	5.31	0	0.0	46	2	3.8	4	32	57.9
Zeier, Eric, Bal.	21	10	47.6	97	4.62	1	4.8	15	1	4.8	4	26	57.0
Klingler, David, Oak.	24	10	41.7	87	3.63	0	0.0	20	0	0.0	4	16	51.9
Foley, Glenn, NY-J	110	54	49.1	559	5.08	3	2.7	46t	7	6.4	9	65	46.7
Lewis, Jeff, Den.	17	9	52.9	58	3.41	0	0.0	11	1	5.9	1	7	35.9
Torretta, Gino, Sea.	16	5	31.3	41	2.56	1	6.3	32t	1	6.3	3	17	35.4
Stewart, Kordell, Pit.	30	11	36.7	100	3.33	0	0.0	15	2	6.7	3	37	18.8

Fewer than 10 attempts	Att.	Comp.	Pct. Comp.	Yds.	Avg. Gain	TD	Pct. TD	Long	Int.	Pct. Int.	Sack	Yds. Lost	Rating Points
Abdul-Jabbar, Karim, Mia.	0	0	—	0	—	0	—	—	0	—	1	3	-1.0
Allen, Marcus, K.C.	1	0	0.0	0	0.00	0	0.0	0	0	0.0	0	0	39.6
Bell, Kerwin, Ind.	5	5	100.0	75	15.00	1	20.0	30	0	0.0	0	0	158.3
Craver, Aaron, Den.	1	0	0.0	0	0.00	0	0.0	0	0	0.0	0	0	39.6
Gelbaugh, Stan, Sea.	2	0	0.0	0	0.00	0	0.0	0	0	0.0	0	0	39.6
Grier, Marrio, N.E.	1	0	0.0	0	0.00	0	0.0	0	0	0.0	1	11	39.6
Hobbs, Daryl, Oak.	1	1	100.0	7	7.00	0	0.0	7	0	0.0	0	0	95.8
Hughes, Danan, K.C.	1	1	100.0	30	30.00	0	0.0	30	0	0.0	0	0	118.8
Meggett, Dave, N.E.	1	0	0.0	0	0.00	0	0.0	0	0	0.0	0	0	39.6
Pickens, Carl, Cin.	1	1	100.0	12	12.00	0	0.0	12	0	0.0	0	0	116.7
Tupa, Tom, N.E.	2	0	0.0	0	0.00	0	0.0	0	0	0.0	0	0	39.6
Van Pelt, Alex, Buf.	5	2	40.0	9	1.80	0	0.0	5	0	0.0	0	0	47.9
Williams, Harvey, Oak.	2	1	50.0	18	9.00	1	50.0	18t	0	0.0	0	0	120.8
Zolak, Scott, N.E.	1	1	100.0	5	5.00	0	0.0	5	0	0.0	0	0	87.5

t = Touchdown
Leader based on rating points, minimum 224 attempts

NFC PASSING—INDIVIDUAL

	Att.	Comp.	Pct. Comp.	Yds.	Avg. Gain	TD	Pct. TD	Long	Int.	Pct. Int.	Sack	Yds. Lost	Rating Points
Young, Steve, S.F.	316	214	67.7	2410	7.63	14	4.4	52	6	1.9	34	160	97.2
Favre, Brett, G.B.	543	325	59.9	3899	7.18	39	7.2	80t	13	2.4	40	241	95.8
Johnson, Brad, Min.	311	195	62.7	2258	7.26	17	5.5	82t	10	3.2	15	119	89.4
Detmer, Ty, Phi.	401	238	59.4	2911	7.26	15	3.7	42	13	3.2	27	171	80.8
Aikman, Troy, Dal.	465	296	63.7	3126	6.72	12	2.6	61	13	2.8	18	120	80.1
Collins, Kerry, Car.	364	204	56.0	2454	6.74	14	3.8	55	9	2.5	18	114	79.4
Frerotte, Gus, Was.	470	270	57.4	3453	7.35	12	2.6	52t	11	2.3	22	134	79.3
Krieg, Dave, Chi.	377	226	59.9	2278	6.04	14	3.7	53t	12	3.2	14	104	76.3
Graham, Kent, Ariz	274	146	53.3	1624	5.93	12	4.4	69	7	2.6	19	120	75.1
Mitchell, Scott, Det.	437	253	57.9	2917	6.68	17	3.9	62t	17	3.9	36	199	74.9
Hebert, Bobby, Atl.	488	294	60.2	3152	6.46	22	4.5	57	25	5.1	27	150	72.9
Banks, Tony, St.L	368	192	52.2	2544	6.91	15	4.1	77t	15	4.1	48	306	71.0
Esiason, Boomer, Ariz	339	190	56.0	2293	6.76	11	3.2	64t	14	4.1	17	109	70.6
Everett, Jim, N.O.	464	267	57.5	2797	6.03	12	2.6	51	16	3.4	19	154	69.4
Moon, Warren, Min.	247	134	54.3	1610	6.52	7	2.8	54t	9	3.6	19	122	68.7
Dilfer, Trent, T.B.	482	267	55.4	2859	5.93	12	2.5	45	19	3.9	28	207	64.8
Brown, Dave, NY-G	398	214	53.8	2412	6.06	12	3.0	37t	20	5.0	49	276	61.3
Nonqualifiers													
Matthews, Shane, Chi.	17	13	76.5	158	9.29	1	5.9	26	0	0.0	1	3	124.1
Rypien, Mark, Phi.	13	10	76.9	76	5.85	1	7.7	16	0	0.0	0	0	116.2
Beuerlein, Steve, Car.	123	69	56.1	879	7.15	8	6.5	40t	2	1.6	18	136	93.5
Martin, Jamie, St.L	34	23	67.6	241	7.09	3	8.8	22t	2	5.9	4	34	92.9
Brohm, Jeff, S.F.	34	21	61.8	189	5.56	1	2.9	49	0	0.0	2	10	86.5
George, Jeff, Atl.	99	56	56.6	698	7.05	3	3.0	67	3	3.0	11	84	76.1
Peete, Rodney, Phi.	134	80	59.7	992	7.40	3	2.2	62	5	3.7	11	53	74.6
Grbac, Elvis, S.F.	197	122	61.9	1236	6.27	8	4.1	40	10	5.1	6	30	72.2
Nussmeier, Doug, N.O.	50	28	56.0	272	5.44	1	2.0	57t	1	2.0	3	17	69.8
Majkowski, Don, Det.	102	55	53.9	554	5.43	3	2.9	27	3	2.9	10	61	67.2
Kramer, Erik, Chi.	150	73	48.7	781	5.21	3	2.0	58t	6	4.0	7	53	54.3
Kanell, Danny, NY-G	60	23	38.3	227	3.78	1	1.7	25	1	1.7	7	48	48.4
Nagle, Browning, Atl.	13	6	46.2	59	4.54	1	7.7	17	2	15.4	4	20	45.5
Wilson, Wade, Dal.	18	8	44.4	79	4.39	0	0.0	20	1	5.6	1	7	34.3
Walsh, Steve, St.L	77	33	42.9	344	4.47	0	0.0	32	5	6.5	4	27	29.4
Fewer than 10 attempts													
Bruce, Isaac, St.L	2	1	50.0	15	7.50	0	0.0	15	1	50.0	0	0	35.4
Conway, Curtis, Chi.	1	1	100.0	33	33.00	1	100.0	33t	0	0.0	0	0	158.3
Garrett, Jason, Dal.	3	3	100.0	44	14.67	0	0.0	32	0	0.0	0	0	118.8
Hentrich, Craig, G.B.	1	0	0.0	0	0.00	0	0.0	0	0	0.0	0	0	39.6
Hoying, Bobby, Phi.	0	0	—	0	—	0	—	—	0	—	0	0	39.6
Hunter, Ernest, N.O.	1	0	0.0	0	0.00	0	0.0	0	0	0.0	1	10	-1.0
Kirby, Terry, S.F.	2	1	50.0	24	12.00	1	50.0	24t	0	0.0	0	0	133.3
McMahon, Jim, G.B.	4	3	75.0	39	9.75	0	0.0	24	0	0.0	0	0	105.2
Milanovich, Scott, T.B.	3	2	66.7	9	3.00	0	0.0	8	0	0.0	0	0	70.1
Mitchell, Brian, Was.	1	0	0.0	0	0.00	0	0.0	0	0	0.0	0	0	39.6
Phillips, Lawrence, St.L	0	0	—	0	—	0	—	—	0	—	1	12	-1.0
Rice, Jerry, S.F.	1	0	0.0	0	0.00	0	0.0	0	0	0.0	0	0	39.6
Royals, Mark, Det.	1	1	100.0	-8	-8.00	0	0.0	-8	0	0.0	0	0	79.2
Sanders, Barry, Det.	1	0	0.0	0	0.00	0	0.0	0	1	100.0	0	0	39.6
Sauerbrun, Todd, Chi.	2	2	100.0	63	31.50	0	0.0	47	0	0.0	0	0	118.8
Stenstrom, Steve, Chi.	4	3	75.0	37	9.25	0	0.0	28	0	0.0	1	5	103.1
Walker, Jay, Min.	2	2	100.0	31	15.50	0	0.0	19	0	0.0	0	0	118.8
Walsh, Chris, Min.	1	0	0.0	0	0.00	0	0.0	0	0	0.0	0	0	39.6
Weldon, Casey, T.B.	9	5	55.6	76	8.44	0	0.0	42	1	11.1	2	10	44.0
Wheatley, Tyrone, NY-G	1	1	100.0	24	24.00	1	100.0	24t	0	0.0	0	0	158.3
Williams, Sherman, Dal.	1	0	0.0	0	0.00	0	0.0	0	0	0.0	0	0	39.6

t = Touchdown
Leader based on rating points, minimum 224 attempts

PASS RECEIVING

Receptions
NFC: 108—Jerry Rice, San Francisco
AFC: 100—Carl Pickens, Cincinnati

Receptions, Game
AFC: 16—Keenan McCardell, Jacksonville at St. Louis, October 20
(232 yards)
AFC: 13—Larry Centers, Arizona vs. St. Louis, September 29
(83 yards - TD)

Yards
NFC: 1338—Isaac Bruce, St. Louis
AFC: 1244—Jimmy Smith, Jacksonville

Yards, Game
AFC: 232—Keenan McCardell, Jacksonville at St. Louis, October 20
(16 receptions)
NFC: 229—Isaac Bruce, St. Louis at Baltimore, October 27
(11 receptions - TD)

Longest
AFC: 95—Quinn Early (from Todd Collins), Buffalo at Indianapolis
December 1 - TD
NFC: 82—Jake Reed (from Brad Johnson), Minnesota at Oakland,
November 17 - TD

Yards Per Reception
NFC: 19.5—Henry Ellard, Washington
AFC: 18.4—Chris Sanders, Houston

Touchdowns
AFC: 14—Michael Jackson, Baltimore
Tony Martin, San Diego
NFC: 11—Irving Fryar, Philadelphia

Team Leaders, Receptions
AFC: BALTIMORE: 76, Michael Jackson; BUFFALO: 66, Andre Reed; CINCIN-
NATI: 100, Carl Pickens; DENVER: 80, Shannon Sharpe; HOUSTON:
53, Frank Wycheck; INDIANAPOLIS: 64, Marvin Harrison; JACK-
SONVILLE: 85, Keenan McCardell; KANSAS CITY: 60, Kimble Anders;
MIAMI: 74, O.J. McDuffie; NEW ENGLAND: 90, Terry Glenn; N.Y. JETS:
84, Wayne Chrebet; OAKLAND: 90, Tim Brown; PITTSBURGH: 72, An-
dre Hastings; SAN DIEGO: 85, Tony Martin; SEATTLE: 57, Joey Gal-
loway
NFC: ARIZONA: 99, Larry Centers; ATLANTA: 75, Bert Emanuel; CAROLINA:
61, Wesley Walls; CHICAGO: 81, Curtis Conway; DALLAS: 64, Michael
Irvin; DETROIT: 106, Herman Moore; GREEN BAY: 56, Antonio Free-
man; MINNESOTA: 96, Cris Carter; NEW ORLEANS: 50, Torrance
Small; N.Y. GIANTS: 53, Chris Calloway, Thomas Lewis; PHILADEL-
PHIA: 88, Irving Fryar; ST. LOUIS: 84, Isaac Bruce; SAN FRANCISCO:
108, Jerry Rice; TAMPA BAY: 65, Mike Alstott; WASHINGTON: 52, Henry
Ellard

NFL TOP TEN PASS RECEIVERS

	No.	Yards	Avg.	Long	TD
Rice, Jerry, S.F.	108	1254	11.6	39	8
Moore, Herman, Det.	106	1296	12.2	50t	9
Pickens, Carl, Cin.	100	1180	11.8	61t	12
Centers, Larry, Ariz	99	766	7.7	39	7
Carter, Cris, Min.	96	1163	12.1	43t	10
Perriman, Brett, Det.	94	1021	10.9	44	5
Brown, Tim, Oak.	90	1104	12.3	42t	9
Glenn, Terry, N.E.	90	1132	12.6	37t	6
Fryar, Irving, Phi.	88	1195	13.6	42	11
Martin, Tony, S.D.	85	1171	13.8	55	14
McCardell, Keenan, Jac.	85	1129	13.3	52	3

NFL TOP TEN RECEIVERS BY YARDS

	Yards	No	Avg.	Long	TD
Bruce, Isaac, St.L	1338	84	15.9	70	7
Reed, Jake, Min.	1320	72	18.3	82t	7
Moore, Herman, Det.	1296	106	12.2	50t	9
Rice, Jerry, S.F.	1254	108	11.6	39	8
Smith, Jimmy, Jac.	1244	83	15.0	62	7
Jackson, Michael, Bal.	1201	76	15.8	86t	14
Fryar, Irving, Phi.	1195	88	13.6	42	11
Pickens, Carl, Cin.	1180	100	11.8	61t	12
Martin, Tony, S.D.	1171	85	13.8	55	14
Carter, Cris, Min.	1163	96	12.1	43t	10

AFC RECEIVERS—INDIVIDUAL

	No.	Yards	Avg.	Long	TD
Pickens, Carl, Cin.	100	1180	11.8	61t	12
Glenn, Terry, N.E.	90	1132	12.6	37t	6
Brown, Tim, Oak.	90	1104	12.3	42t	9
Martin, Tony, S.D.	85	1171	13.8	55	14
McCardell, Keenan, Jac.	85	1129	13.3	52	3
Chrebet, Wayne, NY-J	84	909	10.8	44	3
Smith, Jimmy, Jac.	83	1244	15.0	62	7

	No.	Yards	Avg.	Long	TD
Sharpe, Shannon, Den.	80	1062	13.3	51	10
Jackson, Michael, Bal.	76	1201	15.8	86t	14
McDuffie, O. J., Mia.	74	918	12.4	36	8
Hastings, Andre, Pit.	72	739	10.3	38	6
Reed, Andre, Buf.	66	1036	15.7	67t	6
Harrison, Marvin, Ind.	64	836	13.1	41	8
Johnson, Keyshawn, NY-J	63	844	13.4	50	8
Alexander, Derrick, Bal.	62	1099	17.7	64t	9
Coates, Ben, N.E.	62	682	11.0	84t	9
Fletcher, Terrell, S.D.	61	476	7.8	41	2
Johnson, Charles, Pit.	60	1008	16.8	70t	3
Anders, Kimble, K.C.	60	529	8.8	45	2
Scott, Darnay, Cin.	58	833	14.4	50t	5
Galloway, Joey, Sea.	57	987	17.3	65t	7
Miller, Anthony, Den.	56	735	13.1	46	3
Faulk, Marshall, Ind.	56	428	7.6	30	0
Kinchen, Brian, Bal.	55	581	10.6	29	1
Dawkins, Sean, Ind.	54	751	13.9	42	1
Wycheck, Frank, Hou.	53	511	9.6	29	6
Mitchell, Pete, Jac.	52	575	11.1	30	1
Early, Quinn, Buf.	50	798	16.0	95t	4
Graham, Jeff, NY-J	50	788	15.8	78t	6
Jefferson, Shawn, N.E.	50	771	15.4	42	4
Penn, Chris, K.C.	49	628	12.8	22	5
Sanders, Chris, Hou.	48	882	18.4	83t	4
McCaffrey, Ed, Den.	48	553	11.5	39t	7
Johnson, Lonnie, Buf.	46	457	9.9	33	0
Martin, Curtis, N.E.	46	333	7.2	41	3
Hobbs, Daryl, Oak.	44	423	9.6	29	3
Anderson, Richie, NY-J	44	385	8.8	48	0
Jett, James, Oak.	43	601	14.0	58t	4
Blades, Brian, Sea.	43	556	12.9	80t	2
Dilger, Ken, Ind.	42	503	12.0	51	4
Harmon, Ronnie, Hou.	42	488	11.6	43	2
Jones, Charlie, S.D.	41	524	12.8	63t	4
Warren, Chris, Sea.	40	273	6.8	33	0
Davis, Willie, Hou.	39	464	11.9	49	6
Craver, Aaron, Den.	39	297	7.6	39t	1
Turner, Floyd, Bal.	38	461	12.1	27t	2
McGee, Tony, Cin.	38	446	11.7	22	4
Barnett, Fred, Mia.	36	562	15.6	66	3
Coleman, Andre, S.D.	36	486	13.5	50	2
Davis, Terrell, Den.	36	310	8.6	23	2
Russell, Derek, Hou.	34	421	12.4	29	2
Dudley, Rickey, Oak.	34	386	11.4	62t	4
Jackson, Willie, Jac.	33	486	14.7	58	3
Pritchett, Stanley, Mia.	33	354	10.7	74t	1
Meggett, Dave, N.E.	33	292	8.8	26	0
Gash, Sam, N.E.	33	276	8.4	28	2
Dunn, David, Cin.	32	509	15.9	40	1
Slaughter, Webster, NY-J	32	434	13.6	53	2
Byars, Keith, Mia.-N.E.	32	289	9.0	27	2
Bieniemy, Eric, Cin.	32	272	8.5	42	0
Fenner, Derrick, Oak.	31	252	8.1	23t	4
Byner, Earnest, Bal.	30	270	9.0	40	1
Stewart, James, Jac.	30	177	5.9	21t	2
Drayton, Troy, St.L-Mia.	28	331	11.8	51	0
LaChapelle, Sean, K.C.	27	422	15.6	69	2
Allen, Marcus, K.C.	27	270	10.0	59	0
Crumpler, Carlester, Sea.	26	258	9.9	26	0
Thomas, Thurman, Buf.	26	254	9.8	69	0
Morris, Bam, Bal.	25	242	9.7	52t	1
Pupunu, Alfred, S.D.	24	271	11.3	41	1
Proehl, Ricky, Sea.	23	309	13.4	56	2
George, Eddie, Hou.	23	182	7.9	17	0
Abdul-Jabbar, Karim, Mia.	23	139	6.0	23	0
Warren, Lamont, Ind.	22	174	7.9	17	0
Carter, Ki-Jana, Cin.	22	169	7.7	20	1
Kaufman, Napoleon, Oak.	22	143	6.5	19	1
Williams, Harvey, Oak.	22	143	6.5	20	0
Bettis, Jerome, Pit.	22	122	5.5	16	0
Hill, Randal, Mia.	21	409	19.5	61	4
Tasker, Steve, Buf.	21	372	17.7	62	3
Pritchard, Mike, Sea.	21	328	15.6	44	1
Vanover, Tamarick, K.C.	21	241	11.5	24	1
Brown, Troy, N.E.	21	222	10.6	38	0
Parmalee, Bernie, Mia.	21	189	9.0	17	0
McNair, Todd, K.C.	21	181	8.6	29	1
McPhail, Jerris, Mia.	20	282	14.1	52	0
Moulds, Eric, Buf.	20	279	14.0	47	2
May, Deems, S.D.	19	188	9.9	39	0
Cline, Tony, Buf.	19	117	6.2	15	1

	No.	Yards	Avg.	Long	TD
Bailey, Aaron, Ind.	18	302	16.8	40	0
Fauria, Christian, Sea.	18	214	11.9	23t	1
Stablein, Brian, Ind.	18	192	10.7	30t	1
Johnson, Reginald, K.C.	18	189	10.5	26	1
Stewart, Kordell, Pit.	17	293	17.2	48	3
Hughes, Danan, K.C.	17	167	9.8	26	1
Brown, Derek, Jac.	17	141	8.3	16	0
Van Dyke, Alex, NY-J	17	118	6.9	12	1
Pegram, Erric, Pit.	17	112	6.6	14	0
Murrell, Adrian, NY-J	17	81	4.8	30	1
Smith, Rod, Den.	16	237	14.8	49t	2
Sherrard, Mike, Den.	16	185	11.6	25t	1
Holmes, Darick, Buf.	16	102	6.4	20	1
Green, Eric, Bal.	15	150	10.0	23	1
Brady, Kyle, NY-J	15	144	9.6	25	1
Carswell, Dwayne, Den.	15	85	5.7	11	0
Cash, Keith, K.C.	14	80	5.7	20	0
Russell, Leonard, S.D.	13	180	13.8	35	0
Thomas, Rodney, Hou.	13	128	9.8	33	0
Roche, Brian, S.D.	13	111	8.5	19	0
Groce, Clif, Ind.	13	106	8.2	24	0
Thigpen, Yancey, Pit.	12	244	20.3	39	2
Bruener, Mark, Pit.	12	141	11.8	36	0
Hearst, Garrison, Cin.	12	131	10.9	40	1
Chamberlain, Byron, Den.	12	129	10.8	17	0
Crockett, Zack, Ind.	11	96	8.7	32	1
Thomas, Lamar, Mia.	10	166	16.6	34	1
Floyd, Malcolm, Hou.	10	145	14.5	63t	1
Mitchell, Shannon, S.D.	10	57	5.7	25	0
Miller, Scott, Mia.	9	116	12.9	22	0
Glover, Andrew, Oak.	9	101	11.2	25	1
Strong, Mack, Sea.	9	78	8.7	20	0
Walker, Derrick, K.C.	9	73	8.1	24	1
Smith, Lamar, Sea.	9	58	6.4	22	0
Spikes, Irving, Mia.	8	81	10.1	19	1
Battaglia, Marco, Cin.	8	79	9.9	17	0
Aska, Joe, Oak.	8	63	7.9	22	0
Bennett, Donnell, K.C.	8	21	2.6	10	0
Jordan, Charles, Mia.	7	152	21.7	43	0
Baxter, Fred, NY-J	7	114	16.3	23	0
Mills, Ernie, Pit.	7	92	13.1	22	1
Copeland, Russell, Buf.	7	85	12.1	31	0
Lester, Tim, Pit.	7	70	10.0	19	0
Lewis, Roderick, Hou.	7	50	7.1	18	0
Cothran, Jeff, Cin.	7	49	7.0	14	0
Means, Natrone, Jac.	7	45	6.4	11t	1
Hebron, Vaughn, Den.	7	43	6.1	11	0
Gardner, Carwell, Bal.	7	28	4.0	7	0
Still, Bryan, S.D.	6	142	23.7	56	0
Carter, Dale, K.C.	6	89	14.8	46t	1
Pollard, Marcus, Ind.	6	86	14.3	48t	1
Arnold, Jahine, Pit.	6	76	12.7	26	0
Maston, Le'Shai, Jac.	6	54	9.0	17	0
Broussard, Steve, Sea.	6	26	4.3	9	0
Dawson, Lake, K.C.	5	83	16.6	25	1
Lewis, Jermaine, Bal.	5	78	15.6	24	1
Bailey, Henry, NY-J	5	65	13.0	28	0
Graham, Hason, N.E.	5	64	12.8	23	0
Griffith, Richard, Jac.	5	53	10.6	18	0
Brantley, Chris, Buf.	5	47	9.4	22t	1
Williams, Ronnie, Sea.	5	25	5.0	11	1
McAfee, Fred, Pit.	5	21	4.2	9	0
Carolan, Brett, Mia.	4	48	12.0	21	1
Botkin, Kirk, Pit.	4	36	9.0	17	0
Workman, Vince, Ind.	4	36	9.0	18	0
Cobb, Reggie, NY-J	4	23	5.8	12	0
Davison, Jerone, Oak.	4	21	5.3	8	0
Shedd, Kenny, Oak.	3	87	29.0	51	1
Hill, Greg, K.C.	3	60	20.0	34t	1
Moore, Will, N.E.	3	37	12.3	16	0
Milne, Brian, Cin.	3	29	9.7	15	0
Ellison, 'Omar, S.D.	3	15	5.0	6	0
Sadowski, Troy, Cin.	3	15	5.0	8	0
Horn, Joe, K.C.	2	30	15.0	21	0
Harris, Ronnie, Sea.	2	26	13.0	21	0
Ethridge, Ray, Bal.	2	24	12.0	15	0
Stock, Mark, Ind.	2	24	12.0	13	0
Wilson, Sheddrick, Hou.	2	24	12.0	14	0
Bishop, Harold, Bal.	2	22	11.0	13	0
Richardson, Tony, K.C.	2	18	9.0	17	1
Witman, Jon, Pit.	2	15	7.5	11	0
Hayes, Jonathan, Pit.	2	14	7.0	7	0

	No.	Yards	Avg.	Long	TD
Wilson, Robert, Mia.	2	5	2.5	3t	1
McKnight, James, Sea.	1	73	73.0	73	0
Kinchen, Todd, Den.	1	27	27.0	27	0
Bradley, Freddie, S.D.	1	20	20.0	20	0
Burke, John, N.E.	1	19	19.0	19	0
Hundon, James, Cin.	1	14	14.0	14t	1
Bailey, Victor, K.C.	1	12	12.0	12	0
Coons, Robert, Buf.	1	12	12.0	12	0
Doering, Chris, Ind.	1	10	10.0	10	0
Hayden, Aaron, S.D.	1	10	10.0	10	0
Grier, Marrio, N.E.	1	8	8.0	8	0
Holliday, Corey, Pit.	1	7	7.0	7	0
Davis, Tyrone, NY-J	1	6	6.0	6	0
Gray, Oscar, Sea.	1	5	5.0	5	0
Hallock, Ty, Jac.	1	5	5.0	5	0
Jells, Dietrich, N.E.	1	5	5.0	5	0
Cunningham, Rick, Oak.	1	3	3.0	3t	1
Reeves, Walter, S.D.	1	3	3.0	3	0
Jones, James, Bal.	1	2	2.0	2t	1
Wainright, Frank, Mia.	1	2	2.0	2t	1
Arvie, Herman, Bal.	1	1	1.0	1t	1
Bartrum, Mike, N.E.	1	1	1.0	1t	1
Norgard, Erik, Hou.	1	1	1.0	1t	1
Ogden, Jonathan, Bal.	1	1	1.0	1t	1
Louchiey, Corey, Buf.	1	0	0.0	0	0
Rivers, Reggie, Den.	1	-1	-1.0	-1	0
Tindale, Tim, Buf.	1	-1	-1.0	-1	0

t = Touchdown
Leader based on receptions

NFC RECEIVERS—INDIVIDUAL

	No.	Yards	Avg.	Long	TD
Rice, Jerry, S.F.	108	1254	11.6	39	8
Moore, Herman, Det.	106	1296	12.2	50t	9
Centers, Larry, Ariz	99	766	7.7	39	7
Carter, Cris, Min.	96	1163	12.1	43t	10
Perriman, Brett, Det.	94	1021	10.9	44	5
Fryar, Irving, Phi.	88	1195	13.6	42	11
Bruce, Isaac, St.L	84	1338	15.9	70	7
Conway, Curtis, Chi.	81	1049	13.0	58t	7
Emanuel, Bert, Atl.	75	921	12.3	53	6
Reed, Jake, Min.	72	1320	18.3	82t	7
Jones, Chris T., Phi.	70	859	12.3	38	5
Sanders, Frank, Ariz	69	813	11.8	34	4
Mathis, Terance, Atl.	69	771	11.2	55	7
Alstott, Mike, T.B.	65	557	8.6	29	3
Irvin, Michael, Dal.	64	962	15.0	61	2
Timpson, Michael, Chi.	62	802	12.9	49	0
Walls, Wesley, Car.	61	713	11.7	40t	10
Moore, Rob, Ariz	58	1016	17.5	69	4
Carrier, Mark, Car.	58	808	13.9	39	6
Freeman, Antonio, G.B.	56	933	16.7	51t	9
Morton, Johnnie, Det.	55	714	13.0	62t	6
Kennison, Eddie, St.L	54	924	17.1	77t	9
Metcalf, Eric, Atl.	54	599	11.1	67	6
Lee, Amp, Min.	54	422	7.8	21	2
Calloway, Chris, NY-G	53	739	13.9	36	4
Lewis, Thomas, NY-G	53	694	13.1	34	4
Ellard, Henry, Was.	52	1014	19.5	51	2
Kirby, Terry, S.F.	52	439	8.4	52	1
Watters, Ricky, Phi.	51	444	8.7	36	0
Small, Torrance, N.O.	50	558	11.2	41	2
Anderson, Jamal, Atl.	49	473	9.7	34	1
Bjornson, Eric, Dal.	48	388	8.1	25	3
Rison, Andre, Jac.-G.B.	47	593	12.6	61t	3
Smith, Emmitt, Dal.	47	249	5.3	21	3
Green, Willie, Car.	46	614	13.3	50	3
Hawkins, Courtney, T.B.	46	544	11.8	45	1
Haynes, Michael, N.O.	44	786	17.9	51	4
Turner, Kevin, Phi.	43	409	9.5	41	1
Johnston, Daryl, Dal.	43	278	6.5	23	1
Asher, Jamie, Was.	42	481	11.5	34	4
Carter, Tony, Chi.	41	233	5.7	29	0
Jackson, Keith, G.B.	40	505	12.6	51t	10
Beebe, Don, G.B.	39	699	17.9	80t	4
Green, Harold, St.L	37	246	6.6	19	1
Sanders, Deion, Dal.	36	475	13.2	41	1
Owens, Terrell, S.F.	35	520	14.9	46t	4
Westbrook, Michael, Was.	34	505	14.9	45	1
Jones, Brent, S.F.	33	428	13.0	39	1
Thomas, Robb, T.B.	33	427	12.9	31t	2

	No.	Yards	Avg.	Long	TD
Engram, Bobby, Chi.	33	389	11.8	24	6
Way, Charles, NY-G	32	328	10.3	37t	1
Harris, Raymont, Chi.	32	296	9.3	47	1
Mitchell, Brian, Was.	32	286	8.9	20	0
Allen, Terry, Was.	32	194	6.1	28	0
Levens, Dorsey, G.B.	31	226	7.3	49	5
Neal, Lorenzo, N.O.	31	194	6.3	23	1
Bennett, Edgar, G.B.	31	176	5.7	25t	1
Harris, Jackie, T.B.	30	349	11.6	36	1
Birden, J. J., Atl.	30	319	10.6	57	2
Edwards, Anthony, Ariz	29	311	10.7	31	1
Chmura, Mark, G.B.	28	370	13.2	29	0
Brown, Tyrone, Atl.	28	325	11.6	38	1
Vardell, Tommy, S.F.	28	179	6.4	22	0
Williams, Kevin, Dal.	27	323	12.0	31	1
Moore, Dave, T.B.	27	237	8.8	23	3
Griffith, Howard, Car.	27	223	8.3	21	1
Lusk, Henry, N.O.	27	210	7.8	24	0
Henderson, William, G.B.	27	203	7.5	27	1
Carter, Pat, Ariz	26	329	12.7	36	1
Popson, Ted, S.F.	26	301	11.6	39t	6
Floyd, William, S.F.	26	197	7.6	24	1
Johnson, Anthony, Car.	26	192	7.4	55	0
Whittle, Ricky, N.O.	26	162	6.2	28	0
Muhammad, Muhsin, Car.	25	407	16.3	54t	1
Martin, Kelvin, Dal.	25	380	15.2	60t	1
Sanders, Barry, Det.	24	147	6.1	28	0
Brooks, Robert, G.B.	23	344	15.0	38	4
Shepherd, Leslie, Was.	23	344	15.0	52t	3
Logan, Marc, Was.	23	269	11.7	26	0
Ismail, Qadry, Min.	22	351	16.0	54t	3
Williams, Karl, T.B.	22	246	11.2	25	0
Cross, Howard, NY-G	22	178	8.1	19	1
Evans, Chuck, Min.	22	135	6.1	16	0
Wetnight, Ryan, Chi.	21	223	10.6	38	1
Preston, Roell, Atl.	21	208	9.9	17t	1
Dowdell, Marcus, Ariz	20	318	15.9	64t	2
Jeffires, Haywood, N.O.	20	215	10.8	27t	3
Harper, Alvin, T.B.	19	289	15.2	40t	1
Seay, Mark, Phi.	19	260	13.7	35	0
Jordan, Andrew, Min.	19	128	6.7	15	0
Stokes, J.J., S.F.	18	249	13.8	40	0
Dawsey, Lawrence, NY-G	18	233	12.9	28	0
Ellison, Jerry, T.B.	18	208	11.6	42	0
Hunter, Ernest, Bal.-N.O.	18	163	9.1	25	0
Mickens, Terry, G.B.	18	161	8.9	19	2
Brooks, Bill, Was.	17	224	13.2	31	0
Metzelaars, Pete, Det.	17	146	8.6	20	0
Heyward, Craig, Atl.	16	168	10.5	25	0
Loville, Derek, S.F.	16	138	8.6	44t	2
Dunn, Jason, Phi.	15	332	22.1	58	2
DeRamus, Lee, N.O.	15	182	12.1	28t	1
Johnson, LeShon, Ariz	15	176	11.7	35	1
Conwell, Ernie, St.L	15	164	10.9	26	0
Ross, Jermaine, St.L	15	160	10.7	28	0
Oliver, Winslow, Car.	15	144	9.6	29	0
Smith, Irv, N.O.	15	144	9.6	37	0
Williams, Calvin, Bal.-Phi.	15	93	6.2	19	1
Hampton, Rodney, NY-G	15	82	5.5	16	0
Garner, Charlie, Phi.	14	92	6.6	13	0
Laing, Aaron, St.L	13	116	8.9	22	0
Howard, Desmond, G.B.	13	95	7.3	12	0
Green, Robert, Chi.	13	78	6.0	18	0
Bates, Mario, N.O.	13	44	3.4	15	0
Ismail, Raghib, Car.	12	214	17.8	51	0
Wheatley, Tyrone, NY-G	12	51	4.3	13	2
Pierce, Aaron, NY-G	11	144	13.1	30	1
Hoard, Leroy, Bal.-Min.	11	133	12.1	37	0
Neely, Bobby, Chi.	9	92	10.2	21	0
Zellars, Ray, N.O.	9	45	5.0	12	0
Solomon, Freddie, Phi.	8	125	15.6	23	0
West, Ed, Phi.	8	91	11.4	29	0
Galbraith, Scott, Was.	8	89	11.1	30t	2
Brown, Derek, N.O.	8	54	6.8	18	0
Elias, Keith, NY-G	8	51	6.4	11	0
DeLong, Greg, Min.	8	34	4.3	9	0
Phillips, Lawrence, St.L	8	28	3.5	11t	1
Johnson, Jimmie, Phi.	7	127	18.1	31	0
Green, Paul, N.O.	7	91	13.0	23	0
Uwaezuoke, Iheanyi, S.F.	7	91	13.0	29t	1
Walker, Herschel, Dal.	7	89	12.7	24	0
McWilliams, Johnny, Ariz	7	80	11.4	21	1

	No.	Yards	Avg.	Long	TD
Scott, Freddie, Atl.	7	80	11.4	27	0
Johnson, Tony, N.O.	7	76	10.9	17	1
Sloan, David, Det.	7	51	7.3	18	0
Graham, Scottie, Min.	7	48	6.9	18	0
Thomas, J.T., St.L	7	46	6.6	11	0
Salaam, Rashaan, Chi.	7	44	6.3	11t	1
Smith, Robert, Min.	7	39	5.6	16	0
Jennings, Keith, Chi.	6	56	9.3	20	0
Mayes, Derrick, G.B.	6	46	7.7	12	2
Palmer, David, Min.	6	40	6.7	20	0
McElroy, Leeland, Ariz	5	41	8.2	22t	1
Williams, Sherman, Dal.	5	41	8.2	13	0
Thompson, Leroy, T.B.	5	36	7.2	12	0
Hayes, Mercury, N.O.	4	101	25.3	50	0
Alexander, Kevin, NY-G	4	88	22.0	35	0
Anderson, Stevie, Ariz	4	64	16.0	19	0
Clay, Hayward, St.L	4	51	12.8	34	0
Cash, Kerry, Chi.	4	42	10.5	14	0
Jackson, Jack, Chi.	4	39	9.8	14	0
Walsh, Chris, Min.	4	39	9.8	17	1
Saxton, Brian, NY-G	4	31	7.8	14	0
Harris, Derrick, St.L	4	17	4.3	8	0
Lyons, Mitch, Atl.	4	16	4.0	5	1
Rhett, Errict, T.B.	4	11	2.8	5t	1
Thomason, Jeff, G.B.	3	45	15.0	24	0
Matthews, Aubrey, Det.	3	41	13.7	21	0
Frisch, David, Min.	3	27	9.0	21	1
Bell, William, Was.	3	23	7.7	12	0
Downs, Gary, NY-G	3	20	6.7	13	0
Manuel, Sean, S.F.	3	18	6.0	7	0
Bowie, Larry, Was.	3	17	5.7	8	0
Brooks, Reggie, T.B.	3	13	4.3	9	0
Moore, Jerald, St.L	3	13	4.3	7	0
Smith, Cedric, Ariz	3	3	1.0	2	1
Guess, Terry, N.O.	2	69	34.5	57t	1
Ingram, Mark, Phi.	2	33	16.5	20	0
Rivers, Ron, Det.	2	28	14.0	19	0
Marshall, Marvin, T.B.	2	27	13.5	20	0
Wright, Alexander, St.L	2	24	12.0	13	0
Tobeck, Robbie, Atl.	2	15	7.5	14	1
Lynn, Anthony, S.F.	2	14	7.0	8	0
Armstrong, Tyji, Dal.	2	10	5.0	6	0
Caldwell, Mike, S.F.	2	9	4.5	8	0
Greene, Scott, Car.	2	7	3.5	6	1
Williams, Stepfret, Dal.	1	32	32.0	32	0
Goodwin, Hunter, Min.	1	24	24.0	24	0
Mitchell, Johnny, Dal.	1	17	17.0	17	0
Huntley, Richard, Atl.	1	14	14.0	14	0
Price, Derek, Det.	1	14	14.0	14	0
Toomer, Amani, NY-G	1	12	12.0	12	0
Cooper, Adrian, S.F.	1	11	11.0	11	0
Singleton, Nate, S.F.	1	11	11.0	11	0
Stone, Dwight, Car.	1	11	11.0	11	0
Douglas, Omar, NY-G	1	8	8.0	8	0
Jenkins, James, Was.	1	7	7.0	7	0
Robinson, Greg, St.L	1	6	6.0	6	0
Krieg, Dave, Chi.	1	5	5.0	5	0
Ware, Derek, Dal.	1	5	5.0	5	0
Kozlowski, Brian, NY-G	1	4	4.0	4t	1
McIntyre, Guy, Phi.	1	4	4.0	4	0
Faulkerson, Mike, Chi.	1	1	1.0	1t	1
Flanigan, Jim, Chi.	1	1	1.0	1t	1
Spears, Marcus, Chi.	1	1	1.0	1t	1
Terry, Ryan, Ariz	1	0	0.0	0	0
Hicks, Michael, Chi.	1	-1	-1.0	-1	0
Roberts, Ray, Det.	0	5	—	5	0
Williams, Aeneas, Ariz	0	0	—	—	0

t = Touchdown
Leader based on receptions

INTERCEPTIONS

Interceptions
AFC: 9—Tyrone Braxton, Denver
NFC: 9—Keith Lyle, St. Louis
Interceptions, Game
NFC: 3—Keith Lyle, St. Louis at Atlanta, December 15
AFC: 2—by many
Yards
AFC: 164—Terrell Buckley, Miami
NFC: 152—Keith Lyle, St. Louis
Longest
AFC: 100—Aaron Glenn, N.Y. Jets at Miami, September 15 - TD
NFC: 98—Bennie Blades, Detroit at Tampa Bay, September 29 - TD
Touchdowns
AFC: 2—Jason Belser, Indianapolis
Aaron Glenn, N.Y. Jets
NFC: 2—Anthony Parker, St. Louis

Team Leaders, Interceptions
AFC: BALTIMORE: 5, Antonio Langham, Eric Turner; BUFFALO: 4, Kurt Schulz; CINCINNATI: 8, Ashley Ambrose; DENVER: 9, Tyrone Braxton; HOUSTON: 5, Darryll Lewis; INDIANAPOLIS: 4, Jason Belser; JACKSONVILLE: 2, Travis Davis, Kevin Hardy, Chris Hudson, Dave Thomas; KANSAS CITY: 6, Mark Collins; MIAMI: 6, Terrell Buckley; NEW ENGLAND: 4, Willie Clay; N.Y. JETS: 4, Aaron Glenn; OAKLAND: 5, Terry McDaniel; PITTSBURGH: 6, Rod Woodson; SAN DIEGO: 5, Rodney Harrison; SEATTLE: 5, Darryl Williams.
NFC: ARIZONA: 6, Aeneas Williams; ATLANTA: 2, Brad Edwards; CAROLINA: 5, Chad Cota, Eric Davis; CHICAGO: 6, Donnell Woolford; DALLAS: 5, Kevin Smith, Darren Woodson; DETROIT: 5, Ryan McNeil; GREEN BAY: 6, Eugene Robinson; MINNESOTA: 5, Orlando Thomas; NEW ORLEANS: 3, Greg Jackson, Anthony Newman; N.Y. GIANTS: 5, Jason Sehorn; PHILADELPHIA: 5, Mike Zordich; ST. LOUIS: 9, Keith Lyle; SAN FRANCISCO: 6, Marquez Pope; TAMPA BAY: 5, Donnie Abraham; WASHINGTON: 5, Tom Carter.

Team Champion
AFC: 34—Cincinnati
NFC: 26—Green Bay
St. Louis

AFC INTERCEPTIONS—TEAM

	No.	Yards	Avg.	Long	TD
Cincinnati	34	308	9.1	42t	2
Denver	23	241	10.5	69t	1
New England	23	255	11.1	46t	2
Pittsburgh	23	334	14.5	47t	3
San Diego	22	336	15.3	83t	1
Miami	20	475	23.8	91t	3
Kansas City	17	171	10.1	34	0
Oakland	17	353	20.8	66t	2
Baltimore	15	147	9.8	45t	1
Buffalo	14	113	8.1	31	0
Seattle	14	256	18.3	79t	1
Indianapolis	13	276	21.2	68t	4
Jacksonville	13	114	8.8	27	0
Houston	12	162	13.5	53	1
N.Y. Jets	11	165	15.0	100t	2
AFC Total	271	3706	13.7	100t	23
AFC Average	18.1	247.1	13.7	—	1.5

NFC INTERCEPTIONS—TEAM

	No.	Yards	Avg.	Long	TD
Green Bay	26	524	20.2	90t	3
St. Louis	26	390	15.0	92t	4
Carolina	22	277	12.6	42	0
Minnesota	22	206	9.4	41	1
N.Y. Giants	22	341	15.5	35	3
Washington	21	214	10.2	68t	1
San Francisco	20	176	8.8	55t	1
Dallas	19	168	8.8	24	0
Philadelphia	19	303	15.9	104t	1
Chicago	17	107	6.3	29	1
Tampa Bay	17	139	8.2	26	0
New Orleans	12	114	9.5	33	0
Arizona	11	122	11.1	65t	1
Detroit	11	169	15.4	98t	2
Atlanta	6	41	6.8	21	0
NFC Total	271	3291	12.1	104t	18
NFC Average	18.1	219.4	12.1	—	1.2
League Total	542	6997	—	104t	41
League Average	18.1	233.2	12.9	—	1.4

NFL TOP TEN INTERCEPTORS

	No.	Yards	Avg.	Long	TD
Braxton, Tyrone, Den.	9	128	14.2	69t	1
Lyle, Keith, St.L	9	152	16.9	68	0
Ambrose, Ashley, Cin.	8	63	7.9	31t	1
Buckley, Terrell, Mia.	6	164	27.3	91t	1
Collins, Mark, K.C.	6	45	7.5	23	0
Pope, Marquez, S.F.	6	98	16.3	55t	1
Robinson, Eugene, G.B.	6	107	17.8	39	0
Williams, Aeneas, Ariz	6	89	14.8	65t	1
Woodson, Rod, Pit.	6	121	20.2	43t	1
Woolford, Donnell, Chi.	6	37	6.2	28t	1

AFC INTERCEPTIONS—INDIVIDUAL

	No.	Yards	Avg.	Long	TD
Braxton, Tyrone, Den.	9	128	14.2	69t	1
Ambrose, Ashley, Cin.	8	63	7.9	31t	1
Buckley, Terrell, Mia.	6	164	27.3	91t	1
Woodson, Rod, Pit.	6	121	20.2	43t	1
Collins, Mark, K.C.	6	45	7.5	23	0
McDaniel, Terry, Oak.	5	150	30.0	56t	1
Williams, Darryl, Sea.	5	148	29.6	79t	1
Perry, Darren, Pit.	5	115	23.0	28	1
Lewis, Darryll, Hou.	5	103	20.6	53	1
Langham, Antonio, Bal.	5	59	11.8	28	0
Harrison, Rodney, S.D.	5	56	11.2	29	0
Spencer, Jimmy, Cin.	5	48	9.6	34	0
Turner, Eric, Bal.	5	1	0.2	1	0
Glenn, Aaron, NY-J	4	113	28.3	100t	2
Belser, Jason, Ind.	4	81	20.3	44t	2
Clay, Willie, N.E.	4	50	12.5	35	0
Robertson, Marcus, Hou.	4	44	11.0	27	0
Tovar, Steve, Cin.	4	42	10.5	24	0
Schulz, Kurt, Buf.	4	24	6.0	19	0
Kirkland, Levon, Pit.	4	12	3.0	6	0
Oliver, Louis, Mia.	3	110	36.7	60	0
Jackson, Calvin, Mia.	3	82	27.3	61t	1
Shaw, Terrance, S.D.	3	78	26.0	36	0
Lynch, Lorenzo, Oak.	3	75	25.0	35	0
Thomas, Zach, Mia.	3	64	21.3	27	1
Francis, James, Cin.	3	61	20.3	42t	1
Blackmon, Robert, Sea.	3	48	16.0	38	0
Law, Ty, N.E.	3	45	15.0	38t	1
Gouveia, Kurt, S.D.	3	41	13.7	21	0
Washington, Brian, K.C.	3	39	13.0	34	0
Daniel, Eugene, Ind.	3	35	11.7	35t	1
Bellamy, Jay, Sea.	3	18	6.0	16	0
Carter, Dale, K.C.	3	17	5.7	17	0
Atwater, Steve, Den.	3	11	3.7	11	0
Romanowski, Bill, Den.	3	1	0.3	1	0
Clark, Willie, S.D.	2	83	41.5	83t	1
Gordon, Darrien, S.D.	2	55	27.5	55	0
Davis, Anthony, K.C.	2	37	18.5	30	0
Martin, Emanuel, Buf.	2	35	17.5	31	0
Walker, Bracey, Cin.	2	35	17.5	35	0
Crockett, Ray, Den.	2	34	17.0	34	0
Buchanan, Ray, Ind.	2	32	16.0	32	0

	No.	Yards	Avg.	Long	TD
Green, Victor, NY-J	2	27	13.5	18	0
Hudson, Chris, Jac.	2	25	12.5	21	0
Brown, Chad, Pit.	2	20	10.0	16	0
Smith, Otis, N.E.	2	20	10.0	11	0
Hardy, Kevin, Jac.	2	19	9.5	13	0
Seau, Junior, S.D.	2	18	9.0	10	0
Washington, Lionel, Den.	2	17	8.5	23	0
James, Tory, Den.	2	15	7.5	15	0
Wooden, Shawn, Mia.	2	15	7.5	15	0
Hitchcock, Jimmy, N.E.	2	14	7.0	14	0
Milloy, Lawyer, N.E.	2	14	7.0	14	0
Figures, Deon, Pit.	2	13	6.5	13	0
Morton, Mike, Oak.	2	13	6.5	13	0
Myers, Greg, Cin.	2	10	5.0	10	0
Henderson, Jerome, N.E.	2	7	3.5	7	0
Reynolds, Ricky, N.E.	2	7	3.5	7	0
Ross, Kevin, S.D.	2	7	3.5	7	0
Thomas, Dave, Jac.	2	7	3.5	8	0
Houston, Bobby, NY-J	2	3	1.5	3	0
Jones, Rod W., Cin.	2	2	1.0	2	0
Davis, Travis, Jac.	2	0	0.0	0	0
Lewis, Albert, Oak.	2	0	0.0	0	0
Orlando, Bo, Cin.	2	0	0.0	0	0
Sawyer, Corey, Cin.	2	0	0.0	0	0
Stevens, Matt, Buf.	2	0	0.0	0	0
Herrod, Jeff, Ind.	1	68	68.0	68t	1
Ball, Jerry, Oak.	1	66	66.0	66t	1
Lake, Carnell, Pit.	1	47	47.0	47t	1
McGinest, Willie, N.E.	1	46	46.0	46t	1
Caldwell, Mike, Bal.	1	45	45.0	45t	1
Ray, Terry, N.E.	1	43	43.0	43	0
Jones, Roger, Cin.	1	30	30.0	30	0
Brown, J.B., Mia.	1	29	29.0	29	0
Burris, Jeff, Buf.	1	28	28.0	28	0
Brackens, Tony, Jac.	1	27	27.0	27	0
Hilliard, Randy, Den.	1	27	27.0	27	0
Harris, Corey, Sea.	1	25	25.0	25	0
Coleman, Marcus, NY-J	1	23	23.0	23	0
Trapp, James, Oak.	1	23	23.0	23	0
Edwards, Donnie, K.C.	1	22	22.0	22	0
Carrington, Darren, Oak.	1	21	21.0	21	0
Watts, Damon, Ind.	1	21	21.0	21	0
Hall, Dana, Jac.	1	20	20.0	20	0
Morrison, Steve, Ind.	1	20	20.0	20	0
Alberts, Trev, Ind.	1	19	19.0	19	0
Adams, Vashone, Bal.	1	16	16.0	16	0
Croel, Mike, Bal.	1	16	16.0	16	0
Clark, Vinnie, Jac.	1	15	15.0	15	0
Spielman, Chris, Buf.	1	14	14.0	14	0
Wooden, Terry, Sea.	1	13	13.0	13	0
Hollier, Dwight, Mia.	1	11	11.0	11	0
Dixon, Gerald, Cin.	1	10	10.0	10	0
Moore, Stevon, Bal.	1	10	10.0	10	0
Stargell, Tony, K.C.	1	9	9.0	9	0
Mobley, John, Den.	1	8	8.0	8	0
Collins, Todd, N.E.	1	7	7.0	7	0
Dishman, Cris, Hou.	1	7	7.0	7	0
Wilkinson, Dan, Cin.	1	7	7.0	7	0
Bishop, Blaine, Hou.	1	6	6.0	6	0
Kerner, Marlon, Buf.	1	6	6.0	6	0
Perry, Marlo, Buf.	1	6	6.0	6	0
Olsavsky, Jerry, Pit.	1	5	5.0	5	0
Brown, Larry, Oak.	1	4	4.0	4	0
Robinson, Rafael, Hou.	1	2	2.0	2	0
Simien, Tracy, K.C.	1	2	2.0	2	0
Slade, Chris, N.E.	1	2	2.0	2	0
Kidd, Carl, Oak.	1	1	1.0	1	0
Moss, Winston, Sea.	1	1	1.0	1	0
Washington, Mickey, Jac.	1	1	1.0	1	0
Williams, Willie, Pit.	1	1	1.0	1	0
Beasley, Aaron, Jac.	1	0	0.0	0	0
Fuller, Randy, Pit.	1	0	0.0	0	0
Harper, Dwayne, S.D.	1	0	0.0	0	0
Hill, Sean, Mia.	1	0	0.0	0	0
Jackson, Raymond, Buf.	1	0	0.0	0	0
Johnson, Ted, N.E.	1	0	0.0	0	0
Langford, Jevon, Cin.	1	0	0.0	0	0
Lewis, Ray, Bal.	1	0	0.0	0	0
Sabb, Dwayne, N.E.	1	0	0.0	0	0
Smith, Thomas, Buf.	1	0	0.0	0	0
Young, Lonnie, NY-J	1	0	0.0	0	0
Lee, Shawn, S.D.	1	-1	-1.0	-1	0

	No.	Yards	Avg.	Long	TD
Spindler, Marc, NY-J	1	-1	-1.0	-1	0
Young, Glen, S.D.	1	-1	-1.0	-1	0
Gray, Carlton, Sea.	0	3	—	3	0
Biekert, Greg, Oak.	0	0	—	0	0
Jones, Rod E., Cin.	0	0	—	—	0

t = Touchdown
Leader based on interceptions

NFC INTERCEPTIONS—INDIVIDUAL

	No.	Yards	Avg.	Long	TD
Lyle, Keith, St.L	9	152	16.9	68	0
Robinson, Eugene, G.B.	6	107	17.8	39	0
Pope, Marquez, S.F.	6	98	16.3	55t	1
Williams, Aeneas, Ariz	6	89	14.8	65t	1
Woolford, Donnell, Chi.	6	37	6.2	28t	1
Butler, LeRoy, G.B.	5	149	29.8	90t	1
Evans, Doug, G.B.	5	102	20.4	63	1
Cota, Chad, Car.	5	63	12.6	35	0
Sehorn, Jason, NY-G	5	61	12.2	24	1
Davis, Eric, Car.	5	57	11.4	36	0
Thomas, Orlanda, Min.	5	57	11.4	34	0
Smith, Kevin, Dal.	5	45	9.0	24	0
Lyght, Todd, St.L	5	43	8.6	25t	1
Woodson, Darren, Dal.	5	43	8.6	21	0
Abraham, Donnie, T.B.	5	27	5.4	21	0
Carter, Tom, Was.	5	24	4.8	24	0
McNeil, Ryan, Det.	5	14	2.8	15	0
Parker, Anthony, St.L	4	128	32.0	92t	2
Griffith, Robert, Min.	4	67	16.8	41	0
Zordich, Mike, Phi.	4	54	13.5	28	0
Teague, George, Dal.	4	47	11.8	22	0
Hanks, Merton, S.F.	4	7	1.8	8	0
Vincent, Troy, Phi.	3	144	48.0	90t	1
Green, Darrell, Was.	3	84	28.0	68t	1
Koonce, George, G.B.	3	84	28.0	75t	1
Ellsworth, Percy, NY-G	3	62	20.7	33	0
Richard, Stanley, Was.	3	47	15.7	42	0
Thomas, William, Phi.	3	47	15.7	37	0
Dawkins, Brian, Phi.	3	41	13.7	30	0
Newman, Anthony, N.O.	3	40	13.3	21	0
Carter, Marty, Chi.	3	34	11.3	29	0
Cook, Toi, Car.	3	28	9.3	22	0
Dodge, Dedrick, S.F.	3	27	9.0	26	0
Lynch, John, T.B.	3	26	8.7	25	0
Jackson, Greg, N.O.	3	24	8.0	10	0
Sparks, Phillippi, NY-G	3	23	7.7	19	0
Brady, Jeff, Min.	3	20	6.7	8	0
Terrell, Pat, Car.	3	6	2.0	6	0
Fuller, Corey, Min.	3	3	1.0	2	0
Taylor, Bobby, Phi.	3	-1	-.3	0	0
Blades, Bennie, Det.	2	112	56.0	98t	1
Harper, Roger, Dal.	2	30	15.0	15	0
Washington, Dewayne, Min.	2	27	13.5	27t	1
Patton, Marvcus, Was.	2	26	13.0	23	0
Johnson, Melvin, T.B.	2	24	12.0	24	0
Nickerson, Hardy, T.B.	2	24	12.0	17	0
Armstead, Jessie, NY-G	2	23	11.5	23	0
Newsome, Craig, G.B.	2	22	11.0	20	0
Marshall, Anthony, Chi.	2	20	10.0	20	0
Turner, Scott, Was.	2	16	8.0	12	0
Edwards, Brad, Atl.	2	15	7.5	15	0
Campbell, Jesse, NY-G	2	14	7.0	14	0
McDonald, Tim, S.F.	2	14	7.0	14	0
Pounds, Darryl, Was.	2	11	5.5	11	0
Widmer, Corey, NY-G	2	8	4.0	4	0
Jackson, Alfred M., Min.	2	4	2.0	4	0
McMillian, Mark, N.O.	2	4	2.0	4	0
Alexander, Brent, Ariz	2	3	1.5	3	0
Sanders, Deion, Dal.	2	3	1.5	2	0
Molden, Alex, N.O.	2	2	1.0	2	0
Dimry, Charles, T.B.	2	1	0.5	1	0
Doleman, Chris, S.F.	2	1	0.5	1	0
Carrier, Mark, Chi.	2	0	0.0	0	0
Harris, Walt, Chi.	2	0	0.0	0	0
White, Reggie, G.B.	1	46	46.0	46	0
Lofton, Steve, Car.	1	42	42.0	42	0
Dorn, Torin, St.L	1	40	40.0	40	0
Maxie, Brett, Car.	1	35	35.0	35	0
Poole, Tyrone, Car.	1	35	35.0	35	0
Wooten, Tito, NY-G	1	35	35.0	35	0
Agnew, Ray, NY-G	1	34	34.0	34t	1

	No.	Yards	Avg.	Long	TD
Allen, Eric, N.O.	1	33	33.0	33	0
Douglass, Maurice, NY-G	1	32	32.0	32t	1
Hamilton, Conrad, NY-G	1	29	29.0	29	0
Mincy, Charles, T.B.	1	26	26.0	26	0
Raymond, Corey, Det.	1	24	24.0	24t	1
Smith, Chuck, Atl.	1	21	21.0	21	0
Beamon, Willie, NY-G	1	20	20.0	20	0
Lassiter, Kwamie, Ariz	1	20	20.0	20	0
Wright, Toby, St.L	1	19	19.0	19t	1
Edwards, Dixon, Min.	1	18	18.0	18	0
Stubblefield, Dana, S.F.	1	15	15.0	15	0
Stewart, Ryan, Det.	1	14	14.0	14	0
Willis, James, Phi.	1	14	14.0	14	0
Burton, James, Chi.	1	11	11.0	11	0
Drakeford, Tyronne, S.F.	1	11	11.0	11	0
Tubbs, Winfred, N.O.	1	11	11.0	11	0
Joyner, Seth, Ariz	1	10	10.0	10	0
Mills, Sam, Car.	1	10	10.0	10	0
Talley, Darryl, Min.	1	10	10.0	10	0
Prior, Mike, G.B.	1	7	7.0	7	0
Brooks, Derrick, T.B.	1	6	6.0	6	0
Dowden, Corey, G.B.	1	5	5.0	5	0
Farr, D'Marco, St.L	1	5	5.0	5	0
Malone, Van, Det.	1	5	5.0	5	0
Mayhew, Martin, T.B.	1	5	5.0	5	0
Minter, Barry, Chi.	1	5	5.0	5	0
Fuller, James, Phi.	1	4	4.0	4	0
Morrison, Darryl, Was.	1	4	4.0	4	0
Bennett, Cornelius, Atl.	1	3	3.0	3	0
Israel, Steve, S.F.	1	3	3.0	3	0
Lincoln, Jeremy, St.L	1	3	3.0	3	0
McBurrows, Gerald, St.L	1	3	3.0	3	0
Bush, Devin, Atl.	1	2	2.0	2	0
Harvey, Ken, Was.	1	2	2.0	2	0
Hollinquest, Lamont, G.B.	1	2	2.0	2	0
King, Shawn, Car.	1	1	1.0	1	0
Boutte, Marc, Was.	1	0	0.0	0	0
Bradford, Ronnie, Ariz	1	0	0.0	0	0
Farmer, Ray, Phi.	1	0	0.0	0	0
Fisk, Jason, Min.	1	0	0.0	0	0
Jeffries, Greg, Det.	1	0	0.0	0	0
Jones, Robert, St.L	1	0	0.0	0	0
Pieri, Damon, Car.	1	0	0.0	0	0
Simmons, Wayne, G.B.	1	0	0.0	0	0
Stephens, Rod, Was.	1	0	0.0	0	0
Strickland, Fred, Dal.	1	0	0.0	0	0
Walker, Darnell, Atl.	1	0	0.0	0	0
Walker, Marquis, St.L	1	0	0.0	0	0
Jenkins, Carlos, St.L	1	-3	-3.0	-3	0
Davis, Wendell, Dal.	0	0	—	0	0
Hall, Rhett, Phi.	0	0	—	—	—

t = Touchdown
Leader based on interceptions

PUNTING

Average Yards Per Punt
  AFC: 46.3—John Kidd, Miami
  NFC: 45.1—Matt Turk, Washington
Net Average Yards Per Punt
  NFC: 39.2—Matt Turk, Washington
  AFC: 39.0—Chris Gardocki, Indianapolis
Longest
  AFC: 80—Chris Mohr, Buffalo vs. Miami, October 13
  NFC: 72—Todd Sauerbrun, Chicago at Washington, September 8
Punts
  NFC: 102—Mike Horan, N.Y. Giants
  AFC: 101—Chris Mohr, Buffalo
Punts, Game
  AFC: 12—Chris Gardocki, Indianapolis at Buffalo, October 6
      (551 yards)
  NFC: 10—Mike Horan, N.Y. Giants vs. Buffalo, September 1
      (397 yards)
      Mark Royals, Detroit vs. Tampa Bay, September 8
      (421 yards)
      Tommy Barnhardt, Tampa Bay at Minnesota,
      December 15 (429 yards)
      Klaus Wilmsmeyer, New Orleans at N.Y. Giants,
      December 15 (363 yards)
Team Champion
  AFC: 46.3—Miami
  NFC: 45.1—Washington

AFC PUNTING—TEAM

	Total Punts	Yards	Long	Avg.	TB	Blk.	Opp. Ret.	Return Yards	Inside the 20	Net. Avg.
Miami	78	3611	63	46.3	11	0	48	368	26	38.8
Indianapolis	68	3105	61	45.7	2	0	38	413	23	39.0
San Diego	87	3967	66	45.6	6	0	51	612	23	37.2
N.Y. Jets	74	3293	69	44.5	8	0	40	429	13	36.5
Cincinnati	82	3634	67	44.3	17	1	38	502	16	34.0
Houston	68	2973	68	43.7	7	1	31	251	25	38.0
Jacksonville	69	3016	62	43.7	8	0	44	400	16	35.6
Seattle	86	3746	66	43.6	7	1	52	640	20	34.5
New England	64	2766	62	43.2	7	0	34	334	15	35.8
Baltimore	69	2980	67	43.2	5	1	27	273	23	37.8
Denver	65	2714	57	41.8	5	0	23	261	16	36.2
Kansas City	88	3667	68	41.7	10	0	42	492	25	33.8
Buffalo	101	4194	80	41.5	13	0	40	246	27	36.5
Pittsburgh	72	2931	61	40.7	11	0	32	284	25	33.7
Oakland	79	3169	64	40.1	8	0	38	272	24	34.6
AFC Total	1150	49766	80	—	125	4	578	5777	317	—
AFC Average	76.7	3317.7	—	43.3	8.3	0.3	38.5	385.1	21.1	36.1

NFC PUNTING—TEAM

	Total Punts	Yards	Long	Avg.	TB	Blk.	Opp. Ret.	Return Yards	Inside the 20	Net. Avg.
Washington	77	3470	63	45.1	12	0	35	235	24	38.9
Chicago	78	3491	72	44.8	12	0	42	527	15	34.9
St. Louis	78	3491	70	44.8	9	0	41	495	23	36.1
Arizona	77	3328	68	43.2	6	1	37	403	23	36.4
San Francisco	75	3217	65	42.9	6	2	36	235	20	38.2
Detroit	71	3044	60	42.9	8	1	42	519	12	33.3
Dallas	74	3150	60	42.6	9	0	32	249	22	36.8
Tampa Bay	71	3015	62	42.5	4	1	38	248	24	37.8
Green Bay	68	2886	65	42.4	9	0	29	237	28	36.3
N.Y. Giants	102	4289	63	42.0	10	0	45	432	32	35.9
Atlanta	75	3152	58	42.0	4	0	32	413	22	35.5
Philadelphia	74	3107	60	42.0	9	1	36	330	17	35.1
New Orleans	87	3551	63	40.8	9	0	43	546	16	32.5
Carolina	78	3158	60	40.5	10	0	32	173	21	35.7
Minnesota	90	3616	63	40.2	6	2	37	577	26	32.4
NFC Total	1175	49965	72	—	123	8	557	5619	325	—
NFC Average	78.3	3331.0	—	42.5	8.2	0.5	37.1	374.6	21.7	35.6
NFL Total	2325	99731	80	—	248	12	1135	11396	642	—
NFL Average	77.5	3324.4	—	42.9	8.3	0.4	37.8	379.9	21.4	35.9

NFL TOP TEN PUNTERS

	No.	Yards	Long	Avg.	Total Punts	TB	Blk.	Opp. Ret.	Ret. Yds.	In 20	Net. Avg.
Kidd, John, Mia.	78	3611	63	46.3	78	11	0	48	368	26	38.8
Gardocki, Chris, Ind.	68	3105	61	45.7	68	2	0	38	413	23	39.0
Bennett, Darren, S.D.	87	3967	66	45.6	87	6	0	51	612	23	37.2
Johnson, Lee, Cin.	80	3630	67	45.4	81	17	1	38	502	16	34.4
Turk, Matt, Was.	75	3386	63	45.1	75	11	0	34	224	24	39.2
Landeta, Sean, St.L	78	3491	70	44.8	78	9	0	41	495	23	36.1
Sauerbrun, Todd, Chi.	78	3491	72	44.8	78	12	0	42	527	15	34.9
Hansen, Brian, NY-J	74	3293	69	44.5	74	8	0	40	429	13	36.5
Roby, Reggie, Hou.	67	2973	68	44.4	68	7	1	31	251	25	38.0
Tuten, Rick, Sea.	85	3746	66	44.1	86	7	1	52	640	20	34.5

AFC PUNTERS—INDIVIDUAL

	No.	Yards	Long	Avg.	Total Punts	TB	Blk.	Opp. Ret.	Ret. Yds.	In 20	Net. Avg.
Kidd, John, Mia.	78	3611	63	46.3	78	11	0	48	368	26	38.8
Gardocki, Chris, Ind.	68	3105	61	45.7	68	2	0	38	413	23	39.0
Bennett, Darren, S.D.	87	3967	66	45.6	87	6	0	51	612	23	37.2
Johnson, Lee, Cin.	80	3630	67	45.4	81	17	1	38	502	16	34.4
Hansen, Brian, NY-J	74	3293	69	44.5	74	8	0	40	429	13	36.5
Roby, Reggie, Hou.	67	2973	68	44.4	68	7	1	31	251	25	38.0
Tuten, Rick, Sea.	85	3746	66	44.1	86	7	1	52	640	20	34.5
Montgomery, Greg, Bal.	68	2980	67	43.8	69	5	1	27	273	23	37.8
Barker, Bryan, Jac.	69	3016	62	43.7	69	8	0	44	400	16	35.6
Tupa, Tom, N.E.	63	2739	62	43.5	63	7	0	34	334	14	36.0
Rouen, Tom, Den.	65	2714	57	41.8	65	5	0	23	261	16	36.2
Aguiar, Louie, K.C.	88	3667	68	41.7	88	10	0	42	492	25	33.8
Mohr, Chris, Buf.	101	4194	80	41.5	101	13	0	40	246	27	36.5
Miller, Josh, Pit.	55	2256	61	41.0	55	8	0	24	248	18	33.6
Gossett, Jeff, Oak.	57	2264	64	39.7	57	5	0	28	192	19	34.6
Nonqualifiers											
Edge, Shayne, Pit.	17	675	48	39.7	17	3	0	8	36	7	34.1
Araguz, Leo, Oak.	13	534	52	41.1	13	2	0	6	45	4	34.5
Hobert, Billy Joe, Oak.	9	371	53	41.2	9	1	0	4	35	1	35.1
Vinatieri, Adam, N.E.	1	27	27	27.0	1	0	0	0	0	1	27.0
Pelfrey, Doug, Cin.	1	4	4	4.0	1	0	0	0	0	0	4.0

Leader based on average, minimum 40 punts

NFC PUNTERS—INDIVIDUAL

	No.	Yards	Long	Avg.	Total Punts	TB	Blk.	Opp. Ret.	Ret. Yds.	In 20	Net. Avg.
Turk, Matt, Was.	75	3386	63	45.1	75	11	0	34	224	24	39.2
Landeta, Sean, St.L	78	3491	70	44.8	78	9	0	41	495	23	36.1
Sauerbrun, Todd, Chi.	78	3491	72	44.8	78	12	0	42	527	15	34.9
Thompson, Tommy, S.F.	73	3217	65	44.1	75	6	2	36	235	20	38.2
Feagles, Jeff, Ariz	76	3328	68	43.8	77	6	1	37	403	23	36.4
Royals, Mark, Det.	69	3020	60	43.8	70	8	1	42	519	11	33.4
Barnhardt, Tommy, T.B.	70	3015	62	43.1	71	4	1	38	248	24	37.8
Jett, John, Dal.	74	3150	60	42.6	74	9	0	32	249	22	36.8
Hutton, Tom, Phi.	73	3107	60	42.6	74	9	1	36	330	17	35.1
Hentrich, Craig, G.B.	68	2886	65	42.4	68	9	0	29	237	28	36.3
Horan, Mike, NY-G	102	4289	63	42.0	102	10	0	45	432	32	35.9
Stryzinski, Dan, Atl.	75	3152	58	42.0	75	4	0	32	413	22	35.5
Berger, Mitch, Min.	88	3616	63	41.1	90	6	2	37	577	26	32.4
Wilmsmeyer, Klaus, N.O.	87	3551	63	40.8	87	9	0	43	546	16	32.5
Stark, Rohn, Car.	77	3128	60	40.6	77	9	0	32	173	21	36.0
Nonqualifiers											
Blanton, Scott, Was.	2	84	45	42.0	2	1	0	1	11	0	26.5
Kasay, John, Car.	1	30	30	30.0	1	1	0	0	0	0	10.0
Hanson, Jason, Det.	1	24	24	24.0	1	0	0	0	0	1	24.0

Leader based on average, minimum 40 punts

PUNT RETURNS

Yards Per Return
- NFC: 15.1—Desmond Howard, Green Bay
- AFC: 14.9—Darrien Gordon, San Diego

Yards
- NFC: 875—Desmond Howard, Green Bay
- AFC: 588—David Meggett, New England

Yards, Game
- NFC: 167—Desmond Howard, Green Bay at Detroit, December 15 (5 returns - TD)
- AFC: 141—Ray Buchanan, Indianapolis vs. San Diego November 3 (5 returns)

Longest
- NFC: 92—Desmond Howard, Green Bay at Detroit, December 15 - TD
- AFC: 88—Joey Galloway, Seattle vs. Denver, September 8 - TD

Returns
- NFC: 58—Desmond Howard, Green Bay
- AFC: 52—David Meggett, New England

Returns, Game
- AFC: 7—Rod Smith, Denver vs. Kansas City, October 27 (99 yards)
- NFC: 7—Desmond Howard, Green Bay vs. San Diego, September 15 (118 yards)

Fair Catches
- AFC: 24—O.J. McDuffie, Miami
- NFC: 20—Tyrone Hughes, New Orleans David Palmer, Minnesota

Touchdowns
- NFC: 3—Desmond Howard, Green Bay
- AFC: 1—Joey Galloway, Seattle Darrien Gordon, San Diego David Meggett, New England

Team Champion
- NFC: 15.1—Green Bay
- AFC: 14.7—San Diego

AFC PUNT RETURNS—TEAM

	No.	FC	Yards	Avg.	Long	TD
San Diego.	38	14	559	14.7	81t	1
Denver.	49	19	583	11.9	40	0
New England	52	9	588	11.3	60t	1
Indianapolis	41	15	447	10.9	82	0
Seattle	34	15	352	10.4	88t	1
Jacksonville	34	13	351	10.3	60	0
Buffalo	43	15	423	9.8	45	0
Miami	26	25	251	9.7	19	0
Houston	29	18	279	9.6	40	0
Oakland	42	24	403	9.6	50	0
Baltimore.	38	14	357	9.4	46	0
Kansas City	33	16	282	8.5	24	0
Cincinnati	33	8	217	6.6	62	0
Pittsburgh	40	12	251	6.3	33	0
N.Y. Jets.	28	16	139	5.0	15	0
AFC Total	560	233	5482	9.8	88t	3
AFC Average	37.3	15.5	365.5	9.8	—	0.2

NFC PUNT RETURNS—TEAM

	No.	FC	Yards	Avg.	Long	TD
Green Bay.	58	17	875	15.1	92t	3
St. Louis.	35	16	439	12.5	78t	2
Tampa Bay.	41	9	481	11.7	88t	1
N.Y. Giants	42	23	478	11.4	87t	2
Carolina	55	17	624	11.3	84t	1
Washington	23	16	258	11.2	71	0
Atlanta	31	10	315	10.2	39	0
Minnesota.	32	31	300	9.4	69t	1
Chicago	31	19	282	9.1	34	0
San Francisco	39	21	352	9.0	52	0
Dallas.	44	11	394	9.0	22	0
Arizona	39	9	343	8.8	35	0
Detroit	34	19	284	8.4	33	0
Philadelphia	40	17	330	8.3	56	0
New Orleans	31	20	159	5.1	16	0
NFC Total	575	255	5914	10.3	92t	10
NFC Average	38.3	17.0	394.3	10.3	—	0.7
League Total	1135	488	11396	—	92t	13
League Average	37.8	16.3	379.9	10.0	—	0.4

NFL TOP TEN PUNT RETURNERS

	No.	FC	Yards	Avg.	Long	TD
Howard, Desmond, G.B.	58	16	875	15.1	92t	3
Gordon, Darrien, S.D.	36	13	537	14.9	81t	1
Kennison, Eddie, St.L	29	16	423	14.6	78t	2
Smith, Rod, Den.	23	15	283	12.3	36	0
Kinchen, Todd, Den.	26	4	300	11.5	40	0
Oliver, Winslow, Car.	52	17	598	11.5	84t	1
Meggett, David, N.E.	52	9	588	11.3	60t	1
Mitchell, Brian, Was.	23	16	258	11.2	71	0
Metcalf, Eric, Atl.	27	9	296	11.0	39	0
Hudson, Chris, Jac.	32	12	348	10.9	60	0

AFC—INDIVIDUAL PUNT RETURNERS

	No.	FC	Yards	Avg.	Long	TD
Gordon, Darrien, S.D.	36	13	537	14.9	81t	1
Smith, Rod, Den.	23	15	283	12.3	36	0
Kinchen, Todd, Den.	26	4	300	11.5	40	0
Meggett, Dave, N.E.	52	9	588	11.3	60t	1
Hudson, Chris, Jac.	32	12	348	10.9	60	0
Burris, Jeff, Buf.	27	7	286	10.6	45	0
McDuffie, O. J., Mia.	22	24	212	9.6	19	0
Lewis, Jermaine, Bal.	36	13	339	9.4	46	0
Gray, Mel, Hou.	22	15	205	9.3	40	0
Brown, Tim, Oak.	32	21	272	8.5	36	0
Hastings, Andre, Pit.	37	12	242	6.5	33	0
Chrebet, Wayne, NY-J	28	16	139	5.0	15	0
Nonqualifiers						
Harris, Ronnie, Sea.	19	10	194	10.2	35	0
Harrison, Marvin, Ind.	18	9	177	9.8	31	0
Vanover, Tamarick, K.C.	17	12	116	6.8	24	0
Galloway, Joey, Sea.	15	5	158	10.5	88t	1
Sawyer, Corey, Cin.	15	5	117	7.8	62	0
Penn, Chris, K.C.	14	4	148	10.6	20	0
Copeland, Russell, Buf.	14	7	119	8.5	19	0
Buchanan, Ray, Ind.	12	3	201	16.8	82	0
Hobbs, Daryl, Oak.	10	3	84	8.4	35	0
Myers, Greg, Cin.	9	2	51	5.7	12	0
Floyd, Malcolm, Hou.	7	3	74	10.6	32	0
Dunn, David, Cin.	7	1	54	7.7	20	0
Stablein, Brian, Ind.	6	2	56	9.3	30	0
Stock, Mark, Ind.	5	1	13	2.6	9	0
Buckley, Terrell, Mia.	3	1	24	8.0	13	0
Carter, Dale, K.C.	2	0	18	9.0	15	0
Tasker, Steve, Buf.	2	1	18	9.0	12	0
Arnold, Jahine, Pit.	2	0	6	3.0	5	0
Jones, Charlie, S.D.	1	1	21	21.0	21	0
Alexander, Derrick, Bal.	1	0	15	15.0	15	0
Miller, Scott, Mia.	1	0	15	15.0	15	0
Ethridge, Ray, Bal.	1	0	3	3.0	3	0
Jones, Donta, Pit.	1	0	3	3.0	3	0
McCardell, Keenan, Jac.	1	1	2	2.0	2	0
Pickens, Carl, Cin.	1	0	2	2.0	2	0
Still, Bryan, S.D.	1	0	1	1.0	1	0
Thomas, Dave, Jac.	1	0	1	1.0	1	0
Hundon, James, Cin.	1	0	-7	-7.0	-7	0
Kidd, Carl, Oak.	0	0	47	—	47	0
Hunter, Ernest, Bal.	0	1	0	—	—	0

t = Touchdown
Leader based on average return, minimum 20 returns

NFC—INDIVIDUAL PUNT RETURNERS

	No.	FC	Yards	Avg.	Long	TD
Howard, Desmond, G.B.	58	16	875	15.1	92t	3
Kennison, Eddie, St.L	29	16	423	14.6	78t	2
Oliver, Winslow, Car.	52	17	598	11.5	84t	1
Mitchell, Brian, Was.	23	16	258	11.2	71	0
Metcalf, Eric, Atl.	27	9	296	11.0	39	0
Palmer, David, Min.	22	20	216	9.8	69t	1
Martin, Kelvin, Dal.	41	10	373	9.1	22	0
Engram, Bobby, Chi.	31	19	282	9.1	34	0
Carter, Dexter, S.F.	36	17	317	8.8	52	0
Dowdell, Marcus, Ariz	34	8	297	8.7	35	0
Seay, Mark, Phi.	35	14	305	8.7	56	0
Milburn, Glyn, Det.	34	19	284	8.4	33	0
Hughes, Tyrone, N.O.	30	20	152	5.1	16	0
Nonqualifiers						
Toomer, Amani, NY-G	18	10	298	16.6	87t	2
Silvan, Nilo, T.B.	14	5	113	8.1	17	0
Williams, Karl, T.B.	13	2	274	21.1	88t	1
Marshall, Arthur, NY-G	13	9	144	11.1	36	0
Marshall, Marvin, T.B.	13	1	95	7.3	29	0

	No.	FC	Yards	Avg.	Long	TD
Lee, Amp, Min.	10	11	84	8.4	18	0
Lewis, Thomas, NY-G	10	4	36	3.6	8	0
Edwards, Anthony, Ariz	5	1	46	9.2	20	0
Solomon, Freddie, Phi.	5	3	27	5.4	9	0
O'Berry, Herman, St.L	5	0	16	3.2	8	0
Poole, Tyrone, Car.	3	0	26	8.7	12	0
Mathis, Terance, Atl.	3	1	19	6.3	10	0
Singleton, Nate, S.F.	2	0	32	16.0	21	0
Williams, Kevin, Dal.	2	0	17	8.5	9	0
Guess, Terry, N.O.	1	0	7	7.0	7	0
Sanders, Deion, Dal.	1	1	4	4.0	4	0
Kirby, Terry, S.F.	1	4	3	3.0	3	0
Figaro, Cedric, St.L	1	0	0	0.0	0	0
Heyward, Craig, Atl.	1	0	0	0.0	0	0
Sehorn, Jason, NY-G	1	0	0	0.0	0	0
Hawkins, Courtney, T.B.	1	1	-1	-1.0	-1	0
Davis, Paschall, St.L	0	0	0	—	—	0
Prior, Mike, G.B.	0	1	0	—	—	0
Vincent, Troy, Phi.	0	0	-2	—	-2	0

t = Touchdown
Leader based on average return, minimum 20 returns

KICKOFF RETURNS
Yards Per Return
NFC: 30.2—Michael Bates, Carolina
AFC: 25.9—Tamarick Vanover, Kansas City
Yards
NFC: 1791—Tyrone Hughes, New Orleans
AFC: 1224—Mel Gray, Houston
Yards, Game
NFC: 253—Derrick Witherspoon, Philadelphia at Arizona, November 24 (8 returns - TD)
AFC: 206—Andre Coleman, San Diego at Seattle, October 27 (8 returns)
Longest
AFC: 97—Tamarick Vanover, Kansas City at Denver, October 27 - TD
Eric Moulds, Buffalo vs. N.Y. Jets, November 24 - TD
NFC: 97—Derrick Witherspoon, Philadelphia at Atlanta, September 22 - TD
Returns
NFC: 70—Tyrone Hughes, New Orleans
AFC: 55—Andre Coleman, San Diego
Returns, Game
NFC: 9—Eric Metcalf, Atlanta at San Francisco, September 29 (176 yards)
Eric Metcalf, Atlanta at St. Louis, November 10 (144 yards)
AFC: 8—Andre Coleman, San Diego at Seattle, October 27 (206 yards)
Touchdowns
NFC: 2—Derrick Witherspoon, Philadelphia
AFC: 1—Aaron Bailey, Indianapolis
David Dunn, Cincinnati
Eric Moulds, Buffalo
Erric Pegram, Pittsburgh
Tamarick Vanover, Kansas City
Team Champion
NFC: 26.2—Carolina
AFC: 23.9—Denver

AFC KICKOFF RETURNS—TEAM
	No.	Yards	Avg.	Long	TD
Denver.	50	1195	23.9	59	0
Kansas City	66	1567	23.7	97t	1
Buffalo	58	1341	23.1	97t	1
Indianapolis	61	1403	23.0	95t	1
New England	64	1424	22.3	54	0
Pittsburgh	53	1171	22.1	91t	1
Miami	60	1320	22.0	59	0
Jacksonville	67	1463	21.8	73	0
Seattle	71	1542	21.7	86	0
San Diego.	63	1358	21.6	57	0
Houston	66	1421	21.5	88	0
Oakland	61	1276	20.9	48	0
Cincinnati	70	1459	20.8	90t	1
Baltimore.	86	1734	20.2	44	0
N.Y. Jets	79	1504	19.0	37	0
AFC Total	975	21178	21.7	97t	5
AFC Average	65.0	1411.9	21.7	—	0.3

NFC KICKOFF RETURNS—TEAM
	No.	Yards	Avg.	Long	TD
Carolina	50	1310	26.2	93t	1
Dallas.	53	1339	25.3	89	0
New Orleans	78	1899	24.3	58	0
Detroit	69	1675	24.3	65	0
Chicago	56	1337	23.9	88	0
Tampa Bay.	55	1287	23.4	63	0
Philadelphia	64	1439	22.5	97t	2
Green Bay.	47	1038	22.1	90t	1
Washington	65	1401	21.6	50	0
San Francisco	59	1258	21.3	71	0
Arizona	75	1582	21.1	92	0
Atlanta	87	1825	21.0	55	0
St. Louis.	62	1233	19.9	44	0
N.Y. Giants	66	1287	19.5	47	0
Minnesota.	58	1075	18.5	60	0
NFC Total	944	20985	22.2	97t	4
NFC Average	62.9	1399.0	22.2	—	0.3
League Total	1919	42163	—	97t	9
League Average	64.0	1405.4	—	—	0.3

NFL TOP TEN KICKOFF RETURNERS
	No.	Yards	Avg.	Long	TD
Bates, Michael, Car.	33	998	30.2	93t	1
Walker, Herschel, Dal.	27	779	28.9	89	0
Vanover, Tamarick, K.C.	33	854	25.9	97t	1
Hughes, Tyrone, N.O.	70	1791	25.6	58	0
Milburn, Glyn, Det.	64	1627	25.4	65	0
Gray, Mel, Hou.	50	1224	24.5	88	0
Hebron, Vaughn, Den.	45	1099	24.4	59	0
Spikes, Irving, Mia.	28	681	24.3	59	0
Bailey, Aaron, Ind.	43	1041	24.2	95t	1
Witherspoon, Derrick, Phi.	53	1271	24.0	97t	2

1996 INDIVIDUAL STATISTICS—KICKOFF RETURNS

AFC KICKOFF RETURNERS—INDIVIDUAL

	No.	Yards	Avg.	Long	TD
Vanover, Tamarick, K.C.	33	854	25.9	97t	1
Gray, Mel, Hou.	50	1224	24.5	88	0
Hebron, Vaughn, Den.	45	1099	24.4	59	0
Spikes, Irving, Mia.	28	681	24.3	59	0
Bailey, Aaron, Ind.	43	1041	24.2	95t	1
Woods, Jerome, K.C.	25	581	23.2	66	0
Moulds, Eric, Buf.	52	1205	23.2	97t	1
Meggett, Dave, N.E.	34	781	23.0	54	0
Broussard, Steve, Sea.	43	979	22.8	86	0
Dunn, David, Cin.	35	782	22.3	90t	1
Coleman, Andre, S.D.	55	1210	22.0	57	0
Kaufman, Napoleon, Oak.	25	548	21.9	39	0
Brown, Troy, N.E.	29	634	21.9	51	0
Lewis, Jermaine, Bal.	41	883	21.5	44	0
Kidd, Carl, Oak.	29	622	21.4	48	0
Jordan, Randy, Jac.	26	553	21.3	73	0
Cobb, Reggie, NY-J	23	488	21.2	34	0
Baldwin, Randy, Bal.	20	405	20.3	34	0
Bailey, Henry, NY-J	24	470	19.6	34	0
Nonqualifiers					
Arnold, Jahine, Pit.	19	425	22.4	30	0
Pegram, Erric, Pit.	17	419	24.6	91t	1
Brooks, Bucky, Jac.	17	412	24.2	36	0
McPhail, Jerris, Mia.	15	335	22.3	40	0
Van Dyke, Alex, NY-J	15	289	19.3	37	0
Stock, Mark, Ind.	12	254	21.2	28	0
Sawyer, Corey, Cin.	12	241	20.1	33	0
Harris, Ronnie, Sea.	12	240	20.0	29	0
Hundon, James, Cin.	10	237	23.7	31	0
Hill, Jeff, Cin.	9	173	19.2	29	0
Ethridge, Ray, Bal.	8	171	21.4	29	0
Mills, Ernie, Pit.	8	146	18.3	27	0
Moore, Ronald, NY-J	8	118	14.8	28	0
Harris, Corey, Sea.	7	166	23.7	41	0
Bullard, Kendricke, Jac.	7	157	22.4	36	0
Jackson, Willie, Jac.	7	149	21.3	27	0
Dar Dar, Kirby, Mia.	7	132	18.9	25	0
Copeland, Russell, Buf.	6	136	22.7	47	0
Bell, Ricky, Jac.	6	119	19.8	28	0
Johnson, Charles, Pit.	6	111	18.5	31	0
Carpenter, Ron, NY-J	6	107	17.8	21	0
Thomas, Rodney, Hou.	5	80	16.0	35	0
Still, Bryan, S.D.	4	113	28.3	37	0
Jordan, Charles, Mia.	4	81	20.3	22	0
Harmon, Ronnie, Hou.	4	69	17.3	20	0
Byner, Earnest, Bal.	4	61	15.3	19	0
Brown, Reggie, Sea.	4	51	12.8	24	0
McKnight, James, Sea.	3	86	28.7	55	0
Warren, Lamont, Ind.	3	54	18.0	18	0
Shedd, Kenny, Oak.	3	51	17.0	19	0
Chamberlain, Byron, Den.	3	49	16.3	21	0
Smith, Jimmy, Jac.	2	49	24.5	29	0
Hughes, Danan, K.C.	2	42	21.0	22	0
Anders, Kimble, K.C.	f2	37	18.5	20	0
Manusky, Greg, K.C.	2	32	16.0	17	0
Brady, Kyle, NY-J	f2	26	13.0	16	0
Archie, Mike, Hou.	2	24	12.0	13	0
Griffith, Richard, Jac.	2	24	12.0	16	0
McNair, Todd, K.C.	2	21	10.5	16	0
Sadowski, Troy, Cin.	2	7	3.5	7	0
McKeehan, James, Hou.	2	6	3.0	6	0
Wycheck, Frank, Hou.	2	5	2.5	5	0
Hill, Randal, Mia.	2	4	2.0	4	0
Buckley, Terrell, Mia.	1	48	48.0	48	0
Hastings, Andre, Pit.	1	42	42.0	42	0
Smith, Rod, Den.	1	29	29.0	29	0
Brown, Tim, Oak.	1	24	24.0	24	0
Buchanan, Ray, Ind.	1	20	20.0	20	0
Witman, Jon, Pit.	1	20	20.0	20	0
Kinchen, Brian, Bal.	1	19	19.0	19	0
Groce, Clif, Ind.	1	18	18.0	18	0
Jeffers, Patrick, Den.	1	18	18.0	18	0
Aska, Joe, Oak.	1	17	17.0	17	0
Thomas, Zach, Mia.	1	17	17.0	17	0
Hetherington, Chris, Ind.	1	16	16.0	16	0
Pupunu, Alfred, S.D.	1	15	15.0	15	0
Hobbs, Daryl, Oak.	1	14	14.0	14	0
Alexander, Derrick, Bal.	1	13	13.0	13	0
Roan, Michael, Hou.	1	13	13.0	13	0
Barber, Michael, Sea.	1	12	12.0	12	0
Wilson, Robert, Mia.	1	12	12.0	12	0

	No.	Yards	Avg.	Long	TD
Cothran, Jeff, Cin.	1	11	11.0	11	0
Harrison, Rodney, S.D.	1	10	10.0	10	0
Russell, Leonard, S.D.	1	10	10.0	10	0
Wainright, Frank, Mia.	1	10	10.0	10	0
Gisler, Mike, N.E.	1	9	9.0	9	0
Battaglia, Marco, Cin.	1	8	8.0	8	0
Fauria, Christian, Sea.	1	8	8.0	8	0
Perry, Darren, Pit.	1	8	8.0	8	0
Glenn, Aaron, NY-J	1	6	6.0	6	0
Morris, Bam, Bal.	1	3	3.0	3	0
Isaia, Sale, Bal.	1	2	2.0	2	0
Edwards, Vernon, S.D.	1	0	0.0	0	0
Gossett, Jeff, Oak.	1	0	0.0	0	0
Crumpler, Carlester, Sea.	0	0	—	—	0
Murrell, Adrian, NY-J	0	0	—	—	0
Stablein, Brian, Ind.	0	0	—	—	0
Frederick, Mike, Bal.	0	-1	—	-1	0

t = Touchdown
f = Fair Catch
Leader based on average return, minimum 20 returns

NFC KICKOFF RETURNERS—INDIVIDUAL

	No.	Yards	Avg.	Long	TD
Bates, Michael, Car.	33	998	30.2	93t	1
Walker, Herschel, Dal.	27	779	28.9	89	0
Hughes, Tyrone, N.O.	70	1791	25.6	58	0
Milburn, Glyn, Det.	64	1627	25.4	65	0
Witherspoon, Derrick, Phi.	53	1271	24.0	97t	2
Engram, Bobby, Chi.	25	580	23.2	45	0
Jackson, Jack, Chi.	27	619	22.9	60	0
Mitchell, Brian, Was.	56	1258	22.5	50	0
Williams, Kevin, Dal.	21	471	22.4	39	0
Silvan, Nilo, T.B.	28	626	22.4	54	0
Carter, Dexter, S.F.	41	909	22.2	71	0
Wheatley, Tyrone, NY-G	23	503	21.9	43	0
Thomas, J.T., St.L	30	643	21.4	43	0
Preston, Roell, Atl.	32	681	21.3	50	0
McElroy, Leeland, Ariz	54	1148	21.3	92	0
Metcalf, Eric, Atl.	49	1034	21.1	55	0
Howard, Desmond, G.B.	22	460	20.9	40	0
Kennison, Eddie, St.L	23	454	19.7	44	0
Ismail, Qadry, Min.	28	527	18.8	32	0
Nonqualifiers					
Hamilton, Conrad, NY-G	19	382	20.1	29	0
Beebe, Don, G.B.	15	403	26.9	90t	1
Williams, Karl, T.B.	14	383	27.4	63	0
Palmer, David, Min.	13	292	22.5	60	0
Marshall, Marvin, T.B.	12	264	22.0	37	0
Toomer, Amani, NY-G	11	191	17.4	25	0
Loville, Derek, S.F.	10	229	22.9	35	0
Hunter, Ernest, Bal.-N.O.	10	198	19.8	29	0
Johnson, LeShon, Ariz	10	198	19.8	27	0
Bell, William, Was.	8	130	16.3	27	0
Oliver, Winslow, Car.	7	160	22.9	33	0
Garner, Charlie, Phi.	6	117	19.5	28	0
Morrow, Harold, Min.	6	117	19.5	26	0
Dowdell, Marcus, Ariz	5	122	24.4	31	0
Ismail, Raghib, Car.	5	100	20.0	30	0
Lee, Amp, Min.	5	85	17.0	23	0
Levens, Dorsey, G.B.	5	84	16.8	29	0
Lewis, Thomas, NY-G	4	107	26.8	47	0
Terry, Ryan, Ariz	4	84	21.0	30	0
Anderson, Jamal, Atl.	4	80	20.0	27	0
Phillips, Lawrence, St.L	4	74	18.5	35	0
Faulkerson, Mike, Chi.	4	63	15.8	20	0
Seay, Mark, Phi.	4	51	12.8	22	0
Crawford, Keith, St.L	4	47	11.8	19	0
Marion, Brock, Dal.	3	68	22.7	37	0
Owens, Terrell, S.F.	3	47	15.7	18	0
Brown, Richard, Min.	3	35	11.7	12	0
Saxton, Brian, NY-G	3	31	10.3	12	0
Henderson, William, G.B.	2	38	19.0	23	0
Hayes, Mercury, N.O.	2	30	15.0	17	0
Alexander, Kevin, NY-G	2	27	13.5	14	0
Williams, Charlie, Dal.	2	21	10.5	21	0
Deese, Derrick, S.F.	2	20	10.0	12	0
Way, Charles, NY-G	2	19	9.5	10	0
Smith, Brady, N.O.	2	14	7.0	8	0
Greene, Scott, Car.	2	10	5.0	6	0
Kirby, Terry, S.F.	1	22	22.0	22	0
Uwaezuoke, Iheanyi, S.F.	1	21	21.0	21	0

	No.	Yards	Avg.	Long	TD
Thomason, Jeff, G.B.	1	20	20.0	20	0
Hoard, Leroy, Car.	1	19	19.0	19	0
Heyward, Craig, Atl.	1	18	18.0	18	0
McCleskey, J. J., N.O.	1	18	18.0	18	0
Jervey, Travis, G.B.	1	17	17.0	17	0
Freeman, Antonio, G.B.	1	16	16.0	16	0
Kozlowski, Brian, NY-G	1	16	16.0	16	0
Lusk, Henry, N.O.	1	16	16.0	16	0
McDonald, Devon, Ariz	1	16	16.0	16	0
Laing, Aaron, St.L	1	15	15.0	15	0
Lynch, Eric, Det.	1	15	15.0	15	0
Alstott, Mike, T.B.	1	14	14.0	14	0
Smith, Cedric, Ariz	1	14	14.0	14	0
Washington, Keith, Det.	1	14	14.0	14	0
Asher, Jamie, Was.	1	13	13.0	13	0
Gerak, John, Min.	1	13	13.0	13	0
Bickett, Duane, Car.	1	12	12.0	12	0
Styles, Lorenzo, Atl.	1	12	12.0	12	0
Baker, Myron, Car.	1	11	11.0	11	0
Douglas, Omar, NY-G	1	11	11.0	11	0
Brown, Derek, N.O.	1	10	10.0	10	0
Matthews, Aubrey, Det.	1	10	10.0	10	0
Singleton, Nate, S.F.	1	10	10.0	10	0
Rivers, Ron, Det.	1	8	8.0	8	0
Carter, Cris, Min.	1	3	3.0	3	0
DeLong, Greg, Min.	1	3	3.0	3	0
Metzelaars, Pete, Det.	1	1	1.0	1	0
Brooks, Barrett, Phi.	1	0	0.0	0	0
Marshall, Anthony, Chi.	0	75	—	75	0
Ellison, Jerry, T.B.	0	0	—	0	0

t = Touchdown
f = Fair Catch

FUMBLES

Most Fumbles
- **NFC:** 21—Tony Banks, St. Louis
- **AFC:** 14—Mark Brunell, Jacksonville

Most Fumbles, Game
- **AFC:** 4—Craig Erickson, Miami vs. Seattle, October 6
- **NFC:** 4—Steve Beuerlein, Carolina at Jacksonville, September 29
  Tony Banks, St. Louis at Atlanta, December 15

Own Fumbles Recovered
- **AFC:** 5—Mark Brunell, Jacksonville
  Jeff Hostetler, Oakland
- **NFC:** 5—Brett Favre, Green Bay
  Scott Mitchell, Detroit

Most Own Fumbles Recovered, Game
- **AFC:** 3—Craig Erickson, Miami vs. Seattle, October 6
  Lonnie Johnson, Buffalo vs. Kansas City, December 22
- **NFC:** 2—Jeff George, Atlanta vs. Minnesota, September 8
  Brett Favre, Green Bay vs. Tampa Bay, October 27
  Scott Mitchell, Detroit at Chicago, November 24
  LeShon Johnson, Arizona vs. Dallas, December 8

Opponents' Fumbles Recovered
- **AFC:** 4—Louis Oliver, Miami
- **NFC:** 3—by many

Most Opponents' Fumbles Recovered, Game
- **AFC:** 2—Bill Romanowski, Denver at Seattle, September 8
  Tony Brackens, Jacksonville vs. Carolina, September 29
  Junior Seau, San Diego vs. Denver, December 22
  Terry Wooden, Seattle at Oakland, December 22
- **NFC:** 2—Bryan Cox, Chicago vs. Dallas, September 2 - TD
  Rhett Hall, Philadelphia vs. Dallas, September 30 - TD
  Broderick Thomas, Dallas at Philadelphia, September 30
  Carl Simpson, Chicago at New Orleans, October 13
  Anthony Newman, New Orleans at Tampa Bay, November 24

Yards
- **AFC:** 85—Carnell Lake, Pittsburgh
- **NFC:** 66—Kevin Greene, Carolina

Longest
- **AFC:** 85—Carnell Lake, Pittsburgh vs. Jacksonville, November 17 - TD
- **NFC:** 66—Kevin Greene, Carolina vs. St. Louis, October 13 - TD

AFC FUMBLES—TEAM

	Fum.	Own. Rec.	Fum. OB	TD	Opp. Rec.	TD	Fum. Yards	Tot. Rec.
Kansas City	17	6	1	0	10	1	87	16
Cincinnati	19	7	3	0	10	1	46	17
Baltimore	23	8	2	0	7	0	18	15
Indianapolis	24	11	0	0	10	0	4	21
Seattle	24	10	2	0	18	0	97	28
Buffalo	25	11	2	0	14	1	12	25
New England	25	11	2	0	11	2	93	22
N.Y. Jets	25	7	2	0	15	1	-14	22
Houston	26	10	1	0	14	0	14	24
Denver	27	10	2	0	9	0	27	19
Pittsburgh	27	12	1	0	17	2	160	29
Jacksonville	29	17	2	0	14	0	-1	31
Oakland	30	16	2	0	9	1	5	25
San Diego	30	15	4	0	14	0	-10	29
Miami	31	15	3	2	16	0	12	31
AFC Total	382	166	29	2	188	9	550	354
AFC Average	25.5	11.1	1.9	0.1	12.5	0.6	36.7	23.6

NFC FUMBLES—TEAM

	Fum.	Own. Rec.	Fum. OB	TD	Opp. Rec.	TD	Fum. Yards	Tot. Rec.
San Francisco	16	6	2	0	14	1	89	20
Detroit	21	15	1	0	8	1	-9	23
Washington	21	13	1	0	9	1	-2	22
Atlanta	23	11	1	0	17	0	-10	28
Dallas	24	6	3	0	13	1	72	19
Philadelphia	24	8	2	0	12	3	101	20
Carolina	25	10	1	0	16	3	151	26
Chicago	25	15	1	0	11	2	34	26
Minnesota	26	12	2	0	13	0	7	25
N.Y. Giants	27	12	2	0	13	1	57	25
Tampa Bay	28	11	3	0	12	0	-2	23
Arizona	29	11	4	0	14	1	27	25
New Orleans	30	8	2	0	10	1	38	18
Green Bay	33	19	3	1	12	0	18	31
St. Louis	42	19	2	0	13	0	-38	32
NFC Total	394	176	30	1	187	15	533	363
NFC Average	26.3	11.7	2.0	0.1	12.5	1.0	35.5	24.2
NFL Total	776	342	59	3	375	24	1083	717
NFL Average	25.9	11.4	2.0	0.1	12.5	0.8	36.1	23.9

Fum OB = Fumbled out of bounds, includes fumbled through the end zone.
Fumbled through the end zone, ball awarded to opponents: Dallas (ball awarded to Washington), San Francisco (ball awarded to Carolina).

AFC FUMBLES—INDIVIDUAL

	Fum.	Own. Rec.	Opp. Rec.	Yards	Tot. Rec.
Abdul-Jabbar, Karim, Mia	4	0	0	0	0
Adams, Sam, Sea	0	0	1	2	1
Allen, Marcus, K.C	0	0	0	0	0
Anderson, Darren, K.C.	0	0	1	0	1
Anderson, Richie, NY-J	0	0	1	0	1
Araguz, Leo, Oak	0	1	0	0	1
Armstrong, Trace, Mia.	0	0	2	0	2
Arnold, Jahine, Pit	1	0	0	0	0
Arvie, Herman, Bal	0	1	0	0	1
Aska, Joe, Oak	1	0	0	0	0
Atkins, James, Sea	0	2	0	0	2
Atwater, Steve, Den	1	0	0	0	0
Bailey, Aaron, Ind	3	1	0	0	1
Baldwin, Randy, Bal	1	0	0	0	0
Ball, Jerry, Oak	0	0	1	0	1
Ballard, Howard, Sea	0	1	0	0	1
Barber, Michael, Sea	0	0	1	0	1
Barnett, Fred, Mia	1	0	0	0	0
Barrow, Micheal, Hou	0	0	1	0	1
Battaglia, Marco, Cin.	0	0	1	0	1
Baxter, Fred, NY-J	1	0	0	0	0
Bell, Myron, Pit	0	0	2	0	2
Bell, Ricky, Jac	1	0	0	0	0
Belser, Jason, Ind	0	0	1	0	1
Bettis, Jerome, Pit	7	2	0	0	2
Biekert, Greg, Oak	0	0	1	0	1

	Fum.	Own Rec.	Opp. Rec.	Yards	Tot. Rec.		Fum.	Own Rec.	Opp. Rec.	Yards	Tot. Rec.
Bieniemy, Eric, Cin	1	0	0	0	0	Galloway, Joey, Sea	2	0	0	0	0
Blackmon, Robert, Sea.	0	0	1	5	1	Gannon, Rich, K.C	1	0	0	0	0
Blades, Brian, Sea	1	0	0	0	0	Gardener, Daryl, Mia	0	0	1	0	1
Blake, Jeff, Cin	7	1	0	-5	1	George, Eddie, Hou	3	1	0	0	1
Bledsoe, Drew, N.E	9	1	0	-2	1	Glenn, Terry, N.E	1	0	0	0	0
Boatswain, Harry, NY-J	0	1	0	0	1	Gogan, Kevin, Oak	0	1	0	0	1
Bono, Steve, K.C	5	0	0	0	0	Gordon, Darrien, S.D	3	0	0	0	0
Booker, Vaughn, K.C	0	0	1	0	1	Gossett, Jeff, Oak	1	1	0	-19	1
Boselli, Tony, Jac	0	1	0	0	1	Grant, Steve, Ind	0	0	1	0	1
Bowens, Tim, Mia	0	0	1	0	1	Gray, Carlton, Sea	0	0	1	62	1
Brackens, Tony, Jac	0	0	3	0	3	Gray, Mel, Hou	4	0	0	0	0
Brady, Donny, Bal	0	0	1	0	1	Green, Victor, NY-J	0	0	3	0	3
Brady, Kyle, NY-J	1	0	0	0	0	Grier, Marrio, N.E	0	0	1	4	1
Braxton, Tyrone, Den	0	0	1	20	1	Griffith, Richard, Jac	0	1	0	0	1
Brock, Matt, NY-J	0	0	1	5	1	Groce, Clif, Ind	2	1	0	0	1
Broussard, Steve, Sea.	2	0	0	0	0	Grunhard, Tim, K.C	0	1	0	0	1
Brown, Chad, Pit	1	0	2	0	2	Hall, Dana, Jac	0	1	1	0	2
Brown, Corwin, N.E	0	0	1	42	1	Hamilton, Bobby, NY-J.	0	0	1	7	1
Brown, Tim, Oak	3	1	0	0	1	Hamilton, Rick, NY-J	0	0	1	0	1
Bruce, Aundray, Oak	0	0	1	3	1	Hand, Norman, Mia	0	0	1	8	1
Brunell, Mark, Jac	14	5	0	-14	5	Hansen, Phil, Buf	0	0	2	0	2
Buckley, Terrell, Mia.	1	1	1	0	2	Harbaugh, Jim, Ind	8	4	0	-3	4
Buckner, Brentson, Pit	1	0	1	13	1	Hardy, Kevin, Jac	0	0	1	13	1
Bullard, Kendricke, Jac	1	0	0	0	0	Harris, Anthony, Mia	0	0	1	0	1
Burris, Jeff, Buf	1	0	1	0	1	Harris, Corey, Sea	0	0	3	28	3
Burton, Shane, Mia	0	0	1	0	1	Harrison, Marvin, Ind.	1	0	0	0	0
Burton, Kendrick, Hou.	0	0	1	9	1	Harrison, Rodney, S.D.	1	1	1	4	2
Bush, Lewis, S.D	0	0	2	0	2	Hastings, Andre, Pit	3	1	0	0	1
Butcher, Paul, Oak	0	1	0	0	1	Hasty, James, K.C	0	0	1	80	1
Byner, Earnest, Bal	1	0	0	0	0	Hayden, Aaron, S.D	1	1	0	0	1
Cadrez, Glenn, Den	0	1	0	0	1	Hearst, Garrison, Cin.	1	1	0	0	1
Carter, Dale, K.C	1	1	1	7	2	Hebron, Vaughn, Den	3	1	0	0	1
Carter, Ki-Jana, Cin	2	2	0	-8	2	Henry, Kevin, Pit	0	0	1	4	1
Cascadden, Chad, NY-J.	0	0	1	0	1	Hill, Greg, K.C	1	0	0	0	0
Cash, Keith, K.C	1	0	0	0	0	Hill, Jeff, Cin	1	0	1	0	1
Chalenski, Mike, NY-J.	0	0	1	0	1	Hill, Randal, Mia	1	0	0	0	0
Chamberlain, Byron, Den	1	0	0	0	0	Hill, Sean, Mia	0	1	0	10	1
Chandler, Chris, Hou	8	3	0	-4	3	Hilliard, Randy, Den	0	1	0	0	1
Chrebet, Wayne, NY-J	5	2	0	0	2	Hobbs, Daryl, Oak	4	2	0	0	2
Clark, Willie, S.D	0	0	1	9	1	Hobert, Billy Joe, Oak	6	0	0	0	0
Clay, Willie, N.E	0	0	1	17	1	Holmes, Darick, Buf	2	1	0	0	1
Coates, Ben, N.E	1	0	0	0	0	Hopkins, Brad, Hou	0	1	0	0	1
Coleman, Andre, S.D	4	3	0	0	3	Hostetler, Jeff, Oak	4	5	0	-3	5
Collins, Mark, K.C	0	0	1	0	1	Houston, Bobby, NY-J	0	0	1	0	1
Collins, Todd, Buf	3	0	0	0	0	Hudson, Chris, Jac	3	1	1	0	2
Copeland, Russell, Buf	2	1	0	0	1	Hull, Kent, Buf	0	1	0	1	1
Coryatt, Quentin, Ind.	0	0	2	7	2	Humphries, Stan, S.D	7	4	0	-6	4
Craver, Aaron, Den	1	0	0	0	0	Hundon, James, Cin	1	0	0	0	0
Crockett, Zack, Ind	2	0	0	0	0	Irvin, Ken, Buf	0	0	1	0	1
Crumpler, Carlester, Sea	1	0	0	0	0	Isaia, Sale, Bal	1	1	0	0	1
Cunningham, T.J., Sea.	0	0	1	0	1	Jackson, Calvin, Mia	1	0	0	0	0
Daniel, Eugene, Ind	0	0	1	0	1	Jackson, John, Pit	0	1	0	0	1
Daniels, Phillip, Sea.	0	0	1	0	1	Jackson, Michael, Bal.	0	0	1	0	1
Davey, Don, Jac	0	0	1	0	1	Jackson, Steve, Hou	0	0	1	0	1
Davidson, Kenny, Cin	0	0	1	0	1	James, Tory, Den	0	0	1	15	1
Davis, Reuben, S.D	0	0	1	0	1	Jefferson, Shawn, N.E.	2	0	0	0	0
Davis, Terrell, Den	5	2	0	0	2	Jenkins, DeRon, Bal	0	0	1	0	1
Davis, Travis, Jac	0	1	1	0	2	Johnson, Charles, Pit.	1	0	0	0	0
Davis, Willie, Hou	1	0	0	0	0	Johnson, Lonnie, Buf	1	3	1	0	4
Dawkins, Sean, Ind	1	0	0	0	0	Johnson, Ted, N.E	0	0	1	0	1
Dilger, Ken, Ind	1	0	0	0	0	Johnson, Bill, Pit	0	0	1	0	1
Dishman, Cris, Hou	0	0	2	0	2	Johnstone, Lance, Oak.	0	0	1	1	1
Douglas, Hugh, NY-J	0	0	3	64	3	Jones, Gary, NY-J	0	0	1	0	1
Drayton, Troy, Mia	0	1	0	0	1	Jones, Lenoy, Hou	0	0	1	0	1
Dudley, Rickey, Oak	1	0	0	0	0	Jones, Mike, N.E	0	0	1	31	1
Duffy, Roger, NY-J	0	1	0	0	1	Jordan, Randy, Jac	1	1	0	0	1
Dunn, David, Cin	1	0	0	0	0	Jurkovic, John, Jac	0	0	2	0	2
Eatman, Irv, Hou	0	1	0	0	1	Justin, Paul, Ind	1	1	0	0	1
Elway, John, Den	6	2	0	-4	2	Kaufman, Napoleon, Oak	3	0	0	0	0
Emmons, Carlos, Pit	0	1	0	0	1	Kelly, Jim, Buf	9	0	0	0	0
Emtman, Steve, Mia	0	0	1	0	1	Kennedy, Lincoln, Oak.	0	1	0	0	1
Erickson, Craig, Mia	4	3	0	-3	3	Kidd, Carl, Oak	2	1	0	0	1
Ethridge, Ray, Bal	0	1	0	0	1	Kinchen, Brian, Bal	1	0	0	-20	0
Faulk, Marshall, Ind	2	0	0	0	0	Kinchen, Todd, Den	5	1	0	0	1
Figures, Deon, Pit	0	1	0	0	1	Klingler, David, Oak	1	1	0	0	1
Fina, John, Buf	0	1	1	-1	2	Lake, Carnell, Pit	0	0	2	85	2
Fletcher, Terrell, S.D	1	0	1	0	1	Land, Dan, Oak	0	0	2	0	2
Floyd, Malcolm, Hou	1	0	0	0	0	Lane, Max, N.E	0	3	0	0	3
Foley, Glenn, NY-J	1	0	0	-4	0	Langford, Jevon, Cin	0	0	1	0	1
Francis, James, Cin	0	0	3	0	3	Lester, Tim, Pit	1	0	0	0	0
Friesz, John, Sea	7	2	0	-6	2	Lewis, Jermaine, Bal	4	1	0	0	1

	Fum.	Own Rec.	Opp. Rec.	Yards	Tot. Rec.
Mahlum, Eric, Ind	0	1	0	0	1
Manusky, Greg, K.C	1	1	2	0	3
Marino, Dan, Mia	4	1	0	-3	1
Martin, Curtis, N.E	4	1	0	0	1
Martin, Steve, Ind	0	0	1	0	1
Mathews, Jason, Ind	0	1	0	0	1
Mawae, Kevin, Sea	0	2	0	0	2
May, Deems, S.D	0	0	1	0	1
McCardell, Keenan, Jac	1	3	0	0	3
McCoy, Tony, Ind	0	0	1	0	1
McCrary, Michael, Sea.	0	0	1	0	1
McDuffie, O. J., Mia	6	3	0	0	3
McGinest, Willie, N.E.	0	0	2	0	2
McKnight, James, Sea	0	0	1	0	1
McNair, Steve, Hou	7	4	0	0	4
McPhail, Jerris, Mia	2	1	0	0	1
Means, Natrone, Jac	3	1	0	0	1
Meggett, David, N.E	7	3	1	0	4
Miller, Jim, Pit	1	0	0	-4	0
Miller, Scott, Mia	0	1	0	0	1
Milloy, Lawyer, N.E	0	0	1	0	1
Mills, Ernie, Pit	0	0	1	5	1
Mills, John Henry, Hou	0	0	2	0	2
Mims, Chris, S.D	0	0	2	0	2
Mirer, Rick, Sea	4	0	0	0	0
Mitchell, Pete, Jac	1	0	0	0	0
Mitchell, Shannon, S.D	1	0	0	0	0
Montgomery, Greg, Bal.	1	1	0	0	1
Moore, Stevon, Bal	0	0	1	0	1
Morrison, Steve, Ind	0	0	2	0	2
Moten, Eric, S.D	0	1	0	0	1
Moulds, Eric, Buf	1	0	0	0	0
Murrell, Adrian, NY-J.	6	2	0	-16	2
Musgrave, Bill, Den	3	0	0	-4	0
Myers, Greg, Cin	1	0	0	0	0
Neujahr, Quentin, Bal.	0	1	0	0	1
O'Donnell, Neil, NY-J.	2	0	0	0	0
Oliver, Louis, Mia	1	1	4	7	5
Olsavsky, Jerry, Pit	0	0	1	6	1
Orlando, Bo, Cin	0	1	0	0	1
Ostroski, Jerry, Buf	0	1	0	0	1
Parker, Glenn, Buf	0	2	0	0	2
Parker, Vaughn, S.D	0	1	0	0	1
Parmalee, Bernie, Mia.	1	0	0	0	0
Pegram, Erric, Pit	1	1	0	0	1
Penn, Chris, K.C	3	0	0	0	0
Perry, Darren, Pit	1	1	1	0	2
Perry, Michael Dean, Den	0	0	1	0	1
Pleasant, Anthony, Bal	0	0	1	36	1
Pollard, Marcus, Ind	0	1	0	0	1
Pritchett, Kelvin, Jac	0	0	2	0	2
Pritchett, Stanley, Mia	3	1	0	0	1
Pupunu, Alfred, S.D	1	2	0	0	2
Ravotti, Eric, Pit	0	0	1	9	1
Reed, Andre, Buf	1	0	0	0	0
Reich, Frank, NY-J	9	1	0	-70	1
Richardson, Tony, K.C.	0	1	0	0	1
Rivers, Reggie, Den	0	1	0	0	1
Robbins, Barret, Oak	0	1	0	0	1
Roberson, James, Hou	0	0	1	4	1
Robertson, Marcus, Hou	0	0	1	5	1
Robinson, Eddie, Jac	0	0	1	0	1
Robinson, Rafael, Hou.	0	0	1	0	1
Robinson, Jeff, Den	0	1	0	0	1
Rogers, Sam, Buf	0	0	2	0	2
Romanowski, Bill, Den.	0	0	3	0	3
Ross, Kevin, S.D	0	0	1	0	1
Roye, Orpheus, Pit	0	1	0	0	1
Ruddy, Tim, Mia	1	0	0	-14	0
Russell, Leonard, S.D.	6	2	0	-7	2
Salisbury, Sean, S.D	3	0	0	-10	0
Sawyer, Corey, Cin	2	1	0	0	1
Searcy, Leon, Jac	0	1	0	0	1
Seau, Junior, S.D	0	0	3	0	3
Sharpe, Shannon, Den	1	0	0	0	0
Simien, Tracy, K.C	0	0	1	0	1
Simmons, Clyde, Jac	0	0	1	0	1
Siragusa, Tony, Ind	0	0	1	0	1
Slade, Chris, N.E	1	0	0	0	0
Smith, Anthony, Oak	0	0	1	3	1
Smith, Artie, Cin	0	0	1	0	1
Smith, Bruce, Buf	0	0	1	0	1
Smith, Jimmy, Jac	1	0	0	0	0
Smith, Lamar, Sea	4	1	0	0	1
Smith, Rod, Den	1	0	0	0	0
Spencer, Jimmy, Cin	0	0	1	59	1
Spielman, Chris, Buf	0	0	2	0	2
Spikes, Irving, Mia	1	0	0	0	0
Spindler, Marc, NY-J	0	0	1	0	1
Steed, Joel, Pit	0	0	1	0	1
Stevens, Matt, Buf	0	0	1	0	1
Stewart, James, Jac	2	1	0	0	1
Stewart, Kordell, Pit.	1	0	0	0	0
Still, Bryan, S.D	2	0	0	0	0
Strong, Mack, Sea	0	0	1	0	1
Sullivan, Chris, N.E	0	1	0	0	1
Sutter, Eddie, Bal	0	0	1	0	1
Swilling, Pat, Oak	0	0	1	49	1
Tanuvasa, Maa, Den	0	0	1	0	1
Tasker, Steve, Buf	3	0	0	0	0
Testaverde, Vinny, Bal	9	0	0	-11	0
Thomas, Dave, Jac	1	0	0	0	0
Thomas, Derrick, K.C	0	0	1	0	1
Thomas, Thurman, Buf	1	1	0	0	1
Thomas, Zach, Mia	0	0	2	7	2
Tindale, Tim, Buf	1	0	0	0	0
Tomczak, Mike, Pit	7	2	0	0	2
Tovar, Steve, Cin	1	0	0	0	0
Turk, Dan, Oak	1	0	1	-29	1
Vanover, Tamarick, K.C	1	0	0	0	0
Walker, Derrick, K.C	0	1	0	0	1
Walker, Gary, Hou	0	0	1	0	1
Walter, Joe, Cin	0	1	0	0	1
Warren, Chris, Sea	3	2	0	4	2
Warren, Lamont, Ind	3	1	0	0	1
Washington, Brian, K.C	0	0	1	0	1
Wells, Dean, Sea	0	0	2	0	2
Wheeler, Mark, N.E	0	0	1	0	1
Whigham, Larry, N.E	0	0	1	0	1
White, David, Buf	0	0	2	12	2
Wilkinson, Dan, Cin	1	0	1	0	1
Williams, Alfred, Den.	0	0	1	0	1
Williams, Dan, Den	0	0	1	0	1
Williams, Darryl, Sea.	0	0	1	2	1
Williams, Harvey, Oak.	3	0	0	0	0
Williams, Jerrol, Bal.	1	1	1	13	2
Williams, Ronnie, Sea.	0	0	1	0	1
Williams, Willie, Pit.	0	0	1	0	1
Wohlabaugh, Dave, N.E.	0	2	0	1	2
Wooden, Shawn, Mia	0	1	1	0	2
Wooden, Terry, Sea	0	0	2	0	2
Woods, Jerome, K.C	1	1	0	0	1
Woodson, Rod, Pit	1	1	2	42	3
Wortham, Barron, Hou	0	0	2	0	2
Wycheck, Frank, Hou	2	0	0	0	0
Young, Glen, S.D	0	0	1	0	1
Zeier, Eric, Bal	2	1	0	0	1

Yards includes aborted plays, own recoveries and opponents' recoveries.

NFC FUMBLES—INDIVIDUAL

	Fum.	Own Rec.	Opp. Rec.	Yards	Tot. Rec.
Abraham, Donnie, T.B	0	0	2	3	2
Ahanotu, Chidi, T.B	0	0	1	0	1
Aikman, Troy, Dal	6	2	0	-8	2
Alexander, Derrick, Min	0	0	1	3	1
Allen, Terry, Was	4	0	0	0	0
Alstott, Mike, T.B	4	0	0	0	0
Anderson, Jamal, Atl	4	0	1	0	1
Armstead, Jessie, NY-G	1	0	2	0	2
Arthur, Mike, G.B	1	0	0	0	0
Asher, Jamie, Was	0	2	0	0	2
Baker, Myron, Car	0	1	0	0	1
Banks, Tony, St.L	21	4	0	-17	4
Bankston, Michael, Ariz	0	0	1	0	1
Barnett, Harlon, Min	0	0	1	0	1
Bates, Mario, N.O	4	0	0	0	0
Bates, Michael, Car	2	0	0	0	0
Bates, Patrick, Atl	0	0	1	0	1
Beebe, Don, G.B	1	1	0	0	1
Bennett, Cornelius, Atl	0	0	2	0	2

	Fum.	Own Rec.	Opp. Rec.	Yards	Tot. Rec.
Bennett, Edgar, G.B	2	1	0	0	1
Bercich, Pete, Min	0	0	1	0	1
Beuerlein, Steve, Car.	9	2	0	-7	2
Birden, J. J., Atl	2	0	0	0	0
Bishop, Greg, NY-G	0	1	0	0	1
Bjornson, Eric, Dal	1	0	0	0	0
Bradford, Ronnie, Ariz	0	0	1	0	1
Brady, Jeff, Min	0	0	3	0	3
Bratzke, Chad, NY-G	0	0	2	0	2
Brohm, Jeff, S.F	1	1	0	0	1
Brooks, Barrett, Phi	0	1	0	0	1
Brooks, Reggie, T.B	1	0	0	0	0
Brooks, Bill, Was	0	1	0	0	1
Brown, Dave, NY-G	9	1	0	-3	1
Brown, Dennis, S.F	0	0	1	0	1
Bruce, Isaac, St.L	1	0	0	0	0
Bryant, Junior, S.F	0	1	0	0	1
Buckley, Curtis, S.F	0	1	1	0	2
Burger, Todd, Chi	0	1	0	0	1
Bush, Devin, Atl	0	0	1	0	1
Butler, LeRoy, G.B	0	1	1	2	2
Calloway, Chris, NY-G.	1	1	0	7	1
Campbell, Jesse, NY-G.	0	0	1	0	1
Carrier, Mark, Chi	0	0	1	0	1
Carter, Tony, Chi	1	1	0	0	1
Carter, Cris, Min	1	0	1	0	1
Carter, Dexter, S.F	5	0	0	0	0
Carter, Kevin, St.L	0	1	1	0	2
Centers, Larry, Ariz	1	1	0	0	1
Cherry, Je'Rod, N.O.	0	0	1	0	1
Clay, Hayward, St.L	0	1	0	0	1
Clemons, Duane, Min	0	0	1	8	1
Collins, Kerry, Car	6	1	0	0	1
Compton, Mike, Det	1	0	0	0	0
Conway, Curtis, Chi	1	0	0	0	0
Conwell, Ernie, St.L	0	0	1	0	1
Cook, Toi, Car	0	0	1	3	1
Cooper, Adrian, S.F	1	0	0	0	0
Cota, Chad, Car	1	0	1	0	1
Cox, Bryan, Chi	0	0	3	0	3
Cross, Howard, NY-G	1	0	0	0	0
Dahl, Bob, Was	0	1	0	0	1
Darby, Matt, Ariz	0	0	1	0	1
Davis, Don, N.O	0	0	1	0	1
Dawkins, Brian, Phi	0	0	2	23	2
Dawsey, Lawrence, NY-G	0	1	0	0	1
DeLong, Greg, Min	0	1	0	0	1
Dennis, Mark, Car	0	1	0	0	1
Detmer, Ty, Phi	7	1	0	0	1
Dilfer, Trent, T.B	10	4	0	-4	4
Dimry, Charles, T.B	0	0	1	0	1
Dixon, Ernest, N.O	0	0	1	22	1
Doleman, Chris, S.F	0	0	3	13	3
Donaldson, Ray, Dal	2	0	0	-3	0
Dotson, Earl, G.B	0	1	0	0	1
Dotson, Santana, G.B	0	0	1	8	1
Douglass, Maurice, NY-G	0	0	1	1	1
Dowdell, Marcus, Ariz.	6	0	0	0	0
Downs, Gary, NY-G	1	1	0	0	1
Drakeford, Tyrone, S.F	0	0	1	8	1
Dunn, Jason, Phi	0	1	0	0	1
Edwards, Anthony, Ariz	1	0	1	0	1
Elliott, Matt, Car	0	1	0	0	1
Ellison, Jerry, T.B	2	1	0	0	1
Ellsworth, Percy, NY-G	0	0	1	0	1
Engram, Bobby, Chi	2	0	0	0	0
Esiason, Boomer, Ariz.	5	1	0	-8	1
Evans, Doug, G.B	1	0	1	2	1
Everett, Jim, N.O	10	1	0	-9	1
Farmer, Ray, Phi	1	0	3	10	3
Favre, Brett, G.B	11	5	0	-10	5
Feagles, Jeff, Ariz	1	0	0	-7	0
Fields, Mark, N.O	0	0	1	20	1
Figaro, Cedric, St.L	1	1	0	0	1
Fisk, Jason, Min	0	0	1	0	1
Floyd, William, S.F	4	1	0	0	1
Forbes, Marlon, Chi	0	1	0	0	1
Fortin, Roman, Atl	0	2	0	0	2
Freeman, Antonio, G.B.	3	1	0	14	1
Frerotte, Gus, Was	12	1	0	-12	1
Fuller, William, Phi	0	0	1	0	1
Garcia, Frank, Car	0	2	0	0	2
Gardner, Moe, Atl	0	0	1	0	1
Garner, Charlie, Phi	1	0	0	0	0
Garnett, Dave, Min	0	0	1	0	1
Gaskins, Percell, St.L	0	0	1	0	1
George, Jeff, Atl	3	2	0	-24	2
George, Ron, Atl	0	0	3	14	3
Gerak, John, Min	0	1	0	0	1
Glover, Kevin, Det	0	2	0	0	2
Goeas, Leo, St.L	0	1	0	0	1
Gooch, Jeff, T.B	0	1	0	0	1
Graham, Kent, Ariz	5	0	0	0	0
Green, Darrell, Was	0	0	1	15	1
Green, Harold, St.L	2	1	0	0	1
Green, Robert, Chi	3	3	0	0	3
Greene, Kevin, Car	0	0	3	66	3
Griffith, Howard, Car.	1	0	1	0	1
Griffith, Robert, Min.	1	0	0	0	0
Hall, Rhett, Phi	0	0	2	32	2
Hall, Travis, Atl	0	0	1	0	1
Hampton, Rodney, NY-G.	3	1	0	0	1
Harper, Alvin, T.B	1	0	0	0	0
Harris, Derrick, St.L.	0	1	0	0	1
Harris, Jackie, T.B	1	0	0	0	0
Harris, James, St.L	0	0	1	22	1
Harris, Raymont, Chi	3	0	0	0	0
Harris, Walt, Chi	0	0	2	8	2
Hartings, Jeff, Det	0	1	0	0	1
Harvey, Ken, Was	1	0	2	0	2
Hawkins, Courtney, T.B	1	0	0	0	0
Hayes, Mercury, N.O	1	0	0	0	0
Haynes, Michael, N.O	1	0	0	0	0
Hebert, Bobby, Atl	10	2	0	0	2
Henderson, William, G.B	1	0	0	0	0
Hennings, Chad, Dal	0	0	1	0	1
Hentrich, Craig, G.B	0	1	0	0	1
Hicks, Michael, Chi	1	0	0	0	0
Hoage, Terry, Ariz	0	0	1	0	1
Hoard, Leroy, Min	3	0	0	0	0
Howard, Desmond, G.B	2	1	0	0	1
Hoying, Bobby, Phi	1	0	0	0	0
Hughes, Tyrone, N.O	2	0	0	0	0
Hunter, Ernest, Bal.-N.O	4	1	0	0	1
Hutton, Tom, Phi	0	1	0	0	1
Irvin, Michael, Dal	1	0	0	0	0
Irving, Terry, Ariz	0	0	1	5	1
Ismail, Qadry, Min	2	1	0	0	1
Israel, Steve, S.F	0	0	1	0	1
Jackson, Jack, Chi	2	0	0	0	0
Jackson, Greg, N.O	1	0	0	0	0
Jeffires, Haywood, N.O	1	0	0	0	0
Jenkins, Carlos, St.L.	0	0	2	0	2
Jenkins, James, Was	0	1	0	0	1
Jervey, Travis, G.B	4	1	0	0	1
Johnson, Anthony, Car.	2	0	0	0	0
Johnson, Tre', Was	0	1	0	0	1
Johnson, Brad, Min	5	3	0	-8	3
Johnson, LeShon, Ariz.	5	2	0	0	2
Johnson, Melvin, T.B	0	0	1	0	1
Johnston, Daryl, Dal	1	1	0	0	1
Jones, Brian, N.O	0	0	1	11	1
Jones, Chris T., Phi	1	0	0	0	0
Jones, Sean, G.B	0	0	1	0	1
Jones, Jimmie, St.L	0	0	2	0	2
Joyner, Seth, Ariz	0	0	1	0	1
Kanell, Danny, NY-G	2	0	0	-1	0
Kennison, Eddie, St.L.	5	0	0	0	0
King, Ed, N.O.	0	1	0	0	1
King, Shawn, Car	0	0	1	12	1
Kirby, Terry, S.F	1	0	0	0	0
Koonce, George, G.B	0	0	1	0	1
Kowalkowski, Scott, Det	0	0	1	0	1
Kragen, Greg, Car	0	0	2	0	2
Kramer, Erik, Chi	1	1	0	-1	1
Krieg, Dave, Chi	6	3	0	-9	3
Laing, Aaron, St.L	0	1	0	0	1
Landeta, Sean, St.L	1	1	0	-11	1
Lathon, Lamar, Car	0	0	2	4	2
LeBel, Harper, Atl	0	0	1	0	1
Lee, Amp, Min.	2	1	0	0	1
Lett, Leon, Dal	0	0	2	0	2

	Fum.	Own Rec.	Opp. Rec.	Yards	Tot. Rec.
Levens, Dorsey, G.B	2	1	0	0	1
Lincoln, Jeremy, St.L.	0	1	0	0	1
Logan, Marc, Was	1	0	0	0	0
Lowery, Michael, Chi	0	0	1	0	1
Lusk, Henry, N.O	1	0	0	0	0
Lyght, Todd, St.L	1	0	0	0	0
Lyle, Keith, St.L	1	0	0	0	0
Lynch, Eric, Det	1	0	0	0	0
Lynch, John, T.B	1	0	1	0	1
Majkowski, Don, Det	5	1	0	-6	1
Mamula, Mike, Phi	0	1	2	4	3
Marion, Brock, Dal	1	0	1	45	1
Marshall, Marvin, T.B.	1	0	0	0	0
Martin, Jamie, St.L	2	1	0	-2	1
Martin, Wayne, N.O	0	0	1	0	1
Martin, Kelvin, Dal	1	0	0	0	0
Marts, Lonnie, T.B	0	1	1	0	2
Mathis, Terance, Atl	0	1	0	0	1
Mayberry, Tony, T.B	0	1	0	0	1
McCollum, Andy, N.O	0	1	0	0	1
McDonald, Tim, S.F	0	0	1	0	1
McElroy, Leeland, Ariz	3	1	0	0	1
McGill, Lenny, Atl	0	0	1	0	1
McKyer, Tim, Atl	0	1	1	0	2
McMahon, Jim, G.B	1	1	0	0	1
McMillian, Mark, N.O	0	1	0	-6	1
McNeil, Ryan, Det	0	0	2	0	2
Metcalf, Eric, Atl	3	0	0	0	0
Mickens, Terry, G.B	1	1	0	0	1
Miller, Jamir, Ariz	0	0	1	26	1
Miller, Les, Car	0	0	1	14	1
Mills, Sam, Car	0	0	2	41	2
Mitchell, Brian, Was	1	2	0	0	2
Mitchell, Kevin, S.F	0	0	1	0	1
Mitchell, Scott, Det	9	5	0	-3	5
Moon, Warren, Min	7	2	0	0	2
Morrison, Darryl, Was.	0	1	3	14	4
Morton, Johnnie, Det	1	0	0	0	0
Nagle, Browning, Atl	1	0	0	0	0
Neal, Lorenzo, N.O	1	2	0	0	2
Newman, Anthony, N.O	0	0	2	0	2
Newsome, Craig, G.B	0	1	0	0	1
Nickerson, Hardy, T.B.	0	0	2	0	2
Norton, Ken, S.F	0	0	1	21	1
Nussmeier, Doug, N.O	2	0	0	0	0
O'Berry, Herman, St.L.	1	0	0	0	0
Odom, Jason, T.B	0	1	0	0	1
Oliver, Winslow, Car	4	0	0	0	0
O'Neal, Leslie, St.L	0	0	3	0	3
Owens, Dan, Atl	0	0	1	0	1
Owens, Terrell, S.F	1	0	0	0	0
Palmer, David, Min	3	1	0	0	1
Parker, Anthony, St.L.	0	0	1	0	1
Patton, Joe, Was	0	1	0	0	1
Paul, Tito, Ariz	0	1	0	0	1
Peete, Rodney, Phi	2	1	0	0	1
Perry, Todd, Chi	0	1	0	0	1
Phillips, Lawrence, St.L	2	1	0	0	1
Pierce, Aaron, NY-G	0	1	0	0	1
Poole, Tyrone, Car	0	0	1	0	1
Pope, Marquez, S.F	0	0	1	4	1
Popson, Ted, S.F	0	1	0	0	1
Porcher, Robert, Det	0	0	2	0	2
Pounds, Darryl, Was	0	0	1	0	1
Price, Daryl, S.F	0	0	1	0	1
Randolph, Thomas, NY-G	0	0	1	17	1
Rasby, Walter, Car	0	1	0	0	1
Raymer, Cory, Was	0	1	0	0	1
Redmon, Anthony, Ariz.	0	1	0	0	1
Rhett, Errict, T.B	3	1	0	0	1
Rice, Simeon, Ariz	0	0	1	0	1
Richards, David, Atl	0	1	0	0	1
Rison, Andre, G.B	1	0	0	0	0
Roaf, Willie, N.O	0	1	0	0	1
Roberts, Ray, Det	0	2	0	0	2
Robinson, Greg, St.L	1	0	0	0	0
Ross, Jermaine, St.L	0	0	1	0	1
Royal, Andre, Car	0	1	0	0	1
Royals, Mark, Det	0	1	0	0	1
Salaam, Rashaan, Chi	3	1	0	0	1
Sanders, Barry, Det	4	2	0	0	2
Sanders, Deion, Dal	2	0	3	15	3
Sanders, Frank, Ariz	1	1	0	0	1
Sapp, Warren, T.B	0	0	1	0	1
Saxton, Brian, NY-G	0	1	0	0	1
Scott, Todd, T.B	0	0	1	0	1
Scroggins, Tracy, Det.	0	0	1	0	1
Seay, Mark, Phi	2	0	0	0	0
Sehorn, Jason, NY-G	1	1	0	0	1
Shelley, Elbert, Atl	0	0	1	0	1
Shepherd, Leslie, Was.	0	1	0	0	1
Shuler, Heath, Was	1	0	0	-14	0
Simpson, Carl, Chi	0	0	2	2	2
Sloan, David, Det	0	1	0	0	1
Small, Torrance, N.O	1	0	0	0	0
Smith, Chuck, Atl	0	0	1	0	1
Smith, Emmitt, Dal	5	1	0	0	1
Smith, Fernando, Min	0	0	2	4	2
Smith, Robert, Min	2	1	0	0	1
Smith, Vinson, Chi	0	0	2	34	2
Stephens, Rod, Was	0	0	1	0	1
Steussie, Todd, Min	0	1	0	0	1
Strickland, Fred, Dal.	0	0	1	0	1
Stubblefield, Dana, S.F	0	0	1	0	1
Swann, Eric, Ariz	0	0	3	11	3
Taylor, Aaron, G.B	0	1	0	0	1
Taylor, Bobby, Phi	1	1	1	9	2
Terry, Ryan, Ariz	1	1	0	0	1
Thomas, Broderick, Dal	0	0	3	23	3
Thomas, Henry, Det	0	0	1	0	1
Thomas, J.T., St.L	1	0	0	0	0
Thomas, Mark, Car	0	0	1	18	1
Thomas, Orlando, Min	0	0	1	0	1
Thomas, William, Phi	0	0	1	23	1
Timpson, Michael, Chi.	2	1	0	0	1
Tolbert, Tony, Dal	0	0	2	0	2
Toomer, Amani, NY-G	1	2	0	0	2
Tubbs, Winfred, N.O	0	0	1	0	1
Turk, Matt, Was	1	0	0	-5	0
Turnbull, Renaldo, N.O	0	0	1	0	1
Turner, Kevin, Phi	1	0	0	0	0
Turner, Scott, Was	0	0	1	0	1
Unutoa, Morris, Phi	1	0	0	0	0
Upshaw, Regan, T.B	0	0	1	0	1
Valerio, Joe, St.L	1	0	0	-30	0
Walker, Darnell, Atl	0	1	0	0	1
Walker, Herschel, Dal.	0	1	0	0	1
Walsh, Steve, St.L	1	1	0	0	1
Watters, Ricky, Phi	5	0	0	0	0
Way, Charles, NY-G	0	0	3	0	3
Weldon, Casey, T.B	1	0	0	-1	0
Wells, Mike, Det	0	0	1	0	1
Wheatley, Tyrone, NY-G	6	1	0	-18	1
White, Dwayne, St.L	0	1	0	0	1
White, Reggie, G.B	2	0	3	2	3
Whitfield, Bob, Atl	0	1	0	0	1
Whittle, Ricky, N.O	1	0	0	0	0
Widmer, Corey, NY-G	1	0	1	0	1
Wiegert, Zach, St.L	0	2	0	0	2
Williams, Aeneas, Ariz	0	0	1	0	1
Williams, Brian, G.B	0	0	3	0	3
Williams, Charlie, Dal	1	0	0	0	0
Williams, James, Chi	0	2	0	0	2
Williams, Karl, T.B	2	1	0	0	1
Williams, Sherman, Dal	2	0	0	0	0
Williams, Tyrone, G.B.	0	0	1	0	1
Wilson, Bernard, Ariz.	0	0	1	0	1
Winters, Frank, G.B	0	1	0	0	1
Witherspoon, Derrick, Phi	1	0	0	0	0
Wolf, Joe, Ariz	0	2	0	0	2
Woodard, Marc, Phi	0	1	0	0	1
Woodson, Darren, Dal	1	1	0	0	1
Wooten, Tito, NY-G	0	0	1	54	1
Young, Bryant, S.F	0	0	1	43	1
Young, Steve, S.F	3	1	0	0	1
Zellars, Ray, N.O	2	0	0	0	0
Zgonina, Jeff, Atl	0	0	1	0	1

Yards includes aborted plays, own recoveries, and opponents' recoveries.

SACKS

Most Sacks

NFC: 14.5—Kevin Greene, Carolina

AFC: 13.5—Michael McCrary, Seattle
Bruce Smith, Buffalo

Most Sacks, Game

AFC: 4.5—Chad Brown, Pittsburgh vs. Cincinnati, October 13

NFC: 3.5—John Randle, Minnesota vs. Green Bay, September 22

Team Champion

NFC: 60—Carolina

AFC: 51—Pittsburgh

AFC SACKS—TEAM

	Sacks	Yards
Pittsburgh	51	369
Buffalo	48	341
Seattle	48	285
Denver	40	274
Jacksonville	37	237
Miami	37	233
Houston	35	242
Oakland	34	252
New England	33	252
San Diego	33	201
Cincinnati	32	202
Kansas City	31	193
Baltimore	30	146
Indianapolis	29	182
N.Y. Jets	28	178
AFC Total	546	3587
AFC Average	36.4	239.1

NFC SACKS—TEAM

	Sacks	Yards
Carolina	60	371
San Francisco	45	297
Minnesota	43	263
New Orleans	41	283
Philadelphia	40	264
Dallas	37	219
Green Bay	37	202
Atlanta	36	208
Tampa Bay	35	207
Washington	34	207
Detroit	32	233
St. Louis	32	181
Chicago	30	209
N.Y. Giants	30	178
Arizona	28	185
NFC Total	560	3507
NFC Average	37.3	233.8
League Total	1106	7094
League Average	36.9	236.5

NFL TOP TEN LEADERS

	Total
Greene, Kevin, Car.	14.5
Lathon, Lamar, Car.	13.5
McCrary, Michael, Sea.	13.5
Smith, Bruce, Buf.	13.5
Brown, Chad, Pit.	13.0
Fuller, William, Phi.	13.0
Sinclair, Michael, Sea.	13.0
Thomas, Derrick, K.C.	13.0
Williams, Alfred, Den.	13.0
Barker, Roy, S.F.	12.5
Rice, Simeon, Ariz	12.5

AFC SACKS—INDIVIDUAL

McCrary, Michael, Sea.	13.5	McGlockton, Chester, Oak.	8.0
Smith, Bruce, Buf.	13.5	Cook, Anthony, Hou.	7.5
Brown, Chad, Pit.	13.0	Simmons, Clyde, Jac.	7.5
Sinclair, Michael, Sea.	13.0	Brackens, Tony, Jac.	7.0
Thomas, Derrick, K.C.	13.0	Gildon, Jason, Pit.	7.0
Williams, Alfred, Den.	13.0	Seau, Junior, S.D.	7.0
Armstrong, Trace, Mia.	12.0	Slade, Chris, N.E.	7.0
McGinest, Willie, N.E.	9.5	Dent, Richard, Ind.	6.5
Stubbs, Danny, Mia.	9.0	Wilkinson, Dan, Cin.	6.5
Douglas, Hugh, NY-J	8.0	Barrow, Micheal, Hou.	6.0
Hansen, Phil, Buf.	8.0	Bennett, Tony, Ind.	6.0
Kennedy, Cortez, Sea.	8.0	Mims, Chris, S.D.	6.0
		Paup, Bryce, Buf.	6.0

Smith, Neil, K.C.	6.0	Mobley, John, Den.	1.5
Swilling, Pat, Oak.	6.0	Sawyer, Corey, Cin.	1.5
Adams, Sam, Sea.	5.5	Alexander, Elijah, Ind.	1.0
Hardy, Kevin, Jac.	5.5	Bailey, Robert, Mia.	1.0
Walker, Gary, Hou.	5.5	Bayless, Martin, K.C.	1.0
Geathers, Jumpy, Den.	5.0	Beasley, Aaron, Jac.	1.0
Jeffcoat, Jim, Buf.	5.0	Belser, Jason, Ind.	1.0
McCoy, Tony, Ind.	5.0	Blackmon, Robert, Sea.	1.0
McDonald, Ricardo, Cin.	5.0	Booker, Vaughn, K.C.	1.0
Northern, Gabe, Buf.	5.0	Bush, Lewis, S.D.	1.0
Smeenge, Joel, Jac.	5.0	Collins, Mark, K.C.	1.0
Tanuvasa, Maa, Den.	5.0	Eaton, Chad, N.E.	1.0
Caldwell, Mike, Bal.	4.5	Edwards, Vernon, S.D.	1.0
Hamilton, Bobby, NY-J	4.5	Ford, Henry, Hou.	1.0
Lageman, Jeff, Jac.	4.5	Fortune, Elliott, Bal.	1.0
Bruce, Aundray, Oak.	4.0	Gardener, Daryl, Mia.	1.0
Bruschi, Tedy, N.E.	4.0	Gouveia, Kurt, S.D.	1.0
Coleman, Marco, S.D.	4.0	Grant, Steve, Ind.	1.0
Crockett, Ray, Den.	4.0	Harris, Corey, Sea.	1.0
Kirkland, Levon, Pit.	4.0	Harrison, Rodney, S.D.	1.0
Pleasant, Anthony, Bal.	4.0	Hasty, James, K.C.	1.0
Young, Robert, Hou.	4.0	Hill, Sean, Mia.	1.0
Perry, Michael Dean, Den.	3.5	Hollier, Dwight, Mia.	1.0
Rogers, Sam, Buf.	3.5	Holmberg, Rob, Oak.	1.0
Washington, Ted, Buf.	3.5	Holmes, Earl, Pit.	1.0
Ball, Jerry, Oak.	3.0	Johnson, Bill, Pit.	1.0
Bowden, Joe, Hou.	3.0	Johnstone, Lance, Oak.	1.0
Bowens, Tim, Mia.	3.0	Jones, James, Bal.	1.0
Buckner, Brentson, Pit.	3.0	Jones, Donta, Pit.	1.0
Burnett, Rob, Bal.	3.0	Jones, Marvin, NY-J	1.0
Burton, Shane, Mia.	3.0	Jones, Mike, Oak.	1.0
Cascadden, Chad, NY-J	3.0	Jurkovic, John, Jac.	1.0
Copeland, John, Cin.	3.0	Kerner, Marlon, Buf.	1.0
Croel, Mike, Bal.	3.0	Lee, Shawn, S.D.	1.0
Davis, Reuben, S.D.	3.0	Lloyd, Greg, Pit.	1.0
Francis, James, Cin.	3.0	Lyle, Rick, Bal.	1.0
Goad, Tim, Bal.	3.0	Martin, Steve, Ind.	1.0
Johnson, Raylee, S.D.	3.0	Milloy, Lawyer, N.E.	1.0
Lewis, Albert, Oak.	3.0	Mix, Bryant, Hou.	1.0
Roberson, James, Hou.	3.0	Morton, Mike, Oak.	1.0
Romanowski, Bill, Den.	3.0	Moss, Winston, Sea.	1.0
Sagapolutele, Pio, N.E.	3.0	Orlando, Bo, Cin.	1.0
Thompson, Bennie, Bal.	3.0	Perry, Darren, Pit.	1.0
Tovar, Steve, Cin.	3.0	Ray, Terry, N.E.	1.0
Whittington, Bernard, Ind.	3.0	Raybon, Israel, Pit.	1.0
Williams, Jerrol, Bal.	3.0	Robinson, Eddie, Jac.	1.0
Davis, Anthony, K.C.	2.5	Smith, Artie, Cin.	1.0
Emmons, Carlos, Pit.	2.5	Smith, Otis, N.E.	1.0
Gibson, Oliver, Pit.	2.5	Tate, David, Ind.	1.0
Johnson, Tim, Cin.	2.5	Traylor, Keith, K.C.	1.0
Lewis, Ray, Bal.	2.5	Von Oelhoffen, Kimo, Cin.	1.0
Washington, Marvin, NY-J	2.5	Wells, Dean, Sea.	1.0
Bell, Myron, Pit.	2.0	Wheeler, Mark, N.E.	1.0
Brock, Matt, NY-J	2.0	Williams, Dan, Den.	1.0
Browning, John, K.C.	2.0	Williams, Willie, Pit.	1.0
Daniels, Phillip, Sea.	2.0	Woodson, Rod, Pit.	1.0
Edwards, Antonio, Sea.	2.0	Wyman, Devin, N.E.	1.0
Emtman, Steve, Mia.	2.0	Brady, Donny, Bal.	0.5
Gordon, Darrien, S.D.	2.0	Buchanan, Ray, Ind.	0.5
Green, Victor, NY-J	2.0	Chalenski, Mike, NY-J	0.5
Gunn, Mark, NY-J	2.0	Collons, Ferric, N.E.	0.5
Harrison, Nolan, Oak.	2.0	Davey, Don, Jac.	0.5
Hasselbach, Harald, Den.	2.0	Davis, Travis, Jac.	0.5
Irvin, Ken, Buf.	2.0	Footman, Dan, Bal.	0.5
Jackson, Steve, Hou.	2.0	Hand, Norman, Mia.	0.5
Jones, Mike, N.E.	2.0	Hudson, Chris, Jac.	0.5
Lake, Carnell, Pit.	2.0	Lewis, Mo, NY-J	0.5
Langford, Jevon, Cin.	2.0	McGruder, Mike, N.E.	0.5
Maryland, Russell, Oak.	2.0	Morabito, Tim, Cin.	0.5
Oldham, Chris, Pit.	2.0	Olsavsky, Jerry, Pit.	0.5
Parrella, John, S.D.	2.0	Robinson, Jeff, Den.	0.5
Phillips, Joe, K.C.	2.0	Sabb, Dwayne, N.E.	0.5
Pritchett, Kelvin, Jac.	2.0	Spindler, Marc, NY-J	0.5
Ravotti, Eric, Pit.	2.0	Washington, Brian, K.C.	0.5
Siragusa, Tony, Ind.	2.0	White, David, Buf.	0.5
Smith, Anthony, Oak.	2.0		
Stallings, Ramondo, Cin.	2.0		
Thomas, Zach, Mia.	2.0		
Wortham, Barron, Hou.	2.0		
Hamilton, Rick, NY-J	1.5		
Henry, Kevin, Pit.	1.5		
Jackson, Calvin, Mia.	1.5		
Lodish, Mike, Den.	1.5		

NFC SACKS—INDIVIDUAL

Player	Sacks
Greene, Kevin, Car.	14.5
Lathon, Lamar, Car.	13.5
Fuller, William, Phi.	13.0
Barker, Roy, S.F.	12.5
Rice, Simeon, Ariz	12.5
Tolbert, Tony, Dal.	12.0
Randle, John, Min.	11.5
Young, Bryant, S.F.	11.5
Doleman, Chris, S.F.	11.0
Martin, Wayne, N.O.	11.0
Owens, Rich, Was.	11.0
Porcher, Robert, Det.	10.0
Carter, Kevin, St.L	9.5
Smith, Fernando, Min.	9.5
Harvey, Ken, Was.	9.0
Sapp, Warren, T.B.	9.0
White, Reggie, G.B.	8.5
Mamula, Mike, Phi.	8.0
Spellman, Alonzo, Chi.	8.0
Johnson, Joe, N.O.	7.5
Harrison, Martin, Min.	7.0
Marts, Lonnie, T.B.	7.0
O'Neal, Leslie, St.L	7.0
Butler, LeRoy, G.B.	6.5
Elliss, Luther, Det.	6.5
Matthews, Clay, Atl.	6.5
Turnbull, Renaldo, N.O.	6.5
Hall, Travis, Atl.	6.0
Smith, Chuck, Atl.	6.0
Thomas, Henry, Det.	6.0
Ahanotu, Chidi, T.B.	5.5
Dotson, Santana, G.B.	5.5
Jones, Jimmie, St.L	5.5
Mills, Sam, Car.	5.5
Owens, Dan, Atl.	5.5
Thomas, William, Phi.	5.5
Bratzke, Chad, NY-G	5.0
Flanigan, Jim, Chi.	5.0
Jones, Sean, G.B.	5.0
Joyner, Seth, Ariz	5.0
Nottage, Dexter, Was.	5.0
Strahan, Mike, NY-G	5.0
Swann, Eric, Ariz	5.0
Farr, D'Marco, St.L	4.5
Fontenot, Al, Chi.	4.5
Hall, Rhett, Phi.	4.5
Harris, Robert, NY-G	4.5
Hennings, Chad, Dal.	4.5
Thomas, Broderick, Dal.	4.5
Cook, Toi, Car.	4.0
Thomas, Mark, Car.	4.0
Upshaw, Regan, T.B.	4.0
Alexander, Derrick, Min.	3.5
Edwards, Dixon, Min.	3.5
Lett, Leon, Dal.	3.5
Armstead, Jessie, NY-G	3.0
Bennett, Cornelius, Atl.	3.0
Carver, Shante, Dal.	3.0
Cox, Bryan, Chi.	3.0
Evans, Doug, G.B.	3.0
Gilbert, Sean, Was.	3.0
Hamilton, Keith, NY-G	3.0
King, Shawn, Car.	3.0
Kragen, Greg, Car.	3.0
London, Antonio, Det.	3.0
Mickell, Darren, N.O.	3.0
Miller, Les, Car.	3.0
Nickerson, Hardy, T.B.	3.0
Sehorn, Jason, NY-G	3.0
Wilkins, Gabe, G.B.	3.0
Woodson, Darren, Dal.	3.0
Bailey, Carlton, Car.	2.5
Jefferson, Greg, Phi.	2.5
McCormack, Hurvin, Dal.	2.5
Simmons, Wayne, G.B.	2.5
Tuaolo, Esera, Min.	2.5
Waldroup, Kerwin, Det.	2.5
Woodall, Lee, S.F.	2.5
Archambeau, Lester, Atl.	2.0
Bickett, Duane, Car.	2.0
Bonham, Shane, Det.	2.0
Broughton, Willie, N.O.	2.0
Brown, Dennis, S.F.	2.0
Curry, Eric, T.B.	2.0
Drakeford, Tyronne, S.F.	2.0
Fields, Mark, N.O.	2.0
Fox, Mike, Car.	2.0
George, Ron, Atl.	2.0
Griffith, Robert, Min.	2.0
Harris, James, St.L	2.0
Harvey, Richard, N.O.	2.0
Miller, Corey, NY-G	2.0
Molden, Alex, N.O.	2.0
Patton, Marvcus, Was.	2.0
Scroggins, Tracy, Det.	2.0
Smith, Brady, N.O.	2.0
Thierry, John, Chi.	2.0
Widmer, Corey, NY-G	2.0
Brady, Jeff, Min.	1.5
Culpepper, Brad, T.B.	1.5
Miniefield, Kevin, Chi.	1.5
Minter, Barry, Chi.	1.5
Phifer, Roman, St.L	1.5
Simpson, Carl, Chi.	1.5
Barnett, Harlon, Min.	1.0
Brandon, David, Atl.	1.0
Brown, Gilbert, G.B.	1.0
Cain, Joe, Chi.	1.0
Childress, Ray, Dal.	1.0
Cota, Chad, Car.	1.0
Dawkins, Brian, Phi.	1.0
Farmer, Ray, Phi.	1.0
Fisk, Jason, Min.	1.0
Goss, Antonio, St.L	1.0
Haley, Charles, Dal.	1.0
Harmon, Andy, Phi.	1.0
Johnson, Kevin, Phi.	1.0
Jones, Marcus, T.B.	1.0
Lynch, John, T.B.	1.0
Mangum, John, Chi.	1.0
Mayhew, Martin, T.B.	1.0
McDonald, Tim, S.F.	1.0
McKenzie, Keith, G.B.	1.0
McKyer, Tim, Atl.	1.0
Miller, Jamir, Ariz	1.0
Mitchell, Kevin, S.F.	1.0
Osborne, Chuck, St.L	1.0
Ottis, Brad, Ariz	1.0
Palmer, Sterling, Was.	1.0
Riddick, Louis, Atl.	1.0
Robbins, Austin, N.O.	1.0
Rudolph, Coleman, NY-G	1.0
Smith, Ben, Ariz	1.0
Smith, Darrin, Dal.	1.0
Smith, Rod, Car.	1.0
Smith, Vinson, Chi.	1.0
Stephens, Rod, Was.	1.0
Stokes, Fred, N.O.	1.0
Strickland, Fred, Dal.	1.0
Stubblefield, Dana, S.F.	1.0
Taylor, Bobby, Phi.	1.0
Thomas, Hollis, Phi.	1.0
Tubbs, Winfred, N.O.	1.0
Tuggle, Jessie, Atl.	1.0
Walker, Brian, Was.	1.0
Williams, Aeneas, Ariz	1.0
Williams, Gerald, Car.	1.0
Wilson, Bernard, Ariz	1.0
Woods, Tony, Was.	1.0
Zgonina, Jeff, Atl.	1.0
Agnew, Ray, NY-G	0.5
Bankston, Michael, Ariz	0.5
Bryant, Junior, S.F.	0.5
Clavelle, Shannon, G.B.	0.5
Griffin, Don, Phi.	0.5
Williams, Brian, G.B.	0.5

1996 NFL PAID ATTENDANCE BREAKDOWN

	Games	Attendance	Average
AFC Preseason	9	377,676	41,964
NFC Preseason	8	365,084	45,636
AFC-NFC Preseason, Interconference	46	2,524,494	54,880
NFL Preseason Total	**63**	**3,267,254**	**51,861**
AFC Regular Season	90	5,565,139	61,835
NFC Regular Season	90	5,375,302	59,726
AFC-NFC Regular Season, Interconference	60	3,671,976	61,200
NFL Regular Season Total	**240**	**14,612,417**	**60,885**
AFC Wild Card Playoffs	2		
Jacksonville at Buffalo		68,994	
Indianapolis at Pittsburgh		59,365	
AFC Divisional Playoffs	2		
Jacksonville at Denver		75,151	
Pittsburgh at New England		60,462	
AFC Championship Game	1		
Jacksonville at New England		60,887	
NFC Wild Card Playoffs	2		
Minnesota at Dallas		62,808	
Philadelphia at San Francisco		66,096	
NFC Divisional Playoffs	2		
Dallas at Carolina		72,055	
San Francisco at Green Bay		60,370	
NFC Championship Game	1		
Carolina at Green Bay		60,790	
Super Bowl XXXI at New Orleans, Louisiana	1		
Green Bay vs. New England		72,301	
AFC-NFC Pro Bowl at Honolulu, Hawaii	1	50,031	
NFL Postseason Total	**12**	**769,310**	**64,109**
NFL All Games	**315**	**18,648,981**	**59,203**

ONE MILLION PLUS CLUB

During the 1996 season, 13 clubs drew a combined home and away paid attendance of more than one million. The New York Giants drew an NFL-leading 1,122,298 fans in 1996.

Team	Total Paid Home Attendance	Total Paid Visiting Attendance	Total Paid Attendance
New York Giants	611,906	510,392	1,122,298
Buffalo	593,861	521,161	1,115,022
Kansas City	628,460	475,416	1,103,876
Miami	593,851	503,427	1,097,278
New York Jets	613,184	474,814	1,087,998
Denver	582,236	485,209	1,067,445
Dallas	502,021	558,218	1,060,239
Chicago	527,522	510,202	1,037,724
New England	479,365	551,330	1,030,695
Carolina	572,269	449,318	1,021,587
San Francisco	547,847	473,047	1,020,894
Green Bay	479,202	534,339	1,013,541
Pittsburgh	477,060	536,287	1,013,347

Note: For complete year-by-year paid attendance and attendance records, see page 366.

Inside the Numbers

RECORDS FOR NFL TEAMS FOR MOST POINTS IN A GAME (REGULAR SEASON ONLY)

Note: When the record has been achieved more than once, only the most recent game is shown; summaries are listed in alphabetical order by conference. Bold face indicates team holding record.

BALTIMORE RAVENS
October 6, 1996, at Baltimore

New England	3	17	15	11	— 46
Baltimore	0	14	0	24	— 38

TDs: Balt—Earnest Byner 2, Michael Jackson 2, Derrick Alexander; NE—Shawn Jefferson 2, Ben Coates, Mike Bartrum, Ted Bruschi. TD Passes: Balt—Vinny Testaverde 3; NE—Drew Bledsoe 4. FGs: NE—Adam Vinatieri 3.

BUFFALO BILLS
September 18, 1966, at Buffalo

Miami	3	7	0	14	— 24
Buffalo	21	27	3	7	— 58

TDs: Buff—Bobby Burnett 2, Butch Byrd 2, Jack Spikes 2, Bobby Crockett, Jack Kemp; Mia—Dave Kocourek, Bo Roberson, John Roderick. TD Passes: Buff—Jack Kemp, Daryle Lamonica; Mia—George Wilson 3. FGs: Buff—Booth Lusteg; Mia—Gene Mingo.

CINCINNATI BENGALS
December 17, 1989, at Cincinnati

Houston	0	0	0	7	— 7
Cincinnati	21	10	21	9	— 61

TDs: Cin—Eddie Brown 2, Eric Ball, James Brooks, Ira Hillary, Rodney Holman, Tim McGee, Craig Taylor; Hou—Lorenzo White. TD Passes: Cin—Boomer Esiason 4, Erik Wilhelm. FGs: Cin—Jim Breech 2.

CLEVELAND BROWNS
November 7, 1954, at Cleveland

Washington	0	3	0	0	— 3
Cleveland	13	14	21	14	— 62

TDs: Clev—Darrell Brewster 2, Mo Bassett, Ken Gorgal, Otto Graham, Dub Jones, Dante Lavelli, Curley Morrison. TD Passes: Clev—George Ratterman 3, Otto Graham. FGs: Clev—Lou Groza 2; Wash—Vic Janowicz.

DENVER BRONCOS
October 6, 1963, at Denver

San Diego	13	7	0	14	— 34
Denver	3	14	9	24	— 50

TDs: Den—Lionel Taylor 2, Goose Gonsoulin, Gene Prebola, Donnie Stone; SD—Keith Lincoln 2, Lance Alworth, Paul Lowe, Jacque MacKinnon. TD Passes: Den—John McCormick 3; SD—Tobin Rote 3, John Hadl 2. FGs: Den—Gene Mingo 5.

INDIANAPOLIS COLTS
December 12, 1976, at Baltimore

Buffalo	3	3	7	7	— 20
Baltimore Colts	7	13	28	10	— 58

TDs: Balt—Roger Carr, Raymond Chester, Glenn Doughty, Roosevelt Leaks, Derrel Luce, Lydell Mitchell, Howard Stevens; Buff—Bob Chandler, O.J. Simpson. TD Passes: Balt—Bert Jones 3; Buff—Gary Marangi. FGs: Balt—Toni Linhart 3; Buff—George Jakowenko 2.

JACKSONVILLE JAGUARS
December 10, 1995, at Jacksonville

Indianapolis	14	10	3	14	— 41
Jacksonville	0	7	3	21	— 31

TDs: Jax—Willie Jackson 2, Jimmy Smith, James Stewart; Ind—Aaron Bailey 2, Ken Dilger, Marshall Faulk, Lamont Warren. TD Passes: Jax—Mark Brunell 3; Ind—Craig Erickson 2. FGs: Jax—Mike Hollis; Ind—Cary Blanchard 2.

KANSAS CITY CHIEFS
September 7, 1963, at Denver

Kansas City	14	14	21	10	— 59
Denver	0	7	0	0	— 7

TDs: KC—Chris Burford 2, Frank Jackson 2, Dave Grayson, Abner Haynes, Sherrill Headrick, Curtis McClinton; Den—Lionel Taylor. TD Passes: KC—Len Dawson 4, Curtis McClinton; Den—Mickey Slaughter. FG: KC—Tommy Brooker.

MIAMI DOLPHINS
November 24, 1977, at St. Louis

Miami	14	14	20	7	— 55
St. Louis Cardinals	7	0	0	7	— 14

TDs: Mia—Nat Moore 3, Gary Davis, Duriel Harris, Leroy Harris, Benny Malone, Andre Tillman; StL—Ike Harris, Terry Metcalf. TD Passes: Mia—Bob Griese 6; StL—Jim Hart.

NEW ENGLAND PATRIOTS
September 9, 1979, at New England

New York Jets	3	0	0	0	— 3
New England	14	21	7	14	— 56

TDs: NE—Harold Jackson 3, Stanley Morgan 2, Allan Clark, Andy Johnson, Don Westbrook. TD Passes: NE—Steve Grogan 5, Tom Owen. FG: NYJ—Pat Leahy.

NEW YORK JETS
November 17, 1985, at New York

Tampa Bay	14	7	7	0	— 28
New York Jets	17	24	14	7	— 62

TDs: NYJ—Mickey Shuler 3, Johnny Hector 2, Tony Paige, Al Toon, Wesley Walker; TB—James Wilder 2, Kevin House, Calvin Magee. TD Passes: NYJ—Ken O'Brien 3; TB—Steve DeBerg 2. FGs: NYJ—Pat Leahy 2.

OAKLAND RAIDERS
December 22, 1963, at Oakland

Houston	14	21	14	0	— 49
Oakland	7	28	7	10	— 52

TDs: Oak—Art Powell 4, Clem Daniels, Claude Gibson, Ken Herock; Hou—Willard Dewveall 2, Dave Smith 2, Charley Hennigan, Bob McLeod, Charley Tolar. TD Passes: Oak—Tom Flores 6; Hou—George Blanda 5. FG: Oak—Mike Mercer.

PITTSBURGH STEELERS
November 30, 1952, at Pittsburgh

New York Giants	0	0	7	0	— 7
Pittsburgh	14	14	7	28	— 63

TDs: Pitt—Lynn Chandnois 2, Dick Hensley 2, Jack Butler, George Hays, Ray Mathews, Ed Modzelewski, Elbie Nickel; NYG—Bill Stribling. TD Passes: Pitt—Jim Finks 4, Gary Kerkorian; NYG—Tom Landry.

SAN DIEGO CHARGERS
December 22, 1963, at San Diego

Denver	7	10	3	0	— 20
San Diego	10	16	10	22	— 58

TDs: SD—Paul Lowe 2, Chuck Allen, Bobby Jackson, Dave Kocourek, Keith Lincoln, Jacque MacKinnon; Den—Billy Joe, Donnie Stone. TD Passes: SD—John Hadl, Tobin Rote; Den—Don Breaux. FGs: SD—George Blair 3; Den—Gene Mingo 2.

SEATTLE SEAHAWKS
October 30, 1977, at Seattle

Buffalo	3	0	7	7	— 17
Seattle	14	28	7	7	— 56

TDs: Sea—Steve Largent 2, Duke Ferguson, Al Hunter, David Sims, Sherman Smith, Don Testerman, Jim Zorn; Buff—Joe Ferguson, John Kimbrough. TD Passes: Sea—Jim Zorn 4; Buff—Joe Ferguson. FG: Buff—Carson Long.

TENNESSEE OILERS
December 9, 1990, at Houston

Cleveland	0	7	0	7	— 14
Houston Oilers	14	31	7	6	— 58

TDs: Hou—Lorenzo White 4, Ernest Givins, Leonard Harris, Tony Jones, Terry Kinard; Clev—Eric Metcalf 2. TD Passes: Hou—Warren Moon 2, Cody Carlson; Clev—Bernie Kosar. FG: Hou—Teddy Garcia.

ARIZONA CARDINALS
November 13, 1949, at New York

Chicago Cardinals	7	31	14	13	— 65
New York Bulldogs	7	0	6	7	— 20

TDs: Chi—Red Cochran 2, Pat Harder 2, Bill Dewell, Mel Kutner, Bob Ravensburg, Vic Schwall, Charlie Trippi; NY—Joe Golding, Frank Muehlheuser, Johnny Rauch. TD Passes: Chi—Paul Christman 3, Jim Hardy 3; NY—Bobby Layne. FG: Chi—Pat Harder.

ATLANTA FALCONS
September 16, 1973, at New Orleans

Atlanta	0	24	21	17	— 62
New Orleans	0	0	7	0	— 7

TDs: Atl—Ken Burrow 2, Eddie Ray 2, Wes Chesson, Tom Hayes, Art Malone, Joe Profit; NO—Bill Butler. TD Passes: Atl—Dick Shiner 2, Bob Lee; NO—Archie Manning. FGs: Atl—Nick Mike-Mayer 2.

CAROLINA PANTHERS
October 13, 1996, at Carolina

St. Louis	0	13	0	0	— 13
Carolina	14	14	10	7	— 45

TDs: Car—Wesley Walls 2, Kevin Greene, Muhsin Muhammad, Michael Bates, Dino Philyaw; StL—Anthony Parker, Eddie Kennison. TD Passes: Car—Kerry Collins 3; StL—Tony Banks. FG: Car—John Kasay.

CHICAGO BEARS
December 7, 1980, at Chicago

Green Bay	0	7	0	0	— 7
Chicago	0	28	13	20	— 61

TDs: Chi—Walter Payton 3, Brian Baschnagel, Robin Earl, Roland Harper, Willie McClendon, Len Walterscheid, Rickey Watts; GB—James Lofton. TD Passes: Chi—Vince Evans 3; GB—Lynn Dickey.

DALLAS COWBOYS
October 12, 1980, at Dallas

San Francisco	0	7	0	7	— 14
Dallas	14	24	14	7	— 59

TDs: Dall—Drew Pearson 3, Ron Springs 2, Tony Dorsett, Billy Joe DuPree, Robert Newhouse; SF—Dwight Clark 2. TD Passes: Dall—Danny White 4; SF—Steve DeBerg 2. FG: Dall—Rafael Septien.

DETROIT LIONS
October 26, 1952, at Green Bay

Detroit	14	14	14	10	— 52
Green Bay	7	3	0	7	— 17

TDs: Det—Jug Girard 2, Bob Hoernschemeyer 2, Jack Christiansen, Jim Smith, Bill Swiacki; GB—Billy Howton, Jim Keane. TD Passes: Det—Bobby Layne 3; GB—Babe Parilli, Tobin Rote. FGs: Det—Pat Harder; GB—Bill Reichardt.

GREEN BAY PACKERS
October 7, 1945, at Milwaukee

Detroit	0	7	7	7	— 21
Green Bay	0	41	9	7	— 57

TDs: GB—Don Hutson 4, Charley Brock, Irv Comp, Ted Fritsch, Clyde Goodnight; Det—Chuck Fenenbock, John Greene, Bob Westfall. TD Passes: GB—Tex McKay 4, Lou Brock, Irv Comp; Det—Dave Ryan.

MINNESOTA VIKINGS
October 18, 1970, at Minnesota

Dallas	3	3	0	7	— 13
Minnesota	14	20	17	3	— 54

TDs: Minn—Clint Jones 2, Ed Sharockman 2, John Beasley, Dave Osborn; Dall—Calvin Hill. TD Pass: Minn—Gary Cuozzo. FGs: Minn—Fred Cox 4; Dall—Mike Clark 2.

NEW ORLEANS SAINTS
November 21, 1976, at Seattle

New Orleans	3	17	28	3	— 51
Seattle	6	0	7	14	— 27

TDs: NO—Bobby Douglass 2, Tony Galbreath, Chuck Muncie, Tom Myers, Elex Price; Sea—Sherman Smith 2, Steve Largent, Jim Zorn. TD Pass: Sea—Bill Munson. FGs: NO—Rich Szaro 3.

NEW YORK GIANTS
November 26, 1972, at New York

Philadelphia	3	7	0	0	— 10
New York Giants	14	24	10	14	— 62

TDs: NYG—Don Herrmann 2, Ron Johnson 2, Bob Tucker 2, Randy Johnson; Phil—Harold Jackson. TD Passes: NYG—Norm Snead 3, Randy Johnson 2; Phil—John Reaves 2. FGs: NYG—Pete Gogolak 2; Phil—Tom Dempsey.

PHILADELPHIA EAGLES
November 6, 1934, at Philadelphia

Cincinnati Reds	0	0	0	0	— 0
Philadelphia	26	6	12	20	— 64

TDs: Phil—Joe Carter 3, Swede Hanson 3, Marvin Ellstrom, Roger Kirkman, Ed Matesic, Ed Storm. TD Passes: Phil—Ed Matesic 2, Albert Weiner 2, Marvin Elstrom.

ST. LOUIS RAMS
October 22, 1950, at Los Angeles

Baltimore	13	0	7	7	— 27
Los Angeles Rams	21	14	14	21	— 70

TDs: LA—Bob Boyd 2, Vitamin T. Smith 2, Tom Fears, Elroy (Crazylegs) Hirsch, Dick Hoerner, Ralph

Pasquariello, Dan Towler, Bob Waterfield; Balt—Chet Mutryn 2, Adrian Burk, Billy Stone. TD Passes: LA—Norm Van Brocklin 2, Bob Waterfield 2, Glenn Davis; Balt—Adrian Burk 3.

SAN FRANCISCO 49ERS
October 18, 1992, at San Francisco

Atlanta	7	3	0	7	— 17
San Francisco	21	21	14	0	— 56

TDs: SF—Jerry Rice 3, Ricky Watters 3, Brent Jones, Tom Rathman; Atl—Michael Haynes, Jason Phillips. TD Passes: SF—Steve Young 3; Atl—Chris Miller, Wade Wilson. FG: Atl—Norm Johnson.

TAMPA BAY BUCCANEERS
September 13, 1987, at Tampa Bay

Atlanta	0	3	0	7	— 10
Tampa Bay	14	13	7	14	— 48

TDs: TB—Gerald Carter 2, Cliff Austin, Steve Bartalo, Mark Carrier, Phil Freeman, Calvin Magee; Atl—Stacey Bailey. TD Passes: TB—Steve DeBerg 5; Atl—Scott Campbell. FG: Atl—Mick Luckhurst.

WASHINGTON REDSKINS
November 27, 1966, at Washington

New York Giants	0	14	14	13	— 41
Washington	13	21	14	24	— 72

TDs: Wash—A.D. Whitfield 3, Brig Owens 2, Charley Taylor 2, Rickie Harris, Joe Don Looney, Bobby Mitchell; NYG—Allen Jacobs, Homer Jones, Dan Lewis, Joe Morrison, Aaron Thomas, Gary Wood. TD Passes: Wash—Sonny Jurgensen 3; NYG—Gary Wood 2, Tom Kennedy. FG: Wash—Charlie Gogolak.

TEAMS THAT FINISHED IN FIRST PLACE IN THEIR DIVISION THE SEASON AFTER FINISHING IN LAST PLACE

Season	Team	Record	Previous Season
1967	Houston	9-4-1	*3-11
1968	Minnesota	8-6	3-8-3
1970	Cincinnati	8-6	4-9-1
1970	San Francisco	10-3-1	4-8-2
1972	Green Bay	10-4	4-8-2
1975	Baltimore	10-4	2-12
1979	Tampa Bay	10-6	5-11
1981	Cincinnati	12-4	6-10
1987	Indianapolis	9-6	3-13
1988	Cincinnati	12-4	4-11
1990	Cincinnati	9-7	8-8
1991	Denver	12-4	5-11
1992	San Diego	11-5	4-12
1993	Detroit	10-6	5-11

*tied for last place

RECORDS OF NFL TEAMS, 1987-1996

AFC	W	L	T	Pct.	Division Titles	Playoff Berths	Postseason Record	Super Bowl Record
Buffalo	104	55	0	.654	6	8	11-8	0-4
Denver	91	67	1	.575	4	5	5-5	0-2
Pittsburgh	91	68	0	.572	4	6	5-6	0-1
Kansas City	89	68	2	.566	2	6	3-6	0-0
Miami	89	70	0	.560	2	4	3-4	0-0
Tennessee	87	72	0	.547	2	7	3-7	0-0
Oakland	82	77	0	.516	1	3	2-3	0-0
San Diego	77	82	0	.484	2	3	3-3	0-1
Cleveland	68	74	1	.479	2	4	3-4	0-0
Indianapolis	73	86	0	.459	1	3	2-3	0-0
Seattle	71	89	0	.440	1	2	0-2	0-0
Jacksonville	13	19	0	.406	0	1	2-1	0-0
New England	63	96	0	.396	1	2	2-2	0-1
Cincinnati	62	97	0	.390	2	2	3-2	0-1
N.Y. Jets	54	104	1	.343	0	1	0-1	0-0
Baltimore	4	12	0	.250	0	0	0-0	0-0

Oakland totals include L.A. Raiders, 1987-94
Tennessee totals include Houston, 1987-96

NFC	W	L	T	Pct.	Division Titles	Playoff Berths	Postseason Record	Super Bowl Record
San Francisco	121	38	0	.761	8	9	13-6	3-0
Carolina	19	13	0	.594	1	1	1-1	0-0
Philadelphia	94	65	0	.591	1	6	2-6	0-0
Minnesota	90	69	0	.566	3	7	3-7	0-0
Chicago	88	71	0	.553	3	5	3-5	0-0
Dallas	88	71	0	.553	5	6	12-3	3-0
New Orleans	87	72	0	.547	1	4	0-4	0-0
N.Y. Giants	86	73	0	.541	2	3	4-2	1-0
Washington	83	76	0	.522	2	4	8-2	2-0
Green Bay	80	78	1	.506	2	4	7-3	1-0
Detroit	72	87	0	.453	2	4	1-4	0-0
St. Louis	63	96	0	.396	0	2	2-2	0-0
Arizona	58	101	0	.365	0	0	0-0	0-0
Atlanta	57	102	0	.358	0	2	1-2	0-0
Tampa Bay	52	107	0	.327	0	0	0-0	0-0

Arizona totals include St. Louis, 1987, and Phoenix, 1988-93
St. Louis totals include L.A. Rams, 1987-94

HOME RECORDS, 1987-1996

AFC	W-L-T	Pct.	NFC	W-L-T	Pct.
Buffalo	62-18-0	.775	Carolina	13- 3-0	.813
Denver	60-20-0	.750	San Francisco	61-18-0	.772
Kansas City	56-23-0	.709	Minnesota	54-26-0	.675
Pittsburgh	56-23-0	.709	Chicago	53-27-0	.663
Tennessee	50-29-0	.633	Philadelphia	52-28-0	.650
Miami	49-30-0	.620	Green Bay	49-30-1	.619

AFC	W-L-T	Pct.	NFC	W-L-T	Pct.
Oakland	46-34-0	.575	N.Y. Giants	49-31-0	.613
Jacksonville	9- 7-0	.563	Dallas	46-33-0	.582
Cleveland	38-32-1	.542	New Orleans	46-33-0	.582
San Diego	42-37-0	.532	Washington	46-33-0	.582
Indianapolis	41-39-0	.513	Detroit	43-36-0	.544
Seattle	41-39-0	.513	Atlanta	41-39-0	.513
Baltimore	4- 4-0	.500	Arizona	35-44-0	.443
Cincinnati	39-41-0	.488	St. Louis	35-44-0	.443
New England	37-43-0	.463	Tampa Bay	34-45-0	.430
N.Y. Jets	29-50-1	.369			

Arizona totals include St. Louis, 1987, and Phoenix, 1988-93
Oakland totals include L.A. Raiders, 1987-94
St. Louis totals include L.A. Rams, 1987-94
Tennessee totals include Houston, 1987-96

ROAD RECORDS, 1987-1996

AFC	W-L-T	Pct.	NFC	W-L-T	Pct.
Buffalo	42-37-0	.532	San Francisco	60-20-0	.750
Miami	40-40-0	.500	Philadelphia	42-37-0	.532
Tennessee	37-43-0	.463	Dallas	42-38-0	.525
Oakland	36-43-0	.456	New Orleans	41-39-0	.513
Pittsburgh	35-45-0	.438	N.Y. Giants	37-42-0	.468
San Diego	35-45-0	.438	Washington	37-43-0	.463
Kansas City	33-45-2	.425	Minnesota	36-43-0	.456
Cleveland	30-42-0	.417	Chicago	35-44-0	.443
Indianapolis	32-47-0	.405	Green Bay	31-48-0	.392
Denver	31-47-1	.399	Carolina	6-10-0	.375
Seattle	29-50-0	.367	Detroit	29-51-0	.363
New England	26-53-0	.329	St. Louis	28-52-0	.350
N.Y. Jets	25-54-0	.316	Arizona	23-57-0	.288
Cincinnati	23-56-0	.291	Tampa Bay	18-62-0	.225
Jacksonville	4-12-0	.250	Atlanta	16-63-0	.203
Baltimore	0- 8-0	.000			

Arizona totals include St. Louis, 1987, and Phoenix, 1988-93
Oakland totals include L.A. Raiders, 1987-94
St. Louis totals include L.A. Rams, 1987-94
Tennessee totals include Houston, 1987-96

RECORDS BY MONTHS, 1987-1996

AFC	Sept. W-L-T	Oct. W-L-T	Nov. W-L-T	Dec. W-L-T	Total W-L-T	Pct.
Buffalo	29- 7	26-13	29-14	20-21	104- 55-0	.654
Denver	22-15-1	23-16	27-14	19-22	91- 67-1	.575
Pittsburgh	18-19	23-17	26-16	24-16	91- 68-0	.572
Kansas City	24-14	17-22-1	25-15-1	23-17	89- 68-2	.566
Miami	22-13	25-16	22-20	20-21	89- 70-0	.560
Tennessee	19-18	23-17	21-20	24-17	87- 72-0	.547
Oakland	19-19	24-16	18-22	21-20	82- 77-0	.516
San Diego	18-20	16-24	23-18	20-20	77- 82-0	.484
Cleveland	18-15	22-14	13-23-1	15-22	68- 74-1	.479
Indianapolis	12-23	22-20	17-24	22-19	73- 86-0	.459
Seattle	14-23	20-22	17-22	19-22	70- 89-0	.440
Jacksonville	2- 7	4- 5	2- 4	5- 3	13- 19-0	.406
New England	11-25	14-27	18-23	20-21	63- 96-0	.396
Cincinnati	15-21	11-30	17-24	19-22	62- 97-0	.390
N.Y. Jets	15-23	12-28-1	19-21	8-32	54-104-1	.343
Baltimore	2- 2	1- 3	0- 4	1- 3	4- 12-0	.250

Oakland totals include L.A. Raiders, 1987-94
Tennessee totals include Houston, 1987-96
December totals include January

NFC	Sept. W-L-T	Oct. W-L-T	Nov. W-L-T	Dec. W-L-T	Total W-L-T	Pct.
San Francisco	26-11	31- 9	31-10	33- 8	121- 28-0	.761
Carolina	3- 4	5- 4	5- 3	6- 2	19- 13-0	.594
Philadelphia	20-16	24-16	25-17	25-16	94- 65-0	.591
Minnesota	23-15	18-21	26-16	23-17	90- 69-0	.566
Chicago	24-14	25-13	25-18	14-26	88- 71-0	.553
Dallas	19-17	24-17	23-21	22-16	88- 71-0	.553

	Sept.	Oct.	Nov.	Dec.	Total	
	W-L-T	W-L-T	W-L-T	W-L-T	W-L-T	Pct.
New Orleans	18-20	23-16	23-18	23-18	87-72-0	.547
N.Y. Giants	21-15	21-19	22-21	22-18	86-73-0	.541
Washington	21-16	23-17	15-27	24-16	83-76-0	.522
Green Bay	16-21-1	20-18	22-20	22-19	80-78-1	.506
Detroit	16-23	16-22	16-27	24-15	72-87-0	.453
St. Louis	21-16	12-28	13-28	17-24	63-96-0	.396
Arizona	13-24	16-25	16-26	13-26	58-101-0	.365
Atlanta	12-25	14-26	19-22	12-29	57-102-0	.358
Tampa Bay	13-25	13-27	12-29	14-26	52-107-0	.327

Arizona totals include St. Louis, 1987, and Phoenix, 1988-93
St. Louis totals include L.A. Rams, 1987-94
December totals include January

TAKEAWAYS/GIVEAWAYS IN 1987-1996

	Takeaways			Giveaways			
AFC	Int.	Fum.	Total	Int.	Fum.	Total	Net.Diff.
Kansas City	169	176	345	140	136	276	69
Pittsburgh	219	158	377	164	144	308	69
San Diego	195	120	315	185	123	308	7
Indianapolis	154	147	301	169	133	302	-1
N.Y. Jets	178	155	333	181	153	334	-1
Buffalo	189	148	337	184	159	343	-6
Denver	174	144	318	174	150	324	-6
Cincinnati	173	133	306	173	140	313	-7
Jacksonville	26	25	51	35	23	58	-7
Baltimore	15	7	22	20	13	33	-11
Cleveland	159	111	270	153	133	286	-16
Tennessee	200	151	351	191	180	371	-20
Seattle	169	156	325	200	147	347	-22
Miami	166	125	291	178	146	324	-33
Oakland	145	132	277	181	130	311	-34
New England	170	152	322	216	150	366	-44

Oakland totals include L.A. Raiders, 1987-94
Tennessee totals include Houston, 1987-96

	Takeaways			Giveaways			
NFC	Int.	Fum.	Total	Int.	Fum.	Total	Net.Diff.
Philadelphia	231	171	402	166	154	320	82
San Francisco	202	132	334	136	130	266	68
Minnesota	236	136	372	184	126	310	62
N.Y. Giants	178	133	311	136	127	263	48
New Orleans	179	165	344	171	146	317	27
Washington	206	119	325	189	125	314	11
Carolina	43	32	75	36	30	66	9
Green Bay	187	150	337	182	152	334	3
Chicago	190	121	311	177	145	322	-11
Detroit	171	144	315	192	135	327	-12
Dallas	154	126	280	169	132	301	-21
Arizona	157	154	311	215	142	357	-46
St. Louis	173	125	298	194	154	348	-50
Atlanta	165	135	300	210	143	353	-53
Tampa Bay	163	149	312	235	131	366	-54

Arizona totals include St. Louis, 1987, and Phoenix, 1988-93
St. Louis totals include L.A. Rams, 1987-94

BEST TAKEAWAY/GIVEAWAY DIFFERENTIAL, SEASON

+43 Washington, 1983
+26 Kansas City, 1990
+24 Philadelphia, 1989
+24 Seattle, 1984

HIGH AND LOW SINGLE-GAME YARDAGE TOTALS, 1987-1996

Most Total Yards, Game
676 Washington vs. Detroit, Nov. 4, 1990 (OT)
615 Arizona vs. Washington, Nov. 10, 1996 (OT)
598 San Francisco vs. Buffalo, Sept. 13, 1992
597 N.Y. Jets vs. Miami, Nov. 27, 1988
590 San Francisco vs. Atlanta, Oct. 18, 1992

Fewest Total Yards, Game
53 Pittsburgh vs. Cleveland, Sept. 10, 1989
60 Detroit vs. Minnesota, Nov. 24, 1988
62 Seattle vs. Dallas, Oct. 11, 1992
65 Seattle vs. New England, Dec. 4, 1988
82 Denver vs. Philadelphia, Sept. 20, 1992

Most Yards Rushing, Game
356 L.A. Raiders vs. Seattle, Nov. 30, 1987
315 Buffalo vs. Atlanta, Nov. 22, 1992
310 Kansas City vs. Detroit, Oct. 14, 1990
305 Pittsburgh vs. Miami, Dec. 18, 1988
304 Philadelphia vs. New England, Nov. 4, 1990

Fewest Yards Rushing, Game
0 Buffalo vs. Chicago, Oct. 2, 1988
1 Tampa Bay vs. Washington, Oct. 22, 1989
4 Indianapolis vs. Detroit, Sept. 22, 1991
6 N.Y. Giants vs. L.A. Rams, Nov. 12, 1989
8 Oakland vs. Kansas City, Dec. 3, 1995

Most Yards Passing, Game
521 Miami vs. N.Y. Jets, Oct. 23, 1988
507 Arizona vs. Washington, Nov. 10, 1996 (OT)
505 Houston vs. Kansas City, Dec. 16, 1990
483 Cincinnati vs. L.A. Rams, Oct. 7, 1990
482 Washington vs. Detroit, Nov. 4, 1990 (OT)

Fewest Yards Passing, Game
-13 Cincinnati vs. San Diego, Oct. 4, 1987
4 St. Louis vs. New Orleans, Oct. 11, 1987
12 Carolina vs. Buffalo, Sept. 10, 1995
13 Seattle vs. Oakland, Dec. 22, 1996
15 New England vs. Atlanta, Nov. 29, 1992

NFL INDIVIDUAL LEADERS, 1987-1996

Points		Touchdowns		Field Goals	
1,112	Morten Andersen	145	Jerry Rice	258	Morten Andersen
1,034	Gary Anderson	115	Emmitt Smith	241	Gary Anderson
1,006	Norm Johnson	91	Barry Sanders	228	Nick Lowery
991	Nick Lowery	82	Thurman Thomas	216	Norm Johnson
913	Chip Lohmiller	77	Cris Carter	204	Chip Lohmiller

Rushes		Rushing Yards		Rushing TDs	
2,566	Thurman Thomas	11,725	Barry Sanders	108	Emmitt Smith
2,384	Barry Sanders	10,762	Thurman Thomas	84	Barry Sanders
2,334	Emmitt Smith	10,161	Emmitt Smith	63	Marcus Allen
1,801	Rodney Hampton	7,468	Herschel Walker	62	Thurman Thomas
1,797	Herschel Walker	6,816	Rodney Hampton	54	Terry Allen

Passes		Completions		Passing Yards	
4,854	Dan Marino	2,885	Dan Marino	35,459	Dan Marino
4,701	Jim Everett	2,799	Warren Moon	34,251	Warren Moon
4,685	Warren Moon	2,732	Jim Everett	33,397	John Elway
4,644	John Elway	2,689	John Elway	33,362	Jim Everett
4,299	Jim Kelly	2,589	Jim Kelly	31,874	Jim Kelly

TD Passes		Receptions		Reception Yards	
227	Dan Marino	915	Jerry Rice	13,880	Jerry Rice
215	Jim Kelly	667	Cris Carter	11,029	Henry Ellard
214	Warren Moon	665	Andre Reed	9,508	Andre Reed
194	Jim Everett	637	Henry Ellard	9,500	Michael Irvin
185	John Elway	595	Sterling Sharpe	8,665	Gary Clark

Receiving TDs		Interceptions		Sacks	
136	Jerry Rice	43	Eugene Robinson	134.5	Reggie White
76	Cris Carter	38	Rod Woodson	118.5	Bruce Smith
66	Andre Rison	37	Eric Allen	115.5	Kevin Greene
65	Sterling Sharpe	34	Deion Sanders	112.0	Chris Doleman
64	Andre Reed	33	Vencie Glenn	101.5	Pat Swilling
		33	Terry McDaniel		

NFL GAMES IN WHICH A TEAM HAS SCORED 60 OR MORE POINTS

(Home team in capitals)

Regular Season

WASHINGTON 72, New York Giants 41	November 27, 1966
LOS ANGELES RAMS 70, Baltimore 27	October 22, 1950
Chicago Cardinals 65, NEW YORK BULLDOGS 20	November 13, 1949
LOS ANGELES RAMS 65, Detroit 24	October 29, 1950
PHILADELPHIA 64, Cincinnati 0	November 6, 1934
CHICAGO CARDINALS 63, New York Giants 35	October 17, 1948
AKRON 62, Oorang 0	October 29, 1922
PITTSBURGH 62, New York Giants 7	November 30, 1952
CLEVELAND 62, New York Giants 14	December 6, 1953
CLEVELAND 62, Washington 3	November 7, 1954
NEW YORK GIANTS 62, Philadelphia 10	November 26, 1972
Atlanta 62, NEW ORLEANS 7	September 16, 1973
NEW YORK JETS 62, Tampa Bay 28	November 17, 1985
CHICAGO 61, San Francisco 20	December 12, 1965
Cincinnati 61, HOUSTON 17	December 17, 1972
CHICAGO 61, Green Bay 7	December 7, 1980
CINCINNATI 61, Houston 7	December 17, 1989
ROCK ISLAND 60, Evansville 0	October 15, 1922
CHICAGO CARDINALS 60, Rochester 0	October 7, 1923

Postseason

Chicago Bears 73, WASHINGTON 0	December 8, 1940

YOUNGEST AND OLDEST PLAYERS IN NFL IN 1996

10 Youngest Players	Birthdate	Games	Starts	Position
Andre Davis, Jacksonville	10/7/75	2	0	DT
Regan Upshaw, Tampa Bay	8/12/75	16	16	DE
Willie Anderson, Cincinnati	7/11/75	16	10	T
Ray Lewis, Baltimore	5/15/75	14	13	LB
Lawrence Phillips, St. Louis	5/12/75	15	11	RB
Kevin Alexander, N.Y. Giants	1/23/75	4	0	WR
Tony Brackens, Jacksonville	12/26/74	16	1	DE
Jerald Moore, St. Louis	11/20/74	11	4	RB
Conrad Hamilton, N.Y. Giants	11/5/74	15	1	DB
Jeff Gooch, Tampa Bay	10/31/74	15	0	LB

10 Oldest Players	Birthdate	Games	Starts	Position
Clay Matthews, Atlanta	3/15/56	15	1	DE
Nick Lowery, N.Y. Jets	5/27/56	16	0	K
Warren Moon, Minnesota	11/18/56	8	8	QB
Jeff Gossett, Oakland	1/25/57	12	0	P
Ray Donaldson, Dallas	5/18/58	16	16	C
Dave Krieg, Chicago	10/20/58	13	12	QB
Mike Horan, N.Y. Giants	2/1/59	16	0	P
Wade Wilson, Dallas	2/1/59	3	1	QB
Rohn Stark, Carolina	5/4/59	16	0	P
Sam Mills, Carolina	6/3/59	16	16	LB

YOUNGEST AND OLDEST REGULAR STARTERS BY POSITION IN 1996

Minimum: 8 Games Started

	Youngest		Oldest
QB	12/30/72 Kerry Collins, Car.	11/18/56	Warren Moon, Minn.
RB	5/12/75 Lawrence Phillips, St. L	3/26/60	Marcus Allen, K.C.
WR	7/23/74 Terry Glenn, N.E.	7/21/61	Henry Ellard, Wash.
TE	11/15/73 Jason Dunn, Phil.	5/24/60	Pete Metzelaars, Det.
C	8/26/73 Barret Robbins, Oak.	5/18/58	Ray Donaldson, Dall.
G	7/31/74 Jonathan Ogden, Balt.	8/8/61	Bruce Matthews, Hou.
T	7/11/75 Willie Anderson, Cin.	3/31/60	Mark Tuinei, Dall.
DE	8/12/75 Regan Upshaw, T.B.	10/16/61	Chris Doleman, S.F.
DT	6/13/73 Sam Adams, Sea.	3/4/62	Greg Kragen, Car.
LB	5/15/75 Ray Lewis, Balt.	6/3/59	Sam Mills, Car.
CB	8/10/74 Walt Harris, Chi.	2/15/60	Darrell Green, Wash.
S	11/14/73 Lawyer Milloy, N.E.	1/13/62	Brett Maxie, Car.

MARCUS ALLEN'S CAREER RUSHING VS. EACH OPPONENT

Opponent	Games	Rushes	Yards	Yards Per Rush	Yards Per Game	TD
Arizona	3	33	158	4.8	52.7	1
Atlanta	4	55	241	4.4	60.3	1
Buffalo	9	148	526	3.6	58.4	5
Chicago	5	77	316	4.1	63.2	4
Cincinnati	8	101	363	3.6	45.4	5
Cleveland	5	56	227	4.1	45.4	0
Dallas	4	28	97	3.5	24.3	1
Denver	26	374	1,553	4.2	59.7	11
Detroit	4	61	226	3.7	56.5	4
Green Bay	5	85	317	3.7	63.4	5
Indianapolis	3	40	192	4.8	64.0	0
Kansas City	17	264	961	3.6	56.5	8
Miami	8	110	558	5.1	69.8	7
Minnesota	5	62	239	3.9	47.8	2
New England	3	50	200	4.0	66.7	1
New Orleans	4	70	316	4.5	79.0	3
N.Y. Giants	5	49	203	4.1	40.6	2
N.Y. Jets	2	30	119	4.0	59.5	2
Oakland	8	146	578	4.0	72.3	3
Philadelphia	2	30	82	2.7	41.0	0
Pittsburgh	3	42	151	3.6	50.3	2
St. Louis	4	78	328	4.2	82.0	3
San Diego	25	370	1,468	4.0	58.7	21
San Francisco	4	69	302	4.4	75.5	2
Seattle	27	314	1,370	4.4	50.7	15
Tampa Bay	1	13	79	6.1	79.0	0
Tennessee	8	106	390	3.7	48.8	3
Washington	4	37	178	4.8	44.5	1
Totals	206	2,898	11,738	4.1	57.5	112

Arizona totals include one game vs. St. Louis, one game vs. Phoenix
Oakland totals include four games vs. L.A. Raiders
St. Louis totals include four games vs. L.A. Rams
Tennessee totals include eight games vs. Houston

EMMITT SMITH'S CAREER RUSHING VS. EACH OPPONENT

Opponent	Games	Rushes	Yards	Yards Per Rush	Yards Per Game	TD
Arizona	14	285	1,180	4.1	84.3	19
Atlanta	6	114	586	5.1	97.7	7
Buffalo	1	15	25	1.7	25.0	1
Chicago	2	38	201	5.3	100.5	1
Cincinnati	2	44	154	3.5	77.0	1
Cleveland	2	58	224	3.9	112.0	1
Denver	2	52	176	3.4	88.0	2
Detroit	3	64	276	4.3	92.0	4
Green Bay	5	128	508	4.0	101.6	5
Indianapolis	2	51	205	4.0	102.5	2
Kansas City	2	42	151	3.6	75.5	2
Miami	2	38	125	3.3	62.5	0
Minnesota	2	39	254	6.5	127.0	3
New England	1	27	85	3.1	85.0	0
New Orleans	3	66	271	4.1	90.3	2
N.Y. Giants	13	264	1,226	4.6	94.3	13
N.Y. Jets	2	35	146	4.2	73.0	0
Oakland	2	58	262	4.5	131.0	6
Philadelphia	14	319	1,539	4.8	109.9	11
Pittsburgh	2	63	280	4.4	140.0	2
St. Louis	2	40	134	3.4	67.0	1
San Diego	2	24	70	2.9	35.0	2
San Francisco	5	103	391	3.8	78.2	4
Seattle	1	22	78	3.5	78.0	2
Tampa Bay	2	39	169	4.3	84.5	1
Tennessee	2	39	139	3.6	69.5	1
Washington	12	267	1,305	4.9	108.8	15
Totals	108	2,334	10,160	4.4	94.1	108

Arizona totals include eight games vs. Phoenix
Oakland totals include one game vs. L.A. Raiders
St. Louis totals include two games vs. L.A. Rams
Tennessee totals include two games vs. Houston

BARRY SANDERS'S CAREER RUSHING VS. EACH OPPONENT

Opponent	Games	Rushes	Yards	Yards Per Rush	Yards Per Game	TD
Arizona	3	56	308	5.5	102.7	2
Atlanta	6	129	553	4.3	92.2	5
Buffalo	2	45	153	3.4	76.5	2
Chicago	15	292	1,376	4.7	91.7	9
Cincinnati	2	47	265	5.6	132.5	2
Cleveland	3	76	389	5.1	129.7	4
Dallas	3	79	357	4.5	119.0	0
Denver	1	23	147	6.4	147.0	1
Green Bay	15	291	1,590	5.5	106.0	6
Indianapolis	1	30	179	6.0	179.0	2
Jacksonville	1	22	76	3.5	76.0	2
Kansas City	2	36	167	4.6	83.5	2
Miami	2	44	195	4.4	97.5	0
Minnesota	15	279	1,416	5.1	94.4	11
New England	2	50	279	5.6	139.5	2
New Orleans	4	57	194	3.4	48.5	2
N.Y. Giants	4	65	319	4.9	79.8	1
N.Y. Jets	2	43	241	5.6	120.5	2
Oakland	2	34	212	6.2	106.0	2
Philadelphia	1	16	49	3.1	49.0	2
Pittsburgh	3	47	203	4.3	67.7	1
St. Louis	2	52	148	2.8	74.0	1
San Diego	1	16	51	3.2	51.0	2
San Francisco	5	93	424	4.6	84.8	2
Seattle	3	47	258	5.5	86.0	2
Tampa Bay	15	310	1,763	5.7	117.5	12
Tennessee	3	60	199	3.3	66.3	4
Washington	3	45	214	4.8	71.3	1
Totals	121	2,384	11,725	4.9	96.9	84

Arizona totals include two games vs. Phoenix
Oakland totals include one game vs. L.A. Raiders
St. Louis totals include two games vs. L.A. Rams
Tennessee totals include three games vs. Houston

THURMAN THOMAS'S CAREER RUSHING VS. EACH OPPONENT

Opponent	Games	Rushes	Yards	Yards Per Rush	Yards Per Game	TD
Arizona	1	26	112	4.3	112.0	0
Atlanta	3	51	264	5.2	88.0	1
Carolina	1	22	91	4.1	91.0	1
Chicago	2	30	129	4.3	64.5	1
Cincinnati	4	69	312	4.5	78.0	1

Opponent	Games	Rushes	Yards	Yards Per Rush	Yards Per Game	TD
Cleveland	2	40	144	3.6	72.0	2
Dallas	2	47	126	2.7	63.0	1
Denver	5	84	343	4.1	68.6	3
Detroit	1	17	58	3.4	58.0	0
Green Bay	3	78	302	3.9	100.7	2
Indianapolis	16	276	1,117	4.0	69.8	7
Kansas City	4	66	196	3.0	49.0	1
Miami	16	327	1,452	4.4	90.8	8
Minnesota	2	34	136	4.0	68.0	1
New England	18	372	1,658	4.5	92.1	10
New Orleans	2	40	155	3.9	77.5	2
N.Y. Giants	3	79	279	3.5	93.0	2
N.Y. Jets	18	305	1,439	4.7	79.9	6
Oakland	5	79	356	4.5	71.2	3
Philadelphia	3	53	174	3.3	58.0	1
Pittsburgh	6	118	510	4.3	85.0	1
St. Louis	3	70	337	4.8	112.3	3
San Francisco	3	35	132	3.8	44.0	1
Seattle	4	68	216	3.2	54.0	0
Tampa Bay	2	24	55	2.3	27.5	0
Tennessee	6	100	433	4.3	72.2	2
Washington	3	56	236	4.2	78.7	2
Totals	138	2,566	10,762	4.2	78.0	62

Arizona totals include one game vs. Phoenix
Oakland totals include five games vs. L.A. Raiders
St. Louis totals include two games vs. L.A. Rams
Tennessee totals include six games vs. Houston

DAN MARINO'S CAREER PASSING VS. EACH OPPONENT

Opponent	Games	Att.	Cmp.	Pct.	Yards	Avg. Gain	TD	Int.	Sacked
Arizona	3	84	56	66.7	812	9.67	7	0	3/21
Atlanta	3	130	75	57.7	896	6.89	4	6	1/2
Buffalo	25	865	540	62.4	6,637	7.67	45	31	33/273
Chicago	4	117	63	53.8	855	7.31	6	4	8/1
Cincinnati	6	219	143	65.3	1,680	7.67	11	2	6/1
Cleveland	6	205	126	61.5	1,661	8.10	11	5	4/1
Dallas	4	142	78	54.9	1,033	7.27	7	4	4/36
Denver	1	43	25	58.1	390	9.07	3	0	3/25
Detroit	3	113	65	57.5	706	6.25	2	2	4/28
Green Bay	5	171	112	65.5	1,328	7.77	11	6	6/1
Indianapolis	27	862	527	61.1	6,313	7.32	46	14	24/164
Kansas City	6	212	123	58.0	1,428	6.74	11	4	3/30
Minnesota	2	91	49	53.8	695	7.64	5	6	1/5
New England	25	840	494	58.8	6,142	7.31	39	37	19/150
New Orleans	3	105	65	61.9	650	6.19	5	2	6/1
N.Y. Giants	2	60	30	50.0	324	5.40	1	4	4/25
N.Y. Jets	24	878	520	59.2	7,141	8.13	64	28	31/169
Oakland	8	280	155	55.4	1,945	6.95	15	10	11/90
Philadelphia	3	127	72	56.7	987	7.77	6	2	5/1
Pittsburgh	9	284	179	63.0	2,082	7.33	12	10	9/64
St. Louis	4	156	98	62.8	1,195	7.66	11	5	3/14
San Diego	5	202	128	63.4	1,534	7.59	11	3	6/1
San Francisco	4	144	84	58.3	942	6.54	5	5	8/1
Seattle	2	68	40	58.8	504	7.41	3	4	3/25
Tampa Bay	3	117	74	63.2	875	7.48	7	1	1/10
Tennessee	8	248	137	55.2	1,701	6.86	11	11	10/64
Washington	4	141	76	53.9	1,180	8.37	10	3	2/7
Totals	199	6,904	4,134	59.9	51,636	7.48	369	209	218/1,554

Arizona totals include one game vs. St. Louis, one game vs. Phoenix
Indianapolis totals include two games vs. Baltimore Colts
Oakland totals include seven games vs. L.A. Raiders
St. Louis totals include three games vs. L.A. Rams
Tennessee totals include eight games vs. Houston

JOHN ELWAY'S CAREER PASSING VS. EACH OPPONENT

Opponent	Games	Att.	Cmp.	Pct.	Yards	Avg. Gain	TD	Int.	Sacked
Arizona	3	83	55	66.3	748	9.01	6	5	4/26
Atlanta	3	106	62	58.5	908	8.57	6	3	9/1
Baltimore	1	39	25	64.1	326	8.36	3	1	0/0
Buffalo	6	196	103	52.6	1,336	6.82	6	6	14/108
Chicago	6	150	84	56.0	961	6.41	4	4	13/79
Cincinnati	5	150	92	61.3	1,191	7.94	9	2	11/93
Cleveland	9	251	147	58.6	2,005	7.99	14	7	16/126
Dallas	2	48	23	47.9	352	7.33	5	1	3/24
Detroit	3	88	56	63.6	699	7.94	2	2	7/1
Green Bay	4	153	88	57.5	913	5.97	2	5	5/1
Indianapolis	7	213	118	55.4	1,545	7.25	8	2	17/129
Jacksonville	1	34	22	64.7	286	8.41	4	1	0/0
Kansas City	26	814	452	55.5	5,728	7.04	25	34	70/508

Miami	1	37	18	48.6	250	6.76	0	1	3/24
Minnesota	6	166	111	66.9	1,257	7.57	12	3	16/125
New England	8	249	143	57.4	1,748	7.02	10	6	10/65
New Orleans	2	79	46	58.2	519	6.57	4	2	4/1
N.Y. Giants	3	103	58	56.3	724	7.03	2	3	3/19
N.Y. Jets	5	165	96	58.2	1,177	7.13	6	6	10/61
Oakland	24	744	402	54.0	4,994	6.71	29	27	62/513
Philadelphia	5	105	54	51.4	680	6.48	5	6	16/119
Pittsburgh	7	192	105	54.7	1,366	7.11	6	5	14/109
St. Louis	3	119	63	52.9	742	6.24	7	2	4/29
San Diego	27	843	491	58.2	5,784	6.86	27	32	60/406
San Francisco	3	99	51	51.5	531	5.36	3	4	11/1
Seattle	26	838	471	56.2	6,041	7.21	34	25	61/410
Tampa Bay	2	75	51	68.0	405	5.40	1	2	1/0
Tennessee	4	139	81	58.3	1,081	7.78	8	6	11/109
Washington	3	114	65	57.0	737	6.46	3	2	9/1
Totals	205	6,392	3,633	56.8	45,034	7.05	251	205	464/3,447

Arizona totals include two games vs. Phoenix
Oakland totals include 20 games vs. L.A. Raiders
St. Louis totals include three games vs. L.A. Rams
Tennessee totals include four games vs. Houston

BRETT FAVRE'S CAREER PASSING VS. EACH OPPONENT

Opponent	Games	Att.	Cmp.	Pct.	Yards	Avg. Gain	TD	Int.	Sacked
Atlanta	2	87	62	71.3	597	6.86	3	2	4/26
Buffalo	1	40	22	55.0	214	5.35	3	1	1/9
Chicago	10	309	195	63.1	2,418	7.83	22	8	19/115
Cincinnati	2	82	53	64.6	628	7.66	5	1	6/1
Cleveland	2	61	43	70.5	433	7.10	3	0	4/22
Dallas	4	155	90	58.1	920	5.94	6	1	7/61
Denver	2	70	40	57.1	515	7.36	5	5	1/4
Detroit	10	342	226	66.1	2,645	7.73	20	14	18/119
Jacksonville	1	30	20	66.7	202	6.73	2	1	2/9
Kansas City	2	83	47	56.6	527	6.35	3	4	8/50
Miami	1	51	31	60.8	362	7.10	2	1	4/17
Minnesota	9	268	159	59.3	1,682	6.28	12	10	22/131
New England	1	47	25	53.2	294	6.26	1	2	4/30
New Orleans	2	62	39	62.9	458	7.39	5	0	8/1
N.Y. Giants	2	69	41	59.4	420	6.09	2	3	5/1
N.Y. Jets	1	28	20	71.4	183	6.54	2	0	1/11
Oakland	1	28	14	50.0	190	6.79	1	0	2/9
Philadelphia	4	133	76	57.1	927	6.97	8	6	10/55
Pittsburgh	2	51	37	72.5	511	10.02	4	0	4/27
St. Louis	6	182	112	61.5	1,165	6.40	9	8	13/109
San Diego	2	56	35	62.5	377	6.73	3	2	4/49
San Francisco	1	61	28	45.9	395	6.48	1	2	2/17
Seattle	1	34	20	58.8	209	6.15	4	0	2/7
Tampa Bay	10	329	213	64.7	2,297	6.98	20	5	14/66
Tennessee	1	30	19	63.3	155	5.17	1	1	3/1
Washington	1	5	0	0.0	0	0.00	0	2	1/11
Totals	81	2,693	1,667	61.9	18,724	6.95	147	79	169/1,064

Oakland totals include one game vs. L.A. Raiders
St. Louis totals include four games vs. L.A. Rams
Tennessee totals include one game vs. Houston

WARREN MOON'S CAREER PASSING VS. EACH OPPONENT

Opponent	Games	Att.	Cmp.	Pct.	Yards	Avg. Gain	TD	Int.	Sacked
Arizona	4	151	84	55.6	1,150	7.62	9	4	9/1
Atlanta	4	156	87	55.8	1,189	7.62	9	5	9/1
Buffalo	8	206	117	56.8	1,528	7.42	7	9	12/1
Carolina	1	34	19	55.9	209	6.15	2	1	4/17
Chicago	8	281	168	59.8	2,019	7.19	9	8	19/141
Cincinnati	20	649	383	59.0	4,902	7.55	37	22	37/310
Cleveland	19	590	336	56.9	4,315	7.31	25	22	42/314
Dallas	4	149	89	59.7	1,058	7.10	4	4	19/130
Denver	3	87	50	57.5	777	8.93	5	2	9/1
Detroit	7	223	142	63.7	1,824	8.18	9	8	12/95
Green Bay	6	222	126	56.8	1,291	5.82	8	10	14/133
Indianapolis	7	255	160	62.7	2,156	8.45	13	7	14/97
Kansas City	8	267	166	62.2	2,006	7.51	10	7	26/180
Miami	6	148	102	68.9	1,236	8.35	8	6	11/112
Minnesota	3	95	58	61.1	592	6.23	2	2	14/106
New England	4	136	76	55.9	946	6.96	6	4	5/1
New Orleans	6	202	121	59.9	1,495	7.40	10	4	13/85
N.Y. Giants	4	142	84	59.2	1,008	7.10	4	4	8/56
N.Y. Jets	4	171	118	69.0	1,411	8.25	8	6	10/1
Oakland	4	138	68	49.3	1,004	7.28	6	5	13/115
Philadelphia	1	46	24	52.2	262	5.70	0	0	4/1
Pittsburgh	20	621	350	56.4	4,421	7.12	24	29	42/320
St. Louis	4	157	85	54.1	1,163	7.41	4	7	10/1
San Diego	6	201	108	53.7	1,362	6.78	7	6	10/1

San Francisco	5	167	93	55.7	1,127	6.75	10	8	13/81
Seattle	4	145	87	60.0	970	6.69	5	6	6/44
Tampa Bay	6	216	132	61.1	1,498	6.94	7	7	9/63
Tennessee	1	43	28	65.1	289	6.72	2	2	1/8
Washington	3	102	53	52.0	579	5.68	4	3	6/1
Totals	180	6,000	3,514	58.6	43,787	7.30	254	208	401/3,037

Arizona totals include one game vs. St. Louis, one game vs. Phoenix
Oakland totals include four games vs. L.A. Raiders
St. Louis totals include four games vs. L.A. Rams
Tennessee totals include one game vs. Houston

TROY AIKMAN'S CAREER PASSING VS. EACH OPPONENT

Opponent	Games	Att.	Cmp.	Pct.	Yards	Avg. Gain	TD	Int.	Sacked
Arizona	14	360	228	63.3	3,063	8.51	15	10	15/95
Atlanta	4	93	67	72.0	943	10.14	8	3	3/19
Buffalo	2	78	44	56.4	461	5.91	0	5	2/11
Chicago	2	57	31	54.4	270	4.74	0	1	3/21
Cincinnati	2	55	34	61.8	548	9.96	3	3	1/12
Cleveland	2	73	45	61.6	462	6.33	3	2	4/20
Denver	2	66	43	65.2	427	6.47	5	1	2/9
Detroit	3	106	70	66.0	765	7.22	3	3	4/30
Green Bay	5	158	115	72.8	1,251	7.92	4	4	6/34
Indianapolis	2	55	38	69.1	429	7.80	2	0	2/14
Kansas City	2	58	42	72.4	384	6.62	3	2	3/26
Miami	3	117	86	73.5	805	6.88	5	2	1/4
Minnesota	2	67	43	64.2	454	6.78	2	0	2/13
New England	1	28	16	57.1	169	6.04	0	2	3/25
New Orleans	3	84	53	63.1	532	6.33	1	4	4/46
N.Y. Giants	16	386	261	67.6	2,848	7.38	14	8	18/109
N.Y. Jets	2	67	46	68.7	501	7.48	2	5	6/40
Oakland	2	49	35	71.4	461	9.41	1	0	6/31
Philadelphia	14	362	195	53.9	2,091	5.78	10	15	38/235
Pittsburgh	1	32	21	65.6	245	7.66	1	1	0/0
St. Louis	3	103	58	56.3	754	7.32	7	2	4/25
San Diego	2	59	34	57.6	415	7.03	1	1	6/39
San Francisco	5	143	81	56.6	937	6.55	2	6	10/63
Seattle	1	23	15	65.2	173	7.52	0	2	1/3
Tampa Bay	2	53	30	56.6	332	6.26	2	2	5/38
Tennessee	2	64	38	59.4	488	7.63	2	1	6/22
Washington	14	382	231	60.5	2,525	6.61	14	13	30/216
Totals	113	3,178	2,000	62.9	22,733	7.15	110	98	185/1,200

Arizona totals include eight games vs. Phoenix
Oakland totals include one game vs. L.A. Raiders
St. Louis totals include three games vs. L.A. Rams
Tennessee totals include two games vs. Houston

STEVE YOUNG'S CAREER PASSING VS. EACH OPPONENT

Opponent	Games	Att.	Cmp.	Pct.	Yards	Avg. Gain	TD	Int.	Sacked
Arizona	5	131	69	52.7	885	6.76	5	2	10/71
Atlanta	15	391	260	66.5	3,460	8.85	28	12	19/112
Buffalo	4	124	77	62.1	1,051	8.48	4	4	12/88
Carolina	3	126	82	65.1	996	7.90	6	4	12/47
Chicago	6	136	75	55.1	993	7.30	8	3	9/52
Cincinnati	2	55	32	58.2	453	8.24	2	5	5/29
Cleveland	3	34	19	55.9	274	8.06	0	3	1/8
Dallas	5	85	56	65.9	707	8.32	6	1	10/46
Denver	2	32	20	62.5	350	10.94	3	3	1/8
Detroit	9	218	149	68.3	1,764	8.09	13	3	15/115
Green Bay	5	109	59	54.1	668	6.13	2	6	24/177
Indianapolis	2	65	42	64.6	480	7.38	2	3	8/43
Kansas City	3	58	37	63.8	433	7.47	2	3	9/55
Miami	1	27	19	70.4	220	8.15	2	1	0/0
Minnesota	9	243	154	63.4	1,938	7.98	12	9	28/129
New England	3	81	59	72.8	706	8.72	8	2	7/30
New Orleans	15	323	216	66.9	2,362	7.31	15	4	42/245
N.Y. Giants	5	87	53	60.9	506	5.82	3	1	5/26
N.Y. Jets	2	43	28	65.1	345	8.02	3	0	1/4
Oakland	2	67	37	55.2	525	7.84	4	3	4/20
Philadelphia	4	92	60	65.2	702	7.63	5	2	8/52
Pittsburgh	3	72	48	66.7	493	6.85	6	3	4/21
St. Louis	14	331	225	68.0	2,830	8.55	20	4	18/84
San Diego	3	71	53	74.6	666	9.38	5	0	2/10
Seattle	1	6	4	66.7	49	8.17	1	0	0/0
Tampa Bay	4	87	62	71.3	850	9.77	8	1	5/28
Tennessee	3	30	16	53.3	187	6.23	0	2	2/10
Washington	3	68	48	70.6	586	8.62	1	2	6/28
Totals	136	3,192	2,059	64.5	25,479	7.98	174	85	267/1,538

Arizona totals include two games vs. St. Louis, three games vs. Phoenix
Oakland totals include two games vs. L.A. Raiders
St. Louis totals include 12 games vs. L.A. Rams
Tennessee totals include three games vs. Houston

JERRY RICE'S CAREER RECEIVING VS. EACH OPPONENT

Opponent	Games	Rec.	Yards	Yards Per Rec.	Yards Per Game	TD
Arizona	5	25	465	18.6	93.0	5
Atlanta	23	140	2,150	15.4	93.5	22
Baltimore	1	6	58	9.7	58.0	1
Buffalo	3	11	104	9.5	34.7	1
Carolina	4	34	488	14.4	122.0	1
Chicago	5	24	424	17.7	84.8	7
Cincinnati	4	23	351	15.3	87.8	2
Cleveland	3	19	275	14.5	91.7	4
Dallas	7	43	671	15.6	95.9	4
Denver	3	16	266	16.6	88.7	1
Detroit	8	38	533	14.0	66.6	2
Green Bay	5	30	516	17.2	103.2	6
Indianapolis	3	18	378	21.0	126.0	5
Kansas City	3	13	178	13.7	59.3	2
Miami	3	18	304	16.9	101.3	5
Minnesota	9	50	874	17.5	97.1	10
New England	4	19	294	15.5	73.5	5
New Orleans	24	120	1,751	14.6	76.1	13
N.Y. Giants	7	34	525	15.4	75.0	5
N.Y. Jets	3	15	265	17.7	88.3	2
Oakland	4	18	362	20.1	90.5	2
Philadelphia	6	31	490	15.8	81.7	5
Pittsburgh	4	27	278	10.3	69.5	4
St. Louis	24	134	2,134	15.9	88.9	18
San Diego	3	27	465	17.2	155.0	4
Seattle	3	14	272	19.4	90.7	4
Tampa Bay	7	43	672	15.6	96.0	10
Tennessee	4	28	274	9.8	68.5	2
Washington	6	32	560	17.5	112.0	2
Totals	188	1,050	16,377	15.6	88.0	154

Arizona totals include one game vs. St. Louis, four games vs. Phoenix
Oakland totals include four games vs. L.A. Raiders
St. Louis totals include 20 games vs. L.A. Rams
Tennessee totals include four games vs. Houston

ANDRE REED'S CAREER RECEIVING VS. EACH OPPONENT

Opponent	Games	Rec.	Yards	Yards Per Rec.	Yards Per Game	TD
Arizona	2	0	0	—	0.0	0
Atlanta	2	9	170	18.9	85.0	1
Carolina	1	0	0	—	0.0	0
Chicago	3	14	156	11.1	52.0	0
Cincinnati	6	17	276	16.2	55.2	2
Cleveland	5	25	347	13.9	69.4	2
Dallas	2	6	46	7.7	23.0	0
Denver	6	30	408	13.6	68.0	2
Detroit	2	10	89	8.9	44.5	1
Green Bay	3	21	249	11.9	83.0	3
Indianapolis	22	97	1,346	13.9	64.1	14
Kansas City	6	32	444	13.9	74.0	4
Miami	22	106	1,552	14.6	77.6	10
Minnesota	3	11	105	9.5	35.0	0
New England	20	84	1,416	16.9	74.5	7
New Orleans	2	6	54	9.0	27.0	0
N.Y. Giants	3	12	233	19.4	77.7	2
N.Y. Jets	23	91	1,217	13.4	52.9	10
Oakland	5	28	406	14.5	81.2	1
Philadelphia	4	17	183	10.8	45.8	3
Pittsburgh	8	33	389	11.8	48.6	3
St. Louis	2	10	135	13.5	67.5	1
San Diego	2	9	138	15.3	69.0	0
San Francisco	2	20	259	13.0	129.5	0
Seattle	3	6	123	20.5	41.0	1
Tampa Bay	3	8	119	14.9	39.7	0
Tennessee	9	44	663	15.1	73.7	6
Washington	4	20	361	18.1	120.3	2
Totals	175	766	10,884	14.2	65.6	75

Arizona totals include one game vs. St. Louis, one game vs. Phoenix
Oakland totals include five games vs. L.A. Raiders
St. Louis totals include two games vs. L.A. Rams
Tennessee totals include nine games vs. Houston

MICHAEL IRVIN'S CAREER RECEIVING VS. EACH OPPONENT

Opponent	Games	Rec.	Yards	Yards Per Rec.	Yards Per Game	TD
Arizona	16	66	1,310	19.8	93.6	8
Atlanta	8	41	660	16.1	82.5	3
Buffalo	1	8	115	14.4	115.0	0

Opponent	Games	Rec.	Yards	Yards Per Rec.	Yards Per Game	TD
Chicago	1	5	46	9.2	46.0	0
Cincinnati	3	15	314	20.9	104.7	1
Cleveland	3	18	248	13.8	82.7	1
Denver	2	12	156	13.0	78.0	2
Detroit	3	16	304	19.0	101.3	1
Green Bay	6	34	576	16.9	96.0	4
Indianapolis	1	7	112	16.0	112.0	0
Kansas City	2	17	205	12.1	102.5	1
Miami	2	15	217	14.5	108.5	1
Minnesota	3	18	274	15.2	91.3	2
New England	1	6	76	12.7	76.0	0
New Orleans	5	17	268	15.8	53.6	0
N.Y. Giants	14	59	918	15.6	70.6	4
N.Y. Jets	2	10	184	18.4	92.0	2
Oakland	2	10	163	16.3	81.5	1
Philadelphia	15	49	821	16.8	63.2	4
Pittsburgh	3	19	369	19.4	123.0	2
St. Louis	2	10	239	23.9	119.5	2
San Diego	1	7	103	14.7	103.0	0
San Francisco	6	37	457	12.4	76.2	2
Seattle	1	6	113	18.8	113.0	0
Tampa Bay	2	2	42	21.0	21.0	1
Tennessee	3	11	141	12.8	47.0	1
Washington	15	76	1,069	14.1	71.3	9
Totals	123	591	9,500	16.1	81.2	52

Arizona totals include 10 games vs. Phoenix
Oakland totals include one game vs. L.A. Raiders
St. Louis totals include two games vs. L.A. Rams
Tennessee totals include three games vs. Houston

HERMAN MOORE'S CAREER RECEIVING VS. EACH OPPONENT

Opponent	Games	Rec.	Yards	Yards Per Rec.	Yards Per Game	TD
Arizona	3	14	212	15.1	70.7	1
Atlanta	4	22	480	21.8	120.0	4
Buffalo	2	9	194	21.6	97.0	1
Chicago	12	59	782	13.3	71.1	3
Cincinnati	1	5	86	17.2	86.0	0
Cleveland	2	11	177	16.1	88.5	0
Dallas	3	12	156	13.0	52.0	1
Green Bay	12	45	690	15.3	69.0	9
Indianapolis	1	0	0	—	0.0	0
Jacksonville	1	5	59	11.8	59.0	0
Kansas City	1	7	84	12.0	84.0	0
Miami	2	6	69	11.5	34.5	0
Minnesota	11	48	843	17.6	93.7	5
New England	2	10	141	14.1	70.5	0
New Orleans	1	4	42	10.5	42.0	0
N.Y. Giants	2	13	155	11.9	77.5	2
N.Y. Jets	1	6	70	11.7	70.0	0
Oakland	1	10	109	10.9	109.0	2
Philadelphia	1	6	88	14.7	88.0	0
Pittsburgh	2	15	202	13.5	101.0	1
St. Louis	1	6	120	20.0	120.0	0
San Diego	1	3	39	13.0	39.0	0
San Francisco	6	29	360	12.4	60.0	4
Seattle	2	14	153	10.9	76.5	3
Tampa Bay	9	46	585	12.7	73.1	4
Tennessee	2	9	193	21.4	96.5	3
Washington	2	10	102	10.2	51.0	1
Totals	88	424	6,191	14.6	77.4	44

Arizona totals includes two games vs. Phoenix
St. Louis totals include one game vs. L.A. Rams
Tennessee totals include two games vs. Houston

CRIS CARTER'S CAREER RECEIVING VS. EACH OPPONENT

Opponent	Games	Rec.	Yards	Yards Per Rec.	Yards Per Game	TD
Arizona	11	47	710	15.1	78.9	10
Atlanta	3	13	254	19.5	84.7	5
Buffalo	2	10	121	12.1	60.5	0
Carolina	1	7	90	12.9	90.0	2
Chicago	15	86	920	10.7	65.7	4
Cincinnati	3	20	223	11.2	74.3	3
Cleveland	3	12	166	13.8	55.3	0
Dallas	6	22	252	11.5	42.0	5
Denver	5	20	259	13.0	64.8	3
Detroit	14	69	752	10.9	57.8	6
Green Bay	13	63	746	11.8	67.8	6
Kansas City	3	14	177	12.6	88.5	3
Miami	2	7	81	11.6	40.5	3
Minnesota	2	5	30	6.0	15.0	1
New England	3	16	160	10.0	53.3	0
New Orleans	6	31	362	11.7	60.3	3
N.Y. Giants	9	19	329	17.3	54.8	2
N.Y. Jets	2	12	114	9.5	57.0	2
Oakland	4	21	257	12.2	85.7	1
Philadelphia	1	6	151	25.2	151.0	2
Pittsburgh	2	9	140	15.6	70.0	2
St. Louis	3	8	105	13.1	35.0	0
San Diego	2	9	122	13.6	61.0	0
San Francisco	6	28	240	8.6	40.0	3
Seattle	3	12	217	18.1	72.3	1
Tampa Bay	15	63	865	13.7	57.7	5
Tennessee	3	17	211	12.4	70.3	3
Washington	7	21	313	14.9	44.7	1
Totals	149	667	8,367	12.5	62.4	76

Arizona totals include two games vs. St. Louis, six games vs. Phoenix
Oakland totals include three games vs. L.A. Raiders
St. Louis totals include three games vs. L.A. Rams
Tennessee totals include three games vs. Houston

MORTEN ANDERSEN'S CAREER KICKING VS. EACH OPPONENT

Opponent	Games	FG	FGA	FG%	Long FG	XP	XPA	Pts.
Arizona	10	14	14	100.0	52	26	27	68
Atlanta	25	40	51	78.4	49	56	58	176
Buffalo	4	7	11	63.6	50	7	7	28
Carolina	4	8	10	80.0	51	6	6	30
Chicago	5	3	6	50.0	60	12	12	21
Cincinnati	5	5	8	62.5	49	17	17	32
Cleveland	4	7	8	87.5	53	7	7	28
Dallas	10	18	24	75.0	54	17	17	71
Denver	3	4	7	57.1	55	11	12	23
Detroit	7	8	13	61.5	50	13	13	37
Green Bay	6	10	11	90.9	52	15	15	45
Indianapolis	2	3	4	75.0	46	7	7	16
Jacksonville	1	1	2	50.0	46	2	2	5
Kansas City	4	4	5	80.0	50	7	7	19
Miami	4	4	5	80.0	32	10	10	22
Minnesota	9	15	17	88.2	47	15	15	60
New England	5	8	9	88.9	54	11	11	35
New Orleans	4	10	13	76.9	55	8	8	38
N.Y. Giants	7	13	15	86.7	45	11	11	50
N.Y. Jets	5	9	10	90.0	53	12	12	39
Oakland	4	6	8	75.0	51	7	7	25
Philadelphia	8	15	18	83.3	56	15	15	60
Pittsburgh	5	7	9	77.8	50	9	9	30
St. Louis	27	40	47	85.1	51	66	68	186
San Diego	3	3	7	42.9	35	7	7	16
San Francisco	29	50	61	82.0	59	40	41	190
Seattle	3	5	6	83.3	47	5	5	20
Tampa Bay	13	22	30	73.3	50	31	31	97
Tennessee	5	8	12	66.7	45	11	11	35
Washington	7	8	14	57.1	45	11	11	35
Totals	228	355	455	78.0	60	472	479	1,537

Arizona totals include five games vs. St. Louis, four games vs. Phoenix
Oakland totals include four games vs. L.A. Raiders
St. Louis totals include 23 games vs. L.A. Rams
Tennessee totals include five games vs. Houston

STARTING RECORDS OF ACTIVE NFL QUARTERBACKS

Minimum: 10 starts

	W - L - T	Pct.
Steve Bono	28 - 12	.700
Brett Favre	50 - 27	.649
Stan Humphries	47 - 26	.644
Kerry Collins	16 - 9	.640
Ty Detmer	7 - 4	.636
Steve Young	69 - 41	.627
Dan Marino	123 - 74	.624
John Elway	126 - 76 - 1	.623
Troy Aikman	70 - 43	.619
Jeff Hostetler	49 - 31	.613
Mike Tomczak	41 - 27	.603
Mark Rypien	47 - 31	.603
Neil O'Donnell	39 - 28	.582
Bobby Hebert	56 - 44	.560
Dave Krieg	98 - 77	.560
Drew Bledsoe	32 - 27	.542
Wade Wilson	35 - 31	.530
Jim Harbaugh	53 - 47	.530
Steve Walsh	20 - 18	.526
Erik Kramer	22 - 20	.524
Rodney Peete	34 - 31	.523
Warren Moon	91 - 87	.511
Steve Beuerlein	25 - 25	.500
Rich Gannon	21 - 21	.500
Sean Salisbury	6 - 6	.500
Don Majkowski	26 - 30 - 1	.465
Bubby Brister	33 - 38	.465
Mark Brunell	12 - 14	.462
Scott Mitchell	21 - 25	.457
Boomer Esiason	76 - 92	.452
Jeff Blake	18 - 23	.439
Dave Brown	20 - 27	.426
Gus Frerotte	13 - 18	.419
Jim Everett	63 - 89	.414
Chris Chandler	28 - 42	.400
Craig Erickson	14 - 21	.400
Rick Mirer	20 - 31	.392
Tony Banks	5 - 8	.385
Trent Dilfer	13 - 21	.382
Billy Joe Tolliver	13 - 22	.371
Vinny Testaverde	44 - 75	.370
Jeff George	30 - 54	.357
John Friesz	12 - 24	.333
Kent Graham	4 - 8	.333
Heath Shuler	4 - 9	.308
Browning Nagle	4 - 10	.286
Frank Reich	5 - 13	.278
David Klingler	4 - 20	.167
Stan Gelbaugh	1 - 11	.083

ALL-TIME RANKINGS OF PLAYERS IN FOUR CATEGORIES THAT DETERMINE NFL PASSER RATING

Minimum: 1500 Attempts

COMPLETION PERCENTAGE

	Pct.	Att.	Comp.
Steve Young	64.51	3192	2059
Joe Montana	63.24	5391	3409
Troy Aikman	62.93	3178	2000
Brett Favre	61.90	2693	1667
Jim Kelly	60.14	4779	2874
Dan Marino	59.88	6904	4134
Ken Stabler	59.85	3793	2270
Danny White	59.69	2950	1761
Ken Anderson	59.31	4475	2654
Bernie Kosar	59.26	3365	1994

TOUCHDOWN PERCENTAGE

	Pct.	Att.	TD
Sid Luckman	7.86	1744	137
Frank Ryan	6.99	2133	149
Len Dawson	6.39	3741	239
Daryle Lamonica	6.31	2601	164
Sammy Baugh	6.24	2995	187
Charley Conerly	6.11	2833	173
Bob Waterfield	6.00	1617	97
Earl Morrall	5.99	2689	161
Sonny Jurgensen	5.98	4262	255
Norm Van Brocklin	5.98	2895	173

AVERAGE YARDS PER PASS

	Avg.	Att.	Yards
Otto Graham	8.63	1565	13,499
Sid Luckman	8.42	1744	14,686
Norm Van Brocklin	8.16	2895	23,611
Steve Young	7.98	3192	25,479
Ed Brown	7.85	1987	15,600
Bart Starr	7.85	3149	24,718
Johnny Unitas	7.76	5186	40,239
Earl Morrall	7.74	2689	20,809
Dan Fouts	7.68	5604	43,040
Len Dawson	7.67	3741	28,711

INTERCEPTION PERCENTAGE

	Pct.	Att.	Int.
Neil O'Donnell	2.23	2059	46
Steve Bono	2.45	1554	38
Joe Montana	2.58	5391	139
Bernie Kosar	2.59	3365	87
Steve Young	2.66	3192	85
Ken O'Brien	2.72	3602	98
Jeff Hostetler	2.78	2194	61
Neil Lomax	2.85	3153	90
Jeff George	2.88	2712	78
Jim Harbaugh	2.91	2680	78

HIGHEST NFL POSTSEASON PASSER RATINGS (MINIMUM: 150 ATTEMPTS)

	Games	Att.	Comp.	Pct.	Yds.	Avg. Gain	TD	Int.	Rating
Bart Starr	10	213	130	61.0	1753	8.23	15	3	104.8
Troy Aikman	14	415	276	66.5	3372	8.13	22	13	96.0
Joe Montana	23	734	460	62.7	5772	7.86	45	21	95.6
Brett Favre	10	317	194	61.2	2430	7.67	18	7	94.7
Ken Anderson	6	166	110	66.3	1321	7.96	9	6	93.5
Joe Theismann	10	211	128	60.7	1782	8.45	11	7	89.7
Steve Young	18	334	207	62.0	2381	7.13	15	7	84.9
Warren Moon	10	403	259	64.3	2870	7.12	17	14	84.2
Ken Stabler	13	351	203	57.8	2641	7.52	19	13	83.5
Bernie Kosar	10	270	152	56.3	1953	7.23	16	10	

HIGHEST NFL POSTSEASON PASSER RATINGS, ACTIVE PLAYERS (MINIMUM: 150 ATTEMPTS)

	Games	Att.	Comp.	Pct.	Yds.	Avg. Gain	TD	Int.	Rating
Troy Aikman	14	415	276	66.5	3372	8.13	22	13	96.0
Brett Favre	10	317	194	61.2	2430	7.67	18	7	94.7
Steve Young	18	334	207	62.0	2381	7.13	15	7	89.7
Warren Moon	10	403	259	64.3	2870	7.12	17	14	84.9
Dan Marino	13	518	291	56.2	3600	6.95	29	17	82.8
John Elway	15	469	254	54.2	3547	7.56	21	18	77.7
Wade Wilson	7	185	99	53.5	1322	7.15	7	6	75.6
Neil O'Donnell	7	273	158	57.9	1690	6.19	9	8	74.9
Dave Krieg	12	282	144	51.1	1895	6.72	11	9	72.3
Mark Rypien	8	234	126	53.8	1776	7.54	8	10	72.2

NFL INDIVIDUAL LEADERS OVER RECENT SEASONS

Points

Last 2 Seasons	Last 3 Seasons	Last 4 Seasons
250 John Kasay	372 Emmitt Smith	479 Jason Elam
247 Chris Boniol	361 Chris Boniol	472 John Carney
247 Norm Johnson	360 Jason Elam	454 Norm Johnson
245 Al Del Greco	348 John Carney	452 Morten Andersen
241 Jason Elam	342 Norm Johnson	446 Steve Christie

Touchdowns

40 Emmitt Smith	62 Emmitt Smith	72 Emmitt Smith
32 Terry Allen	41 Jerry Rice	57 Jerry Rice
32 Curtis Martin	40 Terry Allen	47 Ricky Watters
29 Carl Pickens	40 Carl Pickens	46 Carl Pickens
27 Cris Carter	36 Ricky Watters	43 Cris Carter

Field Goals

63 John Kasay	84 John Carney	115 John Carney
59 Chris Boniol	83 John Kasay	109 Morten Andersen
59 Al Del Greco	82 Jason Elam	108 Jason Elam
57 Norm Johnson	81 Morten Andersen	106 John Kasay
55 Cary Blanchard	81 Chris Boniol	104 Al Del Greco
55 Steve Christie		104 Norm Johnson
		104 Doug Pelfrey

Rushes

704 Emmitt Smith	1,072 Emmitt Smith	1,355 Emmitt Smith
690 Ricky Watters	952 Barry Sanders	1,195 Barry Sanders
685 Terry Allen	940 Terry Allen	1,190 Thurman Thomas
684 Curtis Martin	929 Ricky Watters	1,179 Rodney Hampton
621 Barry Sanders	887 Rodney Hampton	1,137 Ricky Watters

Rushing Yards

3,053 Barry Sanders	4,936 Barry Sanders	6,051 Barry Sanders
2,977 Emmitt Smith	4,461 Emmitt Smith	5,947 Emmitt Smith
2,684 Ricky Watters	3,746 Chris Warren	4,818 Chris Warren
2,662 Terry Allen	3,693 Terry Allen	4,522 Jerome Bettis
2,655 Terrell Davis	3,561 Ricky Watters	4,511 Ricky Watters

Rushing TDs

37 Emmitt Smith	58 Emmitt Smith	67 Emmitt Smith
31 Terry Allen	39 Terry Allen	40 Ricky Watters
28 Curtis Martin	30 Ricky Watters	39 Terry Allen
24 Ricky Watters	29 Marshall Faulk	36 Chris Warren
22 Barry Sanders	29 Barry Sanders	33 Marcus Allen
	29 Chris Warren	

Passes

1,259 Drew Bledsoe	1,950 Drew Bledsoe	2,379 Drew Bledsoe
1,116 Jeff Blake	1,695 Brett Favre	2,217 Brett Favre
1,113 Brett Farve	1,571 Jim Everett	2,053 John Elway
1,031 Jim Everett	1,502 John Elway	1,974 Warren Moon
1,020 Scott Mitchell	1,470 Dan Marino	1,845 Jim Everett

Completions

696 Drew Bledsoe	1,096 Drew Bledsoe	1,365 Brett Favre
684 Brett Favre	1,047 Brett Favre	1,310 Drew Bledsoe
634 Jeff Blake	958 Jim Everett	1,258 John Elway
612 Jim Everett	915 Dan Marino	1,185 Warren Moon
603 John Elway	910 John Elway	1,151 Steve Young

Passing Yards

8,312 Brett Favre	12,194 Brett Favre	15,497 Brett Favre
7,593 Drew Bledsoe	12,148 Drew Bledsoe	14,818 John Elway
7,446 Jeff Blake	10,916 Dan Marino	14,642 Drew Bledsoe
7,298 John Elway	10,788 John Elway	13,602 Steve Young
7,255 Scott Mitchell	10,622 Jim Everett	13,587 Warren Moon

Touchdown Passes

77 Brett Favre	110 Brett Favre	129 Brett Favre
52 Jeff Blake	71 Dan Marino	98 Steve Young
52 John Elway	69 Steve Young	93 John Elway
50 Vinny Testaverde	68 John Elway	80 Drew Bledsoe
49 Scott Mitchell	66 Jeff Blake	80 Vinny Testaverde
	66 Vinny Testaverde	

Receptions

230 Jerry Rice	342 Jerry Rice	440 Jerry Rice
229 Herman Moore	340 Cris Carter	426 Cris Carter
218 Cris Carter	301 Herman Moore	362 Herman Moore
203 Isaac Bruce	277 Larry Centers	348 Tim Brown
202 Brett Perriman	270 Carl Pickens	343 Larry Centers

Reception Yards

Last 2 Seasons	Last 3 Seasons	Last 4 Seasons
3,119 Isaac Bruce	4,601 Jerry Rice	6,104 Jerry Rice
3,102 Jerry Rice	4,155 Herman Moore	5,136 Michael Irvin
2,982 Herman Moore	3,806 Michael Irvin	5,090 Herman Moore
2,565 Michael Irvin	3,790 Cris Carter	4,935 Tim Brown
2,534 Cris Carter	3,755 Tim Brown	4,861 Cris Carter

Receiving Touchdowns

29 Carl Pickens	40 Carl Pickens	51 Jerry Rice
27 Cris Carter	36 Jerry Rice	46 Carl Pickens
23 Michael Jackson	34 Cris Carter	43 Cris Carter
23 Herman Moore	34 Herman Moore	40 Herman Moore
23 Jerry Rice	28 Tim Brown	35 Tim Brown

Interceptions

14 Orlando Thomas	21 Aeneas Williams	23 Terry McDaniel
12 Willie Clay	18 Terry McDaniel	23 Aeneas Williams
12 Keith Lyle	16 Merton Hanks	20 Darren Perry
12 Aeneas Williams	16 Darryll Lewis	19 Four players tied
11 Four players tied	16 Darren Perry	

Sacks

26.0 William Fuller	37.5 Kevin Greene	50.0 Kevin Greene
24.0 Wayne Martin	35.5 William Fuller	48.0 John Randle
24.0 Bruce Smith	35.5 John Randle	48.0 Bruce Smith
23.5 Kevin Greene	34.0 Wayne Martin	45.5 William Fuller
23.5 Bryce Paup	34.0 Bruce Smith	44.5 Neil Smith

NFL TEAM LEADERS OVER RECENT SEASONS

Highest Won-Lost Percentage

.750 Green Bay	.750 San Francisco	.719 Dallas
.719 San Francisco	.708 Dallas	.719 San Francisco
.688 Dallas	.688 Green Bay	.656 Green Bay
.688 Kansas City	.688 Pittsburgh	.656 Kansas City
.656 Denver	.646 Kansas City	.656 Pittsburgh
.656 Pittsburgh		

Most Points

860 Green Bay	1,360 San Francisco	1,833 San Francisco
855 San Francisco	1,242 Green Bay	1,582 Green Bay
779 Denver	1,135 Dallas	1,511 Dallas
751 Pittsburgh	1,126 Denver	1,499 Denver
738 Detroit	1,126 Miami	1,475 Miami

Most Total Yards

11,831 Denver	17,653 San Francisco	24,088 San Francisco
11,593 San Francisco	17,318 Denver	22,779 Denver
11,285 Green Bay	16,990 Minnesota	22,771 Miami
11,142 Minnesota	16,959 Miami	21,814 Minnesota
11,126 Detroit	16,602 New England	21,667 New England

Most Rushing Yards

4,357 Denver	6,331 Pittsburgh	8,334 Pittsburgh
4,231 Kansas City	6,259 Seattle	8,274 Seattle
4,175 Seattle	5,963 Kansas City	7,956 Dallas
4,151 Pittsburgh	5,827 Denver	7,668 Buffalo
4,106 Oakland	5,795 Dallas	7,618 Kansas City

Most Passing Yards

8,267 San Francisco	12,430 San Francisco	16,732 San Francisco
8,019 Green Bay	12,187 Minnesota	16,526 Miami
7,863 Minnesota	12,173 Miami	15,473 Atlanta
7,841 Atlanta	11,953 Atlanta	15,387 Minnesota
7,753 Miami	11,936 New England	15,259 Denver

***Fewest Turnovers**

45 Green Bay	67 Green Bay	98 Dallas
45 Kansas City	71 Kansas City	99 Kansas City
46 Indianapolis	75 Detroit	101 Green Bay
48 Washington	76 Dallas	104 N.Y. Giants
51 Detroit	76 San Francisco	104 San Diego

***Fewest Points Allowed**

515 San Francisco	789 Dallas	1,018 Dallas
524 Green Bay	811 Green Bay	1,093 Green Bay
541 Dallas	811 San Francisco	1,099 Pittsburgh
541 Kansas City	818 Pittsburgh	1,106 San Francisco
543 Carolina	839 Kansas City	1,130 Kansas City

Last 2 Seasons		Last 3 Seasons		Last 4 Seasons	

*Fewest Total Yards Allowed

8,923	Pittsburgh	13,249	Pittsburgh	17,780	Pittsburgh
9,059	San Francisco	13,739	Dallas	18,506	Dallas
9,200	Philadelphia	13,898	San Francisco	18,557	Green Bay
9,261	Houston	13,910	Philadelphia	18,895	San Francisco
9,311	Green Bay	14,075	Green Bay	18,929	Philadelphia

*Fewest Rushing Yards Allowed

2,558	San Francisco	3,896	San Francisco	5,556	Pittsburgh
2,736	Pittsburgh	4,188	Pittsburgh	5,696	San Francisco
2,911	Tennessee	4,294	Green Bay	5,876	Green Bay
2,931	Green Bay	4,385	Minnesota	5,921	Minnesota
2,993	Kansas City	4,641	Miami	6,164	San Diego

*Fewest Passing Yards Allowed

5,795	Philadelphia	8,830	Dallas	11,828	Philadelphia
6,078	Dallas	8,889	Philadelphia	11,946	Dallas
6,104	N.Y. Jets	9,061	Pittsburgh	12,224	Pittsburgh
6,187	Pittsburgh	9,145	Tennessee	12,589	Oakland
6,331	Oakland	9,633	N.Y. Jets	12,681	Green Bay

Most Opponents' Turnovers

75	Carolina	109	Minnesota	144	Pittsburgh
75	Minnesota	105	Pittsburgh	143	Minnesota
75	St. Louis	104	Philadelphia	139	Philadelphia
74	Pittsburgh	103	Arizona	136	Kansas City
69	Philadelphia	103	New England	135	N.Y. Jets
		103	San Francisco		

*Carolina and Jacksonville excluded from last 3 seasons and last 4 seasons lists; Baltimore and Cleveland excluded from all lists.

RECORDS OF TEAMS ON OPENING DAY, 1933-1996

AFC	W	L	T	Pct.	Longest W Strk.	Longest L Strk.	Current Streak
Baltimore	1	0	0	1.000	1	0	W-1
Denver	23	13	1	.639	3	4	W-2
Kansas City	22	15	0	.595	7	4	W-7
Oakland	21	16	0	.568	5	5	L-1
San Diego	21	16	0	.568	6	6	W-1
Cleveland	26	20	0	.565	5	5	L-1
Miami	16	14	1	.533	5	5	W-5
Indianapolis	23	21	0	.523	8	8	W-1
Pittsburgh	30	28	4	.517	4	3	L-1
Jacksonville	1	1	0	.500	1	1	W-1
Tennessee	18	19	0	.486	4	3	L-1
Cincinnati	14	15	0	.483	4	4	L-1
New England	17	20	0	.459	6	3	L-1
Buffalo	16	21	0	.432	6	5	W-1
N.Y. Jets	15	22	0	.405	3	5	L-2
Seattle	5	16	0	.238	3	8	L-2

NFC	W	L	T	Pct.	Longest W Strk.	Longest L Strk.	Current Streak
Dallas	27	9	1	.750	17	3	L-1
Chicago	38	25	1	.603	9	6	W-3
N.Y. Giants	35	25	4	.583	4	3	L-2
Minnesota	19	16	1	.543	4	3	W-1
St. Louis	32	27	0	.542	5	6	W-3
Green Bay	32	29	3	.525	5	6	W-1
San Francisco	24	22	1	.522	5	3	W-5
Washington	31	29	4	.517	6	5	L-1
Atlanta	16	15	0	.516	5	3	L-1
Detroit	32	30	2	.516	7	4	L-2
Carolina	1	1	0	.500	1	1	W-1
Arizona	26	36	1	.419	6	6	L-5
Philadelphia	26	36	1	.419	5	9	W-1
Tampa Bay	8	13	0	.381	3	5	L-1
New Orleans	7	23	0	.233	1	6	L-3

Kansas City totals include Dallas Texans, 1960-62.
Oakland totals include L.A. Raiders, 1982-94.
San Diego totals include L.A. Chargers, 1960.
Indianapolis totals include Baltimore, 1953-83.
Tennessee totals include Houston, 1960-96.
New England totals include Boston, 1960-70.
St. Louis totals include Cleveland, 1937-42 and 1944-45, and L.A. Rams, 1946-94.
Detroit totals include Portsmouth, 1933.
Arizona totals include Chi. Cardinals, 1933-59, St. Louis, 1960-87, and Phoenix, 1988-93.
NOTE: All tied games occurred prior to 1972, when calculation of ties in percentages as half-win, half-loss was begun.

OLDEST INDIVIDUAL SINGLE-SEASON OR SINGLE-GAME RECORDS IN NFL RECORD & FACT BOOK

Regular-Season Records That Have Not Been Surpassed or Tied

Most Points, Game—40, Ernie Nevers, Chi. Cardinals vs. Chi. Bears, Nov. 28, 1929 (6-td, 4-pat)

Most Touchdowns Rushing, Game—6, Ernie Nevers, Chi. Cardinals vs. Chi. Bears, Nov. 28, 1929

Highest Punting Average, Season (Qualifiers)—51.40, Sammy Baugh, Washington, 1940 (35-1,799)

Highest Punting Average, Game (minimum: 4 punts)—61.75, Bob Cifers, Detroit vs. Chi. Bears, Nov. 24, 1946 (4-247)

Highest Average Gain, Pass Receptions, Season (minimum: 24 receptions)—32.58, Don Currivan, Boston, 1947 (24-782)

Highest Average Gain, Passing, Game (minimum: 20 passes)—18.58, Sammy Baugh, Washington vs. Boston, Oct. 31, 1948 (24-446)

Most Touchdowns, Fumble Recoveries, Game—2, Fred (Dippy) Evans, Chi. Bears vs. Washington, Nov. 28, 1948

Most Yards Gained, Intercepted Passes, Rookie, Season—301, Don Doll, Detroit, 1949

Most Passes Had Intercepted, Game—8, Jim Hardy, Chi. Cardinals vs. Philadelphia, Sept. 24, 1950

Highest Average Gain, Rushing, Game (minimum: 10 attempts)—17.09, Marion Motley, Cleveland vs. Pittsburgh, Oct. 29, 1950 (11-188)

Highest Kickoff Return Average, Game (minimum: 3 returns)—73.50, Wally Triplett, Detroit vs. Los Angeles, Oct. 29, 1950 (4-294)

Most Pass Receptions, Game—18, Tom Fears, Los Angeles vs. Green Bay, Dec. 3, 1950

Highest Punt Return Average, Season (Qualifiers)—23.00, Herb Rich, Baltimore, 1950 (12-276)

Highest Punt Return Average, Rookie, Season (Qualifiers)—23.00, Herb Rich, Baltimore, 1950 (12-276)

Most Yards Passing, Game—554, Norm Van Brocklin, Los Angeles vs. N.Y. Yanks, Sept. 28, 1951

Most Touchdowns, Punt Returns, Rookie, Season—4, Jack Christiansen, Detroit, 1951

Most Interceptions By, Season—14, Dick (Night Train) Lane, Los Angeles, 1952

Most Interceptions By, Rookie, Season—14, Dick (Night Train) Lane, Los Angeles, 1952

Highest Average Gain, Passing, Season (Qualifiers)—11.17, Tommy O'Connell, Cleveland, 1957 (110-1,229)

Most Points, Season—176, Paul Hornung, Green Bay, 1960 (15-td, 41-pat,15-fg)

Most Yards Gained, Pass Receptions, Rookie, Season—1,473, Bill Groman, Houston, 1960

LARGEST TRADES IN NFL HISTORY

(Based on number of players or draft choices involved)

18—October 13, 1989—RB Herschel Walker from the Dallas Cowboys to Minnesota. Dallas also traded its third-round choice in 1990, its tenth-round choice in 1990, and its third-round choice in 1991 to Minnesota. Minnesota traded LB Jesse Solomon, LB David Howard, CB Issiac Holt, and DE Alex Stewart along with its first-round choice in 1990, its second-round choice in 1990, its sixth-round choice in 1990, its first-round choice in 1991, its second-round choice in 1991, its first-round choice in 1992, its second-round choice in 1992, and its third-round choice in 1992 to Dallas. Minnesota traded RB Darrin Nelson to Dallas, which traded Nelson to San Diego for the Chargers' fifth-round choice in 1990, which Dallas then sent to Minnesota.

15—March 26, 1953—T Mike McCormack, DT Don Colo, LB Tom Catlin, DB John Petitbon, and G Herschell Forester from Baltimore to Cleveland for DB Don Shula, DB Bert Rechichar, DB Carl Taseff, LB Ed Sharkey, E Gern Nagler, QB Harry Agganis, T Dick Batten, T Stu Sheets, G Art Spinney, and G Elmer Willhoite.

15—January 28, 1971—LB Marlin McKeever, first- and third-round choices in 1971, and third-, fourth-, fifth-, sixth-, and seventh-round choices in 1972 from Washington to the Los Angeles Rams for LB Maxie Baughan, LB Jack Pardee, LB Myron Pottios, RB Jeff Jordan, G John Wilbur, DT Diron Talbert, and a fifth-round choice in 1971.

12—June 13, 1952—Selection rights to Les Richter from the Dallas Texans to the Los Angeles Rams for RB Dick Hoerner, DB Tom Keane, DB George Sims, C Joe Reid, HB Billy Baggett, T Jack Halliday, FB Dick McKissack, LB Vic Vasicek, E Richard Wilkins, C Aubrey Phillips, and RB Dave Anderson.

10—March 23, 1959—HB Ollie Matson from the Chicago Cardinals to the Los Angeles Rams for T Frank Fuller, DE Glenn Holtzman, T Ken Panfil, DT Art Hauser, E John Tracey, FB Larry Hickman, HB Don Brown, the Rams second-round choice in 1960, and a player to be delivered during the 1959 training camp.

10—October 31, 1987—RB Eric Dickerson from the Los Angeles Rams to Indianapolis. The rights to LB Cornelius Bennett from Indianapolis to Buffalo. Indianapolis running back Owen Gill and the Colts' first- and second-round choices in 1988 and second-round choice in 1989, plus Bills running back Greg Bell and Buffalo's first-round choice in 1988 and first- and second-round choices in 1989 to the Rams.

RETIRED UNIFORM NUMBERS IN NFL

AFC

Buffalo:	None	
Cincinnati:	Bob Johnson	54
Cleveland:	Otto Graham	14
	Jim Brown	32
	Ernie Davis	45
	Don Fleming	46
	Lou Groza	76
Denver:	Frank Tripucka	18
	Floyd Little	44
Indianapolis:	Johnny Unitas	19
	Buddy Young	22
	Lenny Moore	24
	Art Donovan	70
	Jim Parker	77
	Raymond Berry	82
	Gino Marchetti	89
Kansas City:	Jan Stenerud	3
	Len Dawson	16
	Abner Haynes	28
	Stone Johnson	33
	Mack Lee Hill	36
	Willie Lanier	63
	Bobby Bell	78
	Buck Buchanan	86
Miami:	Bob Griese	12
New England:	Steve Grogan	14
	Gino Cappelletti	20
	Mike Haynes	40
	Steve Nelson	57
	John Hannah	73
	Jim Hunt	79
	Bob Dee	89
New York Jets:	Joe Namath	12
	Don Maynard	13
Oakland:	None	
Pittsburgh:	None	
San Diego:	Dan Fouts	14
Seattle:	"Fans/the twelfth man"	12
	Steve Largent	80
Tennessee:	Earl Campbell	34
	Jim Norton	43
	Mike Munchak	63
	Elvin Bethea	65

NFC

Arizona:	Larry Wilson	8
	Stan Mauldin	77
	J.V. Cain	88
	Marshall Goldberg	99
Atlanta:	Steve Bartowski	10
	William Andrews	31
	Jeff Van Note	57
	Tommy Nobis	60
Chicago:	Bronko Nagurski	3
	George McAfee	5
	George Halas	7
	Willie Galimore	28
	Walter Payton	34
	Gale Sayers	40
	Brian Piccolo	41
	Sid Luckman	42
	Dick Butkus	51
	Bill Hewitt	56
	Bill George	61
	Bulldog Turner	66
	Red Grange	77
Dallas:	None	
Detroit:	Dutch Clark	7
	Bobby Layne	22
	Doak Walker	37
	Joe Schmidt	56
	Chuck Hughes	85
	Charlie Sanders	88
Green Bay:	Tony Canadeo	3
	Don Hutson	14
	Bart Starr	15
	Ray Nitschke	66
Minnesota:	Fran Tarkenton	10
	Alan Page	88
New Orleans:	Jim Taylor	31
	Doug Atkins	81

New York Giants:	Ray Flaherty	1
	Mel Hein	7
	Phil Simms	11
	Y.A. Tittle	14
	Al Blozis	32
	Joe Morrison	40
	Charlie Conerly	42
	Ken Strong	50
	Lawrence Taylor	56
Philadelphia:	Steve Van Buren	15
	Tom Brookshier	40
	Pete Retzlaff	44
	Chuck Bednarik	60
	Al Wistert	70
	Jerome Brown	99
St. Louis:	Bob Waterfield	7
	Merlin Olsen	74
	Jackie Slater	78
San Francisco:	John Brodie	12
	Joe Perry	34
	Jimmy Johnson	37
	Hugh McElhenny	39
	Charlie Krueger	70
	Leo Nomellini	73
	Dwight Clark	87
Tampa Bay:	Lee Roy Selmon	63
Washington:	Sammy Baugh	33

1996 NFL SCORE BY QUARTERS

AFC Offense	1	2	3	4	OT	PTS
New England	79	123	108	105	3	418
Denver	131	132	65	63	0	391
Cincinnati	57	111	65	139	0	372
Baltimore	70	129	64	102	6	371
Tennessee	105	79	67	91	3	345
Pittsburgh	84	115	92	53	0	344
Oakland	42	128	83	87	0	340
Miami	57	120	84	78	0	339
Jacksonville	68	80	80	94	3	325
Buffalo	37	110	77	89	6	319
Indianapolis	57	94	65	98	3	317
Seattle	53	117	57	90	0	317
San Diego	113	79	45	73	0	310
Kansas City	61	108	38	90	0	297
N.Y. Jets	54	100	50	75	0	279

NFC Offense	1	2	3	4	OT	PTS
Green Bay	76	125	136	116	3	456
San Francisco	85	153	50	107	3	398
Carolina	74	102	107	84	0	367
Washington	56	123	97	88	0	364
Philadelphia	98	88	64	113	0	363
Atlanta	52	82	82	93	0	309
St. Louis	55	102	60	86	0	303
Detroit	52	124	69	57	0	302
Arizona	39	70	51	134	6	300
Minnesota	50	93	51	101	3	298
Dallas	60	85	57	81	3	286
Chicago	70	89	57	67	0	283
N.Y. Giants	37	107	45	53	0	242
New Orleans	42	58	38	91	0	229
Tampa Bay	46	76	38	58	3	221

AFC Defense	1	2	3	4	OT	PTS
Pittsburgh	67	85	42	63	0	257
Buffalo	70	63	39	91	3	266
Denver	52	77	78	68	0	275
Oakland	69	65	65	88	6	293
Kansas City	81	76	72	71	0	300
New England	59	105	75	74	0	313
Tennessee	64	78	48	129	0	319
Miami	72	89	71	93	0	325
Indianapolis	60	123	66	82	3	334
Jacksonville	70	117	65	80	3	335
Cincinnati	67	105	86	108	3	369
San Diego	71	125	71	109	0	376
Seattle	85	111	64	116	0	376
Baltimore	88	128	92	130	3	441
N.Y. Jets	51	144	107	152	0	454

NFC Defense	1	2	3	4	OT	PTS
Green Bay	32	96	25	57	0	210
Carolina	62	100	23	33	0	218
Dallas	52	80	51	67	0	250
San Francisco	60	63	55	73	6	257
Tampa Bay	64	91	71	67	0	293
N.Y. Giants	75	90	39	90	3	297
Chicago	48	140	62	55	0	305
Washington	39	110	68	89	6	312
Minnesota	53	88	80	94	0	315
New Orleans	80	105	78	76	0	339
Philadelphia	64	119	73	85	0	341
Detroit	81	130	79	78	0	368
Arizona	56	130	90	121	0	397
St. Louis	68	112	120	100	9	409
Atlanta	100	157	87	117	0	461
NFL Totals	1,960	3,102	2,042	2,656	45	9,805

TEAM LEADERS

Offense	**Most Scored**	**Fewest Scored**
1st Quarter	131 Denver	37 Buff. & N.Y.G.
2nd Quarter	153 San Francisco	58 New Orleans
3rd Quarter	136 Green Bay	38 K.C., N.O. & T. B.
4th Quarter	139 Cincinnati	53 N.Y.G. & Pitt.

Defense	**Most Allowed**	**Fewest Allowed**
1st Quarter	100 Atlanta	32 Green Bay
2nd Quarter	157 Atlanta	63 Buff. & S. F.
3rd Quarter	120 St. Louis	23 Carolina
4th Quarter	152 N.Y.J.	33 Carolina

GREATEST COMEBACKS IN NFL HISTORY
(Most Points Overcome To Win Game)

REGULAR SEASON GAMES

FROM 28 POINTS BEHIND TO WIN:
December 7, 1980, at San Francisco

New Orleans	14	21	0	0	0	— 35
San Francisco	0	7	14	14	3	— 38

NO — Harris 33 pass from Manning (Ricardo kick)
NO — Childs 21 pass from Manning (Ricardo kick)
NO — Holmes 1 run (Ricardo kick)
SF — Solomon 57 punt return (Wersching kick)
NO — Holmes 1 run (Ricardo kick)
NO — Harris 41 pass from Manning (Ricardo kick)
SF — Montana 1 run (Wersching kick)
SF — Clark 71 pass from Montana (Wersching kick)
SF — Solomon 14 pass from Montana (Wersching kick)
SF — Elliott 7 run (Wersching kick)
SF — FG Wersching 36

	N.O.	S.F.
First Downs	27	24
Total Yards	519	430
Yards Rushing	143	176
Yards Passing	376	254
Turnovers	3	0

FROM 25 POINTS BEHIND TO WIN:
November 8, 1987, at St. Louis

Tampa Bay	7	7	14	0	— 28
St. Louis	0	3	28	31	— 31

TB — Carrier 5 pass from DeBerg (Igwebuike kick)
TB — Carter 3 pass from DeBerg (Igwebuike kick)
StL — FG Gallery 31
TB — Smith 34 pass from DeBerg (Igwebuike kick)
TB — Smith 3 run (Igwebuike kick)
StL — Awalt 4 pass from Lomax (Gallery kick)
StL — Noga 23 fumble recovery (Gallery kick)
StL — J. Smith 11 pass from Lomax (Gallery kick)
StL — J. Smith 17 pass from Lomax (Gallery kick)

	T.B.	St.L.
First Downs	26	26
Total Yards	377	415
Yards Rushing	83	137
Yards Passing	294	278
Turnovers	1	2

FROM 24 POINTS BEHIND TO WIN:
October 27, 1946, at Washington

Philadelphia	0	0	14	14	— 28
Washington	10	14	0	0	— 24

Wash — Rosato 2 run (Poillon kick)
Wash — FG Poillon 28
Wash — Rosato 4 run (Poillon kick)
Wash — Lapka recovered fumble in end zone (Poillon kick)
Phil — Steele 1 run (Lio kick)
Phil — Pritchard 45 pass from Thompson (Lio kick)
Phil — Steinke 7 pass from Thompson (Lio kick)
Phil — Ferrante 30 pass from Thompson (Lio kick)

	Phil.	Wash.
First Downs	14	8
Total Yards	262	127
Yards Rushing	34	66
Yards Passing	228	61
Turnovers	6	3

FROM 24 POINTS BEHIND TO WIN:
October 20, 1957, at Detroit

Baltimore	7	14	6	0	— 27
Detroit	0	3	7	21	— 31

Balt — Mutscheller 15 pass from Unitas (Rechichar kick)
Det — FG Martin 47
Balt — Moore 72 pass from Unitas (Rechichar kick)
Balt — Mutscheller 52 pass from Unitas (Rechichar kick)
Balt — Moore 4 pass from Unitas (kick failed)
Det — Junker 14 pass from Rote (Layne kick)
Det — Cassady 26 pass from Layne (Layne kick)
Det — Johnson 1 run (Layne kick)
Det — Cassady 29 pass from Layne (Layne kick)

	Balt.	Det.
First Downs	15	20
Total Yards	322	369
Yards Rushing	117	178
Yards Passing	205	191
Turnovers	6	4

FROM 24 POINTS BEHIND TO WIN:
October 25, 1959, at Minneapolis

Philadelphia	0	0	21	7	— 28
Chicago Cardinals	7	10	7	0	— 24

Cardinals — Crow 10 pass from Roach (Conrad kick)
Cardinals — J. Hill 77 blocked field goal return (Conrad kick)
Cardinals — FG Conrad 15
Cardinals — Lane 37 interception return (Conrad kick)
Phil — Barnes 1 run (Walston kick)
Phil — McDonald 29 pass from Van Brocklin (Walston kick)
Phil — Barnes 2 run (Walston kick)
Phil — McDonald 22 pass from Van Brocklin (Walston kick)

	Phil.	Cardinals
First Downs	22	14
Total Yards	399	313
Yards Rushing	168	163
Yards Passing	231	150
Turnovers	2	6

FROM 24 POINTS BEHIND TO WIN:
October 23, 1960, at Denver

Boston	10	7	7	0	— 24
Denver	0	0	14	17	— 31

Bos — FG Cappelletti 12
Bos — Colclough 10 pass from Songin (Cappelletti kick)
Bos — Wells 6 pass from Songin (Cappelletti kick)
Bos — Miller 47 pass from Songin (Cappelletti kick)
Den — Carmichael 21 pass from Tripucka (Mingo kick)
Den — Jessup 19 pass from Tripucka (Mingo kick)
Den — Carmichael 35 lateral from Taylor, pass from Tripucka (Mingo kick)
Den — Taylor 8 pass from Tripucka (Mingo kick)
Den — FG Mingo 9

	Bos.	Den.
First Downs	19	16
Total Yards	434	326
Yards Rushing	211	65
Yards Passing	223	261
Turnovers	7	4

FROM 24 POINTS BEHIND TO WIN:
December 15, 1974, at Miami

New England	21	3	0	3	— 27
Miami	0	17	7	10	— 34

NE — Hannah recovered fumble in end zone (J. Smith kick)
NE — Sanders 23 interception return (J. Smith kick)
NE — Herron 4 pass from Plunkett (J. Smith kick)
NE — FG J. Smith 46
Mia — Nottingham 1 run (Yepremian kick)
Mia — Baker 37 pass from Morrall (Yepremian kick)
Mia — FG Yepremian 28
Mia — Baker 46 pass from Morrall (Yepremian kick)
NE — FG J. Smith 34
Mia — Nottingham 2 run (Yepremian kick)
Mia — FG Yepremian 40

	N.E.	Mia.
First Downs	18	18

Total Yards	333	333
Yards Rushing	114	61
Yards Passing	219	272
Turnovers	3	4

FROM 24 POINTS BEHIND TO WIN:
December 4, 1977, at Minnesota

San Francisco	0	10	14	3	— 27
Minnesota	0	0	7	21	— 28

SF — Delvin Williams 2 run (Wersching kick)
SF — FG Wersching 31
SF — Dave Williams 80 kickoff return (Wersching kick)
SF — Delvin Williams 5 run (Wersching kick)
Minn — McClanahan 15 pass from Lee (Cox kick)
Minn — Rashad 8 pass from Kramer (Cox kick)
Minn — Tucker 9 pass from Kramer (Cox kick)
SF — FG Wersching 31
Minn — S. White 69 pass from Kramer (Cox kick)

	S.F.	Minn.
First Downs	19	18
Total Yards	243	309
Yards Rushing	196	52
Yards Passing	47	257
Turnovers	2	5

FROM 24 POINTS BEHIND TO WIN:
September 23, 1979, at Denver

Seattle	10	10	14	0	— 34
Denver	0	10	21	6	— 37

Sea — FG Herrera 28
Sea — Doornink 5 run (Herrera kick)
Den — FG Turner 27
Sea — Doornink 5 run (Herrera kick)
Den — Armstrong 2 run (Turner kick)
Sea — FG Herrera 22
Sea — McCullum 13 pass from Zorn (Herrera kick)
Sea — Smith 1 run (Herrera kick)
Den — Studdard 2 pass from Morton (Turner kick)
Den — Moses 11 pass from Morton (Turner kick)
Den — Upchurch 35 pass from Morton (Turner kick)
Den — Lytle 1 run (kick failed)

	Sea.	Den.
First Downs	22	23
Total Yards	350	344
Yards Rushing	153	90
Yards Passing	197	254
Turnovers	4	3

FROM 24 POINTS BEHIND TO WIN:
September 23, 1979, at Cincinnati

Houston	0	10	17	0	3 — 30
Cincinnati	14	10	0	3	0 — 27

Cin — Johnson 1 run (Bahr kick)
Cin — Alexander 2 run (Bahr kick)
Cin — Johnson 1 run (Bahr kick)
Cin — FG Bahr 52
Hou — Burrough 35 pass from Pastorini (Fritsch kick)
Hou — FG Fritsch 33
Hou — Campbell 8 run (Fritsch kick)
Hou — Caster 22 pass from Pastorini (Fritsch kick)
Hou — FG Fritsch 47
Cin — FG Bahr 55
Hou — FG Fritsch 29

	Hou.	Cin.
First Downs	19	21
Total Yards	361	265
Yards Rushing	177	165
Yards Passing	184	100
Turnovers	3	2

FROM 24 POINTS BEHIND TO WIN:
November 22, 1982, at Los Angeles

San Diego	10	14	0	0	— 24
L.A. Raiders	0	7	14	7	— 28

SD — FG Benirschke 19
SD — Scales 29 pass from Fouts (Benirschke kick)
SD — Muncie 2 run (Benirschke kick)
SD — Muncie 1 run (Benirschke kick)
Raiders — Christensen 1 pass from Plunkett (Bahr kick)

Raiders — Allen 3 run (Bahr kick)
Raiders — Allen 6 run (Bahr kick)
Raiders — Hawkins 1 run (Bahr kick)

	S.D.	Raiders
First Downs	26	23
Total Yards	411	326
Yards Rushing	72	181
Yards Passing	339	145
Turnovers	4	2

FROM 24 POINTS BEHIND TO WIN:
September 26, 1988, at Denver

L.A. Raiders	0	0	14	13	3 — 30
Denver	7	17	0	3	0 — 27

Den — Dorsett 1 run (Karlis kick)
Den — Dorsett 1 run (Karlis kick)
Den — Sewell 7 pass from Elway (Karlis kick)
Den — FG Karlis 39
Raiders — Smith 40 pass from Schroeder (Bahr kick)
Raiders — Smith 42 pass from Schroeder (Bahr kick)
Raiders — FG Bahr 28
Raiders — Allen 4 run (Bahr kick)
Den — FG Karlis 25
Raiders — FG Bahr 44
Raiders — FG Bahr 35

	Raiders	Den.
First Downs	20	23
Total Yards	363	398
Yards Rushing	128	189
Yards Passing	235	209
Turnovers	1	5

FROM 24 POINTS BEHIND TO WIN:
December 6, 1992, at Tampa

L.A. Rams	0	3	21	7 — 31
Tampa Bay	6	21	0	0 — 27

TB — FG Murray 34
TB — FG Murray 47
TB — Armstrong 81 pass from Testaverde (Murray kick)
TB — Jones 26 fumble recovery (Murray kick)
Rams — FG Zendejas 18
TB — Carrier 10 pass from Testaverde (Murray kick)
Rams — Anderson 40 pass from Everett (Zendejas kick)
Rams — Chadwick 27 pass from Everett (Zendejas

kick)
Rams — Lang 1 run (Zendejas kick)
Rams — Carter 8 pass from Everett (Zendejas kick)

	Rams	T.B.
First Downs	21	16
Total Yards	405	313
Yards Rushing	63	150
Yards Passing	342	163
Turnovers	3	3

POSTSEASON GAMES

FROM 32 POINTS BEHIND TO WIN:
AFC First-Round Playoff Game
January 3, 1993, at Buffalo

Houston	7	21	7	3	0 — 38
Buffalo	3	0	28	7	3 — 41

Hou — Jeffires 3 pass from Moon (Del Greco kick)
Buff — FG Christie 36
Hou — Slaughter 7 pass from Moon (Del Greco kick)
Hou — Duncan 26 pass from Moon (Del Greco kick)
Hou — Jeffires 27 pass from Moon (Del Greco kick)
Hou — McDowell 58 interception return (Del Greco kick)
Buff — Davis 1 run (Christie kick)
Buff — Beebe 38 pass from Reich (Christie kick)
Buff — Reed 26 pass from Reich (Christie kick)
Buff — Reed 18 pass from Reich (Christie kick)
Buff — Reed 17 pass from Reich (Christie kick)
Hou — FG Del Greco 26
Buff — FG Christie 32

	Hou.	Buff.
First Downs	27	19
Total Yards	429	366
Yards Rushing	82	98
Yards Passing	347	268
Turnovers	2	1

FROM 20 POINTS BEHIND TO WIN:
Western Conference Playoff Game
December 22, 1957, at San Francisco

Detroit	0	7	14	10 — 31
San Francisco	14	10	3	0 — 27

SF — Owens 34 pass from Tittle (Soltau kick)
SF — McElhenny 47 pass from Tittle (Soltau kick)

Det — Junker 4 pass from Rote (Martin kick)
SF — Wilson 12 pass from Tittle (Soltau kick)
SF — FG Soltau 25
SF — FG Soltau 10
Det — Tracy 2 run (Martin kick)
Det — Tracy 58 run (Martin kick)
Det — Gedman 3 run (Martin kick)
Det — FG Martin 14

	Det.	S.F.
First Downs	22	20
Total Yards	324	351
Yards Rushing	129	127
Yards Passing	195	224
Turnovers	5	4

FROM 18 POINTS BEHIND TO WIN:
NFC Divisional Playoff Game
December 23, 1972, at San Francisco

Dallas	3	10	0	17 — 30
San Francisco	7	14	7	0 — 28

SF — Washington 97 kickoff return (Gossett kick)
Dall — FG Fritsch 37
SF — Schreiber 1 run (Gossett kick)
SF — Schreiber 1 run (Gossett kick)
Dall — FG Fritsch 45
Dall — Alworth 28 pass from Morton (Fritsch kick)
SF — Schreiber 1 run (Gossett kick)
Dall — FG Fritsch 27
Dall — Parks 20 pass from Staubach (Fritsch kick)
Dall — Sellers 10 pass from Staubach (Fritsch kick)

	Dall.	S.F.
First Downs	22	13
Total Yards	402	255
Yards Rushing	165	105
Yards Passing	237	150
Turnovers	5	3

FROM 18 POINTS BEHIND TO WIN:
AFC Divisional Playoff Game
January 4, 1986, at Miami

Cleveland	7	7	7	0 — 21
Miami	3	0	14	7 — 24

Mia — FG Reveiz 51
Clev — Newsome 16 pass from Kosar (Bahr kick)
Clev — Byner 21 run (Bahr kick)
Clev — Byner 66 run (Bahr kick)
Mia — Moore 6 pass from Marino (Reveiz kick)

RECORDS OF NFL TEAMS SINCE 1970 AFL-NFL MERGER

AFC	W - L - T	Pct.	Division Titles	Playoff Berths	Post-season Record	Super Bowl Record
Miami	265-141-2	.652	11	16	17-14	2-3
Oakland	251-151-6	.624	9	15	18-12	3-0
Pittsburgh	245-162-1	.602	13	17	20-13	4-1
Denver	230-172-6	.571	8	11	9-11	0-4
Cleveland†	194-195-3	.499	6	10	4-10	0-0
Kansas City	199-202-7	.496	3	8	3-8	0-0
Buffalo	196-210-2	.483	7	8	12-11	0-4
Cincinnati	193-215-0	.473	5	7	5-7	0-2
San Diego	187-216-5	.464	5	7	6-7	0-1
Seattle*	148-176-0	.457	1	4	3-4	0-0
New England	185-223-0	.453	3	7	5-7	0-2
Tennessee	181-225-2	.446	2	10	7-10	0-0
Indianapolis	174-232-2	.429	5	8	6-7	1-0
Jacksonville**	13- 19-0	.406	0	1	2-1	0-0
N.Y. Jets	162-244-2	.400	0	5	3-5	0-0
Baltimore***	4- 12-0	.250	0	0	0-0	0-0

NFC	W - L - T	Pct.	Division Titles	Playoff Berths	Post-season Record	Super Bowl Record
Dallas	261-147-0	.640	14	20	31-15	5-3
San Francisco	248-157-3	.612	15	17	22-12	5-0
Washington	243-164-1	.597	5	13	18-10	3-2
Carolina**	19- 13-0	.594	1	1	1-1	0-0
Minnesota	237-169-2	.583	12	17	11-17	0-3
St. Louis	220-184-4	.544	8	14	10-14	0-1
Chicago	211-196-1	.518	6	10	7-9	1-0
Philadelphia	198-204-6	.493	2	10	5-10	0-1
N.Y. Giants	189-217-2	.466	3	7	10-5	2-0
Green Bay	183-217-8	.458	3	6	8-5	1-0
Detroit	184-220-4	.456	3	7	1-7	0-0
Arizona	170-232-6	.424	2	3	0-3	0-0
New Orleans	165-239-4	.409	1	4	0-4	0-0
Atlanta	163-241-4	.404	1	5	2-5	0-0
Tampa Bay*	100-223-1	.310	2	3	1-3	0-0

*entered NFL in 1976.
**entered NFL in 1995.
***entered NFL in 1996.
† Suspended play in 1996. Will return for 1999 season.
Oakland totals include L.A. Raiders, 1982-94.
Tennessee totals include Houston, 1960-96.
Indianapolis totals include Baltimore, 1970-83.
St. Louis totals include L.A. Rams, 1970-94.
Arizona totals include St. Louis, 1970-87, and Phoenix, 1988-93.
Tie games before 1972 are not calculated in won-lost percentage.
In 1982, because of players' strike, the divisional format was abandoned; L.A. Raiders and Washington won regular-season conference titles, not included in "Division Titles" totals listed above. Sixteen teams were awarded playoff berths, included in totals listed above.

LONGEST WINNING STREAKS SINCE 1970

Regular-Season Games

16	Miami, 1971-73	(1 in 1971, 14 in 1972, 1 in 1973)
16	Miami, 1983-84	(5 in 1983, 11 in 1984)
15	San Francisco, 1989-90	(5 in 1989, 10 in 1990)
14	Oakland, 1976-77	(10 in 1976, 4 in 1977)
13	Minnesota, 1974-75	(3 in 1974, 10 in 1975)
13	Chicago, 1984-85	(1 in 1984, 12 in 1985)
13	N.Y. Giants, 1989-90	(3 in 1989, 10 in 1990)
12	Washington, 1990-91	(1 in 1990, 11 in 1991)
11	Pittsburgh, 1975	
11	Baltimore, 1975-76	(9 in 1975, 2 in 1976)
11	Chicago, 1986-87	(7 in 1986, 4 in 1987)
11	Houston, 1993	
10	Miami, 1973	
10	Pittsburgh, 1976-77	(9 in 1976, 1 in 1977)
10	Denver, 1984	
10	San Francisco, 1994	

NFL PLAYOFF APPEARANCES BY SEASONS

Team	Number of Seasons in Playoffs
Dallas	24
Cleveland	23
N.Y. Giants	23
St. Louis	22
Chicago	21
Minnesota	19
Washington	19
Oakland	18
Pittsburgh	18
San Francisco	18
Green Bay	17
Miami	16
Buffalo	15
Tennessee	15
Philadelphia	14
Indianapolis	13
Detroit	12
Kansas City	12
San Diego	12
Denver	11
New England	8
Cincinnati	7
N.Y. Jets	7
Arizona	5
Atlanta	5
New Orleans	4
Seattle	4
Tampa Bay	3
Carolina	1
Jacksonville	1

TEAMS IN SUPER BOWL CONTENTION, 1978-1996

	With 3 Weeks to Play	With 2 Weeks to Play	With 1 Week to Play
1996	23	21	13
1995	*27	21	*18
1994	25	*22	15
1993	20	18	16
1992	20	16	14
1991	20	18	13
1990	23	20	15
1989	21	18	17
1988	21	18	15
1987	19	19	15
1986	19	17	14
1985	21	18	13
1984	18	14	13
1983	24	19	15
1982	20	17	16
1981	21	20	16
1980	20	14	12
1979	19	15	13
1978	20	17	12

*NFL Record

GAMES DECIDED BY 7 POINTS OR LESS AND 3 POINTS OR LESS (1970-1996)

	Games Decided by 7 Points or Less	Games Decided by 3 Points or Less
1970	59 of 182 (32.4%)	34 of 182 (18.7%)
1971	76 of 182 (41.8%)	35 of 182 (19.2%)
1972	71 of 182 (39.0%)	38 of 182 (20.9%)
1973	60 of 182 (32.9%)	28 of 182 (15.4%)
1974	91 of 182 (50.0%)	37 of 182 (20.3%)
1975	62 of 182 (34.1%)	35 of 182 (19.2%)
1976	73 of 196 (37.2%)	38 of 196 (19.4%)
1977	85 of 196 (43.4%)	36 of 196 (18.4%)
1978	108 of 224 (48.2%)	49 of 224 (21.9%)
1979	104 of 224 (46.4%)	51 of 224 (22.8%)
1980	108 of 224 (48.2%)	58 of 224 (25.9%)
1981	91 of 224 (40.6%)	**60 of 224 (26.8%)
1982	61 of 126 (48.4%)	33 of 126 (26.2%)
1983	106 of 224 (47.3%)	54 of 224 (24.1%)
1984	95 of 224 (42.4%)	58 of 224 (25.9%)
1985	87 of 224 (38.8%)	38 of 224 (17.0%)
1986	106 of 224 (47.3%)	48 of 224 (21.4%)
1987	99 of 210 (47.1%)	40 of 210 (19.0%)
1988	113 of 224 (50.4%)	62 of 224 (27.7%)
1989	107 of 224 (47.8%)	55 of 224 (24.6%)
1990	97 of 224 (43.3%)	54 of 224 (24.1%)
1991	112 of 224 (50.0%)	57 of 224 (25.4%)
1992	88 of 224 (39.3%)	**48 of 224 (21.4%)
1993	*105 of 224 (46.9%)	53 of 224 (23.7%)
1994	115 of 224 (51.3%)	60 of 224 (26.8%)
1995	115 of 240 (47.9%)	61 of 240 (25.4%)
1996	109 of 240 (45.4%)	47 of 240 (19.6%)

*Week record: Dec. 11-13, 1993 (Week 15), 12 of 14 games (86%) decided by 7 points or less.

**Week record: Nov. 8-9, 1981 (Week 10), 8 of 14 games (57%), and Nov. 15-16, 1992 (Week 11), 8 of 14 games (57%) decided by 3 points or less.

1996 RECORDS OF TEAMS IN CLOSE GAMES

AFC	Overall Record	Decided by 8 Pts. or Less	Decided By 3 Pts. or Less
Baltimore	4-12	3-7	0-4
Buffalo	10-6	6-4	4-3
Cincinnati	8-8	5-4	1-2
Denver	13-3	6-2	1-1
Houston	8-8	3-6	2-3
Indianapolis	9-7	7-3	2-1
Jacksonville	9-7	7-5	4-2
Kansas City	9-7	5-2	2-1
Miami	8-8	3-4	3-0
New England	11-5	5-3	3-0
N.Y. Jets	1-15	0-7	0-3
Oakland	7-9	1-8	0-4
Pittsburgh	10-6	2-1	1-0
San Diego	8-8	5-1	1-0
Seattle	7-9	5-3	0-1

NFC	Overall Record	Decided by 8 Pts. or Less	Decided By 3 Pts. or Less
Arizona	7-9	6-3	3-0
Atlanta	3-13	2-6	2-2
Carolina	12-4	3-2	1-2
Chicago	7-9	3-5	3-1
Dallas	10-6	5-2	1-2
Detroit	5-11	2-5	1-1
Green Bay	13-3	2-1	1-0
Minnesota	9-7	6-3	3-1
New Orleans	3-13	2-6	1-3
N.Y. Giants	6-10	3-3	0-2
Philadelphia	10-6	4-4	2-0
St. Louis	6-10	3-3	2-1
San Francisco	12-4	4-3	2-2
Tampa Bay	6-10	3-5	1-1
Washington	9-7	4-4	0-4

SUPER BOWL CHAMPIONS WHO DID NOT MAKE PLAYOFFS THE FOLLOWING YEAR

N.Y. Giants—Super Bowl XXV champions did not make playoffs in the 1991 season.

Washington—Super Bowl XXII champions did not make playoffs in the 1988 season.

N.Y. Giants—Super Bowl XXI champions did not make playoffs in the 1987 season.

San Francisco—Super Bowl XVI champions did not make playoffs in the 1982 season.

Oakland—Super Bowl XV champions did not make playoffs in the 1981 season.

Pittsburgh—Super Bowl XIV champions did not make playoffs in the 1980 season.

Kansas City—Super Bowl IV champions did not make playoffs in the 1970 season.

Green Bay—Super Bowl II champions did not make playoffs in the 1968 season.

NON-DIVISION WINNERS THAT PLAYED IN SUPER BOWL

1992	Buffalo Bills (Lost to Dallas, 52-17)	Super Bowl XXVII
1985	New England Patriots (Lost to Chicago, 46-10)	Super Bowl XX
1980	Oakland Raiders (Defeated Philadelphia, 27-10)	Super Bowl XV
1975	Dallas Cowboys (Lost to Pittsburgh, 21-17)	Super Bowl X
1969	Kansas City Chiefs (Defeated Minnesota, 23-7)	Super Bowl IV

TEAMS AT OR UNDER .500 IN POSTSEASON PLAY

1991	New York Jets	8-8
1990	New Orleans Saints	8-8
1985	Cleveland Browns	8-8
1982	Cleveland Browns	4-5
1982	Detroit Lions	4-5
1969	Houston Oilers	6-6-2

COLDEST NFL GAMES ON RECORD

-13 degrees (-48 degree wind chill)—December 31, 1967, Lambeau Field, Green Bay, Wisconsin, NFL Championship (Green Bay 21, Dallas 17)

-9 degrees (-59 degree wind chill)—January 10, 1982, Riverfront Stadium, Cincinnati, Ohio, AFC Championship (Cincinnati 27, San Diego 7)

0 degrees (-32 degree wind chill)—January 15, 1994, Rich Stadium, Orchard Park, New York, AFC Divisional Playoff (Buffalo 29, Los Angeles Raiders 23)

1 degree (wind chill not recorded)—January 4, 1981, Cleveland Stadium, Cleveland, Ohio, AFC Divisional Playoff (Oakland 14, Cleveland 12)

ALL-TIME REGULAR-SEASON RECORDS OF CURRENT NFL TEAMS

AFC

BALTIMORE RAVENS

	All Games			Home Games			Road Games		
Season	W	L	T	W	L	T	W	L	T
1996	4	12		4	4		0	8	

BUFFALO BILLS

	All Games			Home Games			Road Games		
Season	W	L	T	W	L	T	W	L	T
1960	5	8	1	3	4		2	4	1
1961	6	8		2	5		4	3	
1962	7	6	1	3	3	1	4	3	
1963	7	6	1	4	2	1	3	4	
1964	12	2		6	1		6	1	
1965	10	3	1	5	2		5	1	1
1966	9	4	1	4	2	1	5	2	
1967	4	10		2	5		2	5	
1968	1	12	1	1	6		0	6	1
1969	4	10		4	3		0	7	
1970	3	10	1	1	6		2	4	1
1971	1	13		1	6		0	7	
1972	4	9	1	2	4	1	2	5	
1973	9	5		5	2		4	3	
1974	9	5		5	2		4	3	
1975	8	6		3	4		5	2	
1976	2	12		1	6		1	6	
1977	3	11		1	6		2	5	
1978	5	11		4	4		1	7	
1979	7	9		3	5		4	4	
1980	11	5		6	2		5	3	
1981	10	6		7	1		3	5	
1982	4	5		4	1		0	4	
1983	8	8		3	5		5	3	
1984	2	14		2	6		0	8	

Season	All Games W	L	T	Home Games W	L	T	Road Games W	L	T
1985	2	14		2	6		0	8	
1986	4	12		3	5		1	7	
1987	7	8		4	4		3	4	
1988	12	4		8	0		4	4	
1989	9	7		6	2		3	5	
1990	13	3		8	0		5	3	
1991	13	3		7	1		6	2	
1992	11	5		6	2		5	3	
1993	12	4		6	2		6	2	
1994	7	9		4	4		3	5	
1995	10	6		6	2		4	4	
1996	10	6		7	1		3	5	
Total	261	279	8	149	122	4	112	157	4

CINCINNATI BENGALS

Season	All Games W	L	T	Home Games W	L	T	Road Games W	L	T
1968	3	11		2	5		1	6	
1969	4	9	1	4	3		0	6	1
1970	8	6		5	2		3	4	
1971	4	10		3	4		1	6	
1972	8	6		4	3		4	3	
1973	10	4		7	0		3	4	
1974	7	7		4	3		3	4	
1975	11	3		6	1		5	2	
1976	10	4		6	1		4	3	
1977	8	6		5	2		3	4	
1978	4	12		3	5		1	7	
1979	4	12		4	4		0	8	
1980	6	10		3	5		3	5	
1981	12	4		6	2		6	2	
1982	7	2		4	0		3	2	
1983	7	9		4	4		3	5	
1984	8	8		5	3		3	5	
1985	7	9		5	3		2	6	
1986	10	6		6	2		4	4	
1987	4	11		1	7		3	4	
1988	12	4		8	0		4	4	
1989	8	8		5	3		3	5	
1990	9	7		5	3		4	4	
1991	3	13		3	5		0	8	
1992	5	11		3	5		2	6	
1993	3	13		3	5		0	8	
1994	3	13		2	6		1	7	
1995	7	9		3	5		4	4	
1996	8	8		6	2		2	6	
Total	200	235	1	125	93		75	142	1

CLEVELAND BROWNS

Season	All Games W	L	T	Home Games W	L	T	Road Games W	L	T
1950	10	2		5	1		5	1	
1951	11	1		6	0		5	1	
1952	8	4		4	2		4	2	
1953	11	1		6	0		5	1	
1954	9	3		5	1		4	2	
1955	9	2	1	5	1		4	1	1
1956	5	7		1	5		4	2	
1957	9	2	1	6	0		3	2	1
1958	9	3		4	2		5	1	
1959	7	5		3	3		4	2	
1960	8	3	1	4	2		4	1	1
1961	8	5	1	4	3		4	2	1
1962	7	6	1	4	2	1	3	4	
1963	10	4		5	2		5	2	
1964	10	3	1	5	1	1	5	2	
1965	11	3		5	2		6	1	
1966	9	5		5	2		4	3	
1967	9	5		6	1		3	4	
1968	10	4		5	2		5	2	
1969	10	3	1	5	1	1	5	2	
1970	7	7		4	3		3	4	
1971	9	5		4	3		5	2	
1972	10	4		4	3		6	1	
1973	7	5	2	5	1	1	2	4	1
1974	4	10		3	4		1	6	
1975	3	11		3	4		0	7	
1976	9	5		6	1		3	4	
1977	6	8		2	5		4	3	
1978	8	8		5	3		3	5	
1979	9	7		5	3		4	4	

Season	All Games W	L	T	Home Games W	L	T	Road Games W	L	T
1980	11	5		6	2		5	3	
1981	5	11		3	5		2	6	
1982	4	5		2	2		2	3	
1983	9	7		6	2		3	5	
1984	5	11		2	6		3	5	
1985	8	8		5	3		3	5	
1986	12	4		6	2		6	2	
1987	10	5		5	2		5	3	
1988	10	6		6	2		4	4	
1989	9	6	1	5	2	1	4	4	
1990	3	13		2	6		1	7	
1991	6	10		3	5		3	5	
1992	7	9		4	4		3	5	
1993	7	9		4	4		3	5	
1994	11	5		6	2		5	3	
1995	5	11		3	5		2	6	
Total	374	266	10	202	117	5	172	149	5

DENVER BRONCOS

Season	All Games W	L	T	Home Games W	L	T	Road Games W	L	T
1960	4	9	1	2	4	1	2	5	
1961	3	11		2	5		1	6	
1962	7	7		3	4		4	3	
1963	2	11	1	2	5		0	6	1
1964	2	11	1	2	4	1	0	7	
1965	4	10		2	5		2	5	
1966	4	10		3	4		1	6	
1967	3	11		1	6		2	5	
1968	5	9		3	4		2	5	
1969	5	8	1	4	2	1	1	6	
1970	5	8	1	3	3	1	2	5	
1971	4	9	1	2	4	1	2	5	
1972	5	9		3	4		2	5	
1973	7	5	2	3	3	1	4	2	1
1974	7	6	1	3	3	1	4	3	
1975	6	8		5	2		1	6	
1976	9	5		6	1		3	4	
1977	12	2		6	1		6	1	
1978	10	6		6	2		4	4	
1979	10	6		6	2		4	4	
1980	8	8		4	4		4	4	
1981	10	6		8	0		2	6	
1982	2	7		1	4		1	3	
1983	9	7		6	2		3	5	
1984	13	3		7	1		6	2	
1985	11	5		6	2		5	3	
1986	11	5		7	1		4	4	
1987	10	4	1	7	1		3	3	1
1988	8	8		6	2		2	6	
1989	11	5		6	2		5	3	
1990	5	11		4	4		1	7	
1991	12	4		7	1		5	3	
1992	8	8		7	1		1	7	
1993	9	7		5	3		4	4	
1994	7	9		4	4		3	5	
1995	8	8		6	2		2	6	
1996	13	3		8	0		5	3	
Total	269	269	10	166	102	7	103	167	3

INDIANAPOLIS COLTS*

Season	All Games W	L	T	Home Games W	L	T	Road Games W	L	T
1953	3	9		2	4		1	5	
1954	3	9		2	4		1	5	
1955	5	6	1	4	1	1	1	5	
1956	5	7		4	2		1	5	
1957	7	5		4	2		3	3	
1958	9	3		6	0		3	3	
1959	9	3		4	2		5	1	
1960	6	6		4	2		2	4	
1961	8	6		5	2		3	4	
1962	7	7		3	4		4	3	
1963	8	6		4	3		4	3	
1964	12	2		7	1		5	1	
1965	10	3	1	5	2		5	1	1
1966	9	5		5	2		4	3	
1967	11	1	2	6	0	1	5	1	1
1968	13	1		6	1		7	0	
1969	8	5	1	4	2	1	4	3	
1970	11	2	1	5	1	1	6	1	

Season	All Games W	L	T	Home Games W	L	T	Road Games W	L	T
1971	10	4		5	2		5	2	
1972	5	9		2	5		3	4	
1973	4	10		3	4		1	6	
1974	2	12		0	7		2	5	
1975	10	4		5	2		5	2	
1976	11	3		6	1		5	2	
1977	10	4		6	1		4	3	
1978	5	11		2	6		3	5	
1979	5	11		3	5		2	6	
1980	7	9		2	6		5	3	
1981	2	14		1	7		1	7	
1982	0	8	1	0	3	1	0	5	
1983	7	9		3	5		4	4	
1984	4	12		2	6		2	6	
1985	5	11		4	4		1	7	
1986	3	13		1	7		2	6	
1987	9	6		4	4		5	2	
1988	9	7		6	2		3	5	
1989	8	8		6	2		2	6	
1990	7	9		3	5		4	4	
1991	1	15		0	8		1	7	
1992	9	7		4	4		5	3	
1993	4	12		2	6		2	6	
1994	8	8		5	3		3	5	
1995	9	7		5	3		4	4	
1996	9	7		6	2		3	5	
Total	307	316	7	166	145	5	141	171	2

*includes Baltimore Colts (1953-83).

JACKSONVILLE JAGUARS

Season	All Games W	L	T	Home Games W	L	T	Road Games W	L	T
1995	4	12		2	6		2	6	
1996	9	7		7	1		2	6	
Total	13	19		9	7		4	12	

KANSAS CITY CHIEFS*

Season	All Games W	L	T	Home Games W	L	T	Road Games W	L	T
1960	8	6		5	2		3	4	
1961	6	8		4	3		2	5	
1962	11	3		6	1		5	2	
1963	5	7	2	4	3		1	4	2
1964	7	7		4	3		3	4	
1965	7	5	2	5	2		2	3	2
1966	11	2	1	4	2	1	7	0	
1967	9	5		4	3		5	2	
1968	12	2		6	1		6	1	
1969	11	3		6	1		5	2	
1970	7	5	2	4	1	2	3	4	
1971	10	3	1	7	0		3	3	1
1972	8	6		3	4		5	2	
1973	7	5	2	5	1	1	2	4	1
1974	5	9		1	6		4	3	
1975	5	9		3	4		2	5	
1976	5	9		1	6		4	3	
1977	2	12		1	6		1	6	
1978	4	12		3	5		1	7	
1979	7	9		3	5		4	4	
1980	8	8		3	5		5	3	
1981	9	7		5	3		4	4	
1982	3	6		2	2		1	4	
1983	6	10		5	3		1	7	
1984	8	8		5	3		3	5	
1985	6	10		5	3		1	7	
1986	10	6		6	2		4	4	
1987	4	11		3	4		1	7	
1988	4	11	1	4	4		0	7	1
1989	8	7	1	5	3		3	4	1
1990	11	5		6	2		5	3	
1991	10	6		6	2		4	4	
1992	10	6		7	1		3	5	
1993	11	5		7	1		4	4	
1994	9	7		5	3		4	4	
1995	13	3		8	0		5	3	
1996	9	7		5	3		4	4	
Total	286	250	12	166	103	4	120	147	8

*includes Dallas Texans (1960-62).

MIAMI DOLPHINS

Season	All Games W	L	T	Home Games W	L	T	Road Games W	L	T
1966	3	11		2	5		1	6	
1967	4	10		4	3		0	7	
1968	5	8	1	1	5	1	4	3	
1969	3	10	1	2	4	1	1	6	
1970	10	4		6	1		4	3	
1971	10	3	1	6	1		4	2	1
1972	14	0		7	0		7	0	
1973	12	2		7	0		5	2	
1974	11	3		7	0		4	3	
1975	10	4		5	2		5	2	
1976	6	8		3	4		3	4	
1977	10	4		6	1		4	3	
1978	11	5		7	1		4	4	
1979	10	6		6	2		4	4	
1980	8	8		5	3		3	5	
1981	11	4	1	6	1	1	5	3	
1982	7	2		4	0		3	2	
1983	12	4		7	1		5	3	
1984	14	2		7	1		7	1	
1985	12	4		8	0		4	4	
1986	8	8		4	4		4	4	
1987	8	7		4	3		4	4	
1988	6	10		4	4		2	6	
1989	8	8		4	4		4	4	
1990	12	4		7	1		5	3	
1991	8	8		5	3		3	5	
1992	11	5		6	2		5	3	
1993	9	7		4	4		5	3	
1994	10	6		6	2		4	4	
1995	9	7		5	3		4	4	
1996	8	8		4	4		4	4	
Total	280	180	4	159	69	3	121	111	1

NEW ENGLAND PATRIOTS*

Season	All Games W	L	T	Home Games W	L	T	Road Games W	L	T
1960	5	9		3	4		2	5	
1961	9	4	1	4	2	1	5	2	
1962	9	4	1	6	1		3	3	1
1963	7	6	1	5	1	1	2	5	
1964	10	3	1	4	2	1	6	1	
1965	4	8	2	1	4	2	3	4	
1966	8	4	2	4	2	1	4	2	1
1967	3	10	1	2	4		1	6	1
1968	4	10		2	5		2	5	
1969	4	10		2	5		2	5	
1970	2	12		1	6		1	6	
1971	6	8		5	2		1	6	
1972	3	11		2	5		1	6	
1973	5	9		3	4		2	5	
1974	7	7		3	4		4	3	
1975	3	11		2	5		1	6	
1976	11	3		6	1		5	2	
1977	9	5		6	1		3	4	
1978	11	5		5	3		6	2	
1979	9	7		6	2		3	5	
1980	10	6		6	2		4	4	
1981	2	14		2	6		0	8	
1982	5	4		3	1		2	3	
1983	8	8		5	3		3	5	
1984	9	7		5	3		4	4	
1985	11	5		7	1		4	4	
1986	11	5		4	4		7	1	
1987	8	7		5	3		3	4	
1988	9	7		7	1		2	6	
1989	5	11		3	5		2	6	
1990	1	15		0	8		1	7	
1991	6	10		4	4		2	6	
1992	2	14		1	7		1	7	
1993	5	11		3	5		2	6	
1994	10	6		5	3		5	3	
1995	6	10		3	5		3	5	
1996	11	5		6	2		5	3	
Total	248	291	9	141	126	6	107	165	3

*includes Boston Patriots (1960-70).

NEW YORK JETS*

Season	All Games W	L	T	Home Games W	L	T	Road Games W	L	T
1960	7	7		3	4		4	3	
1961	7	7		5	2		2	5	
1962	5	9		2	5		3	4	
1963	5	8	1	4	2	1	1	6	
1964	5	8	1	5	1		0	7	
1965	5	8	1	3	3	1	2	5	
1966	6	6	2	4	3		2	3	2
1967	8	5	1	4	2	1	4	3	
1968	11	3		6	1		5	2	
1969	10	4		5	2		5	2	
1970	4	10		2	5		2	5	
1971	6	8		4	3		2	5	
1972	7	7		4	3		3	4	
1973	4	10		2	4		2	6	
1974	7	7		3	4		4	3	
1975	3	11		1	6		2	5	
1976	3	11		2	5		1	6	
1977	3	11		1	6		2	5	
1978	8	8		4	4		4	4	
1979	8	8		6	2		2	6	
1980	4	12		2	6		2	6	
1981	10	5	1	6	2		4	3	1
1982	6	3		3	1		3	2	
1983	7	9		2	6		5	3	
1984	7	9		3	5		4	4	
1985	11	5		7	1		4	4	
1986	10	6		5	3		5	3	
1987	6	9		4	4		2	5	
1988	8	7	1	5	2	1	3	5	
1989	4	12		1	7		3	5	
1990	6	10		3	5		3	5	
1991	8	8		4	4		4	4	
1992	4	12		3	5		1	7	
1993	8	8		3	5		5	3	
1994	6	10		4	4		2	6	
1995	3	13		2	6		1	7	
1996	1	15		0	8		1	7	
Total	231	309	8	127	141	5	104	168	3

*includes New York Titans (1960-62).

OAKLAND RAIDERS*

Season	All Games W	L	T	Home Games W	L	T	Road Games W	L	T
1960	6	8		3	4		3	4	
1961	2	12		1	6		1	6	
1962	1	13		1	6		0	7	
1963	10	4		6	1		4	3	
1964	5	7	2	5	2		0	5	2
1965	8	5	1	5	2		3	3	1
1966	8	5	1	3	3	1	5	2	
1967	13	1		7	0		6	1	
1968	12	2		6	1		6	1	
1969	12	1	1	7	0		5	1	1
1970	8	4	2	6	1		2	3	2
1971	8	4	2	5	1	1	3	3	1
1972	10	3	1	5	1	1	5	2	
1973	9	4	1	5	2		4	2	1
1974	12	2		6	1		6	1	
1975	11	3		6	1		5	2	
1976	13	1		7	0		6	1	
1977	11	3		6	1		5	2	
1978	9	7		4	4		5	3	
1979	9	7		6	2		3	5	
1980	11	5		6	2		5	3	
1981	7	9		4	4		3	5	
1982	8	1		4	0		4	1	
1983	12	4		6	2		6	2	
1984	11	5		6	2		5	3	
1985	12	4		7	1		5	3	
1986	8	8		3	5		5	3	
1987	5	10		3	5		2	5	
1988	7	9		3	5		4	4	
1989	8	8		7	1		1	7	
1990	12	4		6	2		6	2	
1991	9	7		5	3		4	4	
1992	7	9		5	3		2	6	
1993	10	6		5	3		5	3	
1994	9	7		4	4		5	3	
1995	8	8		4	4		4	4	
1996	7	9		4	4		3	5	
Total	328	209	11	182	89	3	146	120	8

*includes Los Angeles Raiders (1982-94).

PITTSBURGH STEELERS*

Season	All Games W	L	T	Home Games W	L	T	Road Games W	L	T
1933	3	6	2	2	3		1	3	2
1934	2	10		1	5		1	5	
1935	4	8		2	5		2	3	
1936	6	6		4	1		2	5	
1937	4	7		2	4		2	3	
1938	2	9		0	5		2	4	
1939	1	9	1	1	4		0	5	1
1940	2	7	2	1	2	2	1	5	
1941	1	9	1	1	4		0	5	1
1942	7	4		3	2		4	2	
1945	2	8		1	4		1	4	
1946	5	5	1	4	1		1	4	1
1947	8	4		5	1		3	3	
1948	4	8		4	2		0	6	
1949	6	5	1	3	2	1	3	3	
1950	6	6		2	4		4	2	
1951	4	7	1	1	4	1	3	3	
1952	5	7		2	4		3	3	
1953	6	6		3	3		3	3	
1954	5	7		4	2		1	5	
1955	4	8		3	2		1	6	
1956	5	7		3	3		2	4	
1957	6	6		4	2		2	4	
1958	7	4	1	5	1		2	3	1
1959	6	5	1	3	2	1	3	3	
1960	5	6	1	4	2		1	4	1
1961	6	8		4	3		2	5	
1962	9	5		4	3		5	2	
1963	7	4	3	5	0	2	2	4	1
1964	5	9		2	5		3	4	
1965	2	12		1	6		1	6	
1966	5	8	1	3	3	1	2	5	
1967	4	9	1	1	6		3	3	1
1968	2	11	1	1	6		1	5	1
1969	1	13		1	6		0	7	
1970	5	9		4	3		1	6	
1971	6	8		5	2		1	6	
1972	11	3		7	0		4	3	
1973	10	4		7	1		3	3	
1974	10	3	1	5	2		5	1	1
1975	12	2		6	1		6	1	
1976	10	4		6	1		4	3	
1977	9	5		6	1		3	4	
1978	14	2		7	1		7	1	
1979	12	4		8	0		4	4	
1980	9	7		6	2		3	5	
1981	8	8		5	3		3	5	
1982	6	3		4	0		2	3	
1983	10	6		4	4		6	2	
1984	9	7		6	2		3	5	
1985	7	9		5	3		2	6	
1986	6	10		4	4		2	6	
1987	8	7		4	3		4	4	
1988	5	11		4	4		1	7	
1989	9	7		4	4		5	3	
1990	9	7		6	2		3	5	
1991	7	9		5	3		2	6	
1992	11	5		7	1		4	4	
1993	9	7		6	2		3	5	
1994	12	4		7	1		5	3	
1995	11	5		6	2		5	3	
1996	10	6		7	1		3	5	
Total	402	415	19	241	165	8	161	250	11

*includes Pittsburgh Pirates (1933-40).

SAN DIEGO CHARGERS*

Season	All Games W	L	T	Home Games W	L	T	Road Games W	L	T
1960	10	4		5	2		5	2	
1961	12	2		6	1		6	1	
1962	4	10		3	4		1	6	
1963	11	3		6	1		5	2	
1964	8	5	1	4	3		4	2	1
1965	9	2	3	4	1	2	5	1	1
1966	7	6	1	5	2		2	4	1
1967	8	5	1	5	2	1	3	3	
1968	9	5		4	3		5	2	
1969	8	6		5	2		3	4	
1970	5	6	3	2	3	2	3	3	1
1971	6	8		6	1		0	7	

Season	All Games W	L	T	Home Games W	L	T	Road Games W	L	T
1972	4	9	1	2	5		2	4	1
1973	2	11	1	2	5		0	6	1
1974	5	9		3	4		2	5	
1975	2	12		1	6		1	6	
1976	6	8		3	4		3	4	
1977	7	7		3	4		4	3	
1978	9	7		5	3		4	4	
1979	12	4		7	1		5	3	
1980	11	5		6	2		5	3	
1981	10	6		5	3		5	3	
1982	6	3		3	1		3	2	
1983	6	10		4	4		2	6	
1984	7	9		4	4		3	5	
1985	8	8		6	2		2	6	
1986	4	12		2	6		2	6	
1987	8	7		4	3		4	4	
1988	6	10		3	5		3	5	
1989	6	10		4	4		2	6	
1990	6	10		3	5		3	5	
1991	4	12		3	5		1	7	
1992	11	5		6	2		5	3	
1993	8	8		4	4		4	4	
1994	11	5		5	3		6	2	
1995	9	7		5	3		4	4	
1996	8	8		5	3		3	5	
Total	273	264	11	153	116	5	120	148	6

*includes Los Angeles Chargers (1960).

SEATTLE SEAHAWKS

Season	All Games W	L	T	Home Games W	L	T	Road Games W	L	T
1976	2	12		1	6		1	6	
1977	5	9		3	4		2	5	
1978	9	7		5	3		4	4	
1979	9	7		5	3		4	4	
1980	4	12		0	8		4	4	
1981	6	10		5	3		1	7	
1982	4	5		3	2		1	3	
1983	9	7		5	3		4	4	
1984	12	4		7	1		5	3	
1985	8	8		5	3		3	5	
1986	10	6		7	1		3	5	
1987	9	6		6	2		3	4	
1988	9	7		5	3		4	4	
1989	7	9		3	5		4	4	
1990	9	7		5	3		4	4	
1991	7	9		5	3		2	6	
1992	2	14		1	7		1	7	
1993	6	10		4	4		2	6	
1994	6	10		3	5		3	5	
1995	8	8		5	3		3	5	
1996	7	9		4	4		3	5	
Total	148	176		87	76		61	100	

TENNESSEE OILERS*

Season	All Games W	L	T	Home Games W	L	T	Road Games W	L	T
1960	10	4		6	1		4	3	
1961	10	3	1	6	1		4	2	1
1962	11	3		6	1		5	2	
1963	6	8		4	3		2	5	
1964	4	10		3	4		1	6	
1965	4	10		3	4		1	6	
1966	3	11		3	4		0	7	
1967	9	4	1	5	2		4	2	1
1968	7	7		3	4		4	3	
1969	6	6	2	4	2	1	2	4	1
1970	3	10	1	1	6		2	4	1
1971	4	9	1	3	3	1	1	6	
1972	1	13		1	6		0	7	
1973	1	13		0	7		1	6	
1974	7	7		3	4		4	3	
1975	10	4		5	2		5	2	
1976	5	9		3	4		2	5	
1977	8	6		5	2		3	4	
1978	10	6		5	3		5	3	
1979	11	5		6	2		5	3	
1980	11	5		6	2		5	3	
1981	7	9		5	3		2	6	
1982	1	8		1	4		0	4	
1983	2	14		2	6		0	8	
1984	3	13		2	6		1	7	
1985	5	11		4	4		1	7	
1986	5	11		4	4		1	7	
1987	9	6		5	2		4	4	
1988	10	6		7	1		3	5	
1989	9	7		6	2		3	5	
1990	9	7		6	2		3	5	
1991	11	5		7	1		4	4	
1992	10	6		5	3		5	3	
1993	12	4		7	1		5	3	
1994	2	14		2	6		0	8	
1995	7	9		3	5		4	4	
1996	8	8		2	6		6	2	
Total	251	291	6	149	123	2	102	168	4

*includes Houston Oilers (1960-96).

NFC
ARIZONA CARDINALS*

Season	All Games W	L	T	Home Games W	L	T	Road Games W	L	T
1920	6	2	2	5	1	1	1	1	1
1921	3	3	2	3	3	1	0	0	1
1922	8	3		8	3		0	0	
1923	8	4		8	3		0	1	
1924	5	4	1	5	3	1	0	1	
1925	11	2	1	11	2		0	0	1
1926	5	6	1	3	3		2	3	1
1927	3	7	1	2	3	1	1	4	
1928	1	5		1	1		0	4	
1929	6	6	1	3	2		3	4	1
1930	5	6	2	3	2		2	4	2
1931	5	4		3	0		2	4	
1932	2	6	2	1	2	1	1	4	1
1933	1	9	1	0	4	1	1	5	
1934	5	6		2	2		3	4	
1935	6	4	2	2	2		4	2	2
1936	3	8	1	3	1	1	0	7	
1937	5	5	1	1	3		4	2	1
1938	2	9		1	4		1	5	
1939	1	10		0	4		1	6	
1940	2	7	2	2	1	1	0	6	1
1941	3	7	1	0	3	1	3	4	
1942	3	8		2	2		1	6	
1943	0	10		0	3		0	7	
1945	1	9		0	3		1	6	
1946	6	5		2	2		4	3	
1947	9	3		5	0		4	3	
1948	11	1		5	1		6	0	
1949	6	5	1	2	3	1	4	2	
1950	5	7		3	3		2	4	
1951	3	9		1	5		2	4	
1952	4	8		2	4		2	4	
1953	1	10	1	0	5	1	1	5	
1954	2	10		2	4		0	6	
1955	4	7	1	3	2	1	1	5	
1956	7	5		4	2		3	3	
1957	3	9		0	6		3	3	
1958	2	9	1	1	4	1	1	5	
1959	2	10		2	4		0	6	
1960	6	5	1	3	2	1	3	3	
1961	7	7		3	4		4	3	
1962	4	9	1	2	4	1	2	5	
1963	9	5		3	4		6	1	
1964	9	3	2	4	1	1	5	2	1
1965	5	9		2	5		3	4	
1966	8	5	1	5	1	1	3	4	
1967	6	7	1	3	3	1	3	4	
1968	9	4	1	4	2	1	5	2	
1969	4	9	1	3	4		1	5	1
1970	8	5	1	6	1		2	4	1
1971	4	9	1	1	5	1	3	4	
1972	4	9	1	2	5		2	4	1
1973	4	9	1	2	4	1	2	5	
1974	10	4		5	2		5	2	
1975	11	3		6	1		5	2	
1976	10	4		6	1		4	3	
1977	7	7		4	3		3	4	
1978	6	10		3	5		3	5	
1979	5	11		3	5		2	6	
1980	5	11		2	6		3	5	
1981	7	9		5	3		2	6	
1982	5	4		1	3		4	1	
1983	8	7	1	4	3	1	4	4	
1984	9	7		5	3		4	4	
1985	5	11		4	4		1	7	
1986	4	11	1	3	5		1	6	1
1987	7	8		4	3		3	5	
1988	7	9		4	4		3	5	
1989	5	11		2	6		3	5	
1990	5	11		3	5		2	6	
1991	4	12		2	6		2	6	
1992	4	12		3	5		1	7	
1993	7	9		4	4		3	5	
1994	8	8		5	3		3	5	
1995	4	12		3	5		1	7	
1996	7	9		5	3		2	6	
Total	402	543	39	230	238	22	172	305	17

*includes Chicago Cardinals (1920-59), St. Louis Cardinals (1960-87), and Phoenix Cardinals (1988-93).

ATLANTA FALCONS

Season	All Games W	L	T	Home Games W	L	T	Road Games W	L	T
1966	3	11		1	6		2	5	
1967	1	12	1	1	5	1	0	7	
1968	2	12		1	6		1	6	
1969	6	8		4	3		2	5	
1970	4	8	2	3	4		1	4	2
1971	7	6	1	4	3		3	3	1
1972	7	7		4	3		3	4	
1973	9	5		4	3		5	2	
1974	3	11		2	5		1	6	
1975	4	10		3	4		1	6	
1976	4	10		3	4		1	6	
1977	7	7		4	3		3	4	
1978	9	7		7	1		2	6	
1979	6	10		3	5		3	5	
1980	12	4		6	2		6	2	
1981	7	9		4	4		3	5	
1982	5	4		2	3		3	1	
1983	7	9		4	4		3	5	
1984	4	12		2	6		2	6	
1985	4	12		3	5		1	7	
1986	7	8	1	2	5	1	5	3	
1987	3	12		2	6		1	6	
1988	5	11		2	6		3	5	
1989	3	13		3	5		0	8	
1990	5	11		5	3		0	8	
1991	10	6		6	2		4	4	
1992	6	10		5	3		1	7	
1993	6	10		4	4		2	6	
1994	7	9		5	3		2	6	
1995	9	7		7	1		2	6	
1996	3	13		2	6		1	7	
Total	175	284	5	108	123	2	67	161	3

CAROLINA PANTHERS

Season	All Games W	L	T	Home Games W	L	T	Road Games W	L	T
1995	7	9		5	3		2	6	
1996	12	4		8	0		4	4	
Total	19	13		13	3		6	10	

CHICAGO BEARS*

Season	All Games W	L	T	Home Games W	L	T	Road Games W	L	T
1920	10	1	2	6	0	1	4	1	1
1921	9	1	1	9	1	1	0	0	
1922	9	3		7	1		2	2	
1923	9	2	1	7	1	1	2	1	
1924	6	1	4	5	0	3	1	1	1
1925	9	5	3	7	1	1	2	4	2
1926	12	1	3	10	0	2	2	1	1
1927	9	3	2	7	1	1	2	2	1
1928	7	5	1	6	3		1	2	1
1929	4	9	2	1	5	2	3	4	
1930	9	4	1	5	2	1	4	2	
1931	8	5		6	3		2	2	
1932	7	1	6	6	1	1	1	0	5
1933	10	2	1	6	0		4	2	1

Season	All Games W	L	T	Home Games W	L	T	Road Games W	L	T
1934	13	0		5	0		8	0	
1935	6	4	2	1	2	2	5	2	
1936	9	3		3	1		6	2	
1937	9	1	1	4	1		5	0	1
1938	6	5		2	3		4	2	
1939	8	3		4	1		4	2	
1940	8	3		5	0		3	3	
1941	10	1		5	1		5	0	
1942	11	0		6	0		5	0	
1943	8	1	1	5	0		3	1	1
1944	6	3	1	4	0	1	2	3	
1945	3	7		2	3		1	4	
1946	8	2	1	4	1	1	4	1	
1947	8	4		4	2		4	2	
1948	10	2		5	1		5	1	
1949	9	3		5	1		4	2	
1950	9	3		6	0		3	3	
1951	7	5		3	3		4	2	
1952	5	7		3	3		2	4	
1953	3	8	1	1	4	1	2	4	
1954	8	4		4	2		4	2	
1955	8	4		5	1		3	3	
1956	9	2	1	6	0		3	2	1
1957	5	7		2	4		3	3	
1958	8	4		5	1		3	3	
1959	8	4		4	2		4	2	
1960	5	6	1	4	2		1	4	1
1961	8	6		5	2		3	4	
1962	9	5		4	3		5	2	
1963	11	1	2	6	0	1	5	1	1
1964	5	9		2	5		3	4	
1965	9	5		5	2		4	3	
1966	5	7	2	4	1	2	1	6	
1967	7	6	1	3	3	1	4	3	
1968	7	7		2	5		5	2	
1969	1	13		1	6		0	7	
1970	6	8		3	4		3	4	
1971	6	8		4	3		2	5	
1972	4	9	1	1	5	1	3	4	
1973	3	11		1	6		2	5	
1974	4	10		4	3		0	7	
1975	4	10		3	4		1	6	
1976	7	7		4	3		3	4	
1977	9	5		5	2		4	3	
1978	7	9		4	4		3	5	
1979	10	6		6	2		4	4	
1980	7	9		5	3		2	6	
1981	6	10		4	4		2	6	
1982	3	6		2	2		1	4	
1983	8	8		5	3		3	5	
1984	10	6		6	2		4	4	
1985	15	1		8	0		7	1	
1986	14	2		7	1		7	1	
1987	11	4		6	2		5	2	
1988	12	4		7	1		5	3	
1989	6	10		4	4		2	6	
1990	11	5		7	1		4	4	
1991	11	5		6	2		5	3	
1992	5	11		4	4		1	7	
1993	7	9		3	5		4	4	
1994	9	7		5	3		4	4	
1995	9	7		5	3		4	4	
1996	7	9		6	2		1	7	
Total	598	394	42	352	163	24	246	231	18

*includes Decatur Staleys (1920) and Chicago Staleys (1921).

DALLAS COWBOYS

Season	All Games W	L	T	Home Games W	L	T	Road Games W	L	T
1960	0	11	1	0	6		0	5	1
1961	4	9	1	2	4	1	2	5	
1962	5	8	1	2	4	1	3	4	
1963	4	10		3	4		1	6	
1964	5	8	1	2	4	1	3	4	
1965	7	7		5	2		2	5	
1966	10	3	1	6	1		4	2	1
1967	9	5		5	2		4	3	
1968	12	2		5	2		7	0	
1969	11	2	1	6	0	1	5	2	
1970	10	4		6	1		4	3	
1971	11	3		6	1		5	2	
1972	10	4		5	2		5	2	
1973	10	4		6	1		4	3	
1974	8	6		5	2		3	4	
1975	10	4		5	2		5	2	
1976	11	3		6	1		5	2	
1977	12	2		6	1		6	1	
1978	12	4		7	1		5	3	
1979	11	5		6	2		5	3	
1980	12	4		8	0		4	4	
1981	12	4		8	0		4	4	
1982	6	3		3	2		3	1	
1983	12	4		6	2		6	2	
1984	9	7		5	3		4	4	
1985	10	6		7	1		3	5	
1986	7	9		3	5		4	4	
1987	7	8		3	4		4	4	
1988	3	13		1	7		2	6	
1989	1	15		0	8		1	7	
1990	7	9		5	3		2	6	
1991	11	5		6	2		5	3	
1992	13	3		7	1		6	2	
1993	12	4		6	2		6	2	
1994	12	4		6	2		6	2	
1995	12	4		6	2		6	2	
1996	10	6		6	2		4	4	
Total	328	212	6	180	89	4	148	123	2

DETROIT LIONS*

Season	All Games W	L	T	Home Games W	L	T	Road Games W	L	T
1930	5	6	3	5	1	2	0	5	1
1931	11	3		8	0		3	3	
1932	6	2	4	3	0	2	3	2	2
1933	6	5		4	1		2	4	
1934	10	3		6	2		4	1	
1935	7	3	2	5	0	1	2	3	1
1936	8	4		5	1		3	3	
1937	7	4		4	2		3	2	
1938	7	4		4	3		3	1	
1939	6	5		4	2		2	3	
1940	5	5	1	3	3		2	2	1
1941	4	6	1	3	2		1	4	1
1942	0	11		0	7		0	4	
1943	3	6	1	2	2	1	1	4	
1944	6	3	1	4	2		2	1	1
1945	7	3		4	1		3	2	
1946	1	10		1	5		0	5	
1947	3	9		2	4		1	5	
1948	2	10		2	4		0	6	
1949	4	8		2	4		2	4	
1950	6	6		4	2		2	4	
1951	7	4	1	3	3	1	4	1	
1952	9	3		6	1		3	2	
1953	10	2		5	1		5	1	
1954	9	2	1	5	0	1	4	2	
1955	3	9		3	4		0	5	
1956	9	3		5	1		4	2	
1957	8	4		5	1		3	3	
1958	4	7	1	2	4		2	3	1
1959	3	8	1	2	4		1	4	1
1960	7	5		5	1		2	4	
1961	8	5	1	2	5		6	0	1
1962	11	3		7	0		4	3	
1963	5	8	1	3	3	1	2	5	
1964	7	5	2	3	3	1	4	2	1
1965	6	7	1	2	4	1	4	3	
1966	4	9	1	3	4		1	5	1
1967	5	7	2	3	4		2	3	2
1968	4	8	2	1	4	2	3	4	
1969	9	4	1	5	2		4	2	1
1970	10	4		6	1		4	3	
1971	7	6	1	3	4		4	2	1
1972	8	5	1	5	2		3	3	1
1973	6	7	1	4	3		2	4	1
1974	7	7		5	2		2	5	
1975	7	7		4	3		3	4	
1976	6	8		5	2		1	6	
1977	6	8		5	2		1	6	
1978	7	9		5	3		2	6	
1979	2	14		2	6		0	8	
1980	9	7		6	2		3	5	
1981	8	8		7	1		1	7	
1982	4	5		2	3		2	2	
1983	9	7		6	2		3	5	
1984	4	11	1	2	5	1	2	6	
1985	7	9		6	2		1	7	
1986	5	11		1	7		4	4	
1987	4	11		1	6		3	5	
1988	4	12		2	6		2	6	
1989	7	9		4	4		3	5	
1990	6	10		3	5		3	5	
1991	12	4		8	0		4	4	
1992	5	11		3	5		2	6	
1993	10	6		5	3		5	3	
1994	9	7		6	2		3	5	
1995	10	6		7	1		3	5	
1996	5	11		4	4		1	7	
Total	426	439	32	262	183	14	164	256	18

*includes Portsmouth Spartans (1930-33).

GREEN BAY PACKERS

Season	All Games W	L	T	Home Games W	L	T	Road Games W	L	T
1921	3	2	1	2	1		1	1	1
1922	4	3	3	4	1	1	0	2	2
1923	7	2	1	4	2	1	3	0	
1924	7	4		5	0		2	4	
1925	8	5		6	0		2	5	
1926	7	3	3	4	1	2	3	2	1
1927	7	2	1	6	1		1	1	1
1928	6	4	3	2	2	2	4	2	1
1929	12	0	1	5	0		7	0	1
1930	10	3	1	6	0		4	3	1
1931	12	2		8	0		4	2	
1932	10	3	1	5	0	1	5	3	
1933	5	7	1	3	2	1	2	5	
1934	7	6		4	2		3	4	
1935	8	4		5	2		3	2	
1936	10	1	1	5	1		5	0	1
1937	7	4		3	2		4	2	
1938	8	3		4	2		4	1	
1939	9	2		4	1		5	1	
1940	6	4	1	4	2		2	2	1
1941	10	1		4	1		6	0	
1942	8	2	1	4	1		4	1	1
1943	7	2	1	2	1	1	5	1	
1944	8	2		5	0		3	2	
1945	6	4		4	1		2	3	
1946	6	5		2	3		4	2	
1947	6	5	1	4	2		2	3	1
1948	3	9		2	4		1	5	
1949	2	10		1	5		1	5	
1950	3	9		3	3		0	6	
1951	3	9		2	4		1	5	
1952	6	6		3	3		3	3	
1953	2	9	1	1	5		1	4	1
1954	4	8		2	4		2	4	
1955	6	6		5	1		1	5	
1956	4	8		2	4		2	4	
1957	3	9		1	5		2	4	
1958	1	10	1	1	4	1	0	6	
1959	7	5		4	2		3	3	
1960	8	4		4	2		4	2	
1961	11	3		6	1		5	2	
1962	13	1		7	0		6	1	
1963	11	2	1	6	1		5	1	1
1964	8	5	1	4	3		4	2	1
1965	10	3	1	6	1		4	2	1
1966	12	2		6	1		6	1	
1967	9	4	1	4	2	1	5	2	
1968	6	7	1	2	5		4	2	1
1969	8	6		5	2		3	4	
1970	6	8		4	3		2	5	
1971	4	8	2	3	3	1	1	5	1
1972	10	4		4	3		6	1	
1973	5	7	2	3	2	2	2	5	
1974	6	8		4	3		2	5	
1975	4	10		3	4		1	6	
1976	5	9		4	3		1	6	
1977	4	10		2	5		2	5	
1978	8	7	1	7	1		1	6	1
1979	5	11		4	4		1	7	

Season	All W	L	T	Home W	L	T	Road W	L	T
1980	5	10	1	4	4		1	6	1
1981	8	8		4	4		4	4	
1982	5	3	1	3	1		2	2	1
1983	8	8		5	3		3	5	
1984	8	8		5	3		3	5	
1985	8	8		5	3		3	5	
1986	4	12		1	7		3	5	
1987	5	9	1	2	5	1	3	4	
1988	4	12		2	6		2	6	
1989	10	6		6	2		4	4	
1990	6	10		3	5		3	5	
1991	4	12		2	6		2	6	
1992	9	7		6	2		3	5	
1993	9	7		6	2		3	5	
1994	9	7		7	1		2	6	
1995	11	5		7	1		4	4	
1996	13	3		8	0		5	3	
Total	527	437	36	303	180	16	224	257	20

MINNESOTA VIKINGS

Season	All W	L	T	Home W	L	T	Road W	L	T
1961	3	11		3	4		0	7	
1962	2	11	1	1	5	1	1	6	
1963	5	8	1	3	4		2	4	1
1964	8	5	1	4	3		4	2	1
1965	7	7		2	5		5	2	
1966	4	9	1	2	5		2	4	1
1967	3	8	3	1	4	2	2	4	1
1968	8	6		4	3		4	3	
1969	12	2		7	0		5	2	
1970	12	2		7	0		5	2	
1971	11	3		5	2		6	1	
1972	7	7		3	4		4	3	
1973	12	2		7	0		5	2	
1974	10	4		4	3		6	1	
1975	12	2		7	0		5	2	
1976	11	2	1	6	0	1	5	2	
1977	9	5		5	2		4	3	
1978	8	7	1	5	3		3	4	1
1979	7	9		5	3		2	6	
1980	9	7		5	3		4	4	
1981	7	9		5	3		2	6	
1982	5	4		4	1		1	3	
1983	8	8		3	5		5	3	
1984	3	13		2	6		1	7	
1985	7	9		4	4		3	5	
1986	9	7		5	3		4	4	
1987	8	7		5	3		3	4	
1988	11	5		7	1		4	4	
1989	10	6		8	0		2	6	
1990	6	10		4	4		2	6	
1991	8	8		4	4		4	4	
1992	11	5		5	3		6	2	
1993	9	7		4	4		5	3	
1994	10	6		6	2		4	4	
1995	8	8		6	2		2	6	
1996	9	7		5	3		4	4	
Total	289	236	9	163	101	4	126	135	5

NEW ORLEANS SAINTS

Season	All W	L	T	Home W	L	T	Road W	L	T
1967	3	11		2	5		1	6	
1968	4	9	1	3	4		1	5	1
1969	5	9		3	4		2	5	
1970	2	11	1	2	5		0	6	1
1971	4	8	2	2	4	1	2	4	1
1972	2	11	1	2	5		0	6	1
1973	5	9		5	2		0	7	
1974	5	9		4	3		1	6	
1975	2	12		2	5		0	7	
1976	4	10		2	5		2	5	
1977	3	11		2	5		1	6	
1978	7	9		3	5		4	4	
1979	8	8		3	5		5	3	
1980	1	15		0	8		1	7	
1981	4	12		2	6		2	6	
1982	4	5		2	3		2	2	
1983	8	8		5	3		3	5	
1984	7	9		3	5		4	4	

Season	All W	L	T	Home W	L	T	Road W	L	T
1985	5	11		3	5		2	6	
1986	7	9		4	4		3	5	
1987	12	3		6	1		6	2	
1988	10	6		5	3		5	3	
1989	9	7		5	3		4	4	
1990	8	8		5	3		3	5	
1991	11	5		6	2		5	3	
1992	12	4		6	2		6	2	
1993	8	8		4	4		4	4	
1994	7	9		3	5		4	4	
1995	7	9		4	4		3	5	
1996	3	13		2	6		1	7	
Total	177	268	5	100	124	1	77	144	4

NEW YORK GIANTS

Season	All W	L	T	Home W	L	T	Road W	L	T
1925	8	4		7	2		1	2	
1926	8	4	1	5	2	1	3	2	
1927	11	1	1	7	1		4	0	1
1928	4	7	2	1	2	2	3	5	
1929	13	1	1	7	1		6	0	1
1930	13	4		6	2		7	2	
1931	7	6	1	4	2	1	3	4	
1932	4	6	2	3	2	1	1	4	1
1933	11	3		7	0		4	3	
1934	8	5		5	1		3	4	
1935	9	3		4	2		5	1	
1936	5	6	1	3	3	1	2	3	
1937	6	3	2	4	2	1	2	1	1
1938	8	2	1	6	1		2	1	1
1939	9	1	1	6	0		3	1	1
1940	6	4	1	4	3		2	1	1
1941	8	3		5	2		3	1	
1942	5	5	1	3	2	1	2	3	
1943	6	3	1	4	2		2	1	1
1944	8	1	1	5	1		3	0	1
1945	3	6	1	2	4		1	2	1
1946	7	3	1	5	1	1	2	2	
1947	2	8	2	2	3	1	0	5	1
1948	4	8		2	4		2	4	
1949	6	6		2	4		4	2	
1950	10	2		5	1		5	1	
1951	9	2	1	5	1		4	1	1
1952	7	5		2	4		5	1	
1953	3	9		2	4		1	5	
1954	7	5		4	2		3	3	
1955	6	5	1	4	1	1	2	4	
1956	8	3	1	4	1	1	4	2	
1957	7	5		3	3		4	2	
1958	9	3		5	1		4	2	
1959	10	2		5	1		5	1	
1960	6	4	2	1	3	2	5	1	
1961	10	3	1	4	2	1	6	1	
1962	12	2		6	1		6	1	
1963	11	3		5	2		6	1	
1964	2	10	2	2	5		0	5	2
1965	7	7		3	4		4	3	
1966	1	12	1	1	6		0	6	1
1967	7	7		5	2		2	5	
1968	7	7		3	4		4	3	
1969	6	8		5	2		1	6	
1970	9	5		5	2		4	3	
1971	4	10		1	6		3	4	
1972	8	6		4	3		4	3	
1973	2	11	1	2	4	1	0	7	
1974	2	12		0	7		2	5	
1975	5	9		2	5		3	4	
1976	3	11		3	4		0	7	
1977	5	9		3	4		2	5	
1978	6	10		5	3		1	7	
1979	6	10		4	4		2	6	
1980	4	12		2	6		2	6	
1981	9	7		4	4		5	3	
1982	4	5		2	3		2	2	
1983	3	12	1	1	7		2	5	1
1984	9	7		6	2		3	5	
1985	10	6		6	2		4	4	
1986	14	2		8	0		6	2	
1987	6	9		5	3		1	6	
1988	10	6		5	3		5	3	

Season	All W	L	T	Home W	L	T	Road W	L	T
1989	12	4		7	1		5	3	
1990	13	3		7	1		6	2	
1991	8	8		5	3		3	5	
1992	6	10		4	4		2	6	
1993	11	5		6	2		5	3	
1994	9	7		4	4		5	3	
1995	5	11		3	5		2	6	
1996	6	10		3	5		3	5	
Total	513	424	32	290	196	16	223	228	16

PHILADELPHIA EAGLES

Season	All W	L	T	Home W	L	T	Road W	L	T
1933	3	5	1	2	3	1	1	2	
1934	4	7		2	4		2	3	
1935	2	9		0	5		2	4	
1936	1	11		1	6		0	5	
1937	2	8	1	0	5	1	2	3	
1938	5	6		2	3		3	3	
1939	1	9	1	1	3	1	0	6	
1940	1	10		1	4		0	6	
1941	2	8	1	1	4	1	1	4	
1942	2	9		0	5		2	4	
1943	7	1	2	3	1	2	4	0	
1944	7	3		6	0		1	3	
1945	7	3		6	0		1	3	
1946	6	5		3	2		3	3	
1947	8	4		6	1		2	3	
1948	9	2	1	6	0		3	2	1
1949	11	1		6	0		5	1	
1950	6	6		2	4		4	2	
1951	4	8		1	5		3	3	
1952	7	5		4	2		3	3	
1953	7	4	1	5	0	1	2	4	
1954	7	4	1	5	1		2	3	1
1955	4	7	1	4	2		0	5	1
1956	3	8	1	2	3	1	1	5	
1957	4	8		3	3		1	5	
1958	2	9	1	2	4		0	5	1
1959	6	5		4	1		2	4	
1960	10	2		5	1		5	1	
1961	10	4		5	2		5	2	
1962	3	10	1	2	5		1	5	1
1963	2	10	2	1	5	1	1	5	1
1964	6	8		3	4		3	4	
1965	5	9		2	5		3	4	
1966	9	5		5	2		4	3	
1967	6	7	1	5	2		1	5	1
1968	2	12		1	6		1	6	
1969	4	9	1	2	5		2	4	1
1970	3	10	1	3	3		0	7	
1971	6	7	1	3	4		3	3	1
1972	2	11	1	0	6	1	2	5	
1973	5	8	1	4	3		1	5	1
1974	7	7		5	2		2	5	
1975	4	10		2	5		2	5	
1976	4	10		2	5		2	5	
1977	5	9		4	3		1	6	
1978	9	7		5	3		4	4	
1979	11	5		5	3		6	2	
1980	12	4		7	1		5	3	
1981	10	6		6	2		4	4	
1982	3	6		1	4		2	2	
1983	5	11		1	7		4	4	
1984	6	9	1	5	3		1	6	1
1985	7	9		4	4		3	5	
1986	5	10	1	2	5	1	3	5	
1987	7	8		4	4		3	4	
1988	10	6		5	3		5	3	
1989	11	5		6	2		5	3	
1990	10	6		6	2		4	4	
1991	10	6		4	4		6	2	
1992	11	5		8	0		3	5	
1993	8	8		3	5		5	3	
1994	7	9		5	3		2	6	
1995	10	6		6	2		4	4	
1996	10	6		5	3		5	3	
Total	376	442	23	214	199	12	162	243	11

ST. LOUIS RAMS*

Season	All Games W	L	T	Home Games W	L	T	Road Games W	L	T
1937	1	10		0	5		1	5	
1938	4	7		2	2		2	5	
1939	5	5	1	3	2	1	2	3	
1940	4	6	1	3	1	1	1	5	
1941	2	9		1	4		1	5	
1942	5	6		3	2		2	4	
1944	4	6		1	2		3	4	
1945	9	1		4	0		5	1	
1946	6	4	1	3	2		3	2	1
1947	6	6	.	3	3		3	3	
1948	6	5	1	3	2	1	3	3	
1949	8	2	2	5	1		3	1	2
1950	9	3		5	1		4	2	
1951	8	4		5	2		3	2	
1952	9	3		5	1		4	2	
1953	8	3	1	5	1		3	2	1
1954	6	5	1	3	2	1	3	3	
1955	8	3	1	5	1		3	2	1
1956	4	8		4	2		0	6	
1957	6	6		5	1		1	5	
1958	8	4		4	2		4	2	
1959	2	10		0	6		2	4	
1960	4	7	1	2	3	1	2	4	
1961	4	10		4	3		0	7	
1962	1	12	1	0	7		1	5	1
1963	5	9		3	4		2	5	
1964	5	7	2	3	2	2	2	5	
1965	4	10		3	4		1	6	
1966	8	6		5	2		3	4	
1967	11	1	2	5	1	1	6	0	1
1968	10	3	1	5	2		5	1	1
1969	11	3		5	2		6	1	
1970	9	4	1	3	3	1	6	1	
1971	8	5	1	4	2	1	4	3	
1972	6	7	1	4	3		2	4	1
1973	12	2		7	0		5	2	
1974	10	4		6	1		4	3	
1975	12	2		6	1		6	1	
1976	10	3	1	5	2		5	1	1
1977	10	4		7	0		3	4	
1978	12	4		6	2		6	2	
1979	9	7		4	4		5	3	
1980	11	5		6	2		5	3	
1981	6	10		4	4		2	6	
1982	2	7		1	4		1	3	
1983	9	7		5	3		4	4	
1984	10	6		5	3		5	3	
1985	11	5		6	2		5	3	
1986	10	6		6	2		4	4	
1987	6	9		3	4		3	5	
1988	10	6		4	4		6	2	
1989	11	5		6	2		5	3	
1990	5	11		2	6		3	5	
1991	3	13		2	6		1	7	
1992	6	10		4	4		2	6	
1993	5	11		3	5		2	6	
1994	4	12		3	5		1	7	
1995	7	9		4	4		3	5	
1996	6	10		4	4		2	6	
Total	411	368	20	227	157	10	184	211	10

*includes Cleveland Rams (1937-42, 1944-45) and Los Angeles Rams (1946-94).

SAN FRANCISCO 49ERS

Season	All Games W	L	T	Home Games W	L	T	Road Games W	L	T
1950	3	9		3	3		0	6	
1951	7	4	1	5	1		2	3	1
1952	7	5		3	3		4	2	
1953	9	3		5	1		4	2	
1954	7	4	1	4	2		3	2	1
1955	4	8		2	4		2	4	
1956	5	6	1	3	3		2	3	1
1957	8	4		5	1		3	3	
1958	6	6		4	2		2	4	
1959	7	5		4	2		3	3	
1960	7	5		3	3		4	2	
1961	7	6	1	5	1	1	2	5	
1962	6	8		1	6		5	2	
1963	2	12		2	5		0	7	

Season	All Games W	L	T	Home Games W	L	T	Road Games W	L	T
1964	4	10		3	4		1	6	
1965	7	6	1	4	2	1	3	4	
1966	6	6	2	4	2	1	2	4	1
1967	7	7		3	4		4	3	
1968	7	6	1	3	3	1	4	3	
1969	4	8	2	3	3	1	1	5	1
1970	10	3	1	5	1	1	5	2	
1971	9	5		4	3		5	2	
1972	8	5	1	4	2	1	4	3	
1973	5	9		3	4		2	5	
1974	6	8		3	4		3	4	
1975	5	9		2	5		3	4	
1976	8	6		4	3		4	3	
1977	5	9		3	4		2	5	
1978	2	14		2	6		0	8	
1979	2	14		2	6		0	8	
1980	6	10		4	4		2	6	
1981	13	3		7	1		6	2	
1982	3	6		0	5		3	1	
1983	10	6		4	4		6	2	
1984	15	1		7	1		8	0	
1985	10	6		5	3		5	3	
1986	10	5	1	6	2		4	3	1
1987	13	2		6	1		7	1	
1988	10	6		4	4		6	2	
1989	14	2		6	2		8	0	
1990	14	2		6	2		8	0	
1991	10	6		7	1		3	5	
1992	14	2		7	1		7	1	
1993	10	6		6	2		4	4	
1994	13	3		7	1		6	2	
1995	11	5		6	2		5	3	
1996	12	4		6	2		6	2	
Total	368	285	13	195	131	7	173	154	6

TAMPA BAY BUCCANEERS

Season	All Games W	L	T	Home Games W	L	T	Road Games W	L	T
1976	0	14		0	7		0	7	
1977	2	12		1	6		1	6	
1978	5	11		3	5		2	6	
1979	10	6		5	3		5	3	
1980	5	10	1	2	5	1	3	5	
1981	9	7		6	2		3	5	
1982	5	4		4	1		1	3	
1983	2	14		1	7		1	7	
1984	6	10		6	2		0	8	
1985	2	14		2	6		0	8	
1986	2	14		1	7		1	7	
1987	4	11		2	5		2	6	
1988	5	11		3	5		2	6	
1989	5	11		2	6		3	5	
1990	6	10		4	4		2	6	
1991	3	13		3	5		0	8	
1992	5	11		3	5		2	6	
1993	5	11		3	5		2	6	
1994	6	10		4	4		2	6	
1995	7	9		5	3		2	6	
1996	6	10		5	3		1	7	
Total	100	223	1	65	96	1	35	127	

WASHINGTON REDSKINS*

Season	All Games W	L	T	Home Games W	L	T	Road Games W	L	T
1932	4	4	2	2	3	1	2	1	1
1933	5	5	2	4	2		1	3	2
1934	6	6		4	3		2	3	
1935	2	8	1	2	5		0	3	1
1936	7	5		4	3		3	2	
1937	8	3		4	2		4	1	
1938	6	3	2	3	1	1	3	2	1
1939	8	2	1	5	0	1	3	2	
1940	9	2		6	0		3	2	
1941	6	5		4	2		2	3	
1942	10	1		5	1		5	0	
1943	6	3	1	4	2		2	1	1
1944	6	3	1	4	2		2	1	1
1945	8	2		6	0		2	2	
1946	5	5	1	3	2	1	2	3	
1947	4	8		4	2		0	6	
1948	7	5		4	2		3	3	
1949	4	7	1	3	3		1	4	1
1950	3	9		1	5		2	4	
1951	5	7		2	4		3	3	
1952	4	8		1	5		3	3	
1953	6	5	1	3	3		3	2	1
1954	3	9		3	3		0	6	
1955	8	4		3	3		5	1	
1956	6	6		4	2		2	4	
1957	5	6	1	2	3	1	3	3	
1958	4	7	1	3	2	1	1	5	
1959	4	8		2	4		2	4	
1960	1	9	2	1	4	1	0	5	1
1961	1	12	1	1	6		0	6	1
1962	5	7	2	3	4		2	3	2
1963	3	11		1	6		2	5	
1964	6	8		4	3		2	5	
1965	6	8		3	4		3	4	
1966	7	7		4	3		3	4	
1967	5	6	3	2	4	1	3	2	2
1968	5	9		3	4		2	5	
1969	7	5	2	4	2	1	3	3	1
1970	6	8		4	3		2	5	
1971	9	4	1	4	2	1	5	2	
1972	11	3		6	1		5	2	
1973	10	4		7	0		3	4	
1974	10	4		6	1		4	3	
1975	8	6		5	2		3	4	
1976	10	4		5	2		5	2	
1977	9	5		5	2		4	3	
1978	8	8		5	3		3	5	
1979	10	6		6	2		4	4	
1980	6	10		4	4		2	6	
1981	8	8		5	3		3	5	
1982	8	1		3	1		5	0	
1983	14	2		7	1		7	1	
1984	11	5		7	1		4	4	
1985	10	6		5	3		5	3	
1986	12	4		7	1		5	3	
1987	11	4		6	1		5	3	
1988	7	9		4	4		3	5	
1989	10	6		4	4		6	2	
1990	10	6		7	1		3	5	
1991	14	2		7	1		7	1	
1992	9	7		6	2		3	5	
1993	4	12		3	5		1	7	
1994	3	13		0	8		3	5	
1995	6	10		4	4		2	6	
1996	9	7		5	3		4	4	
Total	448	392	26	258	174	10	190	218	16

*includes Boston Braves (1932) and Boston Redskins (1933-36).

History

The Professional Football Hall of Fame is located in Canton, Ohio, site of the organizational meeting on September 17, 1920, from which the National Football League evolved. The NFL recognized Canton as the Hall of Fame site on April 27, 1961. Canton area individuals, foundations, and companies donated almost $400,000 in cash and services to provide funds for the construction of the original two-building complex, which was dedicated on September 7, 1963. Since that time, the Hall added three buildings with major expansion projects in 1971, 1978, and 1995. The Hall's largest-ever expansion, a $9.1 million project, was completed in early fall 1995. With the new fifth building, the Hall's size is now 82,307-square feet, more than four times its original size.

The expanded Hall represents the sport of pro football in many ways—through (1) GameDay Stadium, a dynamic two-part turntable theater featuring NFL action in Cinemascope for the first time, (2) a standard theater showing NFL films hourly, (3) six large exhibition areas where the history of pro football is detailed in memento, picture, and story form, (4) an extensive library and research center, and (5) a new and enlarged museum store.

In recent years, the Pro Football Hall of Fame has become an extremely popular tourist attraction. At the end of 1996, a total of 6,118,098 fans had visited the Hall of Fame.

New members of the Pro Football Hall of Fame are elected annually by a 36-member National Board of Selectors, made up of media representatives from every league city, five at-large representatives, and a representative of the Pro Football Writers of America. Between four and seven new members are elected each year. An affirmative vote of approximately 80 percent is needed for election.

Any fan may nominate any eligible player or contributor simply by writing to the Pro Football Hall of Fame. Players must be retired five years to be eligible, while a coach need only to be retired with no time limit specified. Contributors (administrators, owners, *et al.*) may be elected while they are still active.

The charter class of 17 enshrinees was elected in 1963 and the honor roll now stands at 189 with the election of a four-man class in 1997. That class consists of Mike Haynes, Wellington Mara, Don Shula, and Mike Webster.

ROSTER OF MEMBERS

HERB ADDERLEY
Defensive back. 6-1, 200. Born in Philadelphia, Pennsylvania, June 8, 1939. Michigan State. Inducted in 1980. 1961-69 Green Bay Packers, 1970-72 Dallas Cowboys. **Highlights:** 48 interceptions, 7 touchdowns. Played in four Super Bowls, five Pro Bowls.

LANCE ALWORTH
Wide receiver. 6-0, 184. Born in Houston, Texas, August 3, 1940. Arkansas. Inducted in 1978. 1962-70 San Diego Chargers, 1971-72 Dallas Cowboys. **Highlights:** 542 receptions for 10,266 yards, 85 touchdowns. All-AFL seven

times, seven All-Star games.

DOUG ATKINS
Defensive end. 6-8, 275. Born in Humboldt, Tennessee, May 8, 1930. Tennessee. Inducted in 1982. 1953-54 Cleveland Browns, 1955-66 Chicago Bears, 1967-69 New Orleans Saints. **Highlights:** Eight Pro Bowls, All-NFL three times. Played for 17 years, 205 games.

MORRIS (RED) BADGRO
End. 6-0, 190. Born in Orilla, Washington, December 1, 1902. Southern California. Inducted in 1981. 1927 New York Yankees, 1930-35 New York Giants, 1936 Brooklyn Dodgers. **Highlights:** All-NFL four times. Scored first touchdown in NFL championship game series.

LEM BARNEY
Cornerback. 6-0, 190. Born in Gulfport, Mississippi, September 8, 1945. Jackson State. Inducted in 1992. 1967-77 Detroit Lions. **Highlights:** 56 interceptions for 1,077 yards, 11 defensive touchdowns. Seven Pro Bowls, All-NFL/NFC three times.

CLIFF BATTLES
Halfback. 6-1, 201. Born in Akron, Ohio, May 1, 1910. West Virginia Wesleyan. Inducted in 1968. 1932 Boston Braves, 1933-36 Boston Redskins, 1937 Washington Redskins. **Highlights:** NFL rushing champion 1932, 1937. First to gain more than 200 yards in a game, 1933.

SAMMY BAUGH
Quarterback. 6-2, 180. Born in Temple, Texas, March 17, 1914. Texas Christian. Inducted in 1963. 1937-52 Washington Redskins. **Highlights:** Charter enshrinee. Six-time NFL passing leader. NFL passing, punting, interception champ, 1943.

CHUCK BEDNARIK
Center-linebacker. 6-3, 230. Born in Bethlehem, Pennsylvania, May 1, 1925. Pennsylvania. Inducted in 1967. 1949-62 Philadelphia Eagles. **Highlights:** Eight Pro Bowls. Missed three games in 14 years. Named NFL all-time center, 1969.

BERT BELL
Team owner. Commissioner. Born in Philadelphia, Pennsylvania, February 25, 1895. Died October 11, 1959. Pennsylvania. Inducted in 1963. 1933-40 Philadelphia Eagles, 1941-42 Pittsburgh Steelers, 1943 Phil-Pitt, 1944 Card-Pitt, 1945-46 Pittsburgh Steelers. Commissioner, 1946-59. **Highlights:** Charter enshrinee. Built NFL image as commissioner, 1946-1959. Set up long-term television policies.

BOBBY BELL
Linebacker. 6-4, 225. Born in Shelby, North Carolina, June 17, 1940. Minnesota. Inducted in 1983. 1963-74 Kansas City Chiefs. **Highlights:** 25 interceptions. All-AFL/AFC nine times. Eight career touchdowns, 1 on onside kick return.

RAYMOND BERRY
End. 6-2, 187. Born in Corpus Christi,

Texas, February 27, 1933. Southern Methodist. Inducted in 1973. 1955-67 Baltimore Colts. **Highlights:** 631 receptions for 9,275 yards, 68 touchdowns. Set NFL title game mark with 12 catches for 178 yards, 1958.

CHARLES W. BIDWILL, SR.
Team owner. Born in Chicago, Illinois, September 16, 1895. Died April 19, 1947. Loyola of Chicago. Inducted in 1967. 1933-43 Chicago Cardinals, 1944 Card-Pitt, 1945-47 Chicago Cardinals. **Highlights:** Guiding light for NFL during depression years. Built famous "Dream Backfield."

FRED BILETNIKOFF
Wide receiver. 6-1, 190. Born in Erie, Pennsylvania, February 23, 1943. Florida State. Inducted in 1988. 1965-78 Oakland Raiders. **Highlights:** 589 receptions for 8,974 yards, 76 touchdowns. 40 catches 10 straight years. MVP, Super Bowl XI.

GEORGE BLANDA
Quarterback-kicker. 6-2, 215. Born in Youngwood, Pennsylvania, September 17, 1927. Kentucky. Inducted in 1981. 1949-58 Chicago Bears, 1950 Baltimore Colts, 1960-66 Houston Oilers, 1967-75 Oakland Raiders. **Highlights:** Record 2,002 career points. 26-season, 340-game career longest in NFL history.

MEL BLOUNT
Cornerback. 6-3, 205. Born in Vidalia, Georgia, April 10, 1948. Southern University. Inducted in 1989. 1970-83 Pittsburgh Steelers. **Highlights:** 57 interceptions for 736 yards. NFL defensive MVP, 1975. Played in five Pro Bowls.

TERRY BRADSHAW
Quarterback. 6-3, 210. Born in Shreveport, Louisiana, September 2, 1948. Louisiana Tech. Inducted in 1989. 1970-83 Pittsburgh Steelers. **Highlights:** 27,989 yards passing, 212 touchdowns. MVP in Super Bowls XIII, XIV.

JIM BROWN
Fullback. 6-2, 228. Born in St. Simons, Georgia, February 17, 1936. Syracuse. Inducted in 1971. 1957-65 Cleveland Browns. **Highlights:** 12,312 yards rushing, 756 points. Led NFL rushers eight years. Nine consecutive Pro Bowls.

PAUL BROWN
Coach. Born in Norwalk, Ohio, September 7, 1908. Died August 5, 1991. Miami (Ohio). Inducted in 1967. 1946-49 Cleveland Browns (AAFC), 1950-62 Cleveland Browns. **Highlights:** Built Cleveland dynasty with 167-53-8 record, four AAFC titles, three NFL crowns. Returned to coaching with Cincinnati Bengals after induction, 1968-1975.

ROOSEVELT BROWN
Tackle. 6-3, 255. Born in Charlottesville, Virginia, October 20, 1932. Morgan State. Inducted in 1975. 1953-65 New York Giants. **Highlights:** All-NFL eight consecutive years, nine Pro Bowls. NFL's Lineman of Year, 1956.

WILLIE BROWN
Cornerback. 6-1, 210. Born in Yazoo City, Mississippi, December 2, 1940. Grambling. Inducted in 1984. 1963-66 Denver Broncos, 1967-78 Oakland Raiders. **Highlights:** 54 interceptions for 472 yards. Scored on 75-yard interception in Super Bowl XI.

BUCK BUCHANAN
Defensive tackle. 6-7, 274. Born in Gainesville, Alabama, September 10, 1940. Died July 16, 1992. Grambling. Inducted in 1990. 1963-75 Kansas City Chiefs. **Highlights:** Led Chiefs defensive efforts in Super Bowl I, IV. Missed one game in 13 years.

DICK BUTKUS
Linebacker. 6-3, 245. Born in Chicago, Illinois, December 9, 1942. Illinois. Inducted in 1979. 1965-73 Chicago Bears. **Highlights:** All-NFL seven years, eight consecutive Pro Bowls. 25 fumble recoveries.

EARL CAMPBELL
Running back. 5-11, 233. Born in Tyler, Texas, March 29, 1955. Texas. Inducted in 1991. 1978-84 Houston Oilers, 1984-85 New Orleans Saints. **Highlights:** 9,407 yards rushing, 74 touchdowns. 1,934 yards rushing in 1980, including four games with at least 200 yards.

TONY CANADEO
Halfback. 5-11, 195. Born in Chicago, Illinois, May 5, 1919. Gonzaga. Inducted in 1974. 1941-44, 1946-52 Green Bay Packers. **Highlights:** Two-way player. Third player to rush for 1,000 yards in single season, 1949.

JOE CARR
NFL president. Born in Columbus, Ohio, October 22, 1880. Died May 20, 1939. Did not attend college. Inducted in 1963. President, 1921-39 National Football League. **Highlights:** Charter enshrinee. NFL co-organizer, 1920. Introduced standard player's contract.

GUY CHAMBERLIN
End. Coach. 6-2, 210. Born in Blue Springs, Nebraska, January 16, 1894. Died April 4, 1967. Nebraska. Inducted in 1965. 1919 Canton Bulldogs, 1920 Decatur Staleys, 1921 Chicago Staleys, player-coach 1922-23 Canton Bulldogs, 1924 Cleveland Bulldogs, 1925-26 Frankford Yellow Jackets, 1927-28 Chicago Cardinals. **Highlights:** Player-coach of four NFL championship teams. Six-year coaching record 56-14-5.

JACK CHRISTIANSEN
Safety. 6-1, 185. Born in Sublette, Kansas, December 20, 1928. Died June 29, 1986. Colorado State. Inducted in 1970. 1951-58 Detroit Lions. **Highlights:** 46 interceptions. NFL interception leader, 1953, 1957. NFL record 8 punt returns for touchdowns.

EARL (DUTCH) CLARK
Quarterback. 6-0, 185. Born in Fowler, Colorado, October 11, 1906. Died August 5, 1978. Colorado College. Inducted in 1963. 1931-32 Portsmouth Spartans, 1934-38 Detroit Lions. **Highlights:** Charter enshrinee. NFL

scoring champion three years. Led Lions to 1935 NFL title.

GEORGE CONNOR
Tackle-linebacker. 6-3, 240. Born in Chicago, Illinois, January 21, 1925. Holy Cross, Notre Dame. Inducted in 1975. 1948-55 Chicago Bears. **Highlights:** All-NFL at three positions—T, DT, LB. All-NFL five years. Played in first four Pro Bowls.

JIMMY CONZELMAN
Quarterback. Coach. Team owner. 6-0, 180. Born in St. Louis, Missouri, March 6, 1898. Died July 31, 1970. Washington of St. Louis. Inducted in 1964. 1920 Decatur Staleys, 1921-22 Rock Island Independents, 1923-24 Milwaukee Badgers; owner-coach 1925-26 Detroit Panthers; player-coach 1927-29, coach 1930 Providence Steam Roller; coach 1940-42, 1946-48 Chicago Cardinals. **Highlights:** Player-coach of four NFL teams in 1920's. Coached Cardinals to 1947 NFL crown.

LOU CREEKMUR
Tackle-guard. 6-4, 255. Born in Hopelawn, New Jersey. January 22, 1927. William & Mary. Inducted in 1996. 1950-59 Detroit Lions. **Highlights:** All-NFL six times, twice at guard and four times at tackle. Selected to eight Pro Bowls and played on three NFL Championship teams.

LARRY CSONKA
Running back. 6-3, 235. Born in Stow, Ohio, December 25, 1946. Syracuse. Inducted in 1987. 1968-74, 1979 Miami Dolphins, 1976-78 New York Giants. **Highlights:** 8,081 yards rushing, 68 touchdowns. MVP Super Bowl VIII. Only 21 fumbles in 1,997 carries.

AL DAVIS
Team, League Administrator. Born in Brockton, Massachusetts, July 4, 1929. Wittenberg, Syracuse. Inducted in 1992. 1963-81, 1995-present Oakland Raiders, 1982-94 Los Angeles Raiders, 1966 American Football League. **Highlights:** Only person to serve in pros as personnel assistant, scout, assistant coach, head coach, general manager, commissioner, team owner/CEO.

WILLIE DAVIS
Defensive end. 6-3, 245. Born in Lisbon, Louisiana, July 24, 1934. Grambling. Inducted in 1981. 1958-59 Cleveland Browns, 1960-69 Green Bay Packers. **Highlights:** All-NFL five seasons, five Pro Bowls. Did not miss game in 12-year career.

LEN DAWSON
Quarterback. 6-0, 190. Born in Alliance, Ohio, June 20, 1935. Purdue. Inducted in 1987. 1957-59 Pittsburgh Steelers, 1960-61 Cleveland Browns, 1962 Dallas Texans, 1963-75 Kansas City Chiefs. **Highlights:** 28,711 yards passing, 239 touchdowns. Four AFL passing crowns. MVP, Super Bowl IV.

DAN DIERDORF
Tackle. 6-3, 290. Born in Canton, Ohio, June 29, 1949. Michigan. Inducted in 1996. 1971-83 St. Louis Cardinals. **Highlights:** All-Pro five times, played

in six Pro Bowls, named NFL's best blocker three times.

MIKE DITKA
Tight end. 6-3, 225. Born in Carnegie, Pennsylvania, October 18, 1939. Pittsburgh. Inducted in 1988. 1961-66 Chicago Bears, 1967-68 Philadelphia Eagles, 1969-72 Dallas Cowboys. **Highlights:** 427 receptions for 5,812 yards, 43 touchdowns. First tight end selected to Hall of Fame. Five consecutive Pro Bowls.

ART DONOVAN
Defensive tackle. 6-3, 265. Born in Bronx, New York, June 5, 1925. Boston College. Inducted in 1968. 1950 Baltimore Colts, 1951 New York Yanks, 1952 Dallas Texans, 1953-61 Baltimore Colts. **Highlights:** Five Pro Bowls. Vital part of Baltimore's climb to powerhouse status in 1950s.

TONY DORSETT
Running back. 5-11, 184. Born in Rochester, Pennsylvania, April 7, 1954. Pittsburgh. Inducted in 1994. 1977-87 Dallas Cowboys, 1988 Denver Broncos. **Highlights:** 12,739 yards rushing, 398 receptions, 90 touchdowns. Ran record 99 yards for touchdown vs. Minnesota, January, 1983.

JOHN (PADDY) DRISCOLL
Quarterback. 5-11, 160. Born in Evanston, Illinois, January 11, 1896. Died June 29, 1968. Northwestern. Inducted in 1965. 1919 Hammond Pros, 1920 Decatur Staleys, 1920-25 Chicago Cardinals, 1926-29 Chicago Bears. **Highlights:** All-NFL six times. Dropkicked record 4 field goals in one game, 1925.

BILL DUDLEY
Halfback. 5-10, 176. Born in Bluefield, Virginia, December 24, 1921. Virginia. Inducted in 1966. 1942, 1945-46 Pittsburgh Steelers, 1947-49 Detroit Lions, 1950-51, 1953 Washington Redskins. **Highlights:** Won NFL rushing, interception, punt return titles, 1946. All-NFL 1942, 1946.

ALBERT GLEN (TURK) EDWARDS
Tackle. 6-2, 260. Born in Mold, Washington, September 28, 1907. Died January 12, 1973. Washington State. Inducted in 1969. 1932 Boston Braves, 1933-36 Boston Redskins, 1937-40 Washington Redskins. **Highlights:** All-NFL 1932-33, 1936, 1937. Steamrolling blocker, smothering tackler.

WEEB EWBANK
Coach. Born in Richmond, Indiana, May 6, 1907. Miami (Ohio). Inducted in 1978. 1954-62 Baltimore Colts, 1963-73 New York Jets. **Highlights:** Only coach to win championships in both NFL, AFL. Led both Colts (1958) and Jets (1968) to championships.

TOM FEARS
End. 6-2, 215. Born in Los Angeles, California, December 3, 1923. Santa Clara, UCLA. Inducted in 1970. 1948-56 Los Angeles Rams. **Highlights:** 400 receptions for 5,397 yards, 38 touchdowns. Led NFL receivers first three seasons. Record 18 recep-

tions in single game.

JIM FINKS
Administrator. Born in St. Louis, Missouri, August 31, 1927. Died May 8, 1994. Tulsa. Inducted 1995. 1964-73 Minnesota Vikings, 1974-82 Chicago Bears, 1986-93 New Orleans Saints. **Highlights:** Developed Vikings, Bears, Saints—all teams with losing records—into winners.

RAY FLAHERTY
Coach. Born in Spokane, Washington, September 1, 1903. Died July 19, 1994. Gonzaga. Inducted in 1976. 1936 Boston Redskins, 1937-42 Washington Redskins, 1946-48 New York Yankees (AAFC), 1949 Chicago Hornets (AAFC). **Highlights:** 80-37-5 coaching record. Introduced screen pass in 1937 title game and platoon system.

LEN FORD
Defensive end. 6-5, 260. Born in Washington, D.C., February 18, 1926. Died March 14, 1972. Morgan State, Michigan. Inducted in 1976. 1948-49 Los Angeles Dons (AAFC), 1950-57 Cleveland Browns, 1958 Green Bay Packers. **Highlights:** All-NFL five times, four Pro Bowls. Recovered 20 opponent's fumbles.

DAN FORTMANN
Guard. 6-0, 210. Born in Pearl River, New York, April 11, 1916. Died May 24, 1995. Colgate. Inducted in 1965. 1936-43 Chicago Bears. **Highlights:** At 19, became youngest starter in NFL. All-NFL six consecutive years.

DAN FOUTS
Quarterback. 6-3, 210. Born in San Francisco, California, June 10, 1951. Oregon. Inducted in 1993. 1973-1987 San Diego Chargers. **Highlights:** 43,040 passing yards, 254 touchdowns. Six Pro Bowls, NFL MVP, 1982.

FRANK GATSKI
Center. 6-3, 240. Born in Farmington, West Virginia, March 18, 1922. Marshall, Auburn. Inducted in 1985. 1946-49 Cleveland Browns (AAFC), 1950-56 Cleveland Browns, 1957 Detroit Lions. **Highlights:** Never missed game in high school, college, or pro football. Played 11 championship games, winning eight.

BILL GEORGE
Linebacker. 6-2, 230. Born in Waynesburg, Pennsylvania, October 27, 1930. Died September 30, 1982. Wake Forest. Inducted in 1974. 1952-65 Chicago Bears, 1966 Los Angeles Rams. **Highlights:** All-NFL eight years, eight consecutive Pro Bowls. 14 years of service, longest of any Bears player.

JOE GIBBS
Coach. Born in Mocksville, North Carolina, November 25, 1940. Cerritos (Calif.) J.C., San Diego State. Inducted in 1996. 1981-92 Washington Redskins. **Highlights:** 124-60-0 record in regular season, 16-5 in postseason, including four Super Bowl appearances—winning three. Won 10 or more games eight times.

FRANK GIFFORD
Halfback. 6-1, 195. Born in Santa Monica, California, August 16, 1930. Southern California. Inducted in 1977. 1952-60, 1962-64 New York Giants. **Highlights:** Starred on both offense and defense. Seven Pro Bowls, 1956 NFL Player of the Year.

SID GILLMAN
Coach. Born in Minneapolis, Minnesota, October 26, 1911. Ohio State. Inducted in 1983. 1955-59 Los Angeles Rams, 1960 Los Angeles Chargers, 1961-69, 1971 San Diego Chargers, 1973-74 Houston Oilers. **Highlights:** 123-104-7 coaching record. First to win division titles in both NFL, AFL.

OTTO GRAHAM
Quarterback. 6-1, 195. Born in Waukegan, Illinois, December 6, 1921. Northwestern. Inducted in 1965. 1946-49 Cleveland Browns (AAFC), 1950-55 Cleveland Browns. **Highlights:** 23,584 passing yards, 174 touchdowns. Guided Browns to 10 division or league crowns in 10 years.

HAROLD (RED) GRANGE
Halfback. 6-0, 185. Born in Forksville, Pennsylvania, June 13, 1903. Died January 28, 1991. Illinois. Inducted in 1963. 1925 Chicago Bears, 1926 New York Yankees (AFL), 1927 New York Yankees, 1929-34 Chicago Bears. **Highlights:** Nicknamed "Galloping Ghost." Name produced first huge pro football crowds.

BUD GRANT
Coach. Born in Superior, Wisconsin, May 20, 1927. Minnesota. Inducted in 1994. 1967-83, 1985 Minnesota Vikings. **Highlights:** 168-108-5 coaching record. Led Vikings to 11 division championships, four Super Bowls.

JOE GREENE
Defensive tackle. 6-4, 260. Born in Temple, Texas, September 24, 1946. North Texas State. Inducted in 1987. 1969-81 Pittsburgh Steelers. **Highlights:** NFL Defensive Player of the Year, 1972, 1974. Four-time Super Bowl champion, 10 Pro Bowls.

FORREST GREGG
Tackle. 6-4, 250. Born in Birthright, Texas, October 18, 1933. Southern Methodist. Inducted in 1977. 1956, 1958-70 Green Bay Packers, 1971 Dallas Cowboys. **Highlights:** Played 188 consecutive games. Nine Pro Bowls. Played on seven NFL championship teams, three Super Bowl winners.

BOB GRIESE
Quarterback. 6-1, 190. Born in Evansville, Indiana, February 3, 1945. Purdue. Inducted in 1990. 1967-80 Miami Dolphins. **Highlights:** 25,092 passing yards, 192 touchdowns. Led Miami to three AFC titles, Super Bowl VII, VIII wins.

LOU GROZA
Tackle-kicker. 6-3, 250. Born in Martins Ferry, Ohio, January 25, 1924. Ohio State. Inducted in 1974. 1946-49 Cleveland Browns (AAFC), 1950-59, 1961-67 Cleveland Browns. **High-**

lights: 1,608 points in 21 years. Nine Pro Bowls, All-NFL six years. NFL Player of the Year, 1954.

JOE GUYON
Halfback. 6-1, 180. Born on White Earth Indian Reservation, Minnesota, November 26, 1892. Died November 27, 1971. Carlisle, Georgia Tech. Inducted in 1966. 1919-20 Canton Bulldogs, 1921 Cleveland Indians, 1922-23 Oorang Indians, 1924 Rock Island Independents, 1924-25 Kansas City Cowboys, 1927 New York Giants. **Highlights:** Touchdown pass gave Giants victory over Bears to win 1927 Championship.

GEORGE HALAS
End. Coach. Team owner. Born in Chicago, Illinois, February 2, 1895. Died October 31, 1983. Illinois. Inducted in 1963. Player-coach 1920 Decatur Staleys, 1921 Chicago Staleys, 1922-29 Chicago Bears; coach 1933-42, 1946-55, 1958-67 Chicago Bears. **Highlights:** Charter enshrinee. 324 coaching wins. Only person associated with NFL throughout first 50 years. Coached Bears 40 seasons, won seven NFL titles.

JACK HAM
Linebacker. 6-1, 225. Born in Johnstown, Pennsylvania, December 23, 1948. Penn State. Inducted in 1988. 1971-82 Pittsburgh Steelers. **Highlights:** Won four Super Bowls, 21 opponent's fumbles recovered, 32 interceptions. Eight consecutive Pro Bowls.

JOHN HANNAH
Guard. 6-3, 265. Born in Canton, Georgia, April 4, 1951. Alabama. Inducted in 1991. 1973-85 New England Patriots. **Highlights:** Renowned as premier guard of era. All-Pro 10 years, eight Pro Bowls.

FRANCO HARRIS
Running back. 6-2, 225. Born in Fort Dix, New Jersey, March 7, 1950. Penn State. Inducted in 1990. 1972-83 Pittsburgh Steelers, 1984 Seattle Seahawks. **Highlights:** 12,120 rushing yards, 100 total touchdowns. 1,556 rushing yards in 19 postseason games. MVP in Super Bowl IX.

MIKE HAYNES
Cornerback. 6-2, 195. Born in Denison, Texas, July 1, 1953. Arizona State. Inducted in 1997. 1976-82 New England Patriots, 1983-89 Los Angeles Raiders. **Highlights:** Defensive Rookie of the Year. Selected to nine Pro Bowls and intercepted 46 passes, plus one pick in Super Bowl XVIII.

ED HEALEY
Tackle. 6-3, 220. Born in Indian Orchard, Massachusetts, December 28, 1894. Died December 9, 1978. Dartmouth. Inducted in 1964. 1920-22 Rock Island Independents, 1922-27 Chicago Bears. **Highlights:** Two-way star. Perennial all-pro with Bears.

MEL HEIN
Center. 6-2, 225. Born in Redding, California, August 22, 1909. Died January

31, 1992. Washington State. Inducted in 1963. 1931-45 New York Giants. **Highlights:** Charter enshrinee. 60-minute regular for 15 years. All-NFL eight consecutive years.

TED HENDRICKS
Linebacker. 6-7, 235. Born in Guatemala City, Guatemala, November 1, 1947. Miami. Inducted in 1990. 1969-73 Baltimore Colts, 1974 Green Bay Packers, 1975-81 Oakland Raiders, 1982-83 Los Angeles Raiders. **Highlights:** 25 blocked field goals or extra points, 26 interceptions. Played in 215 consecutive games.

WILBUR (PETE) HENRY
Tackle. 6-0, 250. Born in Mansfield, Ohio, October 31, 1897. Died February 7, 1952. Washington & Jefferson. Inducted in 1963. 1920-23, 1925-26 Canton Bulldogs, 1927 New York Giants, 1927-28 Pottsville Maroons. **Highlights:** Largest player of his time at 250 pounds. Bulwark of Canton's championship lines.

ARNIE HERBER
Quarterback. 6-0, 200. Born in Green Bay, Wisconsin, April 2, 1910. Died October 14, 1969. Wisconsin, Regis College. Inducted in 1966. 1930-40 Green Bay Packers, 1944-45 New York Giants. **Highlights:** NFL passing leader 1932, 1934, 1936. Came out of retirement to lead 1944 Giants to NFL Eastern crown.

BILL HEWITT
End. 5-11, 191. Born in Bay City, Michigan, October 8, 1909. Died January 14, 1947. Michigan. Inducted in 1971. 1932-36 Chicago Bears, 1937-39 Philadelphia Eagles, 1943 Phil-Pitt. **Highlights:** First to be named all-NFL with two teams—1933, 1934, 1936 Bears; 1937 Eagles.

CLARKE HINKLE
Fullback. 5-11, 201. Born in Toronto, Ohio, April 10, 1909. Died November 9, 1988. Bucknell. Inducted in 1964. 1932-41 Green Bay Packers. **Highlights:** 3,860 yards rushing, 373 points, 43.4 punting average. Fullback on offense, linebacker on defense.

ELROY (CRAZYLEGS) HIRSCH
Halfback-end. 6-2, 190. Born in Wausau, Wisconsin, June 17, 1923. Wisconsin, Michigan. Inducted in 1968. 1946-48 Chicago Rockets (AAFC), 1949-57 Los Angeles Rams. **Highlights:** 387 receptions for 7,029 yards, 60 touchdowns. Key part of Rams' revolutionary "three end" offense, 1949.

PAUL HORNUNG
Halfback. 6-2, 220. Born in Louisville, Kentucky, December 23, 1935. Notre Dame. Inducted in 1986. 1957-62, 1964-66 Green Bay Packers. **Highlights:** 760 points. Led NFL scorers three years, including record 176 points, 1960. Record 19 points scored in 1961 NFL title game.

KEN HOUSTON
Safety. 6-3, 198. Born in Lufkin, Texas, November 12, 1944. Prairie View A&M. Inducted in 1986. 1967-72 Houston

Oilers, 1973-80 Washington Redskins. **Highlights:** 49 interceptions, 898 yards, 9 touchdowns. NFL's premier strong safety of 1970s. 10 Pro Bowls.

ROBERT (CAL) HUBBARD
Tackle. 6-5, 250. Born in Keytesville, Missouri, October 31, 1900. Died October 17, 1977. Centenary, Geneva. Inducted in 1963. 1927-28 New York Giants, 1929-33, 1935 Green Bay Packers, 1936 New York Giants, 1936 Pittsburgh Pirates. **Highlights:** Charter enshrinee. Most feared lineman of his time. All-NFL six years, 1928-33.

SAM HUFF
Linebacker. 6-1, 230. Born in Morgantown, West Virginia, October 4, 1934. West Virginia. Inducted in 1982. 1956-63 New York Giants, 1964-67, 1969 Washington Redskins. **Highlights:** 30 interceptions. Played in six NFL title games, five Pro Bowls. Redskins player-coach, 1969.

LAMAR HUNT
Team owner. Born in El Dorado, Arkansas, August 2, 1932. Southern Methodist. Inducted in 1972. 1960-62 Dallas Texans, 1963-present Kansas City Chiefs. **Highlights:** Driving force behind organization of AFL. Spearheaded merger negotiations with NFL, 1966.

DON HUTSON
End. 6-1, 180. Born in Pine Bluff, Arkansas, January 31, 1913. Alabama. Inducted in 1963. 1935-45 Green Bay Packers. **Highlights:** 488 receptions for 7,991 yards, 99 touchdowns. NFL receiving champion eight years. NFL MVP, 1941, 1942.

JIMMY JOHNSON
Cornerback. 6-2, 187. Born in Dallas, Texas, March 31, 1938. UCLA. Inducted in 1994. 1961-76 San Francisco 49ers. **Highlights:** 47 interceptions for 615 yards. Five Pro Bowls. Opposing passers avoided throwing in his area.

JOHN HENRY JOHNSON
Fullback. 6-2, 225. Born in Waterproof, Louisiana, November 24, 1929. St. Mary's, Arizona State. Inducted in 1987. 1954-56 San Francisco 49ers, 1957-59 Detroit Lions, 1960-65 Pittsburgh Steelers, 1966 Houston Oilers. **Highlights:** 6,803 yards rushing, 48 touchdowns. Member of San Francisco's "Fabulous Foursome" backfield.

CHARLIE JOINER
Wide receiver. 5-11, 180. Born in Many, Louisiana, October 14, 1947. Grambling. Inducted in 1996. 1969-72 Houston Oilers, 1972-75 Cincinnati Bengals, 1976-86 San Diego Chargers. **Highlights:** 750 receptions for 12,146 yards and 65 touchdowns. Played 18 seasons, 239 games, most ever for wide receiver.

DAVID (DEACON) JONES
Defensive end. 6-5, 260. Born in Eatonville, Florida, December 9, 1938. South Carolina State, Mississippi Vocational. Inducted in 1980. 1961-71 Los Angeles Rams, 1972-73 San Diego Chargers, 1974 Washington Redskins. **Highlights:** Specialized in

quarterback 'sacks,' a name he invented. Unanimous all-league six consecutive years.

STAN JONES
Guard-defensive tackle. 6-1, 250. Born in Altoona, Pennsylvania, November 24, 1931. Maryland. Inducted in 1991. 1954-65 Chicago Bears, 1966 Washington Redskins. **Highlights:** Seven consecutive Pro Bowls. First to rely on weightlifting for football preparation.

HENRY JORDAN
Defensive tackle, 6-3, 240. Born in Emporia, Virginia, January 26, 1935. Died February 21, 1977. Virginia. Inducted in 1995. 1957-58 Cleveland Browns, 1959-69 Green Bay Packers. **Highlights:** 11-year fixture at DT. Played in four Pro Bowls, seven NFL title games, Super Bowls I, II.

SONNY JURGENSEN
Quarterback. 6-0, 203. Born in Wilmington, North Carolina, August 23, 1934. Duke. Inducted in 1983. 1957-63 Philadelphia Eagles, 1964-74 Washington Redskins. **Highlights:** 32,224 yards passing, 255 touchdowns, 82.63 passer rating. Surpassed 3,000 yards passing in five seasons.

LEROY KELLY
Running back. 6-0, 205. Born in Philadelphia, Pennsylvania, May 20, 1942. Morgan State. Inducted in 1994. 1964-73 Cleveland Browns. **Highlights:** 7,274 yards rushing, 90 total touchdowns, 1,000-yard rusher first three years as regular starter. Two-time punt return champion.

WALT KIESLING
Guard. Coach. 6-2, 245. Born in St. Paul, Minnesota, March 27, 1903. Died March 2, 1962. St. Thomas (Minnesota). Inducted in 1966. 1926-27 Duluth Eskimos, 1928 Pottsville Maroons, 1929-33 Chicago Cardinals, 1934 Chicago Bears, 1935-36 Green Bay Packers, 1937-38 Pittsburgh Pirates; coach, 1939 Pittsburgh Pirates, 1940-42 Pittsburgh Steelers; co-coach, 1943 Phil-Pitt, 1944 Card-Pitt; coach, 1954-56 Pittsburgh Steelers. **Highlights:** 34-year career as pro player, assistant coach, head coach. Led Steelers to first winning season, 1942.

FRANK (BRUISER) KINARD
Tackle. 6-1, 210. Born in Pelahatchie, Mississippi, October 23, 1914. Died September 7, 1985. Mississippi. Inducted in 1971. 1938-43 Brooklyn Dodgers, 1944 Brooklyn Tigers, 1946-47 New York Yankees (AAFC). **Highlights:** First man to earn both All-NFL, All-AAFC honors. Out because of injury only once.

EARL (CURLY) LAMBEAU
Coach. Born in Green Bay, Wisconsin, April 9, 1898. Died June 1, 1965. Notre Dame. Inducted in 1963. 1919-49 Green Bay Packers, 1950-51 Chicago Cardinals, 1952-53 Washington Redskins. **Highlights:** 229-134-22 coaching record with six NFL championships. Founded pre-NFL Packers, 1919.

JACK LAMBERT
Linebacker. 6-4, 220. Born in Mantua, Ohio, July 8, 1952. Kent State. Inducted in 1990. 1974-84 Pittsburgh Steelers. **Highlights:** Prototype middle linebacker. Two-time NFL Defensive Player of Year, nine Pro Bowls.

TOM LANDRY
Coach. Born in Mission, Texas, September 11, 1924. Texas. Inducted in 1990. 1960-88 Dallas Cowboys. **Highlights:** 270-178-6 coaching record. 20 consecutive winning seasons. Perfected flex defense, shotgun offense.

DICK (NIGHT TRAIN) LANE
Cornerback. 6-2, 210. Born in Austin, Texas, April 16, 1928. Scottsbluff Junior College. Inducted in 1974. 1952-53 Los Angeles Rams, 1954-59 Chicago Cardinals, 1960-65 Detroit Lions. **Highlights:** 68 interceptions for 1,207 yards, 5 touchdowns. Record 14 interceptions as rookie. Six Pro Bowls.

JIM LANGER
Center. 6-2, 255. Born in Little Falls, Minnesota, May 16, 1948. South Dakota State. Inducted in 1987. 1970-79 Miami Dolphins, 1980-81 Minnesota Vikings. **Highlights:** Played every offensive down in Dolphins' perfect 1972 season. Six Pro Bowls.

WILLIE LANIER
Linebacker. 6-1, 245. Born in Clover, Virginia, August 21, 1945. Morgan State. Inducted in 1986. 1967-77 Kansas City Chiefs. **Highlights:** 27 interceptions. Defensive star in Super Bowl IV upset. Nicknamed 'Contact' for ferocious tackling.

STEVE LARGENT
Wide receiver. 5-11, 191. Born in Tulsa, Oklahoma, September 28, 1954. Tulsa. Inducted in 1995. 1976-89 Seattle Seahawks. **Highlights:** 819 receptions for 13,089 yards, 100 touchdowns. Receptions in 177 consecutive games.

YALE LARY
Defensive back-punter. 5-11, 189. Born in Fort Worth, Texas, November 24, 1930. Texas A&M. Inducted in 1979. 1952-53, 1956-64 Detroit Lions. **Highlights:** 50 interceptions. Three NFL punting crowns, three touchdowns on punt returns. Nine Pro Bowls.

DANTE LAVELLI
End. 6-0, 199. Born in Hudson, Ohio, February 23, 1923. Ohio State. Inducted in 1975. 1946-49 Cleveland Browns (AAFC), 1950-56 Cleveland Browns. **Highlights:** 386 receptions for 6,488 yards, 62 touchdowns. 24 catches in six NFL title games.

BOBBY LAYNE
Quarterback. 6-2, 190. Born in Santa Anna, Texas, December 19, 1926. Died December 1, 1986. Texas. Inducted in 1967. 1948 Chicago Bears, 1949 New York Bulldogs, 1950-58 Detroit Lions, 1958-62 Pittsburgh Steelers. **Highlights:** 26,768 yards passing, 196 touchdowns, 2,451 yards rushing. Last-second touch-

down pass won 1953 NFL title game.

ALPHONSE (TUFFY) LEEMANS
Fullback. 6-0, 200. Born in Superior, Wisconsin, November 12, 1912. Died January 19, 1979. Oregon, George Washington. Inducted in 1978. 1936-43 New York Giants. **Highlights:** 3,142 yards rushing, 2,324 yards passing, 442 yards receiving. Led NFL rushers as rookie, 1936.

BOB LILLY
Defensive tackle. 6-5, 260. Born in Olney, Texas, July 26, 1939. Texas Christian. Inducted in 1980. 1961-74 Dallas Cowboys. **Highlights:** 11 Pro Bowls. Missed one game in 14 years. Foundation of great Dallas defensive units.

LARRY LITTLE
Guard. 6-1, 265. Born in Groveland, Georgia, November 2, 1945. Bethune-Cookman. Inducted in 1993. 1967-68 San Diego Chargers, 1969-80 Miami Dolphins. **Highlights:** Five Pro Bowls, started in three Super Bowls. Epitome of powerful Dolphins rushing game of 1970s.

VINCE LOMBARDI
Coach. Born in Brooklyn, New York, June 11, 1913. Died September 3, 1970. Fordham. Inducted in 1971. 1959-67 Green Bay Packers, 1969 Washington Redskins. **Highlights:** 105-35-6 coaching record in 10 years, including five NFL titles and victories in Super Bowl I and II.

SID LUCKMAN
Quarterback. 6-0, 195. Born in Brooklyn, New York, November 21, 1916. Columbia. Inducted in 1965. 1939-50 Chicago Bears. **Highlights:** 139 touchdown passes. All-NFL team five times. League MVP in 1943.

WILLIAM ROY (LINK) LYMAN
Tackle. 6-2, 252. Born in Table Rock, Nebraska, November 30, 1898. Died December 16, 1972. Nebraska. Inducted in 1964. 1922-23, 1925 Canton Bulldogs, 1924 Cleveland Bulldogs, 1925 Frankford Yellow Jackets, 1926-28, 1930-31, 1933-34 Chicago Bears. **Highlights:** Played for four NFL champions. In 16 seasons of college and pro football, played on one losing team.

JOHN MACKEY
Tight end. 6-2, 224. Born in New York, New York, September 24, 1941. Syracuse. Inducted in 1992. 1963-71 Baltimore Colts, 1972 San Diego Chargers. **Highlights:** 331 receptions for 5,236 yards, 38 touchdowns. Second tight end to enter Hall of Fame.

TIM MARA
Team owner. Born in New York, New York, July 29, 1887. Died February 17, 1959. Did not attend college. Inducted in 1963. 1925-59 New York Giants. **Highlights:** Charter enshrinee. Founder of New York Giants. Built team into powerhouse winning three NFL titles, eight division titles.

WELLINGTON MARA
Team owner. Born in New York, New York, August 14, 1916. Fordham. Inducted in 1997. 1937-present New York Giants. **Highlights:** Lifetime contributor to NFL and New York Giants. Worked as Giants' ballboy, secretary, vice-president, president and co-CEO. NFC president 1984-present.

GINO MARCHETTI
Defensive end. 6-4, 245. Born in Smithers, West Virginia, January 2, 1927. San Francisco. Inducted in 1972. 1952 Dallas Texans, 1953-64, 1966 Baltimore Colts. **Highlights:** Named top defensive end of NFL's first 50 years. 11 consecutive Pro Bowls. All-NFL seven times.

GEORGE PRESTON MARSHALL
Team owner. Born in Grafton, West Virginia, October 11, 1897. Died August 9, 1969. Randolph-Macon. Inducted in 1963. 1932 Boston Braves, 1933-36 Boston Redskins, 1937-69 Washington Redskins. **Highlights:** Charter enshrinee. Sponsored progressive rules changes. Organized first team band, pioneered halftime shows.

OLLIE MATSON
Halfback. 6-2, 220. Born in Trinity, Texas, May 1, 1930. San Francisco. Inducted in 1972. 1952, 1954-58 Chicago Cardinals, 1959-62 Los Angeles Rams, 1963 Detroit Lions, 1964-66 Philadelphia Eagles. **Highlights:** NFL-record 9 touchdowns on kickoff, punt returns. Traded for nine players in 1959.

DON MAYNARD
Wide receiver. 6-1, 185. Born in Crosbyton, Texas, January 25, 1935. Texas Western. Inducted in 1987. 1958 New York Giants, 1960-62 New York Titans, 1963-72 New York Jets, 1973 St. Louis Cardinals. **Highlights:** 633 receptions for 11,834 yards, 88 touchdowns. At least 50 catches and 1,000 yards in five different seasons.

GEORGE McAFEE
Halfback. 6-0, 177. Born in Corbin, Kentucky, March 13, 1918. Duke. Inducted in 1966. 1940-41, 1945-50 Chicago Bears. **Highlights:** Two-way star. 21 interceptions, 234 points. Career punt return record of 12.78 yards per return.

MIKE McCORMACK
Tackle. 6-4, 250. Born in Chicago, Illinois, June 21, 1930. Kansas. Inducted in 1984. 1951 New York Yanks, 1954-62 Cleveland Browns. **Highlights:** Excelled as offensive right tackle for eight years. Six Pro Bowls.

HUGH McELHENNY
Halfback. 6-1, 198. Born in Los Angeles, California, December 31, 1928. Washington. Inducted in 1970. 1952-60 San Francisco 49ers, 1961-62 Minnesota Vikings, 1963 New York Giants, 1964 Detroit Lions. **Highlights:** 5,281 rushing yards, 360 points. Scored 40-yard touchdown run on first pro play.

JOHNNY (BLOOD) McNALLY
Halfback. 6-0, 185. Born in New Richmond, Wisconsin, November 27, 1903. Died November 28, 1985. Notre Dame, St. John's (Minnesota). Inducted in 1963. 1925-26 Milwaukee Badgers, 1926-27 Duluth Eskimos, 1928 Pottsville Maroons, 1929-33, 1935-36 Green Bay Packers, 1934 Pittsburgh Pirates; player-coach, 1937-39 Pittsburgh Pirates. **Highlights:** 37 touchdowns, 224 points in 15 seasons with five teams.

MIKE MICHALSKE
Guard. 6-0, 209. Born in Cleveland, Ohio, April 24, 1903. Died October 26, 1983. Penn State. Inducted in 1964. 1926 New York Yankees (AFL), 1927-28 New York Yankees, 1929-35, 1937 Green Bay Packers. **Highlights:** Anchored Packers' championship lines, 1929-1931. First-ever guard enshrined in Canton.

WAYNE MILLNER
End. 6-0, 191. Born in Roxbury, Massachusetts, January 31, 1913. Died November 19, 1976. Notre Dame. Inducted in 1968. 1936 Boston Redskins, 1937-41, 1945 Washington Redskins. **Highlights:** Redskins' all-time leader with 124 catches when retired. 55- and 78-yard touchdown receptions in 1937 NFL championship.

BOBBY MITCHELL
Running back-wide receiver. 6-0, 195. Born in Hot Springs, Arkansas, June 6, 1935. Illinois. Inducted in 1983. 1958-61 Cleveland Browns, 1962-68 Washington Redskins. **Highlights:** 91 touchdowns, including 8 on kickoff and punt returns. 14,078 combined yards.

RON MIX
Tackle. 6-4, 255. Born in Los Angeles, California, March 10, 1938. Southern California. Inducted in 1979. 1960 Los Angeles Chargers, 1961-69 San Diego Chargers, 1971 Oakland Raiders. **Highlights:** All-AFL tackle eight times. Only two holding penalties in 10 years with the Chargers.

LENNY MOORE
Flanker-running back. 6-1, 198. Born in Reading, Pennsylvania, November 25, 1933. Penn State. Inducted in 1975. 1956-67 Baltimore Colts. **Highlights:** From 1963-65, scored touchdowns in record 18 consecutive games. 113 career touchdowns, 12,451 combined net yards.

MARION MOTLEY
Fullback. 6-1, 238. Born in Leesburg, Georgia, June 5, 1920. South Carolina State, Nevada. Inducted in 1968. 1946-49 Cleveland Browns (AAFC), 1950-53 Cleveland Browns, 1955 Pittsburgh Steelers. **Highlights:** AAFC's all-time rushing champion. Led league in rushing in first NFL season.

GEORGE MUSSO
Guard-tackle. 6-2, 270. Born in Collinsville, Illinois. April 8, 1910. Millikin. Inducted in 1982. 1933-44 Chicago Bears. **Highlights:** First play-

er to achieve All-NFL status at two positions—tackle in 1935 and guard in 1937.

BRONKO NAGURSKI
Fullback. 6-2, 225. Born in Rainy River, Ontario, Canada, November 3, 1908. Died January 7, 1990. Minnesota. Inducted in 1963. 1930-37, 1943 Chicago Bears. **Highlights:** Charter enshrinee. 4,031 rushing yards in nine seasons. All-NFL three times.

JOE NAMATH
Quarterback. 6-2, 200. Born in Beaver Falls, Pennsylvania, May 31, 1943. Alabama. Inducted in 1985. 1965-76 New York Jets, 1977 Los Angeles Rams. **Highlights:** First quarterback to pass for more than 4,000 yards in season, 1967. Guaranteed, delivered victory over Colts in Super Bowl III.

EARLE (GREASY) NEALE
Coach. Born in Parkersburg, West Virginia, November 5, 1891. Died November 2, 1973. West Virginia Wesleyan. Inducted in 1969. 1941-42, 1944-50 Philadelphia Eagles; co-coach, 1943 Phil-Pitt. **Highlights:** Turned Eagles into winners with three consecutive division crowns, NFL championships in 1948 and 1949.

ERNIE NEVERS
Fullback. 6-1, 205. Born in Willow River, Minnesota, June 11, 1903. Died May 3, 1976. Stanford. Inducted in 1963. 1926-27 Duluth Eskimos, 1929-31 Chicago Cardinals. **Highlights:** Charter enshrinee. Holds NFL's longest-standing record, 40 points in one game in 1929.

RAY NITSCHKE
Linebacker. 6-3, 235. Born in Elmwood Park, Illinois, December 29, 1936. Illinois. Inducted in 1978. 1958-72 Green Bay Packers. **Highlights:** MVP of 1962 title game. Named NFL's all-time linebacker in 1969.

CHUCK NOLL
Coach. Born in Cleveland, Ohio, January 5, 1932. Dayton. Inducted in 1993. 1969-91 Pittsburgh Steelers. **Highlights:** Coached for 23 years. Only coach to win four Super Bowl titles (IX, X, XIII, XIV).

LEO NOMELLINI
Defensive tackle. 6-3, 264. Born in Lucca, Italy, June 19, 1924. Minnesota. Inducted in 1969. 1950-63 San Francisco 49ers. **Highlights:** Played every 49ers game for 14 seasons. 10 Pro Bowls.

MERLIN OLSEN
Defensive tackle. 6-5, 270. Born in Logan, Utah, September 15, 1940. Utah State. Inducted in 1982. 1962-76 Los Angeles Rams. **Highlights:** Member of the Fearsome Foursome. Named to 14 consecutive Pro Bowls, Rams' all-time team.

JIM OTTO
Center. 6-2, 255. Born in Wausau, Wisconsin, January 5, 1938. Miami. Inducted in 1980. 1960-74 Oakland Raiders. **Highlights:** Named AFL's all-time center. Played in 308 games, 12 all-star games, six AFL/AFC title games.

STEVE OWEN
Tackle. Coach. 6-2, 235. Born in Cleo Springs, Oklahoma, April 21, 1898. Died May 17, 1964. Phillips. Inducted in 1966. 1924-25 Kansas City Cowboys, 1925 Cleveland Bulldogs, 1926-31, 1933 New York Giants; coach, 1931-53 New York Giants. **Highlights:** Both player and coach. Coached Giants to record of 153-108-17, eight divisional titles, two NFL championships.

ALAN PAGE
Defensive tackle. 6-4, 225. Born in Canton, Ohio, August 7, 1945. Notre Dame. Inducted in 1988. 1967-78 Minnesota Vikings, 1978-81 Chicago Bears. **Highlights:** NFL iron man. Played in 236 consecutive games, four Super Bowls. League MVP in 1971.

CLARENCE (ACE) PARKER
Quarterback. 5-11, 168. Born in Portsmouth, Virginia, May 17, 1912. Duke. Inducted in 1972. 1937-41 Brooklyn Dodgers, 1945 Boston Yanks, 1946 New York Yankees (AAFC). **Highlights:** Two-way threat. Two-time All-NFL performer, league MVP in 1940.

JIM PARKER
Guard-tackle. 6-3, 273. Born in Macon, Georgia, April 3, 1934. Ohio State. Inducted in 1973. 1957-67 Baltimore Colts. **Highlights:** First full-time offensive lineman elected to Hall of Fame. All-NFL eight consecutive years, eight Pro Bowls.

WALTER PAYTON
Running back. 5-10, 202. Born in Columbia, Mississippi, July 25, 1954. Jackson State. Inducted in 1993. 1975-87 Chicago Bears. **Highlights:** NFL's all-time leading rusher with 16,726 yards. Holds single-game rushing record of 275 yards.

JOE PERRY
Fullback. 6-0, 200. Born in Stevens, Arkansas, January 22, 1927. Compton Junior College. Inducted in 1969. 1948-49 San Francisco 49ers (AAFC), 1950-60, 1963 San Francisco 49ers, 1961-62 Baltimore Colts. **Highlights:** First player in NFL history to gain 1,000 yards two consecutive seasons. 12,505 combined yards.

PETE PIHOS
End. 6-1, 210. Born in Orlando, Florida, October 22, 1923. Indiana. Inducted in 1970. 1947-55 Philadelphia Eagles. **Highlights:** Three-time NFL receiving champion. Caught winning touchdown in 1949 NFL Championship Game.

HUGH (SHORTY) RAY
Supervisor of officials 1938-52. Born in Highland Park, Illinois, September 21, 1884. Died September 16, 1956. Illinois. Inducted in 1966. **Highlights:** Supervisor of Officials, 1938-1952. Streamlined rules to improve game tempo, player safety.

DAN REEVES
Team owner. Born in New York, New York, June 30, 1912. Died April 15, 1971. Georgetown. Inducted in 1967. 1941-45 Cleveland Rams, 1946-71 Los Angeles Rams. **Highlights:** Moved Rams to Los Angeles in 1946 and opened up west coast to pro football. First post-war owner to sign African-American player.

MEL RENFRO
Cornerback-safety. 6-0, 192. Born in Houston, Texas, December 30, 1941. Oregon. Inducted in 1996. 1964-77 Dallas Cowboys. **Highlights:** 52 interceptions for 626 yards and 3 touchdowns. Also added 849 yards on punt returns, 2,246 yards on kickoff returns. Elected to Pro Bowl first 10 seasons.

JOHN RIGGINS
Running back. 6-2, 240. Born in Seneca, Kansas, August 4, 1949. Kansas. Inducted in 1992. 1971-75 New York Jets, 1976-79, 1981-85 Washington Redskins. **Highlights:** 11,352 rushing yards, 104 touchdowns. MVP of Super Bowl XVII with 166 rushing yards including game-winning 43-yard touchdown.

JIM RINGO
Center. 6-2, 230. Born in Orange, New Jersey, November 21, 1931. Syracuse. Inducted in 1981. 1953-63 Green Bay Packers, 1964-67 Philadelphia Eagles. **Highlights:** Ten-time Pro Bowl selection, six-time All-NFL selection. Started in then-record 182 consecutive games.

ANDY ROBUSTELLI
Defensive end. 6-0, 230. Born in Stamford, Connecticut, December 6, 1925. Arnold College. Inducted in 1971. 1951-55 Los Angeles Rams, 1956-64 New York Giants. **Highlights:** Anchored defense in eight championship games. Named NFL's top player in 1962.

ART ROONEY
Team owner. Born in Coulterville, Pennsylvania, January 27, 1901. Died August 25, 1988. Georgetown, Duquesne. Inducted in 1964. 1933-39 Pittsburgh Pirates, 1940-42, 1945-88 Pittsburgh Steelers, 1943 Phil-Pitt, 1944 Card-Pitt. **Highlights:** Founded Pittsburgh Pirates in 1933 and renamed them Steelers in 1940. Team won four Super Bowls in 1970s.

PETE ROZELLE
Commissioner. Born in South Gate, California, March 1, 1926. Died December 6, 1996. Compton Junior College, San Francisco. Inducted in 1985. Commissioner, 1960-89. **Highlights:** Negotiated first league-wide television contract in 1962. Generally recognized as premiere commissioner in all of sports. Credited with making NFL the nation's most popular sport.

BOB ST. CLAIR
Tackle. 6-9, 265. Born in San Francisco, California, February 18, 1931. San Francisco, Tulsa. Inducted in 1990. 1953-63 San Francisco 49ers. **Highlights:** Exceptional offensive lineman. Also played goal-line defense and had 10 blocked field goals, 1956.

GALE SAYERS
Running back. 6-0, 200. Born in Wichita, Kansas, May 30, 1943. Kansas. Inducted in 1977. 1965-71 Chicago Bears. **Highlights:** Broke into league by scoring rookie-record 22 touchdowns. Led league in rushing in 1966, 1969. MVP of three Pro Bowls.

JOE SCHMIDT
Linebacker. 6-0, 222. Born in Pittsburgh, Pennsylvania, January 18, 1932. Pittsburgh. Inducted in 1973. 1953-65 Detroit Lions. **Highlights:** 24 interceptions. Lions team captain for nine years. Mastered middle linebacker position which evolved in 1950s.

TEX SCHRAMM
Team president-general manager. Born in San Gabriel, California, June 2, 1920. Texas. Inducted in 1991. 1947-56 Los Angeles Rams. 1960-89 Dallas Cowboys. **Highlights:** Played prominent role in AFL-NFL merger. Chairman of Competition Committee from 1966-1988.

LEE ROY SELMON
Defensive end. 6-3, 250. Born in Eufaula, Oklahoma, October 20, 1954. Oklahoma. Inducted in 1995. 1976-84 Tampa Bay Buccaneers. **Highlights:** 78½ sacks, 380 quarterback pressures, forced 28 fumbles. Five consecutive Pro Bowls.

ART SHELL
Tackle. 6-5, 285. Born in Charleston, South Carolina, November 26, 1946. Maryland State-Eastern Shore. Inducted in 1989. 1968-81 Oakland Raiders, 1982 Los Angeles Raiders. **Highlights:** Cornerstone of Raiders' offensive line in 1970s. 207 regular-season games, 24 postseason games, eight Pro Bowls.

DON SHULA
Coach. Born in Painesville, Ohio, January 4, 1930. John Carroll. Inducted in 1997. 1963-69 Baltimore Colts, 1970-1995 Miami Dolphins. **Highlights:** Won more games (347) than any coach in NFL history. Won two Super Bowl titles, including Super Bowl VII when Dolphins recorded NFL's only perfect season (17-0).

O.J. SIMPSON
Running back. 6-1, 212. Born in San Francisco, California, July 9, 1947. City College (San Francisco), Southern California. Inducted in 1985. 1969-77 Buffalo Bills, 1978-79 San Francisco 49ers. **Highlights:** In 1973, became first player to rush for 2,000 yards in season. Finished career with four rushing titles, 11,236 yards.

JACKIE SMITH
Tight end. 6-4, 232. Born in Columbia, Mississippi, February 23, 1940. Northwestern State (Louisiana). Inducted in 1994. 1963-77 St. Louis Cardinals, 1978 Dallas Cowboys. **Highlights:** 480 receptions for 7,918 yards, 40 touchdowns. Third tight end to be elected to Hall of Fame.

BART STARR
Quarterback. 6-1, 200. Born in Montgomery, Alabama, January 9, 1934. Alabama. Inducted in 1977. 1956-71 Green Bay Packers. **Highlights:** Quarterbacked Packers to six division titles, five NFL titles including first two Super Bowls in which he was MVP.

ROGER STAUBACH
Quarterback. 6-3, 202. Born in Cincinnati, Ohio, February 5, 1942. New Mexico Military Institute, Navy. Inducted in 1985. 1969-79 Dallas Cowboys. **Highlights:** Led Cowboys to four NFC titles and victories in Super Bowls VI, XII. When retired, 83.4 career passer rating was best of all time.

ERNIE STAUTNER
Defensive tackle. 6-2, 235. Born in Prinzing-by-Cham, Bavaria, April 20, 1925. Boston College. Inducted in 1969. 1950-63 Pittsburgh Steelers. **Highlights:** Played in nine Pro Bowls and won the best lineman award in 1957. Recorded 3 safeties.

JAN STENERUD
Kicker. 6-2, 190. Born in Fetsund, Norway, November 26, 1942. Montana State. Inducted in 1991. 1967-79 Kansas City Chiefs, 1980-83 Green Bay Packers, 1984-85 Minnesota Vikings. **Highlights:** 1,699 points on 580 extra points, 373 field goals. First pure placekicker to enter Hall of Fame.

KEN STRONG
Halfback. 5-11, 210. Born in West Haven, Connecticut, August 6, 1906. Died October 5, 1979. New York University. Inducted in 1967. 1929-32 Staten Island Stapletons, 1933-35, 1939, 1944-47 New York Giants, 1936-37 New York Yanks (AFL). **Highlights:** Scored 17 points to lead Giants to victory in 1934 'Sneakers' game, led NFL with 64 points, 1933.

JOE STYDAHAR
Tackle. 6-4, 230. Born in Kaylor, Pennsylvania, March 17, 1912. Died March 23, 1977. West Virginia. Inducted in 1967. 1936-42, 1945-46 Chicago Bears. **Highlights:** One of stalwarts of Bears' 'Monsters of the Midway.' Played on five divisional, three NFL championship teams.

FRAN TARKENTON
Quarterback. 6-0, 185. Born in Richmond, Virginia, February 3, 1940. Georgia. Inducted in 1986. 1961-66, 1972-78 Minnesota Vikings, 1967-71 New York Giants. **Highlights:** At retirement, held NFL records for attempts (6,467), completions (3,686), yards (47,003), and touchdowns (342). Four touchdowns passes in first NFL game.

CHARLEY TAYLOR
Running back-wide receiver. 6-3, 210. Born in Grand Prairie, Texas, September 28, 1941. Arizona State. Inducted in 1984. 1964-75, 1977 Washington Redskins. **Highlights:** Won Rookie of Year honors as running back. Switched to wide receiver and won receiving titles in 1966, 1967.

JIM TAYLOR
Fullback. 6-0, 216. Born in Baton Rouge, Louisiana, September 20, 1935. Louisiana State. Inducted in 1976. 1958-66 Green Bay Packers, 1967 New Orleans Saints. **Highlights:** 8,597 rushing yards, 558 points. In 1962, led league in rushing and scoring with 19 touchdowns.

JIM THORPE
Halfback. 6-1, 190. Born in Prague, Oklahoma, May 28, 1888. Died March 28, 1953. Carlisle. Inducted in 1963. 1915-17, 1919-20, 1926 Canton Bulldogs, 1921 Cleveland Indians, 1922-23 Oorang Indians, 1924 Rock Island Independents, 1925 New York Giants, 1928 Chicago Cardinals. **Highlights:** Charter enshrinee. First president of American Professional Football Association, 1920. Played for 12 seasons.

Y.A. TITTLE
Quarterback. 6-0, 200. Born in Marshall, Texas, October 24, 1926. Louisiana State. Inducted in 1971. 1948-49 Baltimore Colts (AAFC), 1950 Baltimore Colts, 1951-60 San Francisco 49ers, 1961-64 New York Giants. **Highlights:** 33,070 yards, 242 touchdowns. 33 touchdown passes in 1962 and 36 in 1963. Two-time league MVP.

GEORGE TRAFTON
Center. 6-2, 235. Born in Chicago, Illinois, December 6, 1896. Died September 5, 1971. Notre Dame. Inducted in 1964. 1920 Decatur Staleys, 1921 Chicago Staleys, 1922-32 Chicago Bears. **Highlights:** First center to snap with one hand. Named top NFL center of 1920s.

CHARLEY TRIPPI
Halfback-quarterback. 6-0, 185. Born in Pittston, Pennsylvania, December 14, 1922. Georgia. Inducted in 1968. 1947-55 Chicago Cardinals. **Highlights:** One of football's most versatile performers. Played halfback five years, quarterback for two, defense for two.

EMLEN TUNNELL
Safety. 6-1, 200. Born in Bryn Mawr, Pennsylvania, March 29, 1925. Died July 22, 1975. Toledo, Iowa. Inducted in 1967. 1948-58 New York Giants, 1959-61 Green Bay Packers. **Highlights:** 79 interceptions. Gained more yards on kickoffs and interceptions (923) in 1952 than that season's NFL rushing leader.

CLYDE (BULLDOG) TURNER
Center. 6-2, 235. Born in Sweetwater, Texas, November 10, 1919. Hardin-Simmons. Inducted in 1966. 1940-52 Chicago Bears. **Highlights:** Anchored defense for four NFL championship teams, including 4 interceptions in five title games.

JOHNNY UNITAS
Quarterback. 6-1, 195. Born in Pittsburgh, Pennsylvania, May 7, 1933. Louisville. Inducted in 1979. 1956-72 Baltimore Colts, 1973 San Diego Chargers. **Highlights:** 40,239 passing yards, 290 touchdowns. Led Colts to two NFL championships. Passed for at least one touchdown in 47 consecutive games.

GENE UPSHAW
Guard. 6-5, 255. Born in Robstown, Texas, August 15, 1945. Texas A & I. Inducted in 1987. 1967-81 Oakland Raiders. **Highlights:** Played in 10 AFL/AFC Championship Games, three Super Bowls, seven Pro Bowls—307 total games.

NORM VAN BROCKLIN
Quarterback. 6-1, 190. Born in Eagle Butte, South Dakota, March 15, 1926. Died May 2, 1983. Oregon. Inducted in 1971. 1949-57 Los Angeles Rams, 1958-60 Philadelphia Eagles. **Highlights:** NFL-record 554 yards passing in 1951 season opener. Guided Eagles to NFL crown as league MVP in 1960.

STEVE VAN BUREN
Halfback. 6-1, 200. Born in La Ceiba, Honduras, December 28, 1920. Louisiana State. Inducted in 1965. 1944-51 Philadelphia Eagles. **Highlights:** Four-time rushing champion. Won 1944 punt return title and was 1945 kick return champion.

DOAK WALKER
Halfback. 5-11, 173. Born in Dallas, Texas, January 1, 1927. Southern Methodist. Inducted in 1986. 1950-55 Detroit Lions. **Highlights:** 534 points. Won two NFL scoring titles. Had winning 67-yard scoring run in 1952 title game.

BILL WALSH
Coach. Born in Los Angeles, California, November 30, 1931. San Jose State. Inducted in 1993. 1979-88 San Francisco 49ers. **Highlights:** 102-63-1 coaching record. Guided 49ers to three Super Bowl titles (XVI, XIX, XXIII) in 10 years.

PAUL WARFIELD
Wide receiver. 6-0, 188. Born in Warren, Ohio, November 28, 1942. Ohio State. Inducted in 1983. 1964-69, 1976-77 Cleveland Browns, 1970-74 Miami Dolphins. **Highlights:** 8,565 yards receiving, 85 touchdowns. Eight-time Pro Bowl player. Key to both Cleveland and Miami offenses.

BOB WATERFIELD
Quarterback. 6-2, 200. Born in Elmira, New York, July 26, 1920. Died March 25, 1983. UCLA. Inducted in 1965. 1945 Cleveland Rams, 1946-52 Los Angeles Rams. **Highlights:** NFL MVP as rookie in 1945 and led Rams to NFL title. Grabbed 20 interceptions in limited defensive duties.

MIKE WEBSTER
Center. 6-2, 260. Born in Tomahawk, Wisconsin, March 18, 1952. Wisconsin. Inducted in 1997. 1974-88 Pittsburgh Steelers, 1989-90 Kansas City Chiefs. **Highlights:** Played in 245 games, nine Pro Bowls, and won four Super Bowls during 17-year career.

ARNIE WEINMEISTER
Defensive tackle. 6-4, 235. Born in Rhein, Saskatchewan, Canada, March 23, 1923. Washington. Inducted in 1984. 1948-49 New York Yankees (AAFC), 1950-53 New York Giants. **Highlights:** Dominant defensive tackle of his time. Four-time All-NFL selection, four Pro Bowls.

RANDY WHITE
Defensive tackle. 6-4, 265. Born in Pittsburgh, Pennsylvania, January 15, 1953. Maryland. Inducted in 1994. 1975-88 Dallas Cowboys. **Highlights:** Missed only one game in 14 seasons. Co-MVP of Super Bowl XII. Nine-time Pro Bowl selection.

BILL WILLIS
Guard. 6-2, 215. Born in Columbus, Ohio, October 5, 1921. Ohio State. Inducted in 1977. 1946-49 Cleveland Browns (AAFC), 1950-53 Cleveland Browns. **Highlights:** Two-way player who excelled on defense. Four-time All-NFL player, played in three Pro Bowls.

LARRY WILSON
Safety. 6-0, 190. Born in Rigby, Idaho, March 24, 1938. Utah. Inducted in 1978. 1960-72 St. Louis Cardinals. **Highlights:** 52 interceptions. Had interception in seven consecutive games in 1966. Made "safety blitz" famous.

KELLEN WINSLOW
Tight end. 6-5, 250. Born in St. Louis, Missouri, November 5, 1957. Missouri. Inducted in 1995. 1979-87 San Diego Chargers **Highlights:** 541 receptions for 6,741 yards, 45 touchdowns. 13 catches, blocked field goal in 1981 playoff win over Miami.

ALEX WOJCIECHOWICZ
Center. 6-0, 235. Born in South River, New Jersey, August 12, 1915. Died July 13, 1992. Fordham. Inducted in 1968. 1938-46 Detroit Lions, 1946-50 Philadelphia Eagles. **Highlights:** One of league's first iron men. Played both ways for eight years with Lions.

WILLIE WOOD
Safety. 5-10, 190. Born in Washington, D.C., December 23, 1936. Southern California. Inducted in 1989. 1960-71 Green Bay Packers. **Highlights:** 48 interceptions. Competed in six NFL championship games including Super Bowls I and II.

ENSHRINEES BY YEAR OF INDUCTION
*Deceased
(Date of enshrinement in parentheses)

1963 CHARTER CLASS
(September 7, 1963)
Sammy Baugh
Bert Bell*
Joe Carr*
Earl (Dutch) Clark*
Harold (Red) Grange*
George Halas*
Mel Hein*
Wilbur (Pete) Henry*
Robert (Cal) Hubbard*
Don Hutson
Earl (Curly) Lambeau*
Tim Mara*
George Preston Marshall*
John (Blood) McNally*
Bronko Nagurski*
Ernie Nevers*
Jim Thorpe*

CLASS OF 1964
(September 6, 1964)
Jimmy Conzelman*
Ed Healey*
Clarke Hinkle*
William Roy (Link) Lyman*
Mike Michalske*
Art Rooney*
George Trafton*

CLASS OF 1965
(September 12, 1965)
Guy Chamberlin*
John (Paddy) Driscoll*
Dan Fortmann*
Otto Graham
Sid Luckman
Steve Van Buren
Bob Waterfield*

CLASS OF 1966
(September 17, 1966)
Bill Dudley
Joe Guyon*
Arnie Herber*
Walt Kiesling*
George McAfee
Steve Owen*
Hugh (Shorty) Ray*
Clyde (Bulldog) Turner

CLASS OF 1967
(August 5, 1967)
Chuck Bednarik
Charles W. Bidwill, Sr.*
Paul Brown*
Bobby Layne*
Dan Reeves*
Ken Strong*
Joe Stydahar*
Emlen Tunnell*

CLASS OF 1968
(August 3, 1968)
Cliff Battles*
Art Donovan
Elroy (Crazylegs) Hirsch
Wayne Millner*
Marion Motley
Charley Trippi
Alex Wojciechowicz*

CLASS OF 1969
(September 13, 1969)
Albert Glen (Turk) Edwards*
Earle (Greasy) Neale*
Leo Nomellini
Joe Perry
Ernie Stautner

CLASS OF 1970
(August 8, 1970)
Jack Christiansen*
Tom Fears
Hugh McElhenny
Pete Pihos

CLASS OF 1971
(July 31, 1971)
Jim Brown
Bill Hewitt*
Frank (Bruiser) Kinard*
Vince Lombardi*
Andy Robustelli
Y. A. Tittle
Norm Van Brocklin*

CLASS OF 1972
(July 29, 1972)
Lamar Hunt
Gino Marchetti
Ollie Matson
Clarence (Ace) Parker

CLASS OF 1973
(July 28, 1973)
Raymond Berry
Jim Parker
Joe Schmidt

CLASS OF 1974
(July 27, 1974)
Tony Canadeo
Bill George*
Lou Groza
Dick (Night Train) Lane

CLASS OF 1975
(August 2, 1975)
Roosevelt Brown
George Connor
Dante Lavelli
Lenny Moore

CLASS OF 1976
(July 24, 1976)
Ray Flaherty*
Len Ford*
Jim Taylor

CLASS OF 1977
(July 30, 1977)
Frank Gifford
Forrest Gregg
Gale Sayers
Bart Starr
Bill Willis

CLASS OF 1978
(July 29, 1978)
Lance Alworth
Weeb Ewbank
Alphonse (Tuffy) Leemans*
Ray Nitschke
Larry Wilson

CLASS OF 1979
(July 28, 1979)
Dick Butkus
Yale Lary
Ron Mix
Johnny Unitas

CLASS OF 1980
(August 2, 1980)
Herb Adderley
David (Deacon) Jones
Bob Lilly
Jim Otto

CLASS OF 1981
(August 1, 1981)
Morris (Red) Badgro
George Blanda
Willie Davis
Jim Ringo

CLASS OF 1982
(August 7, 1982)
Doug Atkins
Sam Huff
George Musso
Merlin Olsen

CLASS OF 1983
(July 30, 1983)
Bobby Bell
Sid Gillman
Sonny Jurgensen
Bobby Mitchell
Paul Warfield

CLASS OF 1984
(July 28, 1984)
Willie Brown
Mike McCormack
Charley Taylor
Arnie Weinmeister

CLASS OF 1985
(August 3, 1985)
Frank Gatski
Joe Namath
Pete Rozelle*
O. J. Simpson
Roger Staubach

CLASS OF 1986
(August 2, 1986)
Paul Hornung
Ken Houston
Willie Lanier
Fran Tarkenton
Doak Walker

CLASS OF 1987
(August 8, 1987)
Larry Csonka
Len Dawson
Joe Greene
John Henry Johnson
Jim Langer
Don Maynard
Gene Upshaw

CLASS OF 1988
(July 30, 1988)
Fred Biletnikoff
Mike Ditka
Jack Ham
Alan Page

CLASS OF 1989
(August 5, 1989)
Mel Blount
Terry Bradshaw
Art Shell
Willie Wood

CLASS OF 1990
(August 4, 1989)
Buck Buchanan*
Bob Griese
Franco Harris
Ted Hendricks
Jack Lambert
Tom Landry
Bob St. Clair

CLASS OF 1991
(July 27, 1991)
Earl Campbell
John Hannah
Stan Jones
Tex Schramm
Jan Stenerud

CLASS OF 1992
(August 1, 1992)
Lem Barney
Al Davis
John Mackey
John Riggins

CLASS OF 1993
(July 31, 1993)
Dan Fouts
Larry Little
Chuck Noll
Walter Payton
Bill Walsh

CLASS OF 1994
(July 30, 1994)
Tony Dorsett
Bud Grant
Jimmy Johnson
Leroy Kelly
Jackie Smith
Randy White

CLASS OF 1995
(July 29, 1995)
Jim Finks*
Henry Jordan*
Steve Largent
Lee Roy Selmon
Kellen Winslow

CLASS OF 1996
(July 27, 1996)
Lou Creekmur
Dan Dierdorf
Joe Gibbs
Charlie Joiner
Mel Renfro

CLASS OF 1997
(July 26, 1997)
Mike Haynes
Wellington Mara
Don Shula
Mike Webster

1869

Rutgers and Princeton played a college soccer football game, the first ever, November 6. The game used modified London Football Association rules. During the next seven years, rugby gained favor with the major eastern schools over soccer, and modern football began to develop from rugby.

1876

At the Massasoit convention, the first rules for American football were written. Walter Camp, who would become known as the father of American football, first became involved with the game.

1892

In an era in which football was a major attraction of local athletic clubs, an intense competition between two Pittsburgh-area clubs, the Allegheny Athletic Association (AAA) and the Pittsburgh Athletic Club (PAC), led to the making of the first professional football player. Former Yale All-America guard William (Pudge) Heffelfinger was paid $500 by the AAA to play in a game against the PAC, becoming the first person to be paid to play football, November 12. The AAA won the game 4-0 when Heffelfinger picked up a PAC fumble and ran 25 yards for a touchdown.

1893

The Pittsburgh Athletic Club signed one of its players, probably halfback Grant Dibert, to the first known pro football contract, which covered all of the PAC's games for the year.

1895

John Brallier became the first football player to openly turn pro, accepting $10 and expenses to play for the Latrobe YMCA against the Jeannette Athletic Club.

1896

The Allegheny Athletic Association team fielded the first completely professional team for its abbreviated two-game season.

1897

The Latrobe Athletic Association football team went entirely professional, becoming the first team to play a full season with only professionals.

1898

A touchdown was changed from four points to five.

1899

Chris O'Brien formed a neighborhood team, which played under the name the Morgan Athletic Club, on the south side of Chicago. The team later became known as the Normals, then the Racine (for a street in Chicago) Cardinals, the Chicago Cardinals, the St. Louis Cardinals, the Phoenix Cardinals, and, in 1994, the Arizona Cardinals. The team remains the oldest continuing operation in pro football.

1900

William C. Temple took over the team payments for the Duquesne Country and Athletic Club, becoming the first known individual club owner.

1902

Baseball's Philadelphia Athletics, managed by Connie Mack, and the Philadelphia Phillies formed professional football teams, joining the Pittsburgh Stars in the first attempt at a pro football league, named the National Football League. The Athletics won the first night football game ever played, 39-0 over Kanaweola AC at Elmira, New York, November 21.

All three teams claimed the pro championship for the year, but the league president, Dave Berry, named the Stars the champions. Pitcher Rube Waddell was with the Athletics, and pitcher Christy Mathewson a fullback for Pittsburgh.

The first World Series of pro football, actually a five-team tournament, was played among a team made up of players from both the Athletics and the Phillies, but simply named New York; the New York Knickerbockers; the Syracuse AC; the Warlow AC; and the Orange (New Jersey) AC at New York's original Madison Square Garden. New York and Syracuse played the first indoor football game before 3,000, December 28. Syracuse, with Glen (Pop) Warner at guard, won 6-0 and went on to win the tournament.

1903

The Franklin (Pa.) Athletic Club won the second and last World Series of pro football over the Oreos AC of Asbury Park, New Jersey; the Watertown Red and Blacks; and the Orange AC.

Pro football was popularized in Ohio when the Massillon Tigers, a strong amateur team, hired four Pittsburgh pros to play in the season-ending game against Akron. At the same time, pro football declined in the Pittsburgh area, and the emphasis on the pro game moved west from Pennsylvania to Ohio.

1904

A field goal was changed from five points to four.

Ohio had at least seven pro teams, with Massillon winning the Ohio Independent Championship, that is, the pro title. Talk surfaced about forming a state-wide league to end spiraling salaries brought about by constant bidding for players and to write universal rules for the game. The feeble attempt to start the league failed.

Halfback Charles Follis signed a contract with the Shelby (Ohio) AC, making him the first known black pro football player.

1905

The Canton AC, later to become known as the Bulldogs, became a professional team. Massillon again won the Ohio League championship.

1906

The forward pass was legalized. The first authenticated pass completion in a pro game came on October 27, when George (Peggy) Parratt of Massillon threw a completion to Dan (Bullet) Riley in a victory over a combined Benwood-Moundsville team.

Arch-rivals Canton and Massillon, the two best pro teams in America, played twice, with Canton winning the first game but Massillon winning the second and the Ohio League championship. A betting scandal and the financial disaster wrought upon the two clubs by paying huge salaries caused a temporary decline in interest in pro football in the two cities and, somewhat, throughout Ohio.

1909

A field goal dropped from four points to three.

1912

A touchdown was increased from five points to six.

Jack Cusack revived a strong pro team in Canton.

1913

Jim Thorpe, a former football and track star at the Carlisle Indian School (Pa.) and a double gold medal winner at the 1912 Olympics in Stockholm, played for the Pine Village Pros in Indiana.

1915

Massillon again fielded a major team, reviving the old rivalry with Canton. Cusack signed Thorpe to play for Canton for $250 a game.

1916

With Thorpe and former Carlisle teammate Pete Calac starring, Canton went 9-0-1, won the Ohio League championship, and was acclaimed the pro football champion.

1917

Despite an upset by Massillon, Canton again won the Ohio League championship.

1919

Canton again won the Ohio League championship, despite the team having been turned over from Cusack to Ralph Hay. Thorpe and Calac were joined in the backfield by Joe Guyon.

Earl (Curly) Lambeau and George Calhoun organized the Green Bay Packers. Lambeau's employer at the Indian Packing Company provided $500 for equipment and allowed the team to use the company field for practices. The Packers went 10-1.

1920

Pro football was in a state of confusion due to three major problems: dramatically rising salaries; players continually jumping from one team to another following the highest offer; and the use of college players still enrolled in school. A league in which all the members would follow the same rules seemed the answer. An organizational meeting, at which the Akron Pros, Canton Bulldogs, Cleveland Indians, and Dayton Triangles were represented, was held at the Jordan and Hupmobile auto showroom in Canton, Ohio, August 20. This meeting resulted in the formation of the American Professional Football Conference.

A second organizational meeting was held in Canton, September 17. The teams were from four states—Akron, Canton, Cleveland, and Dayton from Ohio; the Hammond Pros and Muncie Flyers from Indiana; the Rochester Jeffersons from New York; and the Rock Island Independents, Decatur Staleys, and Racine Cardinals from Illinois. The name of the league was changed to the American Professional Football Association. Hoping to capitalize on his fame, the members elected Thorpe president; Stanley Cofall of Cleveland was elected vice president. A membership fee of $100 per team was charged to give an appearance of respectability, but no team ever paid it. Scheduling was left up to the teams, and there were wide variations, both in the overall number of games played and in the number played against APFA member teams.

Four other teams—the Buffalo All-Americans, Chicago Tigers, Columbus Panhandles, and Detroit Heralds—joined the league sometime during the year. On September 26, the first game featuring an APFA team was played at Rock Island's Douglas Park. A crowd of 800 watched the Independents defeat the St. Paul Ideals 48-0. A week later, October 3, the first game matching two APFA teams was held. At Triangle Park, Dayton defeated Columbus 14-0, with Lou Partlow of Dayton scoring the first touchdown in a game between Association teams. The same day, Rock Island defeated Muncie 45-0.

By the beginning of December, most of the teams in the APFA had abandoned their hopes for a championship, and some of them, including the Chicago Tigers and the Detroit Heralds, had finished their seasons, disbanded, and had their franchises canceled by the Association. Four teams—Akron, Buffalo, Canton, and Decatur—still had championship aspirations, but a series of late-season games among them left Akron as the only undefeated team in the Association. At one of these games, Akron sold tackle Bob Nash to Buffalo for $300 and five percent of the gate receipts—the first APFA player deal.

1921

At the league meeting in Akron, April 30, the championship of the 1920 season was awarded to the Akron Pros. The APFA was reorganized, with Joe Carr of the Columbus Panhandles named president and Carl Storck of Dayton secretary-treasurer. Carr moved the Association's headquarters to Columbus, drafted a league constitution and by-laws, gave teams territorial rights, restricted player movements, developed membership criteria for the franchises, and issued standings for the first time, so that the APFA would have a clear champion.

The Association's membership increased to 22 teams, including the Green Bay Packers, who were awarded to John Clair of the Acme Packing Company.

Thorpe moved from Canton to the Cleveland Indians, but he was hurt early in the season and played very little.

A.E. Staley turned the Decatur Staleys over to player-coach George Halas, who moved the team to Cubs Park in Chicago. Staley paid Halas

$5,000 to keep the name Staleys for one more year. Halas made halfback Ed (Dutch) Sternaman his partner.

Player-coach Fritz Pollard of the Akron Pros became the first black head coach.

The Staleys claimed the APFA championship with a 9-1-1 record, as did Buffalo at 9-1-2. Carr ruled in favor of the Staleys, giving Halas his first championship.

1922

After admitting the use of players who had college eligibility remaining during the 1921 season, Clair and the Green Bay management withdrew from the APFA, January 28. Curly Lambeau promised to obey league rules and then used $50 of his own money to buy back the franchise. Bad weather and low attendance plagued the Packers, and Lambeau went broke, but local merchants arranged a $2,500 loan for the club. A public nonprofit corporation was set up to operate the team, with Lambeau as head coach and manager.

The American Professional Football Association changed its name to the National Football League, June 24. The Chicago Staleys became the Chicago Bears.

The NFL fielded 18 teams, including the new Oorang Indians of Marion, Ohio, an all-Indian team featuring Thorpe, Joe Guyon, and Pete Calac, and sponsored by the Oorang dog kennels.

Canton, led by player-coach Guy Chamberlin and tackles Link Lyman and Wilbur (Pete) Henry, emerged as the league's first true powerhouse, going 10-0-2.

1923

For the first time, all of the franchises considered to be part of the NFL fielded teams. Thorpe played first for Oorang, then for the Toledo Maroons. Against the Bears, Thorpe fumbled, and Halas picked up the ball and returned it 98 yards for a touchdown, a record that would last until 1972.

Canton had its second consecutive undefeated season, going 11-0-1 for the NFL title.

1924

The league had 18 franchises, including new ones in Kansas City, Kenosha, and Frankford, a section of Philadelphia. League champion Canton, successful on the field but not at the box office, was purchased by the owner of the Cleveland franchise, who kept the Canton franchise inactive, while using the best players for his Cleveland team, which he renamed the Bulldogs. Cleveland won the title with a 7-1-1 record.

1925

Five new franchises were admitted to the NFL—the New York Giants, who were awarded to Tim Mara and Billy Gibson for $500; the Detroit Panthers, featuring Jimmy Conzelman as owner, coach, and tailback; the Providence Steam Roller; a new Canton Bulldogs team; and the Pottsville Maroons, who had been perhaps the most successful independent pro team. The NFL es-

tablished its first player limit, at 16 players.

Late in the season, the NFL made its greatest coup in gaining national recognition. Shortly after the University of Illinois season ended in November, All-America halfback Harold (Red) Grange signed a contract to play with the Chicago Bears. On Thanksgiving Day, a crowd of 36,000—the largest in pro football history—watched Grange and the Bears play the Chicago Cardinals to a scoreless tie at Wrigley Field. At the beginning of December, the Bears left on a barnstorming tour that saw them play eight games in 12 days, in St. Louis, Philadelphia, New York City, Washington, Boston, Pittsburgh, Detroit, and Chicago. A crowd of 73,000 watched the game against the Giants at the Polo Grounds, helping assure the future of the troubled NFL franchise in New York. The Bears then played nine more games in the South and West, including a game in Los Angeles, in which 75,000 fans watched them defeat the Los Angeles Tigers in the Los Angeles Memorial Coliseum.

Pottsville and the Chicago Cardinals were the top contenders for the league title, with Pottsville winning a late-season meeting 21-7. Pottsville scheduled a game against a team of former Notre Dame players for Shibe Park in Philadelphia. Frankford lodged a protest not only because the game was in Frankford's protected territory, but because it was being played the same day as a Yellow Jackets home game. Carr gave three different notices forbidding Pottsville to play the game, but Pottsville played anyway, December 12. That day, Carr fined the club, suspended it from all rights and privileges (including the right to play for the NFL championship), and returned its franchise to the league. The Cardinals, who ended the season with the best record in the league, were named the 1925 champions.

1926

Grange's manager, C.C. Pyle, told the Bears that Grange wouldn't play for them unless he was paid a five-figure salary and given one-third ownership of the team. The Bears refused. Pyle leased Yankee Stadium in New York City, then petitioned for an NFL franchise. After he was refused, he started the first American Football League. It lasted one season and included Grange's New York Yankees and eight other teams. The AFL champion Philadelphia Quakers played a December game against the New York Giants, seventh in the NFL, and the Giants won 31-0. At the end of the season, the AFL folded.

Halas pushed through a rule that prohibited any team from signing a player whose college class had not graduated.

The NFL grew to 22 teams, including the Duluth Eskimos, who signed All-America fullback Ernie Nevers of Stanford, giving the league a gate attraction to rival Grange. The 15-member Eskimos, dubbed the Iron Men of the North, played 29 exhibition and league games, 28 on the road, and Nevers played in all but 29 minutes of them.

Frankford edged the Bears for the championship, despite Halas having obtained John (Paddy) Driscoll from the Cardinals. On December 4, the Yellow Jackets scored in the final two minutes to defeat the Bears 7-6 and move ahead of them in the standings.

1927

At a special meeting in Cleveland, April 23, Carr decided to secure the NFL's future by eliminating the financially weaker teams and consolidating the quality players onto a limited number of more successful teams. The new-look NFL dropped to 12 teams, and the center of gravity of the league left the Midwest, where the NFL had started, and began to emerge in the large cities of the East. One of the new teams was Grange's New York Yankees, but Grange suffered a knee injury and the Yankees finished in the middle of the pack. The NFL championship was won by the cross-town rival New York Giants, who posted 10 shutouts in 13 games.

1928

Grange and Nevers both retired from pro football, and Duluth disbanded, as the NFL was reduced to only 10 teams. The Providence Steam Roller of Jimmy Conzelman and Pearce Johnson won the championship, playing in the Cycledrome, a 10,000-seat oval that had been built for bicycle races.

1929

Chris O'Brien sold the Chicago Cardinals to David Jones, July 27.

The NFL added a fourth official, the field judge, July 28.

Grange and Nevers returned to the NFL. Nevers scored six rushing touchdowns and four extra points as the Cardinals beat Grange's Bears 40-6, November 28. The 40 points set a record that remains the NFL's oldest.

Providence became the first NFL team to host a game at night under floodlights, against the Cardinals, November 3.

The Packers added back Johnny Blood (McNally), tackle Cal Hubbard, and guard Mike Michalske, and won their first NFL championship, edging the Giants, who featured quarterback Benny Friedman.

1930

Dayton, the last of the NFL's original franchises, was purchased by William B. Dwyer and John C. Depler, moved to Brooklyn, and renamed the Dodgers. The Portsmouth, Ohio, Spartans entered the league.

The Packers edged the Giants for the title, but the most improved team was the Bears. Halas retired as a player and replaced himself as coach of the Bears with Ralph Jones, who refined the T-formation by introducing wide ends and a halfback in motion. Jones also introduced rookie All-America fullback-tackle Bronko Nagurski.

The Giants defeated a team of former Notre Dame players coached by Knute Rockne 22-0 before 55,000 at the Polo Grounds, December 14. The proceeds went to the New York Unem-

ployment Fund to help those suffering because of the Great Depression, and the easy victory helped give the NFL credibility with the press and the public.

1931

The NFL decreased to 10 teams, and halfway through the season the Frankford franchise folded. Carr fined the Bears, Packers, and Portsmouth $1,000 each for using players whose college classes had not graduated.

The Packers won an unprecedented third consecutive title, beating out the Spartans, who were led by rookie backs Earl (Dutch) Clark and Glenn Presnell.

1932

George Preston Marshall, Vincent Bendix, Jay O'Brien, and M. Dorland Doyle were awarded a franchise for Boston, July 9. Despite the presence of two rookies—halfback Cliff Battles and tackle Glen (Turk) Edwards—the new team, named the Braves, lost money and Marshall was left as the sole owner at the end of the year.

NFL membership dropped to eight teams, the lowest in history. Official statistics were kept for the first time. The Bears and the Spartans finished the season in the first-ever tie for first place. After the season finale, the league office arranged for the first playoff game in NFL history. The game was moved indoors to Chicago Stadium because of bitter cold and heavy snow. The arena allowed only an 80-yard field that came right to the walls. The goal posts were moved from the end lines to the goal lines and, for safety, inbounds lines or hashmarks where the ball would be put in play were drawn 10 yards from the walls that butted against the sidelines. The Bears won 9-0, December 18, scoring the winning touchdown on a two-yard pass from Nagurski to Grange. The Spartans claimed Nagurski's pass was thrown from less than five yards behind the line of scrimmage, violating the existing passing rule, but the play stood.

1933

The NFL, which long had followed the rules of college football, made a number of significant changes from the college game for the first time and began to develop rules serving its needs and the style of play it preferred. The innovations from the 1932 championship game—inbounds line or hashmarks and goal posts on the goal lines—were adopted. Also the forward pass was legalized from anywhere behind the line of scrimmage, February 25.

Marshall and Halas pushed through a proposal that divided the NFL into two divisions, with the winners to meet in an annual championship game, July 8.

Three new franchises joined the league—the Pittsburgh Pirates of Art Rooney, the Philadelphia Eagles of Bert Bell and Lud Wray, and the Cincinnati Reds. The Staten Island Stapletons suspended operations for a year, but never returned to the league.

Halas bought out Sternaman, became sole owner of the Bears, and re-

instated himself as head coach. Marshall changed the name of the Boston Braves to the Redskins. David Jones sold the Chicago Cardinals to Charles W. Bidwill.

In the first NFL Championship Game scheduled before the season, the Western Division champion Bears defeated the Eastern Division champion Giants 23-21 at Wrigley Field, December 17.

1934

G.A. (Dick) Richards purchased the Portsmouth Spartans, moved them to Detroit, and renamed them the Lions.

Professional football gained new prestige when the Bears were matched against the best college football players in the first Chicago College All-Star Game, August 31. The game ended in a scoreless tie before 79,432 at Soldier Field.

The Cincinnati Reds lost their first eight games, then were suspended from the league for defaulting on payments. The St. Louis Gunners, an independent team, joined the NFL by buying the Cincinnati franchise and went 1-2 the last three weeks.

Rookie Beattie Feathers of the Bears became the NFL's first 1,000-yard rusher, gaining 1,004 on 101 carries. The Thanksgiving Day game between the Bears and the Lions became the first NFL game broadcast nationally, with Graham McNamee the announcer for NBC radio.

In the championship game, on an extremely cold and icy day at the Polo Grounds, the Giants trailed the Bears 13-3 in the third quarter before changing to basketball shoes for better footing. The Giants won 30-13 in what has come to be known as the Sneakers Game, December 9.

The player waiver rule was adopted, December 10.

1935

The NFL adopted Bert Bell's proposal to hold an annual draft of college players, to begin in 1936, with teams selecting in an inverse order of finish, May 19. The inbounds line or hashmarks were moved nearer the center of the field, 15 yards from the sidelines.

All-America end Don Hutson of Alabama joined Green Bay. The Lions defeated the Giants 26-7 in the NFL Championship Game, December 15.

1936

There were no franchise transactions for the first year since the formation of the NFL. It also was the first year in which all member teams played the same number of games.

The Eagles made University of Chicago halfback and Heisman Trophy winner Jay Berwanger the first player ever selected in the NFL draft, February 8. The Eagles traded his rights to the Bears, but Berwanger never played pro football. The first player selected to actually sign was the number-two pick, Riley Smith of Alabama, who was selected by Boston.

A rival league was formed, and it became the second to call itself the American Football League. The Boston

Shamrocks were its champions.

Because of poor attendance, Marshall, the owner of the host team, moved the Championship Game from Boston to the Polo Grounds in New York. Green Bay defeated the Redskins 21-6, December 13.

1937

Homer Marshman was granted a Cleveland franchise, named the Rams, February 12. Marshall moved the Redskins to Washington, D.C., February 13. The Redskins signed TCU All-America tailback Sammy Baugh, who led them to a 28-21 victory over the Bears in the NFL Championship Game, December 12.

The Los Angeles Bulldogs had an 8-0 record to win the AFL title, but then the 2-year-old league folded.

1938

At the suggestion of Halas, Hugh (Shorty) Ray became a technical advisor on rules and officiating to the NFL. A new rule called for a 15-yard penalty for roughing the passer.

Rookie Byron (Whizzer) White of the Pittsburgh Pirates led the NFL in rushing. The Giants defeated the Packers 23-17 for the NFL title, December 11.

Marshall, *Los Angeles Times* sports editor Bill Henry, and promoter Tom Gallery established the Pro Bowl game between the NFL champion and a team of pro all-stars.

1939

The New York Giants defeated the Pro All-Stars 13-10 in the first Pro Bowl, at Wrigley Field, Los Angeles, January 15.

Carr, NFL president since 1921, died in Columbus, May 20. Carl Storck was named acting president, May 25.

An NFL game was televised for the first time when NBC broadcast the Brooklyn Dodgers-Philadelphia Eagles game from Ebbets Field to the approximately 1,000 sets then in New York.

Green Bay defeated New York 27-0 in the NFL Championship Game, December 10 at Milwaukee. NFL attendance exceeded 1 million in a season for the first time, reaching 1,071,200.

1940

A six-team rival league, the third to call itself the American Football League, was formed, and the Columbus Bullies won its championship.

Halas's Bears, with additional coaching by Clark Shaughnessy of Stanford, defeated the Redskins 73-0 in the NFL Championship Game, December 8. The game, which was the most decisive victory in NFL history, popularized the Bears' T-formation with a man-in-motion. It was the first championship carried on network radio, broadcast by Red Barber to 120 stations of the Mutual Broadcasting System, which paid $2,500 for the rights.

Art Rooney sold the Pittsburgh franchise to Alexis Thompson, December 9, then bought part interest in the Philadelphia Eagles.

1941

Elmer Layden was named the first Commissioner of the NFL, March 1; Storck, the acting president, resigned, April 5. NFL headquarters were moved to Chicago.

Bell and Rooney traded the Eagles to Thompson for the Pirates, then re-named their new team the Steelers. Homer Marshman sold the Rams to Daniel F. Reeves and Fred Levy, Jr.

The league by-laws were revised to provide for playoffs in case there were ties in division races, and sudden-death overtimes in case a playoff game was tied after four quarters. An official *NFL Record Manual* was published for the first time.

Columbus again won the championship of the AFL, but the two-year-old league then folded.

The Bears and the Packers finished in a tie for the Western Division championship, setting up the first divisional playoff game in league history. The Bears won 33-14, then defeated the Giants 37-9 for the NFL championship, December 21.

1942

Players departing for service in World War II depleted the rosters of NFL teams. Halas left the Bears in midseason to join the Navy, and Luke Johnsos and Heartley (Hunk) Anderson served as co-coaches as the Bears went 11-0 in the regular season. The Redskins defeated the Bears 14-6 in the NFL Championship Game, December 13.

1943

The Cleveland Rams, with co-owners Reeves and Levy in the service, were granted permission to suspend operations for one season, April 6. Levy transferred his stock in the team to Reeves, April 16.

The NFL adopted free substitution, April 7. The league also made the wearing of helmets mandatory and approved a 10-game schedule for all teams.

Philadelphia and Pittsburgh were granted permission to merge for one season, June 19. The team, known as Phil-Pitt (and called the Steagles by fans), divided home games between the two cities, and Earle (Greasy) Neale of Philadelphia and Walt Kiesling of Pittsburgh served as co-coaches. The merger automatically dissolved the last day of the season, December 5.

Ted Collins was granted a franchise for Boston, to become active in 1944.

Sammy Baugh led the league in passing, punting, and interceptions. He led the Redskins to a tie with the Giants for the Eastern Division title, and then to a 28-0 victory in a divisional playoff game. The Bears beat the Redskins 41-21 in the NFL Championship Game, December 26.

1944

Collins, who had wanted a franchise in Yankee Stadium in New York, named his new team in Boston the Yanks. Cleveland resumed operations. The Brooklyn Dodgers changed their name to the Tigers.

Coaching from the bench was

legalized, April 20.

The Cardinals and the Steelers were granted permission to merge for one year under the name Card-Pitt, April 21. Phil Handler of the Cardinals and Walt Kiesling of the Steelers served as co-coaches. The merger automatically dissolved the last day of the season, December 3.

In the NFL Championship Game, Green Bay defeated the New York Giants 14-7, December 17.

1945

The inbounds lines or hashmarks were moved from 15 yards away from the sidelines to nearer the center of the field—20 yards from the sidelines.

Brooklyn and Boston merged into a team that played home games in both cities and was known simply as The Yanks. The team was coached by former Boston head coach Herb Kopf. In December, the Brooklyn franchise withdrew from the NFL to join the new All-America Football Conference; all the players on its active and reserve lists were assigned to The Yanks, who once again became the Boston Yanks.

Halas rejoined the Bears late in the season after service with the U.S. Navy. Although Halas took over much of the coaching duties, Anderson and Johnsos remained the coaches of record throughout the season.

Steve Van Buren of Philadelphia led the NFL in rushing, kickoff returns, and scoring.

After the Japanese surrendered ending World War II, a count showed that the NFL service roster, limited to men who had played in league games, totaled 638, 21 of whom had died in action.

Rookie quarterback Bob Waterfield led Cleveland to a 15-14 victory over Washington in the NFL Championship Game, December 16.

1946

The contract of Commissioner Layden was not renewed, and Bert Bell, the co-owner of the Steelers, replaced him, January 11. Bell moved the league headquarters from Chicago to the Philadelphia suburb of Bala-Cynwyd.

Free substitution was withdrawn and substitutions were limited to no more than three men at a time. Forward passes were made automatically incomplete upon striking the goal posts, January 11.

The NFL took on a truly national appearance for the first time when Reeves was granted permission by the league to move his NFL champion Rams to Los Angeles.

Halfback Kenny Washington (March 21) and end Woody Strode (May 7) signed with the Los Angeles Rams to become the first African-Americans to play in the NFL in the modern era. Guard Bill Willis (August 6) and running back Marion Motley (August 9) joined the AAFC with the Cleveland Browns.

The rival All-America Football Conference began play with eight teams. The Cleveland Browns, coached by Paul Brown, won the AAFC's first championship, defeating the New York Yankees 14-9.

Bill Dudley of the Steelers led the NFL in rushing, interceptions, and punt returns, and won the league's most valuable player award.

Backs Frank Filchock and Merle Hapes of the Giants were questioned about an attempt by a New York man to fix the championship game with the Bears. Bell suspended Hapes but allowed Filchock to play; he played well, but Chicago won 24-14, December 15.

1947

The NFL added a fifth official, the back judge.

A bonus choice was made for the first time in the NFL draft. One team each year would select the special choice before the first round began. The Chicago Bears won a lottery and the rights to the first choice and drafted back Bob Fenimore of Oklahoma A&M.

The Cleveland Browns again won the AAFC title, defeating the New York Yankees 14-3.

Charles Bidwill, Sr., owner of the Cardinals, died April 19, but his wife and sons retained ownership of the team. On December 28, the Cardinals won the NFL Championship Game 28-21 over the Philadelphia Eagles, who had beaten Pittsburgh 21-0 in a playoff.

1948

Plastic helmets were prohibited. A flexible artificial tee was permitted at the kickoff. Officials other than the referee were equipped with whistles, not horns, January 14.

Fred Mandel sold the Detroit Lions to a syndicate headed by D. Lyle Fife, January 15.

Halfback Fred Gehrke of the Los Angeles Rams painted horns on the Rams' helmets, the first modern helmet emblems in pro football.

The Cleveland Browns won their third straight championship in the AAFC, going 14-0 and then defeating the Buffalo Bills 49-7.

In a blizzard, the Eagles defeated the Cardinals 7-0 in the NFL Championship Game, December 19.

1949

Alexis Thompson sold the champion Eagles to a syndicate headed by James P. Clark, January 15. The Boston Yanks became the New York Bulldogs, sharing the Polo Grounds with the Giants.

Free substitution was adopted for one year, January 20.

The NFL had two 1,000-yard rushers in the same season for the first time—Steve Van Buren of Philadelphia and Tony Canadeo of Green Bay.

The AAFC played its season with a one-division, seven-team format. On December 9, Bell announced a merger agreement in which three AAFC franchises—Cleveland, San Francisco, and Baltimore—would join the NFL in 1950. The Browns won their fourth consecutive AAFC title, defeating the 49ers 21-7, December 11.

In a heavy rain, the Eagles defeated the Rams 14-0 in the NFL Championship Game, December 18.

1950

Unlimited free substitution was restored, opening the way for the era of two platoons and specialization in pro football, January 20.

Curly Lambeau, founder of the franchise and Green Bay's head coach since 1921, resigned under fire, February 1.

The name National Football League was restored after about three months as the National-American Football League. The American and National conferences were created to replace the Eastern and Western divisions, March 3.

The New York Bulldogs became the Yanks and divided the players of the former AAFC Yankees with the Giants. A special allocation draft was held in which the 13 teams drafted the remaining AAFC players, with special consideration for Baltimore, which received 15 choices compared to 10 for other teams.

The Los Angeles Rams became the first NFL team to have all of its games—both home and away—televised. The Washington Redskins followed the Rams in arranging to televise their games; other teams made deals to put selected games on television.

In the first game of the season, former AAFC champion Cleveland defeated NFL champion Philadelphia 35-10. For the first time, deadlocks occurred in both conferences and playoffs were necessary. The Browns defeated the Giants in the American and the Rams defeated the Bears in the National. Cleveland defeated Los Angeles 30-28 in the NFL Championship Game, December 24.

1951

The Pro Bowl game, dormant since 1942, was revived under a new format matching the all-stars of each conference at the Los Angeles Memorial Coliseum. The American Conference defeated the National Conference 28-27, January 14.

Abraham Watner returned the Baltimore franchise and its player contracts back to the NFL for $50,000. Baltimore's former players were made available for drafting at the same time as college players, January 18.

A rule was passed that no tackle, guard, or center would be eligible to catch a forward pass, January 18.

The Rams reversed their television policy and televised only road games.

The NFL Championship Game was televised coast-to-coast for the first time, December 23. The DuMont Network paid $75,000 for the rights to the game, in which the Rams defeated the Browns 24-17.

1952

Ted Collins sold the New York Yanks' franchise back to the NFL, January 19. A new franchise was awarded to a group in Dallas after it purchased the assets of the Yanks, January 24. The new Texans went 1-11, with the owners turning the franchise back to the league in midseason. For the last five games of the season, the commissioner's office operated the Texans as a road team, using Hershey, Pennsyl-

vania, as a home base. At the end of the season the franchise was canceled, the last time an NFL team failed.

The Pittsburgh Steelers abandoned the Single-Wing for the T-formation, the last pro team to do so.

The Detroit Lions won their first NFL championship in 17 years, defeating the Browns 17-7 in the title game, December 28.

1953

A Baltimore group headed by Carroll Rosenbloom was granted a franchise and was awarded the holdings of the defunct Dallas organization, January 23. The team, named the Colts, put together the largest trade in league history, acquiring 10 players from Cleveland in exchange for five.

The names of the American and National conferences were changed to the Eastern and Western conferences, January 24.

Jim Thorpe died, March 28.

Mickey McBride, founder of the Cleveland Browns, sold the franchise to a syndicate headed by Dave R. Jones, June 10.

The NFL policy of blacking out home games was upheld by Judge Allan K. Grim of the U.S. District Court in Philadelphia, November 12.

The Lions again defeated the Browns in the NFL Championship Game, winning 17-16, December 27.

1954

The Canadian Football League began a series of raids on NFL teams, signing quarterback Eddie LeBaron and defensive end Gene Brito of Washington and defensive tackle Arnie Weinmeister of the Giants, among others.

Fullback Joe Perry of the 49ers became the first player in league history to gain 1,000 yards rushing in consecutive seasons.

Cleveland defeated Detroit 56-10 in the NFL Championship Game, December 26.

1955

The sudden-death overtime rule was used for the first time in a preseason game between the Rams and Giants at Portland, Oregon, August 28. The Rams won 23-17 three minutes into overtime.

A rule change declared the ball dead immediately if the ball carrier touched the ground with any part of his body except his hands or feet while in the grasp of an opponent.

The Baltimore Colts made an 80-cent phone call to Johnny Unitas and signed him as a free agent. Another quarterback, Otto Graham, played his last game as the Browns defeated the Rams 38-14 in the NFL Championship Game, December 26. Graham had quarterbacked the Browns to 10 championship-game appearances in 10 years.

NBC replaced DuMont as the network for the title game, paying a rights fee of $100,000.

1956

The NFL Players Association was founded.

Grabbing an opponent's facemask (other than the ball carrier) was made

illegal. Using radio receivers to communicate with players on the field was prohibited. A natural leather ball with white end stripes replaced the white ball with black stripes for night games.

The Giants moved from the Polo Grounds to Yankee Stadium.

Halas retired as coach of the Bears, and was replaced by Paddy Driscoll.

CBS became the first network to broadcast some NFL regular-season games to selected television markets across the nation.

The Giants routed the Bears 47-7 in the NFL Championship Game, December 30.

1957

Pete Rozelle was named general manager of the Rams. Anthony J. Morabito, founder and co-owner of the 49ers, died of a heart attack during a game against the Bears at Kezar Stadium, October 28. An NFL-record crowd of 102,368 saw the 49ers-Rams game at the Los Angeles Memorial Coliseum, November 10.

The Lions came from 20 points down to post a 31-27 playoff victory over the 49ers, December 22. Detroit defeated Cleveland 59-14 in the NFL Championship Game, December 29.

1958

The bonus selection in the draft was eliminated, January 29. The last selection was quarterback King Hill of Rice by the Chicago Cardinals.

Halas reinstated himself as coach of the Bears.

Jim Brown of Cleveland gained an NFL-record 1,527 yards rushing. In a divisional playoff game, the Giants held Brown to eight yards and defeated Cleveland 10-0.

Baltimore, coached by Weeb Ewbank, defeated the Giants 23-17 in the first sudden-death overtime in an NFL Championship Game, December 28. The game ended when Colts fullback Alan Ameche scored on a one-yard touchdown run after 8:15 of overtime.

1959

Vince Lombardi was named head coach of the Green Bay Packers, January 28. Tim Mara, the co-founder of the Giants, died, February 17.

Lamar Hunt of Dallas announced his intentions to form a second pro football league. The first meeting was held in Chicago, August 14, and consisted of Hunt representing Dallas; Bob Howsam, Denver; K.S. (Bud) Adams, Houston; Barron Hilton, Los Angeles; Max Winter and Bill Boyer, Minneapolis; and Harry Wismer, New York City. They made plans to begin play in 1960.

The new league was named the American Football League, August 22. Buffalo, owned by Ralph Wilson, became the seventh franchise, October 28. Boston, owned by William H. Sullivan, became the eighth team, November 22. The first AFL draft, lasting 33 rounds, was held, November 22. Joe Foss was named AFL Commissioner, November 30. An additional draft of 20 rounds was held by the AFL, December 2.

NFL Commissioner Bert Bell died of a heart attack suffered at Franklin

Field, Philadelphia, during the last two minutes of a game between the Eagles and the Steelers, October 11. Treasurer Austin Gunsel was named president in the office of the commissioner, October 14.

The Colts again defeated the Giants in the NFL Championship Game, 31-16, December 27.

1960

Pete Rozelle was elected NFL Commissioner as a compromise choice on the twenty-third ballot, January 26. Rozelle moved the league offices to New York City.

Hunt was elected AFL president for 1960, January 26. Minneapolis withdrew from the AFL, January 27, and the same ownership was given an NFL franchise for Minnesota (to start in 1961), January 28. Dallas received an NFL franchise for 1960, January 28. Oakland received an AFL franchise, January 30.

The AFL adopted the two-point option on points after touchdown, January 28. A no-tampering verbal pact, relative to players' contracts, was agreed to between the NFL and AFL, February 9.

The NFL owners voted to allow the transfer of the Chicago Cardinals to St. Louis, March 13.

The AFL signed a five-year television contract with ABC, June 9.

The Boston Patriots defeated the Buffalo Bills 28-7 before 16,000 at Buffalo in the first AFL preseason game, July 30. The Denver Broncos defeated the Patriots 13-10 before 21,597 at Boston in the first AFL regular-season game, September 9.

Philadelphia defeated Green Bay 17-13 in the NFL Championship Game, December 26.

1961

The Houston Oilers defeated the Los Angeles Chargers 24-16 before 32,183 in the first AFL Championship Game, January 1.

Detroit defeated Cleveland 17-16 in the first Playoff Bowl, or Bert Bell Benefit Bowl, between second-place teams in each conference in Miami, January 7.

End Willard Dewveall of the Bears played out his option and joined the Oilers, becoming the first player to move deliberately from one league to the other, January 14.

Ed McGah, Wayne Valley, and Robert Osborne bought out their partners in the ownership of the Raiders, January 17. The Chargers were transferred to San Diego, February 10. Dave R. Jones sold the Browns to a group headed by Arthur B. Modell, March 22. The Howsam brothers sold the Broncos to a group headed by Calvin Kunz and Gerry Phipps, May 26.

NBC was awarded a two-year contract for radio and television rights to the NFL Championship Game for $615,000 annually, $300,000 of which was to go directly into the NFL Player Benefit Plan, April 5.

Canton, Ohio, where the league that became the NFL was formed in 1920, was chosen as the site of the Pro Football Hall of Fame, April 27. Dick Mc-

Cann, a former Redskins executive, was named executive director.

A bill legalizing single-network television contracts by professional sports leagues was introduced in Congress by Representative Emanuel Celler. It passed the House and Senate and was signed into law by President John F. Kennedy, September 30.

Houston defeated San Diego 10-3 for the AFL championship, December 24. Green Bay won its first NFL championship since 1944, defeating the New York Giants 37-0, December 31.

1962

The Western Division defeated the Eastern Division 47-27 in the first AFL All-Star Game, played before 20,973 in San Diego, January 7.

Both leagues prohibited grabbing any player's facemask. The AFL voted to make the scoreboard clock the official timer of the game.

The NFL entered into a single-network agreement with CBS for tele-casting all regular-season games for $4.65 million annually, January 10.

Judge Roszel Thompson of the U.S. District Court in Baltimore ruled against the AFL in its antitrust suit against the NFL, May 21. The AFL had charged the NFL with monopoly and conspiracy in areas of expansion, television, and player signings. The case lasted two and a half years, the trial two months.

McGah and Valley acquired controlling interest in the Raiders, May 24. The AFL assumed financial responsibility for the New York Titans, November 8. With Commissioner Rozelle as referee, Daniel F. Reeves regained the ownership of the Rams, outbidding his partners in sealed-envelope bidding for the team, November 27.

The Dallas Texans defeated the Oilers 20-17 for the AFL championship at Houston after 17 minutes, 54 seconds of overtime on a 25-yard field goal by Tommy Brooker, December 23. The game lasted a record 77 minutes, 54 seconds.

Judge Edward Weinfeld of the U.S. District Court in New York City upheld the legality of the NFL's television blackout within a 75-mile radius of home games and denied an injunction that would have forced the championship game between the Giants and the Packers to be televised in the New York City area, December 28. The Packers beat the Giants 16-7 for the NFL title, December 30.

1963

The Dallas Texans transferred to Kansas City, becoming the Chiefs, February 8. The New York Titans were sold to a five-man syndicate headed by David (Sonny) Werblin, March 28. Weeb Ewbank became the Titans' new head coach and the team's name was changed to the Jets, April 15. They began play in Shea Stadium.

NFL Properties, Inc., was founded to serve as the licensing arm of the NFL.

Rozelle indefinitely suspended Green Bay halfback Paul Hornung and Detroit defensive tackle Alex Karras for placing bets on their own teams and on other NFL games; he also fined five

other Detroit players $2,000 each for betting on one game in which they did not participate, and the Detroit Lions Football Company $2,000 on each of two counts for failure to report information promptly and for lack of sideline supervision.

Paul Brown, head coach of the Browns since their inception, was fired and replaced by Blanton Collier. Don Shula replaced Weeb Ewbank as head coach of the Colts.

The AFL allowed the Jets and Raiders to select players from other franchises in hopes of giving the league more competitive balance, May 11.

NBC was awarded exclusive network broadcasting rights for the 1963 AFL Championship Game for $926,000, May 23.

The Pro Football Hall of Fame was dedicated at Canton, Ohio, September 7.

The U.S. Fourth Circuit Court of Appeals reaffirmed the lower court's finding for the NFL in the $10-million suit brought by the AFL, ending three and a half years of litigation, November 21.

Jim Brown of Cleveland rushed for an NFL single-season record 1,863 yards.

Boston defeated Buffalo 26-8 in the first divisional playoff game in AFL history, December 28.

The Bears defeated the Giants 14-10 in the NFL Championship Game, a record sixth and last title for Halas in his thirty-sixth season as the Bears' coach, December 29.

1964

The Chargers defeated the Patriots 51-10 in the AFL Championship Game, January 5.

William Clay Ford, the Lions' president since 1961, purchased the team, January 10. A group representing the late James P. Clark sold the Eagles to a group headed by Jerry Wolman, January 21. Carroll Rosenbloom, the majority owner of the Colts since 1953, acquired complete ownership of the team, January 23.

The AFL signed a five-year, $36-million television contract with NBC to begin with the 1965 season, January 29.

Commissioner Rozelle negotiated an agreement on behalf of the NFL clubs to purchase Ed Sabol's Blair Motion Pictures, which was renamed NFL Films, March 5.

Hornung and Karras were reinstated by Rozelle, March 16.

CBS submitted the winning bid of $14.1 million per year for the NFL regular-season television rights for 1964 and 1965, January 24. CBS acquired the rights to the championship games for 1964 and 1965 for $1.8 million per game, April 17.

Pete Gogolak of Cornell signed a contract with Buffalo, becoming the first soccer-style kicker in pro football.

Buffalo defeated San Diego 20-7 in the AFL Championship Game, December 26. Cleveland defeated Baltimore 27-0 in the NFL Championship Game, December 27.

1965

The NFL teams pledged not to sign

college seniors until completion of all their games, including bowl games, and empowered the Commissioner to discipline the clubs up to as much as the loss of an entire draft list for a violation of the pledge, February 15.

The NFL added a sixth official, the line judge, February 19. The color of the officials' penalty flags was changed from white to bright gold, April 5.

Atlanta was awarded an NFL franchise for 1966, with Rankin Smith, Sr., as owner, June 30. Miami was awarded an AFL franchise for 1966, with Joe Robbie and Danny Thomas as owners, August 16.

Field Judge Burl Toler became the first black official in NFL history, September 19.

According to a Harris survey, sports fans chose professional football (41 percent) as their favorite sport, overtaking baseball (38 percent) for the first time, October.

Green Bay defeated Baltimore 13-10 in sudden-death overtime in a Western Conference playoff game. Don Chandler kicked a 25-yard field goal for the Packers after 13 minutes, 39 seconds of overtime, December 26. The Packers then defeated the Browns 23-12 in the NFL Championship Game, January 2.

In the AFL Championship Game, the Bills again defeated the Chargers, 23-0, December 26.

CBS acquired the rights to the NFL regular-season games in 1966 and 1967, with an option for 1968, for $18.8 million per year, December 29.

1966

The AFL-NFL war reached its peak, as the leagues spent a combined $7 million to sign their 1966 draft choices. The NFL signed 75 percent of its 232 draftees, the AFL 46 percent of its 181. Of the 111 common draft choices, 79 signed with the NFL, 28 with the AFL, and 4 went unsigned.

Buddy Young became the first African-American to work in the league office when Commissioner Rozelle named him director of player relations, February 1.

The rights to the 1966 and 1967 NFL Championship Games were sold to CBS for $2 million per game, February 14.

Foss resigned as AFL Commissioner, April 7. Al Davis, the head coach and general manager of the Raiders, was named to replace him, April 8.

Goal posts offset from the goal line, painted bright yellow, and with uprights 20 feet above the cross-bar were made standard in the NFL, May 16.

A series of secret meetings regarding a possible AFL-NFL merger were held in the spring between Hunt of Kansas City and Tex Schramm of Dallas. Rozelle announced the merger, June 8. Under the agreement, the two leagues would combine to form an expanded league with 24 teams, to be increased to 26 in 1968 and to 28 by 1970 or soon thereafter. All existing franchises would be retained, and no franchises would be transferred outside their metropolitan areas. While maintaining separate schedules

through 1969, the leagues agreed to play an annual AFL-NFL World Championship Game beginning in January, 1967, and to hold a combined draft, also beginning in 1967. Preseason games would be held between teams of each league starting in 1967. Official regular-season play would start in 1970 when the two leagues would officially merge to form one league with two conferences. Rozelle was named Commissioner of the expanded league setup.

Davis rejoined the Raiders, and Milt Woodard was named president of the AFL, July 25.

The St. Louis Cardinals moved into newly constructed Busch Memorial Stadium.

Barron Hilton sold the Chargers to a group headed by Eugene Klein and Sam Schulman, August 25.

Congress approved the AFL-NFL merger, passing legislation exempting the agreement itself from antitrust action, October 21.

New Orleans was awarded an NFL franchise to begin play in 1967, November 1. John Mecom, Jr., of Houston was designated majority stockholder and president of the franchise, December 15.

The NFL was realigned for the 1967-69 seasons into the Capitol and Century Divisions in the Eastern Conference and the Central and Coastal Divisions in the Western Conference, December 2. New Orleans and the New York Giants agreed to switch divisions in 1968 and return to the 1967 alignment in 1969.

The rights to the Super Bowl for four years were sold to CBS and NBC for $9.5 million, December 13.

1967

Green Bay earned the right to represent the NFL in the first AFL-NFL World Championship Game by defeating Dallas 34-27, January 1. The same day, Kansas City defeated Buffalo 31-7 to represent the AFL. The Packers defeated the Chiefs 35-10 before 61,946 fans at the Los Angeles Memorial Coliseum in the first game between AFL and NFL teams, January 15. The winning players' share for the Packers was $15,000 each, and the losing players' share for the Chiefs was $7,500 each. The game was televised by both CBS and NBC.

The "sling-shot" goal post and a six-foot-wide border around the field were made standard in the NFL, February 22.

Baltimore made Bubba Smith, a Michigan State defensive lineman, the first choice in the first combined AFL-NFL draft, March 14.

The AFL awarded a franchise to begin play in 1968 to Cincinnati, May 24. A group with Paul Brown as part owner, general manager, and head coach, was awarded the Cincinnati franchise, September 27.

Arthur B. Modell, the president of the Cleveland Browns, was elected president of the NFL, May 28.

Defensive back Emlen Tunnell of the New York Giants became the first black player to enter the Pro Football Hall of Fame, August 5.

An AFL team defeated an NFL team

for the first time, when Denver beat Detroit 13-7 in a preseason game, August 5.

Green Bay defeated Dallas 21-17 for the NFL championship on a last-minute 1-yard quarterback sneak by Bart Starr in 13-below-zero temperature at Green Bay, December 31. The same day, Oakland defeated Houston 40-7 for the AFL championship.

1968

Green Bay defeated Oakland 33-14 in Super Bowl II at Miami, January 14. The game had the first $3-million gate in pro football history.

Vince Lombardi resigned as head coach of the Packers, but remained as general manager, January 28.

Werblin sold his shares in the Jets to his partners Don Lillis, Leon Hess, Townsend Martin, and Phil Iselin, May 21. Lillis assumed the presidency of the club, but then died July 23. Iselin was appointed president, August 6.

Halas retired for the fourth and last time as head coach of the Bears, May 27.

The Oilers left Rice Stadium for the Astrodome and became the first NFL team to play its home games in a domed stadium.

The movie *Heidi* became a footnote in sports history when NBC didn't show the last 1:05 of the Jets-Raiders game in order to permit the children's special to begin on time. The Raiders scored two touchdowns in the last 42 seconds to win 43-32, November 17.

Ewbank became the first coach to win titles in both the NFL and AFL when his Jets defeated the Raiders 27-23 for the AFL championship, December 29. The same day, Baltimore defeated Cleveland 34-0.

1969

The AFL established a playoff format for the 1969 season, with the winner in one division playing the runner-up in the other, January 11.

An AFL team won the Super Bowl for the first time, as the Jets defeated the Colts 16-7 at Miami, January 12 in Super Bowl III. The title Super Bowl was recognized by the NFL for the first time.

Vince Lombardi became part owner, executive vice-president, and head coach of the Washington Redskins, February 7.

Wolman sold the Eagles to Leonard Tose, May 1.

Baltimore, Cleveland, and Pittsburgh agreed to join the AFL teams to form the 13-team American Football Conference of the NFL in 1970, May 17. The NFL also agreed on a playoff format that would include one "wild-card" team per conference—the second-place team with the best record.

Monday Night Football was signed for 1970. ABC acquired the rights to televise 13 NFL regular-season Monday night games in 1970, 1971, and 1972.

George Preston Marshall, president emeritus of the Redskins, died at 72, August 9.

The NFL marked its fiftieth year by the wearing of a special patch by each of the 16 teams.

1970

Kansas City defeated Minnesota 23-7 in Super Bowl IV at New Orleans, January 11. The gross receipts of approximately $3.8 million were the largest ever for a one-day sports event.

Four-year television contracts, under which CBS would televise all NFC games and NBC all AFC games (except Monday night games) and the two would divide televising the Super Bowl and AFC-NFC Pro Bowl games, were announced, January 26.

Art Modell resigned as president of the NFL, March 12. Milt Woodard resigned as president of the AFL, March 13. Lamar Hunt was elected president of the AFC and George Halas was elected president of the NFC, March 19.

The merged 26-team league adopted rules changes putting names on the backs of players' jerseys, making a point after touchdown worth only one point, and making the scoreboard clock the official timing device of the game, March 18.

The Players Negotiating Committee and the NFL Players Association announced a four-year agreement guaranteeing approximately $4,535,000 annually to player pension and insurance benefits, August 3. The owners also agreed to contribute $250,000 annually to improve or implement items such as disability payments, widows' benefits, maternity benefits, and dental benefits. The agreement also provided for increased preseason game and per diem payments, averaging approximately $2.6 million annually.

The Pittsburgh Steelers moved into Three Rivers Stadium. The Cincinnati Bengals moved into Riverfront Stadium.

Lombardi died of cancer at 57, September 3.

Tom Dempsey of New Orleans kicked a game-winning NFL-record 63-yard field goal against Detroit, November 8.

1971

Baltimore defeated Dallas 16-13 on Jim O'Brien's 32-yard field goal with five seconds to go in Super Bowl V at Miami, January 17. The NBC telecast was viewed in an estimated 23,980,000 homes, the largest audience ever for a one-day sports event.

The NFC defeated the AFC 27-6 in the first AFC-NFC Pro Bowl at Los Angeles, January 24.

The Boston Patriots changed their name to the New England Patriots, March 25. Their new stadium, Schaefer Stadium, was dedicated in a 20-14 preseason victory over the Giants.

The Philadelphia Eagles left Franklin Field and played their games at the new Veterans Stadium.

The San Francisco 49ers left Kezar Stadium and moved their games to Candlestick Park.

Daniel F. Reeves, the president and general manager of the Rams, died at 58, April 15.

The Dallas Cowboys moved from the Cotton Bowl into their new home, Texas Stadium, October 24.

Miami defeated Kansas City 27-24 in sudden-death overtime in an AFC Divisional Playoff Game, December

25. Garo Yepremian kicked a 37-yard field goal for the Dolphins after 22 minutes, 40 seconds of overtime, as the game lasted 82 minutes, 40 seconds overall, making it the longest game in history.

1972

Dallas defeated Miami 24-3 in Super Bowl VI at New Orleans, January 16. The CBS telecast was viewed in an estimated 27,450,000 homes, the top-rated one-day telecast ever.

The inbounds lines or hashmarks were moved nearer the center of the field, 23 yards, 1 foot, 9 inches from the sidelines, March 23. The method of determining won-lost percentage in standings changed. Tie games, previously not counted in the standings, were made equal to a half-game won and a half-game lost, May 24.

Robert Irsay purchased the Los Angeles Rams and transferred ownership of the club to Carroll Rosenbloom in exchange for the Baltimore Colts, July 13.

William V. Bidwill purchased the stock of his brother Charles (Stormy) Bidwill to become the sole owner of the St. Louis Cardinals, September 2.

The National District Attorneys Association endorsed the position of professional leagues in opposing proposed legalization of gambling on professional team sports, September 28.

Franco Harris's "Immaculate Reception" gave the Steelers their first postseason win ever, 13-7 over the Raiders, December 23.

1973

Rozelle announced that all Super Bowl VII tickets were sold and that the game would be telecast in Los Angeles, the site of the game, on an experimental basis, January 3.

Miami defeated Washington 14-7 in Super Bowl VII at Los Angeles, completing a 17-0 season, the first perfect-record regular-season and post-season mark in NFL history, January 14. The NBC telecast was viewed by approximately 75 million people.

The AFC defeated the NFC 33-28 in the Pro Bowl in Dallas, the first time since 1942 that the game was played outside Los Angeles, January 21.

A jersey numbering system was adopted, April 5: 1-19 for quarterbacks and specialists, 20-49 for running backs and defensive backs, 50-59 for centers and linebackers, 60-79 for defensive linemen and interior offensive linemen other than centers, and 80-89 for wide receivers and tight ends. Players who had been in the NFL in 1972 could continue to use old numbers.

NFL Charities, a nonprofit organization, was created to derive an income from monies generated from NFL Properties' licensing of NFL trademarks and team names, June 26. NFL Charities was set up to support education and charitable activities and to supply economic support to persons formerly associated with professional football who were no longer able to support themselves.

Congress adopted experimental legislation (for three years) requiring

any NFL game that had been declared a sellout 72 hours prior to kickoff to be made available for local televising, September 14. The legislation provided for an annual review to be made by the Federal Communications Commission.

The Buffalo Bills moved their home games from War Memorial Stadium to Rich Stadium in nearby Orchard Park. The Giants tied the Eagles 23-23 in the final game in Yankee Stadium, September 23. The Giants played the rest of their home games at the Yale Bowl in New Haven, Connecticut.

A rival league, the World Football League, was formed and was reported in operation, October 2. It had plans to start play in 1974.

O.J. Simpson of Buffalo became the first player to rush for more than 2,000 yards in a season, gaining 2,003.

1974

Miami defeated Minnesota 24-7 in Super Bowl VIII at Houston, the second consecutive Super Bowl championship for the Dolphins, January 13. The CBS telecast was viewed by approximately 75 million people.

Rozelle was given a 10-year contract effective January 1, 1973, February 27.

Tampa Bay was awarded a franchise to begin operation in 1976, April 24.

Sweeping rules changes were adopted to add action and tempo to games: one sudden-death overtime period was added for preseason and regular-season games; the goal posts were moved from the goal line to the end lines; kickoffs were moved from the 40- to the 35-yard line; after missed field goals from beyond the 20, the ball was to be returned to the line of scrimmage; restrictions were placed on members of the punting team to open up return possibilities; roll-blocking and cutting of wide receivers was eliminated; the extent of downfield contact a defender could have with an eligible receiver was restricted; the penalties for offensive holding, illegal use of the hands, and tripping were reduced from 15 to 10 yards; wide receivers blocking back toward the ball within three yards of the line of scrimmage were prevented from blocking below the waist, April 25.

The Toronto Northmen of the WFL signed Larry Csonka, Jim Kiick, and Paul Warfield of Miami, March 31.

Seattle was awarded an NFL franchise to begin play in 1976, June 4. Lloyd W. Nordstrom, president of the Seattle Seahawks, and Hugh Culverhouse, president of the Tampa Bay Buccaneers, signed franchise agreements, December 5.

The Birmingham Americans defeated the Florida Blazers 22-21 in the WFL World Bowl, winning the league championship, December 5.

1975

Pittsburgh defeated Minnesota 16-6 in Super Bowl IX at New Orleans, the Steelers' first championship since entering the NFL in 1933. The NBC telecast was viewed by approximately

78 million people.

The divisional winners with the highest won-loss percentage were made the home team for the divisional playoffs, and the surviving winners with the highest percentage made home teams for the championship games, June 26.

Referees were equipped with wireless microphones for all preseason, regular-season, and playoff games.

The Lions moved to the new Pontiac Silverdome. The Giants played their home games in Shea Stadium. The Saints moved into the Louisiana Superdome.

The World Football League folded, October 22.

1976

Pittsburgh defeated Dallas 21-17 in Super Bowl X in Miami. The Steelers joined Green Bay and Miami as the only teams to win two Super Bowls; the Cowboys became the first wild-card team to play in the Super Bowl. The CBS telecast was viewed by an estimated 80 million people, the largest television audience in history.

Lloyd Nordstrom, the president of the Seahawks, died at 66, January 20. His brother Elmer succeeded him as majority representative of the team.

The owners awarded Super Bowl XII, to be played on January 15, 1978, to New Orleans. They also adopted the use of two 30-second clocks for all games, visible to both players and fans to note the official time between the ready-for-play signal and snap of the ball, March 16.

A veteran player allocation was held to stock the Seattle and Tampa Bay franchises with 39 players each, March 30-31. In the college draft, Seattle and Tampa Bay each received eight extra choices, April 8-9.

The Giants moved into new Giants Stadium in East Rutherford, New Jersey.

The Steelers defeated the College All-Stars in a storm-shortened Chicago College All-Star Game, the last of the series, July 23. St. Louis defeated San Diego 20-10 in a preseason game before 38,000 in Korakuen Stadium, Tokyo, in the first NFL game outside of North America, August 16.

1977

Oakland defeated Minnesota 32-14 in Super Bowl XI at Pasadena, January 9. The paid attendance was a pro record 103,438. The NBC telecast was viewed by 81.9 million people, the largest ever to view a sports event. The victory was the fifth consecutive for the AFC in the Super Bowl.

The NFL Players Association and the NFL Management Council ratified a collective bargaining agreement extending until 1982, covering five football seasons while continuing the pension plan—including years 1974, 1975, and 1976—with contributions totaling more than $55 million. The total cost of the agreement was estimated at $107 million. The agreement called for a college draft at least through 1986; contained a no-strike, no-suit clause; established a 43-man active player limit; reduced pension vesting to four years; provided for in-

creases in minimum salaries and preseason and postseason pay; improved insurance, medical, and dental benefits; modified previous practices in player movement and control; and reaffirmed the NFL Commissioner's disciplinary authority. Additionally, the agreement called for the NFL member clubs to make payments totaling $16 million the next 10 years to settle various legal disputes, February 25.

The San Francisco 49ers were sold to Edward J. DeBartolo, Jr., March 28.

A 16-game regular season, 4-game preseason was adopted to begin in 1978, March 29. A second wild-card team was adopted for the playoffs beginning in 1978, with the wild-card teams to play each other and the winners advancing to a round of eight postseason series.

The Seahawks were permanently aligned in the AFC Western Division and the Buccaneers in the NFC Central Division, March 31.

The owners awarded Super Bowl XIII, to be played on January 21, 1979, to Miami, to be played in the Orange Bowl; Super Bowl XIV, to be played January 20, 1980, was awarded to Pasadena, to be played in the Rose Bowl, June 14.

Rules changes were adopted to open up the passing game and to cut down on injuries. Defenders were permitted to make contact with eligible receivers only once; the head slap was outlawed; offensive linemen were prohibited from thrusting their hands to an opponent's neck, face, or head; and wide receivers were prohibited from clipping, even in the legal clipping zone.

Rozelle negotiated contracts with the three television networks to televise all NFL regular-season and postseason games, plus selected preseason games, for four years beginning with the 1978 season. ABC was awarded yearly rights to 16 Monday night games, four prime-time games, the AFC-NFC Pro Bowl, and the Hall of Fame games. CBS received the rights to all NFC regular-season and postseason games (except those in the ABC package) and to Super Bowls XIV and XVI. NBC received the rights to all AFC regular-season and postseason games (except those in the ABC package) and to Super Bowls XIII and XV. Industry sources considered it the largest single television package ever negotiated, October 12.

Chicago's Walter Payton set a single-game rushing record with 275 yards (40 carries) against Minnesota, November 20.

1978

Dallas defeated Denver 27-10 in Super Bowl XII, held indoors for the first time, at the Louisiana Superdome in New Orleans, January 15. The CBS telecast was viewed by more than 102 million people, meaning the game was watched by more viewers than any other show of any kind in the history of television. Dallas's victory was the first for the NFC in six years.

According to a Louis Harris Sports Survey, 70 percent of the nation's sports fans said they followed football, compared to 54 percent who followed

baseball. Football increased its lead as the country's favorite, 26 percent to 16 percent for baseball, January 19.

A seventh official, the side judge, was added to the officiating crew, March 14.

The NFL continued a trend toward opening up the game. Rules changes permitted a defender to maintain contact with a receiver within five yards of the line of scrimmage, but restricted contact beyond that point. The pass-blocking rule was interpreted to permit the extending of arms and open hands, March 17.

A study on the use of instant replay as an officiating aid was made during seven nationally televised preseason games.

The NFL played for the first time in Mexico City, with the Saints defeating the Eagles 14-7 in a preseason game, August 5.

Bolstered by the expansion of the regular-season schedule from 14 to 16 weeks, NFL paid attendance exceeded 12 million (12,771,800) for the first time. The per-game average of 57,017 was the third-highest in league history and the most since 1973.

1979

Pittsburgh defeated Dallas 35-31 in Super Bowl XIII at Miami to become the first team ever to win three Super Bowls, January 21. The NBC telecast was viewed in 35,090,000 homes, by an estimated 96.6 million fans.

The owners awarded three future Super Bowl sites: Super Bowl XV to the Louisiana Superdome in New Orleans, to be played on January 25, 1981; Super Bowl XVI to the Pontiac Silverdome in Pontiac, Michigan, to be played on January 24, 1982; and Super Bowl XVII to Pasadena's Rose Bowl, to be played on January 30, 1983, March 13.

NFL rules changes emphasized additional player safety. The changes prohibited players on the receiving team from blocking below the waist during kickoffs, punts, and field-goal attempts; prohibited the wearing of torn or altered equipment and exposed pads that could be hazardous; extended the zone in which there could be no crackback blocks; and instructed officials to quickly whistle a play dead when a quarterback was clearly in the grasp of a tackler, March 16.

Rosenbloom, the president of the Rams, drowned at 72, April 2. His widow, Georgia, assumed control of the club.

1980

Pittsburgh defeated the Los Angeles Rams 31-19 in Super Bowl XIV at Pasadena to become the first team to win four Super Bowls, January 20. The game was viewed in a record 35,330,000 homes.

The AFC-NFC Pro Bowl, won 37-27 by the NFC, was played before 48,060 fans at Aloha Stadium in Honolulu, Hawaii. It was the first time in the 30-year history of the Pro Bowl that the game was played in a non-NFL city.

Rules changes placed greater restrictions on contact in the area of the head, neck, and face. Under the head-

ing of "personal foul," players were prohibited from directly striking, swinging, or clubbing on the head, neck, or face. Starting in 1980, a penalty could be called for such contact whether or not the initial contact was made below the neck area.

CBS, with a record bid of $12 million, won the national radio rights to 26 NFL regular-season games, including Monday Night Football, and all 10 postseason games for the 1980-83 seasons.

The Los Angeles Rams moved their home games to Anaheim Stadium in nearby Orange County, California.

The Oakland Raiders joined the Los Angeles Coliseum Commission's antitrust suit against the NFL. The suit contended the league violated antitrust laws in declining to approve a proposed move by the Raiders from Oakland to Los Angeles.

NFL regular-season attendance of nearly 13.4 million set a record for the third year in a row. The average paid attendance for the 224-game 1980 regular season was 59,787, the highest in the league's 61-year history. NFL games in 1980 were played before 92.4 percent of total stadium capacity.

Television ratings in 1980 were the second-best in NFL history, trailing only the combined ratings of the 1976 season. All three networks posted gains, and NBC's 15.0 rating was its best ever. CBS and ABC had their best ratings since 1977, with 15.3 and 20.8 ratings, respectively. CBS Radio reported a record audience of 7 million for Monday night and special games.

1981

Oakland defeated Philadelphia 27-10 in Super Bowl XV at the Louisiana Superdome in New Orleans, to become the first wild-card team to win a Super Bowl, January 25.

Edgar F. Kaiser, Jr., purchased the Denver Broncos from Gerald and Allan Phipps, February 26.

The owners adopted a disaster plan for re-stocking a team should the club be involved in a fatal accident, March 20.

The owners awarded Super Bowl XVIII to Tampa, to be played in Tampa Stadium on January 22, 1984, June 3.

A CBS-New York Times poll showed that 48 percent of sports fans preferred football to 31 percent for baseball.

The NFL teams hosted 167 representatives from 44 predominantly black colleges during training camps for a total of 289 days. The program was adopted for renewal during each training camp period.

NFL regular-season attendance— 13.6 million for an average of 60,745— set a record for the fourth year in a row. It also was the first time the per-game average exceeded 60,000. NFL games in 1981 were played before 93.8 percent of total stadium capacity.

ABC and CBS set all-time rating highs. ABC finished with a 21.7 rating and CBS with a 17.5 rating. NBC was down slightly to 13.9.

1982

San Francisco defeated Cincinnati 26-21 in Super Bowl XVI at the Pontiac

Silverdome, in the first Super Bowl held in the North, January 24. The CBS telecast achieved the highest rating of any televised sports event ever, 49.1 with a 73.0 share. The game was viewed by a record 110.2 million fans. CBS Radio reported a record 14 million listeners for the game.

The NFL signed a five-year contract with the three television networks (ABC, CBS, and NBC) to televise all NFL regular-season and postseason games starting with the 1982 season.

The owners awarded the 1983, 1984, and 1985 AFC-NFC Pro Bowls to Honolulu's Aloha Stadium.

A jury ruled against the NFL in the antitrust trial brought by the Los Angeles Coliseum Commission and the Oakland Raiders, May 7. The verdict cleared the way for the Raiders to move to Los Angeles, where they defeated Green Bay 24-3 in their first preseason game, August 29.

The 1982 season was reduced from a 16-game schedule to nine as the result of a 57-day players' strike. The strike was called by the NFLPA at midnight on Monday, September 20, following the Green Bay at New York Giants game. Play resumed November 21-22 following ratification of the Collective Bargaining Agreement by NFL owners, November 17 in New York.

Under the Collective Bargaining Agreement, which was to run through the 1986 season, the NFL draft was extended through 1992 and the veteran free-agent system was left basically unchanged. A minimum salary schedule for years of experience was established; training camp and postseason pay were increased; players' medical, insurance, and retirement benefits were increased; and a severance-pay system was introduced to aid in career transition, a first in professional sports.

Despite the players' strike, the average paid attendance in 1982 was 58,472, the fifth-highest in league history.

The owners awarded the sites of two Super Bowls, December 14: Super Bowl XIX, to be played on January 20, 1985, to Stanford University Stadium in Stanford, California, with San Francisco as host team; and Super Bowl XX, to be played on January 26, 1986, to the Louisiana Superdome in New Orleans.

1983

Because of the shortened season, the NFL adopted a format of 16 teams competing in a Super Bowl Tournament for the 1982 playoffs. The NFC's number-one seed, Washington, defeated the AFC's number-two seed, Miami, 27-17 in Super Bowl XVII at the Rose Bowl in Pasadena, January 30.

Super Bowl XVII was the second-highest rated live television program of all time, giving the NFL a sweep of the top 10 live programs in television history. The game was viewed in more than 40 million homes, the largest ever for a live telecast.

Halas, the owner of the Bears and the last surviving member of the NFL's second organizational meeting, died at 88, October 31.

1984

The Los Angeles Raiders defeated Washington 38-9 in Super Bowl XVIII at Tampa Stadium, January 22. The game achieved a 46.4 rating and 71.0 share.

An 11-man group headed by H.R. (Bum) Bright purchased the Dallas Cowboys from Clint Murchison, Jr., March 20. Club president Tex Schramm was designated as managing general partner.

Patrick Bowlen purchased a majority interest in the Denver Broncos from Edgar Kaiser, Jr., March 21.

The Colts relocated to Indianapolis, March 28. Their new home became the Hoosier Dome.

The owners awarded two Super Bowl sites at their May 23-25 meetings: Super Bowl XXI, to be played on January 25, 1987, to the Rose Bowl in Pasadena; and Super Bowl XXII, to be played on January 31, 1988, to San Diego Jack Murphy Stadium.

The New York Jets moved their home games to Giants Stadium in East Rutherford, New Jersey.

Alex G. Spanos purchased a majority interest in the San Diego Chargers from Eugene V. Klein, August 28.

Houston defeated Pittsburgh 23-20 to mark the one-hundredth overtime game in regular-season play since overtime was adopted in 1974, December 2.

On the field, many all-time records were set: Dan Marino of Miami passed for 5,084 yards and 48 touchdowns; Eric Dickerson of the Los Angeles Rams rushed for 2,105 yards; Art Monk of Washington caught 106 passes; and Walter Payton of Chicago broke Jim Brown's career rushing mark, finishing the season with 13,309 yards.

According to a CBS Sports/New York Times survey, 53 percent of the nation's sports fans said they most enjoyed watching football, compared to 18 percent for baseball, December 2-4.

NFL paid attendance exceeded 13 million for the fifth consecutive complete regular season with 13,398,112, an average of 59,813, attended games. The figure was the second-highest in league history. Teams averaged 42.4 points per game, the second-highest total since the 1970 merger.

1985

San Francisco defeated Miami 38-16 in Super Bowl XIX at Stanford Stadium in Stanford, California, January 20. The game was viewed on television by more people than any other live event in history. President Ronald Reagan, who took his second oath of office before tossing the coin for the game, was one of 115,936,000 viewers. The game drew a 46.4 rating and a 63.0 share. In addition, 6 million people watched the Super Bowl in the United Kingdom and a similar number in Italy. Super Bowl XIX had a direct economic impact of $113.5 million on the San Francisco Bay area.

NBC Radio and the NFL entered into a two-year agreement granting NBC the radio rights to a 37-game package in each of the 1985-86 sea-

sons, March 6. The package included 27 regular-season games and 10 post-season games.

The owners awarded two Super Bowl sites at their annual meeting, March 10-15: Super Bowl XXIII, to be played on January 22, 1989, to the proposed Dolphins Stadium in Miami; and Super Bowl XXIV, to be played on January 28, 1990, to the Louisiana Superdome in New Orleans.

Norman Braman, in partnership with Edward Leibowitz, bought the Philadelphia Eagles from Leonard Tose, April 29.

Bruce Smith, a Virginia Tech defensive lineman selected by Buffalo, was the first player chosen in the fiftieth NFL draft, April 30.

A group headed by Tom Benson, Jr., was approved to purchase the New Orleans Saints from John W. Mecom, Jr., June 3.

The NFL owners adopted a resolution calling for a series of overseas preseason games, beginning in 1986, with one game to be played in England/Europe and/or one game in Japan each year. The game would be a fifth preseason game for the clubs involved and all arrangements and selection of the clubs would be under the control of the Commissioner, May 23.

The league-wide conversion to videotape from movie film for coaching study was approved.

Commissioner Rozelle was authorized to extend the commitment to Honolulu's Aloha Stadium for the AFC-NFC Pro Bowl for 1988, 1989, and 1990, October 15.

The NFL set a single-weekend paid attendance record when 902,657 tickets were sold for the weekend of October 27-28.

A Louis Harris poll in December revealed that pro football remained the sport most followed by Americans. Fifty-nine percent of those surveyed followed pro football, compared with 54 percent who followed baseball.

The Chicago-Miami Monday game had the highest rating, 29.6, and share, 46.0, of any prime-time game in NFL history, December 2. The game was viewed in more than 25 million homes.

The NFL showed a ratings increase on all three networks for the season, gaining 4 percent on NBC, 10 on CBS, and 16 on ABC.

1986

Chicago defeated New England 46-10 in Super Bowl XX at the Louisiana Superdome, January 26. The Patriots had earned the right to play the Bears by becoming the first wild-card team to win three consecutive games on the road. The NBC telecast replaced the final episode of M*A*S*H as the most-viewed television program in history, with an audience of 127 million viewers, according to A.C. Nielsen figures. In addition to drawing a 48.3 rating and a 70 percent share in the United States, Super Bowl XX was televised to 59 foreign countries and beamed via satellite to the QE II. An estimated 300 million Chinese viewed a tape delay of the game in March. NBC Radio figures indicated an audience of 10 million for the game.

Super Bowl XX injected more than $100 million into the New Orleans-area economy, and fans spent $250 per day and a record $17.69 per person on game day.

The owners adopted limited use of instant replay as an officiating aid, prohibited players from wearing or otherwise displaying equipment, apparel, or other items that carry commercial names, names of organizations, or personal messages of any type, March 11.

After an 11-week trial, a jury in U.S. District Court in New York awarded the United States Football League one dollar in its $1.7 billion antitrust suit against the NFL. The jury rejected all of the USFL's television-related claims, which were the self-proclaimed heart of the USFL's case, July 29.

Chicago defeated Dallas 17-6 at Wembley Stadium in London in the first American Bowl. The game drew a sellout crowd of 82,699 and the NBC national telecast in this country produced a 12.4 rating and 36 percent share, making it the second-highest-rated daytime preseason game and highest daytime preseason television audience ever with 10.65-million viewers, August 3.

Monday Night Football became the longest-running prime-time series in the history of the ABC network.

Instant replay was used to reverse two plays in 31 preseason games. During the regular season, 374 plays were closely reviewed by replay officials, leading to 38 reversals in 224 games. Eighteen plays were closely reviewed by instant replay in 10 post-season games with three reversals.

1987
The New York Giants defeated Denver 39-20 in Super Bowl XXI and captured their first NFL title since 1956. The game, played in Pasadena's Rose Bowl, drew a sellout crowd of 101,063. According to A.C. Nielsen figures, the CBS broadcast of the game was viewed in the U.S. on television by 122.64-million people, making the telecast the second most-watched television show of all-time behind Super Bowl XX. The game was watched live or on tape in 55 foreign countries and NBC Radio's broadcast of the game was heard by a record 10.1 million people.

The NFL set an all-time paid attendance mark of 17,304,463 for all games, including preseason, regular-season, and postseason. Average regular-season game attendance (60,663) exceeded the 60,000 figure for only the second time in league history.

New three-year TV contracts with ABC, CBS, and NBC were announced for 1987-89 at the NFL annual meeting in Maui, Hawaii, March 15. Commissioner Rozelle and Broadcast Committee Chairman Art Modell also announced a three-year contract with ESPN to televise 13 prime-time games each season. The ESPN contract was the first with a cable network. However, NFL games on ESPN also were scheduled for regular television in the city of the visiting team and in the home city if the game was sold out 72

hours in advance.

Owners also voted to continue in effect for one year the instant replay system used during the 1986 season.

A special payment program was adopted to benefit nearly 1,000 former NFL players who participated in the League before the current Bert Bell NFL Pension Plan was created and made retroactive to the 1959 season. Players covered by the new program spent at least five years in the League and played all or part of their career prior to 1959. Each vested player would receive $60 per month for each year of service in the League for life.

Possible sites for Super Bowl XXV were reduced to five locations by the NFL Super Bowl XXV Site Selection Committee: Anaheim Stadium, Los Angeles Memorial Coliseum, Joe Robbie Stadium, San Diego Jack Murphy Stadium, and Tampa Stadium.

NFL and CBS Radio jointly announced agreement granting CBS the radio rights to a 40-game package in each of the next three NFL seasons, 1987-89, April 7.

NFL owners awarded Super Bowl XXV, to be played on January 27, 1991, to Tampa Stadium, May 20.

Over 400 former NFL players from the pre-1959 era received first payments from NFL owners, July 1.

The NFL's debut on ESPN produced the two highest-rated and most-watched sports programs in basic cable history. The Chicago at Miami game on August 16 drew an 8.9 rating in 3.81 million homes. Those records fell two weeks later when the Los Angeles Raiders at Dallas game achieved a 10.2 cable rating in 4.36 million homes.

Fifty-eight preseason games drew a record paid attendance of 3,116,870.

The 1987 season was reduced from a 16-game season to 15 as the result of a 24-day players' strike. The strike was called by the NFLPA on Tuesday, September 22, following the New England at New York Jets game. Games scheduled for the third weekend were canceled but the games of weeks four, five, and six were played with replacement teams. Striking players returned for the seventh week of the season, October 25.

In a three-team deal involving 10 players and/or draft choices, the Los Angeles Rams traded running back Eric Dickerson to the Indianapolis Colts for six draft choices and two players. Buffalo obtained the rights to linebacker Cornelius Bennett from Indianapolis, sending Greg Bell and three draft choices to the Rams. The Colts added Owen Gill and three draft choices of their own to complete the deal with the Rams, October 31.

The Chicago at Minnesota game became the highest-rated and most-watched sports program in basic cable history when it drew a 14.4 cable rating in 6.5 million homes, December 6.

Instant replay was used to reverse eight plays in 52 preseason games. During the strike-shortened 210-game regular season, 490 plays were closely reviewed by replay officials, leading to 57 reversals. Eighteen plays were closely reviewed by instant replay in

10 postseason games, with three reversals.

1988
Washington defeated Denver 42-10 in Super Bowl XXII to earn its second victory this decade in the NFL Championship Game. The game, played for the first time in San Diego Jack Murphy Stadium, drew a sellout crowd of 73,302. According to A.C. Nielsen figures, the ABC broadcast of the game was viewed in the U.S. on television by 115,000,000 people. The game was seen live or on tape in 60 foreign countries, including the People's Republic of China, and CBS's radio broadcast of the game was heard by 13.7 million people.

A total of 811 players shared in the postseason pool of $16.9 million, the most ever distributed in a single season.

In a unanimous 3-0 decision, the 2nd Circuit Court of Appeals in New York upheld the verdict of the jury that in July, 1986, had awarded the United States Football League one dollar in its $1.7 billion antitrust suit against the NFL. In a 91-page opinion, Judge Ralph K. Winter said the USFL sought through court decree the success it failed to gain among football fans, March 10.

By a 23-5 margin, owners voted to continue the instant replay system for the third consecutive season with the Instant Replay Official to be assigned to a regular seven-man, on-the-field crew. At the NFL annual meeting in Phoenix, Arizona, a 45-second clock was also approved to replace the 30-second clock. For a normal sequence of plays, the interval between plays was changed to 45 seconds from the time the ball is signaled dead until it is snapped on the succeeding play.

NFL owners approved the transfer of the Cardinals' franchise from St. Louis to Phoenix; approved two supplemental drafts each year—one prior to training camp and one prior to the regular season; and voted to initiate an annual series of games in Japan/Asia as early as the 1989 preseason, March 14-18.

The NFL Annual Selection Meeting returned to a separate two-day format and for the first time originated on a Sunday. ESPN drew a 3.6 rating during their seven-hour coverage of the draft, which was viewed in 1.6 million homes, April 24-25.

Art Rooney, founder and owner of the Steelers, died at 87, August 25.

Johnny Grier became the first African-American referee in NFL history, September 4.

Paid and average attendance of 934,271 and 66,734 at 14 games on October 16-17 set single weekend records.

Commissioner Rozelle announced that two teams would play a preseason game as part of the American Bowl series on August 6, 1989, in the Korakuen Tokyo Dome in Japan, December 16.

NFL regular-season paid attendance of 13,535,335 and the average of 60,427 was the third highest all-time. Buffalo set an NFL team single-

season, in-house attendance mark of 622,793.

1989
San Francisco defeated Cincinnati 20-16 in Super Bowl XXIII. The game, played for the first time at Joe Robbie Stadium in Miami, was attended by a sellout crowd of 75,129. NBC's telecast of the game was watched by an estimated 110,780,000 viewers, according to A.C. Nielsen, making it the sixth most-watched program in television history. The game was seen live or on tape in 60 foreign countries, including an estimated 300 million in China. The CBS Radio broadcast of the game was heard by 11.2 million people.

Commissioner Rozelle announced his retirement, pending the naming of a successor, March 22 at the NFL annual meeting in Palm Desert, California.

Following the announcement, AFC president Lamar Hunt and NFC president Wellington Mara announced the formation of a six-man search committee composed of Art Modell, Robert Parins, Dan Rooney, and Ralph Wilson. Hunt and Mara served as co-chairmen.

By a 24-4 margin, owners voted to continue the instant replay system for the fourth straight season. A strengthened policy regarding anabolic steroids and masking agents was announced by Commissioner Rozelle. NFL clubs called for strong disciplinary measures in cases of feigned injuries and adopted a joint proposal by the Long-Range Planning and Finance committees regarding player personnel rules, March 19-23.

Two hundred twenty-nine unconditional free agents signed with new teams under management's Plan B system, April 1.

Jerry Jones purchased a majority interest in the Dallas Cowboys from H.R. (Bum) Bright, April 18.

Tex Schramm was named president of the new World League of American Football to work with a six-man committee of Dan Rooney, chairman; Norman Braman, Lamar Hunt, Victor Kiam, Mike Lynn, and Bill Walsh, April 18.

NFL and CBS Radio jointly announced agreement extending CBS's radio rights to an annual 40-game package through the 1994 season, April 18.

NFL owners awarded Super Bowl XXVI, to be played on January 26, 1992, to Minneapolis, May 24.

As of opening day, September 10, of the 229 Plan B free agents, 111 were active and 23 others were on teams' reserve lists. Ninety-two others were waived and three retired.

Art Shell was named head coach of the Los Angeles Raiders making him the NFL's first black head coach since Fritz Pollard coached the Akron Pros in 1921, October 3.

The site of the New England Patriots at San Francisco 49ers game scheduled for Candlestick Park on October 22 was switched to Stanford Stadium in the aftermath of the Bay Area Earthquake of October 17. The change was announced on October 19.

Paul Tagliabue became the seventh

chief executive of the NFL on October 26 when he was chosen to succeed Commissioner Pete Rozelle on the sixth ballot of a three-day meeting in Cleveland, Ohio.

In all, 12 ballots were required to select Tagliabue. Two were conducted at a meeting in Chicago on July 6, and four at a meeting in Dallas on October 10-11. On the twelfth ballot, with Seattle absent, Tagliabue received more than the 19 affirmative votes required for election from among the 27 clubs present.

The transfer from Commissioner Rozelle to Commissioner Tagliabue took place at 12:01 A.M. on Sunday, November 5.

NFL Charities donated $1 million through United Way to benefit Bay Area earthquake victims, November 6.

NFL paid attendance of 17,399,538 was the highest total in league history. This included a total of 13,625,662 for an average of 60,829—both NFL records—for the 224-game regular season.

1990
San Francisco defeated Denver 55-10 in Super Bowl XXIV at the Louisiana Superdome, January 28. San Francisco joined Pittsburgh as the NFL's only teams to win four Super Bowls.

The NFL announced revisions in its 1990 draft eligibility rules. College juniors became eligible but must renounce their collegiate football eligibility before applying for the NFL Draft, February 16.

Commissioner Tagliabue announced NFL teams will play their 16-game schedule over 17 weeks in 1990 and 1991 and 16 games over 18 weeks in 1992 and 1993, February 27.

The NFL revised its playoff format to include two additional wild-card teams (one per conference).

Commissioner Tagliabue and Broadcast Committee Chairman Art Modell announced a four-year contract with Turner Broadcasting to televise nine Sunday-night games.

New four-year TV agreements were ratified for 1990-93 for ABC, CBS, NBC, ESPN, and TNT at the NFL annual meeting in Orlando, Florida, March 12. The contracts totaled $3.6 billion, the largest in TV history.

The NFL announced plans to expand its American Bowl series of preseason games. In addition to games in London and Tokyo, American Bowl games were scheduled for Berlin, Germany, and Montreal, Canada, in 1990.

For the fifth straight year, NFL owners voted to continue a limited system of Instant Replay. Beginning in 1990, the replay official will have a two-minute time limit to make a decision. The vote was 21-7, March 12.

Commissioner Tagliabue announced the formation of a Committee on Expansion and Realignment, March 13. He also named a Player Advisory Council, comprised of 12 former NFL players, March 14.

One-hundred eighty-four Plan B unconditional free agents signed with new teams, April 2.

Commissioner Tagliabue appointed Dr. John Lombardo as the League's Drug Advisor for Anabolic Steroids,

April 25 and named Dr. Lawrence Brown as the League's Advisor for Drugs of Abuse, May 17.

NFL owners awarded Super Bowl XXVIII, to be played in 1994, to the proposed Georgia Dome, May 23.

Commissioner Tagliabue named NFL referee Jerry Seeman as NFL Director of Officiating, replacing Art McNally, who announced his retirement after 31 years on the field and at the league office, July 12.

NFL International Week was celebrated with four preseason games in seven days in Tokyo, London, Berlin, and Montreal. More than 200,000 fans on three continents attended the four games, August 4-11.

Commissioner Tagliabue announced the NFL Teacher of the Month program in which the League furnishes grants and scholarships in recognition of teachers who provided a positive influence upon NFL players in elementary and secondary schools, September 20.

For the first time since 1957, every NFL club won at least one of its first four games, October 1.

NFL total paid attendance of 17,665,671 was the highest total in League history. The regular-season total paid attendance of 13,959,896 and average of 62,321 for 224 games were the highest ever, surpassing the previous records set in the 1989 season.

1991
The New York Giants defeated Buffalo 20-19 in Super Bowl XXV to capture their second title in five years. The game was played before a sellout crowd of 73,813 at Tampa Stadium and became the first Super Bowl decided by one point, January 26. The ABC broadcast of the game was seen by more than 112-million people in the United States and was seen live or taped in 60 other countries.

NFL playoff games earned the top television rating spot of the week for each week of the month-long playoffs, January 29.

A total of 693 players shared in the postseason pool of $14.9 million.

New York businessman Robert Tisch purchased a 50 percent interest in the New York Giants from Mrs. Helen Mara Nugent and her children, Tim Mara and Maura Mara Concannon, February 2.

Commissioner Tagliabue named Neil Austrian to the newly created position of President of the NFL to be chief operating officer for League-wide business and financial operations, February 27.

NFL clubs voted to continue a limited system of Instant Replay for the sixth consecutive year. The vote was 21-7, March 19.

The NFL launched the World League of American Football, the first sports league to operate on a weekly basis on two separate continents, March 23.

NFL Charities presented a $250,000 donation to the United Service Organization. The donation was the second largest single grant ever by NFL Charities, April 5.

Commissioner Tagliabue named Harold Henderson as Executive Vice

President for Labor Relations and Chairman of the NFL Management Council Executive Committee, April 8.

Russell Maryland, a University of Miami defensive lineman, was selected by Dallas, becoming the first player chosen in the 1991 NFL draft, April 21.

NFL clubs approved a recommendation by the Expansion and Realignment Committee to add two teams for the 1994 season, resulting in six divisions of five teams each, May 22.

NFL clubs awarded Super Bowl XXIX, to be played on January 29, 1995, to Miami, May 23.

"NFL International Week" featured six 1990 playoff teams playing nationally televised games in London, Berlin, and Tokyo on July 28 and August 3-4. The games drew more than 150,000 fans.

Paul Brown, founder of the Cleveland Browns and Cincinnati Bengals, died at age 82, August 5.

NFL clubs approved a resolution establishing an international division, reporting to the President of the NFL. A three-year financial plan for the World League was approved by NFL clubs at a meeting in Dallas, October 23.

1992
The NFL agreed to provide a minimum of $2.5 million in financial support to the NFL Alumni Association and assistance to NFL Alumni-related programs. The agreement included contributions from NFL Charities to the Pre-59ers and Dire Need Programs for former players, January 25.

The Washington Redskins defeated the Buffalo Bills 37-24 in Super Bowl XXVI to capture their third world championship in 10 years, January 26. The game was played before a sellout crowd of 63,130 at the Hubert H. Humphrey Metrodome in Minneapolis and attracted the second largest television audience in Super Bowl history. The CBS broadcast was seen by more than 123 million people nationally, second only to the 127 million who viewed Super Bowl XX.

For the third consecutive season, NFL total paid attendance reached a record level. Total paid attendance was 17,752,139 for the 296 preseason, regular-season, and postseason games, February 3.

The use in officiating of a limited system of Instant Replay for a seventh consecutive year was not approved. The vote was 17-11 in favor of approval (21 votes were required), March 18.

Steve Emtman, a University of Washington defensive lineman, was selected by Indianapolis, becoming the first player chosen in the 1992 NFL draft, April 26.

St. Louis businessman James Orthwein purchased controlling interest in the New England Patriots from Victor Kiam, May 11.

In a Harris Poll taken during the NFL offseason, professional football again was declared the nation's most popular sport. Professional football finished atop similar surveys conducted by Harris in 1985 and 1989, May 23.

NFL clubs accepted the report of the Expansion Committee at a league meeting in Pasadena. The report

names five cities as finalists for the two expansion teams—Baltimore, Charlotte, Jacksonville, Memphis, and St. Louis, May 19.

At a league meeting in Dallas, NFL clubs approved a proposal by the World League Board of Directors to restructure the World League and place future emphasis on its international success, September 17.

1993
The NFL and lawyers for the players announced a settlement of various lawsuits and an agreement on the terms of a seven-year deal that included a new player system to be in place through the 1999 season, January 6.

Commissioner Tagliabue announced the establishment of the "NFL World Partnership Program" to develop amateur football internationally through a series of clinics conducted by former NFL players and coaches, January 14.

As part of Super Bowl XXVII, the NFL announced the creation of the first NFL Youth Education Town, a facility located in south central Los Angeles for inner city youth. January 25.

The Dallas Cowboys defeated the Buffalo Bills 52-17 in Super Bowl XXVII to capture their first NFL title since 1978. The game was played before a crowd of 98,374 at the Rose Bowl in Pasadena, California. The NBC broadcast of the game was the most watched program in television history and was seen by 133,400,000 people in the United States. The game also was seen live or taped in 101 other countries. The rating for the game was 45.1, the tenth highest for any televised sports event, January 31.

A total of 695 players shared in the postseason pool of $14.9 million, February 15.

For the fourth consecutive season, the NFL total paid attendance reached a record level. Total paid attendance was 17,784,354 for the 296 preseason, regular-season, and postseason games, March 4.

NFL clubs awarded Super Bowl XXX to the city of Phoenix, to be played on January 28, 1996, at Sun Devil Stadium, March 23.

Drew Bledsoe, a quarterback from Washington State, was selected by New England, becoming the first player chosen in the 1993 NFL draft, April 25.

The NFL and the NFL Players Association officially signed a 7-year Collective Bargaining Agreement in Washington, D.C., which guarantees more than $1 billion in pension, health, and post-career benefits for current and retired players—the most extensive benefits plan in pro sports. It was the NFL's first CBA since the 1982 agreement expired in 1987, June 29.

Ron Bernard was named president of NFL Enterprises, a newly formed division of the NFL responsible for NFL Films, home video, and special domestic and international television programming, August 19.

NFL announced plans to allow fans, for the first time ever, to join players and coaches in selecting the annual AFC and NFC Pro Bowl teams, October 12.

NFL clubs unanimously awarded

the league's twenty-ninth franchise to the Carolina Panthers at a meeting in Chicago. NFL clubs also awarded Super Bowl XXXI to New Orleans and Super Bowl XXXII to San Diego, October 26.

At the same meeting in Chicago, NFL clubs approved a plan to form a European league with joint venture partners, October 27.

Don Shula became the winningest coach in NFL history when Miami beat Philadelphia to give Shula his 325th victory, one more than George Halas, November 14.

NFL clubs awarded the league's thirtieth franchise to the Jacksonville Jaguars at a meeting in Chicago, November 30.

The NFL announced new 4-year television agreements with ABC, ESPN, TNT, and NFL newcomer FOX, which took over the NFC package from CBS, December 18.

The NFL completed its new TV agreements by announcing that NBC would retain the rights to the AFC package, December 20.

1994

The NFL announced that a regular-season paid attendance record was set in 1993. Attendance averaged 62,354, topping the previous record of 62,321 set in 1990, January 6.

The Dallas Cowboys defeated the Buffalo Bills 30-13 in Super Bowl XXVIII to become the fifth team to win back-to-back Super Bowl titles. The game was viewed by the largest U.S. audience in television history—134.8 million people. The game's 45.5 rating was the highest for a Super Bowl since 1987 and the tenth highest-rated Super Bowl ever, January 30.

NFL clubs unanimously approved the transfer of the New England Patriots from James Orthwein to Robert Kraft at a meeting in Orlando, February 22.

In an effort to increase offensive production, NFL clubs at the league's annual meeting in Orlando adopted a package of changes, including modifications in line play, chucking rules, and the roughing-the-passer rule, plus the adoption of the two-point conversion and moving the spot of the kickoff back to the 30-yard line, March 22.

NFL clubs approved the transfer of the majority interest in the Miami Dolphins from the Robbie family to H. Wayne Huizenga, March 23.

The NFL and FOX announced the formation of a joint venture to create a six-team World League to begin play in Europe in April, 1995, March 23.

The NFL announced a total paid attendance record for the fifth consecutive year, with 17,951,831 in paid attendance for all 1993 games, March 23.

Dan Wilkinson, a defensive tackle from Ohio State, was selected by Cincinnati as the first overall selection in the draft, April 24.

The Carolina Panthers earned the right to select first in the 1995 NFL draft by winning a coin toss with the Jacksonville Jaguars. The Jaguars received the second selection in the 1995 draft, April 24.

NFL clubs approved the transfer of

the Philadelphia Eagles from Norman Braman to Jeffrey Lurie, May 6.

The NFL launched "NFL Sunday Ticket," a new season subscription service for satellite television dish owners, June 1.

Sara Levinson, president/business director of MTV, was named president of NFL Properties, July 12.

An all-time NFL record crowd of 112,376 attended the American Bowl game between Dallas and Houston in Mexico City. It concluded the biggest American Bowl series in NFL history with four games attracting a record 256,666 fans, August 15.

The NFL 75th Anniversary All-Time Team was announced at a press conference at Radio City Music Hall, August 30.

The NFL reached agreement on a new seven-year contract with its game officials, September 22.

The NFL Management Council and the NFL Players Association announced an agreement on the formulation and implementation of the most comprehensive drug and alcohol policy in sports, October 28.

At an NFL meeting in Chicago, Commissioner Tagliabue slotted the two new expansion teams into the AFC Central (Jacksonville Jaguars) and NFC West (Carolina Panthers) for the 1995 season only. He also appointed a special committee on realignment to make recommendations on the 1996 season and beyond, November 2.

The NFL set a regular-season paid attendance record for the second consecutive year, topping 14 million for the first time (14,034,977), December 27.

1995

The San Francisco 49ers became the first team to win five Super Bowls when they defeated the San Diego Chargers 49-26 in Super Bowl XXIX at Joe Robbie Stadium in Miami, January 29.

Carolina and Jacksonville stocked their expansion rosters with a total of 66 players from other NFL teams in a veteran player allocation draft in New York, February 16.

CBS Radio and the NFL agreed to a new four-year contract for an annual 53-game package of games, continuing a relationship that spanned 15 of the past 17 years, February 22.

NFL total paid attendance for all 1994 season games reached a record level for the sixth consecutive year, exceeding 18 million for the first time (18,010,264), March 9.

NFL clubs approved the transfer of the Tampa Bay Buccaneers from the estate of the late Hugh Culverhouse to South Florida businessman Malcolm Glazer, March 13.

A total of $20.3 million, the largest NFL postseason pool ever, was divided among 729 players who participated in the 1994 playoffs, March 13.

A series of safety-related rules changes were adopted at a league meeting in Phoenix, primarily related to the use of the helmet against defenseless players, March 14.

After a two-year hiatus, the World League of American Football returned to action with six teams in Europe, April 8.

The NFL became the first major sports league to establish a site on the

Internet system of on-line computer communication, April 10.

The transfer of the Rams from Los Angeles to St. Louis was approved by a vote of the NFL clubs at a meeting in Dallas, April 12.

ABC's *NFL Monday Night Football* finished the 1994-95 television season as the fifth highest-rated show out of 146 with a 17.8 average rating, the highest finish in the 25-year history of the series, April 18.

Ki-Jana Carter, a running back from Penn State, was selected by the Cincinnati Bengals as the first overall selection in the draft, April 22.

In an ABC News Poll taken during the NFL offseason, America's sports fans chose football as their favorite spectator sport by more than a 2-to-1 margin over basketball and baseball (35%-16%-12%), April 26.

The Frankfurt Galaxy defeated the Amsterdam Admirals 26-22 to win the 1995 World Bowl before a crowd of 23,847 in Amsterdam's Olympic Stadium, June 23.

Former NFL quarterback and Rhein Fire general manager Oliver Luck was named President of the World League, July 13.

The transfer of the Raiders from Los Angeles to Oakland was approved by a vote of the NFL clubs at a meeting in Chicago, July 22.

Jacksonville Municipal Stadium opened before a sold-out crowd of more than 70,000 for the first preseason game in Jaguars history, August 18.

NFL Charities and 50 NFL players donated $1 million to the United Negro College Fund in honor of the fiftieth anniversity of the UNCF and the integration of the modern NFL, September 15.

The Pro Football Hall Of Fame in Canton, Ohio, completed an $8.9 million expansion including a $4 million contribution by the NFL clubs, October 14.

The Trans World Dome opened in St. Louis before a sold-out crowd of 65,598 as the Rams defeated the Carolina Panthers 28-17, November 12.

NFL paid attendance totaled 963,521 for 15 games in Week 12, the highest weekend total in the league's 76-year history, November 19-20.

On the field, many significant records and milestones were achieved: Miami's Dan Marino surpassed Pro Football Hall of Famer Fran Tarkenton in four major passing categories—attempts, completions, yards, and touchdowns—to become the NFL's all-time career leader. San Francisco's Jerry Rice became the all-time reception and receiving-yardage leader with career totals of 942 catches and 15,123 yards. Dallas' Emmitt Smith scored 25 touchdowns, breaking the season record of 24 set by Washington's John Riggins in 1983.

1996

The Dallas Cowboys won their third Super Bowl title in four years when they defeated the Pittsburgh Steelers 27-17 in Super Bowl XXX at Sun Devil Stadium in Tempe, Arizona. The game was viewed by the largest audience in U.S. television history—138.5 million

people, January 28.

An agreement between the NFL and the city of Cleveland regarding the Cleveland Browns' relocation was approved by a vote of the NFL clubs, February 9. According to the agreement, the city of Cleveland retained the Browns' heritage and records, including the name, logo, colors, history, playing records, trophies, and memorabilia, and committed to building a new 72,000-seat stadium for a re-activated Browns' franchise to begin play there no later than 1999. Art Modell received approval to move his franchise to Baltimore and rename it.

NFL total paid attendance for all 1995 games reached a record level for the seventh consecutive year, exceeding 19 million for the first time (19,202,757), March 7.

A total of $21.5 million, the largest NFL postseason pool ever, was divided among 717 players who participated in the 1995 playoffs, March 11.

Keyshawn Johnson, a wide receiver from Southern California, was selected by the New York Jets as the first overall selection in the draft, April 20.

The transfer of the Oilers from Houston to Nashville for the 1998 season was approved by a vote of the NFL clubs at a meeting in Atlanta, April 30.

The Scottish Claymores defeated the Frankfurt Galaxy 32-27 to win the 1996 World Bowl in front of 38,982 at Murrayfield Stadium in Edinburgh, Scotland, June 23.

The NFL returned to Baltimore when the new Baltimore Ravens defeated the Philadelphia Eagles 17-9 in a preseason game before a crowd of 63,804 at Memorial Stadium, August 3.

Ericsson Stadium opened in Charlotte, North Carolina before a crowd of 65,350 as the Carolina Panthers defeated the Chicago Bears 30-12 in a preseason game, August 3.

Points scored totaled 762 and NFL paid attendance totaled 964,079 for 15 games in Week 11, the highest weekend totals in either category in the league's 77-year history, November 10-11.

Former NFL Commissioner Pete Rozelle died at his home in Rancho Santa Fe, California. Rozelle, regarded as the premiere commissioner in sports history, led the NFL for 29 years, from 1960-1989, December 6.

1997

Indianapolis Colts owner Robert Irsay died from complications related to a stroke he suffered in 1995. Irsay acquired the club in 1972 when he traded his Los Angeles Rams to Carrol Rosenbloom for the Colts. He later moved the Colts from Baltimore to Indianapolis in 1984, January 14.

The Green Bay Packers won their first NFL title in 29 years by defeating the New England Patriots 35-21 in Super Bowl XXXI at the Louisiana Superdome in New Orleans. The game was viewed by the fourth-largest audience in U.S. television history—128 million people, January 26.

A total of $24.3 million, the largest NFL postseason pool ever, was divided among 730 players who participated in the 1996 playoffs, March 11.

The rules governing cross-owner-

ship were modified, permitting NFL club owners to also own teams in other sports in their home market or markets without NFL teams. The vote was 24-5 (one abstention) in favor of approval, March 11.

Washington Redskins owner Jack Kent Cooke died at his home in Washington, D.C. Cooke became majority owner in 1974 and the Redskins won three Super Bowls under his leadership, April 6.

Orlando Pace, an offensive tackle from Ohio State, was selected by the St. Louis Rams as the first overall selection in the draft, April 19.

NFL COMMISSIONERS AND PRESIDENTS*

1920 ....Jim Thorpe, President
1921-39..................Joe Carr, President
1939-41 ....Carl Storck, President
1941-46 ....Elmer Layden, Commissioner
1946-59 ....Bert Bell, Commissioner
1960-89 ....Pete Rozelle, Commissioner
1989-present...............Paul Tagliabue, Commissioner

*NFL treasurer Austin Gunsel served as president in the office of the commissioner following the death of Bert Bell (Oct. 11, 1959) until the election of Pete Rozelle (Jan. 26, 1960).

1996

AMERICAN CONFERENCE

Eastern Division

	W	L	T	Pct.	Pts.	OP
New England	11	5	0	.688	418	313
Buffalo*	10	6	0	.625	319	266
Indianapolis*	9	7	0	.563	317	334
Miami	8	8	0	.500	339	325
N.Y. Jets	1	15	0	.063	279	454

Central Division

	W	L	T	Pct.	Pts.	OP
Pittsburgh	10	6	0	.625	344	257
Jacksonville*	9	7	0	.563	325	335
Cincinnati	8	8	0	.500	372	369
Houston	8	8	0	.500	345	319
Baltimore	4	12	0	.250	371	441

Western Division

	W	L	T	Pct.	Pts.	OP
Denver	13	3	0	.813	391	275
Kansas City	9	7	0	.563	297	300
San Diego	8	8	0	.500	310	376
Oakland	7	9	0	.438	340	293
Seattle	7	9	0	.438	317	376

NATIONAL CONFERENCE

Eastern Division

	W	L	T	Pct.	Pts.	OP
Dallas	10	6	0	.625	286	250
Philadelphia*	10	6	0	.625	363	341
Washington	9	7	0	.563	364	312
Arizona	7	9	0	.438	300	397
N.Y. Giants	6	10	0	.375	242	297

Central Division

	W	L	T	Pct.	Pts.	OP
Green Bay	13	3	0	.813	456	210
Minnesota*	9	7	0	.563	298	315
Chicago	7	9	0	.438	283	305
Tampa Bay	6	10	0	.375	221	293
Detroit	5	11	0	.313	302	368

Western Division

	W	L	T	Pct.	Pts.	OP
Carolina	12	4	0	.750	367	218
San Francisco*	12	4	0	.750	398	257
St. Louis	6	10	0	.375	303	409
Atlanta	3	13	0	.188	309	461
New Orleans	3	13	0	.188	229	339

Wild-Card qualifier for playoffs

Jacksonville finished ahead of Indianapolis and Kansas City based on better conference record (7-5 to Colts' 6-6 and Chiefs' 5-7). Indianapolis was third Wild Card based on head-to-head victory over Kansas City (1-0). Cincinnati finished ahead of Houston based on better net division points (19 to Oilers' 11). Oakland finished ahead of Seattle based on better division record (3-5 to Seahawks' 2-6). Dallas finished ahead of Philadelphia based on better record against common opponents (8-5 to Eagles' 7-6). Minnesota was third Wild Card based on better conference record than Washington (8-4 to Redskins' 6-6). Carolina finished ahead of San Francisco based on head-to-head sweep (2-0). Atlanta finished ahead of New Orleans based on head-to-head sweep (2-0).
Wild-Card playoffs: Jacksonville 30, BUFFALO 27; PITTSBURGH 42, Indianapolis 14
Divisional playoffs: Jacksonville 30, DENVER 27; NEW ENGLAND 28, Pittsburgh 3
AFC championship: NEW ENGLAND 20, Jacksonville 6
Wild-Card playoffs: DALLAS 40, Minnesota 15; SAN FRANCISCO 14, Philadelphia 0
Divisional playoffs: GREEN BAY 35, San Francisco 14; CAROLINA 26, Dallas 17
NFC championship: GREEN BAY 30, Carolina 13
Super Bowl XXXI: Green Bay (NFC) 35, New England (AFC) 21, at Louisiana
Superdome, New Orleans, Louisiana

In Past Standings section, home teams in playoff games are indicated by capital letters.

1995

AMERICAN CONFERENCE

Eastern Division

	W	L	T	Pct.	Pts.	OP
Buffalo	10	6	0	.625	350	335
Indianapolis*	9	7	0	.563	331	316
Miami*	9	7	0	.563	398	332
New England	6	10	0	.375	294	377
N.Y. Jets	3	13	0	.188	233	384

Central Division

	W	L	T	Pct.	Pts.	OP
Pittsburgh	11	5	0	.688	407	327
Cincinnati	7	9	0	.438	349	374
Houston	7	9	0	.438	348	324
Cleveland	5	11	0	.313	289	356
Jacksonville	4	12	0	.250	275	404

Western Division

	W	L	T	Pct.	Pts.	OP
Kansas City	13	3	0	.813	358	241
San Diego*	9	7	0	.563	321	323
Seattle	8	8	0	.500	363	366
Denver	8	8	0	.500	388	345
Oakland	8	8	0	.500	348	332

NATIONAL CONFERENCE

Eastern Division

	W	L	T	Pct.	Pts.	OP
Dallas	12	4	0	.750	435	291
Philadelphia*	10	6	0	.625	318	338
Washington	6	10	0	.375	326	359
N.Y. Giants	5	11	0	.313	290	340
Arizona	4	12	0	.250	275	422

Central Division

	W	L	T	Pct.	Pts.	OP
Green Bay	11	5	0	.688	404	314
Detroit*	10	6	0	.625	436	336
Chicago	9	7	0	.563	392	360
Minnesota	8	8	0	.500	412	385
Tampa Bay	7	9	0	.438	238	335

Western Division

	W	L	T	Pct.	Pts.	OP
San Francisco	11	5	0	.688	457	258
Atlanta*	9	7	0	.563	362	349
St. Louis	7	9	0	.438	309	418
Carolina	7	9	0	.438	289	325
New Orleans	7	9	0	.438	319	348

Wild-Card qualifier for playoffs

Indianapolis finished ahead of Miami based on head-to-head sweep (2-0). San Diego was first Wild Card based on head-to-head victory over Indianapolis (1-0). Cincinnati finished ahead of Houston based on better division record (4-4 to Oilers' 3-5). Seattle finished ahead of Denver and Oakland based on best head-to-head record (3-1 to Broncos' 2-2 and Raiders' 1-3). Denver finished ahead of Oakland based on head-to-head sweep (2-0). Philadelphia was first Wild Card ahead of Detroit based on better conference record (9-3 to Lions' 7-5). Atlanta was third Wild Card ahead of Chicago based on better record against common opponents (4-2 to Bears' 3-3). St. Louis finished ahead of Carolina and New Orleans based on best head-to-head record (3-1 to Panthers' 1-3 and Saints' 2-2). Carolina finished ahead of New Orleans based on better conference record (4-8 to 3-9).
Wild-Card playoffs: BUFFALO 37, Miami 22; Indianapolis 35, SAN DIEGO 20
Divisional playoffs: PITTSBURGH 40, Buffalo 21; Indianapolis 10, KANSAS CITY 7
AFC championship: PITTSBURGH 20, Indianapolis 16

Wild-Card playoffs: PHILADELPHIA 58, Detroit 37; GREEN BAY 37, Atlanta 20
Divisional playoffs: Green Bay 27, SAN FRANCISCO 17; DALLAS 30, Philadelphia 11
NFC championship: DALLAS 38, Green Bay 27
Super Bowl XXX: Dallas (NFC) 27, Pittsburgh (AFC) 17, at Sun Devil Stadium,
Tempe, Arizona

1994

AMERICAN CONFERENCE

Eastern Division

	W	L	T	Pct.	Pts.	OP
Miami	10	6	0	.625	389	327
New England*	10	6	0	.625	351	312
Indianapolis	8	8	0	.500	307	320
Buffalo	7	9	0	.438	340	356
N.Y. Jets	6	10	0	.375	264	320

Central Division

	W	L	T	Pct.	Pts.	OP
Pittsburgh	12	4	0	.750	316	234
Cleveland*	11	5	0	.688	340	204
Cincinnati	3	13	0	.188	276	406
Houston	2	14	0	.125	226	352

Western Division

	W	L	T	Pct.	Pts.	OP
San Diego	11	5	0	.688	381	306
Kansas City*	9	7	0	.563	319	298
L.A. Raiders	9	7	0	.563	303	327
Denver	7	9	0	.438	347	396
Seattle	6	10	0	.375	287	323

NATIONAL CONFERENCE

Eastern Division

	W	L	T	Pct.	Pts.	OP
Dallas	12	4	0	.750	414	248
N.Y. Giants	9	7	0	.563	279	305
Arizona	8	8	0	.500	235	267
Philadelphia	7	9	0	.438	308	308
Washington	3	13	0	.188	320	412

Central Division

	W	L	T	Pct.	Pts.	OP
Minnesota	10	6	0	.625	356	314
Green Bay*	9	7	0	.563	382	287
Detroit*	9	7	0	.563	357	342
Chicago*	9	7	0	.563	271	307
Tampa Bay	6	10	0	.375	251	351

Western Division

	W	L	T	Pct.	Pts.	OP
San Francisco	13	3	0	.813	505	296
New Orleans	7	9	0	.438	348	407
Atlanta	7	9	0	.438	317	385
L.A. Rams	4	12	0	.250	286	365

Wild-Card qualifier for playoffs

Miami finished ahead of New England based on a head-to-head sweep (2-0). Kansas City finished ahead of L.A. Raiders based on a head-to-head sweep (2-0). Green Bay was first Wild Card based on best head-to-head record (3-1) vs. Detroit (2-2) and Chicago (1-3) and better conference record (8-4) than N.Y. Giants (6-6). Detroit was second Wild Card based on better division record (4-4) than Chicago (3-5) and head-to-head sweep of N.Y. Giants (1-0). Chicago was third Wild Card based on better record vs. common opponents (4-4) than N.Y. Giants (3-5). New Orleans finished ahead of Atlanta based on a head-to-head sweep (2-0).
Wild-Card playoffs: MIAMI 27, Kansas City 17; CLEVELAND 20, New England 13
Divisional playoffs: PITTSBURGH 29, Cleveland 9; SAN DIEGO 22, Miami 21
AFC championship: San Diego 17, PITTSBURGH 13
Wild-Card playoffs: GREEN BAY 16, Detroit 12; Chicago 35, MINNESOTA 18
Divisional playoffs: SAN FRANCISCO 44, Chicago 15; DALLAS 35, Green Bay 9
NFC championship: SAN FRANCISCO 38, Dallas 28
Super Bowl XXIX: San Francisco (NFC) 49, San Diego (AFC) 26, at Joe Robbie
Stadium, Miami, Florida

1993

AMERICAN CONFERENCE

Eastern Division

	W	L	T	Pct.	Pts.	OP
Buffalo	12	4	0	.750	329	242
Miami	9	7	0	.563	349	351
N.Y. Jets	8	8	0	.500	270	247
New England	5	11	0	.313	238	286
Indianapolis	4	12	0	.250	189	378

Central Division

	W	L	T	Pct.	Pts.	OP
Houston	12	4	0	.750	368	238
Pittsburgh*	9	7	0	.563	308	281
Cleveland	7	9	0	.438	304	307
Cincinnati	3	13	0	.188	187	319

Western Division

	W	L	T	Pct.	Pts.	OP
Kansas City	11	5	0	.688	328	291
L.A. Raiders*	10	6	0	.625	306	326
Denver*	9	7	0	.563	373	284
San Diego	8	8	0	.500	322	290
Seattle	6	10	0	.375	280	314

NATIONAL CONFERENCE

Eastern Division

	W	L	T	Pct.	Pts.	OP
Dallas	12	4	0	.750	376	229
N.Y. Giants*	11	5	0	.688	288	205
Philadelphia	8	8	0	.500	293	315
Phoenix	7	9	0	.438	326	269
Washington	4	12	0	.250	230	345

Central Division

	W	L	T	Pct.	Pts.	OP
Detroit	10	6	0	.625	298	292
Minnesota*	9	7	0	.563	277	290
Green Bay*	9	7	0	.563	340	282
Chicago	7	9	0	.438	234	230
Tampa Bay	5	11	0	.313	237	376

Western Division

	W	L	T	Pct.	Pts.	OP
San Francisco	10	6	0	.625	473	295
New Orleans	8	8	0	.500	317	343
Atlanta	6	10	0	.375	316	385
L.A. Rams	5	11	0	.313	221	367

Wild-Card qualifier for playoffs

Minnesota finished ahead of Green Bay based on a head-to-head sweep (2-0).
Wild-Card playoffs: KANSAS CITY 27, Pittsburgh 24 (OT); L.A. RAIDERS 42, Denver 24
Divisional playoffs: BUFFALO 29, L.A. Raiders 23; Kansas City 28, HOUSTON 20
AFC championship: BUFFALO 30, Kansas City 13
Wild-Card playoffs: Green Bay 28, DETROIT 24; N.Y. GIANTS 17, Minnesota 10
Divisional playoffs: SAN FRANCISCO 44, N.Y. Giants 3; DALLAS 27, Green Bay 17
NFC championship: DALLAS 38, San Francisco 21
Super Bowl XXVIII: Dallas (NFC) 30, Buffalo (AFC) 13, at Georgia Dome, Atlanta,
Georgia

1992

AMERICAN CONFERENCE
Eastern Division

	W	L	T	Pct.	Pts.	OP
Miami	11	5	0	.688	340	281
Buffalo*	11	5	0	.688	381	283
Indianapolis	9	7	0	.563	216	302
N.Y. Jets	4	12	0	.250	220	315
New England	2	14	0	.125	205	363

Central Division

	W	L	T	Pct.	Pts.	OP
Pittsburgh	11	5	0	.688	299	225
Houston*	10	6	0	.625	352	258
Cleveland	7	9	0	.438	272	275
Cincinnati	5	11	0	.313	274	364

Western Division

	W	L	T	Pct.	Pts.	OP
San Diego	11	5	0	.688	335	241
Kansas City*	10	6	0	.625	348	282
Denver	8	8	0	.500	262	329
L.A. Raiders	7	9	0	.438	249	281
Seattle	2	14	0	.125	140	312

NATIONAL CONFERENCE
Eastern Division

	W	L	T	Pct.	Pts.	OP
Dallas	13	3	0	.813	409	243
Philadelphia*	11	5	0	.688	354	245
Washington*	9	7	0	.563	300	255
N.Y. Giants	6	10	0	.375	306	367
Phoenix	4	12	0	.250	243	332

Central Division

	W	L	T	Pct.	Pts.	OP
Minnesota	11	5	0	.688	374	249
Green Bay	9	7	0	.563	276	296
Tampa Bay	5	11	0	.313	267	365
Chicago	5	11	0	.313	295	361
Detroit	5	11	0	.313	273	332

Western Division

	W	L	T	Pct.	Pts.	OP
San Francisco	14	2	0	.875	431	236
New Orleans*	12	4	0	.750	330	202
Atlanta	6	10	0	.375	327	414
L.A. Rams	6	10	0	.375	313	383

*Wild-Card qualifier for playoffs

Miami finished ahead of Buffalo based on better conference record (9-3 to 7-5). Tampa Bay finished ahead of Chicago and Detroit based on better conference record (5-9 to Bears' 4-8 and Lions' 3-9). Atlanta finished ahead of L.A. Rams based on better record versus common opponents (5-7 to 4-8).

Wild-Card playoffs: SAN DIEGO 17, Kansas City 0; BUFFALO 41, Houston 38 (OT)
Divisional playoffs: Buffalo 24, PITTSBURGH 3; MIAMI 31, San Diego 0
AFC championship: Buffalo 29, MIAMI 10
Wild-Card playoffs: Washington 24, MINNESOTA 7;
   Philadelphia 36, NEW ORLEANS 20
Divisional playoffs: SAN FRANCISCO 20, Washington 13; DALLAS 34, Philadelphia 10
NFC championship: Dallas 30, SAN FRANCISCO 20
Super Bowl XXVII: Dallas (NFC) 52, Buffalo (AFC) 17, at Rose Bowl, Pasadena,
   California

1991

AMERICAN CONFERENCE
Eastern Division

	W	L	T	Pct.	Pts.	OP
Buffalo	13	3	0	.813	458	318
N.Y. Jets*	8	8	0	.500	314	293
Miami	8	8	0	.500	343	349
New England	6	10	0	.375	211	305
Indianapolis	1	15	0	.063	143	381

Central Division

	W	L	T	Pct.	Pts.	OP
Houston	11	5	0	.688	386	251
Pittsburgh	7	9	0	.438	292	344
Cleveland	6	10	0	.375	293	298
Cincinnati	3	13	0	.188	263	435

Western Division

	W	L	T	Pct.	Pts.	OP
Denver	12	4	0	.750	304	235
Kansas City*	10	6	0	.625	322	252
L.A. Raiders*	9	7	0	.563	298	297
Seattle	7	9	0	.438	276	261
San Diego	4	12	0	.250	274	342

NATIONAL CONFERENCE
Eastern Division

	W	L	T	Pct.	Pts.	OP
Washington	14	2	0	.875	485	224
Dallas*	11	5	0	.688	342	310
Philadelphia	10	6	0	.625	285	244
N.Y. Giants	8	8	0	.500	281	297
Phoenix	4	12	0	.250	196	344

Central Division

	W	L	T	Pct.	Pts.	OP
Detroit	12	4	0	.750	339	295
Chicago*	11	5	0	.688	299	269
Minnesota	8	8	0	.500	301	306
Green Bay	4	12	0	.250	273	313
Tampa Bay	3	13	0	.188	199	365

Western Division

	W	L	T	Pct.	Pts.	OP
New Orleans	11	5	0	.688	341	211
Atlanta*	10	6	0	.625	361	338
San Francisco	10	6	0	.625	393	239
L.A. Rams	3	13	0	.188	234	390

*Wild-Card qualifiers for playoffs

New York Jets finished ahead of Miami based on head-to-head sweep (2-0). Atlanta finished ahead of San Francisco based on head-to-head sweep (2-0).

Wild-Card playoffs: KANSAS CITY 10, L.A. Raiders 6;
   HOUSTON 17, N.Y. Jets 10
Divisional playoffs: DENVER 26, Houston 24; BUFFALO 37, Kansas City 14
AFC championship: BUFFALO 10, Denver 7
Wild-Card playoffs: Atlanta 27, NEW ORLEANS 20; Dallas 17, CHICAGO 13
Divisional playoffs: WASHINGTON 24, Atlanta 7; DETROIT 38, Dallas 6
NFC championship: WASHINGTON 41, Detroit 10
Super Bowl XXVI: Washington (NFC) 37, Buffalo (AFC) 24, at Hubert H. Humphrey
   Metrodome, Minneapolis, Minnesota

1990

AMERICAN CONFERENCE
Eastern Division

	W	L	T	Pct.	Pts.	OP
Buffalo	13	3	0	.813	428	263
Miami*	12	4	0	.750	336	242
Indianapolis	7	9	0	.438	281	353
N.Y. Jets	6	10	0	.375	295	345
New England	1	15	0	.063	181	446

Central Division

	W	L	T	Pct.	Pts.	OP
Cincinnati	9	7	0	.563	360	352
Houston*	9	7	0	.563	405	307
Pittsburgh	9	7	0	.563	292	240
Cleveland	3	13	0	.188	228	462

Western Division

	W	L	T	Pct.	Pts.	OP
L.A. Raiders	12	4	0	.750	337	268
Kansas City*	11	5	0	.688	369	257
Seattle	9	7	0	.563	306	286
San Diego	6	10	0	.375	315	281
Denver	5	11	0	.313	331	374

NATIONAL CONFERENCE
Eastern Division

	W	L	T	Pct.	Pts.	OP
N.Y. Giants	13	3	0	.813	335	211
Philadelphia*	10	6	0	.625	396	299
Washington*	10	6	0	.625	381	301
Dallas	7	9	0	.438	244	308
Phoenix	5	11	0	.313	268	396

Central Division

	W	L	T	Pct.	Pts.	OP
Chicago	11	5	0	.688	348	280
Tampa Bay	6	10	0	.375	264	367
Detroit	6	10	0	.375	373	413
Green Bay	6	10	0	.375	271	347
Minnesota	6	10	0	.375	351	326

Western Division

	W	L	T	Pct.	Pts.	OP
San Francisco	14	2	0	.875	353	239
New Orleans*	8	8	0	.500	274	275
L.A. Rams	5	11	0	.313	345	412
Atlanta	5	11	0	.313	348	365

*Wild-Card qualifiers for playoffs

Cincinnati won AFC Central title based on best head-to-head record (3-1) vs. Houston (2-2) and Pittsburgh (1-3). Houston was Wild Card based on better conference record (8-4) than Seattle (7-5) and Pittsburgh (6-6). Philadelphia finished second in the NFC East based on better division record (5-3) than Washington (4-4). Tampa Bay was second in NFC Central based on 5-1 record vs. Detroit, Green Bay, and Minnesota. Detroit finished third based on best net division points (minus 8) vs. Green Bay (minus 40) in fourth. Minnesota was fifth based on 4-8 conference record. The Los Angeles Rams finished third in NFC West based on net points in division (plus 1) vs. Atlanta (minus 31).

Wild-Card playoffs: MIAMI 17, Kansas City 16; CINCINNATI 41, Houston 14
Divisional playoffs: BUFFALO 44, Miami 34; L.A. RAIDERS 20, Cincinnati 10
AFC championship: BUFFALO 51, L.A. Raiders 3
Wild-Card playoffs: Washington 20, PHILADELPHIA 6; CHICAGO 16, New Orleans 6
Divisional playoffs: SAN FRANCISCO 28, Washington 10; N.Y. GIANTS 31, Chicago 3
NFC championship: N.Y. Giants 15, SAN FRANCISCO 13
Super Bowl XXV: N.Y. Giants (NFC) 20, Buffalo (AFC) 19, at Tampa Stadium, Tampa,
   Florida

1989

AMERICAN CONFERENCE
Eastern Division

	W	L	T	Pct.	Pts.	OP
Buffalo	9	7	0	.563	409	317
Indianapolis	8	8	0	.500	298	301
Miami	8	8	0	.500	331	379
New England	5	11	0	.313	297	391
N.Y. Jets	4	12	0	.250	253	411

Central Division

	W	L	T	Pct.	Pts.	OP
Cleveland	9	6	1	.594	334	254
Houston*	9	7	0	.563	365	412
Pittsburgh*	9	7	0	.563	265	326
Cincinnati	8	8	0	.500	404	285

Western Division

	W	L	T	Pct.	Pts.	OP
Denver	11	5	0	.688	362	226
Kansas City	8	7	1	.531	318	286
L.A. Raiders	8	8	0	.500	315	297
Seattle	7	9	0	.438	241	327
San Diego	6	10	0	.375	266	290

NATIONAL CONFERENCE
Eastern Division

	W	L	T	Pct.	Pts.	OP
N.Y. Giants	12	4	0	.750	348	252
Philadelphia*	11	5	0	.688	342	274
Washington	10	6	0	.625	386	308
Phoenix	5	11	0	.313	258	377
Dallas	1	15	0	.063	204	393

Central Division

	W	L	T	Pct.	Pts.	OP
Minnesota	10	6	0	.625	351	275
Green Bay	10	6	0	.625	362	356
Detroit	7	9	0	.438	312	364
Chicago	6	10	0	.375	358	377
Tampa Bay	5	11	0	.313	320	419

Western Division

	W	L	T	Pct.	Pts.	OP
San Francisco	14	2	0	.875	442	253
L.A. Rams*	11	5	0	.688	426	344
New Orleans	9	7	0	.563	386	301
Atlanta	3	13	0	.188	279	437

*Wild-Card qualifiers for playoffs

Indianapolis finished ahead of Miami in AFC East because of better conference record (7-5 vs. 6-8). Houston finished ahead of Pittsburgh in AFC Central because of head-to-head sweep (2-0). Minnesota finished ahead of Green Bay in NFC Central because of better division record (6-2 vs. 5-3).

Wild-Card playoff: Pittsburgh 26, HOUSTON 23 (OT)
Divisional playoffs: CLEVELAND 34, Buffalo 30; DENVER 24, Pittsburgh 23
AFC championship: DENVER 37, Cleveland 21
Wild-Card playoff: L.A. Rams 21, PHILADELPHIA 7
Divisional playoffs: L.A. Rams 19, N.Y. GIANTS 13 (OT);
   SAN FRANCISCO 41, Minnesota 13
NFC championship: SAN FRANCISCO 30, L.A. Rams 3
Super Bowl XXIV: San Francisco (NFC) 55, Denver (AFC) 10, at Louisiana
   Superdome, New Orleans, Louisiana

1988

AMERICAN CONFERENCE
Eastern Division

	W	L	T	Pct.	Pts.	OP
Buffalo	12	4	0	.750	329	237
Indianapolis	9	7	0	.563	354	315
New England	9	7	0	.563	250	284
N.Y. Jets	8	7	1	.531	372	354
Miami	6	10	0	.375	319	380

Central Division

	W	L	T	Pct.	Pts.	OP
Cincinnati	12	4	0	.750	448	329
Cleveland*	10	6	0	.625	304	288
Houston*	10	6	0	.625	424	365
Pittsburgh	5	11	0	.313	336	421

Western Division

	W	L	T	Pct.	Pts.	OP
Seattle	9	7	0	.563	339	329
Denver	8	8	0	.500	327	352
L.A. Raiders	7	9	0	.438	325	369
San Diego	6	10	0	.375	231	332
Kansas City	4	11	1	.281	254	320

NATIONAL CONFERENCE
Eastern Division

	W	L	T	Pct.	Pts.	OP
Philadelphia	10	6	0	.625	379	319
N.Y. Giants	10	6	0	.625	359	304
Washington	7	9	0	.438	345	387
Phoenix	7	9	0	.438	344	398
Dallas	3	13	0	.188	265	381

Central Division

	W	L	T	Pct.	Pts.	OP
Chicago	12	4	0	.750	312	215
Minnesota*	11	5	0	.688	406	233
Tampa Bay	5	11	0	.313	261	350
Detroit	4	12	0	.250	220	313
Green Bay	4	12	0	.250	240	315

Western Division

	W	L	T	Pct.	Pts.	OP
San Francisco	10	6	0	.625	369	294
L.A. Rams*	10	6	0	.625	407	293
New Orleans	10	6	0	.625	312	283
Atlanta	5	11	0	.313	244	315

*Wild-Card qualifiers for playoffs

Indianapolis finished second in AFC East on basis of better record versus common opponents (7-5) over New England (6-6). Cleveland gained first AFC Wild-Card position based on better division record (4-2) over Houston (3-3). Philadelphia finished first in NFC East on basis of head-to-head sweep over New York Giants. Washington finished third in NFC East on basis of better division record (4-4) over Phoenix (3-5). Detroit finished fourth in NFC Central on basis of head-to-head sweep over Green Bay. San Francisco finished first in NFC West based on better head-to-head record (3-1) over Los Angeles Rams (2-2) and New Orleans (1-3). Los Angeles Rams finished second in NFC West on basis of better division record (4-2) over New Orleans (3-3) and earned Wild-Card position based on better conference record (8-4) over New York Giants (9-5) and New Orleans (6-6).

Wild-Card playoff: Houston 24, CLEVELAND 23
Divisional playoffs: CINCINNATI 21, Seattle 13; BUFFALO 17, Houston 10
AFC championship: CINCINNATI 21, Buffalo 10
Wild-Card playoff: MINNESOTA 28, Los Angeles Rams 17
Divisional playoffs: CHICAGO 20, Philadelphia 12;
SAN FRANCISCO 34, Minnesota 9
NFC championship: San Francisco 28, CHICAGO 3
Super Bowl XXIII: San Francisco (NFC) 20, Cincinnati (AFC) 16, at Joe Robbie Stadium, Miami, Florida

1987

AMERICAN CONFERENCE
Eastern Division

	W	L	T	Pct.	Pts.	OP
Indianapolis	9	6	0	.600	300	238
New England	8	7	0	.533	320	293
Miami	8	7	0	.533	362	335
Buffalo	7	8	0	.467	270	305
N.Y. Jets	6	9	0	.400	334	360

Central Division

	W	L	T	Pct.	Pts.	OP
Cleveland	10	5	0	.667	390	239
Houston*	9	6	0	.600	345	349
Pittsburgh	8	7	0	.533	285	299
Cincinnati	4	11	0	.267	285	370

Western Division

	W	L	T	Pct.	Pts.	OP
Denver	10	4	1	.700	379	288
Seattle*	9	6	0	.600	371	314
San Diego	8	7	0	.533	253	317
L.A. Raiders	5	10	0	.333	301	289
Kansas City	4	11	0	.267	273	388

NATIONAL CONFERENCE
Eastern Division

	W	L	T	Pct.	Pts.	OP
Washington	11	4	0	.733	379	285
Dallas	7	8	0	.467	340	348
St. Louis	7	8	0	.467	362	368
Philadelphia	7	8	0	.467	337	380
N.Y. Giants	6	9	0	.400	280	312

Central Division

	W	L	T	Pct.	Pts.	OP
Chicago	11	4	0	.733	356	282
Minnesota*	8	7	0	.533	336	335
Green Bay	5	9	1	.367	255	300
Tampa Bay	4	11	0	.267	286	360
Detroit	4	11	0	.267	269	384

Western Division

	W	L	T	Pct.	Pts.	OP
San Francisco	13	2	0	.867	459	253
New Orleans*	12	3	0	.800	422	283
L.A. Rams	6	9	0	.400	317	361
Atlanta	3	12	0	.200	205	436

*Wild-Card qualifiers for playoffs

Houston gained first AFC Wild-Card position on better conference record (7-4) over Seattle (5-6).

Wild-Card playoff: HOUSTON 23, Seattle 20 (OT)
Divisional playoffs: CLEVELAND 38, Indianapolis 21; DENVER 34, Houston 10
AFC championship: DENVER 38, Cleveland 33
Wild-Card playoff: Minnesota 44, NEW ORLEANS 10
Divisional playoffs: Minnesota 36, SAN FRANCISCO 24; Washington 21, CHICAGO 17
NFC championship: WASHINGTON 17, Minnesota 10
Super Bowl XXII: Washington (NFC) 42, Denver (AFC) 10, at San Diego Jack Murphy Stadium, San Diego, California
Note: 1987 regular season was reduced from 16 to 15 games for each team due to players' strike.

1986

AMERICAN CONFERENCE
Eastern Division

	W	L	T	Pct.	Pts.	OP
New England	11	5	0	.688	412	307
N.Y. Jets*	10	6	0	.625	364	386
Miami	8	8	0	.500	430	405
Buffalo	4	12	0	.250	287	348
Indianapolis	3	13	0	.188	229	400

Central Division

	W	L	T	Pct.	Pts.	OP
Cleveland	12	4	0	.750	391	310
Cincinnati	10	6	0	.625	409	394
Pittsburgh	6	10	0	.375	307	336
Houston	5	11	0	.313	274	329

Western Division

	W	L	T	Pct.	Pts.	OP
Denver	11	5	0	.688	378	327
Kansas City*	10	6	0	.625	358	326
Seattle	10	6	0	.625	366	293
L.A. Raiders	8	8	0	.500	323	346
San Diego	4	12	0	.250	335	396

NATIONAL CONFERENCE
Eastern Division

	W	L	T	Pct.	Pts.	OP
N.Y. Giants	14	2	0	.875	371	236
Washington*	12	4	0	.750	368	296
Dallas	7	9	0	.438	346	337
Philadelphia	5	10	1	.344	256	312
St. Louis	4	11	1	.281	218	351

Central Division

	W	L	T	Pct.	Pts.	OP
Chicago	14	2	0	.875	352	187
Minnesota	9	7	0	.563	398	273
Detroit	5	11	0	.313	277	326
Green Bay	4	12	0	.250	254	418
Tampa Bay	2	14	0	.125	239	473

Western Division

	W	L	T	Pct.	Pts.	OP
San Francisco	10	5	1	.656	374	247
L.A. Rams*	10	6	0	.625	309	267
Atlanta	7	8	1	.469	280	280
New Orleans	7	9	0	.438	288	287

*Wild-Card qualifiers for playoffs

New York Jets gained first AFC Wild-Card position on better conference record (8-4) over Kansas City (9-5), Seattle (7-5), and Cincinnati (7-5). Kansas City gained second Wild Card based on better conference record (9-5) over Seattle (7-5) and Cincinnati (7-5).

Wild-Card playoff: NEW YORK JETS 35, Kansas City 15
Divisional playoffs: CLEVELAND 23, New York Jets 20 (OT);
DENVER 22, New England 17
AFC championship: Denver 23, CLEVELAND 20 (OT)
Wild-Card playoff: WASHINGTON 19, Los Angeles Rams 7
Divisional playoffs: Washington 27, CHICAGO 13
NEW YORK GIANTS 49, San Francisco 3
NFC championship: NEW YORK GIANTS 17, Washington 0
Super Bowl XXI: New York Giants (NFC) 39, Denver (AFC) 20, at Rose Bowl, Pasadena, California

1985

AMERICAN CONFERENCE
Eastern Division

	W	L	T	Pct.	Pts.	OP
Miami	12	4	0	.750	428	320
N.Y. Jets*	11	5	0	.688	393	264
New England*	11	5	0	.688	362	290
Indianapolis	5	11	0	.313	320	386
Buffalo	2	14	0	.125	200	381

Central Division

	W	L	T	Pct.	Pts.	OP
Cleveland	8	8	0	.500	287	294
Cincinnati	7	9	0	.438	441	437
Pittsburgh	7	9	0	.438	379	355
Houston	5	11	0	.313	284	412

Western Division

	W	L	T	Pct.	Pts.	OP
L.A. Raiders	12	4	0	.750	354	308
Denver	11	5	0	.688	380	329
Seattle	8	8	0	.500	349	303
San Diego	8	8	0	.500	467	435
Kansas City	6	10	0	.375	317	360

NATIONAL CONFERENCE
Eastern Division

	W	L	T	Pct.	Pts.	OP
Dallas	10	6	0	.625	357	333
N.Y. Giants*	10	6	0	.625	399	283
Washington	10	6	0	.625	297	312
Philadelphia	7	9	0	.438	286	310
St. Louis	5	11	0	.313	278	414

Central Division

	W	L	T	Pct.	Pts.	OP
Chicago	15	1	0	.938	456	198
Green Bay	8	8	0	.500	337	355
Minnesota	7	9	0	.438	346	359
Detroit	7	9	0	.438	307	366
Tampa Bay	2	14	0	.125	294	448

Western Division

	W	L	T	Pct.	Pts.	OP
L.A. Rams	11	5	0	.688	340	277
San Francisco*	10	6	0	.625	411	263
New Orleans	5	11	0	.313	294	401
Atlanta	4	12	0	.250	282	452

*Wild-Card qualifiers for playoffs

New York Jets gained first AFC Wild-Card position on better conference record (9-3) over New England (8-4) and Denver (8-4). New England gained second AFC Wild-Card position based on better record vs. common opponents (4-2) than Denver (3-3). Dallas won NFC Eastern Division title based on better record (4-0) vs. New York Giants (1-3) and Washington (1-3). New York Giants gained first NFC Wild Card position based on better conference record (8-4) over San Francisco (7-5) and Washington (6-6). San Francisco gained second NFC Wild-Card position based on head-to-head victory over Washington.

Wild-Card playoff: New England 26, NEW YORK JETS 14
Divisional playoffs: MIAMI 24, Cleveland 21;
New England 27, LOS ANGELES RAIDERS 20
AFC championship: New England 31, MIAMI 14
Wild-Card playoff: NEW YORK GIANTS 17, San Francisco 3
Divisional playoffs: LOS ANGELES RAMS 20, Dallas 0;
CHICAGO 21, New York Giants 0
NFC championship: CHICAGO 24, Los Angeles Rams 0
Super Bowl XX: Chicago (NFC) 46, New England (AFC) 10, at Louisiana Superdome, New Orleans, Louisiana

1984

AMERICAN CONFERENCE

Eastern Division

	W	L	T	Pct.	Pts.	OP
Miami	14	2	0	.875	513	298
New England	9	7	0	.563	362	352
N.Y. Jets	7	9	0	.438	332	364
Indianapolis	4	12	0	.250	239	414
Buffalo	2	14	0	.125	250	454

Central Division

	W	L	T	Pct.	Pts.	OP
Pittsburgh	9	7	0	.563	387	310
Cincinnati	8	8	0	.500	339	339
Cleveland	5	11	0	.313	250	297
Houston	3	13	0	.188	240	437

Western Division

	W	L	T	Pct.	Pts.	OP
Denver	13	3	0	.813	353	241
Seattle*	12	4	0	.750	418	282
L.A. Raiders*	11	5	0	.688	368	278
Kansas City	8	8	0	.500	314	324
San Diego	7	9	0	.438	394	413

NATIONAL CONFERENCE

Eastern Division

	W	L	T	Pct.	Pts.	OP
Washington	11	5	0	.688	426	310
N.Y. Giants*	9	7	0	.563	299	301
St. Louis	9	7	0	.563	423	345
Dallas	9	7	0	.563	308	308
Philadelphia	6	9	1	.406	278	320

Central Division

	W	L	T	Pct.	Pts.	OP
Chicago	10	6	0	.625	325	248
Green Bay	8	8	0	.500	390	309
Tampa Bay	6	10	0	.375	335	380
Detroit	4	11	1	.281	283	408
Minnesota	3	13	0	.188	276	484

Western Division

	W	L	T	Pct.	Pts.	OP
San Francisco	15	1	0	.938	475	227
L.A. Rams*	10	6	0	.625	346	316
New Orleans	7	9	0	.438	298	361
Atlanta	4	12	0	.250	281	382

Wild-Card qualifiers for playoffs

New York Giants clinched Wild-Card berth based on 3-1 record vs. St. Louis's 2-2 and Dallas's 1-3. St. Louis finished ahead of Dallas based on better division record (5-3 to 3-5).

Wild-Card playoff: SEATTLE 13, Los Angeles Raiders 7
Divisional playoffs: MIAMI 31, Seattle 10; Pittsburgh 24, DENVER 17
AFC championship: MIAMI 45, Pittsburgh 28
Wild-Card playoff: New York Giants 16, LOS ANGELES RAMS 13
Divisional playoffs: SAN FRANCISCO 21, New York Giants 10; Chicago 23, WASHINGTON 19
NFC championship: SAN FRANCISCO 23, Chicago 0
Super Bowl XIX: San Francisco (NFC) 38, Miami (AFC) 16, at Stanford Stadium, Stanford, California

1983

AMERICAN CONFERENCE

Eastern Division

	W	L	T	Pct.	Pts.	OP
Miami	12	4	0	.750	389	250
New England	8	8	0	.500	274	289
Buffalo	8	8	0	.500	283	351
Baltimore	7	9	0	.438	264	354
N.Y. Jets	7	9	0	.438	313	331

Central Division

	W	L	T	Pct.	Pts.	OP
Pittsburgh	10	6	0	.625	355	303
Cleveland	9	7	0	.563	356	342
Cincinnati	7	9	0	.438	346	302
Houston	2	14	0	.125	288	460

Western Division

	W	L	T	Pct.	Pts.	OP
L.A. Raiders	12	4	0	.750	442	338
Seattle*	9	7	0	.563	403	397
Denver*	9	7	0	.563	302	327
San Diego	6	10	0	.375	358	462
Kansas City	6	10	0	.375	386	367

NATIONAL CONFERENCE

Eastern Division

	W	L	T	Pct.	Pts.	OP
Washington	14	2	0	.875	541	332
Dallas*	12	4	0	.750	479	360
St. Louis	8	7	1	.531	374	428
Philadelphia	5	11	0	.313	233	322
N.Y. Giants	3	12	1	.219	267	347

Central Division

	W	L	T	Pct.	Pts.	OP
Detroit	9	7	0	.563	347	286
Green Bay	8	8	0	.500	429	439
Chicago	8	8	0	.500	311	301
Minnesota	8	8	0	.500	316	348
Tampa Bay	2	14	0	.125	241	380

Western Division

	W	L	T	Pct.	Pts.	OP
San Francisco	10	6	0	.625	432	293
L.A. Rams*	9	7	0	.563	361	344
New Orleans	8	8	0	.500	319	337
Atlanta	7	9	0	.438	370	389

Wild-Card qualifiers for playoffs

Seattle and Denver gained Wild-Card berths over Cleveland because of their victories over the Browns.

Wild-Card playoff: SEATTLE 31, Denver 7
Divisional playoffs: Seattle 27, MIAMI 20; LOS ANGELES RAIDERS 38, Pittsburgh 10
AFC championship: LOS ANGELES RAIDERS 30, Seattle 14
Wild-Card playoff: Los Angeles Rams 24, DALLAS 17
Divisional playoffs: SAN FRANCISCO 24, Detroit 23; WASHINGTON 51, L.A. Rams 7
NFC championship: WASHINGTON 24, San Francisco 21
Super Bowl XVIII: Los Angeles Raiders (AFC) 38, Washington (NFC) 9, at Tampa Stadium, Tampa, Florida

1982

AMERICAN CONFERENCE

	W	L	T	Pct.	Pts.	OP
L.A. Raiders	8	1	0	.889	260	200
Miami	7	2	0	.778	198	131
Cincinnati	7	2	0	.778	232	177
Pittsburgh	6	3	0	.667	204	146
San Diego	6	3	0	.667	288	221
N.Y. Jets	6	3	0	.667	245	166
New England	5	4	0	.556	143	157
Cleveland	4	5	0	.444	140	182
Buffalo	4	5	0	.444	150	154
Seattle	4	5	0	.444	127	147
Kansas City	3	6	0	.333	176	184
Denver	2	7	0	.222	148	226
Houston	1	8	0	.111	136	245
Baltimore	0	8	1	.056	113	236

NATIONAL CONFERENCE

	W	L	T	Pct.	Pts.	OP
Washington	8	1	0	.889	190	128
Dallas	6	3	0	.667	226	145
Green Bay	5	3	1	.611	226	169
Minnesota	5	4	0	.556	187	198
Atlanta	5	4	0	.556	183	199
St. Louis	5	4	0	.556	135	170
Tampa Bay	5	4	0	.556	158	178
Detroit	4	5	0	.444	181	176
New Orleans	4	5	0	.444	129	160
N.Y. Giants	4	5	0	.444	164	160
San Francisco	3	6	0	.333	209	206
Chicago	3	6	0	.333	141	174
Philadelphia	3	6	0	.333	191	195
L.A. Rams	2	7	0	.222	200	250

As the result of a 57-day players' strike, the 1982 NFL regular season schedule was reduced from 16 weeks to 9. At the conclusion of the regular season, the NFL conducted a 16-team postseason Super Bowl Tournament. Eight teams from each conference were seeded 1-8 based on their records during the season.

Miami finished ahead of Cincinnati based on better conference record (6-1 to 6-2). Pittsburgh won common games tie-breaker with San Diego (3-1 to 2-1) after New York Jets were eliminated from three-way tie based on conference record (Pittsburgh and San Diego 5-3 vs. Jets 2-3). Cleveland finished ahead of Buffalo and Seattle based on better conference record (4-3 to 3-3 to 3-5). Minnesota (4-1), Atlanta (4-3), St. Louis (5-4), Tampa Bay (3-3) seeds were determined by best won-lost record in conference games. Detroit finished ahead of New Orleans and the New York Giants based on better conference record (4-4 to 3-5 to 3-5).

First round playoff:	MIAMI 28, New England 13
	LOS ANGELES RAIDERS 27, Cleveland 10
	New York Jets 44, CINCINNATI 17
	San Diego 31, PITTSBURGH 28
Second round playoff:	New York Jets 17, LOS ANGELES RAIDERS 14
	MIAMI 34, San Diego 13
AFC championship:	MIAMI 14, New York Jets 0
First round playoff:	WASHINGTON 31, Detroit 7
	GREEN BAY 41, St. Louis 16
	MINNESOTA 30, Atlanta 24
	DALLAS 30, Tampa Bay 17
Second round playoff:	WASHINGTON 21, Minnesota 7
	DALLAS 37, Green Bay 26
NFC championship:	WASHINGTON 31, Dallas 17
Super Bowl XVII:	Washington (NFC) 27, Miami (AFC) 17, at Rose Bowl, Pasadena, California

1981

AMERICAN CONFERENCE

Eastern Division

	W	L	T	Pct.	Pts.	OP
Miami	11	4	1	.719	345	275
N.Y. Jets*	10	5	1	.656	355	287
Buffalo	10	6	0	.625	311	276
Baltimore	2	14	0	.125	259	533
New England	2	14	0	.125	322	370

Central Division

	W	L	T	Pct.	Pts.	OP
Cincinnati	12	4	0	.750	421	304
Pittsburgh	8	8	0	.500	356	297
Houston	7	9	0	.438	281	355
Cleveland	5	11	0	.313	276	375

Western Division

	W	L	T	Pct.	Pts.	OP
San Diego	10	6	0	.625	478	390
Denver	10	6	0	.625	321	289
Kansas City	9	7	0	.563	343	290
Oakland	7	9	0	.438	273	343
Seattle	6	10	0	.375	322	388

NATIONAL CONFERENCE

Eastern Division

	W	L	T	Pct.	Pts.	OP
Dallas	12	4	0	.750	367	277
Philadelphia*	10	6	0	.625	368	221
N.Y. Giants*	9	7	0	.563	295	257
Washington	8	8	0	.500	347	349
St. Louis	7	9	0	.438	315	408

Central Division

	W	L	T	Pct.	Pts.	OP
Tampa Bay	9	7	0	.563	315	268
Detroit	8	8	0	.500	397	322
Green Bay	8	8	0	.500	324	361
Minnesota	7	9	0	.438	325	369
Chicago	6	10	0	.375	253	324

Western Division

	W	L	T	Pct.	Pts.	OP
San Francisco	13	3	0	.813	357	250
Atlanta	7	9	0	.438	426	355
Los Angeles	6	10	0	.375	303	351
New Orleans	4	12	0	.250	207	378

Wild-Card qualifiers for playoffs

San Diego won AFC Western title over Denver on the basis of a better division record (6-2 to 5-3). Buffalo won a Wild-Card playoff berth over Denver as the result of a 9-7 victory in head-to-head competition.

Wild-Card playoff: Buffalo 31, NEW YORK JETS 27
Divisional playoffs: San Diego 41, MIAMI 38 (OT); CINCINNATI 28, Buffalo 21
AFC championship: CINCINNATI 27, San Diego 7
Wild-Card playoff: New York Giants 27, PHILADELPHIA 21
Divisional playoffs: DALLAS 38, Tampa Bay 0; SAN FRANCISCO 38, New York Giants 24
NFC championship: SAN FRANCISCO 28, Dallas 27
Super Bowl XVI: San Francisco (NFC) 26, Cincinnati (AFC) 21, at Silverdome, Pontiac, Michigan

1980

AMERICAN CONFERENCE
Eastern Division

	W	L	T	Pct.	Pts.	OP
Buffalo	11	5	0	.688	320	260
New England	10	6	0	.625	441	325
Miami	8	8	0	.500	266	305
Baltimore	7	9	0	.438	355	387
N.Y. Jets	4	12	0	.250	302	395

Central Division

	W	L	T	Pct.	Pts.	OP
Cleveland	11	5	0	.688	357	310
Houston*	11	5	0	.688	295	251
Pittsburgh	9	7	0	.563	352	313
Cincinnati	6	10	0	.375	244	312

Western Division

	W	L	T	Pct.	Pts.	OP
San Diego	11	5	0	.688	418	327
Oakland*	11	5	0	.688	364	306
Kansas City	8	8	0	.500	319	336
Denver	8	8	0	.500	310	323
Seattle	4	12	0	.250	291	408

NATIONAL CONFERENCE
Eastern Division

	W	L	T	Pct.	Pts.	OP
Philadelphia	12	4	0	.750	384	222
Dallas*	12	4	0	.750	454	311
Washington	6	10	0	.375	261	293
St. Louis	5	11	0	.313	299	350
N.Y. Giants	4	12	0	.250	249	425

Central Division

	W	L	T	Pct.	Pts.	OP
Minnesota	9	7	0	.563	317	308
Detroit	9	7	0	.563	334	272
Chicago	7	9	0	.438	304	264
Tampa Bay	5	10	1	.344	271	341
Green Bay	5	10	1	.344	231	371

Western Division

	W	L	T	Pct.	Pts.	OP
Atlanta	12	4	0	.750	405	272
Los Angeles*	11	5	0	.688	424	289
San Francisco	6	10	0	.375	320	415
New Orleans	1	15	0	.063	291	487

*Wild-Card qualifiers for playoffs
Philadelphia won division title over Dallas on the basis of best net points in division games (plus 84 net points to plus 50). Minnesota won division title because of a better conference record than Detroit (8-4 to 9-5). Cleveland won division title because of a better conference record than Houston (8-4 to 7-5). San Diego won division title over Oakland on the basis of best net points in division games (plus 60 net points to plus 37).
Wild-Card playoff: OAKLAND 27, Houston 7
Divisional playoffs: SAN DIEGO 20, Buffalo 14; Oakland 14, CLEVELAND 12
AFC championship: Oakland 34, SAN DIEGO 27
Wild-Card playoff: DALLAS 34, Los Angeles 13
Divisional playoffs: PHILADELPHIA 31, Minnesota 16; Dallas 30, ATLANTA 27
NFC championship: PHILADELPHIA 20, Dallas 7
Super Bowl XV: Oakland (AFC) 27, Philadelphia (NFC) 10, at Louisiana Superdome, New Orleans, Louisiana

1979

AMERICAN CONFERENCE
Eastern Division

	W	L	T	Pct.	Pts.	OP
Miami	10	6	0	.625	341	257
New England	9	7	0	.563	411	326
N.Y. Jets	8	8	0	.500	337	383
Buffalo	7	9	0	.438	268	279
Baltimore	5	11	0	.313	271	351

Central Division

	W	L	T	Pct.	Pts.	OP
Pittsburgh	12	4	0	.750	416	262
Houston*	11	5	0	.688	362	331
Cleveland	9	7	0	.563	359	352
Cincinnati	4	12	0	.250	337	421

Western Division

	W	L	T	Pct.	Pts.	OP
San Diego	12	4	0	.750	411	246
Denver*	10	6	0	.625	289	262
Seattle	9	7	0	.563	378	372
Oakland	9	7	0	.563	365	337
Kansas City	7	9	0	.438	238	262

NATIONAL CONFERENCE
Eastern Division

	W	L	T	Pct.	Pts.	OP
Dallas	11	5	0	.688	371	313
Philadelphia*	11	5	0	.688	339	282
Washington	10	6	0	.625	348	295
N.Y. Giants	6	10	0	.375	237	323
St. Louis	5	11	0	.313	307	358

Central Division

	W	L	T	Pct.	Pts.	OP
Tampa Bay	10	6	0	.625	273	237
Chicago*	10	6	0	.625	306	249
Minnesota	7	9	0	.438	259	337
Green Bay	5	11	0	.313	246	316
Detroit	2	14	0	.125	219	365

Western Division

	W	L	T	Pct.	Pts.	OP
Los Angeles	9	7	0	.563	323	309
New Orleans	8	8	0	.500	370	360
Atlanta	6	10	0	.375	300	388
San Francisco	2	14	0	.125	308	416

*Wild-Card qualifiers for playoffs
Dallas won division title because of a better conference record than Philadelphia (10-2 to 9-3). Tampa Bay won division title because of a better division record than Chicago (6-2 to 5-3). Chicago won a Wild-Card berth over Washington on the basis of best net points in all games (plus 57 net points to plus 53).
Wild-Card playoff: HOUSTON 13, Denver 7
Divisional playoffs: Houston 17, SAN DIEGO 14; PITTSBURGH 34, Miami 14
AFC championship: PITTSBURGH 27, Houston 13
Wild-Card playoff: PHILADELPHIA 27, Chicago 17
Divisional playoffs: TAMPA BAY 24, Philadelphia 17; Los Angeles 21, DALLAS 19
NFC championship: Los Angeles 9, TAMPA BAY 0
Super Bowl XIV: Pittsburgh (AFC) 31, Los Angeles (NFC) 19, at Rose Bowl, Pasadena, California

1978

AMERICAN CONFERENCE
Eastern Division

	W	L	T	Pct.	Pts.	OP
New England	11	5	0	.688	358	286
Miami*	11	5	0	.688	372	254
N.Y. Jets	8	8	0	.500	359	364
Buffalo	5	11	0	.313	302	354
Baltimore	5	11	0	.313	239	421

Central Division

	W	L	T	Pct.	Pts.	OP
Pittsburgh	14	2	0	.875	356	195
Houston*	10	6	0	.625	283	298
Cleveland	8	8	0	.500	334	356
Cincinnati	4	12	0	.250	252	284

Western Division

	W	L	T	Pct.	Pts.	OP
Denver	10	6	0	.625	282	198
Oakland	9	7	0	.563	311	283
Seattle	9	7	0	.563	345	358
San Diego	9	7	0	.563	355	309
Kansas City	4	12	0	.250	243	327

NATIONAL CONFERENCE
Eastern Division

	W	L	T	Pct.	Pts.	OP
Dallas	12	4	0	.750	384	208
Philadelphia*	9	7	0	.563	270	250
Washington	8	8	0	.500	273	283
St. Louis	6	10	0	.375	248	296
N.Y. Giants	6	10	0	.375	264	298

Central Division

	W	L	T	Pct.	Pts.	OP
Minnesota	8	7	1	.531	294	306
Green Bay	8	7	1	.531	249	269
Detroit	7	9	0	.438	290	300
Chicago	7	9	0	.438	253	274
Tampa Bay	5	11	0	.313	241	259

Western Division

	W	L	T	Pct.	Pts.	OP
Los Angeles	12	4	0	.750	316	245
Atlanta*	9	7	0	.563	240	290
New Orleans	7	9	0	.438	281	298
San Francisco	2	14	0	.125	219	350

*Wild-Card qualifiers for playoffs
New England won division title on the basis of a better division record than Miami (6-2 to 5-3). Minnesota won division title because of a better head-to-head record against Green Bay (1-0-1).
Wild-Card playoff: Houston 17, MIAMI 9
Divisional playoffs: Houston 31, NEW ENGLAND 14; PITTSBURGH 33, Denver 10
AFC championship: PITTSBURGH 34, Houston 5
Wild-Card playoff: ATLANTA 14, Philadelphia 13
Divisional playoffs: DALLAS 27, Atlanta 20; LOS ANGELES 34, Minnesota 10
NFC championship: Dallas 28, LOS ANGELES 0
Super Bowl XIII: Pittsburgh (AFC) 35, Dallas (NFC) 31, at Orange Bowl, Miami, Florida

1977

AMERICAN CONFERENCE
Eastern Division

	W	L	T	Pct.	Pts.	OP
Baltimore	10	4	0	.714	295	221
Miami	10	4	0	.714	313	197
New England	9	5	0	.643	278	217
N.Y. Jets	3	11	0	.214	191	300
Buffalo	3	11	0	.214	160	313

Central Division

	W	L	T	Pct.	Pts.	OP
Pittsburgh	9	5	0	.643	283	243
Houston	8	6	0	.571	299	230
Cincinnati	8	6	0	.571	238	235
Cleveland	6	8	0	.429	269	267

Western Division

	W	L	T	Pct.	Pts.	OP
Denver	12	2	0	.857	274	148
Oakland*	11	3	0	.786	351	230
San Diego	7	7	0	.500	222	205
Seattle	5	9	0	.357	282	373
Kansas City	2	12	0	.143	225	349

NATIONAL CONFERENCE
Eastern Division

	W	L	T	Pct.	Pts.	OP
Dallas	12	2	0	.857	345	212
Washington	9	5	0	.643	196	189
St. Louis	7	7	0	.500	272	287
Philadelphia	5	9	0	.357	220	207
N.Y. Giants	5	9	0	.357	181	265

Central Division

	W	L	T	Pct.	Pts.	OP
Minnesota	9	5	0	.643	231	227
Chicago*	9	5	0	.643	255	253
Detroit	6	8	0	.429	183	252
Green Bay	4	10	0	.286	134	219
Tampa Bay	2	12	0	.143	103	223

Western Division

	W	L	T	Pct.	Pts.	OP
Los Angeles	10	4	0	.714	302	146
Atlanta	7	7	0	.500	179	129
San Francisco	5	9	0	.357	220	260
New Orleans	3	11	0	.214	232	336

*Wild-Card qualifier for playoffs
Baltimore won division title on the basis of a better conference record than Miami (9-3 to 8-4). Chicago won a Wild-Card berth over Washington on the basis of best net points in conference games (plus 48 net points to plus 4).
Divisional playoffs: DENVER 34, Pittsburgh 21; Oakland 37, BALTIMORE 31 (OT)
AFC championship: DENVER 20, Oakland 17
Divisional playoffs: DALLAS 37, Chicago 7; Minnesota 14, LOS ANGELES 7
NFC championship: DALLAS 23, Minnesota 6
Super Bowl XII: Dallas (NFC) 27, Denver (AFC) 10, at Louisiana Superdome, New Orleans, Louisiana

1976

AMERICAN CONFERENCE
Eastern Division

	W	L	T	Pct.	Pts.	OP
Baltimore	11	3	0	.786	417	246
New England*	11	3	0	.786	376	236
Miami	6	8	0	.429	263	264
N.Y. Jets	3	11	0	.214	169	383
Buffalo	2	12	0	.143	245	363

Central Division

	W	L	T	Pct.	Pts.	OP
Pittsburgh	10	4	0	.714	342	138
Cincinnati	10	4	0	.714	335	210
Cleveland	9	5	0	.643	267	287
Houston	5	9	0	.357	222	273

Western Division

	W	L	T	Pct.	Pts.	OP
Oakland	13	1	0	.929	350	237
Denver	9	5	0	.643	315	206
San Diego	6	8	0	.429	248	285
Kansas City	5	9	0	.357	290	376
Tampa Bay	0	14	0	.000	125	412

NATIONAL CONFERENCE
Eastern Division

	W	L	T	Pct.	Pts.	OP
Dallas	11	3	0	.786	296	194
Washington*	10	4	0	.714	291	217
St. Louis	10	4	0	.714	309	267
Philadelphia	4	10	0	.286	165	286
N.Y. Giants	3	11	0	.214	170	250

Central Division

	W	L	T	Pct.	Pts.	OP
Minnesota	11	2	1	.821	305	176
Chicago	7	7	0	.500	253	216
Detroit	6	8	0	.429	262	220
Green Bay	5	9	0	.357	218	299

Western Division

	W	L	T	Pct.	Pts.	OP
Los Angeles	10	3	1	.750	351	190
San Francisco	8	6	0	.571	270	190
Atlanta	4	10	0	.286	172	312
New Orleans	4	10	0	.286	253	346
Seattle	2	12	0	.143	229	429

*Wild-Card qualifier for playoffs
Baltimore won division title on the basis of a better division record than New England (7-1 to 6-2). Pittsburgh won division title because of a two-game sweep over Cincinnati. Washington won Wild-Card berth over St. Louis because of a two-game sweep over Cardinals.
Divisional playoffs: OAKLAND 24, New England 21; Pittsburgh 40, BALTIMORE 14
AFC championship: OAKLAND 24, Pittsburgh 7
Divisional playoffs: MINNESOTA 35, Washington 20; Los Angeles 14, DALLAS 12
NFC championship: MINNESOTA 24, Los Angeles 13
Super Bowl XI: Oakland (AFC) 32, Minnesota (NFC) 14, at Rose Bowl, Pasadena, California

1975

AMERICAN CONFERENCE
Eastern Division

	W	L	T	Pct.	Pts.	OP
Baltimore	10	4	0	.714	395	269
Miami	10	4	0	.714	357	222
Buffalo	8	6	0	.571	420	355
New England	3	11	0	.214	258	358
N.Y. Jets	3	11	0	.214	258	433

Central Division

	W	L	T	Pct.	Pts.	OP
Pittsburgh	12	2	0	.857	373	162
Cincinnati*	11	3	0	.786	340	246
Houston	10	4	0	.714	293	226
Cleveland	3	11	0	.214	218	372

Western Division

	W	L	T	Pct.	Pts.	OP
Oakland	11	3	0	.786	375	255
Denver	6	8	0	.429	254	307
Kansas City	5	9	0	.357	282	341
San Diego	2	12	0	.143	189	345

NATIONAL CONFERENCE
Eastern Division

	W	L	T	Pct.	Pts.	OP
St. Louis	11	3	0	.786	356	276
Dallas*	10	4	0	.714	350	268
Washington	8	6	0	.571	325	276
N.Y. Giants	5	9	0	.357	216	306
Philadelphia	4	10	0	.286	225	302

Central Division

	W	L	T	Pct.	Pts.	OP
Minnesota	12	2	0	.857	377	180
Detroit	7	7	0	.500	245	262
Chicago	4	10	0	.286	191	379
Green Bay	4	10	0	.286	226	285

Western Division

	W	L	T	Pct.	Pts.	OP
Los Angeles	12	2	0	.857	312	135
San Francisco	5	9	0	.357	255	286
Atlanta	4	10	0	.286	240	289
New Orleans	2	12	0	.143	165	360

*Wild-Card qualifier for playoffs
Baltimore won division title on the basis of a two-game sweep over Miami.
Divisional playoffs: PITTSBURGH 28, Baltimore 10; OAKLAND 31, Cincinnati 28
AFC championship: PITTSBURGH 16, Oakland 10
Divisional playoffs: LOS ANGELES 35, St. Louis 23; Dallas 17, MINNESOTA 14
NFC championship: Dallas 37, LOS ANGELES 7
Super Bowl X: Pittsburgh (AFC) 21, Dallas (NFC) 17, at Orange Bowl, Miami, Florida

1974

AMERICAN CONFERENCE
Eastern Division

	W	L	T	Pct.	Pts.	OP
Miami	11	3	0	.786	327	216
Buffalo*	9	5	0	.643	264	244
New England	7	7	0	.500	348	289
N.Y. Jets	7	7	0	.500	279	300
Baltimore	2	12	0	.143	190	329

Central Division

	W	L	T	Pct.	Pts.	OP
Pittsburgh	10	3	1	.750	305	189
Cincinnati	7	7	0	.500	283	259
Houston	7	7	0	.500	236	282
Cleveland	4	10	0	.286	251	344

Western Division

	W	L	T	Pct.	Pts.	OP
Oakland	12	2	0	.857	355	228
Denver	7	6	1	.536	302	294
Kansas City	5	9	0	.357	233	293
San Diego	5	9	0	.357	212	285

NATIONAL CONFERENCE
Eastern Division

	W	L	T	Pct.	Pts.	OP
St. Louis	10	4	0	.714	285	218
Washington*	10	4	0	.714	320	196
Dallas	8	6	0	.571	297	235
Philadelphia	7	7	0	.500	242	217
N.Y. Giants	2	12	0	.143	195	299

Central Division

	W	L	T	Pct.	Pts.	OP
Minnesota	10	4	0	.714	310	195
Detroit	7	7	0	.500	256	270
Green Bay	6	8	0	.429	210	206
Chicago	4	10	0	.286	152	279

Western Division

	W	L	T	Pct.	Pts.	OP
Los Angeles	10	4	0	.714	263	181
San Francisco	6	8	0	.429	226	236
New Orleans	5	9	0	.357	166	263
Atlanta	3	11	0	.214	111	271

*Wild-Card qualifier for playoffs
St. Louis won division title because of a two-game sweep over Washington.
Divisional playoffs: OAKLAND 28, Miami 26; PITTSBURGH 32, Buffalo 14
AFC championship: Pittsburgh 24, OAKLAND 13
Divisional playoffs: MINNESOTA 30, St. Louis 14; LOS ANGELES 19, Washington 10
NFC championship: MINNESOTA 14, Los Angeles 10
Super Bowl IX: Pittsburgh (AFC) 16, Minnesota (NFC) 6, at Tulane Stadium, New Orleans, Louisiana

1973

AMERICAN CONFERENCE
Eastern Division

	W	L	T	Pct.	Pts.	OP
Miami	12	2	0	.857	343	150
Buffalo	9	5	0	.643	259	230
New England	5	9	0	.357	258	300
Baltimore	4	10	0	.286	226	341
N.Y. Jets	4	10	0	.286	240	306

Central Division

	W	L	T	Pct.	Pts.	OP
Cincinnati	10	4	0	.714	286	231
Pittsburgh*	10	4	0	.714	347	210
Cleveland	7	5	2	.571	234	255
Houston	1	13	0	.071	199	447

Western Division

	W	L	T	Pct.	Pts.	OP
Oakland	9	4	1	.679	292	175
Denver	7	5	2	.571	354	296
Kansas City	7	5	2	.571	231	192
San Diego	2	11	1	.179	188	386

NATIONAL CONFERENCE
Eastern Division

	W	L	T	Pct.	Pts.	OP
Dallas	10	4	0	.714	382	203
Washington*	10	4	0	.714	325	198
Philadelphia	5	8	1	.393	310	393
St. Louis	4	9	1	.321	286	365
N.Y. Giants	2	11	1	.179	226	362

Central Division

	W	L	T	Pct.	Pts.	OP
Minnesota	12	2	0	.857	296	168
Detroit	6	7	1	.464	271	247
Green Bay	5	7	2	.429	202	259
Chicago	3	11	0	.214	195	334

Western Division

	W	L	T	Pct.	Pts.	OP
Los Angeles	12	2	0	.857	388	178
Atlanta	9	5	0	.643	318	224
New Orleans	5	9	0	.357	163	312
San Francisco	5	9	0	.357	262	319

*Wild-Card qualifier for playoffs
Cincinnati won division title on the basis of a better conference record than Pittsburgh (8-3 to 7-4). Dallas won division title on the basis of a better point differential vs. Washington (net 13 points).
Divisional playoffs: OAKLAND 33, Pittsburgh 14; MIAMI 34, Cincinnati 16
AFC championship: MIAMI 27, Oakland 10
Divisional playoffs: MINNESOTA 27, Washington 20; DALLAS 27, Los Angeles 16
NFC championship: Minnesota 27, DALLAS 10
Super Bowl VIII: Miami (AFC) 24, Minnesota (NFC) 7, at Rice Stadium, Houston, Texas

1972

AMERICAN CONFERENCE
Eastern Division

	W	L	T	Pct.	Pts.	OP
Miami	14	0	0	1.000	385	171
N.Y. Jets	7	7	0	.500	367	324
Baltimore	5	9	0	.357	235	252
Buffalo	4	9	1	.321	257	377
New England	3	11	0	.214	192	446

Central Division

	W	L	T	Pct.	Pts.	OP
Pittsburgh	11	3	0	.786	343	175
Cleveland*	10	4	0	.714	268	249
Cincinnati	8	6	0	.571	299	229
Houston	1	13	0	.071	164	380

Western Division

	W	L	T	Pct.	Pts.	OP
Oakland	10	3	1	.750	365	248
Kansas City	8	6	0	.571	287	254
Denver	5	9	0	.357	325	350
San Diego	4	9	1	.321	264	344

NATIONAL CONFERENCE
Eastern Division

	W	L	T	Pct.	Pts.	OP
Washington	11	3	0	.786	336	218
Dallas*	10	4	0	.714	319	240
N.Y. Giants	8	6	0	.571	331	247
St. Louis	4	9	1	.321	193	303
Philadelphia	2	11	1	.179	145	352

Central Division

	W	L	T	Pct.	Pts.	OP
Green Bay	10	4	0	.714	304	226
Detroit	8	5	1	.607	339	290
Minnesota	7	7	0	.500	301	252
Chicago	4	9	1	.321	225	275

Western Division

	W	L	T	Pct.	Pts.	OP
San Francisco	8	5	1	.607	353	249
Atlanta	7	7	0	.500	269	274
Los Angeles	6	7	1	.464	291	286
New Orleans	2	11	1	.179	215	361

*Wild-Card qualifier for playoffs
Divisional playoffs: PITTSBURGH 13, Oakland 7; MIAMI 20, Cleveland 14
AFC championship: Miami 21, PITTSBURGH 17
Divisional playoffs: Dallas 30, SAN FRANCISCO 28; WASHINGTON 16, Green Bay 3
NFC championship: WASHINGTON 26, Dallas 3
Super Bowl VII: Miami (AFC) 14, Washington (NFC) 7, at Memorial Coliseum,
   Los Angeles, California

1971

AMERICAN CONFERENCE
Eastern Division

	W	L	T	Pct.	Pts.	OP
Miami	10	3	1	.769	315	174
Baltimore*	10	4	0	.714	313	140
New England	6	8	0	.429	238	325
N.Y. Jets	6	8	0	.429	212	299
Buffalo	1	13	0	.071	184	394

Central Division

	W	L	T	Pct.	Pts.	OP
Cleveland	9	5	0	.643	285	273
Pittsburgh	6	8	0	.429	246	292
Houston	4	9	1	.308	251	330
Cincinnati	4	10	0	.286	284	265

Western Division

	W	L	T	Pct.	Pts.	OP
Kansas City	10	3	1	.769	302	208
Oakland	8	4	2	.667	344	278
San Diego	6	8	0	.429	311	341
Denver	4	9	1	.308	203	275

NATIONAL CONFERENCE
Eastern Division

	W	L	T	Pct.	Pts.	OP
Dallas	11	3	0	.786	406	222
Washington*	9	4	1	.692	276	190
Philadelphia	6	7	1	.462	221	302
St. Louis	4	9	1	.308	231	279
N.Y. Giants	4	10	0	.286	228	362

Central Division

	W	L	T	Pct.	Pts.	OP
Minnesota	11	3	0	.786	245	139
Detroit	7	6	1	.538	341	286
Chicago	6	8	0	.429	185	276
Green Bay	4	8	2	.333	274	298

Western Division

	W	L	T	Pct.	Pts.	OP
San Francisco	9	5	0	.643	300	216
Los Angeles	8	5	1	.615	313	260
Atlanta	7	6	1	.538	274	277
New Orleans	4	8	2	.333	266	347

*Wild-Card qualifier for playoffs
Divisional playoffs: Miami 27, KANSAS CITY 24 (OT); Baltimore 20, CLEVELAND 3
AFC championship: MIAMI 21, Baltimore 0
Divisional playoffs: Dallas 20, MINNESOTA 12; SAN FRANCISCO 24, Washington 20
NFC championship: DALLAS 14, San Francisco 3
Super Bowl VI: Dallas (NFC) 24, Miami (AFC) 3, at Tulane Stadium, New Orleans,
   Louisiana

1970

AMERICAN CONFERENCE
Eastern Division

	W	L	T	Pct.	Pts.	OP
Baltimore	11	2	1	.846	321	234
Miami*	10	4	0	.714	297	228
N.Y. Jets	4	10	0	.286	255	286
Buffalo	3	10	1	.231	204	337
Boston Patriots	2	12	0	.143	149	361

Central Division

	W	L	T	Pct.	Pts.	OP
Cincinnati	8	6	0	.571	312	255
Cleveland	7	7	0	.500	286	265
Pittsburgh	5	9	0	.357	210	272
Houston	3	10	1	.231	217	352

Western Division

	W	L	T	Pct.	Pts.	OP
Oakland	8	4	2	.667	300	293
Kansas City	7	5	2	.583	272	244
San Diego	5	6	3	.455	282	278
Denver	5	8	1	.385	253	264

NATIONAL CONFERENCE
Eastern Division

	W	L	T	Pct.	Pts.	OP
Dallas	10	4	0	.714	299	221
N.Y. Giants	9	5	0	.643	301	270
St. Louis	8	5	1	.615	325	228
Washington	6	8	0	.429	297	314
Philadelphia	3	10	1	.231	241	332

Central Division

	W	L	T	Pct.	Pts.	OP
Minnesota	12	2	0	.857	335	143
Detroit*	10	4	0	.714	347	202
Chicago	6	8	0	.429	256	261
Green Bay	6	8	0	.429	196	293

Western Division

	W	L	T	Pct.	Pts.	OP
San Francisco	10	3	1	.769	352	267
Los Angeles	9	4	1	.692	325	202
Atlanta	4	8	2	.333	206	261
New Orleans	2	11	1	.154	172	347

*Wild-Card qualifier for playoffs
Divisional playoffs: BALTIMORE 17, Cincinnati 0; OAKLAND 21, Miami 14
AFC championship: BALTIMORE 27, Oakland 17
Divisional playoffs: DALLAS 5, Detroit 0; San Francisco 17, MINNESOTA 14
NFC championship: Dallas 17, SAN FRANCISCO 10
Super Bowl V: Baltimore (AFC) 16, Dallas (NFC) 13, at Orange Bowl, Miami, Florida

1969 NFL

EASTERN CONFERENCE
Capitol Division

	W	L	T	Pct.	Pts.	OP
Dallas	11	2	1	.846	369	223
Washington	7	5	2	.583	307	319
New Orleans	5	9	0	.357	311	393
Philadelphia	4	9	1	.308	279	377

Century Division

	W	L	T	Pct.	Pts.	OP
Cleveland	10	3	1	.769	351	300
N.Y. Giants	6	8	0	.429	264	298
St. Louis	4	9	1	.308	314	389
Pittsburgh	1	13	0	.071	218	404

WESTERN CONFERENCE
Coastal Division

	W	L	T	Pct.	Pts.	OP
Los Angeles	11	3	0	.786	320	243
Baltimore	8	5	1	.615	279	268
Atlanta	6	8	0	.429	276	268
San Francisco	4	8	2	.333	277	319

Central Division

	W	L	T	Pct.	Pts.	OP
Minnesota	12	2	0	.857	379	133
Detroit	9	4	1	.692	259	188
Green Bay	8	6	0	.571	269	221
Chicago	1	13	0	.071	210	339

Conference championships: Cleveland 38, DALLAS 14; MINNESOTA 23, Los Angeles 20
NFL championship: MINNESOTA 27, Cleveland 7
Super Bowl IV: Kansas City (AFL) 23, Minnesota (NFL) 7, at Tulane Stadium,
   New Orleans, Louisiana

1969 AFL

EASTERN DIVISION

	W	L	T	Pct.	Pts.	OP
N.Y. Jets	10	4	0	.714	353	269
Houston	6	6	2	.500	278	279
Boston Patriots	4	10	0	.286	266	316
Buffalo	4	10	0	.286	230	359
Miami	3	10	1	.231	233	332

WESTERN DIVISION

	W	L	T	Pct.	Pts.	OP
Oakland	12	1	1	.923	377	242
Kansas City	11	3	0	.786	359	177
San Diego	8	6	0	.571	288	276
Denver	5	8	1	.385	297	344
Cincinnati	4	9	1	.308	280	367

Divisional playoffs: Kansas City 13, N.Y. JETS 6; OAKLAND 56, Houston 7
AFL championship: Kansas City 17, OAKLAND 7

1968 NFL

EASTERN CONFERENCE
Capitol Division

	W	L	T	Pct.	Pts.	OP
Dallas	12	2	0	.857	431	186
N.Y. Giants	7	7	0	.500	294	325
Washington	5	9	0	.357	249	358
Philadelphia	2	12	0	.143	202	351

Century Division

	W	L	T	Pct.	Pts.	OP
Cleveland	10	4	0	.714	394	273
St. Louis	9	4	1	.692	325	289
New Orleans	4	9	1	.308	246	327
Pittsburgh	2	11	1	.154	244	397

WESTERN CONFERENCE
Coastal Division

	W	L	T	Pct.	Pts.	OP
Baltimore	13	1	0	.929	402	144
Los Angeles	10	3	1	.769	312	200
San Francisco	7	6	1	.538	303	310
Atlanta	2	12	0	.143	170	389

Central Division

	W	L	T	Pct.	Pts.	OP
Minnesota	8	6	0	.571	282	242
Chicago	7	7	0	.500	250	333
Green Bay	6	7	1	.462	281	227
Detroit	4	8	2	.333	207	241

Conference championships: CLEVELAND 31, Dallas 20; BALTIMORE 24, Minnesota 14
NFL championship: Baltimore 34, CLEVELAND 0
Super Bowl III: N.Y. Jets (AFL) 16, Baltimore (NFL) 7, at Orange Bowl, Miami, Florida

1968 AFL

EASTERN DIVISION

	W	L	T	Pct.	Pts.	OP
N.Y. Jets	11	3	0	.786	419	280
Houston	7	7	0	.500	303	248
Miami	5	8	1	.385	276	355
Boston Patriots	4	10	0	.286	229	406
Buffalo	1	12	1	.077	199	367

WESTERN DIVISION

	W	L	T	Pct.	Pts.	OP
Oakland	12	2	0	.857	453	233
Kansas City	12	2	0	.857	371	170
San Diego	9	5	0	.643	382	310
Denver	5	9	0	.357	255	404
Cincinnati	3	11	0	.214	215	329

Western Division playoff: OAKLAND 41, Kansas City 6
AFL championship: N.Y. JETS 27, Oakland 23

1967 NFL

EASTERN CONFERENCE
Capitol Division

	W	L	T	Pct.	Pts.	OP
Dallas	9	5	0	.643	342	268
Philadelphia	6	7	1	.462	351	409
Washington	5	6	3	.455	347	353
New Orleans	3	11	0	.214	233	379

Century Division

	W	L	T	Pct.	Pts.	OP
Cleveland	9	5	0	.643	334	297
N.Y. Giants	7	7	0	.500	369	379
St. Louis	6	7	1	.462	333	356
Pittsburgh	4	9	1	.308	281	320

WESTERN CONFERENCE
Coastal Division

	W	L	T	Pct.	Pts.	OP
Los Angeles	11	1	2	.917	398	196
Baltimore	11	1	2	.917	394	198
San Francisco	7	7	0	.500	273	337
Atlanta	1	12	1	.077	175	422

Central Division

	W	L	T	Pct.	Pts.	OP
Green Bay	9	4	1	.692	332	209
Chicago	7	6	1	.538	239	218
Detroit	5	7	2	.417	260	259
Minnesota	3	8	3	.273	233	294

Los Angeles won division title on the basis of advantage in points (58-34) in two games vs. Baltimore.

Conference championships: DALLAS 52, Cleveland 14; GREEN BAY 28, Los Angeles 7
NFL championship: GREEN BAY 21, Dallas 17
Super Bowl II: Green Bay (NFL) 33, Oakland (AFL) 14, at Orange Bowl, Miami, Florida

1967 AFL

EASTERN DIVISION

	W	L	T	Pct.	Pts.	OP
Houston	9	4	1	.692	258	199
N.Y. Jets	8	5	1	.615	371	329
Buffalo	4	10	0	.286	237	285
Miami	4	10	0	.286	219	407
Boston Patriots	3	10	1	.231	280	389

WESTERN DIVISION

	W	L	T	Pct.	Pts.	OP
Oakland	13	1	0	.929	468	233
Kansas City	9	5	0	.643	408	254
San Diego	8	5	1	.615	360	352
Denver	3	11	0	.214	256	409

AFL championship: OAKLAND 40, Houston 7

1966 NFL

EASTERN CONFERENCE

	W	L	T	Pct.	Pts.	OP
Dallas	10	3	1	.769	445	239
Cleveland	9	5	0	.643	403	259
Philadelphia	9	5	0	.643	326	340
St. Louis	8	5	1	.615	264	265
Washington	7	7	0	.500	351	355
Pittsburgh	5	8	1	.385	316	347
Atlanta	3	11	0	.214	204	437
N.Y. Giants	1	12	1	.077	263	501

WESTERN CONFERENCE

	W	L	T	Pct.	Pts.	OP
Green Bay	12	2	0	.857	335	163
Baltimore	9	5	0	.643	314	226
Los Angeles	8	6	0	.571	289	212
San Francisco	6	6	2	.500	320	325
Chicago	5	7	2	.417	234	272
Detroit	4	9	1	.308	206	317
Minnesota	4	9	1	.308	292	304

NFL championship: Green Bay 34, DALLAS 27
Super Bowl I: Green Bay (NFL) 35, Kansas City (AFL) 10, at Memorial Coliseum, Los Angeles, California

1966 AFL

EASTERN DIVISION

	W	L	T	Pct.	Pts.	OP
Buffalo	9	4	1	.692	358	255
Boston Patriots	8	4	2	.677	315	283
N.Y. Jets	6	6	2	.500	322	312
Houston	3	11	0	.214	335	396
Miami	3	11	0	.214	213	362

WESTERN DIVISION

	W	L	T	Pct.	Pts.	OP
Kansas City	11	2	1	.846	448	276
Oakland	8	5	1	.615	315	288
San Diego	7	6	1	.538	335	284
Denver	4	10	0	.286	196	381

AFL championship: Kansas City 31, BUFFALO 7

1965 NFL

EASTERN CONFERENCE

	W	L	T	Pct.	Pts.	OP
Cleveland	11	3	0	.786	363	325
Dallas	7	7	0	.500	325	280
N.Y. Giants	7	7	0	.500	270	338
Washington	6	8	0	.429	257	301
Philadelphia	5	9	0	.357	363	359
St. Louis	5	9	0	.357	296	309
Pittsburgh	2	12	0	.143	202	397

WESTERN CONFERENCE

	W	L	T	Pct.	Pts.	OP
Green Bay	10	3	1	.769	316	224
Baltimore	10	3	1	.769	389	284
Chicago	9	5	0	.643	409	275
San Francisco	7	6	1	.538	421	402
Minnesota	7	7	0	.500	383	403
Detroit	6	7	1	.462	257	295
Los Angeles	4	10	0	.286	269	328

Western Conference playoff: GREEN BAY 13, Baltimore 10 (OT)
NFL championship: GREEN BAY 23, Cleveland 12

1965 AFL

EASTERN DIVISION

	W	L	T	Pct.	Pts.	OP
Buffalo	10	3	1	.769	313	226
N.Y. Jets	5	8	1	.385	285	303
Boston Patriots	4	8	2	.333	244	302
Houston	4	10	0	.286	298	429

WESTERN DIVISION

	W	L	T	Pct.	Pts.	OP
San Diego	9	2	3	.818	340	227
Oakland	8	5	1	.615	298	239
Kansas City	7	5	2	.583	322	285
Denver	4	10	0	.286	303	392

AFL championship: Buffalo 23, SAN DIEGO 0

1964 NFL

EASTERN CONFERENCE

	W	L	T	Pct.	Pts.	OP
Cleveland	10	3	1	.769	415	293
St. Louis	9	3	2	.750	357	331
Philadelphia	6	8	0	.429	312	313
Washington	6	8	0	.429	307	305
Dallas	5	8	1	.385	250	289
Pittsburgh	5	9	0	.357	253	315
N.Y. Giants	2	10	2	.167	241	399

WESTERN CONFERENCE

	W	L	T	Pct.	Pts.	OP
Baltimore	12	2	0	.857	428	225
Green Bay	8	5	1	.615	342	245
Minnesota	8	5	1	.615	355	296
Detroit	7	5	2	.583	280	260
Los Angeles	5	7	2	.417	283	339
Chicago	5	9	0	.357	260	379
San Francisco	4	10	0	.286	236	330

NFL championship: CLEVELAND 27, Baltimore 0

1964 AFL

EASTERN DIVISION

	W	L	T	Pct.	Pts.	OP
Buffalo	12	2	0	.857	400	242
Boston Patriots	10	3	1	.769	365	297
N.Y. Jets	5	8	1	.385	278	315
Houston	4	10	0	.286	310	355

WESTERN DIVISION

	W	L	T	Pct.	Pts.	OP
San Diego	8	5	1	.615	341	300
Kansas City	7	7	0	.500	366	306
Oakland	5	7	2	.417	303	350
Denver	2	11	1	.154	240	438

AFL championship: BUFFALO 20, San Diego 7

1963 NFL

EASTERN CONFERENCE

	W	L	T	Pct.	Pts.	OP
N.Y. Giants	11	3	0	.786	448	280
Cleveland	10	4	0	.714	343	262
St. Louis	9	5	0	.643	341	283
Pittsburgh	7	4	3	.636	321	295
Dallas	4	10	0	.286	305	378
Washington	3	11	0	.214	279	398
Philadelphia	2	10	2	.167	242	381

WESTERN CONFERENCE

	W	L	T	Pct.	Pts.	OP
Chicago	11	1	2	.917	301	144
Green Bay	11	2	1	.846	369	206
Baltimore	8	6	0	.571	316	285
Detroit	5	8	1	.385	326	265
Minnesota	5	8	1	.385	309	390
Los Angeles	5	9	0	.357	210	350
San Francisco	2	12	0	.143	198	391

NFL championship: CHICAGO 14, N.Y. Giants 10

1963 AFL

EASTERN DIVISION

	W	L	T	Pct.	Pts.	OP
Boston Patriots	7	6	1	.538	327	257
Buffalo	7	6	1	.538	304	291
Houston	6	8	0	.429	302	372
N.Y. Jets	5	8	1	.385	249	399

WESTERN DIVISION

	W	L	T	Pct.	Pts.	OP
San Diego	11	3	0	.786	399	255
Oakland	10	4	0	.714	363	282
Kansas City	5	7	2	.417	347	263
Denver	2	11	1	.154	301	473

Eastern Division playoff: Boston 26, BUFFALO 8
AFL championship: SAN DIEGO 51, Boston 10

1962 NFL

EASTERN CONFERENCE

	W	L	T	Pct.	Pts.	OP
N.Y. Giants	12	2	0	.857	398	283
Pittsburgh	9	5	0	.643	312	363
Cleveland	7	6	1	.538	291	257
Washington	5	7	2	.417	305	376
Dallas Cowboys	5	8	1	.385	398	402
St. Louis	4	9	1	.308	287	361
Philadelphia	3	10	1	.231	282	356

WESTERN CONFERENCE

	W	L	T	Pct.	Pts.	OP
Green Bay	13	1	0	.929	415	148
Detroit	11	3	0	.786	315	177
Chicago	9	5	0	.643	321	287
Baltimore	7	7	0	.500	293	288
San Francisco	6	8	0	.429	282	331
Minnesota	2	11	1	.154	254	410
Los Angeles	1	12	1	.077	220	334

NFL championship: Green Bay 16, N.Y. GIANTS 7

1962 AFL

EASTERN DIVISION

	W	L	T	Pct.	Pts.	OP
Houston	11	3	0	.786	387	270
Boston Patriots	9	4	1	.692	346	295
Buffalo	7	6	1	.538	309	272
N.Y. Titans	5	9	0	.357	278	423

WESTERN DIVISION

	W	L	T	Pct.	Pts.	OP
Dallas Texans	11	3	0	.786	389	233
Denver	7	7	0	.500	353	334
San Diego	4	10	0	.286	314	392
Oakland	1	13	0	.071	213	370

AFL championship: Dallas Texans 20, HOUSTON 17 (OT)

1961 NFL

EASTERN CONFERENCE

	W	L	T	Pct.	Pts.	OP
N.Y. Giants	10	3	1	.769	368	220
Philadelphia	10	4	0	.714	361	297
Cleveland	8	5	1	.615	319	270
St. Louis	7	7	0	.500	279	267
Pittsburgh	6	8	0	.429	295	287
Dallas Cowboys	4	9	1	.308	236	380
Washington	1	12	1	.077	174	392

WESTERN CONFERENCE

	W	L	T	Pct.	Pts.	OP
Green Bay	11	3	0	.786	391	223
Detroit	8	5	1	.615	270	258
Baltimore	8	6	0	.571	302	307
Chicago	8	6	0	.571	326	302
San Francisco	7	6	1	.538	346	272
Los Angeles	4	10	0	.286	263	333
Minnesota	3	11	0	.214	285	407

NFL championship: GREEN BAY 37, N.Y. Giants 0

1961 AFL

EASTERN DIVISION

	W	L	T	Pct.	Pts.	OP
Houston	10	3	1	.769	513	242
Boston Patriots	9	4	1	.692	413	313
N.Y. Titans	7	7	0	.500	301	390
Buffalo	6	8	0	.429	294	342

WESTERN DIVISION

	W	L	T	Pct.	Pts.	OP
San Diego	12	2	0	.857	396	219
Dallas Texans	6	8	0	.429	334	343
Denver	3	11	0	.214	251	432
Oakland	2	12	0	.143	237	458

AFL championship: Houston 10, SAN DIEGO 3

1960 NFL

EASTERN CONFERENCE

	W	L	T	Pct.	Pts.	OP
Philadelphia	10	2	0	.833	321	246
Cleveland	8	3	1	.727	362	217
N.Y. Giants	6	4	2	.600	271	261
St. Louis	6	5	1	.545	288	230
Pittsburgh	5	6	1	.455	240	275
Washington	1	9	2	.100	178	309

WESTERN CONFERENCE

	W	L	T	Pct.	Pts.	OP
Green Bay	8	4	0	.667	332	209
Detroit	7	5	0	.583	239	212
San Francisco	7	5	0	.583	208	205
Baltimore	6	6	0	.500	288	234
Chicago	5	6	1	.455	194	299
L.A. Rams	4	7	1	.364	265	297
Dallas Cowboys	0	11	1	.000	177	369

NFL championship: PHILADELPHIA 17, Green Bay 13

1960 AFL

EASTERN CONFERENCE

	W	L	T	Pct.	Pts.	OP
Houston	10	4	0	.714	379	285
N.Y. Titans	7	7	0	.500	382	399
Buffalo	5	8	1	.385	296	303
Boston	5	9	0	.357	286	349

WESTERN CONFERENCE

	W	L	T	Pct.	Pts.	OP
L.A. Chargers	10	4	0	.714	373	336
Dallas Texans	8	6	0	.571	362	253
Oakland	6	8	0	.429	319	388
Denver	4	9	1	.308	309	393

AFL championship: HOUSTON 24, L.A. Chargers 16

1959

EASTERN CONFERENCE

	W	L	T	Pct.	Pts.	OP
N.Y. Giants	10	2	0	.833	284	170
Cleveland	7	5	0	.583	270	214
Philadelphia	7	5	0	.583	268	278
Pittsburgh	6	5	1	.545	257	216
Washington	3	9	0	.250	185	350
Chi. Cardinals	2	10	0	.167	234	324

WESTERN CONFERENCE

	W	L	T	Pct.	Pts.	OP
Baltimore	9	3	0	.750	374	251
Chi. Bears	8	4	0	.667	252	196
Green Bay	7	5	0	.583	248	246
San Francisco	7	5	0	.583	255	237
Detroit	3	8	1	.273	203	275
Los Angeles	2	10	0	.167	242	315

NFL championship: BALTIMORE 31, N.Y. Giants 16

1958

EASTERN CONFERENCE

	W	L	T	Pct.	Pts.	OP
N.Y. Giants	9	3	0	.750	246	183
Cleveland	9	3	0	.750	302	217
Pittsburgh	7	4	1	.636	261	230
Washington	4	7	1	.364	214	268
Chi. Cardinals	2	9	1	.182	261	356
Philadelphia	2	9	1	.182	235	306

WESTERN CONFERENCE

	W	L	T	Pct.	Pts.	OP
Baltimore	9	3	0	.750	381	203
Chi. Bears	8	4	0	.667	298	230
Los Angeles	8	4	0	.667	344	278
San Francisco	6	6	0	.500	257	324
Detroit	4	7	1	.364	261	276
Green Bay	1	10	1	.091	193	382

Eastern Conference playoff: N.Y. GIANTS 10, Cleveland 0
NFL championship: Baltimore 23, N.Y. GIANTS 17 (OT)

1957

EASTERN CONFERENCE

	W	L	T	Pct.	Pts.	OP
Cleveland	9	2	1	.818	269	172
N.Y. Giants	7	5	0	.583	254	211
Pittsburgh	6	6	0	.500	161	178
Washington	5	6	1	.455	251	230
Philadelphia	4	8	0	.333	173	230
Chi. Cardinals	3	9	0	.250	200	299

WESTERN CONFERENCE

	W	L	T	Pct.	Pts.	OP
Detroit	8	4	0	.667	251	231
San Francisco	8	4	0	.667	260	264
Baltimore	7	5	0	.583	303	235
Los Angeles	6	6	0	.500	307	278
Chi. Bears	5	7	0	.417	203	211
Green Bay	3	9	0	.250	218	311

Western Conference playoff: Detroit 31, SAN FRANCISCO 27
NFL championship: DETROIT 59, Cleveland 14

1956

EASTERN CONFERENCE

	W	L	T	Pct.	Pts.	OP
N.Y. Giants	8	3	1	.727	264	197
Chi. Cardinals	7	5	0	.583	240	182
Washington	6	6	0	.500	183	225
Cleveland	5	7	0	.417	167	177
Pittsburgh	5	7	0	.417	217	250
Philadelphia	3	8	1	.273	143	215

WESTERN CONFERENCE

	W	L	T	Pct.	Pts.	OP
Chi. Bears	9	2	1	.818	363	246
Detroit	9	3	0	.750	300	188
San Francisco	5	6	1	.455	233	284
Baltimore	5	7	0	.417	270	322
Green Bay	4	8	0	.333	264	342
Los Angeles	4	8	0	.333	291	307

NFL championship: N.Y. GIANTS 47, Chi. Bears 7

1955

EASTERN CONFERENCE

	W	L	T	Pct.	Pts.	OP
Cleveland	9	2	1	.818	349	218
Washington	8	4	0	.667	246	222
N.Y. Giants	6	5	1	.545	267	223
Chi. Cardinals	4	7	1	.364	224	252
Philadelphia	4	7	1	.364	248	231
Pittsburgh	4	8	0	.333	195	285

WESTERN CONFERENCE

	W	L	T	Pct.	Pts.	OP
Los Angeles	8	3	1	.727	260	231
Chi. Bears	8	4	0	.667	294	251
Green Bay	6	6	0	.500	258	276
Baltimore	5	6	1	.455	214	239
San Francisco	4	8	0	.333	216	298
Detroit	3	9	0	.250	230	275

NFL championship: Cleveland 38, LOS ANGELES 14

1954

EASTERN CONFERENCE

	W	L	T	Pct.	Pts.	OP
Cleveland	9	3	0	.750	336	162
Philadelphia	7	4	1	.636	284	230
N.Y. Giants	7	5	0	.583	293	184
Pittsburgh	5	7	0	.417	219	263
Washington	3	9	0	.250	207	432
Chi. Cardinals	2	10	0	.167	183	347

WESTERN CONFERENCE

	W	L	T	Pct.	Pts.	OP
Detroit	9	2	1	.818	337	189
Chi. Bears	8	4	0	.667	301	279
San Francisco	7	4	1	.636	313	251
Los Angeles	6	5	1	.545	314	285
Green Bay	4	8	0	.333	234	251
Baltimore	3	9	0	.250	131	279

NFL championship: CLEVELAND 56, Detroit 10

1953

EASTERN CONFERENCE

	W	L	T	Pct.	Pts.	OP
Cleveland	11	1	0	.917	348	162
Philadelphia	7	4	1	.636	352	215
Washington	6	5	1	.545	208	215
Pittsburgh	6	6	0	.500	211	263
N.Y. Giants	3	9	0	.250	179	277
Chi. Cardinals	1	10	1	.091	190	337

WESTERN CONFERENCE

	W	L	T	Pct.	Pts.	OP
Detroit	10	2	0	.833	271	205
San Francisco	9	3	0	.750	372	237
Los Angeles	8	3	1	.727	366	236
Chi. Bears	3	8	1	.273	218	262
Baltimore	3	9	0	.250	182	350
Green Bay	2	9	1	.182	200	338

NFL championship: DETROIT 17, Cleveland 16

1952

AMERICAN CONFERENCE

	W	L	T	Pct.	Pts.	OP
Cleveland	8	4	0	.667	310	213
N.Y. Giants	7	5	0	.583	234	231
Philadelphia	7	5	0	.583	252	271
Pittsburgh	5	7	0	.417	300	273
Chi. Cardinals	4	8	0	.333	172	221
Washington	4	8	0	.333	240	287

NATIONAL CONFERENCE

	W	L	T	Pct.	Pts.	OP
Detroit	9	3	0	.750	344	192
Los Angeles	9	3	0	.750	349	234
San Francisco	7	5	0	.583	285	221
Green Bay	6	6	0	.500	295	312
Chi. Bears	5	7	0	.417	245	326
Dallas Texans	1	11	0	.083	182	427

National Conference playoff: DETROIT 31, Los Angeles 21
NFL championship: Detroit 17, CLEVELAND 7

1951

AMERICAN CONFERENCE

	W	L	T	Pct.	Pts.	OP
Cleveland	11	1	0	.917	331	152
N.Y. Giants	9	2	1	.818	254	161
Washington	5	7	0	.417	183	296
Pittsburgh	4	7	1	.364	183	235
Philadelphia	4	8	0	.333	234	264
Chi. Cardinals	3	9	0	.250	210	287

NATIONAL CONFERENCE

	W	L	T	Pct.	Pts.	OP
Los Angeles	8	4	0	.667	392	261
Detroit	7	4	1	.636	336	259
San Francisco	7	4	1	.636	255	205
Chi. Bears	7	5	0	.583	286	282
Green Bay	3	9	0	.250	254	375
N.Y. Yanks	1	9	2	.100	241	382

NFL championship: LOS ANGELES 24, Cleveland 17

1950

AMERICAN CONFERENCE

	W	L	T	Pct.	Pts.	OP
Cleveland	10	2	0	.833	310	144
N.Y. Giants	10	2	0	.833	268	150
Philadelphia	6	6	0	.500	254	141
Pittsburgh	6	6	0	.500	180	195
Chi. Cardinals	5	7	0	.417	233	287
Washington	3	9	0	.250	232	326

NATIONAL CONFERENCE

	W	L	T	Pct.	Pts.	OP
Los Angeles	9	3	0	.750	466	309
Chi. Bears	9	3	0	.750	279	207
N.Y. Yanks	7	5	0	.583	366	367
Detroit	6	6	0	.500	321	285
Green Bay	3	9	0	.250	244	406
San Francisco	3	9	0	.250	213	300
Baltimore	1	11	0	.083	213	462

American Conference playoff: CLEVELAND 8, N.Y. Giants 3
National Conference playoff: LOS ANGELES 24, Chi. Bears 14
NFL championship: CLEVELAND 30, Los Angeles 28

1949

EASTERN DIVISION

	W	L	T	Pct.	Pts.	OP
Philadelphia	11	1	0	.917	364	134
Pittsburgh	6	5	1	.545	224	214
N.Y. Giants	6	6	0	.500	287	298
Washington	4	7	1	.364	268	339
N.Y. Bulldogs	1	10	1	.091	153	368

WESTERN DIVISION

	W	L	T	Pct.	Pts.	OP
Los Angeles	8	2	2	.800	360	239
Chi. Bears	9	3	0	.750	332	218
Chi. Cardinals	6	5	1	.545	360	301
Detroit	4	8	0	.333	237	259
Green Bay	2	10	0	.167	114	329

NFL championship: Philadelphia 14, LOS ANGELES 0

1948

EASTERN DIVISION

	W	L	T	Pct.	Pts.	OP
Philadelphia	9	2	1	.818	376	156
Washington	7	5	0	.583	291	287
N.Y. Giants	4	8	0	.333	297	388
Pittsburgh	4	8	0	.333	200	243
Boston	3	9	0	.250	174	372

WESTERN DIVISION

	W	L	T	Pct.	Pts.	OP
Chi. Cardinals	11	1	0	.917	395	226
Chi. Bears	10	2	0	.833	375	151
Los Angeles	6	5	1	.545	327	269
Green Bay	3	9	0	.250	154	290
Detroit	2	10	0	.167	200	407

NFL championship: PHILADELPHIA 7, Chi. Cardinals 0

1947

EASTERN DIVISION

	W	L	T	Pct.	Pts.	OP
Philadelphia	8	4	0	.667	308	242
Pittsburgh	8	4	0	.667	240	259
Boston	4	7	1	.364	168	256
Washington	4	8	0	.333	295	367
N.Y. Giants	2	8	2	.200	190	309

WESTERN DIVISION

	W	L	T	Pct.	Pts.	OP
Chi. Cardinals	9	3	0	.750	306	231
Chi. Bears	8	4	0	.667	363	241
Green Bay	6	5	1	.545	274	210
Los Angeles	6	6	0	.500	259	214
Detroit	3	9	0	.250	231	305

Eastern Division playoff: Philadelphia 21, PITTSBURGH 0
NFL championship: CHI. CARDINALS 28, Philadelphia 21

1946

EASTERN DIVISION

	W	L	T	Pct.	Pts.	OP
N.Y. Giants	7	3	1	.700	236	162
Philadelphia	6	5	0	.545	231	220
Washington	5	5	1	.500	171	191
Pittsburgh	5	5	1	.500	136	117
Boston	2	8	1	.200	189	273

WESTERN DIVISION

	W	L	T	Pct.	Pts.	OP
Chi. Bears	8	2	1	.800	289	193
Los Angeles	6	4	1	.600	277	257
Green Bay	6	5	0	.545	148	158
Chi. Cardinals	6	5	0	.545	260	198
Detroit	1	10	0	.091	142	310

NFL championship: Chi. Bears 24, N.Y. GIANTS 14

1945

EASTERN DIVISION

	W	L	T	Pct.	Pts.	OP
Washington	8	2	0	.800	209	121
Philadelphia	7	3	0	.700	272	133
N.Y. Giants	3	6	1	.333	179	198
Boston	3	6	1	.333	123	211
Pittsburgh	2	8	0	.200	79	220

WESTERN DIVISION

	W	L	T	Pct.	Pts.	OP
Cleveland	9	1	0	.900	244	136
Detroit	7	3	0	.700	195	194
Green Bay	6	4	0	.600	258	173
Chi. Bears	3	7	0	.300	192	235
Chi. Cardinals	1	9	0	.100	98	228

NFL championship: CLEVELAND 15, Washington 14

1944

EASTERN DIVISION

	W	L	T	Pct.	Pts.	OP
N.Y. Giants	8	1	1	.889	206	75
Philadelphia	7	1	2	.875	267	131
Washington	6	3	1	.667	169	180
Boston	2	8	0	.200	82	233
Brooklyn	0	10	0	.000	69	166

WESTERN DIVISION

	W	L	T	Pct.	Pts.	OP
Green Bay	8	2	0	.800	238	141
Chi. Bears	6	3	1	.667	258	172
Detroit	6	3	1	.667	216	151
Cleveland	4	6	0	.400	188	224
Card-Pitt	0	10	0	.000	108	328

NFL championship: Green Bay 14, N.Y. GIANTS 7

1943

EASTERN DIVISION

	W	L	T	Pct.	Pts.	OP
Washington	6	3	1	.667	229	137
N.Y. Giants	6	3	1	.667	197	170
Phil-Pitt	5	4	1	.556	225	230
Brooklyn	2	8	0	.200	65	234

WESTERN DIVISION

	W	L	T	Pct.	Pts.	OP
Chi. Bears	8	1	1	.889	303	157
Green Bay	7	2	1	.778	264	172
Detroit	3	6	1	.333	178	218
Chi. Cardinals	0	10	0	.000	95	238

Eastern Division playoff: Washington 28, N.Y. GIANTS 0
NFL championship: CHI. BEARS 41, Washington 21

1942

EASTERN DIVISION

	W	L	T	Pct.	Pts.	OP
Washington	10	1	0	.909	227	102
Pittsburgh	7	4	0	.636	167	119
N.Y. Giants	5	5	1	.500	155	139
Brooklyn	3	8	0	.273	100	168
Philadelphia	2	9	0	.182	134	239

WESTERN DIVISION

	W	L	T	Pct.	Pts.	OP
Chi. Bears	11	0	0	1.000	376	84
Green Bay	8	2	1	.800	300	215
Cleveland	5	6	0	.455	150	207
Chi. Cardinals	3	8	0	.273	98	209
Detroit	0	11	0	.000	38	263

NFL championship: WASHINGTON 14, Chi. Bears 6

1941

EASTERN DIVISION

	W	L	T	Pct.	Pts.	OP
N.Y. Giants	8	3	0	.727	238	114
Brooklyn	7	4	0	.636	158	127
Washington	6	5	0	.545	176	174
Philadelphia	2	8	1	.200	119	218
Pittsburgh	1	9	1	.100	103	276

WESTERN DIVISION

	W	L	T	Pct.	Pts.	OP
Chi. Bears	10	1	0	.909	396	147
Green Bay	10	1	0	.909	258	120
Detroit	4	6	1	.400	121	195
Chi. Cardinals	3	7	1	.300	127	197
Cleveland	2	9	0	.182	116	244

Western Division playoff: CHI. BEARS 33, Green Bay 14
NFL championship: CHI. BEARS 37, N.Y. Giants 9

1940

EASTERN DIVISION

	W	L	T	Pct.	Pts.	OP
Washington	9	2	0	.818	245	142
Brooklyn	8	3	0	.727	186	120
N.Y. Giants	6	4	1	.600	131	133
Pittsburgh	2	7	2	.222	60	178
Philadelphia	1	10	0	.091	111	211

WESTERN DIVISION

	W	L	T	Pct.	Pts.	OP
Chi. Bears	8	3	0	.727	238	152
Green Bay	6	4	1	.600	238	155
Detroit	5	5	1	.500	138	153
Cleveland	4	6	1	.400	171	191
Chi. Cardinals	2	7	2	.222	139	222

NFL championship: Chi. Bears 73, WASHINGTON 0

1939

EASTERN DIVISION

	W	L	T	Pct.	Pts.	OP
N.Y. Giants	9	1	1	.900	168	85
Washington	8	2	1	.800	242	94
Brooklyn	4	6	1	.400	108	219
Philadelphia	1	9	1	.100	105	200
Pittsburgh	1	9	1	.100	114	216

WESTERN DIVISION

	W	L	T	Pct.	Pts.	OP
Green Bay	9	2	0	.818	233	153
Chi. Bears	8	3	0	.727	298	157
Detroit	6	5	0	.545	145	150
Cleveland	5	5	1	.500	195	164
Chi. Cardinals	1	10	0	.091	84	254

NFL championship: GREEN BAY 27, N.Y. Giants 0

1938

EASTERN DIVISION

	W	L	T	Pct.	Pts.	OP
N.Y. Giants	8	2	1	.800	194	79
Washington	6	3	2	.667	148	154
Brooklyn	4	4	3	.500	131	161
Philadelphia	5	6	0	.455	154	164
Pittsburgh	2	9	0	.182	79	169

WESTERN DIVISION

	W	L	T	Pct.	Pts.	OP
Green Bay	8	3	0	.727	223	118
Detroit	7	4	0	.636	119	108
Chi. Bears	6	5	0	.545	194	148
Cleveland	4	7	0	.364	131	215
Chi. Cardinals	2	9	0	.182	111	168

NFL championship: N.Y. GIANTS 23, Green Bay 17

1937

EASTERN DIVISION

	W	L	T	Pct.	Pts.	OP
Washington	8	3	0	.727	195	120
N.Y. Giants	6	3	2	.667	128	109
Pittsburgh	4	7	0	.364	122	145
Brooklyn	3	7	1	.300	82	174
Philadelphia	2	8	1	.200	86	177

WESTERN DIVISION

	W	L	T	Pct.	Pts.	OP
Chi. Bears	9	1	1	.900	201	100
Green Bay	7	4	0	.636	220	122
Detroit	7	4	0	.636	180	105
Chi. Cardinals	5	5	1	.500	135	165
Cleveland	1	10	0	.091	75	207

NFL championship: Washington 28, CHI. BEARS 21

1936

EASTERN DIVISION

	W	L	T	Pct.	Pts.	OP
Boston	7	5	0	.583	149	110
Pittsburgh	6	6	0	.500	98	187
N.Y. Giants	5	6	1	.455	115	163
Brooklyn	3	8	1	.273	92	161
Philadelphia	1	11	0	.083	51	206

WESTERN DIVISION

	W	L	T	Pct.	Pts.	OP
Green Bay	10	1	1	.909	248	118
Chi. Bears	9	3	0	.750	222	94
Detroit	8	4	0	.667	235	102
Chi. Cardinals	3	8	1	.273	74	143

NFL championship: Green Bay 21, Boston 6, at Polo Grounds, N.Y.

1935

EASTERN DIVISION

	W	L	T	Pct.	Pts.	OP
N.Y. Giants	9	3	0	.750	180	96
Brooklyn	5	6	1	.455	90	141
Pittsburgh	4	8	0	.333	100	209
Boston	2	8	1	.200	65	123
Philadelphia	2	9	0	.182	60	179

WESTERN DIVISION

	W	L	T	Pct.	Pts.	OP
Detroit	7	3	2	.700	191	111
Green Bay	8	4	0	.667	181	96
Chi. Bears	6	4	2	.600	192	106
Chi. Cardinals	6	4	2	.600	99	97

NFL championship: DETROIT 26, N.Y. Giants 7
One game between Boston and Philadelphia was canceled.

1934

EASTERN DIVISION

	W	L	T	Pct.	Pts.	OP
N.Y. Giants	8	5	0	.615	147	107
Boston	6	6	0	.500	107	94
Brooklyn	4	7	0	.364	61	153
Philadelphia	4	7	0	.364	127	85
Pittsburgh	2	10	0	.167	51	206

WESTERN DIVISION

	W	L	T	Pct.	Pts.	OP
Chi. Bears	13	0	0	1.000	286	86
Detroit	10	3	0	.769	238	59
Green Bay	7	6	0	.538	156	112
Chi. Cardinals	5	6	0	.455	80	84
St. Louis	1	2	0	.333	27	61
Cincinnati	0	8	0	.000	10	243

NFL championship: N.Y. GIANTS 30, Chi. Bears 13

1933

EASTERN DIVISION

	W	L	T	Pct.	Pts.	OP
N.Y. Giants	11	3	0	.786	244	101
Brooklyn	5	4	1	.556	93	54
Boston	5	5	2	.500	103	97
Philadelphia	3	5	1	.375	77	158
Pittsburgh	3	6	2	.333	67	208

WESTERN DIVISION

	W	L	T	Pct.	Pts.	OP
Chi. Bears	10	2	1	.833	133	82
Portsmouth	6	5	0	.545	128	87
Green Bay	5	7	1	.417	170	107
Cincinnati	3	6	1	.333	38	110
Chi. Cardinals	1	9	1	.100	52	101

NFL championship: CHI. BEARS 23, N.Y. Giants 21

1932

	W	L	T	Pct.
Chicago Bears	7	1	6	.875
Green Bay Packers	10	3	1	.769
Portsmouth Spartans	6	2	4	.750
Boston Braves	4	4	2	.500
New York Giants	4	6	2	.400
Brooklyn Dodgers	3	9	0	.250
Chicago Cardinals	2	6	2	.250
Staten Island Stapletons	2	7	3	.222

Chicago Bears and Portsmouth finished regularly scheduled games tied for first place. Bears won playoff game, which counted in standings, 9-0.

1931

	W	L	T	Pct.
Green Bay Packers	12	2	0	.857
Portsmouth Spartans	11	3	0	.786
Chicago Bears	8	5	0	.615
Chicago Cardinals	5	4	0	.556
New York Giants	7	6	1	.538
Providence Steam Roller	4	4	3	.500
Staten Island Stapletons	4	6	1	.400
Cleveland Indians	2	8	0	.200
Brooklyn Dodgers	2	12	0	.143
Frankford Yellow Jackets	1	6	1	.143

1930

	W	L	T	Pct.
Green Bay Packers	10	3	1	.769
New York Giants	13	4	0	.765
Chicago Bears	9	4	1	.692
Brooklyn Dodgers	7	4	1	.636
Providence Steam Roller	6	4	1	.600
Staten Island Stapletons	5	5	2	.500
Chicago Cardinals	5	6	2	.455
Portsmouth Spartans	5	6	3	.455
Frankford Yellow Jackets	4	13	1	.222
Minneapolis Red Jackets	1	7	1	.125
Newark Tornadoes	1	10	1	.091

1929

	W	L	T	Pct.
Green Bay Packers	12	0	1	1.000
New York Giants	13	1	1	.929
Frankford Yellow Jackets	10	4	5	.714
Chicago Cardinals	6	6	1	.500
Boston Bulldogs	4	4	0	.500
Staten Island Stapletons	3	4	3	.429
Providence Steam Roller	4	6	2	.400
Orange Tornadoes	3	5	4	.375
Chicago Bears	4	9	2	.308
Buffalo Bisons	1	7	1	.125
Minneapolis Red Jackets	1	9	0	.100
Dayton Triangles	0	6	0	.000

1928

	W	L	T	Pct.
Providence Steam Roller	8	1	2	.889
Frankford Yellow Jackets	11	3	2	.786
Detroit Wolverines	7	2	1	.778
Green Bay Packers	6	4	3	.600
Chicago Bears	7	5	1	.583
New York Giants	4	7	2	.364
New York Yankees	4	8	1	.333
Pottsville Maroons	2	8	0	.200
Chicago Cardinals	1	5	0	.167
Dayton Triangles	0	7	0	.000

1927

	W	L	T	Pct.
New York Giants	11	1	1	.917
Green Bay Packers	7	2	1	.778
Chicago Bears	9	3	2	.750
Cleveland Bulldogs	8	4	1	.667
Providence Steam Roller	8	5	1	.615
New York Yankees	7	8	1	.467
Frankford Yellow Jackets	6	9	3	.400
Pottsville Maroons	5	8	0	.385
Chicago Cardinals	3	7	1	.300
Dayton Triangles	1	6	1	.143
Duluth Eskimos	1	8	0	.111
Buffalo Bisons	0	5	0	.000

1926

	W	L	T	Pct.
Frankford Yellow Jackets	14	1	2	.933
Chicago Bears	12	1	3	.923
Pottsville Maroons	10	2	2	.833
Kansas City Cowboys	8	3	0	.727
Green Bay Packers	7	3	3	.700
Los Angeles Buccaneers	6	3	1	.667
New York Giants	8	4	1	.667
Duluth Eskimos	6	5	3	.545
Buffalo Rangers	4	4	2	.500
Chicago Cardinals	5	6	1	.455
Providence Steam Roller	5	7	1	.417
Detroit Panthers	4	6	2	.400
Hartford Blues	3	7	0	.300
Brooklyn Lions	3	8	0	.273
Milwaukee Badgers	2	7	0	.222
Akron Pros	1	4	3	.200
Dayton Triangles	1	4	1	.200
Racine Tornadoes	1	4	0	.200
Columbus Tigers	1	6	0	.143
Canton Bulldogs	1	9	3	.100
Hammond Pros	0	4	0	.000
Louisville Colonels	0	4	0	.000

1925

	W	L	T	Pct.
Chicago Cardinals	11	2	1	.846
Pottsville Maroons	10	2	0	.833
Detroit Panthers	8	2	2	.800
New York Giants	8	4	0	.667
Akron Indians	4	2	2	.667
Frankford Yellow Jackets	13	7	0	.650
Chicago Bears	9	5	3	.643
Rock Island Independents	5	3	3	.625
Green Bay Packers	8	5	0	.615
Providence Steam Roller	6	5	1	.545
Canton Bulldogs	4	4	0	.500
Cleveland Bulldogs	5	8	1	.385
Kansas City Cowboys	2	5	1	.286
Hammond Pros	1	4	0	.200
Buffalo Bisons	1	6	2	.143
Duluth Kelleys	0	3	0	.000
Rochester Jeffersons	0	6	1	.000
Milwaukee Badgers	0	6	0	.000
Dayton Triangles	0	7	1	.000
Columbus Tigers	0	9	0	.000

1924

	W	L	T	Pct.
Cleveland Bulldogs	7	1	1	.875
Chicago Bears	6	1	4	.857
Frankford Yellow Jackets	11	2	1	.846
Duluth Kelleys	5	1	0	.833
Rock Island Independents	5	2	2	.714
Green Bay Packers	7	4	0	.636
Racine Legion	4	3	3	.571
Chicago Cardinals	5	4	1	.556
Buffalo Bisons	6	5	0	.545
Columbus Tigers	4	4	0	.500
Hammond Pros	2	2	1	.500
Milwaukee Badgers	5	8	0	.385
Akron Indians	2	6	0	.250
Dayton Triangles	2	6	0	.250
Kansas City Blues	2	7	0	.222
Kenosha Maroons	0	4	1	.000
Minneapolis Marines	0	6	0	.000
Rochester Jeffersons	0	7	0	.000

1923

	W	L	T	Pct.
Canton Bulldogs	11	0	1	1.000
Chicago Bears	9	2	1	.818
Green Bay Packers	7	2	1	.778
Milwaukee Badgers	7	2	3	.778
Cleveland Indians	3	1	3	.750
Chicago Cardinals	8	4	0	.667
Duluth Kelleys	4	3	0	.571
Buffalo All-Americans	5	4	3	.556
Columbus Tigers	5	4	1	.556
Racine Legion	4	4	2	.500
Toledo Maroons	3	3	2	.500
Rock Island Independents	2	3	3	.400
Minneapolis Marines	2	5	2	.286
St. Louis All-Stars	1	4	2	.200
Hammond Pros	1	5	1	.167
Dayton Triangles	1	6	1	.143
Akron Indians	1	6	0	.143
Oorang Indians	1	10	0	.091
Louisville Brecks	0	3	0	.000
Rochester Jeffersons	0	4	0	.000

1922

	W	L	T	Pct.
Canton Bulldogs	10	0	2	1.000
Chicago Bears	9	3	0	.750
Chicago Cardinals	8	3	0	.727
Toledo Maroons	5	2	2	.714
Rock Island Independents	4	2	1	.667
Racine Legion	6	4	1	.600
Dayton Triangles	4	3	1	.571
Green Bay Packers	4	3	3	.571
Buffalo All-Americans	5	4	1	.556
Akron Pros	3	5	2	.375
Milwaukee Badgers	2	4	3	.333
Oorang Indians	3	6	0	.333
Minneapolis Marines	1	3	0	.250
Louisville Brecks	1	3	0	.250
Evansville Crimson Giants	0	3	0	.000
Rochester Jeffersons	0	4	1	.000
Hammond Pros	0	5	1	.000
Columbus Panhandles	0	8	0	.000

1921

	W	L	T	Pct.
Chicago Staleys	9	1	1	.900
Buffalo All-Americans	9	1	2	.900
Akron Pros	8	3	1	.727
Canton Bulldogs	5	2	3	.714
Rock Island Independents	4	2	1	.667
Evansville Crimson Giants	3	2	0	.600
Green Bay Packers	3	2	1	.600
Dayton Triangles	4	4	1	.500
Chicago Cardinals	3	3	2	.500
Rochester Jeffersons	2	3	0	.400
Cleveland Indians	3	5	0	.375
Washington Senators	1	2	0	.333
Cincinnati Celts	1	3	0	.250
Hammond Pros	1	3	1	.250
Minneapolis Marines	1	3	0	.250
Detroit Heralds	1	5	1	.167
Columbus Panhandles	1	8	0	.111
Tonawanda Kardex	0	1	0	.000
Muncie Flyers	0	2	0	.000
Louisville Brecks	0	2	0	.000
New York Giants	0	2	0	.000

1920*

	W	L	T	Pct.
Akron Pros	8	0	3	1.000
Decatur Staleys	10	1	2	.909
Buffalo All-Americans	9	1	1	.900
Chicago Cardinals	6	2	2	.750
Rock Island Independents	6	2	2	.750
Dayton Triangles	5	2	2	.714
Rochester Jeffersons	6	3	2	.667
Canton Bulldogs	7	4	2	.636
Detroit Heralds	2	3	3	.400
Cleveland Tigers	2	4	2	.333
Chicago Tigers	2	5	1	.286
Hammond Pros	2	5	0	.286
Columbus Panhandles	2	6	2	.250
Muncie Flyers	0	1	0	.000

*No official standing was maintained for the 1920 season, and the championship was awarded to the Akron Pros in a League meeting on April 30, 1921. Clubs played schedules which included games against non-league opponents.

RS=REGULAR SEASON
PS=POSTSEASON

*ARIZONA vs. ATLANTA
RS: Cardinals lead series, 12-6
1966—Falcons, 16-10 (A)
1968—Cardinals, 17-12 (StL)
1971—Cardinals, 26-9 (A)
1973—Cardinals, 32-10 (A)
1975—Cardinals, 23-20 (StL)
1978—Cardinals, 42-21 (StL)
1980—Falcons, 33-27 (StL) OT
1981—Falcons, 41-20 (A)
1982—Cardinals, 23-20 (A)
1986—Falcons, 33-13 (A)
1987—Cardinals, 34-21 (A)
1989—Cardinals, 34-20 (P)
1990—Cardinals, 24-13 (A)
1991—Cardinals, 16-10 (P)
1992—Falcons, 20-17 (A)
1993—Cardinals, 27-10 (A)
1994—Falcons, 10-6 (Atl)
1995—Cardinals, 40-37 (Ariz) OT
(RS Pts.—Cardinals 431, Falcons 356)
*Franchise known as Phoenix prior to
1994 and in St. Louis prior to 1988*

*ARIZONA vs. BUFFALO
RS: Series tied, 3-3
1971—Cardinals, 28-23 (B)
1975—Bills, 32-14 (StL)
1981—Cardinals, 24-0 (StL)
1984—Cardinals, 37-7 (StL)
1986—Bills, 17-10 (B)
1990—Bills, 45-14 (B)
(RS Pts.—Cardinals 127, Bills 124)
*Franchise known as Phoenix prior to
1994 and in St. Louis prior to 1988*

ARIZONA vs. CAROLINA
RS: Panthers lead series, 1-0
1995—Panthers, 27-7 (C)
(RS Pts.—Panthers 27, Cardinals 7)

*ARIZONA vs. **CHICAGO
RS: Bears lead series, 52-25-6
(NP denotes Normal Park;
Wr denotes Wrigley Field;
Co denotes Comiskey Park;
So denotes Soldier Field;
all Chicago)
1920—Cardinals, 7-6 (NP)
     Staleys, 10-0 (Wr)
1921—Tie, 0-0 (Wr)
1922—Cardinals, 6-0 (Co)
     Cardinals, 9-0 (Co)
1923—Bears, 3-0 (Wr)
1924—Bears, 6-0 (Wr)
     Bears, 21-0 (Co)
1925—Cardinals, 9-0 (Co)
     Tie, 0-0 (Wr)
1926—Bears, 16-0 (Wr)
     Bears, 10-0 (So)
     Tie, 0-0 (Wr)
1927—Bears, 9-0 (NP)
     Cardinals, 3-0 (Wr)
1928—Bears, 15-0 (NP)
     Bears, 34-0 (Wr)
1929—Tie, 0-0 (Wr)
     Cardinals, 40-6 (Co)
1930—Bears, 32-6 (Co)
     Bears, 6-0 (Wr)
1931—Bears, 26-13 (Wr)
     Bears, 18-7 (Wr)
1932—Tie, 0-0 (Wr)
     Bears, 34-0 (Wr)
1933—Bears, 12-9 (Wr)
     Bears, 22-6 (Wr)
1934—Bears, 20-0 (Wr)
     Bears, 17-6 (Wr)
1935—Tie, 7-7 (Wr)
     Bears, 13-0 (Wr)
1936—Bears, 7-3 (Wr)
     Cardinals, 14-7 (Wr)
1937—Bears, 16-7 (Wr)
     Bears, 42-28 (Wr)
1938—Bears, 16-13 (So)

Bears, 34-28 (Wr)
1939—Bears, 44-7 (Wr)
     Bears, 48-7 (Co)
1940—Cardinals, 21-7 (Co)
     Bears, 31-23 (Wr)
1941—Bears, 53-7 (Wr)
     Bears, 34-24 (Co)
1942—Bears, 41-14 (Wr)
     Bears, 21-7 (Co)
1943—Bears, 20-0 (Wr)
     Bears, 35-24 (Co)
1945—Cardinals, 16-7 (Wr)
     Bears, 28-20 (Co)
1946—Bears, 34-17 (Co)
     Cardinals, 35-28 (Wr)
1947—Cardinals, 31-7 (Co)
     Cardinals, 30-21 (Wr)
1948—Bears, 28-17 (Co)
     Cardinals, 24-21 (Wr)
1949—Bears, 17-7 (Co)
     Bears, 52-21 (Wr)
1950—Bears, 27-6 (Wr)
     Cardinals, 20-10 (Co)
1951—Cardinals, 28-14 (Co)
     Cardinals, 24-14 (Wr)
1952—Cardinals, 21-10 (Co)
     Bears, 10-7 (Wr)
1953—Cardinals, 24-17 (Wr)
1954—Bears, 29-7 (Co)
1955—Cardinals, 53-14 (Co)
1956—Bears, 10-3 (Wr)
1957—Bears, 14-6 (Co)
1958—Bears, 30-14 (Wr)
1959—Bears, 31-7 (So)
1965—Bears, 34-13 (Wr)
1966—Bears, 24-17 (StL)
1967—Bears, 30-3 (Wr)
1969—Cardinals, 20-17 (StL)
1972—Bears, 27-10 (StL)
1975—Bears, 34-20 (So)
1977—Cardinals, 16-13 (StL)
1978—Bears, 17-10 (So)
1979—Bears, 42-6 (So)
1982—Cardinals, 10-7 (So)
1984—Cardinals, 38-21 (StL)
1990—Bears, 31-21 (P)
1994—Bears, 19-16 (A) OT
(RS Pts.—Bears 1,567, Cardinals 1,014)
*Franchise known as Phoenix prior to
1994, in St. Louis prior to 1988,
and in Chicago prior to 1960*
**Franchise in Decatur prior to 1921
and known as Staleys prior to 1922*

*ARIZONA vs. CINCINNATI
RS: Bengals lead series, 3-2
1973—Bengals, 42-24 (C)
1979—Bengals, 34-28 (C)
1985—Cardinals, 41-27 (StL)
1988—Bengals, 21-14 (C)
1994—Cardinals, 28-7 (A)
(RS Pts.—Cardinals 135, Bengals 131)
*Franchise known as Phoenix prior to
1994 and in St. Louis prior to 1988*

*ARIZONA vs. CLEVELAND
RS: Browns lead series, 32-10-3
1950—Browns, 34-24 (Cle)
     Browns, 10-7 (Chi)
1951—Browns, 34-17 (Chi)
     Browns, 49-28 (Cle)
1952—Browns, 28-13 (Cle)
     Browns, 10-0 (Chi)
1953—Browns, 27-7 (Chi)
     Browns, 27-16 (Cle)
1954—Browns, 31-7 (Cle)
     Browns, 35-3 (Chi)
1955—Browns, 26-20 (Cle)
     Browns, 35-24 (Cle)
1956—Cardinals, 9-7 (Chi)
     Cardinals, 24-7 (Cle)
1957—Browns, 17-7 (Chi)
     Browns, 31-0 (Cle)
1958—Browns, 35-28 (Cle)
     Browns, 38-24 (Chi)

1959—Browns, 34-7 (Chi)
     Browns, 17-7 (Cle)
1960—Browns, 28-27 (Cle)
     Tie, 17-17 (StL)
1961—Browns, 20-17 (Cle)
     Browns, 21-10 (StL)
1962—Browns, 34-7 (StL)
     Browns, 38-14 (Cle)
1963—Cardinals, 20-14 (Cle)
     Browns, 24-10 (StL)
1964—Tie, 33-33 (Cle)
     Cardinals, 28-19 (StL)
1965—Cardinals, 49-13 (Cle)
     Browns, 27-24 (StL)
1966—Cardinals, 34-28 (Cle)
     Browns, 38-10 (StL)
1967—Browns, 20-16 (Cle)
     Browns, 20-16 (StL)
1968—Cardinals, 27-21 (Cle)
     Cardinals, 28-21 (StL)
1969—Tie, 21-21 (Cle)
     Browns, 27-21 (StL)
1974—Cardinals, 29-7 (StL)
1979—Browns, 38-20 (StL)
1985—Cardinals, 27-24 (Cle) OT
1988—Browns, 29-21 (P)
1994—Browns, 32-0 (Cle)
(RS Pts.—Browns 1,141, Cardinals 797)
*Franchise known as Phoenix prior to
1994, in St. Louis prior to 1988,
and in Chicago prior to 1960*

*ARIZONA vs. DALLAS
RS: Cowboys lead series, 46-22-1
1960—Cardinals, 12-10 (StL)
1961—Cardinals, 31-17 (D)
     Cardinals, 31-13 (StL)
1962—Cardinals, 28-24 (D)
     Cardinals, 52-20 (StL)
1963—Cardinals, 34-7 (D)
     Cowboys, 28-24 (StL)
1964—Cardinals, 16-6 (D)
     Cowboys, 31-13 (StL)
1965—Cardinals, 20-13 (StL)
     Cowboys, 27-13 (D)
1966—Tie, 10-10 (StL)
     Cowboys, 31-17 (D)
1967—Cowboys, 46-21 (D)
1968—Cowboys, 27-10 (StL)
1969—Cowboys, 24-3 (D)
1970—Cardinals, 20-7 (StL)
     Cardinals, 38-0 (D)
1971—Cowboys, 16-13 (StL)
     Cowboys, 31-12 (D)
1972—Cowboys, 33-24 (D)
     Cowboys, 27-6 (StL)
1973—Cowboys, 45-10 (D)
     Cowboys, 30-3 (StL)
1974—Cardinals, 31-28 (StL)
     Cowboys, 17-14 (D)
1975—Cowboys, 37-31 (D) OT
     Cardinals, 31-17 (StL)
1976—Cardinals, 21-17 (StL)
     Cowboys, 19-14 (D)
1977—Cowboys, 30-24 (StL)
     Cardinals, 24-17 (D)
1978—Cowboys, 21-12 (D)
     Cowboys, 24-21 (StL) OT
1979—Cowboys, 22-21 (StL)
     Cowboys, 22-13 (D)
1980—Cowboys, 27-24 (StL)
     Cowboys, 31-21 (D)
1981—Cowboys, 30-17 (D)
     Cardinals, 20-17 (StL)
1982—Cowboys, 24-7 (StL)
1983—Cowboys, 34-17 (StL)
     Cowboys, 35-17 (D)
1984—Cardinals, 31-20 (D)
     Cowboys, 24-17 (StL)
1985—Cardinals, 21-10 (StL)
     Cowboys, 35-17 (D)
1986—Cowboys, 31-7 (StL)
     Cowboys, 37-6 (D)
1987—Cardinals, 24-13 (StL)

Cowboys, 21-16 (D)
1988—Cowboys, 17-14 (P)
     Cardinals, 19-10 (D)
1989—Cardinals, 19-10 (P)
     Cardinals, 24-20 (P)
1990—Cardinals, 20-3 (P)
     Cowboys, 41-10 (D)
1991—Cowboys, 17-9 (P)
     Cowboys, 27-7 (D)
1992—Cowboys, 31-20 (D)
     Cowboys, 16-10 (P)
1993—Cowboys, 17-10 (P)
     Cowboys, 20-15 (D)
1994—Cowboys, 38-3 (D)
     Cowboys, 28-21 (A)
1995—Cowboys, 34-20 (D)
     Cowboys, 37-13 (A)
1996—Cowboys, 17-3 (D)
     Cowboys, 10-6 (A)
(RS Pts.—Cowboys 1,576, Cardinals 1,220)
*Franchise known as Phoenix prior to
1994 and in St. Louis prior to 1988*

*ARIZONA vs. DENVER
RS: Broncos lead series, 4-0-1
1973—Tie, 17-17 (StL)
1977—Broncos, 7-0 (D)
1989—Broncos, 37-0 (P)
1991—Broncos, 24-19 (D)
1995—Broncos, 38-6 (D)
(RS Pts.—Broncos 123, Cardinals 42)
*Franchise known as Phoenix prior to
1994 and in St. Louis prior to 1988*

*ARIZONA vs. **DETROIT
RS: Lions lead series, 27-17-5
1930—Tie, 0-0 (Port)
     Cardinals, 23-0 (C)
1931—Cardinals, 20-19 (C)
1932—Tie, 7-7 (Port)
1933—Spartans, 7-6 (Port)
1934—Lions, 6-0 (D)
     Lions, 17-13 (C)
1935—Tie, 10-10 (D)
     Lions, 7-6 (C)
1936—Lions, 39-0 (D)
     Lions, 14-7 (C)
1937—Lions, 16-7 (C)
     Lions, 16-7 (D)
1938—Lions, 10-0 (D)
     Lions, 7-3 (C)
1939—Lions, 21-3 (D)
     Lions, 17-3 (C)
1940—Tie, 0-0 (Buffalo)
     Lions, 43-14 (C)
1941—Tie, 14-14 (C)
     Lions, 21-3 (D)
1942—Cardinals, 13-0 (C)
     Cardinals, 7-0 (D)
1943—Lions, 35-17 (D)
     Lions, 7-0 (Buffalo)
1945—Lions, 10-0 (Milwaukee)
     Lions, 26-0 (C)
1946—Cardinals, 34-14 (C)
     Cardinals, 36-14 (D)
1947—Cardinals, 45-21 (C)
     Cardinals, 17-7 (D)
1948—Cardinals, 56-20 (C)
     Cardinals, 28-14 (D)
1949—Lions, 24-7 (C)
     Cardinals, 42-19 (D)
1959—Lions, 45-21 (C)
1961—Lions, 45-14 (StL)
1967—Cardinals, 38-28 (StL)
1969—Lions, 20-0 (D)
1970—Lions, 16-3 (D)
1973—Lions, 20-16 (StL)
1975—Cardinals, 24-13 (D)
1978—Cardinals, 21-14 (StL)
1980—Lions, 20-7 (D)
     Cardinals, 24-23 (StL)
1989—Cardinals, 16-13 (D)
1993—Lions, 26-20 (D)
     Lions, 21-14 (Phx)
1995—Cardinals, 20-17 (D)

(RS Pts.—Lions 823, Cardinals 696)
Franchise known as Phoenix prior to 1994, in St. Louis prior to 1988, and in Chicago prior to 1960
**Franchise in Portsmouth prior to 1934 and known as the Spartans*

*ARIZONA vs. GREEN BAY
RS: Packers lead series, 39-21-4
PS: Packers lead series, 1-0
1921—Tie, 3-3 (C)
1922—Cardinals, 16-3 (C)
1924—Cardinals, 3-0 (C)
1925—Cardinals, 9-6 (C)
1926—Cardinals, 13-7 (GB)
　　　Packers, 3-0 (C)
1927—Packers, 13-0 (GB)
　　　Tie, 6-6 (C)
1928—Packers, 20-0 (GB)
1929—Packers, 9-2 (GB)
　　　Packers, 7-6 (C)
　　　Packers, 12-0 (C)
1930—Packers, 14-0 (GB)
　　　Cardinals, 13-6 (C)
1931—Packers, 26-7 (GB)
　　　Cardinals, 21-13 (C)
1932—Packers, 15-7 (GB)
　　　Packers, 19-9 (C)
1933—Packers, 14-6 (C)
1934—Packers, 15-0 (GB)
　　　Cardinals, 9-0 (Mil)
　　　Cardinals, 6-0 (C)
1935—Cardinals, 7-6 (GB)
　　　Cardinals, 3-0 (Mil)
　　　Cardinals, 9-7 (C)
1936—Packers, 10-7 (GB)
　　　Packers, 24-0 (Mil)
　　　Tie, 0-0 (C)
1937—Cardinals, 14-7 (GB)
　　　Packers, 34-13 (Mil)
1938—Packers, 28-7 (Mil)
　　　Packers, 24-22 (Buffalo)
1939—Packers, 14-10 (GB)
　　　Packers, 27-20 (Mil)
1940—Packers, 31-6 (Mil)
　　　Packers, 28-7 (C)
1941—Packers, 14-13 (Mil)
　　　Packers, 17-9 (GB)
1942—Packers, 17-13 (C)
　　　Packers, 55-24 (GB)
1943—Packers, 28-7 (C)
　　　Packers, 35-14 (Mil)
1945—Packers, 33-14 (GB)
1946—Packers, 19-7 (C)
　　　Cardinals, 24-6 (GB)
1947—Cardinals, 14-10 (GB)
　　　Cardinals, 21-20 (C)
1948—Cardinals, 17-7 (Mil)
　　　Cardinals, 42-7 (C)
1949—Cardinals, 39-17 (Mil)
　　　Cardinals, 41-21 (C)
1955—Packers, 31-14 (GB)
1956—Packers, 24-21 (C)
1962—Packers, 17-0 (Mil)
1963—Packers, 30-7 (StL)
1967—Packers, 31-23 (StL)
1969—Packers, 45-28 (GB)
1971—Tie, 16-16 (StL)
1973—Packers, 25-21 (GB)
1976—Cardinals, 29-0 (StL)
1982—**Packers, 41-16 (GB)
1984—Packers, 24-23 (GB)
1985—Cardinals, 43-28 (StL)
1988—Packers, 26-17 (P)
1990—Packers, 24-21 (P)
(RS Pts.—Packers 1,078, Cardinals 823)
(PS Pts.—Packers 41, Cardinals 16)
Franchise known as Phoenix prior to 1994, in St. Louis prior to 1988, and in Chicago prior to 1960
**NFC First-Round Playoff*

*ARIZONA vs. **INDIANAPOLIS
RS: Series tied, 6-6
1961—Colts, 16-0 (B)

1964—Colts, 47-27 (B)
1968—Colts, 27-0 (B)
1972—Cardinals, 10-3 (B)
1976—Cardinals, 24-17 (StL)
1978—Colts, 30-17 (StL)
1980—Cardinals, 17-10 (B)
1981—Cardinals, 35-24 (B)
1984—Cardinals, 34-33 (I)
1990—Cardinals, 20-17 (P)
1992—Colts, 16-13 (I)
1996—Colts, 20-13 (I)
(RS Pts.—Colts 260, Cardinals 210)
Franchise known as Phoenix prior to 1994 and in St. Louis prior to 1988
**Franchise in Baltimore prior to 1984*

*ARIZONA vs. KANSAS CITY
RS: Chiefs lead series, 4-1-1
1970—Tie, 6-6 (KC)
1974—Chiefs, 17-13 (StL)
1980—Chiefs, 21-13 (StL)
1983—Chiefs, 38-14 (KC)
1986—Cardinals, 23-14 (StL)
1995—Chiefs, 24-3 (A)
(RS Pts.—Chiefs 120, Cardinals 72)
Franchise known as Phoenix prior to 1994 and in St. Louis prior to 1988

*ARIZONA vs. MIAMI
RS: Dolphins lead series, 7-0
1972—Dolphins, 31-10 (M)
1977—Dolphins, 55-14 (StL)
1978—Dolphins, 24-10 (M)
1981—Dolphins, 20-7 (StL)
1984—Dolphins, 36-28 (StL)
1990—Dolphins, 23-3 (M)
1996—Dolphins, 38-10 (A)
(RS Pts.—Dolphins 227, Cardinals 82)
Franchise known as Phoenix prior to 1994 and in St. Louis prior to 1988

*ARIZONA vs. MINNESOTA
RS: Cardinals lead series, 8-6
PS: Vikings lead series, 1-0
1963—Cardinals, 56-14 (M)
1967—Cardinals, 34-24 (M)
1969—Vikings, 27-10 (StL)
1972—Cardinals, 19-17 (M)
1974—Vikings, 28-24 (StL)
　　　**Vikings, 30-14 (M)
1977—Cardinals, 27-7 (M)
1979—Cardinals, 37-7 (StL)
1981—Cardinals, 30-17 (StL)
1983—Cardinals, 41-31 (StL)
1991—Vikings, 34-7 (M)
　　　Vikings, 28-0 (P)
1994—Cardinals, 17-7 (A)
1995—Vikings, 30-24 (A) OT
1996—Vikings, 41-17 (M)
(RS Pts.—Cardinals 343, Vikings 312)
(PS Pts.—Vikings 30, Cardinals 14)
Franchise known as Phoenix prior to 1994 and in St. Louis prior to 1988
**NFC Divisional Playoff*

*ARIZONA vs. **NEW ENGLAND
RS: Cardinals lead series, 6-3
1970—Cardinals, 31-0 (StL)
1975—Cardinals, 24-17 (StL)
1978—Patriots, 16-6 (StL)
1981—Cardinals, 27-20 (NE)
1984—Cardinals, 33-10 (NE)
1990—Cardinals, 34-14 (P)
1991—Cardinals, 24-10 (P)
1993—Patriots, 23-21 (P)
1996—Patriots, 31-0 (NE)
(RS Pts.—Cardinals 200, Patriots 141)
Franchise known as Phoenix prior to 1994 and in St. Louis prior to 1988
**Franchise in Boston prior to 1971*

*ARIZONA vs. NEW ORLEANS
RS: Cardinals lead series, 11-9
1967—Cardinals, 31-20 (StL)
1968—Cardinals, 21-20 (NO)
　　　Cardinals, 31-17 (StL)
1969—Saints, 51-42 (StL)
1970—Cardinals, 24-17 (StL)

1974—Saints, 14-0 (NO)
1977—Cardinals, 49-31 (StL)
1980—Cardinals, 40-7 (NO)
1981—Cardinals, 30-3 (StL)
1982—Cardinals, 21-7 (NO)
1983—Saints, 28-17 (NO)
1984—Saints, 34-24 (NO)
1985—Cardinals, 28-16 (StL)
1986—Saints, 16-7 (StL)
1987—Cardinals, 24-19 (StL)
1990—Saints, 28-7 (NO)
1991—Saints, 27-3 (P)
1992—Saints, 30-21 (P)
1993—Saints, 20-17 (P)
1996—Cardinals, 28-14 (NO)
(RS Pts.—Cardinals 465, Saints 419)
Franchise known as Phoenix prior to 1994 and in St. Louis prior to 1988

*ARIZONA vs. N.Y. GIANTS
RS: Giants lead series, 69-37-2
1926—Giants, 20-0 (NY)
1927—Giants, 28-7 (NY)
1929—Giants, 24-21 (NY)
1930—Giants, 25-12 (NY)
　　　Giants, 13-7 (C)
1935—Cardinals, 14-13 (NY)
1936—Giants, 14-6 (NY)
1938—Giants, 6-0 (NY)
1939—Giants, 17-7 (NY)
1941—Cardinals, 10-7 (NY)
1942—Giants, 21-7 (NY)
1943—Giants, 24-13 (NY)
1946—Giants, 28-24 (NY)
1947—Giants, 35-31 (NY)
1948—Cardinals, 63-35 (NY)
1949—Giants, 41-38 (C)
1950—Cardinals, 17-3 (C)
　　　Giants, 51-21 (NY)
1951—Cardinals, 28-17 (NY)
　　　Giants, 10-0 (C)
1952—Cardinals, 24-23 (NY)
　　　Giants, 28-6 (C)
1953—Giants, 21-7 (NY)
　　　Giants, 23-20 (C)
1954—Giants, 41-10 (C)
　　　Giants, 31-17 (NY)
1955—Cardinals, 28-17 (C)
　　　Giants, 10-0 (NY)
1956—Cardinals, 35-27 (C)
　　　Giants, 23-10 (NY)
1957—Cardinals, 27-14 (NY)
　　　Giants, 28-21 (C)
1958—Giants, 37-7 (Buffalo)
　　　Cardinals, 23-6 (NY)
1959—Giants, 9-3 (NY)
　　　Giants, 30-20 (Minn)
1960—Giants, 35-14 (StL)
　　　Cardinals, 20-13 (NY)
1961—Cardinals, 21-10 (NY)
　　　Giants, 24-9 (StL)
1962—Giants, 31-14 (StL)
　　　Giants, 31-28 (NY)
1963—Giants, 38-21 (StL)
　　　Cardinals, 24-17 (NY)
1964—Giants, 34-17 (NY)
　　　Tie, 10-10 (StL)
1965—Giants, 14-10 (NY)
　　　Giants, 28-15 (StL)
1966—Cardinals, 24-19 (StL)
　　　Cardinals, 20-17 (NY)
1967—Giants, 37-20 (StL)
　　　Giants, 37-14 (NY)
1968—Cardinals, 28-21 (NY)
1969—Cardinals, 42-17 (StL)
　　　Giants, 49-6 (NY)
1970—Giants, 35-17 (NY)
　　　Giants, 34-17 (StL)
1971—Giants, 21-20 (StL)
　　　Cardinals, 24-7 (NY)
1972—Giants, 27-21 (NY)
　　　Cardinals, 13-7 (StL)
1973—Cardinals, 35-27 (StL)
　　　Giants, 24-13 (New Haven)

1974—Cardinals, 23-21 (New Haven)
　　　Cardinals, 26-14 (StL)
1975—Cardinals, 26-14 (StL)
　　　Cardinals, 20-13 (NY)
1976—Cardinals, 27-21 (StL)
　　　Cardinals, 17-14 (NY)
1977—Cardinals, 28-0 (StL)
　　　Giants, 27-7 (NY)
1978—Cardinals, 20-10 (StL)
　　　Giants, 17-0 (NY)
1979—Cardinals, 27-14 (NY)
　　　Cardinals, 29-20 (StL)
1980—Giants, 41-35 (StL)
　　　Cardinals, 23-7 (NY)
1981—Giants, 34-14 (NY)
　　　Giants, 20-10 (StL)
1982—Cardinals, 24-21 (StL)
1983—Tie, 20-20 (StL) OT
　　　Cardinals, 10-6 (NY)
1984—Giants, 16-10 (NY)
　　　Cardinals, 31-21 (StL)
1985—Giants, 27-17 (NY)
　　　Giants, 34-3 (StL)
1986—Giants, 13-6 (StL)
　　　Giants, 27-7 (NY)
1987—Giants, 30-7 (NY)
　　　Cardinals, 27-24 (StL)
1988—Cardinals, 24-17 (P)
　　　Giants, 44-7 (NY)
1989—Giants, 35-7 (NY)
　　　Giants, 20-13 (P)
1990—Giants, 20-19 (NY)
　　　Giants, 24-21 (P)
1991—Giants, 20-9 (NY)
　　　Giants, 21-14 (P)
1992—Giants, 31-21 (NY)
　　　Cardinals, 19-0 (P)
1993—Giants, 19-17 (NY)
　　　Cardinals, 17-6 (P)
1994—Giants, 20-17 (A)
　　　Cardinals, 10-9 (NY)
1995—Giants, 27-21 (NY) OT
　　　Giants, 10-6 (A)
1996—Giants, 16-8 (NY)
　　　Cardinals, 31-23 (A)
(RS Pts.—Giants 2,382, Cardinals 1,846)
Franchise known as Phoenix prior to 1994, in St. Louis prior to 1988, and in Chicago prior to 1960

*ARIZONA vs. N.Y. JETS
RS: Series tied, 2-2
1971—Cardinals, 17-10 (StL)
1975—Cardinals, 37-6 (NY)
1978—Jets, 23-10 (NY)
1996—Jets, 31-21 (A)
(RS Pts.—Cardinals 85, Jets 70)
Franchise known as Phoenix prior to 1994 and in St. Louis prior to 1988

*ARIZONA vs. **OAKLAND
RS: Raiders lead series, 2-1
1973—Raiders, 17-10 (StL)
1983—Cardinals, 34-24 (LA)
1989—Raiders, 16-14 (LA)
(RS Pts.—Cardinals 58, Raiders 57)
Franchise known as Phoenix prior to 1994 and in St. Louis prior to 1988
**Franchise in Los Angeles from 1982-1994*

*ARIZONA vs. PHILADELPHIA
RS: Eagles lead series, 47-46-5
PS: Series tied, 1-1
1935—Cardinals, 12-3 (C)
1936—Cardinals, 13-0 (C)
1937—Tie, 6-6 (P)
1938—Eagles, 7-0 (Erie, Pa.)
1941—Eagles, 21-14 (P)
1945—Eagles, 21-6 (P)
1947—Cardinals, 45-21 (P)
　　　**Cardinals, 28-21 (C)
1948—Cardinals, 21-14 (C)
　　　**Eagles, 7-0 (P)
1949—Eagles, 28-3 (P)
1950—Eagles, 45-7 (C)

Cardinals, 14-10 (P)
1951—Eagles, 17-14 (C)
1952—Eagles, 10-7 (P)
Cardinals, 28-22 (C)
1953—Eagles, 56-17 (C)
Eagles, 38-0 (P)
1954—Eagles, 35-16 (C)
Eagles, 30-14 (P)
1955—Tie, 24-24 (C)
Eagles, 27-3 (P)
1956—Cardinals, 20-6 (P)
Cardinals, 28-17 (C)
1957—Eagles, 38-21 (C)
Cardinals, 31-27 (P)
1958—Tie, 21-21 (C)
Eagles, 49-21 (P)
1959—Eagles, 28-24 (Minn)
Eagles, 27-17 (P)
1960—Eagles, 31-27 (P)
Eagles, 20-6 (StL)
1961—Cardinals, 30-27 (P)
Eagles, 20-7 (StL)
1962—Cardinals, 27-21 (P)
Cardinals, 45-35 (StL)
1963—Cardinals, 28-24 (P)
Cardinals, 38-14 (StL)
1964—Cardinals, 38-13 (P)
Cardinals, 36-34 (StL)
1965—Eagles, 34-27 (P)
Eagles, 28-24 (StL)
1966—Cardinals, 16-13 (StL)
Cardinals, 41-10 (P)
1967—Cardinals, 48-14 (StL)
1968—Cardinals, 45-17 (P)
1969—Eagles, 34-30 (StL)
1970—Cardinals, 35-20 (P)
Cardinals, 23-14 (StL)
1971—Eagles, 37-20 (StL)
Eagles, 19-7 (P)
1972—Tie, 6-6 (P)
Cardinals, 24-23 (StL)
1973—Cardinals, 34-23 (P)
Eagles, 27-24 (StL)
1974—Cardinals, 7-3 (StL)
Cardinals, 13-3 (P)
1975—Cardinals, 31-20 (StL)
Cardinals, 24-23 (P)
1976—Cardinals, 33-14 (StL)
Cardinals, 17-14 (P)
1977—Cardinals, 21-17 (P)
Cardinals, 21-16 (StL)
1978—Cardinals, 16-10 (P)
Eagles, 14-10 (StL)
1979—Eagles, 24-20 (StL)
Eagles, 16-13 (P)
1980—Cardinals, 24-14 (StL)
Eagles, 17-3 (P)
1981—Eagles, 52-10 (StL)
Eagles, 38-0 (P)
1982—Cardinals, 23-20 (P)
1983—Cardinals, 14-11 (P)
Cardinals, 31-7 (StL)
1984—Cardinals, 34-14 (P)
Cardinals, 17-16 (StL)
1985—Eagles, 30-7 (P)
Eagles, 24-14 (StL)
1986—Cardinals, 13-10 (StL)
Tie, 10-10 (P) OT
1987—Eagles, 28-23 (StL)
Cardinals, 31-19 (P)
1988—Eagles, 31-21 (P)
Eagles, 23-17 (Phx)
1989—Eagles, 17-5 (Phx)
Eagles, 31-14 (P)
1990—Cardinals, 23-21 (P)
Eagles, 23-21 (Phx)
1991—Cardinals, 26-10 (P)
Eagles, 34-14 (Phx)
1992—Eagles, 31-14 (Phx)
Eagles, 7-3 (P)
1993—Eagles, 23-17 (P)
Cardinals, 16-3 (Phx)
1994—Eagles, 17-7 (P)

Cardinals, 12-6 (A)
1995—Eagles, 31-19 (A)
Eagles, 21-20 (P)
1996—Cardinals, 36-30 (A)
Eagles, 29-19 (P)
(RS Pts.—Eagles 2,106, Cardinals 1,945)
(PS Pts.—Eagles 28, Cardinals 28)
*Franchise known as Phoenix prior to
1994, in St. Louis prior to 1988,
and in Chicago prior to 1960
**NFL Championship
*ARIZONA vs. **PITTSBURGH
RS: Steelers lead series, 29-22-3
1933—Pirates, 14-13 (C)
1935—Pirates, 17-13 (P)
1936—Cardinals, 14-6 (C)
1937—Cardinals, 13-7 (P)
1939—Cardinals, 10-0 (P)
1940—Tie, 7-7 (P)
1942—Steelers, 19-3 (P)
1945—Steelers, 23-0 (P)
1946—Steelers, 14-7 (P)
1948—Cardinals, 24-7 (P)
1950—Steelers, 28-17 (C)
Steelers, 28-7 (P)
1951—Steelers, 28-14 (C)
1952—Steelers, 34-28 (C)
Steelers, 17-14 (P)
1953—Steelers, 31-28 (P)
Steelers, 21-17 (C)
1954—Cardinals, 17-14 (C)
Steelers, 20-17 (P)
1955—Steelers, 14-7 (P)
Cardinals, 27-13 (C)
1956—Steelers, 14-7 (P)
Cardinals, 38-27 (C)
1957—Steelers, 29-20 (P)
Steelers, 27-2 (C)
1958—Steelers, 27-20 (C)
Steelers, 38-21 (P)
1959—Cardinals, 45-24 (C)
Steelers, 35-20 (P)
1960—Steelers, 27-14 (P)
Cardinals, 38-7 (StL)
1961—Steelers, 30-27 (P)
Cardinals, 20-0 (StL)
1962—Steelers, 26-17 (StL)
Steelers, 19-7 (P)
1963—Steelers, 23-10 (P)
Cardinals, 24-23 (StL)
1964—Cardinals, 34-30 (StL)
Cardinals, 21-20 (P)
1965—Cardinals, 20-7 (P)
Cardinals, 21-17 (StL)
1966—Steelers, 30-9 (P)
Cardinals, 6-3 (StL)
1967—Cardinals, 28-14 (P)
Tie, 14-14 (StL)
1968—Tie, 28-28 (StL)
Cardinals, 20-10 (P)
1969—Cardinals, 27-14 (P)
Cardinals, 47-10 (StL)
1972—Steelers, 25-19 (StL)
1979—Steelers, 24-21 (StL)
1985—Steelers, 23-10 (P)
1988—Cardinals, 31-14 (Phx)
1994—Cardinals, 20-17 (A) OT
(RS Pts.—Steelers 1,038, Cardinals 1,003)
*Franchise known as Phoenix prior to
1994, in St. Louis prior to 1988,
and in Chicago prior to 1960
**Steelers known as Pirates prior to 1941
*ARIZONA vs. **ST. LOUIS
RS: Rams lead series, 23-20-2
PS: Rams lead series, 1-0
1937—Cardinals, 6-0 (Clev)
Cardinals, 13-7 (Chi)
1938—Cardinals, 7-6 (Clev)
Cardinals, 31-17 (Chi)
1939—Rams, 24-0 (Clev)
Rams, 14-0 (Clev)
1940—Rams, 26-14 (Clev)
Cardinals, 17-7 (Chi)

1941—Rams, 10-6 (Clev)
Cardinals, 7-0 (Chi)
1942—Cardinals, 7-0 (Buffalo)
Rams, 7-3 (Chi)
1945—Rams, 21-0 (Clev)
Rams, 35-21 (Chi)
1946—Cardinals, 34-10 (Chi)
Rams, 17-14 (LA)
1947—Rams, 27-7 (LA)
Cardinals, 17-10 (Chi)
1948—Cardinals, 27-22 (LA)
Cardinals, 27-24 (Chi)
1949—Tie, 28-28 (Chi)
Cardinals, 31-27 (LA)
1951—Rams, 45-21 (LA)
1953—Tie, 24-24 (Chi)
1954—Rams, 28-17 (LA)
1958—Rams, 20-14 (Chi)
1960—Cardinals, 43-21 (LA)
1965—Rams, 27-3 (StL)
1968—Rams, 24-13 (StL)
1970—Rams, 34-13 (LA)
1972—Cardinals, 24-14 (StL)
1975—***Rams, 35-23 (LA)
1976—Cardinals, 30-28 (LA)
1979—Rams, 21-0 (LA)
1980—Rams, 21-13 (StL)
1984—Rams, 16-13 (StL)
1985—Rams, 46-14 (LA)
1986—Rams, 16-10 (StL)
1987—Rams, 27-24 (StL)
1988—Cardinals, 41-27 (LA)
1989—Rams, 37-14 (LA)
1991—Cardinals, 24-14 (LA)
1992—Cardinals, 20-14 (LA)
1993—Cardinals, 38-10 (P)
1994—Rams, 14-12 (LA)
1996—Cardinals, 31-28 (A) OT
(RS Pts.—Rams 895, Cardinals 773)
(PS Pts.—Rams 35, Cardinals 23)
*Franchise known as Phoenix prior to
1994, in St. Louis prior to 1988,
and in Chicago prior to 1960
**Franchise in Los Angeles prior to
1995 and in Cleveland prior to 1946
***NFC Divisional Playoff
*ARIZONA vs. SAN DIEGO
RS: Chargers lead series, 6-1
1971—Chargers, 20-17 (SD)
1976—Chargers, 43-24 (SD)
1983—Cardinals, 44-14 (StL)
1987—Chargers, 28-24 (SD)
1989—Chargers, 24-13 (P)
1992—Chargers, 27-21 (P)
1995—Chargers, 28-25 (SD)
(RS Pts.—Chargers 184, Cardinals 168)
*Franchise known as Phoenix prior to
1994, in St. Louis prior to 1988,
*ARIZONA vs. SAN FRANCISCO
RS: 49ers lead series, 10-9
1951—Cardinals, 27-21 (SF)
1957—Cardinals, 20-10 (SF)
1962—49ers, 24-17 (StL)
1964—Cardinals, 23-13 (SF)
1968—49ers, 35-17 (SF)
1971—49ers, 26-14 (StL)
1974—Cardinals, 34-9 (SF)
1976—Cardinals, 23-20 (StL) OT
1978—Cardinals, 16-10 (SF)
1979—Cardinals, 13-10 (StL)
1980—49ers, 24-21 (SF) OT
1982—49ers, 31-20 (StL)
1983—49ers, 42-27 (StL)
1986—49ers, 43-17 (SF)
1987—49ers, 34-28 (SF)
1988—Cardinals, 24-23 (P)
1991—49ers, 14-10 (SF)
1992—Cardinals, 24-14 (P)
1993—49ers, 28-14 (SF)
(RS Pts.—49ers 431, Cardinals 389)
*Franchise known as Phoenix prior to
1994, in St. Louis prior to 1988,
and in Chicago prior to 1960

*ARIZONA vs. SEATTLE
RS: Cardinals lead series, 5-0
1976—Cardinals, 30-24 (S)
1983—Cardinals, 33-28 (StL)
1989—Cardinals, 34-24 (S)
1993—Cardinals, 30-27 (S) OT
1995—Cardinals, 20-14 (A) OT
(RS Pts.—Cardinals 147, Seahawks 117)
*Franchise known as Phoenix prior to
1994 and in St. Louis prior to 1988
*ARIZONA vs. TAMPA BAY
RS: Cardinals lead series, 7-6
1977—Buccaneers, 17-7 (TB)
1981—Buccaneers, 20-10 (TB)
1983—Cardinals, 34-27 (TB)
1985—Buccaneers, 16-0 (TB)
1986—Cardinals, 30-19 (TB)
Cardinals, 21-17 (StL)
1987—Cardinals, 31-28 (StL)
Cardinals, 31-14 (TB)
1988—Cardinals, 30-24 (TB)
1989—Buccaneers, 14-13 (P)
1992—Buccaneers, 23-7 (TB)
Buccaneers, 7-3 (P)
1996—Cardinals, 13-9 (A)
(RS Pts.—Buccaneers 235, Cardinals 230)
*Franchise known as Phoenix prior to
1994 and in St. Louis prior to 1988
*ARIZONA vs. **TENNESSEE
RS: Cardinals lead series, 4-2
1970—Cardinals, 44-0 (StL)
1974—Cardinals, 31-27 (H)
1979—Cardinals, 24-17 (H)
1985—Oilers, 20-10 (StL)
1988—Oilers, 38-20 (H)
1994—Cardinals, 30-12 (H)
(RS Pts.—Cardinals 159, Oilers 114)
*Franchise known as Phoenix prior to
1994 and in St. Louis prior to 1988
**Franchise in Houston prior to 1997
*ARIZONA vs. **WASHINGTON
RS: Redskins lead series, 62-41-2
1932—Cardinals, 9-0 (B)
Braves, 8-6 (C)
1933—Redskins, 10-0 (C)
Tie, 0-0 (B)
1934—Redskins, 9-0 (B)
1935—Cardinals, 6-0 (B)
1936—Redskins, 13-10 (B)
1937—Cardinals, 21-14 (W)
1939—Redskins, 28-7 (W)
1940—Redskins, 28-21 (W)
1942—Redskins, 28-0 (W)
1943—Redskins, 13-7 (W)
1945—Redskins, 24-21 (W)
1947—Redskins, 45-21 (W)
1949—Cardinals, 38-7 (C)
1950—Cardinals, 38-28 (W)
1951—Redskins, 7-3 (C)
Redskins, 20-17 (W)
1952—Redskins, 23-7 (C)
Cardinals, 17-6 (W)
1953—Redskins, 24-13 (C)
Redskins, 28-17 (W)
1954—Cardinals, 38-16 (C)
Redskins, 37-20 (W)
1955—Cardinals, 24-10 (W)
Redskins, 31-0 (C)
1956—Cardinals, 31-3 (W)
Redskins, 17-14 (C)
1957—Redskins, 37-14 (C)
Cardinals, 44-14 (W)
1958—Cardinals, 37-10 (C)
Redskins, 45-31 (W)
1959—Cardinals, 49-21 (C)
Redskins, 23-14 (W)
1960—Cardinals, 44-7 (StL)
Cardinals, 26-14 (W)
1961—Cardinals, 24-0 (StL)
Cardinals, 38-24 (StL)
1962—Redskins, 24-14 (W)
Tie, 17-17 (StL)
1963—Cardinals, 21-7 (W)

293

Cardinals, 24-20 (StL)
1964—Cardinals, 23-17 (W)
Cardinals, 38-24 (StL)
1965—Cardinals, 37-16 (W)
Redskins, 24-20 (StL)
1966—Cardinals, 23-7 (StL)
Redskins, 26-20 (W)
1967—Cardinals, 27-21 (W)
1968—Cardinals, 41-14 (StL)
1969—Redskins, 33-17 (W)
1970—Cardinals, 27-17 (StL)
Redskins, 28-27 (W)
1971—Redskins, 24-17 (StL)
Redskins, 20-0 (W)
1972—Redskins, 24-10 (W)
Redskins, 33-3 (StL)
1973—Cardinals, 34-27 (StL)
Redskins, 31-13 (W)
1974—Cardinals, 17-10 (W)
Cardinals, 23-20 (StL)
1975—Redskins, 27-17 (W)
Cardinals, 20-17 (StL) OT
1976—Redskins, 20-10 (W)
Redskins, 16-10 (StL)
1977—Redskins, 24-14 (W)
Redskins, 26-20 (StL)
1978—Redskins, 28-10 (StL)
Cardinals, 27-17 (W)
1979—Redskins, 17-7 (StL)
Redskins, 30-28 (W)
1980—Redskins, 23-0 (W)
Redskins, 31-7 (StL)
1981—Cardinals, 40-30 (StL)
Redskins, 42-21 (W)
1982—Redskins, 12-7 (StL)
Redskins, 28-0 (W)
1983—Redskins, 38-14 (StL)
Redskins, 45-7 (W)
1984—Cardinals, 26-24 (StL)
Redskins, 29-27 (W)
1985—Redskins, 27-10 (W)
Redskins, 27-16 (StL)
1986—Redskins, 28-21 (W)
Redskins, 20-17 (StL)
1987—Redskins, 28-21 (W)
Redskins, 34-17 (StL)
1988—Cardinals, 30-21 (P)
Redskins, 33-17 (W)
1989—Redskins, 30-28 (W)
Redskins, 29-10 (P)
1990—Redskins, 31-0 (W)
Redskins, 38-10 (P)
1991—Redskins, 34-0 (W)
Redskins, 20-14 (P)
1992—Cardinals, 27-24 (P)
Redskins, 41-3 (W)
1993—Cardinals, 17-10 (W)
Cardinals, 36-6 (P)
1994—Cardinals, 19-16 (W) OT
Cardinals, 17-15 (A)
1995—Redskins, 27-7 (W)
Cardinals, 24-20 (A)
1996—Cardinals, 37-34 (W) OT
Cardinals, 27-26 (A)
(RS Pts.—Redskins 2,299, Cardinals 1,957)
*Franchise known as Phoenix prior to 1994, in St. Louis prior to 1988, and in Chicago prior to 1960
**Franchise in Boston prior to 1937 and known as Braves prior to 1933

ATLANTA vs. ARIZONA
RS: Cardinals lead series, 12-6;
See Arizona vs. Atlanta
ATLANTA vs. BUFFALO
RS: Bills lead series, 4-3
1973—Bills, 17-6 (A)
1977—Bills, 3-0 (B)
1980—Falcons, 30-14 (B)
1983—Falcons, 31-14 (A)
1989—Falcons, 30-28 (A)
1992—Bills, 41-14 (B)
1995—Bills, 23-17 (B)

(RS Pts.—Bills 140, Falcons 128)
ATLANTA vs. CAROLINA
RS: Series tied, 2-2
1995—Falcons, 23-20 (A) OT
Panthers, 21-17 (C)
1996—Panthers, 29-6 (C)
Falcons, 20-17 (A)
(RS Pts.—Panthers 87, Falcons 66)
ATLANTA vs. CHICAGO
RS: Series tied, 9-9
1966—Bears, 23-6 (C)
1967—Bears, 23-14 (A)
1968—Falcons, 16-13 (C)
1969—Falcons, 48-31 (A)
1970—Bears, 23-14 (A)
1972—Falcons, 37-21 (C)
1973—Falcons, 46-6 (A)
1974—Falcons, 13-10 (A)
1976—Falcons, 10-0 (C)
1977—Falcons, 16-10 (A)
1978—Bears, 13-7 (C)
1980—Falcons, 28-17 (A)
1983—Falcons, 20-17 (C)
1985—Bears, 36-0 (C)
1986—Bears, 13-10 (A)
1990—Bears, 30-24 (C)
1992—Bears, 41-31 (C)
1993—Bears, 6-0 (C)
(RS Pts.—Falcons 340, Bears 333)
ATLANTA vs. CINCINNATI
RS: Bengals lead series, 7-2
1971—Falcons, 9-6 (C)
1975—Bengals, 21-14 (A)
1978—Bengals, 37-7 (C)
1981—Bengals, 30-28 (A)
1984—Bengals, 35-14 (C)
1987—Bengals, 16-10 (A)
1990—Falcons, 38-17 (A)
1993—Bengals, 21-17 (C)
1996—Bengals, 41-31 (C)
(RS Pts.—Bengals 224, Falcons 168)
ATLANTA vs. CLEVELAND
RS: Browns lead series, 8-2
1966—Browns, 49-17 (A)
1968—Browns, 30-7 (C)
1971—Falcons, 31-14 (C)
1976—Browns, 20-17 (A)
1978—Browns, 24-16 (A)
1981—Browns, 28-17 (C)
1984—Browns, 23-7 (A)
1987—Browns, 38-3 (C)
1990—Browns, 13-10 (C)
1993—Falcons, 17-14 (A)
(RS Pts.—Browns 253, Falcons 142)
ATLANTA vs. DALLAS
RS: Cowboys lead series, 11-6
PS: Cowboys lead series, 2-0
1966—Cowboys, 47-14 (A)
1967—Cowboys, 37-7 (D)
1969—Cowboys, 24-17 (A)
1970—Cowboys, 13-0 (D)
1974—Cowboys, 24-0 (A)
1976—Falcons, 17-10 (A)
1978—*Cowboys, 27-20 (D)
1980—*Cowboys, 30-27 (A)
1985—Cowboys, 24-10 (D)
1986—Cowboys, 37-35 (D)
1987—Falcons, 21-10 (A)
1988—Cowboys, 26-20 (D)
1989—Falcons 27-21 (A)
1990—Falcons, 26-7 (A)
1991—Cowboys, 31-27 (D)
1992—Cowboys, 41-17 (A)
1993—Falcons, 27-14 (A)
1995—Cowboys, 28-13 (A)
1996—Cowboys, 32-28 (D)
(RS Pts.—Cowboys 424, Falcons 308)
(PS Pts.—Cowboys 57, Falcons 47)
*NFC Divisional Playoff
ATLANTA vs. DENVER
RS: Broncos lead series, 5-3
1970—Broncos, 24-10 (D)
1972—Falcons, 23-20 (A)

1975—Falcons, 35-21 (A)
1979—Broncos, 20-17 (A) OT
1982—Falcons, 34-27 (D)
1985—Broncos, 44-28 (A)
1988—Broncos, 30-14 (D)
1994—Broncos, 32-28 (D)
(RS Pts.—Broncos 218, Falcons 189)
ATLANTA vs. DETROIT
RS: Lions lead series, 19-6
1966—Lions, 28-10 (D)
1967—Lions, 24-3 (D)
1968—Lions, 24-7 (A)
1969—Lions, 27-21 (D)
1971—Lions, 41-38 (D)
1972—Lions, 26-23 (A)
1973—Lions, 31-6 (D)
1975—Lions, 17-14 (A)
1976—Lions, 24-10 (D)
1977—Falcons, 17-6 (A)
1978—Falcons, 14-0 (A)
1979—Lions, 24-23 (D)
1980—Falcons, 43-28 (A)
1983—Lions, 30-14 (D)
1984—Lions, 27-24 (A) OT
1985—Lions, 28-27 (A)
1986—Falcons, 20-6 (D)
1987—Lions, 30-13 (A)
1988—Lions, 31-17 (D)
1989—Lions, 31-24 (A)
1990—Lions, 21-14 (D)
1993—Lions, 30-13 (D)
1994—Lions, 31-28 (D) OT
1995—Falcons, 34-22 (A)
1996—Lions, 28-24 (D)
(RS Pts.—Lions 599, Falcons 497)
ATLANTA vs. GREEN BAY
RS: Packers lead series, 10-9
PS: Packers lead series, 1-0
1966—Packers, 56-3 (Mil)
1967—Packers, 23-0 (Mil)
1968—Packers, 38-7 (A)
1969—Packers, 28-10 (GB)
1970—Packers, 27-24 (GB)
1971—Falcons, 28-21 (A)
1972—Falcons, 10-9 (Mil)
1974—Falcons, 10-3 (A)
1975—Packers, 22-13 (GB)
1976—Packers, 24-20 (A)
1979—Falcons, 25-7 (A)
1981—Falcons, 31-17 (GB)
1982—Packers, 38-7 (A)
1983—Falcons, 47-41 (A) OT
1988—Falcons, 20-0 (A)
1989—Packers, 23-21 (Mil)
1991—Falcons, 35-31 (A)
1992—Falcons, 24-10 (A)
1994—Packers, 21-17 (Mil)
1995—*Packers, 37-20 (GB)
(RS Pts.—Packers 439, Falcons 352)
(PS Pts.—Packers 37, Falcons 20)
*NFC First-Round Playoff
ATLANTA vs. *INDIANAPOLIS
RS: Colts lead series, 10-0
1966—Colts, 19-7 (A)
1967—Colts, 38-31 (B)
Colts, 49-7 (A)
1968—Colts, 28-20 (A)
Colts, 44-0 (B)
1969—Colts, 21-14 (A)
Colts, 13-6 (B)
1974—Colts, 17-7 (A)
1986—Colts, 28-23 (A)
1989—Colts, 13-9 (I)
(RS Pts.—Colts 270, Falcons 124)
*Franchise in Baltimore prior to 1984
ATLANTA vs. JACKSONVILLE
RS: Jaguars lead series, 1-0
1996—Jaguars, 19-17 (J)
(RS Pts.—Jaguars, 19, Falcons 17)
ATLANTA vs. KANSAS CITY
RS: Chiefs lead series, 4-0
1972—Chiefs, 17-14 (A)
1985—Chiefs, 38-10 (KC)

1991—Chiefs, 14-3 (KC)
1994—Chiefs, 30-10 (A)
(RS Pts.—Chiefs 99, Falcons 37)
ATLANTA vs. MIAMI
RS: Dolphins lead series, 6-1
1970—Dolphins, 20-7 (A)
1974—Dolphins, 42-7 (M)
1980—Dolphins, 20-17 (A)
1983—Dolphins, 31-24 (M)
1986—Falcons, 20-14 (A)
1992—Dolphins, 21-17 (M)
1995—Dolphins, 21-20 (M)
(RS Pts.—Dolphins 169, Falcons 112)
ATLANTA vs. MINNESOTA
RS: Vikings lead series, 12-6
PS: Vikings lead series, 1-0
1966—Falcons, 20-13 (M)
1967—Falcons, 21-20 (A)
1968—Vikings, 47-7 (A)
1969—Falcons, 10-3 (A)
1970—Vikings, 37-7 (A)
1971—Vikings, 24-7 (M)
1973—Falcons, 20-14 (A)
1974—Vikings, 23-10 (M)
1975—Vikings, 38-0 (M)
1977—Vikings, 14-7 (A)
1980—Vikings, 24-23 (M)
1981—Falcons, 31-30 (A)
1982—*Vikings, 30-24 (M)
1984—Vikings, 27-20 (M)
1985—Falcons, 14-13 (A)
1987—Vikings, 24-13 (M)
1989—Vikings, 43-17 (M)
1991—Vikings, 20-19 (A)
1996—Vikings, 23-17 (A)
(RS Pts.—Vikings 437, Falcons 263)
(PS Pts.—Vikings 30, Falcons 24)
*NFC First-Round Playoff
ATLANTA vs. NEW ENGLAND
RS: Falcons lead series, 5-3
1972—Patriots, 21-20 (NE)
1977—Patriots, 16-10 (A)
1980—Falcons, 37-21 (NE)
1983—Falcons, 24-13 (A)
1986—Patriots, 25-17 (NE)
1989—Falcons, 16-15 (A)
1992—Falcons, 34-0 (A)
1995—Falcons, 30-17 (A)
(RS Pts.—Falcons 188, Patriots 128)
ATLANTA vs. NEW ORLEANS
RS: Falcons lead series, 31-24
PS: Falcons lead series, 1-0
1967—Saints, 27-24 (NO)
1969—Falcons, 45-17 (A)
1970—Falcons, 14-3 (NO)
Falcons, 32-14 (A)
1971—Falcons, 28-6 (A)
Falcons, 24-20 (NO)
1972—Falcons, 21-14 (NO)
Falcons, 36-20 (A)
1973—Falcons, 62-7 (NO)
Falcons, 14-10 (A)
1974—Saints, 14-13 (NO)
Saints, 13-3 (A)
1975—Falcons, 14-7 (A)
Saints, 23-7 (NO)
1976—Saints, 30-0 (NO)
Falcons, 23-20 (A)
1977—Saints, 21-20 (NO)
Falcons, 35-7 (A)
1978—Falcons, 20-17 (NO)
Falcons, 20-17 (A)
1979—Falcons, 40-34 (NO) OT
Saints, 37-6 (A)
1980—Falcons, 41-14 (NO)
Falcons, 31-13 (A)
1981—Falcons, 27-0 (A)
Falcons, 41-10 (NO)
1982—Falcons, 35-0 (A)
Saints, 35-6 (NO)
1983—Saints, 19-17 (A)
Saints, 27-10 (NO)
1984—Falcons, 36-28 (NO)

Saints, 17-13 (A)
1985—Falcons, 31-24 (A)
Falcons, 16-10 (NO)
1986—Falcons, 31-10 (NO)
Saints, 14-9 (A)
1987—Saints, 38-0 (A)
1988—Saints, 29-21 (A)
Saints, 10-9 (NO)
1989—Saints, 20-13 (NO)
Saints, 26-17 (A)
1990—Falcons, 28-27 (A)
Saints, 10-7 (NO)
1991—Saints, 27-6 (A)
Falcons, 23-20 (NO) OT
*Falcons, 27-20 (NO)
1992—Saints, 10-7 (A)
Saints, 22-14 (NO)
1993—Saints, 34-31 (A)
Falcons, 26-15 (NO)
1994—Saints, 33-32 (NO)
Saints, 29-20 (A)
1995—Falcons, 27-24 (NO) OT
Falcons, 19-14 (A)
1996—Falcons, 17-15 (A)
Falcons, 31-15 (NO)
(RS Pts.—Falcons 1,193, Saints 1,017)
(PS Pts.—Falcons 27, Saints 20)
*NFC First-Round Playoff
ATLANTA vs. N.Y. GIANTS
RS: Series tied, 6-6
1966—Falcons, 27-16 (NY)
1968—Falcons, 24-21 (A)
1971—Giants, 21-17 (A)
1974—Falcons, 14-7 (New Haven)
1977—Falcons, 17-3 (A)
1978—Falcons, 23-20 (A)
1979—Giants, 24-3 (NY)
1981—Giants, 27-24 (A) OT
1982—Falcons, 16-14 (NY)
1983—Giants, 16-13 (A) OT
1984—Giants, 19-7 (A)
1988—Giants, 23-16 (A)
(RS Pts.—Giants 211, Falcons 201)
ATLANTA vs. N.Y. JETS
RS: Falcons lead series, 4-3
1973—Falcons, 28-20 (NY)
1980—Jets, 14-7 (A)
1983—Falcons, 27-21 (NY)
1986—Jets, 28-14 (A)
1989—Jets, 27-7 (NY)
1992—Falcons, 20-17 (A)
1995—Falcons, 13-3 (A)
(RS Pts.—Jets 130, Falcons 116)
ATLANTA vs. *OAKLAND
RS: Raiders lead series, 5-3
1971—Falcons, 24-13 (A)
1975—Raiders, 37-34 (O) OT
1979—Raiders, 50-19 (O)
1982—Raiders, 38-14 (A)
1985—Raiders, 34-24 (A)
1988—Falcons, 12-6 (LA)
1991—Falcons, 21-17 (A)
1994—Raiders, 30-17 (LA)
(RS Pts.—Raiders 225, Falcons 165)
*Franchise in Los Angeles from
1982-1994
ATLANTA vs. PHILADELPHIA
RS: Eagles lead series, 9-7-1
PS: Falcons lead series, 1-0
1966—Eagles, 23-10 (P)
1967—Eagles, 38-7 (A)
1969—Falcons, 27-3 (P)
1970—Tie, 13-13 (P)
1973—Falcons, 44-27 (P)
1976—Eagles, 14-13 (A)
1978—*Falcons, 14-13 (A)
1979—Falcons, 14-10 (P)
1980—Falcons, 20-17 (P)
1981—Eagles, 16-13 (P)
1983—Eagles, 28-24 (A)
1984—Falcons, 26-10 (A)
1985—Eagles, 23-17 (P) OT
1986—Eagles, 16-0 (A)

1988—Falcons, 27-24 (P)
1990—Eagles, 24-23 (A)
1994—Falcons, 28-21 (A)
1996—Eagles, 33-18 (A)
(RS Pts.—Eagles 340, Falcons 324)
(PS Pts.—Falcons 14, Eagles 13)
*NFC First-Round Playoff
ATLANTA vs. PITTSBURGH
RS: Steelers lead series, 10-1
1966—Steelers, 57-33 (A)
1968—Steelers, 41-21 (A)
1970—Falcons, 27-16 (A)
1974—Steelers, 24-17 (P)
1978—Steelers, 31-7 (P)
1981—Steelers, 34-20 (A)
1984—Steelers, 35-10 (P)
1987—Steelers, 28-12 (A)
1990—Steelers, 21-9 (P)
1993—Steelers, 45-17 (A)
1996—Steelers, 20-17 (A)
(RS Pts.—Steelers 352, Falcons 190)
ATLANTA vs. *ST. LOUIS
RS: Rams lead series, 39-19-2
1966—Rams, 19-14 (A)
1967—Rams, 31-3 (A)
Rams, 20-3 (LA)
1968—Rams, 27-14 (LA)
Rams, 17-10 (A)
1969—Rams, 17-7 (LA)
Rams, 38-6 (A)
1970—Tie, 10-10 (LA)
Rams, 17-7 (A)
1971—Tie, 20-20 (LA)
Rams, 24-16 (A)
1972—Falcons, 31-3 (A)
Rams, 20-7 (LA)
1973—Rams, 31-0 (LA)
Falcons, 15-13 (A)
1974—Rams, 21-0 (LA)
Rams, 30-7 (A)
1975—Rams, 22-7 (LA)
Rams, 16-7 (A)
1976—Rams, 30-14 (A)
Rams, 59-0 (LA)
1977—Falcons, 17-6 (A)
Rams, 23-7 (LA)
1978—Rams, 10-0 (LA)
Falcons, 15-7 (A)
1979—Rams, 20-14 (LA)
Rams, 34-13 (A)
1980—Falcons, 13-10 (A)
Rams, 20-17 (LA) OT
1981—Rams, 37-35 (A)
Rams, 21-16 (LA)
1982—Falcons, 34-17 (A)
1983—Rams, 27-21 (A)
Rams, 36-13 (A)
1984—Falcons, 30-28 (LA)
Rams, 24-10 (A)
1985—Rams, 17-6 (LA)
Falcons, 30-14 (A)
1986—Falcons, 26-14 (A)
Rams, 14-7 (LA)
1987—Falcons, 24-20 (A)
Rams, 33-0 (LA)
1988—Rams, 33-0 (A)
Rams, 22-7 (LA)
1989—Rams, 31-21 (A)
Rams, 26-14 (LA)
1990—Rams, 44-24 (LA)
Falcons, 20-13 (A)
1991—Falcons, 31-14 (A)
Falcons, 31-14 (LA)
1992—Falcons, 30-28 (A)
Rams, 38-27 (LA)
1993—Falcons, 30-24 (A)
Falcons, 13-0 (LA)
1994—Falcons, 31-13 (A)
Falcons, 8-5 (LA)
1995—Rams, 21-19 (StL)
Falcons, 31-6 (A)
1996—Rams, 59-16 (StL)
Rams, 34-27 (A)

(RS Pts.—Rams 1,342, Falcons 926)
*Franchise in Los Angeles prior to 1995
ATLANTA vs. SAN DIEGO
RS: Falcons lead series, 4-1
1973—Falcons, 41-0 (SD)
1979—Falcons, 28-26 (SD)
1988—Chargers, 10-7 (A)
1991—Falcons, 13-10 (SD)
1994—Falcons, 10-9 (A)
(RS Pts.—Falcons 99, Chargers 55)
ATLANTA vs. SAN FRANCISCO
RS: 49ers lead series, 37-22-1
1966—49ers, 44-7 (A)
1967—49ers, 38-7 (SF)
49ers, 34-28 (A)
1968—49ers, 28-13 (SF)
49ers, 14-12 (A)
1969—Falcons, 24-12 (A)
Falcons, 21-7 (SF)
1970—Falcons, 21-20 (A)
49ers, 24-20 (SF)
1971—Falcons, 20-17 (A)
49ers, 24-3 (SF)
1972—49ers, 49-14 (A)
49ers, 20-0 (SF)
1973—49ers, 13-9 (A)
Falcons, 17-3 (SF)
1974—49ers, 16-10 (A)
49ers, 27-0 (SF)
1975—Falcons, 17-3 (SF)
Falcons, 31-9 (A)
1976—49ers, 15-0 (SF)
Falcons, 21-16 (A)
1977—Falcons, 7-0 (SF)
49ers, 10-3 (A)
1978—Falcons, 20-17 (SF)
Falcons, 21-10 (A)
1979—49ers, 20-15 (SF)
Falcons, 31-21 (A)
1980—Falcons, 20-17 (SF)
Falcons, 35-10 (A)
1981—Falcons, 34-17 (A)
49ers, 17-14 (SF)
1982—Falcons, 17-7 (SF)
1983—49ers, 24-20 (SF)
Falcons, 28-24 (A)
1984—49ers, 14-5 (SF)
49ers, 35-17 (A)
1985—49ers, 35-16 (SF)
49ers, 38-17 (A)
1986—Tie, 10-10 (A) OT
49ers, 20-0 (SF)
1987—49ers, 25-17 (A)
49ers, 35-7 (SF)
1988—Falcons, 34-17 (SF)
49ers, 13-3 (A)
1989—49ers, 45-3 (SF)
49ers, 23-10 (A)
1990—49ers, 19-13 (SF)
49ers, 45-35 (A)
1991—Falcons, 39-34 (SF)
Falcons, 17-14 (A)
1992—49ers, 56-17 (SF)
49ers, 41-3 (A)
1993—49ers, 37-30 (SF)
Falcons, 27-24 (A)
1994—49ers, 42-3 (A)
49ers, 50-14 (SF)
1995—49ers, 41-10 (SF)
Falcons, 28-27 (A)
1996—49ers, 39-17 (SF)
49ers, 34-10 (A)
(RS Pts.—49ers 1,440, Falcons 962)
ATLANTA vs. SEATTLE
RS: Seahawks lead series, 4-1
1976—Seahawks, 30-13 (S)
1979—Seahawks, 31-28 (A)
1985—Seahawks, 30-26 (S)
1988—Seahawks, 31-20 (A)
1991—Falcons, 26-13 (A)
(RS Pts.—Seahawks 135, Falcons 113)
ATLANTA vs. TAMPA BAY
RS: Falcons lead series, 8-6

1977—Falcons, 17-0 (TB)
1978—Buccaneers, 14-9 (TB)
1979—Buccaneers, 17-14 (A)
1981—Buccaneers, 24-23 (TB)
1984—Buccaneers, 23-6 (TB)
1986—Falcons, 23-20 (TB) OT
1987—Buccaneers, 48-10 (TB)
1988—Falcons, 17-10 (A)
1990—Buccaneers, 23-17 (TB)
1991—Falcons, 43-7 (A)
1992—Falcons, 35-7 (TB)
1993—Buccaneers, 31-24 (A)
1994—Falcons, 34-13 (A)
1995—Falcons, 24-21 (TB)
(RS Pts.—Falcons 299, Buccaneers 255)
ATLANTA vs. *TENNESSEE
RS: Falcons lead series, 5-4
1972—Falcons, 20-10 (A)
1976—Oilers, 20-14 (H)
1978—Falcons, 20-14 (A)
1981—Falcons, 31-27 (H)
1984—Falcons, 42-10 (A)
1987—Oilers, 37-33 (H)
1990—Falcons, 47-27 (A)
1993—Oilers, 33-17 (H)
1996—Oilers, 23-13 (A)
(RS Pts.—Falcons 237, Oilers 201)
*Franchise in Houston prior to 1997
ATLANTA vs. WASHINGTON
RS: Redskins lead series, 13-4-1
PS: Redskins lead series, 1-0
1966—Redskins, 33-20 (W)
1967—Tie, 20-20 (A)
1969—Redskins, 27-20 (W)
1972—Redskins, 24-13 (W)
1975—Redskins, 30-27 (A)
1977—Redskins, 10-6 (W)
1978—Falcons, 20-17 (A)
1979—Redskins, 16-7 (A)
1980—Falcons, 10-6 (A)
1983—Redskins, 37-21 (W)
1984—Redskins, 27-14 (W)
1985—Redskins, 44-10 (A)
1987—Falcons, 21-20 (A)
1989—Redskins, 31-30 (A)
1991—Redskins, 56-17 (W)
*Redskins, 24-7 (W)
1992—Redskins, 24-17 (W)
1993—Redskins, 30-17 (W)
1994—Falcons, 27-20 (W)
(RS Pts.—Redskins 472, Falcons 317)
(PS Pts.—Redskins 24, Falcons 7)
*NFC Divisional Playoff

BALTIMORE vs. CAROLINA
RS: Panthers lead series, 1-0
1996—Panthers, 27-16 (C)
(RS Pts.—Panthers 27, Ravens 16)
BALTIMORE vs. CINCINNATI
RS: Bengals lead series, 2-0
1996—Bengals, 24-21 (B)
Bengals, 21-14 (C)
(RS Pts.—Bengals 45, Ravens 35)
BALTIMORE vs. DENVER
RS: Broncos lead series, 1-0
1996—Broncos, 45-34 (D)
(RS Pts.—Broncos 45, Ravens 34)
BALTIMORE vs. INDIANAPOLIS
RS: Colts lead series, 1-0
1996—Colts, 26-21 (I)
(RS Pts.—Colts 26, Ravens 21)
BALTIMORE vs. JACKSONVILLE
RS: Jaguars lead series, 2-0
1996—Jaguars, 30-27 (J)
Jaguars, 28-25 (B) OT
(RS Pts.—Jaguars 58, Ravens 52)
BALTIMORE vs. NEW ENGLAND
RS: Patriots lead series, 1-0
1996—Patriots, 46-38 (B)
(RS Pts.—Patriots 46, Ravens 38)
BALTIMORE vs. NEW ORLEANS
RS: Ravens lead series, 1-0
1996—Ravens, 17-10 (B)

(RS Pts.—Ravens 17, Saints 10)

BALTIMORE vs. OAKLAND
RS: Ravens lead series, 1-0
1996—Ravens, 19-14 (B)
(RS Pts.—Ravens 19, Raiders 14)

BALTIMORE vs. PITTSBURGH
RS: Series tied, 1-1
1996—Steelers, 31-17 (P)
Ravens, 31-17 (B)
(RS Pts.—Ravens 48, Steelers 48)

BALTIMORE vs. ST. LOUIS
RS: Ravens lead series, 1-0
1996—Ravens, 37-31 (B) OT
(RS Pts.—Ravens 37, Rams 31)

BALTIMORE vs. SAN FRANCISCO
RS: 49ers lead series, 1-0
1996—49ers, 38-20 (SF)
(RS Pts.—49ers 38, Ravens 20)

BALTIMORE vs. *TENNESSEE
RS: Oilers lead series, 2-0
1996—Oilers, 29-13 (H)
Oilers, 24-21 (B)
(RS Pts.—Oilers 53, Ravens 34)
*Franchise in Houston prior to 1997

BUFFALO vs. ARIZONA
RS: Series tied, 3-3;
See Arizona vs. Buffalo

BUFFALO vs. ATLANTA
RS: Bills lead series, 4-3;
See Atlanta vs. Buffalo

BUFFALO vs. CAROLINA
RS: Bills lead series, 1-0
1995—Bills, 31-9 (B)
(RS Pts.—Bills 31, Panthers 9)

BUFFALO vs. CHICAGO
RS: Bears lead series, 4-2
1970—Bears, 31-13 (C)
1974—Bills, 16-6 (B)
1979—Bears, 7-0 (B)
1988—Bears, 24-3 (C)
1991—Bills, 35-20 (B)
1994—Bears, 20-13 (C)
(RS Pts.—Bears 108, Bills 80)

BUFFALO vs. CINCINNATI
RS: Bengals lead series, 9-8
PS: Bengals lead series, 2-0
1968—Bengals, 34-23 (C)
1969—Bills, 16-13 (B)
1970—Bengals, 43-14 (B)
1973—Bengals, 16-13 (B)
1975—Bengals, 33-24 (C)
1978—Bills, 5-0 (B)
1979—Bills, 51-24 (B)
1980—Bills, 14-0 (C)
1981—Bengals, 27-24 (C) OT
*Bengals, 28-21 (C)
1983—Bills, 10-6 (C)
1984—Bengals, 52-21 (C)
1985—Bengals, 23-17 (B)
1986—Bengals, 36-33 (C) OT
1988—Bengals, 35-21 (C)
**Bengals, 21-10 (C)
1989—Bills, 24-7 (B)
1991—Bills, 35-16 (B)
1996—Bills, 31-17 (B)
(RS Pts.—Bengals 382, Bills 376)
(PS Pts.—Bengals 49, Bills 31)
*AFC Divisional Playoff
**AFC Championship

BUFFALO vs. CLEVELAND
RS: Browns lead series, 7-4
PS: Browns lead series, 1-0
1972—Browns, 27-10 (C)
1974—Bills, 15-10 (C)
1977—Browns, 27-16 (B)
1978—Browns, 41-20 (C)
1981—Bills, 22-13 (B)
1984—Browns, 13-10 (B)
1985—Browns, 17-7 (C)
1986—Browns, 21-17 (B)
1987—Browns, 27-21 (C)
1989—*Browns, 34-30 (C)

1990—Bills, 42-0 (C)
1995—Bills, 22-19 (C)
(RS Pts.—Browns 215, Bills 202)
(PS Pts.—Browns 34, Bills 30)
*AFC Divisional Playoff

BUFFALO vs. DALLAS
RS: Series tied, 3-3
PS: Cowboys lead series, 2-0
1971—Cowboys, 49-37 (B)
1976—Cowboys, 17-10 (D)
1981—Cowboys, 27-14 (D)
1984—Bills, 14-3 (B)
1992—*Cowboys, 52-17 (Pasadena)
1993—Bills, 13-10 (D)
**Cowboys, 30-13 (Atlanta)
1996—Bills, 10-7 (B)
(RS Pts.—Cowboys 113, Bills 98)
(PS Pts.—Cowboys 82, Bills 30)
*Super Bowl XXVII
**Super Bowl XXVIII

BUFFALO vs. DENVER
RS: Bills lead series, 17-11-1
PS: Bills lead series, 1-0
1960—Broncos, 27-21 (B)
Tie, 38-38 (D)
1961—Broncos, 22-10 (B)
Bills, 23-10 (D)
1962—Broncos, 23-20 (B)
Bills, 45-38 (D)
1963—Bills, 30-28 (D)
Bills, 27-17 (B)
1964—Bills, 30-13 (B)
Bills, 30-19 (D)
1965—Bills, 30-15 (D)
Bills, 31-13 (B)
1966—Bills, 38-21 (B)
1967—Bills, 17-16 (D)
Broncos, 21-20 (B)
1968—Broncos, 34-32 (D)
1969—Bills, 41-28 (B)
1970—Broncos, 25-10 (B)
1975—Bills, 38-14 (B)
1977—Broncos, 26-6 (D)
1979—Broncos, 19-16 (B)
1981—Bills, 9-7 (B)
1984—Broncos, 37-7 (B)
1987—Bills, 21-14 (B)
1989—Broncos, 28-14 (B)
1990—Bills, 29-28 (B)
1991—*Bills, 10-7 (B)
1992—Bills, 27-17 (B)
1994—Bills, 27-20 (B)
1995—Broncos, 22-7 (D)
(RS Pts.—Bills 694, Broncos 640)
(PS Pts.—Bills 10, Broncos 7)
*AFC Championship

BUFFALO vs. DETROIT
RS: Lions lead series, 3-1-1
1972—Tie, 21-21 (B)
1976—Lions, 27-14 (D)
1979—Bills, 20-17 (D)
1991—Lions, 17-14 (B) OT
1994—Lions, 35-21 (D)
(RS Pts.—Lions 117, Bills 90)

BUFFALO vs. GREEN BAY
RS: Bills lead series, 5-1
1974—Bills, 27-7 (GB)
1979—Bills, 19-12 (B)
1982—Packers, 33-21 (Mil)
1988—Bills, 28-0 (B)
1991—Bills, 34-24 (Mil)
1994—Bills 29-20 (B)
(RS Pts.—Bills 158, Packers 96)

BUFFALO vs. *INDIANAPOLIS
RS: Bills lead series, 29-23-1
1970—Tie, 17-17 (Balt)
Colts, 20-14 (Buff)
1971—Colts, 43-0 (Buff)
Colts, 24-0 (Balt)
1972—Colts, 17-0 (Buff)
Colts, 35-7 (Balt)
1973—Bills, 31-13 (Buff)
Bills, 24-17 (Balt)

1974—Bills, 27-14 (Balt)
Bills, 6-0 (Buff)
1975—Bills, 38-31 (Balt)
Colts, 42-35 (Buff)
1976—Colts, 31-13 (Buff)
Colts, 58-20 (Balt)
1977—Colts, 17-14 (Balt)
Colts, 31-13 (Buff)
1978—Bills, 24-17 (Buff)
Bills, 21-14 (Balt)
1979—Bills, 31-13 (Balt)
Colts, 14-13 (Buff)
1980—Colts, 17-12 (Buff)
Colts, 28-24 (Balt)
1981—Bills, 35-3 (Balt)
Bills, 23-17 (Buff)
1982—Bills, 20-0 (Buff)
1983—Bills, 28-23 (Buff)
Bills, 30-7 (Balt)
1984—Colts, 31-17 (I)
Bills, 21-15 (Buff)
1985—Colts, 49-17 (I)
Bills, 21-9 (Buff)
1986—Bills, 24-13 (Buff)
Colts, 24-14 (I)
1987—Colts, 47-6 (Buff)
Bills, 27-3 (I)
1988—Bills, 34-23 (Buff)
Colts, 17-14 (I)
1989—Colts, 37-14 (I)
Bills, 30-7 (Buff)
1990—Bills, 26-10 (Buff)
Bills, 31-7 (I)
1991—Bills, 42-6 (Buff)
Bills, 35-7 (I)
1992—Bills, 38-0 (Buff)
Colts, 16-13 (I) OT
1993—Bills, 23-9 (Buff)
Bills, 30-10 (I)
1994—Colts, 27-17 (Buff)
Colts, 10-9 (I)
1995—Bills, 20-14 (Buff)
Bills, 16-10 (I)
1996—Bills, 16-13 (Buff) OT
Colts, 13-10 (I) OT
(RS Pts.—Bills 1,085, Colts 990)
*Franchise in Baltimore prior to 1984

BUFFALO vs. JACKSONVILLE
PS: Jaguars lead series, 1-0
1996—*Jaguars 30-27 (B)
(PS Pts.—Jaguars 30, Bills 27)
*AFC First-Round Playoff

BUFFALO vs. *KANSAS CITY
RS: Bills lead series, 17-13-1
PS: Bills lead series, 2-1
1960—Texans, 45-28 (B)
Texans, 24-7 (D)
1961—Bills, 27-24 (B)
Bills, 30-20 (D)
1962—Texans, 41-21 (D)
Bills, 23-14 (B)
1963—Tie, 27-27 (B)
Bills, 35-26 (KC)
1964—Bills, 34-17 (B)
Bills, 35-22 (KC)
1965—Bills, 23-7 (KC)
Bills, 34-25 (B)
1966—Chiefs, 42-20 (B)
Bills, 29-14 (KC)
**Chiefs, 31-7 (B)
1967—Chiefs, 23-13 (KC)
1968—Chiefs, 18-7 (B)
1969—Chiefs, 29-7 (B)
Chiefs, 22-19 (KC)
1971—Chiefs, 22-9 (KC)
1973—Bills, 23-14 (B)
1976—Bills, 50-17 (B)
1978—Bills, 28-13 (B)
Chiefs, 14-10 (KC)
1982—Bills, 14-9 (B)
1983—Bills, 14-9 (KC)
1986—Chiefs, 20-17 (B)
Bills, 17-14 (KC)

1991—Chiefs, 33-6 (KC)
***Bills, 37-14 (B)
1993—Chiefs, 23-7 (KC)
****Bills, 30-13 (B)
1994—Bills, 44-10 (B)
1996—Bills, 20-9 (B)
(RS Pts.—Bills 673, Chiefs 652)
(PS Pts.—Bills 74, Chiefs 58)
*Franchise in Dallas prior to 1963 and known as Texans
**AFL Championship
***AFC Divisional Playoff
****AFC Championship

BUFFALO vs. MIAMI
RS: Dolphins lead series, 40-21-1
PS: Bills lead series, 3-0
1966—Bills, 58-24 (B)
Bills, 29-0 (M)
1967—Bills, 35-13 (B)
Dolphins, 17-14 (M)
1968—Tie, 14-14 (M)
Dolphins, 21-17 (B)
1969—Dolphins, 24-6 (M)
Bills, 28-3 (B)
1970—Dolphins, 33-14 (B)
Dolphins, 45-7 (M)
1971—Dolphins, 29-14 (B)
Dolphins, 34-0 (M)
1972—Dolphins, 24-23 (M)
Dolphins, 30-16 (B)
1973—Dolphins, 27-6 (M)
Dolphins, 17-0 (B)
1974—Dolphins, 24-16 (B)
Dolphins, 35-28 (M)
1975—Dolphins, 35-30 (B)
Dolphins, 31-21 (M)
1976—Dolphins, 30-21 (B)
Dolphins, 45-27 (M)
1977—Dolphins, 13-0 (B)
Dolphins, 31-14 (M)
1978—Dolphins, 31-24 (M)
Dolphins, 25-24 (B)
1979—Dolphins, 9-7 (B)
Dolphins, 17-7 (M)
1980—Bills, 17-7 (B)
Dolphins, 17-14 (M)
1981—Bills, 31-21 (B)
Dolphins, 16-6 (M)
1982—Dolphins, 9-7 (B)
Dolphins, 27-10 (M)
1983—Dolphins, 12-0 (B)
Bills, 38-35 (M) OT
1984—Dolphins, 21-17 (B)
Dolphins, 38-7 (M)
1985—Dolphins, 23-14 (B)
Dolphins, 28-0 (M)
1986—Dolphins, 27-14 (M)
Dolphins, 34-24 (B)
1987—Bills, 34-31 (M) OT
Bills, 27-0 (B)
1988—Bills, 9-6 (B)
Bills, 31-6 (M)
1989—Bills, 27-24 (M)
Bills, 31-17 (B)
1990—Dolphins, 30-7 (M)
Bills, 24-14 (B)
*Bills, 44-34 (B)
1991—Bills, 35-31 (B)
Bills, 41-27 (M)
1992—Dolphins, 37-10 (B)
Bills, 26-20 (M)
**Bills, 29-10 (M)
1993—Dolphins, 22-13 (B)
Bills, 47-34 (M)
1994—Bills, 21-11 (B)
Bills, 42-31 (M)
1995—Dolphins, 23-6 (B)
Bills, 23-20 (B)
***Bills, 37-22 (B)
1996—Dolphins, 21-7 (B)
Dolphins, 16-14 (M)
(RS Pts.—Dolphins 1,417, Bills 1,174)
(PS Pts.—Bills 110, Dolphins 66)

*AFC Divisional Playoff
**AFC Championship
***AFC First-Round Playoff

BUFFALO vs. *NEW ENGLAND
RS: Patriots lead series, 37-35-1
PS: Patriots lead series, 1-0
1960—Bills, 13-0 (Bos)
Bills, 38-14 (Buff)
1961—Patriots, 23-21 (Buff)
Patriots, 52-21 (Bos)
1962—Tie, 28-28 (Buff)
Patriots, 21-10 (Bos)
1963—Bills, 28-21 (Buff)
Patriots, 17-7 (Bos)
**Patriots, 26-8 (Buff)
1964—Patriots, 36-28 (Buff)
Bills, 24-14 (Bos)
1965—Bills, 24-7 (Buff)
Bills, 23-7 (Bos)
1966—Patriots, 20-10 (Buff)
Patriots, 14-3 (Bos)
1967—Patriots, 23-0 (Buff)
Bills, 44-16 (Bos)
1968—Patriots, 16-7 (Buff)
Patriots, 23-6 (Bos)
1969—Bills, 23-16 (Buff)
Patriots, 35-21 (Bos)
1970—Bills, 45-10 (Bos)
Patriots, 14-10 (Buff)
1971—Patriots, 38-33 (NE)
Bills, 27-20 (Buff)
1972—Bills, 38-14 (Buff)
Bills, 27-24 (NE)
1973—Bills, 31-13 (NE)
Bills, 37-13 (Buff)
1974—Bills, 30-28 (Buff)
Bills, 29-28 (NE)
1975—Bills, 45-31 (Buff)
Bills, 34-14 (NE)
1976—Patriots, 26-22 (Buff)
Patriots, 20-10 (NE)
1977—Bills, 24-14 (NE)
Patriots, 20-7 (Buff)
1978—Patriots, 14-10 (Buff)
Patriots, 26-24 (NE)
1979—Patriots, 26-6 (Buff)
Bills, 16-13 (NE) OT
1980—Bills, 31-13 (Buff)
Patriots, 24-2 (NE)
1981—Bills, 20-17 (Buff)
Bills, 19-10 (NE)
1982—Patriots, 30-19 (NE)
1983—Patriots, 31-0 (Buff)
Patriots, 21-7 (NE)
1984—Patriots, 21-17 (Buff)
Patriots, 38-10 (NE)
1985—Patriots, 17-14 (Buff)
Patriots, 14-3 (NE)
1986—Patriots, 23-3 (Buff)
Patriots, 22-19 (NE)
1987—Patriots, 14-7 (NE)
Patriots, 13-7 (Buff)
1988—Bills, 16-14 (NE)
Bills, 23-20 (Buff)
1989—Bills, 31-10 (Buff)
Patriots, 33-24 (NE)
1990—Bills, 27-10 (NE)
Bills, 14-0 (Buff)
1991—Bills, 22-17 (Buff)
Patriots, 16-13 (NE)
1992—Bills, 41-7 (NE)
Bills, 16-7 (Buff)
1993—Bills, 38-14 (Buff)

Bills, 13-10 (NE) OT
1994—Bills, 38-35 (NE)
Patriots, 41-17 (Buff)
1995—Patriots, 27-14 (NE)
Patriots, 35-25 (Buff)
1996—Bills, 17-10 (Buff)
Patriots, 28-25 (NE)
(RS Pts.—Bills 1,476, Patriots 1,451)
(PS Pts.—Patriots 26, Bills 8)
*Franchise in Boston prior to 1971
**Division Playoff

BUFFALO vs. NEW ORLEANS
RS: Bills lead series, 3-2
1973—Saints, 13-0 (NO)
1980—Bills, 35-26 (NO)
1983—Bills, 27-21 (B)
1989—Saints, 22-19 (B)
1992—Bills, 20-16 (NO)
(RS Pts.—Bills 101, Saints 98)

BUFFALO vs. N.Y. GIANTS
RS: Bills lead series, 5-2
PS: Giants lead series, 1-0
1970—Giants, 20-6 (NY)
1975—Giants, 17-14 (B)
1978—Bills, 41-17 (B)
1987—Bills, 6-3 (B) OT
1990—Bills, 17-13 (NY)
*Giants, 20-19 (Tampa)
1993—Bills, 17-14 (B)
1996—Bills, 23-20 (NY) OT
(RS Pts.—Bills 124, Giants 104)
(PS Pts.—Giants 20, Bills 19)
*Super Bowl XXV

BUFFALO vs. *N.Y. JETS
RS: Bills lead series, 41-31
PS: Bills lead series, 1-0
1960—Titans, 27-3 (NY)
Titans, 17-13 (B)
1961—Bills, 41-31 (B)
Titans, 21-14 (NY)
1962—Titans, 17-6 (B)
Bills, 20-3 (NY)
1963—Bills, 45-14 (B)
Bills, 19-10 (NY)
1964—Bills, 34-24 (B)
Bills, 20-7 (NY)
1965—Bills, 33-21 (B)
Jets, 14-12 (NY)
1966—Bills, 33-23 (NY)
Bills, 14-3 (B)
1967—Bills, 20-17 (B)
Jets, 20-10 (NY)
1968—Bills, 37-35 (B)
Jets, 25-21 (NY)
1969—Jets, 33-19 (B)
Jets, 16-6 (NY)
1970—Bills, 34-31 (B)
Bills, 10-6 (NY)
1971—Jets, 28-17 (NY)
Jets, 20-7 (B)
1972—Jets, 41-24 (B)
Jets, 41-3 (NY)
1973—Bills, 9-7 (B)
Bills, 34-14 (NY)
1974—Bills, 16-12 (B)
Jets, 20-10 (NY)
1975—Bills, 42-14 (B)
Bills, 24-23 (NY)
1976—Jets, 17-14 (NY)
Jets, 19-14 (B)
1977—Jets, 24-19 (B)
Bills, 14-10 (NY)
1978—Jets, 21-20 (B)
Jets, 45-14 (NY)
1979—Bills, 46-31 (B)
Bills, 14-12 (NY)
1980—Bills, 20-10 (B)
Bills, 31-24 (NY)
1981—Bills, 31-0 (B)
Jets, 33-14 (NY)
**Bills, 31-27 (NY)
1983—Jets, 34-10 (B)
Bills, 24-17 (NY)

1984—Jets, 28-26 (B)
Jets, 21-17 (NY)
1985—Jets, 42-3 (NY)
Jets, 27-7 (B)
1986—Jets, 28-24 (B)
Jets, 14-13 (NY)
1987—Jets, 31-28 (B)
Bills, 17-14 (NY)
1988—Bills, 37-14 (NY)
Bills, 9-6 (B) OT
1989—Bills, 34-3 (B)
Bills, 37-0 (NY)
1990—Bills, 30-7 (NY)
Bills, 30-27 (B)
1991—Bills, 23-20 (NY)
Bills, 24-13 (B)
1992—Bills, 24-20 (NY)
Jets, 24-17 (B)
1993—Bills, 19-10 (NY)
Bills, 16-14 (B)
1994—Jets, 23-3 (B)
Jets, 22-17 (NY)
1995—Bills, 29-10 (B)
Bills, 28-26 (NY)
1996—Bills, 25-22 (NY)
Bills, 35-10 (B)
(RS Pts.—Bills, 1,507, Jets 1,408)
(PS Pts.—Bills 31, Jets 27)
*Jets known as Titans prior to 1963
**AFC First-Round Playoff

BUFFALO vs. *OAKLAND
RS: Raiders lead series, 15-14
PS: Bills lead series, 2-0
1960—Bills, 38-9 (B)
Raiders, 20-7 (O)
1961—Raiders, 31-22 (B)
Bills, 26-21 (O)
1962—Bills, 14-6 (B)
Bills, 10-6 (O)
1963—Raiders, 35-17 (O)
Bills, 12-0 (B)
1964—Bills, 23-20 (B)
Raiders, 16-13 (O)
1965—Bills, 17-12 (B)
Bills, 17-14 (O)
1966—Bills, 31-10 (O)
1967—Raiders, 24-20 (B)
Raiders, 28-21 (O)
1968—Raiders, 48-6 (B)
Raiders, 13-10 (O)
1969—Raiders, 50-21 (O)
1972—Raiders, 28-16 (O)
1974—Bills, 21-20 (B)
1977—Raiders, 34-13 (O)
1980—Bills, 24-7 (B)
1983—Raiders, 27-24 (B)
1987—Raiders, 34-21 (LA)
1988—Bills, 37-21 (B)
1990—Bills, 38-24 (B)
**Bills, 51-3 (B)
1991—Bills, 30-27 (LA) OT
1992—Raiders, 20-3 (LA)
1993—Raiders, 25-24 (B)
***Bills, 29-23 (B)
(RS Pts.—Raiders 630, Bills 576)
(PS Pts.—Bills 80, Raiders 26)
*Franchise in Los Angeles from
1982-1994
**AFC Championship
***AFC Divisional Playoff

BUFFALO vs. PHILADELPHIA
RS: Series tied, 4-4
1973—Bills, 27-26 (B)
1981—Eagles, 20-14 (B)
1984—Eagles, 27-17 (B)
1985—Eagles, 21-17 (P)
1987—Eagles, 17-7 (P)
1990—Bills, 30-23 (B)
1993—Bills, 10-7 (P)
1996—Bills, 24-17 (P)
(RS Pts.—Eagles 158, Bills 146)

BUFFALO vs. PITTSBURGH
RS: Steelers lead series, 8-7

PS: Steelers lead series, 2-1
1970—Steelers, 23-10 (P)
1972—Steelers, 38-21 (B)
1974—*Steelers, 32-14 (P)
1975—Bills, 30-21 (P)
1978—Steelers, 28-17 (B)
1979—Steelers, 28-0 (P)
1980—Bills, 28-13 (B)
1982—Bills, 13-0 (B)
1985—Steelers, 30-24 (P)
1986—Bills, 16-12 (B)
1988—Bills, 36-28 (B)
1991—Bills, 52-34 (B)
1992—Bills, 28-20 (B)
*Bills, 24-3 (P)
1993—Steelers, 23-0 (P)
1994—Steelers, 23-10 (P)
1995—*Steelers, 40-21 (P)
1996—Steelers, 24-6 (P)
(RS Pts.—Steelers 345, Bills 291)
(PS Pts.—Steelers 75, Bills 59)
*AFC Divisional Playoff

BUFFALO vs. *ST. LOUIS
RS: Bills lead series, 4-3
1970—Rams, 19-0 (B)
1974—Rams, 19-14 (LA)
1980—Bills, 10-7 (B) OT
1983—Rams, 41-17 (LA)
1989—Bills, 23-20 (B)
1992—Bills, 40-7 (B)
1995—Bills, 45-27 (StL)
(RS Pts.—Bills 149, Rams 140)
*Franchise in Los Angeles prior to 1995

BUFFALO vs. *SAN DIEGO
RS: Chargers lead series, 16-7-2
PS: Bills lead series, 2-1
1960—Chargers, 24-10 (B)
Bills, 32-3 (LA)
1961—Chargers, 19-11 (B)
Chargers, 28-10 (SD)
1962—Bills, 35-10 (B)
Bills, 40-20 (SD)
1963—Chargers, 14-10 (SD)
Chargers, 23-13 (B)
1964—Bills, 30-3 (B)
Bills, 27-24 (SD)
**Bills, 20-7 (B)
1965—Chargers, 34-3 (B)
Tie, 20-20 (SD)
**Bills, 23-0 (SD)
1966—Chargers, 27-7 (SD)
Tie, 17-17 (B)
1967—Chargers, 37-17 (B)
1968—Chargers, 21-6 (B)
1969—Chargers, 45-6 (SD)
1971—Chargers, 20-3 (SD)
1973—Chargers, 34-7 (SD)
1976—Chargers, 34-13 (B)
1979—Chargers, 27-19 (SD)
1980—Bills, 26-24 (SD)
***Chargers, 20-14 (SD)
1981—Bills, 28-27 (SD)
1985—Chargers, 14-9 (B)
Chargers, 40-7 (SD)
(RS Pts.—Chargers 589, Bills 406)
(PS Pts.—Bills 57, Chargers 27)
*Franchise in Los Angeles prior to 1961
**AFL Championship
***AFC Divisional Playoff

BUFFALO vs. SAN FRANCISCO
RS: Series tied, 3-3
1972—Bills, 27-20 (B)
1980—Bills, 18-13 (SF)
1983—49ers, 23-10 (B)
1989—49ers, 21-10 (SF)
1992—Bills, 34-31 (SF)
1995—49ers, 27-17 (SF)
(RS Pts.—49ers 135, Bills 116)

BUFFALO vs. SEATTLE
RS: Seahawks lead series, 4-2
1977—Seahawks, 56-17 (S)
1984—Seahawks, 31-28 (S)
1988—Bills, 13-3 (S)

BUFFALO vs. MINNESOTA
RS: Vikings lead series, 5-2
1971—Vikings, 19-0 (M)
1975—Vikings, 35-13 (B)
1979—Vikings, 10-3 (M)
1982—Bills, 23-22 (B)
1985—Vikings, 27-20 (B)
1988—Bills, 13-10 (B)
1994—Vikings, 21-17 (B)
(RS Pts.—Vikings 144, Bills 89)

1989—Seahawks, 17-16 (S)
1995—Bills, 27-21 (B)
1996—Seahawks, 26-18 (S)
(RS Pts.—Seahawks 154, Bills 119)
BUFFALO vs. TAMPA BAY
RS: Buccaneers lead series, 4-2
1976—Bills, 14-9 (TB)
1978—Buccaneers, 31-10 (TB)
1982—Buccaneers, 24-23 (TB)
1986—Buccaneers, 34-28 (TB)
1988—Buccaneers, 10-5 (TB)
1991—Bills, 17-10 (TB)
(RS Pts.—Buccaneers 118, Bills 97)
BUFFALO vs. *TENNESSEE
RS: Oilers lead series, 21-13
PS: Bills lead series, 2-0
1960—Bills, 25-24 (B)
      Oilers, 31-23 (H)
1961—Bills, 22-12 (H)
      Oilers, 28-16 (B)
1962—Oilers, 28-23 (B)
      Oilers, 17-14 (H)
1963—Oilers, 31-20 (B)
      Oilers, 28-14 (H)
1964—Bills, 48-17 (H)
      Bills, 24-10 (B)
1965—Oilers, 19-17 (B)
      Bills, 29-18 (H)
1966—Bills, 27-20 (B)
      Bills, 42-20 (H)
1967—Oilers, 20-3 (B)
      Oilers, 10-3 (H)
1968—Oilers, 30-7 (B)
      Oilers, 35-6 (H)
1969—Oilers, 17-3 (B)
      Oilers, 28-14 (H)
1971—Oilers, 20-14 (B)
1974—Oilers, 21-9 (B)
1976—Oilers, 13-3 (B)
1978—Oilers, 17-10 (H)
1983—Bills, 30-13 (B)
1985—Bills, 20-0 (B)
1986—Oilers, 16-7 (H)
1987—Bills, 34-30 (B)
1988—**Bills, 17-10 (B)
1989—Bills, 47-41 (H) OT
1990—Oilers, 27-24 (H)
1992—Oilers, 27-3 (H)
      ***Bills, 41-38 (B) OT
1993—Bills, 35-7 (B)
1994—Bills, 15-7 (H)
1995—Oilers, 28-17 (B)
(RS Pts.—Oilers 710, Bills 648)
(PS Pts.—Bills 58, Oilers 48)
*Franchise in Houston prior to 1997
**AFC Divisional Playoff
***AFC First-Round Playoff
BUFFALO vs. WASHINGTON
RS: Series tied, 4-4
PS: Redskins lead series, 1-0
1972—Bills, 24-17 (W)
1977—Redskins, 10-0 (B)
1981—Bills, 21-14 (B)
1984—Redskins, 41-14 (W)
1987—Redskins, 27-7 (B)
1990—Redskins, 29-14 (W)
1991—*Redskins, 37-24 (Minneapolis)
1993—Bills, 24-10 (B)
1996—Bills, 38-13 (B)
(RS Pts.—Redskins 161, Bills 142)
(PS Pts.—Redskins 37, Bills 24)
*Super Bowl XXVI

CAROLINA vs. ARIZONA
RS: Panthers lead series, 1-0;
See Arizona vs. Carolina
CAROLINA vs. ATLANTA
RS: Series tied, 2-2;
See Atlanta vs. Carolina
CAROLINA vs. BALTIMORE
RS: Panthers lead series, 1-0
See Baltimore vs. Carolina
CAROLINA vs. BUFFALO

RS: Bills lead series, 1-0;
See Buffalo vs. Carolina
CAROLINA vs. CHICAGO
RS: Bears lead series, 1-0
1995—Bears, 31-27 (Chi)
(RS Pts.—Bears 31, Panthers 27)
CAROLINA vs. DALLAS
PS: Panthers lead series, 1-0
1996—*Panthers, 26-17 (C)
(PS Pts.—Panthers 26, Cowboys 17)
*NFC Divisional Playoff
CAROLINA vs. GREEN BAY
PS: Packers lead series, 1-0
1996—*Packers, 30-13 (GB)
(PS Pts.—Packers 30, Panthers 13)
*NFC Championship
CAROLINA vs. INDIANAPOLIS
RS: Panthers lead series, 1-0
1995—Panthers, 13-10 (C)
(RS Pts.—Panthers 13, Colts 10)
CAROLINA vs. JACKSONVILLE
RS: Jaguars lead series, 1-0
1996—Jaguars, 24-14 (J)
(RS Pts.—Jaguars 24, Panthers 14)
CAROLINA vs. MINNESOTA
RS: Vikings lead series, 1-0
1996—Vikings, 14-12 (M)
(RS Pts.—Vikings 14, Panthers 12)
CAROLINA vs. NEW ENGLAND
RS: Panthers lead series, 1-0
1995—Panthers, 20-17 (NE) OT
(RS Pts.—Panthers 20, Patriots 17)
CAROLINA vs. NEW ORLEANS
RS: Panthers lead series, 3-1
1995—Panthers, 20-3 (C)
      Saints, 34-26 (NO)
1996—Panthers, 22-20 (NO)
      Panthers, 19-7 (C)
(RS Pts.—Panthers 87, Saints 64)
CAROLINA vs. N.Y. GIANTS
RS: Panthers lead series, 1-0
1995—Panthers, 27-17 (C)
(RS Pts.—Panthers 27, Giants 17)
CAROLINA vs. N.Y. JETS
RS: Panthers lead series, 1-0
1995—Panthers, 26-15 (C)
(RS Pts.—Panthers 26, Jets 15)
CAROLINA vs. PHILADELPHIA
RS: Eagles lead series, 1-0
1996—Eagles, 20-9 (P)
(RS Pts.—Eagles 20, Panthers 9)
CAROLINA vs. PITTSBURGH
RS: Panthers lead series, 1-0
1996—Panthers, 18-14 (C)
(RS Pts.—Panthers 18, Steelers 14)
CAROLINA vs. ST. LOUIS
RS: Series tied 2-2
1995—Rams, 31-10 (C)
      Rams, 28-17 (StL)
1996—Panthers, 45-13 (C)
      Panthers, 20-10 (StL)
(RS Pts.—Panthers 92, Rams 82)
CAROLINA vs. SAN FRANCISCO
RS: Panthers lead series, 3-1
1995—Panthers, 13-7 (SF)
      49ers, 31-10 (C)
1996—Panthers, 23-7 (C)
      Panthers, 30-24 (SF)
(RS Pts.—Panthers 76, 49ers 69)
CAROLINA vs. TAMPA BAY
RS: Series tied, 1-1
1995—Buccaneers, 20-13 (C)
1996—Panthers, 24-0 (C)
(RS Pts.—Panthers 37, Buccaneers 20)
CAROLINA vs. *TENNESSEE
RS: Panthers lead series, 1-0
1996—Panthers, 31-6 (H)
(RS Pts.—Panthers 31, Oilers 6)
*Franchise in Houston prior to 1997
CAROLINA vs. WASHINGTON
RS: Redskins lead series, 1-0
1995—Redskins, 20-17 (W)
(RS Pts.—Redskins 20, Panthers 17)

CHICAGO vs. ARIZONA
RS: Bears lead series, 52-25-6;
See Arizona vs. Chicago
CHICAGO vs. ATLANTA
RS: Series tied, 9-9;
See Atlanta vs. Chicago
CHICAGO vs. BUFFALO
RS: Bears lead series, 4-2;
See Buffalo vs. Chicago
CHICAGO vs. CAROLINA
RS: Bears lead series, 1-0;
See Carolina vs. Chicago
CHICAGO vs. CINCINNATI
RS: Bengals lead series, 4-2
1972—Bengals, 13-3 (Chi)
1980—Bengals, 17-14 (Chi) OT
1986—Bears, 44-7 (Cin)
1989—Bears, 17-14 (Chi)
1992—Bengals, 31-28 (Chi) OT
1995—Bengals, 16-10 (Cin)
(RS Pts.—Bears 116, Bengals 98)
CHICAGO vs. CLEVELAND
RS: Browns lead series, 8-3
1951—Browns, 42-21 (Cle)
1954—Browns, 39-10 (Chi)
1960—Browns, 42-0 (Cle)
1961—Bears, 17-14 (Chi)
1967—Browns, 24-0 (Cle)
1969—Browns, 28-24 (Chi)
1972—Bears, 17-0 (Cle)
1980—Browns, 27-21 (Cle)
1986—Bears, 41-31 (Chi)
1989—Browns, 27-7 (Cle)
1992—Browns, 27-14 (Cle)
(RS Pts.—Browns 301, Bears 172)
CHICAGO vs. DALLAS
RS: Cowboys lead series, 8-7
PS: Cowboys lead series, 2-0
1960—Bears, 17-7 (C)
1962—Bears, 34-33 (D)
1964—Cowboys, 24-10 (C)
1968—Cowboys, 34-3 (C)
1971—Bears, 23-19 (C)
1973—Cowboys, 20-17 (C)
1976—Cowboys, 31-21 (D)
1977—*Cowboys, 37-7 (D)
1979—Cowboys, 24-20 (D)
1981—Cowboys, 10-9 (D)
1984—Cowboys, 23-14 (C)
1985—Bears, 44-0 (D)
1986—Bears, 24-10 (D)
1988—Bears, 17-7 (C)
1991–**Cowboys, 17-13 (C)
1992—Cowboys, 27-14 (D)
1996—Bears, 22-6 (C)
(RS Pts.—Bears 289, Cowboys 275)
(PS Pts.—Cowboys 54, Bears 20)
*NFC Divisional Playoff
**NFC First-Round Playoff
CHICAGO vs. DENVER
RS: Broncos lead series, 6-5
1971—Broncos, 6-3 (D)
1973—Bears, 33-14 (D)
1976—Broncos, 28-14 (C)
1978—Broncos, 16-7 (D)
1981—Bears, 35-24 (C)
1983—Bears, 31-14 (C)
1984—Bears, 27-0 (C)
1987—Broncos, 31-29 (D)
1990—Bears, 16-13 (D) OT
1993—Broncos, 13-3 (C)
1996—Broncos, 17-12 (D)
(RS Pts.—Bears 210, Broncos 176)
CHICAGO vs. *DETROIT
RS: Bears lead series, 76-53-5
1930—Spartans, 7-6 (P)
      Bears, 14-6 (C)
1931—Bears, 9-6 (C)
      Spartans, 3-0 (P)
1932—Tie, 13-13 (C)
      Tie, 7-7 (P)
      Bears, 9-0 (C)
1933—Bears, 17-14 (C)

      Bears, 17-7 (P)
1934—Bears, 19-16 (D)
      Bears, 10-7 (C)
1935—Tie, 20-20 (C)
      Lions, 14-2 (D)
1936—Bears, 12-10 (C)
      Lions, 13-7 (D)
1937—Bears, 28-20 (C)
      Bears, 13-0 (D)
1938—Lions, 13-7 (C)
      Lions, 14-7 (D)
1939—Lions, 10-0 (C)
      Bears, 23-13 (D)
1940—Bears, 7-0 (C)
      Lions, 17-14 (D)
1941—Bears, 49-0 (C)
      Bears, 24-7 (D)
1942—Bears, 16-0 (C)
      Bears, 42-0 (D)
1943—Bears, 27-21 (D)
      Bears, 35-14 (C)
1944—Tie, 21-21 (C)
      Lions, 41-21 (D)
1945—Lions, 16-10 (D)
      Lions, 35-28 (C)
1946—Bears, 42-6 (C)
      Bears, 45-24 (D)
1947—Bears, 33-24 (C)
      Bears, 34-14 (D)
1948—Bears, 28-0 (C)
      Bears, 42-14 (D)
1949—Bears, 27-24 (C)
      Bears, 28-7 (D)
1950—Bears, 35-21 (D)
      Bears, 6-3 (C)
1951—Bears, 28-23 (D)
      Lions, 41-28 (C)
1952—Bears, 24-23 (C)
      Lions, 45-21 (D)
1953—Lions, 20-16 (C)
      Lions, 13-7 (D)
1954—Lions, 48-23 (D)
      Bears, 28-24 (C)
1955—Bears, 24-14 (D)
      Bears, 21-20 (C)
1956—Lions, 42-10 (D)
      Bears, 38-21 (C)
1957—Bears, 27-7 (D)
      Lions, 21-13 (C)
1958—Bears, 20-7 (D)
      Bears, 21-16 (C)
1959—Bears, 24-14 (D)
      Bears, 25-14 (C)
1960—Bears, 28-7 (C)
      Lions, 36-0 (D)
1961—Bears, 31-17 (D)
      Lions, 16-15 (C)
1962—Lions, 11-3 (D)
      Bears, 3-0 (C)
1963—Bears, 37-21 (D)
      Bears, 24-14 (C)
1964—Lions, 10-0 (C)
      Bears, 27-24 (D)
1965—Bears, 38-10 (C)
      Bears, 17-10 (D)
1966—Lions, 14-3 (D)
      Tie, 10-10 (C)
1967—Bears, 14-3 (C)
      Bears, 27-13 (D)
1968—Lions, 42-0 (D)
      Lions, 28-10 (C)
1969—Lions, 13-7 (D)
      Lions, 20-3 (C)
1970—Lions, 28-14 (D)
      Lions, 16-10 (C)
1971—Bears, 28-23 (D)
      Lions, 28-3 (C)
1972—Lions, 38-24 (D)
      Lions, 14-0 (C)
1973—Lions, 30-7 (D)
      Lions, 40-7 (C)
1974—Bears, 17-9 (C)
      Lions, 34-17 (D)

1975—Lions, 27-7 (D)
    Bears, 25-21 (C)
1976—Bears, 10-3 (C)
    Lions, 14-10 (D)
1977—Bears, 30-20 (C)
    Bears, 31-14 (D)
1978—Bears, 19-0 (D)
    Lions, 21-17 (C)
1979—Bears, 35-7 (C)
    Lions, 20-0 (D)
1980—Bears, 24-7 (C)
    Bears, 23-17 (D) OT
1981—Lions, 48-17 (D)
    Lions, 23-7 (C)
1982—Lions, 17-10 (D)
    Bears, 20-17 (C)
1983—Lions, 31-17 (D)
    Lions, 38-17 (C)
1984—Bears, 16-14 (C)
    Bears, 30-13 (D)
1985—Bears, 24-3 (C)
    Bears, 37-17 (D)
1986—Bears, 13-7 (C)
    Bears, 16-13 (D)
1987—Bears, 30-10 (C)
1988—Bears, 24-7 (D)
    Bears, 13-12 (C)
1989—Bears, 47-27 (D)
    Lions, 27-17 (C)
1990—Bears, 23-17 (C) OT
    Lions, 38-21 (D)
1991—Bears, 20-10 (C)
    Lions, 16-6 (D)
1992—Bears, 27-24 (C)
    Lions, 16-3 (D)
1993—Bears, 10-6 (D)
    Lions, 20-14 (C)
1994—Lions, 21-16 (D)
    Bears, 20-10 (C)
1995—Lions, 24-17 (C)
    Lions, 27-7 (D)
1996—Lions, 35-16 (D)
    Bears, 31-14 (C)
(RS Pts.—Bears 2,493, Lions 2,287)
*Franchise in Portsmouth prior to 1934
and known as the Spartans
CHICAGO vs. GREEN BAY
RS: Bears lead series, 81-65-6
PS: Bears lead series, 1-0
1921—Staleys, 20-0 (C)
1923—Bears, 3-0 (GB)
1924—Bears, 3-0 (C)
1925—Packers, 14-10 (GB)
    Bears, 21-0 (C)
1926—Tie, 6-6 (GB)
    Bears, 19-13 (C)
    Tie, 3-3 (C)
1927—Bears, 7-6 (GB)
    Bears, 14-6 (C)
1928—Tie, 12-12 (GB)
    Packers, 16-6 (C)
    Packers, 6-0 (C)
1929—Packers, 23-0 (GB)
    Packers, 14-0 (C)
    Packers, 25-0 (C)
1930—Packers, 7-0 (GB)
    Packers, 13-12 (C)
    Bears, 21-0 (C)
1931—Packers, 7-0 (GB)
    Packers, 6-2 (C)
    Bears, 7-6 (C)
1932—Tie, 0-0 (GB)
    Packers, 2-0 (C)
    Bears, 9-0 (C)
1933—Bears, 14-7 (GB)
    Bears, 10-7 (C)
    Bears, 7-6 (C)
1934—Bears, 24-10 (GB)
    Bears, 27-14 (C)
1935—Packers, 7-0 (GB)
    Packers, 17-14 (C)
1936—Bears, 30-3 (GB)
    Packers, 21-10 (C)

1937—Bears, 14-2 (GB)
    Packers, 24-14 (C)
1938—Bears, 2-0 (GB)
    Packers, 24-17 (C)
1939—Packers, 21-16 (GB)
    Bears, 30-27 (C)
1940—Bears, 41-10 (GB)
    Bears, 14-7 (C)
1941—Bears, 25-17 (GB)
    Packers, 16-14 (C)
    **Bears, 33-14 (C)
1942—Bears, 44-28 (GB)
    Bears, 38-7 (C)
1943—Tie, 21-21 (GB)
    Bears, 21-7 (C)
1944—Packers, 42-28 (GB)
    Bears, 21-0 (C)
1945—Packers, 31-21 (GB)
    Bears, 28-24 (C)
1946—Bears, 30-7 (GB)
    Bears, 10-7 (C)
1947—Packers, 29-20 (GB)
    Bears, 20-17 (C)
1948—Bears, 45-7 (GB)
    Bears, 7-6 (C)
1949—Bears, 17-0 (GB)
    Bears, 24-3 (C)
1950—Packers, 31-21 (GB)
    Bears, 28-14 (C)
1951—Bears, 31-20 (GB)
    Bears, 24-13 (C)
1952—Bears, 24-14 (GB)
    Packers, 41-28 (C)
1953—Bears, 17-13 (GB)
    Tie, 21-21 (C)
1954—Bears, 10-3 (GB)
    Bears, 28-23 (C)
1955—Packers, 24-3 (GB)
    Bears, 52-31 (C)
1956—Bears, 37-21 (GB)
    Bears, 38-14 (C)
1957—Packers, 21-17 (GB)
    Bears, 21-14 (C)
1958—Bears, 34-20 (GB)
    Bears, 24-10 (C)
1959—Packers, 9-6 (GB)
    Bears, 28-17 (C)
1960—Bears, 17-14 (GB)
    Packers, 41-13 (C)
1961—Packers, 24-0 (GB)
    Packers, 31-28 (C)
1962—Packers, 49-0 (GB)
    Packers, 38-7 (C)
1963—Bears, 10-3 (GB)
    Bears, 26-7 (C)
1964—Packers, 23-12 (GB)
    Packers, 17-3 (C)
1965—Packers, 23-14 (GB)
    Bears, 31-10 (C)
1966—Packers, 17-0 (C)
    Packers, 13-6 (GB)
1967—Packers, 13-10 (GB)
    Packers, 17-13 (C)
1968—Bears, 13-10 (GB)
    Packers, 28-27 (C)
1969—Packers, 17-0 (GB)
    Packers, 21-3 (C)
1970—Packers, 20-19 (GB)
    Bears, 35-17 (C)
1971—Packers, 17-14 (C)
    Packers, 31-10 (GB)
1972—Packers, 20-17 (GB)
    Packers, 23-17 (C)
1973—Bears, 31-17 (GB)
    Packers, 21-0 (C)
1974—Bears, 10-9 (C)
    Packers, 20-3 (Mil)
1975—Bears, 27-14 (C)
    Packers, 28-7 (GB)
1976—Bears, 24-13 (C)
    Bears, 16-10 (GB)
1977—Bears, 26-0 (GB)
    Bears, 21-10 (C)

1978—Packers, 24-14 (GB)
    Bears, 14-0 (C)
1979—Bears, 6-3 (C)
    Bears, 15-14 (GB)
1980—Packers, 12-6 (GB) OT
    Bears, 61-7 (C)
1981—Packers, 16-9 (C)
    Packers, 21-17 (GB)
1983—Packers, 31-28 (GB)
    Bears, 23-21 (C)
1984—Bears, 9-7 (GB)
    Packers, 20-14 (C)
1985—Bears, 23-7 (C)
    Bears, 16-10 (GB)
1986—Bears, 25-12 (GB)
    Bears, 12-10 (C)
1987—Bears, 26-24 (GB)
    Bears, 23-10 (C)
1988—Bears, 24-6 (GB)
    Bears, 16-0 (C)
1989—Packers, 14-13 (GB)
    Packers, 40-28 (C)
1990—Bears, 31-13 (GB)
    Bears, 27-13 (C)
1991—Bears, 10-0 (GB)
    Bears, 27-13 (C)
1992—Bears, 30-10 (GB)
    Packers, 17-3 (C)
1993—Packers, 17-3 (GB)
    Bears, 30-17 (C)
1994—Packers, 33-6 (C)
    Packers, 40-3 (GB)
1995—Packers, 27-24 (C)
    Packers, 35-28 (GB)
1996—Packers, 37-6 (C)
    Packers, 28-17 (GB)
(RS Pts.—Bears 2,562, Packers 2,330)
(PS Pts.—Bears 33, Packers 14)
*Bears known as Staleys prior to 1922
**Division Playoff
CHICAGO vs. *INDIANAPOLIS
RS: Colts lead series, 21-16
1953—Colts, 13-9 (B)
    Colts, 16-14 (C)
1954—Bears, 28-9 (C)
    Bears, 28-13 (B)
1955—Colts, 23-17 (B)
    Bears, 38-10 (C)
1956—Colts, 28-21 (B)
    Bears, 58-27 (C)
1957—Colts, 21-10 (B)
    Colts, 29-14 (C)
1958—Colts, 51-38 (B)
    Colts, 17-0 (C)
1959—Bears, 26-21 (B)
    Colts, 21-7 (C)
1960—Colts, 42-7 (B)
    Colts, 24-20 (C)
1961—Bears, 24-10 (C)
    Bears, 21-20 (B)
1962—Bears, 35-15 (C)
    Bears, 57-0 (B)
1963—Bears, 10-3 (C)
    Bears, 17-7 (B)
1964—Colts, 52-0 (B)
    Colts, 40-24 (C)
1965—Colts, 26-21 (C)
    Bears, 13-0 (B)
1966—Bears, 27-17 (C)
    Colts, 21-16 (B)
1967—Colts, 24-3 (C)
1968—Colts, 28-7 (B)
1969—Colts, 24-21 (C)
1970—Colts, 21-20 (B)
1975—Colts, 35-7 (C)
1983—Colts, 22-19 (B) OT
1985—Bears, 17-10 (C)
1988—Bears, 17-13 (I)
1991—Bears, 31-17 (I)
(RS Pts.—Colts 770, Bears 742)
*Franchise in Baltimore prior to 1984
CHICAGO vs. JACKSONVILLE
RS: Bears lead series, 1-0

1995—Bears, 30-27 (J)
(RS Pts.—Bears 30, Jaguars 27)
CHICAGO vs. KANSAS CITY
RS: Bears lead series, 4-3
1973—Chiefs, 19-7 (KC)
1977—Bears, 28-27 (C)
1981—Bears, 16-13 (KC) OT
1987—Bears, 31-28 (C)
1990—Chiefs, 21-10 (C)
1993—Bears, 19-17 (KC)
1996—Chiefs, 14-10 (KC)
(RS Pts.—Chiefs 139, Bears 121)
CHICAGO vs. MIAMI
RS: Dolphins lead series, 5-2
1971—Dolphins, 34-3 (M)
1975—Dolphins, 46-13 (C)
1979—Dolphins, 31-16 (M)
1985—Dolphins, 38-24 (M)
1988—Bears, 34-7 (C)
1991—Dolphins, 16-13 (C) OT
1994—Bears, 17-14 (M)
(RS Pts.—Dolphins 186, Bears 120)
CHICAGO vs. MINNESOTA
RS: Vikings lead series, 37-32-2
PS: Bears lead series, 1-0
1961—Vikings, 37-13 (M)
    Bears, 52-35 (C)
1962—Bears, 13-0 (M)
    Bears, 31-30 (C)
1963—Bears, 28-7 (M)
    Tie, 17-17 (C)
1964—Bears, 34-28 (M)
    Vikings, 41-14 (C)
1965—Bears, 45-37 (M)
    Vikings, 24-17 (C)
1966—Bears, 13-10 (M)
    Bears, 41-28 (C)
1967—Bears, 17-7 (M)
    Tie, 10-10 (C)
1968—Bears, 27-17 (M)
    Bears, 26-24 (C)
1969—Vikings, 31-0 (C)
    Vikings, 31-14 (M)
1970—Vikings, 24-0 (C)
    Vikings, 16-13 (M)
1971—Bears, 20-17 (M)
    Vikings, 27-10 (C)
1972—Bears, 13-10 (C)
    Vikings, 23-10 (M)
1973—Vikings, 22-13 (C)
    Vikings, 31-13 (M)
1974—Vikings, 11-7 (M)
    Vikings, 17-0 (C)
1975—Vikings, 28-3 (M)
    Vikings, 13-9 (C)
1976—Vikings, 20-19 (M)
    Bears, 14-13 (C)
1977—Vikings, 22-16 (M) OT
    Bears, 10-7 (C)
1978—Vikings, 24-20 (C)
    Vikings, 17-14 (M)
1979—Bears, 26-7 (C)
    Vikings, 30-27 (M)
1980—Vikings, 34-14 (C)
    Vikings, 13-7 (M)
1981—Vikings, 24-21 (M)
    Bears, 10-9 (C)
1982—Vikings, 35-7 (M)
1983—Vikings, 23-14 (C)
    Bears, 19-13 (M)
1984—Bears, 16-7 (C)
    Bears, 34-3 (M)
1985—Bears, 33-24 (M)
    Bears, 27-9 (C)
1986—Bears, 23-0 (C)
    Vikings, 23-7 (M)
1987—Bears, 27-7 (C)
    Bears, 30-24 (M)
1988—Vikings, 31-7 (M)
    Vikings, 28-27 (M)
1989—Bears, 38-7 (C)
    Vikings, 27-16 (M)
1990—Bears, 19-16 (C)

Vikings, 41-13 (M)
1991—Bears, 10-6 (C)
Bears, 34-17 (M)
1992—Vikings, 21-20 (M)
Vikings, 38-10 (C)
1993—Vikings, 10-7 (M)
Vikings, 19-12 (C)
1994—Vikings, 42-14 (C)
Vikings, 33-27 (M) OT
*Bears, 35-18 (M)
1995—Bears, 31-14 (C)
Bears, 14-6 (M)
1996—Vikings, 20-14 (C)
Bears, 15-13 (M)
(RS Pts.—Vikings 1,430, Bears 1,286)
(PS Pts.—Bears 35, Vikings 18)
*NFC First-Round Playoff

CHICAGO vs. NEW ENGLAND
RS: Patriots lead series, 4-2
PS: Bears lead series, 1-0
1973—Patriots, 13-10 (C)
1979—Patriots, 27-7 (C)
1982—Bears, 26-13 (C)
1985—Bears, 20-7 (C)
*Bears, 46-10 (New Orleans)
1988—Patriots, 30-7 (NE)
1994—Patriots, 13-3 (C)
(RS Pts.—Patriots 113, Bears 73)
(PS Pts.—Bears 46, Patriots 10)
*Super Bowl XX

CHICAGO vs. NEW ORLEANS
RS: Bears lead series, 9-7
PS: Bears lead series, 1-0
1968—Bears, 23-17 (NO)
1970—Bears, 24-3 (NO)
1971—Bears, 35-14 (C)
1973—Saints, 21-16 (NO)
1974—Bears, 24-10 (C)
1975—Bears, 42-17 (NO)
1977—Saints, 42-24 (C)
1980—Bears, 22-3 (C)
1982—Saints, 10-0 (C)
1983—Saints, 34-31 (NO) OT
1984—Bears, 20-7 (C)
1987—Saints, 19-17 (C)
1990—*Bears, 16-6 (C)
1991—Bears, 20-17 (NO)
1992—Saints, 28-6 (NO)
1994—Bears, 17-7 (C)
1996—Saints, 27-24 (NO)
(RS Pts.—Bears 345, Saints 276)
(PS Pts.—Bears 16, Saints 6)
*NFC First-Round Playoff

CHICAGO vs. N.Y. GIANTS
RS: Bears lead series, 25-16-2
PS: Bears lead series, 5-3
1925—Bears, 19-7 (NY)
Giants, 9-0 (C)
1926—Bears, 7-0 (C)
1927—Giants, 13-7 (NY)
1928—Bears, 13-0 (C)
1929—Giants, 26-14 (C)
Giants, 34-0 (NY)
Giants, 14-9 (C)
1930—Giants, 12-0 (C)
Bears, 12-0 (NY)
1931—Bears, 6-0 (C)
Bears, 12-6 (NY)
Giants, 25-6 (C)
1932—Bears, 28-8 (NY)
Bears, 6-0 (C)
1933—Bears, 14-10 (C)
Giants, 3-0 (NY)
*Bears, 23-21 (C)
1934—Bears, 27-7 (C)
Bears, 10-9 (NY)
*Giants, 30-13 (NY)
1935—Bears, 20-3 (NY)
Giants, 3-0 (C)
1936—Bears, 25-7 (NY)
1937—Tie, 3-3 (NY)
1939—Giants, 16-13 (NY)
1940—Bears, 37-21 (NY)

1941—*Bears, 37-9 (C)
1942—Bears, 26-7 (NY)
1943—Bears, 56-7 (NY)
1946—Giants, 14-0 (NY)
*Bears, 24-14 (NY)
1948—Bears, 35-14 (C)
1949—Giants, 35-28 (NY)
1956—Tie, 17-17 (NY)
*Giants, 47-7 (NY)
1962—Giants, 26-24 (C)
1963—*Bears, 14-10 (C)
1965—Bears, 35-14 (NY)
1967—Bears, 34-7 (C)
1969—Giants, 28-24 (NY)
1970—Bears, 24-16 (NY)
1974—Bears, 16-13 (C)
1977—Bears, 12-9 (NY) OT
1985—**Bears, 21-0 (C)
1987—Bears, 34-19 (C)
1990—**Giants, 31-3 (NY)
1991—Bears, 20-17 (C)
1992—Giants, 27-14 (C)
1993—Giants, 26-20 (C)
1995—Bears, 27-24 (NY)
(RS Pts.—Bears 734, Giants 556)
(PS Pts.—Giants 162, Bears 142)
*NFL Championship
**NFC Divisional Playoff

CHICAGO vs. N.Y. JETS
RS: Bears lead series, 4-1
1974—Jets, 23-21 (C)
1979—Bears, 23-13 (C)
1985—Bears, 19-6 (NY)
1991—Bears, 19-13 (C) OT
1994—Bears, 19-7 (NY)
(RS Pts.—Bears 101, Jets 62)

CHICAGO vs. *OAKLAND
RS: Raiders lead series, 5-4
1972—Raiders, 28-21 (O)
1976—Raiders, 28-27 (C)
1978—Raiders, 25-19 (C) OT
1981—Bears, 23-6 (O)
1984—Bears, 17-6 (C)
1987—Bears, 6-3 (LA)
1990—Raiders, 24-10 (LA)
1993—Raiders, 16-14 (C)
1996—Bears, 19-17 (C)
(RS Pts.—Bears 156, Raiders 153)
*Franchise in Los Angeles from 1982-1994

CHICAGO vs. PHILADELPHIA
RS: Bears lead series, 24-4-1
PS: Series tied, 1-1
1933—Tie, 3-3 (P)
1935—Bears, 39-0 (P)
1936—Bears, 17-0 (P)
Bears, 28-7 (P)
1938—Bears, 28-6 (P)
1939—Bears, 27-14 (C)
1941—Bears, 49-14 (P)
1942—Bears, 45-14 (C)
1944—Bears, 28-7 (P)
1946—Bears, 21-14 (C)
1947—Bears, 40-7 (C)
1948—Eagles, 12-7 (P)
1949—Bears, 38-21 (C)
1955—Bears, 17-10 (C)
1961—Eagles, 16-14 (P)
1963—Bears, 16-7 (C)
1968—Bears, 29-16 (P)
1970—Bears, 20-16 (C)
1972—Bears, 21-12 (P)
1975—Bears, 15-13 (C)
1979—*Eagles, 27-17 (P)
1980—Eagles, 17-14 (P)
1983—Bears, 7-6 (P)
Bears, 17-14 (C)
1986—Bears, 13-10 (C) OT
1987—Bears, 35-3 (P)
1988—**Bears, 20-12 (C)
1989—Bears, 27-13 (C)
1993—Bears, 17-6 (P)
1994—Eagles, 30-22 (P)

1995—Bears, 20-14 (C)
(RS Pts.—Bears 674, Eagles 322)
(PS Pts.—Eagles 39, Bears 37)
*NFC First-Round Playoff
**NFC Divisional Playoff

CHICAGO vs. *PITTSBURGH
RS: Bears lead series, 16-5-1
1934—Bears, 28-0 (P)
1935—Bears, 23-7 (P)
1936—Bears, 27-9 (P)
Bears, 26-6 (C)
1937—Bears, 7-0 (P)
1939—Bears, 32-0 (P)
1941—Bears, 34-7 (C)
1945—Bears, 28-7 (C)
1947—Bears, 49-7 (C)
1949—Bears, 30-21 (C)
1958—Steelers, 24-10 (P)
1959—Bears, 27-21 (C)
1963—Tie, 17-17 (P)
1967—Steelers, 41-13 (P)
1969—Bears, 38-7 (C)
1971—Bears, 17-15 (C)
1975—Steelers, 34-3 (P)
1980—Steelers, 38-3 (P)
1986—Bears, 13-10 (C) OT
1989—Bears, 20-0 (C)
1992—Bears, 30-6 (C)
1995—Steelers, 37-34 (C) OT
(RS Pts.—Bears 509, Steelers 314)
*Steelers known as Pirates prior to 1941

CHICAGO vs. *ST. LOUIS
RS: Bears lead series, 46-30-3
PS: Series tied, 1-1
1937—Bears, 20-2 (Clev)
Bears, 15-7 (C)
1938—Rams, 14-7 (C)
Rams, 23-21 (Clev)
1939—Rams, 30-21 (Clev)
Bears, 35-21 (C)
1940—Bears, 21-14 (Clev)
Bears, 47-25 (C)
1941—Bears, 48-21 (Clev)
Bears, 31-13 (C)
1942—Bears, 21-7 (Clev)
Bears, 47-0 (C)
1944—Rams, 19-7 (Clev)
Bears, 28-21 (C)
1945—Rams, 17-0 (Clev)
Rams, 41-21 (C)
1946—Tie, 28-28 (C)
Bears, 27-21 (LA)
1947—Bears, 41-21 (LA)
Rams, 17-14 (C)
1948—Bears, 42-21 (C)
Bears, 21-6 (LA)
1949—Rams, 31-16 (C)
Rams, 27-24 (LA)
1950—Bears, 24-20 (LA)
Bears, 24-14 (C)
**Rams, 24-14 (LA)
1951—Rams, 42-17 (C)
1952—Rams, 31-7 (LA)
Rams, 40-24 (C)
1953—Rams, 38-24 (LA)
Bears, 24-21 (C)
1954—Rams, 42-38 (LA)
Bears, 24-13 (C)
1955—Bears, 31-20 (LA)
Bears, 24-3 (C)
1956—Bears, 35-24 (LA)
Bears, 30-21 (C)
1957—Bears, 34-26 (C)
Bears, 16-10 (LA)
1958—Bears, 31-10 (C)
Rams, 41-35 (LA)
1959—Rams, 28-21 (C)
Bears, 26-21 (LA)
1960—Bears, 34-27 (C)
Tie, 24-24 (LA)
1961—Bears, 21-17 (C)
Bears, 28-24 (C)
1962—Bears, 27-23 (LA)

Bears, 30-14 (C)
1963—Bears, 52-14 (LA)
Bears, 6-0 (C)
1964—Bears, 38-17 (C)
Bears, 34-24 (LA)
1965—Rams, 30-28 (LA)
Bears, 31-6 (C)
1966—Rams, 31-17 (LA)
Bears, 17-10 (C)
1967—Rams, 28-17 (C)
1968—Bears, 17-16 (LA)
1969—Rams, 9-7 (C)
1971—Rams, 17-3 (LA)
1972—Tie, 13-13 (C)
1973—Rams, 26-0 (C)
1975—Rams, 38-10 (LA)
1976—Rams, 20-12 (LA)
1977—Bears, 24-23 (C)
1979—Bears, 27-23 (C)
1981—Rams, 24-7 (C)
1982—Bears, 34-26 (LA)
1983—Bears, 21-14 (LA)
1984—Rams, 29-13 (LA)
1985—***Bears, 24-0 (C)
1986—Rams, 20-17 (LA)
1988—Rams, 23-3 (LA)
1989—Bears, 20-10 (C)
1990—Bears, 38-9 (C)
1993—Rams, 20-6 (LA)
1994—Bears, 27-13 (C)
1995—Rams, 34-28 (StL)
1996—Bears, 35-9 (C)
(RS Pts.—Bears 1,860, Rams 1,615)
(PS Pts.—Bears 38, Rams 24)
*Franchise in Los Angeles prior to 1995 and in Cleveland prior to 1946
**Conference Playoff
***NFC Championship

CHICAGO vs. SAN DIEGO
RS: Chargers lead series, 4-3
1970—Chargers, 20-7 (C)
1974—Chargers, 28-21 (SD)
1978—Chargers, 40-7 (SD)
1981—Bears, 20-17 (C) OT
1984—Chargers, 20-7 (SD)
1993—Bears, 16-13 (SD)
1996—Bears, 27-14 (C)
(RS Pts.—Chargers 152, Bears 105)

CHICAGO vs. SAN FRANCISCO
RS: Series tied, 25-25-1
PS: 49ers lead series, 3-0
1950—Bears, 32-20 (SF)
Bears, 17-0 (C)
1951—Bears, 13-7 (C)
Bears, 20-17 (SF)
1952—49ers, 40-16 (C)
Bears, 20-17 (SF)
1953—49ers, 35-28 (C)
49ers, 24-14 (SF)
1954—49ers, 31-24 (C)
Bears, 31-27 (SF)
1955—49ers, 20-19 (C)
Bears, 34-23 (SF)
1956—Bears, 31-7 (C)
Bears, 38-21 (SF)
1957—49ers, 21-17 (C)
49ers, 21-17 (SF)
1958—Bears, 28-6 (C)
Bears, 27-14 (SF)
1959—49ers, 20-17 (SF)
Bears, 14-3 (C)
1960—Bears, 27-10 (C)
49ers, 25-7 (SF)
1961—Bears, 31-0 (C)
49ers, 41-31 (SF)
1962—Bears, 30-14 (SF)
49ers, 34-27 (C)
1963—49ers, 20-14 (SF)
Bears, 27-7 (C)
1964—49ers, 31-21 (SF)
Bears, 23-21 (C)
1965—49ers, 52-24 (SF)
Bears, 61-20 (C)
1966—Tie, 30-30 (C)

49ers, 41-14 (SF)
1967—Bears, 28-14 (SF)
1968—Bears, 27-19 (C)
1969—49ers, 42-21 (SF)
1970—49ers, 37-16 (C)
1971—49ers, 13-0 (SF)
1972—49ers, 34-21 (C)
1974—Bears, 34-0 (C)
1975—49ers, 31-3 (SF)
1976—Bears, 19-12 (SF)
1978—Bears, 16-13 (SF)
1979—Bears, 28-27 (SF)
1981—49ers, 28-17 (SF)
1983—Bears, 13-3 (C)
1984—*49ers, 23-0 (SF)
1985—Bears, 26-10 (SF)
1987—49ers, 41-0 (SF)
1988—Bears, 10-9 (C)
   *49ers, 28-3 (C)
1989—49ers, 26-0 (SF)
1991—49ers, 52-14 (SF)
1994—**49ers, 44-15 (SF)
(RS Pts.—49ers 1,148, Bears 1,063)
(PS Pts.—49ers 95, Bears 18)
*NFC Championship
**NFC Divisional Playoff
CHICAGO vs. SEATTLE
RS: Seahawks lead series, 4-2
1976—Bears, 34-7 (S)
1978—Seahawks, 31-29 (C)
1982—Seahawks, 20-14 (S)
1984—Seahawks, 38-9 (S)
1987—Seahawks, 34-21 (C)
1990—Bears, 17-0 (C)
(RS Pts.—Seahawks 130, Bears 124)
CHICAGO vs. TAMPA BAY
RS: Bears lead series, 29-9
1977—Bears, 10-0 (TB)
1978—Buccaneers, 33-19 (TB)
   Bears, 14-3 (C)
1979—Buccaneers, 17-13 (C)
   Bears, 14-0 (TB)
1980—Bears, 23-0 (C)
   Bears, 14-13 (TB)
1981—Bears, 28-17 (C)
   Buccaneers, 20-10 (TB)
1982—Buccaneers, 26-23 (TB) OT
1983—Bears, 17-10 (C)
   Bears, 27-0 (TB)
1984—Bears, 34-14 (C)
   Bears, 44-9 (TB)
1985—Bears, 38-28 (C)
   Bears, 27-19 (TB)
1986—Bears, 23-3 (TB)
   Bears, 48-14 (C)
1987—Bears, 20-3 (C)
   Bears, 27-26 (TB)
1988—Bears, 28-10 (C)
   Bears, 27-15 (TB)
1989—Buccaneers, 42-35 (TB)
   Buccaneers, 32-31 (C)
1990—Bears, 26-6 (TB)
   Bears, 27-14 (C)
1991—Bears, 21-20 (TB)
   Bears, 27-0 (C)
1992—Bears, 31-14 (C)
   Buccaneers, 20-17 (TB)
1993—Bears, 47-17 (C)
   Buccaneers, 13-10 (TB)
1994—Bears, 21-9 (C)
   Bears, 20-6 (TB)
1995—Bears, 25-6 (TB)
   Bears, 31-10 (C)
1996—Bears, 13-10 (C)
   Buccaneers, 34-19 (TB)
(RS Pts.—Bears 929, Buccaneers 533)
CHICAGO vs. *TENNESSEE
RS: Oilers lead series, 4-3
1973—Bears, 35-14 (C)
1977—Oilers, 47-0 (H)
1980—Oilers, 10-6 (C)
1986—Bears, 20-7 (H)
1989—Oilers, 33-28 (C)

1992—Oilers, 24-7 (H)
1995—Bears, 35-32 (C)
(RS Pts.—Oilers 167, Bears 131)
*Franchise in Houston prior to 1997
CHICAGO vs. *WASHINGTON
RS: Bears lead series, 18-13-1
PS: Redskins lead series, 4-3
1932—Tie, 7-7 (B)
1933—Bears, 7-0 (C)
   Redskins, 10-0 (B)
1934—Bears, 21-0 (B)
1935—Bears, 30-14 (B)
1936—Bears, 26-0 (B)
1937—**Redskins, 28-21 (C)
1938—Bears, 31-7 (C)
1940—Redskins, 7-3 (W)
   **Bears, 73-0 (W)
1941—Bears, 35-21 (C)
1942—**Redskins, 14-6 (W)
1943—Redskins, 21-7 (W)
   **Bears, 41-21 (C)
1945—Redskins, 28-21 (W)
1946—Bears, 24-20 (C)
1947—Bears, 56-20 (W)
1948—Bears, 48-13 (C)
1949—Bears, 31-21 (W)
1951—Bears, 27-0 (W)
1953—Bears, 27-24 (W)
1957—Redskins, 14-3 (C)
1964—Redskins, 27-20 (W)
1968—Redskins, 38-28 (C)
1971—Bears, 16-15 (C)
1974—Redskins, 42-0 (W)
1976—Bears, 33-7 (C)
1978—Bears, 14-10 (W)
1980—Bears, 35-21 (C)
1981—Redskins, 24-7 (C)
1984—***Bears, 23-19 (W)
1985—Bears, 45-10 (C)
1986—***Redskins, 27-13 (C)
1987—***Redskins, 21-17 (C)
1988—Bears, 34-14 (W)
1989—Redskins, 38-14 (W)
1990—Redskins, 10-9 (W)
1991—Redskins, 20-7 (C)
1996—Redskins, 10-3 (W)
(RS Pts.—Bears 669, Redskins 513)
(PS Pts.—Bears 194, Redskins 130)
*Franchise in Boston prior to 1937 and
known as Braves prior to 1933
**NFL Championship
***NFC Divisional Playoff

CINCINNATI vs. ARIZONA
RS: Bengals lead series, 3-2;
See Arizona vs. Cincinnati
CINCINNATI vs. ATLANTA
RS: Bengals lead series, 7-2;
See Atlanta vs. Cincinnati
CINCINNATI vs. BALTIMORE
RS: Bengals lead series, 2-0;
See Baltimore vs. Cincinnati
CINCINNATI vs. BUFFALO
RS: Bengals lead series, 9-8
PS: Bengals lead series, 2-0;
See Buffalo vs. Cincinnati
CINCINNATI vs. CHICAGO
RS: Bengals lead series, 4-2;
See Chicago vs. Cincinnati
CINCINNATI vs. CLEVELAND
RS: Browns lead series, 27-24
1970—Browns, 30-27 (Cle)
   Bengals, 14-10 (Cin)
1971—Browns, 27-24 (Cin)
   Browns, 31-27 (Cle)
1972—Browns, 27-6 (Cle)
   Browns, 27-24 (Cin)
1973—Browns, 17-10 (Cle)
   Bengals, 34-17 (Cin)
1974—Bengals, 33-7 (Cin)
   Bengals, 34-24 (Cle)
1975—Bengals, 24-17 (Cin)
   Browns, 35-23 (Cle)

1976—Bengals, 45-24 (Cle)
   Bengals, 21-6 (Cin)
1977—Browns, 13-3 (Cin)
   Bengals, 10-7 (Cle)
1978—Browns, 13-10 (Cle) OT
   Bengals, 48-16 (Cin)
1979—Browns, 28-27 (Cle)
   Bengals, 16-12 (Cin)
1980—Browns, 31-7 (Cle)
   Browns, 27-24 (Cin)
1981—Browns, 20-17 (Cin)
   Bengals, 41-21 (Cle)
1982—Bengals, 23-10 (Cin)
1983—Browns, 17-7 (Cle)
   Bengals, 28-21 (Cin)
1984—Bengals, 12-9 (Cin)
   Bengals, 20-17 (Cle) OT
1985—Bengals, 27-10 (Cin)
   Browns, 24-6 (Cle)
1986—Bengals, 30-13 (Cle)
   Browns, 34-3 (Cin)
1987—Browns, 34-0 (Cin)
   Browns, 38-24 (Cle)
1988—Bengals, 24-17 (Cin)
   Browns, 23-16 (Cle)
1989—Bengals, 21-14 (Cin)
   Bengals, 21-0 (Cle)
1990—Bengals, 34-13 (Cle)
   Bengals, 21-14 (Cin)
1991—Browns, 14-13 (Cle)
   Bengals, 23-21 (Cin)
1992—Bengals, 30-10 (Cin)
   Browns, 37-21 (Cle)
1993—Browns, 27-14 (Cin)
   Browns, 28-17 (Cin)
1994—Browns, 28-20 (Cin)
   Browns, 37-13 (Cle)
1995—Bengals, 29-26 (Cin) OT
   Browns, 26-10 (Cle)
(RS Pts.—Bengals 1,053, Browns 1,052)
CINCINNATI vs. DALLAS
RS: Cowboys lead series, 4-2
1973—Cowboys, 38-10 (C)
1979—Cowboys, 38-13 (D)
1985—Bengals, 50-24 (C)
1988—Bengals, 38-24 (D)
1991—Cowboys, 35-23 (D)
1994—Cowboys, 23-20 (C)
(RS Pts.—Cowboys 182, Bengals 154)
CINCINNATI vs. DENVER
RS: Broncos lead series, 12-6
1968—Bengals, 24-10 (C)
   Broncos, 10-7 (D)
1969—Broncos, 30-23 (C)
   Broncos, 27-16 (D)
1971—Bengals, 24-10 (D)
1972—Bengals, 21-10 (C)
1973—Broncos, 28-10 (D)
1975—Bengals, 17-16 (D)
1976—Bengals, 17-7 (C)
1977—Broncos, 24-13 (C)
1979—Broncos, 10-0 (D)
1981—Bengals, 38-21 (C)
1983—Broncos, 24-17 (D)
1984—Broncos, 20-17 (D)
1986—Broncos, 34-28 (D)
1991—Broncos, 45-14 (D)
1994—Broncos, 15-13 (D)
1996—Broncos, 14-10 (C)
(RS Pts.—Broncos 355, Bengals 309)
CINCINNATI vs. DETROIT
RS: Series tied, 3-3
1970—Lions, 38-3 (D)
1974—Lions, 23-19 (C)
1983—Bengals, 17-9 (C)
1986—Bengals, 24-17 (D)
1989—Bengals, 42-7 (C)
1992—Lions, 19-13 (C)
(RS Pts.—Bengals 118, Lions 113)
CINCINNATI vs. GREEN BAY
RS: Series tied, 4-4
1971—Packers, 20-17 (GB)
1976—Bengals, 28-7 (C)

1977—Bengals, 17-7 (Mil)
1980—Packers, 14-9 (GB)
1983—Bengals, 34-14 (C)
1986—Bengals, 34-28 (Mil)
1992—Packers, 24-23 (GB)
1995—Packers, 24-10 (GB)
(RS Pts.—Bengals 172, Packers 138)
CINCINNATI vs. *INDIANAPOLIS
RS: Colts lead series, 9-7
PS: Colts lead series, 1-0
1970—**Colts, 17-0 (B)
1972—Colts, 20-19 (C)
1974—Bengals, 24-14 (B)
1976—Colts, 28-27 (B)
1979—Colts, 38-28 (B)
1980—Bengals, 34-33 (C)
1981—Bengals, 41-19 (B)
1982—Bengals, 20-17 (B)
1983—Colts, 34-31 (C)
1987—Bengals, 23-21 (I)
1989—Colts, 23-12 (C)
1990—Colts, 34-20 (C)
1992—Colts, 21-17 (C)
1993—Colts, 9-6 (C)
1994—Colts, 17-13 (C)
1995—Bengals, 24-21 (I) OT
1996—Bengals, 31-24 (C)
(RS Pts.—Colts 373, Bengals 370)
(PS Pts.—Colts 17, Bengals 0)
*Franchise in Baltimore prior to 1984
**AFC Divisional Playoff
CINCINNATI vs. JACKSONVILLE
RS: Bengals lead series, 3-1
1995—Bengals, 24-17 (C)
   Bengals, 17-13 (J)
1996—Bengals, 28-21 (C)
   Jaguars, 30-27 (J)
(RS Pts.—Bengals 96, Jaguars 81)
CINCINNATI vs. KANSAS CITY
RS: Chiefs lead series, 11-9
1968—Chiefs, 13-3 (KC)
   Chiefs, 16-9 (C)
1969—Bengals, 24-19 (C)
   Chiefs, 42-22 (KC)
1970—Chiefs, 27-19 (C)
1972—Bengals, 23-16 (KC)
1973—Bengals, 14-6 (C)
1974—Bengals, 33-6 (C)
1976—Bengals, 27-24 (KC)
1977—Bengals, 27-7 (KC)
1978—Chiefs, 24-23 (C)
1979—Chiefs, 10-7 (C)
1980—Bengals, 20-6 (KC)
1983—Chiefs, 20-15 (KC)
1984—Chiefs, 27-22 (C)
1986—Bengals, 24-14 (KC)
1987—Bengals, 30-27 (C) OT
1988—Chiefs, 31-28 (KC)
1989—Bengals, 21-17 (KC)
1993—Chiefs, 17-15 (KC)
(RS Pts.—Bengals 396, Chiefs 379)
CINCINNATI vs. MIAMI
RS: Dolphins lead series, 11-3
PS: Dolphins lead series, 1-0
1968—Dolphins, 24-22 (C)
   Bengals, 38-21 (M)
1969—Bengals, 27-21 (C)
1971—Dolphins, 23-13 (C)
1973—*Dolphins, 34-16 (M)
1974—Dolphins, 24-3 (M)
1977—Bengals, 23-17 (C)
1978—Dolphins, 21-0 (M)
1980—Dolphins, 17-16 (M)
1983—Dolphins, 38-14 (M)
1987—Dolphins, 20-14 (C)
1989—Dolphins, 20-13 (C)
1991—Dolphins, 37-13 (M)
1994—Dolphins, 23-7 (C)
1995—Dolphins, 26-23 (C)
(RS Pts.—Dolphins 366, Bengals 242)
(PS Pts.—Dolphins 34, Bengals 16)
*AFC Divisional Playoff
CINCINNATI vs. MINNESOTA

RS: Series tied, 4-4
1973—Bengals, 27-0 (C)
1977—Vikings, 42-10 (M)
1980—Bengals, 14-0 (C)
1983—Vikings, 20-14 (M)
1986—Bengals, 24-20 (C)
1989—Vikings, 29-21 (M)
1992—Vikings, 42-7 (C)
1995—Bengals, 27-24 (C)
(RS Pts.—Vikings 177, Bengals 144)

CINCINNATI vs. *NEW ENGLAND
RS: Patriots lead series, 9-7
1968—Patriots, 33-14 (B)
1969—Patriots, 25-14 (C)
1970—Bengals, 45-7 (C)
1972—Bengals, 31-7 (NE)
1975—Patriots, 27-10 (C)
1978—Patriots, 10-3 (C)
1979—Patriots, 20-14 (C)
1984—Patriots, 20-14 (NE)
1985—Patriots, 34-23 (NE)
1986—Bengals, 31-7 (NE)
1988—Patriots, 27-21 (NE)
1990—Bengals, 41-7 (C)
1991—Bengals, 29-7 (C)
1992—Bengals, 20-10 (C)
1993—Patriots, 7-2 (NE)
1994—Patriots, 31-28 (C)
(RS Pts.—Bengals 357, Patriots 262)
*Franchise in Boston prior to 1971

CINCINNATI vs. NEW ORLEANS
RS: Saints lead series, 5-4
1970—Bengals, 26-6 (C)
1975—Bengals, 21-0 (NO)
1978—Saints, 20-18 (C)
1981—Saints, 17-7 (NO)
1984—Bengals, 24-21 (NO)
1987—Saints, 41-24 (C)
1990—Saints, 21-7 (C)
1993—Saints, 20-13 (NO)
1996—Bengals, 30-15 (C))
(RS Pts.—Bengals 170, Saints 161)

CINCINNATI vs. N.Y. GIANTS
RS: Bengals lead series, 4-1
1972—Bengals, 13-10 (C)
1977—Bengals, 30-13 (C)
1985—Bengals, 35-30 (C)
1991—Bengals, 27-24 (C)
1994—Giants, 27-20 (NY)
(RS Pts.—Bengals 125, Giants 104)

CINCINNATI vs. N.Y. JETS
RS: Jets lead series, 9-6
PS: Jets lead series, 1-0
1968—Jets, 27-14 (NY)
1969—Jets, 21-7 (C)
Jets, 40-7 (NY)
1971—Jets, 35-21 (NY)
1973—Bengals, 20-14 (C)
1976—Bengals, 42-3 (C)
1981—Bengals, 31-30 (NY)
1982—*Jets, 44-17 (C)
1984—Jets, 43-23 (NY)
1985—Jets, 29-20 (C)
1986—Bengals, 52-21 (C)
1987—Jets, 27-20 (NY)
1988—Bengals, 36-19 (C)
1990—Bengals, 25-20 (C)
1992—Jets, 17-14 (NY)
1993—Jets, 17-12 (NY)
(RS Pts.—Jets 363, Bengals 344)
(PS Pts.—Jets 44, Bengals 17)
*AFC First-Round Playoff

CINCINNATI vs. *OAKLAND
RS: Raiders lead series, 15-7
PS: Raiders lead series, 2-0
1968—Raiders, 31-10 (O)
Raiders, 34-0 (C)
1969—Bengals, 31-17 (C)
Raiders, 37-17 (O)
1970—Bengals, 31-21 (C)
1971—Raiders, 31-27 (O)
1972—Raiders, 20-14 (C)
1974—Raiders, 30-27 (O)

1975—Bengals, 14-10 (C)
**Raiders, 31-28 (O)
1976—Raiders, 35-20 (O)
1978—Raiders, 34-21 (C)
1980—Raiders, 28-17 (O)
1982—Bengals, 31-17 (C)
1983—Raiders, 20-10 (C)
1985—Raiders, 13-6 (LA)
1988—Bengals, 45-21 (LA)
1989—Raiders, 28-7 (C)
1990—Raiders, 24-7 (LA)
**Raiders, 20-10 (LA)
1991—Raiders, 38-14 (C)
1992—Bengals, 24-21 (C) OT
1993—Bengals, 16-10 (C)
1995—Raiders, 20-17 (C)
(RS Pts.—Raiders 540, Bengals 406)
(PS Pts.—Raiders 51, Bengals 38)
*Franchise in Los Angeles from
1982-1994
**AFC Divisional Playoff

CINCINNATI vs. PHILADELPHIA
RS: Bengals lead series, 6-1
1971—Bengals, 37-14 (C)
1975—Bengals, 31-0 (P)
1979—Bengals, 37-13 (C)
1982—Bengals, 18-14 (P)
1988—Bengals, 28-24 (P)
1991—Eagles, 17-10 (P)
1994—Bengals, 33-30 (C)
(RS Pts.—Bengals 194, Eagles 112)

CINCINNATI vs. PITTSBURGH
RS: Steelers lead series, 30-23
1970—Steelers, 21-10 (P)
Bengals, 34-7 (C)
1971—Steelers, 21-10 (P)
Steelers, 21-13 (C)
1972—Bengals, 15-10 (C)
Steelers, 40-17 (P)
1973—Bengals, 19-7 (C)
Steelers, 20-13 (P)
1974—Bengals, 17-10 (C)
Steelers, 27-3 (P)
1975—Steelers, 30-24 (C)
Steelers, 35-14 (P)
1976—Steelers, 23-6 (P)
Steelers, 7-3 (C)
1977—Steelers, 20-14 (P)
Bengals, 17-10 (C)
1978—Steelers, 28-3 (C)
Steelers, 7-6 (P)
1979—Bengals, 34-10 (C)
Steelers, 37-17 (P)
1980—Bengals, 30-28 (C)
Bengals, 17-16 (P)
1981—Bengals, 34-7 (C)
Bengals, 17-10 (P)
1982—Steelers, 26-20 (P) OT
1983—Steelers, 24-14 (C)
Bengals, 23-10 (P)
1984—Steelers, 38-17 (P)
Bengals, 22-20 (C)
1985—Bengals, 37-24 (P)
Bengals, 26-21 (C)
1986—Bengals, 24-22 (C)
Steelers, 30-9 (P)
1987—Steelers, 23-20 (P)
Steelers, 30-16 (C)
1988—Bengals, 17-12 (P)
Bengals, 42-7 (C)
1989—Bengals, 41-10 (C)
Bengals, 26-16 (P)
1990—Bengals, 27-3 (C)
Bengals, 16-12 (P)
1991—Steelers, 33-27 (C) OT
Steelers, 17-10 (P)
1992—Steelers, 20-0 (C)
Steelers, 21-9 (C)
1993—Steelers, 34-7 (P)
Steelers, 24-16 (C)
1994—Steelers, 14-10 (P)
Steelers, 38-15 (C)
1995—Bengals, 27-9 (P)

Steelers, 49-31 (C)
1996—Steelers, 20-10 (P)
Bengals, 34-24 (C)
(RS Pts.—Steelers 1,083, Bengals 980)

CINCINNATI vs. *ST. LOUIS
RS: Bengals lead series, 5-3
1972—Rams, 15-12 (LA)
1976—Bengals, 20-12 (C)
1978—Bengals, 20-19 (LA)
1981—Bengals, 24-10 (C)
1984—Rams, 24-14 (C)
1990—Bengals, 34-31 (LA) OT
1993—Bengals, 15-3 (C)
1996—Rams, 26-16 (StL)
(RS Pts.—Bengals 155, Rams 140)
*Franchise in Los Angeles prior to 1995

CINCINNATI vs. SAN DIEGO
RS: Chargers lead series, 14-8
PS: Bengals lead series, 1-0
1968—Chargers, 29-13 (SD)
Chargers, 31-10 (C)
1969—Bengals, 34-20 (C)
Chargers, 21-14 (SD)
1970—Bengals, 17-14 (SD)
1971—Bengals, 31-0 (C)
1973—Bengals, 20-13 (SD)
1974—Chargers, 20-17 (C)
1975—Bengals, 47-17 (C)
1977—Chargers, 24-3 (SD)
1978—Chargers, 22-13 (SD)
1979—Chargers, 26-24 (C)
1980—Chargers, 31-14 (C)
1981—Bengals, 40-17 (SD)
*Bengals, 27-7 (C)
1982—Chargers, 50-34 (SD)
1985—Chargers, 44-41 (C)
1987—Chargers, 10-9 (C)
1988—Bengals, 27-10 (C)
1990—Bengals, 21-16 (SD)
1992—Chargers, 27-10 (SD)
1994—Chargers, 27-10 (SD)
1996—Chargers, 27-14 (SD)
(RS Pts.—Chargers 496, Bengals 463)
(PS Pts.—Bengals 27, Chargers 7)
*AFC Championship

CINCINNATI vs. SAN FRANCISCO
RS: 49ers lead series, 7-1
PS: 49ers lead series, 2-0
1974—Bengals, 21-3 (SF)
1978—49ers, 28-12 (SF)
1981—49ers, 21-3 (C)
*49ers, 26-21 (Detroit)
1984—49ers, 23-17 (SF)
1987—49ers, 27-26 (C)
1988—**49ers, 20-16 (Miami)
1990—49ers, 20-17 (C) OT
1993—49ers, 21-8 (SF)
1996—49ers, 28-21 (SF)
(RS Pts.—49ers 171, Bengals 125)
(PS Pts.—49ers 46, Bengals 37)
*Super Bowl XVI
**Super Bowl XXIII

CINCINNATI vs. SEATTLE
RS: Series tied, 7-7
PS: Bengals lead series, 1-0
1977—Bengals, 42-20 (C)
1981—Bengals, 27-21 (C)
1982—Bengals, 24-10 (C)
1984—Seahawks, 26-6 (C)
1985—Seahawks, 28-24 (C)
1986—Bengals, 34-7 (C)
1987—Bengals, 17-10 (S)
1988—*Bengals, 21-13 (C)
1989—Seahawks, 24-17 (C)
1990—Seahawks, 31-16 (S)
1991—Seahawks, 13-7 (C)
1992—Bengals, 21-3 (S)
1993—Seahawks, 19-10 (C)
1994—Bengals, 20-17 (S) OT
1995—Seahawks, 24-21 (S)
(RS Pts.—Bengals 286, Seahawks 253)
(PS Pts.—Bengals 21, Seahawks 13)
*AFC Divisional Playoff

CINCINNATI vs. TAMPA BAY
RS: Bengals lead series, 3-2
1976—Bengals, 21-0 (C)
1980—Buccaneers, 17-12 (C)
1983—Bengals, 23-17 (TB)
1989—Bengals, 56-23 (C)
1995—Buccaneers, 19-16 (TB)
(RS Pts.—Bengals 128, Buccaneers 76)

CINCINNATI vs. *TENNESSEE
RS: Oilers lead series, 28-27-1
PS: Bengals lead series, 1-0
1968—Oilers, 27-17 (C)
1969—Tie, 31-31 (H)
1970—Oilers, 20-13 (C)
Bengals, 30-20 (H)
1971—Oilers, 10-6 (H)
Bengals, 28-13 (C)
1972—Bengals, 30-7 (C)
Bengals, 61-17 (H)
1973—Bengals, 24-10 (C)
Bengals, 27-24 (H)
1974—Oilers, 34-21 (C)
Oilers, 20-3 (H)
1975—Bengals, 21-19 (H)
Bengals, 23-19 (C)
1976—Bengals, 27-7 (H)
Bengals, 31-27 (C)
1977—Bengals, 13-10 (C) OT
Oilers, 21-16 (H)
1978—Bengals, 28-13 (C)
Oilers, 17-10 (H)
1979—Oilers, 30-27 (C) OT
Oilers, 42-21 (H)
1980—Oilers, 13-10 (C)
Oilers, 23-3 (H)
1981—Oilers, 17-10 (H)
Bengals, 34-21 (C)
1982—Bengals, 27-6 (C)
Bengals, 35-27 (H)
1983—Bengals, 55-14 (H)
Bengals, 38-10 (H)
1984—Bengals, 13-3 (C)
Bengals, 31-13 (H)
1985—Oilers, 44-27 (H)
Bengals, 45-27 (C)
1986—Bengals, 31-28 (C)
Oilers, 32-28 (H)
1987—Bengals, 31-29 (C)
Oilers, 21-17 (H)
1988—Bengals, 44-21 (C)
Oilers, 41-6 (H)
1989—Bengals, 26-24 (C)
Bengals, 61-7 (C)
1990—Oilers, 48-17 (H)
Bengals, 40-20 (C)
**Bengals, 41-14 (C)
1991—Oilers, 30-7 (C)
Oilers, 35-3 (H)
1992—Oilers, 38-24 (C)
Oilers, 26-10 (H)
1993—Oilers, 28-12 (H)
Oilers, 38-3 (C)
1994—Oilers, 20-13 (H)
Bengals, 34-31 (C)
1995—Oilers, 38-28 (C)
Bengals, 32-25 (H)
1996—Oilers, 30-27 (C) OT
Bengals, 21-13 (H)
(RS Pts.—Bengals 1,347, Oilers 1,283)
(PS Pts.—Bengals 41, Oilers 14)
*Franchise in Houston prior to 1997
**AFC First-Round Playoff

CINCINNATI vs. WASHINGTON
RS: Redskins lead series, 4-2
1970—Redskins, 20-0 (W)
1974—Bengals, 28-17 (C)
1979—Redskins, 28-14 (W)
1985—Redskins, 27-24 (W)
1988—Bengals, 20-17 (C) OT
1991—Redskins, 34-27 (C)
(RS Pts.—Redskins 143, Bengals 113)

CLEVELAND vs. ARIZONA

RS: Browns lead series, 32-10-3;
See Arizona vs. Cleveland
CLEVELAND vs. ATLANTA
RS: Browns lead series, 8-2;
See Atlanta vs. Cleveland
CLEVELAND vs. BUFFALO
RS: Browns lead series, 7-4
PS: Browns lead series, 1-0;
See Buffalo vs. Cleveland
CLEVELAND vs. CHICAGO
RS: Browns lead series, 8-3;
See Chicago vs. Cleveland
CLEVELAND vs. CINCINNATI
RS: Browns lead series, 27-24;
See Cincinnati vs. Cleveland
CLEVELAND vs. DALLAS
RS: Browns lead series, 15-9
PS: Browns lead series, 2-1
1960—Browns, 48-7 (D)
1961—Browns, 25-7 (C)
  Browns, 38-17 (D)
1962—Browns, 19-10 (C)
  Cowboys, 45-21 (D)
1963—Browns, 41-24 (D)
  Browns, 27-17 (C)
1964—Browns, 27-6 (C)
  Browns, 20-16 (D)
1965—Browns, 23-17 (C)
  Browns, 24-17 (D)
1966—Browns, 30-21 (C)
  Cowboys, 26-14 (D)
1967—Cowboys, 21-14 (C)
  *Cowboys, 52-14 (D)
1968—Cowboys, 28-7 (C)
  *Browns, 31-20 (C)
1969—Browns, 42-10 (C)
  *Browns, 38-14 (D)
1970—Cowboys, 6-2 (C)
1974—Cowboys, 41-17 (D)
1979—Browns, 26-7 (C)
1982—Cowboys, 31-14 (D)
1985—Cowboys, 20-7 (D)
1988—Browns, 24-21 (C)
1991—Cowboys, 26-14 (C)
1994—Browns, 19-14 (D)
(RS Pts.—Browns 543, Cowboys 455)
(PS Pts.—Cowboys 86, Browns 83)
*Conference Championship
CLEVELAND vs. DENVER
RS: Broncos lead series, 13-5
PS: Broncos lead series, 3-0
1970—Browns, 27-13 (D)
1971—Broncos, 27-0 (C)
1972—Browns, 27-20 (D)
1974—Browns, 23-21 (C)
1975—Broncos, 16-15 (D)
1976—Broncos, 44-13 (D)
1978—Broncos, 19-7 (C)
1980—Broncos, 19-16 (C)
1981—Broncos, 23-20 (D) OT
1983—Broncos, 27-6 (D)
1984—Broncos, 24-14 (C)
1986—*Broncos, 23-20 (C) OT
1987—*Broncos, 38-33 (D)
1988—Broncos, 30-7 (D)
1989—Browns, 16-13 (C)
  *Broncos, 37-21 (D)
1990—Browns, 30-29 (D)
1991—Broncos, 17-7 (C)
1992—Broncos, 12-0 (C)
1993—Broncos, 29-14 (D)
1994—Broncos, 26-14 (D)
(RS Pts.—Broncos 409, Browns 256)
(PS Pts.—Broncos 98, Browns 74)
*AFC Championship
CLEVELAND vs. DETROIT
RS: Lions lead series, 12-3
PS: Lions lead series, 3-1
1952—Lions, 17-6 (D)
  *Lions, 17-7 (D)
1953—*Lions, 17-16 (D)
1954—Lions, 14-10 (C)
  *Browns, 56-10 (C)

1957—Lions, 20-7 (D)
  *Lions, 59-14 (D)
1958—Lions, 30-10 (C)
1963—Lions, 38-10 (D)
1964—Browns, 37-21 (C)
1967—Lions, 31-14 (D)
1969—Lions, 28-21 (C)
1970—Lions, 41-24 (C)
1975—Lions, 21-10 (D)
1983—Browns, 31-26 (D)
1986—Browns, 24-21 (C)
1989—Lions, 13-10 (D)
1992—Lions, 24-14 (D)
1995—Lions, 38-20 (D)
(RS Pts.—Lions 383, Browns 248)
(PS Pts.—Lions 103, Browns 93)
*NFL Championship
CLEVELAND vs. GREEN BAY
RS: Packers lead series, 8-6
PS: Packers lead series, 1-0
1953—Browns, 27-0 (Mil)
1955—Browns, 41-10 (C)
1956—Browns, 24-7 (Mil)
1961—Packers, 49-17 (C)
1964—Packers, 28-21 (Mil)
1965—*Packers, 23-12 (GB)
1966—Packers, 21-20 (C)
1967—Packers, 55-7 (Mil)
1969—Browns, 20-7 (C)
1972—Packers, 26-10 (C)
1980—Browns, 26-21 (C)
1983—Packers, 35-21 (Mil)
1986—Packers, 17-14 (C)
1992—Browns, 17-6 (C)
1995—Packers, 31-20 (C)
(RS Pts.—Packers 313, Browns 285)
(PS Pts.—Packers 23, Browns 12)
*NFL Championship
CLEVELAND vs. *INDIANAPOLIS
RS: Browns lead series, 13-7
PS: Series tied, 2-2
1956—Colts, 21-7 (C)
1959—Browns, 38-31 (B)
1962—Colts, 36-14 (C)
1964—**Browns, 27-0 (C)
1968—Browns, 30-20 (B)
  **Colts, 34-0 (C)
1971—Browns, 14-13 (B)
  ***Colts, 20-3 (C)
1973—Browns, 24-14 (C)
1975—Colts, 21-7 (B)
1978—Browns, 45-24 (B)
1979—Browns, 13-10 (C)
1980—Browns, 28-27 (B)
1981—Browns, 42-28 (C)
1983—Browns, 41-23 (C)
1986—Browns, 24-9 (I)
1987—Colts, 9-7 (C)
  ***Browns, 38-21 (C)
1988—Browns, 23-17 (C)
1989—Colts, 23-17 (I) OT
1991—Browns, 31-0 (I)
1992—Colts, 14-3 (I)
1993—Colts, 23-10 (I)
1994—Browns, 21-14 (I)
(RS Pts.—Browns 439, Colts 377)
(PS Pts.—Colts 75, Browns 68)
*Franchise in Baltimore prior to 1984
**NFL Championship
***AFC Divisional Playoff
CLEVELAND vs. JACKSONVILLE
RS: Jaguars lead series, 2-0
1995—Jaguars, 23-15 (C)
  Jaguars, 24-21 (J)
(RS Pts.—Jaguars 47, Browns 36)
CLEVELAND vs. KANSAS CITY
RS: Browns lead series, 8-7-2
1971—Chiefs, 13-7 (KC)
1972—Chiefs, 31-7 (C)
1973—Tie, 20-20 (KC)
1975—Browns, 40-14 (C)
1976—Chiefs, 39-14 (KC)
1977—Browns, 44-7 (C)

1978—Chiefs, 17-3 (KC)
1979—Browns, 27-24 (KC)
1980—Browns, 20-13 (C)
1984—Chiefs, 10-6 (KC)
1986—Browns, 20-7 (C)
1988—Browns, 6-3 (KC)
1989—Tie, 10-10 (C) OT
1990—Chiefs, 34-0 (KC)
1991—Browns, 20-15 (C)
1994—Chiefs, 20-13 (KC)
1995—Browns, 35-17 (C)
(RS Pts.—Chiefs 294, Browns 292)
CLEVELAND vs. MIAMI
RS: Dolphins lead series, 6-4
PS: Dolphins lead series, 2-0
1970—Browns, 28-0 (M)
1972—*Dolphins, 20-14 (M)
1973—Dolphins, 17-9 (C)
1976—Browns, 17-13 (C)
1979—Browns, 30-24 (C) OT
1985—*Dolphins, 24-21 (M)
1986—Browns, 26-16 (C)
1988—Dolphins, 38-31 (M)
1989—Dolphins, 13-10 (M) OT
1990—Dolphins, 30-13 (C)
1992—Dolphins, 27-23 (C)
1993—Dolphins, 24-14 (C)
(RS Pts.—Dolphins 202, Browns 201)
(PS Pts.—Dolphins 44, Browns 35)
*AFC Divisional Playoff
CLEVELAND vs. MINNESOTA
RS: Vikings lead series, 8-3
PS: Vikings lead series, 1-0
1965—Vikings, 27-17 (C)
1967—Browns, 14-10 (C)
1969—Vikings, 51-3 (M)
  *Vikings, 27-7 (M)
1973—Vikings, 26-3 (M)
1975—Vikings, 42-10 (C)
1980—Vikings, 28-23 (M)
1983—Vikings, 27-21 (C)
1986—Browns, 23-20 (M)
1989—Browns, 23-17 (C) OT
1992—Vikings, 17-13 (M)
1995—Vikings, 27-11 (M)
(RS Pts.—Vikings 292, Browns 161)
(PS Pts.—Vikings 27, Browns 7)
*NFL Championship
CLEVELAND vs. NEW ENGLAND
RS: Browns lead series, 10-4
PS: Browns lead series, 1-0
1971—Browns, 27-7 (C)
1974—Browns, 21-14 (NE)
1977—Browns, 30-27 (C) OT
1980—Patriots, 34-17 (NE)
1982—Browns, 10-7 (C)
1983—Browns, 30-0 (NE)
1984—Patriots, 17-16 (C)
1985—Browns, 24-20 (C)
1987—Browns, 20-10 (NE)
1991—Browns, 20-0 (NE)
1992—Browns, 19-17 (NE)
1993—Patriots, 20-17 (C)
1994—Browns, 13-6 (C)
  *Browns, 20-13 (C)
1995—Patriots, 17-14 (NE)
(RS Pts.—Browns 278, Patriots 196)
(PS Pts.—Browns 20, Patriots 13)
*AFC First-Round Playoff
CLEVELAND vs. NEW ORLEANS
RS: Browns lead series, 9-3
1967—Browns, 42-7 (NO)
1968—Browns, 24-10 (NO)
  Browns, 35-17 (C)
1969—Browns, 27-17 (NO)
1971—Browns, 21-17 (NO)
1975—Browns, 17-16 (C)
1978—Browns, 24-16 (NO)
1981—Browns, 20-17 (C)
1984—Saints, 16-14 (C)
1987—Saints, 28-21 (NO)
1990—Saints, 25-20 (NO)
1993—Browns, 17-13 (C)

(RS Pts.—Browns 282, Saints 199)
CLEVELAND vs. N.Y. GIANTS
RS: Browns lead series, 25-17-2
PS: Series tied, 1-1
1950—Giants, 6-0 (C)
  Giants, 17-13 (NY)
  *Browns, 8-3 (C)
1951—Browns, 14-13 (C)
  Browns, 10-0 (NY)
1952—Giants, 17-9 (C)
  Giants, 37-34 (NY)
1953—Browns, 7-0 (NY)
  Browns, 62-14 (C)
1954—Browns, 24-14 (C)
  Browns, 16-7 (NY)
1955—Browns, 24-14 (C)
  Tie, 35-35 (NY)
1956—Giants, 21-9 (C)
  Browns, 24-7 (NY)
1957—Browns, 6-3 (C)
  Browns, 34-28 (NY)
1958—Giants, 21-17 (C)
  Giants, 13-10 (NY)
  *Giants, 10-0 (NY)
1959—Giants, 10-6 (C)
  Giants, 48-7 (NY)
1960—Giants, 17-13 (C)
  Browns, 48-34 (NY)
1961—Giants, 37-21 (C)
  Tie, 7-7 (NY)
1962—Browns, 17-7 (C)
  Giants, 17-13 (NY)
1963—Browns, 35-24 (NY)
  Giants, 33-6 (C)
1964—Browns, 42-20 (C)
  Browns, 52-20 (NY)
1965—Browns, 38-14 (NY)
  Browns, 34-21 (C)
1966—Browns, 28-7 (NY)
  Browns, 49-40 (C)
1967—Giants, 38-34 (NY)
  Browns, 24-14 (C)
1968—Browns, 45-10 (C)
1969—Browns, 28-17 (C)
  Giants, 27-14 (NY)
1973—Browns, 12-10 (C)
1977—Browns, 21-7 (NY)
1985—Browns, 35-33 (NY)
1991—Giants, 13-10 (NY)
1994—Giants, 16-13 (C)
(RS Pts.—Browns 1,000, Giants 808)
(PS Pts.—Giants 13, Browns 8)
*Conference Playoff
CLEVELAND vs. N.Y. JETS
RS: Browns lead series, 9-6
PS: Browns lead series, 1-0
1970—Browns, 31-21 (C)
1972—Browns, 26-10 (NY)
1976—Browns, 38-17 (C)
1978—Browns, 37-34 (C) OT
1979—Browns, 25-22 (NY) OT
1980—Browns, 17-14 (C)
1981—Jets, 14-13 (C)
1983—Browns, 10-7 (C)
1984—Jets, 24-20 (C)
1985—Jets, 37-10 (NY)
1986—*Browns, 23-20 (C) OT
1988—Jets, 23-3 (C)
1989—Browns, 38-24 (C)
1990—Jets, 24-21 (NY)
1991—Jets, 17-14 (C)
1994—Browns, 27-7 (C)
(RS Pts.—Browns 330, Jets 295)
(PS Pts.—Browns 23, Jets 20)
*AFC Divisional Playoff
CLEVELAND vs. *OAKLAND
RS: Raiders lead series, 8-4
PS: Raiders lead series, 2-0
1970—Raiders, 23-20 (O)
1971—Raiders, 34-20 (C)
1973—Browns, 7-3 (O)
1974—Raiders, 40-24 (C)
1975—Raiders, 38-17 (O)

1977—Raiders, 26-10 (C)
1979—Raiders, 19-14 (O)
1980—**Raiders, 14-12 (C)
1982—***Raiders, 27-10 (LA)
1985—Raiders, 21-20 (C)
1986—Raiders, 27-14 (LA)
1987—Browns, 24-17 (LA)
1992—Browns, 28-16 (LA)
1993—Browns, 19-16 (LA)
(RS Pts.—Raiders 280, Browns 217)
(PS Pts.—Raiders 41, Browns 22)
*Franchise in Los Angeles from 1982-1994
**AFC Divisional Playoff
***AFC First-Round Playoff

CLEVELAND vs. PHILADELPHIA
RS: Browns lead series, 31-12-1
1950—Browns, 35-10 (C)
    Browns, 13-7 (C)
1951—Browns, 20-17 (C)
    Browns, 24-9 (C)
1952—Browns, 49-7 (P)
    Eagles, 28-20 (C)
1953—Browns, 37-13 (C)
    Eagles, 42-27 (P)
1954—Eagles, 28-10 (P)
    Browns, 6-0 (C)
1955—Browns, 21-17 (C)
    Eagles, 33-17 (P)
1956—Browns, 16-0 (P)
    Browns, 17-14 (C)
1957—Browns, 24-7 (C)
    Eagles, 17-7 (P)
1958—Browns, 28-14 (C)
    Browns, 21-14 (P)
1959—Browns, 28-7 (C)
    Browns, 28-21 (P)
1960—Browns, 41-24 (P)
    Eagles, 31-29 (C)
1961—Eagles, 27-20 (P)
    Browns, 45-24 (C)
1962—Eagles, 35-7 (P)
    Tie, 14-14 (C)
1963—Browns, 37-7 (C)
    Browns, 23-17 (P)
1964—Browns, 28-20 (C)
    Browns, 38-24 (C)
1965—Browns, 35-17 (P)
    Browns, 38-34 (C)
1966—Browns, 27-7 (C)
    Eagles, 33-21 (P)
1967—Eagles, 28-24 (P)
1968—Browns, 47-13 (C)
1969—Browns, 27-20 (P)
1972—Browns, 27-17 (C)
1976—Browns, 24-3 (C)
1979—Browns, 24-19 (P)
1982—Eagles, 24-21 (C)
1988—Browns, 19-3 (C)
1991—Eagles, 32-30 (C)
1994—Browns, 26-7 (P)
(RS Pts.—Browns 1,120, Eagles 785)

CLEVELAND vs. PITTSBURGH
RS: Browns lead series, 52-40
PS: Steelers lead series, 1-0
1950—Browns, 30-17 (P)
    Browns, 45-7 (C)
1951—Browns, 17-0 (C)
    Browns, 28-0 (P)
1952—Browns, 21-20 (P)
    Browns, 29-28 (C)
1953—Browns, 34-16 (C)
    Browns, 20-16 (P)
1954—Steelers, 55-27 (P)
    Browns, 42-7 (C)
1955—Browns, 41-14 (C)
    Browns, 30-7 (P)
1956—Browns, 14-10 (P)
    Steelers, 24-16 (C)
1957—Browns, 23-12 (P)
    Browns, 24-0 (C)
1958—Browns, 45-12 (P)
    Browns, 27-10 (C)

1959—Steelers, 17-7 (P)
    Steelers, 21-20 (C)
1960—Browns, 28-20 (C)
    Steelers, 14-10 (P)
1961—Browns, 30-28 (P)
    Steelers, 17-13 (C)
1962—Browns, 41-14 (P)
    Browns, 35-14 (C)
1963—Browns, 35-23 (C)
    Steelers, 9-7 (P)
1964—Steelers, 23-7 (C)
    Browns, 30-17 (P)
1965—Browns, 24-19 (C)
    Browns, 42-21 (P)
1966—Browns, 41-10 (C)
    Steelers, 16-6 (P)
1967—Browns, 21-10 (C)
    Browns, 34-14 (P)
1968—Browns, 31-24 (C)
    Browns, 45-24 (P)
1969—Browns, 42-31 (C)
    Browns, 24-3 (P)
1970—Browns, 15-7 (C)
    Steelers, 28-9 (P)
1971—Browns, 27-17 (C)
    Steelers, 26-9 (P)
1972—Browns, 26-24 (C)
    Steelers, 30-0 (P)
1973—Steelers, 33-6 (P)
    Browns, 21-16 (C)
1974—Steelers, 20-16 (P)
    Steelers, 26-16 (C)
1975—Steelers, 42-6 (C)
    Steelers, 31-17 (P)
1976—Steelers, 31-14 (P)
    Browns, 18-16 (C)
1977—Steelers, 28-14 (C)
    Steelers, 35-31 (P)
1978—Steelers, 15-9 (P) OT
    Steelers, 34-14 (C)
1979—Steelers, 51-35 (C)
    Steelers, 33-30 (P) OT
1980—Browns, 27-26 (C)
    Steelers, 16-13 (P)
1981—Steelers, 13-7 (P)
    Steelers, 32-10 (C)
1982—Browns, 10-9 (C)
    Steelers, 37-21 (P)
1983—Steelers, 44-17 (P)
    Browns, 30-17 (C)
1984—Browns, 20-10 (C)
    Steelers, 23-20 (P)
1985—Browns, 17-7 (C)
    Steelers, 10-9 (P)
1986—Browns, 27-24 (P)
    Browns, 37-31 (C) OT
1987—Browns, 34-10 (C)
    Browns, 19-13 (P)
1988—Browns, 23-9 (P)
    Browns, 27-7 (C)
1989—Browns, 51-0 (C)
    Steelers, 17-7 (P)
1990—Browns, 13-3 (C)
    Steelers, 35-0 (P)
1991—Browns, 17-14 (C)
    Steelers, 17-10 (P)
1992—Browns, 17-9 (C)
    Steelers, 23-13 (P)
1993—Browns, 28-23 (C)
    Steelers, 16-9 (P)
1994—Steelers, 17-10 (C)
    Steelers, 17-7 (P)
    *Steelers, 29-9 (P)
1995—Steelers, 20-3 (P)
    Steelers, 20-17 (C)
(RS Pts.—Browns 1,989, Steelers 1,756)
(PS Pts.—Steelers 29, Browns 9)
*AFC Divisional Playoff

CLEVELAND vs. *ST. LOUIS
RS: Browns lead series, 8-7
PS: Browns lead series, 2-1
1950—**Browns, 30-28 (C)
1951—Browns, 38-23 (LA)

    **Rams, 24-17 (LA)
1952—Browns, 37-7 (C)
1955—**Browns, 38-14 (LA)
1957—Browns, 45-31 (C)
1958—Browns, 30-27 (LA)
1963—Browns, 20-6 (C)
1965—Rams, 42-7 (LA)
1968—Rams, 24-6 (C)
1973—Rams, 30-17 (LA)
1977—Rams, 9-0 (C)
1978—Browns, 30-19 (C)
1981—Rams, 27-16 (LA)
1984—Rams, 20-17 (LA)
1987—Browns, 30-17 (C)
1990—Rams, 38-23 (C)
1993—Browns, 42-14 (LA)
(RS Pts.—Browns 358, Rams 334)
(PS Pts.—Browns 85, Rams 66)
*Franchise in Los Angeles prior to 1995
**NFL Championship

CLEVELAND vs. SAN DIEGO
RS: Chargers lead series, 9-6-1
1970—Chargers, 27-10 (C)
1972—Browns, 21-17 (SD)
1973—Tie, 16-16 (C)
1974—Chargers, 36-35 (SD)
1976—Browns, 21-17 (C)
1977—Chargers, 37-14 (SD)
1981—Chargers, 44-14 (C)
1982—Chargers, 30-13 (C)
1983—Browns, 30-24 (SD) OT
1985—Browns, 21-7 (SD)
1986—Browns, 47-17 (C)
1987—Chargers, 27-24 (SD) OT
1990—Chargers, 24-14 (C)
1991—Browns, 30-24 (SD) OT
1992—Chargers, 14-13 (C)
1995—Chargers, 31-13 (SD)
(RS Pts.—Chargers 392, Browns 336)

CLEVELAND vs. SAN FRANCISCO
RS: Browns lead series, 9-6
1950—Browns, 34-14 (C)
1951—49ers, 24-10 (SF)
1953—Browns, 23-21 (C)
1955—Browns, 38-3 (SF)
1959—49ers, 21-20 (C)
1962—Browns, 13-10 (SF)
1968—Browns, 33-21 (SF)
1970—49ers, 34-31 (SF)
1974—Browns, 7-0 (C)
1978—Browns, 24-7 (C)
1981—Browns, 15-12 (SF)
1984—49ers, 41-7 (C)
1987—49ers, 38-24 (SF)
1990—49ers, 20-17 (SF)
1993—Browns, 23-13 (C)
(RS Pts.—Browns 319, 49ers 279)

CLEVELAND vs. SEATTLE
RS: Seahawks lead series, 9-4
1977—Seahawks, 20-19 (S)
1978—Seahawks, 47-24 (S)
1979—Seahawks, 29-24 (C)
1980—Browns, 27-3 (S)
1981—Seahawks, 42-21 (S)
1982—Browns, 21-7 (S)
1983—Seahawks, 24-9 (C)
1984—Seahawks, 33-0 (S)
1985—Seahawks, 31-13 (S)
1988—Seahawks, 16-10 (S)
1989—Browns, 17-7 (S)
1993—Seahawks, 22-5 (S)
1994—Browns, 35-9 (C)
(RS Pts.—Seahawks 290, Browns 225)

CLEVELAND vs. TAMPA BAY
RS: Browns lead series, 5-0
1976—Browns, 24-7 (TB)
1980—Browns, 34-27 (TB)
1983—Browns, 20-0 (C)
1989—Browns, 42-31 (TB)
1995—Browns, 22-6 (C)
(RS Pts.—Browns 142, Buccaneers 71)

CLEVELAND vs. *TENNESSEE
RS: Browns lead series, 30-21

PS: Oilers lead series, 1-0
1970—Browns, 28-14 (C)
    Browns, 21-10 (H)
1971—Browns, 31-0 (C)
    Browns, 37-24 (H)
1972—Browns, 23-17 (H)
    Browns, 20-0 (C)
1973—Browns, 42-13 (C)
    Browns, 23-13 (H)
1974—Browns, 20-7 (C)
    Oilers, 28-24 (H)
1975—Oilers, 40-10 (C)
    Oilers, 21-10 (H)
1976—Browns, 21-7 (H)
    Browns, 13-10 (C)
1977—Browns, 24-23 (H)
    Oilers, 19-15 (C)
1978—Oilers, 16-13 (C)
    Oilers, 14-10 (H)
1979—Oilers, 31-10 (H)
    Browns, 14-7 (C)
1980—Oilers, 16-7 (C)
    Browns, 17-14 (H)
1981—Oilers, 9-3 (C)
    Oilers, 17-13 (H)
1982—Browns, 20-14 (H)
1983—Browns, 25-19 (C) OT
    Oilers, 34-27 (H)
1984—Browns, 27-10 (C)
    Browns, 27-20 (H)
1985—Browns, 21-6 (H)
    Browns, 28-21 (C)
1986—Browns, 23-20 (H)
    Browns, 13-10 (C) OT
1987—Browns, 15-10 (C)
    Browns, 40-7 (H)
1988—Oilers, 24-17 (H)
    Browns, 28-23 (C)
    **Oilers, 24-23 (C)
1989—Browns, 28-17 (C)
    Browns, 24-20 (H)
1990—Oilers, 35-23 (C)
    Oilers, 58-14 (H)
1991—Oilers, 28-24 (C)
    Oilers, 17-14 (H)
1992—Browns, 24-14 (H)
    Oilers, 17-14 (C)
1993—Oilers, 27-20 (H)
    Oilers, 19-17 (H)
1994—Browns, 11-8 (H)
    Browns, 34-10 (C)
1995—Browns, 14-7 (C)
    Oilers, 37-10 (C)
(RS Pts.—Browns 1,026, Oilers 907)
(PS Pts.—Oilers 24, Browns 23)
*Franchise in Houston prior to 1997
**AFC First-Round Playoff

CLEVELAND vs. WASHINGTON
RS: Browns lead series, 32-9-1
1950—Browns, 20-14 (C)
    Browns, 45-21 (W)
1951—Browns, 45-0 (C)
1952—Browns, 19-15 (C)
    Browns, 48-24 (W)
1953—Browns, 30-14 (W)
    Browns, 27-3 (C)
1954—Browns, 62-3 (C)
    Browns, 34-14 (W)
1955—Redskins, 27-17 (C)
    Browns, 24-14 (W)
1956—Redskins, 20-9 (W)
    Redskins, 20-17 (C)
1957—Browns, 21-17 (C)
    Tie, 30-30 (W)
1958—Browns, 20-10 (W)
    Browns, 21-14 (C)
1959—Browns, 34-7 (C)
    Browns, 31-17 (W)
1960—Browns, 31-10 (W)
    Browns, 27-16 (C)
1961—Browns, 31-7 (C)
    Browns, 17-6 (W)
1962—Redskins, 17-16 (C)

Redskins, 17-9 (W)
1963—Browns, 37-14 (C)
Browns, 27-20 (W)
1964—Browns, 27-13 (W)
Browns, 34-24 (C)
1965—Browns, 17-7 (W)
Browns, 24-16 (C)
1966—Browns, 38-14 (W)
Browns, 14-3 (C)
1967—Browns, 42-37 (C)
1968—Browns, 24-21 (W)
1969—Browns, 27-23 (C)
1971—Browns, 20-13 (W)
1975—Redskins, 23-7 (C)
1979—Redskins, 13-9 (C)
1985—Redskins, 14-7 (C)
1988—Browns, 17-13 (W)
1991—Redskins, 42-17 (W)
(RS Pts.—Browns 1,073, Redskins 667)

DALLAS vs. ARIZONA
RS: Cowboys lead series, 46-22-1;
See Arizona vs. Dallas
DALLAS vs. ATLANTA
RS: Cowboys lead series, 11-6
PS: Cowboys lead series, 2-0;
See Atlanta vs. Dallas
DALLAS vs. BUFFALO
RS: Series tied, 3-3
PS: Cowboys lead series, 2-0;
See Buffalo vs. Dallas
DALLAS vs. CAROLINA
PS: Panthers lead series, 1-0;
See Carolina vs. Dallas
DALLAS vs. CHICAGO
RS: Cowboys lead series, 8-7
PS: Cowboys lead series, 2-0;
See Chicago vs. Dallas
DALLAS vs. CINCINNATI
RS: Cowboys lead series, 4-2;
See Cincinnati vs. Dallas
DALLAS vs. CLEVELAND
RS: Browns lead series, 15-9
PS: Browns lead series, 2-1;
See Cleveland vs. Dallas
DALLAS vs. DENVER
RS: Cowboys lead series, 4-2
PS: Cowboys lead series, 1-0
1973—Cowboys, 22-10 (Den)
1977—Cowboys, 14-6 (Dal)
*Cowboys, 27-10 (New Orleans)
1980—Broncos, 41-20 (Den)
1986—Broncos, 29-14 (Den)
1992—Cowboys, 31-27 (Den)
1995—Cowboys, 31-21 (Dal)
(RS Pts.—Broncos 134, Cowboys 132)
(PS Pts.—Cowboys 27, Broncos 10)
*Super Bowl XII
DALLAS vs. DETROIT
RS: Cowboys lead series, 7-6
PS: Series tied, 1-1
1960—Lions, 23-14 (Det)
1963—Cowboys, 17-14 (Dal)
1968—Cowboys, 59-13 (Dal)
1970—*Cowboys, 5-0 (Dal)
1972—Cowboys, 28-24 (Dal)
1975—Cowboys, 36-10 (Det)
1977—Cowboys, 37-0 (Dal)
1981—Lions, 27-24 (Det)
1985—Lions, 26-21 (Det)
1986—Cowboys, 31-7 (Det)
1987—Lions, 27-17 (Det)
1991—Lions, 34-10 (Det)
*Lions, 38-6 (Det)
1992—Cowboys, 37-3 (Det)
1994—Lions, 20-17 (Dal) OT
(RS Pts.—Cowboys 348, Lions 228)
(PS Pts.—Lions 38, Cowboys 11)
*NFC Divisional Playoff
DALLAS vs. GREEN BAY
RS: Cowboys lead series 9-8
PS: Cowboys lead series, 4-2
1960—Packers, 41-7 (GB)

1964—Packers, 45-21 (D)
1965—Packers, 13-3 (Mil)
1966—*Packers, 34-27 (D)
1967—*Packers, 21-17 (GB)
1968—Packers, 28-17 (D)
1970—Cowboys, 16-3 (D)
1972—Packers, 16-13 (Mil)
1975—Packers, 19-17 (D)
1978—Cowboys, 42-14 (Mil)
1980—Cowboys, 28-7 (Mil)
1982—**Cowboys, 37-26 (D)
1984—Cowboys, 20-6 (D)
1989—Packers, 31-13 (GB)
Packers, 20-10 (D)
1991—Cowboys, 20-17 (Mil)
1993—Cowboys, 36-14 (D)
***Cowboys, 27-17 (D)
1994—Cowboys, 42-31 (D)
***Cowboys, 35-9 (D)
1995—Cowboys, 34-24 (D)
****Cowboys, 38-27 (D)
1996—Cowboys, 21-6 (D)
(RS Pts.—Cowboys 360, Packers 335)
(PS Pts.—Cowboys 181, Packers 134)
*NFL Championship
**NFC Second-Round Playoff
***NFC Divisional Playoff
****NFC Championship
DALLAS vs. *INDIANAPOLIS
RS: Cowboys lead series, 7-3
PS: Colts lead series, 1-0
1960—Colts, 45-7 (D)
1967—Colts, 23-17 (B)
1969—Cowboys, 27-10 (D)
1970—**Colts, 16-13 (Miami)
1972—Cowboys, 21-0 (B)
1976—Cowboys, 30-27 (D)
1978—Cowboys, 38-0 (D)
1981—Cowboys, 37-13 (B)
1984—Cowboys, 22-3 (D)
1993—Cowboys, 27-3 (I)
1996—Colts, 25-24 (D)
(RS Pts.—Cowboys 250, Colts 149)
(PS Pts.—Colts 16, Cowboys 13)
*Franchise in Baltimore prior to 1984
**Super Bowl V
DALLAS vs. KANSAS CITY
RS: Cowboys lead series, 4-2
1970—Cowboys, 27-16 (KC)
1975—Chiefs, 34-31 (D)
1983—Cowboys, 41-21 (D)
1989—Chiefs, 36-28 (KC)
1992—Cowboys, 17-10 (D)
1995—Cowboys, 24-12 (D)
(RS Pts.—Cowboys 168, Chiefs 129)
DALLAS vs. MIAMI
RS: Dolphins lead series, 6-2
PS: Cowboys lead series, 1-0
1971—*Cowboys, 24-3 (New Orleans)
1973—Dolphins, 14-7 (D)
1978—Dolphins, 23-16 (M)
1981—Cowboys, 28-27 (D)
1984—Dolphins, 28-21 (M)
1987—Dolphins, 20-14 (D)
1989—Dolphins, 17-14 (D)
1993—Dolphins, 16-14 (D)
1996—Cowboys, 29-10 (M)
(RS Pts.—Dolphins 155, Cowboys 143)
(PS Pts.—Cowboys 24, Dolphins 3)
*Super Bowl VI
DALLAS vs. MINNESOTA
RS: Cowboys lead series, 9-6
PS: Cowboys lead series, 4-1
1961—Cowboys, 21-7 (D)
Cowboys, 28-0 (M)
1966—Cowboys, 28-17 (D)
1968—Cowboys, 20-7 (M)
1970—Vikings, 54-13 (M)
1971—*Cowboys, 20-12 (M)
1973—**Vikings, 27-10 (D)
1974—Vikings, 23-21 (D)
1975—*Cowboys, 17-14 (M)
1977—Cowboys, 16-10 (M) OT

**Cowboys, 23-6 (D)
1978—Vikings, 21-10 (D)
1979—Cowboys, 36-20 (M)
1982—Vikings, 31-27 (M)
1983—Cowboys, 37-24 (M)
1987—Vikings, 44-38 (D) OT
1988—Vikings, 43-3 (D)
1993—Cowboys, 37-20 (M)
1995—Cowboys, 23-17 (M) OT
1996—***Cowboys, 40-15 (D)
(RS Pts.—Cowboys 358, Vikings 338)
(PS Pts.—Cowboys 110, Vikings 74)
*NFC Divisional Playoff
**NFC Championship
***NFC First-Round Playoff
DALLAS vs. NEW ENGLAND
RS: Cowboys lead series, 7-0
1971—Cowboys, 44-21 (D)
1975—Cowboys, 34-31 (NE)
1978—Cowboys, 17-10 (D)
1981—Cowboys, 35-21 (NE)
1984—Cowboys, 20-17 (D)
1987—Cowboys, 23-17 (NE) OT
1996—Cowboys, 12-6 (D)
(RS Pts.—Cowboys 185, Patriots 123)
DALLAS vs. NEW ORLEANS
RS: Cowboys lead series, 14-3
1967—Cowboys, 14-10 (D)
Cowboys, 27-10 (NO)
1968—Cowboys, 17-3 (NO)
1969—Cowboys, 21-17 (NO)
Cowboys, 33-17 (D)
1971—Saints, 24-14 (NO)
1973—Cowboys, 40-3 (D)
1976—Cowboys, 24-6 (NO)
1978—Cowboys, 27-7 (D)
1982—Cowboys, 21-7 (D)
1983—Cowboys, 21-20 (D)
1984—Cowboys, 30-27 (D) OT
1988—Saints, 20-17 (NO)
1989—Saints, 28-0 (NO)
1990—Cowboys, 17-13 (D)
1991—Cowboys, 23-14 (D)
1994—Cowboys, 24-16 (NO)
(RS Pts.—Cowboys 370, Saints 242)
DALLAS vs. N.Y. GIANTS
RS: Cowboys lead series, 44-23-2
1960—Tie, 31-31 (NY)
1961—Giants, 31-10 (D)
Cowboys, 17-16 (NY)
1962—Giants, 41-10 (D)
Giants, 41-31 (NY)
1963—Giants, 37-21 (D)
Giants, 34-27 (D)
1964—Tie, 13-13 (D)
Cowboys, 31-21 (NY)
1965—Cowboys, 31-2 (D)
Cowboys, 38-20 (NY)
1966—Cowboys, 52-7 (D)
Cowboys, 17-7 (NY)
1967—Cowboys, 38-24 (D)
1968—Giants, 27-21 (D)
Cowboys, 28-10 (NY)
1969—Cowboys, 25-3 (D)
1970—Cowboys, 28-10 (D)
Giants, 23-20 (NY)
1971—Cowboys, 20-13 (D)
Cowboys, 42-14 (NY)
1972—Cowboys, 23-14 (NY)
Giants, 23-3 (D)
1973—Cowboys, 45-28 (D)
Cowboys, 23-10 (New Haven)
1974—Giants, 14-6 (D)
Cowboys, 21-7 (New Haven)
1975—Cowboys, 13-7 (NY)
Cowboys, 14-3 (D)
1976—Cowboys, 24-14 (NY)
Cowboys, 9-3 (D)
1977—Cowboys, 41-21 (D)
Cowboys, 24-10 (NY)
1978—Cowboys, 34-24 (NY)
Cowboys, 24-3 (D)
1979—Cowboys, 16-14 (NY)

Cowboys, 28-7 (D)
1980—Cowboys, 24-3 (D)
Giants, 38-35 (NY)
1981—Cowboys, 18-10 (D)
Giants, 13-10 (NY) OT
1983—Cowboys, 28-13 (D)
Cowboys, 38-20 (NY)
1984—Giants, 28-7 (D)
Giants, 19-7 (D)
1985—Cowboys, 30-29 (NY)
Cowboys, 28-21 (D)
1986—Cowboys, 31-28 (D)
Giants, 17-14 (NY)
1987—Cowboys, 16-14 (NY)
Cowboys, 33-24 (D)
1988—Cowboys, 12-10 (D)
Giants, 29-21 (NY)
1989—Giants, 30-13 (D)
Giants, 15-0 (NY)
1990—Cowboys, 28-7 (D)
Giants, 31-17 (NY)
1991—Cowboys, 21-16 (D)
Giants, 22-9 (NY)
1992—Cowboys, 34-28 (NY)
Cowboys, 30-3 (D)
1993—Cowboys, 31-9 (D)
Cowboys, 16-13 (NY) OT
1994—Cowboys, 38-10 (D)
Giants, 15-10 (NY)
1995—Cowboys, 35-0 (NY)
Cowboys, 21-20 (D)
1996—Cowboys, 27-0 (D)
Giants, 20-6 (D)
(RS Pts.—Cowboys 1,564, Giants 1,205)
DALLAS vs. N.Y. JETS
RS: Cowboys lead series, 5-1
1971—Cowboys, 52-10 (D)
1975—Cowboys, 31-21 (NY)
1978—Cowboys, 30-7 (NY)
1987—Cowboys, 38-24 (NY)
1990—Jets, 24-9 (NY)
1993—Cowboys, 28-7 (NY)
(RS Pts.—Cowboys 188, Jets 93)
DALLAS vs. *OAKLAND
RS: Series tied, 3-3
1974—Raiders, 27-23 (O)
1980—Cowboys, 19-13 (O)
1983—Raiders, 40-38 (D)
1986—Raiders, 17-13 (D)
1992—Cowboys, 28-13 (LA)
1995—Cowboys, 34-21 (O)
(RS Pts.—Cowboys 155, Raiders 131)
*Franchise in Los Angeles from
1982-1994
DALLAS vs. PHILADELPHIA
RS: Cowboys lead series, 44-28
PS: Cowboys lead series, 2-1
1960—Eagles, 27-25 (D)
1961—Eagles, 43-7 (D)
Eagles, 35-13 (P)
1962—Cowboys, 41-19 (D)
Eagles, 28-14 (P)
1963—Eagles, 24-21 (P)
Cowboys, 27-20 (D)
1964—Eagles, 17-14 (D)
Eagles, 24-14 (P)
1965—Eagles, 35-24 (D)
Cowboys, 21-19 (P)
1966—Cowboys, 56-7 (D)
Eagles, 24-23 (P)
1967—Eagles, 21-14 (P)
Cowboys, 38-17 (D)
1968—Cowboys, 45-13 (D)
Cowboys, 34-14 (D)
1969—Cowboys, 38-7 (P)
Cowboys, 49-14 (D)
1970—Cowboys, 17-7 (P)
Cowboys, 21-17 (D)
1971—Cowboys, 42-7 (P)
Cowboys, 20-7 (D)
1972—Cowboys, 28-6 (D)
Cowboys, 28-7 (P)
1973—Eagles, 30-16 (P)

305

Cowboys, 31-10 (D)
1974—Eagles, 13-10 (P)
Cowboys, 31-24 (D)
1975—Cowboys, 20-17 (P)
Cowboys, 27-17 (D)
1976—Cowboys, 27-7 (D)
Cowboys, 26-7 (P)
1977—Cowboys, 16-10 (P)
Cowboys, 24-14 (D)
1978—Cowboys, 14-7 (D)
Cowboys, 31-13 (P)
1979—Eagles, 31-21 (D)
Cowboys, 24-17 (P)
1980—Eagles, 17-10 (P)
Cowboys, 35-27 (D)
*Eagles, 20-7 (P)
1981—Cowboys, 17-14 (P)
Cowboys, 21-10 (D)
1982—Eagles, 24-20 (D)
1983—Cowboys, 37-7 (D)
Cowboys, 27-20 (P)
1984—Cowboys, 23-17 (D)
Cowboys, 26-10 (P)
1985—Eagles, 16-14 (P)
Cowboys, 34-17 (D)
1986—Cowboys, 17-14 (P)
Eagles, 23-21 (D)
1987—Cowboys, 41-22 (D)
Eagles, 37-20 (P)
1988—Eagles, 24-23 (P)
Eagles, 23-7 (D)
1989—Eagles, 27-0 (D)
Eagles, 20-10 (P)
1990—Eagles, 21-20 (P)
Eagles, 17-3 (P)
1991—Eagles, 24-0 (D)
Cowboys, 25-13 (P)
1992—Eagles, 31-7 (P)
Cowboys, 20-10 (D)
**Cowboys, 34-10 (D)
1993—Cowboys, 23-10 (P)
Cowboys, 23-17 (D)
1994—Cowboys, 24-13 (D)
Cowboys, 31-19 (P)
1995—Cowboys, 34-12 (D)
Eagles, 20-17 (P)
**Cowboys, 30-11 (D)
1996—Cowboys, 23-19 (P)
Eagles, 31-21 (D)
(RS Pts.—Cowboys 1,666, Eagles 1,302)
(PS Pts.—Cowboys 71, Eagles 41)
*NFC Championship
**NFC Divisional Playoff
DALLAS vs. PITTSBURGH
RS: Cowboys lead series, 13-11
PS: Steelers lead series, 2-1
1960—Steelers, 35-28 (D)
1961—Cowboys, 27-24 (D)
Steelers, 37-7 (P)
1962—Steelers, 30-28 (D)
Cowboys, 42-27 (P)
1963—Steelers, 27-21 (P)
Steelers, 24-19 (D)
1964—Steelers, 23-17 (P)
Cowboys, 17-14 (D)
1965—Steelers, 22-13 (P)
Cowboys, 24-17 (D)
1966—Cowboys, 52-21 (D)
Cowboys, 20-7 (P)
1967—Cowboys, 24-21 (P)
1968—Cowboys, 28-7 (D)
1969—Cowboys, 10-7 (P)
1972—Cowboys, 17-13 (D)
1975—*Steelers, 21-17 (Miami)
1977—Steelers, 28-13 (P)
1978—**Steelers, 35-31 (Miami)
1979—Steelers, 14-3 (P)
1982—Steelers, 36-28 (D)
1985—Cowboys, 27-13 (D)
1988—Steelers, 24-21 (D)
1991—Cowboys, 20-10 (D)
1994—Cowboys, 26-9 (P)
1995—***Cowboys, 27-17 (Tempe)

(RS Pts.—Cowboys 532, Steelers 490)
(PS Pts.—Cowboys 75, Steelers 73)
*Super Bowl X
**Super Bowl XIII
***Super Bowl XXX
DALLAS vs. *ST. LOUIS
RS: Rams lead series, 9-8
PS: Series tied, 4-4
1960—Rams, 38-13 (D)
1962—Cowboys, 27-17 (LA)
1967—Rams, 35-13 (D)
1969—Rams, 24-23 (LA)
1971—Cowboys, 28-21 (D)
1973—Rams, 37-31 (LA)
**Cowboys, 27-16 (D)
1975—Cowboys, 18-7 (D)
***Cowboys, 37-7 (LA)
1976—**Rams, 14-12 (D)
1978—Rams, 27-14 (LA)
***Cowboys, 28-0 (LA)
1979—Cowboys, 30-6 (D)
Rams, 21-19 (D)
1980—Rams, 38-14 (LA)
****Cowboys, 34-13 (D)
1981—Cowboys, 29-17 (D)
1983—****Rams, 24-17 (D)
1984—Cowboys, 20-13 (LA)
1985—**Rams, 20-0 (LA)
1986—Rams, 29-10 (LA)
1987—Cowboys, 29-21 (LA)
1989—Rams, 35-31 (D)
1990—Cowboys, 24-21 (LA)
1992—Rams, 27-23 (D)
(RS Pts.—Rams 413, Cowboys 377)
(PS Pts.—Cowboys 174, Rams 115)
*Franchise in Los Angeles prior to 1995
**NFC Divisional Playoff
***NFC Championship
****NFC First-Round Playoff
DALLAS vs. SAN DIEGO
RS: Cowboys lead series, 5-1
1972—Cowboys, 34-28 (SD)
1980—Cowboys, 42-31 (D)
1983—Chargers, 24-23 (SD)
1986—Cowboys, 24-21 (SD)
1990—Cowboys, 17-14 (D)
1995—Cowboys, 23-9 (SD)
(RS Pts.—Cowboys 163, Chargers 127)
DALLAS vs. SAN FRANCISCO
RS: 49ers lead series, 11-7-1
PS: Cowboys lead series, 5-2
1960—49ers, 26-14 (D)
1963—49ers, 31-24 (SF)
1965—Cowboys, 39-31 (D)
1967—49ers, 24-16 (SF)
1969—Tie, 24-24 (D)
1970—*Cowboys, 17-10 (SF)
1971—*Cowboys, 14-3 (D)
1972—49ers, 31-10 (D)
**Cowboys, 30-28 (SF)
1974—Cowboys, 20-14 (D)
1977—Cowboys, 42-35 (SF)
1979—Cowboys, 21-13 (SF)
1980—Cowboys, 59-14 (D)
1981—49ers, 45-14 (SF)
*49ers, 28-27 (SF)
1983—49ers, 42-17 (SF)
1985—49ers, 31-16 (D)
1989—49ers, 31-14 (D)
1990—49ers, 24-6 (D)
1992—*Cowboys, 30-20 (SF)
1993—Cowboys, 26-17 (D)
*Cowboys, 38-21 (D)
1994—49ers, 21-14 (SF)
*49ers, 38-28 (SF)
1995—49ers, 38-20 (D)
1996—Cowboys, 20-17 (SF) OT
(RS Pts.—49ers 509, Cowboys 416)
(PS Pts.—Cowboys 184, 49ers 148)
*NFC Championship
**NFC Divisional Playoff
DALLAS vs. SEATTLE
RS: Cowboys lead series, 4-1

1976—Cowboys, 28-13 (S)
1980—Cowboys, 51-7 (D)
1983—Cowboys, 35-10 (S)
1986—Seahawks, 31-14 (D)
1992—Cowboys, 27-0 (D)
(RS Pts.—Cowboys 155, Seahawks 61)
DALLAS vs. TAMPA BAY
RS: Cowboys lead series, 6-0
PS: Cowboys lead series, 2-0
1977—Cowboys, 23-7 (D)
1980—Cowboys, 28-17 (D)
1981—*Cowboys, 38-0 (D)
1982—Cowboys, 14-9 (D)
**Cowboys, 30-17 (D)
1983—Cowboys, 27-24 (D) OT
1990—Cowboys, 14-10 (D)
Cowboys, 17-13 (TB)
(RS Pts.—Cowboys 123, Buccaneers 80)
(PS Pts.—Cowboys 68, Buccaneers 17)
*NFC Divisional Playoff
**NFC First-Round Playoff
DALLAS vs. *TENNESSEE
RS: Cowboys lead series, 5-3
1970—Cowboys, 52-10 (D)
1974—Cowboys, 10-0 (H)
1979—Oilers, 30-24 (H)
1982—Cowboys, 37-7 (H)
1985—Cowboys, 17-10 (H)
1988—Oilers, 25-17 (D)
1991—Oilers, 26-23 (H) OT
1994—Cowboys, 20-17 (D)
(RS Pts.—Cowboys 200, Oilers 125)
*Franchise in Houston prior to 1997
DALLAS vs. WASHINGTON
RS: Cowboys lead series, 40-30-2
PS: Redskins lead series, 2-0
1960—Redskins, 26-14 (W)
1961—Tie, 28-28 (D)
Redskins, 34-24 (W)
1962—Tie, 35-35 (D)
Cowboys, 38-10 (W)
1963—Redskins, 21-17 (W)
Cowboys, 35-20 (D)
1964—Cowboys, 24-18 (D)
Redskins, 28-16 (W)
1965—Cowboys, 27-7 (D)
Redskins, 34-31 (W)
1966—Cowboys, 31-30 (W)
Redskins, 34-31 (D)
1967—Cowboys, 17-14 (W)
Redskins, 27-20 (D)
1968—Cowboys, 44-24 (W)
Cowboys, 29-20 (D)
1969—Cowboys, 41-28 (W)
Cowboys, 20-10 (D)
1970—Cowboys, 45-21 (W)
Cowboys, 34-0 (D)
1971—Redskins, 20-16 (D)
Cowboys, 13-0 (W)
1972—Redskins, 24-20 (W)
Cowboys, 34-24 (D)
*Redskins, 26-3 (W)
1973—Redskins, 14-7 (W)
Cowboys, 27-7 (D)
1974—Redskins, 28-21 (W)
Cowboys, 24-23 (D)
1975—Redskins, 30-24 (W) OT
Cowboys, 31-10 (D)
1976—Cowboys, 20-7 (W)
Redskins, 27-14 (D)
1977—Cowboys, 34-16 (D)
Cowboys, 14-7 (W)
1978—Redskins, 9-5 (W)
Cowboys, 37-10 (D)
1979—Redskins, 34-20 (W)
Cowboys, 35-34 (D)
1980—Cowboys, 17-3 (W)
Cowboys, 14-10 (D)
1981—Cowboys, 26-10 (W)
Cowboys, 24-10 (D)
1982—Cowboys, 24-10 (W)
*Redskins, 31-17 (W)
1983—Cowboys, 31-30 (W)

Redskins, 31-10 (D)
1984—Redskins, 34-14 (W)
Redskins, 30-28 (D)
1985—Cowboys, 44-14 (D)
Cowboys, 13-7 (W)
1986—Cowboys, 30-6 (D)
Redskins, 41-14 (W)
1987—Redskins, 13-7 (D)
Redskins, 24-20 (W)
1988—Redskins, 35-17 (D)
Cowboys, 24-17 (W)
1989—Redskins, 30-7 (D)
Cowboys, 13-3 (W)
1990—Redskins, 19-15 (W)
Cowboys, 27-17 (D)
1991—Redskins, 33-31 (D)
Cowboys, 24-21 (W)
1992—Cowboys, 23-10 (D)
Redskins, 20-17 (W)
1993—Redskins, 35-16 (W)
Cowboys, 38-3 (D)
1994—Cowboys, 34-7 (W)
Cowboys, 31-7 (D)
1995—Redskins, 27-23 (W)
Redskins, 24-17 (D)
1996—Cowboys, 21-10 (D)
Redskins, 37-10 (W)
(RS Pts.—Cowboys, 1,701, Redskins 1,421)
(PS Pts.—Redskins 57, Cowboys 20)
*NFC Championship

DENVER vs. ARIZONA
RS: Broncos lead series, 4-0-1;
See Arizona vs. Denver
DENVER vs. ATLANTA
RS: Broncos lead series, 5-3;
See Atlanta vs. Denver
DENVER vs. BALTIMORE
RS: Broncos lead series, 1-0;
See Baltimore vs. Denver
DENVER vs. BUFFALO
RS: Bills lead series, 17-11-1
PS: Bills lead series, 1-0;
See Buffalo vs. Denver
DENVER vs. CHICAGO
RS: Broncos lead series, 6-5;
See Chicago vs. Denver
DENVER vs. CINCINNATI
RS: Broncos lead series, 12-6;
See Cincinnati vs. Denver
DENVER vs. CLEVELAND
RS: Broncos lead series, 13-5
PS: Broncos lead series, 3-0;
See Cleveland vs. Denver
DENVER vs. DALLAS
RS: Cowboys lead series, 4-2
PS: Cowboys lead series, 1-0;
See Dallas vs. Denver
DENVER vs. DETROIT
RS: Broncos lead series, 4-3
1971—Lions, 24-20 (Den)
1974—Broncos, 31-27 (Det)
1978—Lions, 17-14 (Den)
1981—Broncos, 27-21 (Den)
1984—Broncos, 28-7 (Det)
1987—Broncos, 34-0 (Den)
1990—Lions, 40-27 (Det)
(RS Pts.—Broncos 181, Lions 136)
DENVER vs. GREEN BAY
RS: Broncos lead series, 4-3-1
1971—Packers, 34-13 (Mil)
1975—Broncos, 23-13 (D)
1978—Broncos, 16-3 (D)
1984—Broncos, 17-14 (D)
1987—Tie, 17-17 (Mil) OT
1990—Broncos, 22-13 (D)
1993—Packers, 30-27 (GB)
1996—Packers, 41-6 (GB)
(RS Pts.—Packers 165, Broncos 141)
DENVER vs. *INDIANAPOLIS
RS: Broncos lead series, 9-2
1974—Broncos, 17-6 (B)
1977—Broncos, 27-13 (D)

1978—Colts, 7-6 (B)
1981—Broncos, 28-10 (D)
1983—Broncos, 17-10 (B)
Broncos, 21-19 (D)
1985—Broncos, 15-10 (I)
1988—Colts, 55-23 (I)
1989—Broncos, 14-3 (D)
1990—Broncos, 27-17 (I)
1993—Broncos, 35-13 (D)
(RS Pts.—Broncos 230, Colts 163)
*Franchise in Baltimore prior to 1984

DENVER vs. JACKSONVILLE
RS: Broncos lead series, 1-0
PS: Jaguars lead series, 1-0
1995—Broncos, 31-23 (D)
1996—*Jaguars, 30-27 (D)
(RS Pts.—Broncos 31, Jaguars 23)
(PS Pts.—Jaguars 30, Broncos 27)
*AFC Divisional Playoff

DENVER vs. *KANSAS CITY
RS: Chiefs lead series, 42-31
1960—Texans, 17-14 (D)
Texans, 34-7 (Dal)
1961—Texans, 19-12 (D)
Texans, 49-21 (Dal)
1962—Texans, 24-3 (D)
Texans, 17-10 (Dal)
1963—Chiefs, 59-7 (D)
Chiefs, 52-21 (KC)
1964—Broncos, 33-27 (D)
Chiefs, 49-39 (KC)
1965—Chiefs, 31-23 (D)
Chiefs, 45-35 (KC)
1966—Chiefs, 37-10 (KC)
Chiefs, 56-10 (D)
1967—Chiefs, 52-9 (KC)
Chiefs, 38-24 (D)
1968—Chiefs, 34-2 (KC)
Chiefs, 30-7 (D)
1969—Chiefs, 26-13 (D)
Chiefs, 31-17 (KC)
1970—Broncos, 26-13 (D)
Chiefs, 16-0 (KC)
1971—Chiefs, 16-3 (D)
Chiefs, 28-10 (KC)
1972—Chiefs, 45-24 (D)
Chiefs, 24-21 (KC)
1973—Chiefs, 16-14 (KC)
Broncos, 14-10 (D)
1974—Broncos, 17-14 (KC)
Chiefs, 42-34 (D)
1975—Broncos, 37-33 (D)
Chiefs, 26-13 (KC)
1976—Broncos, 35-26 (KC)
Broncos, 17-16 (D)
1977—Broncos, 23-7 (D)
Broncos, 14-7 (KC)
1978—Broncos, 23-17 (KC) OT
Broncos, 24-3 (D)
1979—Broncos, 24-10 (KC)
Broncos, 20-3 (D)
1980—Chiefs, 23-17 (D)
Chiefs, 31-14 (KC)
1981—Chiefs, 28-14 (KC)
Broncos, 16-13 (D)
1982—Chiefs, 37-16 (D)
1983—Broncos, 27-24 (D)
Chiefs, 48-17 (KC)
1984—Broncos, 21-0 (D)
Chiefs, 16-13 (KC)
1985—Broncos, 30-10 (KC)
Broncos, 14-13 (D)
1986—Broncos, 38-17 (D)
Chiefs, 37-10 (KC)
1987—Broncos, 26-17 (KC)
Broncos, 20-17 (D)
1988—Chiefs, 20-13 (KC)
Broncos, 17-11 (D)
1989—Broncos, 34-20 (D)
Broncos, 16-13 (KC)
1990—Broncos, 24-23 (D)
Chiefs, 31-20 (KC)
1991—Broncos, 19-16 (D)

Broncos, 24-20 (KC)
1992—Broncos, 20-19 (D)
Chiefs, 42-20 (KC)
1993—Chiefs, 15-7 (KC)
Broncos, 27-21 (D)
1994—Chiefs, 31-28 (D)
Broncos, 20-17 (KC) OT
1995—Chiefs, 21-7 (D)
Chiefs, 20-17 (KC)
1996—Chiefs, 17-14 (KC)
Broncos, 34-7 (D)
(RS Pts.—Chiefs 1,794, Broncos 1,364)
*Franchise in Dallas prior to 1963 and
known as Texans

DENVER vs. MIAMI
RS: Dolphins lead series, 5-2-1
1966—Dolphins, 24-7 (M)
Broncos, 17-7 (D)
1967—Dolphins, 35-21 (M)
1968—Broncos, 21-14 (D)
1969—Dolphins, 27-24 (M)
1971—Tie, 10-10 (M)
1975—Dolphins, 14-13 (M)
1985—Dolphins, 30-26 (D)
(RS Pts.—Dolphins 161, Broncos 139)

DENVER vs. MINNESOTA
RS: Vikings lead series, 5-4
1972—Vikings, 23-20 (D)
1978—Vikings, 12-9 (M) OT
1981—Broncos, 19-17 (D)
1984—Broncos, 42-21 (D)
1987—Vikings, 34-27 (M)
1990—Vikings, 27-22 (M)
1991—Broncos, 13-6 (M)
1993—Vikings, 26-23 (D)
1996—Broncos, 21-17 (M)
(RS Pts.—Broncos 196, Vikings 183)

DENVER vs. *NEW ENGLAND
RS: Broncos lead series, 18-12
PS: Broncos lead series, 1-0
1960—Broncos, 13-10 (B)
Broncos, 31-24 (D)
1961—Patriots, 45-17 (B)
Patriots, 28-24 (D)
1962—Patriots, 41-16 (B)
Patriots, 33-29 (D)
1963—Broncos, 14-10 (D)
Patriots, 40-21 (B)
1964—Patriots, 39-10 (D)
Patriots, 12-7 (B)
1965—Broncos, 27-10 (D)
Patriots, 28-20 (D)
1966—Patriots, 24-10 (D)
Broncos, 17-10 (B)
1967—Broncos, 26-21 (D)
1968—Patriots, 20-17 (D)
Broncos, 35-14 (B)
1969—Broncos, 35-7 (D)
1972—Broncos, 45-21 (D)
1976—Patriots, 38-14 (NE)
1979—Broncos, 45-10 (D)
1980—Patriots, 23-14 (NE)
1984—Broncos, 26-19 (D)
1986—Broncos, 27-20 (D)
**Broncos, 22-17 (D)
1987—Broncos, 31-20 (D)
1988—Broncos, 21-10 (D)
1991—Broncos, 9-6 (NE)
Broncos, 20-3 (D)
1995—Broncos, 37-3 (NE)
1996—Broncos, 34-8 (NE)
(RS Pts.—Broncos 692, Patriots 597)
(PS Pts.—Broncos 22, Patriots 17)
*Franchise in Boston prior to 1971
**AFC Divisional Playoff

DENVER vs. NEW ORLEANS
RS: Broncos lead series, 4-2
1970—Broncos, 31-6 (NO)
1974—Broncos, 33-17 (D)
1979—Broncos, 10-3 (D)
1985—Broncos, 34-23 (D)
1988—Saints, 42-0 (NO)
1994—Saints, 30-28 (D)

(RS Pts.—Broncos 136, Saints 121)
DENVER vs. N.Y. GIANTS
RS: Series tied, 3-3
PS: Giants lead series, 1-0
1972—Giants, 29-17 (NY)
1976—Broncos, 14-13 (D)
1980—Broncos, 14-9 (NY)
1986—Broncos, 19-16 (NY)
*Giants, 39-20 (Pasadena)
1989—Giants, 14-7 (D)
1992—Broncos, 27-13 (D)
(RS Pts.—Giants 97, Broncos 95)
(PS Pts.—Giants 39, Broncos 20)
*Super Bowl XXI

DENVER vs. *N.Y. JETS
RS: Broncos lead series, 13-12-1
1960—Titans, 28-24 (NY)
Titans, 30-27 (D)
1961—Titans, 35-28 (NY)
Broncos, 27-10 (D)
1962—Broncos, 32-10 (NY)
Titans, 46-45 (D)
1963—Tie, 35-35 (NY)
Jets, 14-9 (D)
1964—Jets, 30-6 (NY)
Broncos, 20-16 (D)
1965—Broncos, 16-13 (D)
Jets, 45-10 (NY)
1966—Jets, 16-7 (D)
1967—Jets, 38-24 (D)
Broncos, 33-24 (NY)
1968—Broncos, 21-13 (NY)
1969—Broncos, 21-19 (D)
1973—Broncos, 40-28 (NY)
1976—Broncos, 46-3 (D)
1978—Jets, 31-28 (D)
1980—Broncos, 31-24 (D)
1986—Jets, 22-10 (NY)
1992—Broncos, 27-16 (D)
1993—Broncos, 26-20 (NY)
1994—Jets, 25-22 (NY) OT
1996—Broncos, 31-6 (D)
(RS Pts.—Broncos 646, Jets 597)
*Jets known as Titans prior to 1963

DENVER vs. *OAKLAND
RS: Raiders lead series, 48-23-2
PS: Series tied, 1-1
1960—Broncos, 31-14 (D)
Raiders, 48-10 (O)
1961—Raiders, 33-19 (O)
Broncos, 27-24 (O)
1962—Broncos, 44-7 (D)
Broncos, 23-6 (O)
1963—Raiders, 26-10 (D)
Raiders, 35-31 (O)
1964—Raiders, 40-7 (O)
Tie, 20-20 (D)
1965—Raiders, 28-20 (D)
Raiders, 24-13 (O)
1966—Raiders, 17-3 (D)
Raiders, 28-10 (O)
1967—Raiders, 51-0 (O)
Raiders, 21-17 (D)
1968—Raiders, 43-7 (D)
Raiders, 33-27 (O)
1969—Raiders, 24-14 (D)
Raiders, 41-10 (O)
1970—Raiders, 35-23 (D)
Raiders, 24-19 (O)
1971—Raiders, 27-16 (D)
Raiders, 21-13 (O)
1972—Broncos, 30-23 (O)
Raiders, 37-20 (O)
1973—Tie, 23-23 (D)
Raiders, 21-17 (O)
1974—Raiders, 28-17 (D)
Broncos, 20-17 (O)
1975—Raiders, 42-17 (D)
Raiders, 17-10 (O)
1976—Raiders, 17-10 (D)
Raiders, 19-6 (O)
1977—Broncos, 30-7 (O)
Raiders, 24-14 (D)

**Broncos, 20-17 (D)
1978—Broncos, 14-6 (D)
Broncos, 21-6 (O)
1979—Raiders, 27-3 (O)
Raiders, 14-10 (D)
1980—Raiders, 9-3 (O)
Raiders, 24-21 (D)
1981—Broncos, 9-7 (D)
Broncos, 17-0 (O)
1982—Raiders, 27-10 (LA)
1983—Raiders, 22-7 (D)
Raiders, 22-20 (LA)
1984—Broncos, 16-13 (D)
Broncos, 22-19 (LA) OT
1985—Raiders, 31-28 (LA) OT
Raiders, 17-14 (D) OT
1986—Broncos, 38-36 (D)
Raiders, 21-10 (LA)
1987—Broncos, 30-14 (D)
Broncos, 23-17 (LA)
1988—Raiders, 30-27 (D) OT
Raiders, 21-20 (LA)
1989—Broncos, 31-21 (D)
Raiders, 16-13 (LA) OT
1990—Raiders, 14-9 (LA)
Raiders, 23-20 (D)
1991—Raiders, 16-13 (LA)
Raiders, 17-16 (D)
1992—Broncos, 17-13 (D)
Raiders, 24-0 (LA)
1993—Raiders, 23-20 (D)
Raiders, 33-30 (LA) OT
***Raiders, 42-24 (LA)
1994—Raiders, 48-16 (D)
Raiders, 23-13 (LA)
1995—Broncos, 27-0 (D)
Broncos, 31-28 (O)
1996—Broncos, 22-21 (O)
Broncos, 24-19 (D)
(RS Pts.—Raiders 1,656, Broncos 1,304)
(PS Pts.—Raiders 59, Broncos 44)
*Franchise in Los Angeles from
1982-1994
**AFC Championship
***AFC First-Round Playoff

DENVER vs. PHILADELPHIA
RS: Eagles lead series, 6-2
1971—Eagles, 17-16 (P)
1975—Broncos, 25-10 (D)
1980—Eagles, 27-6 (P)
1983—Eagles, 13-10 (D)
1986—Broncos, 33-7 (P)
1989—Eagles, 28-24 (D)
1992—Eagles, 30-0 (P)
1995—Eagles, 31-13 (P)
(RS Pts.—Eagles 163, Broncos 127)

DENVER vs. PITTSBURGH
RS: Broncos lead series, 10-5-1
PS: Series tied, 2-2
1970—Broncos, 16-13 (D)
1971—Broncos, 22-10 (P)
1973—Broncos, 23-13 (P)
1974—Tie, 35-35 (D) OT
1975—Steelers, 20-9 (P)
1977—Broncos, 21-7 (D)
*Broncos, 34-21 (D)
1978—Steelers, 21-17 (P)
*Steelers, 33-10 (P)
1979—Steelers, 42-7 (P)
1983—Broncos, 14-10 (D)
1984—*Steelers, 24-17 (D)
1985—Broncos, 31-23 (P)
1986—Broncos, 21-10 (P)
1988—Steelers, 39-21 (P)
1989—Broncos, 34-7 (D)
*Broncos, 24-23 (D)
1990—Steelers, 34-17 (D)
1991—Broncos, 20-13 (D)
1993—Broncos, 37-13 (D)
(RS Pts.—Broncos 345, Steelers 310)
(PS Pts.—Steelers 101, Broncos 85)
*AFC Divisional Playoff

DENVER vs. *ST. LOUIS

RS: Rams lead series, 4-3
1972—Broncos, 16-10 (LA)
1974—Rams, 17-10 (D)
1979—Rams, 13-9 (D)
1982—Broncos, 27-24 (LA)
1985—Rams, 20-16 (LA)
1988—Broncos, 35-24 (D)
1994—Rams, 27-21 (LA)
(RS Pts.—Rams 135, Broncos 134)
Franchise in Los Angeles prior to 1995

DENVER vs. *SAN DIEGO
RS: Broncos lead series, 38-35-1
1960—Chargers, 23-19 (D)
    Chargers, 41-33 (LA)
1961—Chargers, 37-0 (SD)
    Chargers, 19-16 (D)
1962—Broncos, 30-21 (D)
    Broncos, 23-20 (SD)
1963—Broncos, 50-34 (D)
    Chargers, 58-20 (SD)
1964—Chargers, 42-14 (SD)
    Chargers, 31-20 (D)
1965—Chargers, 34-31 (SD)
    Chargers, 33-21 (D)
1966—Chargers, 24-17 (SD)
    Broncos, 20-17 (D)
1967—Chargers, 38-21 (D)
    Chargers, 24-20 (SD)
1968—Chargers, 55-24 (SD)
    Chargers, 47-23 (SD)
1969—Broncos, 13-0 (D)
    Chargers, 45-24 (SD)
1970—Chargers, 24-21 (SD)
    Tie, 17-17 (D)
1971—Broncos, 20-16 (D)
    Chargers, 45-17 (SD)
1972—Chargers, 37-14 (SD)
    Broncos, 38-13 (D)
1973—Broncos, 30-19 (D)
    Broncos, 42-28 (SD)
1974—Broncos, 27-7 (D)
    Chargers, 17-0 (SD)
1975—Broncos, 27-17 (SD)
    Broncos, 13-10 (D) OT
1976—Broncos, 26-0 (D)
    Broncos, 17-0 (SD)
1977—Broncos, 17-14 (SD)
    Broncos, 17-9 (D)
1978—Broncos, 27-14 (D)
    Chargers, 23-0 (SD)
1979—Broncos, 7-0 (D)
    Chargers, 17-7 (SD)
1980—Chargers, 30-13 (D)
    Broncos, 20-13 (SD)
1981—Broncos, 42-24 (D)
    Chargers, 34-17 (SD)
1982—Chargers, 23-3 (D)
    Chargers, 30-20 (SD)
1983—Broncos, 14-6 (D)
    Chargers, 31-7 (SD)
1984—Broncos, 16-13 (SD)
    Broncos, 16-13 (D)
1985—Chargers, 30-10 (SD)
    Broncos, 30-24 (D) OT
1986—Broncos, 31-14 (SD)
    Chargers, 9-3 (D)
1987—Broncos, 31-17 (SD)
    Broncos, 24-0 (D)
1988—Broncos, 34-3 (D)
    Broncos, 12-0 (SD)
1989—Broncos, 16-10 (D)
    Chargers, 19-16 (SD)
1990—Chargers, 19-7 (SD)
    Broncos, 20-10 (D)
1991—Broncos, 27-19 (D)
    Broncos, 17-14 (SD)
1992—Broncos, 21-13 (D)
    Chargers, 24-21 (SD)
1993—Broncos, 34-17 (D)
    Chargers, 13-10 (SD)
1994—Chargers, 37-34 (D)
    Broncos, 20-15 (SD)
1995—Chargers, 17-6 (SD)

Broncos, 30-27 (D)
1996—Broncos, 28-17 (D)
    Chargers, 16-10 (SD)
(RS Pts.—Chargers 1,571, Broncos 1,483)
Franchise in Los Angeles prior to 1961

DENVER vs. SAN FRANCISCO
RS: Broncos lead series, 4-3
PS: 49ers lead series, 1-0
1970—49ers, 19-14 (SF)
1973—49ers, 36-34 (D)
1979—Broncos, 38-28 (SF)
1982—Broncos, 24-21 (D)
1985—Broncos, 17-16 (D)
1988—Broncos, 16-13 (SF) OT
1989—*49ers, 55-10 (New Orleans)
1994—49ers, 42-19 (SF)
(RS Pts.—49ers 175, Broncos 162)
(PS Pts.—49ers 55, Broncos 10)
Super Bowl XXIV

DENVER vs. SEATTLE
RS: Broncos lead series, 24-15
PS: Seahawks lead series, 1-0
1977—Broncos, 24-13 (S)
1978—Broncos, 28-7 (D)
    Broncos, 20-17 (S) OT
1979—Broncos, 37-34 (D)
    Seahawks, 28-23 (S)
1980—Broncos, 36-20 (D)
    Broncos, 25-17 (S)
1981—Seahawks, 13-10 (S)
    Broncos, 23-13 (D)
1982—Seahawks, 17-10 (D)
    Seahawks, 13-11 (S)
1983—Seahawks, 27-19 (S)
    Broncos, 38-27 (D)
    *Seahawks, 31-7 (S)
1984—Seahawks, 27-24 (D)
    Broncos, 31-14 (S)
1985—Broncos, 13-10 (D) OT
    Broncos, 27-24 (S)
1986—Broncos, 20-13 (D)
    Seahawks, 41-16 (S)
1987—Broncos, 40-17 (D)
    Seahawks, 28-21 (S)
1988—Seahawks, 21-14 (D)
    Seahawks, 42-14 (S)
1989—Broncos, 24-21 (S) OT
    Broncos, 41-14 (D)
1990—Broncos, 34-31 (D) OT
    Seahawks, 17-12 (S)
1991—Broncos, 16-10 (D)
    Seahawks, 13-10 (S)
1992—Seahawks, 16-13 (S) OT
    Broncos, 10-6 (D)
1993—Broncos, 28-17 (D)
    Broncos, 17-9 (S)
1994—Broncos, 16-9 (S)
    Broncos, 17-10 (D)
1995—Seahawks, 27-10 (S)
    Seahawks, 31-27 (D)
1996—Broncos, 30-20 (S)
    Broncos, 34-7 (D)
(RS Pts.—Broncos 863, Seahawks 741)
(PS Pts.—Seahawks 31, Broncos 7)
AFC First-Round Playoff

DENVER vs. TAMPA BAY
RS: Broncos lead series, 3-1
1976—Broncos, 48-13 (D)
1981—Broncos, 24-7 (TB)
1993—Buccaneers, 17-10 (D)
1996—Broncos, 27-23 (D)
(RS Pts.—Broncos 109, Buccaneers 60)

DENVER vs. *TENNESSEE
RS: Oilers lead series, 20-11-1
PS: Broncos lead series, 2-1
1960—Oilers, 45-25 (D)
    Oilers, 20-10 (H)
1961—Oilers, 55-14 (D)
    Oilers, 45-14 (H)
1962—Broncos, 20-10 (D)
    Oilers, 34-17 (H)
1963—Oilers, 20-14 (H)
    Oilers, 33-24 (D)

1964—Oilers, 38-17 (D)
    Oilers, 34-15 (H)
1965—Broncos, 28-17 (D)
    Broncos, 31-21 (H)
1966—Oilers, 45-7 (H)
    Broncos, 40-38 (D)
1967—Oilers, 10-6 (H)
    Oilers, 20-18 (D)
1968—Oilers, 38-17 (H)
1969—Oilers, 24-21 (H)
    Tie, 20-20 (D)
1970—Oilers, 31-21 (H)
1972—Broncos, 30-17 (D)
1973—Oilers, 48-20 (H)
1974—Broncos, 37-14 (D)
1976—Oilers, 17-3 (H)
1977—Broncos, 24-14 (H)
1979—**Oilers, 13-7 (H)
1980—Oilers, 20-16 (D)
1983—Broncos, 26-14 (H)
1985—Broncos, 31-20 (D)
1987—Oilers, 40-10 (D)
    ***Broncos, 34-10 (D)
1991—Oilers, 42-14 (H)
    ***Broncos, 26-24 (D)
1992—Broncos, 27-21 (D)
1995—Oilers, 42-33 (H)
(RS Pts.—Oilers 879, Broncos 678)
(PS Pts.—Broncos 67, Oilers 47)
Franchise in Houston prior to 1997
**AFC First-Round Playoff*
***AFC Divisional Playoff*

DENVER vs. WASHINGTON
RS: Broncos lead series, 4-3
PS: Redskins lead series, 1-0
1970—Redskins, 19-3 (D)
1974—Redskins, 30-3 (W)
1980—Broncos, 20-17 (D)
1986—Broncos, 31-30 (D)
1987—*Redskins, 42-10 (San Diego)
1989—Broncos, 14-10 (W)
1992—Redskins, 34-3 (W)
1995—Broncos, 38-31 (D)
(RS Pts.—Redskins 171, Broncos 112)
(PS Pts.—Redskins 42, Broncos 10)
Super Bowl XXII

DETROIT vs. ARIZONA
RS: Lions lead series, 27-17-5;
See Arizona vs. Detroit
DETROIT vs. ATLANTA
RS: Lions lead series, 19-6;
See Atlanta vs. Detroit
DETROIT vs. BUFFALO
RS: Lions lead series, 3-1-1;
See Buffalo vs. Detroit
DETROIT vs. CHICAGO
RS: Bears lead series, 76-53-5;
See Chicago vs. Detroit
DETROIT vs. CINCINNATI
RS: Series tied, 3-3;
See Cincinnati vs. Detroit
DETROIT vs. CLEVELAND
RS: Lions lead series, 12-3
PS: Lions lead series, 3-1;
See Cleveland vs. Detroit
DETROIT vs. DALLAS
RS: Cowboys lead series, 7-6
PS: Series tied, 1-1;
See Dallas vs. Detroit
DETROIT vs. DENVER
RS: Broncos lead series, 4-3;
See Denver vs. Detroit
*DETROIT vs. GREEN BAY
RS: Packers lead series, 68-58-7
PS: Packers lead series, 2-0
1930—Packers, 47-13 (GB)
    Tie, 6-6 (P)
1932—Packers, 15-10 (GB)
    Spartans, 19-0 (P)
1933—Packers, 17-0 (GB)
    Spartans, 7-0 (P)
1934—Lions, 3-0 (GB)

Packers, 3-0 (D)
1935—Packers, 13-9 (Mil)
    Packers, 31-7 (GB)
    Lions, 20-10 (D)
1936—Packers, 20-18 (GB)
    Packers, 26-17 (D)
1937—Packers, 26-6 (GB)
    Packers, 14-13 (D)
1938—Lions, 17-7 (GB)
    Packers, 28-7 (D)
1939—Packers, 26-7 (GB)
    Packers, 12-7 (D)
1940—Lions, 23-14 (GB)
    Packers, 50-7 (D)
1941—Packers, 23-0 (GB)
    Packers, 24-7 (D)
1942—Packers, 38-7 (Mil)
    Packers, 28-7 (D)
1943—Packers, 35-14 (GB)
    Packers, 27-6 (D)
1944—Packers, 27-6 (Mil)
    Packers, 14-0 (D)
1945—Packers, 57-21 (Mil)
    Lions, 14-3 (D)
1946—Packers, 10-7 (Mil)
    Packers, 9-0 (D)
1947—Packers, 34-17 (GB)
    Packers, 35-14 (D)
1948—Packers, 33-21 (GB)
    Lions, 24-20 (D)
1949—Packers, 16-14 (Mil)
    Lions, 21-7 (D)
1950—Lions, 45-7 (GB)
    Lions, 24-21 (D)
1951—Lions, 24-17 (GB)
    Lions, 52-35 (D)
1952—Lions, 52-17 (GB)
    Lions, 48-24 (D)
1953—Lions, 14-7 (GB)
    Lions, 34-15 (D)
1954—Lions, 21-17 (GB)
    Lions, 28-24 (D)
1955—Packers, 20-17 (GB)
    Lions, 24-10 (D)
1956—Lions, 20-16 (GB)
    Packers, 24-20 (D)
1957—Lions, 24-14 (GB)
    Lions, 18-6 (D)
1958—Tie, 13-13 (GB)
    Lions, 24-14 (D)
1959—Packers, 28-10 (GB)
    Packers, 24-17 (D)
1960—Packers, 28-9 (GB)
    Lions, 23-10 (D)
1961—Lions, 17-13 (Mil)
    Packers, 17-9 (D)
1962—Packers, 9-7 (GB)
    Lions, 26-14 (D)
1963—Packers, 31-10 (Mil)
    Tie, 13-13 (D)
1964—Packers, 14-10 (GB)
    Packers, 30-7 (GB)
1965—Packers, 31-21 (D)
    Lions, 12-7 (GB)
1966—Packers, 23-14 (GB)
    Packers, 31-7 (D)
1967—Tie, 17-17 (GB)
    Packers, 27-17 (D)
1968—Lions, 23-17 (GB)
    Tie, 14-14 (D)
1969—Packers, 28-17 (GB)
    Lions, 16-10 (GB)
1970—Lions, 40-0 (GB)
    Lions, 20-0 (D)
1971—Lions, 31-28 (D)
    Tie, 14-14 (Mil)
1972—Packers, 24-23 (D)
    Packers, 33-7 (GB)
1973—Tie, 13-13 (D)
    Lions, 34-0 (D)
1974—Packers, 21-19 (Mil)
    Lions, 19-17 (D)
1975—Lions, 30-16 (Mil)

Lions, 13-10 (D)
1976—Packers, 24-14 (GB)
Lions, 27-6 (D)
1977—Lions, 10-6 (D)
Packers, 10-9 (GB)
1978—Packers, 13-7 (D)
Packers, 35-14 (Mil)
1979—Packers, 24-16 (Mil)
Packers, 18-13 (D)
1980—Lions, 29-7 (Mil)
Lions, 24-3 (D)
1981—Lions, 31-27 (D)
Packers, 31-17 (GB)
1982—Lions, 30-10 (GB)
Lions, 27-24 (D)
1983—Lions, 38-14 (D)
Lions, 23-20 (Mil) OT
1984—Packers, 41-9 (GB)
Lions, 31-28 (D)
1985—Packers, 43-10 (GB)
Packers, 26-23 (D)
1986—Lions, 21-14 (GB)
Packers, 44-40 (D)
1987—Lions, 19-16 (GB) OT
Packers, 34-33 (D)
1988—Lions, 19-9 (Mil)
Lions, 30-14 (D)
1989—Packers, 23-20 (Mil) OT
Lions, 31-22 (D)
1990—Packers, 24-21 (D)
Lions, 24-17 (GB)
1991—Lions, 23-14 (D)
Lions, 21-17 (GB)
1992—Packers, 27-13 (D)
Packers, 38-10 (Mil)
1993—Packers, 26-17 (Mil)
Lions, 30-20 (D)
**Packers, 28-24 (D)
1994—Packers, 38-30 (Mil)
Lions, 34-31 (D)
**Packers, 16-12 (GB)
1995—Packers, 30-21 (GB)
Lions, 24-16 (D)
1996—Packers, 28-18 (GB)
Packers, 31-3 (D)
(RS Pts.—Packers 2,661, Lions 2,401)
(PS Pts.—Packers 44, Lions 36)
*Franchise in Portsmouth prior to 1934
and known as the Spartans
**NFC First-Round Playoff

DETROIT vs. *INDIANAPOLIS
RS: Series tied, 17-17-2
1953—Lions, 27-17 (B)
Lions, 17-7 (D)
1954—Lions, 35-0 (D)
Lions, 27-3 (B)
1955—Colts, 28-13 (B)
Lions, 24-14 (D)
1956—Lions, 31-14 (B)
Lions, 27-3 (D)
1957—Colts, 34-14 (B)
Lions, 31-27 (D)
1958—Colts, 28-15 (B)
Colts, 40-14 (D)
1959—Colts, 21-9 (B)
Colts, 31-24 (D)
1960—Lions, 30-17 (D)
Lions, 20-15 (B)
1961—Lions, 16-15 (B)
Colts, 17-14 (D)
1962—Lions, 29-20 (B)
Lions, 21-14 (D)
1963—Colts, 25-21 (D)
Colts, 24-21 (B)
1964—Colts, 34-0 (D)
Lions, 31-14 (B)
1965—Colts, 31-7 (B)
Tie, 24-24 (D)
1966—Colts, 45-14 (B)
Lions, 20-14 (D)
1967—Colts, 41-7 (B)
1968—Colts, 27-10 (D)
1969—Tie, 17-17 (B)

1973—Colts, 29-27 (D)
1977—Lions, 13-10 (B)
1980—Colts, 10-9 (D)
1985—Colts, 14-6 (I)
1991—Lions, 33-24 (I)
(RS Pts.—Colts 748, Lions 698)
*Franchise in Baltimore prior to 1984
DETROIT vs. JACKSONVILLE
RS: Lions lead series, 1-0
1995—Lions, 44-0 (D)
(RS Pts.—Lions 44, Jaguars 0)
DETROIT vs. KANSAS CITY
RS: Chiefs lead series, 5-3
1971—Lions, 32-21 (D)
1975—Chiefs, 24-21 (KC) OT
1980—Chiefs, 20-17 (KC)
1981—Lions, 27-10 (D)
1987—Chiefs, 27-20 (D)
1988—Lions, 7-6 (KC)
1990—Chiefs, 43-24 (KC)
1996—Chiefs, 28-24 (D)
(RS Pts.—Chiefs 179, Lions 172)
DETROIT vs. MIAMI
RS: Dolphins lead series, 3-2
1973—Dolphins, 34-7 (M)
1979—Dolphins, 28-10 (D)
1985—Lions, 31-21 (D)
1991—Lions, 17-13 (D)
1994—Dolphins, 27-20 (M)
(RS Pts.—Dolphins 123, Lions 85)
DETROIT vs. MINNESOTA
RS: Vikings lead series, 44-25-2
1961—Lions, 37-10 (M)
Lions, 13-7 (D)
1962—Lions, 17-6 (M)
Lions, 37-23 (D)
1963—Lions, 28-10 (D)
Vikings, 34-31 (M)
1964—Lions, 24-20 (M)
Tie, 23-23 (D)
1965—Lions, 31-29 (M)
Vikings, 29-7 (D)
1966—Lions, 32-31 (M)
Vikings, 28-16 (D)
1967—Tie, 10-10 (M)
Lions, 14-3 (D)
1968—Vikings, 24-10 (M)
Vikings, 13-6 (D)
1969—Vikings, 24-10 (M)
Vikings, 27-0 (D)
1970—Vikings, 30-17 (D)
Vikings, 24-20 (M)
1971—Vikings, 16-13 (D)
Vikings, 29-10 (M)
1972—Vikings, 34-10 (D)
Vikings, 16-14 (M)
1973—Vikings, 23-9 (D)
Vikings, 28-7 (M)
1974—Vikings, 7-6 (D)
Lions, 20-16 (M)
1975—Vikings, 25-19 (M)
Lions, 17-10 (D)
1976—Vikings, 10-9 (D)
Vikings, 31-23 (M)
1977—Vikings, 14-7 (M)
Vikings, 30-21 (D)
1978—Vikings, 17-7 (M)
Lions, 45-14 (D)
1979—Vikings, 13-10 (D)
Vikings, 14-7 (M)
1980—Lions, 27-7 (D)
Vikings, 34-0 (M)
1981—Vikings, 26-24 (M)
Lions, 45-7 (D)
1982—Vikings, 34-31 (D)
1983—Vikings, 20-17 (M)
Lions, 13-2 (D)
1984—Vikings, 29-28 (D)
Lions, 16-14 (M)
1985—Vikings, 16-13 (M)
Lions, 41-21 (D)
1986—Lions, 13-10 (M)
Vikings, 24-10 (D)

1987—Vikings, 34-19 (M)
Vikings, 17-14 (D)
1988—Vikings, 44-17 (M)
Vikings, 23-0 (D)
1989—Vikings, 24-17 (M)
Vikings, 20-7 (D)
1990—Lions, 34-27 (M)
Vikings, 17-7 (D)
1991—Lions, 24-20 (D)
Lions, 34-14 (M)
1992—Lions, 31-17 (D)
Vikings, 31-14 (M)
1993—Lions, 30-27 (M)
Vikings, 13-0 (D)
1994—Vikings, 10-3 (M)
Lions, 41-19 (D)
1995—Vikings, 20-10 (M)
Lions, 44-38 (D)
1996—Vikings, 17-13 (M)
Vikings, 24-22 (D)
(RS Pts.—Vikings 1,455, Lions 1,296)
DETROIT vs. NEW ENGLAND
RS: Series tied, 3-3
1971—Lions, 34-7 (NE)
1976—Lions, 30-10 (D)
1979—Patriots, 24-17 (NE)
1985—Patriots, 23-6 (NE)
1993—Lions, 19-16 (NE) OT
1994—Patriots, 23-17 (D)
(RS Pts.—Lions 123, Patriots 103)
DETROIT vs. NEW ORLEANS
RS: Saints lead series, 7-6-1
1968—Tie, 20-20 (D)
1970—Saints, 19-17 (NO)
1972—Lions, 27-14 (D)
1973—Saints, 20-13 (NO)
1974—Lions, 19-14 (D)
1976—Saints, 17-16 (NO)
1977—Lions, 23-19 (D)
1979—Saints, 17-7 (NO)
1980—Lions, 24-13 (D)
1988—Saints, 22-14 (D)
1989—Lions, 21-14 (D)
1990—Lions, 27-10 (NO)
1992—Saints, 13-7 (D)
1993—Saints, 14-3 (NO)
(RS Pts.—Lions 238, Saints 226)
*DETROIT vs. N.Y. GIANTS
RS: Lions lead series, 18-16-1
PS: Lions lead series, 1-0
1930—Giants, 19-6 (P)
1931—Spartans, 14-6 (P)
Giants, 14-0 (NY)
1932—Spartans, 7-0 (P)
Spartans, 6-0 (NY)
1933—Spartans, 17-7 (P)
Giants, 13-10 (NY)
1934—Lions, 9-0 (D)
1935—**Lions, 26-7 (D)
1936—Giants, 14-7 (NY)
Lions, 38-0 (D)
1937—Lions, 17-0 (NY)
1939—Lions, 18-14 (D)
1941—Giants, 20-13 (NY)
1943—Tie, 0-0 (D)
1945—Giants, 35-14 (NY)
1947—Lions, 35-7 (D)
1949—Lions, 45-21 (NY)
1953—Lions, 27-16 (NY)
1955—Lions, 24-19 (D)
1958—Giants, 19-17 (D)
1962—Giants, 17-14 (NY)
1964—Lions, 26-3 (D)
1967—Lions, 30-7 (NY)
1969—Lions, 24-0 (D)
1972—Lions, 30-16 (D)
1974—Lions, 20-19 (D)
1976—Giants, 24-10 (NY)
1982—Giants, 13-6 (D)
1983—Lions, 15-9 (D)
1988—Giants, 30-10 (NY)
Giants, 13-10 (D) OT
1989—Giants, 24-14 (NY)

1990—Giants, 20-0 (NY)
1994—Lions, 28-25 (NY) OT
1996—Giants, 35-7 (D)
(RS Pts.—Lions 563, Giants 484)
(PS Pts.—Lions 26, Giants 7)
*Franchise in Portsmouth prior to 1934
and known as the Spartans
**NFL Championship
DETROIT vs. N.Y. JETS
RS: Lions lead series, 4-3
1972—Lions, 37-20 (D)
1979—Jets, 31-10 (NY)
1982—Jets, 28-13 (D)
1985—Lions, 31-20 (D)
1988—Jets, 17-10 (D)
1991—Lions, 34-20 (D)
1994—Lions, 18-7 (NY)
(RS Pts.—Lions 153, Jets 143)
DETROIT vs. *OAKLAND
RS: Raiders lead series, 6-2
1970—Lions, 28-14 (D)
1974—Raiders, 35-13 (O)
1978—Raiders, 29-17 (O)
1981—Lions, 16-0 (D)
1984—Raiders, 24-3 (D)
1987—Raiders, 27-7 (LA)
1990—Raiders, 38-31 (D)
1996—Raiders, 37-21 (O)
(RS Pts.—Raiders 204, Lions 136)
*Franchise in Los Angeles from
1982-1994
*DETROIT vs. PHILADELPHIA
RS: Lions lead series, 12-10-2
PS: Eagles lead series, 1-0
1933—Spartans, 25-0 (P)
1934—Lions, 10-0 (P)
1935—Lions, 35-0 (P)
1936—Lions, 23-0 (P)
1938—Eagles, 21-7 (D)
1940—Lions, 21-0 (P)
1941—Lions, 21-17 (D)
1945—Lions, 28-24 (D)
1948—Eagles, 45-21 (P)
1949—Eagles, 22-14 (D)
1951—Lions, 28-10 (P)
1954—Tie, 13-13 (D)
1957—Lions, 27-16 (P)
1960—Eagles, 28-10 (P)
1961—Eagles, 27-24 (D)
1965—Lions, 35-28 (P)
1968—Eagles, 12-0 (D)
1971—Eagles, 23-20 (D)
1974—Eagles, 28-17 (P)
1977—Lions, 17-13 (D)
1979—Eagles, 44-7 (P)
1984—Tie, 23-23 (D) OT
1986—Lions, 13-11 (P)
1995—**Eagles, 58-37 (P)
1996—Eagles, 24-17 (P)
(RS Pts.—Lions 456, Eagles 429)
(PS Pts.—Eagles 58, Lions 37)
*Franchise in Portsmouth prior to 1934
and known as the Spartans
**NFC First-Round Playoff
DETROIT vs. *PITTSBURGH
RS: Lions lead series, 13-12-1
1934—Lions, 40-7 (D)
1936—Lions, 28-3 (D)
1937—Lions, 7-3 (D)
1938—Lions, 16-7 (D)
1940—Pirates, 10-7 (D)
1942—Steelers, 35-7 (D)
1946—Lions, 17-7 (D)
1947—Steelers, 17-10 (P)
1948—Lions, 17-14 (D)
1949—Steelers, 14-7 (P)
1950—Lions, 10-7 (D)
1952—Lions, 31-6 (P)
1953—Lions, 38-21 (D)
1955—Lions, 31-28 (P)
1956—Lions, 45-7 (D)
1959—Tie, 10-10 (P)
1962—Lions, 45-7 (D)

1966—Steelers, 17-3 (P)
1967—Steelers, 24-14 (D)
1969—Steelers, 16-13 (P)
1973—Steelers, 24-10 (P)
1983—Lions, 45-3 (D)
1986—Steelers, 27-17 (P)
1989—Steelers, 23-3 (D)
1992—Steelers, 17-14 (P)
1995—Steelers, 23-20 (P)
(RS Pts.—Lions 505, Steelers 377)
*Steelers known as Pirates prior to 1941

DETROIT vs. *ST. LOUIS
RS: Rams lead series, 39-35-1
PS: Lions lead series, 1-0
1937—Lions, 28-0 (C)
    Lions, 27-7 (D)
1938—Rams, 21-17 (C)
    Lions, 6-0 (D)
1939—Lions, 15-7 (D)
    Rams, 14-3 (C)
1940—Lions, 6-0 (D)
    Rams, 24-0 (C)
1941—Lions, 17-7 (D)
    Lions, 14-0 (C)
1942—Rams, 14-0 (D)
    Rams, 27-7 (C)
1944—Rams, 20-17 (D)
    Lions, 26-14 (C)
1945—Rams, 28-21 (D)
1946—Rams, 35-14 (LA)
    Rams, 41-20 (D)
1947—Rams, 27-13 (D)
    Rams, 28-17 (LA)
1948—Rams, 44-7 (LA)
    Rams, 34-27 (D)
1949—Rams, 27-24 (LA)
    Rams, 21-10 (D)
1950—Rams, 30-28 (D)
    Rams, 65-24 (LA)
1951—Rams, 27-21 (D)
    Lions, 24-22 (LA)
1952—Lions, 17-14 (LA)
    Lions, 24-16 (D)
    **Lions, 31-21 (D)
1953—Rams, 31-19 (D)
    Rams, 37-24 (LA)
1954—Lions, 21-3 (D)
    Lions, 27-24 (LA)
1955—Rams, 17-10 (D)
    Rams, 24-13 (LA)
1956—Lions, 24-21 (D)
    Lions, 16-7 (LA)
1957—Lions, 10-7 (D)
    Rams, 35-17 (LA)
1958—Rams, 42-28 (D)
    Lions, 41-24 (LA)
1959—Lions, 17-7 (LA)
    Lions, 23-17 (D)
1960—Rams, 48-35 (LA)
    Lions, 12-10 (D)
1961—Lions, 14-13 (D)
    Lions, 28-10 (LA)
1962—Lions, 13-10 (D)
    Lions, 12-3 (LA)
1963—Lions, 23-2 (LA)
    Rams, 28-21 (D)
1964—Tie, 17-17 (LA)
    Lions, 37-17 (D)
1965—Lions, 20-0 (D)
    Lions, 31-7 (LA)
1966—Rams, 14-7 (D)
    Rams, 23-3 (LA)
1967—Rams, 31-7 (D)
1968—Rams, 10-7 (LA)
1969—Lions, 28-0 (D)
1970—Lions, 28-23 (LA)
1971—Rams, 21-13 (D)
1972—Lions, 34-17 (LA)
1974—Rams, 16-13 (LA)
1975—Rams, 20-0 (D)
1976—Rams, 20-17 (D)
1980—Lions, 41-20 (LA)
1981—Rams, 20-13 (LA)

1982—Lions, 19-14 (LA)
1983—Rams, 21-10 (LA)
1986—Rams, 14-10 (LA)
1987—Rams, 37-16 (D)
1988—Rams, 17-10 (LA)
1991—Lions, 21-10 (D)
1993—Lions, 16-13 (LA)
(RS Pts.—Rams 1,436, Lions 1,340)
(PS Pts.—Lions 31, Rams 21)
*Franchise in Los Angeles prior to 1995
and in Cleveland prior to 1946
**Conference Playoff

DETROIT vs. SAN DIEGO
RS: Series tied, 3-3
1972—Lions, 34-20 (D)
1977—Lions, 20-0 (D)
1978—Lions, 31-14 (D)
1981—Chargers, 28-23 (SD)
1984—Chargers, 27-24 (SD)
1996—Chargers, 27-21 (SD)
(RS Pts.—Lions 153, Chargers 116)

DETROIT vs. SAN FRANCISCO
RS: 49ers lead series, 28-26-1
PS: Series tied, 1-1
1950—Lions, 24-7 (D)
    49ers, 28-27 (SF)
1951—49ers, 20-10 (D)
    49ers, 21-17 (SF)
1952—49ers, 17-3 (SF)
    49ers, 28-0 (D)
1953—Lions, 24-21 (D)
    Lions, 14-10 (SF)
1954—49ers, 37-31 (D)
    Lions, 48-7 (D)
1955—49ers, 27-24 (D)
    49ers, 38-21 (SF)
1956—Lions, 20-17 (D)
    Lions, 17-13 (SF)
1957—49ers, 35-31 (SF)
    Lions, 31-10 (D)
    *Lions, 31-27 (SF)
1958—49ers, 24-21 (SF)
    Lions, 35-21 (D)
1959—49ers, 34-13 (D)
    49ers, 33-7 (SF)
1960—49ers, 14-10 (D)
    Lions, 24-0 (SF)
1961—49ers, 49-0 (D)
    Tie, 20-20 (SF)
1962—Lions, 45-24 (D)
    Lions, 38-24 (SF)
1963—Lions, 26-3 (D)
    Lions, 45-7 (SF)
1964—Lions, 26-17 (SF)
    Lions, 24-7 (D)
1965—49ers, 27-21 (D)
    49ers, 17-14 (SF)
1966—49ers, 27-24 (D)
    49ers, 41-14 (SF)
1967—Lions, 45-3 (SF)
1968—49ers, 14-7 (D)
1969—49ers, 26-14 (SF)
1970—Lions, 28-7 (D)
1971—49ers, 31-27 (SF)
1973—Lions, 30-20 (D)
1974—Lions, 17-13 (D)
1975—Lions, 28-17 (SF)
1977—49ers, 28-7 (SF)
1978—Lions, 33-14 (D)
1980—Lions, 17-13 (D)
1981—Lions, 24-17 (D)
1983—**49ers, 24-23 (SF)
1984—49ers, 30-27 (D)
1985—Lions, 23-21 (D)
1988—49ers, 20-13 (SF)
1991—49ers, 35-3 (SF)
1992—49ers, 24-6 (SF)
1993—49ers, 55-17 (D)
1994—49ers, 27-21 (D)
1995—Lions, 27-24 (D)
1996—49ers, 24-14 (SF)
(RS Pts.—Lions 1,189, 49ers 1,176)
(PS Pts.—Lions 54, 49ers 51)

*Conference Playoff
**NFC Divisional Playoff
DETROIT vs. SEATTLE
RS: Seahawks lead series, 4-3
1976—Lions, 41-14 (S)
1978—Seahawks, 28-16 (S)
1984—Seahawks, 38-17 (S)
1987—Seahawks, 37-14 (D)
1990—Seahawks, 30-10 (S)
1993—Lions, 30-10 (D)
1996—Lions, 17-16 (D)
(RS Pts.—Seahawks 173, Lions 145)

DETROIT vs. TAMPA BAY
RS: Lions lead series, 21-17
1977—Lions, 16-7 (D)
1978—Lions, 15-7 (TB)
    Lions, 34-23 (D)
1979—Buccaneers, 31-16 (TB)
    Buccaneers, 16-14 (D)
1980—Lions, 24-10 (TB)
    Lions, 27-14 (D)
1981—Buccaneers, 28-10 (TB)
    Buccaneers, 20-17 (D)
1982—Buccaneers, 23-21 (TB)
1983—Lions, 11-0 (TB)
    Lions, 23-20 (D)
1984—Buccaneers, 21-17 (TB)
    Lions, 13-7 (D) OT
1985—Lions, 30-9 (D)
    Buccaneers, 19-16 (TB) OT
1986—Buccaneers, 24-20 (D)
    Lions, 38-17 (TB)
1987—Buccaneers, 31-27 (D)
    Lions, 20-10 (TB)
1988—Buccaneers, 23-20 (D)
    Buccaneers, 21-10 (TB)
1989—Lions, 17-16 (TB)
    Lions, 33-7 (D)
1990—Buccaneers, 38-21 (D)
    Buccaneers, 23-20 (TB)
1991—Lions, 31-3 (D)
    Buccaneers, 30-21 (TB)
1992—Buccaneers, 27-23 (D)
    Lions, 38-7 (TB)
1993—Buccaneers, 27-10 (TB)
    Lions, 23-0 (D)
1994—Buccaneers, 24-14 (TB)
    Lions, 14-9 (D)
1995—Lions, 27-24 (D)
    Lions, 37-10 (TB)
1996—Lions, 21-6 (D)
    Lions, 27-0 (TB)
(RS Pts.—Lions 816, Buccaneers 632)

DETROIT vs. *TENNESSEE
RS: Oilers lead series, 4-3
1971—Lions, 31-7 (H)
1975—Oilers, 24-8 (H)
1983—Oilers, 27-17 (H)
1986—Lions, 24-13 (D)
1989—Oilers, 35-31 (H)
1992—Oilers, 24-21 (D)
1995—Lions, 24-17 (H)
(RS Pts.—Lions 156, Oilers 147)
*Franchise in Houston prior to 1997

***DETROIT vs. **WASHINGTON**
RS: Redskins lead series, 23-8
PS: Redskins lead series, 2-0
1932—Spartans, 10-0 (P)
1933—Spartans, 13-0 (B)
1934—Lions, 24-0 (D)
1935—Lions, 17-7 (B)
    Lions, 14-0 (D)
1938—Redskins, 7-5 (D)
1939—Redskins, 31-7 (W)
1940—Redskins, 20-14 (D)
1942—Redskins, 15-3 (D)
1943—Redskins, 42-20 (W)
1946—Redskins, 17-16 (W)
1947—Lions, 38-21 (D)
1948—Redskins, 46-21 (W)
1951—Lions, 35-17 (D)
1956—Redskins, 18-17 (W)
1965—Lions, 14-10 (D)

1968—Redskins, 14-3 (W)
1970—Redskins, 31-10 (W)
1973—Redskins, 20-0 (D)
1976—Redskins, 20-7 (W)
1978—Redskins, 21-19 (D)
1979—Redskins, 27-24 (W)
1981—Redskins, 33-31 (W)
1982—***Redskins, 31-7 (W)
1983—Redskins, 38-17 (W)
1984—Redskins, 28-14 (W)
1985—Redskins, 24-3 (W)
1987—Redskins, 20-13 (W)
1990—Redskins, 41-38 (D)
1991—Redskins, 45-0 (W)
    ****Redskins, 41-10 (W)
1992—Redskins, 13-10 (W)
1995—Redskins, 36-30 (W) OT
(RS Pts.—Redskins 662, Lions 487)
(PS Pts.—Redskins 72, Lions 17)
*Franchise in Portsmouth prior to 1934
and known as the Spartans.
**Franchise in Boston prior to 1937
***NFC First-Round Playoff
****NFC Championship

GREEN BAY vs. ARIZONA
RS: Packers lead series, 39-21-4
PS: Packers lead series, 1-0;
See Arizona vs. Green Bay
GREEN BAY vs. ATLANTA
RS: Packers lead series, 10-9
PS: Packers lead series, 1-0;
See Atlanta vs. Green Bay
GREEN BAY vs. BUFFALO
RS: Bills lead series, 5-1;
See Buffalo vs. Green Bay
GREEN BAY vs. CAROLINA
PS: Packers lead series, 1-0;
See Carolina vs. Green Bay
GREEN BAY vs. CHICAGO
RS: Bears lead series, 81-65-6
PS: Bears lead series, 1-0;
See Chicago vs. Green Bay
GREEN BAY vs. CINCINNATI
RS: Series tied, 4-4;
See Cincinnati vs. Green Bay
GREEN BAY vs. CLEVELAND
RS: Packers lead series, 8-6
PS: Packers lead series, 1-0;
See Cleveland vs. Green Bay
GREEN BAY vs. DALLAS
RS: Cowboys lead series, 9-8
PS: Cowboys lead series, 4-2;
See Dallas vs. Green Bay
GREEN BAY vs. DENVER
RS: Broncos lead series, 4-3-1;
See Denver vs. Green Bay
GREEN BAY vs. DETROIT
RS: Packers lead series, 68-58-7
PS: Packers lead series, 2-0;
See Detroit vs. Green Bay
GREEN BAY vs. *INDIANAPOLIS
RS: Series tied, 18-18-1
PS: Packers lead series, 1-0
1953—Packers, 37-14 (GB)
    Packers, 35-24 (B)
1954—Packers, 7-6 (B)
    Packers, 24-13 (Mil)
1955—Colts, 24-20 (Mil)
    Colts, 14-10 (B)
1956—Packers, 38-33 (Mil)
    Colts, 28-21 (B)
1957—Colts, 45-17 (Mil)
    Packers, 24-21 (B)
1958—Colts, 24-17 (Mil)
    Colts, 56-0 (B)
1959—Colts, 38-21 (B)
    Colts, 28-24 (Mil)
1960—Packers, 35-21 (GB)
    Colts, 38-24 (B)
1961—Packers, 45-7 (GB)
    Colts, 45-21 (B)
1962—Packers, 17-6 (B)

Packers, 17-13 (GB)
1963—Packers, 31-20 (GB)
Packers, 34-20 (B)
1964—Colts, 21-20 (GB)
Colts, 24-21 (B)
1965—Packers, 20-17 (Mil)
Packers, 42-27 (B)
**Packers, 13-10 (GB) OT
1966—Packers, 24-3 (Mil)
Packers, 14-10 (B)
1967—Colts, 13-10 (B)
1968—Colts, 16-3 (GB)
1969—Colts, 14-6 (B)
1970—Colts, 13-10 (Mil)
1974—Packers, 20-13 (B)
1982—Tie, 20-20 (B) OT
1985—Colts, 37-10 (I)
1988—Colts, 20-13 (GB)
1991—Packers, 14-10 (Mil)
(RS Pts.—Colts 796, Packers 766)
(PS Pts.—Packers 13, Colts 10)
*Franchise in Baltimore prior to 1984
**Conference Playoff

GREEN BAY vs. JACKSONVILLE
RS: Packers lead series, 1-0
1995—Packers, 24-14 (J)
(RS Pts.—Packers 24, Jaguars 14)

GREEN BAY vs. KANSAS CITY
RS: Chiefs lead series, 5-1-1
PS: Packers lead series, 1-0
1966—*Packers, 35-10 (Los Angeles)
1973—Tie, 10-10 (Mil)
1977—Chiefs, 20-10 (KC)
1987—Packers, 23-3 (KC)
1989—Chiefs, 21-3 (GB)
1990—Chiefs, 17-3 (GB)
1993—Chiefs, 23-16 (KC)
1996—Chiefs, 27-20 (KC)
(RS Pts.—Chiefs 121, Packers 85)
(PS Pts.—Packers 35, Chiefs 10)
*Super Bowl I

GREEN BAY vs. MIAMI
RS: Dolphins lead series, 8-0
1971—Dolphins, 27-6 (Mia)
1975—Dolphins, 31-7 (GB)
1979—Dolphins, 27-7 (Mia)
1985—Dolphins, 34-24 (GB)
1988—Dolphins, 24-17 (Mia)
1989—Dolphins, 23-20 (Mia)
1991—Dolphins, 16-13 (Mia)
1994—Dolphins, 24-14 (Mil)
(RS Pts.—Dolphins 206, Packers 108)

GREEN BAY vs. MINNESOTA
RS: Vikings lead series, 36-34-1
1961—Packers, 33-7 (Minn)
Packers, 28-10 (Mil)
1962—Packers, 34-7 (GB)
Packers, 48-21 (Minn)
1963—Packers, 37-28 (Mil)
Packers, 28-7 (GB)
1964—Vikings, 24-23 (GB)
Packers, 42-13 (Minn)
1965—Packers, 38-13 (Mil)
Packers, 24-19 (GB)
1966—Vikings, 20-17 (GB)
Packers, 28-16 (Minn)
1967—Vikings, 10-7 (Mil)
Packers, 30-27 (Minn)
1968—Vikings, 26-13 (Mil)
Vikings, 14-10 (Minn)
1969—Vikings, 19-7 (Minn)
Vikings, 9-7 (Mil)
1970—Packers, 13-10 (Mil)
Vikings, 10-3 (Minn)
1971—Vikings, 24-13 (GB)
Vikings, 3-0 (Minn)
1972—Vikings, 27-13 (GB)
Packers, 23-7 (Minn)
1973—Vikings, 11-3 (Minn)
Vikings, 31-7 (GB)
1974—Vikings, 32-17 (GB)
Packers, 19-7 (Minn)
1975—Vikings, 28-17 (GB)

Vikings, 24-3 (Minn)
1976—Vikings, 17-10 (Mil)
Vikings, 20-9 (Minn)
1977—Vikings, 19-7 (Minn)
Vikings, 13-6 (GB)
1978—Vikings, 21-7 (Minn)
Tie, 10-10 (GB) OT
1979—Vikings, 27-21 (Minn) OT
Packers, 19-7 (Mil)
1980—Packers, 16-3 (GB)
Packers, 25-13 (Minn)
1981—Vikings, 30-13 (Mil)
Packers, 35-23 (Minn)
1982—Packers, 26-7 (Mil)
1983—Vikings, 20-17 (GB) OT
Packers, 29-21 (Minn)
1984—Packers, 45-17 (Mil)
Packers, 38-14 (Minn)
1985—Packers, 20-17 (Mil)
Packers, 27-17 (Minn)
1986—Vikings, 42-7 (Minn)
Vikings, 32-6 (GB)
1987—Packers, 23-16 (Minn)
Packers, 16-10 (Mil)
1988—Packers, 34-14 (Minn)
Packers, 18-6 (GB)
1989—Vikings, 26-14 (Minn)
Packers, 20-19 (Mil)
1990—Packers, 24-10 (Mil)
Vikings, 23-7 (Minn)
1991—Vikings, 35-21 (GB)
Packers, 27-7 (Minn)
1992—Vikings, 23-20 (GB) OT
Vikings, 27-7 (Minn)
1993—Vikings, 15-13 (Minn)
Vikings, 21-17 (Mil)
1994—Packers, 16-10 (GB)
Vikings, 13-10 (M) OT
1995—Packers, 38-21 (GB)
Vikings, 27-24 (M)
1996—Vikings, 30-21 (M)
Packers, 38-10 (GB)
(RS Pts.—Packers 1,386, Vikings 1,257)

GREEN BAY vs. NEW ENGLAND
RS: Patriots lead series, 3-2
PS: Packers lead series, 1-0
1973—Patriots, 33-24 (NE)
1979—Packers, 27-14 (GB)
1985—Patriots, 26-20 (NE)
1988—Packers, 45-3 (Mil)
1994—Patriots, 17-16 (NE)
1996—*Packers, 35-21 (New Orleans)
(RS Pts.—Packers 132, Patriots 93)
(PS Pts.—Packers 35, Patriots 21)
*Super Bowl XXXI

GREEN BAY vs. NEW ORLEANS
RS: Packers lead series, 13-4
1968—Packers, 29-7 (Mil)
1971—Saints, 29-21 (Mil)
1972—Packers, 30-20 (NO)
1973—Packers, 30-10 (Mil)
1975—Saints, 20-19 (NO)
1976—Packers, 32-27 (Mil)
1977—Packers, 24-20 (NO)
1978—Packers, 28-17 (Mil)
1979—Packers, 28-19 (Mil)
1981—Packers, 35-7 (NO)
1984—Packers, 23-13 (NO)
1985—Packers, 38-14 (Mil)
1986—Saints, 24-10 (NO)
1987—Saints, 33-24 (NO)
1989—Packers, 35-34 (GB)
1993—Packers, 19-17 (NO)
1995—Packers, 34-23 (NO)
(RS Pts.—Packers 459, Saints 334)

GREEN BAY vs. N.Y. GIANTS
RS: Packers lead series, 22-20-2
PS: Packers lead series, 4-1
1928—Giants, 6-0 (GB)
Packers, 7-0 (NY)
1929—Packers, 20-6 (NY)
1930—Packers, 14-7 (GB)
Giants, 13-6 (NY)

1931—Packers, 27-7 (GB)
Packers, 14-10 (NY)
1932—Packers, 13-0 (GB)
Giants, 6-0 (NY)
1933—Giants, 10-7 (Mil)
Giants, 17-6 (NY)
1934—Packers, 20-6 (Mil)
Giants, 17-3 (NY)
1935—Packers, 16-7 (GB)
1936—Packers, 26-14 (NY)
1937—Giants, 10-0 (NY)
1938—Giants, 15-3 (NY)
*Giants, 23-17 (NY)
1939—*Packers, 27-0 (Mil)
1940—Giants, 7-3 (NY)
1942—Tie, 21-21 (NY)
1943—Packers, 35-21 (NY)
1944—Giants, 24-0 (NY)
*Packers, 14-7 (NY)
1945—Packers, 23-14 (NY)
1947—Tie, 24-24 (NY)
1948—Giants, 49-3 (Mil)
1949—Giants, 30-10 (GB)
1952—Packers, 17-3 (NY)
1957—Giants, 31-17 (GB)
1959—Giants, 20-3 (NY)
1961—Packers, 20-17 (Mil)
*Packers, 37-0 (GB)
1962—*Packers, 16-7 (NY)
1967—Packers, 48-21 (NY)
1969—Packers, 20-10 (Mil)
1971—Giants, 42-40 (GB)
1973—Packers, 16-14 (New Haven)
1975—Packers, 40-14 (Mil)
1980—Giants, 27-21 (NY)
1981—Packers, 27-14 (NY)
Packers, 26-24 (Mil)
1982—Packers, 27-19 (NY)
1983—Giants, 27-3 (NY)
1985—Packers, 23-20 (GB)
1986—Giants, 55-24 (NY)
1987—Giants, 20-10 (NY)
1992—Giants, 27-7 (NY)
1995—Packers, 14-6 (GB)
(RS Pts.—Giants 752, Packers 704)
(PS Pts.—Packers 111, Giants 37)
*NFL Championship

GREEN BAY vs. N.Y. JETS
RS: Jets lead series, 5-2
1973—Packers, 23-7 (Mil)
1979—Jets, 27-22 (GB)
1981—Jets, 28-3 (NY)
1982—Jets, 15-13 (NY)
1985—Jets, 24-3 (Mil)
1991—Jets, 19-16 (NY) OT
1994—Packers, 17-10 (GB)
(RS Pts.—Jets 130, Packers 97)

GREEN BAY vs. *OAKLAND
RS: Raiders lead series, 5-2
PS: Packers lead series, 1-0
1967—**Packers, 33-14 (Miami)
1972—Raiders, 20-14 (GB)
1976—Raiders, 18-14 (O)
1978—Raiders, 28-3 (GB)
1984—Raiders, 28-7 (LA)
1987—Raiders, 20-0 (GB)
1990—Packers, 29-16 (LA)
1993—Packers, 28-0 (GB)
(RS Pts.—Raiders 130, Packers 95)
(PS Pts.—Packers 33, Raiders 14)
*Franchise in Los Angeles from
1982-1994
**Super Bowl II

GREEN BAY vs. PHILADELPHIA
RS: Packers lead series, 20-8
PS: Eagles lead series, 1-0
1933—Packers, 35-9 (GB)
Packers, 10-0 (P)
1934—Packers, 19-6 (GB)
1935—Packers, 13-6 (P)
1937—Packers, 37-7 (Mil)
1939—Packers, 23-16 (P)
1940—Packers, 27-20 (GB)

1942—Packers, 7-0 (P)
1946—Packers, 19-7 (P)
1947—Eagles, 28-14 (P)
1951—Packers, 37-24 (GB)
1952—Packers, 12-10 (Mil)
1954—Packers, 37-14 (P)
1958—Packers, 38-35 (GB)
1960—*Eagles, 17-13 (P)
1962—Packers, 49-0 (P)
1968—Packers, 30-13 (GB)
1970—Packers, 30-17 (Mil)
1974—Eagles, 36-14 (P)
1976—Packers, 28-13 (GB)
1978—Eagles, 10-3 (P)
1979—Eagles, 21-10 (GB)
1987—Packers, 16-10 (GB) OT
1990—Eagles, 31-0 (P)
1991—Eagles, 20-3 (GB)
1992—Packers, 27-24 (Mil)
1993—Eagles, 20-17 (GB)
1994—Eagles, 13-7 (P)
1996—Packers, 39-13 (GB)
(RS Pts.—Packers 601, Eagles 423)
(PS Pts.—Eagles 17, Packers 13)
*NFL Championship

GREEN BAY vs. *PITTSBURGH
RS: Packers lead series, 18-11
1933—Packers, 47-0 (GB)
1935—Packers, 27-0 (GB)
Packers, 34-14 (P)
1936—Packers, 42-10 (Mil)
1938—Packers, 20-0 (GB)
1940—Packers, 24-3 (Mil)
1941—Packers, 54-7 (P)
1942—Packers, 24-21 (Mil)
1946—Packers, 17-7 (GB)
1947—Steelers, 18-17 (Mil)
1948—Steelers, 38-7 (P)
1949—Steelers, 30-7 (Mil)
1951—Packers, 35-33 (Mil)
Steelers, 28-7 (P)
1953—Steelers, 31-14 (P)
1954—Steelers, 21-20 (GB)
1957—Packers, 27-10 (P)
1960—Packers, 19-13 (P)
1963—Packers, 33-14 (Mil)
1965—Packers, 41-9 (P)
1967—Steelers, 24-17 (GB)
1969—Steelers, 38-34 (P)
1970—Packers, 20-12 (P)
1975—Steelers, 16-13 (Mil)
1980—Steelers, 22-20 (P)
1983—Steelers, 25-21 (GB)
1986—Steelers, 27-3 (P)
1992—Packers, 17-3 (GB)
1995—Packers, 24-19 (GB)
(RS Pts.—Packers 689, Steelers 489)
*Steelers known as Pirates prior to 1941

GREEN BAY vs. *ST. LOUIS
RS: Rams lead series, 43-38-2
PS: Packers lead series, 1-0
1937—Packers, 35-10 (C)
Packers, 35-7 (GB)
1938—Packers, 26-17 (GB)
Packers, 28-7 (C)
1939—Rams, 27-24 (GB)
Packers, 7-6 (C)
1940—Packers, 31-14 (GB)
Tie, 13-13 (C)
1941—Packers, 24-7 (Mil)
Packers, 17-14 (C)
1942—Packers, 45-28 (GB)
Packers, 30-12 (C)
1944—Packers, 30-21 (GB)
Packers, 42-7 (C)
1945—Rams, 27-14 (GB)
Rams, 20-7 (C)
1946—Rams, 21-17 (Mil)
Rams, 38-17 (LA)
1947—Packers, 17-14 (Mil)
Packers, 30-10 (LA)
1948—Packers, 16-0 (GB)
Rams, 24-10 (LA)

1949—Rams, 48-7 (GB)
Rams, 35-7 (LA)
1950—Rams, 45-14 (Mil)
Rams, 51-14 (LA)
1951—Rams, 28-0 (Mil)
Rams, 42-14 (LA)
1952—Rams, 30-28 (Mil)
Rams, 45-27 (LA)
1953—Rams, 38-20 (Mil)
Rams, 33-17 (LA)
1954—Packers, 35-17 (Mil)
Rams, 35-27 (LA)
1955—Packers, 30-28 (Mil)
Rams, 31-17 (LA)
1956—Packers, 42-17 (Mil)
Rams, 49-21 (LA)
1957—Rams, 31-27 (Mil)
Rams, 42-17 (LA)
1958—Rams, 20-7 (GB)
Rams, 34-20 (LA)
1959—Rams, 45-6 (Mil)
Packers, 38-20 (LA)
1960—Rams, 33-31 (Mil)
Packers, 35-21 (LA)
1961—Packers, 35-17 (GB)
Packers, 24-17 (LA)
1962—Packers, 41-10 (Mil)
Packers, 20-17 (LA)
1963—Packers, 42-10 (GB)
Packers, 31-14 (LA)
1964—Rams, 27-17 (Mil)
Tie, 24-24 (LA)
1965—Packers, 6-3 (Mil)
Rams, 21-10 (LA)
1966—Packers, 24-13 (GB)
Packers, 27-23 (LA)
1967—Rams, 27-24 (LA)
**Packers, 28-7 (Mil)
1968—Rams, 16-14 (Mil)
1969—Rams, 34-21 (LA)
1970—Rams, 31-21 (GB)
1971—Rams, 30-13 (LA)
1973—Rams, 24-7 (LA)
1974—Packers, 17-6 (Mil)
1975—Packers, 22-5 (LA)
1977—Rams, 24-6 (Mil)
1978—Rams, 31-14 (LA)
1980—Rams, 51-21 (GB)
1981—Rams, 35-23 (LA)
1982—Packers, 35-23 (Mil)
1983—Packers, 27-24 (Mil)
1984—Packers, 31-6 (Mil)
1985—Rams, 34-17 (LA)
1988—Rams, 34-7 (GB)
1989—Rams, 41-38 (LA)
1990—Packers, 36-24 (GB)
1991—Rams, 23-21 (LA)
1992—Packers, 28-13 (GB)
1993—Packers, 36-6 (Mil)
1994—Packers, 24-17 (GB)
1995—Rams, 17-14 (GB)
1996—Packers, 24-9 (StL)
(RS Pts.—Rams 1,960, Packers 1,841)
(PS Pts.—Packers 28, Rams 7)
*Franchise in Los Angeles prior to 1995
and in Cleveland prior to 1946
**Conference Championship
GREEN BAY vs. SAN DIEGO
RS: Packers lead series, 5-1
1970—Packers, 22-20 (SD)
1974—Packers, 34-0 (GB)
1978—Packers, 24-3 (SD)
1984—Chargers, 34-28 (GB)
1993—Packers, 20-13 (SD)
1996—Packers, 42-10 (GB)
(RS Pts.—Packers 170, Chargers 80)
GREEN BAY vs. SAN FRANCISCO
RS: 49ers lead series, 25-22-1
PS: Packers lead series, 2-0
1950—Packers, 25-21 (GB)
49ers, 30-14 (SF)
1951—49ers, 31-19 (SF)
1952—49ers, 24-14 (SF)

1953—49ers, 37-7 (Mil)
49ers, 48-14 (SF)
1954—49ers, 23-17 (Mil)
49ers, 35-0 (SF)
1955—Packers, 27-21 (Mil)
Packers, 28-7 (SF)
1956—49ers, 17-16 (GB)
49ers, 38-20 (SF)
1957—49ers, 24-14 (Mil)
49ers, 27-20 (SF)
1958—49ers, 33-12 (Mil)
49ers, 48-21 (SF)
1959—Packers, 21-20 (GB)
Packers, 36-14 (SF)
1960—Packers, 41-14 (Mil)
Packers, 13-0 (SF)
1961—Packers, 30-10 (GB)
49ers, 22-21 (SF)
1962—Packers, 31-13 (Mil)
Packers, 31-21 (SF)
1963—Packers, 28-10 (Mil)
Packers, 21-17 (SF)
1964—Packers, 24-14 (Mil)
49ers, 24-14 (SF)
1965—Packers, 27-10 (GB)
Tie, 24-24 (SF)
1966—49ers, 21-20 (SF)
Packers, 20-7 (Mil)
1967—Packers, 13-0 (GB)
1968—49ers, 27-20 (SF)
1969—Packers, 14-7 (Mil)
1970—49ers, 26-10 (SF)
1972—Packers, 34-24 (Mil)
1973—49ers, 20-6 (SF)
1974—49ers, 7-6 (SF)
1976—49ers, 26-14 (GB)
1977—Packers, 16-14 (Mil)
1980—Packers, 23-16 (Mil)
1981—49ers, 13-3 (Mil)
1986—49ers, 31-17 (Mil)
1987—49ers, 23-12 (GB)
1989—Packers, 21-17 (SF)
1990—49ers, 24-20 (GB)
1995—*Packers, 27-17 (SF)
1996—Packers, 23-20 (GB) OT
*Packers, 35-14 (GB)
(RS Pts.—49ers 1,000, Packers 922)
(PS Pts.—Packers 62, 49ers 31)
*NFC Divisional Playoff
GREEN BAY vs. SEATTLE
RS: Packers lead series, 4-3
1976—Packers, 27-20 (Mil)
1978—Packers, 45-28 (Mil)
1981—Packers, 34-24 (GB)
1984—Seahawks, 30-24 (Mil)
1987—Seahawks, 24-13 (S)
1990—Seahawks, 20-14 (Mil)
1996—Packers, 31-10 (S)
(RS Pts.—Packers 188, Seahawks 156)
GREEN BAY vs. TAMPA BAY
RS: Packers lead series, 22-13-1
1977—Packers, 13-0 (TB)
1978—Packers, 9-7 (GB)
Packers, 17-7 (TB)
1979—Buccaneers, 21-10 (GB)
Buccaneers, 21-3 (TB)
1980—Tie, 14-14 (TB) OT
Buccaneers, 20-17 (Mil)
1981—Buccaneers, 21-10 (GB)
Buccaneers, 37-3 (TB)
1983—Packers, 55-14 (GB)
Packers, 12-9 (TB) OT
1984—Buccaneers, 30-27 (TB) OT
Packers, 27-14 (GB)
1985—Packers, 21-0 (GB)
Packers, 20-17 (TB)
1986—Packers, 31-7 (Mil)
Packers, 21-7 (TB)
1987—Buccaneers, 23-17 (Mil)
1988—Packers, 13-10 (GB)
Buccaneers, 27-24 (TB)
1989—Buccaneers, 23-21 (GB)
Packers, 17-16 (TB)

1990—Buccaneers, 26-14 (TB)
Packers, 20-10 (Mil)
1991—Packers, 15-13 (GB)
Packers, 27-0 (TB)
1992—Buccaneers, 31-3 (TB)
Packers, 19-14 (Mil)
1993—Packers, 37-14 (TB)
Packers, 13-10 (GB)
1994—Packers, 30-3 (GB)
Packers, 34-19 (TB)
1995—Packers, 35-13 (GB)
Buccaneers, 13-10 (TB) OT
1996—Packers, 34-3 (TB)
Packers, 13-7 (GB)
(RS Pts.—Packers 703, Buccaneers 524)
GREEN BAY vs. *TENNESSEE
RS: Series tied, 3-3
1972—Packers, 23-10 (H)
1977—Oilers, 16-10 (GB)
1980—Oilers, 22-3 (GB)
1983—Packers, 41-38 (H) OT
1986—Oilers, 31-3 (GB)
1992—Packers, 16-14 (H)
(RS Pts.—Oilers 131, Packers 96)
*Franchise in Houston prior to 1997
GREEN BAY vs. *WASHINGTON
RS: Packers lead series, 13-12-1
PS: Series tied, 1-1
1932—Packers, 21-0 (B)
1933—Tie, 7-7 (GB)
Redskins, 20-7 (B)
1934—Packers, 10-0 (B)
1936—Packers, 31-2 (GB)
Packers, 7-3 (B)
**Packers, 21-6 (New York)
1937—Redskins, 14-6 (W)
1939—Packers, 24-14 (Mil)
1941—Packers, 22-17 (W)
1943—Redskins, 33-7 (Mil)
1946—Packers, 20-7 (W)
1947—Packers, 27-10 (Mil)
1948—Redskins, 23-7 (B)
1949—Redskins, 30-0 (W)
1950—Packers, 35-21 (Mil)
1952—Packers, 35-20 (Mil)
1958—Redskins, 37-21 (W)
1959—Packers, 21-0 (GB)
1968—Packers, 27-7 (W)
1972—Redskins, 21-16 (W)
***Redskins, 16-3 (W)
1974—Redskins, 17-6 (GB)
1977—Redskins, 10-9 (W)
1979—Redskins, 38-21 (W)
1983—Packers, 48-47 (GB)
1986—Redskins, 16-7 (GB)
1988—Redskins, 20-17 (Mil)
(RS Pts.—Packers 459, Redskins 434)
(PS Pts.—Packers 24, Redskins 22)
*Franchise in Boston prior to 1937 and
known as Braves prior to 1933
**NFL Championship
***NFC Divisional Playoff

INDIANAPOLIS vs. ARIZONA
RS: Series tied, 6-6;
See Arizona vs. Indianapolis
INDIANAPOLIS vs. ATLANTA
RS: Colts lead series, 10-0;
See Atlanta vs. Indianapolis
INDIANAPOLIS vs. BALTIMORE
RS: Colts lead series, 1-0;
See Baltimore vs. Indianapolis
INDIANAPOLIS vs. BUFFALO
RS: Bills lead series, 29-23-1;
See Buffalo vs. Indianapolis
INDIANAPOLIS vs. CAROLINA
RS: Panthers lead series, 1-0;
See Carolina vs. Indianapolis
INDIANAPOLIS vs. CHICAGO
RS: Colts lead series, 21-16;
See Chicago vs. Indianapolis
INDIANAPOLIS vs. CINCINNATI
RS: Colts lead series, 9-7

PS: Colts lead series, 1-0;
See Cincinnati vs. Indianapolis
INDIANAPOLIS vs. CLEVELAND
RS: Browns lead series, 13-7
PS: Series tied, 2-2;
See Cleveland vs. Indianapolis
INDIANAPOLIS vs. DALLAS
RS: Cowboys lead series, 7-3
PS: Colts lead series, 1-0;
See Dallas vs. Indianapolis
INDIANAPOLIS vs. DENVER
RS: Broncos lead series, 9-2;
See Denver vs. Indianapolis
INDIANAPOLIS vs. DETROIT
RS: Series tied, 17-17-2;
See Detroit vs. Indianapolis
INDIANAPOLIS vs. GREEN BAY
RS: Series tied, 18-18-1
PS: Packers lead series, 1-0;
See Green Bay vs. Indianapolis
INDIANAPOLIS vs. JACKSONVILLE
RS: Colts lead series, 1-0
1995—Colts, 41-31 (J)
(RS Pts.—Colts 41, Jaguars 31)
INDIANAPOLIS vs. KANSAS CITY
RS: Chiefs lead series, 6-5
PS: Colts lead series, 1-0
1970—Chiefs, 44-24 (B)
1972—Chiefs, 24-10 (KC)
1975—Colts, 28-14 (B)
1977—Colts, 17-6 (KC)
1979—Chiefs, 14-0 (KC)
Chiefs, 10-7 (B)
1980—Colts, 31-24 (KC)
Chiefs, 38-28 (B)
1985—Chiefs, 20-7 (KC)
1990—Colts, 23-19 (I)
1995—**Colts, 10-7 (KC)
1996—Colts, 24-19 (KC)
(RS Pts.—Chiefs 232, Colts 199)
(PS Pts.—Colts 10, Chiefs 7)
*Franchise in Baltimore prior to 1984
**AFC Divisional Playoff
INDIANAPOLIS vs. MIAMI
RS: Dolphins lead series, 36-18
PS: Dolphins lead series, 1-0
1970—Colts, 35-0 (B)
Dolphins, 34-17 (M)
1971—Dolphins, 17-14 (M)
Colts, 14-3 (B)
**Dolphins, 21-0 (M)
1972—Dolphins, 23-0 (B)
Dolphins, 16-0 (M)
1973—Dolphins, 44-0 (M)
Colts, 16-3 (B)
1974—Dolphins, 17-7 (M)
Dolphins, 17-16 (B)
1975—Colts, 33-17 (M)
Colts, 10-7 (B) OT
1976—Colts, 28-14 (B)
Colts, 17-16 (M)
1977—Colts, 45-28 (B)
Dolphins, 17-6 (M)
1978—Dolphins, 42-0 (B)
Dolphins, 26-8 (M)
1979—Dolphins, 19-0 (M)
Dolphins, 28-24 (B)
1980—Colts, 30-17 (M)
Dolphins, 24-14 (B)
1981—Dolphins, 31-28 (B)
Dolphins, 27-10 (M)
1982—Dolphins, 24-20 (M)
Dolphins, 34-7 (B)
1983—Dolphins, 21-7 (B)
Dolphins, 37-0 (M)
1984—Dolphins, 44-7 (M)
Dolphins, 35-17 (I)
1985—Dolphins, 30-13 (M)
Dolphins, 34-20 (I)
1986—Dolphins, 30-10 (M)
Dolphins, 17-13 (I)
1987—Dolphins, 23-10 (I)
Colts, 40-21 (M)

1988—Colts, 15-13 (I)
Colts, 31-28 (M)
1989—Dolphins, 19-13 (M)
Colts, 42-13 (I)
1990—Dolphins, 27-7 (I)
Dolphins, 23-17 (M)
1991—Dolphins, 17-6 (M)
Dolphins, 10-6 (I)
1992—Colts, 31-20 (M)
Dolphins, 28-0 (I)
1993—Dolphins, 24-20 (I)
Dolphins, 41-27 (M)
1994—Dolphins, 22-21 (M)
Colts, 10-6 (I)
1995—Colts, 27-24 (M) OT
Colts, 36-28 (I)
1996—Colts, 10-6 (I)
Dolphins, 37-13 (M)
(RS Pts.—Dolphins 1,223, Colts 868)
(PS Pts.—Dolphins 21, Colts 0)
*Franchise in Baltimore prior to 1984
**AFC Championship
**INDIANAPOLIS vs. MINNESOTA*
RS: Colts lead series, 11-6-1
PS: Colts lead series, 1-0
1961—Colts, 34-33 (B)
Vikings, 28-20 (M)
1962—Colts, 34-7 (M)
Colts, 42-17 (B)
1963—Colts, 37-34 (M)
Colts, 41-10 (B)
1964—Vikings, 34-24 (M)
Colts, 17-14 (B)
1965—Colts, 35-16 (B)
Colts, 41-21 (M)
1966—Colts, 38-23 (M)
Colts, 20-17 (B)
1967—Tie, 20-20 (M)
1968—Colts, 21-9 (B)
**Colts, 24-14 (B)
1969—Vikings, 52-14 (M)
1971—Vikings, 10-3 (M)
1982—Vikings, 13-10 (M)
1988—Vikings, 12-3 (M)
(RS Pts.—Colts 454, Vikings 370)
(PS Pts.—Colts 24, Vikings 14)
*Franchise in Baltimore prior to 1984
**Conference Championship
*INDIANAPOLIS vs. **NEW ENGLAND
RS: Patriots lead series, 31-22
1970—Colts, 14-6 (Bos)
Colts, 27-3 (Balt)
1971—Colts, 23-3 (NE)
Patriots, 21-17 (Balt)
1972—Colts, 24-17 (NE)
Colts, 31-0 (Balt)
1973—Patriots, 24-16 (NE)
Colts, 18-13 (Balt)
1974—Patriots, 42-3 (NE)
Patriots, 27-17 (Balt)
1975—Patriots, 21-10 (NE)
Colts, 34-21 (Balt)
1976—Colts, 27-13 (NE)
Patriots, 21-14 (Balt)
1977—Patriots, 17-3 (NE)
Colts, 30-24 (Balt)
1978—Colts, 34-27 (NE)
Patriots, 35-14 (Balt)
1979—Colts, 31-26 (Balt)
Patriots, 50-21 (NE)
1980—Patriots, 37-21 (Balt)
Patriots, 47-21 (NE)
1981—Colts, 29-28 (NE)
Colts, 23-21 (Balt)
1982—Patriots, 24-13 (Balt)
1983—Colts, 29-23 (NE) OT
Colts, 12-7 (Balt)
1984—Patriots, 50-17 (I)
Patriots, 16-10 (NE)
1985—Patriots, 34-15 (NE)
Patriots, 38-31 (I)
1986—Patriots, 33-3 (NE)
Patriots, 30-21 (I)

1987—Colts, 30-16 (I)
Patriots, 24-0 (NE)
1988—Patriots, 21-17 (NE)
Colts, 24-21 (I)
1989—Patriots, 23-20 (I) OT
Patriots, 22-16 (NE)
1990—Patriots, 16-14 (I)
Colts, 13-10 (NE)
1991—Patriots, 16-7 (I)
Patriots, 23-17 (NE) OT
1992—Patriots, 37-34 (I) OT
Colts, 6-0 (NE)
1993—Colts, 9-6 (I)
Patriots, 38-0 (NE)
1994—Patriots, 12-10 (I)
Patriots, 28-13 (NE)
1995—Colts, 24-10 (NE)
Colts, 10-7 (I)
1996—Patriots, 27-9 (I)
Patriots, 27-13 (NE)
(RS Pts.—Patriots 1,183, Colts 939)
*Franchise in Baltimore prior to 1984
**Franchise in Boston prior to 1971
*INDIANAPOLIS vs. NEW ORLEANS
RS: Series tied, 3-3
1967—Colts, 30-10 (B)
1969—Colts, 30-10 (NO)
1973—Colts, 14-10 (B)
1986—Saints, 17-14 (I)
1989—Saints, 41-6 (NO)
1995—Saints, 17-14 (NO)
(RS Pts.—Colts 108, Saints 105)
*Franchise in Baltimore prior to 1984
*INDIANAPOLIS vs. N.Y. GIANTS
RS: Series tied, 5-5
PS: Colts lead series, 2-0
1954—Colts, 20-14 (B)
1955—Giants, 17-7 (NY)
1958—Giants, 24-21 (NY)
**Colts, 23-17 (NY) OT
1959—**Colts, 31-16 (B)
1963—Giants, 37-28 (B)
1968—Colts, 26-0 (NY)
1971—Colts, 31-7 (NY)
1975—Colts, 21-0 (NY)
1979—Colts, 31-7 (NY)
1990—Giants, 24-7 (I)
1993—Giants, 20-6 (NY)
(RS Pts.—Colts 198, Giants 150)
(PS Pts.—Colts 54, Giants 33)
*Franchise in Baltimore prior to 1984
**NFL Championship
*INDIANAPOLIS vs. N.Y. JETS
RS: Colts lead series, 32-21
PS: Jets lead series, 1-0
1968—**Jets 16-7 (Miami)
1970—Colts, 29-22 (NY)
Colts, 35-20 (B)
1971—Colts, 22-0 (B)
Colts, 14-13 (NY)
1972—Jets, 44-34 (B)
Jets, 24-20 (NY)
1973—Jets, 34-10 (B)
Jets, 20-17 (NY)
1974—Colts, 35-20 (NY)
Jets, 45-38 (B)
1975—Colts, 45-28 (NY)
Colts, 52-19 (B)
1976—Colts, 20-0 (NY)
Colts, 33-16 (B)
1977—Colts, 20-12 (NY)
Colts, 33-12 (B)
1978—Jets, 33-10 (B)
Jets, 24-16 (NY)
1979—Colts, 10-8 (B)
Jets, 30-17 (NY)
1980—Colts, 17-14 (NY)
Colts, 35-21 (B)
1981—Jets, 41-14 (B)
Jets, 25-0 (NY)
1982—Jets, 37-0 (NY)
1983—Colts, 17-14 (NY)
Jets, 10-6 (B)

1984—Jets, 23-14 (I)
Colts, 9-5 (NY)
1985—Jets, 25-20 (NY)
Jets, 35-17 (I)
1986—Jets, 26-7 (I)
Jets, 31-16 (NY)
1987—Colts, 6-0 (I)
Colts, 19-14 (NY)
1988—Colts, 38-14 (I)
Jets, 34-16 (NY)
1989—Colts, 17-10 (NY)
Colts, 27-10 (I)
1990—Colts, 17-14 (I)
Colts, 29-21 (NY)
1991—Jets, 17-6 (I)
Colts, 28-27 (NY)
1992—Colts, 6-3 (I) OT
Colts, 10-6 (NY)
1993—Jets, 31-17 (I)
Colts, 9-6 (NY)
1994—Jets, 16-6 (NY)
Colts, 28-25 (I)
1995—Colts, 27-24 (NY) OT
Colts, 17-10 (I)
1996—Colts, 21-7 (NY)
Colts, 34-29 (I)
(RS Pts.—Colts 1,060, Jets 1,049)
(PS Pts.—Jets 16, Colts 7)
*Franchise in Baltimore prior to 1984
**Super Bowl III
*INDIANAPOLIS vs **OAKLAND
RS: Raiders lead series, 5-2
PS: Series tied, 1-1
1970—***Colts, 27-17 (B)
1971—Colts, 37-14 (O)
1973—Raiders, 34-21 (B)
1975—Raiders, 31-20 (B)
1977—****Raiders, 37-31 (B) OT
1984—Raiders, 21-7 (LA)
1986—Colts, 30-24 (LA)
1991—Raiders, 16-0 (LA)
1995—Raiders, 30-17 (O)
(RS Pts.—Raiders 170, Colts 132)
(PS Pts.—Colts 58, Raiders 54)
*Franchise in Baltimore prior to 1984
**Franchise in Los Angeles from
1982-1994
***AFC Championship
****AFC Divisional Playoff
*INDIANAPOLIS vs. PHILADELPHIA
RS: Colts lead series, 7-6
1953—Eagles, 45-14 (P)
1965—Colts, 34-24 (B)
1967—Colts, 38-6 (P)
1969—Colts, 24-20 (B)
1970—Colts, 29-10 (B)
1974—Eagles, 30-10 (P)
1978—Eagles, 17-14 (B)
1981—Eagles, 38-13 (P)
1983—Colts, 22-21 (P)
1984—Eagles, 16-7 (P)
1990—Colts, 24-23 (P)
1993—Eagles, 20-10 (I)
1996—Colts, 37-10 (I)
(RS Pts.—Eagles 280, Colts 276)
*Franchise in Baltimore prior to 1984
*INDIANAPOLIS vs. PITTSBURGH
RS: Steelers lead series, 11-4
PS: Steelers lead series, 4-0
1957—Steelers, 19-13 (B)
1968—Colts, 41-7 (P)
1971—Colts, 34-21 (P)
1974—Steelers, 30-0 (B)
1975—**Steelers, 28-10 (P)
1976—**Steelers, 40-14 (B)
1977—Colts, 31-21 (B)
1978—Steelers, 35-13 (P)
1979—Steelers, 17-13 (P)
1980—Steelers, 20-17 (B)
1983—Steelers, 24-13 (B)
1984—Colts, 17-16 (I)
1985—Steelers, 45-3 (P)
1987—Steelers, 21-7 (P)

1991—Steelers, 21-3 (I)
1992—Steelers, 30-14 (P)
1994—Steelers, 31-21 (P)
1995—***Steelers, 20-16 (P)
1996—****Steelers, 42-14 (P)
(RS Pts.—Steelers 358, Colts 240)
(PS Pts.—Steelers 130, Colts 54)
*Franchise in Baltimore prior to 1984
**AFC Divisional Playoff
***AFC Championship
****AFC First-Round Playoff
*INDIANAPOLIS vs. **ST. LOUIS
RS: Colts lead series, 21-16-2
1953—Rams, 21-13 (B)
Rams, 45-2 (B)
1954—Rams, 48-0 (B)
Colts, 22-21 (LA)
1955—Tie, 17-17 (B)
Rams, 20-14 (LA)
1956—Colts, 56-21 (B)
Rams, 31-7 (LA)
1957—Colts, 31-14 (B)
Rams, 37-21 (LA)
1958—Colts, 34-7 (B)
Rams, 30-28 (LA)
1959—Colts, 35-21 (B)
Colts, 45-26 (LA)
1960—Colts, 31-17 (B)
Rams, 10-3 (LA)
1961—Colts, 27-24 (B)
Rams, 34-17 (LA)
1962—Colts, 30-27 (B)
Colts, 14-2 (LA)
1963—Rams, 17-16 (LA)
Colts, 19-16 (B)
1964—Colts, 35-20 (B)
Colts, 24-7 (LA)
1965—Colts, 35-20 (B)
Colts, 20-17 (LA)
1966—Colts, 17-3 (B)
Rams, 23-7 (B)
1967—Tie, 24-24 (B)
Rams, 34-10 (LA)
1968—Colts, 27-10 (B)
Colts, 28-24 (LA)
1969—Rams, 27-20 (B)
Colts, 13-7 (LA)
1971—Colts, 24-17 (B)
Rams, 24-13 (LA)
1986—Rams, 24-7 (I)
1989—Rams, 31-17 (LA)
1995—Colts, 21-18 (I)
(RS Pts.—Rams 836, Colts 824)
*Franchise in Baltimore prior to 1984
**Franchise in Los Angeles prior to 1995
*INDIANAPOLIS vs. SAN DIEGO
RS: Chargers lead series, 11-5
PS: Colts lead series, 1-0
1970—Colts, 16-14 (SD)
1972—Chargers, 23-20 (B)
1976—Colts, 37-21 (SD)
1981—Chargers, 43-14 (B)
1982—Chargers, 44-26 (SD)
1984—Chargers, 38-10 (I)
1986—Chargers, 17-3 (I)
1987—Chargers, 16-13 (I)
Colts, 20-7 (SD)
1988—Colts, 16-0 (SD)
1989—Colts, 10-6 (I)
1992—Chargers, 34-14 (I)
Chargers, 26-0 (SD)
1993—Chargers, 31-0 (I)
1995—Chargers, 27-24 (I)
**Colts, 35-20 (SD)
1996—Chargers, 26-19 (I)
(RS Pts.—Chargers 373, Colts 242)
(PS Pts.—Colts 35, Chargers 20)
*Franchise in Baltimore prior to 1984
**AFC First-Round Playoff
*INDIANAPOLIS vs. SAN FRANCISCO
RS: Colts lead series, 22-16
1953—49ers, 38-21 (B)
49ers, 45-14 (SF)

1954—Colts, 17-13 (B)
    49ers, 10-7 (SF)
1955—Colts, 26-14 (B)
    49ers, 35-24 (SF)
1956—49ers, 20-17 (B)
    49ers, 30-17 (SF)
1957—Colts, 27-21 (B)
    49ers, 17-13 (SF)
1958—Colts, 35-27 (B)
    49ers, 21-12 (SF)
1959—Colts, 45-14 (B)
    Colts, 34-14 (SF)
1960—49ers, 30-22 (B)
    49ers, 34-10 (SF)
1961—Colts, 20-17 (B)
    Colts, 27-24 (SF)
1962—49ers, 21-13 (B)
    Colts, 22-3 (SF)
1963—Colts, 20-14 (SF)
    Colts, 20-3 (B)
1964—Colts, 37-7 (B)
    Colts, 14-3 (SF)
1965—Colts, 27-24 (B)
    Colts, 34-28 (SF)
1966—Colts, 36-14 (B)
    Colts, 30-14 (SF)
1967—Colts, 41-7 (B)
    Colts, 26-9 (SF)
1968—Colts, 27-10 (B)
    Colts, 42-14 (SF)
1969—49ers, 24-21 (SF)
    49ers, 20-17 (SF)
1972—49ers, 24-21 (SF)
1986—49ers, 35-14 (SF)
1989—49ers, 30-24 (I)
1995—Colts, 18-17 (I)
(RS Pts.—Colts 892, 49ers 745)
*Franchise in Baltimore prior to 1984
INDIANAPOLIS vs. SEATTLE
RS: Colts lead series, 4-1
1977—Colts, 29-14 (S)
1978—Colts, 17-14 (S)
1991—Seahawks, 31-3 (S)
1994—Colts, 17-15 (I)
    Colts, 31-19 (S)
(RS Pts.—Colts 97, Seahawks 93)
*Franchise in Baltimore prior to 1984
INDIANAPOLIS vs. TAMPA BAY
RS: Colts lead series, 5-3
1976—Colts, 42-17 (B)
1979—Buccaneers, 29-26 (B) OT
1985—Colts, 31-23 (TB)
1987—Colts, 24-6 (I)
1988—Colts, 35-31 (I)
1991—Buccaneers, 17-3 (TB)
1992—Colts, 24-14 (TB)
1994—Buccaneers, 24-10 (TB)
(RS Pts.—Colts 195, Buccaneers 161)
*Franchise in Baltimore prior to 1984
INDIANAPOLIS vs. **TENNESSEE
RS: Series tied, 7-7
1970—Colts, 24-20 (H)
1973—Oilers, 31-27 (B)
1976—Colts, 38-14 (B)
1979—Oilers, 28-16 (B)
1980—Oilers, 21-16 (H)
1983—Colts, 20-10 (B)
1984—Colts, 35-21 (H)
1985—Colts, 34-16 (I)
1986—Oilers, 31-17 (H)
1987—Colts, 51-27 (I)
1988—Oilers, 17-14 (I) OT
1990—Oilers, 24-10 (H)
1992—Oilers, 20-10 (I)
1994—Colts, 45-21 (I)
(RS Pts.—Colts 357, Oilers 301)
*Franchise in Baltimore prior to 1984
**Franchise in Houston prior to 1997
INDIANAPOLIS vs. WASHINGTON
RS: Colts lead series, 16-9
1953—Colts, 27-17 (B)
1954—Redskins, 24-21 (W)
1955—Redskins, 14-13 (B)

1956—Colts, 19-17 (B)
1957—Colts, 21-17 (W)
1958—Colts, 35-10 (B)
1959—Redskins, 27-24 (W)
1960—Colts, 20-0 (B)
1961—Colts, 27-6 (W)
1962—Colts, 34-21 (B)
1963—Colts, 36-20 (W)
1964—Colts, 45-17 (B)
1965—Colts, 38-7 (W)
1966—Colts, 37-10 (B)
1967—Colts, 17-13 (W)
1969—Colts, 41-17 (B)
1973—Redskins, 22-14 (W)
1977—Colts, 10-3 (B)
1978—Colts, 21-17 (B)
1981—Redskins, 38-14 (W)
1984—Redskins, 35-7 (I)
1990—Colts, 35-28 (I)
1993—Redskins, 30-24 (W)
1994—Redskins, 41-27 (I)
1996—Redskins, 31-16 (W)
(RS Pts.—Colts 623, Redskins 482)
*Franchise in Baltimore prior to 1984

JACKSONVILLE vs. ATLANTA
RS: Jaguars lead series, 1-0;
See Atlanta vs. Jacksonville
JACKSONVILLE vs. BALTIMORE
RS: Jaguars lead series, 2-0;
See Baltimore vs. Jacksonville
JACKSONVILLE vs. BUFFALO
PS: Jaguars lead series, 1-0;
See Buffalo vs. Jacksonville
JACKSONVILLE vs. CAROLINA
RS: Jaguars lead series, 1-0;
See Carolina vs. Jacksonville
JACKSONVILLE vs. CHICAGO
RS: Bears lead series, 1-0;
See Chicago vs. Jacksonville
JACKSONVILLE vs. CINCINNATI
RS: Bengals lead series, 3-1;
See Cincinnati vs. Jacksonville
JACKSONVILLE vs. CLEVELAND
RS: Jaguars lead series, 2-0;
See Cleveland vs. Jacksonville
JACKSONVILLE vs. DENVER
RS: Broncos lead series, 1-0
PS: Jaguars lead series, 1-0;
See Denver vs. Jacksonville
JACKSONVILLE vs. DETROIT
RS: Lions lead series, 1-0;
See Detroit vs. Jacksonville
JACKSONVILLE vs. GREEN BAY
RS: Packers lead series, 1-0;
See Green Bay vs. Jacksonville
JACKSONVILLE vs. INDIANAPOLIS
RS: Colts lead series, 1-0;
See Indianapolis vs. Jacksonville
JACKSONVILLE vs. NEW ENGLAND
RS: Patriots lead series, 1-0
PS: Patriots lead series, 1-0
1996—Patriots, 28-25 (NE) OT
    *Patriots, 20-6 (NE)
(RS Pts.—Patriots 28, Jaguars 25)
(PS Pts.—Patriots 20, Jaguars 6)
*AFC Championship
JACKSONVILLE vs. NEW ORLEANS
RS: Saints lead series, 1-0
1996—Saints, 17-13 (NO)
(RS Pts.—Saints 17, Jaguars 13)
JACKSONVILLE vs. N.Y. JETS
RS: Series tied, 1-1
1995—Jets, 27-10 (NY)
1996—Jaguars, 21-17 (J)
(RS Pts.—Jets 44, Jaguars 31)
JACKSONVILLE vs. OAKLAND
RS: Raiders lead series, 1-0
1996—Raiders, 17-3 (O)
(RS Pts.—Raiders 17, Jaguars 3)
JACKSONVILLE vs. PITTSBURGH
RS: Series tied, 2-2
1995—Jaguars, 20-16 (J)

    Steelers, 24-7 (P)
1996—Jaguars, 24-9 (J)
    Steelers, 28-3 (P)
(RS Pts.—Steelers 77, Jaguars 54)
JACKSONVILLE vs. ST. LOUIS
RS: Rams lead series, 1-0
1996—Rams, 17-14 (StL)
(RS Pts.—Rams 17, Jaguars 14)
JACKSONVILLE vs. SEATTLE
RS: Series tied, 1-1
1995—Seahawks, 47-30 (J)
1996—Jaguars, 20-13 (J)
(RS Pts.—Seahawks 60, Jaguars 50)
JACKSONVILLE vs. TAMPA BAY
RS: Buccaneers lead series, 1-0
1995—Buccaneers, 17-16 (TB)
(RS Pts.—Buccaneers 17, Jaguars 16)
JACKSONVILLE vs. *TENNESSEE
RS: Series tied, 2-2
1995—Oilers, 10-3 (J)
    Jaguars, 17-16 (H)
1996—Oilers, 34-27 (J)
    Jaguars, 23-17 (H)
(RS Pts.—Oilers 77, Jaguars 70)
*Franchise in Houston prior to 1997

KANSAS CITY vs. ARIZONA
RS: Chiefs lead series, 4-1-1;
See Arizona vs. Kansas City
KANSAS CITY vs. ATLANTA
RS: Chiefs lead series, 4-0;
See Atlanta vs. Kansas City
KANSAS CITY vs. BUFFALO
RS: Bills lead series, 17-13-1
PS: Bills lead series, 2-1;
See Buffalo vs. Kansas City
KANSAS CITY vs. CHICAGO
RS: Bears lead series, 4-3;
See Chicago vs. Kansas City
KANSAS CITY vs. CINCINNATI
RS: Chiefs lead series, 11-9;
See Cincinnati vs. Kansas City
KANSAS CITY vs. CLEVELAND
RS: Browns lead series, 8-7-2;
See Cleveland vs. Kansas City
KANSAS CITY vs. DALLAS
RS: Cowboys lead series, 4-2;
See Dallas vs. Kansas City
KANSAS CITY vs. DENVER
RS: Chiefs lead series, 42-31;
See Denver vs. Kansas City
KANSAS CITY vs. DETROIT
RS: Chiefs lead series, 5-3;
See Detroit vs. Kansas City
KANSAS CITY vs. GREEN BAY
RS: Chiefs lead series, 5-1-1
PS: Packers lead series, 1-0;
See Green Bay vs. Kansas City
KANSAS CITY vs. INDIANAPOLIS
RS: Chiefs lead series, 6-5
PS: Colts lead series, 1-0;
See Indianapolis vs. Kansas City
KANSAS CITY vs. MIAMI
RS: Chiefs lead series, 10-9
PS: Dolphins lead series, 3-0
1966—Chiefs, 34-16 (KC)
    Chiefs, 19-18 (M)
1967—Chiefs, 24-0 (M)
    Chiefs, 41-0 (KC)
1968—Chiefs, 48-3 (M)
1969—Chiefs, 17-10 (KC)
1971—*Dolphins, 27-24 (KC) OT
1972—Dolphins, 20-10 (KC)
1974—Dolphins, 9-3 (M)
1976—Chiefs, 20-17 (M) OT
1981—Dolphins, 17-7 (KC)
1983—Dolphins, 14-6 (M)
1985—Dolphins, 31-0 (M)
1987—Dolphins, 42-0 (M)
1989—Chiefs, 26-21 (KC)
    Chiefs, 27-24 (M)
1990—**Dolphins, 17-16 (M)
1991—Chiefs, 42-7 (KC)

1993—Dolphins, 30-10 (M)
1994—Dolphins, 45-28 (M)
    **Dolphins, 27-17 (M)
1995—Dolphins, 13-6 (M)
(RS Pts.—Chiefs 368, Dolphins 337)
(PS Pts.—Dolphins 71, Chiefs 57)
*AFC Divisional Playoff
**AFC First-Round Playoff
KANSAS CITY vs. MINNESOTA
RS: Series tied, 3-3
PS: Chiefs lead series, 1-0
1969—*Chiefs, 23-7 (New Orleans)
1970—Vikings, 27-10 (M)
1974—Vikings, 35-15 (KC)
1981—Chiefs, 10-6 (M)
1990—Chiefs, 24-21 (KC)
1993—Vikings, 30-10 (M)
1996—Chiefs, 21-6 (M)
(RS Pts.—Vikings 125, Chiefs 90)
(PS Pts.—Chiefs 23, Vikings 7)
*Super Bowl IV
KANSAS CITY vs. **NEW ENGLAND
RS: Chiefs lead series, 14-7-3
1960—Patriots, 42-14 (B)
    Texans, 34-0 (D)
1961—Patriots, 18-17 (B)
    Patriots, 28-21 (B)
1962—Texans, 42-28 (D)
    Texans, 27-7 (B)
1963—Tie, 24-24 (B)
    Chiefs, 35-3 (KC)
1964—Patriots, 24-7 (B)
    Patriots, 31-24 (KC)
1965—Chiefs, 27-17 (KC)
    Tie, 10-10 (B)
1966—Chiefs, 43-24 (B)
    Tie, 27-27 (KC)
1967—Chiefs, 33-10 (B)
1968—Chiefs, 31-17 (KC)
1969—Chiefs, 31-0 (B)
1970—Chiefs, 23-10 (KC)
1973—Chiefs, 10-7 (NE)
1977—Patriots, 21-17 (NE)
1981—Patriots, 33-17 (NE)
1990—Chiefs, 37-7 (NE)
1992—Chiefs, 27-20 (KC)
1995—Chiefs, 31-26 (KC)
(RS Pts.—Chiefs 609, Patriots 434)
*Franchise located in Dallas prior to
1963 and known as Texans
**Franchise in Boston prior to 1971
KANSAS CITY vs. NEW ORLEANS
RS: Series tied, 3-3
1972—Chiefs, 20-17 (NO)
1976—Saints, 27-17 (KC)
1982—Saints, 27-17 (NO)
1985—Chiefs, 47-27 (NO)
1991—Saints, 17-10 (KC)
1994—Chiefs, 30-17 (NO)
(RS Pts.—Chiefs 141, Saints 132)
KANSAS CITY vs. N.Y. GIANTS
RS: Giants lead series, 6-2
1974—Giants, 33-27 (KC)
1978—Giants, 26-10 (NY)
1979—Giants, 21-17 (KC)
1983—Chiefs, 38-17 (KC)
1984—Giants, 28-27 (NY)
1988—Giants, 28-12 (NY)
1992—Giants, 35-21 (NY)
1995—Chiefs, 20-17 (KC) OT
(RS Pts.—Giants 205, Chiefs 172)
KANSAS CITY vs. **N.Y. JETS
RS: Chiefs lead series, 14-12-1
PS: Series tied, 1-1
1960—Titans, 37-35 (D)
    Titans, 41-35 (NY)
1961—Titans, 28-7 (NY)
    Texans, 35-24 (D)
1962—Texans, 20-17 (D)
    Texans, 52-31 (NY)
1963—Jets, 17-0 (NY)
    Chiefs, 48-0 (KC)
1964—Jets, 27-14 (NY)

Chiefs, 24-7 (KC)
1965—Chiefs, 14-10 (NY)
   Jets, 13-10 (KC)
1966—Chiefs, 32-24 (NY)
1967—Chiefs, 42-18 (KC)
   Chiefs, 21-7 (NY)
1968—Jets, 20-19 (KC)
1969—Chiefs, 34-16 (NY)
   ***Chiefs, 13-6 (NY)
1971—Jets, 13-10 (NY)
1974—Chiefs, 24-16 (KC)
1975—Jets, 30-24 (KC)
1982—Chiefs, 37-13 (KC)
1984—Jets, 17-16 (KC)
   Jets, 28-7 (NY)
1986—****Jets, 35-15 (NY)
1987—Jets, 16-9 (KC)
1988—Tie, 17-17 (NY)
   Chiefs, 38-34 (KC)
1992—Chiefs, 23-7 (NY)
(RS Pts.—Chiefs 647, Jets 528)
(PS Pts.—Jets 41, Chiefs 28)
*Franchise in Dallas prior to 1963 and known as Texans
**Jets known as Titans prior to 1963
***Inter-Divisional Playoff
****AFC First-Round Playoff
*KANSAS CITY vs. **OAKLAND
RS: Raiders lead series, 36-35-2
PS: Chiefs lead series, 2-1
1960—Texans, 34-16 (O)
   Raiders, 20-19 (D)
1961—Texans, 42-35 (O)
   Texans, 43-11 (D)
1962—Texans, 26-16 (O)
   Texans, 35-7 (D)
1963—Raiders, 10-7 (O)
   Raiders, 22-7 (KC)
1964—Chiefs, 21-9 (O)
   Chiefs, 42-7 (KC)
1965—Raiders, 37-10 (O)
   Chiefs, 14-7 (KC)
1966—Chiefs, 32-10 (O)
   Raiders, 34-13 (KC)
1967—Raiders, 23-21 (O)
   Raiders, 44-22 (KC)
1968—Chiefs, 24-10 (KC)
   Raiders, 38-21 (O)
   ***Raiders, 41-6 (O)
1969—Raiders, 27-24 (KC)
   Raiders, 10-6 (O)
   ****Chiefs, 17-7 (O)
1970—Tie, 17-17 (KC)
   Raiders, 20-6 (O)
1971—Tie, 20-20 (O)
   Chiefs, 16-14 (KC)
1972—Chiefs, 27-14 (KC)
   Raiders, 26-3 (O)
1973—Chiefs, 16-3 (KC)
   Raiders, 37-7 (O)
1974—Raiders, 27-7 (O)
   Raiders, 7-6 (KC)
1975—Chiefs, 42-10 (KC)
   Raiders, 28-20 (O)
1976—Raiders, 24-21 (KC)
   Raiders, 21-10 (O)
1977—Raiders, 37-28 (KC)
   Raiders, 21-20 (O)
1978—Raiders, 28-6 (O)
   Raiders, 20-10 (KC)
1979—Chiefs, 35-7 (KC)
   Chiefs, 24-21 (O)
1980—Raiders, 27-14 (KC)
   Chiefs, 31-17 (O)
1981—Chiefs, 27-0 (KC)
   Chiefs, 28-17 (O)
1982—Raiders, 21-16 (KC)
1983—Raiders, 21-20 (LA)
   Raiders, 28-20 (KC)
1984—Raiders, 22-20 (KC)
   Raiders, 17-7 (LA)
1985—Chiefs, 36-20 (KC)
   Raiders, 19-10 (LA)

1986—Raiders, 24-17 (KC)
   Chiefs, 20-17 (LA)
1987—Raiders, 35-17 (LA)
   Chiefs, 16-10 (KC)
1988—Raiders, 27-17 (KC)
   Raiders, 17-10 (LA)
1989—Chiefs, 24-19 (KC)
   Raiders, 20-14 (LA)
1990—Chiefs, 9-7 (KC)
   Chiefs, 27-24 (LA)
1991—Chiefs, 24-21 (KC)
   Chiefs, 27-21 (LA)
   *****Chiefs, 10-6 (KC)
1992—Chiefs, 27-7 (KC)
   Raiders, 28-7 (LA)
1993—Chiefs, 24-9 (KC)
   Chiefs, 31-20 (LA)
1994—Chiefs, 13-3 (KC)
   Chiefs, 19-9 (LA)
1995—Chiefs, 23-17 (KC) OT
   Chiefs, 29-23 (O)
1996—Chiefs, 19-3 (KC)
   Raiders, 26-7 (O)
(RS Pts.—Chiefs 1,454, Raiders 1,391)
(PS Pts.—Raiders 54, Chiefs 33)
*Franchise in Dallas prior to 1963 and known as Texans
**Franchise in Los Angeles from 1982-1994
***Division Playoff
****AFL Championship
*****AFC First-Round Playoff
KANSAS CITY vs. PHILADELPHIA
RS: Series tied, 1-1
1972—Eagles, 21-20 (KC)
1992—Chiefs, 24-17 (KC)
(RS Pts.—Chiefs 44, Eagles 38)
KANSAS CITY vs. PITTSBURGH
RS: Steelers lead series, 14-5
PS: Chiefs lead series, 1-0
1970—Chiefs, 31-14 (P)
1971—Chiefs, 38-16 (KC)
1972—Steelers, 16-7 (P)
1974—Steelers, 34-24 (KC)
1975—Steelers, 28-3 (P)
1976—Steelers, 45-0 (KC)
1978—Steelers, 27-24 (P)
1979—Steelers, 30-3 (KC)
1980—Steelers, 21-16 (P)
1981—Chiefs, 37-33 (P)
1982—Steelers, 35-14 (P)
1984—Chiefs, 37-27 (KC)
1985—Steelers, 36-28 (KC)
1986—Chiefs, 24-19 (P)
1987—Steelers, 17-16 (KC)
1988—Steelers, 16-10 (P)
1989—Steelers, 23-17 (P)
1992—Steelers, 27-3 (KC)
1993—*Chiefs, 27-24 (KC) OT
1996—Steelers, 17-7 (KC)
(RS Pts.—Steelers 481, Chiefs 339)
(PS Pts.—Chiefs 27, Steelers 24)
*AFC First-Round Playoff
*KANSAS CITY vs. *ST. LOUIS
RS: Rams lead series, 4-1
1973—Rams, 23-13 (KC)
1982—Rams, 20-14 (LA)
1985—Rams, 16-0 (KC)
1991—Chiefs, 27-20 (LA)
1994—Rams, 16-0 (KC)
(RS Pts.—Rams 95, Chiefs 54)
*Franchise in Los Angeles prior to 1995
*KANSAS CITY vs. **SAN DIEGO
RS: Chiefs lead series, 37-35-1
PS: Chargers lead series, 1-0
1960—Chargers, 21-20 (LA)
   Texans, 17-0 (D)
1961—Chargers, 26-10 (D)
   Chargers, 24-14 (SD)
1962—Chargers, 32-28 (SD)
   Texans, 26-17 (D)
1963—Chargers, 24-10 (SD)
   Chargers, 38-17 (KC)

1964—Chargers, 28-14 (KC)
   Chiefs, 49-6 (SD)
1965—Tie, 10-10 (SD)
   Chiefs, 31-7 (KC)
1966—Chiefs, 24-14 (KC)
   Chiefs, 27-17 (SD)
1967—Chargers, 45-31 (SD)
   Chargers, 17-16 (KC)
1968—Chiefs, 27-20 (KC)
   Chiefs, 40-3 (SD)
1969—Chiefs, 27-9 (SD)
   Chiefs, 27-3 (KC)
1970—Chiefs, 26-14 (KC)
   Chargers, 31-13 (SD)
1971—Chargers, 21-14 (SD)
   Chiefs, 31-10 (KC)
1972—Chiefs, 26-14 (SD)
   Chargers, 27-17 (KC)
1973—Chiefs, 19-0 (SD)
   Chiefs, 33-6 (KC)
1974—Chiefs, 24-14 (SD)
   Chargers, 14-7 (KC)
1975—Chiefs, 12-10 (SD)
   Chargers, 28-20 (KC)
1976—Chargers, 30-16 (KC)
   Chiefs, 23-20 (SD)
1977—Chargers, 23-7 (KC)
   Chiefs, 21-16 (SD)
1978—Chargers, 29-23 (SD) OT
   Chiefs, 23-0 (KC)
1979—Chargers, 20-14 (KC)
   Chargers, 28-7 (SD)
1980—Chargers, 24-7 (KC)
   Chargers, 20-7 (SD)
1981—Chargers, 42-31 (KC)
   Chargers, 22-20 (SD)
1982—Chiefs, 19-12 (KC)
1983—Chargers, 17-14 (KC)
   Chargers, 41-38 (SD)
1984—Chiefs, 31-13 (KC)
   Chiefs, 42-21 (SD)
1985—Chargers, 31-20 (SD)
   Chiefs, 38-34 (KC)
1986—Chiefs, 42-41 (KC)
   Chiefs, 24-23 (SD)
1987—Chiefs, 20-13 (KC)
   Chargers, 42-21 (SD)
1988—Chargers, 24-23 (KC)
   Chargers, 24-13 (SD)
1989—Chargers, 21-6 (SD)
   Chargers, 20-13 (KC)
1990—Chiefs, 27-10 (KC)
   Chiefs, 24-21 (SD)
1991—Chiefs, 14-13 (SD)
   Chiefs, 20-17 (KC) OT
1992—Chiefs, 24-10 (SD)
   Chiefs, 16-14 (KC)
   ***Chargers, 17-0 (SD)
1993—Chiefs, 17-14 (SD)
   Chiefs, 28-24 (KC)
1994—Chargers, 20-6 (SD)
   Chargers, 14-13 (KC)
1995—Chiefs, 29-23 (KC) OT
   Chiefs, 22-7 (SD)
1996—Chargers, 22-19 (SD)
   Chargers, 28-14 (KC)
(RS Pts.—Chiefs 1,543, Chargers 1,438)
(PS Pts.—Chargers 17, Chiefs 0)
*Franchise in Dallas prior to 1963 and known as Texans
**Franchise in Los Angeles prior to 1961
***AFC First-Round Playoff
KANSAS CITY vs. SAN FRANCISCO
RS: 49ers lead series, 4-2
1971—Chiefs, 26-17 (SF)
1975—49ers, 20-3 (KC)
1982—49ers, 26-13 (KC)
1985—49ers, 31-3 (SF)
1991—49ers, 28-14 (SF)
1994—Chiefs, 24-17 (KC)
(RS Pts.—49ers 139, Chiefs 83)
KANSAS CITY vs. SEATTLE
RS: Chiefs lead series, 24-13

1977—Seahawks, 34-31 (KC)
1978—Seahawks, 13-10 (KC)
   Seahawks, 23-19 (S)
1979—Chiefs, 24-6 (S)
   Chiefs, 37-21 (KC)
1980—Seahawks, 17-16 (KC)
   Chiefs, 31-30 (S)
1981—Chiefs, 20-14 (S)
   Chiefs, 40-13 (KC)
1983—Chiefs, 17-13 (KC)
   Seahawks, 51-48 (S) OT
1984—Seahawks, 45-0 (S)
   Chiefs, 34-7 (KC)
1985—Chiefs, 28-7 (KC)
   Seahawks, 24-6 (S)
1986—Seahawks, 23-17 (S)
   Chiefs, 27-7 (KC)
1987—Seahawks, 43-14 (S)
   Chiefs, 41-20 (KC)
1988—Seahawks, 31-10 (S)
   Chiefs, 27-24 (KC)
1989—Chiefs, 20-16 (S)
   Chiefs, 20-10 (KC)
1990—Seahawks, 19-7 (S)
   Seahawks, 17-16 (KC)
1991—Chiefs, 20-13 (KC)
   Chiefs, 19-6 (S)
1992—Chiefs, 26-7 (KC)
   Chiefs, 24-14 (S)
1993—Chiefs, 31-16 (S)
   Chiefs, 34-24 (KC)
1994—Chiefs, 38-23 (KC)
   Seahawks, 10-9 (S)
1995—Chiefs, 34-10 (S)
   Chiefs, 26-3 (KC)
1996—Chiefs, 35-17 (S)
   Chiefs, 34-16 (KC)
(RS Pts.—Chiefs 890, Seahawks 687)
KANSAS CITY vs. TAMPA BAY
RS: Chiefs lead series, 5-2
1976—Chiefs, 28-19 (TB)
1978—Buccaneers, 30-13 (KC)
1979—Buccaneers, 3-0 (TB)
1981—Chiefs, 19-10 (KC)
1984—Chiefs, 24-20 (KC)
1986—Chiefs, 27-20 (KC)
1993—Chiefs, 27-3 (TB)
1995—Chiefs, 24-3 (KC)
(RS Pts.—Chiefs 138, Buccaneers 105)
*KANSAS CITY vs. **TENNESSEE
RS: Chiefs lead series, 24-17
PS: Chiefs lead series, 2-0
1960—Oilers, 20-10 (H)
   Texans, 24-0 (D)
1961—Texans, 26-21 (D)
   Oilers, 38-7 (H)
1962—Texans, 31-7 (H)
   Oilers, 14-6 (D)
   ***Texans, 20-17 (H) OT
1963—Chiefs, 28-7 (KC)
   Oilers, 28-7 (H)
1964—Chiefs, 28-7 (KC)
   Chiefs, 28-19 (H)
1965—Chiefs, 52-21 (KC)
   Oilers, 38-36 (H)
1966—Chiefs, 48-23 (KC)
1967—Chiefs, 25-20 (H)
   Oilers, 24-19 (KC)
1968—Chiefs, 26-21 (H)
   Chiefs, 24-10 (KC)
1969—Chiefs, 24-0 (KC)
1970—Chiefs, 24-9 (KC)
1971—Chiefs, 20-16 (H)
1973—Chiefs, 38-14 (KC)
1974—Chiefs, 17-7 (H)
1975—Oilers, 17-13 (KC)
1977—Oilers, 34-20 (H)
1978—Oilers, 20-17 (KC)
1979—Oilers, 20-6 (H)
1980—Chiefs, 21-20 (KC)
1981—Chiefs, 23-10 (KC)
1983—Chiefs, 13-10 (H) OT
1984—Oilers, 17-16 (KC)

1985—Oilers, 23-20 (H)
1986—Chiefs, 27-13 (KC)
1988—Oilers, 7-6 (H)
1989—Chiefs, 34-0 (KC)
1990—Oilers, 27-10 (KC)
1991—Oilers, 17-7 (H)
1992—Oilers, 23-20 (H) OT
1993—Oilers, 30-0 (H)
    ****Chiefs, 28-20 (H)
1994—Chiefs, 31-9 (KC)
1995—Chiefs, 20-13 (KC)
1996—Chiefs, 20-19 (H)
(RS Pts.—Chiefs 872, Oilers 693)
(PS Pts.—Chiefs 48, Oilers 37)
*Franchise in Dallas prior to 1963 and known as Texans
**Franchise in Houston prior to 1997
***AFL Championship
****AFC Divisional Playoff

KANSAS CITY vs. WASHINGTON
RS: Chiefs lead series, 4-1
1971—Chiefs, 27-20 (KC)
1976—Chiefs, 33-30 (W)
1983—Redskins, 27-12 (W)
1992—Chiefs, 35-16 (KC)
1995—Chiefs, 24-3 (KC)
(RS Pts.—Chiefs 131, Redskins 96)

MIAMI vs. ARIZONA
RS: Dolphins lead series, 7-0;
See Arizona vs. Miami
MIAMI vs. ATLANTA
RS: Dolphins lead series, 6-1;
See Atlanta vs. Miami
MIAMI vs. BUFFALO
RS: Dolphins lead series, 40-21-1
PS: Bills lead series, 3-0;
See Buffalo vs. Miami
MIAMI vs. CHICAGO
RS: Dolphins lead series, 5-2;
See Chicago vs. Miami
MIAMI vs. CINCINNATI
RS: Dolphins lead series, 11-3
PS: Dolphins lead series, 1-0;
See Cincinnati vs. Miami
MIAMI vs. CLEVELAND
RS: Dolphins lead series, 6-4
PS: Dolphins lead series, 2-0;
See Cleveland vs. Miami
MIAMI vs. DALLAS
RS: Dolphins lead series, 6-2
PS: Cowboys lead series, 1-0;
See Dallas vs. Miami
MIAMI vs. DENVER
RS: Dolphins lead series, 5-2-1;
See Denver vs. Miami
MIAMI vs. DETROIT
RS: Dolphins lead series, 3-2;
See Detroit vs. Miami
MIAMI vs. GREEN BAY
RS: Dolphins lead series, 8-0;
See Green Bay vs. Miami
MIAMI vs. INDIANAPOLIS
RS: Dolphins lead series, 36-18
PS: Dolphins lead series, 1-0;
See Indianapolis vs. Miami
MIAMI vs. KANSAS CITY
RS: Chiefs lead series, 10-9
PS: Dolphins lead series, 3-0;
See Kansas City vs. Miami
MIAMI vs. MINNESOTA
RS: Dolphins lead series, 4-2
PS: Dolphins lead series, 1-0
1972—Dolphins, 16-14 (Minn)
1973—*Dolphins, 24-7 (Houston)
1976—Vikings, 29-7 (Mia)
1979—Dolphins, 27-12 (Minn)
1982—Dolphins, 22-14 (Mia)
1988—Dolphins, 24-7 (Mia)
1994—Vikings, 38-35 (M)
(RS Pts.—Dolphins 131, Vikings 114)
(PS Pts.—Dolphins 24, Vikings 7)
*Super Bowl VIII

MIAMI vs. *NEW ENGLAND
RS: Dolphins lead series, 37-23
PS: Series tied, 1-1
1966—Patriots, 20-14 (M)
1967—Patriots, 41-10 (B)
    Dolphins, 41-32 (M)
1968—Dolphins, 34-10 (B)
    Dolphins, 38-7 (M)
1969—Dolphins, 17-16 (B)
    Patriots, 38-23 (Tampa)
1970—Patriots, 27-14 (B)
    Dolphins, 37-20 (M)
1971—Dolphins, 41-3 (M)
    Patriots, 34-13 (NE)
1972—Dolphins, 52-0 (M)
    Dolphins, 37-21 (NE)
1973—Dolphins, 44-23 (M)
    Dolphins, 30-14 (NE)
1974—Patriots, 34-24 (NE)
    Dolphins, 34-27 (M)
1975—Dolphins, 22-14 (NE)
    Dolphins, 20-7 (M)
1976—Patriots, 30-14 (NE)
    Dolphins, 10-3 (M)
1977—Dolphins, 17-5 (M)
    Patriots, 14-10 (NE)
1978—Patriots, 33-24 (NE)
    Dolphins, 23-3 (M)
1979—Patriots, 28-13 (NE)
    Dolphins, 39-24 (M)
1980—Patriots, 34-0 (NE)
    Dolphins, 16-13 (M) OT
1981—Dolphins, 30-27 (NE) OT
    Dolphins, 24-14 (M)
1982—Patriots, 3-0 (NE)
    **Dolphins, 28-13 (M)
1983—Dolphins, 34-24 (M)
    Patriots, 17-6 (NE)
1984—Dolphins, 28-7 (M)
    Dolphins, 44-24 (NE)
1985—Patriots, 17-13 (NE)
    Dolphins, 30-27 (M)
    ***Patriots, 31-14 (M)
1986—Patriots, 34-7 (NE)
    Patriots, 34-27 (M)
1987—Patriots, 28-21 (NE)
    Patriots, 24-10 (M)
1988—Patriots, 21-10 (NE)
    Patriots, 6-3 (M)
1989—Dolphins, 24-10 (NE)
    Dolphins, 31-10 (M)
1990—Dolphins, 27-24 (NE)
    Dolphins, 17-10 (M)
1991—Dolphins, 20-10 (NE)
    Dolphins, 30-20 (M)
1992—Dolphins, 38-17 (M)
    Dolphins, 16-13 (NE) OT
1993—Dolphins, 17-13 (M)
    Patriots, 33-27 (NE) OT
1994—Dolphins, 39-35 (M)
    Dolphins, 23-3 (NE)
1995—Dolphins, 20-3 (NE)
    Patriots, 34-17 (M)
1996—Dolphins, 24-10 (M)
    Patriots, 42-23 (NE)
(RS Pts.—Dolphins 1,391, Patriots 1,169)
(PS Pts.—Patriots 44, Dolphins 42)
*Franchise in Boston prior to 1971
**AFC First-Round Playoff
***AFC Championship

MIAMI vs. NEW ORLEANS
RS: Dolphins lead series, 4-3
1970—Dolphins, 21-10 (M)
1974—Dolphins, 21-0 (NO)
1980—Dolphins, 21-16 (M)
1983—Saints, 17-7 (NO)
1986—Dolphins, 31-27 (NO)
1992—Saints, 24-13 (NO)
1995—Saints, 33-30 (NO)
(RS Pts.—Dolphins 144, Saints 127)

MIAMI vs. N.Y. GIANTS
RS: Giants lead series, 3-1
1972—Dolphins, 23-13 (NY)

1990—Giants, 20-3 (NY)
1993—Giants, 19-14 (M)
1996—Giants, 17-7 (M)
(RS Pts.—Giants 69, Dolphins 47)

MIAMI vs. N.Y. JETS
RS: Dolphins lead series, 32-29-1
PS: Dolphins lead series, 1-0
1966—Jets, 19-14 (M)
    Jets, 30-13 (NY)
1967—Jets, 29-7 (NY)
    Jets, 33-14 (M)
1968—Jets, 35-17 (NY)
    Jets, 31-7 (M)
1969—Jets, 34-31 (NY)
    Jets, 27-9 (M)
1970—Dolphins, 20-6 (NY)
    Dolphins, 16-10 (M)
1971—Jets, 14-10 (M)
    Dolphins, 30-14 (NY)
1972—Dolphins, 27-17 (NY)
    Dolphins, 28-24 (M)
1973—Dolphins, 31-3 (M)
    Dolphins, 24-14 (NY)
1974—Dolphins, 21-17 (M)
    Jets, 17-14 (NY)
1975—Dolphins, 43-0 (NY)
    Dolphins, 27-7 (M)
1976—Dolphins, 16-0 (M)
    Dolphins, 27-7 (NY)
1977—Dolphins, 21-17 (M)
    Dolphins, 14-10 (NY)
1978—Jets, 33-20 (NY)
    Jets, 24-13 (M)
1979—Jets, 33-27 (M)
    Jets, 27-24 (M)
1980—Jets, 17-14 (NY)
    Jets, 24-17 (M)
1981—Tie, 28-28 (M) OT
    Jets, 16-15 (NY)
1982—Dolphins, 45-28 (NY)
    Dolphins, 20-19 (M)
    *Dolphins, 14-0 (M)
1983—Dolphins, 32-14 (NY)
    Dolphins, 34-14 (M)
1984—Dolphins, 31-17 (NY)
    Dolphins, 28-17 (M)
1985—Jets, 23-7 (NY)
    Dolphins, 21-17 (M)
1986—Jets, 51-45 (NY) OT
    Dolphins, 45-3 (M)
1987—Jets, 37-31 (NY) OT
    Dolphins, 37-28 (M)
1988—Jets, 44-30 (M)
    Jets, 38-34 (NY)
1989—Jets, 40-33 (M)
    Dolphins, 31-23 (NY)
1990—Dolphins, 20-16 (M)
    Dolphins, 17-3 (NY)
1991—Jets, 41-23 (NY)
    Jets, 23-20 (M) OT
1992—Jets, 26-14 (NY)
    Dolphins, 19-17 (M)
1993—Jets, 24-14 (M)
    Jets, 27-10 (NY)
1994—Dolphins, 28-14 (M)
    Dolphins, 28-24 (NY)
1995—Dolphins, 52-14 (M)
    Jets, 17-16 (NY)
1996—Dolphins, 36-27 (M)
    Dolphins, 31-28 (NY)
(RS Pts.—Dolphins 1,471, Jets 1,331)
(PS Pts.—Dolphins 14, Jets 0)
*AFC Championship

MIAMI vs. *OAKLAND
RS: Raiders lead series, 15-5-1
PS: Raiders lead series, 2-1
1966—Raiders, 23-14 (M)
    Raiders, 21-10 (O)
1967—Raiders, 31-17 (O)
1968—Raiders, 47-21 (M)
1969—Raiders, 20-17 (O)
    Tie, 20-20 (M)
1970—Dolphins, 20-13 (M)

    **Raiders, 21-14 (O)
1973—Raiders, 12-7 (O)
    ***Dolphins, 27-10 (M)
1974—**Raiders, 28-26 (O)
1975—Raiders, 31-21 (M)
1978—Dolphins, 23-6 (M)
1979—Raiders, 13-3 (O)
1980—Raiders, 16-10 (O)
1981—Raiders, 33-17 (M)
1983—Raiders, 27-14 (LA)
1984—Raiders, 45-34 (M)
1986—Raiders, 30-28 (M)
1988—Dolphins, 24-14 (LA)
1990—Raiders, 13-10 (M)
1992—Dolphins, 20-7 (M)
1994—Dolphins, 20-17 (M) OT
1996—Raiders, 17-7 (O)
(RS Pts.—Raiders 456, Dolphins 357)
(PS Pts.—Dolphins 67, Raiders 59)
*Franchise in Los Angeles from 1982-1994
**AFC Divisional Playoff
***AFC Championship

MIAMI vs. PHILADELPHIA
RS: Dolphins lead series, 6-3
1970—Eagles, 24-17 (P)
1975—Dolphins, 24-16 (M)
1978—Eagles, 17-3 (P)
1981—Dolphins, 13-10 (M)
1984—Dolphins, 24-23 (M)
1987—Dolphins, 28-10 (P)
1990—Dolphins, 23-20 (M) OT
1993—Dolphins, 19-14 (P)
1996—Eagles, 35-28 (P)
(RS Pts.—Dolphins 179, Eagles 169)

MIAMI vs. PITTSBURGH
RS: Dolphins lead series, 8-7
PS: Dolphins lead series, 2-1
1971—Dolphins, 24-21 (M)
1972—*Dolphins, 21-17 (P)
1973—Dolphins, 30-26 (M)
1976—Steelers, 14-3 (P)
1979—**Steelers, 34-14 (P)
1980—Steelers, 23-10 (P)
1981—Dolphins, 30-10 (M)
1984—Dolphins, 31-7 (P)
    *Dolphins, 45-28 (M)
1985—Dolphins, 24-20 (M)
1987—Dolphins, 35-24 (M)
1988—Steelers, 40-24 (P)
1989—Steelers, 34-14 (M)
1990—Steelers, 28-6 (P)
1993—Steelers, 21-20 (M)
1994—Steelers, 16-13 (P) OT
1995—Dolphins, 23-10 (M)
1996—Steelers, 24-17 (M)
(RS Pts.—Dolphins 326, Steelers 296)
(PS Pts.—Dolphins 80, Steelers 79)
*AFC Championship
**AFC Divisional Playoff

MIAMI vs. *ST. LOUIS
RS: Dolphins lead series, 6-1
1971—Dolphins, 20-14 (LA)
1976—Rams, 31-28 (M)
1980—Dolphins, 35-14 (LA)
1983—Dolphins, 30-14 (M)
1986—Dolphins, 37-31 (LA) OT
1992—Dolphins, 26-10 (M)
1995—Dolphins, 41-22 (StL)
(RS Pts.—Dolphins 217, Rams 136)
*Franchise in Los Angeles prior to 1995

MIAMI vs. SAN DIEGO
RS: Chargers lead series, 10-6
PS: Series tied, 2-2
1966—Chargers, 44-10 (SD)
1967—Chargers, 24-0 (SD)
    Dolphins, 41-24 (M)
1968—Chargers, 34-28 (SD)
1969—Chargers, 21-14 (M)
1972—Dolphins, 24-10 (M)
1974—Dolphins, 28-21 (SD)
1977—Chargers, 14-13 (M)
1978—Dolphins, 28-21 (SD)

1980—Chargers, 27-24 (M) OT
1981—*Chargers, 41-38 (M) OT
1982—**Dolphins, 34-13 (M)
1984—Chargers, 34-28 (SD) OT
1986—Chargers, 50-28 (SD)
1988—Dolphins, 31-28 (M)
1991—Chargers, 38-30 (SD)
1992—*Dolphins, 31-0 (M)
1993—Chargers, 45-20 (SD)
1994—*Chargers, 22-21 (SD)
1995—Dolphins, 24-14 (SD)
(RS Pts.—Chargers 449, Dolphins 371)
(PS Pts.—Dolphins 124, Chargers 76)
*AFC Divisional Playoff
**AFC Second-Round Playoff
MIAMI vs. SAN FRANCISCO
RS: Dolphins lead series, 4-3
PS: 49ers lead series, 1-0
1973—Dolphins, 21-13 (M)
1977—Dolphins, 19-15 (SF)
1980—Dolphins, 17-13 (M)
1983—Dolphins, 20-17 (SF)
1984—*49ers, 38-16 (Stanford)
1986—49ers, 31-16 (M)
1992—49ers, 27-3 (SF)
1995—49ers, 44-20 (M)
(RS Pts.—49ers 160, Dolphins 116)
(PS Pts.—49ers 38, Dolphins 16)
*Super Bowl XIX
MIAMI vs. SEATTLE
RS: Dolphins lead series, 4-2
PS: Series tied, 1-1
1977—Dolphins, 31-13 (M)
1979—Dolphins, 19-10 (M)
1983—*Seahawks, 27-20 (M)
1984—*Dolphins, 31-10 (M)
1987—Seahawks, 24-20 (S)
1990—Dolphins, 24-17 (M)
1992—Dolphins, 19-17 (S)
1996—Seahawks, 22-15 (M)
(RS Pts.—Dolphins 128, Seahawks 103)
(PS Pts.—Dolphins 51, Seahawks 37)
*AFC Divisional Playoff
MIAMI vs. TAMPA BAY
RS: Dolphins lead series, 4-1
1976—Dolphins, 23-20 (TB)
1982—Buccaneers, 23-17 (TB)
1985—Dolphins, 41-38 (M)
1988—Dolphins, 17-14 (TB)
1991—Dolphins, 33-14 (M)
(RS Pts.—Dolphins 131, Buccaneers 109)
MIAMI vs. *TENNESSEE
RS: Dolphins lead series, 12-11
PS: Oilers lead series, 1-0
1966—Dolphins, 20-13 (H)
        Dolphins, 29-28 (M)
1967—Oilers, 17-14 (H)
        Oilers, 41-10 (M)
1968—Oilers, 24-10 (M)
        Dolphins, 24-7 (H)
1969—Oilers, 22-10 (H)
        Oilers, 32-7 (M)
1970—Dolphins, 20-10 (H)
1972—Dolphins, 34-13 (M)
1975—Oilers, 20-19 (H)
1977—Dolphins, 27-7 (M)
1978—Oilers, 35-30 (H)
        **Oilers, 17-9 (M)
1979—Oilers, 9-6 (M)
1981—Dolphins, 16-10 (H)
1983—Dolphins, 24-17 (H)
1984—Dolphins, 28-10 (M)
1985—Oilers, 26-23 (H)
1986—Dolphins, 28-7 (M)
1989—Oilers, 39-7 (H)
1991—Oilers, 17-13 (M)
1992—Dolphins, 19-16 (M)
1996—Dolphins, 23-20 (H)
(RS Pts.—Dolphins 441, Oilers 440)
(PS Pts.—Oilers 17, Dolphins 9)
*Franchise in Houston prior to 1997
**AFC First-Round Playoff
MIAMI vs. WASHINGTON

RS: Dolphins lead series, 5-2
PS: Series tied, 1-1
1972—*Dolphins, 14-7 (Los Angeles)
1974—Redskins, 20-17 (W)
1978—Dolphins, 16-0 (W)
1981—Dolphins, 13-10 (M)
1982—**Redskins, 27-17 (Pasadena)
1984—Dolphins, 35-17 (W)
1987—Dolphins, 23-21 (M)
1990—Redskins, 42-20 (M)
1993—Dolphins, 17-10 (M)
(RS Pts.—Dolphins 141, Redskins 120)
(PS Pts.—Redskins 34, Dolphins 31)
*Super Bowl VII
**Super Bowl XVII

MINNESOTA vs. ARIZONA
RS: Cardinals lead series, 8-6
PS: Vikings lead series, 1-0;
See Arizona vs. Minnesota
MINNESOTA vs. ATLANTA
RS: Vikings lead series, 12-6
PS: Vikings lead series, 1-0;
See Atlanta vs. Minnesota
MINNESOTA vs. BUFFALO
RS: Vikings lead series, 5-2;
See Buffalo vs. Minnesota
MINNESOTA vs. CAROLINA
RS: Vikings lead series, 1-0;
See Carolina vs. Minnesota
MINNESOTA vs. CHICAGO
RS: Vikings lead series, 37-32-2
PS: Bears lead series, 1-0;
See Chicago vs. Minnesota
MINNESOTA vs. CINCINNATI
RS: Series tied, 4-4;
See Cincinnati vs. Minnesota
MINNESOTA vs. CLEVELAND
RS: Vikings lead series, 8-3
PS: Vikings lead series, 1-0;
See Cleveland vs. Minnesota
MINNESOTA vs. DALLAS
RS: Cowboys lead series, 9-6
PS: Cowboys lead series, 4-1;
See Dallas vs. Minnesota
MINNESOTA vs. DENVER
RS: Vikings lead series, 5-4;
See Denver vs. Minnesota
MINNESOTA vs. DETROIT
RS: Vikings lead series, 44-25-2;
See Detroit vs. Minnesota
MINNESOTA vs. GREEN BAY
RS: Vikings lead series, 36-34-1;
See Green Bay vs. Minnesota
MINNESOTA vs. INDIANAPOLIS
RS: Colts lead series, 11-6-1
PS: Colts lead series, 1-0;
See Indianapolis vs. Minnesota
MINNESOTA vs. KANSAS CITY
RS: Series tied, 3-3
PS: Chiefs lead series, 1-0;
See Kansas City vs. Minnesota
MINNESOTA vs. MIAMI
RS: Dolphins lead series, 4-2
PS: Dolphins lead series, 1-0;
See Miami vs. Minnesota
MINNESOTA vs. *NEW ENGLAND
RS: Patriots lead series, 4-2
1970—Vikings, 35-14 (B)
1974—Patriots, 17-14 (M)
1979—Patriots, 27-23 (NE)
1988—Vikings, 36-6 (M)
1991—Patriots, 26-23 (NE) OT
1994—Patriots, 26-20 (NE) OT
(RS Pts.—Vikings 151, Patriots 116)
*Franchise in Boston prior to 1971
MINNESOTA vs. NEW ORLEANS
RS: Vikings lead series, 13-6
PS: Vikings lead series, 1-0
1968—Saints, 20-17 (NO)
1970—Vikings, 26-0 (M)
1971—Vikings, 23-10 (NO)
1972—Vikings, 37-6 (M)

1974—Vikings, 29-9 (M)
1975—Vikings, 20-7 (NO)
1976—Vikings, 40-9 (NO)
1978—Saints, 31-24 (NO)
1980—Vikings, 23-20 (NO)
1981—Vikings, 20-10 (M)
1983—Saints, 17-16 (NO)
1985—Saints, 30-23 (M)
1986—Vikings, 33-17 (M)
1987—*Vikings, 44-10 (NO)
1988—Vikings, 45-3 (M)
1990—Vikings, 32-3 (M)
1991—Saints, 26-0 (NO)
1993—Saints, 17-14 (M)
1994—Vikings, 21-20 (M)
1995—Vikings, 43-24 (M)
(RS Pts.—Vikings 486, Saints 279)
(PS Pts.—Vikings 44, Saints 10)
*NFC First-Round Playoff
MINNESOTA vs. N.Y. GIANTS
RS: Vikings lead series, 7-5
PS: Giants lead series, 1-0
1964—Vikings, 30-21 (NY)
1965—Vikings, 40-14 (M)
1967—Vikings, 27-24 (M)
1969—Giants, 24-23 (NY)
1971—Vikings, 17-10 (NY)
1973—Vikings, 31-7 (New Haven)
1976—Vikings, 24-7 (M)
1986—Giants, 22-20 (M)
1989—Giants, 24-14 (NY)
1990—Giants, 23-15 (NY)
1993—*Giants, 17-10 (NY)
1994—Vikings, 27-10 (NY)
1996—Giants, 15-10 (NY)
(RS Pts.—Vikings 278, Giants 201)
(PS Pts.—Giants 17, Vikings 10)
*NFC First-Round Playoff
MINNESOTA vs. N.Y. JETS
RS: Jets lead series, 4-1
1970—Jets, 20-10 (NY)
1975—Vikings, 29-21 (M)
1979—Jets, 14-7 (NY)
1982—Jets, 42-14 (M)
1994—Jets, 31-21 (M)
(RS Pts.—Jets 128, Vikings 81)
MINNESOTA vs. *OAKLAND
RS: Raiders lead series, 6-3
PS: Raiders lead series, 1-0
1973—Vikings, 24-16 (M)
1976—**Raiders, 32-14 (Pasadena)
1977—Raiders, 35-13 (O)
1978—Raiders, 27-20 (O)
1981—Raiders, 36-10 (M)
1984—Raiders, 23-20 (LA)
1987—Vikings, 31-20 (M)
1990—Raiders, 28-24 (M)
1993—Raiders, 24-7 (LA)
1996—Vikings, 16-13 (O) OT
(RS Pts.—Raiders 222, Vikings 165)
(PS Pts.—Raiders 32, Vikings 14)
*Franchise in Los Angeles from 1982-1994
**Super Bowl XI
MINNESOTA vs. PHILADELPHIA
RS: Vikings lead series, 10-6
PS: Eagles lead series, 1-0
1962—Vikings, 31-21 (M)
1963—Vikings, 34-13 (P)
1968—Vikings, 24-17 (P)
1971—Vikings, 13-0 (P)
1973—Vikings, 28-21 (M)
1976—Vikings, 31-12 (P)
1978—Vikings, 28-27 (M)
1980—Eagles, 42-7 (M)
        *Eagles, 31-16 (P)
1981—Vikings, 35-23 (M)
1984—Eagles, 19-17 (P)
1985—Vikings, 28-23 (P)
        Eagles, 37-35 (M)
1988—Vikings, 23-21 (M)
1989—Eagles, 10-9 (P)
1990—Eagles, 32-24 (P)

1992—Eagles, 28-17 (P)
(RS Pts.—Vikings 384, Eagles 346)
(PS Pts.—Eagles 31, Vikings 16)
*NFC Divisional Playoff
MINNESOTA vs. PITTSBURGH
RS: Vikings lead series, 8-4
PS: Steelers lead series, 1-0
1962—Steelers, 39-31 (P)
1964—Vikings, 30-10 (M)
1967—Vikings, 41-27 (P)
1969—Vikings, 52-14 (M)
1972—Steelers, 23-10 (P)
1974—*Steelers, 16-6 (New Orleans)
1976—Vikings, 17-6 (M)
1980—Steelers, 23-17 (M)
1983—Vikings, 17-14 (P)
1986—Vikings, 31-7 (M)
1989—Steelers, 27-14 (P)
1992—Vikings, 6-3 (P)
1995—Vikings, 44-24 (P)
(RS Pts.—Vikings 310, Steelers 217)
(PS Pts.—Steelers 16, Vikings 6)
*Super Bowl IX
MINNESOTA vs. *ST. LOUIS
RS: Vikings lead series, 15-11-2
PS: Vikings lead series, 5-1
1961—Rams, 31-17 (LA)
        Vikings, 42-21 (M)
1962—Vikings, 38-14 (LA)
        Tie, 24-24 (M)
1963—Rams, 27-24 (LA)
        Vikings, 21-13 (M)
1964—Rams, 22-13 (LA)
        Vikings, 34-13 (M)
1965—Vikings, 38-35 (LA)
        Vikings, 24-13 (M)
1966—Vikings, 35-7 (M)
        Rams, 21-6 (LA)
1967—Rams, 39-3 (LA)
1968—Rams, 31-3 (M)
1969—Vikings, 20-13 (LA)
        **Vikings, 23-20 (M)
1970—Vikings, 13-3 (M)
1972—Vikings, 45-41 (LA)
1973—Vikings, 10-9 (M)
1974—Rams, 20-17 (LA)
        ***Vikings, 14-10 (M)
1976—Tie, 10-10 (M) OT
        ***Vikings, 24-13 (M)
1977—Rams, 35-3 (LA)
        ****Vikings, 14-7 (LA)
1978—Rams, 34-17 (M)
        ****Rams, 34-10 (LA)
1979—Rams, 27-21 (LA) OT
1985—Rams, 13-10 (LA)
1987—Vikings, 21-16 (LA)
1988—*****Vikings, 28-17 (M)
1989—Vikings, 23-21 (M) OT
1991—Vikings, 20-14 (M)
1992—Vikings, 31-17 (LA)
(RS Pts.—Rams 584, Vikings 583)
(PS Pts.—Vikings 113, Rams 101)
*Franchise in Los Angeles prior to 1995
**Conference Championship
***NFC Championship
****NFC Divisional Playoff
*****NFC First-Round Playoff
MINNESOTA vs. SAN DIEGO
RS: Chargers lead series, 4-3
1971—Chargers, 30-14 (SD)
1975—Vikings, 28-13 (M)
1978—Chargers, 13-7 (M)
1981—Vikings, 33-31 (SD)
1984—Chargers, 42-13 (M)
1985—Vikings, 21-17 (M)
1993—Chargers, 30-17 (M)
(RS Pts.—Chargers 176, Vikings 133)
MINNESOTA vs. SAN FRANCISCO
RS: Series tied, 16-16-1
PS: 49ers lead series, 3-1
1961—49ers, 38-24 (M)
        49ers, 38-28 (SF)
1962—49ers, 21-7 (SF)

49ers, 35-12 (M)
1963—Vikings, 24-20 (SF)
Vikings, 45-14 (M)
1964—Vikings, 27-22 (SF)
Vikings, 24-7 (M)
1965—Vikings, 42-41 (SF)
49ers, 45-24 (M)
1966—Tie, 20-20 (SF)
Vikings, 28-3 (SF)
1967—49ers, 27-21 (M)
1968—Vikings, 30-20 (SF)
1969—Vikings, 10-7 (M)
1970—*49ers, 17-14 (M)
1971—Vikings, 13-9 (M)
1972—49ers, 20-17 (SF)
1973—Vikings, 17-13 (SF)
1975—Vikings, 27-17 (M)
1976—49ers, 20-16 (SF)
1977—Vikings, 28-27 (M)
1979—Vikings, 28-22 (M)
1983—49ers, 48-17 (M)
1984—49ers, 51-7 (SF)
1985—Vikings, 28-21 (M)
1986—Vikings, 27-24 (SF) OT
1987—*Vikings, 36-24 (SF)
1988—49ers, 24-21 (SF)
*49ers, 34-9 (SF)
1989—*49ers, 41-13 (SF)
1990—49ers, 20-17 (M)
1991—Vikings, 17-14 (M)
1992—49ers, 20-17 (M)
1993—49ers, 38-19 (SF)
1994—Vikings, 21-14 (M)
1995—49ers, 37-30 (SF)
(RS Pts.—49ers 801, Vikings 729)
(PS Pts.—49ers 116, Vikings 72)
*NFC Divisional Playoff

MINNESOTA vs. SEATTLE
RS: Seahawks lead series, 4-2
1976—Vikings, 27-21 (M)
1978—Seahawks, 29-28 (S)
1984—Seahawks, 20-12 (M)
1987—Seahawks, 28-17 (S)
1990—Vikings, 24-21 (S)
1996—Seahawks, 42-23 (S)
(RS Pts.—Seahawks 161, Vikings 131)

MINNESOTA vs. TAMPA BAY
RS: Vikings lead series, 26-12
1977—Vikings, 9-3 (TB)
1978—Buccaneers, 16-10 (M)
Vikings, 24-7 (TB)
1979—Buccaneers, 12-10 (M)
Vikings, 23-22 (TB)
1980—Vikings, 38-30 (M)
Vikings, 21-10 (TB)
1981—Buccaneers, 21-13 (TB)
Vikings, 25-10 (M)
1982—Vikings, 17-10 (M)
1983—Vikings, 19-16 (TB) OT
Buccaneers, 17-12 (M)
1984—Buccaneers, 35-31 (TB)
Vikings, 27-24 (M)
1985—Vikings, 31-16 (TB)
Vikings, 26-7 (M)
1986—Vikings, 23-10 (TB)
Vikings, 45-13 (M)
1987—Buccaneers, 20-10 (TB)
Vikings, 23-17 (M)
1988—Vikings, 14-13 (M)
Vikings, 49-20 (TB)
1989—Vikings, 17-3 (M)
Vikings, 24-10 (TB)
1990—Buccaneers, 23-20 (M) OT
Buccaneers, 26-13 (TB)
1991—Vikings, 28-13 (M)
Vikings, 26-24 (TB)
1992—Vikings, 26-20 (M)
Vikings, 35-7 (TB)
1993—Vikings, 15-0 (M)
Buccaneers, 23-10 (TB)
1994—Vikings, 36-13 (TB)
Buccaneers, 20-17 (M) OT
1995—Buccaneers, 20-17 (TB) OT

Vikings, 31-17 (M)
1996—Buccaneers, 24-13 (TB)
Vikings, 21-10 (M)
(RS Pts.—Vikings 849, Buccaneers 602)

MINNESOTA vs. *TENNESSEE
RS: Vikings lead series, 4-3
1974—Vikings, 51-10 (M)
1980—Oilers, 20-16 (H)
1983—Vikings, 34-14 (M)
1986—Oilers, 23-10 (H)
1989—Vikings, 38-7 (M)
1992—Oilers, 17-13 (M)
1995—Vikings, 23-17 (M) OT
(RS Pts.—Vikings 185, Oilers 108)
*Franchise in Houston prior to 1997

MINNESOTA vs. WASHINGTON
RS: Redskins lead series, 6-4
PS: Redskins lead series, 3-2
1968—Vikings, 27-14 (M)
1970—Vikings, 19-10 (W)
1972—Redskins, 24-21 (M)
1973—*Vikings, 27-20 (M)
1975—Redskins, 31-30 (W)
1976—*Vikings, 35-20 (M)
1980—Vikings, 39-14 (W)
1982—**Redskins, 21-7 (W)
1984—Redskins, 31-17 (M)
1986—Redskins, 44-38 (W) OT
1987—Redskins, 27-24 (M) OT
***Redskins, 17-10 (W)
1992—Redskins, 15-13 (M)
****Redskins, 24-7 (M)
1993—Vikings, 14-9 (W)
(RS Pts.—Vikings 242, Redskins 219)
(PS Pts.—Redskins 102, Vikings 86)
*NFC Divisional Playoff
**NFC Second-Round Playoff
***NFC Championship
****NFC First-Round Playoff

NEW ENGLAND vs. ARIZONA
RS: Cardinals lead series, 6-3;
See Arizona vs. New England
NEW ENGLAND vs. ATLANTA
RS: Falcons lead series, 5-3;
See Atlanta vs. New England
NEW ENGLAND vs. BALTIMORE
RS: Patriots lead series, 1-0;
See Baltimore vs. New England
NEW ENGLAND vs. BUFFALO
RS: Patriots lead series, 37-35-1
PS: Patriots lead series, 1-0;
See Buffalo vs. New England
NEW ENGLAND vs. CAROLINA
RS: Panthers lead series, 1-0;
See Carolina vs. New England
NEW ENGLAND vs. CHICAGO
RS: Patriots lead series, 4-2
PS: Bears lead series, 1-0;
See Chicago vs. New England
NEW ENGLAND vs. CINCINNATI
RS: Patriots lead series, 9-7;
See Cincinnati vs. New England
NEW ENGLAND vs. CLEVELAND
RS: Browns lead series, 10-4
PS: Browns lead series, 1-0;
See Cleveland vs. New England
NEW ENGLAND vs. DALLAS
RS: Cowboys lead series, 7-0;
See Dallas vs. New England
NEW ENGLAND vs. DENVER
RS: Broncos lead series, 18-12
PS: Broncos lead series, 1-0;
See Denver vs. New England
NEW ENGLAND vs. DETROIT
RS: Series tied, 3-3;
See Detroit vs. New England
NEW ENGLAND vs. GREEN BAY
RS: Patriots lead series, 3-2
PS: Packers lead series, 1-0;
See Green Bay vs. New England
NEW ENGLAND vs. INDIANAPOLIS
RS: Patriots lead series, 31-22;

See Indianapolis vs. New England
NEW ENGLAND vs. JACKSONVILLE
RS: Patriots lead series, 1-0
PS: Patriots lead series, 1-0;
See Jacksonville vs. New England
NEW ENGLAND vs. KANSAS CITY
RS: Chiefs lead series, 14-7-3;
See Kansas City vs. New England
NEW ENGLAND vs. MIAMI
RS: Dolphins lead series, 37-23
PS: Series tied, 1-1;
See Miami vs. New England
NEW ENGLAND vs. MINNESOTA
RS: Patriots lead series, 4-2;
See Minnesota vs. New England
NEW ENGLAND vs. NEW ORLEANS
RS: Patriots lead series, 5-3
1972—Patriots, 17-10 (NO)
1976—Patriots, 27-6 (NE)
1980—Patriots, 38-27 (NO)
1983—Patriots, 7-0 (NE)
1986—Patriots, 21-20 (NO)
1989—Saints, 28-24 (NE)
1992—Saints, 31-14 (NE)
1995—Saints, 31-17 (NE)
(RS Pts.—Patriots 165, Saints 153)
NEW ENGLAND vs. N.Y. GIANTS
RS: Giants lead series, 3-2
1970—Giants, 16-0 (B)
1974—Patriots, 28-20 (New Haven)
1987—Giants, 17-10 (NE)
1990—Giants, 13-10 (NE)
1996—Patriots, 23-22 (NY)
(RS Pts.—Giants 88, Patriots 71)
*Franchise in Boston prior to 1971
***NEW ENGLAND vs. **N.Y. JETS**
RS: Jets lead series, 39-33-1
PS: Patriots lead series, 1-0
1960—Patriots, 28-24 (NY)
Patriots, 38-21 (B)
1961—Titans, 21-20 (B)
Titans, 37-30 (NY)
1962—Patriots, 43-14 (NY)
Patriots, 24-17 (B)
1963—Patriots, 38-14 (B)
Jets, 31-24 (NY)
1964—Patriots, 26-10 (B)
Jets, 35-14 (NY)
1965—Jets, 30-20 (B)
Patriots, 27-23 (NY)
1966—Tie, 24-24 (B)
Jets, 38-28 (NY)
1967—Jets, 30-23 (NY)
Jets, 29-24 (B)
1968—Jets, 47-31 (Birmingham)
Jets, 48-14 (NY)
1969—Jets, 23-14 (B)
Jets, 23-17 (NY)
1970—Jets, 31-21 (B)
Jets, 17-3 (NY)
1971—Patriots, 20-0 (NE)
Jets, 13-6 (NY)
1972—Jets, 41-13 (NE)
Jets, 34-10 (NY)
1973—Jets, 9-7 (NE)
Jets, 33-13 (NY)
1974—Patriots, 24-0 (NY)
Jets, 21-16 (NE)
1975—Jets, 36-7 (NY)
Jets, 30-28 (NE)
1976—Patriots, 41-7 (NE)
Patriots, 38-24 (NY)
1977—Jets, 30-27 (NY)
Patriots, 24-13 (NE)
1978—Patriots, 55-21 (NE)
Patriots, 19-17 (NY)
1979—Patriots, 56-3 (NE)
Jets, 27-26 (NY)
1980—Patriots, 21-11 (NY)
Patriots, 34-21 (NE)
1981—Jets, 28-24 (NY)
Jets, 17-6 (NE)
1982—Jets, 31-7 (NE)

1983—Patriots, 23-13 (NE)
Jets, 26-3 (NY)
1984—Patriots, 28-21 (NY)
Patriots, 30-20 (NE)
1985—Patriots, 20-13 (NE)
Jets, 16-13 (NY) OT
***Patriots, 26-14 (NY)
1986—Patriots, 20-6 (NY)
Jets, 31-24 (NE)
1987—Jets, 43-24 (NY)
Patriots, 42-20 (NE)
1988—Patriots, 28-3 (NE)
Patriots, 14-13 (NY)
1989—Patriots, 27-24 (NE)
Jets, 27-26 (NE)
1990—Patriots, 37-13 (NE)
Jets, 42-7 (NY)
1991—Jets, 28-21 (NE)
Patriots, 6-3 (NY)
1992—Jets, 30-21 (NY)
Patriots, 24-3 (NE)
1993—Jets, 45-7 (NY)
Jets, 6-0 (NE)
1994—Jets, 24-17 (NY)
Patriots, 24-13 (NE)
1995—Patriots, 20-7 (NY)
Patriots, 31-28 (NE)
1996—Patriots, 31-27 (NY)
Patriots, 34-10 (NE)
(RS Pts.—Jets 1,633, Patriots 1,631)
(PS Pts.—Patriots 26, Jets 14)
*Franchise in Boston prior to 1971
**Jets known as Titans prior to 1963
***AFC First-Round Playoff
***NEW ENGLAND vs. **OAKLAND**
RS: Raiders lead series, 13-12-1
PS: Series tied, 1-1
1960—Raiders, 27-14 (O)
Patriots, 34-28 (B)
1961—Patriots, 20-17 (B)
Patriots, 35-21 (O)
1962—Patriots, 26-16 (B)
Raiders, 20-0 (O)
1963—Patriots, 20-14 (O)
Patriots, 20-14 (B)
1964—Patriots, 17-14 (O)
Tie, 43-43 (B)
1965—Patriots, 24-10 (B)
Raiders, 30-21 (O)
1966—Patriots, 24-21 (B)
1967—Raiders, 35-7 (O)
Raiders, 48-14 (B)
1968—Raiders, 41-10 (O)
1969—Raiders, 38-23 (B)
1971—Patriots, 20-6 (NE)
1974—Raiders, 41-26 (O)
1976—Patriots, 48-17 (NE)
***Raiders, 24-21 (O)
1978—Patriots, 21-14 (O)
1981—Raiders, 27-17 (O)
1985—Patriots, 35-20 (NE)
***Patriots, 27-20 (LA)
1987—Patriots, 26-23 (NE)
1989—Raiders, 24-21 (LA)
1994—Raiders, 21-17 (NE)
(RS Pts.—Raiders 659, Patriots 554)
(PS Pts.—Patriots 48, Raiders 44)
*Franchise in Boston prior to 1971
**Franchise in Los Angeles from
1982-1994
***AFC Divisional Playoff
NEW ENGLAND vs. PHILADELPHIA
RS: Eagles lead series, 5-2
1973—Eagles, 24-23 (P)
1977—Patriots, 14-6 (NE)
1978—Patriots, 24-14 (NE)
1981—Eagles, 13-3 (P)
1984—Eagles, 27-17 (P)
1987—Eagles, 34-31 (NE) OT
1990—Eagles, 48-20 (P)
(RS Pts.—Eagles 166, Patriots 132)
NEW ENGLAND vs. PITTSBURGH
RS: Steelers lead series, 10-3

PS: Patriots lead series, 1-0
1972—Steelers, 33-3 (P)
1974—Steelers, 21-17 (NE)
1976—Patriots, 30-27 (P)
1979—Steelers, 16-13 (NE) OT
1981—Steelers, 27-21 (P) OT
1982—Steelers, 37-14 (P)
1983—Patriots, 28-23 (P)
1986—Patriots, 34-0 (P)
1989—Patriots, 28-10 (P)
1990—Steelers, 24-3 (P)
1991—Steelers, 20-6 (P)
1993—Steelers, 17-14 (P)
1995—Steelers, 41-27 (P)
1996—*Patriots, 28-3 (NE)
(RS Pts.—Steelers 314, Patriots 220)
(PS Pts.—Patriots 28, Steelers 3)
*AFC Divisional Playoff
NEW ENGLAND vs. *ST. LOUIS
RS: Series tied, 3-3
1974—Patriots, 20-14 (NE)
1980—Rams, 17-14 (NE)
1983—Patriots, 21-7 (LA)
1986—Patriots, 30-28 (LA)
1989—Rams, 24-20 (NE)
1992—Rams, 14-0 (LA)
(RS Pts.—Patriots 105, Rams 104)
*Franchise in Los Angeles prior to 1995
***NEW ENGLAND vs. **SAN DIEGO**
RS: Patriots lead series, 15-11-2
PS: Chargers lead series, 1-0
1960—Patriots, 35-0 (LA)
       Chargers, 45-16 (B)
1961—Chargers, 38-27 (B)
       Patriots, 41-0 (SD)
1962—Patriots, 24-20 (B)
       Patriots, 20-14 (SD)
1963—Chargers, 17-13 (SD)
       Chargers, 7-6 (B)
       ***Chargers, 51-10 (SD)
1964—Patriots, 33-28 (SD)
       Chargers, 26-17 (B)
1965—Tie, 10-10 (B)
       Patriots, 22-6 (SD)
1966—Chargers, 24-0 (SD)
       Patriots, 35-17 (B)
1967—Chargers, 28-14 (SD)
       Tie, 31-31 (SD)
1968—Chargers, 27-17 (B)
1969—Chargers, 13-10 (B)
       Chargers, 28-18 (SD)
1970—Chargers, 16-14 (B)
1973—Patriots, 30-14 (NE)
1975—Patriots, 33-19 (SD)
1977—Patriots, 24-20 (SD)
1978—Patriots, 28-23 (NE)
1979—Patriots, 27-21 (NE)
1983—Patriots, 37-21 (NE)
1994—Patriots, 23-17 (NE)
1996—Patriots, 45-7 (SD)
(RS Pts.—Patriots 650, Chargers 537)
(PS Pts.—Chargers 51, Patriots 10)
*Franchise in Boston prior to 1971
**Franchise in Los Angeles prior to 1961
***AFL Championship
NEW ENGLAND vs. SAN FRANCISCO
RS: 49ers lead series, 7-1
1971—49ers, 27-10 (SF)
1975—Patriots, 24-16 (NE)
1980—49ers, 21-17 (SF)
1983—49ers, 33-13 (NE)
1986—49ers, 29-24 (NE)
1989—49ers, 37-20 (SF)
1992—49ers, 24-12 (NE)
1995—49ers, 28-3 (SF)
(RS Pts.—49ers 215, Patriots 123)
NEW ENGLAND vs. SEATTLE
RS: Seahawks lead series, 7-6
1977—Patriots, 31-0 (NE)
1980—Patriots, 37-31 (S)
1982—Patriots, 16-0 (S)
1983—Seahawks, 24-6 (S)
1984—Seahawks, 38-23 (NE)

1985—Patriots, 20-13 (S)
1986—Seahawks, 38-31 (NE)
1988—Patriots, 13-7 (NE)
1989—Seahawks, 24-3 (NE)
1990—Seahawks, 33-20 (NE)
1992—Seahawks, 10-6 (NE)
1993—Seahawks, 17-14 (NE)
       Seahawks, 10-9 (S)
(RS Pts.—Patriots 244, Seahawks 230)
NEW ENGLAND vs. TAMPA BAY
RS: Patriots lead series, 3-0
1976—Patriots, 31-14 (TB)
1985—Patriots, 32-14 (TB)
1988—Patriots, 10-7 (NE) OT
(RS Pts.—Patriots 73, Buccaneers 35)
***NEW ENGLAND vs. **TENNESSEE**
RS: Patriots lead series, 17-14-1
PS: Oilers lead series, 1-0
1960—Oilers, 24-10 (B)
       Oilers, 37-21 (H)
1961—Tie, 31-31 (B)
       Oilers, 27-15 (H)
1962—Patriots, 34-21 (B)
       Patriots, 21-17 (H)
1963—Patriots, 45-3 (B)
       Patriots, 46-28 (H)
1964—Patriots, 25-24 (B)
       Patriots, 34-17 (H)
1965—Oilers, 31-10 (H)
       Patriots, 42-14 (B)
1966—Patriots, 27-21 (B)
       Patriots, 38-14 (H)
1967—Patriots, 18-7 (B)
       Oilers, 27-6 (H)
1968—Oilers, 16-0 (B)
       Oilers, 45-17 (H)
1969—Patriots, 24-0 (B)
       Oilers, 27-23 (H)
1971—Patriots, 28-20 (NE)
1973—Patriots, 32-0 (H)
1975—Oilers, 7-0 (NE)
1978—Oilers, 26-23 (NE)
       ***Oilers, 31-14 (NE)
1980—Oilers, 38-34 (H)
1981—Patriots, 38-10 (NE)
1982—Patriots, 29-21 (NE)
1987—Patriots, 21-7 (H)
1988—Oilers, 31-6 (H)
1989—Patriots, 23-13 (NE)
1991—Patriots, 24-20 (NE)
1993—Oilers, 28-14 (NE)
(RS Pts.—Patriots 755, Oilers 656)
(PS Pts.—Oilers 31, Patriots 14)
*Franchise in Boston prior to 1971
**Franchise in Houston prior to 1997
***AFC Divisional Playoff
NEW ENGLAND vs. WASHINGTON
RS: Redskins lead series, 5-1
1972—Patriots, 24-23 (NE)
1978—Redskins, 16-14 (NE)
1981—Redskins, 24-22 (W)
1984—Redskins, 26-10 (NE)
1990—Redskins, 25-10 (NE)
1996—Redskins, 27-22 (NE)
(RS Pts.—Redskins 141, Patriots 102)

NEW ORLEANS vs. ARIZONA
RS: Cardinals lead series, 11-9;
See Arizona vs. New Orleans
NEW ORLEANS vs. ATLANTA
RS: Falcons lead series, 31-24
PS: Falcons lead series, 1-0;
See Atlanta vs. New Orleans
NEW ORLEANS vs. BALTIMORE
RS: Ravens lead series, 1-0;
See Baltimore vs. New Orleans
NEW ORLEANS vs. BUFFALO
RS: Bills lead series, 3-2;
See Buffalo vs. New Orleans
NEW ORLEANS vs. CAROLINA
RS: Panthers lead series, 3-1;
See Carolina vs. New Orleans
NEW ORLEANS vs. CHICAGO

RS: Bears lead series, 9-7
PS: Bears lead series, 1-0;
See Chicago vs. New Orleans
NEW ORLEANS vs. CINCINNATI
RS: Saints lead series, 5-4;
See Cincinnati vs. New Orleans
NEW ORLEANS vs. CLEVELAND
RS: Browns lead series, 9-3;
See Cleveland vs. New Orleans
NEW ORLEANS vs. DALLAS
RS: Cowboys lead series, 14-3;
See Dallas vs. New Orleans
NEW ORLEANS vs. DENVER
RS: Broncos lead series, 4-2;
See Denver vs. New Orleans
NEW ORLEANS vs. DETROIT
RS: Saints lead series, 7-6-1;
See Detroit vs. New Orleans
NEW ORLEANS vs. GREEN BAY
RS: Packers lead series, 13-4;
See Green Bay vs. New Orleans
NEW ORLEANS vs. INDIANAPOLIS
RS: Series tied, 3-3;
See Indianapolis vs. New Orleans
NEW ORLEANS vs. JACKSONVILLE
RS: Saints lead series, 1-0;
See Jacksonville vs. New Orleans
NEW ORLEANS vs. KANSAS CITY
RS: Series tied, 3-3;
See Kansas City vs. New Orleans
NEW ORLEANS vs. MIAMI
RS: Dolphins lead series, 4-3;
See Miami vs. New Orleans
NEW ORLEANS vs. MINNESOTA
RS: Vikings lead series, 13-6
PS: Vikings lead series, 1-0;
See Minnesota vs. New Orleans
NEW ORLEANS vs. NEW ENGLAND
RS: Patriots lead series, 5-3;
See New England vs. New Orleans
NEW ORLEANS vs. N.Y. GIANTS
RS: Giants lead series, 10-8
1967—Giants, 27-21 (NY)
1968—Giants, 38-21 (NY)
1969—Saints, 25-24 (NY)
1970—Saints, 14-10 (NO)
1972—Giants, 45-21 (NY)
1975—Saints, 28-14 (NY)
1978—Saints, 28-17 (NO)
1979—Saints, 24-14 (NO)
1981—Giants, 20-7 (NY)
1984—Saints, 10-3 (NY)
1985—Giants, 21-13 (NO)
1986—Giants, 20-17 (NY)
1987—Saints, 23-14 (NO)
1988—Giants, 13-12 (NO)
1993—Giants, 24-14 (NO)
1994—Saints, 27-22 (NO)
1995—Giants, 45-29 (NY)
1996—Saints 17-3 (NY)
(RS Pts.—Giants 388, Saints 337)
NEW ORLEANS vs. N.Y. JETS
RS: Series tied, 4-4
1972—Jets, 18-17 (NY)
1977—Jets, 16-13 (NO)
1980—Saints, 21-20 (NY)
1983—Jets, 31-28 (NO)
1986—Jets, 28-23 (NY)
1989—Saints, 29-14 (NO)
1992—Saints, 20-0 (NY)
1995—Saints, 12-0 (NY)
(RS Pts.—Saints 163, Jets 127)
NEW ORLEANS vs. *OAKLAND
RS: Raiders lead series, 4-2-1
1971—Tie, 21-21 (NO)
1975—Raiders, 48-10 (O)
1979—Raiders, 42-35 (NO)
1985—Raiders, 23-13 (LA)
1988—Saints, 20-6 (NO)
1991—Saints, 27-0 (NO)
1994—Raiders, 24-19 (LA)
(RS Pts.—Raiders 164, Saints 145)
*Franchise in Los Angeles from

1982-1994
NEW ORLEANS vs. PHILADELPHIA
RS: Eagles lead series, 12-8
PS: Eagles lead series, 1-0
1967—Saints, 31-24 (NO)
       Eagles, 48-21 (P)
1968—Eagles, 29-17 (P)
1969—Eagles, 13-10 (P)
       Saints, 26-17 (NO)
1972—Saints, 21-3 (NO)
1974—Saints, 14-10 (NO)
1977—Eagles, 28-7 (P)
1978—Eagles, 24-17 (NO)
1979—Eagles, 26-14 (NO)
1980—Eagles, 34-21 (NO)
1981—Eagles, 31-14 (NO)
1983—Saints, 20-17 (P) OT
1985—Saints, 23-21 (NO)
1987—Eagles, 27-17 (P)
1989—Saints, 30-20 (NO)
1991—Saints, 13-6 (P)
1992—Eagles, 15-13 (P)
       *Eagles, 36-20 (NO)
1993—Eagles, 37-26 (P)
1995—Eagles, 15-10 (NO)
(RS Pts.—Eagles 445, Saints 365)
(PS Pts.—Eagles 36, Saints 20)
*NFC First-Round Playoff
NEW ORLEANS vs. PITTSBURGH
RS: Steelers lead series, 6-5
1967—Steelers, 14-10 (NO)
1968—Saints, 16-12 (P)
       Saints, 24-14 (NO)
1969—Saints, 27-24 (NO)
1974—Steelers, 28-7 (NO)
1978—Steelers, 20-14 (P)
1981—Steelers, 20-6 (NO)
1984—Saints, 27-24 (NO)
1987—Saints, 20-16 (NO)
1990—Steelers, 9-6 (NO)
1993—Steelers, 37-14 (P)
(RS Pts.—Steelers 218, Saints 171)
NEW ORLEANS vs. *ST. LOUIS
RS: Rams lead series, 30-24
1967—Rams, 27-13 (NO)
1969—Rams, 36-17 (LA)
1970—Rams, 30-17 (NO)
       Rams, 34-16 (LA)
1971—Saints, 24-20 (NO)
       Rams, 45-28 (LA)
1972—Rams, 34-14 (LA)
       Saints, 19-16 (NO)
1973—Rams, 29-7 (LA)
       Rams, 24-13 (NO)
1974—Rams, 24-0 (LA)
       Saints, 20-7 (NO)
1975—Rams, 38-14 (LA)
       Rams, 14-7 (NO)
1976—Rams, 16-10 (NO)
       Rams, 33-14 (LA)
1977—Rams, 14-7 (LA)
       Saints, 27-26 (NO)
1978—Rams, 26-20 (NO)
       Saints, 10-3 (LA)
1979—Rams, 35-17 (NO)
       Saints, 29-14 (LA)
1980—Rams, 45-31 (LA)
       Rams, 27-7 (NO)
1981—Saints, 23-17 (NO)
       Saints, 21-13 (LA)
1983—Rams, 30-27 (NO)
       Rams, 26-24 (NO)
1984—Rams, 28-10 (NO)
       Rams, 34-21 (LA)
1985—Rams, 28-10 (LA)
       Saints, 29-3 (NO)
1986—Saints, 6-0 (NO)
       Rams, 26-13 (LA)
1987—Saints, 37-10 (NO)
       Saints, 31-14 (LA)
1988—Rams, 12-10 (NO)
       Saints, 14-10 (LA)
1989—Saints, 40-21 (LA)

Rams, 20-17 (NO) OT
1990—Saints, 24-20 (LA)
Saints, 20-17 (NO)
1991—Saints, 24-7 (NO)
Saints, 24-17 (LA)
1992—Saints, 13-10 (NO)
Saints, 37-14 (LA)
1993—Saints, 37-6 (LA)
Rams, 23-20 (NO)
1994—Saints, 37-34 (NO)
Saints, 31-15 (LA)
1995—Rams, 17-13 (StL)
Saints, 19-10 (NO)
1996—Rams, 26-10 (NO)
Rams, 14-13 (StL)
(RS Pts.—Rams 1,139, Saints 1,036)
*Franchise in Los Angeles prior to 1995

NEW ORLEANS vs. SAN DIEGO
RS: Chargers lead series, 5-1
1973—Chargers, 17-14 (SD)
1977—Chargers, 14-0 (NO)
1979—Chargers, 35-0 (NO)
1988—Saints, 23-17 (SD)
1991—Chargers, 24-21 (SD)
1994—Chargers, 36-22 (NO)
(RS Pts.—Chargers 143, Saints 80)

NEW ORLEANS vs. SAN FRANCISCO
RS: 49ers lead series, 38-15-2
1967—49ers, 27-13 (SF)
1969—Saints, 43-38 (NO)
1970—Tie, 20-20 (SF)
49ers, 38-27 (NO)
1971—49ers, 38-20 (NO)
Saints, 26-20 (SF)
1972—49ers, 37-2 (NO)
Tie, 20-20 (SF)
1973—49ers, 40-0 (SF)
Saints, 16-10 (NO)
1974—49ers, 17-13 (NO)
49ers, 35-21 (SF)
1975—49ers, 35-21 (SF)
49ers, 16-6 (NO)
1976—49ers, 33-3 (SF)
49ers, 27-7 (NO)
1977—49ers, 10-7 (NO) OT
49ers, 20-17 (SF)
1978—Saints, 14-7 (SF)
Saints, 24-13 (NO)
1979—Saints, 30-21 (SF)
Saints, 31-20 (NO)
1980—49ers, 26-23 (NO)
49ers, 38-35 (SF) OT
1981—49ers, 21-14 (SF)
49ers, 21-17 (NO)
1982—Saints, 23-20 (NO)
1983—49ers, 32-13 (NO)
49ers, 27-0 (SF)
1984—49ers, 30-20 (SF)
49ers, 35-3 (NO)
1985—Saints, 20-17 (SF)
49ers, 31-19 (NO)
1986—49ers, 26-17 (SF)
Saints, 23-10 (NO)
1987—49ers, 24-22 (NO)
Saints, 26-24 (SF)
1988—49ers, 34-33 (NO)
49ers, 30-17 (SF)
1989—49ers, 24-20 (NO)
49ers, 31-13 (SF)
1990—49ers, 13-12 (NO)
Saints, 13-10 (SF)
1991—Saints, 10-3 (NO)
49ers, 38-24 (SF)
1992—49ers, 16-10 (NO)
49ers, 21-20 (SF)
1993—Saints, 16-13 (NO)
49ers, 42-7 (SF)
1994—49ers, 24-13 (SF)
49ers, 35-14 (NO)
1995—49ers, 24-22 (NO)
Saints, 11-7 (SF)
1996—49ers, 27-11 (SF)
49ers, 24-17 (NO)

(RS Pts.—49ers 1,340, Saints 939)
NEW ORLEANS vs. SEATTLE
RS: Saints lead series, 3-2
1976—Saints, 51-27 (S)
1979—Seahawks, 38-24 (S)
1985—Seahawks, 27-3 (NO)
1988—Saints, 20-19 (S)
1991—Saints, 27-24 (NO)
(RS Pts.—Seahawks 135, Saints 125)
NEW ORLEANS vs. TAMPA BAY
RS: Saints lead series, 12-5
1977—Buccaneers, 33-14 (NO)
1978—Saints, 17-10 (TB)
1979—Saints, 42-14 (TB)
1981—Buccaneers, 31-14 (NO)
1982—Buccaneers, 13-10 (NO)
1983—Saints, 24-21 (TB)
1984—Saints, 17-13 (NO)
1985—Saints, 20-13 (NO)
1986—Saints, 38-7 (NO)
1987—Saints, 44-34 (NO)
1988—Saints, 13-9 (NO)
1989—Buccaneers, 20-10 (TB)
1990—Saints, 35-7 (NO)
1991—Saints, 23-7 (NO)
1992—Saints, 23-21 (NO)
1994—Saints, 9-7 (TB)
1996—Buccaneers, 13-7 (TB)
(RS Pts.—Saints 360, Buccaneers 273)
NEW ORLEANS vs. *TENNESSEE
RS: Series tied, 4-4-1
1971—Tie, 13-13 (H)
1976—Oilers, 31-26 (NO)
1978—Oilers, 17-12 (NO)
1981—Saints, 27-24 (H)
1984—Saints, 27-10 (H)
1987—Saints, 24-10 (NO)
1990—Oilers, 23-10 (H)
1993—Saints, 33-21 (NO)
1996—Oilers, 31-14 (NO)
(RS Pts.—Saints 186, Oilers 180)
*Franchise in Houston prior to 1997
NEW ORLEANS vs. WASHINGTON
RS: Redskins lead series, 12-5
1967—Redskins, 30-10 (NO)
Saints, 30-14 (W)
1968—Saints, 37-17 (NO)
1969—Redskins, 26-20 (NO)
Redskins, 17-14 (W)
1971—Redskins, 24-14 (W)
1973—Saints, 19-3 (NO)
1975—Redskins, 41-3 (W)
1979—Saints, 14-10 (W)
1980—Redskins, 22-14 (W)
1982—Redskins, 27-10 (NO)
1986—Redskins, 14-6 (NO)
1988—Redskins, 27-24 (W)
1989—Redskins, 16-14 (NO)
1990—Redskins, 31-17 (W)
1992—Saints, 20-3 (NO)
1994—Redskins, 38-24 (NO)
(RS Pts.—Redskins 360, Saints 290)

N.Y. GIANTS vs. ARIZONA
RS: Giants lead series, 69-37-2;
See Arizona vs. N.Y. Giants
N.Y. GIANTS vs. ATLANTA
RS: Series tied, 6-6;
See Atlanta vs. N.Y. Giants
N.Y. GIANTS vs. BUFFALO
RS: Bills lead series, 5-2
PS: Giants lead series, 1-0;
See Buffalo vs. N.Y. Giants
N.Y. GIANTS vs. CAROLINA
RS: Panthers lead series, 1-0;
See Carolina vs. N.Y. Giants
N.Y. GIANTS vs. CHICAGO
RS: Bears lead series, 25-16-2
PS: Bears lead series, 5-3;
See Chicago vs. N.Y. Giants
N.Y. GIANTS vs. CINCINNATI
RS: Bengals lead series, 4-1;
See Cincinnati vs. N.Y. Giants

N.Y. GIANTS vs. CLEVELAND
RS: Browns lead series, 25-17-2
PS: Series tied, 1-1;
See Cleveland vs. N.Y. Giants
N.Y. GIANTS vs. DALLAS
RS: Cowboys lead series, 44-23-2;
See Dallas vs. N.Y. Giants
N.Y. GIANTS vs. DENVER
RS: Series tied, 3-3
PS: Giants lead series, 1-0;
See Denver vs. N.Y. Giants
N.Y. GIANTS vs. DETROIT
RS: Lions lead series, 18-16-1
PS: Lions lead series, 1-0;
See Detroit vs. N.Y. Giants
N.Y. GIANTS vs. GREEN BAY
RS: Packers lead series, 22-20-2
PS: Packers lead series, 4-1;
See Green Bay vs. N.Y. Giants
N.Y. GIANTS vs. INDIANAPOLIS
RS: Series tied, 5-5
PS: Colts lead series, 2-0;
See Indianapolis vs. N.Y. Giants
N.Y. GIANTS vs. KANSAS CITY
RS: Giants lead series, 6-2;
See Kansas City vs. N.Y. Giants
N.Y. GIANTS vs. MIAMI
RS: Giants lead series, 3-1;
See Miami vs. N.Y. Giants
N.Y. GIANTS vs. MINNESOTA
RS: Vikings lead series, 7-5
PS: Giants lead series, 1-0;
See Minnesota vs. N.Y. Giants
N.Y. GIANTS vs. NEW ENGLAND
RS: Giants lead series, 3-2;
See New England vs. N.Y. Giants
N.Y. GIANTS vs. NEW ORLEANS
RS: Giants lead series, 10-8;
See New Orleans vs. N.Y. Giants
N.Y. GIANTS vs. N.Y. JETS
RS: Series tied, 4-4
1970—Giants, 22-10 (NYJ)
1974—Jets, 26-20 (New Haven) OT
1981—Jets, 26-7 (NYG)
1984—Giants, 20-10 (NYJ)
1987—Giants, 20-7 (NYG)
1988—Jets, 27-21 (NYJ)
1993—Jets, 10-6 (NYG)
1996—Giants, 13-6 (NYJ)
(RS Pts.—Giants 129, Jets 122)
N.Y. GIANTS vs. *OAKLAND
RS: Raiders lead series, 5-2
1973—Raiders, 42-0 (O)
1980—Raiders, 33-17 (NY)
1983—Raiders, 27-12 (LA)
1986—Giants, 14-9 (LA)
1989—Giants, 34-17 (NY)
1992—Raiders, 13-10 (LA)
1995—Raiders, 17-13 (NY)
(RS Pts.—Raiders 158, Giants 100)
*Franchise in Los Angeles from
1982-1994
N.Y. GIANTS vs. PHILADELPHIA
RS: Giants lead series, 64-58-2
PS: Giants lead series, 1-0
1933—Giants, 56-0 (NY)
Giants, 20-14 (P)
1934—Giants, 17-0 (NY)
Eagles, 6-0 (P)
1935—Giants, 10-0 (NY)
Giants, 21-14 (P)
1936—Eagles, 10-7 (P)
Giants, 21-17 (NY)
1937—Giants, 16-7 (P)
Giants, 21-0 (NY)
1938—Eagles, 14-10 (P)
Giants, 17-7 (NY)
1939—Giants, 13-3 (P)
Giants, 27-10 (NY)
1940—Giants, 20-14 (P)
Giants, 17-7 (NY)
1941—Giants, 24-0 (P)
Giants, 16-0 (NY)

1942—Giants, 35-17 (NY)
Giants, 14-0 (P)
1944—Eagles, 24-17 (NY)
Tie, 21-21 (P)
1945—Eagles, 38-17 (NY)
Giants, 28-21 (P)
1946—Eagles, 24-14 (P)
Giants, 45-17 (NY)
1947—Eagles, 23-0 (P)
Eagles, 41-24 (NY)
1948—Eagles, 45-0 (P)
Eagles, 35-14 (NY)
1949—Eagles, 24-3 (NY)
Eagles, 17-3 (P)
1950—Giants, 7-3 (NY)
Giants, 9-7 (P)
1951—Giants, 26-24 (NY)
Giants, 23-7 (P)
1952—Giants, 31-7 (P)
Eagles, 14-10 (NY)
1953—Eagles, 30-7 (NY)
Giants, 37-28 (P)
1954—Giants, 27-14 (NY)
Eagles, 29-14 (P)
1955—Eagles, 27-17 (P)
Giants, 31-7 (NY)
1956—Giants, 20-3 (NY)
Giants, 21-7 (P)
1957—Giants, 24-20 (P)
Giants, 13-0 (NY)
1958—Eagles, 27-24 (P)
Giants, 24-10 (NY)
1959—Eagles, 49-21 (P)
Giants, 24-7 (NY)
1960—Eagles, 17-10 (NY)
Eagles, 31-23 (P)
1961—Giants, 38-21 (NY)
Giants, 28-24 (P)
1962—Giants, 29-13 (P)
Giants, 19-14 (NY)
1963—Giants, 37-14 (P)
Giants, 42-14 (NY)
1964—Eagles, 38-7 (P)
Eagles, 23-17 (NY)
1965—Giants, 16-14 (NY)
Giants, 35-27 (NY)
1966—Eagles, 35-17 (P)
Eagles, 31-3 (NY)
1967—Giants, 44-7 (NY)
1968—Giants, 34-25 (P)
Giants, 7-6 (NY)
1969—Eagles, 23-20 (NY)
1970—Giants, 30-23 (NY)
Eagles, 23-20 (P)
1971—Eagles, 23-7 (P)
Eagles, 41-28 (NY)
1972—Giants, 27-12 (P)
Giants, 62-10 (NY)
1973—Tie, 23-23 (NY)
Eagles, 20-16 (P)
1974—Eagles, 35-7 (P)
Eagles, 20-7 (New Haven)
1975—Giants, 23-14 (P)
Eagles, 13-10 (NY)
1976—Giants, 20-7 (P)
Eagles, 10-0 (NY)
1977—Eagles, 28-10 (NY)
Eagles, 17-14 (P)
1978—Eagles, 19-17 (NY)
Eagles, 20-3 (P)
1979—Eagles, 23-17 (P)
Eagles, 17-13 (NY)
1980—Eagles, 35-3 (P)
Eagles, 31-16 (NY)
1981—Eagles, 24-10 (NY)
Giants, 20-10 (P)
*Giants, 27-21 (P)
1982—Giants, 23-7 (NY)
Giants, 26-24 (P)
1983—Eagles, 17-13 (NY)
Giants, 23-0 (P)
1984—Giants, 28-27 (NY)
Eagles, 24-10 (P)

1985—Giants, 21-0 (NY)
   Giants, 16-10 (P) OT
1986—Giants, 35-3 (NY)
   Giants, 17-14 (P)
1987—Giants, 20-17 (P)
   Giants, 23-20 (NY) OT
1988—Eagles, 24-13 (NY)
   Eagles, 23-17 (NY) OT
1989—Eagles, 21-19 (P)
   Eagles, 24-17 (NY)
1990—Giants, 27-20 (NY)
   Eagles, 31-13 (P)
1991—Eagles, 30-7 (P)
   Eagles, 19-14 (NY)
1992—Eagles, 47-34 (NY)
   Eagles, 20-10 (P)
1993—Giants, 21-10 (NY)
   Giants, 7-3 (P)
1994—Giants, 28-23 (NY)
   Giants, 16-13 (P)
1995—Eagles, 17-14 (NY)
   Eagles, 28-19 (P)
1996—Eagles, 19-10 (NY)
   Eagles, 24-0 (NY)
(RS Pts.—Giants 2,335, Eagles 2,237)
(PS Pts.—Giants 27, Eagles 21)
*NFC First-Round Playoff
N.Y. GIANTS vs. *PITTSBURGH
RS: Giants lead series, 42-27-3
1933—Giants, 23-2 (P)
   Giants, 27-3 (NY)
1934—Giants, 14-12 (P)
   Giants, 17-7 (NY)
1935—Giants, 42-7 (P)
   Giants, 13-0 (NY)
1936—Pirates, 10-7 (P)
1937—Giants, 10-7 (P)
   Giants, 17-0 (NY)
1938—Giants, 27-14 (P)
   Pirates, 13-10 (NY)
1939—Giants, 14-7 (P)
   Giants, 23-7 (NY)
1940—Tie, 10-10 (P)
   Giants, 12-0 (NY)
1941—Giants, 37-10 (P)
   Giants, 28-7 (NY)
1942—Steelers, 13-10 (P)
   Steelers, 17-9 (NY)
1945—Giants, 34-6 (P)
   Steelers, 21-7 (NY)
1946—Giants, 17-14 (P)
   Giants, 7-0 (NY)
1947—Steelers, 38-21 (NY)
   Steelers, 24-7 (P)
1948—Giants, 34-27 (NY)
   Steelers, 38-28 (P)
1949—Steelers, 28-7 (P)
   Steelers, 21-17 (NY)
1950—Giants, 18-7 (P)
   Steelers, 17-6 (NY)
1951—Tie, 13-13 (P)
   Giants, 14-0 (NY)
1952—Steelers, 63-7 (P)
1953—Steelers, 24-14 (P)
   Steelers, 14-10 (NY)
1954—Giants, 30-6 (P)
   Giants, 24-3 (NY)
1955—Steelers, 30-23 (P)
   Steelers, 19-17 (NY)
1956—Giants, 38-10 (P)
   Giants, 17-14 (P)
1957—Giants, 35-0 (NY)
   Steelers, 21-10 (P)
1958—Giants, 17-6 (NY)
   Steelers, 31-10 (P)
1959—Giants, 21-16 (P)
   Steelers, 14-9 (NY)
1960—Giants, 19-17 (P)
   Giants, 27-24 (NY)
1961—Giants, 17-14 (P)
   Giants, 42-21 (NY)
1962—Giants, 31-27 (P)
   Steelers, 20-17 (NY)

1963—Steelers, 31-0 (P)
   Giants, 33-17 (NY)
1964—Steelers, 27-24 (P)
   Steelers, 44-17 (NY)
1965—Giants, 23-13 (P)
   Giants, 35-10 (NY)
1966—Tie, 34-34 (P)
   Steelers, 47-28 (NY)
1967—Giants, 27-24 (P)
   Giants, 28-20 (NY)
1968—Giants, 34-20 (P)
1969—Giants, 10-7 (NY)
   Giants, 21-17 (P)
1971—Steelers, 17-13 (P)
1976—Steelers, 27-0 (NY)
1985—Giants, 28-10 (NY)
1991—Giants, 23-20 (P)
1994—Steelers, 10-6 (P)
(RS Pts.—Giants 1,399, Steelers 1,189)
*Steelers known as Pirates prior to 1941
N.Y. GIANTS vs. *ST. LOUIS
RS: Rams lead series, 21-9
PS: Series tied, 1-1
1938—Giants, 28-0 (NY)
1940—Rams, 13-0 (NY)
1941—Giants, 49-14 (NY)
1945—Rams, 21-17 (NY)
1946—Rams, 31-21 (NY)
1947—Rams, 34-10 (LA)
1948—Rams, 52-37 (NY)
1953—Rams, 21-7 (LA)
1954—Rams, 17-16 (NY)
1959—Giants, 23-21 (LA)
1961—Giants, 24-14 (NY)
1966—Rams, 55-14 (LA)
1968—Rams, 24-21 (LA)
1970—Rams, 31-3 (NY)
1973—Rams, 40-6 (LA)
1976—Rams, 24-10 (LA)
1978—Rams, 20-17 (NY)
1979—Giants, 20-14 (LA)
1980—Rams, 28-7 (NY)
1981—Giants, 10-7 (NY)
1983—Rams, 16-6 (NY)
1984—Rams, 33-12 (LA)
   **Giants, 16-13 (LA)
1985—Giants, 24-19 (NY)
1988—Rams, 45-31 (NY)
1989—Rams, 31-10 (LA)
   ***Rams, 19-13 (NY) OT
1990—Giants, 31-7 (LA)
1991—Rams, 19-13 (NY)
1992—Rams, 38-17 (LA)
1993—Giants, 20-10 (NY)
1994—Rams, 17-10 (LA)
(RS Pts.—Rams 716, Giants 514)
(PS Pts.—Rams 32, Giants 29)
*Franchise in Los Angeles prior to 1995
and in Cleveland prior to 1946
**NFC First-Round Playoff
***NFC Divisional Playoff
N.Y. GIANTS vs. SAN DIEGO
RS: Giants lead series, 4-3
1971—Giants, 35-17 (NY)
1975—Giants, 35-24 (NY)
1980—Chargers, 44-7 (SD)
1983—Chargers, 41-34 (NY)
1986—Giants, 20-7 (NY)
1989—Giants, 20-13 (SD)
1995—Chargers, 27-17 (NY)
(RS Pts.—Chargers 173, Giants 168)
N.Y. GIANTS vs. SAN FRANCISCO
RS: Series tied, 11-11
PS: Series tied, 3-3
1952—Giants, 23-14 (NY)
1956—Giants, 38-21 (SF)
1957—49ers, 27-17 (NY)
1960—Giants, 21-19 (SF)
1963—Giants, 48-14 (NY)
1968—49ers, 26-10 (NY)
1972—Giants, 23-17 (SF)
1975—Giants, 26-23 (SF)
1977—Giants, 20-17 (NY)

1978—Giants, 27-10 (NY)
1979—Giants, 32-16 (NY)
1980—49ers, 12-0 (SF)
1981—49ers, 17-10 (SF)
   *49ers, 38-24 (SF)
1984—49ers, 31-10 (NY)
   *49ers, 21-10 (SF)
1985—**Giants, 17-3 (NY)
1986—Giants, 21-17 (SF)
   *Giants, 49-3 (NY)
1987—49ers, 41-21 (NY)
1988—49ers, 20-17 (NY)
1989—49ers, 34-24 (SF)
1990—49ers, 7-3 (SF)
   ***Giants, 15-13 (SF)
1991—Giants, 16-14 (NY)
1992—49ers, 31-14 (NY)
1993—*49ers, 44-3 (SF)
1995—49ers, 20-6 (SF)
(RS Pts.—49ers 451, Giants 427)
(PS Pts.—49ers 119, Giants 118)
*NFC Divisional Playoff
**NFC First-Round Playoff
***NFC Championship
N.Y. GIANTS vs. SEATTLE
RS: Giants lead series, 5-3
1976—Giants, 28-16 (NY)
1980—Giants, 27-21 (S)
1981—Giants, 32-0 (S)
1983—Seahawks, 17-12 (NY)
1986—Seahawks, 17-12 (S)
1989—Giants, 15-3 (NY)
1992—Giants, 23-10 (NY)
1995—Seahawks, 30-28 (S)
(RS Pts.—Giants 177, Seahawks 114)
N.Y. GIANTS vs. TAMPA BAY
RS: Giants lead series, 8-3
1977—Giants, 10-0 (TB)
1978—Giants, 19-13 (TB)
   Giants, 17-14 (NY)
1979—Giants, 17-14 (NY)
   Buccaneers, 31-3 (TB)
1980—Buccaneers, 30-13 (NY)
1984—Giants, 17-14 (NY)
   Buccaneers, 20-17 (TB)
1985—Giants, 22-20 (NY)
1991—Giants, 21-14 (TB)
1993—Giants, 23-7 (NY)
(RS Pts.—Giants 179, Buccaneers 177)
N.Y. GIANTS vs. *TENNESSEE
RS: Giants lead series, 5-0
1973—Giants, 34-14 (NY)
1982—Giants, 17-14 (NY)
1985—Giants, 35-14 (H)
1991—Giants, 24-20 (NY)
1994—Giants, 13-10 (H)
(RS Pts.—Giants 123, Oilers 72)
*Franchise in Houston prior to 1997
N.Y. GIANTS vs. *WASHINGTON
RS: Giants lead series, 73-52-3
PS: Series tied, 1-1
1932—Braves, 14-6 (B)
   Tie, 0-0 (NY)
1933—Redskins, 21-20 (B)
   Giants, 7-0 (NY)
1934—Giants, 16-13 (B)
   Giants, 3-0 (NY)
1935—Giants, 20-12 (B)
   Giants, 17-6 (NY)
1936—Giants, 7-0 (B)
   Redskins, 14-0 (NY)
1937—Redskins, 13-3 (W)
   Redskins, 49-14 (NY)
1938—Giants, 10-7 (W)
   Giants, 36-0 (NY)
1939—Tie, 0-0 (W)
   Giants, 9-7 (NY)
1940—Redskins, 21-7 (W)
   Giants, 21-7 (NY)
1941—Giants, 17-10 (W)
   Giants, 20-13 (NY)
1942—Giants, 14-7 (W)
   Redskins, 14-7 (NY)

1943—Giants, 14-10 (NY)
   Giants, 31-7 (W)
   **Redskins, 28-0 (NY)
1944—Giants, 16-13 (NY)
   Giants, 31-0 (W)
1945—Redskins, 24-14 (NY)
   Redskins, 17-0 (W)
1946—Redskins, 24-14 (W)
   Giants, 31-0 (NY)
1947—Redskins, 28-20 (W)
   Giants, 35-10 (NY)
1948—Redskins, 41-10 (W)
   Redskins, 28-21 (NY)
1949—Giants, 45-35 (W)
   Giants, 23-7 (NY)
1950—Giants, 21-17 (W)
   Giants, 24-21 (NY)
1951—Giants, 35-14 (W)
   Giants, 28-14 (NY)
1952—Giants, 14-10 (W)
   Redskins, 27-17 (NY)
1953—Redskins, 13-9 (W)
   Redskins, 24-21 (NY)
1954—Giants, 51-21 (W)
   Giants, 24-7 (NY)
1955—Giants, 35-7 (NY)
   Giants, 27-20 (W)
1956—Redskins, 33-7 (W)
   Giants, 28-14 (NY)
1957—Giants, 24-20 (W)
   Redskins, 31-14 (NY)
1958—Giants, 21-14 (W)
   Giants, 30-0 (NY)
1959—Giants, 45-14 (NY)
   Giants, 24-10 (W)
1960—Tie, 24-24 (NY)
   Giants, 17-3 (W)
1961—Giants, 24-21 (W)
   Giants, 53-0 (W)
1962—Giants, 49-34 (NY)
   Giants, 42-24 (W)
1963—Giants, 24-14 (W)
   Giants, 44-14 (NY)
1964—Giants, 13-10 (NY)
   Redskins, 36-21 (W)
1965—Redskins, 23-7 (NY)
   Giants, 27-10 (W)
1966—Giants, 13-10 (NY)
   Redskins, 72-41 (W)
1967—Redskins, 38-34 (W)
1968—Redskins, 48-21 (NY)
   Giants, 13-10 (W)
1969—Redskins, 20-14 (W)
1970—Giants, 35-33 (NY)
   Giants, 27-24 (W)
1971—Redskins, 30-3 (NY)
   Redskins, 23-7 (W)
1972—Redskins, 23-16 (NY)
   Redskins, 27-13 (W)
1973—Redskins, 21-3 (New Haven)
   Redskins, 27-24 (W)
1974—Redskins, 13-10 (New Haven)
   Redskins, 24-3 (W)
1975—Redskins, 49-13 (W)
   Redskins, 21-13 (NY)
1976—Redskins, 19-17 (W)
   Giants, 12-9 (NY)
1977—Giants, 20-17 (NY)
   Giants, 17-6 (W)
1978—Giants, 17-6 (NY)
   Redskins, 16-13 (W) OT
1979—Redskins, 27-0 (W)
   Giants, 14-6 (W)
1980—Redskins, 23-21 (NY)
   Redskins, 16-13 (W)
1981—Giants, 17-7 (W)
   Redskins, 30-27 (NY) OT
1982—Redskins, 27-17 (NY)
   Redskins, 15-14 (W)
1983—Redskins, 33-17 (NY)
   Redskins, 31-22 (W)
1984—Redskins, 30-14 (W)
   Giants, 37-13 (NY)

1985—Giants, 17-3 (NY)
　　　Redskins, 23-21 (W)
1986—Giants, 27-20 (NY)
　　　Giants, 24-14 (W)
　　　***Giants, 17-0 (NY)
1987—Redskins, 38-12 (NY)
　　　Redskins, 23-19 (W)
1988—Giants, 27-20 (NY)
　　　Giants, 24-23 (W)
1989—Giants, 27-24 (W)
　　　Giants, 20-17 (NY)
1990—Giants, 24-20 (W)
　　　Giants, 21-10 (NY)
1991—Redskins, 17-13 (NY)
　　　Redskins, 34-17 (W)
1992—Giants, 24-7 (W)
　　　Redskins, 28-10 (NY)
1993—Giants, 41-7 (W)
　　　Giants, 20-6 (NY)
1994—Giants, 31-23 (NY)
　　　Giants, 21-19 (W)
1995—Giants, 24-15 (W)
　　　Giants, 20-13 (NY)
1996—Redskins, 31-10 (NY)
　　　Redskins, 31-21 (W)
(RS Pts.—Giants 2,557, Redskins 2,299)
(PS Pts.—Redskins 28, Giants 17)
*Franchise in Boston prior to 1937 and known as Braves prior to 1933
**Division Playoff
***NFC Championship

N.Y. JETS vs. ARIZONA
RS: Series tied, 2-2;
See Arizona vs. N.Y. Jets
N.Y. JETS vs. ATLANTA
RS: Falcons lead series, 4-3;
See Atlanta vs. N.Y. Jets
N.Y. JETS vs. BUFFALO
RS: Bills lead series, 41-31
PS: Bills lead series, 1-0;
See Buffalo vs. N.Y. Jets
N.Y. JETS vs. CAROLINA
RS: Panthers lead series, 1-0;
See Carolina vs. N.Y. Jets
N.Y. JETS vs. CHICAGO
RS: Bears lead series, 4-1;
See Chicago vs. N.Y. Jets
N.Y. JETS vs. CINCINNATI
RS: Jets lead series, 9-6
PS: Jets lead series, 1-0;
See Cincinnati vs. N.Y. Jets
N.Y. JETS vs. CLEVELAND
RS: Browns lead series, 9-6
PS: Browns lead series, 1-0;
See Cleveland vs. N.Y. Jets
N.Y. JETS vs. DALLAS
RS: Cowboys lead series, 5-1;
See Dallas vs. N.Y. Jets
N.Y. JETS vs. DENVER
RS: Broncos lead series, 13-12-1;
See Denver vs. N.Y. Jets
N.Y. JETS vs. DETROIT
RS: Lions lead series, 4-3;
See Detroit vs. N.Y. Jets
N.Y. JETS vs. GREEN BAY
RS: Jets lead series, 5-2;
See Green Bay vs. N.Y. Jets
N.Y. JETS vs. INDIANAPOLIS
RS: Colts lead series, 32-21
PS: Jets lead series, 1-0;
See Indianapolis vs. N.Y. Jets
N.Y. JETS vs. JACKSONVILLE
RS: Series tied, 1-1;
See Jacksonville vs. N.Y. Jets
N.Y. JETS vs. KANSAS CITY
RS: Chiefs lead series, 14-12-1
PS: Series tied, 1-1;
See Kansas City vs. N.Y. Jets
N.Y. JETS vs. MIAMI
RS: Dolphins lead series, 32-29-1
PS: Dolphins lead series, 1-0;
See Miami vs. N.Y. Jets

N.Y. JETS vs. MINNESOTA
RS: Jets lead series, 4-1;
See Minnesota vs. N.Y. Jets
N.Y. JETS vs. NEW ENGLAND
RS: Jets lead series, 39-33-1
PS: Patriots lead series, 1-0;
See New England vs. N.Y. Jets
N.Y. JETS vs. NEW ORLEANS
RS: Series tied, 4-4;
See New Orleans vs. N.Y. Jets
N.Y. JETS vs. N.Y. GIANTS
RS: Series tied, 4-4;
See N.Y. Giants vs. N.Y. Jets
***N.Y. JETS vs. **OAKLAND**
RS: Raiders lead series, 16-9-2
PS: Jets lead series, 2-0
1960—Raiders, 28-27 (NY)
　　　Titans, 31-28 (O)
1961—Titans, 14-6 (O)
　　　Titans, 23-12 (NY)
1962—Titans, 28-17 (O)
　　　Titans, 31-21 (NY)
1963—Jets, 10-7 (NY)
　　　Raiders, 49-26 (O)
1964—Jets, 35-13 (NY)
　　　Raiders, 35-26 (O)
1965—Tie, 24-24 (NY)
　　　Raiders, 24-14 (O)
1966—Raiders, 24-21 (NY)
　　　Tie, 28-28 (O)
1967—Jets, 27-14 (NY)
　　　Raiders, 38-29 (O)
1968—Raiders, 43-32 (O)
　　　***Jets, 27-23 (NY)
1969—Raiders, 27-14 (NY)
1970—Raiders, 14-13 (NY)
1972—Raiders, 24-16 (O)
1977—Raiders, 28-27 (NY)
1979—Jets, 28-19 (NY)
1982—****Jets, 17-14 (LA)
1985—Raiders, 31-0 (LA)
1989—Raiders, 14-7 (NY)
1993—Raiders, 24-20 (LA)
1995—Raiders, 47-10 (NY)
1996—Raiders, 34-13 (NY)
(RS Pts.—Raiders 673, Jets 574)
(PS Pts.—Jets 44, Raiders 37)
*Jets known as Titans prior to 1963
**Franchise in Los Angeles from 1982-1994
***AFL Championship
****AFC Second-Round Playoff
N.Y. JETS vs. PHILADELPHIA
RS: Eagles lead series, 6-0
1973—Eagles, 24-23 (P)
1977—Eagles, 27-0 (P)
1978—Eagles, 17-9 (P)
1987—Eagles, 38-27 (NY)
1993—Eagles, 35-30 (NY)
1996—Eagles, 21-20 (NY)
(RS Pts.—Eagles 162, Jets 109)
N.Y. JETS vs. PITTSBURGH
RS: Steelers lead series, 12-1
1970—Steelers, 21-17 (P)
1973—Steelers, 26-14 (P)
1975—Steelers, 20-7 (NY)
1977—Steelers, 23-20 (NY)
1978—Steelers, 28-17 (NY)
1981—Steelers, 38-10 (P)
1983—Steelers, 34-7 (NY)
1984—Steelers, 23-17 (NY)
1986—Steelers, 45-24 (NY)
1988—Jets, 24-20 (NY)
1989—Steelers, 13-0 (NY)
1990—Steelers, 24-7 (NY)
1992—Steelers, 27-10 (P)
(RS Pts.—Steelers 342, Jets 174)
***N.Y. JETS vs. *ST. LOUIS**
RS: Rams lead series, 6-2
1970—Jets, 31-20 (LA)
1974—Rams, 20-13 (NY)
1980—Rams, 38-13 (LA)
1983—Jets, 27-24 (NY) OT

1986—Rams, 17-3 (NY)
1989—Rams, 38-14 (LA)
1992—Rams, 18-10 (LA)
1995—Rams, 23-20 (NY)
(RS Pts.—Rams 198, Jets 131)
*Franchise in Los Angeles prior to 1995
***N.Y. JETS vs. **SAN DIEGO**
RS: Chargers lead series, 17-9-1
1960—Chargers, 21-7 (NY)
　　　Chargers, 50-43 (LA)
1961—Chargers, 25-10 (NY)
　　　Chargers, 48-13 (SD)
1962—Chargers, 40-14 (SD)
　　　Titans, 23-3 (NY)
1963—Chargers, 24-20 (SD)
　　　Chargers, 53-7 (NY)
1964—Tie, 17-17 (NY)
　　　Chargers, 38-3 (SD)
1965—Chargers, 34-9 (NY)
　　　Chargers, 38-7 (SD)
1966—Jets, 17-16 (NY)
　　　Chargers, 42-27 (SD)
1967—Jets, 42-31 (SD)
1968—Jets, 23-20 (NY)
　　　Jets, 37-15 (SD)
1969—Chargers, 34-27 (SD)
1971—Chargers, 49-21 (SD)
1974—Jets, 27-14 (NY)
1975—Chargers, 24-16 (SD)
1983—Jets, 41-29 (SD)
1989—Jets, 20-17 (SD)
1990—Chargers, 39-3 (NY)
　　　Chargers, 38-17 (SD)
1991—Jets, 24-3 (NY)
1994—Chargers, 21-6 (NY)
(RS Pts.—Chargers 783, Jets 521)
*Jets known as Titans prior to 1963
**Franchise in Los Angeles prior to 1961
N.Y. JETS vs. SAN FRANCISCO
RS: 49ers lead series, 6-1
1971—49ers, 24-21 (NY)
1976—49ers, 17-6 (SF)
1980—49ers, 37-27 (NY)
1983—Jets, 27-13 (SF)
1986—49ers, 24-10 (SF)
1989—49ers, 23-10 (NY)
1992—49ers, 31-14 (NY)
(RS Pts.—49ers 169, Jets 115)
N.Y. JETS vs. SEATTLE
RS: Seahawks lead series, 8-4
1977—Seahawks, 17-0 (NY)
1978—Seahawks, 24-17 (NY)
1979—Seahawks, 30-7 (S)
1980—Seahawks, 27-17 (NY)
1981—Seahawks, 19-3 (NY)
　　　Seahawks, 27-23 (S)
1983—Seahawks, 17-10 (NY)
1985—Jets, 17-14 (NY)
1986—Jets, 38-7 (S)
1987—Jets, 30-14 (NY)
1991—Seahawks, 20-13 (S)
1995—Jets, 16-10 (S)
(RS Pts.—Seahawks 226, Jets 191)
N.Y. JETS vs. TAMPA BAY
RS: Jets lead series, 5-1
1976—Jets, 34-0 (NY)
1982—Jets, 32-17 (NY)
1984—Buccaneers, 41-21 (TB)
1985—Jets, 62-28 (NY)
1990—Jets, 16-14 (TB)
1991—Jets, 16-13 (NY)
(RS Pts.—Jets 181, Buccaneers 113)
***N.Y. JETS vs. **TENNESSEE**
RS: Oilers lead series, 20-12-1
PS: Oilers lead series, 1-0
1960—Oilers, 27-21 (H)
　　　Oilers, 42-28 (NY)
1961—Oilers, 49-13 (H)
　　　Oilers, 48-21 (NY)
1962—Oilers, 56-17 (H)
　　　Oilers, 44-10 (NY)
1963—Jets, 24-17 (NY)
　　　Oilers, 31-27 (H)

1964—Jets, 24-21 (NY)
　　　Oilers, 33-17 (H)
1965—Oilers, 27-21 (H)
　　　Jets, 41-14 (NY)
1966—Jets, 52-13 (NY)
　　　Oilers, 24-0 (H)
1967—Tie, 28-28 (NY)
1968—Jets, 20-14 (H)
　　　Jets, 26-7 (NY)
1969—Jets, 26-17 (NY)
　　　Jets, 34-26 (H)
1972—Oilers, 26-20 (H)
1974—Jets, 27-22 (NY)
1977—Oilers, 20-0 (H)
1979—Oilers, 27-24 (H) OT
1980—Jets, 31-28 (NY) OT
1981—Jets, 33-17 (NY)
1984—Oilers, 31-20 (H)
1988—Jets, 45-3 (NY)
1990—Jets, 17-12 (H)
1991—Oilers, 23-20 (NY)
　　　***Oilers, 17-10 (H)
1993—Oilers, 24-0 (H)
1994—Oilers, 24-10 (H)
1995—Oilers, 23-6 (H)
1996—Oilers, 35-10 (NY)
(RS Pts.—Oilers 858, Jets 708)
(PS Pts.—Oilers 17, Jets 10)
*Jets known as Titans prior to 1963
**Franchise in Houston prior to 1997
***AFC First-Round Playoff
N.Y. JETS vs. WASHINGTON
RS: Redskins lead series, 5-1
1972—Redskins, 35-17 (N)
1976—Redskins, 37-16 (NY)
1978—Redskins, 23-3 (W)
1987—Redskins, 17-16 (W)
1993—Jets, 3-0 (W)
1996—Redskins, 31-16 (W)
(RS Pts.—Redskins 143, Jets 71)

OAKLAND vs. ARIZONA
RS: Raiders lead series, 2-1;
See Arizona vs. Oakland
OAKLAND vs. ATLANTA
RS: Raiders lead series, 5-3;
See Atlanta vs. Oakland
OAKLAND vs. BALTIMORE
RS: Ravens lead series, 1-0;
See Baltimore vs. Oakland
OAKLAND vs. BUFFALO
RS: Raiders lead series, 15-14
PS: Bills lead series, 2-0;
See Buffalo vs. Oakland
OAKLAND vs. CHICAGO
RS: Raiders lead series, 5-4;
See Chicago vs. Oakland
OAKLAND vs. CINCINNATI
RS: Raiders lead series, 15-7
PS: Raiders lead series, 2-0;
See Cincinnati vs. Oakland
OAKLAND vs. CLEVELAND
RS: Raiders lead series, 8-4
PS: Raiders lead series, 2-0;
See Cleveland vs. Oakland
OAKLAND vs. DALLAS
RS: Series tied, 3-3;
See Dallas vs. Oakland
OAKLAND vs. DENVER
RS: Raiders lead series, 48-23-2
PS: Series tied, 1-1;
See Denver vs. Oakland
OAKLAND vs. DETROIT
RS: Raiders lead series, 6-2;
See Detroit vs. Oakland
OAKLAND vs. GREEN BAY
RS: Raiders lead series, 5-2
PS: Packers lead series, 1-0;
See Green Bay vs. Oakland
OAKLAND vs. INDIANAPOLIS
RS: Raiders lead series, 5-2
PS: Series tied, 1-1;
See Indianapolis vs. Oakland

OAKLAND vs. JACKSONVILLE
RS: Raiders lead series, 1-0;
See Jacksonville vs. Oakland
OAKLAND vs. KANSAS CITY
RS: Raiders lead series, 36-35-2
PS: Chiefs lead series, 2-1;
See Kansas City vs. Oakland
OAKLAND vs. MIAMI
RS: Raiders lead series, 15-5-1
PS: Raiders lead series, 2-1;
See Miami vs. Oakland
OAKLAND vs. MINNESOTA
RS: Raiders lead series, 6-3
PS: Raiders lead series, 1-0;
See Minnesota vs. Oakland
OAKLAND vs. NEW ENGLAND
RS: Raiders lead series, 13-12-1
PS: Series tied, 1-1;
See New England vs. Oakland
OAKLAND vs. NEW ORLEANS
RS: Raiders lead series, 4-2-1;
See New Orleans vs. Oakland
OAKLAND vs. N.Y. GIANTS
RS: Raiders lead series, 5-2;
See N.Y. Giants vs. Oakland
OAKLAND vs. N.Y. JETS
RS: Raiders lead series, 16-9-2
PS: Jets lead series, 2-0;
See N.Y. Jets vs. Oakland
*OAKLAND vs. PHILADELPHIA
RS: Eagles lead series, 4-3
PS: Raiders lead series, 1-0
1971—Raiders, 34-10 (O)
1976—Raiders, 26-7 (P)
1980—Eagles, 10-7 (P)
　　**Raiders, 27-10 (New Orleans)
1986—Eagles, 33-27 (LA) OT
1989—Eagles, 10-7 (P)
1992—Eagles, 31-10 (P)
1995—Raiders, 48-17 (O)
(RS Pts.—Raiders 159, Eagles 118)
(PS Pts.—Raiders 27, Eagles 10)
**Franchise in Los Angeles from
1982-1994*
**Super Bowl XV
*OAKLAND vs. PITTSBURGH
RS: Raiders lead series, 7-5
PS: Series tied, 3-3
1970—Raiders, 31-14 (O)
1972—Steelers, 34-28 (P)
　　**Steelers, 13-7 (P)
1973—Steelers, 17-9 (O)
　　**Raiders, 33-14 (O)
1974—Raiders, 17-0 (P)
　　***Steelers, 24-13 (O)
1975—***Steelers, 16-10 (P)
1976—Raiders, 31-28 (O)
　　***Raiders, 24-7 (O)
1977—Raiders, 16-7 (P)
1980—Raiders, 45-34 (P)
1981—Raiders, 30-27 (O)
1983—**Raiders, 38-10 (LA)
1984—Steelers, 13-7 (LA)
1990—Raiders, 20-3 (LA)
1994—Steelers, 21-3 (LA)
1995—Steelers, 29-10 (O)
(RS Pts.—Raiders 247, Steelers 227)
(PS Pts.—Raiders 125, Steelers 84)
**Franchise in Los Angeles from
1982-1994*
**AFC Divisional Playoff
***AFC Championship
*OAKLAND vs. **ST. LOUIS
RS: Raiders lead series, 6-2
1972—Raiders, 45-17 (O)
1977—Rams, 20-14 (LA)
1979—Raiders, 24-17 (LA)
1982—Raiders, 37-31 (LA Raiders)
1985—Raiders, 16-6 (LA Rams)
1988—Rams, 22-17 (LA Raiders)
1991—Raiders, 20-17 (LA Raiders)
1994—Raiders, 20-17 (LA Rams)
(RS Pts.—Raiders 193, Rams 147)

**Franchise in Los Angeles from
1982-1994*
**Franchise in Los Angeles prior to 1995
*OAKLAND vs. **SAN DIEGO
RS: Raiders lead series, 44-28-2
PS: Raiders lead series, 1-0
1960—Chargers, 52-28 (LA)
　　Chargers, 41-17 (O)
1961—Chargers, 44-0 (SD)
　　Chargers, 41-10 (O)
1962—Chargers, 42-33 (O)
　　Chargers, 31-21 (SD)
1963—Raiders, 34-33 (SD)
　　Raiders, 41-27 (O)
1964—Chargers, 31-17 (SD)
　　Raiders, 21-20 (O)
1965—Chargers, 17-6 (O)
　　Chargers, 24-14 (SD)
1966—Chargers, 29-20 (O)
　　Raiders, 41-19 (SD)
1967—Raiders, 51-10 (O)
　　Raiders, 41-21 (SD)
1968—Chargers, 23-14 (O)
　　Raiders, 34-27 (SD)
1969—Raiders, 24-12 (SD)
　　Raiders, 21-16 (O)
1970—Tie, 27-27 (SD)
　　Raiders, 20-17 (O)
1971—Raiders, 34-0 (SD)
　　Raiders, 34-33 (O)
1972—Tie, 17-17 (O)
　　Raiders, 21-19 (SD)
1973—Raiders, 27-17 (SD)
　　Raiders, 31-3 (O)
1974—Raiders, 14-10 (SD)
　　Raiders, 17-10 (O)
1975—Raiders, 6-0 (SD)
　　Raiders, 25-0 (O)
1976—Raiders, 27-17 (SD)
　　Raiders, 24-0 (O)
1977—Raiders, 24-0 (O)
　　Chargers, 12-7 (SD)
1978—Raiders, 21-20 (SD)
　　Chargers, 27-23 (O)
1979—Chargers, 30-10 (SD)
　　Raiders, 45-22 (O)
1980—Chargers, 30-24 (SD) OT
　　Raiders, 38-24 (O)
　　***Raiders, 34-27 (SD)
1981—Chargers, 55-21 (O)
　　Chargers, 23-10 (SD)
1982—Raiders, 28-24 (LA)
　　Raiders, 41-34 (SD)
1983—Raiders, 42-10 (SD)
　　Raiders, 30-14 (LA)
1984—Raiders, 33-30 (LA)
　　Raiders, 44-37 (SD)
1985—Raiders, 34-21 (LA)
　　Chargers, 40-34 (SD) OT
1986—Raiders, 17-13 (LA)
　　Raiders, 37-31 (SD) OT
1987—Chargers, 23-17 (LA)
　　Chargers, 16-14 (SD)
1988—Raiders, 24-13 (LA)
　　Raiders, 13-3 (SD)
1989—Raiders, 40-14 (LA)
　　Chargers, 14-12 (SD)
1990—Raiders, 24-9 (SD)
　　Raiders, 17-12 (LA)
1991—Chargers, 21-13 (LA)
　　Raiders, 9-7 (SD)
1992—Chargers, 27-3 (SD)
　　Chargers, 36-14 (LA)
1993—Chargers, 30-23 (LA)
　　Chargers, 12-7 (SD)
1994—Chargers, 26-24 (LA)
　　Raiders, 24-17 (SD)
1995—Raiders, 17-7 (O)
　　Chargers, 12-6 (SD)
1996—Chargers, 40-34 (O)
　　Raiders, 23-14 (SD)
(RS Pts.—Raiders 1,738, Chargers 1,575)
(PS Pts.—Raiders 34, Chargers 27)

**Franchise in Los Angeles from
1982-1994*
**Franchise in Los Angeles prior to 1961
***AFC Championship
*OAKLAND vs. SAN FRANCISCO
RS: Raiders lead series, 5-3
1970—49ers, 38-7 (O)
1974—Raiders, 35-24 (SF)
1979—Raiders, 23-10 (O)
1982—Raiders, 23-17 (SF)
1985—49ers, 34-10 (LA)
1988—Raiders, 9-3 (SF)
1991—Raiders, 12-6 (LA)
1994—49ers, 44-14 (SF)
(RS Pts.—49ers 176, Raiders 133)
**Franchise in Los Angeles from
1982-1994*
*OAKLAND vs. SEATTLE
RS: Raiders lead series, 21-17
PS: Series tied, 1-1
1977—Raiders, 44-7 (O)
1978—Seahawks, 27-7 (S)
　　Seahawks, 17-16 (O)
1979—Seahawks, 27-10 (S)
　　Seahawks, 29-24 (O)
1980—Raiders, 33-14 (O)
　　Raiders, 19-17 (S)
1981—Raiders, 20-10 (O)
　　Raiders, 32-31 (S)
1982—Raiders, 28-23 (LA)
1983—Seahawks, 38-36 (S)
　　Seahawks, 34-21 (LA)
　　**Raiders, 30-14 (LA)
1984—Raiders, 28-14 (LA)
　　Seahawks, 17-14 (S)
　　***Seahawks, 13-7 (S)
1985—Seahawks, 33-3 (S)
　　Raiders, 13-3 (LA)
1986—Raiders, 14-10 (LA)
　　Seahawks, 37-0 (S)
1987—Seahawks, 35-13 (LA)
　　Raiders, 37-14 (S)
1988—Seahawks, 35-27 (S)
　　Seahawks, 43-37 (LA)
1989—Seahawks, 24-20 (LA)
　　Seahawks, 23-17 (S)
1990—Raiders, 17-13 (S)
　　Raiders, 24-17 (LA)
1991—Raiders, 23-20 (S) OT
　　Raiders, 31-7 (LA)
1992—Raiders, 19-0 (S)
　　Raiders, 20-3 (LA)
1993—Raiders, 17-13 (S)
　　Raiders, 27-23 (LA)
1994—Seahawks, 38-9 (LA)
　　Raiders, 17-16 (S)
1995—Raiders, 34-14 (O)
　　Seahawks, 44-10 (S)
1996—Raiders, 27-21 (S)
　　Seahawks, 28-21 (O)
(RS Pts.—Seahawks 819, Raiders 809)
(PS Pts.—Raiders 37, Seahawks 27)
**Franchise in Los Angeles from
1982-1994*
**AFC Championship
***AFC First-Round Playoff
*OAKLAND vs. TAMPA BAY
RS: Raiders lead series, 3-1
1976—Raiders, 49-16 (O)
1981—Raiders, 18-16 (O)
1993—Raiders, 27-20 (LA)
1996—Buccaneers, 20-17 (TB) OT
(RS Pts.—Raiders 111, Buccaneers 72)
**Franchise in Los Angeles from
1982-1994*
*OAKLAND vs. **TENNESSEE
RS: Raiders lead series, 20-13
PS: Raiders lead series, 3-0
1960—Oilers, 37-22 (O)
　　Raiders, 14-13 (H)
1961—Oilers, 55-0 (H)
　　Oilers, 47-16 (O)
1962—Oilers, 28-20 (O)

Oilers, 32-17 (H)
1963—Raiders, 24-13 (H)
　　Raiders, 52-49 (O)
1964—Oilers, 42-28 (H)
　　Raiders, 20-10 (O)
1965—Raiders, 21-17 (O)
　　Raiders, 33-21 (H)
1966—Oilers, 31-0 (H)
　　Raiders, 38-23 (O)
1967—Raiders, 19-7 (H)
　　***Raiders, 40-7 (O)
1968—Raiders, 24-15 (H)
1969—Raiders, 21-17 (O)
　　****Raiders, 56-7 (O)
1971—Raiders, 41-21 (O)
1972—Raiders, 34-0 (H)
1973—Raiders, 17-6 (H)
1975—Oilers, 27-26 (O)
1976—Raiders, 14-13 (H)
1977—Raiders, 34-29 (H)
1978—Raiders, 21-17 (H)
1979—Oilers, 31-17 (H)
1980—*****Raiders, 27-7 (O)
1981—Oilers, 17-16 (H)
1983—Raiders, 20-6 (LA)
1984—Raiders, 24-14 (H)
1986—Raiders, 28-17 (H)
1988—Oilers, 38-35 (H)
1989—Oilers, 23-7 (H)
1991—Oilers, 47-17 (H)
1994—Raiders, 17-14 (LA)
(RS Pts.—Oilers 777, Raiders 737)
(PS Pts.—Raiders 123, Oilers 21)
**Franchise in Los Angeles from
1982-1994*
**Franchise in Houston prior to 1997
***AFL Championship
****Inter-Divisional Playoff
*****AFC First-Round Playoff
*OAKLAND vs. WASHINGTON
RS: Raiders lead series, 6-2
PS: Raiders lead series, 1-0
1970—Raiders, 34-20 (O)
1975—Raiders, 26-23 (W) OT
1980—Raiders, 24-21 (O)
1983—Redskins, 37-35 (W)
　　**Raiders, 38-9 (Tampa)
1986—Redskins, 10-6 (W)
1989—Raiders, 37-24 (LA)
1992—Raiders, 21-20 (W)
1995—Raiders, 20-8 (W)
(RS Pts.—Raiders 203, Redskins 163)
(PS Pts.—Raiders 38, Redskins 9)
**Franchise in Los Angeles from
1982-1994*
**Super Bowl XVIII

PHILADELPHIA vs. ARIZONA
RS: Eagles lead series, 47-46-5
PS: Series tied, 1-1;
See Arizona vs. Philadelphia
PHILADELPHIA vs. ATLANTA
RS: Eagles lead series, 9-7-1
PS: Falcons lead series, 1-0;
See Atlanta vs. Philadelphia
PHILADELPHIA vs. BUFFALO
RS: Series tied, 4-4;
See Buffalo vs. Philadelphia
PHILADELPHIA vs. CAROLINA
RS: Eagles lead series, 1-0;
See Carolina vs. Philadelphia
PHILADELPHIA vs. CHICAGO
RS: Bears lead series, 24-4-1
PS: Series tied, 1-1;
See Chicago vs. Philadelphia
PHILADELPHIA vs. CINCINNATI
RS: Bengals lead series, 6-1;
See Cincinnati vs. Philadelphia
PHILADELPHIA vs. CLEVELAND
RS: Browns lead series, 31-12-1;
See Cleveland vs. Philadelphia
PHILADELPHIA vs. DALLAS
RS: Cowboys lead series, 44-28

PS: Cowboys lead series, 2-1;
See Dallas vs. Philadelphia

PHILADELPHIA vs. DENVER
RS: Eagles lead series, 6-2;
See Denver vs. Philadelphia

PHILADELPHIA vs. DETROIT
RS: Lions lead series, 12-10-2
PS: Eagles lead series, 1-0;
See Detroit vs. Philadelphia

PHILADELPHIA vs. GREEN BAY
RS: Packers lead series, 20-8
PS: Eagles lead series, 1-0;
See Green Bay vs. Philadelphia

PHILADELPHIA vs. INDIANAPOLIS
RS: Colts lead series, 7-6;
See Indianapolis vs. Philadelphia

PHILADELPHIA vs. KANSAS CITY
RS: Series tied, 1-1;
See Kansas City vs. Philadelphia

PHILADELPHIA vs. MIAMI
RS: Dolphins lead series, 6-3;
See Miami vs. Philadelphia

PHILADELPHIA vs. MINNESOTA
RS: Vikings lead series, 10-6
PS: Eagles lead series, 1-0;
See Minnesota vs. Philadelphia

PHILADELPHIA vs. NEW ENGLAND
RS: Eagles lead series, 5-2;
See New England vs. Philadelphia

PHILADELPHIA vs. NEW ORLEANS
RS: Eagles lead series, 12-8
PS; Eagles lead series, 1-0;
See New Orleans vs. Philadelphia

PHILADELPHIA vs. N.Y. GIANTS
RS: Giants lead series, 64-58-2
PS: Giants lead series, 1-0;
See N.Y. Giants vs. Philadelphia

PHILADELPHIA vs. N.Y. JETS
RS: Eagles lead series, 6-0;
See N.Y. Jets vs. Philadelphia

PHILADELPHIA vs. OAKLAND
RS: Eagles lead series, 4-3
PS: Raiders lead series, 1-0;
See Oakland vs. Philadelphia

PHILADELPHIA vs. *PITTSBURGH
RS: Eagles lead series, 43-26-3
PS: Eagles lead series, 1-0
1933—Eagles, 25-6 (Phila)
1934—Eagles, 17-0 (Pitt)
　　　Pirates, 9-7 (Phila)
1935—Pirates, 17-7 (Phila)
　　　Eagles, 17-6 (Pitt)
1936—Pirates, 17-0 (Pitt)
　　　Pirates, 6-0 (Johnstown, Pa.)
1937—Pirates, 27-14 (Pitt)
　　　Pirates, 16-7 (Pitt)
1938—Eagles, 27-7 (Buffalo)
　　　Eagles, 14-7 (Charleston, W. Va.)
1939—Eagles, 17-14 (Phila)
　　　Pirates, 24-12 (Pitt)
1940—Pirates, 7-3 (Pitt)
　　　Eagles, 7-0 (Phila)
1941—Eagles, 10-7 (Pitt)
　　　Tie, 7-7 (Phila)
1942—Eagles, 24-14 (Pitt)
　　　Steelers, 14-0 (Phila)
1945—Eagles, 45-3 (Pitt)
　　　Eagles, 30-6 (Phila)
1946—Steelers, 10-7 (Pitt)
　　　Eagles, 10-7 (Phila)
1947—Steelers, 35-24 (Pitt)
　　　Eagles, 21-0 Phila
　　**Eagles, 21-0 (Pitt)
1948—Eagles, 34-7 (Pitt)
　　　Eagles, 17-0 (Phila)
1949—Eagles, 38-7 (Pitt)
　　　Eagles, 34-17 (Phila)
1950—Eagles, 17-10 (Pitt)
　　　Steelers, 9-7 (Phila)
1951—Eagles, 34-13 (Pitt)
　　　Steelers, 17-13 (Phila)
1952—Eagles, 31-25 (Pitt)
　　　Eagles, 26-21 (Phila)

1953—Eagles, 23-17 (Phila)
　　　Eagles, 35-7 (Pitt)
1954—Eagles, 24-22 (Phila)
　　　Steelers, 17-7 (Pitt)
1955—Steelers, 13-7 (Pitt)
　　　Eagles, 24-0 (Phila)
1956—Eagles, 35-21 (Pitt)
　　　Eagles, 14-7 (Phila)
1957—Steelers, 6-0 (Pitt)
　　　Eagles, 7-6 (Phila)
1958—Steelers, 24-3 (Pitt)
　　　Steelers, 31-24 (Phila)
1959—Eagles, 28-24 (Phila)
　　　Steelers, 31-0 (Pitt)
1960—Eagles, 34-7 (Phila)
　　　Steelers, 27-21 (Pitt)
1961—Eagles, 21-16 (Phila)
　　　Eagles, 35-24 (Pitt)
1962—Steelers, 13-7 (Pitt)
　　　Steelers, 26-17 (Phila)
1963—Tie, 21-21 (Phila)
　　　Tie, 20-20 (Pitt)
1964—Eagles, 21-7 (Phila)
　　　Eagles, 34-10 (Pitt)
1965—Steelers, 20-14 (Phila)
　　　Eagles, 47-13 (Pitt)
1966—Eagles, 31-14 (Pitt)
　　　Eagles, 27-23 (Phila)
1967—Eagles, 34-24 (Phila)
1968—Steelers, 6-3 (Pitt)
1969—Eagles, 41-27 (Phila)
1970—Eagles, 30-20 (Phila)
1974—Steelers, 27-0 (Pitt)
1979—Eagles, 17-14 (Phila)
1988—Eagles, 27-26 (Pitt)
1991—Eagles, 23-14 (Phila)
1994—Steelers, 14-3 (Pitt)
(RS Pts.—Eagles 1,362, Steelers 1,021)
(PS Pts.—Eagles 21, Steelers 0)
*Steelers known as Pirates prior to 1941
**Division Playoff

PHILADELPHIA vs. *ST. LOUIS
RS: Rams lead series, 15-12-1
PS: Series tied, 1-1
1937—Rams, 21-3 (P)
1939—Rams, 35-13 (Colorado Springs)
1940—Rams, 21-13 (C)
1942—Rams, 24-14 (Akron)
1944—Eagles, 26-13 (P)
1945—Eagles, 28-14 (P)
1946—Eagles, 25-14 (LA)
1947—Eagles, 14-7 (P)
1948—Tie, 28-28 (LA)
1949—Eagles, 38-14 (P)
　　**Eagles, 14-0 (LA)
1950—Eagles, 56-20 (P)
1955—Rams, 23-21 (P)
1956—Rams, 27-7 (LA)
1957—Rams, 17-13 (LA)
1959—Eagles, 23-20 (P)
1964—Rams, 20-10 (LA)
1967—Rams, 33-17 (LA)
1969—Rams, 23-17 (P)
1972—Rams, 34-3 (P)
1975—Rams, 42-3 (P)
1977—Rams, 20-0 (LA)
1978—Rams, 16-14 (P)
1983—Eagles, 13-9 (P)
1985—Rams, 17-6 (P)
1986—Eagles, 34-20 (P)
1988—Eagles, 30-24 (P)
1989—***Rams, 21-7 (P)
1990—Eagles, 27-21 (LA)
1995—Eagles, 20-9 (P)
(RS Pts.—Rams 586, Eagles 516)
(PS Pts.—Rams 21, Eagles 21)
*Franchise in Los Angeles prior to 1995
and in Cleveland prior to 1946
**NFL Championship
***NFC First-Round Playoff

PHILADELPHIA vs. SAN DIEGO
RS: Chargers lead series, 4-2
1974—Eagles, 13-7 (SD)

1980—Chargers, 22-21 (SD)
1985—Chargers, 20-14 (SD)
1986—Eagles, 23-7 (P)
1989—Chargers, 20-17 (SD)
1995—Chargers, 27-21 (P)
(RS Pts.—Eagles 109, Chargers 103)

PHILADELPHIA vs. SAN FRANCISCO
RS: 49ers lead series, 13-6-1
PS: 49ers lead series, 1-0
1951—Eagles, 21-14 (P)
1953—49ers, 31-21 (SF)
1956—Tie, 10-10 (P)
1958—49ers, 30-24 (P)
1959—49ers, 24-14 (SF)
1964—49ers, 28-24 (P)
1966—Eagles, 35-34 (SF)
1967—49ers, 28-27 (P)
1969—49ers, 14-13 (SF)
1971—49ers, 31-3 (P)
1973—49ers, 38-28 (SF)
1975—Eagles, 27-17 (P)
1983—Eagles, 22-17 (SF)
1984—49ers, 21-9 (P)
1985—49ers, 24-13 (SF)
1989—49ers, 38-28 (P)
1991—49ers, 23-7 (P)
1992—Eagles, 20-14 (SF)
1993—Eagles, 37-34 (SF) OT
1994—Eagles, 40-8 (SF)
1996—*49ers, 14-0 (SF)
(RS Pts.—49ers 484, Eagles 417)
(PS Pts.—49ers 14, Eagles 0)
*NFC First-Round Playoff

PHILADELPHIA vs. SEATTLE
RS: Eagles lead series, 4-2
1976—Eagles, 27-10 (P)
1980—Eagles, 27-20 (S)
1986—Seahawks, 24-20 (S)
1989—Eagles, 31-7 (P)
1992—Eagles, 20-17 (S) OT
1995—Seahawks, 26-10 (S)
(RS Pts.—Eagles 135, Seahawks 104)

PHILADELPHIA vs. TAMPA BAY
RS: Eagles lead series, 3-2
PS: Buccaneers lead series, 1-0
1977—Eagles, 13-3 (P)
1979—*Buccaneers, 24-17 (TB)
1981—Eagles, 20-10 (P)
1988—Eagles, 41-14 (TB)
1991—Buccaneers, 14-13 (TB)
1995—Buccaneers, 21-6 (P)
(RS Pts.—Eagles 93, Buccaneers 62)
(PS Pts.—Buccaneers 24, Eagles 17)
*NFC Divisional Playoff

PHILADELPHIA vs. *TENNESSEE
RS: Eagles lead series, 6-0
1972—Eagles, 18-17 (H)
1979—Eagles, 26-20 (H)
1982—Eagles, 35-14 (P)
1988—Eagles, 32-23 (P)
1991—Eagles, 13-6 (H)
1994—Eagles, 21-6 (P)
(RS Pts.—Eagles 145, Oilers 86)
*Franchise in Houston prior to 1997

PHILADELPHIA vs. *WASHINGTON
RS: Redskins lead series, 67-51-5
PS: Redskins lead series, 1-0
1934—Redskins, 6-0 (B)
　　　Redskins, 14-7 (P)
1935—Eagles, 7-6 (B)
1936—Redskins, 26-3 (P)
　　　Redskins, 17-7 (B)
1937—Eagles, 14-0 (W)
　　　Redskins, 10-7 (P)
1938—Redskins, 26-23 (P)
　　　Redskins, 20-14 (W)
1939—Redskins, 7-0 (P)
　　　Redskins, 7-6 (W)
1940—Redskins, 34-17 (P)
　　　Redskins, 13-6 (W)
1941—Redskins, 21-17 (P)
　　　Redskins, 20-14 (W)
1942—Redskins, 14-10 (P)

　　　Redskins, 30-27 (W)
1944—Tie, 31-31 (P)
　　　Eagles, 37-7 (W)
1945—Redskins, 24-14 (W)
　　　Eagles, 16-0 (P)
1946—Eagles, 28-24 (W)
　　　Redskins, 27-10 (P)
1947—Eagles, 45-42 (P)
　　　Eagles, 38-14 (W)
1948—Eagles, 45-0 (W)
　　　Eagles, 42-21 (P)
1949—Eagles, 49-14 (P)
　　　Eagles, 44-21 (W)
1950—Eagles, 35-3 (P)
　　　Eagles, 33-0 (W)
1951—Redskins, 27-23 (P)
　　　Eagles, 35-21 (W)
1952—Eagles, 38-20 (P)
　　　Redskins, 27-21 (W)
1953—Tie, 21-21 (P)
　　　Redskins, 10-0 (W)
1954—Eagles, 49-21 (W)
　　　Eagles, 41-33 (P)
1955—Redskins, 31-30 (P)
　　　Redskins, 34-21 (W)
1956—Eagles, 13-9 (P)
　　　Redskins, 19-17 (W)
1957—Eagles, 21-12 (P)
　　　Redskins, 42-7 (W)
1958—Redskins, 24-14 (P)
　　　Redskins, 20-0 (W)
1959—Eagles, 30-23 (P)
　　　Eagles, 34-14 (W)
1960—Eagles, 19-13 (P)
　　　Eagles, 38-28 (W)
1961—Eagles, 14-7 (P)
　　　Eagles, 27-24 (W)
1962—Redskins, 27-21 (P)
　　　Eagles, 37-14 (W)
1963—Eagles, 37-24 (P)
　　　Redskins, 13-10 (P)
1964—Redskins, 35-20 (P)
　　　Redskins, 21-10 (W)
1965—Redskins, 23-21 (W)
　　　Eagles, 21-14 (P)
1966—Redskins, 27-13 (P)
　　　Eagles, 37-28 (W)
1967—Eagles, 35-24 (P)
　　　Tie, 35-35 (W)
1968—Redskins, 17-14 (W)
　　　Redskins, 16-10 (P)
1969—Tie, 28-28 (W)
　　　Redskins, 34-29 (P)
1970—Redskins, 33-21 (P)
　　　Redskins, 24-6 (W)
1971—Tie, 7-7 (W)
　　　Redskins, 20-13 (P)
1972—Redskins, 14-0 (W)
　　　Redskins, 23-7 (P)
1973—Redskins, 28-7 (P)
　　　Redskins, 38-20 (W)
1974—Redskins, 27-20 (P)
　　　Redskins, 26-7 (W)
1975—Eagles, 26-10 (P)
　　　Eagles, 26-3 (W)
1976—Redskins, 20-17 (P) OT
　　　Redskins, 24-0 (W)
1977—Redskins, 23-17 (P)
　　　Redskins, 17-14 (P)
1978—Redskins, 35-30 (W)
　　　Eagles, 17-10 (P)
1979—Eagles, 28-17 (P)
　　　Redskins, 17-7 (W)
1980—Eagles, 24-14 (P)
　　　Eagles, 24-0 (W)
1981—Eagles, 36-13 (P)
　　　Redskins, 15-13 (W)
1982—Redskins, 37-34 (P) OT
　　　Redskins, 13-9 (W)
1983—Redskins, 23-13 (P)
　　　Redskins, 28-24 (W)
1984—Redskins, 20-0 (W)
　　　Eagles, 16-10 (P)

1985—Eagles, 19-6 (W)
Redskins, 17-12 (P)
1986—Redskins, 41-14 (W)
Redskins, 21-14 (P)
1987—Redskins, 34-24 (W)
Eagles, 31-27 (P)
1988—Redskins, 17-10 (W)
Redskins, 20-19 (P)
1989—Eagles, 42-37 (W)
Redskins, 10-3 (P)
1990—Redskins, 13-7 (W)
Eagles, 28-14 (P)
**Redskins, 20-6 (P)
1991—Redskins, 23-0 (W)
Eagles, 24-22 (P)
1992—Redskins, 16-12 (W)
Eagles, 17-13 (P)
1993—Eagles, 34-31 (P)
Eagles, 17-14 (W)
1994—Eagles, 21-17 (P)
Eagles, 31-29 (W)
1995—Eagles, 37-34 (P) (OT)
Eagles, 14-7 (W)
1996—Eagles, 17-14 (W)
Redskins, 26-21 (P)
(RS Pts.—Eagles 2,488, Redskins 2,451)
(PS Pts.—Redskins 20, Eagles 6)
*Franchise in Boston prior to 1937
**NFC First-Round Playoff

PITTSBURGH vs. ARIZONA
RS: Steelers lead series, 29-22-3;
See Arizona vs. Pittsburgh
PITTSBURGH vs. ATLANTA
RS: Steelers lead series, 10-1;
See Atlanta vs. Pittsburgh
PITTSBURGH vs. BALTIMORE
RS: Series tied, 1-1;
See Baltimore vs. Pittsburgh
PITTSBURGH vs. BUFFALO
RS: Steelers lead series, 8-7
PS: Steelers lead series, 2-1;
See Buffalo vs. Pittsburgh
PITTSBURGH vs. CAROLINA
RS: Panthers lead series, 1-0;
See Carolina vs. Pittsburgh
PITTSBURGH vs. CHICAGO
RS: Bears lead series, 16-5-1;
See Chicago vs. Pittsburgh
PITTSBURGH vs. CINCINNATI
RS: Steelers lead series, 30-23;
See Cincinnati vs. Pittsburgh
PITTSBURGH vs. CLEVELAND
RS: Browns lead series, 52-40
PS: Steelers lead series, 1-0;
See Cleveland vs. Pittsburgh
PITTSBURGH vs. DALLAS
RS: Cowboys lead series, 13-11
PS: Steelers lead series, 2-1;
See Dallas vs. Pittsburgh
PITTSBURGH vs. DENVER
RS: Broncos lead series, 10-5-1
PS: Series tied, 2-2;
See Denver vs. Pittsburgh
PITTSBURGH vs. DETROIT
RS: Lions lead series, 13-12-1;
See Detroit vs. Pittsburgh
PITTSBURGH vs. GREEN BAY
RS: Packers lead series, 18-11;
See Green Bay vs. Pittsburgh
PITTSBURGH vs. INDIANAPOLIS
RS: Steelers lead series, 11-4
PS: Steelers lead series, 4-0;
See Indianapolis vs. Pittsburgh
PITTSBURGH vs. JACKSONVILLE
RS: Series tied, 2-2;
See Jacksonville vs. Pittsburgh
PITTSBURGH vs. KANSAS CITY
RS: Steelers lead series, 14-5
PS: Chiefs lead series, 1-0;
See Kansas City vs. Pittsburgh
PITTSBURGH vs. MIAMI
RS: Dolphins lead series, 8-7

PS: Dolphins lead series, 2-1;
See Miami vs. Pittsburgh
PITTSBURGH vs. MINNESOTA
RS: Vikings lead series, 8-4
PS: Steelers lead series, 1-0;
See Minnesota vs. Pittsburgh
PITTSBURGH vs. NEW ENGLAND
RS: Steelers lead series, 10-3
PS: Patriots lead series, 1-0;
See New England vs. Pittsburgh
PITTSBURGH vs. NEW ORLEANS
RS: Steelers lead series, 6-5;
See New Orleans vs. Pittsburgh
PITTSBURGH vs. N.Y. GIANTS
RS: Giants lead series, 42-27-3;
See N.Y. Giants vs. Pittsburgh
PITTSBURGH vs. N.Y. JETS
RS: Steelers lead series, 12-1;
See N.Y. Jets vs. Pittsburgh
PITTSBURGH vs. OAKLAND
RS: Raiders lead series, 7-5
PS: Series tied, 3-3;
See Oakland vs. Pittsburgh
PITTSBURGH vs. PHILADELPHIA
RS: Eagles lead series, 43-26-3
PS: Eagles lead series, 1-0;
See Philadelphia vs. Pittsburgh
***PITTSBURGH vs. **ST. LOUIS**
RS: Rams lead series, 14-5-2
PS: Steelers lead series, 1-0
1938—Rams, 13-7 (New Orleans)
1939—Tie, 14-14 (C)
1941—Rams, 17-14 (Akron)
1947—Rams, 48-7 (LA)
1948—Rams, 31-14 (LA)
1949—Tie, 7-7 (LA)
1952—Rams, 28-14 (LA)
1955—Rams, 27-26 (LA)
1956—Steelers, 30-13 (P)
1961—Rams, 24-14 (LA)
1964—Rams, 26-14 (P)
1968—Rams, 45-10 (LA)
1971—Rams, 23-14 (P)
1975—Rams, 10-3 (LA)
1978—Rams, 10-7 (LA)
1979—***Steelers, 31-19 (Pasadena)
1981—Steelers, 24-0 (P)
1984—Steelers, 24-14 (P)
1987—Rams, 31-21 (LA)
1990—Steelers, 41-10 (P)
1993—Rams, 27-0 (LA)
1996—Steelers, 42-6 (P)
(RS Pts.—Rams 424, Steelers 347)
(PS Pts.—Steelers 31, Rams 19)
*Steelers known as Pirates prior to 1941
**Franchise in Los Angeles prior to
1995 and in Cleveland prior to 1946
***Super Bowl XIV
PITTSBURGH vs. SAN DIEGO
RS: Steelers lead series, 16-5
PS: Chargers lead series, 2-0
1971—Steelers, 21-17 (P)
1972—Steelers, 24-2 (SD)
1973—Steelers, 38-21 (P)
1975—Steelers, 37-0 (SD)
1976—Steelers, 23-0 (P)
1977—Steelers, 10-9 (SD)
1979—Chargers, 35-7 (SD)
1980—Chargers, 26-17 (SD)
1982—*Chargers, 31-28 (P)
1983—Steelers, 26-3 (P)
1984—Steelers, 52-24 (P)
1985—Chargers, 54-44 (SD)
1987—Steelers, 20-16 (SD)
1988—Chargers, 20-14 (SD)
1989—Steelers, 20-17 (P)
1990—Steelers, 36-14 (P)
1991—Steelers, 26-20 (P)
1992—Steelers, 23-6 (SD)
1993—Steelers,.16-3 (P)
1994—Chargers, 37-34 (SD)
**Chargers, 17-13 (P)
1995—Steelers, 31-16 (P)

1996—Steelers, 16-3 (P)
(RS Pts.—Steelers 535, Chargers 343)
(PS Pts.—Chargers 48, Steelers 41)
*AFC First-Round Playoff
**AFC Championship
PITTSBURGH vs. SAN FRANCISCO
RS: 49ers lead series, 9-7
1951—49ers, 28-24 (P)
1952—Steelers, 24-7 (SF)
1954—49ers, 31-3 (SF)
1958—49ers, 23-20 (SF)
1961—Steelers, 20-10 (P)
1965—49ers, 27-17 (SF)
1968—49ers, 45-28 (P)
1973—Steelers, 37-14 (SF)
1977—Steelers, 27-0 (P)
1978—Steelers, 24-7 (SF)
1981—49ers, 17-14 (P)
1984—Steelers, 20-17 (SF)
1987—Steelers, 30-17 (P)
1990—49ers, 27-7 (SF)
1993—49ers, 24-13 (P)
1996—Steelers, 25-15 (P)
(RS Pts.—Steelers 323, 49ers 319)
PITTSBURGH vs. SEATTLE
RS: Seahawks lead series, 6-5
1977—Steelers, 30-20 (P)
1978—Steelers, 21-10 (P)
1981—Seahawks, 24-21 (S)
1982—Seahawks, 16-0 (S)
1983—Steelers, 27-21 (S)
1986—Seahawks, 30-0 (S)
1987—Steelers, 13-9 (P)
1991—Steelers, 27-7 (P)
1992—Steelers, 20-14 (P)
1993—Seahawks, 16-6 (S)
1994—Seahawks, 30-13 (S)
(RS Pts.—Seahawks 217, Steelers 158)
PITTSBURGH vs. TAMPA BAY
RS: Steelers lead series, 4-0
1976—Steelers, 42-0 (P)
1980—Steelers, 24-21 (TB)
1983—Steelers, 17-12 (P)
1989—Steelers, 31-22 (TB)
(RS Pts.—Steelers 114, Buccaneers 55)
PITTSBURGH vs. *TENNESSEE
RS: Steelers lead series, 34-19
PS: Steelers lead series, 3-0
1970—Oilers, 19-7 (P)
Steelers, 7-3 (H)
1971—Steelers, 23-16 (P)
Oilers, 29-3 (H)
1972—Steelers, 24-7 (P)
Steelers, 9-3 (H)
1973—Steelers, 36-7 (H)
Steelers, 33-7 (P)
1974—Steelers, 13-7 (H)
Oilers, 13-10 (P)
1975—Steelers, 24-17 (P)
Steelers, 32-9 (H)
1976—Steelers, 32-16 (P)
Steelers, 21-0 (H)
1977—Oilers, 27-10 (H)
Steelers, 27-10 (P)
1978—Oilers, 24-17 (P)
Steelers, 13-3 (H)
**Steelers, 34-5 (P)
1979—Steelers, 38-7 (P)
Oilers, 20-17 (H)
**Steelers, 27-13 (P)
1980—Steelers, 31-17 (P)
Oilers, 6-0 (H)
1981—Steelers, 26-13 (P)
Oilers, 21-20 (H)
1982—Steelers, 24-10 (H)
1983—Steelers, 40-28 (H)
Steelers, 17-10 (P)
1984—Steelers, 35-7 (P)
Oilers, 23-20 (H) OT
1985—Steelers, 20-0 (P)
Steelers, 30-7 (H)
1986—Steelers, 22-16 (H) OT
Steelers, 21-10 (P)

1987—Oilers, 23-3 (P)
Oilers, 24-16 (H)
1988—Oilers, 34-14 (P)
Steelers, 37-34 (H)
1989—Oilers, 27-0 (H)
Oilers, 23-16 (P)
***Steelers, 26-23 (H) OT
1990—Steelers, 20-9 (P)
Oilers, 34-14 (H)
1991—Steelers, 26-14 (P)
Oilers, 31-6 (H)
1992—Steelers, 29-24 (H)
Steelers, 21-20 (P)
1993—Oilers, 23-3 (H)
Oilers, 26-17 (P)
1994—Steelers, 30-14 (P)
Steelers, 12-9 (H) OT
1995—Steelers, 34-17 (H)
Steelers, 21-7 (P)
1996—Steelers, 30-16 (P)
Oilers, 23-13 (H)
(RS Pts.—Steelers 1,064, Oilers 844)
(PS Pts.—Steelers 87, Oilers 41)
*Franchise in Houston prior to 1997
**AFC Championship
***AFC First-Round Playoff
*PITTSBURGH vs. **WASHINGTON**
RS: Redskins lead series, 42-27-3
1933—Redskins, 21-6 (P)
Pirates, 16-14 (B)
1934—Redskins, 7-0 (P)
Redskins, 39-0 (B)
1935—Pirates, 6-0 (P)
Redskins, 13-3 (B)
1936—Pirates, 10-0 (P)
Redskins, 30-0 (B)
1937—Redskins, 34-20 (W)
Pirates, 21-13 (P)
1938—Redskins, 7-0 (P)
Redskins, 15-0 (W)
1939—Redskins, 44-14 (W)
Redskins, 21-14 (P)
1940—Redskins, 40-10 (P)
Redskins, 37-10 (W)
1941—Redskins, 24-20 (P)
Redskins, 23-3 (W)
1942—Redskins, 28-14 (W)
Redskins, 14-0 (P)
1945—Redskins, 14-0 (P)
Redskins, 24-0 (W)
1946—Tie, 14-14 (W)
Steelers, 14-7 (P)
1947—Redskins, 27-26 (W)
Steelers, 21-14 (P)
1948—Redskins, 17-14 (W)
Steelers, 10-7 (P)
1949—Redskins, 27-14 (W)
Redskins, 27-14 (P)
1950—Steelers, 26-7 (W)
Redskins, 24-7 (P)
1951—Redskins, 22-7 (P)
Steelers, 20-10 (W)
1952—Redskins, 28-24 (P)
Steelers, 24-23 (W)
1953—Redskins, 17-9 (P)
Steelers, 14-13 (W)
1954—Steelers, 37-7 (P)
Redskins, 17-14 (W)
1955—Redskins, 23-14 (P)
Redskins, 28-17 (W)
1956—Steelers, 30-13 (P)
Steelers, 23-0 (W)
1957—Steelers, 28-7 (P)
Redskins, 10-3 (W)
1958—Steelers, 24-16 (P)
Tie, 14-14 (W)
1959—Redskins, 23-17 (P)
Steelers, 27-6 (W)
1960—Tie, 27-27 (W)
Steelers, 22-10 (P)
1961—Steelers, 20-0 (P)
Steelers, 30-14 (W)
1962—Steelers, 23-21 (P)

325

Steelers, 27-24 (W)
1963—Steelers, 38-27 (P)
Steelers, 34-28 (W)
1964—Redskins, 30-0 (P)
Steelers, 14-7 (W)
1965—Redskins, 31-3 (P)
Redskins, 35-14 (W)
1966—Redskins, 33-27 (P)
Redskins, 24-10 (W)
1967—Redskins, 15-10 (P)
1968—Redskins, 16-13 (W)
1969—Redskins, 14-7 (P)
1973—Steelers, 21-16 (P)
1979—Steelers, 38-7 (P)
1985—Redskins, 30-23 (W)
1988—Redskins, 30-29 (W)
1991—Redskins, 41-14 (P)
(RS Pts.—Redskins 1,390, Steelers 1,117)
*Steelers known as Pirates prior to 1941
**Franchise in Boston prior to 1937

ST. LOUIS vs. ARIZONA
RS: Rams lead series, 23-20-2
PS: Rams lead series, 1-0;
See Arizona vs. St. Louis
ST. LOUIS vs. ATLANTA
RS: Rams lead series, 39-19-2;
See Atlanta vs. St. Louis
ST. LOUIS vs. BALTIMORE
RS: Ravens lead series, 1-0;
See Baltimore vs. St. Louis
ST. LOUIS vs. BUFFALO
RS: Bills lead series, 4-3;
See Buffalo vs. St. Louis
ST. LOUIS vs. CAROLINA
RS: Series tied, 2-2;
See Carolina vs. St. Louis
ST. LOUIS vs. CHICAGO
RS: Bears lead series, 46-30-3
PS: Series tied, 1-1;
See Chicago vs. St. Louis
ST. LOUIS vs. CINCINNATI
RS: Bengals lead series, 5-3;
See Cincinnati vs. St. Louis
ST. LOUIS vs. CLEVELAND
RS: Browns lead series, 8-7
PS: Browns lead series, 2-1;
See Cleveland vs. St. Louis
ST. LOUIS vs. DALLAS
RS: Rams lead series, 9-8
PS: Series tied, 4-4;
See Dallas vs. St. Louis
ST. LOUIS vs. DENVER
RS: Rams lead series, 4-3;
See Denver vs. St. Louis
ST. LOUIS vs. DETROIT
RS: Rams lead series, 39-35-1
PS: Lions lead series, 1-0;
See Detroit vs. St. Louis
ST. LOUIS vs. GREEN BAY
RS: Rams lead series, 43-38-2
PS: Packers lead series, 1-0;
See Green Bay vs. St. Louis
ST. LOUIS vs. INDIANAPOLIS
RS: Colts lead series, 21-16-2;
See Indianapolis vs. St. Louis
ST. LOUIS vs. JACKSONVILLE
RS: Rams lead series, 1-0;
See Jacksonville vs. St. Louis
ST. LOUIS vs. KANSAS CITY
RS: Rams lead series, 4-1;
See Kansas City vs. St. Louis
ST. LOUIS vs. MIAMI
RS: Dolphins lead series, 6-1;
See Miami vs. St. Louis
ST. LOUIS vs. MINNESOTA
RS: Vikings lead series, 15-11-2
PS: Vikings lead series, 5-1;
See Minnesota vs. St. Louis
ST. LOUIS vs. NEW ENGLAND
RS: Series tied, 3-3;
See New England vs. St. Louis
ST. LOUIS vs. NEW ORLEANS

RS: Rams lead series, 30-24;
See New Orleans vs. St. Louis
ST. LOUIS vs. N.Y. GIANTS
RS: Rams lead series, 21-9
PS: Series tied, 1-1;
See N.Y. Giants vs. St. Louis
ST. LOUIS vs. N.Y. JETS
RS: Rams lead series, 6-2;
See N.Y. Jets vs. St. Louis
ST. LOUIS vs. OAKLAND
RS: Raiders lead series, 6-2;
See Oakland vs. St. Louis
ST. LOUIS vs. PHILADELPHIA
RS: Rams lead series, 15-12-1
PS: Series tied, 1-1;
See Philadelphia vs. St. Louis
ST. LOUIS vs. PITTSBURGH
RS: Rams lead series, 14-5-2
PS: Steelers lead series, 1-0;
See Pittsburgh vs. St. Louis
*ST. LOUIS vs. SAN DIEGO
RS: Series tied, 3-3
1970—Rams, 37-10 (LA)
1975—Rams, 13-10 (SD) OT
1979—Chargers, 40-16 (LA)
1988—Chargers, 38-24 (LA)
1991—Rams, 30-24 (LA)
1994—Chargers, 31-17 (SD)
(RS Pts.—Chargers 153, Rams 137)
*Franchise in Los Angeles prior to 1995
*ST. LOUIS vs. SAN FRANCISCO
RS: Rams lead series, 48-44-2
PS: 49ers lead series, 1-0
1950—Rams, 35-14 (SF)
Rams, 28-21 (LA)
1951—49ers, 44-17 (SF)
Rams, 23-16 (LA)
1952—Rams, 35-9 (LA)
Rams, 34-21 (SF)
1953—49ers, 31-30 (SF)
49ers, 31-27 (LA)
1954—Tie, 24-24 (LA)
Rams, 42-34 (SF)
1955—Rams, 23-14 (SF)
Rams, 27-14 (LA)
1956—49ers, 33-30 (SF)
Rams, 30-6 (LA)
1957—49ers, 23-20 (SF)
Rams, 37-24 (LA)
1958—Rams, 33-3 (SF)
Rams, 56-7 (LA)
1959—49ers, 34-0 (SF)
49ers, 24-16 (LA)
1960—49ers, 13-9 (SF)
49ers, 23-7 (LA)
1961—49ers, 35-0 (SF)
Rams, 17-7 (LA)
1962—Rams, 28-14 (SF)
49ers, 24-17 (LA)
1963—Rams, 28-21 (LA)
Rams, 21-17 (SF)
1964—Rams, 42-14 (LA)
49ers, 28-7 (SF)
1965—49ers, 45-21 (LA)
49ers, 30-27 (SF)
1966—Rams, 34-3 (LA)
49ers, 21-13 (SF)
1967—49ers, 27-24 (LA)
Rams, 17-7 (SF)
1968—Rams, 24-10 (LA)
Tie, 20-20 (SF)
1969—Rams, 27-21 (SF)
Rams, 41-30 (LA)
1970—49ers, 20-6 (LA)
Rams, 30-13 (SF)
1971—Rams, 20-13 (SF)
Rams, 17-6 (LA)
1972—Rams, 31-7 (LA)
Rams, 26-16 (SF)
1973—Rams, 40-20 (SF)
Rams, 31-13 (LA)
1974—Rams, 37-14 (LA)
Rams, 15-13 (SF)

1975—Rams, 23-14 (SF)
49ers, 24-23 (LA)
1976—49ers, 16-0 (LA)
Rams, 23-3 (SF)
1977—Rams, 34-14 (LA)
Rams, 23-10 (SF)
1978—Rams, 27-10 (LA)
Rams, 31-28 (SF)
1979—Rams, 27-24 (LA)
Rams, 26-20 (SF)
1980—Rams, 48-26 (LA)
Rams, 31-17 (SF)
1981—49ers, 20-17 (SF)
49ers, 33-31 (LA)
1982—49ers, 30-24 (LA)
Rams, 21-20 (SF)
1983—Rams, 10-7 (SF)
49ers, 45-35 (LA)
1984—49ers, 33-0 (LA)
49ers, 19-16 (SF)
1985—49ers, 28-14 (LA)
Rams, 27-20 (SF)
1986—Rams, 16-13 (SF)
49ers, 24-14 (LA)
1987—49ers, 31-10 (LA)
49ers, 48-0 (SF)
1988—49ers, 24-21 (LA)
Rams, 38-16 (SF)
1989—Rams, 13-12 (SF)
49ers, 30-27 (LA)
**49ers, 30-3 (SF)
1990—Rams, 28-17 (SF)
49ers, 26-10 (LA)
1991—49ers, 27-10 (SF)
49ers, 33-10 (LA)
1992—49ers, 27-24 (SF)
49ers, 27-10 (LA)
1993—49ers, 40-17 (SF)
49ers, 35-10 (LA)
1994—49ers, 34-19 (LA)
49ers, 31-27 (SF)
1995—49ers, 44-10 (StL)
49ers, 41-13 (SF)
1996—49ers, 34-0 (SF)
49ers, 28-11 (StL)
(RS Pts.—Rams 2,093, 49ers 2,075)
(PS Pts.—49ers 30, Rams 3)
*Franchise in Los Angeles prior to 1995
**NFC Championship
*ST. LOUIS vs. SEATTLE
RS: Rams lead series, 4-1
1976—Rams, 45-6 (LA)
1979—Rams, 24-0 (S)
1985—Rams, 35-24 (S)
1988—Rams, 31-10 (LA)
1991—Seahawks, 23-9 (S)
(RS Pts.—Rams 144, Seahawks 63)
*Franchise in Los Angeles prior to 1995
*ST. LOUIS vs. TAMPA BAY
RS: Rams lead series, 8-3
PS: Rams lead series, 1-0
1977—Rams, 31-0 (LA)
1978—Rams, 26-23 (LA)
1979—Buccaneers, 21-6 (TB)
**Rams, 9-0 (TB)
1980—Buccaneers, 10-9 (TB)
1984—Rams, 34-33 (TB)
1985—Rams, 31-27 (TB)
1986—Rams, 26-20 (LA) OT
1987—Rams, 35-3 (LA)
1990—Rams, 35-14 (TB)
1992—Rams, 31-27 (TB)
1994—Buccaneers, 24-14 (TB)
(RS Pts.—Rams 278, Buccaneers 202)
(PS Pts.—Rams 9, Buccaneers 0)
*Franchise in Los Angeles prior to 1995
**NFC Championship
*ST. LOUIS vs. **TENNESSEE
RS: Rams lead series, 5-2
1973—Rams, 31-26 (LA)
1978—Rams, 10-6 (H)
1981—Oilers, 27-20 (LA)
1984—Rams, 27-16 (LA)

1987—Oilers, 20-16 (H)
1990—Rams, 17-13 (LA)
1993—Rams, 28-13 (H)
(RS Pts.—Rams 149, Oilers 121)
*Franchise in Los Angeles prior to 1995
**Franchise in Houston prior to 1997
*ST. LOUIS vs. WASHINGTON
RS: Redskins lead series, 17-5-1
PS: Series tied, 2-2
1937—Redskins, 16-7 (C)
1938—Redskins, 37-13 (W)
1941—Redskins, 17-13 (W)
1942—Redskins, 33-14 (W)
1944—Redskins, 14-10 (W)
1945—**Rams, 15-14 (C)
1948—Rams, 41-13 (W)
1949—Rams, 53-27 (LA)
1951—Redskins, 31-21 (W)
1962—Rams, 20-14 (W)
1963—Redskins, 37-14 (LA)
1967—Tie, 28-28 (W)
1969—Rams, 24-13 (W)
1971—Redskins, 38-24 (LA)
1974—Redskins, 23-17 (LA)
***Rams, 19-10 (LA)
1977—Redskins, 17-14 (W)
1981—Redskins, 30-7 (LA)
1983—Redskins, 42-20 (LA)
***Redskins, 51-7 (W)
1986—****Redskins, 19-7 (W)
1987—Rams, 30-26 (W)
1991—Redskins, 27-6 (LA)
1993—Rams, 10-6 (LA)
1994—Redskins, 24-21 (LA)
1995—Redskins, 35-23 (StL)
1996—Redskins, 17-10 (StL)
(RS Pts.—Redskins 571, Rams 434)
(PS Pts.—Redskins 94, Rams 48)
*Franchise in Los Angeles prior to 1995
and in Cleveland prior to 1946
**NFL Championship
***NFC Divisional Playoff
****NFC First-Round Playoff

SAN DIEGO vs. ARIZONA
RS: Chargers lead series, 6-1;
See Arizona vs. San Diego
SAN DIEGO vs. ATLANTA
RS: Falcons lead series, 4-1;
See Atlanta vs. San Diego
SAN DIEGO vs. BUFFALO
RS: Chargers lead series, 16-7-2
PS: Bills lead series, 2-1;
See Buffalo vs. San Diego
SAN DIEGO vs. CHICAGO
RS: Chargers lead series, 4-3;
See Chicago vs. San Diego
SAN DIEGO vs. CINCINNATI
RS: Chargers lead series, 14-8
PS: Bengals lead series, 1-0;
See Cincinnati vs. San Diego
SAN DIEGO vs. CLEVELAND
RS: Chargers lead series, 9-6-1;
See Cleveland vs. San Diego
SAN DIEGO vs. DALLAS
RS: Cowboys lead series, 5-1;
See Dallas vs. San Diego
SAN DIEGO vs. DENVER
RS: Broncos lead series, 38-35-1;
See Denver vs. San Diego
SAN DIEGO vs. DETROIT
RS: Series tied, 3-3;
See Detroit vs. San Diego
SAN DIEGO vs. GREEN BAY
RS: Packers lead series, 5-1;
See Green Bay vs. San Diego
SAN DIEGO vs. INDIANAPOLIS
RS: Chargers lead series, 11-5
PS: Colts lead series, 1-0;
See Indianapolis vs. San Diego
SAN DIEGO vs. KANSAS CITY
RS: Chiefs lead series, 37-35-1
PS: Chargers lead series, 1-0;

See Kansas City vs. San Diego
SAN DIEGO vs. MIAMI
RS: Chargers lead series, 10-6
PS: Series tied, 2-2;
See Miami vs. San Diego
SAN DIEGO vs. MINNESOTA
RS: Chargers lead series, 4-3;
See Minnesota vs. San Diego
SAN DIEGO vs. NEW ENGLAND
RS: Patriots lead series, 15-11-2
PS: Chargers lead series, 1-0;
See New England vs. San Diego
SAN DIEGO vs. NEW ORLEANS
RS: Chargers lead series, 5-1;
See New Orleans vs. San Diego
SAN DIEGO vs. N.Y. GIANTS
RS: Giants lead series, 4-3;
See N.Y. Giants vs. San Diego
SAN DIEGO vs. N.Y. JETS
RS: Chargers lead series, 17-9-1;
See N.Y. Jets vs. San Diego
SAN DIEGO vs. OAKLAND
RS: Raiders lead series, 44-28-2
PS: Raiders lead series, 1-0;
See Oakland vs. San Diego
SAN DIEGO vs. PHILADELPHIA
RS: Chargers lead series, 4-2;
See Philadelphia vs. San Diego
SAN DIEGO vs. PITTSBURGH
RS: Steelers lead series, 16-5
PS: Chargers lead series, 2-0;
See Pittsburgh vs. San Diego
SAN DIEGO vs. ST. LOUIS
RS: Series tied, 3-3
See St. Louis vs. San Diego
SAN DIEGO vs. SAN FRANCISCO
RS: 49ers lead series, 4-3
PS: 49ers lead series, 1-0;
1972—49ers, 34-3 (SF)
1976—Chargers, 13-7 (SD) OT
1979—Chargers, 31-9 (SD)
1982—Chargers, 41-37 (SF)
1988—49ers, 48-10 (SD)
1991—49ers, 34-14 (SF)
1994—49ers, 38-15 (SD)
    *49ers, 49-26 (Miami)
(RS Pts.—49ers 207, Chargers 127)
(PS Pts.—49ers 49, Chargers 26)
*Super Bowl XXIX
SAN DIEGO vs. SEATTLE
RS: Chargers lead series, 20-16
1977—Chargers, 30-28 (S)
1978—Chargers, 24-20 (S)
    Chargers, 37-10 (SD)
1979—Chargers, 33-16 (S)
    Chargers, 20-10 (SD)
1980—Chargers, 34-13 (S)
    Chargers, 21-14 (SD)
1981—Chargers, 24-10 (SD)
    Seahawks, 44-23 (S)
1983—Seahawks, 34-31 (S)
    Chargers, 28-21 (SD)
1984—Seahawks, 31-17 (S)
    Seahawks, 24-0 (SD)
1985—Seahawks, 49-35 (SD)
    Seahawks, 26-21 (S)
1986—Seahawks, 33-7 (S)
    Seahawks, 34-24 (SD)
1987—Seahawks, 34-3 (S)
1988—Chargers, 17-6 (SD)
    Seahawks, 17-14 (S)
1989—Seahawks, 17-16 (SD)
    Seahawks, 10-7 (S)
1990—Chargers, 31-14 (S)
    Seahawks, 13-10 (SD) OT
1991—Seahawks, 20-9 (S)
    Chargers, 17-14 (SD)
1992—Chargers, 17-6 (SD)
    Chargers, 31-14 (S)
1993—Chargers, 18-12 (SD)
    Seahawks, 31-14 (S)
1994—Chargers, 24-10 (S)
    Chargers, 35-15 (SD)

1995—Chargers, 14-10 (SD)
    Chargers, 35-25 (S)
1996—Chargers, 29-7 (SD)
    Seahawks, 32-13 (S)
(RS Pts.—Chargers 763, Seahawks 724)
SAN DIEGO vs. TAMPA BAY
RS: Chargers lead series, 6-1
1976—Chargers, 23-0 (TB)
1981—Chargers, 24-23 (TB)
1987—Chargers, 17-13 (TB)
1990—Chargers, 41-10 (SD)
1992—Chargers, 29-14 (SD)
1993—Chargers, 32-17 (TB)
1996—Buccaneers, 25-17 (SD)
(RS Pts.—Chargers 183, Buccaneers 102)
SAN DIEGO vs. **TENNESSEE
RS: Chargers lead series, 18-13-1
PS: Oilers lead series, 3-0
1960—Oilers, 38-28 (H)
    Chargers, 24-21 (LA)
    ***Oilers, 24-16 (H)
1961—Chargers, 34-24 (SD)
    Oilers, 33-13 (H)
    ***Oilers, 10-3 (SD)
1962—Oilers, 42-17 (SD)
    Oilers, 33-27 (H)
1963—Chargers, 27-0 (SD)
    Chargers, 20-14 (H)
1964—Chargers, 27-21 (SD)
    Chargers, 20-17 (H)
1965—Chargers, 31-14 (SD)
    Chargers, 37-26 (H)
1966—Chargers, 28-22 (H)
1967—Chargers, 13-3 (SD)
    Oilers, 24-17 (H)
1968—Chargers, 30-14 (SD)
1969—Chargers, 21-17 (H)
1970—Tie, 31-31 (SD)
1971—Oilers, 49-33 (H)
1972—Chargers, 34-20 (SD)
1974—Oilers, 21-14 (H)
1975—Oilers, 33-17 (H)
1976—Chargers, 30-27 (SD)
1978—Chargers, 45-24 (H)
1979—****Oilers, 17-14 (SD)
1984—Chargers, 31-14 (SD)
1985—Oilers, 37-35 (H)
1986—Chargers, 27-0 (SD)
1987—Oilers, 33-18 (H)
1989—Oilers, 34-27 (SD)
1990—Oilers, 17-7 (SD)
1992—Oilers, 27-0 (H)
1993—Chargers, 18-17 (SD)
(RS Pts.—Chargers 781, Oilers 747)
(PS Pts.—Oilers 51, Chargers 33)
*Franchise in Los Angeles prior to 1961
**Franchise in Houston prior to 1997
***AFL Championship
****AFC Divisional Playoff
SAN DIEGO vs. WASHINGTON
RS: Redskins lead series, 5-0
1973—Redskins, 38-0 (W)
1980—Redskins, 40-17 (W)
1983—Redskins, 27-24 (SD)
1986—Redskins, 30-27 (SD)
1989—Redskins, 26-21 (W)
(RS Pts.—Redskins 161, Chargers 89)

SAN FRANCISCO vs. ARIZONA
RS: 49ers lead series, 10-9;
See Arizona vs. San Francisco
SAN FRANCISCO vs. ATLANTA
RS: 49ers lead series, 37-22-1;
See Atlanta vs. San Francisco
SAN FRANCISCO vs. BALTIMORE
RS: 49ers lead series, 1-0;
See Baltimore vs. San Francisco
SAN FRANCISCO vs. BUFFALO
RS: Series tied, 3-3;
See Buffalo vs. San Francisco
SAN FRANCISCO vs. CAROLINA
RS: Panthers lead series, 3-1;
See Carolina vs. San Francisco

SAN FRANCISCO vs. CHICAGO
RS: Series tied, 25-25-1
PS: 49ers lead series, 3-0;
See Chicago vs. San Francisco
SAN FRANCISCO vs. CINCINNATI
RS: 49ers lead series, 7-1
PS: 49ers lead series, 2-0;
See Cincinnati vs. San Francisco
SAN FRANCISCO vs. CLEVELAND
RS: Browns lead series, 9-6;
See Cleveland vs. San Francisco
SAN FRANCISCO vs. DALLAS
RS: 49ers lead series, 11-7-1
PS: Cowboys lead series, 5-2;
See Dallas vs. San Francisco
SAN FRANCISCO vs. DENVER
RS: Broncos lead series, 4-3
PS: 49ers lead series, 1-0;
See Denver vs. San Francisco
SAN FRANCISCO vs. DETROIT
RS: 49ers lead series, 28-26-1
PS: Series tied, 1-1;
See Detroit vs. San Francisco
SAN FRANCISCO vs. GREEN BAY
RS: 49ers lead series, 25-22-1
PS: Packers lead series, 2-0;
See Green Bay vs. San Francisco
SAN FRANCISCO vs. INDIANAPOLIS
RS: Colts lead series, 22-16;
See Indianapolis vs. San Francisco
SAN FRANCISCO vs. KANSAS CITY
RS: 49ers lead series, 4-2;
See Kansas City vs. San Francisco
SAN FRANCISCO vs. MIAMI
RS: Dolphins lead series, 4-3
PS: 49ers lead series, 1-0;
See Miami vs. San Francisco
SAN FRANCISCO vs. MINNESOTA
RS: Series tied, 16-16-1
PS: 49ers lead series, 3-1;
See Minnesota vs. San Francisco
SAN FRANCISCO vs. NEW ENGLAND
RS: 49ers lead series, 7-1;
See New England vs. San Francisco
SAN FRANCISCO vs. NEW ORLEANS
RS: 49ers lead series, 38-15-2;
See New Orleans vs. San Francisco
SAN FRANCISCO vs. N.Y. GIANTS
RS: Series tied, 11-11
PS: Series tied, 3-3;
See N.Y. Giants vs. San Francisco
SAN FRANCISCO vs. N.Y. JETS
RS: 49ers lead series, 6-1;
See N.Y. Jets vs. San Francisco
SAN FRANCISCO vs. OAKLAND
RS: Raiders lead series, 5-3;
See Oakland vs. San Francisco
SAN FRANCISCO vs. PHILADELPHIA
RS: 49ers lead series, 13-6-1
PS: 49ers lead series, 1-0;
See Philadelphia vs. San Francisco
SAN FRANCISCO vs. PITTSBURGH
RS: 49ers lead series, 9-7;
See Pittsburgh vs. San Francisco
SAN FRANCISCO vs. ST. LOUIS
RS: Rams lead series, 48-44-2
PS: 49ers lead series, 1-0;
See St. Louis vs. San Francisco
SAN FRANCISCO vs. SAN DIEGO
RS: 49ers lead series, 4-3
PS: 49ers lead series, 1-0;
See San Diego vs. San Francisco
SAN FRANCISCO vs. SEATTLE
RS: 49ers lead series, 4-1
1976—49ers, 37-21 (S)
1979—Seahawks, 35-24 (SF)
1985—49ers, 19-6 (SF)
1988—49ers, 38-7 (S)
1991—49ers, 24-22 (S)
(RS Pts.—49ers 142, Seahawks 91)
SAN FRANCISCO vs. TAMPA BAY
RS: 49ers lead series, 12-1
1977—49ers, 20-10 (SF)

1978—49ers, 6-3 (SF)
1979—49ers, 23-7 (SF)
1980—Buccaneers, 24-23 (SF)
1983—49ers, 35-21 (SF)
1984—49ers, 24-17 (SF)
1986—49ers, 31-7 (TB)
1987—49ers, 24-10 (TB)
1989—49ers, 20-16 (TB)
1990—49ers, 31-7 (SF)
1992—49ers, 21-14 (TB)
1993—49ers, 45-21 (TB)
1994—49ers, 41-16 (SF)
(RS. Pts.—49ers 344, Buccaneers 173)
SAN FRANCISCO vs. **TENNESSEE
RS: 49ers lead series, 6-3
1970—49ers, 30-20 (H)
1975—Oilers, 27-13 (SF)
1978—49ers, 20-19 (H)
1981—49ers, 28-6 (SF)
1984—49ers, 34-21 (SF)
1987—49ers, 27-20 (SF)
1990—49ers, 24-21 (SF)
1993—Oilers, 10-7 (SF)
1996—49ers, 10-9 (H)
(RS Pts.—49ers 192, Oilers 154)
*Franchise in Houston prior to 1997
SAN FRANCISCO vs. WASHINGTON
RS: 49ers lead series, 11-6-1
PS: 49ers lead series, 3-1
1952—49ers, 23-17 (W)
1954—49ers, 41-7 (SF)
1955—Redskins, 7-0 (W)
1961—49ers, 35-3 (SF)
1967—Redskins, 31-28 (W)
1969—Tie, 17-17 (SF)
1970—49ers, 26-17 (SF)
1971—*49ers, 24-20 (SF)
1973—Redskins, 33-9 (W)
1976—Redskins, 24-21 (SF)
1978—Redskins, 38-20 (W)
1981—49ers, 30-17 (W)
1983—**Redskins, 24-21 (W)
1984—49ers, 37-31 (SF)
1985—49ers, 35-8 (SF)
1986—Redskins, 14-6 (W)
1988—49ers, 37-21 (SF)
1990—49ers, 26-13 (SF)
    *49ers, 28-10 (SF)
1992—*49ers, 20-13 (SF)
1994—49ers, 37-22 (SF)
1996—49ers, 19-16 (W) OT
(RS Pts.—49ers 447, Redskins 336)
(PS Pts.—49ers 93, Redskins 67)
*NFC Divisional Playoff
**NFC Championship

SEATTLE vs. ARIZONA
RS: Cardinals lead series, 5-0;
See Arizona vs. Seattle
SEATTLE vs. ATLANTA
RS: Seahawks lead series, 4-1;
See Atlanta vs. Seattle
SEATTLE vs. BUFFALO
RS: Seahawks lead series, 4-2;
See Buffalo vs. Seattle
SEATTLE vs. CHICAGO
RS: Seahawks lead series, 4-2;
See Chicago vs. Seattle
SEATTLE vs. CINCINNATI
RS: Series tied, 7-7
PS: Bengals lead series, 1-0;
See Cincinnati vs. Seattle
SEATTLE vs. CLEVELAND
RS: Seahawks lead series, 9-4;
See Cleveland vs. Seattle
SEATTLE vs. DALLAS
RS: Cowboys lead series, 4-1;
See Dallas vs. Seattle
SEATTLE vs. DENVER
RS: Broncos lead series, 24-15
PS: Seahawks lead series, 1-0;
See Denver vs. Seattle
SEATTLE vs. DETROIT

RS: Seahawks lead series, 4-3;
See Detroit vs. Seattle

SEATTLE vs. GREEN BAY
RS: Packers lead series, 4-3;
See Green Bay vs. Seattle

SEATTLE vs. INDIANAPOLIS
RS: Colts lead series, 4-1;
See Indianapolis vs. Seattle

SEATTLE vs. JACKSONVILLE
RS: Series tied, 1-1;
See Jacksonville vs. Seattle

SEATTLE vs. KANSAS CITY
RS: Chiefs lead series, 24-13;
See Kansas City vs. Seattle

SEATTLE vs. MIAMI
RS: Dolphins lead series, 4-2
PS: Series tied, 1-1;
See Miami vs. Seattle

SEATTLE vs. MINNESOTA
RS: Seahawks lead series, 4-2;
See Minnesota vs. Seattle

SEATTLE vs. NEW ENGLAND
RS: Seahawks lead series, 7-6;
See New England vs. Seattle

SEATTLE vs. NEW ORLEANS
RS: Saints lead series, 3-2;
See New Orleans vs. Seattle

SEATTLE vs. N.Y. GIANTS
RS: Giants lead series, 5-3;
See N.Y. Giants vs. Seattle

SEATTLE vs. N.Y. JETS
RS: Seahawks lead series, 8-4;
See N.Y. Jets vs. Seattle

SEATTLE vs. OAKLAND
RS: Raiders lead series, 21-17
PS: Series tied, 1-1;
See Oakland vs. Seattle

SEATTLE vs. PHILADELPHIA
RS: Eagles lead series, 4-2;
See Philadelphia vs. Seattle

SEATTLE vs. PITTSBURGH
RS: Seahawks lead series, 6-5;
See Pittsburgh vs. Seattle

SEATTLE vs. ST. LOUIS
RS: Rams lead series, 4-1;
See St. Louis vs. Seattle

SEATTLE vs. SAN DIEGO
RS: Chargers lead series, 20-16;
See San Diego vs. Seattle

SEATTLE vs. SAN FRANCISCO
RS: 49ers lead series, 4-1;
See San Francisco vs. Seattle

SEATTLE vs. TAMPA BAY
RS: Seahawks lead series, 4-0
1976—Seahawks, 13-10 (TB)
1977—Seahawks, 30-23 (S)
1994—Seahawks, 22-21 (S)
1996—Seahawks, 17-13 (TB)
(RS Pts.—Seahawks 82, Buccaneers 67)

SEATTLE vs. *TENNESSEE
RS: Seahawks lead series, 6-4
PS: Oilers lead series, 1-0
1977—Oilers, 22-10 (S)
1979—Seahawks, 34-14 (S)
1980—Seahawks, 26-7 (H)
1981—Oilers, 35-17 (H)
1982—Oilers, 23-21 (H)
1987—**Oilers, 23-20 (H) OT
1988—Seahawks, 27-24 (S)
1990—Seahawks, 13-10 (S) OT
1993—Oilers, 24-14 (H)
1994—Seahawks, 16-14 (H)
1996—Seahawks, 23-16 (S)
(RS Pts.—Seahawks 201, Oilers 189)
(PS Pts.—Oilers 23, Seahawks 20)
*Franchise in Houston prior to 1997
**AFC First-Round Playoff

SEATTLE vs. WASHINGTON
RS: Redskins lead series, 5-3
1976—Redskins, 31-7 (W)
1980—Seahawks, 14-0 (W)
1983—Redskins, 27-17 (S)
1986—Redskins, 19-14 (W)

1989—Redskins, 29-0 (S)
1992—Redskins, 16-3 (S)
1994—Seahawks, 28-7 (W)
1995—Seahawks, 27-20 (W)
(RS Pts.—Redskins 149, Seahawks 110)

TAMPA BAY vs. ARIZONA
RS: Cardinals lead series, 7-6;
See Arizona vs. Tampa Bay

TAMPA BAY vs. ATLANTA
RS: Falcons lead series, 8-6;
See Atlanta vs. Tampa Bay

TAMPA BAY vs. BUFFALO
RS: Buccaneers lead series, 4-2;
See Buffalo vs. Tampa Bay

TAMPA BAY vs. CAROLINA
RS: Series tied, 1-1;
See Carolina vs. Tampa Bay

TAMPA BAY vs. CHICAGO
RS: Bears lead series, 29-9;
See Chicago vs. Tampa Bay

TAMPA BAY vs. CINCINNATI
RS: Bengals lead series, 3-2;
See Cincinnati vs. Tampa Bay

TAMPA BAY vs. CLEVELAND
RS: Browns lead series, 5-0;
See Cleveland vs. Tampa Bay

TAMPA BAY vs. DALLAS
RS: Cowboys lead series, 6-0
PS: Cowboys lead series, 2-0;
See Dallas vs. Tampa Bay

TAMPA BAY vs. DENVER
RS: Broncos lead series, 3-1;
See Denver vs. Tampa Bay

TAMPA BAY vs. DETROIT
RS: Lions lead series, 21-17;
See Detroit vs. Tampa Bay

TAMPA BAY vs. GREEN BAY
RS: Packers lead series, 22-13-1;
See Green Bay vs. Tampa Bay

TAMPA BAY vs. INDIANAPOLIS
RS: Colts lead series, 5-3;
See Indianapolis vs. Tampa Bay

TAMPA BAY vs. JACKSONVILLE
RS: Buccaneers lead series, 1-0;
See Jacksonville vs. Tampa Bay

TAMPA BAY vs. KANSAS CITY
RS: Chiefs lead series, 5-2;
See Kansas City vs. Tampa Bay

TAMPA BAY vs. MIAMI
RS: Dolphins lead series, 4-1;
See Miami vs. Tampa Bay

TAMPA BAY vs. MINNESOTA
RS: Vikings lead series, 26-12;
See Minnesota vs. Tampa Bay

TAMPA BAY vs. NEW ENGLAND
RS: Patriots lead series, 3-0;
See New England vs. Tampa Bay

TAMPA BAY vs. NEW ORLEANS
RS: Saints lead series, 12-5;
See New Orleans vs. Tampa Bay

TAMPA BAY vs. N.Y. GIANTS
RS: Giants lead series, 8-3;
See N.Y. Giants vs. Tampa Bay

TAMPA BAY vs. N.Y. JETS
RS: Jets lead series, 5-1;
See N.Y. Jets vs. Tampa Bay

TAMPA BAY vs. OAKLAND
RS: Raiders lead series, 3-1;
See Oakland vs. Tampa Bay

TAMPA BAY vs. PHILADELPHIA
RS: Eagles lead series, 3-2
PS: Buccaneers lead series, 1-0;
See Philadelphia vs. Tampa Bay

TAMPA BAY vs. PITTSBURGH
RS: Steelers lead series, 4-0;
See Pittsburgh vs. Tampa Bay

TAMPA BAY vs. ST. LOUIS
RS: Rams lead series, 8-3
PS: Rams lead series, 1-0;
See St. Louis vs. Tampa Bay

TAMPA BAY vs. SAN DIEGO
RS: Chargers lead series, 6-1;

See San Diego vs. Tampa Bay

TAMPA BAY vs. SAN FRANCISCO
RS: 49ers lead series, 12-1;
See San Francisco vs. Tampa Bay

TAMPA BAY vs. SEATTLE
RS: Seahawks lead series, 4-0;
See Seattle vs. Tampa Bay

TAMPA BAY vs. *TENNESSEE
RS: Oilers lead series, 4-1
1976—Oilers, 20-0 (H)
1980—Oilers, 20-14 (H)
1983—Buccaneers, 33-24 (TB)
1989—Oilers, 20-17 (H)
1995—Oilers, 19-7 (H)
(RS Pts.—Oilers 103, Buccaneers 71)
*Franchise in Houston prior to 1997

TAMPA BAY vs. WASHINGTON
RS: Series tied, 4-4
1977—Redskins, 10-0 (TB)
1982—Redskins, 21-13 (TB)
1989—Redskins, 32-28 (W)
1993—Redskins, 23-17 (TB)
1994—Buccaneers, 26-21 (TB)
        Buccaneers, 17-14 (W)
1995—Buccaneers, 14-6 (TB)
1996—Buccaneers, 24-10 (TB)
(RS Pts.—Buccaneers 139, Redskins 137)

TENNESSEE VS. ARIZONA
RS: Cardinals lead series, 4-2;
See Arizona vs. Tennessee

TENNESSEE vs. ATLANTA
RS: Falcons lead series, 5-4;
See Atlanta vs. Tennessee

TENNESSEE vs. BALTIMORE
RS: Oilers lead series, 2-0;
See Baltimore vs. Tennessee

TENNESSEE vs. BUFFALO
RS: Oilers lead series, 21-13
PS: Bills lead series, 2-0;
See Buffalo vs. Tennessee

TENNESSEE vs. CAROLINA
RS: Panthers lead series, 1-0;
See Carolina vs. Tennessee

TENNESSEE vs. CHICAGO
RS: Oilers lead series, 4-3;
See Chicago vs. Tennessee

TENNESSEE vs. CINCINNATI
RS: Oilers lead series, 28-27-1
PS: Bengals lead series, 1-0;
See Cincinnati vs. Tennessee

TENNESSEE vs. CLEVELAND
RS: Browns lead series, 30-21
PS: Oilers lead series, 1-0;
See Cleveland vs. Tennessee

TENNESSEE vs. DALLAS
RS: Cowboys lead series, 5-3;
See Dallas vs. Tennessee

TENNESSEE vs. DENVER
RS: Oilers lead series, 20-11-1
PS: Broncos lead series, 2-1;
See Denver vs. Tennessee

TENNESSEE vs. DETROIT
RS: Oilers lead series, 4-3;
See Detroit vs. Tennessee

TENNESSEE vs. GREEN BAY
RS: Series tied, 3-3;
See Green Bay vs. Tennessee

TENNESSEE vs. INDIANAPOLIS
RS: Series tied, 7-7;
See Indianapolis vs. Tennessee

TENNESSEE vs. JACKSONVILLE
RS: Series tied, 2-2;
See Jacksonville vs. Tennessee

TENNESSEE vs. KANSAS CITY
RS: Chiefs lead series, 24-17
PS: Chiefs lead series, 2-0;
See Kansas City vs. Tennessee

TENNESSEE vs. MIAMI
RS: Dolphins lead series, 12-11
PS: Oilers lead series, 1-0;
See Miami vs. Tennessee

TENNESSEE vs. MINNESOTA

RS: Vikings lead series, 4-3;
See Minnesota vs. Tennessee

TENNESSEE vs. NEW ENGLAND
RS: Patriots lead series, 17-14-1
PS: Oilers lead series, 1-0;
See New England vs. Tennessee

TENNESSEE vs. NEW ORLEANS
RS: Series tied, 4-4-1;
See New Orleans vs. Tennessee

TENNESSEE vs. N.Y. GIANTS
RS: Giants lead series, 5-0;
See N.Y. Giants vs. Tennessee

TENNESSEE vs. N.Y. JETS
RS: Oilers lead series, 20-12-1
PS: Oilers lead series, 1-0;
See N.Y. Jets vs. Tennessee

TENNESSEE vs. OAKLAND
RS: Raiders lead series, 20-13
PS: Raiders lead series, 3-0;
See Oakland vs. Tennessee

TENNESSEE vs. PHILADELPHIA
RS: Eagles lead series, 6-0;
See Philadelphia vs. Tennessee

TENNESSEE vs. PITTSBURGH
RS: Steelers lead series, 34-19
PS: Steelers lead series, 3-0;
See Pittsburgh vs. Tennessee

TENNESSEE vs. ST. LOUIS
RS: Rams lead series, 5-2;
See St. Louis vs. Tennessee

TENNESSEE vs. SAN DIEGO
RS: Chargers lead series, 18-13-1
PS: Oilers lead series, 3-0;
See San Diego vs. Tennessee

TENNESSEE vs. SAN FRANCISCO
RS: 49ers lead series, 6-3;
See San Francisco vs. Tennessee

TENNESSEE vs. SEATTLE
RS: Seahawks lead series, 6-4
PS: Oilers lead series, 1-0;
See Seattle vs. Tennessee

TENNESSEE vs. TAMPA BAY
RS: Oilers lead series, 4-1;
See Tampa Bay vs. Tennessee

*TENNESSEE vs. WASHINGTON
RS: Series tied, 3-3
1971—Redskins, 22-13 (W)
1975—Oilers, 13-10 (H)
1979—Oilers, 29-27 (W)
1985—Redskins, 16-13 (W)
1988—Oilers, 41-17 (H)
1991—Redskins, 16-13 (W) OT
(RS Pts.—Oilers 122, Redskins 108)
*Franchise in Houston prior to 1997

WASHINGTON vs. ARIZONA
RS: Redskins lead series, 62-41-2;
See Arizona vs. Washington

WASHINGTON vs. ATLANTA
RS: Redskins lead series, 13-4-1
PS: Redskins lead series, 1-0;
See Atlanta vs. Washington

WASHINGTON vs. BUFFALO
RS: Series tied, 4-4
PS: Redskins lead series, 1-0;
See Buffalo vs. Washington

WASHINGTON vs. CAROLINA
RS: Panthers lead series, 1-0;
See Carolina vs. Washington

WASHINGTON vs. CHICAGO
RS: Bears lead series, 18-13-1
PS: Redskins lead series, 4-3;
See Chicago vs. Washington

WASHINGTON vs. CINCINNATI
RS: Redskins lead series, 4-2;
See Cincinnati vs. Washington

WASHINGTON vs. CLEVELAND
RS: Browns lead series, 32-9-1;
See Cleveland vs. Washington

WASHINGTON vs. DALLAS
RS: Cowboys lead series, 40-30-2;
PS: Redskins lead series, 2-0;
See Dallas vs. Washington

WASHINGTON vs. DENVER
RS: Broncos lead series, 4-3
PS: Redskins lead series, 1-0;
See Denver vs. Washington

WASHINGTON vs. DETROIT
RS: Redskins lead series, 23-8
PS: Redskins lead series, 2-0;
See Detroit vs. Washington

WASHINGTON vs. GREEN BAY
RS: Packers lead series, 13-12-1
PS: Series tied, 1-1;
See Green Bay vs. Washington

WASHINGTON vs. INDIANAPOLIS
RS: Colts lead series, 16-9;
See Indianapolis vs. Washington

WASHINGTON vs. KANSAS CITY
RS: Chiefs lead series, 4-1;
See Kansas City vs. Washington

WASHINGTON vs. MIAMI
RS: Dolphins lead series, 5-2
PS: Series tied, 1-1;
See Miami vs. Washington

WASHINGTON vs. MINNESOTA
RS: Redskins lead series, 6-4
PS: Redskins lead series, 3-2;
See Minnesota vs. Washington

WASHINGTON vs. NEW ENGLAND
RS: Redskins lead series, 5-1;
See New England vs. Washington

WASHINGTON vs. NEW ORLEANS
RS: Redskins lead series, 12-5;
See New Orleans vs. Washington

WASHINGTON vs. N.Y. GIANTS
RS: Giants lead series, 73-52-3
PS: Series tied, 1-1;
See N.Y. Giants vs. Washington

WASHINGTON vs. N.Y. JETS
RS: Redskins lead series, 5-1;
See N.Y. Jets vs. Washington

WASHINGTON vs. OAKLAND
RS: Raiders lead series, 6-2
PS: Raiders lead series, 1-0;
See Oakland vs. Washington

WASHINGTON vs. PHILADELPHIA
RS: Redskins lead series, 67-51-5
PS: Redskins lead series, 1-0;
See Philadelphia vs. Washington

WASHINGTON vs. PITTSBURGH
RS: Redskins lead series, 42-27-3;
See Pittsburgh vs. Washington

WASHINGTON vs. ST. LOUIS
RS: Redskins lead series, 17-5-1
PS: Series tied, 2-2;
See St. Louis vs. Washington

WASHINGTON vs. SAN DIEGO
RS: Redskins lead series, 5-0;
See San Diego vs. Washington

WASHINGTON vs. SAN FRANCISCO
RS: 49ers lead series, 11-6-1
PS: 49ers lead series, 3-1;
See San Francisco vs. Washington

WASHINGTON vs. SEATTLE
RS: Redskins lead series, 5-3;
See Seattle vs. Washington

WASHINGTON vs. TAMPA BAY
RS: Series tied, 4-4;
See Tampa Bay vs. Washington

WASHINGTON vs. TENNESSEE
RS: Series tied, 3-3;
See Tennessee vs. Washington

RESULTS

Super Bowl	Date	Winner (Share)	Loser (Share)	Score	Site	Attendance
XXXI	1-26-97	Green Bay ($48,000)	New England ($29,000)	35-21	New Orleans	72,301
XXX	1-28-96	Dallas ($42,000)	Pittsburgh ($27,000)	27-17	Tempe	76,347
XXIX	1-29-95	San Francisco ($42,000)	San Diego ($26,000)	49-26	Miami	74,107
XXVIII	1-30-94	Dallas ($38,000)	Buffalo ($23,500)	30-13	Atlanta	72,817
XXVII	1-31-93	Dallas ($36,000)	Buffalo ($18,000)	52-17	Pasadena	98,374
XXVI	1-26-92	Washington ($36,000)	Buffalo ($18,000)	37-24	Minneapolis	63,130
XXV	1-27-91	N.Y. Giants ($36,000)	Buffalo ($18,000)	20-19	Tampa	73,813
XXIV	1-28-90	San Francisco ($36,000)	Denver ($18,000)	55-10	New Orleans	72,919
XXIII	1-22-89	San Francisco ($36,000)	Cincinnati ($18,000)	20-16	Miami	75,129
XXII	1-31-88	Washington ($36,000)	Denver ($18,000)	42-10	San Diego	73,302
XXI	1-25-87	N.Y. Giants ($36,000)	Denver ($18,000)	39-20	Pasadena	101,063
XX	1-26-86	Chicago ($36,000)	New England ($18,000)	46-10	New Orleans	73,818
XIX	1-20-85	San Francisco ($36,000)	Miami ($18,000)	38-16	Stanford	84,059
XVIII	1-22-84	L.A. Raiders ($36,000)	Washington ($18,000)	38-9	Tampa	72,920
XVII	1-30-83	Washington ($36,000)	Miami ($18,000)	27-17	Pasadena	103,667
XVI	1-24-82	San Francisco ($18,000)	Cincinnati ($9,000)	26-21	Pontiac	81,270
XV	1-25-81	Oakland ($18,000)	Philadelphia ($9,000)	27-10	New Orleans	76,135
XIV	1-20-80	Pittsburgh ($18,000)	Los Angeles ($9,000)	31-19	Pasadena	103,985
XIII	1-21-79	Pittsburgh ($18,000)	Dallas ($9,000)	35-31	Miami	79,484
XII	1-15-78	Dallas ($18,000)	Denver ($9,000)	27-10	New Orleans	75,583
XI	1-9-77	Oakland ($15,000)	Minnesota ($7,500)	32-14	Pasadena	103,438
X	1-18-76	Pittsburgh ($15,000)	Dallas ($7,500)	21-17	Miami	80,187
IX	1-12-75	Pittsburgh ($15,000)	Minnesota ($7,500)	16-6	New Orleans	80,997
VIII	1-13-74	Miami ($15,000)	Minnesota ($7,500)	24-7	Houston	71,882
VII	1-14-73	Miami ($15,000)	Washington ($7,500)	14-7	Los Angeles	90,182
VI	1-16-72	Dallas ($15,000)	Miami ($7,500)	24-3	New Orleans	81,023
V	1-17-71	Baltimore ($15,000)	Dallas ($7,500)	16-13	Miami	79,204
IV	1-11-70	Kansas City ($15,000)	Minnesota ($7,500)	23-7	New Orleans	80,562
III	1-12-69	N.Y. Jets ($15,000)	Baltimore ($7,500)	16-7	Miami	75,389
II	1-14-68	Green Bay ($15,000)	Oakland ($7,500)	33-14	Miami	75,546
I	1-15-67	Green Bay ($15,000)	Kansas City ($7,500)	35-10	Los Angeles	61,946

SUPER BOWL COMPOSITE STANDINGS

	W	L	Pct.	Pts.	OP
San Francisco 49ers	5	0	1.000	188	89
Green Bay Packers	3	0	1.000	103	45
New York Giants	2	0	1.000	59	39
Chicago Bears	1	0	1.000	46	10
New York Jets	1	0	1.000	16	7
Pittsburgh Steelers	4	1	.800	120	100
Oakland/L.A. Raiders	3	1	.750	111	66
Dallas Cowboys	5	3	.625	221	132
Washington Redskins	3	2	.600	122	103
Baltimore Colts	1	1	.500	23	29
Kansas City Chiefs	1	1	.500	33	42
Miami Dolphins	2	3	.400	74	103
Los Angeles Rams	0	1	.000	19	31
Philadelphia Eagles	0	1	.000	10	27
San Diego Chargers	0	1	.000	26	49
Cincinnati Bengals	0	2	.000	37	46
New England Patriots	0	2	.000	31	81
Buffalo Bills	0	4	.000	73	139
Denver Broncos	0	4	.000	50	163
Minnesota Vikings	0	4	.000	34	95

SUPER BOWL MOST VALUABLE PLAYERS*

Super Bowl I — QB Bart Starr, Green Bay
Super Bowl II — QB Bart Starr, Green Bay
Super Bowl III — QB Joe Namath, N.Y. Jets
Super Bowl IV — QB Len Dawson, Kansas City
Super Bowl V — LB Chuck Howley, Dallas
Super Bowl VI — QB Roger Staubach, Dallas
Super Bowl VII — S Jake Scott, Miami
Super Bowl VIII — RB Larry Csonka, Miami
Super Bowl IX — RB Franco Harris, Pittsburgh
Super Bowl X — WR Lynn Swann, Pittsburgh
Super Bowl XI — WR Fred Biletnikoff, Oakland
Super Bowl XII — DT Randy White and
  DE Harvey Martin, Dallas
Super Bowl XIII — QB Terry Bradshaw, Pittsburgh
Super Bowl XIV — QB Terry Bradshaw, Pittsburgh
Super Bowl XV — QB Jim Plunkett, Oakland
Super Bowl XVI — QB Joe Montana, San Francisco
Super Bowl XVII — RB John Riggins, Washington
Super Bowl XVIII — RB Marcus Allen, L.A. Raiders
Super Bowl XIX — QB Joe Montana, San Francisco
Super Bowl XX — DE Richard Dent, Chicago
Super Bowl XXI — QB Phil Simms, N.Y. Giants
Super Bowl XXII — QB Doug Williams, Washington
Super Bowl XXIII — WR Jerry Rice, San Francisco
Super Bowl XXIV — QB Joe Montana, San Francisco
Super Bowl XXV — RB Ottis Anderson, N.Y. Giants
Super Bowl XXVI — QB Mark Rypien, Washington
Super Bowl XXVII — QB Troy Aikman, Dallas
Super Bowl XXVIII — RB Emmitt Smith, Dallas
Super Bowl XXIX — QB Steve Young, San Francisco
Super Bowl XXX — CB Larry Brown, Dallas
Super Bowl XXXI — KR-PR Desmond Howard, Green Bay
* Award named Pete Rozelle Trophy since Super Bowl XXV.

SUPER BOWL XXXI

Louisiana Superdome, New Orleans, Louisiana
January 26, 1997, Attendance: 72,301

GREEN BAY 35, NEW ENGLAND 21— Desmond Howard returned a kickoff 99 yards for a touchdown and Brett Favre threw 2 touchdown passes and ran for a score as the Packers won their first Super Bowl in twenty-nine years. Howard, en route to garnering the MVP trophy, established a Super Bowl record with 244 total return yards. It was Favre's arm that struck first, as he hit Andre Rison for a 54-yard touchdown pass on the Packers' second play from scrimmage to take a 7-0 lead. Two plays later Doug Evans made a diving interception of Drew Bledsoe's pass at the 28-yard line, setting up Chris Jacke's field goal and giving the Packers a 10-0 lead just 6:18 into the Super Bowl. The Patriots answered with touchdowns on their next two possessions. Craig Newsome's pass interference penalty set up the first touchdown and a 44-yard completion from Bledsoe to Terry Glenn preceeding Ben Coates's touchdown gave New England its first and only lead. The 24 combined first quarter points were the most in Super Bowl history. Green Bay struck again 56 seconds into the second quarter as Favre hit Antonio Freeman with a Super Bowl-record 81-yard touchdown bomb. Jacke booted his second field goal on Green Bay's next possession. After a Mike Prior interception, Favre orchestrated a 74-yard, nearly 6-minute drive which concluded with a diving Favre touching the ball against the pylon to give Green Bay a 27-14 halftime lead. Curtis Martin brought the Patriots to within a score by running in from 18 yards out with 3:27 left in the third quarter. But Howard broke the Patriots' spirit by returning the ensuing kickoff a Super Bowl-record 99 yards. Favre found Mark Chmura for the 2-point conversion to finish the scoring. Bledsoe was intercepted twice in the fourth quarter as the Patriots never crossed midfield in 4 fourth-quarter possessions. Reggie White set a Super Bowl record with 3 sacks. Favre completed 14 of 27 passes for 246 yards, 2 touchdowns, 0 interceptions, and 1 rushing TD. Bledsoe completed 11 more passes than Favre, but for just 7 more yards, and threw 4 interceptions.

New England (21)	Offense	Green Bay (35)
Shawn Jefferson	WR	Antonio Freeman
Bruce Armstrong	LT	Bruce Wilkerson
William Roberts	LG	Aaron Taylor
Dave Wohlabaugh	C	Frank Winters
Todd Rucci	RG	Adam Timmerman
Max Lane	RT	Earl Dotson
Ben Coates	TE	Mark Chmura
Terry Glenn	WR	Andre Rison
Drew Bledsoe	QB	Brett Favre
Curtis Martin	RB	Edgar Bennett
Keith Byars	RB	William Henderson
	Defense	
Ferric Collons	DE	Reggie White
Mark Wheeler	DT	Santana Dotson
Pio Sagapolutele	DT	Gilbert Brown
Willie McGinest	DE	Sean Jones
Chris Slade	LLB	Wayne Simmons
Ted Johnson	MLB	Ron Cox
Todd Collins	RLB	Brian Williams
Ty Law	LCB	Craig Newsome
Otis Smith	RCB	Doug Evans
Lawyer Milloy	SS	LeRoy Butler
Willie Clay	FS	Eugene Robinson

SUBSTITUTIONS

NEW ENGLAND—Offense: K—Adam Vinatieri. P—Tom Tupa. RB—Marrio Grier, David Meggett. WR—Vincent Brisby, Hason Graham, Ray Lucas. TE—Mike Bartrum, John Burke. G—Bob Kratch. C—Mike Gisler. Defense: DE—Mike Jones, Chris Sullivan. DT—Chad Eaton. LB—Tedy Bruschi, Marty Moore, Dwayne Sabb. S—Corwin Brown, Terry Ray, Larry Whigham. DNP: CB—Ricky Reynolds.

GREEN BAY—Offense: K—Chris Jacke. P—Craig Hentrich. RB—Travis Jervey, Calvin Jones, Dorsey Lev-

ens. WR—Don Beebe, Desmond Howard, Terry Mickens. TE—Keith Jackson, Jeff Thomason. T—John Michels. G—Lindsay Knapp. C—Jeff Dellenbach. Defense: DE—Keith McKenzie, Gabe Wilkins. DT—Darius Holland. LB—Bernardo Harris, Lamont Hollinquest. CB—Tyrone Williams. S—Chris Hayes, Roderick Mullen, Mike Prior. DNP: QB—Jim McMahon.

OFFICIALS
Referee—Gerald Austin. Umpire—Ron Botchan. Head Linesman—Earnie Frantz. Line Judge—Jeff Bergman. Back Judge—Scott Steenson. Field Judge—Phil Luckett. Side Judge—Tom Fincken.

SCORING
New England (AFC)	14	0	7	0	— 21
Green Bay (NFC)	10	17	8	0	— 35

GB — Rison 54 pass from Favre (Jacke kick) (3:32)
GB — FG Jacke 37 (6:18)
NE — Byars 1 pass from Bledsoe (Vinatieri kick) (8:25)
NE — Coates 4 pass from Bledsoe (Vinatieri kick) (12:27)
GB — Freeman 81 pass from Favre (Jacke kick) (0:56)
GB — FG Jacke 31 (6:45)
GB — Favre 2 run (Jacke kick) (13:49)
NE — Martin 18 run (Vinatieri kick) (11:33)
GB — Howard 99 kick return (Chmura pass from Favre) (11:50)

TEAM STATISTICS
	NE	GB
Total First Downs	16	16
Rushing	3	8
Passing	12	6
Penalty	1	2
Total Net Yardage	257	323
Total Offensive Plays	66	68
Average Gain per Offensive Play	3.9	4.8
Rushes	13	36
Yards Gained Rushing (Net)	43	115
Average Yards per Rush	3.3	3.2
Passes Attempted	48	27
Passes Completed	25	14
Had Intercepted	4	0
Tackled Attempting to Pass	5	5
Yards Lost Attempting to Pass	39	38
Yards Gained Passing (Net)	214	208
Punts	8	7
Average Distance	45.1	42.7
Punt Returns	4	6
Punt Return Yardage	30	90
Kickoff Returns	6	4
Kickoff Return Yardage	135	154
Interception Return Yardage	0	24
Total Return Yardage	165	268
Fumbles	0	0
Own Fumbles Recovered	0	0
Opponent Fumbles Recovered	0	0
Penalties	2	3
Yards Penalized	22	41
Field Goals	0	2
Field Goals Attempted	0	3
Third-Down Efficiency	4/14	3/15
Fourth-Down Efficiency	0/2	0/1
Time of Possession	25:45	34:15

INDIVIDUAL STATISTICS
RUSHING: NE: Martin 11-42, Bledsoe 1-1, Meggett 1-0. GB: Levens 14-61, Bennett 17-40, Favre 4-12, Henderson 1-2.
PASSING: NE: Bledsoe 25-48-253-4. GB: Favre 14-27-246-0.
RECEIVING: NE: Coates 6-67, Glenn 4-62, Byars 4-42, Jefferson 3-34, Martin 3-28, Brisby 2-12, Meggett 3-8. GB: Freeman 3-105, Rison 2-77, Levens 3-23, Henderson 2-14, Chmura 2-13, Jackson 1-10, Bennett 1-4.
KICKOFF RETURNS: NE: Meggett 5-117, Graham 1-18. GB: Howard 4-154.
PUNT RETURNS: NE: Meggett 4-30. GB: Howard 6-90.

PUNTING: NE: Tupa 8-361-45.1. GB: Hentrich 7-299-42.7.
INTERCEPTIONS: NE: None. GB: Evans 1-0, Newsome 1-0, Prior 1-8, B. Williams 1-16.
SACKS: NE: Bruschi 2, Collons 1, McGinest 1, Smith 1. GB: White 3, Butler 1, S. Dotson 1.

SUPER BOWL XXX
Sun Devil Stadium, Tempe, Arizona
January 28, 1996, Attendance: 76,347
DALLAS 27, PITTSBURGH 17—Cornerback Larry Brown's 2 interceptions led to 14 second-half points and helped lift the Cowboys to their third Super Bowl victory in the last four seasons and their record-tying fifth title overall. Brown's interceptions foiled the comeback efforts of the Steelers, and earned him the Pete Rozelle Trophy as the game's most valuable player. Dallas scored on each of its first three possessions, taking a 13-0 lead on Troy Aikman's 3-yard touchdown pass to Jay Novacek and a pair of field goals by Chris Boniol. Neil O'Donnell's 6-yard touchdown pass to Yancey Thigpen 13 seconds before halftime pulled Pittsburgh within 6 points, and the Steelers had the ball near midfield midway through the third quarter. But O'Donnell's third-down pass was intercepted by Brown at the Cowboys' 38-yard line, and his 44-yard return carried to Pittsburgh's 18. After Aikman's 17-yard completion to Michael Irvin, Emmitt Smith ran 1 yard for the touchdown that put Dallas ahead again by 13 points. The Steelers rallied, though, behind Norm Johnson's 46-yard field goal, a successful surprise onside kick, and Byron (Bam) Morris's 1-yard touchdown run with 6:36 to play in the game. And when they forced a punt and took possession at their own 32-yard line trailing only 20-17 with 4:15 remaining, it appeared they might have a chance to break the NFC's recent domination in the Super Bowl. But on second down, Brown struck again, intercepting O'Donnell's pass at the 39 and returning it 33 yards to the 6. Two plays later, Smith barreled over from 4 yards out for the clinching touchdown with 3:43 to go. Pittsburgh limited the Cowboys' powerful running game to only 56 yards and enjoyed a whopping 201-61 advantage in total yards in the second half, but could not overcome the 3 interceptions (another came on the game's final play) thrown by O'Donnell, the NFL's career leader for fewest interceptions per pass attempt. In all, O'Donnell completed 28 of 49 passes for 239 yards. Morris rushed for a game-high 73 yards on 19 carries. For Dallas, Aikman completed 15 of 23 pass attempts for 209 yards. The Cowboys' victory was the twelfth in a row for NFC teams over AFC teams in the Super Bowl.

Dallas (NFC)	10	3	7	7	— 27
Pittsburgh (AFC)	0	7	0	10	— 17

Dall — FG Boniol 42 (2:55)
Dall — Novacek 3 pass from Aikman (Boniol kick) (9:37)
Dall — FG Boniol 35 (8:57)
Pitt — Thigpen 6 pass from O'Donnell (N. Johnson kick) (14:47)
Dall — E. Smith 1 run (Boniol kick) (8:18)
Pitt — FG N. Johnson 46 (3:40)
Pitt — Morris 1 run (N. Johnson kick) (8:24)
Dall — E. Smith 4 run (Boniol kick) (11:17)

SUPER BOWL XXIX
Joe Robbie Stadium, Miami, Florida
January 29, 1995, Attendance: 74,107
SAN FRANCISCO 49, SAN DIEGO 26—Steve Young threw a record 6 touchdown passes, and the 49ers became the first team to win five Super Bowls when they routed the Chargers. Young, the game's most valuable player, directed an explosive offense that generated 7 touchdowns, 28 first downs, and 455 total yards. He completed 24 of 36 passes for 325 yards, and broke former 49ers quarterback Joe Montana's previous record of 5 touchdown passes in Super Bowl XXIV. San Francisco wasted little time scoring, taking the lead for good on Young's 44-yard touchdown pass to Jerry Rice only three plays and 1:24 into the game. The next time they had the ball, the 49ers marched 79 yards in four plays, taking a 14-0 lead when Young teamed with running back

Ricky Watters on a 51-yard touchdown pass with 10:05 still to play in the opening period. San Diego then put together its most impressive possession of the game, a 13-play, 78-yard drive that consumed more than 7 minutes and was capped by Natrone Means's 1-yard touchdown run, to cut its deficit to 14-7 late in the quarter. But San Francisco countered with a 70-yard drive of its own, and Young's 5-yard touchdown pass to fullback William Floyd made it 21-7. Young's fourth touchdown pass of the half, 8 yards to Watters 4:44 before halftime, increased the advantage to 28-7, and the Chargers could get no closer than 18 points after that. Watters, who ran 9 yards for a touchdown in the third quarter, equaled the Super Bowl record with 3 touchdowns. Rice also scored 3 touchdowns (the second time in his career he'd done that in a Super Bowl) while catching 10 passes for 149 yards. He established career records for receptions, yards, and touchdowns in a Super Bowl. Young, who scrambled 21 yards and 15 yards to set up touchdowns in the first half, was the game's leading rusher with 49 yards on 5 carries. San Diego's Means, who rushed for 1,350 yards during the regular season, was limited to 33 yards on 13 attempts. Chargers quarterback Stan Humphries completed 24 of 49 passes for 275 yards. Rookie Andre Coleman became only the third player in Super Bowl history to return a kickoff for a touchdown, going 98 yards in the third quarter. The 75 points scored by the two teams established another record, breaking the previous mark of 69 set in Dallas's 52-17 victory over Buffalo in XXVII. The 49ers' victory was the eleventh straight for NFC teams over AFC teams in the Super Bowl.

San Diego (AFC)	7	3	8	8	— 26
San Francisco (NFC)	14	14	14	7	— 49

SF — Rice 44 pass from S. Young (Brien kick) (1:24)
SF — Watters 51 pass from S. Young (Brien kick) (4:55)
SD — Means 1 run (Carney kick) (12:16)
SF — Floyd 5 pass from S. Young (Brien kick) (1:58)
SF — Watters 8 pass from S. Young (Brien kick) (10:16)
SD — FG Carney 31 (13:16)
SF — Watters 9 run (Brien kick) (5:25)
SF — Rice 15 pass from S. Young (Brien kick) (11:42)
SD — Coleman 98 kickoff return (Seay pass from Humphries) (11:59)
SF — Rice 7 pass from S. Young (Brien kick) (1:11)
SD — Martin 30 pass from Humphries (Pupunu pass from Humphries) (12:35)

SUPER BOWL XXVIII
Georgia Dome, Atlanta, Georgia
January 30, 1994, Attendance: 72,817
DALLAS 30, BUFFALO 13—Emmitt Smith rushed for 132 yards and 2 second-half touchdowns to power the Cowboys to their second consecutive NFL title. By winning, Dallas joined San Francisco and Pittsburgh as the only franchises with four Super Bowl victories. The Bills, meanwhile, extended a dubious string by losing in the Super Bowl for the fourth consecutive year. To win, the Cowboys had to rally from a 13-6 halftime deficit. Buffalo had forged its lead on Thurman Thomas's 4-yard touchdown run and a pair of field goals by Steve Christie, including a 54-yard kick, the longest in Super Bowl history. But just 55 seconds into the second half, Thomas was stripped of the ball by Dallas defensive tackle Leon Lett. Safety James Washington recovered and weaved his way 46 yards for a touchdown to tie the game at 13-13. After forcing the Bills to punt, the Cowboys began their next possession on their 36-yard line and Smith, the game's most valuable player, took over. He carried 7 times for 61 yards on the ensuing 8-play, 64-yard drive, capping the march with a 15-yard touchdown run to give Dallas the lead for good with 8:42 remaining in the third quarter. Early in the fourth quarter, Washington intercepted Jim

Kelly's pass and returned it 12 yards to Buffalo's 34. A penalty moved the ball back to the 39, but Smith carried twice for 10 yards and caught a screen pass for 9, and quarterback Troy Aikman completed a 16-yard pass to Alvin Harper to give the Cowboys a first-and-goal at the 6. Smith took it from there, cracking the end zone on fourth-and-goal from the 1 to put Dallas ahead 27-13 with 9:50 remaining. Eddie Murray's third field goal, from 20 yards with 2:50 left, ended any doubt about the game's outcome. Smith had 30 carries in all, with 19 of his attempts and 92 yards coming after intermission. Washington, normally a reserve who played most of the game because the Cowboys used five defensive backs to combat the Bills' No-Huddle offense, had 11 tackles and forced another fumble by Thomas in the first quarter. Aikman completed 19 of 27 passes for 207 yards. Buffalo's Kelly completed a Super Bowl-record 31 passes in 50 attempts for 260 yards. Dallas, the first team in NFL history to begin the regular season 0-2 and go on to win the Super Bowl, also became the fifth to win back-to-back titles, following Green Bay, Miami, Pittsburgh (the Steelers did it twice), and San Francisco. Buffalo became the third team, along with Minnesota and Denver, to lose four Super Bowls. The Cowboys' victory was the tenth in succession for the NFC over the AFC.

Dallas (NFC)	6	10	14	10	— 30
Buffalo (AFC)	3	10	0	0	— 13

Dall — FG Murray 41 (2:19)
Buff — FG Christie 54 (4:41)
Dall — FG Murray 24 (11:05)
Buff — Thomas 4 run (Christie kick) (2:34)
Buff — FG Christie 28 (15:00)
Dall — Washington 46 fumble return (Murray kick) (0:55)
Dall — E. Smith 15 run (Murray kick) (6:18)
Dall — E. Smith 1 run (Murray kick) (5:10)
Dall — FG Murray 20 (12:10)

SUPER BOWL XXVII

Rose Bowl, Pasadena, California
January 31, 1993, Attendance: 98,374
DALLAS 52, BUFFALO 17—Troy Aikman threw 4 touchdown passes, Emmitt Smith rushed for 108 yards, and the Cowboys converted 9 turnovers into 35 points while coasting to the victory. Dallas's win was its third in its record sixth Super Bowl appearance; the Bills became the first team to drop three in succession. Buffalo led 7-0 until the first 2 of its record number of turnovers helped the Cowboys take the lead for good late in the opening quarter. First, Dallas safety James Washington intercepted a Jim Kelly pass and returned it 13 yards to the Bills' 47, setting up Aikman's 23-yard touchdown pass to tight end Jay Novacek with 1:36 remaining in the period. On the next play from scrimmage, Kelly was sacked by Charles Haley and fumbled at the Bills' 2-yard line where the Cowboys' Jimmie Jones picked up the loose ball and ran 2 yards for a touchdown. Dallas, which recovered 5 fumbles and intercepted 4 passes, struck just as quickly late in the first half, when Aikman tossed 19- and 18-yard touchdown passes to Michael Irvin 15 seconds apart to give the Cowboys a 28-10 lead at intermission. The second score was set up when Bills running back Thurman Thomas lost a fumble at his 19-yard line. Buffalo scored for the last time when backup quarterback Frank Reich, playing because Kelly was injured while attempting to pass midway through the second quarter, threw a 40-yard touchdown pass to Don Beebe on the final play of the third period to trim the deficit to 31-17. But Dallas put the game out of reach by scoring three times in a span of 2:33 of the fourth quarter. Aikman, the game's most valuable player, completed 22 of 30 passes for 273 yards and was not intercepted. The victory was the ninth in succession for the NFC over the AFC.

Buffalo (AFC)	7	3	7	0	— 17
Dallas (NFC)	14	14	3	21	— 52

Buff — Thomas 2 run (Christie kick) (5:00)
Dall — Novacek 23 pass from Aikman (Elliott kick) (13:24)

Dall — J. Jones 2 fumble recovery return (Elliott kick) (13:39)
Buff — FG Christie 21 (11:36)
Dall — Irvin 19 pass from Aikman (Elliott kick) (13:06)
Dall — Irvin 18 pass from Aikman (Elliott kick) (13:24)
Dall — FG Elliott 20 (6:39)
Buff — Beebe 40 pass from Reich (Christie kick) (15:00)
Dall — Harper 45 pass from Aikman (Elliott kick) (4:56)
Dall — E. Smith 10 run (Elliott kick) (6:48)
Dall — Norton 9 fumble recovery return (Elliott kick) (7:29)

SUPER BOWL XXVI

Metrodome, Minneapolis, Minnesota
January 26, 1992, Attendance: 63,130
WASHINGTON 37, BUFFALO 24—Mark Rypien passed for 292 yards and 2 touchdowns as the Redskins overwhelmed the Bills to win their third Super Bowl in the past 10 years. Rypien, the game's most valuable player, completed 18 of 33 passes, including a 10-yard scoring strike to Earnest Byner and a 30-yard touchdown to Gary Clark. The latter came late in the third quarter after Buffalo had trimmed a 24-0 deficit to 24-10, and effectively put the game out of reach. Washington went on to lead by as much as 37-10 before the Bills made it close wih a pair of touchdowns in the final six minutes. Though the Redskins struggled early, converting their first three drives inside the Bills' 20-yard line into only 3 points, they built a 17-0 halftime lead. And they made it 24-0 just 16 seconds into the second half, after Kurt Gouveia intercepted Buffalo quarterback Jim Kelly's pass on the first play of the third quarter and returned it 23 yards to the Bills' 2. One play later, Gerald Riggs scored his second touchdown of the game to make it 24-0. Kelly, forced to bring Buffalo from behind, completed 28 of a Super Bowl-record 58 passes for 275 yards and 2 touchdowns, but was intercepted 4 times. Bills running back Thurman Thomas, who had an AFC-high 1,407 yards rushing and an NFL-best 2,038 total yards from scrimmage during the regular season, ran for only 13 yards on 10 carries and was limited to 27 yards on 4 receptions. Clark had 7 catches for 114 yards and Art Monk added 7 for 113 for the Redskins, who amassed 417 yards of total offense while limiting the explosive Bills to 283. Washington's Joe Gibbs became only the third head coach to win three Super Bowls.

Washington (NFC)	0	17	14	6	— 37
Buffalo (AFC)	0	0	10	14	— 24

Wash — FG Lohmiller 34 (1:58)
Wash — Byner 10 pass from Rypien (Lohmiller kick) (5:06)
Wash — Riggs 1 run (Lohmiller kick) (7:43)
Wash — Riggs 2 run (Lohmiller kick) (0:16)
Buff — FG Norwood 21 (3:01)
Buff — Thomas 1 run (Norwood kick) (9:02)
Wash — Clark 30 pass from Rypien (Lohmiller kick) (13:36)
Wash — FG Lohmiller 25 (0:06)
Wash — FG Lohmiller 39 (3:24)
Buff — Metzelaars 2 pass from Kelly (Norwood kick) (9:01)
Buff — Beebe 4 pass from Kelly (Norwood kick) (11:05)

SUPER BOWL XXV

Tampa Stadium, Tampa, Florida
January 27, 1991, Attendance: 73,813
NEW YORK GIANTS 20, BUFFALO 19—The NFC champion New York Giants won their second Super Bowl in five years with a 20-19 victory over AFC titlist Buffalo. New York, employing its ball-control offense, had possession for 40 minutes, 33 seconds, a Super Bowl record. The Bills, who scored 95 points in their previous two playoff games leading to Super Bowl XXV, had the ball for less than eight minutes in the second half and just 19:27 for the game. Fourteen of New York's 73 plays came on its initial drive of the

third quarter, which covered 75 yards and consumed a Super Bowl-record 9:29 before running back Ottis Anderson ran 1 yard for a touchdown. Giants quarterback Jeff Hostetler kept the long drive going by converting three third-down plays—an 11-yard pass to running back David Meggett on third-and-eight, a 14-yard toss to wide receiver Mark Ingram on third-and-13, and a 9-yard pass to Howard Cross on third-and-four—to give New York a 17-12 lead in the third quarter. Buffalo jumped to a 12-3 lead midway through the second quarter before Hostetler completed a 14-yard scoring strike to wide receiver Stephen Baker to close the score to 12-10 at halftime. Buffalo's Thurman Thomas ran 31 yards for a touchdown on the opening play of the fourth quarter to help Buffalo recapture the lead 19-17. Matt Bahr's 21-yard field goal gave the Giants a 20-19 lead, but Buffalo's Scott Norwood had a chance to win the game with seconds remaining before his 47-yard field-goal attempt sailed wide right. Hostetler completed 20 of 32 passes for 222 yards and 1 touchdown. Anderson rushed 21 times for 102 yards and 1 touchdown to capture the most-valuable-player honors. Thomas totaled 190 scrimmage yards, rushing 15 times for 135 yards and catching 5 passes for 55 yards.

Buffalo (AFC)	3	9	0	7	— 19
N.Y. Giants (NFC)	3	7	7	3	— 20

NYG — FG Bahr 28 (7:46)
Buff — FG Norwood 23 (9:09)
Buff — D. Smith 1 run (Norwood kick) (2:30)
Buff — Safety, B. Smith tackled Hostetler in end zone (6:33)
NYG — Baker 14 pass from Hostetler (Bahr kick) (14:35)
NYG — Anderson 1 run (Bahr kick) (9:29)
Buff — Thomas 31 run (Norwood kick) (0:08)
NYG — FG Bahr 21 (7:40)

SUPER BOWL XXIV

Louisiana Superdome, New Orleans, Louisiana
January 28, 1990, Attendance: 72,919
SAN FRANCISCO 55, DENVER 10—NFC titlist San Francisco won its fourth Super Bowl championship with a 55-10 victory over AFC champion Denver. The 49ers, who also won Super Bowls XVI, XIX, and XXIII, tied the Pittsburgh Steelers for most Super Bowl victories. The Steelers captured Super Bowls IX, X, XIII, and XIV. San Francisco's 55 points broke the previous Super Bowl scoring mark of 46 points by Chicago in Super Bowl XX. San Francisco scored touchdowns on four of its six first-half possessions to hold a 27-3 lead at halftime. Interceptions by Michael Walter and Chet Brooks ended the Broncos' first two possessions of the second half. San Francisco quarterback Joe Montana was named the Super Bowl most valuable player for a record third time. Montana completed 22 of 29 passes for 297 yards and a Super Bowl-record 5 touchdowns. Jerry Rice, Super Bowl XXIII most valuable player, caught 7 passes for 148 yards and three touchdowns. The 49ers' domination included first downs (28 to 12), net yards (461 to 167), and time of possession (39:31 to 20:29).

San Francisco (NFC)	13	14	14	14	— 55
Denver (AFC)	3	0	7	0	— 10

SF — Rice 20 pass from Montana (Cofer kick) (4:54)
Den — FG Treadwell 42 (8:13)
SF — Jones 7 pass from Montana (kick failed) (14:57)
SF — Rathman 1 run (Cofer kick) (7:45)
SF — Rice 38 pass from Montana (Cofer kick) (14:26)
SF — Rice 28 pass from Montana (Cofer kick) (2:12)
SF — Taylor 35 pass from Montana (Cofer kick) (5:16)
Den — Elway 3 run (Treadwell kick) (8:07)
SF — Rathman 3 run (Cofer kick) (0:03)
SF — Craig 1 run (Cofer kick) (1:13)

SUPER BOWL XXIII

Joe Robbie Stadium, Miami, Florida
January 22, 1989, Attendance: 75,129
SAN FRANCISCO 20, CINCINNATI 16—NFC champion San Francisco captured its third Super Bowl of the 1980s by defeating AFC champion Cincinnati 20-16. The 49ers, who also won Super Bowls XVI and XIX, are the first NFC team to win three Super Bowls. Pittsburgh, with four Super Bowl titles (IX, X, XIII, and XIV), and the Oakland/Los Angeles Raiders, with three (XI, XV, and XVIII), lead AFC franchises. Even though San Francisco held an advantage in total net yards (453 to 229), the 49ers found themselves trailing the Bengals late in the game. With the score 13-13, Cincinnati took a 16-13 lead on Jim Breech's 40-yard field goal with 3:20 remaining. It was Breech's third field goal of the day, following earlier successes from 34 and 43 yards. The 49ers started their winning drive at their 8-yard line. Over the next 11 plays, San Francisco covered 92 yards with the decisive score coming on a 10-yard pass from quarterback Joe Montana to wide receiver John Taylor with 34 seconds remaining. At halftime, the score was 3-3, the first time in Super Bowl history the game was tied at intermission. After the teams traded third-period field goals, the Bengals jumped ahead 13-6 on Stanford Jennings's 93-yard kickoff return for a touchdown with 34 seconds remaining in the quarter. The 49ers didn't waste any time coming back as they covered 85 yards in four plays, concluding with Montana's 14-yard scoring pass to Jerry Rice 57 seconds into the final stanza. Rice was named the game's most valuable player after compiling 11 catches for a Super Bowl-record 215 yards. Montana completed 23 of 36 passes for a Super Bowl-record 357 yards and 2 touchdowns.

Cincinnati (AFC)	0	3	10	3	— 16
San Francisco (NFC)	3	0	3	14	— 20

SF — FG Cofer 41 (11:46)
Cin — FG Breech 34 (13:45)
Cin — FG Breech 43 (9:21)
SF — FG Cofer 32 (14:10)
Cin — Jennings 93 kickoff return (Breech kick) (14:26)
SF — Rice 14 pass from Montana (Cofer kick) (0:57)
Cin — FG Breech 40 (11:40)
SF — Taylor 10 pass from Montana (Cofer kick) (14:26)

SUPER BOWL XXII

San Diego Jack Murphy Stadium, San Diego, California
January 31, 1988, Attendance: 73,302
WASHINGTON 42, DENVER 10—NFC champion Washington won Super Bowl XXII and its second NFL championship of the 1980s with a 42-10 decision over AFC champion Denver. The Redskins, who also won Super Bowl XVII, enjoyed a record-setting second quarter en route to the victory. The Broncos broke in front 10-0 when quarterback John Elway threw a 56-yard touchdown pass to wide receiver Ricky Nattiel on the Broncos' first play from scrimmage. Following a Washington punt, Denver's Rich Karlis kicked a 24-yard field goal to cap a seven-play, 61-yard scoring drive. The Redskins then erupted for 35 points on five straight possessions in the second period and coasted thereafter. The 35 points established an NFL postseason mark for most points in a period, bettering the previous total of 21 by San Francisco in Super Bowl XIX and Chicago in Super Bowl XX. Redskins quarterback Doug Williams led the second-period explosion by throwing a Super Bowl record-tying 4 touchdown passes, including 80- and 50-yard passes to wide receiver Ricky Sanders, a 27-yard toss to wide receiver Gary Clark, and an 8-yard pass to tight end Clint Didier. Washington scored 5 touchdowns in 18 plays with total time of possession of only 5:47. Overall, Williams completed 18 of 29 passes for 340 yards and was named the game's most valuable player. His pass-yardage total eclipsed the Super Bowl record of 331 yards by Joe Montana of San Francisco in Super Bowl XIX. Sanders ended with 193 yards on 8 catch-

es, breaking the previous Super Bowl yardage record of 161 yards by Lynn Swann of Pittsburgh in Game X. Rookie running back Timmy Smith was the game's leading rusher with 22 carries for a Super Bowl-record 204 yards, breaking the previous mark of 191 yards by Marcus Allen of Los Angeles in Game XVIII. Smith also scored twice on runs of 58 and 4 yards. Washington's 6 touchdowns and 602 total yards gained also set Super Bowl records. Redskins cornerback Barry Wilburn had 2 of the team's 3 interceptions, and strong safety Alvin Walton had 2 of Washington's 5 sacks.

Washington (NFC)	0	35	0	7	— 42
Denver (AFC)	10	0	0	0	— 10

Den — Nattiel 56 pass from Elway (Karlis kick) (1:57)
Den — FG Karlis 24 (5:51)
Wash — Sanders 80 pass from Williams (Haji-Sheikh kick) (0:53)
Wash — Clark 27 pass from Williams (Haji-Sheikh kick) (4:45)
Wash — Smith 58 run (Haji-Sheikh kick) (8:33)
Wash — Sanders 50 pass from Williams (Haji-Sheikh kick) (11:18)
Wash — Didier 8 pass from Williams (Haji-Sheikh kick) (13:56)
Wash — Smith 4 run (Haji-Sheikh kick) (1:51)

SUPER BOWL XXI

Rose Bowl, Pasadena, California
January 25, 1987, Attendance: 101,063
NEW YORK GIANTS 39, DENVER 20—The NFC champion New York Giants captured their first NFL title since 1956 when they downed the AFC champion Denver Broncos 39-20 in Super Bowl XXI. The victory marked the NFC's fifth NFL title in the past six seasons. The Broncos, behind the passing of quarterback John Elway, who was 13 of 20 for 187 yards in the first half, held a 10-9 lead at intermission, the narrowest half-time margin in Super Bowl history. Denver's Rich Karlis opened the scoring with a Super Bowl record-tying 48-yard field goal. New York drove 78 yards in nine plays on the next series to take a 7-3 lead on quarterback Phil Simms's 6-yard touchdown pass to tight end Zeke Mowatt. The Broncos came right back with a 58-yard scoring drive on six plays capped by Elway's 4-yard touchdown run. The only scoring in the second period was the sack of Elway in the end zone by defensive end George Martin for a New York safety. The Giants produced a key defensive stand early in the second quarter when the Broncos had a first down at the New York 1-yard line, but failed to score on three running plays and Karlis's 23-yard missed field-goal attempt. The Giants took command of the game in the third period en route to a 30-point second surge, the most ever scored in one half of Super Bowl play. New York took the lead for good on tight end Mark Bavaro's 13-yard touchdown catch 4:52 into the third period. The nine-play, 63-yard scoring drive included the successful conversion of a fourth-and-1 play on the New York 46-yard line. Denver was limited to only 2 net yards on 10 offensive plays in the third period. Simms set Super Bowl records for most consecutive completions (10) and highest completion percentage (88 percent on 22 completions in 25 attempts). He also passed for 268 yards and 3 touchdowns and was named the game's most valuable player. New York running back Joe Morris was the game's leading rusher with 20 carries for 67 yards. Denver wide receiver Vance Johnson led all receivers with 5 catches for 121 yards. The Giants defeated their three playoff opponents by a cumulative total of 82 points (New York 105, opponents 23), the largest such margin by a Super Bowl winner.

Denver (AFC)	10	0	0	10	— 20
N.Y. Giants (NFC)	7	2	17	13	— 39

Den — FG Karlis 48 (4:09)
NYG — Mowatt 6 pass from Simms (Allegre kick) (9:33)
Den — Elway 4 run (Karlis kick) (12:54)
NYG — Safety, Martin tackled Elway in end zone (12:14)

NYG — Bavaro 13 pass from Simms (Allegre kick) (4:52)
NYG — FG Allegre 21 (11:06)
NYG — Morris 1 run (Allegre kick) (14:36)
NYG — McConkey 6 pass from Simms (Allegre kick) (4:04)
Den — FG Karlis 28 (8:59)
NYG — Anderson 2 run (kick failed) (10:42)
Den — V. Johnson 47 pass from Elway (Karlis kick) (12:54)

SUPER BOWL XX

Louisiana Superdome, New Orleans, Louisiana
January 26, 1986, Attendance: 73,818
CHICAGO 46, NEW ENGLAND 10—The NFC champion Chicago Bears, seeking their first NFL title since 1963, scored a Super Bowl-record 46 points in downing AFC champion New England 46-10 in Super Bowl XX. The previous record for most points in a Super Bowl was 38, shared by San Francisco in XIX and the Los Angeles Raiders in XVIII. The Bears' league-leading defense tied the Super Bowl record for sacks (7) and limited the Patriots to a record-low 7 rushing yards. New England took the quickest lead in Super Bowl history when Tony Franklin kicked a 36-yard field goal with 1:19 elapsed in the first period. The score came about because of Larry Mc-Grew's fumble recovery at the Chicago 19-yard line. However, the Bears rebounded for a 23-3 first-half lead, while building a yardage advantage of 236 to-tal yards to New England's minus 19. Running back Matt Suhey rushed 8 times for 37 yards, including an 11-yard touchdown run, and caught 1 pass for 24 yards in the first half. After the Patriots first drive of the second half ended with a punt to the Bears' 4-yard line, Chicago marched 96 yards in nine plays with quarterback Jim McMahon's 1-yard scoring run capping the drive. McMahon became the first quarterback in Super Bowl history to rush for a pair of touchdowns. The Bears completed their scoring via a 28-yard interception return by reserve cornerback Reggie Phillips, a 1-yard run by defensive tackle/fullback William Perry, and a safety when defensive end Henry Waechter tackled Patriots quarterback Steve Grogan in the end zone. Bears defensive end Richard Dent became the fourth defender to be named the game's most valuable player after contributing 1½ sacks. The Bears' victory margin of 36 points was the largest in Super Bowl history, bettering the previous mark of 29 by the Los Angeles Raiders when they topped Washington 38-9 in Game XVIII. McMahon completed 12 of 20 passes for 256 yards before leaving the game in the fourth period with a wrist injury. The NFL's all-time leading rusher, Bears running back Walter Payton, carried 22 times for 61 yards. Wide receiver Willie Gault caught 4 passes for 129 yards, the fourth-most receiving yards in a Super Bowl. Chicago coach Mike Ditka became the second man (Tom Flores of Raiders was the other) who played in a Super Bowl and coached a team to a victory in the game.

Chicago (NFC)	13	10	21	2	— 46
New England (AFC)	3	0	0	7	— 10

NE — FG Franklin 36 (1:19)
Chi — FG Butler 28 (5:40)
Chi — FG Butler 24 (13:34)
Chi — Suhey 11 run (Butler kick) (14:37)
Chi — McMahon 2 run (Butler kick) (7:36)
Chi — FG Butler 24 (15:00)
Chi — McMahon 1 run (Butler kick) (7:38)
Chi — Phillips 28 interception return (Butler kick) (8:44)
Chi — Perry 1 run (Butler kick) (11:38)
NE — Fryar 8 pass from Grogan (Franklin kick) (1:46)
Chi — Safety, Waechter tackled Grogan in end zone (9:24)

SUPER BOWL XIX

Stanford Stadium, Stanford, California
January 20, 1985, Attendance: 84,059
SAN FRANCISCO 38, MIAMI 16—The San Francisco 49ers captured their second Super Bowl title with

a dominating offense and a defense that tamed Miami's explosive passing attack. The Dolphins held a 10-7 lead at the end of the first period, which represented the most points scored by two teams in an opening quarter of a Super Bowl. However, the 49ers used excellent field position in the second period to build a 28-16 halftime lead. Running back Roger Craig set a Super Bowl record by scoring 3 touchdowns on pass receptions of 8 and 16 yards and a run of 2 yards. San Francisco's Joe Montana was voted the game's most valuable player. He joined Green Bay's Bart Starr and Pittsburgh's Terry Bradshaw as the only two-time Super Bowl most valuable players. Montana completed 24 of 35 passes for a Super Bowl-record 331 yards and 3 touchdowns, and rushed 5 times for 59 yards, including a 6-yard touchdown. Craig had 58 yards on 15 carries and caught 7 passes for 77 yards. Wendell Tyler rushed 13 times for 65 yards and had 4 catches for 70 yards. Dwight Clark had 6 receptions for 77 yards, while Russ Francis had 5 for 60. San Francisco's 537 total net yards bettered the previous Super Bowl record of 429 yards by Oakland in Super Bowl XI. The 49ers also held a time of possession advantage over the Dolphins of 37:11 to 22:49.

Miami (AFC)	10	6	0	0	—	16
San Francisco (NFC)	7	21	10	0	—	38

Mia — FG von Schamann 37 (7:36)
SF — Monroe 33 pass from Montana (Wersching kick) (11:48)
Mia — D. Johnson 2 pass from Marino (von Schamann kick) (14:15)
SF — Craig 8 pass from Montana (Wersching kick) (3:26)
SF — Montana 6 run (Wersching kick) (8:02)
SF — Craig 2 run (Wersching kick) (12:55)
Mia — FG von Schamann 31 (14:48)
Mia — FG von Schamann 30 (15:00)
SF — FG Wersching 27 (4:48)
SF — Craig 16 pass from Montana (Wersching kick) (8:42)

SUPER BOWL XVIII

Tampa Stadium, Tampa, Florida
January 22, 1984, Attendance: 72,920
LOS ANGELES RAIDERS 38, WASHINGTON 9—The Los Angeles Raiders dominated the Washington Redskins from the beginning in Super Bowl XVIII and achieved the most lopsided victory in Super Bowl history, surpassing Green Bay's 35-10 win over Kansas City in Super Bowl I. The Raiders took a 7-0 lead 4:52 into the game when Derrick Jensen blocked a Jeff Hayes punt and recovered it in the end zone for a touchdown. With 9:14 remaining in the first half, Raiders quarterback Jim Plunkett threw a 12-yard touchdown pass to wide receiver Cliff Branch to complete a three-play, 65-yard drive. Washington cut the Raiders' lead to 14-3 on a 24-yard field goal by Mark Moseley. With seven seconds left in the first half, Raiders linebacker Jack Squirek intercepted a Joe Theismann pass at the Redskins' 5-yard line and ran it in for a touchdown to give Los Angeles a 21-3 halftime lead. In the third period, running back Marcus Allen, who rushed for a Super Bowl-record 191 yards on 20 carries, increased the Raiders' lead to 35-9 on touchdown runs of 5 and 74 yards, the latter erasing the Super Bowl record of 58 yards set by Baltimore's Tom Matte in Game III. Allen was named the game's most valuable player. The victory over Washington raised Raiders coach Tom Flores' playoff record to 8-1, including a 27-10 win against Philadelphia in Super Bowl XV. The 38 points scored by the Raiders were the highest total by a Super Bowl team. The previous high was 35 points by Green Bay in Game I.

Washington (NFC)	0	3	6	0	—	9
L.A. Raiders (AFC)	7	14	14	3	—	38

Raiders — Jensen recovered blocked punt in end zone (Bahr kick) (4:52)
Raiders — Branch 12 pass from Plunkett (Bahr kick) (5:46)
Wash — FG Moseley 24 (11:55)
Raiders — Squirek 5 interception return (Bahr kick) (14:53)

Wash — Riggins 1 run (kick blocked) (4:08)
Raiders — Allen 5 run (Bahr kick) (7:54)
Raiders — Allen 74 run (Bahr kick) (15:00)
Raiders — FG Bahr 21 (12:36)

SUPER BOWL XVII

Rose Bowl, Pasadena, California
January 30, 1983, Attendance: 103,667
WASHINGTON 27, MIAMI 17—Fullback John Riggins ran for a Super Bowl-record 166 yards on 38 carries to spark Washington to a 27-17 victory over AFC champion Miami. It was Riggins's fourth straight 100-yard rushing game during the playoffs, also a record. The win marked Washington's first NFL title since 1942, and was only the second time in Super Bowl history NFL/NFC teams scored consecutive victories (Green Bay did it in Super Bowls I and II and San Francisco won Super Bowl XVI). The Redskins, under second-year head coach Joe Gibbs, used a balanced offense that accounted for 400 total yards (a Super Bowl-record 276 yards rushing and 124 passing), second in Super Bowl history to 429 yards by Oakland in Super Bowl XI. The Dolphins built a 17-10 halftime lead on a 76-yard touchdown pass from quarterback David Woodley to wide receiver Jimmy Cefalo 6:49 into the first period, a 20-yard field goal by Uwe von Schamann with 6:00 left in the half, and a Super Bowl-record 98-yard kickoff return by Fulton Walker with 1:38 remaining. Washington had tied the score at 10-10 with 1:51 left on a four-yard touchdown pass from Joe Theismann to wide receiver Alvin Garrett. Mark Moseley started the Redskins' scoring with a 31-yard field goal late in the first period, and added a 20-yarder midway through the third period to cut the Dolphins' lead to 17-13. Riggins, who was voted the game's most valuable player, gave Washington its first lead of the game with 10:01 left when he ran 43 yards off left tackle for a touchdown in a fourth-and-1 situation. Wide receiver Charlie Brown caught a six-yard scoring pass from Theismann with 1:55 left to complete the scoring. The Dolphins managed only 176 yards (142 in first half). Theismann completed 15 of 23 passes for 143 yards, with 2 touchdowns and 2 interceptions. For Miami, Woodley was 4 of 14 for 97 yards, with 1 touchdown, and 1 interception. Don Strock was 0 for 3 in relief.

Miami (AFC)	7	10	0	0	—	17
Washington (NFC)	0	10	3	14	—	27

Mia — Cefalo 76 pass from Woodley (von Schamann kick) (6:49)
Wash — FG Moseley 31 (0:21)
Mia — FG von Schamann 20 (9:00)
Wash — Garrett 4 pass from Theismann (Moseley kick) (13:09)
Mia — Walker 98 kickoff return (von Schamann kick) (13:22)
Wash — FG Moseley 20 (6:51)
Wash — Riggins 43 run (Moseley kick) (4:59)
Wash — Brown 6 pass from Theismann (Moseley kick) (13:05)

SUPER BOWL XVI

Pontiac Silverdome, Pontiac, Michigan
January 24, 1982, Attendance: 81,270
SAN FRANCISCO 26, CINCINNATI 21—Ray Wersching's Super Bowl record-tying 4 field goals and Joe Montana's controlled passing helped lift the San Francisco 49ers to their first NFL championship with a 26-21 victory over Cincinnati. The 49ers built a game-record 20-0 halftime lead via Montana's 1-yard touchdown run, which capped an 11-play, 68-yard drive; fullback Earl Cooper's 11-yard scoring pass from Montana, which climaxed a Super Bowl record 92-yard drive on 12 plays; and Wersching's 22- and 26-yard field goals. The Bengals rebounded in the second half, closing the gap to 20-14 on quarterback Ken Anderson's 5-yard run and Dan Ross's 4-yard reception from Anderson, who established Super Bowl passing records for completions (25) and completion percentage (73.5 percent on 25 of 34). Wersching added early fourth-period field goals of 40 and 23 yards to increase the 49ers' lead to

26-14. The Bengals managed to score on an Anderson-to-Ross 3-yard pass with only 16 seconds remaining. Ross set a Super Bowl record with 11 receptions for 104 yards. Montana, the game's most valuable player, completed 14 of 22 passes for 157 yards. Cincinnati compiled 356 yards to San Francisco's 275, which marked the first time in Super Bowl history that the team that gained the most yards from scrimmage lost the game.

San Francisco (NFC)	7	13	0	6	—	26
Cincinnati (AFC)	0	0	7	14	—	21

SF — Montana 1 run (Wersching kick) (9:08)
SF — Cooper 11 pass from Montana (Wersching kick) (8:07)
SF — FG Wersching 22 (14:45)
SF — FG Wersching 26 (14:58)
Cin — Anderson 5 run (Breech kick) (3:35)
Cin — Ross 4 pass from Anderson (Breech kick) (4:54)
SF — FG Wersching 40 (9:35)
SF — FG Wersching 23 (13:03)
Cin — Ross 3 pass from Anderson (Breech kick) (14:44)

SUPER BOWL XV

Louisiana Superdome, New Orleans, Louisiana
January 25, 1981, Attendance: 76,135
OAKLAND 27, PHILADELPHIA 10—Jim Plunkett threw 3 touchdown passes, including an 80-yard strike to Kenny King, as the Raiders became the first wild-card team to win the Super Bowl. Plunkett's touchdown bomb to King—the longest play in Super Bowl history—gave Oakland a decisive 14-0 lead with nine seconds left in the first period. Linebacker Rod Martin had set up Oakland's first touchdown, a 2-yard reception by Cliff Branch, with a 17-yard interception return to the Eagles' 30-yard line. The Eagles never recovered from that early deficit, managing only a Tony Franklin field goal (30 yards) and an 8-yard touchdown pass from Ron Jaworski to Keith Krepfle. Plunkett, who became a starter in the sixth game of the season, completed 13 of 21 for 261 yards and was named the game's most valuable player. Oakland won 9 of 11 games with Plunkett starting, but that was good enough only for second place in the AFC West, although they tied division winner San Diego with an 11-5 record. The Raiders, who had previously won Super Bowl XI over Minnesota, had to win three playoff games to get to the championship game. Oakland defeated Houston 27-7 at home followed by road victories over Cleveland (14-12) and San Diego (34-27). Oakland's Mark van Eeghen was the game's leading rusher with 75 yards on 18 carries. Philadelphia's Wilbert Montgomery led all receivers with 6 receptions for 91 yards. Branch had 5 for 67 and Harold Carmichael of Philadelphia 5 for 83. Martin finished the game with 3 interceptions, a Super Bowl record.

Oakland (AFC)	14	0	10	3	—	27
Philadelphia (NFC)	0	3	0	7	—	10

Oak — Branch 2 pass from Plunkett (Bahr kick) (6:04)
Oak — King 80 pass from Plunkett (Bahr kick) (14:51)
Phil — FG Franklin 30 (4:32)
Oak — Branch 29 pass from Plunkett (Bahr kick) (2:36)
Oak — FG Bahr 46 (10:25)
Phil — Krepfle 8 pass from Jaworski (Franklin kick) (1:01)
Oak — FG Bahr 35 (6:31)

SUPER BOWL XIV

Rose Bowl, Pasadena, California
January 20, 1980, Attendance: 103,985
PITTSBURGH 31, LOS ANGELES 19—Terry Bradshaw completed 14 of 21 passes for 309 yards and set two passing records as the Steelers became the first team to win four Super Bowls. Despite 3 interceptions by the Rams, Bradshaw kept his poise and brought the Steelers from behind twice in the second half. Trailing 13-10 at halftime, Pittsburgh went ahead 17-13 when Bradshaw hit Lynn Swann with a 47-yard

touchdown pass after 2:48 of the third quarter. On the Rams' next possession Vince Ferragamo, who completed 15 of 25 passes for 212 yards, responded with a 50-yard pass to Billy Waddy that moved Los Angeles from its 26 to the Steelers' 24. On the following play, Lawrence McCutcheon connected with Ron Smith on a halfback option pass that gave the Rams a 19-17 lead. On Pittsburgh's initial possession of the final period, Bradshaw lofted a 73-yard scoring pass to John Stallworth to put the Steelers in front to stay 24-19. Franco Harris scored on a 1-yard run later in the quarter to seal the verdict. A 45-yard pass from Bradshaw to Stallworth was the key play in the drive to Harris's score. Bradshaw, the game's most valuable player for the second straight year, set career Super Bowl records for most touchdown passes (9) and most passing yards (932). Larry Anderson gave the Steelers excellent field position throughout the game with 5 kickoff returns for a record 162 yards.

Los Angeles (NFC)	7	6	6	0	— 19
Pittsburgh (AFC)	3	7	7	14	— 31

Pitt — FG Bahr 41 (7:29)
LA — Bryant 1 run (Corral kick) (12:16)
Pitt — Harris 1 run (Bahr kick) (2:08)
LA — FG Corral 31 (7:39)
LA — FG Corral 45 (14:46)
Pitt — Swann 47 pass from Bradshaw (Bahr kick) (2:48)
LA — Smith 24 pass from McCutcheon (kick failed) (4:45)
Pitt — Stallworth 73 pass from Bradshaw (Bahr kick) (2:56)
Pitt — Harris 1 run (Bahr kick) (13:11)

SUPER BOWL XIII
Orange Bowl, Miami, Florida
January 21, 1979, Attendance: 79,484
PITTSBURGH 35, DALLAS 31—Terry Bradshaw threw a record 4 touchdown passes to lead the Steelers to victory. The Steelers became the first team to win three Super Bowls, mostly because of Bradshaw's accurate arm. Bradshaw, voted the game's most valuable player, completed 17 of 30 passes for 318 yards, a personal high. Four of those passes went for touchdowns—2 to John Stallworth and the third, with 26 seconds remaining in the second period, to Rocky Bleier for a 21-14 halftime lead. The Cowboys scored twice before intermission on Roger Staubach's 39-yard pass to Tony Hill and a 37-yard fumble return by linebacker Mike Hegman, who stole the ball from Bradshaw. The Steelers broke open the contest with 2 touchdowns in a span of 19 seconds midway through the final period. Franco Harris rambled 22 yards up the middle to give the Steelers a 28-17 lead with 7:10 left. Pittsburgh got the ball right back when Randy White fumbled the kickoff and Dennis Winston recovered for the Steelers. On first down, Bradshaw fired his fourth touchdown pass, an 18-yard pass to Lynn Swann to boost the Steelers' lead to 35-17 with 6:51 to play. The Cowboys refused to let the Steelers run away with the contest. Staubach connected with Billy Joe DuPree on a 7-yard scoring pass with 2:23 left. Then the Cowboys recovered an onside kick and Staubach took them in for another score, passing 4 yards to Butch Johnson with 22 seconds remaining. Bleier recovered another onside kick with 17 seconds left to seal the victory for the Steelers.

Pittsburgh (AFC)	7	14	0	14	— 35
Dallas (NFC)	7	7	3	14	— 31

Pitt — Stallworth 28 pass from Bradshaw (Gerela kick) (5:13)
Dall — Hill 39 pass from Staubach (Septien kick) (15:00)
Dall — Hegman 37 fumble recovery return (Septien kick) (2:52)
Pitt — Stallworth 75 pass from Bradshaw (Gerela kick) (4:35)
Pitt — Bleier 7 pass from Bradshaw (Gerela kick) (14:34)
Dall — FG Septien 27 (12:24)
Pitt — Harris 22 run (Gerela kick) (7:50)

Pitt — Swann 18 pass from Bradshaw (Gerela kick) (8:09)
Dall — DuPree 7 pass from Staubach (Septien kick) (12:37)
Dall — B. Johnson 4 pass from Staubach (Septien kick) (14:38)

SUPER BOWL XII
Louisiana Superdome, New Orleans, Louisiana
January 15, 1978, Attendance: 75,583
DALLAS 27, DENVER 10—The Cowboys evened their Super Bowl record at 2-2 by defeating Denver before a sellout crowd of 75,583, plus 102,010,000 television viewers, the largest audience ever to watch a sporting event. Dallas converted 2 interceptions into 10 points and Efren Herrera added a 35-yard field goal for a 13-0 halftime advantage. In the third period Craig Morton engineered a drive to the Cowboys' 30 and Jim Turner's 47-yard field goal made the score 13-3. After an exchange of punts, Butch Johnson made a spectacular diving catch in the end zone to complete a 45-yard pass from Roger Staubach and put the Cowboys ahead 20-3. Following Rick Upchurch's 67-yard kickoff return, Norris Weese guided the Broncos to a touchdown to cut the Dallas lead to 20-10. Dallas clinched the victory when running back Robert Newhouse threw a 29-yard touchdown pass to Golden Richards with 7:04 remaining in the game. It was the first pass thrown by Newhouse since 1975. Harvey Martin and Randy White, who were named co-most valuable players, led the Cowboys' defense, which recovered 4 fumbles and intercepted 4 passes.

Dallas (NFC)	10	3	7	7	— 27
Denver (AFC)	0	0	10	0	— 10

Dall — Dorsett 3 run (Herrera kick) (10:31)
Dall — FG Herrera 35 (13:29)
Dall — FG Herrera 43 (3:44)
Den — FG Turner 47 (2:28)
Dall — Johnson 45 pass from Staubach (Herrera kick) (8:01)
Den — Lytle 1 run (Turner kick) (9:21)
Dall — Richards 29 pass from Newhouse (Herrera kick) (7:56)

SUPER BOWL XI
Rose Bowl, Pasadena, California
January 9, 1977, Attendance: 103,438
OAKLAND 32, MINNESOTA 14—The Raiders won their first NFL championship before a record Super Bowl crowd plus 81 million television viewers, the largest audience ever to watch a sporting event. The Raiders gained a record-breaking 429 yards, including running back Clarence Davis's 137 rushing yards. Wide receiver Fred Biletnikoff made 4 receptions, which earned him the game's most valuable player trophy. Oakland scored on three successive possessions in the second quarter to build a 16-0 halftime lead. Errol Mann's 24-yard field goal opened the scoring, then the AFC champions put together drives of 64 and 35 yards, scoring on a 1-yard pass from Ken Stabler to Dave Casper and a 1-yard run by Pete Banaszak. The Raiders increased their lead to 19-0 on a 40-yard field goal in the third quarter, but Minnesota responded with a 12-play, 58-yard drive late in the period, with Fran Tarkenton passing 8 yards to wide receiver Sammy White to cut the deficit to 19-7. Two fourth-quarter interceptions clinched the title for the Raiders. One set up Banaszak's second touchdown run, the other resulted in cornerback Willie Brown's Super Bowl-record 75-yard interception return.

Oakland (AFC)	0	16	3	13	— 32
Minnesota (NFC)	0	0	7	7	— 14

Oak — FG Mann 24 (0:48)
Oak — Casper 1 pass from Stabler (Mann kick) (7:50)
Oak — Banaszak 1 run (kick failed) (11:27)
Oak — FG Mann 40 (9:44)
Minn — S. White 8 pass from Tarkenton (Cox kick) (14:13)
Oak — Banaszak 2 run (Mann kick) (7:21)

Oak — Brown 75 interception return (kick failed) (9:17)
Minn — Voigt 13 pass from Lee (Cox kick) (14:35)

SUPER BOWL X
Orange Bowl, Miami, Florida
January 18, 1976, Attendance: 80,187
PITTSBURGH 21, DALLAS 17—The Steelers won the Super Bowl for the second year in a row on Terry Bradshaw's 64-yard touchdown pass to Lynn Swann and an aggressive defense that snuffed out a late rally by the Cowboys with an end-zone interception on the final play of the game. In the fourth quarter, Pittsburgh ran on fourth down and gave up the ball on the Cowboys' 39 with 1:22 to play. Roger Staubach ran and passed for 2 first downs but his last desperation pass was picked off by Glen Edwards. Dallas's scoring was the result of 2 touchdown passes by Staubach, one to Drew Pearson for 29 yards and the other to Percy Howard for 34 yards. Toni Fritsch had a 36-yard field goal. The Steelers scored on 2 touchdown passes by Bradshaw, 1 to Randy Grossman for 7 yards and the long bomb to Swann. Roy Gerela had 36- and 18-yard field goals. Reggie Harrison blocked a punt through the end zone for a safety. Swann set a Super Bowl record by gaining 161 yards on his 4 receptions.

Dallas (NFC)	7	3	0	7	— 17
Pittsburgh (AFC)	7	0	0	14	— 21

Dall — D. Pearson 29 pass from Staubach (Fritsch kick) (4:36)
Pitt — Grossman 7 pass from Bradshaw (Gerela kick) (9:03)
Dall — FG Fritsch 36 (0:15)
Pitt — Safety, Harrison blocked Hoopes's punt through end zone (3:32)
Pitt — FG Gerela 36 (6:19)
Pitt — FG Gerela 18 (8:23)
Pitt — Swann 64 pass from Bradshaw (kick failed) (11:58)
Dall — P. Howard 34 pass from Staubach (Fritsch kick) (13:12)

SUPER BOWL IX
Tulane Stadium, New Orleans, Louisiana
January 12, 1975, Attendance: 80,997
PITTSBURGH 16, MINNESOTA 6—AFC champion Pittsburgh, in its initial Super Bowl appearance, and NFC champion Minnesota, making a third bid for its first Super Bowl title, struggled through a first half in which the only score was produced by the Steelers' defense when Dwight White downed Vikings' quarterback Fran Tarkenton in the end zone for a safety 7:49 into the second period. The Steelers forced another break and took advantage on the second-half kickoff when Minnesota's Bill Brown fumbled and Marv Kellum recovered for Pittsburgh on the Vikings' 30. After Rocky Bleier failed to gain on first down, Franco Harris carried 3 consecutive times for 24 yards, a loss of 3, and a 9-yard touchdown and the 9-0 lead. Though its offense was completely stymied by Pittsburgh's defense, Minnesota managed to move into a threatening position after 4:27 of the final period when Matt Blair blocked Bobby Walden's punt and Terry Brown recovered the ball in the end zone for a touchdown. Fred Cox's kick failed and the Steelers led 9-6. Pittsburgh wasted no time putting the victory away. The Steelers took the ensuing kickoff and marched 66 yards in 11 plays, climaxed by Terry Bradshaw's 4-yard scoring pass to Larry Brown with 3:31 left. Pittsburgh's defense permitted Minnesota only 119 yards total offense, including a Super Bowl low of 17 rushing yards. The Steelers, meanwhile, gained 333 yards, including Harris's record 158 yards on 34 carries.

Pittsburgh (AFC)	0	2	7	7	— 16
Minnesota (NFC)	0	0	0	6	— 6

Pitt — Safety, White downed Tarkenton in end zone (7:49)
Pitt — Harris 9 run (Gerela kick) (1:35)
Minn — T. Brown recovered blocked punt in end zone (kick failed) (4:27)
Pitt — L. Brown 4 pass from Bradshaw (Gerela kick) (11:29)

SUPER BOWL VIII

Rice Stadium, Houston, Texas
January 13, 1974, Attendance: 71,882
MIAMI 24, MINNESOTA 7—The defending NFL champion Dolphins, representing the AFC for the third straight year, scored the first two times they had possession on marches of 62 and 56 yards while the Miami defense limited the Vikings to only seven plays in the first period. Larry Csonka climaxed the initial 10-play drive with a 5-yard touchdown bolt through right guard after 5:27 had elapsed. Four plays later, Miami began another 10-play scoring drive, which ended with Jim Kiick bursting 1 yard through the middle for another touchdown after 13:38 of the period. Garo Yepremian added a 28-yard field goal midway in the second period for a 17-0 Miami lead. Minnesota then drove from its 20 to a second-and-2 situation on the Miami 7 yard line with 1:18 left in the half. But on two plays, Miami limited Oscar Reed to 1 yard. On fourth-and-1 from the 6, Reed went over right tackle, but Dolphins middle linebacker Nick Buoniconti jarred the ball loose and Jake Scott recovered for Miami to halt the Minnesota threat. The Vikings were unable to muster enough offense in the second half to threaten the Dolphins. Csonka rushed 33 times for a Super Bowl-record 145 yards. Bob Griese of Miami completed 6 of 7 passes for 73 yards.

Minnesota (NFC)	0	0	0	7	—	7
Miami (AFC)	14	3	7	0	—	24

Mia — Csonka 5 run (Yepremian kick) (9:33)
Mia — Kiick 1 run (Yepremian kick) (13:38)
Mia — FG Yepremian 28 (8:58)
Mia — Csonka 2 run (Yepremian kick) (6:16)
Minn — Tarkenton 4 run (Cox kick) (1:35)

SUPER BOWL VII

Memorial Coliseum, Los Angeles, California
January 14, 1973, Attendance: 90,182
MIAMI 14, WASHINGTON 7—The Dolphins played virtually perfect football in the first half as their defense permitted the Redskins to cross midfield only once and their offense turned good field position into 2 touchdowns. On its third possession, Miami opened its first scoring drive from the Dolphins' 37 yard line. An 18-yard pass from Bob Griese to Paul Warfield preceded by three plays Griese's 28-yard touchdown pass to Howard Twilley. After Washington moved from its 17 to the Miami 48 with two minutes remaining in the first half, Dolphins linebacker Nick Buoniconti intercepted a Billy Kilmer pass at the Miami 41 and returned it to the Washington 27. Jim Kiick ran for 3 yards, Larry Csonka for 3, Griese passed to Jim Mandich for 19, and Kiick gained 1 to the 1-yard line. With 18 seconds left until intermission, Kiick scored from the 1. Washington's only touchdown came with 2:07 left in the game and resulted from a misplayed field-goal attempt and fumble by Garo Yepremian, with the Redskins' Mike Bass picking the ball out of the air and running 49 yards for the score. Dolphins safety Jake Scott, who had 2 interceptions, including 1 in the end zone to kill a Redskins' drive, was voted the game's most valuable player.

Miami (AFC)	7	7	0	0	—	14
Washington (NFC)	0	0	0	7	—	7

Mia — Twilley 28 pass from Griese (Yepremian kick) (14:59)
Mia — Kiick 1 run (Yepremian kick) (14:42)
Wash — Bass 49 fumble recovery return (Knight kick) (12:53)

SUPER BOWL VI

Tulane Stadium, New Orleans, Louisiana
January 16, 1972, Attendance: 81,023
DALLAS 24, MIAMI 3—The Cowboys rushed for a record 252 yards and their defense limited the Dolphins to a low of 185 yards while not permitting a touchdown for the first time in Super Bowl history. Dallas converted Chuck Howley's recovery of Larry Csonka's first fumble of the season into a 3-0 advantage and led at halftime 10-3. After Dallas received the second-half kickoff, Duane Thomas led

a 71-yard march in eight plays for a 17-3 margin. Howley intercepted Bob Griese's pass at the 50 and returned it to the Miami 9 early in the fourth period, and three plays later Roger Staubach passed 7 yards to Mike Ditka for the final touchdown. Thomas rushed for 95 yards and Walt Garrison gained 74. Staubach, voted the game's most valuable player, completed 12 of 19 passes for 119 yards and 2 touchdowns.

Dallas (NFC)	3	7	7	7	—	24
Miami (AFC)	0	3	0	0	—	3

Dall — FG Clark 9 (13:37)
Dall — Alworth 7 pass from Staubach (Clark kick) (13:45)
Mia — FG Yepremian 31 (14:56)
Dall — D. Thomas 3 run (Clark kick) (5:17)
Dall — Ditka 7 pass from Staubach (Clark kick) (3:18)

SUPER BOWL V

Orange Bowl, Miami, Florida
January 17, 1971, Attendance: 79,204
BALTIMORE 16, DALLAS 13—A 32-yard field goal by rookie kicker Jim O'Brien brought the Baltimore Colts a victory over the Dallas Cowboys in the final five seconds of Super Bowl V. The game between the champions of the AFC and NFC was played on artificial turf for the first time. Dallas led13-6 at the half but interceptions by Rick Volk and Mike Curtis set up a Baltimore touchdown and O'Brien's decisive kick in the fourth period. Earl Morrall relieved an injured Johnny Unitas late in the firsthalf, although Unitas completed the Colts' only scoring pass. It caromed off receiver Eddie Hinton's fingertips, off Dallas defensive back Mel Renfro, and finally settled into the grasp of John Mackey, who went 45 yards to score on a 75-yard play.

Baltimore (AFC)	0	6	0	10	—	16
Dallas (NFC)	3	10	0	0	—	13

Dall — FG Clark 14 (9:28)
Dall — FG Clark 30 (0:08)
Balt — Mackey 75 pass from Unitas (kick blocked) (0:05)
Dall — Thomas 7 pass from Morton (Clark kick) (7:07)
Balt — Nowatzke 2 run (O'Brien kick) (7:25)
Balt — FG O'Brien 32 (14:55)

SUPER BOWL IV

Tulane Stadium, New Orleans, Louisiana
January 11, 1970, Attendance: 80,562
KANSAS CITY 23, MINNESOTA 7—The AFL squared the Super Bowl at two games apiece with the NFL, building a 16-0 halftime lead behind Len Dawson's superb quarterbacking and a powerful defense. Dawson, the fourth consecutive quarterback to be chosen the Super Bowl's top player, called an almost flawless game, completing 12 of 17 passes and hitting Otis Taylor on a 46-yard play for the final Chiefs touchdown. The Kansas City defense limited Minnesota's strong rushing game to 67 yards and had 3 interceptions and 2 fumble recoveries. The crowd of 80,562 set a Super Bowl record, as did the gross receipts of $3,817,872.69.

Minnesota (NFL)	0	0	7	0	—	7
Kansas City (AFL)	3	13	7	0	—	23

KC — FG Stenerud 48 (8:08)
KC — FG Stenerud 32 (1:40)
KC — FG Stenerud 25 (7:08)
KC — Garrett 5 run (Stenerud kick) (9:26)
Minn — Osborn 4 run (Cox kick) (10:28)
KC — Taylor 46 pass from Dawson (Stenerud kick) (13:38)

SUPER BOWL III

Orange Bowl, Miami, Florida
January 12, 1969, Attendance: 75,389
NEW YORK JETS 16, BALTIMORE 7—Jets quarterback Joe Namath "guaranteed" victory on the Thursday before the game, then went out and led the AFL to its first Super Bowl victory over a Baltimore team that had lost only once in 16 games all season. Namath, chosen the outstanding player, completed 17 of 28 passes for 206 yards and directed a steady attack that dominated the NFL champions after the

Jets' defense had intercepted Colts quarterback Earl Morrall 3 times in the first half. The Jets had 337 total yards, including 121 rushing yards by Matt Snell. Johnny Unitas, who had missed most of the season with a sore elbow, came off the bench and led Baltimore to its only touchdown late in the fourth quarter after New York led 16-0.

New York Jets (AFL)	0	7	6	3	—	16
Baltimore (NFL)	0	0	0	7	—	7

NYJ — Snell 4 run (Turner kick) (5:57)
NYJ — FG Turner 32 (4:52)
NYJ — FG Turner 30 (11:02)
NYJ — FG Turner 9 (1:34)
Balt — Hill 1 run (Michaels kick) (11:41)

SUPER BOWL II

Orange Bowl, Miami, Florida
January 14, 1968, Attendance: 75,546
GREEN BAY 33, OAKLAND 14—Green Bay, after winning its third consecutive NFL championship, won the Super Bowl title for the second straight year, defeating the AFL champion Raiders in a game that drew the first $3-million gate in football history. Bart Starr again was chosen the game's most valuable player as he completed 13 of 24 passes for 202 yards and 1 touchdown and directed a Packers attack that was in control all the way after building a 16-7 halftime lead. Don Chandler kicked 4 field goals and all-pro cornerback Herb Adderley capped the Green Bay scoring with a 60-yard interception return. The game marked the last for Vince Lombardi as Packers coach, ending nine years at Green Bay in which he won six Western Conference championships, five NFL championships, and two Super Bowls.

Green Bay (NFL)	3	13	10	7	—	33
Oakland (AFL)	0	7	0	7	—	14

GB — FG Chandler 39 (5:07)
GB — FG Chandler 20 (3:08)
GB — Dowler 62 pass from Starr (Chandler kick) (4:10)
Oak — Miller 23 pass from Lamonica (Blanda kick) (8:45)
GB — FG Chandler 43 (14:59)
GB — Anderson 2 run (Chandler kick) (9:06)
GB — FG Chandler 31 (14:58)
GB — Adderley 60 interception return (Chandler kick) (3:57)
Oak — Miller 23 pass from Lamonica (Blanda kick) (5:47)

SUPER BOWL I

Memorial Coliseum, Los Angeles, California
January 15, 1967, Attendance: 61,946
GREEN BAY 35, KANSAS CITY 10—The Green Bay Packers opened the Super Bowl series by defeating the AFL champion Chiefs behind the passing of Bart Starr, the receiving of Max McGee, and a key interception by all-pro safety Willie Wood. Green Bay broke open the game with 3 second-half touchdowns, the first of which was set up by Wood's 50-yard return of an interception. McGee, filling in for ailing Boyd Dowler after having caught only 4 passes all season, caught 7 from Starr for 138 yards and 2 touchdowns. Elijah Pitts ran for two other scores. The Chiefs' 10 points came in the second quarter, the only touchdown on a 7-yard pass from Len Dawson to Curtis McClinton. Starr completed 16 of 23 passes for 250 yards and 2 touchdowns and was chosen the most valuable player. The Packers collected $15,000 per man and the Chiefs $7,500—the largest single-game shares in the history of team sports.

Kansas City (AFL)	0	10	0	0	—	10
Green Bay (NFL)	7	7	14	7	—	35

GB — McGee 37 pass from Starr (Chandler kick) (8:56)
KC — McClinton 7 pass from Dawson (Mercer kick) (4:20)
GB — Taylor 14 run (Chandler kick) (10:23)
KC — FG Mercer 31 (14:06)
GB — Pitts 5 run (Chandler kick) (2:27)
GB — McGee 13 pass from Starr (Chandler kick) (14:09)
GB — Pitts 1 run (Chandler kick) (8:25)

AFC CHAMPIONSHIP GAME RESULTS
Includes AFL Championship Games (1960-69)

Season	Date	Winner (Share)	Loser (Share)	Score	Site	Attendance
1996	Jan. 12	New England ($29,000)	Jacksonville ($29,000)	20-6	New England	60,190
1995	Jan. 14	Pittsburgh ($27,000)	Indianapolis ($27,000)	20-16	Pittsburgh	61,062
1994	Jan. 15	San Diego ($26,000)	Pittsburgh ($26,000)	17-13	Pittsburgh	61,545
1993	Jan. 23	Buffalo ($23,500)	Kansas City ($23,500)	30-13	Buffalo	76,642
1992	Jan. 17	Buffalo ($18,000)	Miami ($18,000)	29-10	Miami	72,703
1991	Jan. 12	Buffalo ($18,000)	Denver ($18,000)	10-7	Buffalo	80,272
1990	Jan. 20	Buffalo ($18,000)	L.A. Raiders ($18,000)	51-3	Buffalo	80,325
1989	Jan. 14	Denver ($18,000)	Cleveland ($18,000)	37-21	Denver	76,046
1988	Jan. 8	Cincinnati ($18,000)	Buffalo ($18,000)	21-10	Cincinnati	59,747
1987	Jan. 17	Denver ($18,000)	Cleveland ($18,000)	38-33	Denver	76,197
1986	Jan. 11	Denver ($18,000)	Cleveland ($18,000)	23-20*	Cleveland	79,973
1985	Jan. 12	New England ($18,000)	Miami ($18,000)	31-14	Miami	75,662
1984	Jan. 6	Miami ($18,000)	Pittsburgh ($18,000)	45-28	Miami	76,029
1983	Jan. 8	L.A. Raiders ($18,000)	Seattle ($18,000)	30-14	Los Angeles	91,445
1982	Jan. 23	Miami ($18,000)	N.Y. Jets ($18,000)	14-0	Miami	67,396
1981	Jan. 10	Cincinnati ($9,000)	San Diego ($9,000)	27-7	Cincinnati	46,302
1980	Jan. 11	Oakland ($9,000)	San Diego ($9,000)	34-27	San Diego	52,675
1979	Jan. 6	Pittsburgh ($9,000)	Houston ($9,000)	27-13	Pittsburgh	50,475
1978	Jan. 7	Pittsburgh ($9,000)	Houston ($9,000)	34-5	Pittsburgh	50,725
1977	Jan. 1	Denver ($9,000)	Oakland ($9,000)	20-17	Denver	75,044
1976	Dec. 26	Oakland ($8,500)	Pittsburgh ($5,500)	24-7	Oakland	53,821
1975	Jan. 4	Pittsburgh ($8,500)	Oakland ($5,500)	16-10	Pittsburgh	50,609
1974	Dec. 29	Pittsburgh ($8,500)	Oakland ($5,500)	24-13	Oakland	53,800
1973	Dec. 30	Miami ($8,500)	Oakland ($5,500)	27-10	Miami	79,325
1972	Dec. 31	Miami ($8,500)	Pittsburgh ($5,500)	21-17	Pittsburgh	50,845
1971	Jan. 2	Miami ($8,500)	Baltimore ($5,500)	21-0	Miami	76,622
1970	Jan. 3	Baltimore ($8,500)	Oakland ($5,500)	27-17	Baltimore	54,799
1969	Jan. 4	Kansas City ($7,755)	Oakland ($6,252)	17-7	Oakland	53,564
1968	Dec. 29	N.Y. Jets ($7,007)	Oakland ($5,349)	27-23	New York	62,627
1967	Dec. 31	Oakland ($6,321)	Houston ($4,996)	40-7	Oakland	53,330
1966	Jan. 1	Kansas City ($5,309)	Buffalo ($3,799)	31-7	Buffalo	42,080
1965	Dec. 26	Buffalo ($5,189)	San Diego ($3,447)	23-0	San Diego	30,361
1964	Dec. 26	Buffalo ($2,668)	San Diego ($1,738)	20-7	Buffalo	40,242
1963	Jan. 5	San Diego ($2,498)	Boston ($1,596)	51-10	San Diego	30,127
1962	Dec. 23	Dallas ($2,206)	Houston ($1,471)	20-17*	Houston	37,981
1961	Dec. 24	Houston ($1,792)	San Diego ($1,111)	10-3	San Diego	29,556
1960	Jan. 1	Houston ($1,025)	L.A. Chargers ($718)	24-16	Houston	32,183

Sudden death overtime.

AFC CHAMPIONSHIP GAME COMPOSITE STANDINGS

	W	L	Pct.	Pts.	OP
Cincinnati Bengals	2	0	1.000	48	17
Denver Broncos	4	1	.800	125	101
Buffalo Bills	6	2	.750	180	92
Kansas City Chiefs*	3	1	.750	81	61
Miami Dolphins	5	2	.714	152	115
New England Patriots**	2	1	.667	61	71
Pittsburgh Steelers	5	4	.556	186	164
New York Jets	1	1	.500	27	37
Tennessee Oilers##	2	4	.333	76	140
Indianapolis Colts#	1	2	.333	43	58
Oakland/L.A. Raiders	4	8	.333	228	264
San Diego Chargers***	2	6	.250	128	161
Jacksonville Jaguars	0	1	.000	6	20
Seattle Seahawks	0	1	.000	14	30
Cleveland Browns	0	3	.000	74	98

One game played when franchise was in Dallas (Texans). (Won 20-17)

**One game played when franchise was in Boston. (Lost 51-10)*

***One game played when franchise was in Los Angeles. (Lost 24-16)*

#Two games played when franchise was in Baltimore. (Won 27-17, lost 21-0)*

##Six games played when franchise was in Houston. (Won 2, lost 4)*

1996 AFC CHAMPIONSHIP GAME

Foxboro Stadium, Foxboro, Massachusetts
Attendance: 60,190

NEW ENGLAND 20, JACKSONVILLE 6—Otis Smith's 47-yard fumble return with 2:24 remaining gave the Patriots their second Super Bowl berth in franchise history. The Patriots received a couple big plays from their special teams. Jacksonville punted after its opening possession, but the snap was high. Larry Whigham tackled the scrambling Bryan Barker at the 4-yard line, setting up Curtis Martin's 1-yard touchdown. After a Jacksonville field goal, Ray Lucas stripped punt returner Chris Hudson of the ball. Mike Bartrum recovered it at the 20-yard line, and Adam Vinatieri kicked a 29-yard field goal to put New England ahead 10-3. Shawn Jefferson hauled in a 38-yard pass to the Jaguars' 2-yard line with eight seconds left before halftime after Ben Coates's 5-yard reception on fourth-and-2 kept a Patriots' drive alive. Vinatieri's field goal gave the Patriots a 10-point cushion. Eddie Robinson's fumble recovery led to Mike Hollis's 28-yard field goal to pull the Jaguars within 7 points. In the fourth quarter the Jaguars drove to the Patriots' 5-yard line, but Willie Clay intercepted Mark Brunell's pass in the end zone with 3:43 left to preserve the 13-6 lead. The Jaguars forced New England to punt, and Jacksonville got the ball on their own 42-yard line with 2:36 to play. However, Chris Slade stripped James Stewart of the ball, knocking it into Smith's hands. Smith streaked down the right sideline for the score. Tedy Bruschi intercepted Brunell near midfield to quell the Jaguars' third consecutive upset bid.

Jacksonville (6)	Offense	New England (20)
Jimmy Smith	WR-TE	John Burke
Tony Boselli	LT	Bruce Armstrong
Ben Coleman	LG	William Roberts
Dave Widell	C	Dave Wohlabaugh
Rich Tylski	RG	Todd Rucci
Leon Searcy	RT	Max Lane
Derek Brown	TE	Ben Coates
Keenan McCardell	WR-TE	Keith Byars
Mark Brunell	QB	Drew Bledsoe
Natrone Means	RB	Curtis Martin
Pete Mitchell	TE-RB	Marrio Grier
	Defense	
Tony Brackens	DE	Ferric Collons
Clyde Simmons	DT	Mark Wheeler
Paul Frase	NT-DT	Pio Sagapolutele
Don Davey	DT-DE	Willie McGinest
John Jurkovic	DT-LLB	Chris Slade
Jeff Lageman	DE-MLB	Ted Johnson
Brant Boyer	LB-RLB	Todd Collins
Tom McManus	LB-LCB	Ty Law
Robert Massey	DB-RCB	Otis Smith
Dana Hall	SS	Lawyer Milloy
Travis Davis	FS	Willie Clay

SUBSTITUTIONS

Jacksonville—Offense: K—Mike Hollis. P—Bryan Barker. RB—Randy Jordan, Le' Shai Maston, James Stewart. WR—Reggie Barlow, Willie Jackson. TE—Rich Griffith. G—Brian DeMarco. Defense: DT—Kelvin Pritchett. LB—Ty Hallock, Kevin Hardy, Jeff Kopp, Eddie Robinson. CB—Aaron Beasley, Ricky Bell, Bucky Brooks, Mickey Washington. S—Chris Hudson, Darren Studstill. DNP: QB—Rob Johnson. G—Jeff Novak. C—Michael Cheever.

New England—Offense: K—Adam Vinatieri. P—Tom Tupa. RB—David Meggett. WR—Vincent Brisby, Troy Brown, Terry Glenn, Shawn Jefferson, Ray Lucas. TE—Mike Bartrum. G—Bob Kratch. C—Mike Gisler. Defense: DE—Mike Jones, Chris Sullivan. DT—Chad Eaton. LB—Tedy Bruschi, Marty Moore, Dwayne Sabb. CB—Jerome Henderson, Mike McGruder. S—Corwin Brown, Terry Ray, Larry Whigham. DNP: CB—Ricky Reynolds.

OFFICIALS

Referee—Jerry Markbreit. Umpire—Ed Coukart. Head Linesman—George Hayward. Line Judge—Larry Upson. Back Judge—Jim Daopoulos. Field Judge—Don Hakes. Side Judge—Bill Carollo.

SCORING

Jacksonville	0	3	3	0	— 6
New England	7	6	0	7	— 20

NE — Martin 1 run (Vinatieri kick)
Jax — FG Hollis 32
NE — FG Vinatieri 29
NE — FG Vinatieri 20
Jax — FG Hollis 28
NE — Smith 47 fumble return (Vinatieri kick)

337

TEAM STATISTICS	Jax	NE
Total First Downs	18	13
Rushing	6	6
Passing	12	7
Penalty	0	0
Total Net Yardage	289	234
Total Offensive Plays	72	59
Average Gain per Offensive Play	4.0	4.0
Rushes	33	24
Yards Gained Rushing (Net)	101	73
Average Yards per Rush	3.1	3.0
Passes Attempted	38	33
Passes Completed	20	20
Had Intercepted	2	1
Tackled Attempting to Pass	1	2
Yards Lost Attempting to Pass	2	17
Yards Gained Passing (Net)	188	161
Punts	5	6
Average Distance	36.4	39.7
Punt Returns	4	3
Punt Return Yardage	15	29
Kickoff Returns	4	3
Kickoff Return Yardage	69	52
Interception Return Yardage	15	12
Total Return Yardage	99	93
Fumbles	3	2
Own Fumbles Recovered	1	1
Opponents Fumbles Recovered	1	2
Penalties	4	2
Yards Penalized	23	5
Field Goals	2	2
Field Goals Attempted	2	3
Third-Down Efficiency	5/14	2/13
Fourth-Down Efficiency	0/2	1/2
Time of Possession	34:43	25:17

INDIVIDUAL STATISTICS
RUSHING: JAX: Means 19-43, Stewart 7-40, Brunell 6-34, Barker 1-(-16). NE: Martin 19-59, Meggett 3-9, Bledsoe 1-4, Byars 1-1.
PASSING: JAX: Brunell 20-38-190-2. NE: Bledsoe 20-33-178-1.
RECEIVING: JAX: Mitchell 7-63, McCardell 6-62, Smith 3-45, Brown 1-10, Stewart 2-8, Barlow 1-2. NE: Jefferson 4-91, Glenn 5-33, Martin 3-18, Byars 4-16, Meggett 3-15, Coates 1-5.
KICKOFF RETURNS: JAX: Brooks 4-69. NE: Meggett 3-52.
PUNT RETURNS: JAX: Hudson 4-15. NE: Meggett 3-29.
PUNTING: JAX: Barker 5-182-36.4. NE: Tupa 6-238-39.7.
INTERCEPTIONS: JAX: Beasley 1-15. NE: Bruschi 1-12, Clay 1-0.
SACKS: JAX: Davey 1, Robinson 0.5, Simmons 0.5. NE: Slade 1.

NFC CHAMPIONSHIP GAME RESULTS
Includes NFL Championship Games (1933-69)

Season	Date	Winner (Share)	Loser (Share)	Score	Site	Attendance
1996	Jan. 12	Green Bay ($29,000)	Carolina ($29,000)	30-13	Green Bay	60,216
1995	Jan. 14	Dallas ($27,000)	Green Bay ($27,000)	38-27	Dallas	65,135
1994	Jan. 15	San Francisco ($26,000)	Dallas ($26,000)	38-28	San Francisco	69,125
1993	Jan. 23	Dallas ($23,500)	San Francisco ($23,500)	38-21	Dallas	64,902
1992	Jan. 17	Dallas ($18,000)	San Francisco ($18,000)	30-20	San Francisco	64,920
1991	Jan. 12	Washington ($18,000)	Detroit ($18,000)	41-10	Washington	55,585
1990	Jan. 20	N.Y. Giants ($18,000)	San Francisco ($18,000)	15-13	San Francisco	65,750
1989	Jan. 14	San Francisco ($18,000)	L.A. Rams ($18,000)	30-3	San Francisco	65,634
1988	Jan. 8	San Francisco ($18,000)	Chicago ($18,000)	28-3	Chicago	66,946
1987	Jan. 17	Washington ($18,000)	Minnesota ($18,000)	17-10	Washington	55,212
1986	Jan. 11	New York Giants ($18,000)	Washington ($18,000)	17-0	East Rutherford	76,891
1985	Jan. 12	Chicago ($18,000)	L.A. Rams ($18,000)	24-0	Chicago	66,030
1984	Jan. 6	San Francisco ($18,000)	Chicago ($18,000)	23-0	San Francisco	61,336
1983	Jan. 8	Washington ($18,000)	San Francisco ($18,000)	24-21	Washington	55,363
1982	Jan. 22	Washington ($18,000)	Dallas ($18,000)	31-17	Washington	55,045
1981	Jan. 10	San Francisco ($9,000)	Dallas ($9,000)	28-27	San Francisco	60,525
1980	Jan. 11	Philadelphia ($9,000)	Dallas ($9,000)	20-7	Philadelphia	71,522
1979	Jan. 6	Los Angeles ($9,000)	Tampa Bay ($9,000)	9-0	Tampa Bay	72,033
1978	Jan. 7	Dallas ($9,000)	Los Angeles ($9,000)	28-0	Los Angeles	71,086
1977	Jan. 1	Dallas ($9,000)	Minnesota ($9,000)	23-6	Dallas	64,293
1976	Dec. 26	Minnesota ($8,500)	Los Angeles ($5,500)	24-13	Minnesota	48,379
1975	Jan. 4	Dallas ($8,500)	Los Angeles ($5,500)	37-7	Los Angeles	88,919
1974	Dec. 29	Minnesota ($8,500)	Los Angeles ($5,500)	14-10	Minnesota	48,444
1973	Dec. 30	Minnesota ($8,500)	Dallas ($5,500)	27-10	Dallas	64,422
1972	Dec. 31	Washington ($8,500)	Dallas ($5,500)	26-3	Washington	53,129
1971	Jan. 2	Dallas ($8,500)	San Francisco ($5,500)	14-3	Dallas	63,409
1970	Jan. 3	Dallas ($8,500)	San Francisco ($5,500)	17-10	San Francisco	59,364
1969	Jan. 4	Minnesota ($7,930)	Cleveland ($5,118)	27-7	Minnesota	46,503
1968	Dec. 29	Baltimore ($9,306)	Cleveland ($5,963)	34-0	Cleveland	78,410
1967	Dec. 31	Green Bay ($7,950)	Dallas ($5,299)	21-17	Green Bay	50,861
1966	Jan. 1	Green Bay ($9,813)	Dallas ($6,527)	34-27	Dallas	74,152
1965	Jan. 2	Green Bay ($7,819)	Cleveland ($5,288)	23-12	Green Bay	50,777
1964	Dec. 27	Cleveland ($8,052)	Baltimore ($5,571)	27-0	Cleveland	79,544
1963	Dec. 29	Chicago ($5,899)	New York ($4,218)	14-10	Chicago	45,801
1962	Dec. 30	Green Bay ($5,888)	New York ($4,166)	16-7	New York	64,892
1961	Dec. 31	Green Bay ($5,195)	New York ($3,339)	37-0	Green Bay	39,029
1960	Dec. 26	Philadelphia ($5,116)	Green Bay ($3,105)	17-13	Philadelphia	67,325
1959	Dec. 27	Baltimore ($4,674)	New York ($3,083)	31-16	Baltimore	57,545
1958	Dec. 28	Baltimore ($4,718)	New York ($3,111)	23-17*	New York	64,185
1957	Dec. 29	Detroit ($4,295)	Cleveland ($2,750)	59-14	Detroit	55,263
1956	Dec. 30	New York ($3,779)	Chi. Bears ($2,485)	47-7	New York	56,836
1955	Dec. 26	Cleveland ($3,508)	Los Angeles ($2,316)	38-14	Los Angeles	85,693
1954	Dec. 26	Cleveland ($2,478)	Detroit ($1,585)	56-10	Cleveland	43,827
1953	Dec. 27	Detroit ($2,424)	Cleveland ($1,654)	17-16	Detroit	54,577
1952	Dec. 28	Detroit ($2,274)	Cleveland ($1,712)	17-7	Cleveland	50,934
1951	Dec. 23	Los Angeles ($2,108)	Cleveland ($1,483)	24-17	Los Angeles	57,522
1950	Dec. 24	Cleveland ($1,113)	Los Angeles ($686)	30-28	Cleveland	29,751
1949	Dec. 18	Philadelphia ($1,094)	Los Angeles ($739)	14-0	Los Angeles	27,980
1948	Dec. 19	Philadelphia ($1,540)	Chi. Cardinals ($874)	7-0	Philadelphia	36,309
1947	Dec. 28	Chi. Cardinals ($1,132)	Philadelphia ($754)	28-21	Chicago	30,759
1946	Dec. 15	Chi. Bears ($1,975)	New York ($1,295)	24-14	New York	58,346
1945	Dec. 16	Cleveland ($1,469)	Washington ($902)	15-14	Cleveland	32,178
1944	Dec. 17	Green Bay ($1,449)	New York ($814)	14-7	New York	46,016
1943	Dec. 26	Chi. Bears ($1,146)	Washington ($765)	41-21	Chicago	34,320
1942	Dec. 13	Washington ($965)	Chi. Bears ($637)	14-6	Washington	36,006
1941	Dec. 21	Chi. Bears ($430)	New York ($288)	37-9	Chicago	13,341

Season	Date	Winner (Share)	Loser (Share)	Score	Site	Attendance
1940	Dec. 8	Chi. Bears ($873)	Washington ($606)	73-0	Washington	36,034
1939	Dec. 10	Green Bay ($703.97)	New York ($455.57)	27-0	Milwaukee	32,279
1938	Dec. 11	New York ($504.45)	Green Bay ($368.81)	23-17	New York	48,120
1937	Dec. 12	Washington ($225.90)	Chi. Bears ($127.78)	28-21	Chicago	15,870
1936	Dec. 13	Green Bay ($250)	Boston ($180)	21-6	New York	29,545
1935	Dec. 15	Detroit ($313.35)	New York ($200.20)	26-7	Detroit	15,000
1934	Dec. 9	New York ($621)	Chi. Bears ($414.02)	30-13	New York	35,059
1933	Dec. 17	Chi. Bears ($210.34)	New York ($140.22)	23-21	Chicago	26,000

*Sudden death overtime.

NFC CHAMPIONSHIP GAME COMPOSITE STANDINGS

	W	L	Pct.	Pts.	OP
Philadelphia Eagles	4	1	.800	79	48
Baltimore Colts	3	1	.750	88	60
Green Bay Packers	9	3	.750	280	167
Detroit Lions	4	2	.667	139	141
Minnesota Vikings	4	2	.667	108	80
Washington Redskins*	7	5	.583	222	255
Chicago Bears	7	6	.538	286	245
Dallas Cowboys	8	8	.500	361	319
Arizona Cardinals**	1	1	.500	28	28
San Francisco 49ers	5	6	.454	235	199
Cleveland Browns	4	7	.364	224	253
New York Giants	5	11	.313	240	322
St. Louis Rams***	3	9	.250	123	270
Carolina Panthers	0	1	.000	13	30
Tampa Bay Buccaneers	0	1	.000	0	9

*One game played when franchise was in Boston. (Lost 21-6)
**Both games played when franchise was in Chicago. (Won 28-21, lost 7-0)
***One game played when franchise was in Cleveland (Won 15-14), and 11 games when franchise was in Los Angeles (Won 2, lost 9, scored 108 points, allowed 256 points).

1996 NFC CHAMPIONSHIP GAME

Lambeau Field, Green Bay, Wisconsin
January 12, 1997, Attendance: 60,216
GREEN BAY 30, CAROLINA 13—Dorsey Levens combined for 205 total yards of offense, and Brett Favre threw 2 touchdown passes, as the Packers earned their first Super Bowl berth in twenty-nine years. With the wind chill fluctuating between 17- and 25-degrees below zero, the Panthers scored first. Sam Mills intercepted Favre and returned the ball to the 2-yard line, setting up Howard Griffith's touchdown catch. Levens broke off a 35-yard run on third-and-1 late in the first quarter, and then made a spectacular diving catch in the end zone to open the second quarter and tie the game. Lamar Lathon recovered a Favre fumble, setting up John Kasay's go-ahead field goal. Green Bay then scored twice in the final 48 seconds of the first half to turn the game's momentum. Antonio Freeman caught a 6-yard touchdown pass on third-and-3 after Andre Rison's 22-yard catch put the Packers in position. Tyrone Williams then made a diving interception on the Packers' 38-yard line with 35 seconds left in the half. Favre fired a 23-yard pass to Rison and 25-yard bullet to Freeman to set up Chris Jacke's field goal and give Green Bay a 17-10 halftime lead. After an exchange of field goals, Levens turned a screen pass into a 66-yard play, setting up Edgar Bennett's touchdown run. LeRoy Butler recovered Anthony Johnson's fumble on Carolina's next possession, and set up Jacke's last field goal. Green Bay had 201 rushing yards, outgained Carolina 479-251 in total yards, and dominated time of possession (38:03-21:57). The victory gave Green Bay a 9-0 postseason record at Lambeau Field.

Carolina (13)	Offense	Green Bay (30)
Willie Green	WR	Antonio Freeman
Matthew Campbell	LT	Bruce Wilkerson
Matt Elliott	LG	Aaron Taylor
Frank Garcia	C	Frank Winters
Greg Skrepenak	RG	Adam Timmerman
Norberto Garrido	RT	Earl Dotson
Wesley Walls	TE	Mark Chmura
Mark Carrier	WR	Andre Rison
Kerry Collins	QB	Brett Favre
Anthony Johnson	RB	Edgar Bennett
Howard Griffith	RB	William Henderson
Defense		
Mike Fox	DE	Reggie White
Greg Kragen	NT-DT	Santana Dotson
Gerald Williams	DE-DT	Gilbert Brown
Kevin Greene	LOLB-DE	Sean Jones
Sam Mills	LILB-LLB	Wayne Simmons
Carlton Bailey	RILB-MLB	Ron Cox
Lamar Lathon	ROLB-RLB	Brian Williams
Eric Davis	LCB	Craig Newsome
Tyrone Poole	RCB	Doug Evans
Brett Maxie	SS	LeRoy Butler
Pat Terrell	FS	Eugene Robinson

SUBSTITUTIONS

Carolina—Offense: K—John Kasay. P—Rohn Stark. RB—Scott Greene, Winslow Oliver. WR—Michael Bates, Raghib Ismail, Muhsin Muhammad, Dwight Stone. TE—Walter Rasby. T—Blake Brockermeyer. C—Mark Rodenhauser, Curtis Whitley. Defense: DE—Les Miller, Mark Thomas. LB—Myron Baker, Duane Bickett, Andre Royal. CB—Toi Cook, Rod Smith. S—Chad Cota, Damon Pieri. DNP: QB—Steve Beuerlein. CB—Steve Lofton.
Green Bay—Offense: K—Chris Jacke. P—Craig Hentrich. QB—Jim McMahon. RB—Travis Jervey, Calvin Jones, Dorsey Levens. WR—Don Beebe, Desmond Howard, Terry Mickens. TE—Keith Jackson, Jeff Thomason. G—Lindsay Knapp. C—Jeff Dellenbach. Defense: DE—Keith McKenzie, Gabe Wilkins. DT—Darius Holland. LB—Bernardo Harris, Lamont Hollinquest. CB—Tyrone Williams. S—Chris Hayes, Roderick Mullen, Mike Prior.

OFFICIALS

Referee—Bob McElwee. Umpire—Bob Boylston. Head Linesman—Tony Veteri. Line Judge—Ron Baynes. Back Judge—Al Jury. Field Judge—Bobby Skelton. Side Judge—Dean Look.

SCORING

Carolina	7	3	3	0	—	13
Green Bay	0	17	10	3	—	30

Car — Griffith 3 pass from Collins (Kasay kick)
GB — Levens 29 pass from Favre (Jacke kick)
Car — FG Kasay 22
GB — Freeman 6 pass from Favre (Jacke kick)
GB — FG Jacke 31
GB — FG Jacke 32
Car — FG Kasay 23
GB — Bennett 4 run (Jacke kick)
GB — FG Jacke 28

TEAM STATISTICS	Car	GB
Total First Downs	12	22
Rushing	1	10
Passing	11	12
Penalty	0	0
Total Net Yardage	251	479
Total Offensive Plays	53	75
Average Gain per Offensive Play	4.7	6.4
Rushes	14	45
Yards Gained Rushing (Net)	45	201
Average Yards per Rush	3.2	4.5
Passes Attempted	37	29
Passes Completed	19	19
Had Intercepted	2	1
Tackled Attempting to Pass	2	1
Yards Lost Attempting to Pass	9	14
Yards Gained Passing (Net)	206	278
Punts	5	2
Average Distance	36.0	36.0
Punt Returns	1	1
Punt Return Yardage	4	3
Kickoff Returns	7	4
Kickoff Return Yardage	86	104
Interception Return Yardage	10	35
Total Return Yardage	100	142
Fumbles	2	2
Own Fumbles Recovered	0	1
Opponents Fumbles Recovered	1	1
Penalties	4	5
Yards Penalized	25	45
Field Goals	2	3
Field Goals Attempted	2	4
Third-Down Efficiency	5/13	9/17
Fourth-Down Efficiency	0/0	1/1
Time of Possession	21:57	38:03

INDIVIDUAL STATISTICS

RUSHING: CAR: Johnson 11-31, Oliver 2-15, Collins 1-(-1). GB: Bennett 25-99, Levens 10-88, Favre 5-14, Henderson 1-0, McMahon 4-0.
PASSING: CAR: Collins 19-37-215-2. GB: Favre 19-29-292-1.
RECEIVING: CAR: Carrier 4-65, Green 5-51, Walls 3-33, Ismail 1-24, Griffith 4-23, Johnson 1-14, Oliver 1-5. GB: Levens 5-117, Rison 3-53, Freeman 4-43, Jackson 3-30, Beebe 1-29, Chmura 1-15, Bennett 2-5.
KICKOFF RETURNS: CAR: Bates 4-59, S. Greene 1-14, Oliver 1-13, Baker 1-0. GB: Howard 4-104.
PUNT RETURNS: CAR: Oliver 1-4. GB: Howard 1-3, Prior 0-0.
PUNTING: CAR: Stark 5-180-36.0. GB: Hentrich 2-72-36.0.
INTERCEPTIONS: CAR: Mills 1-10. GB: Newsome 1-35, T. Williams 1-0.
SACKS: CAR: Team 1. GB: McKenzie 1, Simmons 1.

AFC DIVISIONAL PLAYOFFS RESULTS

Includes Second-Round Playoff Games (1982), AFC Inter-Divisional Games (1969), and special playoff games to break ties for AFL Division Championships (1963, 1968)

Season	Date	Winner (Share)	Loser (Share)	Score	Site	Attendance
1996	Jan. 5	New England ($14,000)	Pittsburgh ($14,000)	28-3	New England	60,188
	Jan. 4	Jacksonville ($14,000)	Denver ($14,000)	30-27	Denver	75,678
1995	Jan. 7	Indianapolis ($13,000)	Kansas City ($13,000)	10-7	Kansas City	77,594
	Jan. 6	Pittsburgh ($13,000)	Buffalo ($13,000)	40-21	Pittsburgh	59,072
1994	Jan. 8	San Diego ($12,000)	Miami ($12,000)	22-21	San Diego	63,381
	Jan. 7	Pittsburgh ($12,000)	Cleveland ($12,000)	29-9	Pittsburgh	58,185
1993	Jan. 16	Kansas City ($12,000)	Houston ($12,000)	28-20	Houston	64,011
	Jan. 15	Buffalo ($12,000)	L.A. Raiders ($12,000)	29-23	Buffalo	61,923
1992	Jan. 10	Miami ($10,000)	San Diego ($10,000)	31-0	Miami	71,224
	Jan. 9	Buffalo ($10,000)	Pittsburgh ($10,000)	24-3	Pittsburgh	60,407
1991	Jan. 5	Buffalo ($10,000)	Kansas City ($10,000)	37-14	Buffalo	80,182
	Jan. 4	Denver ($10,000)	Houston ($10,000)	26-24	Denver	75,301
1990	Jan. 13	L.A. Raiders ($10,000)	Cincinnati ($10,000)	20-10	Los Angeles	92,045
	Jan. 12	Buffalo ($10,000)	Miami ($10,000)	44-34	Buffalo	77,087
1989	Jan. 7	Denver ($10,000)	Pittsburgh ($10,000)	24-23	Denver	75,477
	Jan. 6	Cleveland ($10,000)	Buffalo ($10,000)	34-30	Cleveland	78,921
1988	Jan. 1	Buffalo ($10,000)	Houston ($10,000)	17-10	Buffalo	79,532
	Dec. 31	Cincinnati ($10,000)	Seattle ($10,000)	21-13	Cincinnati	58,560
1987	Jan. 10	Denver ($10,000)	Houston ($10,000)	34-10	Denver	75,440
	Jan. 9	Cleveland ($10,000)	Indianapolis ($10,000)	38-21	Cleveland	79,372
1986	Jan. 4	Denver ($10,000)	New England ($10,000)	22-17	Denver	75,262
	Jan. 3	Cleveland ($10,000)	N.Y. Jets ($10,000)	23-20*	Cleveland	79,720
1985	Jan. 5	New England ($10,000)	L.A. Raiders ($10,000)	27-20	Los Angeles	87,163
	Jan. 4	Miami ($10,000)	Cleveland ($10,000)	24-21	Miami	74,667
1984	Dec. 30	Pittsburgh ($10,000)	Denver ($10,000)	24-17	Denver	74,981
	Dec. 29	Miami ($10,000)	Seattle ($10,000)	31-10	Miami	73,469
1983	Jan. 1	L.A. Raiders ($10,000)	Pittsburgh ($10,000)	38-10	Los Angeles	90,380
	Dec. 31	Seattle ($10,000)	Miami ($10,000)	27-20	Miami	74,136
1982	Jan. 16	Miami ($10,000)	San Diego ($10,000)	34-13	Miami	71,383
	Jan. 15	N.Y. Jets ($10,000)	L.A. Raiders ($10,000)	17-14	Los Angeles	90,038
1981	Jan. 3	Cincinnati ($5,000)	Buffalo ($5,000)	28-21	Cincinnati	55,420
	Jan. 2	San Diego ($5,000)	Miami ($5,000)	41-38*	Miami	73,735
1980	Jan. 4	Oakland ($5,000)	Cleveland ($5,000)	14-12	Cleveland	78,245
	Jan. 3	San Diego ($5,000)	Buffalo ($5,000)	20-14	San Diego	52,253
1979	Dec. 30	Pittsburgh ($5,000)	Miami ($5,000)	34-14	Pittsburgh	50,214
	Dec. 29	Houston ($5,000)	San Diego ($5,000)	17-14	San Diego	51,192
1978	Dec. 31	Houston ($5,000)	New England ($5,000)	31-14	New England	60,735
	Dec. 30	Pittsburgh ($5,000)	Denver ($5,000)	33-10	Pittsburgh	50,230
1977	Dec. 24	Oakland ($5,000)	Baltimore ($5,000)	37-31*	Baltimore	59,925
	Dec. 24	Denver ($5,000)	Pittsburgh ($5,000)	34-21	Denver	75,059
1976	Dec. 19	Pittsburgh ($)	Baltimore ($)	40-14	Baltimore	59,296
	Dec. 18	Oakland ($)	New England ($)	24-21	Oakland	53,050
1975	Dec. 28	Oakland ($)	Cincinnati ($)	31-28	Oakland	53,030
	Dec. 27	Pittsburgh ($)	Baltimore ($)	28-10	Pittsburgh	49,557
1974	Dec. 22	Pittsburgh ($)	Buffalo ($)	32-14	Pittsburgh	49,841
	Dec. 21	Oakland ($)	Miami ($)	28-26	Oakland	53,023
1973	Dec. 23	Miami ($)	Cincinnati ($)	34-16	Miami	78,928
	Dec. 22	Oakland ($)	Pittsburgh ($)	33-14	Oakland	52,646
1972	Dec. 24	Miami ($)	Cleveland ($)	20-14	Miami	78,916
	Dec. 23	Pittsburgh ($)	Oakland ($)	13-7	Pittsburgh	50,327
1971	Dec. 26	Baltimore ($)	Cleveland ($)	20-3	Cleveland	70,734
	Dec. 25	Miami ($)	Kansas City ($)	27-24*	Kansas City	45,822
1970	Dec. 27	Oakland ($)	Miami ($)	21-14	Oakland	52,594
	Dec. 26	Baltimore ($)	Cincinnati ($)	17-0	Baltimore	49,694
1969	Dec. 21	Oakland ($)	Houston ($)	56-7	Oakland	53,539
	Dec. 20	Kansas City ($)	N.Y. Jets ($)	13-6	New York	62,977
1968	Dec. 22	Oakland ($)	Kansas City ($)	41-6	Oakland	53,605
1963	Dec. 28	Boston ($)	Buffalo ($)	26-8	Buffalo	33,044

Sudden Death Overtime.

$ Players received 1/14 of annual salary for playoff appearances.

1996 AFC DIVISIONAL PLAYOFF GAMES

Foxboro Stadium, Foxboro, Massachusetts
January 12, 1997, Attendance: 60,188
NEW ENGLAND 28, PITTSBURGH 3—Curtis Martin scored three touchdowns and New England's defense stifled Pittsburgh as the Patriots routed the Steelers in the fog in Foxboro. The Patriots broke Pittsburgh's back on their first play from scrimmage as Terry Glenn beat Rod Woodson and, despite heavy fog, caught a 53-yard bomb from Drew Bledsoe. Martin scored on the next play to start the rout. The Patriots next drive lasted 1:59, finishing with Keith Byars's 34-yard touchdown off a screen pass. Martin then raced 78 yards up the right sideline to stake New England to a 21-0 second-quarter lead. The Steelers were forced to punt after each of their first seven possessions. Chad Brown's interception in Patriots' territory set up Norm Johnson's field goal. Martin capped his 166-yard rushing day by scoring on a 23-yard jaunt. Pittsburgh shuffled quarterbacks throughout the game, with Mike Tomczak completing 16 of 29 pass attempts for 110 yards and 2 interceptions, while Kordell Stewart finished a dreadful 0 for 10. Jerome Bettis, hampered by a groin injury, gained just 43 yards. Pittsburgh converted just 3 of 18 third-down opportunities.

Pittsburgh	0	0	3	0	—	3
New England	14	7	0	7	—	28

NE — Martin 2 run (Vinatieri kick)
NE — Byars 34 pass from Bledsoe (Vinatieri kick)
NE — Martin 78 run (Vinatieri kick)
Pitt — FG N. Johnson 29
NE — Martin 23 run (Vinatieri kick)

Mile High Stadium, Denver, Colorado
January 11, 1997, Attendance: 75,678
JACKSONVILLE 30, DENVER 27—Mark Brunell passed for 245 yards and 2 touchdowns to lead the Jaguars to their second consecutive postseason victory. The Broncos, who finished the season 8-0 at home and had home-field advantage throughout the playoffs, blew a 12-0 lead. After Vaughn Hebron's short run began the scoring, Clyde Simmons blocked the extra point attempt. The Broncos failed to convert the 2-point conversion following Shannon Sharpe's touchdown catch late in the first quarter. The Jaguars responded by scoring on their next six possessions. Natrone Means, who carried the ball 21 times for 140 yards, pulled the Jaguars within two points before Mike Hollis's 42-yard field goal with 10 seconds left in the half put Jacksonville ahead 13-12. Brunell, rolling to his left, lofted a perfectly placed 31-yard touchdown

pass to Keenan McCardell in the left corner of the end zone to put the Jaguars ahead 20-12. Jacksonville took 8 minutes, 32 seconds off the clock with its next possession, ending with Hollis's third field goal. The 17-play drive was kept alive when Michael Dean Perry failed to hustle off the field when the Jaguars were punting in a fourth-and-5 situation. Denver got the ball back with less than 11 minutes remaining, and Terrell Davis scored and tallied a 2-point conversion, to cut the deficit to 23-20. Jacksonville calmly marched down field, and Jimmy Smith caught a 16-yard touchdown pass on third-and-5 to put Jacksonville ahead

by 10 points with 3:39 remaining. John Elway quickly led the Broncos to another touchdown, with Ed Mc-Caffrey doing the honors with 1:50 left. However Le'Shai Maston recovered the onside kick and the Jaguars ended the Broncos postseason home-winning streak at 6 games. Neither team committed a turnover.

Jacksonville	0	13	7	10	— 30
Denver	12	0	0	15	— 27

Den — Hebron 1 run (kick blocked)
Den — Sharpe 18 pass from Elway (pass failed)
Jax — FG Hollis 46

Jax — Means 8 run (Hollis kick)
Jax — FG Hollis 42
Jax — McCardell 31 pass from Brunell (Hollis kick)
Jax — FG Hollis 22
Den — Davis 2 run (Davis run)
Jax — Smith 16 pass from Brunell (Hollis kick)
Den — McCaffrey 15 pass from Elway (Elam kick)

NFC DIVISIONAL PLAYOFFS RESULTS

Includes Second-Round Playoff Games (1982), NFL Conference Championship Games (1967-69), and special playoff games to break ties for NFL Division or Conference Championships (1941, 1943, 1947, 1950, 1952, 1957, 1958, 1965)

Season	Date	Winner (Share)	Loser (Share)	Score	Site	Attendance
1996	Jan. 5	Carolina ($14,000)	Dallas ($14,000)	26-17	Carolina	72,808
	Jan. 4	Green Bay ($14,000)	San Francisco ($14,000)	35-14	Green Bay	60,787
1995	Jan. 7	Dallas ($13,000)	Philadelphia ($13,000)	30-11	Dallas	64,371
	Jan. 6	Green Bay ($13,000)	San Francisco ($13,000)	27-17	San Francisco	69,311
1994	Jan. 8	Dallas ($12,000)	Green Bay ($12,000)	35-9	Dallas	64,745
	Jan. 7	San Francisco ($12,000)	Chicago ($12,000)	44-15	San Francisco	64,644
1993	Jan. 16	Dallas ($12,000)	Green Bay ($12,000)	27-17	Dallas	64,790
	Jan. 15	San Francisco ($12,000)	N.Y. Giants ($12,000)	44-3	San Francisco	67,143
1992	Jan. 10	Dallas ($10,000)	Philadelphia ($10,000)	34-10	Dallas	63,721
	Jan. 9	San Francisco ($10,000)	Washington ($10,000)	20-13	San Francisco	64,991
1991	Jan. 5	Detroit ($10,000)	Dallas ($10,000)	38-6	Detroit	78,290
	Jan. 4	Washington ($10,000)	Atlanta ($10,000)	24-7	Washington	55,181
1990	Jan. 13	N.Y. Giants ($10,000)	Chicago ($10,000)	31-3	East Rutherford	77,025
	Jan. 12	San Francisco ($10,000)	Washington ($10,000)	28-10	San Francisco	65,292
1989	Jan. 7	L.A. Rams ($10,000)	N.Y. Giants ($10,000)	19-13*	East Rutherford	76,526
	Jan. 6	San Francisco ($10,000)	Minnesota ($10,000)	41-13	San Francisco	64,918
1988	Jan. 1	San Francisco ($10,000)	Minnesota ($10,000)	34-9	San Francisco	61,848
	Dec. 31	Chicago ($10,000)	Philadelphia ($10,000)	20-12	Chicago	65,534
1987	Jan. 10	Washington ($10,000)	Chicago ($10,000)	21-17	Chicago	65,268
	Jan. 9	Minnesota ($10,000)	San Francisco ($10,000)	36-24	San Francisco	63,008
1986	Jan. 4	N.Y. Giants ($10,000)	San Francisco ($10,000)	49-3	East Rutherford	75,691
	Jan. 3	Washington ($10,000)	Chicago ($10,000)	27-13	Chicago	65,524
1985	Jan. 5	Chicago ($10,000)	N.Y. Giants ($10,000)	21-0	Chicago	65,670
	Jan. 4	L.A. Rams ($10,000)	Dallas ($10,000)	20-0	Anaheim	66,581
1984	Dec. 30	Chicago ($10,000)	Washington ($10,000)	23-19	Washington	55,431
	Dec. 29	San Francisco ($10,000)	N.Y. Giants ($10,000)	21-10	San Francisco	60,303
1983	Jan. 1	Washington ($10,000)	L.A. Rams ($10,000)	51-7	Washington	54,440
	Dec. 31	San Francisco ($10,000)	Detroit ($10,000)	24-23	San Francisco	59,979
1982	Jan. 16	Dallas ($10,000)	Green Bay ($10,000)	37-26	Dallas	63,972
	Jan. 15	Washington ($10,000)	Minnesota ($10,000)	21-7	Washington	54,593
1981	Jan. 3	San Francisco ($5,000)	N.Y. Giants ($5,000)	38-24	San Francisco	58,360
	Jan. 2	Dallas ($5,000)	Tampa Bay ($5,000)	38-0	Dallas	64,848
1980	Jan. 4	Dallas ($5,000)	Atlanta ($5,000)	30-27	Atlanta	59,793
	Jan. 3	Philadelphia ($5,000)	Minnesota ($5,000)	31-16	Philadelphia	70,178
1979	Dec. 30	Los Angeles ($5,000)	Dallas ($5,000)	21-19	Dallas	64,792
	Dec. 29	Tampa Bay ($5,000)	Philadelphia ($5,000)	24-17	Tampa Bay	71,402
1978	Dec. 31	Los Angeles ($5,000)	Minnesota ($5,000)	34-10	Los Angeles	70,436
	Dec. 30	Dallas ($5,000)	Atlanta ($5,000)	27-20	Dallas	63,406
1977	Dec. 26	Dallas ($5,000)	Chicago ($5,000)	37-7	Dallas	63,260
	Dec. 26	Minnesota ($5,000)	Los Angeles ($5,000)	14-7	Los Angeles	70,203
1976	Dec. 19	Los Angeles ($)	Dallas ($)	14-12	Dallas	63,283
	Dec. 18	Minnesota ($)	Washington ($)	35-20	Minnesota	47,466
1975	Dec. 28	Dallas ($)	Minnesota ($)	17-14	Minnesota	48,050
	Dec. 27	Los Angeles ($)	St. Louis ($)	35-23	Los Angeles	73,459
1974	Dec. 22	Los Angeles ($)	Washington ($)	19-10	Los Angeles	77,925
	Dec. 21	Minnesota ($)	St. Louis ($)	30-14	Minnesota	48,150
1973	Dec. 23	Dallas ($)	Los Angeles ($)	27-16	Dallas	63,272
	Dec. 22	Minnesota ($)	Washington ($)	27-20	Minnesota	48,040
1972	Dec. 24	Washington ($)	Green Bay ($)	16-3	Washington	52,321
	Dec. 23	Dallas ($)	San Francisco ($)	30-28	San Francisco	59,746
1971	Dec. 26	San Francisco ($)	Washington ($)	24-20	San Francisco	45,327
	Dec. 25	Dallas ($)	Minnesota ($)	20-12	Minnesota	47,307
1970	Dec. 27	San Francisco ($)	Minnesota ($)	17-14	Minnesota	45,103
	Dec. 26	Dallas ($)	Detroit ($)	5-0	Dallas	69,613
1969	Dec. 28	Cleveland ($)	Dallas ($)	38-14	Dallas	69,321
	Dec. 27	Minnesota ($)	Los Angeles ($)	23-20	Minnesota	47,900
1968	Dec. 22	Baltimore ($)	Minnesota ($)	24-14	Baltimore	60,238
	Dec. 21	Cleveland ($)	Dallas ($)	31-20	Cleveland	81,497
1967	Dec. 24	Dallas ($)	Cleveland ($)	52-14	Dallas	70,786
	Dec. 23	Green Bay ($)	Los Angeles ($)	28-7	Milwaukee	49,861
1965	Dec. 26	Green Bay ($)	Baltimore ($)	13-10*	Green Bay	50,484
1958	Dec. 21	N.Y. Giants (#)	Cleveland (#)	10-0	New York	61,274
1957	Dec. 22	Detroit (#)	San Francisco (#)	31-27	San Francisco	60,118
1952	Dec. 21	Detroit (#)	Los Angeles (#)	31-21	Detroit	47,645
1950	Dec. 17	Los Angeles (#)	Chicago Bears (#)	24-14	Los Angeles	83,501
	Dec. 17	Cleveland (#)	N.Y. Giants (#)	8-3	Cleveland	33,054

PLAYOFF GAMES SUMMARIES

1947	Dec. 21	Philadelphia (#)	Pittsburgh (#)	21-0	Pittsburgh	35,729
1943	Dec. 19	Washington (¢)	N.Y. Giants (¢)	28-0	New York	42,800
1941	Dec. 14	Chicago Bears (¢)	Green Bay (¢)	33-14	Chicago	43,425

* *Sudden Death Overtime.*
$ *Players received 1/14 of annual salary for playoff appearances.*
\# *Players received 1/12 of annual salary for playoff appearances.*
¢ *Players received 1/10 of annual salary for playoff appearances.*

1996 NFC DIVISIONAL PLAYOFF GAMES

Ericsson Stadium, Charlotte, North Carolina
January 5, 1997, Attendance: 72,808
CAROLINA 26, DALLAS 17—The Panthers defense intercepted 3 passes, and John Kasay booted 4 field goals, as Carolina won its first playoff game in franchise history. Dallas, which had won the Super Bowl three of the previous four years, scored on its first possession and went ahead 3-0 on Chris Boniol's field goal. However, the scoring drive was costly because Michael Irvin separated his shoulder making a 23-yard catch and missed the remainder of the game. Carolina responded with a 68-yard scoring drive, keyed by two Cowboys' penalties, and took the lead on Wesley Walls's touchdown catch. After forcing a punt, Collins threw his second touchdown pass, this one to Willie Green, to put the Panthers ahead 14-3. Dallas put its best drive of the game together, with Daryl Johnston's touchdown catch ending the 15-play, eight-minute, 21 second drive. A bad snap over Rohn Stark's head and through the end zone on the following possession pulled Dallas within three points and gave them momentum. However, Chad Cota's interception and 49-yard return set up Kasay's 24-yard field goal three seconds before halftime giving the Panthers a 17-11 lead. Four second-half field goals, 2 by each team, gave the Panthers a 23-17 lead. Dallas got the ball back on a Carolina punt, but with poor field position after Dwight Stone downed it at the 2-yard line. Just as the Cowboys were mounting a possible game-winning drive, Pat Terrell intercepted Aikman and returned the ball 49 yards to set up Kasay's final field goal. Sam Mills's interception in the final minute iced the game. Johnson totaled 104 yards, the first 100-yard rushing game by a Cowboys playoff opponent since Eric Dickerson in 1985.

Dallas	3	8	3	3	— 17
Carolina	7	10	3	6	— 26

Car — Walls 1 pass from Collins (Kasay kick)
Car — W. Green 10 pass from Collins (Kasay kick)
Dall — Johnston 2 pass from Aikman (pass failed)
Dall — Safety, Carolina bad snap on punt went out of end zone
Car — FG Kasay 24
Dall — FG Boniol 21
Car — FG Kasay 40
Car — FG Kasay 40
Dall — FG Boniol 21
Car — FG Kasay 32

Lambeau Field, Green Bay, Wisconsin
January 4, 1997, Attendance: 60,787
GREEN BAY 35, SAN FRANCISCO 14—Desmond Howard had two big punt returns, one for a touchdown and one to set up another, and Edgar Bennett scored twice to lead the Packers to victory at muddy Lambeau Field. Howard's 71-yard punt return for a touchdown 2:15 into the game gave the Packers an early lead. A 46-yard punt return by Howard set up Andre Rison's touchdown catch, Bennett completed a short 15-yard drive, set up by Craig Newsome's interception, with a touchdown to give Green Bay a commanding 21-0 advantage. Two careless turnovers brought the 49ers back into the game. Chris Hayes had a 49ers punt bounce off his foot. Curtis Buckley recovered the ball and Terry Kirby scored 24 seconds before halftime. As Green Bay prepared to receive the opening kickoff to the second half, Howard still was in the locker room changing his pants. Andre Rison ran onto the field as the ball was kicked. Steve Israel beat Rison to the ball, giving the 49ers possession at the 4-yard line. Elvis Grbac's 2-yard run cut the deficit to 21-14. The Packers responded with a long drive, but chaos ensued as they were about to score. Bennett, in his effort to break the end zone plane with the ball, fumbled at the goal line, causing a pileup in the end zone. After sifting through bodies, the referees ruled Antonio Freeman had recovered the ball for a touchdown. Bennett scored the game's final points after Kirby fumbled a punt return at his own 32-yard line. Brett Favre, tempered by the poor weather conditions, attempted just 15 passes, completing 11 for 79 yards. Grbac, who came in during the first quarter after Steve Young's bruised ribs inhibited his performance, completed 19 of 36 passes for 125 yards, 1 touchdown, and 3 interceptions. The teams combined for just 404 total yards and 6 turnovers.

San Francisco	0	7	7	0	— 14
Green Bay	14	7	7	7	— 35

GB — Howard 71 punt return (Jacke kick)
GB — Rison 4 pass from Favre (Jacke kick)
GB — Bennett 2 run (Jacke kick)
SF — Kirby 8 pass from Grbac (Wilkins kick)
SF — Grbac 2 run (Wilkins kick)
GB — Freeman recovered fumble in end zone (Jacke kick)
GB — Bennett 11 run (Jacke kick)

AFC WILD CARD PLAYOFF GAMES RESULTS

Season	Date	Winner (Share)	Loser (Share)	Score	Site	Attendance
1996	Dec. 29	Pittsburgh ($14,000)	Indianapolis ($10,000)	42-14	Pittsburgh	58,078
	Dec. 28	Jacksonville ($10,000)	Buffalo ($10,000)	30-27	Buffalo	70,213
1995	Dec. 31	Indianapolis ($7,500)	San Diego ($7,500)	35-20	San Diego	61,182
	Dec. 30	Buffalo ($13,000)	Miami ($7,500)	37-22	Buffalo	73,103
1994	Jan. 1	Cleveland ($7,500)	New England ($7,500)	20-13	Cleveland	77,452
	Dec. 31	Miami ($12,000)	Kansas City ($7,500)	27-17	Miami	67,487
1993	Jan. 9	L.A. Raiders ($7,500)	Denver ($7,500)	42-24	Los Angeles	65,314
	Jan. 8	Kansas City ($12,000)	Pittsburgh ($7,500)	27-24*	Kansas City	74,515
1992	Jan. 3	Buffalo ($6,000)	Houston ($6,000)	41-38*	Buffalo	75,141
	Jan. 2	San Diego ($10,000)	Kansas City ($6,000)	17-0	San Diego	58,278
1991	Dec. 29	Houston ($10,000)	N.Y. Jets ($6,000)	17-10	Houston	61,485
	Dec. 28	Kansas City ($6,000)	L.A. Raiders ($6,000)	10-6	Kansas City	75,827
1990	Jan. 6	Cincinnati ($10,000)	Houston ($6,000)	41-14	Cincinnati	60,012
	Jan. 5	Miami ($6,000)	Kansas City ($6,000)	17-16	Miami	67,276
1989	Dec. 31	Pittsburgh ($6,000)	Houston ($6,000)	26-23*	Houston	59,406
1988	Dec. 26	Houston ($6,000)	Cleveland ($6,000)	24-23	Cleveland	75,896
1987	Jan. 3	Houston ($6,000)	Seattle ($6,000)	23-20*	Houston	50,519
1986	Dec. 28	N.Y. Jets ($6,000)	Kansas City ($6,000)	35-15	East Rutherford	75,210
1985	Dec. 28	New England ($6,000)	N.Y. Jets ($6,000)	26-14	East Rutherford	75,945
1984	Dec. 22	Seattle ($6,000)	L.A. Raiders ($6,000)	13-7	Seattle	62,049
1983	Dec. 24	Seattle ($6,000)	Denver ($6,000)	31-7	Seattle	64,275
1982	Jan. 9	N.Y. Jets ($6,000)	Cincinnati ($6,000)	44-17	Cincinnati	57,560
	Jan. 9	San Diego ($6,000)	Pittsburgh ($6,000)	31-28	Pittsburgh	53,546
	Jan. 8	L.A. Raiders ($6,000)	Cleveland ($6,000)	27-10	Los Angeles	56,555
	Jan. 8	Miami ($6,000)	New England ($6,000)	28-13	Miami	68,842
1981	Dec. 27	Buffalo ($3,000)	N.Y. Jets ($3,000)	31-27	New York	57,050
1980	Dec. 28	Oakland ($3,000)	Houston ($3,000)	27-7	Oakland	53,333
1979	Dec. 23	Houston ($3,000)	Denver ($3,000)	13-7	Houston	48,776
1978	Dec. 24	Houston ($3,000)	Miami ($3,000)	17-9	Miami	72,445

Sudden death overtime.

1996 AFC WILD CARD PLAYOFF GAMES

Three Rivers Stadium, Pittsburgh, Pennsylvania
December 29, 1996, Attendance: 58,078
PITTSBURGH 42, INDIANAPOLIS 14—Jerome Bettis scored 2 touchdowns, and the Steelers' defense permitted just 8 first downs, 146 yards, and compiled 4 sacks as they advanced to play the New England Patriots. The Colts led 14-13 at halftime on the strength of Eugene Daniel's 59-yard interception return and a 48-yard pass play from Jim Harbaugh to Marvin Harrison. The Steelers opened the second half with a 9:30 drive, with Bettis's first touchdown capping the 16-play march. Late in the third quarter, Carnell Lake forced Marshall Faulk to fumble and recovered the ball at the Colts' 18-yard line. Bettis scored his second touchdown moments later, and the rout was on. Pittsburgh scored a postseason-team record 42 points while totaling 407 yards and controlling the ball for 37:36. Bettis, who eleven times during the season broke the 100-yard barrier, had 25 carries for 102 yards.

Indianapolis	0	14	0	0	—	14
Pittsburgh	10	3	8	21	—	42

Pitt — FG N. Johnson 29
Pitt — Stewart 1 run (N. Johnson kick)
Pitt — FG N. Johnson 50
Ind — Daniel 59 interception return (Blanchard kick)
Ind — Bailey 9 pass from Harbaugh (Blanchard kick)
Pitt — Bettis 1 run (Farquhar pass from Stewart)
Pitt — Bettis 1 run (N. Johnson kick)
Pitt — Witman 31 run (N. Johnson kick)
Pitt — Stewart 3 run (N. Johnson kick)

Rich Stadium, Orchard Park, New York
December 28, 1996, Attendance: 70,213
JACKSONVILLE 30, BUFFALO 27—Mike Hollis's third field goal, a 45-yard boot that caromed off the right upright before going through, with 3:07 remaining gave Jacksonville a playoff victory in its first-ever postseason game. The second-year franchise also pinned the Bills with their first-ever postseason home loss, after having won their first nine playoff games at Rich Stadium. Thurman Thomas scored two first-half touchdowns, but Jacksonville got a defensive touchdown from Clyde Simmons and a 30-yard run by Natrone Means. The teams entered the fourth-quarter tied 20-20 when Buffalo's Jeff Burris intercepted Mark Brunell's tipped pass and raced 38 yards to give the Bills a 27-20 advantage 43 seconds into the final quarter. The Jaguars put a 10-play, 65-yard drive together, keyed by 2 receptions by Keenan McCardell and a fourth-and-1 conversion by Means, to tie the game on Jimmy Smith's 2-yard pass with 8:40 remaining. On the ensuing possession, Chris Hudson sacked a scrambling Jim Kelly, forcing him to fumble and injuring him on the play. Aaron Beasley recovered the ball at the Jaguars' 41 with 7:13 left. Facing third-and-7 from the Bills' 41, Brunell hit McCardell with an 11-yard passing play to set up Hollis's winning kick. Todd Collins replaced the injured Kelly on Buffalo's final two possessions, but the Bills could not move the ball. Means carried 31 times for 175 yards, with 21 carries coming in the second half as the Jaguars won the time of possession battle (33:06-26:54) and total yards (409-308).

Jacksonville	10	7	3	10	—	30
Buffalo	14	3	3	7	—	27

Buff — Thomas 7 pass from Kelly (Christie kick)
Jax — Simmons 20 interception return (Hollis kick)
Buff — Thomas 2 run (Christie kick)
Jax — FG Hollis 27
Jax — Means 30 run (Hollis kick)
Buff — FG Christie 33
Buff — FG Christie 47
Jax — FG Hollis 24
Buff — Burris 38 interception return (Christie kick)
Jax — Smith 2 pass from Brunell (Hollis kick)
Jax — FG Hollis 45

NFC WILD CARD PLAYOFF GAMES RESULTS

Season	Date	Winner (Share)	Loser (Share)	Score	Site	Attendance
1996	Dec. 29	San Francisco ($10,000)	Philadelphia ($10,000)	14-0	San Francisco	56,460
	Dec. 28	Dallas ($14,000)	Minnesota ($10,000)	40-15	Dallas	64,682
1995	Dec. 31	Green Bay ($13,000)	Atlanta ($7,500)	37-20	Green Bay	60,453
	Dec. 30	Philadelphia ($7,500)	Detroit ($7,500)	58-37	Philadelphia	66,099
1994	Jan. 1	Chicago ($7,500)	Minnesota ($12,000)	35-18	Minneapolis	60,347
	Dec. 31	Green Bay ($7,500)	Detroit ($7,500)	16-12	Green Bay	58,125
1993	Jan. 9	N.Y. Giants ($7,500)	Minnesota ($7,500)	17-10	East Rutherford	75,089
	Jan. 8	Green Bay ($7,500)	Detroit ($12,000)	28-24	Detroit	68,479
1992	Jan. 3	Philadelphia ($6,000)	New Orleans ($6,000)	36-20	New Orleans	68,893
	Jan. 2	Washington ($6,000)	Minnesota ($10,000)	24-7	Minneapolis	57,353
1991	Dec. 29	Dallas ($6,000)	Chicago ($6,000)	17-13	Chicago	62,594
	Dec. 28	Atlanta ($6,000)	New Orleans ($10,000)	27-20	New Orleans	68,794
1990	Jan. 6	Chicago ($10,000)	New Orleans ($6,000)	16-6	Chicago	60,767
	Jan. 5	Washington ($6,000)	Philadelphia ($6,000)	20-6	Philadelphia	65,287
1989	Dec. 31	L.A. Rams ($6,000)	Philadelphia ($6,000)	21-7	Philadelphia	65,479
1988	Dec. 26	Minnesota ($6,000)	L.A. Rams ($6,000)	28-17	Minnesota	61,204
1987	Jan. 3	Minnesota ($6,000)	New Orleans ($6,000)	44-10	New Orleans	68,546
1986	Dec. 28	Washington ($6,000)	L.A. Rams ($6,000)	19-7	Washington	54,567
1985	Dec. 29	N.Y. Giants ($6,000)	San Francisco ($6,000)	17-3	East Rutherford	75,131
1984	Dec. 23	N.Y. Giants ($6,000)	L.A. Rams ($6,000)	16-3	Anaheim	67,037
1983	Dec. 26	L.A. Rams ($6,000)	Dallas ($6,000)	24-17	Dallas	62,118
1982	Jan. 9	Dallas ($6,000)	Tampa Bay ($6,000)	30-17	Dallas	65,042
	Jan. 9	Minnesota ($6,000)	Atlanta ($6,000)	30-24	Minnesota	60,560
	Jan. 8	Green Bay ($6,000)	St. Louis ($6,000)	41-16	Green Bay	54,282
	Jan. 8	Washington ($6,000)	Detroit ($6,000)	31-7	Washington	55,045
1981	Dec. 27	N.Y. Giants ($3,000)	Philadelphia ($3,000)	27-21	Philadelphia	71,611
1980	Dec. 28	Dallas ($3,000)	Los Angeles ($3,000)	34-13	Dallas	63,052
1979	Dec. 23	Philadelphia ($3,000)	Chicago ($3,000)	27-17	Philadelphia	69,397
1978	Dec. 24	Atlanta ($3,000)	Philadelphia ($3,000)	14-13	Atlanta	59,403

1996 NFC WILD CARD PLAYOFF GAMES

3Com Park, San Francisco, California
December 29, 1996, Attendance: 56,460
SAN FRANCISCO 14, PHILADELPHIA 0—Steve Young ran for a touchdown and threw for one as the 49ers defeated the Eagles in the mud of 3Com Park. The Eagles blew three scoring chances in the first half. Gary Anderson missed a 40-yard field goal on the Eagles first possession. Trailing 7-0 after a scrambling touchdown run by Young in which he bruised his ribs, the Eagles drove deep into 49ers territory. On third-and-1 from the 8-yard line, Detmer attempted to throw the ball away on a pass attempt. However Marquez Pope grabbed the errant toss for the interception. After a punt, Philadelphia drove to the 49ers' 5-yard line, but Roy Barker intercepted Detmer's third-and-4 pass. Philadelphia got into 49ers territory only once the remainder of the game. Young, who left the game in the second quarter with a rib injury, threw a 36-yard pass to Jerry Rice, who made a spectacular one-handed catch, to set up the duo's third-quarter touchdown. San Francisco garnered its first postseason shutout since the 1984 NFC Championship Game.

Philadelphia	0	0	0	0	—	0
San Francisco	0	7	7	0	—	14

SF — S. Young 9 run (Wilkins kick)
SF — Rice 3 pass from S. Young (Wilkins kick)

Texas Stadium, Irving, Texas
December 28, 1996, Attendance: 64,682
DALLAS 40, MINNESOTA 15—Three big plays by George Teague catapulted Dallas to a 30-0 halftime lead en route to routing the Vikings. With the Cowboys leading 7-0, the Vikings Amp Lee caught a pass over the middle on this way to the end zone. However, Teague lunged at Lee from behind, slapping the ball through the end zone to give Dallas possession at their 20-yard line. Chris Boniol capped the 12-play drive with a 28-yard field goal to put Dallas ahead 10-0. On the next play from scrimmage, Teague forced Leroy Hoard to fumble the ball away. On the next play Emmitt Smith streaked 37 yards for a touchdown. Exactly one minute later, Teague intercepted Brad Johnson's pass and returned it 29 yards for a touchdown, giving the Cowboys 17 points in a one-minute, 32-second span and a 24-0 lead. It was the Vikings seventh consecutive playoff loss, and the fourth under coach Dennis Green. Dallas completely dominated the game statistically, compiling more first downs (27-12), total yards (438-268), time of possession (42:03-17:57), and committing fewer turnovers (5-2).

Minnesota	0	0	7	8	—	15
Dallas	7	23	7	3	—	40

Dall — Aikman 2 run (Boniol kick)
Dall — FG Boniol 28
Dall — E. Smith 37 run (Boniol kick)
Dall — Teague 29 interception return (Boniol kick)
Dall — FG Boniol 31
Dall — FG Boniol 22
Minn — Carter 30 pass from B. Johnson (Sisson kick)
Dall — E. Smith 1 run (Boniol kick)
Dall — FG Boniol 25
Minn — B. Johnson 5 run (Carter pass from B. Johnson)

AFC-NFC PRO BOWL AT A GLANCE RESULTS (1971-1997)

NFC leads series, 15-12

Year	Date	Winner (Share)	Loser (Share)	Score	Site	Attendance
1997	Feb. 2	AFC ($20,000)	NFC ($10,000)	26-23 (OT)	Honolulu	50,031
1996	Feb. 4	NFC ($20,000)	AFC ($10,000)	20-13	Honolulu	50,034
1995	Feb. 5	AFC ($20,000)	NFC ($10,000)	41-13	Honolulu	49,121
1994	Feb. 6	NFC ($20,000)	AFC ($10,000)	17-3	Honolulu	50,026
1993	Feb. 7	AFC ($10,000)	NFC ($5,000)	23-20 (OT)	Honolulu	50,007
1992	Feb. 2	NFC ($10,000)	AFC ($5,000)	21-15	Honolulu	50,209
1991	Feb. 3	AFC ($10,000)	NFC ($5,000)	23-21	Honolulu	50,345
1990	Feb. 4	NFC ($10,000)	AFC ($5,000)	27-21	Honolulu	50,445
1989	Jan. 29	NFC ($10,000)	AFC ($5,000)	34-3	Honolulu	50,113
1988	Feb. 7	AFC ($10,000)	NFC ($5,000)	15-6	Honolulu	50,113
1987	Feb. 1	AFC ($10,000)	NFC ($5,000)	10-6	Honolulu	50,101
1986	Feb. 2	NFC ($10,000)	AFC ($5,000)	28-24	Honolulu	50,101
1985	Jan. 27	AFC ($10,000)	NFC ($5,000)	22-14	Honolulu	50,385
1984	Jan. 29	NFC ($10,000)	AFC ($5,000)	45-3	Honolulu	50,445
1983	Feb. 6	NFC ($10,000)	AFC ($5,000)	20-19	Honolulu	49,883
1982	Jan. 31	AFC ($5,000)	NFC ($2,500)	16-13	Honolulu	50,402
1981	Feb. 1	NFC ($5,000)	AFC ($2,500)	21-7	Honolulu	50,360
1980	Jan. 27	NFC ($5,000)	AFC ($2,500)	37-27	Honolulu	49,800
1979	Jan. 29	NFC ($5,000)	AFC ($2,500)	13-7	Los Angeles	46,281
1978	Jan. 23	NFC ($5,000)	AFC ($2,500)	14-13	Tampa	51,337
1977	Jan. 17	AFC ($2,000)	NFC ($1,500)	24-14	Seattle	64,752
1976	Jan. 26	NFC ($2,000)	AFC ($1,500)	23-20	New Orleans	30,546
1975	Jan. 20	NFC ($2,000)	AFC ($1,500)	17-10	Miami	26,484
1974	Jan. 20	AFC ($2,000)	NFC ($1,500)	15-13	Kansas City	66,918
1973	Jan. 21	AFC ($2,000)	NFC ($1,500)	33-28	Dallas	37,091
1972	Jan. 23	AFC ($2,000)	NFC ($1,500)	26-13	Los Angeles	53,647
1971	Jan. 24	NFC ($2,000)	AFC ($1,500)	27-6	Los Angeles	48,222

1997 AFC-NFC PRO BOWL

Aloha Stadium, Honolulu, Hawaii
February 2, 1997, Attendance: 50,031

AFC 26, NFC 23 (OT)—Cary Blanchard's 37-yard field goal 8:16 into overtime gave the AFC a 26-23 victory. The field goal was an ironic ending to a game that saw Blanchard and NFC kicker John Kasay, who each broke the previous single-season record of 35 field goals, combine to miss 5 of 8 field-goal attempts. The NFC scored on its first two possessions, with Vikings guard Randall McDaniel, who lined up as a fullback, scoring his first professional touchdown to give the NFC a 9-0 lead. However, the follies of the kicking unit began as holder Matt Turk muffed the snap on the extra point attempt. Blanchard booted a 28-yard field goal with 27 seconds left in the half to cut the NFC's lead to 9-3. In the third quarter, Barry Sanders scored from 6 yards out, but Kerry Collins was sacked on the 2-point attempt. A 41-yard pass from Drew Bledsoe to Tony Martin led to Curtis Martin's 3-yard run, and after Ashley Ambrose ran an interception back 54 yards for a touchdown 11 seconds into the fourth quarter, the AFC found itself with a 16-15 lead. The NFC drove for more than six minutes, only to have Kasay miss a 40-yard field goal attempt. After an AFC punt, Cris Carter caught a 47-yard touchdown bomb from Gus Frerotte to put the NFC ahead 23-16. After each team punted, the AFC got the ball on its own 20-yard line with 55 seconds left. Mark Brunell hit Tim Brown with an 80-yard bomb down the right sideline to tie the game with 44 seconds left. Wesley Walls caught a 33-yard pass to give the NFC a chance to win in regulation, but Kasay missed a 39-yard attempt and the game went to overtime. The AFC won the overtime toss, but Blanchard missed a 41-yard field goal attempt. The NFC had to punt after three plays, and Brunell hit Ben Coates with a 43-yard pass on the AFC's first play. After three running plays failed to gain a first down, Blanchard trotted onto the field and made the game-winning kick. The teams combined for a Pro Bowl record 962 total yards. Brunell, who completed 12 of 22 pass attempts for 236 yards, was selected as the player of the game.

AFC (26)	Offense	NFC (23)
Carl Pickens (Cincinnati)	WR	Isaac Bruce (St. Louis)
Richmond Webb (Miami)	LT	Erik Williams (Dallas)
Bruce Matthews (Houston)	LG	Larry Allen (Dallas)
Dermontti Dawson (Pittsburgh)	C	Kevin Glover (Detroit)
Will Shields (Kansas City)	RG	Randall McDaniel (Minnesota)
Bruce Armstrong (New England)	RT	William Roaf (New Orleans)
Shannon Sharpe (Denver)	TE	Wesley Walls (Carolina)
Tony Martin (San Diego)	WR	Herman Moore (Detroit)
Drew Bledsoe (New England)	QB	Brett Favre (Green Bay)
Terrell Davis (Denver)	RB	Barry Sanders (Detroit)
Kimble Anders (Kansas City)	RB	Terry Allen (Washington)

AFC	Defense	NFC
Michael Sinclair (Seattle)	DE	Reggie White (Green Bay)
Cortez Kennedy (Seattle)	DT	John Randle (Minnesota)
Chester McGlockton (Oakland)	DT	Bryant Young (San Francisco)
Alfred Williams (Denver)	DE	Tony Tolbert (Dallas)
Derrick Thomas (Kansas City)	LLB	Kevin Greene (Carolina)
Junior Seau (San Diego)	MLB	Sam Mills (Carolina)
Chad Brown (Pittsburgh)	RLB	Lamar Lathon (Carolina)
Rod Woodson (Pittsburgh)	LCB	Eric Davis (Carolina)
Ashley Ambrose (Cincinnati)	RCB	Aeneas Williams (Arizona)
Carnell Lake (Pittsburgh)	SS	LeRoy Butler (Green Bay)
Eric Turner (Baltimore)	FS	Merton Hanks (San Francisco)

SUBSTITUTIONS

AFC—Offense: K—Cary Blanchard (Indianapolis). P—Chris Gardocki (Indianapolis). QB—Mark Brunell (Jacksonville), Vinny Testaverde (Baltimore). RB—Jerome Bettis (Pittsburgh), Curtis Martin (New England). WR—Tim Brown (Oakland), Keenan McCardell (Jacksonville). TE—Ben Coates (New England). ST—John Henry Mills (Houston). KR—David Meggett (New England). T—Tony Boselli (Jacksonville). G—Ruben Brown (Buffalo). C—Mark Stepnoski (Houston). Defense: DE—Willie McGinest (New England). DT—Michael Dean Perry (Denver). LB—Levon Kirkland (Pittsburgh), Bryce Paup (Buffalo), Bill Romanowski (Denver). CB—Terry McDaniel (Oakland). S—Tyrone Braxton (Denver).
NFC—Offense: K—John Kasay (Carolina). P—Matt Turk (Washington). QB—Kerry Collins (Carolina), Gus Frerotte (Washington). RB—Larry Centers (Arizona), Ricky Watters (Philadelphia). WR—Cris Carter (Minnesota), Irving Fryar (Philadelphia). TE—Keith Jackson (Green Bay). ST—Jim Schwantz (Dallas). KR—Michael Bates (Carolina). T—Lomas Brown (Arizona). G—Nate Newton (Dallas). C—Frank Winters (Green Bay). Defense: DE—William Fuller (Philadelphia). DT— Eric Swann (Arizona). LB—Ken Harvey (Washington), Hardy Nickerson (Tampa Bay), William Thomas (Philadelphia). CB—Darrell Green (Washington). S—Darren Woodson (Dallas).

HEAD COACHES

AFC—Tom Coughlin (Jacksonville).
NFC—Dom Capers (Carolina).

OFFICIALS

Referee—Larry Nemmers. Umpire—Chad Brown. Head Linesman—John Schleyer. Line Judge—Bill Reynolds. Back Judge—Bob Moore. Field Judge—Kirk Dornan. Side Judge—Howard Slavin.

SCORING

AFC	0	3	7	13	3 — 26
NFC	9	0	6	8	0 — 23

NFC — FG Kasay 20
NFC — R. McDaniel 5 pass from Favre (muffed snap)
AFC — FG Blanchard 28
NFC — Sanders 6 run (pass failed)
AFC — Martin 3 run (Blanchard kick)
AFC — Ambrose 54 interception return (pass failed)
NFC — Carter 53 pass from Frerotte (Walls pass from Frerotte)
AFC — T. Brown 80 pass from Brunell (Blanchard kick)
AFC — FG Blanchard 37

TEAM STATISTICS	AFC	NFC
Total First Downs	20	24
Rushing	4	7
Passing	14	14
Penalty	2	3
Total Net Yardage	466	496
Total Offensive Plays	76	79
Average Gain per Offensive Play	6.1	6.3
Rushes	31	35
Yards Gained Rushing (Net)	97	130
Average Yards per Rush	3.1	3.7
Passes Attempted	44	44
Passes Completed	21	23
Had Intercepted	0	2
Tackled Attempting to Pass	1	0
Yards Lost Attempting to Pass	2	0
Yards Gained Passing (Net)	369	366
Punts	6	6
Average Distance	42.3	48.5
Punt Returns	2	2
Punt Return Yardage	51	21
Kickoff Returns	6	5
Kickoff Return Yardage	173	152
Interception Return Yardage	54	0
Total Return Yardage	278	173
Fumbles	2	0
Own Fumbles Recovered	2	0
Opponent Fumbles Recovered	0	0
Penalties	8	5
Yards Penalized	43	32
Field Goals	2	1
Field Goals Attempted	4	4
Third-Down Efficiency	7/18	5/14
Fourth-Down Efficiency	0/2	1/1
Time of Possession	33:29	34:47

INDIVIDUAL STATISTICS

RUSHING: AFC: C. Martin 13-48, Davis 7-21, Bettis 4-9, Testaverde 2-7, Brunell 1-6, T. Brown 1-4, Anders 2-2, Bledsoe 1-0. NFC: Sanders 11-59, Centers 9-38, Allen 6-20, Watters 7-13, Frerotte 2-0.

PASSING: AFC: Brunell 12-22-236-0, Testaverde 6-14-68-0, Bledsoe 3-8-67-0. NFC: Frerotte 13-25-193-1, Favre 6-11-143-0, Collins 4-8-30-1.

RECEIVING: AFC: T. Brown 5-137, Coates 2-46, Sharpe 3-43, T. Martin 1-41, McCardell 3-40, Meggett 2-24, Bettis 1-18, C. Martin 2-8, Anders 1-7, Davis 1-7. NFC: Bruce 7-104, Carter 4-87, Moore 3-48, Walls 2-40, Sanders 1-40, Fryar 2-25, Centers 1-12, R. McDaniel 1-5, Allen 1-5, Watters 1-0.

KICKOFF RETURNS: AFC: Meggett 6-173. NFC: Bates 5-152.

PUNT RETURNS: AFC: Meggett 2-51. NFC: Bruce 1-13, D. Green 1-8.

PUNTING: AFC: Gardocki 6-254-42.3. NFC: Turk 6-291-48.5.

INTERCEPTIONS: AFC: McDaniel 1-0, Ambrose 1-54. NFC: None.

SACKS: AFC: None. NFC: Swann 1.

1996 AFC-NFC PRO BOWL

Aloha Stadium, Honolulu, Hawaii
February 4, 1996, Attendance: 50,034

NFC 20, AFC 13—Jerry Rice had 6 receptions for 82 yards and 1 touchdown to earn player of the game honors in the NFC's victory. The 49ers' wide receiver, who was named to the Pro Bowl for the tenth consecutive year, caught a 1-yard touchdown pass from Packers quarterback Brett Favre 1:41 into the second quarter to cap an 80-yard drive and give the NFC the lead for good at 10-7. The AFC had taken a 7-0 lead 2:26 into the game when Bengals quarterback Jeff Blake connected with Steelers wide receiver Yancey Thigpen on a Pro Bowl-record 93-yard touchdown pass. The NFC increased its advantage to 20-7 at halftime on Redskins linebacker Ken Harvey's 36-yard interception return for a touchdown and Falcons kicker Morten Andersen's 24-yard field goal. The AFC trimmed its deficit to 20-13 when Colts quarterback Jim Harbaugh teamed with Patriots running back Curtis Martin on a 17-yard touchdown pass in the final minute of the third quarter, but its bid to win or tie was rebuffed twice in the final minutes of the fourth quar-

ter. First, 49ers safety Tim McDonald intercepted Harbaugh's pass in the end zone with 1:50 remaining. Then, after the AFC forced a punt and got the ball back near midfield, Harbaugh drove his team to the NFC's 9-yard line in the closing seconds. But he spiked the ball once to stop the clock and threw 3 consecutive incompletions as time ran out. The AFC outgained the NFC 390 total yards to 287, but its quarterbacks suffered 4 interceptions, including 3 off Harbaugh, the NFL's leading passer during the regular season. The NFC raised its edge to 15-11 in Pro Bowl games since the AFL-NFL merger in 1970.

| NFC | 3 | 17 | 0 | 0 | — | 20 |
| AFC | 7 | 0 | 6 | 0 | — | 13 |

AFC — Thigpen 93 pass from Blake (Elam kick)
NFC — FG Andersen 36
NFC — Rice 1 pass from Favre (Andersen kick)
NFC — Harvey 36 interception return (Andersen kick)
NFC — FG Andersen 24
AFC — Martin 17 pass from Harbaugh (kick failed)

1995 AFC-NFC PRO BOWL

Aloha Stadium, Honolulu, Hawaii
February 5, 1995, Attendance: 49,121

AFC 41, NFC 13—Colts rookie Marshall Faulk rushed for a Pro Bowl-record 180 yards to key the AFC's rout of the NFC. Faulk, who earned the Dan McGuire Trophy as the player of the game, averaged nearly 14 yards on his 13 carries and shattered the previous rushing mark of 112 yards set by O.J. Simpson in the 1973 game. Faulk's 49-yard touchdown run from punt formation in the fourth quarter was the longest in Pro Bowl history. The Seahawks' Chris Warren added 127 yards on 14 carries as the AFC amassed records for rushing yards (400) and total yards (552). Steelers tight end Eric Green caught 2 touchdown passes for the victors. The NFC managed only 196 total yards, a large chunk coming when 49ers quarterback Steve Young and Vikings wide receiver Cris Carter teamed on a 51-yard touchdown pass in the first quarter. That gave the NFC a 10-0 advantage, but the AFC rallied in the second quarter and took the lead for good when the Browns' Leroy Hoard scored on a 4-yard touchdown run 2:07 before halftime.

| AFC | 0 | 17 | 3 | 21 | — | 41 |
| NFC | 10 | 0 | 3 | 0 | — | 13 |

NFC — FG Reveiz 28
NFC — Carter 51 pass from Young (Reveiz kick)
AFC — Green 22 pass from Elway (Carney kick)
AFC — FG Carney 22
AFC — Hoard 4 run (Carney kick)
NFC — FG Reveiz 49
AFC — FG Carney 23
AFC — Warren 11 run (Carney kick)
AFC — Green 16 pass from Hostetler (Carney kick)
AFC — Faulk 49 run (Carney kick)

1994 AFC-NFC PRO BOWL

Aloha Stadium, Honolulu, Hawaii
February 6, 1994, Attendance: 50,026

NFC 17, AFC 3—The NFC converted a blocked punt and a fumble recovery into touchdowns just 2:20 apart in the second half of its victory over the AFC. With the score tied 3-3 late in the third quarter, Saints linebacker Renaldo Turnbull deflected a punt by the Oilers' Greg Montgomery, and the NFC took possession at the AFC's 48-yard line. A 32-yard pass from Bobby Hebert to Falcons teammate Andre Rison positioned Rams running back Jerome Bettis for a 4-yard touchdown run with 1:27 left in the third quarter. Moments later, Rams defensive tackle Sean Gilbert recovered a fumble by Oilers quarterback Warren Moon at the AFC's 19. Hebert then teamed with the Vikings' Cris Carter on a 15-yard touchdown pass 53 seconds into the fourth period. The NFC kept the AFC out of the end zone by maintaining possession for more than 38 minutes and forcing 6 turnovers. Rison earned the Dan McGuire Trophy as the player of the game by catching 6 passes for 86 yards. The victory was the fourth in the last six

years for the NFC, which leads the series 14-10.

| NFC | 3 | 0 | 7 | 7 | — | 17 |
| AFC | 0 | 3 | 0 | 0 | — | 3 |

NFC — FG Johnson 35
AFC — FG Anderson 25
NFC — Bettis 4 run (Johnson kick)
NFC — Carter 15 pass from Hebert (Johnson kick)

1993 AFC-NFC PRO BOWL

Aloha Stadium, Honolulu, Hawaii
February 7, 1993, Attendance: 50,007

AFC 23, NFC 20—Nick Lowery's 33-yard field goal 4:09 into overtime gave the American Conference all-stars an unlikely 23-20 victory over the National Conference. Despite being overwhelmed by the NFC in first downs (30-9), and total yards (471-114), the AFC won because it forced 6 turnovers, blocked a pair of field goals (1 of which was returned for a touchdown), and returned an interception for a score. Special-teams star Steve Tasker of the Bills earned the Dan McGuire Trophy as the player of the game for making 4 tackles, forcing a fumble, and blocking a field goal. The block came with eight minutes left in regulation and the game tied at 13-13. The Raiders' Terry McDaniel picked up the loose ball and ran 28 yards for a touchdown and a 20-13 AFC lead. The NFC rallied behind 49ers quarterback Steve Young, whose fourth-down, 23-yard touchdown pass to Giants running back Rodney Hampton tied the game at 20-20 with 10 seconds left in regulation. Young completed 18 of 32 passes for 196 yards but was intercepted 3 times and lost a fumble when sacked in overtime. Raiders defensive end Howie Long fell on that fumble at the NFC 28-yard line, and five plays later, Lowery converted the winning field goal.

| AFC | 0 | 10 | 3 | 7 | 3 | — | 23 |
| NFC | 3 | 10 | 0 | 7 | 0 | — | 20 |

NFC — FG Andersen 27
AFC — Seau 31 interception return (Lowery kick)
NFC — FG Andersen 37
NFC — Irvin 9 pass from Aikman (Andersen kick)
AFC — FG Lowery 42
AFC — FG Lowery 29
AFC — McDaniel 28 blocked field goal return (Lowery kick)
NFC — Hampton 23 pass from Young (Andersen kick)
AFC — FG Lowery 33

1992 AFC-NFC PRO BOWL

Aloha Stadium, Honolulu, Hawaii
February 2, 1992, Attendance: 50,209

NFC 21, AFC 15—Atlanta's Chris Miller threw an 11-yard touchdown pass to San Francisco's Jerry Rice with 4:04 remaining in the game to lift the NFC over the AFC. It was the NFC's thirteenth win in the 22-game series. The AFC had taken a 15-14 lead when the Raiders' Jeff Jaeger kicked a 27-yard field goal 1:49 into the fourth quarter. But the NFC, aided by a key roughing-the-passer penalty on a third-down incompletion from the AFC 24-yard line, drove 85 yards to the winning score. The Cowboys' Michael Irvin, playing in his first Pro Bowl, caught 8 passes for 125 yards, including a 13-yard touchdown in the first quarter, and was named the player of the game. Rice had 7 catches for 77 yards. Mark Rypien of Washington, the Super Bowl most valuable player one week earlier, completed 11 of 18 passes for 165 yards and 2 touchdowns for the NFC, including a 35-yard pass to Redskins teammate Gary Clark just 26 seconds before halftime. Miller completed 7 of his 10 attempts for 85 yards.

| NFC | 7 | 7 | 7 | — | 21 |
| AFC | 7 | 5 | 0 | 3 | — | 15 |

AFC — Clayton 4 pass from Kelly (Jaeger kick)
NFC — Irvin 13 pass from Rypien (Lohmiller kick)
AFC — Safety, Townsend tackled Byner in end zone
AFC — FG Jaeger 48
NFC — Clark 35 pass from Rypien (Lohmiller kick)
AFC — FG Jaeger 27
NFC — Rice 11 pass from Miller (Lohmiller kick)

AFC-NFC PRO BOWL SUMMARIES

1991 AFC-NFC PRO BOWL

Aloha Stadium, Honolulu, Hawaii
February 3, 1991, Attendance: 50,345

AFC 23, NFC 21—Buffalo's Jim Kelly and Houston's Ernest Givins combined for a 13-yard scoring pass late in the fourth quarter to rally the AFC over the NFC. Phoenix rookie Johnny Johnson scored on runs of 1 and 9 yards to put the NFC ahead 14-3 in the third quarter. Buffalo's Andre Reed, who led all receivers with 4 catches for 80 yards, caught a 20-yard scoring reception from Kelly early in the fourth quarter to move the AFC to within 1 point. Barry Sanders ran 22 yards for a touchdown to increase the NFC's lead to 21-13. Miami's Jeff Cross blocked a 46-yard field-goal attempt by New Orleans's Morten Andersen with seven seconds remaining to preserve the win. Buffalo's Bruce Smith recorded 3 sacks and also had a blocked field goal. Kelly, who completed 13 of 19 passes for 210 yards and 2 touchdowns, was presented the Dan McGuire Award as player of the game. The AFC's victory narrowed the NFC's Pro Bowl series lead to 12-9.

AFC	3	0	3	17	— 23
NFC	0	7	7	7	— 21

AFC — FG Lowery 26
NFC — J. Johnson 1 run (Andersen kick)
AFC — FG Lowery 43
NFC — J. Johnson 9 run (Andersen kick)
AFC — Reed 20 pass from Kelly (Lowery kick)
NFC — Sanders 22 run (Andersen kick)
AFC — FG Lowery 34
AFC — Givins 13 pass from Kelly (Lowery kick)

1990 AFC-NFC PRO BOWL

Aloha Stadium, Honolulu, Hawaii
February 4, 1990, Attendance: 50,445

NFC 27, AFC 21—The NFC captured its second straight Pro Bowl as the defense accounted for a pair of touchdowns and forced 5 turnovers before the eleventh consecutive sellout crowd at Aloha Stadium. The AFC held a 7-6 halftime edge on a 1-yard scoring run by Christian Okoye of the Chiefs. The NFC then rallied with 21 unanswered points in the third quarter. David Meggett of the Giants began the comeback with an 11-yard touchdown reception from Philadelphia's Randall Cunningham. The Rams' Jerry Gray followed with a 51-yard interception return for a score and the Vikings' Keith Millard added an 8-yard fumble return for a touchdown four minutes later to give the NFC a commanding 27-7 lead. Seattle's Dave Krieg rallied the AFC with a 5-yard touchdown pass to Miami's Ferrell Edmunds. Cleveland's Mike Johnson then returned an interception 22 yards for a score to pull the AFC to within 27-21. Gray, who was credited with 7 tackles, was given the Dan McGuire Award as player of the game. Krieg led all quarterbacks by completing 15 of 23 for 148 yards and 1 touchdown. Buffalo's Thurman Thomas topped all receivers with 5 catches for 47 yards, while Indianapolis's Eric Dickerson led all rushers with 46 yards on 15 carries. The win gave the NFC a 12-8 advantage in Pro Bowl games since 1971.

NFC	3	3	21	0	— 27
AFC	0	7	0	14	— 21

NFC — FG Murray 23
NFC — FG Murray 41
AFC — Okoye 1 run (Treadwell kick)
NFC — Meggett 11 pass from Cunningham (Murray kick)
NFC — Gray 51 interception return (Murray kick)
NFC — Millard 8 fumble recovery return (Murray kick)
AFC — Edmunds 5 pass from Krieg (Treadwell kick)
AFC — M. Johnson 22 interception return (Treadwell kick)

1989 AFC-NFC PRO BOWL

Aloha Stadium, Honolulu, Hawaii
January 29, 1989, Attendance: 50,113

NFC 34, AFC 3—The NFC scored 34 unanswered points to snap a two-game losing streak to the AFC before the tenth straight sellout crowd in Honolulu's

Aloha Stadium. Bills kicker Scott Norwood provided the AFC's only points on a 38-yard field goal 6:23 into the game. Touchdown runs by Dallas's Herschel Walker (4 yards) and Atlanta's John Settle (1) brought the NFC a 14-3 halftime lead. Walker added a 7-yard scoring run, the Saints' Morten Andersen kicked field goals of 27 and 51 yards, and Los Angeles Rams' wide receiver Henry Ellard caught an 8-yard scoring pass from Minnesota quarterback Wade Wilson in the second half to complete the scoring. Chicago running back Neal Anderson and Philadelphia quarterback Randall Cunningham, who were both appearing in their first Pro Bowl, also played major roles in the NFC's victory. Anderson rushed for 85 yards and had 2 receptions for 17. Cunningham, who was voted the game's outstanding player, completed 10 of 14 passes for 63 yards and rushed for 49 yards. The NFC, which had 5 takeaways, outgained the AFC 355 yards to 167 and held a time-of-possession advantage of 35:18 to 24:42. Houston quarterback Warren Moon completed 13 of 20 passes for 134 yards for the AFC. The win gave the NFC an 11-8 advantage in Pro Bowl games.

AFC	3	0	0	0	— 3
NFC	7	7	10	10	— 34

AFC — FG Norwood 38
NFC — Walker 4 run (Andersen kick)
NFC — Settle 1 run (Andersen kick)
NFC — FG Andersen 27
NFC — Walker 7 run (Andersen kick)
NFC — FG Andersen 51
NFC — Ellard 8 pass from Wilson (Andersen kick)

1988 AFC-NFC PRO BOWL

Aloha Stadium, Honolulu, Hawaii
February 7, 1988, Attendance: 50,113

AFC 15, NFC 6—Led by a tenacious pass rush, the AFC defeated the NFC for the second consecutive year before the ninth straight sellout crowd in Honolulu's Aloha Stadium. Buffalo quarterback Jim Kelly scored the game's lone touchdown on a 1-yard run for a 7-6 halftime lead. Colts kicker Dean Biasucci added field goals from 37 and 30 yards to complete the AFC's scoring. Saints kicker Morten Andersen had 25- and 36-yard field goals to account for the NFC's points. AFC defenders held the NFC to 213 yards and recorded 8 sacks. Bills defensive end Bruce Smith, who had 2 sacks among his 5 tackles, was voted the game's outstanding player. Oilers running back Mike Rozier led all rushers with 49 yards on 9 carries. Jets wide receiver Al Toon had 5 receptions for 75 yards. The AFC generated 341 yards total offense and held a time-of-possession advantage of 34:14 to 25:46. By winning, the AFC cut the NFC's lead in the Pro Bowl series to 10-8.

NFC	0	6	0	0	— 6
AFC	0	7	6	2	— 15

NFC — FG Andersen 25
AFC — Kelly 1 run (Biasucci kick)
NFC — FG Andersen 36
AFC — FG Biasucci 37
AFC — FG Biasucci 30
AFC — Safety, Montana forced out of end zone

1987 AFC-NFC PRO BOWL

Aloha Stadium, Honolulu, Hawaii
February 1, 1987, Attendance: 50,101

AFC 10, NFC 6—The AFC defeated the NFC in the lowest-scoring game in AFC-NFC Pro Bowl history. The AFC took a 10-0 halftime lead on Broncos quarterback John Elway's 10-yard touchdown pass to Raiders tight end Todd Christensen and Patriots kicker Tony Franklin's 26-yard field goal. The AFC defense made the lead stand by forcing the NFC to settle for a pair of field goals from 38 and 19 yards by Saints kicker Morten Andersen after the NFC had first downs at the AFC 31-, 7-, 16-, 15-, 5-, and 7-yard lines. Both AFC scores were set up by fumble recoveries by Seahawks linebacker Fredd Young and Dolphins linebacker John Offerdahl, respectively. Eagles defensive end Reggie White, who tied a Pro Bowl record with 4 sacks among his 7 solo tackles, was voted the game's outstanding player. The AFC victory cut the NFC's lead in the Pro

Bowl series to 10-7.

AFC	7	3	0	0	— 10
NFC	0	0	3	3	— 6

AFC — Christensen 10 pass from Elway (Franklin kick)
AFC — FG Franklin 26
NFC — FG Andersen 38
NFC — FG Andersen 19

1986 AFC-NFC PRO BOWL

Aloha Stadium, Honolulu, Hawaii
February 2, 1986, Attendance: 50,101

NFC 28, AFC 24—New York Giants quarterback Phil Simms brought the NFC back from a 24-7 halftime deficit to defeat the AFC. Simms, who completed 15 of 27 passes for 212 yards and 3 touchdowns, was named the most valuable player of the game. The AFC had taken its first-half lead behind a 2-yard run by Los Angeles Raiders running back Marcus Allen, who also threw a 51-yard scoring pass to San Diego wide receiver Wes Chandler, an 11-yard touchdown catch by Pittsburgh wide receiver Louis Lipps, and a 34-yard field goal by Steelers kicker Gary Anderson. Minnesota's Joey Browner accounted for the NFC's only score before halftime with a 48-yard interception return. After intermission, the NFC blanked the AFC while scoring 3 touchdowns via a 15-yard catch by Washington wide receiver Art Monk, a 2-yard reception by Dallas tight end Doug Cosbie, and a 15-yard catch by Tampa Bay tight end Jimmie Giles with 2:47 remaining in the game. The victory gave the NFC a 10-6 Pro Bowl record against the AFC.

NFC	0	7	7	14	— 28
AFC	7	17	0	0	— 24

AFC — Allen 2 run (Anderson kick)
NFC — Browner 48 interception return (Andersen kick)
AFC — Chandler 51 pass from Allen (Anderson kick)
AFC — FG Anderson 34
AFC — Lipps 11 pass from O'Brien (Anderson kick)
NFC — Monk 15 pass from Simms (Andersen kick)
NFC — Cosbie 2 pass from Simms (Andersen kick)
NFC — Giles 15 pass from Simms (Andersen kick)

1985 AFC-NFC PRO BOWL

Aloha Stadium, Honolulu, Hawaii
January 27, 1985, Attendance: 50,385

AFC 22, NFC 14—Defensive end Art Still of the Kansas City Chiefs recovered a fumble and returned it 83 yards for a touchdown to clinch the AFC's victory over the NFC. Still's touchdown came in the fourth period with the AFC trailing 14-12 and was one of several outstanding defensive plays in a Pro Bowl dominated by two record-breaking defenses. The teams combined for a Pro Bowl-record 17 sacks, including 4 by New York Jets defensive end Mark Gastineau, who was named the game's outstanding player. The AFC's first score came on a safety when Gastineau tackled running back Eric Dickerson of the Los Angeles Rams in the end zone. The AFC's second score, a 6-yard pass from Miami's Dan Marino to Los Angeles Raiders running back Marcus Allen was set up by a partial block of a punt by Seahawks linebacker Fredd Young. The NFC leads the series 9-6.

AFC	0	9	0	13	— 22
NFC	0	0	7	7	— 14

AFC — Safety, Gastineau tackled Dickerson in end zone
AFC — Allen 6 pass from Marino (Johnson kick)
NFC — Lofton 13 pass from Montana (Stenerud kick)
NFC — Payton 1 run (Stenerud kick)
AFC — FG Johnson 33
AFC — Still 83 fumble recovery return (Johnson kick)
AFC — FG Johnson 22

1984 AFC-NFC PRO BOWL

Aloha Stadium, Honolulu, Hawaii
January 29, 1984, Attendance: 50,445
NFC 45, AFC 3—The NFC won its sixth Pro Bowl in the last seven seasons by routing the AFC. The NFC was led by the passing of most valuable player Joe Theismann of Washington, who completed 21 of 27 passes for 242 yards and 3 touchdowns. Theismann set Pro Bowl records for completions and touchdown passes. The NFC established Pro Bowl marks for most points scored and fewest points allowed. Running back William Andrews of Atlanta had 6 carries for 43 yards and caught 4 passes for 49 yards, including scoring receptions of 16 and 2 yards. Los Angeles Rams rookie Eric Dickerson gained 46 yards on 11 carries, including a 14-yard touchdown run, and had 45 yards on 5 catches. Rams safety Nolan Cromwell had a 44-yard interception return for a touchdown early in the third period to give the NFC a commanding 24-3 lead. Green Bay wide receiver James Lofton caught an 8-yard touchdown pass, while tight end teammate Paul Coffman had a 6-yard scoring catch.

NFC	3	14	14	14	—	45
AFC	0	3	0	0	—	3

NFC — FG Haji-Sheikh 23
NFC — Andrews 16 pass from Theismann (Haji-Sheikh kick)
NFC — Andrews 2 pass from Montana (Haji-Sheikh kick)
AFC — FG Anderson 43
NFC — Cromwell 44 interception return (Haji-Sheikh kick)
NFC — Lofton 8 pass from Theismann (Haji-Sheikh kick)
NFC — Coffman 6 pass from Theismann (Haji-Sheikh kick)
NFC — Dickerson 14 run (Haji-Sheikh kick)

1983 AFC-NFC PRO BOWL

Aloha Stadium, Honolulu, Hawaii
February 6, 1983, Attendance: 49,883
NFC 20, AFC 19—Dallas's Danny White threw an 11-yard touchdown pass to the Packers' John Jefferson with 35 seconds remaining to rally the NFC over the AFC. White, who completed 14 of 26 passes for 162 yards, kept the winning 65-yard drive alive with a 14-yard completion to Jefferson on a fourth-and-7 play at the AFC 25. The AFC was ahead 12-10 at halftime and increased the lead to 19-10 in the third period, when Marcus Allen scored on a 1-yard run. San Diego's Dan Fouts, who attempted 30 passes, set Pro Bowl records for most completions (17) and yards (274). Pittsburgh's John Stallworth was the AFC's leading receiver with 7 catches for 67 yards. William Andrews topped the NFC with 5 receptions for 48 yards. Fouts and Jefferson were co-winners of the player of the game award.

AFC	9	3	7	0	—	19
NFC	0	10	0	10	—	20

AFC — Walker 34 pass from Fouts (Benirschke kick)
AFC — Safety, Still tackled Theismann in end zone
NFC — Andrews 3 run (Moseley kick)
NFC — FG Moseley 35
AFC — FG Benirschke 29
AFC — Allen 1 run (Benirschke kick)
NFC — FG Moseley 41
NFC — Jefferson 11 pass from D. White (Moseley kick)

1982 AFC-NFC PRO BOWL

Aloha Stadium, Honolulu, Hawaii
January 31, 1982, Attendance: 50,402
AFC 16, NFC 13—Nick Lowery of Kansas City kicked a 23-yard field goal with three seconds remaining to give the AFC a last-second victory over the NFC. Lowery's kick climaxed a 69-yard drive directed by quarterback Dan Fouts. The NFC gained a 13-13 tie with 2:43 to go when Dallas's Tony Dorsett ran 4 yards for a touchdown. In the drive to the winning field goal, Fouts completed 3 passes, including a 23-yard toss to San Diego teammate Kellen Winslow that put the ball on the NFC's 5-yard line. Two plays later, Lowery kicked the field goal. Winslow, who caught 6 passes for 86 yards, was named co-player of the game along with Tampa Bay defensive end Lee Roy Selmon.

NFC	0	6	0	7	—	13
AFC	0	0	13	3	—	16

NFC — Giles 4 pass from Montana (kick blocked)
AFC — Muncie 2 run (kick failed)
AFC — Campbell 1 run (Lowery kick)
NFC — Dorsett 4 run (Septien kick)
AFC — FG Lowery 23

1981 AFC-NFC PRO BOWL

Aloha Stadium, Honolulu, Hawaii
February 1, 1981, Attendance: 50,360
NFC 21, AFC 7—Eddie Murray kicked 4 field goals and Steve Bartkowski fired a 55-yard scoring pass to Alfred Jenkins to lead the NFC to its fourth straight victory over the AFC and a 7-4 edge in the series. Murray was named the game's most valuable player and missed tying Garo Yepremian's Pro Bowl record of 5 field goals when a 37-yard attempt hit the crossbar with 22 seconds remaining. The AFC's only score came on a 9-yard pass from Brian Sipe to Stanley Morgan in the second period. Bartkowski completed 9 of 21 passes for 173 yards, while Sipe connected on 10 of 15 for 142 yards. Ottis Anderson led all rushers with 70 yards on 10 carries. Earl Campbell, the NFL's leading rusher in 1980, was limited to 24 yards on 8 attempts.

AFC	0	7	0	0	—	7
NFC	3	6	0	12	—	21

NFC — FG Murray 31
AFC — Morgan 9 pass from Sipe (J. Smith kick)
NFC — FG Murray 31
NFC — FG Murray 34
NFC — Jenkins 55 pass from Bartkowski (Murray kick)
NFC — FG Murray 36
NFC — Safety, Shell called for holding in end zone

1980 AFC-NFC PRO BOWL

Aloha Stadium, Honolulu, Hawaii
January 27, 1980, Attendance: 49,800
NFC 37, AFC 27—Running back Chuck Muncie of New Orleans ran for 2 touchdowns and threw a 25-yard option pass for another score to give the NFC its third consecutive victory over the AFC. Muncie, who was selected the game's most valuable player, snapped a 3-3 tie on a 1-yard touchdown run at 1:41 of the second quarter, then scored on an 11-yard run in the fourth quarter for the NFC's final touchdown. Two scoring records were set in the game— 37 points by the NFC, eclipsing the 33 by the AFC in 1973, and the 64 points by both teams, surpassing the 61 scored in 1973.

NFC	3	20	7	7	—	37
AFC	3	7	10	7	—	27

NFC — FG Moseley 37
AFC — FG Fritsch 19
NFC — Muncie 1 run (Moseley kick)
AFC — Pruitt 1 pass from Bradshaw (Fritsch kick)
NFC — D. Hill 13 pass from Manning (kick failed)
NFC — T. Hill 25 pass from Muncie (Moseley kick)
NFC — Henry 86 punt return (Moseley kick)
AFC — Campbell 2 run (Fritsch kick)
AFC — FG Fritsch 29
NFC — Muncie 11 run (Moseley kick)
AFC — Campbell 1 run (Fritsch kick)

1979 AFC-NFC PRO BOWL

Memorial Coliseum, Los Angeles, California
January 29, 1979, Attendance: 46,281
NFC 13, AFC 7—Roger Staubach completed 9 of 15 passes for 125 yards, including the winning touchdown on a 19-yard strike to Dallas Cowboys teammate Tony Hill in the third period. The winning drive began at the AFC's 45-yard line after a shanked punt. Staubach hit Ahmad Rashad with passes of 15 and 17 yards to set up Hill's decisive catch. The victory gave the NFC a 5-4 advantage in Pro Bowl games. Rashad, who accounted for 89 yards on 5 receptions, was named the player of the game. The AFC led 7-6 at halftime on Bob Griese's 8-yard scoring toss to Steve

Largent late in the second quarter. Largent finished the game with 5 receptions for 75 yards. The NFC scored first as Archie Manning marched his team 70 yards in 11 plays, capped by Wilbert Montgomery's 2-yard touchdown run. The AFC's Earl Campbell was the game's leading rusher with 66 yards on 12 carries.

AFC	0	7	0	0	—	7
NFC	0	6	7	0	—	13

NFC — Montgomery 2 run (kick failed)
AFC — Largent 8 pass from Griese (Yepremian kick)
NFC — T. Hill 19 pass from Staubach (Corral kick)

1978 AFC-NFC PRO BOWL

Tampa Stadium, Tampa, Florida
January 23, 1978, Attendance: 51,337
NFC 14, AFC 13—Walter Payton, the NFL's leading rusher in 1977, sparked a second-half comeback to give the NFC the win and tie the series between the two conferences at four victories each. Payton, who was the game's most valuable player, gained 77 yards on 13 carries and scored the tying touchdown on a 1-yard burst with 7:37 left in the game. Efren Herrera kicked the winning extra point. The AFC dominated the first half of the game, taking a 13-0 lead on field goals of 21 and 39 yards by Toni Linhart and a 10-yard touchdown pass from Ken Stabler to Oakland teammate Cliff Branch. On the NFC's first possession of the second half, Pat Haden put together the first touchdown drive after Eddie Brown returned Ray Guy's punt to the AFC 46-yard line. Haden connected on all 4 of his passes on that drive, finally hitting Terry Metcalf with a 4-yard scoring toss. The NFC continued to rally and, with Jim Hart at quarterback, moved 63 yards in 12 plays for the go-ahead score. During the winning drive, Hart completed 5 of 6 passes for 38 yards and Payton picked up 20 more on the ground.

AFC	3	10	0	0	—	13
NFC	0	0	7	7	—	14

AFC — FG Linhart 21
AFC — Branch 10 pass from Stabler (Linhart kick)
AFC — FG Linhart 39
NFC — Metcalf 4 pass from Haden (Herrera kick)
NFC — Payton 1 run (Herrera kick)

1977 AFC-NFC PRO BOWL

Kingdome, Seattle, Washington
January 17, 1977, Attendance: 64,752
AFC 24, NFC 14—O.J. Simpson's 3-yard touchdown burst at 7:03 of the first quarter gave the AFC a lead it would not surrender, breaking a two-game NFC win streak and giving the American Conference stars a 4-3 series lead. The AFC took a 17-7 lead midway through the second period on the first of 2 Ken Anderson touchdown passes, a 12-yard toss to Charlie Joiner. But the NFC mounted a 73-yard drive capped by Lawrence McCutcheon's 1-yard touchdown plunge to pull within 17-14 at the half. Following a scoreless third quarter, player of the game Mel Blount thwarted a possible NFC score when he intercepted Jim Hart's pass in the end zone. Less than three minutes later, Blount again picked off a Hart pass, returning it 16 yards to the NFC 27. That set up Anderson's 27-yard touchdown strike to the Raiders' Cliff Branch for the final score.

NFC	0	14	0	0	—	14
AFC	10	7	0	7	—	24

AFC — Simpson 3 run (Linhart kick)
AFC — FG Linhart 31
NFC — Thomas 15 run (Bakken kick)
AFC — Joiner 12 pass from Anderson (Linhart kick)
NFC — McCutcheon 1 run (Bakken kick)
AFC — Branch 27 pass from Anderson (Linhart kick)

1976 AFC-NFC PRO BOWL

Superdome, New Orleans, Louisiana
January 26, 1976, Attendance: 30,546

NFC 23, AFC 20—Mike Boryla, a late substitute who did not enter the game until 5:39 remained, lifted the National Conference to the victory over the American Football Conference with 2 touchdown passes in the final minutes. It was the second straight NFC win, squaring the series at 3-3. Until Boryla started firing the ball the AFC was in control, leading 13-0 at the half. Boryla entered the game after Billy Johnson had raced 90 yards with a punt to make the score 20-9 in favor of the AFC. He floated a 14-yard touchdown pass to Terry Metcalf and later fired an 8-yard scoring pass to Mel Gray for the winner.

AFC	0	13	0	7	—	20
NFC	0	0	9	14	—	23

AFC — FG Stenerud 20
AFC — FG Stenerud 35
AFC — Burrough 64 pass from Pastorini (Stenerud kick)
NFC — FG Bakken 42
NFC — Foreman 4 pass from Hart (kick blocked)
AFC — Johnson 90 punt return (Stenerud kick)
NFC — Metcalf 14 pass from Boryla (Bakken kick)
NFC — Gray 8 pass from Boryla (Bakken kick)

1975 AFC-NFC PRO BOWL

Orange Bowl, Miami, Florida
January 20, 1975, Attendance: 26,484

NFC 17, AFC 10—Los Angeles quarterback James Harris, who took over the NFC offense after Jim Hart of St. Louis suffered a laceration above his right eye in the second period, threw 2 touchdown passes early in the fourth period to pace the NFC to its second victory in the five-game Pro Bowl series. The NFC win snapped a three-game AFC victory string. Harris, who was named the player of the game, connected with St. Louis's Mel Gray for an 8-yard touchdown 2:03 into the final period. One minute and 24 seconds later, following a fumble recovery by Washington's Ken Houston, Harris tossed another 8-yard scoring pass to Washington's Charley Taylor for the decisive points.

NFC	0	3	0	14	—	17
AFC	0	0	10	0	—	10

NFC — FG Marcol 33
AFC — Warfield 32 pass from Griese (Gerela kick)
AFC — FG Gerela 33
NFC — Gray 8 pass from J. Harris (Marcol kick)
NFC — Taylor 8 pass from J. Harris (Marcol kick)

1974 AFC-NFC PRO BOWL

Arrowhead Stadium, Kansas City, Missouri
January 20, 1974, Attendance: 66,918

AFC 15, NFC 13—Miami's Garo Yepremian's fifth field goal—a 42-yard kick with 21 seconds remaining—gave the AFC its third straight victory since the NFC won the inaugural game following the 1970 season. The field goal by Yepremian, who was voted the game's outstanding player, offset a 21-yard field goal by Atlanta's Nick Mike-Mayer that had given the NFC a 13-12 advantage with 1:41 remaining. The only touchdown in the game was scored by the NFC on a 14-yard pass from Philadelphia's Roman Gabriel to Lawrence McCutcheon of the Los Angeles Rams.

NFC	0	10	0	3	—	13
AFC	3	3	3	6	—	15

AFC — FG Yepremian 16
NFC — FG Mike-Mayer 27
NFC — McCutcheon 14 pass from Gabriel (Mike-Mayer kick)
AFC — FG Yepremian 37
AFC — FG Yepremian 27
AFC — FG Yepremian 41
NFC — FG Mike-Mayer 21
AFC — FG Yepremian 42

1973 AFC-NFC PRO BOWL

Texas Stadium, Irving, Texas
January 21, 1973, Attendance: 37,091

AFC 33, NFC 28—Paced by the rushing and receiving of player of the game O.J. Simpson, the AFC erased a 14-0 first period deficit and built a commanding 33-14 lead midway through the fourth period before the NFC managed 2 touchdowns in the final minute of play. Simpson rushed for 112 yards and caught 3 passes for 58 more to gain unanimous recognition in the balloting for player of the game. John Brockington scored 3 touchdowns for the NFC.

AFC	0	10	10	13	—	33
NFC	14	0	0	14	—	28

NFC — Brockington 1 run (Marcol kick)
NFC — Brockington 3 pass from Kilmer (Marcol kick)
AFC — Simpson 7 run (Gerela kick)
AFC — FG Gerela 18
AFC — FG Gerela 22
AFC — Hubbard 11 run (Gerela kick)
AFC — O. Taylor 5 pass from Lamonica (kick failed)
AFC — Bell 12 interception return (Gerela kick)
NFC — Brockington 1 run (Marcol kick)
NFC — Kwalick 12 pass from Snead (Marcol kick)

1972 AFC-NFC PRO BOWL

Memorial Coliseum, Los Angeles, California
January 23, 1972, Attendance: 53,647

AFC 26, NFC 13—Kansas City's Jan Stenerud kicked 4 field goals to lead the AFC from a 6-0 deficit to victory. The AFC defense picked off 3 passes. Stenerud was selected as the outstanding offensive player and his Kansas City teammate, linebacker Willie Lanier, was the game's outstanding defensive player.

AFC	0	3	13	10	—	26
NFC	0	6	0	7	—	13

NFC — Grim 50 pass from Landry (kick failed)
AFC — FG Stenerud 25
AFC — FG Stenerud 23
AFC — FG Stenerud 48
AFC — Morin 5 pass from Dawson (Stenerud kick)
AFC — FG Stenerud 42
NFC — V. Washington 2 run (Knight kick)
AFC — F. Little 6 run (Stenerud kick)

1971 AFC-NFC PRO BOWL

Memorial Coliseum, Los Angeles, California
January 24, 1971, Attendance: 48,222

NFC 27, AFC 6—Mel Renfro of Dallas broke open the first meeting between the American Football Conference and National Football Conference all-star teams as he returned a pair of punts 82 and 56 yards for touchdowns in the final period to clinch the NFC victory over the AFC. Renfro was voted the game's outstanding back and linebacker Fred Carr of Green Bay the outstanding lineman.

AFC	0	3	3	0	—	6
NFC	0	3	10	14	—	27

AFC — FG Stenerud 37
NFC — FG Cox 13
NFC — Osborn 23 pass from Brodie (Cox kick)
NFC — FG Cox 35
AFC — FG Stenerud 16
NFC — Renfro 82 punt return (Cox kick)
NFC — Renfro 56 punt return (Cox kick)

PRO BOWL ALL-TIME RESULTS

Date	Result	Site (attendance)	Honored players
Jan. 15, 1939	New York Giants 13, Pro All-Stars 10	Wrigley Field, Los Angeles (20,000)	
Jan. 14, 1940	Green Bay 16, NFL All-Stars 7	Gilmore Stadium, Los Angeles (18,000)	
Dec. 29, 1940	Chicago Bears 28, NFL All-Stars 14	Gilmore Stadium, Los Angeles (21,624)	
Jan. 4, 1942	Chicago Bears 35, NFL All-Stars 24	Polo Grounds, New York (17,725)	
Dec. 27, 1942	NFL All-Stars 17, Washington 14	Shibe Park, Philadelphia (18,671)	
Jan. 14, 1951	American Conf. 28, National Conf. 27	Los Angeles Memorial Coliseum (53,676)	Otto Graham, Cleveland, player of the game
Jan. 12, 1952	National Conf. 30, American Conf. 13	Los Angeles Memorial Coliseum (19,400)	Dan Towler, Los Angeles, player of the game
Jan. 10, 1953	National Conf. 27, American Conf. 7	Los Angeles Memorial Coliseum (34,208)	Don Doll, Detroit, player of the game
Jan. 17, 1954	East 20, West 9	Los Angeles Memorial Coliseum (44,214)	Chuck Bednarik, Philadelphia, player of the game
Jan. 16, 1955	West 26, East 19	Los Angeles Memorial Coliseum (43,972)	Billy Wilson, San Francisco, player of the game
Jan. 15, 1956	East 31, West 30	Los Angeles Memorial Coliseum (37,867)	Ollie Matson, Chi. Cardinals, player of the game
Jan. 13, 1957	West 19, East 10	Los Angeles Memorial Coliseum (44,177)	Bert Rechichar, Baltimore, outstanding back Ernie Stautner, Pittsburgh, outstanding lineman
Jan. 12, 1958	West 26, East 7	Los Angeles Memorial Coliseum (66,634)	Hugh McElhenny, San Francisco, outstanding back Gene Brito, Washington, outstanding lineman
Jan. 11, 1959	East 28, West 21	Los Angeles Memorial Coliseum (72,250)	Frank Gifford, N.Y. Giants, outstanding back Doug Atkins, Chi. Bears, outstanding lineman
Jan. 17, 1960	West 38, East 21	Los Angeles Memorial Coliseum (56,876)	Johnny Unitas, Baltimore, outstanding back Gene (Big Daddy) Lipscomb, Baltimore, outstanding lineman
Jan. 15, 1961	West 35, East 31	Los Angeles Memorial Coliseum (62,971)	Johnny Unitas, Baltimore, outstanding back Sam Huff, N.Y. Giants, outstanding lineman
Jan. 7, 1962	AFL West 47, East 27	Balboa Stadium, San Diego (20,973)	Cotton Davidson, Dallas Texans, player of the game
Jan. 14, 1962	NFL West 31, East 30	Los Angeles Memorial Coliseum (57,409)	Jim Brown, Cleveland, outstanding back Henry Jordan, Green Bay, outstanding lineman
Jan. 13, 1963	AFL West 21, East 14	Balboa Stadium, San Diego (27,641)	Curtis McClinton, Dallas Texans, outstanding offensive player Earl Faison, San Diego, outstanding defensive player
Jan. 13, 1963	NFL East 30, West 20	Los Angeles Memorial Coliseum (61,374)	Jim Brown, Cleveland, outstanding back Gene (Big Daddy) Lipscomb, Pittsburgh, outstanding lineman
Jan. 12, 1964	NFL West 31, East 17	Los Angeles Memorial Coliseum (67,242)	Johnny Unitas, Baltimore, player of the game Gino Marchetti, Baltimore, outstanding lineman
Jan. 19, 1964	AFL West 27, East 24	Balboa Stadium, San Diego (20,016)	Keith Lincoln, San Diego, outstanding offensive player Archie Matsos, Oakland, outstanding defensive player
Jan. 10, 1965	NFL West 34, East 14	Los Angeles Memorial Coliseum (60,598)	Fran Tarkenton, Minnesota, outstanding back Terry Barr, Detroit, outstanding lineman
Jan. 16, 1965	AFL West 38, East 14	Jeppesen Stadium, Houston (15,446)	Keith Lincoln, San Diego, outstanding offensive player Willie Brown, Denver, outstanding defensive player
Jan. 15, 1966	AFL All-Stars 30, Buffalo 19	Rice Stadium, Houston (35,572)	Joe Namath, N.Y. Jets, most valuable player, offense Frank Buncom, San Diego, most valuable player, defense
Jan. 15, 1966	NFL East 36, West 7	Los Angeles Memorial Coliseum (60,124)	Jim Brown, Cleveland, outstanding back Dale Meinert, St. Louis, outstanding lineman
Jan. 21, 1967	AFL East 30, West 23	Oakland-Alameda County Coliseum (18,876)	Babe Parilli, Boston, outstanding offensive player Verlon Biggs, N.Y. Jets, outstanding defensive player
Jan. 22, 1967	NFL East 20, West 10	Los Angeles Memorial Coliseum (15,062)	Gale Sayers, Chicago, outstanding back Floyd Peters, Philadelphia, outstanding lineman
Jan. 21, 1968	AFL East 25, West 24	Gator Bowl, Jacksonville, Fla. (40,103)	Joe Namath and Don Maynard, N.Y. Jets, out. off. players Leslie (Speedy) Duncan, San Diego, out. def. player
Jan. 21, 1968	NFL West 38, East 20	Los Angeles Memorial Coliseum (53,289)	Gale Sayers, Chicago, outstanding back Dave Robinson, Green Bay, outstanding lineman
Jan. 19, 1969	AFL West 38, East 25	Gator Bowl, Jacksonville, Fla. (41,058)	Len Dawson, Kansas City, outstanding offensive player George Webster, Houston, outstanding defensive player
Jan. 19, 1969	NFL West 10, East 7	Los Angeles Memorial Coliseum (32,050)	Roman Gabriel, Los Angeles, outstanding back Merlin Olsen, Los Angeles, outstanding lineman
Jan. 17, 1970	AFL West 26, East 3	Astrodome, Houston (30,170)	John Hadl, San Diego, player of the game
Jan. 18, 1970	NFL West 16, East 13	Los Angeles Memorial Coliseum (57,786)	Gale Sayers, Chicago, outstanding back George Andrie, Dallas, outstanding lineman
Jan. 24, 1971	NFC 27, AFC 6	Los Angeles Memorial Coliseum (48,222)	Mel Renfro, Dallas, outstanding back Fred Carr, Green Bay, outstanding lineman
Jan. 23, 1972	AFC 26, NFC 13	Los Angeles Memorial Coliseum (53,647)	Jan Stenerud, Kansas City, outstanding offensive player Willie Lanier, Kansas City, outstanding defensive player
Jan. 21, 1973	AFC 33, NFC 28	Texas Stadium, Irving (37,091)	O.J. Simpson, Buffalo, player of the game
Jan. 20, 1974	AFC 15, NFC 13	Arrowhead Stadium, Kansas City (66,918)	Garo Yepremian, Miami, player of the game
Jan. 20, 1975	NFC 17, AFC 10	Orange Bowl, Miami (26,484)	James Harris, Los Angeles, player of the game
Jan. 26, 1976	NFC 23, AFC 20	Louisiana Superdome, New Orleans (30,546)	Billy Johnson, Houston, player of the game
Jan. 17, 1977	AFC 24, NFC 14	Kingdome, Seattle (64,752)	Mel Blount, Pittsburgh, player of the game
Jan. 23, 1978	NFC 14, AFC 13	Tampa Stadium (51,337)	Walter Payton, Chicago, player of the game
Jan. 29, 1979	NFC 13, AFC 7	Los Angeles Memorial Coliseum (46,281)	Ahmad Rashad, Minnesota, player of the game
Jan. 27, 1980	NFC 37, AFC 27	Aloha Stadium, Honolulu (49,800)	Chuck Muncie, New Orleans, player of the game
Feb. 1, 1981	NFC 21, AFC 7	Aloha Stadium, Honolulu (50,360)	Eddie Murray, Detroit, player of the game
Jan. 31, 1982	AFC 16, NFC 13	Aloha Stadium, Honolulu (50,402)	Kellen Winslow, San Diego, and Lee Roy Selmon, Tampa Bay, players of the game
Feb. 6, 1983	NFC 20, AFC 19	Aloha Stadium, Honolulu (49,883)	Dan Fouts, San Diego, and John Jefferson, Green Bay, players of the game
Jan. 29, 1984	NFC 45, AFC 3	Aloha Stadium, Honolulu (50,445)	Joe Theismann, Washington, player of the game
Jan. 27, 1985	AFC 22, NFC 14	Aloha Stadium, Honolulu (50,385)	Mark Gastineau, N.Y. Jets, player of the game
Feb. 2, 1986	NFC 28, AFC 24	Aloha Stadium, Honolulu (50,101)	Phil Simms, N.Y. Giants, player of the game
Feb. 1, 1987	AFC 10, NFC 6	Aloha Stadium, Honolulu (50,101)	Reggie White, Philadelphia, player of the game
Feb. 7, 1988	AFC 15, NFC 6	Aloha Stadium, Honolulu (50,113)	Bruce Smith, Buffalo, player of the game
Jan. 29, 1989	NFC 34, AFC 3	Aloha Stadium, Honolulu (50,113)	Randall Cunningham, Philadelphia, player of the game
Feb. 4, 1990	NFC 27, AFC 21	Aloha Stadium, Honolulu (50,445)	Jerry Gray, L.A. Rams, player of the game
Feb. 3, 1991	AFC 23, NFC 21	Aloha Stadium, Honolulu (50,345)	Jim Kelly, Buffalo, player of the game
Feb. 2, 1992	NFC 21, AFC 15	Aloha Stadium, Honolulu (50,209)	Michael Irvin, Dallas, player of the game
Feb. 7, 1993	AFC 23, NFC 20 (OT)	Aloha Stadium, Honolulu (50,007)	Steve Tasker, Buffalo, player of the game
Feb. 6, 1994	NFC 17, AFC 3	Aloha Stadium, Honolulu (50,026)	Andre Rison, Atlanta, player of the game
Feb. 5, 1995	AFC 41, NFC 13	Aloha Stadium, Honolulu (49,121)	Marshall Faulk, Indianapolis, player of the game
Feb. 4, 1996	NFC 20, AFC 13	Aloha Stadium, Honolulu (50,034)	Jerry Rice, San Francisco, player of the game
Feb. 2, 1997	AFC 26, NFC 23 (OT)	Aloha Stadium, Honolulu (50,031)	Mark Brunell, Jacksonville, player of the game

PRO FOOTBALL HALL OF FAME GAME

1962	New York Giants 21, St. Louis Cardinals 21
1963	Pittsburgh Steelers 16, Cleveland Browns 7
1964	Baltimore Colts 48, Pittsburgh Steelers 17
1965	Washington Redskins 20, Detroit Lions 3
1966	No game
1967	Philadelphia Eagles 28, Cleveland Browns 13
1968	Chicago Bears 30, Dallas Cowboys 24
1969	Green Bay Packers 38, Atlanta Falcons 24
1970	New Orleans Saints 14, Minnesota Vikings 13
1971	Los Angeles Rams (NFC) 17, Houston Oilers (AFC) 6
1972	Kansas City Chiefs (AFC) 23, New York Giants (NFC) 17
1973	San Francisco 49ers (NFC) 20, New England Patriots (AFC) 7
1974	St. Louis Cardinals (NFC) 21, Buffalo Bills (AFC) 13
1975	Washington Redskins (NFC) 17, Cincinnati Bengals (AFC) 9
1976	Denver Broncos (AFC) 10, Detroit Lions (NFC) 7
1977	Chicago Bears (NFC) 20, New York Jets (AFC) 6
1978	Philadelphia Eagles (NFC) 17, Miami Dolphins (AFC) 3
1979	Oakland Raiders (AFC) 20, Dallas Cowboys (NFC) 13
1980*	San Diego Chargers (AFC) 0, Green Bay Packers (NFC) 0
1981	Cleveland Browns (AFC) 24, Atlanta Falcons (NFC) 10
1982	Minnesota Vikings (NFC) 30, Baltimore Colts (AFC) 14
1983	Pittsburgh Steelers (AFC) 27, New Orleans Saints (NFC) 14
1984	Seattle Seahawks (AFC) 38, Tampa Bay Buccaneers (NFC) 0
1985	New York Giants (NFC) 21, Houston Oilers (AFC) 20
1986	New England Patriots (AFC) 21, St. Louis Cardinals (NFC) 16
1987	San Francisco 49ers (NFC) 20, Kansas City Chiefs (AFC) 7
1988	Cincinnati Bengals (AFC) 14, Los Angeles Rams (NFC) 7
1989	Washington Redskins (NFC) 31, Buffalo Bills (AFC) 6
1990	Chicago Bears (NFC) 13, Cleveland Browns (AFC) 0
1991	Detroit Lions (NFC) 14, Denver Broncos (AFC) 3
1992	New York Jets (AFC) 41, Philadelphia Eagles (NFC) 14
1993	Los Angeles Raiders (AFC) 19, Green Bay Packers (NFC) 3
1994	Atlanta Falcons (NFC) 21, San Diego Chargers (AFC) 17
1995	Carolina Panthers (NFC) 20, Jacksonville Jaguars (AFC) 14
1996	Indianapolis Colts (AFC) 10, New Orleans Saints (NFC) 3

Game called with 5:29 remaining due to severe thunder and lightning.

NFL INTERNATIONAL GAMES

Date	Site	Teams
Aug. 12, 1950	Ottawa, Canada	N.Y. Giants 27, Ottawa Rough Riders 6
Aug. 11, 1951	Ottawa, Canada	N.Y. Giants 41, Ottawa Rough Riders 18
Aug. 5, 1959	Toronto, Canada	Chi. Cardinals 55, Tor. Argonauts 26
Aug. 3, 1960	Toronto, Canada	Pittsburgh 43, Toronto Argonauts 16
Aug. 15, 1960	Toronto, Canada	Chicago 16, N.Y. Giants 7
Aug. 2, 1961	Toronto, Canada	St. Louis 36, Toronto Argonauts 7
Aug. 5, 1961	Montreal, Canada	Chicago 34, Montreal Allouettes 16
Aug. 8, 1961	Hamilton, Canada	Hamilton Tiger-Cats 38, Buffalo 21
Sept. 11, 1969	Montreal, Canada	Pittsburgh 17, N.Y. Giants 13
Aug. 25, 1969	Montreal, Canada	Detroit 22, Boston 9
Aug. 16, 1976	Tokyo, Japan	St. Louis 20, San Diego 10
Aug. 5, 1978	Mexico City, Mexico	New Orleans 14, Philadelphia 7
Aug. 6, 1983	London, England	Minnesota 28, St. Louis 10
*Aug. 3, 1986	London, England	Chicago 17, Dallas 6
*Aug. 9, 1987	London, England	L.A. Rams 28, Denver 27
*July 31, 1988	London, England	Miami 27, San Francisco 21
Aug. 14, 1988	Goteborg, Sweden	Minnesota 28, Chicago 21
Aug. 18, 1988	Montreal, Canada	N.Y. Jets 11, Cleveland 7
*Aug. 5, 1989	Tokyo, Japan	L.A. Rams 16, San Francisco 13 (OT)
*Aug. 6, 1989	London, England	Philadelphia 17, Cleveland 13
*Aug. 4, 1990	Tokyo, Japan	Denver 10, Seattle 7
*Aug. 5, 1990	London, England	New Orleans 17, L.A. Raiders 10
*Aug. 9, 1990	Montreal, Canada	Pittsburgh 30, New England 14
*Aug. 11, 1990	Berlin, Germany	L.A. Rams 19, Kansas City 3
*July 28, 1991	London, England	Buffalo 17, Philadelphia 13
*Aug. 3, 1991	Berlin, Germany	San Francisco 21, Chicago 7
*Aug. 3, 1991	Tokyo, Japan	Miami 19, L.A. Raiders 17
*Aug. 1, 1992	Tokyo, Japan	Houston 34, Dallas 23
*Aug. 15, 1992	Berlin, Germany	Miami 31, Denver 27
*Aug. 16, 1992	London, England	San Francisco 17, Washington 15
*July 31, 1993	Tokyo, Japan	New Orleans 28, Philadelphia 16
*Aug. 1, 1993	Barcelona, Spain	San Francisco 21, Pittsburgh 14
*Aug. 7, 1993	Berlin, Germany	Minnesota 20, Buffalo 6
*Aug. 8, 1993	London, England	Dallas 13, Detroit 13 (OT)
Aug. 14, 1993	Toronto, Canada	Cleveland 12, New England 9
*July 31, 1994	Barcelona, Spain	L.A. Raiders 25, Denver 22
*Aug. 6, 1994	Tokyo, Japan	Minnesota 17, Kansas City 9
*Aug. 13, 1994	Berlin, Germany	N.Y. Giants 28, San Diego 20
*Aug. 15, 1994	Mexico City, Mexico	Houston 6, Dallas 0
*Aug. 5, 1995	Tokyo, Japan	Denver 24, San Francisco 10
*Aug. 12, 1995	Toronto, Canada	Buffalo 9, Dallas 7
*July 27, 1996	Tokyo, Japan	San Diego 20, Pittsburgh 10
*Aug. 5, 1996	Monterrey, Mexico	Kansas City 32, Dallas 6

American Bowl Game

CHICAGO ALL-STAR GAME

Pro teams won 31, lost 9, and tied 2. The game was discontinued after 1976.

Year	Date	Winner	Loser	Attendance
1976*	July 23	Pittsburgh 24	All-Stars 0	52,895
1975	Aug. 1	Pittsburgh 21	All-Stars 14	54,103
1974		No game was played		
1973	July 27	Miami 14	All-Stars 3	54,103
1972	July 28	Dallas 20	All-Stars 7	54,162
1971	July 30	Baltimore 24	All-Stars 17	52,289
1970	July 31	Kansas City 24	All-Stars 3	69,940
1969	Aug. 1	N.Y. Jets 26	All-Stars 24	74,208
1968	Aug. 2	Green Bay 34	All-Stars 17	69,917
1967	Aug. 4	Green Bay 27	All-Stars 0	70,934
1966	Aug. 5	Green Bay 38	All-Stars 0	72,000
1965	Aug. 6	Cleveland 24	All-Stars 16	68,000
1964	Aug. 7	Chicago 28	All-Stars 17	65,000
1963	Aug. 2	All-Stars 20	Green Bay 17	65,000
1962	Aug. 3	Green Bay 42	All-Stars 20	65,000
1961	Aug. 4	Philadelphia 28	All-Stars 14	66,000
1960	Aug. 12	Baltimore 32	All-Stars 7	70,000
1959	Aug. 14	Baltimore 29	All-Stars 0	70,000
1958	Aug. 15	All-Stars 35	Detroit 19	70,000
1957	Aug. 9	N.Y. Giants 22	All-Stars 12	75,000
1956	Aug. 10	Cleveland 26	All-Stars 0	75,000
1955	Aug. 12	All-Stars 30	Cleveland 27	75,000
1954	Aug. 13	Detroit 31	All-Stars 6	93,470
1953	Aug. 14	Detroit 24	All-Stars 10	93,818
1952	Aug. 15	Los Angeles 10	All-Stars 7	88,316
1951	Aug. 17	Cleveland 33	All-Stars 0	92,180
1950	Aug. 11	All-Stars 17	Philadelphia 7	88,885
1949	Aug. 12	Philadelphia 38	All-Stars 0	93,780
1948	Aug. 20	Chi. Cardinals 28	All-Stars 0	101,220
1947	Aug. 22	All-Stars 16	Chi. Bears 0	105,840
1946	Aug. 23	All-Stars 16	Los Angeles 0	97,380
1945	Aug. 30	Green Bay 19	All-Stars 7	92,753
1944	Aug. 30	Chi. Bears 24	All-Stars 21	48,769
1943	Aug. 25	All-Stars 27	Washington 7	48,471
1942	Aug. 28	Chi. Bears 21	All-Stars 0	101,100
1941	Aug. 28	Chi. Bears 37	All-Stars 13	98,203
1940	Aug. 29	Green Bay 45	All-Stars 28	84,567
1939	Aug. 30	N.Y. Giants 9	All-Stars 0	81,456
1938	Aug. 31	All-Stars 28	Washington 16	74,250
1937	Sept. 1	All-Stars 6	Green Bay 0	84,560
1936	Sept. 3	Detroit 7	All-Stars 7 (tie)	76,000
1935	Aug. 29	Chi. Bears 5	All-Stars 0	77,450
1934	Aug. 31	Chi. Bears 0	All-Stars 0 (tie)	79,432

Game shortened due to thunderstorms.

NFL PLAYOFF BOWL

Western Conference won 8, Eastern Conference won 2.
All games played at Miami's Orange Bowl.

1970	Los Angeles Rams 31, Dallas Cowboys 0
1969	Dallas Cowboys 17, Minnesota Vikings 13
1968	Los Angeles Rams 30, Cleveland Browns 6
1967	Baltimore Colts 20, Philadelphia Eagles 14
1966	Baltimore Colts 35, Dallas Cowboys 3
1965	St. Louis Cardinals 24, Green Bay Packers 17
1964	Green Bay Packers 40, Cleveland Browns 23
1963	Detroit Lions 17, Pittsburgh Steelers 10
1962	Detroit Lions 28, Philadelphia Eagles 10
1961	Detroit Lions 17, Cleveland Browns 16

AFC VS. NFC (REGULAR SEASON), 1970-1996

	1970	1971	1972	1973	1974	1975	1976	1977	1978	1979	1980	1981	1982	1983	1984	1985	1986	1987	1988	1989	1990	1991	1992	1993	1994	1995	1996	Totals
Miami	2-1	3-0	3-0	3-0	2-1	3-0	0-2	2-0	3-1	4-0	4-0	3-1	1-1	3-1	4-0	3-1	2-2	3-0	3-1	2-0	2-2	3-1	2-2	3-1	2-2	2-2	1-3	68-25
Oakland	1-2	1-1-1	3-0	2-1	3-0	3-0	3-0	1-1	4-0	4-0	2-2	2-2	3-0	2-2	3-1	3-1	1-3	2-2	1-3	2-2	3-1	2-2	2-2	3-1	3-1	3-1	1-3	63-34-1
Pittsburgh	0-3	1-2	2-1	3-0	3-0	2-1	1-1	2-0	3-1	3-1	4-0	3-1	1-0	2-2	3-1	1-3	2-2	2-2	1-3	3-1	3-1	0-4	1-3	2-2	2-2	2-2	2-2	54-41
Cincinnati	1-2	1-2	2-1	2-1	2-1	3-0	2-0	2-1	2-2	2-2	2-2	2-2	1-0	3-1	2-2	2-2	3-1	1-2	4-0	2-2	1-3	1-3	1-3	2-2	1-3	2-2	4-0	51-44
Kansas City	0-2-1	2-1	2-1	1-1-1	1-2	2-1	1-1	1-1	0-2	0-2	2-0	2-2	0-3	2-2	1-1	2-2	1-1	1-2	0-2	2-0	4-0	2-2	2-2	2-2	3-1	3-1	4-0	43-37-2
Denver	2-2	1-3	1-3	0-3-1	2-2	2-1	2-0	1-1	2-2	3-1	3-1	3-1	2-1	0-2	3-1	3-1	3-1	2-1-1	3-1	2-2	1-3	2-0	1-3	1-3	1-3	2-2	3-1	51-45-2
Buffalo	0-3	0-3	2-0-1	2-1	2-1	1-2	0-2	1-1	1-1	2-2	3-1	1-3	1-2	1-3	1-3	0-2	1-1	1-2	2-2	1-3	3-1	3-1	4-0	4-0	1-3	3-1	4-0	45-44-1
Cleveland	0-3	2-1	1-2	1-2	1-2	1-3	2-0	1-1	4-0	3-1	3-1	3-1	0-2	2-2	1-3	1-3	2-2	2-2	4-0	3-1	1-3	0-4	2-2	3-1	3-1	1-3		47-46
Seattle								1-0	3-1	3-1	1-3	0-2	1-0	1-3	4-0	2-2	3-1	4-0	1-3	0-4	2-2	1-3	0-4	0-2	2-0	3-1	2-2	34-34
Baltimore																											2-2	2-2
San Diego	1-2	2-1	0-3	1-2	1-2	0-3	2-0	1-1	2-2	3-1	2-2	2-2	1-0	2-2	4-0	1-1	0-4	2-0	2-2	2-2	1-1	1-3	2-0	2-2	2-2	3-1	1-3	43-44
Indianapolis	3-0	2-1	0-3	2-1	1-2	2-1	0-2	1-1	2-2	1-1	1-1	0-4	0-1-1	2-0	0-4	3-1	1-3	1-0	2-2	1-3	2-2	0-4	2-0	0-4	0-2	2-2	3-1	34-48-1
New England	0-3	0-3	3-0	2-1	3-0	1-2	1-1	2-0	2-2	3-1	1-3	0-4	0-1	2-2	0-4	3-1	3-1	0-3	2-2	0-4	0-4	1-1	0-4	1-1	4-0	0-4	2-2	36-54
Tennessee	0-3	0-2-1	0-3	0-3	0-3	3-0	2-0	2-0	2-2	2-2	4-0	1-3	0-3	1-3	0-4	1-3	2-2	2-2	3-1	3-1	1-3	1-3	3-1	2-2	0-4	1-3	2-2	38-58-1
N.Y. Jets	2-1	0-3	1-2	0-3	2-1	0-3	0-2	1-1	1-3	3-1	1-3	2-0	4-0	3-1	0-2	2-2	2-2	0-4	2-0	1-3	2-0	2-2	0-4	2-2	1-3	0-4	1-3	35-55
Jacksonville																										0-4	2-2	2-6
Tampa Bay							0-1																					0-1
TOTALS	12-27-1	15-23-2	20-19-1	19-19-2	23-17	23-17	16-12	19-9	31-21	36-16	33-19	24-28	15-14-1	26-26	26-26	27-25	26-26	23-22-1	30-22	24-28	26-26	19-33	22-30	27-25	25-27	27-33	32-28	646-618-8

NFC VS. AFC (REGULAR SEASON), 1970-1996

	1970	1971	1972	1973	1974	1975	1976	1977	1978	1979	1980	1981	1982	1983	1984	1985	1986	1987	1988	1989	1990	1991	1992	1993	1994	1995	1996	Totals
Carolina																										3-1	3-1	6-2
Dallas	3-0	3-0	3-0	2-1	2-1	2-1	2-0	1-1	3-1	1-3	3-1	4-0	2-1	2-2	2-2	3-1	1-3	2-1	0-4	0-2	1-1	3-1	4-0	2-2	3-1	4-0	2-2	60-32
San Francisco	4-0	2-1	2-1	1-2	0-3	1-2	1-1	0-2	1-3	0-4	2-2	3-1	1-3	2-2	3-1	3-1	4-0	3-1	2-2	4-0	4-0	3-1	3-1	2-2	3-1	3-1	4-0	61-38
Washington	2-1	1-2	1-2	2-1	2-1	1-2	1-1	1-1	2-2	2-2	1-3	1-3	1-2	1-3	3-1	3-1	2-2	1-2	2-2	3-1	2-2	1-3	2-2	2-2	2-2	0-4	3-1	51-40
Philadelphia	2-1	1-2	2-1	2-1	2-1	0-3	0-2	1-1	3-1	2-2	3-1	3-1	2-1	1-1	3-1	1-1	2-2	3-1	2-2	3-1	1-3	4-0	3-1	2-2	1-3	1-3	2-2	52-41
St. Louis	2-1	1-2	1-2	3-0	3-1	3-0	1-1	2-0	2-2	2-2	2-2	2-2		4-0	3-1	4-0	3-1	2-1	1-3	2-2	3-1	4-0	2-2	1-3	1-1	1-3	2-2	51-46
N.Y. Giants	3-0	1-2	1-2	1-2	1-2	2-1	0-2	0-2	1-1	1-1	1-3	1-1	1-0	0-4	2-0	2-2	3-1	2-1	1-1	4-0	3-1	3-1	2-2	2-2	3-1	0-4	2-2	43-41
Minnesota	2-1	2-1	1-2	2-1	2-1	4-0	2-0	1-1	1-3	1-3	1-3	1-3	1-3	4-0	0-4	2-0	1-3	2-1	2-2	2-2	2-2	0-2	3-1	2-2	2-2	3-1	1-3	47-47
Chicago	1-2	1-2	1-2	2-2	0-3	0-3	0-2	1-1	0-4	2-2	0-4	4-0	1-1	1-1	2-2	3-1	4-0	2-2	3-1	2-2	2-2	2-2	1-3	2-2	3-1	2-2	2-2	44-51
Detroit	3-0	4-0	2-0-1	0-3	1-2	1-2	2-0	2-0	2-2	0-4	0-2	2-2	0-1	1-3	0-4	2-2	1-3	0-4	1-1	1-3	1-3	4-0	2-2	2-0	2-2	3-1	1-3	40-49-1
Arizona	2-0-1	2-1	1-2	0-2-1	2-1	2-1	1-1	0-2	0-4	1-3	1-1	3-1		3-1	3-1	2-2	1-1	0-1	1-3		2-2	1-1	0-2	1-1	3-1	1-3	0-4	34-45-2
New Orleans	0-3	0-1-2	0-3	1-2	0-3	0-3	1-2	0-2	1-3	0-4	1-3	2-2	1-0	1-3	3-1	0-4	1-3	4-0	4-0	4-0	2-2	3-1	3-1	2-2	1-3	4-0	1-3	40-54-2
Green Bay	2-1	2-1	2-1	1-1-1	2-1	0-3	0-2	0-3	2-2	1-3	1-3	1-1	1-1-1	2-2	0-4	0-4	1-3	1-2-1	1-3	0-2	1-3	1-3	3-1	3-1	1-3	4-0	0-4	36-55-3
Atlanta	1-2	3-0	2-2	2-1	0-3	1-2	0-2	0-2	1-3	1-3	2-2	1-3	1-1	3-1	1-3	0-4	1-3	0-4	1-3	2-2	2-2	3-1	2-2	1-3	1-3	2-2	0-4	34-63
Tampa Bay							0-1	2-0	2-0	1-3	0-4	2-1	1-3	1-1	0-4	1-1	0-2	1-3	0-4	0-2	1-3	0-2	1-3	1-1	2-2	2-2		18-42
Seattle							1-0																					1-0
TOTALS	27-12-1	23-15-2	19-20-1	19-19-2	17-23	17-23	12-16	9-19	21-31	16-36	19-33	28-24	14-15-1	26-26	26-26	25-27	26-26	22-23-1	22-30	28-24	26-26	33-19	30-22	25-27	27-25	33-27	28-32	618-646-8

1996 INTERCONFERENCE GAMES

(Home Team in capital letters)
AFC 32, NFC 28
AFC Victories
INDIANAPOLIS 20, Arizona 13
Buffalo 23, NEW YORK GIANTS 20 (OT)
Miami 38, ARIZONA 10
NEW ENGLAND 31, Arizona 0
Indianapolis 25, DALLAS 24
CINCINNATI 30, New Orleans 15
DENVER 27, Tampa Bay 23
BUFFALO 10, Dallas 7
Seattle 17, TAMPA BAY 13
JACKSONVILLE 24, Carolina 14
BALTIMORE 17, New Orleans 10
OAKLAND 37, Detroit 21
Houston 23, ATLANTA 13
New York Jets 31, ARIZONA 21
Pittsburgh 20, ATLANTA 17
BALTIMORE 37, St. Louis 31 (OT)
Kansas City 21, MINNESOTA 6
PITTSBURGH 42, St. Louis 6
BUFFALO 38, Washington 13
Buffalo 24, PHILADELPHIA 17
DENVER 17, Chicago 12
KANSAS CITY 27, Green Bay 20
Houston 31, NEW ORLEANS 14
SEATTLE 42, Minnesota 23
SAN DIEGO 27, Detroit 21
KANSAS CITY 14, Chicago 10
CINCINNATI 41, Atlanta 31
Denver 21, MINNESOTA 17
Kansas City 28, DETROIT 24
INDIANAPOLIS 37, Philadelphia 10
New England 23, NEW YORK GIANTS 22
JACKSONVILLE 19, Atlanta 17

NFC Victories
ST. LOUIS 26, Cincinnati 16
GREEN BAY 42, San Diego 10
New York Giants 13, NEW YORK JETS 6
Green Bay 31, SEATTLE 10
CHICAGO 19, Oakland 17
WASHINGTON 31, New York Jets 16
NEW ORLEANS 17, Jacksonville 13
Washington 27, NEW ENGLAND 22
SAN FRANCISCO 28, Cincinnati 21
ST. LOUIS 17, Jacksonville 14
PHILADELPHIA 35, Miami 28
Dallas 29, MIAMI 10
WASHINGTON 31, Indianapolis 16
San Francisco 10, HOUSTON 9
TAMPA BAY 20, Oakland 17 (OT)
SAN FRANCISCO 38, Baltimore 20
DETROIT 17, Seattle 16
Tampa Bay 25, SAN DIEGO 17
Minnesota 16, OAKLAND 13 (OT)
Carolina 31, HOUSTON 6
GREEN BAY 41, Denver 6
New York Giants 17, MIAMI 7
Philadelphia 21, NEW YORK JETS 20
CHICAGO 27, San Diego 14
CAROLINA 27, Baltimore 16
DALLAS 12, New England 6
San Francisco 25, PITTSBURGH 15
CAROLINA 18, Pittsburgh 14

REGULAR SEASON INTERCONFERENCE RECORDS, 1970-1996

AMERICAN FOOTBALL CONFERENCE

Eastern Division	W	L	T	Pct.
Miami	68	25	0	.731
Buffalo	45	44	1	.506
Indianapolis	34	48	1	.416
New England	36	54	0	.400
New York Jets	35	55	0	.389
Central Division				
Pittsburgh	54	41	0	.568
Cincinnati	51	44	0	.537
Cleveland	47	46	0	.505
Baltimore	2	2	0	.500
Tennessee	38	58	1	.397
Jacksonville	2	6	0	.250
Western Division				
Oakland	63	34	1	.648
Kansas City	43	37	2	.537
Denver	51	45	2	.531
Seattle*	35	34	0	.507
San Diego	43	44	0	.494

NATIONAL FOOTBALL CONFERENCE

Eastern Division	W	L	T	Pct.
Dallas	60	32	0	.652
Washington	51	40	0	.560
Philadelphia	52	41	0	.559
New York Giants	43	41	0	.512
Arizona	34	45	2	.432
Central Division				
Minnesota	47	47	0	.500
Chicago	44	51	0	.463
Detroit	40	49	1	.450
Green Bay	36	55	3	.399
Tampa Bay*	18	43	0	.295
Western Division				
Carolina	6	2	0	.750
San Francisco	61	38	0	.616
St. Louis	51	46	0	.526
New Orleans	40	54	2	.427
Atlanta	34	63	0	.351

* Records include one game played between Seattle and Tampa Bay, won by the Seahawks 13-10, in their inaugural season (1976) when Seattle competed in the NFC and Tampa Bay in the AFC.

INTERCONFERENCE VICTORIES, 1970-1996

REGULAR SEASON	AFC	NFC	Tie		PRESEASON	AFC	NFC	Tie
1970	12	27	1		1970	21	28	1
1971	15	23	2		1971	28	28	3
1972	20	19	1		1972	27	25	4
1973	19	19	2		1973	23	35	2
1974	23	17	0		1974	35	25	0
1975	23	17	0		1975	30	26	1
1976	16	12	0		1976	30	31	0
1977	19	9	0		1977	38	25	0
1978	31	21	0		1978	20	19	0
1979	36	16	0		1979	25	18	0
1980	33	19	0		1980	22	20	1
1981	24	28	0		1981	18	19	0
1982	15	14	1		1982	25	16	0
1983	26	26	0		1983	15	24	0
1984	26	26	0		1984	16	19	0
1985	27	25	0		1985	10	22	1
1986	26	26	0		1986	22	17	0
1987	23	22	1		1987	22	22	0
1988	30	22	0		1988	23	16	1
1989	24	28	0		1989	16	27	0
1990	26	26	0		1990	15	29	0
1991	19	33	0		1991	19	27	0
1992	22	30	0		1992	30	22	0
1993	27	25	0		1993	17	22	0
1994	25	27	0		1994	22	16	0
1995	27	33	0		1995	19	26	0
1996	32	28	0		1996	27	19	0
Total	**646**	**618**	**8**		**Total**	**615**	**623**	**14**

RECORDS AFTER BYE WEEKS, 1990-96
AFC

Baltimore	1-0		Miami	6-2
Buffalo	7-1		New England	3-5
Cincinnati	2-6		N.Y. Jets	2-6
Cleveland	2-5		Oakland	3-5
Denver	7-1		Pittsburgh	5-3
Indianapolis	4-4		San Diego	4-4
Jacksonville	1-1		Seattle	1-7
Kansas City	6-2		Tennessee	4-4

RECORDS AFTER BYE WEEKS, 1990-96
NFC

Arizona	4-4		New Orleans	3-5
Atlanta	6-2		N.Y. Giants	2-6
Carolina	1-1		Philadelphia	6-2
Chicago	6-2		St. Louis	3-5
Dallas	6-2		San Francisco	3-5
Detroit	4-4		Tampa Bay	2-6
Green Bay	3-5		Washington	2-6
Minnesota	6-2			

MONDAY NIGHT FOOTBALL, 1970-1996

(Home Team in capitals, games listed in chronological order.)

1996
CHICAGO 22, Dallas 6
GREEN BAY 39, Philadelphia 13
PITTSBURGH 24, Buffalo 6
INDIANAPOLIS 10, Miami 6
Dallas 23, PHILADELPHIA 19
Pittsburgh 17, KANSAS CITY 7
GREEN BAY 23, San Francisco 20 (OT)
Oakland 23, SAN DIEGO 14
Chicago 15, MINNESOTA 13
Denver 22, OAKLAND 21
SAN DIEGO 27, Detroit 21
DALLAS 21, Green Bay 6
Pittsburgh 24, MIAMI 17
San Francisco 34, ATLANTA 10
OAKLAND 26, Kansas City 7
MIAMI 16, Buffalo 14
SAN FRANCISCO 24, Detroit 14

1995
Dallas 35, NEW YORK GIANTS 0
Green Bay 27, CHICAGO 24
MIAMI 23, Pittsburgh 10
DETROIT 27, San Francisco 24
Buffalo 22, CLEVELAND 19
KANSAS CITY 29, San Diego 23 (OT)
DENVER 27, Oakland 0
NEW ENGLAND 27, Buffalo 14
Chicago 14, MINNESOTA 6
DALLAS 34, Philadelphia 12
PITTSBURGH 20, Cleveland 3
San Francisco 44, MIAMI 20
SAN DIEGO 12, Oakland 6
DETROIT 27, Chicago 7
MIAMI 13, Kansas City 6
SAN FRANCISCO 37, Minnesota 30
Dallas 37, ARIZONA 13

1994
SAN FRANCISCO 44, Los Angeles Raiders 14
PHILADELPHIA 30, Chicago 22
Detroit 20, DALLAS 17 (OT)
BUFFALO 27, Denver 20
PITTSBURGH 30, Houston 14
Minnesota 27, NEW YORK GIANTS 10
Kansas City 31, DENVER 28
PHILADELPHIA 21, Houston 6
Green Bay 33, CHICAGO 6
DALLAS 38, New York Giants 10
PITTSBURGH 23, Buffalo 10
New York Giants 13, HOUSTON 10
San Francisco 35, NEW ORLEANS 14
Los Angeles Raiders 24, SAN DIEGO 17
MIAMI 45, Kansas City 28
Dallas 24, NEW ORLEANS 16
MINNESOTA 21, San Francisco 14

1993
WASHINGTON 35, Dallas 16
CLEVELAND 23, San Francisco 13
KANSAS CITY 15, Denver 7
Pittsburgh 45, ATLANTA 17
MIAMI 17, Washington 10
BUFFALO 35, Houston 7
Los Angeles Raiders 23, DENVER 20
Minnesota 19, CHICAGO 12
BUFFALO 24, Washington 10
KANSAS CITY 23, Green Bay 16
PITTSBURGH 23, Buffalo 0
SAN FRANCISCO 42, New Orleans 7
San Diego 31, INDIANAPOLIS 0
DALLAS 23, Philadelphia 17
Pittsburgh 21, MIAMI 20
New York Giants 24, NEW ORLEANS 14
SAN DIEGO 45, Miami 20
Philadelphia 37, SAN FRANCISCO 34 (OT)

1992
DALLAS 23, Washington 10
Miami 27, CLEVELAND 23
New York Giants 27, CHICAGO 14
KANSAS CITY 27, Los Angeles Raiders 7
PHILADELPHIA 31, Dallas 7
WASHINGTON 34, Denver 3
PITTSBURGH 20, Cincinnati 0
Buffalo 24, NEW YORK JETS 20
Minnesota 38, CHICAGO 10
San Francisco 41, ATLANTA 3
Buffalo 26, MIAMI 20
NEW ORLEANS 20, Washington 3
SEATTLE 16, Denver 13 (OT)
HOUSTON 24, Chicago 7
MIAMI 20, Los Angeles Raiders 7
Dallas 41, ATLANTA 17
SAN FRANCISCO 24, Detroit 6

1991
NEW YORK GIANTS 16, San Francisco 14
Washington 33, DALLAS 31
HOUSTON 17, Kansas City 7
CHICAGO 19, New York Jets 13 (OT)
WASHINGTON 23, Philadelphia 0
KANSAS CITY 33, Buffalo 6
New York Giants 23, PITTSBURGH 20
BUFFALO 35, Cincinnati 16
KANSAS CITY 24, Los Angeles Raiders 21
PHILADELPHIA 30, New York Giants 7
Chicago 34, MINNESOTA 17
Buffalo 41, MIAMI 27
San Francisco 33, LOS ANGELES RAMS 10
Philadelphia 13, HOUSTON 6
MIAMI 37, Cincinnati 13
NEW ORLEANS 27, Los Angeles Raiders 0
SAN FRANCISCO 52, Chicago 14

1990
San Francisco 13, NEW ORLEANS 12
DENVER 24, Kansas City 23
Buffalo 30, NEW YORK JETS 7
SEATTLE 31, Cincinnati 16
Cleveland 30, DENVER 29
PHILADELPHIA 32, Minnesota 24
Cincinnati 34, CLEVELAND 13
PITTSBURGH 41, Los Angeles Rams 10
New York Giants 24, INDIANAPOLIS 7
PHILADELPHIA 28, Washington 14
Los Angeles Raiders 13, MIAMI 10
HOUSTON 27, Buffalo 24
SAN FRANCISCO 7, New York Giants 3
Los Angeles Raiders 38, DETROIT 31
San Francisco 26, LOS ANGELES RAMS 10
NEW ORLEANS 20, Los Angeles Rams 17

1989
New York Giants 27, WASHINGTON 24
Denver 28, BUFFALO 14
CINCINNATI 21, Cleveland 14
CHICAGO 27, Philadelphia 13
Los Angeles Raiders 14, NEW YORK JETS 7
BUFFALO 23, Los Angeles Rams 20
CLEVELAND 27, Chicago 7
NEW YORK GIANTS 24, Minnesota 14
SAN FRANCISCO 31, New Orleans 13
HOUSTON 26, Cincinnati 24
Denver 14, WASHINGTON 10
SAN FRANCISCO 34, New York Giants 24
SEATTLE 17, Buffalo 16
San Francisco 30, LOS ANGELES RAMS 27
NEW ORLEANS 30, Philadelphia 20
MINNESOTA 29, Cincinnati 21

1988
NEW YORK GIANTS 27, Washington 20
Dallas 17, PHOENIX 14
CLEVELAND 23, Indianapolis 17
Los Angeles Raiders 30, DENVER 27 (OT)
NEW ORLEANS 20, Dallas 17
PHILADELPHIA 24, New York Giants 13
Buffalo 37, NEW YORK JETS 14
CHICAGO 10, San Francisco 9
INDIANAPOLIS 55, Denver 23
HOUSTON 24, Cleveland 17
Buffalo 31, MIAMI 6
SAN FRANCISCO 37, Washington 21
SEATTLE 35, Los Angeles Raiders 27
LOS ANGELES RAMS 23, Chicago 3
MIAMI 38, Cleveland 31
MINNESOTA 28, Chicago 27

1987
CHICAGO 34, New York Giants 19
NEW YORK JETS 43, New England 24
San Francisco 41, NEW YORK GIANTS 21
DENVER 30, Los Angeles Raiders 14
Washington 13, DALLAS 7
CLEVELAND 30, Los Angeles Rams 17
MINNESOTA 34, Denver 27
DALLAS 33, New York Giants 24
NEW YORK JETS 30, Seattle 14
DENVER 31, Chicago 29
Los Angeles Rams 30, WASHINGTON 26
Los Angeles Raiders 37, SEATTLE 14
MIAMI 37, New York Jets 28
SAN FRANCISCO 41, Chicago 0
Dallas 29, LOS ANGELES RAMS 21
New England 24, MIAMI 10

1986
DALLAS 31, New York Giants 28
Denver 21, PITTSBURGH 10
Chicago 25, GREEN BAY 12
Dallas 31, ST. LOUIS 7
SEATTLE 33, San Diego 7
CINCINNATI 24, Pittsburgh 22
NEW YORK JETS 22, Denver 10
NEW YORK GIANTS 27, Washington 20
Los Angeles Rams 20, CHICAGO 17
CLEVELAND 26, Miami 16
WASHINGTON 14, San Francisco 6
MIAMI 45, New York Jets 3
New York Giants 21, SAN FRANCISCO 17
SEATTLE 37, Los Angeles Raiders 0
Chicago 16, DETROIT 13
New England 34, MIAMI 27

1985
DALLAS 44, Washington 14
CLEVELAND 17, Pittsburgh 7
Los Angeles Rams 35, SEATTLE 24
Cincinnati 37, PITTSBURGH 24
WASHINGTON 27, St. Louis 10
NEW YORK JETS 23, Miami 7
CHICAGO 23, Green Bay 7
LOS ANGELES RAIDERS 34, San Diego 21
ST. LOUIS 21, Dallas 10
DENVER 17, San Francisco 16
WASHINGTON 23, New York Giants 21
SAN FRANCISCO 19, Seattle 6
MIAMI 38, Chicago 24
Los Angeles Rams 27, SAN FRANCISCO 20
MIAMI 30, New England 27
L.A. Raiders 16, L.A. RAMS 6

MONDAY NIGHT FOOTBALL

1984
Dallas 20, LOS ANGELES RAMS 13
SAN FRANCISCO 37, Washington 31
Miami 21, BUFFALO 17
LOS ANGELES RAIDERS 33, San Diego 30
PITTSBURGH 38, Cincinnati 17
San Francisco 31, NEW YORK GIANTS 10
DENVER 17, Green Bay 14
Los Angeles Rams 24, ATLANTA 10
Seattle 24, SAN DIEGO 0
WASHINGTON 27, Atlanta 14
SEATTLE 17, Los Angeles Raiders 14
NEW ORLEANS 27, Pittsburgh 24
MIAMI 28, New York Jets 17
SAN DIEGO 20, Chicago 7
Los Angeles Raiders 24, DETROIT 3
MIAMI 28, Dallas 21

1983
Dallas 31, WASHINGTON 30
San Diego 17, KANSAS CITY 14
LOS ANGELES RAIDERS 27, Miami 14
NEW YORK GIANTS 27, Green Bay 3
New York Jets 34, BUFFALO 10
Pittsburgh 24, CINCINNATI 14
GREEN BAY 48, Washington 47
ST. LOUIS 20, New York Giants 20 (OT)
Washington 27, SAN DIEGO 24
DETROIT 15, New York Giants 9
Los Angeles Rams 36, ATLANTA 13
New York Jets 31, NEW ORLEANS 28
MIAMI 38, Cincinnati 14
DETROIT 13, Minnesota 2
Green Bay 12, TAMPA BAY 9 (OT)
SAN FRANCISCO 42, Dallas 17

1982
Pittsburgh 36, DALLAS 28
Green Bay 27, NEW YORK GIANTS 19
LOS ANGELES RAIDERS 28, San Diego 24
TAMPA BAY 23, Miami 17
New York Jets 28, DETROIT 13
Dallas 37, HOUSTON 7
SAN DIEGO 50, Cincinnati 34
MIAMI 27, Buffalo 10
MINNESOTA 31, Dallas 27

1981
San Diego 44, CLEVELAND 14
Oakland 36, MINNESOTA 10
Dallas 35, NEW ENGLAND 21
Los Angeles 24, CHICAGO 7
PHILADELPHIA 16, Atlanta 13
BUFFALO 31, Miami 21
DETROIT 48, Chicago 17
PITTSBURGH 26, Houston 13
DENVER 19, Minnesota 17
DALLAS 27, Buffalo 14
SEATTLE 44, San Diego 23
ATLANTA 31, Minnesota 30
MIAMI 13, Philadelphia 10
OAKLAND 30, Pittsburgh 27
LOS ANGELES 21, Atlanta 16
SAN DIEGO 23, Oakland 10

1980
Dallas 17, WASHINGTON 3
Houston 16, CLEVELAND 7
PHILADELPHIA 35, New York Giants 3
NEW ENGLAND 23, Denver 14
CHICAGO 23, Tampa Bay 0
DENVER 20, Washington 17
Oakland 45, PITTSBURGH 34
NEW YORK JETS 17, Miami 14
CLEVELAND 27, Chicago 21
HOUSTON 38, New England 34
Oakland 19, SEATTLE 17
Los Angeles 27, NEW ORLEANS 7
OAKLAND 9, Denver 3
MIAMI 16, New England 13 (OT)
LOS ANGELES 38, Dallas 14
SAN DIEGO 26, Pittsburgh 17

1979
Pittsburgh 16, NEW ENGLAND 13 (OT)
Atlanta 14, PHILADELPHIA 10
WASHINGTON 27, New York Giants 0
CLEVELAND 26, Dallas 7
GREEN BAY 27, New England 14
OAKLAND 13, Miami 3
NEW YORK JETS 14, Minnesota 7
PITTSBURGH 42, Denver 7
Seattle 31, ATLANTA 28
Houston 9, MIAMI 6
Philadelphia 31, DALLAS 21
LOS ANGELES 20, Atlanta 14
SEATTLE 30, New York Jets 7
Oakland 42, NEW ORLEANS 35
HOUSTON 20, Pittsburgh 17
SAN DIEGO 17, Denver 7

1978
DALLAS 38, Baltimore 0
MINNESOTA 12, Denver 9 (OT)
Baltimore 34, NEW ENGLAND 27
Minnesota 24, CHICAGO 20
WASHINGTON 9, Dallas 5
MIAMI 21, Cincinnati 0
DENVER 16, Chicago 7
Houston 24, PITTSBURGH 17
ATLANTA 15, Los Angeles 7
BALTIMORE 21, Washington 17
Oakland 34, CINCINNATI 21
HOUSTON 35, Miami 30
Pittsburgh 24, SAN FRANCISCO 7
SAN DIEGO 40, Chicago 7
Cincinnati 20, LOS ANGELES 19
MIAMI 23, New England 3

1977
PITTSBURGH 27, San Francisco 0
CLEVELAND 30, New England 27 (OT)
Oakland 37, KANSAS CITY 28
CHICAGO 24, Los Angeles 23
PITTSBURGH 20, Cincinnati 14
LOS ANGELES 35, Minnesota 3
ST. LOUIS 28, New York Giants 0
BALTIMORE 10, Washington 3
St. Louis 24, DALLAS 17
WASHINGTON 10, Green Bay 9
OAKLAND 34, Buffalo 13
MIAMI 17, Baltimore 6
Dallas 42, SAN FRANCISCO 35

1976
Miami 30, BUFFALO 21
Oakland 24, KANSAS CITY 21
Washington 20, PHILADELPHIA 17 (OT)
MINNESOTA 17, Pittsburgh 6
San Francisco 16, LOS ANGELES 0
NEW ENGLAND 41, New York Jets 7
WASHINGTON 20, St. Louis 10
BALTIMORE 38, Houston 14
CINCINNATI 20, Los Angeles 12
DALLAS 17, Buffalo 10
Baltimore 17, MIAMI 16
SAN FRANCISCO 20, Minnesota 16
OAKLAND 35, Cincinnati 20

1975
Oakland 31, MIAMI 21
DENVER 23, Green Bay 13
Dallas 36, DETROIT 10
WASHINGTON 27, St. Louis 17
New York Giants 17, BUFFALO 14
Minnesota 13, CHICAGO 9
Los Angeles 42, PHILADELPHIA 3
Kansas City 34, DALLAS 31
CINCINNATI 33, Buffalo 24
Pittsburgh 32, HOUSTON 9
MIAMI 20, New England 7
OAKLAND 17, Denver 10
SAN DIEGO 24, New York Jets 16

1974
BUFFALO 21, Oakland 20
PHILADELPHIA 13, Dallas 10
WASHINGTON 30, Denver 3
MIAMI 21, New York Jets 17
DETROIT 17, San Francisco 13
CHICAGO 10, Green Bay 9
PITTSBURGH 24, Atlanta 17
Los Angeles 15, SAN FRANCISCO 13
Minnesota 28, ST. LOUIS 24
Kansas City 42, DENVER 34
Pittsburgh 28, NEW ORLEANS 7
MIAMI 24, Cincinnati 3
Washington 23, LOS ANGELES 17

1973
GREEN BAY 23, New York Jets 7
DALLAS 40, New Orleans 3
DETROIT 31, Atlanta 6
WASHINGTON 14, Dallas 7
Miami 17, CLEVELAND 9
DENVER 23, Oakland 23
BUFFALO 23, Kansas City 14
PITTSBURGH 21, Washington 16
KANSAS CITY 19, Chicago 7
ATLANTA 20, Minnesota 14
SAN FRANCISCO 20, Green Bay 6
MIAMI 30, Pittsburgh 26
LOS ANGELES 40, New York Giants 6

1972
Washington 24, MINNESOTA 21
Kansas City 20, NEW ORLEANS 17
New York Giants 27, PHILADELPHIA 12
Oakland 34, HOUSTON 0
Green Bay 24, DETROIT 23
CHICAGO 13, Minnesota 10
DALLAS 28, Detroit 24
Baltimore 24, NEW ENGLAND 17
Cleveland 21, SAN DIEGO 17
WASHINGTON 24, Atlanta 13
MIAMI 31, St. Louis 10
Los Angeles 26, SAN FRANCISCO 16
OAKLAND 24, New York Jets 16

1971
Minnesota 16, DETROIT 13
ST. LOUIS 17, New York Jets 10
Oakland 34, CLEVELAND 20
DALLAS 20, New York Giants 13
KANSAS CITY 38, Pittsburgh 16
MINNESOTA 10, Baltimore 3
GREEN BAY 14, Detroit 14
BALTIMORE 24, Los Angeles 17
SAN DIEGO 20, St. Louis 17
ATLANTA 28, Green Bay 21
MIAMI 34, Chicago 3
Kansas City 26, SAN FRANCISCO 17
Washington 38, LOS ANGELES 24

1970
CLEVELAND 31, New York Jets 21
Kansas City 44, BALTIMORE 24
DETROIT 28, Chicago 14
Green Bay 22, SAN DIEGO 20
OAKLAND 34, Washington 20
MINNESOTA 13, Los Angeles 3
PITTSBURGH 21, Cincinnati 10
Baltimore 13, GREEN BAY 10
St. Louis 38, DALLAS 0
PHILADELPHIA 23, New York Giants 20
Miami 20, ATLANTA 7
Cleveland 21, HOUSTON 10
Detroit 28, LOS ANGELES 23

MONDAY NIGHT WON-LOST RECORDS, 1970-1996

AMERICAN FOOTBALL CONFERENCE

	Balt.	Buff.	Cin.	Clev.	Den.	Ind.	Jax.	K.C.	Mia.	N.E.	N.Y.J.	Oak.	Pitt.	S.D.	Sea.	Tenn.
Total	0-0	15-18	7-16	13-11	14-19-1	10-7	0-0	14-10	32-22	5-12	9-16	33-14-1	25-15	14-12	11-5	11-11
1996		0-2		1-0		1-0		0-2	1-2			2-1	3-0	1-1		
1995		1-1	0-2	1-0				1-1	2-1	1-0		0-2	1-1	1-1		
1994		1-1		0-2				1-1	1-0			1-1	2-0	0-1		0-3
1993		2-1		1-0	0-2	0-1		2-0	1-2			1-0	3-0	2-0		0-1
1992		2-0	0-1	0-1	0-2			1-0	2-1		0-1	0-2	1-0		1-0	1-0
1991		2-1	0-2					2-1	1-1		0-1	0-2	0-1			1-1
1990		1-1	1-1	1-1	1-1	0-1		0-1	0-1			0-1	2-0		1-0	1-0
1989		1-2	1-2	1-1	2-0							0-1	1-0		1-0	1-0
1988		2-0		1-2	0-2	1-1			1-1		0-1	1-1			1-0	1-0
1987				1-0	2-1				1-1	1-1	2-1	1-1			0-2	
1986			1-0	1-0	1-1				1-2	1-0	1-1	0-1	0-2	0-1	2-0	
1985			1-0	1-0	1-0				2-1	0-1	1-0	2-0	0-2	0-1	0-2	
1984		0-1	0-1	1-0					3-0			0-1	2-1	1-1	1-2	2-0
1983		0-1	0-2					0-1	1-1			2-0	1-0	1-0	1-1	
1982		0-1	0-1	0-1					1-1			1-0	1-0	1-0		0-1
1981		1-1		0-1	1-0				1-1	0-1		2-1	1-1	2-1	1-0	0-1
1980				1-1	1-2				1-1	1-2	1-0	3-0	0-2	1-0	0-1	2-0
1979				1-0	0-2				0-2	0-2	1-1	2-0	2-1	1-0	2-0	2-0
1978		1-2		1-1		2-1			2-1	0-2		1-0	1-1	1-0		2-0
1977		0-1	0-1	1-0		1-1		0-1	1-0	0-1		2-0	2-0			
1976		0-2	1-1			2-0		0-1	1-1	1-0	0-1	2-0	0-1			0-1
1975		0-2	1-0	1-1				1-0	1-1	0-1	0-1	2-0	1-0	1-0		0-1
1974		1-0	0-1	0-2				1-0	2-0	0-1		0-1	2-0			
1973		1-0		0-1	0-0-1			1-1	2-0			0-1	0-0-1	1-1		
1972			1-0			1-0		1-0	1-0		0-1	0-1	2-0	0-1		0-1
1971			0-1			1-1		2-0	1-0			0-1	1-0	0-1	1-0	
1970			0-1	2-0		1-1		1-0	1-0			0-1	1-0	1-0	0-1	0-1

NATIONAL FOOTBALL CONFERENCE

	Ariz.	Atl.	Car.	Chi.	Dall.	Det.	G.B.	Minn.	N.O.	N.Y.G.	Phil.	St. L.	S.F.	T.B.	Wash.
Total	5-9-1	5-15	0-0	15-27	29-21	10-11-1	11-12-1	16-16	6-12	14-21-1	14-12	17-20	27-18	1-2	22-21
1996		0-1		2-0	2-1	0-2	2-1	0-1				0-2	2-1		
1995	0-1			1-2	3-0	2-0	1-0	0-2			0-1	0-1	2-1		
1994				0-2	2-1	1-0	1-0	2-0	0-2		1-2	2-0	2-1		
1993		0-1		0-1	1-1		0-1	1-0	0-2	1-0	1-1		1-2		1-2
1992		0-2		0-3	2-1	0-1		1-0	1-0	1-0	1-0		2-0		1-2
1991				2-1	0-1			0-1	1-0	2-1	2-1	0-1	2-1		2-0
1990						0-1		0-1	1-1	1-1	2-1	0-2	3-0		0-1
1989				1-1				1-1	1-1	2-1	1-1	0-2	3-0		0-2
1988	0-1			1-2	1-1			1-0	1-0	1-0	1-1	1-0	1-1		0-2
1987				1-2	2-1			1-0		0-3		1-2	2-0		1-1
1986	0-1			2-1	2-0	0-1	0-1			2-1		1-0	0-2		1-1
1985	1-1			1-1	1-1		0-1				0-1	2-1	1-2		2-1
1984		0-2		0-1	1-1	0-1	0-1		1-0	0-1		1-1	2-0		1-1
1983	0-0-1	0-1		1-1	2-0	2-1	0-1		0-1	1-1-1		1-0	1-0		1-2
1982				1-2	0-1	1-0	1-0			0-1				1-0	
1981		1-2		0-2	2-0	1-0		0-3				1-1	2-0		
1980				1-1	1-1				0-1	0-1	1-0	2-0		0-1	0-2
1979		1-2		0-2			1-0	0-1	0-1	0-1	1-1	1-0			1-0
1978	2-0	1-0		0-3	1-1			2-0				0-2	0-1		1-1
1977	0-1			1-0	1-1		0-1	0-1			0-1	1-1	0-2		1-1
1976	0-1			1-0				1-1		1-0		0-1	1-0		1-0
1975	0-1			0-1	1-1	0-1	0-1	1-0		1-0		0-1	1-0		2-0
1974		0-1		1-0	0-1	1-0	0-1	1-0	0-1			1-0	1-1	0-2	2-0
1973	0-1	1-1		0-1	1-1	1-0	1-1	0-1	0-1	0-1		1-0	1-0		1-1
1972	1-1	0-1		1-0	1-0	0-2	1-0	0-2	0-1	1-0		0-1	1-0		2-0
1971	1-0	1-0		0-1	1-0	0-1-1	0-1-1	2-0		0-1		0-2	0-1		1-0
1970		0-1		0-1	0-1	2-0	1-1	1-0		0-1		1-0	0-2		0-1

THURSDAY-SUNDAY NIGHT FOOTBALL, 1974-1996

(Home Team in capitals, games listed in chronological order.)

1996
Buffalo 23, NEW YORK GIANTS 20 (OT) (Sun.)
Miami 38, ARIZONA 10 (Sun.)
DENVER 27, Tampa Bay 23 (Sun.)
Philadelphia 33, ATLANTA 18 (Sun.)
WASHINGTON 31, New York Jets 16 (Sun.)
Houston 30, CINCINNATI 27 (OT) (Sun.)
INDIANAPOLIS 26, Baltimore 21 (Sun.)
KANSAS CITY 34, Seattle 16 (Thurs.)
NEW ENGLAND 28, Buffalo 25 (Sun.)
San Francisco 24, NEW ORLEANS 17 (Sun.)
CAROLINA 27, New York Giants 17 (Sun.)
Minnesota 16, OAKLAND 13 (OT) (Sun.)
Green Bay 24, ST. LOUIS 9 (Sun.)
New England 45, SAN DIEGO 7 (Sun.)
INDIANAPOLIS 37, Philadelphia 10 (Thurs.)
Minnesota 24, DETROIT 22 (Sun.)
JACKSONVILLE 20, Seattle 13 (Sun.)
SAN DIEGO 16, Denver 10 (Sun.)

1995
DENVER 22, Buffalo 7 (Sun.)
Philadelphia 31, ARIZONA 19 (Sun.)
Dallas 23, MINNESOTA 17 (OT) (Sun.)
Green Bay 24, JACKSONVILLE 14 (Sun.)
Oakland 47, NEW YORK JETS 10 (Sun.)
Denver 37, NEW ENGLAND 3 (Sun.)
ST. LOUIS 21, Atlanta 19 (Thurs.)
Cincinnati 27, PITTSBURGH 9 (Thurs.)
New York Giants 24, WASHINGTON 15 (Sun.)
Miami 24, SAN DIEGO 14 (Sun.)
PHILADELPHIA 31, Denver 13 (Sun.)
KANSAS CITY 20, Houston 13 (Sun.)
NEW ORLEANS 34, Carolina 26 (Sun.)
New York Giants 10, ARIZONA 6 (Thurs.)
SAN FRANCISCO 27, Buffalo 17 (Sun.)
TAMPA BAY 13, Green Bay 10 (OT) (Sun.)
SEATTLE 44, Oakland 10 (Sun.)
INDIANAPOLIS 10, New England 7 (Sat.)

1994
San Diego 17, DENVER 34 (Sun.)
New York Giants 20, ARIZONA 17 (Sun.)
Kansas City 30, ATLANTA 10 (Sun.)
Chicago 19, NEW YORK JETS 7 (Sun.)
Miami 23, CINCINNATI 7 (Sun.)
PHILADELPHIA 21, Washington 17 (Sun.)
Cleveland 11, HOUSTON 8 (Thurs.)
MINNESOTA 13, Green Bay 10 (OT) (Thurs.)
ARIZONA 20, Pittsburgh 17 (OT) (Sun.)
KANSAS CITY 13, Los Angeles Raiders 3 (Sun.)
DETROIT 14, Tampa Bay 9 (Sun.)
SAN FRANCISCO 31, Los Angeles Rams 27 (Sun.)
New England 12, INDIANAPOLIS 10 (Sun.)
MINNESOTA 33, Chicago 27 (OT) (Thurs.)
Buffalo 42, MIAMI 31 (Sun.)
New Orleans 29, ATLANTA 20 (Sun.)
Los Angeles Raiders 17, SEATTLE 16 (Sun.)
MIAMI 27, Detroit 20 (Sun.)

1993
NEW ORLEANS 33, Houston 21 (Sun.)
Los Angeles Raiders 17, SEATTLE 13 (Sun.)
Dallas 17, PHOENIX 10 (Sun.)
NEW YORK JETS 45, New England 7 (Sun.)
BUFFALO 17, New York Giants 14 (Sun.)
GREEN BAY 30, Denver 27 (Sun.)
ATLANTA 30, Los Angeles Rams 24 (Thurs.)
MIAMI 41, Indianapolis 27 (Sun.)
Detroit 30, MINNESOTA 27 (Sun.)
WASHINGTON 30, Indianapolis 24 (Sun.)
Chicago 16, SAN DIEGO 13 (Sun.)
TAMPA BAY 23, Minnesota 10 (Sun.)
HOUSTON 23, Pittsburgh 3 (Sun.)
SAN FRANCISCO 21, Cincinnati 8 (Sun.)
Green Bay 20, SAN DIEGO 13 (Sun.)
Philadelphia 20, INDIANAPOLIS 10 (Sun.)
MINNESOTA 30, Kansas City 10 (Sun.)
HOUSTON 24, New York Jets 0 (Sun.)

1992
DENVER 17, Los Angeles Raiders 13 (Sun.)
Philadelphia 31, PHOENIX 14 (Sun.)

BUFFALO 38, Indianapolis 0 (Sun.)
San Francisco 16, NEW ORLEANS 10 (Sun.)
NEW YORK JETS 30, New England 21 (Sun.)
NEW ORLEANS 13, Los Angeles Rams 10 (Sun.)
MINNESOTA 31, Detroit 14 (Thurs.)
Pittsburgh 27, KANSAS CITY 3 (Sun.)
New York Giants 24, WASHINGTON 7 (Sun.)
Cincinnati 31, CHICAGO 28 (OT) (Sun.)
DENVER 27, New York Giants 13 (Sun.)
Kansas City 24, SEATTLE 14 (Sun.)
SAN DIEGO 27, Los Angeles Raiders 3 (Sun.)
NEW ORLEANS 22, Atlanta 14 (Thurs.)
Los Angeles Rams 31, TAMPA BAY 27 (Sun.)
Green Bay 16, HOUSTON 14 (Sun.)
MIAMI 19, New York Jets 17 (Sun.)
HOUSTON 27, Buffalo 3 (Sun.)

1991
WASHINGTON 45, Detroit 0 (Sun.)
Houston 30, CINCINNATI 7 (Sun.)
NEW ORLEANS 24, Los Angeles Rams 7 (Sun.)
Dallas 17, PHOENIX 9 (Sun.)
Denver 13, MINNESOTA 6 (Sun.)
Pittsburgh 21, INDIANAPOLIS 3 (Sun.)
Los Angeles Raiders 23, SEATTLE 20 (Sun.)
Chicago 10, GREEN BAY 0 (Thurs.)
Washington 17, NEW YORK GIANTS 13 (Sun.)
DENVER 20, Pittsburgh 13 (Sun.)
MIAMI 30, New England 20 (Sun.)
HOUSTON 28, Cleveland 24 (Sun.)
Atlanta 23, NEW ORLEANS 20 (OT) (Sun.)
Los Angeles Raiders 9, SAN DIEGO 7 (Sun.)
Minnesota 26, TAMPA BAY 24 (Sun.)
Buffalo 35, INDIANAPOLIS 7 (Sun.)
SEATTLE 23, Los Angeles Rams 9 (Sun.)

1990
NEW YORK GIANTS 27, Philadelphia 20 (Sun.)
PITTSBURGH 20, Houston 9 (Sun.)
TAMPA BAY 23, Detroit 20 (Sun.)
Washington 38, PHOENIX 10 (Sun.)
BUFFALO 38, Los Angeles Raiders 24 (Sun.)
CHICAGO 38, Los Angeles Rams 9 (Sun.)
MIAMI 17, New England 10 (Thurs.)
ATLANTA 38, Cincinnati 17 (Sun.)
MINNESOTA 27, Denver 22 (Sun.)
San Francisco 24, DALLAS 6 (Sun.)
CINCINNATI 27, Pittsburgh 3 (Sun.)
Seattle 13, SAN DIEGO 10 (Sun.)
MINNESOTA 23, Green Bay 7 (Sun.)
MIAMI 23, Philadelphia 20 (Sun.)
DETROIT 38, Chicago 21 (Sun.)
INDIANAPOLIS 35, Washington 28 (Sat.)
SEATTLE 17, Denver 12 (Sun.)
HOUSTON 34, Pittsburgh 14 (Sun.)

1989
Dallas 13, WASHINGTON 3 (Sun.)
SAN DIEGO 14, Los Angeles Raiders 12 (Sun.)
INDIANAPOLIS 27, New York Jets 10 (Sun.)
Los Angeles Rams 20, NEW ORLEANS 17 (Sun.)
MINNESOTA 27, Chicago 16 (Sun.)
MIAMI 31, New England 10 (Sun.)
SEATTLE 23, Los Angeles Raiders 17 (Sun.)
Cleveland 24, HOUSTON 20 (Sat.)

1988
HOUSTON 41, Washington 17 (Sun.)
Los Angeles Raiders 13, SAN DIEGO 3 (Sun.)
Minnesota 43, DALLAS 3 (Sun.)
New England 6, MIAMI 3 (Sun.)
New York Giants 13, NEW ORLEANS 12 (Sun.)
Pittsburgh 37, HOUSTON 34 (Sun.)
SEATTLE 42, Denver 14 (Sun.)
Los Angeles Rams 38, SAN FRANCISCO 16 (Sun.)

1987
NEW YORK GIANTS 17, New England 10 (Sun.)
SAN DIEGO 16, Los Angeles Raiders 14 (Sun.)
Miami 20, DALLAS 14 (Sun.)
SAN FRANCISCO 38, Cleveland 24 (Sun.)
Chicago 30, MINNESOTA 24 (Sun.)
SEATTLE 28, Denver 21 (Sun.)
MIAMI 23, Washington 21 (Sun.)
SAN FRANCISCO 48, Los Angeles Rams 0 (Sun.)

1986
New England 20, NEW YORK JETS 6 (Thurs.)
Cincinnati 30, CLEVELAND 13 (Thurs.)

Los Angeles Raiders 37, SAN DIEGO 31 (OT) (Thurs.)
LOS ANGELES RAMS 29, Dallas 10 (Sun.)
SAN FRANCISCO 24, Los Angeles Rams 14 (Fri.)

1985
KANSAS CITY 36, Los Angeles Raiders 20 (Thurs.)
Chicago 33, MINNESOTA 24 (Thurs.)
Dallas 30, NEW YORK GIANTS 29 (Sun.)
SAN DIEGO 54, Pittsburgh 44 (Sun.)
Denver 27, SEATTLE 24 (Fri.)

1984
Pittsburgh 23, NEW YORK JETS 17 (Thurs.)
Denver 24, CLEVELAND 14 (Sun.)
DALLAS 30, New Orleans 27 (Sun.)
Washington 31, MINNESOTA 17 (Thurs.)
SAN FRANCISCO 19, Los Angeles Rams 16 (Fri.)

1983
San Francisco 48, MINNESOTA 17 (Thurs.)
CLEVELAND 17, Cincinnati 7 (Thurs.)
Los Angeles Raiders 40, DALLAS 38 (Sun.)
Los Angeles Raiders 42, SAN DIEGO 10 (Thurs.)
MIAMI 34, New York Jets 14 (Fri.)

1982
BUFFALO 23, Minnesota 22 (Thurs.)
SAN FRANCISCO 30, Los Angeles Rams 24 (Thurs.)
ATLANTA 17, San Francisco 7 (Sun.)

1981
MIAMI 30, Pittsburgh 10 (Thurs.)
Philadelphia 20, BUFFALO 14 (Thurs.)
DALLAS 29, Los Angeles 17 (Sun.)
HOUSTON 17, Cleveland 13 (Thurs.)

1980
TAMPA BAY 10, Los Angeles 9 (Thurs.)
DALLAS 42, San Diego 31 (Sun.)
San Diego 27, MIAMI 24 (OT) (Thurs.)
HOUSTON 6, Pittsburgh 0 (Thurs.)

1979
Los Angeles 13, DENVER 9 (Thurs.)
DALLAS 30, Los Angeles 6 (Sun.)
OAKLAND 45, San Diego 22 (Thurs.)
MIAMI 39, New England 24 (Thurs.)

1978
New England 21, OAKLAND 14 (Sun.)
Minnesota 21, DALLAS 10 (Thurs.)
LOS ANGELES 10, Pittsburgh 7 (Sun.)
Denver 21, OAKLAND 6 (Sun.)

1977
Minnesota 30, DETROIT 21 (Sat.)

1976
Los Angeles 20, DETROIT 17 (Sat.)

1975
LOS ANGELES 10, Pittsburgh 3 (Sat.)

1974
OAKLAND 27, Dallas 23 (Sat.)

Compiled by Elias Sports Bureau
*Set or tied NFL all-time record.

MONDAY NIGHT RECORDS

SCORING
TOUCHDOWNS
Most Touchdowns, Game
- 4 Ron Johnson, N.Y. Giants at Philadelphia, Oct. 2, 1972
- 4 Earl Campbell, Houston vs. Miami, Nov. 20, 1978
- 4 Marcus Allen, L.A. Raiders vs. San Diego, Sept. 24, 1984
- 4 Eric Dickerson, Indianapolis vs. Denver, Oct. 31, 1988
- 4 Emmitt Smith, Dallas at N.Y. Giants, Sept. 4. 1995

FIELD GOALS
Most Field Goals, Game
- 7 Chris Boniol, Dallas vs. Green Bay, Nov. 18, 1996*
- 5 Tim Mazzetti, Atlanta vs. Los Angeles, Oct. 30, 1978
- 5 Roger Ruzek, Dallas at L.A. Rams, Dec. 21, 1987
- 5 Rich Karlis, Minnesota vs. Cincinnati, Dec. 25, 1989
- 5 Nick Lowery, Kansas City vs. Denver, Sept. 20, 1993
- 5 Chris Jacke, Green Bay vs. San Francisco, Oct. 14, 1996 (OT)

RUSHING
YARDS GAINED
Most Yards Rushing, Game
- 221 Bo Jackson, L.A. Raiders at Seattle, Nov. 30, 1987
- 214 Thurman Thomas, Buffalo at N.Y. Jets, Sept. 24, 1990
- 199 Earl Campbell, Houston vs. Miami, Nov. 20, 1978

Longest Run From Scrimage, Game
- 99 Tony Dorsett, Dallas at Minnesota, Jan. 3, 1983 (TD)*
- 91 Bo Jackson, L.A. Raiders at Seattle, Nov. 30, 1987 (TD)
- 83 James Lofton, Green Bay at N.Y. Giants, Sept. 30, 1982 (TD)

TOUCHDOWNS
Most Rushing Touchdowns, Game
- 4 Earl Campbell, Houston vs. Miami, Nov. 20, 1978
- 4 Eric Dickerson, Indianapolis vs. Denver, Oct. 31, 1988
- 4 Emmit Smith, Dallas at N.Y. Giants, Sept. 4, 1995

PASSING
YARDS GAINED
Most Yards Passing, Game
- 458 Joe Montana, San Francisco at L.A. Rams, Dec. 11, 1989
- 447 Ken Anderson, Cincinnati vs. Buffalo, Nov. 17, 1975
- 445 Charley Johnson, Denver vs. Kansas City, Nov. 18, 1974

Longest Pass Play
- 99 Brett Favre to Robert Brooks, Green Bay at Chicago, Sept. 11, 1995 (TD)*
- 97 Bernie Kosar to Webster Slaughter, Cleveland vs. Chicago, Oct. 23, 1989 (TD)
- 95 Joe Montana to John Taylor, San Francisco at L.A. Rams, Dec. 11, 1989 (TD)

TOUCHDOWNS
Most Touchdown Passes, Game
- 5 Dave Krieg, Seattle vs. L.A. Raiders, Nov. 28, 1988
- 5 Jim Kelly, Buffalo vs. Cincinnati, Oct. 21, 1991

PASS RECEIVING
RECEPTIONS
Most Pass Receptions, Game
- 14 Herman Moore, Detroit vs. Chicago, Dec. 4, 1995
- 14 Jerry Rice, San Francisco vs. Minnesota, Dec. 18, 1995
- 13 Andre Reed, Buffalo vs. Denver, Sept. 18, 1989

YARDS GAINED
Most Yards on Pass Receptions, Game
- 289 Jerry Rice, San Francisco vs. Minnesota, Dec. 18, 1995
- 286 John Taylor, San Francisco at L.A. Rams, Dec. 11, 1989
- 260 Wes Chandler, San Diego vs. Cincinnati, Dec. 20, 1982

TOUCHDOWNS
Most Touchdown Pass Receptions, Game
- 3 Ron Johnson, N.Y. Giants at Philadelphia, Oct. 2, 1972
- 3 Wesley Walker, N.Y. Jets at Detroit, Dec. 6, 1982
- 3 Steve Largent, Seattle at San Diego, Oct. 29, 1984
- 3 Mark Clayton, Miami vs. Dallas, Dec. 17, 1984
- 3 Jerry Rice, San Francisco vs. Chicago, Dec. 14, 1987
- 3 Jerry Rice, San Francisco vs. Minnesota, Dec. 18, 1995

INTERCEPTIONS BY
Most Interceptions, Game
- 4 Dick Anderson, Miami vs. Pittsburgh, Dec. 3, 1973*
- 3 Johnny Robinson, Kansas City at Baltimore, Sept. 28, 1970
- 3 Charlie Babb, Miami vs. Oakland, Sept. 22, 1975
- 3 Charles Phillips, Oakland vs. Denver, Dec. 8, 1975
- 3 Mark Murphy, Washington at San Diego, Oct. 31, 1983
- 3 Ken Easley, Seattle at San Diego, Oct. 29, 1984
- 3 Dwayne Harper, San Diego vs. Oakland, Nov. 27, 1995

Longest Interception Return
- 102 Eddie Anderson, L.A. Raiders at Miami, Dec. 14, 1992 (TD)
- 94 Nolan Cromwell, L.A. Rams vs. Atlanta, Dec. 14, 1981
- 94 Walker Lee Ashley, Minnesota vs. Chicago, Dec. 19, 1988 (TD)

PUNTING
Longest Punt
- 74 Craig Colquitt, Pittsburgh vs. Oakland, Dec. 7, 1981
- 72 Bill Van Heusen, Denver at Oakland, Oct. 22, 1973
- 71 Jim Arnold, Detroit at San Francisco, Dec. 28, 1992

PUNT RETURNS
Longest Punt Return
- 95 John Taylor, San Francisco vs. Washington, Nov. 21, 1988 (TD)
- 94 Dennis McKinnon, Chicago vs. N.Y. Giants, Sept. 14, 1987 (TD)
- 91 JoJo Townsell, N.Y. Jets vs. Seattle, Nov. 9, 1987 (TD)

KICKOFF RETURNS
Longest Kickoff Return
- 102 Harold Hart, Oakland at Miami, Sept. 22, 1975 (TD)
- 99 Eddie Payton, Minnesota vs. Oakland, Sept. 14, 1981 (TD)
- 99 Gaston Green, L.A. Rams at Pittsburgh, Oct. 29, 1990 (TD)

FUMBLES
Longest Fumble Return
- 99 Don Griffin, San Francisco vs. Chicago, Dec. 23, 1991 (TD)
- 96 Joe Lavender, Philadelphia vs. Dallas, Sept. 23, 1974 (TD)
- 86 Michael Downs, Dallas at Houston, Dec. 13, 1982 (TD)
- 86 Tyrone Hughes, New Orleans vs. San Francisco, Nov. 28, 1994 (TD)

THANKSGIVING DAY RECORDS

SCORING
Most Touchdowns, Game
- 6 Ernie Nevers, Chi. Cardinals vs. Chi. Bears, Nov. 28, 1929*
- 4 Sterling Sharpe, Green Bay at Dallas, Nov. 24, 1994
- 3 By many players

RUSHING
Most Yards Rushing, Game
- 273 O.J. Simpson, Buffalo at Detroit, Nov. 25, 1976
- 198 Bob Hoernschemeyer, Detroit vs. N.Y. Yankees, Nov. 23, 1950
- 195 Earl Campbell, Houston at Dallas, Nov. 22, 1979

PASSING
Most Yards Passing, Game
- 410 Scott Mitchell, Detroit vs. Minnesota, Nov. 23, 1995
- 384 Warren Moon, Minnesota at Detroit, Nov. 23, 1995
- 351 Dave Krieg, Detroit vs. Buffalo, Nov. 24, 1994

PASS RECEIVING
RECEPTIONS
Most Pass Receptions, Game
- 12 Brett Perriman, Detroit vs. Minnesota, Nov. 23, 1995
- 11 Daryl Johnston, Dallas vs. Miami, Nov. 25, 1993
-     Michael Irvin, Dallas vs Kansas City, Nov. 23 1995

YARDS GAINED
Most Yards on Pass Receptions, Game
- 303 Jim Benton, Cleveland at Detroit, Nov. 22, 1945
- 185 Lance Alworth, San Diego vs. Buffalo, Nov. 26, 1964
- 184 Anthony Carter, Minnesota at Dallas, Nov. 26, 1987 (OT)

OVERTIME GAMES

HISTORY OF OVERTIME GAMES

PRESEASON

Aug. 28, 1955	Los Angeles 23, New York Giants 17, at Portland, Oregon
Aug. 24, 1962	Denver 27, Dallas Texans 24, at Fort Worth, Texas
Aug. 10, 1974	San Diego 20, New York Jets 14, at San Diego
Aug. 17, 1974	Pittsburgh 33, Philadelphia 30, at Philadelphia
Aug. 17, 1974	Dallas 19, Houston 13, at Dallas
Aug. 17, 1974	Cincinnati 13, Atlanta 7, at Atlanta
Sept. 6, 1974	Buffalo 23, New York Giants 17, at Buffalo
Aug. 9, 1975	Baltimore 23, Denver 20, at Denver
Aug. 30, 1975	New England 20, Green Bay 17, at Milwaukee
Sept. 13, 1975	Minnesota 14, San Diego 14, at San Diego
Aug. 1, 1976	New England 13, New York Giants 7, at New England
Aug. 2, 1976	Kansas City 9, Houston 3, at Kansas City
Aug. 20, 1976	New Orleans 26, Baltimore 20, at Baltimore
Sept. 4, 1976	Dallas 26, Houston 20, at Dallas
Aug. 13, 1977	Seattle 23, Dallas 17, at Seattle
Aug. 28, 1977	New England 13, Pittsburgh 10, at New England
Aug. 28, 1977	New York Giants 24, Buffalo 21, at East Rutherford, N.J.
Aug. 2, 1979	Seattle 12, Minnesota 9, at Minnesota
Aug. 4, 1979	Los Angeles 20, Oakland 14, at Los Angeles
Aug. 24, 1979	Denver 20, New England 17, at Denver
Aug. 23, 1980	Tampa Bay 20, Cincinnati 14, at Tampa Bay
Aug. 5, 1981	San Francisco 27, Seattle 24, at Seattle
Aug. 29, 1981	New Orleans 20, Detroit 17, at New Orleans
Aug. 28, 1982	Miami 17, Kansas City 17, at Kansas City
Sept. 3, 1982	Miami 16, New York Giants 13, at Miami
Aug. 6, 1983	L.A. Raiders 26, San Francisco 23, at Los Angeles
Aug. 6, 1983	Atlanta 13, Washington 10, at Atlanta
Aug. 13, 1983	St. Louis 27, Chicago 24, at St. Louis
Aug. 18, 1983	New York Jets 20, Cincinnati 17, at Cincinnati
Aug. 27, 1983	Chicago 20, Kansas City 17, at Chicago
Aug. 11, 1984	Pittsburgh 20, Philadelphia 17, at Pittsburgh
Aug. 9, 1985	Buffalo 10, Detroit 10, at Pontiac, Mich.
Aug. 10, 1985	Minnesota 16, Miami 13, at Miami
Aug. 17, 1985	Dallas 27, San Diego 24, at San Diego
Aug. 24, 1985	N.Y. Giants 34, N.Y. Jets 31, at East Rutherford, N.J.
Aug. 15, 1986	Washington 27, Pittsburgh 24, at Washington
Aug. 15, 1986	Detroit 30, Seattle 27, at Detroit
Aug. 23, 1986	Los Angeles Rams 20, San Diego 17, at Anaheim
Aug. 30, 1986	Minnesota 23, Indianapolis 20, at Indianapolis
Aug. 23, 1987	Philadelphia 19, New England 13, at New England
Sept. 5, 1987	Cleveland 30, Green Bay 24, at Milwaukee
Sept. 6, 1987	Kansas City 13, St. Louis 10, at Memphis, Tenn.
Aug. 11, 1988	Seattle 16, Detroit 13, at Detroit
Aug. 19, 1988	Miami 16, Denver 13, at Miami
Aug. 19, 1988	Green Bay 21, Kansas City 21, at Milwaukee
Aug. 20, 1988	Houston 20, Los Angeles Rams 17, at Anaheim
Aug. 21, 1988	Minnesota 19, Phoenix 16, at Phoenix
Aug. 5, 1989	Los Angeles Rams 16, San Francisco 13, at Tokyo, Japan
Aug. 26, 1989	Denver 24, Dallas 21, at Denver
Sept. 1, 1989	N.Y. Jets 15, Kansas City 13, at Kansas City
Aug. 24, 1990	Cincinnati 13, New England 10, at New England
Aug. 16, 1991	Cleveland 24, Washington 21, at Washington
Aug. 17, 1991	Cincinnati 27, Minnesota 24, at Cincinnati
Aug. 23, 1991	Dallas 20, Atlanta 17, at Dallas
Aug. 24, 1991	Cincinnati 19, Green Bay 16, at Green Bay
Aug. 22, 1992	Los Angeles Rams 16, Green Bay 13, at Anaheim
Aug. 8, 1993	Dallas 13, Detroit 13, at London, England
Aug. 12, 1995	Washington 16, Houston 13, at Knoxville, Tenn.
Aug. 19, 1995	Indianapolis 20, Green Bay 17, at Green Bay
Aug. 3, 1996	Minnesota 23, San Diego 20, at Minnesota
Aug. 10, 1996	San Francisco 16, San Diego 13, at San Francisco

REGULAR SEASON

Sept. 22, 1974—Pittsburgh 35, Denver 35, at Denver; Steelers win toss. Gilliam's pass intercepted and returned by Rowser to Denver's 42. Turner misses 41-yard field goal. Walden punts and Greer returns to Broncos' 39. Van Heusen punts and Edwards returns to Steelers' 16. Game ends with Steelers on own 26.

Nov. 10, 1974—New York Jets 26, New York Giants 20, at New Haven, Conn.; Giants win toss. Gogolak misses 42-yard field goal. Namath passes to Boozer for five yards and touchdown at 6:53.

Sept. 28, 1975—Dallas 37, St. Louis 31, at Dallas; Cardinals win toss. Hart's pass intercepted and returned by Jordan to Cardinals' 37. Staubach passes to DuPree for three yards and touchdown at 7:53.

Oct. 12, 1975—Los Angeles 13, San Diego 10, at San Diego; Chargers win toss. Partee punts to Rams' 14. Dempsey kicks 22-yard field goal at 9:27.

Nov. 2, 1975—Washington 30, Dallas 24, at Washington; Cowboys win toss. Staubach's pass intercepted and returned by Houston to Cowboys' 35. Kilmer runs one yard for touchdown at 6:34.

Nov. 16, 1975—St. Louis 20, Washington 17, at St. Louis; Cardinals win toss. Bakken kicks 37-yard field goal at 7:00.

Nov. 23, 1975—Kansas City 24, Detroit 21, at Kansas City; Lions win toss. Chiefs take over on downs at own 38. Stenerud kicks 26-yard field goal at 6:44.

Nov. 23, 1975—Oakland 26, Washington 23, at Washington; Redskins win toss. Bragg punts to Raiders' 42. Blanda kicks 27-yard field goal at 7:13.

Nov. 30, 1975—Denver 13, San Diego 10, at Denver; Broncos win toss. Turner kicks 25-yard field goal at 4:13.

Nov. 30, 1975—Oakland 37, Atlanta 34, at Oakland; Falcons win toss. James punts to Raiders' 16. Guy punts and Herron returns to Falcons' 41. Nick Mike-Mayer misses 45-yard field goal. Guy punts into Falcons' end zone. James punts to Raiders' 39. Blanda kicks 36-yard field goal at 15:00.

Dec. 14, 1975—Baltimore 10, Miami 7, at Baltimore; Dolphins win toss. Seiple punts to Colts' 4. Linhart kicks 31-yard field goal at 12:44.

Sept. 19, 1976—Minnesota 10, Los Angeles 10, at Minnesota; Vikings win toss. Tarkenton's pass intercepted by Monte Jackson and returned to Minnesota 16. Allen blocks Dempsey's 30-yard field goal attempt, ball rolls into end zone for touchback. Clabo punts and Scribner returns to Rams' 20. Rusty Jackson punts to Vikings' 35. Tarkenton's pass intercepted by Kay at Rams' 1, no return. Game ends with Rams on own 3.

*Sept. 27, 1976—Washington 20, Philadelphia 17, at Philadelphia; Eagles win toss. Jones punts and E. Brown loses one yard on return to Redskins' 40. Bragg punts 51 yards into end zone for touchback. Jones punts and E. Brown returns to Redskins' 42. Bragg punts and Marshall returns to Eagles' 41. Boryla's pass intercepted by Dusek at Redskins' 37, no return. Bragg punts and Bradley returns. Philadelphia holding penalty moves ball back to Eagles' 8. Boryla pass intercepted by E. Brown and returned to Eagles' 22. Moseley kicks 29-yard field goal at 12:49.

Oct. 17, 1976—Kansas City 20, Miami 17, at Miami; Chiefs win toss. Wilson punts into end zone for touchback. Bulaich fumbles into Kansas City end zone, Collier recovers for touchdown. Stenerud kicks 34-yard field goal at 14:48.

Oct. 31, 1976—St. Louis 23, San Francisco 20, at St. Louis; Cardinals win toss. Joyce punts and Leonard fumbles on return, Jones recovers at 49ers' 43. Bakken kicks 21-yard field goal at 6:42.

Dec. 5, 1976—San Diego 13, San Francisco 7, at San Diego; Chargers win toss. Morris runs 13 yards for touchdown at 5:12.

Sept. 18, 1977—Dallas 16, Minnesota 10, at Minnesota; Vikings win toss. Dallas starts on Vikings' 47 after a punt early in the overtime period. Staubach scores seven plays later on a four-yard run at 6:14.

*Sept. 26, 1977—Cleveland 30, New England 27, at Cleveland; Browns win toss. Sipe throws a 22-yard pass to Logan at Patriots' 19. Cockroft kicks 35-yard field goal at 4:45.

Oct. 16, 1977—Minnesota 22, Chicago 16, at Minnesota; Bears win toss. Parsons punts 53 yards to Vikings' 18. Minnesota drives to Bears' 11. On a first-and-10, Vikings fake a field goal and holder Krause hits Voigt with a touchdown pass at 6:45.

Oct. 30, 1977—Cincinnati 13, Houston 10, at Cincinnati; Bengals win toss. Bahr kicks a 22-yard field goal at 5:51.

Nov. 13, 1977—San Francisco 10, New Orleans 7, at New Orleans; Saints win toss. Saints fail to move ball and Blanchard punts to 49ers' 41. Wersching kicks a 33-yard field goal at 6:33.

Dec. 18, 1977—Chicago 12, New York Giants 9, at East Rutherford, N.J.; Giants win toss. The ball changes hands eight times before Thomas kicks a 28-yard field goal at 14:51.

Sept. 10, 1978—Cleveland 13, Cincinnati 10, at Cleveland; Browns win toss. Collins returns kickoff 41 yards to Browns' 47. Cockroft kicks 27-yard field goal at 4:30.

*Sept. 11, 1978—Minnesota 12, Denver 9, at Minnesota; Vikings win toss. Danmeier kicks 44-yard field goal at 2:56.

Sept. 24, 1978—Pittsburgh 15, Cleveland 9, at Pittsburgh; Steelers win toss. Cunningham scores on a 37-yard "gadget" pass from Bradshaw at 3:43. Steelers start winning drive on their 21.

Sept. 24, 1978—Denver 23, Kansas City 17, at Kansas City; Broncos win toss. Dilts punts to Kansas City. Chiefs advance to Broncos' 40 where Reed fails to make first down on fourth-and-one situation. Broncos march downfield. Preston scores two-yard touchdown at 10:28.

Oct. 1, 1978—Oakland 25, Chicago 19, at Chicago; Bears win toss. Both teams punt on first possession. On Chicago's second offensive series, Colzie intercepts Avellini's pass and returns it to Bears' 3. Three plays later, Whittington runs two yards for a touchdown at 5:19.

Oct. 15, 1978—Dallas 24, St. Louis 21, at St. Louis; Cowboys win toss. Dallas drives from its 23 into field goal range. Septien kicks 27-yard field goal at 3:28.

Oct. 29, 1978—Denver 20, Seattle 17, at Seattle; Broncos win toss. Ball changes hands four times before Turner kicks 18-yard field goal at 12:59.

Nov. 12, 1978—San Diego 29, Kansas City 23, at San Diego; Chiefs win toss. Fouts hits Jefferson for decisive 14-yard touchdown pass on the last play (15:00) of overtime period.

Nov. 12, 1978—Washington 16, New York Giants 13, at Washington; Redskins win toss. Moseley kicks winning 45-yard field goal at 8:32 after missing first down field goal attempt of 35 yards at 4:50.

Nov. 26, 1978—Green Bay 10, Minnesota 10, at Green Bay; Packers win toss. Both teams have possession of the ball four times.

Dec. 9, 1978—Cleveland 37, New York Jets 34, at Cleveland; Browns win toss. Cockroft kicks 22-yard field goal at 3:07.

Sept. 2, 1979—Atlanta 40, New Orleans 34, at New Orleans; Falcons win toss.

Bartkowski's pass intercepted by Myers and returned to Falcons' 46. Erxleben punts to Falcons' 4. James punts to Chandler on Saints' 43. Erxleben punts and Ryckman returns to Falcons' 28. James punts and Chandler returns to Saints' 36. Erxleben retrieves punt snap on Saints' 1 and attempts pass. Mayberry intercepts and returns six yards for touchdown at 8:22.

Sept. 2, 1979—Cleveland 25, New York Jets 22, at New York; Jets win toss. Leahy's 43-yard field goal attempt goes wide right at 4:41. Evans' punt blocked by Dykes is recovered by Newton. Ramsey punts into end zone for touchback. Evans punts and Harper returns to Jets' 24. Robinson's pass intercepted by Davis and returned 33 yards to Jets' 31. Cockroft kicks 27-yard field goal at 14:45.

***Sept. 3, 1979—Pittsburgh 16, New England 13**, at Foxboro; Patriots win toss. Hare punts to Swann at Steelers' 31. Bahr kicks 41-yard field goal at 5:10.

Sept. 9, 1979—Tampa Bay 29, Baltimore 26, at Baltimore; Colts win toss. Landry fumbles, recovered by Kollar at Colts' 14. O'Donoghue kicks 31-yard, first-down field goal at 1:41.

Sept. 16, 1979—Denver 20, Atlanta 17, at Atlanta; Broncos win toss. Broncos march 65 yards to Falcons' 7. Turner kicks 24-yard field goal at 6:15.

Sept. 23, 1979—Houston 30, Cincinnati 27, at Cincinnati; Oilers win toss. Parsley punts and Lusby returns to Bengals' 33. Bahr's 32-yard field goal attempt is wide right at 8:05. Parsley's punt downed on Bengals' 5. McInally punts and Ellender returns to Bengals' 42. Fritsch's third down, 29-yard field goal attempt hits left upright and bounces through at 14:28.

Sept. 23, 1979—Minnesota 27, Green Bay 21, at Minnesota; Vikings win toss. Kramer throws 50-yard touchdown pass to Rashad at 3:18.

Oct. 28, 1979—Houston 27, New York Jets 24, at Houston; Oilers win toss. Oilers march 58 yards to Jets' 18. Fritsch kicks 35-yard field goal at 5:10.

Nov. 18, 1979—Cleveland 30, Miami 24, at Cleveland; Browns win toss. Sipe passes 39 yards to Rucker for touchdown at 1:59.

Nov. 25, 1979—Pittsburgh 33, Cleveland 30, at Pittsburgh; Browns win toss. Sipe's pass intercepted by Blount on Steelers' 4. Bradshaw pass intercepted by Bolton on Browns' 12. Evans punts and Bell returns to Steelers' 17. Bahr kicks 37-yard field goal at 14:51.

Nov. 25, 1979—Buffalo 16, New England 13, at Foxboro; Patriots win toss. Hare's punt downed on Bills' 38. Jackson punts and Morgan returns to Patriots' 20. Grogan's pass intercepted by Haslett and returned to Bills' 42. Ferguson's 51-yard pass to Butler sets up N. Mike-Mayer's 29-yard field goal at 9:15.

Dec. 2, 1979—Los Angeles 27, Minnesota 21, at Los Angeles; Rams win toss. Clark punts and Miller returns to Vikings' 25. Kramer's pass intercepted by Brown and returned to Rams' 40. Cromwell, holding for 22-yard field goal attempt, runs around left end untouched for winning score at 6:53.

Sept. 7, 1980—Green Bay 12, Chicago 6, at Green Bay; Bears win toss. Parsons punts and Nixon returns 16 yards. Five plays later, Marcol returns own blocked field goal attempt 24 yards for touchdown at 6:00.

Sept. 14, 1980—San Diego 30, Oakland 24, at San Diego; Raiders win toss. Pastorini's first-down pass intercepted by Edwards. Millen intercepts Fouts' first-down pass and returns to San Diego 46. Bahr's 50-yard field goal attempt partially blocked by Williams and recovered on Chargers' 32. Eight plays later, Fouts throws 24-yard touchdown pass to Jefferson at 8:09.

Sept. 14, 1980—San Francisco 24, St. Louis 21, at San Francisco; Cardinals win toss. Swider punts and Robinson returns to 49ers' 32. San Francisco drives 52 yards to St. Louis 16, where Wersching kicks 33-yard field goal at 4:12.

Oct. 12, 1980—Green Bay 14, Tampa Bay 14, at Tampa Bay; Packers win toss. Teams trade punts twice. Lee returns second Tampa Bay punt to Green Bay 42. Dickey completes three passes to Buccaneers' 18, where Birney's 36-yard field goal attempt is wide right as time expires.

Nov. 9, 1980—Atlanta 33, St. Louis 27, at St. Louis; Falcons win toss. Strong runs 21 yards for touchdown at 4:20.

#Nov. 20, 1980—San Diego 27, Miami 24, at Miami; Chargers win toss. Partridge punts into end zone, Dolphins take over on their own 20. Woodley's pass for Nathan intercepted by Lowe and returned 28 yards to Dolphins' 12. Benirschke kicks 28-yard field goal at 7:14.

Nov. 23, 1980—New York Jets 31, Houston 28, at New York; Jets win toss. Leahy kicks 38-yard field goal at 3:58.

Nov. 27, 1980—Chicago 23, Detroit 17, at Detroit; Bears win toss. Williams returns kickoff 95 yards for touchdown at 0:21.

Dec. 7, 1980—Buffalo 10, Los Angeles 7, at Buffalo; Rams win toss. Corral punts and Hooks returns to Bills' 34. Ferguson's 30-yard pass to Lewis sets up N. Mike-Mayer's 30-yard field goal at 5:14.

Dec. 7, 1980—San Francisco 38, New Orleans 35, at San Francisco; Saints win toss. Erxleben's punt downed by Hardy on 49ers' 27. Wersching kicks 36-yard field goal at 7:40.

***Dec. 8, 1980—Miami 16, New England 13**, at Miami; Dolphins win toss. Von Schamann kicks 23-yard field goal at 3:20.

Dec. 14, 1980—Cincinnati 17, Chicago 14, at Chicago; Bengals win toss. Breech kicks 28-yard field goal at 4:23.

Dec. 21, 1980—Los Angeles 20, Atlanta 17, at Los Angeles; Rams win toss. Corral's punt downed at Rams' 37. James punts into end zone for touchback. Corral's punt downed on Falcons' 17. Bartkowski fumbles when hit by Harris, recovered by Delaney. Corral kicks 23-yard field goal on first play of possession at 7:00.

Sept. 27, 1981—Cincinnati 27, Buffalo 24, at Cincinnati; Bills win toss. Cater punts into end zone for touchback. Bengals drive to the Bills' 10 where Breech kicks 28-yard field goal at 9:33.

Sept. 27, 1981—Pittsburgh 27, New England 21, at Pittsburgh; Patriots win toss. Hubach punts and Smith returns five yards to midfield. Four plays later Bradshaw throws 24-yard touchdown pass to Swann at 3:19.

Oct. 4, 1981—Miami 28, New York Jets 28, at Miami; Jets win toss. Teams trade punts twice. Leahy's 48-yard field goal attempt is wide right as time expires.

Oct. 25, 1981—New York Giants 27, Atlanta 24, at Atlanta; Giants win toss. Jennings' punt goes out of bounds at New York 47. Bright returns Atlanta punt to Giants' 14. Woerner fair catches punt at own 28. Andrews fumbles on first play, recovered by Van Pelt. Danelo kicks 40-yard field goal four plays later at 9:20.

Oct. 25, 1981—Chicago 20, San Diego 17, at Chicago; Bears win toss. Teams trade punts. Bears' second punt returned by Brooks to Chargers' 33. Fouts pass intercepted by Fencik and returned 32 yards to San Diego 27. Roveto kicks 27-yard field goal seven plays later at 9:30.

Nov. 8, 1981—Chicago 16, Kansas City 13, at Kansas City; Bears win toss. Teams trade punts. Kansas City takes over on downs on its own 38. Fuller's fumble recovered by Harris on Chicago 36. Roveto's 37-yard field goal wide, but Chiefs penalized for leverage. Roveto's 22-yard field goal attempt three plays later is good at 13:07.

Nov. 8, 1981—Denver 23, Cleveland 20, at Denver; Browns win toss. D. Smith recovers Hill's fumble at Denver 48. Morton's 33-yard pass to Upchurch and 6-yard run by Preston set up Steinfort's 30-yard field goal at 4:10.

Nov. 8, 1981—Miami 30, New England 27, at New England; Dolphins win toss. Orosz punts and Morgan returns six yards to New England 26. Grogan's pass intercepted by Brudzinski who returns 19 yards to Patriots' 26. Von Schamann kicks 30-yard field goal on first down at 7:09.

Nov. 15, 1981—Washington 30, New York Giants 27, at New York; Giants win toss. Nelms returns Giants' punt 26 yards to New York 47. Five plays later Moseley kicks 48-yard field goal at 3:44.

Dec. 20, 1981—New York Giants 13, Dallas 10, at New York; Cowboys win toss and kick off. Jennings punts to Dallas 40. Taylor recovers Dorsett's fumble on second down. Danelo's 33-yard field goal attempt hits right upright and bounces back. White's pass for Pearson intercepted by Hunt and returned seven yards to Dallas 24. Four plays later Danelo kicks 35-yard field goal at 6:19.

Sept. 12, 1982—Washington 37, Philadelphia 34, at Philadelphia; Redskins win toss. Theismann completes five passes for 63 yards to set up Moseley's 26-yard field goal at 4:47.

Sept. 19, 1982—Pittsburgh 26, Cincinnati 20, at Pittsburgh; Bengals win toss. Anderson's pass intended for Kreider intercepted by Woodruff and returned 30 yards to Cincinnati 2. Bradshaw completes two-yard touchdown pass to Stallworth on first down at 1:08.

Dec. 19, 1982—Baltimore 20, Green Bay 20, at Baltimore; Packers win toss. K. Anderson intercepts Dickey's first-down pass and returns to Packers' 42. Miller's 44-yard field goal attempt blocked by G. Lewis. Teams trade punts before Stenerud's 47-yard field goal attempt is wide right. Teams trade punts again before time expires in Colts possession.

Jan. 2, 1983—Tampa Bay 26, Chicago 23, at Tampa; Bears win toss. Parsons punts to T. Bell at Buccaneers' 40. Capece kicks 33-yard field goal at 3:14.

Sept. 4, 1983—Baltimore 29, New England 23, at New England; Patriots win toss. Cooks runs 52 yards with fumble recovery three plays into overtime at 0:30.

Sept. 4, 1983—Green Bay 41, Houston 38, at Houston; Packers win toss. Stenerud kicks 42-yard field goal at 5:55.

Sept. 11, 1983—New York Giants 16, Atlanta 13, at Atlanta; Giants win toss. Dennis returns kickoff 54 yards to Atlanta 41. Haji-Sheikh kicks 30-yard field goal at 3:38.

Sept. 18, 1983—New Orleans 34, Chicago 31, at New Orleans; Bears win toss. Parsons punts and Groth returns five yards to New Orleans 34. Stabler pass intercepted by Schmidt at Chicago 47. Parsons punt downed by Gentry at New Orleans 2. Stabler gains 36 yards in four passes; Wilson 38 on six carries. Andersen kicks 41-yard field goal at 10:57.

Sept. 18, 1983—Minnesota 19, Tampa Bay 16, at Tampa; Vikings win toss. Coleman punts and Bell returns eight yards to Tampa Bay 47. Capece's 33-yard field goal attempt sails wide at 7:26. Dils and Young combine for 48-yard gain to Tampa Bay 27. Ricardo kicks 42-yard field goal at 9:27.

Sept. 25, 1983—Baltimore 22, Chicago 19, at Baltimore; Colts win toss. Allegre kicks 33-yard field goal nine plays later at 4:51.

Sept. 25, 1983—Cleveland 30, San Diego 24, at San Diego; Browns win toss. Walker returns kickoff 33 yards to Cleveland 37. Sipe completes 48-yard touchdown pass to Holt four plays later at 1:53.

Sept. 25, 1983—New York Jets 27, Los Angeles Rams 24, at New York; Jets win toss. Ramsey punts to Irvin who returns to 25 but penalty puts Rams on own 13. Holmes 30-yard interception return sets up Leahy's 26-yard field goal at 3:22.

Oct. 9, 1983—Buffalo 38, Miami 35, at Miami; Dolphins win toss. Von Schamann's 52-yard field goal attempt goes wide at 12:36. Cater punts to Clayton who loses 11 to own 13. Von Schamann's 43-yard field goal attempt sails wide at 5:15. Danelo kicks 36-yard field goal nine plays later at 13:58.

Oct. 9, 1983—Dallas 27, Tampa Bay 24, at Dallas; Cowboys win toss. Septien's 51-yard field goal attempt goes wide but Buccaneers penalized for roughing kicker. Septien kicks 42-yard field goal at 4:38.

Oct. 23, 1983—Kansas City 13, Houston 10, at Houston; Chiefs win toss. Lowery kicks 41-yard field goal 13 plays later at 7:41.

Oct. 23, 1983—Minnesota 20, Green Bay 17, at Green Bay; Packers win toss.

Scribner's punt downed on Vikings' 42. Ricardo kicks 32-yard field goal eight plays later at 5:05.

*Oct. 24, 1983—New York Giants 20, St. Louis 20, at St. Louis; Cardinals win toss. Teams trade punts before O'Donoghue's 44-yard field goal attempt is wide left. Jennings' punt returned by Bird to St. Louis 21. Lomax pass intercepted by Haynes who loses six yards to New York 33. Jennings' punt downed on St. Louis 17. O'Donoghue's 19-yard field goal attempt is wide right. Rutledge's pass intercepted by L. Washington who returns 25 yards to New York 25. O'Donoghue's 42-yard field goal attempt is wide right. Rutledge's pass intercepted by W. Smith at St. Louis 33 to end game.

Oct. 30, 1983—Cleveland 25, Houston 19, at Cleveland; Oilers win toss. Teams trade punts. Nielsen's pass intercepted by Whitwell who returns to Houston 20. Green runs 20 yards for touchdown on first down at 6:34.

Nov. 20, 1983—Detroit 23, Green Bay 20, at Milwaukee; Packers win toss. Scribner punts and Jenkins returns 14 yards to Green Bay 45. Murray's 33-yard field goal attempt is wide left at 9:32. Whitehurst's pass intercepted by Watkins and returned to Green Bay 27. Murray kicks 37-yard field goal four plays later at 8:30.

Nov. 27, 1983—Atlanta 47, Green Bay 41, at Atlanta; Packers win toss. K. Johnson returns interception 31 yards for touchdown at 2:13.

Nov. 27, 1983—Seattle 51, Kansas City 48, at Seattle; Seahawks win toss. Dixon's 47-yard kickoff return sets up N. Johnson's 42-yard field goal at 1:36.

Dec. 11, 1983—New Orleans 20, Philadelphia 17, at Philadelphia; Eagles win toss. Runager punts to Groth who fair catches on New Orleans 32. Stabler completes two passes for 36 yards to Goodlow to set up Andersen's 50-yard field goal at 5:30.

*Dec. 12, 1983—Green Bay 12, Tampa Bay 9, at Tampa; Packers win toss. Stenerud kicks 23-yard field goal 11 plays later at 4:07.

Sept. 9, 1984—Detroit 27, Atlanta 24, at Atlanta; Lions win toss. Murray kicks 48-yard field goal nine plays later at 5:06.

Sept. 30, 1984—Tampa Bay 30, Green Bay 27, at Tampa; Packers win toss. Scribner punts 44 yards to Tampa Bay 2. Epps returns Garcia's punt three yards to Green Bay 27. Scribner's punt downed on Buccaneers' 33. Ariri kicks 46-yard field goal 11 plays later at 10:32.

Oct. 14, 1984—Detroit 13, Tampa Bay 7, at Detroit; Buccaneers win toss. Tampa Bay drives to Lions' 39 before Wilder fumbles. Five plays later Danielson hits Thompson with 37-yard touchdown pass at 4:34.

Oct. 21, 1984—Dallas 30, New Orleans 27, at Dallas; Cowboys win toss. Septien kicks 41-yard field goal eight plays later at 3:42.

Oct. 28, 1984—Denver 22, Los Angeles Raiders 19, at Los Angeles; Raiders win toss. Hawkins fumble recovered by Foley at Denver 7. Teams trade punts. Karlis's 42-yard field goal attempt is wide left. Teams trade punts. Wilson pass intercepted by R. Jackson at Los Angeles 45, returned 23 yards to Los Angeles 22. Karlis kicks 35-yard field goal two plays later at 15:00.

Nov. 4, 1984—Philadelphia 23, Detroit 23, at Detroit; Lions win toss. Lions drive to Eagles' 3 in eight plays. Murray's 21-yard field goal attempt hits right upright and bounces back. Jaworski's pass intercepted by Watkins at Detroit 5. Teams trade punts. Cooper returns Black's punt five yards to Eagles' 14. Time expires four plays later with Eagles on own 21.

Nov. 18, 1984—San Diego 34, Miami 28, at San Diego; Chargers win toss. McGee scores eight plays later on a 25-yard run at 3:17.

Dec. 2, 1984—Cincinnati 20, Cleveland 17, at Cleveland; Browns win toss. Simmons returns Cox's punt 30 yards to Cleveland 35. Breech kicks 35-yard field goal seven plays later at 4:34.

Dec. 2, 1984—Houston 23, Pittsburgh 20, at Houston; Oilers win toss. Cooper kicks 30-yard field goal 16 plays later at 5:53.

Sept. 8, 1985—St. Louis 27, Cleveland 24, at Cleveland; Cardinals win toss. O'Donoghue kicks 35-yard field goal nine plays later at 5:27.

Sept. 29, 1985—New York Giants 16, Philadelphia 10, at Philadelphia; Eagles win toss. Jaworski's pass tipped by Quick and intercepted by Patterson who returns 29 yards for touchdown at 0:55.

Oct. 20, 1985—Denver 13, Seattle 10, at Denver; Seahawks win toss. Teams trade punts twice. Krieg's pass intercepted by Hunter and returned to Seahawks' 15. Karlis kicks 24-yard field goal four plays later at 9:19.

Nov. 10, 1985—Philadelphia 23, Atlanta 17, at Philadelphia; Falcons win toss. Donnelly's 62-yard punt goes out of bounds at Eagles' 1. Jaworski completes 99-yard touchdown pass to Quick two plays later at 1:49.

Nov. 10, 1985—San Diego 40, Los Angeles Raiders 34, at San Diego; Chargers win toss. James scores on 17-yard run seven plays later at 3:44.

Nov. 17, 1985—Denver 30, San Diego 24, at Denver; Chargers win toss. Thomas' 40-yard field goal attempt blocked by Smith and returned 60 yards by Wright for touchdown at 4:45.

Nov. 24, 1985—New York Jets 16, New England 13, at New York; Jets win toss. Teams trade punts twice. Patriots' second punt returned 46 yards by Sohn to Patriots' 15. Leahy kicks 32-yard field goal one play later at 10:05.

Nov. 24, 1985—Tampa Bay 19, Detroit 16, at Tampa; Lions win toss. Teams trade punts. Lions' punt downed on Buccaneers' 38. Igwebuike kicks 24-yard field goal 11 plays later at 12:31.

Nov. 24, 1985—Los Angeles Raiders 31, Denver 28, at Los Angeles; Raiders win toss. Bahr kicks 32-yard field goal six plays later at 2:42.

Dec. 8, 1985—Los Angeles Raiders 17, Denver 14, at Denver; Broncos win toss. Teams trade punts twice. Elway's fumble recovered by Townsend at Broncos' 8. Bahr kicks 26-yard field goal one play later at 4:55.

Sept. 14, 1986—Chicago 13, Philadelphia 10, at Chicago; Eagles win toss.

Crawford's fumble of kickoff recovered by Jackson at Eagles' 35. Butler kicks 23-yard field goal 10 plays later at 5:56.

Sept. 14, 1986—Cincinnati 36, Buffalo 33, at Cincinnati; Bills win toss. Zander intercepts Kelly's first-down pass and returns it to Bills' 17. Breech kicks 20-yard field goal two plays later at 0:56.

Sept. 21, 1986—New York Jets 51, Miami 45, at New York; Jets win toss. O'Brien completes 43-yard touchdown pass to Walker five plays later at 2:35.

Sept. 28, 1986—Pittsburgh 22, Houston 16, at Houston; Oilers win toss. Johnson's punt returned 41 yards by Woods to Oilers' 15. Abercrombie scores on three-yard run three plays later at 2:35.

Sept. 28, 1986—Atlanta 23, Tampa Bay 20, at Tampa; Falcons win toss. Teams trade punts. Luckhurst kicks 34-yard field goal 10 plays later at 12:35.

Oct. 5, 1986—Los Angeles Rams 26, Tampa Bay 20, at Anaheim; Rams win toss. Dickerson scores four plays later on 42-yard run at 2:16.

Oct. 12, 1986—Minnesota 27, San Francisco 24, at San Francisco; Vikings win toss. C. Nelson kicks 28-yard field goal nine plays later at 4:27.

Oct. 19, 1986—San Francisco 10, Atlanta 10, at Atlanta; Falcons win toss. Teams trade punts twice. Donnelly punts to 49ers' 27. The following play Wilson recovers Rice's fumble at 49ers' 46 as time expires.

Nov. 2, 1986—Washington 44, Minnesota 38, at Washington; Redskins win toss. Schroeder completes 38-yard touchdown pass to Clark four plays later at 1:46.

Nov. 20, 1986—Los Angeles Raiders 37, San Diego 31, at San Diego; Raiders win toss. Teams trade punts. Allen scores five plays later on 28-yard run at 8:33.

Nov. 23, 1986—Cleveland 37, Pittsburgh 31, at Cleveland; Browns win toss. Teams trade punts. Six plays later Kosar hits Slaughter with 36-yard touchdown pass at 6:37.

Nov. 30, 1986—Chicago 13, Pittsburgh 10, at Chicago; Bears win toss and kick off. Newsome's punt returned by Barnes to Chicago 49. Butler kicks 42-yard field goal five plays later at 3:55.

Nov. 30, 1986—Philadelphia 33, Los Angeles Raiders 27, at Los Angeles; Eagles win toss. Teams trade punts. Long recovers Cunningham's fumble at Philadelphia 42. Waters returns Allen's fumble 81 yards to Los Angeles 4. Cunningham scores on one-yard run two plays later at 6:53.

Nov. 30, 1986—Cleveland 13, Houston 10, at Cleveland; Oilers win toss and kick off. Gossett punts to Houston 39. Luck's pass intercepted by Minnifield at Cleveland 21. Gossett punts to Houston 34. Luck's pass intercepted by Minnifield at Cleveland 43 who returns 20 yards to Houston 37. Moseley kicks 29-yard field goal nine plays later at 14:44.

Dec. 7, 1986—St. Louis 10, Philadelphia 10, at Philadelphia; Cardinals win toss. White blocks Schubert's 40-yard field goal attempt. Teams trade punts. McFadden's 43-yard field goal attempt is wide left. Schubert's 37-yard field goal attempt is wide right. Cavanaugh's pass intercepted by Carter and returned to Eagles' 48 to end game.

Dec. 14, 1986—Miami 37, Los Angeles Rams 31, at Anaheim; Dolphins win toss. Marino completes 20-yard touchdown pass to Duper six plays later at 3:04.

Sept. 20, 1987—Denver 17, Green Bay 17, at Milwaukee; Packers win toss. Del Greco's 47-yard field goal attempt is short. Teams trade punts. Elway intercepted by Noble who returns 10 yards to Green Bay 34. Davis fumbles on next play and Smith recovers. Two plays later, Karlis's 40-yard field goal attempt is wide left. Time expires two plays later with Packers on own 23.

Oct. 11, 1987—Detroit 19, Green Bay 16, at Green Bay; Lions win toss. Prindle's 42-yard field goal attempt is wide left. Packers punt downed on Detroit 17. Prindle kicks 31-yard field goal 16 plays later at 12:26.

Oct. 18, 1987—New York Jets 37, Miami 31, at New York; Jets win toss. Teams trade punts. Ryan intercepted by Hooper at Jets' 47 who returns 11 yards. Mackey intercepted by Haslett at Jets' 37 who returns 9 yards. Jets punt. Mackey intercepted by Radachowsky who returns 45 yards to Miami 24. Ryan completes eight-yard touchdown pass to Hunter five plays later at 14:26.

Oct. 18, 1987—Green Bay 10, Philadelphia 10, at Green Bay; Packers win toss. Hargrove scores on seven-yard run 10 plays later at 5:04.

Oct. 18, 1987—Buffalo 6, New York Giants 3, at Buffalo; Bills win toss. Schlopy's 28-yard field goal attempt is wide left. Teams trade punts. Rutledge intercepted by Clark who returns 23 yards to Buffalo 40. Schlopy kicks 27-yard field goal nine plays later at 14:41.

Oct. 25, 1987—Buffalo 34, Miami 31, at Miami; Bills win toss. Norwood kicks 27-yard field goal seven plays later at 4:12.

Nov. 1, 1987—San Diego 27, Cleveland 24, at San Diego; Browns win toss. Kosar intercepted by Glenn who returns 20 yards to Browns' 25. Abbott kicks 33-yard field goal three plays later at 2:16.

Nov. 15, 1987—Dallas 23, New England 17, at New England; Cowboys win toss. Walker scores on 60-yard run four plays later at 1:50.

Nov. 26, 1987—Minnesota 44, Dallas 38, at Dallas; Vikings win toss. Coleman's punt downed by Hilton at Cowboys' 37. White intercepted by Studwell who returns 12 yards to Vikings' 37. D. Nelson scores on 24-yard run seven plays later at 7:51.

Nov. 29, 1987—Philadelphia 34, New England 31, at New England; Patriots win toss. Ramsey intercepted by Joyner who returns 29 yards to Eagles' 32. Fryar fair catches Teltschik's punt at Patriots' 13. Franklin's 46-yard field goal attempt is short. McFadden's 39-yard field goal attempt is wide left. Tatupu fumbles on next play and Cobb recovers. McFadden kicks 38-yard field goal four plays later at 12:16.

Dec. 6, 1987—New York Giants 23, Philadelphia 20, at New York; Giants win toss and kick off. Teams trade punts twice. Teltschik's punt is returned 16 yards

by McConkey to Eagles' 33. Three plays later, Allegre's 50-yard field goal attempt is blocked by Joyner and returned 25 yards by Hoage to Eagles' 30. McConkey returns Teltschik's punt four yards to Giants' 44. Allegre kicks 28-yard field goal four plays later at 10:42.

Dec. 6, 1987—Cincinnati 30, Kansas City 27, at Cincinnati; Bengals win toss. Teams trade punts. Breech kicks 32-yard field goal 16 plays later at 9:44.

Dec. 26, 1987—Washington 27, Minnesota 24, at Minnesota; Redskins win toss. Haji-Sheikh kicks 26-yard field goal six plays later at 2:09.

Sept. 4, 1988—Houston 17, Indianapolis 14, at Indianapolis; Colts win toss. Dickerson fumble recovered by Lyles who returns six yards to Colts' 42. Zendejas kicks 35-yard field goal six plays later at 3:51.

***Sept. 26, 1988—Los Angeles Raiders 30, Denver 27,** at Denver; Broncos win toss. Teams trade punts twice. Elway intercepted by Lee who returns 20 yards to Broncos' 31. Bahr kicks 35-yard field goal four plays later at 12:35.

Oct. 2, 1988—New York Jets 17, Kansas City 17, at New York; Chiefs win toss. Chiefs punt goes into end zone for touchback. Leahy's 44-yard field goal attempt is wide right. Chiefs punt is returned by Townsell to Jets' 26. Burruss recovers McNeil's fumble at Chiefs' 11. DeBerg intercepted by Humphery at Jets' 49. Three plays later, time expires.

Oct. 9, 1988—Denver 16, San Francisco 13, at San Francisco; Broncos win toss and kick off. Young intercepted by Haynes at Broncos' 32. Denver punt downed at 49ers' 5. Young intercepted by Wilson who returns seven yards to 49ers' 5. Karlis kicks 22-yard field goal two plays later at 8:11.

Oct. 30, 1988—New York Giants 13, Detroit 10, at Detroit; Lions win toss. James's fumble recovered by Taylor at Lions' 22. Three plays later, McFadden kicks 33-yard field goal at 1:13.

Nov. 20, 1988—Buffalo 9, New York Jets 6, at Buffalo; Jets win toss. Vick's fumble recovered by Bennett at Bills' 32. Norwood kicks 30-yard field goal five plays later at 3:47.

Nov. 20, 1988—Philadelphia 23, New York Giants 17, at New York; Eagles win toss. Philadelphia's punt goes into end zone for touchback. Hostetler intercepted by Hoage who returns 11 yards to Giants' 41. Six plays later, Zendejas's 30-yard field-goal attempt is blocked and ball is recovered behind line of scrimmage by Eagles' Simmons, who runs 15 yards for touchdown at 3:09.

Dec. 11, 1988—New England 10, Tampa Bay 7, at New England; Buccaneers win toss and kick off. Staurovsky kicks 27-yard field goal six plays later at 3:08.

Dec. 17, 1988—Cincinnati 20, Washington 17, at Cincinnati; Bengals win toss. Cincinnati's punt returned by Oliphant to Redskins' 16. Grant recovers Williams's fumble at Redskins' 17. Breech kicks 20-yard field goal three plays later at 7:01.

Sept. 24, 1989—Buffalo 47, Houston 41, at Houston; Oilers win toss. Johnson returns Brady's kickoff 17 yards to Oilers' 19. Oilers drive to Buffalo 25, Zendejas's 37-yard field goal blocked, but Bills offsides and Zendejas's second attempt is wide left. Bills' ball and Kelly completes series of passes, including 28-yard game-winner to Andre Reed, at 8:42.

Oct. 8, 1989—Miami 13, Cleveland 10, at Miami; Browns win toss. Metcalf returns Stoyanovich's kickoff 20 yards to Browns' 28. Browns drive ball 46 yards in eight plays; Bahr wide left on 44-yard field goal attempt. Dolphins ball. Browns called for pass interference on Marino pass to Banks at Cleveland 47. Two plays later, Banks's 20-yard reception at Browns' 23 sets up winning 35-yard field goal by Stoyanovich at 6:23.

Oct. 22, 1989—Denver 24, Seattle 21, at Seattle; Seahawks win toss. Treadwell's 56-yard kickoff returned 18 yards by Jefferson to Seahawks' 27. Seahawks drive to Broncos' 22 in 10 plays, but Johnson's 40-yard field goal attempt wide left. Smith intercepts a Krieg pass and returns it 28 yards to Seahawks' 10. Treadwell kicks winning 27-yard field goal at 7:46.

Oct. 29, 1989—New England 23, Indianapolis 20, at Indianapolis; Patriots win toss. Biasucci kickoff returned 13 yards to Patriots' 23 by Martin. Holding penalty brings ball back to Patriots' 13. After six plays, Feagles punt returned 11 yards by Verdin to Colts' 28. Six plays later, Colts punt to Martin at Patriots' 12. Grogan completes three straight passes to Patriots' 44. Five consecutive runs put New England on Colts' 33. Davis kicks a 51-yard winning field goal for Patriots at 9:46.

Oct. 29, 1989—Green Bay 23, Detroit 20, at Milwaukee; Lions win toss. Sanders touchback on Jacke kickoff. On first play, Murphy intercepts Lions' Peete and returns it three yards to Lions' 26. Fullwood gains five yards on three plays to set up Jacke's 38-yard field goal at 2:14.

Nov. 5, 1989—Minnesota 23, Los Angeles Rams 21, at Minneapolis; Rams win toss. Karlis's kick returned 18 yards by Delpino to Rams' 19. Drive stops at Rams' 28. Merriweather blocks Hatcher's punt at 12. Ball rolls out of end zone for safety.

Nov. 19, 1989—Cleveland 10, Kansas City 10, at Cleveland; Browns win toss. Browns punt three times; Chiefs twice; before Kansas City's Lowery misses 47-yard field goal with 17 seconds remaining in overtime. Kosar's pass intercepted as time expired.

Nov. 26, 1989—Los Angeles Rams 20, New Orleans 17, at New Orleans; Saints win toss. Lansford's kickoff returned 27 yards to Saints' 30. After four plays, Barnhardt punts to Rams' 15. Saints penalized 35 yards for interference to Rams' 43. Three plays later, Everett hits Anderson with 14-yard pass to Saints' 40, then 26-yarder to put Rams in field goal position. Lansford kicks 31-yard field goal at 6:38.

Dec. 3, 1989—Los Angeles Raiders 16, Denver 13, at Los Angeles; Broncos win toss. Bell returns Jaeger kickoff 14 yards to Broncos' 18. Broncos' penalized for illegal block to Broncos' 9. Elway completes three passes for two first downs. On third and eight Elway sacked for 10-yard loss. Horan punts, Adams calls for fair catch at Raiders' 29. Dyal's 26-yard reception moves Raiders to Denver 43. Raiders move ball 34 yards in three plays to set up Jaeger's 26-yard field goal at 7:02.

Dec. 10, 1989—Indianapolis 23, Cleveland 17, at Indianapolis; Browns win toss. Teams trade punts. McNeil returns Colts' punt 42 yards to 42. Seven plays later, Bahr misses 35-yard field goal attempt. Three plays later, Stark punts and McNeil returns ball to 50-yard line. Two plays later, Prior intercepts Kosar's pass at Colts' 42 and returns it 58 yards for touchdown at 10:54.

Dec. 17, 1989—Cleveland 23, Minnesota 17, at Cleveland; Browns win toss. Browns punt to Vikings' 18. Six plays later, Vikings punt to Browns' 22. Nine plays later, Bahr lines up to attempt 31-yard field goal. Holder Pagel takes snap and passes 14 yards to Waiters for touchdown at 9:30.

Sept. 23, 1990—Denver 34, Seattle 31, at Denver; Seahawks win toss. Loville returns kickoff 19 yards to Seahawks' 27. Seahawks drive to Broncos' 26, where Johnson misses 44-yard field goal wide right. Broncos take over and Elway completes series of passes to set up Treadwell's 25-yard field goal at 9:14.

Sept. 30, 1990—Tampa Bay 23, Minnesota 20, at Minnesota; Vikings win toss. Vikings drive to Buccaneers' 31; Igwebuike's 48-yard field goal attempt wide left. Buccaneers drive to Vikings' 43 and punt. Gannon's pass is intercepted at Vikings' 26 by Wayne Haddix. Buccaneers drive to Vikings' 19 to set up Christie's 36-yard field goal at 9:11.

Oct. 7, 1990—Cincinnati 34, Los Angeles Rams 31, at Anaheim; Rams win toss. Berry returns kickoff to Rams' 21. After 3 plays, English punts and Green downs ball at Bengals' 25. After 3 plays, Johnson punts and Sutton downs ball at Rams' 29-yard line. After 3 plays, English punts and Price signals fair catch at Bengals' 47. Esiason completes series of passes to 26-yard line to set up Breech's 44-yard field goal at 11:56.

Nov. 4, 1990—Washington 41, Detroit 38, at Detroit; Redskins win toss. Howard downs kickoff on Redskins' 15. After 3 plays, Mojsiejenko punts to Redskins' 45. After 3 plays, Arnold punts to Redskins' 10. Rutledge completes series of passes to set up Lohmiller's 34-yard field goal at 9:10.

Nov. 18, 1990—Chicago 16, Denver 13, at Denver; Broncos win toss. Ezor returns kickoff to Broncos' 12. Both teams have ball twice and have to punt after each possession. Broncos punt after third possession of overtime and Bailey returns 20 yards to Broncos' 34. Harbaugh completes 10-yard pass to Thornton to set up Butler's 44-yard field goal at 13:14.

Nov. 25, 1990—Seattle 13, San Diego 10, at San Diego; Chargers win toss. Lewis returns kickoff to Chargers' 22. After 2 plays, Cox fumbles and ball is recovered by Porter at Chargers' 23. After two plays, Johnson kicks 40-yard field goal at 3:01.

Dec. 2, 1990—Chicago 23, Detroit 17, at Chicago; Lions win toss. Gray returns kickoff to Lions' 35. After 10 plays, Murray misses 35-yard field goal. Bears take possession at Chicago 20. Harbaugh completes 50-yard game-winning pass to Anderson at 10:57.

Dec. 2, 1990—Seattle 13, Houston 10, at Seattle; Seahawks win toss. Warren returns kickoff to Seahawks' 13. After 5 plays, Donnelly punts to Oilers' 23-yard line. Ford's fumble recovered by Wyman. Seahawks take possession at Oilers' 27. After 2 plays, Johnson kicks 42-yard field goal at 4:25.

Dec. 9, 1990—Miami 23, Philadelphia 20, at Miami; Eagles win toss. After 11 plays, Feagles punts to Dolphins' 26. After 6 plays, Roby punts to Eagles' 14 and Harris returns to 25. After 3 plays, Feagles punts to Dolphins' 43. Marino completes series of passes to Eagles' 22. Stoyanovich kicks 39-yard field goal at 12:32.

Dec. 9, 1990—San Francisco 20, Cincinnati 17, at Cincinnati; 49ers win toss. Carter returns kickoff to 49ers' 19. After 10 plays, Cofer kicks 23-yard field goal at 6:12.

Sept. 23, 1991—Chicago 19, New York Jets 13, at Chicago; Jets win toss. Mathis returns kickoff seven yards to New York's 12. Jets drive to New York 26; Bailey returns punt to Chicago 39. Bears drive to Jets' 44-yard line and punt into the end zone. Jets drive to Bears' 11 where Leahy's 28-yard field goal attempt is wide left. Bears drive from 20 to Jets' 1 where Harbaugh runs for touchdown at 14:42.

Oct. 13, 1991—Los Angeles Raiders 23, Seattle 20, at Seattle. Seahawks win toss. Seahawks begin on 20. After 5 plays, Tuten punts and Brown signals fair catch at Raiders' 24. After 3 plays, Gossett punts and Land downs ball at Seattle 9. After 1 play, Lott intercepts at Seahawks' 19 to set up Jaeger's game-winning 37-yard field goal at 6:37.

Oct. 20, 1991—Cleveland 30, San Diego 24, at San Diego; Chargers win toss. After kickoff, Chargers drive to Browns' 45 and punt to Browns' 6 where Hendrickson downs ball. Browns drive to 38 and punt; Taylor fair catches on Chargers' 14. After 3 plays, Brandon intercepts at Chargers' 30 and scores at 5:58.

Oct. 20, 1991—New England 26, Minnesota 23, at New England; Patriots win toss. Martin returns kickoff 18 yards to New England 22. Patriots drive to Minnesota 19. Staurovsky's 36-yard field goal attempt is wide left. Minnesota drives to the 50 where Newsome punts into end zone. On first play, McMillian intercepts at the 40 for Minnesota. After 2 plays, Marion causes Jordan fumble and Pool recovers at New England 20. New England drives to Minnesota 24 where Staurovsky kicks 42-yard field goal as time expires.

Nov. 3, 1991—New York Jets 19, Green Bay 16, at New York; Packers win toss. Thompson returns kickoff 30 yards to Packers' 39. Green Bay drives to New York 24 where Jacke's 42-yard field goal attempt is wide right. Jets drive to 50. Aguiar's punt is fumbled by Sikahema and recovered by New York at Packers' 23. After 2 plays, Leahy kicks 37-yard field goal at 9:40.

Nov. 3, 1991—Washington 16, Houston 13, at Washington; Redskins win toss. Mitchell returns kickoff 9 yards to Washington 14. After 4 plays, Goodburn punts and Givins returns to Houston 31. After 1 play, Moon's pass is intercepted by

Green at Oilers' 35. After 3 plays, Lohmiller kicks 41-yard field goal at 4:01.

Nov. 10, 1991—Houston 26, Dallas 23, at Houston; Oilers win toss. Pinkett returns kickoff 20 yards to Houston 24. After 6 plays, Montgomery punts and Martin returns to Dallas 24. Cowboys drive to Oilers' 24 where Smith fumbles and McDowell recovers at Oilers' 15. Houston drives to Dallas 5 where Del Greco kicks 23-yard field goal at 14:31.

Nov. 10, 1991—Pittsburgh 33, Cincinnati 27, at Cincinnati; Pittsburgh wins toss. Woodson downs kickoff for touchback. After 3 plays, Stryzinski punts and Barber returns 7 yards to Cincinnati 38. Bengals drive to Pittsburgh 37 where Woods fumbles and Lloyd returns recovery to Cincinnati 44. After 2 plays, O'Donnell passes to Green for 26-yard touchdown at 6:32.

Nov. 24, 1991—Atlanta 23, New Orleans 20, at New Orleans; Atlanta wins toss. Falcons begin at 20. After 3 plays, Fulhage punts and Fenerty signals fair catch at New Orleans 43. After 3 plays, Barnhardt punts and Thompson downs ball at Atlanta 23. After 3 plays, Fulhage punts and Fenerty fair catches at New Orleans 25. Saints drive to Atlanta 38 where Andersen misses 55-yard field-goal attempt. After 1 play, Rozier fumbles and Martin recovers on 50. Saints drive to Atlanta 38 where Barnhardt punts to Falcons' 2. Atlanta drives to New Orleans 33 where Johnson kicks 50-yard field goal at 13:03.

Nov. 24, 1991—Miami 16, Chicago 13, at Chicago; Miami wins toss. Butler kicks to Miami 20 where Paige returns kickoff 15 yards to 35. Miami drives to Chicago 9 where Stoyanovich kicks 27-yard field goal at 4:11.

Dec. 8, 1991—Buffalo 30, Los Angeles Raiders 27, at Los Angeles; Raiders win toss. Daluiso kicks into end zone for touchback. On third play, Kelso intercepts for Buffalo and returns ball to Bills' 36. Bills drive to Los Angeles 24 where Norwood kicks 42-yard field goal at 2:34.

Dec. 8, 1991—Kansas City 20, San Diego 17, at Kansas City; Chiefs win toss. Carney kicks to Kansas City 10 where Stradford returns 23 yards to 33. After 3 plays, Barker punts to San Diego 4. Chargers drive to 40 where Kidd punts 60 yards into end zone for touchback. Kansas City drives to San Diego 39 where Barker punts 38 yards to 1. After 3 plays, Kidd punts 41 yards to San Diego 42 where Stradford returns 12 yards to 30. Chiefs drive to San Diego 1 where Lowery kicks 18-yard field goal at 11:26.

Dec. 8, 1991—New England 23, Indianapolis 17, at New England; Indianapolis wins toss. Baumann kicks off to Indianapolis 2 where Martin returns 23 yards to 25. After 3 downs, Stark punts to New England 17 where Henderson returns 8 yards to 25. New England drives to 50 where McCarthy punts and Prior signals fair catch at Indianapolis 15. After 3 plays, Stark punts to New England 40 where Henderson returns 7 yards to 47. After 2 plays, Millen passes to Timpson for 45-yard touchdown at 8:55.

Dec. 22, 1991—Detroit 17, Buffalo 14, at Buffalo; Detroit wins toss. Daluiso kicks off to Detroit 20 where Dozier returns 15 yards to Lions 35. Lions drive to Bills' 3 where Murray kicks 21-yard field goal at 4:23.

Dec. 22, 1991—New York Jets 23, Miami 20, at Miami; Jets win toss. Aguiar kicks to Miami's 30 where Logan returns 3 yards to the 33. After 4 downs, Stoyanovich punts to Jets' 15 where Baty returns 8 yards to 23. Jets drive to Miami 12 where Allegre kicks 30-yard field goal at 6:33.

Sept. 6, 1992—Minnesota 23, Green Bay 20, at Green Bay. Vikings win toss. Nelson returns kickoff 14 yards to the Minnesota 23. After 5 plays, Newsome punts 49 yards to Green Bay 21 where Brooks returns 12 yards to the 33. After 2 plays, Glenn intercepts pass at the Vikings' 48. On first play, Allen fumbles and Billups recovers at Green Bay 35. After 3 plays, McJulien punts 33 yards to Vikings' 35. Vikings drive to Minnesota 48; Newsome punts 52 yards for touchback. After 3 plays, McJulien punts and Parker returns 10 yards to Green Bay 48. Vikings drive to Packers' 9 where Reveiz kicks 26-yard field goal at 10:20.

Sept. 13, 1992—Cincinnati 24, Los Angeles Raiders 21, at Cincinnati. Raiders win toss. Land returns kickoff 13 yards but fumbles at Los Angeles's 20; ball recovered by Bengals' Bennett at Raiders' 21. After 1 play, Breech kicks 34-yard field goal at 1:01.

Sept. 20, 1992—Houston 23, Kansas City 20, at Houston. Chiefs win toss. Carter returns kickoff 25 yards to Kansas City 28. On third play of drive, Birden fumbles at Kansas City 34; ball recovered by Houston's D. Smith at Chiefs' 23. After one play, Del Greco kicks 39-yard field goal at 1:55.

Oct. 11, 1992—Indianapolis 6, New York Jets 3, at Indianapolis. Colts win toss. Verdin returns kickoff 33 yards to Colts' 36. Colts drive to Jets' 30 where Biasucci kicks 47-yard field goal at 3:01.

Nov. 8, 1992—Cincinnati 31, Chicago 28, at Chicago. Bears win toss. Lewis returns kickoff 22 yards to Chicago's 29. Bears drive to Chicago's 46 where Gardocki punts; fair catch by Wright at the Cincinnati 17. Bengals drive to Bears' 18 where Breech kicks 36-yard field goal at 8:39.

Nov. 15, 1992—New England 37, Indianapolis 34, at Indianapolis. Colts win toss. Verdin returns kickoff 10 yards to Colts' 20; holding penalty brings ball back to Colts' 10. After two plays, Henderson intercepts pass at Colts' 38 and returns it 9 yards to the 29. In three plays, Patriots drive to 1 where Baumann kicks 18-yard field goal at 3:25.

Nov. 29, 1992—Indianapolis 16, Buffalo 13, at Indianapolis. Colts win toss. Verdin returns kickoff 24 yards to Colts' 22. Colts drive to Buffalo 22 where Biasucci kicks 40-yard field goal at 3:51.

***Nov. 30, 1992—Seattle 16, Denver 13,** at Seattle. Seahawks win toss. Daluiso kicks through end zone for touchback. After three plays, Tuten punts 53 yards to Denver 18 where Marshall returns for no gain. After three plays, Rodriguez punts 29 yards to Seattle 45 where Warren signals fair catch. Seahawks drive to Denver 15 where Kasay's 33-yard field goal attempt misses. Broncos take over at Denver 20. After three plays, Rodriguez punts 43 yards to Seattle 38 where Warren signals for fair catch. After four plays, Tuten punts 39 yards to Denver 4 where Daniels downs punt. After three plays, Rodriguez punts 46 yards to Denver 48 where Warren returns 10 yards to the 38. Seahawks drive to Denver 14 where Kasay kicks 32-yard field goal at 11:10.

Dec. 13, 1992—Philadelphia 20, Seattle 17, at Seattle. Eagles win toss. Sydner returns kick 12 yards to Eagles' 16; illegal block penalty brings ball back to 8. Eagles drive to Philadelphia 45 where Feagles punts for a touchback. After 6 plays, Tuten punts 45 yards to Philadelphia 22 where Sydner returns 7 yards to 29. After 6 plays, Feagles punts 44 yards to Seattle 26 where Warren returns 5 yards to 31. After 5 plays, Tuten punts 32 yards to Philadelphia 20 where Sydner signals for fair catch. Eagles drive to Seattle 27 where Ruzek kicks 44-yard field goal with no time remaining.

Dec. 27, 1992—Miami 16, New England 13, at New England. Patriots win toss. Lockwood returns kickoff 15 yards to Patriots' 21. After three plays, McCarthy punts 39 yards to Miami 33 where Miller returns 2 yards to the 35. Miami drives to New England 18 where Stoyanovich kicks 35-yard field goal at 8:17.

Sept. 12, 1993—Detroit 19, New England 16, at New England. Patriots win toss. Patriots begin at 20. After 3 plays, Saxon punts 42 yards to Detroit 29 where Gray returns 12 yards to the 41. After 3 plays, Arnold punts 41 yards to New England 12 where Brown returns 16 yards to the 28. Patriots drive to Detroit 44 where Saxon punts into the end zone for a touchback. Detroit drives to New England 20 where Hanson kicks 38-yard field goal at 11:04.

Nov. 7, 1993—Buffalo 13, New England 10, at New England. Patriots win toss. T. Brown returns kickoff 27 yards to Patriots 30. Patriots drive to Buffalo 48 where Bills take over on downs. Bills drive to New England 25 where Metzelaars fumbles, and C. Brown recovers. After 3 plays, Saxon punts 46 yards to Buffalo 24 where Copeland returns 11 yards to the 35. Bills drive to New England 14 where Christie kicks 32-yard field goal at 9:22.

Dec. 19, 1993—Phoenix 30, Seattle 27, at Seattle. Cardinals win toss. Bailey returns kickoff 14 yards to Cardinals 20. Cardinals drive to Seattle 23 where Davis kicks 41-yard field goal at 6:45.

Jan. 2, 1994—Dallas 16, New York Giants 13, at New York. Giants win toss. Meggett returns kickoff 19 yards to Giants 19. After 6 plays, Horan punts 45 yards to Cowboys 25 where Widmer downs punt. Cowboys drive to Giants' 23 where Murray kicks 41-yard field goal at 10:44.

Jan. 2, 1994—New England 33, Miami 27, at New England. Dolphins win toss. McDuffie returns kickoff 21 yards to Miami 27. After 3 plays, Hatcher punts 43 yards to New England 29 where Harris returns 6 yards to the 35. After 2 plays, Brown intercepts pass from Bledsoe and returns 3 yards to Miami 49. After 3 plays, Hatcher punts 37 yards to New England 14 where Harris returns 18 yards to the 32. After 2 plays, Bledsoe passes 36 yards to Timpson for touchdown at 4:44.

Jan. 2, 1994—Los Angeles Raiders 33, Denver 30, at Los Angeles. Broncos win toss. Delpino returns kickoff 12 yards to Denver 25. Broncos drive to Los Angeles 22 where Elam's 40-yard field goal attempt is wide left. Raiders drive to Denver 29 where Jaeger kicks 47-yard field goal at 7:10.

***Jan. 3, 1994—Philadelphia 37, San Francisco 34,** at San Francisco. 49ers win toss. Walker returns kickoff, 19 yards to San Francisco 27. 49ers drive to Philadelphia 14 where Cofer misses 32-yard field goal. Eagles start at their 20-yard line, and, after 3 plays, Feagles punts 48 yards to San Francisco 36 where Carter fumbles and 49ers recover. After 7 plays, Wilmsmeyer punts 57 yards to Philadelphia 6 where Sikahema returns 16 yards to the 22. Eagles drive to San Francisco 10 where Ruzek kicks 28-yard field goal with no time remaining.

Sept. 4, 1994—Detroit 31, Atlanta 28, at Detroit. Falcons win toss. Falcons start at their own 16 after holding penalty on kickoff. After 3 plays, Alexander punts 41 yards to Detroit 39 where Clay returns 12 yards to Atlanta 49. Detroit drives to Atlanta 20 where Hanson kicks 37-yard field goal with 9:46 remaining.

Sept. 11, 1994—New York Jets 25, Denver 22, at New York. Jets win toss. Murrell returns kickoff 24 yards to New York 33. Jets drive to Denver 22 where Lowery kicks 39-yard field goal with 11:03 remaining.

***Sept. 19, 1994—Detroit 20, Dallas 17,** at Dallas. Lions win toss. Gray returns kickoff 24 yards to Detroit 32. Lions drive to Dallas 34 where Hanson's 51-yard field-goal attempt is blocked by Lett. Cowboys take possession at Dallas 42. Cowboys drive to Detroit 37 where Kennard fumbles and Swilling recovers. Lions take possession at Detroit 45. After 6 plays, Montgomery punts 31 yards to Dallas 16. Cowboys drive to Dallas 49 where Aikman fumbles and Thomas recovers at Dallas 43. Lions drive to Dallas 26 where Hanson kicks 44-yard field goal with 27 seconds remaining.

Oct. 16, 1994—Arizona 19, Washington 16, at Washington. Redskins win toss. Mitchell returns kickoff 27 yards to Washington 41. Redskins drive to Arizona 34 where Lohmiller's 51-yard field-goal attempt is blocked by Joyner and recovered by Williams who returns it to the Washington 37. After 5 plays, Peterson's 45-yard field-goal attempt is wide right. Redskins take possession at the Washington 36. After 3 plays, Roby punts 36 yards to the Arizona 37 where Robinson returns 3 yards to the 40. After 3 plays, Feagles punts 51 yards for a touchback. After 1 play, Shuler's pass is intercepted by Hoage who returns it to the Washington 12. Peterson kicks 29-yard field goal with 5:00 remaining.

Oct. 16, 1994—Miami 20, Los Angeles Raiders 17, at Miami. Dolphins win toss. McDuffie returns kickoff 19 yards to Miami 23. Dolphins drive to Los Angeles 12 where Stoyanovich kicks 29-yard field goal with 9:14 remaining.

#Oct. 20, 1994—Minnesota 13, Green Bay 10, at Minnesota. Vikings win toss. Ismail returns kickoff 22 yards to Minnesota 29. Vikings drive to Green Bay 9 where Fuad Reveiz kicks 27-yard field goal with 10:34 remaining.

Oct. 30, 1994—Detroit 28, New York Giants 25, at New York. Giants win toss. Lewis returns kickoff 16 yards to New York 27. After 3 plays, Horan punts 42 yards to Detroit 24 where Gray calls for fair catch. Detroit drives to New York 6 where Hanson kicks 24-yard field goal with 8:17 remaining.

Oct. 30, 1994—Arizona 20, Pittsburgh 17, at Arizona. Steelers win toss. Johnson returns kickoff 24 yards to Pittsburgh 30 where he fumbles and Arizona's Merritt recovers at Pittsburgh 32. After 3 plays, Davis kicks 51-yard field goal with 13:20 remaining.

Nov. 6, 1994—Cincinnati 20, Seattle 17, at Seattle. Seahawks win toss. Warren returns kickoff 32 yards to Seattle 33. After 3 plays, Tuten punts 37 yards to Cincinnati 28 where Sawyer calls for fair catch. After 3 plays, Johnson punts 64 yards to Seattle 2 where Truitt downs ball. Seahawks drive to Seattle 38 where Tuten punts 50 yards to Cincinnati 12 and Sawyer returns 5 yards to 17. Blake passes to Scott for 76 yards to Seattle 7. Pelfrey kicks 26-yard field goal with 6:46 remaining.

Nov. 6, 1994—Pittsburgh 12, Houston 9, at Houston. Steelers win toss. Stone returns kickoff 15 yards to Pittsburgh 28. After 3 plays, Royals punts 53 yards to Houston 13 where Givins downs ball. After 3 plays, Camarillo punts 57 yards to Pittsburgh 31 where Woodson returns 20 yards to Houston 49. After 3 plays, Royals punts 43 yards to Houston 15 where Coleman returns 3 yards to 18. After 5 plays, Camarillo punts 57 yards to Pittsburgh 12 where Hastings returns 12 yards to 24. Steelers drive to Houston 41 where Royals punts 29 yards to Houston 12, and Coleman calls for fair catch. Brown fumbles on first play and Jones recovers at Houston 22. After 1 play, Anderson kicks 40-yard field goal with 3:36 remaining.

Nov. 13, 1994—New England 26, Minnesota 20, at New England. Patriots win toss. Thompson returns kickoff 27 yards to New England 33. Patriots drive to Minnesota 14 where Bledsoe passes 14 yards to Turner for touchdown with 10:50 remaining.

Nov. 20, 1994—Pittsburgh 16, Miami 13, at Pittsburgh. Steelers win toss. Stone returns kickoff 15 yards to Pittsburgh 16. Steelers drive to Miami 39 where they lose possession on downs. Dolphins drive to Pittsburgh 47 where Arnold punts 35 yards to Pittsburgh 12 and Oliver downs ball. Steelers drive to Miami 21 where Anderson kicks 39-yard field goal with 4:41 remaining.

Nov. 27, 1994—Chicago 19, Arizona 16, at Arizona. Cardinals win toss. Levy returns kickoff 31 yards to Arizona 45. After 5 plays, Feagles punts 38 yards to the end zone for a touchback. Bears drive to Arizona 10 where Butler kicks 27-yard field goal with 6:49 remaining.

Nov. 27, 1994—Tampa Bay 20, Minnesota 17, at Minnesota. Buccaneers win toss. Harris returns kickoff 12 yards to Tampa Bay 38. After 6 plays, Stryzinski punts 40 yards to Minnesota 4 where Guilford muffs punt and Buccaneers' Brady recovers. Husted kicks 22-yard field goal with 12:52 remaining.

#Dec. 1, 1994—Minnesota 33, Chicago 27, at Minnesota. Bears win toss. Lewis returns kickoff 23 yards to Chicago 33. Bears drive to Minnesota 22 where Butler's 40-yard field goal attempt is wide left. After 1 play, Moon passes 65 yards to Carter for touchdown with 9:14 remaining.

Dec. 4, 1994—Denver 20, Kansas City 17, at Kansas City. Broncos win toss. Milburn returns kickoff 24 yards to Denver 29. After 3 plays, Millen fumbles and Phillips recovers at Denver 35. After 4 plays, Allen fumbles and Smith recovers at Denver 27. After 6 plays, Rouen punts 45 yards to Kansas City 25 where Hughes calls for fair catch. After 3 plays, Aguiar punts 33 yards to Denver 42 where Chiefs down ball. Broncos drive to Kansas City 17 where Elam kicks 34-yard field goal with 2:48 remaining.

Sept. 3, 1995—Cincinnati 24, Indianapolis 21, at Indianapolis. Bengals win toss. Dunn returns kickoff 15 yards to Bengals' 17. Cincinnati drives to Indianapolis 29 where Pelfrey kicks 47-yard field goal with 12:24 remaining.

Sept. 3, 1995—Atlanta 23, Carolina 20, at Atlanta. Panthers win toss. Baldwin downs kickoff for touchback. Panthers drive to Carolina 42 where Reich fumbles and ball is recovered by Archambeau at Carolina 31. Falcons drive to Panthers' 16 where Andersen kicks 35-yard field goal with 8:43 remaining.

Sept. 10, 1995—Indianapolis 27, New York Jets 24, at New York. Jets win toss. Carter downs kickoff for touchdown. Jets punt downed at Colts' 37. Colts drive to Jets' 35 where Cofer kicks 52-yard field goal with 10:33 remaining.

Sept. 10, 1995—Kansas City 20, New York Giants 17, at Kansas City. Chiefs win toss. Vanover returns kickoff 30 yards to Chiefs' 28. Aguiar punts to Giants' 3. Horan punts to Chiefs' 49. Chiefs drive to Giants' 6 where Elliott kicks 23-yard field goal with 7:11 left.

Sept. 17, 1995—Dallas 23, Minnesota 17, at Minnesota. Cowboys win toss. K. Williams returns kickoff 23 yards to Cowboys' 27. E. Smith scores on 31-yard run with 12:34 left.

Sept. 17, 1995—Kansas City 23, Oakland 17, at Kansas City. Chiefs win toss. Vanover returns kickoff 28 yards to Chiefs' 41. M. Allen fumbles, ball recovered by Robbins at Raiders' 38. Hasty intercepts pass at Chiefs' 36 and returns it 64 yards for touchdown with 10:33 left.

Sept. 17, 1995—Atlanta 27, New Orleans 24, at Atlanta. Saints win toss. Hughes returns kickoff 21 yards to Saints' 17. Metcalf returns Wilmsmeyer's punt 18 yards to Saints' 39. Stryzinski punts, fair catch by Hughes at Saints' 14. Wilmsmeyer punt downed at Falcons' 6. Falcons drive to Saints' 3 where Andersen kicks 21-yard field goal with 7:02 left.

Oct. 8, 1995—Indianapolis 27, Miami 24, at Miami. Colts win toss. Warren returns kickoff 25 yards to Colts' 39. Colts drive to Dolphins' 10 where Blanchard kicks 27-yard field goal with 10:02 left.

Oct. 8, 1995—New York Giants 27, Arizona 21, at New York. Cardinals win toss. Terry returns kickoff 20 yards to Cardinals' 23. Hamilton recovers Krieg's fumble

at Cardinals' 36. Lynch recovers Brown's fumble at Cardinals' 38. Armstead intercepts pass at Giants' 42 and returns it 58 yards for touchdown with 10:55 left.

Oct. 8, 1995—Minnesota 23, Houston 17, at Minnesota. Vikings win toss. Palmer returns kickoff 10 yards to Vikings' 15. Saxon's punt downed at Oilers' 8. Washington intercepts pass at Vikings' 47 and returns it 25 yards to Oilers' 28. R. Smith scores on 20-yard run with 7:50 left.

Oct. 8, 1995—Philadelphia 37, Washington 34, at Philadelphia. Redskins win toss. Redskins take possession at their 20 after touchback. Turk punt out of bounds at Eagles' 9. Eagles drive to Redskins' 18 where Anderson kicks 35-yard field goal with 4:54 left.

* Oct. 9, 1995—Kansas City 29, San Diego 23, at Kansas City. Chargers win toss. Coleman returns kickoff 24 yards to Chargers' 28. Vanover makes fair catch of Bennett's punt at Chiefs' 15. Coleman makes fair catch of Aguiar's punt at Chargers' 43. Vanover returns Bennett's punt 86 yards for a touchdown with 7:33 left.

Oct. 15, 1995—Tampa Bay 20, Minnesota 17, at Tampa Bay. Buccaneers win toss. Edmonds returns kickoff 19 yards to Buccaneers' 22. A. Lee returns Roby's punt to Vikings' 48. Vikings drive to Tampa Bays' 35 where Reveiz's 53-yard field-goal attempt is wide right. Buccaneers take over at own 43 and drive to Vikings' 33 where Husted kicks 37-yard field goal with 8:37 left.

Oct. 22, 1995—Washington 36, Detroit 30, at Washington. Redskins win toss. B. Mitchell returns kickoff 16 yards to Redskins' 27. Turk's punt downed at Lions' 4. D. Green intercepts S. Mitchell's pass and returns it 7 yards for touchdown with 11:19 left.

Oct. 29, 1995—Carolina 20, New England 17, at New England. Panthers win toss. Baldwin returns kickoff 22 yards to Panthers' 25. Meggett makes fair catch of Barnhardt's punt at Patriots' 9. Guliford returns O'Neill's punt 9 yards to Patriots' 32. Panthers drive to Patriots' 12 where Kasay kicks 29-yard field goal with 7:52 left.

Oct. 29, 1995—Cleveland 29, Cincinnati 26, at Cincinnati. Browns win toss. Hunter returns kickoff 31 yards to Browns' 31. Bieniemy returns Tupa's punt 9 yards to Bengals' 37. McCardell makes fair catch of Johnson's punt at Browns' 12. Bieniemy returns Tupa's punt 0 yards to Bengals' 38. Hall intercepts Blake's pass and returns it 5 yards to Bengals' 45. Browns drive to Bengals' 11 where Stover kicks 28-yard field goal with 8:30 left.

Oct. 29, 1995—Arizona 20, Seattle 14, at Arizona. Cardinals win toss. Dowdell returns kickoff 16 yards to Cardinals' 25. Cardinals drive to Seahawks' 10 where G. Davis' 27-yard field goal attempt is blocked. L. Lynch intercepts Friesz's pass at Cardinals' 28 and returns it 72 yards for a touchdown with 3:44 left.

Nov. 5, 1995—Pittsburgh 37, Chicago 34, at Chicago. Bears win toss. Timpson returns kickoff 23 yards to Bears' 33. Hastings returns Sauerbrun's punt 2 yards to Steelers' 31. Steelers drive to Bears' 6 where N. Johnson kicks 24-yard field goal with 6:41 left.

Nov. 12, 1995—Minnesota 30, Arizona 24, at Arizona. Vikings win toss. A. Lee returns kickoff 20 yards to Vikings' 25. Moon throws 50-yard touchdown pass to Ismail with 12:44 left.

Nov. 26, 1995—Arizona 40, Atlanta 37, at Arizona. Falcons win toss. J. Anderson returns kickoff 20 yards to Falcons' 20. Stryzinski fumbles punt snap. Recovered by England at Falcons' 10 where G. Davis kicks 28-yard field goal with 13:17 left.

Dec. 10, 1995—Tampa Bay 13, Green Bay 10, at Tampa Bay. Buccaneers win toss. Edmonds returns kickoff 24 yards to Buccaneers' 23. Tampa Bay drives to Packers' 29 where Husted kicks 47-yard field goal with 11:14 remaining.

Sept. 1, 1996—Buffalo 23, New York Giants 20, at New York. Bills win toss. Daluiso kick is a touchback. Bills drive to Buffalo 46. Toomer returns Mohr's punt to Giants' 16. Dave Brown's fumble recovered by Spielman at Giants' 33. Bills drive to Giants' 16 where Christie kicks 34-yard field goal with 5:52 remaining.

Sept. 22, 1996—New England 28, Jacksonville 25, at New England. Patriots win toss. T. Brown returns kickoff 18 yards to Patriots' 29. Patriots drive to Jaguars' 22 where Vinatieri kicks 40-yard field goal with 12:24 remaining.

Sept. 29, 1996—Arizona 31, St. Louis 28, at Arizona. Cardinals win toss. Lohmiller kick is a touchback. Cardinals drive to Rams' 7 where G. Davis kicks 24-yard field goal with 13:06 remaining.

Oct. 6, 1996—Buffalo 16, Indianapolis 13, at Buffalo. Colts win toss. Christie kick is a touchback. Colts drive to Indianapolis 32. Burris returns Gardocki's punt to Bills' 35. Bills drive to Colts' 48. Mohr punt out of bounds at Colts' 14. Colts drive to Indianapolis 9. Burris returns Gardocki's punt to Colts' 48. Bills drive to Colts' 22 where Christie kicks 39-yard field goal with 5:38 remaining.

Oct. 6, 1996—Houston 30, Cincinnati 27, at Cincinnati. Bengals win toss. Dunn returns kickoff 23 yards to Bengals' 34. Bengals drive to Cincinnati 36. Floyd returns L. Johnson's punt to Oilers' 18. Oilers drive to Bengals' 31 where Del Greco kicks 49-yard field goal with 7:53 remaining.

* Oct. 14, 1996—Green Bay 23, San Francisco 20, at Green Bay. 49ers win toss. D. Carter returns kickoff 23 yards to 49ers' 22. 49ers drive to San Francisco 25. Howard makes fair catch of Thompson's punt at Packers' 44. Packers drive to 49ers' 35 where Jacke kicks 53-yard field goal with 11:19 remaining.

Oct. 27, 1996—Baltimore 37, St. Louis 31, at Baltimore. Rams win toss. J. Thomas returns kickoff 17 yard to Rams' 17. Rams drive to Ravens' 15. F. Miller fumble in field goal formation recovered by S. Moore at Ravens' 17. Ravens drive to Baltimore 49 and turn ball over on downs. Rams drive to Ravens' 40 and turn ball over on downs. Testaverde throws 22-yard scoring pass to M. Jackson with 10 seconds remaining.

Nov. 10, 1996—Dallas 20, San Francisco 17, at San Francisco. Cowboys win

toss. H. Walker returns kickoff 10 yards to Cowboys' 23. Cowboys drive to 49ers' 11 where Boniol kicks 29-yard field goal with 8:43 remaining.

Nov. 10, 1996—Arizona 37, Washington 34, at Washington. Arizona wins toss. Blanton's kickoff is a touchback. Cardinals drive to Redskins' 15 where Butler misses 32-yard field goal. Redskins drive to Cardinals' 43 where Turk punts for touchback. L. Johnson fumble returned by Morrison to Cardinals' 27. Redskins drive to Cardinals' 31 where Blanton misses 48-yard field goal. Cardinals drive to Redskins' 15 where Butler kicks 32-yard field goal with 33 seconds remaining.

Nov. 10, 1996—Tampa Bay 20, Oakland 17, at Tampa Bay. Tampa Bay wins toss. M. Marshall returns kickoff 15 yards to Bucs' 17. Bucs drive to Tampa Bay 36. T. Brown returns Barnhardt's punt four yards to Raiders' 22. Raiders drive to Oakland 25. M. Marshall returns Gossett's punt nine yards to Bucs' 39. Bucs drive to Raiders' 4 where Husted kicks 23-yard field goal with 3:04 remaining.

Nov. 17, 1996—Minnesota 16, Oakland 13, at Oakland. Oakland wins toss. Kaufman returns kickoff 32 yards to Raiders' 27. Raiders drive to Oakland 46 where Gossett punts to Vikings' 17. Vikings drive to Raiders' 12 where Sisson kicks 31-yard field goal with 3:07 remaining.

Nov. 24, 1996—Jacksonville 28, Baltimore 25, at Baltimore. Jacksonville wins toss. Jordon returns kickoff 16 yards to Jaguars' 30. Jaguars drive to Jacksonville 37. Barker's punt is downed at Ravens' 6. Ravens drive to Jaguars' 37 where Pritchett recovers Byner's fumble. Jaguars drive to Ravens' 15 where Hollis kicks 34-yard field goal with 5:54 remaining.

Nov. 24, 1996—San Francisco 19, Washington 16, at Washington. San Francisco wins toss. D. Carter returns kickoff 20 yards to 49ers' 32. 49ers drive to Redskins' 20 where Wilkins kicks 38-yard field goal with 11:36 remaining.

Dec. 1, 1996—Indianapolis 13, Buffalo 10, at Indianapolis. Buffalo wins toss. Moulds returns kickoff 26 yards to Bills' 25. Bills drive to Buffalo 49. Stock returns Mohr's punt one yard to Colts' 16. Colts drive to Bills' 32 where Blanchard kicks 49-yard field goal with 4:14 remaining.

indicates Monday night game
#indicates Thursday night game

POSTSEASON

Dec. 28, 1958—Baltimore 23, New York Giants 17, at New York in NFL Championship Game. Giants win toss. Maynard returns kickoff to Giants' 20. Chandler punts and Taseff returns one yard to Colts' 20. Colts win at 8:15 on a 1-yard run by Ameche.

Dec. 23, 1962—Dallas Texans 20, Houston Oilers 17, at Houston in AFL Championship Game. Texans win toss and kick off. Jancik returns kickoff to Oilers' 33. Norton punts and Jackson makes fair catch on Texans' 22. Wilson punts and Jancik makes fair catch on Oilers' 45. Robinson intercepts Blanda's pass and returns 13 yards to Oilers' 47. Wilson's punt rolls dead at Oilers' 12. Hull intercepts Blanda's pass and returns 23 yards to midfield. Texans win at 17:54 on a 25-yard field goal by Brooker.

Dec. 26, 1965—Green Bay 13, Baltimore 10, at Green Bay in NFL Divisional Playoff Game. Packers win toss. Moore returns kickoff to Packers' 22. Chandler punts and Haymond returns nine yards to Colts' 41. Gilburg punts and Wood makes fair catch at Packers' 21. Chandler punts and Haymond returns one yard to Colts' 41. Michaels misses 47-yard field goal. Packers win at 13:39 on 25-yard field goal by Chandler.

Dec. 25, 1971—Miami 27, Kansas City 24, at Kansas City in AFC Divisional Playoff Game. Chiefs win toss. Podolak, after a lateral from Buchanan, returns kickoff to Chiefs' 46. Stenerud's 42-yard field goal is blocked. Wilson punts and Podolak makes fair catch at Chiefs' 17. Wilson punts and Scott returns 18 yards to Dolphins' 39. Yepremian misses 62-yard field goal. Scott intercepts Dawson's pass and returns 13 yards to Dolphins' 46. Seiple punts and Podolak loses one yard to Chiefs' 15. Wilson punts and Scott makes fair catch on Dolphins' 30. Dolphins win at 22:40 on a 37-yard field goal by Yepremian.

Dec. 24, 1977—Oakland 37, Baltimore 31, at Baltimore in AFC Divisional Playoff Game. Colts win toss. Raiders start on own 42 following a punt late in the first overtime. Oakland works way into field-goal range on Stabler's 19-yard pass to Branch at Colts' 26. Four plays later, on the second play of the second overtime, Stabler hits Casper with a 10-yard touchdown pass at 15:43.

Jan. 2, 1982—San Diego 41, Miami 38, at Miami in AFC Divisional Playoff Game. Chargers win toss. San Diego drives from its 13 to Miami 8. On second-and-goal, Benirschke misses 27-yard field goal attempt wide left at 9:15. Miami has the ball twice and San Diego twice more before the Dolphins get their third possession. Miami drives from the San Diego 46 to Chargers' 17 and on fourth-and-two, von Schamann's 34-yard field goal attempt is blocked by San Diego's Winslow after 11:27. Fouts then completes four of five passes, including a 39-yarder to Joiner that puts the ball on Dolphins' 10. On first down, Benirschke kicks a 29-yard field goal at 13:52. San Diego's winning drive covered 74 yards in six plays.

Jan. 3, 1987—Cleveland 23, New York Jets 20, at Cleveland in AFC Divisional Playoff Game. Jets win toss. Jets' punt downed at Browns' 26. Moseley's 23-yard field goal attempt is wide right. Teams trade punts. Jets' second punt downed at Browns' 31. First overtime period expires eight plays later with Browns in possession at Jets' 42. Moseley kicks 27-yard field goal four plays into second overtime at 17:02.

Jan. 11, 1987—Denver 23, Cleveland 20, at Cleveland in AFC Championship Game. Browns win toss. Broncos hold Browns on four downs. Browns' punt returned four yards to Denver's 25. Elway completes 22- and 28-yard passes to

set up Karlis's 33-yard field goal nine plays into drive at 5:38.

Jan. 3, 1988—Houston 23, Seattle 20, at Houston in AFC Wild Card Game. Seahawks win toss. Rodriguez punts to K. Johnson who returns one yard to Houston 15. Zendejas kicks 32-yard field goal 12 plays later at 8:05.

Dec. 31, 1989—Pittsburgh 26, Houston 23, at Houston in AFC Wild Card Playoff Game. Steelers win toss. Steelers punt to Oilers. Oilers' fumble recovered by Woodson and returned three yards. Four plays and 13 yards later, Anderson kicks a 50-yard field goal at 3:26.

Jan. 7, 1990—Los Angeles Rams 19, New York Giants 13, at New York in NFC Wild Card Game. Rams win toss. Everett completes two passes to move ball to Giants' 48. White called for pass interference; ball spotted on Giants' 25. Everett hits Anderson with a 30-yard touchdown pass at 1:06.

Jan. 3, 1993—Buffalo 41, Houston 38, at Buffalo in AFC Wild Card Game. Houston wins toss. Oilers begin at 20. After 2 plays, Moon's pass is intercepted by Odomes who returns ball 2 yards to Houston 35. After 2 plays, Christie kicks 32-yard field goal at 3:06.

Jan. 8, 1994—Kansas City 27, Pittsburgh 24, at Kansas City in AFC Wild Card Game. Kansas City wins toss. Hughes returns kickoff 20 yards to Kansas City 25. After 3 plays, Barker punts 48 yards to Pittsburgh 18 where Woodson returns 8 yards to the 26. After 6 plays, Royals punts 30 yards to Kansas City 20. Kansas City drives to Pittsburgh 14 where Lowery kicks 32-yard field goal at 11:03.

NFL POSTSEASON OVERTIME GAMES
(BY LENGTH OF GAME)

Dec. 25, 1971	Miami 27, KANSAS CITY 24	82:40
Dec. 23, 1962	Dallas Texans 20, HOUSTON 17	77:54
Jan. 3, 1987	CLEVELAND 23, New York Jets 20	77:02
Dec. 24, 1977	Oakland 37, BALTIMORE 31	75:43
Jan. 2, 1982	San Diego 41, MIAMI 38	73:52
Dec. 26, 1965	GREEN BAY 13, Baltimore 10	73:39
Jan. 8, 1994	KANSAS CITY 27, Pittsburgh 24	71:03
Dec. 28, 1958	Baltimore 23, N.Y. GIANTS 17	68:15
Jan. 3, 1988	HOUSTON 23, Seattle 20	68:05
Jan. 11, 1987	Denver 23, CLEVELAND 20	65:38
Dec. 31, 1989	Pittsburgh 26, HOUSTON 23	63:26
Jan. 3, 1993	BUFFALO 41, Houston 38	63:06
Jan. 7, 1990	Los Angeles Rams 19, N.Y. GIANTS 13	61:06

Home team in CAPS

OVERTIME WON-LOST RECORDS, 1974-1996
(REGULAR SEASON)

AFC	W	L	T	Pct.
Baltimore	1	1	0	.500
Buffalo	11	5	0	.688
Cincinnati	12	7	0	.632
Cleveland	12	8	1	.595
Denver	12	9	2	.565
Indianapolis	9	7	1	.559
Jacksonville	1	1	0	.500
Kansas City	7	7	2	.500
Miami	8	13	1	.386
New England	8	14	0	.363
New York Jets	9	7	2	.556
Oakland	10	10	0	.500
Pittsburgh	10	4	1	.700
San Diego	7	10	0	.412
Seattle	4	9	0	.308
Tennessee	7	12	0	.368

NFC	W	L	T	Pct.
Arizona	10	6	2	.611
Atlanta	7	9	1	.441
Carolina	1	1	0	.500
Chicago	10	11	0	.476
Dallas	9	5	0	.643
Detroit	9	8	1	.528
Green Bay	6	10	4	.400
Minnesota	13	12	2	.519
New Orleans	2	7	0	.222
New York Giants	7	10	1	.417
Philadelphia	7	8	2	.471
St. Louis	6	7	1	.464
San Francisco	5	7	1	.423
Tampa Bay	9	7	1	.559
Washington	10	7	0	.588

OVERTIME GAMES BY YEAR
(REGULAR SEASON)

1996-14	1990-10	1984- 9	1978-11
1995-21	1989-11	1983-19	1977- 6
1994-16	1988- 9	1982- 4	1976- 5
1993-7	1987-13	1981-10	1975- 9
1992-10	1986-16	1980-13	1974- 2
1991-15	1985-10	1979-12	

OVERTIME GAME SUMMARY—1974-1996
There have been 252 overtime games in regular-season play since the rule was adopted in 1974 (14 in 1996 season). Breakdown follows:

188 (10) times both teams had at least one possession (75%)
124 (8) times the team which won the toss won the game (49%)
115 (6) times the team which lost the toss won the game (46%)
 13 (0) games ended tied (5.2%). Last time: Nov. 19, 1989, Cleveland 10, Kansas City 10, at Cleveland
 64 (4) times the team which won the toss drove for winning score (46 FG, 18 TD) (25%)
175 (13) games were decided by a field goal (69%)
 63 (1) games were decided by a touchdown (25%)
  1 (0) game was decided by a safety (0.4%)

Note: The number in parentheses represents the 1996 season total in each category.

MOST OVERTIME GAMES, SEASON
5 Green Bay Packers, 1983
4 Denver Broncos, 1985
   Cleveland Browns, 1989
   Minnesota Vikings, 1994
   Arizona Cardinals, 1995
   Minnesota Vikings, 1995
3 By many teams, last time: Buffalo Bills, San Francisco 49ers, 1996

LONGEST CONSECUTIVE GAME STREAKS WITHOUT OVERTIME (Current)
35 Denver Broncos (last OT game, 12/4/94 at Kansas City)
30 New York Jets (last OT game, 9/10/95 vs. Indianapolis)
29 New Orleans Saints (last OT games, 9/17/95 vs. Atlanta)
(Record: 110, Phoenix Cardinals, 12/7/86-12/19/93)

SHORTEST OVERTIME GAMES
0:21 Chicago 23, Detroit 17; 11/27/80—only kickoff return for TD
0:30 Baltimore 29, New England 23; 9/4/83
0:55 New York Giants 16, Philadelphia 10; 9/29/85
There have been 13 overtime postseason games dating back to 1958. In 12 cases, both teams had at least one possession. Last time: 1/8/94, Kansas City 27, Pittsburgh 24.

LONGEST OVERTIME GAMES
(ALL POSTSEASON GAMES)
22:40 Miami 27, Kansas City 24; 12/25/71
17:54 Dallas Texans 20, Houston 17; 12/23/62
17:02 Cleveland 23, New York Jets 20; 1/3/87

OVERTIME SCORING SUMMARY
175 were decided by a field goal
 26 were decided by a touchdown pass
 19 were decided by a touchdown run
  9 were decided by interceptions (Atlanta 40, New Orleans 34, 9/2/79; Atlanta 47, Green Bay 41, 11/27/83; New York Giants 16, Philadelphia 10, 9/29/85; Indianapolis 23, Cleveland 17, 12/10/89; Cleveland 30, San Diego 24, 10/20/91; Kansas City 23, Oakland 17, 9/17/95; New York Giants 27, Arizona 21, 10/8/95; Washington 36, Detroit 30, 10/22/95; Arizona 20, Seattle 14, 10/29/95)
  2 were decided on a fake field goal/touchdown pass (Minnesota 22, Chicago 16, 10/16/77; Cleveland 23, Minnesota 17, 12/17/89)
  1 was decided by a kickoff return (Chicago 23, Detroit 17, 11/27/80)
  1 was decided by a punt return (Kansas City 29, San Diego 23, 10/9/95)
  1 was decided by a fumble recovery (Baltimore 29, New England 23, 9/4/83)
  1 was decided on a fake field goal/touchdown run (Los Angeles Rams 27, Minnesota 21, 12/2/79)
  1 was decided on a blocked field goal (Denver 30, San Diego 24, 11/17/85)
  1 was decided on a blocked field goal/recovery by kicker (Green Bay 12, Chicago 6, 9/7/80)
  1 was decided on a blocked field goal/recovery by kicking team (Philadelphia 23, New York Giants 17, 11/20/88)
  1 was decided by a safety (Minnesota 23, Los Angeles Rams 21, 11/5/89)
 13 ended tied

OVERTIME RECORDS
Longest Touchdown Pass
99 Yards — Ron Jaworski to Mike Quick, Philadelphia 23, Atlanta 17 (11/10/85)
65 Yards — Warren Moon to Cris Carter, Minnesota 33, Chicago 27 (12/1/94)
50 Yards — Tommy Kramer to Ahmad Rashad, Minnesota 27, Green Bay 21 (9/23/79)
50 Yards — Jim Harbaugh to Neal Anderson, Chicago 23, Detroit 17 (12/2/90)
50 Yards — Warren Moon to Qadry Ismail, Minnesota 30, Arizona 24 (11/12/95)

Longest Touchdown Run
60 Yards — Herschel Walker, Dallas 23, New England 17 (11/15/87)
42 Yards — Eric Dickerson, Los Angeles Rams 26, Tampa Bay 20 (10/5/86)
31 Yards — Emmitt Smith, Dallas 23, Minnesota 17 (9/17/95)

Longest Field Goal
53 Yards — Chris Jacke, Green Bay 23, San Francisco 20 (10/4/96)
52 Yards — Mike Cofer, Indianapolis 27, N.Y. Jets 24 (9/10/95)
51 Yards — Greg Davis, New England 23, Indianapolis 20 (10/29/89)
          Greg Davis, Arizona 20, Pittsburgh 17 (10/30/94)
          Michael Husted, Tampa Bay 20, Minnesota 17 (10/15/95)

Longest Touchdown Plays
99 Yards — (Pass) Ron Jaworski to Mike Quick, Philadelphia 23, Atlanta 17 (11/10/85)
95 Yards — (Kickoff return) Dave Williams, Chicago 23, Detroit 17 (11/27/80)
86 Yards — (Punt return) Tamarick Vanover, Kansas City 29, San Diego 23 (10/9/95)
72 Yards — (Interception return) Lorenzo Lynch, Arizona 20, Seattle 14 (10/29/95)

NFL PAID ATTENDANCE

For detailed 1996 attendance, see page 236.

Year	Regular Season		Average	Postseason	Total
1996	14,612,417	(240 games)	60,885	769,310 (12)	15,381,727
1995	#15,043,562	(240 games)	#62,682	790,906 (12)	#15,834,468
1994	14,030,435	(224 games)	62,636	779,738 (12)	14,810,173
1993	13,966,843	(224 games)	62,352	814,607 (12)	14,781,450
1992	13,828,887	(224 games)	61,736	815,910 (12)	14,644,797
1991	13,841,459	(224 games)	61,792	813,247 (12)	14,654,706
1990	13,959,896	(224 games)	62,321	847,543 (12)	14,807,439
1989	13,625,662	(224 games)	60,829	685,771 (10)	14,311,433
1988	13,539,848	(224 games)	60,446	658,317 (10)	14,198,165
1987	*11,406,166	(210 games)	54,315	656,977 (10)	12,063,143
1986	13,588,551	(224 games)	60,663	734,002 (10)	14,322,553
1985	13,345,047	(224 games)	59,567	710,768 (10)	14,055,815
1984	13,398,112	(224 games)	59,813	665,194 (10)	14,063,306
1983	13,277,222	(224 games)	59,273	675,513 (10)	13,952,735
1982	**7,367,438	(126 games)	58,472	1,033,153 (16)	8,400,591
1981	13,606,990	(224 games)	60,745	637,763 (10)	14,244,753
1980	13,392,230	(224 games)	59,787	624,430 (10)	14,016,660
1979	13,182,039	(224 games)	58,848	630,326 (10)	13,812,365
1978	12,771,800	(224 games)	57,017	624,388 (10)	13,396,188
1977	11,018,632	(196 games)	56,218	534,925 (8)	11,553,557
1976	11,070,543	(196 games)	56,482	492,884 (8)	11,563,427
1975	10,213,193	(182 games)	56,116	475,919 (8)	10,689,112
1974	10,236,322	(182 games)	56,244	438,664 (8)	10,674,986
1973	10,730,933	(182 games)	58,961	525,433 (8)	11,256,366
1972	10,445,827	(182 games)	57,395	483,345 (8)	10,929,172
1971	10,076,035	(182 games)	55,363	483,891 (8)	10,559,926
1970	9,533,333	(182 games)	52,381	458,493 (8)	9,991,826
1969	6,096,127	(112 games)NFL	54,430	162,279 (3)	6,258,406
	2,843,373	(70 games) AFL	40,620	167,088 (3)	3,010,461
1968	5,882,313	(112 games)NFL	52,521	215,902 (3)	6,098,215
	2,635,004	(70 games) AFL	37,643	114,438 (2)	2,749,442
1967	5,938,924	(112 games)NFL	53,026	166,208 (3)	6,105,132
	2,295,697	(63 games) AFL	36,439	53,330 (1)	2,349,027
1966	5,337,044	(105 games)NFL	50,829	74,152 (1)	5,411,196
	2,160,369	(63 games) AFL	34,291	42,080 (1)	2,202,449
1965	4,634,021	(98 games)NFL	47,286	100,304 (2)	4,734,325
	1,782,384	(56 games) AFL	31,828	30,361 (1)	1,812,745
1964	4,563,049	(98 games)NFL	46,562	79,544 (1)	4,642,593
	1,447,875	(56 games) AFL	25,855	40,242 (1)	1,488,117
1963	4,163,643	(98 games)NFL	42,486	45,801 (1)	4,209,444
	1,208,697	(56 games) AFL	21,584	63,171 (2)	1,271,868
1962	4,003,421	(98 games)NFL	40,851	64,892 (1)	4,068,313
	1,147,302	(56 games) AFL	20,487	37,981 (1)	1,185,283
1961	3,986,159	(98 games)NFL	40,675	39,029 (1)	4,025,188
	1,002,657	(56 games) AFL	17,904	29,556 (1)	1,032,213
1960	3,128,296	(78 games)NFL	40,106	67,325 (1)	3,195,621
	926,156	(56 games) AFL	16,538	32,183 (1)	958,339
1959	3,140,000	(72 games)	43,617	57,545 (1)	3,197,545
1958	3,006,124	(72 games)	41,752	123,659 (2)	3,129,783
1957	2,836,318	(72 games)	39,393	119,579 (2)	2,955,897
1956	2,551,263	(72 games)	35,434	56,836 (1)	2,608,099
1955	2,521,836	(72 games)	35,026	85,693 (1)	2,607,529
1954	2,190,571	(72 games)	30,425	43,827 (1)	2,234,398
1953	2,164,585	(72 games)	30,064	54,577 (1)	2,219,162
1952	2,052,126	(72 games)	28,502	97,507 (2)	2,149,633
1951	1,913,019	(72 games)	26,570	57,522 (1)	1,970,541
1950	1,977,753	(78 games)	25,356	136,647 (3)	2,114,400
1949	1,391,735	(60 games)	23,196	27,980 (1)	1,419,715
1948	1,525,243	(60 games)	25,421	36,309 (1)	1,561,552
1947	1,837,437	(60 games)	30,624	66,268 (2)	1,903,705
1946	1,732,135	(55 games)	31,493	58,346 (1)	1,790,481
1945	1,270,401	(50 games)	25,408	32,178 (1)	1,302,579
1944	1,019,649	(50 games)	20,393	46,016 (1)	1,065,665
1943	969,128	(40 games)	24,228	71,315 (2)	1,040,443
1942	887,920	(55 games)	16,144	36,006 (1)	923,926
1941	1,108,615	(55 games)	20,157	55,870 (2)	1,164,485
1940	1,063,025	(55 games)	19,328	36,034 (1)	1,099,059
1939	1,071,200	(55 games)	19,476	32,279 (1)	1,103,479
1938	937,197	(55 games)	17,040	48,120 (1)	985,317
1937	963,039	(55 games)	17,510	15,878 (1)	978,917
1936	816,007	(54 games)	15,111	29,545 (1)	845,552
1935	638,178	(53 games)	12,041	15,000 (1)	653,178
1934	492,684	(60 games)	8,211	35,059 (1)	527,743

Record

*Players' 24-day strike reduced 224-game schedule to 210 games.
**Players' 57-day strike reduced 224-game schedule to 126 games.

NFL'S TOP 10 PAID ATTENDANCE WEEKENDS

Weekend	Games	Attendance
November 10-11, 1996	15	964,079
December 9-11, 1995	15	963,521
November 19-20, 1995	15	962,523
September 17-18, 105	15	958,105
December 16-18, 1995	15	956,675
December 21-23, 1996	15	952,460
November 30, December 3-4, 1995	15	940,032
December 14-16, 1996	15	937,980
September 3-4, 1995	15	937,747
October 16-17, 1988	14	934,211

NFL'S 10 HIGHEST SCORING WEEKENDS

Point Total	Date	Weekend
762	November 10-11, 1996	11th
761	October 16-17, 1983	7th
739	November 23, 26-27, 1995	13th
736	October 25-26, 1987	7th
734	November 19-20, 1995	12th
732	November 9-10, 1980	10th
725	November 24, 27-28, 1983	13th
714	September 17-18, 1989	2nd
711	November 26, 29-30, 1987	12th
710	November 28, December 1-2, 1985	13th

TOP 10 TELEVISED SPORTS EVENTS OF ALL-TIME

(Based on A.C. Nielsen Figures)

Program	Date	Network	Share	Rating
Super Bowl XVI	1/24/82	CBS	73.0	49.1
Super Bowl XVII	1/30/83	NBC	69.0	48.6
Winter Olympics	2/23/94	CBS	64.0	48.5
Super Bowl XX	1/26/86	NBC	70.0	48.3
Super Bowl XII	1/15/78	CBS	67.0	47.2
Super Bowl XIII	1/21/79	NBC	74.0	47.1
Super Bowl XVIII	1/22/84	CBS	71.0	46.4
Super Bowl XIX	1/20/85	ABC	63.0	46.4
Super Bowl XIV	1/20/80	CBS	67.0	46.3
Super Bowl XXX	1/28/96	NBC	68.0	46.0

TEN MOST WATCHED TV PROGRAMS & ESTIMATED TOTAL NUMBER OF VIEWERS

(Based on A.C. Nielsen Figures)

Program	Date	Network	*Total Viewers
Super Bowl XXX	Jan. 28, 1996	NBC	138,488,000
Super Bowl XXVIII	Jan. 30, 1994	NBC	134,800,000
Super Bowl XXVII	Jan. 31, 1993	NBC	133,400,000
Super Bowl XXXI	Jan. 26, 1997	FOX	128,900,000
Super Bowl XX	Jan. 26, 1986	NBC	127,000,000
Winter Olympics	Feb. 23, 1994	CBS	126,686,000
Super Bowl XXIX	Jan. 29, 1995	ABC	125,216,000
Super Bowl XXI	Jan. 25, 1987	CBS	122,640,000
M*A*S*H (Special)	Feb. 28, 1983	CBS	121,624,000
Winter Olympics	Feb. 25, 1994	CBS	119,900,000

Watched some portion of the broadcast

NFL'S TOP 10 TEAM SINGLE-SEASON HOME PAID ATTENDANCE TOTALS

Year	Club	Games	Attendance
1980	Detroit Lions	8	634,204
1988	Buffalo Bills	8	631,818
1991	Buffalo Bills	8	631,786
1992	Buffalo Bills	8	630,978
1996	Kansas City Chiefs	8	628,460
1994	Kansas City Chiefs	8	626,612
1989	Buffalo Bills	8	626,399
1995	Kansas City Chiefs	8	625,936
1989	Cleveland Browns	8	625,240
1993	Buffalo Bills	8	624,349

NFL'S TOP FIVE PAID ATTENDANCE TOTALS FOR ALL GAMES (Includes Preseason)

Year	Preseason	Regular Season	Postseason	All Games
1995	3,368,289	15,043,562	790,906	19,202,757
1996	3,267,254	14,612,417	769,310	18,648,981
1994	3,200,091	14,030,435	779,738	18,010,264
1993	3,170,381	13,966,843	814,607	17,951,831
1992	3,139,557	13,828,887	815,910	17,784,354

TEN HIGHEST-RATED ABC NFL MONDAY NIGHT FOOTBALL GAMES OF ALL-TIME

(Based on A.C. Nielsen Figures)

Game	Date	Share	Rating
Chicago at Miami	12/2/85	46.0	29.6
N.Y. Giants at San Francisco	12/3/90	42.0	26.9
Dallas at Washington	10/2/78	43.0	26.8
Pittsburgh at San Diego	12/22/80	40.0	25.3
Philadelphia at Miami	11/30/81	40.0	25.3
Pittsburgh at Houston	12/10/79	40.0	25.1
Dallas at Miami	12/17/84	40.0	25.1
Pittsburgh at Dallas	9/13/82	42.0	24.9
Cincinnati at Oakland	12/6/76	40.0	24.7
Dallas at Washington	10/8/73	40.0	24.6
Minnesota at Atlanta	11/19/73	40.0	24.6

NFL'S 10 BIGGEST SINGLE-GAME ATTENDANCE TOTALS

Date	Site	Game	Teams	Attendance
August 15, 1994	Azteca Stadium	American Bowl (Mexico City)	Cowboys vs. Oilers	112,376
August 22, 1947	Soldier Field	College All-Star	Bears vs. All-Stars	105,840
January 20, 1980	Rose Bowl	Super Bowl XIV	Steelers vs. Rams	103,985
January 30, 1983	Rose Bowl	Super Bowl XVII	Redskins vs. Dolphins	103,667
January 9, 1977	Rose Bowl	Super Bowl XI	Raiders vs. Vikings	103,438
November 10, 1957	L.A. Coliseum	Regular Season	49ers at Rams	102,368
January 25, 1987	Rose Bowl	Super Bowl XXI	Giants vs. Broncos	101,643
August 20, 1948	Soldier Field	College All-Star	Cardinals vs. All-Stars	101,220
August 28, 1942	Soldier Field	College All-Star	Bears vs. All-Stars	101,100
November 2, 1958	L.A. Coliseum	Regular Season	Bears at Rams	100,470

NUMBER-ONE DRAFT CHOICES

Season	Date	Team	Player	Position	College
1997	April 19-20	St. Louis	Orlando Pace	T	Ohio State
1996	April 20-21	New York Jets	Keyshawn Johnson	WR	Southern California
1995	April 22-23	Cincinnati	Ki-Jana Carter	RB	Penn State
1994	April 24-25	Cincinnati	Dan Wilkinson	DT	Ohio State
1993	April 25-26	New England	Drew Bledsoe	QB	Washington State
1992	April 26-27	Indianapolis	Steve Emtman	DT	Washington
1991	April 21-22	Dallas	Russell Maryland	DT	Miami
1990	April 22-23	Indianapolis	Jeff George	QB	Illinois
1989	April 23-24	Dallas	Troy Aikman	QB	UCLA
1988	April 24-25	Atlanta	Aundray Bruce	LB	Auburn
1987	April 28-29	Tampa Bay	Vinny Testaverde	QB	Miami
1986	April 29-30	Tampa Bay	Bo Jackson	RB	Auburn
1985	April 30-May 1	Buffalo	Bruce Smith	DE	Virginia Tech
1984	May 1-2	New England	Irving Fryar	WR	Nebraska
1983	April 26-27	Baltimore	John Elway	QB	Stanford
1982	April 27-28	New England	Kenneth Sims	DT	Texas
1981	April 28-29	New Orleans	George Rogers	RB	South Carolina
1980	April 29-30	Detroit	Billy Sims	RB	Oklahoma
1979	May 3-4	Buffalo	Tom Cousineau	LB	Ohio State
1978	May 2-3	Houston	Earl Campbell	RB	Texas
1977	May 3-4	Tampa Bay	Ricky Bell	RB	Southern California
1976	April 8-9	Tampa Bay	Lee Roy Selmon	DE	Oklahoma
1975	January 28-29	Atlanta	Steve Bartkowski	QB	California
1974	January 29-30	Dallas	Ed Jones	DE	Tennessee State
1973	January 30-31	Houston	John Matuszak	DE	Tampa
1972	February 1-2	Buffalo	Walt Patulski	DE	Notre Dame
1971	January 28-29	New England	Jim Plunkett	QB	Stanford
1970	January 27-28	Pittsburgh	Terry Bradshaw	QB	Louisiana Tech
1969	January 28-29	Buffalo (AFL)	O.J. Simpson	RB	Southern California
1968	January 30-31	Minnesota	Ron Yary	T	Southern California
1967	March 14	Baltimore	Bubba Smith	DT	Michigan State
1966	November 27, 1965	Atlanta	Tommy Nobis	LB	Texas
	November 28, 1965	Miami (AFL)	Jim Grabowski	RB	Illinois
1965	November 28, 1964	New York Giants	Tucker Frederickson	RB	Auburn
	November 28, 1964	Houston (AFL)	Lawrence Elkins	E	Baylor
1964	December 2, 1963	San Francisco	Dave Parks	E	Texas Tech
	November 30, 1963	Boston (AFL)	Jack Concannon	QB	Boston College
1963	December 3, 1962	Los Angeles	Terry Baker	QB	Oregon State
	December 1, 1962	Kansas City (AFL)	Buck Buchanan	DT	Grambling
1962	December 4, 1961	Washington	Ernie Davis	RB	Syracuse
	December 2, 1961	Oakland (AFL)	Roman Gabriel	QB	North Carolina State
1961	December 27-28, 1960	Minnesota	Tommy Mason	RB	Tulane
	November 23, 1960	Buffalo (AFL)	Ken Rice	G	Auburn
1960	Secret Draft	Los Angeles	Billy Cannon	RB	Louisiana State
	November 22, December 2, 1959	(AFL had no formal first pick)			
1959	December 2, 1958	Green Bay	Randy Duncan	QB	Iowa
1958	December 2, 1957	Chicago Cardinals	King Hill	QB	Rice
1957	November 27, 1956	Green Bay	Paul Hornung	HB	Notre Dame
1956	November 29, 1955	Pittsburgh	Gary Glick	DB	Colorado A&M
1955	January 27-28	Baltimore	George Shaw	QB	Oregon
1954	January 28	Cleveland	Bobby Garrett	QB	Stanford
1953	January 22	San Francisco	Harry Babcock	E	Georgia
1952	January 17	Los Angeles	Bill Wade	QB	Vanderbilt
1951	January 18-19	New York Giants	Kyle Rote	HB	Southern Methodist
1950	January 21-22	Detroit	Leon Hart	E	Notre Dame
1949	December 21, 1948	Philadelphia	Chuck Bednarik	C	Pennsylvania
1948	December 19, 1947	Washington	Harry Gilmer	QB	Alabama
1947	December 16, 1946	Chicago Bears	Bob Fenimore	HB	Oklahoma A&M
1946	January 14	Boston	Frank Dancewicz	QB	Notre Dame
1945	April 6	Chicago Cardinals	Charley Trippi	HB	Georgia
1944	April 19	Boston	Angelo Bertelli	QB	Notre Dame
1943	April 8	Detroit	Frank Sinkwich	HB	Georgia
1942	December 22, 1941	Pittsburgh	Bill Dudley	HB	Virginia
1941	December 10, 1940	Chicago Bears	Tom Harmon	HB	Michigan
1940	December 9, 1939	Chicago Cardinals	George Cafego	HB	Tennessee
1939	December 8, 1938	Chicago Cardinals	Ki Aldrich	C	Texas Christian
1938	December 12, 1937	Cleveland	Corbett Davis	FB	Indiana
1937	December 12, 1936	Philadelphia	Sam Francis	FB	Nebraska
1936	February 8	Philadelphia	Jay Berwanger	HB	Chicago

Note: From 1947 through 1958, the first selection in the draft was a Bonus pick, awarded to the winner of a random draw. That club, in turn, forfeited its last-round draft choice. The winner of the Bonus choice was eliminated from future draws. The system was abolished after 1958, by which time all clubs had received a Bonus choice.

FIRST-ROUND SELECTIONS

If club had no first-round selection, first player drafted is listed with round in parentheses.

ARIZONA CARDINALS

Year	Player, College, Position
1936	Jim Lawrence, Texas Christian, B
1937	Ray Buivid, Marquette, B
1938	Jack Robbins, Arkansas, B
1939	Charles (Ki) Aldrich, Texas Christian, C
1940	George Cafego, Tennessee, B
1941	John Kimbrough, Texas A&M, B
1942	Steve Lach, Duke, B
1943	Glenn Dobbs, Tulsa, B
1944	Pat Harder, Wisconsin, B
1945	Charley Trippi, Georgia, B
1946	Dub Jones, Louisiana State, B
1947	DeWitt (Tex) Coulter, Army, T
1948	Jim Spavital, Oklahoma A&M, B
1949	Bill Fischer, Notre Dame, G
1950	Jack Jennings, Ohio State, T (2)
1951	Jerry Groom, Notre Dame, C
1952	Ollie Matson, San Francisco, B
1953	Johnny Olszewski, California, B
1954	Lamar McHan, Arkansas, B
1955	Max Boydston, Oklahoma, E
1956	Joe Childress, Auburn, B
1957	Jerry Tubbs, Oklahoma, C
1958	King Hill, Rice, B
	John David Crow, Texas A&M, B
1959	Bill Stacy, Mississippi State, B
1960	George Izo, Notre Dame, QB
1961	Ken Rice, Auburn, T
1962	Fate Echols, Northwestern, DT
	Irv Goode, Kentucky, C
1963	Jerry Stovall, Louisiana State, S
	Don Brumm, Purdue, DE
1964	Ken Kortas, Louisville, DT
1965	Joe Namath, Alabama, QB
1966	Carl McAdams, Oklahoma, LB
1967	Dave Williams, Washington, WR
1968	MacArthur Lane, Utah State, RB
1969	Roger Wehrli, Missouri, DB
1970	Larry Stegent, Texas A&M, RB
1971	Norm Thompson, Utah, CB
1972	Bobby Moore, Oregon, RB-WR
1973	Dave Butz, Purdue, DT
1974	J.V. Cain, Colorado, TE
1975	Tim Gray, Texas A&M, DB
1976	Mike Dawson, Arizona, DT
1977	Steve Pisarkiewicz, Missouri, QB
1978	Steve Little, Arkansas, K
	Ken Greene, Washington State, DB
1979	Ottis Anderson, Miami, RB
1980	Curtis Greer, Michigan, DE
1981	E.J. Junior, Alabama, LB
1982	Luis Sharpe, UCLA, T
1983	Leonard Smith, McNeese State, DB
1984	Clyde Duncan, Tennessee, WR
1985	Freddie Joe Nunn, Mississippi, LB
1986	Anthony Bell, Michigan State, LB
1987	Kelly Stouffer, Colorado State, QB
1988	Ken Harvey, California, LB
1989	Eric Hill, Louisiana State, LB
	Joe Wolf, Boston College, G
1990	Anthony Thompson, Indiana, RB (2)
1991	Eric Swann, No College, DE
1992	Tony Sacca, Penn State, QB (2)
1993	Garrison Hearst, Georgia, RB
	Ernest Dye, South Carolina, T
1994	Jamir Miller, UCLA, LB
1995	Frank Sanders, Auburn, WR (2)
1996	Simeon Rice, Illinois, DE
1997	Tom Knight, Iowa, DB

ATLANTA FALCONS

Year	Player, College, Position
1966	Tommy Nobis, Texas, LB
	Randy Johnson, Texas A&I, QB
1967	Leo Carroll, San Diego State, DE (2)
1968	Claude Humphrey, Tennessee State, DE
1969	George Kunz, Notre Dame, T
1970	John Small, Citadel, LB
1971	Joe Profit, Northeast Louisiana, RB
1972	Clarence Ellis, Notre Dame, DB
1973	Greg Marx, Notre Dame, DT (2)
1974	Gerald Tinker, Kent State, WR (2)
1975	Steve Bartkowski, California, QB
1976	Bubba Bean, Texas A&M, RB
1977	Warren Bryant, Kentucky, T
	Wilson Faumuina, San Jose State, DT
1978	Mike Kenn, Michigan, T
1979	Don Smith, Miami, DE
1980	Junior Miller, Nebraska, TE
1981	Bobby Butler, Florida State, DB
1982	Gerald Riggs, Arizona State, RB
1983	Mike Pitts, Alabama, DE
1984	Rick Bryan, Oklahoma, DT
1985	Bill Fralic, Pittsburgh, T
1986	Tony Casillas, Oklahoma, NT
	Tim Green, Syracuse, LB
1987	Chris Miller, Oregon, QB
1988	Aundray Bruce, Auburn, LB
1989	Deion Sanders, Florida State, DB
	Shawn Collins, Northern Arizona, WR
1990	Steve Broussard, Washington State, RB
1991	Bruce Pickens, Nebraska, DB
	Mike Pritchard, Colorado, WR
1992	Bob Whitfield, Stanford, T
	Tony Smith, Southern Mississippi, RB
1993	Lincoln Kennedy, Washington, T
1994	Bert Emanuel, Rice, WR (2)
1995	Devin Bush, Florida State, DB
1996	Shannon Brown, Alabama, DT (3)
1997	Michael Booker, Nebraska, DB

BALTIMORE RAVENS

Year	Player, College, Position
1996	Jonathan Ogden, UCLA, T
	Ray Lewis, Miami, LB
1997	Peter Boulware, Florida State, DE

BUFFALO BILLS

Year	Player, College, Position
1960	Richie Lucas, Penn State, QB
1961	Ken Rice, Auburn, T
1962	Ernie Davis, Syracuse, RB
1963	Dave Behrman, Michigan State, C
1964	Carl Eller, Minnesota, DE
1965	Jim Davidson, Ohio State, T
1966	Mike Dennis, Mississippi, RB
1967	John Pitts, Arizona State, S
1968	Haven Moses, San Diego State, WR
1969	O.J. Simpson, Southern California, RB
1970	Al Cowlings, Southern California, DE
1971	J.D. Hill, Arizona State, WR
1972	Walt Patulski, Notre Dame, DE
1973	Paul Seymour, Michigan, TE
	Joe DeLamielleure, Michigan State, G
1974	Reuben Gant, Oklahoma State, TE
1975	Tom Ruud, Nebraska, LB
1976	Mario Clark, Oregon, DB
1977	Phil Dokes, Oklahoma State, DT
1978	Terry Miller, Oklahoma State, RB
1979	Tom Cousineau, Ohio State, LB
	Jerry Butler, Clemson, WR
1980	Jim Ritcher, North Carolina State, C
1981	Booker Moore, Penn State, RB
1982	Perry Tuttle, Clemson, WR
1983	Tony Hunter, Notre Dame, TE
	Jim Kelly, Miami, QB
1984	Greg Bell, Notre Dame, RB
1985	Bruce Smith, Virginia Tech, DE
	Derrick Burroughs, Memphis State, DB
1986	Ronnie Harmon, Iowa, RB
	Will Wolford, Vanderbilt, T
1987	Shane Conlan, Penn State, LB
1988	Thurman Thomas, Oklahoma State, RB (2)
1989	Don Beebe, Chadron, Neb., WR (3)
1990	James Williams, Fresno State, DB
1991	Henry Jones, Illinois, DB
1992	John Fina, Arizona, T
1993	Thomas Smith, North Carolina, DB
1994	Jeff Burris, Notre Dame, DB
1995	Ruben Brown, Pittsburgh, G
1996	Eric Moulds, Mississippi State, WR
1997	Antowain Smith, Houston, RB

CAROLINA PANTHERS

Year	Player, College, Position
1995	Kerry Collins, Penn State, QB
	Tyrone Poole, Ft. Valley State, DB
	Blake Brockermeyer, Texas, T
1996	Tim Biakabutuka, Michigan, RB
1997	Rae Carruth, Colorado, WR

CHICAGO BEARS

Year	Player, College, Position
1936	Joe Stydahar, West Virginia, T
1937	Les McDonald, Nebraska, E
1938	Joe Gray, Oregon State, B
1939	Sid Luckman, Columbia, QB
	Bill Osmanski, Holy Cross, B
1940	Clyde (Bulldog) Turner, Hardin-Simmons, C
1941	Tom Harmon, Michigan, B
	Norm Standlee, Stanford, B
	Don Scott, Ohio State, B
1942	Frankie Albert, Stanford, B
1943	Bob Steber, Missouri, B
1944	Ray Evans, Kansas, B
1945	Don Lund, Michigan, B
1946	Johnny Lujack, Notre Dame, QB
1947	Bob Fenimore, Oklahoma State, B
	Don Kindt, Wisconsin, B
1948	Bobby Layne, Texas, QB
	Max Bumgardner, Texas, E
1949	Dick Harris, Texas, C
1950	Chuck Hunsinger, Florida, B
	Fred Morrison, Ohio State, B
1951	Bob Williams, Notre Dame, B
	Billy Stone, Bradley, B
	Gene Schroeder, Virginia, E
1952	Jim Dooley, Miami, B
1953	Billy Anderson, Compton (Calif.) J.C., B
1954	Stan Wallace, Illinois, B
1955	Ron Drzewiecki, Marquette, B
1956	Menan (Tex) Schriewer, Texas, E
1957	Earl Leggett, Louisiana State, T
1958	Chuck Howley, West Virginia, G
1959	Don Clark, Ohio State, B
1960	Roger Davis, Syracuse, G
1961	Mike Ditka, Pittsburgh, E
1962	Ronnie Bull, Baylor, RB
1963	Dave Behrman, Michigan State, C
1964	Dick Evey, Tennessee, DT
1965	Dick Butkus, Illinois, LB
	Gale Sayers, Kansas, RB
	Steve DeLong, Tennessee, T
1966	George Rice, Louisiana State, DT
1967	Loyd Phillips, Arkansas, DE
1968	Mike Hull, Southern California, RB
1969	Rufus Mayes, Ohio State, T
1970	George Farmer, UCLA, WR (3)
1971	Joe Moore, Missouri, RB
1972	Lionel Antoine, Southern Illinois, T
	Craig Clemons, Iowa, DB
1973	Wally Chambers, Eastern Kentucky, DE
1974	Waymond Bryant, Tennessee State, LB
	Dave Gallagher, Michigan, DT
1975	Walter Payton, Jackson State, RB
1976	Dennis Lick, Wisconsin, T
1977	Ted Albrecht, California, T
1978	Brad Shearer, Texas, DT (3)
1979	Dan Hampton, Arkansas, DT
	Al Harris, Arizona State, DE
1980	Otis Wilson, Louisville, LB
1981	Keith Van Horne, Southern California, T
1982	Jim McMahon, Brigham Young, QB
1983	Jim Covert, Pittsburgh, T
	Willie Gault, Tennessee, WR
1984	Wilber Marshall, Florida, LB
1985	William Perry, Clemson, DT
1986	Neal Anderson, Florida, RB
1987	Jim Harbaugh, Michigan, QB
1988	Brad Muster, Stanford, RB
	Wendell Davis, Louisiana State, WR
1989	Donnell Woolford, Clemson, DB
	Trace Armstrong, Florida, DE
1990	Mark Carrier, Southern California, DB

FIRST-ROUND SELECTIONS

1991	Stan Thomas, Texas, T
1992	Alonzo Spellman, Ohio State, DE
1993	Curtis Conway, Southern California, WR
1994	John Thierry, Alcorn State, DE
1995	Rashaan Salaam, Colorado, RB
1996	Walt Harris, Mississippi State, DB
1997	John Allred, Southern California, TE (2)

CINCINNATI BENGALS

Year	Player, College, Position
1968	Bob Johnson, Tennessee, C
1969	Greg Cook, Cincinnati, QB
1970	Mike Reid, Penn State, DT
1971	Vernon Holland, Tennessee State, T
1972	Sherman White, California, DE
1973	Isaac Curtis, San Diego State, WR
1974	Bill Kollar, Montana State, DT
1975	Glenn Cameron, Florida, LB
1976	Billy Brooks, Oklahoma, WR
	Archie Griffin, Ohio State, RB
1977	Eddie Edwards, Miami, DT
	Wilson Whitley, Houston, DT
	Mike Cobb, Michigan State, TE
1978	Ross Browner, Notre Dame, DT
	Blair Bush, Washington, C
1979	Jack Thompson, Washington State, QB
	Charles Alexander, Louisiana State, RB
1980	Anthony Muñoz, Southern California, T
1981	David Verser, Kansas, WR
1982	Glen Collins, Mississippi State, DE
1983	Dave Rimington, Nebraska, C
1984	Ricky Hunley, Arizona, LB
	Pete Koch, Maryland, DE
	Brian Blados, North Carolina, T
1985	Eddie Brown, Miami, WR
	Emanuel King, Alabama, LB
1986	Joe Kelly, Washington, LB
	Tim McGee, Tennessee, WR
1987	Jason Buck, Brigham Young, DE
1988	Rickey Dixon, Oklahoma, DB
1989	Eric Ball, UCLA, RB (2)
1990	James Francis, Baylor, LB
1991	Alfred Williams, Colorado, LB
1992	David Klingler, Houston, QB
	Darryl Williams, Miami, DB
1993	John Copeland, Alabama, DE
1994	Dan Wilkinson, Ohio State, DT
1995	Ki-Jana Carter, Penn State, RB
1996	Willie Anderson, Auburn, T
1997	Reinard Wilson, Florida State, LB

CLEVELAND BROWNS

Year	Player, College, Position
1950	Ken Carpenter, Oregon State, B
1951	Ken Konz, Louisiana State, B
1952	Bert Rechichar, Tennessee, DB
	Harry Agganis, Boston U., QB
1953	Doug Atkins, Tennessee, DE
1954	Bobby Garrett, Stanford, QB
	John Bauer, Illinois, G
1955	Kurt Burris, Oklahoma, C
1956	Preston Carpenter, Arkansas, B
1957	Jim Brown, Syracuse, RB
1958	Jim Shofner, Texas Christian, DB
1959	Rich Kreitling, Illinois, DE
1960	Jim Houston, Ohio State, DE
1961	Bobby Crespino, Mississippi, TE
1962	Gary Collins, Maryland, WR
	Leroy Jackson, Western Illinois, RB
1963	Tom Hutchinson, Kentucky, WR
1964	Paul Warfield, Ohio State, WR
1965	James Garcia, Purdue, T (2)
1966	Milt Morin, Massachusetts, TE
1967	Bob Matheson, Duke, LB
1968	Marvin Upshaw, Trinity, Tex., DT-DE
1969	Ron Johnson, Michigan, RB
1970	Mike Phipps, Purdue, QB
	Bob McKay, Texas, T
1971	Clarence Scott, Kansas State, CB
1972	Thom Darden, Michigan, DB
1973	Steve Holden, Arizona State, WR
	Pete Adams, Southern California, T
1974	Billy Corbett, Johnson C. Smith, T (2)

1975	Mack Mitchell, Houston, DE
1976	Mike Pruitt, Purdue, RB
1977	Robert Jackson, Texas A&M, LB
1978	Clay Matthews, Southern California, LB
	Ozzie Newsome, Alabama, TE
1979	Willis Adams, Houston, WR
1980	Charles White, Southern California, RB
1981	Hanford Dixon, Southern Mississippi, DB
1982	Chip Banks, Southern California, LB
1983	Ron Brown, Arizona State, WR (2)
1984	Don Rogers, UCLA, DB
1985	Greg Allen, Florida State, RB (2)
1986	Webster Slaughter, San Diego State, WR (2)
1987	Mike Junkin, Duke, LB
1988	Clifford Charlton, Florida, LB
1989	Eric Metcalf, Texas, RB
1990	Leroy Hoard, Michigan, RB (2)
1991	Eric Turner, UCLA, DB
1992	Tommy Vardell, Stanford, RB
1993	Steve Everitt, Michigan, C
1994	Antonio Langham, Alabama, DB
	Derrick Alexander, Michigan, WR
1995	Craig Powell, Ohio State, LB

DALLAS COWBOYS

Year	Player, College, Position
1960	None
1961	Bob Lilly, Texas Christian, DT
1962	Sonny Gibbs, Texas Christian, QB (2)
1963	Lee Roy Jordan, Alabama, LB
1964	Scott Appleton, Texas, DT
1965	Craig Morton, California, QB
1966	John Niland, Iowa, G
1967	Phil Clark, Northwestern, DB (3)
1968	Dennis Homan, Alabama, WR
1969	Calvin Hill, Yale, RB
1970	Duane Thomas, West Texas State, RB
1971	Tody Smith, Southern California, DE
1972	Bill Thomas, Boston College, RB
1973	Billy Joe DuPree, Michigan State, TE
1974	Ed (Too Tall) Jones, Tennessee State, DE
	Charley Young, North Carolina State, RB
1975	Randy White, Maryland, LB
	Thomas Henderson, Langston, LB
1976	Aaron Kyle, Wyoming, DB
1977	Tony Dorsett, Pittsburgh, RB
1978	Larry Bethea, Michigan State, DE
1979	Robert Shaw, Tennessee, C
1980	Bill Roe, Colorado, LB (3)
1981	Howard Richards, Missouri, T
1982	Rod Hill, Kentucky State, DB
1983	Jim Jeffcoat, Arizona State, DE
1984	Billy Cannon, Jr., Texas A&M, LB
1985	Kevin Brooks, Michigan, DE
1986	Mike Sherrard, UCLA, WR
1987	Danny Noonan, Nebraska, DT
1988	Michael Irvin, Miami, WR
1989	Troy Aikman, UCLA, QB
1990	Emmitt Smith, Florida, RB
1991	Russell Maryland, Miami, DT
	Alvin Harper, Tennessee, WR
	Kelvin Pritchett, Mississippi, DT
1992	Kevin Smith, Texas A&M, DB
	Robert Jones, East Carolina, LB
1993	Kevin Williams, Miami, WR (2)
1994	Shante Carver, Arizona State, DE
1995	Sherman Williams, Alabama, RB (2)
1996	Kavika Pittman, McNeese State, DE (2)
1997	David LaFleur, Louisiana State, TE

DENVER BRONCOS

Year	Player, College, Position
1960	Roger LeClerc, Trinity, Conn., C
1961	Bob Gaiters, New Mexico State, RB
1962	Merlin Olsen, Utah State, DT
1963	Kermit Alexander, UCLA, CB
1964	Bob Brown, Nebraska, T
1965	Dick Butkus, Illinois, LB (2)
1966	Jerry Shay, Purdue, DT
1967	Floyd Little, Syracuse, RB
1968	Curley Culp, Arizona State, DE (2)
1969	Grady Cavness, Texas-El Paso, DB (2)
1970	Bob Anderson, Colorado, RB

1971	Marv Montgomery, Southern California, T
1972	Riley Odoms, Houston, TE
1973	Otis Armstrong, Purdue, RB
1974	Randy Gradishar, Ohio State, LB
1975	Louis Wright, San Jose State, DB
1976	Tom Glassic, Virginia, G
1977	Steve Schindler, Boston College, G
1978	Don Latimer, Miami, DT
1979	Kelvin Clark, Nebraska, T
1980	Rulon Jones, Utah State, DE (2)
1981	Dennis Smith, Southern California, DB
1982	Gerald Willhite, San Jose State, RB
1983	Chris Hinton, Northwestern, G
1984	Andre Townsend, Mississippi, DE (2)
1985	Steve Sewell, Oklahoma, RB
1986	Jim Juriga, Illinois, T (4)
1987	Ricky Nattiel, Florida, WR
1988	Ted Gregory, Syracuse, NT
1989	Steve Atwater, Arkansas, DB
1990	Alton Montgomery, Houston, DB (2)
1991	Mike Croel, Nebraska, LB
1992	Tommy Maddox, UCLA, QB
1993	Dan Williams, Toledo, DE
1994	Allen Aldridge, Houston, LB (2)
1995	Jamie Brown, Florida A&M, T (4)
1996	John Mobley, Kutztown, LB
1997	Trevor Pryce, Clemson, DT

DETROIT LIONS

Year	Player, College, Position
1936	Sid Wagner, Michigan State, G
1937	Lloyd Cardwell, Nebraska, B
1938	Alex Wojciechowicz, Fordham, C
1939	John Pingel, Michigan State, B
1940	Doyle Nave, Southern California, B
1941	Jim Thomason, Texas A&M, B
1942	Bob Westfall, Michigan, B
1943	Frank Sinkwich, Georgia, B
1944	Otto Graham, Northwestern, B
1945	Frank Szymanski, Notre Dame, C
1946	Bill Dellastatious, Missouri, B
1947	Glenn Davis, Army, B
1948	Y.A. Tittle, Louisiana State, B
1949	John Rauch, Georgia, B
1950	Leon Hart, Notre Dame, E
	Joe Watson, Rice, C
1951	Dick Stanfel, San Francisco, G (2)
1952	Yale Lary, Texas A&M, B (3)
1953	Harley Sewell, Texas, G
1954	Dick Chapman, Rice, T
1955	Dave Middleton, Auburn, B
1956	Hopalong Cassady, Ohio State, B
1957	Bill Glass, Baylor, G
1958	Alex Karras, Iowa, T
1959	Nick Pietrosante, Notre Dame, B
1960	John Robinson, Louisiana State, S
1961	Danny LaRose, Missouri, T (2)
1962	John Hadl, Kansas, QB
1963	Daryl Sanders, Ohio State, T
1964	Pete Beathard, Southern California, QB
1965	Tom Nowatzke, Indiana, RB
1966	Nick Eddy, Notre Dame, RB (2)
1967	Mel Farr, UCLA, RB
1968	Greg Landry, Massachusetts, QB
	Earl McCullouch, Southern California, WR
1969	Altie Taylor, Utah State, RB (2)
1970	Steve Owens, Oklahoma, RB
1971	Bob Bell, Cincinnati, DT
1972	Herb Orvis, Colorado, DE
1973	Ernie Price, Texas A&I, DE
1974	Ed O'Neil, Penn State, LB
1975	Lynn Boden, South Dakota State, G
1976	James Hunter, Grambling, DB
	Lawrence Gaines, Wyoming, RB
1977	Walt Williams, New Mexico State, DB (2)
1978	Luther Bradley, Notre Dame, DB
1979	Keith Dorney, Penn State, T
1980	Billy Sims, Oklahoma, RB
1981	Mark Nichols, San Jose State, WR
1982	Jimmy Williams, Nebraska, LB
1983	James Jones, Florida, RB
1984	David Lewis, California, TE
1985	Lomas Brown, Florida, T

1986	Chuck Long, Iowa, QB
1987	Reggie Rogers, Washington, DE
1988	Bennie Blades, Miami, DB
1989	Barry Sanders, Oklahoma State, RB
1990	Andre Ware, Houston, QB
1991	Herman Moore, Virginia, WR
1992	Robert Porcher, South Carolina State, DE
1993	Ryan McNeil, Miami, DB (2)
1994	Johnnie Morton, Southern California, WR
1995	Luther Elliss, Utah, DT
1996	Reggie Brown, Texas A&M, LB
	Jeff Hartings, Penn State, G
1997	Bryant Westbrook, Texas, DB

GREEN BAY PACKERS

Year	Player, College, Position
1936	Russ Letlow, San Francisco, G
1937	Eddie Jankowski, Wisconsin, B
1938	Cecil Isbell, Purdue, B
1939	Larry Buhler, Minnesota, B
1940	Harold Van Every, Minnesota, B
1941	George Paskvan, Wisconsin, B
1942	Urban Odson, Minnesota, T
1943	Dick Wildung, Minnesota, T
1944	Merv Pregulman, Michigan, G
1945	Walt Schlinkman, Texas Tech, B
1946	Johnny (Strike) Strzykalski, Marquette, B
1947	Ernie Case, UCLA, B
1948	Earl (Jug) Girard, Wisconsin, B
1949	Stan Heath, Nevada, B
1950	Clayton Tonnemaker, Minnesota, C
1951	Bob Gain, Kentucky, T
1952	Babe Parilli, Kentucky, QB
1953	Al Carmichael, Southern California, B
1954	Art Hunter, Notre Dame, T
	Veryl Switzer, Kansas State, B
1955	Tom Bettis, Purdue, G
1956	Jack Losch, Miami, B
1957	Paul Hornung, Notre Dame, B
	Ron Kramer, Michigan, E
1958	Dan Currie, Michigan State, C
1959	Randy Duncan, Iowa, B
1960	Tom Moore, Vanderbilt, RB
1961	Herb Adderley, Michigan State, CB
1962	Earl Gros, Louisiana State, RB
1963	Dave Robinson, Penn State, LB
1964	Lloyd Voss, Nebraska, DT
1965	Donny Anderson, Texas Tech, RB
	Lawrence Elkins, Baylor, E
1966	Jim Grabowski, Illinois, RB
	Gale Gillingham, Minnesota, T
1967	Bob Hyland, Boston College, C
	Don Horn, San Diego State, QB
1968	Fred Carr, Texas-El Paso, LB
	Bill Lueck, Arizona, G
1969	Rich Moore, Villanova, DT
1970	Mike McCoy, Notre Dame, DT
	Rich McGeorge, Elon, TE
1971	John Brockington, Ohio State, RB
1972	Willie Buchanon, San Diego State, DB
	Jerry Tagge, Nebraska, QB
1973	Barry Smith, Florida State, WR
1974	Barty Smith, Richmond, RB
1975	Bill Bain, Southern California, G (2)
1976	Mark Koncar, Colorado, T
1977	Mike Butler, Kansas, DE
	Ezra Johnson, Morris Brown, DE
1978	James Lofton, Stanford, WR
	John Anderson, Michigan, LB
1979	Eddie Lee Ivery, Georgia Tech, RB
1980	Bruce Clark, Penn State, DE
	George Cumby, Oklahoma, LB
1981	Rich Campbell, California, QB
1982	Ron Hallstrom, Iowa, G
1983	Tim Lewis, Pittsburgh, DB
1984	Alphonso Carreker, Florida State, DE
1985	Ken Ruettgers, Southern California, T
1986	Kenneth Davis, Texas Christian, RB (2)
1987	Brent Fullwood, Auburn, RB
1988	Sterling Sharpe, South Carolina, WR
1989	Tony Mandarich, Michigan State, T
1990	Tony Bennett, Mississippi, LB
	Darrell Thompson, Minnesota, RB

1991	Vinnie Clark, Ohio State, DB
1992	Terrell Buckley, Florida State, DB
1993	Wayne Simmons, Clemson, LB
	George Teague, Alabama, DB
1994	Aaron Taylor, Notre Dame, T
1995	Craig Newsome, Arizona State, DB
1996	John Michels, Southern California, T
1997	Ross Verba, Iowa, T

INDIANAPOLIS COLTS

Year	Player, College, Position
1953	Billy Vessels, Oklahoma, B
1954	Cotton Davidson, Baylor, B
1955	George Shaw, Oregon, B
	Alan Ameche, Wisconsin, FB
1956	Lenny Moore, Penn State, B
1957	Jim Parker, Ohio State, G
1958	Lenny Lyles, Louisville, B
1959	Jackie Burkett, Auburn, C
1960	Ron Mix, Southern California, T
1961	Tom Matte, Ohio State, RB
1962	Wendell Harris, Louisiana State, S
1963	Bob Vogel, Ohio State, T
1964	Marv Woodson, Indiana, CB
1965	Mike Curtis, Duke, LB
1966	Sam Ball, Kentucky, T
1967	Bubba Smith, Michigan State, DT
	Jim Detwiler, Michigan, RB
1968	John Williams, Minnesota, G
1969	Eddie Hinton, Oklahoma, WR
1970	Norman Bulaich, Texas Christian, RB
1971	Don McCauley, North Carolina, RB
	Leonard Dunlap, North Texas State, DB
1972	Tom Drougas, Oregon, T
1973	Bert Jones, Louisiana State, QB
	Joe Ehrmann, Syracuse, DT
1974	John Dutton, Nebraska, DE
	Roger Carr, Louisiana Tech, WR
1975	Ken Huff, North Carolina, G
1976	Ken Novak, Purdue, DT
1977	Randy Burke, Kentucky, WR
1978	Reese McCall, Auburn, TE
1979	Barry Krauss, Alabama, LB
1980	Curtis Dickey, Texas A&M, RB
	Derrick Hatchett, Texas, DB
1981	Randy McMillan, Pittsburgh, RB
	Donnell Thompson, North Carolina, DT
1982	Johnie Cooks, Mississippi State, LB
	Art Schlichter, Ohio State, QB
1983	John Elway, Stanford, QB
1984	Leonard Coleman, Vanderbilt, DB
	Ron Solt, Maryland, G
1985	Duane Bickett, Southern California, LB
1986	Jon Hand, Alabama, DE
1987	Cornelius Bennett, Alabama, LB
1988	Chris Chandler, Washington, QB (3)
1989	Andre Rison, Michigan State, WR
1990	Jeff George, Illinois, QB
1991	Shane Curry, Miami, DE (2)
1992	Steve Emtman, Washington, DT
	Quentin Coryatt, Texas A&M, LB
1993	Sean Dawkins, California, WR
1994	Marshall Faulk, San Diego State, RB
	Trev Alberts, Nebraska, LB
1995	Ellis Johnson, Florida, DT
1996	Marvin Harrison, Syracuse, WR
1997	Tarik Glenn, California, T

JACKSONVILLE JAGUARS

Year	Player, College, Position
1995	Tony Boselli, Southern California, T
	James Stewart, Tennessee, RB
1996	Kevin Hardy, Illinois, LB
1997	Renaldo Wynn, Notre Dame, DT

KANSAS CITY CHIEFS

Year	Player, College, Position
1960	Don Meredith, Southern Methodist, QB
1961	E.J. Holub, Texas Tech, C
1962	Ronnie Bull, Baylor, RB
1963	Buck Buchanan, Grambling, DT
	Ed Budde, Michigan State, G
1964	Pete Beathard, Southern California, QB

1965	Gale Sayers, Kansas, RB
1966	Aaron Brown, Minnesota, DE
1967	Gene Trosch, Miami, DE-DT
1968	Mo Moorman, Texas A&M, G
	George Daney, Texas-El Paso, G
1969	Jim Marsalis, Tennessee State, CB
1970	Sid Smith, Southern California, T
1971	Elmo Wright, Houston, WR
1972	Jeff Kinney, Nebraska, RB
1973	Gary Butler, Rice, TE (2)
1974	Woody Green, Arizona State, RB
1975	Elmore Stephens, Kentucky, TE (2)
1976	Rod Walters, Iowa, G
1977	Gary Green, Baylor, DB
1978	Art Still, Kentucky, DE
1979	Mike Bell, Colorado State, DE
	Steve Fuller, Clemson, QB
1980	Brad Budde, Southern California, G
1981	Willie Scott, South Carolina, TE
1982	Anthony Hancock, Tennessee, WR
1983	Todd Blackledge, Penn State, QB
1984	Bill Maas, Pittsburgh, DT
	John Alt, Iowa, T
1985	Ethan Horton, North Carolina, RB
1986	Brian Jozwiak, West Virginia, T
1987	Paul Palmer, Temple, RB
1988	Neil Smith, Nebraska, DE
1989	Derrick Thomas, Alabama, LB
1990	Percy Snow, Michigan State, LB
1991	Harvey Williams, Louisiana State, RB
1992	Dale Carter, Tennessee, DB
1993	Will Shields, Nebraska, G (3)
1994	Greg Hill, Texas A&M, RB
1995	Trezelle Jenkins, Michigan, T
1996	Jerome Woods, Memphis, DB
1997	Tony Gonzalez, California, TE

MIAMI DOLPHINS

Year	Player, College, Position
1966	Jim Grabowski, Illinois, RB
	Rick Norton, Kentucky, QB
1967	Bob Griese, Purdue, QB
1968	Larry Csonka, Syracuse, RB
	Doug Crusan, Indiana, T
1969	Bill Stanfill, Georgia, DE
1970	Jim Mandich, Michigan, TE (2)
1971	Otto Stowe, Iowa State, WR (2)
1972	Mike Kadish, Notre Dame, DT
1973	Chuck Bradley, Oregon, C (2)
1974	Donald Reese, Jackson State, DE
1975	Darryl Carlton, Tampa, T
1976	Larry Gordon, Arizona State, LB
	Kim Bokamper, San Jose State, LB
1977	A.J. Duhe, Louisiana State, DT
1978	Guy Benjamin, Stanford, QB (2)
1979	Jon Giesler, Michigan, T
1980	Don McNeal, Alabama, DB
1981	David Overstreet, Oklahoma, RB
1982	Roy Foster, Southern California, G
1983	Dan Marino, Pittsburgh, QB
1984	Jackie Shipp, Oklahoma, LB
1985	Lorenzo Hampton, Florida, RB
1986	John Offerdahl, Western Michigan, LB (2)
1987	John Bosa, Boston College, DE
1988	Eric Kumerow, Ohio State, DE
1989	Sammie Smith, Florida State, RB
	Louis Oliver, Florida, DB
1990	Richmond Webb, Texas A&M, T
1991	Randal Hill, Miami, WR
1992	Troy Vincent, Wisconsin, DB
	Marco Coleman, Georgia Tech, LB
1993	O.J. McDuffie, Penn State, WR
1994	Tim Bowens, Mississippi, DT
1995	Billy Milner, Houston, T
1996	Daryl Gardener, Baylor, DT
1997	Yatil Green, Miami, WR

MINNESOTA VIKINGS

Year	Player, College, Position
1961	Tommy Mason, Tulane, RB
1962	Bill Miller, Miami, WR (3)
1963	Jim Dunaway, Mississippi, T
1964	Carl Eller, Minnesota, DE

371

1965	Jack Snow, Notre Dame, WR
1966	Jerry Shay, Purdue, DT
1967	Clint Jones, Michigan State, RB
	Gene Washington, Michigan State, WR
	Alan Page, Notre Dame, DT
1968	Ron Yary, Southern California, T
1969	Ed White, California, G (2)
1970	John Ward, Oklahoma State, DT
1971	Leo Hayden, Ohio State, RB
1972	Jeff Siemon, Stanford, LB
1973	Chuck Foreman, Miami, RB
1974	Fred McNeill, UCLA, LB
	Steve Riley, Southern California, T
1975	Mark Mullaney, Colorado State, DE
1976	James White, Oklahoma State, DT
1977	Tommy Kramer, Rice, QB
1978	Randy Holloway, Pittsburgh, DE
1979	Ted Brown, North Carolina State, RB
1980	Doug Martin, Washington, DT
1981	Mardye McDole, Mississippi State, WR (2)
1982	Darrin Nelson, Stanford, RB
1983	Joey Browner, Southern California, DB
1984	Keith Millard, Washington State, DE
1985	Chris Doleman, Pittsburgh, LB
1986	Gerald Robinson, Auburn, DE
1987	D.J. Dozier, Penn State, RB
1988	Randall McDaniel, Arizona State, G
1989	David Braxton, Wake Forest, LB (2)
1990	Mike Jones, Texas A&M, TE (3)
1991	Carlos Jenkins, Michigan State, LB (3)
1992	Robert Harris, Southern University, DE (2)
1993	Robert Smith, Ohio State, RB
1994	DeWayne Washington, N. Carolina St., DB
	Todd Steussie, California, T
1995	Derrick Alexander, Florida State, DE
	Korey Stringer, Ohio State, T
1996	Duane Clemons, California, DE
1997	Dwayne Rudd, Alabama, LB

NEW ENGLAND PATRIOTS

Year	Player, College, Position
1960	Ron Burton, Northwestern, RB
1961	Tommy Mason, Tulane, RB
1962	Gary Collins, Maryland, WR
1963	Art Graham, Boston College, WR
1964	Jack Concannon, Boston College, QB
1965	Jerry Rush, Michigan State, DE
1966	Karl Singer, Purdue, T
1967	John Charles, Purdue, S
1968	Dennis Byrd, North Carolina State, DE
1969	Ron Sellers, Florida State, WR
1970	Phil Olsen, Utah State, DE
1971	Jim Plunkett, Stanford, QB
1972	Tom Reynolds, San Diego State, WR (2)
1973	John Hannah, Alabama, G
	Sam Cunningham, So. California, RB
	Darryl Stingley, Purdue, WR
1974	Steve Corbett, Boston College, G (2)
1975	Russ Francis, Oregon, TE
1976	Mike Haynes, Arizona State, DB
	Pete Brock, Colorado, C
	Tim Fox, Ohio State, DB
1977	Raymond Clayborn, Texas, DB
	Stanley Morgan, Tennessee, WR
1978	Bob Cryder, Alabama, G
1979	Rick Sanford, South Carolina, DB
1980	Roland James, Tennessee, DB
	Vagas Ferguson, Notre Dame, RB
1981	Brian Holloway, Stanford, T
1982	Kenneth Sims, Texas, DT
	Lester Williams, Miami, DT
1983	Tony Eason, Illinois, QB
1984	Irving Fryar, Nebraska, WR
1985	Trevor Matich, Brigham Young, C
1986	Reggie Dupard, Southern Methodist, RB
1987	Bruce Armstrong, Louisville, T
1988	John Stephens, Northwestern St., La., RB
1989	Hart Lee Dykes, Oklahoma State, WR
1990	Chris Singleton, Arizona, LB
	Ray Agnew, North Carolina State, DE
1991	Pat Harlow, Southern California, T
	Leonard Russell, Arizona State, RB
1992	Eugene Chung, Virginia Tech, T

1993	Drew Bledsoe, Washington State, QB
1994	Willie McGinest, Southern California, DE
1995	Ty Law, Michigan, DB
1996	Terry Glenn, Ohio State, WR
1997	Chris Canty, Kansas State, DB

NEW ORLEANS SAINTS

Year	Player, College, Position
1967	Les Kelley, Alabama, RB
1968	Kevin Hardy, Notre Dame, DE
1969	John Shinners, Xavier, G
1970	Ken Burrough, Texas Southern, WR
1971	Archie Manning, Mississippi, QB
1972	Royce Smith, Georgia, G
1973	Derland Moore, Oklahoma, DE (2)
1974	Rick Middleton, Ohio State, LB
1975	Larry Burton, Purdue, WR
	Kurt Schumacher, Ohio State, T
1976	Chuck Muncie, California, RB
1977	Joe Campbell, Maryland, DE
1978	Wes Chandler, Florida, WR
1979	Russell Erxleben, Texas, P-K
1980	Stan Brock, Colorado, T
1981	George Rogers, South Carolina, RB
1982	Lindsay Scott, Georgia, WR
1983	Steve Korte, Arkansas, G (2)
1984	James Geathers, Wichita State, DE
1985	Alvin Toles, Tennessee, LB
1986	Jim Dombrowski, Virginia, T
1987	Shawn Knight, Brigham Young, DT
1988	Craig Heyward, Pittsburgh, RB
1989	Wayne Martin, Arkansas, DE
1990	Renaldo Turnbull, West Virginia, DE
1991	Wesley Carroll, Miami, WR (2)
1992	Vaughn Dunbar, Indiana, RB
1993	Willie Roaf, Louisiana Tech, T
	Irv Smith, Notre Dame, TE
1994	Joe Johnson, Louisville, DE
1995	Mark Fields, Washington State, LB
1996	Alex Molden, Oregon, DB
1997	Chris Naeole, Colorado, G

NEW YORK GIANTS

Year	Player, College, Position
1936	Art Lewis, Ohio U., T
1937	Ed Widseth, Minnesota, T
1938	George Karamatic, Gonzaga, B
1939	Walt Neilson, Arizona, B
1940	Grenville Lansdell, Southern California, B
1941	George Franck, Minnesota, B
1942	Merle Hapes, Mississippi, B
1943	Steve Filipowicz, Fordham, B
1944	Billy Hillenbrand, Indiana, B
1945	Elmer Barbour, Wake Forest, B
1946	George Connor, Notre Dame, T
1947	Vic Schwall, Northwestern, B
1948	Tony Minisi, Pennsylvania, B
1949	Paul Page, Southern Methodist, B
1950	Travis Tidwell, Auburn, B
1951	Kyle Rote, Southern Methodist, B
	Jim Spavital, Oklahoma A&M, B
1952	Frank Gifford, Southern California, B
1953	Bobby Marlow, Alabama, B
1954	Ken Buck, Pacific, C (2)
1955	Joe Heap, Notre Dame, B
1956	Henry Moore, Arkansas, B (2)
1957	Sam DeLuca, South Carolina, T (2)
1958	Phil King, Vanderbilt, B
1959	Lee Grosscup, Utah, B
1960	Lou Cordileone, Clemson, G
1961	Bruce Tarbox, Syracuse, G (2)
1962	Jerry Hillebrand, Colorado, LB
1963	Frank Lasky, Florida, T (2)
1964	Joe Don Looney, Oklahoma, RB
1965	Tucker Frederickson, Auburn, RB
1966	Francis Peay, Missouri, T
1967	Louis Thompson, Alabama, DT (4)
1968	Dick Buzin, Penn State, T (2)
1969	Fred Dryer, San Diego State, DE
1970	Jim Files, Oklahoma, LB
1971	Rocky Thompson, West Texas State, WR
1972	Eldridge Small, Texas A&I, DB
	Larry Jacobson, Nebraska, DE

1973	Brad Van Pelt, Michigan State, LB (2)
1974	John Hicks, Ohio State, G
1975	Al Simpson, Colorado State, T (2)
1976	Troy Archer, Colorado, DE
1977	Gary Jeter, Southern California, DT
1978	Gordon King, Stanford, T
1979	Phil Simms, Morehead State, QB
1980	Mark Haynes, Colorado, DB
1981	Lawrence Taylor, North Carolina, LB
1982	Butch Woolfolk, Michigan, RB
1983	Terry Kinard, Clemson, DB
1984	Carl Banks, Michigan State, LB
	William Roberts, Ohio State, T
1985	George Adams, Kentucky, RB
1986	Eric Dorsey, Notre Dame, DE
1987	Mark Ingram, Michigan State, WR
1988	Eric Moore, Indiana, T
1989	Brian Williams, Minnesota, C-G
1990	Rodney Hampton, Georgia, RB
1991	Jarrod Bunch, Michigan, RB
1992	Derek Brown, Notre Dame, TE
1993	Michael Strahan, Texas Southern, DE (2)
1994	Thomas Lewis, Indiana, WR
1995	Tyrone Wheatley, Michigan, RB
1996	Cedric Jones, Oklahoma, DE
1997	Ike Hilliard, Florida, WR

NEW YORK JETS

Year	Player, College, Position
1960	George Izo, Notre Dame, QB
1961	Tom Brown, Minnesota, G
1962	Sandy Stephens, Minnesota, QB
1963	Jerry Stovall, Louisiana State, S
1964	Matt Snell, Ohio State, RB
1965	Joe Namath, Alabama, QB
	Tom Nowatzke, Indiana, RB
1966	Bill Yearby, Michigan, DT
1967	Paul Seiler, Notre Dame, T
1968	Lee White, Weber State, RB
1969	Dave Foley, Ohio State, T
1970	Steve Tannen, Florida, CB
1971	John Riggins, Kansas, RB
1972	Jerome Barkum, Jackson State, WR
	Mike Taylor, Michigan, LB
1973	Burgess Owens, Miami, DB
1974	Carl Barzilauskas, Indiana, DT
1975	Anthony Davis, Southern California, RB (2)
1976	Richard Todd, Alabama, QB
1977	Marvin Powell, Southern California, T
1978	Chris Ward, Ohio State, T
1979	Marty Lyons, Alabama, DE
1980	Johnny (Lam) Jones, Texas, WR
1981	Freeman McNeil, UCLA, RB
1982	Bob Crable, Notre Dame, LB
1983	Ken O'Brien, Cal-Davis, QB
1984	Russell Carter, Southern Methodist, DB
	Ron Faurot, Arkansas, DE
1985	Al Toon, Wisconsin, WR
1986	Mike Haight, Iowa, T
1987	Roger Vick, Texas A&M, RB
1988	Dave Cadigan, Southern California, T
1989	Jeff Lageman, Virginia, LB
1990	Blair Thomas, Penn State, RB
1991	Browning Nagle, Louisville, QB (2)
1992	Johnny Mitchell, Nebraska, TE
1993	Marvin Jones, Florida State, LB
1994	Aaron Glenn, Texas A&M, DB
1995	Kyle Brady, Penn State, TE
	Hugh Douglas, Central State, Ohio, DE
1996	Keyshawn Johnson, Southern California, WR
1997	James Farrior, Virginia, LB

OAKLAND RAIDERS

Year	Player, College, Position
1960	Dale Hackbart, Wisconsin, CB
1961	Joe Rutgens, Illinois, DT
1962	Roman Gabriel, North Carolina State, QB
1963	George Wilson, Alabama, RB (6)
1964	Tony Lorick, Arizona State, RB
1965	Harry Schuh, Memphis State, T
1966	Rodger Bird, Kentucky, S
1967	Gene Upshaw, Texas A&I, G
1968	Eldridge Dickey, Tennessee State, QB

Year	Player, College, Position
1969	Art Thoms, Syracuse, DT
1970	Raymond Chester, Morgan State, TE
1971	Jack Tatum, Ohio State, S
1972	Mike Siani, Villanova, WR
1973	Ray Guy, Southern Mississippi, P
1974	Henry Lawrence, Florida A&M, T
1975	Neal Colzie, Ohio State, DB
1976	Charles Philyaw, Texas Southern, DT (2)
1977	Mike Davis, Colorado, DB (2)
1978	Dave Browning, Washington, DE (2)
1979	Willie Jones, Florida State, DE (2)
1980	Marc Wilson, Brigham Young, QB
1981	Ted Watts, Texas Tech, DB
	Curt Marsh, Washington, T
1982	Marcus Allen, Southern California, RB
1983	Don Mosebar, Southern California, T
1984	Sean Jones, Northeastern, DE (2)
1985	Jessie Hester, Florida State, WR
1986	Bob Buczkowski, Pittsburgh, DE
1987	John Clay, Missouri, T
1988	Tim Brown, Notre Dame, WR
	Terry McDaniel, Tennessee, DB
	Scott Davis, Illinois, DE
1989	Jeff Francis, Tennessee, QB (6)
1990	Anthony Smith, Arizona, DE
1991	Todd Marinovich, Southern California, QB
1992	Chester McGlockton, Clemson, DE
1993	Patrick Bates, Texas A&M, DB
1994	Rob Fredrickson, Michigan State, LB
1995	Napoleon Kaufman, Washington, RB
1996	Rickey Dudley, Ohio State, TE
1997	Darrell Russell, Southern California, DT

PHILADELPHIA EAGLES

Year	Player, College, Position
1936	Jay Berwanger, Chicago, B
1937	Sam Francis, Nebraska, B
1938	Jim McDonald, Ohio State, B
1939	Davey O'Brien, Texas Christian, B
1940	George McAfee, Duke, B
1941	Art Jones, Richmond, B (2)
1942	Pete Kmetovic, Stanford, B
1943	Joe Muha, Virginia Military, B
1944	Steve Van Buren, Louisiana State, B
1945	John Yonaker, Notre Dame, E
1946	Leo Riggs, Southern California, B
1947	Neill Armstrong, Oklahoma A&M, E
1948	Clyde (Smackover) Scott, Arkansas, B
1949	Chuck Bednarik, Pennsylvania, C
	Frank Tripucka, Notre Dame, B
1950	Harry (Bud) Grant, Minnesota, E
1951	Ebert Van Buren, Louisiana State, B
	Chet Mutryn, Xavier, B
1952	Johnny Bright, Drake, B
1953	Al Conway, Army, B (2)
1954	Neil Worden, Notre Dame, B
1955	Dick Bielski, Maryland, B
1956	Bob Pellegrini, Maryland, C
1957	Clarence Peaks, Michigan State, B
1958	Walt Kowalczyk, Michigan State, B
1959	J.D. Smith, Rice, T (2)
1960	Ron Burton, Northwestern, RB
1961	Art Baker, Syracuse, RB
1962	Pete Case, Georgia, G (2)
1963	Ed Budde, Michigan State, G
1964	Bob Brown, Nebraska, T
1965	Ray Rissmiller, Georgia, T (2)
1966	Randy Beisler, Indiana, DE
1967	Harry Jones, Arkansas, RB
1968	Tim Rossovich, Southern California, DE
1969	Leroy Keyes, Purdue, RB
1970	Steve Zabel, Oklahoma, TE
1971	Richard Harris, Grambling, DE
1972	John Reaves, Florida, QB
1973	Jerry Sisemore, Texas, T
	Charle Young, Southern California, TE
1974	Mitch Sutton, Kansas, DT (3)
1975	Bill Capraun, Miami, T (7)
1976	Mike Smith, Florida, DE (4)
1977	Skip Sharp, Kansas, DB (5)
1978	Reggie Wilkes, Georgia Tech, LB (3)
1979	Jerry Robinson, UCLA, LB
1980	Roynell Young, Alcorn State, DB

Year	Player, College, Position
1981	Leonard Mitchell, Houston, DE
1982	Mike Quick, North Carolina State, WR
1983	Michael Haddix, Mississippi State, RB
1984	Kenny Jackson, Penn State, WR
1985	Kevin Allen, Indiana, T
1986	Keith Byars, Ohio State, RB
1987	Jerome Brown, Miami, DT
1988	Keith Jackson, Oklahoma, TE
1989	Jessie Small, Eastern Kentucky, LB (2)
1990	Ben Smith, Georgia, DB
1991	Antone Davis, Tennessee, T
1992	Siran Stacy, Alabama, RB (2)
1993	Lester Holmes, Jackson State, T
	Leonard Renfro, Colorado, DT
1994	Bernard Williams, Georgia, T
1995	Mike Mamula, Boston College, DE
1996	Jermane Mayberry, Texas A&M-Kingsville, T
1997	Jon Harris, Virginia, DE

PITTSBURGH STEELERS

Year	Player, College, Position
1936	Bill Shakespeare, Notre Dame, B
1937	Mike Basrak, Duquesne, C
1938	Byron (Whizzer) White, Colorado, B
1939	Bill Patterson, Baylor, B (3)
1940	Kay Eakin, Arkansas, B
1941	Chet Gladchuk, Boston College, C (2)
1942	Bill Dudley, Virginia, B
1943	Bill Daley, Minnesota, B
1944	Johnny Podesto, St. Mary's, Calif., B
1945	Paul Duhart, Florida, B
1946	Felix (Doc) Blanchard, Army, B
1947	Hub Bechtol, Texas, E
1948	Dan Edwards, Georgia, E
1949	Bobby Gage, Clemson, B
1950	Lynn Chandnois, Michigan State, B
1951	Butch Avinger, Alabama, B
1952	Ed Modzelewski, Maryland, B
1953	Ted Marchibroda, St. Bonaventure, B
1954	Johnny Lattner, Notre Dame, B
1955	Frank Varrichione, Notre Dame, T
1956	Gary Glick, Colorado A&M, B
	Art Davis, Mississippi State, B
1957	Len Dawson, Purdue, B
1958	Larry Krutko, West Virginia, B (2)
1959	Tom Barnett, Purdue, B (8)
1960	Jack Spikes, Texas Christian, RB
1961	Myron Pottios, Notre Dame, LB (2)
1962	Bob Ferguson, Ohio State, RB
1963	Frank Atkinson, Stanford, T (8)
1964	Paul Martha, Pittsburgh, S
1965	Roy Jefferson, Utah, WR (2)
1966	Dick Leftridge, West Virginia, RB
1967	Don Shy, San Diego State, RB (2)
1968	Mike Taylor, Southern California, T
1969	Joe Greene, North Texas State, DT
1970	Terry Bradshaw, Louisiana Tech, QB
1971	Frank Lewis, Grambling, WR
1972	Franco Harris, Penn State, RB
1973	J.T. Thomas, Florida State, DB
1974	Lynn Swann, Southern California, WR
1975	Dave Brown, Michigan, DB
1976	Bennie Cunningham, Clemson, TE
1977	Robin Cole, New Mexico, LB
1978	Ron Johnson, Eastern Michigan, DB
1979	Greg Hawthorne, Baylor, RB
1980	Mark Malone, Arizona State, QB
1981	Keith Gary, Oklahoma, DE
1982	Walter Abercrombie, Baylor, RB
1983	Gabriel Rivera, Texas Tech, DT
1984	Louis Lipps, Southern Mississippi, WR
1985	Darryl Sims, Wisconsin, DE
1986	John Rienstra, Temple, G
1987	Rod Woodson, Purdue, DB
1988	Aaron Jones, Eastern Kentucky, DE
1989	Tim Worley, Georgia, RB
	Tom Ricketts, Pittsburgh, T
1990	Eric Green, Liberty, TE
1991	Huey Richardson, Florida, DE
1992	Leon Searcy, Miami, T
1993	Deon Figures, Colorado, DB
1994	Charles Johnson, Colorado, WR
1995	Mark Bruener, Washington, TE

Year	Player, College, Position
1996	Jamain Stephens, North Carolina A&T, T
1997	Chad Scott, Maryland, DB

ST. LOUIS RAMS

Year	Player, College, Position
1937	Johnny Drake, Purdue, B
1938	Corbett Davis, Indiana, B
1939	Parker Hall, Mississippi, B
1940	Ollie Cordill, Rice, B
1941	Rudy Mucha, Washington, C
1942	Jack Wilson, Baylor, B
1943	Mike Holovak, Boston College, B
1944	Tony Butkovich, Illinois, B
1945	Elroy (Crazylegs) Hirsch, Wisconsin, B
1946	Emil Sitko, Notre Dame, B
1947	Herman Wedemeyer, St. Mary's, Calif., B
1948	Tom Keane, West Virginia, B (2)
1949	Bobby Thomason, Virginia Military, B
1950	Ralph Pasquariello, Villanova, B
	Stan West, Oklahoma, G
1951	Bud McFadin, Texas, G
1952	Bill Wade, Vanderbilt, QB
	Bob Carey, Michigan State, E
1953	Donn Moomaw, UCLA, C
	Ed Barker, Washington State, E
1954	Ed Beatty, Cincinnati, C
1955	Larry Morris, Georgia Tech, C
1956	Joe Marconi, West Virginia, B
	Charles Horton, Vanderbilt, B
1957	Jon Arnett, Southern California, B
	Del Shofner, Baylor, E
1958	Lou Michaels, Kentucky, T
	Jim Phillips, Auburn, E
1959	Dick Bass, Pacific, B
	Paul Dickson, Baylor, T
1960	Billy Cannon, Louisiana State, RB
1961	Marlin McKeever, Southern California, E-LB
1962	Roman Gabriel, North Carolina State, QB
	Merlin Olsen, Utah State, DT
1963	Terry Baker, Oregon State, QB
	Rufus Guthrie, Georgia Tech, G
1964	Bill Munson, Utah State, QB
1965	Clancy Williams, Washington State, CB
1966	Tom Mack, Michigan, G
1967	Willie Ellison, Texas Southern, RB (2)
1968	Gary Beban, UCLA, QB (2)
1969	Larry Smith, Florida, RB
	Jim Seymour, Notre Dame, WR
	Bob Klein, Southern California, TE
1970	Jack Reynolds, Tennessee, LB
1971	Isiah Robertson, Southern, LB
	Jack Youngblood, Florida, DE
1972	Jim Bertelsen, Texas, RB (2)
1973	Cullen Bryant, Colorado, DB (2)
1974	John Cappelletti, Penn State, RB
1975	Mike Fanning, Notre Dame, DT
	Dennis Harrah, Miami, T
	Doug France, Ohio State, T
1976	Kevin McLain, Colorado State, LB
1977	Bob Brudzinski, Ohio State, LB
1978	Elvis Peacock, Oklahoma, RB
1979	George Andrews, Nebraska, LB
	Kent Hill, Georgia Tech, T
1980	Johnnie Johnson, Texas, DB
1981	Mel Owens, Michigan, LB
1982	Barry Redden, Richmond, RB
1983	Eric Dickerson, Southern Methodist, RB
1984	Hal Stephens, East Carolina, DE (5)
1985	Jerry Gray, Texas, DB
1986	Mike Schad, Queen's University, Canada, T
1987	Donald Evans, Winston-Salem, DE (2)
1988	Gaston Green, UCLA, RB
	Aaron Cox, Arizona State, WR
1989	Bill Hawkins, Miami, DE
	Cleveland Gary, Miami, RB
1990	Bern Brostek, Washington, C
1991	Todd Lyght, Notre Dame, DB
1992	Sean Gilbert, Pittsburgh, DE
1993	Jerome Bettis, Notre Dame, RB
1994	Wayne Gandy, Auburn, T
1995	Kevin Carter, Florida, DE
1996	Lawrence Phillips, Nebraska, RB
	Eddie Kennison, Louisiana State, WR

1997 Orlando Pace, Ohio State, T

SAN DIEGO CHARGERS

Year	Player, College, Position
1960	Monty Stickles, Notre Dame, E
1961	Earl Faison, Indiana, DE
1962	Bob Ferguson, Ohio State, RB
1963	Walt Sweeney, Syracuse, G
1964	Ted Davis, Georgia Tech, LB
1965	Steve DeLong, Tennessee, DE
1966	Don Davis, Cal State-Los Angeles, DT
1967	Ron Billingsley, Wyoming, DE
1968	Russ Washington, Missouri, DT
	Jimmy Hill, Texas A&I, DB
1969	Marty Domres, Columbia, QB
	Bob Babich, Miami, Ohio, LB
1970	Walker Gillette, Richmond, WR
1971	Leon Burns, Long Beach State, RB
1972	Pete Lazetich, Stanford, DE (2)
1973	Johnny Rodgers, Nebraska, WR
1974	Bo Matthews, Colorado, RB
	Don Goode, Kansas, LB
1975	Gary Johnson, Grambling, DT
	Mike Williams, Louisiana State, DB
1976	Joe Washington, Oklahoma, RB
1977	Bob Rush, Memphis State, C
1978	John Jefferson, Arizona State, WR
1979	Kellen Winslow, Missouri, TE
1980	Ed Luther, San Jose State, QB (4)
1981	James Brooks, Auburn, RB
1982	Hollis Hall, Clemson, DB (7)
1983	Billy Ray Smith, Arkansas, LB
	Gary Anderson, Arkansas, WR
	Gill Byrd, San Jose State, DB
1984	Mossy Cade, Texas, DB
1985	Jim Lachey, Ohio State, G
1986	Leslie O'Neal, Oklahoma State, DE
	James FitzPatrick, Southern California, T
1987	Rod Bernstine, Texas A&M, TE
1988	Anthony Miller, Tennessee, WR
1989	Burt Grossman, Pittsburgh, DE
1990	Junior Seau, Southern California, LB
1991	Stanley Richard, Texas, DB
1992	Chris Mims, Tennessee, DE
1993	Darrien Gordon, Stanford, DB
1994	Isaac Davis, Arkansas, G (2)
1995	Terrance Shaw, Stephen F. Austin, DB (2)
1996	Bryan Still, Virginia Tech, WR (2)
1997	Freddie Jones, North Carolina, TE (2)

SAN FRANCISCO 49ERS

Year	Player, College, Position
1950	Leo Nomellini, Minnesota, T
1951	Y.A. Tittle, Louisiana State, B
1952	Hugh McElhenny, Washington, B
1953	Harry Babcock, Georgia, E
	Tom Stolhandske, Texas, E
1954	Bernie Faloney, Maryland, B
1955	Dickie Moegle, Rice, B
1956	Earl Morrall, Michigan State, B
1957	John Brodie, Stanford, B
1958	Jim Pace, Michigan, B
	Charlie Krueger, Texas A&M, T
1959	Dave Baker, Oklahoma, B
	Dan James, Ohio State, C
1960	Monty Stickles, Notre Dame, E
1961	Jimmy Johnson, UCLA, CB
	Bernie Casey, Bowling Green, WR
	Bill Kilmer, UCLA, QB
1962	Lance Alworth, Arkansas, WR
1963	Kermit Alexander, UCLA, CB
1964	Dave Parks, Texas Tech, WR
1965	Ken Willard, North Carolina, RB
	George Donnelly, Illinois, DB
1966	Stan Hindman, Mississippi, DE
1967	Steve Spurrier, Florida, QB
	Cas Banaszek, Northwestern, T
1968	Forrest Blue, Auburn, C
1969	Ted Kwalick, Penn State, TE
	Gene Washington, Stanford, WR
1970	Cedrick Hardman, North Texas State, DE
	Bruce Taylor, Boston U., DB
1971	Tim Anderson, Ohio State, DB

1972	Terry Beasley, Auburn, WR
1973	Mike Holmes, Texas Southern, DB
1974	Wilbur Jackson, Alabama, RB
	Bill Sandifer, UCLA, DT
1975	Jimmy Webb, Mississippi State, DT
1976	Randy Cross, UCLA, C (2)
1977	Elmo Boyd, Eastern Kentucky, WR (3)
1978	Ken MacAfee, Notre Dame, TE
	Dan Bunz, Cal State-Long Beach, LB
1979	James Owens, UCLA, WR (2)
1980	Earl Cooper, Rice, RB
	Jim Stuckey, Clemson, DT
1981	Ronnie Lott, Southern California, DB
1982	Bubba Paris, Michigan, T (2)
1983	Roger Craig, Nebraska, RB (2)
1984	Todd Shell, Brigham Young, LB
1985	Jerry Rice, Mississippi Valley State, WR
1986	Larry Roberts, Alabama, DE (2)
1987	Harris Barton, North Carolina, T
	Terrence Flagler, Clemson, RB
1988	Danny Stubbs, Miami, DE (2)
1989	Keith DeLong, Tennessee, LB
1990	Dexter Carter, Florida State, RB
1991	Ted Washington, Louisville, DT
1992	Dana Hall, Washington, DB
1993	Dana Stubblefield, Kansas, DT
	Todd Kelly, Tennessee, DE
1994	Bryant Young, Notre Dame, DT
	William Floyd, Florida State, RB
1995	J.J. Stokes, UCLA, WR
1996	Israel Ifeanyi, Southern California, DE (2)
1997	Jim Druckenmiller, Virginia Tech, QB

SEATTLE SEAHAWKS

Year	Player, College, Position
1976	Steve Niehaus, Notre Dame, DT
1977	Steve August, Tulsa, G
1978	Keith Simpson, Memphis State, DB
1979	Manu Tuiasosopo, UCLA, DT
1980	Jacob Green, Texas A&M, DE
1981	Ken Easley, UCLA, DB
1982	Jeff Bryant, Clemson, DE
1983	Curt Warner, Penn State, RB
1984	Terry Taylor, Southern Illinois, DB
1985	Owen Gill, Iowa, RB (2)
1986	John L. Williams, Florida, RB
1987	Tony Woods, Pittsburgh, LB
1988	Brian Blades, Miami, WR (2)
1989	Andy Heck, Notre Dame, T
1990	Cortez Kennedy, Miami, DT
1991	Dan McGwire, San Diego State, QB
1992	Ray Roberts, Virginia, T
1993	Rick Mirer, Notre Dame, QB
1994	Sam Adams, Texas A&M, DT
1995	Joey Galloway, Ohio State, WR
1996	Pete Kendall, Boston College, T
1997	Shawn Springs, Ohio State, DB
	Walter Jones, Florida State, T

TAMPA BAY BUCCANEERS

Year	Player, College, Position
1976	Lee Roy Selmon, Oklahoma, DT
1977	Ricky Bell, Southern California, RB
1978	Doug Williams, Grambling, QB
1979	Greg Roberts, Oklahoma, G (2)
1980	Ray Snell, Wisconsin, G
1981	Hugh Green, Pittsburgh, LB
1982	Sean Farrell, Penn State, G
1983	Randy Grimes, Baylor, C (2)
1984	Keith Browner, Southern California, LB (2)
1985	Ron Holmes, Washington, DE
1986	Bo Jackson, Auburn, RB
	Roderick Jones, Southern Methodist, DB
1987	Vinny Testaverde, Miami, QB
1988	Paul Gruber, Wisconsin, T
1989	Broderick Thomas, Nebraska, LB
1990	Keith McCants, Alabama, LB
1991	Charles McRae, Tennessee, T
1992	Courtney Hawkins, Michigan State, WR (2)
1993	Eric Curry, Alabama, DE
1994	Trent Dilfer, Fresno State, QB
1995	Warren Sapp, Miami, DT
	Derrick Brooks, Florida State, LB

1996	Regan Upshaw, California, DE
	Marcus Jones, North Carolina, DT
1997	Warrick Dunn, Florida State, RB
	Reidel Anthony, Florida, WR

TENNESSEE OILERS

Year	Player, College, Position
1960	Billy Cannon, Louisiana State, RB
1961	Mike Ditka, Pittsburgh, E
1962	Ray Jacobs, Howard Payne, DT
1963	Danny Brabham, Arkansas, LB
1964	Scott Appleton, Texas, DT
1965	Lawrence Elkins, Baylor, WR
1966	Tommy Nobis, Texas, LB
1967	George Webster, Michigan State, LB
	Tom Regner, Notre Dame, G
1968	Mac Haik, Mississippi, WR (2)
1969	Ron Pritchard, Arizona State, LB
1970	Doug Wilkerson, N. Carolina Central, G
1971	Dan Pastorini, Santa Clara, QB
1972	Greg Sampson, Stanford, DE
1973	John Matuszak, Tampa, DE
	George Amundson, Iowa State, RB
1974	Steve Manstedt, Nebraska, LB (4)
1975	Robert Brazile, Jackson State, LB
	Don Hardeman, Texas A&I, RB
1976	Mike Barber, Louisiana Tech, TE (2)
1977	Morris Towns, Missouri, T
1978	Earl Campbell, Texas, RB
1979	Mike Stensrud, Iowa State, DE (2)
1980	Angelo Fields, Michigan State, T (2)
1981	Michael Holston, Morgan State, WR (3)
1982	Mike Munchak, Penn State, G
1983	Bruce Matthews, Southern California, T
1984	Dean Steinkuhler, Nebraska, T
1985	Ray Childress, Texas A&M, DE
	Richard Johnson, Wisconsin, DB
1986	Jim Everett, Purdue, QB
1987	Alonzo Highsmith, Miami, RB
	Haywood Jeffires, North Carolina St., WR
1988	Lorenzo White, Michigan State, RB
1989	David Williams, Florida, T
1990	Lamar Lathon, Houston, LB
1991	Mike Dumas, Indiana, DB (2)
1992	Eddie Robinson, Alabama State, LB (2)
1993	Brad Hopkins, Illinois, T
1994	Henry Ford, Arkansas, DE
1995	Steve McNair, Alcorn State, QB
1996	Eddie George, Ohio State, RB
1997	Kenny Holmes, Miami, DE

WASHINGTON REDSKINS

Year	Player, College, Position
1936	Riley Smith, Alabama, B
1937	Sammy Baugh, Texas Christian, B
1938	Andy Farkas, Detroit, B
1939	I.B. Hale, Texas Christian, T
1940	Ed Boell, New York U., B
1941	Forest Evashevski, Michigan, B
1942	Orban (Spec) Sanders, Texas, B
1943	Jack Jenkins, Missouri, B
1944	Mike Micka, Colgate, B
1945	Jim Hardy, Southern California, B
1946	Casl Rossi, UCLA, B*
1947	Casl Rossi, UCLA, B
1948	Harry Gilmer, Alabama, B
	Lowell Tew, Alabama, B
1949	Rob Goode, Texas A&M, B
1950	George Thomas, Oklahoma, B
1951	Leon Heath, Oklahoma, B
1952	Larry Isbell, Baylor, B
1953	Jack Scarbath, Maryland, B
1954	Steve Meilinger, Kentucky, E
1955	Ralph Guglielmi, Notre Dame, B
1956	Ed Vereb, Maryland, B
1957	Don Bosseler, Miami, B
1958	Mike Sommer, George Washington, B (2)
1959	Don Allard, Boston College, B
1960	Richie Lucas, Penn State, QB
1961	Norman Snead, Wake Forest, QB
	Joe Rutgens, Illinois, DT
1962	Ernie Davis, Syracuse, RB
1963	Pat Richter, Wisconsin, TE

1964	Charley Taylor, Arizona State, RB-WR
1965	Bob Breitenstein, Tulsa, T (2)
1966	Charlie Gogolak, Princeton, K
1967	Ray McDonald, Idaho, RB
1968	Jim Smith, Oregon, DB
1969	Eugene Epps, Texas-El Paso, DB (2)
1970	Bill Bundige, Colorado, DT (2)
1971	Cotton Speyrer, Texas, WR (2)
1972	Moses Denson, Maryland State, RB (8)
1973	Charles Cantrell, Lamar, G (5)
1974	Jon Keyworth, Colorado, TE (6)
1975	Mike Thomas, Nevada-Las Vegas, RB (6)
1976	Mike Hughes, Baylor, G (5)
1977	Duncan McColl, Stanford, DE (4)
1978	Tony Green, Florida, RB (6)
1979	Don Warren, San Diego State, TE (4)
1980	Art Monk, Syracuse, WR
1981	Mark May, Pittsburgh, T
1982	Vernon Dean, San Diego State, DB (2)
1983	Darrell Green, Texas A&I, DB
1984	Bob Slater, Oklahoma, DT (2)
1985	Tory Nixon, San Diego State, DB (2)
1986	Markus Koch, Boise State, DE (2)
1987	Brian Davis, Nebraska, DB (2)
1988	Chip Lohmiller, Minnesota, K (2)
1989	Tracy Rocker, Auburn, DT (3)
1990	Andre Collins, Penn State, LB (2)
1991	Bobby Wilson, Michigan State, DT
1992	Desmond Howard, Michigan, WR
1993	Tom Carter, Notre Dame, DB
1994	Heath Shuler, Tennessee, QB
1995	Michael Westbrook, Colorado, WR
1996	Andre Johnson, Penn State, T
1997	Kenard Lang, Miami, DE

Choice lost due to ineligibility

ASSOCIATED PRESS NFL MOST VALUABLE PLAYERS

NFL MOST VALUABLE PLAYERS NAMED BY *ASSOCIATED PRESS* IN BALLOTING BY A NATIONWIDE PANEL OF MEDIA:

YEAR	PLAYER	POS.	TEAM	ACCOMPLISHMENTS
1957	Jim Brown	RB	Cleveland Browns	Rushed for league-leading 942 yards and added 9 TDs as a rookie.
1958	Gino Marchetti	DE	Baltimore Colts	Leader of defense that permitted league-low 1,291 rushing yards and division-low 203 points.
1959	Charley Conerly	QB	New York Giants	Passed for 14 TDs vs. 4 interceptions. Led offense to division-leading 284 points.
1960	Norm Van Brocklin	QB	Philadelphia Eagles	Guided Eagles to first division title since 1949. Passed for 2,471 yards and 24 TDs.
	Joe Schmidt	LB	Detroit Lions	Team went 7-2 after 0-3 start when he returned from injury. Scored 2 defensive TDs.
1961	Paul Hornung	RB	Green Bay Packers	Led league in scoring for second straight season with 146 points (10 TD, 15 FG, 41 PAT).
1962	Jim Taylor	RB	Green Bay Packers	League rushing champion with 1,474 yards. Scored then all-time record 19 touchdowns.
1963	Y.A. Tittle	QB	New York Giants	Set then all-time season record with 36 TD passes. Guided league's top offense (5,024 yards).
1964	Johnny Unitas	QB	Baltimore Colts	Guided Colts to NFL's best record (12-2) and league's top offensive attack (4,779 yards).
1965	Jim Brown	RB	Cleveland Browns	Leader of NFL's top rushing attack. Led league with 1,544 yards, added 21 total TDs.
1966	Bart Starr	QB	Green Bay Packers	Passed for 14 touchdowns vs. 3 interceptions. Led Packers to league-best 12-2 record.
1967	Johnny Unitas	QB	Baltimore Colts	Passed for 3,428 yards and 20 touchdowns. Led Colts to 11-1-2 record.
1968	Earl Morrall	QB	Baltimore Colts	Guided Colts to NFL-best 13-1 record. Led league with 26 touchdown passes.
1969	Roman Gabriel	QB	Los Angeles Rams	Led NFL with 24 touchdown passes. Guided Rams to 11-3 record.
1970	John Brodie	QB	San Francisco 49ers	Took 49ers to first-ever division title. Threw NFL-best 24 TD passes.
1971	Alan Page	DT	Minnesota Vikings	Led defense that allowed NFL-low 139 points. Vikings won fourth straight NFC Central title.
1972	Larry Brown	RB	Washington Redskins	Led conference with 1,216 rushing yards. Redskins had NFC-best 11-3 record.
1973	O.J. Simpson	RB	Buffalo Bills	Rushed for then all-time record 2,003 yards, including three 200-yard performances.
1974	Ken Stabler	QB	Oakland Raiders	Led league with 26 touchdown passes vs. 12 interceptions. Raiders had NFL-best 12-2 record.
1975	Fran Tarkenton	QB	Minnesota Vikings	Tied for league-best 12-2 record. Led NFC with 91.7 passer rating.
1976	Bert Jones	QB	Baltimore Colts	Threw 24 touchdowns vs. 9 interceptions for 102.5 passer rating.
1977	Walter Payton	RB	Chicago Bears	Rushed for league-leading 1,852 yards and 16 total touchdowns.
1978	Terry Bradshaw	QB	Pittsburgh Steelers	Led Steelers to league-leading 14-2 mark. Set team record with 28 TD passes.
1979	Earl Campbell	RB	Houston Oilers	Led league with 1,697 rushing yards and 19 touchdowns.
1980	Brian Sipe	QB	Cleveland Browns	NFL-best 91.4 passer rating. Set Browns' records with 30 TD passes and 4,132 yards.
1981	Ken Anderson	QB	Cincinnati Bengals	Led Bengals to first division title since 1973. NFL-high 98.5 passer rating.
1982	Mark Moseley	K	Washington Redskins	Converted 20 of 21 FGs. Set then consecutive field-goal record at 23 (including last three in '81).
1983	Joe Theismann	QB	Washington Redskins	Leader of offense that scored NFL record 541 points. Redskins had NFL-best 14-2 record.
1984	Dan Marino	QB	Miami Dolphins	Set NFL records with 5,084 yards and 48 TD passes. Led Dolphins to AFC-best 14-2 mark.
1985	Marcus Allen	RB	Los Angeles Raiders	Rushed for league-leading 1,759 yards. Tied for AFC lead with 11 rushing touchdowns.
1986	Lawrence Taylor	LB	New York Giants	Recorded league-high 20.5 sacks, and led Giants' second-ranked defense (297.3).
1987	John Elway	QB	Denver Broncos	In 12 games, passed for 19 TDs and passed four 300-yard games.
1988	Boomer Esiason	QB	Cincinnati Bengals	Led NFL with 97.4 passer rating. Tied for AFC lead with 28 TD passes.
1989	Joe Montana	QB	San Francisco 49ers	Set then NFL record with 112.4 passer rating, including 70.2 completion percentage.
1990	Joe Montana	QB	San Francisco 49ers	Led 49ers to league-best 14-2 record. Completed NFC-high 61.7 percent of passes.
1991	Thurman Thomas	RB	Buffalo Bills	Recorded league-high 2,038 yards from scrimmage (1,407 rushing, 631 receiving).
1992	Steve Young	QB	San Francisco 49ers	NFL's top passer with 107.0 rating. Led 49ers to league-best 14-2 record.
1993	Emmitt Smith	RB	Dallas Cowboys	Led league in rushing (1,486 yards) for third straight year despite missing first two games.
1994	Steve Young	QB	San Francisco 49ers	Compiled NFL all-time best 112.8 passer rating. Completed more than 70 percent of his passes.
1995	Brett Favre	QB	Green Bay Packers	Led league with 38 touchdown passes and NFC with 99.5 passer rating.
1996	Brett Favre	QB	Green Bay Packers	Led Packers to top conference record (13-3). Threw NFL-best 39 TD passes.

Total *Associated Press* NFL MVPs: 41
Two-time Winners: Jim Brown, Brett Favre, Joe Montana, Johnny Unitas, Steve Young

ASSOCIATED PRESS NFL MVP BY POSITION

Quarterback:	25	Defensive End:	1
Running Back:	11	Defensive Tackle:	1
Linebacker:	2	Kicker:	1

ASSOCIATED PRESS MVPs WHO WON SUPER BOWL/NFL CHAMPIONSHIP IN SAME SEASON: 12

1958	Gino Marchetti	Baltimore Colts
1960	Norm Van Brocklin	Philadelphia Eagles
1961	Paul Hornung	Green Bay Packers
1962	Jim Taylor	Green Bay Packers
1966	Bart Starr	Green Bay Packers
1978	Terry Bradshaw	Pittsburgh Steelers
1982	Mark Moseley	Washington Redskins
1986	Lawrence Taylor	New York Giants
1989	Joe Montana	San Francisco 49ers
1993	Emmitt Smith	Dallas Cowboys
1994	Steve Young	San Francisco 49ers
1996	Brett Favre	Green Bay Packers

ASSOCIATED PRESS MVPs BY TEAM

5	Baltimore Colts	1	Chicago Bears
	Green Bay Packers		Dallas Cowboys
	San Francisco 49ers		Denver Broncos
			Detroit Lions
3	Cleveland Browns		Houston Oilers
	New York Giants		Los Angeles Rams
	Washington Redskins		Miami Dolphins
			Philadelphia Eagles
2	Buffalo Bills		Pittsburgh Steelers
	Cincinnati Bengals		
	Minnesota Vikings		
	Oakland/Los Angeles Raiders		

MILLER LITE PLAYERS OF THE YEAR

YEAR	PLAYER	POS.	TEAM
1989	Joe Montana	QB	San Francisco 49ers
1990	Joe Montana	QB	San Francisco 49ers
1991	Thurman Thomas	RB	Buffalo Bills
1992	Steve Young	QB	San Francisco 49ers
1993	Emmitt Smith	RB	Dallas Cowboys
1994	Steve Young	QB	San Francisco 49ers
1995	Brett Favre	QB	Green Bay Packers
1996	Brett Favre	QB	Green Bay Packers

75TH ANNIVERSARY ALL-TIME TEAM

Chosen by a selection committee of media and league personnel.

Position	Name	Team(s)	Ht.	Wt.	College
OFFENSE					
QB	Sammy Baugh	Washington Redskins (1937-52)	6-2	180	Texas Christian
QB	Otto Graham	Cleveland Browns (1946-55)	6-1	195	Northwestern
QB	Joe Montana	San Francisco 49ers (1979-92), Kansas City Chiefs (1993-94)	6-2	195	Notre Dame
QB	Johnny Unitas	Baltimore Colts (1956-72), San Diego Chargers (1973)	6-1	195	Louisville
RB	Jim Brown	Cleveland Browns (1957-65)	6-2	232	Syracuse
RB	Marion Motley	Cleveland Browns (1946-53), Pittsburgh Steelers (1955)	6-1	238	Nevada-Reno
RB	Bronko Nagurski	Chicago Bears (1930-37, 1943)	6-2	225	Minnesota
RB	Walter Payton	Chicago Bears (1975-87)	5-10	202	Jackson State
RB	Gale Sayers	Chicago Bears (1965-71)	6-0	200	Kansas
RB	O.J. Simpson	Buffalo Bills (1969-77), San Francisco 49ers (1978-79)	6-1	212	Southern California
RB	Steve Van Buren	Philadelphia Eagles (1944-51)	6-1	200	Louisiana State
WR	Lance Alworth	San Diego Chargers (1962-70), Dallas Cowboys (1971-72)	6-0	184	Arkansas
WR	Raymond Berry	Baltimore Colts (1955-67)	6-2	187	Southern Methodist
WR	Don Hutson	Green Bay Packers (1935-45)	6-1	180	Alabama
WR	Jerry Rice	San Francisco 49ers (1985-present)	6-2	200	Miss. Valley State
TE	Mike Ditka	Chicago Bears (1961-66), Philadelphia Eagles (1967-68), Dallas Cowboys (1969-72)	6-3	225	Pittsburgh
TE	Kellen Winslow	San Diego Chargers (1979-87)	6-5	250	Missouri
T	Roosevelt Brown	New York Giants (1953-65)	6-3	255	Morgan State
T	Forrest Gregg	Green Bay Packers (1956, 1958-70)	6-4	250	Southern Methodist
T	Anthony Muñoz	Cincinnati Bengals (1980-92)	6-6	285	Southern California
G	John Hannah	New England Patriots (1973-85)	6-3	265	Alabama
G	Jim Parker	Baltimore Colts (1957-67)	6-3	273	Ohio State
G	Gene Upshaw	Oakland Raiders (1967-81)	6-5	255	Texas A&I
C	Mel Hein	New York Giants (1931-45)	6-2	225	Washington State
C	Mike Webster	Pittsburgh Steelers (1974-88), Kansas City Chiefs (1989-90)	6-2	250	Wisconsin
DEFENSE					
DE	David (Deacon) Jones	Los Angeles Rams (1961-71), San Diego Chargers (1972-73), Washington Redskins (1974)	6-5	250	Miss. Vocational
DE	Gino Marchetti	Dallas Texans (1952), Baltimore Colts (1953-64,1966)	6-4	245	San Francisco
DE	Reggie White	Philadelphia Eagles (1985-95), Green Bay Packers (1993-present)	6-5	290	Tennessee
DT	Joe Greene	Pittsburgh Steelers (1969-81)	6-4	260	North Texas State
DT	Bob Lilly	Dallas Cowboys (1961-74)	6-5	260	Texas Christian
DT	Merlin Olsen	Los Angeles Rams (1962-76)	6-5	270	Utah State
LB	Dick Butkus	Chicago Bears (1965-73)	6-3	245	Illinois
LB	Jack Ham	Pittsburgh Steelers (1971-82)	6-1	225	Penn State
LB	Ted Hendricks	Baltimore Colts (1969-73), Green Bay Packers (1974), Oakland/L.A. Raiders (1975-83)	6-7	235	Miami
LB	Jack Lambert	Pittsburgh Steelers (1974-84)	6-4	220	Kent State
LB	Willie Lanier	Kansas City Chiefs (1967-77)	6-1	245	Morgan State
LB	Ray Nitschke	Green Bay Packers (1958-72)	6-3	235	Illinois
LB	Lawrence Taylor	New York Giants (1981-93)	6-3	243	North Carolina
CB	Mel Blount	Pittsburgh Steelers (1970-83)	6-3	205	Southern
CB	Mike Haynes	New England Patriots (1976-82), Los Angeles Raiders (1983-89)	6-2	190	Arizona State
CB	Dick (Night Train) Lane	Los Angeles Rams (1952-53), Chicago Cardinals (1954-59), Detroit Lions (1960-65)	6-2	210	Scottsbluff JC
CB	Rod Woodson	Pittsburgh Steelers (1987-present)	6-0	200	Purdue
S	Ken Houston	Houston Oilers (1967-72), Washington Redskins (1973-80)	6-3	198	Prairie View A&M
S	Ronnie Lott	San Francisco 49ers (1981-90), Los Angeles Raiders (1991-92), New York Jets (1993-94)	6-0	200	Southern California
S	Larry Wilson	St. Louis Cardinals (1960-72)	6-0	190	Utah
SPECIAL TEAMS					
P	Ray Guy	Oakland/L.A. Raiders (1973-86)	6-3	190	Southern Miss.
K	Jan Stenerud	Kansas City Chiefs (1967-79), Green Bay Packers (1980-83), Minnesota Vikings (1984-85)	6-2	190	Montana State
PR	Billy (White Shoes) Johnson	Houston Oilers (1974-80), Atlanta Falcons (1982-87), Washington Redskins (1988)	5-9	170	Widener
KR	Gale Sayers	Chicago Bears (1965-71)	6-0	200	Kansas

75TH ANNIVERSARY ALL-TWO-WAY TEAM
Positions

Quarterback, Defensive Halfback, Punter	Sammy Baugh
Center, Linebacker	Chuck Bednarik
Quarterback, Defensive Halfback, Punter	Earl (Dutch) Clark
Tackle, Defensive Tackle	George Connor
Guard, Defensive Tackle	Danny Fortmann
Center, Defensive Tackle	Mel Hein
Tackle, Defensive Tackle, Punter	Wilbur (Pete) Henry
Back, Defensive Halfback	Bill Hewitt
Fullback, Linebacker, Kicker	Clarke Hinkle
Tackle, Defensive Tackle	Cal Hubbard
End, Defensive Halfback	Don Hutson
Back, Defensive Back	George McAfee
Fullback, Linebacker	Marion Motley
Guard-Tackle, Defensive Tackle	George Musso
Fullback, Linebacker	Bronko Nagurski
Halfback, Defensive Halfback	Ernie Nevers
End, Defensive Back	Pete Pihos
Tackle, Defensive Tackle	Joe Stydahar
Running Back, Defensive Back	Steve Van Buren

50TH ANNIVERSARY TEAM
Chosen by the Hall of Fame Selection Committee in 1969.

Offense

Split End	Don Hutson
Tight End	John Mackey
Tackle	Cal Hubbard
Guard	Jerry Kramer
Center	Chuck Bednarik
Flanker	Elroy Hirsch
Quarterback	Johnny Unitas
Halfback	Jim Thorpe
Halfback	Gale Sayers
Fullback	Jim Brown
Kicker	Lou Groza

Defense

End	Gino Marchetti
Tackle	Leo Nomellini
Linebacker	Ray Nitschke
Cornerback	Dick (Night Train) Lane
Safety	Emlen Tunnell

ALL-TIME AFL TEAM
Chosen by 1969 AFL Hall of Fame Selection Committee members.

Offense

Flanker	Lance Alworth
End	Don Maynard
Tight End	Fred Arbanas
Tackle	Ron Mix
Tackle	Jim Tyrer
Guard	Ed Budde
Guard	Billy Shaw
Center	Jim Otto
Quarterback	Joe Namath
Running Back	Clemon Daniels
Running Back	Paul Lowe

Defense

End	Jerry Mays
End	Gerry Philbin
Tackle	Houston Antwine
Tackle	Tom Sestak
Linebacker	Bobby Bell
Linebacker	George Webster
Linebacker	Nick Buoniconti
Cornerback	Willie Brown
Cornerback	Dave Grayson
Safety	Johnny Robinson
Safety	George Saimes

Special Teams

Kicker	George Blanda
Punter	Jerrel Wilson

SUPER BOWL SILVER ANNIVERSARY TEAM
Chosen by the fans prior to Super Bowl XXV in 1990.

Head Coach	Vince Lombardi

Offense

Quarterback	Joe Montana
Running Back	Franco Harris
Running Back	Larry Csonka
Wide Receiver	Lynn Swann
Wide Receiver	Jerry Rice
Tight End	Dave Casper
Tackle	Art Shell
Tackle	Forrest Gregg
Guard	Gene Upshaw
Guard	Jerry Kramer
Center	Mike Webster

Defense

Defensive End	L.C. Greenwood
Defensive End	Ed (Too Tall) Jones
Defensive Tackle	Joe Greene
Defensive Tackle	Randy White
Inside Linebacker	Jack Lambert
Inside Linebacker	Mike Singletary
Outside Linebacker	Jack Ham
Outside Linebacker	Ted Hendricks
Cornerback	Ronnie Lott
Cornerback	Mel Blount
Safety	Donnie Shell
Safety	Willie Wood

Special Teams

Punter	Ray Guy
Kicker	Jan Stenerud
Kick Returner	John Taylor

All-Decade teams chosen by the Pro Football Hall of Fame Board of Selectors.

1920's ALL-DECADE TEAM

Back	Paddy Driscoll
Halfback	Red Grange
Halfback	Jim Thorpe
Fullback	Ernie Nevers
End	Guy Chamberlin
End	Lavern Dilweg
Tackle	Wilbur (Pete) Henry
Tackle	Cal Hubbard
Guard	Walt Kiesling
Guard	Mike Michalske
Center	George Trafton

1930's ALL-DECADE TEAM

Back	Earl (Dutch) Clark
Halfback	Cliff Battles
Halfback	Clarke Hinkle
Fullback	Bronko Nagurski
End	Bill Hewitt
End	Don Hutson
Tackle	Glen (Turk) Edwards
Tackle	Joe Stydahar
Guard	Grover (Ox) Emerson
Guard	Dan Fortmann
Center	Mel Hein

1940's ALL-DECADE TEAM

Quarterback	Sammy Baugh
Halfback	George McAfee
Halfback	Steve Van Buren
Fullback	Marion Motley
End	Dante Lavelli
End	Pete Pihos
Tackle	George Conner
Tackle	Al Wistert
Guard	Bruno Banducci
Guard	Bill Willis
Center	Clyde (Bulldog) Turner

1950's ALL-DECADE TEAM

Offense

Quarterback	Otto Graham
Halfback	Ollie Matson
Halfback	Hugh McElhenny
Fullback	Joe Perry
End	Raymond Berry
End	Tom Fears
Flanker	Elroy (Crazylegs) Hirsch
Tackle	Roosevelt Brown
Tackle	Bob St. Clair
Guard	Jim Parker
Guard	Dick Stanfel
Center	Chuck Bednarik

Defense

Defensive End	Len Ford
Defensive End	Gino Marchetti
Defensive Tackle	Leo Nomellini
Defensive Tackle	Ernie Stautner
Linebacker	Bill George
Linebacker	Sam Huff
Linebacker	Joe Schmidt
Defensive Halfback	Jack Butler
Defensive Halfback	Dick (Night Train) Lane
Safety	Jack Christiansen
Safety	Emlen Tunnell

Special Teams

Kicker	Lou Groza

1960's ALL-DECADE TEAM

Offense

Quarterback	Johnny Unitas
Halfback	Paul Hornung
Halfback	Gale Sayers
Fullback	Jim Brown
Wide Receiver	Lance Alworth
Wide Receiver	Charley Taylor
Tight End	John Mackey
Tackle	Forrest Gregg
Tackle	Ron Mix
Guard	Jerry Kramer
Guard	Billy Shaw
Center	Jim Otto

Defense

Defensive End	Willie Davis
Defensive End	David (Deacon) Jones
Defensive Tackle	Bob Lilly
Defensive Tackle	Merlin Olsen
Linebacker	Bobby Bell
Linebacker	Dick Butkus
Linebacker	Ray Nitschke
Cornerback	Herb Adderley
Cornerback	Willie Brown
Safety	Johnny Robinson
Safety	Larry Wilson

Special Teams

Punter	Don Chandler
Kicker	Jim Bakken

1970's ALL-DECADE TEAM

Offense

Quarterback	Terry Bradshaw
Running Back	Walter Payton
Running Back	O.J. Simpson
Wide Receiver	Drew Pearson
Wide Receiver	Lynn Swann
Tight End	Dave Casper
Tackle	Art Shell
Tackle	Ron Yary
Guard	Joe DeLamielleure
Guard	Larry Little
Center	Jim Langer

Defense

Defensive End	Carl Eller
Defensive End	Jack Youngblood
Defensive Tackle	Joe Greene
Defensive Tackle	Bob Lilly
Outside Linebacker	Jack Ham
Middle Linebacker	Dick Butkus
Outside Linebacker	Ted Hendricks
Cornerback	Willie Brown
Cornerback	Jimmy Johnson
Safety	Cliff Harris
Safety	Ken Houston

Special Teams

Punter	Ray Guy
Kicker	Garo Yepremian
Kick Returner	Rick Upchurch

1980's ALL-DECADE TEAM

Offense

Quarterback	Joe Montana
Running Back	Eric Dickerson
Running Back	Walter Payton
Wide Receiver	Steve Largent
Wide Receiver	Jerry Rice
Tight End	Kellen Winslow
Tackle	Jim Covert
Tackle	Anthony Muñoz
Guard	Russ Grimm
Guard	John Hannah
Center	Dwight Stephenson

Defense

Defensive End	Howie Long
Defensive End	Reggie White
Defensive Tackle	Dan Hampton
Defensive Tackle	Randy White
Linebacker	Ted Hendricks
Inside Linebacker	Mike Singletary
Outside Linebacker	Lawrence Taylor
Cornerback	Mel Blount
Cornerback	Mike Haynes
Safety	Kenny Easley
Safety	Ronnie Lott

Special Teams

Punter	Sean Landeta
Kicker	Morten Andersen
Punt Returner	Billy (White Shoes) Johnson
Kick Returner	Mike Nelms

Records

ALL-TIME RECORDS

Compiled by Elias Sports Bureau

The following records reflect all available official information on the National Football League from its formation in 1920 to date. Also included are all applicable records from the American Football League, 1960-69.

Individuals eligible for Rookie records are players who were in their first season of professional football and had not been on the roster of another professional football team, including teams in other leagues, for any regular-season or post-season games in a previous season. Eligible players, therefore, include those who were under contract to a National Football League club for a previous season but were terminated prior to their club's first regular-season game and not re-signed, or who were placed on Reserve/Injured (or another category of the Reserve List) prior to their club's first regular-season game and were not activated during the rest of the regular season or postseason.

INDIVIDUAL RECORDS

SERVICE

Most Seasons
- 26 George Blanda, Chi. Bears, 1949, 1950-58; Baltimore, 1950; Houston, 1960-66; Oakland, 1967-75
- 21 Earl Morrall, San Francisco, 1956; Pittsburgh, 1957-58; Detroit, 1958-64; N.Y. Giants, 1965-67; Baltimore, 1968-71; Miami, 1972-76
- 20 Jim Marshall, Cleveland, 1960; Minnesota, 1961-79
- Jackie Slater, L.A. Rams, 1976-94; St. Louis, 1995

Most Seasons, One Club
- 20 Jackie Slater, L.A. Rams, 1976-94; St. Louis, 1995
- 19 Jim Marshall, Minnesota, 1961-79
- 18 Jim Hart, St. Louis, 1966-83
- Jeff Van Note, Atlanta, 1969-86
- Pat Leahy, N.Y. Jets, 1974-91

Most Games Played, Career
- 340 George Blanda, Chi. Bears, 1949, 1950-58; Baltimore, 1950; Houston, 1960-66; Oakland, 1967-75
- 282 Jim Marshall, Cleveland, 1960; Minnesota, 1961-79
- 278 Clay Matthews, Cleveland, 1978-93; Atlanta, 1994-96

Most Consecutive Games Played, Career
- 282 Jim Marshall, Cleveland, 1960; Minnesota, 1961-79
- 240 Mick Tingelhoff, Minnesota, 1962-78
- 234 Jim Bakken, St. Louis, 1962-78

SCORING

Most Seasons Leading League
- 5 Don Hutson, Green Bay, 1940-44
- Gino Cappelletti, Boston, 1961, 1963-66
- 3 Earl (Dutch) Clark, Portsmouth, 1932; Detroit, 1935-36
- Pat Harder, Chi. Cardinals, 1947-49
- Paul Hornung, Green Bay, 1959-61
- 2 Jack Manders, Chi. Bears, 1934, 1937
- Gordy Soltau, San Francisco, 1952-53
- Doak Walker, Detroit, 1950, 1955
- Gene Mingo, Denver, 1960, 1962
- Jim Turner, N.Y. Jets, 1968-69
- Fred Cox, Minnesota, 1969-70
- Chester Marcol, Green Bay, 1972, 1974
- John Smith, New England, 1979-80

Most Consecutive Seasons Leading League
- 5 Don Hutson, Green Bay, 1940-44
- 4 Gino Cappelletti, Boston, 1963-66
- 3 Pat Harder, Chi. Cardinals, 1947-49
- Paul Hornung, Green Bay, 1959-61

POINTS

Most Points, Career
- 2,002 George Blanda, Chi. Bears, 1949, 1950-58; Baltimore, 1950; Houston, 1960-66; Oakland, 1967-75 (9-td, 943-pat, 335-fg)
- 1,711 Nick Lowery, New England, 1978; Kansas City, 1980-93; N.Y. Jets, 1994-96 (562-pat, 383-fg)
- 1,699 Jan Stenerud, Kansas City, 1967-79; Green Bay, 1980-83; Minnesota, 1984-85 (580-pat, 373-fg)

Most Points, Season
- 176 Paul Hornung, Green Bay, 1960 (15-td, 41-pat, 15-fg)
- 161 Mark Moseley, Washington, 1983 (62-pat, 33-fg)
- 155 Gino Cappelletti, Boston, 1964 (7-td, 38-pat, 25-fg)

Most Points, No Touchdowns, Season
- 161 Mark Moseley, Washington, 1983 (62-pat, 33-fg)
- 149 Chip Lohmiller, Washington, 1991 (56-pat, 31-fg)
- 145 Jim Turner, N.Y. Jets, 1968 (43-pat, 34-fg)
- John Kasay, Carolina, 1996 (34-pat, 37-fg)

Most Seasons, 100 or More Points
- 11 Nick Lowery, Kansas City, 1981, 1983-86, 1988-93
- 10 Morten Andersen, New Orleans, 1985-89, 1991-94; Atlanta, 1995
- 9 Gary Anderson, Pittsburgh, 1983-85, 1988, 1991-94; Philadelphia, 1996

Most Points, Rookie, Season
- 144 Kevin Butler, Chicago, 1985 (51-pat, 31-fg)
- 132 Gale Sayers, Chicago, 1965 (22-td)
- 128 Doak Walker, Detroit, 1950 (11-td, 38-pat, 8-fg)
- Chester Marcol, Green Bay, 1972 (29-pat, 33-fg)

Most Points, Game
- 40 Ernie Nevers, Chi. Cardinals vs. Chi. Bears, Nov. 28, 1929 (6-td, 4-pat)
- 36 Dub Jones, Cleveland vs. Chi. Bears, Nov. 25, 1951 (6-td)
- Gale Sayers, Chicago vs. San Francisco, Dec. 12, 1965 (6-td)
- 33 Paul Hornung, Green Bay vs. Baltimore, Oct. 8, 1961 (4-td, 6-pat, 1-fg)

Most Consecutive Games Scoring
- 206 Morten Andersen, New Orleans, 1982-94; Atlanta, 1995-96 (current)
- 186 Jim Breech, Oakland, 1979; Cincinnati, 1980-92
- 155 Ray Wersching, San Francisco, 1977-87

TOUCHDOWNS

Most Seasons Leading League
- 8 Don Hutson, Green Bay, 1935-38, 1941-44
- 3 Jim Brown, Cleveland, 1958-59, 1963
- Lance Alworth, San Diego, 1964-66
- Emmitt Smith, Dallas, 1992, 1994-95
- 2 By many players

Most Consecutive Seasons Leading League
- 4 Don Hutson, Green Bay, 1935-38, 1941-44
- 3 Lance Alworth, San Diego, 1964-66
- 2 By many players

Most Touchdowns, Career
- 165 Jerry Rice, San Francisco, 1985-96 (10-r, 154-p, 1-ret)
- 134 Marcus Allen, L.A. Raiders, 1982-92; Kansas City, 1993-96 (112-r, 21-p, 1-ret)
- 126 Jim Brown, Cleveland, 1957-65 (106-r, 20-p)

Most Touchdowns, Season
- 25 Emmitt Smith, Dallas, 1995 (25-r)
- 24 John Riggins, Washington, 1983 (24-r)
- 23 O.J. Simpson, Buffalo, 1975 (16-r, 7-p)
- Jerry Rice, San Francisco, 1987 (1-r, 22-p)

Most Touchdowns, Rookie, Season
- 22 Gale Sayers, Chicago, 1965 (14-r, 6-p, 2-ret)
- 20 Eric Dickerson, L.A. Rams, 1983 (18-r, 2-p)
- 16 Billy Sims, Detroit, 1980 (13-r, 3-p)

Most Touchdowns, Game
- 6 Ernie Nevers, Chi. Cardinals vs. Chi. Bears, Nov. 28, 1929 (6-r)
- Dub Jones, Cleveland vs. Chi. Bears, Nov. 25, 1951 (4-r, 2-p)
- Gale Sayers, Chicago vs. San Francisco, Dec. 12, 1965 (4-r, 1-p, 1-ret)
- 5 Bob Shaw, Chi. Cardinals vs. Baltimore, Oct. 2, 1950 (5-p)
- Jim Brown, Cleveland vs. Baltimore, Nov. 1, 1959 (5-r)
- Abner Haynes, Dall. Texans vs. Oakland, Nov. 26, 1961 (4-r, 1-p)
- Billy Cannon, Houston vs. N.Y. Titans, Dec. 10, 1961 (3-r, 2-p)
- Cookie Gilchrist, Buffalo vs. N.Y. Jets, Dec. 8, 1963 (5-r)
- Paul Hornung, Green Bay vs. Baltimore, Dec. 12, 1965 (3-r, 2-p)
- Kellen Winslow, San Diego vs. Oakland, Nov. 22, 1981 (5-p)
- Jerry Rice, San Francisco vs. Atlanta, Oct. 14, 1990 (5-p)
- 4 By many players. Last time: Irving Fryar, Philadelphia vs. Miami, Oct. 20, 1996 (4-p)

Most Consecutive Games Scoring Touchdowns
- 18 Lenny Moore, Baltimore, 1963-65
- 14 O.J. Simpson, Buffalo, 1975
- 13 John Riggins, Washington, 1982-83
- George Rogers, Washington, 1985-86
- Jerry Rice, San Francisco, 1986-87

POINTS AFTER TOUCHDOWN

Most Seasons Leading League
- 8 George Blanda, Chi. Bears, 1956; Houston, 1961-62; Oakland, 1967-69, 1972, 1974
- 4 Bob Waterfield, Cleveland, 1945; Los Angeles, 1946, 1950, 1952
- 3 Earl (Dutch) Clark, Portsmouth, 1932; Detroit, 1935-36
- Jack Manders, Chi. Bears, 1933-35
- Don Hutson, Green Bay, 1941-42, 1945

Most (Kicking) Points After Touchdown Attempted, Career
- 959 George Blanda, Chi. Bears, 1949, 1950-58; Baltimore, 1950; Houston, 1960-66; Oakland, 1967-75
- 657 Lou Groza, Cleveland, 1950-59, 1961-67
- 601 Jan Stenerud, Kansas City, 1967-79; Green Bay, 1980-83; Minnesota, 1984-85

Most (Kicking) Points After Touchdown Attempted, Season
- 70 Uwe von Schamann, Miami, 1984
- 65 George Blanda, Houston, 1961
- 63 Mark Moseley, Washington, 1983

Most (Kicking) Points After Touchdown Attempted, Game
- 10 Charlie Gogolak, Washington vs. N.Y. Giants, Nov. 27, 1966
- 9 Pat Harder, Chi. Cardinals vs. N.Y. Giants, Oct. 17, 1948; vs. N.Y. Bulldogs, Nov. 13, 1949

Bob Waterfield, Los Angeles vs. Baltimore, Oct. 22, 1950
Bob Thomas, Chicago vs. Green Bay, Dec. 7, 1980
8 By many players

Most (One-Point) Points After Touchdown, Career
943 George Blanda, Chi. Bears, 1949, 1950-58; Baltimore, 1950; Houston, 1960-66; Oakland, 1967-75
641 Lou Groza, Cleveland, 1950-59, 1961-67
580 Jan Stenerud, Kansas City, 1967-79; Green Bay, 1980-83; Minnesota, 1984-85

Most (One-Point) Points After Touchdown, Season
66 Uwe von Schamann, Miami, 1984
64 George Blanda, Houston, 1961
62 Mark Moseley, Washington, 1983

Most (One-Point) Points After Touchdown, Game
9 Pat Harder, Chi. Cardinals vs. N.Y. Giants, Oct. 17, 1948
Bob Waterfield, Los Angeles vs. Baltimore, Oct. 22, 1950
Charlie Gogolak, Washington vs. N.Y. Giants, Nov. 27, 1966
8 By many players

Most Consecutive (Kicking) Points After Touchdown
234 Tommy Davis, San Francisco, 1959-65
228 Eddie Murray, Detroit, 1988-91; Kansas City, 1992; Tampa Bay, 1992; Dallas, 1993; Philadelphia, 1994; Washington, 1995
221 Jim Turner, N.Y. Jets, 1967-70; Denver, 1971-74

Highest (Kicking) Points After Touchdown Percentage, Career (200 points after touchdown)
99.43 Tommy Davis, San Francisco, 1959-69 (350-348)
99.01 Eddie Murray, Detroit, 1980-91; Kansas City, 1992; Tampa Bay, 1992; Dallas, 1993; Philadelphia, 1994; Washington, 1995 (503-498)
98.99 Gary Anderson, Pittsburgh, 1982-94; Philadelphia, 1995-96 (493-488)

Most (Kicking) Points After Touchdown, No Misses, Season
56 Danny Villanueva, Dallas, 1966
Ray Wersching, San Francisco, 1984
Chip Lohmiller, Washington, 1991
54 Mike Clark, Dallas, 1968
George Blanda, Oakland, 1968
53 Pat Harder, Chi. Cardinals, 1948

Most (Kicking) Points After Touchdown, No Misses, Game
9 Pat Harder, Chi. Cardinals vs. N.Y. Giants, Oct. 17, 1948
Bob Waterfield, Los Angeles vs. Baltimore, Oct. 22, 1950
8 By many players

Most Two-Point Conversions, Career
6 Terance Mathis, Atlanta, 1994-96
4 Gino Cappelletti, Boston, 1960-69
Rob Moore, N.Y. Jets, 1994; Arizona, 1995-96
3 By many players

Most Two-Point Conversions, Season
3 Gino Cappelletti, Boston, 1960
Richie Lucas, Buffalo, 1961
Ronnie Harmon, San Diego, 1994
Haywood Jeffires, Houston, 1994
Tom Tupa, Cleveland, 1994
Terance Mathis, Atlanta, 1995
Lamar Smith, Seattle, 1996
2 By many players

Most Two-Point Conversions, Game
2 Brett Perriman, Detroit vs. Green Bay, Nov. 6, 1994
Michael Jackson, Baltimore vs. New England, Oct. 6, 1996

FIELD GOALS

Most Seasons Leading League
5 Lou Groza, Cleveland, 1950, 1952-54, 1957
4 Jack Manders, Chi. Bears, 1933-34, 1936-37
Ward Cuff, N.Y. Giants, 1938-39, 1943; Green Bay, 1947
Mark Moseley, Washington, 1976-77, 1979, 1982
3 Bob Waterfield, Los Angeles, 1947, 1949, 1951
Gino Cappelletti, Boston, 1961, 1963-64
Fred Cox, Minnesota, 1965, 1969-70
Jan Stenerud, Kansas City, 1967, 1970, 1975

Most Consecutive Seasons Leading League
3 Lou Groza, Cleveland, 1952-54
2 Jack Manders, Chi. Bears, 1933-34
Armand Niccolai, Pittsburgh, 1935-36
Jack Manders, Chi. Bears, 1936-37
Ward Cuff, N.Y. Giants, 1938-39
Clark Hinkle, Green Bay, 1940-41
Cliff Patton, Philadelphia, 1948-49
Gino Cappelletti, Boston, 1963-64
Jim Turner, N.Y. Jets, 1968-69
Fred Cox, Minnesota, 1969-70
Mark Moseley, Washington, 1976-77
Chip Lohmiller, Washington, 1991-92
Pete Stoyanovich, Miami, 1991-92

Most Field Goals Attempted, Career
637 George Blanda, Chi. Bears, 1949, 1950-58; Baltimore, 1950; Houston, 1960-66; Oakland, 1967-75
558 Jan Stenerud, Kansas City, 1967-79; Green Bay, 1980-83; Minnesota, 1984-85
488 Jim Turner, N.Y. Jets, 1964-70; Denver, 1971-79

Most Field Goals Attempted, Season
49 Bruce Gossett, Los Angeles, 1966
Curt Knight, Washington, 1971
48 Chester Marcol, Green Bay, 1972
47 Jim Turner, N.Y. Jets, 1969
David Ray, Los Angeles, 1973
Mark Moseley, Washington, 1983

Most Field Goals Attempted, Game
9 Jim Bakken, St. Louis vs. Pittsburgh, Sept. 24, 1967
8 Lou Michaels, Pittsburgh vs. St. Louis, Dec. 2, 1962
Garo Yepremian, Detroit vs. Minnesota, Nov. 13, 1966
Jim Turner, N.Y. Jets vs. Buffalo, Nov. 3, 1968
7 By many players

Most Field Goals, Career
383 Nick Lowery, New England, 1978; Kansas City, 1980-93; N.Y. Jets, 1994-96
373 Jan Stenerud, Kansas City, 1967-79; Green Bay, 1980-83; Minnesota, 1984-85
356 Gary Anderson, Pittsburgh, 1982-94; Philadelphia, 1995-96

Most Field Goals, Season
37 John Kasay, Carolina, 1996
36 Cary Blanchard, Indianapolis, 1996
35 Ali Haji-Sheikh, N.Y. Giants, 1983
Jeff Jaeger, L.A. Raiders, 1993

Most Field Goals, Rookie, Season
35 Ali Haji-Sheikh, N.Y. Giants, 1983
33 Chester Marcol, Green Bay, 1972
31 Kevin Butler, Chicago, 1985

Most Field Goals, Game
7 Jim Bakken, St. Louis vs. Pittsburgh, Sept. 24, 1967
Rich Karlis, Minnesota vs. L.A. Rams, Nov. 5, 1989 (OT)
Chris Boniol, Dallas vs. Green Bay, Nov. 18, 1996
6 Gino Cappelletti, Boston vs. Denver, Oct. 4, 1964
Garo Yepremian, Detroit vs. Minnesota, Nov. 13, 1966
Jim Turner, N.Y. Jets vs. Buffalo, Nov. 3, 1968
Tom Dempsey, Philadelphia vs. Houston, Nov. 12, 1972
Bobby Howfield, N.Y. Jets vs. New Orleans, Dec. 3, 1972
Jim Bakken, St. Louis vs. Atlanta, Dec. 9, 1973
Joe Danelo, N.Y. Giants vs. Seattle, Oct. 18, 1981
Ray Wersching, San Francisco vs. New Orleans, Oct. 16, 1983
Gary Anderson, Pittsburgh vs. Denver, Oct. 23, 1988
John Carney, San Diego vs. Seattle, Sept. 5, 1993
John Carney, San Diego vs. Houston, Sept. 19, 1993
Doug Pelfrey, Cincinnati vs. Seattle, Nov. 6, 1994 (OT)
Norm Johnson, Atlanta vs. New Orleans, Nov. 13, 1994
Jeff Wilkins, San Francisco vs. Atlanta, Sept. 29, 1996
Steve Christie, Buffalo vs. N.Y. Jets, Oct. 20, 1996
5 By many players

Most Field Goals, One Quarter
4 Garo Yepremian, Detroit vs. Minnesota, Nov. 13, 1966 (second quarter)
Curt Knight, Washington vs. N.Y. Giants, Nov. 15, 1970 (second quarter)
Roger Ruzek, Dallas vs. N.Y. Giants, Nov. 2, 1987 (fourth quarter)
3 By many players

Most Consecutive Games Scoring Field Goals
31 Fred Cox, Minnesota, 1968-70
28 Jim Turner, N.Y. Jets, 1970; Denver, 1971-72
Chip Lohmiller, Washington, 1988-90
23 Morten Andersen, New Orleans, 1986-88

Most Consecutive Field Goals
31 Fuad Reveiz, Minnesota, 1994-95
29 John Carney, San Diego, 1992-93
27 Chris Boniol, Dallas, 1996 (current)

Longest Field Goal
63 Tom Dempsey, New Orleans vs. Detroit, Nov. 8, 1970
60 Steve Cox, Cleveland vs. Cincinnati, Oct. 21, 1984
Morten Andersen, New Orleans vs. Chicago, Oct. 27, 1991
59 Tony Franklin, Philadelphia vs. Dallas, Nov. 12, 1979
Pete Stoyanovich, Miami vs. N.Y. Jets, Nov. 12, 1989
Steve Christie, Buffalo vs. Miami, Sept. 26, 1993
Morten Andersen, Atlanta vs. San Francisco, Dec. 24, 1995

Highest Field Goal Percentage, Career (100 field goals)
81.25 Doug Pelfrey, Cincinnati, 1993-96 (128-104)
79.96 Nick Lowery, New England, 1978; Kansas City, 1980-93; N.Y. Jets, 1994-96 (479-383)
79.87 Matt Stover, Cleveland, 1991-95; Baltimore, 1996 (159-127)

Highest Field Goal Percentage, Season (Qualifiers)
100.00 Tony Zendejas, L.A. Rams, 1991 (17-17)

96.43 Chris Boniol, Dallas, 1995 (28-27)
96.30 Norm Johnson, Atlanta, 1993 (27-26)

Most Field Goals, No Misses, Game
7 Rich Karlis, Minnesota vs. L.A. Rams, Nov. 5, 1989 (OT)
  Chris Boniol, Dallas vs. Green Bay, Nov. 18, 1996
6 Gino Cappelletti, Boston vs. Denver, Oct. 4, 1964
  Joe Danelo, N.Y. Giants vs. Seattle, Oct. 18, 1981
  Ray Wersching, San Francisco vs. New Orleans, Oct. 16, 1983
  Gary Anderson, Pittsburgh vs. Denver, Oct. 23, 1988
  John Carney, San Diego vs. Seattle, Sept. 5, 1993
  John Carney, San Diego vs. Houston, Sept. 19, 1993
  Doug Pelfrey, Cincinnati vs. Seattle, Nov. 6, 1994 (OT)
  Norm Johnson, Atlanta vs. New Orleans, Nov. 13, 1994
  Jeff Wilkins, San Francisco vs. Atlanta, Sept. 29, 1996
5 By many players

Most Field Goals, 50 or More Yards, Career
31 Morten Andersen, New Orleans, 1982-94; Atlanta, 1995-96
22 Nick Lowery, New England, 1978; Kansas City, 1980-93; N.Y. Jets, 1994-96
21 Eddie Murray, Detroit, 1980-91; Kansas City, 1992; Tampa Bay, 1992; Dallas, 1993; Philadelphia, 1994; Washington, 1995

Most Field Goals, 50 or More Yards, Season
8 Morten Andersen, Atlanta, 1995
6 Dean Biasucci, Indianapolis, 1988
  Chris Jacke, Green Bay, 1993
  Tony Zendejas, L.A. Rams, 1993
5 Fred Steinfort, Denver, 1980
  Norm Johnson, Seattle, 1986
  Kevin Butler, Chicago, 1993
  Jason Elam, Denver, 1995
  Cary Blanchard, Indianapolis, 1996

Most Field Goals, 50 or More Yards, Game
3 Morten Andersen, Atlanta vs. New Orleans, Dec. 10, 1995
2 By many players. Last time: John Kasay, Carolina vs. New Orleans, Sept. 8, 1996

SAFETIES
Most Safeties, Career
4 Ted Hendricks, Baltimore, 1969-73; Green Bay, 1974; Oakland, 1975-81; L.A. Raiders, 1982-83
  Doug English, Detroit, 1975-79, 1981-85
3 Bill McPeak, Pittsburgh, 1949-57
  Charlie Krueger, San Francisco, 1959-73
  Ernie Stautner, Pittsburgh, 1950-63
  Jim Katcavage, N.Y. Giants, 1956-68
  Roger Brown, Detroit, 1960-66; Los Angeles, 1967-69
  Bruce Maher, Detroit, 1960-67; N.Y. Giants, 1968-69
  Ron McDole, St. Louis, 1961; Houston, 1962; Buffalo, 1963-70; Washington, 1971-78
  Alan Page, Minnesota, 1967-78; Chicago, 1979-81
  Lyle Alzado, Denver, 1971-78; Cleveland, 1979-81; L.A. Raiders, 1982-85
  Rulon Jones, Denver, 1980-88
  Steve McMichael, New England, 1980; Chicago, 1981-93; Green Bay, 1994
  Kevin Greene, L.A. Rams, 1985-92; Pittsburgh, 1993-95; Carolina 1996
  Burt Grossman, San Diego, 1989-93; Philadelphia, 1994
  Eric Swann, Phoenix, 1991-93; Arizona, 1994-96
2 By many players

Most Safeties, Season
2 Tom Nash, Green Bay, 1932
  Roger Brown, Detroit, 1962
  Ron McDole, Buffalo, 1964
  Alan Page, Minnesota, 1971
  Fred Dryer, Los Angeles, 1973
  Benny Barnes, Dallas, 1973
  James Young, Houston, 1977
  Tom Hannon, Minnesota, 1981
  Doug English, Detroit, 1983
  Don Blackmon, New England, 1985
  Tim Harris, Green Bay, 1988
  Brian Jordan, Atlanta, 1991
  Burt Grossman, San Diego, 1992
  Rod Stephens, Seattle, 1993
  Bryant Young, San Francisco, 1996

Most Safeties, Game
2 Fred Dryer, Los Angeles vs. Green Bay, Oct. 21, 1973

RUSHING
Most Seasons Leading League
8 Jim Brown, Cleveland, 1957-61, 1963-65
4 Steve Van Buren, Philadelphia, 1945, 1947-49
  O.J. Simpson, Buffalo, 1972-73, 1975-76
  Eric Dickerson, L.A. Rams, 1983-84, 1986; Indianapolis, 1988
  Emmitt Smith, Dallas, 1991-93, 1995
3 Earl Campbell, Houston, 1978-80
  Barry Sanders, Detroit, 1990, 1994, 1996

Most Consecutive Seasons Leading League
5 Jim Brown, Cleveland, 1957-61
3 Steve Van Buren, Philadelphia, 1947-49
  Jim Brown, Cleveland, 1963-65
  Earl Campbell, Houston, 1978-80
  Emmitt Smith, Dallas, 1991-93
2 Bill Paschal, N.Y. Giants, 1943-44
  Joe Perry, San Francisco, 1953-54
  Jim Nance, Boston, 1966-67
  Leroy Kelly, Cleveland, 1967-68
  O.J. Simpson, Buffalo, 1972-73; 1975-76
  Eric Dickerson, L.A. Rams, 1983-84

ATTEMPTS
Most Seasons Leading League
6 Jim Brown, Cleveland, 1958-59, 1961, 1963-65
4 Steve Van Buren, Philadelphia, 1947-50
  Walter Payton, Chicago, 1976-79
3 Cookie Gilchrist, Buffalo, 1963-64; Denver, 1965
  Jim Nance, Boston, 1966-67, 1969
  O.J. Simpson, Buffalo, 1973-75
  Eric Dickerson, L.A. Rams, 1983, 1986; Indianapolis, 1988
  Emmitt Smith, Dallas, 1991, 1994-95

Most Consecutive Seasons Leading League
4 Steve Van Buren, Philadelphia, 1947-50
  Walter Payton, Chicago, 1976-79
3 Jim Brown, Cleveland, 1963-65
  Cookie Gilchrist, Buffalo, 1963-64; Denver, 1965
  O.J. Simpson, Buffalo, 1973-75
2 By many players

Most Attempts, Career
3,838 Walter Payton, Chicago, 1975-87
2,996 Eric Dickerson, L.A. Rams, 1983-87; Indianapolis, 1987-91; L.A. Raiders, 1992; Atlanta, 1993
2,949 Franco Harris, Pittsburgh, 1972-83; Seattle, 1984

Most Attempts, Season
407 James Wilder, Tampa Bay, 1984
404 Eric Dickerson, L.A. Rams, 1986
397 Gerald Riggs, Atlanta, 1985

Most Attempts, Rookie, Season
390 Eric Dickerson, L.A. Rams, 1983
378 George Rogers, New Orleans, 1981
368 Curtis Martin, New England, 1995

Most Attempts, Game
45 Jamie Morris, Washington vs. Cincinnati, Dec. 17, 1988 (OT)
43 Butch Woolfolk, N.Y. Giants vs. Philadelphia, Nov. 20, 1983
  James Wilder, Tampa Bay vs. Green Bay, Sept. 30, 1984 (OT)
42 James Wilder, Tampa Bay vs. Pittsburgh, Oct. 30, 1983

YARDS GAINED
Most Yards Gained, Career
16,726 Walter Payton, Chicago, 1975-87
13,259 Eric Dickerson, L.A. Rams, 1983-87; Indianapolis, 1987-91; L.A. Raiders, 1992; Atlanta, 1993
12,739 Tony Dorsett, Dallas, 1977-87; Denver, 1988

Most Seasons, 1,000 or More Yards Rushing
10 Walter Payton, Chicago, 1976-81, 1983-86
8 Franco Harris, Pittsburgh, 1972, 1974-79, 1983
  Tony Dorsett, Dallas, 1977-81, 1983-85
  Barry Sanders, Detroit, 1989-96
  Thurman Thomas, Buffalo, 1989-96
7 Jim Brown, Cleveland, 1958-61, 1963-65
  Eric Dickerson, L.A. Rams, 1983-86; L.A. Rams-Indianapolis, 1987; Indianapolis, 1988-89

Most Consecutive Seasons, 1,000 or More Yards Rushing
8 Barry Sanders, Detroit, 1989-96
  Thurman Thomas, Buffalo, 1989-96
7 Eric Dickerson, L.A. Rams, 1983-86; L.A. Rams-Indianapolis, 1987; Indianapolis, 1988-89
6 Franco Harris, Pittsburgh, 1974-79
  Walter Payton, Chicago, 1976-81
  Emmitt Smith, Dallas, 1991-96

Most Yards Gained, Season
2,105 Eric Dickerson, L.A. Rams, 1984
2,003 O.J. Simpson, Buffalo, 1973
1,934 Earl Campbell, Houston, 1980

Most Yards Gained, Rookie, Season
1,808 Eric Dickerson, L.A. Rams, 1983

1,674   George Rogers, New Orleans, 1981
1,605   Ottis Anderson, St. Louis, 1979

Most Yards Gained, Game
275   Walter Payton, Chicago vs. Minnesota, Nov. 20, 1977
273   O.J. Simpson, Buffalo vs. Detroit, Nov. 25, 1976
250   O.J. Simpson, Buffalo vs. New England, Sept. 16, 1973

Most Games, 200 or More Yards Rushing, Career
6   O.J. Simpson, Buffalo, 1969-77; San Francisco, 1978-79
4   Jim Brown, Cleveland, 1957-65
    Earl Campbell, Houston, 1978-84; New Orleans, 1984-85
3   Eric Dickerson, L.A. Rams, 1983-87; Indianapolis, 1987-91;
    L.A. Raiders, 1992; Atlanta, 1993
    Greg Bell, Buffalo, 1984-87; L.A. Rams, 1987-89; L.A. Raiders, 1990

Most Games, 200 or More Yards Rushing, Season
4   Earl Campbell, Houston, 1980
3   O.J. Simpson, Buffalo, 1973
2   Jim Brown, Cleveland, 1963
    O.J. Simpson, Buffalo, 1976
    Walter Payton, Chicago, 1977
    Eric Dickerson, L.A. Rams, 1984
    Greg Bell, L.A. Rams, 1989

Most Consecutive Games, 200 or More Yards Rushing
2   O.J. Simpson, Buffalo, 1973, 1976
    Earl Campbell, Houston, 1980

Most Games, 100 or More Yards Rushing, Career
77   Walter Payton, Chicago, 1975-87
64   Eric Dickerson, L.A. Rams, 1983-87; Indianapolis, 1987-91;
     L.A. Raiders, 1992; Atlanta, 1993
58   Jim Brown, Cleveland, 1957-65

Most Games, 100 or More Yards Rushing, Season
12   Eric Dickerson, L.A. Rams, 1984
     Barry Foster, Pittsburgh, 1992
11   O.J. Simpson, Buffalo, 1973
     Earl Campbell, Houston, 1979
     Marcus Allen, L.A. Raiders, 1985
     Eric Dickerson, L.A. Rams, 1986
     Emmitt Smith, Dallas, 1995
10   Walter Payton, Chicago, 1977
     Earl Campbell, Houston, 1980
     Walter Payton, Chicago, 1985
     Barry Sanders, Detroit, 1994
     Jerome Bettis, Pittsburgh, 1996

Most Consecutive Games, 100 or More Yards Rushing
11   Marcus Allen, L.A. Raiders, 1985-86
9   Walter Payton, Chicago, 1985
7   O.J. Simpson, Buffalo, 1972-73
    Earl Campbell, Houston, 1979

Longest Run From Scrimmage
99   Tony Dorsett, Dallas vs. Minnesota, Jan. 3, 1983 (TD)
97   Andy Uram, Green Bay vs. Chi. Cardinals, Oct. 8, 1939 (TD)
     Bob Gage, Pittsburgh vs. Chi. Bears, Dec. 4, 1949 (TD)
96   Jim Spavital, Baltimore vs. Green Bay, Nov. 5, 1950 (TD)
     Bob Hoernschemeyer, Detroit vs. N.Y. Yanks, Nov. 23, 1950 (TD)

AVERAGE GAIN
Highest Average Gain, Career (750 attempts)
5.22   Jim Brown, Cleveland, 1957-65 (2,359-12,312)
5.14   Eugene (Mercury) Morris, Miami, 1969-75; San Diego, 1976
       (804-4,133)
5.00   Gale Sayers, Chicago, 1965-71 (991-4,956)

Highest Average Gain, Season (Qualifiers)
8.44   Beattie Feathers, Chi. Bears, 1934 (119-1,004)
7.98   Randall Cunningham, Philadelphia 1990 (118-942)
6.87   Bobby Douglass, Chicago, 1972 (141-968)

Highest Average Gain, Game (10 attempts)
17.09   Marion Motley, Cleveland vs. Pittsburgh, Oct. 29, 1950 (11-188)
16.70   Bill Grimes, Green Bay vs. N.Y. Yanks, Oct. 8, 1950 (10-167)
16.57   Bobby Mitchell, Cleveland vs. Washington, Nov. 15, 1959 (14-232)

TOUCHDOWNS
Most Seasons Leading League
5   Jim Brown, Cleveland, 1957-59, 1963, 1965
4   Steve Van Buren, Philadelphia, 1945, 1947-49
3   Abner Haynes, Dall. Texans, 1960-62
    Cookie Gilchrist, Buffalo, 1962-64
    Paul Lowe, L.A. Chargers, 1960; San Diego, 1961, 1965
    Leroy Kelly, Cleveland, 1966-68
    Emmitt Smith, Dallas, 1992, 1994-95

Most Consecutive Seasons Leading League
3   Steve Van Buren, Philadelphia, 1947-49
    Jim Brown, Cleveland, 1957-59
    Abner Haynes, Dall. Texans, 1960-62
    Cookie Gilchrist, Buffalo, 1962-64

Leroy Kelly, Cleveland, 1966-68

Most Touchdowns, Career
112   Marcus Allen, L.A. Raiders, 1982-92; Kansas City, 1993-96
110   Walter Payton, Chicago, 1975-87
108   Emmitt Smith, Dallas, 1990-96

Most Touchdowns, Season
25   Emmitt Smith, Dallas, 1995
24   John Riggins, Washington, 1983
21   Joe Morris, N.Y. Giants, 1985
     Emmitt Smith, Dallas, 1994
     Terry Allen, Washington, 1996

Most Touchdowns, Rookie, Season
18   Eric Dickerson, L.A. Rams, 1983
15   Ickey Woods, Cincinnati, 1988
14   Gale Sayers, Chicago, 1965
     Barry Sanders, Detroit, 1989
     Curtis Martin, New England, 1995

Most Touchdowns, Game
6   Ernie Nevers, Chi. Cardinals vs. Chi. Bears, Nov. 28, 1929
5   Jim Brown, Cleveland vs. Baltimore, Nov. 1, 1959
    Cookie Gilchrist, Buffalo vs. N.Y. Jets, Dec. 8, 1963
4   By many players

Most Consecutive Games Rushing for Touchdowns
13   John Riggins, Washington, 1982-83
     George Rogers, Washington, 1985-86
11   Lenny Moore, Baltimore, 1963-64
     Emmitt Smith, Dallas, 1994-95
     Emmitt Smith, Dallas, 1995
10   Greg Bell, L.A. Rams, 1988-89
     Terry Allen, Washington, 1995-96

PASSING
Most Seasons Leading League
6   Sammy Baugh, Washington, 1937, 1940, 1943, 1945, 1947, 1949
5   Steve Young San Francisco, 1991-94, 1996
4   Len Dawson, Dall. Texans; 1962; Kansas City, 1964, 1966, 1968
    Roger Staubach, Dallas, 1971, 1973, 1978-79
    Ken Anderson, Cincinnati, 1974-75, 1981-82

Most Consecutive Seasons Leading League
4   Steve Young, San Francisco, 1991-94
2   Cecil Isbell, Green Bay, 1941-42
    Milt Plum, Cleveland, 1960-61
    Ken Anderson, Cincinnati, 1974-75, 1981-82
    Roger Staubach, Dallas, 1978-79

PASS RATING
Highest Pass Rating, Career (1,500 attempts)
96.2   Steve Young, Tampa Bay, 1985-86; San Francisco, 1987-96
92.3   Joe Montana, San Francisco, 1979-90, 1992; Kansas City, 1993-94
88.6   Brett Favre, Atlanta, 1991; Green Bay, 1992-96

Highest Pass Rating, Season (Qualifiers)
112.8   Steve Young, San Francisco, 1994
112.4   Joe Montana, San Francisco, 1989
110.4   Milt Plum, Cleveland, 1960

Highest Pass Rating, Rookie, Season (Qualifiers)
96.0   Dan Marino, Miami, 1983
88.2   Greg Cook, Cincinnati, 1969
84.0   Charlie Conerly, N.Y. Giants, 1948

ATTEMPTS
Most Seasons Leading League
4   Sammy Baugh, Washington, 1937, 1943, 1947-48
    Johnny Unitas, Baltimore, 1957, 1959-61
    George Blanda, Chi. Bears, 1953; Houston, 1963-65
    Dan Marino, Miami, 1984, 1986, 1988, 1992
3   Arnie Herber, Green Bay, 1932, 1934, 1936
    Sonny Jurgensen, Washington, 1966-67, 1969
    Drew Bledsoe, New England, 1994-96
2   By many players

Most Consecutive Seasons Leading League
3   Johnny Unitas, Baltimore, 1959-61
    George Blanda, Houston, 1963-65
    Drew Bledsoe, New England, 1994-96
2   By many players

Most Passes Attempted, Career
6,904   Dan Marino, Miami, 1983-96
6,467   Fran Tarkenton, Minnesota, 1961-66, 1972-78; N.Y. Giants, 1967-71
6,392   John Elway, Denver, 1983-96

Most Passes Attempted, Season
691   Drew Bledsoe, New England, 1994
655   Warren Moon, Houston, 1991
636   Drew Bledsoe, New England, 1995

ALL-TIME RECORDS

Most Passes Attempted, Rookie, Season
  486 Rick Mirer, Seattle, 1993
  439 Jim Zorn, Seattle, 1976
  433 Kerry Collins, Carolina, 1995
Most Passes Attempted, Game
  70 Drew Bledsoe, New England vs. Minnesota, Nov. 13, 1994 (OT)
  68 George Blanda, Houston vs. Buffalo, Nov. 1, 1964
  66 Chris Miller, Atlanta vs. Detroit, Dec. 24, 1989

COMPLETIONS
Most Seasons Leading League
  5 Sammy Baugh, Washington, 1937, 1943, 1945, 1947-48
      Dan Marino, Miami, 1984-86, 1988, 1992
  4 George Blanda, Chi. Bears, 1953; Houston, 1963-65
      Sonny Jurgensen, Philadelphia, 1961; Washington, 1966-67, 1969
  3 Arnie Herber, Green Bay, 1932, 1934, 1936
      Johnny Unitas, Baltimore, 1959-60, 1963
      John Brodie, San Francisco, 1965, 1968, 1970
      Fran Tarkenton, Minnesota, 1975-76, 1978
      Warren Moon, Houston, 1990-91; Minnesota, 1995
Most Consecutive Seasons Leading League
  3 George Blanda, Houston, 1963-65
      Dan Marino, Miami, 1984-86
  2 By many players
Most Passes Completed, Career
  4,134 Dan Marino, Miami, 1983-96
  3,686 Fran Tarkenton, Minnesota, 1961-66, 1972-78; N.Y. Giants, 1967-71
  3,633 John Elway, Denver, 1983-96
Most Passes Completed, Season
  404 Warren Moon, Houston, 1991
  400 Drew Bledsoe, New England, 1994
  385 Dan Marino, Miami, 1994
Most Passes Completed, Rookie, Season
  274 Rick Mirer, Seattle, 1993
  214 Drew Bledsoe, New England, 1993
      Kerry Collins, Carolina, 1995
  208 Jim Zorn, Seattle, 1976
Most Passes Completed, Game
  45 Drew Bledsoe, New England vs. Minnesota, Nov. 13, 1994 (OT)
  42 Richard Todd, N.Y. Jets vs. San Francisco, Sept. 21, 1980
  41 Warren Moon, Houston vs. Dallas, Nov. 10, 1991 (OT)
Most Consecutive Passes Completed
  22 Joe Montana, San Francisco vs. Cleveland (5), Nov. 29, 1987; vs. Green Bay (17), Dec. 6, 1987
  20 Ken Anderson, Cincinnati vs. Houston, Jan. 2, 1983
      Hugh Millen, Denver vs. L.A. Raiders (7), Dec. 11, 1994; vs. San Francisco (13), Dec. 17, 1994
      Steve Young, San Francisco vs. Washington, Nov. 24, 1996
  18 Steve DeBerg, Denver vs. L.A. Rams (17), Dec. 12, 1982; vs. Kansas City (1), Dec. 19, 1982
      Lynn Dickey, Green Bay vs. Houston, Sept. 4, 1983
      Joe Montana, San Francisco vs. L.A. Rams (13), Oct. 28, 1984; vs. Cincinnati (5), Nov. 4, 1984
      Don Majkowski, Green Bay vs. New Orleans, Sept. 18, 1989
      Boomer Esiason, N.Y. Jets vs. Miami (5), Sept. 12, 1993; vs. New England (13), Sept. 26, 1993

COMPLETION PERCENTAGE
Most Seasons Leading League
  8 Len Dawson, Dall. Texans, 1962; Kansas City, 1964-69, 1975
  7 Sammy Baugh, Washington, 1940, 1942-43, 1945, 1947-49
  5 Joe Montana, San Francisco, 1980-81, 1985, 1987, 1989
Most Consecutive Seasons Leading League
  6 Len Dawson, Kansas City, 1964-69
  3 Sammy Baugh, Washington, 1947-49
      Otto Graham, Cleveland, 1953-55
      Milt Plum, Cleveland, 1959-61
      Steve Young, San Francisco, 1994-96
  2 By many players
Highest Completion Percentage, Career (1,500 attempts)
  64.51 Steve Young, Tampa Bay, 1985-86; San Francisco, 1987-96 (3,192-2,059)
  63.24 Joe Montana, San Francisco, 1979-90, 1992; Kansas City, 1993-94 (5,391-3,409)
  62.93 Troy Aikman, Dallas, 1989-96 (3,178-2,000)
Highest Completion Percentage, Season (Qualifiers)
  70.55 Ken Anderson, Cincinnati, 1982 (309-218)
  70.33 Sammy Baugh, Washington, 1945 (182-128)
  70.28 Steve Young, San Francisco, 1994 (461-324)
Highest Completion Percentage, Rookie, Season (Qualifiers)
  58.45 Dan Marino, Miami, 1983 (296-173)
  57.14 Jim McMahon, Chicago, 1982 (210-120)
  56.38 Rick Mirer, Seattle, 1993 (486-274)

Highest Completion Percentage, Game (20 attempts)
  91.30 Vinny Testaverde, Cleveland vs. L.A. Rams, Dec. 26, 1993 (23-21)
  90.91 Ken Anderson, Cincinnati vs. Pittsburgh, Nov. 10, 1974 (22-20)
  90.48 Lynn Dickey, Green Bay vs. New Orleans, Dec. 13, 1981 (21-19)

YARDS GAINED
Most Seasons Leading League
  5 Sonny Jurgensen, Philadelphia, 1961-62; Washington, 1966-67, 1969
      Dan Marino, Miami, 1984-86, 1988, 1992
  4 Sammy Baugh, Washington, 1937, 1940, 1947-48
      Johnny Unitas, Baltimore, 1957, 1959-60, 1963
      Dan Fouts, San Diego, 1979-82
  3 Arnie Herber, Green Bay, 1932, 1934, 1936
      Sid Luckman, Chi. Bears, 1943, 1945-46
      John Brodie, San Francisco, 1965, 1968, 1970
      John Hadl, San Diego, 1965, 1968, 1971
      Joe Namath, N.Y. Jets, 1966-67, 1972
Most Consecutive Seasons Leading League
  4 Dan Fouts, San Diego, 1979-82
  3 Dan Marino, Miami, 1984-86
  2 By many players
Most Yards Gained, Career
  51,636 Dan Marino, Miami, 1983-96
  47,003 Fran Tarkenton, Minnesota, 1961-66, 1972-78; N.Y. Giants, 1967-71
  45,034 John Elway, Denver, 1983-96
Most Seasons, 3,000 or More Yards Passing
  11 Dan Marino, Miami, 1984-92, 1994-95
      John Elway, Denver, 1985-91, 1993-96
  8 Joe Montana, San Francisco, 1981, 1983-85, 1987, 1989-90; Kansas City, 1994
      Jim Kelly, Buffalo, 1986, 1988-89, 1991-95
      Warren Moon, Houston, 1984, 1986, 1989-91, 1993; Minnesota, 1994-95
  7 Boomer Esiason, Cincinnati, 1985-90; N.Y. Jets, 1993
      Jim Everett, L.A. Rams, 1988-92; New Orleans, 1994-95
Most Yards Gained, Season
  5,084 Dan Marino, Miami, 1984
  4,802 Dan Fouts, San Diego, 1981
  4,746 Dan Marino, Miami, 1986
Most Yards Gained, Rookie, Season
  2,833 Rick Mirer, Seattle, 1993
  2,717 Kerry Collins, Carolina, 1995
  2,571 Jim Zorn, Seattle, 1976
Most Yards Gained, Game
  554 Norm Van Brocklin, Los Angeles vs. N.Y. Yanks, Sept. 28, 1951
  527 Warren Moon, Houston vs. Kansas City, Dec. 16, 1990
  522 Boomer Esiason, Arizona vs. Washington, Nov. 10, 1996
Most Games, 400 or More Yards Passing, Career
  13 Dan Marino, Miami, 1983-96
  7 Joe Montana, San Francisco, 1979-90, 1992; Kansas City, 1993-94
  6 Dan Fouts, San Diego, 1973-87
      Warren Moon, Houston, 1984-93; Minnesota, 1994-96
Most Games, 400 or More Yards Passing, Season
  4 Dan Marino, Miami, 1984
  3 Dan Marino, Miami, 1986
  2 By many players
Most Consecutive Games, 400 or More Yards Passing
  2 Dan Fouts, San Diego, 1982
      Dan Marino, Miami, 1984
      Phil Simms, N.Y. Giants, 1985
Most Games, 300 or More Yards Passing, Career
  52 Dan Marino, Miami, 1983-96
  51 Dan Fouts, San Diego, 1973-87
  48 Warren Moon, Houston, 1984-93; Minnesota, 1994-96
Most Games, 300 or More Yards Passing, Season
  9 Dan Marino, Miami, 1984
      Warren Moon, Houston, 1990
  8 Dan Fouts, San Diego, 1980
  7 Dan Fouts, San Diego, 1981
      Bill Kenney, Kansas City, 1983
      Neil Lomax, St. Louis, 1984
      Dan Fouts, San Diego, 1985
      Brett Favre, Green Bay, 1995
Most Consecutive Games, 300 or More Yards Passing
  5 Joe Montana, San Francisco, 1982
  4 Dan Fouts, San Diego, 1979
      Dan Fouts, San Diego, 1980-81
      Bill Kenney, Kansas City, 1983
      Joe Montana, San Francisco, 1985-86
      Joe Montana, San Francisco, 1990
      Warren Moon, Houston, 1990
      Drew Bledsoe, New England, 1993-94
  3 By many players

Longest Pass Completion (All TDs except as noted)

99   Frank Filchock (to Farkas), Washington vs. Pittsburgh, Oct. 15, 1939
     George Izo (to Mitchell), Washington vs. Cleveland, Sept. 15, 1963
     Karl Sweetan (to Studstill), Detroit vs. Baltimore, Oct. 16, 1966
     Sonny Jurgensen (to Allen), Washington vs. Chicago, Sept. 15, 1968
     Jim Plunkett (to Branch), L.A. Raiders vs. Washington, Oct. 2, 1983
     Ron Jaworski (to Quick), Philadelphia vs. Atlanta, Nov. 10, 1985
     Stan Humphries (to Martin), San Diego vs. Seattle, Sept. 18, 1994
     Brett Favre (to Brooks), Green Bay vs. Chicago, Sept. 11, 1995
98   Doug Russell (to Tinsley), Chi. Cardinals vs. Cleveland, Nov. 27, 1938
     Ogden Compton (to Lane), Chi. Cardinals vs. Green Bay, Nov. 13, 1955
     Bill Wade (to Farrington), Chicago Bears vs. Detroit, Oct. 8, 1961
     Jacky Lee (to Dewveall), Houston vs. San Diego, Nov. 25, 1962
     Earl Morrall (to Jones), N.Y. Giants vs. Pittsburgh, Sept. 11, 1966
     Jim Hart (to Moore), St. Louis vs. Los Angeles, Dec. 10, 1972 (no TD)
     Bobby Hebert (to Haynes), Atlanta vs. New Orleans, Sept. 12, 1993
97   Pat Coffee (to Tinsley), Chi. Cardinals vs. Chi. Bears, Dec. 5, 1937
     Bobby Layne (to Box), Detroit vs. Green Bay, Nov. 26, 1953
     George Shaw (to Tarr), Denver vs. Boston, Sept. 21, 1962
     Bernie Kosar (to Slaughter), Cleveland vs. Chicago, Oct. 23, 1989
     Steve Young (to Taylor), San Francisco vs. Atlanta, Nov. 3, 1991

AVERAGE GAIN

Most Seasons Leading League
7   Sid Luckman, Chi. Bears, 1939-43, 1946-47
4   Steve Young, San Francisco, 1991-94
3   Arnie Herber, Green Bay, 1932, 1934, 1936
    Norm Van Brocklin, Los Angeles, 1950, 1952, 1954
    Len Dawson, Dall. Texans, 1962; Kansas City, 1966, 1968
    Bart Starr, Green Bay, 1966-68

Most Consecutive Seasons Leading League
5   Sid Luckman, Chi. Bears, 1939-43
4   Steve Young, San Francisco, 1991-94
3   Bart Starr, Green Bay, 1966-68

Highest Average Gain, Career (1,500 attempts)
8.63   Otto Graham, Cleveland, 1950-55 (1,565-13,499)
8.42   Sid Luckman, Chi. Bears, 1939-50 (1,744-14,686)
8.16   Norm Van Brocklin, Los Angeles, 1949-57; Philadelphia, 1958-60
      (2,895-23,611)

Highest Average Gain, Season (Qualifiers)
11.17   Tommy O'Connell, Cleveland, 1957 (110-1,229)
10.86   Sid Luckman, Chi. Bears, 1943 (202-2,194)
10.55   Otto Graham, Cleveland, 1953 (258-2,722)

Highest Average Gain, Rookie, Season (Qualifiers)
9.411   Greg Cook, Cincinnati, 1969 (197-1,854)
9.409   Bob Waterfield, Cleveland, 1945 (171-1,609)
8.36   Zeke Bratkowski, Chi. Bears, 1954 (130-1,087)

Highest Average Gain, Game (20 attempts)
18.58   Sammy Baugh, Washington vs. Boston, Oct. 31, 1948 (24-446)
18.50   Johnny Unitas, Baltimore vs. Atlanta, Nov. 12, 1967 (20-370)
17.71   Joe Namath, N.Y. Jets vs. Baltimore, Sept. 24, 1972 (28-496)

TOUCHDOWNS

Most Seasons Leading League
4   Johnny Unitas, Baltimore, 1957-60
    Len Dawson, Dall. Texans, 1962; Kansas City, 1963, 1965-66
3   Arnie Herber, Green Bay, 1932, 1934, 1936
    Sid Luckman, Chi. Bears, 1943, 1945-46
    Y.A. Tittle, San Francisco, 1955; N.Y. Giants, 1962-63
    Dan Marino, Miami, 1984-86
    Steve Young, San Francisco, 1992-94
2   By many players

Most Consecutive Seasons Leading League
4   Johnny Unitas, Baltimore, 1957-60
3   Dan Marino, Miami, 1984-86
    Steve Young, San Francisco, 1992-94
2   By many players

Most Touchdown Passes, Career
369   Dan Marino, Miami, 1983-96
342   Fran Tarkenton, Minnesota, 1961-66, 1972-78; N.Y. Giants, 1967-71
290   Johnny Unitas, Baltimore, 1956-72: San Diego, 1973

Most Touchdown Passes, Season
48   Dan Marino, Miami, 1984
44   Dan Marino, Miami, 1986
39   Brett Favre, Green Bay, 1996

Most Touchdown Passes, Rookie, Season
22   Charlie Conerly, N.Y. Giants, 1948
20   Dan Marino, Miami, 1983
19   Jim Plunkett, New England, 1971

Most Touchdown Passes, Game
7   Sid Luckman, Chi. Bears vs. N.Y. Giants, Nov. 14, 1943
    Adrian Burk, Philadelphia vs. Washington, Oct. 17, 1954
    George Blanda, Houston vs. N.Y. Titans, Nov. 19, 1961

    Y.A. Tittle, N.Y. Giants vs. Washington, Oct. 28, 1962
    Joe Kapp, Minnesota vs. Baltimore, Sept. 28, 1969
6   By many players. Last time: Mark Rypien, Washington vs. Atlanta,
    Nov. 10, 1991

Most Games, Four or More Touchdown Passes, Career
20   Dan Marino, Miami, 1983-96
17   Johnny Unitas, Baltimore, 1956-72; San Diego, 1973
13   George Blanda, Chi. Bears, 1949, 1950-58; Baltimore, 1950; Houston,
      1960-66; Oakland, 1967-75

Most Games, Four or More Touchdown Passes, Season
6   Dan Marino, Miami, 1984
5   Dan Marino, Miami, 1986
    Brett Favre, Green Bay, 1996
4   George Blanda, Houston, 1961
    Vince Ferragamo, Los Angeles, 1980

Most Consecutive Games, Four or More Touchdown Passes
4   Dan Marino, Miami, 1984
2   By many players

Most Consecutive Games, Touchdown Passes
47   Johnny Unitas, Baltimore, 1956-60
30   Dan Marino, Miami, 1985-87
28   Dave Krieg, Seattle, 1983-85

HAD INTERCEPTED

Most Consecutive Passes Attempted, None Intercepted
308   Bernie Kosar, Cleveland, 1990-91
294   Bart Starr, Green Bay, 1964-65
279   Jeff George, Indianapolis, 1993; Atlanta, 1994

Most Passes Had Intercepted, Career
277   George Blanda, Chi. Bears, 1949, 1950-58; Baltimore, 1950; Houston,
      1960-66; Oakland, 1967-75
268   John Hadl, San Diego, 1962-72; Los Angeles, 1973-74; Green Bay,
      1974-75; Houston, 1976-77
266   Fran Tarkenton, Minnesota, 1961-66, 1972-78;
      N.Y. Giants, 1967-71

Most Passes Had Intercepted, Season
42   George Blanda, Houston, 1962
35   Vinny Testaverde, Tampa Bay, 1988
34   Frank Tripucka, Denver, 1960

Most Passes Had Intercepted, Game
8   Jim Hardy, Chi. Cardinals vs. Philadelphia, Sept. 24, 1950
7   Parker Hall, Cleveland vs. Green Bay, Nov. 8, 1942
    Frank Sinkwich, Detroit vs. Green Bay, Oct. 24, 1943
    Bob Waterfield, Los Angeles vs. Green Bay, Oct. 17, 1948
    Zeke Bratkowski, Chicago vs. Baltimore, Oct. 2, 1960
    Tommy Wade, Pittsburgh vs. Philadelphia, Dec. 12, 1965
    Ken Stabler, Oakland vs. Denver, Oct. 16, 1977
    Steve DeBerg, Tampa Bay vs. San Francisco, Sept. 7, 1986
6   By many players

Most Attempts, No Interceptions, Game
70   Drew Bledsoe, New England vs. Minnesota, Nov. 13, 1994 (OT)
63   Rich Gannon, Minnesota vs. New England, Oct. 20, 1991 (OT)
60   Davey O'Brien, Philadelphia vs. Washington, Dec. 1, 1940

LOWEST PERCENTAGE, PASSES HAD INTERCEPTED

Most Seasons Leading League, Lowest Percentage, Passes Had Intercepted
5   Sammy Baugh, Washington, 1940, 1942, 1944-45, 1947
3   Charlie Conerly, N.Y. Giants, 1950, 1956, 1959
    Bart Starr, Green Bay, 1962, 1964, 1966
    Roger Staubach, Dallas, 1971, 1977, 1979
    Ken Anderson, Cincinnati, 1972, 1981-82
    Ken O'Brien, N.Y. Jets, 1985, 1987-88
2   By many players

Lowest Percentage, Passes Had Intercepted, Career (1,500 attempts)
2.23   Neil O'Donnell, Pittsburgh, 1991-95; N.Y. Jets, 1996 (2,059-46)
2.45   Steve Bono, Minnesota, 1985-86; Pittsburgh, 1987-88;
      San Francisco, 1989, 1991-93; Kansas City, 1994-96 (1,554-38)
2.58   Joe Montana, San Francisco, 1979-90, 1992; Kansas City, 1993-94
      (5,391-139)

Lowest Percentage, Passes Had Intercepted, Season (Qualifiers)
0.66   Joe Ferguson, Buffalo, 1976 (151-1)
0.90   Steve DeBerg, Kansas City, 1990 (444-4)
1.16   Steve Bartkowski, Atlanta, 1983 (432-5)

Lowest Percentage, Passes Had Intercepted, Rookie, Season (Qualifiers)
2.03   Dan Marino, Miami, 1983 (296-6)
2.10   Gary Wood, N.Y. Giants, 1964 (143-3)
2.82   Bernie Kosar, Cleveland, 1985 (248-7)

TIMES SACKED

Times Sacked has been compiled since 1963.

Most Times Sacked, Career
492   Dave Krieg, Seattle, 1980-91; Kansas City, 1992-93; Detroit, 1994;
     Arizona, 1995; Chicago, 1996

483   Fran Tarkenton, Minnesota, 1963-66, 1972-78; N.Y. Giants, 1967-71
477   Phil Simms, N.Y. Giants, 1979-81, 1983-93

Most Times Sacked, Season

72   Randall Cunningham, Philadelphia, 1986
62   Ken O'Brien, N.Y. Jets, 1985
61   Neil Lomax, St. Louis, 1985

Most Times Sacked, Game

12   Bert Jones, Baltimore vs. St. Louis, Oct. 26, 1980
      Warren Moon, Houston vs. Dallas, Sept. 29, 1985
11   Charley Johnson, St. Louis vs. N.Y. Giants, Nov. 1, 1964
      Bart Starr, Green Bay vs. Detroit, Nov. 7, 1965
      Jack Kemp, Buffalo vs. Oakland, Oct. 15, 1967
      Bob Berry, Atlanta vs. St. Louis, Nov. 24, 1968
      Greg Landry, Detroit vs. Dallas, Oct. 6, 1975
      Ron Jaworski, Philadelphia vs. St. Louis, Dec. 18, 1983
      Paul McDonald, Cleveland vs. Kansas City, Sept. 30, 1984
      Archie Manning, Minnesota vs. Chicago, Oct. 28, 1984
      Steve Pelluer, Dallas vs. San Diego, Nov. 16, 1986
      Randall Cunningham, Philadelphia vs. L.A. Raiders, Nov. 30, 1986 (OT)
      David Norrie, N.Y. Jets vs. Dallas, Oct. 4, 1987
      Troy Aikman, Dallas vs. Philadelphia, Sept. 15, 1991
      Bernie Kosar, Cleveland vs. Indianapolis, Sept. 6, 1992
10   By many players

PASS RECEIVING

Most Seasons Leading League

8   Don Hutson, Green Bay, 1936-37, 1939, 1941-45
5   Lionel Taylor, Denver, 1960-63, 1965
3   Tom Fears, Los Angeles, 1948-50
    Pete Pihos, Philadelphia, 1953-55
    Billy Wilson, San Francisco, 1954, 1956-57
    Raymond Berry, Baltimore, 1958-60
    Lance Alworth, San Diego, 1966, 1968-69
    Sterling Sharpe, Green Bay, 1989, 1992-93

Most Consecutive Seasons Leading League

5   Don Hutson, Green Bay, 1941-45
4   Lionel Taylor, Denver, 1960-63
3   Tom Fears, Los Angeles, 1948-50
    Pete Pihos, Philadelphia, 1953-55
    Raymond Berry, Baltimore, 1958-60

Most Pass Receptions, Career

1,050   Jerry Rice, San Francisco, 1985-96
940   Art Monk, Washington, 1980-93; N.Y. Jets, 1994; Philadelphia, 1995
819   Steve Largent, Seattle, 1976-89

Most Seasons, 50 or More Pass Receptions

11   Jerry Rice, San Francisco, 1986-96
10   Steve Largent, Seattle, 1976, 1978-81, 1983-87
     Gary Clark, Washington, 1985-92; Phoenix, 1993; Arizona, 1994
     Henry Ellard, L.A. Rams, 1985, 1987-91, 1993; Washington, 1994-96
     Andre Reed, Buffalo, 1986-94, 1996
9   Art Monk, Washington, 1980-81, 1984-86, 1988-91
    James Lofton, Green Bay, 1979-81, 1983-86; Buffalo, 1991-92

Most Pass Receptions, Season

123   Herman Moore, Detroit, 1995
122   Cris Carter, Minnesota, 1994
     Cris Carter, Minnesota, 1995
     Jerry Rice, San Francisco, 1995
119   Isaac Bruce, St. Louis, 1995

Most Pass Receptions, Rookie, Season

90   Terry Glenn, New England, 1996
83   Earl Cooper, San Francisco, 1980
81   Keith Jackson, Philadelphia, 1988

Most Pass Receptions, Game

18   Tom Fears, Los Angeles vs. Green Bay, Dec. 3, 1950
17   Clark Gaines, N.Y. Jets vs. San Francisco, Sept. 21, 1980
16   Sonny Randle, St. Louis vs. N.Y. Giants, Nov. 4, 1962
     Jerry Rice, San Francisco vs. L.A. Rams, Nov. 20, 1994
     Keenan McCardell, Jacksonville vs. St. Louis, Oct. 20, 1996

Most Consecutive Games, Pass Receptions

183   Art Monk, Washington, 1980-93; N.Y. Jets, 1994; Philadelphia, 1995
177   Steve Largent, Seattle, 1977-89
175   Jerry Rice, San Francisco, 1985-96 (current)

YARDS GAINED

Most Seasons Leading League

7   Don Hutson, Green Bay, 1936, 1938-39, 1941-44
6   Jerry Rice, San Francisco, 1986, 1989-90, 1993-95
3   Raymond Berry, Baltimore, 1957, 1959-60
    Lance Alworth, San Diego, 1965-66, 1968

Most Consecutive Seasons Leading League

4   Don Hutson, Green Bay, 1941-44
3   Jerry Rice, San Francisco, 1993-95
2   By many players

Most Yards Gained, Career

16,377   Jerry Rice, San Francisco, 1985-96
14,004   James Lofton, Green Bay, 1978-86; L.A. Raiders, 1987-88; Buffalo, 1989-92; L.A. Rams, 1993; Philadelphia, 1993
13,177   Henry Ellard, L.A. Rams, 1983-1993; Washington, 1994-96

Most Seasons, 1,000 or More Yards, Pass Receiving

11   Jerry Rice, San Francisco, 1986-96
8   Steve Largent, Seattle, 1978-81, 1983-86
7   Lance Alworth, San Diego, 1963-69
    Henry Ellard, L.A. Rams, 1983-93; Washington 1994-96

Most Yards Gained, Season

1,848   Jerry Rice, San Francisco, 1995
1,781   Isaac Bruce, St. Louis, 1995
1,746   Charley Hennigan, Houston, 1961

Most Yards Gained, Rookie, Season

1,473   Bill Groman, Houston, 1960
1,231   Bill Howton, Green Bay, 1952
1,132   Terry Glenn, New England, 1996

Most Yards Gained, Game

336   Willie Anderson, L.A. Rams vs. New Orleans, Nov. 26, 1989 (OT)
309   Stephone Paige, Kansas City vs. San Diego, Dec. 22, 1985
303   Jim Benton, Cleveland vs. Detroit, Nov. 22, 1945

Most Games, 200 or More Yards Pass Receiving, Career

5   Lance Alworth, San Diego, 1962-70; Dallas, 1971-72
4   Don Hutson, Green Bay, 1935-45
    Charley Hennigan, Houston, 1960-66
    Jerry Rice, San Francisco, 1985-96
3   Don Maynard, N.Y. Giants, 1958; N.Y. Jets, 1960-72; St. Louis, 1973
    Wes Chandler, New Orleans, 1978-81; San Diego, 1981-87; San Francisco, 1988

Most Games, 200 or More Yards Pass Receiving, Season

3   Charley Hennigan, Houston, 1961
2   Don Hutson, Green Bay, 1942
    Gene Roberts, N.Y. Giants, 1949
    Lance Alworth, San Diego, 1963
    Don Maynard, N.Y. Jets, 1968

Most Games, 100 or More Yards Pass Receiving, Career

61   Jerry Rice, San Francisco, 1985-96
50   Don Maynard, N.Y. Giants, 1958; N.Y. Jets, 1960-72; St. Louis, 1973
43   James Lofton, Green Bay, 1978-86; L.A. Raiders, 1987-88; Buffalo, 1989-92; L.A. Rams, 1993; Philadelphia, 1993

Most Games, 100 or More Yards Pass Receiving, Season

11   Michael Irvin, Dallas, 1995
10   Charley Hennigan, Houston, 1961
     Herman Moore, Detroit, 1995
9   Elroy (Crazylegs) Hirsch, Los Angeles, 1951
    Bill Groman, Houston, 1960
    Lance Alworth, San Diego, 1965
    Don Maynard, N.Y. Jets, 1967
    Stanley Morgan, New England, 1986
    Mark Carrier, Tampa Bay, 1989
    Robert Brooks, Green Bay, 1995
    Isaac Bruce, St. Louis, 1995
    Jerry Rice, San Francisco, 1995

Most Consecutive Games, 100 or More Yards Pass Receiving

7   Charley Hennigan, Houston, 1961
    Bill Groman, Houston, 1961
    Michael Irvin, Dallas, 1995
6   Raymond Berry, Baltimore, 1960
    Pat Studstill, Detroit, 1966
    Isaac Bruce, St. Louis, 1995
5   Elroy (Crazylegs) Hirsch, Los Angeles, 1951
    Bob Boyd, Los Angeles, 1954
    Terry Barr, Detroit, 1963
    Lance Alworth, San Diego, 1966
    Don Maynard, N.Y. Jets, 1968-69
    Harold Jackson, Philadelphia, 1971-72

Longest Pass Reception (All TDs except as noted)

99   Andy Farkas (from Filchock), Washington vs. Pittsburgh, Oct. 15, 1939
     Bobby Mitchell (from Izo), Washington vs. Cleveland, Sept. 15, 1963
     Pat Studstill (from Sweetan), Detroit vs. Baltimore, Oct. 16, 1966
     Gerry Allen (from Jurgensen), Washington vs. Chicago, Sept. 15, 1968
     Cliff Branch (from Plunkett), L.A. Raiders vs. Washington, Oct. 2, 1983
     Mike Quick (from Jaworski), Philadelphia vs. Atlanta, Nov. 10, 1985
     Tony Martin (from Humphries), San Diego vs. Seattle, Sept. 18, 1994
     Robert Brooks (from Favre), Green Bay vs. Chicago, Sept. 11, 1995
98   Gaynell Tinsley (from Russell), Chi. Cardinals vs. Cleveland, Nov. 17, 1938
     Dick (Night Train) Lane (from Compton), Chi. Cardinals vs. Green Bay, Nov. 13, 1955
     John Farrington (from Wade), Chicago vs. Detroit, Oct. 8, 1961
     Willard Dewveall (from Lee), Houston vs. San Diego, Nov. 25, 1962
     Homer Jones (from Morrall), N.Y. Giants vs. Pittsburgh, Sept. 11, 1966

Bobby Moore (from Hart), St. Louis vs. Los Angeles, Dec. 10, 1972 (no TD)
Michael Haynes (from Hebert), Atlanta vs. New Orleans,
 Sept. 12, 1993
97 Gaynell Tinsley (from Coffee), Chi. Cardinals vs. Chi. Bears,
 Dec. 5, 1937
 Cloyce Box (from Layne), Detroit vs. Green Bay, Nov. 26, 1953
 Jerry Tarr (from Shaw), Denver vs. Boston, Sept. 21, 1962
 Webster Slaughter (from Kosar), Cleveland vs. Chicago,
 Oct. 23, 1989
 John Taylor (from Young), San Francisco vs. Atlanta, Nov. 3, 1991

AVERAGE GAIN
Highest Average Gain, Career (200 receptions)
22.26 Homer Jones, N.Y. Giants, 1964-69; Cleveland, 1970 (224-4,986)
20.83 Buddy Dial, Pittsburgh, 1959-63; Dallas, 1964-66 (261-5,436)
20.24 Harlon Hill, Chi. Bears, 1954-61; Pittsburgh, 1962; Detroit, 1962
 (233-4,717)
Highest Average Gain, Season (24 receptions)
32.58 Don Currivan, Boston, 1947 (24-782)
31.44 Bucky Pope, Los Angeles, 1964 (25-786)
28.60 Bobby Duckworth, San Diego, 1984 (25-715)
Highest Average Gain, Game (3 receptions)
60.67 Bill Groman, Houston vs. Denver, Nov. 20, 1960 (3-182)
 Homer Jones, N.Y. Giants vs. Washington, Dec. 12, 1965 (3-182)
60.33 Don Currivan, Boston vs. Washington, Nov. 30, 1947 (3-181)
59.67 Bobby Duckworth, San Diego vs. Chicago, Dec. 3, 1984 (3-179)

TOUCHDOWNS
Most Seasons Leading League
9 Don Hutson, Green Bay, 1935-38, 1940-44
6 Jerry Rice, San Francisco, 1986-87, 1989-91, 1993
3 Lance Alworth, San Diego, 1964-66
Most Consecutive Seasons Leading League
5 Don Hutson, Green Bay, 1940-44
4 Don Hutson, Green Bay, 1935-38
3 Lance Alworth, San Diego, 1964-66
 Jerry Rice, San Francisco, 1989-91
Most Touchdowns, Career
154 Jerry Rice, San Francisco, 1985-96
100 Steve Largent, Seattle, 1976-89
99 Don Hutson, Green Bay, 1935-45
Most Touchdowns, Season
22 Jerry Rice, San Francisco, 1987
18 Mark Clayton, Miami, 1984
 Sterling Sharpe, Green Bay, 1994
17 Don Hutson, Green Bay, 1942
 Elroy (Crazylegs) Hirsch, Los Angeles, 1951
 Bill Groman, Houston, 1961
 Jerry Rice, San Francisco, 1989
 Cris Carter, Minnesota, 1995
 Carl Pickens, Cincinnati, 1995
Most Touchdowns, Rookie, Season
13 Bill Howton, Green Bay, 1952
 John Jefferson, San Diego, 1979
12 Harlon Hill, Chi. Bears, 1954
 Bill Groman, Houston, 1960
 Mike Ditka, Chicago, 1961
 Bob Hayes, Dallas, 1965
10 Bill Swiacki, N.Y. Giants, 1948
 Bucky Pope, Los Angeles, 1964
 Sammy White, Minnesota, 1976
 Daryl Turner, Seattle, 1984
Most Touchdowns, Game
5 Bob Shaw, Chi. Cardinals vs. Baltimore, Oct. 2, 1950
 Kellen Winslow, San Diego vs. Oakland, Nov. 22, 1981
 Jerry Rice, San Francisco vs. Atlanta, Oct. 14, 1990
4 By many players. Last time: Irving Fryar, Philadelphia vs. Miami,
 Oct. 20, 1996
Most Consecutive Games, Touchdowns
13 Jerry Rice, San Francisco, 1986-87
11 Elroy (Crazylegs) Hirsch, Los Angeles, 1950-51
 Buddy Dial, Pittsburgh, 1959-60
10 Carl Pickens, Cincinnati, 1994-95

INTERCEPTIONS BY
Most Seasons Leading League
3 Everson Walls, Dallas, 1981-82, 1985
2 Dick (Night Train) Lane, Los Angeles, 1952; Chi. Cardinals, 1954
 Jack Christiansen, Detroit, 1953, 1957
 Milt Davis, Baltimore, 1957, 1959
 Dick Lynch, N.Y. Giants, 1961, 1963
 Johnny Robinson, Kansas City, 1966, 1970
 Bill Bradley, Philadelphia, 1971-72

Emmitt Thomas, Kansas City, 1969, 1974
Ronnie Lott, San Francisco, 1986; L.A. Raiders, 1991
Most Interceptions By, Career
81 Paul Krause, Washington, 1964-67; Minnesota, 1968-79
79 Emlen Tunnell, N.Y. Giants, 1948-58; Green Bay, 1959-61
68 Dick (Night Train) Lane, Los Angeles, 1952-53; Chi. Cardinals, 1954-59;
 Detroit, 1960-65
Most Interceptions By, Season
14 Dick (Night Train) Lane, Los Angeles, 1952
13 Dan Sandifer, Washington, 1948
 Orban (Spec) Sanders, N.Y. Yanks, 1950
 Lester Hayes, Oakland, 1980
12 By nine players
Most Interceptions By, Rookie, Season
14 Dick (Night Train) Lane, Los Angeles, 1952
13 Dan Sandifer, Washington, 1948
12 Woodley Lewis, Los Angeles, 1950
 Paul Krause, Washington, 1964
Most Interceptions By, Game
4 Sammy Baugh, Washington vs. Detroit, Nov. 14, 1943
 Dan Sandifer, Washington vs. Boston, Oct. 31, 1948
 Don Doll, Detroit vs. Chi. Cardinals, Oct. 23, 1949
 Bob Nussbaumer, Chi. Cardinals vs. N.Y. Bulldogs, Nov. 13, 1949
 Russ Craft, Philadelphia vs. Chi. Cardinals, Sept. 24, 1950
 Bobby Dillon, Green Bay vs. Detroit, Nov. 26, 1953
 Jack Butler, Pittsburgh vs. Washington, Dec. 13, 1953
 Austin (Goose) Gonsoulin, Denver vs. Buffalo, Sept. 18, 1960
 Jerry Norton, St. Louis vs. Washington, Nov. 20, 1960; vs. Pittsburgh,
 Nov. 26, 1961
 Dave Baker, San Francisco vs. L.A. Rams, Dec. 4, 1960
 Bobby Ply, Dall. Texans vs. San Diego, Dec. 16, 1962
 Bobby Hunt, Kansas City vs. Houston, Oct. 4, 1964
 Willie Brown, Denver vs. N.Y. Jets, Nov. 15, 1964
 Dick Anderson, Miami vs. Pittsburgh, Dec. 3, 1973
 Willie Buchanon, Green Bay vs. San Diego, Sept. 24, 1978
 Deron Cherry, Kansas City vs. Seattle, Sept. 29, 1985
Most Consecutive Games, Passes Intercepted By
8 Tom Morrow, Oakland, 1962-63
7 Paul Krause, Washington, 1964
 Larry Wilson, St. Louis, 1966
 Ben Davis, Cleveland, 1968
6 Dick (Night Train) Lane, Chi. Cardinals, 1954-55
 Will Sherman, Los Angeles, 1954-55
 Jim Shofner, Cleveland, 1960
 Paul Krause, Minnesota, 1968
 Willie Williams, N.Y. Giants, 1968
 Kermit Alexander, San Francisco, 1968-69
 Mel Blount, Pittsburgh, 1975
 Lemar Parrish, Washington, 1978-79
 Eric Harris, Kansas City, 1980
 Lester Hayes, Oakland, 1980
 Barry Wilburn, Washington, 1987

YARDS GAINED
Most Seasons Leading League
2 Dick (Night Train) Lane, Los Angeles, 1952; Chi. Cardinals, 1954
 Herb Adderley, Green Bay, 1965, 1969
 Dick Anderson, Miami, 1968, 1970
Most Yards Gained, Career
1,282 Emlen Tunnell, N.Y. Giants, 1948-58; Green Bay, 1959-61
1,207 Dick (Night Train) Lane, Los Angeles, 1952-53; Chi. Cardinals, 1954-59;
 Detroit, 1960-65
1,185 Paul Krause, Washington, 1964-67; Minnesota, 1968-79
Most Yards Gained, Season
349 Charlie McNeil, San Diego, 1961
303 Deion Sanders, San Francisco, 1994
301 Don Doll, Detroit, 1949
Most Yards Gained, Rookie, Season
301 Don Doll, Detroit, 1949
298 Dick (Night Train) Lane, Los Angeles, 1952
275 Woodley Lewis, Los Angeles, 1950
Most Yards Gained, Game
177 Charlie McNeil, San Diego vs. Houston, Sept. 24, 1961
170 Louis Oliver, Miami vs. Buffalo, Oct. 4, 1992
167 Dick Jauron, Detroit vs. Chicago, Nov. 18, 1973
Longest Return (All TDs)
103 Vencie Glenn, San Diego vs. Denver, Nov. 29, 1987
 Louis Oliver, Miami vs. Buffalo, Oct. 4, 1992
102 Bob Smith, Detroit vs. Chi. Bears, Nov. 24, 1949
 Erich Barnes, N.Y. Giants vs. Dall. Cowboys, Oct. 15, 1961
 Gary Barbaro, Kansas City vs. Seattle, Dec. 11, 1977
 Louis Breeden, Cincinnati vs. San Diego, Nov. 8, 1981
 Eddie Anderson, L.A. Raiders vs. Miami, Dec. 14, 1992

Donald Frank, San Diego vs. L.A. Raiders, Oct. 31, 1993
101 Richie Petitbon, Chicago vs Los Angeles, Dec. 9, 1962
Henry Carr, N.Y. Giants vs. Los Angeles, Nov. 13, 1966
Tony Greene, Buffalo vs. Kansas City, Oct. 3, 1976
Tom Pridemore, Atlanta vs. San Francisco, Sept. 20, 1981

TOUCHDOWNS
Most Touchdowns, Career
- 9 Ken Houston, Houston, 1967-72; Washington, 1973-80
- 7 Herb Adderley, Green Bay, 1961-69; Dallas, 1970-72
  Erich Barnes, Chi. Bears, 1958-60; N.Y. Giants, 1961-64; Cleveland, 1965-70
  Lem Barney, Detroit, 1967-77
- 6 Tom Janik, Denver, 1963-64; Buffalo, 1965-68; Boston, 1969-70; New England, 1971
  Miller Farr, Denver, 1965; San Diego, 1965-66; Houston, 1967-69; St. Louis, 1970-72; Detroit, 1973
  Bobby Bell, Kansas City, 1963-74
  Deion Sanders, Atlanta, 1989-93; San Francisco, 1994; Dallas, 1995-96

Most Touchdowns, Season
- 4 Ken Houston, Houston, 1971
  Jim Kearney, Kansas City, 1972
  Eric Allen, Philadelphia, 1993
- 3 Dick Harris, San Diego, 1961
  Dick Lynch, N.Y. Giants, 1963
  Herb Adderley, Green Bay, 1965
  Lem Barney, Detroit, 1967
  Miller Farr, Houston, 1967
  Monte Jackson, Los Angeles, 1976
  Rod Perry, Los Angeles, 1978
  Ronnie Lott, San Francisco, 1981
  Lloyd Burruss, Kansas City, 1986
  Wayne Haddix, Tampa Bay, 1990
  Robert Massey, Phoenix, 1992
  Ray Buchanan, Indianapolis, 1994
  Deion Sanders, San Francisco, 1994
- 2 By many players

Most Touchdowns, Rookie, Season
- 3 Lem Barney, Detroit, 1967
  Ronnie Lott, San Francisco, 1981
- 2 By many players

Most Touchdowns, Game
- 2 Bill Blackburn, Chi. Cardinals vs. Boston, Oct. 24, 1948
  Dan Sandifer, Washington vs. Boston, Oct. 31, 1948
  Bob Franklin, Cleveland vs. Chicago, Dec. 11, 1960
  Bill Stacy, St. Louis vs. Dall. Cowboys, Nov. 5, 1961
  Jerry Norton, St. Louis vs. Pittsburgh, Nov. 26, 1961
  Miller Farr, Houston vs. Buffalo, Dec. 7, 1968
  Ken Houston, Houston vs. San Diego, Dec. 19, 1971
  Jim Kearney, Kansas City vs. Denver, Oct. 1, 1972
  Lemar Parrish, Cincinnati vs. Houston, Dec. 17, 1972
  Dick Anderson, Miami vs. Pittsburgh, Dec. 3, 1973
  Prentice McCray, New England vs. N.Y. Jets, Nov. 21, 1976
  Kenny Johnson, Atlanta vs. Green Bay, Nov. 27, 1983 (OT)
  Mike Kozlowski, Miami vs. N.Y. Jets, Dec. 16, 1983
  Dave Brown, Seattle vs. Kansas City, Nov. 4, 1984
  Lloyd Burruss, Kansas City vs. San Diego, Oct. 19, 1986
  Henry Jones, Buffalo vs. Indianapolis, Sept. 20, 1992
  Robert Massey, Phoenix vs. Washington, Oct. 4, 1992
  Eric Allen, Philadelphia vs. New Orleans, Dec. 26, 1993
  Ken Norton, San Francisco vs. St. Louis, Oct. 22, 1995

PUNTING
Most Seasons Leading League
- 4 Sammy Baugh, Washington, 1940-43
  Jerrel Wilson, Kansas City, 1965, 1968, 1972-73
- 3 Yale Lary, Detroit, 1959, 1961, 1963
  Jim Fraser, Denver, 1962-64
  Ray Guy, Oakland, 1974-75, 1977
  Rohn Stark, Baltimore, 1983; Indianapolis, 1985-86
- 2 By many players

Most Consecutive Seasons Leading League
- 4 Sammy Baugh, Washington, 1940-43
- 3 Jim Fraser, Denver, 1962-64
- 2 By many players

PUNTS
Most Punts, Career
- 1,154 Dave Jennings, N.Y. Giants, 1974-84; N.Y. Jets, 1985-87
- 1,121 Rohn Stark, Baltimore, 1982-83; Indianapolis, 1984-94; Pittsburgh, 1995; Carolina, 1996
- 1,083 John James, Atlanta, 1972-81; Detroit, 1982, Houston, 1982-84

Most Punts, Season
- 114 Bob Parsons, Chicago, 1981
- 109 John James, Atlanta, 1978
- 108 John Teltschik, Philadelphia, 1986
  Rick Tuten, Seattle, 1992

Most Punts, Rookie, Season
- 108 John Teltschik, Philadelphia, 1986
- 99 Lewis Colbert, Kansas City, 1986
- 96 Mike Connell, San Francisco, 1978
  Chris Norman, Denver, 1984

Most Punts, Game
- 15 John Teltschik, Philadelphia vs. N.Y. Giants, Dec. 6, 1987 (OT)
- 14 Dick Nesbitt, Chi. Cardinals vs. Chi. Bears, Nov. 30, 1933
  Keith Molesworth, Chi. Bears vs. Green Bay, Dec. 10, 1933
  Sammy Baugh, Washington vs. Philadelphia, Nov. 5, 1939
  Carl Kinscherf, N.Y. Giants vs. Detroit, Nov. 7, 1943
  George Taliaferro, N.Y. Yanks vs. Los Angeles, Sept. 28, 1951
- 12 By many players. Last time: Chris Gardocki, Indianapolis vs. Buffalo, Oct. 6, 1996

Longest Punt
- 98 Steve O'Neal, N.Y. Jets vs. Denver, Sept. 21, 1969
- 94 Joe Lintzenich, Chi. Bears vs. N.Y. Giants, Nov. 16, 1931
- 93 Shawn McCarthy, New England vs. Buffalo, Nov. 3, 1991

AVERAGE YARDAGE
Highest Average, Punting, Career (250 punts)
- 45.10 Sammy Baugh, Washington, 1937-52 (338-15,245)
- 44.68 Tommy Davis, San Francisco, 1959-69 (511-22,833)
- 44.29 Yale Lary, Detroit, 1952-53, 1956-64 (503-22,279)

Highest Average, Punting, Season (Qualifiers)
- 51.40 Sammy Baugh, Washington, 1940 (35-1,799)
- 48.94 Yale Lary, Detroit, 1963 (35-1,713)
- 48.73 Sammy Baugh, Washington, 1941 (30-1,462)

Highest Average, Punting, Rookie, Season (Qualifiers)
- 45.92 Frank Sinkwich, Detroit, 1943 (12-551)
- 45.66 Tommy Davis, San Francisco, 1959 (59-2,694)
- 45.57 David Lee, Baltimore, 1966 (49-2,233)

Highest Average, Punting, Game (4 punts)
- 61.75 Bob Cifers, Detroit vs. Chi. Bears, Nov. 24, 1946 (4-247)
- 61.60 Roy McKay, Green Bay vs. Chi. Cardinals, Oct. 28, 1945 (5-308)
- 59.50 Darren Bennett, San Diego vs. Pittsburgh, Oct. 1, 1995 (4-238)

PUNTS HAD BLOCKED
Most Consecutive Punts, None Blocked
- 623 Dave Jennings, N.Y. Giants, 1976-83
- 619 Ray Guy, Oakland, 1979-81; L.A. Raiders, 1982-86
- 578 Bobby Walden, Minnesota, 1964-67; Pittsburgh, 1968-72

Most Punts Had Blocked, Career
- 14 Herman Weaver, Detroit, 1970-76; Seattle, 1977-80
  Harry Newsome, Pittsburgh, 1985-89; Minnesota, 1990-93
- 12 Jerrel Wilson, Kansas City, 1963-77; New England, 1978
  Tom Blanchard, N.Y. Giants, 1971-73; New Orleans, 1974-78; Tampa Bay, 1979-81
- 11 David Lee, Baltimore, 1966-78

Most Punts Had Blocked, Season
- 6 Harry Newsome, Pittsburgh, 1988
- 4 Bryan Wagner, Cleveland, 1990
- 3 By many players

PUNT RETURNS
Most Seasons Leading League
- 3 Les (Speedy) Duncan, San Diego, 1965-66; Washington, 1971
  Rick Upchurch, Denver, 1976, 1978, 1982
- 2 Dick Christy, N.Y. Titans, 1961-62
  Claude Gibson, Oakland, 1963-64
  Billy Johnson, Houston, 1975, 1977
  Mel Gray, New Orleans, 1987; Detroit, 1991

PUNT RETURNS
Most Punt Returns, Career
- 301 Tim Brown, L.A. Raiders, 1988-94; Oakland, 1995-96
- 299 David Meggett, N.Y. Giants, 1989-94; New England, 1995-96
- 292 Vai Sikahema, St. Louis, 1986-87; Phoenix, 1988-90; Green Bay, 1991; Philadelphia, 1992-93

Most Punt Returns, Season
- 70 Danny Reece, Tampa Bay, 1979
- 62 Fulton Walker, Miami-L.A. Raiders, 1985
- 58 J.T. Smith, Kansas City, 1979
  Greg Pruitt, L.A. Raiders, 1983
  Leo Lewis, Minnesota, 1988
  Desmond Howard, Green Bay, 1996

Most Punt Returns, Rookie, Season
- 57 Lew Barnes, Chicago, 1986

54 James Jones, Dallas, 1980
53 Louis Lipps, Pittsburgh, 1984
Most Punt Returns, Game
11 Eddie Brown, Washington vs. Tampa Bay, Oct. 9, 1977
10 Theo Bell, Pittsburgh vs. Buffalo, Dec. 16, 1979
Mike Nelms, Washington vs. New Orleans, Dec. 26, 1982
Ronnie Harris, New England vs. Pittsburgh, Dec. 5, 1993
9 Rodger Bird, Oakland vs. Denver, Sept. 10, 1967
Ralph McGill, San Francisco vs. Atlanta, Oct. 29, 1972
Ed Podolak, Kansas City vs. San Diego, Nov. 10, 1974
Anthony Leonard, San Francisco vs. New Orleans, Oct. 17, 1976
Butch Johnson, Dallas vs. Buffalo, Nov. 15, 1976
Larry Marshall, Philadelphia vs. Tampa Bay, Sept. 18, 1977
Nesby Glasgow, Baltimore vs. Kansas City, Sept. 2, 1979
Mike Nelms, Washington vs. St. Louis, Dec. 21, 1980
Leon Bright, N.Y. Giants vs. Philadelphia, Dec. 11, 1982
Pete Shaw, N.Y. Giants vs. Philadelphia, Nov. 20, 1983
Cleotha Montgomery, L.A. Raiders vs. Detroit, Dec. 10, 1984
Phil McConkey, N.Y. Giants vs. Philadelphia, Dec. 6, 1987 (OT)
Andre Hastings, Pittsburgh vs. Cleveland, Nov. 13, 1995

FAIR CATCHES
Most Fair Catches, Career
111 Tim Brown, L.A. Raiders 1988-94; Oakland, 1995-96
106 Mel Gray, New Orleans, 1986-88; Detroit, 1989-94; Houston, 1995-96
Kelvin Martin, Dallas, 1987-92, 1996; Seattle, 1993-94;
Philadelphia, 1995
David Meggett, N.Y. Giants, 1989-94; New England, 1995-96
102 Willie Wood, Green Bay, 1960-71
Most Fair Catches, Season
27 Leo Lewis, Minnesota, 1989
25 Mark Konecny, Philadelphia, 1988
Phil McConkey, N.Y. Giants, 1988
Chris Warren, Seattle, 1992
24 Ken Graham, San Diego, 1969
Brian Mitchell, Washington, 1994
O.J. McDuffie, Miami, 1996
Most Fair Catches, Game
7 Lem Barney, Detroit vs. Chicago, Nov. 21, 1976
Bobby Morse, Philadelphia vs. Buffalo, Dec. 27, 1987
6 Jake Scott, Miami vs. Buffalo, Dec. 20, 1970
Greg Pruitt, L.A. Raiders vs. Seattle, Oct. 7, 1984
Phil McConkey, San Diego vs. Kansas City, Dec. 17, 1989
Gerald McNeil, Houston vs. Pittsburgh, Sept. 16, 1990
Bobby Engram, Chicago vs. Minnesota, Sept. 15, 1996
5 By many players

YARDS GAINED
Most Seasons Leading League
3 Alvin Haymond, Baltimore, 1965-66; Los Angeles, 1969
2 Bill Dudley, Pittsburgh, 1942, 1946
Emlen Tunnell, N.Y. Giants, 1951-52
Dick Christy, N.Y. Titans, 1961-62
Claude Gibson, Oakland, 1963-64
Rodger Bird, Oakland, 1966-67
J.T. Smith, Kansas City, 1979-80
Vai Sikahema, St. Louis, 1986-87
David Meggett, N.Y. Giants, 1989-90
Most Yards Gained, Career
3,317 Billy Johnson, Houston, 1974-80; Atlanta, 1982-87; Washington, 1988
3,201 David Meggett, N.Y. Giants, 1989-94; New England, 1995-96
3,169 Vai Sikahema, St. Louis, 1986-87; Phoenix, 1988-90; Green Bay, 1991;
Philadelphia, 1992-93
Most Yards Gained, Season
875 Desmond Howard, Green Bay, 1996
692 Fulton Walker, Miami-L.A. Raiders, 1985
666 Greg Pruitt, L.A. Raiders, 1983
Most Yards Gained, Rookie, Season
656 Louis Lipps, Pittsburgh, 1984
655 Neal Colzie, Oakland, 1975
608 Mike Haynes, New England, 1976
Most Yards Gained, Game
207 LeRoy Irvin, Los Angeles vs. Atlanta, Oct. 11, 1981
205 George Atkinson, Oakland vs. Buffalo, Sept. 15, 1968
184 Tom Watkins, Detroit vs. San Francisco, Oct. 6, 1963
Longest Punt Return (All TDs)
103 Robert Bailey, L.A. Rams vs. New Orleans, Oct. 23, 1994
98 Gil LeFebvre, Cincinnati vs. Brooklyn, Dec. 3, 1933
Charlie West, Minnesota vs. Washington, Nov. 3, 1968
Dennis Morgan, Dallas vs. St. Louis, Oct. 13, 1974
Terance Mathis, N.Y. Jets vs. Dallas, Nov. 4, 1990
97 Greg Pruitt, L.A. Raiders vs. Washington, Oct. 2, 1983

AVERAGE YARDAGE
Highest Average, Career (75 returns)
13.66 Darrien Gordon, San Diego, 1993-94, 1996 (103-1,407)
13.37 Desmond Howard, Washington, 1992-94; Jacksonville, 1995;
Green Bay, 1996 (92-1,230)
12.78 George McAfee, Chi. Bears, 1940-41, 1945-50 (112-1,431)
Highest Average, Season (Qualifiers)
23.00 Herb Rich, Baltimore, 1950 (12-276)
21.47 Jack Christiansen, Detroit, 1952 (15-322)
21.28 Dick Christy, N.Y. Titans, 1961 (18-383)
Highest Average, Rookie, Season (Qualifiers)
23.00 Herb Rich, Baltimore, 1950 (12-276)
20.88 Jerry Davis, Chi. Cardinals, 1948 (16-334)
20.73 Frank Sinkwich, Detroit, 1943 (11-228)
Highest Average, Game (3 returns)
47.67 Chuck Latourette, St. Louis vs. New Orleans, Sept. 29, 1968 (3-143)
47.33 Johnny Roland, St. Louis vs. Philadelphia, Oct. 2, 1966 (3-142)
45.67 Dick Christy, N.Y. Titans vs. Denver, Sept. 24, 1961 (3-137)

TOUCHDOWNS
Most Touchdowns, Career
8 Jack Christiansen, Detroit, 1951-58
Rick Upchurch, Denver, 1975-83
7 David Meggett, N.Y. Giants, 1989-94; New England, 1995-96
6 Billy Johnson, Houston, 1974-80; Atlanta, 1982-87; Washington, 1988
Brian Mitchell, Washington, 1990-96
Eric Metcalf, Cleveland, 1989-94; Atlanta, 1995-96
Most Touchdowns, Season
4 Jack Christiansen, Detroit, 1951
Rick Upchurch, Denver, 1976
3 Emlen Tunnell, N.Y. Giants, 1951
Billy Johnson, Houston, 1975
LeRoy Irvin, Los Angeles, 1981
Desmond Howard, Green Bay, 1996
2 By many players
Most Touchdowns, Rookie, Season
4 Jack Christiansen, Detroit, 1951
2 By many players
Most Touchdowns, Game
2 Jack Christiansen, Detroit vs. Los Angeles, Oct. 14, 1951; vs. Green
Bay, Nov. 22, 1951
Dick Christy, N.Y. Titans vs. Denver, Sept. 24, 1961
Rick Upchurch, Denver vs. Cleveland, Sept. 26, 1976
LeRoy Irvin, Los Angeles vs. Atlanta, Oct. 11, 1981
Vai Sikahema, St. Louis vs. Tampa Bay, Dec. 21, 1986
Todd Kinchen, L.A. Rams vs. Atlanta, Dec. 27, 1992
Eric Metcalf, Cleveland vs. Pittsburgh, Oct. 24, 1993

KICKOFF RETURNS
Most Seasons Leading League
3 Abe Woodson, San Francisco, 1959, 1962-63
2 Lynn Chandnois, Pittsburgh, 1951-52
Bobby Jancik, Houston, 1962-63
Travis Williams, Green Bay, 1967; Los Angeles, 1971
Mel Gray, Detroit, 1991, 1994

KICKOFF RETURNS
Most Kickoff Returns, Career
412 Mel Gray, New Orleans, 1986-88; Detroit, 1989-94; Houston, 1995-96
275 Ron Smith, Chicago, 1965, 1970-72; Atlanta, 1966-67; Los Angeles,
1968-69; San Diego, 1973; Oakland, 1974
272 Brian Mitchell, Washington, 1990-96
Most Kickoff Returns, Season
70 Tyrone Hughes, New Orleans, 1996
66 Tyrone Hughes, New Orleans, 1995
64 Glyn Milburn, Detroit, 1996
Most Kickoff Returns, Rookie, Season
55 Stump Mitchell, St. Louis, 1981
54 Leeland McElroy, Arizona, 1996
53 Buster Rhymes, Minnesota, 1985
Most Kickoff Returns, Game
9 Noland Smith, Kansas City vs. Oakland, Nov. 23, 1967
Dino Hall, Cleveland vs. Pittsburgh, Oct. 7, 1979
Paul Palmer, Kansas City vs. Seattle, Sept. 20, 1987
Eric Metcalf, Atlanta vs. San Francisco, Sept. 29, 1996;
vs. St. Louis, Nov. 10, 1996
8 By many players

YARDS GAINED
Most Seasons Leading League
3 Bruce Harper, N.Y. Jets, 1977-79
Tyrone Hughes, New Orleans, 1994-96

   2 Marshall Goldberg, Chi. Cardinals, 1941-42
      Woodley Lewis, Los Angeles, 1953-54
      Al Carmichael, Green Bay, 1956-57
      Timmy Brown, Philadelphia, 1961, 1963
      Bobby Jancik, Houston, 1963, 1966
      Ron Smith, Atlanta, 1966-67
      Tyrone Hughes, New Orleans, 1994-95

Most Yards Gained, Career
10,057 Mel Gray, New Orleans, 1986-88; Detroit, 1989-94; Houston, 1995-96
 6,922 Ron Smith, Chicago, 1965, 1970-72; Atlanta, 1966-67; Los Angeles, 1968-69; San Diego, 1973; Oakland, 1974
 6,262 Brian Mitchell, Washington, 1990-96

Most Yards Gained, Season
 1,791 Tyrone Hughes, New Orleans, 1996
 1,627 Glyn Milburn, Detroit, 1996
 1,617 Tyrone Hughes, New Orleans, 1995

Most Yards Gained, Rookie, Season
 1,345 Buster Rhymes, Minnesota, 1985
 1,293 Andre Coleman, San Diego, 1994
 1,292 Stump Mitchell, St. Louis, 1981

Most Yards Gained, Game
  304 Tyrone Hughes, New Orleans vs. L.A. Rams, Oct. 23, 1994
  294 Wally Triplett, Detroit vs. Los Angeles, Oct. 29, 1950
  253 Derrick Witherspoon, Philadelphia vs. Arizona, Nov. 24, 1996

Longest Kickoff Return (All TDs)
  106 Al Carmichael, Green Bay vs. Chi. Bears, Oct. 7, 1956
      Noland Smith, Kansas City vs. Denver, Dec. 17, 1967
      Roy Green, St. Louis vs. Dallas, Oct. 21, 1979
  105 Frank Seno, Chi. Cardinals vs. N.Y. Giants, Oct. 20, 1946
      Ollie Matson, Chi. Cardinals vs. Washington, Oct. 14, 1956
      Abe Woodson, San Francisco vs. Los Angeles, Nov. 8, 1959
      Timmy Brown, Philadelphia vs. Cleveland, Sept. 17, 1961
      Jon Arnett, Los Angeles vs. Detroit, Oct. 29, 1961
      Eugene (Mercury) Morris, Miami vs. Cincinnati, Sept. 14, 1969
      Travis Williams, Los Angeles vs. New Orleans, Dec. 5, 1971
  104 By many players

AVERAGE YARDAGE
Highest Average, Career (75 returns)
 30.56 Gale Sayers, Chicago, 1965-71 (91-2,781)
 29.57 Lynn Chandnois, Pittsburgh, 1950-56 (92-2,720)
 28.69 Abe Woodson, San Francisco, 1958-64; St. Louis, 1965-66 (193-5,538)

Highest Average, Season (Qualifiers)
 41.06 Travis Williams, Green Bay, 1967 (18-739)
 37.69 Gale Sayers, Chicago, 1967 (16-603)
 35.50 Ollie Matson, Chi. Cardinals, 1958 (14-497)

Highest Average, Rookie, Season (Qualifiers)
 41.06 Travis Williams, Green Bay, 1967 (18-739)
 33.08 Tom Moore, Green Bay, 1960 (12-397)
 32.88 Duriel Harris, Miami, 1976 (17-559)

Highest Average, Game (3 returns)
 73.50 Wally Triplett, Detroit vs. Los Angeles, Oct. 29, 1950 (4-294)
 67.33 Lenny Lyles, San Francisco vs. Baltimore, Dec. 18, 1960 (3-202)
 65.33 Ken Hall, Houston vs. N.Y. Titans, Oct. 23, 1960 (3-196)

TOUCHDOWNS
Most Touchdowns, Career
   6 Ollie Matson, Chi. Cardinals, 1952, 1954-58; L.A. Rams, 1959-62; Detroit, 1963; Philadelphia, 1964
      Gale Sayers, Chicago, 1965-71
      Travis Williams, Green Bay, 1967-70; Los Angeles, 1971
      Mel Gray, New Orleans, 1986-88; Detroit, 1989-94; Houston, 1995-96
   5 Bobby Mitchell, Cleveland, 1958-61; Washington, 1962-68
      Abe Woodson, San Francisco, 1958-64; St. Louis, 1965-66
      Timmy Brown, Green Bay, 1959; Philadelphia, 1960-67; Baltimore, 1968
   4 Cecil Turner, Chicago, 1968-73
      Ron Brown, L.A. Rams, 1984-89, 1991; L.A. Raiders, 1990
      Jon Vaughn, New England, 1991-92; Seattle, 1993-94; Kansas City, 1994
      Andre Coleman, San Diego, 1994-96

Most Touchdowns, Season
   4 Travis Williams, Green Bay, 1967
      Cecil Turner, Chicago, 1970
   3 Verda (Vitamin T) Smith, Los Angeles, 1950
      Abe Woodson, San Francisco, 1963
      Gale Sayers, Chicago, 1967
      Raymond Clayborn, New England, 1977
      Ron Brown, L.A. Rams, 1985
      Mel Gray, Detroit, 1994
   2 By many players

Most Touchdowns, Rookie, Season
   4 Travis Williams, Green Bay, 1967
   3 Raymond Clayborn, New England, 1977
   2 By nine players

Most Touchdowns, Game
   2 Timmy Brown, Philadelphia vs. Dallas, Nov. 6, 1966
      Travis Williams, Green Bay vs. Cleveland, Nov. 12, 1967
      Ron Brown, L.A. Rams vs. Green Bay, Nov. 24, 1985
      Tyrone Hughes, New Orleans vs. L.A. Rams, Oct. 23, 1994

COMBINED KICK RETURNS
Most Combined Kick Returns, Career
  645 Mel Gray, New Orleans, 1986-88; Detroit, 1989-94; Houston, 1995-96
  527 Vai Sikahema, St. Louis, 1986-87; Phoenix, 1988-90; Green Bay, 1991; Philadelphia, 1992-93 (p-292, k-235)
  517 David Meggett, N.Y. Giants, 1989-94; New England, 1995-96 (p-218, k-299)

Most Combined Kick Returns, Season
  100 Larry Jones, Washington, 1975 (p-53, k-47)
      Tyrone Hughes, New Orleans, 1996 (p-30, k-70)
   98 Glyn Milburn, Detroit, 1996 (p-34, k-64)
   97 Stump Mitchell, St. Louis, 1981 (p-42, k-55)

Most Combined Kick Returns, Game
   13 Stump Mitchell, St. Louis vs. Atlanta, Oct. 18, 1981 (p-6, k-7)
      Ronnie Harris, New England vs. Pittsburgh, Dec. 5, 1993 (p-10, k-3)
   12 Mel Renfro, Dallas vs. Green Bay, Nov. 29, 1964 (p-4, k-8)
      Larry Jones, Washington vs. Dallas, Dec. 13, 1975 (p-6, k-6)
      Eddie Brown, Washington vs. Tampa Bay, Oct. 9, 1977 (p-11, k-1)
      Nesby Glasgow, Baltimore vs. Denver, Sept. 2, 1979 (p-9, k-3)
   11 By many players

YARDS GAINED
Most Yards Returned, Career
12,649 Mel Gray, New Orleans, 1986-88; Detroit, 1989-94; Houston, 1995-96 (p-2,592, k-10,057)
 8,710 Ron Smith, Chicago, 1965, 1970-72; Atlanta, 1966-67; Los Angeles, 1968-69; San Diego, 1973; Oakland, 1974 (p-1,788, k-6,922)
 8,458 Brian Mitchell, Washington, 1990-96 (p-2,196, k-6,262)

Most Yards Returned, Season
 1,943 Tyrone Hughes, New Orleans, 1996 (p-152, k-1,791)
 1,930 Brian Mitchell, Washington, 1994 (p-452, k-1,478)
 1,911 Glyn Milburn, Detroit, 1996 (p-284, k-1,627)

Most Yards Returned, Game
  347 Tyrone Hughes, New Orleans vs. L.A. Rams, Oct. 23, 1994 (p-43, k-304)
  294 Wally Triplett, Detroit vs. Los Angeles, Oct. 29, 1950 (k-294)
      Woodley Lewis, Los Angeles vs. Detroit, Oct. 18, 1953 (p-120, k-174)
  289 Eddie Payton, Detroit vs. Minnesota, Dec. 17, 1977 (p-105, k-184)

TOUCHDOWNS
Most Touchdowns, Career
   9 Ollie Matson, Chi. Cardinals, 1952, 1954-58; Los Angeles, 1959-62; Detroit, 1963; Philadelphia, 1964-66 (p-3, k-6)
      Mel Gray, New Orleans, 1986-88; Detroit, 1989-94; Houston, 1995-96 (p-3, k-6)
   8 Jack Christiansen, Detroit, 1951-58 (p-8)
      Bobby Mitchell, Cleveland, 1958-61; Washington, 1962-68 (p-3, k-5)
      Gale Sayers, Chicago, 1965-71 (p-2, k-6)
      Rick Upchurch, Denver, 1975-83 (p-8)
      Billy (White Shoes) Johnson, Houston, 1974-80; Atlanta, 1982-87; Washington, 1988 (p-6, k-2)
      Eric Metcalf, Cleveland, 1989-94; Atlanta, 1995-96 (p-6, k-2)
      David Meggett, N.Y. Giants, 1989-94; New England, 1995-96 (p-7, k-1)
   7 Abe Woodson, San Francisco, 1958-64; St. Louis, 1965-66 (p-2, k-5)
      Travis Williams, Green Bay, 1967-70; Los Angeles, 1971 (p-1, k-6)

Most Touchdowns, Season
   4 Jack Christiansen, Detroit, 1951 (p-4)
      Emlen Tunnell, N.Y. Giants, 1951 (p-3, k-1)
      Gale Sayers, Chicago, 1967 (p-1, k-3)
      Travis Williams, Green Bay, 1967 (k-4)
      Cecil Turner, Chicago, 1970 (k-4)
      Billy Johnson, Houston, 1975 (p-3, k-1)
      Rick Upchurch, Denver, 1976 (p-4)
   3 Verda (Vitamin T) Smith, Los Angeles, 1950 (k-3)
      Abe Woodson, San Francisco, 1963 (k-3)
      Raymond Clayborn, New England, 1977 (k-3)
      Billy Johnson, Houston, 1977 (p-2, k-1)
      LeRoy Irvin, Los Angeles, 1981 (p-3)
      Ron Brown, L.A. Rams, 1985 (k-3)
      Tyrone Hughes, New Orleans, 1993 (p-2, k-1)
      Mel Gray, Detroit, 1994 (k-3)
      Tamarick Vanover, Kansas City, 1995 (p-1, k-2)

Desmond Howard, Green Bay, 1996 (p-3)

2 By many players

Most Touchdowns, Game

2 Jack Christiansen, Detroit vs. Los Angeles, Oct. 14, 1951 (p-2); vs. Green Bay, Nov. 22, 1951 (p-2)
Jim Patton, N.Y. Giants vs. Washington, Oct. 30, 1955 (p-1, k-1)
Bobby Mitchell, Cleveland vs. Philadelphia, Nov. 23, 1958 (p-1, k-1)
Dick Christy, N.Y. Titans vs. Denver, Sept. 24, 1961 (p-2)
Al Frazier, Denver vs. Boston, Dec. 3, 1961 (p-1, k-1)
Timmy Brown, Philadelphia vs. Dallas, Nov. 6, 1966 (k-2)
Travis Williams, Green Bay vs. Cleveland, Nov. 12, 1967 (k-2); vs. Pittsburgh, Nov. 2, 1969 (p-1, k-1)
Gale Sayers, Chicago vs. San Francisco, Dec. 3, 1967 (p-1, k-1)
Rick Upchurch, Denver vs. Cleveland, Sept. 26, 1976 (p-2)
Eddie Payton, Detroit vs. Minnesota, Dec. 17, 1977 (p-1, k-1)
LeRoy Irvin, Los Angeles vs. Atlanta, Oct. 11, 1981 (p-2)
Ron Brown, L.A. Rams vs. Green Bay, Nov. 24, 1985 (k-2)
Vai Sikahema, St. Louis vs. Tampa Bay, Dec. 21, 1986 (p-2)
Eric Metcalf, Cleveland vs. Pittsburgh, Oct. 24, 1993 (p-2)
Tyrone Hughes, New Orleans vs. L.A. Rams, Oct. 23, 1994 (k-2)

FUMBLES

Most Fumbles, Career

150 Dave Krieg, Seattle, 1980-91; Kansas City, 1992-93; Detroit, 1994; Arizona, 1995; Chicago, 1996
145 Warren Moon, Houston, 1984-93; Minnesota, 1994-96
122 Boomer Esiason, Cincinnati, 1984-92; N.Y. Jets, 1993-95; Arizona, 1996

Most Fumbles, Season

21 Tony Banks, St. Louis, 1996
18 Dave Krieg, Seattle, 1989
Warren Moon, Houston, 1990
17 Dan Pastorini, Houston, 1973
Warren Moon, Houston, 1984
Randall Cunningham, Philadelphia, 1989

Most Fumbles, Game

7 Len Dawson, Kansas City vs. San Diego, Nov. 15, 1964
6 Sam Etcheverry, St. Louis vs. N.Y. Giants, Sept. 17, 1961
Dave Krieg, Seattle vs. Kansas City, Nov. 5, 1989
5 Paul Christman, Chi. Cardinals vs. Green Bay, Nov. 10, 1946
Charlie Conerly, N.Y. Giants vs. San Francisco, Dec. 1, 1957
Jack Kemp, Buffalo vs. Houston, Oct. 29, 1967
Roman Gabriel, Philadelphia vs. Oakland, Nov. 21, 1976
Randall Cunningham, Philadelphia vs. L.A. Raiders, Nov. 30, 1986 (OT)
Willie Totten, Buffalo vs. Indianapolis, Oct. 4, 1987
Dave Walter, Cincinnati vs. Seattle, Oct. 11, 1987
Dave Krieg, Seattle vs. San Diego, Nov. 25, 1990 (OT)
Andre Ware, Detroit vs. Green Bay, Dec. 6, 1992

FUMBLES RECOVERED

Most Fumbles Recovered, Career, Own and Opponents'

53 Warren Moon, Houston, 1984-93, Minnesota, 1994-96 (53 own)
46 Dave Krieg, Seattle, 1980-91; Kansas City, 1992-93; Detroit, 1994; Arizona, 1995; Chicago, 1996 (46 own)
45 Boomer Esiason, Cincinnati, 1984-92; N.Y. Jets, 1993-95; Arizona, 1996 (45 own)

Most Fumbles Recovered, Season, Own and Opponents'

9 Don Hultz, Minnesota, 1963 (9 opp)
Dave Krieg, Seattle, 1989 (9 own)
8 Paul Christman, Chi. Cardinals, 1945 (8 own)
Joe Schmidt, Detroit, 1955 (8 opp)
Bill Butler, Minnesota, 1963 (8 own)
Kermit Alexander, San Francisco, 1965 (4 own, 4 opp)
Jack Lambert, Pittsburgh, 1976 (1 own, 7 opp)
Danny White, Dallas, 1981 (8 own)
Dan Marino, Miami, 1988 (7 own, 1 opp)
7 By many players

Most Fumbles Recovered, Game, Own and Opponents'

4 Otto Graham, Cleveland vs. N.Y. Giants, Oct. 25, 1953 (4 own)
Sam Etcheverry, St. Louis vs. N.Y. Giants, Sept. 17, 1961 (4 own)
Roman Gabriel, Los Angeles vs. San Francisco, Oct. 12, 1969 (4 own)
Joe Ferguson, Buffalo vs. Miami, Sept. 18, 1977 (4 own)
Randall Cunningham, Philadelphia vs. L.A. Raiders, Nov. 30, 1986 (OT) (4 own)
3 By many players

OWN FUMBLES RECOVERED

Most Own Fumbles Recovered, Career

53 Warren Moon, Houston, 1984-93; Minnesota, 1994-96
46 Dave Krieg, Seattle, 1980-91; Kansas City, 1992-93; Detroit, 1994; Arizona, 1995; Chicago, 1996
45 Boomer Esiason, Cincinnati, 1984-92; N.Y. Jets, 1993-95; Arizona, 1996

Most Own Fumbles Recovered, Season

9 Dave Krieg, Seattle, 1989
8 Paul Christman, Chi. Cardinals, 1945
Bill Butler, Minnesota, 1963
Danny White, Dallas, 1981
7 By many players

Most Own Fumbles Recovered, Game

4 Otto Graham, Cleveland vs. N.Y. Giants, Oct. 25, 1953
Sam Etcheverry, St. Louis vs. N.Y. Giants, Sept. 17, 1961
Roman Gabriel, Los Angeles vs. San Francisco, Oct. 12, 1969
Joe Ferguson, Buffalo vs. Miami, Sept. 18, 1977
Randall Cunningham, Philadelphia vs. L.A. Raiders, Nov. 30, 1986 (OT)
3 By many players

OPPONENTS' FUMBLES RECOVERED

Most Opponents' Fumbles Recovered, Career

29 Jim Marshall, Cleveland, 1960; Minnesota, 1961-79
28 Rickey Jackson, New Orleans, 1981-93; San Francisco, 1994-95
25 Dick Butkus, Chicago, 1965-73

Most Opponents' Fumbles Recovered, Season

9 Don Hultz, Minnesota, 1963
8 Joe Schmidt, Detroit, 1955
7 Alan Page, Minnesota, 1970
Jack Lambert, Pittsburgh, 1976
Ray Childress, Houston, 1988
Rickey Jackson, New Orleans, 1990

Most Opponents' Fumbles Recovered, Game

3 Corwin Clatt, Chi. Cardinals vs. Detroit, Nov. 6, 1949
Vic Sears, Philadelphia vs. Green Bay, Nov. 2, 1952
Ed Beatty, San Francisco vs. Los Angeles, Oct. 7, 1956
Ron Carroll, Houston vs. Cincinnati, Oct. 27, 1974
Maurice Spencer, New Orleans vs. Atlanta, Oct. 10, 1976
Steve Nelson, New England vs. Philadelphia, Oct. 8, 1978
Charles Jackson, Kansas City vs. Pittsburgh, Sept. 6, 1981
Willie Buchanon, San Diego vs. Denver, Sept. 27, 1981
Joey Browner, Minnesota vs. San Francisco, Sept. 8, 1985
Ray Childress, Houston vs. Washington, Oct. 30, 1988
John Thierry, Chicago vs. Houston, Oct. 22, 1995
2 By many players

YARDS RETURNING FUMBLES

Longest Fumble Run (All TDs)

104 Jack Tatum, Oakland vs. Green Bay, Sept. 24, 1972
100 Chris Martin, Kansas City vs. Miami, Oct. 13, 1991
99 Don Griffin, San Francisco vs. Chicago, Dec. 23, 1991

TOUCHDOWNS

Most Touchdowns, Career (Total)

4 Bill Thompson, Denver, 1969-81
Jessie Tuggle, Atlanta, 1987-96
3 Ralph Heywood, Detroit, 1947-48; Boston, 1948; N.Y. Bulldogs, 1949
Leo Sugar, Chi. Cardinals, 1954-59; St. Louis, 1960; Philadelphia, 1961; Detroit, 1962
Bud McFadin, Los Angeles, 1952-56; Denver, 1960-63; Houston, 1964-65
Doug Cline, Houston, 1960-66; San Diego, 1966
Bob Lilly, Dall. Cowboys, 1961-74
Chris Hanburger, Washington, 1965-78
Lemar Parrish, Cincinnati, 1970-77; Washington, 1978-81; Buffalo, 1982
Paul Krause, Washington, 1964-67; Minnesota, 1968-79
Brad Dusek, Washington, 1974-81
David Logan, Tampa Bay, 1979-86; Green Bay, 1987
Thomas Howard, Kansas City, 1977-83; St. Louis, 1984-85
Greg Townsend, L.A. Raiders, 1983-93; Philadelphia, 1994
Les Miller, San Diego, 1987-90, 1994; New Orleans, 1991-94; Carolina, 1996
Chris Martin, New Orleans, 1983; Minnesota, 1984-88; Kansas City, 1989-92; L.A. Rams, 1993-94
Seth Joyner, Philadelphia, 1986-93; Arizona, 1994-96
Derrick Thomas, Kansas City, 1989-96
Tony Bennett, Green Bay, 1990-93; Indianapolis, 1994-96
2 By many players

Most Touchdowns, Season (Total)

2 Harold McPhail, Boston, 1934
Harry Ebding, Detroit, 1937
John Morelli, Boston, 1944
Frank Maznicki, Boston, 1947
Fred (Dippy) Evans, Chi. Bears, 1948
Ralph Heywood, Boston, 1948
Art Tait, N.Y. Yanks, 1951
John Dwyer, Los Angeles, 1952
Leo Sugar, Chi. Cardinals, 1957
Doug Cline, Houston, 1961

Jim Bradshaw, Pittsburgh, 1964
Royce Berry, Cincinnati, 1970
Ahmad Rashad, Buffalo, 1974
Tim Gray, Kansas City, 1977
Charles Phillips, Oakland, 1978
Kenny Johnson, Atlanta, 1981
George Martin, N.Y. Giants, 1981
Del Rodgers, Green Bay, 1982
Mike Douglass, Green Bay, 1983
Shelton Robinson, Seattle, 1983
Erik McMillan, N.Y. Jets, 1989
Les Miller, San Diego, 1990
Seth Joyner, Philadelphia, 1991
Robert Goff, New Orleans, 1992
Willie Clay, Detroit, 1993
Tyrone Hughes, New Orleans, 1994

Most Touchdowns, Career (Own recovered)
2 Ken Kavanaugh, Chi. Bears, 1940-41, 1945-50
Mike Ditka, Chicago, 1961-66; Philadelphia, 1967-68; Dallas, 1969-72
Gail Cogdill, Detroit, 1960-68; Baltimore, 1968; Atlanta, 1969-70
Ahmad Rashad, St. Louis, 1972-73; Buffalo, 1974; Minnesota, 1976-82
Jim Mitchell, Atlanta, 1969-79
Drew Pearson, Dallas, 1973-83
Del Rodgers, Green Bay, 1982, 1984; San Francisco, 1987-88

Most Touchdowns, Season (Own recovered)
2 Ahmad Rashad, Buffalo, 1974
Del Rodgers, Green Bay, 1982
1 By many players

Most Touchdowns, Career (Opponents' recovered)
4 Jessie Tuggle, Atlanta, 1987-96
3 Leo Sugar, Chi. Cardinals, 1954-59; St. Louis, 1960; Philadelphia, 1961; Detroit, 1962
Doug Cline, Houston, 1960-66; San Diego, 1966
Bud McFadin, Los Angeles, 1952-56; Denver, 1960-63; Houston, 1964-65
Bob Lilly, Dall. Cowboys, 1961-74
Chris Hanburger, Washington, 1965-78
Paul Krause, Washington, 1964-67; Minnesota, 1968-79
Lemar Parrish, Cincinnati, 1970-77; Washington, 1978-81; Buffalo, 1982
Bill Thompson, Denver, 1969-81
Brad Dusek, Washington, 1974-81
David Logan, Tampa Bay, 1979-86; Green Bay, 1987
Thomas Howard, Kansas City, 1977-83; St. Louis, 1984-85
Greg Townsend, L.A. Raiders, 1983-93; Philadelphia, 1994
Les Miller, San Diego, 1987-90, 1994; New Orleans, 1991-94, Carolina, 1996
Chris Martin, New Orleans, 1983; Minnesota, 1984-88; Kansas City, 1989-92; L.A. Rams, 1993-94
Seth Joyner, Philadelphia, 1986-93; Arizona, 1994-96
Derrick Thomas, Kansas City, 1989-96
Tony Bennett, Green Bay, 1990-93; Indianapolis, 1994-96
2 By many players

Most Touchdowns, Season (Opponents' recovered)
2 Harold McPhail, Boston, 1934
Harry Ebding, Detroit, 1937
John Morelli, Boston, 1944
Frank Maznicki, Boston, 1947
Fred (Dippy) Evans, Chi. Bears, 1948
Ralph Heywood, Boston, 1948
Art Tait, N.Y. Yanks, 1951
John Dwyer, Los Angeles, 1952
Leo Sugar, Chi. Cardinals, 1957
Doug Cline, Houston, 1961
Jim Bradshaw, Pittsburgh, 1964
Royce Berry, Cincinnati, 1970
Tim Gray, Kansas City, 1977
Charles Phillips, Oakland, 1978
Kenny Johnson, Atlanta, 1981
George Martin, N.Y. Giants, 1981
Mike Douglass, Green Bay, 1983
Shelton Robinson, Seattle, 1983
Erik McMillan, N.Y. Jets, 1989
Les Miller, San Diego, 1990
Seth Joyner, Philadelphia, 1991
Robert Goff, New Orleans, 1992
Willie Clay, Detroit, 1993
Tyrone Hughes, New Orleans, 1994

Most Touchdowns, Game (Opponents' recovered)
2 Fred (Dippy) Evans, Chi. Bears vs. Washington, Nov. 28, 1948

COMBINED NET YARDS GAINED
Rushing, receiving, interception returns, punt returns, kickoff returns, and fumble returns
Most Seasons Leading League
5 Jim Brown, Cleveland, 1958-61, 1964
3 Cliff Battles, Boston, 1932-33; Washington, 1937
Gale Sayers, Chicago, 1965-67
Eric Dickerson, L.A. Rams, 1983-84, 1986
Thurman Thomas, Buffalo, 1989, 1991-92
Brian Mitchell, Washington, 1994-96
2 By many players

Most Consecutive Seasons Leading League
4 Jim Brown, Cleveland, 1958-61
3 Gale Sayers, Chicago, 1965-67
Brian Mitchell, Washington, 1994-96
2 Cliff Battles, Boston, 1932-33
Charley Trippi, Chi. Cardinals, 1948-49
Timmy Brown, Philadelphia, 1962-63
Floyd Little, Denver, 1967-68
James Brooks, San Diego, 1981-82
Eric Dickerson, L.A. Rams, 1983-84
Thurman Thomas, Buffalo, 1991-92

ATTEMPTS
Most Attempts, Career
4,368 Walter Payton, Chicago, 1975-87
3,487 Marcus Allen, L.A. Raiders, 1982-92; Kansas City, 1993-96
3,351 Tony Dorsett, Dallas, 1977-87; Denver, 1988

Most Attempts, Season
496 James Wilder, Tampa Bay, 1984
449 Marcus Allen, L.A. Raiders, 1985
442 Eric Dickerson, L.A. Rams, 1983

Most Attempts, Rookie, Season
442 Eric Dickerson, L.A. Rams, 1983
395 George Rogers, New Orleans, 1981
390 Joe Cribbs, Buffalo, 1980

Most Attempts, Game
48 James Wilder, Tampa Bay vs. Pittsburgh, Oct. 30, 1983
47 James Wilder, Tampa Bay vs. Green Bay, Sept. 30, 1984 (OT)
46 Gerald Riggs, Atlanta vs. L.A. Rams, Nov. 17, 1985

YARDS GAINED
Most Yards Gained, Career
21,803 Walter Payton, Chicago, 1975-87
17,057 Marcus Allen, L.A. Raiders, 1982-92; Kansas City, 1993-96
17,007 Jerry Rice, San Francisco, 1985-96

Most Yards Gained, Season
2,535 Lionel James, San Diego, 1985
2,477 Brian Mitchell, Washington, 1994
2,462 Terry Metcalf, St. Louis, 1975

Most Yards Gained, Rookie, Season
2,317 Tim Brown, L.A. Raiders, 1988
2,272 Gale Sayers, Chicago, 1965
2,212 Eric Dickerson, L.A. Rams, 1983

Most Yards Gained, Game
404 Glyn Milburn, Denver vs. Seattle, Dec. 10, 1995
373 Billy Cannon, Houston vs. N.Y. Titans, Dec. 10, 1961
347 Tyrone Hughes, New Orleans vs. L.A. Rams, Oct. 23, 1994

SACKS
Sacks have been compiled since 1982.
Most Seasons Leading League
2 Mark Gastineau, N.Y. Jets, 1983-84
Reggie White, Philadelphia, 1987-88
Kevin Greene, Pittsburgh, 1994; Carolina, 1996

Most Sacks, Career
165.5 Reggie White, Philadelphia, 1985-92; Green Bay, 1993-96
140 Bruce Smith, Buffalo, 1985-96
133 Richard Dent, Chicago, 1983-93, 1995; San Francisco, 1994; Indianapolis, 1996

Most Sacks, Season
22 Mark Gastineau, N.Y. Jets, 1984
21 Reggie White, Philadelphia, 1987
Chris Doleman, Minnesota, 1989
20.5 Lawrence Taylor, N.Y. Giants, 1986

Most Sacks, Rookie, Season
12.5 Leslie O'Neal, San Diego, 1986
Simeon Rice, Arizona, 1996
12 Charles Haley, San Francisco, 1986
11 Vernon Maxwell, Baltimore, 1983

Most Sacks, Game
- 7   Derrick Thomas, Kansas City vs. Seattle, Nov. 11, 1990
- 6   Fred Dean, San Francisco vs. New Orleans, Nov. 13, 1983
- 5.5 William Gay, Detroit vs. Tampa Bay, Sept. 4, 1983

Most Seasons, 10 or More Sacks
- 10   Reggie White, Philadelphia, 1985-92; Green Bay, 1993, 1995
  - Bruce Smith, Buffalo, 1986-1990, 1992-96
- 8   Richard Dent, Chicago, 1984-88, 1990-91, 1993
- 7   Lawrence Taylor, N.Y. Giants, 1984-1990
  - Greg Townsend, L.A. Raiders, 1983, 1985-86, 1988-91
  - Leslie O'Neal, San Diego, 1986, 1989-90, 1992-95
  - Kevin Greene, L.A. Rams, 1988-90, 1992; Pittsburgh, 1993-94; Carolina, 1996

Most Consecutive Seasons, 10 or More Sacks
- 9   Reggie White, Philadelphia, 1985-92; Green Bay, 1993
- 7   Lawrence Taylor, N.Y. Giants, 1984-1990
- 5   Richard Dent, Chicago, 1984-88
  - Bruce Smith, Buffalo, 1986-1990, 1992-96
  - Simon Fletcher, Denver, 1989-93
  - John Randle, Minnesota, 1992-96

MISCELLANEOUS

Longest Return of Missed Field Goal (All TDs)
- 101   Al Nelson, Philadelphia vs. Dallas, Sept. 26, 1971
- 100   Al Nelson, Philadelphia vs. Cleveland, Dec. 11, 1966
  - Ken Ellis, Green Bay vs. N.Y. Giants, Sept. 19, 1971
- 99   Jerry Williams, Los Angeles vs. Green Bay, Dec. 16, 1951
  - Carl Taseff, Baltimore vs. Los Angeles, Dec. 12, 1959
  - Timmy Brown, Philadelphia vs. St. Louis, Sept. 16, 1962

TEAM RECORDS

CHAMPIONSHIPS

Most Seasons League Champion
- 12   Green Bay, 1929-31, 1936, 1939, 1944, 1961-62, 1965-67, 1996
- 9   Chi. Bears, 1921, 1932-33, 1940-41, 1943, 1946, 1963, 1985
- 6   N.Y. Giants, 1927, 1934, 1938, 1956, 1986, 1990

Most Consecutive Seasons League Champion
- 3   Green Bay, 1929-31
  - Green Bay, 1965-67
- 2   Canton, 1922-23
  - Chi. Bears, 1932-33
  - Chi. Bears, 1940-41
  - Philadelphia, 1948-49
  - Detroit, 1952-53
  - Cleveland, 1954-55
  - Baltimore, 1958-59
  - Houston, 1960-61
  - Green Bay, 1961-62
  - Buffalo, 1964-65
  - Miami, 1972-73
  - Pittsburgh, 1974-75
  - Pittsburgh, 1978-79
  - San Francisco, 1988-89
  - Dallas, 1992-93

Most Times Finishing First, Regular Season
- 18   Clev. Browns, 1950-55, 1957, 1964-65, 1967-69, 1971, 1980, 1985-87, 1989
  - Chi. Bears, 1921, 1932-34, 1937, 1940-43, 1946, 1956, 1963, 1984-88, 1990
  - N.Y. Giants, 1927, 1933-35, 1938-39, 1941, 1944, 1946, 1956, 1958-59, 1961-63, 1986, 1989-90
  - Dallas, 1966-71, 1973, 1976-79, 1981, 1985, 1992-96
- 16   Green Bay, 1929-31, 1936, 1938-39, 1944, 1960-62, 1965-67, 1972, 1995-96
- 15   Cleveland/L.A. Rams, 1945, 1949-51, 1955, 1967, 1969, 1973-79, 1985
  - San Francisco, 1970-72, 1981, 1983-84, 1986-90, 1992-95

Most Consecutive Times Finishing First, Regular Season
- 7   Los Angeles, 1973-79
- 6   Cleveland, 1950-55
  - Dallas, 1966-71
  - Minnesota, 1973-78
  - Pittsburgh, 1974-79
- 5   Oakland, 1972-76
  - Chicago, 1984-88
  - San Francisco, 1986-90
  - Dallas, 1992-96

GAMES WON

Most Consecutive Games Won
- 17   Chi. Bears, 1933-34
- 16   Chi. Bears, 1941-42

-      Miami, 1971-73
-      Miami, 1983-84
- 15   L.A. Chargers/San Diego, 1960-61
  - San Francisco, 1989-90

Most Consecutive Games Without Defeat
- 25   Canton, 1921-23 (won 22, tied 3)
- 24   Chi. Bears, 1941-43 (won 23, tied 1)
- 23   Green Bay, 1928-30 (won 21, tied 2)

Most Games Won, Season
- 15   San Francisco, 1984
  - Chicago, 1985
- 14   Frankford, 1926
  - Miami, 1972
  - Pittsburgh, 1978
  - Washington, 1983
  - Miami, 1984
  - Chicago, 1986
  - N.Y. Giants, 1986
  - San Francisco, 1989
  - San Francisco, 1990
  - Washington, 1991
  - San Francisco, 1992
- 13   By many teams

Most Consecutive Games Won, Season
- 14   Miami, 1972
- 13   Chi. Bears, 1934
- 12   Minnesota, 1969
  - Chicago, 1985

Most Consecutive Games Won, Start of Season
- 14   Miami, 1972, entire season
- 13   Chi. Bears, 1934, entire season
- 12   Chicago, 1985

Most Consecutive Games Won, End of Season
- 14   Miami, 1972, entire season
- 13   Chi. Bears, 1934, entire season
- 11   Chi. Bears, 1942, entire season
  - Cleveland, 1951
  - Houston, 1993

Most Consecutive Games Without Defeat, Season
- 14   Miami, 1972 (won 14)
- 13   Chi. Bears, 1926 (won 11, tied 2)
  - Green Bay, 1929 (won 12, tied 1)
  - Chi. Bears, 1934 (won 13)
  - Baltimore, 1967 (won 11, tied 2)
- 12   Canton, 1922 (won 10, tied 2)
  - Canton, 1923 (won 11, tied 1)
  - Minnesota, 1969 (won 12)
  - Chicago, 1985 (won 12)

Most Consecutive Games Without Defeat, Start of Season
- 14   Miami, 1972 (won 14), entire season
- 13   Chi. Bears, 1926 (won 11, tied 2)
  - Green Bay, 1929 (won 12, tied 1), entire season
  - Chi. Bears, 1934 (won 13), entire season
  - Baltimore, 1967 (won 11, tied 2)
- 12   Canton, 1922 (won 10, tied 2), entire season
  - Canton, 1923 (won 11, tied 1), entire season
  - Chicago, 1985 (won 12)

Most Consecutive Games Without Defeat, End of Season
- 14   Miami, 1972 (won 14), entire season
- 13   Green Bay, 1929 (won 12, tied 1), entire season
  - Chi. Bears, 1934 (won 13), entire season
- 12   Canton, 1922 (won 10, tied 2), entire season
  - Canton, 1923 (won 11, tied 1), entire season

Most Consecutive Home Games Won
- 27   Miami, 1971-74
- 20   Green Bay, 1929-32
- 18   Oakland, 1968-70
  - Dallas, 1979-81

Most Consecutive Home Games Without Defeat
- 30   Green Bay, 1928-33 (won 27, tied 3)
- 27   Miami, 1971-74 (won 27)
- 25   Chi. Bears, 1923-25 (won 19, tied 6)

Most Consecutive Road Games Won
- 18   San Francisco, 1988-90
- 11   L.A. Chargers/San Diego, 1960-61
  - San Francisco, 1987-88
- 10   Chi. Bears, 1941-42
  - Dallas, 1968-69
  - New Orleans, 1987-88

Most Consecutive Road Games Without Defeat
- 18   San Francisco, 1988-90 (won 18)
- 13   Chi. Bears, 1941-43 (won 12, tied 1)
- 12   Green Bay, 1928-30 (won 10, tied 2)

Most Shutout Games Won or Tied, Season

10 Pottsville, 1926 (won 9, tied 1)
   N.Y. Giants, 1927 (won 9, tied 1)
9 Akron, 1921 (won 8, tied 1)
   Canton, 1922 (won 7, tied 2)
   Frankford, 1926 (won 9)
   Frankford, 1929 (won 6, tied 3)
8 By many teams

Most Consecutive Shutout Games Won or Tied

13 Akron, 1920-21 (won 10, tied 3)
7 Pottsville, 1926 (won 6, tied 1)
   Detroit, 1934 (won 7)
6 Buffalo, 1920-21 (won 5, tied 1)
   Frankford, 1926 (won 6)
   Detroit, 1926 (won 4, tied 2)
   N.Y. Giants, 1926-27 (won 5, tied 1)

GAMES LOST

Most Consecutive Games Lost

26 Tampa Bay, 1976-77
19 Chi. Cardinals, 1942-43, 1945
   Oakland, 1961-62
18 Houston, 1972-73

Most Consecutive Games Without Victory

26 Tampa Bay, 1976-77 (lost 26)
23 Rochester, 1922-25 (lost 21, tied 2)
   Washington, 1960-61 (lost 20, tied 3)
19 Dayton, 1927-29 (lost 18, tied 1)
   Chi. Cardinals, 1942-43, 1945 (lost 19)
   Oakland, 1961-62 (lost 19)

Most Games Lost, Season

15 New Orleans, 1980
   Dallas, 1989
   New England, 1990
   Indianapolis, 1991
   N.Y. Jets, 1996
14 By many teams

Most Consecutive Games Lost, Season

14 Tampa Bay, 1976
   New Orleans, 1980
   Baltimore, 1981
   New England, 1990
13 Oakland, 1962
   Pittsburgh, 1969
   Indianapolis, 1986
12 Tampa Bay, 1977

Most Consecutive Games Lost, Start of Season

14 Tampa Bay, 1976, entire season
   New Orleans, 1980
13 Oakland, 1962
   Indianapolis, 1986
12 Tampa Bay, 1977

Most Consecutive Games Lost, End of Season

14 Tampa Bay, 1976, entire season
   New England, 1990
13 Pittsburgh, 1969
11 Philadelphia, 1936
   Detroit, 1942, entire season
   Houston, 1972

Most Consecutive Games Without Victory, Season

14 Tampa Bay, 1976 (lost 14), entire season
   New Orleans, 1980 (lost 14)
   Baltimore, 1981 (lost 14)
   New England, 1990 (lost 14)
13 Washington, 1961 (lost 12, tied 1)
   Oakland, 1962 (lost 13)
   Pittsburgh, 1969 (lost 13)
   Indianapolis, 1986 (lost 13)
12 Dall. Cowboys, 1960 (lost 11, tied 1), entire season
   Tampa Bay, 1977 (lost 12)

Most Consecutive Games Without Victory, Start of Season

14 Tampa Bay, 1976 (lost 14), entire season
   New Orleans, 1980 (lost 14)
13 Washington, 1961 (lost 12, tied 1)
   Oakland, 1962 (lost 13)
   Indianapolis, 1986 (lost 13)
12 Dall. Cowboys, 1960 (lost 11, tied 1), entire season
   Tampa Bay, 1977 (lost 12)

Most Consecutive Games Without Victory, End of Season

14 Tampa Bay, 1976, (lost 14), entire season
   New England, 1990 (lost 14)
13 Pittsburgh, 1969 (lost 13)
12 Dall. Cowboys, 1960 (lost 11, tied 1), entire season

Most Consecutive Home Games Lost

14 Dallas, 1988-89
13 Houston, 1972-73
   Tampa Bay, 1976-77
12 N.Y. Jets, 1995-96 (current)

Most Consecutive Home Games Without Victory

14 Dallas, 1988-89 (lost 14)
13 Houston, 1972-73 (lost 13)
   Tampa Bay, 1976-77 (lost 13)
12 Philadelphia, 1936-38 (lost 11, tied 1)
   N.Y. Jets, 1995-96 (lost 12; current)

Most Consecutive Road Games Lost

23 Houston, 1981-84
22 Buffalo, 1983-86
19 Tampa Bay, 1983-85
   Atlanta, 1988-91

Most Consecutive Road Games Without Victory

23 Houston, 1981-84 (lost 23)
22 Buffalo, 1983-86 (lost 22)
19 Tampa Bay, 1983-85 (lost 19)
   Atlanta, 1988-91 (lost 19)

Most Shutout Games Lost or Tied, Season

8 Frankford, 1927 (lost 6, tied 2)
   Brooklyn, 1931 (lost 8)
7 Dayton, 1925 (lost 6, tied 1)
   Orange, 1929 (lost 4, tied 3)
   Frankford, 1931 (lost 6, tied 1)
6 By many teams

Most Consecutive Shutout Games Lost or Tied

8 Rochester, 1922-24 (lost 8)
7 Hammond, 1922-23 (lost 6, tied 1)
6 Providence, 1926-27 (lost 5, tied 1)
   Brooklyn, 1942-43 (lost 6)

TIE GAMES

Most Tie Games, Season

6 Chi. Bears, 1932
5 Frankford, 1929
4 Chi. Bears, 1924
   Orange, 1929
   Portsmouth, 1932

Most Consecutive Tie Games

3 Chi. Bears, 1932
2 By many teams

SCORING

Most Seasons Leading League

10 Chi. Bears, 1932, 1934-35, 1939, 1941-43, 1946-47, 1956
9 San Francisco, 1953, 1965, 1970, 1987, 1989, 1992-95
7 Green Bay, 1931, 1936-38, 1961-62, 1996

Most Consecutive Seasons Leading League

4 San Francisco, 1992-1996
3 Green Bay, 1936-38
   Chi. Bears, 1941-43
   Los Angeles, 1950-52
   Oakland, 1967-69
2 By many teams

POINTS

Most Points, Season

541 Washington, 1983
513 Houston, 1961
   Miami, 1984
505 San Francisco, 1994

Fewest Points, Season (Since 1932)

37 Cincinnati/St. Louis, 1934
38 Cincinnati, 1933
   Detroit, 1942
51 Pittsburgh, 1934
   Philadelphia, 1936

Most Points, Game

72 Washington vs. N.Y. Giants, Nov. 27, 1966
70 Los Angeles vs. Baltimore, Oct. 22, 1950
65 Chi. Cardinals vs. N.Y. Bulldogs, Nov. 13, 1949
   Los Angeles vs. Detroit, Oct. 29, 1950

Most Points, Both Teams, Game

113 Washington (72) vs. N.Y. Giants (41), Nov. 27, 1966
101 Oakland (52) vs. Houston (49), Dec. 22, 1963
99 Seattle (51) vs. Kansas City (48), Nov. 27, 1983 (OT)

Fewest Points, Both Teams, Game

0 In many games. Last time: N.Y. Giants vs. Detroit, Nov. 7, 1943

Most Points, Shutout Victory, Game

64 Philadelphia vs. Cincinnati, Nov. 6, 1934

62 Akron vs. Oorang, Oct. 29, 1922
60 Rock Island vs. Evansville, Oct. 15, 1922
Chi. Cardinals vs. Rochester, Oct. 7, 1923

Fewest Points, Shutout Victory, Game
2 Green Bay vs. Chi. Bears, Oct. 16, 1932
Chi. Bears vs. Green Bay, Sept. 18, 1938

Most Points Overcome to Win Game
28 San Francisco vs. New Orleans, Dec. 7, 1980 (OT) (trailed 7-35, won 38-35)
25 St. Louis vs. Tampa Bay, Nov. 8, 1987 (trailed 3-28, won 31-28)
24 Philadelphia vs. Washington, Oct. 27, 1946 (trailed 0-24, won 28-24)
Detroit vs. Baltimore, Oct. 20, 1957 (trailed 3-27, won 31-27)
Philadelphia vs. Chi. Cardinals, Oct. 25, 1959 (trailed 0-24, won 28-24)
Denver vs. Boston, Oct. 23, 1960 (trailed 0-24, won 31-24)
Miami vs. New England, Dec. 15, 1974 (trailed 0-24, won 34-27)
Minnesota vs. San Francisco, Dec. 4, 1977 (trailed 0-24, won 28-27)
Denver vs. Seattle, Sept. 23, 1979 (trailed 10-34, won 37-34)
Houston vs. Cincinnati, Sept. 23, 1979 (OT) (trailed 0-24, won 30-27)
L.A. Raiders vs. San Diego, Nov. 22, 1982 (trailed 0-24, won 28-24)
L.A. Raiders vs. Denver, Sept. 26, 1988 (OT) (trailed 0-24, won 30-27)
L.A. Rams vs. Tampa Bay, Dec. 6, 1992 (trailed 3-27, won 31-27)

Most Points Overcome to Tie Game
31 Denver vs. Buffalo, Nov. 27, 1960 (trailed 7-38, tied 38-38)
28 Los Angeles vs. Philadelphia, Oct. 3, 1948 (trailed 0-28, tied 28-28)

Most Points, Each Half
1st: 49 Green Bay vs. Tampa Bay, Oct. 2, 1983
48 Buffalo vs. Miami, Sept. 18, 1966
45 Green Bay vs. Cleveland, Nov. 12, 1967
Indianapolis vs. Denver, Oct. 31, 1988
Houston vs. Cleveland, Dec. 9, 1990
2nd: 49 Chi. Bears vs. Philadelphia, Nov. 30, 1941
48 Chi. Cardinals vs. Baltimore, Oct. 2, 1950
N.Y. Giants vs. Baltimore, Nov. 19, 1950
45 Cincinnati vs. Houston, Dec. 17, 1972

Most Points, Both Teams, Each Half
1st: 70 Houston (35) vs. Oakland (35), Dec. 22, 1963
62 N.Y. Jets (41) vs. Tampa Bay (21), Nov. 17, 1985
59 St. Louis (31) vs. Philadelphia (28), Dec. 16, 1962
2nd: 65 Washington (38) vs. N.Y. Giants (27), Nov. 27, 1966
62 L.A. Raiders (31) vs. San Diego (31), Jan. 2, 1983
58 New England (37) vs. Baltimore (21), Nov. 23, 1980
N.Y. Jets (37) vs. New England (21), Sept. 21, 1987

Most Points, One Quarter
41 Green Bay vs. Detroit, Oct. 7, 1945 (second quarter)
Los Angeles vs. Detroit, Oct. 29, 1950 (third quarter)
37 Los Angeles vs. Green Bay, Sept. 21, 1980 (second quarter)
35 Chi. Cardinals vs. Boston, Oct. 24, 1948 (third quarter)
Green Bay vs. Cleveland, Nov. 12, 1967 (first quarter)
Green Bay vs. Tampa Bay, Oct. 2, 1983 (second quarter)

Most Points, Both Teams, One Quarter
49 Oakland (28) vs. Houston (21), Dec. 22, 1963 (second quarter)
48 Green Bay (41) vs. Detroit (7), Oct. 7, 1945 (second quarter)
Los Angeles (41) vs. Detroit (7), Oct. 29, 1950 (third quarter)
47 St. Louis (27) vs. Philadelphia (20), Dec. 13, 1964 (second quarter)

Most Points, Each Quarter
1st: 35 Green Bay vs. Cleveland, Nov. 12, 1967
31 Buffalo vs. Kansas City, Sept. 13, 1964
28 By seven teams
2nd: 41 Green Bay vs. Detroit, Oct. 7, 1945
37 Los Angeles vs. Green Bay, Sept. 21, 1980
35 Green Bay vs. Tampa Bay, Oct. 2, 1983
3rd: 41 Los Angeles vs. Detroit, Oct. 29, 1950
35 Chi. Cardinals vs. Boston, Oct. 24, 1948
28 By 10 teams
4th: 31 Oakland vs. Denver, Dec. 17, 1960
Oakland vs. San Diego, Dec. 8, 1963
Atlanta vs. Green Bay, Sept. 13, 1981
28 By many teams

Most Points, Both Teams, Each Quarter
1st: 42 Green Bay (35) vs. Cleveland (7), Nov. 12, 1967
35 Dall. Texans (21) vs. N.Y. Titans (14), Nov. 11, 1962
Dallas (28) vs. Philadelphia (7), Oct. 19, 1969
Kansas City (21) vs. Seattle (14), Dec. 11, 1977
Detroit (21) vs. L.A. Raiders (14), Dec. 10, 1990
Dallas (21) vs. Atlanta (14), Dec. 22, 1991
34 Los Angeles (21) vs. Baltimore (13), Oct. 22, 1950
Oakland (21) vs. Atlanta (13), Nov. 30, 1975
2nd: 49 Oakland (28) vs. Houston (21), Dec. 22, 1963
48 Green Bay (41) vs. Detroit (7), Oct. 7, 1945
47 St. Louis (27) vs. Philadelphia (20), Dec. 13, 1964
3rd: 48 Los Angeles (41) vs. Detroit (7), Oct. 29, 1950
42 Washington (28) vs. Philadelphia (14), Oct. 1, 1955
41 Green Bay (21) vs. N.Y. Yanks (20), Oct. 8, 1950

4th: 42 Chi. Cardinals (28) vs. Philadelphia (14), Dec. 7, 1947
Green Bay (28) vs. Chi. Bears (14), Nov. 6, 1955
N.Y. Jets (28) vs. Boston (14), Oct. 27, 1968
Pittsburgh (21) vs. Cleveland (21), Oct. 18, 1969
41 Baltimore (27) vs. New England (14), Sept. 18, 1978
New England (27) vs. Baltimore (14), Nov. 23, 1980
40 Chicago (21) vs. Tampa Bay (19), Nov. 19, 1989

Most Consecutive Games Scoring
306 San Francisco, 1977-96 (current)
274 Cleveland, 1950-71
218 Dallas, 1970-85

TOUCHDOWNS

Most Seasons Leading League, Touchdowns
13 Chi. Bears, 1932, 1934-35, 1939, 1941-44, 1946-48, 1956, 1965
7 Dallas, 1966, 1968, 1971, 1973, 1977-78, 1980
San Francisco, 1953, 1970, 1987, 1992-95
6 Oakland, 1967-69, 1972, 1974, 1977
San Diego, 1963, 1965, 1979, 1981-82, 1985
Green Bay, 1932, 1937-38, 1961-62, 1996

Most Consecutive Seasons Leading League, Touchdowns
4 Chi. Bears, 1941-44
Los Angeles, 1949-52
San Francisco, 1992-95
3 Chi. Bears, 1946-48
Baltimore, 1957-59
Oakland, 1967-69
2 By many teams

Most Touchdowns, Season
70 Miami, 1984
66 Houston, 1961
San Francisco, 1994
64 Los Angeles, 1950

Fewest Touchdowns, Season (Since 1932)
3 Cincinnati, 1933
4 Cincinnati/St. Louis, 1934
5 Detroit, 1942

Most Touchdowns, Game
10 Philadelphia vs. Cincinnati, Nov. 6, 1934
Los Angeles vs. Baltimore, Oct. 22, 1950
Washington vs. N.Y. Giants, Nov. 27, 1966
9 Chi. Cardinals vs. Rochester, Oct. 7, 1923
Chi. Cardinals vs. N.Y. Giants, Oct. 17, 1948
Chi. Cardinals vs. N.Y. Bulldogs, Nov. 13, 1949
Los Angeles vs. Detroit, Oct. 29, 1950
Pittsburgh vs. N.Y. Giants, Nov. 30, 1952
Chicago vs. San Francisco, Dec. 12, 1965
Chicago vs. Green Bay, Dec. 7, 1980
8 By many teams.

Most Touchdowns, Both Teams, Game
16 Washington (10) vs. N.Y. Giants (6), Nov. 27, 1966
14 Chi. Cardinals (9) vs. N.Y. Giants (5), Oct. 17, 1948
Los Angeles (10) vs. Baltimore (4), Oct. 22, 1950
Houston (7) vs. Oakland (7), Dec. 22, 1963
13 New Orleans (7) vs. St. Louis (6), Nov. 2, 1969
Kansas City (7) vs. Seattle (6), Nov. 27, 1983 (OT)
San Diego (8) vs. Pittsburgh (5), Dec. 8, 1985
N.Y. Jets (7) vs. Miami (6), Sept. 21, 1986 (OT)

Most Consecutive Games Scoring Touchdowns
166 Cleveland, 1957-69
97 Oakland, 1966-73
96 Kansas City, 1963-70

POINTS AFTER TOUCHDOWN
Most (One-Point) Points After Touchdown, Season
66 Miami, 1984
65 Houston, 1961
62 Washington, 1983

Fewest (One-Point) Points After Touchdown, Season
2 Chi. Cardinals, 1933
3 Cincinnati, 1933
Pittsburgh, 1934
4 Cincinnati/St. Louis, 1934

Most (One-Point) Points After Touchdown, Game
10 Los Angeles vs. Baltimore, Oct. 22, 1950
9 Chi. Cardinals vs. N.Y. Giants, Oct. 17, 1948
Pittsburgh vs. N.Y. Giants, Nov. 30, 1952
Washington vs. N.Y. Giants, Nov. 27, 1966
8 By many teams

Most (One-Point) Points After Touchdown, Both Teams, Game
14 Chi. Cardinals (9) vs. N.Y. Giants (5), Oct. 17, 1948
Houston (7) vs. Oakland (7), Dec. 22, 1963
Washington (9) vs. N.Y. Giants (5), Nov. 27, 1966

13   Los Angeles (10) vs. Baltimore (3), Oct. 22, 1950
12   In many games

Most Two-Point Conversions, Season
6   Miami, 1994
5   Arizona, 1995
    Baltimore, 1996
    Jacksonville, 1996
4   By many teams

Most Two-Point Conversions, Game
3   Baltimore vs. New England, Oct. 6, 1996
2   Denver vs. Oakland, Oct. 1, 1961
    Oakland vs. San Diego, Sept. 30, 1962
    Kansas City vs. Houston, Oct. 24, 1965
    Houston vs. N.Y. Jets, Dec. 6, 1969
    Seattle vs. Kansas City, Oct. 23, 1994
    Tampa Bay vs. San Francisco, Oct. 23, 1994
    Detroit vs. Green Bay, Nov. 6, 1994
    Washington vs. San Francisco, Nov. 6, 1994
    Carolina vs. New Orleans, Nov. 26, 1995
    Miami vs. Indianapolis, Nov. 26, 1995
    New England vs. Baltimore, Oct. 6, 1996
    Minnesota vs. Seattle, Nov. 10, 1996

Most Two-Point Conversions, Both Teams, Game
5   Baltimore (3) vs. New England (2), Oct. 6, 1996
3   Seattle (2) vs. Kansas City (1), Oct. 23, 1994
    Minnesota (2) vs. Seattle (1), Nov. 10, 1996
2   In many games

FIELD GOALS

Most Seasons Leading League, Field Goals
11   Green Bay, 1935-36, 1940-43, 1946-47, 1955, 1972, 1974
8   Washington, 1945, 1956, 1971, 1976-77, 1979, 1982, 1992
7   N.Y. Giants, 1933, 1937, 1939, 1941, 1944, 1959, 1983

Most Consecutive Seasons Leading League, Field Goals
4   Green Bay, 1940-43
3   Cleveland, 1952-54
2   By many teams

Most Field Goals Attempted, Season
49   Los Angeles, 1966
    Washington, 1971
48   Green Bay, 1972
47   N.Y. Jets, 1969
    Los Angeles, 1973
    Washington, 1983

Fewest Field Goals Attempted, Season (Since 1938)
0   Chi. Bears, 1944
2   Cleveland, 1939
    Card-Pitt, 1944
    Boston, 1946
    Chi. Bears, 1947
3   Chi. Bears, 1945
    Cleveland, 1945

Most Field Goals Attempted, Game
9   St. Louis vs. Pittsburgh, Sept. 24, 1967
8   Pittsburgh vs. St. Louis, Dec. 2, 1962
    Detroit vs. Minnesota, Nov. 13, 1966
    N.Y. Jets vs. Buffalo, Nov. 3, 1968
7   By many teams

Most Field Goals Attempted, Both Teams, Game
11   St. Louis (6) vs. Pittsburgh (5), Nov. 13, 1966
    Washington (6) vs. Chicago (5), Nov. 14, 1971
    Green Bay (6) vs. Detroit (5), Sept. 29, 1974
    Washington (6) vs. N.Y. Giants (5), Nov. 14, 1976
10   In many games

Most Field Goals, Season
37   Carolina, 1996
36   Indianapolis, 1996
35   N.Y. Giants, 1983
    L.A. Raiders, 1993

Fewest Field Goals, Season (Since 1932)
0   Boston, 1932, 1935
    Chi. Cardinals, 1932, 1945
    Green Bay, 1932, 1944
    N.Y. Giants, 1932
    Brooklyn, 1944
    Card-Pitt, 1944
    Chi. Bears, 1944, 1947
    Boston, 1946
    Baltimore, 1950
    Dallas, 1952

Most Field Goals, Game
7   St. Louis vs. Pittsburgh, Sept. 24, 1967
    Minnesota vs. L.A. Rams, Nov. 5, 1989 (OT)

    Dallas vs. Green Bay, Nov. 18, 1996
6   Boston vs. Denver, Oct. 4, 1964
    Detroit vs. Minnesota, Nov. 13, 1966
    N.Y. Jets vs. Buffalo, Nov. 3, 1968
    Philadelphia vs. Houston, Nov. 12, 1972
    N.Y. Jets vs. New Orleans, Dec. 3, 1972
    St. Louis vs. Atlanta, Dec. 9, 1973
    N.Y. Giants vs. Seattle, Oct. 18, 1981
    San Francisco vs. New Orleans, Oct. 16, 1983
    Pittsburgh vs. Denver, Oct. 23, 1988
    San Diego vs. Seattle, Sept. 5, 1993
    San Diego vs. Houston, Sept. 19, 1993
    Cincinnati vs. Seattle, Nov. 6, 1994
    Atlanta vs. New Orleans, Nov. 13, 1994
    San Francisco vs. Atlanta, Sept. 29, 1996
    Buffalo vs. N.Y. Jets, Oct. 20, 1996
5   By many teams

Most Field Goals, Both Teams, Game
9   San Diego (5) vs. Kansas City (4), Sept. 29, 1996
8   Cleveland (4) vs. St. Louis (4), Sept. 20, 1964
    Chicago (5) vs. Philadelphia (3), Oct. 20, 1968
    Washington (5) vs. Chicago (3), Nov. 14, 1971
    Kansas City (5) vs. Buffalo (3), Dec. 19, 1971
    Detroit (4) vs. Green Bay (4), Sept. 29, 1974
    Cleveland (5) vs. Denver (3), Oct. 19, 1975
    New England (4) vs. San Diego (4), Nov. 9, 1975
    San Francisco (6) vs. New Orleans (2), Oct. 16, 1983
    Seattle (5) vs. L.A. Raiders (3), Dec. 18, 1988
    Atlanta (6) vs. New Orleans (2), Nov. 13, 1994
    Indianapolis (4) vs. San Diego (4), Nov. 3, 1996
7   In many games

Most Consecutive Games Scoring Field Goals
31   Minnesota, 1968-70
28   Washington, 1988-90
22   San Francisco, 1988-89

SAFETIES

Most Safeties, Season
4   Cleveland, 1927
    Detroit, 1962
    Seattle, 1993
    San Francisco, 1996
3   By many teams

Most Safeties, Game
3   L.A. Rams vs. N.Y. Giants, Sept. 30, 1984
2   N.Y. Giants vs. Pottsville, Oct. 30, 1927
    Chi. Bears vs. Pottsville, Nov. 13, 1927
    Detroit vs. Brooklyn, Dec. 1, 1935
    N.Y. Giants vs. Pittsburgh, Sept. 17, 1950
    N.Y. Giants vs. Washington, Nov. 5, 1961
    Chicago vs. Pittsburgh, Nov. 9, 1969
    Dallas vs. Philadelphia, Nov. 19, 1972
    Los Angeles vs. Green Bay, Oct. 21, 1973
    Oakland vs. San Diego, Oct. 26, 1975
    Denver vs. Seattle, Jan. 2, 1983
    New Orleans vs. Cleveland, Sept. 13, 1987
    Buffalo vs. Denver, Nov. 8, 1987
    San Francisco vs. St. Louis, Sept. 8, 1996

Most Safeties, Both Teams, Game
3   L.A. Rams (3) vs. N.Y. Giants (0), Sept. 30, 1984
2   Chi. Cardinals (1) vs. Frankford (1), Nov. 19, 1927
    Chi. Cardinals (1) vs. Cincinnati (1), Nov. 12, 1933
    Chi. Bears (1) vs. San Francisco (1), Oct. 19, 1952
    Cincinnati (1) vs. Los Angeles (1), Oct. 22, 1972
    Chi. Bears (1) vs. San Francisco (1), Sept. 19, 1976
    Baltimore (1) vs. Miami (1), Oct. 29, 1978
    Atlanta (1) vs. Detroit (1), Oct. 5, 1980
    Houston (1) vs. Philadelphia (1), Oct. 2, 1988
    Cleveland (1) vs. Seattle (1), Nov. 14, 1993
    Arizona (1) vs. Houston (1), Dec. 4, 1994
    (Also see previous record)

FIRST DOWNS

Most Seasons Leading League
9   Chi. Bears, 1935, 1939, 1941, 1943, 1945, 1947-49, 1955
7   San Diego, 1965, 1969, 1980-83, 1985
6   L.A. Rams, 1946, 1950-51, 1954, 1957, 1973

Most Consecutive Seasons Leading League
4   San Diego, 1980-83
3   Chi. Bears, 1947-49
2   By many teams

Most First Downs, Season
387   Miami, 1984

380 San Diego, 1985
379 San Diego, 1981

Fewest First Downs, Season
51 Cincinnati, 1933
64 Pittsburgh, 1935
67 Philadelphia, 1937

Most First Downs, Game
39 N.Y. Jets vs. Miami, Nov. 27, 1988
 Washington vs. Detroit, Nov. 4, 1990 (OT)
38 Los Angeles vs. N.Y. Giants, Nov. 13, 1966
37 Green Bay vs. Philadelphia, Nov. 11, 1962

Fewest First Downs, Game
0 N.Y. Giants vs. Green Bay, Oct. 1, 1933
 Pittsburgh vs. Boston, Oct. 29, 1933
 Philadelphia vs. Detroit, Sept. 20, 1935
 N.Y. Giants vs. Washington, Sept. 27, 1942
 Denver vs. Houston, Sept. 3, 1966

Most First Downs, Both Teams, Game
62 San Diego (32) vs. Seattle (30), Sept. 15, 1985
59 Miami (31) vs. Buffalo (28), Oct. 9, 1983 (OT)
 Seattle (33) vs. Kansas City (26), Nov. 27, 1983 (OT)
 N.Y. Jets (32) vs. Miami (27), Sept. 21, 1986 (OT)
 N.Y. Jets (39) vs. Miami (20), Nov. 27, 1988
58 Los Angeles (30) vs. Chi. Bears (28), Oct. 24, 1954
 Denver (34) vs. Kansas City (24), Nov. 18, 1974
 Atlanta (35) vs. New Orleans (23), Sept. 2, 1979 (OT)
 Pittsburgh (36) vs. Cleveland (22), Nov. 25, 1979 (OT)
 San Diego (34) vs. Miami (24), Nov. 18, 1984 (OT)
 Cincinnati (32) vs. San Diego (26), Sept. 22, 1985

Fewest First Downs, Both Teams, Game
7 Chi. Cardinals (2) vs. Detroit (5), Sept. 15, 1940
9 Pittsburgh (1) vs. Boston (8), Oct. 27, 1935
 Boston (4) vs. Brooklyn (5), Nov. 24, 1935
 N.Y. Giants (3) vs. Detroit (6), Nov. 7, 1943
 Pittsburgh (4) vs. Chi. Cardinals (5), Nov. 11, 1945
 N.Y. Bulldogs (1) vs. Philadelphia (8), Sept. 22, 1949
10 N.Y. Giants (4) vs. Washington (6), Dec. 11, 1960

Most First Downs, Rushing, Season
181 New England, 1978
177 Los Angeles, 1973
176 Chicago, 1985

Fewest First Downs, Rushing, Season
36 Cleveland, 1942
 Boston, 1944
39 Brooklyn, 1943
40 Philadelphia, 1940
 Detroit, 1945

Most First Downs, Rushing, Game
25 Philadelphia vs. Washington, Dec. 2, 1951
23 St. Louis vs. New Orleans, Oct. 5, 1980
21 Cleveland vs. Philadelphia, Dec. 13, 1959
 Green Bay vs. Philadelphia, Nov. 11, 1962
 Los Angeles vs. New Orleans, Nov. 25, 1973
 Pittsburgh vs. Kansas City, Nov. 7, 1976
 New England vs. Denver, Nov. 28, 1976
 Oakland vs. Green Bay, Sept. 17, 1978
 Buffalo vs. Washington, Nov. 3, 1996

Fewest First Downs, Rushing, Game
0 By many teams. Last time: Minnesota vs. Chicago, Oct. 28, 1996

Most First Downs, Rushing, Both Teams, Game
36 Philadelphia (25) vs. Washington (11), Dec. 2, 1951
31 Detroit (18) vs. Washington (13), Sept. 30, 1951
30 Los Angeles (17) vs. Minnesota (13), Nov. 5, 1961
 New Orleans (17) vs. Green Bay (13), Sept. 9, 1979
 New Orleans (16) vs. San Francisco (14), Nov. 11, 1979
 New England (16) vs. Kansas City (14), Oct. 4, 1981

Fewest First Downs, Rushing, Both Teams, Game
2 Houston (0) vs. Denver (2), Dec. 2, 1962
 N.Y. Jets, (1) vs. St. Louis (1), Dec. 3, 1995
3 Philadelphia (1) vs. Pittsburgh (2), Oct. 27, 1957
 Boston (1) vs. Buffalo (2), Nov. 15, 1964
 Los Angeles (0) vs. San Francisco (3), Dec. 6, 1964
 Pittsburgh (1) vs. St. Louis (2), Nov. 13, 1966
 Seattle (1) vs. New Orleans (2), Sept. 1, 1991
 New Orleans (0) vs. N.Y. Jets (3), Dec. 24, 1995
 Philadelphia (1) vs. Carolina (2), Oct. 27, 1996
4 In many games

Most First Downs, Passing, Season
259 San Diego, 1985
251 Houston, 1990
250 Miami, 1986

Fewest First Downs, Passing, Season
18 Pittsburgh, 1941

23 Brooklyn, 1942
 N.Y. Giants, 1944
24 N.Y. Giants, 1943

Most First Downs, Passing, Game
29 N.Y. Giants vs. Cincinnati, Oct. 13, 1985
27 San Diego vs. Seattle, Sept. 15, 1985
26 Miami vs. Cleveland, Dec. 12, 1988

Fewest First Downs, Passing, Game
0 By many teams. Last time: Houston vs. Kansas City, Oct. 9, 1988

Most First Downs, Passing, Both Teams, Game
43 San Diego (23) vs. Cincinnati (20), Dec. 20, 1982
 Miami (24) vs. N.Y. Jets (19), Sept. 21, 1986 (OT)
42 San Francisco (22) vs. San Diego (20), Dec. 11, 1982
41 San Diego (27) vs. Seattle (14), Sept. 15, 1985
 Miami (26) vs. Cleveland (15), Dec. 12, 1988

Fewest First Downs, Passing, Both Teams, Game
0 Brooklyn vs. Pittsburgh, Nov. 29, 1942
1 Green Bay (0) vs. Cleveland (1), Sept. 21, 1941
 Pittsburgh (0) vs. Brooklyn (1), Oct. 11, 1942
 N.Y. Giants (0) vs. Detroit (1), Nov. 7, 1943
 Pittsburgh (0) vs. Chi. Cardinals (1), Nov. 11, 1945
 N.Y. Bulldogs (0) vs. Philadelphia (1), Sept. 22, 1949
 Chicago (0) vs. Buffalo (1), Oct. 7, 1979
2 In many games

Most First Downs, Penalty, Season
43 Denver, 1994
42 Chicago, 1987
41 Denver, 1986

Fewest First Downs, Penalty, Season
2 Brooklyn, 1940
4 Chi. Cardinals, 1940
 N.Y. Giants, 1942, 1944
 Washington, 1944
 Cleveland, 1952
 Kansas City, 1969
5 Brooklyn, 1939
 Chi. Bears, 1939
 Detroit, 1953
 Los Angeles, 1953
 Houston, 1982

Most First Downs, Penalty, Game
11 Denver vs. Houston, Oct. 6, 1985
9 Chi. Bears vs. Cleveland, Nov. 25, 1951
 Baltimore vs. Pittsburgh, Oct. 30, 1977
 N.Y. Jets vs. Houston, Sept. 18, 1988
8 Philadelphia vs. Detroit, Dec. 2, 1979
 Cincinnati vs. N.Y. Jets, Oct. 6, 1985
 Buffalo vs. Houston, Sept. 20, 1987
 Houston vs. Atlanta, Sept. 9, 1990
 Kansas City vs. L.A. Raiders, Oct. 3, 1993

Most First Downs, Penalty, Both Teams, Game
11 Chi. Bears (9) vs. Cleveland (2), Nov. 25, 1951
 Cincinnati (8) vs. N.Y. Jets (3), Oct. 6, 1985
 Denver (11) vs. Houston (0), Oct. 6, 1985
 Detroit (6) vs. Dallas (5), Nov. 8, 1987
 N.Y. Jets (9) vs. Houston (2), Sept. 18, 1988
 Kansas City (8) vs. L.A. Raiders (3), Oct. 3, 1993
 Detroit (6) vs. San Diego (5), Nov. 11, 1996
10 In many games

NET YARDS GAINED RUSHING AND PASSING
Most Seasons Leading League
12 Chi. Bears, 1932, 1934-35, 1939, 1941-44, 1947, 1949, 1955-56
7 San Diego, 1963, 1965, 1980-83, 1985
6 L.A. Rams, 1946, 1950-51, 1954, 1957, 1973
 Baltimore, 1958-60, 1964, 1967, 1976
 Dall. Cowboys, 1966, 1968-69, 1971, 1974, 1977

Most Consecutive Seasons Leading League
4 Chi. Bears, 1941-44
 San Diego, 1980-83
3 Baltimore, 1958-60
 Houston, 1960-62
 Oakland, 1968-70
2 By many teams

Most Yards Gained, Season
6,936 Miami, 1984
6,744 San Diego, 1981
6,535 San Diego, 1985

Fewest Yards Gained, Season
1,150 Cincinnati, 1933
1,443 Chi. Cardinals, 1934
1,486 Chi. Cardinals, 1933

Most Yards Gained, Game

735 Los Angeles vs. N.Y. Yanks, Sept. 28, 1951
683 Pittsburgh vs. Chi. Cardinals, Dec. 13, 1958
682 Chi. Bears vs. N.Y. Giants, Nov. 14, 1943

Fewest Yards Gained, Game

–7 Seattle vs. Los Angeles, Nov. 4, 1979
–5 Denver vs. Oakland, Sept. 10, 1967
14 Chi. Cardinals vs. Detroit, Sept. 15, 1940

Most Yards Gained, Both Teams, Game

1,133 Los Angeles (636) vs. N.Y. Yanks (497), Nov. 19, 1950
1,102 San Diego (661) vs. Cincinnati (441), Dec. 20, 1982
1,087 St. Louis (589) vs. Philadelphia (498), Dec. 16, 1962

Fewest Yards Gained, Both Teams, Game

30 Chi. Cardinals (14) vs. Detroit (16), Sept. 15, 1940
136 Chi. Cardinals (50) vs. Green Bay (86), Nov. 18, 1934
154 N.Y. Giants (51) vs. Washington (103), Dec. 11, 1960

Most Consecutive Games, 400 or More Yards Gained

11 San Diego, 1982-83
6 Houston, 1961-62
San Diego, 1981
San Francisco, 1987
5 Chi. Bears, 1947
Philadelphia, 1953
Chi. Bears, 1955
Oakland, 1968
New England, 1981
Cincinnati, 1986
San Francisco, 1994

Most Consecutive Games, 300 or More Yards Gained

29 Los Angeles, 1949-51
26 Miami, 1983-85
25 Miami, 1993-95

RUSHING

Most Seasons Leading League

16 Chi. Bears, 1932, 1934-35, 1939-42, 1951, 1955-56, 1968, 1977, 1983-86
7 Buffalo, 1962, 1964, 1973, 1975, 1982, 1991-92
6 Cleveland, 1958-59, 1963, 1965-67

Most Consecutive Seasons Leading League

4 Chi. Bears, 1939-42
Chi. Bears, 1983-86
3 Detroit, 1936-38
San Francisco, 1952-54
Cleveland, 1965-67
2 By many teams

ATTEMPTS

Most Rushing Attempts, Season

681 Oakland, 1977
674 Chicago, 1984
671 New England, 1978

Fewest Rushing Attempts, Season

211 Philadelphia, 1982
219 San Francisco, 1982
225 Houston, 1982

Most Rushing Attempts, Game

72 Chi. Bears vs. Brooklyn, Oct. 20, 1935
70 Chi. Cardinals vs. Green Bay, Dec. 5, 1948
69 Chi. Cardinals vs. Green Bay, Dec. 6, 1936
Kansas City vs. Cincinnati, Sept. 3, 1978

Fewest Rushing Attempts, Game

6 Chi. Cardinals vs. Boston, Oct. 29, 1933
7 Oakland vs. Buffalo, Oct. 15, 1963
Houston vs. N.Y. Giants, Dec. 8, 1985
Seattle vs. L.A. Raiders, Nov. 17, 1991
Green Bay vs. Miami, Sept. 11, 1994
8 Denver vs. Oakland, Dec. 17, 1960
Buffalo vs. St. Louis, Sept. 9, 1984
Detroit vs. San Francisco, Oct. 20, 1991
Atlanta vs. Detroit, Sept. 5, 1993

Most Rushing Attempts, Both Teams, Game

108 Chi. Cardinals (70) vs. Green Bay (38), Dec. 5, 1948
105 Oakland (62) vs. Atlanta (43), Nov. 30, 1975 (OT)
104 Chi. Bears (64) vs. Pittsburgh (40), Oct. 18, 1936

Fewest Rushing Attempts, Both Teams, Game

34 Atlanta (12) vs. Houston (22), Dec. 5, 1993
Atlanta (15) vs. San Francisco (19), Dec. 24, 1995
35 Seattle (15) vs. New Orleans (20), Sept. 1, 1991
36 Houston (15) vs. N.Y. Jets (21), Oct. 13, 1991

YARDS GAINED

Most Yards Gained Rushing, Season

3,165 New England, 1978
3,088 Buffalo, 1973
2,986 Kansas City, 1978

Fewest Yards Gained Rushing, Season

298 Philadelphia, 1940
467 Detroit, 1946
471 Boston, 1944

Most Yards Gained Rushing, Game

426 Detroit vs. Pittsburgh, Nov. 4, 1934
423 N.Y. Giants vs. Baltimore, Nov. 19, 1950
420 Boston vs. N.Y. Giants, Oct. 8, 1933

Fewest Yards Gained Rushing, Game

–53 Detroit vs. Chi. Cardinals, Oct. 17, 1943
–36 Philadelphia vs. Chi. Bears, Nov. 19, 1939
–33 Phil-Pitt vs. Brooklyn, Oct. 2, 1943

Most Yards Gained Rushing, Both Teams, Game

595 Los Angeles (371) vs. N.Y. Yanks (224), Nov. 18, 1951
574 Chi. Bears (396) vs. Pittsburgh (178), Oct. 10, 1934
558 Boston (420) vs. N.Y. Giants (138), Oct. 8, 1933

Fewest Yards Gained Rushing, Both Teams, Game

–15 Detroit (–53) vs. Chi. Cardinals (38), Oct. 17, 1943
4 Detroit (–10) vs. Chi. Cardinals (14), Sept. 15, 1940
62 L.A. Rams (15) vs. San Francisco (47), Dec. 6, 1964

AVERAGE GAIN

Highest Average Gain, Rushing, Season

5.74 Cleveland, 1963
5.65 San Francisco, 1954
5.56 San Diego, 1963

Lowest Average Gain, Rushing, Season

0.94 Philadelphia, 1940
1.45 Boston, 1944
1.55 Pittsburgh, 1935

TOUCHDOWNS

Most Touchdowns, Rushing, Season

36 Green Bay, 1962
33 Pittsburgh, 1976
30 Chi. Bears, 1941
New England, 1978
Washington, 1983

Fewest Touchdowns, Rushing, Season

1 Brooklyn, 1934
2 Chi. Cardinals, 1933
Cincinnati, 1933
Pittsburgh, 1934
Philadelphia, 1935
Philadelphia, 1936
Philadelphia, 1937
Philadelphia, 1938
Pittsburgh, 1940
Philadelphia, 1972
N.Y. Jets, 1995
3 By many teams

Most Touchdowns, Rushing, Game

7 Los Angeles vs. Atlanta, Dec. 4, 1976
6 By many teams

Most Touchdowns, Rushing, Both Teams, Game

8 Los Angeles (6) vs. N.Y. Yanks (2), Nov. 18, 1951
Chi. Bears (5) vs. Green Bay (3), Nov. 6, 1955
Cleveland (6) vs. Los Angeles (2), Nov. 24, 1957
7 In many games

PASSING
ATTEMPTS

Most Passes Attempted, Season

709 Minnesota, 1981
699 New England, 1994
686 New England, 1995

Fewest Passes Attempted, Season

102 Cincinnati, 1933
106 Boston, 1933
120 Detroit, 1937

Most Passes Attempted, Game

70 New England vs. Minnesota, Nov. 13, 1994
68 Houston vs. Buffalo, Nov 1, 1964
66 Atlanta vs. Detroit, Dec. 24, 1989

Fewest Passes Attempted, Game

0 Green Bay vs. Portsmouth, Oct. 8, 1933
Detroit vs. Cleveland, Sept. 10, 1937

Pittsburgh vs. Brooklyn, Nov. 16, 1941
Pittsburgh vs. Los Angeles, Nov. 13, 1949
Cleveland vs. Philadelphia, Dec. 3, 1950

Most Passes Attempted, Both Teams, Game
- 112 New England (70) vs. Minnesota (42), Nov. 13, 1994
- 104 Miami (55) vs. N.Y. Jets (49), Oct. 18, 1987 (OT)
- 102 San Francisco (57) vs. Atlanta (45), Oct. 6, 1985

Fewest Passes Attempted, Both Teams, Game
- 4 Chi. Cardinals (1) vs. Detroit (3), Nov. 3, 1935
  Detroit (0) vs. Cleveland (4), Sept. 10, 1937
- 6 Chi. Cardinals (2) vs. Detroit (4), Sept. 15, 1940
- 8 Brooklyn (2) vs. Philadelphia (6), Oct. 1, 1939

COMPLETIONS

Most Passes Completed, Season
- 432 San Francisco, 1995
- 411 Houston, 1991
- 409 Minnesota, 1994

Fewest Passes Completed, Season
- 25 Cincinnati, 1933
- 33 Boston, 1933
- 34 Chi. Cardinals, 1934
  Detroit, 1934

Most Passes Completed, Game
- 45 New England vs. Minnesota, Nov. 13, 1994 (OT)
- 42 N.Y. Jets vs. San Francisco, Sept. 21, 1980
- 41 Houston vs. Dallas, Nov. 10, 1991 (OT)

Fewest Passes Completed, Game
- 0 By many teams. Last time: Buffalo vs. N.Y. Jets, Sept. 29, 1974

Most Passes Completed, Both Teams, Game
- 71 New England (45) vs. Minnesota (26), Nov. 13, 1994
- 68 San Francisco (37) vs. Atlanta (31), Oct. 6, 1985
- 66 Cincinnati (40) vs. San Diego (26), Dec. 20, 1982

Fewest Passes Completed, Both Teams, Game
- 1 Chi. Cardinals (0) vs. Philadelphia (1), Nov. 8, 1936
  Detroit (0) vs. Cleveland (1), Sept. 10, 1937
  Chi. Cardinals (0) vs. Detroit (1), Sept. 15, 1940
  Brooklyn (0) vs. Pittsburgh (1), Nov. 29, 1942
- 2 Chi. Cardinals (0) vs. Detroit (2), Nov. 3, 1935
  Buffalo (0) vs. N.Y. Jets (2), Sept. 29, 1974
  Chi. Cardinals (0) vs. Green Bay (2), Nov. 18, 1934
- 3 In seven games

YARDS GAINED

Most Seasons Leading League, Passing Yardage
- 10 San Diego, 1965, 1968, 1971, 1978-83, 1985
- 8 Chi. Bears, 1932, 1939, 1941, 1943, 1945, 1949, 1954, 1964
  Washington, 1938, 1940, 1944, 1947-48, 1967, 1974, 1989
- 7 Houston, 1960-61, 1963-64, 1990-92

Most Consecutive Seasons Leading League, Passing Yardage
- 6 San Diego, 1978-83
- 4 Green Bay, 1934-37
- 3 Miami, 1986-88
  Houston, 1990-92

Most Yards Gained, Passing, Season
- 5,018 Miami, 1984
- 4,870 San Diego, 1985
- 4,805 Houston, 1990

Fewest Yards Gained, Passing, Season
- 302 Chi. Cardinals, 1934
- 357 Cincinnati, 1933
- 459 Boston, 1934

Most Yards Gained, Passing, Game
- 554 Los Angeles vs. N.Y. Yanks, Sept. 28, 1951
- 530 Minnesota vs. Baltimore, Sept. 28, 1969
- 521 Miami vs. N.Y. Jets, Oct. 23, 1988

Fewest Yards Gained, Passing, Game
- –53 Denver vs. Oakland, Sept. 10, 1967
- –52 Cincinnati vs. Houston, Oct. 31, 1971
- –39 Atlanta vs. San Francisco, Oct. 23, 1976

Most Yards Gained, Passing, Both Teams, Game
- 884 N.Y. Jets (449) vs. Miami (435), Sept. 21, 1986 (OT)
- 883 San Diego (486) vs. Cincinnati (397), Dec. 20, 1982
- 874 Miami (456) vs. New England (418), Sept. 4, 1994

Fewest Yards Gained, Passing, Both Teams, Game
- –11 Green Bay (–10) vs. Dallas (–1), Oct. 24, 1965
- 1 Chi. Cardinals (0) vs. Philadelphia (1), Nov. 8, 1936
- 7 Brooklyn (0) vs. Pittsburgh (7), Nov. 29, 1942

TIMES SACKED

Most Seasons Leading League, Fewest Times Sacked
- 10 Miami, 1973, 1982-90

- 4 San Diego, 1963-64, 1967-68
  San Francisco, 1964-65, 1970-71
  N.Y. Jets, 1965-66, 1968, 1993
- 3 Houston, 1961-62, 1978
  St. Louis, 1974-76
  Washington, 1966-67, 1991

Most Consecutive Seasons Leading League, Fewest Times Sacked
- 9 Miami, 1982-90
- 3 St. Louis, 1974-76
- 2 By many teams

Most Times Sacked, Season
- 104 Philadelphia, 1986
- 72 Philadelphia, 1987
- 70 Atlanta, 1968

Fewest Times Sacked, Season
- 7 Miami, 1988
- 8 San Francisco, 1970
  St. Louis, 1975
- 9 N.Y. Jets, 1966
  Washington, 1991

Most Times Sacked, Game
- 12 Pittsburgh vs. Dallas, Nov. 20, 1966
  Baltimore vs. St. Louis, Oct. 26, 1980
  Detroit vs. Chicago, Dec. 16, 1984
  Houston vs. Dallas, Sept. 29, 1985
- 11 St. Louis vs. N.Y. Giants, Nov. 1, 1964
  Los Angeles vs. Baltimore, Nov. 22, 1964
  Denver vs. Buffalo, Dec. 13, 1964
  Green Bay vs. Detroit, Nov. 7, 1965
  Buffalo vs. Oakland, Oct. 15, 1967
  Denver vs. Oakland, Nov. 5, 1967
  Atlanta vs. St. Louis, Nov. 24, 1968
  Detroit vs. Dallas, Oct. 6, 1975
  Philadelphia vs. St. Louis, Dec. 18, 1983
  Cleveland vs. Kansas City, Sept. 30, 1984
  Minnesota vs. Chicago, Oct. 28, 1984
  Atlanta vs. Cleveland, Nov. 18, 1984
  Dallas vs. San Diego, Nov. 16, 1986
  Philadelphia vs. Detroit, Nov. 16, 1986
  Philadelphia vs. L.A. Raiders, Nov. 30, 1986 (OT)
  L.A. Raiders vs. Seattle, Dec. 8, 1986
  N.Y. Jets vs. Dallas, Oct. 4, 1987
  Philadelphia vs. Chicago, Oct. 4, 1987
  Dallas vs. Philadelphia, Sept. 15, 1991
  Cleveland vs. Indianapolis, Sept. 6, 1992
- 10 By many teams

Most Times Sacked, Both Teams, Game
- 18 Green Bay (10) vs. San Diego (8), Sept. 24, 1978
- 17 Buffalo (10) vs. N.Y. Titans (7), Nov. 23, 1961
  Pittsburgh (12) vs. Dallas (5), Nov. 20, 1966
  Atlanta (9) vs. Philadelphia (8), Dec. 16, 1984
  Philadelphia (11) vs. L.A. Raiders (6), Nov. 30, 1986 (OT)
- 16 Los Angeles (11) vs. Baltimore (5), Nov. 22, 1964
  Buffalo (11) vs. Oakland (5), Oct. 15, 1967

COMPLETION PERCENTAGE

Most Seasons Leading League, Completion Percentage
- 13 San Francisco, 1952, 1957-58, 1965, 1981, 1983, 1987, 1989, 1992-96
- 11 Washington, 1937, 1939-40, 1942-45, 1947-48, 1969-70
- 7 Green Bay, 1936, 1941, 1961-62, 1964, 1966, 1968

Most Consecutive Seasons Leading League, Completion Percentage
- 5 San Francisco, 1992-96
- 4 Washington, 1942-45
  Kansas City, 1966-69
  San Francisco, 1992-95
- 3 Cleveland, 1953-55

Highest Completion Percentage, Season
- 70.65 Cincinnati, 1982 (310-219)
- 70.25 San Francisco, 1994 (511-359)
- 70.19 San Francisco, 1989 (483-339)

Lowest Completion Percentage, Season
- 22.9 Philadelphia, 1936 (170-39)
- 24.5 Cincinnati, 1933 (102-25)
- 25.0 Pittsburgh, 1941 (168-42)

TOUCHDOWNS

Most Touchdowns, Passing, Season
- 49 Miami, 1984
- 48 Houston, 1961
- 46 Miami, 1986

1,000 YARDS RUSHING IN A SEASON

Year	Player, Team	Att.	Yards	Avg.	Long	TD
1996	Barry Sanders, Detroit[8]	307	1,553	5.1	54	11
	Terrell Davis, Denver[2]	345	1,538	4.5	71	13
	Jerome Bettis, Pittsburgh[3]	320	1,431	4.5	50	11
	Ricky Watters, Philadelphia[3]	353	1,411	4.0	56	13
	*Eddie George, Houston	335	1,368	4.1	76	8
	Terry Allen, Washington[4]	347	1,353	3.9	49	21
	Adrian Murrell, N.Y. Jets	301	1,249	4.1	78	6
	Emmitt Smith, Dallas[6]	327	1,204	3.7	42	12
	Curtis Martin, New England[2]	316	1,152	3.6	57	14
	Anthony Johnson, Carolina	300	1,120	3.7	29	6
	*Karim Abdul-Jabbar, Miami	307	1,116	3.6	29	11
	Jamal Anderson, Atlanta	232	1,055	4.5	32	5
	Thurman Thomas, Buffalo[8]	281	1,033	3.7	36	8
1995	Emmitt Smith, Dallas[5]	377	1,773	4.7	60	25
	Barry Sanders, Detroit[7]	314	1,500	4.8	75	11
	*Curtis Martin, New England	368	1,487	4.0	49	14
	Chris Warren, Seattle[4]	310	1,346	4.3	52	15
	Terry Allen, Washington[3]	338	1,309	3.9	28	10
	Ricky Watters, Philadelphia[2]	337	1,273	3.8	57	11
	Errict Rhett, Tampa Bay[2]	332	1,207	3.6	21	11
	Rodney Hampton, N.Y. Giants[5]	306	1,182	3.9	32	10
	*Terrell Davis, Denver	237	1,117	4.7	60	7
	Harvey Williams, Oakland	255	1,114	4.4	60	9
	Craig Heyward, Atlanta	236	1,083	4.6	31	6
	Marshall Faulk, Indianapolis[2]	289	1,078	3.7	40	11
	*Rashaan Salaam, Chicago	296	1,074	3.6	42	10
	Garrison Hearst, Arizona	284	1,070	3.8	38	1
	Edgar Bennett, Green Bay	316	1,067	3.4	23	3
	Thurman Thomas, Buffalo[7]	267	1,005	3.8	49	6
1994	Barry Sanders, Detroit[6]	331	1,883	5.7	85	7
	Chris Warren, Seattle[3]	333	1,545	4.6	41	9
	Emmitt Smith, Dallas[4]	368	1,484	4.0	46	21
	Natrone Means, San Diego	343	1,350	3.9	25	12
	*Marshall Faulk, Indianapolis	314	1,282	4.1	52	11
	Thurman Thomas, Buffalo[6]	287	1,093	3.8	29	7
	Rodney Hampton, N.Y. Giants[4]	327	1,075	3.3	27	6
	Terry Allen, Minnesota[2]	255	1,031	4.0	45	8
	Jerome Bettis, L.A. Rams[2]	319	1,025	3.2	19	3
	*Errict Rhett, Tampa Bay	284	1,011	3.6	27	7
1993	Emmitt Smith, Dallas[3]	283	1,486	5.3	62	9
	*Jerome Bettis, L.A. Rams	294	1,429	4.9	71	7
	Thurman Thomas, Buffalo[5]	355	1,315	3.7	27	6
	Erric Pegram, Atlanta	292	1,185	4.1	29	3
	Barry Sanders, Detroit[5]	243	1,115	4.6	42	3
	Leonard Russell, New England	300	1,088	3.6	21	7
	Rodney Hampton, N.Y. Giants[3]	292	1,077	3.7	20	5
	Chris Warren, Seattle[2]	273	1,072	3.9	45	7
	*Reggie Brooks, Washington	223	1,063	4.8	85	3
	*Ron Moore, Phoenix	263	1,018	3.9	20	9
	Gary Brown, Houston	195	1,002	5.1	26	6
1992	Emmitt Smith, Dallas[2]	373	1,713	4.6	68	18
	Barry Foster, Pittsburgh	390	1,690	4.3	69	11
	Thurman Thomas, Buffalo[4]	312	1,487	4.8	44	9
	Barry Sanders, Detroit[4]	312	1,352	4.3	55	9
	Lorenzo White, Houston	265	1,226	4.6	44	7
	Terry Allen, Minnesota	266	1,201	4.5	51	13
	Reggie Cobb, Tampa Bay	310	1,171	3.8	25	9
	Harold Green, Cincinnati	265	1,170	4.4	53	2
	Rodney Hampton, N.Y. Giants[2]	257	1,141	4.4	63	14
	Cleveland Gary, L.A. Rams	279	1,125	4.0	63	7
	Herschel Walker, Philadelphia[2]	267	1,070	4.0	38	8
	Chris Warren, Seattle	223	1,017	4.6	52	3
	*Ricky Watters, San Francisco	206	1,013	4.9	43	9
1991	Emmitt Smith, Dallas	365	1,563	4.3	75	12
	Barry Sanders, Detroit[3]	342	1,548	4.5	69	16
	Thurman Thomas, Buffalo[3]	288	1,407	4.9	33	7
	Rodney Hampton, N.Y. Giants	256	1,059	4.1	44	10
	Earnest Byner, Washington[3]	274	1,048	3.8	32	5
	Gaston Green, Denver	261	1,037	4.0	63	4
	Christian Okoye, Kansas City[2]	225	1,031	4.6	48	9
1990	Barry Sanders, Detroit[2]	255	1,304	5.1	45	13
	Thurman Thomas, Buffalo[2]	271	1,297	4.8	80	11
	Marion Butts, San Diego	265	1,225	4.6	52	8
	Earnest Byner, Washington[2]	297	1,219	4.1	22	6
	Bobby Humphrey, Denver[2]	288	1,202	4.2	37	7
	Neal Anderson, Chicago[3]	260	1,078	4.1	52	10
	Barry Word, Kansas City	204	1,015	5.0	53	4
	James Brooks, Cincinnati[3]	195	1,004	5.1	56	5
1989	Christian Okoye, Kansas City	370	1,480	4.0	59	12
	*Barry Sanders, Detroit	280	1,470	5.3	34	14
	Eric Dickerson, Indianapolis[7]	314	1,311	4.2	21	7
	Neal Anderson, Chicago[2]	274	1,275	4.7	73	11
	Dalton Hilliard, New Orleans	344	1,262	3.7	40	13
	Thurman Thomas, Buffalo	298	1,244	4.2	38	6
	James Brooks, Cincinnati[2]	221	1,239	5.6	65	7
	*Bobby Humphrey, Denver	294	1,151	3.9	40	7
	Greg Bell, L.A. Rams[3]	272	1,137	4.2	47	15
	Roger Craig, San Francisco[3]	271	1,054	3.9	27	6
	Ottis Anderson, N.Y. Giants[6]	325	1,023	3.1	36	14
1988	Eric Dickerson, Indianapolis[6]	388	1,659	4.3	41	14
	Herschel Walker, Dallas	361	1,514	4.2	38	5
	Roger Craig, San Francisco[2]	310	1,502	4.8	46	9
	Greg Bell, L.A. Rams[2]	288	1,212	4.2	44	16
	*John Stephens, New England	297	1,168	3.9	52	4
	Gary Anderson, San Diego	225	1,119	5.0	36	3
	Neal Anderson, Chicago	249	1,106	4.4	80	12
	Joe Morris, N.Y. Giants[3]	307	1,083	3.5	27	5
	*Ickey Woods, Cincinnati	203	1,066	5.3	56	15
	Curt Warner, Seattle[4]	266	1,025	3.9	29	10
	John Settle, Atlanta	232	1,024	4.4	62	7
	Mike Rozier, Houston	251	1,002	4.0	28	10
1987	Charles White, L.A. Rams	324	1,374	4.2	58	11
	Eric Dickerson, L.A. Rams-Indianapolis[5]	283	1,288	4.6	57	6
1986	Eric Dickerson, L.A. Rams[4]	404	1,821	4.5	42	11
	Joe Morris, N.Y. Giants[2]	341	1,516	4.4	54	14
	Curt Warner, Seattle[3]	319	1,481	4.6	60	13
	*Rueben Mayes, New Orleans	286	1,353	4.7	50	8
	Walter Payton, Chicago[10]	321	1,333	4.2	41	8
	Gerald Riggs, Atlanta[3]	343	1,327	3.9	31	9
	George Rogers, Washington[4]	303	1,203	4.0	42	18
	James Brooks, Cincinnati	205	1,087	5.3	56	5
1985	Marcus Allen, L.A. Raiders[3]	390	1,759	4.6	61	11
	Gerald Riggs, Atlanta[2]	397	1,719	4.3	50	10
	Walter Payton, Chicago[9]	324	1,551	4.8	40	9
	Joe Morris, N.Y. Giants	294	1,336	4.5	65	21
	Freeman McNeil, N.Y. Jets[2]	294	1,331	4.5	69	3
	Tony Dorsett, Dallas[8]	305	1,307	4.3	60	7
	James Wilder, Tampa Bay[2]	365	1,300	3.6	28	10
	Eric Dickerson, L.A. Rams[3]	292	1,234	4.2	43	12
	Craig James, New England	263	1,227	4.7	65	5
	Kevin Mack, Cleveland	222	1,104	5.0	61	7
	Curt Warner, Seattle[2]	291	1,094	3.8	38	8
	George Rogers, Washington[3]	231	1,093	4.7	35	7
	Roger Craig, San Francisco	214	1,050	4.9	62	9
	Earnest Jackson, Philadelphia[2]	282	1,028	3.6	59	5
	Stump Mitchell, St. Louis	183	1,006	5.5	64	7
	Earnest Byner, Cleveland	244	1,002	4.1	36	8
1984	Eric Dickerson, L.A. Rams[2]	379	2,105	5.6	66	14
	Walter Payton, Chicago[8]	381	1,684	4.4	72	11
	James Wilder, Tampa Bay	407	1,544	3.8	37	13
	Gerald Riggs, Atlanta	353	1,486	4.2	57	13
	Wendell Tyler, San Francisco[3]	246	1,262	5.1	40	7
	John Riggins, Washington[5]	327	1,239	3.8	24	14
	Tony Dorsett, Dallas[7]	302	1,189	3.9	31	6
	Earnest Jackson, San Diego	296	1,179	4.0	32	8
	Ottis Anderson, St. Louis[5]	289	1,174	4.1	24	6
	Marcus Allen, L.A. Raiders[2]	275	1,168	4.2	52	13
	Sammy Winder, Denver	296	1,153	3.9	24	4
	*Greg Bell, Buffalo	262	1,100	4.2	85	7
	Freeman McNeil, N.Y. Jets	229	1,070	4.7	53	5
1983	*Eric Dickerson, L.A. Rams	390	1,808	4.6	85	18
	William Andrews, Atlanta[4]	331	1,567	4.7	27	7
	*Curt Warner, Seattle	335	1,449	4.3	60	13
	Walter Payton, Chicago[7]	314	1,421	4.5	49	6
	John Riggins, Washington[4]	375	1,347	3.6	44	24
	Tony Dorsett, Dallas[6]	289	1,321	4.6	77	8
	Earl Campbell, Houston[5]	322	1,301	4.0	42	12
	Ottis Anderson, St. Louis[4]	296	1,270	4.3	43	5
	Mike Pruitt, Cleveland[4]	293	1,184	4.0	27	10
	George Rogers, New Orleans[2]	256	1,144	4.5	76	5
	Joe Cribbs, Buffalo[3]	263	1,131	4.3	45	3
	Curtis Dickey, Baltimore	254	1,122	4.4	56	4
	Tony Collins, New England	219	1,049	4.8	50	10
	Billy Sims, Detroit[3]	220	1,040	4.7	41	7
	Marcus Allen, L.A. Raiders	266	1,014	3.8	19	9
	Franco Harris, Pittsburgh[8]	279	1,007	3.6	19	5
1981	*George Rogers, New Orleans	378	1,674	4.4	79	13
	Tony Dorsett, Dallas[5]	342	1,646	4.8	75	4
	Billy Sims, Detroit[2]	296	1,437	4.9	51	13
	Wilbert Montgomery, Philadelphia[3]	286	1,402	4.9	41	8
	Ottis Anderson, St. Louis[2]	328	1,376	4.2	28	9
	Earl Campbell, Houston[4]	361	1,376	3.8	43	10
	William Andrews, Atlanta[3]	289	1,301	4.5	29	10
	Walter Payton, Chicago[6]	339	1,222	3.6	39	6

409

Year	Player, Team	Att	Yards	Avg	Long	TD
	Chuck Muncie, San Diego[2]	251	1,144	4.6	73	19
	*Joe Delaney, Kansas City	234	1,121	4.8	82	3
	Mike Pruitt, Cleveland[3]	247	1,103	4.5	21	7
	Joe Cribbs, Buffalo[2]	257	1,097	4.3	35	3
	Pete Johnson, Cincinnati	274	1,077	3.9	39	12
	Wendell Tyler, Los Angeles[2]	260	1,074	4.1	69	12
	Ted Brown, Minnesota	274	1,063	3.9	34	6
1980	Earl Campbell, Houston[3]	373	1,934	5.2	55	13
	Walter Payton, Chicago[5]	317	1,460	4.6	69	6
	Ottis Anderson, St. Louis[2]	301	1,352	4.5	52	9
	William Andrews, Atlanta[2]	265	1,308	4.9	33	4
	*Billy Sims, Detroit	313	1,303	4.2	52	13
	Tony Dorsett, Dallas[4]	278	1,185	4.3	56	11
	*Joe Cribbs, Buffalo	306	1,185	3.9	48	11
	Mike Pruitt, Cleveland[2]	249	1,034	4.2	56	6
1979	Earl Campbell, Houston[2]	368	1,697	4.6	61	19
	Walter Payton, Chicago[4]	369	1,610	4.4	43	14
	*Ottis Anderson, St. Louis	331	1,605	4.8	76	8
	Wilbert Montgomery, Philadelphia[2]	338	1,512	4.5	62	9
	Mike Pruitt, Cleveland	264	1,294	4.9	77	9
	Ricky Bell, Tampa Bay	283	1,263	4.5	49	7
	Chuck Muncie, New Orleans	238	1,198	5.0	69	11
	Franco Harris, Pittsburgh[7]	267	1,186	4.4	71	11
	John Riggins, Washington[3]	260	1,153	4.4	66	9
	Wendell Tyler, Los Angeles	218	1,109	5.1	63	9
	Tony Dorsett, Dallas[3]	250	1,107	4.4	41	6
	*William Andrews, Atlanta	239	1,023	4.3	23	3
1978	*Earl Campbell, Houston	302	1,450	4.8	81	13
	Walter Payton, Chicago[3]	333	1,395	4.2	76	11
	Tony Dorsett, Dallas[2]	290	1,325	4.6	63	7
	Delvin Williams, Miami[2]	272	1,258	4.6	58	8
	Wilbert Montgomery, Philadelphia	259	1,220	4.7	47	9
	Terdell Middleton, Green Bay	284	1,116	3.9	76	11
	Franco Harris, Pittsburgh[6]	310	1,082	3.5	37	8
	Mark van Eeghen, Oakland[3]	270	1,080	4.0	34	9
	*Terry Miller, Buffalo	238	1,060	4.5	60	7
	Tony Reed, Kansas City	206	1,053	5.1	62	5
	John Riggins, Washington[2]	248	1,014	4.1	31	5
1977	Walter Payton, Chicago[2]	339	1,852	5.5	73	14
	Mark van Eeghen, Oakland[2]	324	1,273	3.9	27	7
	Lawrence McCutcheon, Los Angeles[4]	294	1,238	4.2	48	7
	Franco Harris, Pittsburgh[5]	300	1,162	3.9	61	11
	Lydell Mitchell, Baltimore[3]	301	1,159	3.9	64	3
	Chuck Foreman, Minnesota[3]	270	1,112	4.1	51	6
	Greg Pruitt, Cleveland[3]	236	1,086	4.6	78	3
	Sam Cunningham, New England	270	1,015	3.8	31	4
	*Tony Dorsett, Dallas	208	1,007	4.8	84	12
1976	O.J. Simpson, Buffalo[5]	290	1,503	5.2	75	8
	Walter Payton, Chicago	311	1,390	4.5	60	13
	Delvin Williams, San Francisco	248	1,203	4.9	80	7
	Lydell Mitchell, Baltimore[2]	289	1,200	4.2	43	5
	Lawrence McCutcheon, Los Angeles[3]	291	1,168	4.0	40	9
	Chuck Foreman, Minnesota[2]	278	1,155	4.2	46	13
	Franco Harris, Pittsburgh[4]	289	1,128	3.9	30	14
	Mike Thomas, Washington	254	1,101	4.3	28	5
	Rocky Bleier, Pittsburgh	220	1,036	4.7	28	5
	Mark van Eeghen, Oakland	233	1,012	4.3	21	3
	Otis Armstrong, Denver[2]	247	1,008	4.1	31	5
	Greg Pruitt, Cleveland[2]	209	1,000	4.8	64	4
1975	O.J. Simpson, Buffalo[4]	329	1,817	5.5	88	16
	Franco Harris, Pittsburgh[3]	262	1,246	4.8	36	10
	Lydell Mitchell, Baltimore	289	1,193	4.1	70	11
	Jim Otis, St. Louis	269	1,076	4.0	30	5
	Chuck Foreman, Minnesota	280	1,070	3.8	31	13
	Greg Pruitt, Cleveland	217	1,067	4.9	50	8
	John Riggins, N.Y. Jets	238	1,005	4.2	42	8
	Dave Hampton, Atlanta	250	1,002	4.0	22	5
1974	Otis Armstrong, Denver	263	1,407	5.3	43	9
	*Don Woods, San Diego	227	1,162	5.1	56	7
	O.J. Simpson, Buffalo[3]	270	1,125	4.2	41	3
	Lawrence McCutcheon, Los Angeles[2]	236	1,109	4.7	23	3
	Franco Harris, Pittsburgh[2]	208	1,006	4.8	54	5
1973	O.J. Simpson, Buffalo[2]	332	2,003	6.0	80	12
	John Brockington, Green Bay[3]	265	1,144	4.3	53	3
	Calvin Hill, Dallas[2]	273	1,142	4.2	21	6
	Lawrence McCutcheon, Los Angeles	210	1,097	5.2	37	2
	Larry Csonka, Miami[3]	219	1,003	4.6	25	5
1972	O.J. Simpson, Buffalo	292	1,251	4.3	94	6
	Larry Brown, Washington[2]	285	1,216	4.3	38	8
	Ron Johnson, N.Y. Giants[2]	298	1,182	4.0	35	9
	Larry Csonka, Miami[2]	213	1,117	5.2	45	6
	Marv Hubbard, Oakland	219	1,100	5.0	39	4
	*Franco Harris, Pittsburgh	188	1,055	5.6	75	10
	Calvin Hill, Dallas	245	1,036	4.2	26	6
	Mike Garrett, San Diego[2]	272	1,031	3.8	41	6
	John Brockington, Green Bay[2]	274	1,027	3.7	30	8
	Eugene (Mercury) Morris, Miami	190	1,000	5.3	33	12
1971	Floyd Little, Denver	284	1,133	4.0	40	6
	*John Brockington, Green Bay	216	1,105	5.1	52	4
	Larry Csonka, Miami	195	1,051	5.4	28	7
	Steve Owens, Detroit	246	1,035	4.2	23	8
	Willie Ellison, Los Angeles	211	1,000	4.7	80	4
1970	Larry Brown, Washington	237	1,125	4.7	75	5
	Ron Johnson, N.Y. Giants	263	1,027	3.9	68	8
1969	Gale Sayers, Chicago[2]	236	1,032	4.4	28	8
1968	Leroy Kelly, Cleveland[3]	248	1,239	5.0	65	16
	*Paul Robinson, Cincinnati	238	1,023	4.3	87	8
1967	Jim Nance, Boston[2]	269	1,216	4.5	53	7
	Leroy Kelly, Cleveland[2]	235	1,205	5.1	42	11
	Hoyle Granger, Houston	236	1,194	5.1	67	6
	Mike Garrett, Kansas City	236	1,087	4.6	58	9
1966	Jim Nance, Boston	299	1,458	4.9	65	11
	Gale Sayers, Chicago	229	1,231	5.4	58	8
	Leroy Kelly, Cleveland	209	1,141	5.5	70	15
	Dick Bass, Los Angeles[2]	248	1,090	4.4	50	8
1965	Jim Brown, Cleveland[7]	289	1,544	5.3	67	17
	Paul Lowe, San Diego[2]	222	1,121	5.0	59	7
1964	Jim Brown, Cleveland[6]	280	1,446	5.2	71	7
	Jim Taylor, Green Bay[5]	235	1,169	5.0	84	12
	John Henry Johnson, Pittsburgh[2]	235	1,048	4.5	45	7
1963	Jim Brown, Cleveland[5]	291	1,863	6.4	80	12
	Clem Daniels, Oakland	215	1,099	5.1	74	3
	Jim Taylor, Green Bay[4]	248	1,018	4.1	40	9
	Paul Lowe, San Diego	177	1,010	5.7	66	8
1962	Jim Taylor, Green Bay[3]	272	1,474	5.4	51	19
	John Henry Johnson, Pittsburgh	251	1,141	4.5	40	7
	Cookie Gilchrist, Buffalo	214	1,096	5.1	44	13
	Abner Haynes, Dall. Texans	221	1,049	4.7	71	13
	Dick Bass, Los Angeles	196	1,033	5.3	57	6
	Charlie Tolar, Houston	244	1,012	4.1	25	7
1961	Jim Brown, Cleveland[4]	305	1,408	4.6	38	8
	Jim Taylor, Green Bay[2]	243	1,307	5.4	53	15
1960	Jim Brown, Cleveland[3]	215	1,257	5.8	71	9
	Jim Taylor, Green Bay	230	1,101	4.8	32	11
	John David Crow, St. Louis	183	1,071	5.9	57	6
1959	Jim Brown, Cleveland[2]	290	1,329	4.6	70	14
	J.D. Smith, San Francisco	207	1,036	5.0	73	10
1958	Jim Brown, Cleveland	257	1,527	5.9	65	17
1956	Rick Casares, Chi. Bears	234	1,126	4.8	68	12
1954	Joe Perry, San Francisco[2]	173	1,049	6.1	58	8
1953	Joe Perry, San Francisco	192	1,018	5.3	51	10
1949	Steve Van Buren, Philadelphia[2]	263	1,146	4.4	41	11
	Tony Canadeo, Green Bay	208	1,052	5.1	54	4
1947	Steve Van Buren, Philadelphia	217	1,008	4.6	45	13
1934	*Beattie Feathers, Chi. Bears	119	1,004	8.4	82	8

*First season of professional football.

200 YARDS RUSHING IN A GAME

Date	Player, Team, Opponent	Att	Yards	TD
Sept. 22, 1996	LeShon Johnson, Arizona vs. New Orleans	21	214	2
Nov. 13, 1994	Barry Sanders, Detroit vs. Tampa Bay	26	237	0
Dec. 12, 1993	*Jerome Bettis, L.A. Rams vs. New Orleans	28	212	1
Oct. 31, 1993	Emmitt Smith, Dallas vs. Philadelphia	30	237	1
Nov. 24, 1991	Barry Sanders, Detroit vs. Minnesota	23	220	4
Dec. 23, 1990	James Brooks, Cincinnati vs. Houston	20	201	1
Oct. 14, 1990	Barry Word, Kansas City vs. Detroit	18	200	2
Sept. 24, 1990	Thurman Thomas, Buffalo vs. N.Y. Jets	18	214	0
Dec. 24, 1989	Greg Bell, L.A. Rams vs. New England	26	210	1
Sept. 24, 1989	Greg Bell, L.A. Rams vs. Green Bay	28	221	2
Sept. 17, 1989	Gerald Riggs, Washington vs. Philadelphia	29	221	1
Dec. 18, 1988	Gary Anderson, San Diego vs. Kansas City	34	217	1
Nov. 30, 1987	*Bo Jackson, L.A. Raiders vs. Seattle	18	221	2
Nov. 15, 1987	Charles White, L.A. Rams vs. St. Louis	34	213	1
Dec. 7, 1986	Rueben Mayes, New Orleans vs. Miami	28	203	2
Oct. 5, 1986	Eric Dickerson, L.A. Rams vs. Tampa Bay (OT)	30	207	2
Dec. 21, 1985	George Rogers, Washington vs. St. Louis	34	206	1
Dec. 21, 1985	Joe Morris, N.Y. Giants vs. Pittsburgh	36	202	3
Dec. 9, 1984	Eric Dickerson, L.A. Rams vs. Houston	27	215	2
Nov. 18, 1984	*Greg Bell, Buffalo vs. Dallas	27	206	1
Nov. 4, 1984	Eric Dickerson, L.A. Rams vs. St. Louis	21	208	0
Sept. 2, 1984	Gerald Riggs, Atlanta vs. New Orleans	35	202	2
Nov. 27, 1983	*Curt Warner, Seattle vs. Kansas City (OT)	32	207	3
Nov. 6, 1983	James Wilder, Tampa Bay vs. Minnesota	31	219	1
Sept. 18, 1983	Tony Collins, New England vs. N.Y. Jets	23	212	3
Sept. 4, 1983	George Rogers, New Orleans vs. St. Louis	24	206	2
Dec. 21, 1980	Earl Campbell, Houston vs. Minnesota	29	203	1

Nov. 16, 1980	Earl Campbell, Houston vs. Chicago	31	206	0
Oct. 26, 1980	Earl Campbell, Houston vs. Cincinnati	27	202	2
Oct. 19, 1980	Earl Campbell, Houston vs. Tampa Bay	33	203	0
Nov. 26, 1978	*Terry Miller, Buffalo vs. N.Y. Giants	21	208	2
Dec. 4, 1977	*Tony Dorsett, Dallas vs. Philadelphia	23	206	2
Nov. 20, 1977	Walter Payton, Chicago vs. Minnesota	40	275	1
Oct. 30, 1977	Walter Payton, Chicago vs. Green Bay	23	205	2
Dec. 5, 1976	O.J. Simpson, Buffalo vs. Miami	24	203	1
Nov. 25, 1976	O.J. Simpson, Buffalo vs. Detroit	29	273	2
Oct. 24, 1976	Chuck Foreman, Minnesota vs. Philadelphia	28	200	2
Dec. 14, 1975	Greg Pruitt, Cleveland vs. Kansas City	26	214	3
Sept. 28, 1975	O.J. Simpson, Buffalo vs. Pittsburgh	28	227	1
Dec. 16, 1973	O.J. Simpson, Buffalo vs. N.Y. Jets	34	200	1
Dec. 9, 1973	O.J. Simpson, Buffalo vs. New England	22	219	1
Sept. 16, 1973	O.J. Simpson, Buffalo vs. New England	29	250	2
Dec. 5, 1971	Willie Ellison, Los Angeles vs. New Orleans	26	247	1
Dec. 20, 1970	John (Frenchy) Fuqua, Pittsburgh vs. Philadelphia	20	218	2
Nov. 3, 1968	Gale Sayers, Chicago vs. Green Bay	24	205	0
Oct. 30, 1966	Jim Nance, Boston vs. Oakland	38	208	2
Oct. 10, 1964	John Henry Johnson, Pittsburgh vs. Cleveland	30	200	3
Dec. 8, 1963	Cookie Gilchrist, Buffalo vs. N.Y. Jets	36	243	5
Nov. 3, 1963	Jim Brown, Cleveland vs. Philadelphia	28	223	1
Oct. 20, 1963	Clem Daniels, Oakland vs. N.Y. Jets	27	200	2
Sept. 22, 1963	Jim Brown, Cleveland vs. Dallas	20	232	2
Dec. 10, 1961	Billy Cannon, Houston vs. N.Y. Titans	25	216	3
Nov. 19, 1961	Jim Brown, Cleveland vs. Philadelphia	34	237	4
Dec. 18, 1960	John David Crow, St. Louis vs. Pittsburgh	24	203	0
Nov. 15, 1959	Bobby Mitchell, Cleveland vs. Washington	14	232	3
Nov. 24, 1957	*Jim Brown, Cleveland vs. Los Angeles	31	237	4
Dec. 16, 1956	*Tom Wilson, Los Angeles vs. Green Bay	23	223	0
Nov. 22, 1953	Dan Towler, Los Angeles vs. Baltimore	14	205	1
Nov. 12, 1950	Gene Roberts, N.Y. Giants vs. Chi. Cardinals	26	218	2
Nov. 27, 1949	Steve Van Buren, Philadelphia vs. Pittsburgh	27	205	0
Oct. 8, 1933	Cliff Battles, Boston vs. N.Y. Giants	16	215	1

First season of professional football.

TIMES 200 OR MORE
61 times by 42 players...Simpson 6; Brown, Campbell 4; Bell, Dickerson 3; Payton, Riggs, Rogers, Sanders 2.

4,000 YARDS PASSING IN A SEASON

Year	Player, Team	Att.	Comp.	Pct.	Yards	TD	Int.
1996	Mark Brunell, Jacksonville	557	353	63.4	4,367	19	20
	Vinny Testaverde, Baltimore	549	325	59.2	4,177	33	19
	Drew Bledsoe, New England[2]	623	373	59.9	4,086	27	15
1995	Brett Favre, Green Bay	570	359	63.0	4,413	38	13
	Scott Mitchell, Detroit	583	346	59.3	4,338	32	12
	Warren Moon, Minnesota[4]	606	377	62.2	4,228	33	14
	Jeff George, Atlanta	557	336	60.3	4,143	24	11
1994	Drew Bledsoe, New England	691	400	57.9	4,555	25	27
	Dan Marino, Miami[6]	615	385	62.6	4,453	30	17
	Warren Moon, Minnesota[3]	601	371	61.7	4,264	18	19
1993	John Elway, Denver	551	348	63.2	4,030	25	10
	Steve Young, San Francisco	462	314	68.0	4,023	29	16
1992	Dan Marino, Miami[5]	554	330	59.6	4,116	24	16
1991	Warren Moon, Houston[2]	655	404	61.7	4,690	23	21
1990	Warren Moon, Houston	584	362	62.0	4,689	33	13
1989	Don Majkowski, Green Bay	599	353	58.9	4,318	27	20
	Jim Everett, L.A. Rams	518	304	58.7	4,310	29	17
1988	Dan Marino, Miami[4]	606	354	58.4	4,434	28	23
1986	Dan Marino, Miami[3]	623	378	60.7	4,746	44	23
	Jay Schroeder, Washington	541	276	51.0	4,109	22	22
1985	Dan Marino, Miami[2]	567	336	59.3	4,137	30	21
1984	Dan Marino, Miami	564	362	64.2	5,084	48	17
	Neil Lomax, St. Louis	560	345	61.6	4,614	28	16
	Phil Simms, N.Y. Giants	533	286	53.7	4,044	22	18
1983	Lynn Dickey, Green Bay	484	289	59.7	4,458	32	29
	Bill Kenney, Kansas City	603	346	57.4	4,348	24	18
1981	Dan Fouts, San Diego[3]	609	360	59.1	4,802	33	17
1980	Dan Fouts, San Diego[2]	589	348	59.1	4,715	30	24
	Brian Sipe, Cleveland	554	337	60.8	4,132	30	14
1979	Dan Fouts, San Diego	530	332	62.6	4,082	24	24
1967	Joe Namath, N.Y. Jets	491	258	52.5	4,007	26	28

400 YARDS PASSING IN A GAME

Date	Player, Team, Opponent	Att.	Comp.	Yards	TD
Nov. 10, 1996	Boomer Esiason, Arizona vs. Washington (OT)	59	35	522	3
Nov. 3, 1996	Drew Bledsoe, New England vs. Miami	41	30	419	3
Oct. 27, 1996	Vinny Testaverde, Baltimore vs. St. Louis (OT)	51	31	429	3
Oct. 20, 1996	Mark Brunell, Jacksonville vs. St. Louis	52	37	421	0
Sept. 22, 1996	Mark Brunell, Jacksonville vs. New England (OT)	39	23	432	3
Dec. 18, 1995	Steve Young, San Francisco vs. Minnesota	49	30	425	3
Nov. 26, 1995	Dave Krieg, Arizona vs. Atlanta (OT)	43	27	413	4
Nov. 23, 1995	Scott Mitchell, Detroit vs. Minnesota	45	30	410	4
Oct. 1, 1995	Dan Marino, Miami vs. Cincinnati	48	33	450	2
Nov. 20, 1994	Warren Moon, Minnesota vs. N.Y. Jets	50	33	400	2
Nov. 13, 1994	Drew Bledsoe, New England vs. Minnesota (OT)	70	45	426	3
Nov. 6, 1994	Warren Moon, Minnesota vs. New Orleans	57	33	420	3
Sept. 25, 1994	Dan Marino, Miami vs. Minnesota	54	29	431	3
Sept. 4, 1994	Dan Marino, Miami vs. New England (OT)	42	23	473	5
Sept. 4, 1994	Drew Bledsoe, New England vs. Miami (OT)	51	32	421	4
Dec. 19, 1993	Steve Beuerlein, Phoenix vs. Seattle	53	34	431	3
Dec. 5, 1993	Brett Favre, Green Bay vs. Chicago	54	36	402	2
Nov. 28, 1993	Steve Young, San Francisco vs. L.A. Rams	32	26	462	4
Oct. 31, 1993	Jeff Hostetler, L.A. Raiders vs. San Diego	32	20	424	2
Sept. 13, 1992	Steve Young, San Francisco vs. Buffalo	37	26	449	3
Sept. 13, 1992	Jim Kelly, Buffalo vs. San Francisco	33	22	403	3
Nov. 10, 1991	Warren Moon, Houston vs. Dallas (OT)	56	41	432	0
Nov. 10, 1991	Mark Rypien, Washington vs. Atlanta	31	16	442	6
Oct. 13, 1991	Warren Moon, Houston vs. N.Y. Jets	50	35	423	2
Dec. 16, 1990	Warren Moon, Houston vs. Kansas City	45	27	527	3
Nov. 4, 1990	Joe Montana, San Francisco vs. Green Bay	40	25	411	3
Oct. 14, 1990	Joe Montana, San Francisco vs. Atlanta	49	32	476	6
Oct. 7, 1990	Boomer Esiason, Cincinnati vs. L.A. Rams (OT)	45	31	490	3
Dec. 23, 1989	Warren Moon, Houston vs. Cleveland	51	32	414	2
Dec. 11, 1989	Joe Montana, San Francisco vs. L.A. Rams	42	30	458	3
Nov. 26, 1989	Jim Everett, L.A. Rams vs. New Orleans (OT)	51	29	454	1
Nov. 26, 1989	Mark Rypien, Washington vs. Chicago	47	30	401	4
Oct. 2, 1989	Randall Cunningham, Philadelphia vs. Chicago	62	32	401	1
Sept. 24, 1989	Joe Montana, San Francisco vs. Philadelphia	34	25	428	5
Sept. 24, 1989	Dan Marino, Miami vs. N.Y. Jets	55	33	427	3
Sept. 17, 1989	Randall Cunningham, Phil. vs. Washington	46	34	447	5
Dec. 18, 1988	Dave Krieg, Seattle vs. L.A. Raiders	32	19	410	4
Dec. 12, 1988	Dan Marino, Miami vs. Cleveland	50	30	404	4
Oct. 23, 1988	Dan Marino, Miami vs. N.Y. Jets	60	35	521	3
Oct. 16, 1988	Vinny Testaverde, Tampa Bay vs. Indianapolis	42	25	469	2
Sept. 11, 1988	Doug Williams, Washington vs. Pittsburgh	52	30	430	2
Nov. 29, 1987	Tom Ramsey, New England vs. Philadelphia	53	34	402	3
Nov. 22, 1987	Boomer Esiason, Cincinnati vs. Pittsburgh	53	30	409	0
Sept. 20, 1987	Neil Lomax, St. Louis vs. San Diego	61	32	457	3
Dec. 21, 1986	Boomer Esiason, Cincinnati vs. N.Y. Jets	30	23	425	5
Dec. 14, 1986	Dan Marino, Miami vs. L.A. Rams (OT)	46	29	403	5
Nov. 23, 1986	Bernie Kosar, Cleveland vs. Pittsburgh (OT)	46	28	414	2
Nov. 17, 1986	Joe Montana, San Francisco vs. Washington	60	33	441	0
Nov. 16, 1986	Dan Marino, Miami vs. Buffalo	54	39	404	4
Nov. 10, 1986	Bernie Kosar, Cleveland vs. Miami	50	32	401	0
Nov. 2, 1986	Tommy Kramer, Minnesota vs. Washington (OT)	35	20	490	4
Nov. 2, 1986	Ken O'Brien, N.Y. Jets vs. Seattle	32	26	431	4
Oct. 27, 1986	Jay Schroeder, Washington vs. N.Y. Giants	40	22	420	1
Oct. 12, 1986	Steve Grogan, New England vs. N.Y. Jets	42	23	401	3
Sept. 21, 1986	Ken O'Brien, N.Y. Jets vs. Miami (OT)	43	29	479	4
Sept. 21, 1986	Dan Marino, Miami vs. N.Y. Jets (OT)	50	30	448	6
Sept. 21, 1986	Tony Eason, New England vs. Seattle	45	26	414	3
Dec. 20, 1985	John Elway, Denver vs. Seattle	42	24	432	1
Nov. 10, 1985	Dan Fouts, San Diego vs. L.A. Raiders (OT)	41	26	436	4
Oct. 13, 1985	Phil Simms, N.Y. Giants vs. Cincinnati	62	40	513	1
Oct. 13, 1985	Dave Krieg, Seattle vs. Atlanta	51	33	405	4
Oct. 6, 1985	Phil Simms, N.Y. Giants vs. Dallas	36	18	432	3
Oct. 6, 1985	Joe Montana, San Francisco vs. Atlanta	57	37	429	5
Sept. 19, 1985	Tommy Kramer, Minnesota vs. Chicago	55	28	436	3
Sept. 15, 1985	Dan Fouts, San Diego vs. Seattle	43	29	440	4
Dec. 16, 1984	Neil Lomax, St. Louis vs. Washington	46	37	468	2
Dec. 9, 1984	Dan Marino, Miami vs. Indianapolis	41	29	404	4
Dec. 2, 1984	Dan Marino, Miami vs. L.A. Raiders	57	35	470	4
Nov. 25, 1984	Dave Krieg, Seattle vs. Denver	44	30	406	3
Nov. 4, 1984	Dan Marino, Miami vs. N.Y. Jets	42	23	422	2
Oct. 21, 1984	Dan Fouts, San Diego vs. L.A. Raiders	45	24	410	3
Sept. 30, 1984	Dan Marino, Miami vs. St. Louis	36	24	429	3
Sept. 2, 1984	Phil Simms, N.Y. Giants vs. Philadelphia	30	23	409	4
Dec. 11, 1983	Bill Kenney, Kansas City vs. San Diego	41	31	411	4
Nov. 20, 1983	Dave Krieg, Seattle vs. Denver	42	31	418	3
Oct. 9, 1983	Joe Ferguson, Buffalo vs. Miami (OT)	55	38	419	5
Oct. 2, 1983	Joe Theismann, Washington vs. L.A. Raiders	39	23	417	3
Sept. 25, 1983	Richard Todd, N.Y. Jets vs. L.A. Rams (OT)	50	37	446	2
Dec. 26, 1982	Vince Ferragamo, L.A. Rams vs. Chicago	46	30	509	3
Dec. 20, 1982	Dan Fouts, San Diego vs. Cincinnati	40	25	435	1
Dec. 20, 1982	Ken Anderson, Cincinnati vs. San Diego	56	40	416	2
Dec. 11, 1982	Dan Fouts, San Diego vs. San Francisco	48	33	444	5
Nov. 21, 1982	Joe Montana, San Francisco vs. St. Louis	39	26	408	3
Nov. 15, 1981	Steve Bartkowski, Atlanta vs. Pittsburgh	50	33	416	2
Oct. 25, 1981	Brian Sipe, Cleveland vs. Baltimore	41	30	444	4
Oct. 25, 1981	David Woodley, Miami vs. Dallas	37	21	408	3
Oct. 11, 1981	Tommy Kramer, Minnesota vs. San Diego	43	27	444	4
Dec. 14, 1980	Tommy Kramer, Minnesota vs. Cleveland	49	38	456	4

REMOVING TEAM FROM FIELD

No player, coach, or other person affiliated with a club may remove that club's team from the field during the playing of any game, including preseason, except at the direction of the referee. Any club violating this rule will be subject to disciplinary action by the Commissioner, including possible game forfeiture and sole liability for financial losses suffered by the opposing club and any other affected member clubs of the League. [See Section 9.1 (E) of the NFL Constitution and Bylaws.]

280 Park Avenue, New York, New York 10017 (212) 450-2000
NFL Internet Address: http://nfl.com

Commissioner: Paul Tagliabue
President: Neil Austrian

Executive Vice President-Labor Relations/Chairman NFLMC:
Harold Henderson
Executive Vice President & League Counsel: Jeff Pash
Executive Vice President-League & Football Development:
Roger Goodell
Chief Financial Officer: Tom Spock
Senior Vice President-Communications & Government Affairs:
Joe Browne
Senior Vice President-Broadcasting & Network Television:
Val Pinchbeck, Jr.
Senior Vice President-Broadcast Planning: Dennis Lewin

COMMUNICATIONS
Vice President of Public Relations: Greg Aiello
Director of International Public Affairs: Pete Abitante
Director of Media Services: Leslie Hammond
Director of Corporate Communications: Chris Widmaier

BROADCASTING
Vice President-Programming, Marketing & Sales: John Collins
Director of Broadcasting Research: Joe Ferreira
Director of Broadcasting Services: Dick Maxwell

LEAGUE AND FOOTBALL DEVELOPMENT
Vice President-Club Administration &
Stadium Management: Joe Ellis
Senior Director of Security: Milt Ahlerich
Senior Director of Officiating: Jerry Seeman
Director of Strategic Development: Neil Glat
Director of Game Operations: Peter Hadhazy
Director of Football Development: Gene Washington

SPECIAL EVENTS
Vice President of Special Events: Jim Steeg
Director of Special Events Operations: Don Renzulli
Director of Special Events Planning: Sue Robichek

MANAGEMENT COUNCIL
Senior Vice President-General Counsel: Dennis Curran
Senior Vice President-Labor Relations: Peter Ruocco
Vice President of Player & Employee Development: Lem Burnham
Senior Director of Player Personnel/
Football Operations: Joel Bussert
Director of Labor Relations: Lal Heneghan
Director of Compliance: Mike Keenan
Director of Player Programs: Guy Troupe

FINANCE AND ADMINISTRATION
Vice President-Law Enterprises,
Broadcast & Finance: Frank Hawkins
Treasurer: Joe Siclare
Vice President-Internal Audit: Tom Sullivan
Controller: Richard Iandoli
Senior Director of Human Resources
& Administration: John Buzzeo
Senior Director of Systems & Information Processing: Mary Oliveti
Director, Financial Planning & Analysis: Ken Saunders

NFL ENTERPRISES
President: Ron Bernard
Senior Vice President-International: Don Garber
Vice President-NFL Interactive: Ann Kirschner
Vice President-Marketing & Sales: Tola Murphy-Baran
Vice President-International TV Distribution: Anne Murray

NFL FILMS
President: Steve Sabol
Vice President-Cinematography: Steve Andrich
Vice President-In Charge of Production: Jay Gerber
Vice President-Video Operations: Jeff Howard
Vice President-Production Director: Hal Lipman
Vice President-Editor-in-Chief: Bob Ryan
Vice President-Special Projects: Phil Tuckett
Vice President-Finance & Administration: Barry Wolper

NFL PROPERTIES
President: Sara Levinson
Senior Vice President-Consumer Products: Jim Connelly
Senior Vice President-Business Affairs & General Counsel:
Gary Gertzog
Senior Vice President-Marketing: Howard Handler
Senior Vice President-Club Services: Mark Holtzman
Senior Vice President-Corporate Sponsorships: Jim Schwebel
Vice President-Retail Sales: Roger Atkin
Vice President-Advertising & Design: Bruce Burke
Vice President-Corporate Sponsorship: Gary Jacobus
Vice President-Events: David Newman
Vice President-Marketing: Tony Sciolla
Vice President-Publishing: John Wiebusch